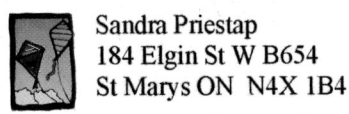

W9-AXB-599

TRAVELING WITH YOUR PET
THE AAA PETBOOK®

The AAA guide to more than 13,000 pet-friendly, AAA-RATED® hotels and campgrounds across the United States and Canada

T
O
P
DOG

11th Edition

SPCA

AAA PUBLISHING

AAA wishes to acknowledge the following for their assistance:
Dogpark.com®
Veterinary Emergency & Critical Care Society

Cover Photos

Cover: Black and White Pooch with blue ball	© BananaStock / age fotostock
Back Cover: Zillie in Gatlinburg, TN	**Photo Contest winners Brian and Joy Peeler**
Spine: Michelob with Morris Island Lighthouse in background from Folly Beach, SC	**Photo Contest winner Mark S. Moore**

Published by AAA Publishing
1000 AAA Drive, Heathrow, Florida 32746

Eleventh Edition Copyright © 2009 AAA Publishing. All rights reserved.
ISBN 10: 1-59508-325-1 ISBN 13: 978-1-59508-325-8 Stock Number 552209
Printed in the USA by Dickinson Press, Inc.

ABOUT THIS BOOK

Welcome to the 11th edition of *Traveling With Your Pet: The AAA PetBook®*. *Traveling With Your Pet* is a must for the traveler who's also an animal lover. This comprehensive book provides all the information you need to know about taking a four-legged friend on the road. Will Spot be a good car passenger? Is it safe to take Snowball on a plane? What are the important rules of pet etiquette? Is pet insurance a good idea? *Traveling With Your Pet* answers all of these questions and more. Here are just some of the features covered:

- Dog parks where you and your furry friends can play, exercise or just relax.

- An extensive listing of emergency animal clinics compiled by the Veterinary Emergency & Critical Care Society. Names, addresses and phone numbers provide valuable information for unexpected or emergency situations, both en route and at your destination.

- A roundup of pet-friendly attractions.

- National public lands in the United States and Canada that allow pets, along with recreation information.

- Border crossing procedures and tips for travelers — both entering Canada from the United States and vice versa.

- Policies pertaining to service animals.

Traveling With Your Pet lists more than 13,000 AAA-RATED® hotels and campgrounds. And the listings show AAA's trustworthy diamond ratings, the traveler's assurance of quality. Other handy features include:

- Informative highway directions.

- Specific information about lodgings' pet policies: deposits and fees (rounded to the nearest dollar), housekeeping service, designated rooms and other stipulations relating to travelers with pets.

- Additional details about the lodgings themselves, including icons for amenities, recreation, dining and accessibility.

- Icons designating AAA's member discount programs.

- Listings for AAA's highest rated campgrounds, including rate and pet policy information and service/amenity icons.

All of this valuable information is packaged in a contemporary, easy-to-read format, making *Traveling With Your Pet: The AAA PetBook®* as indispensable an on-the-road companion as Spot's water dish or Snowball's litter box. Don't leave home without it, and remember: It always pays to *Travel With Someone You Trust®*.

Have some great pictures from traveling with your pet? The AAA PetBook Photo Contest, sponsored by AAA and Best Western®, gives you a chance at winning some great prizes and seeing your pet's photo on a cover of *Traveling With Your Pet: The AAA PetBook®*. Check out some adorable photos of traveling pets in the middle section of this guide. For details on the annual Photo Contest, please refer to the entry form on the next page or visit www.AAA.com/petbook.

AAA PetBook® Photo Contest
Sponsored by Best Western®
Entry Form

The next time you go on vacation with your pet, be sure to take along your camera.

The winning entry in the AAA PetBook Photo Contest will appear on a cover of the 12th edition of **Traveling With Your Pet: The AAA PetBook.** The winner also will receive a $350 AAA VISA Gift Card, five complimentary copies of the book and a Best Western® Travel Card for $150 which can be used at any Best Western® worldwide. The second place entry will appear on the book's spine and the winner will receive a $200 AAA VISA Gift Card and two complimentary copies of the book. Contest rules and entries from previous years are online at www.AAA.com/PetBook.

Name:_____

Address:_____

City: _____ **State:** _____ **Zip code:**_____

Daytime phone: _____ **Evening phone:**_____

Email address:_____

Pet's name/gender: _____ **Animal breed:**_____

Photo taken:_____

Please answer the following questions:

*1. Why do you travel with your pet?_____
_____

*2. What is your favorite place or city to take your pet, and why?_____
_____

3. Tell us about an adventure you had while traveling with your pet._____

*Required answer

AAA PetBook® Photo Contest Official Rules

1. Email **one** digital photo to Petbookcontest@national.aaa.com. Please send the photo as a .jpeg file attachment no larger than 2 MB, and include the information requested on the entry form in the body of the email. The digital photo must have a minimum resolution of 1200 pixels by 1600 pixels. The entry form information (name, address, phone, pet's name/gender, animal breed and answers to questions) must be included in the email for contest consideration. Minor digital enhancement for cropping, red-eye removal, filters and correction functions are permitted, but images that are determined to be significantly altered will be disqualified. Photographers are not permitted to place borders or frames around their image or to place a watermark, signature, date or copyright notices on the image.

     OR

2. Send printed color 8" x 10" unmounted photo that is in focus, along with the completed entry form to:

     AAA PetBook® Photo Contest
     AAA
     1000 AAA Drive, MS 64
     Heathrow, FL 32746

3. Photos must be postmarked by November 27, 2009, and received by November 30, 2009, to be eligible for the contest.

4. Photo must feature at least one pet and convey a travel theme.

5. Only one photo may be entered per household.

6. The entrant must be the person who took the photo and who has full rights to the photo.

7. The entrant must obtain full consent from all models or persons appearing in the photo for full use of the photo, including use and publishing in this contest and the other uses stated herein.

8. All photos entered in the contest, including the prize-winning photo(s), along with all rights of every kind therein, become the sole and exclusive property of AAA and will not be returned.

9. A panel of judges will choose the winning photo based on the following qualities: impact, lighting, composition and effectively conveying the idea that *Traveling With Your Pet: The AAA PetBook®* is about traveling on vacation with your pet. Posed or studio photographs will be disqualified.

10. The winner will be notified **by mail** in early January 2010.

Disclaimer

By participating, entrants agree that: (i) they have read the rules pertaining to the AAA PetBook Photo Contest, and (ii) these rules and the decisions of AAA shall be final in all respects, and (iii) AAA may put the winner's photo on the front or back cover or spine of *Traveling With Your Pet: The AAA PetBook®.* Each entrant grants AAA the right to use his or her name, likeness, portrait, picture, photo, answers on entry form and/or prize information for advertising, publicity and promotional purposes relating to the book, *Traveling With Your Pet: The AAA PetBook®,* and the contest without compensation or permission (unless prohibited by law). Each entrant agrees to hold harmless and release AAA from any injuries, losses or damages of any kind that may result from taking a photo intended to be submitted. AAA is not responsible for late, lost or misdirected entries or mail; for technical, hardware or software malfunctions, lost or unavailable network connections, or failed, incorrect, inaccurate, incomplete, garbled or delayed electronic communications, whether caused by the sender or by any of the equipment or programming associated with or utilized in this promotion, or by any human error that may occur in the processing of entries; or for loss of or damage to any entries. AAA retains the right to not award the prize should no acceptable photos be received. By participating in the contest, each entrant agrees that AAA becomes the owner of each photo submitted and AAA may use said photo in any manner and medium—print, electronic or otherwise—that AAA chooses and entrant relinquishes all rights in and to said photo(s) including, but not limited to, the right to compensation, if any.

Eligibility

No purchase is necessary to enter the contest or claim the prize. Open to U.S. or Canadian residents 18 years or older. **Employees (and their immediate family members) of AAA, CAA and their clubs are not eligible to enter.**

By submitting an entry I agree that I have read the Contest Rules, assent thereto, and submit the enclosed photo in accordance therewith; I attest that I own all rights to the photo and it has not been published or accepted for publication in any medium; and if the photo portrays any living person or persons, I have secured a model release or releases. I further agree that should my entry be chosen as the winning entry I will execute all necessary paperwork/releases as requested by AAA.

Traveling with Your Pet: The AAA PetBook® contains listings for more than 13,000 pet-friendly, AAA-Rated hotels and campgrounds in the United States and Canada. In addition, the AAA PetBook® lists animal hospitals, dog parks, and pet-accessible federal lands, along with information on preparing your pet for travel, how to pack for your pet, and selecting a carrier or crate. *Traveling With Your Pet: The AAA PetBook®* is available at many AAA/CAA offices and at better bookstores.

TABLE OF CONTENTS

AAA PetBook® Photo Contest

Traveling With Pets

Pet-Friendly Places

Pet-Friendly Lodgings

U.S. Lodgings

Canadian Lodgings

Pet-Friendly Campgrounds

Many people view their pets as full-fledged members of the family. Spot and Snowball often have their own beds, premium-quality foods, a basketful of toys and a special place in their humans' heart.

Until it's time to go on vacation, that is. Then the family dog or cat is consigned to "watching the fort" at home while everyone else experiences the joy of traveling. Many animal lovers hesitate to take their pet with them because they don't think they'll be able to find accommodations that accept four-legged guests. Others aren't sure how — or if — their furry friends will adapt.

The truth is, including a pet in the family vacation is fairly easy, so long as you plan ahead. Most pets respond well to travel, a fact that isn't lost on the tourism industry. More than 13,000 AAA-RATED® hotels and campgrounds from coast to coast are pet-friendly, and airline bookings for pet passengers are on the rise. Great companions at home, pets are earning their stripes on the road, too.

So if you've been longing to hit the trail with a canine or feline companion, read the tips on the following pages. You may find that a getaway can be far more enjoyable with than without your pet.

Should Your Pet Travel?

Before you make reservations, determine if your pet is able to travel. Most animals can and do make the most of the experience, but a small percentage simply are not cut out for traveling. Illness, physical condition and temperament are important factors, as is your pet's ability to adjust to such stresses as changes to his environment and routine. When in doubt, check with your veterinarian. If you feel your pet isn't up to the trip, it's better for everyone if he stays home.

❧ **Rule 1: Pets who are very young, very old, pregnant, sick, injured, prone to biting or excessive vocalizing, or who cannot follow basic obedience commands should not travel.**

Even if Spot and Snowball are seasoned travelers, take into account the type of vacation and activities you have planned. No pet is going to be happy (or safe) cooped up in a car or hotel room. Likewise, the family dog may love camping and hiking, but the family cat may not. Putting a little thought toward your animal's needs and safety will pay off in a more enjoyable vacation for everyone.

❧ **Rule 2: If your pet can't actively participate in the trip, she should stay home.**

Most of the information in this book pertains to cats and dogs. If you own a bird, hamster, pig, ferret, lizard or other exotic creature, remember that unusual animals are not always accepted as readily as more conventional pets. Always specify the type of pet you have when making arrangements.

Also check states' animal policies. **Hawaii** imposes 120-day or 5-days-or-less quarantines for all imported dogs, cats and other carnivores to prevent the importation of rabies. Guide dogs and service dogs are exempt from the quarantine provided they have: a standard health certificate issued within 30 days prior to arrival; a current rabies vaccination with documentation of the product name, lot number and lot expiration date; a successful result of an OIE-FAVN rabies blood test conducted after 1 year of age; and an electronic identification microchip implanted and operational. Upon arrival, guide dogs and service dogs still must be examined for external parasites. For additional details, obtain the Hawaii Rabies Quarantine Information Brochure from the Hawaii Department of Agriculture, Animal Quarantine Station, 99-951 Halawa Valley St., Aiea, HI 96701-5602; phone (808) 483-7151 or (808) 837-8092, fax (808) 483-7161. The Web site address is http://www.hawaii.gov/hdoa/ai/aqs/info.

North Carolina has stringent restrictions regarding pets in lodgings. Make certain you understand an accommodation's specific policies before making reservations.

❧ **Rule 3: Be specific when making travel plans that include your pet. Nobody wants unpleasant surprises on vacation.**

If Spot and Snowball stay behind, leave them in good hands while you're gone. **Family, friends and neighbors** make good sitters (provided they're willing), especially if they know your pet and can care for him in your home. Provide detailed instructions for feeding, exercise and medication, as well as phone numbers for your destination, your veterinarian and your local animal emergency clinic.

Professional pet sitters offer a range of services, from feeding and walking your pet daily to full-time house sitting while you are gone. Interview several candidates, and always check credentials and references. For additional information, contact the National Association of Professional Pet Sitters or Pet Sitters International. *(See sidebars on p. 8 and p. 9.)*

Kennels board many animals simultaneously and generally are run by professionals who will provide food and exercise according to your instructions. Pets usually are kept in a run (dogs) or cage (cats and small dogs) and may not get the same level of human interaction as at home. **Veterinary clinics** also board pets and may be the best choice if yours is sick, injured or needs special medical care. For further information on how to select a kennel, contact the Pet Care Services Association.

Veterinarians, fellow pet owners and professional associations are a good source of referrals for sitters and kennels.

❧ **Rule 4: Never leave your pet with someone you don't trust.**

Travelers Who Have Disabilities

Individuals with disabilities who own service animals to assist them with everyday activities undoubtedly face challenges, but traveling should not be one of them. Service animals (the accepted term for animals trained to help people with disabilities) are not pets and thus are not subject to many of the laws or policies pertaining to pets.

The Americans With Disabilities Act (ADA) defines a service animal as "any guide dog, signal dog or other animal individually trained to provide assistance to an individual with a disability." ADA regulations stipulate that public accommodations are required to modify policies, practices and procedures to permit the use of a service animal by an individual with a disability.

The purpose of these regulations is to provide equal access opportunities for people with disabilities and to ensure that they are not separated from their service animals. A tow truck operator, for example, must allow a service animal to ride in the truck with her owner rather than in the towed vehicle.

Public accommodations may charge a fee or deposit to an individual who has a disability — provided that fee or deposit is required of all customers — but no fees or deposits may be charged for the service animal, even those normally charged for pets.

The handler/owner is responsible for the animal's care and behavior; if the dog creates an altercation or poses a direct threat, the handler may be required to remove it from the premises and pay for any resulting damages.

CHOOSING A PET SITTER

Before hiring a pet sitter, ask:
- Is he or she insured (for commercial liability) and bonded?
- What is included in the fee?
- Does the sitter require that your pet have a current vaccination?
- What kind of animals does the sitter typically care for?
- How will a medical, weather or home emergency be handled?
- Does he or she fully understand your pet's medical or dietary needs?
- How much time will be spent with your pet?

The pet sitter should:
- Have a polished, professional attitude.
- Provide references.
- Have a standard contract outlining terms of service.
- Have experience in caring for animals.
- Insist on current vaccinations.
- Ask about your pet's health, temperament, schedule and needs.
- Visit and interact with your pet before you leave.
- Devote time and attention to your pet.
- Be affiliated with pet care organizations.

Be sure you:
- Explain your pet's personality — favorite toys, good and bad habits, hiding spots, general health, etc.
- Leave care instructions, keys, food and water dishes, extra supplies (food, medication, etc.), and phone numbers for your veterinarian and an emergency contact.
- Bring pets inside before leaving.

CHOOSING A KENNEL

Before reserving a kennel, ask:
- What is included in the fee?
- Are current vaccinations required?
- What kind of animals do they board?
- How will a medical or weather emergency be handled?
- Will your pet be kept in a cage or run?
- Will your pet receive daily exercise?
- Does the kennel fully understand your pet's medical or dietary needs?
- How and how often will staff interact with your pet?

The kennel should:
- Require proof of current vaccinations.
- Be clean, well-ventilated and offer adequate protection from the elements.
- Have separate areas for dogs, cats and other animals, with secure fencing and caging.
- Clean and disinfect facilities daily.
- Give your pet his regular food on his regular schedule.
- Provide soft bedding in runs/cages.
- Understand your pet's medical needs.
- Provide or obtain veterinary care if necessary.
- Offer sufficient supervision.
- Have a friendly, animal-loving staff.

Be sure you:
- Notify staff of behavior quirks (dislike of other animals, children, etc.).
- Provide food and medication.
- Leave a familiar object with your pet.
- Leave phone numbers for your veterinarian and an emergency contact.
- Spend time with your pet before boarding him.

The **Delta Society,** an organization devoted to companion and service animals, has information about laws that affect people and service animals in public accommodations. Phone (425) 679-5500 for a catalog, or visit www.deltasociety.org.

Preparing Your Pet for Travel

Happily, many vacations can be planned to include fun activities for pets. Trips to parks, nature trails, the ocean or lakes offer exposure to the world beyond the window or fence at home, as well as the chance to explore new sights and sounds. Even the streets of an unfamiliar city can provide a smorgasbord of discoveries for your animal friend to enjoy.

Once you decide Spot and Snowball are ready to hit the road, plan accordingly:

❧ **Get a clean bill of health from the veterinarian.** Update your pet's vaccinations, check his general physical condition and obtain a health certificate showing proof of up-to-date inoculations, particularly rabies, distemper and kennel cough. Such documentation will be necessary if you cross state or country lines, and also may come in handy in the unlikely event your pet gets lost and must be retrieved from the local shelter. Don't forget to ask the doctor about potential health risks at your destination (Lyme disease, heartworm infection) and the necessary preventive measures.

If your pet is taking prescribed medicine, pack a sufficient supply plus a few days' extra. Also take the prescription in case you need a refill. Be prepared for emergencies by getting the names and numbers of clinics or doctors at your destination from your veterinarian or the American Animal Hospital Association. **Hint:** Obtain these references before you leave and keep them handy throughout the trip.

Make sure your pet is in good physical shape overall, especially if you are planning an active vacation. If your animal is primarily sedentary or overweight, he may not be up to lengthy hikes through the woods.

Note: Some owners believe a sedated animal will travel more easily than one that is fully aware, but this is rarely the case. In fact, tranquilizing an animal can make travel much more stressful. Always consult a veterinarian about what is best for your pet, and administer sedatives only under the doctor's direction. In addition, never give an animal medication that is specifically prescribed for humans. The dosage may be too high for an animal's much smaller body mass, or may cause dangerous side effects.

❧ **Acclimate your pet to car travel.** Even if you're flying, your pet will have to ride in the car to get to the airport or terminal, and you don't want any unpleasant surprises before departure.

CONTACT INFORMATION

The following organizations offer information, tips, brochures and other travel materials designed to help you and your pet enjoy a happy and safe vacation.

American Animal Hospital Association
12575 W. Bayaud Ave., Lakewood, CO 80228
(303) 986-2800 — www.healthypet.com

American Society for the Prevention of Cruelty to Animals
424 E. 92nd St., New York, NY 10128-6804
(212) 876-7700 — www.aspca.org

American Veterinary Medical Association
1931 N. Meacham Rd., Suite 100
Schaumburg, IL 60173
(847) 925-8070 — www.avma.org

Dogpark.com ®
820 Fifth Ave., Suite B, San Rafael, CA 94901
www.dogpark.com

The Humane Society of the United States
2100 L St. N.W., Washington, DC 20037
(202) 452-1100 — www.hsus.org

National Association of Professional Pet Sitters
15000 Commerce Pkwy., Suite C
Mt. Laurel, NJ 08054
(856) 439-0324 — www.petsitters.org

Pet Care Services Association
1702 E. Pikes Peak Ave.
Colorado Springs, CO 80909
(719) 667-1600 — www.petcareservices.org

PetGroomer.com
P.O. Box 2489
Yelm, WA 98597
(360) 446-5348 — www.petgroomer.com

Pet Sitters International
201 E. King St., King, NC 27021
(336) 983-9222 — www.petsit.com

USDA-APHIS
USDA-APHIS-Animal Care
4700 River Rd., Unit 84
Riverdale, MD 20737-1224
(301) 734-7833
www.aphis.usda.gov/animal_welfare/index.shtml

Some animals are used to riding in the car and even enjoy it. But most associate the inside of the carrier or the car with one thing only: the annual visit to the V-E-T. Considering that these visits usually end with a jab from a sharp needle, it's no wonder that some pets forget their training and act up in the car. If this is your situation, you will have to re-train your animal to view a drive as a reward, not a punishment.

Begin by allowing your pet to become used to the car without actually going anywhere. Then take short trips to places that are fun for animals, such as the park or the drive-through window at a fast-food restaurant. (Keep those indulgent snacks to a minimum!) Be sure to praise her for good behavior with words, petting and healthy treats. It shouldn't take long before you and your furry friend are enjoying leisurely drives without incident. *(See Traveling by Car, p. 12.)*

❧ **Brush up on behavior.** Will Snowball make a good travel companion? Or will he be an absolute terror on the road? Don't wait until the vacation is already under way to find out; review general behavioral guidelines with respect to your animal, keeping in mind that the unfamiliarity of travel situations may test the temperament of even the most well-behaved pet.

It's a good idea to socialize Spot by exposing her to other people and animals (especially if she normally stays inside). You're likely to encounter both on your trip, and it is important that she learns to behave properly in the company of strangers. Make her introduction to the outside world gradual, such as a walk in a new neighborhood or taking her along while you run errands. Exposure to new situations will help reduce fear of the unknown and result in more socially acceptable behavior.

Is your pet housebroken? How is he around children? Does he obey vocal commands? Be honest about your animal's ability to cope in unfamiliar surroundings. Depending on the length and nature of the trip and your pet's level of command response, an obedience refresher course might be a good idea.

❧ **Learn about your destination.** Check into quarantines or other restrictions well in advance, and make follow-up calls as your departure date approaches. Find out what types of documentation will be required — not just en route, but on the way home as well.

Be aware of potential safety or health risks where you're going, and plan accordingly. For example, the southeastern United States — particularly Florida — is home to alligators and heartworm-carrying mosquitoes, and many mountainous and wooded areas may harbor ticks that transmit Lyme disease.

Confirm all travel plans within a few days of your departure, especially with lodgings and airlines; their policies may have changed after you made the reservations. If you plan to visit state parks or attractions that accept pets on the premises, obtain their animal regulations in advance.

WHAT TO TAKE

- ❑ Carrier or crate. *(See Selecting a Carrier or Crate, p. 11, for specifications.)*
- ❑ Nylon or leather collar or harness, license tag, ID tag(s) and leash. All should be sturdy and should fit your pet properly.
- ❑ Food and water dishes.
- ❑ Can opener and spoon (for canned food).
- ❑ An ample supply of food, plus a few days' extra.
- ❑ Bottled water from home. (Many animals are finicky about their drinking water.)
- ❑ Cooler with ice.
- ❑ Healthy treats.
- ❑ Medications, if necessary.
- ❑ Health certificate and other required documents.
- ❑ A blanket or other bedding. (If your pet is used to sleeping on the furniture, bring an old blanket or sheet to place on top of the hotel's bedding.)
- ❑ Litter supplies (for cats or other small animals), a scooper and plastic bags (for dogs).
- ❑ Favorite toys.
- ❑ Carpet deodorizer.
- ❑ Chewing preventative.

- ❑ A recent photograph and a written description including name, breed, gender, height, weight, coloring and distinctive markings.
- ❑ Grooming supplies:
  comb/brush
  nail clippers
  shampoo
  cloth and paper towels
  cotton balls/tissues
- ❑ First-aid kit:
  gauze, bandages and adhesive tape
  hydrogen peroxide
  rubbing alcohol
  ointment
  muzzle
  scissors
  tweezers (for removing ticks, burrs, splinters, etc.)
  local emergency phone numbers
  first-aid guide (such as *Pet First Aid: Cats & Dogs,* published by The Humane Society of the United States and the American Red Cross)

❖ **Determine the best mode of transportation.** Most people traveling with pets drive. Many airlines do accept animals in the passenger cabin or cargo hold, and as more people choose to fly with their pet airlines are becoming more pet-conscious. Restrictions vary as to the type and number of pets an airline will carry, however, so inquire about animal shipping and welfare policies before making reservations. If your pet must travel in the cargo hold, heed the cautionary advice in the Traveling by Air section. *(See p. 13.)*

Flying is really the only major option to car travel. Amtrak, as well as Greyhound and other interstate bus lines, do not accept pets. **Note:** Seeing-eye dogs and other service animals are exempt from the regulations prohibiting pets on Amtrak and interstate bus lines. Local rail and bus companies may allow pets in small carriers, but this is an exception rather than a rule.

The only cruise ship that currently permits pets is the Cunard Line's *Queen Mary 2* (on transatlantic crossings); kennels are provided, but animals are accepted on a very limited basis. Some charter and sightseeing boat companies permit pets onboard, however.

A word of advice: Never try to sneak your pet onto any mode of public transportation where she is not permitted. You may face legal action or fines, and the animal may be confiscated if discovered.

❖ **Pack as carefully for your pet as you do for yourself.** *(See What To Take, p. 10.)* Make sure she has a collar with a license tag and ID tag(s) listing her name and yours, along with your address and phone number. As an added precaution, some owners outfit their dog with a second tag listing the name and number of a contact person at home. Popular backup identification methods are to have your animal tattooed with an ID number (usually a social security number) or to implant a microchip under her skin.

If your pet requires medication, make sure that is specified on his tag. This helps others understand your animal's needs and also may prevent people from keeping a found pet or from stealing one to sell.

Note: Choke chains, collars that tighten when they are pulled, may be useful during training sessions, but they do not make good full-time collars. If the chain catches on something, your pet could choke herself trying to pull free. For regular wear, use a harness or a conventional collar made of nylon or leather.

Selecting a Carrier or Crate

This is one of the most important steps in ensuring your pet's safety when traveling. A good-quality carrier not only contains your pet during transit, it also gives him a safe, reassuring place to stay when confinement is necessary at your destination. Acclimate the animal before the trip so he views the crate as a cozy den, not a place of exile.

If you plan to travel by car, a carrier will confine your pet en route, and also may come in handy if Spot or Snowball must stay in the room unsupervised. A secured crate will prevent your pet from escaping from the room when the cleaning staff arrives, or at night if camping in the open. *(See At Your Destination, p. 16.)*

Some airlines allow small pets to travel in the passenger cabin as carry-on luggage. There are no laws dictating the type of carrier to use, but remember that it must be small enough to fit under a standard airplane seat and should not exceed 45 linear inches (length + width + height), or roughly **22 by 14 by 9 inches.** If your pet will be flying in the cargo hold, you must use a carrier that meets U.S. Department of Agriculture Animal and Plant Health Inspection Service (USDA-APHIS) specifications. *(See Traveling by Air, p. 13.)*

Crates are available at pet supply stores; some airlines also sell carriers. Soft-sided travel bags are handy for flyers with small pets. Before you make the investment, make sure your carrier is airline-approved.

Even if you never take to the skies, these common-sense guidelines provide a good rule of thumb in selecting a crate for other uses. USDA-APHIS rules stipulate the following:

❖ The crate must be enclosed, but with ventilation openings occupying at least 14 percent of total wall space, at least one-third of which must be located on the top half of the kennel. A three-quarter-inch lip or rim must surround the exterior to prevent air holes from being blocked.

❖ The crate must open easily, but must be sufficiently strong to hold up during normal cargo transit procedures (loading, unloading, etc.).

❖ The floor must be solid and leakproof, and must be covered with an absorbent lining or material (such as an old towel or litter).

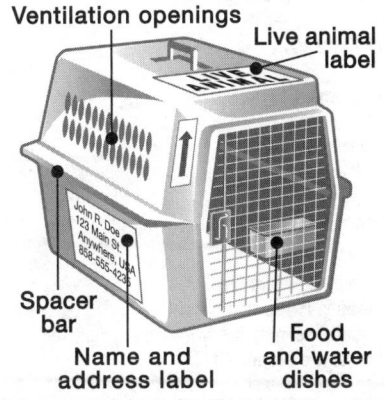

Ventilation openings

Live animal label

Spacer bar

Name and address label

Food and water dishes

HEATSTROKE
AND
HYPOTHERMIA

The best way to treat heatstroke or hypothermia is to prevent it. Do not leave pets unattended in a car, even if only for a few minutes. Also heed airlines' restrictions on pet travel, and carefully investigate animal welfare policies to make certain the airline has safeguards to protect your pet from both conditions.

Other preventive measures are to avoid strenuous exercise — including such activities as hiking and "fetch" — when the sun is strongest (10 a.m.-2 p.m.), and to provide your pet access to clean, fresh drinking water at all times.

Following are the warning signs and basic first aid for heatstroke and hypothermia. Always be alert to your pet's physical condition and watch for symptoms — immediate attention to the situation may mean the difference between life and death. If your pet is struck with either disorder, take him to an animal hospital or veterinarian as fast as safely possible.

HEATSTROKE

Symptoms
- rapid, shallow breathing
- excessive salivation
- heavy panting
- hot to the touch
- glazed eyes
- unsteadiness, dizziness
- deep red or purple tongue or gums
- vomiting
- body temperature of 104 F or higher

First Aid
- place pet in the shade
- quickly dampen with cool water, especially on the head and neck
- give small amounts of water

HYPOTHERMIA

Symptoms
- shivering
- weakness
- lethargy
- cold to the touch
- body temperature of 95 F or lower

First Aid
- place in a warm area
- wrap in towels or a blanket
- quickly warm by gently massaging the head, chest and extremities

❦ The crate must be just large enough to allow the animal to turn freely while standing, and to have a full range of normal movement while standing or lying down.

❦ The crate must offer exterior grips or handles so that handlers do not have to place their hands or fingers inside.

❦ Food and water dishes must be securely attached and accessible without opening the kennel.

❦ If the carrier has wheels, they must be removed or immobilized prior to loading.

❦ One-inch lettering stating "Live Animals" must be placed visibly on the exterior, and must be accompanied by directional arrows showing the crate's proper orientation. It also is a good idea to label the crate with your name, home address and home phone number, as well as an address and phone number where you can be reached during the trip. **Hint:** Use an adhesive label or an indelible marker and write directly on the crate, as paper may be ripped off accidentally in transit.

❦ Attach a list of care instructions (feeding, watering, etc.) for a 24-hour period to the exterior of the carrier. This will help airport workers care for your pet if he is sent to the wrong destination.

❦ If you are traveling with multiple pets, note that crates may contain only one animal whose weight exceeds 20 pounds. Smaller animals may travel together under the following guidelines: one species to a crate, except compatible dogs and cats of similar size; two puppies or kittens under 6 months of age; 15 guinea pigs or rabbits; 50 hamsters. **Note:** These are federal limits; airlines may impose more stringent regulations.

Traveling by Car

The first step in ensuring your pet's well-being during a vacation is to train her to ride in the car. For safety reasons, pets should be confined to the back seat, either in a carrier or a harness attached to the car's seat belt. This keeps the animal from interfering with or distracting the driver, and also may save her life in the event of an accident. And a restrained animal will not be able to break free and run away the second the car door is opened.

To help prevent car sickness, feed your pet a light meal four to six hours before departing. Do not give an animal food or water in a moving vehicle.

Never allow your pet to ride in the bed of a pickup truck. It's illegal in some states; he also can jump out or be thrown, endangering himself and others on the road. Harnessing or leashing him to the truck bed is not advisable either: If he tries to jump out, he could be dragged along the road or the restraint could become a noose.

Avoid placing animals in campers or trailers as well. **If your pet cannot ride in the car with you, leave him at home.**

Don't let your dog stick her head out the window, no matter how enjoyable it seems. Road debris and other flying objects can injure delicate eyes and ears, and the animal is at greater risk for severe injury if the vehicle should stop suddenly or be struck. If it is hot outside, run the air conditioner instead of opening the windows, and be sure that the air flow is reaching your pet.

AAA recommends that drivers stop every two hours to stretch their legs and take a quick break from driving. Your pet will appreciate the same break. Plan to visit a rest stop every four hours or so to let him have a drink and a chance to answer the call of nature. (Cat owners should bring along a litter box; dog owners should clean up afterward.)

Be sure your pet is leashed before opening the car door. This is not merely a courtesy to fellow travelers; it will prevent her from unexpectedly breaking free and running away. Keep in mind that even the most obedient pet may become disoriented during travel or in strange places and set off for home. **Hint:** If your pet is not used to traveling, use a harness instead of a collar; it is more difficult for an animal to wriggle out of a harness.

NEVER leave an animal in a parked car, even if the windows are partially open. Even on pleasant days the temperature inside a car can soar to well over 100 degrees in less than 10 minutes, placing your pet at risk for heatstroke and possibly death. On very cold days, hypothermia is a risk. Also, animals left unattended in parked cars frequently are stolen.

Traveling by Air

(Service animals are normally exempt from most of the regulations and fees specified in this section. Check policies with the airline when making reservations.)

Opinion is divided as to whether air travel is truly safe for pets. Statistically, it is less dangerous than being a passenger in a car, but some experts warn of potentially deadly conditions for animals. The truth lies somewhere in between: Most pets arrive at their destination in fine condition, but death or injury is always a possibility. Before you decide to fly, know the risk factors and the necessary precautions to keep your pet safe.

❧ **Determine whether your pet is fit to fly.** The Animal Welfare Act (AWA), administered by USDA-APHIS, specifies that dogs and cats must be at least 8 weeks old and weaned at least 5 days before air travel. Animals that are very young, very old, pregnant, ill or injured should not fly at all. Cats, snub-nosed dogs (pugs, boxers, etc.) and long-nosed dogs (shelties, collies, etc.) are prone to severe respiratory difficulties in an airplane's poorly ventilated cargo hold and should travel only in the passenger cabin (if size allows) with their owner. Some airlines will not accept snub-nosed breeds if the temperature exceeds 70 degrees anywhere in the routing.

❧ **Decide where your pet will fly.** Most animals fly in the hold as checked baggage when traveling with their owners, or as cargo when they are unaccompanied. The AWA was enacted to ensure animals traveling in this manner are treated humanely and are not subjected to dangerous or life-threatening conditions. For specific requirements pertaining to your animal, check with the airline in advance, as policies vary. Some airlines will not ship dogs as checked baggage, and others will only accept dogs shipped as cargo from "known shippers"; i.e., commercial shippers or licensed pet breeders. Except for service animals, Southwest accepts no pets in the cabin or cargo compartment.

Items classified as "dangerous goods" (dry ice or toxic chemicals, for example) must be transported in a different part of the hold from where live animals are carried. Some planes are designed to have separate hold areas, but so-called "people mover" airlines that are primarily interested in getting human passengers from one point to

---

AIRLINE CONTACT INFORMATION

Following is a list of the major North American airlines and their toll-free reservation numbers.

Web site addresses include information about flying with animals. **Hint:** Look under links for baggage, cargo or special travel needs, or do a site search for "pets."

Air Canada. . . . . (888) 247-2262
www.aircanada.com (only service animals in cabin)

Alaska Airlines. . . . . (800) 252-7522
www.alaskaair.com

American Airlines . . . . (800) 433-7300
www.aa.com

Continental Airlines. . . . . (800) 523-3273
www.continental.com

Delta Airlines. . . . . (800) 221-1212
www.delta.com

Northwest Airlines. . . . . (800) 225-2525
www.nwa.com

Southwest Airlines. . . . . (800) 435-9792
www.southwest.com (accepts service animals only)

United Airlines. . . . . (800) 864-8331
www.united.com

US Airways . . . . (800) 428-4322
www.usairways.com

another as quickly as possible may not give priority to this feature. Check your airline's specific baggage policies so you know exactly where in the hold your pet will be traveling.

Small pets may be taken into the passenger cabin with you as carry-on luggage on most airlines. This places the animal's welfare squarely in your hands but is feasible only if he is very well-behaved and fits comfortably in a container that meets standard carry-on regulations. *(See Selecting a Carrier or Crate, p. 11.)* Keep in mind that the carrier — with the animal inside — must be kept under the seat in front of you throughout the flight. Some airlines charge a fee ($50-$95) for carry-on pets. **Note:** AWA regulations do not apply to animals traveling in the cabin.

❧ **Do your homework.** Investigate the airline's animal transport and welfare policies, especially if you are flying with a small or commuter airline. All airlines are subject to basic AWA regulations, but specific standards of care vary greatly from one company to another. Do your research well in advance and confirm the information 24-48 hours before departing.

The more information an airline provides, the better care your pet is likely to receive. Beware of companies that have vague animal welfare guidelines, or none at all. All major airlines provide information about pet transport on

their Web sites. Also talk to fellow travelers and pet owners about their experiences. Finally, keep in mind that airlines are not required to transport live animals and can refuse to carry them for any reason.

❧ **Protect your investment.** Most people think of their pets as part of the family, but the legal system assigns them the same value as a piece of luggage. Inquire about insurance — an airline that won't insure animals in its care may not be the right one for your pet. (Always read the fine print before purchasing any insurance policy.) Also ask if the airline's workers are trained to handle animals. Few are, but it doesn't hurt to check. Remember, it's up to you to choose an airline that values pets and will treat yours with care.

❧ **Understand the potential hazards.** Because a plane's cargo hold is neither cooled nor heated until take-off, the most dangerous time for your pet is that spent on the ground in this unventilated compartment. In summer the space absorbs heat while the plane sits on the tarmac; the reverse is true in winter, when it is no warmer inside the hold than outside. Both instances expose pets to the possibility of serious injury or death from heatstroke or hypothermia. **Note:** The latter also may be a concern during flight if the hold's heater is disabled or turned off, allowing the temperature to drop to near-freezing levels.

To minimize these risks, USDA-APHIS rules prohibit animals from being kept in the hold or on the tarmac for more than 45 minutes when temperatures are above 85 F or below 45 F. Some airlines impose even tighter temperature restrictions and may not permit animals to fly on planes going to cities where the ground temperatures may exceed these limits. Delta, for example, does not carry animals in the cargo hold May 15 through Sept. 15. (Exceptions may be made for animals whose veterinarians certify they are acclimated to colder temperatures, but never warmer.)

❧ **Make stress-free travel arrangements.** Once you decide to fly, reserve space for Spot or Snowball when you arrange your own tickets, preferably well in advance of your travel date. Airlines accept only a limited number of animals per flight — usually two to four in the passenger cabin and one pet per passenger — on a first-come, first-served basis. More animals are generally allowed in the cargo hold.

Prepare to pay an additional fee, about $75-$100 each way; the cost is often greater for large animals traveling on a flight without their owner. (Unfortunately, pets are not eligible for frequent flyer miles.) Always reconfirm your reservations and flight information 24-48 hours before departure.

If your pet will be flying in the hold, travel on the same plane and reserve a nonstop flight. This not only reduces the danger of heatstroke or hypothermia during layovers, it also eliminates the possibility that she will be placed on the wrong connecting flight. In summer, fly during the

PET INSURANCE

Just like their owners, pets can experience major medical problems at some point in their lifetime — even those that live indoors. And if illness strikes while you're on the road, it may be necessary to obtain care quickly. As a result, more and more people who travel with their devoted companion are considering pet health insurance.

Insurance plans run the gamut from basic coverage and routine care for illness and injury to comprehensive health maintenance, vaccinations and exams. Annual premiums range from less than $100 to more than $350, depending on the type of pet and plan. When choosing your plan, consider the following:

- What are the enrollment guidelines (age, breed, specific restrictions, etc.)?
- Which expenses are covered and which are excluded?
- What is the plan's policy concerning existing health problems?
- Does the plan allow you to use your own veterinarian?
- How are veterinary fees paid?
- Is a multiple pet discount offered?

early morning or late evening when temperatures are cooler. Because of large crowds and the chance of heavy air traffic causing delays, avoid holiday travel whenever possible.

Additional precautions may be necessary when traveling outside the United States and Canada. Other countries may impose lengthy quarantines, and airline workers outside North America may not be bound by animal welfare laws. *(See International Travel, p. 18.)*

❧ **Play an active role in your pet's well-being.** Flying safely with your pet requires careful planning and attention to his welfare. See the veterinarian within 10 days of departure for a health certificate (required by most airlines) and a pre-flight check-up.

Address any concerns you have about your pet traveling by air, especially if you are considering tranquilization. Sedation usually is not recommended for cats and dogs, regardless of whether they fly in the cabin or in the hold. Exposure to increased altitude pressure can create respiratory and cardiovascular problems; animals with short, wide heads are particularly susceptible to disorientation and possible injury. Sedation should never be administered without your veterinarian's approval.

Obtain an airline-approved carrier and acclimate your pet to its presence by leaving it open with a familiar object inside. A sturdy, well-ventilated crate adds an additional measure of protection.

Because animals are classified as luggage, they may be loaded on the plane via conveyor belt. If the crate falls off the belt, your pet could be injured or released. Ask that she be hand-carried on and off the plane, and that you be permitted to watch both procedures. Also ask about "counter-to-counter" shipping, in which the animal is loaded immediately before departure and unloaded immediately after arrival. There usually is an additional fee for this service.

Make sure you will have access to your pet if there is a lengthy layover or delay. Think twice about flying on an airline that won't allow you to check on your animal under such circumstances.

❧ **Prepare for the flight.** Keep in mind that traveling with an animal will require additional pre-flight time and preparation on your part. Exercise your pet before the flight, and arrive at least two but not more than four hours before departure. If he is traveling as carry-on luggage, check-in is normally at the passenger terminal; if he is traveling as checked baggage or as cargo in the cargo hold, proceed to the airline's cargo terminal, which is often in a different location. Find this out when making reservations and again when confirming flight information.

Make sure your animal's crate is properly labeled and secured, but do not lock it in case airline personnel have to provide emergency care. Include an ice pack for extra comfort on a hot day or a hot water bottle on a cold day. **Hint:** Wrap in a towel to prevent leaking.

Do not feed your pet less than four hours before departure, but provide water up until boarding. **Hint:** Freeze water in the bowl so that it melts throughout the trip, providing a constant drinking source.

Spot or Snowball should wear a sturdy collar (breakaway collars are recommended for cats) and two identification tags marked with your name, home address and phone number, and travel address and phone number. It's also a good idea to clip your pet's nails before departure so they won't accidentally get caught on any part of the carrier.

Note: You may be required to take your pet out of the carrier as you pass through security on your way to the gate. Make sure the animal is wearing a collar and leash or harness.

Attach food and water dishes inside the carrier so that airline workers can reach them without opening the door. If the trip will take longer than 12 hours, also attach a plastic bag with at least one meal's worth of dry food. Animals under 16 weeks of age must be fed every 12 hours, adult animals every 24 hours. Water must be provided at least every 12 hours, regardless of the animal's age.

Allow your pet to answer the call of nature before boarding, but do not take her out of the carrier while in the terminal. As a courtesy, wait until you are outside and away from fellow travelers. Keep her leash with you — do not leave it inside or attached to the kennel.

If your pet is traveling as carry-on luggage, let the passenger sitting next to you know. Someone with allergies may want to change seats.

Perhaps the most important precaution is to alert the flight crew and the captain that your pet is aboard. The pilot must activate the heater for the cargo hold; make sure this is done once you are in the air. If there are layovers or delays, ask the flight crew to be sure your pet has adequate shelter and/or ventilation; better yet, ask them to allow you to check in person.

If you have arranged to watch your pet being unloaded, ask a flight attendant to call the baggage handlers and let them know you are on the way. Above all, do not hesitate to voice any concerns you have for your pet's welfare — it is your responsibility to do so.

❧ **Be prepared for emergencies.** In the unlikely event your pet gets lost en route, contact the airline, local humane shelters, animal control agencies or USDA-APHIS. Many airlines can trace a pet that was transferred to the wrong flight. If your pet is injured in transit, proceed to the nearest animal hospital; register any complaints with USDA-APHIS. **Hint:** Carry a list of emergency contact numbers and a current photograph of your pet in your wallet or purse, just in case.

At Your Destination

How well you and your companion behave on the road directly affects the way future furry travelers will be treated. Always clean up after your pet and keep him under your control. This is not only a courtesy to fellow human travelers; it's the surest way to enjoy a safe and happy vacation.

Inquire about pet policies before making lodging reservations. Properties may impose restrictions on the type or size of pet allowed, or they may designate only certain rooms, such as smoking rooms, for travelers with animals. If you have a dog, get a room on the first floor with direct access outside, preferably near a walking area; keep her leashed on any excursion.

Lodgings may have supervision policies requiring that pets be crated when unattended or that they may not be left alone at all. Allow your pet only in designated exercise or animal-approved areas; never take him into such off-limits places as the lobby, pool area, patio or restaurant. Prepare to receive limited housekeeping service, or none at all.

Expect to pay some type of additional charge, which may be per room or per pet and may include any of the following: refundable deposit, non-refundable deposit, daily fee, weekly fee.

If staying with friends or relatives, make certain your pet is a welcome guest. Know and respect their "house rules," especially if they have small children or pets of their own.

Once in the room, check for such hazards as chemically treated toilet water, hiding spaces and electrical cords before freeing your pet. Give her time to adjust to her new surroundings under your supervision.

Above all, practice good "petiquette":

🐾 Try not to leave your pet alone, but if you must, crate or otherwise confine her.

🐾 Crate at night as well.

🐾 To keep your pet and the housekeeper from having an unexpected encounter, leave the "Do Not Disturb" sign on the door when you go out without him.

🐾 Barking dogs make poor hotel neighbors — keep your pet quiet.

🐾 Don't allow your pet on the furniture. If she insists on sleeping on the bed, bring a bedspread or sheet from home and place that on top of the hotel bedding.

🐾 Clean up after your pet immediately — inside the room and out — and leave no trace of him behind when checking out.

🐾 Dispose of litter and other "accidents" properly — check with housekeeping.

🐾 Notify the management immediately if something is damaged, and be ready to pay for repairs.

🐾 Add a little extra to the housekeeping tip.

🐾 When you take your pet out of the room, keep her leashed, especially in wilderness areas and around small children. No matter how obedient she is at home, new stimuli and distractions may cause her to forget or ignore vocal commands. Know and obey animal policies at parks, beaches and other public areas. Check before arriving to make certain animals still are welcome, even if you've been there before — the rules may have changed.

🐾 Look for outdoor cafes when selecting restaurants. For health reasons, pets are not permitted inside eating establishments, but many restaurants allow animals to sit quietly with their owners at outdoor tables. Drive-through restaurants are another alternative.

In Case of Emergency

Be prepared for any turn of events by knowing how to get to the nearest animal hospital. *(See Animal Clinics, p. 51.)* Also have the name and number of a local animal shelter and a local veterinarian handy — ask your veterinarian for a recommendation. Take first-aid supplies with you and know how to use them. An animal in pain may become aggressive, so exercise caution at all times.

Emergency evacuation shelters do not accept pets, and domesticated animals do not fare well if left to weather an emergency on their own, especially when far from home. Avert a potential tragedy by planning in advance where you will go with your pet in case of evacuation. Use the listings in this book to find other lodgings willing to take you and your pet. Above all, don't wait for disaster to strike. Leave as soon as the evacuation order is announced, and take your animal with you.

The Great Outdoors

Travelers planning an active or camping vacation should make some additional preparations. Check in advance to be sure your pet is permitted at campgrounds, parks, beaches, trails and anywhere else you will be visiting. If there are restrictions — and there usually are — follow them. Remember that pets other than service animals usually are not allowed in public buildings.

Note: It is not advisable to take animals other than dogs into wilderness areas. For example, bringing a pet is not recommended at some national parks in Alaska. Also keep in mind that rural areas often have few veterinarians and even fewer boarding kennels.

Use common sense. Clean up after your pet, do not allow excessive vocalizing and keep her under your control. If the property requires your pet to be leashed or crated at all times, do so. Few parks or natural areas will allow a pet to be unattended, even when chained — the risk of disagreeable encounters with other travelers or wildlife is too great. The National Park Service may confiscate pets that harm wildlife or other visitors.

If camping, crate your pet at night to protect him from the elements and predators. (Chaining confines the animal but won't keep him from becoming a midnight snack.)

When hiking, stick to the trail and keep your pet on a short leash. It is all too easy for an unleashed pet to wander off and get lost or fall prey to a larger animal. Keep an eye out for such wildlife as alligators, bears, big cats, porcupines and skunks, and avoid other dogs and small children. Be aware of indigenous poisonous plants, such as English ivy and oleander, or those causing physical injury, such as cactus, poison ivy or stinging nettle. Your veterinarian or local poison control center should be able to give you a full list of hazardous flora.

Before setting out on the trail, make sure both of you are in good physical shape. An animal that rarely exercises at home will not suddenly be ready for a 10-mile trek across uneven terrain. Plan a hike well within the limits of your pet's endurance, and don't push — remember, if Spot gets too tired to make it back on her own, you'll have to carry her.

Carry basic first-aid supplies, including a first-aid guide. *(See What to Take, p. 10.)* Also carry fresh drinking water for both of you — "found" water may contain harmful germs or toxins. Drink often, not just when thirst strikes, and have your pet do the same. Watch for signs of dehydration, leg or foot injuries, heat exhaustion or heatstroke. Stop immediately and return home or to camp if any of these occur.

Note: Dogs can carry their own backpacks (check your local pet store for specially designed packs), but should never carry more than one-third of their body weight. Train the dog to accept the pack beforehand, and only use it with a strong, healthy animal in excellent physical condition.

No matter where or how you spend your vacation, visit the veterinarian when you return home to check for injuries, parasites and general health.

Note: Most campgrounds accept pets. The AAA CampBook guides are an excellent source for obtaining detailed information regarding pet policies, restrictions and extra charges for campgrounds in the United States and Canada. AAA members may obtain complimentary copies of the CampBook guides at their local AAA club.

Traveling Between the United States and Canada

Traveling across the international border with your pet — either from the United States into Canada or from Canada into the United States — should prove largely hassle-free, although some basic regulations need to be kept in mind.

All U.S. and Canadian citizens traveling *by air* between the United States and Canada, Mexico, Bermuda or the Caribbean region are required to show a passport or other accepted secure document. The passport requirement will be extended to land and sea border crossings on June 1, 2009 (a Passport Card also will be accepted for land and sea crossings only). Prior to this date the participating governments also will accept a birth certificate, which must be a certified copy with a raised seal from the government agency that issued it and be accompanied by government-issued photo identification (such as a driver's license). For more information visit www.travel.state.gov or phone (877) 487-2778.

U.S. Customs grants returning U.S. citizens who stay in Canada more than 48 hours an individual $800 duty-free exemption (if not used within the prior 30 days). Any amount over the $800 exemption is subject to duty.

The exemption is based on fair retail value and applies to goods acquired for personal or household use or as gifts but not intended for sale. All items for which the exemption is claimed must accompany you upon return.

A 5 percent goods and services tax (GST) is levied on most items sold and most services rendered in Canada. In New Brunswick, Nova Scotia or Newfoundland and Labrador, a harmonized sales tax (HST) of 13 percent (which includes the GST) is charged on goods and services.

U.S. citizens taking pet cats and dogs 3 months of age and older into Canada must carry a rabies vaccination certificate signed by a licensed veterinarian that describes the animal, provides proof of rabies vaccination and includes documentation of the product name, lot number and lot expiration date. Collar tags are not sufficient proof of immunization. The certificate also is needed to bring a pet dog back into the United States; make sure the vaccination doesn't expire while you're in Canada. **Note:** Pit bulls are not permitted into Ontario.

Service animals are exempt from import restrictions. Also exempt are puppies and kittens under 3 months old; obtain a certificate of health from your veterinarian indicating that the animal is too young to vaccinate. **Note:** For details on pet imports, contact the Canadian Embassy; 501 Pennsylvania Ave. N.W., Washington, DC 20001; phone (202) 682-1740. The Web site address is www.canadianembassy.org.

The Canadian Food Inspection Agency (CFIA) provides additional pet information; phone (613) 225-2342 or visit the Web site at www.inspection.gc.ca. If you need assistance while in Canada, contact the U.S. Embassy, 490 Sussex Dr., P.O. Box 866/Station B, Ottawa, ON, Canada K1N 1G8/K1P 5T1; phone (613) 688-5335.

Canadian Customs allows Canadian citizens to bring back from the United States, duty and tax free, goods valued up to $400 any number of times per year, provided the visit is 48 hours or more. A $50 exemption, excluding alcoholic beverages and tobacco products, may be claimed if the visit is 24 hours or more and no other exemption is being used.

If returning from a visit of 7 days or more (not counting the day of departure from Canada), the exemption goes up to $750.

Canadian travelers may take pet cats and dogs into the United States with no restrictions, but U.S. Customs requires that dogs have proof of rabies vaccination no less than 30 days before arrival. For additional information on U.S. regulations, contact the USDA-APHIS National Center for Import and Export, (301) 734-8364.

International Travel

If you plan to travel abroad with Spot or Snowball, prepare for a lengthy flight and at least a short quarantine period. Be aware that airline and animal workers in other countries may not be bound by the same animal welfare laws that exist in the United States and Canada. Contact the embassy or consulate at your destination for information about documentation and quarantine requirements, animal control laws and animal welfare regulations.

As with any trip, have your pet checked by your regular veterinarian within 10 days of departure to obtain a health certificate showing proof of rabies and other inoculations. If you are traveling with an animal other than a domesticated dog or cat, check with USDA-APHIS for restrictions or additional documentation required.

The booklet "Pets and Wildlife: Licensing and Health Requirements" has general information about traveling abroad with animals; write U.S. Customs & Border Protection, 1300 Pennsylvania Ave. N.W., Washington, DC 20229; phone (202) 354-1000, or visit www.customs.gov.

Note: Island nations such as Australia and the United Kingdom, which are rabies-free, have adopted the Pet Travel Scheme (PETS) to allow entry for dogs and cats from the U.S. and Canada without the usual 6-month quarantine. Pets must be tested and vaccinated for rabies at least 6 months prior to travel, be implanted with microchip identification and receive a certificate of treatment from an official government veterinarian. For information, visit the U.K. Web site for the Department for Environment, Food and Rural Affairs (DEFRA) at www.defra.gov.uk. Hawaii, which has a standard 120-day quarantine for all imported animals except guide dogs, has adopted a similar expedited program of 5 days or less; a pet must have been vaccinated at least *twice* for rabies in its lifetime.

Loss Prevention Tips

Searching the woods or an unfamiliar town for a missing pet is easily prevented by following these helpful tips:

* Have your pet wear a sturdy nylon or leather collar with current ID and rabies tags firmly attached. Be sure the ID tag includes the phone number of an emergency contact. Consider having your pet implanted with microchip identification; it's a simple procedure similar to a vaccination.

* Keep your pet on a leash or harness. Even trained animals can become agitated or disoriented in unfamiliar surroundings and fail to obey vocal commands.

* Attach the leash or harness while your pet is still inside the closed car or crate.

* Do not leave your pet unattended at any time, anywhere. A stolen pet is extremely difficult to recover.

* Escape-proof your hotel room by crating your pet and asking hotel management to make certain no one enters your room while you are gone. (Inform the property that you're traveling with an animal when making reservations.)

* Take along a recent picture and a detailed written description of your pet.

If your pet gets lost these steps will improve your chances of recovery:

* If your pet is lost in transit, contact the airline immediately. Ask to trace the animal via the airline's automated baggage tracking system.

* Contact local police, animal control, animal shelters, humane organizations and veterinary clinics with a description and a recent photograph. Stay in contact until your pet is found, and provide your home and destination phone numbers.

* Post signs and place an ad in the local newspaper so that anyone who comes across your pet knows she is lost and how to reach you.

The Last Word

You are ultimately responsible for your pet's welfare and behavior while traveling. Since animals cannot speak for themselves, it is up to you to focus on your pet's well-being every step of the way. It also is important to make sure he conducts himself properly so that other pets will be welcome visitors in the future. Following the common-sense information in this book will help ensure that both you and your animal companion have a safe and happy trip.

Pet-Friendly Places

in the United States and Canada

Dog Parks
Attractions
National Public Lands
Emergency Animal Clinics

DOG PARKS

A dog park is a place where people and their dogs can play together. These places offer dogs an area to play, exercise and socialize with other dogs while their owners enjoy the park-like setting. Dog park size and features vary greatly from location to location, from several hundred square feet in urban areas to several hundred acres in the suburbs and rural locations. Dog owners should remember to always keep their animal leashed until they reach the dog park entrance, to maintain voice control of their animal at all times, to bring their own supply of bags for picking up after their pet (and to be diligent in doing so), and to always have fresh water available for their dog. Please observe all dog park rules.

This list of dog parks in the United States and Canada is provided by Dogpark.com®. Dogpark.com is all about dogs — all breeds, all mixes of breeds, and all shapes, sizes and dispositions. It provides articles and information about dogs and their care, health and play. Online, visit www.dogpark.com.

The dog parks listed here welcome people who travel with their dogs; private parks or parks requiring local residency are not included. **Note:** Fence types and heights vary, and some areas have no fencing at all, requiring that the dog be under firm voice control.

United States

ARIZONA

Echo Mountain Off Leash Area - Phoenix
phoenix.gov, (602) 262-6696
2302 E. Grovers Ave. (located in Grovers Basin on 20th Street at Cave Creek Road)
Daily 6:30 a.m.-10 p.m.
Fenced, 2.5 acres with grass surface, disposal bags, trash cans, separate areas for large and small dogs; bring your own water.

PETsMART Dog Park at Washington Park - Phoenix
phoenix.gov, (602) 262-6971
21st Avenue north of Mayland, between Bethany Home and Glendale roads
Daily 6:30 a.m.-10 p.m.
Fenced, 2.65 acres with grass surface, double-gated entries, benches, water fountain, two dog-watering stations, disposal bags, trash cans, separate areas for large and small dogs. Access for the disabled.

RJ Dog Park at Pecos Park - Phoenix
phoenix.gov, (602) 262-6111
48th Street and Pecos Parkway (enter from 48th Street via Chandler Boulevard)
Daily 6 a.m.-10 p.m.
Fenced, 2 acres with grass surface, double-gated entry, benches, water fountain, separate areas for large and small dogs. Access for the disabled.

Rose Mofford Sports Complex - Phoenix
phoenix.gov, (602) 262-8011
9833 N. 25th Ave. (north of Dunlap)
Daily 6:30 a.m.-10 p.m.
Fenced, 2.65 acres with grass surface, double-gated entries, benches, trees, water fountain, disposal bags, trash cans, separate areas for large and small dogs. Access for the disabled.

Steele Indian School Park - Phoenix
phoenix.gov
West side of 7th Street, just north of Indian School Road
Daily 6 a.m.-10 p.m.
Fenced, 1.83 acres with granite surface, double-gated entries, disposal bags, trash cans, separate areas for large and small dogs. Access for the disabled.

Chaparral Park - Scottsdale
scottsdaleaz.gov
5401 N. Hayden Rd. at McDonald Drive
Daily 5:30 a.m.-10 p.m., May-Oct.; 6 a.m.-10 p.m., rest of year. Closed for maintenance Tues. and Fri. 8-noon and in wet conditions. Phone (480) 312-9663 for status.
Fenced, 4 acres, benches, shade, restroom, water, separate areas for large and small dogs.

Horizon Park - Scottsdale
scottsdaleaz.gov
15444 N. 100th St. at Thompson Peak Parkway (east of SR 101 off Frank Lloyd Wright Boulevard)
Daily dawn-dusk.
Fenced, lighted, benches, some shade, tables, disposal bags, trash cans, parking, phones, restrooms; bring your own water.

Vista del Camino Park - Scottsdale
scottsdaleaz.gov
7700 E. Pierce St. (take Pierce Street heading west from Hayden Road)
Daily 5:30 a.m.-10 p.m.
Fenced, ½ acre, lighted, grass turf, benches, restrooms nearby, water fountains for dogs and people, mutt mitt stations.

Creamery Park - Tempe
tempe.gov, (480) 350-5200
8th Street and Una Avenue (just south of University Drive near Rural Road)
Daily 6 a.m.-10 p.m.
Fenced, lighted, benches, disposal bags, trash cans, parking, water.

Jaycee Park - Tempe
tempe.gov, (480) 350-5200
5th Street and Hardy Drive
Daily 6 a.m.-10 p.m.
Fenced, lighted, trees, benches, disposal bags, trash cans, parking, water. Access for the disabled.

Mitchell Park - Tempe
tempe.gov, (480) 350-5200
Mitchell Drive and 9th Street
Daily 6 a.m.-10 p.m.
Fenced, lighted, trees, benches, disposal bags, trash cans, parking, water. Access for the disabled.

ARIZONA (CONT'D)

Papago Park - Tempe
tempe.gov, (480) 350-5200
Curry Road and College Avenue
Daily 6 a.m.-10 p.m.
Fenced, lighted, trees, disposal bags, trash cans, parking, water.

Tempe Sports Complex - Tempe
tempe.gov, (480) 350-5200
Warner Road and Hardy Drive
Daily 6 a.m.-10 p.m.
Fenced, lighted, trees, disposal bags, trash cans, parking, water.

Christopher Columbus Park - Tucson
tucsonaz.gov, (520) 791-4873
4600 N. Silverbell Rd.
Daily dawn to 2-3 hours after dusk.
Fenced, ⅓ acre, water fountain for dogs, scrambling area, shaded area with ramada, scooper dispenser.

Gene C. Reid Park - Miko's Corner Playground - Tucson
tucsonaz.gov, (520) 837-8071
Country Club Road and 22nd Street (use Picnic Place or Concert Place entrances off Country Club Road)
Daily 7 a.m.-10 p.m.
Fenced, lighted, three double-entry gates, large turf areas, divided 2-acre site for large and small dogs, dog-friendly potable water fountains, scooper dispenser, ramada with tables. Named after Miko, a Tucson police dog that lost its life in the line of duty.

Jacobs Park - Tucson
tucsonaz.gov, (520) 791-4873
3300 N. Fairview Ave. on the west side of Jacobs Park
Daily 6 a.m.-10:30 p.m.
Fenced, turf area, walkway, picnic table, double-entry gate.

Palo Verde Park - Tucson
tucsonaz.gov, (520) 791-5930
300 S. Mann Ave. (south of Broadway Boulevard, west of Kolb Road)
Daily 6 a.m.-10:30 p.m.
Fenced, separate areas for large and small dogs, both with separate double-entry gates; entire facility lighted; DG/pea gravel surface, no turf; picnic tables; trash cans; water fountains for dogs on each side; scooper dispensers.

Sixth Avenue Dog Park - Tucson
tucsonaz.gov, (520) 791-4873
2075 N. Sixth Ave. (east side of Sixth Avenue across from Northwest Center and Mansfield Park)
Daily 6 a.m.-10:30 p.m.
Fenced, ramada, tables, wash area, double-entry gate.

Udall Park - Tucson
tucsonaz.gov, (520) 791-5930
7290 E. Tanque Verde Rd.
Daily 6 a.m.-10 p.m.
Fenced, 1 acre, trash cans, seating, water for dogs.

CALIFORNIA

Calabasas Bark Park - Calabasas
cityofcalabasas.com
4232 Las Virgenes Rd. (approximately 2 miles west of US 101 on the south side)
Daily 5 a.m.-9 p.m.
Fenced, lighted, trees, benches, scoops, trash cans, paved parking, water fountain for dogs, separate areas for large and small dogs.

Costa Mesa Bark Park - Costa Mesa
cmbarkpark.org, (949) 733-4101 or (714) 754-5041
Arlington Drive and Newport Boulevard (across from the Orange County Fairgrounds Equestrian Center)
Wed.-Mon. dawn-9 p.m.
Fenced, 2.1 acres, night lights dusk-9 p.m., grass turf, trees, benches, tables, disposal bags, trash cans, parking, restrooms, water fountains, water for dogs, separate small dog area. Access for the disabled.

Jacinto Creek Park - Dog Park - Elk Grove
cityofsacramento.org
8600 W. Stockton Blvd.
Daily 5 a.m.-10 p.m.
Fenced, 2 acres, double-gated entry, water fountain for dogs, turf and decomposed granite areas, trees, obstacle course for dogs, benches.

Ernie Smith Dog Park - El Verano
sonoma-county.org
18776 Gilman Dr.
Daily dawn-dusk.
Fenced, ½ acre, double-gated entry, water fountain for dogs, picnic tables, disposal bags, trash can, free parking.

Elizabeth Anne Perrone Dog Park - Glen Ellen
sonoma-county.org
13630 Sonoma Hwy. in Sonoma Valley Regional Park (SR 12 between Arnold Drive and Madrone Road)
Daily dawn-dusk. Parking fee $5 or annual park pass.
Fenced, 1 acre, double-gated entry, covered gazebo, shade trees, water fountain for dogs, disposal bags, trash can.

Huntington Dog Beach - Huntington Beach
dogbeach.org
Pacific Coast Highway between 21st and Seapoint streets
Daily 5 a.m.-10 p.m.; parking lot closes at 10 p.m.
Unfenced, benches and tables on the bluffs above the beach, disposal bags, trash cans, metered parking, restrooms. Dogs may be off leash anywhere on the beach while under an owner's supervision. Access for the disabled to the sand.

Laguna Niguel Pooch Park - Laguna Niguel
ci.laguna-niguel.ca.us
31461 Golden Lantern near Chapparosa Park
Tues.-Thurs. and Sat. 7 a.m.-dusk, Sun. 8 a.m.-dusk, Mon. and Fri. noon-dusk.
Fenced, 1 acre, wood chip ground cover, picnic tables, shelters, disposal bag dispenser, parking, restroom, water faucet with hose, separate fenced area for small dogs.

CALIFORNIA (CONT'D)

Long Beach Recreation Dog Park - Long Beach
geocities.com/lbdogpark
5201 E. 7th St. at Park Avenue
Daily dawn-10 p.m.
Fenced, lighted, trees, crushed-granite surface, benches, tables, disposal bags, trash cans, parking, water, separate fenced area for small dogs. Access for the disabled.

Palm Springs Dog Park - Palm Springs
palmspringsca.gov
3200 E. Tahquitz Canyon Way, behind City Hall
Daily dawn-10 p.m.
Fenced, lighted, double-gated entry, trees, benches, tables, shelter, disposal bags, trash cans, parking, phones, dual-level water fountains, separate areas for large and small dogs, antique fire hydrants, unusual iron fence created by sculptor Phill Evans. Access for the disabled.

Redondo Beach Dog Park - Redondo Beach
rbdogpark.com
Southeast corner of 190th Street and Flagler Lane
Daily dawn-dusk; closed Wed. dawn-noon for maintenance.
Fenced, trees, benches, disposal bags, trash cans, parking, phones, water, separate fenced area for small dogs. Access for the disabled.

Bannon Creek Park - Sacramento
cityofsacramento.org
2780 Azevedo Dr. (near West El Camino Avenue)
Daily 5 a.m.-10 p.m.
Fenced, .6 acres, double-gated entry, benches, disposal bag dispensers, water fountain/faucet for dogs.

Glenbrook Dog Park - Sacramento
cityofsacramento.org
8500 La Riviera Dr. in Glenbrook Park, behind the little league fields
Daily 5 a.m.-10 p.m.
Fenced, 1 acre, double-gated entry, water fountain for dogs, shade, trees, seating, picnic tables.

Granite Dog Park - Sacramento
cityofsacramento.org
Ramona Avenue off Power Inn Road in Granite Regional Park
Daily 5 a.m.-10 p.m.
Fenced, 2 acres, double-gated entry, bench, disposal bags, trash cans, water spigot for dogs. Access for the disabled.

Partner Park - Sacramento
cityofsacramento.org
5699 South Land Park Dr. at Fruitridge Road (behind the Belle Cooledge Community Center)
Daily 5 a.m.-10 p.m.
Fenced, 2 acres, lighted, double-gated entry, landscaped with turf and mature trees, bench, disposal bags, trash cans, water spigot for dogs. Access for the disabled.

Regency Community Park - Dog Park - Sacramento
cityofsacramento.org
5500 Honor Pkwy. in North Natomas
Daily 5 a.m.-10 p.m.
Fenced, 2 acres, double-gated entry, water fountain for dogs, turf and decomposed granite areas, trees, benches.

Tanzanite Community Park - Sacramento
cityofsacramento.org
2220 Tanzanite Way in Tanzanite Community Park
Daily 5 a.m.-10 p.m.
Fenced, 2 acres, double-gated entry, landscaped with turf and native grass, trees, benches, disposal bags, trash cans, water fountain for dogs.

Balboa Park - San Diego
sandiego.gov
Daily 24 hours.
Unfenced, large field.
Two off-leash areas:
(1) Nate's Point at El Prado, on the southwest side of Cabrillo Bridge
(2) Morley Field, northwest of the tennis courts

Cadman Community Park - San Diego
sandiego.gov
4280 Avati Dr.
Daily 7-9:30 a.m. and 5-7:30 p.m., in summer; 7:30-10 a.m. and 4:30-7 p.m., rest of year.
Unfenced.

Capehart Park (Pacific Beach) - San Diego
sandiego.gov
Soledad Mountain Road and Feldspar Street
Daily 24 hours.
Fenced, 1 acre, picnic tables, benches, parking, separate grass-turf areas for large and small dogs, areas to provide water to dogs, water fountain.

Dog Beach - San Diego
sandiego.gov
Voltaire Street in Ocean Beach (enter the parking lot at the west end of Voltaire Street)
Daily 24 hours.
Unfenced, disposal bags, trash cans, water, restrooms nearby. Access for the disabled.

Doyle Community Park - San Diego
sandiego.gov
8175 Regents Rd. (behind the Doyle Recreation Center)
Daily 24 hours.
Fenced, no lights, separate grass-turf areas for large and small dogs.

Fiesta Island - San Diego
sandiego.gov
Part of Mission Bay Park
Daily 6 a.m.-10 p.m.
This island allows dogs anywhere outside the fenced areas.

Grape Street Park - San Diego
sandiego.gov
Grape Street and Granada Avenue
Mon.-Fri. 7:30 a.m.-9 p.m., Sat.-Sun. and holidays 9-9.
Unfenced, 5 acres, lighted, trees, benches, tables, trash cans, parking, restrooms, water.

San Francisco
San Francisco regularly reviews its off-leash ("dog play area") policies. Refer to sfgov.org for the most recent information on dog parks.

CALIFORNIA (CONT'D)

Alamo Square Park - San Francisco
sfgov.org
Scott Street between Hayes and Fulton streets in the western half of the park
Daily 6 a.m.-10 p.m.
Unfenced, 5 acres; dogs must be under firm voice control.

Alta Plaza Park - San Francisco
sfgov.org
Clay Street between Scott and Steiner streets on the second terrace of the park
Daily 6 a.m.-10 p.m.
Unfenced, ½ acre; dogs must be under firm voice control.

Bernal Heights - San Francisco
sfgov.org
Bernal Heights Boulevard at the top of the hill
Daily 6 a.m.-10 p.m.
Unfenced; dogs must be under firm voice control.

Brotherhood Mini Park - San Francisco
sfgov.org
Head Street and Brotherhood Way on Department of Public Works property, improved by Recreation and Parks Dept.
Daily 6 a.m.-10 p.m.
Unfenced; dogs must be under firm voice control.

Buena Vista Park - San Francisco
sfgov.org
Buena Vista West Avenue at Central Avenue
Daily 6 a.m.-10 p.m.
Unfenced; dogs must be under firm voice control.

Corona Heights - San Francisco
sfgov.org
Roosevelt Way and Museum Way in the field next to the Randall Museum
Daily 6 a.m.-10 p.m.
Fenced.

Crocker Amazon Playground - San Francisco
sfgov.org
Between LaGrande and Dublin streets in the northern portion of the park, adjacent to the community garden
Daily 6 a.m.-10 p.m.
Unfenced; dogs must be under firm voice control.

Dolores Park - San Francisco
sfgov.org
Between Church and Dolores streets, south of the tennis courts and soccer field
Daily 6 a.m.-10 p.m.
Unfenced; dogs must be under firm voice control.

Douglass Park - San Francisco
sfgov.org
27th and Douglass streets, upper field
Daily 6 a.m.-10 p.m.
Unfenced; dogs must be under firm voice control.

Eureka Valley Recreation Center - San Francisco
sfgov.org
Collingwood Street, adjacent to the tennis courts and east of the baseball diamond
Daily 6 a.m.-10 p.m.
Fenced.

Golden Gate Park - San Francisco
sfgov.org
Four off-leash areas:
(1) Southeast section bounded by Lincoln Way, King Drive and 5th and 7th avenues
(2) Northeast section at Fulton and Willard streets
(3) South-central area bounded by King Drive, Middle Drive and 34th and 38th avenues
(4) Fenced dog-training area near 38th Avenue and Fulton Street

Jefferson Park - San Francisco
sfgov.org
Eddy and Laguna streets at the northwest end of the park
Daily 6 a.m.-10 p.m.
Unfenced; dogs must be under firm voice control.

Lafayette Park - San Francisco
sfgov.org
Near Sacramento Street between Octavia and Gough streets
Daily 6 a.m.-10 p.m.
Unfenced; dogs must be under firm voice control.

Lake Merced - San Francisco
sfgov.org
Lake Merced Boulevard and Middlefield Drive, northern lake area
Daily 6 a.m.-10 p.m.
Unfenced; dogs must be under firm voice control.

McKinley Square - San Francisco
sfgov.org
San Bruno Avenue and 20th Street, on the west slope
Daily 6 a.m.-10 p.m.
Unfenced; dogs must be under firm voice control.

McLaren Park - San Francisco
sfgov.org
Daily 6 a.m.-10 p.m.
Two off-leash areas:
(1) A 59-acre hilltop bounded by Shelly Drive with trails, open areas, reservoir and fence at roadway. Includes natural area, excludes group picnic facilities, children's play area and custodian housing. Leash restrictions during performances at amphitheater.
(2) South entrance at 1600 block of Geneva Avenue adjacent to natural area with open area fenced on roadway

Mountain Lake Park - San Francisco
sfgov.org
North of Lake Street at 8th Avenue, east end of the park
Daily 6 a.m.-10 p.m.
Unfenced; dogs must be under firm voice control.

Pine Lake Park - San Francisco
sfgov.org
Crestlake and Vale streets, west of and contiguous to Stern Grove and adjacent to the parking lot
Daily 6 a.m.-10 p.m.
Unfenced; dogs must be under firm voice control.

Potrero Hill Mini Park - San Francisco
sfgov.org
22nd Street between Arkansas and Connecticut streets
Daily 6 a.m.-10 p.m.
Unfenced; dogs must be under firm voice control.

CALIFORNIA (CONT'D)

St. Mary's Recreation Center - San Francisco
sfgov.org
Justin and Benton streets, lower terrace of the park
Daily 6 a.m.-10 p.m.
Fenced.

Stern Grove - San Francisco
sfgov.org
Wawona Street between 21st and 23rd avenues, north side
Daily 6 a.m.-10 p.m.
Unfenced; dogs must be under firm voice control.

Upper Noe Recreation Center - San Francisco
sfgov.org
30th Street between Church and Sanchez streets, behind
and along the baseball field
Daily 6 a.m.-10 p.m.
Fenced.

Walter Haas Playground - San Francisco
sfgov.org
Diamond Heights Boulevard, upper terrace of the park
Daily 6 a.m.-10 p.m.
Unfenced; dogs must be under firm voice control.

Field of Dogs - San Rafael
fieldofdogs.org
3540 Civic Center Dr. (near the intersection of US 101 and
North San Pedro Road)
Daily dawn-dusk.
Fenced, double-gated entry, trees, benches, tables, shelter,
disposal bags, trash cans, parking, water. Access for the
disabled.

DeTurk Roundbarn Park - Santa Rosa
ci.santa-rosa.ca.us
819 Donahue St. (between West 8th and 9th streets)
Daily dawn-dusk.
Fenced, water (small neighborhood park).

Doyle Park Dog Park - Santa Rosa
ci.santa-rosa.ca.us
700 Hoen Ave. in Doyle Park (go west on Sonoma Avenue,
turn left on Hoen Avenue and then turn right into the
parking lot; the fenced dog park is behind the stadium)
Daily dawn-dusk.
Fenced, bench, disposal bags, water, separate areas for
large and small dogs.

Galvin Dog Park - Santa Rosa
ci.santa-rosa.ca.us
3330 Yulupa Ave. in Don Galvin Park (next to Bennet Valley
Golf Course)
Daily dawn-dusk.
Fenced, ½ acre, double-gated entry, trees, trash cans,
parking, water, picnic tables, restrooms. Access for the
disabled.

Northwest Community Dog Park - Santa Rosa
ci.santa-rosa.ca.us
2620 W. Steele Ln. in Northwest Community Park (go west
on Gurneville Road, turn right on Marlow Road and then
turn right at the first traffic light into the park's parking lot;
walk east along the path to the dog park on the left)
Daily dawn-dusk.
Fenced, ½ acre, benches, disposal bags, trash cans,
restrooms nearby, water, separate area for small dogs.

Rincon Valley Dog Park - Santa Rosa
ci.santa-rosa.ca.us
5108 Badger Rd. in Rincon Valley Community Park
Daily dawn-dusk.
Fenced, ½ acre, trees, benches, tables, disposal bags,
trash cans, parking, phones, restrooms, water, separate
fenced areas for large and small dogs (area for large dogs
closed during the winter), fenced pond area for dogs (open
year-round). Monitors are present during peak hours to
enforce rules. Access for the disabled.

Off-leash, unfenced, under voice control areas:

700 Doyle Park Drive - Santa Rosa
ci.santa-rosa.ca.us
700 Doyle Park Dr. (go west on Sonoma Avenue, turn
left on Hoen Avenue and then turn right into the parking
lot; the unfenced, off-leash area is to the right of the
fenced dog park)
Daily 6-8 a.m.

Franklin Park - Santa Rosa
ci.santa-rosa.ca.us
2095 Franklin Ave.
Daily 6-8 a.m.

Southwest Community - Santa Rosa
ci.santa-rosa.ca.us
1698 Hearn Ave.
Daily 6-8 a.m.

Youth Community - Santa Rosa
ci.santa-rosa.ca.us
1725 Fulton Rd.
Daily 6-8 a.m.

Remington Dog Park - Sausalito
sausalitodogpark.org
Ebbtide Avenue at Bridgeway Boulevard
Mon.-Fri. 7-7, Sat.-Sun. 8-7
Fenced, lighted, safety-gated entry, picnic tables, benches,
tents for shelter, scoops and scooper cleaning station, trash
cans, parking, water, tennis balls and racquets provided.

Animal Care Center Dog Park - Sebastopol
sonoma-county.org
500 Ragle Rd.
Daily dawn-dusk. Parking fee $5 or annual park pass.
Fenced, ½ acre, double-gated entry, disposal bags, trash
can, water fountain for dogs.

Sierra Madre Dog Park - Sierra Madre
cityofsierramadre.com
611 E. Sierra Madre Blvd. in Sierra Vista Park, south of the
tennis courts
Daily 6 a.m.-10 p.m. Permit required; daily permit $5. Daily
and annual permits are available at City Hall; the Sierra
Madre Police Department, 242 W. Sierra Madre Blvd.; or
the Sierra Madre Community Recreation Center, 611 E.
Sierra Madre Blvd.
Fenced, lighted, double-gated entry, trees, benches,
disposal bags, trash cans, parking, phones, restrooms,
water, separate fenced areas for large/active dogs and
"special needs" dogs. Access for the disabled.

CALIFORNIA (CONT'D)

Baldy View Dog Park - Upland
baldyviewdogpark.com
11th Street between Mountain Avenue and San Antonio Avenue
Daily dawn-dusk.
Fenced, 1.3 acres, double-gated entry and exit, grass turf, shade trees, benches, free parking, separate areas for large and small dogs, water stations for dogs.

COLORADO

Grandview Off-Leash Dog Park - Aurora
auroragov.org, (303) 739-7160
17900 E. Quincy Ave. (just east of Pitkin Street, adjacent to Quincy Reservoir on the lake's west side)
Daily dawn-dusk.
Fenced, trash cans, parking, water.

East Boulder Community - Boulder City
bouldercolorado.gov
5660 Sioux Dr.
Daily dawn-dusk.
Fenced, disposal bags, trash cans, parking, water, fenced-off swimming area. Access for the disabled.

Foothills Community Park - Boulder City
bouldercolorado.gov
Locust Avenue and Lee Hill Road, west of Broadway Street
Daily dawn-dusk.
Fenced, 2 acres, separate areas for large and small dogs, disposal bags, trash cans, parking, water. Access for the disabled.

Howard H. Hueston Park - Boulder City
bouldercolorado.gov
34th Street near O'Neal Parkway
Daily dawn-dusk.
Unfenced, trees, benches, tables, trash cans, parking. Dogs must be under voice control and kept in sight at all times. Access for the disabled.

Valmont Dog Park - Boulder City
bouldercolorado.gov
Valmont and Airport roads
Daily dawn-dusk.
Fenced, 3 acres, disposal bags, trash cans, parking, water (available seasonally). Access for the disabled.

Palmer Park - Colorado Springs
springsgov.com
Maizeland Road and Academy Boulevard
Daily 5 a.m.-11 p.m., May-Oct.; 5 a.m.-9 p.m., rest of year.
Fenced, benches, tables, disposal bags, trash cans, parking, restrooms, water. Access for the disabled.

Rampart Dog Park - Colorado Springs
springsgov.com
8270 Lexington Dr. (from the intersection of Lexington Drive and North Union Boulevard, go north on Lexington, then turn left into the park entrance)
Daily 5 a.m.-11 p.m., May-Oct.; 5 a.m.-9 p.m., rest of year.
Fenced, trees, benches, disposal bags, trash cans, parking, water. Access for the disabled.

Barnum Park - Denver
denvergov.org
Hooker Street and West 5th Avenue
Daily dawn-dusk.
Natural barriers (turf with split-rail fencing to delineate boundaries), 3 acres, trees, disposal bags, trash cans, parking, restroom, bulletin board.

Berkeley Park - Denver
denvergov.org
Sheridan Boulevard and West 46th Avenue, west of the lake
Daily dawn-dusk.
Fenced, 2 acres, turf, double-gate entry, trees, disposal bags, trash cans, parking, bulletin board.

Denver Off-Leash Dog Park - Denver
denvergov.org
678 S. Jason St. (behind the Denver Municipal Animal Shelter)
Daily dawn-dusk.
Fenced, grass turf, parking, toys. Access for the disabled.

Fuller Park - Denver
denvergov.org
Franklin Street and East 29th Avenue, northwest section (enter from 29th Avenue)
Daily dawn-dusk.
Fenced, 1 acre, turf, double-gate entry, disposal bags, trash cans, bulletin board, on-street neighborhood parking only.

Green Valley Ranch East Park - Denver
denvergov.org
Jebel Street and East 45th Avenue, southwest section (dog park accessible from parking lot)
Daily dawn-dusk.
Natural barriers (native vegetation and split-rail fencing to delineate boundaries), 2 acres, disposal bags, trash cans, parking.

Kennedy Park - Denver
denvergov.org
Hampden Avenue and South Dayton Street, southwest section
Daily dawn-dusk.
Natural barriers (native vegetation and split-rail fencing to delineate boundaries), 3 acres, disposal bags, trash cans, bulletin board, very limited parking (complex parking lot not open to dog park visitors).

FLORIDA

Happy Tails Canine Park - Bradenton
geocities.com/happytailspark
51st Street West at G.T. Bray Park, about halfway between Manatee Avenue and Cortez Road
Daily dawn-dusk.
Eight-foot fence, 3 acres, trees, benches, tables, disposal bags, trash cans, parking, restrooms nearby, water.

FLORIDA (CONT'D)

Dr. Paul's Memorial Dog Park - Coral Springs
toppetcare.com/petutopiawelcome.html
Sportsplex Drive in the Sportsplex Regional Park Complex
(park off Sportsplex Drive at the west pedestrian entrance)
Daily dawn-9:30 p.m.
Enclosed, lighted, trees, shaded area, paved running path,
picnic table, gazebo, disposal bag dispensers, trash cans,
indoor restroom, separate areas for large and small dogs,
water fountains for dogs and people, dog shower, dog
statues, weatherproof dog agility equipment.

The Dog Park in Lake Ida Park - Delray Beach
pbcgov.com
2929 Lake Ida Rd. (take the Atlantic Avenue West exit off
I-95, proceed west to Congress Avenue, go north on
Congress for 1 mile, turn right onto Lake Ida Road and
proceed east under I-95; park entrance is on the left)
Daily dawn-dusk; closed Thurs. noon-3 for maintenance.
Fenced, 2.5 acres, partial paved pathway, eight shaded
sitting areas, disposal bag dispensers and receptacles,
restrooms and parking nearby, separate fenced areas for
large and small dogs, two canine drinking stations, dog
washing area, information kiosk.

Pooch Pines Dog Park at Okeeheelee Park - Delray Beach
pbcgov.com
7715 Forest Hill Blvd. (off I-95 exit Forest Hill Boulevard,
west to the main Okeeheelee Park entrance on the north
side of the road; follow the park road to the Pooch Pines
sign, turn right and continue to the top of the hill)
Daily dawn-dusk; closed Wed. noon-3 for maintenance.
Fenced, 5 acres, paved pathways, shaded sitting areas,
disposal bag dispensers and receptacles, trash cans,
restrooms and parking nearby, separate areas for large and
small dogs, canine drinking stations, dog washing area.

Bark Park at Snyder Park - Fort Lauderdale
ci.fort-lauderdale.fl.us
3299 S.W. 4th Ave.
Daily 7 a.m.-7:30 p.m., Apr.-Oct.; 7-6:30, rest of year.
Closed Jan. 1 and Dec. 25.
Entry fee varies; canine beach $7.
Fenced, two open-air pavilions, benches, disposal bags,
trash cans, parking, restrooms, water, separate area for
small dogs, two hose stations, water fountains, agility
equipment, small nature area with more than 20 labeled
native trees, canine swimming in East Lake, canine beach
(hours vary). Access for the disabled. **Note:** Dogs must
remain in the car until arrival at Bark Park and are not
permitted in the remainder of Snyder Park.

Dog Wood Off-Leash Park - Gainesville
dogwoodpark.com, (352) 335-1919
5505 S.W. Archer Rd. (1 mile west of I-75)
Tues.-Thurs. 1-4 p.m., Fri. 4-6 p.m., Sat.-Sun. 9-5; closed
Jan. 1 and Dec. 24-25 and 31.
Fee $9 plus tax for the first dog, $3 plus tax for each
additional dog per family.
Six-foot fence, 15 acres, double-gated entry and exit,
jogging trail, hammocks, gazebo, picnic tables, lounge
chairs, swinging and regular benches, multiple clean-up
stations with disposal bags, indoor restrooms, bottled water
and soft drinks for sale, two large swimming ponds for
dogs, wading pools, dog shower, agility course, sunny and
shady areas for small dogs, park-provided tennis balls. Park
also offers a do-it-yourself dog wash, a doggie boutique,
dog day care, and agility and obedience training. All male
dogs over 7 months must be neutered in order to enter the
park. Children under 4 feet tall are not permitted.

Paw Park of Historic Sanford - Sanford
pawparksanford.org
427 French Ave. (US 17/92) in Sanford's Historic District, 20
minutes north of downtown Orlando. From I-4, take the SR
46 exit (exit 101C, Sanford/Mount Dora), proceed east on
SR 46 approximately 4 miles to French Avenue, turn right
(southbound) and get into the left thru-lane; the Paw Park is
on the left just past the Burger King
Daily 7:30 a.m.-8 p.m.
Fenced, double-gated entry, shaded with mature oak trees,
historic lighting, paved walkway, benches, tables, disposal
bag dispensers, parking, self-watering bowls, water misting
station, dog showers, separate area for small dogs,
community bulletin board. Access for the disabled.

Davis Islands Dog Park - Tampa
tampagov.net
1002 Severn St.
Daily dawn-dusk.
Fenced, with two areas at the south end of the island: a
1-acre dry area and a 1.5-acre beach with more than 200
feet of waterfront. Both areas have double-gated entries,
disposal bags, trash cans and water. Designated off-leash
area on the beach.

Gadsden Park - Tampa
tampagov.net
6901 S. MacDill Ave., southwest corner of the grounds
Daily dawn-dusk.
Fenced, 1 acre, double-gated entry, water, disposal bags,
trash cans, benches, tables, shade trees.

Giddens Park - Tampa
tampagov.net
5202 N. 12th St.
Daily dawn-dusk.
Fenced, 1 acre, double-gated entry, drinking fountains for
dogs and people, disposal bags, trash cans, benches,
tables, shade trees.

James Urbanski Dog Park at Al Lopez Park - Tampa
tampagov.net
4810 N. Himes Ave.
Daily dawn-dusk.
Fenced, separate area for small dogs, double-gated entry,
disposal bags, trash cans, benches, tables, shade trees.

FLORIDA (CONT'D)

Palma Ceia Park - Tampa
tampagov.net
2200 Marti St.
Mon.-Fri. 8 a.m.-dusk or 7:15 p.m. (whichever is earlier),
Sat.-Sun. 9 a.m.-dusk or 7:15 p.m. (whichever is earlier).
Fenced, ¾ acre, double-gated entry, disposal bags, trash
cans, benches, tables, shade trees.

Picnic Island Park - Tampa
tampagov.net
7409 Picnic Island Blvd.
Daily dawn-dusk.
Fenced, double-gated entry, disposal bags, trash cans,
benches, tables, shade trees. Designated off-leash area on
beach.

Rowlett Park - Tampa
tampagov.net
2401 E. Yukon St.
Daily dawn-dusk.
Fenced, 1.75 acre, double-gated entry, disposal bags, trash
cans, benches, tables, shade trees, separate areas for large
and small dogs, agility equipment.

Brohard Beach & Paw Park - Venice
venicegov.com
1600 Harbor Dr. S.
Daily 7 a.m.-dusk
Six-foot fence, trees, benches, tables, shelter, disposal bags,
trash cans, parking, water, dog shower, separate area for
small dogs, community bulletin board. Dog Beach is
accessed by a boardwalk from Paw Park. Dogs are
permitted in a restricted area along Brohard Beach as
indicated by beach signs. Access for the disabled.

Woodmere Park & Woodmere Paw Park - Venice
scgov.net
3951 Woodmere Park Blvd. (2 blocks north of US 41 on
Jacaranda Boulevard)
Daily dawn-dusk.
Fenced, 2.5 acres, double-gated entry, trees, benches,
tables, disposal bags, trash cans, parking, restrooms, water,
double-gated section for small dogs near the front gate, dog
shower, community bulletin board.

ILLINOIS

Rover's Run Dog Park - Homewood
hfparks.com, (708) 957-0300
Near 191st Street and Center Avenue in Apollo Park
Daily dawn-dusk.
Annual membership fee $25 (non-residents); $15
(residents). A list of current vaccinations is required.
Fenced, 3 acres, double-gated entry, separate training area
and entrance, benches, covered picnic tables, free parking,
walking path, water fountain for dogs and people.

MICHIGAN

Orion Oaks Bark Park - Lake Orion
oakgov.com
South of Clarkston Road on Joslyn Road (park at the north
Joslyn Road entrance and follow the signs)
Daily half-hour before dawn to half-hour after dusk, or as
posted.
A park pass is required; a daily pass is available at the
Lake Orion Township office (open Mon.-Fri.) on Joslyn Road
south of the park; or at the Independence Oaks County
Park (open daily) on Sashabaw Road, 2.5 miles north of
I-75.
Day pass per private vehicle $12 (non-resident); $7
(resident); $4 (ages 63+). Annual pass per private vehicle
$46 (non-resident); $30 (resident); $28 (ages 63+).
Fenced, 7 acres, trees, benches, tables, disposal bags,
trash cans, parking, portable toilet, water. A portion of Lake
Sixteen is reserved for canine swimming. Access for the
disabled.

Lyon Oaks Bark Park - Lyon Township
oakgov.com
Pontiac Trail between Wixom and Old Plank roads
Daily half-hour before dawn to half-hour after dusk, or as
posted.
A park pass is required and is available at the park.
Day pass per private vehicle $12 (non-resident); $7
(resident); $4 (ages 63+). Annual pass per private vehicle
$46 (non-resident); $30 (resident); $28 (ages 63+).
Fenced, 13 acres of open fields, benches, tables, disposal
bags, trash cans, parking, restrooms, water pump.

MINNESOTA

Note: In the greater Minneapolis area there are multiple
off-leash sites within a 15-minute drive of downtown
Minneapolis/St. Paul. There are additional sites in
rural/suburban areas of the seven-county metropolitan area.
Some parks require a permit for use. Please read
descriptions carefully.

Alimagnet Dog Park - Burnsville (south metro suburb)
alimagnetdogpark.org
1200 Alimagnet Pkwy. (from central St. Paul, go south on
I-35E to the CR 42 exit, east to CR 11, then north on CR
11 to Alimagnet Parkway and turn right; the dog park is on
the right)
Daily 5 a.m.-10 p.m. Permit required; for more information
visit the Web site or phone the Recreation Department at
(952) 895-4500.
Fenced, 7 acres, double-gated entry, wooded areas, open
fields, mowed prairie-grass trail, benches, tables, disposal
bags, trash cans, parking, phones, restrooms, water, pond.

Coates/Dakota County (south metro rural)
co.dakota.mn.us
Blaine Avenue south of CR 46 (160th Street East) in the
center of Dakota County near Coates
Daily 5 a.m.-10 p.m. Permit required.
Fenced, 16 acres of wooded and open spaces with a
walking trail loop, tables, disposal bag dispensers, trash
cans, parking, portable toilets, no surface water; bring your
own water.

MINNESOTA (CONT'D)

Elm Creek Park Reserve - Dayton (northwest metro rural)
threeriversparkdistrict.org
13080 Territorial Rd.
Daily 5 a.m.-dusk. Permit required; day permits are available at the site. Annual special-use permits may be obtained by phoning Park Guest Services at (763) 559-9000.
Fenced, 30 acres with a mowed trail, trees, tables, trash cans, parking, restrooms.

Battle Creek Off-Leash Site - Maplewood (east central metro)
co.ramsey.mn.us
Lower Afton and McKnight roads
Daily dawn-dusk. No permit required.
Partially fenced, 12 acres, tables, trash cans, parking.

Franklin Terrace - Minneapolis
minneapolisparks.org
Franklin Terrace and 30th Avenue South
Daily 6 a.m.-10 p.m. Permit required.
Fully fenced, 1.6 acres, double-gated entry at the east and west ends of the site, bench, disposal bag dispensers, on-street parking.

Lake of the Isles Park - Minneapolis
minneapolisparks.org
Lake of the Isles Parkway and West 28th Street
Daily 6 a.m.-10 p.m. Permit required.
Fully fenced, 3.6 acres, double-gated entry at the northern end of the site, lighted at the southern end, benches, disposal bag dispensers.

Loring Park - Minneapolis
minneapolisparks.org
Maple Street and Harmon Place
Daily 6 a.m.-10 p.m. Permit required.
Fenced, ¼ acre, disposal bag dispensers, limestone boulders for climbing and sitting, crushed limestone surface.

Minnehaha Park - Minneapolis
minneapolisparks.org
Minnehaha Avenue and East 54th Street
Daily 6 a.m.-10 p.m. Permit required.
Partially fenced, 4.2 acres along the Mississippi River (where dogs can swim), disposal bag dispensers, lighted parking area (parking permit required), portable toilet in parking area.

St. Anthony Parkway - Minneapolis
minneapolisparks.org
St. Anthony Parkway off Central Avenue
Daily 6 a.m.-10 p.m. Permit required.
Fully fenced, 2 acres, double-gated entry at the east and west ends of the park, bench, disposal bag dispensers, parking.

Egan Park's Off-Leash Area - Plymouth
ci.plymouth.mn.us
CR 47 in northwest Plymouth, about 2 blocks west of Dunkirk Lane on the south side of CR 47
Daily dawn-dusk. No permit required.
Unfenced, 10 acres, trash cans; bring your own water and disposal bags.

Cleary Lake Regional Park - Prior Lake (south metro rural)
threeriversparkdistrict.org
18106 Texas Ave.
Daily 5 a.m.-dusk. Permit required; day permits are available at the site. Annual special-use permits may be obtained by phoning Park Guest Services at (763) 559-9000.
Fenced, 35 acres, tables, trash cans, parking, restrooms, pond. Trails are mowed in summer, packed in winter.

Lake Sarah Regional Park - Rockford (west metro rural)
threeriversparkdistrict.org
Lake Sarah Drive, 30 miles west of Minneapolis and east of CR 92 (take US 55 west to CR 92, proceed south to Lake Sarah Drive, turn left and then left again onto the first gravel road; the parking lot for the off-leash area is on the left)
Daily 5 a.m.-dusk. Permit required; day permits are available at the site. Annual special-use permits may be obtained by phoning Park Guest Services at (763) 559-9000.
Unfenced, 30 acres, trees, mowed parking area, trash cans, restrooms.

Crow-Hassan Park Reserve - Rogers (northwest metro rural)
threeriversparkdistrict.org
Sylvan Lake Road west of Rogers (from I-94, take the Rogers exit and go south through town to the T intersection, turn right on CR 116 and proceed to CR 203, turn left and follow CR 203 to the park entrance)
Daily 5 a.m.-dusk. Permit required; day permits are available at the site. Annual special-use permits may be obtained by phoning Park Guest Services at (763) 559-9000.
Fenced, 30 acres with a mowed trail, trees, tables, trash cans, parking, restrooms.

Woodview Dog Park - Roseville (central)
co.ramsey.mn.us
Larpenteur Avenue, just east of Dale Street (access gate to main off-leash area is about 100 yards down the bike trail)
Daily dawn-dusk. No permit required.
Partially fenced (along bike trail only), 3 acres, trees, tables, disposal bags, trash cans, parking, water, separate fenced area for small dogs. Access for the disabled.

Arlington-Arkwright (ArlArk) Dog Park - St. Paul
stpaul.gov
Arkwright Street at Arlington Avenue (from I-35E, take the Maryland Avenue exit east to Arkwright Street, then go north; the park is on the right)
Daily dawn-9 p.m. No permit required.
Fenced, 4.5 acres with trails and woods, tables, disposal bags, trash cans, parking. Park users sometimes leave gates open; keep your dog under voice control to prevent escapes.

Rice Creek Off-Leash Site - Shoreview (northeast metro)
co.ramsey.mn.us
Lexington Avenue, just south of CR J
Daily dawn-dusk. No permit required.
Unfenced, 12 acres of flat prairie vegetation, tables, trash cans, parking, small pond.

MINNESOTA (CONT'D)

Otter Lake Dog Park - White Bear Township (northeast suburban)
co.ramsey.mn.us
Otter Lake Road (take I-35E to the CR J exit, then CR J east to Otter Lake Road, following it south to the dog park; the entrance is next to the boat launch)
Daily dawn-dusk. No permit required.
Partially fenced, 10 acres of rolling hills with wooded and open prairie vegetation, separate 1-acre fenced area for small dogs. The park is fenced adjacent to Otter Lake Road and along most of the south boundary, bounded on the east by a large wetland and on the north by Otter Lake.

NEVADA

All Clark County/Las Vegas dog park areas include water, seating and waste receptacles.

Desert Breeze Park Dog Park - Clark County/Las Vegas (NW)
accessclarkcounty.com
8425 W. Spring Mountain Rd. at Durango Drive
Daily 6 a.m.-11 p.m.
Three runs, trees.

Desert Inn Dog Park - Clark County/Las Vegas (SE)
accessclarkcounty.com
3570 Vista del Monte Dr. (near Lamb Boulevard and Boulder Highway)
Daily 6 a.m.-11 p.m.

Dog Fancier's Park - Clark County/Las Vegas (SE)
accessclarkcounty.com, (702) 455-8200
5800 E. Flamingo Rd. at Jimmy Durante Boulevard
Daily 6 a.m.-11 p.m. Since this 12-acre park also is used for dog shows and training, phone ahead to confirm schedule.

Molasky Park Dog Park - Clark County/Las Vegas (SE)
accessclarkcounty.com
1065 E. Twain Ave. (west of Maryland Parkway; dog run is south of Twain Avenue)
Daily 6 a.m.-11 p.m.
Ten acres.

Shadow Rock Dog Park - Clark County/Las Vegas (NE)
accessclarkcounty.com
2650 Los Feliz St. at Lake Mead Boulevard (east of Hollywood Boulevard; dog run is east of the park area)
Daily 6 a.m.-11 p.m.
Tree, two shade shelters.

Silverado Ranch Park Dog Park - Clark County/Las Vegas (SE)
accessclarkcounty.com
9855 S. Gillespie St.
Daily 6 a.m.-11 p.m.
Two runs, one for dogs under 30 pounds and another for dogs over 29 pounds; lights.

Sunset Park - Clark County/Las Vegas (SE)
accessclarkcounty.com
2601 E. Sunset Rd. (closest parking is off Eastern Avenue between Sunset and Warm Springs roads)
Daily 6 a.m.-11 p.m.
Two runs for large and small dogs.

NEW HAMPSHIRE

Derry Dog Park - Derry
derry.nh.us
45 Fordway St.
Daily dawn-dusk.
Fenced, ½ acre, double-gated entry, gazebo, picnic tables, separate area for small dogs, bone-shaped dog pool (open in summer only). Tunnel, seesaw, tire jump and other agility items are provided. Children under 9 are not permitted. Rules are posted on fence inside and out. Parking is free but somewhat limited after 25 vehicles.

NEW YORK

New York City (Manhattan and boroughs)
urbanhound.com
nycgovparks.org

Canine Court, Van Cortlandt Park - Bronx
West 252nd Street and Broadway (enter on the path on 252nd and follow it about 100 feet to the left)
Daily dawn-dusk.
Fenced with two large runs: a basic dog run and a canine agility playground with teeter-totter, hurdles, ladder, three chutes and a hanging tire.

Ewen Park ("John's Run") - Bronx (Riverdale)
Riverdale to Johnson avenues, south of West 232nd Street and down the steps in the clearing on the right
Daily dawn-dusk.
Unfenced, plastic lawn furniture, scenic views.

Seton Park - Bronx (Riverdale)
West 235th Street and Independence Avenue (west of Independence on 235th Street, near the Spuyten Duyvil Library)
Daily dawn-dusk.

Prospect Park - Brooklyn
fidobrooklyn.org
Grand Army Plaza and Flatbush; off-leash areas may be accessed from all park entrances
Daily 9 p.m.-9 a.m. At all other times, dogs must be on a leash; minimum fine for non-compliance $100.
Trees, restrooms (at Long Meadow only; may not be available early in the morning), water (some fountains equipped with troughs for dogs). No separate area for small dogs. Small swimming area in the Long Meadow near the 9th Street entrance. **Note:** Use of the park is at the owner's risk. Dogs may be off-leash with appropriate supervision in three large meadows at the hours specified above; please observe all off-leash rules. Rules are posted online and at park entrances. Dogs must be on a leash at all other places and times.

Owl's Head Park - Brooklyn (Bay Ridge)
68th Street and Shore Road
Tree, grass surface, disposal bags.

Hillside Park - Brooklyn Heights
Columbia Heights and Middagh Street
Daily 24 hours.
Fenced.

NEW YORK (CONT'D)

Palmetto Playground - Brooklyn Heights
Columbia Place and State Street (in the corner by the Brooklyn-Queens Expressway)
Daily 24 hours.
Benches, one park light, water.

Tompkins Square Park - Manhattan (East Village)
East 9th Street at Avenue B
Daily 6 a.m.-midnight.
Benches, picnic tables, water, a canine memorial.

Madison Square Park - Manhattan (Gramercy/Flatiron/ Union Square)
East 24th Street at Fifth Avenue
Daily 6 a.m.-midnight.
Trees, benches, disposal bags, water.

Thomas Jefferson Park - Manhattan (Harlem)
East 112th Street at First Avenue
Daily 24 hours.
Benches, wood chip surface.

J. Hood Wright Park - Manhattan (Inwood/Ft. George/ Washington Heights)
West 173rd Street between Fort Washington Avenue and Haven Avenue

Fishbridge Park - Manhattan (Lower East Side)
Dover Street at Pearl Street, just south of the Brooklyn Bridge
Daily dawn-dusk.
Benches, water hose, wading pool (open in summer only), lockbox for toys, lockbox with newspapers for picking up after your dog.

Peter Detmold Park - Manhattan (Midtown East)
East 49th Street at FDR Drive (behind Beekman Place)
Daily dawn-9 p.m., June-Sept.; dawn-8 p.m., Mar.-May and Oct.-Nov.; dawn-7 p.m., rest of year.
Trees, benches, historical lamps, disposal bags.

Carl Schurz Park - Manhattan (Upper East Side)
East 86th Street at East End Avenue
Daily dawn-1 a.m.
Benches, scoops, pea gravel surface. A second run for small dogs (past the main run, toward the East River) has a scenic view of the river and the 59th Street Bridge.

Riverside Park at 72nd Street - Manhattan (Upper West Side/Morningside Heights)
West 72nd Street
Daily 6 a.m.-1 a.m.
Bench, hanging flowerpots, disposal bags, scoopers.

Riverside Park at 87th Street - Manhattan (Upper West Side/Morningside Heights)
West 87th Street
Daily dawn-dusk.
Separate areas for large and small dogs, water fountain and hose.

Riverside Park at 105th Street - Manhattan (Upper West Side/Morningside Heights)
riversidedog.org
West 105th Street, Riverside Park Central Promenade
Daily dawn-dusk.
Trees, crushed granite surface, benches, disposal bag dispensers, water fountain, water faucet for dogs, separate area for small dogs.

Theodore Roosevelt Park - Manhattan (Upper West Side/Morningside Heights)
West 81st Street at Columbus Avenue
Daily 8 a.m.-10 p.m.
Shade trees, benches, dog water faucet, separate run for small dogs.

Washington Square Park - Manhattan (West Village)
West 4th Street at Thompson Street
Daily 6 a.m.-midnight.
Trees, pea gravel surface, benches, scoopers, water hose, water bowls.

Doughboy Plaza - Queens (Woodside)
Woodside Avenue from 54th to 56th streets (also south of Woodside at 56th Street) at Windmuller Park
Daily dawn-dusk.
Fenced, trash can.

NORTH CAROLINA

Down East Dog Park - New Bern
newbern-nc.org
303 Glenburnie Dr. in Glenburnie Park
Daily dawn-dusk.
Annual fee $35 for the first dog, $20 for each additional dog. Weekly pass $5. Proof of current rabies vaccination is required. Phone (252) 639-7588 for more information.
Fenced. The main 1-acre area is for large dogs over 25 pounds, but dogs of any size may use it; a separate area is set aside for puppies and small dogs.

OHIO

Mt. Airy Dog Park - Cincinnati
cincinnati-oh.gov
Westwood Northern Boulevard in Mt. Airy Forest's Highpoint Picnic Area, between Montana Avenue and North Bend Road
Daily dawn-dusk.
Fenced, 2 acres, trees, benches, tables, shelter, trash cans, parking, restrooms, water. Access for the disabled.

Big Walnut Dog Park - Columbus
bigwalnutdogpark.com
5000 E. Livingston Ave. in Big Walnut Park (across from Walnut Ridge High School)
Daily 7 a.m.-11 p.m.
Fenced, 3 acres, two double-gated entries, swimming pond, shade trees, picnic tables, paved parking; no restrictions on breeds or spay/neuter.

OREGON

Alton Baker Park - Eugene
eugene-or.gov
South of Leo Harris Parkway (park in the lot south of Autzen Stadium and cross the pedestrian bridge to the dog park)
Daily 6 a.m.-11 p.m.
Fenced, benches, tables, simple shelters for protection from sun and rain, disposal bag receptacles, water.

Amazon Park - Eugene
eugene-or.gov
East of 29th Street and Amazon Parkway
Daily 6 a.m.-11 p.m.
Fenced, benches, tables, simple shelters for protection from sun and rain, disposal bag receptacles, water, parking nearby.

OREGON (CONT'D)

Candlelight Park - Eugene
eugene-or.gov
Royal Avenue and Throne Drive
Daily 6 a.m.-11 p.m.
Fenced, benches, tables, disposal bag receptacles.

Wayne Morse Family Farm - Eugene
eugene-or.gov
Crest Drive and Lincoln Street (park in the main parking area at 595 Crest Dr. and take the trail east)
Daily 6 a.m.-11 p.m.
Fenced, benches, tables, simple shelters for protection from sun and rain, disposal bag receptacles, water.

Brentwood Park - Portland
portlandonline.com
Southeast 60th Avenue and Duke Street
Daily 5 a.m.-midnight.
Fenced.

Chimney Park - Portland
portlandonline.com
9360 N. Columbia Blvd.
Daily 5 a.m.-midnight.
Fenced, 6 acres of off-leash meadow and trails. Dogs should be under excellent voice command.

East Delta Park - Portland
portlandonline.com
North Denver Avenue and Martin Luther King Jr. Boulevard (off I-5 exit 307 across from the East Delta Sports Complex)
Daily 5 a.m.-midnight, May-Oct. (open during dry season only).
Fenced, 5 acres of off-leash field, trees, benches; bring your own water. Dogs are not allowed on the sports fields.

Gabriel Park - Portland
portlandonline.com
Southwest 45th Avenue and Vermont Street
Daily 5 a.m.-midnight, May-Oct. (open during dry season only).
Fenced, off-leash area, trees, picnic tables, water. Dogs must remain leashed when not in the off-leash area.

Normandale Park - Portland
portlandonline.com
Northeast 57th Avenue and Halsey Street
Daily 5 a.m.-midnight.
Fenced.

TEXAS

White Rock Lake Dog Park - Dallas
whiterockdogpark.com
Mockingbird Point within White Rock Lake Park
Daily 5 a.m.-midnight (weather permitting); closed for maintenance second and fourth Mon. of the month.
Fenced, 2.5 acres, trees, benches, disposal bags, trash cans, parking, restrooms, water fountains, separate fenced areas for large and small dogs, fenced swimming area for dogs in White Rock Lake.

Jack Carter Park - Plano
plano.gov
Pleasant Valley Drive and Spring Creek Parkway (½ block north of the intersection on Pleasant Valley Drive)
Daily dawn-dusk (weather permitting); closed for maintenance first and third Tues. of the month.
Fenced, 2 acres, double-gated entry, benches, disposal bags, trash cans, parking, water fountains for dogs and people.

VIRGINIA

Note: Disposal bag receptacles are provided at Alexandria parks; patrons must provide their own bags.

Ben Brenman Park - Alexandria
alexandriava.gov
Cameron Station along Backlick Creek
Daily 6 a.m.-10 p.m.
Fenced, disposal bag receptacles, trash cans, parking.

Dog Park - Alexandria
alexandriava.gov
5000 block of Duke Street east of the Charles E. Beatley Jr. Library
Daily 6 a.m.-10 p.m.
Fenced, disposal bag receptacles, trash cans, parking.

Montgomery Park - Alexandria
alexandriava.gov
Fairfax and 1st streets
Daily 6 a.m.-10 p.m.
Fenced, disposal bag receptacles, trash cans, parking.

Simpson Stadium Park - Alexandria
alexandriava.gov
Monroe Avenue
Daily 6 a.m.-10 p.m.
Fenced, disposal bag receptacles, trash cans, parking, water fountains for dogs.

Off-leash, unfenced, under voice control areas:

Braddock Road - Alexandria
alexandriava.gov
Southeast corner of Braddock Road and Commonwealth Avenue
Daily 6 a.m.-10 p.m.
Unfenced.

Chambliss Street - Alexandria
alexandriava.gov
Chambliss Street at Grigsby Avenue, south of the tennis courts
Daily 6 a.m.-10 p.m.
Unfenced; area is marked by traffic barriers.

Chinquapin Park - Alexandria
alexandriava.gov
King Street at the east end of the loop road
Daily 6 a.m.-10 p.m.
Unfenced; area is marked by traffic barriers.

Edison Street - Alexandria
alexandriava.gov
Edison Street, west of the cul-de-sac between the bike trail and Berkey Photo Processing
Daily 6 a.m.-10 p.m.
Unfenced; area is marked by traffic barriers.

VIRGINIA (CONT'D)

Ft. Williams - Alexandria
alexandriava.gov
Ft. Williams and New Ft. Williams Parkway
Daily 6 a.m.-10 p.m.
Unfenced; area is marked by traffic barriers.

Founders Park - Alexandria
alexandriava.gov
Oronoco Street and Union Street, northeast corner
Daily 6 a.m.-10 p.m.
Unfenced; 100-by-100-foot area is marked by traffic barriers.

Hooff's Run - Alexandria
alexandriava.gov
East of Commonwealth Avenue between Oak and Chapman streets
Daily 6 a.m.-10 p.m.
Unfenced; area is marked by traffic barriers.

Monticello Park - Alexandria
alexandriava.gov
Beverly Drive, east of the entrance
Daily 6 a.m.-10 p.m.
Unfenced; 50-by-200-foot area is marked by traffic barriers.

North Fort Ward Park - Alexandria
alexandriava.gov
Braddock Road, east side of entrance
Daily 6 a.m.-10 p.m.
Unfenced; 100-by-100-foot area is marked by traffic barriers.

Tarleton Park - Alexandria
alexandriava.gov
Mill Run west of Gordon Street
Daily 6 a.m.-10 p.m.
Unfenced.

Timberbranch Parkway - Alexandria
alexandriava.gov
Median to Timberbranch Parkway between Braddock Road and Oakley Place
Daily 6 a.m.-10 p.m.
Unfenced; area is marked by traffic barriers.

Windmill Hill Park - Alexandria
alexandriava.gov
Gibbon and Union streets
Daily 6 a.m.-10 p.m.
Unfenced.

W&OD Railroad - Alexandria
alexandriava.gov
Raymond Avenue (200 feet of the W&OD Railroad right-of-way south of Raymond)
Daily 6 a.m.-10 p.m.
Unfenced; area is marked by traffic barriers.

Benjamin Banneker Park - Arlington County
arlingtondogs.org
1600 block of North Sycamore Street (take I-66 west to Sycamore Street/exit 69, turn left on Sycamore and proceed past the East Falls Church Metro Station, turn right onto North 16th Street and take the first right, which dead-ends at the dog exercise area)
Daily dawn to half-hour after dusk.
Fully fenced, 11 acres, picnic table, benches, water.

Fort Barnard Park - Arlington County
arlingtondogs.org
South Pollard Street and South Walter Reed Drive (from Rte. 50, take Glebe Road south, turn right on South Walter Reed Drive and proceed to Pollard Street; the park is on the right)
Daily dawn to half-hour after dusk.
Fully fenced, picnic table, benches, water.

Glencarlyn Park - Arlington County
arlingtondogs.org
301 S. Harrison St. (from Rte. 50, head west to Carlin Springs Road, exit right and then turn left at the stop sign, pass under Rte. 50 and follow Carlin Springs to 4th Street, turn left on 4th Street and proceed 5 blocks until the road ends at the Glencarlyn Park sign, following the park road until it ends; park and walk over a small bridge and stream to the exercise area)
Daily dawn to half-hour after dusk.
Unfenced area near a creek and woods, picnic table, benches.

Shirlington Park - Arlington County
arlingtondogs.org
2601 S. Arlington Mill Dr., bordering South Four Mile Run between Shirlington Road and South Walter Reed Drive along the bicycle path between a storage facility and the water, near but not in Jennie Dean Park (from South Four Mile Run, turn south onto Nelson and park behind the storage facility; there are no signs indicating the dog park)
Daily dawn to half-hour after dusk.
Partially fenced, picnic table, benches, water.

Towers Park - Arlington County
arlingtondogs.org
801 S. Scott St., behind the tennis courts
Daily dawn to half-hour after dusk.
Fully fenced, 3.5 acres, separate small dog area, parking.

Red Wing Park - Virginia Beach
vbgov.com
1398 General Booth Blvd.
Daily 7:30 a.m.-dusk.
Annual fee for first-time visitors $10; owners must register at the park office, show proof of pet's rabies shot and vaccines, and obtain a city dog license.
Fenced, benches, disposal bags, parking, restrooms, water. Access for the disabled.

Woodstock Community Park - Virginia Beach
vbgov.com
5709 Providence Rd.
Daily 7:30 a.m.-dusk.
Annual fee for first-time visitors $10; owners must register at the park office, show proof of pet's rabies shot and vaccines, and obtain a city dog license.
Fenced, benches, disposal bags, restrooms, parking. Access for the disabled.

WASHINGTON

I-5 Colonnade Park - Seattle
coladog.org
Lakeview Boulevard and Franklin Avenue East in the
Eastlake neighborhood beneath I-5, south of East Howe
Street
Daily 6 a.m.-11 p.m.
Fenced, 1.2 acres, double-gated entry, water fountain for
dogs; the I-5 freeway deck provides shelter from the
elements.

I-90 "Blue Dog Pond" - Seattle
coladog.org
Martin Luther King Jr. Way and South Massachusetts
Street, on the northwest corner
Daily 6 a.m.-11 p.m.
Fenced, 1 acre, parking, water fountain for dogs, Blue Dog
sculpture. No off-leash areas in I-90 Lid Park, just east of
Blue Dog Pond.

Dr. Jose Rizal Park - Seattle
coladog.org
1008 12th Ave. S. on North Beacon Hill; off-leash area is in
the lower portion of the park
Daily 6 a.m.-11 p.m.
Fenced, 4 acres, double-gated entry, parking, water fountain
for dogs, scenic view of downtown.

Genesee Park - Seattle
coladog.org
46th Avenue South and South Genesee Street
Daily 6 a.m.-11 p.m.
Fenced, 3 acres, double-gated entry, parking, water fountain
for dogs.

Golden Gardens Park - Seattle
coladog.org
8498 Seaview Pl. N.W. in Ballard
Daily 6 a.m.-11 p.m.
Fenced, 1 acre, lighted, parking, water fountain for dogs.
The off-leash area is in the upper (eastern) portion of the
park; dogs are not allowed on the lower beach area.

Magnuson Park - Seattle
coladog.org
6500 Sandpoint Way N.E. (enter the park at 74th Street
and drive to the end of the road)
Daily 6 a.m.-11 p.m.
Fenced, 9 acres, double-gated entry, shelter, parking,
separate area for small/shy dogs, water fountain for dogs,
beach access.

Northacres Park - Seattle
coladog.org
North 130th Street, west of I-5; off-leash area is in the
northeast corner of the park at 12530 Third Ave. N.E., north
of the ball field. Parking is available on the west side of the
park along 1st Street Northeast and on the south side along
North 125th Street
Daily 6 a.m.-11 p.m.
Fenced, double-gated entry, parking, water fountain for
dogs.

Plymouth Pillars Park - Seattle
coladog.org
Boren Avenue and Pike Street on Capitol Hill above I-5
Daily 6 a.m.-11 p.m.
Fenced, 9,800 square feet, double-gated entry, water
fountain for dogs, scenic view of downtown Seattle.

Regrade Park - Seattle
coladog.org
3rd Avenue and Bell Street, downtown
Fenced, 13,000 square feet, double-gated entry, water
fountain for dogs.

Westcrest Park - Seattle
coladog.org
8806 8th Ave. S.W. in West Seattle
Daily 6 a.m.-11 p.m.
Fenced, 5 acres, parking, water fountain for dogs. The
off-leash area is along the east side of the reservoir.

Woodland Park - Seattle
coladog.org
West Green Lake Way North, west of the tennis courts
Daily 6 a.m.-11 p.m.
Fenced, 1 acre, double-gated entry, parking, water fountain
for dogs.

SCRAPS Off-Leash Park - Spokane
spokanecounty.org
26715 E. Spokane Bridge Rd. in Gateway Park
Daily dawn-dusk.
Fenced, 3.5 acres, grass and wooded walking area,
double-gated entry, parking, water fountain for dogs (not
available in winter), restrooms, disposal bags, trash cans.
Access for the disabled.

Canada

ALBERTA

91 Street Right of Way - Edmonton
gov.edmonton.ab.ca, (780) 496-1475
Berm east of 91 Street from 10 Avenue north to Whitemud
Freeway and east to 76 Street
Unfenced.

Buena Vista Great Meadow - Edmonton
gov.edmonton.ab.ca, (780) 496-1475
North of Laurier Park and Buena Vista Drive and south of
Melton Ravine in the vicinity of 88 Avenue
Unfenced; area does not include the pedestrian bridge
access trail, Yorath property or the trail north to McKenzie
Ravine. This is a hot-air balloon site, so please leash your
dog during balloon launches.

Hermitage Park North - Edmonton
gov.edmonton.ab.ca, (780) 496-1475
129 Avenue to 137 Avenue; also 22 Street along the
riverbank where signs designate an off-leash area.
Unfenced. This is a multiuse area in the valley north of the
park's fishing pond and picnic area.

Jackie Parker Park - Edmonton
gov.edmonton.ab.ca, (780) 496-1475
Whitemud Freeway and 50th Street
Unfenced. Includes the area south of the 44 Avenue
entrance; dogs are not allowed on the golf course.

Keehewin Blackmud - Edmonton
gov.edmonton.ab.ca, (780) 496-1475
Pipeline corridor, 104 Street and 20 Avenue to the south
end of 109 Street (excludes Bearspaw Drive West and
Blackmud Creek and Ravine)
Unfenced.

Kennedale - Edmonton
gov.edmonton.ab.ca, (780) 496-1475
Ravine west of the 40 Street loop, west to 47 Street and
the top of the bank
Unfenced.

Lauderdale - Edmonton
gov.edmonton.ab.ca, (780) 496-1475
South end of Grand Trunk Park, from 127 to 129 Avenue
and 113A to 109 Street
Unfenced.

Mill Creek Ravine - Edmonton
gov.edmonton.ab.ca, (780) 496-1475
68 Avenue and 93 Street, accessible from the west or north
sides of Argyll Park
Unfenced. A granular trail along the bottom of the ravine
leads to the Whyte (82) Avenue overpass.

Terwillegar Park - Edmonton
gov.edmonton.ab.ca, (780) 496-1475
Rabbit Hill Road
Unfenced. This is a multiuse area.

MANITOBA

Bourkevale Park - Winnipeg
winnipeg.ca
100 Ferry Rd., south of the dike along the riverbank
Daily 6 a.m.-10 p.m.
Unfenced, trash cans, parking; bring your own disposal
bags.

Juba Park & Pioneer Avenue - Winnipeg
winnipeg.ca
Pioneer Avenue, all vacant land west of the walkway to
Juba Park
Daily 6 a.m.-10 p.m.
Unfenced, trash cans, parking; bring your own disposal
bags.

Kil-Cona Park - Winnipeg
winnipeg.ca
Lagimodiere Boulevard in the area north of the west parking
lot
Daily 6 a.m.-10 p.m.
Unfenced, trash cans, parking; bring your own disposal
bags.

King's Park - Winnipeg
winnipeg.ca
King's Drive, south end of the park, south of the lake
Daily 6 a.m.-10 p.m.
Unfenced, trash cans, parking; bring your own disposal
bags.

Little Mountain Park - Winnipeg
winnipeg.ca
West side of the park adjacent to Klimpike Road entrance
Daily 6 a.m.-10 p.m.
Unfenced, trash cans, parking; bring your own disposal
bags.

Maple Grove Park - Winnipeg
winnipeg.ca
Frobisher Road, north area of the park
Daily 6 a.m.-10 p.m.
Unfenced, trash cans, parking; bring your own disposal
bags.

Mazenod Park - Winnipeg
winnipeg.ca
Area surrounding retention pond, bordered by Mazenod
Road, Camiel Sys Street and Beghin Street
Daily 6 a.m.-10 p.m.
Unfenced, trash cans, parking; bring your own disposal
bags.

Westview Park - Winnipeg
winnipeg.ca
Midland Street; entire park is an off-leash area
Daily 6 a.m.-10 p.m.
Unfenced, trash cans, parking; bring your own disposal
bags.

Worosworth Park - Winnipeg
winnipeg.ca
Northeast of King Edward Avenue and Park Lane
Daily 6 a.m.-10 p.m.
Unfenced, trash cans, parking; bring your own disposal
bags.

United States

CALIFORNIA

◈ Disneyland® Resort

(714) 781-4565, 1313 S. Harbor Blvd. via I-5 Disneyland Drive and Disney Way exits, Anaheim
Disneyland® Resort consists of two family-oriented theme parks — Disneyland® and Disney's California Adventure™ — and the shops, restaurants and entertainment of Downtown Disney®. Indoor kennel facilities. Both theme parks are open daily with extended hours during the summer, on some holidays and on weekends. Admission to either park $69; $67 (ages 60+); $59 (ages 3-9). Parking fee. disneyland.disney.go.com

◈ SeaWorld

(619) 226-3901 or (800) 380-3203, 500 SeaWorld Dr., San Diego
SeaWorld offers animal shows, rides and playgrounds, a marina and exhibits featuring marine creatures from around the world. Pet facility provided for a nominal charge on a first-come, first-serve basis. Park open daily at 9 or 10, mid-June through Labor Day; at 10, rest of year. Closing times vary. Hours vary and may be extended during summer and holiday periods; phone ahead. Admission $65; $55 (ages 3-9). Parking fee. www.seaworld.com/

◈ Universal Studios Hollywood

(800) 864-8377, off Hollywood Freeway (US 101) at Lankershim Boulevard, Universal City
In addition to thrill rides and attractions, Universal Studios gives visitors a behind-the-scenes look at the workings of a major film and TV studio. Complimentary kennel service. Park open daily 9-9, in summer; 10-6, rest of year. Box office closes nightly at 5, in summer; at 4, rest of year. Admission $67; $57 (under 48 inches tall). Parking fee. www.universalstudioshollywood.com

DISTRICT OF COLUMBIA

◈ Washington Monument

(202) 426-6841, 15th Street and Constitution Avenue N.W., Washington, D.C.
This instantly recognizable 555-foot marble obelisk commemorates our nation's first president and is surrounded by expansive grounds. Pets on leash. Daily 9-4:45; closed Dec. 25. Free. www.nps.gov/wamo

FLORIDA

◈ Busch Gardens Tampa Bay

(866) 353-8622 or (888) 800-5447, 3000 E. Busch Blvd., Tampa
This African-themed family entertainment park and outstanding zoological facility features all kinds of thrill rides and numerous opportunities for animal observation. Indoor kennel facilities. Generally open daily at 9 or 10; closing times vary. Phone ahead to confirm hours. Admission $67.95; $57.95 (ages 3-9). Parking fee. www.buschgardens.com

◈ SeaWorld Orlando

(407) 351-3600 or (800) 327-2424, 7007 SeaWorld Dr. at I-4 and SR 528 (Beachline Expressway), Orlando
This marine life adventure park presents crowd-pleasing animal shows starring a family of performing killer whales. SeaWorld also features numerous attractions and rides, including a floorless roller coaster, penguin encounter area and simulated helicopter ride. Air-conditioned kennels. Park open daily at 9; closing times vary. Phone ahead to confirm hours. Admission $74.95; $64.95 (ages 3-9). Parking fee. www.seaworld.com

◈ Universal Orlando® Resort

(407) 363-8000, off I-4 exit 75A (eastbound) or 74B (westbound) following signs, Orlando
At Universal Orlando you can "ride the movies" at the Universal Studios® theme park, cavort with superheroes and cartoon characters at Universal's Islands of Adventure® theme park, or visit the specialty shops, themed restaurants and entertainment venues at Universal CityWalk®. Air-conditioned kennels. Theme parks open daily at 9; closing times vary by season. Phone ahead to confirm hours. CityWalk open daily 11 a.m.-2 a.m. One-day admission to either theme park $75; $63 (ages 3-9). Individual CityWalk venue charges vary. Parking fee. www.universalorlando.com

◈ Walt Disney World® Resort

(407) 824-4321 or (407) 934-7639, theme parks accessible from US 192, Osceola Parkway and several I-4 exits, Lake Buena Vista
Walt Disney World has — count 'em — four theme parks: Magic Kingdom® Park, Epcot®, Disney's Animal Kingdom® Theme Park and Disney's Hollywood Studios,™ plus shopping, dining and entertainment at the Downtown Disney® area. Air-conditioned kennels. Theme parks generally open daily at 9; closing times vary. One-day, one-park admission $75; $63 (ages 3-9). Parking fee. www.DisneyWorld.com

GEORGIA

◈ Six Flags Over Georgia

(770) 948-9290, 275 Riverside Pkwy. (off I-20), Austell
Six Flags offers rides, attractions, live shows and a July 4 fireworks display. Kennel facilities. Park open daily at 10, late May to mid-Aug.; Sat.-Sun. at 10:30, mid-Mar. to late May and mid-Aug. to late Sept. Closing times vary. Admission $39.99; $29.99 (under 48 inches tall); free (ages 0-2). Parking fee. www.sixflags.com

ILLINOIS

 Six Flags Great America

(847) 249-4636 or (847) 249-1776, 542 SR 21N, Gurnee
Batman the Ride, Iron Wolf and Raging Bull are among
the thrill rides at this family theme park, which also has a
section of rides and attractions for children under 54
inches tall. Kennel facilities. Park open daily at 10, late
May to mid.-Sept.; Sat.-Sun. at 10, mid-Sept. to late Oct.
Closing times vary; phone ahead to confirm hours.
Admission $58.99; $29.99 (under 48 inches tall); free
(ages 0-2). Parking fee. www.sixflags.com

IOWA

 Pella Historical Village

(641) 628-2409 or (641) 628-4311, 507 Franklin St., Pella
A country store, log cabin, grist mill, windmill, smithy and
other buildings (including Wyatt Earp's boyhood home) are
reminders of this town's Dutch Heritage. Pets on leash
(grounds only). Mon.-Sat. 9-5, Mar.-Dec. Admission $8; $2
(ages 5-18).

MASSACHUSETTS

 Bunker Hill Monument

(617) 242-5641, in Monument Square on Breed's Hill,
Charlestown
Part of Boston National Historical Park, this 221-foot-tall
granite obelisk commemorates the site of the Battle of
Bunker Hill, which occurred on June 17, 1775. Pets on
leash (grounds only); must pick up after pet. Visitor lodge
and exhibits daily 9-5. Free. www.nps.gov/bost/Bunker_Hill/
htm

MISSISSIPPI

 Vicksburg National Military Park

(601) 636-0583, entered via I-20 exit 4B, then .2 miles
west on Clay St. (US 80)
More than 1,260 memorials, monuments, statues, tablets,
bronze portraits and markers honor the Union and
Confederate troops who engaged in the siege of
Vicksburg in 1863. Pets on leash. Grounds open daily
dawn-dusk. Visitor center daily 8-5. Admission $8 per
private vehicle. www.nps.gov/vick

MISSOURI

 The Gateway Arch

(877) 982-1410, Memorial Drive and Market Street, St.
Louis
This curved, stainless steel monument soars 630 feet high
and symbolizes the gateway to the West. A tram ride
takes visitors to an observation deck. Pets on leash
(grounds only). Tram ticket center open daily 8 a.m.-10
p.m., Memorial Day-Labor Day; 9-6, rest of year. Closed
Jan. 1, Thanksgiving and Dec. 25. Tram ride $10; $5
(ages 3-15). www.gatewayarch.com

NORTH CAROLINA

 Carowinds Theme Park

(704) 588-2600, (803) 548-5300 or (800) 888-4386, 10
miles south on I-77 to exit 90, Charlotte
Depicting the past and present of the Carolinas, the
themed areas at this park offer roller coasters, water rides,
children's play areas and other family entertainment.
Air-conditioned kennels. Park open daily at 10, early June
to mid-Aug.; Sat.-Sun. at 10, mid-Mar. to early June and
mid-Aug. to early Oct. Closing times vary; phone ahead to
confirm hours. Admission $37.99; $21.99 (ages 3-6, ages
62+ and under 48 inches tall). Parking fee.
www.carowinds.com

OHIO

 Kings Island

(513) 754-5700 or (800) 288-0808, Kings Island Drive (off
I-71 exits 24 and 25), Kings Mills
Kings Island is a family entertainment park featuring 15
hair-raising roller coasters; Boomerang Bay, a 15-acre
water park; costumed cartoon characters; and a variety of
live shows. Kennel facilities (fee). Park open daily at 10,
May 22-Aug. 30; some Fri., Sat. and Sun., mid-Apr. to
mid-May and early Sept.-Nov. 1 (opening times vary).
Phone ahead to confirm hours. Admission $47.99; $30.99
(ages 3-6, ages 62+ and under 48 inches tall). Prices may
vary. Parking fee. www.visitkingsisland.com

PENNSYLVANIA

 Hersheypark

(800) 437-7439, 100 W. Hersheypark Dr. (just off SR 743
and US 422), Hershey
Hersheypark has more than 65 rides and attractions —
including 11 roller coasters — plus live entertainment.
Visitors can enjoy a marine mammal show, song and
dance reviews and concerts highlighting big-name
performers. Zooamerica North American Wildlife Park
covers 11 acres. Kennel facilities. Park open daily at 10,
Memorial Day-Labor Day; Fri.-Sun. at 10, May 1-Sun.
before Memorial Day weekend; Sat.-Sun. at 10, day after
Labor Day-late Sept. Closing times vary; phone ahead to
confirm hours. Admission (Memorial Day weekend-late
Sept.) $51.95; $30.95 (ages 3-8 and 55-69); $20.95 (ages
70+). Admission (early May-late May) $43.95; $24.95
(ages 3-8 and 55-69); $17.95 (ages 70+). Parking fee.
www.hersheypark.com

TEXAS

 SeaWorld San Antonio

(800) 700-7786, 10500 SeaWorld Dr. (off SR 151 at the junction of Westover Hills Boulevard and Ellison Drive), San Antonio
A 250-acre marine life adventure park, SeaWorld San Antonio entertains and educates with shark exhibits, a penguin habitat and high-energy whale and dolphin shows. Such thrill rides as Journey to Atlantis, the Steel Eel coaster and Texas Splashdown add to the excitement. Outdoor kennel facilities (owner must provide food). Park open daily at 10, early Mar.-late Nov.; closing times vary. Phone ahead to confirm hours. Admission $52.99; $44.99 (ages 3-9). Prices may vary. Parking fee. www.seaworld.com

 Six Flags Over Texas

(817) 530-6000, 2201 Road to Six Flags (at the junction of I-30 and SR 360 exit 30), Arlington
Themed areas, each featuring thrill rides, food and entertainment, depict Texas under six different flags: Spain, France, Mexico, the Republic of Texas, the Confederate States of America and the United States. Air-conditioned kennels (fee). Park open daily, mid-May to late Aug.; Sat.-Sun. and some Fri., Feb. 28-May 10, Sept. 5-Nov. 1 and day after Thanksgiving-Dec. 31. Schedule varies; phone ahead. Admission $49.99; $31 (under 48 inches tall); free (ages 0-2). Prices may vary. Parking fee. www.sixflags.com

VIRGINIA

 Busch Gardens Europe

(800) 343-7946, 3 miles east on US 60 or off I-64 exit 243A, Williamsburg
This European-themed adventure park offers something for the entire family, from thrill rides to dance and music shows to villages representing England, Germany, France and other nations. Kennel facilities (England parking lot); fee $6 per pet per day. Park open daily at 10, Mar.-Dec.; days and closing times vary. Phone ahead to confirm schedule. Admission $59.95; $49.95 (ages 3-9). Parking fee. www.buschgardens.com/va

 Kings Dominion

(804) 876-5000, 16000 Theme Park Way (on SR 30 ½ mile east off I-95 exit 98), Doswell
This 400-acre park features a water park, thrill rides, children's play areas, costumed characters, live shows and specialty shopping. Kennel facilities (fee); water provided, but not food. Park open daily, Memorial Day-Labor Day; Fri.-Sun., late Mar.-day before Memorial Day and first Fri. after Labor Day-late Oct. Hours vary seasonally; phone ahead. Admission $54.99; $31.99 (ages 62+ and under 48 inches tall); free (ages 0-2). Parking fee. www.kingsdominion.com

WASHINGTON

 Hovander Homestead

(360) 384-3444, 1 mile south via Hovander Road, Ferndale
This restored house, dating from 1903 and furnished with antiques, is within a large park encompassing gardens, picnic sites and a children's farm area. Pets on leash (grounds only). Grounds open daily 8 a.m.-dusk. House open Thurs.-Sun. noon-4:30, early June-Labor Day; Sat.-Sun. noon-4:30, in May. House $1; 50 cents (ages 5-12). www.co.whatcom.wa.us/parks/hovander/hovander.jsp

Canada

ONTARIO

Upper Canada Village

(613) 543-4328 or (800) 437-2233, 7 miles (11 kilometers) east on CR 2 off Hwy. 401, Morrisburg
Upper Canada Village re-creates life during the 1860s through a working community of artisans and costumed interpreters who perform chores typical of the era. Pets on leash (grounds only). Daily 9:30-5, late May-early Oct. Village admission $17.95; $16.95 (ages 66+); $11.95 (students with ID); $7.95 (ages 5-12); $2.50 (ages 2-4). www.uppercanadavillage.com

Canada's Wonderland

(905) 832-7000 or (905) 832-8131, off Hwy. 400 (Rutherford Road exit northbound or Major MacKenzie Drive E. exit southbound) at 9580 Jane St., Vaughan
Thrill rides at this theme park include the hair-raising Behemoth rollercoaster and the Backlot Stunt Coaster, while Nickelodeon Central and Hanna-Barbera Land will entertain little ones. Air-conditioned kennels (fee). Park open daily at 10, late May-Labour Day; open some weekends, early to late May and day after Labour Day-late Oct. Closing times vary; phone ahead to confirm hours. Grounds admission $27.26. Passport for grounds admission and most rides $51.40; $26.45 (ages 3-6 and 60+). Parking fee. www.canadaswonderland.com

NATIONAL PUBLIC LANDS

The National Public Lands listed below permit pets on a leash. Keep in mind that animals may be prohibited from entering public buildings and even some areas outdoors, particularly those that are ecologically sensitive. Where swimming is permitted, there are usually no lifeguards on duty; people and pets swim at their own risk. Specific pet policies vary from park to park and are subject to change. Always check in advance regarding any applicable regulations and to confirm that pets are still permitted where you are going.

Be aware of dangers to your pet in natural areas, including snakes, ticks and fast-moving currents in rivers and streams. An unleashed dog may chase after a wild animal and become separated from its owner, increasing the risk of loss or injury. Never leave your pet unattended. Keep him leashed or crated at all times. Follow park guidelines faithfully, and monitor your pet's behavior; the National Park Service may confiscate pets that harm wildlife or other visitors. *For additional information on outdoor vacations, see The Great Outdoors, p. 16.*

United States

ALABAMA

Conecuh National Forest
On the Alabama-Florida border.
(334) 222-2555
🚲 ⛺ 🥾 🧺 🏊

Eufaula National Wildlife Refuge
On the Chattahoochee River.
(334) 687-4065
🏠

Horseshoe Bend National Military Park
12 mi. north of Dadeville on SR 49.
(256) 234-7111
🥾 🧺 🏠

Talladega National Forest
In central Alabama.
(256) 362-2909
⛺ 🥾 🧺 🏊

Tuskegee National Forest
Northeast of Tuskegee.
(334) 727-2652
⛺ 🥾 🧺

William B. Bankhead National Forest
In northwestern Alabama.
(205) 489-5111
🚲 ⛺ 🥾 🧺 🏊 🏠

Wheeler National Wildlife Refuge
Between Decatur and Huntsville.
(256) 350-6639
🚲 🥾 🧺 🏠

ALASKA

Chugach National Forest
Along the Gulf of Alaska from Cape Suckling to Seward.
(907) 743-9500
⛺ 🥾 🧺 🏠

Denali National Park and Preserve
In south-central Alaska.
(907) 683-2294
⛺ 🥾 🧺 🏠 🍴

Glacier Bay National Park and Preserve
North of Cross Sound to the Canadian border.
(907) 697-2230
⛺ 🥾 🏠

Kenai Fjords National Park
Southeastern side of the Kenai Peninsula.
(907) 224-7500 or (907) 224-2132
⛺ 🥾 🧺 🏠

Lake Clark National Park and Preserve
In southern Alaska.
(907) 644-3626
⛺ 🏠

Tongass National Forest
In southeastern Alaska.
(907) 225-3101 or (907) 228-6220
⛺ 🥾 🧺 🏠

Wrangell-St. Elias National Park and Preserve
In southeastern Alaska, northwest of Tongass National Forest.
(907) 822-5234
⛺ 🥾 🧺 🏠

ARIZONA

Apache-Sitgreaves National Forests
In east-central Arizona.
(928) 333-4301
🚲 ⛺ 🥾 🧺 🏠 🍴

Bill Williams River National Wildlife Refuge
Off SR 95 near Parker.
(928) 667-4144
🥾 🧺 🏠

Buenos Aires National Wildlife Refuge
North of Sasabe on SR 286.
(520) 823-4251
⛺ 🥾 🧺 🏠

Coconino National Forest
In north-central Arizona.
(928) 527-3600
🚲 ⛺ 🥾 🧺 🏊 🏠

🚲 Bicycling Trails   ⛺ Camping   🥾 Hiking Trails   🧺 Picnic Facilities
🏊 Swimming   🏠 Visitor Center   🍴 Food Service

Coronado National Forest
In southeastern Arizona and southwestern New Mexico.
(520) 388-8300

Glen Canyon National Recreation Area
In northern Arizona and Southern Utah.
(928) 608-6200 or (928) 608-6404

Grand Canyon National Park
In northwestern Arizona.
(928) 638-7888

Kaibab National Forest
In north-central Arizona.
(928) 635-8200

Lake Mead National Recreation Area
In northwestern Arizona and southeastern Nevada.
(702) 293-8990

Petrified Forest National Park
In east-central Arizona, east of Holbrook.
(928) 524-6228

Prescott National Forest
In central Arizona.
(928) 443-8000

Saguaro National Park
Two districts, 15 mi. east and west of Tucson.
(520) 733-5153 or (520) 733-5158

Tonto National Forest
In central Arizona.
(602) 225-5200

ARKANSAS

Buffalo National River
In northwestern Arkansas.
(870) 741-5443 or (870) 439-2502

Felsenthal National Wildlife Refuge
7 mi. west of Crossett on US 82.
(870) 364-3167

Hot Springs National Park
In western Arkansas.
(501) 620-6701 or TDD (501) 624-2308

Ouachita National Forest
In west-central Arkansas and southeastern Oklahoma.
(501) 321-5202

Ozark-St. Francis National Forests
In northwestern and east-central Arkansas.
(479) 964-7200

Pea Ridge National Military Park
Northeast of Rogers in northwest Arkansas.
(479) 451-8122

CALIFORNIA

Angeles National Forest
In southern California.
(626) 574-5200

Cleveland National Forest
In southwestern California.
(858) 673-6180

Death Valley National Park
Along the Nevada border in east-central California.
(760) 786-2331 for recorded information

Eldorado National Forest
In central California.
(530) 644-6048

Golden Gate National Recreation Area
North of the Golden Gate Bridge and in northern and western San Francisco.
(415) 561-4700

Inyo National Forest
In east-central California.
(760) 873-2400

Joshua Tree National Park
East of Desert Hot Springs.
(760) 367-5500

Klamath National Forest
In northern California.
(530) 842-6131

Lassen National Forest
In northeastern California.
(530) 257-2151

Lassen Volcanic National Park
In northeastern California.
(530) 595-4444

Los Padres National Forest
In southern California.
(805) 968-6640

Mendocino National Forest
In northwestern California.
(530) 934-2350 or (530) 934-3316, or TDD (530) 934-7724
🚲 🏕 🥾 🏞 🏊 👫

Modoc National Forest
In northeastern California.
(530) 233-5811
🚲 🏕 🥾 🏞 🏊 👫

Mojave National Preserve
Between I-15 and I-40 in southeastern California.
(760) 252-6100
🏕 🥾 🏞 👫 🍽

Plumas National Forest
In northern California.
(530) 283-2050
🚲 🏕 🥾 🏞 🏊 👫 🍽

Point Reyes National Seashore
Along the California coast just north of San Francisco.
(415) 464-5100
🚲 🏕 🥾 🏞 👫 🍽

Redwood National and State Parks
On the northern California coast.
(707) 464-6101
🚲 🏕 🥾 🏞 🏊 👫

San Bernardino National Forest
In southern California.
(909) 382-2600
🚲 🏕 🥾 🏞 🏊 👫 🍽

Santa Monica Mountains National Recreation Area
West from Griffith Park in Los Angeles past the Ventura County line.
(805) 370-2301
🚲 🏕 🥾 🏞 👫 🍽

Sequoia and Kings Canyon National Parks
In east-central California.
(559) 565-3341
🏕 🥾 🏞 👫 🍽

Sequoia National Forest
In south-central California.
(559) 784-1500
🚲 🏕 🥾 🏞 🏊

Shasta-Trinity National Forests
In northern California.
(530) 226-2500
🚲 🏕 🥾 🏞 🏊 👫 🍽

Sierra National Forest
In central California.
(559) 297-0706
🚲 🏕 🥾 🏞 🏊 🍽

Six Rivers National Forest
In northwestern California.
(707) 442-1721
🚲 🏕 🥾 🏞 🏊 👫 🍽

Smith River National Recreation Area
Within Six Rivers National Forest in northwestern California.
(707) 457-3131
🚲 🏕 🥾 🏞 🏊 👫

Stanislaus National Forest
In central California.
(209) 532-3671
🚲 🏕 🥾 🏞 🏊 🍽

Tahoe National Forest
In north-central California.
(530) 265-4531
🚲 🏕 🥾 🏞 🏊 👫 🍽

Whiskeytown-Shasta-Trinity National Recreation Area
North and west of Redding.
(530) 246-1225 in Whiskeytown, (530) 275-1589 in Shasta or (530) 623-2121 in Trinity
🚲 🏕 🥾 🏞 🏊 👫

Yosemite National Park
In central California.
(209) 372-0200
🚲 🏕 🥾 🏞 🏊 👫 🍽

COLORADO

Arapaho and Roosevelt National Forests and Pawnee National Grassland
In north-central Colorado.
(970) 295-6700
🚲 🏕 🥾 🏞 👫 🍽

Arapaho National Recreation Area
In north-central Colorado.
(970) 887-4100
🚲 🏕 🥾 🏞 🏊 👫

Black Canyon of the Gunnison National Park
In western Colorado.
(970) 641-2337
🚲 🏕 🥾 🏞 👫

Curecanti National Recreation Area
In south-central Colorado between Gunnison and Montrose, paralleling US 50.
(970) 641-2337
🚲 🏕 🥾 🏞 🏊 👫 🍽

Grand Mesa-Uncompahgre-Gunnison National Forests
In west-central Colorado.
(970) 874-6600
🚲 🏕 🥾 🏞 👫

🚲 Bicycling Trails   🏕 Camping   🥾 Hiking Trails   🏞 Picnic Facilities
🏊 Swimming   👫 Visitor Center   🍽 Food Service

Great Sand Dunes National Park and Preserve
Northeast of Alamosa.
(719) 378-6300
▲ 𝆑 ⛰ ⚓ 🚶

Mesa Verde National Park
In southwestern Colorado.
(970) 529-4465
▲ 𝆑 ⛰ 🚶 🖼

Pike and San Isabel National Forest
In south-central Colorado.
(719) 553-1400
♿ ▲ 𝆑 ⛰ 🚶

Rio Grande National Forest
In south-central Colorado.
(719) 852-5941
♿ ▲ 𝆑 ⛰ 🚶

Rocky Mountain National Park
In north-central Colorado.
(970) 586-1206
▲ 𝆑 ⛰ 🚶

Routt National Forest
In northwestern Colorado.
(970) 870-2299
♿ ▲ 𝆑 ⛰ 🚶

San Juan National Forest
In southwestern Colorado.
(970) 247-4874
♿ ▲ 𝆑 ⛰ ⚓ 🚶

White River National Forest
In west-central Colorado.
(970) 945-2521
♿ ▲ 𝆑 ⛰ ⚓ 🚶

DELAWARE

Bombay Hook National Wildlife Refuge
South of Smyrna.
(302) 653-9345
♿ 𝆑 ⛰ 🚶

Prime Hook National Wildlife Refuge
North of Milton via SR 1.
(302) 684-8419
𝆑 ⛰ 🚶

FLORIDA

Apalachicola National Forest
In northwestern Florida.
(850) 926-3561
♿ ▲ 𝆑 ⛰ ⚓

Biscayne National Park
In southeast Florida.
(305) 230-7275
▲ ⛰ ⚓ 🚶 🖼

J.N. "Ding" Darling National Wildlife Refuge
1 Wildlife Dr. in Sanibel.
(239) 472-1100
♿ 𝆑🚶

Ocala National Forest
In north-central Florida.
(352) 236-0288
♿ ▲ 𝆑 ⛰ ⚓ 🚶 🖼

Osceola National Forest
Near the Georgia border.
(386) 752-2577 or (386) 752-0147
♿ ▲ 𝆑 ⛰ ⚓ 🚶

GEORGIA

Chattahoochee and Oconee National Forests
In central and northern Georgia.
(770) 297-3000
♿ ▲ 𝆑 ⛰ ⚓ 🚶 🖼

Chattahoochee River National Recreation Area
North of Atlanta.
(678) 538-1200
♿ 𝆑 ⛰ ⚓ 🚶

Chickamauga and Chattanooga National Military Park
On the Georgia-Tennessee border.
(706) 866-9241 or (423) 752-5213, ext 123
♿ 𝆑 ⛰ 🚶

Kennesaw Mountain National Battlefield Park
Northwest of Marietta.
(770) 427-4686
𝆑 ⛰ 🚶

IDAHO

Boise National Forest
In southwestern Idaho.
(208) 373-4007
♿ ▲ 𝆑 ⛰ ⚓ 🚶 🖼

Caribou-Targhee National Forest
In southeastern Idaho.
(208) 524-7500
▲ 𝆑 ⛰ ⚓ 🚶

Clearwater National Forest
In northeastern Idaho.
(208) 476-8267
▲ 𝆑 ⛰ ⚓ 🚶 🖼

Hells Canyon National Recreation Area
In western Idaho and northeastern Oregon.
(509) 758-0616
♿ ▲ 𝆑 ⛰ ⚓ 🚶

Idaho Panhandle National Forests
In northern and northwestern Idaho.
(208) 765-7223
♿ ▲ 𝆑 ⛰ ⚓

Nez Perce National Forest
In northwestern Idaho.
(208) 983-1950
♿ ▲ 𝆑 ⛰ ⚓ 🚶 🖼

Payette National Forest
In west-central Idaho.
(208) 634-0700
♿ ▲ 𝆑 ⛰ ⚓ 🚶 🖼

Salmon-Challis National Forest
In east-central Idaho.
(208) 756-5100
🅰 🏇 🎪 ⚘ 🏠

Sawtooth National Forest
In south-central Idaho.
(208) 737-3200 or (800) 260-5970
🚲 🅰 🏇 🎪 ⚘ 🏠 🍴

Sawtooth National Recreation Area
In south-central Idaho.
(208) 727-5013 or (800) 260-5970
🚲 🅰 🏇 🎪 ⚘ 🏠 🍴

ILLINOIS

Chautauqua National Wildlife Refuge
Near Havana.
(309) 535-2290
🚲 🏇 🎪

Shawnee National Forest
In southern Illinois.
(618) 253-7114 or (800) 699-6637
🅰 🏇 🎪 ⚘ 🏠

INDIANA

George Rogers Clark National Historical Park
Off US 50 and US 41 near Vincennes.
(812) 882-1776
🏇 🎪 🏠

Hoosier National Forest
In southern Indiana.
(812) 275-5987
🚲 🅰 🏇 🎪 ⚘

Indiana Dunes National Lakeshore
On the southern shore of Lake Michigan.
(219) 926-7561, ext. 225
🚲 🅰 🏇 🎪 ⚘ 🏠

Muscatatuck National Wildlife Refuge
East of jct. I-65 and US 50 near Seymour.
(812) 522-4352
🚲 🏇 🏠

KANSAS

Kirwin National Wildlife Refuge
702 E. Xavier Rd.
(785) 543-6673
🚲 🏇 🏠

KENTUCKY

Big South Fork National River and Recreation Area
In southeastern Kentucky and northeastern Tennessee.
(423) 286-7275 or (606) 376-5073
🚲 🅰 🏇 🎪 ⚘ 🏠

Cumberland Gap National Historical Park
At the borders of Kentucky, Tennessee and Virginia.
(606) 248-2817
🚲 🅰 🏇 🎪 🏠

Daniel Boone National Forest
Five districts in eastern and southeastern Kentucky.
(859) 745-3100
🚲 🅰 🏇 🎪 ⚘ 🏠

Land Between the Lakes National Recreation Area
In western Kentucky and Tennessee.
(270) 924-2000 or (800) 525-7077
🚲 🅰 🏇 🎪 ⚘ 🏠

Mammoth Cave National Park
In south-central Kentucky 10 mi. west of Cave City.
(270) 758-2180
🚲 🅰 🏇 🎪 🏠 🍴

LOUISIANA

Bayou Sauvage National Wildlife Refuge
Within the New Orleans city limits.
(985) 882-2000
🚲 🏇 🎪

Kisatchie National Forest
In central and northern Louisiana.
(318) 473-7160
🚲 🅰 🏇 🎪 ⚘ 🏠

MAINE

Acadia National Park
Along the Atlantic coast southeast of Bangor.
(207) 288-3338
🚲 🅰 🏇 🎪 ⚘ 🏠 🍴

Moosehorn National Wildlife Refuge
Near Baring and Dennysville.
(207) 454-7161
🚲 🏇

MARYLAND

Assateague Island National Seashore
In southeastern Maryland south of Ocean City.
(410) 641-1441 or (410) 641-3030
🚲 🅰 🏇 🎪 ⚘ 🏠

Chesapeake and Ohio Canal National Historical Park
From Georgetown to Cumberland.
(301) 739-4200
🚲 🅰 🏇 🎪 🏠 🍴

MASSACHUSETTS

Cape Cod National Seashore
Occupies 40 miles along the shoreline.
(508) 255-3421
🚲 🏇 🎪 ⚘ 🏠

🚲 Bicycling Trails   🅰 Camping   🏇 Hiking Trails   🎪 Picnic Facilities
⚘ Swimming   🏠 Visitor Center   🍴 Food Service

MICHIGAN

Hiawatha National Forest
In Michigan's Upper Peninsula.
(906) 786-4062
🚴 🔺 🏍 ⛱ 🛶 🏕 🛶

Huron-Manistee National Forests
In the northern part of the Lower Peninsula.
(231) 775-2421 or (800) 821-6263
🚴 🔺 🏍 ⛱ 🛶 🏕 🛶

Ottawa National Forest
In Michigan's Upper Peninsula.
(906) 932-1330 or (800) 562-1201
🚴 🔺 🏍 ⛱ 🛶 🏕 🛶

Pictured Rocks National Lakeshore
Along Lake Superior in Michigan's Upper Peninsula.
906-387-3700 or (906) 387-2607
🔺 🏍 ⛱ 🛶 🏕

Sleeping Bear Dunes National Lakeshore
Along Lake Michigan in the northwestern part of the Lower Peninsula.
(231) 326-5134
🔺 🏍 ⛱ 🛶 🏕 🛶

MINNESOTA

Chippewa National Forest
In north-central Minnesota.
(218) 335-8600
🚴 🔺 🏍 ⛱ 🛶 🏕 🛶

Minnesota Valley National Wildlife Refuge
3815 E. American Blvd, Bloomington
(952) 854-5900
🚴 🏍 🏕

Superior National Forest
In northeastern Minnesota.
(218) 626-4300
🚴 🔺 🏍 ⛱ 🛶 🏕 🛶

MISSISSIPPI

Bienville National Forest
In central Mississippi.
(601) 469-3811
🔺 🏍 ⛱ 🛶 🏕

Gulf Islands National Seashore
Along the Gulf of Mexico in southern Mississippi.
(228) 875-9057
🚴 🔺 🏍 ⛱ 🏕

MISSOURI

Mark Twain National Forest (Big Bay)
1 mi. southeast of Shell Knob on SR 39, then 3 mi. southeast on CR YY.
(573) 364-4621
🚴 ⛱ 🛶

Mark Twain National Forest (Council Bluff)
13 mi. s. of Potosi on CR P, 4 mi. w. on CR C , then 8 mi. s. on CR DD.
(573) 364-4621
🚴 🔺 🏍 ⛱ 🛶

Mark Twain National Forest (Crane Lake)
12 mi. south of Ironton off SR 49 and CR E.
(573) 364-4621
🚴 🏍 ⛱ 🛶

Mark Twain National Forest (Fourche Lake)
18 mi. west of Doniphan on SR 160.
(573) 364-4621
🏍 ⛱ 🛶

Mark Twain National Forest (Noblett Lake)
8 mi. west of Willow Springs on SR 76, then 1.5 mi. south on SR 181, 3 mi. southeast on CR AP and 1 mi. southwest on FR 857.
(573) 364-4621
🚴 🏍 ⛱

Mark Twain National Forest (Pinewoods Lake)
2 mi. west of Ellsinore on SR 60.
(573) 364-4621
🚴 🏍 ⛱ 🛶

Mark Twain National Forest (Red Bluff)
1 mi. east of Davisville on CR V, then 1 mi. north on FR 2011.
(573) 364-4621
🔺 🏍 ⛱ 🛶

Ozark National Scenic Riverways
In southeastern Missouri.
(573) 323-4236
🔺 🏍 ⛱ 🛶 🏕 🛶

MONTANA

Beaverhead-Deerlodge National Forest
In southwestern Montana.
(406) 683-3900
🚴 🔺 🏍 ⛱ 🛶 🛶

Bighorn Canyon National Recreation Area
In southern Montana and northern Wyoming.
(406) 666-2412
🔺 🏍 ⛱ 🛶 🏕 🛶

Bitterroot National Forest
In western Montana.
(406) 363-7100
🚴 🔺 🏍 ⛱ 🛶 🏕

Custer National Forest
In southeastern Montana.
(406) 657-6200
🚴 🔺 🏍 ⛱ 🛶

Flathead National Forest
In northwestern Montana.
(406) 758-5204
🚴 🔺 🏍 ⛱ 🛶 🏕

Gallatin National Forest
In south-central Montana.
(406) 522-2520
🚲 ⛺ 🥾 🎪 🏊 🏠

Glacier National Park
In northwestern Montana.
(406) 888-7800
🚲 ⛺ 🥾 🎪 🏊 🏠 🍽

Helena National Forest
In west-central Montana.
(406) 449-5201
🚲 ⛺ 🥾 🎪 🏊 🏠

Kootenai National Forest
In northwestern Montana.
(406) 293-6211
🚲 ⛺ 🥾 🎪 🏊 🏠 🍽

Lewis and Clark National Forest
In central Montana.
(406) 791-7700
🚲 ⛺ 🥾 🎪 🏠

NEBRASKA

Fort Niobrara National Wildlife Refuge
East of Valentine on SR 12.
(402) 376-3789
🥾 🎪

Nebraska National Forest
In central and northwestern Nebraska.
(308) 432-0300 or TDD (308) 432-0304
🚲 ⛺ 🥾 🎪

Oglala National Grassland
In northwestern Nebraska, 6 mi. north of Crawford via
SR 2.
(308) 432-0300
⛺ 🥾 🎪

NEVADA

Great Basin National Park
In central Nevada, 5 mi. west of Baker near the
Nevada-Utah border.
(775) 234-7331
⛺ 🥾 🎪 🏠 🍽

Humboldt-Toiyabe National Forest
In central, western, northern and southern Nevada and
eastern California.
(775) 331-6444
🚲 ⛺ 🥾 🎪 🍽

Lake Mead National Recreation Area
In southeastern Nevada and northwestern Arizona.
(702) 293-8990
🚲 ⛺ 🥾 🎪 🏊 🏠 🍽

NEW HAMPSHIRE

White Mountain National Forest
In northern New Hampshire.
(603) 528-8721
🚲 ⛺ 🥾 🎪 🏊 🏠

NEW JERSEY

Edwin B. Forsythe National Wildlife Refuge
US 9 and Great Creek Road near Oceanville
(609) 652-1665
🥾 🎪 🏠

Gateway National Recreation Area (Sandy Hook Unit)
In northeastern New Jersey.
(732) 872-5970
🚲 🥾 🎪 🏊 🏠 🍽

Morristown National Historical Park
Four units in Morristown and southwest.
(973) 539-2016
🥾 🏠

NEW MEXICO

Carson National Forest
In north-central New Mexico.
(575) 758-6200
🚲 ⛺ 🥾 🎪 🏠 🍽

Chaco Culture National Historical Park
In northwestern New Mexico.
(505) 786-7014
🚲 ⛺ 🥾 🎪 🏠

Cibola National Forest
In central New Mexico.
(505) 346-3900
🚲 ⛺ 🥾 🎪 🏊 🏠

Gila National Forest
In southwestern New Mexico.
(575) 388-8201
🚲 ⛺ 🥾 🎪 🏠

Lincoln National Forest
In south-central New Mexico.
(575) 434-7200
🚲 ⛺ 🥾 🎪 🍽

Santa Fe National Forest
In north-central New Mexico between the Jemez
Mountains and the Sangre de Cristo Mountains.
(505) 438-7840
🚲 ⛺ 🥾 🎪 🏠 🍽

NEW YORK

Finger Lakes National Forest
In south-central New York on a ridge between Seneca and
Cayuga lakes, via I-90, I-81 and SR 17.
(607) 546-4470
🚲 ⛺ 🥾 🎪 🏠

🚲 Bicycling Trails   ⛺ Camping   🥾 Hiking Trails   🎪 Picnic Facilities
🏊 Swimming   🏠 Visitor Center   🍽 Food Service

Fire Island National Seashore
In southeastern New York on Fire Island, off the south
shore of Long Island.
(631) 687-4750
🅰 👭 ⛱ 🛈 🍴

Gateway National Recreation Area (Jamaica Bay Unit)
In Brooklyn and Queens boroughs in New York City.
(718) 338-3799
♿ 🅰 👭 ⛱ 🛈 🍴

Gateway National Recreation Area (Staten Island Unit)
On Staten Island borough in New York City.
(718) 354-4500
♿ 🅰 👭 ⛱ 🛈 🍴

Saratoga National Historical Park
8 miles south of Schuylerville on US 4.
(518) 664-9821, ext. 224
♿ 👭 ⛱ 🛈

NORTH CAROLINA

Cape Hatteras National Seashore
In eastern North Carolina along the Outer Banks.
(252) 473-2111
♿ 🅰 👭 ⛱ 🛈 🍴

Croatan National Forest
In southeastern North Carolina.
(252) 638-5628
♿ 🅰 👭 ⛱ 🛈

Great Smoky Mountains National Park
In western North Carolina and eastern Tennessee.
(865) 436-1200
♿ 🅰 👭 ⛱ 🛈

Nantahala National Forest
At North Carolina's southwestern tip.
(828) 257-4200 or (828) 524-6441
♿ 🅰 👭 ⛱ 🛈

Pisgah National Forest
In western North Carolina.
(828) 257-4200
♿ 🅰 👭 ⛱ 🛈 🛈

Pisgah National Forest (Lake Powhatan)
7 mi. southwest of Asheville on SR 191 and FR 3807.
(828) 257-4200
♿ 🅰 👭 ⛱ 🛈

Pisgah National Forest (Rocky Bluff)
3 mi. south of Hot Springs on SR 209.
(828) 257-4200
🅰 👭 ⛱

Uwharrie National Forest
In central North Carolina.
(910) 576-6391
♿ 🅰 👭 ⛱ 🛈 🛈

NORTH DAKOTA

Little Missouri National Grassland
Between the Missouri River and South Dakota.
(701) 227-7800
♿ 🅰 👭 ⛱

Sheyenne National Grassland
Along the Sheyenne River south of Fargo.
(701) 683-4342
🅰 👭 ⛱

Theodore Roosevelt National Park (North Unit)
In western North Dakota.
(701) 842-2333
🅰 👭 ⛱ 🛈

Theodore Roosevelt National Park (South Unit)
In western North Dakota.
(701) 623-4466
🅰 👭 ⛱ 🛈 🍴

OHIO

Cuyahoga Valley National Park
In northeastern Ohio.
(216) 524-1497
♿ 👭 ⛱ 🛈 🍴

Hopewell Culture National Historical Park
About 3 mi. north of Chillicothe on SR 104.
(740) 774-1126
♿ 👭 ⛱ 🛈

Wayne National Forest
In southeast Ohio.
(740) 753-0101
♿ 🅰 👭 ⛱ 🛈 🛈

OKLAHOMA

Chickasaw National Recreation Area
In south-central Oklahoma.
(580) 622-3165
♿ 🅰 👭 ⛱ 🛈 🛈

Ouachita National Forest
In southeastern Oklahoma and west-central Arkansas.
(501) 321-5202
♿ 🅰 👭 ⛱ 🛈 🛈 🍴

Salt Plains National Wildlife Refuge
Off SR 38, 2 mi. south of jct. SRs 11 and 38 at Cherokee.
(580) 626-4794
🅰 👭 🛈

OREGON

Crater Lake National Park
On the crest of the Cascade Range off SR 62.
(541) 594-3100
🅰 👭 ⛱ 🛈 🍴

Deschutes National Forest
In central Oregon 6 mi. south of Bend via US 97.
(541) 383-5300
♿ 🅰 👭 ⛱ 🛈 🛈 🍴

Fremont-Winema National Forests
In south-central Oregon.
(541) 947-2151
[icons]

Hells Canyon National Recreation Area
In northeastern Oregon and western Idaho.
(541) 426-5546
[icons]

Malheur National Forest
In eastern Oregon.
(541) 575-3000
[icons]

Mount Hood National Forest
In northwestern Oregon.
(888) 622-4822
[icons]

Ochoco National Forest
In central Oregon off US 26.
(541) 416-6500
[icons]

Oregon Dunes National Recreation Area
Between North Bend and Florence.
(541) 271-6000
[icons]

Rogue River-Siskiyou National Forest
In southwestern Oregon off I-5 from Medford.
(541) 858-2200
[icons]

Siuslaw National Forest
In western Oregon.
(541) 750-7000
[icons]

Umatilla National Forest
In northeastern Oregon.
(541) 278-3716
[icons]

Umpqua National Forest
In southwestern Oregon 33 mi. east of Roseburg on SR 138.
(541) 672-6601
[icons]

Wallowa-Whitman National Forest
In northeastern Oregon.
(541) 523-6391
[icons]

Willamette National Forest
In western Oregon.
(541) 225-6300
[icons]

PENNSYLVANIA

Allegheny National Forest
In northwestern Pennsylvania.
(814) 723-5150 or TDD (814) 726-2710
[icons]

Delaware Water Gap National Recreation Area
In eastern Pennsylvania and northwestern New Jersey.
(570) 426-2457
[icons]

Gettysburg National Military Park
Surrounding the town of Gettysburg at SR 134.
(717) 334-1124
[icons]

John Heinz National Wildlife Refuge at Tinicum
I-95S exit 14 near Philadelphia
(215) 365-3118
[icons]

Valley Forge National Historical Park
1400 N. Outer Line Dr.
(610) 783-1077
[icons]

SOUTH CAROLINA

Congaree National Park
Southeast of Hopkins.
(803) 776-4396
[icons]

Francis Marion National Forest
On the Coastal Plain north of Charleston.
(803) 561-4000
[icons]

Kings Mountain National Military Park
South of Kings Mountain, N.C., off I-85.
(864) 936-7921
[icons]

Sumter National Forest
In western South Carolina.
(803) 561-4000
[icons]

SOUTH DAKOTA

Badlands National Park
In southwestern South Dakota.
(605) 433-5361, ext. 100
[icons]

Black Hills National Forest
In southwestern South Dakota.
(605) 673-9200 or TDD (605) 673-4954
[icons]

Custer National Forest
In northwestern South Dakota and southeastern Montana.
(605) 797-4432
[icons]

[symbol] Bicycling Trails   [symbol] Camping   [symbol] Hiking Trails   [symbol] Picnic Facilities
[symbol] Swimming   [symbol] Visitor Center   [symbol] Food Service

Wind Cave National Park
In southwestern South Dakota.
(605) 745-4600
🅰 🚶 ⛰ 👪

TENNESSEE

Big South Fork National River and Recreation Area
In northeastern Tennessee and southeastern Kentucky.
(423) 286-7275
🚴 🅰 🚶 ⛰ ⚓ 👪

Cherokee National Forest
In eastern Tennessee.
(423) 476-9700
🚴 🅰 🚶 ⛰ ⚓ 👪

Chickamauga and Chattanooga National Military Park
On the Georgia-Tennessee border.
(706) 866-9241
🚴 🚶 ⛰ 👪

Great Smoky Mountains National Park
In eastern Tennessee and western North Carolina.
(865) 436-1200
🚴 🅰 🚶 ⛰ 👪

Land Between the Lakes National Recreation Area
In western Kentucky and Tennessee.
(270) 924-2000 or (800) 525-7077
🚴 🅰 🚶 ⛰ ⚓ 👪

TEXAS

Amistad National Recreation Area
Northwest of Del Rio via US 90.
(830) 775-7491
🅰 🚶 ⛰ ⚓ 👪

Angelina National Forest
In east Texas.
(936) 897-1068
🅰 🚶 ⛰ ⚓

Big Bend National Park
In southwest Texas.
(432) 477-2251 or (432) 477-1188
🅰 🚶 ⛰ 👪 🍴

Davy Crockett National Forest
In east Texas.
(936) 655-2299
🅰 🚶 ⛰ ⚓ 🍴

Guadalupe Mountains National Park
110 mi. east of El Paso on US 62/180.
(915) 828-3251
🅰 🚶 ⛰ 👪

Lake Meredith National Recreation Area
45 mi. northeast of Amarillo and 9 mi. west of Borger via SR 136.
(806) 857-3151
🅰 ⛰ ⚓ 👪🍴

Padre Island National Seashore
On Padre Island near Corpus Christi.
(361) 949-8173
🚴 🅰 🚶 ⛰ ⚓ 👪 🍴

Sabine National Forest
In east Texas.
(409) 625-1940
🅰 🚶 ⛰ ⚓

Sam Houston National Forest
40 mi. north of Houston in east Texas.
(936) 344-6205 or (888) 361-6908
🚴 🅰 🚶 ⛰ ⚓ 👪 🍴

UTAH

Ashley National Forest
In northeastern Utah.
(435) 789-1181
🚴 🅰 🚶 ⛰ ⚓ 👪 🍴

Canyonlands National Park
In southeastern Utah.
(435) 719-2100
🅰 🚶 ⛰ 👪

Capitol Reef National Park
10 mi. east of Torrey on SR 24.
(435) 425-3791, ext. 111
🅰 🚶 ⛰ 👪

Dixie National Forest
In southwestern Utah.
(435) 865-3700
🚴 🅰 🚶 ⛰ ⚓ 👪 🍴

Fishlake National Forest
In south-central Utah.
(435) 896-9233
🚴 🅰 🚶 ⛰ ⚓ 👪 🍴

Flaming Gorge National Recreation Area
In northeastern Utah.
(435) 784-3445
🚴 🅰 🚶 ⛰ ⚓ 👪 🍴

Glen Canyon National Recreation Area
In south-central Utah.
(928) 608-6200
🅰 🚶 ⛰ ⚓ 👪 🍴

Manti-La Sal National Forest
In southeastern Utah.
(435) 637-2817
🚴 🅰 🚶 ⛰ ⚓ 👪

Uinta-Wasatch-Cache National Forest
In north-central, central and northeastern Utah.
(801) 236-3400 or (801) 466-6411
🚴 🅰 🚶 ⛰ ⚓ 👪 🍴

Zion National Park
In southwestern Utah.
(435) 772-3256
🚴 🅰 🚶 ⛰ 👪 🍴

VERMONT

Green Mountain National Forest
In south-central Vermont.
(802) 747-6700
[A] [Hiking] [Picnic] [Swimming][Visitor]

Marsh-Billings-Rockefeller National Historical Park
Off SR 12 near Woodstock.
(802) 457-3368, ext. 22
[Hiking][Visitor]

VIRGINIA

George Washington and Jefferson National Forests
In western Virginia and the eastern edge of West Virginia.
(540) 265-5100 or (888) 265-0019
[Bicycling][A][Hiking][Picnic][Swimming]

Mount Rogers National Recreation Area
In southwestern Virginia.
(276) 783-5196 or (800) 628-7202
[Bicycling][A][Hiking][Picnic][Swimming][Visitor]

Shenandoah National Park
In northwestern Virginia.
(540) 999-3500
[A][Hiking][Picnic][Visitor][Food]

WASHINGTON

Colville National Forest
In northeastern Washington.
(509) 684-7000
[Bicycling][A][Hiking][Picnic][Swimming]

Gifford Pinchot National Forest
In southwestern Washington.
(360) 891-5001 or (360) 891-5002
[Bicycling][A][Hiking][Picnic][Swimming][Visitor]

Lake Chelan National Recreation Area
In north-central Washington.
(509) 682-2549
[A][Hiking][Picnic][Visitor][Food]

Lake Roosevelt National Recreation Area
In northeastern Washington.
(509) 633-9441
[Bicycling][A][Hiking][Picnic][Swimming][Visitor][Food]

Mount Baker-Snoqualmie National Forest
2 mi. east of Glacier on SR 542.
(425) 783-6000 or (800) 627-0062, ext. 0
[Bicycling][A][Hiking][Picnic][Swimming][Visitor][Food]

Okanogan National Forest
In north-central Washington.
(509) 996-4000
[Bicycling][A][Hiking][Picnic][Swimming][Visitor]

Olympic National Forest
In northwestern Washington.
(360) 956-2400
[Bicycling][A][Hiking][Picnic][Swimming][Visitor][Food]

Ross Lake National Recreation Area
Between the north and south sections of North Cascades National Park.
(360) 854-7200
[A][Hiking][Picnic][Swimming][Visitor]

WEST VIRGINIA

Monongahela National Forest
In eastern West Virginia.
(304) 636-1800
[Bicycling][A][Hiking][Picnic][Swimming][Visitor][Food]

New River Gorge National River
Between Fayetteville and Hinton.
(304) 465-0508
[Bicycling][A][Hiking][Picnic][Visitor]

Spruce Knob-Seneca Rocks National Recreation Area
In east-central West Virginia.
(304) 257-4488
[Bicycling][A][Hiking][Picnic][Visitor]

WISCONSIN

Apostle Islands National Lakeshore
Off northern Wisconsin's Bayfield Peninsula in Lake Superior.
(715) 779-3397
[A][Hiking][Picnic][Swimming][Visitor]

Chequamegon-Nicolet National Forest
In north-central and northeastern Wisconsin.
(715) 762-2461 (Chequamegon) or (715) 362-1300 (Nicolet)
[Bicycling][A][Hiking][Picnic][Swimming]

St. Croix National Scenic Riverway
Running 252 mi. from Cable to Prescott.
(715) 483-2274
[A][Hiking][Picnic][Visitor]

WYOMING

Bighorn Canyon National Recreation Area
In southern Montana and northern Wyoming.
(307) 548-2251
[A][Hiking][Picnic][Swimming][Visitor]

Bighorn National Forest
In north-central Wyoming.
(307) 674-2600
[Bicycling][A][Hiking][Picnic][Visitor][Food]

Devils Tower National Monument
Between Sundance and Hulett.
(307) 467-5283
[A][Hiking][Picnic][Visitor]

Flaming Gorge National Recreation Area
On the Wyoming-Utah border.
(435) 784-3445
[Bicycling][A][Hiking][Picnic][Swimming][Visitor][Food]

[Bicycling] Bicycling Trails [A] Camping [Hiking] Hiking Trails [Picnic] Picnic Facilities
[Swimming] Swimming [Visitor] Visitor Center [Food] Food Service

Fossil Butte National Monument
14 mi. west of Kemmerer on US 30.
(307) 877-4455
🔣 🔣 🔣

Grand Teton National Park
In northwestern Wyoming.
(307) 739-3300
🔣 🔣 🔣 🔣 🔣 🔣 🔣

Medicine Bow National Forest
In southeastern Wyoming.
(307) 745-2300
🔣 🔣 🔣 🔣 🔣

Shoshone National Forest
In northwestern Wyoming.
(307) 527-6241
🔣 🔣 🔣 🔣 🔣 🔣

Yellowstone National Park
In northwestern Wyoming.
(307) 344-7311
🔣 🔣 🔣 🔣 🔣 🔣

Canada

ALBERTA

Banff National Park of Canada
In southwestern Alberta, west of Calgary.
(403) 762-1550
🔣 🔣 🔣 🔣 🔣 🔣

Elk Island National Park of Canada
In central Alberta, east of Edmonton.
(780) 992-2950
🔣 🔣 🔣 🔣 🔣 🔣

Jasper National Park of Canada
In west-central Alberta along the British Columbia border.
(780) 852-6176
🔣 🔣 🔣 🔣 🔣 🔣 🔣

Waterton Lakes National Park of Canada
In Alberta's southwestern corner.
(403) 859-2224
🔣 🔣 🔣 🔣 🔣 🔣 🔣

BRITISH COLUMBIA

Gulf Islands National Park Reserve of Canada
Off the southeast coast of Vancouver Island.
(250) 654-4000
🔣 🔣 🔣 🔣

Glacier National Park of Canada
In southeastern British Columbia.
(250) 837-7500
🔣 🔣 🔣 🔣 🔣

Kootenay National Park of Canada
In southeastern British Columbia.
(250) 347-9505 or (888) 773-8888
🔣 🔣 🔣 🔣 🔣 🔣

Mount Revelstoke National Park of Canada
In southeastern British Columbia.
(250) 837-7500
🔣 🔣 🔣 🔣

Pacific Rim National Park Reserve of Canada
On the southwestern coast of Vancouver Island.
(250) 726-3500
🔣 🔣 🔣 🔣 🔣 🔣

Yoho National Park of Canada
On the British Columbia-Alberta border.
(250) 343-6783
🔣 🔣 🔣 🔣 🔣 🔣

MANITOBA

Riding Mountain National Park of Canada
In southwestern Manitoba.
(204) 848-7275
🔣 🔣 🔣 🔣 🔣 🔣 🔣

NEW BRUNSWICK

Fundy National Park of Canada
On Hwy. 114, 130 km. southwest of Moncton.
(506) 887-6000
🔣 🔣 🔣 🔣 🔣 🔣 🔣

Kouchibouguac National Park of Canada
On Hwy. 134, north of Moncton.
(506) 876-2443 or TDD (506) 876-4205
🔣 🔣 🔣 🔣 🔣 🔣 🔣

NEWFOUNDLAND

Gros Morne National Park of Canada
On Newfoundland's western coast.
(709) 458-2417 or TDD (709) 772-4564
🔣 🔣 🔣 🔣 🔣

Terra Nova National Park of Canada
In eastern Newfoundland.
(709) 533-2801
🔣 🔣 🔣 🔣 🔣 🔣 🔣

NORTHWEST TERRITORIES

Nahanni National Park Reserve of Canada
145 km. west of Fort Simpson in southwestern Northwest Territories.
(867) 695-3151
🔣 🔣 🔣

Wood Buffalo National Park of Canada
On the Northwest Territories-Alberta border.
(867) 872-7960
🔣 🔣 🔣 🔣

NOVA SCOTIA

Cape Breton Highlands National Park of Canada
5 km. northeast of Chéticamp on Cabot Tr.
(902) 224-2306 or (888) 773-8888
🚴 🛆 🚶 🏕 🏊 🛈 🍴

Kejimkujik National Park and National Historic Site of Canada
In southwestern Nova Scotia off Hwy. 8 at Maitland Bridge.
(902) 682-2772
🚴 🛆 🚶 🏕 🏊 🛈 🍴

ONTARIO

Bruce Peninsula National Park of Canada
In southwestern Ontario.
(519) 596-2233
🛆 🚶 🏕 🏊 🛈

Georgian Bay Islands National Park
Along the southeastern portion of Georgian Bay.
(705) 526-9804
🚴 🛆 🚶 🏕 🏊

Point Pelee National Park of Canada
South of Leamington.
(519) 322-2365 or (888) 773-8888
🚴 🚶 🏕 🏊 🛈 🍴

Pukaskwa National Park of Canada
On the north shore of Lake Superior.
(807) 229-0801, ext. 242
🛆 🚶 🏕 🏊 🛈

St. Lawrence Islands National Park of Canada
In the St. Lawrence River between Kingston and Brockville.
(613) 923-5261
🛆 🚶 🏕 🏊 🛈

PRINCE EDWARD ISLAND

Port La Joye-Fort Amherst National Historic Site of Canada
West of Charlottetown on Hwy. 1.
(902) 566-7626
🚶 🏕 🛈 🍴

Prince Edward Island National Park of Canada
Along the island's northern shore.
(902) 672-6350 or TTY (902) 566-7061
🚴 🛆 🚶 🏕 🏊 🛈 🍴

QUEBEC

Forillon National Park of Canada
20 km. northeast of Gaspé via Hwy. 132.
(418) 368-5505 or (888) 773-8888
🚴 🛆 🚶 🏕 🏊 🛈 🍴

La Mauricie National Park of Canada
North of Trois-Rivières via Hwy. 55.
(819) 538-3232 or (888) 773-8888
🚴 🛆 🚶 🏕 🏊 🛈 🍴

SASKATCHEWAN

Grasslands National Park of Canada
Between Val Marie and Killdeer in southern Saskatchewan.
(306) 298-2257
🛆 🚶 🛈

Prince Albert National Park of Canada
In central Saskatchewan.
(306) 663-4522
🚴 🛆 🚶 🏕 🏊 🛈 🍴

YUKON TERRITORY

Kluane National Park of Canada
West of Haines Junction.
(867) 634-7250
🚴 🛆 🚶 🏕 🏊 🛈 🍴

🚴 Bicycling Trails   🛆 Camping   🚶 Hiking Trails   🏕 Picnic Facilities
🏊 Swimming   🛈 Visitor Center   🍴 Food Service

EMERGENCY ANIMAL CLINICS

This list of emergency animal clinics in the United States and Canada is provided by the Veterinary Emergency & Critical Care Society (VECCS) as a service to the community for information purposes only. This is not to be construed as a certification or an endorsement of any clinic listed. For further information, contact the society at (210) 698-5575 or online at www.veccs.org. Note: Hours frequently change, and not all clinics are open 24 hours or in the evening. In addition, not all facilities listed here are emergency clinics. In non-emergency situations, it's best to call first.

If you are traveling to an area not covered in this list, be prepared for an emergency by asking your regular veterinarian to recommend a clinic or veterinarian at your destination. The American Animal Hospital Association also provides a veterinary locator service to clinics that meet the association's high standards for veterinary care. Contact the association at (303) 986-2800 or online at www.healthypet.com.

United States

ALABAMA

Auburn University Small Animal Teaching Hospital
Hoerlein Hall, 1185 Wire Rd., Auburn
(334) 844-4690

Emergency & Specialty Animal Medical Center
2864 Acton Rd., Birmingham
(205) 967-7389

Animal Emergency Clinic of North Alabama
2112 Memorial Pkwy. S.W., Huntsville
(256) 533-7600

ALASKA

Pet Emergency Treatment, Inc.
2320 E. Dowling Rd., Anchorage
(907) 274-5636

After Hours Veterinary Emergency Clinic
8 Bonnie Ave., Fairbanks
(907) 479-2700

ARIZONA

First Regional Animal Hospital
1233 W. Warner Rd., Chandler
(480) 732-0018

Emergency Animal Clinic, PLC
86 W. Juniper, Gilbert
(480) 497-0222

1st Emergency Pet Care
1423 S. Higley Rd. #102, Mesa
(480) 924-1123

Emergency Animal Clinic, PLC
9875 W. Peoria Ave., Peoria
(623) 974-1520

Emergency Animal Clinic, PLC
2260 W. Glendale Ave., Phoenix
(602) 995-3757

North Valley Regional Animal Hospital
520 W. Union Hills Dr. #105, Phoenix
(623) 849-0700

Sonora Veterinary Specialists
4015 E. Cactus Rd., Phoenix
(602) 765-3700

Emergency Animal Clinic, PLC
14202 N. Scottsdale Rd., Suite 163, Scottsdale
(480) 949-8001

Ina Road Animal Hospital
7320 N. La Cholla, Suite 114, Tucson
(520) 544-7700

Pima Pet Clinic - Animal Emergency Service
4832 E. Speedway Blvd., Tucson
(520) 327-5624

Southern Arizona Veterinary Specialty and Emergency Center
141 E. Fort Lowell, Tucson
(520) 888-3177, ext. 1

Southern Arizona Veterinary Specialty and Emergency Center
7474 E. Broadway Blvd., Tucson
(520) 888-3177, ext. 2

Veterinary Specialty Center of Tucson
4909 N. La Canada Dr., Tucson
(520) 795-9955

ARKANSAS

Ft. Smith Animal Emergency Clinic
4301 Regions Park Dr., Suite 3, Fort Smith
(479) 649-3100

After Hours Animal Hospital
290 Smokey Ln., North Little Rock
(501) 955-0911

Animal Emergency & Specialty Clinic
8735 Sheltie Dr., Suite G, North Little Rock
(501) 224-3784

Animal Emergency Clinic of Northwest Arkansas
777 Mathias Dr., Suite B, Springdale
(479) 927-0007

CALIFORNIA

East Bay Veterinary Emergency
1312 Sunset Dr., Antioch
(925) 754-5001

Central Coast Pet Emergency Clinic
1558 W. Branch St., Arroyo Grande
(805) 489-6573

Atascadero Pet Hospital and Emergency Center
9575 El Camino Real, Atascadero
(805) 466-3880

Animal Emergency & Urgent Care
4300 Easton Dr., Suite 1, Bakersfield
(661) 322-6019

Pet Emergency Treatment Service
1048 University Ave., Berkeley
(510) 548-6684

United Emergency Animal Clinic
905 Dell Ave., Campbell
(408) 371-6252

**Pacific Veterinary Specialists and
Emergency Critical Care Center**
1980 41st Ave., Capitola
(831) 476-0667

Sacramento Animal Medical Group
4990 Manzanita Ave., Carmichael
(916) 331-7430

Contra Costa Veterinary Emergency Center
1410 Monument Blvd., Suite 108, Concord
(925) 798-2900

Advanced Critical Care
9599 Jefferson Blvd., Culver City
(310) 558-6100

**UC Davis Veterinary Medical Teaching Hospital
Small Animal Clinic**
One Shields Ave., Davis
(530) 752-1393

Vetcare Emergency & Specialty Care Center
7660 Amador Valley Blvd., Dublin
(925) 556-1234

Emergency Pet Clinic of San Gabriel Valley
3254 Santa Anita Ave., El Monte
(626) 579-4550

North Coast Veterinary and Emergency
414 Encinitas Blvd., Encinitas
(760) 632-1072

Animal Urgent Care
2430 A.S. Escondido Blvd., Escondido
(760) 738-9600

Animal Emergency Center
3954 A Jacobs Ave., Eureka
(707) 443-2776

Solano-Napa Pet Emergency Clinic
4437 Central Pl., Fairfield
(707) 864-1444

VCA All-Care Animal Referral Center
18440 Amistad St., Suite E, Fountain Valley
(714) 963-0909

Ohlone Veterinary Emergency Clinic
1618 Washington Blvd., Fremont
(510) 657-6620

Central California Veterinary Specialty Center
6606 N. Blackstone Ave., Fresno
(559) 451-0800

Veterinary Emergency Service, Inc.
1639 N. Fresno St., Fresno
(559) 486-0520

Orange County Emergency Pet Clinic
12750 Garden Grove Blvd., Garden Grove
(714) 537-3032

Animal Emergency Clinic
12022 La Crosse Ave., Grand Terrace
(909) 825-9350

North Orange County Emergency Pet Clinic
1474 S. Harbor Blvd., La Habra
(714) 441-2925

Pet Emergency and Specialty Center
5232 Jackson Dr. #105, La Mesa
(619) 462-4800

Animal Emergency Clinic
1055 W. Avenue M, Suite 101, Lancaster
(661) 723-3959

Animal Specialty Group
4641 Colorado Blvd., Los Angeles
(818) 244-7977

Animal Surgical and Emergency Center (ASEC)
1535 S. Sepulveda Blvd., Los Angeles
(310) 473-5906

Eagle Rock Emergency Pet Clinic
4254 Eagle Rock Blvd., Los Angeles
(323) 254-7382

VCA West Los Angeles Animal Hospital
1818 S. Sepulveda Blvd., Los Angeles
(310) 473-2951

Animal Urgent Care
2805 Hillcrest, Mission Viejo
(949) 364-6228

Modesto Veterinary Emergency Clinic
1800 Prescott Rd., Modesto
(209) 527-8844

Monterey Peninsula-Salinas Vet Emergency Clinic
20 Lower Ragsdale, Suite 150, Monterey
(831) 373-7374

Central Orange County Emergency Animal Hospital
3720 Campus Dr., Suite D, Newport Beach
(949) 261-7979

Crossroads Animal Emergency and Referral Clinic
11057 E. Rosecrans Ave., Norwalk
(562) 863-2522

Orange Veterinary Hospital
1100 W. Chapman Ave., Orange
(714) 997-8200

South Peninsula Veterinary Emergency Clinic
3045 Middlefield Rd., Palo Alto
(650) 494-1461

Animal Emergency Clinic of Pasadena
2121 E. Foothill Blvd., Pasadena
(626) 564-0704

Animal Emergency Clinic of San Diego
12775 Poway Rd., Poway
(858) 748-7387

Animal Care Center of Sonoma County
6470 Redwood Dr., Rohnert Park
(707) 584-4343

Atlantic St. Veterinary Hospital Pet Emergency Center
1100 Atlantic St., Roseville
(916) 783-4655

El Camino Veterinary Hospital
4000 El Camino Ave., Sacramento
(916) 488-6878

Mueller Pet Medical Center
6420 Freeport Blvd., Sacramento
(916) 428-9202

VCA Sacramento Veterinary Referral Center
9801 Old Winery Pl., Sacramento
(916) 362-3111

Animal E.R. of San Diego
5610 Kearny Mesa Rd., Suite A, San Diego
(858) 569-0600

VCA Emergency Animal Hospital and Referral Center
2317 Hotel Cir. S., San Diego
(619) 299-2400

Veterinary Specialty Hospital
10435 Sorrento Valley Rd., Suite 100, San Diego
(858) 875-7500

All Animals Emergency Hospital
1333 Ninth Ave., San Francisco
(415) 566-0531

Pets Unlimited
2343 Fillmore St., San Francisco
(415) 563-6700

San Francisco Veterinary Specialists & Emergency Services
600 Alabama St., San Francisco
(415) 401-9200

Emergency Animal Clinic of South San Jose
5440 Thornwood Dr., San Jose
(408) 578-5622

Bay Area Veterinary Emergency Clinic
14790 Washington Ave., San Leandro
(510) 352-6080

California Veterinary Specialists
100 N. Rancho Santa Fe Rd., San Marcos
(760) 734-4433

North Peninsula Veterinary Emergency Clinic, Inc.
227 N. Amphlett Blvd., San Mateo
(650) 348-2575

The Pet Emergency and Specialty Center
901 E. Francisco Blvd., Suite C, San Rafael
(415) 456-7372

California Animal Referral & Emergency Hospital
301 E. Haley St., Santa Barbara
(805) 899-2273

Santa Cruz Veterinary Hospital
2585 Soquel Dr., Santa Cruz
(831) 475-5400

Westside Animal Emergency Hospital
1304 Wilshire Blvd., Santa Monica
(310) 451-8962

Emergency Animal Hospital of Santa Rosa
1946 Santa Rosa Ave., Santa Rosa
(707) 544-1647

PetCare Veterinary Hospital
1370 Fulton Rd., Santa Rosa
(707) 579-5900

TLC Pet Medical Centers-South Pasadena
1412 Huntington Dr., South Pasadena
(626) 441-8555

Associated Veterinary Emergency Services
3008 E. Hammer Ln. #115, Stockton
(209) 952-8387

Animal Emergency Centre
11730 Ventura Blvd., Studio City
(818) 760-3882

Pet Emergency Clinic, Inc.
2967 N. Moorpark Rd., Thousand Oaks
(805) 492-2436

Animal Emergency Referral Center
3511 Pacific Coast Hwy., Torrance
(310) 325-3000

Emergency Pet Clinic of South Bay
2325 Torrance Blvd., Torrance
(310) 320-8300

Monte Vista Small Animal Hospital
901 E. Monte Vista Ave., Turlock
(209) 634-0023

Advanced Critical Care & Internal Medicine
3021 Edinger Ave., Tustin
(949) 654-8950

Inland Valley Emergency Pet Clinic
10 W. 7th St., Upland
(909) 931-7871

Pet Emergency Clinic, Inc.
2301 S. Victoria Ave., Ventura
(805) 642-8562

Veterinary Medical and Surgical Group
2199 Sperry Ave., Ventura
(805) 339-2290

Animal Emergency Clinic
12180 Ridgecrest Rd., Suite 122, Victorville
(760) 962-1122

Tulare-Kings Veterinary Emergency Service
4240 W. Mineral King Ave., Visalia
(559) 739-7054

TLC Pet Medical Centers-West Hollywood
8725 Santa Monica Blvd., West Hollywood
(310) 859-4852

COLORADO

Valley Emergency Pet Care
180 Fiou Ln., Suite 101, Basalt
(970) 927-5066

Boulder Emergency Pet Clinic
1658 30th St., Boulder
(303) 440-7722

VCA Douglas County Animal Hospital
531 Jerry St., Castle Rock
(303) 688-2480

Animal Emergency Care Centers, Inc.
3775 Airport Rd., Colorado Springs
(719) 578-9300

Animal Emergency Care Center
5520 N. Nevada Ave., Colorado Springs
(719) 260-7141

VCA Alameda East Veterinary Hospital
9770 E. Alameda Ave., Denver
(303) 366-2639

Central Veterinary Emergency Services
3550 S. Jason St., Englewood
(303) 874-7387

Pet Emergency Treatment Services of N. Colorado
3629 23rd Ave., Evans
(970) 339-8700

Fort Collins Veterinary Emergency Hospital
816 S. Lemay Ave., Fort Collins
(970) 484-8080

James L. Voss Veterinary Teaching Hospital Colorado State University
300 W. Drake Rd., Fort Collins
(970) 221-4535

Grand Valley Veterinary Emergency Center
1660 North Ave., Grand Junction
(970) 255-1911

Animal Hospital Specialty Center
5640 County Line Pl., Suite 1, Highland Ranch
(303) 740-9595

Animal Critical Care & Emergency Services, Inc.
1597 Wadsworth Blvd., Lakewood
(303) 239-1200

Animal E.R.
221 W. County Line Rd., Littleton
(720) 283-9348

Columbine Animal Hospital & Emergency Clinic
5546 W. Canyon Tr., Littleton
(303) 979-4040

Aspen Meadow Veterinary Specialists
104 S. Main St., Longmont
(303) 678-8844

VCA Vet Specialists of Northern Colorado & Emergency Services
201 W. 67th Ct., Loveland
(970) 278-0668

Animal Emergency & Specialty Center
17701 Cottonwood Dr., Parker
(720) 842-5050

Northside Emergency Pet Clinic
945 W. 124th Ave., Westminster
(303) 252-7722

Wheat Ridge Animal Hospital / Wheat Ridge Veterinary Specialists
3695 Kipling St., Wheat Ridge
(303) 424-3325

CONNECTICUT

Farmington Valley Veterinary Emergency Hospital
9 Avonwood Rd., Avon
(860) 674-1886

New Haven Central Hospital for Veterinary Medicine, Inc.
843 State St., New Haven
(203) 865-0878

VCA Veterinary Referral & Emergency Center
123 W. Cedar St., Norwalk
(203) 854-9960

V-E-T-S (Veterinary Emergency Treatment Services)
8 Enterprise Ln., Oakdale
(860) 444-8870

VCA Shoreline Referral & Emergency Center
895 Bridgeport Ave., Shelton
(203) 929-8600

Connecticut Veterinary Center
470 Oakwood Ave., West Hartford
(860) 233-8564

DELAWARE

VCA Newark Animal Hospital Emergency & Specialty Service
1360 Marrows Rd., Newark
(302) 737-8100

Veterinary Emergency Center of Delaware
1212 E. Newport Pike, Wilmington
(302) 691-3647

Wincrest Animal Emergency Hospital
3705 Lancaster Pike, Wilmington
(302) 998-2995

DISTRICT OF COLUMBIA

Friendship Hospital for Animals
4105 Brandywine St., Washington
(202) 363-7300

FLORIDA

Animal Emergency Clinic of Brandon
693 W. Lumsden Rd., Brandon
(813) 684-3013

FVS (Florida Veterinary Specialists)
607 Lumsden Professional Ct., Brandon
(813) 571-3303

Veterinary Emergency Clinic of Central Florida, Inc.
195 Concord Dr., Casselberry
(407) 644-4449

Animal Emergency and Critical Care Services of S. Florida
9410 Stirling Rd., Cooper City
(954) 432-5611

Coral Springs Animal Hospital & Emergency Service
2160 N. University Dr., Coral Springs
(954) 753-1800

Volusia Animal Emergency Clinic
US 92, Daytona Beach
(386) 252-4300

Animal Emergency Clinic of Deerfield Beach
103 N. Powerline Rd., Deerfield Beach
(954) 428-9888

Florida Veterinary Referral Center & 24 Hour Emergency & Critical Care
9220 Estero Park Commons Blvd., Suite 7, Estero
(239) 992-8878

Animal Emergency Trauma Center
2200 W. Oakland Park Blvd., Fort Lauderdale
(954) 731-4228

Pet Emergency Center
921 E. Cypress Creek Rd., Fort Lauderdale
(954) 772-0420

Emergency Veterinary Clinic, Inc.
2045 Collier Ave., Fort Myers
(239) 939-5542

Animal Emergency and Referral Center
3984 S. US 1, Fort Pierce
(772) 466-3441

Affiliated Pet Emergency Services
7314 W. University Ave., Gainesville
(352) 373-4444

Hollywood Animal Hospital
2864 Hollywood Blvd., Hollywood
(954) 920-3556

Animal ER
3444 Southside Blvd., Suite 101, Jacksonville
(904) 642-4357

Emergency Pet Care, LLC
14185 Beach Blvd., Suite 7, Jacksonville
(904) 223-8000

Emergency Pet Care of Jupiter
300 S. Central Blvd., Jupiter
(561) 746-0555

Tampa Bay Veterinary Emergency Service
1501-A Belcher Rd., Suite 1A, Largo
(727) 531-5752

Animal Emergency and Critical Care Center of Brevard
2281 W. Eau Gallie Blvd., Melbourne
(321) 725-5365

AEC-Animal Emergency Clinic South
8429 S.W. 132nd St., Miami
(305) 251-2096

Miami Pet Emergency
11774 S.W. 88th St., Miami
(305) 273-8100

Miami Veterinary Specialists
8601 Sunset Dr., Miami
(305) 665-2820

Snapper Creek Emergency Clinic (Knowles Animal Clinics)
9933 Sunset Dr., Miami
(305) 279-2323

Emergency Pet Hospital of Collier County
6530 Dudley Dr., Naples
(239) 263-8010

Animal ER of SW Florida
15201 N. Cleveland Ave. #1400, North Fort Myers
(239) 995-7755

Clay-Duval Pet Emergency Clinic
275 Corporate Way, Suite 200, Orange Park
(904) 264-8281

Veterinary Emergency Clinic of Central Florida, South Facility
2080 Principal Row, Orlando
(407) 438-4449

Pet Emergency and Critical Care Clinic
3816 Northlake Blvd., Palm Beach Gardens
(561) 691-9999

A.A. Animal ER Center, LLC
36401 US 19N, Palm Harbor
(727) 787-5402

Animal Emergency of Countryside, Inc.
30610 US 19N, Palm Harbor
(727) 786-5755

After Hours Emergency Animal Clinic of Hollywood, Inc.
6602 Pines Blvd., Pembroke Pines
(954) 962-0300

Veterinary Referral Emergency Center
4800 N. Davis Hwy., Pensacola
(850) 477-3914

The Veterinary Emergency Clinic
17829 Murdock Cir., Port Charlotte
(941) 255-5222

Sarasota Veterinary Emergency Hospital
7517 S. Tamiami Tr., Sarasota
(941) 923-7260

Animal Emergency Clinic of St. Petersburg
3165 22nd Ave. N., St. Petersburg
(727) 323-1311

Noahs Animal Hospital and 24 Hour Emergency
2050 62nd Ave. N., St. Petersburg
(727) 522-6640

Pet Emergency of Martin County
2239 S. Kanner Hwy., Stuart
(772) 781-3302

Pet Emergency Center
7110 N. University Dr., Tamarac
(954) 726-0998

FVS (Florida Veterinary Specialists)
3000 Busch Lake Blvd., Tampa
(813) 933-8944

Tampa Bay Veterinary Emergency Service
238 E. Bearss Ave., Tampa
(813) 265-4043

Animal E.R.
8237 Cooper Creek Blvd., University Park
(941) 355-2884

Palm Beach Veterinary Referral and Critical Care Center
3092 Forest Hill Blvd., West Palm Beach
(561) 434-5700

GEORGIA

All Pets Emergency and Referral Center, P.C.
6460 Hwy. 9N, Alpharetta
(678) 366-2125

University of Georgia - Vet Teaching Hospital
College of Veterinary Medicine, Athens
(706) 542-3221

Southern Crescent Animal Emergency Clinic
1270 Hwy. 54 E., Fayetteville
(770) 460-8166

An-Emerg Animal Emergency Center
275 #3 Pearl Nix Pkwy., Gainesville
(770) 534-2911

VCA Animal Emergency & Referral of Gwinnett
1956 Lawrenceville-Suwanee Rd., Lawrenceville
(770) 277-3220

Cobb Emergency Veterinary Clinic
630 Cobb Pkwy. N., Suite C, Marietta
(770) 424-9157

Animal Emergency Center of North Fulton
900 Mansell Rd., Suite 19, Roswell
(770) 594-2266

Animal Emergency Center of Sandy Springs
228 Sandy Springs Pl. N.E., Sandy Springs
(404) 252-7881

Georgia Veterinary Specialists and Emergency Care
455 Abernathy Rd. N.E., Sandy Springs
(404) 459-0903

DeKalb-Gwinnet Animal Emergency Clinic
6430 Lawrenceville Hwy., Tucker
(770) 491-0661

Cherokee Emergency Veterinary Clinic
7800 Hwy. 92, Woodstock
(770) 924-3720

IDAHO

WestVet
5019 N. Sawyer Ave., Garden City
(208) 375-1600

North Idaho Pet Emergency
2700 E. Seltice Way #12, Post Falls
(208) 777-2707

ILLINOIS

Animal E.R. of Arlington Heights
1195 E. Palatine Rd., Arlington Heights
(847) 394-6049

VCA Animal Hospital
2600 W. Galena Blvd., Aurora
(630) 896-8541

Animal Emergency Clinic of McLean County
2505 E. Oakland Ave., Bloomington
(309) 665-5020

Veterinary Specialty Center Emergency & Critical Care
1515 Busch Pkwy., Buffalo Grove
(847) 459-7535

Animal Emergency Clinic of Champaign County
1713 S. State St. #4, Champaign
(217) 359-1977

Chicago Veterinary Emergency Services
3123 N. Clybourne Ave., Chicago
(773) 281-7110

Animal Emergency Center
2005 Mall St., Collinsville
(618) 346-1898

Emergency Veterinary Care South, Assoc.
13715 S. Cicero Ave., Crestwood
(708) 388-3771

Animal Emergency of McHenry County
1095 Pingree Rd., Suite 120, Crystal Lake
(815) 479-9119

Arboretum View Animal Hospital
2551 Warrenville Rd., Downers Grove
(630) 963-0424

Dundee Animal Hospital
199 Penny Ave., Dundee
(847) 428-6114

VCA Franklin Park Animal Hospital
9846 W. Grand Ave., Franklin Park
(847) 455-4922

Animal Emergency & Treatment Center
1810 E. Belvidere Rd., Grayslake
(847) 548-5300

Emergency Veterinary Services
820 Ogden Ave., Lisle
(630) 960-2900

Animal Emergency of Mokena
19110 S. 88th Ave., Mokena
(708) 326-4800

Animal Emergency and Referral Center
1810 Skokie Blvd., Northbrook
(847) 564-5775

Animal Emergency Clinic of Rockford
4236 Maray Dr., Rockford
(815) 229-7791

Animal 911
3735 W. Dempster St., Skokie
(847) 673-9110

Animal Emergency Clinic of Springfield
1333 W. Wabash Ave., Springfield
(217) 698-0870

Emergency Veterinary Services of St. Charles
530 Dunham Rd., St. Charles
(630) 584-7447

University of Illinois College of Veterinary Medicine
1008 W. Hazelwood Dr., Urbana
(217) 333-5300

INDIANA

Northwood Veterinary Hospital
3255 N. SR 9, Anderson
(765) 649-5218

St. Francis Family Pet Health Care
822 W. Plymouth St., Breman
(574) 546-9005

Airport Animal Emergi-Center
5235 W. Washington St., Indianapolis
(317) 248-0832

Indiana Veterinary Specialist & Emergency Center
8250 Bash St., Indianapolis
(317) 849-4925

Indianapolis Veterinary Emergency Center
5425 Victory Dr., Indianapolis
(317) 782-4484

Noahs Animal Hospital, P.C.
5510 Millersville Rd., Indianapolis
(317) 253-1327

Animal Emergency Clinic of Tippecanoe County
1343 Sagamore Pkwy. N., Lafayette
(765) 449-2001

Animal Emergency Clinic
2324 Grape Rd., Mishawaka
(574) 259-8387

Calumet Emergency Veterinary Clinic
150 W. Lincoln Hwy., Schererville
(219) 865-0970

North Central Veterinary Emergency Center
1645 S. US 421, Westville
(219) 785-7300

IOWA

Iowa State University Veterinary Clinical Sciences Teaching Hospital
S. 16th St., Ames
(515) 294-4900

Animal Emergency Center of the Quad Cities
1510 State St., Bettendorf
(563) 344-9599

Eastern Iowa Veterinary Specialty Center
755 Capital Dr. S.W., Cedar Rapids
(319) 841-5161

Iowa Veterinary Specialty
6110 Creston Ave., Des Moines
(515) 280-3051

KANSAS

Kansas State University Vet. Med. Teaching Hospital
1800 Denison Ave., Manhattan
(785) 532-4100

Mission MedVet
5914 Johnson Dr., Mission
(913) 722-5566

Veterinary Specialty & Emergency Center
11950 W. 110th St., Overland Park
(913) 642-9563

Central Kansas Veterinary Center
515 W. Blanchard Ave., South Hutchinson
(620) 663-8387

Animal Emergency Treatment Center
839 S.W. Fairlawn Rd., Topeka
(785) 272-2926

Veterinary Emergency and Specialty Hospital of Wichita
727 S. Washington, Wichita
(316) 262-5321

KENTUCKY

AA Small Animal Emergency Service
150 Dennis Dr., Lexington
(859) 276-2505

Jefferson Animal Hospital and Regional Emergency Center
4504 Outer Loop, Louisville
(502) 966-4104

Louisville Veterinary Specialty and Emergency Services
12905 Shelbyville Rd., Suite 3, Louisville
(502) 244-3036

Greater Cincinnati Veterinary Specialists & Emergency Services
11 Beacon Dr., Wilder
(859) 572-0560

LOUISIANA

Baton Rouge Pet Emergency Hospital
1514 Cottondale Dr., Baton Rouge
(225) 925-5566

Veterinary Emergency and Critical Care
2611 Florida St., Mandeville
(985) 626-4862

Southeast Vet Emergency
3409 Division St., Metairie
(504) 219-0444

MAINE

Eastern Maine Emergency Veterinary Clinic
15 Dirigo Dr., Brewer
(207) 989-6267

Animal Emergency Clinic of Mid-Maine
37 Strawberry Ave., Lewiston
(207) 777-1110

Animal Emergency Clinic
739 Warren Ave., Portland
(207) 878-3121

MARYLAND

Anne Arundel Veterinary Emergency Clinic
808 Bestgate Rd., Annapolis
(410) 224-0331

Harford Emergency Veterinary Services
526 Underwood Ln., Bel Air
(410) 420-8000

Emergency Veterinary Clinic, Inc.
32 Mellor Ave., Catonsville
(410) 788-7040

Emergency Animal Hospital of Ellicott City
10270 Baltimore National Pike (SR 40W), Ellicott City
(410) 750-1177

Frederick Emergency Animal Hospital
434 Prospect Blvd., Frederick
(301) 662-6622

Greenbriar Veterinary Referral & Emergency Center
3051 Thurston Rd., Frederick
(301) 874-8880

VCA Veterinary Referral Associates
15021 Dufief Mill Rd., Gaithersburg
(301) 340-3224

Metropolitan Emergency Animal Clinic
12106 Nebel St., Rockville
(301) 770-5225

Pets ER
329 Tilghman Rd., Suite 100, Salisbury
(410) 543-8400

PET ER
1209 Cromwell Bridge Rd., Towson
(410) 252-8387

VCA Veterinary Referral & Emergency Center
3485 Rockefeller Ct., Waldorf
(301) 638-0988

MASSACHUSETTS

Animal Emergency Care
164 Great Rd., Acton
(978) 263-1742

MSPCA Angell Animal Medical Center
350 S. Huntington Ave., Boston
(617) 522-7282

Cape Cod Veterinary Specialists Emergency Service
11 Bourne Bridge Approach, Buzzards Bay
(508) 759-5125

Wignall Animal Hospital
1837 Bridge St., Dracut
(978) 454-8272

Essex County Veterinary Emergency Hospital
247 Chickering Rd., North Andover
(978) 725-5544

Tufts University Cummings School of Veterinary Medicine
200 Westboro Rd., North Grafton
(508) 839-5395

VCA South Shore Animal Hospital
595 Columbian St., South Weymouth
(781) 337-6622

VCA Boston Road Animal Hospital
1235 Boston Rd., Springfield
(413) 783-1203

TUFTS Veterinary Emergency Treatment and Specialties
525 South St., Walpole
(508) 668-5454

Veterinary Emergency & Specialty Center of New England
180 Bear Hill Rd., Waltham
(781) 684-8387

New England Animal Medical Center
595 W. Center St., West Bridgewater
(508) 580-2515

Massachusetts Veterinary Referral Hospital
20 Cabot Rd., Woburn
(781) 932-5802

Woburn Animal Hospital
373 Russell St., Woburn
(781) 933-0170

MICHIGAN

Animal Emergency Clinic
4126 Packard Rd., Ann Arbor
(734) 971-8774

Ann Arbor Animal Hospital Emergency Service
2150 W. Liberty, Ann Arbor
(734) 662-4474

Michigan Veterinary Specialists
3412 E. Walton Blvd., Auburn Hills
(248) 371-3713

Oakland Veterinary Emergency & Critical Care
1400 Telegraph Rd., Bloomfield Hills
(248) 334-6877

Michigan State University Veterinary Teaching Hospital
Michigan State University, Wilson Rd., East Lansing
(517) 353-5420

Animal Emergency Hospital
1007 S. Ballenger Hwy., Flint
(810) 238 7557

Animal Emergency Hospital
3260 Plainfield Ave. N.E., Grand Rapids
(616) 361-9911

Southwest Michigan Animal Emergency Hospital
3301 S. Burdick, Kalamazoo
(269) 381-5228

Lansing Veterinary Urgent Care
3276 E. Jolly Rd., Lansing
(517) 393-9200

Veterinary Emergency Service-East
28223 John R Rd., Madison Heights
(248) 547-4677

Veterinary Care Specialists
205 Rowe Rd., Milford
(248) 684-0468

Animal Emergency Center
24360 Novi Rd., Novi
(248) 348-1788

Veterinary Emergency Service-West
40850 Ann Arbor Rd., Plymouth
(734) 207-8500

Great Lakes Pet Emergencies
1221 Tittabawassee Rd., Saginaw
(989) 752-1960

Michigan Veterinary Specialists
29080 Inkster Rd., Southfield
(248) 354-6660

Affiliated Veterinary Emergency Service
14085 Northline Rd., Southgate
(734) 284-1700

MINNESOTA

South Metro Animal Emergency Care
14690 Pennock Ave., Apple Valley
(952) 953-3737

Midwest Veterinary Referral & Emergency Center
11850 Aberdeen St., N.E., Blaine
(763) 754-5000

Affiliated Emergency Veterinary Hospital
1615 Coon Rapids Blvd., Coon Rapids
(763) 754-9434

Affiliated Emergency Veterinary Service
2314 W. Michigan St., Duluth
(218) 302-8000

Affiliated Emergency Veterinary Service
7717 Flying Cloud Dr., Eden Prairie
(952) 942-8272

Affiliated Emergency Veterinary Service
4708 Hwy. 55, Golden Valley
(763) 529-6560

Animal Emergency Clinic
7166 10th St. N., Oakdale
(651) 501-3766

Affiliated Emergency Veterinary Service
121 23rd Ave. S.W., Rochester
(507) 424-3976

Affiliated Emergency Veterinary Service
4180 Thielman Ln., St. Cloud
(320) 258-3481

Animal Emergency Clinic
301 University Ave., St. Paul
(651) 293-1800

University of Minnesota, College of Veterinary Medicine
1365 Gortner Ave., St. Paul
(612) 626-8387

MISSOURI

Animal Emergency Clinic
12501 Natural Bridge Rd., Bridgeton
(314) 739-1500

University of Missouri-Columbia Veterinary Med. Teaching Hospital
900 E. Campus Dr., Columbia
(573) 882-4589

Animal Emergency Center
8141 N. Oak Traffic Way, Kansas City
(816) 455-5430

Animal Emergency & Referral Hospital
3495 N.E. Ralph Powell Rd., Lee's Summit
(816) 554-4990

Animal Emergency Clinic
334 Fort Zumwalt Sq., O'Fallon
(636) 240-5496

Emergency Veterinary Clinic of Southwest Missouri
400 S. Glenstone Ave., Springfield
(417) 890-1600

Animal Emergency Clinic
9937 Big Bend Blvd., St. Louis
(314) 822-7600

MONTANA

Western Montana Small Animal Emergency Clinic
1914 S. Reserve St., Missoula
(406) 829-9300

NEBRASKA

Veterinary Emergency Services of Lincoln
3700 S. 9th St., Lincoln
(402) 489-6800

Animal Emergency Clinic
9664 Mockingbird Dr., Omaha
(402) 339-6232

NEVADA

Animal Emergency Center of Las Vegas
3340 E. Patrick Ln., Las Vegas
(702) 457-8050

Las Vegas Animal Emergency Hospital
5231 W. Charleston Blvd., Las Vegas
(702) 822-1045

Animal Emergency Center
6425 S. Virginia St., Reno
(775) 851-3600

NEW HAMPSHIRE

Capital Area Veterinary Emergency Service
22 Bridge St., Concord
(603) 227-1199

Veterinary Emergency Center of Manchester
55 Carl Dr., Manchester
(603) 666-6677

Animal Medical Center of New England
168 Main Dunstable Rd., Nashua
(603) 821-7222

The Veterinary Emergency, Critical Care & Cancer Treatment Center of NH
15 Piscataque Dr., Portsmouth
(603) 431-3600

NEW JERSEY

Veterinary Surgical & Diagnostic Specialists
34 Trenton-Lakewood Rd., Clarksburg
(609) 259-8300

Animal Emergency Referral Associates
1237 Broomfield Ave., Fairfield
(973) 226-3282

Red Bank Veterinary Hospital Hillsborough
210 Rt. 206S, Hillsborough
(908) 359-3161

Central Jersey Veterinary Emergency Services
643 Lincoln Hwy., Iselin
(732) 283-3535

Jersey Shore Veterinary Emergency Service
1000 Rt. 70, Lakewood
(732) 363-3200

Red Bank Veterinary Hospital Linwood
535 Maple Ave., Linwood
(609) 926-5300

Animal Emergency Service of South Jersey
220 Moorestown-Mount Laurel Rd., Mount Laurel
(856) 727-1332

Oradell Animal Hospital
580 Winters Ave., Paramus
(201) 262-0010

Alliance Emergency Veterinary Clinic
540 Rt. 10W, Randolph
(973) 328-2844

Animerge
21 Rt. 206S, Raritan
(908) 707-9077

Garden State Veterinary Specialists
1 Pine St., Tinton Falls
(732) 922-0011

Red Bank Veterinary Hospital
197 Hance Ave., Tinton Falls
(732) 747-3636

NEW MEXICO

Veterinary Medical Clinic
1407 Indian Wells Rd., Alamogordo
(575) 437-3063

Albuquerque Animal Emergency Clinic
4000 Montgomery Blvd. N.E., Albuquerque
(505) 884-3433

VCA Vet Care Animal Hospital & Referral Center
9901 Montgomery Blvd. N.E., Albuquerque
(505) 292-5353

Emergency Veterinary Clinic of Santa Fe
2001 Vivigen Way, Santa Fe
(505) 984-0625

NEW YORK

Greater Buffalo Veterinary Emergency Services
4949 Main St., Amherst
(716) 839-4043

Veterinary Emergency & Critical Care Center
2115 Downer Street Rd., Baldwinsville
(315) 638-3500

Katonah Bedford Veterinary Center
546 N. Bedford Rd., Bedford Hills
(914) 241-7700

Atlantic Coast Veterinary Specialists
3250 Veterans Hwy., Bohemia
(631) 285-7780

Animal Emergency Service
6230-C Jericho Tpke., Commack
(631) 462-6044

Veterinary Medical Center of Central New York
5841 Bridge St., East Syracuse
(315) 446-7933

New York Veterinary Specialty Center
2233 Broadhollow Rd., Farmingdale
(631) 694-3400

Animal Emergency Clinic
1112 Morton Blvd., Kingston
(845) 336-0713

Capital District Animal Emergency Clinic
222 Troy-Schenectady Rd., Latham
(518) 785-1094

Orange County Animal Emergency Service
517 Rt. 211E, Middletown
(845) 692-0260

The Veterinary Referral Center of Ultravet Diagnostics
220 E. Jericho Tpke., Mineola
(516) 294-6680

NYC Veterinary Specialists and Cancer Treatment Center
410 W. 55th St., New York
(212) 767-0099

Orchard Park Veterinary Medical Center
3930 N. Buffalo Rd., Orchard Park
(716) 662-6660

Long Island Veterinary Specialists & Animal Emergency & Critical Care Center
163 S. Service Rd., Plainview
(516) 501-1700

East End Veterinary Emergency Center
67 Commerce Dr., Riverhead
(631) 369-4513

Veterinary Specialists of Rochester and Animal Emergency Service
825 White Spruce Blvd., Rochester
(585) 424-1277 or (585) 424-1260

Animal Emergency Service
280-L Middle Country Rd., Selden
(631) 698-2225

Valley Cottage Animal Hospital
202 Rt. 303, Valley Cottage
(845) 268-9263

Nassau Animal Emergency Group
740 Old Country Rd., Westbury
(516) 333-6262

The Center for Specialized Veterinary Care
609-5 Cantiague Rock Rd., Westbury
(516) 420-0000

NORTH CAROLINA

REACH of Asheville Emergency Animal Hospital
677 Brevard Rd., Asheville
(828) 665-4399

Animal Emergency Clinic of the High Country
1126 Blowing Rock Rd., Suite A, Boone
(828) 268-2833

Animal Emergency Clinic of Cary
220 High House Rd., Cary
(919) 462-8989

Veterinary Specialty Hospital of the Carolinas
6405 Tryon Rd., Cary
(919) 233-4911

Animal Medical Hospital
3832 Monroe Rd., Charlotte
(704) 334-4684

Carolina Veterinary Specialists-Animal Emergency and Trauma Center
2225 Township Rd., Charlotte
(704) 504-9608

Triangle Veterinary Emergency Clinic
3319 Chapel Hill Blvd., Durham
(919) 489-0615

After Hours Veterinary Emergency Clinic
5505 W. Friendly Ave., Greensboro
(336) 851-1990

Carolina Veterinary Specialists-Animal Emergency and Trauma Center
501 Nicholas Rd., Greensboro
(336) 632-0605

After Hours Emergency Veterinary Clinic
126 Hwy. 321 S.W., Hickory
(828) 328-2660

Carolina Veterinary Specialists-Animal Emergency and Trauma Center
12117 Statesville Rd., Huntersville
(704) 949-1100

Cabarrus Emergency Veterinary Clinic
1317 S. Cannon Blvd., Kannapolis
(704) 932-1182

Emergency Veterinary Clinic, PA
2440 Plantation Center Dr., Matthews
(704) 844-6440

After Hours Small Animal Emergency Clinic
409 Vick Ave., Raleigh
(919) 781-5145

Quail Corners Animal Hospital & 24 Hour Emergency Care
1613 E. Millbrook Rd., Raleigh
(919) 876-0739

Veterinary Specialty Hospital-North Raleigh
4640 Paragon Park Rd., Raleigh
(919) 861-0109

Eastern Carolina Veterinary Emergency Treatment Service
4909-D Expressway Dr., Wilson
(252) 265-9920

Carolina Veterinary Specialists-Animal Emergency and Trauma Center
1600 Hanes Mall Blvd., Winston-Salem
(336) 896-0902

OHIO

Akron Veterinary Referral & Emergency Center
1321 Centerview Cir., Akron
(330) 665-4996

Metropolitan Veterinary Hospital
1053 S. Cleveland-Massillon Rd., Akron
(330) 666-2976

Great Lakes Veterinary Specialists
5035 Richmond Rd., Bedford Heights
(216) 831-6789

Animal Emergency Clinic West
5320 W. 140th St., Brook Park
(216) 362-6001

Stark County Veterinary Emergency Clinic, LLC
2705 Fulton Dr. N.W., Canton
(330) 452-5116

Cincinnati Animal Referral and Emergency Center
6995 E. Kemper Rd., Cincinnati
(513) 530-0911

Capital Veterinary Referral & Emergency Clinic
5230 Renner Rd., Columbus
(614) 870-0480

Ohio State University Veterinary Teaching Hospital
601 Vernon L. Tharp St., Columbus
(614) 292-3551

Dayton Emergency Veterinary Clinic
2714 Springboro W., Dayton
(937) 293-2714

After Hours Animal Emergency Clinic, Inc.
2680 W. Liberty St., Girard
(330) 530-8387

Animal Emergency Center, Inc.
5152 Grove Ave., Lorain
(440) 240-1400

Aaron Animal Clinic and Emergency Hospital
7640 Broadview Rd., Parma
(216) 901-9980

Animal Emergency & Critical Care Center of Toledo, Inc.
2785 W. Central Ave., Toledo
(419) 473-0328

Green Animal Medical Center
1620 Corporate Woods Cir., Uniontown
(330) 896-4040

MedVet Associates, Ltd.
300 E. Wilson Bridge Rd., Worthington
(614) 846-5800

OKLAHOMA

Animal Emergency Center
931 S.W. 74th, Oklahoma City
(405) 631-7828

Neel Veterinary Hospital
2700 N. MacArthur, Oklahoma City
(405) 947-8387

Veterinary Emergency and Critical Care Hospital
1800 W. Memorial Rd., Oklahoma City
(405) 749-6989

Animal Emergency Center, Inc.
7220 E. 41st St., Tulsa
(918) 665-0508

OREGON

The Animal Emergency Center of Central Oregon
1245 S.E. 3rd St., Suite C3, Bend
(541) 385-9110

VCA Northwest Veterinary Specialists & Emergency Services
16756 S.E. 82nd Dr., Clackamas
(503) 656-3999

Animal Emergency and Critical Care Center
1562 S.W. 3rd St., Corvallis
(541) 753-5750

Dove Lewis Emergency Animal Hospital
1945 N.W. Pettygroove, Portland
(503) 228-7281

VCA Southeast Portland Animal Hospital
13830 S.E. Stark St., Portland
(503) 255-8139

Salem Veterinary Emergency Clinic
3215 Market St. N.E., Salem
(503) 588-8082

Springfield-Eugene Emergency Veterinary Hospital
103 W. Q St., Springfield
(541) 746-0112

Emergency Veterinary Clinic of Tualatin
19314 S.W. Mohave Ct., Tualatin
(503) 691-7922

PENNSYLVANIA

Center for Animal Referral and Emergency Services
2010 Cabot Blvd. W., Suite D, Langhorne
(215) 750-2774

Veterinary Specialty & Emergency Center
1900 W. Old Lincoln Hwy., Langhorne
(215) 750-7884

Gwynedd Veterinary Hospital and Emergency Service
1615 W. Point Pike, Lansdale
(215) 699-9294

Allegheny Veterinary Emergency Trauma & Specialty
4224 Northern Pike, Monroeville
(412) 373-4200

Emergency Service, Veterinary Hospital of the University of PA
3900 Delancey St., Philadelphia
(215) 898-4685

VCA Castle Shannon Animal Hospital Service
3610 Library Rd., Pittsburgh
(412) 885-2500

Veterinary Emergency Clinic
807 Camp Horn Rd., Pittsburgh
(412) 366-3400

Hickory Veterinary Hospital
2303 Hickory Rd., Plymouth Meeting
(610) 828-3054

Metropolitan Emergency Service
2626 Van Buren Ave., Norristown
(610) 666-0914

Bucks County Veterinary Emergency Trauma Service
978 Easton Rd., Warrington
(215) 918-2200

Animal Emergency Center
395 Susquehanna Tr., Watsontown
(570) 742-7400

Valley Central Emergency Veterinary Hospital
210 Fullerton Ave., Whitehall
(610) 435-5588

RHODE ISLAND

Ocean State Veterinary Specialists
1480 S. County Tr., East Greenwich
(401) 886-6787

SOUTH CAROLINA

South Carolina Veterinary Emergency Care
3924 Fernandina Rd., Columbia
(803) 798-3837

Palmetto Regional Emergency Hospital for Animals
921 Spears Creek Ct., Elgin
(803) 865-1418

Greater Charleston Emergency Veterinary Clinic
930 Pine Hollow Rd., Mt. Pleasant
(843) 216-7554

Animal Emergency Hospital of the Strand
303 Hwy. 15, Suite 1, Myrtle Beach
(843) 445-9797

Greater Charleston Emergency Veterinary Clinic
3163 W. Montague Ave., North Charleston
(843) 744-3372

Spartanburg Veterinary Emergency Clinic
1291 Asheville Hwy., Spartanburg
(864) 591-1923

SOUTH DAKOTA
Veterinary Emergency Hospital
3508 S. Minnesota Ave., Suite 104, Sioux Falls
(605) 977-6200

TENNESSEE
Midland Pet Emergency Center, Inc.
235 Calderwood St., Alcoa
(865) 982-1007

Airport Pet Emergency Clinic
2436 Hwy. 75, Blountville
(423) 279-0574

Pet Emergency Treatment Service
1668 Mallory Ln., Brentwood
(615) 333-1212, ext. 1

Regional Institute for Veterinary Emergency & Referral
2132 Amnicola Hwy., Chattanooga
(423) 698-4612

Animal Emergency Clinic of Maury County, LLC
1900B Shady Brook St., Columbia
(931) 380-1929

PetMed Emergency Center, LLC
830 N. Germantown Pkwy., Suite 105, Cordova
(901) 624-9002

Knoxville Pet Emergency Clinic
1819 Ailor Ave., Knoxville
(865) 637-0114

University of Tennessee Veterinary Teaching Hospital
2407 River Dr., Knoxville
(865) 974-8387

Animal Emergency Center, PC
3767 Summer Ave., Memphis
(901) 323-4563

TEXAS
I-20 Animal Medical Center
5820 W. I-20, Arlington
(817) 478-9238

Austin Vet Care
4106 N. Lamar, Austin
(512) 459-4336

Emergency Animal Hospital of Northwest Austin
12034 Research Blvd., Suite 8, Austin
(512) 331-6121

Emergency Animal Hospital of Northwest Austin - South Branch
4434 Frontier Tr., Austin
(512) 899-0955

Southeast Texas Animal Emergency Clinic
3420 W. Cardinal Dr., Beaumont
(409) 842-3239

North Texas Emergency Pet Clinic
1712 W. Frankford Rd., Suite 108, Carrollton
(972) 323-1310

Emergency Animal Clinic
12101 Greenville Ave., Suite 118, Dallas
(972) 994-9110

The E-Clinic, Inc.
3337 Fitzhugh Ave., Dallas
(214) 520-8388

Denton County Animal Emergency Room
4145 S. I-35E, Suite 101, Denton
(940) 271-1200

El Paso Animal Emergency Center
1220 Airway Blvd., El Paso
(915) 545-1148

Airport Frwy. Animal Emergency Clinic
411 N. Main St., Euless
(817) 571-2088

Metro West Emergency Veterinary Center
3201 Hulen St., Fort Worth
(817) 731-3734

Animal Emergency Hospital of North Texas
2700 W. SR 114, Grapevine
(817) 410-2273

Animal Emergency Center of West Houston
4823 Hwy. 6N, Houston
(832) 593-8387

Animal Emergency Clinic
1111 West Loop S. #200, Houston
(713) 693-1100

Animal Emergency Clinic SH 249
19311 SH 249, Houston
(281) 890-8875

VCA Animal Emergency Hospital Southeast
10331 Gulf Frwy., Houston
(713) 941-8460

Veterinary Emergency Referral Group, Inc.
8921 Katy Frwy., Houston
(713) 932-9589

VCA Metroplex Animal Hospital & Pet Lodge
700 W. Airport Frwy., Irving
(972) 438-7113

After Hours Veterinary Services
2501 S. W.S. Young, Suite 109, Killeen
(254) 628-5017

VCA Animal Emergency Clinic Southeast-Calder Rd.
1108 Gulf Frwy. S., Suite 280, League City
(281) 332-1678

Lake Ray Hubbard Emergency Pet Care Center
4651 N. Beltline Rd., Mesquite
(972) 226-3377

Lake Ray Hubbard Emergency Pet Care Center
9501 Lakeview Pkwy., Rowlett
(972) 475-5349

Angel of Mercy Animal Critical Care, Inc.
8734 Grissom Rd., San Antonio
(210) 684-2105

Animal Emergency Room
4315 Fredericksburg Rd., Suite 2, San Antonio
(210) 737-7380

Emergency Pet Clinic, Inc.
8503 Broadway #105, San Antonio
(210) 822-2873

Northeast Emergency Animal Clinic
8365 Perrin Beitel, San Antonio
(210) 650-3141

Animal Emergency & Urgent Care Center of The Woodlands
27870 I-45N, The Woodlands
(281) 367-5444

Texas Animal Medical Center
4900 Steinbeck Bend, Waco
(254) 753-0901

UTAH

Central Valley Veterinary Hospital
55 E. Miller Ave., Salt Lake City
(801) 487-1325

Pet E.R. - The Pet Emergency Room
6360 S. Highland Dr., Salt Lake City
(801) 278-0505

Animal Emergency Center
2465 N. Main St., Sunset
(801) 776-8118

VERMONT

Burlington Emergency Veterinary Service
200 Commerce St., Williston
(802) 865-1205

VIRGINIA

Alexandria Veterinary Emergency Service
2660 Duke St., Alexandria
(703) 823-3601

Veterinary Emergency Treatment Services, Inc.
370 Greenbrier Dr., Suite A-2, Charlottesville
(434) 973-3519

Greenbrier Veterinary Emergency Center
1100 Eden Way N., Suite 101B, Chesapeake
(757) 366-9000

SouthPaws Veterinary Specialists & Emergency Center
8500 Arlington Blvd., Fairfax
(703) 752-9100

Animal Emergency Critical Care
165 Fort Evans Rd. N.E., Leesburg
(703) 777-5755

Animal Emergency & Critical Care of Lynchburg
3432 Odd Fellows Rd., Lynchburg
(434) 846-1504

Veterinary Referral & Critical Care (VRCC)
1596 Hockett Rd., Manakin Sabot
(804) 784-8722

Prince William Emergency Veterinary Clinic
8610 Centreville Rd., Manassas
(703) 361-8287

Veterinary Emergency Center South
2460 Colony Crossing Pl., Midlothian
(804) 744-9800

Veterinary Emergency Center, Inc.
3312 W. Cary St., Richmond
(804) 353-9000

Emergency Veterinary Services of Roanoke
4902 Frontage Rd. N.W., Roanoke
(540) 563-8575

Regional Veterinary Referral Center
6651 Backlick Rd., Springfield
(703) 451-8900

The Hope Center for Advanced Veterinary Medicine
140 Park St. S.E., Vienna
(703) 281-5121

Beach Veterinary Emergency Center
1124 Lynnhaven Pkwy., Virginia Beach
(757) 468-4900

Tidewater Animal Emergency & Referral Center
364 S. Independence Blvd., Virginia Beach
(757) 499-5463

Woodbridge Animal Hospital
2703 Caton Hill Rd., Woodbridge
(703) 897-5665

Emergency Veterinary Clinic
1120 George Washington Memorial Hwy., Yorktown
(757) 874-8115

WASHINGTON

After Hours Animal Emergency Clinic
718 Auburn Way N., Auburn
(253) 939-6272

Animal Emergency Care
317 Telegraph Rd., Bellingham
(360) 758-2200

Animal Emergency Clinic of Everett
3625 Rucker Ave., Everett
(425) 258-4466

VCA Alpine Animal Hospital
888 N.W. Sammamish Rd., Issaquah
(425) 392-8888

Animal Emergency Service, East
636 7th Ave., Kirkland
(425) 827-8727

VCA Veterinary Specialty Center of Seattle
20115 44th Ave. W., Lynnwood
(425) 697-6106

Pet Emergency Center
14434 Avon Allen Rd., Mount Vernon
(360) 848-5911

Animal Emergency & Trauma Center
320 Lindvig Way, Poulsbo
(360) 697-7771

Washington State University
Veterinary Teaching Hospital, 100 Grimes Way, Pullman
(509) 335-0711

Animal Critical Care & Emergency Services (ACCES)
11536 Lake City Way, N.E., Seattle
(206) 364-1660

Emerald City Emergency Clinic
4102 Stone Way N., Seattle
(206) 634-9000

VCA Five Corners Veterinary Hospital
15707 1st Ave. S., Seattle
(206) 243-2982

PSCVM Small Animal Emergency and Critical Care Center
11308 92nd St. S.E., Snohomish
(360) 568-9111

Pet Emergency Clinic
21 E. Mission Ave., Spokane
(509) 326-6670

The Animal Emergency Clinic
5608 S. Durango St., Tacoma
(253) 474-0791

Columbia River Veterinary Specialists
6818 N.E. 4th Plain Blvd., Suite C, Vancouver
(360) 694-3007

St. Francis 24 Hr. Animal Hospital
12010 N.E. 65th St., Vancouver
(360) 253-5446

WEST VIRGINIA

Kanawha Valley Animal Emergency Clinic
5304 MacCorkle Ave. S.W., Charleston
(304) 768-2911

Animal Urgent Care, Inc.
4201 Wood St., Wheeling
(304) 233-0002

WISCONSIN

Fox Valley Animal Referral Center
4706 New Horizons Blvd., Appleton
(920) 993-9193

Animal Emergency Center & Specialty Services
2100 W. Silver Spring Dr., Glendale
(414) 540-6710

Green Bay Animal Emergency Center
933 Anderson Dr., Suite F, Green Bay
(920) 494-9400

Animal Emergency Center, South
4607 S. 108th St., Greenfield
(414) 427-1731

Emergency Clinic for Animals
229 W. Beltline Hwy., Madison
(608) 274-7772

Emergency Vets of Central Wisconsin, LLC
1420 Kronenwetter Dr., Mosinee
(715) 693-6934

The Animal ER of Kenosha & Racine
4333 S. Green Bay Rd., Racine
(262) 553-9223

Wisconsin Veterinary Referral Center
360 Bluemound Rd., Waukesha
(262) 542-3241

Canada

ALBERTA

Calgary North Veterinary Hospital and Emergency Service
4204 4th St. N.W., Calgary
(403) 277-0135

Animal Emergency Hospital South, Ltd.
3823 99th St. N.W., Edmonton
(780) 436-5880

Edmonton Veterinarians Emergency Clinic
11104 102nd Ave., Edmonton
(780) 433-9505

BRITISH COLUMBIA

Central Animal Emergency Clinic
812 Roderick Ave., Coquitlam
(604) 931-1911

Animal Emergency Clinic of the Fraser Valley
#306-6325 204th St., Langley
(604) 514-1711

Vancouver Animal Emergency Clinic, Ltd.
1590 W. 4th St., Vancouver
(604) 734-5104

Animal Emergency Clinic
760 Roderick St., Victoria
(250) 475-2495

MANITOBA

Winnipeg Animal Emergency Hospital
400 Pembina Hwy., Winnipeg
(204) 452-9427

NOVA SCOTIA

Metro Animal Emergency Clinic
201 Brownlow Ave., Unit 9, Dartmouth
(902) 468-0674

ONTARIO

Veterinary Emergency Clinic of York Region
1210 Journey's End Cir., New Market
(905) 953-5351

Huronia Veterinary Emergency Clinic
115 Bell Farm Rd., Barrie
(705) 722-0377

Emergency Veterinary Clinic
#1 Wexford Rd., Brampton
(905) 495-9907

North Town Veterinary Hospital
496 Main St. N., Brampton
(905) 451-2000

Veterinary Emergency Clinic
41 Adelaide St. N., #43, London
(519) 432-7341

Mississauga-Oakville Veterinary Emergency Hospital & Referral Group
2285 Bristol Cir., Oakville
(905) 829-9444

Alta Vista Animal Hospital
2616 Bank St., Ottawa
(613) 731-9911

Niagara Veterinary Emergency Clinic
3300 Merrittville Hwy., Thorold
(905) 641-3185

Veterinary Emergency Clinic
280 Sheppard Ave. E., Toronto
(416) 226-3663

Veterinary Emergency Clinic & Referral Center
920 Yonge St. #117, Toronto
(416) 920-2002

Animal Emergency Clinic
1910 Dundas St. E., Unit B 101, Whitby
(905) 576-3031

QUEBEC

DMV Veterinary Centre
2300 54th Ave., Lachine
(514) 633-8888

University of Montreal/Companion Animal Clinic
1525 Des Veterinary St., St-Hyacinthe
(450) 778-8111

Pet-Friendly Lodgings

How to Use the Listings

U.S. Lodgings

Canadian Lodgings

Campground Listings

How to Use the Listings

Some 13,000 AAA-RATED® hotels and campgrounds across North America accept traveling pets. This guide provides listings for those lodgings in the United States and Canada that roll out the welcome mat for pets as well as the people who love them.

For the purpose of this book, "pets" are domestic cats or dogs. If you are planning to travel with any other kind of animal — particularly such exotic pets as birds or reptiles — check with the property before making definite plans. Expect to keep nontraditional pets crated at all times.

Note: Always inform the management that you are traveling with an animal; you may be fined if you do not declare your pet. Many properties require guests with pets to sign a waiver or release form and to pay for the room with a credit card. Of course, whether you pay in cash or by credit card, you will be held liable for any damages caused by your pet, even if the property does not charge a deposit or pet fee. It is not a good idea to leave your pet unattended in the room, but if you must, crate him and notify management. When in public areas, keep your pet leashed and do not allow him to disturb other guests.

About the Listings

Geographic listings are used for accuracy and consistency; lodgings are listed under the city or town in which they physically are located — or in some cases under the nearest recognized city or town. For a complete list of all cities within a state or province, see the comprehensive City Index at the beginning of the corresponding section.

U.S. properties are shown first, followed by Canadian properties. Most listings are alphabetically organized by state or province, city and establishment name. Reflecting contemporary travel patterns, properties in some cities or towns may instead be listed within destination cities or areas. Such "vicinity cities" and their listings will be shown alphabetically in the destination city or area, and the vicinity city also will appear in alphabetical order in the City Index, along with the page number on which the listings begin.

Each listing provides the following information *(see sample listing, next page):*

❶ Symbol denoting Official Appointment (OA) properties. The OA program permits properties to display and advertise the 🚗 or 🚗 logo. OAs have a special interest in serving AAA/CAA members. Ask if they offer special member amenities such as free breakfast, early check-in/late check-out, free room upgrade, free local phone calls, etc.

❷ Diamond rating

❸ Property name

❹ Lodging classification
(see next page for descriptions)

❺ Special amenities offered. These properties provide an additional benefit to pets, such as treats, toys or gifts, pet sitting and/or walking, a pet menu, food/water dishes, pet sheets or pillows, pet beds or other extras.

❻ Telephone number

❼ Two-person (2P) rate year-round, and cancellation notice validity period (if more than 48 hours). Rates listed are daily. **Note:** Most properties accept any or all of the major credit cards, including American Express, MasterCard and VISA. If a property accepts only cash, the phrase "(no credit cards)" follows the rates. "Call for rates" indicates rates were not available at time of printing. Please contact property for current rate information.

❽ Physical address and/or highway location, if available

❾ Exterior or interior corridors

❿ Pet policies. If the phrase "pets accepted" appears, the property does accept pets but specific information was unavailable at press time. Otherwise, pet-specific policies are denoted as follows:

Size. "Very small" denotes pets weighing up to 10 pounds; "small," up to 25 pounds; "medium," up to 50 pounds; and "large," up to 100 pounds. If no size is specified, the property accepts pets of all sizes.

Species. "Other" indicates the property accepts animals other than dogs and cats. Always call ahead and specify the type of pet you plan to bring.

Deposits and fees. Includes the dollar amount, the type of charge (refundable deposit or nonrefundable fee), the frequency of the charge and whether the charge is per pet or per room.

Designated rooms. Guests with pets are placed in certain rooms, often smoking rooms or those on the ground floor.

Housekeeping service. The phrase "service with restrictions" denotes properties that require the pet to be crated, removed or attended by the owner during housekeeping service.

Supervision. The pet is required to be supervised at all times.

Crate. The pet must be crated when the owner is not present.

⓫ **Property discounts and amenities:**

[SAVE] Discounted standard room rate or lowest public rate available at time of booking for dates of stay

[ASK] May offer discount

[⊠] Designated non-smoking rooms

[♿] Accessible features
(call property for available services and amenities)

[🗄] Refrigerator

[☕] Coffee maker

[🍽] Restaurant on premises

Pool

Recreational activities

No air conditioning

No TV

No telephones

> Please note: Some in-room amenities represented by the icons in the listings may be available only in selected rooms, and may incur an extra fee. Please inquire when making your reservations.

It is important to remember that animal policies do change; always confirm policies, restrictions and fees with the lodging when making reservations and again 1-2 days before departure.

Listing information is subject to change. All listing information was accurate at press time. However, lodging rates and policies change and the publisher cannot be held liable for changes occurring after publication. AAA cannot guarantee the safety of guests or their pets at any facility.

AAA Diamond Ratings

Before a property is listed by AAA, it must satisfy a set of minimum standards regarding basic lodging needs as identified by AAA members. If a property meets those requirements (determined during an unannounced evaluation by a AAA inspector), it is assigned a Diamond Rating.

Once an establishment becomes AAA Approved, it is then assigned a rating of one to five Diamonds, indicating the extensiveness of its facilities, amenities and services, from basic to moderate to luxury. The Diamond Ratings guide members in selecting establishments appropriately matched to their needs and expectations.

These establishments typically appeal to the budget-minded traveler. They provide essential, no-frills accommodations and basic comfort and hospitality.

These establishments appeal to family travelers seeking affordable yet more than the basic accommodations. Facilities, décor and amenities are modestly enhanced.

These establishments offer a distinguished style. Properties are multifaceted, with marked upgrades in physical attributes, amenities and guest comforts.

These establishments are refined and stylish. Physical attributes are upscale. The fundamental hallmarks at this level include an extensive array of amenities combined with a high degree of hospitality, service, and attention to detail.

These establishments reflect the characteristics of the ultimate in luxury and sophistication. Physical attributes are extraordinary in every manner. Service is meticulous, exceeding guest expectations and maintaining impeccable standards of excellence. Extensive personalized services and amenities provide first-class comfort.

Lodging Classifications

Bed & Breakfast: Typically smaller scale properties emphasizing a high degree of personal touches that provide guests an "at home" feeling. Guest units tend to be individually decorated. Rooms may not include some modern amenities such as televisions and telephones, and may have a shared bathroom. Usually owner-operated with a common room or parlor separate from the innkeeper's living quarters, where guests and operators can interact during evening and breakfast hours. Evening office closures are normal. A continental or full, hot breakfast is served and is included in the room rate.

Cabin/Cottage: Vacation-oriented, small-scale, freestanding houses or cabins. Units vary in design and décor and often contain one or more bedrooms, living room, kitchen, dining area and bathroom. Studio-type

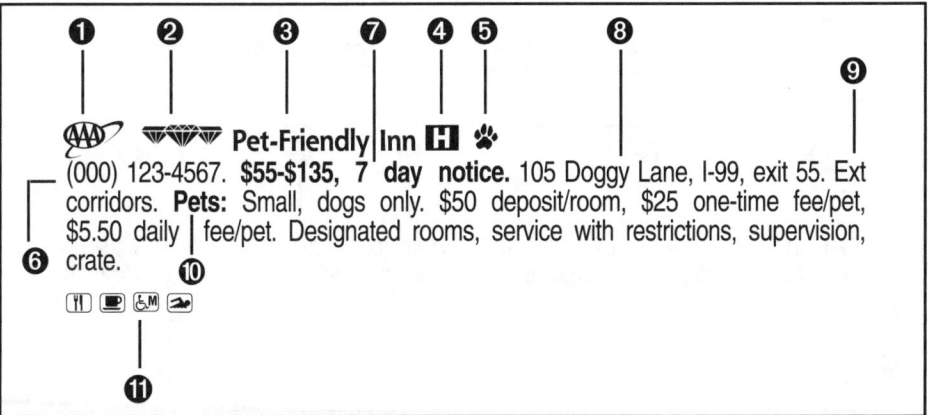

① ② ③ ⑦ ④ ⑤ ⑧ ⑨

Pet-Friendly Inn H ❀
(000) 123-4567. **$55-$135, 7 day notice.** 105 Doggy Lane, I-99, exit 55. Ext corridors. **Pets:** Small, dogs only. $50 deposit/room, $25 one-time fee/pet, $5.50 daily fee/pet. Designated rooms, service with restrictions, supervision, ⑥ crate. ⑩

⑪

models combine the sleeping and living areas into one room. Typically, basic cleaning supplies, kitchen utensils, and complete bed and bath linens are supplied. The guest registration area may be located off-site.

CI Country Inn: Although similar in definition to a bed and breakfast, country inns are usually larger in scale with spacious public areas and offer a dining facility that serves at least breakfast and dinner.

CO Condominium: Vacation-oriented—commonly for extended-stay purposes—apartment-style accommodations of varying design or décor. Routinely available for rent through a management company, units often contain one or more bedrooms, a living room, full kitchen, and an eating area. Studio-type models combine the sleeping and living areas into one room. As a rule, basic cleaning supplies, kitchen utensils, and complete bed and bath linens are supplied. The guest registration area may be located off site.

H Hotel: Commonly, a multistory establishment with interior room entrances offering a variety of guest unit styles. The magnitude of the public areas is determined by the overall theme, location and service level, but may include a variety of facilities such as a restaurant, shops, fitness center, spa, business center, and/or meeting rooms.

M Motel: Commonly, a one- or two-story establishment with exterior room entrances and drive up parking. Typically, guest units have one bedroom with a bathroom of similar décor and design. Public areas and facilities are often limited in size and/or availability.

RA Ranch: Typically a working ranch with an obvious rustic, Western theme featuring equestrian-related activities and a variety of guest unit styles.

VH Vacation Rental House: Vacation-oriented—commonly for extended-stay purposes—typically larger scale, freestanding, and of varying design or décor. Routinely available for rent through a management company, houses often contain two or more bedrooms, a living room, full kitchen, dining room, and multiple bathrooms. As a rule, basic cleaning supplies, kitchen utensils, and complete bed and bath linens are supplied. The guest registration area may be located off site.

Campground Listings

Geographic listings are used for accuracy and consistency. Campgrounds are listed under the city or town in which they physically are located — or in some cases under the nearest recognized city or town. Not all listings include physical addresses. U.S. campgrounds are listed first, followed by Canadian campgrounds. Listings are alphabetically organized by state or province, city and campground name.

Note: Call first before taking your pet on a camping trip, as campground policies regarding pets may change, including any possible fees that may be assessed.

Each listing provides the following information (see sample listing):

❶ Location

❷ Campground name

❸ Symbol denoting Official Appointment (OA) campgrounds. The OA program permits privately operated campgrounds to display and advertise the AAA or CAA logo. OAs have a special interest in serving AAA/CAA members.

❹ Telephone number

❺ Fee range for a specified number of persons, including the fee for an extra person (XP) staying at the campground.

❻ Most campgrounds accept any or all of the major credit cards, including American Express, MasterCard and Visa. If a campground accepts only cash, the phrase "(no credit cards)" appears.

❼ Physical address and/or highway location and mailing address (if available).

❽ Campground discounts and amenities:

    🅂🄳 10% senior discount for members over 59

    🅰 No Tents

    🌀 Pool

    🆇 Recreational activities

    🅶🄼 Accessible features
    (call property for available
    services and amenities)

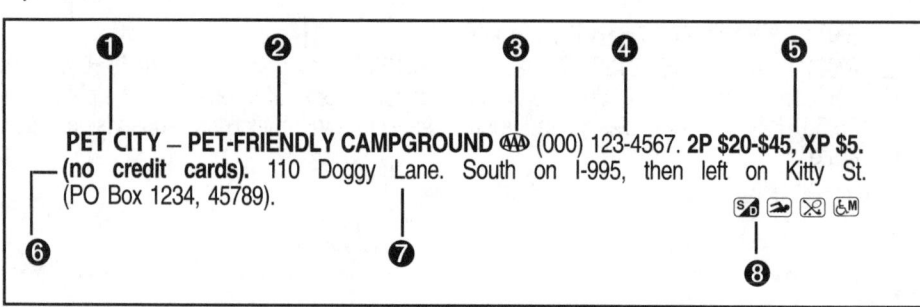

United States Lodgings

ALABAMA

ABBEVILLE

🔶 ▼▼▼ Best Western-Abbeville Inn M
(334) 585-5060. **$59-$89, 3 day notice.** 1237 US Hwy 431. Jct SR 27. Ext corridors. **Pets:** Large, other species. $8 daily fee/pet. Service with restrictions, crate.

SAVE ✖ 🖥 💻 ⌫

ALBERTVILLE

▼▼ Jameson Inn H
(256) 891-2600. **$78-$85.** 315 Martling Rd. On US 431, just e of SR 75. Ext corridors. **Pets:** Small, other species. $15 daily fee/pet. Service with restrictions.

ASK ✖ 🖥 💻 ⌫

▼▼ Microtel Inn & Suites H
(256) 894-4000. **$65-$70.** 220 Hwy 75 N. Jct US 431 and SR 75, just ne. Int corridors. **Pets:** Accepted.

✖ 🖥 💻 ⌫

ALEXANDER CITY

▼▼ Jameson Inn H
(256) 234-7099. **$78-$85.** 4335 US Hwy 280. US 280, just s of jct SR 22; just w of jct SR 63. Ext corridors. **Pets:** Medium, other species. $15 daily fee/pet. Service with restrictions, crate.

ASK ✖ 🖥 💻 ⌫

ANDALUSIA

▼▼ Days Inn M
(334) 427-0050. **Call for rates.** 1604 Dr. MLK Jr Expwy. On US 84 Bypass. Ext corridors. **Pets:** Medium, other species. $10 daily fee/room. Service with restrictions, supervision.

✖ 🖥 💻 ⌫

🔶 ▼ Econo Lodge M
(334) 222-7511. **$57-$90, 3 day notice.** 1421 Dr. MLK Jr Expwy. On US 84 Bypass. Ext corridors. **Pets:** Small. $10 daily fee/pet. Service with restrictions, supervision.

SAVE ✖ 🖥 💻 ⌫

ANNISTON

▼▼ Long Leaf Lodge at McClellan H
(256) 820-9494. **Call for rates.** 74 Exchange Ave. I-20, exit 185, 10 mi n on SR 21, then 1.5 mi e into McClellan-Ballzell Gate. Ext corridors. **Pets:** Accepted.

✖ 🖥 💻 ⌫

▼▼▼ The Victoria, a Country Inn CI
(256) 236-0503. **$89.** 1600 Quintard Ave. I-20, exit 185, 4 mi n on SR 21/US 431. Ext/int corridors. **Pets:** Accepted.

✖ 🖥 💻 🍴 ⌫

ARAB

▼▼ Jameson Inn H
(256) 586-5777. **$78-$85.** 706 N Brindlee Mountain Pkwy. On US 231, 0.5 mi n of jct SR 69. Ext corridors. **Pets:** Accepted.

ASK ✖ 🖥 💻 ⌫

ATHENS

🔶 ▼▼ Best Western Athens Inn H
(256) 233-4030. **$70-$100.** 1329 Hwy 72. I-65, exit 351, just w. Ext corridors. **Pets:** Small. $20 daily fee/pet. Designated rooms, service with restrictions, supervision.

SAVE ✖ 🖥 💻 ⌫

▼▼ Comfort Inn H
(256) 232-2704. **Call for rates.** 1218 Kelli Dr. I-65, exit 351, just e on US 72, then just s. Ext corridors. **Pets:** $30 daily fee/pet. Service with restrictions, crate.

✖ 🖥 💻 ⌫

▼▼ Sleep Inn Athens H
(256) 232-4700. **Call for rates.** 1115 Audubon Ln. I-65, exit 351, just nw. Int corridors. **Pets:** Medium. $10 daily fee/pet. Service with restrictions, supervision.

✖ 🖥 💻 ⌫

ATTALLA

▼▼ Days Inn Attalla H
(256) 538-7861. **Call for rates.** 801 Cleveland Ave. I-59, exit 183 northbound, just e; exit southbound, through first set of lights, then just e. Ext corridors. **Pets:** $15 daily fee/pet. Service with restrictions, supervision.

✖ 🖥 💻 ⌫

🔶 ▼ Econo Lodge H
(256) 570-0117. **Call for rates.** 915 E 5th Ave. I-59, exit 183 southbound, just e; exit northbound, through first set of lights, then just e. Ext corridors. **Pets:** Accepted.

SAVE ✖ 🖥

AUBURN

🔶 ▼▼▼ Best Western University Convention Center H
(334) 821-7001. **$100-$260.** 1577 S College St. I-85, exit 51, 1.4 mi n on US 29/SR 147. Ext corridors. **Pets:** Accepted.

SAVE ✖ 🖥 💻 ⌫

🔶 ▼▼▼ The Hotel at Auburn University & Dixon Conference Center H
(334) 821-8200. **Call for rates.** 241 S College St. I-85, exit 51, 3.5 mi n on US 29/SR 147. Int corridors. **Pets:** Accepted.

SAVE ✖ 🖥 💻 🍴 ⌫ ✖

Jameson Inn H
(334) 502-5020. **$83-$90.** 1212 Mall Pkwy. I-85, exit 58, 1.5 mi n on US 280 W, then 2.1 mi s on US 29/SR 14. Ext corridors. **Pets:** Accepted.
ASK ✕ ☐ ▣ ⇌

Microtel Inn & Suites H
(334) 826-1444. **$56-$199, 14 day notice.** 2174 S College St. I-85, exit 51, just n. Int corridors. **Pets:** Accepted.
SAVE ✕ ☐ ▣

BIRMINGHAM METROPOLITAN AREA

BESSEMER

Best Western Hotel & Suites H ❀
(205) 481-1950. **$99-$250.** 5041 Academy Ln. I-20/59, exit 108, just sw. Int corridors. **Pets:** Medium, other species. $15 daily fee/pet. Designated rooms, service with restrictions, supervision.
SAVE ✕ ☐ ▣ ⇌

Jameson Inn H
(205) 428-3194. **$88-$95.** 5021 Academy Ln. I-20/59, exit 108, just sw. Ext corridors. **Pets:** Medium, other species. $15 daily fee/room. No service, supervision.
ASK ✕ ☐ ▣ ⇌

Sleep Inn H
(205) 424-0000. **$79-$200.** 1259 Greenmor Dr. I-459, exit 6, just s, then just w. Int corridors. **Pets:** Accepted.
ASK ✕ ☐ ▣ ⇌

BIRMINGHAM

Best Western Mountain Brook M
(205) 991-9977. **$80.** 4627 Hwy 280 E. I-459, exit 19 (US 280), 1.4 mi e. Ext corridors. **Pets:** Accepted.
SAVE ✕ ▣ ⇌ ⊠

Clarion Hotel H
(205) 591-7900. **$109-$119, 7 day notice.** 5216 Airport Hwy. I-20/59, exit 129, just n. Int corridors. **Pets:** Accepted.
SAVE ✕ ☐ ▣ ⊓ ⇌

Days Inn H
(205) 324-4510. **$65-$150.** 905 11th Ct W. I-20/59, exit 123, just sw. Ext/int corridors. **Pets:** Other species. $10 daily fee/pet. Service with restrictions.
ASK ✕ ☐ ▣ ⇌

Drury Inn & Suites-Birmingham Southeast H
(205) 967-2450. **$100-$175.** 3510 Grandview Pkwy. I-459, exit 19 (US 280), just e; in Grandview. Int corridors. **Pets:** Other species. Service with restrictions, supervision.
ASK ✕ ☐ ▣ ⇌

Embassy Suites Birmingham H
(205) 879-7400. **$139-$369.** 2300 Woodcrest Pl. Just n of jct US 31 and 280, exit 21st Ave southbound, then 0.3 mi s. Int corridors. **Pets:** Accepted.
✕ ☐ ▣ ⊓ ⇌ ⊠

Homestead Studio Suites Hotel-Birmingham Perimeter Park South H
(205) 967-3800. **$65-$80.** 12 Perimeter Park S. I-459, exit 19 (US 280), 0.5 mi e, then just s. Ext corridors. **Pets:** Other species. $25 daily fee/pet. Service with restrictions, crate.
ASK ✕ ☐ ▣

La Quinta Inn & Suites Birmingham H ❀
(205) 995-9990. **$49-$99.** 513 Cahaba Park Cir. I-459, exit 19 (US 280), 1.2 mi e. Int corridors. **Pets:** Medium, other species. Service with restrictions, supervision.
ASK ✕ ☐ ▣

Residence Inn By Marriott H
(205) 991-8686. **$197-$211.** 3 Greenhill Pkwy. I-459, exit 19 (US 280), 2 mi e. Ext corridors. **Pets:** Accepted.
SAVE ✕ ☐ ▣ ⇌ ⊠

Sheraton Birmingham Hotel H ❀
(205) 324-5000. **$109-$309.** 2101 Richard Arrington Jr Blvd N. I-20/59, exit 22nd St. Int corridors. **Pets:** Medium, dogs only. Designated rooms, service with restrictions, supervision.
SAVE ✕ ▣ ⊓ ⇌ ⊠

CALERA

Holiday Inn Express H
(205) 668-3641. **$99-$119.** 357 Hwy 304. I-65, exit 231, just se. Ext corridors. **Pets:** Accepted.
ASK ✕ ☐ ▣ ⇌

HOMEWOOD

Best Western Carlton Suites H
(205) 940-9990. **$119-$169.** 140 State Farm Pkwy. I-65, exit 255, just w to Wildwood Pkwy, then just n. Int corridors. **Pets:** Small, dogs only. $10 daily fee/pet. No service, supervision.
SAVE ✕ ☐ ▣ ⇌

Drury Inn & Suites-Birmingham Southwest H
(205) 940-9500. **$85-$145.** 160 State Farm Pkwy. I-65, exit 255, 0.5 mi on northwest frontage road. Int corridors. **Pets:** Other species. Service with restrictions, supervision.
ASK ✕ ☐ ▣ ⇌

La Quinta Inn & Suites Birmingham (Homewood) H ❀
(205) 290-0150. **$79-$139.** 60 State Farm Pkwy. I-65, exit 255, 0.9 mi on northwest frontage road. Int corridors. **Pets:** Medium, other species. Service with restrictions, supervision.
ASK ✕ ☐ ▣ ⇌

Residence Inn by Marriott H
(205) 943-0044. **$197-$211.** 50 State Farm Pkwy. I-65, exit 255, 1 mi on northwest frontage road. Int corridors. **Pets:** Accepted.
SAVE ✕ ☐ ▣ ⇌ ⊠

StudioPLUS H
(205) 290-0102. **$65-$80.** 40 State Farm Pkwy. I-65, exit 255, just e on Lakeshore Pkwy, just n on Wildwood Pkwy, then 0.6 mi w. Int corridors. **Pets:** Other species. $25 daily fee/pet. Service with restrictions, crate.
ASK ✕ ☐ ▣ ⇌

Super 8 H
(205) 945-9888. **$47-$70.** 140 Vulcan Rd. I-65, exit 256 northbound; exit 256A southbound, just nw. Int corridors. **Pets:** Small, other species. $5 daily fee/pet. Service with restrictions.
ASK ✕ ☐ ▣

TownePlace Suites by Marriott H
(205) 943-0114. **$172-$184.** 500 Wildwood Cir. I-65, exit 255, 0.6 mi w, then just n. Int corridors. **Pets:** Medium, other species. $75 one-time fee/room. Service with restrictions, supervision.
SAVE ✕ &M ☐ ▣ ⇌

HOOVER

Homewood Suites by Hilton H ❀
(205) 995-9823. **$169-$229.** 215 Inverness Center Dr. I-459, exit 19 (US 280), 1.8 mi e, then just s. Int corridors. **Pets:** Large, other species. $75 one-time fee/room. Designated rooms, service with restrictions.
✕ ☐ ▣ ⇌ ⊠

▼▼▼▼ Riverchase Inn at the Galleria 🄷
(205) 985-7500. **$74-$140.** 1800 Riverchase Dr. I-459, exit 13, 0.5 mi s on US 31, then 0.4 mi w on SR 150. Ext corridors. **Pets:** Very small. $25 daily fee/pet. Designated rooms, service with restrictions.
(A$K) ⊠ 🛉 ⬜ 🌢

IRONDALE

▼▼▼▼ Quality Inn Birmingham East 🄷
(205) 956-4100. **$80-$180.** 3910 Kilgore Memorial Dr. I-20, exit 133, just e. Ext corridors. **Pets:** Small. $20 daily fee/pet. Designated rooms, service with restrictions, supervision.
⊠ 🛉 ⬜ 🌢

LEEDS

(AAA) ▼▼▼▼ Best Western Bass Hotel & Suites 🄷
(205) 640-5300. **$86-$106, 3 day notice.** 1949 Village Dr. I-20, exit 144A westbound; 144B eastbound, just ne. Int corridors. **Pets:** Very small. $10 daily fee/pet. Service with restrictions, supervision.
(SAVE) ⊠ 🛉 ⬜ 🌢

(AAA) ▼▼▼ Days Inn of Leeds 🄼
(205) 699-9833. **$69-$180.** 1838 Ashville Rd. I-20, exit 144A eastbound; exit 144B westbound, just s. Ext corridors. **Pets:** Medium, other species. $7 daily fee/pet. Service with restrictions.
(SAVE) ⊠ 🛉 ⬜ 🌢

ONEONTA

(AAA) ▼▼▼ Best Western Colonial Inn 🄷
(205) 274-2200. **$80-$139.** 293 Valley Rd. On SR 75, 0.5 mi n of jct US 231. Ext corridors. **Pets:** Accepted.
(SAVE) ⊠ 🛉 ⬜ 🌢

PELHAM

(AAA) ▼▼▼ Quality Inn 🄷
(205) 444-9200. **$69-$89, 14 day notice.** 110 Cahaba Valley Pkwy. I-65, exit 246, just nw. Ext corridors. **Pets:** Very small. $25 one-time fee/room. Service with restrictions, supervision.
(SAVE) ⊠ 🛉 ⬜ 🌢

TRUSSVILLE

▼▼▼ Jameson Inn 🄷
(205) 661-9323. **$93-$100.** 4730 Norrell Dr. I-59, exit 141, just e on Chalkville Rd, then just n. Ext corridors. **Pets:** Accepted.
(A$K) ⊠ 🛉 ⬜ 🌢

END METROPOLITAN AREA

CHILDERSBURG

▼▼▼ Key West Inn Childersburg 🄼
(256) 378-0337. **$64.** 32210 US Hwy 280. Just s of jct CR 235. Ext corridors. **Pets:** Very small, dogs only. $25 one-time fee/room. Designated rooms, service with restrictions, crate.
(A$K) ⊠ 🛉 ⬜ 🌢

CLANTON

(AAA) ▼▼▼ Best Western Inn 🄷
(205) 280-1006. **$65-$100, 5 day notice.** 801 Bradberry Ln. I-65, exit 205, 0.5 mi e. Ext corridors. **Pets:** Small. $10 daily fee/pet. Service with restrictions, supervision.
(SAVE) ⊠ 🛉 ⬜ 🌢

(AAA) ▼▼◆ GuestHouse International Inn 🄼
(205) 280-0306. **$60-$72.** 946 Lake Mitchell Rd. I-65, exit 208, just w. Ext corridors. **Pets:** Medium. $10 daily fee/pet. Service with restrictions, supervision.
(SAVE) ⊠ 🛉 ⬜ 🌢

CULLMAN

(AAA) ▼▼◆ Best Western Fairwinds Inn 🄷
(256) 737-5009. **$67-$113, 3 day notice.** 1917 Commerce Ave NW. I-65, exit 310, just e. Ext corridors. **Pets:** Small. $12 daily fee/pet. Service with restrictions, supervision.
(SAVE) ⊠ 🛉 ⬜ 🌢

▼▼ Comfort Inn 🄷
(256) 734-1240. **$90-$121.** 5917 Alabama Hwy 157 NW. I-65, exit 310, just e. Ext corridors. **Pets:** Accepted.
(A$K) ⊠ 🛉 ⬜ 🌢

▼▼ Days Inn 🄷
(256) 739-3800. **$70-$90.** 1841 4th St SW. I-65, exit 308, just e. Ext corridors. **Pets:** Accepted.
(A$K) ⊠ 🛉 ⬜ 🍽 🌢

(AAA) ▼▼ Econo Lodge 🄼 🐾
(256) 734-2691. **$60-$75, 7 day notice.** 1655 CR 437. I-65, exit 304, just e. Ext corridors. **Pets:** Small, other species. $10 daily fee/pet. Designated rooms, service with restrictions, supervision.
(SAVE) ⊠ 🛉 ⬜

DECATUR

(AAA) ▼▼▼ Best Western River City Hotel 🄷
(256) 301-1388. **$77, 3 day notice.** 1305 Front Ave. I-65, exit 334, 8 mi n. Int corridors. **Pets:** Medium. $25 one-time fee/pet. Service with restrictions, crate.
(SAVE) ⊠ 🅛🄼 🛉 ⬜ 🌢

(AAA) ▼▼▼ Comfort Inn & Suites 🄷
(256) 355-1999. **$75-$95.** 2212 Danville Rd SW. SR 67, jct Beltline Rd SW. Ext corridors. **Pets:** Accepted.
(SAVE) ⊠ 🛉 ⬜ 🌢

▼▼▼▼ Holiday Inn Hotel & Suites 🄷
(256) 355-3150. **$95-$135.** 1101 6th Ave NE. Just w of jct US 31, 72A and SR 20. Ext/int corridors. **Pets:** Small. $15 one-time fee/room. Designated rooms, service with restrictions, supervision.
(A$K) ⊠ 🛉 ⬜ 🍽 🌢 ⊠

▼▼ Jameson Inn 🄷 🐾
(256) 355-2229. **$73-$78.** 2120 Jameson Pl SW. SR 67, 1.6 mi s of jct US 72A; 3.9 mi n of jct US 31. Ext corridors. **Pets:** Small, other species. $10 daily fee/room. Service with restrictions.
(A$K) ⊠ 🛉 ⬜ 🌢

▼▼ La Quinta Inn 🄼 🐾
(256) 355-9977. **$50-$117.** 918 Beltline Rd SW. Jct US 31 and SR 67, 1.6 mi w. Int corridors. **Pets:** Medium, other species. Service with restrictions, supervision.
(A$K) ⊠ 🛉 ⬜ 🌢

▼▼ Microtel Inn & Suites 🄷
(256) 301-9995. **$59-$79.** 2226 Beltline Rd SW. On SR 67, 4 mi w of jct US 31. Int corridors. **Pets:** Accepted.
(A$K) ⊠ 🅛🄼 🛉 ⬜ 🌢

DOTHAN

Americas Best Value Inn & Suites [M]
(334) 793-5200. **$45-$99.** 2901 Ross Clark Cir. 0.8 mi s of jct US 84; west end of town. Ext corridors. **Pets:** Very small, dogs only. $10 daily fee/pet. Service with restrictions, supervision.

Clarion [M]
(334) 794-6601. **Call for rates.** 3053 Ross Clark Cir. Just s of jct US 84; west end of town. Ext corridors. **Pets:** Accepted.

Days Inn [M]
(334) 793-2550. **Call for rates.** 2841 Ross Clark Cir. 0.9 mi s of jct US 84; west end of town. Ext corridors. **Pets:** Accepted.

Howard Johnson Inn [M]
(334) 792-3339. **Call for rates.** 2244 Ross Clark Cir. 1.4 mi s of jct SR 52; west end of town. Ext corridors. **Pets:** Accepted.

La Quinta Inns & Suites-Dothan [H]
(334) 793-9090. **Call for rates.** 3593 Ross Clark Cir. Just w of jct US 231; northwest part of town. Int corridors. **Pets:** Medium, other species. Service with restrictions, supervision.

Motel 6 #1233 [M]
(334) 793-6013. **$39-$51.** 2907 Ross Clark Cir. 0.8 mi s of jct US 84; west end of town. Ext corridors. **Pets:** Other species. Service with restrictions, supervision.

Quality Inn [M]
(334) 671-3700. **Call for rates.** 3071 Ross Clark Cir. Just s of jct US 84; west end of town. Ext corridors. **Pets:** Accepted.

ENTERPRISE

Comfort Inn [M]
(334) 393-2304. **$75.** 615 Boll Weevil Cir. On US 84 Bypass. Ext corridors. **Pets:** Accepted.

EUFAULA

Eufaula Comfort Suites [H]
(334) 616-0114. **$100-$110.** 12 Paul Lee Pkwy. 1.7 mi s on US 431 from jct US 82 E, then just e. Int corridors. **Pets:** Other species. $25 one-time fee/room. Service with restrictions, crate.

Jameson Inn [M]
(334) 687-7747. **$83-$90.** 136 Towne Center Blvd. On US 431, 1 mi s of US 82 E. Ext corridors. **Pets:** Accepted.

EVERGREEN

Comfort Inn [M]
(251) 578-4701. **$60-$125.** 1571 Ted Bates Rd. I-65, exit 96, just w. Ext corridors. **Pets:** $10 daily fee/pet. Service with restrictions, supervision.

Days Inn of Evergreen [M]
(251) 578-2100. **Call for rates.** 215 Hwy 83. I-65, exit 96, just w. Ext corridors. **Pets:** Accepted.

FAIRHOPE

Key West Inn [M]
(251) 990-7373. **$69-$109.** 231 S Greeno Rd. On US 98, 1.9 mi s of jct SR 104. Ext corridors. **Pets:** Small. $10 daily fee/pet. Designated rooms, service with restrictions, supervision.

FLORENCE

Jameson Inn [H]
(256) 764-5326. **$88-$95.** 115 Ana Dr. On US 43/72, just nw of jct SR 133 (Cox Creek Pkwy). Ext corridors. **Pets:** Small. $10 daily fee/pet. Service with restrictions, crate.

Marriott Shoals Hotel and Spa [H]
(256) 246-3600. **$148-$180.** 800 Cox Creek Pkwy S. From jct US 43/72 and SR 133 (Cox Creek Pkwy), 1.5 mi s; at Wilson Dam. Int corridors. **Pets:** Small, other species. $75 one-time fee/pet. Designated rooms, service with restrictions, crate.

FOLEY

Key West Inn [M]
(251) 943-1241. **$69-$139.** 2520 S McKenzie St. On SR 59, 1.8 mi s of jct US 98. Ext corridors. **Pets:** Small. $20 daily fee/pet. Designated rooms, service with restrictions, supervision.

Shular Inn & Suites [H]
(251) 943-9100. **$90-$190.** 2682 S McKenzie St. On SR 59, 1.9 mi s of jct US 98. Ext corridors. **Pets:** Accepted.

GADSDEN

Gadsden Inn & Suites [H]
(256) 543-7240. **$59-$159.** 200 Albert Rains Blvd. Jct US 411 and 431/278; enter on 2nd St off US 431. Ext corridors. **Pets:** Small. $20 one-time fee/pet. Service with restrictions, crate.

GENEVA

Briarwood Inn of Geneva [M]
(334) 684-7715. **$69-$102.** 1503 W Magnolia Ave. On SR 52, 0.3 mi w of jct SR 196. Ext corridors. **Pets:** Accepted.

GREENVILLE

Days Inn [M]
(334) 382-3118. **$65-$95, 7 day notice.** 946 Fort Dale Rd. I-65, exit 130, just s on SR 185. Ext corridors. **Pets:** Medium. $10 daily fee/pet. Service with restrictions, supervision.

Jameson Inn [M]
(334) 382-6300. **$78-$85.** 71 Jameson Ln. I-65, exit 130, just n on SR 185, then just w on Cahaba Rd. Ext corridors. **Pets:** Other species. $15 daily fee/room. Service with restrictions, supervision.

GULF SHORES

La Quinta Inn [H]
(251) 967-3500. **$50-$319.** 213 W Fort Morgan Rd. On SR 180, just w of jct SR 59. Int corridors. **Pets:** Medium, other species. Service with restrictions, supervision.

GUNTERSVILLE

Super 8-Guntersville [M]
(256) 582-8444. **Call for rates.** 14341 Hwy 431 S. Jct SR 69, 2 mi s. Ext corridors. **Pets:** Accepted.
⊠ 🛏 💻

HAMILTON

Days Inn [H]
(205) 921-1790. **$59-$89.** 1849 Military St S. US 78, exit 14, 1 mi n, then 1 mi w on US 43. Ext corridors. **Pets:** Other species. $10 daily fee/pet. Service with restrictions, crate.
SAVE ⊠ 🛏 💻 ⋙

HUNTSVILLE

America's Best Inns [M]
(256) 539-9671. **$64-$74.** 1304 N Memorial Pkwy. I-565, exit 19B, 0.5 mi n on US 231/431, exit Cook Ave. Ext corridors. **Pets:** Small. Service with restrictions, crate.
SAVE ⊠ 🛏 💻 ⋙

Extended StayAmerica Huntsville-U.S. Space and Rocket Center [H]
(256) 830-9110. **$73-$83.** 4751 Governors House Dr. I-565, exit 17A, just s, then 0.5 mi w. Ext corridors. **Pets:** Other species. $25 daily fee/pet. Service with restrictions, crate.
ASK ⊠ &M 🛏 💻

Holiday Inn Express Hotel & Suites [H]
(256) 721-1000. **$80-$129.** 3808 University Dr. I-565, exit 17A, just e. Int corridors. **Pets:** Small. $50 one-time fee/room. Service with restrictions, supervision.
⊠ 🛏 💻 ⋙

Holiday Inn Hunstville Downtown [H]
(256) 533-1400. **$99-$162.** 401 Williams Ave SW. Just w of Church St; downtown. Int corridors. **Pets:** Small. $30 one-time fee/room. Designated rooms, service with restrictions, crate.
ASK ⊠ 🛏 💻 ❚❙ ⋙

La Quinta Inn & Suites Huntsville [H] ❧
(256) 830-8999. **$64-$119.** 4890 University Dr NW. I-565, exit 14B, 2.6 mi n on Research Park Blvd, then 1 mi e on US 72. Int corridors. **Pets:** Medium, other species. Service with restrictions, supervision.
ASK ⊠ 🛏 💻 ⋙

La Quinta Inn Huntsville (Research Park) [H] ❧
(256) 830-2070. **$55-$89.** 4870 University Dr NW. I-565, exit 14B, 2.6 mi n on Research Park Blvd, then 1 mi e on US 72. Ext corridors. **Pets:** Medium, other species. Service with restrictions, supervision.
ASK ⊠ 🛏 💻 ⋙

La Quinta Inn Huntsville (Space Center) [H] ❧
(256) 533-0756. **$35-$79.** 3141 University Dr (Hwy 72). I-565, exit 17A, 1.1 mi n on SR 53 (Jordan Ln), then 0.6 mi e on US 72. Ext corridors. **Pets:** Medium, other species. Service with restrictions, supervision.
ASK ⊠ 🛏 💻 ⋙

JACKSON

Econo Lodge [M]
(251) 246-4111. **$70-$83.** 3680 N College Ave. I-65, exit 19, on US 43. Ext corridors. **Pets:** Other species. Service with restrictions, crate.
SAVE ⊠ 🛏 💻

JASPER

Jameson Inn [H]
(205) 387-7710. **$83-$90.** 1100 Hwy 78/118 E. SR 118, 1.8 mi w of jct SR 69. Ext corridors. **Pets:** Accepted.
ASK ⊠ &M 🛏 💻 ⋙

MADISON

Country Hearth Inn & Suites [H]
(256) 772-0701. **Call for rates.** 8716 Madison Blvd. I-565, exit 8, just n on Wall Triana Hwy, then 0.4 mi e. Int corridors. **Pets:** Accepted.
⊠ 🛏 💻 ❚❙ ⋙

MILLBROOK

Key West Inn [M]
(334) 309-2004. **$69-$89.** 2275 Cobbs Ford Rd. I-65, exit 179, just w. Ext corridors. **Pets:** Medium. $10 daily fee/pet. Designated rooms, service with restrictions, supervision.
SAVE ⊠ 🛏 💻 ⋙

MOBILE

Best Western Battleship Inn [M] ❧
(251) 432-2703. **$109-$199, 3 day notice.** 2701 Battleship Pkwy. I-10, exit 27, just e. Ext corridors. **Pets:** Other species. $25 one-time fee/room. Service with restrictions, supervision.
SAVE ⊠ 🛏 💻 ❚❙ ⋙

Drury Inn-Mobile [H]
(251) 344-7700. **$95-$140.** 824 W I-65 Service Rd S. I-65, exit 3 (Airport Blvd), just w, then just s on service road. Int corridors. **Pets:** Other species. Service with restrictions, supervision.
ASK ⊠ 🛏 💻 ⋙

Extended StayAmerica [H]
(251) 344-2514. **$80-$110.** 508 Spring Hill Plaza Ct. I-65, exit 5A, just w, then just n. Ext corridors. **Pets:** Other species. $25 daily fee/pet. Service with restrictions, crate.
ASK ⊠ 🛏 💻

La Quinta Inn Mobile [M] ❧
(251) 343-4051. **$65-$119.** 816 W I-65 Service Rd S. I-65, exit 3 (Airport Blvd), just w, then just s. Ext/int corridors. **Pets:** Medium, other species. Service with restrictions, supervision.
ASK ⊠ 🛏 💻 ⋙

Olsson Motel [M]
(251) 661-5331. **$45-$85, 10 day notice.** 4137 Government Blvd. I-65, exit 1, 2 mi w on US 90. Ext corridors. **Pets:** Very small, dogs only. $15 daily fee/pet, $35 one-time fee/pet. No service, supervision.
SAVE ⊠ 🛏

Residence Inn by Marriott Mobile [H]
(251) 304-0570. **$142-$152.** 950 W I-65 Service Rd S. I-65, exit 3 (Airport Blvd), just w, then 0.4 mi s. Int corridors. **Pets:** Accepted.
⊠ &M 🛏 💻 ⋙ ⊠

TownePlace Suites by Marriott [H]
(251) 345-9588. **$157-$169.** 1075 Montlimar Dr. I-65, exit 3 (Airport Blvd), just w, then 0.5 mi s. Int corridors. **Pets:** Large. $75 one-time fee/room. Service with restrictions, crate.
⊠ 🛏 💻 ⋙

MONROEVILLE

Americas Best Value Inn [M]
(251) 743-3154. **$50-$200.** 50 Hwy 21 S. On SR 21, just s of jct US 84. Ext corridors. **Pets:** Small. $15 daily fee/pet. Designated rooms, no service, supervision.
SAVE ⊠ 🛏

Best Western of Monroeville [M]
(251) 575-9999. **$70.** 4419 S Alabama Ave. On SR 21, 0.5 mi n of jct US 84. Ext corridors. **Pets:** Accepted.
SAVE ⊠ 🛏 💻 ⋙

Days Inn of Monroeville [M]
(251) 743-3297. **$66-$80.** 4389 S Alabama Ave. On SR 21, 0.5 mi n of jct US 84. Ext corridors. **Pets:** Accepted.
ASK ⊠ 🛏 💻 ⋙

Holiday Inn Express H
(251) 743-3333. **$85-$200.** 120 Hwy 21 S. On SR 21, just s of jct US 84. Int corridors. **Pets:** Small. $15 daily fee/pet. Designated rooms, no service, supervision.
SAVE ⊠ ᕒM 🛢 💻 ➔

MONTGOMERY

Days Inn Midtown M
(334) 269-9611. **$59-$64.** 2625 Zelda Rd. I-85, exit 3, just s on Ann St. Ext corridors. **Pets:** $10 daily fee/pet. Service with restrictions, supervision.
SAVE ⊠ 🛢 💻 ➔

Drury Inn & Suites-Montgomery H
(334) 273-1101. **$85-$145.** 1124 Eastern Blvd. I-85, exit 6, just n. Int corridors. **Pets:** Other species. Service with restrictions, supervision.
ASK ⊠ ᕒM 🛢 💻 ➔

Econo Lodge M
(334) 284-3400. **$55-$65.** 4135 Troy Hwy. On US 82/231, 0.7 mi e of jct South and East blvds. Ext corridors. **Pets:** Accepted.
ASK ⊠ 🛢 💻 ➔

Embassy Suites Montgomery Conference Center H ❀
(334) 269-5055. **$149-$179.** 300 Tallapoosa St. Between Motton and Commerce sts; in historic downtown. Int corridors. **Pets:** Small. $35 daily fee/pet. Service with restrictions, supervision.
SAVE ⊠ ᕒM 🛢 💻 ⑪ ➔

Extended StayAmerica Montgomery-Eastern Blvd H
(334) 279-1204. **$65-$75.** 2491 Eastern Blvd. I-85, exit 6, 1.3 mi s on US 231. Ext corridors. **Pets:** Other species. $25 daily fee/pet. Service with restrictions, crate.
ASK ⊠ 🛢 💻

La Quinta Inn & Suites H ❀
(334) 277-6000. **$59-$109.** 5225 Carmichael Rd. I-85, exit 6, just s on Eastern Blvd, then just w. Int corridors. **Pets:** Medium, other species. Service with restrictions, supervision.
ASK ⊠ ᕒM 🛢 💻 ➔

La Quinta Inn Montgomery M ❀
(334) 271-1620. **$39-$89.** 1280 East Blvd. I-85, exit 6, just s. Ext corridors. **Pets:** Medium, other species. Service with restrictions, supervision.
ASK ⊠ 🛢 💻 ➔

The Lexington Hotel by Vantage H
(334) 272-0370. **$55-$79.** 1185 Eastern Blvd. I-85, exit 6, just n. Ext/int corridors. **Pets:** Accepted.
ASK ⊠ ᕒM 🛢 💻 ⑪ ➔ ⊠

Monticello Inn M
(334) 277-4442. **Call for rates.** 5837 Monticello Dr. I-85, exit 6, just n, then just e. Ext corridors. **Pets:** Accepted.
⊠ 🛢 💻 ➔

Motel 6 #4263 M
(334) 280-1866. **$52-$56.** 7760 Slade Plaza Blvd. I-65, exit 164, just s. Int corridors. **Pets:** Medium, other species. Designated rooms, service with restrictions, supervision.
ASK ⊠ 🛢 ➔

Quality Inn & Suites-Convention Center H
(334) 288-2800. **Call for rates.** 2705 E South Blvd. I-85, exit 6, 3.7 mi s on East Blvd. Ext corridors. **Pets:** Accepted.
SAVE ⊠ 🛢 💻 ➔

Residence Inn by Marriott H
(334) 270-3300. **$167-$179.** 1200 Hilmar Ct. I-85, exit 6, just s on Eastern Blvd, then just e. Ext/int corridors. **Pets:** Accepted.
SAVE ⊠ 🛢 💻 ➔ ⊠

StudioPLUS H
(334) 273-0075. **$67-$77.** 5115 Carmichael Rd. I-85, exit 6, 0.5 mi s on US 231. Int corridors. **Pets:** Other species. $25 daily fee/pet. Service with restrictions, crate.
ASK ⊠ 🛢 💻 ➔

TownePlace Suites by Marriott H
(334) 396-5505. **$142-$152.** 5047 Towneplace Dr. I-85, exit 6, just s on Eastern Blvd, then just w on Carmichael Rd. Int corridors. **Pets:** Accepted.
⊠ ᕒM 🛢 💻 ➔

OXFORD

Baymont Inn Anniston/Oxford H
(256) 835-1492. **$69.** 1600 Hwy 21 S. I-20, exit 185, just s. Ext corridors. **Pets:** Accepted.
ASK ⊠ 🛢 💻 ➔

Holiday Inn Express & Suites Anniston/Oxford H ❀
(256) 835-8768. **$95-$105.** 160 Colonial Dr. I-20, exit 188, just n, then w. Int corridors. **Pets:** Medium, other species. $20 daily fee/pet. Supervision.
SAVE ⊠ 🛢 💻 ⊠

Jameson Inn Oxford M
(256) 835-2170. **$88-$95.** 161 Colonial Dr. I-20, exit 188, just n, then w. Ext corridors. **Pets:** Accepted.
ASK ⊠ 🛢 💻 ➔

OZARK

All American Ozark Inn M
(334) 774-5166. **Call for rates.** 2064 Hwy 231 S. 1 mi s of jct SR 249. Ext corridors. **Pets:** Medium, other species. $50 deposit/pet. Service with restrictions, supervision.
SAVE ⊠ 🛢 💻 ➔

Jameson Inn M
(334) 774-0233. **$78-$81.** 1360 S US Hwy 231. 0.3 mi s of jct SR 249. Ext corridors. **Pets:** Very small, dogs only. $15 daily fee/pet. Designated rooms, service with restrictions, supervision.
ASK ⊠ ᕒM 🛢 💻 ➔

PRATTVILLE

Jameson Inn H
(334) 361-6463. **$78-$85.** 104 Jameson Ct. I-65, exit 179, 1 mi w. Ext corridors. **Pets:** Accepted.
ASK ⊠ 🛢 💻 ➔

La Quinta Inn & Suites H 🐾
(334) 358-5454. **$79-$139.** 261 Interstate Commercial Park Loop. I-65, exit 181, just w. Int corridors. **Pets:** Medium, other species. Service with restrictions, supervision.
⊠ 🛢 💻 ➔

PRICEVILLE

Comfort Inn H
(256) 355-1037. **$60-$300.** 3239 Point Mallard Pkwy. I-65, exit 334, just w. Int corridors. **Pets:** Accepted.
ASK ⊠ 🛢 💻 ➔

Days Inn H
(256) 355-3297. **$54-$89.** 63 Marco Dr. I-65, exit 334, just e. Ext corridors. **Pets:** $10 daily fee/room. Service with restrictions, crate.
ASK ⊠ 🛢 💻 ➔

SCOTTSBORO

Jameson Inn H
(256) 574-6666. **$88-$95.** 208 Micah Way. On US 72, just s of jct SR 35. Ext corridors. **Pets:** Accepted.
ASK ⊠ 🛢 💻 ➔

SELMA

▽▽ Jameson Inn Ⓜ
(334) 874-8600. **$78-$85.** 2420 Broad St. On SR 22, just n of jct US 80. Ext corridors. **Pets:** Accepted.

ⒶⓈⓀ ⊠ 🛏 💻 ⌇

▽▽ Ramada Inn Selma Ⓗ
(334) 872-0461. **$60-$100, 3 day notice.** 1710 W Highland Ave. On US 80. Ext corridors. **Pets:** Accepted.

ⒶⓈⓀ ⊠ 🛏 💻 ⫾⫿ ⌇

STEVENSON

▽ Budget Host Inn Ⓜ
(256) 437-2215. **$45-$65.** 42973 US Hwy 72. On US 72, just s of CR 85. Ext corridors. **Pets:** Small. $10 daily fee/pet. Designated rooms, service with restrictions, supervision.

ⒶⓈⓀ ⊠ 🛏 💻

SYLACAUGA

▽▽ Jameson Inn Ⓗ
(256) 245-4141. **$78-$85.** 89 Gene Stewart Blvd. Off US 280, just s. Ext corridors. **Pets:** Accepted.

ⒶⓈⓀ ⊠ 🛏 💻 ⌇

TROY

▽▽ Holiday Inn Express Ⓗ
(334) 670-0012. **$73-$78.** Hwy 231 at US 29. On US 231, just n of jct US 29. Ext corridors. **Pets:** Accepted.

ⒶⓈⓀ ⊠ 🛏 💻

▽▽▽ Holiday Inn of Troy Ⓗ
(334) 566-1150. **$61-$109.** Hwy 231 at US 29. On US 231, just n of jct US 29. Ext corridors. **Pets:** Accepted.

ⒶⓈⓀ ⊠ 🛏 💻 ⫾⫿ ⌇

TUSCALOOSA

ⒶⒶⒶ ▽▽▽ Americas Best Value Inn Ⓗ ❖
(205) 556-7950. **$59-$145, 3 day notice.** 3501 McFarland Blvd. I-59/20, exit 73, just ne on US 82. Ext corridors. **Pets:** Very small, other species. $20 one-time fee/room. Designated rooms, service with restrictions, supervision.

ⓈⒶⓋⒺ ⊠ 🛏 💻 ⌇

ⒶⒶⒶ▽ ▽▽ Comfort Inn Ⓗ
(205) 556-3232. **$81, 30 day notice.** 4700 Doris Pate Dr. I-59/20, exit 76, just n. Int corridors. **Pets:** Medium, other species. $50 one-time fee/room. Designated rooms, service with restrictions, supervision.

ⓈⒶⓋⒺ ⊠ 🛏 💻 ⌇

▽▽ Jameson Inn Ⓗ
(205) 345-5018. **$88-$95.** 5021 Oscar Baxter Dr. I-59/20, exit 71A, just s. Ext corridors. **Pets:** Very small, other species. $15 daily fee/pet. Service with restrictions.

ⒶⓈⓀ ⊠ 🛏 💻 ⌇

▽▽ La Quinta Inn Tuscaloosa Ⓜ ❖
(205) 349-3270. **$44-$165.** 4122 McFarland Blvd E. I-59/20, exit 73, just sw on US 82. Ext corridors. **Pets:** Medium, other species. Service with restrictions, supervision.

ⒶⓈⓀ ⊠ 🛏 💻 ⌇

ⒶⒶⒶ▽ ▽ Masters Inn Ⓜ
(205) 556-2010. **$45-$55.** 3600 McFarland Blvd. I-59/20, exit 73, just nw on US 82. Ext corridors. **Pets:** Very small. $10 one-time fee/room. Designated rooms, service with restrictions, supervision.

ⓈⒶⓋⒺ ⊠ 🛏 ⌇

VANCE

▽▽▽ Baymont Inn & Suites Ⓗ
(205) 556-3606. **$85-$150.** 11170 Will Walker Rd/Daimler Benz Blvd. I-59/20, exit 89 southbound, just s; exit northbound, 0.8 mi n on Mercedes Dr, 0.3 mi w, then just s. Int corridors. **Pets:** Accepted.

ⒶⓈⓀ ⊠ ⎙ᴹ 🛏 💻

ALASKA

ANCHORAGE

▼▼▼ Comfort Inn Ship Creek 🏨
(907) 277-6887. **$127-$289.** 111 W Ship Creek Ave. At 3rd and E sts, 0.3 mi n on E St, across the railway, just e on Ship Creek Ave; downtown. Int corridors. **Pets:** Medium, other species. $15 daily fee/pet. Designated rooms, service with restrictions, supervision.

🅰️$ ✕ ⟨M⟩ 🛏️ 💻 ⤳

▼▼▼ Extended Stay Deluxe Anchorage-Midtown 🏨
(907) 646-4208. **$84-$214.** 700 E 34th Ave. Between Denali St and Old Seward Hwy. Int corridors. **Pets:** Other species. $25 daily fee/pet. Service with restrictions, crate.

🅰️$ ✕ ⟨M⟩ 🛏️ 💻 𝒦

AAA ▼▼▼ Hawthorn Suites Ltd 🏨
(907) 222-5005. **$108-$232, 3 day notice.** 1110 W 8th Ave. Corner of L St and W 8th Ave. Int corridors. **Pets:** Accepted.

SAVE ✕ 🛏️ 💻 ⤳

▼▼▼ Hilton Anchorage 🏨
(907) 272-7411. **$100-$310.** 500 W 3rd Ave. At E St; downtown. Int corridors. **Pets:** Accepted.

✕ ⟨M⟩ 🛏️ 💻 🍴 ⤳ ✕

▼▼▼ Microtel Inn & Suites 🏨
(907) 245-5002. **$75-$170.** 5205 Northwood Dr. Jct International Airport Rd, just n. Int corridors. **Pets:** Other species. $10 daily fee/pet. Designated rooms, service with restrictions, supervision.

🅰️$ ✕ ⟨M⟩ 🛏️ 💻

AAA ▼▼▼ Millennium Alaskan Hotel Anchorage 🏨
(907) 243-2300. **$159-$300.** 4800 Spenard Rd. Jct International Airport Rd, just n. Int corridors. **Pets:** Other species. $20 daily fee/pet. Service with restrictions, supervision.

SAVE ✕ ⟨M⟩ 🛏️ 💻 🍴 ✕

▼▼ Motel 6–4216 Ⓜ
(907) 677-8000. **Call for rates.** 5000 a St. Jct C St, just e on International Airport Rd, then just n. Int corridors. **Pets:** Other species. Service with restrictions, supervision.

✕ ⟨M⟩

AAA ▼▼▼ Quality Inn & Suites 🏨
(907) 243-3131. **$90-$189.** 4615 Spenard Rd. International Airport Rd; just ne of jct Jewel Lake and Spenard rds. Ext/int corridors. **Pets:** Accepted.

SAVE ✕ 🛏️ 💻

AAA ▼▼▼ Ramada Anchorage Downtown 🏨
(907) 272-7561. **$89-$339.** 115 E 3rd Ave. Jct Barrow St; downtown. Ext/int corridors. **Pets:** Dogs only. $100 deposit/room, $10 daily fee/pet. Designated rooms, service with restrictions, crate.

SAVE ✕ 🛏️ 💻

▼▼ Red Roof Inn Ⓜ
(907) 274-1650. **Call for rates.** 1104 E 5th Ave. At Karluk St. Ext/int corridors. **Pets:** Accepted.

✕ ⟨M⟩ 🛏️ 💻

▼▼▼ Residence Inn by Marriott 🏨
(907) 563-9844. **$159-$275.** 1025 E 35th Ave. Corner of SR 1 (Seward Hwy) and 36th Ave. Int corridors. **Pets:** $100 one-time fee/room. Service with restrictions, crate.

✕ 🛏️ 💻 ⤳ ✕

AAA ▼▼▼ Sheraton Anchorage Hotel & SPA 🏨 ❀
(907) 276-8700. **$109-$349.** 401 E 6th Ave. 6th Ave and Denali St. Int corridors. **Pets:** Medium, dogs only. $50 deposit/pet. Service with restrictions, supervision.

SAVE ✕ 🛏️ 💻 🍴

CANTWELL

AAA ▼▼ Backwoods Lodge Ⓜ
(907) 768-2232. **$90-$170, 10 day notice.** Denali Hwy MM 133.8. Parks Hwy, (Milepost 210), just e. Ext corridors. **Pets:** Medium. Service with restrictions, supervision.

SAVE ✕ 🛏️ 💻 𝒦

DENALI NATIONAL PARK AND PRESERVE

AAA ▼▼▼ McKinley Chalet Resort 🏨
(907) 683-8200. **$299, 30 day notice.** Milepost 238 Parks Hwy. Milepost 238.5 on SR 3 (Parks Hwy). Ext/int corridors. **Pets:** Accepted.

SAVE ✕ ⟨M⟩ 🛏️ 💻 🍴

EAGLE RIVER

AAA ▼▼▼ Eagle River Microtel Inn & Suites 🏨
(907) 622-6000. **$120-$180.** 13049 Old Glenn Hwy. Jct Glenn Hwy (SR 1), exit Eagle River, 1.7 mi e. Int corridors. **Pets:** Other species. $25 daily fee/room. Designated rooms, service with restrictions, crate.

SAVE ✕ ⟨M⟩ 🛏️ 💻 𝒦

▼▼ Eagle River Motel Ⓜ
(907) 694-5000. **Call for rates.** 11111 Old Eagle River Rd. Glenn Hwy, exit Eagle River, just e; just s on Monte Rd, then just w. Ext corridors. **Pets:** Accepted.

✕ 🛏️ 💻 𝒦

FAIRBANKS

▼▼ Comfort Inn-Chena River 🏨
(907) 479-8080. **$90-$220.** 1908 Chena Landings Loop. Airport Way, just n on Peger Rd, then just e on Phillips Field Rd, follow signs in wooded area south of road. Int corridors. **Pets:** $10 daily fee/pet. Designated rooms, no service, crate.

🅰️$ ✕ ⟨M⟩ 🛏️ 💻 ⤳

▼▼ Extended Stay Deluxe Fairbanks-Old Airport Way 🏨
(907) 457-2288. **$84-$204.** 4580 Old Airport Rd. Near jct Parks Hwy and Airport Rd. Int corridors. **Pets:** Other species. $25 daily fee/pet. Service with restrictions, crate.

🅰️$ ✕ ⟨M⟩ 🛏️ 💻 ⤳

AAA ▼▼▼ Pike's Waterfront Lodge 🏨 ❀
(907) 456-4500. **$89-$600.** 1850 Hoselton Rd. Jct Airport and Hoselton rds. Ext/int corridors. **Pets:** Other species. $10 daily fee/pet. Designated rooms, service with restrictions.

SAVE ✕ 🛏️ 💻 🍴 ✕

▼▼ Super 8 Motel Ⓜ
(907) 451-8888. **Call for rates.** 1909 Airport Way. Airport Way at Wilbur St. Int corridors. **Pets:** Other species. $10 one-time fee/pet. Service with restrictions.

✕ ⟨M⟩ 🛏️

GUSTAVUS

▼▼▼ Glacier Bay's Bear Track Inn H
(907) 697-3017. **Call for rates.** 255 Rink Creek Rd. 7 mi e of airport; at end of Rink Creek Rd. Int corridors. **Pets:** Accepted.
⊠ ⑪ 𝕂 �𝒲 ☎

HAINES

△△△ ▼ Captain's Choice Inc Motel M
(907) 766-3111. **$84-$192.** 108 2nd Ave N. Jct 2nd Ave and Dalton St. Ext corridors. **Pets:** Other species. $25 one-time fee/room. Service with restrictions, supervision.
SAVE ⊠ 🖥 🖵 𝕂

HOMER

△△△ ▼▼▼ Best Western Bidarka Inn M 🐾
(907) 235-8148. **$89-$199.** 575 Sterling Hwy. 0.3 mi n on SR 1 (Sterling Hwy). Ext/int corridors. **Pets:** Other species. $10 daily fee/pet. Designated rooms, service with restrictions, supervision.
SAVE ⊠ 🖥 🖵 ⑪ 𝕂

JUNEAU

▼▼ Extended Stay Deluxe Juneau H
(907) 790-6435. **$99-$209.** 1800 Shell Simmons Dr. At Juneau International Airport. Int corridors. **Pets:** Other species. $25 daily fee/pet. Service with restrictions, crate.
ASK ⊠ 🖥 🖵 ⊇

△△△ ▼▼▼ Westmark Baranof H
(907) 586-2660. **$149-$279.** 127 N Franklin St. At 2nd and Franklin sts; downtown. Int corridors. **Pets:** Accepted.
SAVE ⊠ 🖥 🖵 ⑪ 𝕂

KETCHIKAN

△△△ ▼▼▼▼ Best Western Landing H 🐾
(907) 225-5166. **$137-$238, 3 day notice.** 3434 Tongass Ave. Across from the Alaska Marine Hwy ferry terminal. Ext/int corridors. **Pets:** Other species. $10 daily fee/pet. Designated rooms, service with restrictions, supervision.
SAVE ⊠ 🖥 🖵 ⑪

△△△ ▼▼▼ Cape Fox Lodge H
(907) 225-8001. **$110-$230.** 800 Venetia Way. Above Creek St (tramway from Creek St). Ext/int corridors. **Pets:** $30 one-time fee/pet. Designated rooms, no service, supervision.
SAVE ⊠ 🖥 🖵 ⑪ 𝕂

KODIAK

△△△ ▼▼▼ Best Western Kodiak Inn H
(907) 486-5712. **$100-$200.** 236 W Rezanof Dr. 0.3 mi w of ferry terminal; center. Ext/int corridors. **Pets:** Accepted.
SAVE ⊠ 🖥 🖵 ⑪ 𝕂

▼▼ Comfort Inn Kodiak H
(907) 487-2700. **$90-$207, 3 day notice.** 1395 Airport Way. Adjacent to airport. Int corridors. **Pets:** Medium, dogs only. $15 daily fee/pet. Designated rooms, service with restrictions, supervision.
ASK ⊠ 🖥 🖵 ⑪ 𝕂

SEWARD

△△△ ▼▼▼ Hotel Seward H
(907) 224-8001. **$79-$359, 7 day notice.** 221 5th Ave. Just n of Alaska SeaLife Center; downtown. Int corridors. **Pets:** Medium, dogs only. $250 deposit/room, $25 daily fee/pet. Designated rooms, service with restrictions, supervision.
SAVE ⊠ 🖥 🖵 𝕂

SITKA

△△△ ▼▼▼ Shee Atika Totem Square Inn H 🐾
(907) 747-3693. **Call for rates.** 201 Katlian St. Center; in Totem Square Complex, near Municipal Office. Int corridors. **Pets:** Small, other species. $50 deposit/pet, $10 daily fee/pet. Service with restrictions, crate.
SAVE ⊠ 🖥 🖵 𝕂

▼▼ Super 8 Motel-Sitka H
(907) 747-8804. **$89-$146.** 404 Sawmill Creek Rd. Just e from corner of Lake St and Halibut Point/Sawmill Creek rds; center. Int corridors. **Pets:** Other species. $10 daily fee/pet. Service with restrictions, crate.
ASK ⊠ 🔊 🖥 🖵

SKAGWAY

△△△ ▼▼▼ Westmark Inn Skagway M
(907) 983-6000. **$135-$145.** 3rd & Spring St. Downtown. Ext/int corridors. **Pets:** Accepted.
SAVE ⊠ 🔊 🖥 🖵 ⑪ 𝕂

TOK

△△△ ▼▼▼ Cleft of the Rock Bed & Breakfast CA 🐾
(907) 883-4219. **$95-$160, 3 day notice.** 122 Sundog Tr. Jct SR 1 and 2 (Alaskan Hwy), 2.5 mi w on SR 2 (Alaskan Hwy) to Sundog Trail, then 0.5 mi n. Ext/int corridors. **Pets:** $10 daily fee/pet. Designated rooms, crate.
SAVE ⊠ 🖥 🖵 ⊠ 𝕂

△△△ ▼▼▼ Westmark Inn Tok M
(907) 883-5174. **$145.** Jct Alaska Hwy & Glenn Hwy. On SR 1; jct SR 2 (Alaskan Hwy). Ext corridors. **Pets:** Accepted.
SAVE ⊠ 🖵 ⑪

TRAPPER CREEK

▼▼ Gate Creek Cabins CA
(907) 733-1393. **$120-$520, 10 day notice.** Mile 10.5 Petersville Rd. From MM 114 (Parks Hwy), 10.5 mi w at Petersville Rd. Ext corridors. **Pets:** Accepted.
ASK ⊠ 🖥 🖵 ⊠ 𝕂 ☎

VALDEZ

《△△△ ▼▼▼ Best Western Valdez Harbor Inn H
(907) 835-3434. **$98-$165, 3 day notice.** 100 N Harbor Dr. Just s at Meals Dr. Int corridors. **Pets:** Accepted.
SAVE ⊠ 🔊 🖥 🖵 ⑪ 𝕂

WASILLA

△△△ ▼▼▼▼ Best Western Lake Lucille Inn H
(907) 373-1776. **Call for rates.** 1300 W Lake Lucille Dr. SR 3 (George Parks Hwy), just w on Hallea Ln; center. Int corridors. **Pets:** Medium. $20 deposit/pet. Supervision.
SAVE ⊠ 🔊 🖥 🖵 ⊠ 𝕂

△△△ ▼▼▼ Grandview Inn & Suites H
(907) 352-1700. **$90-$220.** 2900 E Parks Hwy. 1 mi n of jct SR 3 (George Parks Hwy) and Fairview Loop exit. Int corridors. **Pets:** $50 deposit/pet, $10 daily fee/pet. Designated rooms, service with restrictions, crate.
SAVE ⊠ 🖥 🖵 ⑪ ⊇

ARIZONA

AJO

La Siesta Motel
(520) 387-6569. **$46-$60.** 2561 N Ajo-Gila Bend Hwy. On SR 85, 1.8 mi n of town plaza. Ext corridors. **Pets:** Accepted.

AMADO

Amado Territory Inn
(520) 398-8684. **$105-$155, 7 day notice.** 3001 E Frontage Rd. I-19, exit 48, just e, then just s. Int corridors. **Pets:** Accepted.

ANTHEM

Hampton Inn at Anthem
(623) 465-7979. **$89-$399.** 42415 N 41st Dr. I-17, exit 229 (Anthem Way), just w. Int corridors. **Pets:** Small, dogs only. $50 one-time fee/pet. Designated rooms, service with restrictions, supervision.

BELLEMONT

Americas Best Value Inn
(928) 556-9599. **$55-$150.** 12380 W Interstate Hwy 40. I-40, exit 185, just n. Int corridors. **Pets:** Accepted.

BENSON

Best Western-Quail Hollow Inn
(520) 586-3646. **$73-$150.** 699 N Ocotillo Rd. I-10, exit 304 (Ocotillo Rd), just s. Ext corridors. **Pets:** Accepted.

Super 8
(520) 586-1530. **Call for rates.** 855 N Ocotillo Rd. I-10, exit 304 (Ocotillo Rd), just n. Ext corridors. **Pets:** Other species. $10 one-time fee/room. Service with restrictions, supervision.

BISBEE

Americas Best Value Inn & Suites
(520) 432-2293. **$69-$325.** 1372 Hwy 92. 0.8 mi w of jct Naco Hwy; sw of downtown. Ext corridors. **Pets:** Accepted.

Audrey's Inn
(520) 227-6120. **$105-$110.** 20 Brewery Ave. Just ne of Main St; in historic district. Int corridors. **Pets:** Accepted.

San Jose Lodge
(520) 432-5761. **$69-$145.** 1002 Naco Hwy. SR 92 W, 1.5 mi s. Ext corridors. **Pets:** Dogs only. $10 daily fee/pet. Designated rooms, service with restrictions, supervision.

BULLHEAD CITY

Best Western Bullhead City Inn
(928) 754-3000. **$79-$99.** 1126 Hwy 95. 1.8 mi s of Laughlin Bridge. Ext corridors. **Pets:** Medium. $20 one-time fee/pet. Service with restrictions, supervision.

Budget Host Inn
(928) 763-1002. **$75-$85.** 1616 Hwy 95. Jct SR 68, 3.2 mi s on SR 95. Int corridors. **Pets:** Medium, dogs only. $10 one-time fee/pet. Service with restrictions, supervision.

Lake Mohave Resort Motel
(928) 754-3245. **$90-$125, 3 day notice.** 2690 E Katherine Spur Rd. Jct SR 95, 1.5 mi e on SR 68, 1 mi n, then 5.4 mi e; at Katherine Landing; in Lake Mead National Recreation area. Ext corridors. **Pets:** Other species. $50 deposit/room, $10 daily fee/pet. Service with restrictions, supervision.

Lodge on The River
(928) 758-8080. **$45-$65, 7 day notice.** 1717 Hwy 95. 3.8 mi s of Laughlin Bridge. Ext corridors. **Pets:** Medium. $5 daily fee/pet. Designated rooms, service with restrictions, supervision.

CAMERON

Cameron Trading Post Motel, Restaurant & Gift Shop
(928) 679-2231. **$69-$109.** US 89. 1 mi from east gate turn off. Ext corridors. **Pets:** Accepted.

CAMP VERDE

Comfort Inn-Camp Verde
(928) 567-9000. **$59-$199.** 340 N Goswick Way. I-17, exit 287, just e, then just s. Int corridors. **Pets:** Large, other species. $15 daily fee/pet. Service with restrictions, supervision.

Days Inn & Suites of Camp Verde
(928) 567-3700. **$50-$126.** 1640 W Hwy 260. I-17, exit 287, just e, then just n. Int corridors. **Pets:** Other species. $10 daily fee/pet. Designated rooms, service with restrictions, crate.

AAA ✓ ▼▼ The Lodge At Cliff Castle Casino H
(928) 567-6611. **$89-$209.** 333 Middle Verde Rd. I-17, exit 289, 0.4 mi se.
Ext corridors. **Pets:** Accepted.
SAVE ✕ ☎ ▣ ❒ ≋

AAA ✓ ▼ Super 8 Motel-Camp Verde M
(928) 567-2622. **$54-$149.** 1550 W Hwy 260. I-17, exit 287, just e. Int
corridors. **Pets:** Medium. $15 daily fee/pet. Designated rooms, service with
restrictions, supervision.
SAVE ✕ ☎ ≋

CASA GRANDE

▼▼▼ Francisco Grande Hotel & Golf Resort H
(520) 836-6444. **$79-$219.** 26000 W Gila Bend Hwy (SR 84). I-8, exit 172
(Thornton Rd), 3.5 mi n, then 4.2 mi w. Ext corridors. **Pets:** Small, dogs
only. $25 daily fee/pet. Service with restrictions, supervision.
ASK ✕ ☎ ▣ ❒ ≋ ✕

AAA ✓ ▼▼▼ Holiday Inn Hotel H 🐾
(520) 426-3500. **$81-$169.** 777 N Pinal Ave. I-10, exit 194 (SR 287), 3.9
mi w. Int corridors. **Pets:** $20 one-time fee/pet. Designated rooms, service
with restrictions, supervision.
SAVE ✕ ☎ ▣ ❒ ≋

AAA ✓ ▼▼▼ Super 8 H
(520) 836-8800. **$60-$110.** 2066 E Florence Blvd. I-10, exit 194 (SR 287),
0.6 mi w. Int corridors. **Pets:** $10 daily fee/pet. Service with restrictions,
supervision.
SAVE ✕ ☎ ▣ ≋

COTTONWOOD

AAA ✓ ▼▼▼ Best Western Cottonwood Inn H
(928) 634-5575. **$100-$150, 3 day notice.** 993 S Main St. On SR 89A, at
SR 260. Ext corridors. **Pets:** Accepted.
SAVE ✕ ☎ ▣ ≋

AAA ✓ ▼ Little Daisy Motel M
(928) 634-7865. **$56-$140.** 34 S Main St. On SR 89A, just n. Ext corridors.
Pets: Dogs only. $10 daily fee/room. Service with restrictions, crate.
SAVE ✕ ☎

AAA ✓ ▼▼▼ Pines Motel H
(928) 634-9975. **$59-$129.** 920 S Camino Real. Jct SR 260, just nw on SR
89A, then just s. Ext corridors. **Pets:** $10 daily fee/room. Service with
restrictions, supervision.
SAVE ✕ ☎ ▣ ≋

AAA ✓ ▼▼▼ Quality Inn H
(928) 634-4207. **$80-$120.** 301 W SR 89A. On SR 89A, 1.8 mi s of jct SR
260. Ext corridors. **Pets:** Accepted.
SAVE ✕ ☎ ▣ ❒ ≋

AAA ✓ ▼ The View Motel M
(928) 634-7581. **$54-$125.** 818 S Main St. On SR 89A, 0.4 mi nw of jct SR
260. Ext corridors. **Pets:** Accepted.
SAVE ✕ ☎ ≋

DOUGLAS

▼ Motel 6 #305 M
(520) 364-2457. **$45-$58.** 111 16th St (SR 80). 1.2 mi e of jct SR 191. Ext
corridors. **Pets:** Other species. Service with restrictions, supervision.
✕ ☎ ≋

EAGAR

AAA ✓ ▼▼▼ Best Western Sunrise Inn M
(928) 333-2540. **$95-$125.** 128 N Main St. Jct SR 260, just n; jct US 60,
1.5 mi w. Ext corridors. **Pets:** Other species. $10 one-time fee/pet. Desig-
nated rooms, service with restrictions, supervision.
SAVE ✕ ☎ ▣

EHRENBERG

AAA ✓ ▼▼▼ Best Western Desert Oasis H
(928) 923-9711. **$80-$160, 3 day notice.** S Frontage Rd. I-10, exit 1, just
s; 0.5 mi e of Colorado River. Int corridors. **Pets:** Accepted.
SAVE ✕ ☎ ▣ ≋

ELOY

▼ Motel 6–1263 M
(520) 836-3323. **$49-$65.** 4965 S Sunland Gin Rd. I-10, exit 200, just w.
Ext corridors. **Pets:** Other species. Service with restrictions, supervision.
✕ ☎ ≋

FLAGSTAFF

**AAA ✓ ▼▼▼ Best Western Pony Soldier Inn and
Suites H 🐾**
(928) 526-2388. **$75-$135.** 3030 E Route 66. I-40, exit 201, just n, then 1
mi w. Int corridors. **Pets:** Large. $15 one-time fee/room. Designated rooms,
service with restrictions, supervision.
SAVE ✕ ☎ ▣ ≋

AAA ✓ ▼▼▼ Comfort Inn I-17/I-40 H
(928) 774-2225. **$79-$159.** 2355 S Beulah Blvd. I-40, exit 195, just n to
Forest Meadows St, then 1 blk w. Int corridors. **Pets:** Accepted.
SAVE ✕ ☎ ▣ ≋

AAA ✓ ▼▼ Days Inn East H
(928) 527-1477. **$49-$169.** 3601 E Lockett Rd. I-40, exit 201, just n, 0.5 mi
w on I-40 business loop, then just n. Int corridors. **Pets:** Other species. $20
one-time fee/room. Supervision.
SAVE ✕ ☎ ▣ ≋

AAA ✓ ▼▼▼ Days Inn Route 66 M 🐾
(928) 774-5221. **$46-$130, 7 day notice.** 1000 W Route 66. I-40, exit
195, 1.5 mi n on Milton Rd, then just w. Ext corridors. **Pets:** Other species.
$10 daily fee/pet. Service with restrictions, supervision.
SAVE ✕ ☎ ▣ ≋

AAA ✓ ▼ Econo Lodge-University M
(928) 774-7326. **$49-$99.** 914 S Milton Rd. I-40, exit 195, 1.2 mi n. Ext
corridors. **Pets:** Medium, other species. $10 daily fee/room. Service with
restrictions, crate.
SAVE ✕ ☎ ▣ ≋

AAA ✓ ▼▼ Howard Johnson Inn-Lucky Lane M
(928) 779-5121. **$54-$129.** 2520 E Lucky Ln. I-40, exit 198 (Butler Ave),
just n, then just e. Ext corridors. **Pets:** Accepted.
SAVE ✕ ☎ ▣ ≋

AAA ✓ ▼ King's House Hotel M
(928) 774-7186. **$79-$129.** 1560 E Route 66. I-40, exit 198 (Butler Ave),
just w, just n on Enterprise, then just w. Ext corridors. **Pets:** Large, other
species. $15 daily fee/room. Service with restrictions, supervision.
SAVE ✕ ☎ ▣ ≋

▼▼▼ La Quinta Inn & Suites H 🐾
(928) 556-8666. **$59-$179.** 2015 S Beulah Blvd. I-40, exit 195, just n to
Forest Meadow St, then just w. Int corridors. **Pets:** Medium, other species.
Service with restrictions, supervision.
ASK ✕ ☎ ▣ ≋

▼ Motel 6-Flagstaff West #1000 M
(928) 779-3757. **$45-$65.** 2745 S Woodlands Village Blvd. I-40, exit 195,
just n to Forest Meadows St, w to Beulah Blvd, just s, then just w. Ext
corridors. **Pets:** Other species. Service with restrictions, supervision.
✕ ☎ ≋

AAA ✓ ▼▼▼ Quality Inn I-40/I-17 H
(928) 774-8771. **$54-$124.** 2000 S Milton Rd. I-40, exit 195, just n to
Forest Meadows St, then right. Int corridors. **Pets:** Other species. $10 daily
fee/room. Service with restrictions, supervision.
SAVE ✕ ▣ ≋

▼▼ Ramada Inn **H**
(928) 779-3614. **Call for rates.** 2350 E Lucky Ln. I-40, exit 198 (Butler Ave), just n, then just e. Ext corridors. **Pets:** Accepted.
❌ 🛏 💻 ➰

▼▼▼ Residence Inn by Marriott Flagstaff **M**
(928) 526-5555. **$159-$189.** 3440 N Country Club Dr. I-40, exit 201, 0.5 mi s. Ext/int corridors. **Pets:** Accepted.
❌ 🛏 💻 ➰ ❎

▼▼ Sleep Inn **M**
(928) 556-3000. **Call for rates.** 2765 S Woodlands Village Blvd. I-40, exit 195, just n to Forest Meadows St, w to Beulah Rd, just s, then just w. Int corridors. **Pets:** Accepted.
❌ 🔙ᴹ 🛏 💻 ➰

▼▼ Super 8–Flagstaff Mall **M**
(928) 526-0818. **$50-$120.** 3725 Kasper Ave. I-40, exit 201, just n, 0.5 mi w on I-40 business loop, then just n. Int corridors. **Pets:** Other species. $15 daily fee/pet. Designated rooms, service with restrictions, supervision.
ASK ❌ 🛏 💻

✧✧✧ ▼▼ Super 8-Lucky Lane **M**
(928) 773-4888. **$49-$125.** 2540 E Lucky Ln. I-40, exit 198 (Butler Ave), just n, then just e. Ext corridors. **Pets:** Accepted.
SAVE ❌ 🛏 💻 ➰

✧✧✧ ▼ Travel Inn **M**
(928) 774-3381. **$39-$119, 3 day notice.** 801 W Route 66. I-40, exit 195, 1.2 mi n on Milton Rd, then just w. Ext corridors. **Pets:** Other species. $10 daily fee/room. No service, supervision.
SAVE ❌ 🛏

FLORENCE

▼▼▼▼ Rancho Sonora Inn **M**
(520) 868-8000. **$89-$225, 3 day notice.** 9198 N Hwy 79. On SR 79, 5 mi s of SR 287. Ext corridors. **Pets:** Accepted.
ASK ❌ 🛏 💻 ➰

FOREST LAKES

✧✧✧ ▼ Forest Lakes Lodge **M**
(928) 535-4727. **$54-$79.** 876 AZ Hwy 260. On SR 260; between MM 288 and 289. Ext corridors. **Pets:** Accepted.
SAVE ❌ 🛏 🔖

GILA BEND

▼ America's Choice Inn & Suites **M**
(928) 683-6311. **$65.** 2888 Butterfield Tr. I-8, exit 119, just nw. Int corridors. **Pets:** $10 one-time fee/room. Service with restrictions, supervision.
ASK ❌ 🛏 ➰

✧✧✧ ▼▼ Best Western Space Age Lodge **M**
(928) 683-2273. **$99-$169.** 401 E Pima St. Business Loop I-8; center. Ext corridors. **Pets:** Medium, other species. Service with restrictions.
SAVE ❌ 🛏 💻 🍴 ➰

GLOBE

▼▼ Comfort Inn at Round Mountain Park **M**
(928) 425-7575. **Call for rates.** 1515 South St. On US 60, 1 mi e of town. Ext corridors. **Pets:** Accepted.
❌ 🛏 💻 ➰

GRAND CANYON NATIONAL PARK AREA

GRAND CANYON NATIONAL PARK (SOUTH RIM)

✧✧✧ ▼▼▼▼ Canyon Plaza Resort Grand Canyon **H** ✿
(928) 638-2673. **$83-$268.** 116 Hwy 64. On SR 64; 2 mi s of South Rim entrance. Ext/int corridors. **Pets:** Medium. $50 one-time fee/room. Designated rooms, service with restrictions, supervision.
SAVE ❌ 🛏 💻 🍴 ➰

✧✧✧ ▼▼▼ Red Feather Lodge **H**
(928) 638-2414. **$69-$182.** Hwy 64. On SR 64; 2 mi s of South Rim entrance. Ext/int corridors. **Pets:** Accepted.
SAVE ❌ 🔙ᴹ 🛏 💻 🍴 ➰

END AREA

HEBER

✧✧✧ ▼▼ Best Western Sawmill Inn **M**
(928) 535-5053. **$67-$110.** 1877 Hwy 260. 0.5 mi e of center. Ext corridors. **Pets:** Accepted.
SAVE ❌ 🛏 💻

HOLBROOK

✧✧✧ ▼ American Best Inn **M**
(928) 524-2654. **$41-$56.** 2211 E Navajo Blvd. I-40, exit 289, 1 mi w. Ext corridors. **Pets:** Other species. $10 daily fee/pet. No service.
SAVE ❌ 🛏 💻

✧✧✧ ▼▼ Best Western Adobe Inn **M**
(928) 524-3948. **$59-$109.** 615 W Hopi Dr. I-40, exit 285, 1 mi e on US 180 (Hopi Dr). Ext corridors. **Pets:** Medium, other species. $10 one-time fee/pet. Service with restrictions, supervision.
SAVE ❌ 🛏 💻 ➰

✧✧✧ ▼▼▼ Best Western Arizonian Inn **H**
(928) 524-2611. **$94-$114, 3 day notice.** 2508 Navajo Blvd. I-40, exit 289, 0.5 mi w. Ext corridors. **Pets:** Accepted.
SAVE ❌ 🛏 💻 ➰

✧✧✧ ▼▼ Comfort Inn **H**
(928) 524-6131. **Call for rates.** 2602 E Navajo Blvd. I-40, exit 289, just w. Ext corridors. **Pets:** Accepted.
SAVE ❌ 🛏 💻 ➰

✧✧✧ ▼▼ Econo Lodge **H**
(928) 524-1448. **Call for rates.** 2596 E Navajo Blvd. I-40, exit 289, just w. Ext corridors. **Pets:** Accepted.
SAVE ❌ 🛏 💻 ➰

▼▼ Holbrook Holiday Inn Express **M**
(928) 524-1466. **Call for rates.** 1308 E Navajo Blvd. I-40, exit 286, just e. Int corridors. **Pets:** Accepted.
❌ 🛏 💻 ➰

JEROME

✧✧✧ ▼▼▼▼ Connor Hotel of Jerome **H**
(928) 634-5006. **$90-$165, 3 day notice.** 164 Main St. Center. Int corridors. **Pets:** Accepted.
SAVE ❌ 🛏 💻

KAYENTA

〰️〰️〰️ Hampton Inn of Kayenta �H ❀
(928) 697-3170. **$64-$137.** Hwy 160. Just w. Int corridors. **Pets:** Medium, other species. $10 daily fee/room. Designated rooms, service with restrictions, supervision.
🗙 Ⓜ ▣ 🍴 ⇒

KINGMAN

🅐🅐🅐 〰️〰️〰️ Best Western a Wayfarer's Inn & Suites �H ❀
(928)·753-6271. **$87-$120.** 2815 E Andy Devine Ave. I-40, exit 53, 0.5 mi w on Route 66. Ext corridors. **Pets:** Medium. $10 one-time fee/room. Designated rooms, service with restrictions, supervision.
🆂🅰🆅🅴 🗙 ▯ ▣ ⇒

🅐🅐🅐 〰️〰️〰️ Brunswick Hotel �H
(928) 718-1800. **$30-$125.** 315 E Andy Devine Ave. On Route 66; downtown. Int corridors. **Pets:** $10 one-time fee/room. Designated rooms, service with restrictions, supervision.
🆂🅰🆅🅴 🗙 ▯ 🍴

〰️〰️ Comfort Inn Ⓜ
(928) 718-1717. **$90-$150.** 3129 E Andy Devine Ave. I-40, exit 53, just w on Route 66. Int corridors. **Pets:** Medium, dogs only. $20 one-time fee/pet. Designated rooms, service with restrictions, supervision.
🅐🆂🅺 🗙 ▯ ▣ ⇒

🅐🅐🅐 〰️〰️ Days Inn West Ⓜ
(928) 753-7500. **$50-$120.** 3023 E Andy Devine Ave. I-40, exit 53, just w on Route 66. Ext corridors. **Pets:** Large. $10 daily fee/pet. Service with restrictions, supervision.
🆂🅰🆅🅴 🗙 ▯ ▣ ⇒

🅐🅐🅐 〰️〰️ Hill Top Motel Ⓜ
(928) 753-2198. **$40-$100, 3 day notice.** 1901 E Andy Devine Ave. I-40, exit 53, 2 mi w on Route 66. Ext corridors. **Pets:** Accepted.
🆂🅰🆅🅴 🗙 ▯ ⇒

〰️ Motel 6–1114 Ⓜ
(928) 753-9222. **$45-$58.** 424 W Beale St. I-40, exit 48, just se on Business Loop I-40/US 93. Ext corridors. **Pets:** Other species. Service with restrictions, supervision.
🗙 ⇒

〰️ Motel 6 E–1366 Ⓜ
(928) 757-7151. **$42-$55.** 3351 E Andy Devine Ave. I-40, exit 53, just e on Route 66. Ext corridors. **Pets:** Other species. Service with restrictions, supervision.
🗙 Ⓜ ⇒

🅐🅐🅐 〰️〰️〰️ Super 8 �H
(928) 757-4808. **$50-$100.** 3401 E Andy Devine Ave. I-40, exit 53, just e on Route 66. Int corridors. **Pets:** Accepted.
🆂🅰🆅🅴 🗙 ▯ ▣

KOHLS RANCH

〰️〰️ Kohl's Ranch Lodge 🅒🅞
(928) 478-4211. **Call for rates.** 202 S Kohl's Ranch Lodge Rd. Jct SR 87 and 260 E, 16.6 mi e, just s. Ext/int corridors. **Pets:** Accepted.
🗙 ▯ ▣ 🍴 ⇒ 🆇

LAKE HAVASU CITY

〰️〰️ Americas Best Value Inn Ⓜ
(928) 855-5559. **$49-$99.** 101 London Bridge Rd. Jct SR 95, 0.3 mi nw. Ext corridors. **Pets:** Small, dogs only. $5 daily fee/pet. Service with restrictions, supervision.
🗙 ▯ ▣ ⇒

〰️〰️ Days Inn Lake Havasu Ⓜ ❀
(928) 855-7841. **Call for rates.** 1700 McCulloch Blvd N. Just ne of Lake Havasu Ave; center. Ext corridors. **Pets:** Other species. $25 one-time fee/pet. Service with restrictions.
🗙 ▯ ▣ ⇒

🅐🅐🅐 〰️〰️〰️ Hampton Inn Lake Havasu �H ❀
(928) 855-4071. **$90-$219.** 245 London Bridge Rd. 0.5 mi n of London Bridge. Ext/int corridors. **Pets:** Large, other species. Designated rooms, service with restrictions, supervision.
🆂🅰🆅🅴 🗙 ▯ ▣ ⇒ 🆇

〰️〰️ Island Inn Hotel �H
(928) 680-0606. **$60-$250.** 1300 W McCulloch Blvd. 0.7 mi w of London Bridge/SR 95. Int corridors. **Pets:** Medium. $10 one-time fee/pet. Designated rooms, service with restrictions, supervision.
🅐🆂🅺 🗙 ▯ ▣ 🍴 ⇒

🅐🅐🅐 〰️〰️ Island Suites �H
(928) 855-7333. **$55-$85, 3 day notice.** 236 S Lake Havasu Ave. Just s of jct McCulloch Blvd. Int corridors. **Pets:** Small, dogs only. $10 one-time fee/pet. Designated rooms, service with restrictions, supervision.
🆂🅰🆅🅴 🗙 ▯ ⇒

〰️ Lake Havasu City Super 8 Ⓜ
(928) 855-8844. **$55-$175.** 305 London Bridge Rd. Just w of SR 95, exit Palo Verde; 0.5 mi n of London Bridge. Int corridors. **Pets:** Small. $20 one-time fee/pet. Designated rooms, service with restrictions, supervision.
🅐🆂🅺 🗙 ▯ ▣ ⇒

〰️〰️ Lake Place Inn Ⓜ
(928) 855-2146. **$50-$250.** 31 Wing's Loop. 1 mi e of SR 95 via Swanson Ave; downtown. Ext corridors. **Pets:** Medium. $10 one-time fee/pet. Designated rooms, service with restrictions, supervision.
🅐🆂🅺 🗙 ▯ ▣ ⇒

〰️ Motel 6 Lakeside Ⓜ
(928) 855-3200. **Call for rates.** 111 London Bridge Rd. 0.3 mi n of London Bridge. Int corridors. **Pets:** Other species. Service with restrictions, supervision.
🗙

〰️〰️ Quality Inn & Suites Ⓜ
(928) 855-1111. **$59-$149.** 271 S Lake Havasu Ave. SR 95, just e on Swanson Ave, then just s. Ext corridors. **Pets:** Large, other species. $50 deposit/room, $20 one-time fee/room. Designated rooms, service with restrictions, supervision.
🅐🆂🅺 🗙 ▯ ▣ 🍴 ⇒

🅐🅐🅐 〰️〰️〰️ Travelodge-Lake Havasu City Ⓜ
(928) 680-9202. **$50-$300, 3 day notice.** 480 London Bridge Rd. 1 mi n of London Bridge. Int corridors. **Pets:** Medium. $50 deposit/pet, $10 daily fee/pet. Designated rooms, service with restrictions, supervision.
🆂🅰🆅🅴 🗙 ▯ ▣

MUNDS PARK

🅐🅐🅐 〰️ Motel In The Pines Ⓜ
(928) 286-9699. **$39-$79.** 80 W Pinewood Rd. I-17, exit 322, just e. Ext corridors. **Pets:** Accepted.
🆂🅰🆅🅴 🗙 ▯ ▣

NOGALES

〰️〰️〰️ Holiday Inn Express �H
(520) 281-0123. **$105.** 850 W Shell Rd. I-19, exit 4, just w to Frank Reed, then just nw. Int corridors. **Pets:** Small, other species. $50 daily fee/pet. Supervision.
🅐🆂🅺 🗙 ▯ ▣ ⇒

〰️ Motel 6 Nogales #71 Ⓜ
(520) 281-2951. **$51-$63.** 141 W Mariposa Rd. I-19, exit 4, 0.9 mi e. Ext corridors. **Pets:** Other species. Service with restrictions, supervision.
🗙 ▯ ⇒

PAGE

ⒶⒶⒶ ▽▽ Americas Best Value Inn Ⓜ
(928) 645-2858. **$49-$120.** 75 S 7th Ave. 1 mi e of US 89 via SR 89L; just n of Lake Powell Blvd. Ext corridors. **Pets:** Medium. $15 daily fee/pet. Designated rooms, service with restrictions, supervision.
SAVE ☒ ⊟

ⒶⒶⒶ ▽▽▽ Best Western Arizona Inn Ⓗ
(928) 645-2466. **$59-$119, 3 day notice.** 716 Rimview Dr. 0.7 mi e of US 89 via SR 89L. Int corridors. **Pets:** Large, other species. $10 daily fee/pet. No service, supervision.
SAVE ☒ ⊟ ▣ ⇶

ⒶⒶⒶ ▽▽▽▽ Lake Powell Days Inn & Suites Ⓗ
(928) 645-2800. **$69-$189.** 961 N Hwy 89. On US 89, just s. Int corridors. **Pets:** $10 daily fee/pet. Service with restrictions, supervision.
SAVE ☒ ⊟ ▣ ⇶

ⒶⒶⒶ ▽▽▽▽ Lake Powell Resort and Marina Ⓗ
(928) 645-2433. **$144-$233.** 100 Lakeshore Dr. 4 mi n of Glen Canyon Dam via US 89. Int corridors. **Pets:** $20 daily fee/room. Designated rooms, service with restrictions, supervision.
SAVE ☒ ⊟ ▣ 🍴 ⇶ ☒

▽▽ Linda's Lake Powell Condos ⒸⓄ
(928) 353-4591. **Call for rates.** 1019 Tower Butte. 6 mi n on US 89. Ext corridors. **Pets:** Accepted.
☒ ⊟ ▣

ⒶⒶⒶ ▽▽ Motel 6-Page/Lake Powell #4013 Ⓗ
(928) 645-5888. **$39-$83, 3 day notice.** 637 S Lake Powell Blvd. On Business Loop SR 89L, just e of US 89. Int corridors. **Pets:** Other species. Service with restrictions, supervision.
SAVE ☒ ⇶

ⒶⒶⒶ ▽▽▽ Quality Inn Lake Powell Ⓗ
(928) 645-8851. **$50-$92.** 287 N Lake Powell Blvd. 0.8 mi e of US 89/SR 89L. Int corridors. **Pets:** Accepted.
SAVE ☒ ⊟ ▣ 🍴 ⇶

ⒶⒶⒶ ▽▽▽ Super 8 Gateway to Lake Powell Ⓗ
(928) 645-5858. **$59-$109, 3 day notice.** 649 S Lake Powell Blvd. On SR 89L, just e of US 89. Int corridors. **Pets:** Small. $10 daily fee/pet. Service with restrictions, supervision.
SAVE ☒ ⊟ ▣ ⇶

PARKER

ⒶⒶⒶ ▽▽▽ Best Western Parker Inn Ⓜ
(928) 669-6060. **$70-$150, 7 day notice.** 1012 Geronimo Ave. SR 95, just e. Int corridors. **Pets:** Accepted.
SAVE ☒ ⊟ ▣ ⇶

PAYSON

ⒶⒶⒶ ▽▽ Americas Best Value Inn Ⓜ
(928) 474-2283. **$49-$120.** 811 S Beeline Hwy. On SR 87, 0.7 mi s of SR 260. Ext/int corridors. **Pets:** Small, dogs only. $15 daily fee/pet. Designated rooms, service with restrictions, supervision.
SAVE ☒ ⊟ ▣

ⒶⒶⒶ ▽▽▽ Best Western Payson Inn Ⓜ
(928) 474-3241. **$60-$170.** 801 N Beeline Hwy. On SR 87, 0.6 mi n of SR 260. Ext corridors. **Pets:** $25 daily fee/room. Service with restrictions, supervision.
SAVE ☒ ⊟ ▣ ⇶

ⒶⒶⒶ ▽▽▽ Days Inn & Suites Ⓗ 🐾
(928) 474-9800. **$70-$170.** 301-A S Beeline Hwy. On SR 87, just s of SR 260. Int corridors. **Pets:** Small. $10 daily fee/pet. Designated rooms, service with restrictions, supervision.
SAVE ☒ ⊟ ▣ ⇶

▽▽▽ Majestic Mountain Inn Ⓜ 🐾
(928) 474-0185. **Call for rates.** 602 E Hwy 260. On SR 260, 0.5 mi e of SR 87. Ext corridors. **Pets:** Medium. $25 one-time fee/room. Designated rooms, service with restrictions, supervision.
☒ ⊟ ▣ ⇶

PHOENIX METROPOLITAN AREA

APACHE JUNCTION

ⒶⒶⒶ ▽▽▽ Apache Junction Super 8 Ⓗ 🐾
(480) 288-8888. **$99-$119.** 251 E 29th Ave. US 60, exit 196 (Idaho Rd/SR 88 E), just n. Ext/int corridors. **Pets:** Medium, dogs only. $100 deposit/pet. Service with restrictions, supervision.
SAVE ☒ ⊟ ▣ ⇶

BUCKEYE

ⒶⒶⒶ ▽▽▽ Days Inn-Buckeye Ⓗ
(623) 386-5400. **Call for rates.** 25205 W Yuma Rd. I-10, exit 114 (Miller Rd), just sw. Ext corridors. **Pets:** Accepted.
SAVE ☒ ⊟ ▣ ⇶

CAREFREE

ⒶⒶⒶ ▽▽▽▽ The Boulders Resort and Golden Door Spa Ⓗ
(480) 488-9009. **$129-$699, 7 day notice.** 34631 N Tom Darlington Dr. Scottsdale Rd, 11 mi n of Bell Rd. Ext corridors. **Pets:** Accepted.
SAVE ☒ ⊟ ▣ 🍴 ⇶ ☒

▽▽▽▽ Carefree Resort & Villas Ⓗ
(480) 488-5300. **$90-$1200, 3 day notice.** 37220 Mule Train Rd. SR 101, exit 36 (Pima Rd), 12.2 mi n to Cave Creek Rd, 1 mi w, then 0.4 mi n. Ext/int corridors. **Pets:** Accepted.
ASK ☒ ⊟ ▣ 🍴 ⇶ ☒

CHANDLER

ⒶⒶⒶ ▽▽▽ Chandler Super 8 Ⓗ
(480) 961-3888. **$60-$200.** 7171 W Chandler Blvd. I-10, exit 160 (Chandler Blvd), just e. Int corridors. **Pets:** Accepted.
SAVE ☒ ⊟ ⇶

ⒶⒶⒶ ▽▽▽ Comfort Inn Ⓗ
(480) 705-8882. **$90-$140.** 255 N Kyrene Rd. I-10, exit 160 (Chandler Blvd), 1.5 mi e, then just n. Int corridors. **Pets:** Accepted.
SAVE ☒ Ⓜ ⊟ ▣ ⇶

ⒶⒶⒶ ▽▽▽▽ Crowne Plaza San Marcos Golf Resort Ⓗ
(480) 812-0900. **$129-$299.** 1 San Marcos Pl. Jct Chandler Blvd, just s on Arizona Ave, then just w on Buffalo St; in historic downtown. Ext corridors. **Pets:** Small, dogs only. $50 one-time fee/room. Designated rooms, service with restrictions, crate.
SAVE ☒ ⊟ ▣ 🍴 ⇶ ☒

ⒶⒶⒶ ▽▽▽▽ Hawthorn Suites Chandler Ⓗ
(480) 705-8881. **$79-$199.** 5858 W Chandler Blvd. I-10, exit 160 (Chandler Blvd), 1.5 mi e. Int corridors. **Pets:** Medium. $25 daily fee/pet, $125 one-time fee/room. Supervision.
SAVE ☒ ⊟ ▣ ⇶

▽▽▽▽ Homewood Suites by Hilton Ⓗ
(480) 753-6200. **$499.** 7373 W Detroit St. I-10, exit 160 (Chandler Blvd), 0.4 mi e, n on 54th St, then just w. Int corridors. **Pets:** Small, dogs only. $100 one-time fee/room. Service with restrictions.
☒ Ⓜ ⊟ ▣ ⇶

Red Roof Inn-Chandler
(480) 857-4969. **Call for rates.** 7400 W Boston St. I-10, exit 160 (Chandler Blvd), just e, then s on Southgate Dr. Int corridors. **Pets:** Accepted.

Residence Inn-Chandler Fashion Center
(480) 782-1551. **$139-$209.** 200 N Federal St. I-10, exit 160 (Chandler Blvd), 4.2 mi e, just n on N Metro Blvd, then just e. Int corridors. **Pets:** Accepted.

Sheraton Wild Horse Pass Resort & Spa
(602) 225-0100. **$159-$810, 7 day notice.** 5594 W Wild Horse Pass Blvd. I-10, exit 162, 2.4 mi w. Int corridors. **Pets:** Large, dogs only. Service with restrictions, supervision.

Windmill Suites of Chandler
(480) 812-9600. **$85-$179.** 3535 W Chandler Blvd. I-10, exit 160 (Chandler Blvd), 4 mi e. Int corridors. **Pets:** Other species. Designated rooms, service with restrictions, supervision.

FOUNTAIN HILLS

Comfort Inn
(480) 837-5343. **$59-$159.** 17105 E Shea Blvd. 0.5 mi w of SR 87 (Beeline Hwy). Int corridors. **Pets:** Accepted.

Holiday Inn Hotel & Suites-Fountain Hills/Mayo Clinic
(480) 837-6565. **$109-$159, 5 day notice.** 12800 N Saguaro Blvd. Jct Shea Blvd, 2.2 mi n; center. Int corridors. **Pets:** Accepted.

GLENDALE

Comfort Suites Glendale
(623) 271-9005. **$79-$161.** 9824 W Camelback Rd. Loop 101, exit 5 (Camelback Rd), just w to 99th St, then just n. Int corridors. **Pets:** Accepted.

Ramada
(623) 412-2000. **Call for rates.** 7885 W Arrowhead Towne Center Dr. Loop 101, exit 14 (Bell Rd), 0.3 mi e, then just n on 79th Ave. Ext corridors. **Pets:** Accepted.

Residence Inn by Marriott Glendale
(623) 772-8900. **$149-$229.** 7350 W Zanjero Blvd. Loop 101, exit 7 (Glendale Ave), then e. Int corridors. **Pets:** $100 one-time fee/room. Service with restrictions, supervision.

GOODYEAR

Best Western Phoenix Goodyear Inn
(623) 932-3210. **$79-$179.** 55 N Litchfield Rd. I-10, exit 128, 0.8 mi s. Ext/int corridors. **Pets:** Large, other species. $15 daily fee/room.

Comfort Suites Goodyear
(623) 266-2884. **$120-$400.** 15575 W Roosevelt St. I-10, exit 126, just s on Estrella Pkwy, then just w. Int corridors. **Pets:** Medium. $50 one-time fee/pet. Designated rooms, service with restrictions, supervision.

Hampton Inn & Suites
(623) 536-1313. **$129-$699.** 2000 N Litchfield Rd. I-10, exit 128, 0.5 mi n. Int corridors. **Pets:** Accepted.

Holiday Inn Express
(623) 535-1313. **$99-$199.** 1313 N Litchfield Rd. I-10, exit 128, just n. Int corridors. **Pets:** Service with restrictions, supervision.

Holiday Inn Hotel & Suites
(623) 547-1313. **$109-$189.** 1188 N Dysart Rd. I-10, exit 129 (Dysart Rd), just n. Int corridors. **Pets:** $35 one-time fee/room. Service with restrictions, crate.

Quality Inn & Suites Goodyear
(623) 932-9191. **$79-$169.** 950 N Dysart Rd. I-10, exit 129 (Dysart Rd), just s. Ext corridors. **Pets:** Medium. $50 deposit/pet, $15 daily fee/pet. Service with restrictions, supervision.

Residence Inn by Marriott
(623) 866-1313. **$149-$229.** 2020 N Litchfield Rd. I-10, exit 128, 0.6 mi n. Int corridors. **Pets:** Other species. $100 one-time fee/room.

LITCHFIELD PARK

The Wigwam Golf Resort & Spa
(623) 935-3811. **$119-$629, 7 day notice.** 300 Wigwam Blvd. I-10, exit 128 (Litchfield Rd), 2.4 mi n, then 0.4 mi e. Ext corridors. **Pets:** Designated rooms, service with restrictions, crate.

MESA

Arizona Golf Resort & Conference Center
(480) 832-3202. **$180-$250.** 425 S Power Rd. 1.3 mi n of US 60 (Superstition Frwy), exit 188 (Power Rd); southeast corner of Broadway and Power rds; entrance on Broadway Rd. Ext corridors. **Pets:** $25 one-time fee/room. Service with restrictions.

Best Western Mesa Inn
(480) 964-8000. **$69-$169.** 1625 E Main St. 2 mi n of US 60 (Superstition Frwy), exit Stapley Dr, 0.5 mi e. Ext corridors. **Pets:** Accepted.

Best Western Mezona Inn
(480) 834-9233. **$104-$179, 3 day notice.** 250 W Main St. Just e of Country Club Dr; downtown. Ext corridors. **Pets:** $20 one-time fee/pet. Designated rooms, service with restrictions, supervision.

Best Western Superstition Springs Inn
(480) 641-1164. **$90-$150.** 1342 S Power Rd. Just n of US 60 (Superstition Frwy), exit 188 (Power Rd); northwest corner of Power Rd and Hampton Ave. Ext corridors. **Pets:** Small. $10 daily fee/pet. Designated rooms, service with restrictions, supervision.

Days Hotel
(480) 844-8900. **$65-$180.** 333 W Juanita. US 60 (Superstition Frwy), exit 179 (Country Club Dr), just s, then just e. Int corridors. **Pets:** Accepted.

Days Inn-East Mesa
(480) 981-8111. **Call for rates.** 5531 E Main St. 0.4 mi e of Higley Rd. Ext corridors. **Pets:** Small, dogs only. $10 daily fee/pet. Designated rooms, service with restrictions, crate.

Extended StayAmerica-Phoenix/Mesa
(480) 632-0201. **$64-$119.** 455 W Baseline Rd. US 60 (Superstition Frwy), exit 179 (Country Club Dr), 0.4 mi s on SR 87, then just w. Int corridors. **Pets:** Other species. $25 daily fee/pet. Service with restrictions, crate.

AAA ▼▼▼▼ **Hilton Phoenix East/Mesa** H ❋
(480) 833-5555. **$79-$249.** 1011 W Holmes Ave. US 60 (Superstition Frwy), exit 178 (Alma School Rd), just n, then just e. Int corridors. **Pets:** Large. $75 one-time fee/room. Designated rooms, service with restrictions, supervision.
SAVE ✕ 🛑 💻 🍽 🏊 ✕

AAA ▼▼▼▼ **Holiday Inn Hotel & Suites** H
(480) 964-7000. **$85-$245.** 1600 S Country Club Dr. US 60 (Superstition Frwy), exit 179 (Country Club Dr), just s. Ext/int corridors. **Pets:** Other species. $25 daily fee/room.
SAVE ✕ 🛑 💻 🍽 🏊

▼▼ ▼▼ **Homestead Studio Suites Hotel Phoenix-Mesa** H
(480) 752-2266. **$62-$114.** 1920 W Isabella. Just s of US 60 (Superstition Frwy), exit 177 (Dobson Rd). Ext corridors. **Pets:** Other species. $25 daily fee/pet. Service with restrictions, crate.
ASK ✕ 🛑 💻

▼▼▼▼ **La Quinta Inn & Suites Phoenix (Mesa East)** H ❋
(480) 654-1970. **$74-$199.** 6530 E Superstition Springs Blvd. US 60 (Superstition Frwy), exit 187 (Superstition Springs Blvd) eastbound, just se; exit 188 (Power Rd) westbound, just sw. Int corridors. **Pets:** Medium, other species. Service with restrictions, supervision.
ASK ✕ 🔥M 🛑 💻 🏊

▼▼▼▼ **La Quinta Inn & Suites Phoenix (Mesa West)** H ❋
(480) 844-8747. **$69-$189.** 902 W Grove Ave. US 60 (Superstition Frwy), exit 178 (Alma School Rd), just n, then just e. Int corridors. **Pets:** Medium, other species. Service with restrictions, supervision.
ASK ✕ 🛑 💻 🏊

▼ **Motel 6-Mesa South #1030** M
(480) 834-0066. **$41-$65.** 1511 S Country Club Dr. US 60 (Superstition Frwy), exit 179 (Country Club Dr), northeast corner. Ext corridors. **Pets:** Other species. Service with restrictions, supervision.
✕ 🛑 🏊

AAA ▼▼ ▼▼ **Quality Inn & Suites Mesa/Phoenix** H
(480) 964-2897. **$49-$159.** 1410 S Country Club Dr. US 60, exit 179 (Country Club Dr), just n. Ext corridors. **Pets:** Small, other species. $10 daily fee/pet. Service with restrictions, supervision.
SAVE ✕ 🛑 💻 🏊

▼▼▼▼ **Residence Inn by Marriott Mesa** H
(480) 610-0100. **$136-$246.** 941 W Grove Ave. US 60 (Superstition Frwy), exit 178 (Alma School Rd), just n, then just e. Int corridors. **Pets:** Accepted.
✕ 🔥M 🛑 💻 🏊 ✕

▼▼ ▼▼ **Sleep Inn of Mesa** H
(480) 807-7760. **$80-$325, 21 day notice.** 6347 E Southern Ave. US 60 (Superstition Frwy), exit 188 (Power Rd), 0.8 mi n, then 0.4 mi w to mall entrance. Int corridors. **Pets:** Medium, other species. $10 daily fee/room, $25 one-time fee/room. Designated rooms, service with restrictions, supervision.
ASK ✕ 🛑 💻 🏊

AAA ▼▼ **Super 8-Mesa/Gilbert Rd** H
(480) 545-0888. **Call for rates.** 1550 S Gilbert Rd. US 60 (Superstition Frwy), exit 182 (Gilbert Rd), 1 blk n. Int corridors. **Pets:** Accepted.
SAVE ✕ 🛑 🏊

▼ **Travelodge Suites Mesa** H ❋
(480) 832-5961. **$50-$130.** 4244 E Main St. US 60 (Superstition Frwy), exit 185 (Greenfield Rd), 2 mi n, then just w. Ext corridors. **Pets:** Medium, other species. $10 daily fee/pet. Service with restrictions, supervision.
ASK ✕ 🛑 💻 🏊

AAA ▼▼ ▼▼ **Windemere Hotel and Conference Center** H
(480) 985-3600. **$59-$229.** 5750 E Main St. 0.6 mi e of Higley Rd. Ext corridors. **Pets:** Accepted.
SAVE ✕ 🛑 💻 🏊

PARADISE VALLEY

AAA ▼▼▼▼ ▼▼▼▼ **Sanctuary on Camelback Mountain** H
(480) 948-2100. **Call for rates.** 5700 E McDonald Dr. US 101, exit McDonald Dr, 3.9 mi w; 1.8 mi w of jct Scottsdale Rd. Ext corridors. **Pets:** Accepted.
SAVE ✕ 💻 🍽 🏊 ✕

PEORIA

▼▼ ▼▼ **Comfort Suites by Choice Hotels/Sports Complex** H ❋
(623) 334-3993. **Call for rates.** 8473 W Paradise Ln. Loop 101, exit 14 (Bell Rd), just e to 83rd Ave, just s, then just w. Int corridors. **Pets:** Other species. $50 one-time fee/room. Service with restrictions.
✕ 🛑 💻

▼▼ ▼▼ **Extended StayAmerica Phoenix-Peoria** H
(623) 487-0020. **$74-$159.** 7345 W Bell Rd. Loop 101, exit 14 (Bell Rd), 1.2 mi e. Int corridors. **Pets:** Other species. $25 daily fee/pet. Service with restrictions, crate.
ASK ✕ 🛑 💻

▼▼▼▼ **Holiday Inn Express Hotel & Suites** H
(623) 853-1313. **Call for rates.** 16771 N 84th Ave. Loop 101, exit 14 (Bell Rd), just w, then just s. Int corridors. **Pets:** Accepted.
✕ 🔥M 🛑 💻 🏊

▼▼▼▼ **La Quinta Inn & Suites Phoenix (West/Peoria)** H ❋
(623) 487-1900. **$69-$229.** 16321 N 83rd Ave. Loop 101, exit 14 (Bell Rd), just e, then just s. Int corridors. **Pets:** Medium, other species. Service with restrictions, supervision.
ASK ✕ 🛑 💻 🏊

▼▼▼▼ **Residence Inn by Marriott** H
(623) 979-2074. **$139-$209.** 8435 W Paradise Ln. Loop 101, exit 14 (Bell Rd), just e, just s on 83rd Ave, then just w. Int corridors. **Pets:** Accepted.
✕ 🛑 💻 🏊 ✕

PHOENIX

AAA ▼▼▼▼ ▼▼▼▼ **Arizona Biltmore Resort & Spa** H ❋
(602) 955-6600. **$305-$485.** 2400 E Missouri Ave. Jct Camelback Rd, 0.5 mi n on 24th St, then 0.4 mi e. Int/ext corridors. **Pets:** Small, other species. $50 deposit/room, $50 one-time fee/room. Designated rooms, service with restrictions, supervision.
SAVE ✕ 💻 🍽 🏊 ✕

AAA ▼▼ ▼▼ **Best Western Airport Inn** H
(602) 273-7251. **$79-$199, 3 day notice.** 2425 S 24th St. I-10, exit 150B (24th St) westbound, just s; exit 151 (University Dr) eastbound, just n to I-10 westbound, 1 mi w to exit 150B (24th St), then just s. Ext/int corridors. **Pets:** Accepted.
SAVE ✕ 🛑 💻 🍽 🏊

AAA ▼▼ ▼▼ **Best Western Bell Hotel** H
(602) 993-8300. **$54-$149.** 17211 N Black Canyon Hwy. I-17, exit 212, just e, then just n. Ext corridors. **Pets:** Accepted.
SAVE ✕ 🛑 💻 🏊

AAA ▼▼▼▼ **Best Western InnSuites Phoenix Biltmore Hotel & Suites** H
(602) 997-6285. **$79-$199.** 1615 E Northern Ave. SR 51, exit 7, 0.6 mi w. Ext corridors. **Pets:** Accepted.
SAVE ✕ 🛑 💻 🏊

AAA ▼▼ ▼▼ **Best Western Metrocenter Inn** H
(602) 864-6233. **$79-$169.** 8101 N Black Canyon Hwy. I-17, exit 206 (Northern Ave), just e, then just n; on east side of freeway. Ext corridors. **Pets:** Small. $50 one-time fee/room. Designated rooms, service with restrictions, supervision.
SAVE ✕ 🛑 💻 🏊

▼▼ Candlewood Suites 🅗
(602) 861-4900. **$79-$189.** 11411 N Black Canyon Hwy. I-17, exit 208 (Peoria Ave), just e, then 0.4 mi n. Int corridors. **Pets:** Medium, other species. $75 one-time fee/room. Service with restrictions, supervision.
🄰🄺 ⊠ 🛏 💻 🌊

▼▼▼ Clarion Hotel @ Phoenix Tech Center 🅗
(480) 893-3900. **$69-$189.** 5121 E La Puenta Ave. I-10, exit 157 (Elliot Rd), just w, just n on 51st St, then just e. Ext corridors. **Pets:** Other species. $25 one-time fee/room. Service with restrictions, supervision.
🄰🄺 ⊠ 🛏 💻

▲▲▲ ▼▼▼ Comfort Inn Black Canyon 🅗
(602) 242-8011. **$59-$469.** 5050 N Black Canyon Hwy. I-17, exit 203 (Camelback Rd), just w, then just n; on west side of freeway. Ext corridors. **Pets:** Medium, other species. $35 one-time fee/room. Service with restrictions, supervision.
🆂🅰🆅🅴 ⊠ 🛏 💻 🌊

▲▲▲ ▼▼▼ Comfort Inn I-10 West/Central 🅗
(602) 415-1623. **Call for rates.** 1344 N 27th Ave. I-10, exit 27th Ave eastbound, just n; exit 141 (35th Ave) westbound, just n, 1 mi e on McDowell Rd, then s. Int corridors. **Pets:** Accepted.
🆂🅰🆅🅴 ⊠ 🛏 💻 🌊

▲▲▲ ▼▼▼ Comfort Inn-Phoenix North 🅗
(602) 978-2222. **$60-$160.** 2641 W Union Hills Dr. I-17, exit 214A (Union Hills Dr), just w. Int corridors. **Pets:** Small. $10 daily fee/pet. Service with restrictions, supervision.
🆂🅰🆅🅴 ⊠ 🛏 💻 🍽 🌊

▼▼ Comfort Suites by Choice Hotels 🅗
(602) 861-9900. **Call for rates.** 10210 N 26th Dr. I-17, exit 208 (Peoria Ave), just e, just s on 25th Ave, then 0.3 mi w on W Beryl Ave. Int corridors. **Pets:** Accepted.
⊠ 🅖🅜 🛏 💻 🌊

▼▼ Crossland Economy Studios-Phoenix West 🅗
(602) 272-8571. **$54-$84.** 4861 W McDowell Rd. I-10, exit 139 (51st Ave), just n, then just e. Ext corridors. **Pets:** Other species. $25 daily fee/pet. Service with restrictions, crate.
🄰🄺 ⊠ 🛏 💻

▼▼▼▼ Crowne Plaza Phoenix 🅗
(602) 943-2341. **$69-$499.** 2532 W Peoria Ave. I-17, exit 208 (Peoria Ave), just e, then just n on 25th Ave. Int corridors. **Pets:** Medium, other species. $25 one-time fee/pet. Service with restrictions, supervision.
🄰🄺 ⊠ 🅖🅜 🛏 💻 🍽 🌊 ⊠

▲▲▲ ▼▼▼▼ Crowne Plaza Phoenix Airport 🅗
(602) 273-7778. **$89-$299.** 4300 E Washington St. Loop 202, exit 2 (44th St), 0.7 mi s. Int corridors. **Pets:** Accepted.
🆂🅰🆅🅴 ⊠ 🛏 💻 🍽 🌊

▼▼ Days Inn Phoenix I-17 & Thomas 🅗
(602) 257-0801. **$60-$160.** 2420 W Thomas Rd. I-17, exit 201 (Thomas Rd), just e. Int corridors. **Pets:** Small. $25 one-time fee/pet. Designated rooms, service with restrictions, supervision.
🄰🄺 ⊠ 🛏 💻 🌊

▲▲▲ ▼▼▼▼ Embassy Suites Phoenix Airport at 24th St 🅗 ❀
(602) 957-1910. **$89-$499.** 2333 E Thomas Rd. SR 51, exit 2 (44th St), just e. Ext corridors. **Pets:** $20 daily fee/pet. Service with restrictions.
🆂🅰🆅🅴 ⊠ 🛏 💻 🍽 🌊

▼▼▼▼ Embassy Suites Phoenix-Biltmore 🅗
(602) 955-3992. **$105-$629.** 2630 E Camelback Rd. Just n of Camelback Rd, on 26th St. Int corridors. **Pets:** Medium. $40 one-time fee/room. Service with restrictions, crate.
⊠ 🛏 💻 🍽 🌊

▲▲▲ ▼▼▼▼ Embassy Suites Phoenix North 🅗
(602) 375-1777. **$99-$699.** 2577 W Greenway Rd. I-17, exit 211, just e. Ext corridors. **Pets:** $50 one-time fee/room. Service with restrictions, supervision.
🆂🅰🆅🅴 ⊠ 🛏 💻 🍽 🌊 ⊠

▼▼▼ Extended StayAmerica-Chandler 🅗
(480) 785-0464. **$74-$144.** 14245 S 50th St. I-10, exit 159, just w on Ray Rd, just s, then just e. Int corridors. **Pets:** Other species. $25 daily fee/pet. Service with restrictions, crate.
🄰🄺 ⊠ 🅖🅜 🛏 💻

▼▼▼ Extended StayAmerica-Phoenix Airport 🅗
(602) 438-2900. **$59-$134.** 3421 E Elwood St. I-10, exit 151 (University Dr), just n, then just e. Int corridors. **Pets:** Other species. $25 daily fee/pet. Service with restrictions, crate.
🄰🄺 ⊠ 🛏 💻

▼▼▼ Extended StayAmerica Phoenix/Airport/E Oak St 🅗
(602) 225-2998. **$71-$139.** 4357 E Oak St. Loop 202, exit 2 (44th St), 1 mi n. Ext corridors. **Pets:** Other species. $25 daily fee/pet. Service with restrictions, crate.
🄰🄺 ⊠ 🅖🅜 🛏 💻 🌊

▼▼▼ Extended StayAmerica Phoenix-Chandler-E Chandler Blvd 🅗
(480) 753-6700. **$69-$144.** 5035 E Chandler Blvd. I-10, exit 160 (Chandler Blvd), just w. Ext corridors. **Pets:** Other species. $25 daily fee/pet. Service with restrictions, crate.
🄰🄺 ⊠ 🛏 💻 🌊

▼▼▼ Extended StayAmerica Phoenix-Deer Valley 🅗
(623) 879-6609. **$54-$119.** 20827 N 27th Ave. I-10, exit 215 (Rose Garden Ln), just w; exit 215B southbound, just w, then 0.4 mi s. Int corridors. **Pets:** Other species. $25 daily fee/pet. Service with restrictions, crate.
🄰🄺 ⊠ 🛏 💻

▼▼▼ Extended StayAmerica Phoenix-Metro Center 🅗
(602) 870-2999. **$54-$129.** 11211 N Black Canyon Hwy. I-17, exit 208 (Peoria Ave), just e, then 0.3 mi n; on east side of freeway. Ext corridors. **Pets:** Other species. $25 daily fee/pet. Service with restrictions, crate.
🄰🄺 ⊠ 🛏 💻 🌊

▼▼▼ Extended Stay Deluxe Phoenix-Biltmore 🅗
(602) 265-6800. **$74-$169.** 5235 N 16th St. Jct SR 51, just w on Camelback Rd, then just n. Int corridors. **Pets:** Other species. $25 daily fee/pet. Service with restrictions, crate.
🄰🄺 ⊠ 🛏 💻 🌊

▼▼▼ Extended Stay Deluxe (Phoenix/Midtown) 🅗
(602) 279-9000. **$89-$169.** 217 W Osborn Rd. Just w of Central Ave; between Indian School and Thomas rds. Int corridors. **Pets:** Other species. $25 daily fee/pet. Service with restrictions, crate.
🄰🄺 ⊠ 🅖🅜 🛏 💻 🌊

▼▼▼▼ Hilton Suites-Phoenix 🅗 ❀
(602) 222-1111. **$89-$599.** 10 E Thomas Rd. Just e of Central Ave; in Phoenix Plaza. Int corridors. **Pets:** Large, other species. $50 deposit/room. Service with restrictions, crate.
⊠ 🅖🅜 🛏 💻 🍽 🌊 ⊠

▲▲▲ ▼▼▼▼ Holiday Inn Downtown North 🅗 ❀
(602) 595-4444. **$109-$149.** 212 W Osborn Rd. Just w of Central Ave. Int corridors. **Pets:** Other species. Service with restrictions.
🆂🅰🆅🅴 ⊠ 🛏 💻 🍽 🌊

▲▲▲ ▼▼▼▼ Holiday Inn West 🅗
(602) 484-9009. **$89-$159.** 1500 N 51st Ave. I-10, exit 139 (51st Ave), just n. Int corridors. **Pets:** Accepted.
🆂🅰🆅🅴 ⊠ 🅖🅜 🛏 💻 🍽 🌊

▼▼ Homestead Studio Suites Hotel-Phoenix North/Metro Center M
(602) 944-7828. **$49-$94.** 2102 W Dunlap Ave. I-17, exit 207 (Dunlap Ave), 0.7 mi e. Ext corridors. **Pets:** Other species. $25 daily fee/pet. Service with restrictions, crate.
🅰️🆂🅺 ✕ 🛗 💻

▼▼▼ Homewood Suites by Hilton H
(602) 508-0937. **$119-$575.** 2001 E Highland Ave. Just e of 20th St. Int corridors. **Pets:** Accepted.
✕ 🛗 💻 🏊 ✕

▼▼▼ Homewood Suites Hotel H
(602) 674-8900. **$98-$399.** 2536 Beryl Ave. I-17, exit 208 (Peoria Ave), just e, just s on 25th Ave, then just w. Int corridors. **Pets:** Accepted.
✕ 🅼 🛗 💻 🏊

▼▼▼ La Quinta Inn & Suites Phoenix (Chandler) H ❄️
(480) 961-7700. **$69-$199.** 15241 S 50th St. I-10, exit 160 (Chandler Blvd), just w, then just n. Int corridors. **Pets:** Medium, other species. Service with restrictions, supervision.
🅰️🆂🅺 ✕ 🅼 🛗 💻 🏊

▼▼▼ La Quinta Inn & Suites Phoenix West H ❄️
(602) 595-7601. **$69-$199.** 4929 W McDowell Rd. I-10, exit 139 (51st Ave), just n, then just e. Int corridors. **Pets:** Medium, other species. Service with restrictions, supervision.
🅰️🆂🅺 ✕ 🛗 💻 🏊

▼▼ La Quinta Inn Phoenix Airport North H ❄️
(602) 956-6500. **$63-$144.** 4727 E Thomas Rd. Just w of 48th St. Ext/int corridors. **Pets:** Medium, other species. Service with restrictions, supervision.
🅰️🆂🅺 ✕ 🛗 💻 🏊

▼▼ La Quinta Inn Phoenix (North) H ❄️
(602) 993-0800. **$39-$159.** 2510 W Greenway Rd. I-17, exit 211, just e. Ext corridors. **Pets:** Medium, other species. Service with restrictions, supervision.
🅰️🆂🅺 ✕ 🛗 💻 🏊 ✕

▼▼ La Quinta Inn Phoenix (Thomas Road) M ❄️
(602) 258-6271. **$49-$129.** 2725 N Black Canyon Hwy. I-17, exit 201 (Thomas Rd), just e, then just s; on east side of freeway. Ext corridors. **Pets:** Medium, other species. Service with restrictions, supervision.
🅰️🆂🅺 ✕ 🛗 💻 🏊

▼▼ MainStay Suites H
(602) 395-0900. **$59-$139.** 9455 N Black Canyon Hwy. I-17, exit 207 (Dunlap Ave), just e, then 0.4 mi n. Int corridors. **Pets:** Accepted.
🅰️🆂🅺 ✕ 🛗 💻 🏊

▼ Motel 6 Phoenix East #18 M
(602) 267-8555. **$55-$68.** 5315 E Van Buren St. Loop 202 E, exit 4 (52nd St/Van Buren St) just s, then just e. Ext corridors. **Pets:** Other species. Service with restrictions, supervision.
✕ 🛗 🏊

▼ Motel 6 Phoenix-North #344 M
(602) 993-2353. **$49-$65.** 2330 W Bell Rd. I-17, exit 212, just e. Ext corridors. **Pets:** Other species. Service with restrictions, supervision.
🏊

▼ Motel 6 Phoenix West #696 M
(602) 272-0220. **$48-$71.** 1530 N 52nd Dr. I-10, exit 139 (51st Ave), just n to McDowell Rd, just w, then just s. Ext corridors. **Pets:** Other species. Service with restrictions, supervision.
✕ 🛗 🏊

🅰🅰🅰▼ ▼🔷▼ Pointe Hilton Squaw Peak Resort H
(602) 997-2626. **$99-$399.** 7677 N 16th St. SR 51, exit Glendale Ave, 0.4 mi w, then 0.6 mi n. Ext corridors. **Pets:** Accepted.
🆂🅰🆅🅴 ✕ 🛗 💻 🍴 🏊 ✕

🅰🅰🅰▼ ▼🔷▼ ▼🔷▼ Pointe Hilton Tapatio Cliffs Resort H ❄️
(602) 866-7500. **$99-$399.** 11111 N 7th St. I-17, exit 207 (Dunlap Ave), 3 mi e, then 2 mi n. Ext corridors. **Pets:** $75 one-time fee/room. Service with restrictions, supervision.
🆂🅰🆅🅴 ✕ 🅼 🛗 💻 🍴 🏊 ✕

▼🔷▼ ▼🔷▼ Radisson Hotel Phoenix Airport North H
(602) 220-4400. **Call for rates.** 427 N 44th St. Loop 202, exit 2 (44th St), 0.5 mi s. Int corridors. **Pets:** Accepted.
✕ 🅼 🛗 💻 🍴 🏊

🅰🅰🅰▼ ▼🔷▼ ▼🔷▼ Ramada Plaza Hotel and Suites H
(602) 548-6000. **$59-$118.** 12027 N 28th Dr. I-17, exit 209 (Cactus Rd), just w, then just s. Int corridors. **Pets:** Medium. $35 daily fee/pet. Designated rooms, service with restrictions, crate.
🆂🅰🆅🅴 ✕ 🛗 💻 🍴 🏊

🅰🅰🅰▼ ▼🔷▼ ▼🔷▼ Red Roof Inn H
(602) 233-8004. **$67-$87.** 5215 W Willetta. I-10, exit 139 (51st Ave), just n, just e on McDowell Rd, then just s. Int corridors. **Pets:** Accepted.
🆂🅰🆅🅴 ✕ 🅼 🛗 🏊

🅰🅰🅰▼ ▼🔷▼ ▼🔷▼ Residence Inn by Marriott H
(602) 864-1900. **$159-$249.** 8242 N Black Canyon Hwy. I-17, exit 207 (Dunlap Ave), just w, then 0.8 mi s. Ext/int corridors. **Pets:** Accepted.
🆂🅰🆅🅴 ✕ 🅼 🛗 💻 🏊 ✕

🅰🅰🅰▼ ▼🔷▼ Residence Inn by Marriott Phoenix Airport H ❄️
(602) 273-9220. **$149-$279.** 801 N 44th St. Loop 202, exit 2 (44th St), just s. Int corridors. **Pets:** Medium, other species. $100 one-time fee/room. Service with restrictions.
🆂🅰🆅🅴 ✕ 🅼 🛗 💻 🏊 ✕

▼🔷▼ ▼🔷▼ Residence Inn by Marriott Phoenix North/Happy Valley H ❄️
(623) 580-8833. **$99-$199.** 2035 W Whispering Wind Dr. I-17, exit 128 (Happy Valley Rd), 0.4 mi e to 23rd Ave, just s, then just e. Int corridors. **Pets:** Large, other species. $100 one-time fee/room. Service with restrictions.
✕ 🛗 💻 🏊 ✕

▼🔷▼ ▼🔷▼ The Ritz-Carlton, Phoenix H
(602) 468-0700. **Call for rates.** 2401 E Camelback Rd. Southeast corner of Camelback Rd and 24th St. Int corridors. **Pets:** Accepted.
✕ 🛗 💻 🍴 🏊 ✕

🅰🅰🅰▼ ▼🔷▼ ▼🔷▼ Royal Palms Resort and Spa H
(602) 840-3610. **$169-$599, 7 day notice.** 5200 E Camelback Rd. Just e of 52nd St. Ext/int corridors. **Pets:** Accepted.
🆂🅰🆅🅴 ✕ 🛗 💻 🍴 🏊 ✕

🅰🅰🅰▼ ▼🔷▼ ▼🔷▼ Sheraton Crescent Hotel H ❄️
(602) 943-8200. **Call for rates.** 2620 W Dunlap Ave. I-17, exit 207 (Dunlap Ave), just e. Int corridors. **Pets:** Medium. Designated rooms, service with restrictions.
🆂🅰🆅🅴 ✕ 🅼 🛗 💻 🍴 🏊 ✕

🅰🅰🅰▼ ▼🔷▼ ▼🔷▼ Sleep Inn Phoenix North H
(602) 504-1200. **$69-$259.** 18235 N 27th Ave. I-17, exit 214A (Union Hills Dr), just w, then just s. Int corridors. **Pets:** Small. $100 deposit/room, $15 daily fee/pet. Designated rooms, service with restrictions, crate.
🆂🅰🆅🅴 ✕ 🅼 🛗 💻 🏊

🅰🅰🅰▼ ▼🔷▼ ▼🔷▼ Sleep Inn Sky Harbor Airport H
(480) 967-7100. **$59-$229.** 2621 S 47th Pl. I-10, exit 151 (University Dr), 2 mi n, then just w. Int corridors. **Pets:** Medium. $25 one-time fee/pet. Service with restrictions, supervision.
🆂🅰🆅🅴 ✕ 🛗 💻 🏊

▼▼ **Studio 6 Phoenix-Deer Valley #6030** �H
(602) 843-1151. **$71-$91.** 18405 N 27th Ave. I-17, exit 214A (Union Hills Dr), just w, then just s. Ext corridors. **Pets:** Other species. $10 daily fee/room. Service with restrictions, supervision.

✕ 🖪 🖵

▼▼ **Super 8-Phoenix** �H
(602) 415-0888. **Call for rates.** 1242 N 53rd Ave. I-10, exit 139 (51st Ave), just s to Latham Rd, then just w. Int corridors. **Pets:** Medium. $10 daily fee/pet. Designated rooms, service with restrictions, supervision.

✕ 🖪 🖵 ⇌

▼▼ **TownePlace Suites by Marriott** �H
(602) 943-9510. **$89-$159.** 9425 N Black Canyon Frwy. I-17, exit 207 (Dunlap Ave), just e, then 0.3 mi n. Int corridors. **Pets:** Medium, other species. $75 one-time fee/pet. Service with restrictions, supervision.

✕ 🖪 🖵 ⇌

SCOTTSDALE

🅐🅐🅐 ▼▼▼▼ **Camelback Inn, a JW Marriott Resort & Spa** �H 🐾
(480) 948-1700. **$209-$509, 3 day notice.** 5402 E Lincoln Dr. 0.5 mi e of Tatum Blvd; on north side of Lincoln Dr. Ext corridors. **Pets:** Large. $250 deposit/room. Service with restrictions.

SAVE ✕ 👶M 🖪 🖵 ¶¶ ⇌ ✕

🅐🅐🅐 ▼▼▼▼ **The Canyon Suites at the Phoenician** �H
(480) 423-2880. **Call for rates.** 6000 E Camelback Rd. 0.5 mi w of 64th St; in The Phoenician. Int corridors. **Pets:** Accepted.

SAVE ✕ 👶M ¶¶ ⇌ ✕

🅐🅐🅐 ▼▼▼▼ **Chaparral Suites Resort** �H
(480) 949-1414. **$129-$279.** 5001 N Scottsdale Rd. At Chaparral Rd. Ext corridors. **Pets:** Medium, dogs only. $25 one-time fee/pet. Service with restrictions, supervision.

SAVE ✕ 👶M 🖪 🖵 ¶¶ ⇌ ✕

▼▼ **Comfort Suites by Choice Hotels-Old Town** �H
(480) 946-1111. **Call for rates.** 3275 N Drinkwater Blvd. N of Thomas Rd; just e of Scottsdale Rd. Int corridors. **Pets:** Other species. $25 one-time fee/room. Service with restrictions, supervision.

✕ 👶M 🖪 🖵 ⇌

▼▼▼ **Country Inn & Suites By Carlson** �H
(480) 314-1200. **$99-$153, 3 day notice.** 10801 N 89th Pl. SR 101, exit 41, just e on Shea Blvd, then just n. Int corridors. **Pets:** Medium. $50 one-time fee/room. Designated rooms, service with restrictions, supervision.

ASK ✕ 🖪 🖵 ⇌

🅐🅐🅐 ▼▼▼▼ **DoubleTree Paradise Valley Resort** �H
(480) 947-5400. **$79-$339.** 5401 N Scottsdale Rd. Just n of Chaparral Rd; on east side of Scottsdale Rd. Ext corridors. **Pets:** Small, dogs only. $50 one-time fee/room. Service with restrictions, supervision.

SAVE ✕ 🖪 🖵 ¶¶ ⇌ ✕

▼▼▼ **Extended StayAmerica Scottsdale/Kierland** �H
(480) 607-3767. **$54-$184.** 15501 N Scottsdale Rd. SR 101, exit Frank Lloyd Wright Blvd, 2 mi w, 0.5 mi s on Scottsdale Rd, then just e on Tierra Buena Ln. Ext corridors. **Pets:** Other species. $25 daily fee/pet. Service with restrictions, crate.

ASK ✕ 🖪 🖵

▼▼▼ **Extended Stay Deluxe Phoenix-Scottsdale** �H
(480) 483-1333. **$69-$169.** 10660 N 69th St. Jct Scottsdale Rd, just w on Shea Blvd, then just n. Int corridors. **Pets:** Other species. $25 daily fee/pet. Service with restrictions, crate.

ASK ✕ 🖪 🖵 ⇌ ✕

🅐🅐🅐 ▼▼▼▼ **The Fairmont Scottsdale** �H 🐾
(480) 585-4848. **$129-$1179, 7 day notice.** 7575 E Princess Dr. SR 101, exit 34 (Scottsdale Rd), 0.8 mi s, then just e; 0.6 mi n of Bell Rd. Ext/int corridors. **Pets:** Other species. Service with restrictions.

SAVE ✕ 👶M 🖪 🖵 ¶¶ ⇌ ✕

🅐🅐🅐 ▼▼▼▼ **FireSky Resort & Spa, a Kimpton Hotel** �H
(480) 945-7666. **$115-$469, 3 day notice.** 4925 N Scottsdale Rd. Southeast corner of Scottsdale and Chaparral rds. Int corridors. **Pets:** Accepted.

SAVE ✕ 🖵 ¶¶ ⇌ ✕

🅐🅐🅐 ▼▼▼▼ **Four Seasons Resort Scottsdale at Troon North** �H 🐾
(480) 515-5700. **$205-$5500, 7 day notice.** 10600 E Crescent Moon Dr. SR 101, exit 36 (Pima Rd), 4.7 mi n, 2 mi e on Happy Valley Rd, then 1.5 mi n on Alma School Rd. Ext corridors. **Pets:** Small. Service with restrictions, supervision.

SAVE ✕ 👶M 🖪 🖵 ¶¶ ⇌ ✕

🅐🅐🅐 ▼▼▼▼ **Hilton Scottsdale Resort & Villas** �H 🐾
(480) 948-7750. **$89-$369.** 6333 N Scottsdale Rd. SR 101, exit 45, 2.1 mi w on McDonald Dr, then 0.3 mi n. Int corridors. **Pets:** Large. $75 one-time fee/room.

SAVE ✕ 👶M 🖪 🖵 ¶¶ ⇌ ✕

▼▼ **Homestead Studio Suites Hotel-Phoenix-Scottsdale** �H
(480) 994-0297. **$64-$139.** 3560 N Marshall Way. Just w of Scottsdale Rd on Goldwater, just s. Ext corridors. **Pets:** Other species. $25 daily fee/pet. Service with restrictions, crate.

ASK ✕ 👶M 🖪 🖵 ⇌

🅐🅐🅐 ▼▼▼ **Hotel Indigo Scottsdale** �H
(480) 941-9400. **$79-$329, 3 day notice.** 4415 N Civic Center Plaza. Scottsdale Rd, just e on Camelback Rd, just s on 75th St. Ext/int corridors. **Pets:** Accepted.

SAVE ✕ 👶M 🖪 🖵 ¶¶ ⇌

🅐🅐🅐 ▼▼▼▼ **Hotel Valley Ho** �H 🐾
(480) 248-2000. **$149-$429.** 6850 E Main St. 0.4 mi w of Scottsdale Rd, just s of Indian School Rd; on north side of Main St. Ext/int corridors. **Pets:** Other species. Service with restrictions, supervision.

SAVE ✕ 🖵 ¶¶ ⇌ ✕

🅐🅐🅐 ▼▼▼ **Hyatt Summerfield Suites-Scottsdale** �H
(480) 946-7700. **$79-$449.** 4245 N Drinkwater Blvd. 0.3 mi e of Scottsdale Rd. Ext corridors. **Pets:** Accepted.

SAVE ✕ 🖪 🖵 ⇌ ✕

🅐🅐🅐 ▼▼ **The Inn at Pima, a Condominium Suite Hotel** 🅒🅞
(480) 948-3800. **$59-$338.** 7330 N Pima Rd. 0.4 mi n of Indian Bend Rd; on west side of Pima Rd. Ext/int corridors. **Pets:** $10 daily fee/room. Designated rooms, service with restrictions, supervision.

SAVE ✕ 🖪 🖵 ⇌ ✕

▼▼▼ **La Quinta Inn & Suites Phoenix (Scottsdale)** �H 🐾
(480) 614-5300. **$69-$199.** 8888 E Shea Blvd. SR 101, exit Shea Blvd, northeast corner. Int corridors. **Pets:** Medium, other species. Service with restrictions, supervision.

ASK ✕ 👶M 🖪 🖵 ⇌ ✕

🅐🅐🅐 ▼▼▼ **Millennium Resort Scottsdale McCormick Ranch** �H
(480) 948-5050. **$59-$339, 3 day notice.** 7401 N Scottsdale Rd. 0.8 mi n of Indian Bend Rd. Int corridors. **Pets:** Small, dogs only. $200 deposit/room. Service with restrictions.

SAVE ✕ 🖪 🖵 ¶¶ ⇌ ✕

▼ **Motel 6 Scottsdale #29** 🅜
(480) 946-2280. **$55-$91.** 6848 E Camelback Rd. Just w of Scottsdale Rd. Ext corridors. **Pets:** Other species. Service with restrictions, supervision.

✕ ¶¶ ⇌

The Phoenician H ❀
(480) 941-8200. **$219-$850, 7 day notice.** 6000 E Camelback Rd. 0.5 mi w of 64th St. Ext/int corridors. **Pets:** Medium, dogs only. Designated rooms.
SAVE ☒ 🗗 📖 ⊟ 🍴 ➿ 🌊

Radisson Fort McDowell Resort & Casino H
(480) 789-5300. **$119-$309.** 10438 N Fort McDowell Rd. Jct Shea Blvd, 1.6 mi ne on SR 87. Int corridors. **Pets:** Dogs only. $10 daily fee/room. Service with restrictions, crate.
SAVE ☒ ⅃M 🗗 📖 ⊟ 🍴 ➿ 🌊

Residence Inn by Marriott, Scottsdale/ Paradise Valley H
(480) 948-8666. **$119-$289.** 6040 N Scottsdale Rd. Just n of McDonald Dr. Ext/int corridors. **Pets:** Accepted.
SAVE ☒ ⅃M 🗗 📖 ➿ 🌊

Residence Inn Scottsdale North H ❀
(480) 563-4120. **$129-$289.** 17011 N Scottsdale Rd. SR 101, exit 34 (Scottsdale Rd), 1.1 mi s, then just e on 17050 N. Int corridors. **Pets:** Medium. $100 one-time fee/room. Service with restrictions, crate.
☒ 🗗 📖 ➿ 🌊

Scottsdale Cottonwoods Resort H
(480) 991-1414. **$139-$339.** 6160 N Scottsdale Rd. Just n of McDonald Dr. Ext corridors. **Pets:** Medium. $75 one-time fee/room. Service with restrictions, supervision.
SAVE ☒ ⅃M 🗗 📖 🍴 ➿ 🌊

Scottsdale Marriott at McDowell Mountains H
(480) 502-3836. **$149-$329.** 16770 N Perimeter Dr. SR 101, exit 36 (Princess Dr), just w to N Perimeter Dr, then 0.6 mi s. **Pets:** Accepted.
SAVE ☒ ⅃M 🗗 📖 ⊟ 🍴 ➿ 🌊

Scottsdale Thunderbird Suites H
(480) 951-4000. **$79-$249.** 7515 E Butherus Dr. 0.8 mi n of Thunderbird Rd; 0.5 mi e of Scottsdale Rd. Ext corridors. **Pets:** Other species. $10 daily fee/pet. Service with restrictions.
SAVE ☒ 🗗 📖 🍴 ➿

Sleep Inn H ❀
(480) 998-9211. **$69-$209.** 16630 N Scottsdale Rd. Just s of Bell Rd. Int corridors. **Pets:** Large, other species. $15 daily fee/pet. Crate.
SAVE ☒ ⅃M 🗗 📖 ➿

TownePlace Suites Scottsdale by Marriott H
(480) 551-1100. **$109-$209.** 10740 N 90th St. SR 101, exit Shea Blvd, just e to 90th St, then just n. Int corridors. **Pets:** Accepted.
☒ ⅃M 🗗 📖 ➿

The Westin Kierland Resort & Spa H ❀
(480) 624-1000. **$159-$699, 7 day notice.** 6902 E Greenway Pkwy. 0.5 mi w of Scottsdale Rd. Int corridors. **Pets:** Dogs only. Service with restrictions, supervision.
SAVE ☒ 📖 🍴 ➿ 🌊

SURPRISE

Days Inn & Suites H
(623) 933-4000. **$59-$159.** 12477 W Bell Rd. US 60 (Grand Ave), 1.1 mi e, then just s on Greasewood St. Int corridors. **Pets:** Medium. $25 one-time fee/room. Service with restrictions, supervision.
ASK ☒ 🗗 📖 ➿

Hampton Inn & Suites Surprise H ❀
(623) 537-9122. **$69-$499.** 14783 W Grand Ave. Jct Bell Rd, 2 mi nw. Int corridors. **Pets:** Other species. Service with restrictions, supervision.
SAVE ☒ ⅃M 🗗 📖 ➿

Windmill Suites in Surprise H ❀
(623) 583-0133. **$79-$179.** 12545 W Bell Rd. US 60 (Grand Ave), 1 mi e. Int corridors. **Pets:** Other species. Designated rooms, service with restrictions, supervision.
SAVE ☒ 🗗 📖 ➿ 🌊

TEMPE

Best Western Inn of Tempe H
(480) 784-2233. **$79-$175.** 670 N Scottsdale Rd. SR 202 Loop (Red Mountain Frwy), exit 7 (Rural Rd S), just s. Int corridors. **Pets:** Small. $50 deposit/pet. Designated rooms, service with restrictions.
SAVE ☒ 🗗 📖 ➿

Best Western Tempe by the Mall H
(480) 820-7500. **$69-$139, 3 day notice.** 5300 S Priest Dr. I-10, exit 155 (Baseline Rd), 0.4 mi e, then just s. Int corridors. **Pets:** Medium, other species. $25 one-time fee/pet. Service with restrictions, supervision.
SAVE ☒ 🗗 📖 ➿

Comfort Inn & Suites Tempe/ASU H
(480) 966-7202. **$69-$149, 7 day notice.** 1031 E Apache Blvd. SR 202 Loop (Red Mountain Frwy), exit 7 (Rural Rd S), 1.5 mi s, then just e. Int corridors. **Pets:** Medium. $50 deposit/room.
SAVE ☒ 🗗 📖 ➿ 🌊

Country Inn & Suites By Carlson H
(480) 345-8585. **Call for rates.** 1660 W Elliot Rd. I-10, exit 157, just e. Ext corridors. **Pets:** Accepted.
☒ 🗗 📖 ➿

Country Inn & Suites By Carlson H ❀
(480) 858-9898. **$59-$159.** 808 N Scottsdale Rd. SR 202 Loop (Red Mountain Frwy), exit 7 (Rural Rd S), just n. Int corridors. **Pets:** Medium, other species. $50 one-time fee/room.
ASK ☒ ⅃M 🗗 📖 ➿

Hampton Inn & Suites H
(480) 675-9799. **$139-$249.** 1429 N Scottsdale Rd. SR 202 Loop (Red Mountain Frwy), exit 7 (Rural Rd S), 0.5 mi n. Ext corridors. **Pets:** Accepted.
☒ 🗗 📖 ➿ 🌊

Homestead Studio Suites Hotel-Phoenix/Airport/Tempe H
(480) 557-8880. **$74-$119.** 2165 W 15th St. I-10, exit 153 (Broadway Rd), 0.3 mi ne, just nw on S 52nd St, then just w. Int corridors. **Pets:** Other species. $25 daily fee/pet. Service with restrictions, crate.
ASK ☒ 🗗 📖 ➿

Hotel Tempe/Phoenix Airport InnSuites Hotels & Suites H
(480) 897-7900. **$79-$219.** 1651 W Baseline Rd. I-10, exit 155 (Baseline Rd), just e. Ext corridors. **Pets:** Accepted.
SAVE ☒ 🗗 📖 🍴 ➿ 🌊

La Quinta Inn Phoenix (Sky Harbor South) H ❀
(480) 967-4465. **$59-$159.** 911 S 48th St. I-10, exit 153 (Broadway Rd) eastbound; exit 153A (University Dr) westbound, 0.8 mi n; on south side of University Dr; east side of SR 143 (Hohokam Expwy). Ext/int corridors. **Pets:** Medium, other species. Service with restrictions, supervision.
ASK ☒ 🗗 📖 ➿

Quality Inn-Phoenix Airport-Tempe H
(480) 967-3000. **$49-$155.** 1550 S 52nd St. I-10, exit 153B (Broadway Rd) westbound; exit 153A (48th St) eastbound, 0.3 mi ne. Ext corridors. **Pets:** Accepted.
SAVE ☒ 🗗 📖 ➿

Ramada Inn–Arizona Mills Mall H
(480) 413-1188. **$65-$200.** 1701 W Baseline Rd. I-10, exit 155 (Baseline Rd), just e. Ext corridors. **Pets:** Accepted.
ASK ☒ 🗗 📖 ➿

(AAA) ▼▼▼ Ramada Limited Tempe-University M
(480) 736-1700. **$79-$189.** 1915 E Apache Blvd. US 60 (Superstition Frwy), exit 175, 1.9 mi n on McClintock Dr, then 0.3 mi e. Ext corridors. **Pets:** Medium, other species. $50 deposit/room, $15 daily fee/room. Service with restrictions, supervision.
[SAVE] [X] [B] [▦] [≈]

(AAA) ▼▼▼ Red Roof Inn Phoenix Airport H
(480) 449-3205. **$59-$90.** 2135 W 15th St. I-10, exit 153 (Broadway Rd), just nw on S 52nd St, then just w. Int corridors. **Pets:** Accepted.
[SAVE] [X] [B] [≈]

▼▼▼ Residence Inn by Marriott H
(480) 756-2122. **$149-$259.** 5075 S Priest Dr. I-10, exit 155 (Baseline Rd), 0.4 mi e, then just n. Ext/int corridors. **Pets:** $100 one-time fee/room. Service with restrictions.
[X] [B] [▦] [≈] [X]

(AAA) ▼▼▼ Sheraton Phoenix Airport Hotel-Tempe H ❖
(480) 967-6600. **$89-$419.** 1600 S 52nd St. I-10, exit 153B (Broadway Rd) westbound; exit 153A (48th St) eastbound, 0.3 mi ne. Int corridors. **Pets:** Medium, dogs only. $75 one-time fee/room. Service with restrictions, supervision.
[SAVE] [X] [B] [▦] [⑪] [≈] [X]

▼▼ Studio 6 Extended Stay #6031 H
(602) 414-4470. **$77-$91.** 4909 S Wendler Dr. I-10, exit 155 (Baseline Rd), just w, then 0.4 mi n. Ext corridors. **Pets:** Other species. $10 daily fee/room. Service with restrictions, supervision.
[X] [B] [▦] [≈]

(AAA) ▼▼▼ Tempe Mission Palms Hotel H
(480) 894-1400. **$119-$319, 3 day notice.** 60 E 5th St. Jct University Dr, just n on Mill Ave, then just e; downtown. Int corridors. **Pets:** Small. $100 deposit/room, $25 one-time fee/pet. Service with restrictions, supervision.
[SAVE] [X] [B] [▦] [⑪] [≈] [X]

TOLLESON

(AAA) ▼▼▼ Premier Inns H
(623) 533-4660. **$52-$70.** 8399 W Lynwood St. I-10, exit 135 (83rd Ave), just n, then just w. Ext corridors. **Pets:** Accepted.
[SAVE] [X] [B] [≈]

YOUNGTOWN

(AAA) ▼▼▼ Best Western Inn & Suites of Sun City H ❖
(623) 933-8211. **$70-$170.** 11201 Grand Ave. On US 60, just se of 113th Ave. Ext/int corridors. **Pets:** Small, other species. Designated rooms, service with restrictions, supervision.
[SAVE] [X] [B] [▦] [≈]

END METROPOLITAN AREA

PINETOP-LAKESIDE

(AAA) ▼▼▼ Best Western Inn of Pinetop M
(928) 367-6667. **$89-$119.** 404 E White Mountain Blvd. On SR 260. Ext corridors. **Pets:** Other species. $10 daily fee/pet. Service with restrictions, supervision.
[SAVE] [X] [B] [▦]

(AAA) ▼▼▼ Holiday Inn Express H
(928) 367-6077. **$59-$169, 3 day notice.** 431 E White Mountain Blvd. On SR 260. Int corridors. **Pets:** $25 daily fee/pet. Service with restrictions, supervision.
[SAVE] [X] [B] [▦] [≈] [X]

▼▼▼ Lazy Oaks Resort CA
(928) 368-6203. **$89-$239, 30 day notice.** 1075 Larson Rd. Jct SR 260, 0.8 mi s on Rainbow Lake Dr, then 0.6 mi w. Ext corridors. **Pets:** Accepted.
[B] [▦] [X] [K] [Z]

(AAA) ▼▼ Mountain Hacienda Lodge M
(928) 367-4146. **$49-$64.** 1023 E White Mountain Blvd. On SR 260. Ext corridors. **Pets:** Medium, dogs only. $10 daily fee/pet. Designated rooms, service with restrictions, supervision.
[SAVE] [X] [B] [▦]

▼▼▼ Northwoods Resort CA
(928) 367-2966. **Call for rates.** 165 E White Mountain Blvd. On SR 260. Ext corridors. **Pets:** Other species. $12 daily fee/pet. Service with restrictions, supervision.
[X] [B] [▦] [X] [K] [Z]

▼▼ TimberLodge Inn M ❖
(928) 367-4463. **$45-$99.** 1078 E White Mountain Blvd. On SR 260. Ext corridors. **Pets:** Other species. $10 daily fee/pet. Service with restrictions, crate.
[ASK] [X] [B] [▦] [K]

(AAA) ▼▼▼ Woodland Inn & Suites M
(928) 367-3636. **$74-$169, 3 day notice.** 458 E White Mountain Blvd. On SR 260. Ext corridors. **Pets:** Medium, other species. $10 daily fee/pet. Service with restrictions, supervision.
[SAVE] [X] [B] [▦]

PRESCOTT

▼▼ Americas Best Value Inn M ❖
(928) 776-1282. **$60-$120.** 1105 E Sheldon St. 0.4 mi e of jct SR 89. Int corridors. **Pets:** Dogs only. $15 one-time fee/room. Service with restrictions, supervision.
[ASK] [X] [B] [▦] [≈]

(AAA) ▼▼▼ Best Western Prescottonian Motel M
(928) 445-3096. **$79-$149.** 1317 E Gurley St. On SR 89, just s of jct SR 69. Ext corridors. **Pets:** Accepted.
[SAVE] [X] [B] [▦] [⑪] [≈]

(AAA) ▼▼▼ Comfort Inn of Prescott M
(928) 778-5770. **$65-$250.** 1290 White Spar Rd. On SR 89, 1.5 mi s of town center. Ext corridors. **Pets:** Medium, dogs only. $10 daily fee/pet. Service with restrictions, supervision.
[SAVE] [X] [B] [▦]

▼▼ Motel 6 #0166 M
(928) 776-0160. **$43-$55.** 1111 E Sheldon St. 0.4 mi e of jct SR 89; center. Ext corridors. **Pets:** Other species. Service with restrictions, supervision.
[X] [B] [≈]

▼▼ Prescott Cabin Rentals H
(928) 778-9573. **$89-$428, 31 day notice.** 5555 Onyx Dr. Jct SR 89, 5 mi e on SR 69, 0.4 mi s on dirt/gravel road. Ext corridors. **Pets:** Accepted.
[X] [B] [▦] [X]

Quality Inn & Suites and Conference Center H ❀
(928) 777-0770. **$109-$229.** 4499 Hwy 69. On SR 69, 3.6 mi e of jct SR 89. Int corridors. **Pets:** Medium, other species. $40 one-time fee/room. Service with restrictions, supervision.
[SAVE] [X] [B] [▣] [▥] [≈] [X]

Residence Inn by Marriott H
(928) 775-2232. **$159-$189.** 3599 Lee Cir. Jct SR 69, just n on Lee Blvd, then just e. Int corridors. **Pets:** Accepted.
[SAVE] [X] [&M] [B] [▣] [≈]

PRESCOTT VALLEY

Americas Best Value Inn H
(928) 772-2200. **$65-$155.** 8383 E Hwy 69. On SR 69, just w of N Navajo Dr. Int corridors. **Pets:** $10 one-time fee/pet. Designated rooms, service with restrictions, supervision.
[SAVE] [X] [B] [▣] [≈]

Days Inn/Prescott Valley H
(928) 772-8600. **$79-$129.** 7875 E Hwy 69. On SR 69; corner of Windsong Rd. Ext corridors. **Pets:** Other species. $50 deposit/room. Service with restrictions.
[SAVE] [X] [B] [▣] [≈]

QUARTZSITE

Super 8 Motel-Quartzsite M
(928) 927-8080. **$135-$165.** 2050 W Dome Rock Rd. I-10, exit 17, just s to Frontage Rd, then 0.6 mi w. Int corridors. **Pets:** Other species. $10 daily fee/pet. No service.
[ASK] [X] [B] [▣]

RIO RICO

Esplendor Resort at Rio Rico H ❀
(520) 281-1901. **$134-$249.** 1069 Camino Caralampi. I-19, exit 17 (Rio Rico Dr), just w to Camino Caralampi, then just s. Ext corridors. **Pets:** Small. $25 one-time fee/room. Service with restrictions, supervision.
[SAVE] [X] [&M] [B] [▣] [Ⅱ] [≈] [X]

SAFFORD

Best Western Desert Inn M
(928) 428-0521. **$90-$100.** 1391 W Thatcher Blvd. US 191, 1 mi w on US 70. Ext corridors. **Pets:** Accepted.
[SAVE] [X] [B] [▣] [≈]

Days Inn M
(928) 428-5000. **Call for rates.** 520 E Hwy 70. US 191, 0.5 mi e. Ext corridors. **Pets:** Small. $20 daily fee/pet. Service with restrictions, supervision.
[X] [&M] [B] [▣] [≈]

ST. JOHNS

Days Inn M
(928) 337-4422. **Call for rates.** 125 E Commercial St. On US 191/SR 61; center. Ext corridors. **Pets:** Other species. $10 daily fee/pet. Designated rooms, service with restrictions, supervision.
[X] [B] [▣]

SEDONA

Amara Hotel, Restaurant & Spa H
(928) 282-4828. **$155-$315, 3 day notice.** 310 N Hwy 89A. Jct SR 179, 0.4 mi ne; center. Int corridors. **Pets:** Dogs only. $75 one-time fee/pet. Service with restrictions, supervision.
[SAVE] [X] [B] [▣] [Ⅱ] [≈] [X]

Best Western Inn of Sedona H ❀
(928) 282-3072. **$149-$219, 3 day notice.** 1200 W Hwy 89A. Jct SR 179, 1.2 mi w. Ext corridors. **Pets:** Medium, other species. $20 daily fee/room. Designated rooms, service with restrictions, crate.
[SAVE] [X] [B] [▣] [≈]

Desert Quail Inn H
(928) 284-1433. **$69-$189.** 6626 Hwy 179. Jct Bell Rock Blvd, 0.9 mi s. Ext corridors. **Pets:** Small, dogs only. $15 daily fee/room. Designated rooms, service with restrictions, crate.
[SAVE] [X] [B] [▣] [≈]

El Portal Sedona Luxury Inn H ❀
(928) 203-9405. **$199-$550.** 95 Portal Ln. Jct SR 89A, just s on SR 179, then just w. Ext/int corridors. **Pets:** Other species. Service with restrictions, supervision.
[SAVE] [X] [B]

Hilton Sedona Resort & Spa H ❀
(928) 284-4040. **$139-$369.** 90 Ridge Trail Dr. Jct SR 89A, 7.3 mi s on SR 179. Int corridors. **Pets:** Medium, other species. $75 one-time fee/room. Designated rooms, service with restrictions.
[SAVE] [X] [B] [▣] [Ⅱ] [≈] [X]

King's Ransom Sedona Hotel H ❀
(928) 282-7151. **$125-$225.** 771 Hwy 179. 0.7 mi s of jct SR 89A. Ext/int corridors. **Pets:** Large, other species. $15 daily fee/room. Designated rooms, service with restrictions, supervision.
[SAVE] [X] [B] [▣] [Ⅱ] [≈] [X]

La Quinta Inn Sedona H ❀
(928) 284-0711. **$69-$159.** 6176 Hwy 179. Jct Bell Rock Blvd, just s. Int corridors. **Pets:** Medium, other species. Service with restrictions, supervision.
[SAVE] [X] [&M] [B] [▣] [≈]

L'Auberge de Sedona Inn and Spa H ❀
(928) 282-1661. **$195-$350, 7 day notice.** 301 L'Auberge Ln. Jct SR 179, just n on SR 89A, then ne; down the hill. Ext/int corridors. **Pets:** Dogs only. $35 daily fee/pet. Designated rooms, service with restrictions, supervision.
[SAVE] [X] [B] [▣] [Ⅱ] [X]

The Lodge at Sedona BB ❀
(928) 204-1942. **$189-$339, 14 day notice.** 125 Kallof Pl. Jct SR 179, 1.8 mi w on SR 89A, then just s. Ext/int corridors. **Pets:** Dogs only. $35 daily fee/room. Designated rooms, service with restrictions, supervision.
[ASK] [X] [X] [≈]

Los Abrigados Resort & Spa CO ❀
(928) 282-1777. **$110-$425, 3 day notice.** 160 Portal Ln. Jct SR 89A, just s on SR 179, just w. Ext corridors. **Pets:** Medium, other species. $20 daily fee/pet. Designated rooms.
[ASK] [X] [B] [▣] [Ⅱ] [≈] [X]

Matterhorn Inn M ❀
(928) 282-7176. **$89-$179.** 230 Apple Ave. Jct SR 179, just ne on SR 89A; uptown. Ext corridors. **Pets:** Large. $10 daily fee/pet. Designated rooms, service with restrictions, crate.
[SAVE] [X] [B] [▣] [≈]

Quail Ridge Resort H
(928) 284-9327. **$135-$329, 10 day notice.** 120 Canyon Circle Dr. Jct SR 179, just w on Bell Rock Blvd, then just nw. Ext corridors. **Pets:** Accepted.
[SAVE] [X] [B] [▣] [≈]

Sedona Real Inn & Suites H ❀
(928) 282-1414. **$95-$340.** 95 Arroyo Pinon Dr. Jct SR 179, 3.4 mi w on SR 89A, just sw. Ext corridors. **Pets:** Medium, other species. $30 one-time fee/pet. Designated rooms, service with restrictions, crate.
[SAVE] [X] [B] [▣] [≈]

WWWW Sedona Rouge Hotel & Spa H ❀
(928) 203-4111. **$209-$279, 3 day notice.** 2250 W Hwy 89A. Jct SR 179, 2 mi w. Ext/int corridors. **Pets:** Medium, dogs only. $100 deposit/room, $50 one-time fee/pet. Designated rooms, service with restrictions, crate.
SAVE ✕ 🔋 💻 🍴 ⊇ ⊠

WWWW Sedona Super 8 H
(928) 282-1533. **$80-$130.** 2545 W Hwy 89A. Jct SR 179, 2.4 mi w. Int corridors. **Pets:** Large. $25 one-time fee/pet. Designated rooms, service with restrictions, supervision.
ASK ✕ 🔋 💻 ⊇

WWWW Sky Ranch Lodge M
(928) 282-6400. **$75-$189.** Airport Rd. Jct SR 179, 1 mi w on SR 89A, then 1 mi s. Ext corridors. **Pets:** Large, other species. $10 daily fee/pet. Service with restrictions, supervision.
✕ 🔋 💻 ⊇

WWWW The Views Inn Sedona H
(928) 284-2487. **$89-$129.** 65 E Cortez Dr. Jct Bell Rock Blvd, 0.9 mi s on SR 179, just e. Ext corridors. **Pets:** Other species. $15 daily fee/pet. Service with restrictions, supervision.
ASK ✕ 🔋 💻 ⊇

WWW Village Lodge M
(928) 284-3626. **$49-$59.** 78 Bell Rock Blvd. Jct SR 179, just w. Ext/int corridors. **Pets:** Small, dogs only. $10 daily fee/pet. Designated rooms, service with restrictions, supervision.
SAVE ✕ 🔋 💻

SELIGMAN

WWW Canyon Lodge M
(928) 422-3255. **$60.** 114 E Chino Ave. I-40, exit 121, 1 mi n, then 0.7 mi e on Route 66. Ext corridors. **Pets:** Medium, other species. $25 daily fee/pet. Service with restrictions, supervision.
SAVE ✕ 🔋 💻

WWW Deluxe Inn Motel M
(928) 422-3244. **$42-$52.** 22295 W Old Hwy 66. I-40, exit 121 eastbound, 1 mi n, then 0.7 mi e on Route 66; exit 123 westbound, just ne on I-40 business loop, then 2.4 mi w. Ext corridors. **Pets:** Other species. $10 one-time fee/pet. Designated rooms, service with restrictions, supervision.
SAVE ✕ 🔋

SHOW LOW

WWW Best Western Paint Pony Lodge M
(928) 537-5773. **$80-$220.** 581 W Deuce of Clubs Ave. On US 60 and SR 260. Ext corridors. **Pets:** Accepted.
SAVE ✕ 🔋 💻

WW Days Inn M
(928) 537-4356. **$69-$85.** 480 W Deuce of Clubs Ave. On US 60 and SR 260. Ext/int corridors. **Pets:** Medium. $10 one-time fee/room. Service with restrictions, supervision.
SAVE ✕ 🔋 💻 🍴 ⊇

WW Kiva Motel M
(928) 537-4542. **$58-$68, 3 day notice.** 261 E Deuce of Clubs Ave. On US 60 and SR 260; center. Ext corridors. **Pets:** Small, dogs only. $5 daily fee/pet. Service with restrictions, supervision.
SAVE ✕ 🔋 💻

WWW Sleep Inn H
(928) 532-7323. **$72-$115.** 1751 W Deuce of Clubs Ave. Jct SR 260 and US 60, just w. Int corridors. **Pets:** Other species. $15 daily fee/pet. Supervision.
SAVE ✕ 🔋 💻 ⊇

SIERRA VISTA

WW Americas Best Value Inn M
(520) 459-5380. **$45-$72.** 100 Fab Ave. Jct Business SR 90 and Fry Blvd, then just e of main gate to Fort Huachuca. Ext corridors. **Pets:** Accepted.
SAVE ✕ 🔋 💻 ⊇

WWW Best Western Mission Inn H
(520) 458-8500. **$86.** 3460 E Fry Blvd. Just w of jct SR 90 and 92. Ext corridors. **Pets:** Other species. $10 daily fee/pet. Service with restrictions, supervision.
SAVE ✕ 🔋 🔋 💻 ⊇

WWW Candlewood Suites H
(520) 439-8200. **$119-$152, 14 day notice.** 1904 S Hwy 92. Jct SR 90 and 92, 1.4 mi s. Int corridors. **Pets:** Other species. $75 one-time fee/room. Service with restrictions, crate.
ASK ✕ 🔋

WWWW Holiday Inn Express H ❀
(520) 439-8800. **$108-$119.** 1902 S Hwy 92. Jct SR 90 and 92, 1.4 mi s. Int corridors. **Pets:** Large, other species. Service with restrictions.
ASK ✕ 🔋 💻 ⊇

WWW Quality Inn H
(520) 458-7900. **$84, 5 day notice.** 1631 S Hwy 92. On SR 92, 1 mi s of jct SR 90. Int corridors. **Pets:** Medium. $10 daily fee/pet. Designated rooms, service with restrictions, supervision.
SAVE ✕ 🔋 💻 ⊇

WWW TownePlace Suites by Marriott H
(520) 515-9900. **$107-$131.** 3399 Rodeo Dr. Jct SR 90, 1.5 mi s on SR 92, just w on Avenida Cochise, just s on Oakmont, then just e. Int corridors. **Pets:** Accepted.
✕ 🔋 💻 ⊇

SNOWFLAKE

WW Comfort Inn H
(928) 536-3888. **Call for rates.** 2055 S Main St. SR 77, just s of town. Int corridors. **Pets:** Accepted.
✕ 🔋 💻 ⊇

TAYLOR

WWW Silver Creek Inn-Rodeway Inn M
(928) 536-2600. **$63-$80.** 825 N Main St. On SR 77. Ext corridors. **Pets:** $50 deposit/room, $15 daily fee/room. Service with restrictions, supervision.
SAVE ✕ 🔋 💻

TOMBSTONE

WWW Best Western Lookout Lodge H ❀
(520) 457-2223. **$95-$115.** 781 Hwy 80 W. On SR 80, 1 mi n. Ext corridors. **Pets:** Other species. $20 daily fee/pet. Designated rooms, service with restrictions, crate.
SAVE ✕ 💻 🍴 ⊇

TUBAC

WWWWW Tubac Golf Resort and Spa RA ❀
(520) 398-2211. **$159-$289, 7 day notice.** 1 Otero Rd. I-19, exit 40 (Chavez Siding Rd), on east side, then 2 mi s. Ext corridors. **Pets:** $25 daily fee/pet. Service with restrictions, supervision.
SAVE ✕ 🔋 💻 🍴 ⊇ ⊠

TUBA CITY

WWW Quality Inn Navajo Nation H
(928) 283-4545. **$75-$123.** 10 N Main St. 1 mi n of US 160. Int corridors. **Pets:** Small. $10 daily fee/pet. Service with restrictions, supervision.
SAVE ✕ 🔋 💻 🍴

TUCSON METROPOLITAN AREA

CATALINA

⟨AAA⟩ ▼▼▼ Best Western Catalina Inn **M**
(520) 818-9500. **$96-$130, 3 day notice.** 15691 N Oracle Rd. 4.6 mi n of Tangerine Rd. Ext/int corridors. **Pets:** Small, dogs only. $100 deposit/room, $10 daily fee/pet. Designated rooms, service with restrictions.
(SAVE) ⊠ 📶 💻 ➴

GREEN VALLEY

⟨AAA⟩ ▼▼▼▼ Comfort Inn **H**
(520) 399-3736. **Call for rates.** 90 W Esperanza Blvd. I-19, exit 65, just w. Int corridors. **Pets:** Small, dogs only. $10 daily fee/pet. Designated rooms, service with restrictions, supervision.
(SAVE) ⊠ 📶 💻 ➴

⟨AAA⟩ ▼▼▼ Holiday Inn Express **H**
(520) 625-0900. **$79-$140.** 19200 S I-19 Frontage Rd. I-19, exit 69 (Duval Mine Rd), west side of interstate, then just s. Int corridors. **Pets:** Accepted.
(SAVE) ⊠ 📶 💻

⟨AAA⟩ ▼▼▼ Quality Inn Green Valley **H**
(520) 625-2250. **$65-$159.** 111 S La Canada Dr. I-19, exit 65, just w, then just s. Int corridors. **Pets:** Medium. $10 daily fee/room. Designated rooms, service with restrictions.
(SAVE) ⊠ 📶 💻 🍴 ➴

MARANA

▼▼▼▼ La Quinta Inn & Suites **H** ❀
(520) 572-4235. **$49-$199.** 6020 W Hospitality Rd. I-10, exit 246 (Cortaro Rd), just w, then just n. Int corridors. **Pets:** Medium, other species. Service with restrictions, supervision.
(ASK) ⊠ 🅲ᴹ 📶 💻 ➴

⟨AAA⟩ ▼▼ Red Roof Inn Tucson North **H**
(520) 744-8199. **$62-$118.** 4940 W Ina Rd. I-10, exit 248 (Ina Rd), just w. Int corridors. **Pets:** Accepted.
(SAVE) ⊠ 📶 ➴

▼▼ Super 8 **H**
(520) 572-0300. **Call for rates.** 8351 N Cracker Barrel Rd. I-10, exit 246 (Cortaro Rd), just w. Int corridors. **Pets:** Accepted.
⊠ 📶 💻 ➴

ORO VALLEY

▼▼▼ ▼▼▼ Hilton Tucson El Conquistador Golf & Tennis Resort **H** ❀
(520) 544-5000. **$99-$289.** 10000 N Oracle Rd. I-10, exit 248 (Ina Rd), 4.4 mi n. Ext/int corridors. **Pets:** Large. $75 one-time fee/pet. Designated rooms, service with restrictions, crate.
⊠ 🅰ᴹ 📶 💻 🍴 ➴ ⊠

TUCSON

⟨AAA⟩ ▼▼▼ Americas Best Value Inn-Tucson **M**
(520) 884-5800. **$44-$160.** 810 E Benson Hwy. I-10, exit 262, just s. Ext corridors. **Pets:** Other species. $25 deposit/room. Service with restrictions, crate.
(SAVE) ⊠ 📶 ➴

⟨AAA⟩ ▼▼▼▼ Best Western InnSuites Tucson Foothills Hotel & Suites **H**
(520) 297-8111. **$79-$149.** 6201 N Oracle Rd. I-10, exit 250 (Orange Grove Rd), 4 mi e, then just s. Ext corridors. **Pets:** Accepted.
(SAVE) ⊠ 📶 💻 ➴ ⊠

⟨AAA⟩ ▼▼▼ Comfort Suites **H**
(520) 295-4400. **$79-$189.** 6935 S Tucson Blvd. Just n of Tucson International Airport. Int corridors. **Pets:** Medium. $25 one-time fee/room. Service with restrictions, crate.
(SAVE) ⊠ 📶 💻 ➴

⟨AAA⟩ ▼▼▼ Comfort Suites at Sabino Canyon **H**
(520) 298-2300. **$79-$159.** 7007 E Tanque Verde Rd. Jct Grand Rd, 0.4 mi ne. Ext corridors. **Pets:** $25 daily fee/pet. Service with restrictions, supervision.
(SAVE) ⊠ 📶 💻 ➴

⟨AAA⟩ ▼▼▼ Comfort Suites at Tucson Mall **H** ❀
(520) 888-6676. **$99-$200.** 515 W Auto Mall Dr. I-10, exit 254 (Prince Rd), 1.9 mi e, then 1.2 mi n. Int corridors. **Pets:** Other species. $10 one-time fee/pet. Designated rooms, service with restrictions, supervision.
(SAVE) ⊠ 📶 💻 ➴ ⊠

▼▼ Crossland Economy Studios-Tucson-Butterfield Dr **H**
(520) 745-3612. 4800 S Butterfield Dr. I-10, exit 264B eastbound, just n to Irvington, just e to Hotel Dr, then just n; exit 264 westbound, just n. Ext corridors. **Pets:** Other species. $25 daily fee/pet. Service with restrictions, crate.
(ASK) ⊠ 📶 💻

⟨AAA⟩ ▼▼▼▼ DoubleTree Hotel at Reid Park **H**
(520) 881-4200. **$79-$349.** 445 S Alvernon Way. I-10, exit 259 (22nd St), 4 mi e, then just n. Ext/int corridors. **Pets:** $25 one-time fee/pet. Designated rooms, service with restrictions, supervision.
(SAVE) ⊠ 📶 💻 🍴 ➴ ⊠

⟨AAA⟩ ▼▼ Econo Lodge **M**
(520) 622-6714. **$39-$179.** 1136 N Stone Ave. I-10, exit 257 (Speedway Blvd) eastbound, just e, then just n. Ext corridors. **Pets:** Dogs only. $10 deposit/pet, $5 daily fee/pet, $10 one-time fee/pet. Designated rooms, no service, crate.
(SAVE) ⊠ 📶 ➴

▼▼ Executive Inn & Suites of Tucson **H**
(520) 791-7551. **Call for rates.** 333 W Drachman St. I-10, exit 257 (Speedway Blvd), 0.4 mi e to Main St, then 0.3 mi n. Int corridors. **Pets:** Accepted.
⊠ 📶 💻 ➴

▼▼ Extended StayAmerica-Tucson-Grant Rd **H**
(520) 795-9510. **$44-$162.** 5050 E Grant Rd. 0.5 mi e of Swan Rd. Ext corridors. **Pets:** Other species. $25 daily fee/pet. Service with restrictions, crate.
(ASK) ⊠ 📶 💻

⟨AAA⟩ ▼▼▼ Hampton Inn North **H**
(520) 206-0602. **$84-$174.** 1375 W Grant Rd. I-10, exit 256 (Grant Rd), just w. Int corridors. **Pets:** Accepted.
(SAVE) ⊠ 🅲ᴹ 📶 💻 ➴

⟨AAA⟩ ▼▼▼ Holiday Inn Express Hotel & Suites Tucson Airport **H**
(520) 889-6600. **$99-$189.** 2548 E Medina Rd. 0.5 mi n of Tucson International Airport entrance. Int corridors. **Pets:** Accepted.
(SAVE) ⊠ 🅲ᴹ 📶 💻 ➴

⟨AAA⟩ ▼▼▼▼ The Hotel Arizona **H**
(520) 624-8711. **$67-$139.** 181 W Broadway Blvd. I-10, exit 258 (Broadway Blvd/Congress St), just e. Int corridors. **Pets:** Other species. $50 one-time fee/room. Service with restrictions.
(SAVE) ⊠ 📶 💻 🍴 ➴

AAA ▼▼ Hotel Tucson City Center InnSuites Conference Suite Resort H ☙
(520) 622-3000. **$69-$189.** 475 N Granada Ave. I-10, exit 258 (Broadway Blvd/Congress St), just e, then 0.4 mi n. Ext/int corridors. **Pets:** Large, other species. $25 one-time fee/room. Designated rooms, service with restrictions.
SAVE ✕ 🛢 💻 ⏹ ⤴ ✕

▼▼▼ La Posada Lodge & Casitas H
(520) 887-4800. **$105-$172.** 5900 N Oracle Rd. 0.5 mi s of Orange Grove Rd. Ext corridors. **Pets:** Accepted.
✕ 🛢 💻 ⏹ ⤴

▼▼▼ La Quinta Inn & Suites Tucson Airport H ☙
(520) 573-3333. **$69-$179.** 7001 S Tucson Blvd. Just n of Tucson International Airport. Int corridors. **Pets:** Medium, other species. Service with restrictions, supervision.
ASK ✕ ▣ 🛢 💻 ⤴

AAA ▼▼▼ La Quinta Inn Downtown H ☙
(520) 624-4455. **$59-$129.** 750 W Starr Pass Blvd. I-10, exit 259 (Starr Pass Blvd), just w. Int corridors. **Pets:** Medium, other species. Service with restrictions, supervision.
SAVE ✕ 🛢 💻 ⤴

▼▼ La Quinta Inn Tucson (East) H ☙
(520) 747-1414. **$49-$169.** 6404 E Broadway Blvd. Just e of Wilmot Rd. Ext corridors. **Pets:** Medium, other species. Service with restrictions, supervision.
ASK ✕ 🛢 💻 ⤴

AAA ▼▼▼ ▼▼▼ The Lodge At Ventana Canyon H
(520) 577-1400. **$99-$799, 21 day notice.** 6200 N Clubhouse Ln. I-10, exit 256 (Grant Rd), 8.6 mi e, 0.6 mi e on Tanque Verde Rd, 2 mi n on Sabino Canyon Rd, then 3.2 mi n on Kolb Rd. Ext/int corridors. **Pets:** Accepted.
SAVE ✕ 🛢 💻 ⏹ ⤴ ✕

AAA ▼▼▼ Lodge on the Desert H ☙
(520) 325-3366. **$119-$379.** 306 N Alvernon Way. I-10, exit 258 (Broadway Blvd/Congress St), 4 mi e, then just n. Ext corridors. **Pets:** Medium, dogs only. $50 deposit/pet, $25 daily fee/pet. Designated rooms, service with restrictions.
SAVE ✕ 🛢 💻 ⏹ ⤴

AAA ▼▼▼ ▼▼▼ Loews Ventana Canyon Resort H ☙
(520) 299-2020. **$149-$449, 7 day notice.** 7000 N Resort Dr. I-10, exit 256 (Grant Rd), 8.6 mi e, 0.6 mi ne on Tanque Verde Rd, 2 mi n on Sabino Canyon Rd, then 3.5 mi n on Kolb Rd. Ext/int corridors. **Pets:** Other species. $25 one-time fee/room. Supervision.
SAVE ✕ ▣ 🛢 💻 ⏹ ⤴ ✕

▼▼ Motel 6 Tucson-Congress Street #50 M
(520) 628-1339. **$45-$61.** 960 S Freeway. I-10, exit 258 (Broadway Blvd/Congress St), 0.7 mi s; on west side of interstate. Ext corridors. **Pets:** Other species. Service with restrictions, supervision.
✕ ⤴

▼▼ Motel 6 Tucson North #1127 H
(520) 744-9300. **$49-$65.** 4630 W Ina Rd. I-10, exit 248 (Ina Rd), just e to Camino de Oeste, then just n. Int corridors. **Pets:** Other species. Service with restrictions, supervision.
✕ 🛢 ⤴

AAA ▼▼▼ Quality Inn at Tucson Airport H
(520) 294-2500. **$59-$225.** 2803 E Valencia Rd. 1 mi ne of Tucson International Airport; just e of Tucson Blvd. Ext/int corridors. **Pets:** Medium. $10 daily fee/pet. Service with restrictions, supervision.
SAVE ✕ 🛢 💻 ⤴

AAA ▼▼▼ Quality Inn Tucson H ☙
(520) 623-7792. **$60-$180.** 1025 E Benson Hwy. I-10, exit 262, just s. Int corridors. **Pets:** Other species. $15 one-time fee/room. Service with restrictions.
SAVE ✕ 🛢 💻 ⏹ ⤴

AAA ▼▼▼ Radisson Suites Tucson H
(520) 721-7100. **$109-$269.** 6555 E Speedway Blvd. Just e of Wilmot Rd. Ext corridors. **Pets:** Large, other species. $50 one-time fee/room.
SAVE ✕ 🛢 💻 ⏹ ⤴ ✕

AAA ▼▼▼ Ramada Inn & Suites Foothills Resort H ☙
(520) 886-9595. **$99-$159.** 6944 E Tanque Verde Rd. Jct Campbell Ave, 5.5 mi e on Grant Rd, then just ne. Ext corridors. **Pets:** Small. $25 one-time fee/pet. Designated rooms, service with restrictions, supervision.
SAVE ✕ 🛢 💻 ⤴

AAA ▼▼▼ Randolph Park Hotel and Suites H
(520) 795-0330. **$70-$165, 3 day notice.** 102 N Alvernon Way. Jct Campbell Ave, 2.2 mi e on Broadway Blvd, then just n. Ext/int corridors. **Pets:** Small. $25 one-time fee/pet. Designated rooms, service with restrictions, supervision.
SAVE ✕ 🛢 💻 ⤴ ✕

AAA ▼▼ Red Roof Inn-Tucson South H
(520) 571-1400. **$50-$107.** 3704 E Irvington Rd. I-10, exit 264 westbound; exit 264B eastbound. Ext corridors. **Pets:** Medium, other species. Service with restrictions, supervision.
SAVE ✕ 🛢 ⤴

▼▼▼ Residence Inn by Marriott H ☙
(520) 721-0991. **$169-$259, 3 day notice.** 6477 E Speedway Blvd. Just e of Wilmot Rd. Ext corridors. **Pets:** Other species. $100 one-time fee/room. Designated rooms, service with restrictions, crate.
✕ 🛢 💻 ⤴ ✕

▼▼▼ Residence Inn by Marriott Williams Centre H
(520) 790-6100. **$159-$219.** 5400 E Williams Cir. Jct Campbell Ave, 3.8 mi e on Broadway Blvd, then just s and just e on Williams Blvd. Int corridors. **Pets:** Medium, other species. $100 one-time fee/room. Service with restrictions, crate.
✕ ▣ 🛢 💻 ⤴ ✕

▼▼▼ Residence Inn Tucson Airport H
(520) 294-5522. **$139-$259.** 2660 E Medina Rd. 0.5 mi n of airport entrance on Tucson Blvd, just e. Int corridors. **Pets:** Accepted.
✕ 🛢 💻 ⤴ ✕

▼▼▼ Riverpark Inn H
(520) 239-2300. **$89-$299.** 350 S Freeway. I-10, exit 258 (Broadway Blvd/Congress St), just w, then 0.4 mi s. Ext/int corridors. **Pets:** Medium. $35 one-time fee/pet. Designated rooms, service with restrictions, crate.
ASK ✕ 🛢 💻 ⏹ ⤴ ✕

AAA ▼▼ Rodeway Inn-University of AZ M
(520) 622-6446. **$45-$129.** 1248 N Stone Ave. I-10, exit 257 (Speedway Blvd) eastbound, just e, then just n. Ext corridors. **Pets:** Small. $10 daily fee/pet. Designated rooms, service with restrictions, crate.
SAVE ✕ 🛢 ⤴

AAA ▼▼▼ Sheraton Tucson Hotel & Suites H
(520) 323-6262. **Call for rates.** 5151 E Grant Rd. Jct Campbell Ave, 3.6 mi e. Ext/int corridors. **Pets:** Medium, dogs only. $50 one-time fee/room. Designated rooms, service with restrictions, supervision.
SAVE ✕ ▣ 🛢 💻 ⏹ ⤴ ✕

▼▼ Studio 6 Extended Stay #6002 M
(520) 746-0030. **$57-$87.** 4950 S Outlet Center Dr. I-10, exit 264A eastbound; exit 264B westbound, just s, then just nw on Julian Dr. Ext corridors. **Pets:** Other species. $10 daily fee/room. Service with restrictions, supervision.
✕ 🛢 💻 ⤴

▼▼▼ TownePlace Suites by Marriott H
(520) 292-9697. **$99-$149.** 405 W Rudasill Rd. Jct Orange Grove Rd, 0.5 mi s on Oracle Rd, then just e. Int corridors. **Pets:** Other species. $75 one-time fee/room. Service with restrictions, crate.
✕ 🛢 💻 ⤴

△△△ ▽△▽ ▽△▽ **The Westin La Paloma Resort &**
Spa 🅗 ❖
(520) 742-6000. **$129-$539, 7 day notice.** 3800 E Sunrise Dr. SR 77
(Oracle Rd), 4.6 mi e on Ina Rd via Skyline and Sunrise drs, then just s on
Via Palomita. Ext corridors. **Pets:** Medium, dogs only. Designated rooms,
service with restrictions.
[SAVE] ⊠ 🛋 💻 [ﾔ] ➳ ⊠

△△△ ▽△▽ ▽△▽ **Westward Look Resort** 🅗 ❖
(520) 297-1151. **$99-$369, 7 day notice.** 245 E Ina Rd. I-10, exit 248 (Ina
Rd), 6 mi e, then just n on Westward Look Dr. Ext corridors. **Pets:** Medium.
$75 one-time fee/room. Designated rooms, service with restrictions, crate.
[SAVE] ⊠ 🛋 💻 [ﾔ] ➳ ⊠

△△△ ▽△▽ ▽△▽ **Windmill Suites at St. Philip's Plaza** 🅗
(520) 577-0007. **$99-$199.** 4250 N Campbell Ave. I-10, exit 254 (Prince
Rd), 4 mi e, then 1 mi n. Int corridors. **Pets:** Accepted.
[SAVE] ⊠ 🛋 💻 ➳ ⊠

END METROPOLITAN AREA

WELLTON

▽△▽ ▽△▽ **Microtel Inn & Suites at Coyote Wash** 🅗
(928) 785-3777. **$55-$115.** 28784 Commerce Way. I-8, exit 30, just s. Int
corridors. **Pets:** Medium, other species. Service with restrictions, crate.
[ASK] ⊠ 🛋 💻 ➳

WICKENBURG

△△△ ▽△▽ ▽△▽ **Best Western Rancho Grande** 🅗 ❖
(928) 684-5445. **$75-$116.** 293 E Wickenburg Way. On US 60; center. Ext
corridors. **Pets:** Other species. $8 daily fee/room. Designated rooms, serv-
ice with restrictions, supervision.
[SAVE] ⊠ 🛋 💻 ➳ ⊠

△△△ ▽△▽ ▽△▽ **Super 8 Motel & Suites** 🅜
(928) 684-0808. **$80-$110.** 1021 N Tegner St. 1 mi n of US 60 and 93.
Ext/int corridors. **Pets:** $10 daily fee/pet. Service with restrictions, supervi-
sion.
[SAVE] ⊠ 🛋 💻

△△△ ▽△▽ ▽△▽ **Wickenburg Inn** 🅗
(928) 684-5461. **$69-$95, 5 day notice.** 850 E Wickenburg Way. 1.3 mi
se on US 60. Int corridors. **Pets:** Medium. $7 daily fee/pet. Service with
restrictions, supervision.
[SAVE] ⊠ 🛋 💻 ➳

WILLCOX

△△△ ▽△▽ ▽△▽ **Best Western Plaza Inn** 🅗
(520) 384-3556. **$80.** 1100 W Rex Allen Dr. I-10, exit 340, just s. Ext
corridors. **Pets:** Medium. $15 daily fee/pet. Service with restrictions, super-
vision.
[SAVE] ⊠ 🛋 💻 [ﾔ] ➳

△△△ ▽△▽ ▽△▽ **Days Inn** 🅜
(520) 384-4222. **$70-$80.** 724 N Bisbee Ave. I-10, exit 340, just s. Int
corridors. **Pets:** Medium. $7 daily fee/pet. Service with restrictions, supervi-
sion.
[SAVE] ⊠ 🛋 💻 ➳

▽△▽ **Motel 6 Willcox #410** 🅜
(520) 384-2201. **$45-$58.** 921 N Bisbee Ave. I-10, exit 340, just s. Ext
corridors. **Pets:** Other species. Service with restrictions, supervision.
⊠ 🛋 ➳

▽△▽ ▽△▽ **Super 8** 🅗
(520) 384-0888. **$70-$85.** 1500 W Ft. Grant Rd. I-10, exit 340, just n. Int
corridors. **Pets:** Small, other species. $7 one-time fee/pet. Designated
rooms, service with restrictions, supervision.
[ASK] ⊠ 🅼 🛋 💻 ➳

WILLIAMS

△△△ ▽△▽ ▽△▽ **Americas Best Value Inn of Williams** 🅜
(928) 635-2202. **$35-$84.** 1001 W Route 66. I-40, exit 161, 0.9 mi e. Ext/int
corridors. **Pets:** Medium. $10 daily fee/pet. No service, supervision.
[SAVE] ⊠ ➳

△△△ ▽△▽ ▽△▽ **Best Western Inn of Williams** 🅗
(928) 635-4400. **$159-$209.** 2600 W Route 66. I-40, exit 161, just e. Int
corridors. **Pets:** Accepted.
[SAVE] ⊠ 🛋 💻 ➳

△△△ ▽△▽ ▽△▽ **Days Inn** 🅜
(928) 635-4051. **$59-$175.** 2488 W Route 66. I-40, exit 161, just e. Int
corridors. **Pets:** Accepted.
[SAVE] ⊠ 🛋 ➳

△△△ ▽△▽ **El Rancho Motel** 🅜 ❖
(928) 635-2552. **$38-$88.** 617 E Route 66. I-40, exit 163, 0.6 mi s, then
just e. Ext corridors. **Pets:** $5 daily fee/pet. Designated rooms, service with
restrictions, supervision.
[SAVE] ⊠ 🛋 💻 ➳

▽△▽ ▽△▽ **Holiday Inn Williams** 🅗 ❖
(928) 635-4114. **$95-$170.** 950 N Grand Canyon Blvd. I-40, exit 163, just
s. Int corridors. **Pets:** Large, other species. Service with restrictions, crate.
⊠ 🅼 🛋 💻 [ﾔ] ➳

▽△▽ ▽△▽ **Motel 6–4010** 🅜
(928) 635-9000. **Call for rates.** 831 W Route 66. I-40, exit 161, 1 mi e. Int
corridors. **Pets:** Other species. Service with restrictions, supervision.
⊠ 🛋 ➳

△△△ ▽△▽ ▽△▽ **Quality Inn Mountain Ranch Resort** 🅗 ❖
(928) 635-2693. **$79-$209.** 6701 E Mountain Ranch Rd. I-40, exit 171
(Deer Farm Rd), just s. Ext corridors. **Pets:** Small. $45 one-time fee/room.
Designated rooms, service with restrictions, supervision.
[SAVE] ⊠ 🛋 💻 [ﾔ] ➳ ⊠

△△△ ▽△▽ **Travelodge Williams** 🅜
(928) 635-2651. **$40-$90.** 430 E Route 66. I-40, exit 163, 0.5 mi s, then
just e. Ext corridors. **Pets:** Dogs only. $10 daily fee/pet. Service with restric-
tions, supervision.
[SAVE] ⊠ 🛋 💻 ➳

WINDOW ROCK

△△△ ▽△▽ ▽△▽ **Quality Inn Navajo Nation Capital** 🅗
(928) 871-4108. **$67-$81.** 48 W Hwy 264. Center. Ext corridors.
Pets: Medium, other species. $50 deposit/pet. Service with restrictions,
supervision.
[SAVE] ⊠ 🛋 💻 [ﾔ]

WINSLOW

🐾 💎💎💎 Econo Lodge at I-40 🅷

(928) 289-4687. **$50-$110, 7 day notice.** 1706 N Park Dr. I-40, exit 253, just s. Ext corridors. **Pets:** Medium. $10 one-time fee/room. Service with restrictions, crate.

[SAVE] [✕] 🖥 🖨 🏊

💎💎💎💎 La Posada Hotel 🅷

(928) 289-4366. **$99-$149, 3 day notice.** 303 E 2nd St. I-40, exit 253, 1 mi s to Route 66 (2nd St), then just e; in historic downtown. Int corridors. **Pets:** Other species. $10 one-time fee/room.

[✕] [🔕M] 🖥 [🍽] [🐾]

🐾 💎💎💎 Super 8 Ⓜ

(928) 289-4606. **$63-$95.** 1916 W 3rd St. I-40, exit 252, just s, then just e on Route 66. Int corridors. **Pets:** Accepted.

[SAVE] [✕] 🖥 🖨

YUMA

🐾 💎💎💎 Best Western Coronado Motor Hotel Ⓜ ❀

(928) 783-4453. **$79-$170.** 233 4th Ave. I-8, exit 172 (4th Ave) eastbound, 0.5 mi s; exit 1 (Harold C. Giss Pkwy) westbound, 1 mi w. Ext corridors. **Pets:** Medium. $50 deposit/pet. Designated rooms, service with restrictions, supervision.

[SAVE] [✕] 🖥 🖨 [🍽] 🏊

🐾 💎💎💎💎 Best Western InnSuites Yuma Mall Hotel & Suites 🅷

(928) 783-8341. **$89-$199.** 1450 Castle Dome Ave. I-8, exit 2 (16th St/US 95), just e to Yuma Palms Pkwy, just n, then just w. Ext corridors. **Pets:** Small, other species. $50 one-time fee/pet. Designated rooms, service with restrictions, crate.

[SAVE] [✕] 🖥 🖨 [🍽] 🏊 [✕]

🐾 💎💎💎💎 Clarion Suites 🅷

(928) 726-4830. **$102-$120.** 2600 S 4th Ave. I-8, exit 2 (16 St/US 95) eastbound, 1 mi w, then 1.3 mi s; exit 3 (SR 280) westbound, 0.5 mi s, then 2 mi w. Ext corridors. **Pets:** Accepted.

[SAVE] [✕] 🖥 🖨 🏊

💎💎💎 Comfort Inn 🅷

(928) 782-1200. **$109-$209, 7 day notice.** 1691 S Riley Ave. I-8, exit 2 (16th St/US 95), just w. Int corridors. **Pets:** Large. $10 daily fee/room. Service with restrictions, supervision.

[ASK] [✕] [🔕M] 🖥 🖨 🏊

💎💎💎 Holiday Inn 🅷

(928) 782-9300. **Call for rates.** 1901 E 18th St. I-8, exit 2 (16th St/US 95), 0.4 mi e on 16th St, just s on Pacific Ave, then just w. Int corridors. **Pets:** Medium. $10 one-time fee/pet. Designated rooms, service with restrictions, supervision.

[✕] [🔕M] 🖥 🖨 [🍽] 🏊

💎💎💎💎 Holiday Inn Express 🅷

(928) 317-1400. **$99-$199.** 2044 S Ave 3 E. I-8, exit 3, just n, then just w on Frontage Rd. Int corridors. **Pets:** Small. $15 daily fee/pet. Service with restrictions, supervision.

[ASK] [✕] [🔕M] 🖥 🖨 🏊

🐾 💎💎💎 Howard Johnson Inn 🅷 ❀

(928) 344-1420. **$59-$120.** 3181 S 4th Ave. I-8, exit 3E (SR 280 S), 1 mi s to 32nd St, then 2 mi w. Ext corridors. **Pets:** Other species. $10 daily fee/pet. Service with restrictions, crate.

[SAVE] [✕] 🖥 🖨 🏊

💎💎💎 Microtel Inn & Suites 🅷

(928) 345-1777. **$57-$140.** 11274 S Fortuna Rd. I-8, exit 12 (Fortuna Rd), just s, then w on frontage road. Int corridors. **Pets:** Accepted.

[ASK] [✕] 🖥 🖨 🏊

💎💎 Oak Tree Inn 🅷 🐾

(928) 539-9000. **$69-$179.** 1731 Sunridge Dr. I-8, exit 2 (16th St/US 95), just e, then just s. Int corridors. **Pets:** Other species. Service with restrictions, supervision.

[ASK] [✕] 🖥 🖨 🏊

🐾 💎💎💎 Quality Inn Airport 🅷

(928) 726-4721. **$79-$159.** 711 E 32nd St. I-8, exit 3E (SR 280), 1.2 mi s, then 1.9 mi w. Ext corridors. **Pets:** Accepted.

[SAVE] [✕] 🖥 🖨 [🍽] 🏊

🐾 💎💎💎 Shilo Inn Hotel & Suites-Yuma 🅷 ❀

(928) 782-9511. **$145-$250.** 1550 S Castle Dome Ave. I-8, exit 2 (16th St/US 95), just e to Yuma Palms Pkwy, just n, then just w. Int corridors. **Pets:** Dogs only. $25 one-time fee/room. Designated rooms, service with restrictions, supervision.

[SAVE] [✕] 🖥 🖨 [🍽] 🏊 [✕]

💎💎💎💎 TownePlace Suites by Marriott 🅷

(928) 783-6900. **$129-$149.** 1726 S Sunridge Dr. I-8, exit 2 (16th St/US 95), just e to Sunridge Dr, then just s. Int corridors. **Pets:** Accepted.

[✕] [🔕M] 🖥 🖨 🏊

🐾 💎💎💎 Yuma Cabana Motel Ⓜ

(928) 783-8311. **$46-$130, 3 day notice.** 2151 S 4th Ave. I-8, exit 2 (16th St/US 95), 1 mi w, then 0.5 mi s. Int corridors. **Pets:** Small. $6 daily fee/pet. Service with restrictions, supervision.

[SAVE] [✕] 🖥 🏊

💎💎💎 Yuma Super 8 🅷

(928) 782-2000. **$89-$149, 7 day notice.** 1688 S Riley Ave. I-8, exit 2 (16th St/US 95), just w. Int corridors. **Pets:** Large. $10 daily fee/room. Service with restrictions, supervision.

[ASK] [✕] [🔕M] 🖥 🖨 🏊

ARKANSAS

ALMA

▼▼▼ Comfort Inn & Suites H
(479) 632-4141. **$75-$95.** 439 Hwy 71 N. I-40, exit 13, just n. Ext/int corridors. **Pets:** Small. $25 one-time fee/pet. Designated rooms, service with restrictions, supervision.
ASK ⊗ 📶 💻

ARKADELPHIA

◬◬◬ ▼▼▼ Best Western-Continental Inn H ❀
(870) 246-5592. **$65-$99, 5 day notice.** 136 Valley St. I-30, exit 78, just e. Ext corridors. **Pets:** $10 daily fee/pet. Designated rooms, service with restrictions.
SAVE ⊗ 📶 💻 ⊗

BATESVILLE

▼▼▼ Ramada Inn of Batesville H ❀
(870) 698-1800. **Call for rates.** 1325 N St Louis St. 1 mi n on US 167. Ext corridors. **Pets:** Small. $20 daily fee/pet. Designated rooms, service with restrictions, crate.
⊗ 📶 💻 🍴 ⊗

▼▼ Super 8-Batesville M ❀
(870) 793-5888. **$59-$62.** 1287 N St. Louis St. 1 mi n on US 167. Int corridors. **Pets:** Dogs only. $25 one-time fee/pet. Service with restrictions, supervision.
ASK ⊗ 📶 💻

BEEBE

▼▼ Days Inn H
(501) 882-2008. **$70-$95, 3 day notice.** 100 Tammy Ln. US 67/167, exit 28, just e. Ext corridors. **Pets:** Accepted.
ASK ⊗ 📶 💻 ⊗

BENTON

◬◬◬ ▼▼▼ Best Western Inn H
(501) 778-9695. **$65-$75.** 17036 I-30. I-30, exit 117, just w. Ext corridors. **Pets:** Medium, other species. $10 daily fee/pet. Service with restrictions.
SAVE ⊗ 📶 💻 ⊗

BENTONVILLE

◬◬◬ ◈◈◈◈ Comfort Suites Bentonville/Rogers H
(479) 254-9099. **$79-$139.** 2011 SE Walton Blvd. I-540, exit 85, just w. Int corridors. **Pets:** Accepted.
SAVE ⊗ 📶 💻 ⊗

◈◈◈◈ La Quinta Inn & Suites H ❀
(479) 271-7555. **$74-$179.** 1001 SE Walton Blvd. I-540, exit 85, 0.7 mi w. Int corridors. **Pets:** Medium, other species. Service with restrictions, supervision.
ASK ⊗ 💪M 📶 💻 ⊗

▼▼ Microtel Inn & Suites Bentonville H
(479) 271-6699. **Call for rates.** 911 SE Walton Blvd. I-540, exit 85, 0.8 mi w. Int corridors. **Pets:** Accepted.
⊗ 📶 💻

◈◈◈ TownePlace Suites by Marriott Bentonville/Rogers H ❀
(479) 621-0202. **$130-$158.** 3100 SE 14th St. I-540, exit 86, just e. Int corridors. **Pets:** $100 one-time fee/room. Service with restrictions, supervision.
⊗ 💪M 📶 💻 ⊗

◈◈◈ Wingate by Wyndham H
(479) 418-5400. **$129.** 7400 SW Old Farm Blvd. 7.4 mi w of jct Walton and SW Regional Airport blvds. Int corridors. **Pets:** Accepted.
ASK ⊗ 💪M 📶 💻 ⊗

BLYTHEVILLE

▼▼ Hampton Inn H
(870) 763-5220. **$84.** 301 N Frontage Rd. I-55, exit 67, just nw. Ext corridors. **Pets:** Accepted.
⊗ 📶 💻 🍴 ⊗

▼▼ Holiday Inn H
(870) 763-5800. **Call for rates.** 1121 E Main St. I-55, exit 67, just w. Ext/int corridors. **Pets:** Accepted.
⊗ 📶 💻 🍴 ⊗

▼▼ Quality Inn H
(870) 763-7081. **Call for rates.** 1520 E Main St. I-55, exit 67, just w. Ext corridors. **Pets:** Medium, other species. $15 one-time fee/room. Service with restrictions, supervision.
⊗ 📶 💻 🍴 ⊗

BRYANT

▼▼ Americas Best Value Inn M
(501) 653-7800. **$55-$90.** 407 W Commerce St. I-30, exit 123, just sw. Ext corridors. **Pets:** Medium, dogs only. $10 daily fee/pet. Designated rooms, service with restrictions, supervision.
ASK ⊗ 📶 💻

◬◬◬ ▼▼▼ Comfort Inn & Suites H
(501) 653-4000. **$69-$129.** 209 W Commerce St. I-30, exit 123, just w. Int corridors. **Pets:** Accepted.
SAVE ⊗ 📶 💻 ⊗ ⊗

▼▼ Super 8 M
(501) 847-7888. **$50-$65.** 201 Dell Dr. I-30, exit 123, just e. Ext corridors. **Pets:** Small, dogs only. $20 deposit/room, $10 one-time fee/pet. Designated rooms, service with restrictions, supervision.
ASK ⊗

◬◬◬ ▼▼▼ Vista Inn & Suites H
(501) 847-7120. **$65-$96, 7 day notice.** 210 Office Park Dr. I-30, exit 123, just w. Ext corridors. **Pets:** Medium. $15 daily fee/pet. Crate.
SAVE ⊗ 📶 💻 ⊗

CAMDEN

▼▼▼ Comfort Inn H
(870) 836-9000. **$90-$108.** 1 Ridgecrest Dr. Just w of jct US 79 and 278. Int corridors. **Pets:** Accepted.
ASK ⊗ 💪M 📶 💻 ⊗ ⊗

▼▼▼ **Holiday Inn Express** 🅷
(870) 836-8100. **Call for rates.** 1450 US Hwy 278 W. 1 mi w of jct US 79 and 278. Int corridors. **Pets:** Accepted.
☒ 🅶M 🅗 🖭 ⇌

CLARKSVILLE

🆀🆀🆀 ▼▼▼ **Best Western Sherwood Inn** 🅷
(479) 754-7900. **$49-$78.** 1203 S Rogers Ave. I-40, exit 58, just n. Ext corridors. **Pets:** Other species. Service with restrictions, supervision.
SAVE ☒ 🅗 🖭 ⇌

CONWAY

🆀🆀🆀 ▼▼▼ **Best Western Conway** 🅷
(501) 329-9855. **$69-$74.** 816 E Oak St. I-40, exit 127, just n. Ext corridors. **Pets:** Accepted.
SAVE ☒ 🅗 🖭 ⇌

▼▼▼ **Candlewood Suites** 🅷
(501) 329-8551. **Call for rates.** 2360 Sanders St. I-40, exit 125, just se. Int corridors. **Pets:** Medium, other species. $75 one-time fee/room. Service with restrictions, crate.
☒ 🅗 🖭

🆀🆀🆀 ▼▼▼ **Quality Inn** 🅷
(501) 329-0300. **Call for rates.** 150 Hwy 65 N. I-40, exit 125, just n. Ext corridors. **Pets:** Medium. $25 one-time fee/room. Service with restrictions, crate.
SAVE ☒ 🅗 🖭 ⇌

EL DORADO

▼▼▼▼ **La Quinta Inn El Dorado** 🅷 🐾
(870) 863-6677. **$49-$89.** 2303 Junction City Rd. Just e of jct US 167 and 82B. Ext/int corridors. **Pets:** Medium, other species. Service with restrictions, supervision.
ASK ☒ 🅗 🖭 ⇌

EUREKA SPRINGS

🆀🆀🆀 ▼▼▼▼ **1886 Crescent Hotel & Spa** 🅷
(479) 253-9766. **$169-$219, 3 day notice.** 75 Prospect Ave. 1.3 mi n of jct SR 23 on US 62B Historic Loop. Int corridors. **Pets:** Other species. $10 one-time fee/pet. Designated rooms, no service, supervision.
SAVE ☒ 🅗 🖭 ⑪ ⇌ ☒

🆀🆀🆀 ▼▼▼ **1905 Basin Park Hotel** 🅷
(479) 253-7837. **$89-$149, 3 day notice.** 12 Spring St. 0.7 mi n of jct US 62 via SR 23 N; downtown. Int corridors. **Pets:** Accepted.
SAVE ☒ 🅗 🖭 ⑪

▼▼▼ **Arsenic & Old Lace B&B** 🅱🅱 🐾
(479) 253-5454. **$139-$279, 15 day notice.** 60 Hillside Ave. 1.2 mi n on SR 23, just sw; downtown. Ext/int corridors. **Pets:** Dogs only. $30 one-time fee/room. Designated rooms, service with restrictions, crate.
ASK ☒

▼▼▼ **Bavarian Inn** 🅷
(479) 253-8128. **Call for rates.** 325 W Van Buren St. 1 mi w of jct US 62 and SR 23. Ext corridors. **Pets:** Accepted.
☒ 🅗 🖭 ⇌

🆀🆀🆀 ▼▼▼ **Best Western-Eureka Inn** 🅷
(479) 253-9551. **$69-$139.** 101 E Van Buren St. Just w of jct US 62 and SR 23 N. Ext/int corridors. **Pets:** Small, dogs only. $6 daily fee/pet. Designated rooms, service with restrictions, crate.
SAVE ☒ 🅗 🖭 ⑪ ☒

🆀🆀🆀 ▼▼▼ **Best Western Inn of the Ozarks** 🅷 🐾
(479) 253-9768. **$59-$149, 3 day notice.** 207 W Van Buren St. On US 62, 0.5 mi w of jct SR 23. Ext corridors. **Pets:** Medium, dogs only. $10 daily fee/pet. Service with restrictions, supervision.
SAVE ☒ 🅗 🖭 ⑪ ⇌ ☒

▼▼ ▼▼ **Brackenridge Lodge** 🅼
(479) 253-6803. **$42-$149, 7 day notice.** 352 W Van Buren St. 1 mi w of jct US 62 and SR 23. Ext corridors. **Pets:** Very small, dogs only. Designated rooms, no service, supervision.
ASK ☒ 🅗 🖭 ⇌ ☑

🆀🆀🆀 ▼▼▼ **Colonial Inn** 🅷
(479) 253-7300. **$48-$150, 3 day notice.** 154 Huntsville Rd. Just s of jct US 62 and SR 23. Ext/int corridors. **Pets:** Small. $4 daily fee/pet. Designated rooms, service with restrictions, crate.
SAVE ☒ 🅗 🖭 ⇌

▼▼▼ **Days Inn** 🅼 🐾
(479) 253-8863. **$49-$179, 3 day notice.** 120 W Van Buren St. On US 62, just w of jct SR 23 N. Ext corridors. **Pets:** Medium, dogs only. $15 daily fee/room. Service with restrictions, supervision.
ASK ☒ 🅗 🖭 ⇌

▼▼▼ **Howard Johnson Express** 🅷
(479) 253-6665. **Call for rates.** 4042 E Van Buren St. 1.8 mi e of jct US 62 and SR 23. Ext corridors. **Pets:** Accepted.
☒ 🅗 🖭 ⇌

▼▼ **Roadrunner Inn** 🅼
(479) 253-8166. **$69-$275, 30 day notice.** 3034 Mundell Rd. On US 62, 4.3 mi w, 3.9 mi s on SR 187, then 3 mi se. Ext corridors. **Pets:** Large. $10 daily fee/pet. Designated rooms, service with restrictions, supervision.
ASK ☒ 🅗 🖭 ☑

▼▼ **Travelodge** 🅷
(479) 253-8992. **Call for rates.** 110 Huntsville Dr. Jct US 62 and SR 23. Ext corridors. **Pets:** Accepted.
☒ 🅗 🖭 ⇌

FAYETTEVILLE

🆀🆀🆀 ▼▼▼ **Best Western Windsor Suites** 🅷
(479) 587-1400. **$77-$86.** 1122 S Futrall Dr. I-540, exit 62, just se. Ext corridors. **Pets:** Small. $10 one-time fee/room. Service with restrictions.
SAVE ☒ 🅗 🖭 ⇌

▼▼▼ **Sleep Inn by Choice Hotels** 🅷
(479) 587-8700. **Call for rates.** 728 Millsap Rd. I-540, exit 67, 1.6 mi e, then just s on US 71B. Int corridors. **Pets:** Large, other species. $25 one-time fee/room. Service with restrictions.
☒ 🅗 🖭

FORDYCE

▼▼▼ **Days Inn** 🅷
(870) 352-2400. **Call for rates.** 2500 W 4th St. US 79/167; 1 mi w. Ext/int corridors. **Pets:** Small. $10 daily fee/pet. Service with restrictions, supervision.
☒ 🅗 🖭 ⇌

FORREST CITY

🆀🆀🆀 ▼▼ **Best Western Colony Inn** 🅷
(870) 633-0870. **$70-$73, 45 day notice.** 2333 N Washington St. I-40, exit 241A, just s. Ext corridors. **Pets:** Medium, other species. Service with restrictions, supervision.
SAVE ☒ 🅗 🖭 ⇌

▼▼▼ **Holiday Inn** 🅷
(870) 633-6300. **$81-$90.** 200 Holiday Dr. I-40, exit 241B, just n. Ext corridors. **Pets:** Accepted.
☒ 🅗 🖭 ⑪ ⇌

FORT SMITH

▼▼▼ **Aspen Hotel & Suites** 🅷
(479) 452-9000. **$109-$120.** 2900 S 68th St. I-540, exit 8B (Rogers Ave), just e. Int corridors. **Pets:** Other species. Service with restrictions, crate.
ASK ☒ 🅗 🖭 ⇌

▼▼ **Baymont Inn & Suites Fort Smith** H
(479) 484-5770. **$89-$199.** 2123 Burnham Rd. I-540, exit 8A (Rogers Ave), just w. Int corridors. **Pets:** Other species. No service.
[ASK] [X] [🛏] [🖥] [🏊]

▼▼ **Comfort Inn** H
(479) 484-0227. **$99-$169.** 2120 Burnham Rd. I-540, exit 8A (Rogers Ave), just w. Int corridors. **Pets:** Accepted.
[ASK] [X] [🛏] [🖥] [🏊] [X]

▲▲▲ ▼▼▼ **Courtyard by Marriott Downtown Fort Smith** H
(479) 783-2100. **$125-$153.** 900 Rogers Ave. Just s of US 64 (Garrison Ave); downtown. Int corridors. **Pets:** Accepted.
[SAVE] [X] [🛏M] [🛏] [🖥] [🍴] [🏊] [X]

▼▼ **GuestHouse Inn** H
(479) 646-5100. **$79-$94.** 3600 Grinnell Ave. I-540, exit 12, 0.5 mi se. Int corridors. **Pets:** Small, dogs only. $20 daily fee/pet. Designated rooms, service with restrictions, supervision.
[ASK] [X] [🛏] [🖥] [🏊]

▲▲▲ ▼▼▼ **Holiday Inn City Center Fort Smith** H
(479) 783-1000. **$109-$149.** 700 Rogers Ave. Just s of US 64 (Garrison Ave); downtown. Int corridors. **Pets:** Accepted.
[SAVE] [X] [🛏M] [🛏] [🖥] [🍴] [🏊] [X]

▼▼▼ **Holiday Inn Express** H
(479) 452-7500. **$100-$119.** 6813 Phoenix Ave. I-540, exit 8A (Rogers Ave), 0.6 mi e, then 0.5 mi s. Int corridors. **Pets:** Accepted.
[X] [🛏] [🖥] [🏊]

▼▼▼ **Residence Inn by Marriott** H
(479) 478-8300. **$121-$147.** 3005 S 74th. I-540, exit 8A (Rogers Ave), 0.8 mi e. Int corridors. **Pets:** Large. $75 one-time fee/room. Service with restrictions.
[X] [🛏] [🖥] [🏊] [X]

GENTRY

▼▼▼ **Apple Crest Inn Bed & Breakfast** BB
(479) 736-8201. **$110-$180, 14 day notice.** 12758 S Hwy 59. On SR 59, 1 mi s. Int corridors. **Pets:** Other species. $10 one-time fee/room. Designated rooms, service with restrictions.
[ASK] [X]

HARRISON

▼▼ **Comfort Inn** H
(870) 741-7676. **$70-$96.** 1210 Hwy 62/65 N. 1 mi n on US 62/65/412. Ext/int corridors. **Pets:** Small. Service with restrictions, supervision.
[ASK] [X] [🛏] [🖥] [🏊]

▼▼▼ **Holiday Inn Express Hotel & Suites** H
(870) 741-3636. **$80-$125.** 117 Hwy 43 E. Just e from jct US 62/65/412 and SR 43. Int corridors. **Pets:** Small. $25 daily fee/pet. Service with restrictions, supervision.
[ASK] [X] [🛏] [🖥] [🏊] [X]

HOPE

▲▲▲ ▼▼ **Best Western of Hope** H
(870) 777-9222. **$80-$90, 3 day notice.** 1800 Holiday Dr. I-30, exit 30, just nw. Ext corridors. **Pets:** Other species. $10 daily fee/room. Service with restrictions, supervision.
[SAVE] [X] [🛏] [🖥] [🏊]

HOT SPRINGS

▲▲▲ ▼▼▼▼ **Clarion Resort** H
(501) 525-1391. **$89-$229.** 4813 Central Ave. 5.5 mi s of jct US 270 and SR 7. Int corridors. **Pets:** Medium. $10 daily fee/room, $25 one-time fee/room. Designated rooms, service with restrictions, supervision.
[SAVE] [X] [🛏] [🖥] [🍴] [🏊] [X]

▲▲▲ ▼▼▼ **Embassy Suites Hot Springs-Hotel & Spa** H ✿
(501) 624-9200. **$109-$259.** 400 Convention Blvd. Just w of jct US 70. Int corridors. **Pets:** Medium, other species. $35 daily fee/room. Supervision.
[SAVE] [X] [🛏M] [🛏] [🖥] [🍴] [🏊] [X]

JONESBORO

▲▲▲ ▼▼▼ **Comfort Inn & Suites** H
(870) 972-9000. **$70-$78.** 2911 Gilmore Dr. US 63, exit Stadium Blvd/Caraway Rd, just n. Int corridors. **Pets:** Accepted.
[SAVE] [X] [🛏] [🖥] [🏊]

▼▼▼ **Holiday Inn Express** H
(870) 932-5554. **Call for rates.** 2407 Phillips Dr. US 63, exit Stadium Blvd/Caraway Rd, just n. Int corridors. **Pets:** Accepted.
[X] [🛏] [🖥] [🏊]

▼▼▼ **Holiday Inn of Jonesboro** H
(870) 935-2030. **$70-$80.** 3006 S Caraway Rd. US 63, exit Stadium Blvd/Caraway Rd, just n. Ext/int corridors. **Pets:** Medium. $15 daily fee/pet. Service with restrictions, supervision.
[ASK] [X] [🛏] [🖥] [🍴] [🏊] [X]

LITTLE ROCK

▼▼ **Airport Travelodge** H
(501) 490-2200. **Call for rates.** 7615 Fluid Dr. I-440, exit 5, just n. Ext corridors. **Pets:** Accepted.
[X] [🛏] [🖥]

▲▲▲ ▼▼▼ **Best Western Luxury Inn & Suites** H
(501) 562-4448. **$80-$90.** 8219 I-30. I-30, exit 133, just ne on E Service Rd. Ext corridors. **Pets:** Accepted.
[SAVE] [X] [🛏] [🖥] [🏊]

▲▲▲ ▼▼▼ **Comfort Inn & Suites, Downtown Little Rock @ The Clinton Library** H
(501) 687-7700. **$89-$139.** 707 I-30. I-30, exit 140A, just e. Int corridors. **Pets:** Medium. $25 one-time fee/room. Service with restrictions, supervision.
[SAVE] [X] [🛏M] [🛏] [🖥] [🏊]

▲▲▲ ▼▼▼ **Embassy Suites Hotel Little Rock** H
(501) 312-9000. **$119-$219.** 11301 Financial Centre Pkwy. Jct I-430 and 630, just w. Int corridors. **Pets:** Accepted.
[SAVE] [X] [🛏M] [🛏] [🖥] [🍴] [🏊] [X]

▼▼ **La Quinta Inn at Rodney Parham Rd** H ✿
(501) 225-7007. **$59-$79.** 1010 Breckenridge Rd. I-430, exit 8, just e to Breckenridge Rd, then just s. Int corridors. **Pets:** Medium, other species. Service with restrictions, supervision.
[ASK] [X] [🛏] [🖥]

▼▼ **La Quinta Inn Little Rock (West)** H ☂
(501) 224-0900. **$55-$79.** 200 S Shackleford Rd. I-430, exit 6; I-630, exit Shackleford Rd N; jct I-430 and 630. Ext corridors. **Pets:** Medium, other species. Service with restrictions, supervision.
[ASK] [X] [🛏] [🖥] [🏊]

▲▲▲ ▼▼▼ **Residence Inn by Marriott** H
(501) 312-0200. **$143-$175.** 1401 S Shackleford Rd. I-430, exit 5, just n. Int corridors. **Pets:** Medium. $100 one-time fee/room. Service with restrictions, supervision.
[SAVE] [X] [🛏] [🖥] [🏊] [X]

LONOKE

▲▲▲ ▼▼▼ **Days Inn** H
(501) 676-5138. **$60-$75.** 105 Dee Dee Ln. I-40, exit 175, just n. Ext corridors. **Pets:** Small, other species. $10 daily fee/pet. Designated rooms, service with restrictions, supervision.
[SAVE] [X] [🛏] [🖥] [🏊]

AAA **▽▽▽▽** Holiday Inn Express Hotel & Suites **H**
(501) 676-7800. **$99-$140.** 104 Dee Dee Ln. I-40, exit 175, just n. Int corridors. **Pets:** Small, other species. $25 one-time fee/room. Designated rooms, service with restrictions, supervision.
SAVE **✕** **🖒M** **🛈** **💷** **⊗**

AAA **▽▽▽▽** Super 8 **H**
(501) 676-8880. **$70-$80.** 102 Dee Dee Ln. I-40, exit 175, just n. Int corridors. **Pets:** Medium. $10 daily fee/pet. Designated rooms, service with restrictions, supervision.
SAVE **✕** **🛈** **💷** **⊗**

MARION

AAA **▽▽▽** Best Western-Regency Motor Inn **H**
(870) 739-3278. **$63-$66.** 3635 I-55. I-55, exit 10, just nw. Ext corridors. **Pets:** Medium. $5 daily fee/room. Service with restrictions, supervision.
SAVE **✕** **🛈** **💷** **⊗**

MCGEHEE

AAA **▽▽▽** Best Western McGehee **M**
(870) 222-3564. **$64-$71.** 1202 Hwy 65 N. Center. Ext corridors. **Pets:** Very small, dogs only. $5 daily fee/pet. Designated rooms, service with restrictions, supervision.
SAVE **✕** **🛈** **💷** **⊗**

MOUNTAIN HOME

AAA **▽▽▽** Comfort Inn **H** ❀
(870) 424-9000. **$64-$150, 3 day notice.** 1031 Highland Cir. 1.5 mi e on US 62B. Ext/int corridors. **Pets:** Small, dogs only. $25 one-time fee/room. Service with restrictions, supervision.
SAVE **✕** **🖒M** **🛈** **💷** **⊗**

▽▽▽ Days Inn **H**
(870) 425-1010. **$69-$77.** 1746 E Hwy 62B. On US 62B, 2.3 mi e. Int corridors. **Pets:** Small, other species. $8 daily fee/pet. Service with restrictions, crate.
ASK **✕** **🖒M** **🛈** **💷** **⊗**

▽▽▽▽ Holiday Inn Express **H**
(870) 425-6200. **Call for rates.** 1005 Coley Dr. 1.4 mi e on US 62B. Int corridors. **Pets:** Accepted.
✕ **🖒M** **🛈** **💷** **⊗**

▽▽▽ Super 8-Mountain Home **M**
(870) 424-5600. **$65.** 865 Hwy 62 E. On US 62B, 1.3 mi e. Int corridors. **Pets:** Accepted.
ASK **✕** **🛈** **💷**

AAA **▽▽▽▽** Teal Point Resort **CA**
(870) 492-5145. **$73-$399, 45 day notice.** 715 Teal Point Rd. 7 mi e on US 62, 0.6 mi n on CR 406, follow signs. Ext corridors. **Pets:** Other species. $7 daily fee/pet. Service with restrictions, supervision.
SAVE **🛈** **⊗** **✕** **🔇**

MOUNTAIN VIEW

AAA **▽▽▽** Best Western Fiddlers Inn **M**
(870) 269-2828. **$60-$90, 3 day notice.** 601 Sylomore Ave. 1 mi n on SR 5, 9 and 14. Ext corridors. **Pets:** Dogs only. $10 daily fee/pet. Service with restrictions, supervision.
SAVE **✕** **🛈** **💷** **⊗**

NORTH LITTLE ROCK

▽▽▽▽ Holiday Inn-North **H**
(501) 758-1851. **$120-$130.** 120 W Pershing Blvd. I-40, exit 152 westbound; exit 153A eastbound. Int corridors. **Pets:** Accepted.
ASK **✕** **🛈** **💷** **🍽** **⊗**

▽▽▽ La Quinta Inn **H** 🐾
(501) 758-8888. **$59-$85.** 4100 E McCain Blvd. Jct US 67/167, exit 1A northbound; exit 1 southbound. Ext corridors. **Pets:** Medium, other species. Service with restrictions, supervision.
ASK **✕** **🛈** **💷** **⊗**

▽▽▽ La Quinta Inn & Suites **H** 🐾
(501) 945-0808. **$75-$95.** 4311 Warden Rd. US 67/167, exit 1B northbound; exit 1 southbound. Int corridors. **Pets:** Medium, other species. Service with restrictions, supervision.
ASK **✕** **🛈** **💷** **⊗**

▽▽▽ Red Roof Inn **H**
(501) 945-0080. **$68-$85.** 5711 Pritchard Dr. I-40, exit 157, just s. Int corridors. **Pets:** Medium. Designated rooms, service with restrictions, crate.
ASK **✕** **🛈** **⊗**

▽▽▽▽ Residence Inn by Marriott-North **H**
(501) 945-7777. **$135-$165.** 4110 Healthcare Dr. I-40, exit 156. Int corridors. **Pets:** Accepted.
✕ **🛈** **💷** **⊗** **✕**

PINE BLUFF

AAA **▽▽▽▽** Best Western Presidential Hotel **H**
(870) 535-6300. **$62-$89.** 3104 Market St. I-530, exit 46, just n. Int corridors. **Pets:** Small, dogs only. $10 daily fee/pet. Service with restrictions, supervision.
SAVE **✕** **🛈** **💷** **⊗**

▽▽▽ Comfort Inn **H**
(870) 535-5300. **$55-$99.** 2809 Pines Mall Dr. I-530, exit 46, just n. Int corridors. **Pets:** Small. Service with restrictions, supervision.
ASK **✕** **🛈** **💷** **⊗**

▽▽▽ Days Inn & Suites **H**
(870) 534-1800. **Call for rates.** 406 N Blake St. Just n of jct US 65B and 79B. Ext corridors. **Pets:** Accepted.
✕ **🛈** **💷** **⊗**

▽▽▽▽ Holiday Inn Express Hotel & Suites **H** 🐾
(870) 879-3800. **Call for rates.** 3620 Camden Rd. I-530, exit 39, just sw. Int corridors. **Pets:** Small, other species. $25 one-time fee/room. Service with restrictions, supervision.
✕ **🖒M** **🛈** **💷** **⊗**

▽▽▽ La Quinta Inn & Suites **H** 🐾
(870) 850-7444. **Call for rates.** 3103 E Market St. I-530, exit 46, just n. Ext corridors. **Pets:** Medium, other species. Service with restrictions, supervision.
✕ **🖒M** **🛈** **💷** **⊗**

POCAHONTAS

▽▽▽ Days Inn & Suites **H**
(870) 892-9500. **Call for rates.** 2805 Hwy 67 S. 1.7 mi s. Int corridors. **Pets:** Accepted.
✕ **🛈** **💷** **⊗** **✕**

ROGERS

AAA **▽▽▽▽** aloft Rogers-Bentonville **H**
(479) 268-6799. **Call for rates.** 1103 S 52nd St. I-540, exit 83, just nw. Int corridors. **Pets:** Accepted.
SAVE **✕** **🛈** **💷** **⊗**

▽▽▽ Candlewood Suites **H**
(479) 636-2783. **$114-$133.** 4601 W Rozell St. I-540, exit 85, 0.5 mi n on 46th St. Int corridors. **Pets:** Accepted.
ASK **✕** **🛈** **💷** **⊗**

Embassy Suites Northwest Arkansas H ❀
(479) 254-8400. **$109-$259.** 3303 Pinnacle Hills Pkwy. I-540, exit 83, just w, then 0.6 mi s. Int corridors. **Pets:** Medium, other species. $75 one-time fee/room. Service with restrictions, crate.

Microtel Inn & Suites H
(479) 636-5551. **Call for rates.** 909 S 8th St. 0.5 mi s of jct Walnut St. Int corridors. **Pets:** Accepted.

Residence Inn by Marriott H
(479) 636-5900. **$134-$164.** 4611 W Locust St. I-540, exit 85, 0.4 mi n on 46th St. Int corridors. **Pets:** Medium. $75 one-time fee/room. Service with restrictions, crate.

RUSSELLVILLE

Holiday Inn H
(479) 968-4300. **$95-$125.** 2407 N Arkansas Ave. I-40, exit 81, just s. Ext corridors. **Pets:** Accepted.

Motel 6 Russellville #265 M
(479) 968-3666. **$45-$59.** 215 W Birch St. I-40, exit 81, just n. Ext corridors. **Pets:** Other species. Service with restrictions, supervision.

Quality Inn H
(479) 967-7500. **$65-$90.** 3019 E Parkway Dr. I-40, exit 84, just s. Ext corridors. **Pets:** Accepted.

SEARCY

Hampton Inn H
(501) 268-0654. **$89-$129.** 3204 E Race Ave. US 67, exit 46, just w. Ext/int corridors. **Pets:** Medium, other species. $25 daily fee/room. Designated rooms, service with restrictions, supervision.

SILOAM SPRINGS

Super 8 M
(479) 524-8898. **$63-$70.** 1800 Hwy 412 W. Center. Ext corridors. **Pets:** Very small, dogs only. $25 daily fee/room. Designated rooms, service with restrictions, supervision.

SPRINGDALE

Hampton Inn & Suites H
(479) 756-3500. **$84-$119.** 1700 S 48th St. I-540, exit 72, just e. Int corridors. **Pets:** Medium, other species. $50 one-time fee/room. Service with restrictions.

Holiday Inn Northwest AR Hotel & Convention Center H
(479) 751-8300. **$129, 14 day notice.** 1500 S 48th St. I-540, exit 72, just e on US 412. Int corridors. **Pets:** Accepted.

La Quinta Inn & Suites H ❀
(479) 751-2626. **Call for rates.** 1300 S 48th St. I-540, exit 72, just e. Int corridors. **Pets:** Medium, other species. Service with restrictions, supervision.

Residence Inn by Marriott H
(479) 872-9100. **$121-$147.** 1740 S 48th St. I-540, exit 72, just e to 48th St, then just s. Int corridors. **Pets:** Other species. $75 one-time fee/room. Service with restrictions, crate.

STAR CITY

Super 8-Star City H
(870) 628-6883. **Call for rates.** 1308 N Lincoln St. Just n on US 425. Int corridors. **Pets:** Accepted.

STUTTGART

Days Inn & Suites H
(870) 673-3616. **$77-$150.** 708 W Michigan St. Just w on US 63/79. Ext corridors. **Pets:** Small, other species. $10 daily fee/pet. Service with restrictions, crate.

TEXARKANA

La Crosse Hotel H
(870) 774-3521. **$109.** 5100 N State Line Ave. I-30, exit 223B, just n. Int corridors. **Pets:** Small. $50 one-time fee/pet. Designated rooms, service with restrictions, crate.

La Quinta Inn & Suites H ❀
(870) 773-1000. **$59-$89.** 5102 N State Line Ave. I-30, exit 223B, just n. Int corridors. **Pets:** Medium, other species. Service with restrictions, supervision.

TRUMANN

Days Inn & Suites H
(870) 483-8383. **$75.** 400 Commerce Dr. US 63, exit 29, just e. Ext/int corridors. **Pets:** Other species. $10 daily fee/pet. Service with restrictions, supervision.

VAN BUREN

Best Western Van Buren Inn H
(479) 474-8100. **$83, 7 day notice.** 1903 N 6th St. I-40, exit 5, just n. Ext corridors. **Pets:** Accepted.

WEST MEMPHIS

Best Western West Memphis Inn H
(870) 735-7185. **$73-$120, 7 day notice.** 3401 Service Loop Rd. I-55, exit 4, just nw. Int corridors. **Pets:** Very small. Service with restrictions, supervision.

CALIFORNIA

CITY INDEX

ALAMEDA

▼▼▼ **Extended StayAmerica Oakland-Alameda** H
(510) 864-1333. **$131-$141.** 1350 Marina Village Pkwy. I-880, exit Broadway W, through Webster Tube, s on Atlantic Ave, e on Challenger Dr, then s. Int corridors. **Pets:** Other species. $25 daily fee/pet. Service with restrictions, crate.

ASK ⊠ &M 🛁 💻

ALTURAS

ΔΔΔ ▼▼▼ **Best Western Trailside Inn** M
(530) 233-4111. **$90-$105.** 343 N Main St. Jct US 395 and W 4th St; center. Ext corridors. **Pets:** Small, dogs only. $10 daily fee/pet. Designated rooms, service with restrictions, supervision.

SAVE ⊠ 🛁 💻 ➤

ΔΔΔ ▼ **Rim Rock Motel** M
(530) 233-5455. **$58-$75.** Hwy 299. Jct SR 299 and US 395, 0.7 mi ne on US 395. Ext corridors. **Pets:** Very small, dogs only. $10 daily fee/pet. Designated rooms, service with restrictions, supervision.

SAVE ⊠ 🛁 💻

ANAHEIM

▼▼▼▼ **Anabella Hotel** H
(714) 905-1050. **$109-$369, 3 day notice.** 1030 W Katella Ave. I-5, exit 109 (Katella Ave/Disney Way) northbound; exit 109A (Katella Ave/ Orangewood Ave) southbound, 1.2 mi w. Ext corridors. **Pets:** Accepted.

ASK ⊠ 🛁 💻 🍴 ➤

▼▼▼▼ **Anaheim Candlewood Suites** H
(714) 808-9000. **$149-$199.** 1733 S Anaheim Blvd. I-5, exit 109 (Katella Ave/Disney Way) northbound; 109A (Katella Ave/Orangewood Ave) southbound, just w, then just n. Int corridors. **Pets:** Accepted.

ASK ⊠ &M 🛁 💻 🍴

▼▼▼ **Anaheim Plaza Hotel & Suites** H
(714) 772-5900. **$89-$218.** 1700 S Harbor Blvd. I-5, exit 110 (Harbor Blvd/Ball Rd) northbound; exit 110A (Harbor Blvd) southbound, 0.6 mi s. Ext corridors. **Pets:** Medium. $12 daily fee/pet. Designated rooms, service with restrictions, supervision.

ASK ⊠ 🛁 💻 🍴 ➤

ΔΔΔ ▼▼▼ **Clarion Hotel Anaheim Resort** H
(714) 750-3131. **$79-$209.** 616 Convention Way. I-5, exit 109 (Katella Ave/Disney Way) northbound; exit 109A (Katella Ave/Orangewood Ave) southbound, 0.8 mi w to Harbor Blvd, just s, then just w. Int corridors. **Pets:** Small, other species. $75 one-time fee/pet. Designated rooms, service with restrictions.

SAVE ⊠ 🛁 💻 🍴 ➤

▼▼▼ **Embassy Suites Hotel Anaheim-North** H ☀
(714) 632-1221. **$129-$249.** 3100 E Frontera St. SR 91, exit 31 (Kramer Blvd/Glasset St) eastbound; exit 32 westbound just s, then just e. Int corridors. **Pets:** Other species. $35 daily fee/room. Designated rooms, service with restrictions.

⊠ 🛁 💻 🍴 ➤

▼▼ **Extended StayAmerica-Orange County-Anaheim Convention Center** H
(714) 502-9988. **$76-$117.** 1742 S Clementine St. I-5, exit 109 (Katella Ave/Disney Way) northbound; exit 109A (Katella Ave/Orangewood Ave) southbound, just w, then just n. Int corridors. **Pets:** Other species. $25 daily fee/pet. Service with restrictions, crate.

ASK ⊠ 🛁 💻 ➤

▼▼ **Extended StayAmerica-Orange County-Anaheim Hills** H
(714) 630-4006. **$76-$117.** 1031 N Pacificenter Dr. SR 91, exit 33 (Tustin Ave), just n, then just w. Int corridors. **Pets:** Other species. $25 daily fee/pet. Service with restrictions, crate.

ASK ⊠ 🛁 💻

▼▼▼▼ **Hotel Menage** H
(714) 758-0900. **$129-$299.** 1221 S Harbor Blvd. I-5, exit 110 (Harbor Blvd/Ball Rd) northbound; exit 110A (Harbor Blvd) southbound, just n. Ext corridors. **Pets:** Accepted.

ASK ⊠ 💻 🍴 ➤

▼▼ **La Quinta Inn & Suites** H ☀
(714) 635-5000. **$59-$199.** 1752 S Clementine St. I-5, exit 109 (Katella Ave/Disney Way) northbound; exit 109A (Katella Ave/Orangewood Ave) southbound, just w, then just n. Int corridors. **Pets:** Medium, other species. Service with restrictions, supervision.

ASK ⊠ 🛁 💻 ➤ ✕

▼▼ **Lemon Tree Hotel** M
(714) 772-0200. **$89-$139.** 1600 E Lincoln Ave. I-5, exit 111 (Lincoln Ave), 2 mi e. Ext/int corridors. **Pets:** Small, dogs only. $15 daily fee/pet. Service with restrictions, supervision.

ASK ⊠ 🛁 💻 ➤

▼▼ **Motel 6 Anaheim-Maingate #1066** M
(714) 520-9696. **$73-$95.** 100 Disney Way. I-5, exit 109 (Katella Ave/ Disney Way) northbound; exit 109B (Disney Way/Anaheim Blvd) southbound, just w, just n on Anaheim Blvd, then just w on Disney Way. Ext corridors. **Pets:** Other species. Service with restrictions, supervision.

⊠ 🛁 ➤

▼▼▼▼ **Residence Inn by Marriott Anaheim Maingate** H ☀
(714) 533-3555. **$188-$230.** 1700 S Clementine St. I-5, exit 109 (Katella Ave/Disney Way) northbound; exit 109A (Katella Ave/Orangewood Ave) southbound, just w on Katella Ave, then just n. Ext corridors. **Pets:** Medium, other species. $100 one-time fee/room. Service with restrictions, crate.

⊠ &M 🛁 💻 ➤ ✕

ΔΔΔ ▼▼▼▼ **Sheraton Anaheim Hotel** H ☀
(714) 778-1700. **$145-$295.** 900 S Disneyland Dr. I-5, exit 110 (Harbor Blvd/Ball Rd) northbound; exit 110A (Harbor Blvd) southbound, just n on Harbor Blvd, just w on Ball Rd, then just n. Int corridors. **Pets:** Other species. $25 one-time fee/room. Service with restrictions, supervision.

SAVE ⊠ 🛁 💻 🍴 ➤ ✕

ΔΔΔ ▼▼▼▼ **Sheraton Park Hotel at the Anaheim Resort** H ☀
(714) 750-1811. **Call for rates.** 1855 S Harbor Blvd. I-5, exit 109 (Katella Ave/Disney Way) northbound; exit 109A (Katella Ave/Orangewood Ave) southbound, 0.8 mi w, then just s. Int corridors. **Pets:** Medium, dogs only. Designated rooms, service with restrictions, crate.

SAVE ⊠ 🛁 💻 ➤

▼▼▼▼ **Staybridge Suites by Holiday Inn-Anaheim Resort** H
(714) 748-7700. **Call for rates.** 1855 S Manchester Ave. I-5, exit 109 (Katella Ave/Disney Way) northbound; exit 109A (Katella Ave/Orangewood Ave) southbound, just w on Katella Ave, then 0.3 mi s; adjacent to west side of freeway. Int corridors. **Pets:** Accepted.

⊠ &M 🛁 💻 ➤ ✕

ΔΔΔ ▼▼▼ **TownePlace Suites By Marriott** M
(714) 939-9700. **$79-$179.** 1730 S State College Blvd. I-5, exit 109 (Katella Ave/Disney Way) northbound; exit 109A (Katella Ave/Orangewood Ave) southbound, 0.7 mi e, then just n. Int corridors. **Pets:** Accepted.

SAVE ⊠ 🛁 💻 ➤ ✕

ANAHEIM HILLS

ΔΔΔ ▼▼▼▼ **Best Western Anaheim Hills** M ☀
(714) 779-0252. **$74-$129.** 5710 E La Palma Ave. SR 91, exit 36 (SR 90 W/Imperial Hwy), 0.3 mi n. Ext/int corridors. **Pets:** Large, other species. $15 daily fee/pet. Service with restrictions.

SAVE ⊠ 🛁 💻 ➤ ✕

ANDERSON

AAA⁄ ▼▼▼ Best Western Knights Inn H
(530) 365-2753. **$65-$149.** 2688 Gateway Dr. I-5, exit 668 (Central Anderson) eastbound; exit Lassen Park westbound, just e. Ext corridors. **Pets:** Accepted.
[SAVE] [X] [H] [▯] [≈]

ANGELS CAMP

AAA⁄ ▼▼▼ Angels Inn Motel H
(209) 736-4242. **$109-$189.** 600 N Main St. SR 49, north end of town. Ext corridors. **Pets:** Dogs only. $50 deposit/room, $10 daily fee/pet. Designated rooms, service with restrictions, supervision.
[SAVE] [X] [H] [▯] [≈]

AAA⁄ ▼▼▼▼ Best Western Cedar Inn & Suites H ❀
(209) 736-4000. **$99-$329.** 444 S Main St. On SR 49; center. Ext/int corridors. **Pets:** $15 daily fee/pet. Designated rooms, service with restrictions, supervision.
[SAVE] [X] [&M] [H] [▯] [≈]

▼▼ Gold Country Inn M
(209) 736-4611. **$60-$190.** 720 S Main St. 1 mi s of jct SR 49 and 4. Ext corridors. **Pets:** $10 daily fee/pet. Service with restrictions, supervision.
[ASK] [X] [H] [▯]

AAA⁄ ▼▼ Jumping Frog Motel M
(209) 736-2191. **$60-$150, 3 day notice.** 330 Murphys Grade Rd. Just e of jct SR 49 and Murphys Grade Rd. Ext corridors. **Pets:** Small, dogs only. $10 daily fee/pet. Designated rooms, service with restrictions, supervision.
[SAVE] [X] [H] [▯]

ANTIOCH

AAA⁄ ▼▼▼▼ Best Western Heritage Inn H
(925) 778-2000. **$80-$88.** 3210 Delta Fair Blvd. SR 4, exit Somersville Rd. Ext corridors. **Pets:** $20 one-time fee/pet. Service with restrictions, supervision.
[SAVE] [X] [H] [▯] [≈]

APTOS

▼▼ Bayview Hotel CI
(831) 688-8654. **Call for rates.** 8041 Soquel Dr. SR 1, exit State Park Dr E, 0.8 mi s. Int corridors. **Pets:** Accepted.
[X] [Y]

ARCATA

AAA⁄ ▼ Arcata Super 8 H
(707) 822-8888. **Call for rates.** 4887 Valley West Blvd. US 101, exit Giuntoli Ln/Janes Rd, just e, then just s. Int corridors. **Pets:** Accepted.
[SAVE] [X] [H] [▯]

AAA⁄ ▼▼▼ Best Western Arcata Inn M ❀
(707) 826-0313. **$79-$169.** 4827 Valley West Blvd. US 101, exit Giuntoli Ln/Janes Rd, just e, then just s. Ext corridors. **Pets:** Dogs only. $20 one-time fee/room. Designated rooms, service with restrictions, supervision.
[SAVE] [X] [H] [▯] [≈]

AAA⁄ ▼▼▼ Comfort Inn M ❀
(707) 826-2827. **$65-$185.** 4701 Valley West Blvd. US 101, exit Giuntoli Ln/Janes Rd, just e, then 0.3 mi s. Ext corridors. **Pets:** Medium, dogs only. $15 daily fee/pet. Designated rooms, service with restrictions, supervision.
[SAVE] [X] [&M] [H] [▯] [≈]

▼▼ Days Inn H
(707) 822-4861. **Call for rates.** 4975 Valley West Blvd. US 101, exit Giuntoli Ln/Janes Rd, just e, then s. Int corridors. **Pets:** Large. $35 one-time fee/pet. Service with restrictions, supervision.
[X] [H] [▯] [Y] [≈]

AAA⁄ ▼▼▼ Quality Inn Arcata H
(707) 822-0409. **$94-$200.** 3535 Janes Rd. US 101, exit Giuntoli Ln/Janes Rd, just w. Int corridors. **Pets:** Accepted.
[SAVE] [X] [H] [▯] [≈] [X]

ARROYO GRANDE

AAA⁄ ▼▼▼ Premier Inns M
(805) 481-4774. **$40-$80.** 555 Camino Mercado. US 101, exit 188 (Oak Park Rd), just e, then 0.3 mi s. Ext corridors. **Pets:** Accepted.
[SAVE] [X] [H] [≈]

AUBURN

AAA⁄ ▼▼▼▼ Best Western Golden Key H ❀
(530) 885-8611. **$85-$160.** 13450 Lincoln Way. I-80, exit 121 (Foresthill-Auburn Ravine rds), just e, then n. Ext corridors. **Pets:** Other species. $15 one-time fee/pet. Designated rooms, service with restrictions, supervision.
[SAVE] [X] [&M] [H] [▯] [≈]

AAA⁄ ▼▼ Foothills Motel M
(530) 885-8444. **$65-$98.** 13431 Bowman Rd. I-80, exit 121 (Foresthill-Auburn Ravine rds), just w, then just n. Ext corridors. **Pets:** Dogs only. $50 deposit/room, $10 daily fee/room. Designated rooms, service with restrictions, supervision.
[SAVE] [X] [&M] [H] [▯] [≈]

AAA⁄ ▼▼▼▼ Holiday Inn-Auburn H
(530) 887-8787. **$139-$179.** 120 Grass Valley Hwy. I-80, exit SR 49, just nw. Int corridors. **Pets:** Accepted.
[SAVE] [X] [&M] [H] [▯] [Y] [≈]

▼ Motel 6 #4152 M
(530) 888-7829. **Call for rates.** 1819 Auburn Ravine Rd. I-80, exit 121 (Foresthill-Auburn Ravine rds), just w. Int corridors. **Pets:** Other species. Service with restrictions, supervision.
[X] [&M] [H] [≈]

AAA⁄ ▼▼▼ Travelodge M
(530) 885-7025. **$70-$140.** 13490 Lincoln Way. I-80, exit 121 (Foresthill-Auburn Ravine rds), just e, then just n. Ext/int corridors. **Pets:** Very small. $15 daily fee/pet. Designated rooms, service with restrictions, supervision.
[SAVE] [X] [&M] [H] [▯] [≈]

AVILA BEACH

▼▼▼ Avila Village Inn H ❀
(805) 627-1810. **$150-$350.** 6655 Bay Laurel Dr. US 101, exit 195 (Avila Beach Dr), 1.2 mi w to San Luis Bay Dr, just n, then just w. Int corridors. **Pets:** Medium, other species. $25 daily fee/room. Designated rooms, service with restrictions, supervision.
[ASK] [X] [&M] [H] [▯]

BAKERSFIELD

AAA⁄ ▼▼▼ Bakersfield Red Lion Hotel H
(661) 327-0681. **$99-$139.** 2400 Camino Del Rio Ct. SR 99, exit 26 (SR 58 W/Rosedale Hwy), just w, then just s. Ext/int corridors. **Pets:** Other species. $20 one-time fee/room. Service with restrictions, supervision.
[SAVE] [X] [H] [▯] [Y] [≈]

AAA⁄ ▼▼▼ Best Western Crystal Palace Inn & Suites H
(661) 327-9651. **$77-$110, 3 day notice.** 2620 Buck Owens Blvd. SR 99, exit 26B (Buck Owens Blvd) northbound, just s; exit 26 (SR 58 W/SR 178 E) southbound, just e, then just n. Int corridors. **Pets:** Other species. $10 daily fee/room. Designated rooms, service with restrictions, supervision.
[SAVE] [X] [&M] [H] [▯] [Y] [≈]

AAA⁄ ▼▼▼ Best Western Heritage Inn M
(661) 764-6268. **$85-$95.** 253 Trask St. I-5, exit 253 (Stockdale Hwy), just e. Ext corridors. **Pets:** Small. $10 daily fee/pet. Designated rooms, service with restrictions, supervision.
[SAVE] [X] [&M] [H] [▯] [≈]

Best Western Hill House 🅷 ❀
(661) 327-4064. **$89-$149, 3 day notice.** 700 Truxton Ave. SR 99, exit 25 (California Ave), 1.2 mi e, 0.4 mi n on Chester Ave, then 0.4 mi e. Int corridors. **Pets:** Medium. $15 daily fee/pet. Designated rooms, service with restrictions, supervision.
SAVE ⊠ 🛢 💻 🍴 ⊇

California Best Inn Ⓜ
(661) 834-3377. **$59-$69.** 1030 Wible Rd. SR 99, exit 23 (Ming Ave), just e, then 0.7 mi n. Ext corridors. **Pets:** Large. $10 daily fee/pet. Service with restrictions, supervision.
SAVE ⊠ 🛢 💻 ⊇

DoubleTree Hotel Bakersfield 🅷 ❀
(661) 323-7111. **$120-$205.** 3100 Camino Del Rio Ct. SR 99, exit 26 (SR 58 W/Rosedale Hwy), just w, then just s. Int corridors. **Pets:** Other species. $50 one-time fee/room. Service with restrictions, supervision.
⊠ 🐾ᴹ 🛢 💻 🍴 ⊇ ⊠

Extended StayAmerica-Bakersfield-California Avenue 🅷
(661) 322-6888. **$65-$86.** 3318 California Ave. SR 99, exit 25 (California Ave), on east side of freeway, just n. Int corridors. **Pets:** Other species. $25 daily fee/pet. Service with restrictions, crate.
ASK ⊠ 🛢 💻

Extended Stay Deluxe 🅷
(661) 328-8181. **$100-$126.** 3600 Chester Ln. SR 99, exit 25 (California Ave), just w to Real Rd, just s, then just w. Int corridors. **Pets:** Other species. $25 daily fee/pet. Service with restrictions, crate.
ASK ⊠ 🛢 💻

La Quinta Inn & Suites 🅷 ❀
(661) 393-7775. **$93-$125.** 8858 Spectrum Park Way. SR 99, exit 30 (SR 65) northbound, just n to 7th Standard Rd, just w, then just s; exit 31 (7th Standard Rd) southbound, just e, then just s. Int corridors. **Pets:** Medium, other species. Service with restrictions, supervision.
SAVE ⊠ 🐾ᴹ 🛢 💻 ⊇

La Quinta Inn Bakersfield Ⓜ ❀
(661) 325-7400. **$49-$139.** 3232 Riverside Dr. SR 99, exit 26B (SR 58 W/Rosedale Hwy) southbound, just e, then just n; exit 26B (Buck Owens Blvd) northbound, just s. Ext corridors. **Pets:** Medium, other species. Service with restrictions, supervision.
ASK ⊠ 🐾ᴹ 🛢 💻 ⊇

Ramada Limited-Central Ⓜ ❀
(661) 831-1922. **$59-$199.** 830 Wible Rd. SR 99, exit 23 (Ming Ave), just e, then 0.8 mi n. Ext corridors. **Pets:** Medium. $10 daily fee/pet, $10 one-time fee/pet. Service with restrictions, supervision.
SAVE ⊠ 🛢 💻 ⊇

Residence Inn by Marriott 🅷 ❀
(661) 321-9800. **$161-$197.** 4241 Chester Ln. SR 99, exit 25 (California Ave), 0.5 mi w, then just n. Ext corridors. **Pets:** Other species. $100 one-time fee/room. Service with restrictions, supervision.
⊠ 🛢 💻 ⊇ ⊠

Rodeway Inn Ⓜ
(661) 764-5221. **$65-$75.** 200 Trask St. I-5, exit 253 (Stockdale Hwy), just e. Ext corridors. **Pets:** Medium, other species. $5 daily fee/pet. Service with restrictions, supervision.
SAVE ⊠ 🛢 💻 ⊇

Sleep Inn 🅷
(661) 399-2100. **$69-$189.** 6257 Knudson Dr. SR 99, exit 28 (Olive Dr), just w, then just n. Int corridors. **Pets:** $10 daily fee/pet. Service with restrictions, crate.
SAVE ⊠ 🐾ᴹ 🛢 💻

Super 8 Ⓜ
(661) 833-1000. **$55-$85.** 3620 Wible Rd. SR 99, exit 21 (White Ln), just w, then 0.3 mi n. Ext corridors. **Pets:** Small, other species. $5 daily fee/pet. Service with restrictions, supervision.
SAVE ⊠ 🛢 💻 ⊇

Super 8 Bakersfield Ⓜ
(661) 322-1012. **$65-$85.** 901 Real Rd. SR 99, exit 25 (California Ave), just w, then just s. Ext corridors. **Pets:** Small. $10 daily fee/pet. Designated rooms, service with restrictions, supervision.
SAVE ⊠ 🛢 💻 ⊇

Travelodge of Bakersfield Ⓜ
(661) 325-0772. **$64-$72.** 1011 Oak St. SR 99, exit 25 (California Ave), just e, then just s. Ext/int corridors. **Pets:** Other species. $10 daily fee/pet. Designated rooms, service with restrictions, supervision.
ASK ⊠ 🛢 💻 ⊇

Vagabond Inn South Ⓜ
(661) 831-9200. **$45-$65.** 6501 Colony St. SR 99, exit 20 (Panama Ln), just e, then just s. Ext corridors. **Pets:** Accepted.
SAVE ⊠ 🛢 💻 ⊇

BANNING

Banning Travelodge Ⓜ
(951) 849-1000. **$66-$299.** 1700 W Ramsey St. I-10, exit 99 (22nd St), just n, then 0.5 mi e. Ext corridors. **Pets:** Medium, dogs only. $10 daily fee/pet. Designated rooms, service with restrictions, supervision.
SAVE ⊠ 🛢 💻 ⊇

Days Inn Ⓜ
(951) 849-0092. **Call for rates.** 2320 W Ramsey St. I-10, exit 99 (22nd St), just n, then just w. Ext corridors. **Pets:** Accepted.
⊠ 🛢 💻

Super 8 Ⓜ
(951) 849-8888. **$66-$300.** 1690 W Ramsey St. I-10, exit 99 (22nd St), just n, then 0.4 mi e. Int corridors. **Pets:** Medium, dogs only. $10 daily fee/pet. Designated rooms, service with restrictions, supervision.
SAVE ⊠ 🛢 💻 ⊇

BARSTOW

Barstow-Super 8 Ⓜ
(760) 256-8443. **$72-$77.** 170 Coolwater Ln. I-15, exit 184B (E Main St) northbound; exit 184 (E Main St/I-40 E/Needles) southbound, 0.3 mi w, then just s; I-40 westbound, exit 1 (E Main St), 0.7 mi w, then just s. Ext corridors. **Pets:** Large, other species. $5 daily fee/pet. Service with restrictions, supervision.
SAVE ⊠ 🛢 💻 ⊇

Best Western Desert Villa Inn Ⓜ
(760) 256-1781. **$72-$129, 3 day notice.** 1984 E Main St. I-15, exit 184B (E Main St) northbound; exit 184 (E Main St/I-40/Needles) southbound, 0.5 mi e; I-40 westbound, exit 1 (E Main St), just w. Ext corridors. **Pets:** $15 daily fee/pet. Supervision.
SAVE ⊠ 🐾ᴹ 🛢 💻 ⊇

Days Inn Ⓜ
(760) 256-1737. **$59-$69.** 1590 Coolwater Ln. I-15, exit 184B (E Main St) northbound; exit 184 (E Main St/I-40 E/Needles) southbound, just w, then just s; I-40, exit 1 (E Main St) westbound, 0.7 mi w, then just s. Ext corridors. **Pets:** Accepted.
SAVE ⊠ 🛢 💻 ⊇

Days Inn South at Lenwood Ⓜ
(760) 253-2121. **Call for rates.** 2551 Commerce Pkwy. I-15, exit 178 (Lenwood Rd), just w; 8 mi s of town. Ext corridors. **Pets:** Medium. $5 daily fee/pet. Service with restrictions, supervision.
SAVE ⊠ 🛢 ⊇

Hampton Inn & Suites 🅷
(760) 253-2600. **$139-$159.** 2710 Lenwood Rd. I-15, exit 178 (Lenwood Rd), just e, then 0.4 mi s. Int corridors. **Pets:** Other species. Service with restrictions, crate.
⊠ 🐾ᴹ 💻 ⊇

▼▼▼ Holiday Inn Express, Barstow-Historic Route 66 **H**
(760) 256-1300. **$72-$119.** 1861 W Main St. I-15, exit 181 (L St), 0.5 mi n, then just e. Int corridors. **Pets:** Accepted.
ASK ✕ 🛢 💻 🏊

▼▼▼ Holiday Inn Express Hotel & Suites **H**
(760) 253-9200. **$155-$202.** 2700 Lenwood Rd. I-15, exit 178 (Lenwood Rd), just e, then 0.5 mi s. Int corridors. **Pets:** Other species. $25 deposit/room. Supervision.
✕ ⓜ 🛢 💻 🏊 ✕

▼ Motel 6 Barstow #1355 **M**
(760) 256-1752. **$45-$55.** 150 N Yucca Ave. I-15, exit 184B (E Main St) northbound; exit 184 (E Main St/I-40 E/Needles) southbound, 0.5 mi w, then just n; I-40, exit 1 (E Main St) westbound, 1 mi w, then just n. Ext corridors. **Pets:** Other species. Service with restrictions, supervision.
✕ 🏊

🅰🅰🅰 ▼▼▼ Quality Inn **M**
(760) 256-6891. **$89-$190.** 1520 E Main St. I-15, exit 184B (E Main St) northbound; exit 184 (E Main St/I-40 E/Needles) southbound, 0.3 mi w; I-40, exit 1 (E Main St) westbound, 0.8 mi w. Ext corridors. **Pets:** Accepted.
SAVE ✕ 🛢 💻 🍴 🏊

▼▼▼ Ramada Inn **H**
(760) 256-5673. **$95-$120.** 1511 E Main St. I-15, exit 184B (E Main St) northbound; exit 184 (E Main St/I-40 E/Needles) southbound, 0.3 mi w; I-40, exit 1 (E Main St) westbound, 0.8 mi w. Int corridors. **Pets:** Medium. $20 one-time fee/room. Service with restrictions, supervision.
ASK ✕ 🛢 💻 🍴 🏊

🅰🅰🅰 ▼▼▼ Rodeway Inn **M**
(760) 256-7581. **$43-$80.** 1261 E Main St. I-15, exit 184B (E Main St) northbound; exit 184 (E Main St/I-40 E/Needles) southbound, 0.8 mi w; I-40, exit 1 (E Main St) westbound, 1.3 mi w. Ext corridors. **Pets:** Accepted.
SAVE ✕ 🛢 🏊

🅰🅰🅰 ▼ Stardust Inn **M**
(760) 256-7116. **$40-$60.** 901 E Main St. I-15, exit 183 (Barstow Rd), 0.8 mi n, then 0.4 mi e. Ext corridors. **Pets:** Small, dogs only. $5 daily fee/pet. Designated rooms, service with restrictions, supervision.
SAVE ✕ 🛢 🏊

▼ Travelodge **M**
(760) 256-8931. **$55-$85.** 1630 E Main St. I-15, exit 184B (E Main St) northbound; exit 184 (E Main St/I-40 E/Needles) southbound, just e; I-40 westbound, exit 1 (E Main St), just w. Ext corridors. **Pets:** Accepted.
ASK ✕ 🛢 🏊

BASS LAKE

▼▼ The Pines Resort Chalets **CA**
(559) 642-3121. **$119-$369, 7 day notice.** 54432 Rd 432. 6 mi e of SR 41, exit CR 222, e on CR 274, then s on CR 434. Ext corridors. **Pets:** Accepted.
ASK ✕ 🛢 💻 🍴 🏊 ✕

BEAUMONT

🅰🅰🅰 ▼ Americas Best Value Inn **M**
(951) 845-2185. **$70-$199.** 625 E 5th St. I-10, exit 94 (SR 79/Beaumont Ave), just n. Ext corridors. **Pets:** Medium. $5 daily fee/pet. Service with restrictions, supervision.
SAVE ✕ 🛢 🏊

🅰🅰🅰 ▼▼▼ Best Western El Rancho Motor Inn **M**
(951) 845-2176. **$86-$105.** 480 E 5th St. I-10, exit 94 (SR 79/Beaumont Ave), just n, then just e. Ext corridors. **Pets:** Small. $25 daily fee/pet. Service with restrictions, supervision.
SAVE ✕ 🛢 💻 🍴 🏊

BENICIA

🅰🅰🅰 ▼▼▼ Best Western Heritage Inn **H**
(707) 746-0401. **$109-$159, 3 day notice.** 1955 E 2nd St. I-780, exit Central Benicia/E 2nd St, just e. Int corridors. **Pets:** Accepted.
SAVE ✕ 🛢 💻 🏊

BEN LOMOND

🅰🅰🅰 ▼▼▼ Coast Redwood Inn & Suites **M** 🐾
(831) 336-2292. **$70-$230, 7 day notice.** 9733 Hwy 9. SR 9, 0.3 mi n; on San Lorenzo River. Ext corridors. **Pets:** Small, dogs only. $10 daily fee/pet, $25 one-time fee/pet. Designated rooms, service with restrictions, supervision.
SAVE ✕ 🛢 💻 🏊

BERKELEY

🅰🅰🅰 ▼ Best Value Golden Bear Inn **M**
(510) 525-6770. **$80-$160.** 1620 San Pablo Ave. I-80, exit Gilman E, 2 mi s. Ext corridors. **Pets:** Other species. $10 daily fee/pet. Service with restrictions, supervision.
SAVE ✕ 🛢 💻

🅰🅰🅰 ▼▼▼ Claremont Resort and Spa **H**
(510) 843-3000. **$209-$389.** 41 Tunnel Rd. SR 13 and 24, exit SR 24 (Claremont Ave), 1 mi n; in Berkeley Hills. Int corridors. **Pets:** Medium, dogs only. $99 one-time fee/pet. Designated rooms, service with restrictions, crate.
SAVE ✕ 💻 🍴 🏊 ✕

🅰🅰🅰 ▼▼▼ Hotel Durant **H**
(510) 845-8981. **Call for rates.** 2600 Durant Ave. E off I-80 on Ashby to Telegraph, n to Durant Ave; westbound from SR 13 and 24, exit Berkeley, w on Ashby to Telegraph, then n to Durant Ave at Bowditch. Int corridors. **Pets:** Accepted.
SAVE ✕ 🛢 💻 🍴

BERRY CREEK

▼▼▼ Lake Oroville Bed & Breakfast **BB** 🐾
(530) 589-0700. **$145-$200, 5 day notice.** 240 Sunday Dr. From Oroville; follow SR 162, 15 mi e to Bell Ranch Rd, then 1.4 mi nw. Int corridors. **Pets:** Other species. $25 daily fee/pet. Supervision.
ASK ✕ ⓜ

BIG BEAR LAKE

▼▼ Bear Manor Cabins **CA**
(909) 866-6800. **$89-$399, 30 day notice.** 40393 Big Bear Blvd. SR 18, 0.8 mi w of village. Ext corridors. **Pets:** Small, dogs only. $150 deposit/room. Designated rooms, no service, supervision.
✕ 🛢 💻 🎾

🅰🅰🅰 ▼ Big Bear Lakefront Lodge **M**
(909) 866-8271. **Call for rates.** 40360 Lakeview Dr. SR 18, 0.5 mi w of Pine Knot Ave, 0.5 mi nw. Ext/int corridors. **Pets:** Accepted.
SAVE ✕ 🛢 💻 ✕ 🎾 🐕

▼▼ Cozy Hollow Lodge **CA**
(909) 866-9694. **$59-$189, 15 day notice.** 40409 Big Bear Blvd. SR 18, 0.8 mi w. Ext corridors. **Pets:** Accepted.
ASK ✕ 🛢 💻 🎾

▼▼ Eagle's Nest Bed & Breakfast **BB**
(909) 866-6465. **$120-$185, 5 day notice.** 41675 Big Bear Blvd. SR 18, 1 mi e of Pine Knot Ave. Ext/int corridors. **Pets:** Accepted.
ASK ✕ 🛢 💻

▼▼ Golden Bear Cottages **CA**
(909) 866-2010. **$99-$799, 90 day notice.** 39367 Big Bear Blvd. SR 18, 2 mi w of village. Ext corridors. **Pets:** Accepted.
ASK ✕ 🛢 💻 🏊 ✕ 🎾

Grey Squirrel Resort 🅲🅰 ❖
(909) 866-4335. **$94, 14 day notice.** 39372 Big Bear Blvd. SR 18, 2.5 mi w of village. Ext corridors. **Pets:** Cats only. $10 daily fee/pet. Service with restrictions, supervision.

Pine Knot Guest Ranch 🅲🅰 ❖
(909) 866-6500. **$89-$199.** 908 Pine Knot Ave. Just s of SR 18 and downtown area. Ext corridors. **Pets:** Other species. $10 daily fee/pet. Service with restrictions.

Sleepy Forest Cottages 🅲🅰
(909) 866-7444. **$99-$299, 15 day notice.** 426 Eureka Dr. SR 18, 0.7 mi e of Pine Knot Ave, then just n. Ext corridors. **Pets:** Accepted.

Timber Haven Lodge 🅲🅰 ❖
(909) 866-7207. **$99-$320, 7 day notice.** 877 Tulip Ln. SR 18, 1.8 mi w of Pine Knot Ave, 0.4 mi s. Ext corridors. **Pets:** Dogs only. $20 daily fee/pet. Designated rooms, service with restrictions, supervision.

BIG PINE

Big Pine Motel Ⓜ
(760) 938-2282. **Call for rates.** 370 S Main St. On US 395. Ext corridors. **Pets:** Accepted.

Bristlecone Motel Ⓜ 🐾
(760) 938-2067. **$55-$80.** 101 N Main St. On US 395. Ext corridors. **Pets:** Other species. $5 daily fee/room. Service with restrictions, supervision.

BISHOP

Best Western Bishop Holiday Spa Lodge Ⓜ
(760) 873-3543. **$85-$300.** 1025 N Main St. On US 395. **Pets:** Accepted.

Comfort Inn Ⓜ
(760) 873-4284. **Call for rates.** 805 N Main St. On US 395. Ext corridors. **Pets:** Accepted.

Holiday Inn Express Hotel & Suites 🅷
(760) 872-2423. **$109-$279.** 636 N Main St. On US 395. Int corridors. **Pets:** Medium, dogs only. $25 daily fee/pet. Designated rooms, service with restrictions, supervision.

La Quinta Inn-Bishop 🅷 ❖
(760) 873-6380. **$90-$260.** 651 N Main St. On US 395. Int corridors. **Pets:** Medium, other species. Service with restrictions, supervision.

Motel 6-#4094 Ⓜ
(760) 873-8426. **Call for rates.** 1005 N Main St. On US 395. **Pets:** Other species. Service with restrictions, supervision.

Ramada Limited Ⓜ
(760) 872-1771. **$80-$150.** 155 E Elm St. On US 395, just e. **Pets:** Accepted.

Rodeway Inn Ⓜ
(760) 873-3564. **$70-$150.** 150 E Elm St. On US 395, just e. Ext/int corridors. **Pets:** Large. $5 daily fee/room. Service with restrictions, crate.

Super 8 Ⓜ
(760) 872-1386. **Call for rates.** 535 S Main St. On US 395. Ext corridors. **Pets:** Accepted.

Thunderbird Motel Ⓜ
(760) 873-4215. **$50-$120.** 190 W Pine St. Just w of US 395. Ext corridors. **Pets:** Accepted.

Vagabond Inn Ⓜ
(760) 873-6351. **$80-$150.** 1030 N Main St. On US 395. Ext corridors. **Pets:** Accepted.

BLYTHE

Best Western Sahara Motel Ⓜ
(760) 922-7105. **$89-$169.** 825 W Hobsonway. I-10, exit 239 (Lovekin Blvd), just n, then just w. Ext corridors. **Pets:** Small. $10 one-time fee/room. Service with restrictions, supervision.

Comfort Suites Ⓜ
(760) 922-9209. **$80-$150.** 545 E Hobsonway. I-10, exit 240 (7th St), just n, then just w. Ext corridors. **Pets:** Accepted.

Days Inn Ⓜ
(760) 922-5101. **$69-$179.** 9274 E Hobsonway. I-10, exit 241 (Intake Blvd), just n, then just w. Ext corridors. **Pets:** Medium. $10 one-time fee/room. Service with restrictions, crate.

Regency Inn & Suites Ⓜ
(760) 922-4146. **$89-$169.** 903 W Hobsonway. I-10, exit 239 (Lovekin Blvd), just n, then just w. Ext corridors. **Pets:** Accepted.

Super 8 Ⓜ
(760) 922-8881. **$70-$140.** 550 W Donlon St. I-10, exit 239 (Lovekin Blvd), just e. Int corridors. **Pets:** Medium, other species. $10 daily fee/pet. No service, supervision.

Travelers Inn Express Ⓜ
(760) 922-3334. **$59-$149, 3 day notice.** 1781 E Hobsonway. I-10, exit 241 (Intake Blvd), just n, then just w. Ext corridors. **Pets:** Medium, other species. $10 daily fee/room. Designated rooms, service with restrictions, supervision.

BORREGO SPRINGS

Borrego Ranch Resort & Spa 🅷 🐾
(760) 767-5323. **$240-$785, 3 day notice.** 3845 Yaqui Pass Rd. 5.5 mi se on CR S-3; jct Yaqui Pass and Borrego Springs rds. Ext corridors. **Pets:** Medium, dogs only. $150 one-time fee/room. Designated rooms, service with restrictions.

Borrego Springs Resort Hotel 🅷
(760) 767-5700. **$100-$175.** 1112 Tilting T Dr. SR 22, 1.5 mi s on Borrego Valley Rd, just w. Int corridors. **Pets:** Accepted.

BREA

Homestead Studio Suites Hotel-Orange County-Brea Ⓜ
(714) 528-2500. **$79-$129.** 3050 E Imperial Hwy. SR 57, exit 9 (SR 90), 1.4 mi e on Imperial Hwy. Ext corridors. **Pets:** Other species. $25 daily fee/pet. Service with restrictions, crate.

Woodfin Suite Hotel M
(714) 579-3200. **$129-$299.** 3100 E Imperial Hwy. SR 57, exit 9 (SR 90), 1.5 mi e on Imperial Hwy. Ext corridors. **Pets:** Accepted.
[SAVE] [X] [i] [P] [≈]

BRIDGEPORT

Redwood Motel M ❀
(760) 932-7060. **$59-$250.** 425 Main St. On US 395; on north side of town. Ext corridors. **Pets:** Large. $10 daily fee/pet. Designated rooms, service with restrictions, supervision.
[SAVE] [X] [i] [P]

Ruby Inn M ❀
(760) 932-7241. **$125-$200.** 333 Main St. On US 395; center. Ext corridors. **Pets:** Medium, dogs only. Service with restrictions, supervision.
[SAVE] [X] [i] [P]

Silver Maple Inn M
(760) 932-7383. **$70-$120.** 310 Main St. On US 395; center. Ext corridors. **Pets:** Other species. Supervision.
[SAVE] [X] [i] [P] [♬]

Walker River Lodge M ❀
(760) 932-7021. **$70-$220.** 100 Main St. On US 395; at south end of town. Ext corridors. **Pets:** Other species. Supervision.
[SAVE] [X] [i] [P] [≈]

BUELLTON

Quality Inn Solvang/Buellton M
(805) 688-0022. **Call for rates.** 630 Ave of the Flags. US 101, exit 140B (Ave of the Flags) southbound, just s; exit 140A (SR 246) northbound, just w, then just n. Ext/int corridors. **Pets:** Accepted.
[SAVE] [X] [i] [P]

Santa Ynez Valley Marriott H ❀
(805) 688-1000. **$149-$169.** 555 McMurray Rd. US 101, exit 140A (SR 246), just e, then just n. Int corridors. **Pets:** Large, other species. $75 one-time fee/room. Designated rooms, service with restrictions.
[SAVE] [X] [i] [P] [♬] [≈] [X]

BUENA PARK

Red Roof Inn M
(714) 670-9000. **$60-$100.** 7121 Beach Blvd. SR 91, exit 23B (Beach Blvd/SR 39), just n. Ext corridors. **Pets:** Accepted.
[SAVE] [X] [i] [≈] [X]

BURNEY

Charm Motel M ❀
(530) 335-2254. **$69-$99, 3 day notice.** 37363 Main St. Jct Hudson St and SR 299, 0.5 mi ne on SR 299; town center. Ext corridors. **Pets:** Other species. $10 daily fee/pet. Service with restrictions, supervision.
[SAVE] [X] [i] [P]

Green Gables Motel M ❀
(530) 335-2264. **$69-$129, 3 day notice.** 37385 Main St. Jct Hudson St and SR 299, 0.5 mi ne on SR 299; town center. Ext corridors. **Pets:** Other species. $10 daily fee/pet. Service with restrictions, supervision.
[SAVE] [X] [i] [P] [≈]

BUTTONWILLOW

Super 8 Motel M
(661) 764-5117. **Call for rates.** 20681 Tracy Ave. I-5, exit 257 (SR 58), just e, then just n. Ext corridors. **Pets:** Accepted.
[X] [♬] [i] [P] [≈]

CALEXICO

Best Western John Jay Inn M
(760) 768-0442. **$89-$124, 30 day notice.** 2421 Scaroni Rd. I-8, exit 118A (SR 111 S), 5.5 mi s, just w on W Cole Rd, then just n. Int corridors. **Pets:** Dogs only. $100 deposit/room, $10 daily fee/pet. Designated rooms, service with restrictions, supervision.
[SAVE] [X] [♬] [i] [P] [≈]

CALIMESA

Calimesa Inn Motel M
(909) 795-2536. **$60-$150.** 1205 Calimesa Blvd. I-10, exit 88 (Calimesa Blvd), just ne. Ext corridors. **Pets:** Small. $25 daily fee/pet. Designated rooms, service with restrictions, supervision.
[SAVE] [X] [i] [P] [≈]

CALIPATRIA

Calipatria Inn & Suites M
(760) 348-7348. **$100-$135.** 700 N Sorenson Ave. On SR 111. Ext corridors. **Pets:** $20 one-time fee/room. Service with restrictions, supervision.
[SAVE] [X] [i] [P] [♬] [≈]

CAMBRIA

Blue Dolphin Inn H
(805) 927-3300. **$122-$333.** 6470 Moonstone Beach Dr. SR 1, exit Moonstone Beach Dr, 0.7 mi n. Int corridors. **Pets:** Accepted.
[ASK] [X] [i] [P] [♬]

Cambria Shores Inn M ❀
(805) 927-8644. **$150-$350, 7 day notice.** 6276 Moonstone Beach Dr. SR 1, exit Moonstone Beach Dr, just w, then 0.8 mi s. Ext corridors. **Pets:** Dogs only. $15 daily fee/pet. Supervision.
[X] [i] [P]

Fog Catcher Inn M ❀
(805) 927-1400. **$139-$500.** 6400 Moonstone Beach Dr. SR 1, exit Moonstone Beach Dr, just w, then 0.7 mi s. Ext corridors. **Pets:** $25 daily fee/room. Designated rooms, service with restrictions.
[ASK] [X] [i] [P] [≈] [♬]

Mariners Inn by the Sea M ❀
(805) 927-4624. **$89-$289, 3 day notice.** 6180 Moonstone Beach Dr. SR 1, exit Moonstone Beach Dr, just w, then 1 mi s. Ext corridors. **Pets:** Dogs only. $15 daily fee/pet. Designated rooms, service with restrictions, supervision.
[SAVE] [X] [i] [♬]

Sand Pebbles Inn H
(805) 927-5600. **$109-$299.** 6252 Moonstone Beach Dr. SR 1, exit Moonstone Beach Dr, just w, then 0.9 mi s. Int corridors. **Pets:** Accepted.
[ASK] [X] [i] [P] [♬]

Sea Otter Inn M
(805) 927-5888. **$99-$299, 3 day notice.** 6656 Moonstone Beach Dr. SR 1, exit Moonstone Beach Dr, just w, then 0.5 mi s. Ext corridors. **Pets:** $25 daily fee/pet. Designated rooms, service with restrictions, supervision.
[ASK] [X] [i] [P] [≈] [♬]

CAMPBELL

Larkspur Landing Campbell H
(408) 364-1514. **$99-$199.** 550 W Hamilton Ave. SR 17, exit Hamilton Ave, 1 mi w. Int corridors. **Pets:** Accepted.
[SAVE] [X] [♬] [i] [P]

Residence Inn by Marriott-San Jose H ❀
(408) 559-1551. **$188-$230.** 2761 S Bascom Ave. SR 17, exit Camden Ave E, just n. Ext corridors. **Pets:** Other species. $100 one-time fee/room. Service with restrictions, crate.
[X] [i] [P] [≈]

▼▼▼ TownePlace Suites by Marriott-San Jose/Campbell 🅷 ❀
(408) 370-4510. **$170-$208.** 700 E Campbell Ave. SR 17, exit Hamilton Ave E, 0.3 mi to Bascom Ave, 0.3 mi s, then 0.3 mi w. Int corridors. **Pets:** Other species. $75 one-time fee/room. Service with restrictions.

CARLSBAD

🆔 ▼▼▼▼▼ Four Seasons Resort Aviara 🅷 ❀
(760) 603-6800. **$405-$4800, 3 day notice.** 7100 Four Seasons Point. I-5, exit 45 (Poinsettia Ln/Aviara Pkwy), 1 mi e on Poinsettia Ln, then 1 mi s on Aviara Pkwy. Int corridors. **Pets:** Very small, dogs only. Service with restrictions, supervision.

🆔 ▼▼▼▼ Homewood Suites by Hilton Carlsbad-North San Diego County 🅷
(760) 431-2266. **$219-$249.** 2223 Palomar Airport Rd. I-5, exit 47 (Palomar Airport Rd), 3.1 mi e. Int corridors. **Pets:** Accepted.

▼▼▼▼ La Quinta Inn Carlsbad 🅼 ❀
(760) 438-2828. **$79-$199.** 760 Macadamia Dr. I-5, exit 45 (Poinsettia Ln/Aviara Pkwy), just w to Ave Encinas, just n, then just e. Ext corridors. **Pets:** Medium, other species. Service with restrictions, supervision.

▼▼▼▼ Quality Inn & Suites 🅷
(760) 931-1185. **$74-$189.** 751 Raintree Dr. I-5, exit 45 (Poinsettia Ln), just w to Ave Encinas, then just n. Ext corridors. **Pets:** Large, other species. $10 daily fee/pet. Service with restrictions, supervision.

🆔 ▼▼▼ Ramada Inn & Suites 🅼 ❀
(760) 438-2285. **$84-$289.** 751 Macadamia Dr. I-5, exit 45 (Poinsettia Ln), just w to Ave Encinas, then 0.3 mi n. Ext corridors. **Pets:** Medium. $25 daily fee/room. Designated rooms, service with restrictions, supervision.

▼▼▼▼ West Inn & Suites 🅷 ❀
(760) 448-4500. **$169-$399, 3 day notice.** 4970 Avenida Encinas. I-5, exit 48 (Cannon Rd), just w, then just n. Int corridors. **Pets:** $75 one-time fee/room. Designated rooms, supervision.

CARPINTERIA

🆔 ▼▼▼▼▼ Holiday Inn Express Hotel & Suites 🅷
(805) 566-9499. **$109-$239.** 5606 Carpinteria Ave. US 101, exit 86A (Casitas Pass Rd), just s, then just e. Int corridors. **Pets:** Large, other species. $10 daily fee/room. Designated rooms, service with restrictions, supervision.

CASSEL

▼▼▼▼ Burney Mountain Guest Ranch 🆁🅰
(530) 335-4087. **Call for rates.** 22800 Hat Creek Powerhouse #2. Jct SR 89 and 299, 2.7 mi ne on SR 299, 0.3 mi se on Hat Creek Powerhouse to jct with Guest Ranch Rd; up unmaintained Guest Ranch Rd, 0.9 mi se. Ext corridors. **Pets:** Accepted.

CASTAIC

🆔 ▼▼▼ Days Inn 🅼
(661) 295-1070. **$54-$149.** 31410 Castaic Rd. I-5, exit 176A (Parker Rd) northbound, just e on Ridge Route Rd, then just s; exit 176 (Lake Hughes Rd/Castaic) southbound, just s on The Old Rd, just e on Sloan Canyon Rd, then 0.6 mi s. Ext corridors. **Pets:** Small, dogs only. $15 daily fee/pet. Designated rooms, service with restrictions, supervision.

▼▼▼ Rodeway Inn 🅼
(661) 295-1100. **$60-$100.** 31558 Castaic Rd. I-5, exit 175A (Parker Rd) northbound, just e on Ridge Route Rd, then just n; exit 176 (Lake Hughes Rd/Castaic) southbound, just s on The Old Rd, just e on Sloan Canyon Rd, then 0.4 mi s. Ext corridors. **Pets:** Accepted.

CASTRO VALLEY

▼▼▼▼ Holiday Inn Express 🅷
(510) 538-9501. **Call for rates.** 2532 Castro Valley Blvd. I-580, exit Castro Valley Blvd, 0.3 mi n. Int corridors. **Pets:** Accepted.

CATHEDRAL CITY

▼▼▼▼ Doral Desert Princess Resort, Palm Springs 🅷
(760) 322-7000. **$99-$359, 3 day notice.** 67-967 Vista Chino. I-10, exit 126 (Date Palm Dr), 0.5 mi s, then 1 mi w. Int corridors. **Pets:** Accepted.

▼▼▼▼ Quality Inn & Suites–Date Palm 🅼
(760) 324-5939. **$69-$279.** 69-151 E Palm Canyon Dr. I-10, exit 126 (Date Palm Dr), 5 mi s, then just e. Ext corridors. **Pets:** Small, dogs only. $50 deposit/pet, $20 one-time fee/pet. Service with restrictions, supervision.

CAYUCOS

▼▼▼▼ Beachwalker Inn 🅼
(805) 995-2133. **Call for rates.** 501 S Ocean Ave. On SR 1 business route. Ext corridors. **Pets:** Other species. $10 one-time fee/pet. Designated rooms, service with restrictions, supervision.

▼▼▼▼ Cayucos Beach Inn 🅼
(805) 995-2828. **$85-$215, 3 day notice.** 333 S Ocean Ave. On SR 1 business route. Ext corridors. **Pets:** Accepted.

🆔 ▼▼▼ Cypress Tree Motel 🅼 ❀
(805) 995-3917. **$50-$117.** 125 S Ocean Ave. On SR 1 business route. Ext corridors. **Pets:** Other species. $10 one-time fee/room. Service with restrictions.

🆔 ▼▼▼ Estero Bay Motel 🅼
(805) 995-3614. **$60-$160, 3 day notice.** 25 S Ocean Ave. On SR 1 business route. Ext corridors. **Pets:** Medium, dogs only. $10 daily fee/pet. Designated rooms, service with restrictions, supervision.

🆔 ▼▼▼▼ Shoreline Inn...On The Beach 🅼
(805) 995-3681. **$105-$205.** 1 N Ocean Ave. On SR 1 business route. Ext corridors. **Pets:** Accepted.

CEDARVILLE

🆔 ▼▼▼ Sunrise Motel 🅼
(530) 279-2161. **$65-$75, 7 day notice.** 62271 Hwy 299 W. Jct SR 299 and CR 1, 0.6 mi w on CR 1. Ext corridors. **Pets:** Medium. $5 daily fee/pet. Designated rooms, service with restrictions, supervision.

CHESTER

🆔 ▼▼▼▼ Almanor Lakeside Resort 🅲🅰
(530) 596-4530. **$125-$195, 30 day notice.** 325 Peninsula Dr. Jct SR 36 and A13, 2.1 mi se on A13 to Peninsula Dr, then 1.3 mi s on Peninsula Dr; on east side of city. Ext corridors. **Pets:** Accepted.

△△△ ▽▽▽▽ Best Western Rose Quartz Inn 🏨 ❖
(530) 258-2002. **$97-$114, 3 day notice.** 306 Main St. On SR 36; center. Int corridors. **Pets:** Medium, dogs only. $30 daily fee/pet. Designated rooms, service with restrictions, supervision.
SAVE ✕ &M 🛢 🖵 🖵

CHICO

△△△ ▽▽▽▽ Best Western Heritage Inn-Chico 🏨
(530) 894-8600. **$95-$130.** 25 Heritage Ln. Just e of SR 99, via Cohasset Rd. Int corridors. **Pets:** Medium, other species. $30 one-time fee/room. Designated rooms, service with restrictions, supervision.
SAVE ✕ &M 🛢 🖵 🖵 ⇔

△△△ ▽▽▽ Heritage Inn Express Ⓜ
(530) 343-4527. **$89-$109.** 725 Broadway. SR 99, exit SR 32, 1.1 mi w; downtown. Ext corridors. **Pets:** $20 one-time fee/room. Designated rooms, service with restrictions, supervision.
SAVE ✕ 🛢 🖵 ⇔

△△△ ▽▽▽ Holiday Inn of Chico 🏨
(530) 345-2491. **Call for rates.** 685 Manzanita Ct. SR 99, exit 387A (Mangrove Ave/Cohasset Rd), follow Mangrove Ave, just sw. Int corridors. **Pets:** Accepted.
SAVE ✕ &M 🛢 🖵 🍽 ⇔

▽▽▽ Music Express Inn Bed & Breakfast 🅱🅱
(530) 345-8376. **$76-$125, 3 day notice.** 1145 El Monte Ave. SR 99, exit 385 (SR 32), 1 mi e to El Monte Ave, then just n. Ext/int corridors. **Pets:** Large, dogs only. $15 daily fee/pet. Service with restrictions, crate.
ASK ✕ 🛢 🄯

▽▽▽ Oxford Suites 🏨 ❖
(530) 899-9090. **$129-$169.** 2035 Business Ln. SR 99, exit 384 (E 20th St), just e, then just s. Int corridors. **Pets:** Medium. $35 one-time fee/room. Designated rooms, service with restrictions, supervision.
ASK ✕ &M 🛢 🖵 ⇔ ✕

▽▽▽ Residence Inn 🏨
(530) 894-5500. **$116-$142.** 2485 Carmichael Dr. SR 99, exit Park Ave, 0.5 mi nw. Int corridors. **Pets:** Accepted.
✕ 🛢 🖵 ⇔ ✕

△△△ ▽▽▽ Super 8 🏨
(530) 345-2533. **$60-$200.** 655 Manzanita Ct. SR 99, exit 387A (Mangrove Ave/Cohasset Rd) follow Mangrove Ave, then just se. Int corridors. **Pets:** Medium. $10 daily fee/pet. Service with restrictions, supervision.
SAVE ✕ 🛢 🖵 ⇔

CHOWCHILLA

△△△ ▽▽▽ Days Inn Ⓜ
(559) 665-4821. **$59-$89.** 220 E Robertson Blvd. SR 99, exit Robertson Blvd W. Ext corridors. **Pets:** Other species. $10 daily fee/pet. Service with restrictions, crate.
SAVE ✕ 🛢 🖵 ⇔

CLIO

▽▽▽▽ Molly's Bed & Breakfast 🅱🅱
(530) 836-4436. **$95-$120, 7 day notice.** 276 Lower Main St. Just n of SR 89; center. Int corridors. **Pets:** Accepted.
ASK ✕ 🄯 🄯

COALINGA

△△△ ▽▽▽ Best Western Big Country Inn Ⓜ
(559) 935-0866. **$95-$149.** 25020 W Dorris Ave. I-5, exit SR 198/Hanford-Lemoore, just w. Ext corridors. **Pets:** Medium. $20 daily fee/pet. Designated rooms, service with restrictions, supervision.
SAVE ✕ 🛢 🖵 ⇔

COLUMBIA

▽▽▽ Columbia Gem Motel Ⓜ
(209) 532-4508. **$89-$149.** 22131 Parrotts Ferry Rd. 3 mi n of Sonora; 1 mi from Columbia State Historic Park. Ext corridors. **Pets:** Dogs only. Service with restrictions, supervision.
✕ 🛢 🖵 🄯

CONCORD

△△△ ▽▽▽ Best Western Heritage Inn 🏨
(925) 686-4466. **$80-$130.** 4600 Clayton Rd. 3 mi e at Wharton Way. Ext corridors. **Pets:** Medium. Service with restrictions, crate.
SAVE ✕ 🛢 🖵 ⇔

▽▽▽▽ Crowne Plaza Hotel Concord/Walnut Creek 🏨
(925) 825-7700. **$109-$249.** 45 John Glenn Dr. I-680, exit Concord Ave, just e. Int corridors. **Pets:** Accepted.
ASK ✕ &M 🛢 🖵 🍽 ⇔

△△△ ▽▽▽ Holiday Inn Concord 🏨
(925) 687-5500. **$85-$169.** 1050 Burnett Ave. I-680, exit E Concord Ave, just e. Ext/int corridors. **Pets:** Dogs only. $10 daily fee/room. Designated rooms, service with restrictions, crate.
SAVE ✕ 🛢 🖵 🍽 ⇔

△△△ ▽▽▽ Premier Inns 🏨
(925) 674-0888. **$52-$72.** 1581 Concord Ave. SR 242, exit Clayton Rd northbound; exit Concord Ave southbound, just e. Ext corridors. **Pets:** Accepted.
SAVE ✕ 🛢 ⇔

CORNING

△△△ ▽▽▽ Best Western Inn Corning Ⓜ ❖
(530) 824-2468. **$75-$119.** 2165 Solano St. I-5, exit 631 (Central Corning), just e. Ext corridors. **Pets:** Small. $10 daily fee/pet. Designated rooms, service with restrictions, supervision.
SAVE ✕ &M 🛢 🖵 ⇔

△△△ ▽▽▽ Comfort Inn 🏨 🐾
(530) 824-5200. **$64-$149.** 910 Hwy 99 W. I-5, exit 631 (Central Corning), just e. Int corridors. **Pets:** Other species. $10 one-time fee/pet. Designated rooms, service with restrictions, supervision.
SAVE ✕ &M 🛢 🖵 ⇔

△△△ ▽▽▽ Holiday Inn Express Hotel & Suites 🏨 ❖
(530) 824-6400. **Call for rates.** 3350 Sunrise Way. I-5, exit 630 (South Ave), just s. Int corridors. **Pets:** Other species. $10 one-time fee/pet.
SAVE ✕ 🛢 🖵 ⇔ ✕

△△△ ▽▽▽ Ramada Inn & Suites 🏨
(530) 824-8300. **$99-$129.** 2645 Barham Ave. I-5, exit 628 (Liberal Ave/99 W), just w, then just n. Int corridors. **Pets:** Other species. $10 one-time fee/pet. Designated rooms, service with restrictions.
SAVE ✕ 🛢 🖵 ⇔

CORONA

▽▽▽ Hotel Paseo Ⓜ
(951) 371-7185. **$89-$150.** 1805 W 6th St. SR 91, exit 48 (Maple St/W 6th St) eastbound; exit 48 (Maple St) westbound, just s. Ext corridors. **Pets:** Small. $20 daily fee/pet. Designated rooms, service with restrictions.
ASK ✕ 🖵 ⇔

▽▽▽ Residence Inn by Marriott Corona 🏨 🐾
(951) 371-0107. **$167-$204.** 1015 Montecito Dr. I-15, exit 95 (Magnolia Ave), just e, just n on El Camino, just w on Carly Way, then just n. Int corridors. **Pets:** Other species. $100 one-time fee/room. Service with restrictions, crate.
✕ &M 🛢 🖵 ⇔ ✕

COSTA MESA

◆◆◆◆ Hilton Orange County/Costa Mesa 🏨
(714) 540-7000. **$109-$329.** 3050 Bristol St. I-405, exit 9B (Bristol St), just s. Int corridors. **Pets:** Accepted.
⊠ 🖶 🖵 ¶¶ ☞ ⊠

ⓐⓐⓐ ◆◆◆◆ Holiday Inn-Costa Mesa/Orange County Airport 🏨
(714) 557-3000. **$89-$219.** 3131 Bristol St. I-405, exit 9B (Bristol St), just s. Int corridors. **Pets:** Medium. $50 one-time fee/pet. Service with restrictions, supervision.
SAVE ⊠ 🖶 🖵 ¶¶ ☞

◆◆◆◆ La Quinta Inn Costa Mesa (John Wayne/Orange Co. Airport) 🅼 ❖
(714) 957-5841. **$69-$139.** 1515 S Coast Dr. I-405, exit 11B (Harbor Blvd), just n, then just w. Ext corridors. **Pets:** Medium, other species. Service with restrictions, supervision.
ASK ⊠ 🖶 🖵 ☞

ⓐⓐⓐ ◆◆◆ Ramada Limited & Suites 🏨 ❖
(949) 645-2221. **$85-$195.** 1680 Superior Ave. Just w of SR 55 (Newport Blvd) at 17th St. Ext corridors. **Pets:** Medium. $150 deposit/room, $5 daily fee/room. Designated rooms, service with restrictions, supervision.
SAVE ⊠ 🖶 🖶 🖵 ☞

◆◆◆◆ Residence Inn by Marriott 🏨
(714) 241-8800. **$206-$252.** 881 W Baker St. SR 73, exit 17B (Bear St); SR 55, exit 5B (Baker St). Ext corridors. **Pets:** Accepted.
⊠ 🖶 🖵 ☞ ⊠

ⓐⓐⓐ ◆ Travelodge-Orange County Airport 🅼
(714) 557-8700. **$75-$125.** 1400 Bristol St. Adjacent to SR 73, just w of Red Hill Ave. Ext corridors. **Pets:** Small. $50 deposit/pet. Designated rooms, service with restrictions.
SAVE ⊠ 🖶 🖶 🖵

◆ Vagabond Inn 🅼
(714) 557-8360. **$69-$119.** 3205 Harbor Blvd. I-405, exit 11 (Harbor Blvd), just s; entrance from Gisler Ave, just w of Harbor. Ext corridors. **Pets:** Accepted.
ASK ⊠ 🖶 🖶 🖵 ☞

ⓐⓐⓐ ◆◆◆◆ The Westin South Coast Plaza Hotel 🏨
(714) 540-2500. **$139-$375.** 686 Anton Blvd. I-405, exit 9B (Bristol St), just n, then just e. Int corridors. **Pets:** Accepted.
SAVE ⊠ 🖶 🖶 🖵 ¶¶ ☞ ⊠

ⓐⓐⓐ ◆◆◆◆ Wyndham Orange County Airport 🏨 ❖
(714) 751-5100. **$209-$269.** 3350 Ave of the Arts. I-405, exit 9B (Bristol St), n to Anton Blvd, just e, then just n. Int corridors. **Pets:** Other species. Service with restrictions, crate.
SAVE ⊠ 🖶 🖵 ¶¶ ☞

CRESCENT CITY

ⓐⓐⓐ ◆ Americas Best Value Inn 🅼
(707) 464-4141. **$50-$125.** 440 Hwy 101 N. Center. Ext corridors. **Pets:** Medium, dogs only. $10 daily fee/pet. Designated rooms, service with restrictions, supervision.
SAVE ⊠ 🖶 🖵 ℀

◆ Hiouchi Motel 🅼
(707) 458-3041. **$65-$81.** 2097 Hwy 199. On US 199, 5.5 mi e of jct US 101. Ext corridors. **Pets:** Accepted.
ASK ⊠ 🖶 ℀ ⊠

ⓐⓐⓐ ◆ Pacific Inn 🅼
(707) 464-9553. **$59-$109.** 220 M St. On US 101; between 2nd and 3rd sts; center. Ext corridors. **Pets:** Accepted.
SAVE ⊠ 🖶 🖵 ℀

ⓐⓐⓐ ◆◆ Quality Inn & Suites 🏨
(707) 464-3885. **$94-$210.** 100 Walton St. Just w of US 101. Ext corridors. **Pets:** Accepted.
SAVE ⊠ 🖶 🖵

ⓐⓐⓐ ◆ Super 8 🅼 ❖
(707) 464-4111. **$55-$150.** 685 Hwy 101 S. On US 101. Ext corridors. **Pets:** Small, dogs only. $10 daily fee/pet. Designated rooms, service with restrictions, supervision.
SAVE ⊠ 🖶 🖵 ℀

CUPERTINO

ⓐⓐⓐ ◆◆◆◆ Cypress Hotel 🏨
(408) 253-8900. **$129-$309.** 10050 S De Anza Blvd. I-280, exit De Anza Blvd, just s. Int corridors. **Pets:** Accepted.
SAVE ⊠ 🖶 🖶 ¶¶ ☞

CYPRESS

◆◆ Homestead Studio Suites Hotel-Orange County-Cypress 🏨
(714) 761-2766. **$55-$132.** 5990 Corporate Ave. I-605, exit 1D (Katella Ave) southbound; exit 1B (Katella Ave/Willow St) northbound, 3 mi e, 0.4 mi n on Valley View Ave, then just w. Int corridors. **Pets:** Other species. $25 daily fee/pet. Service with restrictions, crate.
ASK ⊠ 🖶 🖵

ⓐⓐⓐ ◆◆◆ Woodfin Suite Hotel-Cypress 🏨
(714) 828-4000. **$154-$164.** 5905 Corporate Ave. I-605, exit 1D (Katella Ave) southbound; exit 1B (Katella Ave/Willow St) northbound, 3 mi e, 0.4 mi n on Valley View Ave, then just w. Int corridors. **Pets:** Accepted.
SAVE ⊠ 🖶 🖵 ☞

DANA POINT

◆◆◆◆ DoubleTree Guest Suites Doheny Beach 🏨
(949) 661-1100. **$139-$369.** 34402 Pacific Coast Hwy. I-5, exit 79 (Beach Cities Dr) northbound; exit 79 (Pacific Coast Hwy) southbound, 0.6 mi w, U-turn at Doheny Park Plaza Dr, then 0.8 mi s. Int corridors. **Pets:** Accepted.
⊠ 🖶 🖵 ¶¶ ☞ ⊠

ⓐⓐⓐ ◆◆◆◆ Holiday Inn Express Hotel & Suites 🏨
(949) 248-1000. **$119-$399.** 34280 Pacific Coast Hwy. I-5, exit 79 (Pacific Coast Hwy) southbound; exit 79 (Beach Cities Dr) northbound, 0.6 mi w, then 0.5 mi n. Ext/int corridors. **Pets:** Large, other species. $75 one-time fee/room. Service with restrictions, supervision.
SAVE ⊠ 🖶 🖵 ☞

ⓐⓐⓐ ◆◆◆◆◆ St. Regis Resort, Monarch Beach 🏨 ❖
(949) 234-3200. **$345-$6000, 7 day notice.** One Monarch Beach Resort. I-5, exit 79 (Pacific Coast Hwy) northbound, 3 mi n; exit 86 (Crown Valley Pkwy) southbound, 3 mi w, 1 mi s on Pacific Coast Hwy, then 0.5 mi e on Niguel Rd. Int corridors. **Pets:** Small, dogs only. $150 one-time fee/pet. Designated rooms, no service, supervision.
SAVE ⊠ 🖶 ¶¶ ☞ ⊠

DAVIS

ⓐⓐⓐ ◆◆ Best Western University Lodge 🏨
(530) 756-7890. **$110-$180.** 123 B St. I-80, exit 72B (Richards Blvd), westbound, just nw to First St, just w to B St, then just n; exit 72 (Richards Blvd) eastbound , just nw to First St, just w to B St, then just n; at 2nd and B sts.. Ext corridors. **Pets:** Medium. $20 daily fee/pet. Service with restrictions, supervision.
SAVE ⊠ 🖶 🖶 🖵 ⊠

ⓐⓐⓐ ◆◆◆ University Park Inn & Suites 🏨
(530) 756-0910. **$80-$119.** 1111 Richards Blvd. I-80, exit 72B (Richards Blvd) westbound, just nw; exit 72 (Richards Blvd) eastbound, just nw. Ext corridors. **Pets:** Medium. $10 daily fee/pet. Designated rooms, service with restrictions, supervision.
SAVE ⊠ 🖶 🖶 🖵 ☞

DEATH VALLEY NATIONAL PARK

▼ Stovepipe Wells Village M
(760) 786-2387. $95-$114. SR 190. On SR 190; 24 mi nw of visitor center. Ext corridors. Pets: Accepted.
✕ ⟨M⟩ 🖪 ⟨†⟩ ⟨⟩ ⟨⟩

DELANO

⟨AAA⟩ ▼▼ Rodeway Inn M
(661) 725-1022. $69-$89. 2211 Girard St. SR 99, exit 58 (County Line Rd), just e, then just s. Ext corridors. Pets: Accepted.
(SAVE) ✕ 🖪 ⟨⟩ ⟨⟩

DESERT HOT SPRINGS

▼▼ Desert Hot Springs Spa Hotel H
(760) 329-6000. $59-$119, 3 day notice. 10-805 Palm Dr. I-10, exit 123 (Gene Autry Tr/Palm Dr), 6.7 mi n. Ext corridors. Pets: Medium, dogs only. $100 deposit/pet. Designated rooms, service with restrictions.
(ASK) ✕ 🖪 ⟨⟩ ⟨†⟩ ⟨⟩

DINUBA

▼▼▼ Reedley Country Inn BB ✿
(559) 638-2585. $85-$95, 3 day notice. 43137 Rd 52. SR 99, exit 121 (Manning Ave), 10 mi e, then 1 mi s. Ext/int corridors. Pets: Small. $20 daily fee/pet. Designated rooms.
✕

DIXON

⟨AAA⟩ ▼▼▼ Best Western Inn Dixon H
(707) 678-1400. $89-$179. 1345 Commercial Way. I-80, exit 64 (Pitt School Rd), just se. Ext/int corridors. Pets: $25 one-time fee/room. Service with restrictions, supervision.
(SAVE) ✕ ⟨M⟩ 🖪 ⟨⟩ ⟨⟩ ⟨⟩

⟨AAA⟩ ▼▼ Microtel Inn & Suites M
(707) 693-0606. $59-$129. 1480 Ary Ln. I-80, exit 64 (Pitt School Rd), just s, then just w. Int corridors. Pets: Medium. $10 daily fee/pet. Service with restrictions, supervision.
(SAVE) ✕ ⟨M⟩ 🖪 ⟨⟩ ⟨⟩

▼▼ Super 8 H
(707) 678-3399. Call for rates. 2500 Plaza Ct. I-80, exit West a St, follow signs for West a St, just n on Gateway Dr. Int corridors. Pets: Accepted.
✕ 🖪 ⟨⟩ ⟨⟩

DORRIS

⟨AAA⟩ ▼ Golden Eagle Motel M
(530) 397-3114. $39-$99. 100 N Main St. US 97; center. Ext corridors. Pets: Medium. $6 daily fee/pet. Designated rooms, service with restrictions, supervision.
(SAVE) ✕ 🖪

DOWNIEVILLE

⟨AAA⟩ ▼▼ Riverside Inn M
(530) 289-1000. $80-$104, 3 day notice. 206 Commercial St (SR 49). SR 49; center. Ext corridors. Pets: Accepted.
(SAVE) ✕ 🖪 ⟨⟩ ⟨K⟩ ⟨⟩

DUNNIGAN

⟨AAA⟩ ▼▼ Americas Best Value Inn H
(530) 724-3333. $66-$85. 3930 Rd 89. I-5, exit 556 (Dunnigan), just ne. Int corridors. Pets: $20 one-time fee/room. Service with restrictions, supervision.
(SAVE) ✕ ⟨M⟩ 🖪 ⟨⟩

⟨AAA⟩ ▼▼▼ Best Western Country M
(530) 724-3471. $82-$120. 3930 Rd 89. I-5, exit 556 (Dunnigan), just ne. Ext corridors. Pets: Other species. $20 one-time fee/room. Service with restrictions, supervision.
(SAVE) ✕ ⟨M⟩ 🖪 ⟨⟩ ⟨⟩

DUNSMUIR

⟨AAA⟩ ▼▼▼▼ Caboose Motel-Railroad Park Resort M ✿
(530) 235-4440. $105-$110, 3 day notice. 100 Railroad Park Rd. I-5, exit 728 (Railroad Park Rd), just nw; follow signs. Ext corridors. Pets: Medium, dogs only. $15 daily fee/pet. Designated rooms, service with restrictions, supervision.
(SAVE) ✕ 🖪 ⟨⟩ ⟨†⟩ ⟨⟩

⟨AAA⟩ ▼ Cedar Lodge Motel M ✿
(530) 235-4331. $50-$74. 4201 Dunsmuir Ave. I-5, exit 732, just w, then sw. Ext corridors. Pets: Medium, dogs only. $10 daily fee/pet. Service with restrictions, supervision.
(SAVE) ✕ 🖪 ⟨⟩

EAST PALO ALTO

▼▼ ▼▼ Four Seasons Hotel Silicon Valley at East Palo Alto H
(650) 566-1200. $355-$480. 2050 University Ave. US 101, exit University Ave. Int corridors. Pets: Accepted.
✕ ⟨M⟩ ⟨⟩ ⟨†⟩ ⟨⟩ ⟨⟩

EL CENTRO

▼▼ Barbara Worth Golf Resort H ✿
(760) 356-2806. $109-$278. 2050 Country Club Dr. I-8, exit 120 (Bowker Rd), 2 mi n, then 3 mi e on CR S-80; 9 mi e of SR 86. Ext/int corridors. Pets: Small, other species. $150 deposit/pet. Service with restrictions, crate.
(ASK) ✕ 🖪 ⟨⟩ ⟨†⟩ ⟨⟩ ⟨⟩

▼▼ Comfort Inn & Suites M
(760) 335-3502. $90-$170. 2354 S 4th St. I-8, exit 115 (4th St/SR 86), just s. Int corridors. Pets: Small, dogs only. $10 daily fee/pet. Service with restrictions, supervision.
(ASK) ✕ 🖪 ⟨⟩ ⟨⟩ ⟨⟩

⟨AAA⟩ ▼▼ Ramada El Centro M
(760) 352-5152. $59-$99. 1455 Ocotillo Dr. I-8, exit 114 (Imperial Ave), just n, then just e. Ext corridors. Pets: Accepted.
(SAVE) ✕ ⟨M⟩ 🖪 ⟨⟩ ⟨†⟩ ⟨⟩

⟨AAA⟩ ▼▼▼ Rodeway Inn & Suites M
(760) 352-6620. $50-$75. 455 W Wake Ave. I-8, exit 115 (4th St/SR 86), just s, then just w. Ext corridors. Pets: Small. $5 daily fee/pet. Service with restrictions, supervision.
(SAVE) ✕ 🖪 ⟨⟩ ⟨⟩

▼▼ Vacation Inn & Suites M
(760) 352-9700. $60-$95. 2015 Cottonwood Cir. I-8, exit 114 (Imperial Ave), just n, then just w. Ext corridors. Pets: Small, dogs only. Designated rooms, service with restrictions, supervision.
(ASK) ✕ 🖪 ⟨⟩ ⟨†⟩ ⟨⟩

ELK GROVE

▼▼ Extended StayAmerica-Sacramento-Elk Grove H
(916) 683-3753. $89-$99. 2201 Longport Ct. I-5, exit Laguna Blvd, 0.5 mi e, just s on Harbour Point Dr, then just w. Int corridors. Pets: Other species. $25 daily fee/pet. Service with restrictions, crate.
(ASK) ✕ 🖪 ⟨⟩

EL PORTAL

⟨AAA⟩ ▼▼▼ Yosemite View Lodge H
(209) 379-2681. $95-$729, 14 day notice. 11136 Hwy 140. Just w of Yosemite National Park West Gate. Ext corridors. Pets: Accepted.
(SAVE) ✕ ⟨M⟩ 🖪 ⟨⟩ ⟨⟩ ⟨⟩

EMERYVILLE

AAA **◆◆◆◆** Woodfin Suite Hotel San Francisco Bay Bridge **H**
(510) 601-5880. **$159-$249.** 5800 Shellmound St. I-80, exit Powell St. Int corridors. **Pets:** Accepted.
SAVE ⊠ 🛏 🖵 🍴 🏊

ENCINITAS

AAA **◆◆◆** Best Western Encinitas Inn & Suites at Moonlight Beach **M**
(760) 942-7455. **$130-$215, 3 day notice.** 85 Encinitas Blvd. I-5, exit 41B (Encinitas Blvd), just w. Ext corridors. **Pets:** Accepted.
SAVE ⊠ 🛏 🖵 🍴 🏊

AAA **◆◆◆** Econo Lodge Encinitas **M**
(760) 436-4999. **$69-$299.** 410 N Coast Hwy 101. I-5, exit 41B (Encinitas Blvd), 0.6 mi w, then 0.6 mi n. Int corridors. **Pets:** Small, other species. $100 deposit/pet, $20 daily fee/pet. Designated rooms, service with restrictions, supervision.
SAVE ⊠ 🛏 🖵 🏊

◆◆ Quality Inn & Suites North Coast **M** 🐾
(760) 944-0301. **$69-$350.** 186 N Coast Hwy. I-5, exit 41B (Encinitas Blvd), 0.6 mi w, then just n. Ext corridors. **Pets:** Medium. $10 daily fee/pet. Service with restrictions.
ASK ⊠ 🛏 🖵

ESCONDIDO

AAA **◆◆◆** Best Western Escondido **H**
(760) 740-1700. **$99-$189, 3 day notice.** 1700 Seven Oaks Rd. I-15, exit 33 (El Norte Pkwy), just e. Int corridors. **Pets:** Small. $25 one-time fee/pet. Service with restrictions, supervision.
SAVE ⊠ 🖵 🏊

AAA **◆◆◆** Comfort Inn San Diego/Escondido **H**
(760) 489-1010. **$99-$399.** 1290 W Valley Pkwy. I-15, exit 31 (Valley Pkwy), just w. Int corridors. **Pets:** Other species. $10 daily fee/pet. Service with restrictions.
SAVE ⊠ 🛏 🖵 🏊 🐾

AAA **◆◆** Rodeway Inn **M**
(760) 746-0441. **$54-$129.** 250 W El Norte Pkwy. I-15, exit 33 (El Norte Pkwy), 1 mi e. Ext corridors. **Pets:** Accepted.
SAVE ⊠ 🛏 🖵

EUREKA

AAA **◆◆** Americas Best Value Inn & Suites **M** 🐾
(707) 443-9751. **$55-$150.** 129 4th St. On US 101 southbound; corner of C St. Ext corridors. **Pets:** Small, dogs only. $10 daily fee/pet, $10 one-time fee/pet. Designated rooms, service with restrictions, supervision.
SAVE ⊠ 🛏 🖵 🗶

AAA **◆◆◆** Best Western Bayshore Inn **M**
(707) 268-8005. **$99-$199.** 3500 Broadway. US 101; south end of town. Ext corridors. **Pets:** Accepted.
SAVE ⊠ 🛏 🖵 🍴 🏊 🐾

AAA **◆◆◆◆** Carter House Inns **CI** 🐾
(707) 444-8062. **$190-$612, 3 day notice.** 301 L St. Just w of US 101 S. Int corridors. **Pets:** Medium, other species. $50 one-time fee/room. Designated rooms, service with restrictions, supervision.
SAVE ⊠ 🛏 🍴 🗶

AAA **◆◆** Eureka Town House Motel **M**
(707) 443-4536. **$55-$150.** 933 4th St. On US 101 southbound; corner of K St. Ext corridors. **Pets:** Medium, dogs only. $10 one-time fee/room. Designated rooms, service with restrictions, supervision.
SAVE ⊠ 🛏 🖵 🗶

◆◆ Eureka Travelodge **M**
(707) 443-6345. **Call for rates.** 4 4th St. On US 101; corner of 4th and B sts. Ext corridors. **Pets:** Accepted.
⊠ 🛏 🖵 🏊 🗶

AAA **◆◆◆** Quality Inn Eureka **M**
(707) 443-1601. **$78-$250.** 1209 4th St. On US 101 southbound; between M and N sts. Ext corridors. **Pets:** Accepted.
SAVE ⊠ 🛏 🖵 🏊 🗶

AAA **◆◆◆** Red Lion Hotel Eureka **H**
(707) 445-0844. **Call for rates.** 1929 4th St. On US 101 southbound; between T and V sts. Int corridors. **Pets:** Other species. $20 one-time fee/room. Service with restrictions, supervision.
SAVE ⊠ 🛏 🖵 🍴 🏊

FAIRFIELD

AAA **◆◆◆** Days Inn **M**
(707) 864-1728. **$65.** 4376 Central Pl. I-80, exit Suisun Valley Rd, just e. Ext corridors. **Pets:** Accepted.
SAVE ⊠ 🛏 🖵 🏊

◆◆◆ Extended StayAmerica-Fairfield-Napa Valley **H**
(707) 438-0932. **$95-$105.** 1019 Oliver Rd. I-80, exit Texas St, just w. Int corridors. **Pets:** Other species. $25 daily fee/pet. Service with restrictions, crate.
ASK ⊠ 🛏 🖵

AAA **◆◆◆◆** Homewood Suites Fairfield-Napa Valley Area **H** 🐾
(707) 863-0300. **$169.** 4755 Business Center Dr. I-80, exit Green Valley Rd/Suisun Valley Rd, n on Green Valley Rd, then just e. Int corridors. **Pets:** Medium. $100 one-time fee/room. Service with restrictions, crate.
SAVE ⊠ 🛁 🛏 🖵 🏊 🗶

◆◆◆ Staybridge Suites Fairfield-Napa Valley Area **H**
(707) 863-0900. **$144.** 4755 Business Center Dr. I-80, exit Green Valley Rd/Suisun Valley Rd, n on Green Valley Rd, then just e. Int corridors. **Pets:** Accepted.
ASK ⊠ 🛁 🛏 🖵 🏊

FALLBROOK

◆◆◆ Pala Mesa Resort **H**
(760) 728-5881. **$149-$225, 3 day notice.** 2001 Old Hwy 395. I-15, exit 46 (SR 76/Pala/Oceanside), just w, then 2 mi n. Ext corridors. **Pets:** Accepted.
ASK ⊠ 🛏 🖵 🍴 🏊 🗶

FALL RIVER MILLS

AAA **◆◆◆** Hi-Mont Motel **M** 🐾
(530) 336-5541. **$69-$99, 3 day notice.** 43021 Bridge St. Jct SR 299 and Main St; at Town Center; 0.4 mi sw on SR 299. Ext corridors. **Pets:** Other species. $10 daily fee/pet. Service with restrictions, supervision.
SAVE ⊠ 🛏

FERNDALE

◆◆◆ Collingwood Inn Bed & Breakfast **BB**
(707) 786-9219. **Call for rates.** 831 Main St. Center. Int corridors. **Pets:** Accepted.
⊠ 🗶 📺 🖉

AAA **◆◆◆◆** Shaw House Inn Bed & Breakfast **BB** 🐾
(707) 786-9958. **$125-$275, 15 day notice.** 703 Main St. Center. Ext/int corridors. **Pets:** Medium, other species. $30 daily fee/pet. Designated rooms, service with restrictions, supervision.
SAVE ⊠ 🗶 🖉

FILLMORE

◢◤ ▼▼◆ Best Western La Posada Motel Ⓜ
(805) 524-0440. **$95-$120, 3 day notice.** 827 Ventura Ave. On SR 126. Ext corridors. **Pets:** Medium. $15 one-time fee/pet. Service with restrictions, supervision.
[SAVE] [X] [🗄] [▣] [⇌]

FIREBAUGH

◢◤ ▼▼◆ Best Western Apricot Inn Ⓜ
(559) 659-1444. **$73-$109.** 46290 W Panoche Rd. I-5, exit W Panoche Rd, just w. Ext corridors. **Pets:** Accepted.
[SAVE] [X] [🗄] [▣] [⇌]

FISH CAMP

◢◤ ▼▼◆ Apple Tree Inn Ⓗ ❀
(559) 683-5111. **$99-$259.** 1110 Hwy 41. 2 mi from South Gate to Yosemite National Park. Ext corridors. **Pets:** Medium. $50 one-time fee/pet. Designated rooms, service with restrictions, supervision.
[SAVE] [X] [&M] [🗄] [▣] [⇌] [X] [AC]

▼▼ The Narrow Gauge Inn Ⓗ ❀
(559) 683-7720. **$79-$250, 4 day notice.** 48571 Hwy 41. 4 mi from South Gate to Yosemite National Park. Ext corridors. **Pets:** Medium, other species. $25 one-time fee/pet. Designated rooms, service with restrictions, supervision.
[X] [▣] [🍴] [⇌]

◢◤ ▼▼◆ Tenaya Lodge at Yosemite Ⓗ ❀
(559) 683-6555. **$129-$389, 7 day notice.** 1122 Hwy 41. 2 mi from South Gate to Yosemite National Park. Int corridors. **Pets:** Dogs only. $75 one-time fee/room. Designated rooms, service with restrictions, supervision.
[SAVE] [X] [&M] [🗄] [▣] [🍴] [⇌] [X]

FOLSOM

◢◤ ▼▼◆ Lake Natoma Inn Ⓗ
(916) 351-1500. **$89-$169.** 702 Gold Lake Dr. 3 mi n, 0.5 mi e on Riley St; behind The Lakes Specialty Shopping Center. Int corridors. **Pets:** Other species. $15 daily fee/pet, $45 one-time fee/room. Service with restrictions, crate.
[SAVE] [X] [&M] [🗄] [▣] [🍴] [⇌] [X]

◢◤ ▼▼▼ Larkspur Landing Folsom Ⓗ
(916) 355-1616. **$99-$179.** 121 Iron Point Rd. US 50, exit Folsom Blvd, 0.5 mi n to Iron Point Rd, then 0.3 mi e. Int corridors. **Pets:** Accepted.
[SAVE] [X] [🗄] [▣] [⇌] [X]

▼▼▼ Residence Inn by Marriott Ⓗ
(916) 983-7289. **$170-$180.** 2555 Iron Point Rd. US 50, exit Bidwell St, just e. Int corridors. **Pets:** Other species. $100 one-time fee/room. Service with restrictions, supervision.
[X] [&M] [🗄] [▣] [⇌] [X]

FORTUNA

◢◤ ▼▼▼ Best Western Country Inn Ⓜ ❀
(707) 725-6822. **$79-$145.** 2025 Riverwalk Dr. US 101, exit 687 (Kenmar Rd), just w. Ext corridors. **Pets:** Small, dogs only. $20 one-time fee/pet. Designated rooms, service with restrictions, supervision.
[SAVE] [X] [&M] [🗄] [▣] [⇌]

◢◤ ▼▼◆ Fortuna Super 8 Ⓜ
(707) 725-2888. **$80-$155.** 1805 Alamar Way. US 101, exit 687 (Kenmar Rd), 0.3 mi w on Riverwalk Dr to Alamar Way. Ext corridors. **Pets:** Medium, dogs only. $15 daily fee/pet. Designated rooms, service with restrictions, supervision.
[SAVE] [X] [🗄] [▣]

▼▼▼ Holiday Inn Express Ⓜ ❀
(707) 725-5500. **$90-$140.** 1859 Alamar Way. US 101, exit 687 (Kenmar Rd), 0.3 mi w on Riverwalk Dr to Alamar Way. Ext corridors. **Pets:** Small, dogs only. $20 daily fee/pet. Designated rooms, service with restrictions, supervision.
[ASK] [X] [🗄] [▣] [⇌]

FOUNTAIN VALLEY

▼▼▼ Residence Inn by Marriott Ⓗ
(714) 965-8000. **$233-$285.** 9930 Slater Ave. I-405, exit 14 (Brookhurst St), just n, then just w. Ext corridors. **Pets:** Accepted.
[X] [🗄] [▣] [⇌] [X]

FREMONT

◢◤ ▼▼▼ Best Western Garden Court Inn Ⓗ 🐾
(510) 792-4300. **$90-$210.** 5400 Mowry Ave. I-880, exit Mowry Ave, just e. Int corridors. **Pets:** Medium. $15 one-time fee/pet. Designated rooms, service with restrictions, supervision.
[SAVE] [X] [🗄] [▣] [⇌]

▼ Extended StayAmerica-Fremont Ⓗ
(510) 979-1222. **$84-$94.** 46312 Mission Blvd. I-680, exit Mission Blvd (SR 262), just w. Int corridors. **Pets:** Other species. $25 daily fee/pet. Service with restrictions, crate.
[ASK] [X] [▣]

▼ Extended StayAmerica-Fremont-Newark Ⓗ
(510) 794-8040. **$84-$94.** 5355 Farwell Pl. I-880, exit Mowry Ave, just e. Int corridors. **Pets:** Other species. $25 daily fee/pet. Service with restrictions, crate.
[ASK] [X] [&M] [▣]

▼▼ Extended Stay Deluxe-Fremont-Newark Ⓗ
(510) 794-9693. **$95-$105.** 5375 Farwell Pl. I-880, exit Mowry Ave, just e. Int corridors. **Pets:** Other species. $25 daily fee/pet. Service with restrictions, crate.
[ASK] [X] [&M] [▣] [⇌]

▼▼◆ Fremont Marriott Ⓗ
(510) 413-3700. **$242-$296.** 46100 Landing Pkwy. I-880, exit Fremont Blvd/Cushing Pkwy, then w. Int corridors. **Pets:** Accepted.
[X] [🗄] [▣] [🍴] [⇌]

▼▼ Homestead Studio Suites Hotel-Fremont Blvd South Ⓗ
(510) 353-1664. **$89-$99.** 46080 Fremont Blvd. I-880, exit Fremont Blvd/Cushing Pkwy, just w. Int corridors. **Pets:** Other species. $25 daily fee/pet. Service with restrictions, crate.
[ASK] [X] [&M] [▣]

▼▼◆ La Quinta Inn & Suites Fremont Ⓗ ❀
(510) 445-0808. **$49-$159.** 46200 Landing Pkwy. I-880, exit Fremont Blvd/Cushing Pkwy, just w. Int corridors. **Pets:** Medium, other species. Service with restrictions, supervision.
[ASK] [X] [&M] [🗄] [▣] [⇌]

▼▼▼ Residence Inn by Marriott Ⓗ
(510) 794-5900. **$161-$197.** 5400 Farwell Pl. I-880, exit Mowry Ave, just e. Ext corridors. **Pets:** Accepted.
[X] [&M] [▣] [⇌] [X]

FRESNO

◢◤ ▼▼▼ Ambassador Inn & Suites Ⓜ
(559) 442-1082. **$55-$90.** 1804 W Olive Ave. I-41, exit Olive Ave, just w. Ext corridors. **Pets:** Accepted.
[SAVE] [X] [🗄] [▣] [⇌]

▼ Crossland Economy Studios Fresno-West Ⓗ
(559) 277-8700. **$63-$73.** 3460 W Shaw Ave. SR 99, exit Shaw Ave, 1.8 mi e. Ext corridors. **Pets:** Other species. $25 daily fee/pet. Service with restrictions, crate.
[ASK] [X] [&M] [🗄] [▣]

Days Inn Jensen & 99 H
(559) 237-6644. **$80-$110.** 2640 S Second St. SR 99, exit Jensen Ave, just e. Ext corridors. **Pets:** Small. $10 daily fee/pet. Service with restrictions, supervision.
SAVE ⊠ 🖥 💻 🏊

Days Inn-Parkway M
(559) 268-6211. **Call for rates.** 1101 N Parkway Dr. SR 99, exit Olive Ave, just w. Ext corridors. **Pets:** Accepted.
⊠ 🖥 💻 🏊

Extended StayAmerica Fresno-North H
(559) 438-7105. **$100-$110.** 7135 N Fresno St. SR 41, exit Herndon Ave, just e, then just n. Ext corridors. **Pets:** Other species. $25 daily fee/pet. Service with restrictions, crate.
ASK ⊠ 🖥 💻

La Quinta Inn & Suites H ☘
(559) 449-0928. **$109-$189.** 330 E Fir Ave. SR 41, exit Herndon Ave, just e. Int corridors. **Pets:** Medium, other species. Service with restrictions, supervision.
SAVE ⊠ 🖥 💻 🏊

La Quinta Inn Fresno/Yosemite H ☘
(559) 442-1110. **$59-$139.** 2926 Tulare St. SR 99, exit Fresno St, 1 mi e to R St, then s, then just e. Ext/int corridors. **Pets:** Medium, other species. Service with restrictions, supervision.
ASK ⊠ 🖥 💻

Quality Inn M
(559) 275-2727. **$89-$159, 3 day notice.** 4278 W Ashlan Ave. SR 99, exit Ashlan Ave, just w. Ext corridors. **Pets:** Medium, dogs only. $30 one-time fee/room. Service with restrictions, supervision.
ASK ⊠ 🖥 💻

Red Roof Inn M
(559) 276-1910. **$50-$80.** 5021 N Barcus Ave. SR 99, exit Shaw Ave, just e. Ext corridors. **Pets:** Accepted.
⊠ 🖥 🏊

Residence Inn by Marriott H
(559) 222-8900. **$170-$208.** 5322 N Diana St. SR 41, exit Shaw Ave, 0.3 mi w, n on Blackstone Ave, then e on Barstow Ave. Int corridors. **Pets:** Other species. $100 one-time fee/pet. Service with restrictions, supervision.
⊠ 🖥 💻 🏊

Rodeway Inn H
(559) 431-3557. **$60-$150.** 6730 N Blackstone Ave. SR 41, exit Herndon Ave, then w. Ext corridors. **Pets:** Accepted.
SAVE ⊠ 💻 🏊

Super 8-Parkway M
(559) 268-0741. **$57-$89.** 1087 N Parkway Dr. SR 99, exit Olive Ave, just w. Ext corridors. **Pets:** Medium. $10 daily fee/pet. Service with restrictions, supervision.
SAVE ⊠ 🖥 💻 🏊

TownePlace Suites by Marriott H
(559) 435-4600. **$79-$179.** 7127 N Fresno St. SR 41, exit Herndon Ave E. Int corridors. **Pets:** Medium, other species. $100 one-time fee/room. Service with restrictions, supervision.
SAVE ⊠ 🖥 💻 🏊

University Inn H
(559) 294-0224. **$59-$99.** 2655 E Shaw Ave. SR 168, exit Shaw Ave, just w. Ext corridors. **Pets:** Accepted.
SAVE ⊠ 🖥 🏊

Valley Inn M
(559) 233-3913. **$45-$65.** 933 N Parkway Dr. SR 99, exit Olive Ave, then w. Ext corridors. **Pets:** Small, dogs only. $5 daily fee/room. Designated rooms, service with restrictions, crate.
SAVE ⊠ 🖥

FULLERTON

Fullerton Marriott Hotel at California State Univ H ☘
(714) 738-7800. **$161-$197.** 2701 E Nutwood Ave. SR 57, exit 7 (Nutwood Ave) northbound; exit 7 (Nutwood Ave/Chapman Ave) southbound, just w. Int corridors. **Pets:** Medium. $35 daily fee/room. Service with restrictions.
⊠ 🖥 💻 🍴 🏊 🍽

GARBERVILLE

Best Western Humboldt House Inn M
(707) 923-2771. **$109-$179.** 701 Redwood Dr. US 101, exit Garberville, just e. Ext corridors. **Pets:** Small, dogs only. $10 one-time fee/pet. Designated rooms, service with restrictions, supervision.
SAVE ⊠ 🖥 💻 🏊

GARDEN GROVE

Anaheim Marriott Suites H ☘
(714) 750-1000. **$188-$230.** 12015 Harbor Blvd. I-5, exit 107B (Chapman Ave) northbound, 1.5 mi w on Chapman Ave, then just s; exit 107C (State College/The City Dr) southbound, just s on State College Blvd, 1.5 mi w on Chapman Ave, then just s. Int corridors. **Pets:** Other species. $35 daily fee/pet. Designated rooms, service with restrictions, supervision.
SAVE ⊠ 🖥 💻 🍴 🏊 🍽

Candlewood Suites Anaheim-South H ☘
(714) 539-4200. **$90-$140.** 12901 Garden Grove Blvd. SR 22, exit 13 (Haster St) westbound; exit 13 (Fairview St) eastbound, just n, then just w. Int corridors. **Pets:** Other species. $75 one-time fee/room.
ASK ⊠ 🖥 💻

Residence Inn Anaheim Resort Area H
(714) 591-4000. **$188-$230.** 11931 Harbor Blvd. I-5, exit 107B (Chapman Ave) northbound, 1.5 mi w, then just n; exit 107C (State College/The City Dr) southbound, just s on State College Blvd, 1.5 mi w on Chapman Ave, then just n. Int corridors. **Pets:** Small. $75 one-time fee/pet. Service with restrictions, supervision.
⊠ 🖥 💻 🏊 🍽

GILROY

Best Western Forest Park Inn H
(408) 848-5144. **$100-$260.** 375 Leavesley Rd. US 101, exit Leavesley Rd, just w. Int corridors. **Pets:** Accepted.
SAVE ⊠ 🖥 💻 🏊 🍽

Quality Inn & Suites H
(408) 847-5500. **$69-$249.** 8430 Murray Ave. US 101, exit Leavesley Rd, just w. Ext corridors. **Pets:** Accepted.
SAVE ⊠ 🖥 💻 🏊

Super 8 H
(408) 848-4108. **$69-$89.** 8435 San Ysidro Ave. US 101, exit Leavesley Rd, just e. Int corridors. **Pets:** Small. $10 daily fee/pet. Designated rooms, service with restrictions, supervision.
SAVE ⊠ 🖥 💻 🏊

GLENNVILLE

The Bunkhouse Motel M
(661) 536-9100. **$65-$75.** 12044 Hwy 155 S. On SR 155 at Granite Rd. Ext corridors. **Pets:** Accepted.
ASK ⊠ 🖥 💻 🍴

GRAEAGLE

Chalet View Lodge H ☘
(530) 832-5528. **$92-$325, 7 day notice.** 72056 Hwy 70. Jct SR 70 and 89, 5.7 mi e on SR 70. Ext corridors. **Pets:** $25 daily fee/room. Designated rooms, service with restrictions, supervision.
ASK ⊠ 🖥 💻 🍴 🏊 🍽

GRASS VALLEY

Alta Sierra Village Inn Ⓜ
(530) 273-9102. **$69-$195, 7 day notice.** 11858 Tammy Way. 6 mi s, 1.2 mi e on Alta Sierra Dr, 0.8 mi w on Norlene, then 0.5 mi e; follow signs to Alta Sierra Country Club. Ext corridors. **Pets:** Other species. $10 one-time fee/room. Designated rooms, service with restrictions, supervision.
[SAVE] [X] [&M] [⊟] [▣] [Z]

Best Western Gold Country Inn Ⓜ
(530) 273-1393. **$110-$146.** 11972 Sutton Way. SR 20 and 49, exit Brunswick Rd, just e; midway between Grass Valley and Nevada City. Ext corridors. **Pets:** Accepted.
[SAVE] [X] [&M] [⊟] [▣] [≃]

Coach N' Four Motel Ⓜ ❖
(530) 273-8009. **$61-$260, 3 day notice.** 628 S Auburn St. SR 49, exit E Empire St, 0.3 mi e, then just s. Ext corridors. **Pets:** Other species. $100 deposit/pet, $15 one-time fee/pet. Service with restrictions, supervision.
[SAVE] [X] [&M]

Golden Chain Resort Motel Ⓜ
(530) 273-7279. **$55-$99.** 13413 State Hwy 49. On SR 49, 2.5 mi s. Ext corridors. **Pets:** Accepted.
[SAVE] [X] [&M] [⊟] [▣] [≃]

Grass Valley Courtyard Suites Ⓗ ❖
(530) 272-7696. **$145-$330, 3 day notice.** 210 N Auburn St. SR 49, exit SR 174 (Colfax Ave), just n. Ext corridors. **Pets:** Dogs only. $50 one-time fee/pet. Supervision.
[SAVE] [X] [&M] [▣] [≃] [X]

Stagecoach Motel Ⓜ
(530) 272-3701. **$70-$109, 3 day notice.** 405 S Auburn St. SR 49, exit SR 174 (Colfax Ave), 0.4 mi s. Ext corridors. **Pets:** Accepted.
[SAVE] [X] [&M] [⊟] [▣]

GROVELAND

Groveland Hotel at Yosemite National Park Ⓒ ❖
(209) 962-4000. **$145-$285.** 18767 Main St. Center. Int corridors. **Pets:** Other species. $15 daily fee/pet. Service with restrictions, supervision.
[SAVE] [X] [▣] [¶]

HANFORD

Irwin Street Inn ⒷⒷ
(559) 583-8000. **Call for rates.** 522 N Irwin St. Downtown. Ext corridors. **Pets:** Accepted.
[X] [⊟] [¶]

Sequoia Inn Ⓗ
(559) 582-0338. **$79.** 1655 Mall Dr. SR 198, exit 12th Ave, then n. Int corridors. **Pets:** Other species. $100 deposit/room. Service with restrictions, crate.
[SAVE] [X] [⊟] [▣] [≃] [X]

HAYWARD

Comfort Inn Ⓗ
(510) 538-4466. **$89-$170.** 24997 Mission Blvd. 1.8 mi e of I-880, exit SR 92 (Jackson St), 0.5 mi s on SR 238 (Mission Blvd). Ext corridors. **Pets:** Small. $100 deposit/room, $15 daily fee/pet. Designated rooms, service with restrictions, supervision.
[ASK] [X] [⊟] [▣]

La Quinta Inn & Suites Hayward/Oakland Airport Ⓗ ❖
(510) 732-6300. **$69-$189.** 20777 Hesperian Blvd. I-880, exit a St, 0.5 mi w. Int corridors. **Pets:** Medium, other species. Service with restrictions, supervision.
[ASK] [X] [⊟] [▣] [≃]

HEMET

Best Western Inn of Hemet Ⓜ
(951) 925-6605. **$99-$129.** 2625 W Florida Ave. 2.4 mi w of SR 79 N (San Jacinto St) on SR 74/79. Ext corridors. **Pets:** Small. $50 one-time fee/room. Designated rooms, service with restrictions, supervision.
[SAVE] [X] [⊟] [▣] [≃]

Coach Light Motel Ⓜ
(951) 658-3237. **$60-$80.** 1640 W Florida Ave. 1.7 mi w of SR 79 N (San Jacinto St) on SR 74/79. Ext corridors. **Pets:** Dogs only. $5 daily fee/pet. No service, supervision.
[SAVE] [X] [≃]

Quality Inn Ⓜ
(951) 766-1902. **$98-$119.** 1201 W Florida Ave. 1.5 mi w of SR 79 N (San Jacinto St) on SR 74/79. Ext corridors. **Pets:** Small. $20 daily fee/pet. Service with restrictions, supervision.
[SAVE] [X] [&M] [⊟] [▣] [≃]

HESPERIA

Days Inn Suites-Hesperia/Victorville Ⓜ
(760) 948-0600. **Call for rates.** 14865 Bear Valley Rd. I-15, exit 147 (Bear Valley Rd), 0.5 mi e of Victor Valley Mall. Ext corridors. **Pets:** Accepted.
[X] [⊟] [▣]

Econo Lodge Ⓜ
(760) 949-1515. **$59-$99.** 11976 Mariposa Rd. I-15, exit 147 (Bear Valley Rd), just e, then just s. Ext corridors. **Pets:** Small, dogs only. $10 daily fee/pet. Service with restrictions, supervision.
[SAVE] [X] [⊟] [▣]

Holiday Inn Express Hotel & Suites Ⓗ
(760) 244-7674. **$79-$99.** 9750 Key Pointe Dr. I-15, exit 143 (Hesperia/Main St), just w on Main St, then just n. Int corridors. **Pets:** Medium. $25 daily fee/room. Service with restrictions, supervision.
[SAVE] [X] [&M] [⊟] [▣] [≃]

La Quinta Inn & Suites Victorville Ⓗ ❖
(760) 949-9900. **$80-$100.** 12000 Mariposa Rd. I-15, exit 147 (Bear Valley Rd), just e, then just s. Int corridors. **Pets:** Medium, other species. Service with restrictions, supervision.
[SAVE] [X] [&M] [⊟] [▣] [≃] [X]

Super 8 Ⓜ
(760) 949-3231. **$76-$90.** 12033 Oakwood Ave. I-15, exit 147 (Bear Valley Rd), just se. Ext corridors. **Pets:** Accepted.
[ASK] [X] [⊟] [▣] [≃]

HUNTINGTON BEACH

Extended StayAmerica-Orange County/Huntington Beach Ⓗ
(714) 799-4887. **$110-$138.** 5050 Skylab W Cir. I-405, exit 21 (SR 22/Valley View Blvd) northbound, 1.8 mi s; exit 18 (Bolsa Ave) southbound, 2 mi s. Int corridors. **Pets:** Other species. $25 daily fee/pet. Service with restrictions, crate.
[ASK] [X] [&M] [⊟] [▣]

Hilton Waterfront Beach Resort Ⓗ ❖
(714) 845-8000. **$179-$419.** 21100 Pacific Coast Hwy. I-405, exit 16 (Beach Blvd), 6 mi s, then just w. Int corridors. **Pets:** Large. $75 daily fee/pet. Service with restrictions, supervision.
[SAVE] [X] [&M] [⊟] [▣] [¶] [≃] [X]

IDYLLWILD

Cedar Street Inn Ⓒ
(951) 659-4789. **$89-$160, 10 day notice.** 25880 Cedar St. From SR 243 and town center, 0.3 mi ne on N Circle Dr. Ext corridors. **Pets:** Accepted.
[ASK] [X] [⊟] [▣] [X] [Z]

Fern Valley Inn and Cabins CA
(951) 659-2205. **$85-$175, 10 day notice.** 25240 Fern Valley Rd. From SR 243 and town center, 0.8 mi ne on N Circle Dr, just s on S Circle Dr, then 0.4 mi ne. Ext corridors. **Pets:** Accepted.

Fireside Inn CA ❀
(951) 659-2966. **$65-$130, 10 day notice.** 54540 N Circle Dr. From SR 243 and town center, 0.3 mi ne. Ext corridors. **Pets:** Dogs only. $10 one-time fee/room. Designated rooms, crate.

Quiet Creek Inn M ❀
(951) 659-6110. **$117-$165, 14 day notice.** 26345 Delano Dr. From SR 243, 0.8 mi sw of town center, 0.4 mi w on Toll Gate Rd, then just n. Ext corridors. **Pets:** Other species. $35 one-time fee/room. Designated rooms, supervision.

Woodland Park Manor M
(951) 659-2657. **$95-$195, 10 day notice.** 55350 S Circle Dr. From SR 243 and town center, 1 mi ne. Ext corridors. **Pets:** Other species. Designated rooms, no service, supervision.

INDEPENDENCE

Independence Courthouse Motel M
(760) 878-2732. **$55-$80.** 157 N Edwards. On US 395. Ext corridors. **Pets:** Accepted.

INDIAN WELLS

Hyatt Grand Champions Resort H
(760) 341-1000. **$89-$499, 7 day notice.** 44-600 Indian Wells Ln. I-10, exit 136 (Cook St), 4.4 mi s, 1.5 mi e on SR 111, then just n. Ext/int corridors. **Pets:** Accepted.

Miramonte Resort and Spa H
(760) 341-2200. **$199-$419, 3 day notice.** 45-000 Indian Wells Ln. I-10, exit 136 (Cook St), 4.4 mi s, 1.5 mi e, then just s. Ext/int corridors. **Pets:** Small, dogs only. $50 one-time fee/room. Designated rooms, service with restrictions, supervision.

INDIO

Best Western Date Tree Hotel M ❀
(760) 347-3421. **$59-$360, 3 day notice.** 81-909 Indio Blvd. I-10, exit 139 (Jefferson St/Indio Blvd) westbound, 2 mi se; eastbound, south across freeway, then 2.8 mi e. Int corridors. **Pets:** $10 daily fee/pet. Service with restrictions, supervision.

**Indian Palms Country Club &
Resort** H ❀
(760) 775-4444. **$84-$209.** 48-630 Monroe St. I-10, exit 142 (Monroe St), 2 mi s. Ext corridors. **Pets:** Medium. $15 daily fee/room. Service with restrictions, crate.

Quality Inn M
(760) 347-4044. **$79-$350.** 43-505 Monroe St. I-10, exit 142 (Monroe St), 0.5 mi s. Int corridors. **Pets:** Medium, dogs only. $10 daily fee/pet. Service with restrictions, supervision.

Super 8 Motel M
(760) 342-0264. **$55-$275.** 81-753 Hwy 111. I-10, exit 142 (Monroe St), 1.5 mi s, then 0.5 mi w. Ext corridors. **Pets:** Small. $50 deposit/room, $15 daily fee/pet. Service with restrictions, supervision.

IRVINE

Hilton Irvine/Orange County Airport H
(949) 833-9999. **$120-$350.** 18800 MacArthur Blvd. I-405, exit 8 (MacArthur Blvd/John Wayne Airport), 0.5 mi s. Int corridors. **Pets:** Medium. $50 one-time fee/room. Service with restrictions, supervision.

**La Quinta Inn Irvine Spectrum (Old Historic
Site)** M ❀
(949) 551-0909. **$79-$149.** 14972 Sand Canyon Ave. I-5, exit 96 (Sand Canyon Ave) northbound; exit 96A (Sand Canyon Ave) southbound, just w. Ext/int corridors. **Pets:** Medium, other species. Service with restrictions, supervision.

**Residence Inn by Marriott Irvine John Wayne
Airport** H ❀
(949) 261-2020. **$251-$307.** 2855 Main St. I-405, exit 7 (Jamboree Blvd), just n, then just e. Int corridors. **Pets:** Other species. $100 one-time fee/room. Service with restrictions.

Residence Inn by Marriott-Irvine Spectrum H
(949) 380-3000. **$233-$285.** 10 Morgan. I-5, exit 94B (Alton Pkwy) northbound; exit 94 (Alton Pkwy) southbound, 2 mi e. Ext corridors. **Pets:** Small. $100 one-time fee/room. Service with restrictions.

JACKSON

Best Western Amador Inn H ❀
(209) 223-0211. **$69-$129.** 200 S Hwy 49. On SR 49. Int corridors. **Pets:** Other species. $10 daily fee/pet. Designated rooms, service with restrictions, supervision.

The Jackson Lodge M
(209) 223-0486. **$59-$154.** 850 N Hwy 49/88. On SR 49 and 88, 0.5 mi w. Ext corridors. **Pets:** Small. Designated rooms, service with restrictions, supervision.

JAMESTOWN

**1859 Historic National Hotel, a Country
Inn** CI ❀
(209) 984-3446. **$140-$160, 3 day notice.** 18183 Main St. Downtown. Int corridors. **Pets:** Medium, dogs only. $25 daily fee/pet. Service with restrictions, crate.

**Americas Best Value Inn Royal Carriage
Inn** H
(209) 984-5271. **Call for rates.** 18239 Main St. SR 108 and 49, exit Central Business District. Ext/int corridors. **Pets:** Accepted.

Country Inn Sonora M
(209) 984-0315. **$48-$189.** 18730 Hwy 108. SR 108 and 49, 1 mi e of town. Ext corridors. **Pets:** Large. $10 daily fee/pet. Designated rooms, service with restrictions, supervision.

Jamestown Railtown Motel M
(209) 984-3332. **$40-$80, 3 day notice.** 10301 Willow St. Center. Ext corridors. **Pets:** Small, dogs only. $10 daily fee/pet. No service.

Victorian Gold Bed & Breakfast BB
(209) 984-3429. **$110-$185, 5 day notice.** 10382 Willow St. Center. Int corridors. **Pets:** Accepted.

JUNE LAKE

△△△ ▽▽◈▽ **Double Eagle Resort/Spa** [CA]
(760) 648-7004. **$169-$369, 30 day notice.** 5587 Hwy 158. On SR 158; 3 mi w of village. Ext corridors. **Pets:** Large. $15 daily fee/room. Designated rooms, service with restrictions, supervision.
[SAVE] [✕] [🖢M] [🛏] [💻] [🍴] [🏊] [✕] [🐾]

▽▽ ▽▽ **Gull Lake Lodge** [M]
(760) 648-7516. **$79-$204, 7 day notice.** 132 Leonard Ave. Just n of SR 158, via Knoll and Bruce sts; in village. Ext corridors. **Pets:** Other species. Designated rooms, service with restrictions, supervision.
[ASK] [✕] [🛏] [💻] [🐾] [🐾]

▽▽ ▽▽ **June Lake Villager** [M] ❖
(760) 648-7712. **$65-$95.** 2640 Hwy 158 Dr. On SR 158; center of village. Ext corridors. **Pets:** Other species. Service with restrictions, supervision.
[ASK] [✕] [🛏] [💻] [🐾]

KERNVILLE

△△△ ▽▽ ▽▽ **Barewood Inn & Suites** [M] ❖
(760) 376-1910. **$75-$195.** 7013 Wofford Blvd. In Wofford Heights. Ext corridors. **Pets:** Dogs only. Service with restrictions, supervision.
[ASK] [✕] [🛏] [💻]

▽▽ ▽▽ **River View Lodge** [M]
(760) 376-6019. **Call for rates.** 2 Sirretta St. On Kernville Rd; at the bridge. Ext corridors. **Pets:** Accepted.
[✕] [🛏]

KETTLEMAN CITY

△△△ ▽▽ ▽▽ **Best Western Kettleman Inn & Suites** [M]
(559) 386-0804. **$84-$89.** 33410 Powers Dr. E of and adjacent to I-5, exit SR 41 N, 0.3 mi to Bernard, then 0.3 mi n. Ext corridors. **Pets:** Accepted.
[SAVE] [✕] [🛏] [💻] [🏊]

△△△ ▽▽ ▽▽ **Super 8** [M]
(559) 386-9530. **$59-$119.** 33415 Powers Dr. E of and adjacent to I-5, exit SR 41 N, 0.3 mi to Bernard, then 0.3 mi n. Ext corridors. **Pets:** Accepted.
[SAVE] [✕] [🛏] [💻] [🏊]

KLAMATH

△△△ ▽▽ **Motel Trees** [M]
(707) 482-3152. **$66-$130.** 15495 Hwy 101 N. On US 101, 4.5 mi n. Ext corridors. **Pets:** $25 daily fee/pet. Designated rooms, service with restrictions, supervision.
[SAVE] [✕] [🛏] [💻] [🍴] [🐾]

LAGUNA BEACH

△△△ ▽▽ ▽▽ **Aliso Creek Inn** [H]
(949) 499-2271. **$139-$402.** 31106 S Coast Hwy. SR 133, 3 mi s on SR 1, then 0.3 mi e. Ext corridors. **Pets:** Accepted.
[SAVE] [✕] [🛏] [💻] [🍴] [🏊] [✕] [🐾]

△△△ ▽▽◈▽▽ **Best Western Laguna Brisas Spa Hotel** [H]
(949) 497-7272. **$119-$529, 3 day notice.** 1600 S Coast Hwy. SR 133, 1 mi s on SR 1. Ext/int corridors. **Pets:** Small. $50 daily fee/pet. Designated rooms, service with restrictions, supervision.
[SAVE] [✕] [🛏] [💻] [🏊]

▽▽▽▽ **The Carriage House-Bed & Breakfast** [BB]
(949) 494-8945. **$150-$195.** 1322 Catalina St. SR 133, 1 mi s on S Coast Hwy to Cress St, then just e. Ext corridors. **Pets:** Other species. $15 daily fee/pet. Supervision.
[✕] [🛏] [💻] [🐾] [🐾]

▽▽▽▽ **Casa Laguna Inn** [BB] ❖
(949) 494-2996. **$150-$650, 5 day notice.** 2510 S Coast Hwy. SR 133, 1.3 mi s on SR 1. Ext corridors. **Pets:** Medium, dogs only. $25 daily fee/pet. Service with restrictions, supervision.
[ASK] [✕] [🛏] [💻] [🏊]

▽▽◈▽▽ **Montage Laguna Beach** [H] ❖
(949) 715-6000. **Call for rates.** 30801 S Coast Hwy. SR 133, 3 mi s. Ext/int corridors. **Pets:** Small. $100 one-time fee/room. Designated rooms, service with restrictions, supervision.
[✕] [🍴] [🏊] [✕]

LAGUNA HILLS

△△△ ▽▽◈▽▽ **Holiday Inn Laguna Hills** [H] ❖
(949) 586-5000. **$129-$229.** 25205 La Paz Rd. I-5, exit 89 (La Paz Rd), just w. Int corridors. **Pets:** Medium. $100 one-time fee/pet. Designated rooms, service with restrictions, supervision.
[SAVE] [✕] [🖢M] [🛏] [💻] [🍴] [🏊]

LAKE ARROWHEAD

△△△ ▽▽◈▽▽ **Arrowhead Saddleback Inn** [CI]
(909) 336-3571. **$137-$648, 7 day notice.** Hwy 173. On SR 173, jct SR 189; across from entrance to Lake Arrowhead Village. Ext/int corridors. **Pets:** Other species. $8 daily fee/pet. Designated rooms, service with restrictions, crate.
[SAVE] [✕] [🛏] [💻] [🍴]

△△△ ▽▽ ▽▽ **Arrowhead Tree Top Lodge** [M]
(909) 337-2311. **$69-$217, 7 day notice.** 27992 Rainbow Dr. 0.3 mi s of Lake Arrowhead Village on SR 173. Ext corridors. **Pets:** Medium, dogs only. $8 daily fee/pet. Designated rooms, service with restrictions, supervision.
[SAVE] [✕] [🛏] [💻] [🏊] [🐾] [🐾]

▽▽◈▽▽ **Lake Arrowhead Resort and Spa** [H] ❖
(909) 336-1511. **$159-$429, 3 day notice.** 27984 Hwy 189. Just w of SR 173; in Lake Arrowhead Village. Int corridors. **Pets:** Small. $20 daily fee/pet. Designated rooms, service with restrictions, supervision.
[ASK] [✕] [🖢M] [💻] [🍴] [🏊] [✕]

▽▽◈▽▽ **Storybook Inn** [BB]
(909) 337-0011. **$99-$299, 7 day notice.** 28717 SR 18. SR 18, 1.1 mi e of jct SR 173. Ext/int corridors. **Pets:** Accepted.
[ASK] [✕] [🛏] [💻] [🍴] [🐾]

LAKE FOREST

▽▽▽▽ **Staybridge Suites Irvine East/Lake Forest** [H]
(949) 462-9500. **$149-$399.** 2 Orchard. I-5, exit Bake Pkwy northbound; exit 1B (Bake Pkwy) southbound, 4.7 mi e, then just s on Rancho Pkwy S. Int corridors. **Pets:** Accepted.
[ASK] [✕] [🛏] [💻] [🏊] [✕]

LAKE TAHOE AREA

SOUTH LAKE TAHOE

△△△ ▽▽ ▽▽ **Alpenrose Inn** [H]
(530) 544-2985. **$65-$165, 7 day notice.** 4074 Pine Blvd. 0.3 mi n of US 50 via Park Ave, 3 blks from casino area. Ext corridors. **Pets:** Accepted.
[SAVE] [✕] [🛏] [💻]

△△△ ▽▽ **Ambassador Motor Lodge** [M]
(530) 544-6461. **$45-$300.** 4130 Manzanita Ave. Just s of US 50 on Stateline Ave. Ext corridors. **Pets:** Accepted.
[SAVE] [✕] [🛏] [💻] [🏊] [🐾]

(AAA) ▽▽▽▽ Best Western Timber Cove Lodge 🅷
(530) 541-6722. **$91-$305, 14 day notice.** 3411 Lake Tahoe Blvd. 1.5 mi w of casino area; 0.5 mi w of Ski Run Blvd. Ext corridors. **Pets:** Medium, other species. $100 deposit/room, $25 daily fee/pet. Designated rooms, service with restrictions, supervision.
[SAVE] [✕] [&M] [🛏] [💻] [🍴] [➰] [✕]

(AAA) ▽▽▽ Big Pines Mountain House of Tahoe 🅼
(530) 541-5155. **$75-$209.** 4083 Cedar Ave. US 50, exit Friday Ave, toward the lake; near casino area. Ext corridors. **Pets:** Large, other species. $25 deposit/room, $10 daily fee/room. Service with restrictions, supervision.
[SAVE] [✕] [&M] [🛏] [💻] [➰] [🅺]

(AAA) ▽ Capri Motel 🅼
(530) 544-3665. **$35-$300.** 932 Stateline Ave. Just s of US 50; in casino area. Ext corridors. **Pets:** Accepted.
[SAVE] [✕] [🛏] [💻] [➰] [🅺]

(AAA) ▽▽▽▽ Fireside Lodge–A Premier Bed & Breakfast 🅱🅱 🐾
(530) 544-5515. **$99-$199.** 515 Emerald Bay Rd. 1 mi n of jct US 50 and SR 89. Ext corridors. **Pets:** Other species. $20 daily fee/pet.
[SAVE] [✕] [🛏] [💻] [🅺]

(AAA) ▽ Pistantes Coyote Den 🅼
(530) 541-2282. **$55-$375, 4 day notice.** 1211 Emerald Bay Rd. US 50, 0.5 mi n of airport. Ext corridors. **Pets:** Accepted.
[SAVE] [✕] [🛏] [🅺]

(AAA) ▽▽▽▽ Tahoe Keys Resort 🆑 🐾
(530) 544-5397. **$112-$1300.** 599 Tahoe Keys Blvd. US 50, 1 mi n on Tahoe Keys Blvd. Ext corridors. **Pets:** Dogs only. $100 deposit/pet, $25 one-time fee/pet. Designated rooms, service with restrictions, supervision.
[SAVE] [✕] [🛏] [💻] [➰] [✕] [🅺]

(AAA) ▽▽▽ Tahoe Valley Lodge 🅼
(530) 541-0353. **$125-$495, 7 day notice.** 2241 Lake Tahoe Blvd. 0.5 mi e of jct US 50 and SR 89. Ext corridors. **Pets:** Very small, dogs only. $15 daily fee/pet. Designated rooms, service with restrictions, supervision.
[SAVE] [✕] [🛏] [💻] [➰]

TAHOE CITY

▽▽▽▽ Cottage Inn at Lake Tahoe 🅱🅱
(530) 581-4073. **$158-$340, 14 day notice.** 1690 W Lake Blvd. SR 89, 2 mi s. Ext corridors. **Pets:** Accepted.
[✕] [&M] [🛏] [💻] [🅺] [✉]

(AAA) ▽▽▽ Mother Nature's Inn 🅼 🐾
(530) 581-4278. **$59-$125, 7 day notice.** 551 N Lake Blvd. SR 28, 0.5 mi e of jct SR 89; behind Mother Nature's Store. Int corridors. **Pets:** Other species. $15 daily fee/room. Supervision.
[SAVE] [✕] [🛏] [💻]

TAHOE VISTA

▽▽▽ Holiday House 🅼 🐾
(530) 546-2369. **$125-$225, 14 day notice.** 7276 N Lake Blvd. SR 28, 1 mi w of SR 267. Ext corridors. **Pets:** Other species. $30 one-time fee/pet. Supervision.
[✕] [&M] [🛏] [💻] [🅺]

TRUCKEE

(AAA) ▽▽▽▽ Best Western Truckee Tahoe Inn 🅷
(530) 587-4525. **$139-$189, 3 day notice.** 11331 Brockway Rd. I-80, exit 188, westbound; 188B (SR 267) eastbound, then 1.5 mi se. Int corridors. **Pets:** Accepted.
[SAVE] [✕] [🛏] [💻] [🍴] [➰] [✕]

▽▽▽▽ The Cedar House Sport Hotel 🅷 🐾
(530) 582-5655. **$170-$320, 3 day notice.** 10918 Brockway Rd. I-80, exit 188 westbound; 188B (SR 267)eastbound, 1.5 mi s. Int corridors. **Pets:** Medium, dogs only. $50 one-time fee/pet. Designated rooms, supervision.
[ASK] [✕] [🛏] [💻]

END AREA

LANCASTER

(AAA) ▽▽▽ Antelope Valley Inn 🅼
(661) 948-4651. **$159.** 44055 N Sierra Hwy. SR 14, exit 42 (Ave K), 2.3 mi e. Ext/int corridors. **Pets:** Large. $35 one-time fee/room. Service with restrictions, supervision.
[SAVE] [✕] [🛏] [💻] [🍴] [➰]

▽▽▽▽ Comfort Inn & Suites 🅷
(661) 723-2001. **$109-$209.** 1825 W Ave J-12. SR 14, exit 42 (Ave K), just w, then just n. Int corridors. **Pets:** Small, other species. $50 one-time fee/pet. Supervision.
[ASK] [✕] [&M] [🛏] [💻] [➰] [✕]

(AAA) ▽▽▽▽ Holiday Inn Express 🅷
(661) 951-8848. **$145-$189.** 43719 17th St W. SR 14, exit 42 (Ave K), just e, then just n. Int corridors. **Pets:** Dogs only. $100 deposit/room, $10 daily fee/pet. Designated rooms, service with restrictions, supervision.
[SAVE] [✕] [&M] [🛏] [💻] [➰]

▽▽▽▽ Oxford Inn & Suites 🅼 🐾
(661) 949-3423. **$119-$159.** 1651 W Ave K. SR 14, exit 42 (Ave K), just w. Int corridors. **Pets:** Dogs only. $50 one-time fee/pet. Service with restrictions, supervision.
[ASK] [✕] [&M] [🛏] [💻] [➰]

LA PALMA

▽▽▽▽ La Quinta Inn & Suites Orange County (Buena Park) 🅷 🐾
(714) 670-1400. **$79-$139.** 3 Center Pointe Dr. SR 91, exit 21 (Orangethorpe Ave/Valley View St) eastbound; exit 22 (Orangethorpe Ave/Valley View St) westbound, just n. Int corridors. **Pets:** Medium, other species. Service with restrictions, supervision.
[ASK] [✕] [🛏] [💻] [➰]

LATHROP

▽▽ Days Inn 🅷
(209) 982-1959. **Call for rates.** 14750 S Harlan Rd. I-5, exit Lathrop Rd, just e. Int corridors. **Pets:** Accepted.
[✕] [&M] [🛏] [💻] [➰]

LEBEC

(AAA) ▽▽▽ Best Rest Inn 🅼
(661) 248-2700. **$79-$109.** 51541 N Peace Valley Rd. I-5, exit 205 (Frazier Park), just w. Int corridors. **Pets:** Accepted.
[SAVE] [✕] [&M] [🛏] [💻] [➰]

(AAA) ▽▽▽▽ Ramada Limited Grapevine 🅼
(661) 248-1530. **$69-$99.** 9000 Country Side Ct. I-5, exit 215 (Grapevine Rd), just w. Ext corridors. **Pets:** Accepted.
[SAVE] [✕] [🛏] [💻] [➰]

LEE VINING

ᏯᏯᏯ ▼▼▼▼ Lake View Lodge M
(760) 647-6543. **$59-$159.** 51285 Hwy 395. US 395; in town. Ext corridors.
Pets: Accepted.
[SAVE] [✕] [🛏] [🖳]

ᏯᏯᏯ ▼▼▼ Murphey's Motel M
(760) 647-6316. **$58-$113.** 51493 Hwy 395. US 395; in town. Ext corridors.
Pets: Medium. $5 one-time fee/room. Designated rooms, service with restrictions, supervision.
[SAVE] [✕] [🖳]

LEMOORE

ᏯᏯᏯ ▼▼▼ Days Inn Lemoore M
(559) 924-1261. **$66-$135.** 877 E "D" St. SR 198, exit Houston St, 0.8 mi nw. Ext corridors. **Pets:** Accepted.
[SAVE] [✕] [🕭M] [🛏] [🖳] [🏊]

LINDSAY

ᏯᏯᏯ ▼▼▼ Super 8 Motel M
(559) 562-5188. **$85-$99.** 390 N Hwy 65. SR 65. Ext corridors.
Pets: Small, dogs only. $10 daily fee/pet. Service with restrictions, supervision.
[SAVE] [✕] [🛏] [🖳] [🏊]

LIVERMORE

▼▼▼ La Quinta Inn H 🐾
(925) 373-9600. **$59-$149.** 7700 Southfront Rd. I-580, exit Greenville Rd, just s. Int corridors. **Pets:** Medium, other species. Service with restrictions, supervision.
[ASK] [✕] [🛏] [🖳] [🏊] [✕]

▼▼▼ Residence Inn by Marriott H
(925) 373-1800. **$161-$197.** 1000 Airway Blvd. I-580, exit Airway Blvd/Collier Canyon Rd, just n. Ext corridors. **Pets:** Other species. $75 one-time fee/room. Service with restrictions.
[✕] [🛏] [🖳] [🏊] [✕]

LODI

▼ El Rancho Motel M 🐾
(209) 368-0651. **$60-$65.** 603 N Cherokee Ln. SR 99, exit Turner Rd, just s. Ext corridors. **Pets:** Small. $10 one-time fee/pet. Service with restrictions, supervision.
[ASK] [✕] [🕭M] [🛏] [🏊]

ᏯᏯᏯ ▼▼▼ Microtel Inn & Suites H
(209) 367-9700. **$69-$99.** 6428 W Banner St. I-5, exit SR 12, just e. Int corridors. **Pets:** Accepted.
[SAVE] [✕] [🕭M] [🛏] [🖳] [🏊]

▼▼▼ Wine & Roses Hotel and Restaurant CI
(209) 334-6988. **$169-$495, 3 day notice.** 2505 W Turner Rd. I-5, exit Turner Rd, 5 mi e; SR 99, exit Turner Rd, 2 mi w. Int corridors. **Pets:** Medium. $45 daily fee/pet. Designated rooms, service with restrictions, crate.
[ASK] [✕] [🕭M] [🛏] [🖳] [🍴]

LOMA LINDA

ᏯᏯᏯ ▼ Loma Linda Inn M
(909) 583-2500. **$75-$85.** 24532 University Ave. I-10, exit 74 (Anderson St/Tippecanoe Ave), 1 mi s, just w on Stewart, just s on Campus, then just w. Ext corridors. **Pets:** Large. $35 one-time fee/pet. Service with restrictions, supervision.
[SAVE] [✕] [🛏] [🖳]

LOMPOC

ᏯᏯᏯ ▼▼▼ Americas Best Value Inn M 🐾
(805) 735-3737. **$60-$130.** 1200 N H St. SR 1, 1.3 mi n of Ocean Ave. Ext corridors. **Pets:** $10 daily fee/pet. Service with restrictions, crate.
[SAVE] [✕] [🕭M] [🛏] [🚗]

ᏯᏯᏯ ▼▼▼ Days Inn M
(805) 735-7744. **$99-$199.** 1122 N H St. SR 1, 1.2 mi n of Ocean Ave. Ext/int corridors. **Pets:** $25 one-time fee/room. Service with restrictions, crate.
[SAVE] [✕] [🛏] [🖳] [🏊]

▼▼▼ O'Cairns Inn M
(805) 735-6444. **Call for rates.** 1020 E Ocean Ave. SR 1, 1.5 mi w of H St. Ext corridors. **Pets:** Accepted.
[✕] [🛏] [🖳]

ᏯᏯᏯ ▼▼▼ Quality Inn & Executive Suites H
(805) 735-8555. **$109-$219.** 1621 N H St. SR 1, 1.8 mi n of Ocean Ave. Int corridors. **Pets:** Medium, dogs only. $25 daily fee/pet. Designated rooms, service with restrictions, supervision.
[SAVE] [✕] [🛏] [🖳] [🏊]

▼▼▼ White Oaks Hotel M
(805) 733-5000. **$80-$149.** 3955 Apollo Way. SR 1, exit 211 (Constellation Blvd), just e; 3.5 mi n of Ocean Ave. Ext/int corridors. **Pets:** Accepted.
[ASK] [✕] [🛏] [🖳] [🍴] [🏊] [✕] [🗶]

LONE PINE

ᏯᏯᏯ ▼▼▼▼ Best Western Frontier Motel M
(760) 876-5571. **$75-$124.** 1008 S Main St. US 395; at south end of town. Ext corridors. **Pets:** Other species. Service with restrictions, supervision.
[SAVE] [✕] [🕭M] [🛏] [🖳] [🏊]

ᏯᏯᏯ ▼▼▼▼ Comfort Inn H
(760) 876-8700. **$69-$225.** 1920 S Main St. US 395, 1.5 mi s of town. Int corridors. **Pets:** Other species. $20 daily fee/pet. Designated rooms, service with restrictions, supervision.
[SAVE] [✕] [🛏] [🖳] [🏊]

ᏯᏯᏯ ▼▼▼▼ Dow Villa Motel M
(760) 876-5521. **$72-$145.** 310 S Main St. US 395. Ext corridors.
Pets: Medium. $50 deposit/room. Designated rooms, service with restrictions, supervision.
[SAVE] [✕] [🕭M] [🛏] [🖳] [🏊]

▼ Lone Pine Budget Inn Motel M
(760) 876-5655. **$45-$99, 3 day notice.** 138 W Willow St. US 395, just w. Ext corridors. **Pets:** Small, dogs only. $10 daily fee/pet. Designated rooms, service with restrictions, supervision.
[✕] [🛏] [🖳]

ᏯᏯᏯ ▼ Timberline Motel M
(760) 876-4555. **$45-$99.** 215 E Post St. US 395, just e. Ext corridors.
Pets: Small, dogs only. $10 daily fee/pet. Designated rooms, service with restrictions, supervision.
[SAVE] [✕] [🛏] [🖳] [🔷]

ᏯᏯᏯ ▼▼ Trails Motel M
(760) 876-5555. **$49-$99, 3 day notice.** 633 S Main St. US 395. Ext corridors. **Pets:** Very small, dogs only. $10 daily fee/pet. Designated rooms, no service, supervision.
[SAVE] [✕] [🛏] [🖳] [🏊]

LOS ALAMITOS

▼▼▼▼ Residence Inn by Marriott-Cypress/Los Alamitos H 🐾
(714) 484-5700. **$169-$179.** 4931 Katella Ave. I-605, exit 1D (Katella Ave) southbound; exit 1B (Katella Ave/Willow St) northbound, 1.5 mi e. Int corridors. **Pets:** Small, other species. $100 one-time fee/room. Service with restrictions.
[✕] [🛏] [🖳] [🏊] [✕]

LOS ALTOS

▼▼▼▼ Residence Inn-Palo Alto/Los Altos ⊞
(650) 559-7890. **$233-$285.** 4460 El Camino Real. US 101, exit San
Antonio Rd, 2 mi w to SR 82, then just n. Int corridors. **Pets:** Accepted.
⊠ ⚐ 🖭 ⊲ ⊠

LOS ANGELES METROPOLITAN AREA

ALHAMBRA

AAA⁷ ▼▼▼ Super 8 Ⓜ
(323) 225-2310. **$69-$85.** 5350 Huntington Dr. I-10, exit 22 (Fremont Ave),
2.5 mi n, then 0.5 mi w. Ext corridors. **Pets:** Large. $20 daily fee/pet.
Designated rooms, no service, supervision.
SAVE ⊠ ⚐ 🖭 🖭

ARCADIA

▼▼ Extended StayAmerica-Los Angeles-Arcadia ⊞
(626) 446-6422. **$105-$132.** 401 E Santa Clara St. I-210, exit 33 (Huntington Dr), just w to 5th, just n, then just w. Int corridors. **Pets:** Other species.
$25 daily fee/pet. Service with restrictions, crate.
ASK ⊠ ⚐ 🖭 🖭

▼▼▼▼ Residence Inn by Marriott ⊞
(626) 446-6500. **$199-$309.** 321 E Huntington Dr. I-210, exit 33 (Huntington Dr), 0.5 mi w, then just n on Gateway Dr. Ext corridors. **Pets:** Accepted.
⊠ ⚐ 🖭 🖭 ⊲ ⊠

BEVERLY HILLS

▼▼▼▼ Avalon Hotel ⊞
(310) 277-5221. **Call for rates.** 9400 W Olympic Blvd. I-10, exit 6 (Robertson Blvd), 1.7 mi n, then 0.8 mi w. Ext/int corridors. **Pets:** Accepted.
⊠ 🖭 🖭 ⊲

▼▼▼▼ The Beverly Hills Hotel & Bungalows ⊞ ✿
(310) 276-2251. **$595-$7780.** 9641 Sunset Blvd. I-405, exit 57 (Sunset
Blvd), 3.7 mi e. Int corridors. **Pets:** Small. $250 one-time fee/room. Desig-
nated rooms, service with restrictions.
ASK ⊠ ⚐ 🖭 🖭 ⊲ ⊠

▼▼▼▼ The Beverly Hilton ⊞
(310) 274-7777. **$235-$500.** 9876 Wilshire Blvd. I-405, exit 55 (Wilshire
Blvd), 2.2 mi e. Int corridors. **Pets:** Accepted.
⊠ ⚐ 🖭 ⊲ ⊠

**▼▼▼ ▼▼▼ Beverly Wilshire Beverly Hills a Four Seasons
Hotel** ⊞
(310) 275-5200. **$595-$625.** 9500 Wilshire Blvd. I-405, exit 55 (Wilshire
Blvd), 4.5 mi e. Int corridors. **Pets:** Accepted.
⊠ ⚐ 🖭 ⊲ ⊠

AAA⁷ ▼▼▼▼▼ The Peninsula Beverly Hills ⊞ ✿
(310) 551-2888. **$555-$5000.** 9882 S Santa Monica Blvd. I-405, exit 55A
(Santa Monica Blvd), 2.2 mi e at Wilshire Blvd. Int corridors. **Pets:** Other
species. $35 daily fee/pet.
SAVE ⊠ ⚐ 🖭 🖭 ⊲ ⊠

AAA⁷ ▼▼▼▼▼ Raffles L'Ermitage Beverly Hills ⊞ ✿
(310) 278-3344. **$383-$1350.** 9291 Burton Way. I-10, exit 6 (Robertson
Blvd), 3.1 mi n, then just w. Int corridors. **Pets:** Medium. $150 one-time
fee/room. Service with restrictions, supervision.
SAVE ⊠ ⚐ 🖭 🖭 ⊲ ⊠

BURBANK

**▼▼▼▼▼ Burbank Airport Marriott Hotel & Convention
Center** ⊞ ✿
(818) 843-6000. **$224-$274.** 2500 Hollywood Way. I-5, exit 149 (Hollywood
Way), 1 mi s. Int corridors. **Pets:** Small, dogs only. $200 one-time fee/room.
Service with restrictions, crate.
⊠ ⚐ ⚐ 🖭 🖭 ⊲

**▼▼ ▼▼ Extended StayAmerica-Los Angeles-Burbank
Airport** ⊞
(818) 567-0952. **$130-$161.** 2200 Empire Ave. I-5, exit 146B (Burbank
Blvd), just w, then 0.7 mi n on Victory Pl. Int corridors. **Pets:** Other species.
$25 daily fee/pet. Service with restrictions, crate.
ASK ⊠ ⚐ 🖭

AAA⁷ ▼▼▼▼ Hotel Amarano Burbank ⊞
(818) 842-8887. **$330-$585.** 322 N Pass Ave. SR 134, exit 2 (Hollywood
Way) westbound, just w on Alameda Ave, then 0.5 mi n; exit 2 (Pass Ave)
eastbound, 0.5 mi n. Ext corridors. **Pets:** Accepted.
SAVE ⊠ ⚐ ⚐ 🖭 🖭 ⊲ ⊠

▼▼▼▼ Residence Inn by Marriott Burbank Downtown ⊞
(818) 260-8787. **$249-$309.** 321 S First St. I-5, exit 146A (Olive Ave)
northbound, just e on Angeleno Ave, then just s; exit 146A (Verdugo Ave)
southbound, just s on Front St, just e on Verdugo Ave, then just n. Int
corridors. **Pets:** Large, other species. $100 one-time fee/room. Service with
restrictions.
⊠ ⚐ 🖭 ⊲

AAA⁷ ▼▼▼▼ Safari Inn, a Coast Hotel Ⓜ
(818) 845-8586. **$129-$299.** 1911 W Olive Ave. I-5, exit 146A (Olive Ave),
1.3 mi sw. Ext corridors. **Pets:** Large, other species. $200 deposit/room,
$25 one-time fee/room. Service with restrictions, supervision.
SAVE ⊠ ⚐ 🖭 🖭 ⊲

CARSON

▼▼▼ Extended StayAmerica-Los Angeles/Carson ⊞
(310) 323-2080. **$85-$109.** 401 E Albertoni St. SR 91, exit 7B (Avalon
Blvd) just s, then just w. Int corridors. **Pets:** Other species. $25 daily fee/pet.
Service with restrictions, crate.
ASK ⊠ ⚐ ⚐ 🖭

CERRITOS

**AAA⁷ ▼▼▼▼ Sheraton Cerritos Hotel at Towne
Center** ⊞ ✿
(562) 809-1500. **$119-$219.** 12725 Center Court Dr. SR 91, exit 19B
(Artesia/Bloomfield Dr), just s to Town Center Dr, just e, then just s. Int
corridors. **Pets:** Medium, dogs only. $50 deposit/room. Service with restric-
tions, crate.
SAVE ⊠ 🖭 🖭 ⊲

CHATSWORTH

▼▼▼ Ramada Inn ⊞
(818) 998-5289. **$89-$120.** 21340 Devonshire St. SR 118, exit 35 (De Soto
Ave), 1.5 mi s, then 0.5 mi w. Int corridors. **Pets:** Small. $50 deposit/room,
$10 daily fee/pet. Designated rooms, service with restrictions, supervision.
ASK ⊠ ⚐ 🖭 🖭 ⊲

CHINO

**▼▼▼ Extended StayAmerica Los Angeles-Chino
Valley** ⊞
(909) 597-8675. **$89-$119.** 4325 Corporate Center Ave. SR 71, exit Chino
Hills Pkwy, just e to Ramona Ave, just n, then just w. Int corridors.
Pets: Other species. $25 daily fee/pet. Service with restrictions, crate.
ASK ⊠ ⚐ ⚐ 🖭

CLAREMONT

▼▼ Hotel Claremont & Tennis Club M ❀
(909) 621-4831. **$89-$109.** 840 S Indian Hill Blvd. I-10, exit 47 (Indian Hill Blvd), just s; enter on Auto Center Dr. Ext corridors. **Pets:** Medium, other species. $50 deposit/room. Service with restrictions, supervision.

ASK ☒ �ⓜ 🛏 💻 ➳ ⊠

COMMERCE

◈◈◈ DoubleTree Los Angeles/Commerce H
(323) 887-8100. **$99-$219.** 5757 Telegraph Rd. I-5, exit 128B (Washington Blvd), just e, then just s. Int corridors. **Pets:** Accepted.

☒ ⓜ 💻 ▯ ➳ ⊠

◈◈◈ ▼▼ Ramada Commerce H
(562) 806-4777. **$69-$119.** 7272 E Gage Ave. I-5, exit 126B (Slauson Ave), just e, then just s. Int corridors. **Pets:** Small. $30 one-time fee/room. Designated rooms, service with restrictions, supervision.

SAVE ☒ 🛏 💻 ➳

CULVER CITY

◈◈◈ ▼▼▼ Four Points by Sheraton Culver City H
(310) 641-7740. **$165-$220.** 5990 Green Valley Cir. I-405, exit 49 (Howard Hughes Pkwy), just n, then just e. Int corridors. **Pets:** Accepted.

SAVE ☒ 🛏 💻 ▯ ➳

▼▼▼ Radisson Hotel-LA Westside H
(310) 649-1776. **$109-$229.** 6161 W Centinela Ave. I-405, exit 50 (Jefferson Blvd), just s, then just nw. Int corridors. **Pets:** Medium, other species. $50 one-time fee/room. Designated rooms, supervision.

ASK ☒ 🛏 💻 ▯ ➳

DOWNEY

▼▼ Embassy Suites Hotel H
(562) 861-1900. **$119-$209.** 8425 Firestone Blvd. I-605, exit 10 (Firestone Blvd), 2 mi w. Int corridors. **Pets:** Accepted.

☒ ⓜ 🛏 💻 ▯ ➳ ⊠

EL SEGUNDO

▼▼▼ Embassy Suites-LAX South H
(310) 640-3600. **$139-$259.** 1440 E Imperial Ave. I-405, exit 45B (Imperial Hwy), 1.6 mi w. Int corridors. **Pets:** Small, other species. $25 daily fee/pet. Supervision.

☒ ⓜ 🛏 💻 ▯ ➳

▼▼ Homestead Studio Suites Hotel-Los Angeles-LAX Airport-El Segundo M
(310) 607-4000. **$140-$172.** 1910 E Mariposa Ave. I-105, exit 1B (Sepulveda Blvd), 1 mi s. Ext corridors. **Pets:** Other species. $25 daily fee/pet. Service with restrictions, crate.

ASK ☒ ⓜ 🛏 💻

◈◈◈ ▼▼▼ Hyatt Summerfield Suites-El Segundo H
(310) 725-0100. **$99-$499.** 810 S Douglas St. I-405, exit 43 (Rosecrans Ave), 0.5 mi e, then just n. Ext/int corridors. **Pets:** Small, dogs only. $200 one-time fee/room. Service with restrictions.

SAVE ☒ ⓜ 🛏 💻 ➳ ⊠

▼▼▼ Residence Inn by Marriott-LAX/El Segundo H
(310) 333-0888. **$206-$252.** 2135 E El Segundo Blvd. I-405, exit 44 (El Segundo Blvd), 1.4 mi w. Int corridors. **Pets:** Accepted.

☒ ⓜ 🛏 💻 ➳ ⊠

GLENDALE

◈◈◈ ▼▼▼ ▼▼▼ Hilton Los Angeles North/Glendale & Executive Meeting Center H
(818) 956-5466. **$149-$329.** 100 W Glenoaks Blvd. SR 134, exit 7B (Brand Blvd), just n, then just w. Int corridors. **Pets:** Accepted.

SAVE ☒ ⓜ 🛏 💻 ▯ ➳ ⊠

▼▼▼ Homestead Studio Suites Hotel-Los Angeles-Glendale H
(818) 956-6665. **$130-$161.** 1377 W Glenoaks Blvd. I-5, exit 145A (Western Ave), 0.4 mi e, then 0.6 mi s. Int corridors. **Pets:** Other species. $25 daily fee/pet. Service with restrictions, crate.

ASK ☒ ⓜ 🛏 💻

▼▼ Los Angeles Days Inn-Glendale H
(818) 956-0202. **$94-$149, 7 day notice.** 450 W Pioneer Dr. SR 134, exit 7A (Pacific Ave), just s, then just e. Int corridors. **Pets:** Small. $50 deposit/room. Designated rooms, service with restrictions, supervision.

ASK ☒ 🛏 💻 ▯ ➳

◈◈◈ ▼▼▼ Vagabond Inn Glendale M
(818) 240-1700. **$76-$94.** 120 W Colorado St. SR 134, exit 7B (Brand Blvd), 1 mi s, then just w. Ext corridors. **Pets:** Accepted.

SAVE ☒ 🛏 💻 ➳

HAWTHORNE

▼▼ TownePlace Suites by Marriott M
(310) 725-9696. **$194-$199.** 14400 Aviation Blvd. I-405, exit 43 (Rosecrans Ave), 0.4 mi w. Int corridors. **Pets:** Other species. $100 one-time fee/room.

☒ 🛏 💻 ➳

HOLLYWOOD

◈◈◈ ▼▼▼ Best Western Hollywood Hills Hotel M
(323) 464-5181. **$149-$245.** 6141 Franklin Ave. US 101, exit Gower St, just n, then just e. Ext/int corridors. **Pets:** Medium. $25 daily fee/pet. Designated rooms, service with restrictions.

SAVE ☒ 🛏 💻 ▯ ➳

◈◈◈ ▼▼▼ Hollywood Hotel Near Universal Studios-A Ramada Hotel H
(323) 315-1800. **$90-$189.** 1160 N Vermont Ave. US 101, exit 6A (Vermont Ave), 0.5 mi n. Int corridors. **Pets:** Medium. $50 daily fee/pet. Service with restrictions, supervision.

SAVE ☒ ⓜ 🛏 💻 ▯ ➳

INDUSTRY

▼▼▼ Pacific Palms Resort H ❀
(626) 810-4455. **Call for rates.** One Industry Hills Pkwy. SR 60, exit 18 (Azusa Ave), 1.3 mi n, 0.5 mi w. Int corridors. **Pets:** Medium. $25 daily fee/pet. Service with restrictions, supervision.

☒ ⓜ 💻 ▯ ➳ ⊠

LA MIRADA

▼▼ Extended StayAmerica-Los Angeles-La Mirada H
(714) 670-8579. **$85-$109.** 14775 Firestone Blvd. I-5, exit 118 (Valley View Ave), just n, then 0.7 mi e. Int corridors. **Pets:** Other species. $25 daily fee/pet. Service with restrictions, crate.

ASK ☒ 🛏 💻

▼▼▼ Residence Inn by Marriott H
(714) 523-2800. **$152-$186.** 14419 Firestone Blvd. I-5, exit 118 (Valley View Ave), just n, then 0.5 mi e. Ext corridors. **Pets:** Accepted.

☒ ⓜ 🛏 💻 ➳ ⊠

LONG BEACH

▼▼▼ The Coast Long Beach Hotel H
(562) 435-7676. **Call for rates.** 700 Queensway Dr. I-710, exit 14 (Harbor Scenic Dr/Queen Mary), 1 mi s. Ext corridors. **Pets:** Accepted.

☒ 🛏 💻 ▯ ➳ ⊠

◈◈◈ ▼▼▼ Colonial Pool and Spa Motel M
(562) 591-8327. **$60-$80.** 802 E Pacific Coast Hwy. I-710, exit 2 (SR 1), 1.8 mi e. Ext corridors. **Pets:** Accepted.

SAVE ☒ 🛏 ➳

▼▼ **Extended StayAmerica-Los Angeles-Long Beach** 🅗
(562) 989-4601. **$100-$126.** 4105 E Willow St. I-405, exit 27 (Lakewood Blvd), 0.3 mi sw. Int corridors. **Pets:** Other species. $25 daily fee/pet. Service with restrictions, crate.
A$K ✕ ⓦM 🛏 🖵

◈ ▼▼◈ **GuestHouse Hotel Long Beach** Ⓜ
(562) 597-1341. **$109-$169.** 5325 E Pacific Coast Hwy. I-405, exit 23 (SR 22/Long Beach) northbound, 2 mi nw; exit 27 (Lakewood Blvd) southbound, 2 mi se on SR 1. Ext corridors. **Pets:** Accepted.
SAVE ✕ 🛏 🖵 ⤳

▼◈▼ **Hilton Long Beach** 🅗 🐾
(562) 983-3400. **$150-$357.** Two World Trade Center. I-710, exit Downtown/Broadway, just e to Daisy Ave, just s to Ocean Blvd, then just w. Int corridors. **Pets:** Medium, other species. $25 daily fee/pet. Designated rooms, service with restrictions, supervision.
✕ ⓦM 🖵 ¶¶ ✕̶

◈ ▼◈▼ **Holiday Inn-Long Beach Airport** 🅗
(562) 597-4401. **$129-$279.** 2640 Lakewood Blvd. I-405, exit 27 (Lakewood Blvd), just s. Ext/int corridors. **Pets:** Small. $100 deposit/room, $25 daily fee/room. Designated rooms, service with restrictions, crate.
SAVE ✕ 🛏 🖵 ¶¶ ⤳

▼◈▼ **Renaissance Long Beach Hotel** 🅗
(562) 437-5900. **$215-$263.** 111 E Ocean Blvd. I-710, exit Downtown/Broadway, 0.8 mi e to Long Beach Blvd, just s, then just w. Int corridors. **Pets:** $75 one-time fee/room. Service with restrictions, supervision.
✕ ⓦM 🖵 ¶¶ ⤳ ✕̶

▼◈▼ **Residence Inn by Marriott Long Beach** 🅗
(562) 595-0909. **$179-$219.** 4111 E Willow St. I-405, exit 27 (Lakewood Blvd), just s, then just w. Ext corridors. **Pets:** Accepted.
✕ ⓦM 🛏 🖵 ⤳ ✕̶

◈ ▼◈▼ **The Westin Long Beach** 🅗
(562) 436-3000. **$149-$499.** 333 E Ocean Blvd. I-710, exit Downtown/Broadway, 0.8 mi e to Long Beach Blvd, then just s. Int corridors. **Pets:** Accepted.
SAVE 🖵 ¶¶ ⤳ ✕̶

LOS ANGELES

◈ ▼ **Beverly Laurel Motor Hotel** Ⓜ
(323) 651-2441. **$114-$155.** 8018 Beverly Blvd. I-10, exit 7B (Fairfax Ave), 2.8 mi n, then just w. Ext corridors. **Pets:** $25 daily fee/pet. Service with restrictions, crate.
SAVE ✕ 🛏 ¶¶ ⤳

▼▼ **Extended StayAmerica-Los Angeles/LAX Airport** 🅗
(310) 568-9337. **$125-$155.** 6531 S Sepulveda Blvd. I-405, exit 49 (Howard Hughes Pkwy), 0.9 mi w, then just n. Int corridors. **Pets:** Other species. $25 daily fee/pet. Service with restrictions, crate.
A$K ✕ ⓦM 🛏 🖵

◈ ▼◈▼◈ **Four Seasons Hotel Los Angeles at Beverly Hills** 🅗 🐾
(310) 273-2222. **$495-$6950.** 300 S Doheny Dr. I-10, exit 6 (Robertson Blvd), 3 mi n to Burton Way, then just w. Int corridors. **Pets:** Small. Service with restrictions, supervision.
SAVE ✕ ⓦM 🖵 ¶¶ ⤳ ✕̶

▼◈▼ **Hotel Bel-Air** 🅗
(310) 472-1211. **$465-$6500, 3 day notice.** 701 Stone Canyon Rd. I-405, exit 57 (Sunset Blvd), 2 mi e, then 0.8 mi n. Ext corridors. **Pets:** Accepted.
✕ 🛏 ¶¶ ⤳

◈ ▼◈▼ **Hotel Palomar la Westwood** 🅗
(310) 475-8711. **$209-$559.** 10740 Wilshire Blvd. I-405, exit 55B (Wilshire Blvd), 1 mi w; in Westwood. Int corridors. **Pets:** Accepted.
SAVE ✕ 🖵 ¶¶ ⤳

◈ ▼▼ ▼◈▼ **Hyatt Regency Century Plaza** 🅗 🐾
(310) 228-1234. **$179-$499.** 2025 Avenue of the Stars. I-10, exit 6 (Robertson Blvd), 2.7 mi n to Olympic Blvd, 1.9 mi w, then just n. Int corridors. **Pets:** Small, dogs only. $35 daily fee/pet. Service with restrictions, supervision.
SAVE ✕ ⓦM 🖵 ¶¶ ⤳ ✕̶

▼◈▼ **La Quinta Inn & Suites–LAX** 🅗 🐾
(310) 645-2200. **$89-$199.** 5249 W Century Blvd. I-405, exit 46 (Century Blvd), just w. Int corridors. **Pets:** Medium, other species. Service with restrictions, supervision.
A$K ✕ 🛏 🖵 ¶¶ ⤳

◈ ▼◈▼ **Los Angeles Airport Hilton & Towers** 🅗 🐾
(310) 410-4000. **$119-$249.** 5711 W Century Blvd. I-405, exit 46 (Century Blvd), 0.8 mi w. Int corridors. **Pets:** Medium. $50 one-time fee/room. Service with restrictions.
SAVE ✕ 🛏 🖵 ¶¶ ⤳ ✕̶

▼◈▼ **Luxe Hotel Sunset Boulevard** 🅗
(310) 476-6571. **$490.** 11461 Sunset Blvd. I-405, exit 57 (Sunset Blvd), just w. Int corridors. **Pets:** Accepted.
A$K ✕ 🛏 🖵 ¶¶ ⤳ ✕̶

◈ ▼◈▼◈ **Omni Los Angeles Hotel** 🅗
(213) 617-3300. **$289-$680.** 251 S Olive St. SR 110, exit 4th St southbound; exit 6th St northbound, just e, then just n. Int corridors. **Pets:** Accepted.
SAVE ✕ ⓦM 🛏 🖵 ¶¶ ⤳

▼◈▼ **The Orlando** 🅗
(323) 658-6600. **$279-$329.** 8384 W 3rd St. I-10, exit 7A (La Cienega Blvd), 2.3 mi n, then just e. Int corridors. **Pets:** Very small. $50 daily fee/pet. Designated rooms, service with restrictions, supervision.
A$K ✕ 🛏 🖵 ¶¶ ⤳ ✕̶

▼◈▼ **Radisson Hotel at Los Angeles Airport** 🅗
(310) 670-9000. **Call for rates.** 6225 W Century Blvd at Sepulveda Blvd. I-405, exit 46 (Century Blvd), 1.6 mi w. Int corridors. **Pets:** Accepted.
✕ 🖵 ¶¶ ⤳ ✕̶

▼◈▼ **Residence Inn by Marriott-Beverly Hills** 🅗 🐾
(310) 277-4427. **$239-$249.** 1177 S Beverly Dr. I-10, exit 6 (Robertson Blvd), 1.6 mi n to Pico Blvd, then 0.6 mi w. Int corridors. **Pets:** Large. $10 daily fee/pet, $100 one-time fee/room. Service with restrictions, supervision.
✕ ⓦM 🛏 🖵

◈ ▼◈▼ **Sheraton Gateway Hotel, Los Angeles Airport** 🅗 🐾
(310) 642-1111. **$99-$399.** 6101 W Century Blvd. I-405, exit 46 (Century Blvd), 1.3 mi w. Int corridors. **Pets:** Medium, dogs only. $25 one-time fee/room. Service with restrictions, supervision.
SAVE ✕ ⓦM 🖵 ¶¶ ⤳

◈ ▼◈▼ **Sheraton Los Angeles Downtown** 🅗
(213) 488-3500. **Call for rates.** 711 S Hope St. SR 110, exit 6th St southbound, just e, then just s. Int corridors. **Pets:** Medium, other species. Service with restrictions, supervision.
SAVE ✕ ⓦM 🖵 ¶¶

▼◈▼ **Sofitel Los Angeles** 🅗
(310) 278-5444. **$535-$2000, 3 day notice.** 8555 Beverly Blvd. I-10, exit 7A (La Cienega Blvd), 2.5 mi n. Int corridors. **Pets:** Accepted.
A$K ✕ ¶¶ ⤳ ✕̶

▼◈▼ **The Tower–Beverly Hills** 🅗 🐾
(310) 277-2800. **$269-$369.** 1224 S Beverwil Dr. I-10, exit 6 (Robertson Blvd), 1.8 mi n, then 0.7 mi e. Int corridors. **Pets:** Other species. $100 deposit/room. Supervision.
A$K ✕ ⓦM 🖵 ¶¶ ⤳

Travelodge Hotel at Lax H ❀
(310) 649-4000. **$75-$120.** 5547 W Century Blvd. I-405, exit 46 (Century Blvd), 0.5 mi w. Ext/int corridors. **Pets:** Other species. $10 daily fee/pet. Designated rooms, service with restrictions, supervision.
SAVE ✕ 🛢 💻 🍽 🏊

Vagabond Inn Los Angeles-USC M
(213) 746-1531. **$84-$149.** 3101 S Figueroa St. SR 110, exit Adams Blvd, 0.5 mi s. Ext corridors. **Pets:** Medium. $10 daily fee/pet. Designated rooms, service with restrictions, supervision.
SAVE ✕ 🛢 💻 🏊

The Westin Bonaventure Hotel & Suites H ❀
(213) 624-1000. **$119-$949.** 404 S Figueroa St. SR 110, exit 6th St, just n on Figueroa St, e on 4th St, then s on Flower. Int corridors. **Pets:** Medium, other species. Supervision.
SAVE ✕ 🛢M 🛢 💻 🍽 🏊

The Westin Hotel-Los Angeles Airport H
(310) 216-5858. **$139-$289.** 5400 W Century Blvd. I-405, exit 46 (Century Blvd), just w. Int corridors. **Pets:** Accepted.
SAVE ✕ 🛢M 💻 🍽 🏊 🐾

MANHATTAN BEACH

The Belamar, a Larkspur Collection Hotel H
(310) 750-0300. **$189-$499.** 3501 S Sepulveda Blvd. I-405, exit 43 (Rosecrans Ave), 1.5 mi w, then just s. Int corridors. **Pets:** Accepted.
SAVE ✕ 🛢M 🛢 💻 🍽 🏊 🐾

Residence Inn by Marriott H
(310) 421-3100. **$189-$199.** 1700 N Sepulveda Blvd. I-405, exit 43B (Rosecrans Ave), 1.5 mi w, then 1 mi s on SR 1. Ext corridors. **Pets:** Accepted.
✕ 🛢M 🛢 💻 🏊 🐾

MARINA DEL REY

The Ritz-Carlton, Marina del Rey H
(310) 823-1700. **$489-$3200.** 4375 Admiralty Way. SR 90 (Marina Frwy), just s on Lincoln Blvd (SR 1), just w on Bali Way. Int corridors. **Pets:** Accepted.
✕ 🛢M 💻 🍽 🏊 🐾

MONROVIA

Homestead Studio Suites Hotel-Los Angeles-Monrovia H
(626) 256-6999. **$110-$138.** 930 S Fifth Ave. I-210, exit 33 (Huntington Dr), just w, then just n. Int corridors. **Pets:** Other species. $25 daily fee/pet. Service with restrictions, crate.
ASK ✕ 🛢 💻

NORTHRIDGE

Extended StayAmerica-Los Angeles/Northridge H
(818) 734-1787. **$95-$121.** 19325 Londelius St. SR 118, exit 37 (Tampa Ave), 3 mi s. Int corridors. **Pets:** Other species. $25 daily fee/pet. Service with restrictions, crate.
ASK ✕ 🛢M 🛢 💻

PASADENA

The Langham Huntington Hotel & Spa H
(626) 568-3900. **$199-$595.** 1401 S Oak Knoll Ave. I-210, exit 26B (Lake Ave), 2 mi s. Ext/int corridors. **Pets:** Accepted.
ASK ✕ 🛢M 🛢 💻 🍽 🏊 🐾

Quality Inn Pasadena M
(626) 796-9291. **$85-$250.** 3321 E Colorado Blvd. I-210, exit 29B (Madre St), just s, then 0.3 mi e. Ext corridors. **Pets:** Other species. $20 daily fee/pet. Designated rooms, service with restrictions, supervision.
ASK ✕ 🛢 💻 🏊 🐾

Sheraton Pasadena Hotel H
(626) 449-4000. **Call for rates.** 303 E Cordova St. I-210, exit 26B (Lake Ave), 0.7 mi s, then just w. Int corridors. **Pets:** Accepted.
SAVE ✕ 🛢M 🛢 💻 🍽 🏊 🐾

Super 8 M
(626) 449-3020. **$78-$250, 30 day notice.** 2863 E Colorado Blvd. I-210, exit 29A (San Gabriel Blvd)), 0.3 mi s, then just e. Ext corridors. **Pets:** Very small. $25 daily fee/pet. Designated rooms, service with restrictions, supervision.
SAVE ✕ 🛢 🏊

Vagabond Inn Executive M
(626) 449-3170. **$90-$130.** 1203 E Colorado Blvd. I-210, exit 27A (Hill Ave), just s, then just w. Ext/int corridors. **Pets:** Accepted.
SAVE ✕ 🛢M 🛢 💻 🏊

The Westin-Pasadena H
(626) 792-2727. **Call for rates.** 191 N Los Robles Ave. I-210, exit Los Robles Ave, just s; in Plaza Las Fuentes. Int corridors. **Pets:** Accepted.
SAVE ✕ 🛢M 🛢 💻 🍽 🏊 🐾

Westway Inn M
(626) 304-9678. **$75-$350, 30 day notice.** 1599 E Colorado Blvd. I-210, exit 27B (Allen Ave) westbound; exit 27 (Hill Ave) eastbound, 0.8 mi s. Ext corridors. **Pets:** Accepted.
SAVE ✕ 🛢 💻 🏊

POMONA

Sheraton Suites Fairplex H
(909) 622-2220. **$119-$274.** 601 W McKinley Ave. I-10, exit 45A (White Ave) eastbound, 0.5 mi n, then just w; exit 43 (Fairplex Dr) westbound, 1 mi n, then 0.7 mi e. Int corridors. **Pets:** Medium, other species. Designated rooms, service with restrictions, supervision.
SAVE ✕ 🛢M 🛢 💻 🍽 🏊 🐾

SAN DIMAS

Red Roof Inn M
(909) 599-2362. **Call for rates.** 204 N Village Ct. SR 57, exit 45 (Arrow Hwy), just e, then just n. Ext corridors. **Pets:** Accepted.
✕ 🛢M 🛢 🏊

SAN PEDRO

Vagabond Inn San Pedro M
(310) 831-8911. **$69-$109.** 215 S Gaffey St. I-110, exit Gaffey St, just s of terminus. Ext corridors. **Pets:** Small. $25 one-time fee/pet. Designated rooms, service with restrictions, supervision.
SAVE ✕ 🛢 💻 🏊

SANTA CLARITA

Best Western Valencia Inn M
(661) 255-0555. **Call for rates.** 27413 Wayne Mills Pl. I-5, exit 170 (Magic Mountain Pkwy), just e. Ext corridors. **Pets:** Accepted.
SAVE ✕ 🛢 💻 🏊

Comfort Suites H ❀
(661) 254-7700. **$90-$126.** 25380 The Old Road. I-5, exit 167 (Lyons Ave), just w. Int corridors. **Pets:** Medium. $5 daily fee/pet, $50 one-time fee/pet. Service with restrictions, supervision.
ASK ✕ 🛢M 🛢 💻 🏊

Extended StayAmerica Los Angeles-Valencia H
(661) 255-1044. **$90-$115.** 24940 W Pico Canyon Rd. I-5, exit 167 (Lyons Ave), just w. Int corridors. **Pets:** Other species. $25 daily fee/pet. Service with restrictions, crate.
ASK ✕ 🛢 💻

▼▼▼▼ La Quinta Inn & Suites Stevenson Ranch 🅷 ❀
(661) 286-1111. **$99-$159.** 25201 The Old Rd. I-5, exit 167 (Lyons Ave),
just w to Chiquella Ln, just n, then just w. Int corridors. **Pets:** Medium, other
species. Service with restrictions, supervision.
🆊 ⊠ 🛏 💻 ⊃

▼▼▼ Residence Inn by Marriott 🅷
(661) 290-2800. **$134-$164.** 25320 The Old Rd. I-5, exit 167 (Lyons Ave),
just w. Int corridors. **Pets:** Accepted.
⊠ ⅃M 🛏 💻 ⊃ ⊠

SANTA MONICA

🆊 ▼▼▼ ▼▼▼ The Fairmont Miramar Hotel Santa
Monica 🅷 ❀
(310) 576-7777. **$279-$1287.** 101 Wilshire Blvd. I-10, exit 1B (Lincoln
Blvd), 0.6 mi n, then 0.6 mi w. Ext/int corridors. **Pets:** No service.
🆂🅰🆅🅴 ⊠ ⅃M 🍴 ⊃ ⊠

▼▼▼ The Georgian 🅷 ❀
(310) 395-9945. **$252-$528.** 1415 Ocean Ave. I-10, exit 1B (Lincoln Blvd),
just n, then 0.5 mi w on Broadway. Int corridors. **Pets:** Medium. $150
one-time fee/pet. Service with restrictions, supervision.
🆊 ⊠

▼▼▼ ▼▼▼ Le Merigot–A JW Marriott Beach Hotel &
Spa 🅷 ❀
(310) 395-9700. **$338-$413.** 1740 Ocean Ave. I-10, exit 1B (Lincoln Blvd),
0.3 mi s, 0.6 mi w on Pico Blvd, then just n. Int corridors. **Pets:** Accepted.
⊠ ⅃M 💻 🍴 ⊃ ⊠

🆊 ▼▼▼ ▼▼▼ Loews Santa Monica Beach
Hotel 🅷 ❀
(310) 458-6700. **$299-$2600.** 1700 Ocean Ave. I-10, exit 1B (Lincoln Blvd),
0.3 mi s, 0.6 mi w on Pico Blvd, then just n. Int corridors. **Pets:** Other
species. $25 daily fee/room. Service with restrictions.
🆂🅰🆅🅴 ⊠ ⅃M 💻 🍴 ⊃ ⊠

🆊 ▼▼▼ Sheraton Delfina Santa Monica 🅷
(310) 399-9344. **Call for rates.** 530 Pico Blvd. I-10, exit 1B (Lincoln Blvd),
just s. Int corridors. **Pets:** Accepted.
🆂🅰🆅🅴 ⊠ 🛏 💻 🍴 ⊃

🆊 ▼▼▼ Travelodge-Santa Monica/Pico Blvd 🅼
(310) 450-5766. **$109-$199.** 3102 W Pico Blvd. I-10, exit 2 (Centinela
Ave), just n, then just w. Ext corridors. **Pets:** Small. Designated rooms,
service with restrictions, supervision.
🆂🅰🆅🅴 ⊠ 🛏 💻

▼▼▼ Viceroy Santa Monica 🅷
(310) 260-7500. **$399-$550.** 1819 Ocean Blvd. I-10, exit 1B (Lincoln Blvd),
0.3 mi s, 0.6 mi w on Pico Blvd, then just n. Int corridors. **Pets:** Accepted.
⊠ ⅃M 🍴 ⊃

SEAL BEACH

🆊 ▼▼▼ The Pacific Inn 🅷 ❀
(562) 493-7501. **$119-$189.** 600 Marina Dr. SR 1 (Pacific Coast Hwy), just
s. Ext/int corridors. **Pets:** Other species. $50 one-time fee/room. Designated
rooms, service with restrictions, supervision.
🆂🅰🆅🅴 ⊠ 🛏 💻 ⊃ ⊠

SHERMAN OAKS

🆊 ▼▼▼ Best Western Carriage Inn 🅼
(818) 787-2300. **$115-$299.** 5525 Sepulveda Blvd. I-405, exit 64 (Burbank
Blvd), just e, then just s. Ext/int corridors. **Pets:** Accepted.
🆂🅰🆅🅴 ⊠ ⅃M 🛏 💻 🍴 ⊃

SOUTH EL MONTE

▼▼▼ Rodeway Inn South El Monte 🅼
(626) 579-4490. **$60-$99.** 1228 N Durfee Rd. SR 60, exit 11 (Peck Rd),
just s, then just e. Ext corridors. **Pets:** Small. $10 daily fee/pet. Designated
rooms, service with restrictions, supervision.
🆊 ⊠ 🛏 💻 ⊃

TARZANA

🆊 ▼▼▼ St. George Inn & Suites 🅼
(818) 345-6911. **$80-$110.** 19454 Ventura Blvd. US 101, exit 24 (Tampa
Ave), just s, then just w. Ext corridors. **Pets:** Medium. $150 deposit/room.
Designated rooms, service with restrictions, supervision.
🆂🅰🆅🅴 ⊠ 🛏 💻 ⊃

TORRANCE

▼▼▼ Extended StayAmerica-Los Angeles-Torrance 🅷
(310) 540-5442. **$100-$126.** 3525 Torrance Blvd. I-405, exit 42A (Hawthorne Blvd), 3.5 mi s, then 0.4 mi e. Int corridors. **Pets:** Other species. $25
daily fee/pet. Service with restrictions, crate.
🆊 ⊠ ⅃M 🛏 💻

▼▼▼ Extended StayAmerica-Los Angeles/Torrance Harbor
Gateway 🅷
(310) 328-6000. **$105-$132.** 19200 Harborgate Way. I-405, exit 38A (Normandie Ave), just s, then just w via 190th St. Int corridors. **Pets:** Other
species. $25 daily fee/pet. Service with restrictions, crate.
🆊 ⊠ ⅃M 🛏 💻

▼▼▼ Holiday Inn Torrance 🅷
(310) 781-9100. **$119-$209.** 19800 S Vermont Ave. I-110, exit 9 (190th St)
just e, then 0.4 mi n. Int corridors. **Pets:** Other species. $50 deposit/room.
Service with restrictions, crate.
🆊 ⊠ ⅃M 🛏 💻 🍴 ⊃ ⊠

▼▼▼ Homestead Studio Suites Hotel-Los
Angeles-Torrance 🅷
(310) 543-0048. **$120-$149.** 3995 Carson St. I-405, exit 42A (Hawthorne
Blvd), 3.6 mi s; I-110, exit 7B (Carson St), 4.5 mi w. Int corridors.
Pets: Other species. $25 daily fee/pet. Service with restrictions, crate.
🆊 ⊠ ⅃M 🛏 💻

🆊 ▼▼▼ Ramada Inn 🅼 ❀
(310) 325-0660. **$109-$119.** 2880 Pacific Coast Hwy. I-405, exit 39 (Cren-
shaw Blvd), just s, then just w. Ext corridors. **Pets:** Medium. $50 deposit/
room, $10 daily fee/pet. Service with restrictions, supervision.
🆂🅰🆅🅴 ⊠ 🛏 💻 ⊃

▼▼▼ Residence Inn by Marriott 🅷 ❀
(310) 543-4566. **$179-$219.** 3701 Torrance Blvd. I-405, exit 42A (Hawthorne Blvd), 3.2 mi s, then just e. Ext corridors. **Pets:** Medium, other
species. Service with restrictions, supervision.
⊠ 🛏 💻 ⊃ ⊠

▼▼▼ Staybridge Suites 🅼
(310) 371-8525. **Call for rates.** 19901 Prairie Ave. I-405, exit 39 (Cren-
shaw Blvd), just s to 190th St, 1 mi w, then just s. Ext/int corridors.
Pets: Accepted.
⊠ 🛏 💻 ⊃ ⊠

UNIVERSAL CITY

🆊 ▼▼▼ Sheraton Universal Hotel, at Universal
Studios 🅷 ❀
(818) 980-1212. **$189-$409.** 333 Universal Hollywood Dr. US 101, exit 12A
(Lankershim Blvd), just n, then just e. Int corridors. **Pets:** Other species.
Service with restrictions, supervision.
🆂🅰🆅🅴 ⊠ 🛏 💻 🍴 ⊃

WALNUT

▼▼▼▼ Quality Inn & Suites **H**
(909) 594-9999. **$100-$190.** 1170 Fairway Dr. SR 60, exit 21 (Fairway Dr), 0.3 mi s. Int corridors. **Pets:** Small, other species. $200 deposit/room, $35 daily fee/pet. Designated rooms, service with restrictions, supervision.

(ASK) (X) (&M) (🛏) (💻) (🏊) (X)

WEST HOLLYWOOD

(AAA) ▼▼▼▼ The Grafton on Sunset **H**
(323) 654-4600. **$185-$335.** 8462 Sunset Blvd. I-10, exit 7A (La Cienega Blvd), 4.4 mi n, then just e. Int corridors. **Pets:** Accepted.

(SAVE) (X) (🍴) (🏊)

▼▼▼▼ Le Montrose Suite Hotel **H**
(310) 855-1115. **Call for rates.** 900 Hammond St at Cynthia St. I-10, exit 7A (La Cienega Blvd), 2.6 mi n to San Vicente Blvd, 1.3 mi nw, then just w on Cynthia St. Int corridors. **Pets:** Accepted.

(X) (🛏) (💻) (🍴) (🏊) (X)

▼▼▼▼ Le Parc Suite Hotel **H**
(310) 855-8888. **$249-$499.** 733 N West Knoll Dr. I-10, exit 7A (La Cienega Blvd), 3.5 mi n, just w on Melrose Ave, then just n. Int corridors. **Pets:** Accepted.

(ASK) (X) (🛏) (💻) (🍴) (🏊) (X)

(AAA) ▼▼▼▼ ▼▼▼▼ The London West Hollywood **H**
(310) 854-1111. **$249-$399, 3 day notice.** 1020 N San Vicente Blvd. I-10, exit 7A (La Cienega Blvd), 2.6 mi n, then 1.5 mi nw. Int corridors. **Pets:** Accepted.

(SAVE) (X) (💻) (🍴) (🏊)

WHITTIER

(AAA) ▼▼▼▼ Radisson Hotel Whittier **H**
(562) 945-8511. **$79-$159, 3 day notice.** 7320 Greenleaf Ave. I-605, exit 15 (Whittier Blvd), 2.5 mi e, then 0.6 mi n. Int corridors. **Pets:** Accepted.

(SAVE) (X) (&M) (🛏) (🍴) (🏊)

▼▼ Vagabond Inn **M**
(562) 698-9701. **$70-$120.** 14125 E Whittier Blvd. I-605, exit 15 (Whittier Blvd), 3.5 mi e. Ext corridors. **Pets:** Medium. $15 daily fee/pet. Designated rooms, service with restrictions, supervision.

(X) (🛏) (💻) (🏊)

WOODLAND HILLS

▼▼ ▼▼ Extended StayAmerica-Los Angeles-Woodland Hills **H**
(818) 710-1170. **$95-$121.** 20205 Ventura Blvd. US 101, exit 25 (Winnetka Ave), just s, then just w. Int corridors. **Pets:** Other species. $25 daily fee/pet. Service with restrictions, crate.

(ASK) (X) (🛏) (💻)

▼▼▼▼ Warner Center Marriott Hotel **H** 🐾
(818) 887-4800. **$233-$285.** 21850 Oxnard St. US 101, exit 27A (Topanga Canyon Blvd N), 0.6 mi n, then just e. Int corridors. **Pets:** Other species. $75 one-time fee/room. Service with restrictions, supervision.

(X) (&M) (🛏) (💻) (🍴) (🏊) (X)

END METROPOLITAN AREA

LOS BANOS

(AAA) ▼▼ ▼▼ Best Western Executive Inn **H**
(209) 827-0954. **$70-$99.** 301 W Pacheco Blvd. On SR 152. Int corridors. **Pets:** Small, dogs only. $20 daily fee/pet. Service with restrictions, supervision.

(SAVE) (X) (&M) (🛏) (💻) (🏊) (X)

(AAA) ▼▼ ▼▼ Los Banos Motel **M**
(209) 826-2700. **$55-$75.** 2509 E Pacheco Blvd. East end of town. Ext corridors. **Pets:** Other species. $10 daily fee/pet. Service with restrictions, supervision.

(SAVE) (X) (&M) (🛏) (💻)

LOS GATOS

(AAA) ▼▼▼▼ Los Gatos Lodge **H** 🐾
(408) 354-3300. **$139-$199.** 50 Los Gatos/Saratoga Rd. SR 17, exit E Los Gatos, just e. Ext/int corridors. **Pets:** Medium. $30 one-time fee/room. Designated rooms, service with restrictions, supervision.

(SAVE) (X) (&M) (🛏) (💻) (🍴) (🏊)

(AAA) ▼▼▼▼ Toll House, a Larkspur Collection Hotel **H** 🐾
(408) 395-7070. **$188-$450.** 140 S Santa Cruz Ave. SR 17, exit SR 9, 0.5 mi w. Int corridors. **Pets:** Medium. $75 one-time fee/room. Designated rooms, service with restrictions, crate.

(SAVE) (X) (🛏) (💻) (🍴) (X)

MADERA

(AAA) ▼▼▼▼ Madera Valley Inn **H**
(559) 664-0100. **$69-$99.** 317 North G St. SR 99, exit Central Madera, just e. Int corridors. **Pets:** Accepted.

(SAVE) (X) (🛏) (💻) (🍴) (🏊)

▼▼ Super 8 **M**
(559) 661-1131. **$69-$79.** 1855 W Cleveland Ave. SR 99, exit Cleveland Ave, just w. Ext corridors. **Pets:** $5 daily fee/pet. Service with restrictions, supervision.

(ASK) (X) (🛏) (💻) (🏊)

MAMMOTH LAKES

▼▼ ▼▼ Econo Lodge Wildwood Inn **M**
(760) 934-6855. **$99-$239, 3 day notice.** 3626 Main St. On SR 203, 0.7 mi w of Old Mammoth Rd. Ext corridors. **Pets:** Small. $10 daily fee/pet. Service with restrictions, supervision.

(ASK) (X) (🛏) (💻) (🏊) (🎿)

▼▼▼▼ Mammoth Mountain Inn **H**
(760) 934-2581. **$99-$269, 14 day notice.** 1 Minaret Rd. 5 mi w of town on SR 203. Int corridors. **Pets:** Accepted.

(ASK) (X) (🛏) (💻) (🍴) (🏊) (X) (🎿)

▼▼ Mammoth Ski & Racquet Club **CO**
(760) 934-7368. **$110-$485, 30 day notice.** 248 Mammoth Slopes Dr. From Old Mammoth Rd, 1 mi w on SR 203, just n; Canyon Blvd, 0.8 mi w, then just s. Int corridors. **Pets:** Accepted.

(ASK) (X) (🛏) (💻) (🏊) (X) (🎿)

(AAA) ▼▼ ▼▼ Shilo Inn Suites-Mammoth Lakes **H** 🐾
(760) 934-4500. **$110-$280.** 2963 Main St. On SR 203, just e of Old Mammoth Rd. Int corridors. **Pets:** Dogs only. $25 one-time fee/room. Designated rooms, service with restrictions, supervision.

(SAVE) (X) (🛏) (💻) (🏊) (X)

(AAA) ▼▼ ▼▼ Sierra Lodge **H**
(760) 934-8881. **$69-$199.** 3540 Main St. On SR 203, 0.6 mi w of Old Mammoth Rd. Int corridors. **Pets:** $10 daily fee/pet. Designated rooms, service with restrictions.

(SAVE) (X) (🛏) (🎿)

▼▼ ▼▼ **Sierra Nevada Rodeway Inn** �H
(760) 934-2515. **$109-$129.** 164 Old Mammoth Rd. Just s of SR 203. Ext/int corridors. **Pets:** Accepted.
[A$K] [✕] [🛏] [🔲] [🛏] [🎾]

▼▼ **The Westin Monache Resort** �H 🐾
(760) 934-0400. **$149-$529, 7 day notice.** 50 Hillside Dr. SR 203, 1 mi w to Minaret Rd, 0.3 mi n to Forest Tr, just w, then just nw. Int corridors. **Pets:** Service with restrictions, supervision.
[SAVE] [✕] [&M] [🛏] [🔲] [🍴] [🛏]

MANTECA

▼▼▼▼ **Best Western Executive Inn & Suites** �H
(209) 825-1415. **$82-$116.** 1415 E Yosemite Ave. Jct SR 99 and 120, exit E Yosemite Ave. Ext corridors. **Pets:** $30 one-time fee/room. Service with restrictions, supervision.
[SAVE] [✕] [&M] [🛏] [🔲] [🛏]

MARIPOSA

▼▼ ▼▼ **Americas Best Value Inn–Mariposa Lodge** �H
(209) 966-3607. **$59-$149.** 5052 Hwy 140. Center. Ext corridors. **Pets:** Accepted.
[SAVE] [✕] [🛏] [🔲] [🛏]

▼▼ ▼▼ **Best Western Yosemite Way Station Motel** �H
(209) 966-7545. **$59-$149.** 4999 Hwy 140. SR 140 at SR 49 S. Ext corridors. **Pets:** Medium, dogs only. $10 daily fee/pet. Designated rooms, service with restrictions, supervision.
[SAVE] [✕] [&M] [🔲] [🛏]

▼▼ ▼▼ **Comfort Inn Yosemite Valley Gateway** �H
(209) 966-4344. **$79-$126.** 4994 Bullion St. Jct SR 140 and 49 S, just e. Ext corridors. **Pets:** Small, other species. $15 daily fee/pet. Service with restrictions, crate.
[SAVE] [✕] [&M] [🔲] [🛏]

▼▼ ▼▼ **Miners Inn** �H
(209) 742-7777. **$63-$174.** 5181 Hwy 49 N. On SR 49, n at SR 140. Ext/int corridors. **Pets:** $10 daily fee/pet. Designated rooms, service with restrictions, supervision.
[SAVE] [✕] [🔲] [🍴] [🛏]

MARYSVILLE

▼▼▼▼ **Baymont Inn & Suites** �H
(530) 742-2700. **$69-$199.** 1111 N Beale Rd. SR 70, exit 20A (Feather River Blvd/Yuba College) northbound; exit 20B southbound, just w. Int corridors. **Pets:** Accepted.
[SAVE] [✕] [&M] [🛏] [🔲] [🛏]

▼▼▼▼ **Comfort Suites** �H
(530) 742-9200. **$90-$175.** 1034 N Beale Rd. SR 70, exit 20A (Feather River Blvd/Yuba College) northbound, just w; exit 20B southbound, N Beale Rd, just w. Int corridors. **Pets:** Medium. $100 deposit/room, $10 one-time fee/pet. Designated rooms, service with restrictions, supervision.
[SAVE] [✕] [🛏] [🔲] [🛏]

MERCED

▼▼▼▼ **Merced-Yosemite Travelodge** 🅜
(209) 722-6224. **$65-$95.** 1260 Yosemite Pkwy. SR 99, exit SR 140, just e. Ext corridors. **Pets:** Accepted.
[SAVE] [✕] [&M] [🛏] [🔲] [🛏]

▼▼▼▼ **Ramada Inn** �H
(209) 723-3121. **$72-$126.** 2010 E Childs Ave. SR 99, exit E Childs Ave, just e. Ext/int corridors. **Pets:** Accepted.
[A$K] [✕] [🛏] [🔲] [🛏]

MILPITAS

▼▼▼▼ **Best Western Brookside Inn** �H
(408) 263-5566. **$99-$149.** 400 Valley Way. I-880, exit Calaveras Blvd (SR 237), just e. Ext/int corridors. **Pets:** Small. $15 daily fee/pet. Service with restrictions, supervision.
[SAVE] [✕] [🛏] [🔲] [🛏] [🎾]

▼▼▼▼ **Beverly Heritage Hotel** �H
(408) 943-9080. **$79-$209.** 1820 Barber Ln. Northwest quadrant of I-880 and Montague Expwy. Int corridors. **Pets:** Small. $25 one-time fee/pet. Service with restrictions, supervision.
[SAVE] [✕] [🛏] [🔲] [🍴] [🛏] [🎾]

▼▼▼▼ **Embassy Suites Milpitas/Silicon Valley** �H
(408) 942-0400. **$119-$259.** 901 E Calaveras Blvd. I-680, exit Calaveras Blvd (SR 237), just w. Int corridors. **Pets:** $50 one-time fee/pet. Service with restrictions, supervision.
[✕] [🛏] [🔲] [🍴] [🛏] [🎾]

▼▼ **Extended StayAmerica-San Jose/Milpitas** �H
(408) 941-9977. **$100-$110.** 1000 Hillview Ct. I-680, exit Calaveras Blvd W (SR 237), just n. Int corridors. **Pets:** Other species. $25 daily fee/pet. Service with restrictions, crate.
[A$K] [✕] [🛏]

▼▼ **Homestead Studio Suites Hotel-San Jose-Milpitas** �H
(408) 433-9700. **$142-$152.** 330 Cypress Dr. SR 237, exit McCarthy S. Ext/int corridors. **Pets:** Other species. $25 daily fee/pet. Service with restrictions, crate.
[A$K] [✕] [🛏] [🔲]

▼▼▼▼ **Larkspur Landing Milpitas/San Jose** �H
(408) 719-1212. **$99-$229.** 40 Ranch Dr. SR 237, exit McCarthy, just n. Int corridors. **Pets:** Medium. $75 one-time fee/room. Designated rooms, service with restrictions, crate.
[SAVE] [✕] [&M] [🔲]

▼▼▼▼ **Residence Inn by Marriott** �H
(408) 941-9222. **$206-$252.** 1501 California Cir. I-880, exit Dixon Landing Rd E, just s. Int corridors. **Pets:** Accepted.
[✕] [🛏] [🔲] [🛏] [🎾]

▼▼▼▼ **Sheraton San Jose Hotel** �H
(408) 943-0600. **$99-$329.** 1801 Barber Ln. 4 mi n of San Jose International Airport; 0.3 mi nw of I-880 and Montague Expwy. Ext/int corridors. **Pets:** Accepted.
[SAVE] [✕] [🛏] [🔲] [🍴] [🛏] [🎾]

▼▼▼▼ **TownePlace Suites by Marriott** �H
(408) 719-1959. **$179-$219.** 1428 Falcon Dr. I-680, exit Montague Expwy, just w, then just n. Int corridors. **Pets:** Accepted.
[✕] [&M] [🔲] [🛏]

MIRANDA

▼▼ ▼▼ **Miranda Gardens Resort** 🅒🅐
(707) 943-3011. **$105-$265, 7 day notice.** 6766 Ave of the Giants. US 101, exit 650 (Miranda), just e on French Rd, 0.3 mi s on Maple Hills Rd, then 1.5 mi e. Ext corridors. **Pets:** Medium. $150 deposit/room, $15 daily fee/pet. Designated rooms, service with restrictions, supervision.
[SAVE] [✕] [🛏] [🔲] [🛏] [🎾] [🖊]

MI-WUK VILLAGE

▼▼ ▼▼ **Christmas Tree Inn** �H
(209) 586-1005. **$89-$129, 3 day notice.** 24685 Hwy 108. On SR 108, 15 mi e of Sonora. Ext corridors. **Pets:** Medium, dogs only. $20 daily fee/room. Designated rooms, service with restrictions, supervision.
[SAVE] [✕] [🛏] [🔲] [🛏]

MODESTO

AAA ▼▼▼▼ **Clarion Hotel** H
(209) 521-1612. **$79-$239.** 1612 Sisk Rd. SR 99, exit Briggsmore Ave, just e. Int corridors. **Pets:** Small. $50 one-time fee/pet. Service with restrictions, supervision.
SAVE X &M H ■ ▯ ⑪ ⌒ ☒

▼▼▼▼ **Days Inn** H
(209) 527-1010. **$69-$109.** 1312 McHenry Ave. SR 99, exit Briggsmore Ave, 2.3 mi e, then 0.5 mi s. Ext/int corridors. **Pets:** Accepted.
A$K X &M

AAA ▼▼ ▼ **Microtel Inn & Suites** H
(209) 538-6466. **$66-$110.** 1760 Herndon Rd. SR 99, exit Hatch Rd E, just s. Int corridors. **Pets:** Very small. $50 deposit/room. Designated rooms, service with restrictions, supervision.
SAVE X &M H ■ ▯ ⌒

AAA ▼▼ ▼ **Ramada Inn** H
(209) 521-9000. **$72-$89.** 2001 W Orangeburg Ave. SR 99, exit Briggsmore Ave, just s. Ext corridors. **Pets:** Accepted.
SAVE X &M H ■ ▯ ⌒

MOJAVE

AAA ▼▼ ▼ **Americas Best Value Inn** M
(661) 824-9317. **$60-$65.** 16352 Sierra Hwy. On SR 14 and 58. Ext corridors. **Pets:** Accepted.
SAVE X H ■ ▯ ⌒

AAA ▼▼▼▼ **Best Western Desert Winds** M
(661) 824-3601. **$94-$120.** 16200 Sierra Hwy. On SR 14 and 58. Ext corridors. **Pets:** Small, other species. $10 daily fee/room. Designated rooms, service with restrictions, supervision.
SAVE X H ■ ▯ ⌒

AAA ▼▼▼▼ **Days Inn-Mojave** M ❀
(661) 824-2421. **$70-$200.** 16100 Sierra Hwy. On SR 14. Ext corridors. **Pets:** Small. $10 daily fee/pet. Designated rooms, service with restrictions, supervision.
SAVE X H ■ ▯ ⌒

AAA ▼▼▼▼ **Desert Inn** M
(661) 824-2518. **$45-$65.** 1954 Hwy 58. Just e of SR 14. Ext corridors. **Pets:** Medium. Service with restrictions, supervision.
SAVE X H ■ ▯

▼▼▼ **Econo Lodge** M ❀
(661) 824-2463. **$49-$62.** 2145 Hwy 58. Just e of SR 14. Ext corridors. **Pets:** Small. $5 daily fee/pet. Service with restrictions, supervision.
A$K X H ■ ▯

AAA ▼▼▼▼ **Mariah Country Inn & Suites** H
(661) 824-4980. **$110-$135.** 1385 Hwy 58. 1.5 mi e of SR 14. Int corridors. **Pets:** Small, other species. $10 daily fee/room. Service with restrictions, supervision.
SAVE X &M H ■ ▯ ⑪ ⌒

CARMEL-BY-THE-SEA

AAA ▼▼▼▼ **Briarwood Inn** BB
(831) 626-9056. **$105-$285, 7 day notice.** San Carlos St. 3 blks n of Ocean Ave; at jct 4th Ave. Ext corridors. **Pets:** Accepted.
SAVE X H ■ ▯ ⓚ

▼▼▼▼ **Carmel Country Inn** BB ❀
(831) 625-3263. **$275-$425, 7 day notice.** Dolores St & 3rd Ave. 4 blks n of Ocean Ave. Ext corridors. **Pets:** Other species. $20 daily fee/pet. Service with restrictions, supervision.
X H ■ ▯ ⓚ

AAA ▼▼▼▼ **Carmel Fireplace Inn Bed & Breakfast** BB
(831) 624-4862. **$105-$295, 7 day notice.** San Carlos St & 4th Ave. 3 blks n of Ocean Ave. Ext corridors. **Pets:** Accepted.
SAVE X H ■ ▯ ⓚ

AAA ▼▼▼▼ **Carmel Mission Inn** H
(831) 624-1841. **$129-$529.** 3665 Rio Rd. 1 mi s on SR 1. Ext/int corridors. **Pets:** Medium. $35 one-time fee/room. Designated rooms, service with restrictions, crate.
SAVE X H ■ ▯ ⑪ ⌒

▼▼ ▼ **Carmel River Inn** M ❀
(831) 624-1575. **$99-$369, 3 day notice.** Hwy One. 1 mi s on SR 1; n of Carmel River Bridge at Oliver Rd. Ext corridors. **Pets:** Other species. $25 daily fee/pet. Designated rooms, service with restrictions, supervision.
A$K X H ■ ▯ ⌒ ⓚ

AAA ▼▼▼▼ **Coachman's Inn** H
(831) 624-6421. **$145-$435, 3 day notice.** San Carlos St at 7th Ave. Just s of Ocean Ave on San Carlos St; between 7th and 8th aves. Ext corridors. **Pets:** Dogs only. $25 daily fee/pet. Designated rooms, service with restrictions, supervision.
SAVE X &M H ■ ▯ ⓚ

▼▼▼▼ **Cypress Inn** H ❀
(831) 624-3871. **$130-$625, 7 day notice.** Lincoln & 7th Ave. Just s off Ocean Ave. Ext/int corridors. **Pets:** $30 daily fee/room. Supervision.
X ⑪ ⓚ

AAA ▼▼ ▼ **Hofsas House** H
(831) 624-2745. **$100-$400, 3 day notice.** San Carlos St. 3 blks n off Ocean Ave; between 3rd and 4th aves. Ext corridors. **Pets:** Dogs only. $25 daily fee/pet. Designated rooms, supervision.
SAVE X H ■ ▯ ⌒ ⓚ

AAA ▼▼▼▼ **Horizon Inn & Ocean View Lodge** H
(831) 624-5327. **$129-$350, 3 day notice.** 3rd Ave & Junipero Ave. 4 blks n off Ocean Ave. **Pets:** Medium, dogs only. $20 daily fee/pet. Designated rooms, service with restrictions, supervision.
SAVE X ■ ▯ ⓚ

AAA ▼▼▼▼ **Quail Lodge** H ❀
(831) 624-2888. **$440-$680, 3 day notice.** 8205 Valley Greens Dr. 3.5 mi e of SR 1, via Carmel Valley Rd. Ext corridors. **Pets:** Other species. $35 daily fee/pet. Service with restrictions, supervision.
SAVE X ■ ▯ ⑪ ⌒ ☒

▼▼▼▼ **Tradewinds Carmel** H ❀
(831) 624-2776. **$225-$550, 3 day notice.** Mission St and 3rd Ave. 4 blks n off Ocean Ave. Ext corridors. **Pets:** Medium. $25 daily fee/pet. Designated rooms, service with restrictions, supervision.
A$K X H ■ ▯ ⓚ

CARMEL VALLEY

▼▼▼▼ **Los Laureles Lodge** H ❀
(831) 659-2233. **$125-$650, 3 day notice.** 313 W Carmel Valley Rd. 10.5 mi e of SR 1. Ext corridors. **Pets:** Small, dogs only. $20 daily fee/pet. Service with restrictions, supervision.
X H ■ ▯ ⑪ ⌒ ⓚ

MONTEREY

AAA ▼▼▼▼ **Bay Park Hotel** H ❀
(831) 649-1020. **$99-$350.** 1425 Munras Ave. SR 1, exit Soledad Dr/Munras Ave, just w. Int corridors. **Pets:** Medium, other species. $20 daily fee/pet. Designated rooms, service with restrictions, supervision.
SAVE X &M H ■ ▯ ⑪ ⌒

Best Western Beach Resort Monterey 🅷 ❀
(831) 394-3321. **$100-$500.** 2600 Sand Dunes Dr. SR 1, exit Del Rey Oaks, just w. Ext corridors. **Pets:** Other species. $25 daily fee/room. Designated rooms, service with restrictions.
[SAVE] [✕] [🛏] [💻] [🍴] [🏊]

Best Western Victorian Inn 🅷 ❀
(831) 373-8000. **$109-$379, 3 day notice.** 487 Foam St. SR 1, exit Monterey, 3.4 mi w. Ext/int corridors. **Pets:** Other species. $30 daily fee/room. Designated rooms, service with restrictions.
[SAVE] [✕] [🛗ᴹ] [🛏] [💻] [𝒦]

Casa Munras, a Larkspur Collection Hotel 🅷
(831) 375-2411. **$119-$349, 3 day notice.** 700 Munras Ave. SR 1, exit Soledad Dr/Munras Ave, 0.8 mi w. Ext/int corridors. **Pets:** Accepted.
[SAVE] [✕] [🛏] [💻] [🍴] [🏊] [𝒦]

El Adobe Inn Ⓜ
(831) 372-5409. **$49-$199, 3 day notice.** 936 Munras Ave. SR 1, exit Soledad Dr/Munras Ave, 0.6 mi w. Ext corridors. **Pets:** Medium, dogs only. $15 daily fee/pet. Designated rooms, service with restrictions, supervision.
[SAVE] [✕] [🛏] [💻] [𝒦]

Hyatt Regency-Monterey Resort & Spa on Del Monte Golf Course 🅷
(831) 372-1234. **$99-$439, 3 day notice.** 1 Old Golf Course Rd. SR 1, exit Aguajito Rd northbound; exit Monterey southbound, just e. Int corridors. **Pets:** Accepted.
[SAVE] [✕] [🛗ᴹ] [🛏] [💻] [🍴] [🏊] [✕] [𝒦]

La Quinta Inn 🅷 ❀
(831) 373-7100. **$69-$289.** 2401 Del Monte Ave. SR 1, exit Del Rey Oaks, just e. Int corridors. **Pets:** Medium, other species. Service with restrictions, supervision.
[SAVE] [✕] [🛏] [💻]

Mariposa Inn 🅷 ❀
(831) 649-1414. **$149-$419, 3 day notice.** 1386 Munras Ave. SR 1, exit Soledad Dr/Munras Ave, just w. Ext/int corridors. **Pets:** Medium, dogs only. $40 daily fee/pet. Service with restrictions, supervision.
[ASK] [✕] [🛏] [💻] [🏊]

Monterey Bay Lodge 🅷
(831) 372-8057. **$68-$245.** 55 Camino Aguajito. SR 1, exit Aguajito Rd, just w. Ext corridors. **Pets:** Medium, dogs only. $15 daily fee/pet. Designated rooms, service with restrictions, supervision.
[SAVE] [✕] [🛏] [💻] [🍴] [🏊]

Monterey Bay Travelodge 🅷
(831) 373-3381. **$169.** 2030 N Fremont St. Jct SR 1 and Fremont St, at SR 68. Ext/int corridors. **Pets:** Small, dogs only. $20 daily fee/pet. Service with restrictions, supervision.
[SAVE] [✕] [🛏] [💻] [🍴] [🏊] [𝒦]

Monterey Fireside Lodge Ⓜ
(831) 373-4172. **$69-$599, 3 day notice.** 1131 10th St. SR 1, exit Aguajito Rd or Monterey, just w. Ext corridors. **Pets:** Other species. $20 daily fee/pet. Designated rooms, service with restrictions, supervision.
[SAVE] [✕] [🛏] [𝒦]

PACIFIC GROVE

Bide-A-Wee Inn & Cottages Ⓜ ❀
(831) 372-2330. **$69-$319, 3 day notice.** 221 Asilomar Ave. 1 mi n of SR 68. Ext corridors. **Pets:** Medium. $15 daily fee/pet. Designated rooms, service with restrictions, supervision.
[SAVE] [✕] [🛏] [💻] [𝒦]

Deer Haven Inn & Suites 🅷
(831) 373-7784. **$79-$209, 3 day notice.** 740 Crocker Ave. Just e of SR 68 via Sinex Ave. Ext corridors. **Pets:** Medium, other species. $20 daily fee/pet. Service with restrictions, supervision.
[ASK] [✕] [🛏] [💻] [𝒦]

Olympia Lodge 🅷
(831) 373-2777. **$99-$375, 3 day notice.** 1140 Lighthouse Ave. 1 mi w. Ext corridors. **Pets:** Accepted.
[ASK] [✕] [🛏] [💻] [🏊] [𝒦]

Pacific Gardens Inn 🅷
(831) 646-9414. **$81-$198, 7 day notice.** 701 Asilomar Blvd. Just n of SR 68; across conference grounds. Ext corridors. **Pets:** Other species. Designated rooms, service with restrictions.
[SAVE] [✕] [🛏] [💻] [𝒦]

Sea Breeze Inn and Cottages 🅷 ❀
(831) 372-7771. **$79-$399.** 1100 Lighthouse Ave. Just w of Seventeen Mile Dr; jct Lighthouse Ave and Grove Acre. Ext/int corridors. **Pets:** Other species. $25 one-time fee/pet. Designated rooms, service with restrictions, crate.
[✕] [🛏] [💻] [🍴] [𝒦]

Sea Breeze Lodge Ⓜ ❀
(831) 372-3431. **$79-$399.** 1101 Lighthouse Ave. Just w of Seventeen Mile Dr. Ext corridors. **Pets:** Other species. $25 one-time fee/pet. Designated rooms, service with restrictions, crate.
[✕] [🛏] [💻] [🏊] [𝒦]

PEBBLE BEACH

The Lodge at Pebble Beach 🅷
(831) 624-3811. **$675-$3275, 3 day notice.** 1700 Seventeen Mile Dr. Off SR 1. Ext/int corridors. **Pets:** Accepted.
[✕] [🛗ᴹ] [💻] [🍴] [🏊] [✕] [𝒦]

SEASIDE

Econo Lodge Bay Breeze Ⓜ
(831) 899-7111. **$60-$120.** 2049 Fremont Blvd. SR 1, exit Sand City/Seaside, just e. Ext/int corridors. **Pets:** Accepted.
[SAVE] [✕] [🛏] [💻] [𝒦]

Thunderbird Motel Ⓜ
(831) 394-6797. **$39-$199, 3 day notice.** 1933 Fremont Blvd. SR 1 business route, 0.3 mi n. Ext corridors. **Pets:** Medium. $50 deposit/pet. Service with restrictions, supervision.
[SAVE] [✕] [🛏] [🏊] [𝒦]

END AREA

MORENO VALLEY

Comfort Inn Ⓜ
(951) 242-0699. **$70-$139.** 23330 Sunnymead Blvd. SR 60, exit 62 (Perris Blvd) westbound, just s, then 1.3 mi w; eastbound, 1 mi w. Ext/int corridors. **Pets:** Medium, other species. $50 deposit/pet, $10 daily fee/pet. Service with restrictions, supervision.
[SAVE] [✕] [🛏] [💻] [🏊]

MORGAN HILL

Extended StayAmerica-Morgan Hill 🅷
(408) 779-9660. **$84-$94.** 605 Jarvis Dr. US 101, exit Cochrane W, s on Sutter Blvd, then just e. Int corridors. **Pets:** Other species. $25 daily fee/pet. Service with restrictions, crate.
[ASK] [✕] [🛏] [💻]

AAA **WWW** Quality Inn **H**
(408) 779-0447. **$69-$129.** 16525 Condit Rd. US 101, exit Tennant or E Dunne aves, just e. Int corridors. **Pets:** Small, dogs only. $15 daily fee/pet, $15 one-time fee/pet. Designated rooms, service with restrictions, supervision.
SAVE ✕ 🗄 💻 🏊

WWWW Residence Inn by Marriott **H** 🐾
(408) 782-8311. **$165-$170.** 18620 Madrone Pkwy. US 101, exit Cochrane W, just n. Int corridors. **Pets:** Medium, other species. $100 one-time fee/ room. Designated rooms, service with restrictions.
✕ 🗄 💻 🏊

MORRO BAY

AAA **WWWW** Best Western El Rancho **M**
(805) 772-2212. **$65-$195.** 2460 Main St. SR 1, exit SR 41, 0.5 mi n. Ext corridors. **Pets:** Accepted.
SAVE ✕ ♿ 🗄 💻 🏊 🎾

AAA **WWW** Days Inn **M**
(805) 772-2711. **$69-$179, 3 day notice.** 1095 Main St. SR 1, exit Morro Bay Blvd, 0.7 mi w, then just n. Ext corridors. **Pets:** Accepted.
SAVE ✕ 🗄 💻 🎾

WWW Econo Lodge South **M**
(805) 772-7503. **$50-$200, 3 day notice.** 540 Main St. SR 1, exit Morro Bay Blvd, 0.7 mi w, then 0.4 mi s. Ext corridors. **Pets:** Accepted.
ASK ✕ 🗄 💻 🎾

AAA **WWWW** Sea Pines Golf Resort **M**
(805) 528-5252. **$124-$219.** 1945 Solano St. SR 1, exit Los Osos/ Baywood Park, 4 mi s on S Bay Blvd, 1.6 mi w on Los Osos Valley Rd, 0.3 mi n on Pecho Rd, then just w on Skyline Dr; in Los Osos. Ext corridors. **Pets:** Dogs only. $25 daily fee/room. Designated rooms, service with restrictions, supervision.
SAVE ✕ 🗄 💻 🍴 ✕

MOUNTAIN VIEW

WWW Homestead Studio Suites Hotel-San Jose, Mountain View **H**
(650) 962-1500. **$136-$146.** 190 E El Camino Real. SR 82, just w of SR 85. Ext corridors. **Pets:** Other species. $25 daily fee/pet. Service with restrictions, crate.
ASK ✕ ♿ 🗄 💻

MOUNT SHASTA

AAA **WW** A-1 Choice Inn **M**
(530) 926-4811. **$69-$149, 3 day notice.** 1340 S Mount Shasta Blvd. I-5, exit 737 (Mount Shasta City), 0.9 mi n. Ext corridors. **Pets:** Very small, dogs only. $10 daily fee/pet. Designated rooms, service with restrictions, supervision.
SAVE ✕ 🗄 💻 🏊

AAA **WWWW** Best Western Tree House Motor Inn **H** 🐾
(530) 926-3101. **$119-$209.** 111 Morgan Way. I-5, exit 738 (Central Mount Shasta), just e. Ext/int corridors. **Pets:** Large, other species. $15 daily fee/pet. Supervision.
SAVE ✕ 🗄 💻 🍴 🎾

AAA **WW** Cold Creek Inn **M** 🐾
(530) 926-9851. **$69-$129, 3 day notice.** 724 N Mount Shasta Blvd. I-5, exit 738 (Central Mount Shasta), 0.5 mi ne on W Lake St, then 0.4 mi nw. Ext corridors. **Pets:** Other species. $10 daily fee/pet. Service with restrictions, supervision.
SAVE ✕ 🗄 💻

WW Mt Shasta Ranch Bed & Breakfast **BB**
(530) 926-3870. **$80-$125, 3 day notice.** 1008 W a Barr Rd. I-5, exit 738 (Central Mount Shasta), 1.5 mi w. Ext/int corridors. **Pets:** $10 one-time fee/pet. Supervision.
ASK ✕ 🗄 💻 🖊

AAA **WW** Swiss Holiday Lodge **M** 🐾
(530) 926-3446. **$65-$180.** 2400 S Mount Shasta Blvd. I-5, exit 737 (Mount Shasta City), just e, then s. Ext corridors. **Pets:** Small. $10 daily fee/pet. Designated rooms, service with restrictions, supervision.
SAVE ✕ 🗄 🎾

MYERS FLAT

AAA **WWWW** Myers Inn **BB**
(707) 943-3259. **$165-$225, 14 day notice.** 12913 Ave of the Giants. US 101, exit Myers Flat, just w. Int corridors. **Pets:** Medium, dogs only. $20 daily fee/room. Designated rooms, service with restrictions, supervision.
SAVE ✕ 🗄 🖊

NEEDLES

WW **WW** Americas Best Value Inn **M** 🐾
(760) 326-4501. **$36-$77, 3 day notice.** 1102 E Broadway. I-40, exit 144 (US 95/E Broadway), just sw. Ext corridors. **Pets:** Other species. $5 one-time fee/room.
ASK ✕ 🗄 💻 🎾

AAA **WWW** Best Western Colorado River Inn **M**
(760) 326-4552. **$72-$189.** 2371 W Broadway. I-40, exit 141 (W Broadway/ River Rd), 0.3 mi e; on Business Loop I-40. Ext corridors. **Pets:** Accepted.
SAVE ✕ 🗄 💻 🎾

AAA **WWW** Best Western Royal Inn **M** 🐾
(760) 326-5660. **$72-$169, 3 day notice.** 1111 Pashard St. I-40, exit 141 (W Broadway/River Rd). Ext corridors. **Pets:** Large, other species. $25 deposit/room. Designated rooms, service with restrictions.
SAVE ✕ 🗄 💻 🎾

WW Travelers Inn **M**
(760) 326-4900. **Call for rates.** 1195 3rd St Hill. I-40, exit 142 (J St), just e, then just s. Ext corridors. **Pets:** Other species. $10 one-time fee/room. Service with restrictions, supervision.
✕ 🗄 🎾

NEVADA CITY

AAA **WWW** Nevada City Inn **M**
(530) 265-2253. **$55-$99.** 760 Zion St. SR 20 and 49, exit Gold Flat/Ridge Rd, 0.3 mi n, then 0.3 mi n. Ext corridors. **Pets:** Medium, other species. $10 daily fee/pet. Service with restrictions, supervision.
SAVE ✕ ♿ 🗄 💻

WW Northern Queen Inn **H**
(530) 265-5824. **$99-$600.** 400 Railroad Ave. SR 20 and 49, exit Sacramento St, 0.5 mi w. Ext corridors. **Pets:** Accepted.
✕ ♿ 🗄 💻 🍴 🎾

NEWARK

AAA **WWWW** Chase Suites by Woodfin **H**
(510) 795-1200. **$119-$129.** 39150 Cedar Blvd. I-880, exit Mowry Ave, just w, then 0.3 mi s. Ext corridors. **Pets:** Accepted.
SAVE ✕ 🗄 🎾

WWWW Homewood Suites by Hilton **H**
(510) 791-7700. **$89-$189.** 39270 Cedar Blvd. I-880, exit Mowry Ave, w to Cedar Blvd, then 0.3 mi s. Int corridors. **Pets:** Medium, other species. $10 daily fee/pet, $50 one-time fee/room. Service with restrictions, crate.
✕ 🗄 💻 🎾 ✕

WWW Residence Inn by Marriott Newark/Silicon Valley **H** 🐾
(510) 739-6000. **$188-$230.** 35466 Dumbarton Ct. SR 84, exit Newark Blvd, just s. Int corridors. **Pets:** $100 one-time fee/room. Service with restrictions, supervision.
✕ ♿ 🗄 💻 🎾 ✕

NEWPORT BEACH

AAA ▼▼▼▼ **The Balboa Bay Club & Resort** H ❀
(949) 645-5000. **$250-$559.** 1221 W Coast Hwy. SR 73, exit 15 (Jamboree Rd), 3.5 mi s, then just w. Int corridors. **Pets:** Small. $100 deposit/room. Designated rooms, service with restrictions, supervision.
SAVE ✕ 🔥M 🛏 💻 🍴 🐾 ✕

AAA ▼▼▼ **Best Western Newport Beach Inn** M
(949) 642-8252. **$169-$399, 3 day notice.** 6208 W Coast Hwy. SR 55, 1 mi nw on SR 1. Int corridors. **Pets:** Small, dogs only. $50 one-time fee/pet. Designated rooms, service with restrictions.
SAVE ✕ 💻 🐾

▼▼ **Extended StayAmerica-Orange County/John Wayne Airport** H
(949) 851-2711. **$110-$138.** 4881 Birch St. I-405, exit 8 (MacArthur Blvd), 0.8 mi s, then just e. Int corridors. **Pets:** Other species. $25 daily fee/pet. Service with restrictions, crate.
ASK ✕ 🔥M 🛏 💻

▼▼ ▼▼ **Fairmont Newport Beach** H ❀
(949) 476-2001. **Call for rates.** 4500 MacArthur Blvd. I-405, exit 8 (MacArthur Blvd), 1 mi s. Int corridors. **Pets:** $25 daily fee/pet. Service with restrictions, supervision.
✕ 🔥M 💻 🍴 🐾 ✕

AAA ▼▼▼▼ **The Island Hotel Newport Beach** H ❀
(949) 759-0808. **$420-$5000.** 690 Newport Center Dr. SR 73, exit 14 (MacArthur Blvd) northbound, 3 mi s to San Joaquin Hills Rd, then 0.5 mi w; exit 15 (Jamboree Rd) southbound, 2.5 mi s to San Joaquin Hills Rd, then 0.5 mi e. Int corridors. **Pets:** Medium. $100 one-time fee/room. Service with restrictions, supervision.
SAVE ✕ 🔥M 💻 🍴 🐾 ✕

NIPOMO

▼▼ **Kaleidoscope Inn & Gardens B&B** BB
(805) 929-5444. **$125-$160, 7 day notice.** 130 E Dana St. US 101, exit 179 (Tefft St), 0.7 mi e, just s on Thompson Rd, then just e. Ext/int corridors. **Pets:** Other species. Designated rooms, service with restrictions, supervision.
✕ 🎵

NOVATO

AAA ▼▼▼ **Inn Marin** H ❀
(415) 883-5952. **$129-$329.** 250 Entrada Dr. US 101, exit Ignacio Blvd, just w, then just n on Enfrente Rd. Ext corridors. **Pets:** Other species. $20 one-time fee/pet. Service with restrictions, crate.
SAVE ✕ 🔥M 🛏 💻 🍴 🐾

AAA ▼▼▼ **Novato Days Inn** H
(415) 897-7111. **$71-$96.** 8141 Redwood Blvd. US 101, exit San Marin Dr, 1 mi n. Ext corridors. **Pets:** Dogs only. $10 daily fee/pet. Designated rooms, service with restrictions, supervision.
SAVE ✕ 🔥M 🛏 💻 🍴 🐾

AAA ▼ **Travelodge** M
(415) 892-7500. **$69-$89.** 7600 Redwood Blvd. US 101, exit San Marin Dr, just sw. Ext corridors. **Pets:** Small, dogs only. $10 daily fee/pet. Designated rooms, no service, supervision.
SAVE ✕ 🛏 💻 🐾

OAKDALE

AAA ▼ **Holiday Motel** M ❀
(209) 847-7023. **$50-$140.** 950 East F St. 1 mi e on SR 108 and 120. Ext corridors. **Pets:** $20 daily fee/pet. Supervision.
SAVE ✕ 🛏 🐾

OAKHURST

AAA ▼▼▼ **Americas Best Value Inn** H
(559) 658-5500. **$59-$259.** 48800 Royal Oaks Dr. SR 41, just s of SR 49. Int corridors. **Pets:** Very small. $15 daily fee/room. Designated rooms, service with restrictions, supervision.
SAVE ✕ 🔥M 🛏 💻 🐾

AAA ▼▼▼ **Best Western Yosemite Gateway Inn** H
(559) 683-2378. **Call for rates.** 40530 Hwy 41. SR 49, 0.8 mi n. Ext corridors. **Pets:** Accepted.
SAVE ✕ 🔥M 🛏 💻 🍴 🐾 ✕

AAA ▼▼▼▼ **Chateau du Sureau** CI
(559) 683-6860. **$385-$585, 14 day notice.** 48688 Victoria Ln. Just w of jct SR 41 and 49. Int corridors. **Pets:** Accepted.
SAVE ✕ 🍴 🐾

AAA ▼▼▼ **Comfort Inn Yosemite Area** H
(559) 683-8282. **$59-$159.** 40489 Hwy 41. SR 49, 0.5 mi n. Ext corridors. **Pets:** Other species. $20 daily fee/room. Designated rooms, service with restrictions, supervision.
SAVE ✕ 💻 🐾

AAA ▼▼▼ **Shilo Inn Suites-Oakhurst** H ❀
(559) 683-3555. **$70-$230.** 40644 Hwy 41. SR 49, 0.8 mi n. Int corridors. **Pets:** Dogs only. $25 one-time fee/room. Designated rooms, service with restrictions, supervision.
SAVE ✕ 🔥M 🛏 💻 🐾 ✕

OAKLAND

▼▼▼▼ **Hilton Oakland Airport** H
(510) 635-5000. **$109-$259.** 1 Hegenberger Rd. I-880, exit Hegenberger Rd, 1 mi w; 1.3 mi e of Metropolitan Oakland International Airport. Int corridors. **Pets:** Accepted.
✕ 🔥M 🛏 💻 🍴 🐾

AAA ▼▼▼ **Homewood Suites** H
(510) 663-2700. **$99-$179.** 1103 Embarcadero. I-880, exit 16th Ave/Embarcadero southbound; exit 5th Ave/Embarcadero northbound, just w. Int corridors. **Pets:** Medium. $50 one-time fee/room. Service with restrictions.
SAVE ✕ 🛏 💻 🐾

AAA ▼▼▼ **La Quinta Inn Oakland Airport Coliseum** H ❀
(510) 632-8900. **$80-$150.** 8465 Enterprise Way. I-880, exit Hegenberger Rd, just e. Int corridors. **Pets:** Medium, other species. Service with restrictions, supervision.
SAVE ✕ 🔥M 🛏 💻 🐾

AAA ▼▼ **Quality Inn** H
(510) 562-4888. **$69-$129.** 8471 Enterprise Way. I-880, exit Hegenberger Rd, just e. Ext corridors. **Pets:** Small. $100 deposit/room, $10 daily fee/pet. Service with restrictions.
SAVE ✕ 🛏 💻 🐾

OCEANO

AAA ▼▼ **Oceano Inn** M
(805) 473-0032. **$69-$219, 3 day notice.** 1252 Pacific Blvd. On SR 1. Ext corridors. **Pets:** Very small. $15 one-time fee/pet. Service with restrictions, supervision.
SAVE ✕ 🔥M 🛏 💻

OCEANSIDE

AAA ▼▼▼ **Best Western Marty's Valley Inn** M
(760) 757-7700. **$85-$155, 7 day notice.** 3240 E Mission Ave. I-5, exit 53 (Mission Ave), 2 mi e. Ext/int corridors. **Pets:** Medium, other species. $10 daily fee/pet. Designated rooms, service with restrictions, supervision.
SAVE ✕ 🛏 💻 🐾

▼▼▼ Extended StayAmerica-San Diego/Oceanside 🅗
(760) 439-1499. **$92-$189.** 3190 Vista Way. I-5, exit 51B (SR 78 E) 1.5 mi e to El Camino Real, just n, then just e. Int corridors. **Pets:** Other species. $25 daily fee/pet. Service with restrictions, crate.
Ⓐ𝕊𝕂 ⊠ 𝕃ᴹ 🛏 🖵

㊿ ▼▼▼ La Quinta Inn 🅗 ❁
(760) 450-0730. **$69-$346.** 937 N Coast Hwy. I-5, exit 54 (Coast Hwy), just w. Int corridors. **Pets:** Medium, other species. Service with restrictions, supervision.
🆂🅰🆅🅴 ⊠ 🛏 🖵

㊿ ▼▼▼ Motel 6 #4208 🅜
(760) 721-1543. **$70-$110, 7 day notice.** 909 N Coast Hwy. I-5, exit 54B (Coast Hwy), just w. Int corridors. **Pets:** Other species. Service with restrictions, supervision.
🆂🅰🅅🅴 ⊠ 𝕃ᴹ 🛏 🖘

▼▼▼ Residence Inn by Marriott San Diego/Oceanside 🅗 ❁
(760) 722-9600. **$189-$249.** 3603 Ocean Ranch Blvd. I-5, exit 52 (Oceanside Blvd), 3.3 mi e, then 0.5 mi n. Int corridors. **Pets:** Other species. $100 one-time fee/pet. Service with restrictions, supervision.
⊠ 🛏 🖵 🖘

OJAI

㊿ ▼▼▼ Best Western Casa Ojai 🅜 ❁
(805) 646-8175. **$90-$180, 3 day notice.** 1302 E Ojai Ave. 0.8 mi e on SR 150. Ext corridors. **Pets:** Dogs only. $25 daily fee/pet. Designated rooms, service with restrictions, supervision.
🆂🅰🅅🅴 ⊠ 🛏 🖵

▼▼▼ Blue Iguana Inn 🅜
(805) 646-5277. **$119-$269, 7 day notice.** 11794 N Ventura Ave. 2.5 mi w of town on SR 33. Ext corridors. **Pets:** Accepted.
Ⓐ𝕊𝕂 ⊠ 🛏 🖵 🖘 🖾

㊿ ▼▼▼ Oakridge Inn 🅜
(805) 649-4018. **$65-$140, 3 day notice.** 780 N Ventura Ave. 4 mi s on SR 33; 2 mi e of Lake Casitas; in Oak View. Ext corridors. **Pets:** Accepted.
🆂🅰🅅🅴 ⊠ 🛏 🖵

㊿ ▼▼▼▼ Ojai Valley Inn & Spa 🅗 ❁
(805) 646-1111. **$400-$3000, 3 day notice.** 905 Country Club Rd. 1 mi w on SR 150, 0.3 mi s. Ext/int corridors. **Pets:** Large, other species. Service with restrictions, supervision.
🆂🅰🅅🅴 ⊠ 𝕃ᴹ 🛏 🖵 🍴 🖘 🖾

ONTARIO

㊿ ▼▼▼ Best Western InnSuites Hotel & Suites Ontario/LA 🅗 ❁
(909) 466-9600. **$71-$169, 3 day notice.** 3400 Shelby St. I-10, exit 56 (Haven Ave), just n to Inland Empire Blvd, just w, then just se. Ext corridors. **Pets:** Medium, other species. $50 one-time fee/room. Designated rooms, service with restrictions, supervision.
🆂🅰🅅🅴 ⊠ 🛏 🖵 🍴 🖘 🖾

▼▼▼ Country Inn & Suites by Carlson 🅜
(909) 937-6000. **$110-$214.** 231 N Vineyard Ave. I-10, exit 54 (Vineyard Ave), just s. Ext corridors. **Pets:** Accepted.
Ⓐ𝕊𝕂 ⊠ 🛏 🖵 🖘

▼▼▼ DoubleTree Hotel Ontario 🅗
(909) 937-0900. **$99-$225.** 222 N Vineyard Ave. I-10, exit 54 (Vineyard Ave), 0.4 mi s. Int corridors. **Pets:** Accepted.
⊠ 🛏 🖵 🍴 🖘

▼▼ Extended StayAmerica-Los Angeles-Ontario Airport 🅗
(909) 944-8900. **$89-$143.** 3990 E Inland Empire Blvd. I-10, exit 56 (Haven Ave), just n, then 0.5 mi e. Int corridors. **Pets:** Other species. $25 daily fee/pet. Service with restrictions, crate.
Ⓐ𝕊𝕂 ⊠ 🛏 🖘

▼▼▼ Hilton Ontario Airport 🅗
(909) 980-0400. **$99-$249.** 700 N Haven Ave. I-10, exit 56 (Haven Ave), just n. Int corridors. **Pets:** Accepted.
⊠ 🛏 🖵 🍴 🖘

▼▼▼ La Quinta Inn & Suites Ontario (Airport) 🅗 ❁
(909) 476-1112. **$79-$169.** 3555 Inland Empire Blvd. I-10, exit 56 (Haven Ave), just n, then just e. Int corridors. **Pets:** Medium, other species. Service with restrictions, supervision.
Ⓐ𝕊𝕂 ⊠ 𝕃ᴹ 🛏 🖵 🖘 🖾

▼▼▼ Residence Inn by Marriott 🅗
(909) 937-6788. **$152-$186.** 2025 Convention Center Way. I-10, exit 54 (Vineyard Ave), just s, then 1 blk e. Ext corridors. **Pets:** Accepted.
⊠ 𝕃ᴹ 🛏 🖵 🖘 🖾

㊿ ▼▼▼▼ Sheraton Ontario Airport Hotel 🅗 ❁
(909) 937-8000. **Call for rates.** 429 N Vineyard Ave. I-10, exit 54 (Vineyard Ave), just s. Int corridors. **Pets:** Small. Service with restrictions, crate.
🆂🅰🅅🅴 ⊠ 🛏 🖵 🍴 🖘

ORANGE

▼▼▼▼ DoubleTree Hotel Anaheim/Orange County 🅗
(714) 634-4500. **$129-$239.** 100 The City Dr. I-5, exit 107B (Chapman Ave) northbound, just w; exit 107C (State College/The City Dr) southbound, just s on State College Blvd, then just w. Int corridors. **Pets:** Large. $75 one-time fee/pet.
⊠ 🛏 🖵 🍴 🖘 🖾

▼▼▼ Hilton Suites Anaheim/Orange 🅗
(714) 938-1111. **$99-$249.** 400 N State College Blvd. I-5, exit 107C (State College Blvd/The City Dr), just s. Int corridors. **Pets:** Accepted.
⊠ 🛏 🖵 🖘 🖾

ORLAND

▼▼ Amber Light Inn Motel 🅜
(530) 865-7655. **$54-$65.** 828 Newville Rd. I-5, exit 619 (SR 32), 0.3 mi e. Ext corridors. **Pets:** Medium. $5 daily fee/pet. No service, supervision.
Ⓐ𝕊𝕂 ⊠ 🛏 🖘

㊿ ▼▼ Orland Inn 🅜
(530) 865-7632. **$59-$69.** 1052 South St. I-5, exit 618 (CR 16/South St), just ne; in Stony Creek Shopping Center. Ext corridors. **Pets:** Medium, other species. $5 one-time fee/pet. Service with restrictions, crate.
🆂🅰🅅🅴 ⊠ 𝕃ᴹ 🛏 🖘

OROVILLE

㊿ ▼▼▼ Americas Best Value Inn 🅜
(530) 533-7070. **$60-$155.** 580 Oro Dam Blvd. SR 70, exit SR 162 (Oroville Dam Blvd), 0.3 mi e. Ext corridors. **Pets:** Large, other species. $10 daily fee/pet. Designated rooms, service with restrictions, supervision.
🆂🅰🅅🅴 ⊠ 𝕃ᴹ 🛏 🖵

㊿ ▼▼▼ Comfort Inn 🅗
(530) 533-9673. **$85-$175.** 1470 Feather River Blvd. SR 70, exit Montgomery St, just e, then s. Int corridors. **Pets:** Dogs only. $100 deposit/room, $10 daily fee/pet. Designated rooms, service with restrictions, supervision.
🆂🅰🅅🅴 ⊠ 𝕃ᴹ 🛏 🖵 🖘 🖾

㊿ ▼▼▼ Days Inn-Oroville 🅜
(530) 533-3297. **$75-$149.** 1745 Feather River Blvd. SR 70, exit E Montgomery St, just e to Feather River Blvd, then 0.5 mi s. Ext corridors. **Pets:** Medium. $10 daily fee/pet. Service with restrictions, supervision.
🆂🅰🅅🅴 ⊠ 🛏 🖵 🖘

㊿ ▼▼▼ Sunset Inn 🅜
(530) 533-8201. **$55-$150.** 1835 Feather River Blvd. SR 70, exit E Montgomery St, 0.5 mi s. Ext corridors. **Pets:** Accepted.
🆂🅰🅅🅴 ⊠ 🛏 🖵 🖘

OXNARD

▼▼▼▼ Comfort Inn Oxnard M
(805) 201-6000. **$89-$179.** 1001 E Channel Islands Blvd. US 101, exit 61 (Rose Ave), 3.5 mi s, then 1.5 mi w. Ext corridors. **Pets:** Accepted.
ASK ✕ 🛅 💻 ➿ ✕

▼▼▼▼ Residence Inn At River Ridge H
(805) 278-2200. **$159-$179.** 2101 W Vineyard Ave. US 101, exit 62A (Vineyard Ave), 1.8 mi w. Ext corridors. **Pets:** Accepted.
✕ ♿ 🛅 💻 ➿ ✕

◈◈◈ ▼▼▼ Vagabond Inn Oxnard M ✿
(805) 983-0251. **$66-$80.** 1245 N Oxnard Blvd. US 101, exit 62A (Vineyard Ave) northbound; exit 62B (Oxnard Blvd) southbound, 1.5 mi s. Ext corridors. **Pets:** Other species. $5 one-time fee/pet. Service with restrictions, supervision.
SAVE ✕ ♿ 🛅 💻 ➿

PALMDALE

▼▼▼▼ Residence Inn by Marriott H
(661) 947-4204. **$167-$204.** 514 W Ave P. SR 14, exit Ave P, just w. Int corridors. **Pets:** Medium, other species. $100 one-time fee/room. Service with restrictions, crate.
✕ ♿ 🛅 💻 ➿ ✕

▼▼ Super 8 M
(661) 273-8000. **Call for rates.** 200 W Palmdale Blvd. SR 14, exit 35 (Palmdale Blvd), just e. Int corridors. **Pets:** Accepted.
✕ 🛅 ➿

PALM DESERT

◈◈◈ ▼▼▼▼ Best Western Palm Desert Resort M
(760) 340-4441. **$79-$249.** 74-695 Hwy 111. I-10, exit 134 (Cook St), 4.4 mi s, then 0.3 mi w. Ext corridors. **Pets:** Other species. $10 daily fee/room. Service with restrictions, crate.
SAVE ✕ ♿ 🛅 💻 ➿ ✕

◈◈◈ ▼▼▼▼ Comfort Suites M ✿
(760) 360-3337. **$89-$349.** 39-585 Washington St. I-10, exit 137 (Washington St), just n. Int corridors. **Pets:** Medium, other species. $100 deposit/room, $20 daily fee/room. Service with restrictions, supervision.
SAVE ✕ ♿ 🛅 💻 ➿ ✕

▼▼▼▼ Embassy Suites Hotel H
(760) 340-6600. **$99-$269.** 74-700 Hwy 111. I-10, exit 134 (Cook St), 4.4 mi s, then 0.3 mi w. Ext corridors. **Pets:** Medium, other species. $50 one-time fee/room. Designated rooms, service with restrictions, crate.
✕ 🛅 💻 🍴 ➿ ✕

◈◈◈ ▼▼▼ The Inn at Deep Canyon M
(760) 346-8061. **$63-$127, 3 day notice.** 74-470 Abronia Tr. I-10, exit 134 (Cook St), 4.4 mi s to SR 111, 0.5 mi w, then just s on Deep Canyon Rd. Ext corridors. **Pets:** Large, other species. $10 daily fee/pet. Designated rooms, service with restrictions.
SAVE ✕ 🛅 💻 ➿

▼▼▼▼ Residence Inn by Marriott H
(760) 776-0050. **$119-$219.** 38-305 Cook St. I-10, exit 134 (Cook St), 0.8 mi s. Ext corridors. **Pets:** Small, other species. $75 one-time fee/room. Service with restrictions, supervision.
✕ 🛅 💻 ➿ ✕

PALM SPRINGS

▼▼ A Place In The Sun M ✿
(760) 325-0254. **$79-$299, 7 day notice.** 754 San Lorenzo Rd. Just e of Palm Canyon Dr via Mesquite Ave and Random Rd. Ext corridors. **Pets:** Other species. $15 daily fee/pet.
✕ 🛅 💻 ➿

▼▼ Casa Cody Country Inn M
(760) 320-9346. **$79-$429, 3 day notice.** 175 S Cahuilla Rd. SR 111, just w of Palm Canyon Dr on Tahquitz Canyon Way, then just s. Ext corridors. **Pets:** Accepted.
✕ 🛅 💻 ➿

▼▼▼▼ Hilton Palm Springs H
(760) 320-6868. **$80-$315.** 400 E Tahquitz Canyon Way. Just e of Indian Canyon Dr. Int corridors. **Pets:** Large, other species. $100 deposit/pet, $25 one-time fee/pet. Designated rooms, service with restrictions.
✕ 🛅 💻 🍴 ➿ ✕

▼▼▼▼ Holiday Inn Palm Springs-City Center H ✿
(760) 323-1711. **$89-$325.** 1800 E Palm Canyon Dr. 2 mi se of Tahquitz Canyon Way. Ext/int corridors. **Pets:** Medium, dogs only. $20 daily fee/room. Designated rooms, service with restrictions, supervision.
ASK ✕ 🛅 💻 🍴 ➿

▼▼▼ Hotel California M
(760) 322-8855. **$89-$250, 3 day notice.** 424 E Palm Canyon Dr. 1.5 mi s of Tahquitz Canyon Way. Ext corridors. **Pets:** Accepted.
ASK ✕ 🛅 💻 ➿

▼▼▼▼ Hotel Zoso H
(760) 325-9676. **$109-$349, 3 day notice.** 150 S Indian Canyon Dr. Just s of Tahquitz Canyon Way. Int corridors. **Pets:** Medium, dogs only. $100 deposit/pet, $50 one-time fee/pet. Service with restrictions.
ASK ✕ 🛅 💻 🍴 ➿

▼▼▼▼ Quality Inn Palm Springs M
(760) 323-2775. **$59-$189.** 1269 E Palm Canyon Dr. 2.3 mi se of Tahquitz Canyon Way. Ext corridors. **Pets:** Accepted.
ASK ✕ 🛅 💻 ➿

◈◈◈ ▼▼▼ Ramada Palm Springs M
(760) 320-0555. **$59-$229.** 2000 N Palm Canyon Dr. 1.5 mi n of Tahquitz Canyon Way. Ext/int corridors. **Pets:** Accepted.
SAVE ✕ 🛅 💻 ➿

◈◈◈ ▼▼▼▼ Shilo Inn Suites M ✿
(760) 320-7676. **$115-$255.** 1875 N Palm Canyon Dr. 1.5 mi n of Tahquitz Canyon Way. Int corridors. **Pets:** Dogs only. $25 one-time fee/room. Designated rooms, service with restrictions, supervision.
SAVE ✕ 🛅 💻 ➿ ✕

◈◈◈ ▼▼▼ Vagabond Inn Palm Springs M
(760) 325-7211. **$49-$179.** 1699 S Palm Canyon Dr. 1.5 mi s of Tahquitz Canyon Way. Ext corridors. **Pets:** Accepted.
SAVE ✕ 🛅 💻 ➿

PALO ALTO

◈◈◈ ▼▼▼▼ Crowne Plaza Cabana Hotel H
(650) 857-0787. **$179-$305.** 4290 El Camino Real. US 101, exit San Antonio Rd, 0.4 mi n. Ext/int corridors. **Pets:** Medium. $50 one-time fee/pet. Designated rooms, no service, supervision.
SAVE ✕ ♿ 🛅 💻 🍴 ➿

◈◈◈ ◈◈ Days Inn M
(650) 493-4222. **$55-$150.** 4238 El Camino Real. US 101, exit San Antonio Rd, 2 mi w to SR 82, then 1 mi n. Ext corridors. **Pets:** Small. $15 daily fee/pet. Service with restrictions, supervision.
SAVE ✕ ♿ 🛅 💻

◈◈◈ ▼▼▼▼ Sheraton Palo Alto Hotel H
(650) 328-2800. **$109-$489.** 625 El Camino Real. US 101, exit Embarcadero, 1.8 mi w, then just n on SR 82. Int corridors. **Pets:** Accepted.
SAVE ✕ ♿ 🛅 💻 ➿

◈◈◈ ▼▼▼▼ The Westin Palo Alto H ✿
(650) 321-4422. **$149-$569.** 675 El Camino Real. US 101, exit Embarcadero, 1.8 mi w, then just n on SR 82. Int corridors. **Pets:** Large, dogs only. Service with restrictions, supervision.
SAVE ✕ ♿ 💻 🍴 ➿ ✕

PARADISE

AAA ◈◈◈ Comfort Inn H
(530) 876-0191. **$84-$159.** 5475 Clark Rd. SR 191, 0.5 mi s of Pearson Rd. Int corridors. **Pets:** Dogs only. $100 deposit/room, $10 daily fee/pet. Service with restrictions, supervision.
SAVE ⊠ 🕭M 🛏 🖳 🏊

AAA ◈◈◈ Lantern Inn M
(530) 877-5553. **$65-$98.** 5799 Wildwood Ln. Just n of jct Pearson Rd and Skyway, then 1 blk w off Skyway. Ext corridors. **Pets:** Accepted.
SAVE ⊠ 🛏 🖳 🏊

AAA ◈◈◈ Paradise Inn M
(530) 877-2127. **$58-$65.** 5423 Skyway. Jct Pearson Rd, 1.5 mi w. Ext corridors. **Pets:** $10 daily fee/pet.
SAVE ⊠ 🛏 🖳 🏊

AAA ◈◈◈ Ponderosa Gardens Motel M 🐾
(530) 872-9094. **$89-$139.** 7010 Skyway. 2 blks e; center. Ext corridors. **Pets:** Other species. $10 daily fee/pet. Designated rooms, service with restrictions, supervision.
SAVE ⊠ 🕭M 🛏 🖳 🏊

PASO ROBLES

AAA ◈◈◈ Hampton Inn & Suites H
(805) 226-9988. **$119-$179.** 212 Alexa Ct. US 101, exit 228 (SR 46 W), just sw. Int corridors. **Pets:** Small. $50 deposit/room. Service with restrictions, supervision.
SAVE ⊠ 🕭M 🛏 🖳 🏊

◈◈◈ La Quinta Inn & Suites H 🐾
(805) 239-3004. **$99-$219.** 2615 Buena Vista Dr. US 101, exit 234 northbound; exit 231B (SR 46 E) southbound, 0.3 mi e, then just n. Int corridors. **Pets:** Medium, other species. Service with restrictions, supervision.
ASK ⊠ 🛏 🖳 🏊

PATTERSON

AAA ◈◈◈ Best Western Villa Del Lago Inn H
(209) 892-5300. **$79-$139.** 2959 Speno Dr. I-5, exit Sperry Rd, just e. Int corridors. **Pets:** Large, other species. Designated rooms, service with restrictions, supervision.
SAVE ⊠ 🛏 🖳 🍴 🏊 ⊠

PHELAN

AAA ◈◈◈ Best Western Cajon Pass M
(760) 249-6777. **$70-$95.** 8317 Hwy 138. I-15, exit 131 (SR 138/Palmdale), just w. Ext corridors. **Pets:** Accepted.
SAVE ⊠ 🛏 🖳 🏊

PISMO BEACH

◈◈◈ Cliffs Resort H
(805) 773-5000. **$139-$359, 3 day notice.** 2757 Shell Beach Rd. US 101, exit 193 (Spyglass Dr) northbound; exit 193 (Shell Beach Rd) southbound, just w, then just n. Int corridors. **Pets:** Accepted.
ASK ⊠ 🛏 🖳 🍴 🏊 ⊠

◈◈◈ Cottage Inn by the Sea M
(805) 773-4617. **$109-$429.** 2351 Price St. US 101, exit 191B (Shell Beach Rd) northbound, just w, 0.5 mi s; exit 191B (Price St) southbound, just w, then just s. Ext corridors. **Pets:** Accepted.
⊠ 🕭M 🛏 🖳 🏊 🐾

AAA ◈◈◈ Oxford Suites H 🐾
(805) 773-3773. **$109-$259.** 651 Five Cities Dr. US 101, exit 189 (4th St), just w, then just s. Ext corridors. **Pets:** Medium. $15 daily fee/pet. Designated rooms, service with restrictions, supervision.
SAVE ⊠ 🛏 🖳 🏊 ⊠

◈◈◈ Sandcastle Inn M
(805) 773-2422. **Call for rates.** 100 Stimson Ave. US 101, exit 190 (Price St) northbound, 0.3 mi s, then just w; exit 190B (Hinds Ave) southbound, just w, then just s. Ext/int corridors. **Pets:** Dogs only. $20 daily fee/room. Designated rooms, service with restrictions.
⊠ 🕭M 🛏 🖳

◈◈ Sea Gypsy Motel CO
(805) 773-1801. **$55-$250.** 1020 Cypress St. US 101, exit 191A (Wadsworth Ave) northbound, 0.3 mi w to Cypress St, then just s; exit 191A (SR 1) southbound, just w on Wadsworth Ave, then just s. Ext/int corridors. **Pets:** Other species. $15 daily fee/pet. Service with restrictions, supervision.
⊠ 🛏 🖳 🏊 🐾

◈◈ Shell Beach Inn M
(805) 773-4373. **$65-$225.** 653 Shell Beach Rd. US 101, exit 191B (Shell Beach Rd) northbound, just w, then 1.2 mi s; exit 191B (Price St) southbound, just w, then 1 mi n. Ext corridors. **Pets:** Dogs only. $20 one-time fee/pet. Service with restrictions, supervision.
ASK ⊠ 🛏 🖳 🏊 🐾

◈◈◈ Spyglass Inn H
(805) 773-4855. **$109-$399.** 2705 Spyglass Dr. US 101, exit 193 (Spyglass Dr) northbound; exit 193 (Shell Beach Rd) southbound, just w, then just n. Ext corridors. **Pets:** Accepted.
⊠ 🕭M 🛏 🖳 🍴 🏊 🐾

PLACENTIA

◈◈◈ Residence Inn by Marriott H
(714) 996-0555. **$206-$252.** 700 W Kimberly Ave. SR 57, exit 6 (Orangethorpe Ave) southbound; exit 6A (Orangethorpe Ave) northbound, just w, just n on Placentia Ave, then just e. Ext corridors. **Pets:** Medium, other species. $100 one-time fee/pet. Service with restrictions, supervision.
⊠ 🛏 🖳 🏊 ⊠

PLACERVILLE

AAA ◈◈◈ Best Western Placerville Inn H
(530) 622-9100. **$89-$289, 3 day notice.** 6850 Green Leaf Dr. US 50, exit 44A (Missouri Flat Rd S), just e. Int corridors. **Pets:** Accepted.
SAVE ⊠ 🕭M 🛏 🖳 🏊

AAA ◈◈ Mother Lode Motel M
(530) 622-0895. **$48-$78, 3 day notice.** 1940 Broadway. US 50, exit 49 (Point View Dr), just e. Ext corridors. **Pets:** Accepted.
SAVE ⊠ 🕭M 🛏 🖳 🏊

PLEASANT HILL

◈◈ Extended StayAmerica-Pleasant Hill H
(925) 945-6788. **$121-$131.** 3220 Buskirk Ave. I-680, exit Treat Blvd/Geary Rd E, just n. Int corridors. **Pets:** Other species. $25 daily fee/pet. Service with restrictions, crate.
ASK ⊠ 🛏 🖳

AAA ◈◈◈ Hyatt Summerfield Suites H 🐾
(925) 934-3343. **$104-$319.** 2611 Contra Costa Blvd. I-680, exit Contra Costa Blvd, then w. Int corridors. **Pets:** Large. $150 one-time fee/room. Service with restrictions, crate.
SAVE ⊠ 🕭M 🛏 🖳 🏊 ⊠

◈◈◈ Residence Inn by Marriott-Pleasant Hill H
(925) 689-1010. **$224-$274.** 700 Ellinwood Way. I-680, exit Willow Pass Rd W to S Contra Costa Blvd, e on Ellinwood Dr, then n. Ext/int corridors. **Pets:** $100 one-time fee/room. Service with restrictions, crate.
⊠ 🖳 🏊

PLEASANTON

AAA ◈◈◈ Best Western Pleasanton Inn H
(925) 463-1300. **$99-$129, 7 day notice.** 5375 Owens Ct. I-580, exit Hopyard Rd, just s. Ext corridors. **Pets:** Other species. $20 daily fee/pet. Designated rooms, service with restrictions.
SAVE ⊠ 🛏 🖳 🏊

Extended Stay Deluxe Pleasanton-Chabot Dr 🅷
(925) 730-0000. **$121-$131.** 4555 Chabot Dr. I-580, exit Hopyard Rd, 1 mi s, e on Stoneridge Dr, then s. Int corridors. **Pets:** Other species. $25 daily fee/pet. Service with restrictions, crate.

Hyatt Summerfield Suites 🅷
(925) 730-0070. **$99-$499.** 4545 Chabot Dr. I-580, exit Hopyard Rd, 1 mi s, e on Stoneridge Dr, then s. Ext corridors. **Pets:** Accepted.

Larkspur Landing Home Suite Hotel Pleasanton 🅷
(925) 463-1212. **$189-$229.** 5535 Johnson Dr. I-580, exit Hopyard Rd S, w on Owen. Int corridors. **Pets:** Medium, other species. $75 one-time fee/pet. Service with restrictions, supervision.

Residence Inn by Marriott 🅷
(925) 227-0500. **$197-$241.** 11920 Dublin Canyon Rd. I-580, exit Foothill Blvd S, then w. Int corridors. **Pets:** Accepted.

Sheraton Pleasanton Hotel 🅷
(925) 463-3330. **Call for rates.** 5990 Stoneridge Mall Rd. Jct I-580 and 680, 0.5 mi sw; I-580, exit Foothill Rd, 0.3 mi s, then 0.3 mi e on Canyon Way. Int corridors. **Pets:** Medium, dogs only. Designated rooms, service with restrictions, crate.

PORTOLA

Sleepy Pines Motel 🅼
(530) 832-4291. **$72-$180, 3 day notice.** 74631 Hwy 70. 1 mi w of center on SR 70. Ext corridors. **Pets:** Accepted.

RAMONA

Ramona Valley Inn 🅼
(760) 789-6433. **$75-$125.** 416 Main St. On SR 78, 0.5 mi e of jct SR 67. Ext corridors. **Pets:** Accepted.

RANCHO CORDOVA

Comfort Inn & Suites 🅷
(916) 351-1213. **$70-$90, 4 day notice.** 12249 Folsom Blvd. US 50, exit Hazel Ave, just s, then just w. Ext corridors. **Pets:** $20 daily fee/room. Designated rooms, service with restrictions, supervision.

Extended StayAmerica-Sacramento-White Rock Rd 🅷
(916) 635-2363. **$79-$89.** 10721 White Rock Rd. US 50, exit Zinfandel Dr, just s. Ext corridors. **Pets:** Other species. $25 daily fee/pet. Service with restrictions, crate.

Hawthorn Suites 🅷
(916) 351-9192. **$119.** 12180 Tributary Point Dr. US 50, exit Hazel Ave, just n. Int corridors. **Pets:** Medium. $50 one-time fee/room. Service with restrictions, supervision.

Holiday Inn Rancho Cordova 🅷
(916) 635-4040. **$109-$159.** 11269 Point East Dr. US 50, exit Sunrise Blvd S, e on Folsom Blvd, then just n. Int corridors. **Pets:** Accepted.

La Quinta Inn & Suites 🅷
(916) 638-1111. **$59-$159.** 11131 Folsom Blvd. US 50, exit Sunrise Blvd, just s, then just w. Int corridors. **Pets:** Medium, other species. Service with restrictions, supervision.

Red Roof Inn-Rancho Cordova-Sacramento East 🅼
(916) 638-2500. **$55-$80.** 10800 Olson Dr. US 50, exit Zinfandel Dr, just n. Ext corridors. **Pets:** Large. $50 deposit/room. Supervision.

Residence Inn by Marriott 🅷
(916) 851-1550. **$153-$187.** 2779 Prospect Park Dr. US 50, exit Zinfandel Dr, just s, then e. Int corridors. **Pets:** Small. $100 one-time fee/room. Service with restrictions, supervision.

Vagabond Inn Executive-Rancho Cordova 🅷
(916) 631-7500. **$62-$90.** 10713 White Rock Rd. US 50, exit Zinfandel Dr, just s; 11 mi e of Sacramento. Ext/int corridors. **Pets:** Dogs only. Designated rooms, service with restrictions, crate.

RANCHO CUCAMONGA

Homewood Suites 🅷
(909) 481-6480. **$99-$295.** 11433 Mission Vista Dr. I-15, exit 110 (4th St), just w to Richmond Pl, just n, then just w. Int corridors. **Pets:** Medium. $75 one-time fee/room. Service with restrictions.

TownePlace Suites by Marriott 🅷
(909) 466-1100. **$79-$179.** 9625 Milliken Ave. I-10, exit 57 (Milliken Ave), 0.6 mi n. Int corridors. **Pets:** Small. $100 one-time fee/room. Service with restrictions, supervision.

RANCHO MIRAGE

The Westin Mission Hills Resort & Spa 🅷
(760) 328-5955. **$99-$550, 7 day notice.** 71-333 Dinah Shore Dr. I-10, exit 130 (Ramon Rd), 0.3 mi w on Ramon Rd, 1 mi s on Bob Hope Dr, then 0.6 mi w. Ext corridors. **Pets:** Medium, dogs only. No service, supervision.

RED BLUFF

Best Western Antelope Inn 🅷
(530) 527-8882. **$86-$161.** 203 Antelope Blvd. I-5, exit 649 (SR 36), just e. Int corridors. **Pets:** Other species. $10 daily fee/pet. Designated rooms, service with restrictions, supervision.

Comfort Inn 🅷
(530) 529-7060. **$89-$200.** 90 Sale Ln. I-5, exit 649, Central Red Bluff/Antelope Blvd (SR 36), 0.3 mi e. Int corridors. **Pets:** Large, dogs only. $15 daily fee/pet. Service with restrictions, supervision.

Sportsman Lodge 🅼
(530) 527-2888. **$55-$150, 3 day notice.** 768 Antelope Blvd. I-5, exit 649 (SR 36), 1.5 mi e. Ext corridors. **Pets:** Medium. $7 deposit/pet. Designated rooms, service with restrictions, supervision.

Super 8 Red Bluff 🅼
(530) 529-2028. **$55-$150.** 30 Gilmore Rd. I-5, exit 649 (SR 36), just w. Ext corridors. **Pets:** Medium. $8 daily fee/pet. Designated rooms, service with restrictions, supervision.

REDCREST

AAA ◆ Redcrest Resort **CA** ☼
(707) 722-4208. **$60-$205, 14 day notice.** 26459 Ave of the Giants. US 101, exit Redcrest southbound; exit Redcrest/Holmes northbound, just e, then just n. Ext corridors. **Pets:** Large. $7 daily fee/pet. Service with restrictions, supervision.
SAVE ✕ 🛏 💻 ✕ 🅰 🐾

REDDING

AAA ◆◆◆ Baymont Inn & Suites Redding **H**
(530) 722-9100. **$99-$199.** 2600 Larkspur Ln. I-5, exit 677 (Cypress Ave), just e, then just s. Int corridors. **Pets:** Accepted.
SAVE ✕ 🦽 🛏 💻 ≈

AAA ◆◆◆ Best Western Twin View Inn & Suites **H**
(530) 241-5500. **$99-$249.** 1080 Twin View Blvd. I-5, exit 681 (Twin View Blvd), just w. Int corridors. **Pets:** Medium. $30 daily fee/room. Designated rooms, service with restrictions, supervision.
SAVE ✕ 🦽 🛏 💻 ≈

AAA ◆◆◆ Comfort Inn **H**
(530) 221-4472. **$89-$112.** 850 Mistletoe Ln. I-5, exit 677 (Cypress Ave), 0.8 mi n on Hilltop Dr, then just e. Int corridors. **Pets:** Medium. $10 daily fee/pet. Designated rooms, service with restrictions, supervision.
SAVE ✕ 🛏 💻 ≈

AAA ◆◆◆ Holiday Inn **H**
(530) 221-7500. **$134-$169.** 1900 Hilltop Dr. I-5, exit 677 (Cypress Ave), just e, then 0.8 mi n. Int corridors. **Pets:** Dogs only. $100 deposit/room, $10 daily fee/pet. Designated rooms, service with restrictions, supervision.
SAVE ✕ 🛏 💻 🍴 ≈

◆◆◆ La Quinta Inn Redding **H** ☼
(530) 221-8200. **$69-$149.** 2180 Hilltop Dr. I-5, exit 677 (Cypress Ave), just e, then just n. Int corridors. **Pets:** Medium, other species. Service with restrictions, supervision.
ASK ✕ 🛏 💻 ≈

AAA ◆◆◆◆ Oxford Suites **H** 🐾
(530) 221-0100. **$105-$159.** 1967 Hilltop Dr. I-5, exit 677 (Cypress Ave), just e, then just n. Ext/int corridors. **Pets:** Medium. $25 one-time fee/pet. Designated rooms, service with restrictions, supervision.
SAVE ✕ 🛏 💻 ≈

AAA ◆◆◆ Quality Inn **M**
(530) 221-6530. **$85-$140.** 2059 Hilltop Dr. I-5, exit 677 (Cypress Ave), just e, then 0.3 mi n. Ext corridors. **Pets:** Accepted.
SAVE ✕ 🛏 💻 ≈

AAA ◆◆◆ Redding Travelodge **H**
(530) 243-5291. **$68-$135.** 540 N Market St. I-5, exit Lake Blvd northbound, just w, 0.5 mi to Market St, then 0.5 mi s; exit Market St southbound, 2 mi s. Ext corridors. **Pets:** Other species. $8 daily fee/pet. Designated rooms, service with restrictions, supervision.
SAVE ✕ 🛏 💻 ≈

◆◆◆ Red Lion Hotel Redding **H**
(530) 221-8700. **$109-$189.** 1830 Hilltop Dr. I-5, exit 678 (SR 44/Hilltop Dr) southbound; exit 677 (Cypress Ave) northbound, just e, then 0.6 mi n. Int corridors. **Pets:** Other species. $20 one-time fee/room. Service with restrictions, supervision.
ASK ✕ 🦽 🛏 💻 🍴 ≈

REDLANDS

◆◆◆ Dynasty Suites-Redlands **M**
(909) 793-6648. **$89-$159, 3 day notice.** 1235 W Colton Ave. I-10, exit 77C (Tennessee St) eastbound; exit 77B (Tennessee St) westbound, just s, then just w. Ext corridors. **Pets:** Small. $15 daily fee/pet. Designated rooms, service with restrictions, supervision.
ASK ✕ 🛏 💻 ≈ ✕

◆◆ Howard Johnson Inn **M**
(909) 793-2001. **$54-$199.** 1120 W Colton Ave. I-10, exit 77C (Tennessee St) eastbound; exit 77B (Tennessee St) westbound, just s, then just e. Ext corridors. **Pets:** Accepted.
ASK ✕ 🛏 💻 ≈

REDWAY

AAA ◆◆◆ Dean Creek Resort **M** ☼
(707) 923-2555. **$80-$140.** 4112 Redwood Dr. US 101, exit Redwood Dr northbound; exit Redway/Shelter Cove southbound, just w. Ext corridors. **Pets:** Medium, dogs only. $10 daily fee/pet. Designated rooms, service with restrictions, supervision.
SAVE ✕ 🛏 💻 ≈ ✕

REDWOOD CITY

AAA ◆◆◆◆ Sofitel San Francisco Bay **H**
(650) 598-9000. **$250-$599.** 223 Twin Dolphin Dr. US 101, exit Marine Pkwy E, 0.5 mi s. Int corridors. **Pets:** Other species.
SAVE ✕ 🦽 🍴 ≈

◆◆◆◆ TownePlace Suites by Marriott **H**
(650) 593-4100. **$179-$219.** 1000 Twin Dolphin Dr. US 101, exit Redwood Shores Pkwy, 0.3 mi e, then just s. Int corridors. **Pets:** Medium. $75 one-time fee/room. Service with restrictions.
✕ 🦽 💻

REEDLEY

AAA ◆◆◆ Edgewater Inn **M**
(559) 637-7777. **$75-$79.** 1977 W Manning Ave. 12 mi e of SR 99 via Manning Ave. Ext corridors. **Pets:** Dogs only. $8 daily fee/pet. Service with restrictions, supervision.
SAVE ✕ 🛏 💻 ≈

RIALTO

AAA ◆◆◆ Empire Inn & Suites **M**
(909) 877-0690. **$78-$115, 3 day notice.** 475 W Valley Blvd. I-10, exit 68 (Riverside Ave), just n, then 0.5 mi w. Ext corridors. **Pets:** $15 daily fee/pet. Service with restrictions, supervision.
SAVE ✕ 🛏 💻 🍴 ≈

RIDGECREST

AAA ◆◆◆ Best Western China Lake Inn **M**
(760) 371-2300. **$90-$105, 3 day notice.** 400 S China Lake Blvd. On US 395 business route. Ext corridors. **Pets:** Medium. $25 daily fee/pet. Service with restrictions, supervision.
SAVE ✕ 🦽 🛏 💻 ≈

AAA ◆◆◆ Carriage Inn **M**
(760) 446-7910. **$109-$149.** 901 N China Lake Blvd. On SR 178 and US 395 business route. Ext corridors. **Pets:** Small. $25 one-time fee/pet. Service with restrictions, crate.
SAVE ✕ 🦽 🛏 💻 🍴 ≈ ✕

AAA ◆◆◆ Comfort Inn **M**
(760) 375-9731. **$89-$139.** 507 S China Lake Blvd. On US 395 business route. Ext corridors. **Pets:** Small. $25 daily fee/pet. Designated rooms, service with restrictions, supervision.
SAVE ✕ 🛏 💻 ≈

AAA ◆◆◆ Econo Lodge Inn & Suites **M** ☼
(760) 446-2551. **$70-$97.** 201 Inyokern Rd. On SR 178 and US 395 business route, just w of China Lake Blvd. Ext corridors. **Pets:** Small. Service with restrictions, supervision.
SAVE ✕ 🛏 💻 ≈

AAA ◆◆◆ Heritage Inn & Suites **H**
(760) 446-7951. **$78-$90.** 1050 N Norma. On US 395 business route, just w. Int corridors. **Pets:** $100 deposit/pet. Service with restrictions, crate.
SAVE ✕ 🦽 🛏 💻 🍴 ≈

▼▼ **Rodeway Inn** M
(760) 384-3575. **$49-$99.** 131 W Upjohn Ave. On US 395 business route, just w. Ext corridors. **Pets:** Accepted.
ASK ✕ 🔔 💻

◈ ▼▼ **Vagabond Inn** M
(760) 375-2220. **$65-$89.** 426 China Lake Blvd. On US 395 business route. Ext corridors. **Pets:** Other species. $10 one-time fee/pet. Designated rooms, supervision.
SAVE ✕ &M 🔔 💻

RIO DELL

◈ ▼ **Humboldt Gables Motel** M
(707) 764-5609. **$55-$135.** 40 W Davis St. US 101, exit Wildwood Ave, 0.5 mi w. Ext corridors. **Pets:** Small, dogs only. $20 daily fee/pet. Supervision.
SAVE ✕ &M 🔔 💻 🗶

RIPON

◈ ▼▼▼ **La Quinta Inn & Suites** H ❖
(209) 599-8999. **$74-$116.** 1524 Colony Rd. SR 99, exit Jack Tone Rd, just e. Int corridors. **Pets:** Medium, other species. Service with restrictions, supervision.
SAVE ✕ 🔔 💻 🗨

RIVERSIDE

▼▼ **Comfort Inn-University** M
(951) 683-6000. **$90-$110.** 1590 University Ave. I-215 and SR 60, exit 32 (University Ave), 0.5 mi w. Ext corridors. **Pets:** Accepted.
ASK ✕ 🔔 💻 🗨

◈ ▼▼ **Rodeway Inn of Riverside** M
(951) 359-0770. **Call for rates.** 10518 Magnolia Ave. SR 91, exit 56 (Tyler St), 0.5 mi nw, then 0.3 mi sw. Ext corridors. **Pets:** Accepted.
SAVE ✕ 🔔 💻 🗨

ROCKLIN

◈ ▼▼ **Heritage Inn Express, Rocklin** H
(916) 632-3366. **$69-$99.** 4480 Rocklin Rd. I-80, exit Rocklin Rd, just w, then just s. Int corridors. **Pets:** Accepted.
SAVE ✕ 🔔 💻 🗨

◈ ▼▼ **Howard Johnson Hotel** H
(916) 624-4500. **$81-$100.** 4420 Rocklin Rd. I-80, exit Rocklin Rd, just w, then just s. Int corridors. **Pets:** Accepted.
SAVE ✕ &M 🔔 💻 🏊

ROSEVILLE

◈ ▼▼ **Best Western Roseville Inn** H
(916) 782-4434. **$81-$90, 3 day notice.** 220 Harding Blvd. I-80, exit 103 westbound; exit 103B eastbound, just w, then just n. Ext corridors. **Pets:** Accepted.
SAVE ✕ &M 🔔 💻 🗨

▼▼ **Extended StayAmerica-Sacramento-Roseville** H
(916) 781-9001. **$95-$105.** 1000 Lead Hill Blvd. I-80, exit 103 westbound; exit 103B eastbound, just w, then 0.6 mi n on Harding Blvd. Int corridors. **Pets:** Other species. $25 daily fee/pet. Service with restrictions, crate.
ASK ✕ 🔔 💻

▼▼▼ **Homewood Suites by Hilton** H
(916) 783-7455. **$119-$174.** 401 Creekside Ridge Ct. I-80, exit SR 65, 1 mi w to Galleria Blvd, 0.5 mi s to Antelope Creek Rd, then just e to Creekside Ridge Ct. Int corridors. **Pets:** Small. $75 one-time fee/room. Service with restrictions, supervision.
✕ &M 🔔 💻 🗨 🗶

◈ ▼▼▼ **Larkspur Landing Roseville** H
(916) 773-1717. **$109-$169.** 1931 Taylor Rd. I-80, exit Eureka/Taylor Rd, 0.3 mi ne. Int corridors. **Pets:** Medium. $75 one-time fee/pet. Designated rooms, service with restrictions, crate.
SAVE ✕ &M 🔔 💻

◈ ▼▼▼ **Orchid Suites Roseville** H
(916) 784-2222. **$119-$209.** 130 N Sunrise Ave. I-80, exit Douglas Blvd, just e, then 0.3 mi n. Ext/int corridors. **Pets:** Accepted.
SAVE ✕ &M 🔔 💻 🏊

▼▼▼ **Residence Inn by Marriott** H
(916) 772-5500. **$161-$197.** 1930 Taylor Rd. I-80, exit 105A (Atlantic St/Eureka Rd), just n. Int corridors. **Pets:** Accepted.
✕ &M 🔔 💻 🗨 🗶

SACRAMENTO

◈ ▼▼▼ **Best Western Sandman Motel** H
(916) 443-6515. **$89-$130, 3 day notice.** 236 Jibboom St. I-5, exit Richards Blvd, just w. Ext corridors. **Pets:** Accepted.
SAVE ✕ &M 🔔 💻 🍴 🗨

◈ ▼▼▼ **Clarion Hotel Mansion Inn** H
(916) 444-8000. **$89-$169, 3 day notice.** 700 16th St. At 16th and H sts; downtown. Int corridors. **Pets:** Medium. No service, supervision.
SAVE ✕ &M 🔔 💻 🍴 🗨

◈ ▼▼▼ **DoubleTree Hotel** H
(916) 929-8855. **$100-$220.** 2001 Point West Way. Business Rt I-80, exit via Arden Way, then just e. Int corridors. **Pets:** Accepted.
SAVE ✕ &M 🔔 💻 🍴 🗨

◈ ▼ **Econo Lodge** M
(916) 443-6631. **$59-$129.** 711 16th St. Business Rt I-80, exit 15th St eastbound; exit 16th St westbound; I-5, exit J St (Old Sacramento); jct H and 16th sts; downtown. Ext corridors. **Pets:** Accepted.
SAVE ✕ &M 🔔 💻

▼▼ **Extended StayAmerica-Sacramento-Arden Way** H
(916) 921-9942. **$89-$99.** 2100 Harvard St. I-80 business route, exit Arden Way, just w. Ext corridors. **Pets:** Other species. $25 daily fee/pet. Service with restrictions, crate.
ASK ✕ 🔔 💻

◈ ▼▼▼ **Hawthorn Suites** H
(916) 441-1200. **$99-$199.** 321 Bercut Dr. I-5, exit Richards Blvd, just e. Int corridors. **Pets:** Medium, other species. $50 one-time fee/room. Service with restrictions.
SAVE ✕ &M 🔔 💻 🗨 🗶

◈ ▼▼▼ **Holiday Inn Express Sacramento** H
(916) 444-4436. **$89-$199, 3 day notice.** 728 16th St. Jct H and 16th sts; downtown. Int corridors. **Pets:** Medium. No service, supervision.
SAVE ✕ &M 🔔 💻

▼▼ **Holiday Inn Sacramento Northeast** H
(916) 338-5800. **$109-$179.** 5321 Date Ave. I-80, exit Madison Ave, 0.3 mi e, then just n. Int corridors. **Pets:** Accepted.
ASK ✕ &M 🔔 💻 🍴 🗨

▼▼ **Homestead Studio Suites Hotel-Sacramento-S. Natomas** H
(916) 564-7500. **$95-$105.** 2810 Gateway Oaks Dr. I-5, exit El Camino Ave, just w, then 0.4 mi n; I-80, exit W El Camino Ave, 1 mi e, then 0.4 mi n. Ext corridors. **Pets:** Other species. $25 daily fee/pet. Service with restrictions, crate.
ASK ✕ &M 🔔 💻

▼▼▼ **La Quinta Inn Sacramento (Downtown)** H ❖
(916) 448-8100. **$55-$149.** 200 Jibboom St. I-5, exit Richards Blvd, just w. Ext corridors. **Pets:** Medium, other species. Service with restrictions, supervision.
ASK ✕ &M 🔔 💻 🗨

▼▼▼▼ La Quinta Inn Sacramento (North) 🅷 ❀
(916) 348-0900. **$59-$149.** 4604 Madison Ave. I-80, exit Madison Ave, 0.3 mi e. Ext corridors. **Pets:** Medium, other species. Service with restrictions, supervision.
(ASK) ⊠ (&M) 🛢 💷 ➢

▲▲▲ ▼▼▼▼ Larkspur Landing Sacramento 🅷
(916) 646-1212. **$99-$179.** 555 Howe Ave. US 50, exit Howe Ave, 1.5 mi n. Int corridors. **Pets:** Other species. $75 one-time fee/room. Designated rooms, service with restrictions, crate.
(SAVE) ⊠ (&M) 🛢 💷 ⊠

▼▼▼▼ Lions Gate Hotel 🅷 ❀
(916) 643-6222. **$109.** 3410 Westover St. I-80, exit Watt Ave, 1.5 mi n to Palm St, just w, then just s; in McClellan Business Park. Ext/int corridors. **Pets:** Large, other species. $50 one-time fee/room. Designated rooms, service with restrictions, crate.
(ASK) ⊠ (&M) 🛢 💷 🍴 ➢

▲▲▲ ▼▼▼ Quality Inn Natomas 🅷
(916) 927-7117. **$72.** 3796 Northgate Blvd. I-80, exit Northgate Blvd, just s. Ext corridors. **Pets:** Small. $50 one-time fee/pet. Designated rooms, service with restrictions, supervision.
(SAVE) ⊠ (&M) 🛢 💷 ➢

▲▲▲ ▼▼▼▼ Radisson Hotel 🅷
(916) 922-2020. **$89-$209.** 500 Leisure Ln. Business Rt I-80, exit Cal Expo, 0.4 mi w on Exposition Blvd; SR 160, exit Exposition Blvd; just e. Ext corridors. **Pets:** Accepted.
(SAVE) ⊠ (&M) 🛢 💷 🍴 ➢ ⊠

▲▲▲ ▼▼▼▼ Ramada Limited-Discovery Park 🅷
(916) 442-6971. **$69-$150.** 350 Bercut Dr. I-5, exit Richards Blvd, just e, then just n. Ext corridors. **Pets:** Medium. $20 daily fee/room. Designated rooms, service with restrictions, supervision.
(SAVE) ⊠ (&M) 🛢 💷 ➢

▼▼▼▼ Red Lion Hotel at Arden Village 🅷
(916) 922-8041. **$150-$249.** 1401 Arden Way. I-80 business route, exit Arden Way; adjacent to Arden Fair Mall. Ext/int corridors. **Pets:** Other species. $20 one-time fee/room. Service with restrictions, supervision.
(ASK) ⊠ (&M) 🛢 💷 🍴 ➢

▼▼▼▼ Residence Inn By Marriott- Cal Expo 🅷 ❀
(916) 920-9111. **$152-$186.** 1530 Howe Ave. 2.5 mi n of jct SR 16 and US 50, exit Howe Ave. Ext corridors. **Pets:** $100 one-time fee/room.
⊠ (&M) 🛢 💷 ➢ ⊠

▼▼▼▼ Residence Inn By Marriott-Sacramento Airport Natomas 🅷
(916) 649-1300. **$170-$208.** 2410 W El Camino Ave. I-5, exit W El Camino Ave. Ext corridors. **Pets:** Accepted.
⊠ (&M) 🛢 💷 ➢ ⊠

▼▼▼▼ Residence Inn by Marriott- Sacramento at Capitol Park 🅷
(916) 443-0500. **$224-$274.** 1121 15th St. Jct 15th and L sts; just e of state capitol; downtown. Int corridors. **Pets:** Accepted.
⊠ 🛢 💷 ➢

▼▼▼▼ Staybridge Suites Sacramento 🅷
(916) 575-7907. **Call for rates.** 140 Promenade Cir. I-80, exit Truxel Rd, just nw, n on Gateway Park Blvd, e on N Freeway Blvd, then just s. Int corridors. **Pets:** Accepted.
⊠ (&M) 🛢 💷 ➢

▲▲▲ ▼▼▼▼ TownePlace Suites by Marriott Sacramento Cal Expo 🅷
(916) 920-5400. **$140-$171.** 1784 Tribute Rd. Business Rt I-80, exit Exposition Blvd, just w. Int corridors. **Pets:** Accepted.
(SAVE) ⊠ 🛢 💷 ➢

▲▲▲ ▼▼▼ Vagabond Executive Inn Old Town 🅷
(916) 446-1481. **$99-$169.** 909 3rd St. I-5, exit J St (Old Sacramento); 8 blks w of state capitol; jct J and 3rd sts; downtown. Ext corridors. **Pets:** Small. $10 daily fee/pet. Designated rooms, service with restrictions, supervision.
(SAVE) ⊠ (&M) 🛢 💷 ➢

SALIDA

▲▲▲ ▼▼▼▼ La Quinta Inn & Suites 🅷 ❀
(209) 579-8723. **$74-$129.** 4909 Sisk Rd. SR 99, exit SR 219, just e. Int corridors. **Pets:** Medium, other species. Service with restrictions, supervision.
(SAVE) ⊠ (&M) 🛢 💷 ➢

SALINAS

▲▲▲ ▼▼▼ Econo Lodge Ⓜ
(831) 422-5111. **Call for rates.** 180 S Sanborn Rd. US 101, exit Sanborn Rd or Fairview Ave, just e. Ext corridors. **Pets:** $10 daily fee/room. Service with restrictions, supervision.
(SAVE) ⊠ 🛢

▼▼▼▼ Residence Inn by Marriott-Salinas 🅷
(831) 775-0410. **$190-$200.** 17215 El Rancho Way. US 101, exit Laurel Dr, just w. Int corridors. **Pets:** Accepted.
⊠ (&M) 🛢 💷 ➢ ⊠

▼▼ Vagabond Inn Ⓜ
(831) 758-4693. **Call for rates.** 131 Kern St. US 101, exit Market St, just e. Ext corridors. **Pets:** Accepted.
⊠ (&M) 🛢 💷 ➢

SAN ANDREAS

▼▼▼▼ The Robins Nest 🅱🅱 ❀
(209) 754-1076. **$150-$175, 7 day notice.** 247 W St. Charles St. SR 49; north end of town. Int corridors. **Pets:** Large, other species. Designated rooms, service with restrictions, crate.
(ASK) ⊠ 🛢 💷

SAN BERNARDINO

▼▼ Econo Lodge Ⓜ
(909) 383-1188. **Call for rates.** 606 N "H" St. I-215, exit 44 (SR 66 W/5th St) southbound; exit 44A (SR 66 W/5th St) northbound, just e, then just n. Ext corridors. **Pets:** Accepted.
⊠ 🛢 💷 ➢

▼▼▼▼ Hilton-San Bernardino 🅷
(909) 889-0133. **$109-$209.** 285 E Hospitality Ln. I-10, exit 73 (Waterman Ave) westbound; exit 73B (Waterman Ave) eastbound, just n, then just w. Int corridors. **Pets:** Accepted.
⊠ 🛢 💷 🍴 ➢ ⊠

▼▼▼▼ La Quinta Inn San Bernardino Ⓜ ❀
(909) 888-7571. **$49-$99.** 205 E Hospitality Ln. I-10, exit 73 (Waterman Ave) westbound; 73B (Waterman Ave N) eastbound, just n, then 0.3 mi w. Ext corridors. **Pets:** Medium, other species. Service with restrictions, supervision.
(ASK) ⊠ 🛢 💷 ➢

▲▲▲ ▼▼▼ Quality Inn Hospitality Lane Area Ⓜ ❀
(909) 888-4827. **$89-$169.** 1750 S Waterman Ave. I-10, exit 73 (Waterman Ave), 0.5 mi n. Ext corridors. **Pets:** Medium, dogs only. $25 one-time fee/pet. Service with restrictions, supervision.
(SAVE) ⊠ 🛢 💷 ➢

▼▼▼▼ Residence Inn San Bernardino 🅷 ❀
(909) 382-4564. **$171-$209.** 1040 E Harriman Pl. I-10, exit 74 (Tippecanoe Ave) eastbound; exit 74 (Anderson St/Tippecanoe Ave) westbound, just n, then just w. Int corridors. **Pets:** Other species. $75 one-time fee/room. Service with restrictions, supervision.
⊠ 🛢 💷 ➢ ⊠

SAN CLEMENTE

◇◇◇◇ Best Western Casablanca Inn **H**
(949) 361-1644. **$89-$209.** 1601 N El Camino Real. I-5, exit 76 (Avenida Pico), 0.8 mi sw, then just s. Ext corridors. **Pets:** $25 daily fee/room. Designated rooms, service with restrictions.
[SAVE] [X] [H] [▤] [≈]

◇◇◇◇ Holiday Inn Express **H**
(949) 498-8800. **$109-$229.** 35 Via Pico Plaza. I-5, exit 76 (Avenida Pico), just w, then just s. Int corridors. **Pets:** Accepted.
[SAVE] [X] [&M] [H] [▤] [≈]

◇◇◇◇ Holiday Inn-San Clemente Resort **H**
(949) 361-3000. **$139-$250.** 111 S Avenida de la Estrella. I-5, exit 75 (Avenida Palizada) southbound; exit 75 (Avenida Presidio) northbound, just s, then just w. Int corridors. **Pets:** Accepted.
[ASK] [X] [&M] [H] [▤] [¶¶] [≈]

SAN DIEGO METROPOLITAN AREA

CHULA VISTA

◇◇◇◇ La Quinta Inn San Diego (Chula Vista) **M** 🐾
(619) 691-1211. **$79-$169.** 150 Bonita Rd. I-805, exit 7C (E St/Bonita Rd), just w. Ext corridors. **Pets:** Medium, other species. Service with restrictions, supervision.
[ASK] [X] [H] [▤] [≈]

CORONADO

◇◇ Crown City Inn **M** 🐾
(619) 435-3116. **$100-$300.** 520 Orange Ave. I-5, exit 14A (Coronado Bridge), 1.5 mi w, then just s. Ext corridors. **Pets:** Other species. $8 daily fee/pet. Designated rooms, service with restrictions, supervision.
[X] [&M] [H] [▤] [¶¶] [≈]

◇◇◇◇ Loews Coronado Bay Resort **H** 🐾
(619) 424-4000. **$199-$459, 3 day notice.** 4000 Coronado Bay Rd. I-5, exit 14A (Coronado Bridge), 1.7 mi w to Orange Ave, 1 mi sw to Silver Strand Blvd, then 4.5 mi s to Coronado Cays. Ext/int corridors. **Pets:** Other species. $25 one-time fee/room.
[SAVE] [X] [H] [▤] [¶¶] [≈] [X]

DEL MAR

◇◇◇ Best Western Stratford Inn **M**
(858) 755-1501. **Call for rates.** 710 Camino Del Mar. I-5, exit 34 (Del Mar Heights Rd), 1 mi w, then 0.3 mi n. Int corridors. **Pets:** Accepted.
[SAVE] [X] [&M] [H] [▤] [≈]

◇◇◇◇ DoubleTree Hotel Del Mar **H**
(858) 481-5900. **$109-$350.** 11915 El Camino Real. I-5, exit 33 (Carmel Valley Rd), 0.3 mi e. Int corridors. **Pets:** Accepted.
[X] [H] [▤] [¶¶] [≈]

◇◇◇◇ Hilton San Diego Del Mar **H** 🐾
(858) 792-5200. **$134-$799.** 15575 Jimmy Durante Blvd. I-5, exit 36 (Via de la Valle), just w. Int corridors. **Pets:** Medium. $50 one-time fee/room. Service with restrictions, crate.
[X] [H] [▤] [¶¶] [≈]

EL CAJON

◇◇◇◇ Best Western Courtesy Inn **M**
(619) 440-7378. **$60-$100, 7 day notice.** 1355 E Main St. I-8, exit 19 (2nd St), 0.5 mi s, then just e. Ext corridors. **Pets:** Small. $6 daily fee/pet. Designated rooms, service with restrictions, supervision.
[SAVE] [X] [H] [▤] [≈]

◇◇ Quality Inn & Suites San Diego East County **H**
(619) 588-8808. **$75-$285.** 1250 El Cajon Blvd. I-8, exit 14C (Severin Dr) westbound, 1 mi e on Murray Rd; exit 15 (El Cajon Blvd) eastbound, 0.5 mi w. Ext corridors. **Pets:** Accepted.
[ASK] [X] [H] [▤] [≈]

LA JOLLA

◇◇◇◇ Hilton La Jolla/Torrey Pines **H** 🐾
(858) 558-1500. **$179-$499.** 10950 N Torrey Pines Rd. I-5, exit 29 (Genesee Ave), 0.8 mi w, then just n. Int corridors. **Pets:** Other species. $75 one-time fee/room. Service with restrictions.
[X] [&M] [▤] [¶¶] [≈] [X]

◇◇◇◇ Hotel La Jolla At The Shores **H**
(858) 459-0261. **$159-$249.** 7955 La Jolla Shores Dr. I-5, exit 28 (La Jolla Village Dr) southbound, 1 mi w to Torrey Pines Rd, 1.7 mi sw, then just n; exit 26A (La Jolla Pkwy) northbound, 1.5 mi n to Torrey Pines Rd, just w, then just n. Ext corridors. **Pets:** Accepted.
[ASK] [X] [&M] [H] [▤] [≈] [X]

◇◇◇◇ La Jolla Cove Suites **H**
(858) 459-2621. **$149-$615, 3 day notice.** 1155 Coast Blvd. I-5, exit 28 (La Jolla Village Dr), 1 mi w to Torrey Pines Rd, 2.5 mi to Prospect St, 0.5 mi s to Girard Ave, then just w. Ext corridors. **Pets:** Medium. $25 daily fee/pet. Designated rooms, service with restrictions, supervision.
[SAVE] [X] [H] [▤] [≈] [X]

◇◇◇◇ La Valencia Hotel **H** 🐾
(858) 454-0771. **$275-$795.** 1132 Prospect St. I-5, exit 26A (La Jolla Pkwy) northbound, 1.5 mi w to Torrey Pines Rd, 1 mi w, then 0.6 mi sw; exit 28 (La Jolla Village Dr) southbound, 1 mi w to Torrey Pines Rd, 2.7 mi sw, then 0.6 mi sw. Ext/int corridors. **Pets:** Large. $25 deposit/room. Service with restrictions.
[ASK] [X] [H] [▤] [¶¶] [≈] [X]

◇◇◇◇ Residence Inn by Marriott La Jolla **H** 🐾
(858) 587-1770. **$279-$299.** 8901 Gilman Dr. I-5, exit 27 (Gilman Dr), 1.5 mi nw. Ext corridors. **Pets:** Other species. $100 one-time fee/room. Service with restrictions.
[X] [&M] [H] [▤] [≈] [X]

◇◇◇◇ San Diego Marriott La Jolla **H**
(858) 587-1414. **$299-$350.** 4240 La Jolla Village Dr. I-5, exit 28 (La Jolla Village Dr), 0.5 mi e. Int corridors. **Pets:** Accepted.
[X] [&M] [H] [▤] [¶¶] [≈]

◇◇◇ ◇◇◇◇ Sheraton La Jolla Hotel **H**
(858) 453-5500. **Call for rates.** 3299 Holiday Ct. I-5, exit 28 (La Jolla Village Dr), w to Villa La Jolla Dr, then just s; at top of hill. Int corridors. **Pets:** Medium, dogs only. $75 one-time fee/room. Service with restrictions, supervision.
[SAVE] [X] [&M] [H] [▤] [¶¶] [≈]

POWAY

◇◇◇ ◇◇◇◇ Best Western Country Inn **M**
(858) 748-6320. **$89-$199.** 13845 Poway Rd. I-15, exit 18 (Poway Rd), 4 mi e. Ext corridors. **Pets:** Dogs only. $50 one-time fee/pet. Service with restrictions, crate.
[SAVE] [X] [H] [▤] [≈]

▼▼▼ **Ramada Hotel** H
(858) 748-7311. **$79-$209.** 12448 Poway Rd. I-15, exit 18 (Poway Rd), 3 mi e. Ext corridors. **Pets:** Accepted.
ASK ✕ 🛏 📶 🐾

RANCHO BERNARDO

▼▼▼ **La Quinta Inn San Diego (Rancho Penasquitos)** H ✿
(858) 484-8800. **$69-$169.** 10185 Paseo Montril. I-15, exit 18 (Rancho Penasquitos Blvd), just w. Ext corridors. **Pets:** Medium, other species. Service with restrictions, supervision.
ASK ✕ 🛏 📶 🐾

▼▼▼ **Staybridge Suites Carmel Mountain** H
(858) 487-0900. **Call for rates.** 11855 Ave of Industry. I-15, exit 21 (Carmel Mountain Rd), 1 mi ne to second Rancho Carmel Dr, just w to Innovation Dr, just n, then just e. Int corridors. **Pets:** Accepted.
✕ 🛗ᴹ 🛏 📶 🐾 🗙

SAN DIEGO

🔷 ▼▼▼ **Best Western Lamplighter Inn & Suites** M ✿
(619) 582-3088. **$90-$195.** 6474 El Cajon Blvd. I-8, exit 11 (70th St), 0.5 mi s, then 1 mi w. Ext corridors. **Pets:** Medium. $15 daily fee/pet. Service with restrictions, supervision.
SAVE ✕ 🛏 📶 🐾

🔷 ▼▼▼▼ **Best Western Mission Bay Inn** M
(619) 275-5700. **$109-$189, 3 day notice.** 2575 Clairemont Dr. I-5, exit 22 (Clairemont Dr/Mission Bay Dr), just e. Ext corridors. **Pets:** Small, dogs only. $15 daily fee/pet. Designated rooms, service with restrictions, supervision.
SAVE ✕ 🛏 📶 🐾

▼▼▼▼ **DoubleTree Hotel San Diego-Mission Valley** H
(619) 297-5466. **$159-$459.** 7450 Hazard Center Dr. SR 163, exit 4 (Friars Rd), 0.3 mi e to Frazee Rd, then just s. Int corridors. **Pets:** $75 one-time fee/room. Service with restrictions.
✕ 🛗ᴹ 🛏 📶 🍴 🐾 🗙

▼▼▼ **Extended StayAmerica-San Diego/Hotel Circle** H
(619) 296-5570. **$90-$164.** 2087 Hotel Cir S. I-8, exit 4A (Hotel Cir), south side. Int corridors. **Pets:** Other species. $25 daily fee/pet. Service with restrictions, crate.
ASK ✕ 🛗ᴹ 🛏 📶

▼▼▼ **Extended StayAmerica–San Diego/Mission Valley Stadium** H
(858) 292-8927. **$95-$141.** 3860 Murphy Canyon Dr. I-15, exit 8 (Aero Dr), just w, then 1 mi n. Int corridors. **Pets:** Other species. $25 daily fee/pet. Service with restrictions, crate.
ASK ✕ 🛗ᴹ 🛏 📶

🔷 ▼▼▼▼ **Four Points by Sheraton San Diego** H
(858) 277-8888. **$90-$275.** 8110 Aero Dr. SR 163, exit 7B (Balboa Ave E) southbound, 1 mi se via Kearny Villa Rd; exit 10 (Kearny Villa Rd) northbound, 0.8 mi ne. Int corridors. **Pets:** Accepted.
SAVE ✕ 🛗ᴹ 🛏 📶 🍴 🐾 🗙

▼▼▼ ▼▼▼ **The Grand Del Mar** H
(858) 314-2000. **$355-$575, 7 day notice.** 5300 Grand Del Mar Way. I-5, exit 33 (Carmel Valley Rd), 1.9 mi e, 0.8 mi s, then just e. Int corridors. **Pets:** Accepted.
ASK ✕ 🛏 📶 🍴 🐾 🗙

▼▼▼ ▼▼▼ **Hawthorn Suites** M
(619) 299-3501. **$149-$249.** 1335 Hotel Cir S. I-8, exit 4A (Hotel Cir), south side. Ext/int corridors. **Pets:** Accepted.
ASK ✕ 🛏 📶 🗙

▼ ▼ **The Hillcrest Bed and Breakfast @ Kasa Korbett** BB
(619) 291-3962. **$119-$139, 7 day notice.** 4050 Front St. SR 163, exit 2B (Washington St), 0.4 mi w to 1st Ave, just n to Montecito St, just w, then just s. Int corridors. **Pets:** Small, dogs only. $50 deposit/pet. Designated rooms, service with restrictions, supervision.
ASK ✕ 🛏 🐕 🐾 🐾

🔷 ▼▼▼▼ **Hilton San Diego Mission Valley** H
(619) 543-9000. **$159-$409.** 901 Camino del Rio S. I-8, exit 5 (Mission Center Rd), just s. Int corridors. **Pets:** Accepted.
SAVE ✕ 🛗ᴹ 🛏 📶 🍴 🐾 🗙

▼▼▼ **Holiday Inn on the Bay** H
(619) 232-3861. **$149-$249.** 1355 N Harbor Dr at Ash St. I-5, exit 17 (Hawthorn St) northbound, 0.4 mi w, then 0.4 mi s; exit 17 (Front St) southbound, 0.5 mi s to Ash St, then just w. Int corridors. **Pets:** Accepted.
✕ 🛏 📶 🍴 🐾

▼▼ **Homestead Studio Suites Hotel-San Diego/Mission Valley** M
(619) 299-2292. **$90-$154.** 7444 Mission Valley Rd. SR 163, exit 4 (Friars Rd), just n on Mission Center Dr, then 0.5 mi w. Ext corridors. **Pets:** Other species. $25 daily fee/pet. Service with restrictions, crate.
ASK ✕ 🛏 📶

▼▼ **Homestead Studio Suites Hotel-San Diego/Sorrento Mesa** M
(858) 623-0100. **$104-$167.** 9880 Pacific Heights Blvd. I-805, exit 27 (Mira Mesa Blvd), 1 mi e. Ext corridors. **Pets:** Other species. $25 daily fee/pet. Service with restrictions, crate.
ASK ✕ 🛏 📶

▼▼▼▼ **La Quinta Inn Mission Valley** M ✿
(619) 295-6886. **$79-$199.** 641 Camino Del Rio S. I-8, exit 5 (Mission Center Rd), just s, then just w. Ext corridors. **Pets:** Medium, other species. Service with restrictions, supervision.
ASK ✕ 🛗ᴹ 🛏 📶 🐾

▼▼▼ **La Quinta Inn Old Town** M ✿
(619) 291-9100. **$89-$269.** 2380 Moore St. I-5, exit 19 (Old Town Ave), just n via Frontage Rd on west side of freeway. Ext/int corridors. **Pets:** Medium, other species. Service with restrictions, supervision.
ASK ✕ 🛗ᴹ 🛏 📶 🐾

🔷 ▼▼▼▼ **Manchester Grand Hyatt San Diego** H ✿
(619) 232-1234. **$159-$499, 7 day notice.** One Market Pl. I-5, exit 17 (Front St), 1.3 mi s, then just w. Int corridors. **Pets:** Medium. $30 daily fee/pet. Designated rooms, service with restrictions, crate.
SAVE ✕ 🛗ᴹ 📶 🍴 🐾 🗙

▼▼▼ **Mission Valley Resort** H
(619) 298-8281. **$99-$179.** 875 Hotel Cir S. I-8, exit 4A (Hotel Cir), south side. Ext corridors. **Pets:** Accepted.
ASK ✕ 🛏 📶 🍴 🐾 🗙

▼▼ **Mission Valley Travelodge** M
(619) 297-2271. **$99-$139.** 1201 Hotel Cir S. I-8, exit 4A (Hotel Cir), south side. Ext corridors. **Pets:** Accepted.
ASK ✕ 🛏 📶 🐾

▼▼▼ **Ocean Villa Inn** M ✿
(619) 224-3481. **$99-$399.** 5142 W Point Loma Blvd. I-8, exit Sunset Cliff Blvd, 1.5 mi sw. Ext corridors. **Pets:** Dogs only. $25 one-time fee/room. Designated rooms, service with restrictions.
ASK ✕ 🛏 📶 🐾

🔷 ▼▼▼ **Old Town Inn** M
(619) 260-8024. **$74-$199.** 4444 Pacific Hwy. I-5, exit 21 (SeaWorld Dr), just w, then 1 mi s. Ext corridors. **Pets:** Medium, other species. $15 daily fee/pet. Service with restrictions, supervision.
SAVE ✕ 🛏 📶 🐾

▼▼▼ ▼▼▼ **Omni San Diego Hotel** H ❧
(619) 231-6664. **$270-$288.** 675 L St. I-5, exit 17 (Front St/Civic Center), 0.3 mi s, 0.3 mi e on a St, 0.6 mi s on Sixth Ave, then just e; connected via skybridge to Petco Park. Int corridors. **Pets:** Medium. $50 one-time fee/pet. Service with restrictions.

A$K ✕ ᵫM ▤ ⬛ ⅋⅋ ⇌ ✕

▼▼ ▼▼ **Pacific Inn Hotel & Suites** M
(619) 232-6391. **$59-$289.** 1655 Pacific Hwy. I-5, exit 17 (Front St) southbound, just s to Cedar St, 0.5 mi w, then just n; exit 17 (Hawthorn St) northbound, 0.6 mi w, then just s. Ext corridors. **Pets:** Medium, other species. $20 daily fee/pet. Designated rooms, service with restrictions, supervision.

SAVE ✕ ▤ ⬛ ⇌

▲▲▲ ▼▼ **Pacific Shores Inn** M
(858) 483-6300. **$109-$269, 3 day notice.** 4802 Mission Blvd. I-5, exit 23 (Garnet Ave), 2.5 mi w, then 0.3 mi n. Ext corridors. **Pets:** Medium, dogs only. $35 one-time fee/room. Service with restrictions, crate.

SAVE ✕ ▤ ⬛ ⇌

▼▼▼ ▼ **Porto Vista Hotel & Suites** H ❧
(619) 544-0164. **$129-$199.** 1835 Columbia St. I-5, exit 17 (Front St) southbound, just w on Cedar St, then just n on State St; exit 17 (Hawthorn St) northbound, just e, then just s. Ext/int corridors. **Pets:** $25 daily fee/room. Service with restrictions, supervision.

A$K ✕ ▤ ⬛ ⅋⅋

▲▲▲ ▼ **Premier Inns Mission Valley/Hotel Circle** M
(619) 291-8252. **$50-$109.** 2484 Hotel Circle Pl. I-8, exit 3 (Taylor St), just n. Ext corridors. **Pets:** Medium. Designated rooms, service with restrictions, supervision.

SAVE ✕ ▤ ⬛ ⇌

▲▲▲ ▼ **Premier Inns-Sports Arena/Mission Bay** M
(619) 223-9500. **$55-$175.** 3333 Channel Way. I-5/8, exit 20 (Rosecrans St), 0.5 mi s, 1 mi nw on Sports Arena Blvd, then just e. Ext corridors. **Pets:** Other species. $5 daily fee/room. Service with restrictions, supervision.

SAVE ✕ ᵫM ▤ ⬛ ⇌

▼▼▼▼ **Residence Inn by Marriott-San Diego Central** H
(858) 278-2100. **$199-$249.** 5400 Kearny Mesa Rd. SR 163, exit 8 (Clairemont Mesa Blvd). Ext corridors. **Pets:** Medium, other species. $75 one-time fee/room. Service with restrictions.

✕ ▤ ⬛ ⇌ ✕

▼▼▼▼ **Residence Inn by Marriott San Diego Downtown** H
(619) 338-8200. **$279-$289.** 1747 Pacific Hwy. I-5, exit 17 (Front St) southbound, just s to Grape St, 0.3 mi w, then just n; exit 17 (Hawthorn St) northbound, 0.4 mi w, then just s. Int corridors. **Pets:** Accepted.

✕ ᵫM ▤ ⬛ ⇌

▼▼▼ **Residence Inn San Diego/Mission Valley/SeaWorld Area** H
(619) 881-3600. **$188-$230.** 1865 Hotel Cir S. I-8, exit 4A (Hotel Cir), south side. Int corridors. **Pets:** Large, other species. $75 one-time fee/room. Service with restrictions.

✕ ᵫM ▤ ⬛ ⇌ ✕

▼▼▼ **Residence Inn San Diego Ranch Bernardo/Scripps Poway** H ❧
(858) 635-5724. **$219-$229.** 12011 Scripps Highland Dr. I-805, exit 17 (Mercy Rd/Scripps Poway Pkwy), just e, then just n. Int corridors. **Pets:** Other species. $75 one-time fee/room. Service with restrictions, supervision.

✕ ᵫM ▤ ⬛ ⇌ ✕

▼▼▼ **Residence Inn San Diego-Sorrento Mesa** H
(858) 552-9100. **$279-$299.** 5995 Pacific Mesa Ct. I-805, exit 27 (Mira Mesa Blvd), 1.5 mi e. Int corridors. **Pets:** Accepted.

✕ ▤ ⬛ ⇌ ✕

▼▼▼ ▼▼▼ **San Diego Marriott Hotel & Marina** H ❧
(619) 234-1500. **$302-$369.** 333 W Harbor Dr. I-5, exit 17 (Front St), 1.3 mi s, then just w. Int corridors. **Pets:** Dogs only. $75 one-time fee/room. Designated rooms, no service, supervision.

✕ ▤ ⬛ ⅋⅋ ⇌ ✕

▲▲▲ ▼▼▼ **Sheraton San Diego Hotel and Marina** H ❧
(619) 291-2900. **Call for rates.** 1380 Harbor Island Dr. I-5, exit 17 (Hawthorn St) northbound, just e to Harbor Dr, 1.5 mi w, then just s; exit 18A (Kettern/Hancock) southbound, just s to Laurel St, just w to Harbor Dr, 1.5 mi w, then just s. Ext/int corridors. **Pets:** Medium.

SAVE ✕ ⬛ ⅋⅋ ⇌ ✕

▲▲▲ ▼▼▼ **Sheraton San Diego Hotel, Mission Valley** H
(619) 260-0111. **$139-$269.** 1433 Camino del Rio S. I-8, exit 5 (Mission Center Rd), south side. Int corridors. **Pets:** Accepted.

SAVE ✕ ᵫM ⬛ ⅋⅋ ⇌

▲▲▲ ▼▼▼ **Sheraton Suites San Diego** H ❧
(619) 696-9800. **$169-$399.** 701 a St/7th Ave. I-5, exit 17 (Front St), 0.5 mi s. Int corridors. **Pets:** Medium, other species. Service with restrictions, supervision.

SAVE ✕ ᵫM ▤ ⬛ ⅋⅋ ⇌ ✕

▲▲▲ ▼▼▼ **The Sofia Hotel** H ❧
(619) 234-9200. **$171.** 150 W Broadway. I-5, exit 17 (Front St), 1 mi s. Int corridors. **Pets:** Other species. $50 one-time fee/pet. Service with restrictions, supervision.

SAVE ✕ ᵫM ▤ ⬛ ⅋⅋

▼▼▼ **Sommerset Suites Hotel** H
(619) 692-5200. **$149-$269.** 606 Washington St. SR 163, exit 2B (Washington St), just w. Ext/int corridors. **Pets:** Small. $50 one-time fee/pet. Service with restrictions, supervision.

A$K ✕ ▤ ⬛ ⇌

▼▼▼ **Staybridge Suites by Holiday Inn-Sorrento Mesa** H
(858) 453-5343. **Call for rates.** 6639 Mira Mesa Blvd. I-805, exit 27 (Mira Mesa Blvd), 2.3 mi e. Int corridors. **Pets:** Accepted.

✕ ᵫM ▤ ⬛ ⇌

▲▲▲ ▼▼▼ **The US Grant** H
(619) 232-3121. **$249-$569.** 326 Broadway. I-5, exit 17 (Front St) southbound, 0.9 mi s to Broadway, just e; exit 16B (6th Ave) northbound, 0.6 mi s, just w. Int corridors. **Pets:** Accepted.

SAVE ✕ ᵫM ▤ ⬛ ⅋⅋ ✕

▲▲▲ ▼▼▼ **Vagabond Inn-Point Loma** M
(619) 224-3371. **$79-$305.** 1325 Scott St. I-8, exit Nimitz Blvd, 2 mi s to Rosecrans St, just w to Jarvis St, then just s; in Point Loma area. Ext corridors. **Pets:** Medium. $10 daily fee/pet. Designated rooms, service with restrictions, supervision.

SAVE ✕ ▤ ⬛ ⇌

▲▲▲ ▼▼▼ **Vagabond Inn SeaWorld** M
(619) 297-1691. **$49-$289.** 625 Hotel Cir S. I-8, exit 4A (Hotel Cir), south side. Ext corridors. **Pets:** Medium, other species. $20 daily fee/pet. Designated rooms, service with restrictions, supervision.

SAVE ✕ ▤ ⬛ ⇌

▲▲▲ ▼▼▼ **The Westin Gaslamp Quarter** H
(619) 239-2200. **$189-$449, 3 day notice.** 910 Broadway Cir. I-5, exit 17 (Front St) southbound, 0.9 mi s to Broadway, just e, then just s; exit 16B (6th Ave) northbound, 0.6 mi s, just w, then just s. Int corridors. **Pets:** Accepted.

SAVE ✕ ᵫM ▤ ⬛ ⅋⅋ ⇌ ✕

▲▲▲ ▼▼▼ ▼▼▼ **The Westin San Diego** H
(619) 239-4500. **Call for rates.** 400 W Broadway. Between Columbia and State sts. Int corridors. **Pets:** Accepted.

SAVE ✕ ᵫM ▤ ⬛ ⅋⅋ ⇌ ✕

(AAA) ▼▼▼▼ Woodfin Suite Hotel H
(858) 597-0500. **$139-$399.** 10044 Pacific Mesa Blvd. I-805, exit 27 (Mira Mesa Blvd), 1.1 mi e, then just n. Int corridors. **Pets:** Accepted.
[SAVE] [X] [&M] [🛏] [💻] [🍽] [🐾]

END METROPOLITAN AREA

SAN FRANCISCO METROPOLITAN AREA

BELMONT

(AAA) ▼▼▼ Hyatt Summerfield Suites-Belmont/Redwood Shores H
(650) 591-8600. **$119-$219.** 400 Concourse Dr. US 101, exit Marine World Pkwy, just e, then just n on Oracle Pkwy. Ext corridors. **Pets:** Accepted.
[SAVE] [X] [&M] [💻] [🐾]

BRISBANE

▼▼▼ Homewood Suites By Hilton H
(650) 589-1600. **$129-$209.** 2000 Shoreline Ct. US 101, exit Sierra Point Pkwy, just e. Int corridors. **Pets:** Accepted.
[X] [&M] [💻] [🐾]

BURLINGAME

▼▼▼ Crowne Plaza H ❀
(650) 342-9200. **$99-$209.** 1177 Airport Blvd. US 101, exit Broadway-Burlingame or Old Bayshore Hwy, just e. Int corridors. **Pets:** Medium, other species. $100 deposit/room, $25 one-time fee/room. Designated rooms, service with restrictions, supervision.
[ASK] [X] [&M] [🛏] [💻] [🍽] [🐾]

(AAA) ▼▼▼ DoubleTree Hotel-San Francisco Airport H
(650) 344-5500. **$99-$209.** 835 Airport Blvd. US 101, exit Broadway-Burlingame or Anza Blvd, just e. Int corridors. **Pets:** Accepted.
[SAVE] [X] [&M] [🛏] [💻] [🍽]

▼▼▼ Embassy Suites-San Francisco Airport-Burlingame H
(650) 342-4600. **$129-$269.** 150 Anza Blvd. US 101, exit Broadway-Burlingame, just e. Int corridors. **Pets:** Accepted.
[X] [&M] [🛏] [💻] [🍽] [🐾] [🐕]

(AAA) ▼▼▼ Red Roof Inn M
(650) 342-7772. **$70-$120.** 777 Airport Blvd. US 101, exit Broadway-Burlingame or E Anza Blvd; just s of airport. Ext corridors. **Pets:** Medium. Service with restrictions, supervision.
[SAVE] [X] [&M] [🛏] [🐾]

▼▼▼ ▼▼▼ San Francisco Airport Marriott H
(650) 692-9100. **$224-$274.** 1800 Old Bayshore Hwy. US 101, exit Millbrae Ave, just e. Int corridors. **Pets:** Other species. $75 one-time fee/room.
[X] [&M] [🛏] [💻] [🍽] [🐾] [🐕]

(AAA) ▼▼▼ Sheraton Gateway Hotel-S.F.O. H
(650) 340-8500. **$119-$369.** 600 Airport Blvd. US 101, exit Broadway-Burlingame or Anza Blvd, 0.3 mi e. Int corridors. **Pets:** Accepted.
[SAVE] [X] [&M] [🛏] [💻] [🍽] [🐾]

(AAA) ▼▼▼ Vagabond Inn-SFO H
(650) 692-4040. **$69-$199.** 1640 Bayshore Hwy. US 101, exit Millbrae Ave, just e. Ext corridors. **Pets:** Very small, dogs only. $10 daily fee/pet. Designated rooms, service with restrictions, supervision.
[SAVE] [X] [&M] [🛏] [💻]

CORTE MADERA

(AAA) ▼▼▼ Marin Suites Hotel H ❀
(415) 924-3608. **$159-$209.** 45 Tamal Vista Blvd. US 101, exit Tamalpais Rd/Paradise Dr. Ext corridors. **Pets:** Medium, other species. $20 daily fee/pet. Designated rooms, service with restrictions, crate.
[SAVE] [X] [&M] [🛏] [💻] [🐾] [🐕] [🐈]

HALF MOON BAY

(AAA) ▼▼▼▼ Comfort Inn Half Moon Bay H ❀
(650) 712-1999. **$89-$249.** 2930 N Cabrillo Hwy. On SR 1, 2 mi n of jct SR 92 and 1. Ext corridors. **Pets:** $10 daily fee/pet. Designated rooms, service with restrictions, supervision.
[SAVE] [X] [&M] [🛏] [💻]

(AAA) ▼▼ Days Inn M
(650) 726-9700. **$70-$300.** 3020 N Cabrillo Hwy. 2 mi n of jct SR 92 and 1; w of SR 1. Ext corridors. **Pets:** Medium, dogs only. $15 daily fee/pet. Service with restrictions, supervision.
[SAVE] [X] [&M] [🛏] [💻]

▼▼ Harbor View Inn M
(650) 726-2329. **$86-$275.** 51 Ave Alhambra. 4 mi n of jct SR 92 and 1; e of SR 1. Ext corridors. **Pets:** Accepted.
[ASK] [X] [&M] [🛏] [🐈]

(AAA) ▼▼▼▼ Holiday Inn Express H ❀
(650) 726-3400. **$98-$169.** 230 S Cabrillo Hwy. On SR 1, just s of SR 92. Ext corridors. **Pets:** Large, other species. $10 daily fee/pet. Designated rooms, service with restrictions, supervision.
[SAVE] [X] [&M] [🛏] [💻]

▼▼▼ Landis Shores Oceanfront Inn BB
(650) 726-6642. **$225-$395, 7 day notice.** 211 Mirada Rd. 3 mi n of jct SR 92 and 1, exit SR 1 W at Medio Ave, just n. Int corridors. **Pets:** Accepted.
[X] [&M] [🛏] [🐈]

▼▼▼▼ ▼▼ The Ritz-Carlton, Half Moon Bay H ❀
(650) 712-7000. **$329-$4000.** 1 Miramontes Point Rd. 3 mi s of jct SR 92 and 1; w of SR 1 at Miramontes Point Rd. Ext/int corridors. **Pets:** Medium. $125 one-time fee/pet. Designated rooms, service with restrictions.
[ASK] [X] [💻] [🍽] [🐾] [🐕]

MILLBRAE

▼▼▼ Clarion Hotel-San Francisco Airport H
(650) 692-6363. **Call for rates.** 401 E Millbrae Ave. US 101, exit Millbrae Ave, just e. Int corridors. **Pets:** Accepted.
[X] [&M] [🛏] [💻] [🍽] [🐾]

(AAA) ▼▼▼ The Westin Hotel-San Francisco Airport H ❀
(650) 692-3500. **$139-$349.** 1 Old Bayshore Hwy. Just e of US 101, exit Millbrae Ave. Int corridors. **Pets:** Medium, dogs only. Service with restrictions, supervision.
[SAVE] [X] [&M] [💻] [🍽] [🐾] [🐕]

MILL VALLEY

Acqua Hotel �H
(415) 380-0400. **$189-$279.** 555 Redwood Hwy. US 101, exit Seminary Dr. Ext/int corridors. **Pets:** Accepted.
[SAVE] [X] [&M] [H]

SAN BRUNO

Regency Inn 🅜
(650) 589-7535. **$89-$99.** 411 E San Bruno Ave. US 101, exit San Bruno Ave, 0.4 mi w. Ext corridors. **Pets:** Small. $15 daily fee/pet. Service with restrictions, supervision.
[SAVE] [X] [&M] [H] [▣]

Staybridge Suites �H
(650) 588-0770. **$199-$279.** 1350 Huntington Ave. I-380, exit El Camino Real N, e on Sneath Ln. Ext corridors. **Pets:** Other species. $150 one-time fee/room.
[SAVE] [X] [&M] [H] [▣] [☞] [X]

SAN CARLOS

Homestead Studio Suites Hotel-San Francisco San Carlos �H
(650) 368-2600. **$105-$115.** 3 Circle Star Way. US 101, exit Whipple Ave, w to Industrial, then just n. Int corridors. **Pets:** Other species. $25 daily fee/pet. Service with restrictions, crate.
[ASK] [X] [&M] [H] [▣]

SAN FRANCISCO

Argonaut Hotel �H 🐾
(415) 563-0800. **$209-$429, 3 day notice.** 495 Jefferson St. Fisherman's Wharf; adjacent to The Cannery. Int corridors. **Pets:** Small. $250 deposit/room. Service with restrictions, supervision.
[SAVE] [X] [&M] [▣] [▥]

Beresford Arms Hotel �H 🐾
(415) 673-2600. **$108-$259.** 701 Post St. 3 blks w of Union Square. Int corridors. **Pets:** Other species. $25 one-time fee/pet. Designated rooms, service with restrictions, crate.
[SAVE] [X] [&M] [H] [▣] [Ƙ]

Beresford Hotel �H 🐾
(415) 673-9900. **$89-$159.** 635 Sutter St. 1 blk nw of Union Square at Mason St. Int corridors. **Pets:** Other species. $25 one-time fee/pet. Designated rooms, service with restrictions, crate.
[SAVE] [X] [&M] [▥] [Ƙ]

Best Western Americania �H
(415) 626-0200. **$149-$229.** 121 7th St. Just s of Market St. Ext corridors. **Pets:** Accepted.
[SAVE] [X] [H] [▣] [▥] [☞] [Ƙ]

Best Western Tuscan Inn at Fisherman's Wharf �H 🐾
(415) 561-1100. **$189-$279, 3 day notice.** 425 Northpoint St. Just s of Fisherman's Wharf at Mason St. Int corridors. **Pets:** Medium, other species. Designated rooms, service with restrictions.
[SAVE] [X] [▣] [▥]

Campton Place, a Taj Hotel �H 🐾
(415) 781-5555. **Call for rates.** 340 Stockton St. Just n of Union Square. Int corridors. **Pets:** Other species. $100 one-time fee/room. Crate.
[X] [&M] [▥]

The Fairmont San Francisco �H 🐾
(415) 772-5000. **$199-$999.** 950 Mason St (atop Nob Hill). Atop Nob Hill at California St. Int corridors. **Pets:** Small. $25 one-time fee/pet. Service with restrictions, supervision.
[SAVE] [X] [&M] [▥]

Four Seasons San Francisco �H 🐾
(415) 633-3000. **$525-$595.** 757 Market St. Between 3rd and 4th sts. Int corridors. **Pets:** Other species. Service with restrictions, crate.
[X] [&M] [H] [▣] [▥] [☞] [X]

Galleria Park Hotel �H
(415) 781-3060. **$169-$649.** 191 Sutter St. 2 blks ne of Union Square. Int corridors. **Pets:** Accepted.
[SAVE] [X] [&M] [▣] [▥]

good hotel �H
(415) 621-7001. **$99-$199.** 112 7th St. Just s of Market St. Int corridors. **Pets:** Accepted.
[SAVE] [X] [▣] [▥]

Harbor Court Hotel �H 🐾
(415) 882-1300. **Call for rates.** 165 Steuart St. On Embarcadero; between Howard and Mission sts. Int corridors. **Pets:** Other species. Service with restrictions, crate.
[SAVE] [X] [&M] [▥]

Hilton San Francisco �H
(415) 771-1400. **$149-$449.** 333 O'Farrell St. Just w of Union Square at Mason St. Int corridors. **Pets:** Accepted.
[X] [&M] [▣] [▥] [☞] [X]

Hilton San Francisco Financial District �H
(415) 433-6600. **$169-$449.** 750 Kearny St. Between Clay and Washington sts. Int corridors. **Pets:** Accepted.
[X] [&M] [H] [▣] [▥]

Holiday Inn Civic Center �H
(415) 626-6103. **$99-$389.** 50 8th St. 2 blks from Civic Auditorium; just s of Market St and BART Station. Int corridors. **Pets:** Accepted.
[SAVE] [X] [&M] [H] [▥] [☞]

Hotel Carlton �H 🐾
(415) 673-0242. **$89-$249.** 1075 Sutter St. 0.5 mi w of Union Square; between Hyde and Larkin sts. Int corridors. **Pets:** Medium. $35 daily fee/pet. Designated rooms, service with restrictions, supervision.
[SAVE] [X] [H] [▣] [▥] [Ƙ]

Hotel Diva �H
(415) 885-0200. **$129-$369.** 440 Geary St. Just w of Union Square. Int corridors. **Pets:** Medium, dogs only. $250 deposit/room, $75 one-time fee/room. Service with restrictions, supervision.
[SAVE] [X] [▥]

Hotel Frank �H
(415) 986-2000. **$149-$399.** 386 Geary St. Just w of Union Square at Mason St. Int corridors. **Pets:** Medium, dogs only. $250 deposit/room, $75 one-time fee/room. Service with restrictions, supervision.
[SAVE] [X] [H] [▣] [▥]

Hotel Kabuki �H
(415) 922-3200. **$149-$329.** 1625 Post St. Jct Laguna St; in Japan Center. Int corridors. **Pets:** Small. $35 daily fee/room. Service with restrictions, supervision.
[SAVE] [X] [&M] [▣] [▥]

Hotel Metropolis �H 🐾
(415) 775-4600. **$89-$269.** 25 Mason St. Jct Market St. Int corridors. **Pets:** Medium, dogs only. $75 one-time fee/pet. Service with restrictions, supervision.
[SAVE] [X] [&M] [H] [▣] [Ƙ]

Hotel Monaco �H
(415) 292-0100. **Call for rates.** 501 Geary St. Just w of Union Square at Taylor St. Int corridors. **Pets:** Accepted.
[SAVE] [X] [&M] [▥] [▥] [X]

Hotel Nikko San Francisco H
(415) 394-1111. **Call for rates.** 222 Mason St. Just w of Union Square. Int corridors. **Pets:** Accepted.
[SAVE] [X] [&M] [▭] [¶] [≈] [⊠]

Hotel Palomar H
(415) 348-1111. **Call for rates.** 12 Fourth St. At Market St. Int corridors. **Pets:** Accepted.
[SAVE] [X] [&M] [¶]

Hotel Rex H ❄
(415) 433-4434. **$189-$409.** 562 Sutter St. Just nw of Union Square. Int corridors. **Pets:** Large. $100 one-time fee/room. Service with restrictions, supervision.
[SAVE] [X] [&M] [¶]

Hotel Triton H
(415) 394-0500. **$129-$369.** 342 Grant Ave. Near Union Square at Bush St. Int corridors. **Pets:** Accepted.
[SAVE] [X] [&M] [▭]

Hotel Union Square H
(415) 397-3000. **$129-$369.** 114 Powell St. US 101 (Van Ness Ave), exit Market St E to Powell St; just n of cable car turnaround. Int corridors. **Pets:** Accepted.
[SAVE] [X] [🛏] [▭] [AC]

Hotel Vertigo H
(415) 885-6800. **$119-$349.** 940 Sutter St. Just w of Union Square. Int corridors. **Pets:** Medium, dogs only. $250 deposit/room, $75 one-time fee/room. Service with restrictions, supervision.
[SAVE] [X] [&M] [▭] [AC]

Hotel Vitale H ❄
(415) 278-3700. **$399-$799.** 8 Mission St. At Embarcadero. Int corridors. **Pets:** Small, dogs only. $35 daily fee/room. Service with restrictions, supervision.
[ASK] [X] [&M] [¶] [⊠]

InterContinental San Francisco H ❄
(415) 616-6500. **$189-$689.** 888 Howard St. Between 4th and 5th sts; in the SoMa District; s of Market. Int corridors. **Pets:** Medium, dogs only. $50 daily fee/pet. Designated rooms, service with restrictions, supervision.
[X] [&M] [▭] [¶] [≈] [⊠]

JW Marriott San Francisco H ❄
(415) 771-8600. **$260-$318.** 500 Post St. Just w of Union Square at Mason St. Int corridors. **Pets:** Small. $75 one-time fee/pet. Service with restrictions, supervision.
[X] [&M] [▭] [¶]

Kensington Park Hotel H ❄
(415) 788-6400. **Call for rates.** 450 Post St. Just w of Union Square. Int corridors. **Pets:** Medium, dogs only. $75 one-time fee/room. Designated rooms, service with restrictions, supervision.
[SAVE] [X] [🛏] [▭] [¶] [AC]

Larkspur Hotel Union Square H ❄
(415) 421-2865. **$145-$229.** 524 Sutter St. Union Square at Powell St. Int corridors. **Pets:** Medium. Service with restrictions.
[SAVE] [X] [&M]

The Laurel Inn H
(415) 567-8467. **$219-$249.** 444 Presidio Ave. 1 mi w of US 101 (Van Ness Ave); 1 mi e of Park Presidio Blvd (SR 1) at California St. Int corridors. **Pets:** Service with restrictions, supervision.
[SAVE] [X] [&M] [🛏] [▭] [AC]

Le Meridien San Francisco H
(415) 296-2900. **Call for rates.** 333 Battery St. At Clay St; in financial district. Int corridors. **Pets:** Accepted.
[SAVE] [X] [&M] [🛏] [¶]

Mandarin Oriental, San Francisco H ❄
(415) 276-9888. **$345-$4200.** 222 Sansome St. US 101, 1.2 mi e on Bush St, then just n. Int corridors. **Pets:** Small, dogs only. $25 daily fee/pet. Service with restrictions.
[ASK] [X] [▭] [¶] [⊠]

Omni San Francisco Hotel H ❄
(415) 677-9494. **$209-$799.** 500 California St. At Montgomery St; in financial district. Int corridors. **Pets:** Small. $50 one-time fee/pet. Service with restrictions, crate.
[ASK] [X] [&M] [▭] [¶]

The Opal San Francisco H
(415) 673-4711. **$129-$269.** 1050 Van Ness Ave. On US 101 (Van Ness Ave). Int corridors. **Pets:** Accepted.
[SAVE] [X] [&M] [🛏] [▭]

Palace Hotel H
(415) 512-1111. **Call for rates.** 2 New Montgomery St. Just e of Union Square at Market St. Int corridors. **Pets:** Accepted.
[SAVE] [X] [&M] [🛏] [¶] [≈] [⊠]

Parc 55 Hotel San Francisco H ❄
(415) 392-8000. **$159-$329, 3 day notice.** 55 Cyril Magnin St. Corner of Cyril Magnin and Eddy sts; 3 blks sw of Union Square. Int corridors. **Pets:** Small. $250 deposit/pet.
[SAVE] [X] [&M] [🛏] [▭] [¶]

The Powell Hotel H
(415) 398-3200. **$129-$145.** 28 Cyril Magnin St. At Powell St cable car turnaround. Int corridors. **Pets:** Accepted.
[ASK] [X] [&M] [▭] [¶] [AC]

The Prescott Hotel H
(415) 563-0303. **Call for rates.** 545 Post St. Just w of Union Square. Int corridors. **Pets:** Accepted.
[SAVE] [X] [¶]

The Ritz-Carlton, San Francisco H
(415) 296-7465. **$499-$749.** 600 Stockton St. Just n of Union Square at California St. Int corridors. **Pets:** Accepted.
[SAVE] [X] [&M] [▭] [¶] [≈] [⊠]

St. Regis Hotel San Francisco H
(415) 284-4000. **$329-$1800.** 125 3rd St. At Mission St. Int corridors. **Pets:** Accepted.
[SAVE] [X] [&M] [¶] [⊠]

San Francisco Marriott Fisherman's Wharf H
(415) 775-7555. **$199-$249.** 1250 Columbus Ave. Just s of Fisherman's Wharf at Bay St. Int corridors. **Pets:** Other species. $100 one-time fee/room. Service with restrictions, supervision.
[SAVE] [X] [&M] [🛏] [▭] [¶]

Serrano Hotel H
(415) 885-2500. **$139-$329.** 405 Taylor St. Just w of Union Square at O'Farrell St. Int corridors. **Pets:** Accepted.
[SAVE] [X] [&M] [¶] [⊠]

Sheraton Fisherman's Wharf H
(415) 362-5500. **$129-$459.** 2500 Mason St. Just se of Fisherman's Wharf at Beach St. Int corridors. **Pets:** Accepted.
[SAVE] [X] [&M] [🛏] [▭] [¶] [≈]

Sir Francis Drake Hotel H
(415) 392-7755. **$139-$439.** 450 Powell St. Just n of Union Square at Sutter St. Int corridors. **Pets:** Accepted.
[SAVE] [X] [&M] [¶] [⊠]

▼▼▼▼ **The Stanford Court, a Renaissance Hotel** 🄷
(415) 989-3500. **$269-$329.** 905 California St. Atop Nob Hill; corner of California and Powell sts. Int corridors. **Pets:** Small, dogs only. $25 one-time fee/pet. Service with restrictions, crate.
☒ ♿ 🛋

🆑 ▼▼▼ **Travelodge By The Bay** 🄼
(415) 673-0691. **$59-$359.** 1450 Lombard St. On US 101 (Lombard St). Ext/int corridors. **Pets:** Accepted.
SAVE ☒ ♿ 🛋 🖥

🆑 ▼▼▼▼ **Villa Florence, a Larkspur Collection Hotel** 🄷 🐾
(415) 397-7700. **$179-$349.** 225 Powell St. Just s of Union Square; between O'Farrell and Geary sts. Int corridors. **Pets:** Medium, other species. Service with restrictions.
SAVE ☒ ♿ 🖥 🍴

🆑 ▼▼▼▼▼ **The Westin St. Francis** 🄷 🐾
(415) 397-7000. **$159-$489.** 335 Powell St. On Union Square. Int corridors. **Pets:** Medium, dogs only. Service with restrictions, supervision.
SAVE ☒ ♿ 🖥 🍴 ☒

🆑 ▼▼▼▼▼ **Westin San Francisco Market Street** 🄷
(415) 974-6400. **Call for rates.** 50 3rd St. Just n of Moscone Convention Center. Int corridors. **Pets:** Accepted.
SAVE ☒ ♿ 🖥

🆑 ▼▼▼▼ **W San Francisco** 🄷
(415) 777-5300. **Call for rates.** 181 3rd St. At Howard St. Int corridors. **Pets:** Accepted.
SAVE ☒ 🛋 🖥 🍴 🌊 ☒

SAN MATEO

🆑 ▼▼▼▼ **Best Western Coyote Point** 🄷
(650) 347-9990. **$79-$159, 3 day notice.** 480 N Bayshore Blvd. US 101, exit Dore Ave northbound; exit 3rd Ave E southbound; re-enter US 101, then exit Dore Ave. Int corridors. **Pets:** Very small. $100 deposit/room, $10 daily fee/pet. Service with restrictions.
SAVE ☒ ♿ 🛋 🖥

▼▼▼ **Comfort Inn** 🄷
(650) 344-6376. **Call for rates.** 350 N Bayshore Blvd. US 101, exit Dore Ave northbound; exit 3rd Ave E southbound; re-enter US 101, then exit Dore Ave. Ext/int corridors. **Pets:** Accepted.
☒ ♿ 🛋 🖥

▼▼ **Homestead Studio Suites Hotel-San Francisco-SFO** 🄷
(650) 574-1744. **$115-$125.** 1830 Gateway Dr. SR 92, exit Edgewater Blvd; se of jct US 101 and SR 92. Ext corridors. **Pets:** Other species. $25 daily fee/pet. Service with restrictions, crate.
ASK ☒ ♿ 🛋 🖥

▼▼▼▼ **Residence Inn by Marriott** 🄷
(650) 574-4700. **$206-$252.** 2000 Winward Way. 0.8 mi se from jct US 101 and SR 92; exit SR 92 via Edgewater Blvd. Ext corridors. **Pets:** Accepted.
☒ ♿ 🛋 🖥 🌊 ☒

SAN RAFAEL

▼▼▼ **Gerstle Park Inn** 🄱🄱
(415) 721-7611. **$189-$275, 3 day notice.** 34 Grove St. US 101, exit Central San Rafael, 0.5 mi w on 4th St, 0.5 mi s on D St, then just w on San Rafael Ave. Ext/int corridors. **Pets:** Accepted.
☒ ♿

SOUTH SAN FRANCISCO

▼▼▼▼ **Embassy Suites San Francisco Airport-South San Francisco** 🄷 🐾
(650) 589-3400. **$140-$260.** 250 Gateway Blvd. US 101, exit Grand Ave, just e. Int corridors. **Pets:** Medium, other species. $50 one-time fee/pet. Service with restrictions, supervision.
☒ ♿ 🛋 🖥 🍴 🌊 ☒

▼▼▼ **La Quinta Inn San Francisco (Airport)** 🄷 🐾
(650) 583-2223. **$69-$139.** 20 Airport Blvd. US 101, exit S Airport Blvd, just w. Int corridors. **Pets:** Medium, other species. Service with restrictions, supervision.
ASK ☒ ♿ 🛋 🖥 🌊

🆑 ▼▼▼▼ **Larkspur Landing South San Francisco** 🄷
(650) 827-1515. **$109-$199.** 690 Gateway Blvd. US 101, exit Grand Ave, just e. Int corridors. **Pets:** Accepted.
SAVE ☒ ♿ 🖥

▼▼▼▼ **Residence Inn by Marriott at Oyster Point** 🄷 🐾
(650) 837-9000. **$206-$252.** 1350 Veterans Blvd. US 101, exit Oyster Point, just e. Int corridors. **Pets:** Medium. $100 one-time fee/room. Supervision.
☒ ♿ 🛋 🖥 🌊 ☒

TIBURON

🆑 ▼▼▼ **The Lodge at Tiburon, a Larkspur Collection Hotel** 🄷
(415) 435-3133. **$149-$469, 3 day notice.** 1651 Tiburon Blvd. US 101, exit Tiburon-Belvedere, 4 mi e; in village; 1 blk from bay. Ext corridors. **Pets:** Medium, dogs only. $75 one-time fee/room. Designated rooms, service with restrictions.
SAVE ☒ ♿ 🛋 🖥 🍴 🌊

END METROPOLITAN AREA

SAN JOSE

▼▼▼ **Crowne Plaza San Jose–Downtown** 🄷
(408) 998-0400. **Call for rates.** 282 Almaden Blvd. I-280, exit Almaden-Vine, 6 blks n. Int corridors. **Pets:** Accepted.
☒ ♿ 🛋 🖥 🍴

🆑 ▼▼▼▼ **DoubleTree Hotel San Jose** 🄷 🐾
(408) 453-4000. **$89-$309.** 2050 Gateway Pl. 0.3 mi e of San Jose International Airport via Airport Blvd; w of US 101, exit N 1st St; US 101 northbound, exit Brokaw Rd. Int corridors. **Pets:** Other species. $50 deposit/room. Service with restrictions, supervision.
SAVE ☒ 🛋 🖥 🍴 🌊

▼▼▼ **Extended Stay Deluxe-San Jose-Downtown** 🄷
(408) 453-3000. **$121-$131.** 55 E Brokaw Rd. US 101, exit 1st St/Brokaw Rd, just e. Int corridors. **Pets:** Other species. $25 daily fee/pet. Service with restrictions, crate.
ASK ☒ 🌊

▼▼▼ **Extended Stay Deluxe San Jose–South-Edenvale** 🄷
(408) 229-9188. **$121-$131.** 6189 San Ignacio Ave. US 101, exit Bernal Rd E, just n. Int corridors. **Pets:** Other species. $25 daily fee/pet. Service with restrictions, crate.
ASK ☒ ♿ 🛋 🖥 🌊

▼▼▼ Fairfield Inn and Suites 🅷
(408) 453-3133. **$161-$197.** 1755 N 1st St. US 101, exit N 1st St, just w.
Int corridors. **Pets:** Accepted.
⊠ 🛢 💻 ⇌

▼▼▼ ▼▼▼ The Fairmont San Jose 🅷
(408) 998-1900. **$149-$369.** 170 S Market St. At Fairmont Plaza. Int corridors. **Pets:** Accepted.
(ASK) ⊠ 💻 (🍴) ⇌ (🐾)

⚔⚔⚔ ▼▼▼ Hilton San Jose 🅷
(408) 287-2100. **$109-$319.** 300 Almaden Blvd.. Int corridors.
Pets: Accepted.
(SAVE) ⊠ (🅼) 🛢 💻 (🍴) ⇌

⚔⚔⚔ ▼▼▼ Holiday Inn 🅷
(408) 793-3300. **$79-$209.** 1740 N 1st St. W of US 101, exit N 1st St; 0.5
mi e of San Jose International Airport via Airport Pkwy. Int corridors.
Pets: Accepted.
(SAVE) ⊠ 🛢 💻 (🍴) ⇌ (🐾)

▼▼ ▼▼ Homestead Studio Suites Hotel-San
Jose-Downtown 🅷
(408) 573-0648. **$121-$131.** 1560 N 1st St. 1 mi e of San Jose International Airport; US 101, exit N 1st St, then s. Int corridors. **Pets:** Other
species. $25 daily fee/pet. Service with restrictions, crate.
(ASK) ⊠

▼▼▼ Homewood Suites by Hilton 🅷
(408) 428-9900. **$109-$249.** 10 W Trimble Rd. 2 mi ne of San Jose
International Airport; US 101, exit Trimble Rd, 1.3 mi e. Ext/int corridors.
Pets: Small, dogs only.
⊠ (🅼) 🛢 💻 ⇌ (🐾)

⚔⚔⚔ ▼▼▼ ▼▼▼ Hotel De Anza 🅷
(408) 286-1000. **$129-$399.** 233 W Santa Clara St. SR 87, exit Santa
Clara St, just e. Int corridors. **Pets:** Small. $50 one-time fee/room. Desig-
nated rooms, service with restrictions.
(SAVE) ⊠ 💻 (🍴)

⚔⚔⚔ ▼▼▼ Howard Johnson Inn 🅼
(408) 280-5300. **$79-$225, 14 day notice.** 1215 S 1st St. Jct I-280 and
SR 82, 0.8 mi s. Ext corridors. **Pets:** Other species. $10 daily fee/pet.
Service with restrictions.
(SAVE) ⊠ 🛢 💻

▼▼▼ La Quinta Inn San Jose Airport 🅷 ❀
(408) 435-8800. **$69-$149, 7 day notice.** 2585 Seaboard Ave. US 101,
exit Trimble Rd E; 1 mi ne of San Jose International Airport. Int corridors.
Pets: Medium, other species. Service with restrictions, supervision.
(ASK) ⊠ 🛢 💻 ⇌

▼▼▼ Residence Inn by Marriott 🅷 ❀
(408) 226-7676. **$161-$197.** 6111 San Ignacio Ave. US 101, exit Bernal
Rd, then e. Int corridors. **Pets:** Medium. $100 one-time fee/room. Service
with restrictions, crate.
⊠ (🅼) 🛢 💻 ⇌ (🐾)

▼▼▼ Staybridge Suites San Jose 🅷
(408) 436-1600. **Call for rates.** 1602 Crane Ct. US 101, exit 1st St/Brokaw
Rd, 0.4 mi e to Bering S, then 0.5 mi. Ext corridors. **Pets:** Accepted.
⊠ 🛢 💻 ⇌

▼▼▼ TownePlace Suites by Marriott San
Jose/Cupertino 🅷
(408) 984-5903. **$179-$219.** 440 Saratoga Ave. I-280, exit Saratoga Ave,
just n. Int corridors. **Pets:** Accepted.
⊠ (🅼) 🛢 💻 ⇌

SAN JUAN BAUTISTA

⚔⚔⚔ ▼ San Juan Inn 🅼
(831) 623-4380. **$69-$99.** 410 The Alameda. Jct SR 156. Ext corridors.
Pets: Other species. $15 daily fee/pet. Service with restrictions.
(SAVE) ⊠ 🛢 💻 ⇌

SAN JUAN CAPISTRANO

⚔⚔⚔ ▼▼▼ Best Western Capistrano Inn 🅼
(949) 493-5661. **$90-$160, 3 day notice.** 27174 Ortega Hwy. I-5, exit 82
(SR 74/Ortega Hwy), just e. Ext corridors. **Pets:** Medium, other species.
$25 one-time fee/room. Service with restrictions.
(SAVE) ⊠ 🛢 💻 ⇌

SAN LUIS OBISPO

⚔⚔⚔ ▼▼▼ Best Western Royal Oak Hotel 🅼
(805) 544-4410. **$89-$259.** 214 Madonna Rd. US 101, exit 201 (Madonna
Rd), just s. Ext/int corridors. **Pets:** $15 one-time fee/pet. Service with restric-
tions, supervision.
(SAVE) ⊠ (🅼) 🛢 💻 ⇌

⚔⚔⚔ ▼▼▼ Days Inn-San Luis Obispo 🅼
(805) 549-9911. **$69-$219.** 2050 Garfield St. US 101, exit 204 (Monterey
St), just sw. Ext corridors. **Pets:** Small, dogs only. $50 deposit/room, $10
daily fee/pet. Designated rooms, service with restrictions, supervision.
(SAVE) ⊠ (🅼) 🛢 💻 ⇌

▼▼ Heritage Inn Bed & Breakfast 🅱🅱 ❀
(805) 544-7440. **$85-$200, 7 day notice.** 978 Olive St. US 101, exit 203B
(SR 1/Morro Bay) northbound, just w on Santa Rosa St, then just s; exit
203A (Santa Rosa St) southbound, just ne. Int corridors. **Pets:** Medium,
other species. $100 deposit/room. Designated rooms, service with restric-
tions, supervision.
⊠ (🎬) (📺) (🖤)

▼▼▼ Holiday Inn Express 🅷 ❀
(805) 544-8600. **Call for rates.** 1800 Monterey St. US 101, exit 204
(Monterey St), just w. Int corridors. **Pets:** Other species. $30 one-time
fee/room. Designated rooms, service with restrictions, supervision.
⊠ (🅼) 🛢 💻 ⇌

⚔⚔⚔ ▼▼ ▼ Ramada Inn Olive Tree 🅼
(805) 544-2800. **$79-$399.** 1000 Olive St. US 101, exit 203B (Morro Bay)
northbound, just w on Santa Rosa St, then just s; exit 203A (Santa Rosa St)
southbound, just ne. Ext corridors. **Pets:** Small, dogs only. $100 deposit/
room, $10 daily fee/pet. Designated rooms, service with restrictions, super-
vision.
(SAVE) ⊠ (🅼) 🛢 💻 ⇌

⚔⚔⚔ ▼▼▼ Sands Suites & Motel 🅼
(805) 544-0500. **$79-$249.** 1930 Monterey St. US 101, exit 204 (Monterey
St), just sw. Ext corridors. **Pets:** Other species. $25 one-time fee/pet. Des-
ignated rooms, service with restrictions, supervision.
(SAVE) ⊠ (🅼) 🛢 💻 ⇌ (🐾)

⚔⚔⚔ ▼▼ ▼ Super 8 🅼
(805) 544-6888. **$49-$299.** 1951 Monterey St. US 101, exit 204 (Monterey
St), just e. Ext corridors. **Pets:** Accepted.
(SAVE) ⊠ 🛢 💻 ⇌

SAN MARCOS

⚔⚔⚔ ▼▼▼ Lake San Marcos Resort 🅷
(760) 744-0120. **$129-$469.** 1025 La Bonita Dr. SR 78, exit Rancho Santa
Fe Rd, 2 mi s, then 0.5 mi e via Lake San Marcos and San Marino drs; at
Lake San Marcos. Ext/int corridors. **Pets:** Accepted.
(SAVE) ⊠ 🛢 💻 (🍴) ⇌ (🐾)

SAN RAMON

▼▼ ▼ Homestead Studio Suites Hotel-San Ramon-Bishop
Ranch 🅷
(925) 277-0833. **$100-$110.** 18000 San Ramon Valley Blvd. I-680, exit
Bollinger Canyon Rd E, just n. Ext corridors. **Pets:** Other species. $25 daily
fee/pet. Service with restrictions, crate.
(ASK) ⊠ 🛢 💻

▼▼▼ Residence Inn by Marriott 🅷
(925) 277-9292. **$215-$263.** 1071 Market Pl. I-680, exit Bollinger Canyon
Rd E, 0.5 mi e. Ext corridors. **Pets:** Accepted.
⊠ 🛢 💻 ⇌ (🐾)

▼▼▼▼ San Ramon Marriott at Bishop Ranch H
(925) 867-9200. **$251-$307.** 2600 Bishop Dr. I-680, exit Bollinger Canyon Rd E, n on Sunset, then just w. Int corridors. **Pets:** Medium, dogs only. $75 one-time fee/pet. Service with restrictions, supervision.
⊠ 🛄 💻 🍴 ⊠

SAN SIMEON

▲▲▲ ▼▼▼ Best Western Cavalier Oceanfront Resort H ✿
(805) 927-4688. **$99-$319, 3 day notice.** 9415 Hearst Dr. SR 1, exit Pico W, just s; exit Vista del Mar W, just n. Ext corridors. **Pets:** Other species. Service with restrictions, supervision.
SAVE ⊠ 🛄 🛄 💻 🍴 ⇆ ⊠ 🏋

▲▲▲ ▼▼ Courtesy Inn M
(805) 927-4691. **$89-$119.** 9450 Castillo Dr. East side of SR 1. Ext corridors. **Pets:** Dogs only. $20 daily fee/pet. Designated rooms, service with restrictions, supervision.
SAVE ⊠ 🛄 💻 ⇆

▲▲▲ ▼▼ San Simeon Lodge H
(805) 927-4601. **$50-$210, 3 day notice.** 9520 Castillo Dr. On SR 1. Ext corridors. **Pets:** Accepted.
SAVE ⊠ 🛄 💻 🍴 ⇆ 🏋

▲▲▲ ▼▼ Silver Surf Motel M
(805) 927-4661. **$59-$189.** 9390 Castillo Dr. Just e of SR 1. Ext corridors. **Pets:** Other species. $10 daily fee/pet. Designated rooms, service with restrictions, supervision.
SAVE ⊠ 🛄 💻 ⇆ 🏋

SANTA ANA

▼▼▼▼ La Quinta Inn & Suites Santa Ana M ✿
(714) 540-1111. **$69-$159.** 2721 Hotel Terrace Dr. SR 55, exit 8 (Dyer Rd) northbound; exit 8B (Dyer Rd W) southbound, just w, then just s. Ext corridors. **Pets:** Medium, other species. Service with restrictions, supervision.
ASK ⊠ 🛄 💻 ⇆

▼ Motel 6 #738 M
(714) 558-0500. **$51-$61.** 1623 E 1st St. I-5, exit 103C (1st St/4th St) northbound; exit 104A (1st St/4th St) southbound, just w. Ext corridors. **Pets:** Other species. Service with restrictions, supervision.
⊠ 🛄

▼ ▼ Red Roof Inn M
(714) 542-0311. **$67-$70.** 2600 N Main St. I-5, exit 105B (Main St), 0.3 mi n. Ext/int corridors. **Pets:** Medium, other species. Designated rooms, service with restrictions, supervision.
⊠ 🛄 ⇆

SANTA BARBARA

▼ Blue Sands Motel M
(805) 965-1624. **$85-$275, 3 day notice.** 421 S Milpas St. US 101, exit 96A (Milpas St), 0.3 mi s. Ext corridors. **Pets:** Accepted.
⊠ 🛄 💻 ⇆ 🏋

▼ ▼ Extended StayAmerica Santa Barbara-Calle Real H
(805) 692-1882. **$125-$164.** 4870 Calle Real. US 101, exit Turnpike Rd, just e, then just n. Int corridors. **Pets:** Other species. $25 daily fee/pet. Service with restrictions, crate.
ASK ⊠ 🛄 🛄 💻

▲▲▲ ▼▼▼▼ Fess Parker's DoubleTree Resort H
(805) 564-4333. **$200-$510.** 633 E Cabrillo Blvd. US 101, exit 96A (Milpas St), just s, then just w. Ext/int corridors. **Pets:** Accepted.
SAVE ⊠ 🛄 🛄 💻 🍴 ⇆ ⊠

▼▼▼▼ Four Seasons Biltmore Santa Barbara H ✿
(805) 969-2261. **$550-$4600, 3 day notice.** 1260 Channel Dr. US 101, exit 94A (Olive Mill Rd), 0.3 mi s. Ext corridors. **Pets:** Small, other species. Designated rooms, service with restrictions, supervision.
⊠ 🛄 🛄 💻 🍴 ⇆ ⊠

▲▲▲ ▼▼▼▼ Harbor House Inn M
(805) 962-9745. **$129-$349.** 104 Bath St. US 101, exit 94B (Cabrillo Blvd) (left hand exit), 3 mi n, then just e; exit 97 (Castillo St) southbound, 0.4 mi w, just s on Cabrillo Blvd, then just e. Ext corridors. **Pets:** Medium, dogs only. $15 daily fee/pet. Designated rooms, service with restrictions, supervision.
SAVE ⊠ 🛄 💻 🏋

▲▲▲ ▼▼▼▼ Hotel MarMonte H
(805) 963-0744. **$179-$304, 3 day notice.** 1111 E Cabrillo Blvd. US 101, exit 96A (Milpas St), 0.3 mi s, then just e. Int corridors. **Pets:** Dogs only. $75 one-time fee/pet. Designated rooms, service with restrictions, crate.
SAVE ⊠ 🛄 💻 🍴 ⇆ ⊠

▼▼▼ Marina Beach Motel M
(805) 963-9311. **$99-$324.** 21 Bath St. US 101, exit 96B (Garden St), 0.3 mi w to Cabrillo Blvd, 0.4 mi n to Bath St, then just e. Ext corridors. **Pets:** Small. $15 daily fee/pet. Designated rooms, service with restrictions, supervision.
ASK ⊠ 🛄 💻

▼▼▼ Pacifica Suites H
(805) 683-6722. **$179-$389.** 5490 Hollister Ave. US 101, exit 104A (Patterson Ave), 0.5 mi w, then 0.5 mi n. Ext/int corridors. **Pets:** Accepted.
⊠ 🛄 💻

▼▼▼ The Parkside Inn M
(805) 963-0744. **Call for rates.** 424 Por La Mar. US 101, exit 96A (Milpas St), 0.3 mi s, just e on Cabrillo Blvd, then just n. Int corridors. **Pets:** Accepted.
⊠ 🛄 💻 ⇆ ⊠

SANTA CATALINA ISLAND

▲▲▲ ▼▼▼▼ Catalina Canyon Resort & Spa M
(310) 510-0325. **$109-$329, 3 day notice.** 888 Country Club Dr. In Avalon; 0.5 mi from harbor via Sumner Ave. Ext corridors. **Pets:** Medium, other species. $50 one-time fee/room. Designated rooms, service with restrictions, supervision.
SAVE ⊠ 🛄 💻 🍴 ⇆ ⊠

SANTA CLARA

▲▲▲ ▼▼ ▼ Quality Inn & Suites M
(408) 241-3010. **$109-$169.** 2930 El Camino Real. SR 82, 0.5 mi w of San Tomas Expwy; US 101, exit S Bowers Ave. Ext corridors. **Pets:** Accepted.
SAVE ⊠ 🛄 🛄 💻 ⇆

▼▼▼ Santa Clara Marriott Hotel H
(408) 988-1500. **$260-$318.** 2700 Mission College Blvd. 0.5 mi e off US 101, exit Great America Pkwy; 0.8 mi s of Great America Theme Park. Int corridors. **Pets:** Medium. $75 one-time fee/pet. Service with restrictions, supervision.
⊠ 🛄 🛄 💻 🍴 ⇆ ⊠

▲▲▲ ▼▼ ▼ The Vagabond Inn M
(408) 241-0771. **$69-$199.** 3580 El Camino Real. On SR 82, southeast corner of Lawrence Expwy Cloverleaf. Ext corridors. **Pets:** Accepted.
SAVE ⊠ 🛄 💻 ⇆

SANTA CRUZ

▲▲▲ ▼▼ ▼ GuestHouse International Pacific Inn H
(831) 425-3722. **$70-$220.** 330 Ocean St. 1 mi from jct SR 1 and 17. Int corridors. **Pets:** Accepted.
SAVE ⊠ 🛄 💻 ⇆

W Hilton Santa Cruz/Scotts Valley 🅷 ❄
(831) 440-1000. **$169-$309.** 6001 La Madrona Dr. SR 17, exit Mt. Hermon Rd. Int corridors. **Pets:** Dogs only. $50 deposit/room, $50 one-time fee/pet. Service with restrictions, supervision.
✕ ⬛M 🛏 💻 🍴 ⤳

W The Inn at Pasatiempo 🅷 ❄
(831) 423-5000. **$109-$275.** 555 Hwy 17. 0.8 mi n of jct SR 1 and 17; exit SR 17, exit Pasatiempo Dr. Ext corridors. **Pets:** Small, dogs only. $25 daily fee/pet. Designated rooms, service with restrictions, supervision.
SAVE ✕ 🛏 💻 🍴 🅺

W Santa Cruz Beach Inn 🅷
(831) 458-9660. **$80-$400, 3 day notice.** 600 Riverside Ave. 4 blks from beach. Ext corridors. **Pets:** Dogs only. $15 daily fee/pet. Designated rooms, service with restrictions, supervision.
SAVE ✕ 🛏 💻 ⤳ 🅺

SANTA MARIA

W Best Western Big America Ⓜ
(805) 922-5200. **$125-$189.** 1725 N Broadway. US 101, exit 173 (SR 135/S Broadway), 0.5 mi s. Ext corridors. **Pets:** Service with restrictions, supervision.
SAVE ✕ 🛏 💻 ⤳

W Comfort Inn Ⓜ
(805) 922-5891. **$122-$126.** 210 S Nicholson Ave. US 101, exit 171 (Main St), just e, then just s. Int corridors. **Pets:** Medium, dogs only. $25 one-time fee/room. Service with restrictions, supervision.
SAVE ✕ 🛏 💻 ⤳

W Historic Santa Maria Inn 🅷 🐾
(805) 928-7777. **$124-$169.** 801 S Broadway. US 101, exit 171 (Main St), 1 mi w, then 0.5 mi s. Int corridors. **Pets:** Small, other species. $50 one-time fee/room. Designated rooms, service with restrictions, supervision.
A$K ✕ 🛏 💻 🍴 ⤳ ✕

W Holiday Inn Hotel & Suites 🅷 ❄
(805) 928-6000. **$135-$229.** 2100 N Broadway. US 101, exit 173 (SR 135/S Broadway), just s. Int corridors. **Pets:** Medium. $25 daily fee/pet. Designated rooms, service with restrictions, supervision.
SAVE ✕ ⬛M 🛏 💻 🍴 ⤳

SANTA NELLA

W Holiday Inn Express 🅷
(209) 826-8282. **$79-$129.** 28976 Plaza Dr. I-5, exit 407 (SR 33), just e. Ext corridors. **Pets:** $8 one-time fee/pet. Designated rooms, service with restrictions, supervision.
SAVE ✕ 🛏 💻 ⤳

W Ramada Mission de Oro Ⓜ
(209) 826-4444. **$75-$106.** 13070 State Hwy 33. I-5, exit 407 (SR 33), just w. Ext/int corridors. **Pets:** Accepted.
SAVE ✕ 🛏 💻 🍴 ⤳

W Super 8 Motel 🅷
(209) 827-8700. **$69-$99.** 28821 W Gonzaga Rd. 2.5 mi w of I-5; SR 152, exit Gonzaga Rd, just s. Ext corridors. **Pets:** Small. $25 one-time fee/pet. Designated rooms, no service, supervision.
SAVE ✕ 🛏 💻 ⤳

SANTA PAULA

W Glen Tavern Inn 🅷
(805) 933-5550. **$89-$99.** 134 N Mill St. SR 126, exit 12 (10th St) northbound, 0.5 mi w, then just s. Int corridors. **Pets:** Accepted.
SAVE ✕ 🛏 💻 🍴 ⤳

SCOTTS VALLEY

W Best Western Inn Scotts Valley 🅷
(831) 438-6666. **$108-$155.** 6020 Scotts Valley Dr. SR 17, exit Granite Creek, just w. Ext corridors. **Pets:** Medium, other species. $100 deposit/pet. Designated rooms, service with restrictions, supervision.
SAVE ✕ ⬛M 🛏 💻 ⤳

SELMA

W Holiday Inn-Swan Court 🅷 ❄
(559) 891-8000. **$105-$135.** 2950 Pea Soup Anderson Blvd. SR 99, exit Floral Ave, just w. Int corridors. **Pets:** Small. $50 one-time fee/room. No service, crate.
SAVE ✕ 🛏 💻 🍴 ⤳

W Super 8 Motel 🅷
(559) 896-2800. **$90-$145.** 3142 S Highland Ave. SR 99, exit Floral Ave. Int corridors. **Pets:** Accepted.
SAVE ✕ 🛏 💻 ⤳

SHASTA LAKE

W Bridge Bay Resort Ⓜ
(530) 275-3021. **$85-$190, 3 day notice.** 10300 Bridge Bay Rd. I-5, exit 690, just w. Ext corridors. **Pets:** Accepted.
SAVE ✕ 🛏 💻 🍴 ⤳ ✕

W Fawndale Lodge & RV Resort Ⓜ
(530) 275-8000. **$63-$115.** 15215 Fawndale Rd. I-5, exit 689, exit Fawndale Rd; just e; 10 mi n of Redding; 1 mi s of Shasta Lake. Ext corridors. **Pets:** $10 one-time fee/room. Supervision.
SAVE ✕ 🛏 💻 ⤳ ✕

SHELTER COVE

W Inn of the Lost Coast Ⓜ
(707) 986-7521. **$160-$260.** 205 Wave Dr. US 101, exit Shelter Cove, 1.7 mi s on Redwood Dr, 21.1 mi w on Briceland Rd/Shelter Cove Rd, 0.4 mi n on Upper Pacific Rd, then just w on Lower Pacific Rd. Ext corridors. **Pets:** Other species. $10 daily fee/pet. Designated rooms, service with restrictions, supervision.
A$K ✕ 🛏 💻 🍴 🅺 ✆

SIERRA CITY

W Herrington's Sierra Pines Ⓜ ❄
(530) 862-1151. **$79-$140, 10 day notice.** 104 Main St. 0.5 mi w on SR 49; 12 mi n of Downieville; center. Ext corridors. **Pets:** Other species. Supervision.
SAVE ✕ 🛏 💻 🍴 ✕ 🅺 ✆

SIMI VALLEY

W Extended StayAmerica-Los Angeles-Simi Valley 🅷
(805) 584-8880. **$100-$126.** 2498 Stearns St. SR 118, exit Stearns St, just s. Int corridors. **Pets:** Other species. $25 daily fee/pet. Service with restrictions, crate.
A$K ✕ 🛏 💻

SMITH RIVER

W Ship Ashore Motel Ⓜ
(707) 487-3141. **$54-$105.** 12370 Hwy 101. On US 101, 3.7 mi s of Oregon border. Ext corridors. **Pets:** Very small. Service with restrictions, supervision.
✕ 🛏 💻 🍴 🅺

SOLEDAD

W Valley Harvest Inn 🅷
(831) 678-3833. **$89-$189.** 1155 Front St. US 101, exit Soledad, just e. Ext/int corridors. **Pets:** Small, dogs only. $300 deposit/pet, $10 daily fee/pet. Designated rooms, service with restrictions, supervision.
SAVE ✕ 🛏 💻 🍴 ⤳

SOLVANG

▼▼ Meadowlark Inn M
(805) 688-4631. **$150-$350, 14 day notice.** 2644 Mission Dr. On SR 246, 1.6 mi e. Ext corridors. **Pets:** Accepted.
ASK ⊠ ▯ 🖵 🛋

▲▲▲ ▼▼ Royal Copenhagen Inn M
(805) 688-5561. **$85-$275, 3 day notice.** 1579 Mission Dr. On SR 246. Ext/int corridors. **Pets:** $25 daily fee/pet. Designated rooms, service with restrictions, supervision.
SAVE ⊠ ▯ 🖵 🛋

▲▲▲ ▼▼▼ Wine Valley Inn & Cottages H
(805) 688-2111. **$119-$409, 30 day notice.** 1564 Copenhagen Dr. SR 246, just s on 5th St. Ext/int corridors. **Pets:** Other species. $25 daily fee/pet. Service with restrictions, crate.
SAVE ⊠ ▯ 🖵 🛋 ⊠

SONORA

▲▲▲ ▼▼ Aladdin Motor Inn H
(209) 533-4971. **$79-$87.** 14260 Mono Way (Hwy 108). On SR 108, 3.5 mi e. Ext/int corridors. **Pets:** Large, other species. $15 one-time fee/room. Designated rooms, service with restrictions, supervision.
SAVE ⊠ ▯ 🖵 🛋

▲▲▲ ▼▼◆ Best Western Sonora Oaks H
(209) 533-4400. **$110-$140.** 19551 Hess Ave. 3.5 mi e on SR 108. Ext/int corridors. **Pets:** Accepted.
SAVE ⊠ ▯ 🖵 🛋

▲▲▲ ▼ Miners Motel M
(209) 532-7850. **$40-$80, 3 day notice.** 18740 SR 108. SR 49 and 108, 1 mi e of Jamestown. Ext corridors. **Pets:** Medium, dogs only. $10 daily fee/pet. No service.
SAVE ⊠ ▯ 🖵 🛋

▲▲▲ ▼▼ Sonora Days Inn H
(209) 532-2400. **$64-$144.** 160 S Washington St. Downtown. Ext/int corridors. **Pets:** Dogs only. $10 daily fee/pet. Designated rooms, supervision.
SAVE ⊠ ▯ 🖵 🛋

▼ Sonora Gold Lodge M
(209) 532-3952. **$39-$99.** 480 Stockton St. 0.5 mi sw on SR 49 and 108 business route. Ext corridors. **Pets:** Accepted.
ASK ⊠ ▯ 🖵 🛋

▼▼▼ Union Hill Inn BB
(209) 533-1494. **$150-$195, 3 day notice.** 21645 Parrotts Ferry Rd. Jct SR 49 and Parrotts Ferry Rd; 3 mi n of downtown. Ext corridors. **Pets:** Accepted.
ASK ⊠ ▯ 🖵 🛋 🗲

STOCKTON

▲▲▲ ▼▼ Comfort Inn H
(209) 478-4300. **Call for rates.** 2654 W March Ln. I-5, exit March Ln, just e. Ext corridors. **Pets:** Other species. $15 one-time fee/room. Designated rooms, service with restrictions.
SAVE ⊠ 🔥 ▯ 🖵 🛋

▲▲▲ ▼ Econo Lodge of Stockton H
(209) 466-5741. **$49-$69.** 2210 S Manthey Rd. I-5, exit 8th St W, 0.3 mi s of jct SR 4. Int corridors. **Pets:** Very small, dogs only. $20 one-time fee/pet. Designated rooms, service with restrictions, supervision.
SAVE ⊠ ▯ 🖵 🛋

▼ Extended StayAmerica-Stockton-March Lane H
(209) 472-7588. **$105-$115.** 2844 W March Ln. I-5, exit March Ln, just w. Int corridors. **Pets:** Other species. $25 daily fee/pet. Service with restrictions, crate.
ASK ⊠ ▯ 🖵

▼▼▼ Holiday Inn H
(209) 474-3301. **$99-$149, 3 day notice.** 111 E March Ln. I-5, exit March Ln, 2.5 mi e; corner of El Dorado St. Int corridors. **Pets:** Accepted.
ASK ⊠ 🔥 ▯ 🖵 🍴 🛋

▼▼▼ Howard Johnson Express Inn-Marina H
(209) 948-6151. **$65-$99.** 33 N Center St. 1 blk n; w off El Dorado St via Weber; SR 99, exit Wilson Way southbound; exit northbound, w via Mariposa Rd to Charter Way; I-5, exit downtown. Ext corridors. **Pets:** Small. $10 daily fee/pet. Designated rooms, service with restrictions, supervision.
ASK ⊠ 🔥 ▯ 🖵 🛋

▼▼▼ La Quinta Inn Stockton H 🐾
(209) 952-7800. **$69-$139.** 2710 W March Ln. I-5, exit March Ln, just w. Ext corridors. **Pets:** Medium, other species. Service with restrictions, supervision.
ASK ⊠ 🔥 ▯ 🖵 🛋

▲▲▲ ▼ Red Roof Inn Stockton M
(209) 466-7777. **$63-$75.** 1707 W Fremont St. I-5, exit Fremont St southbound; exit Pershing Ave northbound, just w. Ext corridors. **Pets:** Large, other species. $50 deposit/room. Service with restrictions, supervision.
SAVE ⊠ 🔥 ▯ 🛋

▼▼▼ Residence Inn by Marriott H
(209) 472-9800. **$170-$208.** 3240 W March Ln. I-5, exit March Ln, 0.5 mi w. Int corridors. **Pets:** Accepted.
⊠ 🔥 ▯ 🖵 🛋 ⊠

▼▼▼ Sheraton Stockton at Regent Pointe H
(209) 944-1140. **Call for rates.** 110 W Fremont St. I-5, exit Fremont St, e on Fremont St. Int corridors. **Pets:** Accepted.
⊠ 🔥 🖵 🍴 🛋

SUNNYVALE

▼▼◆ Homestead Studio Suites Hotel-San Jose-Sunnyvale H
(408) 734-3431. **$121-$131.** 1255 Orleans Dr. N of SR 237, exit Mathilda Ave, e on Moffett Park Dr. Ext corridors. **Pets:** Other species. $25 daily fee/pet. Service with restrictions, crate.
ASK ⊠ 🔥

▲▲▲ ▼▼▼ Larkspur Landing Sunnyvale H 🐾
(408) 733-1212. **$89-$269.** 748 N Mathilda Ave. US 101, exit Mathilda Ave, just s. Int corridors. **Pets:** Medium. $10 daily fee/pet, $75 one-time fee/room. Service with restrictions, crate.
SAVE ⊠ 🔥

▲▲▲ ▼▼▼ Maple Tree Inn H 🐾
(408) 720-9700. **$109-$169.** 711 E El Camino Real. On SR 82; between Fair Oaks and Wolfe Rd; 2.5 mi w of US 101. Int corridors. **Pets:** Medium. $10 daily fee/pet. Service with restrictions, crate.
SAVE ⊠ 🔥 ▯ 🖵 🛋

▼▼▼ Quality Inn-Sunnyvale H
(408) 744-1100. **$70-$250.** 1280 Persian Dr. US 101, exit Lawrence Expwy N, 1 mi n to Persian Dr, then 0.3 mi w. Int corridors. **Pets:** Small. $100 deposit/room, $10 daily fee/pet. Designated rooms, service with restrictions, supervision.
ASK ⊠ 🔥 ▯ 🖵 🛋

▲▲▲ ▼▼▼ Ramada Inn-Silicon Valley H
(408) 245-5330. **$99-$159.** 1217 Wildwood Ave. US 101, exit Lawrence Expwy N, just n. Ext corridors. **Pets:** Medium. $200 deposit/room, $15 daily fee/pet. Service with restrictions, supervision.
SAVE ⊠ 🔥 ▯ 🖵 🍴 🛋

▼▼▼ Residence Inn by Marriott H 🐾
(408) 720-8893. **$224-$274.** 1080 Stewart Dr. US 101, exit Lawrence Expwy S, w on Duane Ave W. Ext corridors. **Pets:** Other species. $100 one-time fee/room.
⊠ 🔥 ▯ 🖵 🛋 ⊠

Residence Inn by Marriott H
(408) 720-1000. **$224-$274.** 750 Lakeway Dr. US 101, exit Lawrence Expwy S, e on Oakmead. Ext corridors. **Pets:** Accepted.

Staybridge Suites H
(408) 745-1515. **Call for rates.** 900 Hamlin Ct. SR 237, exit Mathilda Ave S, w on Ross Dr. Ext corridors. **Pets:** Accepted.

TownePlace Suites by Marriott Sunnyvale/Mountain View H
(408) 733-4200. **$179-$219.** 606 S Bernardo Ave. SR 85, exit SR 82, 0.5 mi s. Int corridors. **Pets:** Accepted.

Vagabond Inn M
(408) 734-4607. **$59-$259.** 816 Ahwanee Ave. US 101, exit Mathilda Ave S, then s. Ext corridors. **Pets:** Other species. $10 daily fee/pet. Service with restrictions, supervision.

SUSANVILLE

America's Best Inns M
(530) 257-4522. **Call for rates.** 2705 Main St. Jct SR 36 and 139, 0.7 mi se on SR 36. Ext corridors. **Pets:** Accepted.

River Inn M
(530) 257-6051. **$75.** 1710 Main St. Jct SR 36 and SR 139, just se on SR 36. Ext corridors. **Pets:** Accepted.

The Roseberry House Bed & Breakfast BB
(530) 257-5675. **$110-$135, 5 day notice.** 609 North St. Jct SR 36 and 139, 0.7 mi nw to N Lassen St, then just ne. Int corridors. **Pets:** Other species. $10 daily fee/pet. No service, supervision.

Super 8 M
(530) 257-2782. **Call for rates.** 2975 Johnstonville Rd. Jct SR 36 and 139, 0.9 mi se on SR 139. Ext corridors. **Pets:** $10 daily fee/pet. Designated rooms, supervision.

TEHACHAPI

Best Western Mountain Inn M
(661) 822-5591. **$85-$99.** 418 W Tehachapi Blvd. SR 58, exit 148 (SR 202), 1 mi s, then e. Ext corridors. **Pets:** Other species. Designated rooms, service with restrictions, supervision.

Holiday Inn Express & Suites H
(661) 822-9837. **$99-$112.** 901 Capital Hills Pkwy. SR 58, exit 149 (Mill St), just n. Int corridors. **Pets:** Accepted.

La Quinta Inn & Suites M ❖
(661) 823-8000. **$79-$119.** 500 Steuber Rd. SR 58, exit 151 (Monolith/ Tehachapi Blvd), just s. Int corridors. **Pets:** Medium, other species. Service with restrictions, supervision.

TEMECULA

Extended StayAmerica-Temecula-Wine Country M
(951) 587-8881. **$90-$174.** 27622 Jefferson Ave. I-15, exit 61 (SR 79 N), just w on Winchester Rd, then 0.4 mi s. Int corridors. **Pets:** Other species. $25 daily fee/pet. Service with restrictions, crate.

La Quinta Inn & Suites Temecula H ❖
(951) 296-1003. **$79-$179.** 27330 Jefferson Ave. I-15, exit 61 (SR 79 N), just w on Winchester Rd, then just n. Int corridors. **Pets:** Medium, other species. Service with restrictions, supervision.

Quality Inn Temecula Wine Country M
(951) 296-3788. **$85-$199.** 27338 Jefferson Ave. I-15, exit 61 (SR 79 N), just w on Winchester Rd, then just n. Ext corridors. **Pets:** Dogs only. $20 daily fee/pet. Designated rooms, service with restrictions, crate.

THOUSAND OAKS

La Quinta Inn & Suites M ❖
(805) 499-5910. **$69-$159.** 1320 Newbury Rd. US 101, exit 46 (Ventu Park Rd), just se. Ext corridors. **Pets:** Medium, other species. Service with restrictions, supervision.

Motel 6 #1360 Thousand Oaks M
(805) 499-0711. **$55-$65.** 1516 Newbury Rd. US 101, exit 46 (Ventu Park Rd), just w, then just n. Ext corridors. **Pets:** Other species. Service with restrictions, supervision.

Premier Inns M
(805) 499-0755. **$54.** 2434 W Hillcrest Dr. US 101, exit 47A (Borchard Rd), just e, then just n. Ext corridors. **Pets:** Accepted.

Quality Inn & Suites M
(805) 495-7011. **$99-$149.** 12 Conejo Blvd. US 101, exit 44 (Moorpark Rd), just n to Thousand Oaks Blvd, then just w. Ext/int corridors. **Pets:** Accepted.

TownePlace Suites by Marriott H
(805) 499-3111. **$148-$180.** 1712 Newbury Rd. US 101, exit 46 (Ventu Park Rd), just s, then just w. Int corridors. **Pets:** Accepted.

THOUSAND PALMS

Red Roof Inn M
(760) 343-1381. **$49-$129.** 72-215 Varner Rd. I-10, exit 130 (Ramon Rd), just n, then just w. Ext corridors. **Pets:** $25 deposit/room. Service with restrictions, supervision.

THREE RIVERS

Americas Best Value Inn–Lazy J Ranch M
(559) 561-4449. **$100-$115, 3 day notice.** 39625 Sierra Dr. SR 198, 3 mi sw of town center. Ext corridors. **Pets:** Other species. $10 one-time fee/pet. Service with restrictions, supervision.

Buckeye Tree Lodge M 🐾
(559) 561-5900. **$78-$143, 7 day notice.** 46000 Sierra Dr. SR 198, 6 mi ne of town center; 0.5 mi sw of entrance to Sequoia National Park. Ext corridors. **Pets:** Other species. $10 daily fee/pet. Service with restrictions, supervision.

Comfort Inn & Suites M
(559) 561-9000. **$59-$225.** 40820 Sierra Dr. SR 198, 1.5 mi sw of town center. Ext/int corridors. **Pets:** Small, dogs only. $35 one-time fee/room. Designated rooms, service with restrictions, supervision.

▼▼ Gateway Lodge **M**
(559) 561-4133. **$79-$179, 3 day notice.** 45978 Sierra Dr. SR 198, 6 mi ne of town center; 0.5 mi sw of entrance to Sequoia National Park. Ext corridors. **Pets:** Other species. $10 daily fee/pet. Service with restrictions.
[ASK] [X] [🛏] [💻] [🍽] [🅩]

▼▼ Sequoia River Dance Bed & Breakfast **BB**
(559) 561-4411. **$95-$135, 10 day notice.** 40534 Cherokee Oaks Dr. SR 198, 2 mi sw of town center, then 0.3 mi e. Int corridors. **Pets:** Other species. $10 daily fee/pet. Supervision.
[ASK] [X] [W] [🅩]

◈ ▼▼ Sequoia Village Inn **CA** ☙
(559) 561-3652. **$77-$305, 7 day notice.** 45971 Sierra Dr. SR 198, 6 mi ne of town center; 0.5 mi sw of entrance to Sequoia National Park. Ext corridors. **Pets:** Other species. $10 daily fee/pet. Service with restrictions, supervision.
[SAVE] [X] [🛏] [💻] [🏊] [🅩]

◈ ▼▼ Western Holiday Lodge Three Rivers **M**
(559) 561-4119. **$59-$199.** 40105 Sierra Dr. SR 198, 2 mi sw of town center. Ext corridors. **Pets:** Dogs only. $15 daily fee/pet. Designated rooms, supervision.
[SAVE] [X] [🛏] [💻] [🏊] [X]

TRACY

◈ ▼▼ Best Western Luxury Inn **H**
(209) 832-0271. **$80-$120, 3 day notice.** 811 W Clover Rd. I-205, exit Central Tracy, just s, then just w. Int corridors. **Pets:** Other species. $10 daily fee/pet. Service with restrictions, supervision.
[SAVE] [X] [🛏] [🛏] [💻] [🏊]

◈ ▼▼ Quality Inn-Tracy **H**
(209) 835-1335. **$50-$90.** 3511 N Tracy Blvd. I-205, exit Central Tracy/ Tracy Blvd, just s. Ext/int corridors. **Pets:** Small. $10 daily fee/pet. Designated rooms, service with restrictions, crate.
[SAVE] [X] [🛏] [💻] [🏊]

TRINIDAD

◈ ▼ Bishop Pine Lodge **CA**
(707) 677-3314. **$110-$150, 7 day notice.** 1481 Patrick's Point Dr. US 101, exit Seawood Dr, just w, then 0.8 mi s. Ext corridors. **Pets:** Accepted.
[SAVE] [X] [🛏] [💻] [K]

◈ ▼▼ Trinidad Inn **H**
(707) 677-3349. **$110-$180.** 1170 Patrick's Point Dr. US 101, exit Trinidad, just w on Main St, then 1.3 mi n. Ext corridors. **Pets:** Dogs only. $10 daily fee/pet. Supervision.
[SAVE] [X] [🛏] [💻]

TULARE

◈ ▼▼▼ Best Western Town & Country Lodge **M**
(559) 688-7537. **$85-$199, 3 day notice.** 1051 N Blackstone St. SR 99, exit 88 (Prosperity Ave/Blackstone St), just w. Int corridors. **Pets:** Medium. $20 one-time fee/room. Service with restrictions, supervision.
[SAVE] [X] [🛏] [💻] [🏊]

▼▼▼ Charter Inn & Suites **H** ☙
(559) 685-9500. **$89-$149.** 1016 E Prosperity Ave. SR 99, exit 88 (Prosperity Ave/Blackstone St), just e. Int corridors. **Pets:** Small. $100 deposit/ room, $10 daily fee/pet. Service with restrictions, crate.
[ASK] [X] [🛏] [🛏] [💻] [🏊]

◈ ▼▼▼ Quality Inn **M**
(559) 686-3432. **$79-$149.** 1010 E Prosperity Ave. SR 99, exit 88 (Prosperity Ave/Blackstone St), just e. Int corridors. **Pets:** Small, dogs only. $10 daily fee/pet. No service, supervision.
[SAVE] [X] [🛏] [💻] [🏊] [X]

TURLOCK

◈ ▼▼▼ Best Western Orchard Inn **H**
(209) 667-2827. **$89-$109.** 5025 N Golden State Blvd. SR 99, exit Taylor Rd, just e. Ext corridors. **Pets:** Other species. $25 one-time fee/room. Service with restrictions, crate.
[SAVE] [X] [🛏] [🛏] [💻] [🏊]

◈ ▼ Travelodge **H**
(209) 668-3400. **$69-$109.** 201 W Glenwood Ave. SR 99, exit Lander W. Ext corridors. **Pets:** Accepted.
[SAVE] [X] [🛏] [🛏] [💻] [🏊]

TWAIN HARTE

◈ ▼▼ ▼▼ McCaffrey House Bed & Breakfast
Inn **BB**
(209) 586-0757. **$139-$169, 7 day notice.** 23251 Hwy 108. 0.5 mi on SR 108; just beyond 4000' elevation marker. Int corridors. **Pets:** $25 daily fee/pet. Designated rooms, supervision.
[SAVE] [X]

TWENTYNINE PALMS

◈ ▼▼▼ Roughley Manor **BB**
(760) 367-3238. **$135-$160, 3 day notice.** 74744 Joe Davis Rd. SR 62, 0.5 mi n on Utah Tr, 0.5 mi e on Joe Davis Rd, then just n. Ext/int corridors. **Pets:** Dogs only. Designated rooms, service with restrictions, supervision.
[SAVE] [X] [🛏] [💻] [🏊] [🅩]

▼▼ Sunnyvale Garden Suites Hotel **CO** ☙
(760) 361-3939. **$97.** 73843 Sunnyvale Dr. SR 62, 0.7 mi n on Adobe Rd, just e on S Slope, just n on Ocotillo, then just e. Ext corridors. **Pets:** Large, other species. $50 one-time fee/pet. Service with restrictions.
[ASK] [X] [🛏] [💻] [X]

UNION CITY

▼▼ Extended StayAmerica-Union City **H**
(510) 441-9616. **$95-$105.** 31950 Dyer St. I-880, exit Alvarado-Niles Rd, just w, then just n; in Union Landing Shopping Center. Int corridors. **Pets:** Other species. $25 daily fee/pet. Service with restrictions, crate.
[ASK] [X] [🛏] [💻] [🏊]

VACAVILLE

◈ ▼▼ Best Western Heritage Inn **M**
(707) 448-8453. **$80-$97.** 1420 E Monte Vista Ave. I-80, exit Monte Vista Ave, just n. Ext corridors. **Pets:** Accepted.
[SAVE] [X] [🛏] [🛏] [💻] [🏊]

▼▼ Extended StayAmerica-Sacramento-Vacaville **H**
(707) 469-1371. **$89-$99.** 799 Orange Dr. I-80, exit Leisure Town Rd, just s; just e of I-505 interchange. Int corridors. **Pets:** Other species. $25 daily fee/pet. Service with restrictions, crate.
[ASK] [X] [🛏] [💻]

▼▼▼ Residence Inn by Marriott **H**
(707) 469-0300. **$164-$198.** 360 Orange Dr. I-80, exit Orange Dr eastbound, 0.5 mi; exit Monte Vista westbound, freeway overpass to E Nut Tree Pkwy. Int corridors. **Pets:** Accepted.
[X] [🛏] [🛏] [💻] [🏊] [X]

VALLEJO

◈ ▼▼▼ Best Western Inn & Suites at Discovery
Kingdom **H**
(707) 554-9655. **$69-$169.** 1596 Fairgrounds Dr. I-80, exit SR 37 (Marine World Pkwy) N, 0.3 mi w. Int corridors. **Pets:** Dogs only. $35 one-time fee/pet. Designated rooms, service with restrictions, supervision.
[SAVE] [X] [🛏] [🛏] [💻] [🏊]

▼▼▼ Courtyard by Marriott **H**
(707) 644-1200. **$119-$149.** 1000 Fairgrounds Dr. I-80, exit SR 37 (Marine World Pkwy), 0.3 mi n. Int corridors. **Pets:** Accepted.
[X] [🛏] [🛏] [💻] [🍽] [🏊]

▼▼ **Ramada Inn** H
(707) 643-2700. **$62-$129.** 1000 Admiral Callaghan Ln. I-80, exit Columbus Pkwy, 0.5 mi w. Ext corridors. **Pets:** Medium. $50 one-time fee/room. Service with restrictions.
ASK ⊠ &M 🔒 💻 ⚓

VENTURA

▼▼▼▼ **Crowne Plaza Ventura Beach Resort** H
(805) 648-2100. **$99-$239, 3 day notice.** 450 E Harbor Blvd. US 101, exit 70A (California St) northbound, just s; exit 71 (Main St) southbound, 0.5 mi e to California St, then just s. Int corridors. **Pets:** Accepted.
ASK ⊠ 🔒 💻 ﹖ ⚓

∰ ▼▼▼▼ **Four Points by Sheraton Ventura Harbortown** H
(805) 658-1212. **$125-$245.** 1050 Schooner Dr. US 101, exit 68 (Seaward Ave), just w, then 1.5 mi s; at Ventura Harbor. Ext corridors. **Pets:** $75 one-time fee/room. Designated rooms, service with restrictions, supervision.
SAVE ⊠ 🔒 💻 ﹖ ⚓ ⊠

▼▼▼▼ **La Quinta Inn Ventura** M ☙
(805) 658-6200. **$69-$139.** 5818 Valentine Rd. US 101, exit 64 (Victoria Ave), just s, then just n. Ext/int corridors. **Pets:** Medium, other species. Service with restrictions, supervision.
ASK ⊠ &M 🔒 💻 ⚓

▼▼▼▼ **Marriott Ventura Beach Hotel** H
(805) 643-6000. **$169-$219.** 2055 E Harbor Blvd. US 101, exit 68 (Seaward Ave), just w, then 0.5 mi n. Int corridors. **Pets:** $75 one-time fee/room. Service with restrictions, supervision.
⊠ &M 🔒 💻 ﹖ ⚓

▼▼ ▼▼ **Vagabond Inn Ventura** M
(805) 648-5371. **$79-$249.** 756 E Thompson Blvd. US 101, exit 70A (California St) northbound, just n, then just e; exit 70A (Ventura Ave) southbound, 0.6 mi e. Ext corridors. **Pets:** Accepted.
ASK ⊠ 🔒 💻 ﹖ ⚓

VICTORVILLE

∰ ▼▼▼▼ **Comfort Suites Hotel** H
(760) 245-6777. **$89-$149.** 12281 Mariposa Rd. I-15, exit 147 (Bear Valley Rd), just e, then just n. Int corridors. **Pets:** Medium, other species. $15 one-time fee/pet. Service with restrictions, supervision.
SAVE ⊠ &M 🔒 💻 ⚓

▼▼▼▼ **Hawthorn Suites by Hyatt** H
(760) 949-4700. **Call for rates.** 11750 Dunia Rd. I-15, exit 147 (Bear Valley Rd), just w, just s on Amargosa Rd, then just w. Int corridors. **Pets:** Accepted.
⊠ &M 🔒 💻 ⚓ ⊠

∰ ▼▼▼▼ **Hotel Extended Studio** H
(760) 843-3800. **$99-$159.** 14786 Monarch Blvd. I-15, exit 147 (Bear Valley Rd), just e to Mariposa Rd, just n, then just e. Int corridors. **Pets:** Accepted.
SAVE ⊠ 🔒 💻 ⚓ ⊠

▼▼ ▼▼ **Red Roof Inn** M ☙
(760) 241-1577. **$74-$78.** 13409 Mariposa Rd. I-15, exit 147 (Bear Valley Rd) northbound, just e, then 1.5 mi n; exit 150 (SR 18 W/Palmdale Rd) southbound, just e, then 1.5 mi s. Ext corridors. **Pets:** Large. $50 deposit/room. Service with restrictions, supervision.
ASK ⊠ 🔒 💻 ⚓

∰ ▼▼ ▼▼ **Travelodge Victorville** M
(760) 241-7200. **$59-$89.** 12175 Mariposa Rd. I-15, exit 147 (Bear Valley Rd), just e, then just n. Ext corridors. **Pets:** Small, dogs only. $10 one-time fee/pet. No service, supervision.
SAVE ⊠ 🔒 ⚓

VISALIA

▼▼▼ **Ben Maddox House** BB ☙
(559) 739-0721. **$140-$185, 7 day notice.** 601 N Encina St. SR 198, exit 107A (Central Visalia/SR 63 N), 0.4 mi n to Murray St, just w, then just n. Ext/int corridors. **Pets:** Large. Service with restrictions, crate.
ASK ⊠ 🔒 💻 ⚓ ⊠

∰ ▼▼▼▼ **Holiday Inn Hotel & Conference Center** H
(559) 651-5000. **$89-$149.** 9000 W Airport Dr. SR 198, exit 102 (Plaza Dr), then just s. Int corridors. **Pets:** Other species. $25 daily fee/pet. Service with restrictions, crate.
SAVE ⊠ &M 🔒 💻 ﹖ ⚓

∰ ▼▼▼ **Lamp Liter Inn** M
(559) 732-4511. **$79-$129.** 3300 W Mineral King Ave. SR 198, exit 105B (SR 63 S/Mooney Blvd) westbound, 0.5 mi w; exit eastbound, just n, then 0.5 mi w. Ext corridors. **Pets:** Accepted.
SAVE ⊠ 🔒 💻 ﹖ ⚓

▼▼▼▼ **La Quinta Inn & Suites** H ☙
(559) 739-9800. **$79-$119.** 5438 W Cypress Ave. SR 198, exit 104 (Akers St), just s, then just w. Int corridors. **Pets:** Medium, other species. Service with restrictions, supervision.
ASK ⊠ 🔒 💻 ⚓

▼▼▼ **Rodeway Inn** M
(559) 732-4561. **$69-$140.** 623 W Main St. SR 198, exit 105B (SR 63 S/Mooney Blvd), just n, then 0.9 mi e. Ext corridors. **Pets:** Accepted.
ASK ⊠ 🔒 💻 ⚓

VISTA

▼▼▼ **La Quinta Inn San Diego (Vista)** M ☙
(760) 727-8180. **$59-$139.** 630 Sycamore Ave. SR 78, exit Sycamore Ave, just sw. Ext/int corridors. **Pets:** Medium, other species. Service with restrictions, supervision.
ASK ⊠ 🔒 💻 ⚓

WALNUT CREEK

∰ ▼▼▼▼ **Holiday Inn Express Walnut Creek** H
(925) 932-3332. **$109-$189.** 2730 N Main St. I-680, exit N Main St, just n. Int corridors. **Pets:** Accepted.
SAVE ⊠ 🔒 💻 ﹖ ⚓

WATSONVILLE

∰ ▼▼▼▼ **Best Western Rose Garden Inn** H ☙
(831) 724-3367. **$89-$359.** 740 Freedom Blvd. On SR 152. Ext corridors. **Pets:** $15 daily fee/pet. Designated rooms, service with restrictions, supervision.
SAVE ⊠ 🔒 💻 ⚓

∰ ▼▼▼ **Comfort Inn Watsonville** H
(831) 728-2300. **$79-$450.** 112 Airport Blvd. SR 1, exit Airport Blvd, 1 mi e. Int corridors. **Pets:** Medium. $15 daily fee/pet. Designated rooms, service with restrictions, supervision.
SAVE ⊠ 🔒 💻

∰ ▼▼▼ **Red Roof Inn** H
(831) 740-4520. **$72-$113.** 1620 W Beach St. SR 1, exit Riverside Dr (SR 129), just w. Int corridors. **Pets:** Accepted.
SAVE ⊠ &M 🔒 💻 ⚓

WEAVERVILLE

∰ ▼▼▼ **49er Gold Country Inn** M
(530) 623-4937. **$50-$99, 3 day notice.** 880 Main St (Hwy 299). Jct SR 3 and 299, just se on SR 299. Ext corridors. **Pets:** Dogs only. $5 daily fee/pet. Service with restrictions, supervision.
SAVE ⊠ 🔒 💻 ⚓

$\Diamond\Diamond\Diamond$ $\Diamond\Diamond$ Motel Trinity M
(530) 623-2129. **$70-$95, 3 day notice.** 1270 Main St. Jct SR 3 and 299, 0.7 mi se on SR 299. Ext corridors. **Pets:** Dogs only. $5 one-time fee/pet. Service with restrictions, supervision.
(SAVE) (X) (🔌) (💻) (🏊)

$\Diamond\Diamond$ Red Hill Motel CA
(530) 623-4331. **$42-$90, 7 day notice.** Red Hill Rd. Jct SR 3 and SR 299, just nw on SR 299, then just n. Ext corridors. **Pets:** Medium, other species. $5 one-time fee/pet. Service with restrictions, supervision.
(🔌) (💻)

$\Diamond\Diamond\Diamond\Diamond$ Weaverville Victorian Inn M
(530) 623-4432. **$79-$169.** 2051 Main St. Jct SR 3 and 299, 1.5 mi se on SR 299. Ext corridors. **Pets:** Accepted.
(ASK) (X) (🔌) (💻) (🍴) (🏊)

WEED

$\Diamond\Diamond\Diamond$ $\Diamond\Diamond\Diamond$ Comfort Inn H
(530) 938-1982. **$79-$159.** 1844 Shastina Dr. I-5, exit 745, just ne. Int corridors. **Pets:** Dogs only. $10 daily fee/pet. Designated rooms, service with restrictions, supervision.
(SAVE) (X) (🔌) (💻) (🏊)

$\Diamond\Diamond\Diamond$ $\Diamond\Diamond\Diamond$ Quality Inn & Suites H
(530) 938-1308. **$80-$105.** 1830 Black Butte Dr. I-5, exit 745, just ne. Int corridors. **Pets:** Other species. $10 daily fee/pet. Designated rooms, service with restrictions, supervision.
(SAVE) (X) (🔌) (💻)

$\Diamond\Diamond\Diamond$ $\Diamond$ Sis-Q-Inn Motel M 🐾
(530) 938-4194. **$65-$150.** 1825 Shastina Dr. I-5, exit 745, just ne. Int corridors. **Pets:** Small. $10 daily fee/pet. Designated rooms, service with restrictions, supervision.
(SAVE) (X) (🔌)

WESTLAKE VILLAGE

$\Diamond\Diamond\Diamond$ $\Diamond\Diamond\Diamond\Diamond$ Four Seasons Hotel Westlake Village H
(818) 575-3000. **$235-$4500.** Two Dole Dr. US 101, exit Lindero Canyon Rd, just e, then just n on Via Colinas. Int corridors. **Pets:** Accepted.
(SAVE) (X) (🔌) (💻) (🍴) (🏊)

$\Diamond\Diamond\Diamond$ Residence Inn by Marriott H
(818) 707-4411. **$170-$208.** 30950 Russell Ranch Rd.. Int corridors. **Pets:** Accepted.
(X) (🔌) (💻) (🏊) (X)

WESTLEY

$\Diamond\Diamond\Diamond$ $\Diamond\Diamond$ Econo Lodge M
(209) 894-3900. **$55-$95, 3 day notice.** 7100 McCracken Rd. I-5, exit Westley, just e. Ext corridors. **Pets:** Medium. $10 daily fee/pet. No service, supervision.
(SAVE) (X) (🔌) (💻) (🏊)

$\Diamond\Diamond\Diamond$ $\Diamond\Diamond\Diamond$ Holiday Inn Express H
(209) 894-8940. **$74-$119.** 4525 Howard Rd. I-5, exit Westley, just e. Int corridors. **Pets:** Accepted.
(SAVE) (X) (🔌) (💻) (🏊)

WESTMORLAND

$\Diamond\Diamond$ Americas Best Value Inn M
(760) 351-7100. **$90-$100.** 351 W Main St. On SR 86. Int corridors. **Pets:** Accepted.
(ASK) (X) (🔌) (💻) (🏊)

WEST SACRAMENTO

$\Diamond\Diamond$ Extended StayAmerica-Sacramento-West Sacramento H
(916) 371-1270. **$95-$105.** 795 Stillwater Ave. I-80, exit Reed Ave, just sw. Int corridors. **Pets:** Other species. $25 daily fee/pet. Service with restrictions, crate.
(ASK) (X) (🔌) (💻)

$\Diamond\Diamond\Diamond$ $\Diamond\Diamond\Diamond$ Ramada Inn & Plaza Harbor Conference Center H
(916) 371-2100. **$89-$119.** 1250 Halyard Dr. Business Rt I-80 (Capital City Frwy), exit Harbour Blvd, just s. Ext/int corridors. **Pets:** Small. $25 one-time fee/pet. Service with restrictions, supervision.
(SAVE) (X) (🔌) (🔌) (💻) (🍴) (🏊) (X)

$\Diamond\Diamond\Diamond$ $\Diamond$ Rodeway Inn Capitol M ✿
(916) 371-6983. **$55-$90.** 817 W Capitol Ave. I-80 business route, exit Jefferson Blvd, 0.3 mi n, then just e. Ext corridors. **Pets:** Medium, dogs only. Service with restrictions, supervision.
(SAVE) (X) (🔌) (💻)

WILLIAMS

$\Diamond\Diamond\Diamond$ $\Diamond\Diamond$ Comfort Inn M
(530) 473-2381. **$79-$149.** 400 C St. I-5, exit 577 (Williams), just w on E St (SR 20 business route), just n on 4th St; at Union 76, then just e. Ext corridors. **Pets:** $15 daily fee/pet. Designated rooms, service with restrictions, supervision.
(SAVE) (X) (🔌) (🔌) (💻) (🏊)

$\Diamond\Diamond\Diamond$ $\Diamond\Diamond\Diamond$ Granzella's Inn M
(530) 473-3310. **$85-$110.** 391 6th St. I-5, exit 577 (Williams), 0.5 mi w. Int corridors. **Pets:** Other species. $10 one-time fee/room. Service with restrictions, supervision.
(SAVE) (X) (🔌) (🔌) (💻) (🍴) (🏊)

$\Diamond\Diamond\Diamond$ $\Diamond\Diamond\Diamond$ Holiday Inn Express Hotel & Suites M
(530) 473-5120. **$109-$139.** 374 Ruggieri Way. I-5, exit 577 (Williams), just e. Int corridors. **Pets:** $25 one-time fee/pet. Service with restrictions, crate.
(SAVE) (X) (🔌) (🔌) (💻)

$\Diamond\Diamond\Diamond$ $\Diamond$ Stage Stop Inn M
(530) 473-2281. **$45-$55.** 330 7th St. I-5, exit 577 (Williams), just w on E St (SR 20 business route), then just n. Ext corridors. **Pets:** Accepted.
(SAVE) (X) (🔌) (💻) (🏊)

WILLOW CREEK

$\Diamond\Diamond\Diamond$ $\Diamond$ Bigfoot Motel M
(530) 629-2142. **$65-$150.** 39039 Hwy 299. On SR 299; just e of SR 96; center. Ext corridors. **Pets:** Accepted.
(SAVE) (X) (🔌) (🏊)

WILLOWS

$\Diamond\Diamond\Diamond$ $\Diamond\Diamond$ Baymont Inns & Suites Willows H
(530) 934-9700. **$70-$150.** 199 N Humboldt Ave. I-5, exit 603 (SR 162 Willows Oroville), just e, then s. Int corridors. **Pets:** Accepted.
(SAVE) (X) (🔌) (💻) (🏊)

$\Diamond\Diamond\Diamond$ $\Diamond\Diamond$ Days Inn M
(530) 934-4444. **$60-$100.** 475 N Humboldt Ave. I-5, exit 603 (SR 162 Willows Oroville), just e, then just n. Ext corridors. **Pets:** Accepted.
(SAVE) (X) (🔌) (🔌) (💻) (🏊)

$\Diamond\Diamond\Diamond$ $\Diamond$ Economy Inn M
(530) 934-4224. **$50-$75.** 435 N Tehama St. I-5, exit 603 (SR 162 Willows Oroville), 1 mi e, then just n. Ext corridors. **Pets:** Small. $5 daily fee/pet. Designated rooms, service with restrictions, supervision.
(SAVE) (X) (🔌)

AAA ◈ Motel 6 #4273 **M**
(530) 934-7026. **$55-$99.** 452 N Humboldt Ave. I-5, exit 603 (SR 162 Willows Oroville), just e, then just n. Ext corridors. **Pets:** Other species. Service with restrictions, supervision.
[SAVE] [X] [🐾] [🏊]

AAA ◈ Super 8 of Willows **H**
(530) 934-2871. **$54-$118.** 457 Humboldt Ave. I-5, exit 603 (SR 162/ Willows Oroville), just e, then just n. Int corridors. **Pets:** Accepted.
[SAVE] [X] [🐾] [🏊]

WINE COUNTRY AREA

ALBION

◈◈ Fensalden Inn **BB**
(707) 937-4042. **$139-$253, 7 day notice.** 33810 Navarro Ridge Rd. 1.5 mi s on SR 1, 0.5 mi e. Ext/int corridors. **Pets:** Large, dogs only. $50 one-time fee/pet. Designated rooms, service with restrictions, supervision.
[ASK] [X] [🐾] [💻] [K] [W] [Z]

CALISTOGA

AAA ◈◈◈ Brannan Cottage Inn **BB** ❀
(707) 942-4200. **$165-$250.** 109 Wapoo Ave. At Lincoln Ave. Ext corridors. **Pets:** Other species. $100 deposit/room, $25 daily fee/pet. Designated rooms, service with restrictions, crate.
[SAVE] [X] [🐾] [Z]

◈◈◈ Garnett Creek Inn **BB**
(707) 942-9797. **$108-$325, 7 day notice.** 1139 Lincoln Ave. On SR 29. Int corridors. **Pets:** Accepted.
[ASK] [X] [&M] [💻]

CLOVERDALE

AAA ◈◈◈ Old Crocker Inn **BB** ❀
(707) 894-4000. **$155-$245, 8 day notice.** 1126 Old Crocker Inn Rd. US 101, exit Citrus Fair Dr, just e 0.5 mi n on Asti Rd, 0.8 mi e on Crocker Rd 3.8 mi s on River Rd, 1.1 mi e on Asti Ridge Rd, then just n. Ext corridors. **Pets:** Dogs only. Designated rooms, service with restrictions, supervision.
[SAVE] [X] [🐾] [Z]

FORT BRAGG

AAA ◈◈◈ Beachcomber Motel **M** ❀
(707) 964-2402. **$119-$269, 3 day notice.** 1111 N Main St. 1 mi n on SR 1. Ext corridors. **Pets:** Medium, other species. $20 daily fee/pet. Designated rooms, supervision.
[SAVE] [X] [🐾] [💻] [K]

AAA ◈◈◈ Beach House Inn **M**
(707) 961-1700. **$69-$159.** 100 Pudding Creek Rd. 0.7 mi n on SR 1. Int corridors. **Pets:** Accepted.
[SAVE] [X] [🐾] [💻] [K]

AAA ◈◈◈ Emerald Dolphin Inn & Mini Golf **H** ❀
(707) 964-6699. **$63-$200, 7 day notice.** 1211 S Main St. On SR 1. Ext corridors. **Pets:** Dogs only. $10 daily fee/room. Designated rooms, service with restrictions, supervision.
[SAVE] [X] [&M] [🐾] [💻] [X] [K]

AAA ◈◈◈ Quality Inn & Suites/Tradewinds **H** ❀
(707) 964-4761. **$89-$259, 3 day notice.** 400 S Main St. 6 blks s on SR 1. Ext corridors. **Pets:** Large, dogs only. $10 daily fee/pet. Designated rooms, service with restrictions, supervision.
[SAVE] [X] [&M] [🐾] [💻] [↑↓] [🏊] [K]

AAA ◈◈◈ Seabird Lodge **M**
(707) 964-4731. **$80-$155.** 191 South St. 0.8 mi n of Noyo River Bridge; 1 blk e off SR 1. Ext corridors. **Pets:** Medium, other species. $10 daily fee/pet. Designated rooms, service with restrictions, supervision.
[SAVE] [X] [🐾] [💻] [🏊] [K]

◈◈◈ Super 8 **M**
(707) 964-4003. **$56-$140.** 888 S Main St. 0.5 mi s on SR 1; north end of Noyo River Bridge. Ext corridors. **Pets:** Medium, dogs only. $10 one-time fee/pet. Designated rooms, service with restrictions, supervision.
[ASK] [X] [&M] [🐾] [💻]

AAA ◈◈◈ Surf Motel and Gardens **M** ❀
(707) 964-5361. **$55-$159, 3 day notice.** 1220 S Main St. 1 mi s on SR 1; s of Noyo River Bridge; 0.3 mi n of jct SR 20. Ext corridors. **Pets:** Dogs only. $15 daily fee/pet. Designated rooms, service with restrictions, supervision.
[SAVE] [X] [🐾] [💻] [K]

GUALALA

◈◈ Gualala Country Inn **M**
(707) 884-4343. **$95-$190, 3 day notice.** 47955 Center St. South end of town on east side of SR 1. Ext/int corridors. **Pets:** Accepted.
[ASK] [X] [🐾] [💻] [K]

AAA ◈◈◈◈ North Coast Country Inn **BB** ❀
(707) 884-4537. **$164-$245, 3 day notice.** 34591 S SR 1. On SR 1, 4.5 mi n. Ext corridors. **Pets:** Dogs only. $25 daily fee/pet. service with restrictions, supervision.
[SAVE] [X] [🐾] [💻] [K] [W] [Z]

AAA ◈◈◈ Surf Motel **M** ❀
(707) 884-3571. **$79-$199.** 39170 S SR 1. Center. Ext/int corridors. **Pets:** Large, other species. $10 daily fee/pet. Service with restrictions, supervision.
[SAVE] [X] [🐾] [💻] [K]

GUERNEVILLE

AAA ◈◈◈ Ferngrove Cottages **CA** ❀
(707) 869-8105. **$89-$269, 3 day notice.** 16650 SR 116. Just w of downtown. Ext corridors. **Pets:** Large, other species. $25 daily fee/pet. Designated rooms, service with restrictions, supervision.
[SAVE] [X] [🐾] [💻] [🏊] [K] [Z]

HEALDSBURG

AAA ◈◈◈ Americas Best Value Inn & Suites **M**
(707) 433-5548. **$79-$249.** 74 Healdsburg Ave. US 101, exit Central Healdsburg, just se. Ext corridors. **Pets:** $200 deposit/room, $20 daily fee/pet. Service with restrictions, supervision.
[SAVE] [X] [&M] [💻] [🏊]

AAA ◈◈◈ Best Western Dry Creek Inn **H** ❀
(707) 433-0300. **$119-$325.** 198 Dry Creek Rd. US 101, exit Dry Creek Rd, just se. Ext corridors. **Pets:** Large. $30 daily fee/room. Designated rooms, service with restrictions, supervision.
[SAVE] [X] [&M] [🐾] [💻] [🏊] [X]

◈◈◈ Hotel Healdsburg **H**
(707) 431-2800. **Call for rates.** 25 Matheson St. On the Plaza. Int corridors. **Pets:** Accepted.
[X] [&M] [🐾] [💻] [↑↓] [🏊] [X]

JENNER

AAA ◈◈◈ Jenner Inn & Cottages **CI** ❀
(707) 865-2377. **$118-$378, 10 day notice.** 10400 Hwy 1. On SR 1 at SR 116. Ext corridors. **Pets:** Other species. $35 one-time fee/pet. Designated rooms, service with restrictions, supervision.
[SAVE] [X] [&M] [🐾] [💻] [↑↓] [K] [W]

LAKEPORT

▼▼▼ Konocti Vista Casino Resort & Marina Ⓜ
(707) 262-1900. **Call for rates.** 2755 Mission Rancheria Rd. Jct SR 175, 1.7 mi se on Soda Bay Rd, then 0.4 mi n. Ext corridors. **Pets:** Accepted.
✖ 💻 ⌇

LEGGETT

ⓐⓐⓐ ▼ Redwoods River Resort ⒸⒶ ❧
(707) 925-6249. **$95-$165, 7 day notice.** 75000 Hwy 101. 6.5 mi n of jct SR 1. Ext corridors. **Pets:** Other species. $10 daily fee/pet. Designated rooms, no service, supervision.
ⓈⒶⓋⒺ ✖ 🔒 💻 ⌇ ✖ 🐾 ☎

LITTLE RIVER

ⓐⓐⓐ ▼▼▼ Auberge Mendocino-Rachel's Inn ⒷⒷ ❧
(707) 937-0088. **$189-$355, 21 day notice.** 8200 N SR 1. On SR 1, 0.3 mi n of Van Damme State Park entrance. Ext/int corridors. **Pets:** Medium, dogs only. $100 deposit/room, $35 one-time fee/pet. Designated rooms, service with restrictions, supervision.
ⓈⒶⓋⒺ ✖ 🔒 💻 🐾 ☎

▼▼▼ The Inn at Schoolhouse Creek ⒷⒷ ❧
(707) 937-5525. **$145-$399, 14 day notice.** 7051 N SR 1. On SR 1, 0.8 mi s of Van Damme State Park entrance. Ext corridors. **Pets:** Other species. $50 one-time fee/room. Service with restrictions.
ⒶⓈⓀ ✖ 🔒 💻 ✖ 🐾

▼▼▼ Little River Inn Ⓒ❚ ❧
(707) 937-5942. **$95-$325, 5 day notice.** 7901 N SR 1. On SR 1, just s of Van Damme State Park entrance. Ext/int corridors. **Pets:** Other species. $25 daily fee/pet. Designated rooms, service with restrictions, supervision.
ⒶⓈⓀ ✖ 🔒 💻 🍴 ✖ 🐾

▼▼▼ ▼▼▼ Stevenswood Spa Resort Ⓒ❚
(707) 937-2810. **$159-$965.** 8211 N Hwy 1. On SR 1, 0.4 mi n of Van Damme State Park entrance. Int corridors. **Pets:** Accepted.
ⒶⓈⓀ ✖ 🔒 💻 🍴 ✖ 🐾

MENDOCINO

▼▼ Abigail's Bed & Breakfast ⒷⒷ
(707) 937-0934. **$99-$319, 14 day notice.** 951 Ukiah St. Just e of Lansing St; center. Ext/int corridors. **Pets:** Accepted.
ⒶⓈⓀ ✖ 🔒 💻 🐾 ☎

▼▼▼ Agate Cove Inn ⒸⒶ ❧
(707) 937-0551. **$159-$339, 14 day notice.** 11201 N Lansing St. Just w on Little Lake Rd from jct SR 1, then 0.6 mi n. Ext corridors. **Pets:** $20 one-time fee/room. Designated rooms.
ⒶⓈⓀ ✖ 🔒 💻 🐾 ☎

ⓐⓐⓐ ▼▼ Blackberry Inn Ⓜ ❧
(707) 937-5281. **$145-$275, 14 day notice.** 44951 Larkin Rd. 0.5 mi n on SR 1, then just e. Ext corridors. **Pets:** $10 daily fee/pet. Designated rooms, supervision.
ⓈⒶⓋⒺ ✖ 🔒 💻 🐾

▼▼▼ Hill House Inn Ⓗ
(707) 937-0554. **Call for rates.** 10701 Pallette Dr. Just w on Little Lake St from jct SR 1, just n on Lansing St. Ext corridors. **Pets:** Medium. $25 one-time fee/pet. Designated rooms, service with restrictions, supervision.
✖ 🔒 💻 🐾

▼▼▼ MacCallum House Inn Ⓒ❚ ❧
(707) 937-0289. **$175-$475, 7 day notice.** 45020 Albion St. Just w of Lansing St; center. Ext/int corridors. **Pets:** Other species. $35 daily fee/pet. Designated rooms, service with restrictions, supervision.
ⒶⓈⓀ ✖ 🔒 💻 🍴 ✖ 🐾

▼▼ Mendocino Hotel & Garden Suites Ⓗ
(707) 937-0511. **Call for rates.** 45080 Main St. 0.4 mi w on Main St from jct SR 1. Ext/int corridors. **Pets:** Medium. $25 one-time fee/pet. Designated rooms, service with restrictions, supervision.
✖ 💻 🍴 🐾

ⓐⓐⓐ ▼▼▼ Mendocino Seaside Cottage ⒷⒷ ❧
(707) 485-0239. **$187-$299, 7 day notice.** 10940 Lansing St. Just w on Little Lake Rd from jct SR 1, then 0.3 mi n. Ext/int corridors. **Pets:** Large. $25 one-time fee/pet. No service, supervision.
ⓈⒶⓋⒺ ✖ 🔒 💻 🐾

ⓐⓐⓐ ▼▼▼ ▼▼▼ Stanford Inn by the Sea & Spa Ⓒ❚ ❧
(707) 937-5615. **$215-$475, 7 day notice.** 44850 Comptche-Ukiah Rd. SR 1, exit Comptche-Ukiah Rd, just e. Ext corridors. **Pets:** Other species. $35 one-time fee/pet. Supervision.
ⓈⒶⓋⒺ ✖ 🔒 💻 🍴 🐾 ✖ 🐾

▼▼▼ Whitegate Inn ⒷⒷ
(707) 937-4892. **$159-$319, 14 day notice.** 499 Howard St. Just e of Lansing St; corner of Ukiah St; center. Ext/int corridors. **Pets:** Accepted.
ⒶⓈⓀ ✖ 🔒 🐾

NAPA

ⓐⓐⓐ ▼▼ The Chablis Inn Ⓜ ❧
(707) 257-1944. **$89-$250, 3 day notice.** 3360 Solano Ave. Just w off SR 29 via Redwood Rd, then just s. Ext corridors. **Pets:** Dogs only. $10 daily fee/pet. Service with restrictions, supervision.
ⓈⒶⓋⒺ ✖ 🔒 💻 🐾

ⓐⓐⓐ ▼▼▼ Embassy Suites Napa Valley Ⓗ
(707) 253-9540. **$149-$349.** 1075 California Blvd. SR 29, exit 1st St E. Ext/int corridors. **Pets:** Accepted.
ⓈⒶⓋⒺ ✖ ⓈⓂ 🔒 💻 🍴 🐾 ✖

ⓐⓐⓐ ▼▼▼ The Napa Inn ⒷⒷ
(707) 257-1444. **$120-$295, 10 day notice.** 1137 Warren St. SR 29, exit 1st St, 0.5 mi e, then 0.3 mi n. Int corridors. **Pets:** Accepted.
ⓈⒶⓋⒺ ✖ ⓈⓂ 🔒 💻

▼▼▼ Napa River Inn Ⓗ ❧
(707) 251-8500. **$219-$599.** 500 Main St. Downtown. Int corridors. **Pets:** Large. $25 daily fee/pet. Designated rooms, service with restrictions, supervision.
ⒶⓈⓀ ✖ ⓈⓂ 🔒 💻

ⓐⓐⓐ ▼ Napa Valley Redwood Inn Ⓜ ❧
(707) 257-6111. **$67-$150, 3 day notice.** 3380 Solano Ave. Just w off SR 29 via Redwood Rd, just s. Ext corridors. **Pets:** Other species. Service with restrictions, crate.
ⓈⒶⓋⒺ ✖ ⓈⓂ 🔒 ⌇

OCCIDENTAL

ⓐⓐⓐ ▼▼ Occidental Lodge Ⓜ
(707) 874-3623. **$94-$145.** 3610 Bohemian Hwy. In the village. Ext corridors. **Pets:** Medium. $10 daily fee/pet. Service with restrictions, supervision.
ⓈⒶⓋⒺ ✖ ⓈⓂ 🔒 💻 ⌇

PETALUMA

ⓐⓐⓐ ▼▼▼ Best Western Petaluma Inn Ⓗ
(707) 763-0994. **$89-$169.** 200 S McDowell Blvd. US 101, exit Washington St, 1 blk e. Ext corridors. **Pets:** Large. $20 one-time fee/room. Service with restrictions, supervision.
ⓈⒶⓋⒺ ✖ ⓈⓂ 🔒 💻 ⌇

ⓐⓐⓐ ▼▼▼ Quality Inn-Petaluma Ⓗ
(707) 664-1155. **$99-$219, 7 day notice.** 5100 Montero Way. US 101, exit Old Redwood Hwy-Penngrove northbound; exit Petaluma Blvd N-Penngrove southbound (east side). Ext/int corridors. **Pets:** Other species. $15 daily fee/room. Service with restrictions, supervision.
ⓈⒶⓋⒺ ✖ ⓈⓂ 🔒 💻 ⌇ ✖

AAA **WWW** **Sheraton Sonoma County-Petaluma** **H**
(707) 283-2888. **$129-$269.** 745 Baywood Dr. US 101, exit SR 116 (Lakeville Hwy), just se. Int corridors. **Pets:** Accepted.
[SAVE] [X] [&M] [H] [I] [TI] [~] [X]

POINT ARENA

WWWW **Wharf Master's Inn** **H**
(707) 882-3171. **$79-$395, 3 day notice.** 785 Port Rd. 1 mi w on Iverson Ave from jct SR 1; at wharf. Ext corridors. **Pets:** Accepted.
[X] [H] [I] [X]

ROHNERT PARK

AAA **WWW** **Best Western Inn** **H**
(707) 584-7435. **$89-$130, 3 day notice.** 6500 Redwood Dr. US 101, exit Rohnert Park Expwy, just w. Ext corridors. **Pets:** $10 one-time fee/room. Service with restrictions, supervision.
[SAVE] [X] [&M] [H] [I] [~]

AAA **WWWW** **WWW** **DoubleTree Hotel Sonoma Wine Country** **H** ❀
(707) 584-5466. **$99-$289.** One DoubleTree Dr. US 101, exit Golf Course Dr; 3 mi s of Santa Rosa. Int corridors. **Pets:** Medium, dogs only. $35 daily fee/pet. Designated rooms, service with restrictions, crate.
[SAVE] [X] [&M] [H] [I] [TI] [~] [X]

ST. HELENA

AAA **WWW** **El Bonita Motel** **H**
(707) 963-3216. **$99-$290, 3 day notice.** 195 Main St. 0.8 mi s on SR 29. Ext corridors. **Pets:** Medium, other species. $15 daily fee/pet. Service with restrictions, crate.
[SAVE] [X] [&M] [H] [I] [~]

WWWW **Harvest Inn** **H** ❀
(707) 963-9463. **$249-$749, 7 day notice.** One Main St. 1.5 mi s on SR 29. Ext corridors. **Pets:** Small. $75 one-time fee/room. Designated rooms, service with restrictions, crate.
[ASK] [X] [&M] [H] [I] [~] [X]

SANTA ROSA

AAA **WWW** **Americas Best Value Inn** **M**
(707) 523-3480. **$70-$179.** 1800 Santa Rosa Ave. US 101, exit Baker Ave northbound; exit Corby Ave southbound. Ext corridors. **Pets:** Accepted.
[SAVE] [X] [&M] [H]

AAA **WWWW** **Best Western Garden Inn** **H** 🐾
(707) 546-4031. **$89-$149.** 1500 Santa Rosa Ave. US 101, exit Baker Ave northbound; exit Corby Ave southbound. Ext corridors. **Pets:** Dogs only. $15 daily fee/pet. Designated rooms, no service, supervision.
[SAVE] [X] [&M] [H] [I] [TI] [~]

AAA **WWW** **Days Inn** **H**
(707) 568-1011. **$69-$139.** 3345 Santa Rosa Ave. US 101, exit Todd Rd, 0.5 mi ne. Ext corridors. **Pets:** Accepted.
[SAVE] [X] [&M] [H] [I] [~]

AAA **WWWW** **Hillside Inn Motel** **M**
(707) 546-9353. **$84-$99, 3 day notice.** 2901 4th St. US 101, 2.5 mi e on SR 12; at Farmers Ln and 4th St. Ext corridors. **Pets:** Accepted.
[SAVE] [X] [&M] [I] [TI] [~]

AAA **WWWW** **Hilton Sonoma Wine Country** **H** ❀
(707) 523-7555. **$119-$369.** 3555 Round Barn Blvd. 2.5 mi n on US 101, exit Mendocino Ave/Old Redwood Hwy; just ne at top of hill. Int corridors. **Pets:** $50 one-time fee/room. Designated rooms, service with restrictions, supervision.
[SAVE] [X] [&M] [H] [I] [TI] [~]

AAA **WWW** **Holiday Inn Express** **H**
(707) 545-9000. **$129-$299.** 870 Hopper Ave. US 101, exit Mendocino Ave/Old Redwood Hwy northbound, just w; exit Hopper Ave southbound. Ext corridors. **Pets:** Medium, dogs only. $25 one-time fee/room. Designated rooms, service with restrictions, supervision.
[SAVE] [X] [&M] [H] [I] [~]

AAA **WWW** **Sandman Inn** **H** ❀
(707) 544-8570. **$89-$125, 3 day notice.** 3421 Cleveland Ave. US 101, exit W Mendocino Ave/Old Redwood Hwy. Ext corridors. **Pets:** $25 one-time fee/pet. Service with restrictions, supervision.
[SAVE] [X] [&M] [H] [I] [~]

WWW **Santa Rosa Downtown Travelodge** **M**
(707) 544-4141. **Call for rates.** 635 Healdsburg Ave. US 101, exit College Ave, 0.3 mi e, then just s; at Mendocino Ave. Ext corridors. **Pets:** Accepted.
[X] [H] [I] [~]

AAA **WWW** **Travelodge** **M**
(707) 542-3472. **$65-$180.** 1815 Santa Rosa Ave. 1.5 mi s on US 101 business route; US 101, exit Baker Ave northbound; exit Corby Ave southbound. Ext corridors. **Pets:** $15 daily fee/pet. Service with restrictions, supervision.
[SAVE] [X] [&M] [H] [I] [~]

SONOMA

AAA **WWWW** **Best Western Sonoma Valley Inn** **H** ❀
(707) 938-9200. **$139-$380, 3 day notice.** 550 2nd St W. 1 blk w of town plaza. Ext corridors. **Pets:** $35 daily fee/pet. Designated rooms, supervision.
[SAVE] [X] [&M] [H] [I] [~]

AAA **WWWW** **WWW** **The Lodge at Sonoma, a Renaissance Resort & Spa** **H**
(707) 935-6600. **$249-$329, 7 day notice.** 1325 Broadway. On SR 12, 1 mi s of Sonoma Plaza. Ext/int corridors. **Pets:** Accepted.
[SAVE] [X] [&M] [H] [I] [TI] [~] [X]

UKIAH

AAA **WWW** **Americas Best Value Inn** **M**
(707) 462-6657. **$49-$109.** 1070 S State St. US 101, exit Talmage Rd, 0.4 mi w , then just n. Ext corridors. **Pets:** Other species. $10 daily fee/pet. Service with restrictions, supervision.
[SAVE] [X] [~]

WWW **Comfort Inn & Suites** **H** ❀
(707) 462-3442. **$89-$189.** 1220 Airport Park Blvd. US 101, exit Talmage Rd, just w, then just s. Int corridors. **Pets:** Medium. $20 daily fee/pet. Designated rooms, service with restrictions, supervision.
[ASK] [X] [&M] [H] [I] [~]

AAA **WWW** **Days Inn** **M**
(707) 462-7584. **$69-$199, 7 day notice.** 950 N State St. US 101, exit N State St, 0.5 mi s. Ext corridors. **Pets:** Medium, other species. $10 daily fee/pet. Designated rooms, service with restrictions, supervision.
[SAVE] [X] [H] [I] [~]

AAA **WWW** **Discovery Inn** **H**
(707) 462-8873. **$79-$110.** 1340 N State St. US 101, exit N State St, just sw. Ext corridors. **Pets:** Accepted.
[SAVE] [X] [&M] [H] [I] [~]

AAA **WWW** **Quality Inn** **M**
(707) 462-2906. **$79-$139.** 1050 S State St. US 101, exit Talmage Rd, 0.4 mi w, then just n. Ext corridors. **Pets:** Dogs only. $15 daily fee/pet. Service with restrictions, supervision.
[SAVE] [X] [H] [I] [~]

AAA **WWW** **Super 8 Ukiah** **M** ❀
(707) 468-8181. **$49-$119.** 693 S Orchard Ave. US 101, exit Gobbi St W, just nw. Ext corridors. **Pets:** Other species. $10 daily fee/pet. Service with restrictions, supervision.
[SAVE] [X] [H] [I] [TI] [~]

UPPER LAKE

ⓐⓐⓐ ▼▼▼ Super 8 Ⓜ
(707) 275-0888. **$59-$169, 3 day notice.** 450 E Hwy 20. Jct SR 29, 0.5 mi e. Ext corridors. **Pets:** Dogs only. $10 daily fee/pet. Service with restrictions, crate.

[SAVE] [✕] [🛏] [💻] [≈]

▼▼▼ Tallman Hotel Ⓗ ❀
(707) 275-2244. **$119-$229, 3 day notice.** 9550 Main St. Just n of SR 20; downtown. Ext/int corridors. **Pets:** Small, dogs only. $25 daily fee/pet. Designated rooms, service with restrictions, supervision.

[ASK] [✕] [🛏] [💻] [🍴] [≈]

WILLITS

ⓐⓐⓐ ▼▼▼▼ Baechtel Creek Inn & Spa Ⓗ
(707) 459-9063. **$89-$199.** 101 Gregory Ln. US 101, just w. Ext corridors. **Pets:** Small, dogs only. $20 daily fee/pet. Designated rooms, service with restrictions, supervision.

[SAVE] [✕] [🛏] [💻] [≈]

YOUNTVILLE

ⓐⓐⓐ ▼▼▼▼ Vintage Inn Ⓗ
(707) 944-1112. **$265-$700, 7 day notice.** 6541 Washington St. SR 29, exit Yountville; center. Ext corridors. **Pets:** Accepted.

[SAVE] [✕] [⚹M] [🛏] [💻] [≈] [✕]

END AREA

WOODLAND

ⓐⓐⓐ ▼▼▼ Days Inn Ⓗ
(530) 666-3800. **$75-$109.** 1524 E Main St. I-5, exit Main St (Woodland) northbound; exit SR 113 (Davis) southbound, just w. Int corridors. **Pets:** $10 daily fee/pet. Designated rooms, service with restrictions, supervision.

[SAVE] [✕] [⚹M] [🛏] [💻] [≈]

YERMO

ⓐⓐⓐ ▼▼▼ Oak Tree Inn Ⓗ
(760) 254-1148. **$65-$75.** 35450 Yermo Rd. I-15, exit 191 (Ghost Town Rd), just e, then just s. Int corridors. **Pets:** Accepted.

[SAVE] [✕] [🛏] [💻] [🍴] [≈]

YOSEMITE NATIONAL PARK

▼▼▼ The Redwoods In Yosemite ⓋⒽ
(209) 375-6666. **$131-$798, 30 day notice.** 8038 Chilnualna Falls Rd. 6 mi inside the southern entrance via SR 41 and Chilnualna Falls Rd. Ext corridors. **Pets:** Accepted.

[ASK] [✕] [🛏] [💻]

YREKA

ⓐⓐⓐ ▼▼▼▼ Baymont Inn & Suites Ⓗ
(530) 841-1300. **$69-$140.** 148 Moonlit Oaks Ave. I-5, exit 773, just w. Int corridors. **Pets:** Medium. $20 one-time fee/room. Designated rooms, service with restrictions, supervision.

[SAVE] [✕] [🛏] [💻] [≈] [✕]

ⓐⓐⓐ ▼▼▼▼ Best Western Miner's Inn Ⓜ ❀
(530) 842-4355. **$92-$154.** 122 E Miner St. I-5, exit 776 southbound, just w to N Main St, then just s; exit 775 northbound, just w to N Main St, then just n. Ext corridors. **Pets:** Medium. $10 daily fee/pet. Designated rooms, service with restrictions, supervision.

[SAVE] [✕] [🛏] [💻] [✕]

▼▼▼▼ Comfort Inn Ⓗ
(530) 842-1612. **$59-$149.** 1804-B Fort Jones Rd. I-5, exit 773, just w. Int corridors. **Pets:** Accepted.

[ASK] [✕] [🛏] [💻] [≈]

ⓐⓐⓐ ▼▼ Econo Lodge Inn & Suites Ⓜ
(530) 842-4404. **$49-$149.** 526 S Main St. I-5, exit 775, just w to Main St, then just s. Ext corridors. **Pets:** Medium, other species. $10 daily fee/pet. Designated rooms, service with restrictions, supervision.

[SAVE] [✕] [🛏] [💻] [≈]

ⓐⓐⓐ ▼▼ Mountain View Inn/Motel Ⓜ
(530) 842-1940. **$48-$68.** 801 N Main St. I-5, exit 776, just w. Ext corridors. **Pets:** Very small. $6 daily fee/pet. Designated rooms, service with restrictions, supervision.

[SAVE] [✕] [🛏] [💻]

ⓐⓐⓐ ▼▼ Rodeway Inn Ⓜ ❀
(530) 842-4412. **$47-$67.** 1235 S Main St. I-5, exit 775 southbound, just w to Main St, then 0.9 mi s; exit 773 northbound, just w to Main St, then 1.1 mi n. Ext corridors. **Pets:** $8 daily fee/pet. Service with restrictions, supervision.

[SAVE] [✕] [🛏] [💻] [≈]

ⓐⓐⓐ ▼▼▼ Super 8-Yreka Ⓜ
(530) 842-5781. **$59-$95.** 136 Montague Rd. I-5, exit 776, just w. Ext corridors. **Pets:** $10 daily fee/pet. Service with restrictions, supervision.

[SAVE] [✕] [🛏] [💻] [≈]

YUBA CITY

ⓐⓐⓐ ▼▼▼ Econo Lodge Inn & Suites Ⓜ
(530) 674-1592. **$66-$150.** 730 Palora Ave. 0.5 mi s of jct SR 99 and 20, just e on Bridge St, then just n. Int corridors. **Pets:** Medium, other species. $50 deposit/room, $10 daily fee/pet. Designated rooms, service with restrictions, supervision.

[SAVE] [✕] [⚹M] [🛏] [💻] [≈]

ⓐⓐⓐ ▼▼▼ Quality Inn & Suites Ⓗ
(530) 674-0201. **$89-$329.** 4228 S Hwy 99. On SR 99, 4.5 mi s of SR 20. Ext corridors. **Pets:** Other species. Supervision.

[SAVE] [✕] [⚹M] [🛏] [💻] [🍴] [≈]

YUCCA VALLEY

▼▼ Americas Best Value Inn & Suites-Oasis of Eden Ⓜ
(760) 365-6321. **Call for rates.** 56377 Twentynine Palms Hwy. 1 mi w of jct SR 62 and 247. Ext corridors. **Pets:** Accepted.

[✕] [🛏] [💻] [≈]

ⓐⓐⓐ ▼▼ Super 8 Ⓜ
(760) 228-1773. **$69-$129.** 57096 Twentynine Palms Hwy. On SR 62, 0.3 mi w of jct SR 247. Int corridors. **Pets:** Accepted.

[SAVE] [✕] [🛏] [💻] [≈]

COLORADO

ALAMOSA

Best Western Alamosa Inn
(719) 589-2567. **Call for rates.** 2005 W Main St. 1 mi w on US 160 and 285. Ext corridors. **Pets:** Small, dogs only. $15 one-time fee/pet. Designated rooms, service with restrictions, supervision.

Holiday Inn Express Hotel
(719) 589-4026. **$75-$150.** 3418 Mariposa St. 1.8 mi w on US 160. Int corridors. **Pets:** Accepted.

Super 8
(719) 589-6447. **Call for rates.** 2505 Main St. 1.3 mi w on US 160. Int corridors. **Pets:** Accepted.

ASPEN

Aspen Meadows Resort, a Dolce Resort
(970) 925-4240. **$175-$600, 30 day notice.** 845 Meadows Rd. 3 blks n of SR 82 via 7th Ave, just w. Ext/int corridors. **Pets:** $100 one-time fee/room. Designated rooms, service with restrictions, supervision.

Aspen Mountain Lodge
(970) 925-7650. **$116-$435, 7 day notice.** 311 W Main St. Just w on SR 82; between 2nd and 3rd sts. Int corridors. **Pets:** Dogs only. $20 daily fee/pet. Supervision.

Hotel Jerome
(970) 920-1000. **$180-$1850, 30 day notice.** 330 E Main St. On SR 82; downtown. Int corridors. **Pets:** Other species. $75 one-time fee/room. Service with restrictions.

Hotel Lenado
(970) 925-6246. **Call for rates.** 200 S Aspen St. Just s of SR 82 via Aspen St at jct Hopkins St. Ext/int corridors. **Pets:** Accepted.

The Little Nell
(970) 920-4600. **$250-$5900, 30 day notice.** 675 E Durant Ave. Beside the gondola at base of Aspen Mountain. Int corridors. **Pets:** $100 one-time fee/room. Service with restrictions.

Molly Gibson Lodge
(970) 925-3434. **Call for rates.** 101 W Main St. Just w on SR 82. Ext/int corridors. **Pets:** Accepted.

St. Regis Resort, Aspen
(970) 920-3300. **$160-$2045, 60 day notice.** 315 E Dean St. SR 82, s on Monarch St, then just e. Int corridors. **Pets:** Dogs only. $100 one-time fee/room. Service with restrictions, supervision.

Sky Hotel
(970) 925-6760. **$179-$709, 30 day notice.** 709 E Durant Ave. At base of Aspen Mountain. Ext/int corridors. **Pets:** Dogs only. Service with restrictions, supervision.

AVON

Comfort Inn-Vail/Beaver Creek
(970) 949-5511. **$79-$219.** 161 W Beaver Creek Blvd. I-70, exit 167, just s on Avon Rd, then just w. Int corridors. **Pets:** Medium. $50 one-time fee/pet. Designated rooms, service with restrictions, supervision.

BEAVER CREEK

The Ritz-Carlton, Bachelor Gulch
(970) 748-6200. **$273-$1295, 30 day notice.** 130 Daybreak Ridge. I-70, exit 167, s on Avon and Village rds (beyond gatehouse), w on Prater Rd, follow signs to Bachelor Gulch Village. Int corridors. **Pets:** Accepted.

BOULDER

Best Western Boulder Inn
(303) 449-3800. **$108-$145.** 770 28th St. US 36 (28th St) at Baseline Rd. Int corridors. **Pets:** Medium. $100 deposit/room. Designated rooms, supervision.

Boulder Broker Inn
(303) 444-3330. **$79-$299.** 555 30th St. US 36 (28th St), exit Baseline Rd, 0.3 mi e to 30th St, then just s. Int corridors. **Pets:** Accepted.

Boulder Outlook Hotel & Suites
(303) 443-3322. **$89-$259.** 800 28th St. US 36 (28th St), exit Baseline Rd via Frontage Rd. Ext/int corridors. **Pets:** Accepted.

QQQ WWWW Boulder University Inn M ❀
(303) 417-1700. **$60-$119.** 1632 Broadway. US 36 (28th St), exit Baseline Rd, 0.3 mi s, then 3 mi nw. Ext corridors. **Pets:** Medium, other species. $100 deposit/room, $15 daily fee/pet. Designated rooms, service with restrictions, supervision.
SAVE X 🔒 🖵 ⊅

QQQ WWW Foot of The Mountain Motel M ❀
(303) 442-5688. **$75-$90.** 200 Arapahoe Ave. 1.8 mi w of US 36 (28th St). Ext corridors. **Pets:** $50 deposit/room, $5 daily fee/pet. Designated rooms, service with restrictions, supervision.
SAVE X 🔒 🖵 ℀

WWW WWW Holiday Inn Express H
(303) 442-6600. **$114-$199.** 4777 N Broadway. 3 mi n of Pearl Street Pedestrian Mall; jct US 36 (28th St), 0.3 mi s. Int corridors. **Pets:** Other species. $25 daily fee/room. Service with restrictions, supervision.
ASK X 🔒 🖵 ⊅

WWWWW Homewood Suites by Hilton H ❀
(303) 499-9922. **$109-$359.** 4950 Baseline Rd. 1.2 mi e of US 36 (28th St); Jct SR 157 (Foothills Pkwy), just w; entry off Baseline Rd. Ext/int corridors. **Pets:** Other species. $50 one-time fee/room.
X 🔒 🖵 ⊅ ⊠

QQQ WWWWW Millennium Harvest House Boulder H ❀
(303) 443-3850. **$109-$265.** 1345 28th St. Just s of jct Arapahoe Ave and US 36 (28th St). Int corridors. **Pets:** Other species. $250 deposit/room, $25 daily fee/room. Designated rooms, service with restrictions.
SAVE X 🔒 🖵 ⑪ ⊅ ⊠

QQQ WWWW Quality Inn & Suites Boulder Creek H ❀
(303) 449-7550. **$79-$149.** 2020 Arapahoe Ave. US 36 (28th St), 0.5 mi w. Ext/int corridors. **Pets:** Medium, other species. $100 deposit/room, $15 daily fee/pet. Designated rooms, service with restrictions, supervision.
SAVE X 🔒 🖵 ⊅ ⊠

WWWW Residence Inn by Marriott H
(303) 449-5545. **$209-$219.** 3030 Center Green Dr. 0.5 mi e of US 36 (28th St), e on Valmont Rd; from Foothills Pkwy, just w on Valmont Rd. Ext corridors. **Pets:** Accepted.
X 🔒 🖵 ⊅ ⊠

BRECKENRIDGE

WWWW Great Divide Lodge H
(970) 547-5550. **$90-$450, 21 day notice.** 550 Village Rd. Jct Main St, just w on S Park Ave, then just sw. Int corridors. **Pets:** Accepted.
ASK X ⅏ 🔒 🖵 ⑪ ⊅ ⊠ ℀

BROOMFIELD

QQQ WWWW WWWW Omni Interlocken Resort H
(303) 438-6600. **$119-$389.** 500 Interlocken Blvd. US 36 (Boulder Tpke), exit Interlocken Loop, 0.4 mi s, then 0.4 mi e. Int corridors. **Pets:** Accepted.
SAVE X ⅏ 🔒 🖵 ⑪ ⊅ ⊠

WWW WWW TownePlace Suites by Marriott Boulder/Broomfield H
(303) 466-2200. **$139-$169.** 480 Flatiron Blvd. US 36 (Boulder Tpke), exit Interlocken Loop, 0.4 mi s, just w on Interlocken Blvd, then just s. Int corridors. **Pets:** Accepted.
X ⅏ 🔒 🖵 ⊅

BRUSH

WW WW Microtel Inn H
(970) 842-4241. **$62-$82, 7 day notice.** 975 N Colorado Ave. I-76, exit 90A, just s. Int corridors. **Pets:** Accepted.
ASK X 🔒 🖵 ⊅

BUENA VISTA

WWW WWW Super 8 M
(719) 395-8888. **Call for rates.** 530 N US 24. On US 24, 0.3 mi n. Ext/int corridors. **Pets:** Accepted.
X 🔒 🖵 ⊅

BURLINGTON

QQQ WWW Chaparral Motor Inn M
(719) 346-5361. **$49-$65.** 405 S Lincoln St. I-70, exit 437, just n on jct US 385. Ext corridors. **Pets:** Small. $7 daily fee/pet, $7 one-time fee/pet. Designated rooms, service with restrictions, supervision.
SAVE X 🔒 🖵 ⊅

WWW WWW Comfort Inn Burlington H
(719) 346-7676. **$80-$140.** 282 S Lincoln St. I-70, exit 437, just n on US 385. Int corridors. **Pets:** Accepted.
ASK X 🔒 🖵 ⊅

CANON CITY

WWW WW Comfort Inn H
(719) 276-6900. **Call for rates.** 311 Royal Gorge Blvd. On US 50; just w of downtown. Int corridors. **Pets:** Accepted.
X 🔒 🖵 ⊅

WWWW Holiday Inn Express H
(719) 275-2400. **$100-$115, 7 day notice.** 110 Latigo Ln. 2.5 mi e of SR 115 on US 50. Int corridors. **Pets:** $15 daily fee/pet. Designated rooms, service with restrictions, supervision.
ASK X 🔒 🖵 ⊅

CARBONDALE

QQQ WWWW Comfort Inn & Suites H
(970) 963-8880. **$119-$240.** 920 Cowen Dr. Jct of SR 82 and 133, just s via signs. Int corridors. **Pets:** Accepted.
SAVE X 🔒 🖵 ⊅ ⊠

QQQ WWW Days Inn H
(970) 963-9111. **$109-$209, 3 day notice.** 950 Cowen Dr. Jct SR 82 and 133. Int corridors. **Pets:** $10 daily fee/pet. Service with restrictions, supervision.
SAVE X 🔒 ⊅ ⊠

CASTLE ROCK

QQQ WWW Best Western Inn & Suites of Castle Rock H ❀
(303) 814-8800. **$90-$150, 7 day notice.** 595 Genoa Way. I-25, exit 184 (Meadows Pkwy), just w to Castleton Way, just s, then e. Int corridors. **Pets:** Medium. $15 daily fee/pet. Designated rooms, service with restrictions, supervision.
SAVE X 🔒 🖵 ⊅

WWW WW Castle Rock Days Inn and Suites H
(303) 814-5825. **$54-$99, 30 day notice.** 4961 Castleton Way. I-25, exit 184 (Meadows Pkwy), 0.5 mi e, just s on Castleton Way, then just se. Int corridors. **Pets:** Accepted.
ASK X 🔒 🖵 ⊅

WWWW Comfort Suites H
(303) 814-9999. **$64-$119.** 4755 Castleton Way. I-25, exit 184 (Meadows Pkwy), w to Castleton Way; entrance on east side. Int corridors. **Pets:** Accepted.
ASK X ⅏ 🔒 🖵 ⊅ ⊠

WWWW Hampton Inn H
(303) 660-9800. **$139.** 4830 Castleton Way. I-25, exit 184 (Meadows Pkwy), sw to N Castleton Rd, just s, then e. Int corridors. **Pets:** Other species. $5 daily fee/room, $25 one-time fee/room. Designated rooms, service with restrictions.
X ⅏ 🔒 🖵 ⊅

▼▼▼▼ Holiday Inn Express 🅷
(303) 660-9733. **$79-$139.** 884 Park St. I-25, exit 182, just w. Int corridors.
Pets: Accepted.
(ASK) (✕) 🛋 💻 ➴

CEDAREDGE

◈◈◈ ▼▼▼ Howard Johnson Express Inn 🅷
(970) 856-7824. **$79-$99.** 530 S Grand Mesa Dr. Just s on SR 65. Int corridors. **Pets:** $10 daily fee/pet. Designated rooms, service with restrictions.
(SAVE) (✕) 🛋 💻 ➴

COLORADO SPRINGS METROPOLITAN AREA

CHIPITA PARK

▼▼▼ Chipita Lodge B&B 🅱🅱
(719) 684-8454. **$100-$175, 7 day notice.** 9090 Chipita Park Rd. Jct US 24, just s on Fountain Blvd (Pine Peak Hwy), then 1.5 mi w; go right at fork. Ext/int corridors. **Pets:** Dogs only. $25 one-time fee/pet. Designated rooms, no service.
(ASK) (✕) 🛋 💻 🐾

COLORADO SPRINGS

▼▼▼ Airport Value Inn & Suites 🅷
(719) 596-5588. **$60-$90.** 6875 Space Village Ave. I-25, exit 141, 1 mi e on Cimarron Ave, 0.7 mi n on Wahsatch Ave, 6.3 mi e on Platte Ave, then exit Space Village Ave. Ext/int corridors. **Pets:** Accepted.
(ASK) (✕) (⬥M) 🛋 💻

▼▼◈▼ Antlers Hilton Colorado Springs 🅷 🐾
(719) 473-5600. **$85-$235.** 4 S Cascade Ave. I-25, exit 142 (Bijou St), just e, then just s on Cascade Ave; downtown. Int corridors. **Pets:** Medium. $75 one-time fee/room. Designated rooms, service with restrictions, crate.
(✕) (⬥M) ◈▼ 🍴 ➴ (✕)

◈◈◈ ▼▼▼ Apollo Park Executive Suites (CO)
(719) 634-0286. **$49-$105.** 805 S Circle Dr, 2-B. I-25, exit 138, 2.5 mi e. Int corridors. **Pets:** Accepted.
(SAVE) (✕) 🛋 💻 ➴

◈◈◈ ▼▼▼ Best Western Airport Inn 🅷
(719) 574-7707. **$60-$120, 3 day notice.** 1780 Aeroplaza Dr. I-25, exit 139, 4.5 mi e on US 24 Bypass. Int corridors. **Pets:** Small, dogs only. $50 deposit/pet, $10 daily fee/pet. Designated rooms, service with restrictions, crate.
(SAVE) (✕) (⬥M) 🛋 💻 ➴

◈◈◈ ▼▼▼ Best Western Executive Inn & Suites 🅷
(719) 576-2371. **$59-$149.** 1440 Harrison Rd. I-25, exit 138, just w; on northwest corner of interchange; entrance through restaurant. Int corridors. **Pets:** Medium. $10 daily fee/pet. Designated rooms, no service, supervision.
(SAVE) (✕) (⬥M) 🛋 💻 ➴

◈◈◈ ▼▼▼ Best Western The Academy Hotel 🅷
(719) 598-5770. **Call for rates.** 8110 N Academy Blvd. I-25, exit 150, just s. Int corridors. **Pets:** Accepted.
(SAVE) (✕) 🛋 💻 🍴 ➴ (✕)

◈◈◈ ▼▼◈▼▼ The Broadmoor 🅷 🐾
(719) 634-7711. **$290-$2500, 7 day notice.** 1 Lake Ave. I-25, exit 138, 3 mi w on Circle Dr (which becomes Lake Ave). Int corridors. **Pets:** Other species. $100 one-time fee/pet. Designated rooms, service with restrictions, supervision.
(SAVE) (✕) (⬥M) 🛋 💻 🍴 ➴ (✕)

◈◈◈ ▼▼◈▼ Cheyenne Mountain Resort 🅷 🐾
(719) 538-4000. **$109-$299.** 3225 Broadmoor Valley Rd. I-25, exit 138, 1.4 mi w to SR 115, 0.5 mi s, just w on Cheyenne Mountain Dr, then just s. Ext/int corridors. **Pets:** Medium, dogs only. $35 one-time fee/pet. Service with restrictions, supervision.
(SAVE) (✕) (⬥M) 🛋 💻 🍴 ➴ (✕)

◈◈◈ ▼▼▼ Comfort Inn North 🅷
(719) 262-9000. **$69-$129.** 6450 Corporate Dr. I-25, exit 149 (Woodmen Rd), just w, then 0.3 mi s. Int corridors. **Pets:** $10 daily fee/pet. Designated rooms, service with restrictions, crate.
(SAVE) (✕) (⬥M) 🛋 💻 ➴

◈◈◈ ▼▼▼ Comfort Inn South 🅷 🐾
(719) 579-6900. **$69-$149.** 1410 Harrison Rd. I-25, exit 138, just w to Rand Rd, then ne. Int corridors. **Pets:** Medium. $25 one-time fee/pet. Designated rooms, service with restrictions, supervision.
(SAVE) (✕) 🛋 💻 ➴

◈◈◈ ▼▼▼ Crowne Plaza Colorado Springs 🅷 🐾
(719) 576-5900. **$89-$199.** 2886 S Circle Dr. I-25, exit 138, just e. Int corridors. **Pets:** Large, other species. $50 one-time fee/pet. Service with restrictions, crate.
(SAVE) (✕) 💻 🍴 ➴ (✕)

◈◈◈ ▼▼◈▼▼ DoubleTree Hotel Colorado Springs, World Arena 🅷 🐾
(719) 576-8900. **$105-$205.** 1775 E Cheyenne Mountain Blvd. I-25, exit 138, just w. Int corridors. **Pets:** Medium, other species. $15 one-time fee/room. Service with restrictions, supervision.
(SAVE) (✕) (⬥M) 🛋 💻 🍴 ➴ (✕)

▼▼◈▼ Drury Inn-Pikes Peak 🅷
(719) 598-2500. **$58-$138.** 8155 N Academy Blvd. I-25, exit 150, just s, then e. Int corridors. **Pets:** Other species. Service with restrictions, supervision.
(ASK) (✕) 🛋 💻 ➴

▼▼◈▼▼ Fairfield Inn by Marriott-South 🅷
(719) 576-1717. **$119-$139.** 2725 Geyser Dr. I-25, exit 138, just w to E Cheyenne Mountain Blvd, then just s. Int corridors. **Pets:** Accepted.
(✕) (⬥M) 🛋 💻 ➴

◈◈◈ ▼▼◈▼ Holiday Inn Express Air Force Academy 🅷
(719) 592-9800. **$89-$199.** 7110 Commerce Center Dr. I-25, exit 149 (Woodman Rd), just w, then just n. Int corridors. **Pets:** Large, dogs only. $25 daily fee/pet. Designated rooms, service with restrictions, supervision.
(SAVE) (✕) (⬥M) 🛋 💻 ➴ (✕)

▼▼◈▼▼ Homewood Suites by Hilton Colorado Springs Airport 🅷
(719) 574-2701. **$99-$129.** 2875 Zeppelin Rd. I-25, exit 139, 4 mi e on US 24 Bypass, 1.1 mi s on Powers Blvd, then just e. Int corridors. **Pets:** Medium. $50 one-time fee/pet. Service with restrictions, crate.
(✕) 🛋 💻 ➴ (✕)

▼▼◈▼▼ Homewood Suites by Hilton Colorado Springs-North 🅷
(719) 265-6600. **$119-$179.** 9130 Explorer Dr. I-25, exit 151 (Briargate Pkwy), 0.8 mi e; across from Focus on the Family. Int corridors. **Pets:** Medium, other species. $25 one-time fee/room. Service with restrictions, crate.
(✕) (⬥M) 🛋 💻 ➴

◈◈◈ ▼▼◈▼ Hyatt Summerfield Suites 🅷
(719) 268-9990. **$109-$399.** 5805 Delmonico Dr. I-25, exit 148 (Rockrimmon Blvd), just w, then e on Delmonico Dr; entry around the bank. Int corridors. **Pets:** Accepted.
(SAVE) (✕) 🛋 💻 (✕)

▼▼▼ **La Quinta Inn & Suites Colorado Springs (South/Airport)** 🅷 ❀
(719) 527-4788. **$69-$169.** 2750 Geyser Dr. I-25, exit 138, just w to Cheyenne Mountain Blvd, then just s. Int corridors. **Pets:** Medium, other species. Service with restrictions, supervision.
⊠ 🐾ᴹ 🛏 📺 ➤

▼▼ **La Quinta Inn Colorado Springs (Garden of the Gods)** 🅷 ❀
(719) 528-5060. **$49-$139.** 4385 Sinton Rd. I-25, exit 146 (Garden of the Gods Rd), just e. Ext/int corridors. **Pets:** Medium, other species. Service with restrictions, supervision.
(ASK) ⊠ 🛏 📺 ➤

▼▼ **Microtel Inn & Suites** 🅷
(719) 598-7500. **$59-$120.** 7265 Commerce Center Dr. I-25, exit 149 (Woodman Rd), just w, then n. Int corridors. **Pets:** Medium. $20 one-time fee/room. Designated rooms, service with restrictions, supervision.
⊠ 🐾ᴹ 🛏 📺 ➤

💵📖 ▼▼💵▼ **Radisson Hotel Colorado Springs Airport** 🅷
(719) 597-7000. **$119-$185.** 1645 N Newport Rd. I-25, exit 139, 4.5 mi e on US 24 Bypass. Int corridors. **Pets:** Medium. $100 deposit/room, $25 one-time fee/pet. Designated rooms, service with restrictions, crate.
(SAVE) ⊠ 🐾ᴹ 🛏 📺 ¶ ➤ ⊠

💵📖 ▼▼▼ **Rainbow Lodge and Inn** Ⓜ
(719) 632-4551. **$52-$195, 7 day notice.** 3709 W Colorado Ave. I-25, exit 141, 2.5 mi w on US 24, just n on 31st St, then 0.7 mi w. Ext corridors. **Pets:** Small, dogs only. $25 deposit/room. Designated rooms, service with restrictions, supervision.
(SAVE) ⊠ 🛏 ➤

▼▼ **Ramada Limited East-Airport** 🅷
(719) 596-7660. **$59-$99.** 520 N Murray Blvd. I-25, exit 141, 1 mi e on Cimarron Ave, 0.7 mi n on Wahsatch Ave, 3.7 mi e on Platte Ave, then just n. Ext/int corridors. **Pets:** Accepted.
(ASK) ⊠ 🛏 📺 ➤

💵📖 ▼▼💵▼ **Residence Inn by Marriott-Central** 🅷
(719) 574-0370. **$149-$179.** 3880 N Academy Blvd. I-25, exit 146, 4.5 mi e on Garden of the Gods/Austin Bluffs Pkwy, then 0.3 mi s. Ext corridors. **Pets:** Accepted.
(SAVE) ⊠ 🛏 📺 ➤ ⊠

▼▼▼ **Residence Inn by Marriott Colorado Springs North at Interquest Pkwy** 🅷
(719) 388-9300. **$129-$149.** 9805 Federal Dr. I-25, exit 153, just e, then s. Int corridors. **Pets:** Medium. $75 one-time fee/pet. Service with restrictions, crate.
⊠ 🐾ᴹ 🛏 📺 ➤ ⊠

▼▼💵▼ **Residence Inn by Marriott-Colorado Springs South** 🅷 ❀
(719) 576-0101. **$139-$169.** 2765 Geyser Dr. I-25, exit 138, just w to E Cheyenne Mountain Blvd, then just s. Int corridors. **Pets:** Medium. $75 one-time fee/room. Service with restrictions, crate.
⊠ 🐾ᴹ 🛏 📺 ➤ ⊠

💵📖 ▼▼▼ **Sleep Inn** 🅷
(719) 260-6969. **$49-$149.** 1075 Kelly Johnson Blvd. I-25, exit 150, just s on Academy Blvd to Kelly Johnson Blvd, then w. Int corridors. **Pets:** Small. $10 daily fee/pet. Designated rooms, service with restrictions, supervision.
(SAVE) ⊠ 🐾ᴹ 📺

💵📖 ▼ **Stagecoach Motel** Ⓜ ❀
(719) 633-3894. **$39-$69, 4 day notice.** 1647 S Nevada Ave. I-25, exit 140, just s. Ext corridors. **Pets:** Small. $10 daily fee/room. Service with restrictions, crate.
(SAVE) ⊠ 🛏

💵📖 ▼▼▼ **Staybridge Suites-Air Force Academy** 🅷
(719) 590-7829. **$119-$179.** 7130 Commerce Center Dr. I-25, exit 149 (Woodmen Rd), just w, then n. Int corridors. **Pets:** Large, other species. $75 one-time fee/pet. Designated rooms, service with restrictions, crate.
(SAVE) ⊠ 🐾ᴹ 🛏 📺 ➤ ⊠

▼▼ **TownePlace Suites by Marriott-Colorado Springs** 🅷 ❀
(719) 594-4447. **$109-$124.** 4760 Centennial Blvd. I-25, exit 146 (Garden of the Gods Rd), 1 mi w on, just n on Centennial Blvd, then first left. Int corridors. **Pets:** Other species. $100 one-time fee/room. Service with restrictions.
⊠ 🐾ᴹ 🛏 📺 ➤

▼▼▼ **TownePlace Suites Colorado Springs South** 🅷
(719) 638-0800. **$99-$129.** 1530 N Newport Rd. I-25, exit 139, 5 mi e on US 24 Bypass, then just n. Int corridors. **Pets:** Accepted.
⊠ 🛏 📺 ➤

💵📖 ▼▼ **Travel Inn** Ⓜ
(719) 636-3986. **$40-$99.** 512 S Nevada Ave. I-25, exit 141, 0.7 mi e to Nevada Ave, then just s. Ext/int corridors. **Pets:** Other species. $20 deposit/room, $5 daily fee/pet, $5 one-time fee/pet. Service with restrictions, supervision.
(SAVE) ⊠ 🛏

💵📖 ▼▼ **Travelodge** 🅷
(719) 632-4600. **$50-$95.** 2625 Ore Mill Rd. I-25, exit 141, 2.3 mi nw on US 24; entry via 26th St. Int corridors. **Pets:** Medium. $20 one-time fee/pet. Service with restrictions, supervision.
(SAVE) ⊠ 🛏 📺 ➤

MANITOU SPRINGS

💵📖 ▼▼ **El Colorado Lodge** ⒸⒶ
(719) 685-5485. **$56-$136, 7 day notice.** 23 Manitou Ave. I-25, exit 141, 4 mi w on US 24, then just ne on US 24 business route. Ext corridors. **Pets:** Large. $75 deposit/room. Designated rooms, service with restrictions, crate.
(SAVE) ⊠ 🛏 📺 ➤ ⊠

💵📖 ▼▼ **Park Row Lodge** Ⓜ
(719) 685-5216. **$49-$79.** 54 Manitou Ave. I-25, exit 141, 4 mi w on US 24, then just ne on US 24 business route. Ext corridors. **Pets:** Accepted.
(SAVE) ⊠ 🛏

💵📖 ▼ **Red Wing Motel** Ⓜ
(719) 685-5656. **$39-$119.** 56 El Paso Blvd. I-25, exit 141, 4 mi w on US 24, just ne on US 24 business route/Manitou Ave, then just w on Beckers Ln. Ext corridors. **Pets:** Other species. $7 one-time fee/room. Service with restrictions.
(SAVE) ⊠ 🛏 📺 ➤

END METROPOLITAN AREA

CORTEZ

▼▼▼▼ Best Western Turquoise Inn & Suites H ❀
(970) 565-3778. **$100-$175, 14 day notice.** 535 E Main St. On US 160. Ext corridors. **Pets:** $15 one-time fee/room. Designated rooms, service with restrictions, supervision.

[SAVE] [X] [🛏] [💻] [🏊]

▼▼▼▼ Budget Host Inn M
(970) 565-3738. **$42-$108.** 2040 E Main St. 1.3 mi e on US 160, w of jct SR 145. Ext corridors. **Pets:** Other species. $10 daily fee/pet. Designated rooms, service with restrictions, supervision.

[SAVE] [X] [🛏] [💻] [🏊]

▼▼▼▼ Comfort Inn H ❀
(970) 565-3400. **Call for rates.** 2321 E Main St. 1.3 mi e on US 160. Ext/int corridors. **Pets:** Other species. $10 one-time fee/room. Designated rooms, service with restrictions, supervision.

[SAVE] [X] [💻] [🏊]

▼▼▼ Econo Lodge M
(970) 565-3474. **$50-$150.** 2020 E Main St. 1.3 mi e on US 160. Ext corridors. **Pets:** $10 daily fee/pet. Designated rooms, service with restrictions, supervision.

[ASK] [X] [🛏] [💻] [🏊]

▼▼▼▼ Holiday Inn Express H
(970) 565-6000. **$114-$159.** 2121 E Main St. 1.3 mi e on US 160. Int corridors. **Pets:** Medium. $150 one-time fee/pet. Designated rooms, service with restrictions, supervision.

[SAVE] [X] [🛏] [💻] [🍴] [🏊] [X]

▼▼▼ Tomahawk Lodge M
(970) 565-8521. **$49-$99.** 728 S Broadway. 1 mi sw on US 160 and 491. Ext corridors. **Pets:** Dogs only. $25 deposit/pet. Designated rooms, service with restrictions, supervision.

[SAVE] [X] [💻] [🏊]

CRAIG

▼▼▼▼ Best Western Deer Park Inn & Suites H ❀
(970) 824-9282. **$89-$199.** 262 Commerce St (Hwy 13). Jct US 40, 0.3 mi s on SR 13. Int corridors. **Pets:** $100 deposit/room, $10 one-time fee/room. Service with restrictions, crate.

[SAVE] [X] [🛏] [💻] [🏊]

▼▼▼▼ Holiday Inn & Suites H
(970) 824-4000. **$109-$209.** 300 S Hwy 13. Jct US 40, 0.3 mi s. Int corridors. **Pets:** Accepted.

[ASK] [X] [🛏] [💻] [🍴] [🏊] [X]

CRESTED BUTTE

▼▼▼ Grand Lodge Crested Butte H ❀
(970) 349-8000. **$93-$265, 3 day notice.** 6 Emmons Loop. 2.5 mi n on SR 135. Int corridors. **Pets:** $30 daily fee/pet. Designated rooms, service with restrictions, supervision.

[X] [🛏] [💻] [🍴] [🏊] [X] [🐾]

▼▼▼ Old Town Inn M ❀
(970) 349-6184. **$82-$149, 14 day notice.** 708 6th St. Se on SR 135. Int corridors. **Pets:** $10 daily fee/room. Supervision.

[ASK] [X] [🛏]

DELTA

▼▼▼▼ Best Western Sundance H
(970) 874-9781. **$106-$116, 30 day notice.** 903 Main St. 0.5 mi s on US 50. Ext corridors. **Pets:** $10 daily fee/pet. Service with restrictions, crate.

[SAVE] [X] [🛏] [💻] [🍴] [🏊]

▼▼▼ Comfort Inn H
(970) 874-1000. **$80-$190.** 180 Gunnison River Dr. Just n, then just w of jct US 50 and 92. Int corridors. **Pets:** Other species. $10 daily fee/pet. Service with restrictions, supervision.

[ASK] [X] [🛏] [💻]

▼▼▼ Riverwood Inn M
(970) 874-5787. **$55-$98, 3 day notice.** 677 US 50. 0.5 mi n. Int corridors. **Pets:** Accepted.

[SAVE] [X] [🛏] [💻]

▼▼▼ Rodeway Inn M
(970) 874-9726. **$56-$90.** 2124 S Main St. 1.5 mi s on US 50. Ext corridors. **Pets:** Medium. $10 daily fee/pet. Designated rooms, service with restrictions, supervision.

[SAVE] [X] [🛏] [💻] [🏊]

DENVER METROPOLITAN AREA

AURORA

▼▼▼▼ Best Western Gateway Inn & Suites H
(720) 748-4800. **$95-$150, 4 day notice.** 800 S Abilene St. I-225, exit 7 (Mississippi Ave), just e, then 0.3 mi n. Int corridors. **Pets:** Small. $15 daily fee/pet. Service with restrictions, crate.

[SAVE] [X] [♿M] [🛏] [💻] [🏊] [X]

▼▼ Comfort Inn Denver Southeast H
(303) 755-8000. **$69-$179.** 14071 E Iliff Ave. I-225, exit 5 (E Iliff Ave), just e. Int corridors. **Pets:** Accepted.

[X] [♿M] [🛏] [💻]

▼▼▼ Comfort Inn DIA Airport H
(303) 367-5000. **$69-$129.** 16921 E 32nd Ave. I-70, exit 285, just s on Airport Blvd; on southeast corner. Int corridors. **Pets:** Medium, other species. $10 daily fee/pet. Designated rooms, no service, supervision.

[SAVE] [X] [♿M] [🛏] [💻] [🏊]

▼▼ Crestwood Suites Extended Stay Hotels H
(303) 481-0379. **Call for rates.** 14090 E Evans Ave. I-225, exit 5 (E Iliff Ave), e to Blackhawk St, then 0.4 mi nw. Int corridors. **Pets:** Small. $15 one-time fee/pet. Designated rooms, service with restrictions, crate.

[X] [🛏] [💻]

▼▼▼▼ Crowne Plaza Denver International Airport H
(303) 371-9494. **$89-$199.** 15500 E 40th Ave. I-70, exit 283 (Chambers Rd), just n, then just e. Int corridors. **Pets:** Accepted.

[SAVE] [X] [♿M] [🛏] [💻] [🍴] [🏊] [X]

▼▼▼ Crystal Inn DIA H ❀
(303) 340-3800. **$99-$169.** 3300 N Ouray St. I-70, exit 285, just s on Airport Blvd, then w on 32nd Ave. Int corridors. **Pets:** $20 daily fee/pet. Service with restrictions, supervision.

[SAVE] [X] [♿M] [🛏] [💻] [🏊]

▼▼ Extended Stay Deluxe H
(303) 337-7000. **$67-$95.** 14095 E Evans Ave. I-225, exit 5 (E Iliff Ave), just e to Blackhawk St, then 0.4 mi nw. Int corridors. **Pets:** Other species. $25 daily fee/pet. Service with restrictions, crate.

[ASK] [X] [♿M] [🛏] [💻] [🏊]

▼▼ La Quinta Inn Denver (Aurora) M ❀
(303) 337-0206. **$49-$139.** 1011 S Abilene St. I-225, exit 7 (Mississippi Ave), just e, then n. Ext corridors. **Pets:** Medium, other species. Service with restrictions, supervision.

[X] [♿M] [💻] [🏊]

▼▼ Sleep Inn Denver International Airport 🅷
(303) 373-1616. **$70-$175.** 15900 E 40th Ave. I-70, exit 283 (Chambers Rd); from airport, Pena Blvd S to 40th Ave W. Int corridors. **Pets:** Other species. $25 deposit/room, $10 daily fee/room. Designated rooms, supervision.
A$K ✕ ⓜ 🛏 🖵 ⇌

CENTENNIAL

◈ ▼▼▼ Candlewood Suites 🅷 🐾
(303) 792-5393. **$66-$130.** 6780 S Galena St. I-25, exit 197 (Arapahoe Rd), 0.7 mi e, then just s. Int corridors. **Pets:** Medium, other species. $25 daily fee/pet, $150 one-time fee/room. Service with restrictions, crate.
SAVE ✕ 🛏 🖵

▼▼ Days Inn Denver Tech Center 🅷
(303) 768-9400. **Call for rates.** 9719 E Geddes Ave. I-25, exit 196 (Dry Creek Rd), just e to S Clinton St, just n, then just e. Int corridors. **Pets:** Accepted.
✕ ⓜ 🛏 🖵

◈ ▼▼▼ Embassy Suites Denver Tech Center 🅷
(303) 792-0433. **$99-$239.** 10250 E Costilla Ave. I-25, exit 197 (Arapahoe Rd), 1 mi e, 0.3 mi s on Havana St, then w. Int corridors. **Pets:** Accepted.
SAVE ✕ ⓜ 🛏 🖵 🍽 ⇌

▼▼▼ Staybridge Suites Denver Tech Center 🅷
(303) 858-9990. **$79-$169.** 7150 S Clinton St. I-25, exit 197 (Arapahoe Rd), just e to S Clinton St, then just s. Int corridors. **Pets:** Accepted.
✕ ⓜ 🛏 🖵 ⇌

DENVER

◈ ▼▼▼▼ Brown Palace Hotel and Spa 🅷 🐾
(303) 297-3111. **$189-$569.** 321 17th St. I-25, exit 210 (E Colfax Ave) to Lincoln St, just n on Lincoln St, just w on 18th St, then s. Int corridors. **Pets:** Medium, dogs only. $75 one-time fee/room. Supervision.
SAVE ✕ 🛏 🖵 🍽

◈ ▼▼▼ Comfort Inn Central 🅷 🐾
(303) 297-1717. **$95-$117.** 401 E 58th Ave. I-25, exit 215, just e, then n on Logan St; connected to Denver Merchandise Mart. Int corridors. **Pets:** Large, other species. $10 daily fee/pet. Designated rooms, service with restrictions, crate.
SAVE ✕ ⓜ 🛏 🖵 🍽 ⇌

▼▼▼ Comfort Inn Downtown Denver 🅷 🐾
(303) 296-0400. **$99-$259.** 401 17th St. I-25, exit 210 (E Colfax Ave) to Lincoln St, n to 18th St, then just w; opposite Brown Palace Hotel & Spa. Int corridors. **Pets:** Medium, dogs only. $75 one-time fee/room. Supervision.
A$K ✕ 🛏 🖵 🍽

▼▼▼ Courtyard by Marriott 🅷
(303) 333-3303. **$149-$159.** 7415 E 41st Ave. I-70, exit 278, s on Quebec St, exit Smith Rd, then e to Frontage Rd; I-270, exit 4. Int corridors. **Pets:** Accepted.
✕ 🛏 🖵 🍽 ⇌

▼▼▼ DoubleTree Hotel Denver 🅷
(303) 321-3333. **$89-$249.** 3203 Quebec St. I-70, exit 278, 0.5 mi s; I-270, exit 4. Int corridors. **Pets:** Accepted.
✕ 🛏 🖵 ⇌ 🐾

▼▼▼ Drury Inn-Denver East 🅷
(303) 373-1983. **$80-$131.** 4380 Peoria St. I-70, exit 281, just n. Int corridors. **Pets:** Other species. Service with restrictions, supervision.
A$K ✕ 🛏 🖵 ⇌

◈ ▼▼▼ Embassy Suites Denver-Aurora 🅷
(303) 375-0400. **$109-$229.** 4444 N Havana St. I-70, exit 280, just n. Int corridors. **Pets:** Accepted.
SAVE ✕ ⓜ 🛏 🖵 🍽 ⇌ 🐾

◈ ▼▼▼ The Four Points by Sheraton Denver Southeast 🅷
(303) 758-7000. **$95-$250.** 6363 E Hampden Ave. I-25, exit 201, just e. Ext/int corridors. **Pets:** Medium. Service with restrictions, supervision.
SAVE ✕ ⓜ 🛏 🖵 🍽 ⇌

▼▼▼ Hampton Inn & Suites Denver Tech Center 🅷
(303) 804-9900. **$69-$179.** 5001 S Ulster St. I-25, exit 199, e to Ulster St, then just n. Int corridors. **Pets:** Other species. Service with restrictions.
✕ ⓜ 🛏 🖵 ⇌

◈ ▼▼▼ Hampton Inn DIA 🅷
(303) 371-0200. **$115-$140.** 6290 Tower Rd. I-70, exit 286 (Tower Rd), 3.5 mi n. Int corridors. **Pets:** Accepted.
SAVE ✕ ⓜ 🖵 ⇌

◈ ▼▼▼ Holiday Chalet a Victorian Bed & Breakfast 🅱🅱 🐾
(303) 437-8245. **$94-$160.** 1820 E Colfax Ave. I-25, exit 210 (Colfax Ave), 2.3 mi e on US 40. Int corridors. **Pets:** Other species. $5 daily fee/room. Crate.
SAVE ✕ 🛏 🖵

▼▼ Holiday Inn-Denver Central 🅷
(303) 292-9500. **$79-$249.** 4849 Bannock St. I-25, exit 215 northbound; exit 214B southbound, just w to Broadway, then 1.2 mi s. Ext/int corridors. **Pets:** Accepted.
A$K ✕ ⓜ 🛏 🖵 🍽 ⇌

◈ ▼▼▼▼ Hotel Monaco Denver 🅷 🐾
(303) 296-1717. **$199-$379.** 1717 Champa St. I-25, exit 210A (W Colfax Ave), 1 mi e to Kalamath St, 0.7 mi ne, just nw on 18th St, then just sw. Int corridors. **Pets:** Other species. Designated rooms, service with restrictions, supervision.
SAVE ✕ ⓜ 🖵 🍽 ✕

◈ ▼▼▼▼ Hotel Teatro 🅷 🐾
(303) 228-1100. **$199-$1500.** 1100 14th St. I-25, exit 212B (Speer Blvd) southbound, just ne on Lawrence St, then e to 14th St; exit 212A (Speer Blvd) northbound. Int corridors. **Pets:** Dogs only.
SAVE ✕ 🛏 🖵 🍽 ✕

▼▼ Hotel VQ 🅷
(303) 433-8331. **$49-$169.** 1975 Bryant St. I-25, exit 210B, just w. Int corridors. **Pets:** Accepted.
A$K ✕ 🛏 🖵 ⇌

◈ ▼▼▼ The Inn at Cherry Creek 🅷 🐾
(303) 350-4440. **$189-$345.** 233 Clayton St. Between 2nd and 3rd aves; in Cherry Creek Village; entrance on Clayton St. Int corridors. **Pets:** Medium. $35 daily fee/room. Service with restrictions, supervision.
SAVE ✕ 🛏 🖵 🍽

▼▼▼ JW Marriott Denver At Cherry Creek 🅷
(303) 316-2700. **$309-$319.** 150 Clayton Ln. I-25, exit 205 (University Blvd), 2.4 mi n to 1st Ave, just e, then just n. Int corridors. **Pets:** Accepted.
✕ ⓜ 🛏 🍽 ✕

▼▼▼ La Quinta Inn & Suites Denver (Airport/DIA) 🅷 🐾
(303) 371-0888. **$59-$199.** 6801 Tower Rd. I-70, exit 286 (Tower Rd), 4.2 mi n; 0.8 mi s of Pena Blvd. Int corridors. **Pets:** Medium, other species. Service with restrictions, supervision.
A$K ✕ ⓜ 🛏 🖵 ⇌

▼▼ La Quinta Inn Denver (Central) 🅷 🐾
(303) 458-1222. **$59-$159.** 3500 Park Ave W. I-25, exit 213, just s on Park Ave W, then just e on Globeville Rd. Ext/int corridors. **Pets:** Medium, other species. Service with restrictions, supervision.
A$K ✕ ⓜ 🛏 🖵 ⇌

▼▼ ▼▼ La Quinta Inn Denver (Cherry Creek) H ✿
(303) 758-8886. **$59-$159.** 1975 S Colorado Blvd. I-25, exit 204, just s. Ext corridors. **Pets:** Medium, other species. Service with restrictions, supervision.
ASK ⊠ 🛢 💻 �

ΛΛΛ⁷ ▼▼▼ Microtel Inn D.I.A H
(303) 371-8300. **$66-$89.** 18600 E 63rd Ave. I-70, exit 286 (Tower Rd), 3.6 mi n. Int corridors. **Pets:** Accepted.
SAVE ⊠ ⑤M

▼▼▼▼ The Oxford Hotel H
(303) 628-5400. **Call for rates.** 1600 17th St. Corner of 17th and Wazee sts. Int corridors. **Pets:** Accepted.
⊠ 🍴 🔀

ΛΛΛ⁷ ▼▼ Quality Inn & Suites H
(303) 371-5300. **$69-$149.** 6890 Tower Rd. I-70, exit 286 (Tower Rd), 4.2 mi n; 0.8 mi s of Pena Blvd. Int corridors. **Pets:** Accepted.
SAVE ⊠ ⑤M 🛢 💻 ➥

ΛΛΛ⁷ ▼▼ Quality Inn Denver East H
(303) 371-5640. **$70-$110.** 3975 Peoria Way. I-70, exit 281 eastbound; exit 282 westbound, just s. Ext corridors. **Pets:** Small. $10 one-time fee/pet. Designated rooms, service with restrictions, supervision.
SAVE ⊠ 🛢 💻 ➥

▼▼▼▼ Radisson Hotel Denver Stapleton Plaza H
(303) 321-3500. **$129-$199.** 3333 Quebec St. I-70, exit 278, 0.3 mi s; I-270, exit 4. Int corridors. **Pets:** Accepted.
ASK ⊠ ⑤M 💻 🍴 ➥ 🔀

▼▼ ▼▼ Ramada Inn Denver Downtown H
(303) 831-7700. **$79-$119.** 1150 E Colfax Ave. I-25, exit 210 (E Colfax Ave), 1 mi e on US 40; 0.5 mi e of State Capitol. Int corridors. **Pets:** Accepted.
ASK ⊠ 🛢 💻 🍴 ➥

ΛΛΛ⁷ ▼▼▼ Ramada Suites at Denver International Airport H
(303) 373-1600. **$109-$139.** 7020 Tower Rd. I-70, exit 286 (Tower Rd), 4.5 mi n. Int corridors. **Pets:** Accepted.
SAVE ⊠ ⑤M 🛢 💻 ➥

▼▼▼▼ Red Lion Denver Central H
(303) 321-6666. **$69-$219.** 4040 Quebec St. I-70, exit 278, s on Quebec St, exit Smith Rd, then e to Frontage Rd; I-270, exit 4. Int corridors. **Pets:** Other species. $20 one-time fee/room. Service with restrictions, supervision.
ASK ⊠ 🛢 💻 🍴 ➥

▼▼▼▼ Residence Inn by Marriott Denver City Center H
(303) 296-3444. **$259-$299.** 1725 Champa St. I-25, exit 212B (Speer Blvd) southbound, 1.3 mi s to Stout St, 0.6 mi e, just n on 18th St, then just s; exit 212A (Speer Blvd) northbound. Int corridors. **Pets:** Accepted.
⊠ 🛢 💻

▼▼▼▼ Residence Inn by Marriott Denver Downtown H
(303) 458-5318. **$242-$296.** 2777 Zuni St. I-25, exit 212B, just w, then just n. Ext corridors. **Pets:** Accepted.
⊠ 🛢 💻 ➥

▼▼▼ ▼▼▼ The Ritz-Carlton, Denver H
(303) 312-3800. **$229-$399.** 1881 Curtis St. I-25, exit 212C (20th St), 1 mi se on 20th St, just sw on Arapahoe St, then just se on 17th St; jct 18th and Curtis sts. Int corridors. **Pets:** Accepted.
⊠ ⑤M 💻 🍴 ➥ 🔀

▼▼▼ ▼▼▼ TownePlace Suites by Marriott Downtown Denver H
(303) 722-2322. **$179-$229.** 685 Speer Blvd. I-25, exit 212A (Speer Blvd), 2.2 mi s, stay in right lane, just past second Bannock St, exit towards Broadway, then right on Acoma St. Int corridors. **Pets:** Accepted.
⊠ ⑤M 🛢 💻

ΛΛΛ⁷ ▼▼▼▼ Warwick Denver Hotel H
(303) 861-2000. **$129-$499.** 1776 Grant St. I-25, exit 210 a (E Colfax Ave), 1.7 mi to Logan St, just n to 18th St, then just w. Int corridors. **Pets:** Accepted.
SAVE ⊠ 🛢 💻 🍴 ➥

ΛΛΛ⁷ ▼▼▼ ▼▼▼ The Westin Tabor Center Denver H ✿
(303) 572-9100. **$159-$379.** 1672 Lawrence St. I-25, exit 212B (Speer Blvd) southbound, 1 mi s to Lawrence St, then e; exit 212A (Speer Blvd) northbound. Int corridors. **Pets:** Medium, dogs only. Service with restrictions, supervision.
SAVE ⊠ ⑤M 💻 🍴 ➥ 🔀

ENGLEWOOD

ΛΛΛ⁷ ▼▼▼▼ Comfort Suites Denver Tech Center H
(303) 858-0700. **Call for rates.** 7374 S Clinton St. I-25, exit 196 (Dry Creek Rd), just e, then n. Int corridors. **Pets:** Accepted.
SAVE ⊠ ⑤M 🛢 💻 ➥

▼▼▼ ▼▼ Drury Inn & Suites-Denver Near the Tech Center H
(303) 694-3400. **$73-$150.** 9445 E Dry Creek Rd. I-25, exit 196 (Dry Creek Rd), just w, on northwest corner. Int corridors. **Pets:** Other species. Service with restrictions, supervision.
ASK ⊠ 🛢 💻 ➥

▼▼ ▼▼ Extended Stay Deluxe-Denver Tech Center South H
(303) 858-0292. **$78-$107.** 9604 E Easter Ave. I-25, exit 197 (Arapahoe Rd), just e to Clinton St, 0.5 mi s, then just e. Int corridors. **Pets:** Other species. $25 daily fee/pet. Service with restrictions, crate.
⊠ 🛢 💻 ➥

▼▼▼▼ Holiday Inn Express Hotel & Suites H
(303) 662-0777. **$124-$135.** 7380 S Clinton St. I-25, exit 196 (Dry Creek Rd), e to S Clinton St, then just n. Int corridors. **Pets:** Small. $50 one-time fee/room. Service with restrictions, crate.
ASK ⊠ 🛢 💻 ➥

▼▼ ▼▼ Hotel Gold Crown H
(303) 790-7770. **Call for rates.** 7770 S Peoria St. I-25, exit 197 (Arapahoe Rd), 2 mi e, then 1.3 mi s; follow signs. Int corridors. **Pets:** Accepted.
⊠ 🛢 💻 ➥

▼▼▼▼ Residence Inn by Marriott-Denver Tech Center H
(303) 740-7177. **$166-$202.** 6565 S Yosemite St. I-25, exit 197 (Arapahoe Rd), just w, then n. Ext corridors. **Pets:** Accepted.
⊠ 🛢 💻 ➥ 🔀

▼▼▼▼ Residence Inn Park Meadows H
(720) 895-0200. **$169-$179.** 8322 S Valley Hwy. I-25, exit 195 (County Line Rd), just e to S Valley Hwy, then just s. Int corridors. **Pets:** Accepted.
⊠ ⑤M 🛢 💻 ➥ 🔀

▼▼▼ ▼▼ TownePlace Suites Denver Tech Center H
(720) 875-1113. **$129-$179.** 7877 S Chester St. I-25, exit 196 (Dry Creek Rd), just w to Chester St, then 0.3 mi s. Int corridors. **Pets:** Other species. $100 one-time fee/room.
⊠ ⑤M 🛢 💻 ➥

GLENDALE

▼▼▼ Crossland Studios-Denver/Cherry Creek M
(303) 333-2545. **$52-$78.** 4850 Leetsdale Dr. I-25, exit 204, 1.2 mi n, just e on Alameda, then 0.3 mi se. Ext corridors. **Pets:** Other species. $25 daily fee/pet. Service with restrictions, crate.
ASK ⊠ 🛢 💻

ΛΛΛ⁷ ▼▼▼ ▼▼▼ Loews Denver Hotel H ✿
(303) 782-9300. **$179-$279.** 4150 E Mississippi Ave. I-25, exit 204, 0.8 mi n on Colorado Blvd, then just e. Int corridors. **Pets:** Large, other species. $25 one-time fee/room. Designated rooms.
SAVE ⊠ ⑤M 🛢 💻 🍴

▼▼▼▼ **Staybridge Suites Denver/Cherry Creek** H
(303) 321-5757. **$99-$209.** 4220 E Virginia Ave. I-25, exit 204, 1.5 mi n on Colorado Blvd to Virginia Ave, then just e. Int corridors. **Pets:** Accepted.
A$K ✕ 🖥 🖥 ⊠

GOLDEN

AAA ▼▼▼▼ **The Golden Hotel, an Ascend Collection hotel** H 🐾
(303) 279-0100. **$165-$285.** 800 11th St. At 11th St and Washington Ave; downtown. Int corridors. **Pets:** Medium, other species. $15 daily fee/room. Designated rooms, service with restrictions, supervision.
SAVE ✕ 🖥 🖥 🍴

▼▼ **La Quinta Inn Denver (Golden)** H 🐾
(303) 279-5565. **$49-$139.** 3301 Youngfield Service Rd. I-70, exit 264 (32nd Ave) westbound, just w, then n; exit eastbound, just e, n on 32nd, then just e. Ext corridors. **Pets:** Medium, other species. Service with restrictions, supervision.
A$K ✕ 🖥 🖥 ⌁

▼▼▼▼ **Residence Inn by Marriott Denver West/Golden** H
(303) 271-0909. **$149-$164.** 14600 W 6th Ave Frontage Rd. US 6, exit Indiana Ave, just s to frontage road, just e. Int corridors. **Pets:** Accepted.
✕ 🖥 🖥 ⊠

AAA ▼▼▼▼ **Table Mountain Inn** H
(303) 277-9898. **$121-$209.** 1310 Washington Ave. US 6, exit 19th St, 0.5 mi n to Washington Ave, 0.5 mi w; downtown, just s of arch. Int corridors. **Pets:** Accepted.
SAVE ✕ 🖥 🖥 🍴

GREENWOOD VILLAGE

▼▼▼▼ **Hampton Inn Denver Southeast** H
(303) 792-9999. **$104-$146.** 9231 E Arapahoe Rd. I-25, exit 197 (Arapahoe Rd), just e. Int corridors. **Pets:** Accepted.
✕ 🖥 🖥 ⌁

▼▼ **Homestead Studio Suites Hotel-Denver/Tech Center South-Greenwood Village** H
(303) 858-1669. **$67-$91.** 9253 E Costilla Ave. I-25, exit 197 (Arapahoe Rd), just e, just se on Clinton St to Costilla St, then w. Int corridors. **Pets:** Other species. $25 daily fee/pet. Service with restrictions, crate.
A$K ✕ 🖥 🖥 ⌁

AAA ▼▼▼▼ **Hyatt Summerfield Suites Hotel** H
(303) 706-1945. **$89-$299.** 9280 E Costilla Ave. I-25, exit 197 (Arapahoe Rd), e to Clinton St, then just s. Int corridors. **Pets:** Accepted.
SAVE ✕ 🖥 🖥 ⌁

▼▼▼▼ **La Quinta Inn & Suites Denver Tech Center** H 🐾
(303) 649-9969. **$69-$169.** 7077 S Clinton St. I-25, exit 197 (Arapahoe Rd), e to Clinton St, then s. Int corridors. **Pets:** Medium, other species. Service with restrictions, supervision.
A$K ✕ 🖥 🖥 ⌁

▼▼▼▼ **La Quinta Inn & Suites Englewood** H 🐾
(303) 799-4555. **$69-$169.** 9009 E Arapahoe Rd. I-25, exit 197 (Arapahoe Rd), just e to Boston, n to Southtech, then just w. Int corridors. **Pets:** Medium, other species. Service with restrictions, supervision.
A$K ✕ 🖥 🖥 ⌁ ⊠

AAA ▼▼▼▼ **Sheraton Denver Tech Center Hotel** H 🐾
(303) 799-6200. **$79-$299.** 7007 S Clinton St. I-25, exit 197 (Arapahoe Rd), just e, then s. Int corridors. **Pets:** Medium, dogs only. Supervision.
SAVE ✕ 🖥 🖥 🍴 ⌁

HIGHLANDS RANCH

▼▼▼▼ **Residence Inn Denver South Highlands Ranch** H 🐾
(303) 683-5500. **$197-$241.** 93 Centennial Blvd. SR 470, exit Broadway, just s, then w. Int corridors. **Pets:** Large. $100 one-time fee/room. Service with restrictions, supervision.
✕ 🖥 🖥 🖥 ⌁ ⊠

LAKEWOOD

AAA ▼▼▼▼ **Best Western-Denver Southwest** H
(303) 989-5500. **$84-$119.** 3440 S Vance St. Just ne of jct US 285 (Hampden Ave) and S Wadsworth Blvd, e on Girton Dr, then just s. Int corridors. **Pets:** Designated rooms, service with restrictions, supervision.
SAVE ✕ 🖥 🖥 ⌁

▼▼▼ **Comfort Suites-Lakewood/Golden** H
(303) 231-9929. **$99-$149.** 11909 W 6th Ave. US 6, exit Simms St/Union Blvd, westbound travelers must turn right at stop light, but do not use right turn lane, follow signs to frontage road. Int corridors. **Pets:** Accepted.
A$K ✕ 🖥 🖥 ⌁ ⊠

AAA ▼▼▼▼ **Holiday Inn Lakewood** H
(303) 980-9200. **$99-$139.** 7390 W Hampden Ave. US 285 (W Hampden Ave), exit Wadsworth Blvd, just e on Jefferson Ave, then n on Vance. Int corridors. **Pets:** Accepted.
SAVE ✕ 🖥 🖥 🍴 ⌁ ⊠

▼▼ **Lakewood Comfort Suites** H
(303) 988-8600. **$80-$150.** 7260 W Jefferson Ave. Just se of US 285 (W Hampden Ave) and Wadsworth Blvd, then e. Int corridors. **Pets:** Accepted.
A$K ✕ 🖥 🖥 ⌁

▼▼▼▼ **La Quinta Inn & Suites Denver (Southwest/Lakewood)** M 🐾
(303) 969-9700. **$59-$169.** 7190 W Hampden Ave. Just se of jct US 285 (W Hampden Ave) and Wadsworth Blvd, e on Jefferson Ave, just n, then e on frontage road. Int corridors. **Pets:** Medium, other species. Service with restrictions, supervision.
A$K ✕ 🖥 🖥 🖥 ⌁

▼▼▼▼ **Residence Inn by Marriott Denver SW/Lakewood** H
(303) 985-7676. **$129-$169.** 7050 W Hampden Ave. Just se of jct US 285 (W Hampden Ave) and Wadsworth Blvd, e on Jefferson Ave, then n on frontage road. Int corridors. **Pets:** Accepted.
✕ 🖥 🖥 ⌁ ⊠

AAA ▼▼▼▼ **Sheraton-Denver West Hotel** H 🐾
(303) 987-2000. **$219.** 360 Union Blvd. US 6, exit Simms St/Union Blvd, s on Union Blvd; I-70, exit 261, 3 mi e. Int corridors. **Pets:** Medium, dogs only. Service with restrictions, supervision.
SAVE ✕ 🖥 🖥 🍴 ⊠

▼▼ **TownePlace Suites by Marriott-Denver West/Federal Center** H
(303) 232-7790. **$109-$149.** 800 Tabor St. US 6, exit Simms St/Union Blvd, just n to 8th St, then w. Int corridors. **Pets:** Accepted.
✕ 🖥 🖥 ⌁

LITTLETON

AAA ▼▼▼▼ **Holiday Inn Express** H
(720) 981-1000. **$99-$129.** 12683 W Indore Pl. I-70 to SR 470 and Ken Caryl Ave; I-25 to SR 470 and Ken Caryl Ave, to Shaffer Ave, just n, then w. Int corridors. **Pets:** Accepted.
SAVE ✕ 🖥 🖥 ⌁

LONE TREE

▼▼▼▼ **Staybridge Suites Denver South-Lone Tree** H
(303) 649-1010. **Call for rates.** 7820 Park Meadows Dr. I-25, exit 195 (County Line Rd), w to Acres Green, s to E Park Meadows Dr, then just w; SR 470, exit Quebec St, just s, then just e. Int corridors. **Pets:** Accepted.
✕ 🖥 🖥 ⌁ ⊠

THORNTON

▼▼ Sleep Inn North Denver 🅷 ❄
(303) 280-9818. **$64-$159.** 12101 Grant St. I-25, exit 223, e to Grant St, then n. Int corridors. **Pets:** Other species. $5 daily fee/pet. Designated rooms, service with restrictions.
🅰🆂🅺 ⊠ � 🔧 💻 ⤳

WESTMINSTER

⚫ ▼▼ Comfort Inn Northwest 🅷
(303) 428-3333. **$79-$210.** 8500 Turnpike Dr. US 36 (Boulder Tpke), exit Sheridan Ave, just s, left on Turnpike Dr at 87th Ave, then 0.4 mi. Int corridors. **Pets:** Other species. $10 daily fee/pet. Designated rooms, service with restrictions.
[SAVE] ⊠ � 🔧 💻 ⤳

▼▼ Denver North-Westminster-Super 8 🅷
(303) 451-7200. **$56-$81, 3 day notice.** 12055 Melody Dr. I-25, exit 223, just w. Int corridors. **Pets:** $5 daily fee/pet. Service with restrictions, supervision.
🅰🆂🅺 ⊠ 🔧 💻 ⊠

⚫ ▼▼ DoubleTree Hotel Denver North 🅷 ❄
(303) 427-4000. **$109-$239.** 8773 Yates Dr. US 36 (Boulder Tpke), exit Sheridan Ave, n to 92nd Ave, e to Yates Dr, then 0.5 mi s. Int corridors. **Pets:** $25 one-time fee/room. Service with restrictions, supervision.
[SAVE] ⊠ 💻 🍴 ⤳

⚫ ▼▼ La Quinta Inn & Suites Westminster (Promenade) 🅷 ❄
(303) 438-5800. **$59-$159.** 10179 Church Ranch Way. US 36 (Boulder Tpke), exit Church Ranch Blvd, just s to 103rd Pl, then e. Int corridors. **Pets:** Medium, other species. Service with restrictions, supervision.
[SAVE] ⊠ � 🔧 💻 ⤳

▼▼ La Quinta Inn Denver (Northglenn) 🅷 ❄
(303) 252-9800. **$49-$139.** 345 W 120th Ave. I-25, exit 223, just w. Ext/int corridors. **Pets:** Medium, other species. Service with restrictions, supervision.
🅰🆂🅺 ⊠ 🔧 💻 ⤳

▼▼ La Quinta Inn Denver (Westminster Mall) 🅷 ❄
(303) 425-9099. **$49-$139.** 8701 Turnpike Dr. US 36 (Boulder Tpke), exit Sheridan Ave, just s, then left on Turnpike Dr at 87th Ave. Ext/int corridors. **Pets:** Medium, other species. Service with restrictions, supervision.
🅰🆂🅺 ⊠ � 🔧 💻 ⤳

▼▼ Residence Inn by Marriott 🅷
(303) 427-9500. **$135-$160.** 5010 W 88th Pl. US 36 (Boulder Tpke), exit Sheridan Ave, n to 92nd Ave, e to Yates Dr, then s. Int corridors. **Pets:** Accepted.
⊠ � 🔧 💻 ⤳ ⊠

⚫ ▼▼▼▼ The Westin Westminster 🅷
(303) 410-5000. **$119-$349.** 10600 Westminster Blvd. US 36 (Boulder Tpke), exit 104th Ave, just n. Int corridors. **Pets:** Accepted.
[SAVE] ⊠ � 🔧 💻 🍴 ⤳ ⊠

WHEAT RIDGE

▼▼▼▼ Holiday Inn Express Hotel & Suites 🅷
(303) 424-8300. **Call for rates.** 10101 W 48th Ave. I-70, exit 267, just sw. Int corridors. **Pets:** Accepted.
⊠ 🔧 💻 ⤳

END METROPOLITAN AREA

DILLON

⚫ ▼▼ Best Western Ptarmigan Lodge 🅷
(970) 468-2341. **$75-$180.** 652 Lake Dillon Dr. I-70, exit 205, 1.3 mi se on US 6, then 0.3 mi s. Ext/int corridors. **Pets:** $15 one-time fee/pet. Designated rooms, service with restrictions, crate.
[SAVE] ⊠ 🔧 💻 ⊠ 🅜

DURANGO

▼ Caboose Motel 🅼
(970) 247-1191. **$58-$190.** 3363 Main Ave. On US 550, 2.5 mi n. Ext corridors. **Pets:** Small, dogs only. $12 daily fee/pet. Designated rooms, service with restrictions, supervision.
🅰🆂🅺 ⊠ 🔧 💻

▼▼▼ DoubleTree Hotel Durango 🅷
(970) 259-6580. **$79-$214.** 501 Camino Del Rio. Jct US 160 and 550. Int corridors. **Pets:** Accepted.
⊠ 🔧 💻 🍴 ⤳ ⊠

▼▼ Holiday Inn 🅷
(970) 247-5393. **Call for rates.** 800 Camino Del Rio. On US 550, just n of jct US 160. Ext corridors. **Pets:** Accepted.
⊠ 💻 🍴 ⤳ ⊠

▼▼ Quality Inn 🅼 ❄
(970) 259-5373. **$70-$180.** 2930 N Main Ave. On US 550, 2.1 mi n. Ext corridors. **Pets:** Medium, dogs only. $10 one-time fee/pet. Designated rooms, service with restrictions, supervision.
🅰🆂🅺 ⊠ 💻 ⤳

▼▼▼ Residence Inn by Marriott 🅷
(970) 259-6200. **$175-$213.** 21691 Hwy 160 W. On US 160, just w. Int corridors. **Pets:** Accepted.
⊠ � 🔧 💻 ⤳ ⊠

▼▼▼▼ The Rochester Hotel 🅱🅱 ❄
(970) 385-1920. **$119-$369, 14 day notice.** 726 E 2nd Ave. Just e of Main Ave via 7th St, then just n. Int corridors. **Pets:** Dogs only. $20 daily fee/pet. Designated rooms, service with restrictions, supervision.
🅰🆂🅺 ⊠ 🔧 💻

▼ Siesta Motel 🅼
(970) 247-0741. **$58-$145.** 3475 N Main Ave. On US 550, 2.6 mi n. Ext corridors. **Pets:** Medium, dogs only. $10 daily fee/pet. Designated rooms, service with restrictions, supervision.
🅰🆂🅺 ⊠ 🔧 💻

EAGLE

⚫ ▼▼ Best Western Eagle Lodge & Suites 🅷
(970) 328-6316. **$105-$275.** 200 Loren Ln. I-70, exit 147, just s. Int corridors. **Pets:** Accepted.
[SAVE] 🔧 💻 ⤳ ⊠

EDWARDS

⚫ ▼▼▼ Inn and Suites at Riverwalk 🅷 ❄
(970) 926-0606. **$100-$800, 14 day notice.** 27 Main St. I-70, exit 163, 0.3 mi s. Int corridors. **Pets:** Large. $5 daily fee/pet, $25 one-time fee/pet. Designated rooms, service with restrictions, crate.
[SAVE] ⊠ 🔧 💻 🍴 ⤳

ESTES PARK

♦♦♦ ▼▼◆ Castle Mountain Lodge 🅒🅐
(970) 586-3664. **$70-$575, 30 day notice.** 1520 Fall River Rd. 1 mi w on US 34. Ext corridors. **Pets:** Dogs only. $15 daily fee/pet. Designated rooms, service with restrictions, supervision.
SAVE ✕ 🛏 🖳 ⊠ 🐾 🐾

▼▼◆ Holiday Inn Rocky Mountain Park 🄷 🐾
(970) 586-2332. **Call for rates.** 101 S St Vrain Ave. 0.5 mi se; on SR 7 at US 36. Int corridors. **Pets:** Other species. $30 one-time fee/room. Designated rooms.
✕ 🕭 🛏 🖳 🍴 🐾 🐾

▼▼ McGregor Mountain Lodge 🅒🅐
(970) 586-3457. **$95-$385, 30 day notice.** 2815 Fall River Rd. 3.5 mi w on US 34. Ext corridors. **Pets:** Accepted.
✕ 🛏 🖳 🐾 🐾 🐾

▼▼▼ Mountain Shadows Resort 🄼
(970) 577-0397. **$174, 14 day notice.** 871 Riverside Dr. 1.8 mi sw on US 36, just s on Mary's Lake Rd to Riverside Dr, then just e. Ext corridors. **Pets:** Accepted.
ASK ✕ 🛏 🖳 🐾

♦♦♦ ▼▼◆ Silver Moon Inn 🄼
(970) 586-6006. **$80-$229.** 175 Spruce Dr. Just w on US 34, then just ne. Ext corridors. **Pets:** Accepted.
SAVE ✕ 🛏 🖳 🐾 🐾

EVANS

▼▼ Select Stay 🄷
(970) 356-2180. **$59-$135.** 3025 8th Ave. Just sw of jct US 34 and 85 Bypass. Int corridors. **Pets:** Accepted.
ASK ✕ 🕭 🛏 🖳 🐾

EVERGREEN

▼▼▼ Quality Suites at Evergreen Parkway 🄷 🐾
(303) 526-2000. **$109-$189, 3 day notice.** 29300 US Hwy 40. I-70, exit 252 (Evergreen Pkwy), on west side of El Rancho Restaurant; exit 251 eastbound. Int corridors. **Pets:** $50 deposit/pet. Designated rooms, service with restrictions, supervision.
ASK ✕ 🕭 🛏 🖳 🐾 🐾

FORT COLLINS

♦♦♦ ▼▼◆ AmericInn Lodge & Suites of Fort Collins South 🄷 🐾
(970) 226-1232. **$89-$169.** 7645 Westgate Dr. I-25, exit 262, just se off SR 392. Int corridors. **Pets:** Medium. $10 daily fee/room. Designated rooms, service with restrictions, supervision.
SAVE ✕ 🕭 🛏 🖳 🐾

♦♦♦ ▼▼▼ Best Western University Inn 🄼
(970) 484-1984. **$69-$159.** 914 S College Ave. I-25, exit 268, 4 mi w to College Ave, then just n on US 287. Ext/int corridors. **Pets:** Other species. $15 daily fee/pet. Designated rooms, service with restrictions, supervision.
SAVE ✕ 🛏 🖳 🐾

▼▼◆ Comfort Suites by Choice Hotels 🄷
(970) 206-4597. **Call for rates.** 1415 Oakridge Dr. I-25, exit 265, 3.3 mi w to McMurray Ave, just s, then w. Int corridors. **Pets:** Accepted.
✕ 🛏 🖳 🐾

▼▼◆ Hampton Inn 🄷 🐾
(970) 229-5927. **$109-$199.** 1620 Oakridge Dr. I-25, exit 265, 3.3 mi w, s on McMurray Ave to Oakridge Dr, then just e. Int corridors. **Pets:** Other species. $25 one-time fee/room. Supervision.
✕ 🕭 🛏 🖳 🐾

♦♦♦ ▼▼▼ Hilton Ft Collins 🄷
(970) 482-2626. **$109-$229.** 425 W Prospect Rd. I-25, exit 268, 4.3 mi w. Int corridors. **Pets:** Accepted.
SAVE ✕ 🛏 🖳 🍴 🐾 🐾

▼▼◆ Homewood Suites by Hilton Fort Collins 🄷
(970) 225-2400. **$99-$199.** 1521 Oakridge Dr. I-25, exit 265, 3 mi w, just s on McMurry, then just w. Int corridors. **Pets:** Accepted.
✕ 🛏 🖳 🐾 🐾

♦♦♦ ▼▼◆ La Quinta Inn 🄷 🐾
(970) 493-7800. **$55-$159.** 3709 E Mulberry St. I-25, exit 269B, just w, then just sw on frontage road. Int corridors. **Pets:** Medium, other species. Service with restrictions, supervision.
SAVE ✕ 🛏 🖳 🐾 🐾

♦♦♦ ▼▼◆ Quality Inn & Suites 🄷
(970) 282-9047. **$89-$209.** 4001 S Mason St. I-25, exit 265, 4.6 mi w to Mason St, then 0.5 mi n. Int corridors. **Pets:** Other species. $25 one-time fee/room. Designated rooms, service with restrictions, supervision.
SAVE ✕ 🕭 🛏 🖳 🐾

▼▼ Sleep Inn 🄷
(970) 484-5515. **$89-$129.** 3808 E Mulberry St. I-25, exit 269B, just nw. Int corridors. **Pets:** Large. $10 one-time fee/room. Service with restrictions, crate.
ASK ✕ 🛏 🖳

▼▼ Super 8 🄷
(970) 493-7701. **$52-$150, 14 day notice.** 409 Centro Way. I-25, exit 269B, just w. Int corridors. **Pets:** Medium, other species. $10 daily fee/pet. No service, supervision.
✕ 🛏 🖳 🐾

FORT MORGAN

♦♦♦ ▼▼▼ Best Western Park Terrace Inn 🄷 🐾
(970) 867-8256. **$75-$87.** 725 Main St. I-76, exit 80, 0.5 mi s. Ext corridors. **Pets:** Large. $15 one-time fee/room. Designated rooms, service with restrictions, supervision.
SAVE ✕ 🛏 🖳 🍴 🐾

♦♦♦ ▼▼▼ Central Motel 🄼
(970) 867-2401. **$52-$69.** 201 W Platte Ave. I-76, exit 80, 0.6 mi s, then w on US 34. Ext corridors. **Pets:** Other species. $10 one-time fee/room. Service with restrictions, supervision.
SAVE ✕ 🛏 🖳

▼▼ Rodeway Inn 🄼 🐾
(970) 867-9481. **$79-$129.** 1409 Barlow Rd. I-76, exit 82 (Barlow Rd), just n. Ext/int corridors. **Pets:** Small. $10 daily fee/room. Service with restrictions, supervision.
ASK ✕ 🛏 🖳 🍴

FRISCO

♦♦♦ ▼▼▼ Best Western Lake Dillon Lodge 🄷
(970) 668-5094. **$96-$211, 3 day notice.** 1202 Summit Blvd. I-70, exit 203, just s. Int corridors. **Pets:** Other species. $15 one-time fee/room. Designated rooms, service with restrictions, supervision.
SAVE ✕ 🛏 🖳 🍴 🐾 🐾

▼▼ Hotel Frisco 🄷 🐾
(970) 668-5009. **$59-$319, 14 day notice.** 308 Main. I-70, exit 201, 0.7 mi e; center. Ext/int corridors. **Pets:** Other species. $10 daily fee/pet. No service.
ASK ✕ 🛏 🖳 ⊠

♦♦♦ ▼▼◆ New Summit Inn 🄷
(970) 668-3220. **$49-$159, 15 day notice.** 1205 N Summit Blvd. I-70, exit 203, just s, then just e. Int corridors. **Pets:** Dogs only. $10 daily fee/pet. Service with restrictions, supervision.
SAVE ✕ 🛏 🖳

Ramada Limited Frisco 🅷 ✿
(970) 668-8783. **Call for rates.** 990 Lakepoint Dr. I-70, exit 203, just s. Int corridors. **Pets:** Other species. $10 daily fee/room. Designated rooms, no service, supervision.
(SAVE) ✕ (&M) ⊟ 🖵

Snowshoe Motel Ⓜ
(970) 668-3444. **$49-$140.** 521 Main St. I-70, exit 203 westbound, 1 mi s to Main St, then just w; exit 201 eastbound, then 0.8 mi e. Ext corridors. **Pets:** $10 one-time fee/pet. Designated rooms, service with restrictions, supervision.
(SAVE) ✕ ⊟ 🖵 🎾

FRUITA

Balanced Rock Motel Ⓜ ✿
(970) 858-7333. **$55-$65, 3 day notice.** 126 S Coulson. I-70, exit 19, just n to Aspen Ave, then just w. Ext corridors. **Pets:** $5 daily fee/pet. Designated rooms, service with restrictions, supervision.
(ASK) ✕ ⊟

Comfort Inn 🅷
(970) 858-1333. **$55-$199.** 400 Jurassic Ave. I-70, exit 19, 0.3 mi s; just e of Dinosaur Journey Museum. Int corridors. **Pets:** Other species. Designated rooms, supervision.
(SAVE) ✕ ⊟ 🖵 🏊

La Quinta Inn & Suites 🅷 ✿
(970) 858-8850. **$79-$199.** 570 Raptor Rd. I-70, exit 19, 0.3 mi s; next to Dinosaur Journey Museum. Int corridors. **Pets:** Medium, other species. Service with restrictions, supervision.
(ASK) ✕ ⊟ 🖵 🏊

Super 8 🅷
(970) 858-0808. **$55-$85.** 399 Jurassic Ave. I-70, exit 19, 0.3 mi s; just e of Dinosaur Journey Museum. Int corridors. **Pets:** Accepted.
(SAVE) ✕ ⊟ 🖵 🏊

GLENWOOD SPRINGS

AmericInn Lodge & Suites of Glenwood Springs 🅷
(970) 928-8188. **$155-$235.** 52000 Two Rivers Plaza Rd. I-70, exit 116, just w on US 6 and 24. Int corridors. **Pets:** Accepted.
(ASK) ✕ ⊟ 🖵 🏊 🐾

Hotel Colorado 🅷
(970) 945-6511. **$169-$799, 3 day notice.** 526 Pine St. I-70, exit 116, just ne. Int corridors. **Pets:** Accepted.
(SAVE) ✕ ⊟ 🖵 🍽 🐾 🎾

Hotel Denver 🅷 ✿
(970) 945-6565. **Call for rates.** 402 7th St. I-70, exit 116; across from historic train station; in town center. Int corridors. **Pets:** Dogs only. Service with restrictions, crate.
✕ ⊟ 🖵 🍽

Quality Inn & Suites 🅷
(970) 945-5995. **$99-$169.** 2650 Gilstrap. I-70, exit 114, just s, then w. Int corridors. **Pets:** Small, other species. $10 daily fee/pet, $10 one-time fee/pet. Designated rooms, service with restrictions, supervision.
(ASK) ✕ ⊟ 🖵 🏊

Ramada Inn & Suites 🅷
(970) 945-2500. **$115-$200.** 124 W 6th St. I-70, exit 116, just w. Ext/int corridors. **Pets:** Accepted.
(ASK) ✕ ⊟ 🖵 🍽 🏊

GRAND JUNCTION

Americas Best Value Inn Ⓜ
(970) 245-1410. **$66-$120.** 754 Horizon Dr. I-70, exit 31, 0.3 mi n. Ext corridors. **Pets:** Other species. Service with restrictions, supervision.
(SAVE) ✕ ⊟ 🖵 🏊

Best Western Sandman Motel 🅷 ✿
(970) 243-4150. **$65-$130, 3 day notice.** 708 Horizon Dr. I-70, exit 31, 0.3 mi s. Ext corridors. **Pets:** Small, dogs only. $25 one-time fee/pet. Designated rooms, service with restrictions, supervision.
(SAVE) ✕ ⊟ 🖵 🏊

Clarion Inn 🅷
(970) 243-6790. **$89-$109.** 755 Horizon Dr. I-70, exit 31, just s. Ext/int corridors. **Pets:** Other species. Designated rooms, service with restrictions, supervision.
(SAVE) ✕ ⊟ 🖵 🍽 🏊 🎾

Grand Vista Hotel 🅷
(970) 241-8411. **$79-$109.** 2790 Crossroads Blvd. I-70, exit 31, 0.3 mi n. Int corridors. **Pets:** $10 daily fee/room. Designated rooms, service with restrictions, supervision.
(SAVE) ✕ ⊟ 🖵 🍽 🏊 🎾

Hawthorn Suites 🅷
(970) 242-2525. **Call for rates.** 225 Main St. At 2nd and Main sts; downtown. Int corridors. **Pets:** Accepted.
✕ ⊟ 🖵 🏊 🎾

La Quinta Inn & Suites 🅷 ✿
(970) 241-2929. **$69-$199.** 2761 Crossroads Blvd. I-70, exit 31, n to Crossroads Blvd, then just w. Int corridors. **Pets:** Medium, other species. Service with restrictions, supervision.
(ASK) ✕ ⊟ 🖵 🏊

Quality Inn of Grand Junction 🅷
(970) 245-7200. **$79-$199.** 733 Horizon Dr. I-70, exit 31, just s. Int corridors. **Pets:** Medium. $10 daily fee/room. Designated rooms, service with restrictions, supervision.
(SAVE) ✕ ⊟ 🖵 🍽 🏊

Residence Inn by Marriott 🅷 ✿
(970) 263-4004. **$129-$179.** 767 Horizon Dr. I-70, exit 31, just n. Int corridors. **Pets:** Other species. $100 one-time fee/room. Service with restrictions, crate.
✕ ⊟ 🖵 🏊

Super 8 🅷
(970) 248-8080. **$69-$97.** 728 Horizon Dr. I-70, exit 31, just s. Int corridors. **Pets:** Accepted.
(SAVE) ✕ 🖵 🏊

GRAND LAKE

Spirit Lake Lodge Ⓜ
(970) 627-3344. **$55-$200, 7 day notice.** 829 Grand Ave. Just e of US 34; downtown. Ext corridors. **Pets:** $15 daily fee/pet. No service, supervision.
(SAVE) ✕ ⊟ 🖵

GREAT SAND DUNES NATIONAL PARK AND PRESERVE

Great Sand Dunes Lodge Ⓜ
(719) 378-2900. **$89-$95.** 7900 Hwy 150 N. From Alamosa, 16 mi e on US 160, then 16 mi n. Ext corridors. **Pets:** Medium, dogs only. $10 daily fee/pet. Designated rooms, service with restrictions, supervision.
✕ ⊟ 🖵 🏊

GREELEY

Clarion Hotel & Conference Center 🅷
(970) 353-8444. **Call for rates.** 701 8th St. On US 85 business route; downtown. Int corridors. **Pets:** Accepted.
✕ (&M) ⊟ 🖵 🍽 🏊

Comfort Inn-Greeley 🅷
(970) 330-6380. **$90-$130.** 2467 W 29th St. US 34 Bypass, exit 23rd Ave, just sw. Int corridors. **Pets:** Other species. $15 daily fee/pet. Service with restrictions, supervision.
(ASK) ✕ ⊟ 🖵 🏊

 Country Inn & Suites By Carlson **H** ❀
(970) 330-3404. **$95-$107.** 2501 W 29th St. US 34 Bypass, exit 23rd Ave, just s, then w. Int corridors. **Pets:** Medium. $25 daily fee/pet. Service with restrictions, supervision.

⌖ ⊠ 🔥 🛏 💻 🏊

Days Inn **H**
(970) 392-1530. **Call for rates.** 5630 W 10th St. 5 mi w on US 34 business route; entry via 54th Ave off 10th St. Int corridors. **Pets:** $15 daily fee/pet. Service with restrictions, supervision.

⊠ 🔥 🛏 💻

GUNNISON

 ABC Motel **M**
(970) 641-2400. **$56-$99.** 212 E Tomichi Ave. On US 50; near Western State College. Ext corridors. **Pets:** Dogs only. $10 one-time fee/pet. Designated rooms, service with restrictions, supervision.

⌂ ⊠ 🛏

Affordable Inns at Tomichi Village **H**
(970) 641-1131. **$55-$149.** 41883 Hwy 50 E. Jct SR 135, 2 mi e. Ext corridors. **Pets:** Accepted.

⌂ ⊠ 🛏 💻 🏊

Alpine Inn **M**
(970) 641-2804. **$39-$170.** 1011 W Rio Grande. Jct US 50 and SR 135, 1.1 mi w. Int corridors. **Pets:** Accepted.

⌖ ⊠ 🛏 💻 🏊

Gunnison Inn **M** ❀
(970) 641-0700. **$55-$85.** 412 E Tomichi Ave. On US 50; near Western State College. Ext corridors. **Pets:** $10 daily fee/pet. Service with restrictions, crate.

⌂ ⊠ 🛏

Rodeway Inn **H** ❀
(970) 641-0500. **$55-$109.** 37760 W Hwy 50. US 50, 2.3 mi w. Ext corridors. **Pets:** Small. $10 daily fee/pet. Designated rooms, service with restrictions, supervision.

⌖ ⊠ 🛏 💻

Super 8 **M**
(970) 641-3068. **$55-$135.** 411 E Tomichi Ave. On US 50; near Western State College. Int corridors. **Pets:** Medium, other species. $15 daily fee/pet. Designated rooms, service with restrictions, supervision.

⌖ ⊠ 🛏 💻

Water Wheel Inn **H**
(970) 641-1650. **$69-$109.** 37478 W Hwy 50. Jct SR 135, 2.5 mi w. Ext/int corridors. **Pets:** $5 daily fee/pet. Designated rooms, service with restrictions, supervision.

⌂ ⊠ 🛏 💻

HOT SULPHUR SPRINGS

Canyon Motel **M**
(970) 725-3395. **$49-$99.** 221 Byers Ave. On US 40. Ext corridors. **Pets:** Dogs only. $10 daily fee/room. Designated rooms, no service, supervision.

⌂ ⊠ 🛏 💻 🐾

JULESBURG

Budget Host Platte Valley Inn **H**
(970) 474-3336. **$53-$65.** 15225 Hwy 385. I-76, exit 180, just n. Ext corridors. **Pets:** Dogs only. $7 daily fee/pet. Designated rooms, service with restrictions, supervision.

⌂ ⊠ 🛏 💻 🍴 🏊

KEYSTONE

The Inn at Keystone **H** ❀
(970) 496-4825. **$109-$319, 21 day notice.** 23044 Hwy 6. I-70, exit 205, 6.5 mi e on US 6; at Keystone Ski area. Int corridors. **Pets:** Other species. $25 daily fee/room. Service with restrictions.

⌂ ⊠ 🛏 💻 🍴 🐾 🐾

LA JUNTA

Holiday Inn Express **M**
(719) 384-2900. **$109-$124.** 27994 US Hwy 50 Frontage Rd. On US 50, 0.8 mi w. Int corridors. **Pets:** $20 daily fee/room. Service with restrictions, supervision.

⌖ ⊠ 🛏 💻 🏊

LAKE CITY

Matterhorn Mountain Motel **M**
(970) 944-2210. **$89-$135, 14 day notice.** 409 Bluff St. Just w of SR 149 via 4th St. Ext corridors. **Pets:** Medium, dogs only. $20 one-time fee/pet. Designated rooms, no service, supervision.

⊠ 🛏 💻 🐾 🐾

LAKE GEORGE

Mule Creek Outfitters/M Lazy C Ranch **RA**
(719) 748-3398. **$75-$110, 30 day notice.** 801 CR 453. 5 mi w on US 24, 0.8 mi n on dirt road. Ext corridors. **Pets:** Dogs only. $50 deposit/pet. Designated rooms, no service, supervision.

⌂ ⊠ 🛏 💻 🐾 🐾 🐾 🐾

LAMAR

Blue Spruce Motel **M**
(719) 336-7454. **$50-$85.** 1801 S Main St. 1.3 mi s on US 287 and 385. Ext corridors. **Pets:** Other species. $5 daily fee/pet. Designated rooms, no service, supervision.

⌂ ⊠ 🛏 💻 🏊

Chek Inn **M**
(719) 336-4331. **$45-$75.** 1210 S Main St. 1 mi s on US 287 and 385. Ext corridors. **Pets:** Other species. $5 daily fee/pet. Designated rooms, no service, supervision.

⌂ ⊠ 🛏 💻 🏊

LAS ANIMAS

Best Western Bent's Fort Inn **M**
(719) 456-0011. **$64-$82, 3 day notice.** 10950 E US 50. On US 50, 1.5 mi e on frontage road. Int corridors. **Pets:** Accepted.

⌂ ⊠ 💻 🍴 🏊

LEADVILLE

Alps Motel **M**
(719) 486-1223. **$60-$85, 5 day notice.** 207 Elm St. Just s on US 24. Int corridors. **Pets:** $18 daily fee/pet. Service with restrictions, supervision.

⌂ ⊠ 🛏 💻 🐾

LIMON

Best Western Limon Inn **H**
(719) 775-0277. **$70-$120.** 925 T Ave. I-70, exit 359, just s. Int corridors. **Pets:** Accepted.

⌂ ⊠ 🛏 💻 🏊

Safari Motel **M**
(719) 775-2363. **$45-$110.** 637 Main St. I-70, exit 361, 0.8 mi w. Ext corridors. **Pets:** Other species. $5 one-time fee/pet. Designated rooms, service with restrictions, supervision.

⌂ ⊠ 🛏 💻 🏊

LONGMONT

WW WWW Hawthorn Suites H
(303) 774-7100. **$89-$189.** 2000 Sunset Way. Jct US 287, 1.3 mi w on SR 119, just n on Sunset St, then just w on Korte Pkwy. Int corridors. **Pets:** Medium, other species. $50 deposit/pet. Service with restrictions, supervision.
SAVE ✕ ⑤M 🔌 🖵 ⊶ ⊠

WW WWWW Radisson Hotel & Conference Center
Longmont-Boulder H
(303) 776-2000. **$139-$189.** 1900 Ken Pratt Blvd. Jct US 287, 1.3 mi sw on SR 119. Int corridors. **Pets:** Accepted.
SAVE ✕ 🔌 🖵 ⑪ ⊶

WWWW Residence Inn by Marriott Boulder/Longmont H
(303) 702-9933. **$149-$169.** 1450 Dry Creek Dr. Jct Main St and Ken Pratt Blvd (SR 119), 2.2 mi w on SR 119, just n, then just ne; jct Hoover Rd and SR 119. Int corridors. **Pets:** Large, other species. $100 one-time fee/room. Service with restrictions, supervision.
✕ ⑤M 🔌 🖵 ⊶ ⊠

WW WW Super 8 Motel M
(303) 772-0888. **Call for rates.** 10805 Turner Blvd. I-25, exit 240, just w, then s. Int corridors. **Pets:** Accepted.
✕ 🔌 🖵

WW WW Super 8 Twin Peaks, Longmont H
(303) 772-8106. **$57-$125.** 2446 N Main St. I-25, exit 240, 6.9 mi w to US 287 (Main St), then 3.5 mi n at jct SR 66. Int corridors. **Pets:** $10 daily fee/pet. Designated rooms, service with restrictions, supervision.
SAVE ✕ 🔌 🖵

LOUISVILLE

WW WW Comfort Inn in Boulder County H ❀
(303) 604-0181. **$60-$150.** 1196 Dillon Rd. US 36 (Boulder Tpke), exit Superior (SR 170), just n on McCaslin Blvd, then just w. Int corridors. **Pets:** Large, dogs only. $15 daily fee/pet. Supervision.
SAVE ✕ ⑤M 🔌 🖵

WWW La Quinta Inn & Suites Denver
(Louisville/Boulder) H ❀
(303) 664-0100. **$59-$169.** 902 Dillon Rd. US 36 (Boulder Tpke), exit Superior (SR 170), just n on McCaslin Blvd, then e. Int corridors. **Pets:** Medium, other species. Service with restrictions, supervision.
ASK ✕ ⑤M 🔌 🖵 ⊶

WW WW Quality Inn & Suites H
(303) 327-1215. **Call for rates.** 960 W Dillon Rd. US 36 (Boulder Tpke), exit Superior (SR 170), just n on McCaslin Blvd to Dillon Rd, then just e. Int corridors. **Pets:** Accepted.
✕ 🔌 🖵 ⊶

WWWW Residence Inn by Marriott-Boulder/Louisville H
(303) 665-2661. **$169-$189.** 845 Coal Creek Cir. US 36 (Boulder Tpke), exit Superior (SR 170), n on McCaslin Blvd to Dillon Rd, then 0.6 mi e. Int corridors. **Pets:** Accepted.
✕ ⑤M 🔌 🖵 ⊶ ⊠

LOVELAND

WW WWW Best Western Crossroads Inn & Conference
Center H ❀
(970) 667-7810. **$79-$149.** 5542 E US Hwy 34. I-25, exit 257B, just w. Ext/int corridors. **Pets:** Other species. $15 daily fee/pet. Supervision.
SAVE ✕ 🔌 🖵 ⑪ ⊶

WWWW Residence Inn By Marriott Loveland H
(970) 622-7000. **$149-$169.** 5450 McWhinney Blvd. I-25, exit 257B, 0.5 mi w to Outlet Mall entry, just n, then just e. Int corridors. **Pets:** Medium, other species. Service with restrictions, crate.
✕ 🔌 🖵 ⊶ ⊠

MESA VERDE NATIONAL PARK

WW WWW Far View Lodge in Mesa Verde M
(970) 529-4421. **$99-$149, 3 day notice.** 1 Navajo Hill, MM 15. 15 mi from park gate; near park visitors center. Ext corridors. **Pets:** Medium. $50 deposit/room, $10 one-time fee/room. Designated rooms, no service, supervision.
SAVE ✕ 🔌 🖵 ⑪ ☒

MONTE VISTA

WW WWW Best Western Movie Manor H
(719) 852-5921. **$70-$140, 7 day notice.** 2830 W Hwy 160. On US 160, 2 mi w. Ext corridors. **Pets:** Accepted.
SAVE ✕ 🖵 ⑪

MONTROSE

WW WWW Best Western Red Arrow H ❀
(970) 249-9641. **$69-$129.** 1702 E Main St. 1 mi e on US 50. Ext/int corridors. **Pets:** $10 daily fee/pet. Designated rooms, service with restrictions, supervision.
SAVE ✕ 🔌 🖵 ⊶ ⊠

WWWW Hampton Inn H ❀
(970) 252-3300. **$108-$158.** 1980 N Townsend Ave. On US 550, just n of jct US 50. Int corridors. **Pets:** Medium. Designated rooms, service with restrictions, supervision.
✕ 🖵 ⊶ ⊠

WW WWW Holiday Inn Express Hotel &
Suites H ❀
(970) 240-1800. **$109-$139.** 1391 S Townsend Ave. 1 mi s on US 550, e on Niagara Ave. Int corridors. **Pets:** Other species. Designated rooms, crate.
SAVE ✕ ⑤M 🔌 🖵 ⊶

WWWW Quality Inn & Suites H
(970) 249-1011. **$79-$139, 7 day notice.** 2751 Commercial Way. 2 mi s on US 550, w on O'Delle. Int corridors. **Pets:** Medium. $10 daily fee/pet. Service with restrictions, supervision.
ASK ✕ 🔌 🖵 ⊶

WW WWW Uncompahgre Bed & Breakfast BB
(970) 240-4000. **$90-$150.** 21049 Uncompahgre Rd. 8 mi s on US 550. Int corridors. **Pets:** Medium, dogs only. Designated rooms, service with restrictions, supervision.
ASK ✕ 🔌 ☒

WW Western Motel M
(970) 249-3481. **$50-$150.** 1200 E Main St. 0.8 mi e on US 50. Ext corridors. **Pets:** Accepted.
ASK ✕ 🔌 ⊶

NEDERLAND

WW WWW Best Western Lodge at Nederland H
(303) 258-9463. **$126-$136, 30 day notice.** 55 Lakeview Dr. SR 119; across street from Visitor's Center. Int corridors. **Pets:** Accepted.
SAVE ✕ 🔌 🖵

NEW CASTLE

WW WW Rodeway Inn H
(970) 984-2363. **$90-$179.** 781 Burning Mountain Ave. I-70, exit 105, just n, then w. Int corridors. **Pets:** Other species. $20 daily fee/pet. Crate.
SAVE ✕ 🔌 🖵 ⊶

OURAY

Best Western Twin Peaks Lodge & Hot Springs 🅷 ❀
(970) 325-4427. **$73-$250.** 125 3rd Ave. Just w of US 550. Ext corridors. **Pets:** Medium. $10 daily fee/pet. Designated rooms, service with restrictions, supervision.

Comfort Inn 🅼
(970) 325-7203. **$64-$169.** 191 5th Ave. Just w of US 550. Ext corridors. **Pets:** Accepted.

Ouray Riverside Inn & Cabins 🅼
(970) 325-4061. **$55-$195.** 1804 N Main St. 1 mi n on US 550. Ext corridors. **Pets:** Accepted.

Ouray Victorian Inn 🅼
(970) 325-7222. **$65-$199.** 50 3rd Ave. Just w of US 550. Ext corridors. **Pets:** Large. $10 daily fee/room. Service with restrictions, supervision.

River's Edge Motel 🅼 ❀
(970) 325-4621. **$59-$249.** 110 7th Ave. Just w of US 550. Ext corridors. **Pets:** Medium. $10 one-time fee/pet. Service with restrictions, supervision.

PAGOSA SPRINGS

Alpine Inn 🅼 ❀
(970) 731-4005. **$55-$109.** 8 Solomon Dr. 2.5 mi w on US 160. Ext/int corridors. **Pets:** Other species. $10 daily fee/pet. Designated rooms, supervision.

Americas Best Value High Country Lodge 🅷
(970) 264-4181. **Call for rates.** 3821 E Hwy 160. On US 160, 3 mi e. Ext corridors. **Pets:** Dogs only. $25 daily fee/room. Service with restrictions, supervision.

Fireside Inn Cabins 🅲🅰 ❀
(970) 264-9204. **$105-$180, 30 day notice.** 1600 E Hwy 160. On US 160, 1.3 mi e. Ext corridors. **Pets:** Dogs only. $8 daily fee/pet. Designated rooms, no service, crate.

Oak Ridge Lodge 🅷
(970) 264-4173. **$59-$189, 3 day notice.** 158 Hot Springs Blvd. Just s of US 160. Int corridors. **Pets:** Other species. $100 deposit/room, $15 one-time fee/pet. Designated rooms, service with restrictions, supervision.

Pagosa Lodge 🅷
(970) 731-4141. **$95-$125.** 3505 W Hwy 160. On US 160, 3.5 mi w. Int corridors. **Pets:** Small, dogs only. $75 one-time fee/pet. Designated rooms, service with restrictions, supervision.

Pagosa Springs Inn & Suites 🅷
(970) 731-3400. **$65-$179.** 519 Village Dr. 3.8 mi w on US 160. Int corridors. **Pets:** Medium. $10 daily fee/pet. Designated rooms, service with restrictions, supervision.

PARKER

Super 8-Parker 🅷
(720) 851-2644. **$89-$99.** 6230 E Pine Ln. E-470 toll road, exit 5 (Parker Rd/SR 83), 0.4 mi se, then just e. Int corridors. **Pets:** Accepted.

PLACERVILLE

The Blue Jay Lodge & Cafe 🅷
(970) 728-0830. **$110-$215.** 22332 Hwy 145. Just n on SR 145, 13.5 mi s of Telluride. Int corridors. **Pets:** Other species. $30 one-time fee/pet. Designated rooms, supervision.

PUEBLO

Best Western Eagle Ridge Inn & Suites 🅷
(719) 543-4644. **$95-$135.** 4727 N Elizabeth St. I-25, exit 102, just w, then just n. Int corridors. **Pets:** Other species. $15 daily fee/pet. Designated rooms, service with restrictions, supervision.

La Quinta Inn & Suites Pueblo 🅷 ❀
(719) 542-3500. **$59-$169.** 4801 N Elizabeth St. I-25, exit 102, just nw. Int corridors. **Pets:** Medium, other species. Service with restrictions, supervision.

Microtel Inn & Suites 🅷
(719) 242-2020. **$65-$99.** 3343 Gateway Dr. I-25, exit 94, just w, then just s. Int corridors. **Pets:** Other species. $50 deposit/room, $10 one-time fee/room. Service with restrictions.

The Ramada of Pueblo 🅷
(719) 544-4700. **$69-$119.** 4703 N Freeway. I-25, exit 102, just w. Ext corridors. **Pets:** Medium. $15 one-time fee/room. Designated rooms, service with restrictions.

RIDGWAY

Ridgway-Ouray Lodge & Suites 🅷 ❀
(970) 626-5444. **$70-$118.** 373 Palomino Tr. US 550, just ne on SR 62, then just e. Int corridors. **Pets:** Large. $15 daily fee/pet. Designated rooms, service with restrictions, supervision.

RIFLE

La Quinta Inns & Suites 🅷 ❀
(970) 625-2676. **$99-$169.** 600 Wapiti Ct. I-70, exit 90, just s, then just e. Int corridors. **Pets:** Medium, other species. Service with restrictions, supervision.

Rusty Cannon Motel 🅼
(970) 625-4004. **$92-$100.** 701 Taughenbaugh Blvd. I-70, exit 90, just s. Ext corridors. **Pets:** Medium, dogs only. $25 one-time fee/pet. Designated rooms, service with restrictions, supervision.

SALIDA

Aspen Leaf Lodge 🅼 ❀
(719) 539-6733. **$59-$109.** 7350 W Hwy 50. Just w of Hot Springs Pool. Ext corridors. **Pets:** Medium, other species. $5 daily fee/pet. Service with restrictions, supervision.

Chalets at Tudor Rose 🆅🅷
(719) 539-2002. **$200, 30 day notice.** 6720 CR 104. Just e on US 50, s on CR 104, 0.5 mi up the hill, then follow signs. Ext corridors. **Pets:** Dogs only. $25 deposit/pet, $10 daily fee/pet. Designated rooms, no service, crate.

Circle R Motel 🅼
(719) 539-6296. **$49-$105.** 304 E US Hwy 50. On US 50. Ext corridors. **Pets:** Dogs only. $5 daily fee/pet. Service with restrictions, supervision.

▼▼ Gateway Inn & Suites H
(719) 539-2895. **$39-$179.** 1310 E Hwy 50. On US 50, just e; between Blake and Palmer sts. Ext corridors. **Pets:** Medium, dogs only. $10 daily fee/pet. Designated rooms, supervision.
(ASK) (X) 🔒 💻

◈ ▼▼ Great Western Colorado Lodge H
(719) 539-2514. **$39-$89.** 352 W Rainbow Blvd. On US 50. Ext corridors. **Pets:** Small. $10 daily fee/pet. Designated rooms, service with restrictions, supervision.
(SAVE) (X) 🔒 💻 ➰

◈ ▼▼ Silver Ridge Lodge M ❖
(719) 539-2553. **$49-$119, 3 day notice.** 545 W Rainbow Blvd. On US 50, just w of Chamber of Commerce. Ext corridors. **Pets:** Small, dogs only. $10 daily fee/pet. Designated rooms, service with restrictions, supervision.
(SAVE) (X) 🔒 💻 ➰

▼▼ Super 8 M
(719) 539-6689. **$69-$149.** 525 W Rainbow Blvd. On US 50. Ext corridors. **Pets:** Medium. Service with restrictions, crate.
(ASK) (X) 🔒 💻 ➰

◈ ▼▼ Travelodge M
(719) 539-2528. **Call for rates.** 7310 Hwy 50. On US 50 W, just w of Hot Springs Pool. Ext corridors. **Pets:** Accepted.
(SAVE) (X) 🔒 💻 ➰

◈ ▼▼ Woodland Motel M ❖
(719) 539-4980. **$50-$155.** 903 W 1st St. Center of historic downtown, 0.5 mi w on 1st St (SR 291). Ext corridors. **Pets:** Other species.
(SAVE) (X) 🔒 💻

SILVERTHORNE

▼▼ Quality Inn & Suites H
(970) 513-1222. **$89-$209.** 530 Silverthorne Ln. I-70, exit 205, just n on SR 9, just e on Rainbow Dr, then just e on Tanglewood Ln. Int corridors. **Pets:** Accepted.
(ASK) (X) 🔒M 🔒 💻 ➰

SILVERTON

◈ ▼▼▼ Silverton's Inn of the Rockies at the Historic Alma House BB
(970) 387-5336. **$89-$139, 7 day notice.** 220 E 10th St. On 10th St, just se of Greene St (Main St). Int corridors. **Pets:** Accepted.
(SAVE) (X) (K) (☎)

▼▼ Villa Dallavalle B & B BB
(970) 387-5555. **$89-$125.** 1257 Blair St. Corner of 13th and Blair sts. Int corridors. **Pets:** Dogs only. $15 daily fee/pet. Supervision.
(ASK) (X) 💻 (K)

SOUTH FORK

▼▼ Americas Best Value Inn Wolf Creek Lodge M
(719) 873-5547. **$64-$139.** 31042 Hwy 160 W. On US 160. Ext corridors. **Pets:** Accepted.
(ASK) (X) 🔒 💻

▼ Ute Bluff Lodge M ❖
(719) 873-5595. **$49-$208, 14 day notice.** 27680 W Hwy 160. 2.5 mi e of jct US 160 and SR 149. Ext corridors. **Pets:** Medium, dogs only. $7 daily fee/pet. Designated rooms, service with restrictions, supervision.
(ASK) (X) 🔒 💻 (K)

STEAMBOAT SPRINGS

▼▼ Comfort Inn H
(970) 879-6669. **$79-$499, 3 day notice.** 1055 Walton Creek Rd. 2.8 mi e on US 40. Int corridors. **Pets:** Dogs only. $20 daily fee/pet. Designated rooms, no service, supervision.
(ASK) (X) 🔒M 🔒 💻 ➰

▼▼ Fairfield Inn & Suites by Marriott H
(970) 870-9000. **$99-$219.** 3200 S Lincoln Ave. 3 mi e on US 40. Int corridors. **Pets:** $25 one-time fee/room. Designated rooms, service with restrictions, crate.
(X) 🔒M 🔒 💻 ➰

◈ ▼▼ Holiday Inn Steamboat Springs H ❖
(970) 879-2250. **$119-$239, 3 day notice.** 3190 S Lincoln Ave. 3 mi e on US 40. Int corridors. **Pets:** Other species. $25 deposit/room, $10 daily fee/pet. Designated rooms, service with restrictions, supervision.
(SAVE) (X) 🔒M 🔒 💻 ¶¶ ➰ ⊠

▼▼ Nordic Lodge M
(970) 879-0531. **$69-$299, 14 day notice.** 1036 Lincoln Ave. Between 10th and 11th sts; downtown. Ext corridors. **Pets:** $10 daily fee/room. Service with restrictions, supervision.
(ASK) (X) 🔒 ➰

◈ ▼▼ Rabbit Ears Motel M
(970) 879-1150. **$89-$189, 3 day notice.** 201 Lincoln Ave. Just e on US 40. Ext corridors. **Pets:** $15 one-time fee/pet. Service with restrictions, supervision.
(SAVE) (X) 🔒 💻

◈ ▼▼▼ Sheraton Steamboat Resort H
(970) 879-2220. **$219-$499, 3 day notice.** 2200 Village Inn Ct. 2.3 mi e on US 40, 1 mi n on Mt Werner Rd; at ski area. Int corridors. **Pets:** Medium, dogs only. $35 one-time fee/pet. Designated rooms, service with restrictions, supervision.
(SAVE) (X) 🔒 💻 ¶¶ ➰ ⊠

▼▼ Steamboat Hotel H
(970) 879-5230. **$59-$115.** 3195 S Lincoln Ave. 3 mi e on US 40. Int corridors. **Pets:** Accepted.
(ASK) (X) 🔒 💻 ➰ ⊠

STERLING

◈ ▼▼▼ Best Western Sundowner M
(970) 522-6265. **$89-$120, 3 day notice.** 125 Overland Trail St. I-76, exit 125, just w. Ext/int corridors. **Pets:** Accepted.
(SAVE) (X) 🔒 💻 ➰

▼▼ Ramada Inn H
(970) 522-2625. **$77-$120.** 22140 E Hwy 6. I-76, exit 125, 0.5 mi e on US 6. Ext/int corridors. **Pets:** Other species. $25 deposit/room. Designated rooms, service with restrictions, supervision.
(ASK) (X) 🔒 💻 ¶¶ ➰ ⊠

STRATTON

◈ ▼▼ Best Western Golden Prairie Inn H
(719) 348-5311. **$96-$120.** 700 Colorado Ave. I-70, exit 419, just n. Ext corridors. **Pets:** $10 one-time fee/pet. Designated rooms, service with restrictions, supervision.
(SAVE) (X) 🔒 💻 ¶¶ ➰

TELLURIDE

▼▼▼▼ Fairmont Heritage Place Franz Klammer Lodge CO
(970) 728-3318. **$250-$2200, 45 day notice.** 567 Mountain Village Blvd. SR 145 S, take left on Mountain Village Blvd, then 2.3 mi to entrance; SR 145 N, take right on Mountain Village Blvd, then 2.3 mi to entrance. Int corridors. **Pets:** Accepted.
(X) 🔒 💻 ➰ ⊠ (K)

◈ ▼▼▼ Hotel Columbia H ❖
(970) 728-0660. **$215-$1555, 30 day notice.** 301 W San Juan Ave. Just s of SR 145 (Colorado Ave); corner of Aspen St and San Juan Ave; opposite gondola. Int corridors. **Pets:** Dogs only. $20 daily fee/room. Designated rooms, service with restrictions.
(SAVE) (X) 🔒 💻 ¶¶ ⊠

AAA ◆◆◆ The Hotel Telluride **H** ❀
(970) 369-1188. **$189-$499.** 199 N Cornet St. Just n of jct SR 145 (Colorado Ave). Int corridors. **Pets:** Other species. $100 one-time fee/room. Crate.
[SAVE] [X] [&M] [📧] [💻] [🍴] [🐾]

AAA ◆◆◆ Peaks Resort & Golden Door Spa **H**
(970) 728-6800. **$129-$599, 30 day notice.** 136 Country Club Dr. 1.8 mi s of jct SR 145 (Colorado Ave) and 145 Spur, 2.5 mi e on Mountain Village Blvd, follow ski area signs; in Telluride Mountain Village. Ext/int corridors. **Pets:** Accepted.
[SAVE] [X] [&M] [📧] [💻] [🍴] [🏊] [🐾] [🐾]

TRINIDAD

AAA ◆◆◆ Best Western Trinidad Inn **M**
(719) 846-2215. **$69-$109.** 900 W Adams St. I-25, exit 13A northbound; exit Cross Bridge southbound, just ne. Ext corridors. **Pets:** Accepted.
[SAVE] [X] [📧] [💻] [🏊]

AAA ◆ Budget Host Derrick Motel **M**
(719) 846-3307. **$79-$99.** 10301 Santa Fe Trail Dr. I-25, exit 11, 0.5 mi ne. Ext corridors. **Pets:** Medium. $10 daily fee/pet. Service with restrictions, supervision.
[SAVE] [X] [📧] [💻]

AAA ◆◆ Quality Inn Trinidad **H**
(719) 846-4491. **$79-$129.** 3125 Toupal Dr. I-25, exit 11, just w. Int corridors. **Pets:** Accepted.
[SAVE] [X] [📧] [💻] [🍴] [🏊]

◆◆ Super 8 **M**
(719) 846-8280. **$60-$110.** 1924 Freedom Rd. I-25, exit 15, just ne. Int corridors. **Pets:** Very small. $15 one-time fee/pet. Service with restrictions, supervision.
[ASK] [X] [📧] [💻]

VAIL

◆◆◆◆ Evergreen Lodge at Vail **H**
(970) 476-7810. **Call for rates.** 250 S Frontage Rd W. I-70, exit 176, just w. Int corridors. **Pets:** Small, other species. $20 daily fee/pet. Designated rooms, service with restrictions, supervision.
[X] [📧] [💻] [🍴] [🏊] [🐾] [🐾]

◆◆◆ Holiday Inn Apex Vail **H**
(970) 476-2739. **$109-$599, 30 day notice.** 2211 N Frontage Rd. I-70, exit 173, just e. Int corridors. **Pets:** Medium, dogs only. $25 daily fee/pet. Designated rooms, supervision.
[ASK] [X] [&M] [📧] [💻] [🍴] [🏊] [🐾]

AAA ◆◆◆ The Lodge at Vail, a
RockResort **H** ❀
(970) 476-5011. **$149-$866, 45 day notice.** 174 E Gore Creek Dr. I-70, exit 176, s on Vail Rd to center of village. Ext/int corridors. **Pets:** Dogs only. $50 daily fee/pet. Designated rooms.
[SAVE] [X] [📧] [💻] [🍴] [🏊] [🐾]

WALSENBURG

AAA ◆◆ Best Western Rambler **H** ❀
(719) 738-1121. **$86-$201.** 457 US Hwy 85-87. I-25, exit 52, just w. Ext/int corridors. **Pets:** Medium. $10 daily fee/pet. Designated rooms, service with restrictions, supervision.
[SAVE] [X] [📧] [💻] [🏊]

WELLINGTON

◆◆◆ Comfort Inn Wellington **H**
(970) 568-0444. **Call for rates.** 7860 6th St. I-25, exit 278, just w, then just s. Int corridors. **Pets:** Accepted.
[X] [📧] [💻] [🏊]

WINDSOR

◆◆ Super 8 **H**
(970) 686-5996. **$65-$125.** 1265 Main St. I-25, exit 262, 3.8 mi e; in shopping/restaurant complex. Int corridors. **Pets:** Other species. $15 daily fee/pet. Service with restrictions, supervision.
[ASK] [X] [&M] [📧] [💻]

WINTER PARK

AAA ◆◆ Best Western Alpenglo Lodge **H**
(970) 726-8088. **$78-$175, 30 day notice.** 78665 US Hwy 40. On US 40; center. Int corridors. **Pets:** Accepted.
[SAVE] [X] [&M] [📧] [💻]

YAMPA

◆◆ Oak Tree Inn **H**
(970) 638-1000. **$85-$125.** 98 Moffat Ave. Just off SR 131. Int corridors. **Pets:** Accepted.
[ASK] [X] [📧] [💻] [🍴]

CONNECTICUT

BETHEL

▼▼ ▼▼ **Microtel Inn & Suites** 🅷 ❀
(203) 748-8318. **$79-$99.** 80 Benedict Rd. I-84, exit 8, 1 mi e on US 6. Int corridors. **Pets:** $100 deposit/pet, $11 daily fee/pet. Service with restrictions, crate.
(ASK) ✖ 🔋 💻

BRIDGEPORT

▼▼◆▼▼ **Bridgeport Holiday Inn & Convention Center** 🅷
(203) 334-1234. **$159-$179.** 1070 Main St. SR 8, exit 2 northbound, 0.7 mi se; exit southbound, just s, then just e. Int corridors. **Pets:** Accepted.
(ASK) ✖ ᴸ🇲 🔋 💻 🍴 🌊

BROOKFIELD

▼▼ ▼▼ **The Newbury Inn** 🅼
(203) 775-0220. **$89-$99.** 1030 Federal Rd (Rt 7 & 202). Jct SR 25, 0.9 mi nw. Ext/int corridors. **Pets:** Accepted.
(ASK) ✖ 🔋 💻

DANBURY

▼▼◆▼▼ **Danbury Plaza Hotel & Conference Center** 🅷 ❀
(203) 794-0600. **$89-$149.** 18 Old Ridgebury Rd. I-84, exit 2 eastbound; exit 2A westbound. Int corridors. **Pets:** Large.
(ASK) ✖ 🔋 💻 🍴 🌊

▼▼◆▼▼ **Ethan Allen Hotel** 🅷 ❀
(203) 744-1776. **$95-$144.** 21 Lake Ave Extension. I-84, exit 4, 0.3 mi w on US 6 and 202. Int corridors. **Pets:** Large. $15 daily fee/room. Designated rooms, service with restrictions, crate.
(ASK) ✖ 🔋 💻 🍴 🌊

▲▲▲ ▼▼◆▼▼ **Holiday Inn** 🅷
(203) 792-4000. **$99-$159.** 80 Newtown Rd. I-84, exit 8 (Newtown Rd), 0.5 mi s on US 6 W. Int corridors. **Pets:** Large. $15 daily fee/pet. Designated rooms, service with restrictions, supervision.
(SAVE) ✖ 🔋 💻 🍴 🌊

▲▲▲ ▼▼◆▼▼ **Maron Hotel & Suites** 🅷
(203) 791-2200. **$89-$189.** 42 Lake Ave Extension. I-84, exit 4, 0.5 mi w on US 6 and 202. Int corridors. **Pets:** $25 daily fee/room. Designated rooms, service with restrictions, crate.
(SAVE) ✖ ᴸ🇲 🔋 💻 🍴

▼▼◆▼▼ **Residence Inn by Marriott** 🅷
(203) 797-1256. **$209-$219.** 22 Segar St. I-84, exit 4 eastbound, just n; exit westbound, just e on Lake Ave Extension, then just s. Int corridors. **Pets:** Accepted.
✖ 🔋 💻 🌊

DAYVILLE

▼▼◆▼▼ **Holiday Inn Express** 🅷 ❀
(860) 779-3200. **$120-$145.** 16 Tracy Rd. I-395, exit 94, just w. Int corridors. **Pets:** Medium. $10 daily fee/pet. Service with restrictions, supervision.
✖ ᴸ🇲 🔋 💻 🌊

EAST HAVEN

▲▲▲ ▼▼◆▼▼ **Quality Inn** 🅷
(203) 469-5321. **$69-$249.** 30 Frontage Rd. I-95, exit 51 eastbound, 0.5 mi e; exit westbound, 0.8 mi w on N Frontage Rd to overpass, then 0.8 mi e. Ext/int corridors. **Pets:** Other species. $15 daily fee/room. Designated rooms, service with restrictions, crate.
(SAVE) ✖ 🔋 💻 🌊

FAIRFIELD

▲▲▲ ▼▼◆▼▼ **Best Western Black Rock Inn** 🅷
(203) 659-2200. **$129-$169, 3 day notice.** 100 Kings Hwy Cutoff. I-95, exit 24, just sw. Int corridors. **Pets:** Small, dogs only. $20 daily fee/room. Designated rooms, service with restrictions, supervision.
(SAVE) ✖ ᴸ🇲 🔋 💻

GREENWICH

▲▲▲ ▼▼◆▼▼ **The Stanton House Inn** 🅱🅱
(203) 869-2110. **$169-$249, 7 day notice.** 76 Maple Ave. Just n of US 1; center. Ext/int corridors. **Pets:** Small, dogs only. $100 deposit/pet, $25 daily fee/pet. Designated rooms, service with restrictions, supervision.
(SAVE) ✖ 🔋 🌊

HAMDEN

▼▼◆▼▼ **Clarion Hotel & Suites Hamden-New Haven** 🅼
(203) 288-3831. **$129-$179, 7 day notice.** 2260 Whitney Ave. Just n off SR 15, exit 61. Int corridors. **Pets:** Small, dogs only. Designated rooms, service with restrictions, supervision.
(ASK) ✖ ᴸ🇲 🔋 💻 🌊

HARTFORD METROPOLITAN AREA

AVON

▲▲▲ ▼▼◆▼▼ **Avon Old Farms Hotel** 🅷
(860) 677-1651. **$129-$229.** 279 Avon Mountain Rd. Jct US 44 and SR 10. Ext/int corridors. **Pets:** Other species. Designated rooms, service with restrictions.
(SAVE) ✖ 🔋 💻 🍴 🌊 ⊗

▼▼▼▼ **Residence Inn by Marriott Hartford-Avon** 🅷
(860) 678-1666. **$189-$199.** 55 Simsbury Rd (SR 202). Jct US 44, just n. Int corridors. **Pets:** Accepted.
✖ ᴸ🇲 🔋 💻 🌊 ⊗

CROMWELL

◉◉◉ ▽▽◆ Comfort Inn ℍ
(860) 635-4100. **$70-$140.** 111 Berlin Rd. I-91, exit 21, just e on SR 372. Int corridors. **Pets:** Accepted.
[SAVE] [✕] [⊟] [▣]

EAST HARTFORD

◉◉◉ ▽▽◆ Holiday Inn ℍ
(860) 528-9611. **$89-$119.** 363 Roberts St. I-84, exit 58, just w. Int corridors. **Pets:** Other species. $35 one-time fee/room. Designated rooms, service with restrictions, supervision.
[SAVE] [✕] [⊟] [▣] [⊞] [⊠]

◉◉◉ ▽▽◆ Sheraton Hartford Hotel ℍ ❀
(860) 528-9703. **$105-$179.** 100 E River Dr. I-84, exit 53 eastbound, just s; exit 54 westbound to exit 3 (Darlin St), just n. Int corridors. **Pets:** Other species. Designated rooms, service with restrictions, supervision.
[SAVE] [✕] [⅃M] [⊟] [▣] [⊞] [⊠]

EAST WINDSOR

◉◉◉ ▽▽◆ Holiday Inn Express East Windsor–Airport Ⓜ
(860) 627-6585. **Call for rates.** 260 Main St (US 5). I-91, exit 44, just s. Int corridors. **Pets:** Accepted.
[SAVE] [✕] [⅃M] [⊟] [▣]

ENFIELD

▽▽◆ Red Roof Inn # 7105 Ⓜ
(860) 741-2571. **$57-$109.** 5 Hazard Ave. I-91, exit 47E. Ext corridors. **Pets:** Accepted.
[ASK] [✕] [⅃M] [⊟]

FARMINGTON

◉◉◉ ▽▽◆ Centennial Inn Suites ⒸⓄ
(860) 677-4647. **$121-$181.** 5 Spring Ln. US 6, 0.3 mi e of jct SR 177. Ext/int corridors. **Pets:** Other species. $15 daily fee/pet. Service with restrictions.
[SAVE] [✕] [⅃M] [⊟] [▣] [⊠]

◆◆ Extended StayAmerica Deluxe Hartford-Farmington ℍ
(860) 676-2790. **$96-$129.** 1 Batterson Park Rd. I-84, exit 37, just ne. Int corridors. **Pets:** Other species. $25 daily fee/pet. Service with restrictions, crate.
[ASK] [✕] [⊟] [▣]

▽▽◆ Homewood Suites by Hilton ℍ
(860) 321-0000. **$119-$199.** 2 Farm Glen Blvd. I-84, exit 39, 0.6 mi e on SR 4. Int corridors. **Pets:** Accepted.
[✕] [⅃M] [⊟] [▣] [⊠]

GLASTONBURY

◉◉◉ ▽▽◆ Homewood Suites by Hilton Hartford South-Glastonbury ℍ
(860) 652-8111. **$110-$179.** 65 Glastonbury Blvd. SR 3, exit Main St, just se. Int corridors. **Pets:** Medium. $15 daily fee/pet. Service with restrictions, supervision.
[SAVE] [✕] [⅃M] [⊟] [▣] [⊠]

HARTFORD

▽▽◆ Crowne Plaza Hartford Downtown ℍ
(860) 549-2400. **$129-$209.** 50 Morgan St. I-91, exit 32B; I-84, exit 50 eastbound; exit 52 westbound. Int corridors. **Pets:** Small. $50 one-time fee/room. Service with restrictions, crate.
[ASK] [✕] [⅃M] [⊟] [▣] [⊞] [⊠]

◉◉◉ ▽▽◆ The Goodwin Hotel ℍ
(860) 246-7500. **$129-$1200.** 1 Haynes St. Downtown; entrance on Asylum St. Int corridors. **Pets:** Accepted.
[SAVE] [✕] [⅃M] [⊟] [▣] [⊞]

▽▽◆ Holiday Inn Express Downtown Hartford ℍ
(860) 246-9900. **$99-$189.** 440 Asylum St. I-84, exit 48, just se via Spring St. Int corridors. **Pets:** Accepted.
[ASK] [✕] [⊟] [▣]

▽▽◆ Holiday Inn Express Hotel & Suites Hartford ℍ
(860) 525-1000. **Call for rates.** 185 Brainard Rd. I-91, exit 27, just e, then just s. Int corridors. **Pets:** Small, dogs only. $25 one-time fee/pet. Designated rooms, service with restrictions, crate.
[✕] [⊟] [▣] [⊠]

▽▽◆ Homewood Suites by Hilton Hartford Downtown ℍ
(860) 524-0223. **$149-$179.** 338 Asylum St. Between Ann and High sts; downtown. Int corridors. **Pets:** Accepted.
[✕] [⅃M] [⊟] [▣]

▽▽◆ Residence Inn by Marriott Downtown Hartford ℍ
(860) 524-5550. **$239-$249.** 942 Main St. I-91, exit 29A northbound; exit 31 southbound. Int corridors. **Pets:** Accepted.
[✕] [⊟] [▣]

MANCHESTER

▽▽◆ Extended StayAmerica Hartford-Manchester ℍ
(860) 643-5140. **$79-$119.** 340 Tolland Tpke. I-84, exit 63, 0.3 mi se on SR 30, then just sw. Int corridors. **Pets:** Other species. $25 daily fee/pet. Service with restrictions, crate.
[ASK] [✕] [⅃M] [⊟] [▣]

◉◉◉ ▽▽◆ Residence Inn Manchester ℍ
(860) 432-4242. **$177-$185.** 201 Hale Rd. I-84, exit 63, 0.5 mi nw, then 0.6 mi sw. Int corridors. **Pets:** Accepted.
[SAVE] [✕] [⅃M] [⊟] [▣] [⊠] [⊠]

NEW BRITAIN

▽▽▽◆ La Quinta Inn & Suites New Britain/South Hartford ℍ ❀
(860) 348-1463. **$59-$109.** 65 Columbus Blvd. SR 9, exit 26 northbound; exit 27 southbound, then just nw. Int corridors. **Pets:** Medium, other species. Service with restrictions, supervision.
[ASK] [✕] [⅃M] [⊟] [▣] [⊞]

ROCKY HILL

▽▽◆ Residence Inn by Marriott Hartford-Rocky Hill ℍ
(860) 257-7500. **$175-$213.** 680 Cromwell Ave. I-91, exit 23, 0.4 mi w on West St, then just n. Int corridors. **Pets:** Accepted.
[✕] [⅃M] [⊟] [▣] [⊠] [⊠]

SIMSBURY

▽▽◆ Simsbury 1820 House ⒸⒾ
(860) 658-7658. **$139-$229.** 731 Hopmeadow St. US 202/SR 10, 2 mi n of jct SR 185; center. Ext/int corridors. **Pets:** Accepted.
[ASK] [✕] [⊟] [▣] [⊞]

SOUTHINGTON

◉◉◉ ▽▽◆ Residence Inn by Marriott ℍ
(860) 621-4440. **$144-$179.** 778 West St. I-84, exit 31, just s. Int corridors. **Pets:** Accepted.
[SAVE] [✕] [⅃M] [⊟] [▣] [⊠] [⊠]

VERNON

◉◉◉ ▽▽◆ Quality Inn & Conference Center ℍ
(860) 646-5700. **Call for rates.** 51 Hartford Tpke (SR 83). I-84, exit 64, se on SR 30, then 0.8 mi s. Int corridors. **Pets:** Accepted.
[SAVE] [✕] [⅃M] [⊟] [▣] [⊠] [⊠]

WETHERSFIELD

WWWW Comfort Inn H
(860) 563-2311. **$109-$159.** 1330 Silas Deane Hwy. I-91, exit 24, 0.4 mi n. Int corridors. **Pets:** Accepted.
[SAVE] [X] [&M] [🛏] [💻] [🏊] [🐾]

WINDSOR

WWWW The Residence Inn by Marriott Hartford-Windsor H
(860) 688-7474. **$170-$208.** 100 Dunfey Ln. I-91, exit 37, just w on SR 305 to Dunfey Ln, then 0.3 mi n. Ext corridors. **Pets:** Accepted.
[X] [&M] [🛏] [💻] [🏊] [🐾]

WINDSOR LOCKS

WWWW Candlewood Suites H
(860) 623-2000. **$149-$159.** 149 Ella T Grasso Tpke. I-91, exit 40, 2.5 mi w on SR 20, then 0.6 mi n on SR 75. Int corridors. **Pets:** Medium, other species. $75 one-time fee/pet. Service with restrictions, crate.
[ASK] [X] [&M] [🛏] [💻] [🏊]

WWWW Homewood Suites by Hilton H
(860) 627-8463. **$159-$179.** 65 Ella T Grasso Tpke. I-91, exit 40, 2.5 mi w on SR 20, then just n on SR 75. Ext/int corridors. **Pets:** Accepted.
[X] [&M] [🛏] [💻] [🏊] [🐾]

WWWW La Quinta Inn Hartford-Airport H ❀
(860) 623-3336. **$65-$129.** 64 Ella T Grasso Tpke. I-91, exit 40, 2.5 mi w on SR 20, then just n on SR 75. Int corridors. **Pets:** Medium, other species. Service with restrictions, supervision.
[ASK] [X] [&M] [🛏] [💻]

WW Ramada Inn Bradley International Airport H
(860) 623-9494. **Call for rates.** 5 Ella T Grasso Tpke. I-91, exit 40, 2.5 mi w on SR 20, then just n on SR 75. Int corridors. **Pets:** Accepted.
[X] [🛏] [💻] [🍴] [🏊]

WWWW Sheraton Hotel At Bradley International Airport H ❀
(860) 627-5311. **$299-$359, 3 day notice.** 1 Bradley International Airport. At Bradley International Airport terminal. Int corridors. **Pets:** Medium. Service with restrictions, crate.
[SAVE] [X] [&M] [🛏] [💻] [🍴] [🏊]

END METROPOLITAN AREA

IVORYTON

WWWW The Copper Beech Inn CI
(860) 767-0330. **$225-$400, 14 day notice.** 46 Main St. SR 9, exit 3, 1.7 mi w. Int corridors. **Pets:** Accepted.
[SAVE] [X] [🍴]

LAKEVILLE

WW Inn at Iron Masters M
(860) 435-9844. **$120-$220, 3 day notice.** 229 Main St (Rt 44 & 41). 0.5 mi ne. Ext corridors. **Pets:** Accepted.
[ASK] [X] [💻] [🏊]

WWWW Interlaken Inn Resort and Conference Center H ❀
(860) 435-9878. **$169-$259, 7 day notice.** 74 Interlaken Rd. On SR 112, 0.5 mi w of jct SR 41. Ext/int corridors. **Pets:** Dogs only. $15 daily fee/room. Designated rooms, service with restrictions, supervision.
[SAVE] [X] [🛏] [💻] [🍴] [🏊] [🐾]

LEDYARD

WW Almost In Mystic/Mares Inn BB
(860) 572-7556. **$125-$225, 14 day notice.** 333 Colonel Ledyard Hwy. I-95, exit 89, 1 mi ne to Gold Star Hwy, 0.6 mi w, then 0.7 mi n. Int corridors. **Pets:** Accepted.
[ASK] [X] [🛏] [💻] [🗇]

LITCHFIELD

WWWW Litchfield Inn CI
(860) 567-4503. **$200-$336, 3 day notice.** 432 Bantam Rd. 1.5 mi w on US 202. Int corridors. **Pets:** Medium, other species. $25 daily fee/pet. Designated rooms, service with restrictions, supervision.
[SAVE] [X] [🛏] [💻] [🍴]

MERIDEN

WW Extended StayAmerica Hartford-Meriden H
(203) 630-1927. **$84-$124.** 366 Bee St. I-91, exit 17 northbound, just e on E Main St, then 0.7 mi n; exit 19 southbound, 0.5 mi w on Baldwin Ave, then 0.6 mi s. Int corridors. **Pets:** Other species. $25 daily fee/pet. Service with restrictions, crate.
[ASK] [X] [🛏] [💻]

WWWW Residence Inn by Marriott H
(203) 634-7770. **$148-$180.** 390 Bee St. I-91, exit 16 northbound, just e on E Main St, then 0.7 mi n; exit 19 southbound, 0.5 mi w on Baldwin Ave, then 0.5 mi s. Ext/int corridors. **Pets:** Accepted.
[SAVE] [X] [&M] [🛏] [💻] [🏊] [🐾]

MILFORD

WWWW Residence Inn by Marriott H ❀
(203) 283-2100. **$179-$194.** 62 Rowe Ave. I-95, exit 35, just nw. Int corridors. **Pets:** Medium. $100 one-time fee/room. Service with restrictions, crate.
[X] [🛏] [💻] [🏊]

MYSTIC

WWWW Comfort Inn of Mystic H
(860) 572-8531. **$99-$209.** 48 Whitehall Ave. I-95, exit 90, just n on SR 27. Int corridors. **Pets:** Small, other species. $75 one-time fee/pet. Service with restrictions, crate.
[SAVE] [X] [&M] [🛏] [💻] [🏊]

WWWW Inn at Mystic M
(860) 536-9604. **$95-$315.** 3 Williams Ave. On US 1 at SR 27. Ext/int corridors. **Pets:** $15 daily fee/pet. Designated rooms, service with restrictions, supervision.
[SAVE] [X] [🛏] [💻] [🍴] [🏊] [🐾]

WWWW Residence Inn by Marriott H
(860) 536-5150. **$169-$229.** 40 Whitehall Ave. I-95, exit 90, just n on SR 27. Int corridors. **Pets:** Other species. $100 one-time fee/room. Service with restrictions, crate.
[SAVE] [X] [🛏] [💻] [🏊] [🐾]

NEW HAVEN

▼▼ La Quinta Inn & Suites 🅷 ❀
(203) 562-1111. **$99-$199.** 400 Sargent Dr. I-95, exit 46. Int corridors.
Pets: Medium, other species. Service with restrictions, supervision.
[ASK] [✕] 🖪 🖵 [¶] 🏊

◆◆◆◆ **▼▼▼▼ Omni New Haven Hotel at Yale** 🅷 ❀
(203) 772-6664. **$219-$459.** 155 Temple St. Center of downtown. Int corridors. **Pets:** Small. $50 one-time fee/pet. Service with restrictions, supervision.
[SAVE] [✕] [&M] 🖪 🖵 [¶]

NEW LONDON

▼▼ Red Roof Inn #7145 🅼
(860) 444-0001. **$55-$100.** 707 Colman St. I-95, exit 82A northbound, 0.4 mi e, then just n; exit 83 southbound, 0.6 mi s. Ext corridors. **Pets:** Small, other species. Service with restrictions, supervision.
[ASK] [✕] 🖪

NEW MILFORD

▼▼ The Homestead Inn 🅱🅱
(860) 354-4080. **$105-$220.** 5 Elm St. Just e of village green off Main St; center. Ext/int corridors. **Pets:** Other species. $10 one-time fee/room. Designated rooms, service with restrictions, supervision.
[ASK] [✕] 🖪

NIANTIC

▼ Motel 6–1063 🅼
(860) 739-6991. **$45-$65.** 269 Flanders Rd. I-95, exit 74, just s. Ext corridors. **Pets:** Other species. Service with restrictions, supervision.
[✕] 🖪 🏊

NORTH STONINGTON

▼▼▼ The Inn at Lower Farm B & B 🅱🅱
(860) 535-9075. **$105-$185, 7 day notice.** 119 Mystic Rd. I-95, exit 90, 1.5 mi n on SR 27, 1.4 mi e on SR 184, then 3.4 mi n on SR 201. Int corridors. **Pets:** Medium. $10 daily fee/room. Designated rooms, service with restrictions, supervision.
[✕] [📶] [✆]

NORWALK

◆◆◆ **▼▼▼▼ Four Points by Sheraton Norwalk** 🅷
(203) 849-9828. **$80-$225.** 426 Main Ave. I-95, exit 15, 3.5 mi n via US 7, just e, then 0.7 mi s. Int corridors. **Pets:** Medium, dogs only. $25 one-time fee/room. Designated rooms, service with restrictions, supervision.
[SAVE] [✕] [&M] 🖪 🖵 [¶]

▼▼ Homestead Studio Suites Hotel-Norwalk 🅷
(203) 847-6888. **$82-$168.** 400 Main Ave. I-95, exit 15, 3.5 mi n via US 7, just e, then 1 mi s. Int corridors. **Pets:** Other species. $25 daily fee/pet. Service with restrictions, crate.
[ASK] [✕] 🖪 🖵

◆◆◆ **▼▼ The Silvermine Tavern** 🅒🅘
(203) 847-4558. **$140-$190, 3 day notice.** 194 Perry Ave. Merritt Pkwy, exit 40A, 0.5 mi s on Main Ave, then 1.7 mi ne. Int corridors. **Pets:** Accepted.
[SAVE] [✕] 🖪 🖵 [¶] [📶]

OLD SAYBROOK

◆◆◆ **▼▼▼ Days Inn** 🅼
(860) 388-3453. **$59-$199.** 1430 Boston Post Rd. I-95, exit 66, 0.3 mi s on SR 166, then 0.5 mi e on US 1 N. Ext corridors. **Pets:** Medium, dogs only. $15 daily fee/pet. Designated rooms, service with restrictions, supervision.
[SAVE] [✕] 🖪 🖵

◆◆◆ **▼▼ Liberty Inn** 🅼
(860) 388-1777. **$58-$130.** 55 Spring Brook Rd. I-95, exit 68 southbound; exit 67 northbound, 0.9 mi n on US 1, then w. Ext corridors. **Pets:** Medium, dogs only. $10 daily fee/pet. Service with restrictions, supervision.
[SAVE] [✕] 🖪 🖵

◆◆◆ **▼▼▼ ▼▼▼ Saybrook Point Inn & Spa** 🅷 ❀
(860) 395-2000. **$229-$899, 3 day notice.** 2 Bridge St. On SR 154, 2.2 mi s of jct US 1; at Saybrook Point. Int corridors. **Pets:** Medium, dogs only. $50 daily fee/room. Designated rooms, service with restrictions, supervision.
[SAVE] [✕] [&M] 🖪 🖵 [¶] 🏊 [🏊]

RIVERTON

▼▼ Old Riverton Inn 🅒🅘
(860) 379-8678. **$99-$225, 10 day notice.** 436 E River Rd (SR 20). Center. Int corridors. **Pets:** Accepted.
[✕] 🖪 [¶]

SHELTON

▼▼ Homestead Studio Suites Hotel-Shelton-Fairfield County 🅷
(203) 926-6868. **$89-$159.** 945 Bridgeport Ave. SR 8, exit 11, 0.5 mi w. Int corridors. **Pets:** Other species. $25 daily fee/pet. Service with restrictions, crate.
[ASK] [✕] [&M] 🖪 🖵

▼▼▼ Residence Inn by Marriott 🅷
(203) 926-9000. **$179-$219.** 1001 Bridgeport Ave. SR 8, exit 11, 0.3 mi w. Ext corridors. **Pets:** Accepted.
[✕] [&M] 🖪 🖵 🏊 [🏊]

SOUTHBURY

▼▼▼ Cornucopia at Oldfield Bed and Breakfast 🅱🅱
(203) 267-6772. **$150-$250, 14 day notice.** 782 Main St N. I-84, exit 15, 1.5 mi n. Int corridors. **Pets:** Small, dogs only. $25 daily fee/pet. Designated rooms, service with restrictions, supervision.
[ASK] [✕] 🏊 [✆]

◆◆◆ **▼▼▼ Crowne Plaza Southbury** 🅷
(203) 598-7600. **$109-$185.** 1284 Strongtown Rd. I-84, exit 16, just n on SR 188. Int corridors. **Pets:** Accepted.
[SAVE] [✕] [&M] 🖪 🖵 [¶] 🏊 [🏊]

▼▼▼ The Heritage Hotel 🅷
(203) 264-8200. **$190.** 522 Heritage Rd. I-84, exit 15, 0.4 mi n on SR 67, then 1 mi w. Int corridors. **Pets:** Small, dogs only. $50 deposit/pet. Designated rooms, no service, supervision.
[ASK] [✕] [&M] 🖪 🖵 [¶] 🏊 [🏊]

STAMFORD

◆◆◆ **▼▼▼ Amsterdam Hotel–Greenwich/Stamford** 🅷
(203) 327-4300. **$90-$170.** 19 Clarks Hill Ave. I-95, exit 8 northbound, just n on Atlantic St, 0.6 mi ne on Tresser Blvd, then just s; exit southbound, just nw on Elm St, ne on Main St, then just s. Int corridors. **Pets:** $20 daily fee/pet. Designated rooms, service with restrictions, supervision.
[SAVE] [✕] [&M] 🖪 🖵

▼▼▼ Hilton Stamford Hotel & Executive Meeting Center 🅷 ❀
(203) 967-2222. **$115-$305.** 1 First Stamford Pl. I-95, exit 7 northbound, just s on Greenwich Ave, then just w; exit 6 southbound, just s on West Ave, 0.3 mi w on Baxter Ave, just n on Fairfield Ave, then just e. Int corridors. **Pets:** $75 one-time fee/room. Service with restrictions, crate.
[✕] 🖪 🖵 [¶] 🏊 [🏊]

◆◆◆ **▼▼▼ Holiday Inn Stamford Downtown** 🅷
(203) 358-8400. **$199-$250.** 700 Main St. I-95, exit 8 southbound, just n on Elm; exit northbound, n on Atlantic St, 0.3 mi e on Tresser Blvd, then just n on Elm; downtown. Int corridors. **Pets:** Accepted.
[SAVE] [✕] 🖪 🖵 [¶] 🏊

▼▼ La Quinta Inn & Suites Stamford 🄷 ❀
(203) 357-7100. **$79-$199.** 135 Harvard Ave. I-95, exit 6 northbound, just s; exit southbound, just w on Grenhart Rd, then just s. Int corridors. **Pets:** Medium, other species. Service with restrictions, supervision.
(ASK) ⊠ ᕵᴹ 🛢 💻 🍽 🐾

▼▼▼ Marriott Stamford Hotel & Spa 🄷
(203) 357-9555. **$299-$319.** 243 Tresser Blvd. I-95, exit 8, just n under viaduct, then n. Int corridors. **Pets:** Other species. $49 one-time fee/room. Supervision.
⊠ ᕵᴹ 🛢 💻 🍽 🐾 ⊠

▲▲▲ ▼▼▼ Sheraton Stamford Hotel 🄷
(203) 359-1300. **$119-$319.** 2701 Summer St. I-95, exit 8 northbound, 1.7 mi w on Atlantic and Bedford sts; exit 7 southbound, n on Atlantic and Bedford sts. Int corridors. **Pets:** Accepted.
(SAVE) ⊠ 🛢 💻 🍽 🐾 ⊠

STONINGTON

▲▲▲ ▼▼▼ Another Second Penny Inn 🄱🄱 ❀
(860) 535-1710. **$99-$215, 7 day notice.** 870 Pequot Tr. I-95, exit 91, 0.8 mi s on SR 234. Int corridors. **Pets:** Medium, other species. $25 one-time fee/pet. Designated rooms, service with restrictions, supervision.
(SAVE) ⊠ 🛢

STRATFORD

▼▼▼ Homewood Suites by Hilton 🄷
(203) 377-3322. **$129-$199.** 6905 Main St. SR 15, exit 53, just n. Int corridors. **Pets:** Accepted.
⊠ ᕵᴹ 🛢 💻 🐾

WALLINGFORD

▼▼▼ Homewood Suites by Hilton
NewHaven/Wallingford 🄷
(203) 284-2600. **$99-$169.** 90 Miles Dr. I-91, exit 15, nw on SR 68, then just s. Int corridors. **Pets:** Medium. $100 one-time fee/room. No service, supervision.
⊠ ᕵᴹ 🛢 💻 🐾 ⊠

WATERBURY

▼▼▼ House on the Hill Bed & Breakfast 🄱🄱
(203) 757-9901. **$150-$250, 14 day notice.** 92 Woodlawn Terr. I-84, exit 21, 0.6 mi n on Meadow St, then 0.4 mi ne on Pine St. Int corridors. **Pets:** Service with restrictions, supervision.
(ASK) ⊠ 🛢 💻

WATERFORD

▲▲▲ ▼ Oakdell Motel 🄼
(860) 442-9446. **$60-$150.** 983 Hartford Tpke. I-95, exit 82, 2 mi n on SR 85. Ext/int corridors. **Pets:** Large, dogs only. $25 deposit/room.
(SAVE) ⊠ 🛢 🐾

▼ Rodeway Inn at Crossroad 🄼
(860) 442-7227. **$60-$150.** 211 Parkway N. I-95, exit 81 northbound, just nw; exit southbound, 0.6 mi w. Ext corridors. **Pets:** Other species. $20 daily fee/pet. Designated rooms.
(ASK) ⊠ 🛢 🐾

WESTPORT

▼▼▼ The Westport Inn 🄼
(203) 259-5236. **Call for rates.** 1595 Post Rd E. I-95, exit 18 northbound, n to US 1, then 1.5 mi e; exit 19 southbound, 1 mi w. Ext/int corridors. **Pets:** Accepted.
⊠ 🛢 💻 🍽 🐾

WOODSTOCK

▼▼▼ Inn At Woodstock Hill 🄲🄸
(860) 928-0528. **$135-$220, 3 day notice.** 94 Plaine Hill Rd. 0.8 mi n on SR 169. Int corridors. **Pets:** $15 daily fee/pet. Crate.
⊠ 🛢 💻 🍽

DELAWARE

DEWEY BEACH

Atlantic Oceanside Motel
(302) 227-8811. **$45-$269, 7 day notice.** 1700 Coastal Hwy. Jct SR 1 and McKinley St. Ext corridors. **Pets:** Dogs only. $5 daily fee/pet. Service with restrictions, supervision.

Bellbuoy Motel
(302) 227-6000. **$55-$375, 3 day notice.** 21 Van Dyke St. SR 1, on oceanside block of Van Dyke St. Ext corridors. **Pets:** Large, dogs only. $10 daily fee/pet. Designated rooms, service with restrictions.

Sea-Esta Motel I
(302) 227-7666. **$49-$199.** 2306 Coastal Hwy. SR 1 at Houston St. Ext corridors. **Pets:** Other species. $8 daily fee/pet. Service with restrictions, crate.

Sea-Esta Motel III
(302) 227-4343. **$45-$229.** 1409 Coastal Hwy. Jct SR 1 and Rodney St. Ext corridors. **Pets:** Other species. $8 daily fee/pet. Service with restrictions, crate.

DOVER

Comfort Inn-Dover
(302) 674-3300. **$79-$119.** 222 S DuPont Hwy. SR 1, exit 95, 2 mi n on US 113, then 0.3 mi n on US 13. Ext corridors. **Pets:** Accepted.

Sheraton Dover Hotel
(302) 678-8500. **$99-$199.** 1570 N DuPont Hwy. SR 1, exit 104, 1 mi s on US 13. Int corridors. **Pets:** Accepted.

GEORGETOWN

Comfort Inn & Suites-Georgetown
(302) 854-9400. **$90-$280, 3 day notice.** 20530 DuPont Blvd. On US 113, 0.5 mi n of jct SR 404. Int corridors. **Pets:** Small. $15 daily fee/pet. Designated rooms, service with restrictions, supervision.

HARRINGTON

AmericInn Lodge & Suites of Harrington
(302) 398-3900. **$99-$139.** 1259 Corn Crib Rd. On US 13, 0.6 mi s of jct SR 14. Int corridors. **Pets:** Dogs only. $20 daily fee/room. Service with restrictions, crate.

LEWES

The Inn at Canal Square
(302) 644-3377. **$105-$310, 7 day notice.** 122 Market St. On the canal. Int corridors. **Pets:** Medium. Designated rooms, service with restrictions, supervision.

Sleep Inn & Suites
(302) 645-6464. **$59-$259.** 18451 Coastal Hwy. On SR 1, 1.5 mi s. Int corridors. **Pets:** $35 daily fee/pet. Designated rooms, service with restrictions, crate.

LONG NECK

Sea-Esta II
(302) 945-5900. **$100-$169.** 100 Rudder Rd. On SR 23, 1.1 mi s of jct SR 24, 5 and 23. Ext corridors. **Pets:** Accepted.

MILLSBORO

Atlantic Inn-Millsboro
(302) 934-6711. **$69-$189.** 28534 DuPont Blvd. US 113, just s of SR 24. Ext corridors. **Pets:** Other species. $20 daily fee/pet. Designated rooms, service with restrictions, crate.

NEWARK

Days Inn Wilmington/Newark
(302) 368-2400. **$59-$299.** 900 Churchmans Rd. I-95, exit 4B, 0.3 mi n on SR 7, exit 166, then 0.3 mi w on SR 58 (Churchmans Rd). Ext corridors. **Pets:** Accepted.

Hilton Wilmington/Christiana
(302) 454-1500. **$109-$279.** 100 Continental Dr. I-95, exit 4B, 0.3 mi n on SR 7, exit 166, then 0.4 mi w on SR 58 (Churchmans Rd). Int corridors. **Pets:** Accepted.

Homestead Studio Suites Hotel-Newark/Christiana
(302) 283-0800. **$109-$169.** 333 Continental Dr. I-95, exit 4B, 0.3 mi n on SR 7, exit 166, then 0.4 mi w on SR 58 (Churchmans Rd). Int corridors. **Pets:** Other species. $25 daily fee/pet. Service with restrictions, crate.

Homewood Suites by Hilton Newark/Wilmington South
(302) 453-9700. **$109-$199.** 640 S College Ave. I-95, exit 1B southbound; exit 1 northbound, 0.8 mi n on SR 896. Int corridors. **Pets:** Small. $25 daily fee/room. Service with restrictions, crate.

Howard Johnson Inn & Suites-Wilmington/Newark
(302) 368-8521. **$59-$299.** 1119 S College Ave. I-95, exit 1B southbound; exit 1 northbound, 0.3 mi n on SR 896. Int corridors. **Pets:** Accepted.

Quality Inn University
(302) 731-3131. **$59-$349.** 1120 S College Ave. I-95, exit 1B southbound; exit 1 northbound, 0.3 mi n on SR 896. Ext corridors. **Pets:** Other species. $10 daily fee/pet. Designated rooms, service with restrictions.

Red Roof Inn-Wilmington
(302) 292-2870. **$66-$83.** 415 Stanton Christiana Rd. I-95, exit 4B, 0.5 mi n on SR 7. Ext corridors. **Pets:** Medium. Service with restrictions, crate.

▼▼▼ Residence Inn by Marriott H
(302) 453-9200. **$179-$219.** 240 Chapman Rd. I-95, exit 3 southbound; exit 3A northbound, 0.3 mi e on SR 273 E, then 0.5 mi s. Ext corridors. **Pets:** Accepted.

⊠ 🖥 💻 ⊇ ⊠

▼▼▼ Staybridge Suites-Newark/Wilmington H
(302) 366-8097. **$190-$200.** 270 Chapman Rd. I-95, exit 3 southbound; exit 3A northbound, 0.3 mi e on SR 273 E, then just n. Int corridors. **Pets:** Accepted.

ASK ⊠ 🔊ᴹ 🖥 💻 ⊇

⊕ ▼▼▼ TownePlace Suites by
            Marriott-Wilmington/Newark H
(302) 369-6212. **$161-$197.** 410 Eagle Run Rd. I-95, exit 3 southbound; exit 3A northbound, just e. Int corridors. **Pets:** Medium. $100 one-time fee/room. Designated rooms, service with restrictions, crate.

SAVE ⊠ 🔊ᴹ 🖥 💻 ⊇

NEW CASTLE

⊕ ▼▼▼ Quality Inn & Suites M
(302) 328-6666. **$119-$194.** 147 N DuPont Hwy. I-95, exit 5A, 0.8 mi s on SR 141, exit 1B, then 0.5 mi s on US 13, 40 and 301; I-295, exit New Castle Airport/US 13 S, 1.8 mi s on US 13, 40 and 301. Ext/int corridors. **Pets:** Accepted.

SAVE ⊠ 🔊ᴹ 🖥 💻 ⊇

▼▼ Super 8 M
(302) 322-9480. **$63-$72.** 215 S DuPont Hwy. I-95, exit 3A, 4.3 mi e on SR 273, then 0.8 mi s on US 13. Int corridors. **Pets:** Accepted.

ASK ⊠ 🖥

REHOBOTH BEACH

▼▼ AmericInn Lodge & Suites of Rehoboth
            Beach H 🐾
(302) 226-0700. **$69-$249, 3 day notice.** 329Z Airport Rd. Just w of SR 1; just w on Miller Rd, then just s. Int corridors. **Pets:** Medium, dogs only. $20 daily fee/pet. Designated rooms, service with restrictions.

ASK ⊠ 🔊ᴹ 🖥 💻 ⊇

▼▼ The Atlantis Inn M
(302) 227-9446. **$69-$299, 7 day notice.** 154 Rehoboth Ave. At Rehoboth Ave and 2nd St; downtown. Ext corridors. **Pets:** Accepted.

ASK ⊠ 🖥 💻 ⊇

▼▼▼ The Breakers Hotel & Suites M 🐾
(302) 227-6688. **Call for rates.** 105 2nd St. Just n of Rehoboth Ave. Ext corridors. **Pets:** Dogs only. $50 daily fee/pet. Designated rooms, service with restrictions.

⊠ 🖥 💻 ⊇

⊕ ▼▼ Sea-Esta IV M
(302) 227-5882. **$47-$189.** 20902 Coastal Hwy. 1 mi s. Ext corridors. **Pets:** Other species. $8 daily fee/pet. Service with restrictions, crate.

SAVE ⊠ 🖥 💻 ⊇

⊕ ▼▼▼ Sea Witch, Bewitched & Bedazzled BB
(302) 226-9482. **Call for rates.** 771 Lake Ave. Jct Rehoboth Ave, just ne. Int corridors. **Pets:** Accepted.

SAVE ⊠ 🖥

WILMINGTON

⊕ ▼▼▼ Best Western Brandywine Valley Inn H
(302) 656-9436. **$102-$149, 3 day notice.** 1807 Concord Pike. I-95, exit 8, 1 mi n on US 202. Ext corridors. **Pets:** Accepted.

SAVE ⊠ 🖥 💻 ⊇

⊕ ▼▼▼ Hotel du Pont H
(302) 594-3100. **$139-$565.** 1007 Market St. I-95, exit 7, 0.5 mi se; downtown at 11th St. Int corridors. **Pets:** Accepted.

SAVE ⊠ 💻 🍴 ⊠

DISTRICT OF COLUMBIA

District of Columbia Metropolitan Area

WASHINGTON

Capitol Hill Suites H
(202) 543-6000. **$139-$659.** 200 C St SE. 2 blks from Capitol grounds; at 2nd and C sts SE. Int corridors. **Pets:** Accepted.

DoubleTree Guest Suites, Washington DC H
(202) 785-2000. **$129-$359.** 801 New Hampshire Ave NW. Just sw at Washington Circle. Int corridors. **Pets:** Accepted.

The Fairfax at Embassy Row, Washington, D.C .–The Luxury Collection H
(202) 293-2100. **$199-$759.** 2100 Massachusetts Ave NW. Just w of Dupont Circle; at 21st St. Int corridors. **Pets:** Accepted.

The Fairmont Washington, D.C. H
(202) 429-2400. **$189-$749.** 2401 M St NW. 24th and M sts NW. Int corridors. **Pets:** Accepted.

Four Seasons Hotel Washington D.C. H
(202) 342-0444. **$635-$1975.** 2800 Pennsylvania Ave NW. In Georgetown. Int corridors. **Pets:** Accepted.

Hamilton Crowne Plaza Hotel Washington DC H
(202) 682-0111. **$99-$650.** 1001 14th St NW. 14th and K sts NW. Int corridors. **Pets:** Accepted.

The Hay-Adams H
(202) 638-6600. **$800-$1200.** 800 16th St NW. 16th and H sts NW; just n of the White House. Int corridors. **Pets:** Accepted.

Hilton Washington H
(202) 483-3000. **$99-$399.** 1919 Connecticut Ave NW. Just n of Dupont Circle at T St NW. Int corridors. **Pets:** Accepted.

The Hotel George H
(202) 347-4200. **$169-$529.** 15 E St NW. On Capitol Hill, just n of Capitol grounds. Int corridors. **Pets:** Accepted.

Hotel Helix-A Kimpton Hotel H
(202) 462-9001. **Call for rates.** 1430 Rhode Island Ave NW. Just e of Scott Circle. Int corridors. **Pets:** Accepted.

Hotel Madera H 🐾
(202) 296-7600. **Call for rates.** 1310 New Hampshire Ave NW. Between 20th and N sts NW. Int corridors. **Pets:** Other species. Service with restrictions, crate.

Hotel Monaco Washington DC H 🐾
(202) 628-7177. **$169-$1200.** 700 F St NW. Between 7th and 8th sts NW. Int corridors. **Pets:** Other species. Service with restrictions, supervision.

Hotel Palomar-A Kimpton Hotel H 🐾
(202) 448-1800. **Call for rates.** 2121 P St NW. Between 21st and 22nd sts NW; just w of Dupont Circle. Int corridors. **Pets:** Service with restrictions, crate.

Hotel Rouge-A Kimpton Hotel H
(202) 232-8000. **$139-$409.** 1315 16th St NW. Just n of Scott Circle. Int corridors. **Pets:** Accepted.

L'Enfant Plaza Hotel H
(202) 484-1000. **$119-$579.** 480 L'Enfant Plaza SW. I-395, exit L'Enfant Plaza/12th St. Int corridors. **Pets:** Large. $25 deposit/pet. Service with restrictions, supervision.

The Liaison Capitol Hill, An Affinia Hotel H
(202) 638-1616. **$119-$799.** 415 New Jersey Ave NW. On Capitol Hill. Int corridors. **Pets:** Accepted.

The Loews Madison Hotel H
(202) 862-1600. **$189-$459.** 1177 15th St NW. 15th and M sts NW. Int corridors. **Pets:** Accepted.

Mandarin Oriental, Washington D.C. H 🐾
(202) 554-8588. **$495-$8000.** 1330 Maryland Ave SW. Jct Independence Ave SW, just s on 12th St SW. Int corridors. **Pets:** Medium, dogs only. $50 daily fee/room, $50 one-time fee/room. Service with restrictions, supervision.

Marriott Wardman Park Hotel H
(202) 328-2000. **$349-$429.** 2660 Woodley Rd NW. Just w of Connecticut Ave; at Woodley Park/Zoo Metro Station. Int corridors. **Pets:** Accepted.

The Mayflower-A Renaissance Hotel H
(202) 347-3000. **$399-$479.** 1127 Connecticut Ave NW. Just n of K St NW; in business district. Int corridors. **Pets:** Accepted.

The Melrose Hotel, Washington DC H
(202) 955-6400. **$189-$449.** 2430 Pennsylvania Ave NW. Between 24th and 25th sts NW. Int corridors. **Pets:** Accepted.

Omni Shoreham Hotel H
(202) 234-0700. **$199-$699.** 2500 Calvert St NW. Just w of Connecticut Ave. Int corridors. **Pets:** Accepted.

Park Hyatt Washington, D.C. H
(202) 789-1234. **$249-$575, 3 day notice.** 1201 24th St NW. 24th and M sts NW. Int corridors. **Pets:** Accepted.

The Quincy H
(202) 223-4320. **$139-$339.** 1823 L St NW. Between 18th and 19th sts NW. Int corridors. **Pets:** Small. $150 one-time fee/pet. Supervision.

(AAA) ▼▼ ◆◆ Red Roof Inn Downtown Washington, D.C. H
(202) 289-5959. **Call for rates.** 500 H St NW. At 5th and H sts NW; in Chinatown. Int corridors. **Pets:** Accepted.
[SAVE] [✕] [🖥] [💻]

▼▼◆▼◆ Residence Inn by Marriott Capitol H
(202) 484-8280. **$289-$379.** 333 E St SW. Between 3rd and 4th sts SW. Int corridors. **Pets:** Accepted.
[✕] [&M] [🖥] [💻] [≈]

▼▼◆▼◆ Residence Inn by Marriott-Dupont Circle H
(202) 466-6800. **$299-$389.** 2120 P St NW. Between 21st and 22nd sts NW; just w of Dupont Circle. Int corridors. **Pets:** Accepted.
[✕] [&M] [🖥] [💻]

▼▼◆▼◆ Residence Inn by Marriott-Washington DC-Vermont Ave H
(202) 898-1100. **$289-$379.** 1199 Vermont Ave NW. Jct 14th St and Vermont Ave NW, at Thomas Circle. Int corridors. **Pets:** Accepted.
[✕] [&M] [🖥] [💻]

▼▼◆▼◆▼ The Ritz-Carlton, Georgetown H
(202) 912-4100. **Call for rates.** 3100 South St NW. Just s of jct M St and Wisconsin Ave; in Georgetown. Int corridors. **Pets:** Accepted.
[✕] [🖥] [🍴] [✕]

▼▼◆▼◆▼ The Ritz-Carlton, Washington, D.C. H
(202) 835-0500. **Call for rates.** 1150 22nd St NW. At 22nd and M sts NW. Int corridors. **Pets:** Accepted.
[✕] [💻] [🍴] [≈] [✕]

(AAA) ▼▼◆▼◆ St. Regis, Washington, D.C. H
(202) 638-2626. **$350-$845.** 923 16th St NW. 16th and K sts; just n of the White House. Int corridors. **Pets:** Accepted.
[SAVE] [✕] [🍴]

▼▼◆▼◆▼ Sofitel Lafayette Square Washington DC H
(202) 730-8800. **Call for rates.** 806 15th St NW. Jct 15th and H sts NW. Int corridors. **Pets:** Accepted.
[✕] [&M] [🍴]

(AAA) ▼▼◆▼◆ Topaz Hotel-A Kimpton Hotel H
(202) 393-3000. **Call for rates.** 1733 N St NW. Just e of Connecticut Ave. Int corridors. **Pets:** Accepted.
[SAVE] [✕] [🍴]

(AAA) ▼▼◆▼◆ Washington Suites Georgetown H
(202) 333-8060. **$169-$424.** 2500 Pennsylvania Ave NW. Jct 25th St NW and Pennsylvania Ave; 2 blks from Foggy Bottom metro station. Int corridors. **Pets:** Small. $20 daily fee/pet. Designated rooms, service with restrictions.
[SAVE] [✕] [&M] [🖥] [💻]

(AAA) ▼▼◆▼◆ The Westin Grand H
(202) 429-0100. **Call for rates.** 2350 M St NW. 24th and M sts NW. Int corridors. **Pets:** Accepted.
[SAVE] [✕] [💻] [🍴] [≈]

(AAA) ▼▼◆▼◆ The Westin Washington DC City Center Hotel H
(202) 429-1700. **Call for rates.** 1400 M St NW. Just w of Thomas Circle. Int corridors. **Pets:** Accepted.
[SAVE] [✕] [💻] [🍴]

▼▼◆▼◆▼ The Willard InterContinental H
(202) 628-9100. **$299-$959.** 1401 Pennsylvania Ave NW. Just e of the White House. Int corridors. **Pets:** Medium, dogs only. $100 one-time fee/room. Designated rooms, service with restrictions, crate.
[✕] [&M] [💻] [🍴] [✕]

END METROPOLITAN AREA

FLORIDA

ALACHUA

AAA ▼▼ Econo Lodge 🅷
(386) 462-2414. **$85-$160, 7 day notice.** 15920 NW Hwy 441. I-75, exit 399, just e. Ext corridors. **Pets:** Dogs only. $10 daily fee/pet. Designated rooms, service with restrictions, supervision.
SAVE ⊠ 🛢 💻 ➥

APALACHICOLA

AAA ▼▼▼ Coombs House Inn 🅱🅱
(850) 653-9199. **$99-$229, 7 day notice.** 80 Sixth St (Hwy 98). Corner of US 98 and 6th St; center. Int corridors. **Pets:** Medium, dogs only. $25 one-time fee/pet. Designated rooms, service with restrictions, supervision.
SAVE ⊠ 🛢 💻

AAA ▼▼▼ Gibson Inn 🅲🅸
(850) 653-2191. **$105-$250, 14 day notice.** 51 Ave C. On US 98 at west end of bridge. Int corridors. **Pets:** Other species. $25 daily fee/pet. Designated rooms, service with restrictions, supervision.
SAVE ⊠ 🍽

▼▼▼ Water Street Hotel & Marina 🅲🅾
(850) 653-3700. **$129-$325, 7 day notice.** 329 Water St. Jct Ave I and Water St. Ext corridors. **Pets:** Dogs only. $20 daily fee/pet. Service with restrictions.
ASK ⊠ &M 🛢 💻 ➥ ⊠

ARCADIA

AAA ▼▼ Best Western Arcadia Inn 🅼
(863) 494-4884. **$69-$129.** 504 S Brevard Ave. 0.6 mi s of SR 70; on US 17. Ext corridors. **Pets:** Accepted.
SAVE ⊠ 🛢 💻 ➥

AVON PARK

AAA ▼▼ Econo Lodge 🅼
(863) 453-2000. **$69-$110.** 2511 US Hwy 27 S. On US 27; 2.5 mi s of jct SR 17 and 64. Ext corridors. **Pets:** Other species. $10 daily fee/room. Service with restrictions, crate.
SAVE ⊠ ➥

AAA ▼ Reeds Motel & Oasis Banquet Hall 🅼
(863) 453-3194. **$79-$199.** 102 US Hwy 27 S. Just n of SR 64 (W Main St). Ext corridors. **Pets:** Accepted.
SAVE ⊠ 🛢 💻 ➥

BOCA RATON

AAA ▼▼▼ Boca Raton Bridge Hotel 🅷
(561) 368-9500. **$89-$409, 3 day notice.** 999 E Camino Real. Just w of SR A1A, 1 mi s of jct SR 798 (Palmetto Park Rd). Int corridors. **Pets:** Small. $75 one-time fee/room. Designated rooms, service with restrictions, supervision.
SAVE ⊠ 🛢 💻 🍽 ➥ ⊠

▼▼ Homestead Studio Suites Hotel-Boca Raton/Commerce 🅼
(561) 994-2599. **$60-$150.** 501 NW 77th St. I-95, exit 50, just s on Congress Ave to NW 6th Ave. Ext corridors. **Pets:** Other species. $25 daily fee/pet. Service with restrictions, crate.
ASK ⊠ 🛢 💻

AAA ▼▼▼ Residence Inn-By Marriott-Boca Raton 🅷
(561) 994-3222. **$164-$298.** 525 NW 77th St. I-95, exit 50, w on Congress Ave to NW 6th Ave, then to NW 77th St. Ext corridors. **Pets:** Other species. $100 one-time fee/room. Service with restrictions, supervision.
SAVE ⊠ 🛢 💻 ➥ ⊠

AAA ▼▼▼ TownePlace Suites by Marriott 🅷
(561) 994-7232. **$195-$308.** 5110 NW 8th Ave. I-95, exit 48B (Yamato Rd), just w; in Arvida Corporate Park. Int corridors. **Pets:** Accepted.
SAVE ⊠ &M 🛢 💻 ➥

BONITA SPRINGS

▼▼▼▼ AmericInn Hotel & Suites 🅗
(239) 495-9255. **$69-$179.** 28600 Trails Edge Blvd. US 41 0.7 mi s of jct CR 865 (Bonita Beach Rd SE), just w; in Woods Edge. Int corridors. **Pets:** Accepted.
(A$K) (✕) (&M) (❚) (▣) (≈)

◈◈ ▼▼▼▼ Hyatt Regency Coconut Point Resort & Spa 🅗
(239) 444-1234. **$129-$569, 3 day notice.** 5001 Coconut Rd. I-75, exit 123, 1.9 mi w on CR 850 (Corkscrew Rd), 2.3 mi s on US 41, then 1.5 mi w. Int corridors. **Pets:** Accepted.
(SAVE) (✕) (❚) (▣) (❙❙) (≈) (✕)

◈◈ ▼▼▼▼ Inn at the Springs 🅗
(239) 949-5913. **$79-$249, 3 day notice.** 8901 Highland Woods Blvd. I-75, exit 116, 3.5 mi w on CR 865 (Bonita Beach Rd SE), 1.4 mi n on US 41 (Tamiami Tr), then e. Int corridors. **Pets:** Accepted.
(SAVE) (✕) (&M) (❚) (▣) (≈)

BRADENTON

◈◈ ▼▼ ▼▼ Howard Johnson Express Inn Ⓜ
(941) 756-8399. **$49-$149.** 6511 14th St W. On US 41, 1.5 mi s of jct SR 70. Ext corridors. **Pets:** Accepted.
(SAVE) (✕) (❚) (▣) (≈)

◈◈ ▼▼ ▼▼ Quality Inn North Ⓜ
(941) 758-7199. **$59-$189.** 6727 14th St W. On US 41, 2 mi s of jct SR 70. Ext corridors. **Pets:** Small, dogs only. $10 daily fee/pet. Designated rooms, service with restrictions, supervision.
(SAVE) (✕) (❚) (▣) (≈)

BRADENTON BEACH

◈◈ ▼▼▼▼ Tortuga Inn Beach Resort Ⓒⓞ
(941) 778-6611. **Call for rates.** 1325 Gulf Dr N. On Sarasota Bay and Anna Maria Island; on SR 789, 0.3 mi n of jct SR 684. Ext corridors. **Pets:** Accepted.
(SAVE) (✕) (❚) (▣) (≈)

◈◈ ▼▼▼▼ Tradewinds Resort ⒸⒶ
(941) 779-0010. **Call for rates.** 1603 Gulf Dr N. On Sarasota Bay and Anna Maria Island; on SR 789, 0.5 mi n of jct SR 684. Ext corridors. **Pets:** Accepted.
(SAVE) (✕) (❚) (▣) (≈)

BROOKSVILLE

◈◈ ▼▼ ▼▼ Best Western Brooksville I-75 Ⓜ
(352) 796-9481. **$59-$129.** 30307 Cortez Blvd. I-75, exit 301, just w on US 98/SR 50. Ext corridors. **Pets:** Large, other species. $25 one-time fee/room. Designated rooms, service with restrictions, supervision.
(SAVE) (✕) (&M) (▣) (❙❙) (≈)

◈◈ ▼▼ ▼▼ Days Inn Heritage Inn Ⓜ
(352) 796-9486. **$79-$99.** 6320 Windmere Rd. I-75, exit 301, just e on US 98/SR 50. Ext corridors. **Pets:** Other species. $15 one-time fee/pet. Service with restrictions, crate.
(SAVE) (✕) (&M) (❚) (▣) (≈)

CAPE CANAVERAL

◈◈ ▼▼▼▼ Residence Inn by Marriott Cape Canaveral/ Cocoa Beach 🅗
(321) 323-1100. **$177-$190.** 8959 Astronaut Blvd. On SR A1A, 0.3 mi s of jct SR 528. Int corridors. **Pets:** Other species. $75 one-time fee/room. Service with restrictions.
(SAVE) (✕) (❚) (▣) (≈) (✕)

CAPE CORAL

◈◈ ▼▼ ▼▼ Dockside Inn Ⓜ 🐾
(239) 542-0061. **$95-$165, 3 day notice.** 3817 Del Prado Blvd. 1.2 mi n of jct Cape Coral Pkwy. Ext corridors. **Pets:** Other species. $25 one-time fee/room.
(SAVE) (✕) (❚) (≈) (✕)

▼▼▼▼ Quality Hotel 🅗
(239) 542-2121. **$75-$175.** 1538 Cape Coral Pkwy. Jct Del Prado Blvd. Int corridors. **Pets:** Small. $15 daily fee/pet. Designated rooms, service with restrictions, supervision.
(A$K) (✕) (❚) (▣) (≈)

CEDAR KEY

◈◈ ▼▼ ▼▼ Park Place Motel & Condominiums Ⓜ
(352) 543-5737. **$65-$120.** 211 2nd St. At a St. Ext corridors. **Pets:** Accepted.
(SAVE) (✕) (❚) (▣)

▼▼▼▼ Seahorse Landing Condominiums Ⓒⓞ
(352) 543-5860. **$160-$185, 3 day notice.** 4050 G St. Just w on 6th St. Ext corridors. **Pets:** Medium, dogs only. $15 daily fee/room. Designated rooms, no service, supervision.
(✕) (❚) (▣) (≈) (✕)

CHARLOTTE HARBOR

▼▼ Banana Bay On Charlotte Harbor Ⓜ
(941) 743-4441. **$59-$129.** 23285 Bayshore Rd. Jct US 41. Ext corridors. **Pets:** Accepted.
(A$K) (✕) (❚) (▣) (≈)

CHIEFLAND

◈◈ ▼▼ ▼▼ Best Western Suwannee Valley Inn 🅗 🐾
(352) 493-0663. **$84-$97, 3 day notice.** 1125 N Young Blvd. On US 19/98, just n of jct US 129. Ext corridors. **Pets:** Small. $25 daily fee/pet. Designated rooms, service with restrictions, supervision.
(SAVE) (✕) (❚) (▣) (≈)

▼▼ ▼▼ Holiday Inn Express 🅗
(352) 493-9400. **$77-$139.** 809 NW 21st Ave. US 19/98, 1.5 mi n of jct US 129. Ext corridors. **Pets:** Medium, other species. $20 daily fee/pet. Designated rooms, service with restrictions.
(A$K) (✕) (&M) (❚) (▣) (≈)

CHIPLEY

▼▼ ▼▼ Super 8 Ⓜ 🐾
(850) 638-8530. **Call for rates.** 1150 Motel Dr. I-10, exit 120, just n. Ext corridors. **Pets:** $10 daily fee/pet. No service.
(✕) (❚) (▣)

COCOA

◈◈ ▼▼ ▼▼ Econo Lodge-Space Center 🅗
(321) 632-4561. **$59-$99.** 3220 N Cocoa Blvd. US 1, just n of jct SR 528. Ext corridors. **Pets:** Medium, other species. $50 deposit/room, $15 one-time fee/room. Designated rooms, service with restrictions, supervision.
(SAVE) (✕) (❚) (▣) (≈)

COCOA BEACH

◈◈ ▼▼ ▼▼ Best Western Ocean Beach Hotel & Suites 🅗 🐾
(321) 783-7621. **$89-$289.** 5600 N Atlantic Ave. SR A1A, 0.8 mi n of jct SR 520. Ext/int corridors. **Pets:** Medium. $25 one-time fee/room. Designated rooms, service with restrictions, supervision.
(SAVE) (✕) (&M) (❚) (▣) (≈)

🌀 ▽▽▽ Days Inn Cocoa Beach 🅷 ❖
(321) 784-2550. **$75-$169.** 5500 N Atlantic Ave. SR A1A, 0.8 mi n of jct SR 520. Ext corridors. **Pets:** Medium. $50 deposit/room. Designated rooms, service with restrictions, supervision.
[SAVE] [X] [🛏] [💻] [⊇]

🌀 ▽▽▽▽ Four Points by Sheraton Cocoa Beach 🅷
(321) 783-8717. **$90-$195.** 4001 N Atlantic Ave. SR A1A, just s of jct SR 520. Int corridors. **Pets:** Accepted.
[SAVE] [X] [🛏] [💻] [🍴] [⊇]

🌀 ▽▽▽ Holiday Inn Cocoa Beach Oceanfront Resort 🅷 ❖
(321) 783-2271. **$99-$189.** 1300 N Atlantic Ave. SR A1A, 1.8 mi s of jct SR 520. Ext corridors. **Pets:** Medium, other species. $25 deposit/pet, $10 daily fee/pet, $25 one-time fee/pet. Service with restrictions.
[SAVE] [X] [🛏] [💻] [🍴] [⊇] [X]

🌀 ▽▽▽ La Quinta Inn Cocoa Beach 🅷 ❖
(321) 783-2252. **$59-$179.** 1275 N Atlantic Ave. On SR A1A, 1.7 mi s. Ext corridors. **Pets:** Medium, other species. Service with restrictions, supervision.
[SAVE] [X] [🛏] [💻] [🍴] [⊇]

▽▽▽▽ Quality Suites Cocoa Beach 🅷
(321) 783-6868. **$79-$189.** 3655 N Atlantic Ave. SR A1A, 0.3 mi s of jct SR 520. Int corridors. **Pets:** Accepted.
[ASK] [X] [♿] [🛏] [💻]

▽▽▽ Surf Studio Beach Resort 🅼
(321) 783-7100. **$100-$215, 7 day notice.** 1801 S Atlantic Ave. SR A1A northbound, 5 mi s of jct SR 520 at Francis St; 1.3 mi n of Patrick AFB. Ext corridors. **Pets:** Medium. $20 daily fee/pet. Service with restrictions, supervision.
[🛏] [💻] [⊇]

CRESCENT BEACH

🌀 ▽▽▽ Beacher's Lodge Oceanfront Suites 🄲🄾
(904) 471-8849. **$89-$225, 3 day notice.** 6970 A1A S. Just s of jct SR 206. Ext corridors. **Pets:** Small, other species. $50 one-time fee/pet. Designated rooms, service with restrictions.
[SAVE] [X] [🛏] [💻] [⊇]

CRESCENT CITY

▽▽ Lake View Motel 🅼
(386) 698-1090. **$60-$100.** 1004 N Summit St. 1 mi n on US 17. Ext corridors. **Pets:** Accepted.
[X] [🛏] [💻] [⊇]

CRESTVIEW

▽▽ Jameson Inn 🅷
(850) 683-1778. **$93-$100.** 151 Cracker Barrel Dr. I-10, exit 56, just s. Int corridors. **Pets:** Accepted.
[ASK] [X] [🛏] [💻] [⊇]

🌀 ▽▽ Super 8 🅼
(850) 682-9649. **$53-$78.** 3925 S Ferdon Blvd. I-10, exit 56, 0.3 mi s. Ext corridors. **Pets:** Accepted.
[SAVE] [X] [🛏] [💻]

CRYSTAL RIVER

🌀 ▽▽▽ Best Western Crystal River Resort 🅷
(352) 795-3171. **$118-$165.** 614 NW Hwy 19. On US 19/98, 0.8 mi n of jct SR 44. Ext corridors. **Pets:** Other species. $3 daily fee/pet. Service with restrictions, supervision.
[SAVE] [X] [🛏] [💻] [⊇] [X]

▽▽ Days Inn 🅷
(352) 795-2111. **$65-$140.** 2380 NW Hwy 19. US 19, 2.2 mi n of jct SR 44. Ext corridors. **Pets:** Other species. $15 daily fee/pet. Designated rooms, no service, supervision.
[ASK] [X] [🛏] [💻] [🍴]

CUTLER BAY

▽▽▽ La Quinta Inn & Suites 🅷 ❖
(305) 278-0001. **$59-$179.** 10821 Caribbean Blvd. Florida Tpke, exit 12 (US 1), northwest corner. Int corridors. **Pets:** Medium, other species. Service with restrictions, supervision.
[ASK] [X] [♿] [🛏] [💻] [⊇]

DAYTONA BEACH

🌀 ▽ Days Inn Speedway 🅼
(386) 255-0541. **$45-$349.** 2900 W International Speedway Blvd. I-95, exit 261B southbound; exit 261 northbound, just w on US 92. Ext corridors. **Pets:** Other species. $15 daily fee/pet. Designated rooms, service with restrictions, supervision.
[SAVE] [X] [🛏] [💻] [🍴] [⊇]

▽▽▽ Extended Stay Deluxe Daytona Beach-International Speedway 🅷
(386) 257-4311. **$75-$250.** 255 Bill France Blvd. I-95, exit 261, 2.5 mi e, then just n. Int corridors. **Pets:** Other species. $25 daily fee/pet. Service with restrictions, crate.
[ASK] [X] [♿] [🛏] [💻] [⊇]

▽▽▽ Homewood Suites by Hilton Daytona Speedway/Airport 🅷 ❖
(386) 258-2828. **$74-$499.** 165 Bill France Blvd. I-95, exit 261, 2.5 mi e, then just n. Int corridors. **Pets:** Medium. $100 one-time fee/room. Service with restrictions, supervision.
[X] [♿] [🛏] [💻] [⊇] [X]

🌀 ▽▽▽ Plaza Ocean Club Hotel 🅷
(386) 239-9800. **$89-$499, 3 day notice.** 640 N Atlantic Ave. On SR A1A, 1 mi n of jct SR 90. Int corridors. **Pets:** Small, other species. $50 deposit/room, $20 daily fee/pet. Designated rooms, service with restrictions, crate.
[SAVE] [X] [♿] [🛏] [💻] [🍴] [⊇]

▽▽▽ Ramada Inn Speedway 🅷 ❖
(386) 255-2422. **$89, 30 day notice.** 1798 W International Speedway Blvd. I-95, exit 261A southbound; exit 261 northbound, 2 mi e on US 92. Ext corridors. **Pets:** Medium. $25 one-time fee/room. No service.
[ASK] [X] [🛏] [💻] [🍴] [⊇]

🌀 ▽▽▽ Residence Inn by Marriott 🅷
(386) 252-3949. **$205-$236.** 1725 Richard Petty Blvd. I-95, exit 261, 2.6 mi e, then just s. Int corridors. **Pets:** Large. $75 one-time fee/room. Service with restrictions.
[SAVE] [X] [♿] [🛏] [💻] [⊇] [X]

▽▽ Scottish Inns 🅼
(386) 258-5742. **$39-$250, 15 day notice.** 1515 S Ridgewood Ave. I-95, exit 260A, 2.5 mi e on SR 400, then just n on US 1. Ext corridors. **Pets:** Accepted.
[ASK] [X] [🛏] [⊇]

DAYTONA BEACH SHORES

🌀 ▽▽ Atlantic Ocean Palm Inn 🅼
(386) 761-8450. **$59-$139, 30 day notice.** 3247 S Atlantic Ave. On SR A1A, 5 mi s of jct US 92. Ext corridors. **Pets:** Small. $15 daily fee/pet. Designated rooms, service with restrictions, supervision.
[SAVE] [X] [🛏] [⊇]

🌀 ▽▽▽ The Shores Resort & Spa 🅷 ❖
(386) 767-7350. **$99-$499, 3 day notice.** 2637 S Atlantic Ave. On SR A1A, 3.2 mi s of jct US 92. Int corridors. **Pets:** Small. $250 deposit/room, $25 daily fee/room. Designated rooms, service with restrictions, supervision.
[SAVE] [X] [♿] [💻] [🍴] [⊇] [X]

DE FUNIAK SPRINGS

AAA **WW** Best Western Crossroads Inn **H**
(850) 892-5111. **$80-$99, 7 day notice.** 2343 Freeport Rd. I-10, exit 85, just s. Ext/int corridors. **Pets:** Small. $20 one-time fee/room. Designated rooms, service with restrictions, supervision.
[SAVE] [X] [•] [•] [¶] [≈]

DELAND

AAA **WW** University Inn **M**
(386) 734-5711. **$79-$199.** 644 N Woodland Blvd. US 17, 0.9 mi n of jct SR 44. Ext corridors. **Pets:** Medium. $10 daily fee/pet. Designated rooms, service with restrictions, supervision.
[SAVE] [X] [•] [≈]

DELRAY BEACH

AAA **WWW** Colony Hotel & Cabana Club **H** ❀
(561) 276-4123. **$125-$349, 3 day notice.** 525 E Atlantic Ave. On SR 806 (Atlantic Ave) at US 1 northbound; center. Int corridors. **Pets:** Other species. $25 daily fee/pet.
[SAVE] [X] [≈]

AAA **WWW** Residence Inn Delray Beach **H**
(561) 276-7441. **$179-$369.** 1111 E Atlantic Ave. I-95, exit 52 (SR 806/ Atlantic Ave), 1.7 mi e. Int corridors. **Pets:** $100 one-time fee/room. Service with restrictions, crate.
[SAVE] [X] [&M] [•] [•] [≈]

DELTONA

AAA **WW** Best Western Deltona Inn **H**
(386) 860-3000. **$80-$369, 3 day notice.** 481 Deltona Blvd. I-4, exit 108, just ne. Ext corridors. **Pets:** Small. Designated rooms, service with restrictions, supervision.
[SAVE] [X] [•] [•] [¶] [≈]

DESTIN

WW Beachside Inn **H** ❀
(850) 650-9099. **$79-$199.** 2931 Scenic Hwy 98. 1 mi s of US 98. Ext corridors. **Pets:** Other species. $25 one-time fee/pet. Designated rooms, service with restrictions.
[ASK] [X] [•] [•] [¶] [≈]

WWW Hilton Sandestin Beach Golf Resort & Spa **H**
(850) 267-9500. **$89-$549.** 4000 S Sandestin Blvd. 10 mi e at Sandestin Blvd. Int corridors. **Pets:** Accepted.
[X] [•] [•] [¶] [≈] [X]

WWW Residence Inn Sandestin at Grand Boulevard **H**
(850) 650-7811. **$164-$246.** 300 Grand Blvd. 6 mi w on US 98 from jct US 331. Int corridors. **Pets:** Accepted.
[X] [&M] [•] [•] [≈] [X]

ELKTON

AAA **WW** Quality Inn St. Augustine **M**
(904) 829-3435. **$64-$109.** 2625 SR 207. I-95, exit 311, just w. Ext corridors. **Pets:** Accepted.
[SAVE] [X] [•] [•] [≈]

ELLENTON

AAA **WW** Sleep Inn & Suites Riverfront **H** ❀
(941) 721-4933. **$79-$179.** 5605 18th St E. I-75, exit 224, just n on US 301, just e on 19th St E, then 0.3 mi sw. Int corridors. **Pets:** Medium. $20 daily fee/room. Designated rooms, service with restrictions, supervision.
[SAVE] [X] [&M] [•] [•] [≈]

FLAGLER BEACH

AAA **W** Topaz Motel **H**
(386) 439-3301. **$70-$185, 14 day notice.** 1224 S Oceanshore Blvd. On SR A1A, 0.5 mi s of SR 100. Ext/int corridors. **Pets:** Medium, dogs only. $15 one-time fee/pet. Service with restrictions, supervision.
[SAVE] [X] [•] [•] [¶] [≈]

FLORAL CITY

WW Moonrise Resort **CA**
(352) 726-2553. **$75-$1800 (no credit cards), 14 day notice.** 8801 E Moonrise Ln, Lot 18. Just e on CR 48, then 1.5 mi n on Old Floral City Rd. Ext corridors. **Pets:** Dogs only. $20 daily fee/pet. No service.
[•] [•] [X] [Z]

THE FLORIDA KEYS AREA

ISLAMORADA

AAA **WW** Sands of Islamorada **M** ❀
(305) 664-2791. **$120-$315, 3 day notice.** 80051 Overseas Hwy. US 1 at MM 80. Ext corridors. **Pets:** Other species. $20 daily fee/pet. Supervision.
[SAVE] [•] [•] [≈] [X]

KEY LARGO

AAA **WWW** Hilton Key Largo Beach Resort **H**
(305) 852-5553. **$99-$399.** 97000 S Overseas Hwy. US 1 at MM 97. Ext corridors. **Pets:** Accepted.
[SAVE] [X] [•] [•] [¶] [≈] [X]

AAA **WW** Marina Del Mar Resort & Marina **H**
(305) 451-4107. **$99-$299, 3 day notice.** 527 Caribbean Dr. US 1 at MM 100. Ext corridors. **Pets:** Accepted.
[SAVE] [X] [•] [•] [¶] [≈] [X]

KEY WEST

WWW Ambrosia Too At Fleming St **BB** ❀
(305) 296-9838. **$209-$609, 30 day notice.** 622 Fleming St. Just n of Simonton St; in Old Town. Ext corridors. **Pets:** Other species. $35 one-time fee/pet. Crate.
[ASK] [X] [•] [•] [≈]

WWW Banana Bay Resort-Key West **M**
(305) 296-6925. **Call for rates.** 2319 N Roosevelt Blvd. On US 1, 1 mi s of entrance to island. Ext corridors. **Pets:** Accepted.
[X] [•] [•] [≈] [X]

AAA **WWWW** Casa Marina Resort & Beach Club **H**
(305) 296-3535. **$149-$599.** 1500 Reynolds St. 4 mi s on Flagler (CR 5A) from jct SR A1A. Ext/int corridors. **Pets:** Accepted.
[SAVE] [X] [•] [•] [¶] [≈] [X]

WWW Center Court Historic Inn & Cottages **BB**
(305) 296-9292. **$118-$608, 30 day notice.** 1075 Duval, C-19 St. Just e of Truman Ave; in Duval Square. Ext/int corridors. **Pets:** Other species. $15 daily fee/pet. Designated rooms, service with restrictions.
[X] [•] [≈]

AAA **WWWW** Chelsea House Pool & Gardens **BB**
(305) 296-2211. **$119-$389, 7 day notice.** 709 Truman Ave. Corner of Elizabeth St and Truman Ave. Ext/int corridors. **Pets:** $25 daily fee/room. Designated rooms, service with restrictions, crate.
[SAVE] [X] [•] [•] [≈]

◬ ▼▼◈ Courtney's Place Historic Cottages &
Inn 🅲🅰 ❖
(305) 294-3480. **$109-$349, 21 day notice.** 720 Whitmarsh Ln. Just e of jct Petronia and Simonton sts; in Old Town. Ext corridors. **Pets:** Other species. $25 one-time fee/room. Designated rooms.
(SAVE) (✕) (🛏) (💻) (≈)

▼▼◈ The Cuban Club Suites 🎏
(305) 294-5269. **Call for rates.** 1108 Duval St. Corner of Duval and Amelia sts; in Old Town. Int corridors. **Pets:** Accepted.
(✕) (🛏)

◬ ▼▼▼◈ Curry Mansion Inn 🆑🆑
(305) 294-5349. **$225-$375, 14 day notice.** 511 Caroline St. Just n of jct Duval St; in Old Town. Ext/int corridors. **Pets:** Very small. Service with restrictions, supervision.
(SAVE) (✕) (🛏) (≈)

◬ ▼▼▼◈ Frances Street Bottle Inn 🆑🆑 ❖
(305) 294-8530. **$125-$500, 14 day notice.** 535 Frances St. US 1/Roosevelt Blvd, w on White St, then just s on Southard St; corner of Frances and Southard sts; in Old Town. Ext/int corridors. **Pets:** Other species. $50 one-time fee/room. Designated rooms.
(SAVE) (✕) (🛏) (💻) (🗟)

◬ ▼▼▼◈ Hyatt Key West Resort & Spa 🎏
(305) 809-1234. **$236-$645, 7 day notice.** 601 Front St. Simonton and Front sts; just n of Mallory Square; in Old Town. Ext corridors. **Pets:** Accepted.
(SAVE) (✕) (🛏) (💻) (🍴) (≈) (✕)

◬ ▼▼◈ The Palms Hotel 🆑🆑 ❖
(305) 294-3146. **$120-$420, 7 day notice.** 820 White St. Just w of Truman Ave. Ext corridors. **Pets:** Small. Service with restrictions, crate.
(SAVE) (✕) (🛏) (💻) (≈)

◬ ▼▼▼◈ The Reach Resort 🎏
(305) 296-5000. **$149-$649.** 1435 Simonton St. Just s of jct Truman Ave and Simonton St. Ext corridors. **Pets:** Accepted.
(SAVE) (✕) (🛏) (💻) (🍴) (≈) (✕)

◬ ▼▼▼◈ Sheraton Suites-Key West 🎏
(305) 292-9800. **$189-$399, 3 day notice.** 2001 S Roosevelt Blvd. Jct US 1 and SR A1A, 3 mi s. Ext/int corridors. **Pets:** Accepted.
(SAVE) (✕) (♿) (🛏) (💻) (🍴) (≈) (✕)

◬ ▼▼▼ ▼▼◈ The Westin Key West Resort &
Marina 🎏 ❖
(305) 294-4000. **Call for rates.** 245 Front St. Adjacent to Mallory Square; in Old Town. Ext/int corridors. **Pets:** Medium, dogs only. Service with restrictions, supervision.
(SAVE) (✕) (♿) (🛏) (💻) (🍴) (≈) (✕)

END AREA

FORT LAUDERDALE METROPOLITAN AREA

CORAL SPRINGS

▼▼▼◈ La Quinta Inn Coral Springs North 🎏 ❖
(954) 753-9000. **$55-$179.** 3701 University Dr. SR 817, just n of jct SR 834 (Sample Rd). Int corridors. **Pets:** Medium, other species. Service with restrictions, supervision.
(ASK) (✕) (♿) (🛏) (💻) (≈)

▼▼◈ La Quinta Inn South 🎏 ❖
(954) 344-2200. **$65-$179.** 3100 N University Dr. SR 817, just s of jct SR 834 (Sample Rd). Int corridors. **Pets:** Medium, other species. Service with restrictions, supervision.
(ASK) (✕) (🛏) (💻) (≈)

▼▼◈ Studio 6 #6027 🎏
(954) 796-0011. **$77-$91.** 5645 University Dr. SR 869 (Sawgrass Expwy), exit 12 (University Dr), just s. Ext corridors. **Pets:** Other species. $10 daily fee/room. Service with restrictions, supervision.
(✕) (🛏) (💻)

DANIA BEACH

▼▼◈ Motel 6 E. Dania Beach Blvd #376 🎏
(954) 921-5505. **$65-$95.** 825 E Dania Beach Blvd. I-95, exit 22, 1.1 mi e on Stirling Rd, just n on US 1 (Federal Hwy), then 0.8 mi e. Ext corridors. **Pets:** Other species. Service with restrictions, supervision.
(✕) (≈)

◬ ▼▼▼◈ Sheraton Fort Lauderdale Airport Hotel 🎏
(954) 920-3500. **$119-$359.** 1825 Griffin Rd. I-95, exit 23. Int corridors. **Pets:** Accepted.
(SAVE) (✕) (♿) (🛏) (💻) (🍴) (≈) (✕)

DAVIE

▼▼◈ Homestead Studio Suites Hotel-Fort
Lauderdale-Plantation 🎏
(954) 476-1211. **$75-$150.** 7550 SR 84 E. I-595, exit 5, 0.3 mi. Ext corridors. **Pets:** Other species. $25 daily fee/pet. Service with restrictions, crate.
(ASK) (✕) (♿) (🛏) (💻)

DEERFIELD BEACH

◬ ▼▼▼◈ Comfort Inn-Oceanside 🎏 ❖
(954) 428-0650. **$70-$250, 3 day notice.** 50 S Ocean Dr. SR A1A, jct SR 810 (Hillsboro Blvd). Int corridors. **Pets:** Cats only. $25 daily fee/pet. Designated rooms, service with restrictions, supervision.
(SAVE) (✕) (🛏) (💻) (≈) (✕)

◬ ▼▼▼◈ Comfort Suites 🎏
(954) 570-8887. **$69-$189.** 1040 E Newport Center Dr. I-95, exit 41, jct SW 10th St to SW 12th Ave, then s; in Newport Center Complex. Ext corridors. **Pets:** Small. $10 daily fee/room, $50 one-time fee/room. Designated rooms, service with restrictions, supervision.
(SAVE) (✕) (🛏) (💻) (≈)

◬ ▼▼▼◈ Embassy Suites-Deerfield Beach Resort &
Spa 🎏
(954) 426-0478. **$139-$799, 3 day notice.** 950 Ocean Dr (SR A1A). SR A1A, 0.5 mi s of jct SR 810 (Hillsboro Blvd). Int corridors. **Pets:** Accepted.
(SAVE) (✕) (🛏) (💻) (🍴) (≈) (✕)

▼▼◈ Extended StayAmerica-Deerfield Beach 🎏
(954) 428-5997. **$55-$135.** 1200 FAU Research Park Blvd. I-95, exit 41, just e to FAU Research Park Rd, then just s. Int corridors. **Pets:** Other species. $25 daily fee/pet. Service with restrictions, crate.
(ASK) (✕) (♿) (🛏) (💻)

▼▼▼ La Quinta Inn & Suites 🏨 ❖
(954) 428-0661. **$59-$189.** 100 SW 12th Ave. I-95, exit 42B, just w on SR 810 (Hillsboro Blvd), then just s. Int corridors. **Pets:** Medium, other species. Service with restrictions, supervision.

(ASK) ☒ ☕ 🛏 💻 🌊

▼▼ La Quinta Inn Ft. Lauderdale (Deerfield Beach) 🅼 ❖
(954) 421-1004. **$55-$179.** 351 W Hillsboro Blvd. I-95, exit 42A, 0.3 mi e on SR 810. Ext corridors. **Pets:** Medium, other species. Service with restrictions, supervision.

(ASK) ☒ ☕ 🛏 💻 🌊

FORT LAUDERDALE

▼▼▼ Angela's Beach Resort 🅼
(954) 563-7926. **$65-$250, 14 day notice.** 3016 Windamar St. On SR A1A, 6 blks s of SR 838 (Sunrise Blvd); west corner of Breakers Ave and Windamar St. Ext corridors. **Pets:** Accepted.

(ASK) ☒ 🛏 💻 🌊

▼▼▼ Candlewood Suites Fort Lauderdale Air/Seaport 🏨
(954) 522-8822. **$139-$269, 3 day notice.** 1120 W State Rd 84. I-95, exit 25. Int corridors. **Pets:** Large, other species. $75 one-time fee/pet. Service with restrictions, crate.

(ASK) ☒ 🛏 💻

▼ Crossland Studios-Fort Lauderdale/Commercial Blvd 🅼
(954) 484-5115. **$53-$105.** 3031 W Commercial Blvd. I-95, exit 32 SR 870 (Commercial Blvd), 2 mi w; Florida Tpke, exit 62, 1.5 mi e. Ext corridors. **Pets:** Other species. $25 daily fee/pet. Service with restrictions, crate.

(ASK) ☒ 🛏

▼▼▼ Embassy Suites-Fort Lauderdale 🏨
(954) 527-2700. **$140-$340.** 1100 SE 17th St. On SR A1A, just e of jct US 1 (Federal Hwy). Int corridors. **Pets:** Accepted.

☒ 🛏 💻 🍴 🌊 ⊠

▼▼ Extended StayAmerica-Cypress Creek/Andrews Ave 🅼
(954) 776-9447. **$60-$125.** 5851 N Andrews Ave Ext. I-95, exit 33 (Cypress Creek), just w, 0.3 mi s on N Andrews Ave, then left. Ext corridors. **Pets:** Other species. $25 daily fee/pet. Service with restrictions, crate.

(ASK) ☒ 🛏 💻

▼▼ Extended StayAmerica-Marina/Convention Center 🏨
(954) 761-9055. **$95-$170.** 1450 SE 17th St Cswy. 1 mi e of US 1 (Federal Hwy) on SR A1A. Int corridors. **Pets:** Other species. $25 daily fee/pet. Service with restrictions, crate.

(ASK) ☒ 🛏 💻

▼▼ Extended Stay Deluxe–Fort Lauderdale/Cypress Creek 🏨
(954) 772-3155. **$70-$155.** 6001 NW 6th Way. I-95, exit 33 (Cypress Creek), 0.4 mi w, then just s. Int corridors. **Pets:** Other species. $25 daily fee/pet. Service with restrictions, crate.

(ASK) ☒ ☕ 🛏 💻 🌊

🛡 ▼▼▼ Fort Lauderdale Grande Hotel & Yacht Club 🏨 ❖
(954) 463-4000. **$89-$489.** 1881 SE 17th St Cswy. SR A1A, 1 mi e of jct US 1 (Federal Hwy). Ext/int corridors. **Pets:** Small, dogs only. $125 daily fee/pet. Designated rooms, service with restrictions.

(SAVE) ☒ 🛏 💻 🍴 🌊 ⊠

▼▼▼ Hampton Inn Fort Lauderdale Airport North 🏨
(954) 524-9900. **$179-$269.** 2301 SW 12th Ave. I-95, exit 25 (SR 84), 0.7 mi e to SW 12th Ave, then just n. Int corridors. **Pets:** Accepted.

☒ ☕ 🛏 💻 🌊

▼▼▼ La Quinta Inn Fort Lauderdale (Cypress Creek/I-95) 🏨 ❖
(954) 491-7666. **$69-$199.** 999 W Cypress Creek Rd. I-95, exit 33 southbound, 0.8 mi; exit 33B northbound, at Powerline Rd. Int corridors. **Pets:** Medium, other species. Service with restrictions, supervision.

(ASK) ☒ 🛏 💻 🌊

▼▼▼ La Quinta Inn-Fort Lauderdale NE 🏨 ❖
(954) 491-2500. **$69-$179.** 5727 N Federal Hwy. 0.5 mi n on US 1 (Federal Hwy) from SR 870 (Commercial Blvd). Ext corridors. **Pets:** Medium, other species. Service with restrictions, supervision.

(ASK) ☒ ☕ 🛏 💻 🌊

▼ Motel 6–Ft Lauderdale #55 🏨
(954) 760-7999. **$65-$85.** 1801 SR 84. I-95, exit 25 (SR 84 E), just e, then u-turn at light. Int corridors. **Pets:** Other species. Service with restrictions, supervision.

☒ 🌊

▼▼ Red Roof Inn 🏨
(954) 776-6333. **$49-$129.** 4800 Powerline Rd. I-95, exit 32, just w of jct Commercial Blvd, then n. Int corridors. **Pets:** Medium, other species. No service, supervision.

(ASK) ☒ 🛏 🌊

🛡 ▼▼▼ Renaissance Fort Lauderdale Hotel 🏨
(954) 626-1700. **$164-$359.** 1617 SE 17th St Cswy. SR A1A, just e of US 1 (Federal Hwy). Int corridors. **Pets:** Accepted.

(SAVE) ☒ ☕ 🛏 💻 🍴 🌊

🛡 ▼▼▼▼ Ritz Carlton Fort Lauderdale 🏨 ❖
(954) 465-2300. **$239-$3059.** 1 N Ft Lauderdale Beach Blvd. On SR A1A, 1 mi s of SR 838 (Sunrise Blvd). Int corridors. **Pets:** Small, dogs only. $250 one-time fee/pet. Service with restrictions, supervision.

(SAVE) ☒ ☕ 🛏 💻 🍴 🌊 ⊠

🛡 ▼▼ Royal Saxon Apartments 🅼
(954) 566-7424. **$65-$175, 30 day notice.** 551 Breakers Ave. Just w of SR A1A, 0.5 mi s of SR 838 (Sunrise Blvd); corner of Breakers Ave and Terramar St. Ext corridors. **Pets:** Accepted.

(SAVE) ☒ 🛏 🌊

🛡 ▼▼▼ Sheraton Suites Cypress Creek 🏨 ❖
(954) 772-5400. **$109-$379.** 555 NW 62nd St. I-95, exit 33B northbound, then w; exit 33 southbound, then w on SR 811 (Cypress Creek Rd). Int corridors. **Pets:** Small, dogs only. $25 daily fee/room. Designated rooms, service with restrictions, supervision.

(SAVE) ☒ 🛏 💻 🍴 🌊 ⊠

🛡 ▼▼▼ Sheraton Yankee Clipper Hotel 🏨 ❖
(954) 524-5551. **$109-$759.** 1140 Seabreeze Blvd (A1A). SR A1A, just s of Bahia Mar Marina. Ext/int corridors. **Pets:** Large, dogs only. Service with restrictions, supervision.

(SAVE) ☒ ☕ 🛏 💻 🍴 🌊

🛡 ▼▼▼ TownePlace Suites by Marriott 🏨
(954) 484-2214. **$195-$298.** 3100 Prospect Rd. I-95, exit 33, 2.7 mi w, then 0.5 mi s on NW 31st St. Int corridors. **Pets:** Large, other species. $100 one-time fee/room. Service with restrictions.

(SAVE) ☒ 🛏 💻 🌊

🛡 ▼▼▼ Westin, Fort Lauderdale 🏨
(954) 772-1331. **$99-$339.** 400 Corporate Dr. I-95, exit 33 southbound, then e; exit 33A northbound; in Radice Corporate Park. Int corridors. **Pets:** Accepted.

(SAVE) ☒ 🛏 💻 🍴 🌊 ⊠

HOLLYWOOD

🛡 ▼▼ Comfort Inn-Airport/Cruise Port South 🏨
(954) 922-1600. **$79-$299.** 2520 Stirling Rd. I-95, exit 22, just e; 2 mi s of airport. Ext corridors. **Pets:** Small. $50 deposit/pet, $25 one-time fee/pet. Designated rooms, service with restrictions, crate.

(SAVE) ☒ ☕ 🛏 💻 🌊

▼▼▼ **Days Inn Fort Lauderdale/Hollywood Airport South** 🄷
(954) 923-7300. **$98-$299.** 2601 N 29th Ave. I-95, exit 21, just nw on SR 822 (Sheridan St). Int corridors. **Pets:** Accepted.
ASK ✕ 🅗 ▣ ⇌

▼▼▼ **La Quinta Inn & Suites Ft. Lauderdale (Airport)** 🄷 ❀
(954) 922-2295. **$99-$259.** 2620 N 26th Ave. I-95, exit 21, just e to Oakwood, then just left. Int corridors. **Pets:** Medium, other species. Service with restrictions, supervision.
ASK ✕ ♿M 🅗 ▣ ⇌

▼▼▼ **Quality Inn & Suites Hollywood Blvd** Ⓜ
(954) 981-1800. **Call for rates.** 4900 Hollywood Blvd. I-95, exit 20, 1.6 mi w; Florida Tpke, exit 49, 1.3 mi e. Ext corridors. **Pets:** Accepted.
✕ 🅗 ▣ ⇌

▼ **Sandy Shores Motel & Family Lodging** Ⓜ
(954) 923-3750. **Call for rates.** 342 Van Buren St. From SR 820 (Hollywood Blvd), just s on SR A1A (S Ocean Dr), then e. Ext corridors. **Pets:** Accepted.
✕ 🅗 ▣

AAA ▼▼▼ **Seminole Hard Rock Hotel & Casino Hollywood** 🄷 ❀
(954) 327-7625. **$299-$399.** 1 Seminole Way. I-95, exit 22, 2.9 mi w, then just n on SR 7/US 441; Florida Tpke, exit 53, 0.5 mi e, then 0.8 mi s. Int corridors. **Pets:** Small. $100 one-time fee/room. Designated rooms, service with restrictions, crate.
SAVE ✕ ♿M 🅗 ▣ 🍴 ⇌ ✕

LAUDERDALE-BY-THE-SEA

AAA ▼▼▼ **Buena Vista Hotel & Beach Club** 🄷
(954) 489-9870. **$99-$279, 30 day notice.** 4225 El Mar Dr. Just s of SR 870 (Commercial Blvd). Ext/int corridors. **Pets:** Small. $25 daily fee/pet. Service with restrictions, crate.
SAVE ✕ 🅗 ▣

▼▼▼ **Courtyard Villa On The Ocean** Ⓜ
(954) 776-1164. **$125-$359, 30 day notice.** 4312 El Mar Dr. SR 870 (Commercial Blvd), just s. Ext corridors. **Pets:** Small. $25 daily fee/pet. Service with restrictions, crate.
ASK ✕ 🅗 ▣ ✕

MIRAMAR

▼▼▼ **Residence Inn by Marriott Fort Lauderdale SW/Miramar** 🄷 ❀
(954) 450-2717. **$174-$277.** 14700 Hotel Rd. I-75, exit 7A (Miramar Pkwy), just e to SW 145th Ave, then n. Int corridors. **Pets:** Medium, other species. $100 one-time fee/room. Service with restrictions, crate.
✕ ♿M 🅗 ▣ ⇌

PLANTATION

▼▼ **Extended StayAmerica-Fort Lauderdale/Plantation** 🄷
(954) 382-8888. **$80-$155.** 7755 SW 6th St. Just w of SR 817 (University Dr). Int corridors. **Pets:** Other species. $25 daily fee/pet. Service with restrictions, crate.
ASK ✕ 🅗 ▣ ⇌

▼▼▼ **Holiday Inn Express Hotel & Suites Plantation** 🄷 ❀
(954) 472-5600. **$149-$259.** 1701 N University Dr. SR 817 (University Dr), just s of jct SR 838 (Sunrise Blvd). Int corridors. **Pets:** Other species. $10 daily fee/pet. Designated rooms, service with restrictions, crate.
ASK ✕ 🅗 ▣ ⇌

▼▼▼ **La Quinta Inn** 🄷 ❀
(954) 473-8257. **$79-$189.** 7901 SW 6th St. 0.3 mi w of SR 817 (University Dr); 0.5 mi sw of jct SR 842 (Broward Blvd). Int corridors. **Pets:** Medium, other species. Service with restrictions, supervision.
ASK ✕ 🅗 ▣ ⇌

▼▼▼ **La Quinta Inn & Suites Ft. Lauderdale (Plantation)** 🄷 ❀
(954) 476-6047. **$69-$199.** 8101 Peters Rd. I-595, exit 5 (SR 817 N/University Dr), just n, then just w; in Crossroad Office Park. Int corridors. **Pets:** Medium, other species. Service with restrictions, supervision.
ASK ✕ ♿M 🅗 ▣ ⇌

AAA ▼▼▼ **Plantation Hotel & Conference Center** 🄷
(954) 556-8200. **$65-$149.** 1711 N University Dr. On SR 817 (University Dr), just s of Sunrise Blvd (SR 838). Ext corridors. **Pets:** Medium. $25 one-time fee/pet. Service with restrictions.
SAVE ✕ 🅗 ▣ 🍴 ⇌

▼▼▼ **Residence Inn by Marriott–Ft Lauderdale Plantation** 🄷
(954) 723-0300. **$189-$299.** 130 N University Dr. I-95, exit 27 (Broward Blvd), 5.2 mi e, then just n. Int corridors. **Pets:** Medium. $100 one-time fee/room. Service with restrictions, crate.
✕ ♿M 🅗 ▣ ⇌ ✕

AAA ▼▼▼ **Sheraton Suites-Plantation** 🄷
(954) 424-3300. **$115-$409.** 311 N University Dr. I-595, exit 5 (SR 817/University Dr), 0.7 mi n; 0.3 mi n of jct Broward Blvd (SR 842); at Fashion Mall. Int corridors. **Pets:** Accepted.
SAVE ✕ 🅗 ▣ 🍴 ⇌ ✕

▼▼▼ **Staybridge Suites Ft Lauderdale-Plantation** 🄷
(954) 577-9696. **$230-$450, 7 day notice.** 410 N Pine Island Rd. I-595, exit 4 (Pine Island Rd), 1.7 mi n. Int corridors. **Pets:** Accepted.
ASK ✕ ♿M 🅗 ▣ ⇌

POMPANO BEACH

▼▼▼ **Extended Stay Deluxe–Cypress Creek Park North** 🄷
(954) 783-1050. **$80-$160.** 1401 SW 15th St. I-95, exit 33B (Cypress Creek Rd) to Andrews Ave, just s, then left on McNab St. Int corridors. **Pets:** Other species. $25 daily fee/pet. Service with restrictions, crate.
ASK ✕ 🅗 ▣ ⇌

AAA ▼▼▼ **The Ocean Sands Resort and Spa** 🄷 ❀
(954) 590-1000. **$129-$529.** 1350 N Ocean Blvd. On SR A1A, 1.4 mi n of SR 814 (Atlantic Blvd). Ext/int corridors. **Pets:** Large. $25 deposit/room. Service with restrictions, supervision.
SAVE ✕ ♿M 🅗 ▣ 🍴 ⇌ ✕

SUNRISE

▼▼ **La Quinta Inn & Suites Sunrise** 🄷 ❀
(954) 845-9929. **$79-$199.** 13600 NW 2nd St. SW 136th Ave, 0.3 mi n of jct I-595, exit 1A and SR 84; 0.5 mi e of jct I-75 and SR 869 (Sawgrass Expwy). Int corridors. **Pets:** Medium, other species. Service with restrictions, supervision.
ASK ✕ 🅗 ▣ ⇌

▼▼▼ **La Quinta Inn-Sawgrass Mills Outlet Mall** 🄷 ❀
(954) 846-1200. **$69-$189.** 13651 NW 2nd St. SW 136th Ave, 0.3 mi n of jct I-595, exit 1A and SR 84; 0.5 mi e of jct I-75 and SR 869 (Sawgrass Expwy). Int corridors. **Pets:** Medium, other species. Service with restrictions, supervision.
ASK ✕ 🅗 ▣ ⇌

TAMARAC

▼▼ ▼▼ Homestead Studio Suites Hotel-Ft Lauderdale-Tamarac M
(954) 733-6644. **$55-$120.** 3873 W Commercial Blvd. SR 870 (Commercial Blvd), 0.7 mi e of Florida Tpke, exit 62; just e of jct US 441 and SR 7. Ext corridors. **Pets:** Other species. $25 daily fee/pet. Service with restrictions, crate.

ASK ⊠ 🛏 💻

▼▼▼ La Quinta Inn & Suites H ❖
(954) 484-6909. **$65-$169.** 5070 N SR 7. SR 7 and US 441, just n of jct SR 870 (Commercial Blvd); 0.5 mi e of Florida Tpke, exit 62, then n. Int corridors. **Pets:** Medium, other species. Service with restrictions, supervision.

ASK ⊠ 🛏 💻 ⊷

WESTON

◀◀◀▷ ▼▼▼▼ Hawthorn Suites Weston H
(954) 659-1555. **$100-$300.** 2201 N Commerce Pkwy. I-75, exit 15, 0.5 mi w on Arvida Pkwy to Weston Rd, n to N Commerce Pkwy, then just e. Int corridors. **Pets:** Small. $10 daily fee/pet. Service with restrictions, crate.

SAVE ⊠ ♿ 🛏 💻 ⊷

◀◀◀▷ ▼▼▼▼ Hyatt Regency Bonaventure Conference Center and Spa H
(954) 616-1234. **$99-$639.** 250 Racquet Club Rd. I-75, exit 21 (Indian Trace) southbound, 1.6 mi e on SR 84 to E Mall Dr, then just s; exit northbound, U-turn to SR 84, 1.6 mi to E Mall Dr, then just s. Ext corridors. **Pets:** Medium. $50 one-time fee/room. Designated rooms, service with restrictions.

SAVE ⊠ 🛏 💻 🍴 ⊷ ✗

▼▼▼ Residence Inn by Marriott Weston H
(954) 659-8585. **$277-$318.** 2605 Weston Rd. I-75, exit 15 to Weston Rd, just s. Int corridors. **Pets:** Other species. $100 one-time fee/room. Service with restrictions.

⊠ ♿ 🛏 💻 ⊷ ✗

▼▼▼ TownePlace Suites by Marriott Weston H
(954) 659-2234. **$226-$267.** 1545 Three Village Rd. I-75, exit 15, 1 mi e on Arvida Pkwy to Bonaventure Blvd, n to Three Village Rd, then w. Int corridors. **Pets:** Accepted.

⊠ ♿ 🛏 💻 ⊷

END METROPOLITAN AREA

FORT MYERS

◀◀◀▷ ▼▼ ▼▼ Best Western Airport Inn H ❖
(239) 561-7000. **$80-$190.** 8955 Daniels Pkwy. I-75, exit 131, 0.6 mi w, on CR 879 (Daniels Pkwy). Int corridors. **Pets:** Small. $15 daily fee/pet. Designated rooms, service with restrictions, supervision.

SAVE ⊠ 🛏 💻 ⊷ ✗

◀◀◀▷ ▼▼▼ Best Western Springs Resort M ❖
(239) 267-7900. **$89-$159, 7 day notice.** 18051 S Tamiami Tr. On US 41 at Constitution Blvd. Ext corridors. **Pets:** Large, other species. $20 daily fee/pet. Service with restrictions, supervision.

SAVE ⊠ 🛏 💻 🍴 ⊷

◀◀◀▷ ▼▼▼▼ Candlewood Suites H
(239) 344-4400. **Call for rates.** 3626 Colonial Ct. I-75, exit 136, just e on CR 884 (Colonial Blvd), then just s; in Colonial Plaza. Int corridors. **Pets:** Accepted.

SAVE ⊠ ♿ 🛏 💻

▼▼ ▼▼ Comfort Suites Airport/University M ❖
(239) 768-0005. **$60-$170.** 13651 Indian Paint Ln. I-75, exit 131, just w on CR 879 (Daniels Pkwy). Int corridors. **Pets:** Small, other species. $10 daily fee/pet. Service with restrictions, supervision.

ASK ⊠ 🛏 💻 ⊷

◀◀◀▷ ▼▼▼▼ Country Inn & Suites By Carlson Sanibel-Gateway H ❖
(239) 454-9292. **$109-$249.** 13901 Shell Point Plaza. Just w of jct McGregor Blvd. Int corridors. **Pets:** Small, other species. $20 daily fee/pet. Designated rooms, service with restrictions, supervision.

SAVE ⊠ ♿ 🛏 💻

▼▼▼▼ Holiday Inn Downtown Historic District H
(239) 332-3232. **Call for rates.** 2431 Cleveland Ave. On US 41, just s of jct Edison Ave. Int corridors. **Pets:** Accepted.

⊠ ♿ 🛏 💻 🍴 ⊷

▼▼▼▼ Homewood Suites by Hilton-Ft. Myers H
(239) 275-6000. **$109-$339.** 5255 Big Pine Way. Just e of jct US 41; just n of jct Daniels Pkwy; in Bell Tower Shops. Int corridors. **Pets:** Large. $75 one-time fee/room. Service with restrictions, supervision.

⊠ ♿ 🛏 💻 ⊷

▼▼▼▼ La Quinta Inn & Suites H ❖
(239) 466-1200. **$69-$199.** 20091 Summerlin Rd SW. Jct John Morris Rd. Ext corridors. **Pets:** Medium, other species. Service with restrictions, supervision.

ASK ⊠ 🛏 💻 ⊷

▼▼▼▼ La Quinta Inn & Suites-Airport H ❖
(239) 466-0012. **$70-$260.** 9521 Marketplace Rd. I-75, exit 131, 0.4 mi w on Daniels Pkwy, then just n on Danport Blvd. Int corridors. **Pets:** Medium, other species. Service with restrictions, supervision.

⊠ ♿ 🛏 💻 ⊷

▼▼▼▼ La Quinta Inn Fort Myers M ❖
(239) 275-3300. **$49-$169.** 4850 S Cleveland Ave. On US 41, just s of jct N Airport Rd. Ext corridors. **Pets:** Medium, other species. Service with restrictions, supervision.

ASK ⊠ ♿ 🛏 💻 ⊷

▼▼▼▼ Residence Inn by Marriott H ❖
(239) 936-0110. **$164-$267.** 2960 Colonial Blvd. I-75, exit 136, 3.5 mi w on SR 884. Int corridors. **Pets:** Other species. $100 one-time fee/room.

⊠ ♿ 🛏 💻 ⊷ ✗

▼▼▼▼ Suburban Extended Stay Hotel H
(239) 938-0100. **$70-$144.** 10150 Metro Pkwy. I-75, exit 136, 3.4 mi w on SR 884 (Colonial Blvd); just s on SR 739. Int corridors. **Pets:** Medium. $15 daily fee/pet, $110 one-time fee/pet. Designated rooms, service with restrictions, supervision.

ASK ⊠ ♿ 🛏 💻 ⊷

▼▼▼▼ Wynstar Inn & Suites H
(239) 791-5000. **$69-$259.** 10150 Daniels Pkwy. I-75, exit 131, just e on CR 879 (Daniels Pkwy). Int corridors. **Pets:** Accepted.

ASK ⊠ ♿ 🛏 💻 ⊷

FORT MYERS BEACH

◀◀◀▷ ▼▼ ▼▼ Best Western Beach Resort H
(239) 463-6000. **$139-$299, 30 day notice.** 684 Estero Blvd. 0.4 mi n of Matanzas Pass Bridge (SR 865). Ext corridors. **Pets:** Small, other species. $20 daily fee/pet. Designated rooms, service with restrictions, supervision.

SAVE ⊠ 🛏 💻 ⊷ ✗

▼▼ ▼▼ Casa Playa All Suite Resort CO
(239) 765-0510. **$109-$199, 14 day notice.** 510 Estero Blvd. 0.5 mi n of Matanzas Pass Bridge (SR 865) via 5th St. Ext corridors. **Pets:** Accepted.

ASK ⊠ 🛏 💻 ⊷

AAA ▼▼ Lighthouse Resort Inn & Suites **H**
(239) 463-9392. **Call for rates.** 1051 5th St. Jct Matanzas Pass Bridge (SR 865). Ext corridors. **Pets:** Small. $25 daily fee/pet. Service with restrictions, supervision.
[SAVE] [X] [🔒] [💻] [🍽] [🌊]

FORT PIERCE

AAA ▼▼ Dockside Inn & Resort **H**
(772) 468-3555. **$75-$155.** 1160 Seaway Dr. SR A1A southbound, 2 mi e of jct US 1. Ext corridors. **Pets:** Medium, other species. $50 one-time fee/room. Designated rooms, service with restrictions.
[SAVE] [X] [🔒] [💻] [🌊] [🚫]

▼ Fountain Resort **M**
(772) 466-7041. **$69-$139, 3 day notice.** 4889 N US 1. I-95, exit 138 (Indrio Rd), 5.5 mi e, then just n. Ext corridors. **Pets:** Small. $25 one-time fee/room. No service.
[ASK] [X] [🔒] [💻] [🌊]

▼▼ Holiday Inn Express **H**
(772) 464-5000. **$90-$149.** 7151 Okeechobee Rd. I-95, exit 129, 0.7 mi w on SR 70; Florida Tpke, exit 152. Ext corridors. **Pets:** Accepted.
[ASK] [X] [🔒] [💻]

▼ Motel 6-Fort Pierce #1207 **M**
(772) 461-9937. **$45-$55.** 2500 Peters Rd. I-95, exit 129, just w, then n. Ext corridors. **Pets:** Other species. Service with restrictions, supervision.
[X] [🔒] [🌊]

AAA ▼ Royal Inn **M** 🐾
(772) 464-0405. **$79-$129.** 222 Hernando St. 2.5 mi e on SR A1A southbound to Hernando St, then just s. Ext corridors. **Pets:** Medium. Designated rooms, crate.
[SAVE] [X] [🔒]

AAA ▼▼ The Sandhurst Hotel & Suites **H** 🐾
(772) 595-0711. **$99-$199.** 1230 Seaway Dr. Jct US 1 and SR A1A southbound, 2 mi e. Int corridors. **Pets:** Large, other species. $50 one-time fee/room. Service with restrictions, supervision.
[SAVE] [X] [🔒] [💻] [🌊] [🚫]

GAINESVILLE

AAA ▼▼▼ Best Western Gateway Grand **H** 🐾
(352) 331-3336. **$114-$164.** 4200 NW 97th Blvd. I-75, exit 390, just n of SR 222, then just w. Int corridors. **Pets:** Small, other species. $25 one-time fee/pet. Designated rooms, supervision.
[SAVE] [X] [🔒] [💻] [🍽] [🌊] [🚫]

AAA ▼▼ Comfort Inn **H**
(352) 373-6500. **$68-$143.** 2435 SW 13th St. I-75, exit 382, 2 mi ne on SR 331, then 1 mi n on US 441. Ext corridors. **Pets:** Medium. $10 daily fee/pet. Service with restrictions, crate.
[SAVE] [X] [🔒] [💻] [🌊]

▼▼▼ Comfort Inn West **H** 🐾
(352) 264-1771. **$99-$229.** 3440 SW 40th Blvd. I-75, exit 384, just e, then just n. Int corridors. **Pets:** $10 one-time fee/room. Designated rooms, service with restrictions, supervision.
[ASK] [X] [🔒] [💻] [🌊]

▼▼ Extended StayAmerica **H**
(352) 375-0073. **$60-$95.** 3600 SW 42nd St. I-75, exit 384, just e. Ext corridors. **Pets:** Other species. $25 daily fee/pet. Service with restrictions, crate.
[ASK] [X] [🔒] [💻]

AAA ▼▼▼ Holiday Inn Express **H**
(352) 376-0004. **$109-$119.** 3905 SW 43rd St. I-75, exit 384, just w; behind Cracker Barrel Restaurant. Int corridors. **Pets:** Accepted.
[SAVE] [X] [🔒] [🔒] [💻] [🌊]

▼▼▼ Homewood Suites **H**
(352) 335-3133. **$144-$189.** 3333 SW 42nd St. I-75, exit 384, just e. Int corridors. **Pets:** Accepted.
[ASK] [X] [🔒] [🔒] [💻] [🌊] [🚫]

AAA ▼▼▼ Red Roof Inn-Gainesville **H**
(352) 336-3311. **Call for rates.** 3500 SW 42nd St. I-75, exit 384, just e. Int corridors. **Pets:** Medium. Service with restrictions, supervision.
[SAVE] [X] [🔒] [🔒] [🌊]

HAINES CITY

AAA ▼▼▼ Rodeway Inn **M**
(863) 421-6929. **Call for rates.** 605 B Moore Rd. On US 27, just s of jct SR 544; 2 mi s of jct US 17-92. Ext corridors. **Pets:** Accepted.
[SAVE] [X] [🔒] [🔒] [💻] [🌊] [🚫]

HERNANDO

AAA ▼▼▼ Best Western Citrus Hills Lodge **H**
(352) 527-0015. **$95-$115.** 350 E Norvell Bryant Hwy. CR 486 at Citrus Hills Blvd, 3.3 mi w of US 41. Ext corridors. **Pets:** Accepted.
[SAVE] [X] [🔒] [🔒] [💻] [🍽] [🌊]

HOLMES BEACH

AAA ▼▼▼ Haley's Motel **M** 🐾
(941) 778-5405. **$89-$259, 30 day notice.** 8102 Gulf Dr N. On Anna Maria Island; SR 789, 1.2 mi n of jct SR 64, jct Palm Dr. Ext corridors. **Pets:** Other species. $30 one-time fee/room.
[SAVE] [X] [🔒] [🌊]

HORSESHOE BEACH

▼▼▼ Horseshoe Beach-Vacation Rentals **VH**
(352) 498-2400. **$250-$435, 30 day notice.** 130 Main St. 20 mi s of US 19; north side of town. Ext corridors. **Pets:** Accepted.
[X] [🔒] [💻]

INDIALANTIC

▼▼▼ DoubleTree Guest Suites Melbourne Beach Oceanfront **H**
(321) 723-4222. **$169-$269.** 1665 N SR A1A. On SR A1A, 1.5 mi n of jct US 192. Ext corridors. **Pets:** Accepted.
[X] [🔒] [💻] [🍽] [🌊]

▼▼▼ Oceanfront Cottages **CA**
(321) 725-8474. **$159-$175, 60 day notice.** 612 Wavecrest Ave. Just s of east end of US 192. Ext corridors. **Pets:** Small. $30 one-time fee/room. Supervision.
[X] [🔒] [🌊]

INDIAN HARBOUR BEACH

AAA ▼▼▼ Lexington Hotel on the Island **H**
(321) 773-0325. **$89-$139.** 1894 S Patrick Dr. I-95, exit 183 (SR 518), 8 mi e on Eau Gallie Blvd, then 1 mi n on SR 513. Ext/int corridors. **Pets:** Medium, other species. $35 one-time fee/pet. Designated rooms, service with restrictions, crate.
[SAVE] [X] [🔒] [💻] [🌊]

INGLIS

AAA ▼▼▼ Pine Lodge Bed & Breakfast **BB**
(352) 447-7463. **$106-$150, 7 day notice.** 649 Hwy 40 W. 1.5 mi w of US 19. Ext/int corridors. **Pets:** Large. $25 one-time fee/pet. Designated rooms, service with restrictions, supervision.
[SAVE] [X] [🔒] [💻] [🌊] [Z]

JACKSONVILLE METROPOLITAN AREA

BALDWIN

(AAA) ▼▼ Best Western Baldwin Inn M ❀
(904) 266-9759. **$75, 15 day notice.** 1088 US 301 S. I-10, exit 343, just s. Ext corridors. **Pets:** $10 daily fee/pet. Designated rooms, service with restrictions, supervision.
SAVE ⊗ 🛏 💻 🌊

FERNANDINA BEACH

(AAA) ▼▼▼ ▼▼▼ Amelia Island Plantation-Inn & Beach Club H
(904) 261-6161. **$259-$429, 7 day notice.** 6800 First Coast Hwy. In Fernandina Beach; SR A1A, 6.5 mi s of the bridge. Ext corridors. **Pets:** Accepted.
SAVE ⊗ 💻 🍴 🌊 ❌

(AAA) ▼▼ Best Western Inn Amelia Island H
(904) 277-2300. **$70-$180.** 2707 Sadler Rd. In Fernandina Beach; I-95, exit 373, 12.3 mi e, then 1.2 mi. Ext corridors. **Pets:** Medium. $25 daily fee/room. Designated rooms, service with restrictions.
SAVE ⊗ 🛏 💻 🌊 ❌

▼▼ Hampton Inn Amelia Island H
(904) 321-1111. **$93-$143.** 2549 Sadler Rd. In Fernandina Beach; just w' of jct SR A1A and Sadler Rd. Int corridors. **Pets:** Accepted.
⊗ 🔥ᴹ 🛏 💻 🌊

▼▼ Hoyt House BB
(904) 277-4300. **Call for rates.** 804 Atlantic Ave. In Fernandina Beach; on Atlantic Ave/SR 200 at Centre and S 8th sts; in historic district. Int corridors. **Pets:** Accepted.
⊗ 🌊

JACKSONVILLE

(AAA) ▼▼▼ Best Western Hotel JTB/Southpoint H ❀
(904) 281-0900. **$79-$169.** 4660 Salisbury Rd. I-95, exit 344 (SR 202), just ne, then just s. Int corridors. **Pets:** Small. $10 daily fee/pet. Designated rooms, service with restrictions, crate.
SAVE ⊗ 🛏 💻 🌊 ❌

(AAA) ▼▼▼ Best Western Jacksonville Airport H
(904) 741-4980. **$79-$159, 3 day notice.** 1170 Airport Entrance Rd. I-95, exit 363B, just w, then just s on Duval Rd. Ext corridors. **Pets:** Medium. $20 daily fee/pet. Designated rooms, service with restrictions, supervision.
SAVE ⊗ 🔥ᴹ 🛏 💻 🌊

▼▼ Candlewood Suites H
(904) 296-7785. **$90.** 4990 Belfort Rd. I-95, exit 344 (SR 202), ne to Belfort Rd, then just s. Int corridors. **Pets:** Accepted.
ASK ⊗ 🔥ᴹ 🛏 💻

▼▼ Extended StayAmerica-Jacksonville-Butler Blvd H
(904) 296-0181. **$60-$80.** 6961 Lenoir Ave. I-95, exit 344 (SR 202), just sw, then 0.3 mi n. Int corridors. **Pets:** Other species. $25 daily fee/pet. Service with restrictions, crate.
ASK ⊗ 🛏 💻

▼▼ Extended Stay Deluxe-Butler Blvd H
(904) 332-6512. **$80-$100.** 4699 Lenoir Ave S. I-95, exit 344 (SR 202), just sw, then just n. Int corridors. **Pets:** Other species. $25 daily fee/pet. Service with restrictions, crate.
ASK ⊗ 🛏 💻 🌊

▼▼ Extended Stay Deluxe (Jacksonville/Deerwood Park) H
(904) 620-9008. **$90-$110.** 8801 Perimeter Park Blvd. I-95, exit 344 (SR 202), 2.5 mi e on J Turner Butler Blvd to Southside Blvd, then just n on west side of road. Int corridors. **Pets:** Other species. $25 daily fee/pet. Service with restrictions, crate.
ASK ⊗ 🔥ᴹ 🛏 💻 🌊

▼▼▼▼ Holiday Inn Express & Suites Jacksonville H ❀
(904) 696-3333. **$109-$259.** 10148 New Berlin Rd. I-95, exit 362A southbound, 4.9 mi s on SR 9A to Heckscher Dr, then just w; exit 358A northbound, 5.8 mi ne on Heckscher Dr; 0.6 mi from Jaxport Cruise Terminal. Int corridors. **Pets:** Other species. $30 one-time fee/room. Service with restrictions, supervision.
ASK ⊗ 🛏 💻 🌊

▼▼▼▼ Homestead Jacksonville-Southside-St Johns Towne Center M
(904) 642-9911. **$57-$80.** 10020 Skinner Lake Dr. I-95, exit 344 (SR 202), 3.5 mi e on J Turner Butler Blvd to Gate Pkwy, just n, then just w. Ext corridors. **Pets:** Other species. $25 daily fee/pet. Service with restrictions, crate.
ASK ⊗ 🔥ᴹ 🛏 💻

▼▼▼▼ Homewood Suites by Hilton Jacksonville South/Town Center H
(904) 641-7988. **$109-$179.** 10434 Midtown Pkwy. I-95, exit 344 (SR 202), 3.5 mi e on J Turner Butler Blvd to Gate Blvd, 0.3 mi n to Town Center Pkwy, 0.5 mi e to Midtown Pkwy, then 0.3 mi s. Int corridors. **Pets:** Small. $125 one-time fee/room. Service with restrictions, crate.
⊗ 🛏 💻 🌊 ❌

▼▼ Howard Johnson Inn & Suites M
(904) 281-0198. **$60-$120.** 4300 Salisbury Rd N. I-95, exit 344 (SR 202), just nw to Salisbury Rd, then just n. Ext corridors. **Pets:** Accepted.
ASK ⊗ 🛏 💻 🌊

▼▼ Jameson Inn H
(904) 296-0968. **$93-$100.** 7030 Bonneval Rd. I-95, exit 344 (SR 202), just w. Int corridors. **Pets:** Accepted.
ASK ⊗ 🛏 💻 🌊

▼▼ La Quinta Inn H ❀
(904) 268-9999. **$52-$119.** 3199 Hartley Rd. I-295, exit 5A northbound; exit 5 southbound at SR 13. Int corridors. **Pets:** Medium, other species. Service with restrictions, supervision.
ASK ⊗ 🛏 💻 🌊

▼▼▼▼ La Quinta Inn & Suites Jacksonville (Butler Blvd) H ❀
(904) 296-0703. **$59-$189.** 4686 Lenoir Ave S. I-95, exit 344 (SR 202), just sw, then just nw. Int corridors. **Pets:** Medium, other species. Service with restrictions, supervision.
ASK ⊗ 🔥ᴹ 🛏 💻 🌊

▼▼ La Quinta Inn Jacksonville (Airport/Cruise Port) H ❀
(904) 751-6960. **$49-$119.** 812 Dunn Ave. I-95, exit 360, southwest corner. Ext corridors. **Pets:** Medium, other species. Service with restrictions, supervision.
ASK ⊗ 🛏 💻 🌊

▼▼ La Quinta Inn Jacksonville (Orange Park) H ❀
(904) 778-9539. **$49-$119.** 8555 Blanding Blvd. I-295, exit 12, just s on SR 21. Ext corridors. **Pets:** Medium, other species. Service with restrictions, supervision.
ASK ⊗ 🛏 💻 🌊

▼▼ ▼▼ Microtel Inn & Suites Butler Blvd/Southpoint H
(904) 281-2244. **$49-$79.** 4940 Mustang Rd. I-95, exit 344 (SR 202), just sw, then just nw. Int corridors. **Pets:** Medium, other species. $15 daily fee/pet. Service with restrictions, supervision.

(ASK) (X) (&M) (🔒) (💻)

AAA▼ ▼▼▼ ▼▼▼ Omni Jacksonville Hotel H
(904) 355-6664. **$299-$349.** 245 Water St. Corner of Pearl and Water sts; on north side of St. Johns River; downtown; adjacent to The Landing. Int corridors. **Pets:** Accepted.

(SAVE) (X) (🔒) (💻) (🍽) (🌊)

▼▼ ▼▼ Ramada Conference Center Mandarin H
(904) 268-8080. **$99-$119.** 3130 Hartley Rd. I-295, exit 5A northbound; exit 5 southbound, just n on SR 13. Ext corridors. **Pets:** Medium, other species. $30 one-time fee/room. Designated rooms, service with restrictions, supervision.

(ASK) (X) (🔒) (💻) (🍽) (🌊)

AAA▼ ▼▼▼ Residence Inn by Marriott H
(904) 733-8088. **$195-$205.** 8365 Dix Ellis Tr. I-95, exit 341 (SR 152), just w to Freedom Commerce Pkwy, then just s. Ext corridors. **Pets:** Accepted.

(SAVE) (X) (🔒) (💻) (🌊) (X)

▼▼▼ ▼▼▼ Residence Inn by Marriott H 🐾
(904) 996-8900. **$256-$275.** 10551 Deerwood Park Blvd. I-95, exit 344 (SR 202), 3.5 mi e on J Turner Butler Blvd to Gate Blvd, just s, then just w. Int corridors. **Pets:** Other species. $100 one-time fee/room. Service with restrictions.

(X) (&M) (🔒) (💻) (🌊) (X)

JACKSONVILLE BEACH

AAA▼ ▼▼▼ ▼ Quality Suites Oceanfront H 🐾
(904) 435-3535. **$179-$349.** 11 1st St N. Just n of Beach Blvd (US 90). Int corridors. **Pets:** Medium. $35 daily fee/pet. Service with restrictions, supervision.

(SAVE) (X) (🔒) (💻) (🌊) (X)

ORANGE PARK

▼▼ ▼▼ Comfort Inn H
(904) 644-4444. **$65-$109.** 341 Park Ave. I-295, exit 10 (US 17), just s. Ext corridors. **Pets:** Other species. $30 one-time fee/pet. Service with restrictions, supervision.

(ASK) (X) (🔒) (💻) (🌊)

▼▼ ▼▼ Howard Johnson Inn H 🐾
(904) 264-9513. **$69-$89.** 150 Park Ave. I-295, exit 10 (US 17), just s. Ext corridors. **Pets:** $30 one-time fee/room. Service with restrictions.

(ASK) (X) (🔒) (💻) (🍽) (🌊)

PONTE VEDRA BEACH

▼▼▼ ▼▼▼ Ponte Vedra Beach Oceanfront Homes & Condominiums CO
(904) 285-2882. **Call for rates.** 574 Ponte Vedra Blvd. Jct J Turner Butler Blvd, 1.7 mi s on SR A1A, on Solana Rd. Ext corridors. **Pets:** Accepted.

(X) (🔒) (💻)

AAA▼ ▼▼▼ ▼ Sawgrass Marriott Resort & Spa H
(904) 285-7777. **$164-$246.** 1000 PGA Tour Blvd. 2.5 mi s of J Turner Butler Blvd. Ext/int corridors. **Pets:** Accepted.

(SAVE) (X) (🔒) (💻) (🍽) (🌊) (X)

YULEE

▼▼ ▼▼ Comfort Inn H
(904) 225-2600. **Call for rates.** 76043 Sidney Pl. I-95, exit 373, just e on SR 200/A1A. Int corridors. **Pets:** Accepted.

(X) (🔒) (💻) (🌊)

END METROPOLITAN AREA

JUPITER

▼▼▼ ▼▼▼ Fairfield Inn & Suites by Marriott H
(561) 748-5252. **$133-$256.** 6748 W Indiantown Rd. I-95, exit 87A, 0.8 mi e on SR 706 (Indiantown Rd). Int corridors. **Pets:** Accepted.

(X) (🔒) (💻) (🌊)

LAKE CITY

AAA▼ ▼▼▼ Best Western Lake City Inn H
(386) 752-3801. **$76-$130.** 3598 W Hwy 90. I-75, exit 427, just w. Ext corridors. **Pets:** Accepted.

(SAVE) (X) (🔒) (💻) (🌊) (X)

AAA▼ ▼▼▼ Days Inn I-10 H
(386) 758-4224. **$59-$120.** 3430 N Hwy 441. I-10, exit 303, just s. Ext corridors. **Pets:** $10 daily fee/pet. Service with restrictions, crate.

(SAVE) (X) (🔒) (💻) (🌊)

AAA▼ ▼▼▼ Driftwood Inn M 🐾
(386) 755-3545. **$42-$70.** 2764 W Hwy 90. I-75, exit 427, 0.7 mi e. Ext corridors. **Pets:** Small, dogs only. $10 daily fee/pet. Designated rooms, no service, supervision.

(SAVE) (X) (🔒)

AAA▼ ▼▼▼ Rodeway Inn M
(386) 755-5203. **$49-$59.** 205 SW Commerce Dr. I-75, exit 427, just e. Ext corridors. **Pets:** Designated rooms, service with restrictions, supervision.

(SAVE) (X) (🔒) (💻)

LAKE HELEN

▼▼▼ ▼▼▼ The Ann Stevens House BB
(386) 228-0310. **$130-$170, 7 day notice.** 201 E Kicklighter Rd. I-4, exit 116, 1 mi e on Main St, 0.5 mi s on CR 4139, turn left on Ohio St, right on Pleasant Rd, then right. Ext/int corridors. **Pets:** Accepted.

(ASK) (X)

LAKELAND

▼▼ ▼▼ Howard Johnson Inn Executive Center M
(863) 688-7972. **Call for rates.** 3311 US Hwy 98 N. I-4, exit 32, just s. Ext corridors. **Pets:** Accepted.

(X) (🔒) (💻) (🍽) (🌊)

▼▼ ▼▼ Jameson Inn H
(863) 858-9070. **$98-$105.** 4375 Lakeland Park Dr. I-4, exit 33, just nw. Int corridors. **Pets:** Accepted.

(ASK) (X) (&M) (🔒) (💻) (🌊)

▼▼▼ ▼▼▼ Lakeland Residence Inn by Marriott H
(863) 680-2323. **$159-$164.** 3701 Harden Blvd. I-4, exit 27 (Polk Pkwy), se on SR 570 (toll road) to exit 5, then just n. Int corridors. **Pets:** Accepted.

(X) (🔒) (💻) (🌊) (X)

▼▼▼ ▼▼▼ La Quinta Inn & Suites Lakeland H 🐾
(863) 859-2866. **$79-$400.** 1024 Crevasse St. I-4, exit 32, just n on US 98. Int corridors. **Pets:** Medium, other species. Service with restrictions, supervision.

(ASK) (X) (&M) (🔒) (💻) (🌊)

▼▼ La Quinta Inn East H ❀
(863) 815-0606. **$59-$109.** 4315 Lakeland Park Dr. I-4, exit 33; jct SR 33, just nw. Int corridors. **Pets:** Medium, other species. Service with restrictions, supervision.
ASK ✕ ᏳM ᐧ ▣ ⇌

LANTANA

▼ Motel 6 Lantana #688 M
(561) 585-5833. **$59-$71.** 1310 W Lantana Rd. I-95, exit 61 (SR 812), just e, then s. Ext corridors. **Pets:** Other species. Service with restrictions, supervision.
✕ ⇌

◈◈◈ ▼▼ Super 8 Lantana M
(561) 585-3970. **$59-$139.** 1255 Hypoluxo Rd. I-95, exit 60 (Hypoluxo Rd), just e on north side. Ext corridors. **Pets:** Medium, other species. $10 daily fee/room. Service with restrictions.
SAVE ✕ ᏳM ᐧ ▣ ⇌

LIVE OAK

◈◈◈ ▼▼ Econo Lodge H
(386) 362-7459. **$62-$85.** 6811 N US 129 & I-10. I-10, exit 283, just s. Ext corridors. **Pets:** Large, other species. $10 one-time fee/pet. Service with restrictions, supervision.
SAVE ✕ ᐧ ▣ ⇌

◈◈◈ ▼▼ Suwannee River Best Western Inn H
(386) 362-6000. **$56-$140, 3 day notice.** 6819 US 129 N. I-10, exit 283, 0.3 mi s. Ext corridors. **Pets:** Small, other species. $50 deposit/room, $20 daily fee/pet. Service with restrictions, supervision.
SAVE ✕ ᐧ ▣ ⇌

LONGBOAT KEY

▼▼▼ Cedars Tennis Resort CO
(941) 383-4621. **Call for rates.** 645 Cedars Ct, Suite A. Just e of jct SR 789 (Gulf of Mexico Dr), on Companion Way. Ext corridors. **Pets:** Medium. $200 one-time fee/pet.
✕ ᐧ ⇌ ⌧

▼▼ Sandpiper Inn M
(941) 383-2552. **$139-$249, 30 day notice.** 5451 Gulf of Mexico Dr. On SR 789, 5 mi se of jct SR 684 (Cortez Rd). Ext corridors. **Pets:** Small. $100 deposit/pet, $15 daily fee/pet. No service, supervision.
ASK ✕ ᐧ ⇌

LYNN HAVEN

▼▼▼ Wingate Inn H
(850) 248-8080. **$95-$150.** 2610 Lynn Haven Pkwy. Jct 23rd St, 2.3 mi n on SR 77. Int corridors. **Pets:** Medium, dogs only. $60 one-time fee/pet. Designated rooms, service with restrictions, crate.
ASK ✕ ᐧ ▣ ⇌ ⌧

MACCLENNY

◈◈◈ ▼▼ Econo Lodge M
(904) 259-3000. **$58-$80.** 151 Woodlawn Rd. I-10, exit 335, just s of jct SR 121. Ext corridors. **Pets:** Accepted.
SAVE ✕ ᐧ ▣ ⇌

MANALAPAN

◈◈◈ ▼▼▼▼ The Ritz-Carlton, Palm Beach H
(561) 533-6000. **$175-$749, 15 day notice.** 100 S Ocean Blvd. On SR A1A; 9 mi s of Palm Beach. Int corridors. **Pets:** Accepted.
SAVE ✕ ▣ ᐧ⬩ ⇌ ⌧

MARIANNA

◈◈◈ ▼▼ Americas Best Value Inn H ❀
(850) 526-5666. **$65-$95.** 2086 Hwy 71 S. I-10, exit 142, 0.3 mi s. Ext corridors. **Pets:** Medium. $10 daily fee/pet. Service with restrictions, supervision.
SAVE ✕ ᐧ ▣ ⇌

▼▼ Quality Inn H
(850) 526-5600. **$55-$89.** 2175 Hwy 71 S. I-10, exit 142, just n. Ext corridors. **Pets:** Accepted.
ASK ✕ ᐧ ▣ ⇌

MELBOURNE

▼▼◈▼ Crane Creek Inn Waterfront Bed & Breakfast BB ❀
(321) 768-6416. **$149-$229, 14 day notice.** 907 E Melbourne Ave. Jct US 192, just s on Babcock, 0.9 mi e. Ext/int corridors. **Pets:** Dogs only. $10 daily fee/pet. Supervision.
✕ ᐧ ▣ ⇌ ⌧

▼▼◈▼ Hilton Melbourne Rialto Place H ❀
(321) 768-0200. **$95-$199.** 200 Rialto Pl. 1 mi w of US 1, 0.8 mi n of US 192 via Airport Blvd. Int corridors. **Pets:** Medium, other species. $50 one-time fee/room. Designated rooms, service with restrictions, crate.
✕ ᏳM ᐧ ▣ ⬩ ⇌ ⌧

▼▼ La Quinta Inn & Suites Melbourne H ❀
(321) 242-9400. **$59-$159.** 7200 George T Edwards Dr. I-95, exit 191 (CR 509), just w. Int corridors. **Pets:** Medium, other species. Service with restrictions, supervision.
ASK ✕ ᐧ ▣ ⇌

<hr/>

MIAMI-MIAMI BEACH METROPOLITAN AREA

AVENTURA

◈◈◈ ▼▼◈▼◈ The Fairmont Turnberry Isle Resort & Club H
(305) 932-6200. **$179-$5800, 3 day notice.** 19999 W Country Club Dr. 0.5 mi w of SR A1A via SR 856; from US 1 at NE 199th St and Biscayne Blvd. Ext/int corridors. **Pets:** Accepted.
SAVE ✕ ᏳM ᐧ ▣ ⬩ ⇌ ⌧

◈◈◈ ▼▼◈▼ Residence Inn by Marriott-Aventura Mall H ❀
(786) 528-1001. **$179-$299.** 19900 W Country Club Dr. 0.5 mi w of SR A1A via SR 856; from US 1 at NE 199th St and Biscayne Blvd. Int corridors. **Pets:** Medium. $100 one-time fee/room. Service with restrictions.
SAVE ✕ ᏳM ᐧ ▣ ⇌

COCONUT GROVE

◈◈◈ ▼▼◈▼ Mayfair Hotel & Spa H
(305) 441-0000. **$139-$339.** 3000 Florida Ave. At Florida Ave and Virginia St; center. Ext/int corridors. **Pets:** Accepted.
SAVE ✕ ▣ ⬩ ⇌ ⌧

▼▼◈▼ Residence Inn by Marriott H
(305) 285-9303. **$153-$215.** 2835 Tigertail Ave. S Bayshore Dr, w on SW 27th Ave/Cornelia Dr, then s. Ext corridors. **Pets:** $100 one-time fee/room. Service with restrictions, supervision.
✕ ᐧ ▣ ⇌

CORAL GABLES

▼▼▼▼ **The Biltmore Hotel Coral Gables** H
(305) 445-1926. **$169-$399.** 1200 Anastasia Ave. 1 mi w of Le Jeune Rd. Int corridors. **Pets:** Accepted.
⊠ 🔒 🍽 ➯ ⊠

△△△ ▼▼▼ **Chateaubleau Hotel** H
(305) 448-2634. **$99-$169.** 1111 Ponce de Leon. Corner of Antilla and Ponce de Leon Blvd. Ext/int corridors. **Pets:** Accepted.
SAVE ⊠ 🔒 💻 🍽 ➯

▼▼ ▼▼ **Extended StayAmerica-Miami-Coral Gables** H
(305) 443-7444. **$95-$170.** 3640 Coral Way/SW 22nd St. Just e of Douglas Rd. Int corridors. **Pets:** Other species. $25 daily fee/pet. Service with restrictions, crate.
ASK ⊠ 🔒M 🔒 💻

CUTLER RIDGE

△△△ ▼▼▼▼ **Best Western Floridian Hotel** H
(305) 253-9960. **$79-$259.** 10775 Caribbean Blvd. Florida Tpke, exit 12 (US 1), then w. Ext corridors. **Pets:** Accepted.
SAVE ⊠ 🔒M 🔒 💻 ➯

FLORIDA CITY

△△△ ▼▼▼ **Coral Roc Motel** M
(305) 246-2888. **$39-$159.** 1100 N Krome Ave. On SR 997; just w of US 1; 0.5 mi s of Homestead. Ext corridors. **Pets:** Medium, dogs only. $50 deposit/pet. Service with restrictions, supervision.
SAVE ⊠ 🔒 ➯

▼▼▼▼ **Ramada Inn Florida City** M
(305) 247-8833. **$69-$139.** 124 E Palm Dr. On US 1, 0.3 mi s of Florida Tpke terminus. Ext corridors. **Pets:** Accepted.
ASK ⊠ 🔒 ➯

△△△ ▼▼▼ **Travelodge** M
(305) 248-9777. **$65-$225.** 409 SE 1st Ave. On US 1, just s of Florida Tpke terminus. Ext corridors. **Pets:** Medium. $10 daily fee/pet. Service with restrictions, supervision.
SAVE ⊠ 🔒M 🔒 💻 ➯

HOMESTEAD

△△△ ▼ **Everglades Motel** M
(305) 248-3560. **$39-$129.** 605 S Krome Ave. Just w of US 1; between Lucy and 6th sts; on SR 997, 0.5 mi s of center of town. Ext corridors. **Pets:** Medium, other species. $10 daily fee/pet. Service with restrictions, crate.
SAVE ⊠ 🔒 ➯

KEY BISCAYNE

▼▼▼▼ **The Ritz-Carlton, Key Biscayne** H
(305) 365-4500. **Call for rates.** 455 Grand Bay Dr. Crandon Blvd, just e. Int corridors. **Pets:** Accepted.
⊠ 🔒M 🔒 💻 🍽 ➯ ⊠

MIAMI

▼▼▼▼ **Candlewood Suites Miami Airport West** H
(305) 591-9099. **Call for rates.** 8855 NW 27th St. SR 826 (Palmetto Expwy), 0.8 mi w on nw 36th St, 0.4 mi s. Int corridors. **Pets:** Accepted.
⊠ 🔒M 🔒 💻 ➯

▼▼ ▼▼ **Extended StayAmerica-Miami-Brickell-Port of Miami** H
(305) 856-3700. **$95-$170.** 298 SW 15th Rd. I-95, exit 1B (SW 7th St) to SW 8th St, then e, s on SW 2nd Ave, then w. Int corridors. **Pets:** Other species. $25 daily fee/pet. Service with restrictions, crate.
ASK ⊠ 🔒M 🔒 💻

▼▼ ▼▼ **Extended Stay Deluxe-Miami Airport** H
(305) 716-9005. **$95-$160.** 7750 NW 25th St. From SR 836 (Dolphin Expwy), exit NW 25th St, then w; turn into The Shoppes at MICC Center. Int corridors. **Pets:** Other species. $25 daily fee/pet. Service with restrictions, crate.
ASK ⊠ 🔒M 🔒 💻 ➯

△△△ ▼▼▼▼▼ **Four Seasons Hotel Miami** H ❀
(305) 358-3535. **$350-$575.** 1435 Brickell Ave. On US 1; jct 14th St. Int corridors. **Pets:** Small, dogs only. Service with restrictions, supervision.
SAVE ⊠ 🔒M 🔒 💻 🍽 ➯ ⊠

▼▼ ▼▼ **Homestead Studio Suites Hotel-Miami/Airport at Doral** M
(305) 436-1811. **$75-$140.** 8720 NW 33rd St. SR 826 (Palmetto Expwy), 0.8 mi w on NW 36th St, just s. Ext corridors. **Pets:** Other species. $25 daily fee/pet. Service with restrictions, crate.
ASK ⊠ 🔒 💻 ➯

▼▼ ▼▼ **Homestead Studio Suites Hotel–Miami Airport–Blue Lagoon** M
(305) 260-0085. **$70-$130.** 6605 NW 7th St. SR 836 (Dolphin Expwy), exit Milam Dairy Rd S, 0.3 mi e; in Blue Lagoon Office Park. Ext corridors. **Pets:** Other species. $25 daily fee/pet. Service with restrictions, crate.
ASK ⊠ 🔒 💻

△△△ ▼▼▼▼ **Hyatt Summerfield Suites-Miami Airport** H
(305) 269-1922. **$129-$399.** 5710 Blue Lagoon Dr. Se of jct SR 836 (Dolphin Expwy), exit Red Rd, just w. Int corridors. **Pets:** Large. $150 one-time fee/room. Service with restrictions, crate.
SAVE ⊠ 🔒M 🔒 💻 ➯

▼▼▼▼ **La Quinta Inn & Suites Miami (Airport West)** H ❀
(305) 436-0830. **$95-$219.** 8730 NW 27th St. SR 836 (Dolphin Expwy), just n on 87th NW Ave. Int corridors. **Pets:** Medium, other species. Service with restrictions, supervision.
ASK ⊠ 🔒M 🔒 💻 ➯

▼▼ ▼▼ **La Quinta Inn Miami (Airport North)** M ❀
(305) 599-9902. **$55-$189.** 7401 NW 36th St. Just e of jct SR 826 (Palmetto Expwy). Ext corridors. **Pets:** Medium, other species. Service with restrictions, supervision.
ASK ⊠ 🔒M 🔒 💻 ➯

△△△ ▼▼▼▼ ▼▼ **Mandarin Oriental, Miami** H ❀
(305) 913-8288. **$465-$6500.** 500 Brickell Key Dr. US 1 (Brickell Ave), just e on SE 8th St (Brickell Key Dr). Int corridors. **Pets:** Small. $100 deposit/room, $100 one-time fee/room. Supervision.
SAVE ⊠ 🔒M 🔒 💻 🍽 ➯ ⊠

△△△ ▼▼▼▼ **Miami Mart Airport Hotel** H
(305) 261-3800. **$129-$259.** 711 NW 72nd Ave. At Milam Dairy Rd off SR 836 (Dolphin Expwy). Int corridors. **Pets:** Accepted.
SAVE ⊠ 🔒 💻 🍽 ➯

▼▼ ▼▼ **Miami River Inn** BB
(305) 325-0045. **$89-$299, 7 day notice.** 118 SW South River Dr. I-95, exit 1B (SW 7th St), just w to SW 5th Ave, just n to SW 2nd St, then e. Ext/int corridors. **Pets:** Medium. $25 one-time fee/pet. Service with restrictions, supervision.
ASK ⊠ ➯

△△△ ▼▼▼▼ **Quality Inn-South at The Falls** M ❀
(305) 251-2000. **$82-$199.** 14501 S Dixie Hwy (US 1). US 1 at SW 145th St. Ext corridors. **Pets:** Medium. $10 daily fee/room. Service with restrictions.
SAVE ⊠ 🔒 💻 🍽 ➯

▼▼▼▼ **Residence Inn by Marriott** H
(305) 591-2211. **$129-$199.** 1212 NW 82nd Ave. SR 836 (Dolphin Expwy), exit 87th Ave NW, just n to NW 82nd Ave, then e. Ext corridors. **Pets:** Other species. $100 one-time fee/room. Service with restrictions, supervision.
⊠ 🔒 💻 ➯ ⊠

▼▼ ▼▼▼ Sofitel Miami �H
(305) 264-4888. **$430-$540.** 5800 Blue Lagoon Dr. Just sw of jct SR 836 (Dolphin Expwy), exit Red Rd. Int corridors. **Pets:** Accepted.
(ASK) ☒ 🛏 🍴 🏊 ⊠

▼▼▼▼ Staybridge Suites Miami/Doral Area �H ❀
(305) 500-9100. **Call for rates.** 3265 NW 87th Ave. 0.4 mi s of jct NW 36th St. Int corridors. **Pets:** Medium. $150 one-time fee/pet. Service with restrictions, crate.
☒ 🛏 🖵 🏊

₳₳₳ ▼▼▼▼ TownePlace Suites by Marriott �H ❀
(305) 718-4144. **$153-$205.** 10505 NW 36th St. Florida Tpke, exit 29, 1.2 mi e to 107th Ave, then just s. Int corridors. **Pets:** Other species. $100 one-time fee/pet. Service with restrictions, supervision.
(SAVE) ☒ 🛏 🖵 🏊

MIAMI BEACH

₳₳₳ ▼▼▼ ▼▼▼ Fontainebleau Resort �H ❀
(305) 538-2000. **$203-$510, 3 day notice.** 4441 Collins Ave. On SR A1A. Int corridors. **Pets:** Large, other species. $75 one-time fee/room. Designated rooms, service with restrictions, crate.
(SAVE) ☒ 🛏 🖵 🏊 ⊠

₳₳₳▽ ▼▼ Greenview Hotel �H
(305) 531-6588. **Call for rates.** 1671 Washington Ave. From SR A1A (Collins Ave), just e on Lincoln Rd, then just n. Int corridors. **Pets:** Accepted.
(SAVE)

▼▼▼▼ Hotel Ocean �H
(305) 672-2579. **$139-$749.** 1230 Ocean Dr. E of jct SR A1A (Collins Ave) and 12th St. Int corridors. **Pets:** Medium. $45 daily fee/pet. Service with restrictions.
(ASK) ☒ 🛏 🍴

₳₳₳▽ ▼▼▼▼ Hotel Victor �H
(305) 428-1234. **$199-$799, 3 day notice.** 1144 Ocean Dr. Corner of Ocean Dr and 11th St. Int corridors. **Pets:** Accepted.
(SAVE) ☒ 🛏 🍴 🏊

▼▼▼ The Kent Hotel �H
(305) 604-5068. **$75-$250, 3 day notice.** 1131 Collins Ave. On SR A1A, jct Collins Ave and 11th St. Int corridors. **Pets:** Accepted.
(ASK) ☒ 🛏

₳₳₳▽ ▼▼▼ ▼▼▼ Loews Miami Beach Hotel �H ❀
(305) 604-1601. **$239-$599, 3 day notice.** 1601 Collins Ave. On SR A1A, jct Collins and 16th aves. Int corridors. **Pets:** Other species. $25 one-time fee/room. Service with restrictions, supervision.
(SAVE) ☒ 🕭 🛏 🖵 🍴 🏊 ⊠

▼▼▼ The Marlin �H
(305) 604-0096. **Call for rates.** 1200 Collins Ave. On SR A1A, at Collins Ave and 12th St. Int corridors. **Pets:** Accepted.
🛏 🖵

₳₳₳▽ ▼▼▼ ▼▼▼ Marriott South Beach �H ❀
(305) 536-7700. **$236-$411, 3 day notice.** 161 Ocean Dr. Just e of SR A1A (Collins Ave); just s of 2nd St. Int corridors. **Pets:** Large, dogs only. $150 one-time fee/pet. Service with restrictions, supervision.
(SAVE) ☒ 🛏 🖵 🍴 🏊 ⊠

▼▼▼ ▼▼▼ The Ritz-Carlton, South Beach �H
(786) 276-4000. **$275-$825, 7 day notice.** 1 Lincoln Rd. Jct SR A1A. Int corridors. **Pets:** Accepted.
☒ 🕭 🛏 🖵 🍴 🏊 ⊠

▼▼ ▼▼▼ The Setai �H
(305) 520-6000. **Call for rates.** 2001 Collins Ave. On SR A1A (Collins Ave); at 20th St. Int corridors. **Pets:** Accepted.
☒ 🕭 🛏 🖵 🍴 🏊 ⊠

MIAMI LAKES

▼▼▼▼ La Quinta Inn & Suites �H ❀
(305) 821-8274. **$75-$209.** 7925 NW 154th St. Jct SR 826 (Palmetto Expwy), just w. Int corridors. **Pets:** Medium, other species. Service with restrictions, supervision.
(ASK) ☒ 🛏 🖵 🏊

₳₳₳▽ ▼▼▼ ▼▼▼ TownePlace Suites by Marriott �H
(305) 512-9191. **$143-$195.** 8079 NW 154th St. SR 826 (Palmetto Expwy), exit 154th St, 0.4 mi w. Int corridors. **Pets:** $100 one-time fee/room. Service with restrictions.
(SAVE) ☒ 🕭 🛏 🖵 🏊

MIAMI SPRINGS

▼▼▼ ▼▼▼ Homestead Studio Suites Hotel-Miami/Airport/Miami Springs �H
(305) 870-0448. **$95-$170.** 101 Fairway Dr. I-95 to SR 112 W, exit NW 36th St, then w, right on Palmetto Dr, then w; between Le Jeune Rd and SR 826 (Palmetto Expwy); behind Clarion Hotel. Int corridors. **Pets:** Other species. $25 daily fee/pet. Service with restrictions, crate.
(ASK) ☒ 🛏 🖵 🏊

▼▼▼ ▼▼▼ La Quinta Inn &Suites �H ❀
(305) 871-1777. **$59-$199.** 3501 NW Le Jeune Rd. SR 953 (Le Jeune Rd) at jct SR 112. Int corridors. **Pets:** Medium, other species. Service with restrictions, supervision.
(ASK) ☒ 🛏 🖵 🏊

₳₳₳▽ ▼▼▼ ▼▼▼ Red Roof Inn Miami Airport �H
(305) 871-4221. **$89-$149.** 3401 NW Lejeane Rd. On SR 953 (Le Jeune Rd) at SR 112; 0.5 mi n of airport entrance. Int corridors. **Pets:** Medium. Service with restrictions, supervision.
(SAVE) ☒ 🛏 🏊

SUNNY ISLES BEACH

▼▼▼ ▼▼▼ Acqualina Resort and Spa �H
(305) 918-8000. **Call for rates.** 17875 Collins Ave. On SR A1A (Collins Ave); corner of 178th St; just s of William Lehman Cswy. Int corridors. **Pets:** Accepted.
☒ 🕭 🛏 🖵 🍴 🏊 ⊠

₳₳₳▽ ▼▼▼ ▼▼▼ Le Meridien Sunny Isles Beach Miami CO
(305) 503-6000. **$150-$1500.** 18683 Collins Ave. From north, just s from William Lehman Cswy, U-turn at 186th St, then just n; from south, SR 826, 1.3 mi n. Int corridors. **Pets:** Accepted.
(SAVE) ☒ 🛏 🖵 🍴 🏊 ⊠

₳₳₳▽ ▼▼▼ ▼▼▼ Newport Beachside Hotel & Resort �H
(305) 949-1300. **$99-$299, 3 day notice.** 16701 Collins Ave. SR A1A, jct SR 826 and Sunny Isles Blvd. Int corridors. **Pets:** Accepted.
(SAVE) ☒ 🛏 🖵 🍴 🏊 ⊠

END METROPOLITAN AREA

MILTON

AAA ⬦⬦⬦ **Comfort Inn** H
(850) 623-1511. **$80-$120.** 8936 S Hwy 87. I-10, exit 31, just s. Int corridors. **Pets:** Small. $15 daily fee/room. Service with restrictions, supervision.
SAVE ✕ &M 🛏 💻 ➡

AAA ⬦⬦⬦ **Red Roof Inn & Suites** H 🐾
(850) 995-6100. **$65-$90.** 2672 Avalon Blvd. I-10, exit 22, just s. Int corridors. **Pets:** Designated rooms, service with restrictions, supervision.
SAVE ✕ &M 🛏 💻 ➡

MOSSY HEAD

⬦⬦ **Rodeway Inn** M
(850) 951-9780. **Call for rates.** 326 Green Acres Dr. I-10, exit 70, just s. Ext corridors. **Pets:** Medium. $15 daily fee/pet. Designated rooms, service with restrictions, crate.
✕ 💻 🍴

NAPLES

AAA ⬦⬦⬦⬦ **Hawthorn Suites Hotel of Naples** H 🐾
(239) 593-1300. **$139-$329.** 3557 Pine Ridge Rd. I-75, exit 107, 0.5 mi w on CR 896. Int corridors. **Pets:** Other species. $125 one-time fee/room. Designated rooms, service with restrictions, supervision.
SAVE ✕ &M 🛏 💻 ➡ 🐾

AAA ⬦⬦⬦⬦ **Hilton Naples** H 🐾
(239) 430-4900. **$124-$344.** 5111 Tamiami Tr N. Just s of jct CR 896 (Pine Ridge Rd). Int corridors. **Pets:** Dogs only. $200 deposit/room, $75 one-time fee/pet. Supervision.
SAVE ✕ &M 🛏 💻 🍴 ➡ 🐾

⬦⬦⬦⬦ **Holiday Inn of Naples** M 🐾
(239) 263-3434. **$89-$219.** 1100 Tamiami Tr N. On US 41 (Tamiami Tr), jct 13th Ave n. Ext corridors. **Pets:** Medium. $25 daily fee/room. Designated rooms, service with restrictions.
SAVE ✕ 🛏 💻 🍴 ➡

⬦⬦⬦⬦ **La Quinta Inn & Suites** H 🐾
(239) 352-8400. **$59-$159.** 185 Bedzel Cir. I-75, exit 101, just w on SR 84 (Davis Blvd). Int corridors. **Pets:** Medium, other species. Service with restrictions, supervision.
ASK ✕ &M 🛏 💻 ➡

⬦⬦⬦⬦ **La Quinta Inn & Suites** H 🐾
(239) 793-4646. **$69-$179.** 1555 5th Ave S. Just w of Jct SR 84 (Davis Blvd) and US 41. Int corridors. **Pets:** Medium, other species. Service with restrictions, supervision.
ASK ✕ 🛏 💻 ➡

AAA ⬦⬦ **Red Roof Inn** H
(239) 774-3117. **$65-$170.** 1925 Davis Blvd. Just e of jct US 41 (Tamiami Tr). Ext corridors. **Pets:** Accepted.
SAVE ✕ 🛏 💻 ➡

⬦⬦⬦ **Residence Inn by Marriott, Naples** H 🐾
(239) 659-1300. **$205-$339.** 4075 Tamiami Tr N. I-75, exit 107, 3.8 mi w on CR 896 (Pine Ridge Rd), then 1 mi s on US 41. Int corridors. **Pets:** Large, other species. $75 one-time fee/room. Service with restrictions.
✕ &M 🛏 💻 ➡ 🐾

AAA ⬦⬦⬦⬦⬦ **The Ritz-Carlton Golf Resort** H
(239) 593-2000. **$189-$649, 7 day notice.** 2600 Tiburon Dr. I-75, exit 111, 1.6 mi w on CR 846 (Immokalee Rd), 1.3 mi s on CR 31 (Airport-Pulling Rd), then just e. Int corridors. **Pets:** Accepted.
SAVE ✕ &M 💻 🍴 ➡ 🐾

⬦⬦⬦ **Staybridge Suites by Holiday Inn** H
(239) 643-8002. **Call for rates.** 4805 Tamiami Tr N. I-75, exit 107, 3.8 mi w on CR 896 (Pine Ridge Rd), then 0.9 mi s on US 41. Int corridors. **Pets:** Accepted.
✕ &M 🛏 💻 ➡

NEW SMYRNA BEACH

⬦⬦ **Buena Vista Inn** M 🐾
(386) 428-5565. **$75-$130, 14 day notice.** 500 N Causeway. 2 mi e on SR Business Rt 44; at west end North Causeway Bridge. Ext corridors. **Pets:** Other species. $5 daily fee/pet. No service.
✕ 🛏 💻 ❌

AAA ⬦⬦⬦ **Longboard Inn** BB
(386) 428-3499. **$115-$160, 14 day notice.** 312 Washington St. 0.25 mi w of jct N Riverside Dr. Ext corridors. **Pets:** Other species. $10 daily fee/room. Designated rooms, supervision.
SAVE ✕ 🛏

⬦⬦⬦ **Night Swan Intracoastal Bed & Breakfast** BB
(386) 423-4940. **$120-$220, 3 day notice.** 512 S Riverside Dr. Just s of SR 44 Intracoastal Waterway bridge; west side of Intracoastal Waterway. Ext/int corridors. **Pets:** Accepted.
ASK ✕ 🛏 💻 ❌

NORTH FORT MYERS

AAA ⬦⬦⬦ **Best Western Fort Myers Waterfront** H
(239) 997-5511. **$129-$209.** 13021 N Cleveland Ave. On US 41, 0.6 mi s of SR 78A (Pondella Rd), jct N Bay Dr and Caloosahatchee Bridge. Ext corridors. **Pets:** Small, dogs only. $35 one-time fee/room. Designated rooms, service with restrictions, crate.
SAVE ✕ 🛏 💻 🍴 ➡ ❌

OCALA

AAA ⬦⬦⬦ **Budget Host Inn** M
(352) 732-6940. **$40-$95.** 4013 NW Bonnie Heath Blvd. I-75, exit 354, 0.3 mi n on US 27. Ext corridors. **Pets:** Medium. $10 daily fee/pet. Service with restrictions, supervision.
SAVE ✕

AAA ⬦⬦ **Days Inn** H
(352) 629-7041. **$60-$110, 3 day notice.** 3811 NW Bonnie Heath Blvd. I-75, exit 354, just n on US 27. Ext/int corridors. **Pets:** Other species. $5 daily fee/pet. Service with restrictions, supervision.
SAVE ✕ 🛏 💻 ➡

AAA ⬦⬦⬦ **Hilton Ocala** H
(352) 854-1400. **$99-$229.** 3600 SW 36th Ave. I-75, exit 350, 0.3 mi e on SR 200. Int corridors. **Pets:** Accepted.
SAVE ✕ 🛏 💻 🍴 ➡ ❌

AAA ⬦⬦⬦ **Howard Johnson Inn & Restaurant** M
(352) 629-7021. **$60-$200.** 3951 NW Bonnie Heath Blvd. I-75, exit 354, just w. Ext corridors. **Pets:** Accepted.
SAVE ✕ 🛏 💻 🍴 ➡ ❌

⬦⬦⬦ **La Quinta Inn & Suites Ocala** H 🐾
(352) 861-1137. **$79-$139.** 3530 SW 36th Ave. I-75, exit 350, just e on SR 200. Int corridors. **Pets:** Medium, other species. Service with restrictions, supervision.
ASK ✕ &M 🛏 💻 ➡

AAA ⬦⬦⬦ **Quality Inn Ocala Hotel and Conference Center** H
(352) 629-0381. **$59-$150.** 3621 W Silver Springs Blvd. I-75, exit 352, just e on SR 40. Ext corridors. **Pets:** Accepted.
SAVE ✕ 🛏 💻 🍴 ➡

AAA ⬦⬦⬦ **Ramada Inn & Conference Center** H
(352) 732-3131. **$56-$104.** 3810 NW Bonnie Heath Blvd. I-75, exit 354, just w. Ext corridors. **Pets:** Accepted.
SAVE ✕ 🛏 💻 🍴 ➡ ❌

AAA ⬦⬦⬦ **Red Roof Inn & Suites** H
(352) 732-4590. **$60-$150.** 120 NW 40th Ave. I-75, exit 352, just w. Int corridors. **Pets:** Accepted.
SAVE ✕ 🛏 💻 ➡

▼▼▼▼ Residence Inn by Marriott Ocala 🅷 ❖
(352) 547-1600. **$174-$184.** 3610 SW 38th Ave. I-75, exit 350, just w on SR 200, then n. Int corridors. **Pets:** Medium. $75 one-time fee/room. Service with restrictions.
✕ 🛅 💻 🏊 ✕

▼▼▼▼ Seven Sisters Inn 🅱🅱
(352) 867-1170. **$119-$279, 7 day notice.** 820 SE Fort King St. Just s of jct SR 40 on SE Winona Ave; in downtown historic district. Int corridors. **Pets:** Accepted.
✕ 💻

(AAA) ▼▼ Travelodge Ocala 🅷
(352) 629-8850. **$69-$129.** 4040 W Silver Springs Blvd. I-75, exit 352, just w on SR 40. Ext corridors. **Pets:** Small. $10 daily fee/pet. Service with restrictions, supervision.
SAVE ✕ 🛅 💻 🏊

OLD TOWN

(AAA) ▼▼ Suwanee Gables Motel 🅼
(352) 542-7752. **$98-$210, 3 day notice.** 27659 SE Hwy 19, Alt 27. US 19, 98 and 27A; 2 mi s of jct SR 349. Ext corridors. **Pets:** Accepted.
SAVE ✕ 🛅 🏊

ORANGE CITY

(AAA) ▼▼ Comfort Inn 🅼
(386) 775-7444. **$79-$249.** 445 S Volusia Ave. I-4, exit 114, 2.8 mi w on SR 472, then 2 mi s on US 17-92. Ext corridors. **Pets:** Medium. $10 daily fee/pet. Service with restrictions, crate.
SAVE ✕ 🛅 💻 🏊

ORLANDO METROPOLITAN AREA

ALTAMONTE SPRINGS

▼▼ Candlewood Suites 🅷
(407) 767-5757. **Call for rates.** 644 Raymond Ave. I-4, exit 92, just w to Douglas Ave, 0.8 mi n to Central Pkwy, then just e. Int corridors. **Pets:** Accepted.
✕ &M 🛅 💻 🏊

(AAA) ▼▼▼▼ Clarion-Orlando North 🅷
(407) 862-4455. **$99-$169.** 230 W SR 436. I-4, exit 92, just sw. Ext/int corridors. **Pets:** Accepted.
SAVE ✕ &M 🛅 💻 🍽 🏊

(AAA) ▼▼▼ Days Inn & Suites 🅷
(407) 788-1411. **$69-$120.** 150 S Westmonte Dr. I-4, exit 92, 0.3 mi w on SR 436, then just s. Ext corridors. **Pets:** $10 daily fee/pet. Designated rooms, service with restrictions, supervision.
SAVE ✕ 🛅 💻 🏊

(AAA) ▼▼▼ Embassy Suites Orlando North 🅷 ❖
(407) 834-2400. **$119-$239.** 225 Shorecrest Dr. I-4, exit 92, 0.3 mi e on SR 436, then just n on North Lake Blvd. Int corridors. **Pets:** Medium. $20 daily fee/pet. Designated rooms, service with restrictions, supervision.
SAVE ✕ &M 🛅 💻 🍽 🏊 ✕

▼▼ Homestead Studio Suites Hotel-Orlando/Altamonte Springs 🅷
(407) 332-9300. **$70-$90.** 302 North Lake Blvd. I-4, exit 92, just e, then 0.3 mi s. Int corridors. **Pets:** Other species. $25 daily fee/pet. Service with restrictions, crate.
A$K ✕ &M 🛅 💻

▼▼▼ Residence Inn by Marriott 🅷
(407) 788-7991. **$187-$201.** 270 Douglas Ave. I-4, exit 92, just w on SR 436, then just n. Ext corridors. **Pets:** $75 one-time fee/room. Service with restrictions, supervision.
✕ &M 🛅 💻 🏊 ✕

CLERMONT

(AAA) ▼▼▼▼ Fairfield Inn & Suites Clermont 🅷 ❖
(352) 394-6585. **$99-$154.** 1750 Hunt Trace Blvd. Jct US 27 and SR 50, 0.5 mi e on SR 50, just n. Int corridors. **Pets:** Medium. $75 one-time fee/pet. Designated rooms, service with restrictions, supervision.
SAVE ✕ 🛅 💻 🏊

DAVENPORT

(AAA) ▼▼ Best Western Main Gate South 🅷
(863) 424-2596. **$51-$68, 4 day notice.** 2425 Frontage Rd. I-4, exit 55, just s on US 27. Ext corridors. **Pets:** Accepted.
SAVE ✕ &M 🛅 💻 🏊

▼▼▼ Calabay Parc-The Florida Store 🆅🅷
(407) 846-1722. **$129-$189, 30 day notice.** 325 Calabay Parc Blvd. Jct US 192 and 27, 4 mi s. Ext corridors. **Pets:** Accepted.
A$K ✕ 🛅 💻 🏊

▼▼▼▼ Hampton Inn Orlando-South of Walt Disney World Resorts 🅷
(863) 420-9898. **$99-$149.** 44117 Hwy 27. I-4, exit 55, just nw. Int corridors. **Pets:** Accepted.
✕ &M 🛅 💻 🏊

(AAA) ▼▼▼▼ Hampton Lakes-The Florida Store 🆅🅷
(407) 846-1722. **$129-$189, 30 day notice.** 1740 Bloomingdale Dr. I-4, exit 68, 3.5 mi s on SR 535, then 3.8 mi e on US 192. Ext corridors. **Pets:** $75 one-time fee/pet. Service with restrictions.
SAVE ✕ 🛅 💻 🏊

(AAA) ▼▼▼▼ Omni Orlando Resort at ChampionsGate 🅷
(407) 390-6664. **Call for rates.** 1500 Masters Blvd. I-4, exit 58, 0.3 mi w. Int corridors. **Pets:** Accepted.
SAVE ✕ &M 🛅 💻 🍽 🏊 ✕

▼▼▼▼ Southern Dunes-The Florida Store 🆅🅷
(407) 846-1722. **$129-$189, 30 day notice.** 2684 Hemingway Dr. I-4, exit 68, 3.5 mi s on SR 535, then 3.8 mi e on US 192. Ext corridors. **Pets:** Accepted.
A$K ✕ 🛅 💻 🍽 🏊 ✕

▼▼ Super 8 Motel Maingate South 🅷
(863) 420-8888. **$49-$89.** 44199 Hwy 27. I-4, exit 55, 0.5 mi n. Ext corridors. **Pets:** Accepted.
A$K ✕ 🛅 💻 🏊

KISSIMMEE

(AAA) ▼▼ Baymont Inn Kissimmee 🅷
(407) 994-1900. **$59-$99.** 4156 W Vine St. I-4, exit 64A, 6 mi e. Ext corridors. **Pets:** Accepted.
SAVE ✕ 🛅 💻 🏊

(AAA) ▼▼▼ Clarion Resort & Water Park-Conference Center 🅷
(407) 846-2221. **$100-$140.** 2261 E Irlo Bronson Memorial Pkwy. Florida Tpke, exit 244, then just w. Ext corridors. **Pets:** Accepted.
SAVE ✕ 🛅 💻 🍽 🏊 ✕

▼▼▼ FL Hotel & Suites Maingate East 🅷
(407) 870-2000. **Call for rates.** 4018 W Vine St. I-4, exit 64A, 7 mi e on US 192. Ext corridors. **Pets:** Accepted.
✕ 🛅 💻 🏊 ✕

(AAA) ▼▼ Howard Johnson Maingate Resort West H ❀
(407) 396-4500. **$39-$109.** 8660 W Irlo Bronson Memorial Hwy. I-4, exit 64B, 5.6 mi w on US 192. Ext corridors. **Pets:** Medium. $25 daily fee/room. Designated rooms, service with restrictions.
[SAVE] [X] [🛏] [🖥] [🍴] [🏊] [X]

▼▼▼ Indian Creek-The Florida Store VH
(352) 243-2853. **Call for rates.** 8009 Bow Creek Rd. I-4, exit 64B, 3.2 mi on US 192 to Formosa Gardens Blvd, then 1.2 mi s. Ext corridors. **Pets:** Other species. $75 one-time fee/pet. No service.
[X] [🛏] [🖥] [🏊]

(AAA) ▼▼ Masters Inn-Main Gate H
(407) 396-7743. **$45-$150, 3 day notice.** 2945 Entry Point Blvd. I-4, exit 25, 2.5 mi w on US 192; 1 mi w of Disney World main gate. Ext corridors. **Pets:** Small. $20 one-time fee/pet. Service with restrictions, crate.
[SAVE] [X] [🛏] [🖥] [🏊]

▼ Motel 6-#0436 H
(407) 396-6422. **$45-$55.** 7455 W Irlo Bronson Memorial Hwy. I-4, exit 64B, 1.3 mi w on US 192. Ext corridors. **Pets:** Other species. Service with restrictions, supervision.
[X] [🏊]

▼ Motel 6-#0464 M
(407) 396-6333. **$45-$55.** 5731 W Hwy 192. I-4, exit 64A, 2 mi e. Ext corridors. **Pets:** Other species. Service with restrictions, supervision.
[X] [♿] [🏊]

(AAA) ▼▼▼ The Palms Hotel and Villas by 3 Palms CO
(407) 396-2229. **$89-$139.** 3100 Parkway Blvd. I-4, exit 64A, 0.3 mi e on US 192, then 0.5 mi n. Ext/int corridors. **Pets:** Medium. $100 one-time fee/room. Service with restrictions.
[SAVE] [X] [🛏] [🖥] [🏊] [X]

▼▼ Rodeway Inn Eastgate M
(407) 396-1212. **$35-$89.** 4559 W Hwy 192. I-4, exit 68, 4 mi s on SR 535, then 3 mi e. Ext corridors. **Pets:** Small. $50 deposit/room, $5 daily fee/pet. Designated rooms, service with restrictions, crate.
[ASK] [X] [🛏] [🖥] [🏊]

(AAA) ▼▼ Rodeway Inn Maingate H
(407) 396-4300. **$39-$99.** 5995 W Irlo Bronson Memorial Hwy. I-4, exit 64A, 1 mi e. Ext corridors. **Pets:** Accepted.
[SAVE] [X] [🛏] [🖥] [🏊]

(AAA) ▼▼ Seralago Hotel & Suites Main Gate East H ❀
(407) 396-4488. **$50-$109.** 5678 W Irlo Bronson Memorial MM 9. I-4, exit 64A; between MM 9 and 10. Ext corridors. **Pets:** Medium, dogs only. $40 one-time fee/room. Designated rooms, service with restrictions.
[SAVE] [X] [♿] [🛏] [🖥] [🍴] [🏊] [X]

▼▼▼ Venetian Bay-Ventura Resort Rentals CO
(407) 273-8770. **$115-$199, 15 day notice.** 4008 San Gallo Dr. SR 417, exit 11, 3 mi s on Orange Blossom Tr, then 2 mi w on West Carroll. Ext corridors. **Pets:** Small, other species. $100 one-time fee/pet. Designated rooms, service with restrictions.
[ASK] [🛏] [🖥] [🏊]

LADY LAKE

(AAA) ▼▼▼ Comfort Suites in the Villages H
(352) 259-6578. **$99-$119.** 1202 Avenida Central N. Just n on US 441. Int corridors. **Pets:** Accepted.
[SAVE] [X] [🛏] [🖥] [🏊]

(AAA) ▼▼▼ Holiday Inn Express Hotel & Suites H
(352) 750-3888. **$99-$155.** 1205 Avenida Central N. Just n on US 441. Int corridors. **Pets:** Accepted.
[SAVE] [X] [🛏] [🖥] [🏊]

▼▼ Microtel Inn & Suites H
(352) 259-0184. **$59-$99.** 850 US 27/441. 1 mi s. Int corridors. **Pets:** Medium. $50 one-time fee/pet. Supervision.
[ASK] [X] [🛏] [🖥] [🏊]

▼▼▼ TownePlace Suites by Marriott at the Villages H
(352) 753-8686. **$112-$153.** 1141 Alonzo Ave. US 441/27 to Main St. Int corridors. **Pets:** Accepted.
[X] [♿] [🛏] [🖥] [🏊]

LAKE BUENA VISTA

(AAA) ▼▼ Comfort Inn Lake Buena Vista H ❀
(407) 996-7300. **$59-$89.** 8442 Palm Pkwy. I-4, exit 68, 0.6 mi n on SR 535, then 0.5 mi e. Ext corridors. **Pets:** Medium. $50 deposit/room, $10 daily fee/pet. Designated rooms, service with restrictions, supervision.
[SAVE] [X] [♿] [🛏] [🖥] [🍴] [🏊]

▼▼ Extended Stay Deluxe Orlando Lake Buena Vista H
(407) 239-4300. **$110-$125.** 8100 Palm Pkwy. I-4, exit 68, 0.6 mi n on SR 535, then 0.7 mi e. Int corridors. **Pets:** Other species. $25 daily fee/pet. Service with restrictions, crate.
[ASK] [X] [🛏] [🖥] [🏊] [X]

▼▼▼ Holiday Inn Express Lake Buena Vista H
(407) 239-8400. **$99-$189.** 8686 Palm Pkwy. I-4, exit 68, 0.5 mi n on CR 535, then 0.3 mi e. Int corridors. **Pets:** Small. $50 one-time fee/pet. Service with restrictions, supervision.
[ASK] [X] [🛏] [🖥] [🏊] [X]

▼▼▼ Residence Inn Orlando Lake Buena Vista H
(407) 465-0075. **$187-$201, 3 day notice.** 11450 Marbella Palms Ct. I-4, exit 68, 0.4 mi n on SR 535, then 0.5 mi e on Palm Pkwy. Int corridors. **Pets:** Accepted.
[X] [♿] [🛏] [🖥] [🏊] [X]

(AAA) ▼▼▼ Sheraton Safari Hotel & Suites H
(407) 239-0444. **$89-$219.** 12205 Apopka-Vineland Rd. I-4, exit 68, 0.5 mi n on SR 535. Ext/int corridors. **Pets:** Large, dogs only. Service with restrictions, supervision.
[SAVE] [X] [♿] [🛏] [🖥] [🍴] [🏊] [X]

LAKE MARY

▼▼▼ Candlewood Suites Lake Mary-Heathrow H
(407) 585-3000. **Call for rates.** 1130 Greenwood Blvd. I-4, exit 98, just e to Lake Emma Rd, 0.5 mi s to Greenwood Blvd, then 0.6 mi w. Int corridors. **Pets:** Accepted.
[X] [🛏] [🖥] [🏊]

▼▼▼ Extended StayAmerica-Lake Mary-Heathrow H
(407) 833-0011. **$75-$90.** 1036 Greenwood Blvd. I-4, exit 98, just e to Lake Emma Rd, then 0.5 mi. Int corridors. **Pets:** Other species. $25 daily fee/pet. Service with restrictions, crate.
[ASK] [X] [🛏] [🖥]

▼▼ Homestead Studio Suites-Orlando/Lake Mary-Heathrow H
(407) 829-2332. **$82-$97.** 1040 Greenwood Blvd. I-4, exit 98, 0.5 mi s on Lake Emma Rd; in Commerce Park. Int corridors. **Pets:** Other species. $25 daily fee/pet. Service with restrictions, crate.
[ASK] [X] [♿] [🛏] [🖥] [🏊]

LEESBURG

(AAA) ▼▼ Leesburg Super 8 H
(352) 787-6363. **$50-$175, 3 day notice.** 1392 North Blvd W. Jct US 27 and 441. Int corridors. **Pets:** Medium. $10 daily fee/pet. Service with restrictions, supervision.
[SAVE] [X] [♿] [🛏] [🏊]

MAITLAND

▼▼ Extended Stay Deluxe-Maitland 🅷
(407) 475-1675. **$75-$95.** 1776 Pembrook Dr. I-4, exit 90B, 0.5 mi w. Int corridors. **Pets:** Other species. $25 daily fee/pet. Service with restrictions, crate.
A$K ☒ 🗂 🖥 ⌘

◈◈◈ ▼▼▼ Homewood Suites by Hilton Orlando North 🅷
(407) 875-8777. **$89-$199.** 290 Southhall Ln. I-4, exit 90, just w, then just s on Lake Destiny. Int corridors. **Pets:** Accepted.
SAVE ☒ 🕭 🗂 🖥 ⌘

◈◈◈ ▼▼▼▼ Sheraton Orlando North 🅷
(407) 660-9000. **Call for rates.** 600 N Lake Destiny Dr. I-4, exit 90B, just w. Int corridors. **Pets:** Accepted.
SAVE ☒ 🕭 🗂 🖥 🍴 ⌘ ⊠

MOUNT DORA

▼▼▼ ◈◈◈ Heron Cay Lakeview Bed & Breakfast 🅱🅱
(352) 383-4050. **$175-$295, 15 day notice.** 495 Old Hwy 441. On CR 441 (Old US 441), 0.3 mi w. Int corridors. **Pets:** Large, other species. $25 daily fee/room. Designated rooms, service with restrictions, supervision.
A$K ☒ 🗂 ☎

OCOEE

◈◈◈ ▼▼▼ Best Western Turnpike West-Orlando 🅷
(407) 656-5050. **$79-$94, 3 day notice.** 10945 W Colonial Dr. I-4, exit 84, 10 mi w on SR 50; 0.5 mi e of Florida Tpke, exit 267B. Ext corridors. **Pets:** Accepted.
SAVE ☒ 🗂 🖥 🍴 ⌘

▼▼ ▼ Red Roof Inn Orlando West 🅷
(407) 347-0140. **Call for rates.** 11241 W Colonial Dr. I-4, exit 84, 10 mi w on SR 50; 0.6 mi e of Florida Tpke, exit 267. Int corridors. **Pets:** Accepted.
☒ 🗂 ⌘

ORLANDO

◈◈◈ ▼▼▼ AmeriSuites Orlando Airport/Northeast 🅷
(407) 240-3939. **Call for rates.** 7500 Augusta National Dr. SR 528 (Beachline Expwy), exit 11, 0.5 mi n on SR 436, just e on TG Lee Blvd, then just s. Int corridors. **Pets:** Accepted.
SAVE ☒ 🗂 🖥 ⌘

◈◈◈ ▼▼▼ Baymont Inn & Suites Florida Mall 🅷
(407) 851-8200. **$80-$159.** 8820 S Orange Blossom Tr. Florida Tpke, exit 254, just n. Int corridors. **Pets:** Medium. $10 daily fee/room. Designated rooms, service with restrictions, crate.
SAVE ☒ 🕭 🗂 🖥 ⌘

◈◈◈ ▼▼▼ Best Western Orlando West 🅷
(407) 841-8600. **$69-$125, 7 day notice.** 2014 W Colonial Dr. I-4, exit 84, 1.5 mi w on SR 50; 0.4 mi e of SR 423. Int corridors. **Pets:** Accepted.
SAVE ☒ 🗂 🖥 🍴 ⌘

◈◈◈ ▼▼▼▼ Clarion Hotel Universal 🅷
(407) 351-5009. **$89-$149.** 7299 Universal Blvd. I-4, exit 75A, just e of International Dr. Int corridors. **Pets:** Accepted.
SAVE ☒ 🕭 🗂 🖥 🍴 ⌘ ⊠

◈◈◈ ▼▼▼ Comfort Inn Universal Studios 🅷
(407) 363-7886. **$69.** 6101 Sand Lake Rd. I-4, exit 74A, 0.3 mi e on SR 482 (Sand Lake Rd), at Universal Blvd. Ext corridors. **Pets:** Accepted.
SAVE ☒ 🕭 🗂 🖥 ⌘

◈◈◈ ▼▼▼ Comfort Suites Orlando 🅷
(407) 351-5050. **$99-$149.** 9350 Turkey Lake Rd. I-4, exit 74A, just w on SR 482 (Sand Lake Rd), then 1.5 mi s. Ext corridors. **Pets:** Medium. $49 one-time fee/room. Designated rooms, service with restrictions, crate.
SAVE ☒ 🕭 🗂 🖥 ⌘

▼▼▼ Country Inn & Suites by Carlson-Orlando International Airport 🅷
(407) 856-8896. **Call for rates.** 5440 Forbes Pl. SR 528 (Beachline Expwy), exit 11, 0.6 mi n on SR 436, then just w. Int corridors. **Pets:** Accepted.
☒ 🗂 🖥 ⌘

◈◈◈ ▼▼▼▼ Courtyard by Marriott Orlando International Airport 🅷
(407) 240-7200. **$179-$226.** 7155 N Frontage Rd. SR 436, 0.3 mi n of SR 528 (Beachline Expwy). Int corridors. **Pets:** Other species. $25 one-time fee/pet. Service with restrictions, crate.
SAVE ☒ 🕭 🗂 🖥 🍴 ⌘

▼▼ ▼ Crestwood Suites Orlando 🅷
(407) 587-1800. **Call for rates.** 8010 Presidents Dr. I-4, exit 79, 4.3 mi s on SR 423 (John Young Pkwy), then 0.6 mi e on SR 482 (Sand Lake Rd). Int corridors. **Pets:** Accepted.
☒ 🗂 🖥

▼ Crossland Economy Studios-University of Central Florida
(407) 282-7112. **$72-$87.** 12350 E Colonial Dr. SR 417, exit 34, 4 mi e. Ext corridors. **Pets:** Other species. $25 daily fee/pet. Service with restrictions, crate.
A$K ☒ 🗂 🖥

▼▼ ▼ Extended StayAmerica/Orlando Convention Center/ Westwood Blvd
(407) 352-3454. **$60-$75.** 6451 Westwood Blvd. I-4, exit 72, just e on SR 528 (Beachline Expwy) to exit 1 (International Dr), just s, then just w. Int corridors. **Pets:** Other species. $25 daily fee/pet. Service with restrictions, crate.
A$K ☒ 🗂 🖥

▼▼ ▼ Extended StayAmerica-Orlando Universal Studios 🅷
(407) 351-1788. **$64-$79.** 5620 Major Blvd. I-4, exit 75B, just n, then just e. Int corridors. **Pets:** Other species. $25 daily fee/pet. Service with restrictions, crate.
A$K ☒ 🗂 🖥

▼▼▼ Extended Stay Deluxe Orlando Convention Center/ Pointe Orlando 🅷
(407) 903-1500. **$105-$120.** 8750 Universal Blvd. I-4, exit 74A, 0.5 mi e on SR 482 (Sand Lake Rd), then 0.7 mi s. Int corridors. **Pets:** Other species. $25 daily fee/pet. Service with restrictions, crate.
A$K ☒ 🕭 🗂 🖥 ⌘ ⊠

▼▼ ▼ Extended Stay Deluxe/Orlando Convention Center/ Westwood Blvd. 🅷
(407) 351-1982. **$85-$100.** 6443 Westwood Blvd. I-4, exit 72, just e on SR 528 (Beachline Expwy) to exit 1 (International Dr), just s, then just w. Int corridors. **Pets:** Other species. $25 daily fee/pet. Service with restrictions, crate.
A$K ☒ 🗂 🖥 ⌘

▼▼▼ Extended Stay Deluxe Orlando-John Young Parkway 🅷
(407) 248-8010. **$70-$90.** 8687 Commodity Cir. Just sw of jct SR 423 (John Young Pkwy) and 482 (Sand Lake Rd). Int corridors. **Pets:** Other species. $25 daily fee/pet. Service with restrictions, crate.
A$K ☒ 🗂 🖥 ⌘

▼▼ ▼ Extended Stay Deluxe Orlando-Universal Studios 🅷
(407) 370-4428. **$74-$89.** 5610 Vineland Rd. I-4, exit 75B, just n, then e. Int corridors. **Pets:** Other species. $25 daily fee/pet. Service with restrictions, crate.
A$K ☒ 🕭 🗂 🖥 ⌘

Floridays Resort Orlando ⬛
(407) 238-7700. **$150-$450.** 12550 Floridays Resort Dr. I-4, exit 72, just e on SR 528 (Beachline Expwy), exit 1, then 3 mi s. Ext corridors. **Pets:** Medium, other species. $250 one-time fee/room. Service with restrictions, supervision.

The Grand Bohemian Hotel ⬛
(407) 313-9000. **$199-$599.** 325 S Orange Ave. Corner of Jackson St. Int corridors. **Pets:** Small, dogs only. $125 one-time fee/pet. Supervision.

Hawthorn Suites Orlando Airport ⬛ ✿
(407) 438-2121. **$89-$229.** 7450 Augusta National Dr. SR 528 (Beachline Expwy), exit 11, 0.5 mi n on SR 436, just e, then just s. Int corridors. **Pets:** Medium. $25 daily fee/room. Designated rooms, service with restrictions, supervision.

Holiday Inn Express Orlando International Airport ⬛
(407) 581-7900. **$99-$149, 14 day notice.** 7900 Conway Rd. SR 528 (Beachline Expwy), exit 9, just n. Int corridors. **Pets:** Accepted.

Holiday Inn-International Drive Resort ⬛
(407) 351-3500. **$79-$169.** 6515 International Dr. I-4, exit 74A, just e on SR 482 (Sand Lake Rd), then 0.5 mi n. Ext/int corridors. **Pets:** Accepted.

Homestead Studio Suites Hotel-Orlando/John Young Parkway ⬛
(407) 352-5577. **$65-$80.** 4101 Equity Row. Just sw of jct SR 423 (John Young Pkwy) and 482 (Sand Lake Rd). Int corridors. **Pets:** Other species. $25 daily fee/pet. Service with restrictions, crate.

Howard Johnson Inn ⬛
(407) 851-1050. **Call for rates.** 9393 S Orange Blossom Tr. Florida Tpke, exit 254, just s. Ext corridors. **Pets:** Accepted.

Hyatt Place Orlando Airport ⬛
(407) 816-7800. **Call for rates.** 5435 Forbes Pl. SR 528 (Beachline Expwy), exit 11, 0.5 mi n on SR 436, then just w. Int corridors. **Pets:** Accepted.

La Quinta Inn & Suites Orlando (Convention Center) ⬛ ✿
(407) 345-1365. **$79-$159.** 8504 Universal Blvd. I-4, exit 74A, 0.5 mi e on SR 482 (Sand Lake Rd), then 0.5 mi s. Int corridors. **Pets:** Medium, other species. Service with restrictions, supervision.

La Quinta Inn & Suites Orlando (U.C.F.) ⬛ ✿
(407) 737-6075. **$69-$139.** 11805 Research Pkwy. Just se of jct University Blvd and SR 434 (Alafaya Tr). Int corridors. **Pets:** Medium, other species. Service with restrictions, supervision.

La Quinta Inn International Dr North ⬛ ✿
(407) 351-4100. **$50-$130.** 5825 International Dr. I-4, exit 75A, just w. Int corridors. **Pets:** Medium, other species. Service with restrictions, supervision.

La Quinta Inn Orlando (Airport West) ⬛ ✿
(407) 857-9215. **$55-$125.** 7931 Daetwyler Dr. SR 528 (Beachline Expwy), exit 9 (Tradeport), via McCoy Rd. Ext corridors. **Pets:** Medium, other species. Service with restrictions, supervision.

La Quinta Inn Orlando (International Drive) ⬛ ✿
(407) 351-1660. **$49-$129.** 8300 Jamaican Ct. I-4, exit 74A, just e on SR 482 (Sand Lake Rd), then just s on International Dr. Ext corridors. **Pets:** Medium, other species. Service with restrictions, supervision.

Motel 6 Orlando-International Drive #1079 ⬛
(407) 351-6500. **$51-$65.** 5909 American Way. I-4, exit 75A, just w of SR 435, then just n. Int corridors. **Pets:** Other species. Service with restrictions, supervision.

Quality Inn & Suites ⬛
(407) 996-4600. **$90-$200.** 8700 S Orange Blossom Tr. On US 17-92 and 441, 0.5 mi n of SR 528 and Florida Tpke, exit 254. Ext corridors. **Pets:** Small. $10 daily fee/pet. Designated rooms, service with restrictions, crate.

Quality Inn International ⬛ ✿
(407) 996-1600. **$59-$109.** 7600 International Dr. I-4, exit 74A, just e on SR 482 (Sand Lake Rd), then just n. Ext corridors. **Pets:** Medium, other species. $10 daily fee/pet. Designated rooms, service with restrictions.

Quality Inn Plaza ⬛ ✿
(407) 996-8585. **$49-$129.** 9000 International Dr. I-4, exit 74A, just e on SR 482 (Sand Lake Rd), then 1 mi s. Ext corridors. **Pets:** Medium, other species. $50 deposit/pet, $10 daily fee/pet. Service with restrictions, crate.

Red Roof Inn Convention Center ⬛
(407) 352-1507. **$50-$126, 3 day notice.** 9922 Hawaiian Ct. I-4, exit 72, 0.9 mi e on SR 528 (Beachline Expwy) to exit 1, then just n. Ext corridors. **Pets:** Accepted.

Residence Inn by Marriott Orlando Convention Center ⬛
(407) 226-0288. **$143-$164, 3 day notice.** 8800 Universal Blvd. I-4, exit 74A, 0.5 mi e on SR 482 (Sand Lake Rd), then 0.8 mi s. Int corridors. **Pets:** Accepted.

Residence Inn by Marriott Orlando International Airport ⬛
(407) 856-2444. **$174-$215.** 7024 Augusta National Dr. SR 528 (Beach Line Expwy), exit 11, 1 mi n; 1 mi e of Orlando International Airport. Int corridors. **Pets:** Accepted.

Residence Inn by Marriott-Orlando International Dr ⬛
(407) 345-0117. **$119-$249.** 7975 Canada Ave. I-4, exit 74A, just e on SR 482 (Sand Lake Rd). Ext corridors. **Pets:** Small, other species. $75 one-time fee/room. Service with restrictions, crate.

Residence Inn SeaWorld International Center ⬛
(407) 313-3600. **$339-$370.** 11000 Westwood Blvd. I-4, exit 72. Int corridors. **Pets:** Accepted.

Rodeway Inn International ⬛
(407) 996-4444. **$50-$90.** 6327 International Dr. I-4, exit 75A, just e on SR 482 (Sand Lake Rd), then 0.7 mi n. Ext/int corridors. **Pets:** Medium. $10 daily fee/pet. Designated rooms, service with restrictions, supervision.

Sheraton Orlando Downtown Hotel ⬛
(407) 425-4455. **Call for rates.** 60 S Ivanhoe Blvd. I-4, exit Ivanhoe Blvd. Int corridors. **Pets:** Accepted.

Sheraton Suites Orlando Airport
(407) 240-5555. **Call for rates.** 7550 Augusta National Dr. 2 mi n of airport terminal via SR 436 and TG Lee Blvd. Int corridors. **Pets:** Accepted.

TownePlace Suites by Marriott Orlando East/UCF
(407) 243-6100. **$177-$190.** 11801 High Tech Ave. 2.2 mi e of SR 417 on University Blvd. Int corridors. **Pets:** Large, other species. $25 daily fee/room. Service with restrictions, crate.

Universal's Hard Rock Hotel
(407) 503-2000. **$234-$519, 5 day notice.** 5800 Universal Blvd. I-4, exit 75A, 1 mi n, follow signs. Int corridors. **Pets:** Other species. $25 one-time fee/pet. Designated rooms, service with restrictions.

Universal's Loews Portofino Bay Hotel
(407) 503-1000. **$274-$559, 5 day notice.** 5601 Universal Blvd. I-4, exit 74B westbound; exit 75A eastbound, 1 mi n, follow signs. Int corridors. **Pets:** Other species. $25 one-time fee/room. Designated rooms, service with restrictions.

Universal's Loews Royal Pacific Resort
(407) 503-3000. **$219-$469, 5 day notice.** 6300 Hollywood Way. I-4, exit 74B, just n. Int corridors. **Pets:** Other species. $25 one-time fee/room. Designated rooms, service with restrictions.

Ventura Cove-Ventura Country Club-Ventura Resort Rentals
(407) 273-8770. **$79-$199, 15 day notice.** 3763 Ventura Club. 0.6 mi e of SR 436. Ext corridors. **Pets:** Small, other species. $100 one-time fee/pet. Designated rooms, service with restrictions.

Wyndham Orlando Resort
(407) 351-2420. **$83-$194, 3 day notice.** 8001 International Dr. I-4, exit 74A, just e at SR 482 (Sand Lake Rd). Ext/int corridors. **Pets:** Large. $50 one-time fee/room. Service with restrictions, crate.

ST. CLOUD

Budget Inn of St Cloud
(407) 892-2858. **$35-$90, 3 day notice.** 602 13th St. On US 192, 0.5 mi e of The Water Tower, 2 mi w of jct CR 15. Ext corridors. **Pets:** Very small, dogs only. $10 daily fee/pet. Service with restrictions.

TAVARES

Best Western Lake County Inn & Suites
(352) 253-2378. **$79-$199.** 1380 E Burleigh Blvd. On US 441 N. Int corridors. **Pets:** Medium, other species. $25 daily fee/pet. Service with restrictions, crate.

Budget Inn
(352) 343-4666. **Call for rates.** 101 W Burleigh Blvd. On US 441, 0.3 mi e of jct SR 19 S. Ext corridors. **Pets:** Accepted.

END METROPOLITAN AREA

ORMOND BEACH

Jameson Inn
(386) 672-3675. **$83-$90.** 175 Interchange Blvd. I-95, exit 268, just w, then just s. Int corridors. **Pets:** Other species. $15 daily fee/room. Service with restrictions, supervision.

PALATKA

Sleep Inn & Suites
(386) 325-8889. **Call for rates.** 3805 Reid St. 2 mi n on SR 100, jct SR 19. Int corridors. **Pets:** Small. $100 deposit/room, $15 daily fee/pet. Designated rooms, service with restrictions, supervision.

PALM BAY

Jameson Inn
(321) 725-2952. **$123-$135.** 890 Palm Bay Rd. I-95, exit 176. Int corridors. **Pets:** Accepted.

PALM BEACH

The Brazilian Court
(561) 655-7740. **$270-$3000, 7 day notice.** 301 Australian Ave. From Royal Palm Way (SR 704), s on Cocoanut Row, 2 blks to Australian Ave, then just e; corner of Hibiscus and Australian aves. Int corridors. **Pets:** Accepted.

The Four Seasons Resort, Palm Beach
(561) 582-2800. **$359-$3870, 14 day notice.** 2800 S Ocean Blvd. SR A1A, 0.3 mi n of jct SR 802. Int corridors. **Pets:** Accepted.

PALM BEACH GARDENS

PGA National Resort & Spa
(561) 627-2000. **$149-$369, 3 day notice.** 400 Ave of the Champions. I-95, exit 79AB, 2 mi w; Florida Tpke, exit 109, just w. Int corridors. **Pets:** Medium. $150 one-time fee/pet. Designated rooms, service with restrictions, supervision.

PALM BEACH SHORES

SeaSpray Beach Resort
(561) 844-0233. **$90-$250.** 123 S Ocean Ave. On Singer Island; 0.5 mi s of SR A1A. Int corridors. **Pets:** Small, other species. $15 deposit/pet. Service with restrictions, supervision.

PALM COAST

Microtel Inn & Suites
(386) 445-8976. **Call for rates.** 16 Kingswood Dr. I-95, exit 289, 0.5 mi se via Old Kings Rd. Int corridors. **Pets:** Accepted.

Palm Coast Villas
(386) 445-3525. **$69-$79, 7 day notice.** 5454 N Oceanshore Blvd. I-95, exit 289, 2.8 mi e to SR A1A, then 1.8 mi n. Ext corridors. **Pets:** Dogs only. $5 daily fee/room. Service with restrictions, supervision.

PANAMA CITY

AAA ◆◆ **Comfort Inn & Conference Center** Ⓗ
(850) 769-6969. **$79-$159.** 1013 E 23rd St. SR 368, just w of jct US 231.
Ext corridors. **Pets:** Other species. $50 deposit/room, $10 one-time fee/
room. Designated rooms, service with restrictions, supervision.
⬛⬛⬛⬛⬛⬛

◆◆◆ **La Quinta Inn & Suites Panama City** Ⓗ 🐾
(850) 914-0022. **$79-$139.** 1030 E 23rd St. Jct US 231 and SR 390. Int
corridors. **Pets:** Medium, other species. Service with restrictions, supervision.
⬛⬛⬛⬛⬛⬛

◆ **Super 8** Ⓜ
(850) 784-1988. **$49-$129.** 207 Hwy 231 N. Just n of jct US 98. Ext/int
corridors. **Pets:** Small, dogs only. $15 daily fee/pet. Service with restrictions,
crate.
⬛⬛⬛⬛

PANAMA CITY BEACH

◆◆◆ **La Quinta Inn & Suites Panama City
Beach** Ⓗ 🐾
(850) 234-3133. **$69-$194.** 7115 Coastal Palms Blvd. 2 mi s of US 98. Int
corridors. **Pets:** Medium, other species. Service with restrictions, supervision.
⬛⬛⬛⬛⬛⬛

PENSACOLA

AAA ◆◆◆ **Americas Best Value Inn & Suites** Ⓗ
(850) 479-1099. **$59-$89.** 8240 N Davis Hwy. I-10, exit 13, 0.8 mi n. Ext/int
corridors. **Pets:** Accepted.
⬛⬛⬛⬛⬛

◆◆ **Ashton Inn & Suites** Ⓗ
(850) 454-0280. **Call for rates.** 4 New Warrington Rd. Just n of jct US 98
and SR 295. Int corridors. **Pets:** Accepted.
⬛⬛⬛⬛

◆◆ **Extended StayAmerica-Pensacola-University Mall** Ⓗ
(850) 473-9323. **$70-$85.** 809 Bloodworth Ln. I-10, exit 13, just s on Davis
Hwy, then e. Int corridors. **Pets:** Other species. $25 daily fee/pet. Service
with restrictions, crate.
⬛⬛⬛

◆◆ **La Quinta Inn Pensacola** Ⓗ 🐾
(850) 474-0411. **$69-$139.** 7750 N Davis Hwy. I-10, exit 13, just n. Ext
corridors. **Pets:** Medium, other species. Service with restrictions, supervision.
⬛⬛⬛⬛⬛

◆ **Motel 6 #1105** Ⓜ
(850) 474-1060. **$39-$51.** 7226 Plantation Rd. I-10, exit 13, sw on Mall Rd.
Ext corridors. **Pets:** Other species. Service with restrictions, supervision.
⬛⬛

◆ **Motel 6 Pensacola North #1183** Ⓜ
(850) 476-5386. **$39-$48.** 7827 N Davis Hwy. I-10, exit 13, 0.3 mi n. Ext
corridors. **Pets:** Other species. Service with restrictions, supervision.
⬛⬛

AAA ◆◆◆ **Red Roof Inn** Ⓜ
(850) 476-7960. **Call for rates.** 7340 Plantation Rd. I-10, exit 13, just s.
Ext corridors. **Pets:** Accepted.
⬛⬛⬛

◆◆◆ **Residence Inn By Marriott** Ⓗ
(850) 479-1000. **$184-$195.** 7230 Plantation Rd. I-10, exit 13, just s. Ext
corridors. **Pets:** Accepted.
⬛⬛⬛⬛⬛⬛

PERRY

AAA ◆ **Best Budget Inn** Ⓜ
(850) 584-6231. **$56-$62.** 2220 US 19 S. US 19 and 98, 0.4 mi s of jct US
221. Ext corridors. **Pets:** $10 daily fee/pet. Service with
restrictions, supervision.
⬛⬛⬛⬛

PORT CHARLOTTE

AAA ◆◆◆ **Days Inn of Port Charlotte** Ⓗ 🐾
(941) 627-8900. **$59-$139.** 1941 Tamiami Tr. On US 41, 2.3 mi s of jct
Toledo Blade Blvd (CR 779). Ext corridors. **Pets:** Medium. $10 daily fee/
room. Designated rooms, service with restrictions, supervision.
⬛⬛⬛⬛⬛

PORT ST. JOE

AAA ◆◆◆ **MainStay Suites** Ⓗ 🐾
(850) 229-6246. **$90-$200.** 3951 E Hwy 98. 2 mi e of center. Int corridors.
Pets: Small, other species. $25 daily fee/pet. Designated rooms, supervi-
sion.
⬛⬛⬛⬛⬛⬛

PORT ST. LUCIE

◆◆ **Holiday Inn-Port St Lucie** Ⓗ
(772) 337-2200. **$129-$249.** 10120 S Federal Hwy, Rt 1. US 1, 0.5 mi n of
jct SR 716 (Port St Lucie Blvd). Int corridors. **Pets:** $50 one-time fee/room.
Designated rooms, service with restrictions, supervision.
⬛⬛⬛⬛⬛⬛

◆◆ **MainStay Suites at PGA Village** Ⓗ
(772) 460-8882. **$89-$199.** 8501 Champions Way. I-95, exit 121, just w. Int
corridors. **Pets:** Small. $50 one-time fee/pet. Designated rooms, no service,
supervision.
⬛⬛⬛⬛⬛

PUNTA GORDA

AAA ◆◆◆ **Best Western Waterfront** Ⓗ
(941) 639-1165. **Call for rates.** 300 Retta Esplanade. Jct US 41 southbound, just s of jct US 41 northbound. Int corridors. **Pets:** Small, other
species. $25 one-time fee/room. Designated rooms, service with restric-
tions.
⬛⬛⬛⬛⬛⬛

QUINCY

◆◆◆ **Allison House Inn** Ⓑ 🐾
(850) 875-2511. **$80-$165, 21 day notice.** 215 N Madison St. Just e of
town center; in historic district. Int corridors. **Pets:** Small, dogs only. Designated rooms, service with restrictions, crate.
⬛⬛

ST. AUGUSTINE

◆◆◆ **Bayfront Westcott House** Ⓑ
(904) 824-4301. **$119-$279, 7 day notice.** 146 Avenida Menendez. 1 blk
s of Bridge of Lions. Ext/int corridors. **Pets:** Other species. $15 daily fee/
pet. Designated rooms.
⬛⬛

AAA ◆◆◆ **Best Western St. Augustine I-95** Ⓜ
(904) 829-1999. **$75-$130, 7 day notice.** 2445 SR 16. I-95, exit 318, just
w. Ext corridors. **Pets:** Accepted.
⬛⬛⬛

AAA ◆◆◆ **Casablanca Inn on the Bay** Ⓑ
(904) 829-0928. **$99-$379, 7 day notice.** 24 Avenida Menendez. US 1
business route and SR A1A, then just n. Int corridors. **Pets:** Other species.
$30 daily fee/pet. Designated rooms, service with restrictions, supervision.
⬛⬛⬛⬛

Casa Monica Hotel 🅗 ❖
(904) 827-1888. **$189-$379, 3 day notice.** 95 Cordova St. Downtown; across from Lightner Museum and Flagler College. Int corridors. **Pets:** Small, dogs only. $150 one-time fee/pet. Designated rooms, service with restrictions, crate.

The Cozy Inn 🅜
(904) 824-2449. **$49-$209, 30 day notice.** 202 San Marco Ave. 0.3 mi s of jct SR 16. Ext corridors. **Pets:** $15 one-time fee/room. Service with restrictions.

The Inn At Camachee Harbor 🆑 ❖
(904) 825-0003. **$109-$179.** 201 Yacht Club Dr. On Intracoastal Waterway at west side of Usine Bridge; 1 mi e of jct N SR A1A and San Marco Blvd. Ext/int corridors. **Pets:** Medium, other species. $15 daily fee/pet. Designated rooms, service with restrictions, supervision.

La Quinta Inn & Suites 🅗 ❖
(904) 209-2580. **$79-$249.** 250 Belz Outlet Blvd. I-95, exit 318 (SR 16), just e, then n. Int corridors. **Pets:** Medium, other species. Service with restrictions, supervision.

Rodeway Inn 🅗 ❖
(904) 829-6581. **$70-$120.** 2800 N Ponce de Leon Blvd. US 1 at SR 16; in historic district. Ext corridors. **Pets:** Medium, dogs only. $10 daily fee/pet. Designated rooms, service with restrictions.

St. Francis Inn 🅱🅱
(904) 824-6068. **$109-$319, 7 day notice.** 279 St George St. Just s; in historic district. Ext/int corridors. **Pets:** Medium, other species. $15 daily fee/pet. Designated rooms, service with restrictions, crate.

ST. AUGUSTINE BEACH

Comfort Inn at St. Augustine Beach 🅗
(904) 471-1474. **Call for rates.** 901 A1A Beach Blvd. On Business Rt SR A1A, 1.6 mi s of jct SR 312 and A1A. Ext corridors. **Pets:** Other species. $10 daily fee/pet. No service, supervision.

Holiday Inn-St Augustine Beach 🅗 ❖
(904) 471-2555. **$114-$209.** 860 A1A Beach Blvd. On Business Rt SR A1A, 1.8 mi s of jct SR 312 and A1A. Int corridors. **Pets:** Medium. $20 daily fee/pet. Designated rooms, service with restrictions, supervision.

House of Sea and Sun 🅱🅱 ❖
(904) 461-1716. **$99-$225, 7 day notice.** 2 B St. Jct SR 312 and A1A, 1 mi e, s on A1A Beach Blvd. Ext/int corridors. **Pets:** Other species. $25 one-time fee/room. Designated rooms, service with restrictions.

St Augustine Island Inn 🅗
(904) 471-1440. **$59-$249, 7 day notice.** 894 A1A Beach Blvd. On Business Rt SR A1A, 2 mi s of jct SR 312 and A1A. Int corridors. **Pets:** Small. $20 daily fee/pet. Designated rooms, service with restrictions, supervision.

SANTA ROSA BEACH

A Highlands House Bed & Breakfast Inn 🅱🅱
(850) 267-0110. **$165-$275.** 4193 W Scenic CR 30A. US 98, 2 mi s on CR 393, just e. Int corridors. **Pets:** Accepted.

SARASOTA

Comfort Inn, Sarasota I-75 🅗
(941) 921-7750. **$69-$189.** 5778 Clark Rd. I-75, exit 205, just w on SR 72. Int corridors. **Pets:** Medium, other species. $10 daily fee/room. Designated rooms, service with restrictions, supervision.

Hibiscus Suites Inn 🆑
(941) 921-5797. **$119-$289, 3 day notice.** 1735 Stickney Point Rd. On SR 72, 0.3 mi sw of jct US 41. Ext corridors. **Pets:** Accepted.

Holiday Inn Express Sarasota Siesta Key 🅗
(941) 924-4900. **$99-$375, 3 day notice.** 6600 S Tamiami Tr. On US 41, just s of jct SR 72 (Clark Rd/Stickney Point Rd). Ext corridors. **Pets:** Accepted.

Homewood Suites by Hilton 🅗
(941) 365-7300. **$99-$229.** 3470 Fruitville Rd. I-75, exit 210, 3.2 mi w on SR 780 (Fruitville Rd). Int corridors. **Pets:** Medium. $100 one-time fee/room. Service with restrictions, crate.

Hotel Indigo 🅗
(941) 487-3800. **$169-$289.** 1223 Boulevard of the Arts. Jct US 41 (N Tamiami Tr). Int corridors. **Pets:** Accepted.

Hyatt Regency Sarasota on Sarasota Bay 🅗 ❖
(941) 953-1234. **$199-$459, 3 day notice.** 1000 Boulevard of the Arts. Just w of jct US 41 (Tamiami Tr). Int corridors. **Pets:** Medium. $150 one-time fee/pet. Service with restrictions, supervision.

La Quinta Inn & Suites Sarasota Airport 🅗 ❖
(941) 366-5128. **$75-$189.** 1803 N Tamiami Tr. On US 41, 1 mi n of jct SR 780 (Fruitville Rd). Int corridors. **Pets:** Medium, other species. Service with restrictions, supervision.

The Ritz-Carlton, Sarasota 🅗 ❖
(941) 309-2000. **$362-$549.** 1111 Ritz-Carlton Dr. On US 41, jct John Ringling Blvd. Int corridors. **Pets:** Small. $125 one-time fee/room. Designated rooms, service with restrictions, supervision.

SEBRING

Four Points by Sheraton Sebring Chateau Elan 🅗
(863) 655-7200. **Call for rates.** 150 Midway Dr. From US 27, 2.2 mi e on US 98; at entrance to Sebring International Raceway. Int corridors. **Pets:** Accepted.

Inn On The Lakes 🅗 ❖
(863) 471-9400. **$89-$219, 3 day notice.** 3100 Golfview Rd. On US 27, 1.5 mi n of jct SR 17. Ext/int corridors. **Pets:** Other species. $40 one-time fee/room. Designated rooms, service with restrictions.

Kenilworth Lodge 🅗
(863) 385-0111. **$75-$205, 3 day notice.** 1610 Lakeview Dr. On US 27, 1 mi e on SR 17. Ext/int corridors. **Pets:** Other species. $15 daily fee/pet. Designated rooms, service with restrictions.

Residence Inn by Marriott–Sebring H
(863) 314-9100. **$133-$184.** 3221 Tubbs Rd. On US 27, 1 mi n of jct SR 17. Int corridors. **Pets:** Other species. Designated rooms, service with restrictions, crate.

SIESTA KEY

Tropical Breeze Resort & Spa of Siesta Key CO
(941) 349-1125. **$99-$365.** 153 Avenida Messina. Jct Ocean Blvd; in Siesta Village. Ext corridors. **Pets:** Other species. $35 one-time fee/room. Designated rooms, no service, crate.

Tropical Breeze Vacations M
(941) 349-1125. **$99-$495.** 153 Avenida Messina. Jct Ocean Blvd; in Siesta Village. Ext corridors. **Pets:** Other species. $35 one-time fee/room. Designated rooms, no service, crate.

SPRING HILL

Quality Inn Weeki Wachee M
(352) 596-2007. **$89-$149.** 6172 Commercial Way. On US 19, jct SR 50 (Cortez Blvd). Ext corridors. **Pets:** $15 daily fee/pet. Designated rooms, service with restrictions, supervision.

STARKE

Best Western Starke H
(904) 964-6744. **$81-$125, 15 day notice.** 1290 N Temple Ave. 1 mi n on US 301 from jct SR 100. Ext corridors. **Pets:** Small. $10 daily fee/pet. Service with restrictions, supervision.

STEINHATCHEE

Steinhatchee Landing Resort CO
(352) 498-3513. **$140-$612, 14 day notice.** SR 51. SR 51, 8 mi w of jct US 19/98. Ext corridors. **Pets:** Medium, dogs only. $150 deposit/room. Designated rooms, service with restrictions, crate.

STUART

Monterey Inn & Marina M
(772) 283-3500. **$99-$149, 7 day notice.** 300 SW Monterey Rd. Jct SR 76 and CR 714, just w. Ext corridors. **Pets:** Other species. $25 one-time fee/room. No service.

Pirates Cove Resort & Marina H
(772) 287-2500. **$130-$200.** 4307 SE Bayview St. 0.3 mi e of SR A1A. Ext corridors. **Pets:** Large, other species. $20 daily fee/pet. Designated rooms, service with restrictions, supervision.

TALLAHASSEE

Best Western Pride Inn & Suites H
(850) 656-6312. **$70-$200.** 2016 Apalachee Pkwy. 1 mi se of US 27. Ext corridors. **Pets:** Medium, other species. $10 daily fee/pet. Service with restrictions.

Best Western Seminole Inn M
(850) 656-2938. **$70-$150, 3 day notice.** 6737 Mahan Dr. I-10, exit 209A, just w on US 90. Ext corridors. **Pets:** Small. $10 daily fee/pet. Service with restrictions, crate.

Days Inn H
(850) 222-3219. **$50-$190.** 1350 W Tennessee St. 1.6 mi w of US 27. Int corridors. **Pets:** Accepted.

Econo Lodge M
(850) 385-6155. **$55-$95.** 2681 N Monroe St. I-10, exit 199, 0.5 mi s. Ext corridors. **Pets:** Large, other species. $10 one-time fee/pet. Service with restrictions, supervision.

Holiday Inn Capital East H
(850) 877-3171. **$109-$249, 30 day notice.** 1355 Apalachee Pkwy. 1.3 mi se on US 27. Int corridors. **Pets:** Medium, other species. $50 one-time fee/room. Service with restrictions, crate.

Homewood Suites by Hilton H
(850) 402-9400. **$169-$249.** 2987 Apalachee Pkwy. US 27, 3.5 mi s. Int corridors. **Pets:** Large, other species. $75 one-time fee/room.

La Quinta Inn Tallahassee (North) H
(850) 385-7172. **$54-$109.** 2905 N Monroe St. I-10, exit 199, just s on US 27. Ext corridors. **Pets:** Medium, other species. Service with restrictions, supervision.

La Quinta Inn Tallahassee (South) H
(850) 878-5099. **$49-$109.** 2850 Apalachee Pkwy. 3 mi se on US 27. Ext corridors. **Pets:** Medium, other species. Service with restrictions, supervision.

Motel 6 #1073 H
(850) 877-6171. **$39-$51.** 1027 Apalachee Pkwy. 1 mi se on US 27. Ext corridors. **Pets:** Other species. Service with restrictions, supervision.

Motel 6 #1191 H
(850) 386-7878. **$35-$45.** 2738 N Monroe St. I-10, exit 199, just s on US 27. Ext corridors. **Pets:** Other species. Service with restrictions, supervision.

Motel 6 #420 M
(850) 668-2600. **$39-$51.** 1481 Timberlane Rd. I-10, exit 203, just n, then w. Ext corridors. **Pets:** Other species. Service with restrictions, supervision.

Ramada Conference Center H
(850) 386-1027. **$59-$189.** 2900 N Monroe St. I-10, exit 199, just s. Ext/int corridors. **Pets:** $15 daily fee/room. Designated rooms.

Residence Inn by Marriott Tallahassee Universities at the Capitol H
(850) 329-9080. **$215-$256.** 600 W Gaines St. 0.5 mi w of S Monroe St; downtown. Int corridors. **Pets:** Accepted.

Staybridge Suites Tallahassee H
(850) 219-7000. **$89-$399.** 1600 Summit Lake Dr. I-10, exit 209B, just n. Int corridors. **Pets:** Large, other species. $10 daily fee/room, $50 one-time fee/room. Service with restrictions, crate.

StudioPLUS-Tallahassee-Killearn H
(850) 383-1700. **$70-$145.** 1950 Raymond Diehl Rd. I-10, exit 203, 2.4 mi s, then just n. Int corridors. **Pets:** Other species. $25 daily fee/pet. Service with restrictions, crate.

TAMPA BAY METROPOLITAN AREA

BRANDON

♥♥ Homestead Studio Suites Hotel-Tampa/Brandon M
(813) 643-5900. **$65-$120.** 330 Grand Regency Blvd. I-75, exit 257, just e on SR 60, then 0.4 mi n; in Regency Corporate Park. Ext corridors. **Pets:** Other species. $25 daily fee/pet. Service with restrictions, crate.
ASK ✕ &M 🛏 💻

♥♥♥ La Quinta Inn & Suites Tampa Bay (Brandon) H ❖
(813) 643-0574. **$79-$129.** 310 Grand Regency Blvd. I-75, exit 257, just e on SR 60, then 0.5 mi n; in Regency Corporate Office. Int corridors. **Pets:** Medium, other species. Service with restrictions, supervision.
ASK ✕ &M 🛏 💻 🌊

CLEARWATER

♥♥♥ Candlewood Suites Clearwater-St Petersburg H
(727) 573-3344. **Call for rates.** 13231 49th St N. I-275, exit 31 southbound, 3 mi w on SR 688, then just s; exit 30 northbound, 1.4 mi w on SR 686, 1.6 mi w on SR 688 (Ulmerton Rd), then just s. Int corridors. **Pets:** Accepted.
✕ &M 🛏 💻 🌊

♣ ♥♥♥ Days Inn Clearwater/St. Petersburg Airport H
(727) 573-3334. **$59-$109.** 3910 Ulmerton Rd. I-275, exit 31 southbound, 2 mi w on SR 688; exit 30 northbound, 1.4 mi w on SR 686, 0.7 mi w. Int corridors. **Pets:** Accepted.
SAVE ✕ &M 🛏 💻 🌊

♥♥ Extended StayAmerica-St. Petersburg-Clearwater H
(727) 561-9032. **$50-$100.** 3089 Executive Dr. I-275, exit 31 southbound; exit 30 northbound, 1.8 mi w on SR 699, just n on 34th St N, then 0.3 mi ne. Int corridors. **Pets:** Other species. $25 daily fee/pet. Service with restrictions, crate.
ASK ✕ 🛏 💻

♥♥ Homestead Studio Suites Hotel-St Petersburg-Clearwater M
(727) 572-4800. **$50-$100.** 2311 Ulmerton Rd. I-275, exit 31 southbound, 1.3 mi w on SR 688; exit 30 northbound, 1.4 mi w on SR 686; 0.6 mi on SR 688. Ext corridors. **Pets:** Other species. $25 daily fee/pet. Service with restrictions, crate.
ASK ✕ 🛏 💻 🌊

♥♥♥ Homewood Suites by Hilton H
(727) 573-1500. **$99-$209.** 2233 Ulmerton Rd. I-275, exit 31 southbound, 1.3 mi w on SR 688 (Ulmerton Rd); exit 30 northbound, 1.4 mi w on SR 686, 0.6 mi e on SR 688. Int corridors. **Pets:** Accepted.
✕ &M 🛏 💻 🌊

♥♥ Howard Johnson Inn & Suites M
(727) 796-0135. **$60-$130.** 27988 US Hwy 19 N. On US 19, 0.6 mi n of jct SR 580. Ext corridors. **Pets:** Small, other species. $10 daily fee/pet. Designated rooms, service with restrictions, supervision.
ASK ✕ 🛏 💻 🌊

♥♥♥ La Quinta Inn Tampa Bay (Clearwater-Airport) H ❖
(727) 572-7222. **$49-$500.** 3301 Ulmerton Rd. I-275, exit 31 southbound; exit 30 northbound, 1.7 mi w on SR 688; in The Centres Office Park. Int corridors. **Pets:** Medium, other species. Service with restrictions, supervision.
ASK ✕ 🛏 💻 🌊 ✕

♣ ♥♥♥ Radisson Hotel Clearwater Central H
(727) 799-1181. **Call for rates.** 20967 US 19 N. On US 19, just n of jct SR 60. Ext/int corridors. **Pets:** Other species. $50 one-time fee/room. Service with restrictions.
SAVE ✕ &M 🛏 💻 🍴 🌊 ✕

♣ ♥♥♥ Residence Inn by Marriott St. Petersburg/Clearwater H ❖
(727) 573-4444. **$195-$226.** 5050 Ulmerton Rd. I-275, exit 31 southbound, 3.1 mi w on SR 688; exit 30 northbound, 1.4 mi w on SR 686, then 1.7 mi w on SR 688. Ext corridors. **Pets:** Medium. $100 one-time fee/room. Service with restrictions.
SAVE ✕ 🛏 💻 🌊 ✕

♣ ♥♥♥ Super 8 Clearwater/St. Petersburg Airport/ Tampa Bay H
(727) 572-8881. **$50-$200.** 13260 34th St N. I-275, exit 31 southbound; 1.8 mi w on SR 688; exit 30 northbound, 1.4 mi w on SR 686. Int corridors. **Pets:** Medium, dogs only. $10 daily fee/pet. Designated rooms, service with restrictions, supervision.
SAVE ✕ 🛏 💻 🌊

♥♥♥ TownePlace Suites by Marriott St. Petersburg/Clearwater H
(727) 299-9229. **$143-$205.** 13200 49th St N. I-275, exit 31 southbound; exit 30 northbound, 3 mi w on SR 688, then just s; in Turtle Creek. Int corridors. **Pets:** Accepted.
✕ &M 🛏 💻 🌊

INDIAN ROCKS BEACH

♥♥ Sea Star Motel & Apartments M ❖
(727) 596-2525. **$75-$130, 30 day notice.** 1805 Gulf Blvd. On SR 699, 1.2 mi n of jct SR 688 (Walsingham Rd). Ext corridors. **Pets:** Other species. $10 daily fee/pet. No service.
✕ 🛏 💻 ✕ ✕

INDIAN SHORES

♣ ♥♥♥ Sea Club Resort Condominiums CO ❖
(727) 596-2046. **$55-$110 (no credit cards), 45 day notice.** 19725 Gulf Blvd. On SR 699, 1.1 mi n of jct CR 694. Ext corridors. **Pets:** Small. $50 one-time fee/pet. Designated rooms, service with restrictions, supervision.
SAVE ✕ 🛏 🌊 ✕

LARGO

♣ ♥♥♥ Hampton Inn & Suites H
(727) 585-3333. **$109-$399.** 100 E Bay Dr. On SR 686, 3.4 mi w of jct US 19; at jct Alt US 19. Int corridors. **Pets:** Service with restrictions, crate.
SAVE ✕ &M 🛏 💻 🌊

LUTZ

♣ ♥♥♥ Residence Inn by Marriott Tampa Suncoast at NorthPointe Village H
(813) 792-8400. **$164-$205.** 2101 NorthPointe Pkwy. Just s of jct SR 54; Suncoast Pkwy, exit 19, just e; in NorthPointe at Suncoast Crossings. Int corridors. **Pets:** Small, dogs only. $100 one-time fee/pet. Service with restrictions, crate.
SAVE ✕ &M 🛏 💻 🌊

MADEIRA BEACH

♣ ♥♥♥ Snug Harbor Inn Waterfront Bed & Breakfast M ❖
(727) 395-9256. **$67-$500, 21 day notice.** 13655 Gulf Blvd. On SR 699, 0.9 mi s of jct Tom Stuart Cswy. Ext corridors. **Pets:** Other species. Service with restrictions.
SAVE ✕ 🛏 💻 🌊 ✕

NEW PORT RICHEY

Riverside Inn M
(727) 845-4990. **$50-$100.** 7631 US 19. On US 19, 0.8 mi n of jct Main St. Ext corridors. **Pets:** Medium. $6 daily fee/room. Designated rooms, no service, supervision.

OLDSMAR

Residence Inn Tampa/Oldsmar H
(813) 818-9400. **$184-$251.** 4012 Tampa Rd. On SR 580; jct St. Pete Dr. Int corridors. **Pets:** Medium, other species. $100 one-time fee/room. Service with restrictions, supervision.

PALM HARBOR

Best Western Lake Tarpon Hotel H
(727) 942-0358. **$90-$160, 3 day notice.** 37611 US 19 N. On US 19, 3 mi s of jct SR 582. Ext corridors. **Pets:** Medium, other species. $10 daily fee/pet. Designated rooms, service with restrictions, crate.

Innisbrook Resort & Golf Club CO
(727) 942-2000. **$109-$509, 3 day notice.** 36750 US Hwy 19 N. On US 19, 2.8 mi s of jct SR 582; at jct Olde Post Rd, follow signs. Int corridors. **Pets:** Small. $200 one-time fee/pet. Service with restrictions.

Knights Inn-Clearwater/Palm Harbor M
(727) 789-2002. **$45-$85.** 34106 US 19 N. On US 19, 1.8 mi n of CR 752 (Tampa Rd). Ext corridors. **Pets:** Small, other species. $10 daily fee/room. Service with restrictions, supervision.

Red Roof Inn M
(727) 786-2529. **$49-$126.** 32000 US 19 N. On US 19, 0.4 mi s of jct CR 752 (Tampa Rd). Ext corridors. **Pets:** Accepted.

PINELLAS PARK

La Quinta Inn Tampa (Pinellas Park/Clearwater) H
(727) 545-5611. **$49-$500.** 7500 US Hwy 19 N. I-275, exit 28, 1.4 mi s on Gandy Blvd (SR 694), then just n. Ext/int corridors. **Pets:** Medium, other species. Service with restrictions, supervision.

PLANT CITY

Comfort Inn of Plant City H
(813) 707-6000. **$69-$339.** 2003 S Frontage Rd. I-4, exit 22, just ne on Park Rd. Int corridors. **Pets:** Medium. $20 daily fee/pet. Service with restrictions, crate.

Red Rose Inn & Suites M
(813) 752-3141. **Call for rates.** 2011 N Wheeler St. I-4, exit 21, 0.4 mi ne; at jct SR 39. Ext corridors. **Pets:** Accepted.

PORT RICHEY

Comfort Inn M
(727) 863-3336. **Call for rates.** 11810 US 19. On US 19, just s of jct SR 52. Ext corridors. **Pets:** Accepted.

RUSKIN

Southern Comfort Bed & Breakfast BB
(813) 645-6361. **$75-$195, 30 day notice.** 2409 Ravine Dr W. Jct US 41, 1.1 mi sw on 1st St, just s on 24th Ave SW, then just s. Ext/int corridors. **Pets:** $20 daily fee/pet. Designated rooms, crate.

ST. PETE BEACH

Bayview Plaza Waterfront Resort M
(727) 367-2791. **$55-$229, 14 day notice.** 4321 Gulf Blvd. On SR 699; 0.6 mi n of Pinellas Bayway. Ext/int corridors. **Pets:** Medium, other species. $10 daily fee/pet. Designated rooms.

Beach House Suites By The Don Cesar H
(727) 363-0001. **$169-$524, 3 day notice.** 3860 Gulf Blvd. On SR 699, 0.4 mi n of jct Pinellas Bayway. Ext corridors. **Pets:** Accepted.

Don CeSar Beach Resort, a Loews Hotel H
(727) 360-1881. **$169-$669, 3 day notice.** 3400 Gulf Blvd. On SR 699, jct Pinellas Bayway. Int corridors. **Pets:** Large, other species. $25 one-time fee/pet. Designated rooms, service with restrictions, supervision.

ST. PETERSBURG

Best Western Gateway Inn H
(727) 525-1800. **$100, 3 day notice.** 6638 4th St N. I-275, exit 26, 1.7 mi e on 54th Ave N (CR 202), 0.8 mi n. Int corridors. **Pets:** Medium. $25 daily fee/pet. Designated rooms, service with restrictions, supervision.

La Quinta Inn Tampa Bay Area (St. Petersburg) M
(727) 527-8421. **$49-$125.** 4999 34th St N. I-275, exit 26 southbound; exit 26B northbound, just w on 54th Ave N, then just s on US 19. Ext corridors. **Pets:** Medium, other species. Service with restrictions, supervision.

Mansion House B & B BB
(727) 821-9391. **$159-$260, 7 day notice.** 105 5th Ave NE. 0.5 mi n at 1st St N. Ext/int corridors. **Pets:** Accepted.

Ramada Inn Mirage M
(727) 525-1181. **$80-$90.** 5005 34th St N. I-275, exit 26 southbound; exit 26B northbound, 0.8 mi w on 54th Ave N, then 0.3 mi s on US 19. Ext corridors. **Pets:** Large, other species. $25 one-time fee/room. Designated rooms, crate.

SEFFNER

Hampton Inn & Suites Tampa-East H
(813) 630-4321. **$129-$169.** 11740 Tampa Gateway Blvd. I-4, exit 10, just n of CR 579. Int corridors. **Pets:** Accepted.

TAMPA

AmeriSuites Tampa/Sabal Park M
(813) 622-8557. **Call for rates.** 10007 Princess Palm Ave. I-75, exit 260 southbound; exit 260B northbound, 0.5 mi w on SR 574 (Dr. Martin Luther King Jr Blvd), just s on Falkenburg Rd, then just w; in Sabal Corporate Park. Int corridors. **Pets:** Accepted.

(AAA) ▼▼ ▼▼ Best Western Brandon Hotel & Conference Center M
(813) 621-5555. **$99-$129.** 9331 Adamo Dr. I-75, exit 257, 1.2 mi w on SR 60. Ext corridors. **Pets:** Small. $25 one-time fee/room. Designated rooms, service with restrictions, crate.
[SAVE] [⊠] [🛏] [▣] [¶] [⊜]

(AAA) ▼▼▼▼ Chase Suite Hotel by Woodfin M
(813) 281-5677. **$149-$399.** 3075 N Rocky Point Dr. I-275, exit 39 southbound; exit 39B northbound, 3 mi w on SR 60, then just n; in Rocky Point Harbor. Ext corridors. **Pets:** Accepted.
[SAVE] [⊠] [&M] [🛏] [▣] [⊜] [⊠]

(AAA) ▼▼▼▼ Clarion Hotel & Conference Center Tampa M
(813) 971-4710. **$99-$199, 3 day notice.** 2701 E Fowler Ave. I-275, exit 51, 1.5 mi e on SR 582. Ext/int corridors. **Pets:** Accepted.
[SAVE] [⊠] [&M] [🛏] [▣] [¶] [⊜]

▼▼▼ Comfort Inn Hotel & Suites Tampa Stadium/Airport M
(813) 877-6061. **Call for rates.** 4732 N Dale Mabry Hwy. I-275, exit 41B, 2 mi n. Ext corridors. **Pets:** $25 one-time fee/pet. Service with restrictions, supervision.
[⊠] [&M] [🛏] [▣] [⊜] [⊠]

▼▼▼ Extended StayAmerica-Tampa Airport-West Shore H
(813) 873-2850. **$70-$115.** 4312 W Spruce St. I-275, exit 40B, 0.6 mi n on Lois Ave, then just w. Int corridors. **Pets:** Other species. $25 daily fee/pet. Service with restrictions, crate.
[ASK] [⊠] [&M] [🛏] [▣]

▼▼▼ Extended Stay Deluxe Tampa–Airport H
(813) 886-5253. **$65-$115.** 4811 Memorial Hwy. Veteran's Expwy, exit 3, just sw on CR 576. Int corridors. **Pets:** Other species. $25 daily fee/pet. Service with restrictions, crate.
[ASK] [⊠] [&M] [🛏] [▣] [⊜]

▼▼▼ Extended Stay Deluxe-Tampa-Airport-N West Shore Blvd H
(813) 637-8990. **$80-$125.** 1805 N Westshore Blvd. I-275, exit 40A southbound, 0.5 mi nw; exit 39A northbound, 1 mi e on Kennedy Blvd, then 1.3 mi w. Int corridors. **Pets:** Other species. $25 daily fee/pet. Service with restrictions, crate.
[ASK] [⊠] [&M] [🛏] [▣] [⊜]

(AAA) ▼▼▼▼ Grand Hyatt Tampa Bay H ❀
(813) 874-1234. **$109-$399.** 2900 Bayport Dr. SR 60, east end of Courtney Campbell Cswy. Ext/int corridors. **Pets:** Medium, dogs only. $75 one-time fee/room. Designated rooms, service with restrictions.
[SAVE] [⊠] [🛏] [▣] [¶] [⊜] [⊠]

▼▼▼ Hampton Inn Veterans Expressway H
(813) 901-5900. **$99-$199.** 5628 W Waters Ave. SR 589 (Veteran's Expwy), exit 6A, just e on CR 584. Int corridors. **Pets:** Medium, other species. $10 daily fee/room. Service with restrictions, supervision.
[ASK] [⊠] [&M] [🛏] [▣] [⊜]

(AAA) ▼▼▼▼ Hilton Tampa Airport Westshore H
(813) 877-6688. **$109-$349.** 2225 N Lois Ave. I-275, exit 40B, 0.8 mi n. Int corridors. **Pets:** Accepted.
[SAVE] [⊠] [&M] [🛏] [▣] [¶] [⊜] [⊠]

(AAA) ▼▼▼▼ Holiday Inn Express Hotel & Suites H
(813) 910-7171. **$99-$179.** 8310 Galbraith Rd. I-75, exit 270, 0.3 mi n on CR 581 (Bruce B Downs Blvd), just w on Highwoods Preserve Pkwy, then just n; in Highwoods Preserve. Int corridors. **Pets:** Accepted.
[SAVE] [⊠] [&M] [🛏] [▣] [⊜] [⊠]

▼▼ ▼▼ Homestead Studio Suites Hotel-Tampa/North Airport M
(813) 243-1913. **$50-$95.** 5401 Beaumont Ctr Blvd E. SR 589 (Veterans Expwy), exit 4, just w on SR 580. Ext/int corridors. **Pets:** Other species. $25 daily fee/pet. Service with restrictions, crate.
[ASK] [⊠] [&M] [🛏] [▣]

▼▼▼ Homewood Suites Brandon/Tampa H
(813) 685-7099. **$109-$179.** 10240 Palm River Rd. I-75, exit 257, 0.4 mi w on SR 60, just s on S Falkenburg Rd, then 0.3 mi e. Int corridors. **Pets:** Other species. $100 one-time fee/room.
[⊠] [&M] [🛏] [▣] [⊜] [⊠]

▼▼▼ Howard Johnson Plaza Downtown Tampa H
(813) 223-1351. **$99-$169, 7 day notice.** 111 W Fortune St. I-275, exit 44, just s on Ashley Dr. Int corridors. **Pets:** Accepted.
[ASK] [⊠] [&M] [🛏] [▣] [⊜]

(AAA) ▼▼▼▼ Hyatt Place Tampa Airport/Westshore H
(813) 282-1037. **$109-$259.** 4811 W Main St. I-275, exit 40A, 0.5 mi n on Westshore Blvd; exit 39A northbound, 1 mi e on Kennedy Blvd, 1 mi n on Westshore Blvd, then just w. Int corridors. **Pets:** Accepted.
[SAVE] [⊠] [&M] [🛏] [▣] [¶] [⊜]

▼▼▼ La Quinta Inn & Suites Tampa Bay (Airport) M ❀
(813) 287-0440. **$59-$650.** 4730 W Spruce St. I-275, exit 40A, 0.7 mi n on Westshore Blvd; exit 39A northbound, 1 mi e on Kennedy Blvd, 1.2 mi n on Westshore Blvd, then just w. Ext corridors. **Pets:** Medium, other species. Service with restrictions, supervision.
[ASK] [⊠] [🛏] [▣] [⊜]

▼▼▼ La Quinta Inn & Suites Tampa Bay (U.S.F./Near Busch Gardens) H ❀
(813) 910-7500. **$79-$500.** 3701 E Fowler Ave. I-275, exit 51, 2.2 mi e on SR 582. Int corridors. **Pets:** Medium, other species. Service with restrictions, supervision.
[ASK] [⊠] [&M] [🛏] [▣] [⊜]

▼▼▼ La Quinta Inn Tampa East Fairgrounds H ❀
(813) 626-0885. **$49-$500.** 4811 US 301 N. I-4, exit 6 westbound; exit 6A eastbound, just se. Int corridors. **Pets:** Medium, other species. Service with restrictions, supervision.
[ASK] [⊠] [🛏] [▣] [⊜]

▼▼▼ La Quinta Inn Tampa South H ❀
(813) 835-6262. **$99-$159.** 4620 W Gandy Blvd. Just e of jct S Westshore Blvd. Int corridors. **Pets:** Medium, other species. Service with restrictions, supervision.
[ASK] [⊠] [&M] [🛏] [▣] [⊜]

▼▼▼ La Quinta Inn West Tampa-Brandon H ❀
(813) 684-4007. **$69-$500.** 602 S Falkenburg Rd. I-75, exit 257, just w on SR 60, then just n. Int corridors. **Pets:** Medium, other species. Service with restrictions, supervision.
[ASK] [⊠] [🛏] [▣] [⊜]

▼▼▼ Mainsail Suites Hotel & Conference Center H
(813) 243-2600. **$125-$250.** 5108 Eisenhower Blvd. SR 589 (Veteran's Expwy), exit 4, just w on SR 580; main entrance on Hillsborough Ave. Ext corridors. **Pets:** Accepted.
[⊠] [&M] [🛏] [▣] [¶] [⊜] [⊠]

▼▼ Motel 6 #1192 M
(813) 628-0888. **$49-$65.** 6510 US 301 N. I-4, exit 7 westbound; exit 7B eastbound, 0.7 mi n. Ext corridors. **Pets:** Other species. Service with restrictions, supervision.
[⊠] [⊜]

▼▼ ▼▼ Red Roof Inn-Brandon H
(813) 681-8484. **$69-$110.** 10121 Horace Ave. I-75, exit 257, just w on SR 60 (Adamo Dr), just n on Falkenburg Rd, then just e. Ext corridors. **Pets:** Medium, other species. Service with restrictions.
[⊠] [&M] [🛏] [⊜]

Red Roof Inn-Fairgrounds H
(813) 623-5245. **$61-$300.** 5001 N US 301. I-4, exit 7 westbound; exit 7A eastbound, just se. Ext corridors. **Pets:** Medium. Service with restrictions, supervision.

Residence Inn by Marriott Sabal Park H ❖
(813) 627-8855. **$148-$190.** 9719 Princess Palm Ave. I-75, exit 260 southbound; exit 260B northbound, just w on SR 574 (Dr. Martin Luther King Jr Blvd), just s on Falkenburg Rd, then 0.4 mi w; in Sabal Corporate Center. Int corridors. **Pets:** Other species. $112 one-time fee/room. Service with restrictions.

Seminole Hard Rock Hotel and Casino Tampa H
(813) 627-7625. **$219-$399.** 5223 N Orient Rd. I-4, exit 6, just w. Int corridors. **Pets:** Accepted.

Sheraton Suites Tampa Airport H
(813) 873-8675. **Call for rates.** 4400 W Cypress St. I-275, exit 40A southbound, just nw on CR 587; exit 39A northbound, just nw on Westshore Blvd (CR 587), then just e. Int corridors. **Pets:** Accepted.

Sheraton Tampa Riverwalk H
(813) 223-2222. **$109-$339.** 200 N Ashley Dr. I-275, exit 44, 0.8 mi s. Int corridors. **Pets:** Accepted.

Staybridge Suites Tampa-Sabal Park H
(813) 227-4000. **Call for rates.** 3624 N Falkenburg Rd. I-75, exit 260 southbound; exit 260B northbound, just w on SR 574 (Dr. Martin Luther King Blvd), then just s. Int corridors. **Pets:** Medium. $75 one-time fee/pet. Service with restrictions, crate.

Tahitian Inn H
(813) 877-6721. **$129-$259.** 601 S Dale Mabry Hwy. I-275, exit 41A, 1.1 mi s. Ext/int corridors. **Pets:** Accepted.

The Westin Tampa Harbour Island H
(813) 229-5000. **$159-$419.** 725 S Harbour Island Blvd. I-275, exit 44 eastbound, 2 mi s on Tampa St, follow signs to Convention Center and Harbour Island; exit 45A westbound. Int corridors. **Pets:** Accepted.

TEMPLE TERRACE

Extended Stay Tampa North H
(813) 989-2264. **$65-$120.** 12242 Morris Bridge Rd. I-75, exit 266, just w on Fletcher Ave (CR 582A). Int corridors. **Pets:** Other species. $25 daily fee/pet. Service with restrictions, crate.

TREASURE ISLAND

Residence Inn St. Petersburg/Treasure Island H
(727) 367-2761. **$149-$269.** 11908 Gulf Blvd. On SR 699, 0.7 mi n of jct Treasure Island Cswy. Ext/int corridors. **Pets:** Accepted.

END METROPOLITAN AREA

TITUSVILLE

Best Western Space Shuttle Inn Kennedy Space Center H
(321) 269-9100. **Call for rates.** 3455 Cheney Hwy. I-95, exit 215 (SR 50), just e. Ext corridors. **Pets:** Accepted.

Comfort Inn Titusville H
(321) 269-7110. **$69-$250.** 3655 Cheney Hwy. I-95, exit 215 (SR 50), just w. Ext corridors. **Pets:** Other species. $20 daily fee/pet. Designated rooms, service with restrictions, supervision.

Days Inn Titusville H
(321) 269-4480. **$59-$159, 14 day notice.** 3755 Cheney Hwy. I-95, exit 215 (SR 50). Ext corridors. **Pets:** Accepted.

Ramada Inn & Suites-Kennedy Space Center H
(321) 269-5510. **$79-$89.** 3500 Cheney Hwy. I-95, exit 215 (SR 50), just e. Int corridors. **Pets:** Other species. $15 daily fee/pet. Service with restrictions, supervision.

VENICE

Holiday House Venice M
(941) 485-5411. **$69-$179.** 455 US 41 Bypass N. 0.5 mi s of jct US 41. Ext/int corridors. **Pets:** Accepted.

Holiday Inn Express Hotel & Suites H ❖
(941) 584-6800. **$99-$145.** 380 Commercial Ct. I-75, exit 193, just w on Jacaranda Blvd (CR 765), then just n. Int corridors. **Pets:** Other species. $30 one-time fee/room. Designated rooms, service with restrictions.

Horse and Chaise Inn a Bed & Breakfast BB
(941) 488-2702. **$115-$169, 7 day notice.** 317 Ponce de Leon. Just s of jct Venice Ave on Nassau St, just sw; downtown. Ext/int corridors. **Pets:** Large. $10 one-time fee/room. Designated rooms, service with restrictions, crate.

WEST MELBOURNE

Extended Stay Deluxe H
(321) 733-6050. **$70-$105.** 1701 Evans Rd. I-95, exit 180 (US 192), 3 mi e, then 0.3 mi n. Int corridors. **Pets:** Other species. $25 daily fee/pet. Service with restrictions, crate.

Fairfield Inn & Suites by Marriott H ❖
(321) 722-2220. **$131-$140.** 4355 W New Haven Ave. I-95, exit 180, just e. Int corridors. **Pets:** Small. $50 deposit/room, $50 one-time fee/room. Designated rooms, service with restrictions, supervision.

WEST PALM BEACH

Comfort Inn & Conference Center M
(561) 689-6100. **$109-$199.** 1901 Palm Beach Lakes Blvd. I-95, exit 71, just w. Int corridors. **Pets:** Small, other species. $10 daily fee/room, $25 one-time fee/room. Service with restrictions, supervision.

Extended Stay Deluxe-Northpoint Corporate Park H
(561) 683-5332. **$70-$165.** 700 Northpoint Pkwy. I-95, exit 74 (45th St), just w, then n. Int corridors. **Pets:** Other species. $25 daily fee/pet. Service with restrictions, crate.

▼▼▼ **Hibiscus House Bed & Breakfast** BB
(561) 863-5633. **$89-$210, 14 day notice.** 501 30th St. 1.2 mi n on Flagler Dr from jct Palm Beach Lakes Blvd, 0.3 mi w. Int corridors. **Pets:** Other species.

ASK ✕ 🖬 ⚞

◈◈◈ ▼▼▼ **Red Roof Inn-West Palm Beach** M
(561) 697-7710. **Call for rates.** 2421 Metrocentre Blvd E. I-95, exit 74 (45th St), just w on CR 702; in Metrocentre Corporate Park. Ext/int corridors. **Pets:** Accepted.

SAVE ✕ ⟨M 🖬 ⚞

◈◈◈ ▼▼▼ **Residence Inn by Marriott West Palm Beach** H
(561) 687-4747. **$120-$140.** 2461 Metrocentre Blvd. I-95, exit 74, just w on 45th St; in Metrocentre Corporate Park. Int corridors. **Pets:** Accepted.

SAVE ✕ ⟨M 🖬 ▣ ⚞ ✕

WINTER HAVEN

◈◈◈ ▼▼▼ **Best Western Admiral's Inn and Conference Center** H ✿
(863) 324-5950. **$90-$325, 4 day notice.** 5665 Cypress Gardens Blvd. SR 540, 3 mi e of jct US 17; 3.9 mi w of jct US 27. Ext/int corridors. **Pets:** Medium, other species. $15 daily fee/pet. Designated rooms, service with restrictions, crate.

SAVE ✕ 🖬 ▣ ⟨¶ ⚞

▼▼▼ **Clarion of Winter Haven** H
(863) 294-4451. **Call for rates.** 1150 Third St SW. 0.8 mi s on US 17. Ext corridors. **Pets:** Accepted.

✕ ⟨M 🖬 ▣ ⟨¶ ⚞

GEORGIA

CITY INDEX

ADAIRSVILLE

◈◈ ▼▼▼ Comfort Inn 🅷
(770) 773-2886. **$60-$90.** 107 Princeton Blvd. I-75, exit 306, just w. Ext corridors. **Pets:** Small. $10 daily fee/pet. Service with restrictions, supervision.
[SAVE] [X] [🔥M] [🅱] [💻] [🏊]

▼▼ Ramada Limited 🅷 🐾
(770) 769-9726. **Call for rates.** 500 Georgia North Cir. I-75, exit 306, 0.3 mi w. Ext corridors. **Pets:** Medium. $10 daily fee/pet. Designated rooms, service with restrictions, supervision.
[X] [🔥M] [🅱] [💻] [🏊]

ADEL

◈◈ ▼▼▼▼ Hampton Inn 🅷
(229) 896-3099. **$71-$99.** 1500 W 4th St. I-75, exit 39, just w. Int corridors. **Pets:** Accepted.
[SAVE] [X] [🔥M] [🅱] [💻] [🏊]

▼▼ Super 8 I-75 🅼
(229) 896-2244. **$45-$69.** 1103 W 4th St. I-75, exit 39, just e. Ext corridors. **Pets:** Accepted.
[ASK] [X] [🅱] [🏊]

ALBANY

▼▼ Jameson Inn 🅷
(229) 435-3737. **$78-$85.** 2720 Dawson Rd. 0.5 mi s of jct US 82 and SR 520. Ext corridors. **Pets:** Small, other species. $15 daily fee/room. Designated rooms, service with restrictions, supervision.
[ASK] [X] [🅱] [💻] [🏊]

▼▼ Quality Inn-Merry Acres 🅼
(229) 435-7721. **$65-$85.** 1500 Dawson Rd. 3.3 mi w. Ext corridors. **Pets:** Medium, dogs only. $10 daily fee/room. Designated rooms, service with restrictions, crate.
[ASK] [X] [🅱] [💻] [🏊]

▼▼▼▼ Wingate Inn 🅷
(229) 883-9800. **$86.** 2735 Dawson Rd. Jct US 82 and SR 520, 0.4 mi s. Int corridors. **Pets:** Other species. $50 one-time fee/room. Service with restrictions, supervision.
[ASK] [X] [🔥M] [🅱] [💻] [🏊]

ALMA

▼▼ Days Inn 🅼
(912) 632-7000. **$53-$63.** 930 S Pierce St. Jct SR 32/US 1, 0.4 mi s on US 1. Ext corridors. **Pets:** Accepted.
[ASK] [X] [🅱] [💻] [🏊]

AMERICUS

◈◈◈ ▼▼▼▼ 1906 Pathway Inn Bed & Breakfast 🅱🅱
(229) 928-2078. **$99-$145, 3 day notice.** 501 S Lee St. 0.5 mi s of US 280 on SR 377. Int corridors. **Pets:** Small. $50 deposit/room, $20 daily fee/pet. Designated rooms, service with restrictions, supervision.
[SAVE] [X]

▼▼ Holiday Inn Express 🅷
(229) 928-5400. **$70-$95.** 1611 E Lomar St. On US 280, just w of jct US 27. Ext corridors. **Pets:** Accepted.
[ASK] [X] [🅱] [💻] [🏊]

▼▼ Quality Inn 🅷
(229) 924-4431. **$84.** 1205 Martin Luther King Jr Blvd. On US 19 S, 1 mi w of downtown. Ext corridors. **Pets:** Small. $10 daily fee/pet. Designated rooms, service with restrictions, crate.
[ASK] [X] [🅱] [💻] [🍴] [🏊]

ASHBURN

◈◈◈ ▼▼▼▼ Best Western Ashburn Inn 🅷
(229) 567-0080. **$59-$75.** 820 Shoney's Dr. I-75, exit 82, just w. Ext corridors. **Pets:** Small. $15 daily fee/pet. Designated rooms, service with restrictions, supervision.
[SAVE] [X] [🅱] [💻] [🏊]

◈◈◈ ▼▼▼ Days Inn 🅷
(229) 567-3346. **$55-$65.** 823 E Washington Ave. I-75, exit 82, just w on SR 112. Ext corridors. **Pets:** Small. $15 daily fee/pet. Designated rooms, service with restrictions, supervision.
[SAVE] [X] [🅱] [🏊]

▼▼ Super 8 🅷
(229) 567-4688. **$45-$65.** 749 E Washington Ave. I-75, exit 82, just w. Ext corridors. **Pets:** Small. $5 daily fee/pet. Supervision.
[ASK] [X] [🅱] [💻]

ATHENS

⟨AAA⟩ ▼▼▼ Best Western-Colonial Inn M
(706) 546-7311. **$70-$240, 14 day notice.** 170 N Milledge Ave. Jct US 78 business route (Broad St), 0.5 mi w on SR 15. Ext corridors. **Pets:** Accepted.
[SAVE] [X] [🛏] [💻] [🏊]

⟨AAA⟩ ▼▼▼ Comfort Suites Athens H
(706) 995-4000. **$89-$109.** 255 North Ave. SR 10 Loop, exit 11B (Dougherty St/North Ave); 1 mi n of downtown. Int corridors. **Pets:** Small. $25 daily fee/pet. Service with restrictions, supervision.
[SAVE] [X] [🛏] [💻] [🏊]

⟨AAA⟩ ▼▼▼ Microtel Inn H
(706) 548-5676. **$54-$130.** 1050 Ultimate Dr. US 78 business route (Broad St) and SR 10 Loop, 1.4 mi e. Int corridors. **Pets:** Medium, dogs only. $25 one-time fee/room. Designated rooms, service with restrictions, supervision.
[SAVE] [X] [🛁M] [🛏] [💻]

ATLANTA METROPOLITAN AREA

ACWORTH

⟨AAA⟩ ▼▼▼ America's Best Inn M
(770) 974-5400. **$45-$50, 7 day notice.** 5320 Cherokee St. I-75, exit 278, just w. Ext corridors. **Pets:** Dogs only. $5 one-time fee/pet. Designated rooms, service with restrictions, supervision.
[SAVE] [X] [🛏] [🏊]

⟨AAA⟩ ▼▼▼ Best Western Acworth Inn M
(770) 974-0116. **$55-$80.** 5155 Cowan Rd. I-75, exit 277, just w. Ext corridors. **Pets:** Accepted.
[SAVE] [X] [🛏] [💻] [🏊]

⟨AAA⟩ ▼▼▼ Econo Lodge M
(770) 974-1922. **$55-$65.** 4980 Cowan Rd. I-75, exit 277, just w. Ext corridors. **Pets:** Accepted.
[SAVE] [X] [🛏] [💻] [🏊]

▼▼ Motel 6 M
(770) 974-1700. **$45-$65.** 5035 Cowan Rd. I-75, exit 277, just w. Ext corridors. **Pets:** Accepted.
[ASK] [X] [🛏] [💻] [🏊]

⟨AAA⟩ ▼▼▼ Super 8 M
(770) 966-9700. **$60-$80.** 4970 Cowan Rd. I-75, exit 277, just w. Ext corridors. **Pets:** Medium. $10 daily fee/pet. Service with restrictions, supervision.
[SAVE] [X] [🛏] [💻] [🏊]

ALPHARETTA

▼▼ Extended StayAmerica H
(770) 475-2676. **$57-$72.** 1950 Rock Mill Rd. SR 400, exit 9, just e. Int corridors. **Pets:** Other species. $25 daily fee/pet. Service with restrictions, crate.
[ASK] [🛁M] [🛏] [💻]

▼▼▼ Extended Stay Deluxe
Atlanta-Alpharetta-Northpoint H
(770) 569-1730. **$72-$87.** 3329 Old Milton Pkwy. SR 400, exit 10, just e. Int corridors. **Pets:** Other species. $25 daily fee/pet. Service with restrictions, crate.
[ASK] [X] [🛁M] [🛏] [💻] [🏊]

▼▼▼ Homewood Suites H
(770) 998-1622. **$79-$149.** 10775 Davis Dr. SR 400, exit 8, northwest corner. Int corridors. **Pets:** Accepted.
[X] [🛁M] [🛏] [💻] [🏊]

⟨AAA⟩ ▼▼▼ Hotel Sierra Alpharetta H
(678) 339-0505. **$139-$199.** 12505 Cingular Way. SR 400, exit 11, 0.5 mi w. Int corridors. **Pets:** Accepted.
[SAVE] [X] [🛁M] [🛏] [💻] [🏊]

▼▼▼ La Quinta Inn & Suites Atlanta
(Alpharetta) H 🐾
(770) 754-7800. **$55-$139.** 1350 North Point Dr. SR 400, exit 9, 0.5 mi e. Int corridors. **Pets:** Medium, other species. Service with restrictions, supervision.
[ASK] [X] [🛁M] [🛏] [💻] [🏊]

⟨AAA⟩ ▼▼▼▼ Residence Inn by Marriott H
(770) 664-0664. **$197-$211.** 5465 Windward Pkwy W. SR 400, exit 11, 0.4 mi w. Ext/int corridors. **Pets:** Accepted.
[SAVE] [X] [🛁M] [🛏] [💻] [🏊] [X]

▼▼▼▼ Staybridge Suites H
(770) 569-7200. **$135-$171.** 3980 North Point Pkwy. SR 400, exit 10, 0.5 mi e. Int corridors. **Pets:** Accepted.
[ASK] [X] [🛁M] [🛏] [💻] [🏊] [X]

▼▼▼ StudioPLUS H
(770) 475-7871. **$62-$77.** 3331 Old Milton Pkwy. SR 400, exit 10, just e. Int corridors. **Pets:** Other species. $25 daily fee/pet. Service with restrictions, crate.
[ASK] [X] [🛁M] [🛏] [💻] [🏊]

▼▼▼ TownePlace Suites by Marriott H
(770) 664-1300. **$142-$152.** 7925 S Westside Pkwy. SR 400, exit 9, 0.3 mi w. Int corridors. **Pets:** Accepted.
[X] [🛁M] [🛏] [💻] [🏊]

▼▼▼ Wingate Inn H
(770) 649-0955. **$114.** 1005 Kingswood Pl. SR 400, exit 8, 0.7 mi w. Int corridors. **Pets:** Accepted.
[ASK] [X] [🛁M] [🛏] [💻]

ATLANTA

⟨AAA⟩ ▼▼▼▼ Best Western Granada Suite Hotel H 🐾
(404) 876-6100. **$109-$209.** 1302 W Peachtree St. I-75/85, exit 250 (14th St), just e, then just n on W Peachtree St to 16th St. Int corridors. **Pets:** Medium. $50 one-time fee/room. Service with restrictions.
[SAVE] [X] [🛏] [💻]

▼▼▼ Beverly Hills Inn BB
(404) 233-8520. **$129-$249, 3 day notice.** 65 Sheridan Dr NE. Jct Piedmont and Peachtree rds, 1.1 mi s on Peachtree Rd to Sheridan Dr, then just e. Int corridors. **Pets:** Accepted.
[ASK] [🛏] [💻]

▼▼▼ Crowne Plaza Atlanta Perimeter NW H
(770) 955-1700. **$69-$219.** 6345 Powers Ferry Rd NW. I-285, exit 22, southeast corner. Int corridors. **Pets:** Accepted.
[ASK] [X] [🛁M] [🛏] [💻] [🍴] [🏊]

▼▼ Extended StayAmerica H
(404) 679-4333. **$70-$87.** 3115 Clairmont Rd. I-85, exit 91, 0.6 mi w. Int corridors. **Pets:** Other species. $25 daily fee/pet. Service with restrictions, crate.
[ASK] [X] [🛁M] [🛏] [💻]

▼▼ Extended StayAmerica 🔲
(770) 396-5600. **$65-$90.** 905 S Crestline Pkwy. I-285, exit 28 westbound, 0.7 mi n; exit 26 eastbound, 0.5 mi n to Hammond Dr, 0.5 mi e, then 0.3 mi n. Int corridors. **Pets:** Other species. $25 daily fee/pet. Service with restrictions, crate.

ASK ✕ 💧 🔲 🖥

▼▼▼ Extended Stay Deluxe 🔲
(770) 436-1511. **$70-$80.** 2474 Cumberland Pkwy SE. I-285, exit 18, just e. Int corridors. **Pets:** Other species. $25 daily fee/pet. Service with restrictions, crate.

ASK ✕ 💧 🔲 🖥 🌊

▼▼▼ Extended Stay Deluxe Atlanta-Lenox 🔲
(404) 237-9100. **$80-$100.** 3967 Peachtree Rd. I-85, exit 89, 2.8 mi w. Int corridors. **Pets:** Other species. $25 daily fee/pet. Service with restrictions, crate.

ASK ✕ 💧 🔲 🖥 🌊

▼▼▼ Extended Stay Deluxe (Atlanta/Marietta/Powers Ferry Rd) 🔲
(770) 933-8010. **$75-$85.** 2010 Powers Ferry Rd. I-75, exit 260 (Windy Hill Rd), 0.5 mi e, then just s. Int corridors. **Pets:** Other species. $25 daily fee/pet. Service with restrictions, crate.

ASK ✕ 💧 🔲 🖥 🌊

▼▼▼ Extended Stay Deluxe (Atlanta/Marietta/Windy Hill/Int. N Pkwy) 🔲
(770) 226-0242. **$77-$87.** 2225 Interstate North Pkwy. I-75, exit 260 (Windy Hill Rd), just e to Interstate North Pkwy, then just s. Int corridors. **Pets:** Other species. $25 daily fee/pet. Service with restrictions, crate.

ASK ✕ 💧 🔲 🖥 🌊

▼▼▼ Extended Stay Deluxe Atlanta-Perimeter 🔲
(770) 379-0111. **$78-$92.** 6330 Peachtree-Dunwoody Rd NE. I-285, exit 28 westbound, 0.7 mi n; exit 26 eastbound, 0.5 mi n to Hammond Dr, 0.5 mi e, then 0.3 mi n. Int corridors. **Pets:** Other species. $25 daily fee/pet. Service with restrictions, crate.

ASK ✕ 💧 🔲 🖥 🌊

◈◈◈ ▼▼▼▼ Four Seasons Hotel Atlanta 🔲
(404) 881-9898. **$430-$4700.** 75 14th St. I-75/85, exit 250 (14th St), 0.3 mi e. Int corridors. **Pets:** Accepted.

✕ 💧 🍴 🌊 🗙

▼▼▼ The Glenn Hotel 🔲
(404) 521-2250. **$129-$389, 3 day notice.** 110 Marietta St NW. I-75/85, exit 248C northbound, 0.8 mi w, then just n; exit 249A southbound, just s to Baker St, just w, then just n. Int corridors. **Pets:** Accepted.

ASK ✕ 💧 🔲 🍴

◈◈◈ ▼▼▼ ▼▼▼ Grand Hyatt Atlanta 🔲 🐾
(404) 237-1234. **$139-$499.** 3300 Peachtree Rd NE. Corner of Peachtree and Piedmont rds. Int corridors. **Pets:** $100 one-time fee/room. Service with restrictions, supervision.

SAVE ✕ 💧 🔲 🖥 🍴 🌊 🗙

◈◈◈ ▼▼▼ Hawthorn Suites-Atlanta NW 🔲
(770) 952-9595. **$129-$149.** 1500 Parkwood Cir. I-75, exit 260 (Windy Hill Rd), 0.5 mi e, then 0.3 mi s on Powers Ferry Rd. Ext corridors. **Pets:** Accepted.

SAVE ✕ 🔲 🖥 🌊 🗙

▼▼▼ Hilton Atlanta 🔲
(404) 659-2000. **$99-$299.** 255 Courtland St NE. I-75/85, exit 249A southbound; exit 248C northbound, just w to Piedmont Ave, just n to Baker St, then just w. Int corridors. **Pets:** Accepted.

✕ 🔲 🍴 🌊 🗙

▼▼▼ Holiday Inn Select Atlanta Perimeter 🔲
(770) 457-6363. **$69-$139.** 4386 Chamblee-Dunwoody Rd. I-285, exit 30 eastbound, just s; exit westbound, follow access road 1.3 mi to Chamblee-Dunwoody Rd, then just s. Int corridors. **Pets:** Accepted.

ASK ✕ 💧 🔲 🖥 🍴 🌊

▼▼ Homestead Studio Suites Hotel-Atlanta/North Druid Hills 🔲
(404) 325-1223. **$58-$70.** 1339 Executive Park Dr NE. I-85, exit 89, just e to Executive Park Dr, then just s. Ext corridors. **Pets:** Other species. $25 daily fee/pet. Service with restrictions, crate.

ASK ✕ 💧 🔲 🖥

▼▼▼ Homestead Studio Suites Hotel-Atlanta/Perimeter 🔲
(770) 522-0025. **$60-$83.** 1050 Hammond Dr. I-285, exit 26 eastbound, 0.5 mi n to Hammond Dr, then 0.5 mi e; exit 28 westbound, just n to Hammond Dr, then just w. Ext corridors. **Pets:** Other species. $25 daily fee/pet. Service with restrictions, crate.

ASK ✕ 💧 🔲 🖥

▼▼▼▼ Homewood Suites-Atlanta Buckhead 🔲 🐾
(404) 365-0001. **$189-$250.** 3566 Piedmont Rd. SR 400, exit 2, just s to Piedmont Rd, then 1 mi w. Int corridors. **Pets:** Medium. $100 one-time fee/room. Service with restrictions, supervision.

ASK ✕ 💧 🔲 🖥 🌊

▼▼▼ Homewood Suites-Cumberland 🔲
(770) 988-9449. **$89-$169.** 3200 Cobb Pkwy SW. I-285, exit 19 eastbound; exit 20 westbound, 0.7 mi se on US 41 (Cobb Pkwy). Ext/int corridors. **Pets:** Accepted.

✕ 💧 🔲 🖥 🌊 🗙

▼▼▼ Hotel Indigo 🔲 🐾
(404) 874-9200. **Call for rates.** 683 Peachtree St NE. I-75/85, exit 249D, 0.5 mi e to Peachtree St, then just n. Int corridors. **Pets:** Other species. Service with restrictions.

✕ 💧 🔲 🖥 🍴

▼▼▼ Inn at the Peachtrees 🔲
(404) 577-6970. **$99-$119, 7 day notice.** 330 W Peachtree St. I-75/85, exit 248C northbound, 0.4 mi w to Peachtree St, then 0.3 mi n; exit 249C southbound, just s to Peachtree Pl, then just e. Ext/int corridors. **Pets:** Accepted.

✕ 🔲 🖥

◈◈◈ ▼▼▼▼ InterContinental Buckhead Atlanta 🔲
(404) 946-9000. **$219-$499.** 3315 Peachtree Rd NE. Jct Piedmont and Peachtree rds NE, just e. Int corridors. **Pets:** Accepted.

SAVE ✕ 💧 🔲 🍴 🌊 🗙

▼▼▼ La Quinta Inn & Suites Atlanta (Paces Ferry/Vinings) 🔲 🐾
(770) 801-9002. **$69-$144.** 2415 Paces Ferry Rd SE. I-285, exit 18, just w. Int corridors. **Pets:** Medium, other species. Service with restrictions, supervision.

ASK ✕ 💧 🔲 🖥 🌊

▼▼▼ La Quinta Inn & Suites Atlanta (Perimeter/Medical Center) 🔲 🐾
(770) 350-6177. **$55-$149.** 6260 Peachtree-Dunwoody. I-285, exit 28 westbound, 0.7 mi n; exit 26 eastbound, 0.5 mi n to Hammond Dr, 0.7 mi e, then 0.5 mi n. Int corridors. **Pets:** Medium, other species. Service with restrictions, supervision.

ASK ✕ 💧 🔲 🖥 🌊

▼▼▼ La Quinta Inn-Buckhead 🔲 🐾
(404) 321-0999. **$64-$109.** 2535 Chantilly Dr NE. I-85, exit 88 southbound; exit 86 northbound, 2 mi on Buford Hwy to Lenox Rd, then just e under highway. Int corridors. **Pets:** Medium, other species. Service with restrictions, supervision.

ASK ✕ 🔲 🖥

◈◈◈ ▼▼▼▼ ▼▼▼▼ Omni Hotel at CNN Center 🔲
(404) 659-0000. **$159-$289.** 100 CNN Center. I-75/85, exit 248C northbound, 0.8 mi w; exit 249C southbound to International Blvd, then 0.5 mi w. Int corridors. **Pets:** Accepted.

SAVE ✕ 🔲 🖥 🍴 🌊 🗙

▼▼ Red Roof Inn Atlanta Downtown 🅷
(404) 659-4545. **Call for rates.** 311 Courtland St NE. I-75/85, exit 249A southbound; exit 249B northbound. Ext/int corridors. **Pets:** Accepted.
⊠ 🛆ᴹ ⇌

▼▼ Red Roof Inn-Druid Hills Ⓜ
(404) 321-1653. **$60-$100, 14 day notice.** 1960 N Druid Hills Rd. I-85, exit 89, just w. Ext corridors. **Pets:** Accepted.
[SAVE] ⊠ 🔒

▼▼▼ Residence Inn Atlanta Midtown at 17th Street 🅷
(404) 745-1000. **$195-$215.** 1365 Peachtree St. I-75/85, exit 250 (14th St), 0.5 mi e to Peachtree St, then 0.3 mi n. Int corridors. **Pets:** Accepted.
⊠ 🛆ᴹ 🔒 💻

ⒶⒶⒶ ▼▼▼ Residence Inn-Buckhead/Lenox 🅷
(404) 467-1660. **$227-$243.** 2220 Lake Blvd. I-85, exit 89, 1.6 mi w on N Druid Hills (becomes E Roxboro), then just n on Lenox Park Blvd. Int corridors. **Pets:** Accepted.
[SAVE] ⊠ 🛆ᴹ 🔒 💻 ⇌ ⊠

ⒶⒶⒶ ▼▼▼ Residence Inn by Marriott-Atlanta/Buckhead 🅷
(404) 239-0677. **$227-$243.** 2960 Piedmont Rd NE. Jct Piedmont and Pharr rds, just s. Ext corridors. **Pets:** Accepted.
[SAVE] ⊠ 🔒 💻 ⇌ ⊠

ⒶⒶⒶ ▼▼▼ Residence Inn by Marriott-Atlanta Downtown 🅷
(404) 522-0950. **$205-$236.** 134 Peachtree St NW. I-75/85, exit 248C northbound, 0.4 mi w, then just s; exit 249A southbound to International Blvd, just w, then just s. Int corridors. **Pets:** Medium. $75 one-time fee/room. Crate.
[SAVE] ⊠ 🔒 💻

ⒶⒶⒶ ▼▼▼ Residence Inn by Marriott Atlanta Dunwoody 🅷
(770) 455-4446. **$177-$190.** 1901 Savoy Dr. I-285, exit 30, just e. Ext corridors. **Pets:** Accepted.
[SAVE] ⊠ 🔒 💻 ⇌ ⊠

▼▼▼ Residence Inn by Marriott Midtown 🅷
(404) 872-8885. **$220-$251.** 1041 W Peachtree St. I-75/85, exit 250 (10th St), just e to W Peachtree St, then just n; corner of 11th St. Int corridors. **Pets:** Large. $100 one-time fee/room. Service with restrictions, crate.
⊠ 🛆ᴹ 🔒 💻

ⒶⒶⒶ ▼▼▼ Residence Inn by Marriott-Perimeter Center 🅷
(404) 252-5066. **$236-$253.** 6096 Barfield Rd. I-285, exit 26 eastbound, 0.5 mi n on Glenridge to Hammond Dr, then 0.3 mi e to Barfield Rd; exit 28 westbound (Peachtree-Dunwoody Rd), 0.5 mi n to Hammond Dr, then just w. Ext corridors. **Pets:** Accepted.
[SAVE] ⊠ 🔒 💻 ⇌ ⊠

ⒶⒶⒶ ▼▼▼▼ The Ritz-Carlton, Atlanta 🅷
(404) 659-0400. **Call for rates.** 181 Peachtree St NE. I-75/85, exit 248C northbound, 0.4 mi w, then just s; exit 249A southbound, just s to International Blvd, just w, then just s. Int corridors. **Pets:** Accepted.
[SAVE] ⊠ 🛆ᴹ 🔒 💻 🍴 ⊠

ⒶⒶⒶ ▼▼▼▼ The Ritz-Carlton, Buckhead 🅷 🐾
(404) 237-2700. **$369-$479.** 3434 Peachtree Rd NE. I-85, exit 86, 1.8 mi n on Cheshire Bridge-Lenox Rd. Int corridors. **Pets:** Small. $250 one-time fee/room. Designated rooms, service with restrictions, supervision.
[SAVE] ⊠ 🔒 💻 🍴 ⇌ ⊠

ⒶⒶⒶ ▼▼▼▼ Sheraton Atlanta Hotel 🅷
(404) 659-6500. **$119-$399.** 165 Courtland St. I-75/85, exit 249A southbound; exit 248C northbound, just w. Int corridors. **Pets:** Accepted.
[SAVE] ⊠ 💻 🍴 ⇌

ⒶⒶⒶ ▼▼▼▼ Sheraton Suites Galleria 🅷
(770) 955-3900. **Call for rates.** 2844 Cobb Pkwy SE. I-285, exit 20 westbound; exit 19 eastbound, just s on US 41 (Cobb Pkwy). Int corridors. **Pets:** Accepted.
[SAVE] ⊠ 🛆ᴹ 🔒 💻 🍴 ⇌

▼▼▼ Staybridge Suites 🅷
(404) 842-0800. **$169-$269.** 540 Pharr Rd. Jct Pharr and Piedmont rds, just w. Int corridors. **Pets:** Small. $75 one-time fee/room. Service with restrictions, supervision.
[ASK] ⊠ 🔒 💻 ⇌

▼▼▼ Staybridge Suites-Atlanta-Mt. Vernon 🅷
(404) 250-0110. **Call for rates.** 760 Mt Vernon Hwy NE. I-285, exit 25, 0.8 mi n on Roswell Rd, then 1 mi e. Ext/int corridors. **Pets:** Accepted.
⊠ 🔒 💻 ⇌ ⊠

▼▼▼ Staybridge Suites Atlanta Perimeter 🅷
(678) 320-0111. **Call for rates.** 4601 Ridgeview Rd. I-285, exit 29 (Ashford-Dunwoody Rd), 0.5 mi n, 0.5 mi w on Perimeter Center W to Crowne Pointe Dr, then just n. Int corridors. **Pets:** Accepted.
⊠ 🛆ᴹ 🔒 💻 ⇌

▼▼ Super 8 Ⓜ
(404) 873-5731. **$79-$109.** 1641 Peachtree St NE. I-75/85, exit 250, 0.3 mi e to W Peachtree St, then 1 mi n. Ext/int corridors. **Pets:** $10 one-time fee/pet. Service with restrictions, supervision.
[ASK] ⊠ 🔒 💻

▼▼▼ TownePlace Suites Atlanta Buckhead 🅷
(404) 949-4820. **$197-$211.** 820 Sidney Marcus Blvd. I-85, exit 86 northbound, 1.9 mi n to Sidney Marcus Blvd, then just w; exit 88 southbound, just w to Sidney Marcus Blvd, then just w. Int corridors. **Pets:** Accepted.
⊠ 🛆ᴹ 🔒 💻

ⒶⒶⒶ ▼▼▼ University Inn at Emory 🅷 🐾
(404) 634-7327. **$135-$250.** 1767 N Decatur Rd. I-85, exit 91, 3.8 mi s on Clairmont Rd to N Decatur Rd, then 0.8 mi w. Ext corridors. **Pets:** Large, other species. $25 daily fee/room. Designated rooms, service with restrictions.
[SAVE] ⊠ 🔒 💻 ⇌

ⒶⒶⒶ ▼▼▼▼ W Atlanta Midtown 🅷
(404) 892-6000. **$199-$539.** 188 14th St NE. I-75/85, exit 250, 0.5 mi. Int corridors. **Pets:** Accepted.
[SAVE] ⊠ 🛆ᴹ 💻 🍴 ⇌ ⊠

ⒶⒶⒶ ▼▼▼ W Atlanta Perimeter 🅷 🐾
(770) 396-6800. **$109-$519.** 111 Perimeter Center W. I-285 E, exit 29 (Ashford-Dunwoody Rd), 0.5 mi n. Int corridors. **Pets:** Medium. $25 daily fee/pet, $100 one-time fee/pet. Designated rooms, service with restrictions, supervision.
[SAVE] ⊠ 🛆ᴹ 🔒 💻 🍴 ⇌

ⒶⒶⒶ ▼▼▼▼ The Westin Atlanta North 🅷
(770) 395-3900. **$99-$399.** 7 Concourse Pkwy. I-285, exit 28 westbound; exit 26 eastbound, 0.5 mi n to Hammond Dr, then 0.4 mi e. Int corridors. **Pets:** Accepted.
[SAVE] ⊠ 🔒 💻 🍴 ⇌ ⊠

ⒶⒶⒶ ▼▼▼▼ The Westin Buckhead Atlanta 🅷
(404) 365-0065. **$169-$459.** 3391 Peachtree Rd NE. Adjacent to Lenox Square Mall. Int corridors. **Pets:** Accepted.
[SAVE] ⊠ 💻 🍴 ⇌ ⊠

ⒶⒶⒶ ▼▼▼▼ The Westin Peachtree Plaza 🅷
(404) 659-1400. **$119-$405.** 210 Peachtree St. I-75/85, exit 248C northbound, 0.4 mi w; exit 249C southbound, 0.5 mi s. Int corridors. **Pets:** Accepted.
[SAVE] ⊠ 💻 🍴 ⇌

AUSTELL

▼▼▼ Baymont Inn-Six Flags 🄷
(770) 944-2110. **$60-$76.** 7377 Six Flags Dr. I-20, exit 46 eastbound; exit 46B westbound, just n. Ext/int corridors. **Pets:** Medium. $10 daily fee/pet. Service with restrictions, supervision.

(ASK) ⊠ 🛢 💻 ⊇

COLLEGE PARK

▼▼ Econo Lodge 🄼
(404) 768-1241. **$50-$55.** 4874 Old National Hwy. I-285, exit 62, just n. Ext corridors. **Pets:** Accepted.

(ASK) ⊠ ⊇

▼▼▼ Holiday Inn Express-Atlanta Airport 🄷 ❁
(404) 761-6500. **$79-$159.** 4601 Best Rd. I-85, exit 71, northwest corner. Int corridors. **Pets:** Medium, dogs only. $250 deposit/room, $50 one-time fee/room. Service with restrictions, supervision.

(ASK) ⊠ 🕭 🛢 💻 ⊇

⁓⁓⁓ ▼▼▼ La Quinta Inn & Suites Atlanta Airport 🄷 ❁
(770) 996-0000. **$80-$190.** 4820 Massachusetts Blvd. I-85, exit 71, just e to Airport Rd, then just s. Int corridors. **Pets:** Medium, other species. Service with restrictions, supervision.

(SAVE) ⊠ 🛢 💻 ⊇

⁓⁓⁓ ▼▼▼ Microtel Inn-Atlanta Airport 🄷
(770) 994-3003. **$69-$89.** 4839 Massachusetts Blvd. I-85, exit 71, just e to Airport Rd, then just s; I-285, exit 60 (Riverdale Rd N), 1 mi to Sullivan Rd, then just s. Int corridors. **Pets:** Accepted.

(SAVE) ⊠ 🕭 🛢 💻

⁓⁓⁓ ▼▼▼ Sheraton Gateway Hotel, Atlanta Airport 🄷 ❁
(770) 997-1100. **$89-$269.** 1900 Sullivan Rd. I-85, exit 71, just e to Airport Rd, then just s. Int corridors. **Pets:** Small, other species. $100 deposit/room. Service with restrictions, crate.

(SAVE) ⊠ 🛢 💻 🍴 ⊇

⁓⁓⁓ ▼▼▼ The Westin Hotel-Atlanta Airport 🄷
(404) 762-7676. **$99-$529.** 4736 Best Rd. I-85, exit 71, just w, se on access road to Best Rd, then just s. Int corridors. **Pets:** Accepted.

(SAVE) ⊠ 💻 🍴 ⊇

DECATUR

▼▼▼ America's Best Inn & Suites 🄼
(404) 286-2500. **$65.** 4095 Covington Hwy. I-285, exit 43, just w. Ext corridors. **Pets:** $10 daily fee/pet. Service with restrictions, supervision.

(ASK) ⊠ 🕭 🛢 💻

▼▼▼ Holiday Inn Select 🄷
(404) 371-0204. **Call for rates.** 130 Clairmont Ave. Downtown. Int corridors. **Pets:** Accepted.

⊠ 🛢 💻 🍴 ⊇

DORAVILLE

⁓⁓⁓ ▼▼▼ Holiday Inn Northeast/Doraville 🄷
(770) 455-3700. **$99-$134.** 2001 Clearview Ave. I-285, exit 32, southeast corner. Int corridors. **Pets:** Small. $100 one-time fee/room. Service with restrictions, supervision.

(SAVE) ⊠ 🛢 💻 🍴 ⊇

⁓⁓⁓ ▼▼▼ Super 8 Atlanta NE 🄼
(770) 458-2671. **$46-$65.** 2822 Chamblee Tucker Rd. I-85, exit 94, just w. Ext corridors. **Pets:** Accepted.

(SAVE) ⊠ 🛢 💻

DOUGLASVILLE

⁓⁓⁓ ▼▼▼ Best Western Garden Inn & Suites 🄷
(770) 489-4863. **$85-$95, 3 day notice.** 8304 Cherokee Blvd. I-20, exit 37, just n to Cherokee Blvd, then just e. Int corridors. **Pets:** $15 daily fee/pet. Service with restrictions, supervision.

(SAVE) ⊠ 🕭 🛢 💻 ⊇

▼▼ Days Inn 🄼
(770) 949-1499. **$50-$95.** 5489 Westmoreland Plaza. I-20, exit 37, just n. Ext corridors. **Pets:** Medium. $20 daily fee/pet. Service with restrictions.

(ASK) ⊠ 🛢 💻 ⊇

▼▼▼ La Quinta Inn & Suites 🄷 ❁
(770) 577-3838. **$69-$135.** 1000 Linnenkohl Dr. I-20, exit 34, just n. Int corridors. **Pets:** Medium, other species. Service with restrictions, supervision.

⊠ 🕭 🛢 💻 ⊇

DULUTH

▼▼▼ Candlewood Suites-Atlanta 🄷
(678) 380-0414. **Call for rates.** 3665 Shackleford Rd. I-85, exit 104, just e, then just s. Int corridors. **Pets:** Accepted.

⊠ 🕭 🛢 💻

▼▼ Days Inn Gwinnett Place 🄷
(770) 476-8700. **Call for rates.** 1920 Pleasant Hill Rd. I-85, exit 104; northwest corner. Int corridors. **Pets:** Accepted.

⊠ 💻

▼▼▼ Extended Stay Deluxe 🄷
(770) 623-6800. **$75-$90.** 3390 Venture Pkwy NW. I-85, exit 104, just w to Venture Pkwy, then just n. Int corridors. **Pets:** Other species. $25 daily fee/pet. Service with restrictions, crate.

(ASK) ⊠ 🕭 🛢 💻 ⊇

▼▼ Holiday Inn Express 🄷
(770) 935-7171. **$79-$119.** 3670 Shackleford Rd. I-85, exit 104, just e to Shackleford Rd, then just s. Int corridors. **Pets:** Medium. $50 one-time fee/pet. Service with restrictions, supervision.

(ASK) ⊠ 🛢 💻 ⊇

▼▼▼ Holiday Inn-Gwinnett Center 🄷
(770) 476-2022. **$84-$169.** 6310 Sugarloaf Pkwy. I-85, exit 108, just w. Int corridors. **Pets:** Accepted.

(ASK) ⊠ 🕭 🛢 💻 🍴 ⊇

⁓⁓⁓ ▼▼▼ La Quinta Inn Duluth 🄷 ❁
(678) 957-0500. **$59-$139.** 2370 Stephen Center Dr. I-85, exit 107, just w. Int corridors. **Pets:** Medium, other species. Service with restrictions, supervision.

(SAVE) ⊠ 🕭 🛢 💻 ⊇

▼▼ Quality Inn-Gwinnett Mall 🄷
(770) 623-9300. **$60-$129.** 3500 Venture Pkwy. I-85, exit 104, just w to Venture Pkwy, then just n. Ext/int corridors. **Pets:** Accepted.

(ASK) ⊠ 🕭 🛢 💻 ⊇

▼▼▼ Residence Inn-Atlanta Gwinnett 🄷
(770) 921-2202. **$188-$202.** 1760 Pineland Rd. I-85, exit 104, just e to Shackleford Rd, just s to Pineland Rd, then just e. Int corridors. **Pets:** Medium, other species. $100 one-time fee/room. Service with restrictions, supervision.

⊠ 🕭 🛢 💻 ⊇ 🐾

▼▼ Studio 6 #6023 🄷
(770) 931-3113. **$57-$63.** 3525 Breckinridge Blvd. I-85, exit 104, just e to Breckinridge Blvd, then just s. Ext corridors. **Pets:** Other species. $10 daily fee/room. Service with restrictions, supervision.

⊠ 🕭 🛢 💻

EAST POINT

▼▼ ▼▼ Comfort Inn & Suites Atlanta Airport Camp Creek H
(404) 762-5566. $79-$119, 30 day notice. 3601 N Desert Dr. I-285, exit 2, just e. Int corridors. Pets: Accepted.
[ASK] [X] [&M] [🔒] [📖] [🐾]

▼▼▼▼ Crowne Plaza Hotel and Resort Atlanta Airport H
(404) 768-6660. $89-$209. 1325 Virginia Ave. I-85, exit 73 southbound; exit 73B northbound, just w. Int corridors. Pets: Accepted.
[ASK] [X] [&M] [🔒] [📖] [🍴] [🏊]

▼▼▼▼ Drury Inn & Suites-Atlanta Airport H
(404) 761-4900. $90-$170. 1270 Virginia Ave. I-85, exit 73 southbound; exit 73A northbound, just e. Int corridors. Pets: Other species. Service with restrictions, supervision.
[ASK] [X] [&M] [🔒] [📖] [🏊]

🟡 ▼▼▼▼ Ramada Atlanta Airport Conference Center H ❀
(404) 762-8411. $109-$159. 1380 Virginia Ave. I-85, exit 73 southbound; exit 73B northbound, just w. Ext/int corridors. Pets: $50 one-time fee/room. Service with restrictions, supervision.
[SAVE] [X] [&M] [📖] [🍴] [🏊]

▼▼ ▼▼ Red Roof Inn-Atlanta Airport North H
(404) 209-1800. $71-$81. 1200 Virginia Ave. I-85, exit 73 southbound; exit 73A northbound, just e. Int corridors. Pets: Accepted.
[ASK] [X] [&M] [🔒] [📖] [🐾]

FOREST PARK

▼▼ ▼▼ Days Inn-Airport East M
(404) 768-6400. $53-$95. 5116 Hwy 85. I-75, exit 237A southbound; exit 237 northbound, 0.5 mi w. Ext corridors. Pets: Small, other species. $25 daily fee/pet. Designated rooms, service with supervision.
[ASK] [X] [🔒] [📖] [🐾]

▼▼ ▼▼ Econo Lodge M ❀
(404) 363-6429. $40-$53. 5060 Frontage Rd. I-75, exit 237, just e to Frontage Rd, then just s. Ext corridors. Pets: Other species. $15 daily fee/pet. Service with restrictions, supervision.
[ASK] [X] [🔒]

▼▼ ▼▼ Super 8 M
(404) 363-8811. $50-$100. 410 Old Dixie Way. I-75, exit 235, just e. Ext corridors. Pets: Small, dogs only. $10 daily fee/pet. Service with restrictions, supervision.
[ASK] [X] [🔒] [📖] [🐾]

HAPEVILLE

▼▼▼ ▼▼▼ Hilton Atlanta Airport H
(404) 767-9000. $99-$229. 1031 Virginia Ave. I-85, exit 73 southbound; exit 73A northbound, just e. Int corridors. Pets: Accepted.
[X] [&M] [🔒] [📖] [🍴] [🐾] [🐾]

🟡 ▼▼▼▼ Residence Inn Atlanta Airport H ❀
(404) 761-0511. $246-$264. 3401 International Blvd. I-85, exit 73 southbound; exit 73A northbound, 0.5 mi e to International Blvd, then just n. Ext/int corridors. Pets: Other species. $75 one-time fee/room. No service.
[SAVE] [X] [🔒] [📖] [🐾] [🐾]

JONESBORO

🟡 ▼▼▼▼ Holiday Inn Atlanta South Jonesboro H
(770) 968-4300. $75-$175. 6288 Old Dixie Hwy. I-75, exit 235, just w. Int corridors. Pets: Accepted.
[SAVE] [X] [&M] [🔒] [📖] [🍴] [🐾]

KENNESAW

🟡 ▼▼▼ Best Western Kennesaw Inn H
(770) 424-7666. $90-$100. 3375 Busbee Dr. I-75, exit 271, just e. Ext corridors. Pets: Medium, other species. $10 daily fee/pet. Designated rooms, no service, supervision.
[SAVE] [X] [🔒] [📖] [🐾]

▼▼ ▼▼ Days Inn H
(770) 419-1576. $55-$79, 7 day notice. 760 Cobb Place Blvd. I-75, exit 269, just w. Ext corridors. Pets: Accepted.
[ASK] [X] [&M] [🔒] [📖] [🐾]

▼▼ ▼▼ Extended StayAmerica H
(770) 422-1403. $55-$70. 3000 George Busbee Pkwy. I-75, exit 269, just e to George Busbee Pkwy, then 0.8 mi n. Int corridors. Pets: Other species. $25 daily fee/pet. Service with restrictions, crate.
[ASK] [X] [&M] [🔒] [📖]

🟡 ▼▼▼ Green Roof Inn & Suites M
(770) 529-3370. $45-$120. 3027 Cobb Pkwy NW. I-75, exit 271, 2.5 mi w, then 2.2 mi n on US 41. Ext corridors. Pets: Other species. $10 daily fee/room. Designated rooms, service with supervision.
[SAVE] [X] [&M] [🔒] [📖]

▼▼▼ ▼▼ La Quinta Inn H ❀
(770) 426-0045. $69-$150. 2625 George Busbee Pkwy. I-75, exit 269, just e to George Busbee Pkwy, then just n. Int corridors. Pets: Medium, other species. Service with restrictions, supervision.
[ASK] [X] [&M] [🔒] [📖] [🐾]

▼▼ ▼▼ Quality Inn H
(770) 419-1530. $55-$80, 7 day notice. 750 Cobb Place Blvd. I-75, exit 269, just w. Ext corridors. Pets: Accepted.
[ASK] [X] [&M] [🔒] [📖] [🐾]

🟡 ▼▼▼ Red Roof Inn-Town Center Mall M ❀
(770) 429-0323. $50-$100, 14 day notice. 520 Roberts Ct NW. I-75, exit 269, just e. Ext corridors. Pets: Small. No service, supervision.
[SAVE] [X] [&M] [🔒]

🟡 ▼▼▼▼ Residence Inn by Marriott Town Center H
(770) 218-1018. $177-$190. 3443 Busbee Dr. I-75, exit 271, just e. Int corridors. Pets: Accepted.
[SAVE] [X] [&M] [🔒] [📖] [🐾] [🐾]

▼▼ ▼▼ StudioPLUS H
(770) 425-6101. $55-$75. 3316 Busbee Dr. I-75, exit 271, just e to Busbee Dr, then just s. Int corridors. Pets: Other species. $25 daily fee/pet. Service with restrictions, crate.
[ASK] [X] [&M] [🔒] [📖] [🐾]

▼▼ ▼▼ Travelodge M
(770) 590-0519. $49-$79. 1460 George Busbee Pkwy. I-75, exit 273, just e. Ext corridors. Pets: Accepted.
[ASK] [X] [🔒] [📖] [🐾]

LAWRENCEVILLE

🟡 ▼▼▼ Best Western Lawrenceville Inn H
(770) 513-0028. $66-$86. 571 Budford Dr. Jct SR 316 and 20/124, 0.5 mi s. Int corridors. Pets: Accepted.
[SAVE] [X] [&M] [🔒] [📖] [🏊]

🟡 ▼▼▼ Days Inn M
(770) 995-7782. $70-$121. 731 Duluth Hwy. Jct SR 316, just e on SR 120. Ext corridors. Pets: Other species. $20 one-time fee/pet. Crate.
[SAVE] [X] [🔒] [📖]

▼▼ ▼▼ Extended StayAmerica Atlanta-Lawrenceville H
(770) 962-5660. $55-$65. 474 W Pike St. SR 316, exit SR 120, 0.8 mi s. Ext corridors. Pets: Other species. $25 daily fee/pet. Service with restrictions, crate.
[ASK] [X] [&M] [🔒] [📖]

♦♦♦ **Hampton Inn** Ⓗ
(770) 338-9600. **$79-$139.** 1135 Lakes Pkwy. SR 316, exit Riverside Pkwy, just n. Int corridors. **Pets:** Accepted.
⊠ ♿M ▣ ☕ 🏊

LITHONIA

Ⓐ ♦♦ **Red Roof Inn** Ⓗ
(770) 332-1400. **$70-$90.** 5400 Fairington Rd. I-20, exit 71, just s to Fairington Rd, then just ne. Int corridors. **Pets:** Small, other species. Service with restrictions, supervision.
SAVE ⊠ ♿M ▣

MARIETTA

♦♦♦ **Comfort Inn-Marietta** Ⓗ
(770) 952-3000. **$69-$109.** 2100 Northwest Pkwy. I-75, exit 261, 0.3 mi w to Franklin Rd, then just s. Ext corridors. **Pets:** Small. $10 one-time fee/pet. Designated rooms, service with restrictions, crate.
A$K ⊠ ▣ ☕ 🏊

Ⓐ ♦♦♦ **Crowne Plaza Atlanta-Marietta** Ⓗ
(770) 428-4400. **$79-$189.** 1775 Parkway Pl NW. I-75, exit 263, just w. Int corridors. **Pets:** Accepted.
SAVE ⊠ ♿M ▣ ☕ 🍴 🏊

♦♦♦ **Drury Inn & Suites-Atlanta Northwest** Ⓗ
(770) 612-0900. **$70-$110.** 1170 Powers Ferry Pl. I-75, exit 261, just e. Int corridors. **Pets:** Other species. Service with restrictions, supervision.
A$K ⊠ ♿M ▣ ☕ 🏊

♦♦ **Econo Lodge Northwest** Ⓗ
(770) 952-0052. **Call for rates.** 1940 Leland Dr. I-75, exit 260, just e, then 0.3 mi n. Ext/int corridors. **Pets:** Accepted.
⊠ ▣ ☕

♦♦ **Extended StayAmerica Atlanta-Marietta Windy Hill** Ⓗ
(770) 690-9477. **$55-$65.** 1967 Leland Dr. I-75, exit 260, just e to Leland Dr, then just n. Int corridors. **Pets:** Other species. $25 daily fee/pet. Service with restrictions, crate.
A$K ⊠ ♿M ▣ ☕

♦♦♦ **Homestead Studio Suites Hotel-Atlanta-Marietta-Powers Ferry Rd** Ⓗ
(770) 303-0043. **$70-$80.** 2239 Powers Ferry Rd. I-285, exit 22, just n. Int corridors. **Pets:** Other species. $25 daily fee/pet. Service with restrictions, crate.
A$K ⊠ ♿M ▣ ☕

♦♦ **Hometown Inn** Ⓗ
(770) 499-9550. **Call for rates.** 1051 Canton Rd. I-75, exit 267A northbound, 1.8 mi w. Ext corridors. **Pets:** Accepted.
⊠ ▣ ☕

Ⓐ ♦♦♦ **Hyatt Regency Suites Perimeter Northwest** Ⓗ
(770) 956-1234. **$79-$329, 3 day notice.** 2999 Windy Hill Rd. I-75, exit 260, 0.5 mi e at Powers Ferry Rd. Int corridors. **Pets:** Small, other species. Service with restrictions, supervision.
SAVE ⊠ ♿M ▣ ☕ 🍴 🏊

♦♦♦ **La Quinta Inn** Ⓗ 🐾
(770) 951-0026. **$39-$79.** 2170 Delk Rd. I-75, exit 261, 0.3 mi w. Ext/int corridors. **Pets:** Medium, other species. Service with restrictions, supervision.
A$K ⊠ ▣ ☕ 🏊

Ⓐ ♦ **Masters Inn Marietta** Ⓜ
(770) 951-2005. **$45-$52, 5 day notice.** 2682 Windy Hill Rd. I-75, exit 260, just w to Circle 75 Pkwy, then just s. Ext corridors. **Pets:** Small, other species. $20 one-time fee/pet. Designated rooms, service with restrictions, crate.
SAVE ⊠ ▣

MORROW

Ⓐ ♦♦ **Best Western Southlake Inn** Ⓗ
(770) 961-6300. **$59-$99.** 6437 Jonesboro Rd. I-75, exit 233, just e. Ext corridors. **Pets:** Small. $10 daily fee/pet. Service with restrictions, crate.
SAVE ⊠ ▣ ☕ 🏊

♦♦♦ **Drury Inn & Suites-Atlanta South** Ⓗ
(770) 960-0500. **$85-$140, 3 day notice.** 6520 S Lee St. I-75, exit 233, just e. Int corridors. **Pets:** Other species. Service with restrictions, supervision.
A$K ⊠ ♿M ▣ ☕ 🏊

♦♦ **Extended StayAmerica-Atlanta-Morrow** Ⓗ
(770) 472-0727. **$60-$75.** 2265 Mt. Zion Pkwy. I-75, exit 231, just w, then 1.3 mi s. Int corridors. **Pets:** Other species. $25 daily fee/pet. Service with restrictions, crate.
A$K ⊠ ▣ ☕

Ⓐ ♦♦ **Red Roof Inn-South** Ⓜ 🐾
(770) 968-1483. **$50-$90, 14 day notice.** 1348 Southlake Plaza Dr. I-75, exit 233, just e to Southlake Plaza Dr, then just n. Ext corridors. **Pets:** Medium, other species. Service with restrictions, supervision.
SAVE ⊠ ▣

♦♦ **Sleep Inn** Ⓗ
(770) 472-9800. **$55-$90.** 2185 Mt. Zion Pkwy. I-75, exit 231, just w to Mt. Zion Pkwy, then just s. Int corridors. **Pets:** Accepted.
A$K ⊠ ♿M ▣ ☕ 🏊

NORCROSS

♦♦ **America's Best Inn** Ⓗ
(770) 449-7322. **$59-$79.** 6045 Oakbrook Pkwy. I-85, exit 99, just e to Live Oak Pkwy, 1 mi n, then w. Ext/int corridors. **Pets:** Accepted.
A$K ⊠ ▣ ☕

♦♦♦ **Baymont Inn & Suites** Ⓗ
(770) 449-5144. **Call for rates.** 5375 Peachtree Industrial Blvd. I-285, exit 31B, 5.5 mi n; I-85, exit 99, 4 mi w to Peachtree Industrial Blvd, then 1.5 mi n. Ext/int corridors. **Pets:** Accepted.
⊠ ▣ ☕ 🏊

Ⓐ ♦♦♦ **Best Western North Atlanta-Norcross Inn** Ⓗ
(770) 448-8686. **$55-$99, 7 day notice.** 6187 Dawson Blvd. I-85, exit 99, just e to McDonough Dr, then just s. Ext corridors. **Pets:** Accepted.
SAVE ⊠ ▣ ☕ 🏊

♦♦♦ **Comfort Inn & Suites** Ⓗ
(770) 263-8883. **$79-$99.** 5200 Peachtree Industrial Blvd. I-285, exit 31B, 5.5 mi n; I-85, exit 99, 4 mi w to Peachtree Industrial Blvd, then 1.5 mi n. Int corridors. **Pets:** $20 daily fee/pet. Supervision.
A$K ⊠ ♿M ▣ ☕ 🏊

Ⓐ ♦♦♦ **Comfort Inn & Suites Conference Centre** Ⓗ
(770) 662-8175. **$74-$99.** 5985 Oakbrook Pkwy. I-85, exit 99, 0.5 mi e to Live Oak Pkwy, 0.8 mi n, then w. Int corridors. **Pets:** Accepted.
SAVE ⊠ ▣ ☕ 🏊

♦♦ **Days Inn & Suites** Ⓗ
(770) 416-9021. **$48-$99.** 5385 Peachtree Industrial Blvd. I-285, exit 31B, 5.5 mi n; I-85, exit 99, 4 mi w to Peachtree Industrial Blvd, then 1.5 mi n. Int corridors. **Pets:** Accepted.
A$K ⊠ ♿M ▣ ☕ 🏊

Ⓐ ♦♦ **Days Inn Atlanta NE** Ⓜ
(770) 368-0218. **$56-$70.** 5990 Western Hills Dr. I-85, exit 99, 0.8 mi w to Norcross Tucker Rd to Western Hills Dr, then just n. Ext corridors. **Pets:** Very small. $25 daily fee/pet. Designated rooms, service with restrictions, supervision.
SAVE ⊠ ▣ ☕ 🏊

▼▼▼▼ Drury Inn & Suites-Atlanta Northeast 🅷
(770) 729-0060. **$70-$125.** 5655 Jimmy Carter Blvd. I-85, exit 99, just w. Int corridors. **Pets:** Other species. Service with restrictions, supervision.
A$K ☒ &M 🛏 💻 ⟋

▼▼ Extended StayAmerica Atlanta-Jimmy Carter Blvd. 🅷
(770) 446-9245. **$50-$65.** 6295 Jimmy Carter Blvd. I-85, exit 99, 2.5 mi w. Ext corridors. **Pets:** Other species. $25 daily fee/pet. Service with restrictions, crate.
A$K ☒ &M 🛏 💻

▼▼ Extended StayAmerica Atlanta-Norcross 🅷
(770) 729-8100. **$58-$70.** 200 Lawrenceville St. Downtown; behind post office. Ext corridors. **Pets:** Other species. $25 daily fee/pet. Service with restrictions, crate.
A$K ☒ &M 🛏 💻

⟨AAA⟩ ▼▼ GuestHouse Inn 🅷
(770) 564-0492. **$49-$89.** 2050 Willowtrail Pkwy. I-85, exit 101, just e. Ext corridors. **Pets:** Accepted.
SAVE ☒ 🛏 💻 ⟋

▼▼▼ Hilton Atlanta Northeast 🅷
(770) 447-4747. **$94-$199.** 5993 Peachtree Industrial Blvd. I-285, exit 31B, 4.5 mi ne. Int corridors. **Pets:** Medium. $50 one-time fee/pet. Service with restrictions.
☒ &M 🛏 💻 🍴 ⟋ ☒

▼▼ Homestead Studio Suites Hotel-Atlanta/Peachtree Corners 🅷
(770) 449-9966. **$55-$65.** 7049 Jimmy Carter Blvd. I-85, exit 99, 4 mi n; I-285, exit 31B, 4 mi n. Ext corridors. **Pets:** Other species. $25 daily fee/pet. Service with restrictions, crate.
A$K ☒ &M 🛏 💻

▼▼▼ Homewood Suites by Hilton 🅷
(770) 448-4663. **$69-$129.** 450 Technology Pkwy. I-85, exit 99, 4 mi w to Peachtree Industrial Blvd, 0.4 mi n, w on Holcomb Bridge Rd, then 2 blks n on Peachtree Pkwy; I-285, exit 31B, 5 mi n on SR 141. Ext/int corridors. **Pets:** Accepted.
☒ &M 🛏 💻 ⟋ ☒

⟨AAA⟩ ▼▼▼▼ La Quinta Inn 🅷 🐾
(770) 368-9400. **$59-$134.** 5945 Oakbrook Pkwy. I-85, exit 99, 0.5 mi e to Live Oak Pkwy, then 0.8 mi w. Int corridors. **Pets:** Medium, other species. Service with restrictions, supervision.
SAVE ☒ 🛏 💻 ⟋

▼▼ Red Roof Inn & Suites 🅷
(770) 446-2882. **$48-$52.** 5395 Peachtree Industrial Blvd. I-285, exit 31B, 5.5 mi n; I-85, exit 99, 4 mi w to Peachtree Industrial Blvd, then 1.5 mi n. Int corridors. **Pets:** Accepted.
A$K ☒ 🛏 💻 ⟋

▼▼ Red Roof Inn-Indian Trail Ⓜ
(770) 448-8944. **$45-$90, 14 day notice.** 5171 Brook Hollow Pkwy. I-85, exit 101, just w to Brook Hollow Pkwy, then just s. Ext corridors. **Pets:** Accepted.
☒

▼▼ StudioPlus 🅷
(770) 582-9984. **$60-$75.** 7065 Jimmy Carter Blvd. I-85, exit 99, 4 mi n; I-285, exit 31B, 4 mi n. Int corridors. **Pets:** Other species. $25 daily fee/pet. Service with restrictions, crate.
A$K ☒ &M 🛏 💻 ⟋

ROSWELL

▼▼ Brookwood Inn 🅷
(770) 587-5161. **Call for rates.** 9995 Old Dogwood Rd. SR 400, exit 7B, just w to Old Dogwood Rd, then just n. Ext corridors. **Pets:** Accepted.
☒ 🛏 💻 ⟋

▼▼▼ La Quinta Inn 🅷 🐾
(770) 552-0200. **$44-$79.** 575 Old Holcomb Bridge Rd. SR 400, exit 7B, just w. Int corridors. **Pets:** Medium, other species. Service with restrictions, supervision.
A$K ☒ &M 🛏 💻 ⟋

▼▼ Studio 6 #6025 🅷
(770) 992-9449. **$61-$68.** 9955 Old Dogwood Rd. SR 400, exit 7B, just w. Ext corridors. **Pets:** Other species. $10 daily fee/room. Service with restrictions, supervision.
&M 🛏 💻

SMYRNA

▼▼ Baymont Inn & Suites 🅷
(404) 794-1600. **Call for rates.** 5130 S Cobb Dr. I-285, exit 15, 0.3 mi w. Int corridors. **Pets:** Accepted.
☒ &M 🛏 💻 ⟋ ☒

⟨AAA⟩ ▼▼▼▼ Holiday Inn Express Atlanta / Smyrna Cobb Galleria Center 🅷
(770) 435-4990. **$80-$100.** 2855 Springhill Pkwy. I-285, exit 20 westbound; exit 19 eastbound, just n on US 41 (Cobb Pkwy), then just w on Spring Rd. Int corridors. **Pets:** Other species. Crate.
SAVE ☒ &M 🛏 💻 ⟋ ☒

▼▼ Homestead Studio Suites Hotel-Atlanta/Cumberland Mall 🅷
(770) 432-4000. **$60-$70.** 3103 Sports Ave. I-285, exit 20 westbound; exit 19 eastbound, just n to Spring Rd, then 0.3 mi w. Ext corridors. **Pets:** Other species. $25 daily fee/pet. Service with restrictions, crate.
A$K ☒ &M 🛏 💻

⟨AAA⟩ ▼▼▼ Red Roof Inn-North Ⓜ
(770) 952-6966. **$50-$100, 14 day notice.** 2200 Corporate Plaza. I-75, exit 260, just w to Corporate Plaza, then just s. Ext corridors. **Pets:** Accepted.
SAVE ☒ &M 🛏

⟨AAA⟩ ▼▼▼ Residence Inn-Atlanta Cumberland 🅷
(770) 433-8877. **$177-$190.** 2771 Cumberland Blvd. I-285, exit 20 westbound; exit 19 eastbound, just n to Spring Rd, 0.3 mi w to Cumberland Blvd, then just n. Ext corridors. **Pets:** Accepted.
SAVE ☒ &M 🛏 💻 ⟋ ☒

SNELLVILLE

▼▼ Crestwood Suites 🅷
(770) 982-5250. **$50-$70.** 1784 Presidential Cir. Jct Ronald Reagan Pkwy and SR 124, just w. Int corridors. **Pets:** Small. $15 daily fee/pet, $50 one-time fee/pet. Designated rooms, service with restrictions, crate.
A$K ☒ 🛏 💻

⟨AAA⟩ ▼▼▼ Super 8 Motel 🅷
(770) 736-4723. **$74-$120.** 2971 W Main St. Jct US 78 and SR 124, 0.6 mi w. Int corridors. **Pets:** Accepted.
SAVE ☒ &M 🛏 💻 ⟋

STONE MOUNTAIN

⟨AAA⟩ ▼▼▼ Best Western Stone Mountain 🅷
(770) 465-1022. **$80-$115, 3 day notice.** 1595 E Park Place Blvd. US 78, exit E Park Place Blvd, just n. Ext corridors. **Pets:** Medium. $25 daily fee/pet. Designated rooms, service with restrictions, supervision.
SAVE ☒ 🛏 💻 ⟋

SUWANEE

⟨AAA⟩ ▼▼▼ Best Western Gwinnett Inn 🅷 🐾
(770) 271-5559. **$80-$110.** 77 Gwinco Blvd. I-85, exit 111, just e to Gwinco Blvd, then just s. Int corridors. **Pets:** Large, other species. $15 daily fee/pet. Service with restrictions, crate.
SAVE ☒ &M 🛏 💻 ⟋

AAA ▼▼▼ **Comfort Inn** H
(770) 945-1608. **$75-$129.** 2945 Hwy 317. I-85, exit 111, just e. Ext corridors. **Pets:** Other species. $25 one-time fee/room. Service with restrictions.
SAVE ✕ 🛈 🖵 ⌁

TUCKER

AAA ▼▼▼▼ **Atlanta Northlake TownePlace Suites** H
(770) 938-0408. **$157-$169.** 3300 Northlake Pkwy. I-285, exit 36 southbound, just w; exit 37 northbound, just w to Parklake Dr, 0.5 mi n, then just w. Int corridors. **Pets:** Other species. $75 one-time fee/room.
SAVE ✕ 🛄 🛈 🖵 ⌁

▼▼▼▼ **DoubleTree Hotel NE/Northlake** H
(770) 938-1026. **$89-$199.** 4156 La Vista Rd. I-285, exit 37, just w. Int corridors. **Pets:** Accepted.
✕ 🛄 🖵 🍽 ⌁

AAA ▼▼ **Econo Lodge** M
(770) 939-8440. **$50-$70.** 1820 Mountain Industrial Blvd. US 78, exit 4, just n. Int corridors. **Pets:** Small. $10 daily fee/pet. Designated rooms, service with restrictions, supervision.
SAVE ✕ 🛈 🖵

AAA ▼▼ **Masters Inn Tucker** M
(770) 938-3552. **$42-$75.** 1435 Montreal Rd. I-285, exit 38, just w. Ext corridors. **Pets:** Small. $10 daily fee/pet. Designated rooms, service with restrictions, crate.
SAVE ✕ 🛈 ⌁

▼▼ **Motel 6 #2007** M
(770) 496-1311. **$35-$41.** 2810 Lawrenceville Hwy. I-285, exit 38, just w. Ext corridors. **Pets:** Other species. Service with restrictions, supervision.
✕

AAA ▼▼▼ **Quality Inn Atlanta/Northlake** H
(770) 491-7444. **$75-$99.** 2155 Ranchwood Dr. I-285, exit 37, 0.4 mi w, then just n. Ext/int corridors. **Pets:** Small. $10 daily fee/pet. Designated rooms, service with restrictions.
SAVE ✕ 🛄 🛈 🖵 ⌁

UNION CITY

▼▼ **Days Inn Shannon Mall** H
(770) 306-6067. **$55-$85.** 6840 Shannon Pkwy S. I-85, exit 64, 0.3 mi w to Shannon Pkwy, then just s. Ext corridors. **Pets:** Medium, dogs only. $15 daily fee/pet. Service with restrictions, crate.
ASK ✕ 🛈 🖵 ⌁

AAA ▼▼ **Microtel Inn & Suites** H
(770) 306-3800. **$50-$70.** 6690 Shannon Pkwy. I-85, exit 64, 0.3 mi w to Shannon Pkwy, then just n. Int corridors. **Pets:** Small. $50 deposit/room. Designated rooms, service with restrictions, supervision.
SAVE ✕ 🛈 🖵

END METROPOLITAN AREA

AUGUSTA

AAA ▼▼▼ **Comfort Inn Medical Center** H
(706) 722-2224. **$75.** 1455 Walton Way. I-20, exit 199 (Washington Rd), 4.5 mi e on SR 28, then just sw on 15th St. Ext corridors. **Pets:** Other species. $25 one-time fee/room. Service with restrictions, crate.
SAVE ✕ 🛈 🖵 ⌁

▼▼▼ **DoubleTree Hotel Augusta** H
(706) 855-8100. **$110-$199.** 2651 Perimeter Pkwy. I-520, exit 1C (Wheeler Rd), just w to Perimeter Pkwy, then just n. Int corridors. **Pets:** Accepted.
ASK ✕ 🛄 🛈 🖵 🍽 ⌁ ✕

▼▼▼ **Holiday Inn Gordon Highway at Bobby Jones** H
(706) 737-2300. **$111.** 2155 Gordon Hwy. I-520, exit 3A (US 78), just w. Ext corridors. **Pets:** Accepted.
ASK ✕ 🛈 🖵 🍽 ⌁

▼▼ **La Quinta Inn Augusta** H 🐾
(706) 733-2660. **$49-$99.** 3020 Washington Rd. I-20, exit 199 (Washington Rd), just w. Ext/int corridors. **Pets:** Medium, other species. Service with restrictions, supervision.
ASK ✕ 🛄 🛈 🖵 ⌁

AAA ▼▼▼▼ **Marriott Augusta Hotel & Suites** H
(706) 722-8900. **$187-$201.** 2 10th St. I-20, exit 200 (River Watch Pkwy), 5.4 mi se, then just n; downtown. Int corridors. **Pets:** Medium. $50 one-time fee/room. Service with restrictions, crate.
SAVE ✕ 🛄 🛈 🖵 🍽 ⌁ ✕

AAA ▼▼▼▼ **The Partridge Inn** H
(706) 737-8888. **$99-$249.** 2110 Walton Way. 1.3 mi w off 15th St. Int corridors. **Pets:** Accepted.
SAVE ✕ 🛈 🖵 🍽 ⌁

BAINBRIDGE

▼▼ **Jameson Inn** H
(229) 243-7000. **$88-$93.** 1403 Tallahassee Hwy. Just s of US 84 Bypass on US 27. Ext corridors. **Pets:** Accepted.
ASK ✕ 🛈 🖵 ⌁

BARNESVILLE

▼▼ **Country Hearth Inn** H
(770) 358-0967. **Call for rates.** 648 Hwy 341 S. Jct US 341 and 41, 2.3 mi s. Int corridors. **Pets:** Accepted.
✕ 🛈 🖵

BLUE RIDGE

AAA ▼▼▼ **Douglas Inn & Suites** M
(706) 258-3600. **$45-$69.** 1192 Windy Ridge Rd. Just off SR 515 and US 76. Ext corridors. **Pets:** Accepted.
SAVE ✕ 🛈 🖵 ⌁

BRASELTON

AAA ▼▼▼ **Best Western Braselton Inn** H
(706) 654-3081. **$89-$165.** 303 Zion Church Rd. I-85, exit 129, 0.3 mi n. Ext corridors. **Pets:** Medium. $15 daily fee/pet. Designated rooms, service with restrictions, crate.
SAVE ✕ 🛈 🖵 ⌁

AAA ▼▼▼ **Chateau Elan Lodge by Holiday Inn Express** H 🐾
(770) 867-8100. **$90-$130.** 2069 Hwy 211 NW. I-85, exit 126, just w. Int corridors. **Pets:** $20 one-time fee/room. Service with restrictions, supervision.
SAVE 🛈 🖵 ⌁

BREMEN

AAA ▼▼ **Days Inn** H 🐾
(770) 537-4646. **$65.** 35 Price Creek Rd. I-75, exit 11, just n. Ext corridors. **Pets:** Large, dogs only. $10 daily fee/pet. Service with restrictions, supervision.
SAVE ✕ 🛈 🖵 ⌁

AAA ▼▼▼▼ **Holiday Inn Express Hotel & Suites** H
(770) 537-3770. **$90-$100.** 125 US Hwy 27 Bypass. I-20, exit 11, just n. Int corridors. **Pets:** Accepted.
SAVE ✕ 🛄 🛈 🖵 ⌁

AAA **WWW** **Microtel Inn & Suites** H
(770) 537-8000. **Call for rates.** 104 Price Creek Rd. I-20, exit 11, just n. Int corridors. **Pets:** Small. $25 one-time fee/room. Designated rooms, no service, supervision.
SAVE X &M H P ~

BRUNSWICK

AAA **WWW** **Best Western Brunswick Inn** H *
(912) 264-0144. **$75-$135.** 5323 New Jesup Hwy. I-95, exit 36B (New Jesup Hwy/US 25), just nw. Ext corridors. **Pets:** Small, other species. Service with restrictions, supervision.
SAVE X H P ¶1 ~

AAA **WWW** **Hampton Inn** H *
(912) 261-0002. **$89-$109.** 230 Warren Mason Blvd. I-95, exit 36A (New Jesup Hwy/US 25), just se, then just sw on Tourist Dr. Ext/int corridors. **Pets:** Small. $25 deposit/room. Designated rooms, service with restrictions.
SAVE X H P ~

WWW **Jameson Inn Brunswick** H
(912) 267-0800. **$78-$85.** 661 Scranton Rd. I-95, exit 38 (Golden Isles Pkwy), 1.6 mi se, then just sw. Ext corridors. **Pets:** Medium, other species. $15 daily fee/pet. Service with restrictions, crate.
ASK X H P ~

WWW **La Quinta Inn & Suites Brunswick** H *
(912) 265-7725. **$39-$79.** 165 Warren Mason Blvd. I-95, exit 36A (New Jesup Hwy/US 25), just se, then sw on Tourist Dr. Int corridors. **Pets:** Medium, other species. Service with restrictions, supervision.
ASK X H P ~

AAA **WW** **Super 8** H
(912) 264-8800. **$45-$125.** 5280 New Jesup Hwy. I-95, exit 36B (New Jesup Hwy/US 25), just nw. Int corridors. **Pets:** $10 daily fee/pet. Service with restrictions, supervision.
SAVE X H

BYRON

AAA **WWW** **Best Western Inn & Suites** H
(478) 956-3056. **$63-$69.** 101 Dunbar Rd. I-75, exit 149 (SR 49), just ne. Ext corridors. **Pets:** $10 daily fee/pet. Designated rooms, service with restrictions, supervision.
SAVE X H P ~

WWW **Quality Inn** H
(478) 956-1600. **$70-$115.** 115 Chapman Rd. I-75, exit 149 (SR 49), just sw, then n. Ext corridors. **Pets:** Accepted.
ASK X H P ~

CAIRO

AAA **WWW** **Best Western Executive Inn** H
(229) 377-8000. **$60-$100.** 2800 Hwy 84 E. 2 mi e. Ext corridors. **Pets:** Small. $10 daily fee/pet. Designated rooms, service with restrictions, crate.
SAVE X H P ¶1 ~

CALHOUN

WWW **Comfort Inn** H
(706) 629-8271. **$60-$70.** 742 Hwy 53 SE. I-75, exit 312, just w. Ext corridors. **Pets:** Large, other species. $10 daily fee/pet. Service with restrictions, supervision.
ASK X H P ¶1 ~

WWW **Country Inn & Suites** H
(706) 625-6500. **$76-$149.** 1033 Fairmount Hwy. I-75, exit 312, just e. Int corridors. **Pets:** Small. Service with restrictions, supervision.
ASK X &M H P ~

WWW **Jameson Inn** H
(706) 629-8133. **$83-$90.** 189 Jameson St. I-75, exit 312, just w. Ext corridors. **Pets:** Medium, other species. $15 daily fee/room. Service with restrictions, supervision.
ASK X H P ~

WWW **Quality Inn Calhoun** H
(706) 629-9501. **$55-$75.** 915 Hwy 53 E SE. I-75, exit 312, just e. Ext corridors. **Pets:** Accepted.
ASK X H P ¶1 ~

WWW **Ramada Limited** M
(706) 629-9207. **$55-$100.** 1204 Red Bud Rd NE. I-75, exit 315, just w. Ext corridors. **Pets:** $7 daily fee/pet. Service with restrictions, supervision.
ASK X H P ~

AAA **WWW** **Smith Motel** M *
(706) 629-8427. **$30-$33.** 1437 US Hwy 41 N. I-75, exit 318, just w. Ext corridors. **Pets:** Medium. $5 daily fee/pet. Service with restrictions.
SAVE X H

CARROLLTON

WWW **Jameson Inn** H
(770) 834-2600. **$78-$85.** 700 S Park St. On US 27, just s of downtown. Ext corridors. **Pets:** Accepted.
ASK X &M H P ~

CARTERSVILLE

AAA **WWWW** **Best Western Garden Inn & Suites** H
(770) 386-1569. **$60-$85.** 5663 Hwy 20 NE. I-75, exit 290, 0.3 mi e. Ext corridors. **Pets:** Medium. $10 daily fee/pet. Designated rooms, service with restrictions, supervision.
SAVE X &M H P ~

AAA **WWW** **Comfort Inn** M
(770) 387-1800. **$60-$70.** 28 SR 20 Spur. I-75, exit 290, 0.3 mi se. Ext corridors. **Pets:** $5 daily fee/pet. Service with restrictions, supervision.
SAVE X H P ~

WWWW **Country Inn & Suites by Carlson** H
(770) 386-5888. **$81-$149.** 43 SR 20 Spur. I-75, exit 290, 0.3 mi se. Ext corridors. **Pets:** Small. Service with restrictions, supervision.
ASK X &M H P ~

AAA **WW** **Days Inn** H
(770) 382-1824. **$55-$60.** 5618 Hwy 20 SE. I-75, exit 290, just w. Ext corridors. **Pets:** Other species. $10 daily fee/pet. Designated rooms, service with restrictions, supervision.
SAVE X H P ~

WWW **Holiday Inn** H
(770) 386-0830. **Call for rates.** 2336 Hwy 411. I-75, exit 293, southwest corner. Int corridors. **Pets:** Medium. $10 one-time fee/pet. Service with restrictions, supervision.
X &M H P ¶1 ~

WWW **Howard Johnson Express** M
(770) 386-0700. **Call for rates.** 25 Carson Loop NW. I-75, exit 296, just w. Ext corridors. **Pets:** $5 daily fee/pet. Designated rooms, no service, supervision.
X H P ¶1 ~

AAA **WWW** **Knights Inn** M
(770) 386-7263. **$55-$75.** 420 E Church St. I-75, exit 288, 1.5 mi w. Ext corridors. **Pets:** Medium. $10 one-time fee/pet. Service with restrictions, crate.
SAVE X H ~

WW **Motel 6–4046** M
(770) 386-1449. **$43-$47, 3 day notice.** 5657 Hwy 20 NE. I-75, exit 290, 0.3 mi e. Ext corridors. **Pets:** Other species. Service with restrictions, supervision.
 X ~

▼▼ Quality Inn �H
(770) 386-0510. **Call for rates.** 235 Dixie Ave. I-75, exit 288, 2.5 mi w. Ext corridors. **Pets:** Accepted.
✕ 🛢 💻 🍽 🌊

▲▲ ▼▼▼ Sleep Inn �H
(770) 386-9259. **$90.** 11 Kent Dr. I-75, exit 296, just e. Int corridors. **Pets:** Medium, other species. $10 daily fee/pet. Designated rooms, service with restrictions, supervision.
🆂🅰🆅🅴 ✕ 🌡 🛢 💻 🌊

▲▲ ▼▼▼ Super 8 M
(770) 382-8881. **$48-$65.** 41 SR 20 Spur SE. I-75, exit 290, 0.3 mi e. Int corridors. **Pets:** $5 daily fee/pet. Service with restrictions, supervision.
🆂🅰🆅🅴 ✕ 🛢 🌊

CEDARTOWN

▼▼ Country Hearth Inn �H
(770) 749-9951. **Call for rates.** 925 N Main St. 1.5 mi n on US 27. Int corridors. **Pets:** Other species. $10 one-time fee/pet. Service with restrictions, supervision.
✕ 🌡 🛢 💻

CHATSWORTH

▲▲ ▼▼▼ Best Western Fairwinds Inn & Suites M
(706) 695-1411. **$79-$89.** 613 S 3rd Ave. On US 411/SR 76, 0.3 mi s. Ext corridors. **Pets:** Accepted.
🆂🅰🆅🅴 ✕ 🌡 🛢 💻 🌊

▼▼ Key West Inn M
(706) 517-1155. **Call for rates.** 501 Gl Maddox Pkwy. Jct SR 76 and US 411. Ext corridors. **Pets:** Accepted.
✕ 🛢

CLAYTON

▼▼ Americas Best Value Inn �H
(706) 782-4702. **$45-$95, 21 day notice.** 698 Hwy 441 S. 0.8 mi s. Int corridors. **Pets:** Very small. $10 daily fee/pet. No service, supervision.
🅰🆂🅺 ✕ 🛢 💻

▼▼▼ Beechwood Inn 🄲🄸
(706) 782-5485. **$199-$229, 14 day notice.** 220 Beechwood Dr. Jct US 76 and 441, just e on US 76 to Beechwood Dr, then just n. Int corridors. **Pets:** Accepted.
✕ 💻 🍽 🎦

▼▼ Days Inn �H
(706) 782-4258. **$56-$100.** 54 Hwy 441. Center. Ext corridors. **Pets:** Very small. $10 daily fee/pet. No service, supervision.
🅰🆂🅺 ✕ 🛢 💻 🍽 🌊

▲▲ ▼ Regal Inn M
(706) 782-4269. **$37-$95.** 707 Hwy 441 S. 0.8 mi s. Ext corridors. **Pets:** Small, dogs only. $5 daily fee/pet. Designated rooms, service with restrictions, supervision.
🆂🅰🆅🅴 ✕ 🛢

COLUMBUS

▼▼ Extended StayAmerica-Columbus-Airport �H
(706) 653-0131. **$70-$85.** 5020 Armour Rd. I-185, exit 8, 1.5 mi e, then 0.5 mi n. Ext corridors. **Pets:** Other species. $25 daily fee/pet. Service with restrictions, crate.
🅰🆂🅺 ✕ 🛢 💻

▼▼ Extended StayAmerica-Columbus-Bradley Park �H
(706) 653-9938. **$65-$85.** 1721 Rollins Way. I-185, exit 10 (US 80 and SR 22), 1.5 mi w on US 80, exit 3A, just s to Whittlesey Rd, 0.3 mi e to Rollins Way, then just n. Int corridors. **Pets:** Other species. $25 daily fee/pet. Service with restrictions, crate.
🅰🆂🅺 ✕ 🛢 💻

▼▼ Howard Johnson Express Inn & Suites �H
(706) 322-6641. **$65-$99.** 1011 Veterans Pkwy. I-185, exit 7 southbound; exit 7A northbound, 1.2 mi w to Veterans Pkwy, then 3.2 mi s. Ext corridors. **Pets:** Other species. $15 one-time fee/room. Service with restrictions.
🅰🆂🅺 ✕ 🛢 💻 🍽 🌊

▼▼ La Quinta Inn Columbus Midtown �H 🐾
(706) 568-1740. **$59-$99.** 3201 Macon Rd. I-185, exit 6, just w. Ext/int corridors. **Pets:** Medium, other species. Service with restrictions, supervision.
🅰🆂🅺 ✕ 🛢 💻 🌊

▼▼ La Quinta Inn Columbus State University �H 🐾
(706) 323-4344. **$79-$129.** 2919 Warm Springs Rd. I-185, exit 7 southbound; exit 7A northbound, just e. Int corridors. **Pets:** Medium, other species. Service with restrictions, supervision.
🅰🆂🅺 ✕ 🛢 💻 🌊

▼ Motel 6 #58 M
(706) 687-7214. **$49-$59.** 3050 Victory Dr. I-185, exit 1B, 3 mi w. Ext corridors. **Pets:** Other species. Service with restrictions, supervision.
✕ 🌊

▼▼▼ Rothschild-Pound House Inn 🄲🄸
(706) 322-4075. **$175-$365, 14 day notice.** 201 7th St. Jct US 27 (Veterans Pkwy/7th St), just w; downtown. Ext/int corridors. **Pets:** Other species. Designated rooms, no service.
🅰🆂🅺 ✕ 🛢 💻 🍽 🎦

COMMERCE

▲▲ ▼▼ Best Western Commerce Inn �H
(706) 335-3640. **$55-$160.** 157 Eisenhower Dr. I-85, exit 149, just ne. Int corridors. **Pets:** Small. $20 daily fee/pet. Designated rooms, service with restrictions, supervision.
🆂🅰🆅🅴 ✕ 🌡 🛢 💻 🌊

▼▼ Comfort Inn M
(706) 335-9001. **$70-$150.** 165 Eisenhower Dr. I-85, exit 149, just ne. Ext corridors. **Pets:** Other species. $10 daily fee/pet. Service with restrictions, supervision.
🅰🆂🅺 ✕ 🛢 💻 🌊

▼▼ Howard Johnson Inn & Suites M
(706) 335-5581. **$53-$140.** 148 Eisenhower Dr. I-85, exit 149, just ne. Ext corridors. **Pets:** Medium. $10 one-time fee/pet. Service with restrictions, supervision.
🅰🆂🅺 ✕ 🛢 💻 🌊

▼▼ Super 8 M
(706) 336-8008. **$49-$140.** 152 Eisenhower Dr. I-85, exit 149, just ne. Ext corridors. **Pets:** Medium. $10 one-time fee/pet. Service with restrictions, supervision.
🅰🆂🅺 ✕ 💻

CONYERS

▼▼▼ Comfort Inn �H
(770) 760-0300. **$79-$129, 7 day notice.** 1363 Klondike Rd. I-20, exit 80, just s. Int corridors. **Pets:** Small. $25 one-time fee/pet. No service, crate.
🅰🆂🅺 ✕ 🌡 🛢 💻 🌊

▼▼▼ Hampton Inn �H
(770) 483-8838. **$104-$145.** 1340 Dogwood Dr. I-20, exit 82, just n, then just e. Int corridors. **Pets:** Accepted.
✕ 🌡 🛢 💻 🌊

▼▼ Jameson Inn �H
(770) 760-1230. **$88-$95.** 1164 Dogwood Dr. I-20, exit 82, just n, then just w. Ext corridors. **Pets:** Very small. Service with restrictions, supervision.
🅰🆂🅺 ✕ 🛢 💻 🌊

WWW La Quinta Inn & Suites Atlanta (Conyers) 🅷 ❀
(770) 918-0092. **$74-$139.** 1184 Dogwood Dr. I-20, exit 82, just n, then just w. Int corridors. **Pets:** Medium, other species. Service with restrictions, supervision.
[ASK] [X] [&M] [🛏] [💻] [≋]

CORDELE

AAA WWW Best Western Colonial Inn 🅷
(229) 273-5420. **$62-$69, 10 day notice.** 1706 E 16th Ave (US 280). I-75, exit 101 (US 280), just w. Ext/int corridors. **Pets:** Accepted.
[SAVE] [X] [🛏] [💻] [≋]

AAA WWWW Country Inn & Suites 🅷
(229) 273-7117. **$59-$209.** 2803 Frontage Rd. I-75, exit 99 (SR 300), just w, then n. Int corridors. **Pets:** Other species. Service with restrictions.
[SAVE] [X] [&M] [🛏] [💻] [≋]

AAA WWWW Lake Blackshear Resort & Golf Club 🅷 ❀
(229) 276-1004. **$99-$199, 7 day notice.** 2459-H US 280 W. I-75, exit 101 (US 280), 10 mi w. Ext/int corridors. **Pets:** Other species. $50 one-time fee/room. Service with restrictions, supervision.
[SAVE] [X] [&M] [🛏] [💻] [🍴] [≋] [X]

AAA WWW Ramada Inn 🅷 ❀
(229) 273-5000. **$69-$79.** 2016 E 16th Ave (US 280). I-75, exit 101 (US 280), just e. Ext corridors. **Pets:** Medium. $10 daily fee/pet. Service with restrictions, supervision.
[SAVE] [X] [🛏] [💻] [≋]

AAA WW Travelodge 🄼
(229) 273-2456. **$45-$60.** 1618 16th Ave E (US 280). I-75, exit 101 (US 280), just w. Ext corridors. **Pets:** Other species. $5 deposit/pet. No service.
[SAVE] [X] [🛏]

CORNELIA

WW Comfort Inn 🅷
(706) 778-9573. **$79-$109.** 2965 J Warren Rd. Jct SR 365 and US 441 business route, just w. Int corridors. **Pets:** Medium. $25 daily fee/pet. Designated rooms, service with restrictions, crate.
[ASK] [X] [&M] [🛏] [💻] [≋]

COVINGTON

AAA WWW Baymont Inn & Suites 🄼
(770) 787-4900. **$70-$150.** 10111 Alcovy Rd. I-20, exit 92, just n. Ext corridors. **Pets:** Small. $10 daily fee/pet. Service with restrictions, supervision.
[SAVE] [X] [&M] [🛏] [💻] [≋]

WWW Super 8-Covington 🄼
(770) 786-5800. **$55-$150, 3 day notice.** 10130 Alcovy Rd. I-20, exit 92, just n. Ext corridors. **Pets:** Accepted.
[ASK] [X] [🛏] [💻]

DAHLONEGA

AAA WWW Econo Lodge 🄼
(706) 864-6191. **$55-$130.** 619 N Grove St. 0.5 mi n on US 19 business route. Ext corridors. **Pets:** Small, dogs only. $10 daily fee/pet. Designated rooms, service with restrictions, supervision.
[SAVE] [X] [🛏] [💻] [≋]

WWW Super 8 🄼
(706) 864-4343. **Call for rates.** 20 Mountain Dr. 0.5 mi s on US 19 and SR 60. Ext corridors. **Pets:** Accepted.
[X] [🛏] [≋]

DALLAS

WWW Days Inn 🄼 ❀
(770) 505-4567. **$59-$70.** 1007 Old Harris Rd. Jct Business Rt SR 6 (Atlanta Hwy). Ext corridors. **Pets:** $15 daily fee/pet. Supervision.
[ASK] [X] [&M] [🛏] [💻]

DALTON

AAA WWW America's Best Inn 🄼
(706) 226-1100. **$44-$69.** 1529 W Walnut Ave. I-75, exit 333, just e. Ext corridors. **Pets:** Other species. $10 daily fee/pet. Designated rooms, service with restrictions, supervision.
[SAVE] [X] [🛏] [💻] [≋]

AAA WWW Best Western Inn of Dalton 🅷
(706) 226-5022. **$59-$74.** 2106 Chattanooga Rd. I-75, exit 336, just w. Ext corridors. **Pets:** Small, dogs only. $5 one-time fee/pet. Service with restrictions, supervision.
[SAVE] [X] [&M] [🛏] [💻] [≋]

WWWW Comfort Inn & Suites 🅷
(706) 259-2583. **$89-$219.** 905 Westbridge Rd. I-75, exit 333, just w to Westbridge Rd, then just s. Int corridors. **Pets:** Medium. $15 daily fee/pet. Designated rooms, service with restrictions, supervision.
[ASK] [X] [🛏] [💻] [≋]

AAA WWW Econo Lodge 🄼
(706) 278-4300. **$43-$100.** 2007 Tampico Way. I-75, exit 336, just e. Int corridors. **Pets:** Accepted.
[SAVE] [X] [🛏] [💻] [≋]

WWW Jameson Inn 🅷
(706) 281-1880. **$73-$78.** 790 College Dr. I-75, exit 333, just w, then 0.3 mi n. Ext corridors. **Pets:** Other species. $15 daily fee/room. Service with restrictions, supervision.
[ASK] [X] [🛏] [💻] [≋]

WWWW La Quinta Inn & Suites 🅷 ❀
(706) 272-9099. **$89-$169.** 715 College Dr. I-75, exit 333, just w to Holiday Dr, then 0.5 mi n. Int corridors. **Pets:** Medium, other species. Service with restrictions, supervision.
[ASK] [X] [🛏] [💻] [≋]

DARIEN

AAA WWW Comfort Inn 🅷
(912) 437-4200. **$85-$250.** 703 Frontage Rd. I-95, exit 49 (SR 251), just nw. Int corridors. **Pets:** Large. $15 daily fee/pet. Designated rooms, service with restrictions, supervision.
[SAVE] [X] [🛏] [💻] [≋]

WW Quality Inn 🅷
(912) 437-5373. **Call for rates.** GA Hwy 251 & I-95 exit 49. I-95, exit 49 (SR 251), just w. Int corridors. **Pets:** Large. $10 one-time fee/room. Service with restrictions, supervision.
[X] [🛏] [💻] [≋]

DAWSONVILLE

AAA WWW Best Western Dawson Village Inn 🅷
(706) 216-4410. **$70-$90, 7 day notice.** 76 N Georgia Ave. Jct SR 400/53, 0.5 mi s. Int corridors. **Pets:** Accepted.
[SAVE] [X] [&M] [🛏] [💻] [≋]

WWWW Comfort Inn 🅷
(706) 216-1900. **$71-$134, 15 day notice.** 127 Beartooth Pkwy. Jct SR 400/53, 0.5 mi s. Int corridors. **Pets:** Large, other species. $15 daily fee/pet.
[ASK] [X] [&M] [🛏] [💻] [≋]

WWW Super 8 🅷
(706) 216-6801. **$49-$99.** 205 N 400 Center Ln. Jct SR 400/53, just n. Int corridors. **Pets:** Accepted.
[ASK] [X] [&M] [🛏] [💻] [≋]

DILLARD

ⓐⓐⓐ ▼▼▼▼ **Dillard House** 🅷
(706) 746-5348. **$59-$149, 3 day notice.** 768 Franklin St. US 441, just e via Old Dillard Rd. Ext corridors. **Pets:** Small, dogs only. $10 one-time fee/pet. Designated rooms, service with restrictions, crate.
[SAVE] [✕] [🛏] [▦] [🍴] [🏊] [⊠]

▼▼ **Knights Inn** Ⓜ ❀
(706) 746-5321. **$60-$140.** 3 Best Inn Way. Center. Ext corridors. **Pets:** Small. $10 daily fee/pet. Designated rooms, service with restrictions, supervision.
[ASK] [✕] [🛏] [▦] [🏊]

ⓐⓐⓐ ▼▼▼ **Mountain Valley Inn** Ⓜ
(706) 746-5373. **$35-$98.** 13 Royalty Ln. Just n of town center. Ext corridors. **Pets:** Medium, dogs only. $6 daily fee/pet. Service with restrictions, supervision.
[SAVE] [✕] [🛏] [▦] [🏊]

DUBLIN

▼▼ **Comfort Inn** 🅷
(478) 274-8000. **$55-$90.** 2110 Hwy 441 S. I-16, exit 51 (US 441), 0.6 mi n. Ext corridors. **Pets:** Accepted.
[ASK] [✕] [♿] [🛏] [▦] [🏊]

▼▼ **Jameson Inn** Ⓜ
(478) 275-3008. **$78-$85.** 100 PM Watson Dr. I-16, exit 51 (US 441), just n. Ext corridors. **Pets:** Accepted.
[ASK] [✕] [🛏] [▦] [🏊]

▼▼▼▼ **La Quinta Inn & Suites** 🅷 ❀
(478) 272-3110. **$59-$129.** 101 Travel Center Blvd. I-16, exit 51 (US 441), just s. Int corridors. **Pets:** Medium, other species. Service with restrictions, supervision.
[ASK] [✕] [🛏] [▦] [🏊]

ⓐⓐⓐ ▼▼ **Travelodge Suites and Conference Center** 🅷
(478) 275-2650. **$50-$60, 3 day notice.** 2121 Hwy 441 S. I-16, exit 51 (US 441), 0.5 mi n. Ext corridors. **Pets:** $15 daily fee/pet. Designated rooms, service with restrictions, supervision.
[SAVE] [✕] [🛏] [▦] [🏊]

EAST ELLIJAY

ⓐⓐⓐ ▼▼▼ **Best Western Mountain View Inn** 🅷
(706) 515-1500. **$79-$150.** 43 Coosawattee Dr. 0.8 mi s on SR 515. Int corridors. **Pets:** Accepted.
[SAVE] [✕] [♿] [🛏] [▦] [🏊]

ⓐⓐⓐ ▼▼ **Stratford Motor Inn** 🅷
(706) 276-1080. **$60-$100.** 79 Maddox Cir. Jct Maddox Cir and SR 515; behind KFC. Ext corridors. **Pets:** Medium, other species. $10 one-time fee/pet. Designated rooms, service with restrictions, supervision.
[SAVE] [✕] [🛏] [🏊]

FITZGERALD

▼▼ **Country Hearth Inn** 🅷
(229) 409-9911. **$50-$90.** 125 Stuart Way. Just n of US 319/107, just e. Int corridors. **Pets:** Other species. Service with restrictions, supervision.
[ASK] [✕] [🛏]

▼▼ **Western Motel** 🅷
(229) 424-9500. **Call for rates.** 111 Bull Run Rd. Just n of US 319/107, on US 129. Ext corridors. **Pets:** Small. $10 daily fee/pet. Service with restrictions, supervision.
[✕] [🛏] [▦] [🏊]

FORSYTH

ⓐⓐⓐ ▼▼ **Best Western Hilltop Inn** Ⓜ
(478) 994-9260. **$60-$116.** 951 Hwy 42 N. I-75, exit 188 (SR 42), just ne via Frontage Rd. Ext corridors. **Pets:** Medium. $15 one-time fee/pet. Service with restrictions, supervision.
[SAVE] [✕] [🛏] [▦] [🏊]

ⓐⓐⓐ ▼▼ **Comfort Inn** 🅷
(478) 994-3400. **$69-$99.** 333 Harold G Clark Pkwy. I-75, exit 185 (SR 18), just w. Ext corridors. **Pets:** Accepted.
[SAVE] [✕] [🛏] [▦] [🏊]

ⓐⓐⓐ ▼▼ **Econo Lodge** Ⓜ 🐾
(478) 994-5603. **$50-$80.** 320 Cabiness Rd. I-75, exit 187 (SR 83), just ne. Int corridors. **Pets:** Medium. $10 daily fee/pet. No service, supervision.
[SAVE] [🛏] [▦] [🏊]

▼▼▼ **Holiday Inn Express** 🅷
(478) 994-9697. **$109-$169.** 520 Holiday Cir. I-75, exit 186 (Juliette Rd), just w, then just s on Aaron St. Int corridors. **Pets:** Small, other species. $10 one-time fee/pet. Designated rooms, service with restrictions, supervision.
[ASK] [✕] [♿] [🛏] [▦]

▼▼▼ **Holiday Inn Forsyth** 🅷
(478) 994-5691. **$96.** 480 Holiday Cir. I-75, exit 186 (Juliette Rd), just w, then just s on Aaron St. Ext corridors. **Pets:** Large. $10 daily fee/pet. Designated rooms, service with restrictions, supervision.
[ASK] [✕] [🛏] [▦] [🍴] [🏊]

ⓐⓐⓐ ▼▼ **Super 8 Motel** 🅷
(478) 994-5101. **$58-$100.** 436 Tift College Dr. I-75, exit 186 (Juliette Rd), just w. Ext/int corridors. **Pets:** Small, dogs only. $15 daily fee/pet. Designated rooms, service with restrictions, supervision.
[SAVE] [✕] [🛏] [▦] [🏊]

GAINESVILLE

ⓐⓐⓐ ▼▼ **Days Inn** 🅷
(770) 535-8100. **$55-$80.** 520 Queen City Pkwy SW. I-985, exit 20, 1.8 mi nw on SR 60/Queen City Pkwy. Ext corridors. **Pets:** Accepted.
[SAVE] [✕] [🛏] [▦] [🏊]

ⓐⓐⓐ ▼▼ **Quality Inn & Suites** 🅷
(770) 536-4451. **Call for rates.** 726 Jessie Jewell Pkwy. I-985, exit 20, 1.9 mi w to Jesse Jewell Pkwy, then just s. Ext corridors. **Pets:** Small. Service with restrictions, crate.
[SAVE] [✕] [♿] [🛏] [▦] [🍴] [🏊]

▼▼ **Ramada Limited** Ⓜ
(770) 287-3205. **$56-$60.** 766 Jesse Jewell Pkwy. I-985, exit 20, 1.9 mi w to Jesse Jewell Pkwy, then just s. Ext corridors. **Pets:** Accepted.
[ASK] [✕] [🛏] [▦]

GARDEN CITY

▼▼ **Baymont Inn & Suites** 🅷
(912) 964-8669. **Call for rates.** 357 Main St. I-95, exit 109 (SR 21), 6.5 mi se to Spur SR 21 (Brampton Rd), 0.3 mi n to Coastal Hwy/Main St, then just se. Int corridors. **Pets:** Accepted.
[✕] [🛏] [▦] [🏊]

GLENNVILLE

ⓐⓐⓐ ▼ **Cheeri-O Inn** Ⓜ
(912) 654-2176. **$45-$50.** 820 S Downing Musgrove St. 0.8 mi s on US 25 and 301. Ext corridors. **Pets:** Medium. $7 daily fee/pet. Service with restrictions, supervision.
[SAVE] [✕] [🛏] [▦]

GOLDEN ISLES AREA

JEKYLL ISLAND

Quality Inn & Suites 🔲 ❀
(912) 635-2202. **$99-$169.** 700 N Beachview Dr. Jct Ben Fortson Pkwy (SR 520)/Beachview Dr, 1.5 mi n. Ext corridors. **Pets:** Medium. $10 daily fee/pet. Service with restrictions, supervision.

END AREA

GREENSBORO

The Ritz-Carlton Lodge, Reynolds Plantation 🔲
(706) 467-0600. **$219-$559.** One Lk Oconee Tr. I-20, exit 130, 7.2 mi sw on SR 44 (Old Eatonton Rd), 1.5 mi e on Linger Longer Rd, then 2 mi ne. Ext/int corridors. **Pets:** Accepted.

GROVETOWN

Super 8 Motel-Augusta 🔲
(706) 396-1600. **$80-$425.** 456 Park West Dr. I-20, exit 194 (SR 383), just s, then w. Int corridors. **Pets:** Accepted.

HARTWELL

Best Western Lake Hartwell Inn & Suites 🔲
(706) 376-4700. **$80.** 1357 E Franklin St. I-85, exit 177, 2 mi on US 29 E. Int corridors. **Pets:** Medium. $20 one-time fee/room. Service with restrictions, supervision.

HELEN

Chalet Kristy Motel & Cabins 🅼
(706) 878-2155. **$45-$139, 3 day notice.** 134 River St. Just w off Main St. Ext corridors. **Pets:** Accepted.

The Helendorf River Inn & Conference Center 🔲
(706) 878-2271. **$34-$159, 10 day notice.** 33 Munichstrasse. SR 17 and 75; center. Ext corridors. **Pets:** Other species. $10 daily fee/pet. Designated rooms, service with restrictions, supervision.

Kountry Peddler Tanglewood Resort Cabins 🅲🅰
(706) 878-3286. **$89-$169, 14 day notice.** 3387 Hwy 356. 1 mi n on SR 75, then 3 mi ne. Ext corridors. **Pets:** Accepted.

Premier Vacation Rentals 🅲🅰
(706) 348-8323. **$99-$495, 14 day notice.** 5156 Helen Hwy. 3.5 mi s on SR 75. Ext corridors. **Pets:** Accepted.

Quality Inn & Suites 🅼 ❀
(706) 878-2268. **$49-$209, 3 day notice.** 15 Yonah St. Just w of Mack St. Ext corridors. **Pets:** Small, other species. $20 daily fee/pet. Service with restrictions, supervision.

HIAWASSEE

Enota B & B, Cabins & Conference Lodge 🅲🅰
(706) 896-9966. **$80-$165.** 1000 Hwy 180. E on US 76 to SR 75/17, 6 mi s to SR 180, then 3 mi w. Ext corridors. **Pets:** Other species. $15 daily fee/pet. No service, supervision.

HINESVILLE

Best Western Ft. Stewart Inn & Suites 🔲 ❀
(912) 408-4444. **$70-$110.** 773 Frank Cochran Dr. Jct SR 119/196, 1 mi sw on SR 196, then just nw. Int corridors. **Pets:** Small. $5 daily fee/pet, $25 one-time fee/pet. Designated rooms, service with restrictions, supervision.

HIRAM

Country Inn & Suites by Carlson 🔲
(770) 222-0456. **$75-$120.** 70 Enterprise Path. Jct SR 92/6 and US 278, 0.3 mi w. Int corridors. **Pets:** Small. $10 daily fee/pet. Service with restrictions, supervision.

HOGANSVILLE

Key West Inn & Suites 🅼
(706) 637-9395. **$60-$120.** 1888 E Main St. I-85, exit 28, just w. Ext corridors. **Pets:** Small, dogs only. $20 daily fee/pet. Designated rooms, service with restrictions, supervision.

JASPER

Super 8 🅼
(706) 253-3297. **Call for rates.** 100 Whitfield Dr. Jct SR 515/53; in Lawsons Crossing. Ext corridors. **Pets:** Accepted.

JESUP

Jameson Inn of Jesup 🅼
(912) 427-6800. **$73-$78.** 205 N Hwy 301. Jct US 341, just n. Ext corridors. **Pets:** Accepted.

KINGSLAND

Econo Lodge 🅼
(912) 673-7336. **$62.** 1135 E King Ave. I-95, exit 3 (SR 40), just nw. Ext corridors. **Pets:** Medium. $5 daily fee/pet. Service with restrictions, supervision.

Hawthorn Suites 🔲
(912) 882-4170. **$99-$119.** 1323 E King Ave. I-95, exit 3 (SR 40), just w. Int corridors. **Pets:** Accepted.

♦♦ Jameson Inn M
(912) 729-9600. **$78-$85.** 105 May Creek Blvd. I-95, exit 3 (SR 40), just w, then s at Boone Ave. Ext corridors. **Pets:** Other species. Service with restrictions.
ASK ☒ ✍M 🛏 🖵 ≈

♠ ♦♦ Magnolia Inn M
(912) 576-4777. **$60-$100, 3 day notice.** 1325 Hospitality Ave. I-95, exit 3 (SR 40), 0.5 mi e, then just n on JSJ Ave. Ext corridors. **Pets:** Small. $10 daily fee/pet. Designated rooms, service with restrictions, supervision.
SAVE ☒ 🛏 🖵

♠ ♦♦ Microtel Inn & Suites H
(912) 729-1555. **$49-$79.** 1325 E King Ave. I-95, exit 3 (SR 40), just ne. Int corridors. **Pets:** Medium. $10 daily fee/pet. Service with restrictions, supervision.
SAVE ☒ 🛏 🖵

♠♦ Super 8 M
(912) 729-6888. **$50-$100.** 120 Robert L Edenfield Dr. I-95, exit 3 (SR 40), just se. Int corridors. **Pets:** Other species. $10 daily fee/pet. Service with restrictions.
SAVE ☒ 🛏 🖵

LA FAYETTE

♠ ♦♦ Days Inn M
(706) 639-9362. **$50-$65.** 2209 N Main St. 2.5 mi n on US 27. Ext corridors. **Pets:** $10 daily fee/pet. Service with restrictions, supervision.
SAVE ☒ 🛏 🖵 ≈

♦♦ Key West Inn M
(706) 638-6800. **$47-$60, 3 day notice.** 2221 N Main St. 2.5 mi n on US 27. Ext corridors. **Pets:** Accepted.
ASK ☒ ✍M 🛏 ≈

LAGRANGE

♠ ♦♦ Days Inn-LaGrange/Callaway Gardens H
(706) 882-8881. **$60.** 2606 Whitesville Rd. I-85, exit 13, just e. Ext corridors. **Pets:** Medium, other species. $15 daily fee/pet. No service, supervision.
SAVE ☒ 🛏 🖵 ≈

♦♦ Jameson Inn H
(706) 882-8700. **$78-$85.** 110 Jameson Dr. I-85, exit 18 (Lafayette Pkwy), 0.3 mi w. Ext corridors. **Pets:** Small, other species. $15 daily fee/pet. No service, supervision.
ASK ☒ ✍M 🛏 🖵 ≈

LAKE PARK

♠ ♦♦ Days Inn H
(229) 559-0229. **$59-$89.** 4913 Timber Dr. I-75, exit 5, just nw. Ext corridors. **Pets:** Accepted.
SAVE ☒ 🛏 🖵 ≈

♠ ♦♦ Quality Inn H
(229) 559-5181. **$59-$115.** 1198 Lakes Blvd. I-75, exit 5, just e. Ext corridors. **Pets:** Accepted.
SAVE ☒ 🛏 🖵 ≈

♠ ♦♦ Super 8 H
(229) 559-8111. **$55-$75.** 4907 Timber Dr. I-75, exit 5, just w, then n. Ext corridors. **Pets:** Small, dogs only. $10 daily fee/pet. Service with restrictions, supervision.
SAVE ☒ 🛏

LAVONIA

♠ ♦♦ Best Western Regency Inn & Suites M
(706) 356-4000. **$63-$120.** 13705 Jones St. I-85, exit 173, just e. Ext corridors. **Pets:** Medium, other species. $15 one-time fee/pet. Service with restrictions, supervision.
SAVE ☒ 🛏 🖵 ≈

♦♦ Super 8-Lavonia H
(706) 356-8848. **$48-$90.** 14227 Jones St. I-85, exit 173, just w. Ext corridors. **Pets:** Accepted.
ASK ☒ ✍M 🛏 🖵 ≈

LOCUST GROVE

♦♦ Econo Lodge M
(770) 957-2601. **Call for rates.** 4829 Bill Gardner Pkwy. I-75, exit 212, just e. Ext corridors. **Pets:** Accepted.
☒ 🛏 🖵

♠ ♦♦♦ La Quinta Inn & Suites H
(678) 583-0004. **$69-$110.** 4832 Bill Gardner Pkwy. I-75, exit 212, just e. Int corridors. **Pets:** Large. Service with restrictions, supervision.
SAVE ☒ ✍M 🛏 🖵 ≈

MACON

♦♦ The Baymont Inn and Suites of Macon M
(478) 474-8004. **$70-$140.** 150 Plantation Inn Dr. I-475, exit 9 (Zebulon Rd), just e to Peake Rd, then just s. Ext corridors. **Pets:** Accepted.
ASK ☒ 🛏 🖵 ≈

♠ ♦♦ Best Western Inn & Suites of Macon M ✿
(478) 781-5300. **$71-$83.** 4681 Chambers Rd. I-475, exit 3 (Eisenhower Pkwy/US 80), just ne, then just se. Ext corridors. **Pets:** Small, other species. $10 daily fee/room. Service with restrictions.
SAVE ☒ 🛏 🖵 ≈

♠ ♦♦ Best Western Riverside Inn H ✿
(478) 743-6311. **$60-$75.** 2400 Riverside Dr. I-75, exit 167 (Riverside Dr), just w, then 0.4 mi se. Int corridors. **Pets:** Medium. $10 daily fee/pet. Service with restrictions, crate.
SAVE ☒ 🛏 🖵 🍴 ≈

♦♦♦ La Quinta Inn & Suites Macon H ✿
(478) 475-0206. **$79-$139.** 3944 River Place Dr. I-75, exit 169 (Arkwright Rd), just n, then e. Int corridors. **Pets:** Medium, other species. Service with restrictions, supervision.
ASK ☒ ✍M 🛏 🖵 ≈

♠ ♦♦ Rodeway Inn M ✿
(478) 781-4343. **$49-$59.** 4999 Eisenhower Pkwy. I-475, exit 3 (Eisenhower Pkwy/US 80), just ne. Ext corridors. **Pets:** Medium. $5 daily fee/pet. Service with restrictions, crate.
SAVE ☒ 🛏 🖵 ≈

♠ ♦♦ Sleep Inn I-475 H
(478) 476-8111. **$59-$99.** 140 Plantation Inn Dr. I-475, exit 9 (Zebulon Rd), just e to Peake Rd, then just s. Int corridors. **Pets:** Small. $10 daily fee/pet. Designated rooms, service with restrictions, supervision.
SAVE ☒ ✍M 🛏 🖵 ≈

MCDONOUGH

♠ ♦♦ Comfort Inn H ✿
(770) 954-9110. **$85-$175.** 80 Hwy 81 W. I-75, exit 218, just nw. Ext corridors. **Pets:** Medium. $10 daily fee/pet. Service with restrictions, supervision.
SAVE ☒ 🛏 🖵 ≈

♦♦ Days Inn H
(770) 957-5261. **$59-$120.** 744 Hwy 155 S. I-75, exit 216, just e. Ext corridors. **Pets:** Other species. $7 daily fee/pet. Designated rooms, service with restrictions, crate.
ASK ☒ 🛏 🖵 ≈

♦ Econo Lodge M
(770) 957-2651. **Call for rates.** 1279 Hwy 20 W. I-75, exit 218, just w. Ext corridors. **Pets:** Medium. $10 daily fee/pet. Designated rooms, supervision.
☒ 🛏 🖵

(AAA) ▼▼▼ **Quality Inn & Suites Conference Center M**
(770) 957-5291. **$79-$199.** 930 Hwy 155 S. I-75, exit 216, just w. Ext corridors. **Pets:** Other species. $10 daily fee/room. Service with restrictions.
[SAVE] [✕] [&M] [🔒] [💻] [🍽] [🏊]

MILLEDGEVILLE

▼▼▼▼ **Holiday Inn Express Hotel & Suites H**
(478) 454-9000. **Call for rates.** 1839 N Columbia St. US 441, 2 mi n of downtown. Int corridors. **Pets:** Accepted.
[✕] [&M] [🔒] [💻] [🏊]

NEWNAN

(AAA) ▼▼▼ **Best Western-Shenandoah Inn H**
(770) 304-9700. **$59-$109, 7 day notice.** 620 Hwy 34 E. I-85, exit 47, just w. Ext corridors. **Pets:** Medium, other species. $10 daily fee/pet. Service with restrictions, supervision.
[SAVE] [✕] [&M] [🔒] [💻] [🏊]

▼▼▼ **Howard Johnson Inn M**
(770) 683-1499. **$50-$75.** 1310 Hwy 29 S. I-85, exit 41, just w. Ext corridors. **Pets:** Small. $15 daily fee/pet. Service with restrictions, supervision.
[ASK] [✕] [🔒] [💻] [🏊]

OAKWOOD

▼▼▼ **Country Inn & Suites by Carlson H**
(770) 535-8080. **Call for rates.** 4535 Oakwood Rd. I-985, exit 16, just sw. Int corridors. **Pets:** Accepted.
[✕] [🔒] [💻] [🏊]

PEACHTREE CITY

(AAA) ▼▼▼ **Best Western Inn & Suites M**
(770) 632-9700. **$90-$130.** 976 Crosstown Dr. Jct SR 74 and 54, 2.1 mi s on SR 74. Ext corridors. **Pets:** Small. $25 daily fee/pet. Designated rooms, service with restrictions, supervision.
[SAVE] [✕] [&M] [🔒] [💻] [🏊]

PERRY

(AAA) ▼▼▼ ▼▼ **Henderson Village CI**
(478) 988-8696. **$159-$297, 3 day notice.** 125 S Langston Cir. I-75, exit 127 (SR 26), 1.3 mi w. Ext/int corridors. **Pets:** Accepted.
[SAVE] [✕] [🔒] [💻] [🍽] [🏊] [✕]

▼▼ **New Perry Hotel H**
(478) 987-1000. **$59-$125.** 800 Main St. I-75, exit 136 (Sam Nunn Blvd) southbound, 1.2 mi se on US 341, then just w; exit 135 (US 41) northbound, 1.5 mi ne, then just s. Ext/int corridors. **Pets:** $15 daily fee/pet. Service with restrictions, crate.
[ASK] [✕] [🔒] [💻] [🍽] [🏊]

(AAA) ▼▼▼ **Quality Inn M**
(478) 987-1345. **$65-$95, 30 day notice.** 1504 Sam Nunn Blvd. I-75, exit 136 (Sam Nunn Blvd), just w. Ext corridors. **Pets:** Accepted.
[SAVE] [✕] [🔒] [💻] [🍽] [🏊]

(AAA) ▼▼▼ **Super 8 Motel H**
(478) 987-0999. **Call for rates.** 102 Plaza Dr. I-75, exit 136 (Sam Nunn Blvd), just e. Ext corridors. **Pets:** Medium. $10 daily fee/pet. Service with restrictions, crate.
[SAVE] [✕] [🔒] [🏊]

PINE MOUNTAIN

(AAA) ▼▼▼▼ **Mountain Creek Inn at Callaway Gardens M**
(706) 663-2281. **$129-$171, 7 day notice.** 17800 Hwy 27. Jct SR 354, 1.5 mi s on US 27/SR 1; in Callaway Gardens. Ext corridors. **Pets:** Accepted.
[SAVE] [✕] [&M] [🔒] [💻] [🍽] [🏊]

▼▼ **White Columns Motel M** ✿
(706) 663-2312. **$59-$80, 3 day notice.** 524 S Main Ave. Jct SR 354, just n on US 27/SR 1. Ext corridors. **Pets:** Medium. $10 daily fee/pet. Designated rooms, service with restrictions, supervision.
[ASK] [✕] [🔒]

POOLER

(AAA) ▼▼▼ **Best Western Bradbury Suites H**
(912) 330-0330. **$79-$189.** 155 Bourne Ave. I-95, exit 102 (US 80), just e. Int corridors. **Pets:** Medium. $10 daily fee/pet. Designated rooms, service with restrictions, supervision.
[SAVE] [✕] [&M] [🔒] [💻] [🏊] [✕]

▼▼▼ **Holiday Inn Savannah West H** 🐾
(912) 330-5100. **$125-$165.** 103 San Dr. I-95, exit 102 (US 80), just w. Int corridors. **Pets:** Medium, other species. $35 one-time fee/room. Designated rooms, service with restrictions, supervision.
[ASK] [✕] [🔒] [💻] [🍽] [🏊]

▼▼▼ **Jameson Inn H**
(912) 748-0017. **$93-$100.** 125 Bourne Ave. I-95, exit 102 (US 80), just e. Int corridors. **Pets:** Accepted.
[ASK] [✕] [🔒] [💻] [🏊]

▼▼▼ **La Quinta Inn & Suites H** ✿
(912) 748-3771. **$69-$139.** 414 Gray St. I-95, exit 102 (US 80), just w. Int corridors. **Pets:** Medium, other species. Service with restrictions, supervision.
[✕] [🔒] [💻] [🏊]

(AAA) ▼▼▼ **Travelodge Suites H** ✿
(912) 748-6363. **$59-$149.** 130 Continental Blvd. I-95, exit 102 (US 80), just e. Int corridors. **Pets:** Medium, other species. $10 deposit/pet. Service with restrictions, supervision.
[SAVE] [✕] [🔒] [💻] [🏊]

PORT WENTWORTH

(AAA) ▼▼▼ **Wingate Inn H**
(912) 964-0840. **$69-$129.** 115 O' Leary Rd. I-95, exit 109 (SR 21), just e, then just n. Int corridors. **Pets:** Medium. $20 daily fee/pet. Designated rooms, no service, supervision.
[SAVE] [✕] [&M] [🔒] [💻]

RICHMOND HILL

(AAA) ▼▼▼ **Best Western Richmond Hill Inn H**
(912) 756-7070. **$79-$129.** 4564 Hwy 17. I-95, exit 87 (Ocean Hwy/US 17), just w. Int corridors. **Pets:** Accepted.
[SAVE] [✕] [🔒] [💻] [🏊]

(AAA) ▼▼▼ **Comfort Suites H**
(912) 756-6668. **$89-$109, 14 day notice.** 4601 Hwy 17. I-95, exit 87 (Ocean Hwy/US 17), 0.4 mi sw. Int corridors. **Pets:** Medium, other species. $20 daily fee/pet. Designated rooms, service with restrictions, supervision.
[SAVE] [✕] [🔒] [💻] [🏊] [✕]

RINGGOLD

(AAA) ▼▼▼ **Comfort Inn H**
(706) 935-4000. **$79-$119.** 177 Industrial Blvd. I-75, exit 348, just w. Int corridors. **Pets:** Small. $15 daily fee/pet. Designated rooms, service with restrictions, supervision.
[SAVE] [✕] [🔒] [💻] [🏊]

(AAA) ▼▼▼ **Hometown Inn H** ✿
(706) 937-7070. **$60-$75.** 22 Gateway Business Park Dr. I-75, exit 350, just e. Int corridors. **Pets:** $10 one-time fee/pet. Service with restrictions, supervision.
[SAVE] [✕] [&M] [🔒] [💻] [🏊]

▼▼ Super 8 **M**
(706) 965-7080. **Call for rates.** 5400 Alabama Hwy. I-75, exit 348, just e. Ext corridors. **Pets:** Accepted.
⊠ ⅙M 🖥 💻

ROCKMART

▼▼ Days Inn **M**
(770) 684-9955. **Call for rates.** 105 GTM Pkwy. Jct US 278 and SR 101, just n. Ext corridors. **Pets:** Accepted.
⊠ ⅙M 🖥 💻

ROME

▼▼▼ Jameson Inn **H**
(706) 291-7797. **$93-$100.** 40 Grace Dr. On US 411, 2.2 mi e. Int corridors. **Pets:** Accepted.
ASK ⊠ ⅙M 🖥 💻 ⌁

SANDERSVILLE

▼▼ Days Inn Sandersville **M**
(478) 553-0393. **Call for rates.** 128 Commerce St. On SR 15 at jct SR 77, just s. Ext corridors. **Pets:** Accepted.
⊠ ⅙M 🖥 💻 ⌁

SAVANNAH

▼▼▼ Catherine Ward House Inn **BB**
(912) 234-8564. **$369, 3 day notice.** 118 E Waldburg St. Between Drayton and Abercorn sts. Ext/int corridors. **Pets:** Dogs only. $25 one-time fee/room. Designated rooms, service with restrictions.
ASK ⊠

Ⓐ ▼▼▼ Clarion Inn & Suites **H**
(912) 920-3200. **$79-$169.** 16 Gateway Blvd E. I-95, exit 94 (SR 204/ Abercorn St), just e. Int corridors. **Pets:** Accepted.
SAVE ⊠ ⅙M 🖥 💻 ⌁

▼▼▼ Comfort Suites Savannah Airport **H**
(912) 721-9100. **$109-$129.** 1 Yvette Johnson Hagins Dr. I-95, exit 104, 0.4 mi e. **Pets:** Medium, other species. $50 one-time fee/room. Designated rooms, service with restrictions, crate.
ASK ⊠ 🖥 💻 ⌁

Ⓐ ▼▼▼ East Bay Inn **CI**
(912) 238-1225. **$189-$269, 7 day notice.** 225 E Bay St. I-16, exit 167 (Montgomery St), 0.8 mi ne, then 0.4 mi se; in historic district. Int corridors. **Pets:** Accepted.
SAVE ⊠ 💻 🛎

▼▼ Extended StayAmerica-Midtown **H**
(912) 692-0076. **$70-$185.** 5511 Abercorn St. Jct SR 21 and 204 (Abercorn St), just s. Int corridors. **Pets:** Other species. $25 daily fee/pet. Service with restrictions, crate.
ASK ⊠ 🖥 💻

Ⓐ ▼▼ ▼▼ Foley House Inn **BB**
(912) 232-6622. **$225-$410, 10 day notice.** 14 W Hull St on Chippewa Square. Between Bull and Whitaker sts; in historic district. Ext/int corridors. **Pets:** Other species. $50 one-time fee/pet. Service with restrictions.
SAVE ⊠

▼▼▼ The Forsyth Park Inn **BB**
(912) 233-6800. **$175-$275, 14 day notice.** 102 W Hall St. Between Whitaker and Howard sts; on Forsyth Park. Int corridors. **Pets:** Accepted.
ASK ⊠ 🖥

Ⓐ ▼▼▼ Four Points by Sheraton **H**
(912) 629-1500. **Call for rates.** 15 Jay R Turner Dr. I-95, exit 104, 0.4 mi e. Int corridors. **Pets:** Medium. $75 one-time fee/room. Service with restrictions, supervision.
SAVE ⊠ 🖥 💻 🛎 ⌁

Ⓐ ▼▼▼ ▼▼ Hamilton-Turner Inn **BB**
(912) 233-1833. **$189-$369, 10 day notice.** 330 Abercorn St. Between E Charlton and E Harris sts; overlooking Lafayette Square; in historic district. Ext/int corridors. **Pets:** Small, other species. $50 one-time fee/room. Designated rooms, supervision.
SAVE ⊠

▼▼▼▼ Homewood Suites by Hilton **H**
(912) 353-8500. **$139-$229.** 5820 White Bluff Rd. Jct SR 21 and 204 (Abercorn St), 0.5 mi s. Ext/int corridors. **Pets:** Medium. $75 one-time fee/room. Service with restrictions, crate.
⊠ 🖥 💻 🛎 ⊠

▼▼ Joan's on Jones B & B **BB** 🐾
(912) 234-3863. **$175-$195 (no credit cards), 7 day notice.** 17 W Jones St. Between Whitaker and Bull sts. Ext corridors. **Pets:** Dogs only. $50 one-time fee/room. Designated rooms.
⊠ 🖥 💻

▼▼ La Quinta Inn & Suites **H** 🐾
(912) 927-7660. **$59-$149.** 8484 Abercorn St. 2.4 mi s of jct SR 21 and 204 (Abercorn St). Int corridors. **Pets:** Medium, other species. Service with restrictions, supervision.
ASK ⊠ 🖥 💻 ⌁

▼▼ La Quinta Inn Savannah (I-95) **H** 🐾
(912) 925-9505. **$55-$109.** 6 Gateway Blvd S. I-95, exit 94 (SR 204/ Abercorn St), just e, then s. Ext corridors. **Pets:** Medium, other species. Service with restrictions, supervision.
ASK ⊠ ⅙M 🖥 💻 ⌁

▼▼ La Quinta Inn Savannah (Midtown) **H** 🐾
(912) 355-3004. **$59-$129.** 6805 Abercorn St. 1 mi s of jct SR 21 and 204 (Abercorn St). Ext/int corridors. **Pets:** Medium, other species. Service with restrictions, supervision.
ASK ⊠ 🖥 💻 ⌁

Ⓐ ▼▼▼ ▼▼ The Mansion on Forsyth Park **H**
(912) 238-5158. **$229-$509, 3 day notice.** 700 Drayton St. Between E Hall and E Gwinnett sts; on Forsyth Park. Ext corridors. **Pets:** Accepted.
SAVE ⊠ 🖥 💻 🍴 ⌁

Ⓐ ▼▼▼ Olde Harbour Inn **BB**
(912) 234-4100. **$199-$309, 7 day notice.** 508 E Factors Walk. Lincoln St ramp off E Bay St; in historic riverfront district. Ext corridors. **Pets:** Small, dogs only. $35 one-time fee/pet. Service with restrictions, crate.
SAVE ⊠ 🖥 💻

▼▼ Red Roof Inn **H**
(912) 920-3535. **$45-$107.** 405 Al Henderson Blvd. I-95, exit 94 (SR 204/Abercorn St), just e. Int corridors. **Pets:** Accepted.
ASK ⊠ ⅙M 🖥 💻 ⌁

▼▼▼ Residence Inn by Marriott Savannah **H**
(912) 356-3266. **$159-$169.** 5710 White Bluff Rd. Jct SR 21, 0.5 mi s. Int corridors. **Pets:** Small. $100 one-time fee/room. Service with restrictions, supervision.
⊠ 🖥 💻 🛎 ⊠

Ⓐ ▼▼▼ Staybridge Suites Savannah Historic
District **H** 🐾
(912) 721-9000. **$120-$140, 90 day notice.** 301 E Bay St. Corner of Lincoln St; in historic district. Int corridors. **Pets:** Medium, other species. $75 one-time fee/room. Service with restrictions, crate.
SAVE ⊠ ⅙M 🖥 💻

▼▼ The Thunderbird Inn **M**
(912) 232-2661. **Call for rates.** 611 W Oglethorpe Ave. Just w of Martin Luther King Jr Blvd. Ext corridors. **Pets:** Medium, other species. $25 daily fee/room. Designated rooms, service with restrictions, supervision.
⊠ 🖥 💻

TownePlace Suites Savannah Airport 🅷 ❖
(912) 629-7775. **$123-$132.** 4 Jay R Turner Dr. I-95, exit 104, just e. Int corridors. **Pets:** Other species. $25 daily fee/room.
⊠ ⓜ 🍴 ▣ ⇌

Travelodge Ⓜ
(912) 925-2640. **$40-$299.** 1 Fort Argyle Rd. I-95, exit 94 (SR 204/Abercorn St), just w. Ext corridors. **Pets:** $10 daily fee/pet. Designated rooms, crate.
⟨SAVE⟩ ⊠ 🍴 ▣ ⇌

Westin Savannah Harbor Golf Resort and Spa 🅷
(912) 201-2000. **$169-$439.** 1 Resort Dr. On Hutchinson Island; 1 mi se of first exit after Eugene Talmadge Memorial Bridge and US 17. Int corridors. **Pets:** Accepted.
⟨SAVE⟩ ⊠ ⓜ 🍴 ▣ 🍴 ⇌ ⊠

STATESBORO

Best Western University Inn Ⓜ
(912) 681-7900. **$62-$69.** 1 Jameson Ave. Jct US 25/301 and SR 67, 0.9 mi s on US 25/301. Ext corridors. **Pets:** Medium. $20 one-time fee/pet. Service with restrictions.
⟨SAVE⟩ ⊠ 🍴 ▣ ⇌

La Quinta Inn Statesboro 🅷 ❖
(912) 871-2525. **$63-$119.** 225 Lanier Dr. Jct US 301 Bypass and SR 67, 1.2 mi w on US 301, just n of Georgia Southern University. Int corridors. **Pets:** Medium, other species. Service with restrictions, supervision.
⟨ASK⟩ ⊠ ⓜ 🍴 ▣ ⇌

Quality Inn & Suites 🅷 ❖
(912) 489-3995. **Call for rates.** 230 S Main St. On US 301/25, 0.8 mi s of center; near downtown. Ext corridors. **Pets:** Medium. $15 daily fee/room. Designated rooms, service with restrictions, crate.
⟨SAVE⟩ ⊠ 🍴 ▣ 🍴 ⇌

Statesboro Inn & Restaurant Ⓒ
(912) 489-8628. **Call for rates.** 106 S Main St. US 301/25, just s of town center; downtown. Int corridors. **Pets:** Accepted.
⊠ 🍴 ▣ 🍴

Trellis Garden Inn 🅷
(912) 489-8781. **$75-$105.** 107 S Main St (US 301/25). On US 301/25, just s of center; downtown. Ext corridors. **Pets:** Service with restrictions, supervision.
⟨ASK⟩ ⊠ 🍴 ⇌

STOCKBRIDGE

Baymont Inn & Suites Ⓜ
(770) 507-6500. **$59-$99.** 100 N Park Ct. I-75, exit 224, just e, then just n on Rock Quarry Rd. Int corridors. **Pets:** Medium. $10 daily fee/pet. Service with restrictions, supervision.
⟨SAVE⟩ ⊠ 🍴 ▣ ⇌

La Quinta Inn & Suites 🅷 ❖
(770) 506-9991. **$74-$134.** 3581 Cameron Pkwy. I-75, exit 228, just e on SR 138, then just n; I-675, exit 1, just w on SR 138, then just n. Int corridors. **Pets:** Medium, other species. Service with restrictions, supervision.
⟨SAVE⟩ ⊠ ⓜ 🍴 ▣ ⇌ ⊠

Sleep Inn & Suites 🅷
(770) 474-3870. **$60-$149.** 7423 Davidson Cir W. I-675, exit 1, just e, then just s; I-75, exit 228, 1 mi e on SR 138, then just s. Int corridors. **Pets:** $25 one-time fee/pet. Service with restrictions, supervision.
⟨ASK⟩ ⊠ ⓜ 🍴 ▣ ⇌

Super 8 Atlanta South Ⓜ
(770) 474-5758. **$54-$60.** 1451 Hudson Bridge Rd. I-75, exit 224, just w. Ext corridors. **Pets:** Accepted.
⟨SAVE⟩ ⊠ 🍴 ▣ ⇌

SWAINSBORO

Best Western Bradford Inn Ⓜ
(478) 237-2400. **$60-$65.** 688 S Main St. I-16, exit 90 (US 1), 12.4 mi n. Ext corridors. **Pets:** Accepted.
⟨SAVE⟩ ⊠ 🍴 ▣ ⇌

THOMASTON

Jameson Inn 🅷 ❖
(706) 648-2232. **$73-$80.** 1010 Hwy 19 N. Jct SR 74, 2.3 mi n. Ext corridors. **Pets:** Medium. Designated rooms, service with restrictions, supervision.
⟨ASK⟩ ⊠ 🍴 ▣ ⇌

THOMASVILLE

Comfort Inn Ⓜ
(229) 228-5555. **$65-$83.** 14866 US 19 S. Jct SR 300/US 19 and 84/SR 122. Ext corridors. **Pets:** Medium. $45 deposit/room. Service with restrictions, crate.
⟨ASK⟩ ⊠ 🍴 ▣ ⇌

Jameson Inn Ⓜ
(229) 227-9500. **$78-$81.** 1470 Remington Ave. US 19, just w on CR 122. Ext corridors. **Pets:** Accepted.
⟨ASK⟩ ⊠ ⓜ 🍴 ▣ ⇌

Quality Inn & Suites Ⓜ
(229) 225-2134. **$55-$69.** 15138 Hwy 19 S. 0.3 mi s of US 319. Ext corridors. **Pets:** Medium, dogs only. $10 daily fee/pet. Designated rooms, no service, supervision.
⟨SAVE⟩ ⊠ ⓜ 🍴 ▣ 🍴 ⇌

THOMSON

Best Western White Columns Inn 🅷 ❖
(706) 595-8000. **$82, 3 day notice.** 1890 Washington Rd. I-20, exit 172 (US 78), just s. Ext corridors. **Pets:** Small. $10 daily fee/pet. Designated rooms, service with restrictions, supervision.
⟨SAVE⟩ ⊠ 🍴 ▣ 🍴 ⇌ ⊠

TIFTON

Days Inn & Suites 🅷 ❖
(229) 382-8505. **$59-$89.** 1199 Hwy 82 W. I-75, exit 62, just w. Int corridors. **Pets:** Other species. $10 daily fee/pet. Service with restrictions, supervision.
⟨ASK⟩ ⊠ 🍴 ▣ ⇌

Hampton Inn 🅷
(229) 382-8800. **$95-$175.** 720 Hwy 319 S. I-75, exit 62, just e. Ext corridors. **Pets:** Accepted.
⊠ 🍴 ▣ ⇌

Holiday Inn 🅷
(229) 382-6687. **$80-$109.** 1208 Hwy 82 W. I-75, exit 62, at jct US 82 and 319. Ext corridors. **Pets:** Designated rooms, service with restrictions, supervision.
⟨SAVE⟩ ⊠ 🍴 ▣ 🍴 ⇌

Ramada Limited and Conference Center 🅷
(229) 382-8500. **$59-$109.** 1211 Hwy 82 W. I-75, exit 62, just w. Ext corridors. **Pets:** Other species. $10 daily fee/pet.
⟨ASK⟩ ⊠ 🍴 ▣ ⇌

TRENTON

Days Inn 🅷
(706) 657-2550. **$57-$70.** 95 Killian Ave. I-59, exit 11, just e. Ext corridors. **Pets:** Accepted.
⟨ASK⟩ ⊠ ⓜ 🍴 ▣ ⇌

VALDOSTA

Best Western King of the Road 🅷 ❀
(229) 244-7600. **$69-$89, 7 day notice.** 1403 N St Augustine Rd. I-75, exit 18, just w off of SR 94. Ext corridors. **Pets:** Medium. $10 daily fee/room. Designated rooms, service with restrictions, supervision.
SAVE ⊠ 🛏 💻 🍴 ⇨

Comfort Inn Conference Center 🅷
(229) 242-1212. **$95-$100.** 2101 W Hill Ave. I-75, exit 16, just w. Ext/int corridors. **Pets:** Small, other species. Designated rooms, supervision.
SAVE ⊠ 🛏 💻 🍴 ⇨ ⊠

Days Inn I-75 North 🅷
(229) 244-4460. **$54-$79.** 4598 N Valdosta Rd. I-75, exit 22, just w. Ext corridors. **Pets:** Large, other species. $10 daily fee/pet. Service with restrictions, supervision.
ASK ⊠ 🛏 💻 ⇨

Econo Lodge 🅷
(229) 671-1511. **Call for rates.** 3022 James Rd. I-75, exit 18, just w. Int corridors. **Pets:** Accepted.
⊠ 🛏 💻 ⇨

La Quinta Inn & Suites Valdosta 🅷 ❀
(229) 247-7755. **$89-$149.** 1800 Clubhouse Dr. I-75, exit 18, 0.3 mi e, then just s off SR 94. Int corridors. **Pets:** Medium, other species. Service with restrictions, supervision.
SAVE ⊠ 🛏 💻 ⇨

Quality Inn North 🅷
(229) 244-8510. **$55-$75.** 1209 St Augustine Rd. I-75, exit 18, 0.3 mi e on SR 94. Ext corridors. **Pets:** Small, dogs only. $10 daily fee/pet. Service with restrictions, supervision.
SAVE ⊠ 🛏 💻 ⇨

Quality Inn South 🅷
(229) 244-4520. **$50-$90.** 1902 W Hill Ave. I-75, exit 16, just e on US 84. Ext corridors. **Pets:** Medium, other species. $8 daily fee/pet. Service with restrictions, crate.
ASK ⊠ 🛏 💻 ⇨

Ramada Limited Ⓜ
(229) 242-1225. **Call for rates.** 2008 W Hill Ave. I-75, exit 16, just e on US 84. Ext corridors. **Pets:** Accepted.
⊠ 🛏 💻 ⇨

VIDALIA

Days Inn 🅷
(912) 537-9251. **$69-$79, 7 day notice.** 1503 Lyons Hwy E. 1 mi e on US 280. Ext corridors. **Pets:** $5 daily fee/pet. Service with restrictions, supervision.
SAVE ⊠ 🛏 💻 ⇨

Holiday Inn Express 🅷
(912) 537-9000. **$79-$102.** 2619 E First St. 2.5 mi e on US 280. Ext corridors. **Pets:** Accepted.
ASK ⊠ 🛏 💻 ⇨

VILLA RICA

Days Inn 🅷
(770) 459-8888. **$55-$115.** 195 Hwy 61 Connector. I-20, exit 24, just n. Int corridors. **Pets:** Dogs only. $10 daily fee/pet. Designated rooms, service with restrictions, supervision.
ASK ⊠ 🛦 💻 ⇨

Super 8 🅷
(770) 459-8000. **Call for rates.** 128 Hwy 61 Connector. I-20, exit 24, just n. Ext corridors. **Pets:** Accepted.
SAVE ⊠ 🛏 💻 ⇨

WARNER ROBINS

Best Western Peach Inn 🅷
(478) 953-3800. **$49-$69, 7 day notice.** 2739 Watson Blvd. I-75, exit 146 (SR 247C), 4.1 mi e. Ext corridors. **Pets:** Medium. $10 daily fee/pet. Service with restrictions, supervision.
SAVE ⊠ 🛏 💻 ⇨

Comfort Inn & Suites 🅷
(478) 922-7555. **$82-$150.** 95 S Hwy 247. Jct SR 247C and US 129/SR 247, 1.6 mi s on US 129/SR 247. Ext/int corridors. **Pets:** Medium. $10 daily fee/room. Designated rooms, service with restrictions, crate.
ASK ⊠ 🛏 💻 ⇨

Jameson Inn-Warner Robins 🅷
(478) 953-5522. **$78-$85.** 2731 Watson Blvd. I-75, exit 146 (SR 247C), 4.1 mi e. Ext corridors. **Pets:** Very small. $15 daily fee/room. Designated rooms, service with restrictions, supervision.
⊠ 🛏 💻 ⇨

WASHINGTON

Lafayette Manor Inn 🅒
(706) 678-5922. **$125-$175, 14 day notice.** 219 E Robert Toombs Ave (SR 17). Downtown; just e of town square. Int corridors. **Pets:** Accepted.
SAVE ⊠ 🛏 💻 🍴 🐾

WAYCROSS

Jameson Inn Ⓜ
(912) 283-3800. **$73-$78.** 950 City Blvd. Between US 1 and 82, east of city. Ext corridors. **Pets:** Accepted.
ASK ⊠ 🅼 🛏 💻 ⇨

WAYNESBORO

Jameson Inn Ⓜ
(706) 437-0500. **$78-$85.** 1436 N Liberty St. 0.9 mi n of downtown center on US 25. Ext corridors. **Pets:** Accepted.
ASK ⊠ 🛏 💻 ⇨

WINDER

Best Western Winder Hotel 🅷
(770) 868-5303. **$67-$121, 15 day notice.** 177 W Athens St. Jct Broad St, 0.8 mi n; downtown. Int corridors. **Pets:** Accepted.
SAVE ⊠ 🅼 🛏 💻 ⇨

Jameson Inn Ⓜ
(770) 867-1880. **$83-$90.** 9 Stafford St. Jct SR 81, 11, 53 and 8; center. Ext corridors. **Pets:** Small. $10 daily fee/room. Service with restrictions, supervision.
ASK ⊠ 🛏 💻 ⇨

YOUNG HARRIS

Brasstown Valley Resort 🅷
(706) 379-9900. **Call for rates.** 6321 US Hwy 76. US 76 and US 76/SR 515. Int corridors. **Pets:** Accepted.
⊠ 🛏 💻 🍴 ⇨ ⊠

HAWAII

HONOLULU

AAA ◆◆◆ ◆◆◆ The Kahala Hotel & Resort 🏨 ❀
(808) 739-8888. **$395-$4700, 3 day notice.** 5000 Kahala Ave. E of
Diamond Head at end of Kahala Ave. Int corridors. **Pets:** Small, dogs only.
$150 one-time fee/room.
[SAVE] [✕] [&M] [🛏] [💻] [¶¶] [➡] [✕]

KAANAPALI

AAA ◆◆◆ ◆◆◆ The Westin Maui Resort & Spa 🏨 ❀
(808) 667-2525. **Call for rates.** 2365 Kaanapali Pkwy. Off SR 30, via
Kaanapali Pkwy; in Kaanapali Beach resort area. Int corridors.
Pets: Medium, dogs only. Service with restrictions, supervision.
[SAVE] [✕] [&M] [🛏] [💻] [¶¶] [➡] [✕]

KAUPULEHU

◆◆◆ ◆◆◆ Four Seasons Resort Hualalai at Historic
Ka'upulehu 🏨
(808) 325-8000. **$725-$1215, 21 day notice.** 100 Ka'upulehu Dr. Off SR
19, 6 mi n of Kona International Airport. Ext corridors. **Pets:** Accepted.
[✕] [&M] [🛏] [💻] [¶¶] [➡] [✕]

KOHALA COAST

AAA ◆◆◆ ◆◆◆ The Fairmont Orchid, Hawaii 🏨 ❀
(808) 885-2000. **$449-$6799, 14 day notice.** 1 N Kaniku Dr. On SR 19,
20 mi n of Kona International Airport, 2 mi w; in Mauna Lani resort area. Int
corridors. **Pets:** Small. $25 daily fee/pet. Designated rooms, service with
restrictions, supervision.
[SAVE] [✕] [&M] [🛏] [💻] [¶¶] [➡] [✕]

LANAI CITY

◆◆◆ ◆◆◆ Four Seasons Resort Lanai at Manele
Bay 🏨 ❀
(808) 565-2000. **$445-$7000, 21 day notice.** 1 Manele Bay Rd. From
airport, 4 mi e on Kaumalapau Hwy to Lanai City, 7 mi s on SR 440. Ext
corridors. **Pets:** Very small, other species. Service with restrictions, supervision.
[✕] [&M] [🛏] [💻] [¶¶] [➡] [✕]

◆◆◆ ◆◆◆ Four Seasons Resort Lanai, The Lodge at
Koele 🏨 ❀
(808) 565-4000. **$345-$1600, 21 day notice.** One Keomoku Hwy. From
airport, 4 mi e on Kaumalapau Hwy to Lanai City, 2 mi n on SR 440, follow
signs. Int corridors. **Pets:** Very small, other species. Service with restrictions, supervision.
[✕] [&M] [🛏] [💻] [¶¶] [➡] [✕]

WAILEA

AAA ◆◆◆ ◆◆◆ ◆◆◆ Four Seasons Resort, Maui at
Wailea 🏨
(808) 874-8000. **$495-$14000, 21 day notice.** 3900 Wailea Alanui Dr.
From end of SR 31, 0.5 mi s. Int corridors. **Pets:** Accepted.
[SAVE] [✕] [&M] [🛏] [💻] [¶¶] [➡] [✕]

IDAHO

AHSAHKA

AAA **WWWW** **The High Country Inn** BB
(208) 476-7570. **$95-$125, 7 day notice.** 4231 Old Ahsahka Grade Rd. 0.5 mi w to Dworshak Visitors Center Rd, 2 mi n, just w. Ext/int corridors. **Pets:** $25 one-time fee/room. Service with restrictions, supervision.

BLACKFOOT

AAA **WWW** **Best Western Blackfoot Inn** H
(208) 785-4144. **$89-$129.** 750 Jensen Grove Dr. I-15, exit 93, just e on Bergener, then 0.4 mi n on Parkway Dr. Int corridors. **Pets:** Other species. Service with restrictions, supervision.

WW **Super 8** H
(208) 785-9333. **$66-$85.** 1279 Parkway Dr. I-15, exit 93, just e; shared driveway with McDonald's. Int corridors. **Pets:** Other species. $10 one-time fee/room. Service with restrictions, crate.

BLISS

WW **Amber Inn Motel** H
(208) 352-4441. **Call for rates.** 17286 US Hwy 30. I-84, exit 141, just s. Int corridors. **Pets:** Accepted.

BOISE

AAA **WW** **Best Western Airport Inn** H
(208) 384-5000. **$70-$110, 3 day notice.** 2660 Airport Way. I-84, exit 53 (Vista Ave), just s. Ext corridors. **Pets:** Accepted.

WWW **DoubleTree Club Hotel** H
(208) 345-2002. **$75-$179.** 475 W Parkcenter Blvd. I-84, exit 54 (Broadway Ave), 2 mi n, then 0.3 mi e on Beacon St and Parkcenter Blvd. Int corridors. **Pets:** Accepted.

WW **Fairfield Inn by Marriott** H 🐾
(208) 331-5656. **$107-$131.** 3300 S Shoshone St. I-84, exit 53 (Vista Ave), just n to Elder St, then just w. Int corridors. **Pets:** Small. $20 daily fee/pet. Designated rooms, service with restrictions, supervision.

WWW **Hampton Inn** H
(208) 331-5600. **$119-$149.** 3270 S Shoshone St. I-84, exit 53 (Vista Ave), just n to Elder St, then just w. Int corridors. **Pets:** Small, other species. Service with restrictions, supervision.

WWW **Holiday Inn Boise Airport** H 🐾
(208) 343-4900. **$89-$159.** 3300 Vista Ave. I-84, exit 53 (Vista Ave), just n. Int corridors. **Pets:** Other species. $25 one-time fee/room. Service with restrictions, supervision.

WW **Holiday Inn Express** H
(208) 388-0800. **$119-$129.** 2613 S Vista Ave. I-84, exit 53 (Vista Ave), 0.5 mi n. Int corridors. **Pets:** $20 one-time fee/room. Designated rooms, supervision.

AAA **WWWW** **Oxford Suites** H
(208) 322-8000. **$109-$169.** 1426 S Entertainment Ave. I-84, exit 50A westbound; exit 50B eastbound, just s to Spectrum St, just w, then just n. Int corridors. **Pets:** Other species. $25 one-time fee/room. Designated rooms, service with restrictions, supervision.

WWW **Red Lion Hotel Boise Downtowner** H
(208) 344-7691. **$72-$135.** 1800 Fairview Ave. I-184, exit 3 (Fairview Ave), 1 mi n. Int corridors. **Pets:** Other species. $20 one-time fee/room. Service with restrictions, supervision.

WWW **Residence Inn by Marriott-Boise Central** H
(208) 344-1200. **$152-$186.** 1401 S Lusk Ave. I-84, exit 53 (Vista Ave), 2.4 mi n, just w on Ann Morrison, then just s on Lois Ave. Ext corridors. **Pets:** Large, other species. $75 one-time fee/pet. Service with restrictions, crate.

WWW **Residence Inn by Marriott-Boise West** H
(208) 385-9000. **$143-$175.** 7303 W Denton St. I-84, exit 50A westbound; exit 50B eastbound, 2 mi n on Cole Rd, then just w. Int corridors. **Pets:** Other species. $100 one-time fee/room. Service with restrictions, supervision.

AAA **WWW** **Safari Inn Downtown** H
(208) 344-6556. **$79-$99.** 1070 Grove St. At 11th and Grove sts; center. Int corridors. **Pets:** $10 one-time fee/room. Designated rooms, service with restrictions, supervision.

AAA **WWWW** **Shilo Inn Suites-Boise Airport** H 🐾
(208) 343-7662. **$80-$170.** 4111 Broadway Ave. I-84, exit 54 (Broadway Ave), just sw. Int corridors. **Pets:** Dogs only. $25 one-time fee/room. Designated rooms, service with restrictions, supervision.

WWW **SpringHill Suites by Marriott-Boise ParkCenter** H
(208) 342-1044. **$116-$142.** 424 E ParkCenter Blvd. I-84, exit 54 (Broadway Ave), 2.3 mi n, then just e on Beacon and Parkcenter blvds. Int corridors. **Pets:** $50 one-time fee/room. Designated rooms, service with restrictions.

BONNERS FERRY

AAA **WWWW** **Best Western Kootenai River Inn Casino & Spa** H
(208) 267-8511. **$126-$151.** 7169 Plaza St. On US 95; city center. Int corridors. **Pets:** Accepted.

BURLEY

Best Western Burley Inn & Convention Center H ❄
(208) 678-3501. **$66-$90.** 800 N Overland Ave. I-84, exit 208, just s. Ext/int corridors. **Pets:** Medium. $8 daily fee/pet. Designated rooms, service with restrictions, supervision.
SAVE ✕ 🛢 💻 🍴 🏊

Budget Motel M ❄
(208) 678-2200. **$56-$73.** 900 N Overland Ave. I-84, exit 208, just s. Ext corridors. **Pets:** Medium. $8 daily fee/pet. Designated rooms, service with restrictions, supervision.
SAVE ✕ 🛢 🏊

Super 8–Burley H
(208) 678-7000. **$75-$110.** 336 S 600 W. I-84, exit 208, just n. Int corridors. **Pets:** Accepted.
SAVE ✕ 🛢 🏊

CALDWELL

Best Western Caldwell Inn & Suites M ❄
(208) 454-7225. **$72-$99.** 908 Specht Ave. I-84, exit 29, just s. Int corridors. **Pets:** Other species. $10 daily fee/room. Service with restrictions, crate.
SAVE ✕ 🛢 💻 🏊

La Quinta Inn Caldwell H ❄
(208) 454-2222. **$59-$109.** 901 Specht Ave. I-84, exit 29, just s. Int corridors. **Pets:** Medium, other species. Service with restrictions, supervision.
SAVE ✕ 🛢 💻 🏊

COEUR D'ALENE

Best Western Coeur d'Alene Inn & Conference Center H ❄
(208) 765-3200. **$119-$189.** W 506 Appleway Ave. I-90, exit 12, just nw. Int corridors. **Pets:** Large, dogs only. $25 daily fee/pet. Service with restrictions, supervision.
SAVE ✕ 🏊 🛢 💻 🍴 🏊

The Coeur d'Alene Resort H
(208) 765-4000. **$119-$485, 7 day notice.** 115 S 2nd St. I-90, exit 11, 2 mi s. Ext/int corridors. **Pets:** Medium, other species. $75 one-time fee/room. Supervision.
SAVE ✕ 💻 🍴 🏊 🏊

Comfort Inn H ❄
(208) 664-1649. **$64-$259.** 2303 N 4th St. I-90, exit 13, just n. Int corridors. **Pets:** Medium, other species. $30 one-time fee/room. Service with restrictions, supervision.
SAVE ✕ 🛢 💻 🏊

Days Inn-Coeur d'Alene H ❄
(208) 667-8668. **$65-$170.** 2200 Northwest Blvd. I-90, exit 11, just se. Int corridors. **Pets:** Other species. $5 daily fee/pet. Service with restrictions, supervision.
SAVE ✕ 🏊 🛢 💻

Guest House Inn & Suites H
(208) 765-3011. **Call for rates.** 330 W Appleway Ave. I-90, exit 12, just n, then just e. Int corridors. **Pets:** Accepted.
✕ 🛢 💻

Holiday Inn Express Hotel & Suites Coeur d'Alene H
(208) 667-3100. **Call for rates.** 2300 W Seltice Way. I-90, exit 11, just s. Int corridors. **Pets:** Accepted.
✕ 🛢 💻 🏊

La Quinta Inn & Suites Coeur D'Alene (East) H ❄
(208) 667-6777. **$69-$189.** 2209 E Sherman Ave. I-90, exit 15 (Sherman Ave), just s. Int corridors. **Pets:** Medium, other species. Service with restrictions, supervision.
SAVE ✕ 🏊 🛢 💻 🏊

La Quinta Inn Coeur D'Alene (Appleway) H ❄
(208) 765-5500. **$79-$159.** 280 W Appleway Ave. I-90, exit 12, just ne. Int corridors. **Pets:** Medium, other species. Service with restrictions, supervision.
ASK ✕ 🏊 🛢 💻 🏊 ✕

The Roosevelt Inn, Inc BB
(208) 765-5200. **$89-$319, 14 day notice.** 105 Wallace Ave. I-90, exit 13, 2 mi s, then just w; downtown. Int corridors. **Pets:** Accepted.
SAVE ✕ ✕ 🅦 🎵

Shilo Inn Suites–Coeur d'Alene H ❄
(208) 664-2300. **$90-$200.** 702 W Appleway Ave. I-90, exit 12, just n, then just w. Int corridors. **Pets:** Dogs only. $25 one-time fee/room. Designated rooms, service with restrictions, supervision.
SAVE ✕ 🏊 🛢 💻 🏊 ✕

HAGERMAN

Hagerman Valley Inn M
(208) 837-6196. **$63-$108.** 661 Frog's Landing. South end of town on US 30. Ext/int corridors. **Pets:** $7 daily fee/pet. Designated rooms, service with restrictions, supervision.
SAVE ✕ 🛢

HAILEY

Airport Inn M
(208) 788-2477. **Call for rates.** 820 4th Ave S. Just n of SR 75 at 4th Ave; near airport. Ext corridors. **Pets:** Accepted.
✕ 🛢 💻

AmericInn Lodge & Suites of Hailey H
(208) 788-7950. **$89-$209.** 51 Cobblestone Ln. Just n on SR 75, then just e. Int corridors. **Pets:** Dogs only. $15 one-time fee/room. Designated rooms, service with restrictions, supervision.
SAVE ✕ 🏊 🛢 💻 🏊 ✕

Wood River Inn H
(208) 578-0600. **$106-$143.** 603 N Main St. Just n of downtown on SR 75. Int corridors. **Pets:** $25 one-time fee/room. Designated rooms, service with restrictions, supervision.
ASK ✕ 🏊 🛢 💻 🏊 ✕

HAYDEN

Holiday Inn Express Hotel & Suites H ❄
(208) 772-7900. **$90-$370.** 151 W Orchard Ave. I-90, exit 12, 3.5 mi n. Int corridors. **Pets:** Large, other species. $10 daily fee/pet. Supervision.
ASK ✕ 🏊 🛢 💻 🏊 ✕

IDAHO FALLS

Best Western Driftwood Inn H ❄
(208) 523-2242. **$69-$139.** 575 River Pkwy. I-15, exit 118 (Broadway), 0.5 mi e, then 0.3 mi n. Ext corridors. **Pets:** Other species. $10 daily fee/pet. Service with restrictions, supervision.
SAVE ✕ 🛢 💻 🏊 ✕

GuestHouse Inn & Suites H
(208) 523-6260. **$59-$150.** 850 Lindsay Blvd. I-15, exit 119, just e. Ext/int corridors. **Pets:** Accepted.
ASK ✕ 🛢 💻 🍴 🏊

Le Ritz Hotel & Suites H
(208) 528-0880. **$105-$129.** 720 Lindsay Blvd. I-15, exit 118 (Broadway), 0.5 mi e, then just n. Int corridors. **Pets:** Accepted.
SAVE ✕ 🛢 💻 🏊

♦♦ ♦♦ Red Lion Hotel on the Falls **H**
(208) 523-8000. **Call for rates.** 475 River Pkwy. I-15, exit 118 (Broadway), 0.5 mi e, then just n. Ext/int corridors. **Pets:** Other species. $20 one-time fee/room. Service with restrictions, supervision.
⊠ 🛏 🖥 🍴 ➰ 🖾

(AAA) ♦♦♦ Shilo Inn Suites Hotel-Idaho Falls **H** ❖
(208) 523-0088. **$95-$190.** 780 Lindsay Blvd. I-15, exit 119, just se. Int corridors. **Pets:** Dogs only. $25 one-time fee/room. Designated rooms, service with restrictions, supervision.
SAVE ⊠ 🛏 🖥 🍴 ➰ 🖾

JACKSON HOLE AREA (NEARBY WYOMING)

DRIGGS

♦♦ Teton Valley Cabins **CA**
(208) 354-8153. **$79-$109, 7 day notice.** 34 Ski Hill Rd. 0.8 mi e on Little Ave from SR 33 E. Ext corridors. **Pets:** Accepted.
⊠ 🛏 🖥 🖾 🎿

END AREA

JEROME

(AAA) ♦♦♦♦ Best Western Sawtooth Inn and Suites **H** ❖
(208) 324-9200. **$90-$210, 3 day notice.** 2653 S Lincoln Ave. I-84, exit 168, just n on SR 79. Int corridors. **Pets:** Other species. $100 deposit/room. Designated rooms, service with restrictions, crate.
SAVE ⊠ 🛏 🖥 ➰

KELLOGG

(AAA) ♦♦♦ Baymont Inn & Suites **H** ❖
(208) 783-1234. **$60-$109.** 601 Bunker Ave. I-90, exit 49, 0.5 mi se. Int corridors. **Pets:** Other species. $20 deposit/pet, $5 daily fee/pet. Designated rooms, service with restrictions.
SAVE ⊠ 🔊 🛏 🖥 ➰

♦♦♦♦ Morning Star Lodge **M**
(208) 783-0202. **$143-$590.** 602 Bunker Ave. I-90, exit 49, 0.5 mi se. Int corridors. **Pets:** Other species. $30 one-time fee/room. Designated rooms, service with restrictions.
ASK ⊠ 🛏 🖥 🍴 🖾

♦♦ Silverhorn Motor Inn **H** ❖
(208) 783-1151. **$69-$89.** 699 W Cameron Ave. I-90, exit 49, just ne. Int corridors. **Pets:** Other species. Supervision.
ASK ⊠ 🛏 🍴

KETCHUM

(AAA) ♦♦♦♦ Best Western Tyrolean Lodge **H**
(208) 726-5336. **$89-$169, 3 day notice.** 260 Cottonwood St. South end of town; just w of SR 75 (Main St) on Rivers St, then just s on 3rd Ave. Int corridors. **Pets:** Accepted.
SAVE ⊠ 🛏 🖥 ➰ 🖾

♦♦ Tamarack Lodge **M**
(208) 726-3344. **$89-$164, 3 day notice.** 291 Walnut Ave N. Just ne on Sun Valley Rd from jct SR 75 (Main St); downtown. Ext/int corridors. **Pets:** Accepted.
ASK ⊠ 🛏 🖥 ➰

KOOSKIA

♦♦♦ River Dance Lodge **CA** ❖
(208) 926-4300. **$129-$159, 45 day notice.** 7743 Hwy 12. On US 12, 16 mi e. Ext corridors. **Pets:** Dogs only. $50 deposit/room, $10 daily fee/pet. Designated rooms, service with restrictions, supervision.
⊠ 🛏 🖥 🍴 🖾 🎿 🐾 🍴

LEWISTON

♦♦ Comfort Inn **H**
(208) 798-8090. **$70-$150.** 2128 8th Ave. 1.2 mi s on US 12 from jct US 95, just s on 21st St. Int corridors. **Pets:** Medium. $10 daily fee/room. Service with restrictions, supervision.
ASK ⊠ 🔊 🛏 🖥 ➰

(AAA) ♦♦♦♦ Holiday Inn Express **H** ❖
(208) 750-1600. **$79-$189.** 2425 Nez Perce Dr. 1.2 mi s on US 12 from jct US 95, 1.2 mi s on 21st St, then just e. Int corridors. **Pets:** Large, other species. $10 one-time fee/room. Service with restrictions, crate.
SAVE ⊠ 🔊 🛏 🖥 ➰ 🖾

♦♦ Super 8 **H**
(208) 743-8808. **$53-$71.** 3120 North & South Hwy. Just e on US 12 from jct US 95. Int corridors. **Pets:** $10 one-time fee/pet. Service with restrictions, supervision.
ASK ⊠ 🔊 🛏

LOWER STANLEY

(AAA) ♦♦ Salmon River Cabins & Motel **CA**
(208) 774-3566. **$70-$135, 7 day notice.** 55 Lower Stanley (US Hwy 75). 1 mi n on US 75 from jct SR 21. Ext corridors. **Pets:** Dogs only. $10 daily fee/pet. Service with restrictions, supervision.
SAVE ⊠ 🛏 🖥 🎿

MCCALL

(AAA) ♦♦♦ AmericInn Lodge & Suites of McCall **H** ❖
(208) 634-2230. **$130-$140.** 211 S 3rd St. On SR 55; south end of town. Int corridors. **Pets:** Other species. $10 daily fee/pet. Service with restrictions, supervision.
SAVE ⊠ 🔊 🛏 🖥 ➰ 🖾

(AAA) ♦♦♦ Super 8–McCall **M** ❖
(208) 634-4637. **$89-$109.** 303 S 3rd St. On SR 55; south end of town. Int corridors. **Pets:** $10 daily fee/pet. Designated rooms, service with restrictions, supervision.
SAVE ⊠ 🔊 🛏 🖥

(AAA) ♦♦♦ Western Mountain Lodge **H**
(208) 634-6300. **$94-$160.** 415 N 3rd St. SR 55, just s of jct Lake St. Int corridors. **Pets:** Accepted.
SAVE ⊠ 🔊 🛏 🖥 ➰

MONTPELIER

(AAA) ♦♦♦ Clover Creek Inn **H**
(208) 847-1782. **$79-$85.** 243 N 4th St. Just n on US 30 from jct US 89 S. Ext corridors. **Pets:** Accepted.
SAVE ⊠ 🛏 🖥

MOSCOW

◊◊◊◊ **▼▼▼** Best Western University Inn **H**
(208) 882-0550. **$104-$109, 3 day notice.** 1516 Pullman Rd. Jct US 95, 1 mi w on SR 8. Int corridors. **Pets:** Small. $25 daily fee/room. Service with restrictions, crate.
SAVE ✕ &M ⬛ 💻 ¶¶ ⤳ ✕

▼▼▼ La Quinta Inn **H** ❀
(208) 882-5365. **$89-$159.** 185 Warbonnet Dr. 1.6 mi w on SR 8 from jct US 93, just n. Int corridors. **Pets:** Medium, other species. Service with restrictions, supervision.
ASK ✕ ⬛ 💻 ⤳

▼▼ Super 8 **H**
(208) 883-1503. **Call for rates.** 175 Peterson Dr. Jct US 95, 0.8 mi w on SR 8, just n. Int corridors. **Pets:** $10 daily fee/pet. Service with restrictions, supervision.
✕ ⬛ 💻

MOUNTAIN HOME

◊◊◊◊ **▼▼▼** Best Western Foothills Motor Inn **H**
(208) 587-8477. **$85-$120, 3 day notice.** 1080 Hwy 20. I-84, exit 95, just n. Ext corridors. **Pets:** Accepted.
SAVE ✕ &M ⬛ 💻 ⤳

▼▼ Sleep Inn **H**
(208) 587-9743. **$70-$95.** 1180 Hwy 20. I-84, exit 95, just n. Int corridors. **Pets:** Accepted.
ASK ✕ ⬛ 💻

NAMPA

◊◊◊◊ **▼▼▼▼** Shilo Inn Suites Hotel-Nampa **H** ❀
(208) 465-3250. **$90-$170.** 1401 Shilo Dr. I-84, exit 36, just nw. Int corridors. **Pets:** Dogs only. $25 one-time fee/room. Service with restrictions, supervision.
SAVE ✕ ⬛ 💻 ¶¶ ⤳ ✕

OROFINO

◊◊◊◊ **▼▼▼▼** Best Western Lodge at River's Edge **H**
(208) 476-9999. **$80-$126.** 615 Main St. Downtown. Int corridors. **Pets:** Accepted.
SAVE ✕ ⬛ 💻 ¶¶ ⤳ ✕

◊◊◊◊ **▼▼▼** Konkolville Motel **M**
(208) 476-5584. **$60-$90.** 2000 Konkolville Rd. 2.7 mi e on Michigan Ave. Ext corridors. **Pets:** Other species. $10 daily fee/pet. Designated rooms, service with restrictions, supervision.
SAVE ✕ &M ⬛ 💻 ⤳

POCATELLO

◊◊◊◊ **▼▼▼▼** Best Western CottonTree Inn **H**
(208) 237-7650. **$86-$110.** 1415 Bench Rd. I-15, exit 71, just e. Int corridors. **Pets:** Accepted.
SAVE ✕ ⬛ 💻 ⤳

◊◊◊◊ **▼▼▼** Comfort Inn **H**
(208) 237-8155. **$70-$100.** 1333 Bench Rd. I-15, exit 71, just e. Int corridors. **Pets:** Medium, dogs only. $10 daily fee/pet. Designated rooms, service with restrictions, supervision.
SAVE ✕ ⬛ 💻 ⤳

▼▼▼▼ Holiday Inn-Pocatello **H**
(208) 237-1400. **$79-$99.** 1399 Bench Rd. I-15, exit 71, just e. Ext/int corridors. **Pets:** Other species. $10 daily fee/room. Designated rooms, service with restrictions, crate.
ASK ✕ ⬛ 💻 ¶¶ ⤳ ✕

◊◊◊◊ **▼▼▼** Pocatello Super 8 Motel **H**
(208) 234-0888. **$65-$115.** 1330 Bench Rd. I-15, exit 71, just e. Int corridors. **Pets:** Other species. $10 one-time fee/room. Designated rooms, service with restrictions, supervision.
SAVE ✕ ⬛ 💻

▼▼▼ Ramada Inn & Convention Center **H**
(208) 237-0020. **Call for rates.** 133 W Burnside Ave. I-86, exit 61, just n. Int corridors. **Pets:** Accepted.
✕ ⬛ 💻 ¶¶ ⤳ ✕

◊◊◊◊ **▼▼▼** Red Lion Hotel Pocatello **H**
(208) 233-2200. **$130.** 1555 Pocatello Creek Rd. I-15, exit 71, just e. Int corridors. **Pets:** Other species. $20 one-time fee/room. Service with restrictions, supervision.
SAVE ✕ ⬛ 💻 ¶¶ ⤳ ✕

▼▼ Thunderbird Motel **M**
(208) 232-6330. **$40-$69.** 1415 S 5th Ave. I-15, exit 67, 1.3 mi n; just s of Idaho State University. Ext corridors. **Pets:** Other species. $5 daily fee/pet. Service with restrictions, supervision.
ASK ✕ ⬛ ⤳

▼▼▼▼ TownePlace Suites by Marriott **H**
(208) 478-7000. **$98-$120.** 2376 Via Caporatti Dr. I-15, exit 69 (Clark St), just e. Int corridors. **Pets:** Large, other species. $100 one-time fee/room. Service with restrictions, supervision.
✕ &M ⬛ ⤳

PONDERAY

◊◊◊◊ **▼▼▼** Motel 6 **H**
(208) 263-5383. **$50-$120.** 477255 Hwy 95 N. 1.2 mi n on US 95 from jct SR 200. Int corridors. **Pets:** Accepted.
SAVE ✕ &M ⬛

▼▼ Super 8 **H**
(208) 263-2210. **Call for rates.** 476841 Hwy 95 N. 0.7 mi n on US 95 from jct SR 200. Int corridors. **Pets:** Accepted.
✕ &M ⬛

POST FALLS

◊◊◊◊ **▼▼▼▼** Comfort Inn Post Falls **H**
(208) 773-8900. **$61-$249.** 3175 E Seltice Way. I-90, exit 7, just sw. Int corridors. **Pets:** Accepted.
SAVE ✕ &M ⬛ 💻

▼▼ Howard Johnson Express **H**
(208) 773-4541. **$59-$139.** 3647 W 5th Ave. I-90, exit 2, just ne. Int corridors. **Pets:** Other species. $10 daily fee/pet. Service with restrictions, supervision.
ASK ✕ &M ⬛ 💻 ⤳

◊◊◊◊ **▼▼▼▼** Red Lion Templin's Hotel on the River–Post Falls **H**
(208) 773-1611. **$99-$190.** 414 E First Ave. I-90, exit 5 eastbound, just s to First Ave; exit 6 westbound, 0.7 mi w on Seltice Way to Spokane St, 0.5 mi s, then just e. Int corridors. **Pets:** Other species. $20 one-time fee/room. Service with restrictions, supervision.
SAVE ✕ &M ⬛ 💻 ¶¶ ⤳ ✕

▼▼ Sleep Inn **H**
(208) 777-9394. **$59-$139, 7 day notice.** 157 S Pleasant View Rd. I-90, exit 2, just s. Int corridors. **Pets:** Dogs only. $15 one-time fee/room. Service with restrictions, supervision.
ASK ✕ &M ⬛ 💻 ⤳

PRIEST RIVER

▼▼ Eagle's Nest Motel **M**
(208) 448-2000. **$52-$100.** 1007 Albeni Hwy (US 2). US 2, 0.5 mi w. Ext corridors. **Pets:** Accepted.
ASK ✕ &M ⬛ 💻

REXBURG

AmericInn Lodge & Suites of Rexburg 🅷
(208) 356-5333. **$80-$210.** 1098 Golden Beauty Dr. US 20, exit 332 (S Rexburg). Int corridors. **Pets:** $20 one-time fee/room. Designated rooms, crate.

SAVE ⊠ 🍴 🖃 🕭 ⊠

Best Western Mountain View Inn 🅷
(208) 356-4646. **$75-$150.** 450 W 4th St S. US 20, exit 332 (S Rexburg), 1 mi e. Int corridors. **Pets:** Accepted.

SAVE ⊠ 🍴 🖃 🕭

Comfort Inn 🅷
(208) 359-1311. **$79-$129.** 885 W Main St. US 20, exit 333 (Salmon), just e. Int corridors. **Pets:** Other species. Service with restrictions, supervision.

SAVE ⊠ 🍴 🖃 🕭

RIGGINS

Best Western Salmon Rapids Lodge 🅷 ❋
(208) 628-2743. **$95-$198.** 1010 S Main St. Just e of US 95; downtown. Int corridors. **Pets:** Other species. $15 daily fee/pet. Designated rooms, service with restrictions, supervision.

SAVE ⊠ ⎙ 🍴 🖃 🕭

Pinehurst Resort Cabins 🅲🅰 ❋
(208) 628-3323. **$55-$95.** 5604 Hwy 95. On US 95, 13 mi s. Ext corridors. **Pets:** Dogs only. $10 daily fee/room. Designated rooms with restrictions, supervision.

ASK ⊠ 🍴 🖃 🗷 🔁

SAGLE

Bottle Bay Resort & Marina 🅲🅰
(208) 263-5916. **Call for rates.** 115 Resort Rd. 8.3 mi e on Bottle Bay Rd from US 95. Ext corridors. **Pets:** Accepted.

🍴 🖃 🍽 ⊠ 🗷 🔁

SALMON

Stagecoach Inn 🅼
(208) 756-2919. **$61-$85, 7 day notice.** 201 Hwy 93 N. Just n on US 93 from jct SR 28. Int corridors. **Pets:** Other species. $15 daily fee/pet. Designated rooms, service with restrictions, supervision.

ASK ⊠ 🍴 🖃 🕭

SANDPOINT

Best Western Edgewater Resort 🅷
(208) 263-3194. **$109-$299.** 56 Bridge St. Just e of US 95 N; downtown. Int corridors. **Pets:** Other species. $10 daily fee/pet. Service with restrictions, supervision.

SAVE ⊠ 🍴 🖃 🍽 🕭 ⊠

The K2 Inn 🅼
(208) 263-3441. **$69-$139.** 501 N Fourth Ave. US 95, just e. Ext corridors. **Pets:** Medium, dogs only. $15 one-time fee/pet. Designated rooms, service with restrictions, supervision.

ASK ⊠ 🍴

La Quinta Inn Sandpoint 🅷 ❋
(208) 263-9581. **$89-$299.** 415 Cedar St. Jct US 2 and 95; downtown. Ext/int corridors. **Pets:** Medium, other species. Service with restrictions, supervision.

ASK ⊠ ⎙ 🍴 🖃 🍽 🕭

Quality Inn Sandpoint 🅷
(208) 263-2111. **$79-$189.** 807 N 5th Ave. US 2 and 95, just s of jct SR 200. Int corridors. **Pets:** Other species. $10 daily fee/pet. Service with restrictions, supervision.

ASK ⊠ 🍴 🖃 🍽 🕭

TWIN FALLS

Best Western Twin Falls Hotel 🅷
(208) 736-8000. **$90-$130.** 1377 Blue Lakes Blvd N. I-84, exit 173, 3.9 mi s on US 93. Int corridors. **Pets:** Small, other species. $20 daily fee/pet. Designated rooms, service with restrictions, supervision.

SAVE ⊠ ⎙ 🍴 🖃 🕭 ⊠

Comfort Inn 🅷
(208) 734-7494. **$79-$200.** 1893 Canyon Springs Rd. I-84, exit 173, 3.5 mi s on US 93. Int corridors. **Pets:** Accepted.

ASK ⊠ 🍴 🖃 🕭

Days Inn 🅷
(208) 324-6400. **$74-$94.** 1200 Centennial Spur. I-84, exit 173, just n on US 93. Int corridors. **Pets:** Accepted.

ASK ⊠ 🍴 🖃

Red Lion Hotel Canyon Springs 🅷
(208) 734-5000. **$90-$169.** 1357 Blue Lakes Blvd N. I-84, exit 173, 4 mi s on US 93. Int corridors. **Pets:** Other species. $20 one-time fee/room. Service with restrictions, supervision.

SAVE ⊠ ⎙ 🍴 🖃 🍽 🕭

Shilo Inn Suites Hotel-Twin Falls 🅷 ❋
(208) 733-7545. **$100-$210.** 1586 Blue Lakes Blvd N. I-84, exit 173, 3.7 mi s on US 93. Int corridors. **Pets:** Dogs only. $25 one-time fee/room. Designated rooms, service with restrictions, supervision.

SAVE ⊠ 🍴 🖃 🕭 ⊠

Twin Falls Super 8 🅼
(208) 734-5801. **Call for rates.** 1260 Blue Lakes Blvd N. I-84, exit 173, 4.1 mi s on US 93. Int corridors. **Pets:** Accepted.

⊠ 🍴 🖃

WALLACE

Stardust Motel 🅼
(208) 752-1213. **$52-$130.** 410 Pine St. I-90, exit 61 (Business Rt 90), 0.7 mi e; downtown. Ext corridors. **Pets:** Other species. $20 daily fee/pet. Service with restrictions, supervision.

SAVE ⊠ 🍴 🖃

The Wallace Inn 🅷
(208) 752-1252. **$88-$124, 3 day notice.** 100 Front St. I-90, exit 61 (Business Rt 90), just se. Int corridors. **Pets:** Other species. $25 daily fee/pet, $25 one-time fee/pet. Service with restrictions, supervision.

SAVE ⊠ ⎙ 🍴 🖃 🍽 🕭 ⊠

WHITE BIRD

Hells Canyon Jet Boat Trips & Lodging 🅼
(208) 839-2255. **$70-$80, 7 day notice.** 3252 Waterfront Dr. 1 mi s of White Bird on Old Hwy 95. Ext corridors. **Pets:** $15 daily fee/pet. Service with restrictions, supervision.

⊠ 🍴 🖃 ⊠ 🔁

WORLEY

Coeur d'Alene Casino Resort Hotel 🅷
(208) 686-0248. **Call for rates.** 27068 S Hwy 95. On US 95, 3 mi n. Int corridors. **Pets:** $25 deposit/room, $15 daily fee/pet. Designated rooms, service with restrictions, supervision.

⊠ 🍴 🖃 🍽 🕭 ⊠

ILLINOIS

ALTON

▼▼ Comfort Inn H
(618) 465-9999. **$85-$99.** 11 Crossroads Ct. Off SR 3, jct SR 140. Int corridors. **Pets:** Other species. Service with restrictions, supervision.
ASK ✕ &M 🗋 💷 ➬

▼ Super 8 Motel H
(618) 465-8885. **$54-$80.** 1800 Homer Adams Pkwy. On SR 111, 1.8 mi e of jct US 67. Int corridors. **Pets:** $50 deposit/room. Service with restrictions, supervision.
ASK ✕ &M 🗋 💷

ANNAWAN

▲▲▲ ▼▼▼▼ Best Western Annawan Inn H
(309) 935-6565. **$80-$110.** 315 N Canal St. I-80, exit 33, just s. Int corridors. **Pets:** $10 daily fee/pet. Service with restrictions, supervision.
SAVE ✕ &M 🗋 💷 ➬

ARCOLA

▼▼ Comfort Inn H
(217) 268-4000. **$45-$120.** 610 E Springfield Rd. I-57, exit 203 (SR 133), just w. Int corridors. **Pets:** Small. $10 daily fee/pet. Service with restrictions, supervision.
ASK ✕ 🗋 💷 ➬

BELLEVILLE

▲▲▲ ▼ The Shrine Hotel H
(618) 397-1162. **$70-$85.** 451 S Demazenod Dr. I-255, exit 17A, 1 mi e on SR 15; in Shrine of Our Lady of the Snows Complex. Int corridors. **Pets:** Medium, other species. Service with restrictions, crate.
SAVE ✕ 🗋 💷 🍴 ✕

BLOOMINGTON

▲▲▲ ▼▼▼ Baymont Inn & Suites H
(309) 662-2800. **$62-$92.** 604 1/2 IAA Dr. I-55, exit 167 southbound, follow I-55 business route (Veterans Pkwy), 2.8 mi s to jct SR 9, just e, then just n via service road; exit 157B (Veterans Pkwy) northbound, 4 mi n to SR 9. Int corridors. **Pets:** Other species. $10 daily fee/pet. Service with restrictions, supervision.
SAVE ✕ 🗋 💷 ➬

▼▼▼ Comfort Inn by Choice Hotels H
(309) 828-6000. **Call for rates.** 505 Brock Dr. I-55/74, exit 160 (SR 9), just e. Int corridors. **Pets:** Accepted.
✕ 🗋 💷

▲▲▲ ▼▼▼▼ Country Inn & Suites By Carlson Bloomington/Normal-Airport H
(309) 662-3100. **$89-$139.** 2403 E Empire St. Jct I-55 business route (Veterans Pkwy) and SR 9, 0.8 mi e. Int corridors. **Pets:** Small, other species. $15 daily fee/pet. Service with restrictions, supervision.
SAVE ✕ 🗋 💷 ➬ ✕

▲▲▲ ▼▼▼▼ DoubleTree Hotel Bloomington H
(309) 664-6446. **$99-$189.** 10 Brickyard Dr. I-55 business route (Veterans Pkwy), just n of US 150. Int corridors. **Pets:** Other species. $50 one-time fee/pet. Service with restrictions, supervision.
SAVE ✕ 🗋 💷 🍴 ➬ ✕

▼▼ Eastland Suites Hotel & Conference Center H
(309) 662-0000. **$99-$169.** 1801 Eastland Dr. Jct I-55 business route (Veterans Pkwy) and SR 9, just s to Eastland Dr, then just e. Ext/int corridors. **Pets:** Small, other species. $50 deposit/pet. Designated rooms, service with restrictions, crate.
ASK ✕ 🗋 💷 ➬

▼▼ Econo Lodge by Choice Hotels M
(309) 829-3100. **$45-$105.** 403 Brock Dr. I-55/74, exit 160 (SR 9), just e. Ext corridors. **Pets:** Large. $10 one-time fee/pet. Service with restrictions, supervision.
ASK ✕ 🗋 💷

▼▼ Extended StayAmerica Bloomington-Normal H
(309) 662-8533. **$59-$109.** 1805 S Veterans Pkwy. I-74/55, exit 134B, 2.8 mi n on US 55 business route. Int corridors. **Pets:** Other species. $25 daily fee/pet. Service with restrictions, crate.
ASK ✕ 🗋 💷

▼▼ Ramada Limited & Suites Bloomington/Normal-West H
(309) 828-0900. **$69-$129.** 919 Maple Hill Rd. I-55/74, exit 160 (SR 9), 0.3 mi w to Wylie Dr, just n, then just e. Int corridors. **Pets:** Large, other species. $10 daily fee/pet. Service with restrictions, crate.
ASK ✕ 🗋 💷 ➬

CARBONDALE

▼▼▼▼ Hampton Inn ☐
(618) 549-6900. **$149.** 2175 Reed Station Pkwy. I-57, exit 54B, 11.7 mi w on SR 13. Int corridors. **Pets:** Accepted.
☒ ☐ ☐ ☐ ☐

▼▼▼▼ Holiday Inn Hotel and Conference Center ☐
(618) 549-2600. **$119-$149.** 2300 Reed Station Pkwy. I-57, exit 54B, 12 mi w. Int corridors. **Pets:** Accepted.
(ASK) ☒ ☐ ☐ ☐ ☐ ☐ ☐

▼▼▼ Super 8 Motel ☐
(618) 457-8822. **$56-$95.** 1180 E Main St. I-57, exit 54B, 13.9 mi w on SR 13. Int corridors. **Pets:** Service with restrictions, supervision.
(ASK) ☒ ☐ ☐

CARLINVILLE

◭◭◭⁷ ▼▼▼ Best Western Carlinville Inn ☐
(217) 324-2100. **$90-$97.** 19067 W Frontage Rd. I-55, exit 60 (SR 108), just w. Int corridors. **Pets:** Small. $10 one-time fee/room. Service with restrictions, supervision.
(SAVE) ☒ ☐ ☐ ☐ ☐ ☐

CHAMPAIGN

◭◭◭⁷ ▼▼▼ Baymont Inn & Suites ☐
(217) 356-8900. **$79-$199.** 302 W Anthony Dr. I-74, exit 182 (Neil St), just nw. Int corridors. **Pets:** Medium. $10 daily fee/pet. Designated rooms, service with restrictions, supervision.
(SAVE) ☒ ☐ ☐

◭◭◭⁷ ▼▼▼▼ Country Inn & Suites by Carlson ☐
(217) 355-6666. **$100.** 602 W Marketview Dr. I-74, exit 181 (Prospect Ave), just n, then just e. Int corridors. **Pets:** Small, other species. $15 daily fee/room. Service with restrictions, crate.
(SAVE) ☒ ☐ ☐ ☐

▼▼▼▼ Drury Inn & Suites-Champaign ☐
(217) 398-0030. **$100-$170.** 905 W Anthony Dr. I-74, exit 181 (Prospect Ave), just n. Int corridors. **Pets:** Other species. Service with restrictions, supervision.
(ASK) ☒ ☐ ☐ ☐ ☐

▼▼▼ Extended StayAmerica-Champaign-Urbana ☐
(217) 351-8899. **$59-$129.** 610 W Marketview Dr. I-74, exit 181 (Prospect Ave), just n, then just e. Int corridors. **Pets:** Other species. $25 daily fee/pet. Service with restrictions, crate.
(ASK) ☒ ☐ ☐

◭◭◭⁷ ▼▼▼▼ Hawthorn Suites Champaign ☐
(217) 398-3400. **Call for rates.** 101 Trade Centre Dr. I-74, exit 182 (Neil St), 2.5 mi s. Int corridors. **Pets:** Other species. $25 one-time fee/room. Service with restrictions, crate.
(SAVE) ☒ ☐ ☐ ☐ ☐ ☐

▼▼▼ La Quinta Inn Champaign ☐ ❀
(217) 356-4000. **$59-$119.** 1900 Center Dr. I-74, exit 182B (Neil St), just n. Int corridors. **Pets:** Medium, other species. Service with restrictions, supervision.
(ASK) ☒ ☐ ☐ ☐ ☐

CHESTER

◭◭◭⁷ ▼▼▼ Best Western Reids' Inn ☐
(618) 826-3034. **$80-$90.** 2150 State St. SR 150, 1 mi e of SR 3. Int corridors. **Pets:** Accepted.
(SAVE) ☒ ☐ ☐ ☐ ☐

CHICAGO METROPOLITAN AREA

ALGONQUIN

▼▼▼▼ Holiday Inn Express Hotel & Suites ☐
(847) 458-6000. **Call for rates.** 2595 Bunker Hill Rd. I-90, exit Randall Rd N, 6.1 mi n to Bunker Hill Rd, then just w. Int corridors. **Pets:** Accepted.
☒ ☐ ☐ ☐ ☐ ☐

ALSIP

▼▼▼ Baymont Inn-Midway South ☐
(708) 597-3900. **$89-$139.** 12801 S Cicero Ave. I-294, exit SR 50 (Cicero Ave S). Int corridors. **Pets:** Medium. $50 deposit/room, $10 one-time fee/room. Service with restrictions, crate.
(ASK) ☒ ☐ ☐

ANTIOCH

◭◭◭⁷ ▼▼▼ Comfort Inn & Suites by Choice Hotels ☐
(847) 395-3606. **$90-$150.** 350 Rt 173. SR 173, 0.5 mi w of jct SR 83. Int corridors. **Pets:** Medium. $15 daily fee/pet. Designated rooms, service with restrictions, supervision.
(SAVE) ☒ ☐ ☐ ☐

ARLINGTON HEIGHTS

▼▼▼▼ DoubleTree Hotel Chicago-Arlington Heights ☐ ❀
(847) 364-7600. **$99-$209.** 75 W Algonquin Rd. I-90, exit Arlington Heights Rd, just n to Algonquin Rd, then just w. Int corridors. **Pets:** Large. $100 deposit/room. Designated rooms, service with restrictions, crate.
☒ ☐ ☐ ☐ ☐ ☐ ☐

▼▼▼ Jameson Suites ☐
(847) 956-1400. **Call for rates.** 2111 S Arlington Heights Rd. I-90, exit Arlington Heights Rd, 0.6 mi n. Int corridors. **Pets:** Medium, other species. $15 daily fee/pet. Service with restrictions.
☒ ☐ ☐ ☐

▼▼▼ La Quinta Inn Chicago (Arlington Heights) ☐ ❀
(847) 253-8777. **$69-$119.** 1415 W Dundee Rd. SR 53, exit Dundee Rd, just e. Int corridors. **Pets:** Medium, other species. Service with restrictions, supervision.
(ASK) ☒ ☐ ☐ ☐

▼▼▼ Motel 6–1048 ☐
(847) 806-1230. **$51-$61.** 441 W Algonquin Rd. I-90, exit Arlington Heights Rd, 0.5 mi n, then 0.5 mi w. Int corridors. **Pets:** Other species. Service with restrictions, supervision.
☒ ☐ ☐

◭◭◭⁷ ▼▼ Red Roof Inn #7102 ☐
(847) 228-6650. **$60-$90.** 22 W Algonquin Rd. I-90, exit Arlington Heights Rd, 0.5 mi n, then just w. Ext corridors. **Pets:** Other species. Service with restrictions.
(SAVE) ☒

◭◭◭⁷ ▼▼▼▼ Sheraton Chicago Northwest and CoCo Key Water Resort ☐
(847) 394-2000. **$139-$319.** 3400 W Euclid Ave. SR 53, exit Euclid Ave, just e. Int corridors. **Pets:** Accepted.
(SAVE) ☒ ☐ ☐ ☐ ☐ ☐

AURORA

▼▼ Staybridge Suites by Holiday Inn Aurora/Naperville �H
(630) 978-2222. **$169-$199.** 4320 Meridian Pkwy. I-88, exit SR 59, 2 mi s to Meridian Pkwy, then just w. Int corridors. **Pets:** Accepted.

🅰️🆂🅺 ✖ 🕭 🖥 🚾 ✖

BANNOCKBURN

▼▼▼ La Quinta Inn & Suites Deerfield �H ✿
(847) 317-7300. **$79-$189.** 2000 S Lakeside Dr. I-94, exit Half Day Rd (SR 22), just e to Lakeside Dr, then just s. Int corridors. **Pets:** Medium, other species. Service with restrictions, supervision.

🅰️🆂🅺 ✖ 🕭 🖥 🚾 ✖

BEDFORD PARK

▼▼ Extended StayAmerica Chicago-Midway �H
(708) 496-8211. **$99-$139.** 7524 State Rd. Jct SR 50, just w. Int corridors. **Pets:** Other species. $25 daily fee/pet. Service with restrictions, crate.

🅰️🆂🅺 ✖ 🕭 🖥

BLOOMINGDALE

🆎 ▼▼▼ Hilton Chicago Indian Lakes Resort �H
(630) 529-0200. **$99-$249.** 250 W Schick Rd. I-355, exit US 20 (Lake St), 2.5 mi w, just s on Bloomingdale Rd, then 0.6 mi w. Int corridors. **Pets:** Accepted.

🆂🅰🆅🅴 ✖ 🖥 🍴 🚾 ✖

▼▼▼ Residence Inn by Marriott �H
(630) 893-9200. **$140-$150.** 295 Knollwood Dr. I-355, exit Army Trail Rd, 4 mi w, then just n. Int corridors. **Pets:** Accepted.

✖ 🕭 🖥 🚾 ✖

BOLINGBROOK

🆎 ▼▼▼ AmericInn Lodge & Suites of Bolingbrook �H ✿
(630) 378-5300. **$89-$119.** 175 W Remington Blvd. I-55, exit 267, just n on SR 53. Int corridors. **Pets:** Medium, dogs only. Service with restrictions.

🆂🅰🆅🅴 ✖ 🕭 🖥 🚾

▼▼ La Quinta Inn Chicago-Bolingbrook �H ✿
(630) 226-0000. **$89-$189.** 225 W South Frontage Rd. I-55, exit 267, 0.5 mi sw. Int corridors. **Pets:** Medium, other species. Service with restrictions, supervision.

🅰️🆂🅺 ✖ 🕭 🖥 🚾

BRIDGEVIEW

🆎 ▼ Days Inn Bridgeview �H
(708) 430-1818. **Call for rates.** 9625 S 76th Ave. I-294, exit 95th St, just s. Int corridors. **Pets:** Accepted.

🆂🅰🆅🅴 ✖ 🕭 🖥

BUFFALO GROVE

▼▼ Extended StayAmerica-Chicago-Buffalo Grove-Deerfield �H
(847) 215-0641. **$85-$115.** 1525 Busch Pkwy. I-94, exit Lake Cook Rd, 2 mi w to Milwaukee Ave (US 45/SR 21), then 1.3 mi n. Int corridors. **Pets:** Other species. $25 daily fee/pet. Service with restrictions, crate.

🅰️🆂🅺 ✖ 🕭 🖥

BURR RIDGE

▼▼ Extended StayAmerica Chicago-Burr Ridge �H
(630) 323-6630. **$70-$100.** 15 W 122nd S Frontage Rd. I-55, exit 276A (County Line Rd), just sw. Int corridors. **Pets:** Other species. $25 daily fee/pet. Service with restrictions, crate.

🅰️🆂🅺 ✖ 🕭 🖥

▼▼ The Oaks Hotel & Conference Center �H
(630) 325-2900. **Call for rates.** 300 S Frontage Rd. I-55, exit 276A (County Line Rd), just sw. Int corridors. **Pets:** Accepted.

✖ 🕭 🖥 🍴 🚾 ✖

CHICAGO

🆎 ▼▼▼▼ Affinia Chicago �H
(312) 787-6000. **$229-$499.** 166 E Superior St. Just e of Michigan Ave. Int corridors. **Pets:** Accepted.

🆂🅰🆅🅴 ✖ 🕭 🖥 🍴 ✖

🆎 ▼▼▼ Allegro Chicago, a Kimpton Hotel �H ✿
(312) 236-0123. **$199-$559.** 171 W Randolph St. Jct La Salle St; in theater district. Int corridors. **Pets:** Large, other species. Service with restrictions, crate.

🆂🅰🆅🅴 ✖ 🕭 🖥 🍴

▼▼▼ Amalfi Hotel Chicago �H
(312) 395-9000. **$149-$649.** 20 W Kinzie St. Between State and Dearborn sts. Int corridors. **Pets:** Accepted.

🅰️🆂🅺 ✖ 🅼 🕭 🖥 ✖

🆎 ▼▼▼ Avenue Hotel Chicago �H ✿
(312) 787-2900. **$259-$499.** 160 E Huron St. Just e of N Michigan Ave. Int corridors. **Pets:** Small, dogs only. $75 deposit/pet. Service with restrictions, supervision.

🆂🅰🆅🅴 ✖ 🕭 🖥 🍴 🚾

🆎 ▼▼▼ Carlton Inn Midway 🅼 ✿
(773) 582-0900. **$109-$159.** 4944 S Archer Ave. I-55, exit 287 (Pulaski), 1.8 mi s to Archer Ave, then just e. Ext corridors. **Pets:** Medium. $50 deposit/pet, $5 daily fee/pet. Designated rooms, service with restrictions, supervision.

🆂🅰🆅🅴 ✖ 🕭 🖥

🆎 ▼▼▼▼ Conrad Chicago �H ✿
(312) 645-1500. **$255-$555.** 521 N Rush St. Jct Grand Ave. Int corridors. **Pets:** Small, other species. Designated rooms, service with restrictions, crate.

🆂🅰🆅🅴 ✖ 🅼 🕭 🖥 🍴 ✖

🆎 ▼▼▼▼ Crowne Plaza Chicago Metro �H ✿
(312) 829-5000. **$139-$459.** 733 W Madison St. I-90/94, exit 51D (Madison St), at jct Halsted St. Int corridors. **Pets:** Medium, other species. $50 one-time fee/room. Service with restrictions, crate.

🆂🅰🆅🅴 ✖ 🖥 🍴

▼▼▼▼ The Drake Hotel, Chicago �H
(312) 787-2200. **$139-$529.** 140 E Walton Pl. Jct N Michigan Ave and Lake Shore Dr. Int corridors. **Pets:** Accepted.

✖ 🕭 🖥 🍴

🆎 ▼▼▼▼ Fairmont Chicago �H
(312) 565-8000. **$153-$494.** 200 N Columbus Dr. Jct Michigan Ave and Wacker Dr, just e. Int corridors. **Pets:** Accepted.

🆂🅰🆅🅴 ✖ 🅼 🖥 🍴

🆎 ▼▼▼▼▼ Four Seasons Hotel Chicago �H ✿
(312) 280-8800. **$495-$850.** 120 E Delaware Pl. Jct Michigan Ave; just nw of John Hancock building. Int corridors. **Pets:** Very small. Designated rooms, service with restrictions, crate.

🆂🅰🆅🅴 ✖ 🅼 🕭 🖥 🍴 🚾 ✖

🆎 ▼▼▼ ▼▼ Hard Rock Hotel Chicago-A Preferred Hotel �H
(312) 345-1000. **$129-$559.** 230 N Michigan Ave. Between Lake St and Wacker Dr. Int corridors. **Pets:** Accepted.

🆂🅰🆅🅴 ✖ 🅼 🖥 🍴 ✖

Hilton Chicago 🏨
(312) 922-4400. **$254-$459.** 720 S Michigan Ave. I-290 (Congress Pkwy), exit Michigan Ave, just s. Int corridors. **Pets:** Large, other species. $75 one-time fee/pet. Service with restrictions, crate.

Hilton Chicago O'Hare Airport 🏨
(773) 686-8000. **$234-$439.** O'Hare Intl Airport. Opposite and connected to terminal buildings at Chicago O'Hare International Airport, accessed via I-190. Int corridors. **Pets:** Medium, other species. $50 one-time fee/room. Service with restrictions, supervision.

Holiday Inn Chicago O'Hare 🏨
(773) 693-5800. **Call for rates.** 5615 N Cumberland Ave. I-90, exit 79B (N Cumberland Ave S), just s. Int corridors. **Pets:** Accepted.

Hotel Burnham Chicago 🏨
(312) 782-1111. **Call for rates.** One W Washington St. Jct State St. Int corridors. **Pets:** Other species. Designated rooms, service with restrictions.

Hotel Indigo Chicago-Gold Coast 🏨
(312) 787-4980. **$119-$409.** 1244 N Dearborn St. Just n of Division St. Int corridors. **Pets:** Medium. $75 one-time fee/pet. Designated rooms, service with restrictions, supervision.

Hotel Monaco Chicago 🏨
(312) 960-8500. **$169-$599.** 225 N Wabash Ave. Jct Wacker Dr. Int corridors. **Pets:** Other species. Designated rooms, service with restrictions.

Hotel Sax Chicago 🏨
(312) 245-0333. **$169-$849.** 333 N Dearborn St. Between Dearborn and State sts. Int corridors. **Pets:** Accepted.

InterContinental Chicago 🏨
(312) 944-4100. **$159-$2700.** 505 N Michigan Ave. Just n of Chicago River. Int corridors. **Pets:** $50 deposit/room, $50 one-time fee/room. Service with restrictions, crate.

The James 🏨
(312) 337-1000. **$239-$599.** 55 E Ontario St. Just w of N Michigan Ave. Int corridors. **Pets:** Accepted.

Omni Chicago Hotel 🏨
(312) 944-6664. **$329-$579.** 676 N Michigan Ave. Jct Huron St. Int corridors. **Pets:** Accepted.

The Palmer House Hilton 🏨
(312) 726-7500. **$174-$534.** 17 E Monroe St. Between State St and Wabash Ave. Int corridors. **Pets:** Accepted.

Park Hyatt Chicago 🏨
(312) 335-1234. **$299-$799, 3 day notice.** 800 N Michigan Ave. Jct Chicago Ave at Water Tower Square. Int corridors. **Pets:** Accepted.

The Peninsula Chicago 🏨
(312) 337-2888. **$395-$1195.** 108 E Superior St. Jct Michigan Ave. Int corridors. **Pets:** Accepted.

Renaissance Chicago Hotel 🏨
(312) 372-7200. **$299-$439.** One W Wacker Dr. Jct State St. Int corridors. **Pets:** Accepted.

Residence Inn by Marriott Chicago Downtown/ Magnificent Mile 🏨
(312) 943-9800. **$199-$299.** 201 E Walton Pl. Just e of Michigan Ave at Mies van der Rohe. Int corridors. **Pets:** Other species. $100 one-time fee/pet.

Residence Inn by Marriott River North 🏨
(312) 494-9301. **$169-$249.** 410 N Dearborn St. Between W Kinzie and W Hubbard sts. Int corridors. **Pets:** Large. $100 one-time fee/room. Designated rooms, service with restrictions, crate.

Sheraton Chicago Hotel & Towers 🏨
(312) 464-1000. **$149-$549.** 301 E North Water St. Columbus Dr at Chicago River; just e of Michigan Ave. Int corridors. **Pets:** Accepted.

Sofitel Chicago Water Tower 🏨
(312) 324-4000. **$245-$530, 3 day notice.** 20 E Chestnut St. Jct Wabash Ave and Chestnut St, 1/2 blk w of Rush St. Int corridors. **Pets:** Small. $200 deposit/room. Service with restrictions.

The Sutton Place Hotel 🏨
(312) 266-2100. **$270-$590.** 21 E Bellevue Pl. Jct Rush St. Int corridors. **Pets:** $50 one-time fee/room. Service with restrictions.

W Chicago-City Center 🏨
(312) 332-1200. **$199-$629.** 172 W Adams St. Between La Salle and Wells sts. Int corridors. **Pets:** Small. $25 daily fee/room, $100 one-time fee/room.

W Chicago Lakeshore 🏨
(312) 943-9200. **$699.** 644 N Lakeshore Dr. Jct Ontario St. Int corridors. **Pets:** Medium. $25 daily fee/room, $100 one-time fee/room.

The Westin Chicago River North 🏨
(312) 744-1900. **$149-$599.** 320 N Dearborn St. Just n of Chicago River; between Dearborn and Clark sts. Int corridors. **Pets:** Small, dogs only. Service with restrictions, crate.

The Westin Michigan Avenue Chicago 🏨
(312) 943-7200. **$559-$569.** 909 N Michigan Ave. Across from John Hancock Center. Int corridors. **Pets:** Service with restrictions, supervision.

CRESTWOOD

Hampton Inn-Chicago/Crestwood 🏨
(708) 597-3330. **$89-$179.** 13330 S Cicero Ave. On SR 50 and 83, 0.8 mi s of jct I-294. Int corridors. **Pets:** Accepted.

CRYSTAL LAKE

Comfort Inn by Choice Hotels 🏨
(815) 444-0040. **$79-$100.** 595 E Tracy Tr. Jct US 14 and SR 31, 0.4 mi w, then just s on Pingree St. Int corridors. **Pets:** Accepted.

Holiday Inn Chicago-Crystal Lake 🏨
(815) 477-7000. **$99-$169.** 800 S SR 31. At Three Oaks Rd, 0.3 mi s of jct US 14. Int corridors. **Pets:** Small. $25 one-time fee/pet. Designated rooms, service with restrictions, crate.

DARIEN

▼▼ ▼▼ Extended StayAmerica Chicago-Darien 🄷
(630) 985-4708. **$70-$100.** 2345 Sokol Ct. I-55, exit 271A, 0.5 mi s to Westgate Rd, then 0.5 mi ne via frontage road. Int corridors. **Pets:** Other species. $25 daily fee/pet. Service with restrictions, crate.
A$K ☒ 🄷 💻

DEERFIELD

⟨AAA⟩ ▼▼ Red Roof Inn #7188 Ⓜ
(847) 205-1755. **$66-$78.** 340 S Waukegan Rd. I-94, exit SR 43 (Waukegan Rd). Ext corridors. **Pets:** Medium. Service with restrictions, supervision.
SAVE ☒ 🄷

DES PLAINES

⟨AAA⟩ ▼▼▼ Comfort Inn O'Hare 🄷
(847) 635-1300. **$90-$300.** 2175 E Touhy Ave. I-294, exit Touhy Ave westbound, just w; exit Golf Rd (SR 58) eastbound, 0.3 mi w to River Rd, then 5.5 mi s. Int corridors. **Pets:** Medium. $20 daily fee/pet. Designated rooms, service with restrictions, supervision.
SAVE ☒ 🄷 💻

▼▼▼ Extended StayAmerica-Chicago-O'Hare 🄷
(847) 294-9693. **$75-$105.** 1201 E Touhy Ave. At SR 72 (Higgins Rd), 0.6 mi, w of US 12/45 (Mannheim Rd). Int corridors. **Pets:** Other species. $25 daily fee/pet. Service with restrictions, crate.
A$K ☒ 🄬ᴹ 🄷 💻

▼▼▼ Extended Stay Deluxe Chicago-O'Hare 🄷
(847) 768-0395. **$85-$115.** 1207 E Touhy Ave. At SR 72 (Higgins Rd), 0.6 mi w of US 12/45 (Mannheim Rd). Int corridors. **Pets:** Other species. $25 daily fee/pet. Service with restrictions, crate.
A$K ☒ 🄬ᴹ 🄷 💻

⟨AAA⟩ ▼▼▼▼ Hilton Garden Inn Chicago-O'Hare Airport 🄷
(847) 296-8900. **$95-$229.** 2930 S River Rd. I-294, exit Touhy Ave westbound, just s on River Rd, then 0.3 mi s; exit Golf Rd (SR 58) eastbound, 0.3 mi w to River Rd, then 6 mi s. Int corridors. **Pets:** $50 one-time fee/room. Service with restrictions, supervision.
SAVE ☒ 🄬ᴹ 🄷 💻 🍴 🏊

DOWNERS GROVE

⟨AAA⟩ ▼▼ Comfort Inn by Choice Hotels 🄷
(630) 515-1500. **Call for rates.** 3010 Finley Rd. I-355, exit Butterfield Rd (SR 56), just e. Int corridors. **Pets:** Medium. $40 one-time fee/room. Designated rooms, service with restrictions, crate.
SAVE ☒ 🄷 💻 🏊

⟨AAA⟩ ▼▼ Red Roof Inn #7087 Ⓜ
(630) 963-4205. **$65-$83.** 1113 Butterfield Rd. I-355, exit Butterfield Rd (SR 56), on frontage road; I-88, exit Highland Ave N, just w. Ext corridors. **Pets:** Other species. Service with restrictions, crate.
SAVE ☒ 🄷

ELGIN

⟨AAA⟩ ▼▼▼ Quality Inn-Elgin 🄷
(847) 608-7300. **$75-$100.** 500 Tollgate Rd. I-90, exit SR 31 N, just n. Int corridors. **Pets:** Accepted.
SAVE ☒ 🄬ᴹ 🄷 💻

ELK GROVE VILLAGE

⟨AAA⟩ ▼▼ Baymont Inn & Suites 🄷
(847) 803-9400. **$49-$99.** 2881 Touhy Ave. Jct SR 72 (Higgins Rd) and 83 (Busse Rd), 1.5 mi e on SR 72 (Higgins Rd). Int corridors. **Pets:** Small, other species. Designated rooms, service with restrictions, supervision.
SAVE ☒ 🄷 💻

⟨AAA⟩ ▼▼ Days Inn 🄷
(847) 895-2085. **$49-$99.** 1000 W Devon Ave. I-290, exit Thorndale Ave, 0.5 mi w to Rohlwing Rd, 0.3 mi n to Devon Ave, then 0.3 mi e. Int corridors. **Pets:** Medium. Service with restrictions, crate.
SAVE ☒ 🄷 💻

⟨AAA⟩ ▼▼▼ La Quinta Inn Chicago/O'Hare 🄷 🐾
(847) 439-6767. **$69-$139.** 1900 E Oakton St. Jct SR 72 (Higgins Rd) and 83 (Busse Rd). Int corridors. **Pets:** Medium, other species. Service with restrictions, supervision.
SAVE ☒ 🄷 💻 🏊

⟨AAA⟩ ▼▼▼ Quality Inn & Suites O'Hare/Elk Grove 🄷
(847) 593-8600. **$79-$300.** 100 Busse Rd. Just n of jct SR 72 (Higgins Rd). Int corridors. **Pets:** Accepted.
SAVE ☒ 🄬ᴹ 🄷 💻

⟨AAA⟩ ▼▼▼ Super 8 O'Hare 🄷
(847) 827-3133. **$59-$89.** 2951 Touhy Ave. Jct SR 72 (Higgins Rd) and 83 (Busse Rd), 1.5 mi e on SR 72 (Higgins Rd). Int corridors. **Pets:** Accepted.
SAVE ☒ 🄬ᴹ 🄷 💻 🏊

ELMHURST

▼▼▼ Extended StayAmerica Chicago-Elmhurst-O'Hare 🄷
(630) 530-4353. **$65-$95.** 550 W Grand Ave. Jct US 20 (Lake St), 0.4 mi ne; adjacent to I-290 overpass. Int corridors. **Pets:** Other species. $25 daily fee/pet. Service with restrictions, crate.
A$K ☒ 🄬ᴹ 🄷 💻

EVANSTON

⟨AAA⟩ ▼▼▼ ▼▼▼ Hotel Orrington 🄷 🐾
(847) 866-8700. **$119-$339.** 1710 Orrington Ave. Jct Church St. Int corridors. **Pets:** Small. $50 one-time fee/room. Designated rooms, service with restrictions, crate.
SAVE ☒ 🄬ᴹ 🄷 💻 🍴

GLENVIEW

▼▼▼▼ Staybridge Suites 🄷
(847) 657-0002. **$100-$190.** 2600 Lehigh Ave. I-294, exit Willow Rd, 2.4 mi e. Int corridors. **Pets:** Accepted.
A$K ☒ 🄬ᴹ 🄷 💻 🏊

GURNEE

▼▼▼ Comfort Suites by Choice Hotels 🄷
(847) 782-0890. **$79-$199.** 5430 Grand Ave. I-94, exit Grand Ave (SR 132 E), 0.5 mi e. Int corridors. **Pets:** Accepted.
A$K ☒ 🄬ᴹ 🄷 💻 🏊

▼▼▼▼ Country Inn & Suites By Carlson 🄷
(847) 625-9700. **$79-$179.** 5420 Grand Ave. I-94, exit Grand Ave (SR 132 E), 0.5 mi e. Int corridors. **Pets:** Medium, dogs only. $50 one-time fee/room. Service with restrictions, supervision.
A$K ☒ 🄬ᴹ 🄷 💻 🏊

▼▼▼ La Quinta Inn Chicago-Gurnee 🄷 🐾
(847) 662-7600. **$59-$159.** 5688 Northridge Dr. I-94, exit Grand Ave (SR 132 E), just e via service road. Int corridors. **Pets:** Medium, other species. Service with restrictions, supervision.
A$K ☒ 🄬ᴹ 🄷 💻 🏊

HANOVER PARK

▼▼▼ Extended StayAmerica-Chicago-Hanover Park 🄷
(630) 893-4823. **$65-$95.** 1075 Lake St. On US 20; between Gary Ave and Elgin-O'Hare Expwy. Int corridors. **Pets:** Other species. $25 daily fee/pet. Service with restrictions, crate.
A$K ☒ 🄷 💻

HARVEY

▼▼ Sleep Inn by Choice Hotels-Chicago Southland ⊞
(708) 331-3400. $60-$85. 16940 Halsted St. I-80/294, exit Halsted St, just
n. Int corridors. **Pets:** Accepted.

(A$K) (✕) (💻)

HILLSIDE

◈ ▼▼▼ Best Western Chicago Hillside ⊞
(708) 544-9300. $99-$139, 3 day notice. 4400 Frontage Rd. I-290, exit
US 12/45, just n to Frontage Rd, then 0.5 mi w. Int corridors.
Pets: Accepted.

(SAVE) (✕) (🛏) (💻) (¶¶) (🏊)

HOFFMAN ESTATES

▼▼ La Quinta Inn Chicago (Hoffman Estates) ⊞ 🐾
(847) 882-3312. $59-$129. 2280 Barrington Rd. I-90, exit Barrington Rd
westbound, 0.3 mi s; exit SR 59 eastbound, 0.5 mi n to SR 72 (Higgins
Rd), 2 mi e to Barrington Rd, then just n. Int corridors. **Pets:** Medium, other
species. Service with restrictions, supervision.

(A$K) (✕) (🛏) (💻) (🏊)

◈ ▼ Red Roof Inn #7199 Ⓜ
(847) 885-7877. $63-$89. 2500 Hassell Rd. I-90, exit Barrington Rd westbound, 0.3 mi s; exit SR 59 eastbound, 0.5 mi n to SR 72 (Higgins Rd), 2
mi e to Barrington Rd, then just n. Ext corridors. **Pets:** Medium, other
species. Service with restrictions, supervision.

(SAVE) (✕) (🛏)

ITASCA

▼▼ Extended StayAmerica-Chicago-Itasca ⊞
(630) 250-1111. $65-$95. 1181 Rohlwing Rd. I-290, exit Thorndale Ave, 0.5
mi w. Int corridors. **Pets:** Other species. $25 daily fee/pet. Service with
restrictions, crate.

(A$K) (✕) (♿) (🛏) (💻)

◈ ▼▼▼▼ The Westin Chicago Northwest ⊞
(630) 773-4000. $349. 400 Park Blvd. I-290, exit Thorndale Ave, just e. Int
corridors. **Pets:** Accepted.

(SAVE) (✕) (🛏) (💻) (¶¶) (🏊) (✕)

JOLIET

▼▼ Comfort Inn by Choice Hotels North ⊞
(815) 436-5141. **Call for rates.** 3235 Norman Ave. I-55, exit 257, just e. Int
corridors. **Pets:** Accepted.

(✕) (🛏) (💻) (🏊)

▼▼ Comfort Inn by Choice Hotels-South ⊞
(815) 744-1770. **Call for rates.** 135 S Larkin Ave. I-80, exit 130B, 0.5 mi n.
Int corridors. **Pets:** Accepted.

(✕) (🛏) (💻) (🏊)

◈ ▼▼▼ Holiday Inn Convention Center-Joliet ⊞
(815) 729-2000. $94-$159. 411 S Larkin Ave. I-80, exit 130B, just nw. Int
corridors. **Pets:** Accepted.

(SAVE) (✕) (♿) (🛏) (💻) (¶¶) (🏊)

◈ ▼ Red Roof Inn #7071 Ⓜ
(815) 741-2304. $55-$74. 1750 McDonough St. I-80, exit 130B, just off
Larkin Ave. Ext corridors. **Pets:** Accepted.

(SAVE) (✕) (🛏)

◈ ▼▼▼ TownePlace Suites by Marriott
Joliet ⊞ 🐾
(815) 741-2400. $125-$153. 1515 Riverboat Center Dr. I-80, exit 127, just
n. Int corridors. **Pets:** Large, other species. $100 one-time fee/room. Serv-
ice with restrictions, crate.

(SAVE) (✕) (♿) (🛏) (💻) (🏊)

LANSING

▼▼ Extended StayAmerica-Chicago-Lansing ⊞
(708) 895-6402. $75-$105. 2520 173rd St. I-80/94, exit 161 (Torrence Ave),
just n. Int corridors. **Pets:** Other species. $25 daily fee/pet. Service with
restrictions, crate.

(A$K) (✕) (♿) (🛏) (💻)

◈ ▼ Red Roof Inn #7078 Ⓜ
(708) 895-9570. $56-$84. 2450 E 173rd St. I-80/94, exit 161 (Torrence
Ave), just n. Ext corridors. **Pets:** Medium. Supervision.

(SAVE) (✕) (🛏)

LIBERTYVILLE

▼▼▼ Holiday Inn Express Hotel & Suites ⊞
(847) 549-7878. **Call for rates.** 77 Buckley Rd. I-94, exit SR 137 (Buckley
Rd), 2.3 mi w. Int corridors. **Pets:** Accepted.

(✕) (🛏) (💻) (🏊)

LINCOLNSHIRE

▼▼▼ Homewood Suites by Hilton
Chicago-Lincolnshire ⊞
(847) 945-9300. $89-$159. 10 Westminster Way. I-94, exit Half Day Rd,
just w. Int corridors. **Pets:** Accepted.

(✕) (🛏) (💻) (🏊) (✕)

▼▼▼ Staybridge Suites Lincolnshire ⊞ 🐾
(847) 821-0002. $159-$199. 100 Barclay Blvd. I-94, exit Half Day Rd, 2.2
mi w to Barclay Blvd, then just s; just w of jct US 45 and SR 21; in
Lincolnshire Corporate Center. Int corridors. **Pets:** Other species. $10 daily
fee/room, $50 one-time fee/room. Service with restrictions.

(A$K) (✕) (♿) (🛏) (💻) (🏊)

LISLE

▼▼ Extended StayAmerica-Chicago-Lisle ⊞
(630) 434-7710. $60-$90. 445 Warrenville Rd. I-355, exit Ogden Ave E. Int
corridors. **Pets:** Other species. $25 daily fee/pet. Service with restrictions,
crate.

(A$K) (✕) (🛏) (💻)

◈ ▼▼▼ Hilton Lisle/Naperville ⊞ 🐾
(630) 505-0900. $109-$344. 3003 Corporate West Dr. I-88, exit Naperville
Rd, just n, then 0.3 mi e on Warrenville Rd. Int corridors. **Pets:** Medium.
$75 one-time fee/pet. Service with restrictions, supervision.

(SAVE) (✕) (🛏) (💻) (¶¶) (🏊)

LOMBARD

◈ ▼▼▼ Embassy Suites Hotel Chicago-Lombard/Oak
Brook ⊞
(630) 969-7500. $99-$239. 707 E Butterfield Rd. I-88, exit Highland Ave,
just n to Butterfield Rd (SR 56), then 0.5 mi e. Int corridors. **Pets:** Other
species. $50 one-time fee/room. Service with restrictions.

(SAVE) (✕) (♿) (🛏) (💻) (¶¶) (🏊) (✕)

▼▼ Extended Stay Deluxe-Chicago-Lombard-Oak
Brook ⊞
(630) 424-1000. $70-$100. 260 E 22nd St. I-88, exit Highland Ave, 0.8 mi
n to 22nd St, then just e. Int corridors. **Pets:** Other species. $25 daily
fee/pet. Service with restrictions, crate.

(A$K) (✕) (♿) (🛏) (💻) (✕)

▼▼ Homestead Studio Suites Hotel-Chicago/Lombard-Oak
Brook ⊞
(630) 928-0202. $60-$90. 2701 Technology Dr. I-88, exit Highland Ave, just
n, 0.6 mi e on Butterfield Rd (SR 56), then just s. Int corridors. **Pets:** Other
species. $25 daily fee/pet. Service with restrictions, crate.

(A$K) (✕) (♿) (🛏) (💻)

(AAA) ▼▼▼▼ Residence Inn by Marriott Chicago Lombard [H]
(630) 629-7800. **$149-$169.** 2001 S Highland Ave. I-88, exit Highland Ave, 0.8 mi n. Ext corridors. **Pets:** Other species. $75 one-time fee/room. Service with restrictions.
[SAVE] [X] [🐾] [▣] [🛏] [≋] [✕]

(AAA) ▼▼▼ TownePlace Suites by Marriott Chicago Lombard [H] 🐾
(630) 932-4400. **$124-$139.** 455 E 22nd St. I-88, exit Highland, 0.8 mi, then 0.3 mi. Int corridors. **Pets:** $75 one-time fee/room. Service with restrictions, crate.
[SAVE] [X] [♿] [▣] [🛏] [≋]

(AAA) ▼▼▼▼ The Westin Lombard Yorktown Center [H] 🐾
(630) 719-8000. **Call for rates.** 70 Yorktown Center. Jct Highland Ave and Butterfield Rd (SR 56), just e. Int corridors. **Pets:** Medium, dogs only. Service with restrictions, supervision.
[SAVE] [X] [♿] [🐾] [▣] [🛏] [≋] [✕]

MATTESON

(AAA) ▼▼▼▼ Holiday Inn Chicago-Matteson [H]
(708) 747-3500. **Call for rates.** 500 Holiday Plaza Dr. I-57, exit 340A, just e. Int corridors. **Pets:** Medium. $15 daily fee/room. Service with restrictions, crate.
[SAVE] [X] [🐾] [▣] [🛏] [≋] [✕]

▼▼ La Quinta Inn Chicago-Matteson [H] 🐾
(708) 503-0999. **$55-$125.** 5210 W Southwick Dr. I-57, exit 340A, 0.3 mi e on US 30, then 0.3 mi s on Cicero Ave (SR 50). Int corridors. **Pets:** Medium, other species. Service with restrictions, supervision.
[ASK] [X] [🐾] [▣]

MORTON GROVE

(AAA) ▼▼▼ Best Western Morton Grove Inn-Chicago [H]
(847) 965-6400. **$69-$159.** 9424 Waukegan Rd. On SR 43, just s of Gold Rd (SR 58). Ext corridors. **Pets:** Accepted.
[SAVE] [X] [🐾] [▣]

MUNDELEIN

(AAA) ▼▼▼▼ Comfort Inn Chicago-Mundelein [H]
(847) 566-5400. **$69-$199.** 517 SR 83 E. Jct US 45. Int corridors. **Pets:** Accepted.
[SAVE] [X] [🐾] [▣] [≋] [✕]

▼▼▼▼ Crowne Plaza Chicago North Shore [H] 🐾
(847) 949-5100. **$100-$300.** 510 SR 83 E. Jct US 45. Int corridors. **Pets:** Other species. Designated rooms, service with restrictions, crate.
[ASK] [X] [🐾] [▣] [🍴] [≋]

NAPERVILLE

(AAA) ▼▼ Baymont Inn & Suites [H]
(630) 357-0022. **$49-$90.** 1585 Naperville/Wheaton Rd. I-88, exit Naperville Rd, 0.5 mi s. Int corridors. **Pets:** Medium. $50 deposit/pet, $10 daily fee/pet. Designated rooms, service with restrictions, supervision.
[SAVE] [X] [🐾] [▣]

▼▼ Extended StayAmerica-Chicago-Naperville [H]
(630) 983-0000. **$65-$95.** 1575 Bond St. I-88, exit SR 59, just s. Int corridors. **Pets:** Other species. $25 daily fee/pet. Service with restrictions, crate.
[ASK] [X] [🐾] [▣]

▼▼ Homestead Studio Suites Hotel-Chicago-Naperville [H]
(630) 577-0200. **$60-$90.** 1827 Centre Point Cir. I-88, exit Naperville Rd, just s to Diehl Rd, 0.8 mi w, then just n. Int corridors. **Pets:** Other species. $25 daily fee/pet. Service with restrictions, crate.
[ASK] [X] [♿] [🐾] [▣]

(AAA) ▼▼ Red Roof Inn #7195 [M]
(630) 369-2500. **$60-$90.** 1698 W Diehl Rd. I-88, exit SR 59, just s. Ext corridors. **Pets:** Accepted.
[SAVE] [X] [🐾]

▼▼ TownePlace Suites by Marriott Naperville [H]
(630) 548-0881. **$140-$150.** 1843 W Diehl Rd. I-88, exit SR 59, just s to Diehl Rd, then just w. Int corridors. **Pets:** $100 one-time fee/room. Service with restrictions.
[X] [🐾] [▣] [≋] [✕]

NORTHBROOK

▼▼▼▼ Hilton Chicago Northbrook [H]
(847) 480-7500. **$109-$334.** 2855 N Milwaukee Ave. On SR 21, s of jct US 45 and Willow Rd. Int corridors. **Pets:** Accepted.
[X] [🐾] [▣] [🍴] [≋] [✕]

▼▼▼▼ Radisson Hotel Northbrook [H]
(847) 298-2525. **$169-$219.** 2875 N Milwaukee Ave. I-294, exit Willow Rd, 1 mi w to SR 21 and US 45, then 0.6 mi s. Int corridors. **Pets:** Accepted.
[ASK] [X] [🐾] [▣] [🍴] [≋] [✕]

OAK BROOK

▼▼▼▼ Residence Inn by Marriott Chicago/Oak Brook [H]
(630) 571-1200. **$180-$200.** 790 Jorie Blvd. I-88, exit Midwest Rd eastbound, just n to 22nd St (Cermak Rd), 1.7 mi e to Jorie Blvd, then just sw; exit 22nd St (Cermak Rd) westbound, 0.4 mi e to Jorie Blvd. Int corridors. **Pets:** Large, other species. $100 one-time fee/room. Service with restrictions, crate.
[X] [♿] [🐾] [▣] [≋]

OAKBROOK TERRACE

▼▼ La Quinta Inn Chicago (Oak Brook) [H] 🐾
(630) 495-4600. **$69-$125.** 1 S 666 Midwest Rd. I-88, exit Midwest Rd eastbound, 0.4 mi n, then just n of 22nd St (Cermak Rd); exit 22nd St (Cermak Rd) westbound, 1.1 mi w to Midwest Rd, then just n. Int corridors. **Pets:** Medium, other species. Service with restrictions, supervision.
[ASK] [X] [🐾] [▣] [≋]

▼▼▼ Staybridge Suites Chicago-Oakbrook Terrace [H]
(630) 953-9393. **Call for rates.** 200 Royce Blvd. I-88, exit Midwest Rd eastbound to 22nd St (Cermak Rd), 0.4 mi w to Butterfield Rd (SR 56), just n, then just n on Renaissance Blvd; exit 22nd St (Cermak) westbound, 2.5 mi w on 22nd St to SR 56, just n, then just n on Renaissance Blvd. Int corridors. **Pets:** Large, other species. $75 one-time fee/pet. Service with restrictions, supervision.
[X] [🐾] [🐾] [▣]

PALATINE

▼▼▼ Holiday Inn Express Palatine/Arlington Heights [H]
(847) 934-4900. **$94-$169.** 1550 E Dundee Rd. SR 53, exit Dundee Rd (SR 68), just w. Int corridors. **Pets:** Accepted.
[ASK] [X] [♿] [🐾] [▣] [≋] [✕]

▼▼▼ Hotel Indigo Chicago-Schaumburg North [H] 🐾
(847) 359-6900. **$119-$179.** 920 E Northwest Hwy (US 14). SR 53, exit Northwest Hwy (US 14), just w. Int corridors. **Pets:** Medium. $25 daily fee/pet. Service with restrictions, supervision.
[ASK] [X] [♿] [🐾] [▣] [🍴] [≋]

PROSPECT HEIGHTS

(AAA) ▼▼ Super 8-Prospect Heights [H]
(847) 459-0545. **Call for rates.** 540 Milwaukee Ave. Jct SR 21 and US 45. Int corridors. **Pets:** Accepted.
[SAVE] [X] [🐾] [▣]

RICHMOND

▼▼ Save Inn Richmond/Geneva Lakes ⚓
(815) 678-4711. **$79-$149.** 11200 N Rt 12. 0.5 mi n or jct SR 173. Int corridors. **Pets:** Medium. $50 deposit/room, $10 daily fee/pet. Designated rooms, service with restrictions.

ASK ⊠ 🖥 💻 ➹

ROLLING MEADOWS

▼▼▼ Holiday Inn Rolling Meadows ⚓
(847) 259-5000. **$109-$295.** 3405 Algonquin Rd. On SR 62, just e of SR 53, 0.3 mi ne of I-90. Ext/int corridors. **Pets:** Accepted.

ASK ⊠ 🖥 💻 🍴 ➹ 🐾

ROMEOVILLE

⚐ ▼▼ Best Western Romeoville Inn ⚓
(815) 372-1000. **$80-$100.** 1280 W Normantown Rd. I-55, exit 263, just s. Int corridors. **Pets:** Other species. $25 one-time fee/pet. Service with restrictions, crate.

SAVE ⊠ 🖥 💻 ➹

▼▼ Extended StayAmerica Chicago-Romeoville ⚓
(630) 226-8966. **$70-$100.** 1225 Lakeview Dr. I-55, exit 263, just n. Int corridors. **Pets:** Other species. $25 daily fee/pet. Service with restrictions, crate.

ASK ⊠ 🖥 💻

ROSEMONT

⚐ ▼▼▼ aloft Chicago O'Hare ⚓
(847) 671-4444. **$109-$259, 3 day notice.** 9700 Balmoral Ave. I-190, exit 1B, just s. Int corridors. **Pets:** Accepted.

SAVE ⊠ 🖥 🖥 💻 ➹

⚐ ▼▼▼ Crowne Plaza Chicago O'Hare Hotel & Conference Center ⚓
(847) 671-6350. **$89-$309.** 5440 N River Rd. I-190, exit 1B (River Rd), just s. Int corridors. **Pets:** Small, other species. $50 one-time fee/pet. Service with restrictions, supervision.

SAVE ⊠ 🖥 🖥 💻 🍴 ➹

⚐ ▼▼▼ DoubleTree Hotel Chicago O'Hare Airport-Rosemont ⚓
(847) 292-9100. **$109-$229.** 5460 N River Rd. I-190, exit 1B (River Rd), just s. Int corridors. **Pets:** Medium. $75 deposit/room, $25 one-time fee/room. Service with restrictions, supervision.

SAVE ⊠ 🖥 💻 🍴 ➹ 🐾

⚐ ▼▼▼ Embassy Suites Hotel O'Hare Rosemont ⚓
(847) 678-4000. **$129-$249.** 5500 N River Rd. I-190, exit 1B (River Rd), just s. Int corridors. **Pets:** Medium, other species. $100 deposit/room, $25 one-time fee/room. Service with restrictions, supervision.

SAVE ⊠ 🖥 💻 🍴 ➹

▼▼▼ Residence Inn by Marriott Chicago-O'Hare ⚓
(847) 375-9000. **$188-$230.** 7101 Chestnut St. Jct US 12 and 45 and Touhy Ave. Int corridors. **Pets:** Accepted.

⊠ 🖥 💻 ➹ 🐾

⚐ ▼▼▼ Sheraton Gateway Suites O'Hare ⚓
(847) 699-6300. **$99-$349.** 6501 N Mannheim Rd. On US 12 and 45, at SR 72 (Higgins Rd). Int corridors. **Pets:** Accepted.

SAVE ⊠ 🖥 💻 🍴 ➹ 🐾

⚐ ▼▼▼▼ The Westin O'Hare ⚓ ❀
(847) 698-6000. **$99-$349.** 6100 N River Rd. I-190, exit 1B (River Rd), just n. Int corridors. **Pets:** Small, dogs only. Service with restrictions, supervision.

SAVE ⊠ 🖥 💻 🍴 ➹ 🐾

ST. CHARLES

⚐ ▼▼▼ Best Western Inn of St. Charles ⚓ ❀
(630) 584-4550. **$80-$120.** 1635 E Main St. On SR 64, 0.5 mi e of SR 25. Ext/int corridors. **Pets:** Dogs only. $10 daily fee/pet. Designated rooms, service with restrictions, supervision.

SAVE ⊠ 🖥 💻 ➹

▼▼▼ Courtyard by Marriott Chicago-St Charles ⚓ ❀
(630) 377-6370. **$139-$149.** 700 Courtyard Dr. Jct SR 59 and 64, 3.4 mi w on SR 64, just n on Kirk Rd, then just w on Foxfield. Int corridors. **Pets:** Medium. $75 one-time fee/pet. Service with restrictions, crate.

⊠ 🖥 🖥 💻 🍴 ➹ 🐾

▼▼ Days Inn ⚓
(630) 513-6500. **$70-$170.** 100 S Tyler Rd. Jct SR 25, 0.5 mi e on SR 64, then just s. Int corridors. **Pets:** Accepted.

ASK ⊠ 🖥 💻 ➹

⚐ ▼▼▼ Holiday Inn Express ⚓
(630) 584-5300. **$89-$139.** 1600 E Main St. On SR 64, 0.5 mi e of SR 25. Int corridors. **Pets:** Accepted.

SAVE ⊠ 🖥 💻 ➹

⚐ ▼▼▼ Pheasant Run Resort ⚓
(630) 584-6300. **$109-$199.** 4051 E Main St. On SR 64, 2.4 mi w of SR 59. Ext/int corridors. **Pets:** Accepted.

SAVE ⊠ 🖥 💻 🍴 ➹ 🐾

⚐ ▼▼ Super 8-St. Charles ⚓
(630) 377-8388. **$70-$80.** 1520 E Main St. On SR 64, 1 mi e. Int corridors. **Pets:** Small. $15 daily fee/pet. Designated rooms, service with restrictions, supervision.

SAVE ⊠ 🖥 💻

SCHAUMBURG

▼▼ Extended StayAmerica #4190 Chicago-Schaumburg-Convention Center ⚓
(847) 882-7011. **$75-$105.** 2000 N Roselle Rd. I-90, exit Roselle Rd, just sw. Int corridors. **Pets:** Other species. $25 daily fee/pet. Service with restrictions, crate.

ASK ⊠ 🖥 💻

▼▼ Extended StayAmerica-Chicago-Woodfield ⚓
(847) 517-7255. **$80-$110.** 1200 American Ln. I-290, exit SR 72 (Higgins Rd), 0.5 mi w to Meacham Rd, 0.5 mi n to American Ln, then just w. Int corridors. **Pets:** Other species. $25 daily fee/pet. Service with restrictions, crate.

ASK ⊠ 🖥 💻

▼▼ Homestead Studio Suites #9653 HSD-Chicago-Schaumburg-Convention Center ⚓
(847) 882-6900. **$70-$100.** 51 E State Pkwy. I-90, exit Roselle Rd, 0.8 mi s, then just e. Int corridors. **Pets:** Other species. $25 daily fee/pet. Service with restrictions, crate.

ASK ⊠ 🖥 💻

▼▼▼ Homewood Suites by Hilton-Schaumburg ⚓
(847) 605-0400. **$99-$139.** 815 E American Ln. I-290, exit SR 72 (Higgins Rd), 1.5 mi w, then 0.4 mi n on Plum Grove Rd. Ext/int corridors. **Pets:** Medium, dogs only. $100 one-time fee/room. Designated rooms, service with restrictions, crate.

⊠ 🖥 🖥 💻 ➹ 🐾

⚐ ▼▼▼▼ Hyatt Summerfield Suites ⚓ ❀
(847) 706-9007. **$109-$399.** 1251 E American Ln. I-290, exit SR 72 (Higgins Rd), 0.5 mi w to Meacham Rd, 0.5 mi n to American Ln, then just w. Int corridors. **Pets:** Small. $75 one-time fee/room. Designated rooms, service with restrictions, supervision.

SAVE ⊠ 🖥 🖥 💻 ➹ 🐾

▼▼ ▼▼ La Quinta Inn (Schaumburg) ⊞ ❀
(847) 517-8484. **$59-$129.** 1730 E Higgins Rd. I-290, exit SR 72 (Higgins Rd), just w. Int corridors. **Pets:** Medium, other species. Service with restrictions, supervision.
ASK ⊠ 🛏 💻 🏊

⏢ ▼▼▼ Quality Inn ⊞
(847) 517-7737. **$75-$109.** 600 N Martingale Rd. I-290, exit SR 72 (Higgins Rd), just w, then just n. Int corridors. **Pets:** Accepted.
SAVE ⊠ 🛏 💻 🏊

▼▼▼ Residence Inn by Marriott-Chicago/Schaumburg ⊞ ❀
(847) 517-9200. **$170-$190.** 1610 McConnor Pkwy. I-290, exit 1A (Woodfield Rd/Golf Rd) northbound, follow signs just n to Golf Rd, just w to McConnor Pkwy, then 0.8 mi n; exit 1B (Woodfield Rd/Golf Rd) southbound. Int corridors. **Pets:** Other species. $100 one-time fee/room. Service with restrictions, crate.
⊠ 🖒M 🛏 💻 🏊 ✖

▼▼▼▼ Staybridge Suites Chicago/Schaumburg ⊞
(847) 619-6677. **Call for rates.** 901 E Woodfield Office Ct. I-290, exit SR 72 (Higgins Rd), 1.5 mi w, then 0.3 mi n on Plum Grove Rd. Ext/int corridors. **Pets:** Accepted.
⊠ 🛏 💻 🏊 ✖

SCHILLER PARK

▼▼▼▼ Comfort Suites by Choice Hotels at O'Hare ⊞
(847) 233-9000. **Call for rates.** 4200 N River Rd. Jct SR 19 (Irving Park Rd) and Des Plaines St/River Rd, just n. Int corridors. **Pets:** Accepted.
⊠ 🖒M 🛏 💻 🍴

⏢ ▼▼▼▼ Four Points by Sheraton Chicago O'Hare Airport ⊞
(847) 671-6000. **$85-$250.** 10249 W Irving Park Rd. Jct US 12, 45 and SR 19 (Irving Park Rd). Int corridors. **Pets:** Accepted.
SAVE ⊠ 🖒M 🛏 💻 🍴 🏊 ✖

SKOKIE

▼▼ ▼▼ Extended StayAmerica-Chicago-Skokie ⊞
(847) 663-9031. **$99-$129.** 5211 Old Orchard Rd. I-94, exit 35 (Old Orchard Rd). Int corridors. **Pets:** Other species. $25 daily fee/pet. Service with restrictions, crate.
ASK ⊠ 🛏 💻

▼▼▼▼ Holiday Inn Chicago North Shore ⊞
(847) 679-8900. **$129-$359.** 5300 W Touhy Ave. I-94, exit 39A, 0.5 mi w. Ext/int corridors. **Pets:** Accepted.
ASK ⊠ 🛏 💻 🍴 🏊 ✖

TINLEY PARK

▼▼ ▼▼ La Quinta Inn & Suites Chicago-Tinley Park ⊞ ❀
(708) 633-1200. **$59-$129.** 7255 W 183rd St. I-80, exit 148B, 0.5 mi n to 183rd St, then just w to North Creek Business Center. Int corridors. **Pets:** Medium, other species. Service with restrictions, supervision.
ASK ⊠ 🖒M 🛏 💻 🏊

VERNON HILLS

▼▼ ▼▼ Holiday Inn Express ⊞
(847) 367-8031. **$139-$299.** 975 Lakeview Pkwy. Jct SR 21 (Milwaukee Ave), 0.7 mi w on SR 60 (Town Line Rd) to Lakeview Pkwy, then just n. Int corridors. **Pets:** Accepted.
ASK ⊠ 🖒M 🛏 💻 🏊 ✖

▼▼ ▼▼ Homestead Studio Suites Hotel-Chicago/Vernon Hills-Lincolnshire ⊞
(847) 955-1111. **$85-$115.** 675 Woodlands Pkwy. I-94, exit SR 60 (Town Line Rd), 2.1 mi w to SR 21 (Milwaukee Ave), 1.9 mi s to Woodlands Pkwy, then just w. Int corridors. **Pets:** Other species. $25 daily fee/pet. Service with restrictions, crate.
⊠ 🛏 💻

WARRENVILLE

▼▼▼▼ Residence Inn by Marriott Chicago Naperville/Warrenville ⊞
(630) 393-3444. **$179-$199.** 28500 Bella Vista Pkwy. I-88, exit Winfield Rd, just n to Ferry Rd, then just e. Int corridors. **Pets:** Accepted.
⊠ 🖒M 🛏 💻 🏊 ✖

WAUKEGAN

⏢ ▼▼▼ America's Best Value Inn & Suites ⊞
(847) 244-6100. **$60-$160.** 411 S Green Bay Rd. I-94, exit SR 120 (Belvidere Rd) eastbound, 2.3 mi e to Green Bay Rd, then just n. Ext/int corridors. **Pets:** Small, dogs only. $10 daily fee/pet. Designated rooms, no service, supervision.
SAVE ⊠ 🛏 💻 🏊

▼▼▼ Candlewood Suites Chicago/Waukegan ⊞
(847) 578-5250. **$64-$108.** 1151 S Waukegan Rd. I-94, exit SR 137 (Buckley Rd), 0.5 mi e to SR 43 (Waukegan Rd), then 1.9 mi n. Int corridors. **Pets:** Medium. $150 one-time fee/room. Designated rooms, service with restrictions, crate.
ASK ⊠ 🛏 💻

⏢ ▼▼▼ Comfort Inn by Choice Hotels ⊞
(847) 623-1400. **$59-$139.** 3031 SR 120 (Belvidere) Rd. I-94, exit SR 120 (Belvidere Rd), 2.3 mi e. Int corridors. **Pets:** Accepted.
SAVE ⊠ 🛏 💻

▼▼ Crossland Studios-Chicago-Waukegan Ⓜ
(847) 688-0402. **$55-$85.** 1177 S Northpoint Blvd. At US 41; between US 41 and SR 43. Ext corridors. **Pets:** Other species. $25 daily fee/pet. Service with restrictions, crate.
ASK ⊠ 🛏 💻

⏢ ▼▼▼▼ Residence Inn by Marriott-Waukegan/Gurnee ⊞ ❀
(847) 689-9240. **$149-$189.** 1440 S White Oak Dr. I-94, exit SR 137 (Buckley Rd), 0.5 mi e to SR 43 (Waukegan Rd), 1.5 mi n to Lakeside Dr, then just e. Int corridors. **Pets:** Medium, other species. $100 one-time fee/room. Service with restrictions.
SAVE ⊠ 🖒M 🛏 💻 🏊 ✖

WEST DUNDEE

⏢ ▼▼▼ TownePlace Suites by Marriott-Chicago/Elgin ⊞
(847) 608-6320. **$99-$114.** 2185 Marriott Dr. I-90, exit SR 31, 0.4 mi n to Marriott Dr, then just e. Int corridors. **Pets:** Large, other species. $100 one-time fee/room. Service with restrictions, supervision.
SAVE ⊠ 🛏 💻 🏊

WESTMONT

⏢ ▼▼▼ ClubHouse Inn & Suites ⊞
(630) 920-2200. **$89-$129.** 630 Pasquinelli Dr. Just off US 34 (Ogden Ave), 0.3 mi nw of jct SR 83. Int corridors. **Pets:** Accepted.
SAVE ⊠ 🛏 💻 ✖

▼▼ ▼▼ Homestead Studio Suites Hotel-Chicago/Westmont-Oak Brook ⊞
(630) 323-9292. **$70-$100.** 855 Pasquinelli Dr. SR 83, exit US 34 (Ogden Ave), just w to Pasquinelli Dr, then 0.5 mi n. Int corridors. **Pets:** Other species. $25 daily fee/pet. Service with restrictions, crate.
ASK ⊠ 🖒M 🛏 💻

WHEELING

⏢ ▼▼▼▼ The Westin Chicago North Shore ⊞
(847) 777-6500. **$349-$374.** 601 N Milwaukee Ave. Jct Lake Cook Rd, just s. Int corridors. **Pets:** Accepted.
SAVE ⊠ 🖒M 🛏 💻 🍴 🏊 ✖

WILLOWBROOK

⚛ ☂ Red Roof Inn #7167 M
(630) 323-8811. **$54-$77.** 7535 Kingery Hwy. I-55, exit 274, 0.5 mi n on SR 83. Ext corridors. **Pets:** Medium. Service with restrictions, crate.
[SAVE] ⊠ █

WOODSTOCK

☂ Super 8 H
(815) 337-8808. **Call for rates.** 1220 Davis Rd. On SR 47, s of jct US 14. Int corridors. **Pets:** Accepted.
⊠ █ 💻

END METROPOLITAN AREA

COLLINSVILLE

☂☂ Drury Inn-St. Louis/Collinsville H
(618) 345-7700. **$80-$118.** 602 N Bluff Rd. I-55/70, exit 11 (SR 157), just n. Int corridors. **Pets:** Other species. Service with restrictions, supervision.
[ASK] ⊠ [&M] █ 💻 ⇌

DANVILLE

⚛ ☂☂ Best Western Regency Inn H
(217) 446-2111. **$60-$135.** 360 Eastgate Dr. I-74, exit 220 (Lynch Dr), just n. Ext/int corridors. **Pets:** Small, dogs only. $12 daily fee/pet. Designated rooms, service with restrictions, supervision.
[SAVE] ⊠ █ 💻 ⇌

☂☂ Comfort Inn by Choice Hotels H
(217) 443-8004. **Call for rates.** 383 Lynch Dr. I-74, exit 220 (Lynch Dr), just n. Int corridors. **Pets:** Accepted.
⊠ █ 💻 ⇌

☂☂ Sleep Inn & Suites H 🐾
(217) 442-6600. **Call for rates.** 361 Lynch Dr. I-74, exit 220 (Lynch Dr), just n. Int corridors. **Pets:** Small. $15 daily fee/room. Designated rooms.
⊠ █ 💻 ⇌

☂☂ Super 8 H
(217) 443-4499. **Call for rates.** 377 Lynch Dr. I-74, exit 220 (Lynch Dr), just n. Int corridors. **Pets:** Accepted.
⊠ █ 💻

DECATUR

☂☂☂ Decatur Conference Center & Hotel H
(217) 422-8800. **$99, 3 day notice.** 4191 W Hwy 36. I-72, exit 133A (US 36), 1 mi e. Int corridors. **Pets:** Large. $35 one-time fee/room. Service with restrictions, supervision.
[ASK] ⊠ [&M] █ 💻 [🍴] ⇌ ⊠

☂☂☂ Holiday Inn Express Hotel & Suites H
(217) 875-5500. **$104-$121, 7 day notice.** 5170 Wingate Dr. I-72, exit 141, 0.5 mi n on US 51, then just e. Int corridors. **Pets:** Medium, other species. $10 one-time fee/room. Service with restrictions, supervision.
[ASK] ⊠ [&M] █ 💻 ⇌ ⊠

☂☂ Sleep Inn H
(217) 872-7700. **Call for rates.** 3920 E Hospitality Ln. I-72, exit 144 (SR 48), just s to Brush College Rd, then just e. Int corridors. **Pets:** Accepted.
⊠ █ 💻 ⇌

DEKALB

⚛ ☂☂ Best Western DeKalb Inn & Suites H
(815) 758-8661. **$99, 3 day notice.** 1212 W Lincoln Hwy. I-88, exit Annie Glidden Rd, 2 mi n to W Lincoln Hwy (SR 38), then just w. Ext/int corridors. **Pets:** Medium, dogs only. $50 deposit/room, $10 daily fee/pet. Designated rooms, service with restrictions, supervision.
[SAVE] ⊠ █ 💻 ⇌

☂☂ Magnuson Inn & Suites H
(815) 748-4800. **Call for rates.** 1314 W Lincoln Hwy. I-88, exit Annie Glidden Rd, 2 mi n to W Lincoln Hwy (SR 38), then 0.4 mi w. Int corridors. **Pets:** Accepted.
⊠ [&M] █ 💻 ⇌

DIXON

⚛ ☂☂ Comfort Inn by Choice Hotels H
(815) 284-0500. **$74-$159.** 136 Plaza Dr. I-88, exit SR 26, just n, then just e. Int corridors. **Pets:** Medium. $15 daily fee/pet. Service with restrictions, supervision.
[SAVE] ⊠ █ 💻 ⇌

⚛ ☂☂ Quality Inn & Suites by Choice Hotels H
(815) 288-2001. **$79-$169.** 154 Plaza Dr. I-88, exit SR 26, just n, then just e. Int corridors. **Pets:** Medium. $15 daily fee/pet. Service with restrictions, supervision.
[SAVE] ⊠ █ 💻 ⇌ ⊠

EAST MOLINE

☂☂☂ Comfort Inn & Suites H
(309) 792-4660. **$70-$100, 30 day notice.** 2209 John Deere Expy. I-74, exit 4B (John Deere Rd), 5 mi e; I-80, exit 4A, 6 mi w. Int corridors. **Pets:** Accepted.
[ASK] ⊠ [&M] █ 💻 ⇌

☂ Super 8 Motel-East Moline H
(309) 796-1999. **$54-$60, 4 day notice.** 2201 John Deere Rd. I-74, exit 4B (John Deere Rd), 5.5 mi e on SR 5. Int corridors. **Pets:** Small, dogs only. $10 daily fee/pet. Designated rooms, service with restrictions, crate.
[ASK] ⊠ █ 💻

EAST PEORIA

☂☂ Super 8 H
(309) 698-8889. **$57-$97.** 725 Taylor St. I-74, exit 96, just e. Int corridors. **Pets:** Small. $50 deposit/room. Designated rooms, service with restrictions, supervision.
[ASK] ⊠ █ 💻

EFFINGHAM

⚛ ☂☂ Best Western Raintree Inn H
(217) 342-4121. **$59-$70.** 1811 W Fayette Ave. I-57/70, exit 159, just n. Ext/int corridors. **Pets:** Other species. Designated rooms, service with restrictions, supervision.
[SAVE] ⊠ █ 💻 ⇌

☂ Comfort Inn H
(217) 347-5050. **$60-$80.** 1304 W Evergreen Dr. I-57/70, exit 160 (SR 32/33), just e, then just n. Int corridors. **Pets:** Other species. $5 daily fee/pet. Designated rooms, service with restrictions, supervision.
[ASK] ⊠ [&M] █ 💻 ⇌ ⊠

☂☂☂ Comfort Suites H
(217) 342-3151. **$64-$99.** 1310 W Fayette Ave. I-57/70, exit 159, 0.4 mi e. Int corridors. **Pets:** Accepted.
[ASK] ⊠ [&M] █ 💻 ⇌

⚛ ☂☂ Days Inn H
(217) 347-7131. **$44-$79.** 1205 N Keller Dr. I-57/70, exit 160 (SR 32/33), just n. Int corridors. **Pets:** $10 daily fee/pet. Service with restrictions, supervision.
[SAVE] ⊠ █ 💻

⚛ ☂☂ Econo Lodge M
(217) 342-9271. **$39-$79.** 1412 W Fayette Ave. I-57/70, exit 159, just e. Ext corridors. **Pets:** Accepted.
[SAVE] ⊠ █ 💻 ⇌

△△△ ▼▼▼ **Fairfield Inn & Suites** 🄷
(217) 540-5454. **$98-$120.** 1111 Henritta St. I-57/70, exit 160 (SR 32/33), just se. Int corridors. **Pets:** Medium. $10 one-time fee/room. Service with restrictions, supervision.
SAVE ✕ ♿M 🛄 ▣ 🌊

▼▼▼ **Holiday Inn Express** 🄷
(217) 540-1111. **Call for rates.** 1103 Ave of Mid-America. I-57/70, exit 160 (SR 32/33), just n. Int corridors. **Pets:** Accepted.
✕ ♿M 🛄 ▣

△△△ ▼▼ **Rodeway Inn** Ⓜ
(217) 347-7515. **$42-$120.** 1205A N Keller Dr. I-57/70, exit 160 (SR 32/33), just n. Ext corridors. **Pets:** Other species. $10 daily fee/pet. Service with restrictions, supervision.
SAVE ✕ 🛄 ▣ 🌊 ✕

▼▼ **Super 8 Motel-Effingham** Ⓜ
(217) 342-6888. **$59-$88.** 1400 Thelma Keller Ave. I-57/70, exit 160 (SR 32/33), 0.5 mi n. Int corridors. **Pets:** Other species. Service with restrictions, supervision.
ASK ✕ 🛄 ▣

FAIRFIELD

▼ **Briarwood Inn** Ⓜ
(618) 842-3667. **$73-$100.** 116 N Market Ave. West end of town. Int corridors. **Pets:** Accepted.
ASK ✕ ♿M 🛄 ▣ 🌊

FAIRVIEW HEIGHTS

▼▼▼ **Comfort Suites** 🄷
(618) 394-0202. **$100-$140.** 137 Ludwig Dr. I-64, exit 12 (SR 159), just n to Ludwig Dr, then 0.4 mi w. Int corridors. **Pets:** Medium, other species. $10 daily fee/pet. Service with restrictions, supervision.
ASK ✕ ♿M 🛄 ▣ 🌊

▼▼▼ **Drury Inn & Suites-Fairview Heights** 🄷
(618) 398-8530. **$80-$137.** 12 Ludwig Dr. I-64, exit 12 (SR 159). Int corridors. **Pets:** Other species. Service with restrictions, supervision.
ASK ✕ 🛄 ▣ 🌊

△△△ ▼▼ **Ramada Inn Fairview Heights** 🄷
(618) 632-4747. **$67-$81.** 6900 N Illinois St. I-64, exit 12 (SR 159), just n. Int corridors. **Pets:** Medium. $25 one-time fee/room. Service with restrictions, supervision.
SAVE ✕ 🛄 ▣ 🍴 🌊 ✕

FLORA

△△△ ▼▼ **Best Western Lorson Inn** 🄷
(618) 662-3054. **$70-$90, 3 day notice.** 201 Hagen Ave. Jct US 45 and 50. Int corridors. **Pets:** Large. $8 one-time fee/pet. Service with restrictions, supervision.
SAVE ✕ ♿M 🛄 ▣ ✕

FREEPORT

△△△ ▼▼▼ **Baymont Inn & Suites-Freeport** 🄷
(815) 599-8510. **$79-$150.** 1060 Riverside Dr. Jct US 20 Bypass and SR 26, just s. Int corridors. **Pets:** $25 one-time fee/room. Service with restrictions, supervision.
SAVE ✕ 🛄 ▣ 🌊

△△△ ▼▼▼ **Hampton Inn** 🄷
(815) 232-7100. **$95-$105.** 109 S Galena Ave. Jct Main St; downtown. Int corridors. **Pets:** Medium, dogs only. Designated rooms, service with restrictions, crate.
SAVE ✕ ♿M 🛄 ▣ 🌊

GALENA

△△△ ▼▼▼▼ **Eagle Ridge Resort & Spa** 🄷
(815) 777-5000. **$159-$2509, 7 day notice.** 444 Eagle Ridge Dr. 6 mi e on US 20, 4.5 mi n. Ext/int corridors. **Pets:** Medium, dogs only. $75 one-time fee/room. Service with restrictions, crate.
SAVE ✕ 🛄 ▣ 🍴 🌊 ✕

GALESBURG

△△△ ▼▼▼ **Best Western Prairie Inn** 🄷
(309) 343-7151. **$119-$200.** 300 S Soangetaha Rd. I-74, exit 48 (Main St), just e, then just s. Int corridors. **Pets:** Medium. $25 daily fee/room. Designated rooms, service with restrictions, supervision.
SAVE ✕ 🛄 ▣ 🌊 ✕

▼▼ **Comfort Inn by Choice Hotels** 🄷
(309) 344-5445. **Call for rates.** 907 W Carl Sandburg Dr. US 34, exit US 150 E. Int corridors. **Pets:** Accepted.
✕ ♿M 🛄 ▣

▼▼ **Holiday Inn Express** 🄷 🐾
(309) 343-7100. **$82-$159.** 2285 Washington St. I-74, exit 48A (US 150), just w to Michigan Ave, just s to Washington St, then just e. Int corridors. **Pets:** Other species. $25 one-time fee/room. Service with restrictions, supervision.
ASK ✕ ♿M 🛄 ▣ 🌊 ✕

GILMAN

△△△ ▼▼ **Super 8** 🄷
(815) 265-7000. **$63-$85.** 1301 S Crescent St. I-57, exit 283, 0.3 mi e. Int corridors. **Pets:** Small, other species. $25 deposit/pet, $10 daily fee/pet. Service with restrictions, supervision.
SAVE ✕ 🛄 ▣

△△△ ▼▼ **Travel Inn** Ⓜ
(815) 265-7283. **$60-$70.** 834 US 24 W. I-57, exit 283, just e. Ext/int corridors. **Pets:** $5 daily fee/pet. Designated rooms, no service, supervision.
SAVE ✕ 🌊

GRAYVILLE

▼▼ **Super 8 Motel** 🄷
(618) 375-7288. **Call for rates.** 2060 CR 2450 N. I-64, exit 130 (SR 1), just n. Int corridors. **Pets:** Accepted.
✕ ♿M 🛄 ▣

▼▼ **Windsor Oaks Inn** 🄷
(618) 375-7930. **$77-$150.** 2200 S Court St. I-64, exit 130 (SR 1), just n. Int corridors. **Pets:** $5 daily fee/pet. Designated rooms, service with restrictions, supervision.
ASK ✕ 🛄 ▣ 🍴 🌊

GREENVILLE

▼▼ **Super 8 Motel-Greenville** 🄷
(618) 664-0800. **$56-$66.** 1700 Rt 127 S. I-70, exit 45, just n. Int corridors. **Pets:** $10 daily fee/room. Service with restrictions, supervision.
ASK ✕ 🛄 ▣

HIGHLAND

△△△ ▼▼▼ **Michael's Swiss Inn & Coffee Shop** Ⓜ
(618) 654-8646. **$75-$85, 3 day notice.** 425 Broadway. On SR 160, 1.8 mi s of jct US 40/SR 143. Ext corridors. **Pets:** Other species. Service with restrictions.
SAVE ✕ 🛄 ▣ 🍴 🌊

JACKSONVILLE

Starlite Motel Ⓜ
(217) 245-7184. **$40-$65.** 1910 W Morton Ave. I-72, exit 64, 2.3 mi n on SR 267 (Main St) to SR 104 (Morton Ave), then 1.8 mi w. Ext corridors. **Pets:** Small, other species. $7 daily fee/pet. Service with restrictions, supervision.
[SAVE] [✕] [🖥]

Super 8 Ⓗ
(217) 479-0303. **$45-$90.** 1003 W Morton Ave. I-72, exit 64, 2.3 mi n on SR 267 (Main St) to SR 104 (Morton Ave), then 0.8 mi w. Int corridors. **Pets:** Medium. $10 daily fee/pet. Service with restrictions, crate.
[ASK] [✕] [🖥] [💻]

LINCOLN

Hampton Inn–Lincoln Ⓗ
(217) 732-6729. **$84-$99.** 1019 N Heitmann Dr. I-55, exit 126 (US 121), just e. Int corridors. **Pets:** Other species. $100 deposit/room.
[SAVE] [✕] [&M] [🖥] [💻] [🏊]

Holiday Inn Express Ⓗ
(217) 735-5800. **Call for rates.** 130 Olson Dr. I-55, exit 126 (US 121), just e to Heitman Dr, just w to Olson Dr, then just n. Int corridors. **Pets:** Accepted.
[✕] [🖥] [💻] [🏊]

LITCHFIELD

Hampton Inn Ⓗ
(217) 324-4441. **$84-$99.** 11 Thunderbird Cir. I-55, exit 52 (SR 16), on Corvette Dr, then just e. Int corridors. **Pets:** Medium. $100 deposit/room. Service with restrictions, supervision.
[SAVE] [✕] [&M] [🖥] [💻] [🏊]

Holiday Inn Express Ⓗ
(217) 324-4556. **$84-$99.** 1405 W Hudson Dr. I-55, exit 52 (SR 16), just e to Ohren Ln, just s to W Hudson Dr, then just w. Int corridors. **Pets:** Other species. Designated rooms, service with restrictions, supervision.
[✕] [🖥] [💻] [🏊]

LOVES PARK

Holiday Inn Express Hotel & Suites Rockford North Ⓗ
(815) 654-4100. **$100-$160.** 7552 Park Pl. I-90, exit E Riverside Blvd, just nw. Int corridors. **Pets:** Accepted.
[✕] [&M] [🖥] [💻] [🏊] [✕]

Quality Inn & Suites Rockford/Loves Park Ⓗ
(815) 282-9300. **$70-$200.** 4313 Bell School Rd. I-39/90, exit E Riverside Blvd, just nw. Int corridors. **Pets:** Small, other species. $10 daily fee/pet. Designated rooms, no service, supervision.
[ASK] [✕] [&M] [🖥] [💻] [🏊]

MACOMB

Rodeway Inn-Macomb Ⓗ
(309) 837-2220. **Call for rates.** 1646 N Lafayette St. Jct US 67 and 136, 1.9 mi n on US 67. Int corridors. **Pets:** Accepted.
[✕] [🖥] [💻] [🏊]

Super 8 Motel Ⓗ
(309) 836-8888. **Call for rates.** 313 University Dr. 1.1 mi n on US 67 to University Dr, 0.5 mi w. Int corridors. **Pets:** Accepted.
[✕] [🖥] [💻]

MANTENO

Country Inn & Suites by Carlson Ⓗ
(815) 468-2600. **$79-$199.** 380 S Cypress St. I-57, exit 322, just se via frontage road. Int corridors. **Pets:** Accepted.
[SAVE] [✕] [&M] [🖥] [💻] [🏊]

MARION

Drury Inn-Marion Ⓗ
(618) 997-9600. **$82-$136.** 2706 W DeYoung St. I-57, exit 54B (SR 13), 0.5 mi w. Int corridors. **Pets:** Other species. Service with restrictions, supervision.
[ASK] [✕] [&M] [🖥] [💻] [🏊]

Super 8 Ⓗ
(618) 993-5577. **$60-$90.** 2601 W DeYoung St. I-57, exit 54B (SR 13), just w. Int corridors. **Pets:** Accepted.
[ASK] [✕] [🖥] [💻]

MATTOON

Holiday Inn Express Hotel & Suites Ⓗ
(217) 235-2060. **Call for rates.** 121 Swords Dr. I-57, exit 190B, just w. Int corridors. **Pets:** Medium. $25 one-time fee/room. Designated rooms, service with restrictions, supervision.
[✕] [&M] [🖥] [💻] [🏊]

Super 8 Motel Ⓜ
(217) 235-8888. **$59-$79.** 205 McFall Rd. I-57, exit 190B, just w. Int corridors. **Pets:** Accepted.
[ASK] [✕] [🖥] [💻]

MONMOUTH

AmericInn Lodge & Suites of Monmouth Ⓗ 🐾
(309) 734-9958. **$90-$170.** 1 AmericInn Way. US 34 and jct N Main St, just s; 18 mi w of jct I-74 and US 34. Int corridors. **Pets:** Small, dogs only. $75 one-time fee/room. Designated rooms, service with restrictions, supervision.
[ASK] [✕] [&M] [🖥] [💻] [🏊] [✕]

MONTICELLO

Best Western Monticello Gateway Inn Ⓗ
(217) 762-9436. **$50-$110, 7 day notice.** 805 Iron Horse Pl. I-72, exit 166, just s. Ext/int corridors. **Pets:** Other species. $10 daily fee/pet. Designated rooms, service with restrictions, supervision.
[SAVE] [✕] [🖥] [💻] [🏊]

MORRIS

Comfort Inn by Choice Hotels Ⓗ
(815) 942-1433. **Call for rates.** 70 Gore Rd W. I-80, exit 112 (SR 47), 0.3 mi nw. Int corridors. **Pets:** Accepted.
[✕] [🖥] [💻] [🏊]

Holiday Inn Ⓗ
(815) 942-6600. **Call for rates.** 200 Gore Rd. I-80, exit 112 (SR 47), 0.3 mi nw. Int corridors. **Pets:** Accepted.
[✕] [💻] [🏊] [✕]

MORTON

Baymont Inn & Suites by Wyndham Ⓗ
(309) 266-8888. **$75-$120.** 210 E Ashland St. I-74, exit 102, 0.4 mi ne. Int corridors. **Pets:** Accepted.
[SAVE] [✕] [🖥] [💻] [🏊]

Best Western Ashland House Inn & Conference Center Ⓗ
(309) 263-5116. **$99-$109.** 201 E Ashland St. I-74, exit 102, 0.3 mi ne. Int corridors. **Pets:** Accepted.
[SAVE] [✕] [🖥] [💻] [🍴] [🏊]

Quality Inn by Choice Hotels Ⓗ
(309) 266-8310. **Call for rates.** 115 E Ashland St. I-74, exit 102B, just w. Ext/int corridors. **Pets:** Accepted.
[✕] [🖥] [💻]

MOUNT VERNON

🛆🛆🛆 **▼▼▼** Holiday Inn **H**
(618) 244-7100. **$94-$125.** 222 Potomac Blvd. I-57/64, exit 95 (SR 15), just w to Potomac Blvd, then just n. Int corridors. **Pets:** Accepted.
SAVE ⊠ ⴲ🖙 🖥 ⵏ 🛏 ⊠

NASHVILLE

🛆🛆🛆 **▼** Best Western U.S. Inn **H**
(618) 478-5341. **$65-$85.** 11640 SR 127. I-64, exit 50 (SR 127), 0.3 mi s. Int corridors. **Pets:** Small. $10 daily fee/pet. Designated rooms, service with restrictions, supervision.
SAVE ⊠ ⴲ🖙 🖥 🖥 🛏

NORMAL

🛆🛆🛆 **▼▼▼** Best Western University Inn **H** 🐾
(309) 454-4070. **$70-$95.** 6 Traders Cir. I-55, exit 165A (US 51), just s, then return on frontage road. Int corridors. **Pets:** Other species. $10 daily fee/room. Service with restrictions.
SAVE ⊠ 🖥 🖥 🛏

▼▼ Comfort Suites by Choice Hotels
Bloomington/Normal **H**
(309) 452-8588. **Call for rates.** 310 B Greenbriar Dr. I-55, exit 167, follow I-55 business route (Veterans Pkwy), 1.3 mi s; jct Fort Jesse Rd. Int corridors. **Pets:** Medium, other species. $20 daily fee/room. Service with restrictions, supervision.
⊠ 🖙 🖥 🖥 🛏

▼▼▼ Holiday Inn Express Hotel & Suites
Bloomington/Normal **H** 🐾
(309) 862-1600. **$79-$129.** 1715 Parkway Plaza Dr. I-55, exit 167, follow I-55 business route (Veterans Pkwy), 1.7 mi s to Parkway Plaza Dr, then just e. Int corridors. **Pets:** Medium, other species. $15 daily fee/room. Service with restrictions.
ASK ⊠ 🖥 🖥 🛏 ⊠

O'FALLON

▼▼▼ Candlewood Suites **H**
(618) 622-9555. **$79-$119.** 1332 Park Plaza Dr. I-64, exit 14 (US 50), just s on Lincoln Hwy, 0.5 mi w on Hartman Ln, then just n on 2nd entrance to Park Plaza Dr. Int corridors. **Pets:** Medium. $75 one-time fee/pet. Service with restrictions, supervision.
⊠ 🖙 🖥 🖥

▼▼▼ Drury Inn & Suites-O'Fallon **H**
(618) 624-2211. **$82-$165.** 1118 Central Park Dr. I-64, exit 16, just s. Int corridors. **Pets:** Other species. Service with restrictions, supervision.
ASK ⊠ 🖙 🖥 🖥 🛏 ⊠

▼▼ Extended StayAmerica-O'Fallon Illinois **H**
(618) 624-1757. **$59-$109.** 154 Regency Park Dr. I-64, exit 14 (US 50), just w to Regency Park Dr, then 0.4 mi s. Int corridors. **Pets:** Other species. $25 daily fee/pet. Service with restrictions, crate.
⊠ 🖙 🖥 🖥

🛆🛆🛆 **▼▼▼** Settle Inn & Suites **H**
(618) 624-6060. **$69-$149.** 1100 Eastgate Dr. I-64, exit 19B (SR 158), 0.5 mi n, then just sw. Int corridors. **Pets:** Other species. $50 deposit/pet. Service with restrictions, crate.
SAVE ⊠ 🖥 🖥 🛏

OGLESBY

▼▼ Holiday Inn Express **H**
(815) 883-3535. **Call for rates.** 900 Holiday St. I-39, exit 54, just e. Int corridors. **Pets:** Accepted.
⊠ 🖥 🖥 🛏

OTTAWA

▼▼▼ Hampton Inn-Starved Rock Area **H**
(815) 434-6040. **$104-$124.** 4115 Holiday Ln. I-80, exit 90 (SR 23), just n. Int corridors. **Pets:** Small. Designated rooms, service with restrictions, supervision.
⊠ 🖙 🖥 🖥 🛏

▼▼ Holiday Inn Express **H**
(815) 433-0029. **$119-$199.** 120 W Stevenson Rd. I-80, exit 90 (SR 23), just n. Int corridors. **Pets:** Accepted.
ASK ⊠ 🖥 🖥 🛏

PEORIA

▼▼ Baymont Inn & Suites **H** 🐾
(309) 686-7600. **Call for rates.** 2002 W War Memorial Dr. I-74, exit 89 (US 150/War Memorial Dr), just n; entrance through Northwoods Mall. Ext/int corridors. **Pets:** Medium. $20 one-time fee/room. Designated rooms, service with restrictions, supervision.
⊠ 🖥 🖥 🛏

▼▼ Candlewood Suites Peoria at Grand Prairie **H**
(309) 691-1690. **$119-$199.** 5300 Landens Way. SR 6, exit 2 (War Memorial Dr/US 150), follow US 150 NW to Summershade Cir, then just w. Int corridors. **Pets:** Accepted.
ASK ⊠ 🖙 🖥 🖥

▼▼▼ Comfort Suites by Choice Hotels **H**
(309) 688-3800. **Call for rates.** 1812 W War Memorial Dr. I-74, exit 89 (US 150/War Memorial Dr), just e, then just s. Int corridors. **Pets:** Other species. $25 one-time fee/room. Service with restrictions.
⊠ 🖥 🖥 🛏

▼▼▼ Country Inn & Suites by Carlson Peoria North **H**
(309) 589-0044. **$179.** 5309 W Landens Way. SR 6, exit 2 (War Memorial Dr), just n. Int corridors. **Pets:** Medium. $75 one-time fee/pet. Service with restrictions, supervision.
ASK ⊠ 🖙 🖥 🖥 🛏

▼ Red Roof Inn #7057 **M**
(309) 685-3911. **$74-$99.** 1822 W War Memorial Dr. I-74, exit 89 (US 150/War Memorial Dr), just e. Ext corridors. **Pets:** Accepted.
ASK ⊠ 🖥

▼▼▼ Residence Inn by Marriott **H**
(309) 681-9000. **$160-$180.** 2000 W War Memorial Dr. I-74, exit 89 (US 150/War Memorial Dr), just w; entrance through Northwoods Mall. Int corridors. **Pets:** Other species. $25 one-time fee/room. Service with restrictions, crate.
⊠ 🖥 🖥 🛏 ⊠

▼ Super 8 **H**
(309) 688-8074. **$61-$90.** 1816 W War Memorial Dr. I-74, exit 89 (US 150/War Memorial Dr), just e. Int corridors. **Pets:** Accepted.
ASK ⊠ 🖥 🖥

▼▼▼ Wingate by Wyndham Peoria **H**
(309) 589-0033. **$119-$139.** 7708 N Rt 91. SR 6, exit 2, just w on US 150 (War Memorial Dr), then 0.3 mi n. Int corridors. **Pets:** Accepted.
ASK ⊠ 🖙 🖥 🖥 🛏 ⊠

PERU

▼▼ La Quinta Inn Peru **H** 🐾
(815) 224-9000. **$79-$119.** 4389 Venture Dr. I-80, exit 75 (SR 251), 0.4 mi s to 38th St, just w to Venture Dr, then 0.4 mi nw. Int corridors. **Pets:** Medium, other species. Service with restrictions, supervision.
ASK ⊠ 🖥 🖥 🛏

QUAD CITIES AREA

MOLINE

▼▼ Comfort Inn by Choice Hotels 🏠
(309) 762-7000. **Call for rates.** 2600 52nd Ave. I-280/74, exit 18A eastbound; exit 5B westbound, just s on US 6 and 150, then 0.5 mi nw on 27th St. Int corridors. **Pets:** Accepted.
⊠ 🛏 💻 🏊

▼▼ Fairfield Inn by Marriott 🏠
(309) 762-9083. **$80-$95.** 2705 48th Ave. I-280/74, exit 5B westbound; exit 18A eastbound, just s on US 6 to traffic light, then 1 mi nw on 27th St. Int corridors. **Pets:** Accepted.
⊠ 🛏 💻 🏊

▼▼ Fifth Season Hotel & Convention Center 🏠
(309) 762-8811. **$76-$81.** 6902 27th St. I-280/74, exit 18A eastbound; exit 5B westbound, just s on US 6 and 150, then just nw. Int corridors. **Pets:** Accepted.
ASK ⊠ 🛏 💻 🍴 🏊 ⊠

▼▼ Holiday Inn Express-Moline Airport 🏠
(309) 762-8300. **Call for rates.** 6910 27th St. I-280/74, exit 18A eastbound; exit 5B westbound, just s on US 6 and 150, then just nw. Int corridors. **Pets:** Accepted.
⊠ 🛏 💻

▼▼▼ La Quinta Inn Moline 🏠 🐾
(309) 762-9008. **$49-$89.** 5450 27th St. I-280/74, exit 18A eastbound; exit 5B westbound, just s on US 6 and 150 to traffic light, then just nw. Int corridors. **Pets:** Medium, other species. Service with restrictions, supervision.
ASK ⊠ 🛏 💻 🏊

AAA ▼ Super 8 🏠
(309) 797-5580. **$52-$72.** 2501 52nd Ave. I-280/74, exit 18A eastbound; exit 5B westbound, just s on US 6 and 150, then 1 mi nw on 27th St. Int corridors. **Pets:** Other species. Supervision.
SAVE ⊠ 🛏 💻

ROCK ISLAND

AAA ▼▼▼ Holiday Inn Rock Island Hotel & Conference Center 🏠
(309) 794-1212. **$109-$139, 30 day notice.** 226 17th St. Just e of Centennial Bridge; at 3rd Ave and 17th St; downtown. Int corridors. **Pets:** Accepted.
SAVE ⊠ 🛏 💻 🍴 🏊 ⊠

END AREA

QUINCY

▼▼ Comfort Inn by Choice Hotels 🏠
(217) 228-2700. **Call for rates.** 4122 Broadway. I-172, exit 14 (SR 104), 1.3 mi w. Int corridors. **Pets:** $10 daily fee/pet. Service with restrictions, supervision.
⊠ 🛏 💻 🏊

▼▼▼ Country Inn & Suites By Carlson 🏠
(217) 222-8949. **$95-$500.** 110 N 54th St. I-172, exit 14 (SR 104), just w. Int corridors. **Pets:** Accepted.
ASK ⊠ 🛏 💻 🏊 ⊠

▼ Super 8 Motel 🏠
(217) 228-8808. **$63-$70, 7 day notice.** 224 N 36th St. I-172, exit 14 (SR 104), 1.8 mi w, then just s. Int corridors. **Pets:** Accepted.
ASK ⊠ 🛏 💻

RANTOUL

AAA ▼▼ Best Western Heritage Inn 🏠
(217) 892-9292. **$62, 3 day notice.** 520 S Murray Rd. I-57, exit 250 (US 136), 0.5 mi e, then just s. Ext corridors. **Pets:** Medium. $8 daily fee/pet. Service with restrictions, supervision.
SAVE ⊠ 🛏 💻 🏊

▼▼ Super 8 Motel 🏠
(217) 893-8888. **$50-$150.** 207 S Murray Rd. I-57, exit 250 (US 136), just e. Int corridors. **Pets:** Small, dogs only. $10 daily fee/pet. Service with restrictions, supervision.
ASK ⊠ 🛏 💻

ROBINSON

AAA ▼▼▼ Best Western Robinson Inn 🏠
(618) 544-8448. **$75-$85.** 1500 W Main St. 1.2 mi w on SR 33. Int corridors. **Pets:** Other species. $5 daily fee/room.
SAVE ⊠ 🛏 💻

ROCHELLE

AAA ▼▼ Baymont Inn & Suites 🏠
(815) 562-9530. **$79-$159.** 567 E Hwy 38. I-39, exit 99 (SR 38), 1 mi w. Int corridors. **Pets:** Large. $10 one-time fee/pet. Service with restrictions.
SAVE ⊠ 🛏 💻 🏊

ROCKFORD

▼▼ Baymont Inn & Suites Rockford 🏠 🐾
(815) 229-8200. **$69-$150.** 662 N Lyford Rd. I-90, exit US 20 business route, just e, then just n. Int corridors. **Pets:** Medium, other species. Service with restrictions, supervision.
ASK ⊠ 🛏 💻 🏊

▼▼ Candlewood Suites 🏠
(815) 229-9300. **$119-$149.** 7555 Walton St. I-90, exit US 20 business route, 0.3 mi e to Bell School Rd, just s to Walton St, then just e. Int corridors. **Pets:** Accepted.
ASK ⊠ 🛏 💻

▼▼ Comfort Inn by Choice Hotels 🏠
(815) 398-7061. **$80-$140.** 7392 Argus Dr. I-90, exit US 20 business route, just w to Bell School Rd, then just n. Int corridors. **Pets:** Large, other species. $25 one-time fee/room. Service with restrictions.
ASK ⊠ 🛏 💻

AAA ▼ Days Inn Rockford 🏠
(815) 332-4915. **$49-$119.** 220 S Lyford Rd. I-90, exit US 20 business route, just e, then just s. Int corridors. **Pets:** Accepted.
SAVE ⊠ 🛏 💻

▼▼ Extended StayAmerica-Rockford East 🏠
(815) 226-8969. **$75-$105.** 653 Clark Dr. I-90, exit US 20 business route, just w. Int corridors. **Pets:** Other species. $25 daily fee/pet. Service with restrictions, crate.
ASK ⊠ 🛏 💻

▼▼ Quality Suites 🏠
(815) 227-1300. **Call for rates.** 7401 Walton St. I-90, exit US 20 business route, just w to Bell School Rd, then just s. Int corridors. **Pets:** Small, other species. $25 daily fee/room. Service with restrictions, crate.
⊠ 🛏 💻 🏊 ⊠

◈ ▼ Red Roof Inn #7035 M ❄
(815) 398-9750. **$55-$90.** 7434 E State St. I-90, exit US 20 business route, just w. Ext corridors. **Pets:** Small. Service with restrictions, supervision.
SAVE ✕ 🏢

▼▼ Residence Inn by Marriott H
(815) 227-0013. **$150-$160.** 7542 Colosseum Dr. I-90, exit US 20 business route, just w. Int corridors. **Pets:** Accepted.
✕ 🏢 🖳 ⊃ ✕

◈ ▼▼ Sleep Inn-Rockford H
(815) 398-8900. **$79-$179, 14 day notice.** 725 Clark Dr. I-90, exit US 20 business route, just w to Bell School Rd, just n to Clark Dr, then 0.4 mi ne. Int corridors. **Pets:** Accepted.
SAVE ✕ 🏢 🖳

▼▼ StudioPLUS Deluxe Studios H
(815) 397-8316. **$70-$110.** 747 N Bell School Rd. I-90, exit US 20 business route, just w to Bell School Rd, then 0.3 mi n. Int corridors. **Pets:** Other species. $25 daily fee/pet. Service with restrictions, crate.
ASK ✕ 🏢 🖳

SALEM

▼ Super 8 Motel of Salem H
(618) 548-5882. **$60-$87.** 118 Woods Ln. I-57, exit 116 (US 50), just w. Ext/int corridors. **Pets:** Large. Service with restrictions, supervision.
ASK ✕ ⬛ 🏢 🖳

SAVOY

◈ ▼▼ Best Western Paradise Inn H
(217) 356-1824. **$63-$74, 3 day notice.** 709 N Dunlap Ave. I-57, exit 229, 1 mi e to US 45, then 2.5 mi n. Ext corridors. **Pets:** Small. $5 daily fee/pet. Service with restrictions, crate.
SAVE ✕ 🏢 🖳 ⊃

SOUTH BELOIT

◈ ▼▼ Best Western Legacy Inn & Suites H
(815) 389-4211. **$89-$149.** 5910 Technology Dr. I-90/39, exit 1, just sw. Int corridors. **Pets:** Medium. $25 one-time fee/pet. Service with restrictions, supervision.
SAVE ✕ 🏢 🖳 ⊃

SOUTH JACKSONVILLE

◈ ▼▼▼ Comfort Inn-South Jacksonville H
(217) 245-8372. **$89-$109.** 200 Comfort Dr. I-72, exit 64, just n. Int corridors. **Pets:** $15 daily fee/pet. Service with restrictions, crate.
SAVE ✕ 🏢 ⊃

▼▼ Econo Lodge Inn & Suites by Choice Hotels H
(217) 245-9575. **$65-$70.** 1914 Southbrooke Rd. I-72, exit 64, just n. Int corridors. **Pets:** Accepted.
ASK ✕ ⬛ 🏢 🖳

SPRINGFIELD

◈ ▼▼ Baymont Inn & Suites Springfield H
(217) 529-6655. **$85-$95.** 5871 S 6th St. I-55, exit 90 (Toronto Rd), just e to 6th St, then just n. Int corridors. **Pets:** Small. $10 daily fee/pet. Designated rooms, service with restrictions, supervision.
SAVE ✕ ⬛ 🏢 🖳 ⊃

◈ ▼▼ Best Western Clearlake Plaza H
(217) 525-7420. **$79-$110.** 3440 E Clearlake Ave. I-55, exit 98B, just w. Int corridors. **Pets:** Large, other species. $35 one-time fee/pet. Service with restrictions, supervision.
SAVE ✕ ⬛ 🏢 🖳 ⊃

▼▼▼ Drury Inn & Suites-Springfield H
(217) 529-3900. **$90-$131.** 3180 S Dirksen Pkwy. I-55, exit 94 (Stevenson Dr), just w to Dirksen Pkwy, then just n. Int corridors. **Pets:** Other species. Service with restrictions, supervision.
ASK ✕ ⬛ 🏢 🖳 ⊃

◈ ▼▼▼ Holiday Inn Express Hotel & Suites H
(217) 529-7771. **$89-$111.** 3050 S Dirksen Pkwy. I-55, exit 94 (Stevenson Dr), just w to S Dirksen Pkwy, then 0.4 mi n. Int corridors. **Pets:** Other species. $25 one-time fee/room. Service with restrictions, supervision.
SAVE ✕ ⬛ 🏢 🖳

◈ ▼▼▼ Mansion View Inn & Suites H
(217) 544-7411. **$89.** 529 S 4th St. I-55, exit 92 (6th St), 3.9 mi n to Edwards St, then just w, follow signs. Ext/int corridors. **Pets:** Accepted.
SAVE ✕ 🏢 🖳

▼▼ Microtel Inn & Suites H
(217) 753-2636. **$69-$99.** 2636 Sunrise Dr. I-55, exit 94 (Stevenson Dr), just w to Dirksen Pkwy, then 0.4 mi n. Int corridors. **Pets:** Small. $5 daily fee/pet. Service with restrictions, supervision.
ASK ✕ ⬛ 🏢 🖳 ⊃

▼▼ Pear Tree Inn by Drury-Springfield H
(217) 529-9100. **$45-$78.** 3190 S Dirksen Pkwy. I-55, exit 94 (Stevenson Dr), just w. Int corridors. **Pets:** Other species. Service with restrictions, supervision.
ASK ✕ 🖳

▼ Red Roof Inn #7040 M
(217) 753-4302. **$47-$90.** 3200 Singer Ave. I-55, exit 96B, just w. Ext corridors. **Pets:** Medium, other species. Service with restrictions, supervision.
ASK ✕

▼▼ Sleep Inn by Choice Hotels H
(217) 787-6200. **Call for rates.** 3470 Freedom Dr. I-72, exit 93 (Veterans Pkwy), 0.7 mi n to Lindbergh Blvd, just w to Freedom Dr, then just s. Int corridors. **Pets:** Other species. $25 one-time fee/room. Service with restrictions, supervision.
✕ 🏢 🖳

▼▼▼ Staybridge Suites Springfield South H
(217) 793-6700. **$134-$189.** 4231 Schooner Dr. I-72, exit 93 (Veterans Pkwy), 0.4 mi se. Int corridors. **Pets:** Medium. $75 one-time fee/room. Service with restrictions, supervision.
ASK ✕ ⬛ 🏢 🖳 ⊃ ✕

STAUNTON

▼ Staunton Super 8 H
(618) 635-5353. **$54.** 1527 Herman Rd. I-55, exit 41, 0.5 mi w. Int corridors. **Pets:** Medium. $10 one-time fee/room. Service with restrictions, supervision.
ASK ✕ 🏢 🖳

STOCKTON

▼▼▼ Country Inn & Suites By Carlson H
(815) 947-6060. **$88-$140.** 200 Dillon Ave. On US 20, just e of SR 78. Int corridors. **Pets:** Other species. $20 daily fee/pet. Designated rooms, service with restrictions, crate.
✕ ⬛ 🏢 🖳 ⊃

SYCAMORE

▼▼ Americas Best Value Inn & Suites H
(815) 899-6500. **Call for rates.** 1860 Dekalb Ave. On SR 23, 0.9 mi s of Peace Rd. Int corridors. **Pets:** Accepted.
✕ ⬛ 🏢 🖳

TUSCOLA

▼▼ Baymont Inn & Suites H
(217) 253-3500. **$79-$112.** 1006 Southline Rd. I-57, exit 212 (US 36), 0.3 mi w. Int corridors. **Pets:** Accepted.
ASK ✕ ⬛ 🏢 🖳 ⊃

♦♦ **Holiday Inn Express** 🏨
(217) 253-6363. **$95-$125.** 1201 Tuscola Blvd. I-57, exit 212 (US 36), 0.3 mi w to Progress Blvd, just s to Tuscola Blvd, then 0.4 mi se. Int corridors. **Pets:** Accepted.

ASK ⊠ 🔒 🖥 🐾

♦♦ **Super 8 Motel-Tuscola** 🏨
(217) 253-5488. **Call for rates.** 1007 E Southline Rd. I-57, exit 212 (US 36), 0.4 mi w. Int corridors. **Pets:** Other species. $10 daily fee/pet. Designated rooms, no service, supervision.

⊠ 🔒 🖥

URBANA

AAA ♦♦♦ **Ramada-Urbana/Champaign** 🏨
(217) 328-4400. **$94-$135.** 902 W Killarney St. I-74, exit 183 (Lincoln Ave), just s to Killarney St, then just w. Int corridors. **Pets:** Medium. $10 daily fee/pet. Service with restrictions, crate.

SAVE ⊠ 🔒 🖥 🐾

♦♦♦ **Sleep Inn** 🏨
(217) 367-6000. **$55-$129.** 1908 N Lincoln Ave. I-74, exit 183 (Lincoln Ave), 0.5 mi s. Int corridors. **Pets:** Accepted.

SAVE ⊠ 🔒 🖥 🐾

VANDALIA

AAA ♦♦♦ **Days Inn-Vandalia** Ⓜ
(618) 283-4400. **$69-$81.** 1920 Kennedy Blvd. I-70, exit 63 (US 51), 0.6 mi n. Ext corridors. **Pets:** Other species. $10 deposit/room. Service with restrictions, crate.

SAVE ⊠ 🔒 🖥 🐾

♦♦♦ **Holiday Inn Express Hotel & Suites** 🏨
(618) 283-0010. **Call for rates.** 21 Mattes Ave. I-70, exit 61, just s. Int corridors. **Pets:** Large, other species. $20 one-time fee/room. Designated rooms, service with restrictions, supervision.

⊠ ♿ 🔒 🖥 🐾

AAA ♦♦ **Jay's Inn** Ⓜ
(618) 283-1200. **$56-$65.** 720 Gochenour St. I-70, exit 63 (US 51), just s. Ext corridors. **Pets:** Other species. Service with restrictions, crate.

SAVE ⊠ 🔒 🖥

♦♦ **Ramada Vandalia** 🏨
(618) 283-1400. **$60-$100.** 2707 Veterans Ave. I-70, exit 61, just s. Int corridors. **Pets:** Other species. $10 daily fee/pet. Designated rooms, no service, crate.

ASK ⊠ 🔒 🖥 🐾

WASHINGTON

♦♦ **Super 8** 🏨
(309) 444-8881. **$46-$62, 10 day notice.** 1884 Washington Rd. On Business Rt US 24, 1.5 mi w. Int corridors. **Pets:** Accepted.

ASK ⊠ 🔒 🖥

WATSEKA

AAA ♦♦♦ **Super 8** 🏨
(815) 432-6000. **$63-$85.** 710 W Walnut St. On US 24; center of downtown. Int corridors. **Pets:** Small. $25 deposit/pet, $10 daily fee/pet. Service with restrictions, supervision.

SAVE ⊠ 🔒 🖥

WENONA

♦♦ **Super 8** 🏨
(815) 853-4371. **$64-$69.** 5 Cavalry Dr. I-39, exit 35. Int corridors. **Pets:** $5 daily fee/pet. Designated rooms, supervision.

ASK ⊠ 🔒 🖥

INDIANA

ANGOLA

▼▼▼ Ramada Inn H
(260) 665-9471. **$75-$155.** 3855 N SR 127. I-69, exit 154, just e, then 0.4 mi s. Int corridors. **Pets:** Other species. $25 one-time fee/room. Service with restrictions, supervision.

ASK ⊠ 🛏 💻 ⛱ 🐾

AUBURN

🔺🔻 ▼▼▼ Best Western Auburn Inn H
(260) 925-6363. **$80-$130.** 225 Touring Dr. I-69, exit 129 (SR 8), just e, then just s. Int corridors. **Pets:** Medium, other species. $50 deposit/room, $20 one-time fee/room. Designated rooms, service with restrictions, crate.

SAVE ⊠ 🛏 💻 ⛱

🔺🔻 ▼▼▼ Holiday Inn Express H
(260) 925-1900. **$79-$109.** 404 Touring Dr. I-69, exit 129 (SR 8), just e, then just s. Int corridors. **Pets:** Other species. Service with restrictions, supervision.

SAVE ⊠ 🖑 🛏 💻 ⛱

▼▼ La Quinta Inn Auburn H 🐾
(260) 920-1900. **$60-$200.** 306 Touring Dr. I-69, exit 129 (SR 8), 0.5 mi e. Int corridors. **Pets:** Medium, other species. Service with restrictions, supervision.

ASK ⊠ 🛏 💻 ⛱

▼▼ Super 8-Auburn H
(260) 927-8800. **Call for rates.** 503 Ley Dr. I-69, exit 129 (SR 8), just e, then just s. Int corridors. **Pets:** Accepted.

⊠ 🛏 💻

BEDFORD

🔺🔻 ▼▼▼ Bedford Comfort Inn H
(812) 279-8111. **$90-$249.** 911 Constitution Ave. Jct SR 37 and 58, just s on SR 37. Int corridors. **Pets:** Medium. $25 one-time fee/pet. Designated rooms, service with restrictions, supervision.

SAVE ⊠ 🖑 🛏 💻 🍴 ⛱

▼▼ Bedford Super 8 H
(812) 275-8881. **$65-$125, 3 day notice.** 501 Bell Back Rd. Jct SR 37 and 58, just e on SR 58. Int corridors. **Pets:** $10 daily fee/pet. Service with restrictions.

ASK ⊠ 🛏 💻 ⛱ 🐾

BERNE

▼▼ Black Bear Inn & Suites H
(260) 589-8955. **$68-$73.** 1335 US 27 N. On US 27, 1 mi n. Int corridors. **Pets:** Other species. $5 one-time fee/pet. Designated rooms, service with restrictions, crate.

ASK ⊠ 🛏 💻 ⛱

BLOOMINGTON

▼▼▼ Comfort Inn Bloomington H
(812) 650-0010. **$89-$289.** 1700 N Kinser Pike. On SR 45 and 45 Bypass, 1 mi e of jct SR 37. Int corridors. **Pets:** Small. $25 one-time fee/pet. Designated rooms, service with restrictions, crate.

ASK ⊠ 💻

▼▼▼ Crowne Plaza H
(812) 334-3252. **$119-$329, 3 day notice.** 1710 N Kinser Pike. On SR 45 and 46 Bypass, 1 mi e of jct SR 37. Int corridors. **Pets:** Small. $75 one-time fee/room. Service with restrictions, crate.

ASK ⊠ 🖑 💻 🍴

▼▼ Fairfield Inn by Marriott H
(812) 331-1122. **$98-$120.** 120 Fairfield Dr. Just e from SR 37 at 3rd St. Int corridors. **Pets:** Accepted.

⊠ 🖑 🛏 💻 ⛱

▼▼ Hampton Inn H
(812) 334-2100. **$109-$339.** 2100 N Walnut St. 1 mi e of jct SR 37 on SR 45/46 Bypass, then just s on College Ave/Walnut St. Int corridors. **Pets:** Accepted.

⊠ 🛏 💻 ⛱

▼▼ TownePlace Suites By Marriott H
(812) 334-1234. **$119-$139.** 105 S Franklin Rd. Just e from SR 37 at 3rd St, then 0.3 mi n. Int corridors. **Pets:** Accepted.

⊠ 🛏 💻 ⛱

CHESTERTON

▼▼▼ Gray Goose Inn BB 🐾
(219) 926-5781. **$110-$195, 3 day notice.** 350 Indian Boundary Rd. I-94, exit 26A, 0.6 mi s, then just w. Int corridors. **Pets:** $25 one-time fee/pet. Service with restrictions, supervision.

ASK ⊠

CINCINNATI METROPOLITAN AREA (NEARBY OHIO)

LAWRENCEBURG

▼▼▼ Comfort Inn & Suites H
(812) 539-3600. **$80-$200.** 1610 Flossie Dr. I-275, exit 16, 0.3 mi e. Int corridors. **Pets:** Accepted.

ASK ⊠ 🖑 🛏 💻 ⛱

▼▼ Quality Inn & Suites H
(812) 539-4770. **Call for rates.** 1000 E Eads Pkwy. I-275, exit 16, 0.5 mi w on US 50. Int corridors. **Pets:** Accepted.

⊠ 🛏 💻 ⛱

END METROPOLITAN AREA

CLARKSVILLE

Best Western Green Tree Inn M
(812) 288-9281. **$85-$275.** 1425 Broadway St. I-65, exit 4, just w. Ext corridors. **Pets:** Small, dogs only. Service with restrictions, crate.
SAVE ⊠ 🛅 💻 ⌦

CLOVERDALE

Super 8 Cloverdale/Greencastle H
(765) 795-7373. **$63-$150.** 1020 N Main St. I-70, exit 41, just s on US 231. Int corridors. **Pets:** Dogs only. $10 daily fee/room. Service with restrictions, supervision.
ASK ⊠ 🛅 💻 ⌦

COLUMBUS

Columbus Holiday Inn and Conference Center H
(812) 372-1541. **Call for rates.** 2480 Jonathan Moore Pike. I-65, exit 68, just e on SR 46. Ext/int corridors. **Pets:** Medium, other species. $25 one-time fee/pet. Designated rooms, service with restrictions, supervision.
⊠ 🛅 💻 ⌦ ⌦

Hotel Indigo H
(812) 375-9100. **$149-$169.** 400 Brown St. Jct 4th St. Int corridors. **Pets:** Large. $35 daily fee/pet. Service with restrictions.
ASK ⊠ 🛅 💻 ⌦

CRAWFORDSVILLE

Comfort Inn H
(765) 361-0665. **$89-$175, 7 day notice.** 2991 N Gandhi Dr. I-74, exit 34, just s on US 231. Int corridors. **Pets:** $15 daily fee/pet. Service with restrictions, supervision.
SAVE ⊠ 🛅 💻 ⌦

Holiday Inn-Crawfordsville H
(765) 362-8700. **$76-$145.** 2500 N Lafayette Rd. I-74, exit 34, 0.3 mi s on US 231. Ext corridors. **Pets:** Small, other species. $15 daily fee/room. Designated rooms, service with restrictions, supervision.
ASK ⊠ 🛅 💻 ⌦

DALE

Baymont Inn & Suites Dale H
(812) 937-7000. **Call for rates.** 1339 N Washington St. I-64, exit 57 (US 231), just s. Int corridors. **Pets:** Accepted.
⊠ 🛅 💻 ⌦

DECATUR

Americas Best Value Inn M
(260) 728-2196. **$55-$69.** 1033 N 13th St. On US 27 and 33, 0.5 mi n of jct US 224. Ext/int corridors. **Pets:** Dogs only. $10 daily fee/pet. Service with restrictions, supervision.
ASK ⊠ 🛅 💻 ⌦

Baymont Inn & Suites H
(260) 728-4600. **$84.** 1201 S 13th St. On US 27 and 33, 1 mi s of jct US 224. Int corridors. **Pets:** $25 deposit/pet. Service with restrictions, supervision.
ASK ⊠ 🛅 💻 ⌦

Comfort Inn of Decatur H
(260) 724-8888. **$75-$95, 7 day notice.** 1302 S 13th St. 1 mi s on US 27 and 33. Int corridors. **Pets:** $10 daily fee/room. Service with restrictions, supervision.
ASK ⊠ 🛅 💻 ⌦

ELKHART

Candlewood Suites H
(574) 262-8600. **$85-$260.** 300 Northpointe Blvd. I-80/90, exit 92, just n on SR 19, then just w. Int corridors. **Pets:** Accepted.
⊠ 🛅 🛅 💻

Jameson Inn Elkhart H
(574) 264-7222. **Call for rates.** 3010 Brittany Ct. I-80/90, exit 92, 0.3 mi s on SR 19. Int corridors. **Pets:** Medium, other species. $15 daily fee/room. Service with restrictions, supervision.
⊠ 🛅 🛅 💻 ⌦

EVANSVILLE

Baymont Inn & Suites Evansville East H
(812) 477-2677. **$79.** 8005 E Division St. I-164, exit 7B (SR 66/Lloyd Expwy), 0.5 mi w to Cross Pointe Blvd, just n to Division St, then 0.5 mi e. Int corridors. **Pets:** Accepted.
SAVE ⊠ 🛅 🛅 💻 ⌦

Best Western Gateway Inn & Suites H
(812) 868-8000. **$67-$120.** 324 Rusher Creek Rd. I-64, exit 25A (US 41), 0.5 mi s, then just w. Int corridors. **Pets:** Large, other species. $15 one-time fee/pet. Service with restrictions, supervision.
SAVE ⊠ 🛅 🛅 💻 ⌦

Casino Aztar Hotel H
(812) 433-4000. **$109-$159.** 421 NW Riverside Dr. SR 62 (Lloyd Expwy), just s on Fulton. Int corridors. **Pets:** Small. $100 deposit/pet. Service with restrictions.
SAVE ⊠ 🛅 🛅 💻 ⌦

Comfort Inn East H
(812) 476-3600. **$79-$249.** 8331 E Walnut St. I-164, exit 7B (SR 66/Lloyd Expwy), 0.5 mi w to Eagle Crest Blvd, 0.3 mi se to Fuquay St, just s to Walnut St, then 0.4 mi e. Int corridors. **Pets:** Accepted.
ASK ⊠ 🛅 🛅 💻 ⌦

Comfort Inn North H
(812) 867-1600. **$56-$90.** 19622 Elpers Rd. I-64, exit 25A (US 41), 0.5 mi s, then just w. Int corridors. **Pets:** Accepted.
ASK ⊠ 🛅 💻 ⌦

Drury Inn & Suites-Evansville East H
(812) 471-3400. **$87-$145.** 100 Cross Pointe Blvd. I-164, exit 7B (SR 66/Lloyd Expwy), 0.5 mi w. Int corridors. **Pets:** Other species. Service with restrictions, supervision.
ASK ⊠ 🛅 🛅 💻 ⌦ ⌦

Drury Inn & Suites-Evansville North H
(812) 423-5818. **$75-$130.** 3901 US 41 N. On US 41, 2.5 mi n of jct SR 62 and 66 (Lloyd Expwy), 3.3 mi sw of Regional Airport entrance. Int corridors. **Pets:** Other species. Service with restrictions, supervision.
ASK ⊠ 🛅 💻 ⌦

Holiday Inn Express–Evansville West H
(812) 421-9773. **$95-$209.** 5737 Pearl Dr. Jct US 41 and SR 62, 5.7 mi w on SR 62, then just s on Boehne Camp Rd. Int corridors. **Pets:** Accepted.
SAVE ⊠ 🛅 🛅 💻 ⌦

HomeLife Studios & Suites M
(812) 475-1700. **Call for rates.** 100 S Green River Rd. I-164, exit 7B (SR 66/Lloyd Expwy), 2 mi w to Green River Rd, then just s. Ext corridors. **Pets:** Accepted.
⊠ 🛅 💻 ⌦

▼▼▼ Jameson Inn Evansville 🅗
(812) 476-9626. **Call for rates.** 1101 N Green River Rd. I-164, exit 9 (SR 62 E/Morgan Ave), 1.5 mi w on SR 62, then just s. Int corridors. **Pets:** Accepted.
⊠ ♿ 📱 💻 🏊

▼▼▼ Residence Inn by Marriott Evansville East 🅗
(812) 471-7191. **$134-$164.** 8283 E Walnut St. I-164, exit 7B (SR 66/Lloyd Expwy), 0.5 mi w to Eagle Crest Blvd, 0.3 mi se to Fuquay St, then 0.3 mi e. Int corridors. **Pets:** Other species. $100 one-time fee/room. Service with restrictions, crate.
⊠ ♿ 🔒 📱 💻 🏊 ⊠

▼ ▼ Studio Plus Evansville East 🅗
(812) 479-0103. **$52-$78.** 301 Eagle Crest Dr. I-164, exit 7B (SR 66/Lloyd Expwy), 0.5 mi w to Eagle Crest Blvd, 0.5 mi s, then just e. Int corridors. **Pets:** Other species. $25 daily fee/pet. Service with restrictions, crate.
ASK ⊠ 🔒 🏊

FERDINAND

▼▼▼ Comfort Inn 🅗
(812) 367-1122. **$69-$399.** 440 S Main St. I-64, exit 63. Int corridors. **Pets:** Medium, other species. $20 daily fee/pet. Designated rooms, service with restrictions, supervision.
ASK ⊠ ♿ 🔒 📱 🏊

FORT WAYNE

▼▼ Baymont Inn Fort Wayne 🅗 🐾
(260) 489-6900. **$68-$99.** 1005 W Washington Center Rd. I-69, exit 111B, just n on SR 3, then 0.4 mi e. Int corridors. **Pets:** Other species. $50 deposit/room. Service with restrictions, supervision.
ASK ⊠ 🔒 📱

◈◈◈ ▼▼▼ Best Western Luxbury Inn Fort Wayne 🅗
(260) 436-0242. **$88-$94.** 5501 Coventry Ln. I-69, exit 102. Int corridors. **Pets:** Other species. $15 daily fee/pet. Designated rooms, supervision.
SAVE ⊠ 🔒 📱

▼▼▼ Candlewood Suites 🅗
(260) 484-1400. **Call for rates.** 5250 Distribution Dr. I-69, exit 111A, just e. Int corridors. **Pets:** Accepted.
⊠ ♿ 🔒 📱 🏊

▼▼▼ Don Hall's Guesthouse 🅗
(260) 489-2524. **$89-$99.** 1313 W Washington Center Rd. I-69, exit 111B, just n on SR 3, then 0.3 mi e. Ext/int corridors. **Pets:** Dogs only. $10 daily fee/pet. No service, supervision.
ASK ⊠ 🔒 📱 🍽 🏊 ⊠

▼▼ Extended StayAmerica-Fort Wayne-South 🅗
(260) 432-1916. **$47-$78.** 8309 W Jefferson Blvd. I-69, exit 102, 0.4 mi e on US 24, then 0.6 mi s. Int corridors. **Pets:** Other species. $25 daily fee/pet. Service with restrictions, crate.
ASK ⊠ 🔒 📱

◈◈◈ ▼▼▼ Hilton Fort Wayne at Grand Wayne Convention Center 🅗 🐾
(260) 420-1100. **$99-$189.** 1020 S Calhoun St. Jct Jefferson Blvd; center. Int corridors. **Pets:** Medium. $50 one-time fee/room. Service with restrictions, supervision.
SAVE ⊠ ♿ 🔒 📱 🍽 🏊

▼▼▼ Residence Inn by Marriott Fort Wayne 🅗
(260) 484-4700. **$161-$197.** 4919 Lima Rd. I-69, exit 111A, 0.4 mi s on US 27. Ext corridors. **Pets:** Other species. $100 one-time fee/room. Service with restrictions.
⊠ 🔒 📱 🏊 ⊠

▼▼▼ Residence Inn Southwest 🅗
(260) 432-8000. **$125-$153.** 7811 W Jefferson Blvd. I-69, exit 102, 0.5 mi e. Int corridors. **Pets:** Accepted.
⊠ 🔒 📱 🏊 ⊠

▼▼▼ Staybridge Suites 🅗 🐾
(260) 432-2427. **Call for rates.** 5925 Ellison Rd. I-69, exit 102, just w. Int corridors. **Pets:** Medium. $150 one-time fee/room. Service with restrictions, supervision.
⊠ ♿ 🔒 📱 🏊 ⊠

FRENCH LICK

◈◈◈ ▼▼▼ ▼▼▼ French Lick Resort 🅗
(812) 936-9300. **$129-$399, 3 day notice.** 8670 W SR 56. Jct SR 145. Int corridors. **Pets:** Dogs only. $50 one-time fee/room. Service with restrictions, crate.
SAVE ⊠ ♿ 🔒 📱 🍽 🏊 ⊠

GOSHEN

◈◈◈ ▼▼▼ Best Western Inn 🅜 🐾
(574) 533-0408. **$99, 7 day notice.** 900 Lincolnway E. 1 mi se on US 33. Ext corridors. **Pets:** Service with restrictions, crate.
SAVE ⊠ 🔒 📱

GREENCASTLE

◈◈◈ ▼ College Inn 🅜
(765) 653-4167. **$35-$75.** 315 Bloomington St. I-70, exit 41, 8 mi n on US 231. Ext corridors. **Pets:** Accepted.
SAVE ⊠ 🔒

GREENSBURG

▼▼▼ Holiday Inn Express 🅗 🐾
(812) 663-5500. **$99-$169.** 915 Ann Blvd. I-74, exit 134A, 1.4 mi s on SR 3. Int corridors. **Pets:** Other species. $25 deposit/pet. Service with restrictions, supervision.
ASK ⊠ ♿ 🔒 📱 🏊

HAMMOND

◈◈◈ ▼▼▼ Best Western Northwest Indiana Inn 🅗
(219) 844-2140. **$100-$120, 30 day notice.** 3830 179th St. I-80/94, exit 5, 0.6 mi s on Cline Ave (SR 912), then 0.6 mi n on frontage road (179th St). Int corridors. **Pets:** Accepted.
SAVE ⊠ 🔒 📱 🍽 🏊

▼▼▼ Residence Inn by Marriott Chicago Southeast 🅗
(219) 844-8440. **$179-$189.** 7740 Corinne Dr. I-80/94, exit 3 (Kennedy Ave S), just s. Int corridors. **Pets:** Large. $100 one-time fee/room.
⊠ ♿ 🔒 📱 🏊 ⊠

HUNTINGTON

▼▼ Super 8 🅗
(260) 358-8888. **Call for rates.** 2801 Guilford St. US 24, just n. Int corridors. **Pets:** Accepted.
⊠ 🔒 🏊

▼▼ Vista Inn & Suites Huntington 🅗
(260) 359-9000. **Call for rates.** 2820 Hotel Ave. 0.6 mi nw of jct US 24/224 and SR 5. Int corridors. **Pets:** Accepted.
⊠ 🔒 📱 🏊

INDIANAPOLIS METROPOLITAN AREA

CARMEL

▼▼▼ Jameson Inn Carmel Ⓗ
(317) 816-1616. **Call for rates.** 10201 N Meridian St. I-465, exit 31, 0.3 mi n on US 31. Int corridors. **Pets:** Other species. $15 daily fee/pet. Service with restrictions.
☒ 🔊 🖥 💻 🌊 ☒

▼▼▼ Residence Inn by Marriott Indianapolis/Carmel Ⓗ
(317) 846-2000. **$149-$159.** 11895 N Meridian St. I-465, exit 31, 2 mi n on US 31, just e on 116th St, then just n on Pennsylvania Rd. Int corridors. **Pets:** Accepted.
☒ 🔊 🖥 💻 🌊 ☒

EDINBURGH

AAA ▼▼ Best Western Horizon Inn Ⓗ
(812) 526-9883. **$99-$129, 3 day notice.** 11780 N US 31. I-65, exit 76B, just n. Int corridors. **Pets:** Medium. $20 one-time fee/room. Designated rooms, supervision.
SAVE ☒ 🖥 💻 🌊

FISHERS

AAA ▼▼▼ Comfort Suites Ⓗ
(317) 578-1200. **$70-$180.** 9760 Crosspoint Blvd. I-69, exit 3, just w on 96th St, then just n. Int corridors. **Pets:** Medium. $10 daily fee/pet. Service with restrictions.
SAVE ☒ 🖥 💻 🌊

▼▼▼ Hotel Indigo Ⓗ ✿
(317) 558-4100. **$159-$500.** 9791 North by Northeast Blvd. I-69, exit 3, just ne. Int corridors. **Pets:** Other species. $25 one-time fee/pet. Service with restrictions, crate.
ASK ☒ 🔊 🖥 💻 🍴 🌊 ☒

▼▼▼ Residence Inn by Marriott Indianapolis/Fishers Ⓗ ✿
(317) 842-1111. **$149-$159.** 9765 Crosspoint Blvd. I-69, exit 3, just nw. Int corridors. **Pets:** Other species. $100 one-time fee/room. Service with restrictions, crate.
☒ 🔊 🖥 💻 🌊 ☒

▼▼▼ Staybridge Suites Indianapolis-Fishers Ⓗ ✿
(317) 577-9500. **Call for rates.** 9780 Crosspoint Blvd. I-69, exit 3, just nw. Int corridors. **Pets:** Medium. $75 one-time fee/room. Service with restrictions, crate.
☒ 🔊 🖥 💻 🌊 ☒

GREENWOOD

AAA ▼▼ Red Roof Inn Ⓜ
(317) 887-1515. **$59-$75.** 110 Sheek Rd. I-65, exit 99, just w. Ext corridors. **Pets:** Very small, dogs only. $10 one-time fee/pet. Designated rooms, service with restrictions, supervision.
SAVE ☒ 🖥 💻 🌊

INDIANAPOLIS

AAA ▼▼▼ Baymont Inn & Suites Ⓗ
(317) 322-2000. **$89-$159, 3 day notice.** 1540 Brookville Crossing Way. I-465, exit 47, 0.3 mi e. Int corridors. **Pets:** Other species. Service with restrictions, crate.
SAVE ☒ 🔊 🖥 💻 🌊

AAA ▼▼▼ Best Western Airport Suites Ⓗ
(317) 246-1505. **$79-$249, 30 day notice.** 55 S High School Rd. I-465, exit 13B, just w. Int corridors. **Pets:** Small, other species. $10 daily fee/pet. Service with restrictions, supervision.
SAVE ☒ 🖥 💻

AAA ▼▼▼ Best Western Castleton Inn Ⓗ
(317) 842-9190. **$59-$99.** 8300 Craig St. I-69, exit 1, 0.5 mi w. Int corridors. **Pets:** Small, other species. $25 one-time fee/pet. Service with restrictions, crate.
SAVE ☒ 💻 🌊

▼▼▼ Candlewood Suites Ⓗ ✿
(317) 595-9292. **$89-$189.** 8111 Bash St. I-69, exit 1, just w. Int corridors. **Pets:** Large, other species. $25 one-time fee/room.
ASK ☒ 🖥 💻 🌊 ☒

AAA ▼▼▼▼ Conrad Indianapolis Ⓗ ✿
(317) 713-5000. **$179-$409.** 50 W Washington St. Jct Illinois St. Int corridors. **Pets:** Small, dogs only. $100 deposit/room, $150 one-time fee/room. Service with restrictions, crate.
SAVE ☒ 🔊 🖥 💻 🍴 🌊 ☒

▼▼ Drury Inn-Indianapolis Ⓗ
(317) 876-9777. **$75-$115.** 9320 N Michigan Rd. I-465, exit 27, just s. Int corridors. **Pets:** Other species. Service with restrictions, supervision.
ASK ☒ 🖥 💻 🌊

▼▼ Extended StayAmerica Castleton Ⓗ
(317) 596-1288. **$44-$125.** 7940 N Shadeland Ave. I-69, exit 1, 0.5 mi s. Int corridors. **Pets:** Other species. $25 daily fee/pet. Service with restrictions, crate.
ASK ☒ 🖥 💻

▼▼ Extended StayAmerica-Indianapolis North Ⓗ
(317) 843-1181. **$45-$140.** 9750 Lakeshore Dr. I-465, exit 33, 0.4 mi n on Keystone Dr, 0.6 mi e on 96th St, then just n on Bauer Dr. Int corridors. **Pets:** Other species. $25 daily fee/pet. Service with restrictions, crate.
ASK ☒ 🖥 💻 🌊

▼▼ Extended StayAmerica-Indianapolis-Northwest-College Park Ⓗ
(317) 872-3090. **$47-$140.** 9030 Wesleyan Rd. I-465, exit 27, just s to Depauw Blvd, just e, then just s. Int corridors. **Pets:** Other species. $25 daily fee/pet. Service with restrictions, crate.
ASK ☒ 🖥 💻

AAA ▼▼▼ Hilton Indianapolis Ⓗ ✿
(317) 972-0600. **$119-$499.** 120 W Market St. Jct Illinois St. Int corridors. **Pets:** Large. $75 one-time fee/room. Service with restrictions, crate.
SAVE ☒ 🔊 🖥 💻 🍴 🌊 ☒

▼▼ Homestead Studio Suites Hotel-Indianapolis/Northwest Ⓗ
(317) 334-7829. **$52-$175.** 8520 Northwest Blvd. I-465, exit 23, just e. Int corridors. **Pets:** Other species. $25 daily fee/pet. Service with restrictions, crate.
ASK ☒ 🔊 🖥 💻 🌊

▼▼▼ Indianapolis Marriott East Ⓗ
(317) 352-1231. **$143-$175.** 7202 E 21st St. I-70, exit 89, 0.3 mi se; 0.5 mi w of jct I-465. Int corridors. **Pets:** Accepted.
☒ 🔊 🖥 💻 🍴 🌊

▼▼▼ Jameson Inn Indianapolis Castleton Ⓗ
(317) 849-8555. **Call for rates.** 8380 Kelly Ln. I-465, exit 35 (Allisonville Rd), just s. Int corridors. **Pets:** Accepted.
☒ 🖥 💻 🌊

▼▼▼ Jameson Inn of Indianapolis South Ⓗ
(317) 784-7006. **Call for rates.** 4402 E Creekview Dr. I-65, exit 103, just w. Int corridors. **Pets:** Accepted.
☒ 🖥 💻 🌊

▼▼◆ La Quinta Inn & Suites Indianapolis-Airport 🄷 ❀
(317) 244-8100. **$55-$129.** 2650 Executive Dr. I-465, exit 11A southbound; exit 11B northbound, 0.3 mi e. Int corridors. **Pets:** Medium, other species. Service with restrictions, supervision.
Ⓐ§Ⓚ ⓧ 𝄞ᴹ 🄷 🄸🄿

▼▼ La Quinta Inn Indianapolis Airport 🄷 ❀
(317) 247-4281. **$55-$129.** 5316 W Southern Ave. I-465, exit 11A, 0.5 mi e on Airport Expwy to Lynhurst Dr. Int corridors. **Pets:** Medium, other species. Service with restrictions, supervision.
Ⓐ§Ⓚ ⓧ 🄷 🄸🄿 🔁

▼▼ La Quinta Inn Indianapolis (East) 🄷 ❀
(317) 359-1021. **$59-$149.** 7304 E 21st St. I-70, exit 89, just s, then just e; 0.5 mi w of jct I-465. Int corridors. **Pets:** Medium, other species. Service with restrictions, supervision.
Ⓐ§Ⓚ ⓧ 🄷 🄸🄿 🔁

◆◆◆ ▼▼▼▼ Omni Severin Hotel 🄷
(317) 634-6664. **$129-$299.** 40 W Jackson Pl. Opposite Union Station. Int corridors. **Pets:** Accepted.
Ⓢ🄰ᴠᴇ ⓧ 🄷 🄸🄿 ⌘⌘ 🔁

▼▼ Quality Inn & Suites Airport 🄷
(317) 381-1000. **$70-$190.** 2631 S Lynhurst Dr. I-465, exit 11A, 0.5 mi e on Airport Expwy. Int corridors. **Pets:** Other species. $10 daily fee/pet. Designated rooms, service with restrictions, supervision.
Ⓐ§Ⓚ ⓧ 🄷 🄸🄿 🔁

▼▼ Quality Inn Downtown South 🄷
(317) 788-4774. **Call for rates.** 4502 S Harding St. I-465, exit 4, just n. Int corridors. **Pets:** Medium. $10 daily fee/room. Service with restrictions, supervision.
ⓧ 🄸🄿

▼▼▼ Radisson Hotel Indianapolis Airport 🄷
(317) 244-3361. **$99-$299.** 2500 S High School Rd. I-465, exit 11B, just w. Int corridors. **Pets:** Accepted.
Ⓐ§Ⓚ ⓧ 🄷 🄸🄿 ⌘⌘

▼▼ Ramada Limited 🄷
(317) 297-1848. **$79-$199, 30 day notice.** 3851 Shore Dr. I-465, exit 17, just w on 38th St, then just n. Ext corridors. **Pets:** Other species. $15 daily fee/pet. No service, crate.
Ⓐ§Ⓚ ⓧ 🄷 🄸🄿 🔁

▼▼▼▼ Residence Inn by Marriott Indianapolis Airport 🄷
(317) 244-1500. **$152-$186.** 5224 W Southern Ave. I-465, exit 11A, 0.5 mi e on Airport Expwy to Lynhurst Dr. Int corridors. **Pets:** Small, other species. $100 one-time fee/room. Service with restrictions, supervision.
ⓧ 𝄞ᴹ 🄷 🄸🄿 🔁 ⊠

▼▼▼▼ Residence Inn by Marriott Indianapolis Downtown on the Canal 🄷
(317) 822-0840. **$170-$208.** 350 W New York St. Jct Senate Ave. Int corridors. **Pets:** Accepted.
ⓧ 𝄞ᴹ 🄷 🄸🄿 🔁

▼▼▼▼ Residence Inn by Marriott Northwest-Indianapolis 🄷
(317) 275-6000. **$130-$158.** 6220 Digital Way. I-465, exit 21, just w. Int corridors. **Pets:** Accepted.
ⓧ 𝄞ᴹ 🄷 🄸🄿 🔁 ⊠

◆◆◆ ▼▼▼▼ Sheraton Indianapolis City Centre 🄷
(317) 635-2000. **$189-$349, 4 day notice.** 31 W Ohio St. Jct Meridian St; just n of Monument Cir. Int corridors. **Pets:** Accepted.
Ⓢ🄰ᴠᴇ ⓧ 𝄞ᴹ 🄷 🄸🄿 ⌘⌘ 🔁

◆◆◆ ▼▼▼▼ Sheraton Indianapolis Hotel & Suites 🄷 ❀
(317) 846-2700. **$169-$219.** 8787 Keystone Crossing. I-465, exit 33, 0.5 mi s on SR 431, just e on 86th St, then just n. Int corridors. **Pets:** Medium, dogs only. Service with restrictions, supervision.
Ⓢ🄰ᴠᴇ ⓧ 𝄞ᴹ 🄷 🄸🄿 ⌘⌘ 🔁

▼▼▼▼ Staybridge Suites City Centre 🄷 ❀
(317) 536-7500. **$139-$399, 3 day notice.** 535 S West St. Just s of South St. Int corridors. **Pets:** Medium. $75 one-time fee/room. Service with restrictions.
ⓧ 𝄞ᴹ 🄷 🄸🄿 🔁

▼▼ Suburban Extended Stay Hotel 🄷
(317) 598-1914. **$69-$79.** 8055 Bash St. I-69, exit 1, just w. Int corridors. **Pets:** Accepted.
Ⓐ§Ⓚ ⓧ 𝄞ᴹ 🄷 🄸🄿

▼▼ TownePlace Suites by Marriott Keystone 🄷
(317) 255-3700. **$107-$131.** 8468 Union Chapel Rd. I-465, exit 33, 0.5 mi s on SR 431, just e on 86th St, then just s. Int corridors. **Pets:** Accepted.
ⓧ 🄷 🄸🄿 🔁

▼▼ TownePlace Suites by Marriott Park 100 🄷
(317) 290-8900. **$107-$131.** 5802 W 71st St. I-465, exit 21, 0.3 mi e. Int corridors. **Pets:** Accepted.
ⓧ 🄷 🄸🄿 🔁

◆◆◆ ▼▼▼▼ The Westin Indianapolis 🄷 ❀
(317) 262-8100. **$129-$349.** 50 S Capitol Ave. Jct Washington and Maryland sts. Int corridors. **Pets:** Medium. Service with restrictions, supervision.
Ⓢ🄰ᴠᴇ ⓧ 𝄞ᴹ 🄸🄿 ⌘⌘ 🔁 ⊠

▼▼▼ Wingate Inn-Airport 🄷
(317) 243-8310. **$89-$109.** 5797 Rockville Rd. I-465, exit 13A, just e. Int corridors. **Pets:** Other species. $25 one-time fee/room. Service with restrictions, crate.
Ⓐ§Ⓚ ⓧ 𝄞ᴹ 🄷 🄸🄿 🔁

LEBANON

◆◆◆ ▼▼ Comfort Inn 🄷
(765) 482-4800. **$75-$169, 7 day notice.** 210 N Sam Ralston Rd. I-65, exit 140. Int corridors. **Pets:** Accepted.
Ⓢ🄰ᴠᴇ ⓧ 🄷 🄸🄿 🔁

▼▼▼ Holiday Inn Express 🄷
(765) 483-4100. **$95-$195.** 335 N Mt Zion Rd. I-65, exit 140, just w. Int corridors. **Pets:** Medium. $10 daily fee/pet. Designated rooms, service with restrictions, supervision.
ⓧ 𝄞ᴹ 🄷 🄸🄿 🔁

▼▼ Super 8 🄷
(765) 482-9999. **Call for rates.** 405 N Mt Zion Rd. I-65, exit 140, just w. Int corridors. **Pets:** Accepted.
ⓧ 🄷 🄸🄿 🔁

MARTINSVILLE

◆◆◆ ▼▼ Best Western Martinsville Inn 🄷
(765) 342-1842. **$70-$150.** 50 Bill's Blvd. SR 37 to Ohio St, just w. Int corridors. **Pets:** $10 daily fee/pet. No service, supervision.
Ⓢ🄰ᴠᴇ ⓧ 𝄞ᴹ 🄷 🄸🄿

NOBLESVILLE

▼▼ Quality Inn & Suites 🄷 ❀
(317) 770-6772. **Call for rates.** 16025 Prosperity Dr. I-69, exit 5, 4 mi n on SR 37. Int corridors. **Pets:** Large, other species. $20 daily fee/room. Designated rooms, service with restrictions, crate.
ⓧ 🄷 🄸🄿 🔁

PLAINFIELD

▼▼▼▼ Staybridge Suites Indianapolis Airport 🅷 ❀
(317) 839-2700. **$124-$295, 4 day notice.** 6295 Cambridge Way. I-70, exit 66, 0.4 mi n on SR 267, just e on Hadley Rd, then just s. Int corridors. **Pets:** Other species. $75 one-time fee/room. Service with restrictions, supervision.

(ASK) ⊠ � 🔋 ▦ ➫

END METROPOLITAN AREA

JASPER

⬙⬙⬙ ▼▼▼ Days Inn Jasper 🅷
(812) 482-6000. **Call for rates.** 272 Brucke Strasse. Jct SR 164, just w. Ext/int corridors. **Pets:** Accepted.

(SAVE) ⊠ 🔋 ▦ ⑪ ➫ ⊠

JEFFERSONVILLE

▼▼▼ Comfort Suites Louisville North 🅷
(812) 282-2100. **$90-$325.** 360 Eastern Blvd. I-65, exit 2 (Eastern Blvd), just e. Int corridors. **Pets:** Accepted.

(ASK) ⊠ ⅏M 🔋 ▦

▼▼ TownePlace Suites by Marriott 🅷
(812) 280-8200. **$95-$116.** 703 N Shore Dr. I-65, exit 0, just w. Int corridors. **Pets:** Accepted.

⊠ 🔋 ▦ ➫

KENDALLVILLE

⬙⬙⬙ ▼▼▼ Best Western Kendallville Inn 🅷
(260) 347-5263. **$77-$80, 3 day notice.** 621 Professional Way. 1 mi e on US 6. Int corridors. **Pets:** Large, dogs only. $25 one-time fee/room. Service with restrictions, supervision.

(SAVE) ⊠ 🔋 ▦ ➫ ⊠

▼▼▼ Holiday Inn Express Kendallville 🅷
(260) 343-0000. **$75-$110.** 1917 Dowling St. I-69, exit 134, 9.3 mi e on US 6. Int corridors. **Pets:** Accepted.

(ASK) ⊠ ⅏M 🔋 ▦ ➫ ⊠

KOKOMO

▼▼ Comfort Inn by Choice Hotels 🅷
(765) 452-5050. **Call for rates.** 522 Essex Dr. Jct US 35, 0.3 mi n on US 31. Int corridors. **Pets:** Accepted.

⊠ 🔋 ▦ ➫

▼▼ Days Inn & Suites 🅼
(765) 453-7100. **$56-$80.** 264 S 00 EW. US 31, 2.8 mi s of jct US 35. Ext corridors. **Pets:** Medium. $10 one-time fee/room. Service with restrictions, supervision.

(ASK) ⊠ 🔋 ▦ ⑪ ➫

▼▼▼ Hampton Inn & Suites 🅷
(765) 455-2900. **$89-$119.** 2920 S Reed Rd (US Hwy 31). US 31, 2 mi s of jct US 35. Int corridors. **Pets:** Other species. Designated rooms, service with restrictions, crate.

⊠ ⅏M 🔋 ▦ ➫ ⊠

LAFAYETTE

⬙⬙⬙ ▼▼▼ Best Western Lafayette Executive Plaza & Conference Center 🅷
(765) 447-0575. **$89-$289, 30 day notice.** 4343 SR 26 E. I-65, exit 172, just w. Int corridors. **Pets:** Small. $25 daily fee/room. Designated rooms, service with restrictions, supervision.

(SAVE) ⊠ ⅏M 🔋 ▦ ⑪ ➫ ⊠

▼▼ ▼▼ Days Inn & Suites 🅷 ❀
(765) 446-8558. **$80-$90, 7 day notice.** 151 Frontage Rd. I-65, exit 172, just e. Int corridors. **Pets:** $75 deposit/pet. Service with restrictions, supervision.

(ASK) ⊠ 🔋 ▦

⬙⬙⬙ ▼▼▼▼ Holiday Inn Express 🅷
(765) 449-4808. **Call for rates.** 201 Frontage Rd. I-65, exit 172, just e on SR 26, then just n. Int corridors. **Pets:** Accepted.

(SAVE) ⊠ 🔋 ▦

▼▼▼ Homewood Suites by Hilton 🅷
(765) 448-9700. **$86-$229.** 3939 SR 26 E. I-65, exit 172, 0.8 mi w. Ext/int corridors. **Pets:** Medium, other species. $250 deposit/room, $10 daily fee/pet, $50 one-time fee/pet. Service with restrictions, crate.

⊠ 🔋 ▦ ➫ ⊠

▼▼▼ Loeb House Inn 🅱🅱
(765) 420-7737. **$109-$189, 5 day notice.** 708 Cincinnati St. SR 38, 0.4 mi n on 9th St, then just w. Int corridors. **Pets:** Accepted.

(ASK) ⊠

▼▼ Motel 6 🅼
(765) 447-7566. **$50-$119.** 139 Frontage Rd. I-65, exit 172. Ext corridors. **Pets:** Other species. Service with restrictions, supervision.

(ASK) ⊠ 🔋

▼▼ Red Roof Inn-Lafayette #7062 🅼
(765) 448-4671. **$51-$95.** 4201 SR 26 E. I-65, exit 172, 0.3 mi w. Ext corridors. **Pets:** Accepted.

(ASK) ⊠ 🔋

▼▼▼ TownePlace Suites by Marriott 🅷
(765) 446-8668. **$134-$164.** 163 Frontage Rd. I-65, exit 172, just e. Int corridors. **Pets:** Small. $75 one-time fee/room. Service with restrictions, supervision.

⊠ 🔋 ▦ ➫

LOGANSPORT

▼▼ Ramada 🅷
(574) 753-6351. **$85-$95.** 3550 E Market St. 2.5 mi e on Business Rt US 24. Int corridors. **Pets:** Accepted.

(ASK) ⊠ 🔋 ▦ ⑪ ➫

MADISON

⬙⬙⬙ ▼▼▼ Country Hearth Inn 🅷
(812) 273-0757. **Call for rates.** 308 Demaree Dr. Jct SR 7 and 62, 2 mi e on SR 62. Int corridors. **Pets:** Accepted.

(SAVE) ⊠ 🔋 ▦

MARION

▼▼▼ Comfort Suites-Marion 🅷
(765) 651-1006. **$79-$125.** 1345 N Baldwin Ave. 1.5 mi n of jct SR 9 and 18. Int corridors. **Pets:** Other species. $10 one-time fee/pet. Designated rooms, service with restrictions, supervision.

(ASK) ⊠ 🔋 ▦ ➫ ⊠

MERRILLVILLE

♦♦♦ Candlewood Suites 🅷 ✿
(219) 791-9100. **$99-$114.** 8339 Ohio St. I-65, exit 253, 0.3 mi e, just s on Mississippi St, 0.4 mi w on 83rd Ave, then just s. Int corridors. **Pets:** Medium. $75 one-time fee/pet. Service with restrictions, supervision.

ASK ⊠ 🛏 💻

♦♦ Extended StayAmerica-Merrillville-US Rte 30 🅷
(219) 769-4740. **$70-$100.** 1355 E 83rd Ave. I-65, exit 253, 0.3 mi e on US 30, just s on Mississippi St, then 0.4 mi w. Int corridors. **Pets:** Other species. $25 daily fee/pet. Service with restrictions, crate.

ASK ⊠ 🛏 💻

♦♦♦♦ Residence Inn by Marriott Merrillville 🅷
(219) 791-9000. **$153-$187.** 8018 Delaware Pl. I-65, exit 253, 0.3 mi nw. Int corridors. **Pets:** Accepted.

⊠ 🖂M 🛏 💻 ⇆ 🞋

🅐🅐🅐 ♦ Super 8 🅷
(219) 736-8383. **$45-$80.** 8300 Louisiana St. I-65, exit 253, 0.3 mi e, just s on Mississippi St, then just w on 83rd Ave. Int corridors. **Pets:** Medium, other species. $20 deposit/pet. Designated rooms, service with restrictions, supervision.

SAVE ⊠ 🖂M 🛏 💻

MISHAWAKA

♦♦♦♦ Residence Inn by Marriott South Bend/Mishawaka 🅷
(574) 271-9283. **$149-$159.** 231 Park Pl. I-80/90, exit 83, just n on SR 331 to SR 23, 1.6 mi sw, then 1.3 mi s. Int corridors. **Pets:** Accepted.

⊠ 🖂M 🛏 💻 ⇆ 🞋

MONTGOMERY

♦♦ Gasthof Amish Village Inn 🅷
(812) 486-2600. **Call for rates.** 6747 E Garth of Village Rd E. US 50, 0.8 mi n on First St. Int corridors. **Pets:** Accepted.

⊠ 🛏 💻 🍽 ⇆ 🞋

MOUNT VERNON

♦♦ Four Seasons Motel Ⓜ
(812) 838-4821. **$56-$100.** 70 Hwy 62 W. 1.8 mi w. Ext corridors. **Pets:** Accepted.

ASK ⊠ 🛏 💻 ⇆

MUNCIE

♦♦ Days Inn Muncie 🅷
(765) 288-2311. **$54-$120.** 3509 N Everbrook Ln. I-69, exit 41, 6.3 mi e on SR 332, then just n. Int corridors. **Pets:** $10 one-time fee/pet. Service with restrictions, supervision.

ASK ⊠ 🛏 💻

♦♦♦♦ Signature Inn-Muncie 🅷
(765) 284-4200. **Call for rates.** 3400 N Chadam Ln. I-69, exit 41, 6.3 mi e on SR 332. Int corridors. **Pets:** Accepted.

⊠ 🛏 💻 ⇆

♦♦ Super 8 🅷
(765) 286-4333. **$45-$95.** 3601 W Fox Ridge Ln. I-69, exit 41, 6.3 mi e on SR 332. Int corridors. **Pets:** Medium, dogs only. $10 one-time fee/pet. Service with restrictions, supervision.

ASK ⊠ 🛏 💻

NEW ALBANY

🅐🅐🅐 ♦♦♦♦ Holiday Inn Express 🅷
(812) 945-2771. **$100-$400.** 411 W Spring St. I-64, exit 123. Int corridors. **Pets:** Accepted.

SAVE ⊠ 🛏 💻 ⇆

NEW CASTLE

🅐🅐🅐 ♦♦ Raintree Inn 🅷
(765) 521-0100. **$69-$129.** 2836 S SR 3. I-70, exit 123, 2.8 mi n. Ext/int corridors. **Pets:** Accepted.

SAVE ⊠ 🛏 💻 ⇆

NORTH VERNON

♦♦♦ Comfort Inn 🅷
(812) 352-9999. **$84-$109.** 150 FDR Dr. Jct US 50, 0.6 mi n on SR 7. Int corridors. **Pets:** Accepted.

ASK ⊠ 🛏 💻 ⇆

PERU

🅐🅐🅐 ♦♦♦ Best Western Circus City Inn 🅷
(765) 473-8800. **$87-$97, 3 day notice.** 2642 Business Rt US 31 S. Just e of jct US 31. Int corridors. **Pets:** Other species. $50 deposit/pet, $5 daily fee/pet. Supervision.

SAVE ⊠ 🛏 💻 ⇆

PLYMOUTH

♦♦ Super 8 🅷
(574) 936-8856. **$55-$135.** 2160 N Oak Rd. US 30, just s. Int corridors. **Pets:** Medium. $10 daily fee/pet. Service with restrictions, supervision.

ASK ⊠ 🛏 💻 ⇆

PORTAGE

♦♦ Comfort Inn 🅷
(219) 763-7177. **$69-$179.** 2300 Willow Creek Rd. I-80/90, exit 23; I-94, exit 19, 1.5 mi s on CR 249. Int corridors. **Pets:** Accepted.

ASK ⊠ 🛏 💻

♦♦ Super 8 Portage 🅷
(219) 762-8857. **Call for rates.** 6118 Melton Rd. I-94, exit 19, just s on CR 249, then just w on US 20; I-80, exit 23, 1.2 mi n on CR 249, then just w on US 20. Int corridors. **Pets:** Accepted.

⊠ 🛏 💻

PRINCETON

♦♦♦♦ Fairfield Inn by Marriott 🅷
(812) 385-4300. **$77-$94.** 2828 Dixon St. Jct US 41 and SR 64, 0.3 mi w. Int corridors. **Pets:** Accepted.

⊠ 🖂M 🛏 💻 ⇆

RICHMOND

♦♦ Days Inn Ⓜ
(765) 966-4900. **$45-$70.** 5775 National Rd E. I-70, exit 156A, just s. Ext corridors. **Pets:** $10 daily fee/pet. Designated rooms, service with restrictions, supervision.

ASK ⊠ 🛏 💻

♦♦♦♦ Holiday Inn-Richmond 🅷
(765) 966-7511. **$89-$325.** 5501 National Rd E. I-70, exit 156A, 0.3 mi w. Int corridors. **Pets:** Accepted.

ASK ⊠ 🖂M 🛏 💻 🍽 ⇆ 🞋

🅐🅐🅐 ♦♦ Knights Inn Ⓜ
(765) 966-1505. **$55-$89.** 3020 E Main St. I-70, exit 156A, 2 mi w. Ext corridors. **Pets:** Small. $8 daily fee/pet. Service with restrictions, supervision.

SAVE ⊠ 🛏 💻

🅐🅐🅐 ♦♦ Lees Inn & Suites 🅷
(765) 966-6559. **$99, 7 day notice.** 6030 National Rd E. I-70, exit 156A, jct US 40. Int corridors. **Pets:** Medium. Designated rooms, service with restrictions.

SAVE ⊠ 🖂M 🛏 💻 ⇆

Motel 6 Richmond #4170 **M**
(765) 966-6682. **$39-$89, 10 day notice.** 419 Commerce Dr. I-70, exit 156A, just s on US 40. Ext corridors. **Pets:** Other species. Service with restrictions, supervision.

ROCKVILLE

Parke Bridge Motel **M**
(765) 569-3525. **$45-$80, 3 day notice.** 304 E Ohio St. US 36, just e of center, 0.5 mi e of jct US 41. Ext corridors. **Pets:** Accepted.

RUSHVILLE

Comfort Inn **H**
(765) 932-2999. **Call for rates.** 320 Conrad Harcourt Way. Just e of SR 3. Int corridors. **Pets:** Medium, dogs only. Service with restrictions, supervision.

SCOTTSBURG

Mariann Travel Inn **M**
(812) 752-3396. **$59-$69.** I-65 & SR 56. I-65, exit 29A, just e. Ext corridors. **Pets:** Large. Service with restrictions, supervision.

SELLERSBURG

Home Lodge **H**
(812) 246-6332. **$69.** 363 Triangle Dr. I-65, exit 9, just e. Int corridors. **Pets:** Accepted.

Ramada Limited & Suites **H**
(812) 246-3131. **$79.** 360 Triangle Dr. I-65, exit 9, just e. Int corridors. **Pets:** Medium, other species. $25 one-time fee/room. Service with restrictions, supervision.

SEYMOUR

Motel 6 Seymour #4153 **H**
(812) 524-7443. **$40-$66.** 365 Tanger Blvd. I-65, exit 50A. Int corridors. **Pets:** Other species. Service with restrictions, supervision.

Seymour Quality Inn **H**
(812) 522-6767. **$79-$99.** 2025 E Tipton St. I-65, exit 50B, 0.5 mi w on US 50. Ext corridors. **Pets:** Other species. Service with restrictions.

SOUTH BEND

Comfort Suites South Bend **H**
(574) 272-1500. **$100-$165.** 52939 SR 933 N. I-80/90, exit 77, just e to Business Rt US 31/SR 933, then 1 mi n. Int corridors. **Pets:** $10 daily fee/pet. Designated rooms, no service, crate.

Cushing Manor Inn **BB**
(574) 288-1990. **$95-$165, 7 day notice.** 508 W Washington St. 0.4 mi w of jct SR 933 and Business Rt US 31. Int corridors. **Pets:** Accepted.

The English Rose Bed & Breakfast Guest House **BB**
(574) 288-1990. **Call for rates.** 116 S Taylor St. Business Rt US 31, 0.3 mi w on Washington St to Taylor St, then just s. Int corridors. **Pets:** Accepted.

Oliver Inn Bed & Breakfast **BB**
(574) 232-4545. **$135-$339, 14 day notice.** 630 W Washington St. 0.3 mi w of SR 933 and Business Rt US 31. Int corridors. **Pets:** $10 one-time fee/room. Designated rooms, service with restrictions, supervision.

Quality Inn & Suites **H**
(574) 288-3800. **$69-$299.** 4124 Lincolnway W. I-80/90, exit 72, 1.5 mi s on US 31 to South Bend Regional Airport exit, then 2 mi e. Int corridors. **Pets:** Small. $10 daily fee/pet. Service with restrictions, supervision.

Sleep Inn **H**
(574) 232-3200. **$80-$260.** 4134 Lincolnway W. I-80/90, exit 72, 1.5 mi s on US 31 to South Bend Regional Airport exit, then 2 mi e. Int corridors. **Pets:** Medium. $10 daily fee/pet. Service with restrictions, crate.

Super 8–South Bend **H**
(574) 243-0200. **$79-$249, 30 day notice.** 4124 Ameritech Dr. I-80/90, exit 72, 0.7 mi n on US 31, just e on Cleveland Rd, then just s. Int corridors. **Pets:** Small. $10 daily fee/pet. Designated rooms, service with restrictions, supervision.

Waterford Estates Lodge **H**
(574) 272-5220. **$98-$107.** 52890 SR 933 N. I-80/90, exit 77, 1 mi n. Int corridors. **Pets:** $30 one-time fee/pet. Service with restrictions, crate.

TAYLORSVILLE

Red Roof Inn **M**
(812) 526-9747. **$49-$125.** 10330 US 31. I-65, exit 76A, just s. Ext corridors. **Pets:** Small, other species. Designated rooms, service with restrictions, crate.

TELL CITY

Holiday Inn Express **H**
(812) 547-0800. **Call for rates.** 310 Orchard Hill Dr. Just off SR 66, 1.7 mi se of jct SR 37. Int corridors. **Pets:** Accepted.

Ramada Limited **H**
(812) 547-3234. **$69-$99.** 235 Orchard Hill Dr. Just off SR 66, 1.7 mi se of jct SR 37. Int corridors. **Pets:** Medium, other species. $10 daily fee/room. Designated rooms, service with restrictions, supervision.

TERRE HAUTE

Drury Inn-Terre Haute **H**
(812) 238-1206. **$100-$140.** 3040 Hwy 41 S. I-70, exit 7 (US 41/150), just n. Int corridors. **Pets:** Other species. Service with restrictions, supervision.

Holiday Inn **H**
(812) 232-6081. **$115-$180.** 3300 US 41 S. I-70, exit 7 (US 41/150), just s. Int corridors. **Pets:** $25 one-time fee/room. Service with restrictions, supervision.

Pear Tree Inn by Drury-Terre Haute **H**
(812) 234-4268. **$60-$83.** 3050 US 41 S. I-70, exit 7 (US 41/150), just n. Int corridors. **Pets:** Other species. Service with restrictions, supervision.

Super 8-Terre Haute **H**
(812) 232-4890. **$44-$69.** 3089 S 1st St. I-70, exit 7 (US 41/150), just nw. Int corridors. **Pets:** $10 one-time fee/room. Service with restrictions, supervision.

VALPARAISO

 **Best Western Valparaiso Inn** 🅷

(219) 464-8555. **$79-$85.** 760 Morthland Dr. On US 30, 0.3 mi w of jct SR 2. Ext/int corridors. **Pets:** Medium, dogs only. $25 daily fee/pet. Designated rooms, service with restrictions, crate.

`SAVE` `X` `🛏` `🖵`

 **Courtyard by Marriott Valparaiso** 🅷

(219) 465-1700. **$109-$119.** 2301 E Morthland Dr. On US 30, just w of jct SR 49. Int corridors. **Pets:** Other species. $50 one-time fee/room. Service with restrictions, supervision.

`X` `🛏` `🖵` `≥`

WARREN

 **Comfort Inn Warren** 🅷

(260) 375-4800. **$49-$145, 7 day notice.** 7275 S 75 E. I-69, exit 78, just n on SR 5. Int corridors. **Pets:** Small. $10 daily fee/pet. Designated rooms, service with restrictions, supervision.

`ASK` `X` `&M` `🛏` `🖵` `≥`

WARSAW

Comfort Inn & Suites-Warsaw 🅷

(574) 269-6655. **$69-$199.** 3328 E Center St. 3.2 mi e of SR 15 on US 30. Int corridors. **Pets:** Small. $10 daily fee/pet. Designated rooms, no service, crate.

`X` `🛏` `🖵` `≥` `X`

Ramada Plaza of Warsaw 🅷 ❀

(574) 269-2323. **$99-$110.** 2519 E Center St. 2.8 mi e of SR 15 on US 30, just s. Int corridors. **Pets:** Large, other species. Service with restrictions, crate.

`ASK` `X` `🛏` `🖵` `❙❙` `≥` `X`

WASHINGTON

Baymont Inn & Suites Washington 🅷

(812) 254-7000. **$80-$104.** 7 Cumberland Dr. Just ne of jct US 50 and SR 257. Int corridors. **Pets:** Medium. $50 deposit/room. Service with restrictions, supervision.

`ASK` `X` `🛏` `🖵` `≥` `X`

Holiday Inn Express 🅷

(812) 254-6666. **Call for rates.** 1808 E National Hwy. On US 50 business route, 0.4 mi e of SR 257. Int corridors. **Pets:** Accepted.

`X` `🛏` `🖵` `≥`

WEST BADEN SPRINGS

  **West Baden Springs Hotel** 🅷

(812) 936-1902. **$180-$325, 3 day notice.** 8538 W Baden Ave. On SR 56. Int corridors. **Pets:** Accepted.

`SAVE` `X` `&M` `🛏` `🖵` `❙❙` `≥` `X`

IOWA

ALBIA

 **Indian Hills Inn** 🅷
(641) 932-7181. **$72-$110.** 100 Hwy 34 E. Just e of jct US 34 and SR 5. Ext/int corridors. **Pets:** Accepted.
❌ 🅗 🖵 🍴 ➰

ALGONA

▽▽ **AmericInn Lodge & Suites of Algona** 🅷
(515) 295-3333. **Call for rates.** 600 Hwy 18 W. Just w of jct US 169/18. Int corridors. **Pets:** Designated rooms, service with restrictions, crate.
❌ 🅐🅼 🅗 🖵 ➰ 🚫

ALTOONA

▽▽▽ **Motel 6 Des Moines East #1420** 🅷
(515) 967-5252. **$45-$65.** 3225 Adventureland Dr. I-80, exit 142A. Int corridors. **Pets:** Other species. Service with restrictions, supervision.
❌ 🅗 ➰

▽▽▽ **Settle Inn & Suites-Altoona** 🅷
(515) 967-7888. **$79-$99.** 2101 Adventureland Dr. I-80, exit 142A, just se. Int corridors. **Pets:** Small, dogs only. $15 daily fee/pet. Designated rooms, service with restrictions, supervision.
🅐🆂🅺 ❌ 🅗 🖵 ➰

AMES

▽▽▽ **AmericInn of Ames** 🅷
(515) 233-1005. **Call for rates.** 2507 SE 16th St. I-35, exit 111B, just w on US 30, then exit 150. Int corridors. **Pets:** Accepted.
❌ 🅐🅼 🅗 🖵 ➰ 🚫

🆀🅐🅐 ▽▽▽ **Best Western University Park** 🅷
(515) 296-2500. **$90-$140.** 2500 University Blvd. I-35, exit 111B, 3.5 mi w on US 30, exit 146 (Elwood Dr), then just s. Int corridors. **Pets:** Medium. Service with restrictions, supervision.
🆂🅰🆅🅴 ❌ 🅗 🖵 ➰

🆀🅐🅐 ▽▽▽ **Comfort Inn-Ames** 🅷 ❀
(515) 232-0689. **$69-$125, 7 day notice.** 1605 S Dayton Ave. I-35, exit 111B, just w on US 30, then exit 150. Int corridors. **Pets:** Medium. $10 daily fee/pet. Service with restrictions, supervision.
🆂🅰🆅🅴 ❌ 🅗 🖵 ➰

▽▽▽ **Gateway Hotel & Conference Center** 🅷
(515) 292-8600. **$119-$159.** 2100 Green Hills Dr. I-35, exit 111B, 3.5 mi w on US 30, exit 146 (Elwood Dr). Int corridors. **Pets:** Designated rooms, service with restrictions, crate.
🅐🆂🅺 ❌ 🅐🅼 🅗 🖵 🍴 ➰ 🚫

▽▽▽ **GrandStay Residential Suites** 🅷
(515) 232-8363. **$77-$87.** 1606 S Kellogg Ave. I-35, exit 111, 1 mi w, then just nw on Duff Ave to Kellogg Ave. Int corridors. **Pets:** $25 daily fee/room. Service with restrictions, supervision.
🅐🆂🅺 ❌ 🅐🅼 🅗 🖵 ➰ 🚫

🆀🅐🅐 ▽◆◆◆ **Holiday Inn Ames Conference Center-ISU** 🅷
(515) 268-8808. **$99-$199.** 2609 University Blvd. I-35, exit 111B, 3.5 mi w on US 30, exit 146 (Elwood Dr), then just s. Int corridors. **Pets:** Accepted.
🆂🅰🆅🅴 ❌ 🅐🅼 🅗 🖵 🍴 ➰

▽▽▽ **Microtel Inn & Suites** 🅷 ❀
(515) 233-4444. **$49-$149.** 2216 SE 16th St. I-35, exit 111B, just w on US 30, then exit 150. Int corridors. **Pets:** $10 daily fee/pet. Service with restrictions, crate.
🅐🆂🅺 ❌ 🅐🅼 🅗 🖵

🆀🅐🅐 ▽▽▽ **Quality Inn & Suites Starlite Village Conference Center** 🅷 🐾
(515) 232-9260. **$99-$159.** 2601 E 13th St. I-35, exit 113 (13th St), 0.5 mi w. Int corridors. **Pets:** Medium. $10 daily fee/pet. Designated rooms, service with restrictions, supervision.
🆂🅰🆅🅴 ❌ 🅗 🖵 🍴 ➰ 🚫

ANAMOSA

▽▽ **Super 8-Anamosa** 🅷
(319) 462-3888. **$55-$68.** 100 Grant Wood Dr. Just e on US 64 from US 151 (exit 54). Int corridors. **Pets:** Medium. $10 one-time fee/pet. Service with restrictions, supervision.
🅐🆂🅺 ❌ 🅗 ➰

ANKENY

🆀🅐🅐 ▽▽▽ **Comfort Inn** 🅷
(515) 963-1100. **$69-$189.** 2602 SE Creekview Dr. I-35, exit 90, just ne. Int corridors. **Pets:** Small, dogs only. $10 daily fee/pet. Designated rooms, no service, supervision.
🆂🅰🆅🅴 ❌ 🅗 🖵 ➰

ARNOLDS PARK

🆀🅐🅐 ▽▽▽ **Bridges Bay Resort** 🅒🅞
(712) 332-2202. **$99-$699, 7 day notice.** 630 Linden Dr. Just e of US 71. Int corridors. **Pets:** Other species. Service with restrictions, crate.
🆂🅰🆅🅴 ❌ 🅗 🖵 ➰ 🚫

▼▼ Fillenwarth Beach M
(712) 332-5646. **$77-$1000 (no credit cards), 60 day notice.** 87 Lake Shore Dr. Just w of US 71; on West Lake Okoboji. Ext corridors. **Pets:** Other species.
⊠ 📶 🖥 ≈ ⊠

ATLANTIC

▼▼ Days Inn H
(712) 243-4067. **$55-$90.** 64968 Boston Rd. I-80, exit 60 (US 71), 0.5 mi s. Int corridors. **Pets:** Medium, other species. $5 one-time fee/room. Designated rooms, service with restrictions, supervision.
ASK ⊠ 📶 🖥 ≈

▼▼ Super 8 H
(712) 243-4723. **$60-$99.** 1902 E 7th St. I-80, exit 60 (US 71), 6 mi s, then 2 mi w; east side of town. Int corridors. **Pets:** Accepted.
ASK ⊠ 📶 🖥 ≈

BURLINGTON

◈◈ ▼▼▼ Comfort Suites Hotel & Conference Center H
(319) 753-1300. **$99-$112.** 1780 Stonegate Center Dr. On US 61, 2 mi s of US 34. Int corridors. **Pets:** Medium, other species. $15 daily fee/pet. Designated rooms, service with restrictions.
SAVE ⊠ ♿ 📶 🖥 ⁙ ≈ ⊠

◈◈ ▼▼▼ Quality Inn H
(319) 753-0000. **$60-$90.** 3051 Kirkwood Ave. Jct US 61 and 34, just n. Int corridors. **Pets:** $10 daily fee/pet. Supervision.
SAVE ⊠ 📶 🖥 ≈

▼▼ Super 8 H
(319) 752-9806. **$45-$79.** 3001 Kirkwood St. Jct US 61 and 34, just n. Int corridors. **Pets:** Medium, other species. $10 daily fee/pet. Service with restrictions, supervision.
ASK ⊠ 📶 🖥

CARROLL

▼▼ Super 8 H
(712) 792-4753. **$56-$70.** 1757 US 71 N. Just n of jct US 30 and 71. Int corridors. **Pets:** Accepted.
ASK ⊠ 📶 🖥

CARTER LAKE

◈◈ ▼▼▼ Holiday Inn Express Hotel & Suites H
(402) 505-4900. **$89-$259.** 2510 Abbott Plaza. I-480 W, exit 4 to 10th St, 2 mi n, follow Eppley Airfield signs. Int corridors. **Pets:** Medium, other species. $100 deposit/room, $10 daily fee/room. Service with restrictions, crate.
SAVE ⊠ ♿ 📶 🖥 ≈

▼▼▼ La Quinta Inn & Suites H ✿
(712) 347-6595. **$69-$189.** 1201 Ave H. I-480 W, exit 4 to 10th St, 2 mi n, follow Eppley Airfield signs. Int corridors. **Pets:** Medium, other species. Service with restrictions, supervision.
ASK ⊠ ♿ 📶 🖥 ≈

▼▼ Super 8 H
(712) 347-5588. **$77-$154.** 3000 Airport Dr. I-480 W, exit 4 to 10th St, 2.3 mi n, follow Eppley Airfield signs. Int corridors. **Pets:** $10 one-time fee/room. Service with restrictions, supervision.
ASK ⊠ 📶 🖥 ≈

CEDAR FALLS

▼▼▼ Comfort Suites H
(319) 273-9999. **Call for rates.** 7402 Nordic Dr. US 20, exit 225, just nw. Int corridors. **Pets:** Accepted.
⊠ ♿ 📶 🖥 ≈

▼▼ Days Inn H
(319) 266-1222. **Call for rates.** 5826 University Ave, Suite 2. 0.7 mi e of jct SR 58. Int corridors. **Pets:** Accepted.
⊠ 📶 🖥

◈◈ ▼▼ University Inn H
(319) 277-1412. **$46-$76.** 4711 University Ave. 1.6 mi e of jct SR 58. Ext/int corridors. **Pets:** Medium, dogs only. $30 deposit/pet. Designated rooms, service with restrictions, supervision.
SAVE ⊠ 📶 🖥

CEDAR RAPIDS

◈◈ ▼▼▼ Baymont Inn & Suites H ✿
(319) 378-8000. **$80-$125.** 1220 Park Place NE. I-380, exit 24A (SR 100/Collins Rd), 0.9 mi e, then just n. Int corridors. **Pets:** Medium. $10 daily fee/pet. Designated rooms, service with restrictions, supervision.
SAVE ⊠ ♿ 📶 🖥 ≈

◈◈ ▼▼▼ Best Western Cooper's Mill Hotel & Restaurant H
(319) 366-5323. **$110-$130.** 100 F Ave NW. I-380, exit 19C northbound, take right at end of exit, make immediate U-turn and go under I-380; exit 20A southbound, cross river, right on 1st St NW. Int corridors. **Pets:** Medium. $10 daily fee/pet. Service with restrictions, crate.
SAVE ⊠ 📶 🖥 ⁙ ≈ ⊠

◈◈ ▼▼▼ Best Western Longbranch Hotel & Convention Center H
(319) 377-6386. **$110-$130.** 90 Twixt Town Rd NE. I-380, exit 24A (SR 100/Collins Rd), 2.5 mi e, then just n. Int corridors. **Pets:** Medium, other species. $10 daily fee/room. Designated rooms, service with restrictions, supervision.
SAVE ⊠ 📶 🖥 ⁙ ≈ ⊠

◈◈ ▼▼ Clarion Hotel & Convention Center H
(319) 366-8671. **$95-$125.** 525 33rd Ave SW. I-380, exit 17 (33rd Ave SW), just w. Int corridors. **Pets:** Other species. $15 daily fee/room. Service with restrictions, crate.
SAVE ⊠ 📶 🖥 ⁙ ≈ ⊠

▼▼ Comfort Inn by Choice Hotels North H
(319) 393-8247. **Call for rates.** 5055 Rockwell Dr NE. I-380, exit 24A (SR 100/Collins Rd), 1 mi e. Int corridors. **Pets:** Small. $10 daily fee/room. Designated rooms, service with restrictions, crate.
⊠ 📶 🖥

▼▼ Comfort Inn by Choice Hotels South H
(319) 363-7934. **Call for rates.** 390 33rd Ave SW. I-380, exit 17 (33rd Ave SW), just w. Int corridors. **Pets:** Accepted.
⊠ 📶 🖥

◈◈ ▼▼▼ Country Inn & Suites Cedar Rapids Airport H
(319) 363-3789. **$109-$149.** 9100 Atlantic Dr SW. I-380, exit 13, just w. Int corridors. **Pets:** $10 one-time fee/pet. Service with restrictions, crate.
SAVE ⊠ ♿ 📶 🖥 ≈

▼▼▼ Hawthorn Suites H
(319) 294-8700. **$122-$144.** 4444 Czech Ln NE. I-380, exit 24A (SR 100/Collins Rd), just s. Int corridors. **Pets:** Other species. Service with restrictions, crate.
ASK ⊠ ♿ 📶 🖥 ≈

◈◈ ▼▼ Howard Johnson M
(319) 366-2475. **Call for rates.** 616 33rd Ave SW. I-380, exit 17 (33rd Ave SW), 0.3 mi w. Int corridors. **Pets:** Medium. $25 deposit/pet. Service with restrictions, supervision.
SAVE ⊠ 📶 🖥

◈◈ ▼▼▼ Mainstay Suites H
(319) 363-7829. **Call for rates.** 5145 Rockwell Dr NE. I-380, exit 24A (SR 100/Collins Rd), 1 mi e, then just n. Int corridors. **Pets:** Accepted.
SAVE ⊠ ♿ 📶 🖥 ≈ ⊠

▼▼ Motel 6 #1485 **M**
(319) 366-7523. **$39-$55.** 3325 Southgate Ct SW. I-380, exit 17 (33rd Ave SW), just sw. Ext corridors. **Pets:** Other species. Service with restrictions, supervision.

⊠ ㋖ 🔒

▼▼ Quality Inn & Suites **H**
(319) 378-8888. **$75-$125.** 2025 Werner Ave NE. I-380, exit 24A (SR 100/Collins Rd), just se. Int corridors. **Pets:** Small. $10 daily fee/pet. Service with restrictions, supervision.

A$K ⊠ 🔒 🖵 ➴

▼▼ Quality Inn of Cedar Rapids **H**
(319) 393-8800. **Call for rates.** 4747 1st Ave SE. I-380, exit 24A (SR 100/Collins Rd), 2.5 mi e, then 1st Ave SE. Int corridors. **Pets:** Accepted.

⊠ ㋖ 🔒 🖵 ➴

▼▼ Ramada Limited **H**
(319) 396-5000. **$80-$135.** 4011 16th Ave SW. I-380, exit 16 (US 30), 2.4 mi w, 1.4 mi n (exit 250) on Edgewood Rd to 16th Ave, then just w. Int corridors. **Pets:** Accepted.

A$K ⊠ 🔒 🖵 ➴

◆▼◆▼ Residence Inn by Marriott **H** ❖
(319) 395-0111. **$140-$170.** 1900 Dodge Rd NE. I-380, exit 24A (SR 100/Collins Rd), just e. Int corridors. **Pets:** Other species. $75 one-time fee/room.

⊠ ㋖ 🔒 🖵 ➴ ⊠

▼▼ Super 8 **H**
(319) 362-6002. **Call for rates.** 720 33rd Ave SW. I-380, exit 17 (33rd Ave SW), 0.4 mi w. Int corridors. **Pets:** Accepted.

⊠ 🔒 🖵

▼▼ Super 8 **H**
(319) 363-1755. **Call for rates.** 400 33rd Ave SW. I-380, exit 17 (33rd Ave SW), just w. Int corridors. **Pets:** Accepted.

⊠ 🔒

CHARLES CITY

▼ Hartwood Inn **M**
(641) 228-4352. **$40-$60, 4 day notice.** 1312 Gilbert St. US 218/18, exit 212, 2.2 mi e. Ext corridors. **Pets:** Accepted.

A$K ⊠ 🔒 🖵 ➴

◆▼◆▼ Sleep Inn & Suites **H**
(641) 257-6700. **$64-$199.** 1416 S Grand Ave. US 218/18, exit 218, 0.7 mi n on US 218 business route; south side of town. Int corridors. **Pets:** $10 daily fee/pet. Designated rooms, service with restrictions, supervision.

A$K ⊠ 🔒 🖵 ➴

▼▼ Super 8–Charles City **H** ❖
(641) 228-2888. **$55-$74.** 1411 S Grand Ave. US 218/18, exit 218, 0.8 mi n on US 218 business route; south side of town. Int corridors. **Pets:** Medium. $10 one-time fee/pet. Service with restrictions, crate.

A$K ⊠ ㋖ 🔒 🖵

CHEROKEE

◆◆◆ ▼◆▼ Best Western La Grande Hacienda **H**
(712) 225-5701. **$80-$90, 3 day notice.** 1401 N 2nd St. Just s of jct SR 3 and US 59 (N 2nd St). Int corridors. **Pets:** Accepted.

SAVE ⊠ ㋖ 🖵 ¶ ➴

CLARINDA

▼▼ Clarinda Super 8 **H**
(712) 542-6333. **$55-$88.** 1203 S 12th St. Jct US 71 and SR 2, just e. Int corridors. **Pets:** No service, crate.

A$K ⊠ ㋖ 🔒 🖵 ➴

CLEAR LAKE

▼▼ AmericInn Lodge & Suites of Clear Lake **H**
(641) 357-8954. **$91-$111.** 1406 N 25th St. I-35, exit 194 (US 18), just nw. Int corridors. **Pets:** Accepted.

A$K ⊠ 🔒 🖵 ➴

◆◆◆ ▼▼ Best Western Holiday Lodge **H**
(641) 357-5253. **$74-$99.** 2023 7th Ave N. I-35, exit 194 (US 18), 0.3 mi w. Ext/int corridors. **Pets:** Other species. $10 daily fee/room. Service with restrictions, supervision.

SAVE ⊠ ㋖ 🔒 🖵 ¶ ➴ ⊠

◆◆◆ ▼▼ Budget Inn **M**
(641) 357-8700. **$40-$90.** 1306 N 25th St. I-35, exit 194 (US 18), just nw. Int corridors. **Pets:** Accepted.

SAVE ⊠ 🔒 ➴

▼ Lake Country Inn **M**
(641) 357-2184. **$49-$69.** 518 US 18. I-35, exit 194 (US 18), 1.9 mi w. Ext corridors. **Pets:** Other species. $5 daily fee/pet. Designated rooms, service with restrictions, supervision.

⊠ 🔒

▼▼ Microtel Inn **H**
(641) 357-0966. **$65-$98.** 1305 N 25th St. I-35, exit 194 (US 18), just nw. Int corridors. **Pets:** Accepted.

A$K ⊠ ㋖ 🔒 🖵

▼▼ Super 8 **H**
(641) 357-7521. **$45-$90.** 2809 4th Ave S. I-35, exit 193, just se. Int corridors. **Pets:** Accepted.

A$K ⊠ 🖵

CLINTON

◆◆◆ ▼▼ Best Western-Frontier **H** ❖
(563) 242-7112. **$86-$126.** 2300 Lincoln Way. On US 30, just e of jct US 30 and 67. Int corridors. **Pets:** Medium. $10 daily fee/pet. Service with restrictions, crate.

SAVE ⊠ 🔒 🖵 ¶ ➴ ⊠

◆◆◆ ◆▼◆▼ Country Inn & Suites By Carlson **H**
(563) 244-9922. **$89-$119.** 2224 Lincoln Way. On US 30, just e of jct US 30 and 67. Int corridors. **Pets:** $10 daily fee/pet. Service with restrictions, supervision.

SAVE ⊠ ㋖ 🔒 🖵 ➴

◆◆◆ ▼▼ Oak Tree Inn **H**
(563) 243-1000. **$65-$77.** 2300 Valley West Ct. Just n of jct US 30 and 67, west side of town. Int corridors. **Pets:** Accepted.

SAVE ⊠ ㋖ 🔒 🖵

▼▼ Super 8-Clinton **H** ❖
(563) 242-8870. **$50-$70.** 1711 Lincoln Way. On US 30, 0.7 mi e of jct US 67. Int corridors. **Pets:** Other species. $10 one-time fee/pet. Service with restrictions, crate.

A$K ⊠ ㋖ 🔒

CLIVE

◆◆◆ ▼◆▼ Best Western Des Moines West **H**
(515) 221-2345. **$89-$119.** 1450 NW 118th St. I-80/35, exit 124 (University Ave), just nw. Int corridors. **Pets:** Other species. $10 daily fee/pet. Service with restrictions, supervision.

SAVE ⊠ ㋖ 🔒 🖵 ➴ ⊠

◆◆◆ ▼◆▼ Chase Suite Hotel by Woodfin **H** ❖
(515) 223-7700. **$109-$129.** 11428 Forest Ave. I-80/35, exit 124 (University Ave), just ne. Ext corridors. **Pets:** Other species. $10 daily fee/pet. Service with restrictions.

SAVE ⊠ ㋖ 🔒 🖵 ➴ ⊠

▼▼ **La Quinta Inn & Suites West Des Moines-Clive** H ❀
(515) 221-9200. **$49-$99.** 1390 NW 118th St. I-80/35, exit 124 (University Ave). Int corridors. **Pets:** Medium, other species. Service with restrictions, supervision.
ASK ⊠ ᏜM ⊞ ▣ ⇌ ⊠

COLFAX

𝔸𝔸𝔻 ▼▼ **Comfort Inn** H
(515) 674-4455. **$67-$169.** 1402 N Walnut. I-80, exit 155 (SR 117), just ne. Int corridors. **Pets:** Other species. $13 daily fee/pet. Service with restrictions, supervision.
SAVE ⊠ ᏜM ⊞ ▣ ⇌

𝔸𝔸𝔻 ▼▼▼ **Microtel Inn & Suites** H
(515) 674-0600. **$69-$79.** 11000 Federal Ave. I-80, exit 155 (SR 117). Int corridors. **Pets:** Other species. $10 daily fee/room. Service with restrictions, supervision.
SAVE ⊠ ⊞ ▣

CORALVILLE

𝔸𝔸𝔻 ▼▼▼ **Baymont Inn & Suites** H ❀
(319) 337-9797. **$80-$115.** 200 6th St. I-80, exit 242, just s, then right on 6th St. Int corridors. **Pets:** $25 daily fee/pet. Service with restrictions, crate.
SAVE ⊠ ⊞ ▣ ⇌

𝔸𝔸𝔻 ▼▼▼ **Best Western-Cantebury Inn & Suites** H
(319) 351-0400. **$69-$169, 7 day notice.** 704 1st Ave. I-80, exit 242, just s. Int corridors. **Pets:** Medium. $10 one-time fee/pet. Designated rooms, service with restrictions, supervision.
SAVE ⊠ ⊞ ▣ ⊺⫙ ⇌ ⊠

▼▼ **Comfort Inn by Choice Hotels** H
(319) 351-8144. **Call for rates.** 209 W 9th St. I-80, exit 242, just s. Int corridors. **Pets:** Accepted.
⊠ ᏜM ⊞ ▣ ⇌

▼▼ **Days Inn** M
(319) 354-4400. **$63-$140.** 205 2nd St. I-80, exit 242, 1 mi s to 2nd St, then just w. Ext corridors. **Pets:** Accepted.
ASK ⊠ ⊞ ▣

𝔸𝔸𝔻 ▼▼▼ **Hampton Inn** H
(319) 351-6600. **$139.** 1200 1st Ave. I-80, exit 242, just n. Int corridors. **Pets:** Accepted.
SAVE ⊠ ᏜM ⊞ ▣ ⊺⫙ ⇌

𝔸𝔸𝔻 ▼▼▼ **Holiday Inn** H ❀
(319) 351-5049. **$89-$269.** 1220 1st Ave. I-80, exit 242, just n. Int corridors. **Pets:** $20 one-time fee/room. Designated rooms, service with restrictions, supervision.
SAVE ⊠ ᏜM ⊞ ▣ ⊺⫙ ⇌

▼▼ **Super 8** H ❀
(319) 337-8388. **$60-$130.** 611 1st Ave. I-80, exit 242, 0.4 mi s. Int corridors. **Pets:** $10 daily fee/pet. Designated rooms, service with restrictions, supervision.
ASK ⊠ ᏜM ⊞

COUNCIL BLUFFS

▼▼ **Days Inn** H
(712) 366-9699. **Call for rates.** 3208 S 7th St. I-29/80, exit 3 (US 92), just sw. Int corridors. **Pets:** Accepted.
⊠ ⊞ ▣

▼▼ **Days Inn** H
(712) 323-2200. **Call for rates.** 3619 9th Ave. I-29, exit 53A (9th Ave). Int corridors. **Pets:** Accepted.
⊠ ⊞ ▣

▼ **Super 8** H
(712) 322-2888. **$69-$95.** 2712 S 24th St. I-29/80, exit 1B (24th St), just nw. Int corridors. **Pets:** Service with restrictions, supervision.
ASK ⊠ ᏜM ▣

𝔸𝔸𝔻 ▼▼ **Western Inn** H
(712) 322-4499. **$59-$109.** 1842 Madison Ave. I-80, exit 5 (Madison Ave), just s. Int corridors. **Pets:** Small. $10 one-time fee/pet. Service with restrictions, supervision.
SAVE ⊠ ⇌

CRESCO

𝔸𝔸𝔻 ▼ **Cresco Motel** M
(563) 547-2240. **$53-$81.** 620 2nd Ave SE (SR 9) SE. On SR 9; east side of town. Ext corridors. **Pets:** Dogs only. Service with restrictions, supervision.
SAVE ⊠ ᏜM ⊞

CRESTON

▼▼ **Super 8-Creston** H
(641) 782-6541. **$55-$75.** 804 W Taylor. Jct US 34 and SR 25, on US 34. Int corridors. **Pets:** Small. $10 daily fee/pet. Designated rooms, no service, crate.
ASK ⊠ ᏜM ⊞ ▣

DENISON

▼▼ **Denison Super 8** H
(712) 263-5081. **$75-$85.** 502 Boyer Valley Rd. Jct US 30/59 and SR 141, 0.3 mi sw. Int corridors. **Pets:** Accepted.
ASK ⊠ ⊞ ▣

DES MOINES

𝔸𝔸𝔻 ▼▼▼ **Best Western Des Moines Airport Hotel** H ❀
(515) 287-6464. **$120-$170.** 1810 Army Post Rd. Across from airport. Int corridors. **Pets:** Medium. $25 one-time fee/room. Designated rooms, service with restrictions, crate.
SAVE ⊠ ᏜM ⊞ ▣ ⊺⫙ ⇌

▼▼ **Comfort Inn by Choice Hotels** H ❀
(515) 287-3434. **Call for rates.** 5231 Fleur Dr. Opposite the airport. Int corridors. **Pets:** Medium. $5 daily fee/room. Designated rooms.
⊠ ᏜM ⊞ ▣ ⇌

𝔸𝔸𝔻 ▼▼▼ **Econo Lodge** H
(515) 278-8858. **$54-$70.** 4755 Merle Hay Rd. I-80/35, exit 131 (Merle Hay Rd), just s. Int corridors. **Pets:** $10 daily fee/pet. Service with restrictions, supervision.
SAVE ⊠ ⊞

▼▼ **Motel 6-30** M
(515) 287-6364. **$45-$55.** 4817 Fleur Dr. Opposite the airport. Ext corridors. **Pets:** Other species. Service with restrictions, supervision.
⊠

𝔸𝔸𝔻 ▼▼▼ **Quality Inn & Suites Event Center** H
(515) 282-5251. **$70-$275.** 929 3rd St. I-235, exit 3rd St; downtown. Int corridors. **Pets:** Medium. $10 daily fee/pet. Service with restrictions, supervision.
SAVE ⊠ ⊞ ▣ ⊺⫙ ⇌

𝔸𝔸𝔻 ▼▼ **Red Roof Inn & Suites** H
(515) 266-6800. **$67-$76.** 4950 NE 14th St. I-80, exit 136 (US 69). Int corridors. **Pets:** Accepted.
SAVE ⊠ ᏜM ⊞ ▣ ⇌

DE SOTO

Edgetowner Motel
(515) 834-2641. **$48.** 804 Guthrie. I-80, exit 110, just s. Ext corridors.
Pets: Dogs only. Service with restrictions, supervision.

DUBUQUE

Best Western Midway Hotel
(563) 557-8000. **$90-$210.** 3100 Dodge St. US 20, 2.3 mi w of jct US
52/61/151 and Mississippi Bridge. Int corridors. **Pets:** Accepted.

Comfort Inn by Choice Hotels
(563) 556-1000. **$70-$105.** 4055 McDonald Dr. US 20, 3.8 mi w of jct US
52/61/151 and Mississippi Bridge. Int corridors. **Pets:** Medium. $10 one-
time fee/pet. Service with restrictions, supervision.

Days Inn
(563) 583-3297. **$70-$100.** 1111 Dodge St. US 20, 0.8 mi w of jct US
52/61/151 and Mississippi Bridge, exit Hill/Bryant. Ext corridors. **Pets:** Other
species. $10 one-time fee/pet. Service with restrictions.

Holiday Inn Dubuque/Galena
(563) 556-2000. **$129-$169.** 450 Main St. At Main and 4th sts; downtown.
Int corridors. **Pets:** $25 one-time fee/room. Service with restrictions, super-
vision.

MainStay Suites
(563) 557-7829. **$79-$170.** 1275 Associates Dr. Just n of jct US 20 and
NW Arterial Rd; west side of town. Int corridors. **Pets:** Small, other species.
$100 deposit/room, $20 daily fee/room. Designated rooms, no service,
crate.

DYERSVILLE

Comfort Inn-Dyersville
(563) 875-7700. **$79-$180.** 527 16th Ave SE. US 20, exit 294 (SR 136),
just nw. Int corridors. **Pets:** Medium. $15 daily fee/room. Designated rooms,
service with restrictions, supervision.

Super 8 Motel-Dyersville
(563) 875-8885. **$50-$99.** 925 15th Ave SE. US 20, exit 294 (SR 136), just
n. Int corridors. **Pets:** Accepted.

ELDRIDGE

Quality Inn & Suites
(563) 285-4600. **$59-$159.** 1000 E Iowa St. I-80, exit 295B (US 61), 4 mi
n to exit 127 (CR F45). Int corridors. **Pets:** Accepted.

ELK HORN

AmericInn Lodge & Suites of Elkhorn
(712) 764-4000. **$85-$130.** 4037 Main St. I-80, exit 54 (SR 173), 6.4 mi n.
Int corridors. **Pets:** Other species. $10 daily fee/room. Designated rooms,
service with restrictions, supervision.

EMMETSBURG

Super 8
(712) 852-2667. **Call for rates.** 3501 Main St. Jct US 18 and SR 4, 0.8 mi
w. Int corridors. **Pets:** Accepted.

ESTHERVILLE

Sleep Inn & Suites
(712) 362-5522. **$79-$149.** 2008 Central Ave. Jct SR 4 and 9, 1 mi e. Int
corridors. **Pets:** Large, other species. $25 one-time fee/room. Service with
restrictions, supervision.

Super 8
(712) 362-2400. **$50-$70.** 1919 Central Ave. Jct SR 4 and 9, 1 mi e. Int
corridors. **Pets:** Small. $4 daily fee/pet. Designated rooms, supervision.

EVANSDALE

Days Inn
(319) 235-1111. **Call for rates.** 450 Evansdale Dr. I-380/20, exit 68, just n.
Int corridors. **Pets:** Accepted.

FAIRFIELD

Best Western Fairfield Inn
(641) 472-2200. **$84-$94, 3 day notice.** 2200 W Burlington Ave. On US
34, 1 mi w of jct SR 1. Int corridors. **Pets:** $25 one-time fee/pet. Designated
rooms, service with restrictions.

Super 8
(641) 469-2000. **$73-$125.** 3001 W Burlington Ave. On US 34, 1.5 mi w of
jct SR 1. Int corridors. **Pets:** Medium. $50 deposit/room, $5 daily fee/pet.
Service with restrictions, supervision.

FORT DODGE

**AmericInn Lodge & Suites of Fort
Dodge**
(515) 576-2100. **$100-$190.** 100 Kenyon Rd W. 3 mi n of jct US 20 and
169. Int corridors. **Pets:** Medium, other species. $10 daily fee/room. Desig-
nated rooms, service with restrictions, crate.

Comfort Inn
(515) 573-5000. **$90-$150.** 2938 5th Ave S. US 20, exit 124 (Coalville), 3.5
mi n on CR P59, then 1.3 mi w on 5th Ave and Business Rt US 20. Int
corridors. **Pets:** Accepted.

Days Inn
(515) 576-8000. **$64-$74.** 3040 5th Ave S. US 20, exit 124 (Coalville), 3.5
mi n on CR P59, then 1.2 mi w on Business Rt US 20. Int corridors.
Pets: Medium. $25 one-time fee/pet. Designated rooms, service with
restrictions, supervision.

FORT MADISON

Comfort Inn & Suites
(319) 372-6800. **$85-$141.** 6169 Reve Ct. Just e of jct US 61 and SR 2,
on US 61. Int corridors. **Pets:** $25 daily fee/pet. Service with restrictions,
supervision.

Knights Inn
(319) 372-7740. **$65-$105.** 3440 Ave L. 2.1 mi e of jct US 61 and SR 2.
Ext corridors. **Pets:** Small. $10 daily fee/pet. Designated rooms, service
with restrictions, supervision.

Super 8-Ft Madison
(319) 372-8500. **$50-$69.** US 61 W, 5107 Ave O. 1 mi e of jct US 61 and
SR 2. Int corridors. **Pets:** $10 daily fee/room. Service with restrictions,
supervision.

GRIMES

▼▼▼ **AmericInn Lodge & Suites of Grimes** 🅷
(515) 986-9900. **$95-$100.** 251 Gateway Cir. Just sw of jct US 44 and SR 141. Int corridors. **Pets:** Medium, dogs only. $50 deposit/room, $10 daily fee/room. Designated rooms, service with restrictions, supervision.
☒ ⓶Ⓜ 🛅 💻 ⇌ ☒

GRINNELL

▼▼▼ **Comfort Inn & Suites** 🅷
(641) 236-5236. **$99-$189.** 1630 West St S. I-80, exit 182, 0.7 mi n. Int corridors. **Pets:** Accepted.
(A$K) ☒ ⓶Ⓜ 🛅 💻 ⇌ ☒

HAMPTON

▼▼ **AmericInn Lodge & Suites of Hampton** 🅷 🐾
(641) 456-5559. **$80-$160.** 702 Central Ave W. On SR 3 (Central Ave W), 0.7 mi w of jct US 65 and SR 3. Int corridors. **Pets:** Medium. $50 deposit/pet, $10 daily fee/pet. Service with restrictions, supervision.
(A$K) ☒ 🛅 💻 ⇌ ☒

IDA GROVE

▼ **Delux Motel** Ⓜ
(712) 364-3317. **$45-$60.** 5981 US Hwy 175. Jct US 59 S and 175. Ext/int corridors. **Pets:** $10 daily fee/pet. Designated rooms, service with restrictions, supervision.
☒ 🛅

INDEPENDENCE

▼▼▼ **Super 8** 🅷
(319) 334-7041. **$66-$125.** 2000 1st St W. US 20, exit 252, 1.4 mi n. Int corridors. **Pets:** Accepted.
(A$K) ☒ ⓶Ⓜ 🛅 💻

IOWA CITY

🔺🔺 ▼▼▼ **Alexis Park Inn & Suites** 🅷 🐾
(319) 337-8665. **$75-$220, 3 day notice.** 1165 S Riverside Dr. I-80, exit 239 (US 218), 5 mi s, 2 mi e on US 6, then just s. Ext corridors. **Pets:** $10 daily fee/pet. Designated rooms, service with restrictions, crate.
(SAVE) ☒ 🛅 💻 ⇌

▼▼▼▼ **hotelVetro conference center** 🅷
(319) 337-4961. **$159-$329.** 201 S Linn St. I-80, exit 244, s on Dubuque St, e on Washington St, then s. Int corridors. **Pets:** Accepted.
(A$K) ☒ 🛅 💻 ⇌

🔺🔺 ▼▼▼▼ **Quality Inn & Suites** 🅷 🐾
(319) 354-2000. **$79-$169.** 2525 N Dodge. I-80, exit 246, just ne. Int corridors. **Pets:** $10 daily fee/room. Service with restrictions, supervision.
(SAVE) ☒ 🛅 💻 🍽 ⇌ ☒

🔺🔺 ▼▼▼▼ **Sheraton Iowa City Hotel** 🅷
(319) 337-4058. **$119-$239.** 210 S Dubuque St. Dubuque and Burlington sts (SR 1); downtown. Int corridors. **Pets:** Accepted.
(SAVE) ☒ 🛅 💻 🍽 ⇌ ☒

IOWA FALLS

▼▼ **Iowa Falls Super 8** 🅷
(641) 648-4618. **Call for rates.** 839 S Oak St. Jct US 65 and Washington Ave, 1 mi s; US 20, exit 168, 3.8 mi n. Int corridors. **Pets:** Accepted.
☒ ⓶Ⓜ 🛅 💻 ⇌

JOHNSTON

▼▼▼ **TownePlace Suites by Marriott Des Moines/Urbandale** 🅷
(515) 727-4066. **$116-$142.** 8800 Northpark Dr. I-35/80, exit 129 (86th St), just nw. Int corridors. **Pets:** Other species. $100 one-time fee/room. Service with restrictions.
☒ 🛅 💻 ⇌

KEOKUK

▼▼▼ **Hampton Inn** 🅷
(319) 524-6700. **$69-$89.** 3201 Main St. 1.8 mi n of jct US 136. Int corridors. **Pets:** Accepted.
☒ ⓶Ⓜ 💻 ⇌

▼▼▼ **Holiday Inn Express** 🅷
(319) 524-8000. **$80-$89.** 325 Main St. 4th and Main sts; downtown. Int corridors. **Pets:** Dogs only. $15 daily fee/pet. Designated rooms, service with restrictions, supervision.
☒ ⓶Ⓜ 🛅 💻 ⇌ ☒

▼▼ **Super 8-Keokuk** 🅷
(319) 524-3888. **$50-$79.** 3511 Main St. On Business US 61/218, 2 mi n of jct US 136. Int corridors. **Pets:** $10 daily fee/pet. Service with restrictions, supervision.
(A$K) ☒ ⓶Ⓜ 🛅 💻

LE CLAIRE

🔺🔺 ▼▼▼ **Comfort Inn & Suites-Riverview** 🅷 🐾
(563) 289-4747. **$75-$170.** 902 Mississippi View Ct. I-80, exit 306 (US 67), 0.5 mi n to Eagle Ridge Rd, then just sw. Int corridors. **Pets:** Medium. $10 daily fee/pet. Service with restrictions, crate.
(SAVE) ☒ ⓶Ⓜ 🛅 💻 ⇌

🔺🔺 ▼▼▼ **Holiday Inn Express** 🅷
(563) 289-9978. **$80-$200.** 1201 Canal Shore Dr. I-80, exit 306 (US 67), just n. Int corridors. **Pets:** Medium. $12 one-time fee/room. Designated rooms, service with restrictions, supervision.
(SAVE) ☒ 🛅 💻 ⇌

🔺🔺 ▼▼▼ **Super 8 of LeClaire** 🅷 🐾
(563) 289-5888. **$66-$113.** 1552 Welcome Center Dr. I-80, exit 306 (US 67), 0.5 mi n to Eagle Ridge Rd, then just sw to Mississippi View Ct. Int corridors. **Pets:** Medium. $10 daily fee/pet. Service with restrictions, crate.
(SAVE) ☒ ⓶Ⓜ 🛅 💻

LE MARS

▼▼ **Super 8** 🅷
(712) 546-8800. **Call for rates.** 1201 Hawkeye Ave SW. US 75, exit 116, 1.6 mi ne. Int corridors. **Pets:** $10 daily fee/pet. Service with restrictions, supervision.
☒ ⓶Ⓜ 🛅 💻 ⇌

MANCHESTER

🔺🔺 ▼▼▼ **Super 8** 🅷
(563) 927-2533. **$55-$65.** 1020 W Main St. Jct US 20 and SR 13, exit 275, 1.3 mi n, then 0.3 mi e. Int corridors. **Pets:** Other species. $10 one-time fee/room.
(SAVE) ☒ 🛅 💻

MARION

▼▼ **Microtel Inn & Suites** 🅷
(319) 373-7400. **$55-$85.** 5500 Dyer Ave. Jct US 151 and SR 13. Int corridors. **Pets:** Accepted.
(A$K) ☒ ⓶Ⓜ 🛅 💻

MARQUETTE

▼ **The Frontier Motel** Ⓜ
(563) 873-3497. **$55-$120.** 101 S 1st St. Just s of jct US 18 and SR 76; between Mississippi River Bridge and casino. Ext corridors. **Pets:** Accepted.
☒ 🛅 💻 ⇌

MARSHALLTOWN

▼▼ **AmericInn Motel & Suites of Marshalltown** 🅷
(641) 752-4844. **Call for rates.** 115 Iowa Ave W. Just nw of jct US 30 and SR 14. Int corridors. **Pets:** Accepted.
☒ ⓶Ⓜ 🛅 💻 ⇌ ☒

AAA ▼▼▼▼ **Best Western Regency Inn** �H ❀
(641) 752-6321. **$68-$90.** 3303 S Center St. Jct US 30 and SR 14. Int corridors. **Pets:** Other species. $10 daily fee/room. Service with restrictions.
SAVE ✕ 🛏 🖥 🍽 ⊘

▼▼ **Comfort Inn** �H
(641) 752-6000. **$70-$100.** 2613 S Center St. 0.5 mi n of jct US 30 and SR 14. Int corridors. **Pets:** Accepted.
ASK ✕ 🛏 🖥 ⊘

▼▼ **Days Inn** �H
(641) 753-8181. **$50-$60, 7 day notice.** 18 E Berle Rd. Just n of jct US 30 and SR 14. Int corridors. **Pets:** Accepted.
ASK ✕ 🛏 🖥

▼▼ **Super 8** �H
(641) 753-3333. **$53-$63.** 3315 S Center St. Just n of jct US 30 and SR 14. Int corridors. **Pets:** Accepted.
ASK ✕ 🛏 🖥

MASON CITY

▼ **Days Inn Mason City** �H
(641) 424-0210. **$54-$110.** 2301 4th St SW. I-35, exit 194 (SR 122), 6 mi e. Int corridors. **Pets:** $10 one-time fee/room. Service with restrictions, crate.
ASK ✕ 🛏 🖥

AAA ▼▼▼ **Holiday Inn** �H ❀
(641) 423-1640. **$89-$169.** 2101 4th St SW (Hwy 122). I-35, exit 194 (SR 122), 6 mi e. Ext/int corridors. **Pets:** $25 one-time fee/room. Service with restrictions, crate.
SAVE ✕ 🛏 🖥 🍽 ⊘ ⊘

▼▼ **Mason City Super 8** �H
(641) 423-8855. **$65-$80.** 3010 4th St SW. I-35, exit 194 (SR 122), 5.3 mi e. Int corridors. **Pets:** Other species. $10 daily fee/pet. Service with restrictions, supervision.
ASK ✕ 🛏 🖥

MISSOURI VALLEY

AAA ▼▼ **Oak Tree Inn** �H
(712) 642-3000. **$63-$84.** 128 S Willow Rd. I-29, exit 75, 0.4 mi ne. Int corridors. **Pets:** Other species. $5 daily fee/pet. Service with restrictions, supervision.
SAVE ✕ 🛏 🖥

MONTICELLO

▼▼ **The Blue Inn** �H
(319) 465-6116. **$30-$100.** 250 N Main St. North end of town on Business Rt US 151. Int corridors. **Pets:** Accepted.
ASK ✕ 🛏 🖥 🍽

MOUNT PLEASANT

▼▼ **Brazelton Hotel & Suites** �H
(319) 385-0571. **Call for rates.** 1200 E Baker. US 218/27, exit 45, 0.6 mi s on Grand Ave. Int corridors. **Pets:** Accepted.
✕ 🛏 🖥 ⊘

▼▼ **Super 8** �H
(319) 385-8888. **$55-$65.** 1000 N Grand Ave. US 218/27, exit 45, 0.6 mi s. Int corridors. **Pets:** Small. $10 daily fee/pet. Service with restrictions, supervision.
ASK ✕ 🛏 🖥

MOUNT VERNON

AAA ▼▼▼ **Sleep Inn & Suites** �H
(319) 895-0055. **$79-$149.** 310 Virgil Ave. Jct US 30 and SR 1, just se. Int corridors. **Pets:** Medium. $13 one-time fee/room. Service with restrictions, supervision.
SAVE ✕ 🛏 🖥

MUSCATINE

▼▼ **AmericInn Lodge & Suites of Muscatine** �H
(563) 263-0880. **Call for rates.** 3115 Hwy 61 N. Jct US 61 and SR 38, just n. Int corridors. **Pets:** Accepted.
✕ 🛏 🖥 ⊘

▼ **Muscatine Super 8** �H
(563) 263-9100. **$53-$64.** 2900 N Hwy 61. Jct US 61 and SR 38. Int corridors. **Pets:** Small. $10 daily fee/pet. Designated rooms, no service, crate.
ASK ✕ 🛏 🖥

NEW HAMPTON

▼▼▼ **Super 8-New Hampton** �H
(641) 394-3838. **$68-$80.** 825 S Linn Ave. US 63, exit 201, 1.5 mi ne on US 63 business route. Int corridors. **Pets:** Dogs only. $15 one-time fee/pet. Designated rooms, service with restrictions, supervision.
ASK ✕ 🛏 🖥 ⊘

NEWTON

▼▼ **Days Inn of Newton** �H
(641) 792-2330. **$55-$150.** 1605 W 19th St S. I-80, exit 164 (SR 14), just n. Int corridors. **Pets:** Other species. $10 daily fee/pet. Service with restrictions, supervision.
ASK ✕ 🛏 🖥

▼▼ **Holiday Inn Express** �H
(641) 792-3333. **Call for rates.** 208 W 4th St N. Downtown. Int corridors. **Pets:** Accepted.
✕ 🛏 🖥 ⊘

▼▼ **Quality Inn of Newton Iowa** �H
(641) 792-7722. **Call for rates.** 1700 W 19th St S. I-80, exit 164 (SR 14), just nw. Int corridors. **Pets:** Accepted.
✕ 🛏 🖥

NORTH LIBERTY

AAA ▼▼▼ **Sleep Inn & Suites** �H
(319) 665-2700. **$79-$129.** 485 Madison Ave N. I-380, exit 4. Int corridors. **Pets:** Accepted.
SAVE ✕ 🛏 🖥 ⊘

NORTHWOOD

AAA ▼▼▼ **Country Inn & Suites By Carlson** �H
(641) 323-7000. **$100-$105, 14 day notice.** 711 Diamond Jo Ln. I-35, exit 214, just nw. Int corridors. **Pets:** Accepted.
SAVE ✕ 🛏 🖥 ⊘

OELWEIN

▼▼ **Super 8-Oelwein** 🅼
(319) 283-2888. **$65-$95.** 210 10th St SE. Jct SR 3 and 150, 1 mi s on SR 150; south end of downtown. Int corridors. **Pets:** Accepted.
ASK ✕ 🛏 🖥

OKOBOJI

▼▼ **AmericInn Lodge & Suites of Okoboji** �H
(712) 332-9000. **$79-$269, 7 day notice.** 1005 Brooks Park Dr. Jct US 71 and SR 9, 2.5 mi s on US 71. Int corridors. **Pets:** Medium, dogs only. $25 one-time fee/pet. Service with restrictions, supervision.
✕ 🛏 🖥 ⊘

AAA ▼▼▼ **Arrowwood Resort & Conference Center by ClubHouse** �H
(712) 332-2161. **$81-$171, 7 day notice.** 1405 US 71 S. Jct US 71 and SR 9, 3 mi s. Ext/int corridors. **Pets:** Other species. Service with restrictions, crate.
SAVE ✕ 🛏 🖥 🍽 ⊘ ⊘

OSCEOLA

▼▼ AmericInn Lodge & Suites of Osceola 🅗
(641) 342-9400. **$90-$160.** 111 Ariel Cir. I-35, exit 33. Int corridors.
Pets: Accepted.
🄰🅂🄺 ⊠ 🦽ᴹ 🛏 💻 ⇆

▼▼ Days Inn 🅗
(641) 342-6666. **$70-$110.** 710 Warren Ave. I-35, exit 33, just e. Int corridors. **Pets:** $10 daily fee/pet. Designated rooms, supervision.
🄰🅂🄺 ⊠ 🦽ᴹ 💻 ⇆

OSKALOOSA

▼▼ Americas Best Value Inn 🅜
(641) 673-8351. **Call for rates.** 1315 a Ave E. On SR 92, just w of jct SR 23. Ext/int corridors. **Pets:** Accepted.
⊠ 🛏 💻

▼▼ Comfort Inn 🅗
(641) 676-6000. **$90-$175.** 2401 a Ave W. SR 163, exit 57 (SR 92), just e. Int corridors. **Pets:** Accepted.
🄰🅂🄺 ⊠ 🛏 💻 ⇆

▼▼ Super 8-Oskaloosa 🅗
(641) 673-8481. **$59-$95.** 306 S 17th St. Just s of SR 92 and 23. Int corridors. **Pets:** Accepted.
🄰🅂🄺 ⊠ 🦽ᴹ 🛏 💻

PELLA

▼▼ Super 8 🅗
(641) 628-8181. **$45-$65.** 105 E Oskaloosa St. SR 163, exit 42, 1 mi n, then 0.5 mi e. Int corridors. **Pets:** Small. $10 daily fee/pet. Designated rooms, no service, crate.
🄰🅂🄺 ⊠ 🦽ᴹ 🛏 💻

PERCIVAL

▼▼ Americas Best Value Inn & Suites 🅗
(712) 382-2100. **$73-$110.** 2113 Sapp Brothers Dr. I-29, exit 10 (SR 2), just w. Int corridors. **Pets:** Very small, dogs only. $10 daily fee/pet. Designated rooms, service with restrictions, supervision.
🄰🅂🄺 ⊠ 🛏 💻 ⇆

🆔 ▼▼ Nebraska City Super 8 🅗
(712) 382-2828. **$62-$69.** 2103 249th St. I-29, exit 10 (SR 2), just w. Int corridors. **Pets:** Other species. $10 one-time fee/room. Service with restrictions, supervision.
🆂🄰🆅🄴 ⊠ 🦽ᴹ 🛏 💻

PLEASANT HILL

🆔 ▼▼ Sleep Inn & Suites 🅗
(515) 299-9922. **$95-$169.** 5850 Morning Star Ct. US 65, exit 79 (SR 163/E University Ave), just e. Int corridors. **Pets:** Other species. $13 daily fee/room. Service with restrictions, supervision.
🆂🄰🆅🄴 ⊠ 🦽ᴹ 🛏 💻 ⇆

QUAD CITIES AREA

BETTENDORF

▼▼▼ The Lodge-Hotel & Conference Center 🅗
(563) 359-7141. **$95.** 900 Spruce Hills Dr. I-74, exit 2, just e. Int corridors.
Pets: Accepted.
🄰🅂🄺 ⊠ 🛏 💻 🍽 ⇆ 🐾

🆔 ▼▼▼ Ramada Inn 🅗
(563) 355-7575. **$90-$110.** 3020 Utica Ridge Rd. I-74, exit 2, just e. Int corridors. **Pets:** Medium. $10 daily fee/pet. Designated rooms, service with restrictions, supervision.
🆂🄰🆅🄴 ⊠ 🦽ᴹ 🛏 💻 ⇆ 🐾

DAVENPORT

▼▼ Baymont Inn & Suites Davenport 🅗
(563) 386-1600. **Call for rates.** 400 Jason Way Ct. I-80, exit 295A (US 61), just s to 65th St, then 0.5 mi ne on frontage road. Int corridors.
Pets: Accepted.
⊠ 🛏 💻 ⇆

🆔 ▼▼▼ Best Western SteepleGate Inn 🅗 ❀
(563) 386-6900. **$100-$190, 3 day notice.** 100 W 76th St. I-80, exit 295A (US 61), 0.5 mi s to 65th St and west frontage road entrance, then just nw. Int corridors. **Pets:** Small. $10 daily fee/pet. Designated rooms, service with restrictions, supervision.
🆂🄰🆅🄴 ⊠ 🛏 💻 🍽 ⇆

🆔 ▼▼▼ Clarion Hotel & Conference Center 🅗
(563) 391-1230. **$79-$159.** 5202 Brady St. I-80, exit 295A (US 61), 1.6 mi s. Int corridors. **Pets:** Medium, other species. $10 daily fee/pet. Designated rooms, service with restrictions, crate.
🆂🄰🆅🄴 ⊠ 🦽ᴹ 🛏 💻 🍽 ⇆ 🐾

🆔 ▼▼▼ Comfort Inn & Suites-Davenport 🅗
(563) 324-8300. **$99-$149.** 8300 Northwest Blvd. I-80, exit 292, just n. Int corridors. **Pets:** Small, dogs only. $50 one-time fee/room. Service with restrictions, crate.
🆂🄰🆅🄴 ⊠ 🦽ᴹ 🛏 💻

▼▼ Country Inn & Suites by Carlson 🅗
(563) 388-6444. **Call for rates.** 140 E 55th St. I-80, exit 295A (US 61), 1.4 mi s. Int corridors. **Pets:** Medium. $25 one-time fee/pet. Service with restrictions, supervision.
⊠ 🦽ᴹ 🛏 💻 ⇆

▼▼ Econo Lodge Inn & Suites 🅗
(563) 391-8222. **$50-$80.** 7222 Northwest Blvd. I-80, exit 292 (Northwest Blvd), 0.3 mi s. Ext corridors. **Pets:** Small, other species. $5 daily fee/pet. Service with restrictions, supervision.
🄰🅂🄺 ⊠ 🛏 💻

▼▼ Fairfield Inn by Marriott 🅗
(563) 355-2264. **$80-$90.** 3206 E Kimberly Rd. I-74, exit 2, just w. Int corridors. **Pets:** Accepted.
⊠ 🛏 💻 ⇆

🆔 ▼▼▼ La Quinta Inn 🅗 ❀
(563) 359-3921. **$64-$150.** 3330 E Kimberly Rd. I-74, exit 2, just w, then just s. Int corridors. **Pets:** Medium, other species. Service with restrictions, supervision.
🆂🄰🆅🄴 ⊠ 🛏 💻 ⇆

▼▼ Residence Inn by Marriott 🅗
(563) 391-8877. **$130-$140.** 120 E 55th St. I-80, exit 295A (US 61), 1.4 mi s. Int corridors. **Pets:** Medium, other species. $100 one-time fee/room. Service with restrictions, crate.
⊠ 🦽ᴹ 🛏 💻 ⇆ 🐾

▼▼ Super 8 🅗
(563) 388-9810. **Call for rates.** 410 E 65th St. I-80, exit 295A (US 61), 0.5 mi s, then just e. Int corridors. **Pets:** Accepted.
⊠ 🛏 💻

🆔 ▼▼ Travelodge 🅗
(563) 386-6350. **Call for rates.** 6310 N Brady Ave. I-80, exit 295A (US 61), 0.5 mi s; use frontage road on west side. Int corridors. **Pets:** Accepted.
🆂🄰🆅🄴 ⊠ 🛏 💻

END AREA

SIBLEY

◆◆ Super 8 🅷
(712) 754-3603. **$60-$100.** 1108 2nd Ave. SR 60, exit 48, 1 mi w. Int corridors. **Pets:** $8 daily fee/room. Supervision.
(ASK) (✕) 🛆 💻

SIOUX CENTER

◆◆ Econo Lodge 🅷
(712) 722-4000. **Call for rates.** 86 9th Street Cir NE. On US 75, 1 mi n of jct SR 840; north side of town. Ext/int corridors. **Pets:** Accepted.
(✕) 🛆ᴹ 🛆 💻

SIOUX CITY

◆◆ AmericInn Lodge & Suites of Sioux City 🅷
(712) 255-1800. **$85-$155.** 4230 S Lewis Blvd. I-29, exit 143, just e. Int corridors. **Pets:** Other species. $10 daily fee/room. Designated rooms, service with restrictions, supervision.
(ASK) (✕) 🛆ᴹ 🛆 💻 ➣ ✕

◆◆ Comfort Inn by Choice Hotels 🅷
(712) 274-1300. **Call for rates.** 4202 S Lakeport St. I-29, exit 144A, 1 mi e on US 20, then just s. Int corridors. **Pets:** Accepted.
(✕) 🛆 💻 ➣

◆◆ Holiday Inn Express 🅷 🐾
(712) 274-1400. **Call for rates.** 4230 S Lakeport St. I-29, exit 144A, 1 mi e on US 20, then just s. Int corridors. **Pets:** Medium. $10 daily fee/room. Service with restrictions, supervision.
(✕) 🛆ᴹ 🛆 💻

◆◆ Ramada City Centre 🅷
(712) 277-1550. **$55-$100, 30 day notice.** 130 Nebraska St. I-29, exit 147B, just w on Gordon Dr, then just n. Int corridors. **Pets:** Other species. $10 daily fee/room. Designated rooms, service with restrictions, supervision.
(ASK) (✕) 🛆 💻 ➣

◆◆ Super 8 🅷
(712) 274-1520. **$54-$78.** 4307 Stone Ave. I-29, exit 144A northbound, US 75 to exit 4B, 1.5 mi w on Gordon Dr; exit 147B southbound to Gordon Dr, 3 mi e. Int corridors. **Pets:** Small. $10 daily fee/pet. Designated rooms, service with restrictions, supervision.
(ASK) (✕) 🛆ᴹ 🛆 💻

SLOAN

◆◆ Winna Vegas Inn 🅷
(712) 428-4280. **Call for rates.** 1862 Hwy 141. I-29, exit 127, just e. Int corridors. **Pets:** Accepted.
(✕) 🛆ᴹ 🛆 💻

SPIRIT LAKE

◆◆ Ramada 🅷
(712) 336-3984. **$79-$199, 3 day notice.** 2704 17th St. Jct US 71 and SR 9, just w. Int corridors. **Pets:** $200 deposit/room, $50 one-time fee/room. Service with restrictions, supervision.
(ASK) (✕) 🛆 💻 ➣ ✕

◆ Shamrock Inn 🅼
(712) 336-2668. **$49-$114, 3 day notice.** 1905 18th St. 0.6 mi e on SR 9 from jct US 71. Ext/int corridors. **Pets:** $10 daily fee/room. Designated rooms, service with restrictions, supervision.
(ASK) (✕) 🛆 💻 ➣

◆◆ Spirit Lake Super 8 🅷 🐾
(712) 336-4901. **$64-$139, 3 day notice.** 2203 Circle Dr W. Jct US 71 and SR 9. Int corridors. **Pets:** $10 one-time fee/room. Service with restrictions, crate.
(ASK) (✕) 🛆ᴹ 🛆 💻

SPRINGDALE

◆◆ Econo Lodge 🅼
(319) 627-2171. **$60.** 1943 Garfield Ave. I-80, exit 259, just sw. Ext corridors. **Pets:** Accepted.
(SAVE) (✕) 💻

STORY CITY

◆◆ Comfort Inn 🅷
(515) 733-6363. **Call for rates.** 425 Timberland Dr. I-35, exit 124, just sw. Int corridors. **Pets:** Other species. $13 daily fee/room. Service with restrictions, supervision.
(SAVE) (✕) 🛆ᴹ 🛆 💻 ➣ ✕

◆◆ Super 8 🅷
(515) 733-5281. **$51-$66.** 515 Factory Outlet Dr. I-35, exit 124, just sw. Int corridors. **Pets:** Accepted.
(ASK) (✕) 🛆ᴹ 🛆 💻

◆◆ Viking Hotel 🅼
(515) 733-4306. **Call for rates.** 1520 Broad St. I-35, exit 124, just w. Int corridors. **Pets:** Accepted.
(✕) 🛆

STUART

◆◆ AmericInn Lodge & Suites of Stuart 🅷
(515) 523-9000. **$70-$99.** 420 SW 8th St. I-80, exit 93, just w. Int corridors. **Pets:** Accepted.
(ASK) (✕) 🛆ᴹ 🛆 💻 ➣ ✕

◆◆ Super 8 Motel 🅷
(515) 523-2888. **Call for rates.** 203 SE 7th St. I-80, exit 93. Int corridors. **Pets:** Accepted.
(✕) 🛆ᴹ 🛆 💻 ➣

TOLEDO

◆◆ Designer Inn & Suites 🅷
(641) 484-5678. **$53-$69.** 403 US 30 W. On US 30, just w of jct US 63 and 30. Int corridors. **Pets:** Accepted.
(ASK) (✕) 🛆 ➣

◆◆ Super 8-Toledo 🅷
(641) 484-5888. **Call for rates.** 207 Hwy 30 W. On US 30, just w of jct US 63 and 30. Ext/int corridors. **Pets:** Accepted.
(✕) 🛆ᴹ 🛆 💻

URBANA

◆◆ Urbana Inn & Suites 🅷
(319) 443-8888. **$59-$71.** 5369 Hutton Dr. I-380, exit 43, just s on east access road. Int corridors. **Pets:** Small. $15 one-time fee/room. Service with restrictions, supervision.
(ASK) (✕) 🛆 💻 ➣ ✕

URBANDALE

◆◆ Extended StayAmerica 🅷
(515) 276-1929. **$69-$109.** 3940 114th St. I-35/80, exit 126 (Douglas Ave), just e to 114th St, then 0.4 mi nw. Int corridors. **Pets:** Other species. $25 daily fee/pet. Service with restrictions, crate.
(ASK) (✕) 🛆ᴹ 🛆 💻

Holiday Inn Hotel & Suites Northwest H
(515) 278-4755. **Call for rates.** 4800 Merle Hay Rd. I-35/80, exit 131 (Merle Hay Rd), just s. Int corridors. **Pets:** Accepted.

Sleep Inn H
(515) 270-2424. **$79-$119.** 11211 Hickman Rd. I-35/80, exit 125 (Hickman Rd), just ne. Int corridors. **Pets:** Other species. $10 daily fee/pet. Service with restrictions, supervision.

WALNUT

Super 8 H
(712) 784-2221. **$50-$100.** 2109 Antique City Dr. I-80, exit 46, just n. Int corridors. **Pets:** Medium, other species. $5 one-time fee/pet. Designated rooms, service with restrictions, supervision.

WASHINGTON

Super 8-Washington M
(319) 653-6621. **Call for rates.** 119 Westview Dr. 1.5 mi w on SR 1 and 92. Int corridors. **Pets:** Accepted.

WATERLOO

Baymont Inn & Suites H
(319) 233-9191. **Call for rates.** 2141 LaPorte Rd. I-380, exit 72 (E San Marnan Dr). Int corridors. **Pets:** Medium. $10 daily fee/pet. Service with restrictions, supervision.

Candlewood Suites H
(319) 235-7000. **Call for rates.** 2056 LaPorte Rd. I-218, exit 72 (E San Marnan Dr), just sw. Int corridors. **Pets:** Accepted.

Comfort Inn by Choice Hotels H
(319) 234-7411. **$80-$95.** 1945 LaPorte Rd. I-380, exit 72 (E San Marnan Dr). Int corridors. **Pets:** Other species. Designated rooms, service with restrictions, supervision.

Ramada Hotel & Convention Center H
(319) 233-7560. **Call for rates.** 205 W 4th St. 4th and Commercial sts; downtown. Int corridors. **Pets:** Accepted.

Super 8 H
(319) 233-1800. **Call for rates.** 1825 LaPorte Rd. I-380, exit 72 (E San Marnan Dr), just nw. Int corridors. **Pets:** Accepted.

WAVERLY

Comfort Inn H
(319) 352-0399. **$80-$169.** 404 29th Ave SW. US 218, exit 198, 0.7 mi n. Int corridors. **Pets:** Medium, dogs only. $10 daily fee/pet. Designated rooms, service with restrictions, supervision.

Super 8 Waverly H
(319) 352-0888. **$65-$129.** 301 13th Ave SW. US 218, exit 198, 1.4 mi n. Int corridors. **Pets:** Medium, other species. $10 daily fee/pet. Designated rooms, service with restrictions, supervision.

WEBSTER CITY

AmericInn Motel & Suites of Webster City H
(515) 832-3999. **Call for rates.** 411 Closz Dr. Just s of jct US 20 and SR 17. Int corridors. **Pets:** Accepted.

Super 8 H
(515) 832-2000. **$50-$75.** 305 Closz Dr. Just s of jct US 20 and SR 17. Int corridors. **Pets:** Medium. $6 daily fee/pet. Service with restrictions, supervision.

WEST BEND

Park View Inn & Suites and Conference Center H
(515) 887-3611. **Call for rates.** 13 4th St NE. Jct CR B63, 1 mi n on SR 15, then just w. Int corridors. **Pets:** Small. $10 one-time fee/room. Designated rooms, service with restrictions, supervision.

WEST BURLINGTON

AmericInn Lodge & Suites of Burlington H
(319) 758-9000. **$70-$150.** 628 S Gear Ave. US 34, exit 260 (Gear Ave), just ne. Int corridors. **Pets:** Medium. $10 daily fee/pet. Designated rooms, supervision.

WEST DES MOINES

Candlewood Suites-West Des Moines H
(515) 221-0001. **Call for rates.** 7625 Office Plaza Dr N. I-80, exit 121 (Jordan Creek Pkwy), just sw. Int corridors. **Pets:** Accepted.

Motel 6–1408 H
(515) 267-8885. **$45-$59.** 7655 Office Plaza Dr N. I-80, exit 121 (Jordan Creek Pkwy), just sw. Int corridors. **Pets:** Other species. Service with restrictions, supervision.

Residence Inn-Des Moines West H
(515) 267-0338. **$150-$170.** 160 S Jordan Creek Pkwy. I-35, exit 70 (Mills Civic Pkwy), 1.2 mi w to 68th St, then just nw. Int corridors. **Pets:** Medium. $100 one-time fee/room. Service with restrictions, crate.

Sheraton West Des Moines H
(515) 223-1800. **$99-$199.** 1800 50th St. I-80/35, exit 124 (University Ave), just e. Int corridors. **Pets:** Medium. $75 one-time fee/room. Designated rooms, service with restrictions, crate.

Staybridge Suites H
(515) 223-0000. **$99-$229.** 6905 Lake Dr. I-80, exit 121 (Jordan Creek Pkwy), just ne. Int corridors. **Pets:** Small. $50 one-time fee/pet. Service with restrictions.

West Des Moines Marriott H
(515) 267-1500. **$170-$208.** 1250 Jordan Creek Pkwy. I-80, exit 121 (Jordan Creek Pkwy), just sw. Int corridors. **Pets:** $100 one-time fee/room. Service with restrictions, supervision.

WILLIAMS

Best Western Norseman Inn M
(515) 854-2281. **$67-$78.** 3086 220th St. I-35, exit 144, just e. Int corridors. **Pets:** Medium, dogs only. $10 daily fee/pet. Designated rooms, service with restrictions, supervision.

WILLIAMSBURG

▼▼▼ Amana Holiday Inn 🅷
(319) 668-1175. **$99-$249.** 2211 U Ave. I-80, exit 225 (US 151). Int corridors. **Pets:** Accepted.
A$K ☒ 🛏 💻 🍽 ⊅ ☒

AAA ▼▼▼ Best Western Cozy House Suites 🅷
(319) 668-9777. **$90-$160.** 1708 N Highland St. I-80, exit 220, 0.8 mi n. Int corridors. **Pets:** $17 daily fee/pet. Designated rooms, service with restrictions, supervision.
SAVE ☒ 🛏 💻 ⊅

AAA ▼▼ Crest Country Inn 🅼
(319) 668-1522. **$60-$85.** 340 W Evans St. I-80, exit 220, just nw. Ext corridors. **Pets:** Accepted.
SAVE ☒

▼▼ Heritage Inn Hotel & Suites Amana Colonies 🅷 🐾
(319) 668-2700. **$77-$160.** 2185 U Ave. I-80, exit 225 (US 151), just n. Int corridors. **Pets:** Medium, other species. $10 daily fee/pet. Designated rooms, no service, supervision.
A$K ☒ 🛎M 🛏 💻 ⊅

▼▼ Super 8 🅷
(319) 668-9718. **$70-$80.** 1708 N Highland St. I-80, exit 220, 0.8 mi n. Ext/int corridors. **Pets:** $17 daily fee/pet. Designated rooms, service with restrictions, supervision.
A$K ☒ 🛏 💻

ABILENE

AAA ♦♦ Americas Best Value Inn /President's Inn M 🐾
(785) 263-2050. **Call for rates.** 2210 N Buckeye. I-70, exit 275, just s. Ext corridors. **Pets:** Medium, dogs only. $25 deposit/room, $7 daily fee/room. Service with restrictions, supervision.
SAVE ⊠ 🕭M 🛏 💻 🍴 🏊

AAA ♦ Diamond Motel M
(785) 263-2360. **$40-$75.** 1407 NW 3rd St. I-70, exit 275, 1.3 mi s, then 1 mi w. Ext corridors. **Pets:** Small. $7 one-time fee/pet. Service with restrictions, supervision.
SAVE ⊠ 🛏

♦♦♦ Holiday Inn Express Hotel & Suites H
(785) 263-4049. **$91.** 110 E Lafayette Ave. I-70, exit 275, just n. Int corridors. **Pets:** Medium, other species. $20 daily fee/pet. Service with restrictions, supervision.
ASK ⊠ 🕭M 🛏 💻 🏊 ⊠

♦♦ Super 8 Motel H 🐾
(785) 263-4545. **Call for rates.** 2207 N Buckeye. I-70, exit 275, just s. Int corridors. **Pets:** Other species. $13 daily fee/pet. Designated rooms, service with restrictions, supervision.
⊠ 🕭M 🛏 💻

ANDOVER

AAA ♦♦ Andover Express Inn M
(316) 733-8881. **$57-$63.** 222 W US Hwy 54. 2.2 mi e of jct SR 96. Ext corridors. **Pets:** Medium. $5 daily fee/pet. Service with restrictions, supervision.
SAVE ⊠ 🛏 🏊

ATCHISON

♦♦ AmericInn Lodge & Suites of Atchison H
(913) 367-4000. **$74-$85.** 500 US 73. Just s at US 59 and 73. Int corridors. **Pets:** Accepted.
ASK ⊠ 🕭M 🛏 💻 🏊

BAXTER SPRINGS

♦♦ Baxter Inn-4-Less H
(620) 856-2106. **$39-$60.** 2451 Military Ave. On US 69 alternate route, 1 mi s of jct US 166. Int corridors. **Pets:** Very small. Service with restrictions, supervision.
ASK ⊠ 🛏

BELLEVILLE

♦♦ Americas Best Value Inn M
(785) 527-2231. **$63.** 215 Hwy 36. Jct US 81 and 36; northwest corner; just up hill. Ext corridors. **Pets:** Accepted.
ASK ⊠ 🛏 💻 🏊

♦♦ Super 8 Motel H
(785) 527-2112. **$62-$101.** 1410 28th St. On US 36, 0.5 mi e of jct US 81. Int corridors. **Pets:** Other species. $10 daily fee/pet. Service with restrictions, supervision.
ASK ⊠ 🛏 💻

BELOIT

♦♦ Super 8 Motel H
(785) 738-4300. **$54-$99, 3 day notice.** 3018 US 24 Hwy. Just e of jct SR 14. Ext/int corridors. **Pets:** Medium. $5 daily fee/pet. Designated rooms, service with restrictions, supervision.
⊠ 🕭M 🛏 💻

BURLINGTON

♦♦ Country Haven Inn H
(620) 364-8260. **$60-$70.** 207 Cross St. Just e of US 75; 1 mi n of center. Int corridors. **Pets:** Very small. $50 deposit/pet. Service with restrictions, supervision.
ASK ⊠ 🛏 💻

CHANUTE

♦ Chanute Safari Inn M
(620) 431-9460. **$40-$50.** 3428 S Santa Fe. US 169, exit 35th St, 1.5 mi e. Ext corridors. **Pets:** Accepted.
ASK ⊠ 🛏 🏊

♦ Guest House Motor Inn M
(620) 431-0600. **$40-$50.** 1814 S Santa Fe. US 169, exit 35th St, 2.5 mi ne. Ext corridors. **Pets:** Accepted.
ASK ⊠ 🛏 🏊

CLAY CENTER

♦♦ Cedar Court Motel M
(785) 632-2148. **$49-$75.** 905 Crawford St. On US 24, just e of jct SR 15. Ext corridors. **Pets:** Small. $5 daily fee/pet. Designated rooms, service with restrictions, crate.
ASK ⊠ 🕭M 🛏 💻 🍴 🏊

COLBY

♦♦ Comfort Inn H 🐾
(785) 462-3833. **$84-$130.** 2225 S Range Rd. I-70, exit 53 (SR 25), just s. Int corridors. **Pets:** Large, other species. $5 daily fee/pet. Designated rooms, service with restrictions, supervision.
ASK ⊠ 🕭M 🛏 💻 🍴 🏊

AAA ♦♦ Crown Inn M
(785) 462-3943. **$55-$80.** 2320 S Range Rd. I-70, exit 53 (SR 25), just s. Ext corridors. **Pets:** Accepted.
SAVE ⊠ 🛏

AAA ▼▼▼ Days Inn H
(785) 462-8691. **Call for rates.** 1925 S Range Rd. I-70, exit 53 (SR 25), 0.3 mi n. Int corridors. **Pets:** Medium, dogs only. $10 daily fee/pet. Designated rooms, service with restrictions, supervision.
SAVE ✕ 🛢 🖵 ⊇

AAA ▼▼▼▼ Holiday Inn Express Hotel & Suites H
(785) 462-8787. **Call for rates.** 645 W Willow St. I-70, exit 53 (SR 25), just ne. Int corridors. **Pets:** Other species. $10 daily fee/pet. Service with restrictions, supervision.
SAVE ✕ �&M 🛢 🖵 ⊇ ✕

AAA ▼ Motel 6 #4245 H
(785) 462-8201. **Call for rates.** 1985 S Range Rd. I-70, exit 53 (SR 25), just n. Ext/int corridors. **Pets:** Other species. Service with restrictions, supervision.
SAVE ✕ 🛢

AAA ▼▼ Quality Inn H
(785) 462-3933. **$60-$90, 7 day notice.** 1950 S Range Rd. I-70, exit 53 (SR 25), just n. Ext/int corridors. **Pets:** Accepted.
SAVE ✕ 🛢 🖵 ⊺⊺ ⊇

▼▼ Super 8 Motel H
(785) 462-8248. **Call for rates.** 1040 Zelfer Ave. I-70, exit 53 (SR 25), 0.3 mi n, then just w. Int corridors. **Pets:** Accepted.
✕ 🛢 🖵

CONCORDIA

AAA ▼ Super 8 Motel-Concordia H
(785) 243-4200. **$60-$65.** 1320 Lincoln St. On US 81, 1 mi s of center. Ext/int corridors. **Pets:** Accepted.
SAVE ✕ 🛢 🖵

COTTONWOOD FALLS

AAA ▼▼▼▼ Grand Central Hotel CI
(620) 273-6763. **$160-$190.** 215 Broadway. Just w of US 177; center of downtown. Int corridors. **Pets:** Service with restrictions, supervision.
SAVE ✕ 🛢 ⊺⊺

COUNCIL GROVE

AAA ▼▼▼ The Cottage House Hotel & Motel H
(620) 767-6828. **$50-$175, 7 day notice.** 25 N Neosho. Just n of Main St; downtown. Int/int corridors. **Pets:** Accepted.
SAVE ✕ 🛢 🖵

DODGE CITY

AAA ▼▼▼ Best Western Country Inn & Suites H
(620) 225-7378. **$90-$130, 21 day notice.** 506 N 14th Ave. Just n of jct US 50 business route (Wyatt Earp Blvd). Ext/int corridors. **Pets:** Medium, dogs only. $25 daily fee/pet. Designated rooms, service with restrictions, supervision.
SAVE ✕ &M 🛢 🖵 ⊇

▼▼▼ Holiday Inn Express H
(620) 227-5000. **$109-$129.** 2320 W Wyatt Earp Blvd. 1.4 mi w on US 50 business route. Int corridors. **Pets:** Large, other species. $25 one-time fee/room. Service with restrictions, supervision.
ASK ✕ 🛢 🖵 ⊇

▼▼▼ LaQuinta Inn & Suites H ❀
(620) 225-7373. **$89-$139.** 2400 W Wyatt Earp Blvd. 1.4 mi w on US 50 business route. Int corridors. **Pets:** Medium, other species. Service with restrictions, supervision.
✕ &M 🛢 🖵 ⊇

▼▼ Super 8 H
(620) 225-3924. **$75-$150.** 1708 W Wyatt Earp Blvd. 1.2 mi w on US 50 business route. Int corridors. **Pets:** Medium. $25 one-time fee/room. Service with restrictions, crate.
ASK ✕ 🛢 🖵 ⊇

EL DORADO

AAA ▼▼▼ Best Western Red Coach Inn H
(316) 321-6900. **$70-$130, 7 day notice.** 2525 W Central Ave. I-35, exit 71, 0.5 mi e. Ext corridors. **Pets:** Accepted.
SAVE ✕ 🛢 🖵 ⊺⊺ ⊇

▼ Super 8-El Dorado M
(316) 321-4888. **$45-$95.** 2530 W Central Ave. I-35, exit 71, 0.5 mi e. Int corridors. **Pets:** Small. $15 daily fee/pet. Designated rooms, no service, supervision.
ASK ✕ 🛢 🖵

ELLSWORTH

AAA ▼ Americas Best Value Inn H
(785) 472-3116. **Call for rates.** 1414 Foster Rd. Jct SR 140 and 156. Ext/int corridors. **Pets:** Accepted.
SAVE ✕ &M 🛢 🖵 ⊇

EMPORIA

AAA ▼ Americas Best Value Inn M
(620) 342-7567. **$45-$65.** 2913 W Hwy 50. I-35, exit 127, 0.8 mi e. Int corridors. **Pets:** Dogs only. $15 one-time fee/room. Designated rooms, supervision.
SAVE ✕ 🖵

AAA ▼▼▼ Best Western Hospitality House H
(620) 342-7587. **$65-$140.** 3021 W Hwy 50. I-35, exit 127, just e. Ext/int corridors. **Pets:** Accepted.
SAVE ✕ 🛢 🖵 ⊺⊺ ⊇

▼▼ Candlewood Suites H ❀
(620) 343-7756. **$79.** 2602 Candlewood Dr. I-35, exit 128 (Industrial St), just n, then e. Int corridors. **Pets:** Other species. $75 one-time fee/room.
ASK ✕ 🛢 🖵

▼▼ Comfort Inn H
(620) 342-9700. **$60-$120.** 2836 W 18th Ave. I-35, exit 128 (Industrial St), just nw. Int corridors. **Pets:** Accepted.
ASK ✕ 🛢 🖵 ⊇

FORT SCOTT

▼▼ Fort Scott Inn H
(620) 223-0100. **Call for rates.** 101 State St. On US 69 Bypass, exit US 54 southbound; exit 3rd St northbound. Ext/int corridors. **Pets:** Accepted.
✕ 🛢 🖵 ⊺⊺ ⊇ ✕

GARDEN CITY

▼▼ AmericInn Lodge & Suites of Garden City H
(620) 272-9860. **$89-$165.** 3020 E Kansas Ave. Jct US 50, 83 and SR 156. Int corridors. **Pets:** Medium, dogs only. $100 deposit/room, $10 daily fee/pet. Designated rooms, service with restrictions, supervision.
ASK ✕ 🛢 🖵 ⊇ ✕

AAA ▼▼▼ Best Western Red Baron Hotel H
(620) 275-4164. **$71-$80.** 2205 E Hwy 50. 2.3 mi e on US 50 business route, at US 83 Bypass. Ext corridors. **Pets:** Accepted.
SAVE ✕ 🛢 🖵

AAA ▼▼▼ Best Western Wheat Lands Hotel H
(620) 276-2387. **$65-$89.** 1311 E Fulton St. 1 mi e on US 50 business route. Ext corridors. **Pets:** Other species. $25 deposit/room. Service with restrictions, crate.
SAVE ✕ 🛢 🖵 ⊇

AAA ▼▼▼ Comfort Inn H
(620) 275-5800. **$70-$199.** 2608 E Kansas Ave. Jct US 50, 83 and SR 156. Int corridors. **Pets:** Medium. $10 daily fee/pet. Service with restrictions, supervision.
SAVE ✕ 🛢 🖵 ⊇ ✕

WWWW **Holiday Inn Express Hotel & Suites** [H]
(620) 275-5900. **Call for rates.** 2502 E Kansas Ave. Jct US 50, 83 and SR 156. Int corridors. **Pets:** Accepted.
[X] [🐾] [💻] [🏊]

GARNETT

WWW **Garnett Inn & Suites & RV Park** [H]
(785) 448-6800. **$60-$78.** 109 Prairie Plaza Pkwy. On US 169, 1.6 mi n of jct US 59. Int corridors. **Pets:** Accepted.
[A$K] [X] [🐾M] [🐾] [💻]

GODDARD

(AAA) WW **Express Inn** [M]
(316) 794-3366. **$50-$66.** 19941 W Kellogg Dr. Just se of jct US 54/400 and 199th St. Ext corridors. **Pets:** Small. $10 daily fee/pet. Service with restrictions, supervision.
[SAVE] [X] [🐾]

GOODLAND

WW **Comfort Inn** [H]
(785) 899-7181. **Call for rates.** 2519 Enterprise Rd. I-70, exit 17 (SR 27), just n. Int corridors. **Pets:** Small. $15 one-time fee/pet. Designated rooms, service with restrictions, supervision.
[X] [🐾M] [🐾] [💻] [🏊]

WWW **Holiday Inn Express Hotel & Suites** [H]
(785) 890-9060. **Call for rates.** 2631 Enterprise Rd. I-70, exit 17 (SR 27), just s. Int corridors. **Pets:** $15 one-time fee/pet. Designated rooms, service with restrictions, crate.
[X] [🐾M] [🐾] [💻] [🏊]

WW **Super 8 Motel-Goodland** [H]
(785) 890-7566. **Call for rates.** 2520 Commerce Rd. I-70, exit 17 (SR 27), just n. Ext corridors. **Pets:** Accepted.
[X] [🐾] [💻]

GREAT BEND

(AAA) WW **Best Western Angus Inn** [H]
(620) 792-3541. **$65-$73, 3 day notice.** 2920 10th St. 0.8 mi w on US 56 and SR 96/156. Ext/int corridors. **Pets:** $5 daily fee/pet. Designated rooms, service with restrictions, crate.
[SAVE] [X] [🐾] [💻] [🍴] [🐾] [X]

(AAA) WWW **Highland Hotel & Convention Center** [H]
(620) 792-2431. **$64-$85.** 3017 W 10th St. 1 mi w on US 56 and SR 96/156. Ext/int corridors. **Pets:** Large. $10 daily fee/room. Designated rooms, service with restrictions, supervision.
[SAVE] [X] [🐾] [💻] [🍴] [🐾] [X]

HAYS

WW **Americas Best Value Inn** [M]
(785) 625-2511. **$66-$163.** 2524 Vine St. I-70, exit 159 (US 183), 1 mi s. Ext corridors. **Pets:** Service with restrictions, supervision.
[A$K] [X] [🐾] [💻] [🍴] [🐾]

(AAA) WW **Baymont Inn & Suites** [H]
(785) 625-8103. **Call for rates.** 3801 N Vine St. I-70, exit 159 (US 183), just sw. Ext/int corridors. **Pets:** Accepted.
[SAVE] [X] [💻]

HERINGTON

WW **Herington Inn & Suites** [H]
(785) 258-3300. **$65-$86.** 565 Hwy 77. US 77, just w. Int corridors. **Pets:** Very small, dogs only. $25 one-time fee/pet. Designated rooms, service with restrictions, supervision.
[A$K] [X] [🐾M] [🐾] [💻]

HESSTON

WW WW **AmericInn Lodge & Suites of Hesston** [H]
(620) 327-2053. **$80-$150.** 2 Leonard Ct. I-135, exit 40, just e. Int corridors. **Pets:** Medium. $50 deposit/room. Service with restrictions, supervision.
[A$K] [X] [🐾] [💻] [🏊]

HILLSBORO

WW **Country Haven Inn** [H]
(620) 947-2929. **$62-$75.** 804 Western Heights. On US 56; center. Int corridors. **Pets:** Small, other species. $15 one-time fee/room. Designated rooms, service with restrictions, supervision.
[A$K] [X] [🐾]

HUTCHINSON

(AAA) WW **Americas Best Value Inn** [H]
(620) 662-6394. **$50-$70.** 1315 E 11th Ave. Just se of jct SR 61. Int corridors. **Pets:** Accepted.
[SAVE] [X] [💻]

WW **Comfort Inn** [H]
(620) 663-7822. **Call for rates.** 1621 Super Plaza. Just w of jct SR 61 and N 17th Ave. Int corridors. **Pets:** Small, other species. $15 one-time fee/room. Designated rooms, service with restrictions, supervision.
[X] [🐾] [💻] [🐾]

WWW **Holiday Inn Express Hotel & Suites** [H] ❀
(620) 669-5200. **$96-$153.** 1601 Super Plaza. Just w of jct SR 61 and N 17th Ave. Int corridors. **Pets:** Other species. $25 one-time fee/room. Service with restrictions.
[A$K] [X] [🐾M] [🐾] [💻] [🐾]

WW **Microtel Inn & Suites** [H]
(620) 665-3700. **$65-$85.** 1420 N Lorraine St. Just nw of jct SR 61 and N 11th Ave. Int corridors. **Pets:** Accepted.
[A$K] [X] [🐾] [💻]

INDEPENDENCE

WW **Appletree Inn** [H]
(620) 331-5500. **$95-$140.** 201 N 8th St. At 8th and Laurel sts. Ext/int corridors. **Pets:** Accepted.
[X] [🐾] [💻] [🏊]

WW **Microtel Inn & Suites** [H]
(620) 331-0088. **Call for rates.** 2917 W Main St. 1.2 mi e of jct US 75 and 160. Int corridors. **Pets:** Accepted.
[X] [🐾M] [💻]

WW **Super 8** [H]
(620) 331-8288. **$61-$76.** 2800 W Main St. 1.3 mi e of jct US 160 and 75. Int corridors. **Pets:** Small. $15 daily fee/pet. Designated rooms, service with restrictions, supervision.
[A$K] [X] [🐾] [💻] [🐾]

IOLA

(AAA) WWW **Best Western Inn** [M]
(620) 365-5161. **$66-$82.** 1315 N State St. Jct US 54 and 169, 1.5 mi w on US 54, then 0.8 mi n. Ext corridors. **Pets:** Small, dogs only. $10 daily fee/pet. Designated rooms, service with restrictions, supervision.
[SAVE] [X] [🐾M] [🐾] [💻] [🍴] [🐾]

WW **Super 8 Iola** [H]
(620) 365-3030. **Call for rates.** 200 Bills Way. Jct US 54 and 169. Int corridors. **Pets:** Very small. $10 daily fee/pet. Service with restrictions, supervision.
[X] [🐾M] [🐾] [💻] [🐾]

JUNCTION CITY

Best Western J.C. Inn H
(785) 210-1212. **$85-$160.** 604 E Chestnut St. I-70, exit 298, just w. Int corridors. **Pets:** Accepted.
[SAVE] [X] [&M] [H] [IP] [≈]

Candlewood Suites H
(785) 238-1454. **$109-$149.** 100 S Hammons Dr. I-70, exit 298, just w. Int corridors. **Pets:** Accepted.
[ASK] [X] [&M] [H] [IP]

Courtyard by Marriott Junction City H
(785) 210-1500. **$98-$120.** 310 Hammons Dr. I-70, exit 298, just w. Int corridors. **Pets:** Medium. $75 one-time fee/room. Designated rooms, service with restrictions, crate.
[SAVE] [X] [&M] [H] [IP] [≈]

Holiday Inn Express H
(785) 762-4200. **$105.** 120 N East St. I-70, exit 298, just nw. Int corridors. **Pets:** Small, other species. $50 deposit/room, $5 daily fee/pet. Service with restrictions, supervision.
[ASK] [X] [&M] [H] [IP] [≈]

KANSAS CITY METROPOLITAN AREA

GARDNER

Super 8 Motel H
(913) 856-8887. **$65-$150.** 2001 E Santa Fe. I-35, exit 210. Int corridors. **Pets:** Accepted.
[ASK] [X] [&M] [H] [≈]

KANSAS CITY

Best Western Inn and Conference Center H
(913) 677-3060. **$89-$99, 7 day notice.** 501 Southwest Blvd. I-35, exit 234 (7th St), just s. Int corridors. **Pets:** $30 one-time fee/room. Service with restrictions, supervision.
[SAVE] [X] [H] [IP] [≈]

Candlewood Suites H
(913) 788-9929. **$109-$400.** 10920 Parallel Pkwy. I-435, exit 14B, just w. Int corridors. **Pets:** Medium. $15 daily fee/room. Service with restrictions, crate.
[ASK] [X] [&M] [H] [IP]

Days Inn Kansas Speedway H
(913) 334-3028. **$60-$95.** 7721 Elizabeth Ave. I-70, exit 414 (78th St N), just ne. Int corridors. **Pets:** Accepted.
[ASK] [X] [H] [IP] [≈]

LENEXA

Extended Stay Deluxe-Kansas City-Lenexa-87th St H
(913) 894-5550. **$65-$109.** 8015 Lenexa Dr. I-35, exit 227 (75th St), 1 mi s on east frontage road. Ext corridors. **Pets:** Other species. $25 daily fee/pet. Service with restrictions, crate.
[ASK] [X] [&M] [H] [IP] [≈]

La Quinta Inn Kansas City (Lenexa) H 🐾
(913) 492-5500. **$52-$99.** 9461 Lenexa Dr. I-35, exit 224 (95th St), just ne; entrance left on Monrovia Rd, off 95th St. Int corridors. **Pets:** Medium, other species. Service with restrictions, supervision.
[ASK] [X] [H] [IP] [≈]

Super 8 Motel-Lenexa H
(913) 888-8899. **$60-$70.** 9601 Westgate Dr. I-35, exit 224 (95th St), just se. Int corridors. **Pets:** Small. $10 daily fee/pet. Designated rooms, no service, crate.
[ASK] [X] [&M] [H] [IP]

MERRIAM

Comfort Inn-Merriam H
(913) 262-2622. **$44-$99.** 6401 E Frontage Rd. I-35, exit 228B (Shawnee Mission Pkwy), just se. Int corridors. **Pets:** Accepted.
[SAVE] [X] [H] [IP] [≈]

Drury Inn-Merriam/Shawnee Mission Parkway H
(913) 236-9200. **$80-$111.** 9009 W Shawnee Mission Pkwy. I-35, exit 228B (Shawnee Mission Pkwy). Int corridors. **Pets:** Other species. Service with restrictions, supervision.
[ASK] [X] [&M] [H] [IP] [≈]

Homestead Studio Suites Hotel-Kansas City-Shawnee Mission M
(913) 236-6006. **$59-$109.** 6451 E Frontage Rd. I-35, exit 228B (Shawnee Mission Pkwy), just se. Ext corridors. **Pets:** Other species. $25 daily fee/pet. Service with restrictions, crate.
[ASK] [X] [&M] [H] [IP]

Quality Inn H
(913) 262-4448. **$39-$179.** 6601 E Frontage Rd. I-35, exit 228A, just ne. Ext/int corridors. **Pets:** Medium. $10 daily fee/pet. Designated rooms, service with restrictions, supervision.
[SAVE] [X] [&M] [H] [IP] [≈]

OLATHE

Holiday Inn H
(913) 829-4000. **$86-$139.** 101 W 151st St. I-35, exit 215 (151st St). Int corridors. **Pets:** Accepted.
[ASK] [X] [H] [IP] [TI] [≈] [X]

Microtel Inn Olathe H
(913) 397-9455. **Call for rates.** 1501 S Hamilton Cir. I-35, exit 215 (151st St), jct 151st St and CR 7 N, just nw of jct I-35. Int corridors. **Pets:** Accepted.
[X] [&M] [≈]

Sleep Inn H
(913) 390-9500. **$80-$85.** 20662 W 151st St. I-35, exit 215 (151st St), 0.4 mi sw, follow signs. Int corridors. **Pets:** Other species. $10 daily fee/pet. Service with restrictions.
[SAVE] [X] [&M] [H] [IP] [≈]

OVERLAND PARK

Candlewood Suites H
(913) 469-5557. **$95-$115.** 11001 Oakmont St. I-435, exit 82 (Quivira Rd), 0.5 mi s, 0.3 mi w on College Ave, then just n. Int corridors. **Pets:** Accepted.
[ASK] [X] [&M] [H] [IP]

Chase Suites by Woodfin H
(913) 491-3333. **$182-$242.** 6300 W 110th St. I-435, exit 79 (Metcalf Ave/US 169), 0.3 mi s on US 169, 0.5 mi e on College Blvd to Lamar Ave, then just n. Ext corridors. **Pets:** Accepted.
[SAVE] [X] [H] [IP] [≈] [X]

Comfort Inn & Suites H
(913) 648-7858. **$79-$200.** 7200 W 107th St. I-435, exit 79 (Metcalf Ave/US 169), just nw. Int corridors. **Pets:** Accepted.
[ASK] [X] [&M] [H] [IP]

Drury Inn & Suites-Overland Park H
(913) 345-1500. **$85-$145.** 10963 Metcalf Ave. I-435, exit 79 (Metcalf Ave/US 169), just se. Int corridors. **Pets:** Other species. Service with restrictions, supervision.
[ASK] [X] [&M] [H] [IP] [≈] [X]

▼▼ ▼▼ Extended StayAmerica-Kansas City-Overland Park 🔳
(913) 661-9299. **$65-$125.** 10750 Quivira Rd. I-435, exit 82 (Quivira Rd), just sw. Int corridors. **Pets:** Other species. $25 daily fee/pet. Service with restrictions, crate.
(ASK) (X) (&M) 🔳 🔳

▼▼ ▼▼ Extended Stay Deluxe Kansas City-Overland Park-Metcalf 🔳
(913) 642-2299. **$69-$139.** 7201 W 106th St. I-435, exit 79 (Metcalf Ave/US 169), just nw. Int corridors. **Pets:** Other species. $25 daily fee/pet. Service with restrictions, crate.
(ASK) (X) (&M) 🔳 🔳

▼▼▼▼ Holtze Executive Village 🔳
(913) 344-8100. **$79-$219.** 11400 College Blvd. I-435, exit 82 (Quivira Rd), 0.5 mi s, then just e. Ext/int corridors. **Pets:** Small, dogs only. $250 deposit/room. Service with restrictions, supervision.
(ASK) (X) (&M) 🔳 🔳 (≈) (X)

▼▼▼▼ Homestead Studio Suites Hotel-Kansas City-Overland Park 🔳
(913) 661-7111. **$59-$119.** 5401 W 110th St. I-435, exit 77B (Nall Ave), just s. Int corridors. **Pets:** Other species. $25 daily fee/pet. Service with restrictions, crate.
(ASK) (X) (&M) 🔳 🔳

◈◈◈ ▼▼▼▼ Hyatt Place Metcalf 🔳
(913) 451-2553. **$69-$189.** 6801 W 112th St. I-435, exit 79 (Metcalf Ave/US 169), 0.6 mi s. Int corridors. **Pets:** Accepted.
(SAVE) (X) (&M) 🔳 🔳 (≈)

▼▼▼▼ La Quinta Inn & Suites 🔳 ❖
(913) 648-5555. **$54-$159.** 10610 Marty St. I-435, exit 79 (Metcalf Ave/US 169), just nw. Int corridors. **Pets:** Medium, other species. Service with restrictions, supervision.
(ASK) (X) 🔳 🔳 (≈)

▼▼▼▼ Pear Tree Inn by Drury-Overland Park 🔳
(913) 451-0200. **$65-$95.** 10951 Metcalf Ave. I-435, exit 79 (Metcalf Ave/US 169), just se. Int corridors. **Pets:** Other species. Service with restrictions, supervision.
(ASK) (X) (&M) 🔳 🔳 (≈)

▼▼▼▼ Ramada Overland Park-Mission 🔳
(913) 262-3010. **$89-$139.** 7240 Shawnee Mission Pkwy. I-35, exit 228B (Shawnee Mission Pkwy), 1 mi e. Ext/int corridors. **Pets:** Accepted.
(ASK) (X) (&M) 🔳 🔳 (¶) (≈) (X)

◈◈◈ ▼▼▼▼ Red Roof Inn-Overland Park 🅜
(913) 341-0100. **$58-$100.** 6800 W 108th St. I-435, exit 79 (Metcalf Ave/US 169), just ne. Ext corridors. **Pets:** Large. Service with restrictions, supervision.
(SAVE) (X) (&M)

▼▼▼▼ Residence Inn by Marriott 🔳
(913) 491-4444. **$179-$219.** 12010 Blue Valley Pkwy. I-435, exit 79 (Metcalf Ave/US 169), 1.3 mi s. Int corridors. **Pets:** Accepted.
(X) (&M) 🔳 🔳 (≈) (X)

◈◈◈ ▼▼▼▼ Sheraton Overland Park Hotel at the Convention Center 🔳 ❖
(913) 234-2100. **$99-$339.** 6100 College Blvd. I-435, exit 79 (Metcalf Ave/US 169), just s to College Blvd, then 0.6 mi e. Int corridors. **Pets:** Medium, dogs only. Service with restrictions, supervision.
(SAVE) (X) (&M) 🔳 🔳 (¶) (≈)

◈◈◈ ▼▼▼▼ Super 8 Motel 🔳
(913) 341-4440. **$55-$65.** 10750 Barkley St. I-435, exit 79 (Metcalf Ave/US 169), just n to 107th St, then just e. Int corridors. **Pets:** Other species. $10 daily fee/pet. Service with restrictions, supervision.
(SAVE) (X) (&M) 🔳 🔳 (≈)

END METROPOLITAN AREA

LANSING

▼▼ ▼▼ Econo Lodge 🔳
(913) 727-2777. **$60-$76, 3 day notice.** 504 N Main. I-70, exit 224 (Leavenworth), 10 mi n on US 73 and SR 7. Int corridors. **Pets:** Small. $10 daily fee/pet. Designated rooms, service with restrictions, supervision.
(ASK) (X) 🔳 🔳

LARNED

◈◈◈ ▼▼ ▼▼ Best Western Townsman Inn 🔳
(620) 285-3114. **$55-$63.** 123 E 14th St. Jct US 56 and SR 156. Ext corridors. **Pets:** Accepted.
(SAVE) (X) 🔳 🔳 (≈)

LAWRENCE

◈◈◈ ▼▼ ▼▼ Americas Best Value Inn 🔳 ❖
(785) 842-5721. **$50-$90.** 515 McDonald Dr. I-70, exit 202, 0.8 mi s, then just w. Int corridors. **Pets:** Dogs only. $15 one-time fee/room. Service with restrictions, supervision.
(SAVE) (X) 🔳

◈◈◈ ▼▼ ▼▼ Best Western Lawrence 🔳
(785) 843-9100. **$69-$109.** 2309 Iowa St. On US 59; jct SR 10. Ext/int corridors. **Pets:** Small, dogs only. $8 daily fee/pet. Designated rooms, no service, supervision.
(SAVE) (X) (&M) 🔳 🔳 (≈)

▼▼ ▼▼ Econo Lodge 🔳
(785) 842-7030. **$55-$150.** 2222 W 6th St. I-70, exit 202, 1 mi s. Int corridors. **Pets:** Other species. $10 daily fee/room. Service with restrictions, crate.
(ASK) (X) 🔳 🔳 (¶) (≈)

◈◈◈ ▼▼▼▼ Holiday Inn 🔳
(785) 841-7077. **Call for rates.** 200 McDonald Dr. I-70, exit 202, 0.5 mi s on US 59. Int corridors. **Pets:** Other species. $25 one-time fee/pet. Service with restrictions.
(SAVE) (X) 🔳 🔳 (¶) (≈) (X)

◈◈◈ ▼▼▼▼ Holiday Inn Express Hotel & Suites 🔳
(785) 749-7555. **$99-$129.** 3411 SW Iowa St. I-70, exit 197 (SR 10), 8.4 mi e on SR 10 to US 59, then just n. Int corridors. **Pets:** Accepted.
(SAVE) (X) (&M) 🔳 🔳 (≈) (X)

◈◈◈ ▼▼▼▼ Quality Inn 🅜
(785) 842-5100. **$69-$149.** 801 Iowa St. I-70, exit 202, 1 mi s on US 59. Ext/int corridors. **Pets:** Medium, dogs only. $8 daily fee/pet. Designated rooms, no service, supervision.
(SAVE) (X) 🔳 🔳 (≈)

LIBERAL

◈◈◈ ▼▼ Americas Best Value Inn 🅜
(620) 624-6203. **$54-$64.** 564 E Pancake Blvd. 0.8 w of jct US 54 and 83. Ext corridors. **Pets:** $10 daily fee/pet. Service with restrictions, supervision.
(SAVE) (X) 🔳 🔳

 Liberal Inn 🏨
(620) 624-7254. **$65-$79.** 603 E Pancake Blvd. 0.5 mi w of jct US 54 and 83. Int corridors. **Pets:** Medium. Designated rooms, service with restrictions, crate.
🖫 ⊠ 🛅 🖵 🍽 🏊

MANHATTAN

🔷🔷🔷 Best Western Manhattan Inn 🏨
(785) 537-8300. **Call for rates.** 601 E Poyntz Ave. SR 177, 0.4 mi e on US 24 (Frontage Rd). Int corridors. **Pets:** Accepted.
🖫 ⊠ �ᏝM 🖵 🏊

🔷🔷🔷 Clarion Hotel 🏨
(785) 539-5311. **Call for rates.** 530 Richards Dr. On SR 18 (Ft. Riley Blvd), 0.3 mi e of jct SR 113. Ext/int corridors. **Pets:** Small, other species. $25 deposit/room. Service with restrictions, crate.
⊠ 🛅 🖵 🍽 🏊 ⊠

🔷🔷🔷 Holiday Inn at the Campus 🏨
(785) 539-7531. **$130-$300.** 1641 Anderson Ave. 1 mi n of SR 18 (Ft. Riley Blvd). Int corridors. **Pets:** Medium, other species. $25 one-time fee/room. Service with restrictions, supervision.
🅰🆂🅺 ⊠ 🛅 🖵 🍽 🏊

🔷 Motel 6–152 Ⓜ
(785) 537-1022. **$45-$61.** 510 Tuttle Creek Blvd. 0.3 mi ne on US 24 (Frontage Rd) and SR 177. Ext corridors. **Pets:** Other species. Service with restrictions, supervision.
⊠ ᏝM 🏊

🔷🔷 Super 8 Motel-Manhattan 🏨
(785) 537-8468. **$65-$125.** 200 Tuttle Creek Blvd. Jct US 24 (Frontage Rd) and SR 177. Int corridors. **Pets:** Small. $25 one-time fee/pet. Designated rooms, no service, crate.
🅰🆂🅺 ⊠ 🛅 🖵

MARYSVILLE

🔷🔷 Heritage Inn Express 🏨
(785) 562-5588. **$55-$90.** 1155 Pony Express Hwy. 2 mi e on US 36 (Pony Express Hwy). Int corridors. **Pets:** Accepted.
🅰🆂🅺 ⊠ 🛅 🖵

🔷🔷 Surf Motel Ⓜ
(785) 562-2354. **$45-$86.** 2105 Center St. 1 mi e on US 36 (Pony Express Hwy). Ext/int corridors. **Pets:** $10 daily fee/room. Designated rooms, service with restrictions, crate.
🅰🆂🅺 ⊠ 🛅 🖵 ⊠

MCPHERSON

🔷🔷🔷 Americas Best Value Inn 🏨
(620) 241-8881. **$56-$96, 3 day notice.** 2110 E Kansas Ave. I-135, exit 60, just w. Int corridors. **Pets:** Accepted.
🖫 ⊠ ᏝM 🖵

🔷🔷🔷 Best Western Holiday Manor Motel 🏨
(620) 241-5343. **$70-$120.** 2211 E Kansas Ave. I-135, exit 60, just w. Ext/int corridors. **Pets:** $10 daily fee/pet. Service with restrictions, supervision.
🖫 ⊠ 🛅 🖵 🍽 🏊

NEWTON

🔷🔷🔷 Best Western Red Coach Inn 🏨
(316) 283-9120. **$77-$110.** 1301 E 1st St. I-135, exit 31, just w. Ext/int corridors. **Pets:** Accepted.
🖫 ⊠ 🛅 🖵 🍽 🏊 ⊠

🔷🔷 Days Inn Newton 🏨
(316) 283-3330. **Call for rates.** 105 Manchester St. I-135, exit 31, just e. Int corridors. **Pets:** Accepted.
⊠ 🛅 🖵 🏊

OTTAWA

🔷🔷🔷 Best Western Ottawa Inn 🏨
(785) 242-2224. **$75-$110, 3 day notice.** 212 E 23rd St. I-35, exit 183 (US 59). Ext/int corridors. **Pets:** Small. $15 daily fee/pet. Service with restrictions, supervision.
🖫 ⊠ ᏝM 🛅 🖵 🏊

🔷🔷🔷 Econo Lodge 🏨
(785) 242-3400. **$60-$150.** 2331 S Cedar Rd. I-35, exit 183 (US 59). Int corridors. **Pets:** Accepted.
🖫 ⊠ 🛅 🖵 🏊

PAOLA

🔷🔷 Best Western 🏨
(913) 294-3700. **$95-$115, 7 day notice.** 1600 E Hedge Lane Ct. US 169, exit 127 (Baptiste Dr), just w. Int corridors. **Pets:** Medium. $10 daily fee/pet. Designated rooms.
🖫 ⊠ ᏝM 🛅 🖵 🏊

PARK CITY

🔷🔷🔷 Best Western Hotel & Suites 🏨
(316) 832-9387. **$71-$89.** 915 E 53rd St N. I-135, exit 13, just w. Ext/int corridors. **Pets:** Other species. $20 one-time fee/room. Service with restrictions, crate.
🖫 ⊠ 🛅 🖵 🍽 🏊 ⊠

🔷 Super 8-Wichita North/Park City Ⓜ
(316) 744-2071. **$45-$84.** 6075 Air Cap Dr. I-135, exit 14, just sw. Int corridors. **Pets:** $10 daily fee/pet. Service with restrictions, supervision.
🅰🆂🅺 ⊠ 🛅

PARSONS

🔷🔷🔷 Best Western Parsons Inn 🏨
(620) 423-0303. **$75, 3 day notice.** 101 E Main St. 1.5 mi e. Int corridors. **Pets:** Other species. $5 daily fee/pet.
🖫 ⊠ 🛅 🖵 🏊

PHILLIPSBURG

🔷🔷 Cottonwood Inn Ⓜ
(785) 543-2125. **$65-$99, 7 day notice.** 1200 State St. 1 mi e on US 36/183. Ext corridors. **Pets:** Accepted.
🅰🆂🅺 ⊠ 🏊

PITTSBURG

🔷🔷 Econo Lodge 🏨
(620) 231-8300. **$50-$95.** 2408 S Broadway. Jct US 69 and Broadway; south side of town. Ext corridors. **Pets:** Small, dogs only. $10 daily fee/pet. Designated rooms, service with restrictions, crate.
🅰🆂🅺 ⊠ 🛅 🏊

🔷🔷🔷 Lamplighter Inn & Suites 🏨
(620) 231-8700. **$69-$99.** 4020 Parkview Dr. 2.3 mi n on US 69 from jct SR 126. Ext/int corridors. **Pets:** Accepted.
🖫 ⊠ ᏝM 🛅 🖵 🏊

🔷🔷 Super 8 Motel 🏨
(620) 232-1881. **$53-$69.** 3108 N Broadway St. 2.1 mi n on US 69 from jct SR 126. Int corridors. **Pets:** Small. $10 daily fee/pet. Designated rooms, no service, crate.
🅰🆂🅺 ⊠ 🛅 🖵

PRATT

🔷 Evergreen Inn Ⓜ
(620) 672-6431. **$54-$100.** 20001 W US Hwy 54. On US 54, 3 mi w. Ext corridors. **Pets:** $5 one-time fee/room. Designated rooms, supervision.
⊠ 🛅 🏊

▼▼ Regency Inn & Suites 🅷
(620) 672-9433. **$78.** 1401 W US Hwy 54. US 54, 2 mi w. Int corridors.
Pets: $25 one-time fee/room. Service with restrictions, supervision.
🅰🆂🅺 ⊠ 🛏 💻 🏊

RUSSELL

▼▼▼ AmericInn Lodge & Suites of Russell 🅷 ❖
(785) 483-4200. **$80-$95.** 1430 S Fossil St. I-70, exit 184 (US 281), just n.
Int corridors. **Pets:** Large. $10 one-time fee/pet. Designated rooms, service
with restrictions, supervision.
🅰🆂🅺 ⊠ &ᴹ 🛏 💻 🏊 ⊠

▼ Days Inn 🅼
(785) 483-6660. **Call for rates.** 1225 S Fossil St. I-70, exit 184 (US 281),
just n. Ext corridors. **Pets:** Accepted.
⊠ 🛏 💻 🏊

SABETHA

▼▼ Country Inn 🅷
(785) 284-2300. **$59-$92.** 1423 S Old US 75. South side of town. Int
corridors. **Pets:** $35 one-time fee/room. Service with restrictions, supervi-
sion.
⊠ 🛏

SALINA

▼▼ America's Best Inn 🅷
(785) 825-2500. **$56-$79.** 429 W Diamond Dr. I-70, exit 252, just n. Int
corridors. **Pets:** $10 daily fee/pet. No service, supervision.
🅰🆂🅺 ⊠ &ᴹ 🛏

▼▼ Baymont Inn & Suites 🅷
(785) 493-9800. **$63-$82.** 745 W Schilling Rd. I-135, exit 89 (Schilling Rd),
just w. Int corridors. **Pets:** Accepted.
🅰🆂🅺 ⊠ &ᴹ 🛏 💻 🏊 ⊠

▼▼▼ Best Western Heart of America Inn 🅷
(785) 827-9315. **$78-$93.** 632 Westport Blvd. I-135, exit 92, just e. Ext
corridors. **Pets:** Large, other species. Designated rooms, service with
restrictions, supervision.
🆂🅰🆅🅴 ⊠ 💻 🏊

▼▼▼ Best Western Mid-America Inn 🅼
(785) 827-0356. **$66-$95.** 1846 N 9th St. I-70, exit 252, just s. Ext corridors. **Pets:** Accepted.
🆂🅰🆅🅴 ⊠ &ᴹ 💻 🍽 🏊

▼▼▼ Candlewood Suites 🅷 ❖
(785) 823-6939. **$59-$129.** 2650 Planet Ave. I-135, exit 89 (Schilling Rd),
just e to S 9th St, 0.5 mi n to Belmont, then just w. Int corridors.
Pets: Medium, other species. $20 one-time fee/pet. Service with restric-
tions, crate.
🅰🆂🅺 ⊠ &ᴹ 🛏 💻

▼▼ Comfort Inn 🅷
(785) 826-1711. **$60-$120.** 1820 W Crawford St. I-135, exit 92, just e. Int
corridors. **Pets:** Small. $20 one-time fee/pet. Service with restrictions,
supervision.
🅰🆂🅺 ⊠ &ᴹ 🛏 💻 🏊

▼▼ Days Inn 🅷
(785) 823-9791. **$55-$129.** 407 W Diamond Dr. I-70, exit 252, just n. Int
corridors. **Pets:** Medium. $15 one-time fee/pet. Designated rooms, no serv-
ice, supervision.
🅰🆂🅺 ⊠ 🛏 💻 🏊

▼▼▼ Holiday Inn Express Hotel & Suites 🅷
(785) 827-9000. **$89-$149.** 201 E Diamond Dr. I-70, exit 252, just ne. Int
corridors. **Pets:** Other species. $20 one-time fee/pet. Designated rooms,
service with restrictions, crate.
⊠ &ᴹ 🛏 💻 🏊

▲▲▲ ▼▼▼ Quality Inn & Suites 🅷
(785) 825-2111. **Call for rates.** 2110 W Crawford St. I-135, exit 92, just w.
Int corridors. **Pets:** Accepted.
🆂🅰🆅🅴 ⊠ &ᴹ 🛏 💻 🍽 🏊 ⊠

▲▲▲ ▼▼▼ Super 8 🅷
(785) 823-8808. **Call for rates.** 120 E Diamond Dr. I-70, exit 252, just ne.
Int corridors. **Pets:** Accepted.
🆂🅰🆅🅴 ⊠ &ᴹ 🛏 💻 🏊

SHARON SPRINGS

▼▼ Oak Tree Inn 🅷
(785) 852-4664. **$73-$79.** 801 N Hwy 27. Jct US 40 and SR 27. Ext/int
corridors. **Pets:** Small, other species. $10 daily fee/pet. Service with restric-
tions, supervision.
🅰🆂🅺 ⊠ &ᴹ 🛏 💻 🍽

SMITH CENTER

▼ U.S. Center Motel 🅼
(785) 282-6611. **Call for rates.** 116 E Hwy 36. Jct US 36 and 281. Ext
corridors. **Pets:** Accepted.
⊠ 🛏 🏊

TOPEKA

▲▲▲ ▼▼▼ Best Western Topeka Inn & Suites 🅷
(785) 228-2223. **Call for rates.** 700 SW Fairlawn Rd. I-70, exit 357A, just
ne. Int corridors. **Pets:** Accepted.
🆂🅰🆅🅴 ⊠ 🛏 💻 🏊

▼▼ Candlelight Inn Hotel 🅷
(785) 272-9550. **Call for rates.** 2831 SW Fairlawn Rd. I-470, exit 3. Ext
corridors. **Pets:** Accepted.
⊠ 🛏 💻 🏊 ⊠

▲▲▲ ▼▼▼▼ Capitol Plaza Hotel 🅷
(785) 431-7200. **$79-$149.** 1717 SW Topeka Blvd. I-70, exit SE 8th Ave,
1.6 mi s; I-470, exit Topeka Blvd, 2.9 mi n. Int corridors. **Pets:** Medium. $50
one-time fee/pet. Service with restrictions, crate.
🆂🅰🆅🅴 ⊠ &ᴹ 🛏 💻 🍽 🏊 ⊠

▲▲▲ ▼▼▼▼ ClubHouse Inn & Suites 🅷
(785) 273-8888. **$105-$125.** 924 SW Henderson. I-70, exit 356 (Wanamaker Rd). Int corridors. **Pets:** Accepted.
🆂🅰🆅🅴 ⊠ 🛏 💻 🏊

▼▼ Comfort Inn by Choice Hotels 🅷
(785) 273-5365. **Call for rates.** 1518 SW Wanamaker Rd. I-470, exit 1
(Wanamaker Rd). Int corridors. **Pets:** Accepted.
⊠ 🛏 💻 🏊

▼▼▼▼ Country Inn & Suites By Carlson-Topeka-West 🅷
(785) 478-9800. **$75-$125.** 6020 SW 10th St. I-70, exit 356 (Wanamaker
Rd), just sw. Int corridors. **Pets:** Medium. $10 daily fee/room. Designated
rooms, service with restrictions, supervision.
🅰🆂🅺 ⊠ &ᴹ 🛏 💻 🏊

▼▼ Quality Inn 🅷
(785) 273-6969. **$50-$120.** 1240 SW Wanamaker Rd. I-470, exit 1 (Wanamaker Rd), just ne; I-70, exit 356A (Wanamaker Rd), 1 mi s. Int corridors.
Pets: Accepted.
🅰🆂🅺 ⊠ 🛏 💻 🏊

▼▼ Ramada Hotel & Convention Center 🅷
(785) 234-5400. **$89-$115.** 420 SE 6th Ave. I-70, exit 362B, just e. Int
corridors. **Pets:** Medium. $20 one-time fee/room. Service with restrictions,
crate.
🅰🆂🅺 ⊠ &ᴹ 🛏 💻 🍽 🏊 ⊠

▼▼▼ Residence Inn by Marriott 🅷
(785) 271-8903. **$150-$160.** 1620 SW Westport Dr. I-470, exit 1 (Wanamaker Rd), just se. Int corridors. **Pets:** Accepted.
⊠ &ᴹ 🛏 💻 🏊 ⊠

WWWW The Senate Luxury Suites ⊞
(785) 233-5050. **$80-$120.** 900 SW Tyler St. Just w of state capitol; downtown. Int corridors. **Pets:** Accepted.

ASK ✕ ⊟ ▢

WW Sleep Inn & Suites ⊞
(785) 228-2500. **$69-$119.** 1024 SW Wanamaker Rd. I-70, exit 356 (Wanamaker Rd), just s. Int corridors. **Pets:** Medium, other species. $10 daily fee/pet. Service with restrictions, supervision.

ASK ✕ ᔍM ⊟ ▢ ☇

AAA WW Super 8 at Forbes Landing ⊞ ❀
(785) 862-2222. **$70-$140.** 5922 S Topeka Blvd. I-470, exit 6, 2.2 mi s. Int corridors. **Pets:** Dogs only. $20 one-time fee/room. Service with restrictions, crate.

SAVE ✕ ᔍM ⊟ ▢ ☇

ULYSSES

WW Single Tree Inn ⊞
(620) 356-1500. **Call for rates.** 2033 W Oklahoma St. 1.5 mi w on US 160. Int corridors. **Pets:** Accepted.

✕ ⊟ ▢

UNIONTOWN

W Wyatt Earp Inn & B&B ⊞ ❀
(620) 756-4990. **$65-$150, 30 day notice.** 100 5th St. On SR 3; west side of town. Int corridors. **Pets:** $10 daily fee/pet. Designated rooms, supervision.

ASK ✕

WAKEENEY

AAA WWWW Best Western Wakeeney Inn & Suites ⊞
(785) 743-2700. **Call for rates.** 525 S 1st St. I-70, exit 127, just n. Int corridors. **Pets:** Large. $10 daily fee/pet. Designated rooms, service with restrictions, supervision.

SAVE ✕ ᔍM ⊟ ▢ ☇

AAA WWW Super 8 Motel ⊞ ❀
(785) 743-6442. **$59.** 709 S 13th St. I-70, exit 128, just n. Int corridors. **Pets:** Medium. $10 one-time fee/pet. Designated rooms, service with restrictions, supervision.

SAVE ✕ ⊟ ▢

WAMEGO

AAA W Simmer Motel Ⓜ ❀
(785) 456-2304. **$46-$100.** 1215 Hwy 24 W. Jct SR 99, 0.5 mi w. Ext corridors. **Pets:** Other species. $10 one-time fee/pet. Designated rooms, service with restrictions.

SAVE ✕ ⊟ ▢ ☇

WICHITA

AAA WWW Best Western Airport Inn & Conference Center ⊞
(316) 942-5600. **$91-$115.** 6815 W Kellogg. I-235, exit 7, 0.6 mi w on US 54 (S Frontage Rd). Int corridors. **Pets:** Small. Service with restrictions, supervision.

SAVE ✕ ⊟ ▢ 🍴 ☇ ✕

AAA WWW Best Western Governors Inn & Suites ⊞
(316) 522-0775. **$70-$90.** 4742 S Emporia. I-135, exit 1 A/B (47th St S), just sw. Int corridors. **Pets:** Accepted.

SAVE ✕ ⊟ ▢ ☇

WW Candlewood Suites ⊞
(316) 942-0400. **$79-$159.** 570 S Julia. I-235, exit 7, 0.4 mi nw on Dugan Rd. Int corridors. **Pets:** Accepted.

ASK ✕ ⊟ ▢

WW Candlewood Suites-Wichita Northeast ⊞
(316) 634-6070. **Call for rates.** 3141 N Webb Rd. SR 96, exit Webb Rd, just nw. Int corridors. **Pets:** Accepted.

✕ ᔍM ⊟ ▢

AAA WWWW Clarion Inn & Suites ⊞
(316) 942-7911. **$90.** 5805 W Kellogg. I-235, exit 7A, just w. Int corridors. **Pets:** Medium. $35 one-time fee/room. Designated rooms, service with restrictions, supervision.

SAVE ✕ ⊟ ▢ ☇

AAA WWW Comfort Inn ⊞
(316) 522-1800. **$79-$109, 3 day notice.** 4849 S Laura. I-135, exit 1A/B (47th St S), just e. Int corridors. **Pets:** Other species. $10 daily fee/room. Service with restrictions, supervision.

SAVE ✕ ⊟ ▢ ☇

WW Comfort Inn by Choice Hotels ⊞
(316) 686-2844. **Call for rates.** 9525 E Corporate Hills Dr. I-35, exit 50, just ne. Int corridors. **Pets:** Accepted.

✕ ⊟ ▢ ☇

WW Cresthill Suites Hotel ⊞
(316) 689-8000. **$108.** 12111 E Central Ave. 1.7 mi e of jct Webb Rd. Int corridors. **Pets:** Accepted.

ASK ✕ ⊟ ▢ ☇

AAA WWWW Hawthorn Suites at Reflection Ridge ⊞
(316) 729-5700. **$109-$139, 3 day notice.** 2405 N Ridge Rd. I-235, exit 10, 1.7 mi w on Zoo Blvd/21st St N, then just n. Int corridors. **Pets:** Accepted.

SAVE ✕ ⊟ ▢

AAA WWWW Holiday Inn ⊞
(316) 686-7131. **$90-$130.** 549 S Rock Rd. I-35, exit 50, 0.5 mi w. Ext/int corridors. **Pets:** Accepted.

SAVE ✕ ⊟ ▢ 🍴 ☇ ✕

WW Holiday Inn Express ⊞
(316) 529-4848. **$75-$94.** 4848 S Laura. I-135, exit 1 A/B (47th St S), just ne. Int corridors. **Pets:** Accepted.

ASK ✕ ▢ ☇

AAA WWWW Holiday Inn Hotel & Suites Convention Center ⊞
(316) 269-2090. **Call for rates.** 221 E Kellogg. Just sw of jct US 54/400 and Broadway. Int corridors. **Pets:** Accepted.

SAVE ✕ ᔍM ⊟ ▢ 🍴 ☇ ✕

WWW Homewood Suites by Hilton@The Waterfront ⊞ ❀
(316) 260-8844. **$119-$169.** 1550 N Waterfront Pkwy. Just e of Jct 13th and Webb rds. Int corridors. **Pets:** Large. $50 deposit/room, $25 one-time fee/room. Designated rooms, service with restrictions, crate.

✕ ᔍM ⊟ ▢ ☇ ✕

AAA WWWW Hyatt Regency Wichita ⊞
(316) 293-1234. **$89-$229.** 400 W Waterman. Just w of jct Main St and Waterman; downtown. Int corridors. **Pets:** Accepted.

SAVE ✕ ⊟ ▢ 🍴 ☇

AAA WWW Quality Suites Airport ⊞
(316) 945-2600. **$90-$129, 3 day notice.** 658 Westdale Dr. Jct I-235 and US 54. Int corridors. **Pets:** Small. Supervision.

SAVE ✕ ⊟ ▢ ☇

WWW Residence Inn by Marriott at Plazzio ⊞
(316) 682-7300. **$148-$180.** 1212 N Greenwich. SR 96, exit 13th St, 0.5 mi sw. Int corridors. **Pets:** Medium, other species. $75 one-time fee/room. Service with restrictions, crate.

✕ ᔍM ⊟ ▢ ☇ ✕

◆◆ **Super 8-Wichita/East** 🄷
(316) 686-3888. **$51-$73.** 527 S Webb Rd. I-35, exit 50, just e. Int corridors. **Pets:** Small. $10 daily fee/pet. Designated rooms, no service, crate.
ASK ✕ 🛢 💻

◆◆ **TownePlace Suites by Marriott** 🄷
(316) 631-3773. **$107-$131.** 9444 E 29th St N. SR 96, exit Webb Rd, just sw. Int corridors. **Pets:** Other species. $75 one-time fee/room. Service with restrictions, supervision.
✕ 🛢 💻

◆◆ **Wesley Inn** 🄷
(316) 858-3343. **$87.** 3343 E Central Ave. Just e of jct Hillside St. Int corridors. **Pets:** Small, dogs only. $25 one-time fee/room. Service with restrictions, crate.
ASK ✕ 🛢 💻

WINFIELD

◆◆◆ **Comfort Inn** 🄷
(620) 221-7529. **Call for rates.** Hwy 77 at Quail Ridge Dr. On US 77, 1 mi s. Ext/int corridors. **Pets:** Accepted.
✕ 🛢 💻 🏊

◆◆ **Econo Lodge** 🄼
(620) 221-9050. **$55-$85.** 1710 Main St. 0.5 mi s of jct US 77 and 160. Ext corridors. **Pets:** Small. $10 daily fee/pet. Designated rooms, supervision.
ASK ✕ 🛢 💻

KENTUCKY

ASHLAND

ⓐⓐⓐ ▼▼▼▼ Best Western River Cities 🅷
(606) 326-0357. **$79-$105.** 31 Russell Plaza Dr. I-64, exit 185, 6 mi nw on US 60, then 3 mi n on US 23. Int corridors. **Pets:** Small, dogs only. $5 daily fee/pet. Designated rooms, service with restrictions, supervision.
🆂🅰🆅🅴 ✕ ♿ 🛏 🖵 🏊

▼▼▼ Holiday Inn Express Hotel & Suites 🅷
(606) 929-1720. **$100-$150.** 13131 Slone Ct. I-64, exit 185, just n. Int corridors. **Pets:** Medium. $25 daily fee/pet. Service with restrictions, crate.
✕ ♿ 🛏 🖵 🏊

▼▼▼ Quality Inn 🅷
(606) 325-8989. **$70-$90.** 4708 Winchester Ave. I-64, exit 191, 4.8 mi n on US 23. Ext corridors. **Pets:** Medium. $15 daily fee/pet. Service with restrictions, crate.
🅰🆂🅺 ✕ ♿ 🛏 🖵 🏊

BARDSTOWN

ⓐⓐⓐ ▼▼▼ Bardstown-Parkview Motel Ⓜ
(502) 348-5983. **$45-$80.** 418 E Stephen Foster Ave. 0.5 mi e on US 150; e of jct US 62. Ext corridors. **Pets:** Accepted.
🆂🅰🆅🅴 ✕ 🛏 🍴 🏊

ⓐⓐⓐ ▼▼ Best Western General Nelson Inn 🅷
(502) 348-3977. **$60-$119, 30 day notice.** 411 W Stephen Foster Ave. 0.5 mi w on US 62. Ext corridors. **Pets:** Small. $10 one-time fee/room. Service with restrictions, crate.
🆂🅰🆅🅴 ✕ 🛏 🖵 🏊

▼▼▼ Hampton Inn 🅷
(502) 349-0100. **$81-$139.** 985 Chambers Blvd. Just s of US 245. Int corridors. **Pets:** Accepted.
✕ ♿ 🛏 🖵 🏊

BENTON

▼▼▼ Comfort Inn & Suites 🅷
(270) 527-5300. **Call for rates.** 173 Carroll Rd. Purchase Pkwy, exit 47. Int corridors. **Pets:** Accepted.
✕ ♿ 🛏 🖵 🏊

BEREA

ⓐⓐⓐ ▼▼▼ Boone Tavern Hotel & Restaurant of Berea College 🅷
(859) 985-3700. **$102-$142.** 100 Main St. I-75, exit 76, 1.5 mi ne on SR 21. Int corridors. **Pets:** Medium, other species. $50 one-time fee/pet. Service with restrictions, crate.
🆂🅰🆅🅴 ✕ 🖵 🍴

▼▼▼ Comfort Inn & Suites 🅷
(859) 985-5500. **$59-$99.** 1003 Paint Lick Rd. I-75, exit 76, just w. Int corridors. **Pets:** Small. $10 daily fee/pet. Service with restrictions, supervision.
🅰🆂🅺 ✕ ♿ 🛏 🖵 🏊

BOWLING GREEN

ⓐⓐⓐ ▼▼▼▼ Candlewood Suites 🅷 ❁
(270) 843-5505. **$109-$209.** 540 Wall St. I-65, exit 22 (Scottsville Rd), just n. Int corridors. **Pets:** Medium, other species. $100 one-time fee/room. Service with restrictions, supervision.
🆂🅰🆅🅴 ✕ ♿ 🛏 🖵 🏊

ⓐⓐⓐ ▼▼▼ Country Hearth Inn 🅷
(270) 783-4443. **$45-$90.** 395 Corvette Dr. I-65, exit 28, just w. Int corridors. **Pets:** Small. $5 daily fee/room. No service, supervision.
🆂🅰🆅🅴 ✕ ♿ 🛏 🖵

ⓐⓐⓐ ▼▼▼ Drury Inn-Bowling Green 🅷
(270) 842-7100. **$95-$134.** 3250 Scottsville Rd. I-65, exit 22 (Scottsville Rd), just w. Int corridors. **Pets:** Other species. Service with restrictions, supervision.
🅰🆂🅺 ✕ ♿ 🛏 🖵 🏊

ⓐⓐⓐ ▼▼▼▼ Holiday Inn University Plaza 🅷
(270) 745-0088. **$99-$149.** 1021 Wilkinson Trace. I-65, exit 22 (Scottsville Rd), 2.5 mi w, then just n. Int corridors. **Pets:** Accepted.
🆂🅰🆅🅴 ✕ 🛏 🖵 🍴 🏊 ✕

ⓐⓐⓐ ▼▼▼ News Inn of Bowling Green Ⓜ
(270) 781-3460. **$49-$119.** 3160 Scottsville Rd. I-65, exit 22 (Scottsville Rd). Ext corridors. **Pets:** Large. $5 daily fee/pet. Service with restrictions, supervision.
🆂🅰🆅🅴 ✕ 🛏 🖵 🏊

ⓐⓐⓐ ▼▼▼ Red Roof Inn 🅷
(270) 781-6550. **$50-$130.** 3140 Scottsville Rd. I-65, exit 22 (Scottsville Rd), 0.3 mi w. Ext corridors. **Pets:** Medium. Designated rooms, service with restrictions, crate.
🆂🅰🆅🅴 ✕ 🛏

CALVERT CITY

▼▼ Super 8 Calvert City/KY Lake 🅷
(270) 395-5566. **$62-$70.** 86 Campbell Dr. I-24, exit 27 (US 62), just n. Int corridors. **Pets:** Small, dogs only. $10 daily fee/pet.
🅰🆂🅺 ✕ ♿ 🛏 🖵 🏊

CAMPBELLSVILLE

▼▼▼ Holiday Inn Express 🅷
(270) 465-2727. **Call for rates.** 102 Plantation Dr. Jct US 68 and SR 55, 0.5 mi n. Int corridors. **Pets:** Accepted.
✕ ♿ 🛏 🖵 🏊

CARROLLTON

ⓐⓐⓐ ▼▼▼ Best Western Executive Inn 🅷
(502) 732-8444. **$65-$119.** 10 Slumber Ln. I-71, exit 44, just nw. Int corridors. **Pets:** Accepted.
🆂🅰🆅🅴 ✕ ♿ 🛏 🖵 🏊

Super 8 Carrollton H
(502) 732-0252. **Call for rates.** 130 Slumber Ln. I-71, exit 44, just nw. Int corridors. **Pets:** Accepted.

CATLETTSBURG

Ramada Limited Hotel H
(606) 739-5700. **$84-$94.** 6000 Crider Dr. I-64, exit 191, 0.5 mi n on US 23. Int corridors. **Pets:** Other species. $10 daily fee/pet. Designated rooms, service with restrictions, supervision.

CAVE CITY

Best Western Kentucky Inn H
(270) 773-3161. **$50-$100, 14 day notice.** 1009 Doyle Ave. I-65, exit 53, just e. Ext corridors. **Pets:** Small, dogs only. $10 daily fee/pet. Designated rooms, service with restrictions, supervision.

Comfort Inn H
(270) 773-2030. **$30-$140, 3 day notice.** 801 Mammoth Cave St. I-65, exit 53, just ne. Ext corridors. **Pets:** Small. $10 daily fee/pet. Designated rooms, service with restrictions, supervision.

Super 8 H
(270) 773-2500. **$49-$99.** 799 Mammoth Cave St. I-65, exit 53, just ne. Ext corridors. **Pets:** Medium. $10 daily fee/pet. Service with restrictions, supervision.

CORBIN

Best Western-Corbin Inn H
(606) 528-2100. **$70-$100, 7 day notice.** 2630 Cumberland Falls Hwy. I-75, exit 25. Ext corridors. **Pets:** Small. $10 daily fee/pet. Service with restrictions, supervision.

COVINGTON

Embassy Suites Cincinnati RiverCenter H
(859) 261-8400. **$119-$189.** 10 E RiverCenter Blvd. I-71/75, exit 192, 0.8 mi e on 5th St, then 0.3 mi n on Madison Ave. Int corridors. **Pets:** Accepted.

Extended StayAmerica H
(859) 581-3000. **$89-$179.** 650 W 3rd St. I-71/75, exit 192, 0.5 mi ne on SR 8. Int corridors. **Pets:** Other species. $25 daily fee/pet. Service with restrictions, crate.

DANVILLE

Best Western Danville Inn H
(859) 236-5525. **Call for rates.** 210 Brenda Ave. Just e on US 127 Bypass and 150 (Perryville Rd). Int corridors. **Pets:** Accepted.

Holiday Inn Express-Danville H
(859) 236-8600. **$69-$109.** 96 Daniel Dr. Just e of US 127 on 150 Bypass. Int corridors. **Pets:** Other species. $50 deposit/pet. Service with restrictions, supervision.

DRY RIDGE

Holiday Inn Express H
(859) 824-7121. **$79-$99.** 1050 Fashion Ridge Rd. I-75, exit 159, just nw. Int corridors. **Pets:** $10 one-time fee/pet. Designated rooms, service with restrictions, supervision.

EDDYVILLE

Eddy Creek Marina Resort M
(270) 388-2271. **$74-$170, 45 day notice.** 7612 SR 93 S. I-24, exit 45, 4 mi s. Ext corridors. **Pets:** Medium, dogs only. $15 daily fee/pet. No service, crate.

ELIZABETHTOWN

Best Western Atrium Gardens H
(270) 769-3030. **$100-$132.** 1043 Executive Dr. I-65, exit 94, just nw. Int corridors. **Pets:** Other species. $25 one-time fee/room. Service with restrictions, supervision.

Comfort Inn H
(270) 765-4166. **Call for rates.** 2009 N Mulberry St. I-65, exit 94, just sw. Int corridors. **Pets:** Medium. $10 daily fee/pet. Designated rooms, service with restrictions, supervision.

Country Hearth Inn & Suites H
(270) 769-2344. **$77-$107.** 1058 N Mulberry St. I-65, exit 94, just nw. Ext corridors. **Pets:** Accepted.

Holiday Inn Express H
(270) 769-1334. **$65-$119.** 107 Buffalo Creek Dr. I-65, exit 94, just w. Int corridors. **Pets:** Small. $25 daily fee/pet. Designated rooms, service with restrictions, supervision.

La Quinta Inn Elizabethtown H 🐾
(270) 765-4747. **$69-$159.** 210 Commerce Dr. I-65, exit 94, just nw. Int corridors. **Pets:** Medium, other species. Service with restrictions, supervision.

ERLANGER

Comfort Inn-Cincinnati Airport H
(859) 727-3400. **$65-$95.** 630 Donaldson Rd. I-71/75, exit 184, off SR 236 southbound; exit 184B northbound. Int corridors. **Pets:** $10 daily fee/pet. No service, supervision.

Residence Inn by Marriott, Cincinnati Airport H
(859) 282-7400. **$184-$200.** 2811 Circleport Dr. I-275, exit 2. Int corridors. **Pets:** $100 one-time fee/pet. Service with restrictions.

FLORENCE

Ashley Quarters H 🐾
(859) 525-9997. **Call for rates.** 4880 Houston Rd. I-71/75, exit 182, 0.6 mi w on Turfway and Houston rds. Int corridors. **Pets:** Other species. $75 one-time fee/room.

Best Western Inn Florence H 🐾
(859) 525-0090. **$60-$125.** 7821 Commerce Dr. I-71/75, exit 181, just ne. Int corridors. **Pets:** Dogs only. $15 daily fee/pet. Service with restrictions, supervision.

Extended StayAmerica H
(859) 282-0172. **$59-$129.** 7350 Turfway Rd. I-71/75, exit 182, just w. Int corridors. **Pets:** Other species. $25 daily fee/pet. Service with restrictions, crate.

Florence Super 8 H
(859) 283-1221. **$59-$89.** 7928 Dream St. I-71/75, exit 180, just e on US 42, then just n. Int corridors. **Pets:** Accepted.

▼▼▼▼ La Quinta Inn & Suites �H ❀
(859) 282-8212. **$89-$169.** 350 Meijer Dr. I-71/75, exit 182, 0.4 mi sw. Int corridors. **Pets:** Medium, other species. Service with restrictions, supervision.
[ASK] [✕] [🔥M] [📶] [📺] [🏊]

🔺🔺🔺 ▼▼▼ Red Roof Inn M
(859) 647-2700. **Call for rates.** 7454 Turfway Rd. I-71/75, exit 182, 0.8 mi sw. Int corridors. **Pets:** Medium. Service with restrictions, supervision.
[SAVE] [✕] [📶]

FRANKFORT

🔺🔺🔺 ▼ Americas Best Value Inn �H
(502) 875-3220. **$60-$80.** 1225 US Hwy 127 S. I-64, exit 53B, 1.2 mi n. Int corridors. **Pets:** Large, dogs only. $15 one-time fee/room. Service with restrictions, crate.
[SAVE] [✕] [📶] [📺]

🔺🔺🔺 ▼▼▼▼ Best Western Parkside Inn �H
(502) 695-6111. **$80-$150.** 80 Chenault Rd. I-64, exit 58. Ext/int corridors. **Pets:** Medium. $20 daily fee/pet. Designated rooms, service with restrictions, supervision.
[SAVE] [✕] [📶] [📺] [🏊]

▼▼▼▼ Capital Plaza Hotel �H
(502) 227-5100. **$83-$89.** 405 Wilkinson Blvd. Adjacent to Frankfort Convention Center. Int corridors. **Pets:** $25 one-time fee/room. Service with restrictions, supervision.
[ASK] [✕] [🔥M] [📶] [📺] [🏊]

FRANKLIN

🔺🔺🔺 ▼▼▼ Comfort Inn �H
(270) 586-6100. **$50-$100.** 3794 Nashville Rd. I-65, exit 2. Ext corridors. **Pets:** Small. $20 daily fee/pet. Service with restrictions, supervision.
[SAVE] [✕] [🔥M] [📶] [📺] [🏊]

GLASGOW

▼▼ Comfort Inn �H
(270) 651-9099. **$60-$129.** 210 Calvary Dr. Cumberland Pkwy, exit 11, just n. Ext corridors. **Pets:** $10 daily fee/pet. Designated rooms, no service, supervision.
[ASK] [✕] [📶] [📺] [🏊]

GRAND RIVERS

🔺🔺🔺 ▼▼▼ Best Western Kentucky-Barkley Lakes Inn �H
(270) 928-2700. **$47-$130.** 720 Complex Dr. I-24, exit 31 (SR 453), just s. Ext/int corridors. **Pets:** Accepted.
[SAVE] [✕] [📶] [📺] [🏊]

▼▼▼ Microtel Inn & Suites �H
(270) 928-2740. **$55-$80, 7 day notice.** 1017 Dover Rd. I-24, exit 31 (SR 453), just n. Int corridors. **Pets:** Small, other species. $10 one-time fee/pet. Service with restrictions, supervision.
[ASK] [✕] [🔥M] [📶] [🏊]

GRAYSON

▼▼ Quality Inn-Grayson, KY �H
(606) 474-7854. **Call for rates.** 205 SR 1947. I-64, exit 172, just n. Ext corridors. **Pets:** Accepted.
[✕] [🔥M] [📶] [📺] [🏊]

▼▼ Super 8 �H
(606) 474-8811. **$58-$98.** 125 Super 8 Ln. I-64, exit 172, just s. Int corridors. **Pets:** Small, other species. $10 daily fee/pet. Designated rooms, service with restrictions, supervision.
[ASK] [✕] [🔥M] [📶] [📺]

HARLAN

▼▼▼▼ Holiday Inn Express Harlan �H
(606) 573-3385. **$69-$99.** 2608 S Hwy 421. On US 421, 2.8 mi s. Int corridors. **Pets:** Small. $7 daily fee/room. Designated rooms, service with restrictions, supervision.
[ASK] [✕] [📶] [📺] [🏊]

HARRODSBURG

▼▼ Country Hearth Inn �H
(859) 734-2400. **$61-$97.** 105 Commercial Dr. 0.6 mi n on College St. Int corridors. **Pets:** Small. $20 one-time fee/pet. Service with restrictions, supervision.
[ASK] [✕] [📶] [📺]

HEBRON

🔺🔺🔺 ▼▼▼▼ Sheraton Cincinnati Airport Hotel �H
(859) 371-6166. **Call for rates.** 2826 Terminal Dr. I-71/75 via I-275, 4 mi w, exit 4B from I-275 (SR 212), then 1.3 mi w on SR 212. Int corridors. **Pets:** Accepted.
[SAVE] [✕] [🔥M] [📶] [📺] [🍴] [🏊]

HOPKINSVILLE

▼▼▼▼ Holiday Inn �H
(270) 886-4413. **$86-$128.** 2910 Ft Campbell Blvd. Pennyrile Pkwy, exit 7A, 0.6 mi n on US 41A. Int corridors. **Pets:** Large, other species. $50 one-time fee/room. Service with restrictions, supervision.
[ASK] [✕] [📶] [📺] [🍴] [🏊] [✕🐾]

🔺🔺🔺 ▼▼▼▼ Hopkinsville Best Western �H
(270) 886-9000. **$67-$82.** 4101 Ft Campbell Blvd. Pennyrile Pkwy, exit 7A, just s on US 41A. Int corridors. **Pets:** Accepted.
[SAVE] [✕] [📶] [📺] [🏊]

KUTTAWA

▼▼ Days Inn �H ❀
(270) 388-4060. **$60-$140.** 139 Days Inn Dr. I-24, exit 40 (US 62), just s. Ext corridors. **Pets:** Large, other species. $10 one-time fee/room. Service with restrictions, supervision.
[ASK] [✕] [🔥M] [📶] [📺] [🏊]

🔺🔺🔺 ▼ Relax Inn M
(270) 388-2285. **$45-$70.** 224 New Circle Dr. I-24, exit 40 (US 62), just e. Ext corridors. **Pets:** Very small, dogs only. $6 one-time fee/pet. Designated rooms, service with restrictions, supervision.
[SAVE] [✕] [📶]

LEBANON

▼▼▼▼ Hampton Inn Lebanon �H
(270) 699-4000. **$89-$104.** 1125 Loretto Rd. Jct SR 49 and 84. Int corridors. **Pets:** Small. $25 one-time fee/room. Service with restrictions, crate.
[ASK] [✕] [🔥M] [📶] [📺] [🏊]

LEITCHFIELD

▼▼ Hatfield Inn �H
(270) 259-0464. **$78-$125.** 769 White St. Western Kentucky Pkwy, exit 107, just nw. Int corridors. **Pets:** Other species. $10 daily fee/pet. Service with restrictions, supervision.
[ASK] [✕] [📶]

LEWISPORT

🔺🔺🔺 ▼▼▼▼ Best Western Hancock Inn M
(270) 295-3234. **$79-$129, 7 day notice.** 9040 US Hwy 60 W. On US 60. Int corridors. **Pets:** Accepted.
[SAVE] [✕] [📶] [📺] [🏊]

LEXINGTON

▼▼ Days Inn-South �H
(859) 263-3100. **$45-$60.** 5575 Athens-Boonesboro Rd. I-75, exit 104, just e. Ext corridors. **Pets:** $10 daily fee/pet. Service with restrictions, supervision.
🅰️🆂🅺 ⊠ 🅼 🔒 💻

▼▼▼ DoubleTree Guest Suites Lexington �H
(859) 268-0060. **$99-$299.** 2601 Richmond Rd. I-75, exit 104, 5.5 mi w. Int corridors. **Pets:** Medium, dogs only. $75 one-time fee/pet. Service with restrictions, supervision.
🅰️🆂🅺 ⊠ 🅼 🔒 💻 🍽 🏊

▼▼ Extended StayAmerica-Nicholasville Rd �H
(859) 278-9600. **$59-$99.** 2650 Wilhite Dr. Jct US 27 and SR 4. Ext corridors. **Pets:** Other species. $25 daily fee/pet. Service with restrictions, crate.
🅰️🆂🅺 ⊠ 🅼 🔒 💻

▼▼ Extended StayAmerica-Tates Creek �H
(859) 271-6160. **$64-$104.** 3575 Tates Creek Rd. New Circle Rd (SR 4), exit 18, 0.4 mi s. Int corridors. **Pets:** Other species. $25 daily fee/pet. Service with restrictions, crate.
🅰️🆂🅺 ⊠ 🔒 💻

⚠️ ▼▼▼ Four Points Sheraton Hotel �H
(859) 259-1311. **Call for rates.** 1938 Stanton Way. I-75/64, exit 115, just se on SR 922. Int corridors. **Pets:** Other species. $100 one-time fee/pet. Service with restrictions, supervision.
🆂🅰🆅🅴 ⊠ 🅼 🔒 💻 🍽 🏊

▼▼▼ Griffin Gate Marriott Resort �H
(859) 231-5100. **$226-$267.** 1800 Newtown Pike. I-75/64, exit 115, 0.5 mi sw. Int corridors. **Pets:** Accepted.
⊠ 🅼 🔒 💻 🍽 🏊 ⊠

▼▼▼ Hampton Inn I-75 �H
(859) 299-2613. **$94-$142.** 2251 Elkhorn Rd. I-75, exit 110, 0.4 mi nw. Int corridors. **Pets:** Service with restrictions, supervision.
⊠ 🅼 🔒 💻 🏊

▼▼▼ Holiday Inn Express Hotel & Suites-Lexington �H
(859) 389-6800. **$89-$189.** 1000 Export St. I-75, exit 113, 4.5 mi s, then just e. Int corridors. **Pets:** Accepted.
🅰️🆂🅺 ⊠ 🅼 🔒 💻 🏊

⚠️ ▼▼▼ Holiday Inn-Lexington North �H
(859) 233-0512. **$119-$189.** 1950 Newtown Pike. I-75/64, exit 115, just s. Ext/int corridors. **Pets:** Accepted.
🆂🅰🆅🅴 ⊠ 🅼 🔒 💻 🍽 🏊 ⊠

⚠️ ▼▼▼ Lexington Downtown Hotel & Conference Center �H
(859) 231-9000. **$89-$499.** 369 W Vine St. Corner of Vine St and Broadway. Int corridors. **Pets:** Accepted.
🆂🅰🆅🅴 ⊠ 🅼 🔒 💻 🍽 🏊 ⊠

⚠️ ▼▼ Red Roof Inn-North �H
(859) 293-2626. **$50-$80, 14 day notice.** 1980 Haggard Ct. I-75/64, exit 113, 0.3 mi nw. Ext corridors. **Pets:** Accepted.
🆂🅰🆅🅴 ⊠

⚠️ ▼▼ Red Roof Inn South �H
(859) 277-9400. **$50-$80, 14 day notice.** 2651 Wilhite Dr. Jct US 27 and SR 4. Ext corridors. **Pets:** Accepted.
🆂🅰🆅🅴 ⊠ 🅼 🔒

▼▼ Red Roof Inn Southeast �H
(859) 543-1877. **Call for rates.** 100 Canebrake Dr. I-75, exit 104, just e. Int corridors. **Pets:** Accepted.
⊠ 🔒 💻 🏊

▼▼▼ Residence Inn by Marriott �H 🐾
(859) 231-6191. **$144-$499.** 1080 Newtown Pike. I-75/64, exit 115, 1 mi s on SR 922. Ext corridors. **Pets:** Other species. $75 one-time fee/room. Service with restrictions.
⊠ 🔒 💻 🏊 ⊠

▼▼▼ Residence Inn South @ Hamburg �H 🐾
(859) 263-9979. **$137-$147.** 2688 Pink Pigeon Pkwy. I-75, exit 108, just se. Int corridors. **Pets:** Other species. $75 one-time fee/room. Service with restrictions, crate.
⊠ 🅼 🔒 💻 🍽 🏊 ⊠

▼▼ Sleep Inn Lexington �H 🐾
(859) 543-8400. **$79-$149.** 1920 Plaudit Pl. I-75, exit 108, just sw. Int corridors. **Pets:** $15 one-time fee/pet. Service with restrictions, crate.
🅰️🆂🅺 ⊠ 🔒 💻 🏊

LONDON

▼▼ Budget Host Westgate Inn �H 🐾
(606) 878-7330. **$40-$62, 3 day notice.** 254 Russell Dyche Memorial Hwy. I-75, exit 41, just w on SR 80. Ext/int corridors. **Pets:** Small. Designated rooms, service with restrictions, supervision.
🅰️🆂🅺 ⊠ 🅼 🔒 🏊

▼▼ Econo Lodge �H
(606) 877-9700. **$60-$80.** 105 Melcon Ln. I-75, exit 41, southeast corner. Int corridors. **Pets:** Accepted.
🅰️🆂🅺 ⊠ 🅼 🔒 💻 🏊

▼▼▼ Holiday Inn Express �H
(606) 862-0077. **$110.** 506 Minton Dr. I-75, exit 38, just e. Int corridors. **Pets:** Accepted.
⊠ 🅼 🔒 💻 🏊

▼▼ Red Roof Inn �H
(606) 862-8844. **$50-$85.** 110 Melcon Ln. I-75, exit 41, southwest corner. Int corridors. **Pets:** Medium. Designated rooms, service with restrictions, supervision.
🅰️🆂🅺 ⊠ 🅼 🔒 💻 🏊

LOUISA

▼▼ Super 8-Louisa �H
(606) 638-7888. **$56-$69.** 191 Falls Creek Dr. Jct US 23 and SR 3. Int corridors. **Pets:** Accepted.
🅰️🆂🅺 ⊠ 🅼 🔒

LOUISVILLE METROPOLITAN AREA

BROOKS

▼▼ Comfort Inn �H
(502) 957-6900. **$59-$265.** 149 Willabrook Dr. I-65, exit 121, just nw. Int corridors. **Pets:** $10 daily fee/pet. No service, supervision.
🅰️🆂🅺 ⊠ 🔒 💻 🏊 ⊠

HURSTBOURNE

▼▼▼ Drury Inn & Suites-Louisville �H
(502) 326-4170. **$82-$145.** 9501 Blairwood Rd. I-64, exit 15. Int corridors. **Pets:** Other species. Service with restrictions, supervision.
🅰️🆂🅺 ⊠ 🅼 🔒 💻 🏊

AAA ▼▼ **Red Roof Inn Louisville–East #034** 🅷
(502) 426-7621. **$50-$80, 14 day notice.** 9330 Blairwood Rd. I-64, exit 15, 0.3 mi nw of Hurstbourne Pkwy. Ext corridors. **Pets:** Accepted.
[SAVE] [✕] [♿M] [🛏]

JEFFERSONTOWN

AAA ▼▼▼ **Holiday Inn-Hurstbourne** 🅷
(502) 426-2600. **$95-$190.** 1325 S Hurstbourne Pkwy. I-64, exit 15, just n. Ext/int corridors. **Pets:** Accepted.
[SAVE] [✕] [♿M] [🛏] [💻] [🍴] [🌊] [✕]

▼▼▼ **Homestead Studio Suites Louisville–Alliant Drive** 🅷
(502) 267-4454. **$69-$259.** 1650 Alliant Dr. I-64, exit 17, just s. Int corridors. **Pets:** Other species. $25 daily fee/pet. Service with restrictions, crate.
[ASK] [✕] [♿M] [🛏] [💻] [🌊]

▼▼▼ **Jameson Inn Louisville East** 🅷
(502) 267-8100. **$83.** 1301 Kentucky Mills Dr. I-64, exit 17. Ext/int corridors. **Pets:** Medium. $15 daily fee/pet. Designated rooms, service with restrictions, supervision.
[ASK] [✕] [♿M] [🛏] [💻] [🌊] [✕]

AAA ▼▼ **Microtel Inn Louisville East** 🅷
(502) 266-6590. **$50-$65.** 1221 Kentucky Mills Dr. I-64, exit 17. Int corridors. **Pets:** Medium. $20 one-time fee/pet. Designated rooms, service with restrictions, supervision.
[SAVE] [✕] [♿M]

▼▼ **Super 8 Motel & Suites** 🅷
(502) 267-8889. **$50-$350.** 1501 Alliant Ave. I-64, exit 17, just e. Int corridors. **Pets:** Medium, other species. $20 daily fee/pet. Designated rooms, no service, supervision.
[ASK] [✕] [♿M] [🛏] [💻] [🌊]

LA GRANGE

▼▼▼ **Comfort Suites** 🅷
(502) 225-4125. **$63-$252, 14 day notice.** 1500 Crystal Dr E. I-71, exit 22, just e. Int corridors. **Pets:** Accepted.
[ASK] [✕] [♿M] [🛏] [💻] [🌊] [✕]

AAA ▼▼▼ **Holiday Inn Express** 🅷
(502) 222-5678. **$106.** 1001 Paige Pl. I-71, exit 22, just se. Int corridors. **Pets:** Accepted.
[SAVE] [✕] [🛏] [💻] [🌊]

LOUISVILLE

▼▼ ▼▼ **21C Museum Hotel** 🅷
(502) 217-6300. **$129-$299.** 700 W Main St. Jct 7th and Main sts. Int corridors. **Pets:** Accepted.
[ASK] [✕] [♿M] [💻] [🍴] [✕]

▼▼▼ **Aleksander House Bed and Breakfast** 🅱🅱 ❀
(502) 637-4985. **$109-$185, 3 day notice.** 1213 S 1st St. I-65, exit 135 (St Catherine St), just s. Int corridors. **Pets:** $25 one-time fee/pet. Designated rooms, service with restrictions, crate.
[ASK] [✕] [🛏] [💻]

AAA ▼▼ **Best Western Airport East Expo Center** 🅷 ❀
(502) 456-4411. **$69-$200.** 1921 Bishop Ln. I-264, exit 15B, westbound, 0.3 mi s; exit 15 eastbound. Int corridors. **Pets:** Other species. $25 one-time fee/pet. Service with restrictions, supervision.
[SAVE] [✕] [♿M] [🛏] [💻] [🌊]

▼▼▼ **Crowne Plaza Louisville** 🅷
(502) 367-2251. **$179.** 830 Phillips Ln. I-264, exit 11 (Fairgrounds/Expo Center Main Gate). Int corridors. **Pets:** $100 daily fee/pet. Service with restrictions, crate.
[ASK] [✕] [🛏] [💻] [🍴] [🌊]

▼▼▼ **Holiday Inn South-Airport** 🅷
(502) 964-3311. **$100-$160.** 2715 Fern Valley Rd. I-65, exit 128 (Fern Valley Rd), northeast corner. Int corridors. **Pets:** $35 one-time fee/room. Service with restrictions, crate.
[ASK] [✕] [♿M] [🛏] [💻] [🍴] [🌊]

▼▼▼ **Homewood Suites** 🅷
(502) 429-9070. **$79-$599.** 9401 Hurstbourne Trace. I-64, exit 15, 2.5 mi n. Int corridors. **Pets:** Large, other species. $100 one-time fee/room. Service with restrictions, crate.
[✕] [♿M] [🛏] [💻] [🌊] [✕]

▼▼▼ **Jameson Inn Airport South** 🅷
(502) 968-4100. **$93-$100.** 6515 Signature Dr. I-65, exit 128 (Fern Valley Rd), southeast corner. Int corridors. **Pets:** Accepted.
[ASK] [✕] [🛏] [💻] [🌊]

AAA ▼▼▼ **La Quinta Inn & Suites Airport & Expo-Louisville** 🅷 ❀
(502) 368-0007. **$64-$389.** 4125 Preston Hwy. I-65, exit 130, 1 mi n. Int corridors. **Pets:** Medium, other species. Service with restrictions, supervision.
[SAVE] [✕] [♿M] [🛏] [💻] [🌊]

▼▼▼ **Ramada Limited & Suites** 🅷
(502) 637-6336. **$60-$430.** 2912 Crittenden Dr. I-264, exit 11 (Fairgrounds/Expo Center Main Gate), 0.6 mi n. Int corridors. **Pets:** Other species. $15 one-time fee/room. Service with restrictions, supervision.
[ASK] [✕] [🛏] [💻] [🌊]

AAA ▼▼ **Red Roof Inn-Airport-Fairgrounds** 🅷
(502) 968-0151. **$50-$80, 14 day notice.** 4704 Preston Hwy. I-65, exit 130, northeast corner. Ext corridors. **Pets:** Accepted.
[SAVE] [✕] [🛏]

AAA ▼▼ **Red Roof Inn-Southeast-Fairgrounds** 🅷
(502) 456-2993. **$50-$80, 14 day notice.** 3322 Red Roof Inn Pl. I-264, 15B westbound, 0.3 mi s; exit 15 eastbound. Ext corridors. **Pets:** Medium, other species. Service with restrictions, crate.
[SAVE] [✕] [🛏]

▼▼▼ **Residence Inn by Marriott-Louisville Airport** 🅷
(502) 363-8800. **$195-$514.** 700 Phillips Ln. I-264, exit 11 (Fairgrounds/Expo Center Main Gate), 0.4 mi w. Int corridors. **Pets:** Other species. $100 one-time fee/room. Service with restrictions, crate.
[✕] [♿M] [🛏] [💻] [🌊] [✕]

▼▼▼ **Residence Inn by Marriott Louisville Downtown** 🅷
(502) 589-8998. **$170-$210.** 333 E Market St. Corner of Preston and E Market. Int corridors. **Pets:** Accepted.
[✕] [♿M] [🛏] [💻] [🌊]

▼▼▼ **Residence Inn by Marriott-Louisville NE** 🅷
(502) 412-1311. **$187-$201.** 3500 Springhurst Commons Dr. I-265, exit 32, 0.5 mi w on Westport Rd, then just n. Int corridors. **Pets:** Accepted.
[✕] [♿M] [🛏] [💻] [🌊] [✕]

▼▼▼ **Residence Inn Louisville East** 🅷
(502) 425-1821. **$157-$169.** 120 N Hurstbourne Pkwy. I-64, exit 15, 1.8 mi n. Ext corridors. **Pets:** Accepted.
[✕] [🛏] [💻] [🌊] [✕]

AAA ▼▼ ▼▼ **The Seelbach Hilton Louisville** 🅷 ❀
(502) 585-3200. **$109-$2000.** 500 4th St. I-65, exit 136C (Muhammad Ali), 0.3 mi w, then just s. Int corridors. **Pets:** Medium. $65 one-time fee/room. Service with restrictions, crate.
[SAVE] [✕] [♿M] [🛏] [💻] [🍴] [✕]

▼▼ ▼▼ **Sleep Inn Fairgrounds** 🅷 ❀
(502) 368-9597. **$69-$325.** 3330 Preston Hwy. I-264, exit 11 (Fairgrounds/Expo Center Main Gate), 0.5 mi e on Phillips Ln, then just n. Int corridors. **Pets:** Other species. $10 daily fee/room. Service with restrictions.
[ASK] [✕] [🛏] [💻] [🌊]

▼▼▼▼ Staybridge Suites by Holiday Inn H
(502) 244-9511. **$130-$140.** 11711 Gateworth Way. I-64, exit 17, just n. Int corridors. **Pets:** Accepted.
ASK ✕ ⟨M⟩ ⊟ ⟨⟩ ⟨⟩

SHEPHERDSVILLE

⟨AAA⟩ ▼▼▼▼ Best Western South H
(502) 543-7097. **$77-$89.** 211 S Lakeview Dr. I-65, exit 117 (SR 44 W), just se. Int corridors. **Pets:** Small. Service with restrictions, supervision.
SAVE ✕ ⊟ ⟨⟩ ⟨⟩

▼▼ Super 8 H
(502) 543-8870. **$46-$225, 14 day notice.** 275 Keystone Crossroads. I-65, exit 117 (SR 44 W), just w. Int corridors. **Pets:** Medium, dogs only. $10 daily fee/pet. No service, supervision.
ASK ✕ ⊟ ⟨⟩ ⟨⟩

SHIVELY

▼▼▼ Holiday Inn-Southwest H
(502) 448-2020. **Call for rates.** 4110 Dixie Hwy. I-264, exit 8B, just n on US 31 W and 60. Int corridors. **Pets:** Accepted.
✕ ⊟ ⟨⟩ ⟨†⟩ ⟨⟩

END METROPOLITAN AREA

MAYSVILLE

⟨AAA⟩ ▼▼▼ Best Western Maysville Inn H
(606) 759-5696. **$70, 7 day notice.** 1428 a US 68. Jct US 68 and SR 9 (AA Hwy). Ext corridors. **Pets:** Accepted.
SAVE ✕ ⟨M⟩ ⊟ ⟨⟩ ⟨⟩

▼▼ Super 8, Maysville KY H
(606) 759-8888. **$54-$113.** 550 Tucker Dr. Just e of US 68. Int corridors. **Pets:** Accepted.
ASK ✕ ⊟ ⟨⟩

MOREHEAD

⟨AAA⟩ ▼▼▼ Comfort Inn & Suites H
(606) 780-7378. **$72-$159.** 2650 Kentucky 801 N. I-64, exit 133, just s. Int corridors. **Pets:** Accepted.
SAVE ✕ ⟨M⟩ ⊟ ⟨⟩ ⟨⟩

⟨AAA⟩ ▼▼▼ Holiday Inn Express of Morehead H
(606) 784-5796. **$79-$119.** 110 Toms Dr. I-64, exit 137 (SR 32), just sw. Int corridors. **Pets:** Accepted.
SAVE ✕ ⟨M⟩ ⊟ ⟨⟩ ⟨⟩

MORTONS GAP

⟨AAA⟩ ▼▼▼ Best Western Pennyrile Inn H 🐾
(270) 258-5201. **$50-$64, 5 day notice.** White City Rd. Pennyrile Pkwy, exit 37 (US 41). Ext corridors. **Pets:** Medium. $7 one-time fee/pet. Service with restrictions, supervision.
SAVE ✕ ⊟ ⟨⟩ ⟨⟩

MOUNT VERNON

▼▼ Days Inn-Renfro Valley H
(606) 256-3300. **$45-$80.** 1630 Richmond St. I-75, exit 62, just n. Ext corridors. **Pets:** Small. $10 one-time fee/pet. Service with restrictions, supervision.
ASK ✕ ⊟ ⟨⟩

MUNFORDVILLE

▼▼▼ Super 8 H
(270) 524-4888. **Call for rates.** 88 Bull Run Rd. I-65, exit 65, 0.5 mi s. Int corridors. **Pets:** Accepted.
✕ ⊟ ⟨⟩

MURRAY

⟨AAA⟩ ▼▼▼ Best Western University Inn H
(270) 753-5353. **$60-$110.** 1503 N 12th St. 1.9 mi n on US 641. Ext corridors. **Pets:** Small, dogs only. $10 one-time fee/room. No service, crate.
SAVE ✕ ⊟ ⟨⟩ ⟨⟩

▼▼ Days Inn-Murray, KY H
(270) 753-6706. **$80-$100.** 517 S 12th St. 1 mi s on US 641. Ext corridors. **Pets:** Accepted.
✕ ⊟ ⟨⟩ ⟨⟩

OAK GROVE

▼▼▼ Holiday Inn Express H
(270) 439-0022. **$89, 7 day notice.** 12759 Ft Campbell Blvd. I-24, exit 86. Int corridors. **Pets:** Small. $10 daily fee/pet. Service with restrictions, supervision.
ASK ✕ ⟨M⟩ ⊟ ⟨⟩ ⟨⟩

⟨AAA⟩ ▼▼▼ Quality Inn @ Ft. Campbell H
(270) 439-3311. **$69-$89.** 201 Auburn St. I-24, exit 86, just s. Ext corridors. **Pets:** Medium. $20 daily fee/pet. Designated rooms, no service, supervision.
SAVE ✕ ⟨M⟩ ⊟ ⟨⟩ ⟨⟩

OWENSBORO

▼▼ Motel 6 #205 H
(270) 686-8606. **$37-$45.** 4585 Frederica St. US 60 Bypass, exit 4 at US 431, just n. Ext corridors. **Pets:** Other species. Service with restrictions, supervision.
✕ ⟨M⟩ ⊟ ⟨⟩

▼▼ Super 8-Owensboro H
(270) 685-3388. **$55-$90.** 1027 Goetz Dr. US 60 Bypass, exit 4 at US 431. Int corridors. **Pets:** Medium, dogs only. $10 daily fee/pet. Designated rooms, service with restrictions, supervision.
ASK ✕ ⟨M⟩ ⊟ ⟨⟩

OWINGSVILLE

▼▼ Super 8 Owingsville H
(606) 674-2200. **Call for rates.** 201 Williams Ave. I-64, exit 121, just n. Int corridors. **Pets:** Accepted.
✕ ⟨M⟩ ⊟

PADUCAH

⟨AAA⟩ ▼▼▼ Americas Best Value Inn H
(270) 575-9605. **$60-$70.** 5125 Old Cairo Rd. I-24, exit 3 (SR 305), just e. Ext corridors. **Pets:** Accepted.
SAVE ✕ ⊟

▼▼ Days Inn H
(270) 442-7500. **$50-$100.** 3901 Hinkleville Rd. I-24, exit 4 (US 60), just e. Ext corridors. **Pets:** Accepted.
ASK ✕ ⊟ ⟨⟩ ⟨⟩

▼▼▼ Drury Inn-Paducah H
(270) 443-3313. **$85-$124.** 3975 Hinkleville Rd. I-24, exit 4 (US 60), just e. Int corridors. **Pets:** Other species. Service with restrictions, supervision.
ASK ✕ ⊟ ⟨⟩ ⟨⟩

▼▼▼ Drury Suites-Paducah H
(270) 441-0024. **$100-$130.** 2930 James-Sanders Blvd. I-24, exit 4 (US 60), just w. Int corridors. **Pets:** Other species. Service with restrictions, supervision.
ASK ✕ ⟨M⟩ ⊟ ⟨⟩ ⟨⟩

▼▼▼▼ Holiday Inn Express **H**
(270) 442-8874. **Call for rates.** 3994 Hinkleville Rd. I-24, exit 4 (US 60), just e. Int corridors. **Pets:** Small, other species. Service with restrictions, supervision.

✕ 🕽 💻 ⊃

▼▼ Pear Tree Inn-Paducah **H**
(270) 444-7200. **$81-$101.** 5006 Hinkleville Rd. I-24, exit 4 (US 60), just w. Int corridors. **Pets:** Other species. Service with restrictions, supervision.

ASK ✕ &M 💻 ⊃

▼▼▼ Residence Inn by Marriott-Paducah **H** ❀
(270) 444-3966. **$123-$132.** 3900 Coleman Crossing Cir. I-24, exit 4 (US 60), just n. Int corridors. **Pets:** Other species. $75 one-time fee/room. Crate.

✕ &M 🕽 💻 ⊃ ✕

▼▼ Thrifty Inn **H**
(270) 444-0157. **$57-$90.** 5002 Hinkleville Rd. I-24, exit 4 (US 60), just w. Ext corridors. **Pets:** Other species. Service with restrictions, supervision.

ASK ✕ 💻 ⊃

RICHMOND

▼▼▼▼ Holiday Inn Express Hotel & Suites **H**
(859) 624-4055. **$89-$159.** 1990 Colby Taylor Dr. I-75, exit 87, just w. Int corridors. **Pets:** Accepted.

ASK ✕ &M 🕽 💻 ⊃

▼▼ Jameson Inn **H**
(859) 623-0063. **$83-$90.** 1007 Colby Taylor Dr. I-75, exit 87, just w. Int corridors. **Pets:** Accepted.

ASK ✕ &M 🕽 💻 ⊃

AAA▷ ▼▼ Super 8 **H** ❀
(859) 624-1550. **$60-$65, 7 day notice.** 107 N Keeneland Dr. I-75, exit 90. Int corridors. **Pets:** Very small. $10 daily fee/pet. Designated rooms, service with restrictions, supervision.

SAVE ✕ &M 🕽 💻

SCOTTSVILLE

AAA▷ ▼▼ Executive Inn **H**
(270) 622-7770. **$54.** 57 Burnley Rd. US 31 E, jct SR 231. Ext corridors. **Pets:** Small. $6 daily fee/pet. Service with restrictions.

SAVE ✕ 🕽 ⊃

SHELBYVILLE

AAA▷ ▼▼▼ Best Western Shelbyville Lodge **H**
(502) 633-4400. **$73-$109, 30 day notice.** 115 Isaac Shelby Dr. I-64, exit 32, 0.5 mi n on SR 55. Int corridors. **Pets:** $10 one-time fee/room. Service with restrictions, supervision.

SAVE ✕ 🕽 💻 ⊃

AAA▷ ▼▼▼ Holiday Inn Express **H**
(502) 647-0109. **$90, 14 day notice.** 110 Club House Dr. I-64, exit 35, just s. Int corridors. **Pets:** $20 one-time fee/room. Service with restrictions, crate.

SAVE ✕ &M 🕽 💻 ⊃

▼▼▼ Ramada **H**
(502) 633-9933. **$79-$129, 3 day notice.** 251 Breighton Cir. I-64, exit 32, just s. Int corridors. **Pets:** Accepted.

✕ &M 🕽 💻 ⊃

SMITHS GROVE

AAA ▼▼▼ Bryce Inn **M**
(270) 563-5141. **$49-$65.** 592 S Main St. I-65, exit 38, 0.3 mi w. Ext corridors. **Pets:** Medium, dogs only. $10 one-time fee/pet. Designated rooms, service with restrictions, supervision.

SAVE ✕ 🕽 💻 ⊃

SPARTA

▼▼▼ Ramada at the Kentucky Speedway **H**
(859) 567-7223. **$79-$129, 3 day notice.** 525 Dale Dr. I-71, exit 57, just w. Int corridors. **Pets:** Medium, other species. $25 one-time fee/room. Service with restrictions, crate.

ASK ✕ &M 🕽 💻 ⊃

VERSAILLES

▼▼▼ 1823 Historic Rose Hill Inn **BB**
(859) 873-5957. **$129-$184, 7 day notice.** 233 Rose Hill. Just s on SR 33 (S Main St), then just w. Ext/int corridors. **Pets:** Dogs only. $15 one-time fee/room. Designated rooms.

✕ 🕽 💻

WEST LIBERTY

▼▼ Days Inn **H**
(606) 743-4206. **Call for rates.** 1613 W Main St. Jct SR 519 and 460, just w. Int corridors. **Pets:** Accepted.

✕ &M 💻

WILLIAMSBURG

▼▼▼ Cumberland Inn **H**
(606) 539-4100. **$94.** 649 S 10th St. I-75, exit 11. Int corridors. **Pets:** Medium. $25 one-time fee/room. Designated rooms, service with restrictions, supervision.

ASK ✕ &M 🕽 💻 🍴 ⊃

WINCHESTER

AAA▷ ▼▼▼ Best Western-Country Squire **H**
(859) 744-7210. **$59-$109.** 1307 W Lexington Rd. I-64, exit 94 (US 60), 0.9 mi se. Ext corridors. **Pets:** Very small. $20 daily fee/pet. Designated rooms, service with restrictions, supervision.

SAVE ✕ 🕽 💻 ⊃

LOUISIANA

ALEXANDRIA

▼▼▼ La Quinta Inn & Suites Alexandria 🅷 ❋
(318) 442-3700. **$79-$129.** 6116 W Calhoun Dr. I-49, exit 90 (Air Base Rd), just w. Int corridors. **Pets:** Medium, other species. Service with restrictions, supervision.
(ASK) ✕ ♿M 🛏 💻 🐾

ⒶⒶⒶ ▼▼ Ramada Limited 🅷
(318) 448-1611. **$75-$93.** 742 MacArthur Dr. 0.4 mi s of jct SR 28 and US 71/165 (MacArthur Dr). Ext corridors. **Pets:** Accepted.
(SAVE) ✕ 🛏 💻 🐾

BATON ROUGE

ⒶⒶⒶ ▼▼▼ Best Western Richmond Suites Hotel–Baton Rouge 🅷
(225) 924-6500. **$109-$209.** 5668 Hilton Ave. I-10, exit 158, just ne. Int corridors. **Pets:** Medium. $100 one-time fee/room. Service with restrictions, crate.
(SAVE) ✕ 🛏 💻 🐾 ✕

ⒶⒶⒶ ▼▼▼ Chase Suites by Woodfin 🅷 ❋
(225) 927-5630. **$149-$209.** 5522 Corporate Blvd. I-10, exit 158, just n on College Dr, then just e. Ext corridors. **Pets:** Large, other species. $250 deposit/pet. Designated rooms, service with restrictions, supervision.
(SAVE) ✕ 🛏 💻 🐾 ✕

▼▼▼ Crowne Plaza Executive Center 🅷
(225) 925-2244. **$149-$209.** 4728 Constitution Ave. I-10, exit 158, just se on frontage road. Int corridors. **Pets:** Accepted.
(ASK) ✕ ♿M 🛏 💻 🍴 🐾

▼▼ La Quinta Inn Baton Rouge-Siegen Lane 🅷 ❋
(225) 291-6600. **$79-$109.** 10555 Rieger Rd. I-10, exit 163 (Siegen Ln), just n, then just e. Int corridors. **Pets:** Medium, other species. Service with restrictions, supervision.
(ASK) ✕ 🛏 💻 🐾

▼▼ La Quinta Inn Baton Rouge-University Area 🅷 ❋
(225) 924-9600. **$59-$115.** 2333 S Acadian Thruway. I-10, exit 157B. Ext corridors. **Pets:** Medium, other species. Service with restrictions, supervision.
(ASK) ✕ 🛏 💻 🐾

ⒶⒶⒶ ▼▼▼ Red Lion Hotel & Conference Center Baton Rouge 🅷
(225) 236-4000. **$129-$279, 3 day notice.** 2445 S Acadian Thruway. I-10, exit 157B, just n. Int corridors. **Pets:** Other species. $20 one-time fee/room. Service with restrictions, supervision.
(SAVE) ✕ 🛏 💻 🍴 🐾 ✕

▼▼▼ Residence Inn by Marriott-Baton Rouge-Siegen Lane 🅷
(225) 293-8700. **$187-$201.** 10333 N Mall Dr. I-10, exit 163 westbound, just s on Siegen Ln, then just e; exit eastbound, 0.5 mi to S Mall Dr, just e to Andrea (at Lowe's), then just n. Int corridors. **Pets:** Large, other species. $100 one-time fee/room. Service with restrictions, supervision.
✕ ♿M 🛏 💻 🐾 ✕

▼▼▼ Residence Inn by Marriott Baton Rouge-Towne Center at Cedar Lodge 🅷
(225) 925-9100. **$157-$169.** 7061 Commerce Cir. I-10, exit 158 (College), just n to Corporate Blvd, then 1.8 mi e. Int corridors. **Pets:** Medium, other species. $75 one-time fee/room. Service with restrictions, supervision.
✕ 🛏 💻 🐾 ✕

ⒶⒶⒶ ▼▼▼▼ Sheraton Baton Rouge Convention Center Hotel 🅷 ❋
(225) 242-2600. **$90-$226.** 102 France St. I-110, exit 1A (Government St), 0.8 mi w to St. James, then just s. Int corridors. **Pets:** Medium. No service.
(SAVE) ✕ 🛏 💻 🍴 🐾

▼▼ TownePlace Suites by Marriott 🅷
(225) 819-2112. **$167-$179.** 8735 Summa Ave. I-10, exit 162 (Bluebonnet Blvd), just s to Picardy, just w to Summa Ave, then 0.5 mi nw. Int corridors. **Pets:** Large, other species. $75 one-time fee/room. Service with restrictions, crate.
✕ ♿M 🛏 💻 🐾

BOSSIER CITY

▼▼▼ Hampton Inn 🅷
(318) 752-1112. **$94-$159.** 1005 Gould Dr. I-20, exit 21, 0.5 mi ne on service road. Int corridors. **Pets:** Small. Service with restrictions, crate.
✕ ♿M 🛏 💻 🐾

▼▼ Howard Johnson 🅷
(318) 742-6000. **Call for rates.** 1984 Airline Dr. I-20, exit 22 (Airline Dr), just n. Ext corridors. **Pets:** Accepted.
✕ 🛏 💻 🍴 🐾

▼▼ La Quinta Inn Bossier City 🅷 ❋
(318) 747-4400. **$49-$109.** 309 Preston Blvd. I-20, exit 21, just n. Ext corridors. **Pets:** Medium, other species. Service with restrictions, supervision.
(ASK) ✕ 🛏 💻 🐾

▼▼ Microtel Inn & Suites 🅷
(318) 742-1840. **$65-$119.** 2713 Village Ln. I-20, exit 22 (Airline Dr), just s, then just w. Int corridors. **Pets:** Medium, other species. $25 one-time fee/pet. Service with restrictions, supervision.
(ASK) ✕ ♿M 🛏 💻

▼▼ Quality Inn & Suites 🅷
(318) 742-7890. **$94-$195.** 2717 Village Ln. I-20, exit 22 (Airline Dr), just s, then just w. Int corridors. **Pets:** Medium, other species. $25 one-time fee/pet. No service, supervision.
(ASK) ✕ ♿M 🛏 💻 🐾

▼▼▼ Residence Inn by Marriott-Shreveport/Bossier City 🅷
(318) 747-6220. **$197-$211.** 1001 Gould Dr. I-20, exit 21, just ne. Ext corridors. **Pets:** Accepted.
✕ 🛏 💻 🐾 ✕

BREAUX BRIDGE

▼▼ Holiday Inn Express of Breaux Bridge 🅷
(337) 667-8913. **Call for rates.** 2942 H Grand Point Hwy. I-10, exit 115, just n. Int corridors. **Pets:** Accepted.
✕ ♿M 🛏 💻 🐾

CONVENT

AAA  **Poche Plantation Bed & Breakfast and RV Resort** BB
(225) 562-7728. **$119-$198, 15 day notice.** 6554 Louisiana Hwy 44. Jct SR 44 and 641; 10.1 mi s of Sunshine Bridge (SR 70), then 10.2 mi n. Ext/int corridors. **Pets:** $25 one-time fee/pet. Service with restrictions, supervision.
SAVE ⊠ 🛏 🖵 🖘

DELHI

AAA ▼▼▼ **Best Western Delhi Inn** M
(318) 878-5126. **$65-$85.** 135 Snider Rd.. Ext corridors. **Pets:** Dogs only. $10 daily fee/pet. Service with restrictions, supervision.
SAVE ⊠ 🛏 🖵 🖘

DERIDDER

AAA ▼▼▼ **Stagecoach Inn** H
(337) 462-0022. **$75.** 505 E 1st St. 2 mi on east side; between US 171 and 190. Ext corridors. **Pets:** Small, dogs only. $25 daily fee/pet. Service with restrictions, supervision.
SAVE ⊠ ᵭᴹ 🛏 🖵 🖘

HAMMOND

AAA ▼▼ **Best Western University Inn** H
(985) 345-0003. **$85-$115, 3 day notice.** 46053 N Puma Dr. I-55, exit 32 (Wardline/University), just e. Ext corridors. **Pets:** Accepted.
SAVE ⊠ 🛏 🖵 🖘

AAA ▼▼▼ **Michabelle Inn** CI
(985) 419-0550. **$75-$125, 4 day notice.** 1106 S Holly St. I-12, exit 40 (US 51), 0.8 mi n, just e on Old Covington Hwy, then n, follow signs. Ext/int corridors. **Pets:** Accepted.
SAVE ⊠ 🛏 🖵 ⊪ ☎

HOUMA

▼▼▼ **La Quinta Inn & Suites Houma** H ❀
(985) 879-1646. **$59-$139.** 189 Synergy Center Blvd. US 90, exit 202, 3.4 mi s on Main St to Martin Luther King Jr Blvd, then just w. Int corridors. **Pets:** Medium, other species. Service with restrictions, supervision.
⊠ ᵭᴹ 🛏 🖵 🖘

KINDER

AAA ▼▼▼ **Best Western Inn At Coushatta** H
(337) 738-4800. **$89-$129.** 12102 US Hwy 165 N. 5 mi n of jct US 190/165. Int corridors. **Pets:** Small, other species. $25 deposit/pet. Service with restrictions, supervision.
SAVE ⊠ 🛏 🖵 🖘

LAFAYETTE

▼▼▼▼ **Drury Inn & Suites-Lafayette** H
(337) 262-0202. **$75-$145.** 120 Alcide Dominique. I-10, exit 101 (SR 182), just s on University Ave, then just w. Int corridors. **Pets:** Other species. Service with restrictions, supervision.
ASK ⊠ ᵭᴹ 🛏 🖵 🖘

AAA ▼▼▼ **Holiday Inn Lafayette** H
(337) 233-6815. **Call for rates.** 2032 NE Evangeline Thruway. I-10, exit 103A, just s. Ext/int corridors. **Pets:** Medium. $30 one-time fee/room. Designated rooms, no service, supervision.
SAVE ⊠ 🛏 🖵 ⊪ 🖘 ⊠

▼▼ **Jameson Inn of Lafayette** H
(337) 291-2916. **$93-$100.** 2200 NE Evangeline Thruway. I-10, exit 103A, just s. Int corridors. **Pets:** Accepted.
ASK ⊠ 🛏 🖵 🖘

▼▼▼▼ **La Quinta Inn & Suites Lafayette Oil Center** H ❀
(337) 291-1088. **$89-$115.** 1015 W Pinhook Rd. I-10, exit 101 (University Ave), 3.5 mi to SR 182 (Pinhook Rd), then 0.5 mi w. Int corridors. **Pets:** Medium, other species. Service with restrictions, supervision.
ASK ⊠ 🛏 🖵 🖘

▼▼ **Pear Tree Inn By Drury** H
(337) 289-9907. **$75-$105.** 126 Alcide Dominique. I-10, exit 101, just s. Int corridors. **Pets:** Other species. Service with restrictions, supervision.
ASK ⊠ 🖵 🖘

▼▼ **Ramada Inn** H
(337) 235-0858. **$75-$105.** 120 E Kaliste Saloom Rd. I-10, exit 103A, 4.4 mi e on US 90 (Evangeline Thruway), then 1 mi s. Ext corridors. **Pets:** Small. $20 daily fee/pet. No service, supervision.
ASK ⊠ 🛏 🖵 🖘

LAKE CHARLES

▼▼ **America's Best Suites** H
(337) 439-2444. **$99-$160.** 401 Lakeshore Dr. I-10, exit 29 (business district/tourist bureau) eastbound; exit 30B (Ryan St business district) westbound, just s to Pine, then just w. Int corridors. **Pets:** Accepted.
ASK ⊠ 🛏 🖵 🖘

▼▼ **Baymont Inn & Suites** H
(337) 310-7666. **Call for rates.** 1004 MLK Hwy (171 N). I-10, exit 33, just n. Ext corridors. **Pets:** Accepted.
⊠ 🛏 🖵

AAA ▼▼▼ **Best Western Richmond Suites Hotel** H
(337) 433-5213. **$98, 5 day notice.** 2600 Moeling St. I-10, exit 33, just n. Ext/int corridors. **Pets:** Medium. $75 one-time fee/pet. Designated rooms, service with restrictions, supervision.
SAVE ⊠ 🛏 🖵 🖘 ⊠

LIVONIA

▼▼ **Oak Tree Inn** H
(225) 637-2590. **$59.** 7875 Airline Hwy. Jct SR 77 and US 190, 0.3 mi w. Ext corridors. **Pets:** Accepted.
ASK ⊠ 🛏 🖵

MANY

AAA ▼▼▼ **Cypress Bend Resort Golf, Spa & Conference Center** H
(318) 590-1500. **$129-$159, 7 day notice.** 2000 Cypress Bend Pkwy. 13 mi w on SR 6, 3 mi s on SR 191, 3 mi w on Cypress Bend Dr, then 1.5 mi w. Int corridors. **Pets:** Small. $50 one-time fee/room. Service with restrictions, supervision.
SAVE ⊠ ᵭᴹ 🛏 🖵 ⊪ 🖘 ⊠

MINDEN

AAA ▼▼ **Best Western Minden Inn** H
(318) 377-1001. **$80-$90.** 1411 Sibley Rd. I-20, exit 47, just n. Ext corridors. **Pets:** Large. $15 daily fee/pet. Service with restrictions, supervision.
SAVE ⊠ 🛏 🖵 🖘

MONROE

▼▼ **Holiday Inn Hotel & Suites Conference Center** H
(318) 387-5100. **$69-$149.** 1051 Hwy 165 Bypass. I-20, exit 118B, just ne on US 165 service road. Ext/int corridors. **Pets:** Other species. $20 one-time fee/room. No service.
⊠ 🛏 🖵 ⊪ 🖘 ⊠

▼▼ **La Quinta Inn Monroe** H ❀
(318) 322-3900. **$52-$79.** 1035 Martin Luther King Dr. I-20, exit 118B, just ne on US 165 service road. Ext corridors. **Pets:** Medium, other species. Service with restrictions, supervision.
ASK ⊠ 🛏 🖵 🖘

▼▼▼▼ Residence Inn by Marriott 🄷
(318) 387-0210. **$137-$147.** 4960 Millhaven Rd. I-20, exit 120, just n of Pecanland Mall. Int corridors. **Pets:** Accepted.
⊠ 🄼 🛏 💻 ⇌ 🐾

MORGAN CITY

▼▼▼▼ Holiday Inn-Morgan City 🄷 ❀
(985) 385-2200. **$92-$119.** 520 Roderick St. 1.5 mi s of jct US 90 and SR 70. Ext corridors. **Pets:** Medium, other species. $50 one-time fee/room. Service with restrictions, supervision.
ASK ⊠ 🄼 🛏 💻 ¶¶ ⇌

NATCHITOCHES

AAA⁷ ▼▼▼ Best Western Natchitoches Inn 🄷
(318) 352-6655. **$81.** 5131 University Pkwy. I-49, exit 138, just e. Int corridors. **Pets:** Accepted.
SAVE ⊠ 🛏 💻 ⇌

NEW ORLEANS METROPOLITAN AREA

GRETNA

▼▼▼ La Quinta Inn New Orleans (West Bank) 🄷 ❀
(504) 368-5600. **$65-$109.** 50 Terry Pkwy. S US 90 business route, exit 9A (Terry Pkwy); N US 90 (Westbank Expwy), exit 9 (Terry Pkwy/General DeGaulle). Ext corridors. **Pets:** Medium, other species. Service with restrictions, supervision.
ASK ⊠ 🛏 💻 ⇌

KENNER

▼▼▼▼ La Quinta Inn New Orleans (Airport) 🄷 ❀
(504) 466-1401. **$69-$119.** 2610 Williams Blvd. I-10, exit 223A (Williams Blvd), 0.3 mi s. Int corridors. **Pets:** Medium, other species. Service with restrictions, supervision.
ASK ⊠ 🛏 💻 ⇌

LA PLACE

AAA⁷ ▼▼▼ Best Western La Place Inn 🄷
(985) 651-4000. **$120, 3 day notice.** 4289 Main St. I-10, exit 209, just s. Ext corridors. **Pets:** Medium. $25 daily fee/pet. Service with restrictions, supervision.
SAVE ⊠ 🛏 💻 ⇌

METAIRIE

▼▼▼ La Quinta Inn New Orleans (Causeway) 🄷 ❀
(504) 835-8511. **$59-$99.** 3100 I-10 Service Rd. I-10, exit 228 (Causeway Blvd), just s. Ext corridors. **Pets:** Medium, other species. Service with restrictions, supervision.
ASK ⊠ 🛏 💻 ⇌

▼▼▼ La Quinta Inn New Orleans (Veterans) 🄷 ❀
(504) 456-0003. **$59-$89.** 5900 Veterans Memorial Blvd. I-10, exit 225, just n. Ext corridors. **Pets:** Medium, other species. Service with restrictions, supervision.
ASK ⊠ 💻 ⇌

AAA⁷ ▼▼▼▼ Residence Inn by Marriott-Metairie 🄷
(504) 832-0888. **$206-$221.** 3 Galleria Blvd. I-10, exit 228 (Causeway Blvd), just se to 36th St, then just e. Int corridors. **Pets:** Accepted.
SAVE ⊠ 🛏 💻 ⇌ 🐾

AAA⁷ ▼▼▼▼ Sheraton Metairie New Orleans 🄷
(504) 837-6707. **$99-$159.** 4 Galleria Blvd. I-10, exit 228 (Causeway Blvd), just s to 36th St, just e, then just n. Int corridors. **Pets:** Accepted.
SAVE ⊠ 💻 ¶¶

NEW ORLEANS

AAA⁷ ▼▼▼▼ Best Western St. Christopher Hotel 🄷
(504) 648-0444. **$79-$299, 3 day notice.** 114 Magazine St. Between Canal and Common sts. Int corridors. **Pets:** $50 one-time fee/room. Service with restrictions, supervision.
SAVE ⊠ 💻

AAA⁷ ▼▼▼▼ The Bienville House Hotel 🄷
(504) 529-2345. **$79-$209, 3 day notice.** 320 Decatur St. Between Conti and Bienville sts. Ext/int corridors. **Pets:** Accepted.
SAVE ⊠ 🛏 💻 ⇌

▼▼▼▼ Drury Inn & Suites-New Orleans 🄷
(504) 529-7800. **$90-$221.** 820 Poydras St. Between Baronne and Carondelet sts. Int corridors. **Pets:** Other species. Service with restrictions, supervision.
ASK ⊠ 🄼 🛏 💻 ⇌

AAA⁷ ▼▼▼▼ Elysian Fields Inn 🄱🄱
(504) 948-9420. **$109-$269, 15 day notice.** 930 Elysian Fields Ave. I-610, exit 3 (Elysian Fields Ave), 1.2 mi s. Int corridors. **Pets:** $25 daily fee/pet. Service with restrictions, crate.
SAVE ⊠

AAA⁷ ▼▼▼▼ Hilton New Orleans Riverside 🄷
(504) 561-0500. **$99-$419, 3 day notice.** 2 Poydras St. At the Mississippi River. Int corridors. **Pets:** Small. $75 one-time fee/room. Service with restrictions, supervision.
SAVE ⊠ 🄼 🛏 💻 ¶¶ ⇌ 🐾

AAA⁷ ▼▼▼ ▼▼▼ Hotel Monteleone 🄷 ❀
(504) 523-3341. **$119-$399, 3 day notice.** 214 Royal St. Between Iberville and Bienville sts. Int corridors. **Pets:** Medium. $100 one-time fee/room. Designated rooms, service with restrictions, crate.
SAVE ⊠ 🛏 💻 ¶¶ ⇌

AAA⁷ ▼▼▼ ▼▼▼ The Iberville Suites 🄷
(504) 523-2400. **$89-$449, 3 day notice.** 910 Iberville St. Between Burgundy and Dauphine sts. Int corridors. **Pets:** Accepted.
SAVE ⊠ 🛏 💻 ⇌

▼▼▼▼ La Quinta Inn & Suites New Orleans–Downtown Flagship 🄷 ❀
(504) 598-9977. **$69-$169.** 301 W Camp St. Corner of Gravier and Camp sts. Int corridors. **Pets:** Medium, other species. Service with restrictions, supervision.
ASK ⊠ 🄼 🛏 💻 ⇌

▼▼▼▼ Lexington Hotel O & Suites 🄷
(504) 299-9900. **Call for rates.** 1300 Canal St. Jct Saratoga St. Int corridors. **Pets:** Accepted.
⊠ 🛏 💻

AAA⁷ ▼▼▼ ▼▼▼ Loews New Orleans Hotel 🄷 ❀
(504) 595-3300. **$149-$279.** 300 Poydras St. Corner of S Peters St. Int corridors. **Pets:** Other species. $25 one-time fee/room. Designated rooms, service with restrictions, supervision.
SAVE ⊠ 💻 ¶¶ ⇌ 🐾

AAA⁷ ▼▼▼▼ Omni Royal Crescent Hotel 🄷
(504) 527-0006. **$109-$299, 3 day notice.** 535 Gravier St. 0.3 mi w of Canal St. Int corridors. **Pets:** Accepted.
SAVE ⊠ 🛏 💻 🐾

▲▲▲ ▼▼▼ ▼▼▼ Omni Royal Orleans Hotel H ❖
(504) 529-5333. **$109-$359, 3 day notice.** 621 St. Louis St. At Royal and St. Louis sts. Int corridors. **Pets:** Other species. $50 one-time fee/room. Service with restrictions, crate.
SAVE ✕ 🖥 💻 🍽 🐾

▲▲▲ ▼▼▼ Residence Inn by Marriott H
(504) 522-1300. **$143-$215.** 345 St. Joseph St. Jct Tchoupitoulas St; in Warehouse District. Int corridors. **Pets:** Large. $100 one-time fee/room. Service with restrictions, supervision.
SAVE ✕ ⬛M 🖥 💻 🐾 🐾

▲▲▲ ▼▼▼ ▼▼▼ The Ritz-Carlton New Orleans H ❖
(504) 524-1331. **$459, 3 day notice.** 921 Canal St. Between Dauphine and Burgundy sts. Int corridors. **Pets:** Other species. Service with restrictions, crate.
SAVE ✕ ⬛M 💻 🍽 🐾

▲▲▲ ▼▼▼ ▼▼▼ Royal Sonesta Hotel New Orleans H
(504) 586-0300. **$129-$329, 3 day notice.** 300 Bourbon St. Garage entrance on Conti or Bienville sts. Int corridors. **Pets:** Small. $50 one-time fee/room. Service with restrictions, supervision.
SAVE ✕ ⬛M 🖥 🍽 🐾

▼▼▼ St. James Hotel H
(504) 304-4000. **Call for rates.** 330 Magazine St. Jct Magazine and Natchez sts. Int corridors. **Pets:** Accepted.
✕ 💻 🍽

▲▲▲ ▼▼▼ ▼▼▼ The Sheraton New Orleans Hotel H ❖
(504) 525-2500. **$89-$429.** 500 Canal St. Between Camp and Magazine sts. Int corridors. **Pets:** Medium. Service with restrictions, supervision.
SAVE ✕ ⬛M 💻 🍽 🐾 🐾

▲▲▲ ▼▼▼ ▼▼▼ Westin New Orleans Canal Place H ❖
(504) 566-7006. **$99-$309.** 100 Iberville St. At Canal Place, near Mississippi River. Int corridors. **Pets:** Medium. Designated rooms, service with restrictions, supervision.
SAVE ✕ 🖥 💻 🍽 🐾

▲▲▲ ▼▼▼ ▼▼▼ W French Quarter H
(504) 581-1200. **Call for rates.** 316 Chartres St. Between Conti and Bienville sts. Int corridors. **Pets:** Accepted.
SAVE ✕ 🍽 🐾

▲▲▲ ▼▼▼ ▼▼▼ Windsor Court Hotel H ❖
(504) 523-6000. **$199-$600.** 300 Gravier St. Between Magazine and Tchoupitoulas sts. Int corridors. **Pets:** Small, dogs only. $250 deposit/room. Service with restrictions.
SAVE ✕ 🖥 🍽 🐾 🐾

▲▲▲ ▼▼▼ ▼▼▼ W New Orleans H
(504) 525-9444. **Call for rates.** 333 Poydras St. Jct Poydras and S Peters sts; close to Riverfront area/convention center. Int corridors. **Pets:** Accepted.
SAVE ✕ ⬛M 🍽 🐾

SLIDELL

▼▼▼ ▼▼▼ La Quinta Inn New Orleans/Slidell H ❖
(985) 643-9770. **$59-$99.** 794 E I-10 Service Rd. I-10, exit 266 (Gause Blvd), just se. Ext corridors. **Pets:** Medium, other species. Service with restrictions, supervision.
ASK ✕ 🖥 💻 🐾

END METROPOLITAN AREA

OAKDALE

▲▲▲ ▼▼▼ ▼▼▼ Best Western Oakdale Inn H
(318) 335-3155. **$89-$150.** 2030 US Hwy 165 S. 1.7 mi s of jct US 165 and SR 10. Int corridors. **Pets:** Accepted.
SAVE ✕ 🖥 💻 🐾

PONCHATOULA

▼▼ ▼▼ Microtel Inn & Suites H
(985) 370-7378. **$69-$109.** 727 W Pine St. I-55, exit 26, just e on SR 22. Int corridors. **Pets:** Accepted.
ASK ✕ ⬛M 🖥 💻 🐾

PORT ALLEN

▲▲▲ ▼▼ ▼▼ Best Western Magnolia Manor H
(225) 344-3638. **$80-$100.** 234 Lobdell Hwy. I-10, exit 151, just n. Int corridors. **Pets:** Accepted.
SAVE ✕ 🖥 💻 🐾

ST. FRANCISVILLE

▼▼ ▼▼ Lake Rosemound Inn Bed & Breakfast BB
(225) 635-3176. **$80-$135.** 10473 Lindsey Ln. 13 mi n on SR 61, then 3 mi w using Rosemound Loop, Sligo Rd, Lake Rosemound Rd and Lindsey Ln, follow signs. Ext/int corridors. **Pets:** No service.
✕ 🐾

SCOTT

▲▲▲ ▼▼ ▼▼ Howard Johnson H
(337) 593-0849. **Call for rates.** 103 Harold Gauthe Dr. I-10, exit 97. Int corridors. **Pets:** Medium. $10 daily fee/pet. Designated rooms, service with restrictions, supervision.
SAVE ✕ 🖥 💻 🐾

SHREVEPORT

▼▼ ▼▼ ▼▼ Holiday Inn Downtown H
(318) 222-7717. **$95-$133.** 102 Lake St. I-20, exit 19A (Spring St), just n. Int corridors. **Pets:** Accepted.
ASK ✕ ⬛M 🖥 💻 🍽 🐾

▼▼ ▼▼ ▼▼ Holiday Inn Financial Plaza H
(318) 688-3000. **$100-$160.** 5555 Financial Plaza. I-20, exit 10 (Pines Rd), 1 mi e on frontage road. Int corridors. **Pets:** Accepted.
ASK ✕ 🖥 💻 🍽 🐾 🐾

▼▼ ▼▼ La Quinta Inn & Suites Shreveport H ❖
(318) 671-1100. **$69-$119.** 6700 Financial Cir. I-20, exit 10 (Pines Rd), 0.5 mi e on frontage road. Int corridors. **Pets:** Medium, other species. Service with restrictions, supervision.
ASK ✕ ⬛M 🖥 💻 🐾

▼▼ ▼▼ Ramada Inn H
(318) 631-2000. **$99-$169, 3 day notice.** 5101 Westwood Park Dr. I-20, exit 13 (Monkhouse Dr), just ne. Int corridors. **Pets:** Accepted.
ASK ✕ 🖥 💻 🐾

▼▼ ▼▼ ▼▼ Residence Inn by Marriott H
(318) 635-8000. **$128-$137.** 4910 W Monkhouse Dr. I-20, exit 13, just nw. Int corridors. **Pets:** Medium. $100 one-time fee/room. Service with restrictions, crate.
✕ ⬛M 🖥 💻 🐾 🐾

SPRINGFIELD

▼▼ ▼▼ ▼▼ The Villas at Carter Plantation H
(225) 294-7555. **Call for rates.** 23475 Carter Trace. I-12, exit 32, 2.7 mi s on SR 43, 1.1 mi e on SR 42, then 1.5 mi s on Carter Cemetery Rd. Ext corridors. **Pets:** Accepted.
✕ 🖥 💻 🍽 🐾

VILLE PLATTE

Best Western Ville Platte H
(337) 360-9961. **$78-$86.** 1919 E Main St (Hwy 167). Jct SR 1168. Int corridors. **Pets:** Small, dogs only. $5 daily fee/pet. Service with restrictions, crate.

SAVE ⊠ 🛢 🔲 🏊

WEST MONROE

Jameson Inn H
(318) 361-0750. **$85-$105.** 213 Constitution Dr. I-20, exit 114 (Thomas Rd), just s to Constitution Dr, then just w. Int corridors. **Pets:** Small, other species. $15 one-time fee/pet. Service with restrictions, supervision.

ASK ⊠ 🛢 🔲 🏊

Quality Inn & Suites-West Monroe H
(318) 387-2711. **$70-$115.** 503 Constitution Dr. I-20, exit 114 (Thomas Rd), just s to Constitution Dr, then 0.6 mi w. Int corridors. **Pets:** Medium, other species. $25 one-time fee/room. Service with restrictions, crate.

ASK ⊠ 🅜 🛢 🔲 🏊

WINNFIELD

Best Western Winnfield Inn M
(318) 628-3993. **Call for rates.** 700 W Court St. Jct US 84 and 167, just e. Ext corridors. **Pets:** Other species. $10 daily fee/pet. Service with restrictions, crate.

SAVE ⊠ 🛢 🔲 🍴 🏊

WINNSBORO

Best Western Winnsboro M
(318) 435-2000. **$65-$85, 3 day notice.** 4198 Front St. Just nw of jct SR 15 and 864. Ext corridors. **Pets:** Accepted.

SAVE ⊠ 🛢 🔲 🏊

ZACHARY

Best Western Zachary Inn H
(225) 658-2550. **$86-$91, 3 day notice.** 4030 Hwy 19. Just s of jct SR 64. Int corridors. **Pets:** Medium, other species. $50 one-time fee/room. Service with restrictions, supervision.

SAVE ⊠ 🛢 🔲 🏊

MAINE

AUBURN

▼▼ A Fireside Inn & Suites 🅷
(207) 777-1777. **$90-$250.** 1777 Washington St. I-95 (Maine Tpke), exit 75, 0.5 mi s on US 202, SR 4 and 100. Ext/int corridors. **Pets:** Dogs only. $10 daily fee/pet. Designated rooms, service with restrictions, supervision.
🆎 ⊠ 🕻 💻 🍽 ⊷

▼ Sleepy Time Motel Ⓜ ✿
(207) 783-1435. **$72-$99.** 46 Danville Corner Rd. I-95 (Maine Tpke), exit 75, 0.5 mi ne on US 202, then just e. Ext corridors. **Pets:** Medium. $10 daily fee/room. Service with restrictions, supervision.
🆎 ⊠ 🕻

AUGUSTA

⟨AAA⟩ ▼▼▼ Best Western Senator Inn & Spa 🅷
(207) 622-5804. **$109-$279.** 284 Western Ave. I-95, exit 109 (Augusta-Winthrop) northbound; exit 109A southbound, on US 202, SR 11 and 100. Ext/int corridors. **Pets:** Small. $50 deposit/room, $9 one-time fee/pet. Designated rooms, service with restrictions, supervision.
💾 ⊠ 🕻 💻 🍽 ⊷ ⊠

▼▼ Comfort Inn 🅷
(207) 623-1000. **$89-$199.** 281 Civic Center Dr. I-95, exit 112B northbound; exit 112 southbound. Int corridors. **Pets:** Designated rooms, service with restrictions.
🆎 ⊠ 🕻 💻 ⊷

▼▼ Holiday Inn 🅷
(207) 622-4751. **$95-$199, 3 day notice.** 110 Community Dr. I-95, exit 112A northbound; exit 112 southbound, just s on SR 8, 11 and 27. Int corridors. **Pets:** Other species. $100 deposit/room. Designated rooms, service with restrictions, supervision.
🆎 ⊠ 🕻 🕻 💻 🍽 ⊷

BANGOR

▼▼ A Fireside Inn & Suites 🅷 ✿
(207) 942-1234. **$89-$169, 7 day notice.** 570 Main St. I-395, exit 3B. Int corridors. **Pets:** Medium, other species. $10 daily fee/pet. Designated rooms, service with restrictions, supervision.
🆎 ⊠ 🕻 💻 🍽

⟨AAA⟩ ▼▼▼ Best Western White House 🅷 ✿
(207) 862-3737. **$125-$160.** 155 Littlefield Ave. I-95, exit 180 (Coldbrook Rd), 5.5 mi s of downtown. Ext/int corridors. **Pets:** Large. $10 daily fee/pet. Designated rooms, service with restrictions, supervision.
💾 ⊠ 🕻 💻 ⊷ ⊠

▼▼ Comfort Inn Bangor 🅷
(207) 942-7899. **$89-$149.** 750 Hogan Rd. I-95, exit 187 (Hogan Rd), 0.5 mi nw. Int corridors. **Pets:** $10 one-time fee/pet. Service with restrictions, supervision.
🆎 ⊠ 🕻 💻

▼▼ Econo Lodge Ⓜ
(207) 945-0111. **$65-$149, 14 day notice.** 327 Odlin Rd. I-95, exit 182B, just e on US 2 and SR 100. Int corridors. **Pets:** Accepted.
🆎 ⊠ 🕻 🕻 💻 ⊷

⟨AAA⟩ ▼▼▼▼ Four Points by Sheraton Bangor 🅷
(207) 947-6721. **$140-$190.** 308 Godfrey Blvd. At Bangor International Airport. Int corridors. **Pets:** Accepted.
💾 ⊠ 🕻 🕻 💻 🍽 ⊷

▼▼ Holiday Inn-Bangor 🅷
(207) 947-0101. **$119-$169.** 404 Odlin Rd. I-95, exit 182B, jct Odlin Rd and I-395. Int corridors. **Pets:** Designated rooms, service with restrictions, supervision.
🆎 ⊠ 🕻 🕻 💻 🍽 ⊷

▼▼ Howard Johnson Inn 🅷
(207) 942-5251. **Call for rates.** 336 Odlin Rd. I-95, exit 182B, jct Odlin Rd and I-395. Int corridors. **Pets:** Accepted.
⊠ 🕻 💻 🍽 ⊷

▼▼ Ramada 🅷
(207) 947-6961. **Call for rates.** 357 Odlin Rd. I-95, exit 182B, jct Odlin Rd and I-395. Int corridors. **Pets:** Accepted.
⊠ 🕻 💻 🍽 ⊷

▼▼ Riverside Inn 🅷
(207) 973-4100. **Call for rates.** 495 State St. Adjacent to Eastern Maine Medical Center. Int corridors. **Pets:** Medium. $5 daily fee/pet. Designated rooms, service with restrictions, supervision.
⊠ 🕻 💻

BAR HARBOR

⟨AAA⟩ ▼ Anchorage Motel Ⓜ
(207) 288-3959. **$69-$139, 4 day notice.** 51 Mt Desert St. In town on SR 3. Ext corridors. **Pets:** $15 daily fee/pet. Service with restrictions, supervision.
💾 ⊠ 🕻

⟨AAA⟩ ▼▼▼ Atlantic Oakes By-The-Sea 🅷 ✿
(207) 288-5801. **$78-$209, 14 day notice.** 119 Eden St. 1.8 mi w on SR 3. Ext/int corridors. **Pets:** Small. $35 one-time fee/room. Designated rooms, service with restrictions, supervision.
💾 ⊠ 🕻 💻 ⊷ ⊠

▼▼ A Wonder View Inn & Suites 🅷
(207) 288-3358. **$59-$249, 3 day notice.** 50 Eden St. 0.5 mi w on SR 3. Ext corridors. **Pets:** Accepted.
⊠ 🕻 💻 🍽 ⊷

⟨AAA⟩ ▼▼▼ Balance Rock Inn 1903 🅱🅱
(207) 288-2610. **$155-$625, 14 day notice.** 21 Albert Meadow. S on Main St, just e; center. Ext/int corridors. **Pets:** Other species. $35 daily fee/pet. Designated rooms, service with restrictions, supervision.
💾 ⊠ ⊷

(AAA) ▼▼▼ Best Western Inn 🇭
(207) 288-5823. **$90-$160.** 452 State Hwy 3. 4.8 mi w. Ext corridors. **Pets:** Medium, dogs only. $10 daily fee/room. Designated rooms, service with restrictions, supervision.

⟨SAVE⟩ ⟨✕⟩ 🛠 💻 ⟨≈⟩

▼▼ Days Inn 🇲
(207) 288-3321. **Call for rates.** 120 Eden St. 1 mi w on SR 3. Ext corridors. **Pets:** Accepted.

⟨✕⟩ 🛠 💻

▼ Hutchins Mountain View Cottages 🇨🇦 ❀
(207) 288-4833. **$64-$98, 14 day notice.** 286 State Rt 3. On SR 3, 4 mi w. Ext corridors. **Pets:** Other species. Service with restrictions.

⟨✕⟩ 🛠 💻 ⟨≈⟩ ⟨X⟩ ⟨Z⟩

BATH

(AAA) ▼▼▼ Holiday Inn Bath/Brunswick 🇭
(207) 443-9741. **Call for rates.** 139 Richardson St. 0.3 mi s on US 1. Int corridors. **Pets:** Designated rooms, service with restrictions, crate.

⟨SAVE⟩ ⟨✕⟩ ⟨&M⟩ 🛠 💻 ⟨¶⟩ ⟨≈⟩ ⟨X⟩

BELFAST

▼▼ Belfast Harbor Inn 🇭 ❀
(207) 338-2740. **$59-$159.** 91 Searsport Ave (Rt 1). On US 1, 1.2 mi n from jct SR 3. Ext/int corridors. **Pets:** Dogs only. $10 daily fee/pet. Designated rooms, service with restrictions, supervision.

⟨ASK⟩ ⟨✕⟩ ⟨≈⟩

▼▼▼ Comfort Inn Ocean's Edge 🇭
(207) 338-2090. **$79-$389.** 159 Searsport Ave. On US 1, 2 mi n from jct SR 3. Int corridors. **Pets:** $10 daily fee/pet. Designated rooms, service with restrictions, supervision.

⟨ASK⟩ ⟨✕⟩ ⟨&M⟩ 🛠 💻 ⟨¶⟩ ⟨≈⟩ ⟨X⟩

▼ Gull Motel 🇲 ❀
(207) 338-4030. **$59-$99, 3 day notice.** 196 Searsport Ave. On US 1, 3 mi n from jct SR 3. Ext corridors. **Pets:** Medium, dogs only.

⟨ASK⟩ ⟨✕⟩ 🛠

▼▼ Seascape Motel & Cottages 🇲
(207) 338-2130. **$59-$189, 3 day notice.** 202 Searsport Ave. US 1, 3 mi n from jct SR 3. Ext corridors. **Pets:** Small, dogs only. $20 one-time fee/pet. Designated rooms, service with restrictions, supervision.

⟨✕⟩ 🛠 💻 ⟨≈⟩

BETHEL

▼▼▼ Briar Lea Inn & The Jolly Drayman English Pub 🇨🇮
(207) 824-4717. **$99-$159, 14 day notice.** 150 Mayville Rd (US 2). 1 mi n of jct US 2, SR 5 and 26. Int corridors. **Pets:** Accepted.

⟨ASK⟩ ⟨✕⟩ ⟨¶⟩

▼▼ The Inn At the Rostay 🇲
(207) 824-3111. **$65-$140, 14 day notice.** 186 Mayville Rd (US 2). On US 2, 2 mi e. Ext corridors. **Pets:** Large, other species. $10 daily fee/pet. Designated rooms, no service, supervision.

⟨ASK⟩ ⟨✕⟩ 🛠 ⟨¶⟩ ⟨≈⟩

BIDDEFORD

▼▼▼ Comfort Suites-Biddeford 🇭 ❀
(207) 294-6464. **$69-$299.** 45 Barra Rd. I-95 (Maine Tpke), exit 32 (SR 111), 0.4 mi ne, then just n. Int corridors. **Pets:** Large, other species. $45 one-time fee/room. Designated rooms, service with restrictions.

⟨ASK⟩ ⟨✕⟩ ⟨&M⟩ 🛠 💻 ⟨≈⟩

BOOTHBAY

▼▼ The Boothbay Resort 🇲 ❀
(207) 633-3411. **$99-$229, 30 day notice.** 301 Adams Pond Rd. US 1, 9 mi s on SR 27, then just w. Ext/int corridors. **Pets:** Dogs only. Designated rooms, service with restrictions, crate.

⟨✕⟩ 🛠 💻 ⟨≈⟩ ⟨Z⟩

▼▼▼ Kenniston Hill Inn B & B Inc 🇧🇧
(207) 633-2159. **$140-$180, 14 day notice.** 988 Wiscasset Rd. US 1 to SR 27, 10 mi s; jct SR 27 S and Country Club Rd. Ext/int corridors. **Pets:** Small, dogs only. $45 one-time fee/room. Designated rooms, service with restrictions, supervision.

⟨ASK⟩ ⟨✕⟩ ⟨Z⟩

(AAA) ▼ White Anchor Inn 🇲
(207) 633-3788. **$59-$95.** 609 Wiscasset Rd. US 1 to SR 27, 7.5 mi s. Ext/int corridors. **Pets:** Large, other species. $15 one-time fee/pet. Designated rooms, service with restrictions, supervision.

⟨SAVE⟩ ⟨✕⟩ 🛠

BOOTHBAY HARBOR

(AAA) ▼▼ Flagship Inn 🇲
(207) 633-5094. **$74-$144, 3 day notice.** 200 Townsend Ave. On SR 27, just n of jct SR 96. Ext corridors. **Pets:** Medium. $10 daily fee/pet. Designated rooms, service with restrictions, supervision.

⟨SAVE⟩ ⟨✕⟩ 🛠 ⟨≈⟩

▼▼▼ Welch House Inn 🇧🇧
(207) 633-3431. **Call for rates.** 56 McKown St. Center. Ext/int corridors. **Pets:** Accepted.

⟨✕⟩

BRIDGTON

▼▼ Pleasant Mountain Inn 🇲 ❀
(207) 647-4505. **$70-$195, 7 day notice.** 656 N High St. On US 302, 3 mi w of center. Ext corridors. **Pets:** Dogs only. $10 daily fee/pet. Service with restrictions, crate.

⟨ASK⟩ ⟨✕⟩ 🛠 💻 ⟨¶⟩

BRUNSWICK

(AAA) ▼▼▼ Captain Daniel Stone Inn 🇭
(207) 725-9898. **Call for rates.** 10 Water St. Just n of center. Int corridors. **Pets:** Accepted.

⟨SAVE⟩ ⟨✕⟩ 🛠 💻

(AAA) ▼▼ Days Inn Brunswick 🇭
(207) 725-8883. **$65-$175.** 224 Bath Rd. US 1, exit Cooks Corner, left on Bath Rd, then 0.3 mi w. Int corridors. **Pets:** Dogs only. $25 daily fee/pet. Designated rooms, service with restrictions, supervision.

⟨SAVE⟩ ⟨✕⟩ ⟨&M⟩ 🛠 💻

▼▼ Viking Motor Inn 🇲
(207) 729-6661. **Call for rates.** 287 Bath Rd. US 1, exit Cooks Corner, left on Bath Rd, then 1 mi w. Ext/int corridors. **Pets:** Accepted.

⟨✕⟩ 🛠 💻

BRYANT POND

▼ Mollyockett Motel & Swim Spa 🇲
(207) 674-2345. **$70-$95.** 1132 S Main St. 1.3 mi n on SR 26 from jct SR 219. Ext/int corridors. **Pets:** Dogs only. Service with restrictions, supervision.

⟨ASK⟩ ⟨✕⟩ 🛠 💻 ⟨¶⟩ ⟨≈⟩ ⟨X⟩

BUCKSPORT

▼ Bucksport Motor Inn 🇲
(207) 469-3111. **$59-$109.** 70 Main St. On US 1; center. Ext corridors. **Pets:** $10 one-time fee/room. Designated rooms, service with restrictions, supervision.

⟨ASK⟩ ⟨✕⟩ 🛠 💻

CAMDEN

The Camden Riverhouse Hotel & Inns H ❀
(207) 236-0500. **$109-$250, 14 day notice.** 11 Tannery Ln. Center. Int corridors. **Pets:** Dogs only. $15 daily fee/pet. Designated rooms, service with restrictions, supervision.
SAVE ⊠ 🛏 ⬛ 🏊

The Inns at Blackberry Common BB
(207) 236-6060. **$125-$285, 14 day notice.** 82 Elm St. Center. Ext/int corridors. **Pets:** Medium, dogs only. $25 one-time fee/pet. Designated rooms, service with restrictions, supervision.
⊠ 🛏 ⬛ 🌀

Lord Camden Inn H ❀
(207) 236-4325. **$119-$299, 4 day notice.** 24 Main St. Center. Int corridors. **Pets:** Dogs only. $25 daily fee/pet. Service with restrictions, supervision.
SAVE ⊠ 🛏 ⬛

CAPE ELIZABETH

Inn By The Sea H ❀
(207) 799-3134. **$199-$819, 14 day notice.** 40 Bowery Beach Rd (SR 77). On SR 77, 7 mi s. Ext/int corridors. **Pets:** Other species. Designated rooms, service with restrictions, supervision.
SAVE ⊠ 🛏M 🛏 ⬛ 🏊 🌀

CARIBOU

Caribou Inn & Convention Center H
(207) 498-3733. **$98-$146.** 19 Main St. 3 mi s on US 1. Int corridors. **Pets:** Other species. Service with restrictions.
SAVE ⊠ 🛏 ⬛ 🍴 🏊 🌀

Crown Park Inn H
(207) 493-3311. **$64-$94.** 30 Access Hwy. On SR 89, 0.4 mi e of jct US 1. Int corridors. **Pets:** Accepted.
ASK ⊠ 🛏

CASTINE

Pentagoet Inn CI
(207) 326-8616. **$95-$245, 14 day notice.** 26 Main St. Center. Int corridors. **Pets:** Accepted.
⊠ 🍴 🐾 🌀 🌀

DEDHAM

The Lucerne Inn CI
(207) 843-5123. **$79-$219.** 2517 Main Rd. On US 1A. Int corridors. **Pets:** Medium. $25 daily fee/pet. Designated rooms, service with restrictions.
SAVE ⊠ 🛏 ⬛ 🍴 🏊

EAGLE LAKE

Overlook Motel & Lakeside Cabins M
(207) 444-4535. **$76.** 3232 Aroostook Rd. On SR 11; center. Ext/int corridors. **Pets:** Other species. $5 daily fee/pet. Supervision.
⊠ 🛏 ⬛ 🌀

EDGECOMB

Sheepscot Harbour Village & Resort H ❀
(207) 882-6343. **$79-$349, 7 day notice.** 306 Eddy Rd. 1 mi w on US 1; on east side of Davies Bridge, 1 mi e of Wiscasset. Ext/int corridors. **Pets:** Other species. $15 daily fee/room. Service with restrictions.
ASK ⊠ 🛏 ⬛ 🍴

ELLSWORTH

Holiday Inn-Acadia Park Hotel H
(207) 667-9341. **$59-$199.** 215 High St. Jct US 1, 1A and SR 3. Int corridors. **Pets:** $20 daily fee/pet. Service with restrictions, supervision.
SAVE ⊠ 🛏M 🛏 ⬛ 🍴 🏊 🌀

Jasper's Motel H
(207) 667-5318. **$53-$116, 3 day notice.** 200 High St. 1 mi e on US 1 and SR 3. Ext corridors. **Pets:** Accepted.
SAVE ⊠ 🛏 🍴

Twilite Motel M ❀
(207) 667-8165. **$54-$120.** 147 Bucksport Rd. Jct US 1A, 1.5 mi w on US 1/SR 3. Ext corridors. **Pets:** Small. $10 daily fee/room. Designated rooms, service with restrictions, supervision.
SAVE ⊠ 🛏 ⬛

FREEPORT

Best Western Freeport Inn H ❀
(207) 865-3106. **$99-$209.** 31 US 1 S. I-295, exit 17, 1 mi n. Ext/int corridors. **Pets:** Other species. Designated rooms, service with restrictions.
SAVE ⊠ 🛏 ⬛ 🍴 🏊

Captain Briggs House B & B BB
(207) 865-1868. **$100-$230, 5 day notice.** 8 Maple Ave. Just n of downtown, then just w. Int corridors. **Pets:** Dogs only. No service.
ASK ⊠ 🌀

Econo Lodge M
(207) 865-3777. **$59-$169.** 537 US Rt 1. I-295, exit 20, 0.3 mi s. Ext corridors. **Pets:** Large. $10 daily fee/room. No service.
SAVE ⊠

White Cedar Inn BB ❀
(207) 865-9099. **$130-$230, 7 day notice.** 178 Main St. I-295, exit 22, 0.5 mi e, then just n on US 1. Ext/int corridors. **Pets:** Dogs only. $25 one-time fee/room. Designated rooms, service with restrictions, supervision.
⊠ 🌀

GREENVILLE

Chalet Moosehead Lakefront Motel M
(207) 695-2950. **$73-$145, 7 day notice.** 12 N Birch St. 1.5 mi w on SR 15. Ext corridors. **Pets:** Accepted.
⊠ 🛏 ⬛ 🌀

Kineo View Motor Lodge M
(207) 695-4470. **$69-$199.** 50 Overlook Dr. 2.5 mi s on SR 15; gravel access road from highway. Ext corridors. **Pets:** Other species. $10 daily fee/room. Designated rooms, service with restrictions, supervision.
SAVE ⊠ 🛏 ⬛

HANCOCK

Le Domaine Inn CI
(207) 422-3395. **$150-$225, 14 day notice.** US Rt 1, #1513. On US 1, 9 mi e of Ellsworth; center. Ext corridors. **Pets:** Accepted.
⊠ 🍴 🐾

HOULTON

Shiretown Inn & Suites H
(207) 532-9421. **$89-$135.** 282 North St. I-95, exit 302, 0.3 mi n on US 1. Ext/int corridors. **Pets:** $10 daily fee/pet. Designated rooms, service with restrictions, crate.
ASK ⊠ 🛏 ⬛ 🍴 🏊

KENNEBUNK

ᗺᗺᗺ ᗫᗫᗫ The Lodge at Kennebunk Ⓜ ❖
(207) 985-9010. **$59-$150, 3 day notice.** 95 Alewive Rd. I-95 (Maine Tpke), exit 25 (Kennebunk), just n on SR 35. Ext corridors. **Pets:** Other species. $15 daily fee/pet. Designated rooms, service with restrictions, supervision.
ⓈⒶⓋⒺ ⊠ 🛏 💻 ⊶ ⊠

ᗫᗫᗫ Turnpike Motel Ⓜ
(207) 985-4404. **Call for rates.** 77 Old Alewive Rd. I-95 (Maine Tpke), exit 25, just e on SR 35, then just n. Ext/int corridors. **Pets:** Accepted.
ⓈⒶⓋⒺ ⊠ 🛏 💻

KENNEBUNKPORT

ᗺᗺᗺ ᗫᗫᗫ The Captain Jefferds Inn 🅱🅱 ❖
(207) 967-2311. **$130-$375, 14 day notice.** 5 Pearl St. From Dock Square, 0.3 mi s on Ocean Ave, just ne; corner of Pearl and Pleasant sts. Ext/int corridors. **Pets:** Dogs only. $30 daily fee/pet. Designated rooms.
ⓈⒶⓋⒺ ⊠ 🛏

ᗺᗺᗺ ᗫᗫᗫ The Colony Hotel Ⓗ ❖
(207) 967-3331. **$199-$500, 7 day notice.** 140 Ocean Ave. From Dock Square, 1 mi s. Int corridors. **Pets:** Other species. $25 daily fee/pet.
ⓈⒶⓋⒺ ⊠ 🛏 🍴 ⊶ ⊠

ᗫᗫᗫᗫ Lodge At Turbat's Creek Ⓜ
(207) 967-8700. **$79-$199, 14 day notice.** 7 Turbat Rd. From Dock Square, 0.5 mi se on Maine St, 0.6 mi ne on Wildes, then just se. Ext corridors. **Pets:** Large. $25 one-time fee/room. Designated rooms, service with restrictions, supervision.
ⒶⓈⓀ ⊠ ♿ 🛏 ⊶

ᗺᗺᗺ ᗫᗫᗫ The Yachtsman Lodge & Marina Ⓜ
(207) 967-2511. **$179-$450, 14 day notice.** 57 Ocean Ave. From Dock Square, just s. Ext corridors. **Pets:** Accepted.
ⓈⒶⓋⒺ ⊠ 🛏 💻 ⊠

KITTERY

ᗺᗺᗺ ᗫᗫᗫ The Coachman Inn Ⓗ
(207) 439-4434. **$73-$169.** 380 US Rt 1. I-95, exit 2, 1 mi n. Ext/int corridors. **Pets:** $10 daily fee/pet. Designated rooms, service with restrictions, supervision.
ⓈⒶⓋⒺ ⊠ ♿ 🛏 ⊶

LINCOLNVILLE

ᗫᗫ Abbingtons Seaview Motel & Cottages Ⓜ ❖
(207) 236-3471. **$69-$149, 5 day notice.** 4 Seaview Dr. US 1, 1.2 mi s of jct SR 173. Ext corridors. **Pets:** Other species. $15 daily fee/pet. Designated rooms, service with restrictions, supervision.
ⒶⓈⓀ ⊠ 🛏 💻 ⊶

ᗫᗫ Pine Grove Cottages Ⓒ🅰 ❖
(207) 236-2929. **$85-$195, 7 day notice.** 2076 Atlantic Hwy. US 1, 2 mi s of jct SR 173. Ext corridors. **Pets:** Other species. $5 daily fee/pet. Service with restrictions, crate.
⊠ 🛏 💻

LUBEC

ᗫᗫ The Eastland Motel Ⓜ
(207) 733-5501. **$68-$78.** 395 County Rd. Jct US 1 and SR 189, 8.4 mi e on SR 189. Ext/int corridors. **Pets:** Accepted.
⊠ 🛏

MACHIAS

ᗺᗺᗺ ᗫᗫ The Bluebird Motel Ⓜ
(207) 255-3332. **$75-$85, 7 day notice.** Dublin St. On US 1, 1 mi s. Ext corridors. **Pets:** Medium, other species. Designated rooms, service with restrictions, supervision.
ⓈⒶⓋⒺ ⊠ ♿ 🛏

ᗺᗺᗺ ᗫᗫᗫ Machias Motor Inn Ⓜ
(207) 255-4861. **$69-$109.** 103 Main St. 0.5 mi e on US 1. Ext corridors. **Pets:** Dogs only. $5 daily fee/pet. Designated rooms, service with restrictions, supervision.
ⓈⒶⓋⒺ ⊠ 🛏 💻

MEDWAY

ᗫᗫ Katahdin Shadows Motel Ⓜ
(207) 746-5162. **Call for rates.** 2166 Medway Rd. I-95, exit 244, 1.5 mi w on SR 157. Ext corridors. **Pets:** Accepted.
⊠ 🛏 ⊶ ⊠

MILFORD

ᗫᗫ Milford Motel On The River Ⓜ
(207) 827-3200. **$59-$115, 3 day notice.** 174 Main Rd. 0.5 mi n on US 2. Ext/int corridors. **Pets:** Medium, dogs only. $50 deposit/room. Service with restrictions, supervision.
ⒶⓈⓀ ⊠ 🛏 💻

MILLINOCKET

ᗫᗫ America's Best Value Heritage Inn Ⓗ
(207) 723-9777. **$79-$119.** 935 Central St. 0.8 mi e on SR 11 and 157. Int corridors. **Pets:** Medium. $10 daily fee/pet. Service with restrictions, supervision.
ⒶⓈⓀ ⊠ 🛏 💻 ⊶

NAPLES

ᗫᗫᗫ Augustus Bove House 🅱🅱
(207) 693-6365. **$99-$250, 30 day notice.** 11 Sebago Rd. Corner of US 302 and SR 114. Int corridors. **Pets:** Medium, dogs only. $10 daily fee/pet. Designated rooms, service with restrictions, supervision.
ⒶⓈⓀ ⊠ 🛏 💻

NEWCASTLE

ᗫᗫᗫ The Newcastle Inn Ⓒ🅸 ❖
(207) 563-5685. **$155-$255, 14 day notice.** 60 River Rd. From jct US 1 and River Rd, 0.5 mi nw. Ext/int corridors. **Pets:** Medium, dogs only. $100 deposit/pet, $25 daily fee/pet. Designated rooms, service with restrictions, crate.
⊠ 🍴 ⓩ

OGUNQUIT

ᗫᗫ Studio East Motor Inn Ⓜ
(207) 646-7297. **$59-$199, 7 day notice.** 267 Main St. On US 1; center. Ext corridors. **Pets:** Accepted.
⊠ 🛏 ⊶

OLD ORCHARD BEACH

ᗺᗺᗺ ᗫᗫ Sea View Motel Ⓗ
(207) 934-4180. **$55-$300, 14 day notice.** 65 W Grand Ave. 0.5 mi w on SR 9 (W Grand Ave). Ext corridors. **Pets:** Medium, dogs only. $100 deposit/pet, $10 daily fee/pet. Designated rooms, supervision.
ⓈⒶⓋⒺ ⊠ 🛏 💻 ⊶

ORONO

ᗺᗺᗺ ᗫᗫᗫ Best Western Black Bear Inn & Conference Center Ⓗ
(207) 866-7120. **$99-$169.** 4 Godfrey Dr. I-95, exit 193 (Stillwater Ave). Int corridors. **Pets:** $10 daily fee/pet. Service with restrictions, supervision.
ⓈⒶⓋⒺ ⊠ ♿ 🛏 💻

ᗫᗫ University Inn Academic Suites Ⓗ
(207) 866-4921. **$69-$119.** 5 College Ave. I-95, exit 191, 1.6 mi n on US 2; 8 mi n of Bangor. Int corridors. **Pets:** Dogs only. Designated rooms, supervision.
⊠ 🛏 💻 ⊶

PORTLAND

◇◇◇ ▼▼▼▼ Clarion Portland H
(207) 774-5611. **$129-$229.** 1230 Congress St. I-295, exit 5, w on SR 22. Int corridors. **Pets:** $50 one-time fee/pet. Supervision.
SAVE ✕ ⑤M 🔒 🖵 ¶¶ ➰

◇◇◇ ▼▼▼▼ Eastland Park Hotel H ❀
(207) 775-5411. **$71-$207.** 157 High St. At Congress Square; center. Int corridors. **Pets:** $30 daily fee/room. Service with restrictions.
SAVE ✕ 🔒 🖵 ¶¶ ✕

◇◇◇ ▼▼▼▼ Embassy Suites Hotel H
(207) 775-2200. **$110-$290.** 1050 Westbrook St. At Portland International Jetport. Int corridors. **Pets:** Medium. $50 one-time fee/pet. Designated rooms, service with restrictions, crate.
SAVE ✕ ⑤M 🔒 🖵 ¶¶ ➰ ✕

▼▼▼▼ Hilton Garden Inn Portland Downtown Waterfront H ❀
(207) 780-0780. **$159-$359.** 65 Commercial St. In the Old Port; across from Casco Bay ferry terminal. Int corridors. **Pets:** $50 one-time fee/room. Designated rooms, service with restrictions, supervision.
✕ ⑤M 🔒 🖵 ¶¶ ➰

◇◇◇ ▼▼▼▼ Holiday Inn-West H
(207) 774-5601. **$120-$220.** 81 Riverside St. I-95, exit 48. Int corridors. **Pets:** $35 one-time fee/room. Service with restrictions, supervision.
SAVE ✕ ⑤M 🔒 🖵 ¶¶ ➰ ✕

▼▼▼▼ Howard Johnson Plaza Hotel H
(207) 774-5861. **$80-$225.** 155 Riverside St. I-95 (Maine Tpke), exit 48, jct SR 25. Int corridors. **Pets:** $50 deposit/room. Service with restrictions.
✕ 🔒 🖵 ¶¶ ➰

▼▼▼▼ La Quinta Inn & Suites Portland H ❀
(207) 871-0611. **$55-$179.** 340 Park Ave. I-295, exit 5A southbound; exit 5 northbound, e on SR 22. Int corridors. **Pets:** Medium, other species. Service with restrictions, supervision.
ASK ✕ ⑤M 🔒 🖵 ➰

◇◇◇ ▼▼▼▼ ▼▼▼▼ Portland Harbor Hotel H
(207) 775-9090. **$179-$379.** 468 Fore St. In the Old Port. Int corridors. **Pets:** Accepted.
SAVE ✕ ⑤M 🔒 ¶¶

PRESQUE ISLE

◇◇◇ ▼▼▼ Presque Isle Inn & Convention Center H
(207) 764-3321. **$88-$150.** 116 Main St. 1 mi s on US 1. Int corridors. **Pets:** Other species. Service with restrictions.
SAVE ✕ 🔒 🖵 ¶¶ ➰

RANGELEY

◇◇◇ ▼▼▼ Rangeley Saddleback Inn H ❀
(207) 864-3434. **$85-$225.** 2303 Main St. On SR 4, just s of village. Ext corridors. **Pets:** Large. $10 daily fee/room. Designated rooms, service with restrictions, supervision.
SAVE ✕ ⑤M 🔒 🖵 ¶¶ ➰

ROCKLAND

◇◇◇ ▼▼▼ Trade Winds Motor Inn H
(207) 596-6661. **$64-$224.** 2 Park Dr. On US 1; center. Ext/int corridors. **Pets:** Dogs only. $100 deposit/room. Designated rooms, service with restrictions, supervision.
SAVE ✕ 🖵 ¶¶ ➰ ✕

ROCKPORT

◇◇◇ ▼▼▼ The Country Inn At Camden/Rockport H ❀
(207) 236-2725. **$99-$219.** 8 Country Inn Way. Jct SR 90, 0.9 mi n on US 1. Ext/int corridors. **Pets:** Medium, other species. $10 daily fee/pet. Designated rooms, service with restrictions, supervision.
SAVE ✕ 🔒 🖵 ➰ ✕

◇◇◇ ▼▼▼ Glen Cove Inn & Suites M
(207) 594-4062. **$69-$199.** 866 Commercial St. Jct SR 90, 3 mi s on US 1. Ext corridors. **Pets:** Dogs only. $100 deposit/room. Designated rooms, service with restrictions, supervision.
SAVE ✕ 🔒 ➰

RUMFORD

◇◇◇ ▼▼▼ Linnell Motel & RestInn Conference Center H
(207) 364-4511. **$55-$95.** 986 Prospect Ave. 2 mi w, just off US 2. Ext/int corridors. **Pets:** Accepted.
SAVE ✕ 🔒 🖵 ✕

SACO

◇◇◇ ▼▼▼▼ Hampton Inn H
(207) 282-7222. **$79-$199.** 48 Industrial Park Rd. I-95 (Maine Tpke), exit 36 (I-195), exit 1 (Industrial Park Rd), just ne. Int corridors. **Pets:** Other species. Designated rooms, service with restrictions, supervision.
SAVE ✕ ⑤M 🔒 🖵

◇◇◇ ▼▼▼▼ Holiday Inn Express Hotel & Suites H
(207) 286-9600. **$80-$309.** 352 North St (SR 112). I-95 (Maine Tpke), exit 36 (I-195), exit 1 (Industrial Park Rd), 0.6 mi sw to SR 112, then 0.4 mi nw. Int corridors. **Pets:** Accepted.
SAVE ✕ ⑤M 🔒 🖵 ➰

◇◇◇ ▼▼ Saco Motel M
(207) 284-6952. **$50-$90, 3 day notice.** 473 Main St. I-95 (Maine Tpke), exit 36 (I-195), exit 2A (US 1), just sw. Ext corridors. **Pets:** Medium, dogs only. $10 daily fee/pet. Service with restrictions, supervision.
SAVE ✕ 🔒 ➰

▼▼ Wagon Wheel Motel M
(207) 284-6387. **Call for rates.** 726 Portland Rd (US 1). I-95 (Maine Tpke), exit 36 (I-195), 1.5 mi se to US 1, then 0.7 mi ne. Ext corridors. **Pets:** Accepted.
✕ 🔒 🖵 ➰

SANFORD

▼▼ Super 8 H
(207) 324-8823. **Call for rates.** 1892 Main St (Rt 109). I-95 (Maine Tpke), exit 19, 7 mi nw. Int corridors. **Pets:** Accepted.
✕ 🔒 🖵

SCARBOROUGH

▼▼ Extended StayAmerica Portland-Scarborough H
(207) 883-0554. **$52-$119.** 2 Ashley Dr. I-95, exit 42, just n. Int corridors. **Pets:** Other species. $25 daily fee/pet. Service with restrictions, crate.
ASK ✕ 🔒 🖵

◇◇◇ ▼▼▼▼ Homewood Suites Portland H ❀
(207) 775-2700. **$139-$229.** 200 Southborough Dr. I-95, exit 45, left on Maine Mall Rd (becomes Payne Rd), then left. Int corridors. **Pets:** Other species. $25 daily fee/room. Designated rooms, service with restrictions, crate.
SAVE ✕ ⑤M 🔒 🖵 ➰ ✕

▼▼ Pride Motel & Cottages CA
(207) 883-4816. **$65-$215, 7 day notice.** 677 US Rt 1. I-95 (Maine Tpke), exit 36, 0.5 mi e to US 1, then 4.5 mi n. Ext corridors. **Pets:** Other species. $15 daily fee/room. Service with restrictions, supervision.
✕ 🔒 ➰ ✕

WWW Residence Inn by Marriott H
(207) 883-0400. **$159-$204.** 800 Roundwood Dr. I-95 (Maine Tpke), exit 42, 1.5 mi n on Payne Rd. Int corridors. **Pets:** Accepted.
X ⅄M 🖥 💻 ➿ ⊠

WWW TownePlace Suites by Marriott H ✿
(207) 883-6800. **$99-$179.** 700 Roundwood Dr. I-95 (Maine Tpke), exit 42, 1.5 mi n on Payne Rd. Int corridors. **Pets:** Other species. $75 one-time fee/room. Service with restrictions, crate.
X ⅄M 🖥 💻 ➿

SKOWHEGAN

AAA WWW Belmont Motel M
(207) 474-8315. **$60-$100.** 273 Madison Ave. 1 mi n on US 201. Ext corridors. **Pets:** Accepted.
SAVE X ⅄M 🖥 💻 ➿

SOUTHPORT

AAA WWW Ocean Gate Resort H
(207) 633-3321. **$89-$399, 7 day notice.** 70 Ocean Gate Rd. SR 27, 2.5 mi s of Boothbay Harbor, 0.5 mi s of bridge to Southport Island. Ext corridors. **Pets:** Accepted.
SAVE X 🖥 💻 ➿ ⊠

SOUTH PORTLAND

AAA WWWW Best Western Merry Manor Inn H
(207) 774-6151. **$110-$190.** 700 Main St. I-95 (Maine Tpke), exit 45, 1.3 mi e to US 1. Ext/int corridors. **Pets:** Accepted.
SAVE X ⅄M 🖥 💻 ⑪ ➿ ⊠

AAA WWW Comfort Inn H
(207) 775-0409. **$89-$209.** 90 Maine Mall Rd. I-95 (Maine Tpke), exit 45, 1 mi n. Int corridors. **Pets:** Other species. $25 one-time fee/room. Service with restrictions, supervision.
SAVE X ⅄M 🖥 💻

AAA WWW Days Inn Portland-South Portland H
(207) 772-3450. **$49-$189.** 461 Maine Mall Rd. I-95 (Maine Tpke), exit 45. Int corridors. **Pets:** Accepted.
SAVE X 🖥 💻 ➿

WWWW Hampton Inn Hotel H
(207) 773-4400. **$89-$259.** 171 Philbrook Ave. I-95 (Maine Tpke), exit 45, just ne. Int corridors. **Pets:** Medium, other species. Designated rooms, service with restrictions, supervision.
X ⅄M 🖥 💻 ➿ ⊠

WWWW Holiday Inn Express & Suites H ✿
(207) 775-3900. **Call for rates.** 303 Sable Oaks Dr. I-95 (Maine Tpke), exit 45, just n on Maine Mall Rd, then just w on Running Hill Rd. Int corridors. **Pets:** Other species. $20 one-time fee/room. Service with restrictions, supervision.
X 🖥 💻 ➿

WWW Howard Johnson Hotel H
(207) 775-5343. **$84-$189.** 675 Main St. I-95 (Maine Tpke), exit 45, 1.3 mi e to US 1. Int corridors. **Pets:** Accepted.
ASK X 🖥 💻 ➿

AAA WWWW Portland Marriott Hotel & Golf Resort H
(207) 871-8000. **$179-$209.** 200 Sable Oaks Dr. I-95 (Maine Tpke), exit 45, just n on Maine Mall Rd, then just w on Running Hill Rd. Int corridors. **Pets:** Large, dogs only. $35 one-time fee/room. Designated rooms, service with restrictions, supervision.
SAVE X ⅄M 🖥 💻 ⑪ ➿ ⊠

AAA WWWW Wyndham Portland Airport Hotel H ✿
(207) 775-6161. **$99-$339.** 363 Maine Mall Rd. I-95 (Maine Tpke), exit 45. Int corridors. **Pets:** $50 deposit/room. Service with restrictions, supervision.
SAVE X 💻 ⑪ ➿ ⊠

SPRUCE HEAD

WWW Craignair Inn CI ✿
(207) 594-7644. **$82-$160, 14 day notice.** 5 Third St. 2.5 mi w on SR 73, 1.5 mi s on Clark Island Rd; 10 mi s of Rockland. Ext/int corridors. **Pets:** $10 daily fee/room. Designated rooms, service with restrictions, supervision.
X ⑪

WATERVILLE

AAA WWWW Best Western Waterville Inn H
(207) 873-3335. **$89-$170.** 356 Main St. I-95, exit 130 (Main St). Int corridors. **Pets:** Other species. Designated rooms, service with restrictions, supervision.
SAVE X 🖥 💻 ⑪ ➿ ⊠

WELLS

WWW Ne'r Beach Motel M ✿
(207) 646-2636. **$49-$229, 14 day notice.** 395 Post Rd (Rt 1). I-95 (Maine Tpke), exit 19, jct SR 109/US 1, 2.7 mi s. Ext corridors. **Pets:** Medium, other species. $200 deposit/room, $10 one-time fee/pet. Designated rooms, supervision.
ASK X 🖥 💻 ➿ ⊠

WEST FORKS

AAA WWW Inn by the River CI
(207) 663-2181. **Call for rates.** 2777 US Rt 201. Center. Int corridors. **Pets:** Accepted.
SAVE X 💻 ⑪ ⊠ ⊠

WESTPORT

WWW The Squire Tarbox Inn CI
(207) 882-7693. **$115-$199, 14 day notice.** 1181 Main Rd. Jct US 1 and SR 144; in Wiscasset; 8.5 mi s on SR 144, follow signs. Ext/int corridors. **Pets:** Accepted.
X ⑪ ⊠ ⊠ ⊠

YARMOUTH

WW Down-East Village Motel M
(207) 846-5161. **$77-$125.** 705 US Rt 1. I-295, exit 15 northbound; exit 17 southbound. Ext corridors. **Pets:** Accepted.
ASK X 🖥 💻 ⑪ ➿

YORK HARBOR

WWW Inn At Harmon Park BB
(207) 363-2031. **$69-$139 (no credit cards), 7 day notice.** 415 York St. I-95, exit 7 (York Ogunquit), 0.3 mi s on US 1, then 1.5 mi n, to York Village on US 1A. Int corridors. **Pets:** Service with restrictions, supervision.
X Ⓚ ⊠

MARYLAND

BALTIMORE METROPOLITAN AREA

ABERDEEN

▼▼▼ Clarion Aberdeen 🏨
(410) 273-6300. **$89-$129.** 980 Hospitality Way. I-95, exit 85, just e on SR 22. Int corridors. **Pets:** Accepted.

⟨AAA⟩ ▼▼▼ La Quinta Inn Aberdeen 🏨 ✦
(410) 272-6000. **$69-$149.** 793 W Bel Air Ave. I-95, exit 85, just e. Int corridors. **Pets:** Medium, other species. Service with restrictions, supervision.

⟨AAA⟩ ▼▼ Red Roof Inn Ⓜ
(410) 273-7800. **$50-$80.** 988 Hospitality Way. I-95, exit 85, just e on SR 22. Ext corridors. **Pets:** Accepted.

▼▼▼ Residence Inn by Marriott Aberdeen 🏨 ✦
(410) 272-0444. **$152-$186.** 830 Long Dr. I-95, exit 85, 0.5 mi w on SR 22, then 0.5 mi n. Int corridors. **Pets:** Large. $75 one-time fee/room. Service with restrictions, crate.

⟨AAA⟩ ▼▼ Super 8 Motel Aberdeen 🏨
(410) 272-5420. **$55-$80.** 1008 Beards Hill Rd. I-95, exit 85, just e on SR 22. Int corridors. **Pets:** Accepted.

ANNAPOLIS

⟨AAA⟩ ▼▼▼ DoubleTree Hotel Annapolis 🏨
(410) 224-3150. **$119-$299.** 210 Holiday Ct. 2.3 mi sw on US 50 and 301, exit 22 to Riva Rd, 0.3 mi n. Int corridors. **Pets:** Accepted.

▼▼ Extended StayAmerica-Annapolis/Naval Academy 🏨
(410) 571-9988. **$89-$170.** 1 Womack Dr. 2.3 mi sw on US 50 and 301, exit 22, just s on Admiral Cochrane Dr, then just n on Spruill Rd. Int corridors. **Pets:** Other species. $25 daily fee/pet. Service with restrictions, crate.

▼▼ Homestead Studio Suites Hotel-Annapolis 🏨
(410) 571-6600. **$99-$180.** 120 Admiral Cochrane Dr. 2.3 mi sw on US 50 and 301, exit 22, just s, then just e. Int corridors. **Pets:** Other species. $25 daily fee/pet. Service with restrictions, crate.

⟨AAA⟩ ▼▼▼▼ Loews Annapolis Hotel 🏨 🐾
(410) 263-7777. **$143-$323.** 126 West St. US 50 and 301, exit 24 eastbound; exit 24A westbound, 1.4 mi s on SR 70, just sw on Calvert St, then just w. Int corridors. **Pets:** Other species. $25 one-time fee/room. Supervision.

▼▼▼ Residence Inn by Marriott-Annapolis 🏨
(410) 573-0300. **$179-$189.** 170 Admiral Cochrane Dr. 2.3 mi sw on US 50 and 301, exit 22 to Riva Rd, just s on Riva Rd, then just e. Ext corridors. **Pets:** Accepted.

⟨AAA⟩ ▼▼▼▼ Sheraton Annapolis Hotel 🏨
(410) 266-3131. **Call for rates.** 173 Jennifer Rd. North side of US 50 and 301, exit 23B westbound; exit 23 eastbound. Int corridors. **Pets:** Medium, dogs only. $50 one-time fee/room. Service with restrictions.

⟨AAA⟩ ▼▼▼▼ The Westin Annapolis 🏨
(410) 972-4300. **$119-$409.** 100 Westgate Cir. US 50 and 301, exit 24 eastbound; exit 24A westbound, 0.7 mi s on SR 70; then 0.8 mi e on SR 435, 0.5 mi n of Church Cir. Int corridors. **Pets:** Accepted.

BALTIMORE

▼▼▼ Admiral Fell Inn 🏨
(410) 522-7377. **$149-$269.** 888 S Broadway St. Corner of Broadway and Thames sts; facing the waterfront. Int corridors. **Pets:** Accepted.

▼▼ Baltimore's Tremont Park Hotel 🏨
(410) 576-1200. **Call for rates.** 8 E Pleasant St. Just s of US 40 E, off Charles St. Int corridors. **Pets:** Small. $20 one-time fee/pet. Service with restrictions, crate.

▼▼ Brookshire Suites 🏨
(410) 625-1300. **$129-$249.** 120 E Lombard St. Corner of Calvert and Lombard sts. Int corridors. **Pets:** Accepted.

▼▼▼ Pier 5 Hotel 🏨
(410) 539-2000. **$179-$299.** 711 Eastern Ave. On the Inner Harbor, at Pier 5. Int corridors. **Pets:** Accepted.

▼▼▼ Residence Inn by Marriott-Baltimore Downtown/Inner Harbor 🏨
(410) 962-1220. **$209-$249.** 17 Light St. Between Mercer and E Redwood sts. Int corridors. **Pets:** Accepted.

⟨AAA⟩ ▼▼▼▼ Sheraton Baltimore City Center Hotel 🏨
(410) 752-1100. **Call for rates.** 101 W Fayette St. Between Charles and Liberty sts. Int corridors. **Pets:** Accepted.

Sheraton Inner Harbor Hotel 🅷 ❖
(410) 962-8300. **$149-$454.** 300 S Charles St. At Conway St. Int corridors.
Pets: Medium, dogs only. $150 one-time fee/room. Designated rooms, supervision.
SAVE ✖ 🔧 📺 🍴 🌊

BELCAMP

Extended StayAmerica-Bel Air 🅷
(410) 273-0194. **$79-$129.** 1361 James Way. I-95, exit 80 (SR 543), just ne. Int corridors. **Pets:** Other species. $25 daily fee/pet. Service with restrictions, crate.
ASK ✖ 🔧 📺

Wingate by Wyndham Aberdeen 🅷
(410) 272-2929. **$89-$139.** 1326 Policy Dr. I-95, exit 80 (SR 543), 0.3 mi s on SR 543. Int corridors. **Pets:** $25 one-time fee/pet. Supervision.
SAVE ✖ 🔧 📺 🌊

COLUMBIA

Extended StayAmerica-Columbia 100 Parkway 🅷
(410) 772-8800. **$89-$145.** 8870 Columbia 100 Pkwy. I-95, exit 43B, 4 mi w on SR 100, exit 1B, then just e. Int corridors. **Pets:** Other species. $25 daily fee/pet. Service with restrictions, crate.
ASK ✖ 🔧 📺

Extended Stay Deluxe Columbia Corporate Park 🅷
(410) 872-2994. **$99-$160.** 8890 Stanford Blvd. I-95, exit 41B, 1.3 mi w on SR 175 (Little Patuxent Pkwy), 0.5 mi s on Snowden River Pkwy, just w on McGaw Rd, then 0.3 mi nw. Int corridors. **Pets:** Other species. $25 daily fee/pet. Service with restrictions, crate.
ASK ✖ 🔧 📺 🌊

Hilton Columbia 🅷
(410) 997-1060. **$99-$239.** 5485 Twin Knolls Rd. Just e on SR 175 (Little Patuxent Pkwy) from jct US 29, just s on Thunder Hill Rd, then 0.3 mi w on Twin Knolls Rd, 5th entrance. Int corridors. **Pets:** Accepted.
SAVE ✖ 🔧 📺 🍴 🌊 ☒

Homewood Suites by Hilton Columbia 🅷
(410) 872-9200. **$109-$209.** 8320 Benson Dr. I-95, exit 41B, 0.5 mi w on SR 175 (Little Patuxent Pkwy), just nw on SR 108, then just w on Lark Brown Rd. Int corridors. **Pets:** Other species. $75 one-time fee/pet.
✖ 🔧 📺 🌊 ☒

Sheraton Columbia Town Center Hotel 🅷
(410) 730-3900. **$119-$299.** 10207 Wincopin Cir. 1.2 mi w on SR 175 (Little Patuxent Pkwy) from jct US 29, then just s; center. Int corridors. **Pets:** Accepted.
SAVE ✖ 🔧 📺 🍴 🌊 ☒

Staybridge Suites Baltimore-Columbia 🅷
(410) 964-9494. **Call for rates.** 8844 Columbia 100 Pkwy. I-95, exit 43B, 4 mi w on SR 100, exit 1B, then just e. Int corridors. **Pets:** Accepted.
✖ 🔧 📺

StudioPLUS Columbia Gateway Drive 🅷
(410) 312-1557. **$79-$139.** 6620 Eli Whitney Dr. I-95, exit 41, 1 mi w on SR 175 (Little Patuxent Pkwy), then just se on Columbia Gateway Dr. Int corridors. **Pets:** Other species. $25 daily fee/pet. Service with restrictions, crate.
ASK ✖ 🔧 📺

EDGEWOOD

Best Western Invitation Inn 🅼
(410) 679-9700. **$75-$95, 3 day notice.** 1709 Edgewood Rd. I-95, exit 77A, just e on SR 24. Ext corridors. **Pets:** Other species. $15 daily fee/room. Service with restrictions, crate.
SAVE ✖ 🔧 📺 🌊

ELLICOTT CITY

Residence Inn by Marriott Columbia 🅷
(410) 997-7200. **$219-$229.** 4950 Beaver Run Way. I-95, exit 43B, 4 mi w on SR 100, exit 1B (Executive Park Dr). Int corridors. **Pets:** Accepted.
✖ 🔧 🔧 📺 🌊 ☒

ESSEX

Super 8 Baltimore/Essex 🅷
(410) 780-0030. **$82-$128.** 98 Stemmers Run Rd. I-695, exit 36 (SR 702 S) to SR 150 E (Chase exit). Int corridors. **Pets:** Small. $10 daily fee/pet. Service with restrictions, supervision.
ASK ✖ 🔧 📺

GLEN BURNIE

Days Inn-Glen Burnie 🅷
(410) 761-8300. **$79-$129.** 6600 Ritchie Hwy. I-695, exit 3B eastbound; exit 2 westbound, 0.5 mi s on SR 2. Ext corridors. **Pets:** Accepted.
SAVE ✖ 🔧 📺 🌊

Extended StayAmerica Baltimore-Glen Burnie 🅷
(410) 761-2708. **$105-$155.** 104 Chesapeake Centre Ct. I-695, exit 3B, 0.9 mi s on SR 2, just e on E Ordance Rd, then just s. Int corridors. **Pets:** Other species. $25 daily fee/pet. Service with restrictions, crate.
ASK ✖ 🔧 📺

HANOVER

Red Roof Inn-BWI Parkway 🅼
(410) 712-4070. **$63-$96.** 7306 Parkway Dr S. I-95, exit 43A, 2 mi e on SR 100, exit 8 (Coca-Cola Dr), then 0.5 mi se. Ext corridors. **Pets:** Service with restrictions, supervision.
✖ 🔧

Residence Inn by Marriott-Arundel Mills/BWI 🅷 ❖
(410) 799-7332. **$209-$219.** 7035 Arundel Mills Cir. I-95, exit 43A, 3.6 mi e on SR 100, exit 10A (Arundel Mills Blvd). Int corridors. **Pets:** Medium, other species. $100 one-time fee/room. Service with restrictions, crate.
✖ 🔧 🔧 📺 🌊 ☒

JESSUP

Extended StayAmerica-Baltimore-Laurel 🅷
(301) 725-3877. **$79-$135.** 8550 Washington Blvd. I-95, exit 38A, 1.4 mi e on SR 32, 0.5 mi n on US 1. Int corridors. **Pets:** Other species. $25 daily fee/pet. Service with restrictions, crate.
ASK ✖ 🔧 📺

La Quinta Inn & Suites-Columbia/Jessup 🅷 ❖
(410) 799-1500. **$69-$159.** 7300 Crestmount Rd. I-95, exit 41A, just s of jct US 1 and SR 175. Int corridors. **Pets:** Medium, other species. Service with restrictions, supervision.
ASK ✖ 🔧 🔧 📺

Red Roof Inn-Columbia/Jessup 🅼
(410) 796-0380. **$70-$90.** 8000 Washington Blvd. I-95, exit 41A, 0.3 mi s of jct US 1 and SR 175. Ext corridors. **Pets:** Large, other species. Service with restrictions, supervision.
✖ 🔧

LINTHICUM HEIGHTS

Candlewood Suites-BWI 🅷 ❖
(410) 850-9214. **$135.** 1247 Winterson Rd. I-695, exit 7A, 1 mi s on SR 295, 1.3 mi e on W Nursery Rd, then 0.3 mi w. Int corridors. **Pets:** Medium, other species. $75 one-time fee/pet. Service with restrictions, crate.
ASK ✖ 🔧 📺

Comfort Inn Airport 🅷
(410) 789-9100. **$109-$189.** 6921 Baltimore Annapolis Blvd. I-695, exit 6A eastbound; exit 5 westbound, at SR 170 and 648. Int corridors. **Pets:** Accepted.
ASK ✖ 🔧 🔧 📺 🍴 ☒

▼▼▼▼ **Comfort Suites-BWI Airport** H
(410) 691-1000. **$89-$229.** 815 Elkridge Landing Rd. I-695, exit 7A, 1 mi s on SR 295, then 1.3 mi e on W Nursery Rd. Int corridors. **Pets:** Accepted.
ASK ⊗ ⚒ⁿ 🛏 💻

ⓐⓐ ▼▼▼▼ **Four Points by Sheraton BWI Airport** H ❀
(410) 859-3300. **Call for rates.** 7032 Elm Rd. I-195, exit 1A, 0.5 mi n on SR 170, then just e. Int corridors. **Pets:** Other species. $25 daily fee/pet. Service with restrictions, supervision.
SAVE ⊗ 🛏 💻 ⑪ ⋙

▼▼▼▼ **Hampton Inn BWI Airport** H
(410) 850-0600. **$109-$199.** 829 Elkridge Landing Rd. I-695, exit 7A, 1 mi s on SR 295, 1.3 mi e on W Nursery Rd, then just w. Int corridors. **Pets:** Accepted.
⊗ ⚒ⁿ 🛏 💻

ⓐⓐ ▼▼▼▼ **Holiday Inn-BWI Airport Conference Center** H
(410) 859-8400. **$109-$229.** 890 Elkridge Landing Rd. I-695, exit 7A, 1 mi s on SR 295, 1.3 mi e on W Nursery Rd, then 0.5 mi w. Int corridors. **Pets:** Accepted.
SAVE ⊗ ⚒ⁿ 🛏 💻 ⑪ ⋙

▼▼ **Homestead Studio Suites Hotel-Baltimore-BWI Airport** H
(410) 691-2500. **$79-$139.** 939 International Dr. I-695, exit 7A, 1 mi s on SR 295, then 0.6 mi e on W Nursery Rd. Ext corridors. **Pets:** Other species. $25 daily fee/pet. Service with restrictions, crate.
ASK ⊗ ⚒ⁿ 🛏 💻

▼▼ **La Quinta Inn & Suites BWI Airport** H ❀
(410) 859-2333. **$79-$179.** 1734 W Nursery Rd. SR 295, exit Nursery Rd, 1.2 mi n. Int corridors. **Pets:** Medium, other species. Service with restrictions, supervision.
ASK ⊗ 🛏 💻 ⋙

▼ **Motel 6 Baltimore-Linthicum Heights #1201** M
(410) 636-9070. **$65-$78.** 5179 Raynor Ave. I-695, exit 8, just e on SR 168. Ext corridors. **Pets:** Other species. Service with restrictions, supervision.
⊗ ⋙

▼▼ **Red Roof Inn-BWI Airport** M
(410) 850-7600. **Call for rates.** 827 Elkridge Landing Rd. I-695, exit 7A, 1 mi s on SR 295, 1.3 mi e on W Nursery Rd, then just w. Ext corridors. **Pets:** Accepted.
⊗ 🛏

▼▼▼ **Residence Inn by Marriott-BWI Airport** H
(410) 691-0255. **$209-$219.** 1160 Winterson Rd. I-695, exit 7A, 1 mi s on SR 295, 0.7 mi e on W Nursery Rd, then just n. Int corridors. **Pets:** $75 one-time fee/room. Service with restrictions, crate.
⊗ ⚒ⁿ 🛏 💻 ⋙ ✗

ⓐⓐ ▼▼▼▼ **Sheraton Baltimore Washington Airport Hotel** H ❀
(443) 577-2100. **Call for rates.** 1100 Old Elkridge Landing Rd. I-695, exit 7A, 1 mi s on SR 295, 1.3 mi e on W Nursery Rd, then 0.4 mi w on Winterson Rd. Int corridors. **Pets:** Large. $25 daily fee/room. Designated rooms, service with restrictions, supervision.
SAVE ⊗ 🛏 💻 ⑪ ⋙ ✗

▼▼ **Sleep Inn & Suites Airport** H
(410) 789-7223. **$99-$189, 30 day notice.** 6055 Belle Grove Rd. I-695, exit 6A eastbound; exit 5 westbound, 0.3 mi n to jct SR 170/648. Int corridors. **Pets:** Accepted.
ASK ⊗ ⚒ⁿ 🛏 💻

▼▼▼▼ **Staybridge Suites BWI** H
(410) 850-5666. **$189-$699, 12 day notice.** 1301 Winterson Rd. I-695, exit 7A, 1 mi s on SR 295, 1.3 mi e on Nursery Rd, then 0.4 mi w. Int corridors. **Pets:** Small. $100 one-time fee/pet. Service with restrictions, crate.
ASK ⊗ ⚒ⁿ 🛏 💻 ⋙

ⓐⓐ ▼▼▼▼ **TownePlace Suites by Marriott Baltimore/BWI Airport** H ❀
(410) 694-0060. **$199-$209.** 1171 Winterson Rd. I-695, exit 7A, 1 mi s on SR 295, 0.7 mi e on W Nursery Rd, then just n. Int corridors. **Pets:** $100 one-time fee/room. Service with restrictions, crate.
SAVE ⊗ ⚒ⁿ 🛏 💻 ⋙

ⓐⓐ ▼▼▼▼ **The Westin-Baltimore Washington Airport** H
(443) 577-2300. **Call for rates.** 1110 Old Elkridge Landing Rd. I-695, exit 7A, 1 mi s on SR 295, 1.3 mi e on W Nursery Rd, then 0.4 mi w on Winterson Rd. Int corridors. **Pets:** Small, dogs only. Designated rooms, service with restrictions, supervision.
SAVE ⊗ ⚒ⁿ 💻 ⑪ ⋙

ROSEDALE

▼▼ ▼▼ **La Quinta Inn & Suites Baltimore North** H ❀
(410) 574-8100. **$79-$169.** 4 Philadelphia Ct. I-695, exit 34, just n. Int corridors. **Pets:** Medium, other species. Service with restrictions, supervision.
ASK ⊗ 🛏 💻 ⋙

SYKESVILLE

▼▼▼▼ **Inn at Norwood** BB ❀
(410) 549-7868. **$135-$225, 7 day notice.** 7514 Norwood Ave. I-70, exit 80 (SR 32), 8 mi n, just w on Main St, then just w on Church St. Int corridors. **Pets:** Dogs only. $20 one-time fee/pet. Designated rooms, no service, crate.
ASK ⊗ 🛏 💻 🖉

TIMONIUM

▼▼ ▼▼ **Extended StayAmerica-Timonium** H
(410) 628-1088. **$89-$139.** 9704 Beaver Dam Rd. I-83, exit 17, just e, follow signs to Beaver Dam Rd. Int corridors. **Pets:** Other species. $25 daily fee/pet. Service with restrictions, crate.
ASK ⊗ ⚒ⁿ 🛏 💻

▼▼ ▼▼ **Red Roof Inn-Timonium** M
(410) 666-0380. **$70-$110.** 111 W Timonium Rd. I-83, exit 16A northbound; exit 16 southbound, just e. Ext corridors. **Pets:** Accepted.
⊗ 🛏

TOWSON

▼▼ ▼▼ **Holiday Inn Baltimore-Towson** H ❀
(410) 823-4410. **Call for rates.** 1100 Cromwell Bridge Rd. I-695, exit 29A, just s. Int corridors. **Pets:** Medium. $40 one-time fee/room. Service with restrictions, supervision.
⊗ 🛏 💻 ⑪ ⋙

ⓐⓐ ▼▼▼▼ **Sheraton Baltimore North Hotel** H
(410) 321-7400. **Call for rates.** 903 Dulaney Valley Rd. I-695, exit 27A, 0.3 mi s. Int corridors. **Pets:** Medium, dogs only. Designated rooms, service with restrictions, supervision.
SAVE ⊗ 🛏 💻 ⑪ ⋙ ✗

WESTMINSTER

▼▼ The Boston Inn **M**
(410) 848-9095. **$47-$75.** 533 Baltimore Blvd. 0.9 mi se on SR 97/140 from jct SR 27. Ext corridors. **Pets:** Dogs only. $50 deposit/room. Service with restrictions, supervision.
(ASK) (✕) 🛢 ⇌

WHITE MARSH

▼▼▼ Residence Inn by Marriott Baltimore/White Marsh **H**
(410) 933-9554. **$152-$186.** 4980 Mercantile Rd. I-95, exit 67B, 0.5 mi w on SR 43 (White Marsh Blvd), just s to Mercantile Rd, then just e. Int corridors. **Pets:** Other species. $75 one-time fee/pet. Service with restrictions, crate.
(✕) (&M) 🛢 💻 ⇌ (✕)

END METROPOLITAN AREA

CAMBRIDGE

AAA ▼▼▼ ▼▼▼ Hyatt Regency Chesapeake Bay Golf Resort, Spa and Marina **H**
(410) 901-1234. **$139-$459, 3 day notice.** 100 Heron Blvd. US 50 E, 1.2 mi e of Frederick C Malkus Jr Bridge. Int corridors. **Pets:** Accepted.
(SAVE) (✕) (&M) 🛢 💻 (¶) ⇌ (✕)

CUMBERLAND

▼▼▼ Holiday Inn **H**
(301) 724-8800. **$109-$159, 3 day notice.** 100 S George St. I-68, exit 43C, just n; downtown. Int corridors. **Pets:** Accepted.
(ASK) (✕) 🛢 💻 (¶) ⇌

DISTRICT OF COLUMBIA METROPOLITAN AREA

BELTSVILLE

AAA ▼▼▼ Sheraton Washington North Hotel **H** ❀
(301) 937-4422. **$99-$299, 3 day notice.** 4095 Powder Mill Rd. I-95, exit 29B, just w on SR 212; 2 mi n of I-495. Int corridors. **Pets:** Medium, dogs only. Designated rooms, service with restrictions, supervision.
(SAVE) (✕) (&M) 🛢 💻 (¶) ⇌

BETHESDA

▼▼▼ Residence Inn by Marriott-Bethesda Downtown **H** ❀
(301) 718-0200. **$319-$339.** 7335 Wisconsin Ave. I-495, exit 34, 2.5 mi s on SR 355; entrance on Waverly St. Int corridors. **Pets:** Medium. $10 daily fee/pet, $200 one-time fee/room. Designated rooms, service with restrictions, supervision.
(✕) 🛢 💻 ⇌

BOWIE

▼▼▼ Comfort Inn Hotel & Conference Center-Bowie **H**
(301) 464-0089. **$135-$160.** 4500 NW Crain Hwy. US 50, exit 13A, jct US 50/301 and SR 3. Int corridors. **Pets:** Medium, other species. $15 daily fee/pet. Designated rooms, service with restrictions, supervision.
(ASK) (✕) (&M) 🛢 💻 (¶) ⇌ (✕)

AAA ▼▼▼ Hampton Inn-Bowie **H**
(301) 809-1800. **$115-$179.** 15202 Major Lansdale Blvd. US 50, exit 11, 0.4 mi s on SR 197. Int corridors. **Pets:** Accepted.
(SAVE) (✕) (&M) 🛢 💻 ⇌

CHEVY CHASE

▼▼▼ Holiday Inn-Washington/Chevy Chase **H**
(301) 656-1500. **Call for rates.** 5520 Wisconsin Ave. Jct SR 191, 0.8 mi s on SR 355. Int corridors. **Pets:** Accepted.
🛢 💻 (¶) ⇌

COLLEGE PARK

▼▼ Super 8-College Park **H**
(301) 474-0894. **Call for rates.** 9150 Baltimore Ave. I-95/495, exit 25 northbound; exit 25B southbound, 0.9 mi s on US 1. Int corridors. **Pets:** Accepted.
(✕) 🛢 💻

GAITHERSBURG

AAA ▼▼▼ Comfort Inn Shady Grove **H** ❀
(301) 330-0023. **$79-$169.** 16216 Frederick Rd. I-270, exit 8, 1 mi e on Shady Grove Rd at SR 355. Int corridors. **Pets:** Large, other species. $15 daily fee/pet. Service with restrictions, crate.
(SAVE) (✕) 🛢 💻 ⇌

▼▼ Extended Stay Deluxe-Washington, DC-Gaithersburg **H**
(301) 963-3539. **$99-$159.** 201 Professional Dr. I-270, exit 11, 0.4 mi e, then 0.9 mi n on SR 355. Int corridors. **Pets:** Other species. $25 daily fee/pet. Service with restrictions, crate.
(ASK) (✕) 🛢 💻

AAA ▼▼▼ Hilton Washington DC North/Gaithersburg **H**
(301) 977-8900. **$99-$259.** 620 Perry Pkwy. I-270, exit 11, then e. Int corridors. **Pets:** Accepted.
(SAVE) (✕) 🛢 💻 (¶) ⇌

AAA ▼▼▼ Holiday Inn-Gaithersburg **H**
(301) 948-8900. **$129-$259.** 2 Montgomery Village Ave. I-270, exit 11, 0.3 mi e. Int corridors. **Pets:** Medium. Service with restrictions, supervision.
(SAVE) (✕) (&M) 🛢 💻 (¶) ⇌ (✕)

▼▼ Homestead Studio Suites Hotel-Gaithersburg/Rockville **H**
(301) 987-9100. **$95-$189.** 2621 Research Blvd. I-270, exit 8, just w, then just n. Int corridors. **Pets:** Other species. $25 daily fee/pet. Service with restrictions, crate.
(ASK) (✕) (&M) 🛢 💻

AAA ▼▼▼ Hyatt Summerfield Suites-Gaithersburg **H**
(301) 527-6000. **$119-$399.** 200 Skidmore Blvd. I-370, exit SR 355, just n to Westland Rd. Ext corridors. **Pets:** Small. $150 one-time fee/pet. Designated rooms, service with restrictions, supervision.
(SAVE) (✕) (&M) 🛢 💻 ⇌ (✕)

▼▼▼ Residence Inn by Marriott-Gaithersburg **H**
(301) 590-3003. **$215-$263.** 9721 Washingtonian Blvd. I-270, exit 9B (I-370/Sam Eig Hwy), just w to Fields Rd, 0.8 mi se, then just ne. Int corridors. **Pets:** Accepted.
(✕) (&M) 🛢 💻 ⇌ (✕)

 **TownePlace Suites by Marriott-Gaithersburg** 🅗 ❀
(301) 590-2300. **$219-$239.** 212 Perry Pkwy. I-270, exit 10 northbound, just e; exit 11 southbound, just e on SR 124 to SR 355, 0.3 mi s, then 0.5 mi sw. Int corridors. **Pets:** Medium, other species. $100 one-time fee/room. Service with restrictions, supervision.
〔SAVE〕⊠ 𝄫ᴹ 🛏 🖵 ⌁

GERMANTOWN

▼▼ **Extended StayAmerica-Washington, DC-Germantown** 🅗
(301) 540-9369. **$69-$129.** 12450 Milestone Center Dr. I-270, exit 16, 0.6 mi e on SR 27 (Father Hurley Blvd), 0.7 mi n on Observation Dr, then just w. Int corridors. **Pets:** Other species. $25 daily fee/pet. Service with restrictions, crate.
〔ASK〕⊠ 𝄫ᴹ 🛏 🖵

▼▼ **Homestead Studio Suites Hotel-Germantown** 🅗
(301) 515-4500. **$79-$139.** 20141 Century Blvd. I-270, exit 15B (SR 118 S/Germantown Rd), just w to Aircraft Dr, then just n. Ext corridors. **Pets:** Other species. $25 daily fee/pet. Service with restrictions, crate.
〔ASK〕⊠ 𝄫ᴹ 🛏 🖵

GREENBELT

▼▼▼ **Residence Inn by Marriott-Greenbelt** 🅗
(301) 982-1600. **$179-$219.** 6320 Golden Triangle Dr. I-95/495, exit 23, 0.5 mi sw of jct SR 201; off SR 193 (Greenbelt Rd), just n on Walker Dr. Int corridors. **Pets:** Accepted.
〔SAVE〕⊠ 𝄫ᴹ 🛏 🖵 ⌁ ⌖

LAUREL

▼▼▼ **Holiday Inn Laurel-West** 🅗
(301) 776-5300. **$99-$159, 3 day notice.** 15101 Sweitzer Ln. I-95, exit 33B, just w on SR 198. Ext/int corridors. **Pets:** Accepted.
〔SAVE〕⊠ 🛏 🖵 🍴 ⌁

▼▼ **Quality Inn & Suites Laurel** 🅗
(301) 725-8800. **$79-$179.** One Second St. On US 1, 0.5 mi n of jct SR 198. Ext/int corridors. **Pets:** Small, other species. $35 daily fee/pet. Designated rooms, service with restrictions.
〔SAVE〕⊠ 🛏 🖵 ⌁

ROCKVILLE

▼▼▼ **Best Western Rockville Hotel & Suites** 🅗
(301) 424-4940. **$89-$169.** 1251 W Montgomery Ave. I-270, exit 6B, just w on SR 28. Int corridors. **Pets:** Medium. $22 daily fee/pet. Designated rooms, service with restrictions, supervision.
〔SAVE〕⊠ 🛏 🖵 🍴 ⌁

▼▼▼ **Chase Suite Hotel Rockville** 🅗 ❀
(301) 590-9880. **$79-$249, 3 day notice.** 1380 Piccard Dr. I-270, exit 8 (Shady Grove Rd), 0.3 mi s; 1 mi w of SR 355 via Redland Rd. Ext corridors. **Pets:** Medium, other species. $100 one-time fee/room. Service with restrictions, supervision.
〔SAVE〕⊠ 🛏 🖵 🍴 ⌁ ⌖

▼▼▼ **Red Roof Inn-Rockville** 🅗
(301) 987-0965. **$77-$145.** 16001 Shady Grove Rd. I-270, exit 8 (Shady Grove Rd), 0.5 mi e. Ext corridors. **Pets:** Accepted.
〔SAVE〕⊠ 𝄫ᴹ 🛏

▼▼▼ **Sheraton Rockville** 🅗
(240) 912-8200. **Call for rates.** 920 King Farm Blvd. I-270, exit 8 northbound (Redland Rd), left on Piccard, then left on King Farm Blvd. Int corridors. **Pets:** Accepted.
〔SAVE〕⊠ 𝄫ᴹ 🛏 🖵 🍴 ⌁ ⌖

▼▼▼ **Sleep Inn-Rockville** 🅗
(301) 948-8000. **$100-$150.** 2 Research Ct. I-270, exit 8 (Shady Grove Rd), just sw. Int corridors. **Pets:** Medium, other species. $15 daily fee/pet. Designated rooms, service with restrictions, crate.
〔SAVE〕⊠ 𝄫ᴹ 🛏 🖵

SILVER SPRING

▼▼▼ **Residence Inn by Marriott Silver Spring** 🅗 ❀
(301) 572-2322. **$229-$249.** 12000 Plum Orchard Dr. I-95, exit 29B, 1.2 mi w on SR 212, then 1 mi n on Cherry Hill Rd. Int corridors. **Pets:** Other species. $100 one-time fee/room. Service with restrictions.
⊠ 𝄫ᴹ 🛏 🖵 ⌁ ⌖

END METROPOLITAN AREA

ELKTON

▼▼▼ **Hawthorn Suites** 🅗
(410) 620-9494. **Call for rates.** 304 Belle Hill Rd. I-95, exit 109A, just e. Int corridors. **Pets:** Accepted.
〔SAVE〕⊠ 𝄫ᴹ 🛏 🖵 ⌁

EMMITSBURG

▼▼ **Sleep Inn & Suites in Emmitsburg** 🅗
(301) 447-0044. **$85-$199.** 501 Silo Hill Pkwy. US 15, exit SR 140, just w, then just n on Silo Hill Pkwy. Int corridors. **Pets:** Large, other species. $25 daily fee/room. Service with restrictions, crate.
〔SAVE〕⊠ 🛏 🖵 ⌁

FREDERICK

▼▼▼ **Comfort Inn** 🅗
(301) 668-7272. **Call for rates.** 7300 Executive Way. I-270, exit 31B, 0.9 mi sw on SR 85. Int corridors. **Pets:** Accepted.
〔SAVE〕⊠ 𝄫ᴹ 🛏 🖵

▼▼ **Extended StayAmerica-Frederick-Westview Dr** 🅗
(301) 668-0808. **$90-$140.** 5240 Westview Dr. I-270, exit 31B, 0.5 mi sw on SR 85, then 0.4 mi n. Int corridors. **Pets:** Other species. $25 daily fee/pet. Service with restrictions, crate.
〔ASK〕⊠ 🛏 🖵

▼▼▼ **Frederick Residence Inn by Marriott** 🅗 ❀
(301) 360-0010. **$161-$197.** 5230 Westview Dr. I-270, exit 31B, 0.5 mi sw on SR 85, then 0.3 mi n on Crestwood Blvd. Int corridors. **Pets:** $100 one-time fee/room. Service with restrictions, crate.
⊠ 🛏 🖵 ⌁ ⌖

▼▼▼ **Hampton Inn** 🅗 ❀
(301) 698-2500. **$119-$139.** 5311 Buckeystown Pike (SR 85). I-270, exit 31B, 0.6 mi w. Int corridors. **Pets:** Medium. Designated rooms, service with restrictions, supervision.
〔SAVE〕⊠ 🛏 🖵 🍴 ⌁

▼▼▼ **Holiday Inn & Conference Center** 🅗
(301) 694-7500. **Call for rates.** 5400 Holiday Dr. I-270, exit 31A, just se of SR 85. Int corridors. **Pets:** Accepted.
⊠ 🛏 🖵 🍴 ⌁ ⌖

▼▼/◆◆ Holiday Inn Express-FSK Mall ℍ
(301) 695-2881. **Call for rates.** 5579 Spectrum Dr. I-270, exit 31A, just e on SR 85. Int corridors. **Pets:** Accepted.

⊠ 🛢 💻

🆑 ▼▼▼▼ MainStay Suites ℍ
(301) 668-4600. **$100-$149.** 7310 Executive Way. I-270, exit 31B, 0.7 mi sw on SR 85. Int corridors. **Pets:** Medium, other species. $10 daily fee/pet. Designated rooms, service with restrictions, supervision.

SAVE ⊠ 🛢 💻 ⇨

🆑 ▼▼▼ Travelodge Frederick ℍ
(301) 663-0500. **$68-$88.** 200 E Walser Dr. I-70, exit 54, just n. Int corridors. **Pets:** Medium, dogs only. $25 deposit/pet. Designated rooms, supervision.

SAVE ⊠ 🛢 💻

FROSTBURG

🆑 ▼▼ Days Inn & Suites ℍ
(301) 689-2050. **$79-$149.** 11100 New Georges Creek Rd. I-68, exit 34, 1 mi n on SR 36. Int corridors. **Pets:** Accepted.

SAVE ⊠ 🛢 💻 ⊠

GRANTSVILLE

▼▼▼ The Stonebow Inn ᴮᴮ ❖
(301) 895-4250. **$160-$200, 14 day notice.** 146 Casselman Rd. I-68, exit 22 westbound, 0.5 mi n on US 219, then 2.1 mi w on US 40; exit 19 eastbound, just n, then 0.9 mi e on US 40; behind Penn Alps Restaurant. Ext/int corridors. **Pets:** Designated rooms, service with restrictions, crate.

ASK ⊠ 💻 ⊠

GRASONVILLE

🆑 ▼▼ Best Western Kent Narrows Inn Ⓜ ❖
(410) 827-6767. **$79-$219.** 3101 Main St. US 50 and 301, exit 42; at Kent Narrows Bridge. Ext corridors. **Pets:** Medium, other species. $10 daily fee/pet. Service with restrictions.

SAVE ⊠ 🛢 💻 ⇨ ⊠

HAGERSTOWN

▼▼/◆◆ Halfway Hagerstown Super 8 ℍ
(301) 582-1992. **$63-$71.** 16805 Blake Rd. I-81, exit 5B, just w. Int corridors. **Pets:** Accepted.

ASK ⊠ 🛢 💻

🆑 ▼▼ Sleep Inn & Suites ℍ
(301) 766-9449. **$80-$139.** 18216 Col Henry K Douglas Dr. I-70, exit 29, just s. Int corridors. **Pets:** Accepted.

SAVE ⊠ 🛢 💻 ⇨

HANCOCK

🆑 ▼ Super 8 ℍ
(301) 678-6101. **Call for rates.** 118 Limestone Rd. I-70, exit 1B, just s. Ext/int corridors. **Pets:** $10 daily fee/pet. Service with restrictions, supervision.

SAVE ⊠ 🛢 💻

INDIAN HEAD

🆑 ▼▼▼ Super 8 Motel ℍ
(301) 753-8100. **$66-$96.** 4694 Indian Head Hwy. SR 210, 0.6 mi s of jct SR 225. Int corridors. **Pets:** Small, dogs only. $10 daily fee/pet. Service with restrictions, supervision.

SAVE ⊠ ♿ᴹ 🛢 💻

LA VALE

🆑 ▼▼/◆◆ Best Western Braddock Motor Inn ℍ
(301) 729-3300. **$100-$126, 3 day notice.** 1268 National Hwy. On US 40, jct SR 53, adjacent to I-68, exit 39W/40E. Int corridors. **Pets:** Medium, other species. $25 deposit/room, $25 one-time fee/room. Designated rooms, supervision.

SAVE ⊠ 🛢 💻 🍴 ⇨ ⊠

🆑 ▼▼/◆◆ Red Roof Inn ℍ
(301) 729-6700. **$60-$90.** 12310 Winchester Rd SW. I-68, exit 40, 0.6 mi s. Ext/int corridors. **Pets:** Accepted.

SAVE ⊠ 🛢

🆑 ▼ Super 8 Ⓜ
(301) 729-6265. **$55-$130.** 1301 National Hwy. I-68, exit 40, 0.4 mi n. Int corridors. **Pets:** Small, other species. $10 daily fee/pet. Service with restrictions, supervision.

SAVE ⊠ 🛢 💻

LEXINGTON PARK

▼▼ Extended StayAmerica Lexington Park-Pax River ℍ
(240) 725-0100. **$99-$159.** 46565 Expedition Park Dr. SR 235, just s to Lexington Park. Int corridors. **Pets:** Other species. $25 daily fee/pet. Service with restrictions, crate.

ASK ⊠ ♿ᴹ 🛢 💻

▼ Super 8 Motel ℍ
(301) 862-9822. **$76.** 22801 Three Notch Rd. On SR 235, 3.3 mi n of jct SR 246. Int corridors. **Pets:** Medium, other species. $10 daily fee/pet. Service with restrictions, supervision.

ASK ⊠ 🛢 💻

MCHENRY

▼▼/◆◆ Wisp Mountain Resort/Hotel & Conference Center ℍ
(301) 387-5581. **$79-$369, 14 day notice.** 290 Marsh Hill Rd. 1 mi s on US 219 from jct SR 42, just w on Sang Run Rd, then 0.3 mi s. Int corridors. **Pets:** Accepted.

ASK ⊠ 🛢 💻 🍴 ⇨ ⊠

NORTH EAST

🆑 ▼▼/◆◆ Comfort Inn & Suites North East ℍ
(410) 287-7100. **$89-$189, 7 day notice.** 1 Center Dr. I-95, exit 100 southbound; exit 100A northbound, just e on SR 272. Int corridors. **Pets:** Small, dogs only. $20 daily fee/pet. Service with restrictions, supervision.

SAVE ⊠ 🛢 💻 ⇨

OCEAN CITY

🆑 ▼▼▼ Clarion Resort Fontainebleau Hotel ℍ ❖
(410) 524-3535. **$89-$399, 3 day notice.** 10100 Coastal Hwy. 101st St and the ocean. Int corridors. **Pets:** Large. $35 daily fee/pet. Designated rooms, service with restrictions, supervision.

SAVE ⊠ 🛢 💻 🍴 ⇨ ⊠

PERRYVILLE

🆑 ▼▼ Ramada Perryville Ⓜ ❖
(410) 642-2866. **$70-$87.** 61 Heather Ln. I-95, exit 93, just e. Ext corridors. **Pets:** Medium. $20 daily fee/room. Designated rooms, service with restrictions, crate.

SAVE ⊠ 🛢 💻

POCOMOKE CITY

▼▼▼ Holiday Inn Express-Pocomoke ℍ
(410) 957-6444. **Call for rates.** 125 Newtowne Blvd. On SR 756 at US 13, 0.8 mi nw on US 13 from jct US 113. Int corridors. **Pets:** Small. $25 daily fee/pet. Service with restrictions, supervision.

⊠ ♿ᴹ 🛢 💻 ⇨

PRINCE FREDERICK

◆◆ **Super 8 Motel-Prince Frederick** ⊞
(410) 535-8668. **Call for rates.** 40 Commerce Ln. Off SR 2/4, just s of jct SR 402. Int corridors. **Pets:** Small. $11 daily fee/pet. Service with restrictions, supervision.
⊠ ⯃ ⌸

ROCK HALL

◆◆◆ **Inn at Huntingfield Creek** ⒷⒷ
(410) 639-7779. **Call for rates.** 4928 Eastern Neck Rd. 1.8 mi s on SR 445 from jct SR 20. Ext/int corridors. **Pets:** Dogs only. $25 daily fee/room. Designated rooms, service with restrictions, crate.
⊠ ⯃ ⌸ ⇌ ⌧

◆ **Mariners Motel** Ⓜ
(410) 639-2291. **$70-$85.** 5681 S Hawthorne Ave. 0.3 mi e of SR 20. Ext corridors. **Pets:** Accepted.
⊠ ⯃ ⌸ ⇌

ST. MICHAELS

◆◆ **The Parsonage Inn** ⒷⒷ
(410) 745-5519. **Call for rates.** 210 N Talbot St. 0.3 mi w on SR 33. Ext/int corridors. **Pets:** Accepted.
⊠ ⌧

SALISBURY

AAA◇ ◆◆ **Best Western Salisbury Plaza** Ⓜ
(410) 546-1300. **$55-$135.** 1735 N Salisbury Blvd. US 13 business route, 0.5 mi s of US 50 Bypass. Ext corridors. **Pets:** $10 daily fee/pet. Service with restrictions, crate.
SAVE ⊠ ⯃ ⌸ ⇌

AAA◇ ◆◆ **Comfort Inn Salisbury** ⊞ ❀
(410) 543-4666. **$49-$159.** 2701 N Salisbury Blvd. US 13, 0.5 mi n of jct US 13 business route and Bypass. Int corridors. **Pets:** Service with restrictions, supervision.
SAVE ⊠ ⯃ ⌸

AAA◇ ◆◆ **Holiday Inn Conference Center** ⊞
(410) 546-4400. **$99-$250.** 300 S Salisbury Blvd. US 13 business route, 0.4 mi s of jct Business US 50; downtown. Int corridors. **Pets:** Accepted.
SAVE ⊠ ⯃ ⌸ ⌑ ⇌

◆◆◆ **Residence Inn by Marriott Salisbury** ⊞ ❀
(410) 543-0033. **$119-$129.** 140 Centre Rd. Just off US 13 business route at US 50. Int corridors. **Pets:** Other species. $100 one-time fee/room. Service with restrictions, crate.
⊠ ⯒ ⯃ ⌸ ⇌ ⌧

SNOW HILL

AAA◇ ◆◆◆ **River House Inn** ⒷⒷ ❀
(410) 632-2722. **$125-$300, 7 day notice.** 201 E Market St. 1 mi w on SR 394 from jct SR 113. Ext/int corridors. **Pets:** Dogs only. $10 daily fee/pet. Designated rooms, service with restrictions.
SAVE ⊠ ⯃ ⌸ ⇌ ⌧

THURMONT

◆ **Super 8-Thurmont** Ⓜ
(301) 271-7888. **Call for rates.** 300 Tippin Dr. US 15, just w on SR 806. Int corridors. **Pets:** Accepted.
⊠ ⯃ ⌸

WALDORF

◆◆ **La Quinta Inn Waldorf** ⊞ ❀
(301) 645-0022. **$59-$199.** 11770 Business Park Dr. 1 mi n on US 301 from jct SR 228. Int corridors. **Pets:** Medium, other species. Service with restrictions, supervision.
ASK ⊠ ⯃ ⌸

WILLIAMSPORT

AAA◇ ◆◆ **Red Roof Inn** ⊞
(301) 582-3500. **Call for rates.** 310 E Potomac St. I-81, exit 2, 0.3 mi sw on US 11. Ext corridors. **Pets:** Medium. Service with restrictions, supervision.
SAVE ⊠ ⯃

MASSACHUSETTS

CITY INDEX

AMHERST

▼▼ University Lodge M
(413) 256-8111. **$59-$159.** 345 N Pleasant St. 0.6 mi n. Ext corridors.
Pets: Accepted.
ASK ✕ ◻ ▯

AUBURN

▼▼ Comfort Inn H
(508) 832-8300. **$80-$139.** 426 Southbridge St. I-90, exit 10, 1 mi n on SR
12; I-290, exit 9 to SR 12. Int corridors. **Pets:** $20 one-time fee/room.
Service with restrictions, supervision.
ASK ✕ ⚄ ◻ ▯

▼▼ La Quinta Inn H ❁
(508) 832-7000. **$65-$129.** 446 Southbridge St. I-90, exit 10, 1.2 mi n on
SR 12. Int corridors. **Pets:** Medium, other species. Service with restrictions,
supervision.
ASK ✕ ◻ ▯

BARRE

▼▼ Jenkins Inn CI
(978) 355-6444. **$180-$260, 7 day notice.** 7 West St. On SR 122 and 32.
Int corridors. **Pets:** Dogs only. $5 daily fee/pet. Service with restrictions,
supervision.
✕ ◻ ▯ ⑪

BOSTON METROPOLITAN AREA

ANDOVER

▼▼ Andover Inn CI
(978) 475-5903. **Call for rates.** 4 Chapel Ave. I-495, exit 41A, 2.3 mi s via
SR 28. Int corridors. **Pets:** Accepted.
✕ ⑪

🅰🅰🅰 ▼▼▼ Comfort Suites H
(978) 475-6000. **$99-$149.** 4 Riverside Dr. I-93, exit 45, 0.5 mi e. Int
corridors. **Pets:** Accepted.
SAVE ✕ ⚄ ◻ ▯ ⇆ ✕

▼▼▼ La Quinta Inn & Suites H ❁
(978) 685-6200. **$79-$119.** 131 River Rd. I-93, exit 45, just w; I-495, exit
40B, 2 mi n. Int corridors. **Pets:** Medium, other species. Service with
restrictions, supervision.
ASK ✕ ◻ ▯ ⇆

▼▼▼ Residence Inn by Marriott
Boston-Andover H ❁
(978) 683-0382. **$149-$179.** 500 Minuteman Rd. I-93, exit 45, 0.3 mi w,
then 0.5 mi n. Int corridors. **Pets:** $100 one-time fee/room. Service with
restrictions, crate.
✕ ⚄ ◻ ▯ ⇆ ✕

▼▼▼ Staybridge Suites Boston/Andover H
(978) 686-2000. **$99-$199.** 4 Tech Dr. I-93, exit 45, just sw via Shattuck
Rd. Int corridors. **Pets:** Accepted.
ASK ✕ ⚄ ◻ ▯ ⇆

🅰🅰🅰 ▼▼▼ Wyndham Boston/Andover Hotel H ❁
(978) 975-3600. **$109-$199.** 123 Old River Rd. I-93, exit 45, just e on River
Rd. Int corridors. **Pets:** Small, other species. $50 one-time fee/room. Des-
ignated rooms, no service, supervision.
SAVE ✕ ◻ ▯ ⑪ ⇆ ✕

ARLINGTON

▼▼▼ Homewood Suites by Hilton H
(781) 643-7258. **$159-$269.** 1 Massachusetts Ave. On SR 2A, just n of SR
16. Int corridors. **Pets:** Accepted.
✕ ⚄ ◻ ▯

BILLERICA

▼▼▼ Homewood Suites by Hilton H
(978) 670-7111. **$109-$199.** 35 Middlesex Tpke. I-95, exit 32B, 2.5 mi n.
Int corridors. **Pets:** Accepted.
✕ ⚄ ◻ ▯ ⇆

BOSTON

🅰🅰🅰 ▼▼▼ Best Western Roundhouse Suites H
(617) 989-1000. **Call for rates.** 891 Massachusetts Ave. I-93, exit 18, just
sw; just n of Newmarket Square. Int corridors. **Pets:** Accepted.
SAVE ✕ ⚄ ◻ ▯

🅰🅰🅰 ▼▼▼▼ Boston Harbor Hotel H
(617) 439-7000. **$290-$650.** 70 Rowes Wharf. At Rowes Wharf. Int corridors. **Pets:** Accepted.
SAVE ✕ ⑪ ⇆ ✕

🅰🅰🅰 ▼▼▼ Boston Omni Parker House Hotel H
(617) 227-8600. **$159-$599.** 60 School St. Corner of Tremont and School
sts; northeast corner of Boston Common. Int corridors. **Pets:** Medium. $50
one-time fee/pet.
SAVE ✕ ◻ ▯ ⑪

The Boston Park Plaza Hotel & Towers
(617) 426-2000. **$129-$369.** 50 Park Plaza at Arlington St. Just s of Boston Common and Public Gardens. Int corridors. **Pets:** Accepted.

Bulfinch Hotel
(617) 624-0202. **Call for rates.** 107 Merrimac St. At Lancaster St. Int corridors. **Pets:** Accepted.

The Colonnade Hotel Boston
(617) 424-7000. **Call for rates.** 120 Huntington Ave. Just s of Copley Square. Int corridors. **Pets:** Accepted.

Comfort Inn Boston
(617) 287-9200. **$109-$199.** 900 William T Morrissey Blvd. I-93, exit 13 northbound, 0.5 mi sw; exit 12 southbound, follow signs. Int corridors. **Pets:** Service with restrictions, supervision.

DoubleTree Guest Suites-Boston/Cambridge
(617) 783-0090. **$109-$419.** 400 Soldiers Field Rd. I-90, exit 20 westbound; exit 18 eastbound. Int corridors. **Pets:** Designated rooms, service with restrictions.

The Eliot Hotel
(617) 267-1607. **$355-$645.** 370 Commonwealth Ave. Corner of Commonwealth and Massachusetts aves. Int corridors. **Pets:** Service with restrictions, supervision.

The Fairmont Copley Plaza Boston
(617) 267-5300. **$209-$579.** 138 St. James Ave. At Copley Square. Int corridors. **Pets:** $25 daily fee/room. Service with restrictions, supervision.

Fifteen Beacon
(617) 670-1500. **$395-$1400.** 15 Beacon St. Just e of State House; just ne of Boston Common; center. Int corridors. **Pets:** Medium, dogs only. Service with restrictions, supervision.

Four Seasons Hotel Boston
(617) 338-4400. **$450-$700.** 200 Boylston St. Between Arlington and Charles sts. Int corridors. **Pets:** Accepted.

Hilton Boston Back Bay
(617) 236-1100. **$199-$639.** 40 Dalton St. At Dalton and Belvidere sts. Int corridors. **Pets:** Accepted.

Hilton Boston Logan Airport
(617) 568-6700. **$169-$539.** One Hotel Dr. At General Edward Lawrence Logan International Airport. Int corridors. **Pets:** Large, other species. $25 one-time fee/room. Service with restrictions, crate.

Hotel Commonwealth
(617) 933-5000. **$209-$498.** 500 Commonwealth Ave. On SR 2; at Beacon St and Brookline Ave. Int corridors. **Pets:** Dogs only. $125 one-time fee/room. Service with restrictions, supervision.

Howard Johnson Hotel Fenway
(617) 267-8300. **$89-$239.** 1271 Boylston St. I-90, exit Brookline Ave S, backing onto Fenway Park. Int corridors. **Pets:** Service with restrictions, supervision.

Hyatt Regency Boston
(617) 912-1234. **$159-$599.** One Ave de Lafayette. Just e of Boston Common at Lafayette Pl. Int corridors. **Pets:** Other species. Service with restrictions, crate.

InterContinental Boston
(617) 747-1000. **$200-$900.** 510 Atlantic Ave. I-93, exit 23 southbound; exit 20 northbound; at Pearl St. Int corridors. **Pets:** Accepted.

The Langham, Boston
(617) 451-1900. **$195-$535.** 250 Franklin St. on Post Office Square; center. Int corridors. **Pets:** Accepted.

The Lenox Hotel
(617) 536-5300. **$195-$465.** 61 Exeter St. I-90, exit 22, just n at Boylston. Int corridors. **Pets:** Accepted.

The Liberty Hotel
(617) 224-4000. **$295-$650.** 215 Charles St. I-93, exit 26 (Storrow Dr). Int corridors. **Pets:** Large, dogs only. $100 one-time fee/room. Designated rooms, service with restrictions, supervision.

The Midtown Hotel
(617) 262-1000. **$99-$309.** 220 Huntington Ave. 3 blks sw of Copley Pl; just n of Symphony Hall and Massachusetts Ave. Int corridors. **Pets:** Medium. $30 one-time fee/pet. Service with restrictions, supervision.

Nine Zero Hotel
(617) 772-5800. **$249-$599.** 90 Tremont St. Just ne of Boston Common; motor entrance on Bosworth, just s of property; center. Int corridors. **Pets:** Other species.

Onyx Hotel
(617) 557-9955. **Call for rates.** 155 Portland St. Just n of corner of Merrimac and Traverse sts; 3 blks s of TD Bank North Garden. Int corridors. **Pets:** Accepted.

Ramada Boston
(617) 287-9100. **$109-$189.** 800 William T Morrissey Blvd. I-93, exit 13 northbound, 0.5 mi sw; exit 12 southbound, follow signs. Int corridors. **Pets:** Service with restrictions, supervision.

Residence Inn by Marriott Boston Harbor on Tudor Wharf
(617) 242-9000. **$299-$399.** 34-44 Charles River Ave. Just se of SR 99 at Charlestown Bridge. Int corridors. **Pets:** Medium, other species. $150 one-time fee/room. Service with restrictions, supervision.

The Ritz-Carlton, Boston Common
(617) 574-7100. **$395-$795.** 10 Avery St. At Washington and Avery sts; 1 blk e of Boston Common. Int corridors. **Pets:** Medium, other species. $125 one-time fee/room. Service with restrictions, crate.

Seaport Hotel
(617) 385-4000. **$179-$499.** 1 Seaport Ln. At Seaport World Trade Center; MBTA-Silverline, World Trade Center Shop. Int corridors. **Pets:** Medium, other species. Designated rooms, service with restrictions, supervision.

Sheraton Boston
(617) 236-2000. **$369-$1500.** 39 Dalton St. I-90, exit 22. Int corridors. **Pets:** Medium. Service with restrictions, supervision.

▼▼▼ ▼▼▼ Taj Boston H ❖
(617) 536-5700. **Call for rates.** 15 Arlington St. At Arlington and Newbury sts; overlooks the Public Gardens. Int corridors. **Pets:** Small. $125 one-time fee/room. Service with restrictions, supervision.
⊠ ⁂ ⊠

ⱯⱯⱯ ▼▼▼ ▼▼▼ Westin Boston Waterfront H
(617) 532-4600. **$189-$599.** 425 Summer St. I-93, exit 23, se via Purchase St to Summer St. Int corridors. **Pets:** Accepted.
SAVE ⊠ ⁂ ⁂ ⊠

**ⱯⱯⱯ ▼▼▼ ▼▼▼ The Westin Copley Place
Boston H ❖**
(617) 262-9600. **$529-$569.** 10 Huntington Ave. I-90, exit 22, at Copley Square. Int corridors. **Pets:** Medium. Designated rooms, service with restrictions, supervision.
SAVE ⊠ ⁂ ⁂ ⊠ ⊠

BOXBOROUGH

▼▼▼▼ Holiday Inn Boxborough Woods H ❖
(978) 263-8701. **$99-$169.** 242 Adams Pl. I-495, exit 28, just e on SR 111. Int corridors. **Pets:** Small. $25 daily fee/pet. Service with restrictions, supervision.
ASK ⊠ ⁂ ⁂ ⁂ ⊠

BRAINTREE

▼▼▼▼ Candlewood Suites Boston–Braintree H
(781) 849-7450. **Call for rates.** 235 Wood Rd. I-93, exit 6, just n on SR 37, then 0.5 mi w. Int corridors. **Pets:** Accepted.
⊠ ⁂ ⁂

▼▼▼▼ Extended StayAmerica Boston-Braintree H
(781) 356-8333. **$93-$119.** 20 Rockdale St. I-93, exit 6, just se. Int corridors. **Pets:** Other species. $25 daily fee/pet. Service with restrictions, crate.
ASK ⊠ ⁂ ⁂ ⁂

ⱯⱯⱯ ▼▼▼ ▼▼▼ Hampton Inn Braintree H ❖
(781) 380-3300. **$149-$209.** 215 Wood Rd. I-93, exit 6, just n on SR 37, then 0.5 mi w. Int corridors. **Pets:** Small. Service with restrictions, supervision.
SAVE ⊠ ⁂ ⁂ ⁂ ⊠

ⱯⱯⱯ ▼▼▼ ▼▼▼ Sheraton Braintree Hotel H
(781) 848-0600. **$99-$349.** 37 Forbes Rd. I-93, exit 6, just s on SR 37, then just w. Int corridors. **Pets:** Accepted.
SAVE ⊠ ⁂ ⁂ ⁂ ⊠ ⊠

BROOKLINE

ⱯⱯⱯ ▼▼▼ ▼▼▼ Holiday Inn Brookline H
(617) 277-1200. **$139-$349.** 1200 Beacon St. 1 mi sw of Kenmore Square; at Beacon and St. Paul sts. Int corridors. **Pets:** Accepted.
SAVE ⊠ ⁂ ⁂ ⁂ ⁂ ⊠

BURLINGTON

▼▼▼▼ Candlewood Suites Boston-Burlington H
(781) 229-4300. **Call for rates.** 130 Middlesex Tpke. I-95, exit 32B, just n. Int corridors. **Pets:** Accepted.
⊠ ⁂ ⁂ ⊠

▼▼▼▼ Hilton Garden Inn Boston/Burlington H
(781) 272-8800. **$89-$209.** 5 Wheeler Rd. I-95, exit 32B, just s on Middlesex Tpke. Int corridors. **Pets:** Accepted.
⊠ ⁂ ⁂ ⁂ ⁂ ⊠

ⱯⱯⱯ ▼▼▼ ▼▼▼ Hyatt Summerfield Suites H
(781) 270-0800. **$99-$299.** 2 Van de Graaff Dr. I-95, exit 33A, just s on US 3, then 0.5 mi w on Wayside Rd. Int corridors. **Pets:** Accepted.
SAVE ⊠ ⁂ ⁂ ⁂ ⊠ ⊠

CAMBRIDGE

ⱯⱯⱯ ▼▼▼ ▼▼▼ Best Western Hotel Tria H
(617) 491-8000. **$139-$299.** 220 Alewife Brook Pkwy. Jct SR 2, 16 and US 3; in North Cambridge; I-90 (Massachusetts Tpke), exit Cambridge/Allston to SR 2 W (Fresh Pond Pkwy). Int corridors. **Pets:** Accepted.
SAVE ⊠ ⁂ ⁂ ⁂ ⊠

ⱯⱯⱯ ▼▼▼ ▼▼▼ The Charles Hotel, Harvard Square H
(617) 864-1200. **$199-$700.** One Bennett St. Just s of Harvard Square, at Eliot St. Int corridors. **Pets:** Accepted.
SAVE ⊠ ⁂ ⁂ ⁂ ⊠ ⊠

ⱯⱯⱯ ▼▼▼ ▼▼▼ Hotel Marlowe H
(617) 868-8000. **$179-$689.** 25 Edwin H Land Blvd. Just sw of jct SR 28. Int corridors. **Pets:** Accepted.
SAVE ⊠ ⁂ ⁂ ⊠

ⱯⱯⱯ ▼▼▼ ▼▼▼ Hyatt Regency Cambridge H
(617) 492-1234. **$99-$529.** 575 Memorial Dr. On US 3 and SR 2. Int corridors. **Pets:** Accepted.
SAVE ⊠ ⁂ ⁂ ⁂ ⁂ ⊠

ⱯⱯⱯ ▼▼▼ ▼▼▼ Le Meridien Cambridge H
(617) 577-0200. **$139-$499, 3 day notice.** 20 Sidney St. On SR 2A, 1 mi n of the river. Int corridors. **Pets:** Large, other species. Service with restrictions.
SAVE ⊠ ⁂ ⁂ ⁂ ⁂

▼▼▼▼ Residence Inn by Marriott Cambridge H ❖
(617) 349-0700. **$259-$549.** 6 Cambridge Center. Corner of Ames St and Broadway. Int corridors. **Pets:** Large. $150 one-time fee/room. Service with restrictions, crate.
⊠ ⁂ ⁂ ⁂ ⊠

ⱯⱯⱯ ▼▼▼ ▼▼▼ Sheraton Commander Hotel H
(617) 547-4800. **$129-$724.** 16 Garden St. Just n of Harvard Square. Int corridors. **Pets:** Accepted.
SAVE ⊠ ⁂ ⁂ ⁂

CONCORD

ⱯⱯⱯ ▼▼▼ ▼▼▼ Best Western at Historic Concord H
(978) 369-6100. **$129-$189.** 740 Elm St. 1.8 mi w, just off SR 2 and 2A. Int corridors. **Pets:** Other species. $10 daily fee/pet. Designated rooms, service with restrictions, supervision.
SAVE ⊠ ⁂ ⁂ ⊠

DANVERS

ⱯⱯⱯ ▼▼▼ ▼▼▼ Comfort Inn North Shore H
(978) 777-1700. **$79-$199.** 50 Dayton St. Just w of US 1; 0.8 mi n of jct SR 114, exit Center St northbound, w under US 1; exit Dayton St southbound. Int corridors. **Pets:** Medium. $10 daily fee/pet, $25 one-time fee/room. Service with restrictions, supervision.
SAVE ⊠ ⁂ ⁂ ⁂ ⊠

▼▼▼ ▼▼▼ Extended StayAmerica Boston-Danvers H
(978) 762-7414. **$62-$93.** 102 Newbury St. On US 1 southbound. Int corridors. **Pets:** Other species. $25 daily fee/pet. Service with restrictions, crate.
ASK ⊠ ⁂ ⁂ ⊠

▼▼▼ ▼▼▼ Residence Inn by Marriott H
(978) 777-7171. **$154-$169.** 51 Newbury St. US 1 N, just s of jct SR 114. Ext corridors. **Pets:** Accepted.
⊠ ⁂ ⁂ ⊠ ⊠

**ⱯⱯⱯ ▼▼▼ ▼▼▼ Sheraton Ferncroft Hotel and Coco Key Water
Resort H**
(978) 777-2500. **$89-$439.** 50 Ferncroft Rd. I-95, exit 50, follow signs for US 1 S to Ferncroft Village. Int corridors. **Pets:** Accepted.
SAVE ⊠ ⁂ ⁂ ⁂ ⁂ ⊠ ⊠

▼▼▼▼ **TownePlace Suites by Marriott** 🅷
(978) 777-6222. **$119-$149.** 238 Andover St. Southwest corner of jct US 1 and SR 114; SR 114 eastbound, enter just w of US 1 (no westbound entrance); US 1 southbound, enter through shopping center. Int corridors. **Pets:** Accepted.
✕ 🛎ᴹ 🛏 💻 🏊

DEDHAM

𝔸𝔸𝔸▷ ▼▼▼▼ **Hilton Boston Dedham** 🅷
(781) 329-7900. **$109-$269.** 25 Allied Dr. I-95, exit 14, just e. Int corridors. **Pets:** Accepted.
🆂🅰🆅🅴 ✕ 🛏 💻 🍴 🏊 ✕

𝔸𝔸𝔸▷ ▼▼▼▼ **Residence Inn by Marriott** 🅷
(781) 407-0999. **$179-$209.** 259 Elm St. I-95, exit 15A, just n, then 0.4 mi e. Int corridors. **Pets:** Medium. $75 one-time fee/room. Service with restrictions, supervision.
🆂🅰🆅🅴 ✕ 🛏 💻 🏊 ✕

FOXBORO

▼▼▼▼ **Foxborough Residence Inn by Marriott** 🅷
(508) 698-2800. **$189-$209.** 250 Foxborough Blvd. I-95, exit 7A, 0.6 mi s on SR 140, 0.7 mi e, then just n. Int corridors. **Pets:** Accepted.
✕ 🛎ᴹ 🛏 💻 🏊 ✕

FRAMINGHAM

𝔸𝔸𝔸▷ ▼▼▼ **Best Western Framingham** 🅷
(508) 872-8811. **$100-$150.** 130 Worcester Rd. I-90, exit 13, 0.5 mi s to SR 9; 1 mi w of Speen St; just w of Shopper's World Mall. Int corridors. **Pets:** Designated rooms, service with restrictions, supervision.
🆂🅰🆅🅴 ✕ 🛏 💻 🍴 🏊

𝔸𝔸𝔸▷ ▼▼ **Red Roof Inn #7068** Ⓜ
(508) 872-4499. **$86-$117.** 650 Cochituate Rd. I-90, exit 13, follow SR 30 E. Ext corridors. **Pets:** Accepted.
🆂🅰🆅🅴 ✕ 🛏 💻

𝔸𝔸𝔸▷ ▼▼▼▼ **Residence Inn by Marriott** 🅷 🐾
(508) 370-0001. **$188-$230.** 400 Staples Dr. SR 9 W to Crossing Blvd, then s. Int corridors. **Pets:** Medium, other species. $100 one-time fee/room. Service with restrictions, crate.
🆂🅰🆅🅴 ✕ 🛎ᴹ 🛏 💻 🏊

𝔸𝔸𝔸▷ ▼▼▼▼ **Sheraton Framingham Hotel & Conference Center** 🅷 🐾
(508) 879-7200. **$95-$289.** 1657 Worcester Rd. I-90, exit 12, follow signs to SR 9 W. Int corridors. **Pets:** Large, dogs only. Designated rooms, service with restrictions, supervision.
🆂🅰🆅🅴 ✕ 🛏 💻 🍴 🏊 ✕

FRANKLIN

▼▼▼▼ **Franklin Residence Inn by Marriott** 🅷
(508) 541-8188. **$189-$209.** 4 Forge Pkwy. I-495, exit 17, 0.7 mi nw off SR 140 N. Int corridors. **Pets:** Large, other species. $100 one-time fee/room. Service with restrictions, crate.
✕ 🛎ᴹ 🛏 💻 🏊 ✕

𝔸𝔸𝔸▷ ▼▼▼▼ **Hawthorn Suites Ltd** 🅷
(508) 553-3500. **Call for rates.** 835 Upper Union St. I-495, exit 16, just s, then 0.3 mi e. Int corridors. **Pets:** Accepted.
🆂🅰🆅🅴 ✕ 🛎ᴹ 🛏 💻 🏊 ✕

GLOUCESTER

▼ **Cape Ann Motor Inn** Ⓜ 🐾
(978) 281-2900. **$80-$170, 7 day notice.** 33 Rockport Rd. 2 mi n of terminus of SR 128 via SR 127A. Ext corridors. **Pets:** Service with restrictions, supervision.
✕ 🛏 🐾

HAVERHILL

𝔸𝔸𝔸▷ ▼▼▼▼ **Best Western Merrimack Valley** 🅷
(978) 373-1511. **$89-$169.** 401 Lowell Ave. I-495, exit 49 (SR 110). Int corridors. **Pets:** Medium. $20 daily fee/pet. Designated rooms, service with restrictions, supervision.
🆂🅰🆅🅴 ✕ 🛏 💻 🏊

𝔸𝔸𝔸▷ ▼▼▼▼ **Comfort Suites** 🅷
(978) 374-7755. **$70-$150.** 106 Bank Rd. I-495, exit 49 (SR 110), 0.5 mi s. Int corridors. **Pets:** Medium. $10 daily fee/room, $25 one-time fee/pet. Designated rooms, service with restrictions, supervision.
🆂🅰🆅🅴 ✕ 🛏 💻

LAWRENCE

𝔸𝔸𝔸▷ ▼▼▼▼ **Holiday Inn Express** 🅷
(978) 975-4050. **$69-$129.** 224 Winthrop Ave. I-495, exit 42A, just s on SR 114. Int corridors. **Pets:** Accepted.
🆂🅰🆅🅴 ✕ 🛎ᴹ 🛏 💻

LEXINGTON

▼▼ **Quality Inn & Suites** 🅷
(781) 861-0850. **Call for rates.** 440 Bedford St. I-95, exit 31B, just n on SR 4 and 225, continue n and use jug handle to reverse direction. Ext corridors. **Pets:** Medium. $25 one-time fee/pet. Designated rooms, service with restrictions, crate.
✕ 🛎ᴹ 🛏 💻 🏊

LOWELL

▼▼▼ **DoubleTree Riverfront Hotel** 🅷
(978) 452-1200. **$89-$189.** 50 Warren St. I-495, exit 35C, via Gorham and Church sts, follow signs; 0.5 mi from end of Lowell connector; center. Int corridors. **Pets:** Accepted.
✕ 🛏 💻 🍴 🏊 ✕

MARLBOROUGH

▼▼▼▼ **Courtyard by Marriott Marlborough** 🅷
(508) 480-0015. **$197-$241.** 75 Felton St. I-495, exit 24B, just w; just off US 20. Int corridors. **Pets:** Large. $79 one-time fee/room. Service with restrictions, crate.
✕ 🛎ᴹ 🛏 💻 🍴 🏊

▼▼▼▼ **Embassy Suites Hotel-Boston Marlborough** 🅷
(508) 485-5900. **$110-$220.** 123 Boston Post Rd W. I-495, exit 24B, 0.5 mi w; just off US 20. Int corridors. **Pets:** Accepted.
✕ 🛎ᴹ 🛏 💻 🍴 🏊 ✕

▼▼▼▼ **Residence Inn By Marriott Boston Marlborough** 🅷
(508) 481-1500. **$161-$197.** 112 Donald Lynch Blvd. I-290, exit 25B, 3 mi ne. Int corridors. **Pets:** Accepted.
✕ 🛎ᴹ 🛏 💻 🏊 ✕

NATICK

▼▼▼▼ **Crowne Plaza Boston-Natick** 🅷
(508) 653-8800. **Call for rates.** 1360 Worcester St. I-90, exit 12, 5 mi e; SR 9, 4 mi e of Framingham Center. Int corridors. **Pets:** Accepted.
✕ 🛎ᴹ 🛏 💻 🍴

NEEDHAM

𝔸𝔸𝔸▷ ▼▼▼▼ **Sheraton Needham Hotel** 🅷 🐾
(781) 444-1110. **$99-$369.** 100 Cabot St. I-95, exit 19A, just e. Int corridors. **Pets:** Medium, dogs only. Designated rooms, service with restrictions, supervision.
🆂🅰🆅🅴 ✕ 🛏 💻 🍴 🏊 ✕

NEWTON

▼▼▼▼ Hotel Indigo Boston-Newton Riverside 🄷
(617) 969-5300. **$159-$259.** 399 Grove St. I-95, exit 22, just e; 0.3 mi s of I-90. Int corridors. **Pets:** Accepted.
ASK ⊠ 🕮 💻 ¶ ⇒

ⒶⒶⒶ ▼▼▼▼ Sheraton Newton Hotel 🄷 ❖
(617) 969-3010. **$99-$349.** 320 Washington St. I-90, exit 17. Int corridors. **Pets:** Large, dogs only. Service with restrictions, crate.
SAVE ⊠ 🕮 💻 ¶ ⇒

NORTH CHELMSFORD

ⒶⒶⒶ ▼▼▼▼ Hawthorn Suites 🄷
(978) 256-5151. **Call for rates.** 25 Research Pl. US 3, exit 32, 0.3 mi ne on SR 4. Int corridors. **Pets:** Accepted.
SAVE ⊠ 🕭 🕮 💻

NORWOOD

▼▼▼▼ Hampton Inn 🄷
(781) 769-7000. **$94-$209.** 434 Boston Providence Hwy. I-95, exit 15B, 2.3 mi s. Int corridors. **Pets:** Small. $25 one-time fee/room. Service with restrictions, supervision.
⊠ 🕭 🕮 💻 ⇒

ⒶⒶⒶ ▼▼▼▼ Residence Inn Boston-Norwood 🄷
(781) 278-9595. **$169-$209.** 275 Norwood Park S. I-95, exit 15B, 4 mi s on US 1. Int corridors. **Pets:** Accepted.
SAVE ⊠ 🕭 🕮 💻 ⇒ ⊠

PEABODY

▼▼▼▼ Homewood Suites by Hilton 🄷
(978) 536-5050. **$109-$169.** 57 Newbury St. On US 1 northbound. Int corridors. **Pets:** Accepted.
⊠ 🕭 🕮 💻 ⇒

REVERE

▼▼▼▼ Comfort Inn & Suites Boston Airport 🄷 ❖
(781) 485-3600. **$99-$239.** 85 American Legion Hwy. Jct SR 1A and 60, 3 mi n of General Edward Lawrence Logan International Airport. Int corridors. **Pets:** Other species. $25 daily fee/pet. Designated rooms, service with restrictions.
ASK ⊠ 🕮 💻 ¶ ⇒

▼▼▼▼ Hampton Inn Boston Logan Airport 🄷
(781) 286-5665. **$109-$199.** 230 Lee Burbank Hwy. On SR 1A, 1.9 mi n of General Edward Lawrence Logan International Airport; 0.6 mi s of terminus SR 60. Int corridors. **Pets:** Accepted.
⊠ 🕭 🕮 💻 ¶ ⇒

ROCKPORT

▼▼▼▼ Inn on Cove Hill/Caleb Norwood Jr Guest House 🄱🄱
(978) 546-2701. **$120-$165, 10 day notice.** 37 Mt. Pleasant St. Just s on SR 127A. Ext/int corridors. **Pets:** Accepted.
⊠ 🗷

SALEM

▼▼▼▼ Hawthorne Hotel 🄷 ❖
(978) 744-4080. **$114-$224, 3 day notice.** 18 Washington Square W. On SR 1A. Int corridors. **Pets:** Medium, other species. $10 one-time fee/pet. Service with restrictions, supervision.
ASK ⊠ 🕮 ¶

▼▼▼▼ The Salem Inn 🄱🄱
(978) 741-0680. **$119-$305, 7 day notice.** 7 Summer St. On SR 114 at Essex St; SR 128, exit 25A, 3 mi e. Int corridors. **Pets:** Other species. $15 daily fee/pet. Designated rooms, service with restrictions.
ASK ⊠ 🕮 💻

SAUGUS

ⒶⒶⒶ ▼▼▼ Red Roof Inn #7305 🄷
(781) 941-1400. **$85-$110.** 920 Broadway. I-95, exit 44 northbound, 3.2 mi s on US 1; exit Main St/Saugus southbound to U-turn. Int corridors. **Pets:** Accepted.
SAVE ⊠ 🕭 🄼 🕮

SOMERVILLE

▼▼▼▼ La Quinta Inn & Suites Boston/ Somerville 🄷 ❖
(617) 625-5300. **$89-$219.** 23 Cummings St. I-93, exit 29 northbound, just ne on SR 28, then just s on Middlesex Ave; exit 31 southbound, 1 mi e on SR 16, then 0.5 mi s on SR 28 to Middlesex Ave. Int corridors. **Pets:** Medium, other species. Service with restrictions, supervision.
ASK ⊠ 🄼 🕮 💻

SUDBURY

▼▼▼ Clarion Carriage House Inn 🄷 ❖
(978) 443-2223. **$129-$279.** 738 Boston Post Rd. I-495, exit 24A, 7.5 mi e on US 20; 4.7 mi w of jct SR 27 on US 20. Int corridors. **Pets:** Medium, dogs only. $10 daily fee/pet. Service with restrictions, supervision.
ASK ⊠ 🕮 💻

TEWKSBURY

▼▼▼▼ Extended StayAmerica Boston-Tewksbury 🄷
(978) 863-9888. **$67-$93.** 1910 Andover St. I-93, exit 43B, just w; I-495, exit 39, just e. Int corridors. **Pets:** Other species. $25 daily fee/pet. Service with restrictions, crate.
ASK ⊠ 🕮 💻

ⒶⒶⒶ ▼▼▼ Holiday Inn Tewksbury-Andover 🄷
(978) 640-9000. **$85-$160.** 4 Highwood Dr. I-495, exit 39, just w on SR 133. Int corridors. **Pets:** Accepted.
SAVE ⊠ 🕮 💻 ¶ ⇒ ⊠

▼▼▼ Motel 6 Boston-Tewksbury #1403 🄼
(978) 851-8677. **$71-$84.** 95 Main St. I-495, exit 38, just s on SR 38. Ext corridors. **Pets:** Other species. Service with restrictions, supervision.
⊠ ⇒

▼▼▼▼ Residence Inn by Marriott Boston-Tewksbury 🄷
(978) 640-1003. **$149-$179.** 1775 Andover St. I-495, exit 39, 0.3 mi w on SR 133. Ext corridors. **Pets:** Accepted.
⊠ 🄼 🕭 🕮 💻 ⇒ ⊠

▼▼▼▼ TownePlace Suites by Marriott 🄷
(978) 863-9800. **$119-$144.** 20 International Pl. I-495, exit 39, 0.3 mi nw. Int corridors. **Pets:** Accepted.
⊠ 🄼 🕭 🕮 💻 ⇒

WAKEFIELD

ⒶⒶⒶ ▼▼▼▼ Sheraton Colonial Hotel Boston North & Conference Center 🄷 ❖
(781) 245-9300. **$95-$235.** 1 Audubon Rd. I-95, exit 42, just n. Int corridors. **Pets:** Large, other species. Service with restrictions, supervision.
SAVE ⊠ 🕭 🕮 💻 ¶ ⇒ ⊠

WALTHAM

▼▼▼▼ Courtyard by Marriott Boston-Waltham 🄷
(781) 419-0900. **$188-$230.** 387 Winter St. I-95, exit 27A, on northeast corner. Int corridors. **Pets:** Accepted.
⊠ 🄼 🕭 🕮 💻 ¶ ⊠

▼▼▼▼ Extended Stay Deluxe Boston-Waltham 🄷
(781) 622-1900. **$88-$108.** 32 Fourth Ave. I-95, exit 27A, just se. Int corridors. **Pets:** Other species. $25 daily fee/pet. Service with restrictions, crate.
ASK ⊠ 🄼 🕭 🕮 💻 ⇒

Hilton Garden Inn Boston/Waltham H
(781) 890-0100. **$89-$259.** 420 Totten Pond Rd. I-95, exit 27A, just e. Int corridors. **Pets:** Large. $100 one-time fee/room. Service with restrictions.

Holiday Inn Express Boston/Waltham H
(781) 890-2800. **$119-$179.** 385 Winter St. I-95, exit 27A, just ne. Ext/int corridors. **Pets:** $50 one-time fee/room. Service with restrictions, crate.

Home Suites Inn of Boston-Waltham H
(781) 890-3000. **$109-$169.** 455 Totten Pond Rd. I-95, exit 27A, just s. Int corridors. **Pets:** Accepted.

The Westin Waltham-Boston H
(781) 290-5600. **$349.** 70 Third Ave. I-95, exit 27A, just se. Int corridors. **Pets:** Accepted.

WESTFORD

Residence Inn by Marriott H
(978) 392-1407. **$152-$186.** 7 Lan Dr. I-495, exit 32, just s, then 0.5 w on SR 110. Int corridors. **Pets:** Accepted.

WOBURN

Best Western New Englander H
(781) 935-8160. **Call for rates.** 1 Rainin Rd. I-93, exit 36, just e. Int corridors. **Pets:** Small. $25 daily fee/pet. Designated rooms, no service, supervision.

Extended Stay Deluxe Boston-Woburn H
(781) 938-3737. **$73-$103.** 831 Main St. I-95, exit 35, just n on SR 38. Int corridors. **Pets:** Other species. $25 daily fee/pet. Service with restrictions, crate.

Hilton Boston/Woburn H
(781) 932-0999. **$100-$240.** 2 Forbes Rd. I-95, exit 36, 0.5 mi s via Washington St, then just e at Lukoil; jct Cedar St. Int corridors. **Pets:** Accepted.

Holiday Inn H
(781) 935-8760. **$99-$189.** 15 Middlesex Canal Park Rd. I-95, exit 35, s via SR 38. Int corridors. **Pets:** Medium. $50 one-time fee/room. Designated rooms, service with restrictions, supervision.

Red Roof Inn Woburn #238 H
(781) 935-7110. **$90-$130.** 19 Commerce Way. I-95, exit 36, just n, then just w on Mishawum Rd. Int corridors. **Pets:** Medium. Service with restrictions, supervision.

Residence Inn by Marriott-Boston/Woburn H
(781) 376-4000. **$209-$249.** 300 Presidential Way. I-93, exit 37C, just nw. Int corridors. **Pets:** Accepted.

END METROPOLITAN AREA

BROCKTON

Quality Inn H
(508) 588-3333. **Call for rates.** 1005 Belmont St. SR 24, exit 17A, just e on SR 123. Int corridors. **Pets:** Accepted.

Residence Inn by Marriott H
(508) 583-3600. **$99-$159.** 124 Liberty St. SR 24, exit 17B, just w, just s on Pearl St, then 0.3 mi se via Mill St connector. Int corridors. **Pets:** Large. $100 one-time fee/room. Service with restrictions, supervision.

CAPE COD AREA

BUZZARDS BAY

Bay Motor Inn CA
(508) 759-3989. **$62-$139, 7 day notice.** 223 Main St. SR 25, 0.5 mi w of Bourne rotary, exit 3. Ext corridors. **Pets:** $15 daily fee/room. Service with restrictions, supervision.

EAST FALMOUTH

Capewind Waterfront Resort M
(508) 548-3400. **$68-$254, 30 day notice.** 34 Maravista Extension. 2.2 mi e via SR 28, then just s, follow signs. Ext corridors. **Pets:** Accepted.

FALMOUTH

Mariner Motel M
(508) 548-1331. **$69-$189, 14 day notice.** 555 Main St. 0.5 mi e on SR 28. Ext corridors. **Pets:** Accepted.

HYANNIS

Cape Cod Harbor House Inn M
(508) 771-1880. **Call for rates.** 119 Ocean St. Opposite ferry docks. Ext corridors. **Pets:** Accepted.

Comfort Inn H
(508) 771-4804. **$89-$210.** 1470 Iyannough Rd. US 6, exit 6, 1.3 mi se on SR 132. Ext/int corridors. **Pets:** Other species. $25 daily fee/room. Designated rooms, service with restrictions, supervision.

ORLEANS

Governor Prence Inn M
(508) 255-1216. **$99-$169, 10 day notice.** 66 SR 6A. 0.5 mi w of rotary. Ext corridors. **Pets:** Accepted.

Orleans Inn CI
(508) 255-2222. **$250-$450.** 21 Rt 6A. On SR 28 and 6A, exit rotary, just w. Int corridors. **Pets:** Accepted.

(AAA) ▼▼▼ Skaket Beach Motel **M**
(508) 255-1020. **$65-$175, 10 day notice.** 203 Cranberry Hwy (Rt 6A). US 6, exit 12, just e. Ext corridors. **Pets:** Dogs only. $12 daily fee/pet. Service with restrictions, supervision.
[SAVE] [X] 🔋 💻 🏊

PROVINCETOWN

▼▼ Bayshore & Chandler **CO** ✿
(508) 487-9133. **Call for rates.** 493 Commercial St. 0.8 mi e of Town Hall. Ext corridors. **Pets:** Dogs only. $20 daily fee/room. Service with restrictions.
[X] 🔋

▼▼▼ Surfside Hotel & Suites **H** ✿
(508) 487-1726. **$129-$329.** 542-543 Commercial St. 1 mi e of Town Hall. Ext/int corridors. **Pets:** Dogs only. $40 daily fee/room. Designated rooms, service with restrictions.
[ASK] [X] 🔋 💻 🏊

▼▼▼▼ White Wind Inn **BB**
(508) 487-1526. **$85-$295, 14 day notice.** 174 Commercial St. Just w of Town Hall. Int corridors. **Pets:** Accepted.
[X] 🔋 💻

SANDWICH

▼ Shady Nook Inn & Motel **M**
(508) 888-0409. **$87-$143.** 14 Old Kings Hwy (SR 6A). On SR 6A, 1.5 mi w. Ext corridors. **Pets:** Accepted.
[X] 🔋 🏊

SOUTH YARMOUTH

(AAA) ▼▼▼▼ Best Western Blue Rock Resort **M** ✿
(508) 398-6962. **$99-$220, 10 day notice.** 39 Todd Rd. SR 28, 1 mi ne via N Main St and High Bank Rd, then 0.5 mi nw on Country Club Dr, follow signs. Ext corridors. **Pets:** Medium, dogs only. $25 daily fee/pet. Designated rooms, service with restrictions, crate.
[SAVE] [X] 🔋 💻 🍴 🏊

(AAA) ▼▼▼▼ Best Western Blue Water on The
Ocean **H** ✿
(508) 398-2288. **$100-$440, 10 day notice.** 291 S Shore Dr. 1 mi s off SR 28. Ext/int corridors. **Pets:** $25 daily fee/pet. Designated rooms, service with restrictions, supervision.
[SAVE] [X] 🔋 💻 🍴 🏊

WEST DENNIS

▼▼ Inn at Swan River **M**
(508) 394-5415. **$69-$165, 10 day notice.** 829 Main St. On SR 28, just w of SR 134. Ext corridors. **Pets:** Accepted.
[ASK] [X] 🔋 🏊

END AREA

CHICOPEE

(AAA) ▼▼▼ Quality Inn-Chicopee **H**
(413) 592-6171. **$69-$99.** 463 Memorial Dr. I-90 (Massachusetts Tpke), exit 5, just ne; upon exiting, use jug handle overpass to SR 33 N. Int corridors. **Pets:** Accepted.
[SAVE] [X] 🔋 💻 🏊

EAST WAREHAM

(AAA) ▼▼ Atlantic Motel **M**
(508) 295-0210. **$69-$199, 10 day notice.** 7 Depot St. Between east-bound and westbound lanes of US 6/SR 28; jct SR 25, exit 1. Ext corridors. **Pets:** Medium, dogs only. $20 daily fee/pet. Designated rooms, service with restrictions, supervision.
[SAVE] [X] 🔋 🏊

FAIRHAVEN

▼▼▼ Seaport Inn L.L.C **H**
(508) 997-1281. **$89-$159.** 110 Middle St. I-195, exit 15, 1 mi s, then just off US 6. Int corridors. **Pets:** Other species. $10 one-time fee/room. Service with restrictions, crate.
[ASK] [X] 🔋 💻

GARDNER

▼▼▼ Colonial Hotel **H**
(978) 630-2500. **$99-$139.** 625 Betty Spring Rd. SR 2, exit 24 eastbound; exit 24B, 0.9 mi n on SR 140, then 0.5 mi w. Int corridors. **Pets:** Other species. $25 one-time fee/room. Designated rooms, crate.
[ASK] [X] 🔋 💻 🍴 🏊 ✕

▼▼ Super 8 **M**
(978) 630-2888. **$79-$110.** 22 Pearson Blvd. SR 2, exit 23, just n. Int corridors. **Pets:** Medium. $16 daily fee/pet. Service with restrictions, super-vision.
[X] 🔋 💻

GREAT BARRINGTON

(AAA) ◆ Monument Mountain Motel **M**
(413) 528-3272. **$59-$199, 14 day notice.** 247 Stockbridge Rd (Rt 7). On US 7, 1.2 mi s of jct SR 183. Ext corridors. **Pets:** Dogs only. $20 daily fee/pet. Designated rooms, service with restrictions, supervision.
[SAVE] [X] 🔋 💻 🏊

GREENFIELD

▼▼▼ The Brandt House B&B **BB** ✿
(413) 774-3329. **$95-$295, 30 day notice.** 29 Highland Ave. I-91, exit 26, 1.8 mi e on SR 2A, then se via Crescent St. Int corridors. **Pets:** Dogs only. $25 one-time fee/room. Service with restrictions, supervision.
[ASK] [X] 🔋

HADLEY

(AAA) ▼▼ Comfort Inn **H**
(413) 584-9816. **$75-$205.** 237 Russell St (SR 9). I-91, exit 19 northbound; exit 20 southbound, 3 mi e on SR 9. Int corridors. **Pets:** Medium, dogs only. $25 daily fee/pet. Designated rooms, service with restrictions, supervision.
[SAVE] [X] 🔋 💻 🏊

▼▼ Howard Johnson Inn **H**
(413) 586-0114. **$79-$179.** 401 Russell St. I-91, exit 19 northbound, 4.3 mi e on SR 9; exit 24 southbound, 10 mi s on SR 116, then just w on SR 9. Int corridors. **Pets:** Dogs only. $20 daily fee/room. Designated rooms, service with restrictions.
[ASK] [X] 🔋 🔋 💻 🏊

HOLLAND

▼▼▼ The Inn at Restful Paws **BB** ✿
(413) 245-7792. **$174, 14 day notice.** 70 Allen Hill Rd. SR 20, 2.1 mi s on E Brimfield Rd, 0.4 mi on Alexander Rd, then 0.7 mi n. Int corridors. **Pets:** No service, supervision.
[ASK] [X] 💻 📺 ✕

HOLYOKE

ⒶⒶⒶ ◆◆◆ Homewood Suites by Hilton Holyoke-Springfield 🅷
(413) 532-3100. **$96-$154.** 375 Whitney Ave. I-91, exit 15, just w on Lower Westfield Rd, then 0.4 mi s. Int corridors. **Pets:** Large, other species. $100 one-time fee/room. Service with restrictions, crate.
ⓈⒶⓋⒺ ✕ ♿ 🛅 🖵 🐾 ✕

KINGSTON

◆◆ Plymouth Bay Inn & Suites 🅼 ❖
(781) 585-3831. **$79-$149.** 149 Main St. SR 3, exit 9, just w. Int corridors. **Pets:** Medium. Designated rooms, service with restrictions, supervision.
ⒶⓈⓀ ✕ ♿ 🛅 🐾

LENOX

◆◆◆◆ Blantyre 🅲🅸
(413) 637-3556. **$600-$1850, 30 day notice.** 16 Blantyre Rd. US 20, 1 mi s from jct SR 183. Int corridors. **Pets:** Accepted.
✕ 🛅 🖵 🍽 🐾 ✕

ⒶⒶⒶ ◆◆◆◆ Cranwell Resort, Spa & Golf Club 🅷
(413) 637-1364. **$205-$395, 7 day notice.** 55 Lee Rd. I-90 (Massachusetts Tpke), exit 2, 3.5 mi n on US 7/20. Ext/int corridors. **Pets:** Accepted.
ⓈⒶⓋⒺ ✕ 🛅 🖵 🍽 🐾 ✕

◆◆◆ The Kemble Inn 🅱🅱
(413) 637-4113. **$115-$455, 15 day notice.** 2 Kemble St. Jct SR 183 and 7A. Int corridors. **Pets:** $45 daily fee/pet. Designated rooms, service with restrictions, supervision.
ⒶⓈⓀ ✕

LEOMINSTER

ⒶⒶⒶ ◆◆◆ Super 8 🅼
(978) 537-2800. **$69-$96.** 482 N Main St. SR 2, exit 31B, just n on SR 12. Int corridors. **Pets:** Accepted.
ⓈⒶⓋⒺ ✕ ♿ 🛅

MANSFIELD

◆◆◆ Holiday Inn Mansfield 🅷
(508) 339-2200. **$110-$190.** 31 Hampshire St. I-95, exit 7A, 0.5 mi s on SR 140, then 1 mi w on Forbes Rd; I-495, exit 12, 2 mi n on SR 140, then w on Forbes Rd. Int corridors. **Pets:** Medium, dogs only. $10 daily fee/pet. Designated rooms, service with restrictions, supervision.
ⒶⓈⓀ ✕ 🛅 🖵 🍽 🐾 ✕

MARTHA'S VINEYARD AREA

EDGARTOWN

ⒶⒶⒶ ◆◆◆ Colonial Inn of Martha's Vineyard 🅲🅸
(508) 627-4711. **$95-$425, 14 day notice.** 38 N Water St. Just n from Main St. Int corridors. **Pets:** Dogs only. $30 daily fee/room. Designated rooms, service with restrictions, crate.
ⓈⒶⓋⒺ ✕ 🛅 🖵 🍽

OAK BLUFFS

ⒶⒶⒶ ◆◆◆ The Dockside Inn 🅱🅱
(508) 693-2966. **$150-$450, 21 day notice.** 9 Circuit Ave Ext. Center. Ext corridors. **Pets:** Medium, dogs only. $20 daily fee/room. Designated rooms, service with restrictions, supervision.
ⓈⒶⓋⒺ ✕ 🛅 🖵

VINEYARD HAVEN

ⒶⒶⒶ ◆◆◆ The Doctor's House 🅱🅱
(508) 696-0859. **$150-$340, 4 day notice.** 60 Mt. Aldworth Rd. 0.4 mi sw to road to Edgartown, 1 blk e. Int corridors. **Pets:** Accepted.
ⓈⒶⓋⒺ ✕ ☎

END AREA

MIDDLEBORO

ⒶⒶⒶ ◆◆ Days Inn-Plymouth/Middleboro 🅷
(508) 946-4400. **$69-$99.** 30 E Clark St. I-495, exit 4, at SR 105. Int corridors. **Pets:** Accepted.
ⓈⒶⓋⒺ ✕ 🛅 🖵 🐾

MILFORD

◆◆◆ DoubleTree Hotel Boston/Milford 🅷
(508) 478-7010. **$99-$199.** 11 Beaver St. I-495, exit 19, jct SR 109. Int corridors. **Pets:** Accepted.
✕ 🛅 🖵 🍽 🐾

ⒶⒶⒶ ◆◆◆ Holiday Inn Express 🅷
(508) 634-1054. **$99-$159.** 50 Fortune Blvd. I-495, exit 20, just sw on SR 85, then just se. Int corridors. **Pets:** Medium. $25 one-time fee/room. Designated rooms, service with restrictions, supervision.
ⓈⒶⓋⒺ ✕ ♿ 🛅 🖵 🐾

◆◆◆ La Quinta Inn 🅷 ❖
(508) 478-8243. **$75-$139.** 24 Beaver St. I-495, exit 19, just w on SR 109. Int corridors. **Pets:** Medium, other species. Service with restrictions, supervision.
ⒶⓈⓀ ✕ 🖵

NANTUCKET ISLAND

ⒶⒶⒶ ◆◆◆ Seven Sea Street Inn 🅱🅱
(508) 228-3577. **$99-$329, 15 day notice.** 7 Sea St. Center. Int corridors. **Pets:** Accepted.
ⓈⒶⓋⒺ ✕ 🛅 🖵

NORTH ADAMS

ⒶⒶⒶ ◆◆◆ Jae's Inn 🅱🅱
(413) 664-0100. **$95-$160, 3 day notice.** 1111 S State St. 2 mi s on SR 8; center. Int corridors. **Pets:** Other species. $20 daily fee/pet. Designated rooms, service with restrictions, supervision.
ⓈⒶⓋⒺ ✕ 🛅 🐾 ✕

NORTHAMPTON

▼▼ ▼▼ Clarion Hotel & Conference Center ⬛
(413) 586-1211. **$89-$175.** One Atwood Dr. I-91, exit 18, just s on US 5. Int corridors. **Pets:** Dogs only. $20 daily fee/room. Designated rooms, service with restrictions.

(ASK) ⊠ 🏃ᴹ 🛏 ➡ 🍴 ⇌ ⊠

NORTH DARTMOUTH

ⱲⱲⱲ ▼▼ Comfort Inn ⬛
(508) 996-0800. **$89-$169.** 171 Faunce Corner Rd. I-195, exit 12A westbound; exit 12 eastbound, then s. Int corridors. **Pets:** Very small. $50 one-time fee/room. Service with restrictions.

(SAVE) ⊠ 🛏 ➡ ⇌

ⱲⱲⱲ ▼▼▼ Residence Inn by Marriott ⬛
(508) 984-5858. **$120-$190.** 181 Faunce Corner Rd. I-195, exit 12A westbound; exit 12 eastbound, just s. Int corridors. **Pets:** Medium. $75 one-time fee/pet. Service with restrictions, supervision.

(SAVE) ⊠ 🏃ᴹ 🛏 ➡ ⇌ ⊠

NORTON

▼▼ ▼▼ Extended StayAmerica-Foxboro-Norton ⬛
(508) 285-7800. **$62-$103.** 280 S Washington St. I-495, exit 9, 0.3 mi se on Bay St, then 0.5 mi nw via Industrial Park Rd. Int corridors. **Pets:** Other species. $25 daily fee/pet. Service with restrictions, crate.

(ASK) ⊠ 🏃ᴹ 🛏 ➡

ORANGE

ⱲⱲⱲ ▼ Executive Inn Ⓜ ❋
(978) 544-8864. **$45-$80, 7 day notice.** 110 Daniel Shay Hwy. US 202, exit 16, just n of jct SR 2. Ext/int corridors. **Pets:** $7 daily fee/pet. Service with restrictions, supervision.

(SAVE) ⊠ 🛏

PITTSFIELD

▼▼▼ Crowne Plaza Hotel and Resort Pittsfield Berkshires ⬛
(413) 499-2000. **$119-$349, 14 day notice.** 1 West St, Berkshire Common. Center. Int corridors. **Pets:** Small. $50 one-time fee/pet. Designated rooms, service with restrictions, supervision.

(ASK) ⊠ 🏃ᴹ 🛏 ➡ 🍴 ⇌ ⊠

ⱲⱲⱲ ▼▼▼▼ Patriot Suites Hotel ⬛
(413) 997-3300. **$145-$295, 3 day notice.** 8 Dan Fox Dr. I-90, exit 2, 9 mi nw on US 20, then just w. Int corridors. **Pets:** Small. $75 one-time fee/room. Designated rooms, service with restrictions, supervision.

(SAVE) ⊠ 🏃ᴹ 🛏 ➡ ⇌

RAYNHAM

ⱲⱲⱲ ▼▼ ▼▼ Quality Inn of Raynham-Taunton Ⓜ
(508) 824-8647. **$80-$130.** 164 New State Hwy. SR 24, exit 13B, 0.8 mi w on US 44. Ext/int corridors. **Pets:** $10 daily fee/pet. Designated rooms, service with restrictions, supervision.

(SAVE) ⊠ 🛏 ➡ ⇌

REHOBOTH

▼▼▼ Five Bridge Inn Bed & Breakfast 🅱🅱
(508) 252-3190. **$98-$145, 3 day notice.** 154 Pine St. 1.6 mi n of US 44; 3.3 mi w of jct SR 118; US 44, n on Blanding, e on Broad, n on Salisbury, then w. Int corridors. **Pets:** Accepted.

(ASK) ⊠ 🛏 ➡ ⇌ ⊠

RICHMOND

▼▼▼ The Inn at Richmond 🅱🅱
(413) 698-2566. **$160-$380, 15 day notice.** 802 State Rd (SR 41). 2.5 mi s of jct US 20. Ext/int corridors. **Pets:** Dogs only. $25 one-time fee/room. Designated rooms, service with restrictions, supervision.

(ASK) ⊠ 🛏 ➡ ⊠

ROCKLAND

ⱲⱲⱲ ▼▼▼ Best Western Rockland ⬛ ❋
(781) 871-5660. **$109-$169.** 909 Hingham St. SR 3, exit 14, 0.3 mi sw on SR 228. Int corridors. **Pets:** $20 daily fee/pet. Designated rooms, service with restrictions.

(SAVE) ⊠ 🛏 ➡

SEEKONK

▼ Motel 6–1289 Ⓜ
(508) 336-7800. **$55-$85.** 821 Fall River Ave. I-195, exit 1, just n on SR 114A. Int corridors. **Pets:** Other species. Service with restrictions, supervision.

⊠

▼▼ ▼▼ Ramada Inn-Providence ⬛ ❋
(508) 336-7300. **$89-$150.** 940 Fall River Ave. I-195, exit 1, just s. Int corridors. **Pets:** $10 daily fee/pet. Designated rooms, service with restrictions.

(ASK) ⊠ 🛏 ➡ 🍴 ⇌ ⊠

SOMERSET

ⱲⱲⱲ ▼▼▼ Quality Inn-Fall River/Somerset ⬛ ❋
(508) 678-4545. **$67-$209.** 1878 Wilbur Ave. Jct SR 103 and I-195, exit 4 eastbound; exit 4A westbound. Int corridors. **Pets:** Large. $50 deposit/room. Designated rooms, service with restrictions, supervision.

(SAVE) ⊠ 🛏 ➡ ⇌ ⊠

SOUTHBOROUGH

ⱲⱲⱲ ▼▼▼ Red Roof Inn # 7075 Ⓜ
(508) 481-3904. **$66-$100.** 367 Turnpike Rd. I-495, exit 23A, just e on SR 9. Ext corridors. **Pets:** Accepted.

(SAVE) ⊠ 🛏

SPRINGFIELD

▼▼▼▼ Holiday Inn ⬛
(413) 781-0900. **Call for rates.** 711 Dwight St. I-291, exit 2A, just e. Int corridors. **Pets:** Medium, other species. $35 one-time fee/room.

⊠ 🏃ᴹ 🛏 ➡ 🍴 ⇌ ⊠

ⱲⱲⱲ ▼▼▼▼ Sheraton Springfield Monarch Place ⬛
(413) 781-1010. **$99-$229.** 1 Monarch Pl. I-91, exit 6 northbound; exit 7 southbound, just n; downtown. Int corridors. **Pets:** Accepted.

(SAVE) ⊠ 🏃ᴹ 🛏 ➡ 🍴 ⇌ ⊠

STURBRIDGE

ⱲⱲⱲ ▼▼▼ Comfort Inn & Suites Colonial ⬛
(508) 347-3306. **$89-$269.** 215 Charlton Rd. I-90 (Massachusetts Tpke), exit 9, 0.5 mi e; I-84, exit 3A. Ext/int corridors. **Pets:** Accepted.

(SAVE) ⊠ 🏃ᴹ 🛏 ➡ ⇌

▼▼ ▼▼ Days Inn Ⓜ
(508) 347-3391. **$49-$149, 7 day notice.** 66-68 Haynes St (SR 15). I-84, exit 2, 0.5 mi n, follow signs to SR 131, on I-84 service road. Ext/int corridors. **Pets:** Medium. $10 daily fee/pet. Service with restrictions, supervision.

(ASK) ⊠ 🛏 ➡ ⇌

▼▼ ▼▼ Publick House Historic Inn & Country Lodge ⬛
(508) 347-3313. **$79-$209.** 295 Main St. I-90 (Massachusetts Tpke), exit 9; I-84, exit 3B, 0.5 mi s of jct US 20. Ext/int corridors. **Pets:** Accepted.

(ASK) ⊠ 🛏 ➡ 🍴 ⇌

ⱲⱲⱲ ▼▼▼ Sturbridge Host Hotel and Conference Center on Cedar Lake ⬛
(508) 347-7393. **$115-$199.** 366 Main St. I-90 (Massachusetts Tpke), exit 9, just w on US 20; I-84, exit 3B. Int corridors. **Pets:** Accepted.

(SAVE) ⊠ 🛏 ➡ 🍴 ⇌ ⊠

AAA WWW Super 8 M
(508) 347-9000. **$49-$149.** 358 Main St. I-90 (Massachusetts Tpke), exit 9; I-84, exit 3B on US 20. Ext corridors. **Pets:** Accepted.
SAVE X ⊟ ▣ ➾

AAA WWW Travelodge H ❖
(508) 347-1978. **$60-$130.** 400 Haynes Rd (SR 15). I-84, exit 1, 0.5 mi w. Int corridors. **Pets:** Medium. $10 daily fee/pet. Designated rooms, no service, supervision.
SAVE X ⊟ ▣ ➾

WESTBOROUGH

WW Comfort Inn-Westborough H
(508) 366-0202. **$89-$149.** 399 Turnpike Rd. I-495, exit 23B, 4.8 mi w. Int corridors. **Pets:** Medium. $10 daily fee/pet. Designated rooms, service with restrictions, supervision.
ASK X ⊟ ▣

WW Extended Stay Deluxe-Boston-Westborough H
(508) 616-9213. **$72-$98.** 180 E Main St. I-495, exit 23B, 1.4 mi w, then just sw on SR 30. Int corridors. **Pets:** Other species. $25 daily fee/pet. Service with restrictions, crate.
ASK X ⚹M ⊟ ▣

WW Extended Stay Deluxe Boston-Westborough-Computer Dr H
(508) 366-6100. **$72-$98.** 1800 Computer Dr. I-495, exit 23B, just w; north side of SR 9. Int corridors. **Pets:** Other species. $25 daily fee/pet. Service with restrictions, crate.
ASK X ⚹M ⊟ ▣ ➾

AAA WWW Residence Inn by Marriott Boston/Westborough H
(508) 366-7700. **$197-$241.** 25 Connector Rd. I-495, exit 23B, just w on SR 9, exit Computer/Research Dr, then 0.3 mi s. Ext/int corridors. **Pets:** Accepted.
SAVE X ⚹M ⊟ ▣ ➾ ⊠

WESTFIELD

AAA WWW Econo Lodge & Suites H
(413) 568-2821. **$64-$129.** 2 Southampton Rd. I-90, exit 3, at US 202 and SR 10. Ext/int corridors. **Pets:** Medium. $25 one-time fee/pet. Designated rooms, service with restrictions, supervision.
SAVE X ⊟ ▣ ➾

WESTMINSTER

AAA WWW Wachusett Village Inn & Conference Center H
(978) 874-2000. **$99-$169.** 9 Village Inn Rd. 0.7 mi w on Village Inn Rd; SR 2, exit 27 westbound, 0.3 mi e; exit 26 eastbound. Ext/int corridors. **Pets:** Small. $50 deposit/room. Designated rooms, service with restrictions, crate.
SAVE X ⊟ ▣ ❰❱ ➾ ⊠

WEST SPRINGFIELD

AAA WWW Candlewood Suites H
(413) 739-1122. **$108-$118.** 572 Riverdale St. I-91, exit 13B, 1.3 mi s. Int corridors. **Pets:** $25 daily fee/room. Service with restrictions, crate.
SAVE X ⚹M ⊟ ▣ ➾

AAA WWW Hampton Inn H ❖
(413) 732-1300. **$189.** 1011 Riverdale St (US 5). I-91, exit 13B, 0.3 mi s. Int corridors. **Pets:** Medium, dogs only. $50 one-time fee/room. Supervision.
SAVE X ⚹M ⊟ ▣ ➾

AAA WWW Quality Inn H
(413) 739-7261. **$59-$169.** 1150 Riverdale St. I-91, exit 13B, jct US 5. Int corridors. **Pets:** $25 one-time fee/room. No service, supervision.
SAVE X ⊟ ▣ ❰❱ ➾

WWW Residence Inn by Marriott H
(413) 732-9543. **$150-$190.** 64 Border Way. I-91, exit 13A, on US 5. Int corridors. **Pets:** Accepted.
X ⚹M ⊟ ▣ ➾ ⊠

WEST STOCKBRIDGE

AAA WW Pleasant Valley Motel M
(413) 232-8511. **$45-$165, 15 day notice.** 42 Stockbridge Rd. I-90 (Massachusetts Tpke), exit B3 eastbound, 0.5 mi s on SR 22, then 3.5 mi e on SR 102; exit 1 westbound, 0.4 mi e. Ext corridors. **Pets:** Designated rooms, service with restrictions, supervision.
SAVE X ➾

WILLIAMSTOWN

WW Cozy Corner Motel M
(413) 458-8006. **$50-$135, 10 day notice.** 284 Sand Springs Rd (US 7). On US 7, 1.5 mi n of jct SR 2. Ext corridors. **Pets:** Other species. $10 daily fee/pet. Service with restrictions, supervision.
X ⊟

WWW Maple Terrace Motel M ❖
(413) 458-9677. **$57-$155, 10 day notice.** 555 Main St. On SR 2, 1 mi e of jct US 7. Ext corridors. **Pets:** Dogs only. $15 one-time fee/pet. Service with restrictions, supervision.
X ⊟ ▣ ➾

AAA WW The Villager Motel M
(413) 458-4046. **$55-$125, 14 day notice.** 953 Simonds Rd. On US 7, 1.7 mi n of jct SR 2. Ext corridors. **Pets:** Accepted.
SAVE X ⊟

WORCESTER

AAA WWW Beechwood Hotel H
(508) 754-5789. **$245-$325.** 363 Plantation St. I-290, exit 22 westbound, 0.5 mi w on Lincoln St, then 1.5 mi s; exit 21 eastbound, 1.3 mi s. Int corridors. **Pets:** Accepted.
SAVE X ⚹M ⊟ ▣ ❰❱ ⊠

WWW Crowne Plaza Hotel H ❖
(508) 791-1600. **$119-$199.** 10 Lincoln Square. I-290, exit 17 eastbound; exit 18 westbound, 0.3 mi s. Int corridors. **Pets:** Medium, other species. $25 daily fee/pet. Service with restrictions, supervision.
ASK X ⚹M ⊟ ▣ ❰❱ ➾ ⊠

WWW Residence Inn by Marriott Worcester H
(508) 753-6300. **$189-$209.** 503 Plantation St. I-290, exit 21, 0.5 mi sw. Int corridors. **Pets:** $100 one-time fee/room. Service with restrictions, crate.
X ⚹M ⊟ ▣ ➾

CITY INDEX

ADRIAN

▼▼ Super 8 🅗
(517) 265-8888. **Call for rates.** 1091 W US 223. Jct US 223 and SR 52, just w. Int corridors. **Pets:** Accepted.

⊠ 🛢 🖵

ALGONAC

▼▼ Linda's Lighthouse Inn 🅱🅱
(810) 794-2992. **$95-$135, 14 day notice.** 5965 Pointe Tremble Rd (SR 29). I-94, exit 243 (23 Mile Rd), 14.3 mi e. Int corridors. **Pets:** Accepted.

⊠ ⊠ 🕅 🗷

ALLEGAN

▼▼▼ Castle In The Country B & B Inn 🅱🅱
(269) 673-8054. **$115-$245, 7 day notice.** 340 SR 40 S. SR 40 S, 6 mi s. Int corridors. **Pets:** Accepted.

⊠ ⊠ 🗷

ALLENDALE

▼▼ Sleep Inn & Suites 🅗 ❀
(616) 892-8000. **$69-$179.** 4869 Becker Dr. I-96, exit 16, 6 mi s, then 2.5 mi e on SR 45. Int corridors. **Pets:** Other species. $10 daily fee/pet. Designated rooms, service with restrictions, supervision.

ⒶⓈⓀ ⊠ 🖢 🛢 🖵 🐾

ALPENA

⚫⚫⚫ ▼▼ Best Western of Alpena Ⓜ
(989) 356-9087. **$79-$87.** 1286 Hwy M-32 W. 2.3 mi w of jct US 23. Ext/int corridors. **Pets:** Large, dogs only. $5 daily fee/pet. Designated rooms, service with restrictions, supervision.

Ⓢ🄰🄳ⓔ ⊠ 🛢 🖵 🐾

▼▼ Days Inn 🅗
(989) 356-6118. **$80-$120.** 1496 Hwy 32 W. 2.5 mi w of jct US 23. Int corridors. **Pets:** Dogs only. $5 daily fee/room. Service with restrictions, supervision.

ⒶⓈⓀ ⊠ 🛢 🖵 🐾 ⊠

▼▼ Holiday Inn 🅗
(989) 356-2151. **$89-$119.** 1000 Hwy 23 N. On US 23, 1 mi n. Int corridors. **Pets:** Accepted.

ⒶⓈⓀ ⊠ 🛢 🖵 🍴 🐾 ⊠

ANN ARBOR

▼▼ Candlewood Suites 🅗
(734) 663-2818. **Call for rates.** 701 Waymarket Way. I-94, exit 175 (Ann Arbor/Saline Rd), just e on Eisenhower Rd. Int corridors. **Pets:** Accepted.

⊠ 🖢 🛢 🖵

▼▼ Extended StayAmerica 🅗
(734) 332-1980. **$48-$90.** 1501 Briarwood Cir Dr. I-94, exit 177 (State St), just ne. Int corridors. **Pets:** Other species. $25 daily fee/pet. Service with restrictions, crate.

⊠ 🖢 🛢 🖵

▼▼ Extended Stay Deluxe Detroit-Ann Arbor 🅗
(734) 997-7623. **$55-$95.** 3265 Boardwalk St. I-94, exit 177 (State St), just n, then just e on Victors Way. Int corridors. **Pets:** Other species. $25 daily fee/pet. Service with restrictions, crate.

⊠ 🛢 🖵

▼▼▼ Hampton Inn-North 🅗
(734) 996-4444. **$89-$259.** 2300 Green Rd. US 23, exit 41 (Plymouth Rd), just nw. Int corridors. **Pets:** Large. $25 one-time fee/room. Service with restrictions, supervision.

⊠ 🖢 🛢 🖵 🍴 🐾

▼▼▼ Hawthorn Suites 🅗
(734) 327-0011. **$125-$250.** 3535 Green Ct. US 23, exit 41 (Plymouth Rd), just sw. Int corridors. **Pets:** Small. $100 one-time fee/room. Service with restrictions, supervision.

ⒶⓈⓀ ⊠ 🖢 🛢 🖵 🐾 ⊠

⚫⚫⚫ ▼▼▼ Red Roof Inn #7045 Ⓜ
(734) 996-5800. **$70-$151.** 3621 Plymouth Rd. US 23, exit 41 (Plymouth Rd), just nw. Ext corridors. **Pets:** Medium. $100 one-time fee/room. Service with restrictions, supervision.

Ⓢ🄰🄳ⓔ ⊠ 🛢

▼▼ Residence Inn by Marriott 🅗
(734) 996-5666. **$159-$169.** 800 Victors Way. I-94, exit 177 (State St), just ne. Ext/int corridors. **Pets:** Accepted.

⊠ 🛢 🖵 🐾 ⊠

AU GRES

▼▼ Econo Lodge Inn 🅗
(989) 876-4060. **Call for rates.** 510 W US 23. On US 23, just w. Int corridors. **Pets:** Accepted.

⊠ 🛢 🖵 🐾

BAD AXE

▼▼ Econo Lodge Inns & Suites **H**
(989) 269-3200. **$63-$80.** 898 N Van Dyke Rd. Just s of jct SR 142 and 53 (Van Dyke Rd). Int corridors. **Pets:** Small. $10 daily fee/pet. Service with restrictions, supervision.
[ASK] [X] [♦] [▣] [≈]

BATTLE CREEK

▼▼ Baymont Inn & Suites-Battle Creek **H**
(269) 979-5400. **Call for rates.** 4725 Beckley Rd. I-94, exit 97 (Capital Ave), just sw. Int corridors. **Pets:** Accepted.
[X] [♦] [▣] [≈]

BAY VIEW

▲▲ **▼▼** Comfort Inn **H** ❀
(231) 347-3220. **$50-$250.** 1314 US 31 N. Jct US 31 and SR 119. Int corridors. **Pets:** Other species. $5 daily fee/room. Service with restrictions, supervision.
[SAVE] [X] [♦] [▣]

BEAR LAKE

▲▲ **▼** Bella Vista Inn **M**
(231) 864-3000. **$55-$106.** 12273 US 31. On US 31; center. Ext corridors. **Pets:** Medium, dogs only. $12 daily fee/pet. Service with restrictions, supervision.
[SAVE] [X] [♦] [≈]

BEULAH

▲▲ **▼▼** Best Western Scenic Hill Resort **H** ❀
(231) 882-7754. **$50-$215.** 1400 US 31 Hwy. 0.8 mi e on US 31. Int corridors. **Pets:** Large, other species. $20 daily fee/pet. Designated rooms, service with restrictions, supervision.
[SAVE] [X] [♦] [▣] [≈] [☒]

BIG RAPIDS

▼▼ Holiday Inn Hotel & Conference Center **H**
(231) 796-4400. **$99-$150.** 1005 Perry St. US 131, exit 139, 1.3 mi e on SR 20. Int corridors. **Pets:** Accepted.
[ASK] [X] [&M] [♦] [▣] [¶¶] [≈] [☒]

▲▲ **▼▼** Quality Inn & Suites **M** ❀
(231) 592-5150. **$59-$159.** 1705 S State St. US 131, exit 139, 2.1 mi e on SR 20, then 1 mi s. Ext/int corridors. **Pets:** Medium. $10 daily fee/pet. Designated rooms, supervision.
[SAVE] [X] [♦] [▣] [≈]

BIRCH RUN

▲▲ **▼▼** Best Western Birch Run-Frankenmuth **H**
(989) 624-9395. **$79-$149.** 9087 Birch Run Rd. I-75, exit 136 (Birch Run Rd), just e. Ext/int corridors. **Pets:** Accepted.
[SAVE] [X] [&M] [♦] [▣] [¶¶] [≈] [☒]

▼▼ Super 8 **H**
(989) 624-4440. **$50-$150.** 9235 E Birch Run Rd. I-75, exit 136 (Birch Run Rd), just e. Int corridors. **Pets:** Accepted.
[ASK] [X] [♦] [▣] [☒]

BRIDGEPORT

▲▲ **▼▼** Baymont Inn & Suites-Frankenmuth/Bridgeport **H**
(989) 777-3000. **Call for rates.** 6460 Dixie Hwy. I-75, exit 144A. Int corridors. **Pets:** Accepted.
[SAVE] [X] [♦] [▣] [≈]

BROOKLYN

▼▼ Super 8 **H**
(517) 592-0888. **$75-$135.** 155 Wamplers Rd. Jct Main St (SR 50) and SR 124; downtown. Int corridors. **Pets:** Accepted.
[ASK] [X] [&M] [♦] [▣]

CADILLAC

▲▲ **▼** Econo Lodge **H**
(231) 775-6700. **$55-$95.** 2501 Sunnyside Dr. Jct SR 55 and 115. Ext/int corridors. **Pets:** Accepted.
[SAVE] [X] [♦] [▣]

▼▼ McGuires Resort **H**
(231) 775-9947. **$79-$99, 7 day notice.** 7880 Mackinaw Tr. US 131, exit 177, 0.7 mi n, then 0.5 mi w. Int corridors. **Pets:** Other species. $20 daily fee/room. Designated rooms, service with restrictions, crate.
[ASK] [X] [♦] [▣] [¶¶] [≈] [☒]

CALUMET

▼▼ AmericInn Lodge & Suites of Calumet **H**
(906) 337-6463. **$95-$146.** 56925 S 6th St. On US 41, just w of Visitors Center. Int corridors. **Pets:** Medium, dogs only. $20 one-time fee/room. Designated rooms, service with restrictions, supervision.
[X] [♦] [▣] [≈] [☒]

CASCADE

▼▼ Baymont Inn-Grand Rapids Airport **H**
(616) 956-3300. **Call for rates.** 2873 Kraft Ave SE. I-96, exit 43B, just e. Int corridors. **Pets:** Accepted.
[X] [♦] [▣]

▲▲ **▼▼** Best Western Hospitality Hotel & Suites **H**
(616) 949-8400. **$54-$140.** 5500 28th St SE. I-96, exit 43B, just e on SR 11. Int corridors. **Pets:** Accepted.
[SAVE] [X] [♦] [▣] [≈] [☒]

▼▼ Clarion Inn & Suites Grand Rapids Airport **H**
(616) 956-9304. **$69-$149.** 4981 28th St SE. I-96, exit 43A, 0.5 mi w on SR 11. Int corridors. **Pets:** Accepted.
[ASK] [X] [♦] [▣]

▼▼ Country Inn & Suites by Carlson **H** ❀
(616) 977-0909. **$79-$114.** 5399 28th St. I-96, exit 43B, just e on SR 11. Int corridors. **Pets:** Other species. Service with restrictions, crate.
[ASK] [X] [&M] [♦] [▣] [≈]

▼▼▼ Crowne Plaza Grand Rapids **H**
(616) 957-1770. **$129-$189.** 5700 28th St SE. I-96, exit 43B, 0.3 mi e on SR 11. Int corridors. **Pets:** Small. $50 deposit/room, $10 daily fee/room. Designated rooms, service with restrictions.
[ASK] [X] [&M] [♦] [▣] [¶¶] [≈] [☒]

▼▼ Holiday Inn Express Suites Airport **H**
(616) 940-8100. **Call for rates.** 5401 28th St SE. I-96, exit 43B, just e on SR 11. Int corridors. **Pets:** Accepted.
[X] [&M] [♦] [▣] [≈] [☒]

▲▲ **▼** Super 8 **H**
(616) 957-3000. **$46-$66.** 4855 28th St SE. I-96, exit 43A, 0.5 mi w on SR 11. Int corridors. **Pets:** Large. Designated rooms, service with restrictions, supervision.
[SAVE] [X] [♦] [▣]

CHARLEVOIX

▼▼ AmericInn Lodge & Suites of Charlevoix **H**
(231) 237-0988. **$65-$200.** 11800 US 31 N. On US 31, 2.4 mi n. Int corridors. **Pets:** Accepted.
[X] [&M] [♦] [▣] [≈]

CHARLOTTE

▼▼ Super 8 **H**
(517) 543-8288. **$75-$90.** 828 E Shepherd St. I-69, exit 60 (SR 50), just w. Int corridors. **Pets:** Accepted.
ASK ⊠ 🔒 💻

CHEBOYGAN

ⒶⒶⒶ ▼▼ Best Western River Terrace Motel **M**
(231) 627-5688. **$79-$209.** 847 S Main St. 1 mi s on SR 27. Ext/int corridors. **Pets:** Medium, dogs only. $10 daily fee/pet. Designated rooms, service with restrictions, supervision.
SAVE ⊠ 🔒 💻 ≈ ⊠

▼ Birch Haus Motel **M**
(231) 627-5862. **$40-$80.** 1301 Mackinaw Ave. On US 23, 0.8 mi nw. Ext corridors. **Pets:** Small, dogs only. $5 daily fee/pet. Service with restrictions, supervision.
ASK ⊠ 🔒

▼ Continental Inn **M**
(231) 627-7164. **$39-$99.** 613 N Main St. Jct US 23 and SR 27. Ext corridors. **Pets:** Other species. $10 daily fee/room. Designated rooms, service with restrictions, supervision.
ASK ⊠ 🔒 ≈

CHELSEA

▼▼▼ Chelsea Comfort Inn & Village Conference Center **H**
(734) 433-8000. **$99-$299.** 1645 Commerce Park Dr. I-94, exit 159 (SR 52/Main St), just n. Int corridors. **Pets:** Medium. $20 daily fee/room. Designated rooms, service with restrictions.
ASK ⊠ 🔒 🔒 💻 ≈

CHESANING

ⒶⒶⒶ ▼ Colonial Motel **M**
(989) 845-3292. **$60-$130.** 9475 E M-57. On SR 57, 0.5 mi e. Ext corridors. **Pets:** Other species. $10 daily fee/pet. Designated rooms, service with restrictions, supervision.
SAVE ⊠ 💻

CLARE

▼▼ Days Inn **H**
(989) 802-0144. **$59-$180.** 10100 S Clare Ave. On Business Rt US 10 and 127, just w of jct US 127 and Old US 27. Int corridors. **Pets:** $10 one-time fee/room. Service with restrictions, supervision.
ASK ⊠ 🔒 🔒 💻 ⊠

COLDWATER

ⒶⒶⒶ ▼▼ Red Roof Inn **H**
(517) 279-1199. **$60-$70.** 348 S Willowbrook Rd. I-69, exit 13 (US 12), just e. Int corridors. **Pets:** Accepted.
SAVE ⊠ 🔒 🔒 💻

▼▼ Super 8 **H**
(517) 278-8833. **Call for rates.** 600 Orleans Blvd. I-69, exit 13 (US 12), 0.3 mi w on E Chicago St, just n on N Michigan Ave, then just e. Int corridors. **Pets:** $15 one-time fee/room. Service with restrictions, supervision.
⊠ 🔒 🔒 💻

COPPER HARBOR

▼ Lake Fanny Hooe Resort **M**
(906) 289-4451. **$85-$125, 7 day notice.** 505 2nd St. Just s on Manganese Rd. Ext corridors. **Pets:** Other species. $8 daily fee/pet. Service with restrictions, supervision.
⊠ 🔒 💻 ⊠ 🐾 🗲

DETROIT METROPOLITAN AREA

ALLEN PARK

ⒶⒶⒶ ▼▼▼ Best Western Greenfield Inn **H**
(313) 271-1600. **$105-$110.** 3000 Enterprise Dr. I-94, exit 206 (Oakwood Blvd), just s, then just w. Int corridors. **Pets:** Medium, dogs only. $100 deposit/room. Designated rooms, service with restrictions, supervision.
SAVE ⊠ 🔒 💻 🍴 ≈ ⊠

AUBURN HILLS

▼▼ Candlewood Suites **H**
(248) 373-3342. **Call for rates.** 1650 N Opdyke Rd. I-75, exit 79 (University Dr), just w, then 0.4 mi n. Int corridors. **Pets:** Accepted.
⊠ 🔒 💻

▼▼ Homestead Studio Suites Hotel-Detroit/Auburn Hills **H**
(248) 340-8888. **$55-$90.** 3315 University Dr. I-75, exit 79 (University Dr), 0.9 mi e. Int corridors. **Pets:** Other species. $25 daily fee/pet. Service with restrictions, crate.
ASK ⊠ 🔒 💻

▼▼▼ Staybridge Suites **H**
(248) 322-4600. **$130-$450.** 2050 Featherstone Rd. I-75, exit 79 (University Dr), just w, 0.5 mi s on Opdyke Rd, then just e. Int corridors. **Pets:** Large. $75 one-time fee/room. Service with restrictions, crate.
ASK ⊠ 🔒 🔒 💻 ≈

BELLEVILLE

ⒶⒶⒶ ▼▼ Red Roof Inn Metro Airport #7183 **M**
(734) 697-2244. **$56-$78, 7 day notice.** 45501 N I-94 Service Dr. I-94, exit 190 (Belleville Rd), just n. Ext corridors. **Pets:** Small, other species. Service with restrictions, supervision.
SAVE ⊠ 🔒

BIRMINGHAM

▼▼▼ Barclay Inn Birmingham **H**
(248) 646-7300. **Call for rates.** 34952 Woodward Ave. On SR 1, jct Woodward Ave and Maple Rd; center. Ext/int corridors. **Pets:** Accepted.
⊠ 🔒 🔒 💻

ⒶⒶⒶ ▼▼▼ Holiday Inn Express–Birmingham **H**
(248) 642-6200. **$139-$169.** 35270 Woodward Ave. Jct Woodward Ave and Maple Rd; center. Int corridors. **Pets:** Small, other species. $50 one-time fee/pet. Designated rooms, service with restrictions, supervision.
SAVE ⊠ 🔒 💻

ⒶⒶⒶ ▼▼▼ ▼▼ The Townsend Hotel **H**
(248) 642-7900. **$299-$369.** 100 Townsend St. Center. Int corridors. **Pets:** Accepted.
SAVE ⊠ 🔒 🔒 💻 🍴 ⊠

CANTON

▼▼ La Quinta Inn **H** 🐾
(734) 981-1808. **$52-$109.** 41211 Ford Rd. I-275, exit 25 (Ford Rd), just w to jct Haggerty Rd. Int corridors. **Pets:** Medium, other species. Service with restrictions, supervision.
ASK ⊠ 🔒 💻

▼▼ Super 8-Canton **H**
(734) 722-8880. **$51-$54.** 3933 Lotz Rd. I-275, exit 22 (Michigan Ave), just e on US 12, then just s. Int corridors. **Pets:** $10 daily fee/pet. Service with restrictions, crate.
ASK ⊠ 🔒 💻

DEARBORN

▼▼ ▼▼ Extended StayAmerica Detroit Dearborn 🅷
(313) 336-0021. **$65-$105.** 260 Towne Center Dr. SR 39 (Southfield Frwy); between Ford Rd and Michigan Ave exits; just w of jct Service and Hubbard drs. Int corridors. **Pets:** Other species. $25 daily fee/pet. Service with restrictions, crate.
⊠ ♿M 🛏 💻

🆔 ▼▼ Red Roof Inn-Dearborn #7182 Ⓜ
(313) 278-9732. **$82-$105.** 24130 Michigan Ave. Jct US 24 (Telegraph Rd) and 12 (Michigan Ave). Ext corridors. **Pets:** Other species. Service with restrictions, supervision.
SAVE ⊠ ♿M 🛏

🆔 ▼▼▼ ▼▼▼ The Ritz-Carlton, Dearborn 🅷
(313) 441-2000. **$269-$319.** 300 Town Center Dr. SR 39 (Southfield Frwy); between Ford Rd and Michigan Ave exits, on Service Dr. Int corridors. **Pets:** Accepted.
SAVE ⊠ ♿M 💻 🍴 🏊 ⊠

▼▼ ▼▼ TownePlace Suites 🅷
(313) 271-0200. **$130-$140.** 6141 Mercury Dr. SR 39 (Southfield Frwy), exit 7 (Ford Rd), just e, then 0.8 mi n. Int corridors. **Pets:** Accepted.
⊠ ♿M 🛏 💻 🏊

DETROIT

▼▼▼ ▼▼▼ Detroit Riverside Hotel 🅷 🌸
(313) 965-0200. **$119-$600.** 2 Washington Blvd. Opposite Cobo Hall. Int corridors. **Pets:** Medium. $50 one-time fee/room. No service, supervision.
ASK ⊠ 🛏 💻 🍴 🏊

▼▼▼ ▼▼▼ Hilton Garden Inn Detroit/Downtown 🅷
(313) 967-0900. **$109-$429.** 351 Gratiot Ave. Jct Randolph St and Gratiot Ave, just e; in Harmonie Park. Int corridors. **Pets:** Accepted.
⊠ ♿M 🛏 💻 🍴 🏊

▼▼▼ ▼▼▼ Holiday Inn Express 🅷
(313) 887-7000. **Call for rates.** 1020 Washington Blvd. Corner of Washington Blvd and Michigan Ave. Int corridors. **Pets:** Accepted.
⊠ 🛏 💻 🍴 🏊

🆔 ▼▼▼ ▼▼▼ MotorCity Casino Hotel 🅷
(313) 237-7711. **$199-$599.** 2901 Grand River Ave. Jct SR 10 (Lodge Frwy). Int corridors. **Pets:** Accepted.
SAVE ⊠ ♿M 💻 🍴 ⊠

▼▼▼ ▼▼▼ Omni Detroit River Place 🅷
(313) 259-9500. **$179-$499.** 1000 River Place Dr. 1.5 mi on E Jefferson Ave, 4 blks s on McDougall. Int corridors. **Pets:** Small. $25 one-time fee/room. Service with restrictions, crate.
ASK ⊠ 💻 🍴

🆔 ▼▼▼ ▼▼▼ Residence Inn By Marriott-Dearborn 🅷
(313) 441-1700. **$143-$175.** 5777 Southfield Service Dr. SR 39 (Southfield Frwy), exit Ford Rd, just w. Ext corridors. **Pets:** Accepted.
SAVE ⊠ 🛏 💻 🏊 ⊠

▼▼ ▼▼ Woodbridge Star Bed & Breakfast 🅱🅱 🌸
(313) 831-9668. **$125-$175, 10 day notice.** 3985 Trumbull St. Jct Alexandrine St. Int corridors. **Pets:** Medium, other species. Service with restrictions, supervision.
ASK ⊠ 🖨

FARMINGTON HILLS

▼▼ ▼▼ Candlewood Suites 🅷
(248) 324-0540. **$110-$259.** 37555 Hills Tech Dr. I-696, exit I-96 E/I-275 S/SR 5, just s to SR 5 N, 2 mi n to 12 Mile Rd, 1.3 mi e, then 0.3 mi s on Halsted Rd. Int corridors. **Pets:** Large, other species. $150 one-time fee/room. Service with restrictions.
ASK ⊠ ♿M 🛏 💻

▼▼ ▼▼ Extended StayAmerica Farmington Hills 🅷
(248) 473-4000. **$55-$80.** 27775 Stansbury Blvd. I-696, exit 5 (Orchard Lake Rd), just n, just e on 12 Mile Rd, then just s. Int corridors. **Pets:** Other species. $25 daily fee/pet. Service with restrictions, crate.
ASK ⊠ ♿M 🛏 💻

🆔 ▼▼ ▼▼ Red Roof Inn-Farmington Hills #7038 Ⓜ
(248) 478-8640. **$48-$73.** 24300 Sinacola Ct. I-96/275 and SR 5, exit 165 (Grand River Ave), just w. Ext corridors. **Pets:** Medium, other species.
SAVE ⊠ ♿M 🛏

LAKE ORION

🆔 ▼▼▼ ▼▼▼ Best Western Palace Inn 🅷
(248) 391-2755. **$99-$129, 3 day notice.** 2755 N Lapeer Rd. I-75, exit 81 (Lapeer Rd), 3.3 mi n. Ext/int corridors. **Pets:** Accepted.
SAVE ⊠ ♿M 🛏 💻 🏊

LIVONIA

🆔 ▼▼▼ ▼▼▼ Hyatt Place Detroit/Livonia 🅷
(734) 953-9224. **$89-$209.** 19300 Haggerty Rd. I-275, exit 169 (7 Mile Rd), just w. Int corridors. **Pets:** Accepted.
SAVE ⊠ ♿M 🛏 💻 🏊

▼▼▼ ▼▼▼ Livonia Marriott 🅷
(734) 462-3100. **$188-$230.** 17100 Laurel Park Dr N. I-275, exit 170 (6 Mile Rd), just w. Int corridors. **Pets:** Accepted.
⊠ 🛏 💻 🍴 🏊

🆔 ▼▼▼ ▼▼▼ Radisson Hotel and Conference Center Detroit-Livonia 🅷 🌸
(734) 464-1300. **$119-$199.** 17123 Laurel Park Dr N. I-275, exit 170 (6 Mile Rd), just e. Int corridors. **Pets:** Medium. $50 deposit/pet. Service with restrictions, supervision.
SAVE ⊠ ♿M 🛏 💻 🍴 🏊 ⊠

🆔 ▼▼▼ ▼▼▼ Residence Inn Detroit-Livonia 🅷
(734) 462-4201. **$170-$208.** 17250 Fox Dr. I-275, exit 170 (6 Mile Rd), just w. Int corridors. **Pets:** Accepted.
SAVE ⊠ ♿M 🛏 💻 🏊 ⊠

▼▼▼ ▼▼▼ TownePlace Suites by Marriott 🅷
(734) 542-7400. **$125-$153.** 17450 Fox Dr. I-275, exit 170 (6 Mile Rd), just nw. Int corridors. **Pets:** Accepted.
⊠ ♿M 🛏 💻 🏊

MADISON HEIGHTS

▼▼ Motel 6 Madison Heights #1109 Ⓜ
(248) 583-0500. **$45-$55.** 32700 Barrington Rd. I-75, exit 65A (14 Mile Rd), just e. Ext corridors. **Pets:** Other species. Service with restrictions, supervision.
⊠ ♿M

🆔 ▼▼ ▼▼ Red Roof Inn #7084 Ⓜ
(248) 583-4700. **$55-$80.** 32511 Concord Dr. I-75, exit 65A (14 Mile Rd), just e, then just s. Ext corridors. **Pets:** Large, other species. Service with restrictions.
SAVE ⊠ 🛏

▼▼▼ ▼▼▼ Residence Inn by Marriott-Detroit Troy/Madison Heights 🅷
(248) 583-4322. **$113-$138.** 32650 Stephenson Hwy. I-75, exit 65B (14 Mile Rd), just w, then just s. Ext corridors. **Pets:** Other species. $75 one-time fee/room. Service with restrictions, crate.
⊠ 🛏 💻 🏊 ⊠

NOVI

▼▼ ▼▼ Extended StayAmerica-Detroit-Novi 🅷
(248) 305-9955. **$55-$95.** 21555 Haggerty Rd. I-275, exit 167 (8 Mile Rd), just w, then 0.5 mi n. Int corridors. **Pets:** Other species. $25 daily fee/pet. Service with restrictions, crate.
ASK ⊠ ♿M 🛏 💻

▼▼▼ **Residence Inn by Marriott-Detroit/Novi** H
(248) 735-7400. **$161-$197.** 27477 Caberet Dr. I-96, exit 162 (Novi Rd), just n to 12 Mile Rd, then just w. Int corridors. **Pets:** $100 one-time fee/room. Service with restrictions, crate.
⊗ ⑤M 🛈 💻 ⊃

◈ ▼▼▼ **Sheraton-Detroit-Novi** H
(248) 349-4000. **$89-$229.** 21111 Haggerty Rd. I-275, exit 167 (8 Mile Rd), just w to Haggerty Rd, then just n. Int corridors. **Pets:** Accepted.
SAVE ⊗ ⑤M 🛈 💻 ⑪ ⊃

▼▼ **TownePlace Suites** H ❖
(248) 305-5533. **$125-$153.** 42600 11 Mile Rd. I-96, exit 162 (Novi Rd), just s, 0.5 mi e on Crescent Dr, then just s on Town Center Dr. Int corridors. **Pets:** Small. $250 one-time fee/room. Service with restrictions, supervision.
⊗ 🛈 💻 ⊃

PLYMOUTH

◈ ▼▼ **Red Roof Inn-Plymouth #7016** M
(734) 459-3300. **$55-$110.** 39700 Ann Arbor Rd. I-275, exit 28 (Ann Arbor Rd), just e. Ext corridors. **Pets:** Medium, other species. Service with restrictions, supervision.
SAVE ⊗ 🛈

PONTIAC

▼▼▼ **Residence Inn by Marriott Detroit Pontiac/Auburn Hills** H
(248) 858-8664. **$143-$175.** 3333 Centerpoint Pkwy. I-75, exit 75 (Square Lake Rd), w via Opdyke Rd. Int corridors. **Pets:** Accepted.
⊗ 🛈 💻 ⊃ ⊗

ROCHESTER HILLS

◈ ▼▼ **Red Roof Inn #7191** M
(248) 853-6400. **$65-$70.** 2580 Crooks Rd. Jct Hall Rd (SR 59). Ext corridors. **Pets:** Medium. Service with restrictions, crate.
SAVE ⊗ 🛈

ROMULUS

▼▼ **Americas Best Value Inn & Suites** H
(734) 595-7400. **Call for rates.** 9095 Wickham Rd. I-94, exit 198 (Merriman Rd), just n, then just w. Int corridors. **Pets:** Accepted.
⊗ 🛈 💻

▼▼ **Baymont Inn & Suites Detroit-Airport** H
(734) 722-6000. **Call for rates.** 9000 Wickham Rd. I-94, exit 198 (Merriman Rd), just n, then just w. Int corridors. **Pets:** Accepted.
⊗ 🛈 💻

◈ ▼▼▼ **Clarion Hotel Detroit Metro Airport** H
(734) 728-7900. **$89-$149.** 8600 Merriman Rd. I-94, exit 198 (Merriman Rd), just n. Int corridors. **Pets:** Accepted.
SAVE ⊗ 💻 ⑪ ⊃

▼▼ **Days Inn** H
(734) 946-4300. **$70-$130.** 9501 Middlebelt Rd. I-94, exit 199 (Middlebelt Rd), 0.4 mi s. Int corridors. **Pets:** Small. $20 daily fee/pet. Designated rooms, service with restrictions, supervision.
ASK ⊗ 🛈 💻 ⑪

▼▼▼ **Detroit Metro Airport Marriott** H
(734) 729-7555. **$170-$208.** 30559 Flynn Dr. I-94, exit 198 (Merriman Rd), just n, then 0.3 mi e. Int corridors. **Pets:** Accepted.
⊗ ⑤M 🛈 💻 ⑪ ⊃

▼▼ **Extended StayAmerica Detroit-Metro Airport** H
(734) 722-7780. **$45-$80.** 30325 Flynn Dr. I-94, exit 198 (Merriman Rd), just n, then 0.4 mi e. Int corridors. **Pets:** Other species. $25 daily fee/pet. Service with restrictions, crate.
ASK ⊗ 🛈 💻

◈ ▼▼▼▼ **Four Points by Sheraton Detroit Metro Airport** H
(734) 729-9000. **$150-$175.** 8800 Wickham Rd. I-94, exit 198 (Merriman Rd), just n, then just e. Int corridors. **Pets:** Accepted.
SAVE ⊗ 🛈 💻 ⑪ ⊃

▼▼▼ **La Quinta Inn Detroit-Metro Airport** H ❖
(734) 641-9006. **$80-$120.** 7680 Merriman Rd. I-94, exit 198 (Merriman Rd), 0.4 mi n. Int corridors. **Pets:** Medium, other species. Service with restrictions, supervision.
⊗ 🛈 💻

▼▼▼ **Romulus Quality Inn & Suites** H
(734) 946-1400. **$69-$134.** 9555 Middlebelt Rd. I-94, exit 199 (Middlebelt Rd), 0.4 mi s. Int corridors. **Pets:** Accepted.
ASK ⊗ 🛈 💻

◈ ▼▼▼ ▼▼ **The Westin Detroit Metropolitan Airport** H
(734) 942-6500. **$99-$289.** 2501 Worldgateway Pl. I-94, exit 198 (Merriman Rd); at McNamara Terminal. Int corridors. **Pets:** Accepted.
SAVE ⊗ 🛈 💻 ⑪ ⊃

ROSEVILLE

◈ ▼▼ **Baymont Inn & Suites Detroit-Roseville** H
(586) 296-6910. **$59-$69.** 20675 13 Mile Rd. I-94, exit 232 (Little Mack Ave), just s. Int corridors. **Pets:** Accepted.
SAVE ⊗ 🛈 💻

◈ ▼▼▼ **Best Western Georgian Inn** M
(586) 294-0400. **$84-$119.** 31327 Gratiot Ave. I-94, exit 232 (Little Mack Ave), just s, 0.5 mi n on 13 Mile Rd, then just n. Ext corridors. **Pets:** Medium, dogs only. $8 daily fee/pet. Service with restrictions, crate.
SAVE ⊗ 🛈 💻 ⑪ ⊃

◈ ▼▼ **Red Roof Inn #7012** M
(586) 296-0310. **$55-$70.** 31800 Little Mack Ave. I-94, exit 232 (Little Mack Ave), just n. Ext corridors. **Pets:** Medium, other species. Service with restrictions, crate.
SAVE ⊗ 🛈

SOUTHFIELD

▼▼ **Candlewood Suites** H
(248) 945-0010. **$93-$113.** 1 Corporate Dr. SR 10 (Northwestern Hwy), exit Lasher Rd, just e. Int corridors. **Pets:** Large. $75 one-time fee/pet. Service with restrictions, crate.
ASK ⊗ ⑤M 🛈 💻

◈ ▼▼ **Hawthorn Suites** H
(248) 352-8900. **Call for rates.** 26700 Central Park Blvd. I-696, exit 11 (Evergreen Rd), just sw of jct 11 Mile and Evergreen rds. Ext corridors. **Pets:** Accepted.
SAVE ⊗ ⑤M 🛈 💻 ⊃ ⊗

◈ ▼▼▼ **Holiday Inn Express Hotel & Suites** H
(248) 350-2400. **$119-$169.** 25100 Northwestern Hwy. SR 10 (Northwestern Hwy), exit 10 Mile Rd. Int corridors. **Pets:** Accepted.
SAVE ⊗ ⑤M 🛈 💻 ⊃

▼▼ **Marvin's Garden Inn** M
(248) 353-6777. **Call for rates.** 27650 Northwestern Hwy. I-696, exit 9 (Telegraph Rd), just nw. Ext/int corridors. **Pets:** Accepted.
⊗ 🛈 💻

▼▼ **Red Roof Inn-Southfield #7133** M
(248) 353-7200. **$61-$79.** 27660 Northwestern Hwy. I-696, exit 9 (Telegraph Rd), just nw. Ext corridors. **Pets:** Medium, other species. Supervision.
ASK ⊗ ⑤M 🛈

◆◆◆ ◆◆ ◆◆ Westin Hotel Southfield-Detroit H
(248) 827-4000. **$99-$309.** 1500 Town Center. SR 10 (Northwestern Hwy), exit 10 (Mile/Evergreen rds), 0.3 mi n. Int corridors. **Pets:** Accepted.
SAVE ✕ ⊟ ⛄ ◻ ☞

SOUTHGATE

◆◆◆◆ La Quinta Inn & Suites Detroit-Southgate H ❀
(734) 374-3000. **$59-$109.** 12888 Reeck Rd. I-75, exit 37 (Northline Rd), just w. Int corridors. **Pets:** Medium, other species. Service with restrictions, supervision.
ASK ✕ ⊟ ◻

◆◆ ◆◆ Motel 6 Detroit-Southgate M ❀
(734) 287-8340. **$39-$139.** 18777 Northline Rd. I-75, exit 37 (Northline Rd), just w. Ext corridors. **Pets:** Medium. Designated rooms, no service, supervision.
ASK ✕ ⊟ ☞

STERLING HEIGHTS

◆◆ ◆◆ TownePlace Suites H
(586) 566-0900. **$120-$130.** 14800 Lakeside Cir. 1 mi e of jct SR 53 (Van Dyke Ave) and 59 (Hall Rd). Int corridors. **Pets:** Other species. $75 one-time fee/room. Supervision.
✕ ⛄ ⊟ ◻ ☞

TAYLOR

◆◆◆ ◆◆ Red Roof Inn-Taylor #7189 M
(734) 374-1150. **$45-$71.** 21230 Eureka Rd. I-75, exit 36 (Eureka Rd), just w. Ext corridors. **Pets:** Large. Service with restrictions, supervision.
SAVE ✕ ⊟

TROY

◆◆◆◆ Drury Inn & Suites-Troy H
(248) 528-3330. **$80-$221.** 575 W Big Beaver Rd. I-75, exit 69 (Big Beaver Rd), just e. Int corridors. **Pets:** Other species. Service with restrictions, supervision.
ASK ✕ ⊟ ◻ 🍴 ☞

◆◆◆◆ Hilton Detroit/Troy H ❀
(248) 879-2100. **$89-$209.** 5500 Crooks Rd. I-75, exit 72 (Crooks Rd), just n. Int corridors. **Pets:** Very small. $50 one-time fee/room. Designated rooms, service with restrictions, supervision.
✕ ⛄ ⊟ ◻ 🍴 ☞

◆◆ ◆◆ Holiday Inn-Troy H
(248) 689-7500. **$72-$134.** 2537 Rochester Ct. I-75, exit 67 (Rochester Rd), 0.3 mi sw, then just w. Int corridors. **Pets:** Dogs only. $30 one-time fee/room. Service with restrictions, crate.
ASK ✕ ⊟ ◻ 🍴 ☞

◆◆◆ ◆◆ ◆◆ Red Roof Inn-Troy #7021 M
(248) 689-4391. **$53-$63.** 2350 Rochester Ct. I-75, exit 67 (Rochester Rd), 0.3 mi sw. Ext corridors. **Pets:** Large, other species. Service with restrictions, crate.
SAVE ✕ ⛄ ⊟

◆◆◆ Residence Inn by Marriott H
(248) 689-6856. **$152-$186.** 2600 Livernois Rd. I-75, exit 69 (Big Beaver Rd), 0.5 mi e to Livernois Rd, then 0.5 mi s. Ext corridors. **Pets:** Accepted.
✕ ⊟ ◻ ☞ ✕

UTICA

◆◆◆ ◆◆ Comfort Inn H
(586) 739-7111. **$89-$149.** 11401 Hall Rd. Jct Van Dyke Ave (SR 53). Int corridors. **Pets:** Accepted.
SAVE ✕ ⊟ ◻

◆◆◆◆ La Quinta Inn & Suites H ❀
(586) 731-4700. **$69-$169.** 45311 Park Ave. Jct Van Dyke Ave (SR 53) and Hall Rd (SR 59), just n. Int corridors. **Pets:** Medium, other species. Service with restrictions, supervision.
ASK ✕ ⊟ ◻ ☞

◆◆◆◆ Staybridge Suites-Utica H ❀
(586) 323-0101. **$129-$189.** 46155 Utica Park Blvd. Jct Van Dyke Ave (SR 53) and Hall Rd (SR 59), just n. Int corridors. **Pets:** Large. $75 one-time fee/room. Service with restrictions, supervision.
ASK ✕ ⛄ ⊟ ◻ ☞

WARREN

◆◆ ◆◆ Extended Stay Deluxe Detroit-Warren H
(586) 558-5554. **$50-$90.** 30125 N Civic Center Blvd. I-696, exit 23 (Van Dyke Ave), 1.5 mi n, then just e. Int corridors. **Pets:** Other species. $25 daily fee/pet. Service with restrictions, crate.
ASK ✕ ⛄ ⊟ ◻

◆◆◆ ◆◆ Hawthorn Suites H
(586) 558-7870. **Call for rates.** 30180 N Civic Center Blvd. I-696, exit 23 (Van Dyke Ave), 1.8 mi n. Ext/int corridors. **Pets:** Accepted.
✕ ⛄ ⊟ ◻ ☞

◆◆ ◆◆ La Quinta Inn H ❀
(586) 574-0550. **$45-$99.** 30900 Van Dyke Ave. I-696, exit 23 (Van Dyke Ave), 1.8 mi n on SR 53. Int corridors. **Pets:** Medium, other species. Service with restrictions, supervision.
ASK ✕ ⊟ ◻

◆◆ ◆◆ Red Roof Inn-Warren #7070 M
(586) 573-4300. **$62-$70.** 26300 Dequindre Rd. I-696, exit 20 (Dequindre Rd), just ne. Ext corridors. **Pets:** Large. Service with restrictions, supervision.
ASK ✕ ⛄ ⊟

◆◆◆ ◆◆◆◆ TownePlace Suites by Marriott-Warren H
(586) 264-8800. **$116-$142.** 7601 Chicago Rd. I-696, exit 23 (Van Dyke Ave), 2 mi n. Int corridors. **Pets:** Small, other species. $100 one-time fee/room. Service with restrictions, supervision.
SAVE ✕ ⛄ ⊟ ◻ ☞

WATERFORD

◆◆◆ ◆◆ Comfort Inn H
(248) 666-8555. **Call for rates.** 7076 Highland Rd. Jct SR 59 (Highland Rd) and Airport Rd, 1 mi w. Int corridors. **Pets:** Large, dogs only. $25 daily fee/pet. Service with restrictions, supervision.
✕ ⊟ ◻ ☞

END METROPOLITAN AREA

DEWITT

◆◆◆ ◆◆ Sleep Inn H
(517) 669-8823. **$59-$109.** 1101 Commerce Park Dr. I-69, exit 87 (Old US 27), 0.8 mi n. Int corridors. **Pets:** Small, dogs only. $10 daily fee/pet. Service with restrictions, supervision.
SAVE ✕ ⊟ ◻ ☞

DIMONDALE

◆◆◆ ◆◆ Comfort Inn & Suites of Lansing H
(517) 721-0000. **$70-$100.** 9742 Woodlane Dr. I-96, exit 98B (Lansing Rd N), just n. Int corridors. **Pets:** Large, other species. $25 daily fee/pet. Designated rooms, service with restrictions, supervision.
SAVE ✕ ⛄ ⊟ ◻ ☞

DOUGLAS

▼▼ AmericInn Lodge & Suites of Douglas 🅷 ❅
(269) 857-8581. **$90-$260, 7 day notice.** 2905 Blue Star Hwy. I-196, exit 36, 0.3 mi n. Int corridors. **Pets:** Medium, dogs only. $20 daily fee/room. Designated rooms, service with restrictions, supervision.
ⒶⓈⓀ ✕ ☾ℳ ⬛ 🖵 ≈

DOWAGIAC

⚛ ▼▼ Baymont Inn & Suites of Dowagiac 🅷
(269) 782-4270. **$89-$169.** 29291 Amerihost Dr. 0.4 mi s of jct SR 51 and 62. Int corridors. **Pets:** $20 deposit/room. Designated rooms, service with restrictions.
ⓈⒶⓋⒺ ✕ ☾ℳ ⬛ 🖵 ≈

EAST LANSING

▼▼▼ Candlewood Suites 🅷 ❅
(517) 351-8181. **$79-$149.** 3545 Forest Rd. I-496, exit 11 (Jolly Rd), just e to Collins Rd, 0.3 mi n, then just e. Int corridors. **Pets:** Large. $75 one-time fee/room. Service with restrictions, crate.
ⒶⓈⓀ ✕ ☾ℳ ⬛ 🖵 ⑪

▼▼▼ Residence Inn by Marriott 🅷 ❅
(517) 332-7711. **$140-$171.** 1600 E Grand River Ave. US 127, exit Grand River Ave, 2.6 mi se on SR 43. Ext corridors. **Pets:** $75 one-time fee/room. Service with restrictions, supervision.
✕ ⬛ 🖵 ≈ ⊠

EAST TAWAS

⚛ ▼▼ Tawas Bay Beach Resort 🅷
(989) 362-8601. **$70-$186, 3 day notice.** 300 E Bay St. On US 23 W. Int corridors. **Pets:** Small. $30 one-time fee/room. Designated rooms, service with restrictions, supervision.
ⓈⒶⓋⒺ ✕ ⬛ 🖵 ⑪ ≈ ⊠

ESCANABA

⚛ ▼ Hiawatha Motel Ⓜ
(906) 786-1341. **$50-$125.** 2400 Ludington St. 0.5 mi w on US 2/41. Ext corridors. **Pets:** Other species. $5 daily fee/room. No service, supervision.
ⓈⒶⓋⒺ ✕ ⬛

FENTON

▼▼▼ Holiday Inn Express Hotel & Suites 🅷
(810) 714-7171. **Call for rates.** 17800 Silver Pkwy. US 23, exit 78 (Owen Rd), just w, then 0.4 mi n. Int corridors. **Pets:** Accepted.
✕ ☾ℳ ⬛ 🖵 ≈

FLINT

▼▼ AmericInn Motel & Suites of Flint 🅷
(810) 233-9000. **Call for rates.** 6075 Hill 23 Dr. US 23, exit 90 (Hill Rd), just w. Int corridors. **Pets:** Accepted.
✕ ☾ℳ ⬛ 🖵 ≈ ⊠

▼▼ Baymont Inn & Suites-Flint 🅷
(810) 732-2300. **$70-$120.** 4160 Pier North Blvd. I-75, exit 122 (Pierson Rd), just w. Int corridors. **Pets:** Other species. $10 one-time fee/room. Service with restrictions, supervision.
ⒶⓈⓀ ✕ ⬛ 🖵 ≈

⚛ ▼▼▼ Holiday Inn Express 🅷
(810) 238-7744. **$89-$149.** 1150 Robert T Longway Blvd. I-475, exit 8A (Robert T Longway Blvd), just w. Int corridors. **Pets:** Medium. $25 daily fee/pet. Designated rooms, service with restrictions, supervision.
ⓈⒶⓋⒺ ✕ ☾ℳ ⬛ 🖵

▼▼▼ Residence Inn by Marriott 🅷
(810) 424-7000. **$140-$270.** 2202 W Hill Rd. US 23, exit 90 (Hill Rd), just e. Int corridors. **Pets:** Accepted.
✕ ☾ℳ ⬛ 🖵 ⊠

FRANKENMUTH

▼▼ Drury Inn & Suites-Frankenmuth 🅷
(989) 652-2800. **$80-$173.** 260 S Main St. On SR 83; downtown. Int corridors. **Pets:** Other species. Service with restrictions, supervision.
ⒶⓈⓀ ✕ ☾ℳ ⬛ 🖵 ≈

GAYLORD

⚛ ▼▼ Alpine Lodge 🅷 🐾
(989) 732-2431. **$69-$109.** 833 W Main St. I-75, exit 282, 0.3 mi e on SR 32. Ext/int corridors. **Pets:** Medium, dogs only. Designated rooms, service with restrictions, supervision.
ⓈⒶⓋⒺ ✕ ⬛ 🖵 ⑪ ≈ ⊠

⚛ ▼ Downtown Motel Ⓜ
(989) 732-5010. **$46-$80.** 208 S Otsego Ave. I-75, exit 282, 0.5 mi e, then 0.3 mi s on I-75 business loop. Ext corridors. **Pets:** $5 daily fee/pet. Service with restrictions, supervision.
ⓈⒶⓋⒺ ✕ ⬛

⚛ ▼▼ Quality Inn 🅷 ❅
(989) 732-7541. **$70-$120.** 137 West St. I-75, exit 282, 0.3 mi e on SR 32. Int corridors. **Pets:** Other species. $10 daily fee/room. Designated rooms, service with restrictions, supervision.
ⓈⒶⓋⒺ ✕ ⬛ 🖵 ⑪ ≈ ⊠

⚛ ▼▼ Royal Crest Motel 🅷 ❅
(989) 732-6451. **$59-$109, 14 day notice.** 803 S Otsego Ave. I-75, exit 279, 2.3 mi ne on I-75 business loop. Int corridors. **Pets:** Small, dogs only. Designated rooms, service with restrictions, supervision.
ⓈⒶⓋⒺ ✕ ⬛ 🖵 ≈ ⊠

GRAND MARAIS

▼ Voyageur's Motel Ⓜ
(906) 494-2389. **$75-$85.** 21914 E Wilson St. 0.5 mi e of SR 77. Ext corridors. **Pets:** Medium, dogs only. $20 daily fee/pet. Designated rooms, supervision.
✕ ⬛ 🖵 ⊠ 🅰

GRAND RAPIDS

▼▼▼ Homewood Suites by Hilton 🅷
(616) 285-7100. **$79-$139.** 3920 Stahl Dr SE. I-96, exit 43A (28th St SW), 1.5 mi w to E Paris Ave, then just n. Int corridors. **Pets:** $60 one-time fee/room. Service with restrictions, supervision.
✕ ☾ℳ ⬛ 🖵 ≈

▼▼ Radisson Hotel Grand Rapids Riverfront 🅷
(616) 363-9001. **$92-$129.** 270 Ann St NW. US 131, exit 88, 1.8 mi n. Int corridors. **Pets:** Small. $25 one-time fee/pet. Service with restrictions, crate.
ⒶⓈⓀ ✕ ⬛ 🖵 ⑪ ≈ ⊠

GRANDVILLE

▼▼ Comfort Suites-Grandville 🅷
(616) 667-0733. **$94-$250.** 4520 Kenowa Ave SW. I-196, exit 67, just sw. Int corridors. **Pets:** Accepted.
ⒶⓈⓀ ✕ ☾ℳ ⬛ 🖵 ≈

⚛ ▼▼ Residence Inn by Marriott Grand Rapids West 🅷
(616) 538-1100. **$116-$142.** 3451 Rivertown Point Ct SW. I-196, exit 67, 1.7 mi e. Int corridors. **Pets:** Large. $75 one-time fee/room. Service with restrictions, supervision.
ⓈⒶⓋⒺ ✕ ☾ℳ ⬛ 🖵 ≈ ⊠

GRAYLING

⚛ ▼ North Country Lodge Ⓜ
(989) 348-8471. **$57-$180.** 617 N I-75 Business Loop. 1 mi n. Ext corridors. **Pets:** Other species. Designated rooms, crate.
ⓈⒶⓋⒺ ✕ ⬛

▼▼ **Ramada Inn of Grayling** H
(989) 348-7611. **$70-$110.** 2650 S Business Loop. I-75 business loop, 0.8 mi s. Ext/int corridors. **Pets:** Service with restrictions, supervision.

ASK ✕ ⟐ᴹ 🛏 🖵 ¶¶ ⇝ ⚡

▼▼ **Super 8** H
(989) 348-8888. **Call for rates.** 5828 Nelson a Miles Pkwy. I-75, exit 251, just w. Int corridors. **Pets:** Accepted.

✕ 🛏 🖵 ⇝ ⚡

GREENVILLE

▼▼▼ **AmericInn Lodge and Suites of Greenville** H
(616) 754-4500. **$90-$100.** 2525 W Washington. US 131, exit 101 (SR 57), 13 mi e. Int corridors. **Pets:** Accepted.

ASK ✕ ⟐ᴹ 🛏 🖵 ⇝ ⚡

HANCOCK

▲▲▷ ▼▼ **Best Western Copper Crown Motel** H
(906) 482-6111. **$68-$74.** 235 Hancock St. On US 41 S; downtown. Ext/int corridors. **Pets:** $10 daily fee/room. Designated rooms, service with restrictions, supervision.

SAVE ✕ 🖵 ⇝ ⚡

HARRISON

▲▲▷ ◈ **Lakeside Motel & Cottages** M ❀
(989) 539-3796. **$62-$99.** 515 E Park St, Business US 127, M-61. US 127, exit US 127 business route/SR 61, 2.2 mi w. Ext corridors. **Pets:** Other species. Service with restrictions, crate.

SAVE ✕ 🛏 🖵 ⚡

HOLLAND

▼▼ **Microtel Inn & Suites** H
(616) 392-3235. **$54-$89.** 643 Hastings Ave. Just w of US 31 and 32nd St. Int corridors. **Pets:** Other species. $20 one-time fee/room. Designated rooms, service with restrictions, supervision.

ASK ✕ ⟐ᴹ 🛏 🖵

▼▼▼ **Residence Inn by Marriott** H
(616) 393-6900. **$109-$139.** 631 Southpoint Ridge Rd. I-196, exit 49, 0.7 mi n on SR 40. Int corridors. **Pets:** Accepted.

✕ ⟐ᴹ 🛏 🖵 ⇝ ⚡

HOUGHTON

▲▲▷ ▼▼▼ **Best Western-Franklin Square Inn** H
(906) 487-1700. **$90-$110, 3 day notice.** 820 Shelden Ave. On US 41; downtown. Int corridors. **Pets:** Small, other species. $10 daily fee/room. Designated rooms, service with restrictions, crate.

SAVE ✕ 🛏 🖵 ¶¶ ⇝ ⚡

▲▲▷ ▼▼▼▼ **Country Inn & Suites** H ❀
(906) 487-6700. **$99-$209.** 919 Razorback Dr. 1.3 mi w on SR 26. Int corridors. **Pets:** Medium, dogs only. $10 daily fee/room. Designated rooms, service with restrictions, supervision.

SAVE ✕ ⟐ᴹ 🛏 🖵 ⇝ ⚡

HOUGHTON LAKE

▼▼ **Super 8** H
(989) 422-3119. **$59-$109.** 9580 W Lake City Rd. Jct US 127 and SR 55. Int corridors. **Pets:** $10 daily fee/pet. Service with restrictions, supervision.

ASK ✕ 🛏 🖵 ⇝ ⚡

HOWELL

▼▼▼▼ **Baymont Inn & Suites-Howell** H
(517) 546-0712. **$70-$100.** 4120 Lambert Dr. I-96, exit 133 (US 59/Grand River Ave), just n, then 0.5 mi e. Int corridors. **Pets:** $50 deposit/room, $10 daily fee/pet. Service with restrictions, crate.

ASK ✕ ⟐ᴹ 🛏 🖵 ⇝

▲▲▲ ▼▼▼ **Best Western Howell** M
(517) 548-2900. **$85-$155.** 1500 Pinckney Rd. I-96, exit 137 (Pickney Rd), just s on CR D19. Ext corridors. **Pets:** Accepted.

SAVE ✕ 🛏 🖵 ¶¶ ⇝

HUDSONVILLE

▼▼ **Quality Inn-Hudsonville** H
(616) 662-4000. **Call for rates.** 3301 Highland Dr. I-196, exit 62 (32nd Ave), just nw. Int corridors. **Pets:** Accepted.

✕ 🛏 🖵 ⇝

▼▼ **Super 8** H
(616) 896-6710. **Call for rates.** 3005 Corporate Grove Dr. I-196, exit 62 (32nd Ave), just se. Int corridors. **Pets:** Accepted.

✕ 🛏 🖵 ⇝

IMLAY CITY

▲▲▷ ▼▼▼ **Days Inn** H
(810) 724-8005. **$69-$139.** 6692 Newark Rd. I-69, exit 168 (SR 53/Van Dyke Rd), just n, then just w. Int corridors. **Pets:** $50 deposit/pet, $12 daily fee/pet. Service with restrictions, supervision.

SAVE ✕ 🛏 🖵 ⇝

▼▼ **Super 8-Imlay City** H
(810) 724-8700. **$59-$99.** 6951 Newark Rd. I-69, exit 168 (SR 53/Van Dyke Rd), just n, then just e. Int corridors. **Pets:** $10 one-time fee/room. Service with restrictions, supervision.

✕ 🛏 🖵

IONIA

▼▼ **Super 8** H
(616) 527-2828. **Call for rates.** 7245 S State Rd. I-96, exit 67 (SR 66). Int corridors. **Pets:** Accepted.

✕ ⟐ᴹ 🛏 🖵

IRON MOUNTAIN

▲▲▷ ◈ **Budget Host Inn** M ❀
(906) 774-6797. **$52-$60.** 1663 N Stephenson Ave. 1.5 mi nw on US 2 and 141. Ext corridors. **Pets:** Medium. $5 one-time fee/room. Designated rooms, service with restrictions, supervision.

SAVE ✕ 🛏

▼▼▼▼ **Country Inn & Suites** H
(906) 774-1900. **$81.** 2005 S Stephenson Ave. Jct SR 141, 0.8 mi w on US 2. Int corridors. **Pets:** Medium, dogs only. $20 one-time fee/room. Designated rooms, service with restrictions, crate.

ASK ✕ ⟐ᴹ 🛏 🖵 ⇝

IRON RIVER

▼▼ **AmericInn Lodge & Suites of Iron River** H
(906) 265-9100. **$84-$136.** 40 E Adams St. On US 2; downtown. Int corridors. **Pets:** Accepted.

ASK ✕ 🛏 🖵 ⇝ ⚡

IRONWOOD

▲▲▷ ▼▼ **AmericInn of Ironwood** H ❀
(906) 932-7200. **$69-$109.** 1117 E Cloverland Dr. 0.8 mi e on US 2. Int corridors. **Pets:** Other species. $30 daily fee/room. Designated rooms, service with restrictions, supervision.

SAVE ✕ ⟐ᴹ 🛏 🖵 ⇝ ⚡

▼ **Super 8** H
(906) 932-3395. **$109-$114.** 160 E Cloverland Dr. Jct US 2 and 2 business route. Int corridors. **Pets:** Other species. $10 one-time fee/pet. Designated rooms, service with restrictions, supervision.

ASK ✕ 🛏 🖵 ⚡

ISHPEMING

♨ ▼▼▼ Best Western Country Inn 🏨
(906) 485-6345. **$78-$108.** 850 US 41 W. US 41, just n of town. Int corridors. **Pets:** Designated rooms, service with restrictions, supervision.
🅂🄰🅅🄴 ⊠ 🖥 🛏 ☎

JACKSON

▼▼ Baymont Inn-Jackson 🏨
(517) 789-6000. **$89-$189, 7 day notice.** 2035 Holiday Inn Dr. I-94, exit 138 (US 127), just nw. Int corridors. **Pets:** Accepted.
🄰🅂🄺 ⊠ 🖥 💻

▼ Motel 6–1088 Ⓜ
(517) 789-7186. **$39-$49.** 830 Royal Dr. I-94, exit 138 (US 127), just se. Ext corridors. **Pets:** Other species. Service with restrictions, supervision.
⊠ 🖥 ☎

KALAMAZOO

▼▼ Baymont Inn & Suites-Kalamazoo 🏨
(269) 372-7999. **Call for rates.** 2203 S 11th St. US 131, exit 36B (Stadium Dr), just w. Int corridors. **Pets:** Accepted.
⊠ 🖥 💻

▼▼▼ Hawthorn Suites 🏨
(269) 353-2547. **Call for rates.** 2575 S 11th St. US 131, exit 36B (Stadium Dr), just w. Int corridors. **Pets:** Accepted.
⊠ 🄼 🖥 💻 ☎

♨ ▼▼▼▼ Holiday Inn-West 🏨
(269) 375-6000. **$129-$179.** 2747 S 11th St. US 131, exit 36B (Stadium Dr), just w. Int corridors. **Pets:** Small, other species. $25 one-time fee/pet. Service with restrictions, supervision.
🅂🄰🅅🄴 ⊠ 🄼 🖥 💻 🛏 ☎

♨ ▼▼▼ Quality Inn 🏨
(269) 381-7000. **$60-$140.** 3820 Sprinkle Rd. I-94, exit 80 (Sprinkle Rd), 0.3 mi s. Int corridors. **Pets:** Medium. $15 one-time fee/room. Service with restrictions, supervision.
🅂🄰🅅🄴 ⊠ 🖥 💻 ☎

▼▼ Red Roof Inn-West #7025 🏨
(269) 375-7400. **$60-$75.** 5425 W Michigan Ave. US 131, exit 36B (Stadium Dr), just nw. Ext corridors. **Pets:** Accepted.
🄰🅂🄺 ⊠ 🄼 🖥

▼▼▼ Residence Inn by Marriott 🏨
(269) 349-0855. **$134-$164.** 1500 E Kilgore Rd. I-94, exit 78 (Portage Rd), just n, then just w. Int corridors. **Pets:** Accepted.
⊠ 🄼 🖥 💻 ☎ 🗶

▼▼▼ Staybridge Suites-Kalamazoo 🏨 🐾
(269) 372-8000. **$129-$199.** 2001 Seneca Ln. US 131, exit 36A (Stadium Dr), 0.3 mi e. Int corridors. **Pets:** Medium. $25 daily fee/room. Service with restrictions, supervision.
🄰🅂🄺 ⊠ 🄼 🖥 💻 ☎

▼▼▼ TownePlace Suites by Marriott Kalamazoo 🏨
(269) 353-1500. **$129-$139.** 5683 S 9th St. I-94, exit 72 (9th St), just s. Int corridors. **Pets:** Accepted.
⊠ 🄼 🖥 💻 ☎

KENTWOOD

▼▼ Comfort Inn 🏨
(616) 957-2080. **$66-$140.** 4155 28th St SE. I-96, exit 43A, 1.5 mi w on SR 11. Int corridors. **Pets:** $20 one-time fee/pet. No service, supervision.
🄰🅂🄺 ⊠ 🖥 💻

♨ ▼▼▼▼ Hilton Grand Rapids Airport 🏨
(616) 957-0100. **$89-$175.** 4747 28th St SE. I-96, exit 43A, 0.5 mi w on SR 11. Int corridors. **Pets:** Accepted.
🅂🄰🅅🄴 ⊠ 🖥 💻 🛏 ☎ 🗶

▼▼ Residence Inn by Marriott East 🏨
(616) 957-8111. **$152-$186.** 2701 E Beltline Ave. Jct SR 11 and E Beltline Ave (SR 37). Ext corridors. **Pets:** Accepted.
⊠ 🖥 💻 ☎ 🗶

▼▼ Staybridge Suites by Holiday Inn 🏨
(616) 464-3200. **$79-$189.** 3000 Lake Eastbrook Blvd SE. I-96, exit 43A, 2 mi w on SR 11, then just s. Int corridors. **Pets:** Other species. $10 daily fee/room. Service with restrictions, supervision.
🄰🅂🄺 ⊠ 🄼 🖥 💻 ☎

LAKESIDE

▼▼▼ White Rabbit Inn 🅱🅱
(269) 469-4620. **Call for rates.** 14634 Red Arrow Hwy. I-94, exit 6 (Union Pier Rd), 1 mi w, then 2 mi n. Ext corridors. **Pets:** Accepted.
⊠ 🖥 💻 🆉

LANSING

♨ ▼▼▼ Best Western Midway Hotel 🏨
(517) 627-8471. **$85-$110, 3 day notice.** 7711 W Saginaw Hwy. I-96, exit 93B (SR 43/Saginaw Hwy), just e. Int corridors. **Pets:** Accepted.
🅂🄰🅅🄴 ⊠ 🖥 💻 🛏 ☎ 🗶

♨ ▼▼▼ Hampton Inn of Lansing 🏨
(517) 627-8381. **$89-$99.** 525 N Canal Rd. I-96, exit 93B (SR 43/Saginaw Hwy), just e. Int corridors. **Pets:** Other species. $100 deposit/room. Designated rooms, service with restrictions, crate.
🅂🄰🅅🄴 ⊠ 🖥 💻

▼ Motel 6 Lansing West #1089 Ⓜ
(517) 321-1444. **$45-$55.** 7326 W Saginaw Hwy. I-96, exit 93B (SR 43/Saginaw Hwy), just e. Ext corridors. **Pets:** Other species. Service with restrictions, supervision.
⊠ 🖥 ☎

♨ ▼▼▼▼ Quality Suites Hotel 🏨
(517) 886-0600. **$99-$119.** 901 Delta Commerce Dr. I-96, exit 93B (SR 43/Saginaw Hwy), 0.3 mi e to Bennigan's Restaurant, then just n. Int corridors. **Pets:** Other species. $25 one-time fee/room. Service with restrictions.
🅂🄰🅅🄴 ⊠ 🖥 💻 🗶

♨ ▼▼▼ Red Roof Inn-West #7020 🏨
(517) 321-7246. **$44-$65.** 7412 W Saginaw Hwy. I-96, exit 93B (SR 43/Saginaw Hwy), just e. Ext corridors. **Pets:** Small, other species. Designated rooms, service with restrictions, supervision.
🅂🄰🅅🄴 ⊠ 🖥

▼▼▼ Residence Inn by Marriott West 🏨
(517) 886-5030. **$115-$130.** 922 Delta Commerce Dr. I-96, exit 93B (SR 43/Saginaw Hwy), 0.4 mi e; behind Bennigans. Int corridors. **Pets:** Accepted.
⊠ 🄼 🖥 💻 ☎ 🗶

♨ ▼▼▼▼ Sheraton Lansing Hotel 🏨 🐾
(517) 323-7100. **$190-$300.** 925 S Creyts Rd. I-496, exit 1 (Creyts Rd), just n. Int corridors. **Pets:** Medium, dogs only. $30 one-time fee/room. Service with restrictions, supervision.
🅂🄰🅅🄴 ⊠ 🖥 💻 🛏 ☎ 🗶

LAPEER

▼▼ Fairfield Inn by Marriott Flint-Lapeer 🏨
(810) 245-7700. **$80-$98.** 927 Demille Rd. I-69, exit 155 (SR 24), 1.2 mi n, then just e. Int corridors. **Pets:** Accepted.
⊠ 🄼 🖥 💻 ☎

LUDINGTON

♨ ▼▼▼ Best Western Splash Park Inn 🏨
(231) 843-2140. **$69-$269, 3 day notice.** 5005 W US 10. Jct US 31, 1 mi w. Int corridors. **Pets:** Accepted.
🅂🄰🅅🄴 ⊠ 🖥 💻 ☎ 🗶

▼▼ Holiday Inn Express 🅗 ☸
(231) 845-7004. **$89-$249.** 5323 W US 10. Jct US 31, 1.3 mi w. Int corridors. **Pets:** $10 daily fee/pet. Designated rooms, service with restrictions, supervision.
ASK ✕ 🛈 ▣ ➤ ✕

MACKINAW CITY

▼▼ Baymont Inn & Suites-Mackinaw City 🅗
(231) 436-7737. **$69-$259.** 109 S Nicolet St. I-75, exit 338 southbound, just n. Int corridors. **Pets:** Medium, other species. $10 daily fee/pet. Designated rooms, service with restrictions, supervision.
ASK ✕ 🛈 ▣ ➤

▼ Beachcomber Motel on the Water 🅜 ☸
(231) 436-8451. **$39-$125, 3 day notice.** 1011 S Huron Ave. 1 mi s on US 23. Ext corridors. **Pets:** Small, dogs only. $5 daily fee/pet. Designated rooms, service with restrictions, supervision.
ASK ✕ 🛈

▼ The Beach House 🅲🅰
(231) 436-5353. **Call for rates.** 11490 W US 23. 1.3 mi s. Ext corridors. **Pets:** Accepted.
✕ 🛈 ➤ ✕ ☎

▲▲ ▼▼ Days Inn & Suites "Bridgeview Lodge" 🅜
(231) 436-8961. **$39-$279.** 206 N Nicolet St. I-75, exit 339; at bridge. Ext/int corridors. **Pets:** Small, dogs only. $50 deposit/room. Designated rooms, supervision.
SAVE ✕ 🛈 ▣ ➤

▲▲ ▼▼▼ Days Inn Lakeview 🅜
(231) 436-5557. **$39-$198, 3 day notice.** 825 S Huron Ave. I-75, exit 337 northbound, 0.5 mi n to US 23, then 0.3 mi e; exit 338 southbound, 0.8 mi se on US 23. Ext corridors. **Pets:** Medium. $100 deposit/room. Supervision.
SAVE ✕ 🛈 ▣ ➤

▼ Econo Lodge at the Bridge 🅜
(231) 436-5026. **$49-$189.** 412 N Nicolet St. I-75, exit 339. Ext corridors. **Pets:** Accepted.
ASK ✕ 🛈 ▣

▲▲ ▼▼ Econo Lodge Bayview 🅜
(231) 436-5777. **$38-$178, 3 day notice.** 712 S Huron Ave. I-75, exit 337 northbound, 0.5 mi n to US 23, 0.3 mi e, then just n; exit 338 southbound, 0.8 mi se on US 23, then just n. Ext corridors. **Pets:** Medium. $100 deposit/room. Supervision.
SAVE ✕ 🛈 ▣ ➤

▲▲ ▼▼▼ Holiday Inn Express at the Bridge 🅗
(231) 436-7100. **$49-$299.** 364 Louvingny. I-75, exit 339. Int corridors. **Pets:** Small, dogs only. $50 deposit/room. Designated rooms, supervision.
SAVE ✕ 🅼 🛈 ▣ ➤ ✕

▲▲ ▼▼▼ Super 8-Beachfront 🅜
(231) 436-7111. **$38-$198, 3 day notice.** 519 S Huron Ave. I-75, exit 337 northbound, 0.5 mi n to US 23, 0.3 mi e, then just n; exit 338 southbound, 0.8 mi se on US 23, then just n. Ext corridors. **Pets:** Medium. $100 deposit/room. Supervision.
SAVE ✕ 🛈 ▣ ➤

▲▲ ▼▼ Super 8 Bridgeview 🅗
(231) 436-5252. **$38-$198, 3 day notice.** 601 N Huron Ave. I-75, exit 339 northbound, just n, then just e. Ext/int corridors. **Pets:** Medium. $100 deposit/room. Supervision.
SAVE ✕ 🛈 ▣ ➤ ✕

MANISTIQUE

▲▲ ▼ Beachcomber Motel 🅜
(906) 341-2567. **Call for rates.** 751 E Lakeshore Dr. 1 mi e on US 2. Ext corridors. **Pets:** Accepted.
SAVE ✕ 🛈

▼▼ Comfort Inn 🅗
(906) 341-6981. **$79-$159.** 617 E Lakeshore Dr. 0.5 mi e on US 2. Int corridors. **Pets:** Accepted.
ASK ✕ 🛈 ▣ ✕

▼▼ Econo Lodge Lakeshore 🅜
(906) 341-6014. **$59-$119.** 1101 E Lakeshore Dr. 1.5 mi e on US 2. Ext/int corridors. **Pets:** Accepted.
ASK ✕ 🛈 ▣ ✕

MARQUETTE

▲▲ ▼ Birchmont Motel 🅜
(906) 228-7538. **$46-$76.** 2090 US 41 S. On US 41 and SR 28, 4.3 mi s. Ext corridors. **Pets:** Other species. $8 daily fee/pet. Designated rooms, service with restrictions, supervision.
SAVE ✕ 🛈 ➤

▼▼ Holiday Inn 🅗
(906) 225-1351. **$114-$125.** 1951 US 41 W. On US 41 and SR 28, 1.8 mi w. Int corridors. **Pets:** Accepted.
ASK ✕ 🅼 🛈 ▣ 🍴 ➤ ✕

▲▲ ▼ Travelodge 🅗
(906) 249-1712. **$50-$138.** 1010 M-28 E. Jct US 41 S and SR 28 E. Int corridors. **Pets:** Accepted.
SAVE ✕ 🛈 ▣ ➤

MARSHALL

▲▲ ▼ Arbor Inn of Historic Marshall 🅜
(269) 781-7772. **$45-$69.** 15435 W Michigan Ave. I-69, exit 36 (Michigan Ave), just w. Ext corridors. **Pets:** Other species. $5 daily fee/pet. Designated rooms, service with restrictions, supervision.
SAVE ✕ 🛈 ➤

MENOMINEE

▼▼ Econo Lodge On The Bay 🅗 ☸
(906) 863-4431. **$50-$150.** 2516 10th St. 1 mi n on US 41. Int corridors. **Pets:** Other species. $10 daily fee/pet. Designated rooms, service with restrictions, supervision.
ASK ✕ 🛈 ▣

MIDLAND

▲▲ ▼▼ Best Western Valley Plaza Resort 🅗
(989) 496-2700. **$90-$200.** 5221 Bay City Rd. US 10, exit Midland/Bay City Rd. Int corridors. **Pets:** Small. Service with restrictions, crate.
SAVE ✕ 🛈 ▣ 🍴 ➤ ✕

▼▼ Fairview Inn & Suites 🅗
(989) 631-0070. **$89-$125.** 2200 W Wackerly St. Jct US 10 and Eastman Rd. Int corridors. **Pets:** Accepted.
ASK ✕ 🛈 ▣ ➤

▼▼ Sleep Inn of Midland 🅗
(989) 837-1010. **$85-$100.** 2100 W Wackerly St. Jct US 10 and Eastman Rd. Int corridors. **Pets:** Other species. $10 daily fee/room. Service with restrictions, supervision.
ASK ✕ 🅼 🛈 ▣ ➤

▼▼ Wyndham 🅗
(989) 631-4220. **$110-$200.** 1500 W Wackerly St. Jct US 10 and Eastman Rd. Ext/int corridors. **Pets:** Accepted.
✕ 🛈 ▣ 🍴 ➤ ✕

MIO

▼ Mio Motel 🅜
(989) 826-3248. **$60-$75, 3 day notice.** 415 N Morenci St. Just n on SR 33 and 72. Ext corridors. **Pets:** Accepted.
✕ 🛈

MONROE

AAA ▼▼▼▼ Best Western Prestige Inn **M**
(734) 289-2330. **$64-$110, 30 day notice.** 1900 Welcome Way. I-75, exit 15 (SR 50), just e. Ext corridors. **Pets:** Dogs only. $10 daily fee/pet. Service with restrictions, supervision.
[SAVE] ☒ ☐ 🖥 ⊇

MOUNT PLEASANT

▼▼▼ Comfort Inn & Suites Hotel and Conference
Center **H** ❀
(989) 772-4000. **$99-$182.** 2424 S Mission St. 2 mi s on US 127 business route. Int corridors. **Pets:** Other species. $15 daily fee/room. Designated rooms, service with restrictions, supervision.
[ASK] ☒ 🖥 🖥 ⊇

▼▼▼ Fairfield Inn and Suites **H**
(989) 775-5000. **$107-$131.** 2525 S University Park Dr. 2 mi s on US 127 business route. Int corridors. **Pets:** Other species. $15 one-time fee/room. Service with restrictions, supervision.
☒ 🞰 🖥 🖥 ⊇ ☒

AAA ▼▼▼▼ Soaring Eagle Inn & Conference Center **H**
(989) 772-2905. **$89-$279.** 5665 E Pickard Ave. Jct US 127 and SR 20 E. Ext/int corridors. **Pets:** Designated rooms, service with restrictions, supervision.
[SAVE] ☒ 🖥 🖥 🖥 🍴 ⊇ ☒

▼▼ Super 8 **H**
(989) 773-8888. **$69-$149.** 2323 S Mission St. 1.8 mi s on US 127 business route. Int corridors. **Pets:** Accepted.
[ASK] ☒ 🖥 🖥 🖥

MUNISING

AAA ▼ Alger Falls Motel **M**
(906) 387-3536. **$45-$75.** E9427 E Hwy M-28. 2 mi e on SR 28 and 94. Ext corridors. **Pets:** Small, dogs only. $10 daily fee/room. Designated rooms, service with restrictions, supervision.
[SAVE] ☒ 🖥

AAA ▼▼ AmericInn Lodge & Suites of Munising **H**
(906) 387-2000. **$70-$170.** E9926 E Hwy M-28. On SR 28, 2.7 mi e. Int corridors. **Pets:** $10 daily fee/pet. Designated rooms, service with restrictions, supervision.
[SAVE] ☒ 🖥 🖥 🖥 ⊇ ☒

AAA ▼ Sunset Motel on the Bay **M** ❀
(906) 387-4574. **$55-$91.** 1315 Bay St. 1 mi e on E Munising Ave (CR H58). Ext corridors. **Pets:** Medium, dogs only. $10 one-time fee/pet. Designated rooms, service with restrictions, supervision.
[SAVE] ☒ 🖥 🖥 ☒

AAA ▼ Terrace Motel **M**
(906) 387-2735. **$40-$60, 3 day notice.** 420 Prospect St. 0.5 mi e, just off SR 28. Ext corridors. **Pets:** Accepted.
[SAVE] ☒ ☒ 🗷 🖀

NEW BUFFALO

▼▼▼ Holiday Inn Express Hotel & Suites **H**
(269) 469-1400. **$99-$350.** 11500 Holiday Dr. I-94, exit 1 (La Porte Rd), just w. Int corridors. **Pets:** Accepted.
[ASK] ☒ 🖥 🖥 🖥 ⊇

NORWAY

▼▼ AmericInn Lodge & Suites of Norway **H** ❀
(906) 563-7500. **$81-$88.** W 6002 US Hwy 2. 0.7 mi w. Int corridors. **Pets:** Medium. $10 one-time fee/room. Designated rooms, service with restrictions, crate.
[ASK] ☒ 🖥 🖥 ⊇ ☒

OKEMOS

▼▼▼ Comfort Inn-E. Lansing/Okemos **H**
(517) 347-6690. **$89-$189.** 2187 University Park Dr. I-96, exit 110 (Okemos Rd), just n, then just e. Int corridors. **Pets:** Large, dogs only. $25 one-time fee/room. Designated rooms, service with restrictions, crate.
[ASK] ☒ 🖥 🖥 🖥

▼▼▼ Holiday Inn Express & Suites **H**
(517) 349-8700. **$88-$105.** 2209 University Park Dr. I-96, exit 110 (Okemos Rd), just n, then just e. Int corridors. **Pets:** Medium, dogs only. $25 one-time fee/room. Service with restrictions, crate.
[ASK] ☒ 🖥 🖥 🖥 ⊇ ☒

PAW PAW

▼▼ Comfort Inn & Suites **H** ❀
(269) 655-0303. **$59-$119.** 153 Ampey Rd. I-94, exit 60 (SR 40), just nw. Int corridors. **Pets:** Other species. Service with restrictions, crate.
[ASK] ☒ 🖥 🖥 🖥 ⊇

AAA ▼▼ Super 8 **H**
(269) 657-1111. **$55-$169.** 111 Ampey Rd. I-94, exit 60 (SR 40). Int corridors. **Pets:** Medium. $15 one-time fee/room. Service with restrictions, supervision.
[SAVE] ☒ 🖥 🖥 🖥 ⊇

PELLSTON

▼▼ Holiday Inn Express Pellston **H**
(231) 539-7000. **$59-$199.** 1600 US 31 N. 1.2 mi n. Int corridors. **Pets:** Accepted.
[ASK] ☒ 🖥 🖥 ⊇ ☒

PETOSKEY

AAA ▼ Days Inn Petoskey **M**
(231) 348-3900. **$49-$149.** 1420 Spring St. 1.3 mi s. Ext corridors. **Pets:** Other species. $9 daily fee/pet. Service with restrictions.
[SAVE] ☒ 🖥 🖥 🍴

AAA ▼ Econo Lodge **M**
(231) 348-3324. **$49-$135.** 1859 US 131 S. 2 mi s of US 31. Ext corridors. **Pets:** Other species. $10 daily fee/pet. Designated rooms, service with restrictions, supervision.
[SAVE] ☒ 🖥 🖥 ⊇

AAA ▼▼▼ Holiday Inn Express Hotel & Suites **H**
(231) 487-0991. **$69-$299.** 1751 S US 131. I-75, exit 282, w on M-32 to US 131 N. Int corridors. **Pets:** Small, dogs only. Designated rooms, service with restrictions, supervision.
[SAVE] ☒ 🖥 🖥 ⊇ ☒

PLAINWELL

AAA ▼▼▼▼ Comfort Inn **H**
(269) 685-9891. **$90-$200.** 622 Allegan St. US 131, exit 49A, just e. Int corridors. **Pets:** Large. $15 daily fee/pet. Service with restrictions, supervision.
[SAVE] ☒ 🖥 🖥 ⊇

PORT HURON

AAA ▼▼▼ Baymont Inn & Suites **H**
(810) 364-8000. **$59-$89.** 1611 Range Rd. I-94, exit 269 (Range Rd), just w. Int corridors. **Pets:** $15 daily fee/pet. Designated rooms, service with restrictions, supervision.
[SAVE] ☒ 🖥 🖥 ⊇

▼▼ Comfort Inn **H**
(810) 982-5500. **$80-$199.** 1700 Yeager St. I-94, exit 274 (Water St), just s, then just w. Int corridors. **Pets:** Other species. Supervision.
[ASK] ☒ 🖥 🖥 ⊇

PORTLAND

⚡ 〰〰 Best Western American Heritage Inn �H
(517) 647-2200. **$69-$149.** 1681 Grand River Ave. I-96, exit 77, just n. Int corridors. **Pets:** Small, dogs only. $10 daily fee/pet. Service with restrictions, supervision.
SAVE ✕ &M 🛗 💻 ⤳

SAGINAW

⚡ 〰〰 Best Western–Saginaw �H
(989) 755-0461. **$59-$109, 3 day notice.** 1408 S Outer Dr. I-75, exit 149B (SR 46). Int corridors. **Pets:** Large, other species. $25 one-time fee/room. Service with restrictions, supervision.
SAVE ✕ 🛗 💻 🍴 ⤳ 🖾

〰〰 Comfort Suites by Choice Hotels �H
(989) 797-8000. **Call for rates.** 5180 Fashion Square Blvd. I-675, exit 6, 0.6 mi w on Tittabawassee Rd. Int corridors. **Pets:** Accepted.
✕ &M 🛗 💻 ⤳

〰 Motel 6 Saginaw #4354 🇲
(989) 754-8414. **$43-$80.** 966 S Outer Dr. I-75, exit 149B (SR 46). Ext corridors. **Pets:** Other species. Service with restrictions, supervision.
✕ 🛗

〰〰 Ramada Inn & Suites �H
(989) 793-7900. **$69-$149.** 3325 Davenport Ave. I-675, exit 3, 2 mi w on SR 58. Int corridors. **Pets:** Medium. $20 daily fee/room. Designated rooms, service with restrictions, supervision.
ASK ✕ 🛗 💻 🍴

〰〰〰 Residence Inn by Marriott �H
(989) 799-9000. **$139-$149.** 5230 Fashion Square Blvd. I-675, exit 6, 0.8 mi w, then just n. Int corridors. **Pets:** Accepted.
✕ 🛗 💻 ⤳ 🖾

⚡ 〰〰 Quality Inn Lakefront 🇲
(906) 643-7581. **$48-$174, 3 day notice.** 1021 N State St. 2.3 mi n of bridge tollgate on I-75 business route. Ext corridors. **Pets:** Small, dogs only. $10 one-time fee/room. Designated rooms, service with restrictions, supervision.
SAVE ✕ 🛗 💻 ⤳

ST. IGNACE

⚡ 〰〰 Budget Host Inn & Suites �H
(906) 643-9666. **$64-$152.** 700 N State St. 1.8 mi n of bridge tollgate on I-75 business route. Ext/int corridors. **Pets:** Other species. $40 deposit/room. Service with restrictions, supervision.
SAVE ✕ 🛗 ⤳ 🖾

SAULT STE. MARIE

⚡ 〰〰 Best Western Sault Ste. Marie �H
(906) 632-2170. **$76-$175.** 4335 I-75 Business Spur. I-75, exit 392, 0.3 mi ne. Int corridors. **Pets:** Accepted.
SAVE ✕ 🛗 💻 ⤳ 🖾

⚡ 〰 Budget Host Crestview Inn 🇲
(906) 635-5213. **$59-$79.** 1200 Ashmun St. I-75, exit 392, 2.8 mi ne on I-75 business loop. Ext corridors. **Pets:** Large, other species. $5 daily fee/room. Designated rooms, service with restrictions, supervision.
SAVE ✕ 🛗

⚡ 〰〰 Comfort Inn �H
(906) 635-1118. **$70-$200, 30 day notice.** 4404 I-75 Business Spur. I-75, exit 392, at I-75 business loop. Int corridors. **Pets:** Other species. Designated rooms, service with restrictions, supervision.
SAVE ✕ 🛗 💻 ⤳ 🖾

⚡ 〰〰 Days Inn �H
(906) 635-5200. **$69-$199.** 3651 I-75 Business Spur. I-75, exit 392, 0.8 mi ne on I-75 business loop. Int corridors. **Pets:** $5 daily fee/pet. Designated rooms, service with restrictions, supervision.
SAVE ✕ 🛗 💻 ⤳ 🖾

⚡ 〰 La France Terrace Motel 🇲
(906) 632-7823. **$45-$75, 7 day notice.** 1608 Ashmun St. I-75, exit 392, 2.3 mi ne on I-75 business loop. Ext corridors. **Pets:** Accepted.
SAVE ✕ 🛗 ⤳

〰 Park Inn �H
(906) 632-6000. **$65-$115.** 3525 I-75 Business Spur. I-75, exit 392, 0.7 mi ne. Int corridors. **Pets:** Accepted.
ASK ✕ &M 🛗 💻 ⤳ 🖾

〰〰 Quality Inn & Suites �H
(906) 635-6918. **$59-$159.** 3290 I-75 Business Loop. I-75, exit 392, 1 mi ne. Int corridors. **Pets:** Accepted.
ASK ✕ 🛗 💻 🍴 ⤳ 🖾

〰 Super 8 �H
(906) 632-8882. **Call for rates.** 3826 I-75 Business Loop. I-75, exit 392, 0.5 mi ne. Int corridors. **Pets:** Accepted.
✕ 🛗 💻

SILVER CITY

〰 Mountain View Lodges 🇨🇦
(906) 885-5256. **$134-$165, 30 day notice.** 34042 M-107. Jct SR 64, 0.8 mi w. Ext corridors. **Pets:** Dogs only. $60 one-time fee/pet. Designated rooms, no service, supervision.
✕ 🛗 💻 🄰

SOUTH HAVEN

⚡ 〰〰 Comfort Suites �H
(269) 639-2014. **$79-$209.** 1755 Phoenix St. I-196, exit 20, 0.5 mi e. Int corridors. **Pets:** $25 daily fee/pet. Service with restrictions, crate.
SAVE ✕ &M 🛗 💻 ⤳

SPRING LAKE

〰〰 Grand Haven Waterfront Holiday Inn �H ✿
(616) 846-1000. **$100-$200, 3 day notice.** 940 W Savidge St. On SR 104, just e of US 31. Int corridors. **Pets:** Dogs only. $10 daily fee/pet. Designated rooms, service with restrictions, supervision.
ASK ✕ 🛗 💻 🍴 ⤳ 🖾

STEVENSVILLE

〰〰 Candlewood Suites �H
(269) 428-4400. **Call for rates.** 2567 W Marquette Woods Rd. I-94, exit 23 (Red Arrow Hwy), just w. Int corridors. **Pets:** Accepted.
✕ &M 🛗 💻

〰〰 Hampton Inn of St. Joseph I-94 �H ✿
(269) 429-2700. **$84-$149.** 5050 Red Arrow Hwy. I-94, exit 23 (Red Arrow Hwy), just se. Int corridors. **Pets:** Large, other species. Service with restrictions, supervision.
✕ &M 🛗 💻 ⤳

SUTTONS BAY

〰 Red Lion Motor Lodge 🇲
(231) 271-6694. **$59-$195.** 4290 S West Bay Shore Rd. 5 mi s on SR 22. Ext corridors. **Pets:** Other species. $20 one-time fee/room. Service with restrictions, supervision.
✕ 🛗 💻 🄯

TAWAS CITY

〰 Tawas Motel-Resort 🇲
(989) 362-3822. **Call for rates.** 1124 US 23 S. On US 23, 1.8 mi s. Ext corridors. **Pets:** Medium. $10 one-time fee/pet. Service with restrictions, crate.
✕ 🛗 💻 ⤳ 🖾

THREE RIVERS

▼▼ Super 8 🅗
(269) 279-8888. **$77-$82.** 711 US 131. Jct US 131 and SR 60 (W Broadway St). Int corridors. **Pets:** Accepted.
(A$K) (✕) (&M) 🛢 💻 🐾

TRAVERSE CITY

▼▼ Baymont Inn & Suites-Traverse City 🅗
(231) 933-4454. **$70-$300.** 2326 N US 31 S. 3.5 mi s on SR 37. Int corridors. **Pets:** Small, dogs only. Designated rooms, service with restrictions, supervision.
(A$K) (✕) 🛢 💻 🐾 (✕)

▼▼ Best Western Four Seasons 🆁 ❖
(231) 946-8424. **$49-$259.** 305 Munson Ave. 2 mi e on US 31. Ext/int corridors. **Pets:** $10 daily fee/room. Service with restrictions, supervision.
(SAVE) (✕) 🛢 💻 🐾

▼▼ Days Inn & Suites 🅗
(231) 941-0208. **$55-$210.** 420 Munson Ave. 2 mi e on US 31. Int corridors. **Pets:** Accepted.
(A$K) (✕) 🛢 💻 🐾 (✕)

▼▼▼ Holiday Inn, West Bay 🅗 ❖
(231) 947-3700. **$90-$250, 3 day notice.** 615 E Front St. 0.5 mi e on US 31. Int corridors. **Pets:** Other species. $15 daily fee/pet. Designated rooms, service with restrictions, supervision.
(SAVE) (✕) (&M) 🛢 💻 🍴 🐾 (✕)

▼▼ Park Place Hotel 🅗
(231) 946-5000. **$99-$329.** 300 E State St. Corner of E State and Park sts; downtown. Int corridors. **Pets:** Accepted.
(A$K) (✕) 🛢 💻 🍴 🐾 (✕)

▼▼ Quality Inn 🅗 ❖
(231) 929-4423. **$50-$190.** 1492 US 31 N. On US 31, 3.3 mi e. Ext/int corridors. **Pets:** Other species. $10 daily fee/room. Designated rooms, service with restrictions, supervision.
(SAVE) (✕) 🛢 💻 🐾

▼▼ Traverse Victorian Inn 🅗
(231) 947-5525. **$69-$189.** 461 Munson Ave. 2.4 mi e on US 31. Int corridors. **Pets:** Small, dogs only. $25 one-time fee/pet. Supervision.
(SAVE) (✕) 🛢 💻 🐾

WALKER

▼▼ Baymont Inn & Suites-Grand Rapids North 🅗
(616) 735-9595. **$75-$109.** 2151 Holton Ct NW. I-96, exit 28 (Walker Ave), just s. Int corridors. **Pets:** Other species. Service with restrictions, supervision.
(A$K) (✕) 🛢 💻 🐾

▼▼ Quality Inn Grand Rapids North 🅗
(616) 791-8500. **$65-$149.** 2171 Holton Ct. I-96, exit 28 (Walker Ave), just s. Int corridors. **Pets:** Accepted.
(A$K) (✕) 🛢 💻 🐾

WATERSMEET

▼▼ Dancing Eagles Resort Lac Vieux Desert Casino 🅗
(906) 358-4949. **$50-$90.** N5384 US Hwy 45. 1.8 mi n of US 2. Int corridors. **Pets:** Accepted.
(A$K) (✕) 🛢 💻 🐾 (✕)

WHITMORE LAKE

▼▼ Best Western Whitmore Lake 🆁
(734) 449-2058. **$69-$99.** 9897 Main St. US 23, exit 53, just e. Ext corridors. **Pets:** $25 daily fee/pet. Designated rooms, service with restrictions, crate.
(SAVE) (✕) 🛢 💻 🐾

WYOMING

▼▼ Howard Johnson Plaza Hotel 🅗
(616) 241-6444. **$65.** 255 28th St SW. On SR 11, 0.3 mi e of jct US 131, exit 28th St. Int corridors. **Pets:** Other species. $25 one-time fee/room. Service with restrictions, supervision.
(SAVE) (✕) 🛢 💻 🍴 🐾 (✕)

▼ Super 8 🅗
(616) 530-8588. **$60-$100.** 727 44th St SW. US 131, exit 79. Int corridors. **Pets:** Accepted.
(A$K) (✕) 🛢 💻

MINNESOTA

AITKIN

Ripple River Motel & RV Park M
(218) 927-3734. **$55-$90.** 701 Minnesota Ave S. US 169, 0.8 mi s of jct SR 210. Ext corridors. **Pets:** $10 daily fee/pet. Designated rooms, service with restrictions, supervision.

ALBERT LEA

Albert Lea Countryside Inn Motel M
(507) 373-2446. **Call for rates.** 2102 E Main St. I-35, exit 11, 1.3 mi w on CR 46. Ext/int corridors. **Pets:** Accepted.

Comfort Inn H
(507) 377-1100. **$80-$110.** 810 Happy Trails Ln. I-35, exit 11, just se. Int corridors. **Pets:** $10 one-time fee/pet. Designated rooms, supervision.

Country Inn & Suites By Carlson H
(507) 373-5513. **$98-$159.** 2214 E Main St. I-35, exit 12 southbound; exit 11 northbound, 1 mi w. Int corridors. **Pets:** Small. $20 one-time fee/room. Designated rooms, service with restrictions, supervision.

ALEXANDRIA

Country Inn & Suites By Carlson H
(320) 763-9900. **$78-$141.** 5304 Hwy 29 S. I-94, exit 103, just sw. Int corridors. **Pets:** Other species. $50 deposit/room, $10 one-time fee/room. Designated rooms, service with restrictions, supervision.

Holiday Inn Alexandria H
(320) 763-6577. **$95-$160.** 5637 State Hwy 29 S. I-94, exit 103, just s. Int corridors. **Pets:** Designated rooms, service with restrictions, crate.

Super 8 H
(320) 763-6552. **$66-$96.** 4620 Hwy 29 S. I-94, exit 103, 0.3 mi nw. Int corridors. **Pets:** Medium, dogs only. $10 daily fee/pet. Designated rooms, service with restrictions, crate.

AUSTIN

Days Inn H
(507) 433-8600. **Call for rates.** 700 16th Ave NW. I-90, exit 178A (4th St NW), just nw. Int corridors. **Pets:** Accepted.

Holiday Inn & Austin Conference Center H
(507) 433-1000. **$92-$149, 3 day notice.** 1701 4th St NW. I-90, exit 178A (4th St NW), just nw. Int corridors. **Pets:** Other species. $25 one-time fee/room. Designated rooms, service with restrictions, crate.

BABBITT

Timber Bay Lodge & Houseboats CA
(218) 827-3682. **$155-$750, 60 day notice.** 8347 Timber Bay Rd. 2.8 mi e of jct CR 21 via CR 70 and 623. Ext corridors. **Pets:** $15 daily fee/pet. No service, crate.

BAUDETTE

AmericInn Lodge & Suites of Baudette H
(218) 634-3200. **$72-$129.** 1179 Main St W. 0.5 mi w on SR 11. Int corridors. **Pets:** Accepted.

BAXTER

Country Inn & Suites by Carlson H
(218) 828-2161. **$95-$139.** 15058 Dellwood Dr N. Jct SR 371 and 210, 1 mi n on SR 371. Int corridors. **Pets:** Small, dogs only. Service with restrictions, supervision.

BEMIDJI

AmericInn Lodge & Suites of Bemidji H
(218) 751-3000. **$70-$135.** 1200 Paul Bunyan Dr NW. 0.5 mi e of northwest jct US 2, 71 and SR 197. Int corridors. **Pets:** Medium, dogs only. $30 one-time fee/pet. Designated rooms, service with restrictions, supervision.

Best Western Bemidji H
(218) 751-0390. **$59-$135, 3 day notice.** 2420 Paul Bunyan Dr. Jct US 71 N and SR 197. Int corridors. **Pets:** $10 daily fee/room. Designated rooms, supervision.

(AAA) ▼▼▼▼ Ruttger's Birchmont Lodge CA
(218) 444-3463. **$48-$375, 30 day notice.** 7598 Bemidji Rd NE. Jct SR 197, 3.6 mi n on CR 21 (Bemidji Ave N). Ext/int corridors. **Pets:** Large, other species. $10 daily fee/pet. Designated rooms, service with restrictions, crate.
[SAVE] [X] 🛡 🖥 ❌ 🛱 ❌

BRAINERD

▼▼▼▼ Red Roof Inn H
(218) 829-1441. **$50-$83.** 2115 S 6th St. On SR 371 business route, 1.8 mi s of jct SR 210. Ext/int corridors. **Pets:** Accepted.
[X] [&M] 🛡 🖥 🛱 🛱 ❌

BRECKENRIDGE

▼▼ Select Inn of Breckenridge/Wahpeton H
(218) 643-9201. **Call for rates.** 821 Hwy 75 N. Just sw of jct US 75 N and 210. Int corridors. **Pets:** Accepted.
[X] 🛡 🖥 🛱

CANNON FALLS

(AAA) ▼▼▼ Best Western Saratoga Inn H
(507) 263-7272. **$69-$135, 3 day notice.** 31591 64th Ave. Jct SR 19, 1 mi sw on US 52. Int corridors. **Pets:** Accepted.
[SAVE] [X] 🛡 🖥 🛱

CLOQUET

▼▼▼ AmericInn Lodge & Suites of Cloquet H 🐾
(218) 879-1231. **Call for rates.** 111 Big Lake Rd. I-35, exit 237 (SR 33), 2 mi nw. Int corridors. **Pets:** Dogs only. $50 deposit/room, $10 daily fee/room. Designated rooms, service with restrictions, supervision.
[X] 🛡 🖥 🛱 ❌

▼▼ Super 8 H 🐾
(218) 879-1250. **$62-$135.** 121 Big Lake Rd. I-35, exit 237 (SR 33), 2 mi nw. Int corridors. **Pets:** Dogs only. $50 deposit/room, $10 daily fee/room. Designated rooms, service with restrictions, supervision.
[ASK] [X] [&M] 🛡 🖥

COOK

▼▼▼ Ludlow's Island Resort VH
(218) 666-5407. **$395-$600, 90 day notice.** 8166 Ludlow Dr. US 53, 3.5 mi ne on CR 24, 5.1 mi e on CR 78 and 540. Ext corridors. **Pets:** Other species. $30 daily fee/pet. Designated rooms, service with restrictions, crate.
🛡 🖥 ❌

▼▼ Spring Bay Resort CA
(218) 666-5607. **Call for rates.** 3045 Vermilion Dr. CR 24, 8 mi ne of jct US 53. Ext corridors. **Pets:** Accepted.
[X] 🛡 🖥 ❌ 🎟 📷

CROOKSTON

▼▼ Northland Inn of Crookston H
(218) 281-5210. **$59-$89.** 2200 University Ave. On US 2 W and 75 N, 1.5 mi n. Int corridors. **Pets:** Accepted.
[ASK] [X] 🛡 🖥 🛱

CROSSLAKE

▼▼▼ Pine Peaks Lodge and Suites H 🐾
(218) 692-7829. **$80-$180, 3 day notice.** 14047 Swann Dr. Jct CR 66 and Swann Dr. Int corridors. **Pets:** Small, other species. $15 daily fee/room. Designated rooms, service with restrictions, supervision.
[ASK] [X] 🛡 🖥 🛱 🛱 ❌

DEER RIVER

(AAA) ▼▼▼ White Oak Inn & Suites H
(218) 246-9400. **$57-$160.** 201 4th Ave NW. On US 2. Int corridors. **Pets:** Accepted.
[SAVE] [X] 🛡 🖥 🛱 ❌

DEERWOOD

▼▼▼ Country Inn By Carlson H
(218) 534-3101. **$79-$109.** 23884 Front St. On SR 6 and 210, e of jct CR 12. Int corridors. **Pets:** Other species. $10 daily fee/room. Service with restrictions, supervision.
[ASK] [X] [&M] 🛡 🖥 🛱

DETROIT LAKES

(AAA) ▼▼▼ AmericInn Lodge & Suites of Detroit Lakes H
(218) 847-8795. **$75-$180.** 777 Hwy 10 E. 1.4 mi se. Int corridors. **Pets:** Other species. $10 daily fee/pet. Supervision.
[SAVE] [X] [&M] 🛡 🖥 🛱 ❌

(AAA) ▼▼▼ Best Western Holland House & Suites H 🐾
(218) 847-4483. **$89-$219, 3 day notice.** 615 Hwy 10 E. 1.3 mi se. Ext/int corridors. **Pets:** Medium. $15 daily fee/pet. Designated rooms, service with restrictions, supervision.
[SAVE] [X] 🛡 🖥 🛱

(AAA) ▼▼▼ Budget Host Inn M
(218) 847-4454. **$52-$130.** 895 Hwy 10 E. 1.5 mi se. Ext corridors. **Pets:** Accepted.
[SAVE] [X] 🛡 🖥

(AAA) ▼▼▼ Country Inn & Suites By Carlson H
(218) 847-2000. **$75-$165.** 1330 Hwy 10 E. Just e of jct US 10 and CR 54 E. Int corridors. **Pets:** Accepted.
[SAVE] [X] [&M] 🛡 🖥 🛱

DULUTH

(AAA) ▼▼▼ AmericInn Hotel & Suites of Duluth South H
(218) 624-1026. **$85-$210.** 185 US 2. Jct I-35 and US 2, 0.8 mi n. Int corridors. **Pets:** Accepted.
[SAVE] [X] 🛡 🖥 🎟 🛱

(AAA) ▼▼▼ Best Western Downtown Motel M
(218) 727-6851. **$49-$135.** 131 W 2nd St. 2nd St at 2nd Ave W; center. Ext/int corridors. **Pets:** Accepted.
[SAVE] [X] 🛡 🖥

(AAA) ▼▼▼ Country Inn & Suites By Carlson H
(218) 628-0668. **$85-$170.** 9330 W Skyline Pkwy. I-35, exit 249 (Boundary Ave), just se. Int corridors. **Pets:** Accepted.
[SAVE] [X] 🛡 🖥 🛱 ❌

(AAA) ▼▼▼ Country Inn & Suites-Duluth North H 🐾
(218) 740-4500. **$109-$229.** 4257 Haines Rd. Just n of US 53. Int corridors. **Pets:** Medium, other species. $10 daily fee/pet. Designated rooms, service with restrictions, supervision.
[SAVE] [X] 🛡 🖥 🛱 ❌

▼▼ Days Inn-Duluth H
(218) 727-3110. **Call for rates.** 909 Cottonwood Ave. SR 194, just n of jct US 53. Int corridors. **Pets:** Other species. $5 daily fee/room. Service with restrictions, supervision.
[X] 🛡 🖥

⚞⚟ ▼▼▼ Duluth Spirit Mountain Red Roof Inn 🄷
(218) 628-3691. **$69-$229, 3 day notice.** 9315 Westgate Blvd. I-35, exit 249 (Boundary Ave), just sw. Int corridors. **Pets:** Medium, dogs only. $25 daily fee/pet. Designated rooms, service with restrictions, supervision.
〖SAVE〗 ⊠ 🛢 💻 🏊 ⊠

⚞⚟ ▼▼▼ Econo Lodge Airport 🄷 🐾
(218) 722-5522. **$76-$166.** 4197 Haines Rd. West side on US 53 and SR 194. Int corridors. **Pets:** Medium, dogs only. $10 one-time fee/pet. Designated rooms, service with restrictions, supervision.
〖SAVE〗 ⊠ 🛢 💻 🏊 ⊠

⚞⚟ ▼▼◈ Edgewater Resort & Waterpark 🄷
(218) 728-3601. **$79-$329.** 2400 London Rd. I-35, exit 258 (21st Ave E), just nw. Ext/int corridors. **Pets:** Accepted.
〖SAVE〗 ⊠ 🛢 💻 🍽 🏊 ⊠

⚞⚟ ▼▼◈ The Inn on Lake Superior 🄷 🐾
(218) 726-1111. **$109-$329.** 350 Canal Park Dr. In Canal Park area. Int corridors. **Pets:** Medium, other species. $25 daily fee/room. Designated rooms, service with restrictions, supervision.
〖SAVE〗 ⊠ &M 🛢 💻 🏊 ⊠

▼▼▼ Radisson Hotel Duluth-Harborview 🄷
(218) 727-8981. **$109-$209.** 505 W Superior St. At 5th Ave W; center. Int corridors. **Pets:** Accepted.
〖ASK〗 ⊠ 🛢 💻 🍽 🏊 ⊠

⚞⚟ ▼▼◈▼ Sheraton Duluth Hotel 🄷
(218) 733-5660. **$99-$289.** 301 E Superior St. I-35, exit 256B (Lake Ave), just nw. Int corridors. **Pets:** Accepted.
〖SAVE〗 ⊠ &M 🛢 💻 🍽 🏊

⚞⚟ ▼▼◈▼ The Suites Hotel at Waterfront Plaza 🄷
(218) 727-4663. **$99-$394.** 325 Lake Ave S. In Canal Park area. Int corridors. **Pets:** Accepted.
〖SAVE〗 ⊠ &M 🛢 💻 🍽 🏊 ⊠

▼▼ Voyageur Lakewalk Inn 🄼
(218) 722-3911. **$45-$74.** 333 E Superior St. I-35, exit 256 (Superior St), just n at jct 4th Ave E and Superior St. Ext corridors. **Pets:** Accepted.
〖ASK〗 ⊠ 🛢 💻

ELY

⚞⚟ ▼▼◈▼ Grand Ely Lodge Resort and Conference Center 🄷 🐾
(218) 365-6565. **$107-$290, 14 day notice.** 400 N Pioneer Rd. SR 169 to Central Ave, just n to Pioneer Rd, then 1 mi n. Ext/int corridors. **Pets:** $15 daily fee/pet. Designated rooms, service with restrictions, crate.
〖SAVE〗 ⊠ 🛢 💻 🍽 🏊 ⊠

⚞⚟ ▼ Motel Ely-Budget Host 🄼
(218) 365-3237. **$60-$120, 3 day notice.** 1047 E Sheridan St. SR 1 and 169. Ext corridors. **Pets:** Dogs only. $10 one-time fee/room. Designated rooms, service with restrictions, supervision.
〖SAVE〗 ⊠ 💻

EVELETH

▼▼ Super 8 🄷
(218) 744-1661. **$70-$140.** 1080 Industrial Park Dr. On US 53, 0.5 mi n of jct SR 37. Int corridors. **Pets:** Accepted.
〖ASK〗 ⊠ &M 🛢 💻 🏊 ⊠

FAIRMONT

▼▼ Comfort Inn 🄷
(507) 238-5444. **Call for rates.** 2225 N State St. I-90, exit 102 (SR 15), just sw. Int corridors. **Pets:** Designated rooms, service with restrictions, supervision.
⊠ 🛢 💻 🏊

▼▼▼▼ Holiday Inn 🄷
(507) 238-4771. **$95-$175.** 1200 Torgerson Dr. I-90, exit 102 (SR 15), just se. Int corridors. **Pets:** Small, other species. Service with restrictions, supervision.
〖ASK〗 ⊠ 🛢 💻 🍽 🏊 ⊠

▼▼ Super 8 🄷
(507) 238-9444. **$63-$73.** 1200 Torgerson Dr. I-90, exit 102 (SR 15), just se. Int corridors. **Pets:** Small, other species. Service with restrictions, supervision.
〖ASK〗 ⊠ 🛢

FARIBAULT

⚞⚟ ▼▼▼ AmericInn Motel & Suites of Faribault 🄷
(507) 334-9464. **$100-$190.** 1801 Lavender Dr. I-35, exit 59 (SR 21), 0.3 mi e. Int corridors. **Pets:** Large, other species. $25 one-time fee/room. Designated rooms, service with restrictions, supervision.
〖SAVE〗 ⊠ 🛢 💻 🏊 ⊠

▼▼ Days Inn & Suites 🄷
(507) 334-6835. **$70-$100.** 1920 Cardinal Ln. I-35, exit 59 (SR 21), just ne. Int corridors. **Pets:** Accepted.
〖ASK〗 ⊠ &M 🛢 💻 🏊

FERGUS FALLS

⚞⚟ ▼▼◈ AmericInn Lodge & Suites of Fergus Falls 🄷 🐾
(218) 739-3900. **$77-$150.** 526 Western Ave N. I-94, exit 54 (SR 210), just se. Int corridors. **Pets:** Large, other species. $50 deposit/room, $10 one-time fee/room. Designated rooms, service with restrictions, supervision.
〖SAVE〗 ⊠ &M 🛢 💻 🏊 ⊠

▼▼ Comfort Inn 🄷
(218) 736-5787. **Call for rates.** 425 Western Ave. I-94, exit 54 (SR 210), just se. Int corridors. **Pets:** Accepted.
⊠ 🛢 💻 🏊 ⊠

▼ Motel 7 🄼
(218) 736-2554. **Call for rates.** 616 Frontier Dr. I-94, exit 54 (SR 210), just ne. Int corridors. **Pets:** Accepted.
⊠ 🛢

FINLAYSON

▼▼ Americas Best Value Inn 🄷
(320) 245-5284. **$53-$73.** 60671 State Hwy 23. I-35, exit 195 (SR 23), just ne. Int corridors. **Pets:** Accepted.
〖ASK〗 ⊠ 🛢

FOSSTON

▼▼ Super 8 🄷
(218) 435-1088. **$59-$125.** 108 S Amber Ave. US 2, 0.5 mi e. Int corridors. **Pets:** Dogs only. $100 deposit/pet, $5 daily fee/pet. Supervision.
〖ASK〗 ⊠ 🛢 💻

GARRISON

▼▼▼ Garrison Inn & Suites by Ruttger's 🄷
(320) 692-4050. **$75-$149.** 9243 Hwy 169. SR 169, just s of jct SR 18. Int corridors. **Pets:** $50 deposit/room, $10 daily fee/pet. Designated rooms, service with restrictions, supervision.
⊠ 🛢 💻 🏊

GAYLORD

▼▼ Gold Leaf Inn & Suites 🄼
(507) 237-5860. **$60-$115.** 330 Main Ave E. 1.5 mi e. Int corridors. **Pets:** Small. Designated rooms, service with restrictions, supervision.
⊠ 🛢

GRAND MARAIS

▼▼▼▼ Best Western Superior Inn & Suites 🅷 ❀
(218) 387-2240. **$89-$319, 3 day notice.** 104 1st Ave E. SR 61, just ne of center. Int corridors. **Pets:** Medium. $15 daily fee/pet. Designated rooms, service with restrictions, supervision.
(SAVE) ⊠ 🛏 💻

▼▼▼ Gunflint Lodge 🆅🅷 ❀
(218) 388-2294. **$109-$599, 31 day notice.** 143 S Gunflint Lake. 43 mi n of town; 0.8 mi e of jct CR 12 (Gunflint Tr) and 50. Ext corridors. **Pets:** Other species. $20 daily fee/pet. Service with restrictions, crate.
🅼 🛏 💻 🍴 ⊠ 🐾 ☎

▼▼ Nor'Wester Lodge and Outfitter 🅲🅰
(218) 388-2252. **Call for rates.** 7778 Gunflint Tr. 30 mi nw on CR 12 (Gunflint Tr) from jct SR 61. Ext corridors. **Pets:** Accepted.
🛏 💻 ⊠ 🐾 🐾 ☎

▼ Outpost Motel 🅼
(218) 387-1833. **$49-$109, 7 day notice.** 2935 SR 61 E. SR 61, 9 mi ne. Ext corridors. **Pets:** Other species. $10 daily fee/pet. Designated rooms, supervision.
⊠ 🛏 💻 ⊠ 🐾

▼▼ Wedgewood Motel 🅼
(218) 387-2944. **$55-$79.** 1663 E Hwy 61. SR 61, 2.5 mi ne. Ext corridors. **Pets:** Dogs only. $5 daily fee/pet. Designated rooms, supervision.
(SAVE) ⊠ 🛏 🐾 ☎

GRAND RAPIDS

▼▼▼ Budget Host Inn 🅼 ❀
(218) 326-3457. **$60-$86.** 311 E Hwy 2. Jct US 2 E and 169 N. Ext/int corridors. **Pets:** Designated rooms, service with restrictions, crate.
(SAVE) ⊠ 🛏

▼▼▼ Country Inn By Carlson 🅷 ❀
(218) 327-4960. **$95-$139.** 2601 S Hwy 169. US 2, 2 mi s. Int corridors. **Pets:** Medium, dogs only. Supervision.
(ASK) ⊠ 🅼 🛏 💻 ☎

▼▼▼ Sawmill Inn 🅷
(218) 326-8501. **$69-$109.** 2301 S Hwy 169. US 2, 2 mi s on US 169. Ext/int corridors. **Pets:** Service with restrictions, supervision.
(SAVE) ⊠ 🛏 💻 🍴 ⊠ ⊠

GRANITE FALLS

▼▼ Granite Falls Super Motel 🅷
(320) 564-4075. **Call for rates.** 845 W SR 212. 0.5 mi w of Jct SR 23. Int corridors. **Pets:** Accepted.
⊠ 🅼 🛏 ☎

HIBBING

▼▼ Super 8 🅷
(218) 263-8982. **Call for rates.** 1411 E 40th St. Just e of US 169 and SR 37. Int corridors. **Pets:** Accepted.
⊠ 🛏 💻

HINCKLEY

▼▼▼ Days Inn 🅷
(320) 384-7751. **$60-$130, 5 day notice.** 104 Grindstone Ct. I-35, exit 183 (SR 48), just e. Int corridors. **Pets:** Small. $10 daily fee/pet. Designated rooms, service with restrictions, supervision.
(SAVE) ⊠ 🛏 💻 ☎

HOYT LAKES

▼▼▼ Country Inn of Hoyt Lakes 🅷
(218) 225-3555. **$80-$180, 3 day notice.** 99 Kennedy Memorial Dr. On SR 110. Int corridors. **Pets:** Medium, dogs only. $10 daily fee/room. Service with restrictions, supervision.
(ASK) ⊠ 🅼 🛏 💻 ☎

HUTCHINSON

▼▼▼ Best Western Victorian Inn 🅷
(320) 587-6030. **$73-$120.** 1000 Hwy 7 W. SR 15, 1 mi w. Int corridors. **Pets:** Medium, dogs only. $10 daily fee/room. Service with restrictions, supervision.
(SAVE) ⊠ 🛏 💻 ☎

INTERNATIONAL FALLS

▼▼▼ Hilltop Motel 🅼
(218) 283-2505. **$49-$84.** 2002 2nd Ave W. US 53, 1 mi s of jct US 53 and SR 11. Ext corridors. **Pets:** Small, dogs only. $10 one-time fee/pet. Service with restrictions, supervision.
(SAVE) ⊠

▼▼▼ Holiday Inn 🅷
(218) 283-8000. **$99-$119.** 1500 US 71 W. 1.5 mi w on US 71 and SR 11 W. Int corridors. **Pets:** Accepted.
⊠ 🛏 💻 🍴 ☎ ⊠

JACKSON

▼▼▼▼ AmericInn Lodge & Suites of Jackson 🅷
(507) 847-2444. **$75-$159.** 110 Belmont Ln. I-90, exit 73 (US 71), just sw. Int corridors. **Pets:** Small, dogs only. $50 deposit/room, $10 one-time fee/pet. Designated rooms, service with restrictions, supervision.
(SAVE) ⊠ 🅼 🛏 💻 ☎

▼▼ Econo Lodge 🅷
(507) 847-3110. **$60-$95.** 2007 US 71 N. I-90, exit 73 (US 71), just nw. Ext/int corridors. **Pets:** Other species. $10 daily fee/pet. Designated rooms, service with restrictions, supervision.
(ASK) ⊠ 🛏 💻 🍴 ☎

LAMBERTON

▼ Lamberton Motel 🅼
(507) 752-7242. **Call for rates.** 601 1st Ave W. Just s of jct US 14 and Ilex St. Ext corridors. **Pets:** Accepted.
⊠ 🛏 💻

LITCHFIELD

▼▼ ScotWood Motel 🅼
(320) 693-2496. **$50-$100.** 1017 E Frontage Rd. On US 12. Int corridors. **Pets:** Medium. $10 daily fee/pet. Designated rooms, service with restrictions, supervision.
(ASK) ⊠ 🛏 ☎

LONG PRAIRIE

▼▼▼ Budget Host Inn 🅼
(320) 732-6118. **$62-$81.** 417 Lake St. On US 71 and SR 27, just s of jct SR 287. Ext corridors. **Pets:** Designated rooms, service with restrictions, supervision.
(SAVE) ⊠ 🛏 💻

LUTSEN

▼▼▼ Cascade Lodge 🅲🅸
(218) 387-1112. **$55-$275, 14 day notice.** 3719 W Hwy 61. SR 61, 7 mi ne of jct CR 4 (Caribou Tr). Ext/int corridors. **Pets:** Small, other species. $10 daily fee/pet. Designated rooms, no service, supervision.
(SAVE) ⊠ 🛏 💻 🍴 ⊠

(AAA) ▽▽ ◈ Solbakken Resort Ⓜ
(218) 663-7566. **$55-$95, 14 day notice.** 4874 W SR 61. SR 61, 1.3 mi n of jct CR 4 (Caribou Tr). Ext corridors. **Pets:** Large, other species. $10 daily fee/pet. Designated rooms, no service, supervision.
[SAVE] [✕] [🛏] [📶] [📺] [🐾] [Ⓐⓒ]

MAHNOMEN

(AAA) ▽▽ ◈ Shooting Star Casino Hotel & Events Center Ⓗ
(218) 935-2701. **Call for rates.** 777 Casino Rd. 1 mi s on SR 59. Int corridors. **Pets:** Accepted.
[SAVE] [✕] [♿] [🛏] [📶] [🍽] [🐾] [✕]

MANKATO

(AAA) ▽▽ ◈ AmericInn Hotel & Conference Center Ⓗ
(507) 345-8011. **$89-$189.** 240 Stadium Rd. From jct US 14, 2 mi s on SR 22, 0.4 mi w on SR 83, just s on Victory Dr, then 1.5 mi w. Int corridors. **Pets:** Accepted.
[ASK] [✕] [♿] [🛏] [📶] [🐾] [✕]

(AAA) ▽▽ ◈ Best Western Hotel & Restaurant Ⓗ
(507) 625-9333. **$80-$195.** 1111 Range St. 0.6 mi s of jct US 169 and 14. Int corridors. **Pets:** Designated rooms, service with restrictions, supervision.
[SAVE] [✕] [🛏] [📶] [🍽] [🐾] [✕]

▽▽ ◈ Comfort Inn by Choice Hotels Ⓗ
(507) 388-5107. **Call for rates.** 131 Apache Pl. Just s of jct US 14 and SR 22 S. Int corridors. **Pets:** $10 daily fee/room. Service with restrictions, supervision.
[✕] [🛏] [📶] [🐾]

▽▽ ◈ Days Inn Ⓗ ❀
(507) 387-3332. **$60-$90, 14 day notice.** 1285 Range St. 0.3 mi s of jct US 169 and 14. Int corridors. **Pets:** Other species. $10 daily fee/pet. Designated rooms, no service, supervision.
[ASK] [✕] [🛏] [📶] [🐾]

▽▽▽ ◈ GrandStay Residential Suites Ⓗ
(507) 388-8688. **Call for rates.** 1000 Raintree Rd. 0.4 mi se of jct US 14 and CR 3. Int corridors. **Pets:** Small. $25 daily fee/room. Designated rooms, service with restrictions, supervision.
[✕] [🛏] [📶] [🐾]

▽▽ ◈ Holiday Inn Ⓗ
(507) 345-1234. **$90-$120.** 101 E Main St. Main St at Riverfront Dr; downtown. Int corridors. **Pets:** Service with restrictions, supervision.
[ASK] [✕] [♿] [🛏] [📶] [🍽] [🐾] [✕]

▽▽ ◈ Microtel Inn & Suites Ⓗ ❀
(507) 388-2818. **$59-$81.** 200 St. Andrews Dr. US 14, exit CR 3, 0.4 mi n. Int corridors. **Pets:** Other species. $15 one-time fee/pet. Service with restrictions, supervision.
[ASK] [✕] [🛏] [📶]

▽▽ ◈ Super 8 Ⓗ
(507) 387-0600. **$68-$98.** 51578 US Hwy 169 N. Jct US 169 and 14, just n. Int corridors. **Pets:** Dogs only. Service with restrictions, supervision.
[ASK] [✕] [🛏] [📶]

MARSHALL

(AAA) ▽▽▽ ◈ Best Western Marshall Inn Ⓗ
(507) 532-3221. **Call for rates.** 1500 E College Dr. SR 19, just w of jct SR 23. Int corridors. **Pets:** Other species. $10 daily fee/pet. Designated rooms, service with restrictions.
[SAVE] [✕] [🛏] [📶] [🍽] [🐾] [✕]

▽▽ ◈ Comfort Inn Ⓗ
(507) 532-3070. **$80-$120.** 1511 E College Dr. SR 19, w of jct SR 23. Int corridors. **Pets:** Large. $10 daily fee/pet. Service with restrictions, crate.
[ASK] [✕] [🛏] [📶] [🐾]

▽▽ ◈ Super 8 Motel Ⓗ
(507) 537-1461. **Call for rates.** 1106 E Main St. 0.3 mi se on US 59 from jct SR 23. Int corridors. **Pets:** Accepted.
[✕] [🛏] [📶]

MCGREGOR

▽▽ ◈ Country Meadows Inn Ⓗ
(218) 768-7378. **$65-$114.** 403 Meadows Dr. Jct SR 65 and 210. Int corridors. **Pets:** Other species. $6 daily fee/pet. Designated rooms, service with restrictions, supervision.
[✕] [🛏] [📶] [🐾]

MILACA

▽▽ ◈ Super 8 Ⓗ
(320) 983-2660. **Call for rates.** 215 10th Ave SE. Jct SR 23 and 169. Int corridors. **Pets:** Accepted.
[✕] [♿] [🛏] [📶]

MINNEAPOLIS-ST. PAUL METROPOLITAN AREA

ANNANDALE

▽▽ ◈ AmericInn Lodge & Suites of Annandale Ⓗ
(320) 274-3006. **$70-$120.** 620 Elm St E. On SR 55. Int corridors. **Pets:** Other species. $50 deposit/room. Designated rooms, service with restrictions, crate.
[ASK] [✕] [♿] [🛏] [📶] [🐾]

BECKER

(AAA) ▽▽▽ ◈ Sleep Inn & Suites Ⓗ
(763) 262-7700. **$80-$100.** 14435 Bank St. Just e on US 10. Int corridors. **Pets:** Accepted.
[SAVE] [✕] [🛏] [📶] [🐾] [✕]

BLAINE

(AAA) ▽▽▽ ◈ Comfort Suites Ⓗ
(763) 792-0750. **$89-$199.** 10580 Baltimore St NE. 1.5 mi n of jct SR 65 and US 10 to 107th Ave NE, just e to Baltimore St NE, then just s. Int corridors. **Pets:** Small, dogs only. $25 one-time fee/pet. Designated rooms, service with restrictions, supervision.
[SAVE] [✕] [♿] [🛏] [📶] [🐾]

▽▽ ◈ Super 8 Ⓗ
(763) 786-8888. **Call for rates.** 9410 Baltimore St NE. Just n of jct US 10 and SR 65 to 93 Ln (Post Office), just e to Baltimore St NE, then just n. Int corridors. **Pets:** Medium, dogs only. $100 deposit/room, $10 daily fee/pet. Designated rooms, crate.
[✕] [♿] [🛏] [📶] [🐾]

BLOOMINGTON

▽▽ ◈ Extended StayAmerica Minneapolis-Bloomington Ⓗ
(952) 884-1400. **$74-$114.** 7956 Lyndale Ave. I-494, exit 4B (Lyndale Ave), just sw. Int corridors. **Pets:** Other species. $25 daily fee/pet. Service with restrictions, crate.
[ASK] [✕] [🛏] [📶]

(AAA) ▽▽ ◈ Hilton Minneapolis South/Bloomington Ⓜ ❀
(952) 893-9500. **$119-$259.** 3900 American Blvd W. I-494, exit France Ave. Int corridors. **Pets:** Medium, dogs only. $50 one-time fee/room. Service with restrictions, supervision.
[SAVE] [✕] [🛏] [📶] [🍽] [🐾]

ⓐⓐⓐ ◈◈◈ Homewood Suites by Hilton 🅗
(952) 854-0900. **$109-$189.** 2261 Killebrew Dr. I-494, exit 2A (24th Ave), 1 mi s, then just w. Int corridors. **Pets:** Accepted.
[SAVE] [✕] [🛏] [💻] [🐾]

◈◈ La Quinta Inn Bloomington West 🅗 🐾
(952) 830-1300. **Call for rates.** 5151 American Blvd W. I-494, exit 6B (France Ave), just se of SR 100, 1 mi w on frontage road. Int corridors. **Pets:** Medium, other species. Service with restrictions, supervision.
[✕] [🛏] [💻] [🍴] [🐾] [✕]

◈◈ La Quinta Inn Minneapolis-Airport
(Bloomington) 🅗 🐾
(952) 881-7311. **$49-$105.** 7815 Nicollet Ave S. I-494, exit 4A (Nicollet Ave), just s. Int corridors. **Pets:** Medium, other species. Service with restrictions, supervision.
[ASK] [✕] [🛏] [💻]

ⓐⓐⓐ ◈◈◈ Le Bourget Aero Suites 🅗
(952) 893-9999. **$99-$215.** 7770 Johnson Ave. I-494, exit 6B (France Ave), 0.5 mi nw on frontage road (78th St). Int corridors. **Pets:** Other species. $10 daily fee/room. Service with restrictions, supervision.
[SAVE] [✕] [♿] [🛏] [💻] [🍴] [🐾]

◈◈◈◈ Park Plaza Hotel Bloomington 🅗
(952) 831-3131. **$79-$189.** 4460 W 78th St Cir. I-494, exit 6B (France Ave), 0.5 mi nw. Int corridors. **Pets:** Accepted.
[✕] [🛏] [💻] [🍴] [🐾] [✕]

ⓐⓐⓐ ◈◈◈ Ramada Mall of America–Airport 🅗
(952) 854-3411. **$59-$129, 14 day notice.** 2300 E American Blvd. I-494, exit 2A (24th Ave), just s. Int corridors. **Pets:** Accepted.
[SAVE] [✕] [🛏] [💻] [🍴] [🐾]

◈◈◈◈ Residence Inn by Marriott 🅗
(952) 876-0900. **$170-$208.** 7850 Bloomington Ave S. I-494, exit 3, on south frontage road. Int corridors. **Pets:** Accepted.
[✕] [🛏] [💻] [🐾]

ⓐⓐⓐ ◈◈◈◈ Sheraton Bloomington Hotel Minneapolis
South 🅗
(952) 835-7800. **Call for rates.** 7800 Normandale Blvd. I-494, exit 7A (SR 100). Int corridors. **Pets:** Accepted.
[SAVE] [✕] [🛏] [💻] [🍴] [🐾] [✕]

ⓐⓐⓐ ◈◈◈◈ Sofitel Minneapolis 🅗
(952) 835-1900. **$109-$299.** 5601 W 78th St. Just nw of jct I-494 and SR 100, access via SR 100 and Industrial Blvd. Int corridors. **Pets:** Other species. Service with restrictions, crate.
[SAVE] [✕] [♿] [🛏] [🍴]

◈◈◈◈ Staybridge Suites 🅗
(952) 831-7900. **$159-$299.** 5150 American Blvd. I-494, exit 6B (France Ave), just se of SR 100, then 1 mi w on frontage road. Int corridors. **Pets:** Medium. $150 one-time fee/room. Service with restrictions, supervision.
[✕] [♿] [🛏] [💻] [🐾] [✕]

ⓐⓐⓐ ◈◈ Super 8 🅗
(952) 888-8800. **$59-$85.** 7800 S 2nd Ave. I-494, exit 4A (Nicollet Ave), just se. Int corridors. **Pets:** Small. $10 daily fee/pet. Service with restrictions, supervision.
[SAVE] [✕] [🛏] [💻] [✕]

BROOKLYN CENTER

◈◈ Comfort Inn by Choice Hotels 🅗
(763) 560-7464. **Call for rates.** 1600 James Cir N. I-94/694, exit 34 (Shingle Creek Pkwy), just ne. Int corridors. **Pets:** Large. $20 one-time fee/pet. Designated rooms.
[✕] [♿] [🛏] [💻]

ⓐⓐⓐ ◈◈◈ Crowne Plaza Minneapolis North 🅗
(763) 566-8000. **$129-$154.** 2200 Freeway Blvd. I-94/694, exit 34 (Shingle Creek Pkwy). Int corridors. **Pets:** Accepted.
[SAVE] [✕] [♿] [🛏] [💻] [🍴] [🐾] [✕]

◈◈ Extended StayAmerica-Minneapolis-Brooklyn
Center 🅗
(763) 549-5571. **$69-$109.** 2701 Freeway Blvd. I-94/694, exit 34 (Shingle Creek Pkwy), 0.5 mi nw. Int corridors. **Pets:** Other species. $25 daily fee/pet. Service with restrictions, crate.
[ASK] [✕] [🛏] [💻]

BROOKLYN PARK

ⓐⓐⓐ ◈◈◈ La Quinta Inn & Suites 🅗 🐾
(763) 971-8000. **$59-$165.** 7011 Northland Cir. I-94/694, exit 30 (Boone Ave), just ne. Int corridors. **Pets:** Medium, other species. Service with restrictions, supervision.
[SAVE] [✕] [♿] [🛏] [💻] [🐾]

BURNSVILLE

ⓐⓐⓐ ◈◈ Americas Best Value Inn 🅜 🐾
(952) 894-3400. **$63-$83.** 1101 Burnsville Pkwy. I-35W, exit 2 (Burnsville Pkwy), just sw. Int corridors. **Pets:** Medium, dogs only. $15 one-time fee/room. Designated rooms, service with restrictions, supervision.
[SAVE] [✕] [💻]

◈◈◈ Holiday Inn Burnsville/Apple Valley 🅗
(952) 435-2100. **$89-$159.** 14201 Nicollet Ave S. Just n of jct I-35W and CR 42. Int corridors. **Pets:** Small. $75 one-time fee/room. Designated rooms, service with restrictions, crate.
[ASK] [✕] [🛏] [💻] [🍴] [🐾] [✕]

CHANHASSEN

ⓐⓐⓐ ◈◈◈ AmericInn of Chanhassen 🅗
(952) 934-3888. **$99-$195.** 570 Pond Promenade. Just se of jct SR 5 and 101 S. Int corridors. **Pets:** Medium. $100 deposit/pet, $30 one-time fee/pet. Designated rooms, service with restrictions.
[SAVE] [✕] [♿] [🛏] [💻] [🐾] [✕]

CHASKA

ⓐⓐⓐ ◈◈◈ Best Western Chaska River Inn &
Suites 🅗 🐾
(952) 448-7877. **$79-$139.** One Riverbend. Jct US 212, 0.3 mi s on SR 41. Int corridors. **Pets:** Medium. $20 daily fee/pet. Designated rooms, service with restrictions, supervision.
[SAVE] [✕] [♿] [🛏] [💻] [🍴] [🐾] [✕]

◈◈◈ Super 8 🅜
(952) 448-7030. **Call for rates.** 830 Yellow Brick Rd. Jct US 212 and SR 41, just e, then n. Int corridors. **Pets:** Accepted.
[✕] [🛏] [💻]

COON RAPIDS

◈◈◈ Country Suites By Carlson 🅗 🐾
(763) 780-3797. **$110-$229.** 155 Coon Rapids Blvd. SR 10, exit Foley Blvd, 0.8 mi s to Coon Rapids Blvd, 0.5 mi e to Springbrook Dr, then just n. Int corridors. **Pets:** Large, other species. $20 daily fee/pet. Designated rooms, service with restrictions, crate.
[ASK] [✕] [🛏] [💻] [🐾]

ⓐⓐⓐ ◈◈◈ Quality Inn-Northtown 🅗
(763) 785-4746. **$59-$199.** 9052 University Ave NW. US 10, exit Foley Blvd, 0.6 mi. Int corridors. **Pets:** Other species. $10 daily fee/pet. Designated rooms, service with restrictions, supervision.
[SAVE] [✕] [🛏] [💻] [🐾]

AAA PetBook® Photo Contest Entries

Each year, the winning entry in AAA's PetBook® Photo Contest appears on a cover of *Traveling With Your Pet: The AAA PetBook®* and also receives other great prizes. You have already met Zillie on the back cover and Michelob on the spine of this book. Here are more great entries that we just had to make room for!

Check out AAA.com/PetBook for pictures, contest rules and an entry form for next year's contest.

"Kodiak"
Elise Cormier, Hopkinton, MA

"Tahoe"
John Pendergast, Las Vegas, NV

"Mr. Bojangles"
Scott and Emily Huddle, Wake Forest, NC

"Ariel"
Brianna Kovnas, Martinez, CA

"Ellie"
Katie Morris, Ann Arbor, MI

"Bikini"
Amanda Lusk, Branson, MO

"Remy"
Lee Landers, Newport News, VA

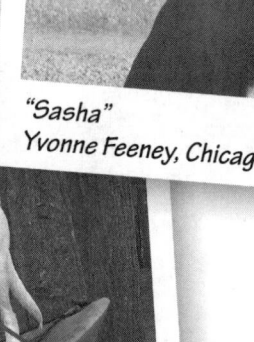

"Sasha"
Yvonne Feeney, Chicago, IL

"Sugar Bear"
Larry Powell and Alicia Hodges, White Lake, MI

"Rigel Orion"
Cynthia Franke, Vancouver, WA

"Amber"
Susie Kim, Los Gatos, CA

"Moby"
Brad Presner, San Francisco, CA

"Andy"
Lisa Mason, Chehalis, WA

"Ayla and Kora"
Mary Schinzel, Queen Creek, AZ

"Fergus"
Kate Hoyt, Seattle, WA

"Ariel"
Linda Bates, North Easton, MA

"Brie"
Jerry and Andrea Pierce, Boise, ID

"Bunker Tee"
Pam Adams and Mindy Adair, Denver, CO

"Winston, Stella and Newman"
Richard Daschner, Roseville, CA

"Murphy"
Amanda Lindberg, San Francisco, CA

"Bailey"
Ranelle Brew, Otsego, MI

"Dolci"
Hanh Nghi, Rowland Heights, CA

"Willie"
John Pitocco, Chepachet, RI

"Sailor"
Anita Fleming, Belchertown, MA

"Ace Marie"
Jeanette Gilbert and Josh Gnaizda, Cotati, CA

"Sula"
Amy Ballentine, Cataumet, MA

"Chloe"
LiB Shore, Horse Shoe, NC

"Trumper"
Mick Gast, San Francisco, CA

"Lucy"
Nicole Collins, San Carlos, CA

"Liberty and Belle"
Daniel and Elizabeth Conrad, West Bridgewater, MA

"Lily"
Laura Jelemensky, Austin, TX

"Jack"
Art Trevena and Joyce Tanihara, Cedaredge, CO

"Sophie"
Denice Watkins, Pleasant Hill, CA

"Apollo"
Gregory S. Wunz, Windber, PA

"Haley"
Jane Best, Morganton, NC

"Brody"
Gaytha McVay, Lake Leelanau, MI

A few more tail-wagging travelers

1) "Paloma Grace (Gracie)", Jessica Kay Ruhle, Raleigh, NC 2) "Skye", Diana Witherspoon, Boulder, CO 3) "Shorewillow Lucinda Lou (Lucy)", Margaret L. Hanson, Park City, UT 4) "Timmy", James C. Forbes, Pittsboro, NC 5) "Harkin", Allan Brouillet, Bay City, MI 6) "CoCo and Boo", Melissa Combs, Verona, KY 7) "Emma", Debra Jo Chiapuzio, Anaheim, CA 8) "Bennie", Kimi and Steve Rohrer, Santa Cruz, CA

EAGAN

Best Western Dakota Ridge 🅗
(651) 452-0100. **$80-$200.** 3450 Washington Dr. I-35E, exit 97B (Yankee Doodle Rd), just sw. Int corridors. **Pets:** $20 one-time fee/room. Service with restrictions, supervision.

Days Inn 🅗
(651) 681-1770. **$69-$149.** 4510 Erin Dr. Just ne of jct SR 77 and Cliff Rd. Int corridors. **Pets:** Other species. $100 deposit/room, $5 daily fee/pet. Designated rooms, service with restrictions, crate.

Extended StayAmerica Minneapolis-Airport-Eagan 🅗
(651) 681-9991. **$74-$114.** 3384 Norwest Ct. I-35E, exit 97, just nw. Int corridors. **Pets:** Other species. $25 daily fee/pet. Service with restrictions, crate.

Homestead Studio Suites Hotel-Minneapolis-Airport-Eagan 🅗
(651) 905-1778. **$74-$114.** 3015 Denmark Ave. I-35E, exit 98 (Lone Oak Rd), just se. Int corridors. **Pets:** Other species. $25 daily fee/pet. Service with restrictions, crate.

Microtel Inn & Suites 🅗
(651) 405-0988. **$59-$89, 14 day notice.** 3000 Denmark Ave. I-35E, exit 98 (Lone Oak Rd), just se. Int corridors. **Pets:** Medium. $15 daily fee/room. Service with restrictions, supervision.

Residence Inn by Marriott-Mpls/St. Paul Airport 🅗
(651) 688-0363. **$189-$199.** 3040 Eagandale Pl. I-35E, exit 98 (Lone Oak Rd), just sw. Ext corridors. **Pets:** Accepted.

Staybridge Suites 🅗 🐾
(651) 994-7810. **$129-$299.** 4675 Rahncliff Rd. I-35E, exit 93 (Cliff Rd), just w, then just s. Int corridors. **Pets:** Medium. $150 one-time fee/room. Service with restrictions, crate.

TownePlace Suites 🅗
(651) 994-4600. **$131-$142.** 3615 Crestridge Dr. I-35E, exit 97A (Pilot Knob Rd), just se. Int corridors. **Pets:** Accepted.

EDEN PRAIRIE

Best Western Eden Prairie Inn 🅗
(952) 829-0888. **$90-$110, 3 day notice.** 11500 W 78th St. I-494, exit 11A, just sw. Int corridors. **Pets:** Small, dogs only. $10 daily fee/pet. Service with restrictions, supervision.

Extended StayAmerica Minneapolis-Eden Prairie 🅗
(952) 941-1113. **$79-$119.** 7550 Office Ridge Cir. I-494, exit 12, just se. Int corridors. **Pets:** Other species. $25 daily fee/pet. Service with restrictions, crate.

Homestead Studio Suites Hotel-Minneapolis-Eden Prairie 🅗
(952) 942-6818. **$79-$119.** 11905 Technology Dr. Just sw of jct I-494 and US 212 (Flying Cloud Dr). Int corridors. **Pets:** Other species. $25 daily fee/pet. Service with restrictions, crate.

Residence Inn by Marriott-Minneapolis SW 🅗
(952) 829-0033. **$159-$189.** 7780 Flying Cloud Dr. I-494, exit 11A, on US 169 S and 212 (Flying Cloud Dr). Int corridors. **Pets:** $75 one-time fee/pet. Service with restrictions, crate.

EDINA

Residence Inn Minneapolis-Edina 🅗
(952) 893-9300. **$179-$189.** 3400 Edinborough Way. I-494, exit 6B (France Ave), 0.3 mi n to Minnesota Dr, then just e. Int corridors. **Pets:** Small, dogs only. $75 one-time fee/room. Designated rooms, service with restrictions, crate.

ELK RIVER

AmericInn Lodge & Suites of Elk River Ⓜ
(763) 441-8554. **Call for rates.** 17432 Hwy 10. 1.5 mi se on US 10/169. Int corridors. **Pets:** Accepted.

FOREST LAKE

AmericInn Motel of Forest Lake 🅗
(651) 464-1930. **$72-$119.** 1291 W Broadway Ave. I-35, exit 131 (CR 2), just ne. Int corridors. **Pets:** Accepted.

HASTINGS

AmericInn Lodge & Suites of Hastings 🅗
(651) 437-8877. **$89-$140.** 2400 Vermillion St. 1.5 mi s on US 61. Int corridors. **Pets:** Medium, dogs only. $15 one-time fee/room. Supervision.

Country Inn & Suites By Carlson 🅗
(651) 437-8870. **$79-$97.** 300 33rd St. 1.7 mi s on US 61, just e. Int corridors. **Pets:** Accepted.

MAPLE GROVE

Extended StayAmerica Minneapolis-Maple Grove 🅗
(763) 694-9747. **$74-$114.** 12970 63rd Ave N. I-494, exit 26, just ne. Int corridors. **Pets:** Other species. $25 daily fee/pet. Service with restrictions, crate.

Select Inn 🅗
(763) 493-2277. **$69-$119.** 7285 Forestview Ln N. I-94, exit 28 (CR 61/Hemlock Ln), just se. Int corridors. **Pets:** Accepted.

Staybridge Suites Minneapolis-Maple Grove 🅗
(763) 494-8856. **$169-$499.** 7821 Elm Creek Blvd. Just ne of jct I-94/494/694. Int corridors. **Pets:** Medium. $150 one-time fee/room. Service with restrictions, crate.

MAPLEWOOD

Emerald Inn 🅗
(651) 777-8131. **$65-$90.** 2025 E County Rd D. I-694, exit 50 (White Bear Ave), just se. Int corridors. **Pets:** $10 daily fee/pet. Designated rooms, service with restrictions, supervision.

MINNEAPOLIS

aloft Minneapolis 🅗
(612) 455-8400. **$119-$379.** 900 Washington Ave S. Jct 9th Ave. Int corridors. **Pets:** Accepted.

Days Hotel on University 🅷
(612) 623-3999. **$89-$169.** 2407 University Ave SE. I-35 W, exit University Ave, 1 mi se. Int corridors. **Pets:** $25 one-time fee/pet. Service with restrictions, supervision.
[SAVE] [✕] [🛏] [💻]

Graves 601 Hotel 🅷
(612) 677-1100. **$149-$359.** 601 1st Ave N. Between 6th and 7th sts. Int corridors. **Pets:** Accepted.
[SAVE] [✕] [🛏] [🍴] [✕]

Hilton Minneapolis 🅷 🐾
(612) 376-1000. **$119-$309.** 1001 Marquette Ave S. Between S 10th and S 11th sts. Int corridors. **Pets:** Medium. $45 one-time fee/pet. Designated rooms, service with restrictions, supervision.
[SAVE] [✕] [🛏] [💻] [🍴] [🏊] [✕]

Hotel Ivy 🅷
(612) 746-4600. **Call for rates.** 201 S 11th St. 2nd Ave and 11th St. Int corridors. **Pets:** Accepted.
[SAVE] [✕] [🍴]

The Marquette Hotel 🅷 🐾
(612) 333-4545. **$109-$339.** 710 Marquette Ave. Jct Marquette Ave and S 7th St. Int corridors. **Pets:** Large, other species. $100 deposit/room. Service with restrictions.
[SAVE] [✕] [🛏] [💻] [🍴]

Radisson Plaza Hotel Minneapolis 🅷
(612) 339-4900. **$89-$399.** 35 S 7th St. Between Nicollet and Hennepin aves. Int corridors. **Pets:** Accepted.
[SAVE] [✕] [ᴍ] [🛏] [💻] [🍴] [✕]

Residence Inn by Marriott Minneapolis Downtown City Center 🅷
(612) 677-1000. **$224-$274.** 45 S 8th St. At 8th St and LaSalle Ave. Int corridors. **Pets:** $100 one-time fee/pet. Service with restrictions, supervision.
[SAVE] [✕] [🛏] [💻]

Residence Inn Milwaukee Road Depot 🅷
(612) 340-1300. **$199-$249.** 425 S 2nd St. Jct S 2nd St and 5th Ave S. Int corridors. **Pets:** Large, other species. $100 one-time fee/room. Service with restrictions, crate.
[✕] [🛏] [💻]

Sheraton Minneapolis Midtown Hotel 🅷
(612) 821-7600. **$109-$299.** 2901 Chicago Ave S. At Lake St. Int corridors. **Pets:** Accepted.
[SAVE] [✕] [ᴍ] [🛏] [💻] [🍴] [🏊]

The Westin Minneapolis 🅷 🐾
(612) 333-4006. **$129-$679.** 88 S 6th St. At Marquette Ave. Int corridors. **Pets:** Medium, dogs only. Service with restrictions.
[SAVE] [✕] [🍴] [🏊] [✕]

MINNETONKA

Minneapolis Marriott-Southwest 🅷
(952) 935-5500. **$159-$179.** 5801 Opus Pkwy. Just nw of jct US 169 and Cross Town SR 62, exit Bren Rd. Int corridors. **Pets:** Accepted.
[SAVE] [✕] [🛏] [💻] [🍴] [🏊] [✕]

Sheraton Minneapolis West Hotel 🅷 🐾
(952) 593-0000. **$89-$279.** 12201 Ridgedale Dr. I-394, exit 1C (Plymouth Rd), 0.3 mi s. Int corridors. **Pets:** Service with restrictions, supervision.
[SAVE] [✕] [🛏] [💻] [🍴] [🏊]

MONTICELLO

Best Western Chelsea Inn & Suites 🅷
(763) 271-8880. **$90-$120.** 89 Chelsea Rd. I-94, exit 193, 0.3 mi se. Int corridors. **Pets:** Small, other species. $10 daily fee/pet. Designated rooms, service with restrictions, supervision.
[SAVE] [✕] [🛏] [💻] [🏊] [✕]

Days Inn 🅷
(763) 295-1111. **$59-$79.** 200 E Oakwood Dr. I-94, exit 193, 0.3 mi se. Int corridors. **Pets:** Other species. $10 daily fee/pet, $10 one-time fee/pet. Service with restrictions, supervision.
[SAVE] [✕] [🛏] [💻]

NORTH BRANCH

AmericInn Lodge & Suites of North Branch 🅷 🐾
(651) 674-8627. **$79-$180.** 38675 14th Ave. I-35, exit 147 (SR 95), just e, s on Oakview, then w on Oak St. Int corridors. **Pets:** $30 one-time fee/room. Service with restrictions, supervision.
[SAVE] [✕] [🛏] [💻] [🏊] [✕]

OAKDALE

Wingate by Wyndham 🅷
(651) 578-8466. **Call for rates.** 970 Helena Ave N. I-694, exit 57, just e, then just s. Int corridors. **Pets:** Small. $25 one-time fee/room. Designated rooms, service with restrictions, crate.
[SAVE] [✕] [ᴍ] [🛏] [💻]

OAK PARK HEIGHTS

AmericInn Lodge & Suites of Oak Park Heights 🅷 🐾
(651) 275-0980. **Call for rates.** 13025 60th St N. SR 36 at Stillwater Blvd, just se. Int corridors. **Pets:** Large, other species. $15 daily fee/room. Service with restrictions, crate.
[✕] [🛏] [💻] [🏊] [✕]

PLYMOUTH

Best Western Kelly Inn 🅷
(763) 553-1600. **$99-$139, 3 day notice.** 2705 N Annapolis Ln. I-494, exit 22 (SR 55), just e. Int corridors. **Pets:** Designated rooms, service with restrictions, supervision.
[SAVE] [✕] [🛏] [💻] [🍴] [🏊] [✕]

Radisson Hotel & Conference Center Minneapolis 🅷 🐾
(763) 559-6600. **$99-$239.** 3131 Campus Dr. I-494, exit 22 (SR 55), just e to CR 61 (Northwest Blvd), then 0.8 mi nw. Int corridors. **Pets:** $50 deposit/room. Service with restrictions, supervision.
[SAVE] [✕] [💻] [🍴] [🏊] [✕]

Red Roof Inn 🅼
(763) 553-1751. **$56-$72, 7 day notice.** 2600 Annapolis Ln N. I-494, exit 22 (SR 55), just se. Ext corridors. **Pets:** Medium. Service with restrictions, supervision.
[SAVE] [✕] [🛏]

Residence Inn by Marriott 🅷 🐾
(763) 577-1600. **$143-$175.** 2750 Annapolis Cir. I-494, exit 22 (SR 55), just e to CR 61, just nw. Int corridors. **Pets:** Large, other species. $100 one-time fee/room. Service with restrictions, crate.
[✕] [🛏] [💻] [🏊]

RICHFIELD

Candlewood Suites 🅷
(612) 869-7704. **$99-$124.** 351 W 77th St. I-494, exit 4B (Lyndale Ave), just ne. Int corridors. **Pets:** Medium. $75 one-time fee/pet. Service with restrictions.
[SAVE] [✕] [ᴍ] [🛏] [💻]

ROGERS

AmericInn Lodge & Suites of Rogers 🅷 🐾
(763) 428-4346. **$87-$148.** 21800 Industrial Blvd. I-94, exit 207 (SR 101), just sw. Int corridors. **Pets:** Medium. $10 daily fee/room. Designated rooms, service with restrictions, crate.
[ASK] [✕] [🛏] [💻] [🏊]

🔺 ▽▽▽▽ **Hampton Inn & Suites** 🅷
(763) 425-0044. **$79-$129.** 13550 Commerce Blvd. I-94, exit 207 (SR 101), 0.4 mi ne. Int corridors. **Pets:** Accepted.
[SAVE] [✕] [⛾ᴹ] [📱] [💻] [🔜]

ROSEVILLE

▽▽▽▽ **Residence Inn** 🅷
(651) 636-0680. **$179-$189.** 2985 Centre Pointe Dr. I-35W, exit 25A (CR D), just se. Int corridors. **Pets:** Accepted.
[✕] [⛾ᴹ] [📱] [💻] [🔜] [✕]

ST. LOUIS PARK

▽▽▽▽ **DoubleTree Hotel Minneapolis Park Place** 🅷
(952) 542-8600. **$99-$219.** 1500 Park Place Blvd. I-394, exit 5 (Park Place Blvd), just sw. Int corridors. **Pets:** Small, other species. $15 daily fee/pet. Service with restrictions, crate.
[✕] [📱] [💻] [🍴] [🔜]

▽▽▽▽ **TownePlace Suites-Minneapolis West** 🅷
(952) 847-6900. **$130-$170.** 1400 Zarthan Ave S. I-394, exit 5 (Park Place Blvd), 0.3 mi w on 16th, then just n. Int corridors. **Pets:** Accepted.
[✕] [📱] [💻] [🔜]

ST. PAUL

🔺 ▽▽▽▽ **Best Western Kelly Inn** 🅷
(651) 227-8711. **$99-$159.** 161 St. Anthony Ave. Jct I-35E and 94. Int corridors. **Pets:** Other species. No service, supervision.
[SAVE] [✕] [📱] [💻] [🍴] [🔜]

🔺 ▽▽▽ **Super 8** 🅷
(651) 771-5566. **Call for rates.** 1739 Old Hudson Rd. I-94, exit 245 (White Bear Ave), just nw. Int corridors. **Pets:** Accepted.
[SAVE] [✕] [📱] [💻]

SHAKOPEE

🔺 ▽▽▽▽ **AmericInn Lodge & Suites of Shakopee** 🅷
(952) 445-6775. **$85-$190.** 4100 12th Ave E. Just ne of US 169. Int corridors. **Pets:** Other species. $30 one-time fee/pet. Service with restrictions, supervision.
[SAVE] [✕] [📱] [💻] [🔜] [✕]

🔺 ▽▽▽▽ **Country Inn & Suites By Carlson** 🅷
(952) 445-0200. **$95-$125.** 1204 Ramsey St. Just ne of US 169. Int corridors. **Pets:** Small. $100 deposit/room, $30 one-time fee/pet. Service with restrictions, crate.
[SAVE] [✕] [⛾ᴹ] [📱] [💻] [🔜]

▽▽ **Sandalwood Studios & Suites** 🅷
(952) 277-0100. **$39-$109.** 3910 12th Ave E. Just nw of US 169. Int corridors. **Pets:** Accepted.
[ASK] [✕] [📱]

STILLWATER

🔺 ▽▽▽ **Americas Best Value Inn** 🅷
(651) 430-1300. **Call for rates.** 1750 W Frontage Rd. SR 36 at Washington Ave, just ne. Int corridors. **Pets:** Accepted.
[SAVE] [✕] [⛾ᴹ] [📱] [💻] [🔜]

▽▽▽ **Super 8** 🅷
(651) 430-3990. **$56-$99.** 2190 W Frontage Rd. SR 36 at Washington Ave. Int corridors. **Pets:** Accepted.
[ASK] [✕] [📱] [💻]

WACONIA

🔺 ▽▽▽▽ **AmericInn Lodge & Suites of Waconia** 🅷 ❀
(952) 442-8787. **$85-$169.** 550 Cherry Dr. Just nw from jct SR 5. Int corridors. **Pets:** Small, dogs only. $10 daily fee/pet. Service with restrictions, crate.
[SAVE] [✕] [📱] [💻] [🔜]

▽▽▽ **Super 8** 🅼
(952) 442-5147. **Call for rates.** 301 E Frontage Rd. On SR 5 at jct CR 10. Int corridors. **Pets:** Accepted.
[✕] [📱] [💻]

WHITE BEAR LAKE

🔺 ▽▽▽▽ **Best Western White Bear Country Inn** 🅷
(651) 429-5393. **$79-$109, 3 day notice.** 4940 N Hwy 61. Jct SR 96, 1 mi n. Int corridors. **Pets:** Service with restrictions, supervision.
[SAVE] [✕] [📱] [💻] [🍴] [🔜] [✕]

WOODBURY

▽▽ ▽▽ **Extended StayAmerica-Minneapolis-Woodbury** 🅷
(651) 501-1085. **$74-$114.** 10020 Hudson Rd. I-94, exit 251, just se. Int corridors. **Pets:** Other species. $25 daily fee/pet. Service with restrictions, crate.
[ASK] [✕] [📱] [💻]

🔺 ▽▽▽▽ **Holiday Inn Express Hotel & Suites** 🅷
(651) 702-0200. **Call for rates.** 9840 Norma Ln. I-94, exit 251, just sw. Int corridors. **Pets:** Medium. $10 daily fee/room. Service with supervision.
[SAVE] [✕] [📱] [💻] [🔜]

▽▽ ▽▽ **Red Roof Inn #7063** 🅼
(651) 738-7160. **Call for rates.** 1806 Wooddale Dr. I-494, exit 59 (Valley Creek Rd), just se. Ext corridors. **Pets:** Service with restrictions, supervision.
[✕]

END METROPOLITAN AREA

MONTEVIDEO

▽▽▽▽ **Country Inn & Suites By Carlson** 🅷
(320) 269-8000. **$84-$149, 30 day notice.** 1805 E SR 7. On SR 7, east of downtown. Int corridors. **Pets:** Other species. $200 deposit/room. Designated rooms, supervision.
[ASK] [✕] [📱] [💻] [🔜]

MOORHEAD

🔺 ▽▽ **Super 8** 🅷
(218) 233-8880. **$55-$62.** 3621 S 8th St. I-94, exit 1A (US 75), 0.5 mi s. Int corridors. **Pets:** Other species. Designated rooms, service with restrictions, supervision.
[SAVE] [✕] [📱] [💻]

▽▽▽ **Travelodge & Suites** 🅷
(218) 233-5333. **$49-$159.** 3027 S Frontage Rd. Just s of US 10 E; east of downtown. Int corridors. **Pets:** Accepted.
[ASK] [✕] [⛾ᴹ] [📱] [💻] [🔜]

MOOSE LAKE

▽▽▽▽ **AmericInn Lodge & Suites of Moose Lake** 🅷
(218) 485-8885. **$75-$175.** 400 Park Place Dr. I-35, exit 214 (SR 73), just sw. Int corridors. **Pets:** Other species. $10 daily fee/room. Designated rooms, service with restrictions, supervision.
[ASK] [✕] [📱] [💻] [🔜]

NEW ULM

▼▼▼▼ Holiday Inn �H
(507) 359-2941. **Call for rates.** 2101 S Broadway. SR 15/68, 1.8 mi se. Int corridors. **Pets:** Accepted.
⊠ 🛇 🖵 🍴 ⇌ ⊠

◊◊◊ ▼▼ Microtel Inn & Suites �H
(507) 354-9800. **$60-$105.** 424 20th St S. Just e of jct SR 15/68 and CR 37. Int corridors. **Pets:** $10 daily fee/room. Service with restrictions.
🆂🅰🆅🅴 ⊠ ⛟ᴹ 🛇 🖵 ⇌

NISSWA

◊◊◊ ▼▼ Nisswa Motel Ⓜ
(218) 963-7611. **$59-$102, 5 day notice.** 5370 Merrill Ave. Just sw of Main St; center. Ext corridors. **Pets:** Medium, dogs only. $10 daily fee/pet. Designated rooms, service with restrictions, crate.
🆂🅰🆅🅴 ⊠ 🛇 🖵

NORTHFIELD

▼▼ Super 8 �H
(507) 663-0371. **Call for rates.** 1420 Riverview Dr. 1.3 mi w of jct SR 19 and 3. Int corridors. **Pets:** Accepted.
⊠ 🛇 🖵 ⇌

ONAMIA

▼▼ Econo Lodge �H
(320) 532-3838. **Call for rates.** 40847 US 169. On US 169; 6 mi n. Int corridors. **Pets:** Accepted.
⊠ 🛇 🖵

ORR

▼▼▼ AmericInn Lodge & Suites of Orr �H
(218) 757-3613. **$85-$230.** 4675 Hwy 53. Just n. Int corridors. **Pets:** Accepted.
🅰🆂🅺 ⊠ 🛇 🖵 🍴 ⇌ ⊠

▼▼ North Country Inn �H
(218) 757-3778. **$68-$94.** 4483 Hwy 53. 0.3 mi s. Int corridors. **Pets:** Accepted.
⊠ ⛟ᴹ 🛇

OWATONNA

▼▼ AmericInn of Owatonna �H
(507) 455-1142. **$85-$95.** 245 Florence Ave. I-35, exit 41 (Bridge St), 0.3 mi ne. Int corridors. **Pets:** $10 one-time fee/pet. Service with restrictions, supervision.
🅰🆂🅺 ⊠ 🛇 🖵 ⇌ ⊠

▼▼▼ Comfort Inn �H
(507) 444-0818. **$90-$140.** 2345 43rd St NW. I-35, exit 45 (Clinton Falls), just sw. Int corridors. **Pets:** Accepted.
🅰🆂🅺 ⊠ ⛟ᴹ 🛇 🖵 ⇌

▼▼ Microtel Inn & Suites �H
(507) 446-0228. **Call for rates.** 150 St. John Dr NW. I-35, exit 41 (Bridge St), just nw. Int corridors. **Pets:** Accepted.
⊠ ⛟ᴹ 🖵

PARK RAPIDS

▼▼ C'mon Inn �H
(218) 732-1471. **$85-$174.** 1009 1st St E. SR 34, 0.8 mi e of jct US 71. Int corridors. **Pets:** Dogs only. Designated rooms, service with restrictions, crate.
🅰🆂🅺 ⊠ 🛇 🖵 ⇌

PEQUOT LAKES

▼▼ ▼▼ AmericInn Lodge & Suites of Pequot Lakes �H
(218) 568-8400. **$75-$205.** 32912 Paul Bunyan Trail Dr (SR 371/CR 16). SR 371; 2 mi n of downtown. Int corridors. **Pets:** Small, dogs only. $10 daily fee/pet. Designated rooms, service with restrictions, supervision.
🅰🆂🅺 ⊠ 🛇 🖵 ⇌ ⊠

PERHAM

▼▼ Super 8 �H
(218) 346-7888. **$66-$83.** 106 Jake St SE. SR 78, just nw of jct US 10. Int corridors. **Pets:** Accepted.
🅰🆂🅺 ⊠ 🛇 🖵

PINE RIVER

▼▼ Rodeway Inn Ⓜ
(218) 587-4499. **$60-$90.** 2684 State 371 SW. 1 mi s. Ext corridors. **Pets:** Medium, dogs only. $10 daily fee/pet. Service with restrictions, supervision.
🅰🆂🅺 ⊠ 🛇 🖵 ⊠

RED WING

◊◊◊ ▼▼ Best Western Rivertown Inn & Suites �H
(651) 388-1577. **$90-$180.** 752 Withers Harbor Dr. 1.5 mi nw on US 61, at Withers Harbor Dr; opposite side of US 61 from Pottery Mall. Ext/int corridors. **Pets:** Small. $15 daily fee/pet. Designated rooms, service with restrictions, supervision.
🆂🅰🆅🅴 ⊠ ⛟ᴹ 🛇 🖵 ⇌

▼▼ Days Inn Ⓜ
(651) 388-3568. **$54-$131.** 955 E 7th St. US 61/63, 1.7 mi se. Ext corridors. **Pets:** Accepted.
🅰🆂🅺 ⊠ 🛇 🖵 ⇌

ROCHESTER

▼▼▼ Extended StayAmerica-Rochester North �H
(507) 289-7444. **$59-$99.** 2814 43rd St NW. Just nw from jct US 52. Int corridors. **Pets:** Other species. $25 daily fee/pet. Service with restrictions, crate.
🅰🆂🅺 ⊠ 🛇 🖵

▼▼▼ Holiday Inn South �H
(507) 288-1844. **Call for rates.** 1630 S Broadway. 0.5 mi s of jct US 14 and 63 (Broadway). Ext/int corridors. **Pets:** Accepted.
⊠ 🛇 🖵 🍴 ⇌ ⊠

◊◊◊ ▼▼▼▼ International Hotel �H
(507) 328-8000. **$450-$3000.** 20 SW 2nd Ave. Opposite Mayo Clinic and Methodist Hospital; 12th Floor of Kahler Grand Hotel. Int corridors. **Pets:** Accepted.
🆂🅰🆅🅴 ⊠ 🛇 🖵 ⇌ ⊠

◊◊◊ ▼▼▼▼ The Kahler Grand Hotel �H
(507) 282-2581. **$99-$139.** 20 SW 2nd Ave. Opposite Mayo Clinic and Methodist Hospital. Int corridors. **Pets:** Other species. Designated rooms, service with restrictions, supervision.
🆂🅰🆅🅴 ⊠ 🛇 🖵 🍴 ⇌ ⊠

▼▼ Kahler Inn & Suites �H
(507) 289-8646. **$89-$119.** 9 NW 3rd Ave. Just n of Mayo Clinic. Int corridors. **Pets:** Accepted.
🅰🆂🅺 ⊠ 🛇 🖵 🍴 ⇌ ⊠

▼▼▼ Marriott Hotel �H
(507) 280-6000. **$233-$285.** 101 1st Ave SW. Just e of Mayo Clinic. Int corridors. **Pets:** Medium. $75 one-time fee/room. Designated rooms, service with restrictions.
⊠ 🛇 🖵 ⇌ ⊠

▼▼ Microtel Inn & Suites �H
(507) 286-8780. **Call for rates.** 4210 Hwy 52 N. US 52, exit 58 (41st St NW), just w. Int corridors. **Pets:** Accepted.
⊠ ⛟ᴹ 🛇 🖵

(AAA) ▼▼▼▼ Quality Inn & Suites 🅷 ❄
(507) 282-8091. **$77-$209.** 1620 1st Ave SE. On US 63 (Broadway) from jct US 14, 0.5 mi s, just e on 16th St, then just s. Ext/int corridors. **Pets:** $10 daily fee/pet. Supervision.
[SAVE] [✕] [🔧] [💻]

▼▼▼▼ Radisson Plaza Hotel 🅷
(507) 281-8000. **$159-$179.** 150 S Broadway. On US 63 (Broadway); downtown. Int corridors. **Pets:** Medium, dogs only. Designated rooms, service with restrictions.
[ASK] [✕] [🔧] [💻] [🍴] [🏊] [✕]

▼▼▼▼ Staybridge Suites 🅷
(507) 289-6600. **$149-$234.** 1211 2nd St SW. US 52/14, exit 55B (2nd St SW), just e. Int corridors. **Pets:** Medium. $150 one-time fee/room. Service with restrictions, crate.
[✕] [♿M] [🔧] [💻] [🏊]

ROSEAU

▼▼ AmericInn Lodge & Suites of Roseau 🅷
(218) 463-1045. **$67-$82.** 1110 3rd St NW. 1 mi w on SR 11. Int corridors. **Pets:** $25 one-time fee/room.
[ASK] [✕] [♿M] [🔧] [💻] [🏊] [✕]

▼▼ North Country Inn 🅷
(218) 463-9444. **Call for rates.** 902 3rd St NW. 0.8 mi w on SR 11. Int corridors. **Pets:** Accepted.
[✕] [🔧] [💻] [🏊]

ST. CLOUD

(AAA) ▼▼▼ AmericInn Lodge & Suites of St. Cloud 🅷 ❄
(320) 253-6337. **$72-$135.** 4385 Clearwater Rd. I-94, exit 171 (CR 75), just ne. Int corridors. **Pets:** Medium. $10 daily fee/pet. Designated rooms, service with restrictions, supervision.
[SAVE] [✕] [♿M] [🔧] [💻] [🏊]

(AAA) ▼▼▼▼ Best Western Americanna Inn & Conference Center 🅷
(320) 252-8700. **$67-$95.** 520 S US Hwy 10. Jct SR 23, 0.3 mi s. Ext/int corridors. **Pets:** Accepted.
[SAVE] [✕] [🔧] [💻] [🍴] [🏊] [✕]

(AAA) ▼▼▼▼ Best Western Kelly Inn 🅷
(320) 253-0606. **$100-$125, 3 day notice.** 100 4th Ave S. SR 23 at 4th Ave S; center. Int corridors. **Pets:** Service with restrictions, supervision.
[SAVE] [✕] [♿M] [🔧] [💻] [🏊] [✕]

▼▼▼▼ Country Inn & Suites By Carlson 🅷
(320) 259-8999. **$99-$140.** 235 S Park Ave. Jct SR 15 and 23 W, just w. Int corridors. **Pets:** Accepted.
[ASK] [✕] [♿M] [🔧] [💻] [🏊]

(AAA) ▼▼▼ Days Inn Hotel and Waterslide 🅷
(320) 253-4444. **$75-$90.** 70 37th Ave S. Jct SR 15 and 23, just e. Int corridors. **Pets:** $10 daily fee/pet. Designated rooms, service with restrictions, supervision.
[SAVE] [✕] [♿M] [🔧] [💻] [🏊]

▼▼▼ GrandStay Residential Suites 🅷
(320) 251-5400. **Call for rates.** 213 6th Ave S. SR 23 at 6th Ave S; center. Int corridors. **Pets:** Accepted.
[✕] [🔧] [💻] [🏊] [✕]

▼▼▼ Holiday Inn Express 🅷
(320) 240-8000. **Call for rates.** 4322 Clearwater Rd. I-94, exit 171 (CR 75), just ne. Int corridors. **Pets:** Accepted.
[✕] [♿M] [🔧] [💻] [🏊]

▼▼▼ Holiday Inn Hotel & Suites 🅷
(320) 253-9000. **$95-$135.** 75 S 37th Ave. Jct SR 15 and 23. Int corridors. **Pets:** Accepted.
[ASK] [✕] [🔧] [💻] [🍴] [🏊] [✕]

▼▼ Quality Inn 🅷
(320) 251-1500. **$70-$149, 7 day notice.** 4040 2nd St S. Jct SR 15 and 23 W, just w. Int corridors. **Pets:** Small, other species. $10 one-time fee/room. Designated rooms, service with restrictions, crate.
[ASK] [✕] [♿M] [🔧] [💻] [🍴] [🏊] [✕]

▼▼▼▼ Radisson Suite Hotel-St Cloud 🅷
(320) 654-1661. **Call for rates.** 404 W St. Germain. Just n of SR 23; center. Int corridors. **Pets:** Accepted.
[✕] [♿M] [🔧] [💻] [🏊] [✕]

▼ Thrifty Motel 🅼
(320) 253-6320. **$38-$80.** 130 14th Ave NE. Jct US 10 and SR 23, 0.3 mi e. Int corridors. **Pets:** Other species. $5 daily fee/pet. Supervision.
[✕] [🔧]

SAUK CENTRE

(AAA) ▼▼ AmericInn Lodge & Suites of Sauk Centre 🅷 ❄
(320) 352-2800. **$74-$149.** 1230 Timberlane Dr. I-94, exit 127, just ne. Int corridors. **Pets:** Medium, dogs only. $10 one-time fee/pet. Designated rooms, service with restrictions, crate.
[SAVE] [✕] [🔧] [💻] [🏊] [✕]

SILVER BAY

▼▼▼ AmericInn Lodge & Suites of Silver Bay 🅷
(218) 226-4300. **$85-$170.** 150 Mensing Dr. On SR 61, 0.5 mi ne of jct SR 61 and Outer Dr. Int corridors. **Pets:** Accepted.
[✕] [♿M] [🔧] [💻] [🏊] [✕]

(AAA) ▼▼▼ Mariner Motel 🅼 ❄
(218) 226-4488. **$55-$75, 3 day notice.** 46 Outer Dr. Just w off SR 61; at traffic signal. Ext corridors. **Pets:** Dogs only. $5 daily fee/pet. Service with restrictions, supervision.
[SAVE] [✕] [🔧] [💻] [🅐🅒]

SLEEPY EYE

▼▼ Inn of Seven Gables 🅷
(507) 794-5390. **$69-$99.** 1100 E Main St. US 14, 0.8 mi e of jct CR 4 and US 14. Int corridors. **Pets:** Accepted.
[ASK] [✕] [🔧] [💻] [🏊]

SPICER

▼▼ Northern Inn Hotel & Suites 🅷
(320) 796-2091. **$60-$110.** 154 Lake Ave S. Just e of jct SR 23 and CR 10. Int corridors. **Pets:** Other species. $10 one-time fee/pet. Designated rooms, service with restrictions, crate.
[✕] [🔧] [💻] [🏊]

SPRING VALLEY

(AAA) ▼▼▼ Spring Valley Inn & Suites 🅷
(507) 346-7788. **$77-$111.** 745 N Broadway. Just w on US 63. Int corridors. **Pets:** Other species. $10 one-time fee/pet. Designated rooms, service with restrictions, crate.
[SAVE] [✕] [♿M] [🔧] [💻]

TOFTE

▼▼▼ AmericInn Lodge & Suites of Tofte 🅷
(218) 663-7899. **$80-$130.** 7231 W SR 61. On SR 61. Int corridors. **Pets:** $10 daily fee/pet. Designated rooms, service with restrictions, crate.
[ASK] [✕] [🔧] [💻] [🏊] [✕]

(AAA) ▼▼▼▼ Bluefin Bay on Lake Superior 🅒🅞 ❄
(218) 663-7296. **$69-$565, 7 day notice.** 7198 W Hwy 61. On SR 61. Ext corridors. **Pets:** Other species. $20 daily fee/room. Designated rooms, service with restrictions, supervision.
[SAVE] [✕] [🔧] [💻] [🍴] [🏊] [✕] [🅐🅒]

▼▼▼ Surfside on Lake Superior CO
(218) 663-6870. **$159-$595, 7 day notice.** 10 Surfside Dr (Hwy 61). On SR 61. Ext corridors. **Pets:** Accepted.
✕ 🛏 💻 🏊 ✕

TWO HARBORS

▼▼ AmericInn Lodge & Suites of Two Harbors H
(218) 834-3000. **$85-$175.** 1088 SR 61 N. On SR 61, 0.7 mi s. Int corridors. **Pets:** Accepted.
ASK ✕ ᴹ 🛏 💻 🏊 ✕

▼▼▼ Superior Shores Resort CO ✿
(218) 834-5671. **$49-$479, 14 day notice.** 1521 Superior Shores Dr. On SR 61, 1.5 mi n of center. Ext/int corridors. **Pets:** $20 one-time fee/room. Designated rooms, service with restrictions, supervision.
ASK ✕ 🛏 💻 🍴 🏊 ✕

VERGAS

▼▼▼ The Log House & Homestead on Spirit Lake BB
(218) 342-2318. **$115-$235, 8 day notice.** 44854 Fredholm Rd. 5 mi sw on CR 4. Ext/int corridors. **Pets:** Accepted.
✕ 🛏 💻 ✕ W Z

VIRGINIA

▼▼ AmericInn of Virginia Lodge & Suites of Virginia H ✿
(218) 741-7839. **$100-$180.** 5480 Mountain Iron Dr. US 53, just s of jct US 169. Int corridors. **Pets:** Medium, dogs only. $10 daily fee/pet. Service with restrictions, supervision.
✕ ᴹ 🛏 💻 🏊 ✕

◈◈◈ ▼ Budget Host–Virginia M ✿
(218) 741-6145. **$50-$95.** 1 Midway Dr. US 53, just e on Cuyuna Dr. Ext/int corridors. **Pets:** Medium, other species. $10 daily fee/pet. Designated rooms, service with restrictions, supervision.
SAVE ✕ 🛏 💻

▼ Lakeshor Motor Inn M ✿
(218) 741-3360. **$40-$104.** 404 6th Ave N. Just n of Chestnut St; center. Ext corridors. **Pets:** Dogs only. $5 daily fee/room. Service with restrictions, supervision.
ASK ✕ 🛏 💻

◈◈◈ ▼ Pine View Inn M
(218) 741-8918. **$59-$109.** 903 N 17th St. Jct US 53 and 169, 0.5 mi n on US 53, 0.7 mi e on 9th St N, then 0.5 mi n on 9th Ave W. Ext/int corridors. **Pets:** Dogs only. $50 deposit/room. Service with restrictions, supervision.
SAVE ✕ 💻

WABASHA

▼▼ AmericInn Lodge & Suites of Wabasha H
(651) 565-5366. **$71-$180.** 150 Commerce Dr. Just ne of jct US 61 and SR 60. Int corridors. **Pets:** Accepted.
ASK ✕ ᴹ 🛏 💻 🏊 ✕

WALKER

▼▼▼ Country Inn & Suites By Carlson H
(218) 547-1400. **$74-$145.** 442 Walker Bay Blvd. 1 mi s on SR 371. Int corridors. **Pets:** Dogs only. $25 one-time fee/room. Service with restrictions, supervision.
ASK ✕ ᴹ 🛏 💻 🏊

WARROAD

▼▼ Can-Am Motel H
(218) 386-3807. **Call for rates.** 406 Main Ave NE. 0.5 mi w on SR 11. Int corridors. **Pets:** Accepted.
✕ ᴹ

▼▼ The Patch Motel H
(218) 386-2723. **Call for rates.** 801 State Ave N. 0.6 mi w on SR 11. Int corridors. **Pets:** Accepted.
✕ ᴹ 🛏 🍴

WILLMAR

▼▼ AmericInn Motel of Willmar H
(320) 231-1962. **Call for rates.** 2404 E US 12. 2 mi e on US 12. Int corridors. **Pets:** Accepted.
✕ 🛏 💻 🏊

▼▼ Comfort Inn H
(320) 231-2601. **$80-$110.** 2200 E US 12. 1.8 mi e. Int corridors. **Pets:** $5 daily fee/pet. Service with restrictions, supervision.
ASK ✕ 🛏 💻 🏊

▼▼ Days Inn-Willmar H
(320) 231-1275. **$60-$80.** 225 28th St SE. 2.3 mi e on US 12. Int corridors. **Pets:** $5 daily fee/pet. Service with restrictions, supervision.
ASK ✕ 🛏 💻

▼▼▼ Holiday Inn & Willmar Conference Center H
(320) 235-6060. **$90-$120.** 2100 US 12 E. 1.8 mi e. Int corridors. **Pets:** $10 daily fee/pet. Service with restrictions, supervision.
✕ 🛏 💻 🍴 🏊 ✕

WINONA

▼▼ Express Suites Riverport Inn H
(507) 452-0606. **$69-$149.** 900 Bruski Dr. Jct US 14/61 and SR 43, just ne. Int corridors. **Pets:** $25 daily fee/room. Designated rooms, service with restrictions, supervision.
ASK ✕ 🛏 💻 🍴 🏊

▼▼▼ Holiday Inn Hotel and Suites H
(507) 453-0303. **$95-$205.** 1025 Hwy 61 E. Jct SR 43, just sw. Int corridors. **Pets:** $25 daily fee/room. Designated rooms, service with restrictions, crate.
ASK ✕ ᴹ 🛏 💻 🍴 🏊 ✕

◈◈◈ ▼▼ Quality Inn H
(507) 454-4390. **$69-$99.** 956 Mankato Ave. Jct US 14/61 and SR 43, just ne. Ext/int corridors. **Pets:** Medium, other species. $10 daily fee/room. Designated rooms, service with restrictions, crate.
SAVE ✕ 🛏 💻 🍴 🏊 ✕

WORTHINGTON

◈◈◈ ▼▼▼ AmericInn Lodge and Suites of Worthington H
(507) 376-4500. **$80-$150.** 1475 Darling Dr. I-90, exit 43 (US 59), just se. Int corridors. **Pets:** Other species. $10 one-time fee/room. Service with restrictions, supervision.
SAVE ✕ 🛏 💻 🏊 ✕

MISSISSIPPI

ABERDEEN

Best Western Aberdeen Inn M
(662) 369-4343. **$70-$100, 7 day notice.** 801 E Commerce St. On US 45, just n of jct SR 25 and Tenn-Tom Bridge. Ext corridors. **Pets:** Accepted.

AMORY

Best Western Amory M
(662) 256-2120. **$76, 3 day notice.** 915 Hwy 278 E. Jct SR 25 (Main St), 0.6 mi e. Ext corridors. **Pets:** Accepted.

BATESVILLE

Comfort Inn H
(662) 563-1188. **$65-$95.** 290 Power Dr. I-55, exit 243B, just ne on frontage road. Ext corridors. **Pets:** Accepted.

BILOXI

Edgewater Inn H
(228) 388-1100. **$109-$169, 3 day notice.** 1936 Beach Blvd. I-110, exit 1B, 3.4 mi w on US 90. Ext corridors. **Pets:** Accepted.

Hard Rock Hotel & Casino Biloxi H
(228) 374-7625. **$89-$479.** 777 Beach Blvd. I-110, exit 1A (US 90), just e. Int corridors. **Pets:** Small, other species. $75 one-time fee/room. No service, supervision.

BOONEVILLE

Best Western College Inn M
(662) 728-2244. **$45-$60.** 805 N 2nd St. Jct US 45 and SR 4/30, 1.7 mi e to SR 145, then 1.1 mi s. Ext corridors. **Pets:** Accepted.

Super 8 H
(662) 720-1688. **$55-$65.** 110 Hospitality Ave. Jct US 45 and SR 4/30, 1.7 mi e to SR 145, then 0.5 mi s. Int corridors. **Pets:** Accepted.

CANTON

Americas Best Value Inn H
(601) 859-2643. **$55-$65.** 119 Soldier Colony Rd. I-55, exit 119, just se. Ext corridors. **Pets:** Medium, dogs only. $10 daily fee/pet. Service with restrictions, supervision.

Best Western-Canton Inn H
(601) 859-8600. **Call for rates.** 137 Soldier Colony Rd. I-55, exit 119, just se. Int corridors. **Pets:** Accepted.

Comfort Inn H
(601) 859-7575. **$70-$100, 14 day notice.** 145 Soldier Colony Rd. I-55, exit 119, just se. Int corridors. **Pets:** Large, other species. $25 one-time fee/pet. Service with restrictions, supervision.

CLEVELAND

Comfort Inn of Cleveland H
(662) 846-1525. **$79-$119, 7 day notice.** 807 N Davis Ave. 1 mi n of jct US 61 and SR 8. Int corridors. **Pets:** Accepted.

Econo Lodge of Cleveland M
(662) 843-4060. **$49-$79, 7 day notice.** 721 N Davis Ave. On US 61, 1 mi n of jct US 61 and SR 8. Ext corridors. **Pets:** Accepted.

CLINTON

Best Western Ridgeland Inn H
(601) 926-4323. **Call for rates.** 102 Clinton Loop Dr. I-20, exit 36, just s, then just w on Clinton Center Dr. Int corridors. **Pets:** Accepted.

CORINTH

Comfort Inn H
(662) 287-4421. **Call for rates.** 2101 Hwy 72 W. Jct US 72 and 45, just e. Ext corridors. **Pets:** Accepted.

FOREST

Americas Best Value Inn H
(601) 469-2640. **Call for rates.** 1846 Hwy 35 S. I-20, exit 88, just n. Ext corridors. **Pets:** Accepted.

Econo Lodge Inn & Suites H
(601) 469-2100. **$60-$75, 15 day notice.** 1250 Hwy 35 S. I-20, exit 88, just n. Ext corridors. **Pets:** Very small. Designated rooms, service with restrictions, supervision.

GREENVILLE

Days Inn H
(662) 334-1818. **Call for rates.** 2701 Hwy 82 E. 3 mi e on US 82. Ext corridors. **Pets:** Small. $15 daily fee/pet. Designated rooms, service with restrictions, supervision.

Econo Lodge of Greenville H
(662) 378-4976. **$49-$79, 7 day notice.** 3080 US 82 E. 3 mi e of center. Ext corridors. **Pets:** Accepted.

GREENWOOD

▼▼ Econo Lodge Inn & Suites 🄷
(662) 453-5974. **$49-$79, 7 day notice.** 401 Hwy 82 W. 0.4 mi w of Main St. Ext corridors. **Pets:** Accepted.
(ASK) (✕) (🛏) (💻) (➿)

GRENADA

▼▼▼ Country Inn & Suites by Carlson 🄷
(662) 227-8444. **$78-$130.** 255 SW Frontage Rd. I-55, exit 206, just sw. Int corridors. **Pets:** Other species. $25 one-time fee/room. Service with restrictions, crate.
(ASK) (✕) (🛏) (💻) (➿)

GULFPORT

▼▼ Americas Best Value Inn 🄷
(228) 868-8500. **$80-$140.** 9375 Hwy 49. I-10, exit 34A, just sw. Ext corridors. **Pets:** Medium, other species. $10 daily fee/pet. Service with restrictions, crate.
(ASK) (✕) (🛏) (💻) (➿)

⚇ ▼▼ Best Western Seaway Inn 🄷
(228) 864-0050. **$79-$179, 3 day notice.** 9475 Hwy 49. I-10, exit 34A, just sw. Ext corridors. **Pets:** Medium. $10 daily fee/pet. Service with restrictions, supervision.
(SAVE) (✕) (🛏) (💻) (➿)

▼▼ Holiday Inn Airport 🄷
(228) 868-8200. **Call for rates.** 9415 Hwy 49. I-10, exit 34A, 0.6 mi s. Ext corridors. **Pets:** Accepted.
(✕) (🛏) (💻) (🍴) (➿)

▼ Motel 6 #416 Ⓜ
(228) 863-1890. **$57-$75.** 9355 US Hwy 49. I-10, exit 34A, just s. Ext corridors. **Pets:** Other species. Service with restrictions, supervision.
(✕) (➿)

▼▼ Quality Inn Gulfport 🄷
(228) 864-7222. **Call for rates.** 9435 Hwy 49. I-10, exit 34A, 0.6 mi s. Ext corridors. **Pets:** Small. $15 daily fee/pet. Service with restrictions, crate.
(✕) (🛏) (💻)

HATTIESBURG

▼▼▼ Candlewood Suites 🄷
(601) 264-9666. **$99-$179.** 9 Gateway Dr. I-59, exit 67B, just nw to Classic Dr, then just sw. Int corridors. **Pets:** Accepted.
(ASK) (✕) (🛏) (💻)

▼▼ Comfort Inn University 🄷
(601) 264-1881. **$89-$149.** 6541 US Hwy 49. I-59, exit 67A, just s. Ext/int corridors. **Pets:** Accepted.
(ASK) (✕) (🛏) (💻) (➿)

▼▼ La Quinta Inn 🄷 🐾
(601) 268-2850. **$59-$159.** 6563 Hwy 49 N. I-59, exit 67A, just se. Int corridors. **Pets:** Medium, other species. Service with restrictions, supervision.
(ASK) (✕) (🛏) (💻) (➿)

⚇ ▼▼ Ramada Hattiesburg 🄷
(601) 599-2001. **$79-$120.** 6595 Hwy 49 N. I-59, exit 67A, just se. Ext corridors. **Pets:** Accepted.
(SAVE) (✕) (🛏) (💻) (🍴) (➿)

HOLLY SPRINGS

▼▼▼ Le' Brooks Inn 🄷
(662) 252-5444. **Call for rates.** 100 Brooks Rd. US 78, exit 30, just sw. Int corridors. **Pets:** Accepted.
(✕) (🛏) (💻) (➿)

HORN LAKE

▼▼▼ Drury Inn & Suites-Memphis South 🄷
(662) 349-6622. **$90-$155.** 735 Goodman Rd W. I-55, exit 289, just sw. Int corridors. **Pets:** Other species. Service with restrictions, supervision.
(ASK) (✕) (🛗) (🛏) (💻) (➿)

JACKSON

⚇ ▼▼▼ Best Western Executive Inn 🄷
(601) 969-6555. **$79-$119, 14 day notice.** 725 Larson St. I-55, exit 96B (High St), e to Greymont Ave, then just n. Int corridors. **Pets:** Accepted.
(SAVE) (✕) (🛏) (💻) (➿)

▼▼▼ Clarion Hotel 🄷
(601) 366-9411. **Call for rates.** 5075 I-55 N. I-55, exit 102A, s on west frontage road. Ext/int corridors. **Pets:** Accepted.
(✕) (🛏) (💻) (🍴) (➿)

▼▼▼ The Edison Walthall Hotel 🄷
(601) 948-6161. **$109-$195.** 225 E Capitol St. I-55, exit 96A (Pearl St), 0.8 mi w; between West and Lamar sts; downtown. Ext/int corridors. **Pets:** Accepted.
(ASK) (✕) (🛏) (💻) (🍴) (➿)

▼▼ Extended StayAmerica Jackson-North 🄷
(601) 956-4312. **$58-$73.** 5354 I-55 N. I-55, exit 100, just n. Ext corridors. **Pets:** Other species. $25 daily fee/pet. Service with restrictions, crate.
(ASK) (✕) (🛏) (💻)

▼▼ Jameson Inn 🄷
(601) 206-8923. **$88-$95.** 585 E Beasley Rd. I-55, exit 102, just w. Int corridors. **Pets:** Large, other species. $15 daily fee/pet. Service with restrictions, supervision.
(ASK) (✕) (🛗) (🛏) (💻) (➿)

▼▼ La Quinta Inn Jackson (North) 🄷 🐾
(601) 957-1741. **$39-$79.** 616 Briarwood Dr. I-55, exit 102A northbound, just ne on Frontage Rd. Ext corridors. **Pets:** Medium, other species. Service with restrictions, supervision.
(ASK) (✕) (🛗) (🛏) (💻) (➿)

▼ Red Roof Inn Fairgrounds #131 Ⓜ
(601) 969-5006. **Call for rates.** 700 Larson St. I-55, exit 96B (High St), e to Greymont Ave, then just ne. Ext corridors. **Pets:** Accepted.
(✕) (🛏)

⚇ ▼▼▼ Regency Hotel & Conference Center 🄷
(601) 969-2141. **Call for rates.** 400 Greymont Ave. I-55, exit 96B, just w, then just s. Ext/int corridors. **Pets:** Accepted.
(SAVE) (✕) (🛗) (🛏) (💻) (🍴) (➿)

⚇ ▼▼▼ Residence Inn by Marriott 🄷 🐾
(601) 355-3599. **$172-$184.** 881 E River Pl. I-55, exit 96C, just e. Ext corridors. **Pets:** Medium, other species. $75 one-time fee/pet. Service with restrictions.
(SAVE) (✕) (🛏) (💻) (➿) (✕)

KOSCIUSKO

⚇ ▼▼ Americas Best Value Inn Ⓜ
(662) 289-6252. **$55-$65.** 1052 Veterans Memorial Dr/Hwy 35 Bypass. Just sw of jct SR 35 and Natchez Trace Pkwy. Ext corridors. **Pets:** Accepted.
(SAVE) (✕) (🛏) (💻) (➿)

MACON

⚇ ▼▼ Best Western Oak Tree Inn Ⓜ
(662) 726-4334. **$62-$76.** 12710 Hwy 45. Jct SR 14, just s. Ext corridors. **Pets:** Accepted.
(SAVE) (✕) (🛗) (🛏) (💻) (➿)

MCCOMB

Hawthorn Inn & Suites H
(601) 684-8655. **$90.** 2001 Veteran's Blvd. I-55, exit 18, just off interstate. Int corridors. **Pets:** Medium. $125 one-time fee/room. Service with restrictions, crate.

SAVE ✕ ⑤M 🛢 💻 ⚓

MERIDIAN

Best Western of Meridian H
(601) 693-3210. **$65-$75.** 2219 S Frontage Rd. I-20/59, exit 153, just sw. Ext/int corridors. **Pets:** Small, dogs only. $10 daily fee/pet. Service with restrictions, crate.

SAVE ✕ 🛢 💻 ⚓

Econo Lodge M
(601) 693-9393. **Call for rates.** 2405 S Frontage Rd. I-20/59, exit 153, 0.5 mi sw. Ext corridors. **Pets:** Accepted.

✕ 🛢 💻

Holiday Inn Meridian H
(601) 485-5101. **$89-$105.** 111 US 11 & 80. I-20/59, exit 154 westbound, just n to frontage road, then just e; exit 154B eastbound. Ext corridors. **Pets:** Medium, other species. $25 one-time fee/room. Service with restrictions, crate.

SAVE ✕ ⑤M 🛢 💻 ⚓

Jameson Inn H
(601) 483-3315. **$83-$90.** 524 Bonita Lakes Dr. I-20/59, exit 154 southbound; exit 154A northbound, just s. Ext corridors. **Pets:** Accepted.

ASK ✕ ⑤M 🛢 💻 ⚓

Motel 6 #0424 M
(601) 482-1182. **$39-$51.** 2309 S Frontage Rd. I-20/59, exit 153, 0.5 mi sw. Ext corridors. **Pets:** Other species. Service with restrictions, supervision.

✕ ⚓

MOSS POINT

Quality Inn H 🐾
(228) 475-2477. **$59-$89.** 6800 Hwy 63 N. I-10, exit 69, just s. Ext corridors. **Pets:** Small, other species. $10 daily fee/pet. Service with restrictions, crate.

SAVE ✕ 🛢 💻 ⚓

NATCHEZ

Days Inn of Natchez H
(601) 445-8291. **$74-$125.** 109 US Hwy 61 S. Just se of jct US 61, 84 and 98. Ext corridors. **Pets:** Small, other species. $10 daily fee/pet. Service with restrictions, crate.

SAVE ✕ 🛢 💻 ⚓

Econo Lodge M
(601) 442-3686. **Call for rates.** 271 D'Evereaux Dr. Just n of jct US 61/84. Ext corridors. **Pets:** Medium. $10 daily fee/pet. Service with restrictions, crate.

✕ 🛢 💻

NEWTON

Days Inn M
(601) 683-3361. **$75-$85.** 261 Eastside Dr. I-20, exit 109, just s on SR 15. Ext corridors. **Pets:** Accepted.

ASK ✕ 🛢 💻 ⚓

OCEAN SPRINGS

Quality Inn Ocean Springs H
(228) 875-7555. **$70-$150.** 7304 Washington Ave. I-10, exit 50, 0.4 mi s on SR 609. Ext corridors. **Pets:** Medium, other species. $20 daily fee/room. Designated rooms, service with restrictions, crate.

ASK ✕ ⑤M 🛢 💻 ⚓

Ramada Limited H
(228) 872-2323. **$64-$159, 7 day notice.** 8011 Tucker Rd. I-10, exit 50, just n. Ext corridors. **Pets:** Accepted.

✕ 🛢 💻 ⚓

OLIVE BRANCH

Comfort Inn H
(662) 895-0456. **$84-$94.** 7049 Enterprise Dr. US 78, exit 2 (SR 302) just w. Int corridors. **Pets:** Accepted.

ASK ✕ 🛢 💻 ⚓

PASCAGOULA

LaFont Inn H
(228) 762-7111. **Call for rates.** 2703 Denny Ave. I-10, exit 69, 3.5 mi s on SR 63, then 2 mi w on US 90. Ext corridors. **Pets:** Accepted.

✕ 🛢 💻 🍴 ⚓ ✕

PEARL

Jameson Inn of Pearl H
(601) 932-6030. **$98-$105.** 434 Riverwind Dr. I-20, exit 48, just nw. Int corridors. **Pets:** Accepted.

ASK ✕ ⑤M 🛢 💻 ⚓

La Quinta Inn & Suites Jackson Airport (Pearl) H 🐾
(601) 664-0065. **$64-$109.** 501 S Pearson Rd. I-20, exit 48, just s. Int corridors. **Pets:** Medium, other species. Service with restrictions, supervision.

ASK ✕ 🛢 💻

PHILADELPHIA

Deluxe Inn & Suites H
(601) 656-0052. **Call for rates.** 1004 Central Dr. Jct SR 15 and 16. Ext corridors. **Pets:** Accepted.

✕ ⑤M 🛢 💻 ⚓

PICAYUNE

Days Inn H
(601) 799-1339. **Call for rates.** 450 S Lofton Ave. I-59, exit 4, just nw. Ext corridors. **Pets:** Accepted.

✕ 🛢 💻 ⚓

RICHLAND

Executive Inn & Suites H
(601) 664-3456. **$49-$59.** 390 Hwy 49 S. I-20, exit 47, just s. Ext corridors. **Pets:** Small, dogs only. $20 deposit/room. Service with restrictions, supervision.

ASK ✕ 🛢 💻 ⚓

RIDGELAND

Drury Inn & Suites-Jackson, MS H
(601) 956-6100. **$90-$149.** 610 E County Line Rd. I-55, exit 103 (County Line Rd), just w. Int corridors. **Pets:** Other species. Service with restrictions, supervision.

ASK ✕ ⑤M 🛢 💻 ⚓ ✕

Econo Lodge M
(601) 956-7740. **Call for rates.** 839 Ridgewood Rd. I-55, exit 103 (County Line Rd), just e, then just n. Ext corridors. **Pets:** Accepted.

✕ 🛢 💻

Homewood Suites by Hilton H
(601) 899-8611. **$102-$139.** 853 Centre St. I-55, exit 103 (County Line Rd), just e to Ridgewood Rd, 0.4 mi ne, then just e. Int corridors. **Pets:** Small, dogs only. $100 one-time fee/room. Supervision.

ASK ✕ ⑤M 🛢 💻 ⚓

▼▼ Quality Inn North H
(601) 956-6203. **Call for rates.** 839 Ridgewood Rd. I-55, exit 103 (County Line Rd), just ne. Ext corridors. **Pets:** Accepted.
⊠ 🖥 🛏 💻 ⊅

▼▼▼ Residence Inn by Marriott H ❀
(601) 206-7755. **$147-$158.** 855 Centre St. I-55, exit 103 (County Line Rd), just e to Ridgewood Rd, then just e. Int corridors. **Pets:** Medium, other species. $75 one-time fee/room. Service with restrictions, crate.
⊠ ᵬM 🛏 💻 ⊅ ⊠

RIPLEY

⚜⚜ ▼▼ Best Western Ripley M
(662) 837-0002. **$68-$72.** 922 City Ave S. Jct US 4 and 15, 0.5 mi s. Ext corridors. **Pets:** Accepted.
ⓈAVE ⊠ 🛏 💻 ⊅

SOUTHAVEN

▼▼▼ Residence Inn Memphis Southaven H
(662) 996-1500. **$147-$158.** 7165 Sleepy Hollow Dr. I-55, exit 289, just ne. Int corridors. **Pets:** Accepted.
⊠ 🛏 💻 ⊅

STARKVILLE

▼▼▼ Comfort Suites Starkville H
(662) 324-9595. **Call for rates.** 801 Russell St. 0.5 mi w of jct US 82 and SR 12. Int corridors. **Pets:** Accepted.
⊠ 🛏 💻 ⊅

⚜⚜ ▼▼ Days Inn & Suites H
(662) 324-5555. **$105-$125.** 119 Hwy 12 W. SR 12, 1.5 mi w of jct US 82. Ext corridors. **Pets:** Small. $25 daily fee/pet. Service with restrictions, supervision.
ⓈAVE ⊠ 🛏 💻 ⊅

TUNICA

▼ Key West Inn Tunica M
(662) 363-0021. **$50-$150.** 11635 Hwy 61 N. US 61, 0.3 mi n of SR 304. Ext corridors. **Pets:** Small, dogs only. $10 daily fee/pet. Service with restrictions, supervision.
ASK ⊠ 🛏 💻

TUPELO

▼▼ America's Best Inn M
(662) 842-4403. **Call for rates.** 897 Harmony Ln. US 45, exit Barnes Crossing, 0.5 mi sw, then just e. Ext corridors. **Pets:** Accepted.
⊠ ᵬM 🛏 💻 ⊅

▼▼ Baymont Inn & Suites H
(662) 844-7660. **Call for rates.** 625 Spicer Dr. On SR 145, 0.4 mi n of McCullough Blvd. Int corridors. **Pets:** Accepted.
⊠ ᵬM 🛏 💻 ⊠

▼▼ Comfort Inn H
(662) 842-5100. **$70-$77.** 1190 N Gloster St. Jct McCullough Blvd and SR 145, 1.3 mi s to McCullough Blvd, w to N Gloster St, then 0.3 mi n. Ext corridors. **Pets:** Small. $25 one-time fee/pet. Service with restrictions, crate.
ASK ⊠ 🛏 💻

⚜⚜ ▼▼ Days Inn M
(662) 842-0088. **$53-$95.** 1015 N Gloster St. Jct McCullough Blvd and SR 145, 1.3 mi s to McCullough Blvd, w to N Gloster St, then just n. Ext corridors. **Pets:** Small, dogs only. $20 one-time fee/room. Designated rooms, service with restrictions, crate.
ⓈAVE ⊠ ᵬM 🛏 💻

▼▼ Jameson Inn H
(662) 840-2380. **$83-$90.** 879 Mississippi Dr. US 45, exit Barnes Crossing, 1 mi sw. Ext corridors. **Pets:** Accepted.
ASK ⊠ 🛏 💻 ⊅

⚜⚜ ▼▼ Super 8 M
(662) 842-0448. **$55-$124.** 3898 McCullough Blvd. US 78, exit 81, just sw. Ext corridors. **Pets:** Medium, dogs only. $10 one-time fee/pet. Service with restrictions, supervision.
ⓈAVE ⊠ 🛏 💻 ⊅

VICKSBURG

▼▼▼ Annabelle Bed & Breakfast BB
(601) 638-2000. **$99-$195, 7 day notice.** 501 Speed St. I-20, exit 1A, 2.3 mi n on Washington St, just w. Ext/int corridors. **Pets:** Accepted.
⊠ 🛏 💻 ⊅

⚜⚜ ▼▼ Battlefield Inn H
(601) 638-5811. **$65-$79.** 4137 I-20 Frontage Rd. I-20, exit 4B, 1 mi ne. Ext/int corridors. **Pets:** Other species. $10 daily fee/pet. Service with restrictions.
ⓈAVE ⊠ 🛏 💻 🍴 ⊅ ⊠

⚜⚜ ▼▼▼ Cedar Grove Mansion CI
(601) 636-1000. **$100-$215, 3 day notice.** 2200 Oak St. I-20, exit 1A, 2.3 mi n on Washington St, then w on Klein St; to gated entrance. Ext/int corridors. **Pets:** Accepted.
ⓈAVE ⊠ 🛏 💻 🍴 ⊅

▼▼▼ Corners Mansion Bed & Breakfast Inn BB
(601) 636-7421. **$121-$209, 3 day notice.** 601 Klein St. I-20, exit 1A, 2.3 mi n on Washington St, then just w. Ext/int corridors. **Pets:** Accepted.
ASK ⊠ 🛏 💻

▼▼ Jameson Inn H
(601) 619-7799. **$93-$100.** 3975 S Frontage Rd. I-20, exit 4A, on southeast frontage road. Ext corridors. **Pets:** Very small. Service with restrictions, crate.
ASK ⊠ ᵬM 🛏 💻 ⊅

▼ Motel 6 #4189 H
(601) 638-5077. **Call for rates.** 4127 N Frontage Rd. I-20, exit 4B (Clay St), just ne. Int corridors. **Pets:** Other species. Service with restrictions, supervision.
⊠ ⊅

▼▼▼ Quality Inn & Suites M
(601) 636-0804. **$80-$155.** 3332 Clay St. I-20, exit 4B (Clay St), just n. Ext corridors. **Pets:** Other species. $15 one-time fee/room. Service with restrictions, supervision.
ASK ⊠ 🛏 💻 ⊅

▼▼ Travel Inn H
(601) 630-0100. **$45-$100.** 1675 N Frontage Rd. I-20, exit 1C, on northeast frontage road. Ext corridors. **Pets:** Small, dogs only. $20 daily fee/pet. Designated rooms, service with restrictions, supervision.
ASK ⊠ 🛏 ⊅

MISSOURI

AVA

▼▼ Ava Super 8 H
(417) 683-1343. **$70-$90.** 1711 S Jefferson St. Jct SR 5 S and 76; 1.5 mi s of SR 14. Int corridors. **Pets:** Other species. $10 one-time fee/room. Designated rooms, service with restrictions, supervision.
[ASK] [X] [&M] [H] [IP]

BETHANY

▼▼ Comfort Inn H
(660) 425-8006. **$75-$139.** 496 S 39th St. I-35, exit 92, just nw. Int corridors. **Pets:** Medium. $10 daily fee/pet. Designated rooms, service with restrictions, supervision.
[SAVE] [X] [H] [IP] [≈]

▼▼ Family Budget Inn M
(660) 425-7915. **$45-$54.** 4014 Miller St. I-35, exit 92. Int corridors. **Pets:** $5 daily fee/pet. Designated rooms, service with restrictions, supervision.
[SAVE] [X] [H] [≈]

BOONVILLE

▼ Boonville Comfort Inn H ☀
(660) 882-5317. **$49-$139.** 2427 Mid America Industrial Dr. I-70, exit 101, just sw. Int corridors. **Pets:** Small, dogs only. $10 daily fee/pet. Designated rooms, service with restrictions, supervision.
[SAVE] [X] [H] [IP] [≈]

BRANSON METROPOLITAN AREA

BRANSON

▼▼ AmazInn & Suites M
(417) 334-2300. **$50-$199.** 3311 Shepard of the Hills Expwy. Jct Gretna Rd (Blue Route), 1.1 mi e. Ext corridors. **Pets:** Small, other species. $10 daily fee/pet. Designated rooms, service with restrictions.
[SAVE] [X] [&M] [H] [≈]

▼▼ ▼▼ Chateau on the Lake Resort Spa & Convention Center H
(417) 334-1161. **$109-$354, 3 day notice.** 415 N State Hwy 265. Just n of jct SR 165 and 265. Int corridors. **Pets:** Small, dogs only. $25 one-time fee/room. Designated rooms, service with restrictions, crate.
[SAVE] [X] [&M] [H] [IP] [TI] [≈] [X]

▼▼ Dockers Inn M
(417) 334-3600. **$50-$79.** 3060 Green Mountain Dr. SR 376, 0.7 mi e on SR 76 (Country Music Blvd), just s. Ext corridors. **Pets:** Accepted.
[ASK] [X] [IP] [≈]

▼ Eagle's Lodge H
(417) 336-2666. **$45-$85.** 3221 Shepherd of the Hills Expy. 0.3 mi e of jct SR 76 (Country Music Blvd). Ext corridors. **Pets:** Accepted.
[SAVE] [X] [H] [IP] [≈]

▼▼ ▼▼ Fall Creek Inn & Suites H ☀
(417) 348-1683. **$39-$69.** 995 Hwy 165. Jct SR 76 (Country Music Blvd), 1.5 mi s on SR 165. Ext corridors. **Pets:** Medium, other species. $50 deposit/pet, $8 daily fee/pet. Designated rooms, service with restrictions.
[SAVE] [X] [H] [IP] [≈]

▼▼ Foxborough Inn & Suites M
(417) 335-4369. **$60-$90.** 235 Expressway Ln. US 65, exit Shepherd of the Hills Expwy, 2.3 mi w, just sw. Ext corridors. **Pets:** $25 one-time fee/pet. Designated rooms, no service, crate.
[ASK] [X] [&M] [H] [IP] [≈]

▼ Golden Arrow Resort M
(417) 338-2245. **$42-$154, 21 day notice.** 2869 Indian Point Rd. Jct SR 76 and 265, 0.6 mi w, then 2.8 mi s. Ext corridors. **Pets:** Medium. $10 daily fee/pet. Designated rooms, no service, crate.
[H] [IP] [≈] [X]

▼▼ Grand Crowne Resorts CO
(417) 332-8330. **$99-$619, 5 day notice.** 405 Hwy 165 S. Just sw of jct Wildwood Dr. Ext corridors. **Pets:** Accepted.
[ASK] [X] [&M] [H] [IP] [≈] [X]

▼▼ ▼▼ Hilton Branson Convention Center H ☀
(417) 336-5400. **$69-$229.** 200 E Main St. Main St; at Branson Landing Shopping Complex. Int corridors. **Pets:** Medium. $75 one-time fee/room. Designated rooms, service with restrictions, supervision.
[SAVE] [X] [&M] [H] [TI] [≈]

▼▼ Howard Johnson H
(417) 336-5151. **$73-$92.** 3027-A W Hwy 76. On SR 76 (Country Music Blvd), 3.5 mi w of jct US 65. Ext corridors. **Pets:** Accepted.
[ASK] [X] [H] [IP] [≈]

▼▼ La Quinta Inn Branson (Music City Centre) H ☀
(417) 332-1575. **$49-$110.** 1835 W Hwy 76. 1.6 mi w of jct US 65. Ext/int corridors. **Pets:** Medium, other species. Service with restrictions, supervision.
[SAVE] [X] [H] [IP] [≈] [X]

▼▼ Quality Inn & Suites on the Strip 🏨
(417) 334-1194. **$49-$99.** 2834 W Hwy 76. Jct US 65, 2 mi w. Ext corridors. **Pets:** Other species. $10 daily fee/room. Service with restrictions, crate.
ASK ✕ 🛄 💻 🏊

▼▼ Ramada Resort & Conference Center 🏨
(417) 334-1000. **$59-$109.** 1700 Hwy 76 W. Jct SR 76 (Country Music Blvd) and US 65, 1.5 mi w. Ext corridors. **Pets:** Accepted.
ASK ✕ 🛄 💻 🍴 🏊 ✕

▼▼ Residence Inn by Marriott 🏨
(417) 336-4077. **$89-$139.** 280 Wildwood Dr S. 2 mi w on SR 76 (Country Music Blvd), just s. Int corridors. **Pets:** Other species. $100 one-time fee/room. Service with restrictions, crate.
✕ 🛄M 🛄 💻 🏊 ✕

▼ Rock View Resort Ⓜ
(417) 334-4678. **$60-$98, 21 day notice.** 1049 Park View Dr. Jct US 65, 4.4 mi w on SR 165, 0.3 mi s via Dale Dr, then 0.7 mi w. Ext corridors. **Pets:** Medium. $8 daily fee/pet. No service, crate.
✕ 🛄 💻 🏊 ✕ 🎾

AAA ▼▼ Scenic Hills Inn 🏨 🐾
(417) 336-8855. **$45-$120.** 2422 Shepherd of the Hills Expwy. Jct SR 76 (Country Music Blvd), 1.1 mi e. Int corridors. **Pets:** Medium, other species. $10 daily fee/room. Designated rooms, service with restrictions.
SAVE ✕ 🛄 💻 🏊

AAA ▼▼ Settle Inn Resort & Conference Center 🏨
(417) 335-4700. **$69-$119.** 3050 Green Mountain Dr. Jct SR 76 (Country Music Blvd) and US 65, 3 mi w on SR 76, 0.8 mi s. Int corridors. **Pets:** $12 daily fee/pet. Designated rooms, service with restrictions, supervision.
SAVE ✕ 🛄 💻 🏊 ✕

▼▼ Super 8 Central of Branson 🏨
(417) 336-3300. **$45-$80.** 3490 Keeter St. SR 76, just s; w of Gretna Rd (SR 165). Ext corridors. **Pets:** Very small.
ASK ✕ 🛄M 🛄 💻 🏊

AAA ▼▼▼ The Village At Indian Point Ⓒ
(417) 338-8800. **$100-$245.** 24 Village Tr. 2.5 mi s of jct SR 76 on Indian Point Rd. Ext corridors. **Pets:** Medium, dogs only. $10 daily fee/room. Designated rooms, no service, supervision.
SAVE ✕ 🛄 💻 🏊 ✕

AAA ▼▼▼ Westgate Branson Woods Resort Ⓒ
(417) 334-2324. **$59-$149, 7 day notice.** 2201 Roark Valley Rd. US 65, exit SR 248 (Shepherd of the Hills Expwy), 3.7 mi w, just n. Ext corridors. **Pets:** Accepted.
SAVE ✕ 🛄 💻 🏊 ✕

BRANSON WEST

AAA ▼▼▼ StoneBridge Resort Ⓒ
(417) 332-1373. **$69-$599, 7 day notice.** 50 Stonebridge Pkwy. 1.9 mi w of jct SR 76 and 265. Ext corridors. **Pets:** Accepted.
SAVE ✕ 🛄 💻 🍴 🏊 ✕

HOLLISTER

AAA ▼▼▼ Westgate Branson Lakes at Emerald Pointe Ⓒ
(417) 334-4944. **$59-$209, 7 day notice.** 750 Emerald Pointe Dr. Jct US 65 and SR 265, 1 mi w to Hill Haven Rd, then 2 mi s. Ext corridors. **Pets:** Accepted.
SAVE ✕ 🛄M 🛄 💻 🏊 ✕

END METROPOLITAN AREA

BROOKFIELD

AAA ▼▼ Best Western Brookfield 🏨
(660) 258-4900. **$87-$95.** 28622 Hwy 11. US 36, exit Business Rt 36, just se. Int corridors. **Pets:** $25 daily fee/room. Designated rooms, service with restrictions.
SAVE ✕ 🛄M 🛄 💻 🏊

CAMERON

AAA ▼▼ Best Western Acorn Inn Ⓜ
(816) 632-2187. **$79-$90.** 2210 E US 36. I-35, exit 54, 0.3 mi e. Ext corridors. **Pets:** Other species. Service with restrictions, supervision.
SAVE ✕ 🛄 💻 🏊

AAA ▼▼ Comfort Inn 🏨
(816) 632-5655. **$84-$129.** 1803 Comfort Ln. I-35, exit 54, just e. Int corridors. **Pets:** Other species. $25 deposit/room. Designated rooms, service with restrictions, supervision.
SAVE ✕ 🛄M 🛄 💻 🏊 ✕

AAA ▼▼ Econo Lodge 🏨 🐾
(816) 632-6571. **$60-$79.** 220 E Grand. I-35, exit 54, 0.5 mi w on US 36, then just s on US 69. Ext corridors. **Pets:** Medium. $110 daily fee/pet. Designated rooms, service with restrictions, supervision.
SAVE ✕ 🛄 🏊

▼ Super 8 🏨
(816) 632-8888. **$62-$78.** 1710 N Walnut St. I-35, exit 54, 0.5 mi w on US 36. Int corridors. **Pets:** Small. $10 one-time fee/pet. Designated rooms, service with restrictions, supervision.
ASK ✕ 🛄 💻 🏊

CANTON

▼▼ Comfort Inn Canton 🏨
(573) 288-8800. **$69-$89.** 1701 Oak St. US 61, exit US 61 business route/CR P, just e. Int corridors. **Pets:** Accepted.
ASK ✕ 🛄 💻 🏊

CAPE GIRARDEAU

▼▼▼ Drury Lodge-Cape Girardeau 🏨
(573) 334-7151. **$85-$120.** 104 S Vantage Dr. I-55, exit 96 (William St), just e. Ext/int corridors. **Pets:** Other species. Service with restrictions, supervision.
ASK ✕ 🛄 💻 🍴 🏊

▼▼▼ Drury Suites-Cape Girardeau 🏨
(573) 339-9500. **$95-$135.** 3303 Campster Dr. I-55, exit 96 (William St), just w. Int corridors. **Pets:** Other species. Service with restrictions, supervision.
ASK ✕ 🛄M 🛄 💻 🏊

▼▼ Hampton Inn-Cape Girardeau 🏨
(573) 651-3000. **$81.** 103 Cape W Pkwy. I-55, exit 96 (William St), 0.3 mi sw. Int corridors. **Pets:** Accepted.
✕ 🛄M 🛄 💻

▼ Pear Tree Inn by Drury-Cape Girardeau 🏨
(573) 334-3000. **$70-$95.** 3248 William St. I-55, exit 96 (William St), just e. Int corridors. **Pets:** Other species. Service with restrictions, supervision.
ASK ✕ 🛄 💻 🏊

▼ Victorian Inn & Suites 🏨
(573) 651-4486. **$60-$109.** 3265 William St. I-55, exit 96 (William St), just e. Ext/int corridors. **Pets:** Medium, other species. $50 deposit/pet. Service with restrictions, crate.
ASK ✕ 🛄M 🛄 💻 🏊 ✕

CARTHAGE

AAA **▼▼▼** Best Western Precious Moments
Hotel 🅷 ❀
(417) 359-5900. **$72-$132.** 2701 Hazel St. Just e of jct US 71 and SR HH. Int corridors. **Pets:** Medium, dogs only. $10 daily fee/room. Service with restrictions, crate.
[SAVE] [✕] 🛢 💻 🥢

AAA **▼▼▼** Econo Lodge 🅷
(417) 358-3900. **$56-$149.** 1441 W Central. On SR 96; jct US 71. Ext/int corridors. **Pets:** Accepted.
[SAVE] [✕] 🛢 🥢

AAA **▼▼▼** Super 8 🅷
(417) 359-9000. **Call for rates.** 416 W Fir Rd. Just e of jct US 71 and SR HH. Int corridors. **Pets:** Accepted.
[SAVE] [✕]

CHILLICOTHE

AAA **▼▼▼** Best Western Inn 🅷
(660) 646-0572. **$60-$80, 14 day notice.** 1020 S Washington St. Jct US 36 and 65 (Washington St). Ext/int corridors. **Pets:** $10 one-time fee/pet. Designated rooms, service with restrictions.
[SAVE] [✕] [♿M] 🛢 💻 🥢

▼▼ Chillicothe Super 8 Motel 🅷
(660) 646-7888. **$59-$72.** 580 Old Hwy 36 E. Jct US 36 and 65 (Washington St), 0.8 mi e. Int corridors. **Pets:** Medium. $10 daily fee/pet. Service with restrictions, supervision.
[ASK] [✕] 🛢 💻

CLINTON

AAA **▼▼▼** Best Western Colonial Motel 🅼
(660) 885-2206. **$59-$69.** 106 S Baird St. Jct SR 7 and 13. Ext corridors. **Pets:** Medium, dogs only. $10 daily fee/pet. Designated rooms, service with restrictions, supervision.
[SAVE] [✕] 🛢 💻 🏊

AAA **▼▼** Motel USA Inn 🅼
(660) 885-2267. **$35-$55.** 1508 N 2nd St. Jct SR 7 and 13. Ext corridors. **Pets:** Small, dogs only. $10 daily fee/pet. Designated rooms, service with restrictions, supervision.
[SAVE] [✕] 🛢

COLUMBIA

AAA **▼▼▼** Best Western Columbia Inn 🅷
(573) 474-6161. **$70-$120.** 3100 I-70 Dr SE. I-70, exit 128A, just s, then just e. Int corridors. **Pets:** Other species. $10 daily fee/room. Designated rooms, service with restrictions.
[SAVE] [✕] [♿M] 🛢 💻 🥢

▼▼▼ Candlewood Suites 🅷
(573) 817-0525. **$99-$129, 13 day notice.** 3100 Wingate Ct. I-70, exit 128A, just s on US 63, just e on I-70 Dr SE, then just s on Keene St. Int corridors. **Pets:** Accepted.
[ASK] [✕] [♿M] 🛢 💻

▼▼▼ Drury Inn-Columbia 🅷
(573) 445-1800. **$86-$155.** 1000 Knipp St. I-70, exit 124 (Stadium Blvd), just s. Int corridors. **Pets:** Other species. Service with restrictions, supervision.
[ASK] [✕] 🛢 💻 🥢

▼▼ Extended StayAmerica-Columbia-Stadium Blvd 🅷
(573) 445-6800. **$54-$124.** 2000 W Business Loop 70. I-70, exit 124 (Stadium Blvd), just ne. Int corridors. **Pets:** Other species. $25 daily fee/pet. Service with restrictions, crate.
[ASK] [✕] 🛢 💻

▼▼ Super 8-Clark Lane in Columbia 🅼 ❀
(573) 474-8488. **$57-$104.** 3216 Clark Ln. I-70, exit 128A, northeast corner. Int corridors. **Pets:** Small. $15 daily fee/pet. Service with restrictions, supervision.
[ASK] [✕] 🛢 💻

CUBA

AAA **▼▼▼** Best Western Cuba Inn 🅼
(573) 885-7707. **Call for rates.** 246 Hwy P. I-44, exit 208, just n on SR 19, then just e. Ext corridors. **Pets:** Small. $10 one-time fee/pet. Designated rooms, service with restrictions, supervision.
[SAVE] [✕] 🛢 💻 🥢

▼▼▼ Super 8 🅼
(573) 885-2087. **Call for rates.** 28 Hwy P. I-44, exit 208 (SR 19), just n, then just w. Ext/int corridors. **Pets:** $20 one-time fee/pet. Designated rooms, service with restrictions, supervision.
[✕] 🛢 💻

FESTUS

▼▼ Comfort Inn Festus 🅷
(636) 937-2888. **Call for rates.** 1303 Veterans Blvd. I-55, exit 175, just w. Int corridors. **Pets:** Accepted.
[✕] 🛢 💻

▼▼ Drury Inn-Festus 🅷
(636) 933-2400. **$75-$125.** 1001 Veterans Blvd. I-55, exit 175, just e. Int corridors. **Pets:** Other species. Service with restrictions, supervision.
[ASK] [✕] 🛢 💻 🥢

FULTON

▼▼▼ Loganberry Inn Bed & Breakfast 🅱🅱 ❀
(573) 642-9229. **$99-$189, 14 day notice.** 310 W 7th St. Jct US 54, exit CR F, 1 mi e, just n to Westminster, then just e. Int corridors. **Pets:** Large, dogs only. $10 one-time fee/pet. Designated rooms, service with restrictions, crate.
[ASK] [✕] 🛢 💻

HANNIBAL

AAA **▼▼▼** Quality Inn & Suites 🅷
(573) 221-4001. **$79-$129.** 120 Lindsey Dr. 2 mi w on US 36, exit Shinn Ln to south service road, then 0.6 mi e. Int corridors. **Pets:** Small. $10 daily fee/pet. Designated rooms, service with restrictions, supervision.
[SAVE] [✕] 🛢 💻 🥢 [✕]

▼▼▼ Super 8 Motel 🅼
(573) 221-5863. **$55-$120.** 120 Huckleberry Heights Dr. Jct US 36, 1.5 mi s on US 61. Int corridors. **Pets:** Accepted.
[ASK] [✕] 🛢 💻 🥢

HARRISONVILLE

AAA **▼▼▼** Harrisonville Inn & Suites 🅼
(816) 884-3200. **$55-$98.** 2201 Rockhaven Rd. Just n of jct US 71 and SR 291. Ext corridors. **Pets:** Very small. $10 daily fee/pet. Designated rooms, service with restrictions, supervision.
[SAVE] [✕] 🛢 💻 🥢

HAYTI

▼▼ Drury Inn & Suites-Hayti Caruthersville 🅷
(573) 359-2702. **$70-$115.** 1317 Hwy 84. I-55, exit 19 (US 412/SR 84), just w. Int corridors. **Pets:** Other species. Service with restrictions, supervision.
[ASK] [✕] 🛢 💻 🥢

HIGGINSVILLE

▼▼ Super 8-Higginsville 🅷
(660) 584-7781. **Call for rates.** 6471 Oakview Ln. I-70, exit 49 (SR 13), just se. Int corridors. **Pets:** Accepted.
[✕] 🛢 💻

JACKSON

▼▼▼▼ **Drury Inn & Suites-Jackson, MO** 🅗
(573) 243-9200. **$75-$115.** 225 Drury Ln. I-55, exit 105 (SR 61), 0.3 mi w.
Int corridors. **Pets:** Other species. Service with restrictions, supervision.
A$K ⊠ &M 🖬 ▦ 🌊

JANE

▼▼ **Booneslick Lodge** 🅗
(417) 226-1888. **$64-$79.** 21140 US Hwy 71. Just s on US 71. Int corridors. **Pets:** $10 one-time fee/pet. Designated rooms, service with restric-
tions, supervision.
A$K ⊠ 🖬 🌊

JEFFERSON CITY

🐾 ▼▼▼▼ **Capitol Plaza Hotel and Convention Center** 🅗
(573) 635-1234. **$129-$139.** 415 W McCarthy St. On US 50 and 63 S, just
e of jct US 54. Int corridors. **Pets:** Other species. $20 one-time fee/room.
Service with restrictions.
SAVE ⊠ &M 🖬 ▦ 🍴 🌊 🐾

▼▼ **Super 8 Motel-Jefferson City** 🅗
(573) 636-5456. **$50-$89.** 1710 Jefferson St. US 54, exit Ellis Blvd, 0.3 mi
nw on frontage road. Int corridors. **Pets:** $10 daily fee/pet. Designated
rooms, no service, supervision.
A$K ⊠ 🖬 ▦

🐾 ▼▼ **Truman Hotel & Conference Center** 🅗
(573) 635-7171. **$80-$92.** 1510 Jefferson St. US 54, exit Ellis Blvd, 0.5 mi
nw. Ext/int corridors. **Pets:** Accepted.
SAVE ⊠ 🖬 ▦ 🍴 🌊

JOPLIN

🐾 ▼▼ **Best Western Oasis Inn & Suites** 🅗
(417) 781-6776. **$69-$99, 3 day notice.** 3508 S Range Line Rd. I-44, exit
8B, just nw. Ext corridors. **Pets:** $10 daily fee/pet. Designated rooms,
service with restrictions, crate.
SAVE ⊠ 🖬 ▦ 🌊

🐾 ▼▼▼▼ **Candlewood Suites** 🅗 ❀
(417) 623-9595. **$89-$129.** 3512 S Range Line Rd. I-44, exit 8B, just nw.
Int corridors. **Pets:** Large, other species. $75 one-time fee/room. Service
with restrictions, crate.
SAVE ⊠ &M 🖬 ▦

▼▼▼▼ **Drury Inn & Suites-Joplin** 🅗
(417) 781-8000. **$85-$140.** 3601 Range Line Rd. I-44, exit 8B, just ne. Int
corridors. **Pets:** Other species. Service with restrictions, supervision.
A$K ⊠ &M 🖬 ▦ 🌊 🐾

🐾 ▼▼▼▼ **Holiday Inn** 🅗 ❀
(417) 782-1000. **$75-$149.** 3615 Range Line Rd. I-44, exit 8B, just ne. Int
corridors. **Pets:** Large, other species. $25 deposit/room. Service with
restrictions, supervision.
SAVE ⊠ 🖬 ▦ 🍴 🌊 🐾

▼▼▼▼ **La Quinta Inn** 🅗 ❀
(417) 781-0500. **Call for rates.** 3320 S Range Line Rd. I-40, exit 8B, just
n. Int corridors. **Pets:** Medium, other species. Service with restrictions,
supervision.
⊠ 🖬 ▦ 🌊

🐾 ▼▼▼▼ **Residence Inn by Marriott-Joplin** 🅗 ❀
(417) 782-0908. **$119-$129.** 3128 E Hammons Blvd. I-44, exit 8B, just ne.
Int corridors. **Pets:** Large, other species. $75 one-time fee/room. Service
with restrictions, supervision.
SAVE ⊠ &M 🖬 ▦ 🌊 🐾

🐾 ▼▼▼ **Sleep Inn** 🅗
(417) 782-1212. **Call for rates.** 4100 Hwy 43 S. I-44, exit 4, just s. Int
corridors. **Pets:** Accepted.
SAVE ⊠ ▦

▼▼▼▼ **TownPlace Suites By Marriott Joplin** 🅗
(417) 659-8111. **$80-$98.** 4026 Arizona Ave. I-44, exit 8A, just sw. Int
corridors. **Pets:** Accepted.
⊠ &M 🖬 ▦ 🌊

KANSAS CITY METROPOLITAN AREA

BLUE SPRINGS

▼▼▼▼ **Hampton Inn Blue Springs** 🅗 ❀
(816) 220-3844. **$89-$119.** 900 NW South Outer Rd. I-70, exit 20, just s on
SR 7, then just w. Int corridors. **Pets:** Other species. Service with restrictions, supervision.
⊠ 🖬 ▦ 🌊

INDEPENDENCE

🐾 ▼▼▼ **Best Western Truman Inn** 🅜
(816) 254-0100. **$50-$110.** 4048 S Lynn Court Dr. I-70, exit 12, just n on
Noland Rd, then just w. Ext corridors. **Pets:** Medium, other species. $10
daily fee/pet. Supervision.
SAVE ⊠ 🖬 ▦ 🌊

🐾 ▼▼▼▼ **Comfort Suites** 🅗 ❀
(816) 373-9880. **$79-$139.** 19751 E Valley View Pkwy. I-70, exit 17, just s
on Little Blue Pkwy, then just w. Int corridors. **Pets:** Medium, other species.
$25 one-time fee/room. Service with restrictions, supervision.
SAVE ⊠ &M 🖬 ▦ 🌊

🐾 ▼▼▼ **Holiday Inn Express Hotel & Suites** 🅗 ❀
(816) 795-8889. **$99-$149.** 19901 E Valley View Pkwy. I-70, exit 17 (Little
Blue Pkwy), just e, then w on E Valley View Pkwy (Eastland Business
Park). Int corridors. **Pets:** Large, other species. $25 one-time fee/room.
Service with restrictions, supervision.
SAVE ⊠ &M 🖬 ▦ 🌊

🐾 ▼▼▼ **Super 8 Independence** 🅗
(816) 833-1888. **$40-$100.** 4032 S Lynn Court Dr. I-70, exit 12, just n on
Noland Rd, then just w. Int corridors. **Pets:** Medium, other species. $10
daily fee/pet. Supervision.
SAVE ⊠ 🖬 ▦ 🌊

KANSAS CITY

🐾 ▼▼▼ **Best Western Country Inn–KCI Airport** 🅗
(816) 464-2002. **$60-$90, 3 day notice.** 11900 NW Plaza Cir. I-29, exit
13, just e on Rt D, then just s. Ext corridors. **Pets:** Small, dogs only. $10
deposit/pet. Service with restrictions, supervision.
SAVE ⊠ 🖬 ▦

🐾 ▼▼▼▼ **Best Western Country Inn-North** 🅜
(816) 459-7222. **$50-$150.** 2633 NE 43rd St. I-35, exit 8C (Antioch Rd),
just s on SR 1, then just e. Ext corridors. **Pets:** Small. $10 daily fee/pet.
Designated rooms, service with restrictions, supervision.
SAVE ⊠ 🖬 ▦ 🌊

🐾 ▼▼▼▼ **Chase Suites by Woodfin** 🅗
(816) 891-9009. **$99-$129.** 9900 NW Prairie View Rd. I-29, exit 10, just w,
then just n. Ext corridors. **Pets:** Accepted.
SAVE ⊠ 🖬 ▦ 🌊 🐾

▼▼▼▼ **Drury Inn & Suites-Kansas City Airport** H
(816) 880-9700. **$70-$165.** 7900 NW Tiffany Springs Pkwy. I-29, exit 10, just w. Int corridors. **Pets:** Other species. Service with restrictions, supervision.

ASK ⊠ ⅂M 🛏 💻 ➔ ⊠

▼▼▼▼ **Drury Inn & Suites-Kansas City Stadium** H
(816) 923-3000. **$74-$139.** 3830 Blue Ridge Cutoff. I-70, exit 9 (Blue Ridge Cutoff), just nw. Int corridors. **Pets:** Other species. Service with restrictions, supervision.

ASK ⊠ ⅂M 🛏 💻 ➔

⚬⚬⚬ ▼▼▼▼ **Embassy Suites Hotel KCI Airport** H
(816) 891-7788. **$119-$209.** 7640 NW Tiffany Springs Pkwy. I-29, exit 10, just e. Int corridors. **Pets:** Accepted.

SAVE ⊠ ⅂M 🛏 💻 ⁌ ➔ ⊠

▼ **Extended StayAmerica-Kansas City Airport** H
(816) 270-7829. **$59-$129.** 11712 NW Plaza Cir. I-29, exit 13, just e on CR D, just s on Ambassador Dr, then just w. Int corridors. **Pets:** Other species. $25 daily fee/pet. Service with restrictions, crate.

ASK ⊠ 🛏 💻

▼ **Extended StayAmerica-Kansas City South** H
(816) 943-1315. **$59-$109.** 550 E 105th St. I-435, exit 74, just s on Holmes Rd, then just w. Int corridors. **Pets:** Other species. $25 daily fee/pet. Service with restrictions, crate.

ASK ⊠ 🛏 💻

⚬⚬⚬ ▼▼▼▼ **Four Points by Sheraton Kansas City Airport** H ✿
(816) 464-2345. **$75-$195, 3 day notice.** 11832 NW Plaza Cir. I-29, exit 13, e on CR D, just s on Ambassador Dr, then just w. Int corridors. **Pets:** Small, other species. $25 deposit/pet. Service with restrictions, supervision.

SAVE ⊠ ⅂M 🛏 💻 ⁌ ➔

⚬⚬⚬ ▼▼▼▼ **Hilton Kansas City Airport** H
(816) 891-8900. **$99-$199.** 8801 NW 112th St. I-29, exit 12, just se. Int corridors. **Pets:** Accepted.

SAVE ⊠ ⅂M 🛏 💻 ⁌ ➔ ⊠

▼▼▼ **Holiday Inn At The Plaza, Kansas City** H
(816) 753-7400. **Call for rates.** One E 45th St. Jct Main St; in Country Club Plaza. Int corridors. **Pets:** Accepted.

⊠ ⅂M 🛏 💻 ⁌ ➔

▼▼▼ **Holiday Inn Express Westport** H
(816) 931-1000. **Call for rates.** 801 Westport Rd. Jct Main St, 0.5 mi w; in Westport Plaza area. Int corridors. **Pets:** Accepted.

⊠ ⅂M 🛏 💻

⚬⚬⚬ ▼▼▼▼ **Holiday Inn Kansas City Northeast** H ✿
(816) 455-1060. **$89-$127.** 7333 NE Parvin Rd. I-435, exit 54, just w. Int corridors. **Pets:** Other species. $20 daily fee/room. Service with restrictions, crate.

SAVE ⊠ ⅂M 🛏 💻 ⁌ ➔ ⊠

⚬⚬⚬ ▼▼▼▼ **Holiday Inn KCI & Expo Center** H
(816) 801-8400. **$89-$149.** 11728 N Ambassador Dr. I-29, exit 13, just e on CR D, then just s. Int corridors. **Pets:** Small. $35 one-time fee/room. Service with restrictions, supervision.

SAVE ⊠ ⅂M 🛏 💻 ⁌ ➔

▼▼▼ **Holiday Inn-Sports Complex** H
(816) 353-5300. **$72-$170.** 4011 Blue Ridge Cutoff. I-70, exit 9 (Blue Ridge Cutoff), just se. Int corridors. **Pets:** Accepted.

ASK ⊠ ⅂M 🛏 💻 ⁌ ➔

▼▼ **Homestead Studio Suites Hotel-Kansas City/Country Club Plaza** H
(816) 531-2212. **$89-$139.** 4535 Main St. Jct 45th St, just s; just ne of Country Club Plaza. Int corridors. **Pets:** Other species. $25 daily fee/pet. Service with restrictions, crate.

ASK ⊠ ⅂M 🛏 💻

⚬⚬⚬ ▼▼▼▼ **Homewood Suites by Hilton** H
(816) 880-9880. **$99-$159.** 7312 NW Polo Dr. I-29, exit 10, just e. Int corridors. **Pets:** $50 one-time fee/pet. Service with restrictions.

SAVE ⊠ 🛏 💻 ➔ ⊠

⚬⚬⚬ ▼▼▼ ▼▼▼ **Hotel Phillips** H
(816) 221-7000. **$169-$269.** 106 W 12th St. Jct Wyandotte St, just e. Int corridors. **Pets:** Accepted.

SAVE ⊠ 💻 ⁌

⚬⚬⚬ ▼▼▼ ▼▼▼ **The InterContinental Kansas City at the Plaza** H ✿
(816) 756-1500. **$149-$449.** 401 Ward Pkwy. Jct Wornall Rd; in Country Club Plaza. Int corridors. **Pets:** Small. $100 one-time fee/pet. Service with restrictions, crate.

SAVE ⊠ 💻 ⁌ ➔ ⊠

▼▼▼ **La Quinta Inn & Suites–Northeast** H ✿
(816) 483-7900. **$72-$92.** 1051 N Cambridge Ave. I-435, exit 57, just w, then just s. Int corridors. **Pets:** Medium, other species. Service with restrictions, supervision.

ASK ⊠ 🛏 💻 ➔ ⊠

⚬⚬⚬ ▼▼ ▼▼ **Microtel Inn & Suites** H
(816) 270-1200. **$55-$65.** 11831 NW Plaza Cir. I-29, exit 13, just e on CR D, then just s. Int corridors. **Pets:** Accepted.

SAVE ⊠ 🛏 💻

▼▼▼ **Q Hotel & Spa** H
(816) 931-0001. **Call for rates.** 560 Westport Rd. Jct Main St, 0.4 mi w; in Westport Plaza area. Int corridors. **Pets:** Accepted.

⊠ 🛏 💻

▼▼▼ **Radisson Hotel Kansas City Airport** H
(816) 464-2423. **Call for rates.** 11828 NW Plaza Cir. I-29, exit 13, just e on CR D, just s on Ambassador Dr, then just w. Int corridors. **Pets:** Accepted.

⊠ ⅂M 🛏 💻 ⁌ ➔

▼▼ **Red Roof Inn-North-Worlds of Fun** M
(816) 452-8585. **$43-$100.** 3636 NE Randolph Rd. I-435, exit 55B northbound; exit 55 southbound, just e on SR 210, then just n. Ext corridors. **Pets:** Accepted.

ASK ⊠ ⅂M

▼▼▼ **Residence Inn by Marriott Downtown/Union Hill** H
(816) 561-3000. **$143-$175.** 2975 Main St. Jct 31st St, just n. Ext corridors. **Pets:** Large. $100 one-time fee/room. Service with restrictions.

⊠ 🛏 💻 ➔

⚬⚬⚬ ▼▼▼ ▼▼ **Residence Inn by Marriott, Kansas City Airport** H
(816) 741-2300. **$161-$197.** 10300 N Ambassador Dr. I-29, exit 10, just ne, then 1.5 mi. Int corridors. **Pets:** Medium, other species. $75 one-time fee/room. Designated rooms, service with restrictions.

SAVE ⊠ ⅂M 🛏 💻 ➔ ⊠

▼▼▼ **Residence Inn by Marriott Kansas City Country Club Plaza** H
(816) 753-0033. **$189-$209.** 4601 Broadway Blvd. Jct JC Nichols Pkwy, just w on 46th Terr; in Country Club Plaza. Int corridors. **Pets:** Small. $100 one-time fee/room. Service with restrictions, crate.

⊠ 🛏 💻 ➔ ⊠

⚬⚬⚬ ▼▼▼ ▼▼ **Sheraton Kansas City Sports Complex Hotel** H ✿
(816) 737-0200. **Call for rates.** 9103 E 39th St. I-70, exit 9 (Blue Ridge Cutoff), just ne. Int corridors. **Pets:** Large, dogs only. $75 deposit/room. Service with restrictions.

SAVE ⊠ 💻 ⁌ ➔ ⊠

(AAA) ▼▼▼ Sheraton Suites Country Club Plaza H ❀
(816) 931-4400. **$129-$400.** 770 W 47th St. Jct Summit St; in Country Club Plaza. Int corridors. **Pets:** Medium, dogs only. Service with restrictions, crate.
SAVE ✕ ⬥M ⊟ ▣ ❚❙ ⊃

(AAA) ▼▼▼ ▼▼▼ The Westin Crown Center H ❀
(816) 474-4400. **$129-$329.** 1 E Pershing Rd. 0.5 mi s. Int corridors. **Pets:** Medium. $25 one-time fee/room. Service with restrictions, supervision.
SAVE ✕ ⬥M ▣ ❚❙ ⊃ ✕

KEARNEY

▼▼ Kearney Inn H
(816) 628-5000. **Call for rates.** 601 Centerville Ave. I-35, exit 26, just w. Int corridors. **Pets:** Other species. $10 daily fee/pet. Designated rooms, supervision.
✕ ⊟ ▣ ⊃

▼▼ Kearney Super 8 Motel H ❀
(816) 628-6800. **$60-$90.** 210 Platte Clay Way. I-35, exit 26, just e on SR 92, then just n. Int corridors. **Pets:** Dogs only. $10 daily fee/pet. Designated rooms, service with restrictions, supervision.
ASK ✕ ⊟ ▣

LEE'S SUMMIT

▼▼ Comfort Inn by Choice Hotels H
(816) 524-8181. **Call for rates.** 607 SE Oldham Pkwy. Jct US 50 and SR 291 N. Int corridors. **Pets:** Medium. $25 one-time fee/pet. No service, crate.
✕ ⬥M ⊟ ▣ ⊃

(AAA) ▼▼▼ Lee's Summit Holiday Inn Express H
(816) 795-6400. **Call for rates.** 4825 NE Lakewood Way. I-470, exit 14, just e on Bowlin Rd, then 0.4 mi s. Int corridors. **Pets:** Small. $25 one-time fee/pet. Service with restrictions, crate.
SAVE ✕ ⬥M ⊟ ▣ ⊃

NORTH KANSAS CITY

▼▼ La Quinta Inn Kansas City North H ❀
(816) 221-1200. **$69-$99.** 2214 Taney Rd. I-29/35, exit 6A, just e on SR 210, then just n. Int corridors. **Pets:** Medium, other species. Service with restrictions, supervision.
ASK ✕ ⊟ ▣

OAK GROVE (JACKSON COUNTY)

(AAA) ▼▼ Econo Lodge M
(816) 690-3681. **$59-$89.** 410 SE 1st St. I-70, exit 28, just s on Broadway St, just e on SE 4th St, then just n. Ext corridors. **Pets:** Small. $10 daily fee/pet. Service with restrictions, supervision.
SAVE ✕ ⊟

PLATTE CITY

(AAA) ▼▼▼ Best Western Airport Inn & Suites KCI North H
(816) 858-0200. **$73-$100.** 2512 NW Prairie View Rd. I-29, exit 18, just e, then just s. Int corridors. **Pets:** Small, other species. $25 one-time fee/room. Designated rooms, service with restrictions, supervision.
SAVE ✕ ⬥M ⊟ ▣ ⊃ ✕

END METROPOLITAN AREA

KIRKSVILLE

▼▼ Super 8 Motel-Kirksville M
(660) 665-8826. **$56-$73.** 1101 Country Club Dr. On US 63 and SR 6. Int corridors. **Pets:** Other species. $10 daily fee/pet. Designated rooms, service with restrictions, supervision.
ASK ✕ ⊟ ▣

LAMAR

▼▼ Super 8-Lamar H
(417) 682-6888. **Call for rates.** 45 SE 1st Ln. Jct US 71 and 160. Int corridors. **Pets:** Accepted.
✕ ⊟ ▣ ⊃

LEBANON

(AAA) ▼▼ Best Western Wyota Inn H
(417) 532-6171. **$73-$103.** 1221 Mill Creek Rd. I-44, exit 130, just nw. Ext corridors. **Pets:** Small. $15 daily fee/room. Designated rooms, service with restrictions, crate.
SAVE ✕ ⊟ ▣ ⊃

▼▼ Holiday Inn Express H
(417) 532-1111. **$95-$110.** 1955 W Elm St. I-44, exit 127, just n. Int corridors. **Pets:** Accepted.
ASK ✕ ⊟ ▣ ⊃

LICKING

▼▼ Scenic Rivers Inn M
(573) 674-4809. **$54-$60.** 209 S Hwy 63. On US 63. Ext corridors. **Pets:** Medium. $10 daily fee/pet. Designated rooms, service with restrictions, supervision.
ASK ✕ ⊟ ▣ ⊃

MACON

▼▼ Super 8 Motel H
(660) 385-5788. **$64.** 203 E Briggs Dr. Jct US 36 and 63. Int corridors. **Pets:** Other species. $10 daily fee/pet. Service with restrictions, supervision.
ASK ✕ ⊟ ▣

MARSHFIELD

▼▼ Holiday Inn Express H
(417) 859-6000. **$89-$109, 7 day notice.** 1301 Banning St. I-44, exit 100 (SR 38), on southeast corner. Int corridors. **Pets:** Medium. $25 one-time fee/pet. Service with restrictions, supervision.
ASK ✕ ⬥M ⊟ ▣ ⊃

MARYVILLE

▼▼ Super 8 H
(660) 582-8088. **$55-$61.** 222 Summit Dr. On Business Rt US 71; just n of US 71 Bypass. Int corridors. **Pets:** Other species. $25 deposit/pet. Service with restrictions, supervision.
ASK ✕ ⊟ ▣

MINER

(AAA) ▼▼▼ Best Western Coach House Inn H
(573) 471-9700. **$80-$110.** 220 S Interstate Dr. I-55, exit 67, just ne. Int corridors. **Pets:** Small. $25 one-time fee/room. Designated rooms, service with restrictions, supervision.
SAVE ✕ ⬥M ⊟ ▣ ⊃

▼▼ Drury Inn-Sikeston H
(573) 471-4100. **$80-$122.** 2602 E Malone Ave. I-55, exit 67, just sw. Int corridors. **Pets:** Other species. Service with restrictions, supervision.
ASK ✕ ⬥M ⊟ ▣ ⊃

▼▼ **Pear Tree Inn by Drury-Sikeston** H
(573) 471-8660. **$60-$84.** 2602 E Malone Ave. I-55, exit 67, just sw. Ext corridors. **Pets:** Other species. Service with restrictions, supervision.
[ASK] [X] [&M] [■] [≈]

MOUNTAIN GROVE

▼ **Days Inn of Mountain Grove** H
(417) 926-5555. **$56-$59.** 300 E 19th St. Jct US 60 and 95, just se. Ext corridors. **Pets:** Accepted.
[ASK] [X] [■] [■] [≈]

▼ **Travelodge** M
(417) 926-3152. **Call for rates.** 111 E 17th St. Jct US 60 and 95, just s. Ext corridors. **Pets:** Accepted.
[X] [■] [≈]

NEOSHO

♦♦♦ ▼▼ **Best Western Big Spring Lodge** H
(417) 455-2300. **$89, 3 day notice.** 1810 Southern View Dr. 0.9 mi e of jct US 60 and 71. Int corridors. **Pets:** Accepted.
[SAVE] [X] [■] [■] [≈]

▼▼ **Super 8-Neosho** H
(417) 455-1888. **$60-$65.** 3085 Gardner/Edgewood Dr. Just s of jct US 60B and 71B. Int corridors. **Pets:** Small. $10 daily fee/pet. Designated rooms, no service, crate.
[ASK] [X] [■] [■]

NEW FLORENCE

▼▼ **Days Inn Booneslick Lodge** H
(573) 835-7777. **Call for rates.** 403 Booneslick Rd. I-70, exit 175, just w. Int corridors. **Pets:** Accepted.
[X] [■] [■] [≈]

NIXA

▼ **Super 8** H
(417) 725-0880. **Call for rates.** 418 Massey Blvd. 0.5 mi n of jct SR 14 and 160; US 65, 4.7 mi w on SR 14, then 0.4 mi n on SR 160. Int corridors. **Pets:** Accepted.
[X] [&M] [■] [■] [≈]

OSAGE BEACH

▼▼ **Dogwood Hills Resort** H 🐾
(573) 348-1735. **$52-$114.** 1252 State Hwy KK. 0.5 mi n, off US 54. Ext corridors. **Pets:** Other species. $25 one-time fee/pet. No service, supervision.
[ASK] [X] [■] [■] [ɪɪ] [≈]

OZARK

♦♦♦ ▼ **Americas Best Value Inn** H
(417) 581-8800. **$53-$58.** 299 N 20th. US 65, exit SR 14, just w to 20th St, then just s. Ext/int corridors. **Pets:** Small, other species. $10 daily fee/pet. Designated rooms, service with restrictions, crate.
[SAVE] [X] [■] [≈]

PACIFIC

♦♦♦ ▼▼▼ **Comfort Inn** H
(636) 257-4600. **$75-$109.** 1320 Thornton St. I-44, exit 257, just ne. Int corridors. **Pets:** Accepted.
[SAVE] [X] [■] [■] [≈] [X]

♦♦♦ ▼ **Quality Inn Near Six Flags** H
(636) 257-8400. **$69-$109.** 1400 W Osage St. I-44, exit 257, just se. Ext/int corridors. **Pets:** Small, other species. $15 daily fee/pet. Service with restrictions.
[SAVE] [X] [■] [■] [≈]

POPLAR BLUFF

♦♦♦ ▼▼ **Comfort Inn by Choice Hotels** H
(573) 686-5200. **Call for rates.** 2582 N Westwood Blvd. 1.3 mi s from jct US 60 E. Int corridors. **Pets:** Small. $20 one-time fee/room. Service with restrictions, supervision.
[SAVE] [X] [&M] [■] [■] [≈]

▼▼ **Drury Inn-Poplar Bluff** H
(573) 686-2451. **$65-$101.** 2220 N Westwood Blvd. On US 67, 1.4 mi s from jct US 60 E. Int corridors. **Pets:** Other species. Service with restrictions, supervision.
[ASK] [X] [■] [■] [≈]

▼ **Pear Tree Inn by Drury-Poplar Bluff** M
(573) 785-7100. **$60-$75.** 2218 N Westwood Blvd. On US 67, 1.4 mi s from jct US 60 E. Ext corridors. **Pets:** Other species. Service with restrictions, supervision.
[ASK] [X] [■] [≈]

▼ **Super 8** H
(573) 785-0176. **Call for rates.** 2831 N Westwood Blvd. On US 67, 0.8 mi s from jct US 60 E. Int corridors. **Pets:** Accepted.
[X] [■] [■]

POTOSI

▼ **Potosi Super 8** H
(573) 438-8888. **Call for rates.** 820 E High St. Jct SR 8 and 21. Ext/int corridors. **Pets:** Accepted.
[X] [■] [■]

REPUBLIC

▼▼ **AmericInn Lodge & Suites of Republic** H 🐾
(417) 732-5335. **$74-$85.** 950 Austin Ln. I-44, exit 67, 4.4 mi s to SR 174 (flashing red light-4-way stop), then 0.7 mi e to Highland Park Town Center; just nw of jct US 60, SR 413 and 174. Int corridors. **Pets:** Small. $50 deposit/room, $10 daily fee/pet. Service with restrictions, crate.
[X] [■] [■] [≈]

ROLLA

♦♦♦ ▼▼ **Baymont Inn & Suites** H
(573) 364-7000. **$76-$95.** 1801 Martin Springs Dr. I-44, exit 184, just sw. Int corridors. **Pets:** Supervision.
[SAVE] [X] [&M] [■] [■] [≈]

♦♦♦ ▼▼ **Best Western Coachlight** M
(573) 341-2511. **Call for rates.** 1403 Martin Springs Dr. Jct I-44 and Business Rt 44 S, exit 184. Ext corridors. **Pets:** Accepted.
[SAVE] [X] [■] [≈]

▼▼ **Drury Inn-Rolla** H
(573) 364-4000. **$73-$95.** 2006 N Bishop Ave. I-44, exit 186 (US 63), just ne. Int corridors. **Pets:** Other species. Service with restrictions, supervision.
[ASK] [X] [■] [■] [≈]

ST. CLAIR

♦♦♦ ▼▼ **Budget Lodging** M
(636) 629-1000. **$69-$79.** 866 S Outer Rd W. I-44, exit 240, just w. Ext corridors. **Pets:** Other species. $10 daily fee/room. Designated rooms, service with restrictions, crate.
[SAVE] [X] [■] [■] [≈]

ST. JOSEPH

♦♦♦ ▼▼ **Best Western Classic Inn** M
(816) 232-2345. **$65-$105.** 4502 SE US 169. I-29, exit 44, just e. Ext corridors. **Pets:** Accepted.
[SAVE] [X] [&M] [■] [■] [≈]

▼▼▼▼ Drury Inn & Suites-St. Joseph H
(816) 364-4700. **$75-$135.** 4213 Frederick Blvd. I-29, exit 47, just e. Int corridors. **Pets:** Other species. Service with restrictions, supervision.
ASK ⊠ ᴙᴹ 🛏 💻 ➿ ⊠

▼▼▼ Ramada Inn H
(816) 233-6192. **$81-$149.** 4016 Frederick Blvd. I-29, exit 47, just w. Int corridors. **Pets:** Accepted.
ASK ⊠ 🛏 💻 ¶¶ ➿ ⊠

AAA ▼▼▼▼ St. Joseph Holiday Inn-Riverfront H ✿
(816) 279-8000. **$85-$99.** 102 S Third St. I-229, exit Edmond St northbound; exit Felix St southbound; downtown. Int corridors. **Pets:** Large. $20 one-time fee/pet. Service with restrictions, supervision.
SAVE ⊠ ᴙᴹ 🛏 💻 ¶¶ ➿ ⊠

ST. LOUIS METROPOLITAN AREA

BRIDGETON

▼▼ StudioPlus–Earth City H
(314) 209-1011. **$59-$109.** 3125 Rider Tr S. I-70, exit 231B (Earth City Expwy), just n, then 0.7 mi e. Int corridors. **Pets:** Other species. $25 daily fee/pet. Service with restrictions, crate.
ASK ⊠ 🛏 💻

CHESTERFIELD

▼▼▼▼ Drury Plaza Hotel-Chesterfield H
(636) 532-3300. **$110-$285.** 355 Chesterfield Center E. I-64/US 40, exit 19B (Clarkson Rd/Olive Blvd); jct I-64/US 40 and Clarkson Rd; southwest corner. Int corridors. **Pets:** Other species. Service with restrictions, supervision.
ASK ⊠ ᴙᴹ 🛏 💻 ¶¶ ➿

▼▼▼▼ Homewood Suites by Hilton H
(636) 530-0305. **$99-$149.** 840 North Chesterfield Pkwy W. I-64, exit 20, 1 mi n. Int corridors. **Pets:** Accepted.
⊠ 🛏 💻 ➿

CLAYTON

AAA ▼▼▼▼ Crowne Plaza St. Louis-Clayton H ✿
(314) 726-5400. **$119-$299.** 7750 Carondelet Ave. I-64, exit 32B (Hanley Rd), 1.3 mi n, then just w. Int corridors. **Pets:** Medium. Designated rooms, service with restrictions, crate.
SAVE ⊠ 💻 ¶¶ ➿ ⊠

AAA ▼▼▼▼ ▼▼▼▼ The Ritz-Carlton, St. Louis H
(314) 863-6300. **$425-$525.** 100 Carondelet Plaza. I-64, exit 32B (Hanley Rd), 1.2 mi n, then just e. Int corridors. **Pets:** Accepted.
SAVE ⊠ ¶¶ ➿ ⊠

AAA ▼▼▼▼ Sheraton Clayton Plaza Hotel H
(314) 863-0400. **Call for rates.** 7730 Bonhomme Ave. I-64, exit 31 (Brentwood Blvd), 1.3 mi n, then 0.7 mi e. Int corridors. **Pets:** Accepted.
SAVE ⊠ 🛏 💻 ¶¶ ➿

CREVE COEUR

▼▼▼▼ Drury Inn & Suites-Creve Coeur H
(314) 989-1100. **$95-$166.** 11980 Olive Blvd. I-270, exit 14 (Olive Blvd). Int corridors. **Pets:** Other species. Service with restrictions, supervision.
ASK ⊠ ᴙᴹ 🛏 💻 ➿ ⊠

EARTH CITY

AAA ▼▼▼▼ Residence Inn St. Louis Airport/Earth City H
(314) 209-0995. **$161-$197.** 3290 Rider Tr S. I-70, exit 231B (Earth City Expwy N), just n, then just e. Int corridors. **Pets:** Accepted.
SAVE ⊠ ᴙᴹ 🛏 💻 ➿ ⊠

EDMUNDSON

▼▼▼▼ Drury Inn-St. Louis Airport H
(314) 423-7700. **$90-$165.** 10490 Natural Bridge Rd. I-70, exit 236 (Lambert Airport), just s, then just e. Int corridors. **Pets:** Other species. Service with restrictions, supervision.
ASK ⊠ ᴙᴹ 🛏 💻 ➿

EUREKA

▼▼▼▼ Holiday Inn at Six Flags H
(636) 938-6661. **$109-$269, 3 day notice.** 4901 Six Flags Rd. I-44, exit 261 (Allenton Rd). Ext/int corridors. **Pets:** Large, other species. $25 daily fee/room. Service with restrictions, crate.
ASK ⊠ 🛏 💻 ¶¶ ➿ ⊠

FENTON

▼▼▼ Drury Inn & Suites-Fenton H
(636) 343-7822. **$70-$145.** 1088 S Highway Dr. I-44, exit 274 (Bowles Ave), just se. Int corridors. **Pets:** Other species. Service with restrictions, supervision.
ASK ⊠ 🛏 💻 ➿

▼▼▼ Pear Tree Inn by Drury-Fenton H
(636) 343-8820. **$62-$98.** 1100 S Highway Dr. I-44, exit 274 (Bowles Ave), just s. Int corridors. **Pets:** Other species. Service with restrictions, supervision.
ASK ⊠ 🛏 💻 ➿

▼▼▼ TownePlace Suites by Marriott H
(636) 305-7000. **$107-$131.** 1662 Fenton Business Park Ct. I-44, exit 275 westbound; exit 274 eastbound to S Highway Dr, just s. Int corridors. **Pets:** Other species. $100 one-time fee/room. Service with restrictions, crate.
⊠ ᴙᴹ 🛏 💻 ➿

FORISTELL

AAA ▼▼▼ Best Western West 70 Inn H ✿
(636) 673-2900. **$60-$95, 7 day notice.** 12 Hwy W. I-70, exit 203 (CR W), just n. Int corridors. **Pets:** Other species. $15 one-time fee/pet. Service with restrictions, supervision.
SAVE ⊠ 🛏 💻 ➿

HAZELWOOD

▼▼▼ La Quinta Inn St. Louis (Airport) H ✿
(314) 731-3881. **$49-$109.** 5781 Campus Ct. I-270, exit 23 (McDonnell Blvd), just s, just w on Campus Pkwy, then just n. Int corridors. **Pets:** Medium, other species. Service with restrictions, supervision.
ASK ⊠ 🛏 💻 ➿

▼▼▼ Studio Plus–St Louis Airport H
(314) 731-2707. **$54-$104.** 155 Chapel Ridge Dr. I-270, exit 25A, 0.6 mi s on Lindbergh Blvd, then just w. Int corridors. **Pets:** Other species. $25 daily fee/pet. Service with restrictions, crate.
ASK ⊠ 🛏 💻 ➿

KIRKWOOD

AAA ▼▼▼ Best Western Kirkwood Inn H ✿
(314) 821-3950. **$90-$130.** 1200 S Kirkwood Rd. I-44, exit 277B (Lindbergh Blvd), just n. Int corridors. **Pets:** Large, other species. $10 daily fee/pet. Designated rooms, service with restrictions, supervision.
SAVE ⊠ 🛏 💻 ¶¶ ➿

MARYLAND HEIGHTS

◆◆◇ ▼▼▼▼ DoubleTree Hotel St. Louis at Westport 🅷
(314) 434-0100. **$85-$209.** 1973 Craigshire Rd. I-270, exit 16A (Page Ave), just e to Lackland Rd, then 0.4 mi sw on Lackland and Craigshire rds. Int corridors. **Pets:** Accepted.
SAVE ✕ ⚴ 🛢 💻 ❚❙ ⇌ ✕

▼▼ Drury Inn & Suites-St. Louis-Westport 🅷
(314) 576-9966. **$70-$145.** 12220 Dorsett Rd. I-270, exit 17 (Dorsett Rd), just e. Int corridors. **Pets:** Other species. Service with restrictions, supervision.
ASK ✕ 🛢 💻 ⇌

◆◆◇ ▼▼▼▼ Residence Inn by Marriott–Westport 🅷
(314) 469-0060. **$152-$186.** 1881 Craigshire Rd. I-270, exit 16A (Page Ave), 0.8 mi e, just w on Lackland Rd, just s on Craig Rd, then just w. Ext corridors. **Pets:** Accepted.
SAVE ✕ 🛢 💻 ⇌ ✕

◆◆◇ ▼▼▼▼ The Sheraton Westport Plaza Tower 🅷
(314) 878-1500. **Call for rates.** 900 Westport Plaza. I-270, exit 16A (Page Ave), 0.8 mi e; exit Lackland Rd, just w, then just n. Int corridors. **Pets:** Accepted.
SAVE ✕ ⚴ 🛢 💻 ❚❙ ⇌ ✕

▼▼▼▼ Staybridge Suites 🅷
(314) 878-1555. **Call for rates.** 1855 Craigshire Rd. I-270, exit 16A (Page Ave), 0.8 mi e, exit Lackland Rd, 1 mi w, 0.4 mi s on Craig Rd, then just e. Ext/int corridors. **Pets:** Accepted.
✕ 🛢 💻 ⇌ ✕

MEHLVILLE

▼▼▼▼ Holiday Inn St. Louis-South I-55 🅷
(314) 894-0700. **$89-$129.** 4234 Butler Hill Rd. I-55, exit 195 (Butler Hill Rd), just e, then just s. Ext/int corridors. **Pets:** Small, dogs only. $150 deposit/room. Service with restrictions, supervision.
ASK ✕ 🛢 💻 ❚❙ ⇌ ✕

O'FALLON

◆◆◇ ▼▼▼▼ Hilton Garden Inn St. Louis/O'Fallon 🅷
(636) 625-2700. **$79-$169.** 2310 Technology Dr. US 40/61, exit 6 (Wing Haven Blvd/CR DD), just ne; I-70, exit 216 (Bryan Rd), 4.2 mi s. Int corridors. **Pets:** Accepted.
SAVE ✕ ⚴ 🛢 💻 ❚❙ ⇌

▼▼▼▼ Staybridge Suites O'Fallon 🅷
(636) 300-0999. **Call for rates.** 1155 Technology Dr. US 40/64, exit 9 (CR K), just nw. Int corridors. **Pets:** Medium, other species. $75 one-time fee/room. Service with restrictions, crate.
✕ ⚴ 🛢 💻 ⇌

RICHMOND HEIGHTS

▼▼▼▼ Residence Inn By Marriott-St. Louis Galleria 🅷
(314) 862-1900. **$169-$179.** 1100 McMorrow Ave. I-170, exit 1C (Brentwood Blvd) northbound; exit 1D southbound, just s, just e on Galleria Pkwy, then just s. Ext corridors. **Pets:** Accepted.
✕ ⚴ 🛢 💻 ⇌ ✕

ST. ANN

▼▼▼▼ Hampton Inn-St. Louis Airport 🅷
(314) 429-2000. **$109-$450.** 10820 Pear Tree Ln. I-70, exit 236 (Airport Dr), just sw. Int corridors. **Pets:** Accepted.
✕ 🛢 💻 ⇌

▼▼ Pear Tree Inn by Drury-St. Louis Airport 🅷
(314) 427-3400. **$75-$116.** 10810 Pear Tree Ln. I-70, exit 236 (Airport Dr), just sw. Int corridors. **Pets:** Other species. Service with restrictions, supervision.
ASK ✕ 🛢 💻 ⇌

ST. CHARLES

▼▼▼▼ Boone's Lick Trail Inn Bed & Breakfast 🅱🅱
(636) 947-7000. **$125-$295, 10 day notice.** 1000 S Main St. Jct Boone's Lick Tr and S Main St; downtown. Ext/int corridors. **Pets:** Dogs only. $35 one-time fee/pet. Designated rooms, service with restrictions, supervision.
✕ 🛢 💻

▼▼▼▼ Comfort Suites-St. Charles 🅷 🐾
(636) 949-0694. **$100-$140.** 1400 S 5th St. I-70, exit 229 (5th St), just ne. Int corridors. **Pets:** Medium, other species. Service with restrictions, supervision.
ASK ✕ 🛢 💻 ⇌

◆◆◇ ▼▼▼▼ Country Inn & Suites St. Charles 🅷
(636) 724-5555. **$120-$152.** 1190 S Main St. I-70, exit 229A (5th St S), to S Main St, then 0.7 mi ne. Int corridors. **Pets:** Small. $25 one-time fee/pet. Designated rooms, service with restrictions, supervision.
SAVE ✕ 🛢 💻 ⇌ ✕

▼▼ TownePlace Suites by Marriott 🅷
(636) 949-6800. **$89-$99.** 1800 Zumbehl Rd. I-70, exit 227 (Zumbehl Rd), 0.6 mi s, adjacent to Zumbehl Crossing Shopping Center, just se. Int corridors. **Pets:** Accepted.
✕ 🛢 💻 ⇌

ST. LOUIS

◆◆◇ ▼▼▼ Best Western St. Louis Inn 🅷
(314) 416-7639. **Call for rates.** 6224 Heimos Industrial Park Dr. I-55, exit 193, just e on Meramec Bottom Rd, then just n. Int corridors. **Pets:** Medium, other species. $10 daily fee/pet. Designated rooms, service with restrictions, supervision.
SAVE ✕ 🛢 💻 ⇌

▼▼▼▼ Drury Inn & Suites Near Forest Park 🅷
(314) 646-0770. **$90-$215.** 2111 Sulphur Ave. I-44, exit 286, just s. Int corridors. **Pets:** Other species. Service with restrictions, supervision.
ASK ✕ ⚴ 🛢 💻 ❚❙ ⇌

▼▼▼▼ Drury Inn & Suites-St. Louis-Convention Center 🅷
(314) 231-8100. **$113-$173.** 711 N Broadway. I-70, exit 250B (Stadium/Memorial Dr), at convention center. Int corridors. **Pets:** Other species. Service with restrictions, supervision.
ASK ✕ 🛢 💻 ❚❙ ⇌ ✕

▼▼▼▼ Drury Inn-St. Louis/Union Station 🅷
(314) 231-3900. **$103-$166.** 201 S 20th St. Just e of Jefferson Ave; between Market St and Clark Ave. Int corridors. **Pets:** Other species. Service with restrictions, supervision.
ASK ✕ 🛢 💻 ❚❙ ⇌

◆◆◇ ▼▼▼▼ Drury Plaza Hotel-St. Louis At the Arch 🅷
(314) 231-3003. **$103-$271.** 4th & Market Sts. I-70, 250B (Stadium/Memorial Dr), just w on Pine St to Broadway, just s to Walnut St, just e to 4th St, then just n. Int corridors. **Pets:** Other species. Service with restrictions, supervision.
SAVE ✕ ⚴ 🛢 💻 ❚❙ ⇌

◆◆◇ ▼▼▼▼▼ Four Seasons Hotel St. Louis 🅷 🐾
(314) 881-5800. **$245-$3000.** 999 N 2nd St. I-70, exit 250A, just s, 1.1 mi e, then just s. Int corridors. **Pets:** Large. Service with restrictions, supervision.
SAVE ✕ ⚴ ❚❙ ⇌ ✕

▼▼▼▼ Hampton Inn-St. Louis/Union Station 🅷
(314) 241-3200. **$137.** 2211 Market St. I-64/US 40, exit 39, just n on Jefferson Ave, then just e. Int corridors. **Pets:** Accepted.
✕ 🛢 💻 ❚❙ ⇌

▼▼ Millennium Hotel St. Louis 🅷 🐾
(314) 241-9500. **$99-$299.** 200 S 4th St. Jct Market St, just s. Int corridors. **Pets:** Medium. Designated rooms, service with restrictions.
ASK ✕ 💻 ❚❙ ⇌

▼▼▼▼ Omni Majestic Hotel 🅗
(314) 436-2355. **Call for rates.** 1019 Pine St. Jct N Broadway, just w; at 10th St. Int corridors. **Pets:** Accepted.
☒ 🖵 🍽

ⱮⱮⱮ ▼▼▼▼ Sheraton St. Louis City Center Hotel & Suites 🅗
(314) 231-5007. **$115-$429.** 400 S 14th St. I-64, exit 39B (14th St) eastbound, just n; exit 40A westbound, just n, just w on Clark Ave, then just s. Int corridors. **Pets:** Accepted.
SAVE ☒ ♿ 🛡 🖵 🍽 ⚊

ⱮⱮⱮ ▼▼▼▼ ▼▼▼▼ The Westin St. Louis 🅗 ❀
(314) 621-2000. **$169-$399, 7 day notice.** 811 Spruce St. I-64, exit 39C eastbound, just n on 11th St, then just e; exit 40A westbound, just n, just e on Clark Ave, just s on 8th St, then just w. Int corridors. **Pets:** Medium, dogs only. Service with restrictions, supervision.
SAVE ☒ ♿ 🖵 🍽

ST. PETERS

▼▼▼▼ Drury Inn St. Peters 🅗
(636) 397-9700. **$80-$146.** 170 Westfield Dr. I-70, exit 222 (Mid Rivers Mall Dr), just se. Int corridors. **Pets:** Other species. Service with restrictions, supervision.
ASK ☒ ♿ 🛡 🖵 ⚊

SUNSET HILLS

ⱮⱮⱮ ▼▼▼▼ Holiday Inn-Southwest & Viking Conference Center 🅗
(314) 821-6600. **$104-$139.** 10709 Watson Rd. I-44, exit 277B, just s. Int corridors. **Pets:** Large, other species. $25 one-time fee/room. Service with restrictions, supervision.
SAVE ☒ 🛡 🖵 🍽 ⚊ ☒

VALLEY PARK

▼▼▼▼ Drury Inn & Suites-St. Louis Southwest 🅗
(636) 861-8300. **$75-$160.** 5 Lambert Drury Pl. I-44, exit 272 (SR 141), just sw. Int corridors. **Pets:** Other species. Service with restrictions, supervision.
ASK ☒ 🛡 🖵 ⚊

▼▼▼▼ Hampton Inn-St. Louis Southwest 🅗
(636) 529-9020. **$98-$114.** 9 Lambert Drury Pl. I-44, exit 272 (SR 141), just sw. Int corridors. **Pets:** Medium. Service with restrictions, supervision.
☒ 🛡 🖵 ⚊

END METROPOLITAN AREA

ST. ROBERT

▼▼▼▼ Baymont Inn & Suites Ft. Leonard Wood-St. Robert 🅗
(573) 336-5050. **$80-$153.** 139 Carmel Valley Way. I-44, exit 161, just nw. Int corridors. **Pets:** Very small. $50 deposit/pet, $10 daily fee/pet. Designated rooms, service with restrictions, supervision.
ASK ☒ 🛡 🖵 ⚊

ⱮⱮⱮ ▼▼▼ Best Western Montis Inn 🅗
(573) 336-4299. **$77.** 14086 Hwy Z. I-44, exit 163, just s. Ext corridors. **Pets:** Very small, dogs only. $10 one-time fee/pet. Service with restrictions, supervision.
SAVE ☒ 🛡 🖵 ⚊

▼▼▼▼ MainStay Suites 🅗
(573) 451-2700. **$80-$100.** 227 St. Robert Blvd. I-44, exit 159, 0.8 mi nw. Ext/int corridors. **Pets:** Other species. $15 daily fee/room. Service with restrictions.
ASK ☒ 🛡 🖵 ⚊

▼▼ ▼▼ Microtel Inn & Suites 🅗
(573) 336-7705. **$60-$80.** 562 Old Route 66. I-44, exit 161 westbound to Business Loop 44/Old Route 66, 0.9 mi w; exit 159 eastbound, 0.4 mi se. Int corridors. **Pets:** Accepted.
ASK ☒ ♿ 🛡 🖵

ⱮⱮⱮ ▼▼ Motel 6 #4211 🅗
(573) 336-3610. **$50-$65.** 545 Hwy Z. I-44, exit 161, just s, then 0.3 mi e on frontage road. Int corridors. **Pets:** Other species. Service with restrictions, supervision.
SAVE ☒ ♿

SEDALIA

ⱮⱮⱮ ▼▼▼ Best Western State Fair Inn 🅗
(660) 826-6100. **$74-$149.** 3120 S Limit Ave. 1.5 mi s on US 65 from jct US 50. Ext/int corridors. **Pets:** Other species. Designated rooms, service with restrictions, crate.
SAVE ☒ 🛡 🖵 🍽 ⚊ ☒

▼▼▼▼ Hotel Bothwell, a Clarion Collection 🅗
(660) 826-5588. **Call for rates.** 103 E 4th St. Corner of 4th and S Ohio sts; downtown. Int corridors. **Pets:** $25 one-time fee/pet. Service with restrictions, crate.
☒ 🖵 🍽 ☒

SPRINGFIELD

ⱮⱮⱮ ▼▼▼ Baymont Inn & Suites 🅗
(417) 889-8188. **$76-$106.** 3776 S Glenstone Ave. On US 60. Int corridors. **Pets:** Accepted.
SAVE ☒ ♿ 🛡 🖵 ⚊

ⱮⱮⱮ ▼▼▼ Best Western Coach House Inn 🅗
(417) 862-0701. **$69-$99, 3 day notice.** 2535 N Glenstone Ave. I-44, exit 80A, just s. Ext corridors. **Pets:** Accepted.
SAVE ☒ 🛡 🖵 ⚊

▼▼▼▼ Candlewood Suites South 🅗
(417) 881-8500. **$89-$129.** 1035 E Republic Rd. SR 60, exit National ave, just s. Int corridors. **Pets:** Accepted.
ASK ☒ ♿ 🛡 🖵

ⱮⱮⱮ ▼▼▼▼ Candlewood Suites Springfield I-44 🅗
(417) 866-4242. **$89-$129.** 1920 E Kerr St. I-44, exit 80A (Glenstone Ave), just e to Evergreen St. Int corridors. **Pets:** Accepted.
SAVE ☒ ♿ 🛡 🖵

ⱮⱮⱮ ▼▼▼ Courtyard by Marriott Airport 🅗
(417) 869-6700. **$121-$147.** 3527 W Kearney. I-44, exit 75 (US 160 W Bypass), just se to SR 744, then just w. Int corridors. **Pets:** Accepted.
SAVE ☒ ♿ 🛡 🖵 ⚊

ⱮⱮⱮ ▼▼▼ Days Inn Battlefield 🅗 ❀
(417) 882-9484. **$66-$87.** 3260 E Montclair St. US 65, exit Battlefield Rd, just w to Moulder Ave, then just sw. Int corridors. **Pets:** Other species. Designated rooms, service with restrictions, supervision.
SAVE ☒ ♿ 🛡 🖵 ⚊

▼▼▼▼ Drury Inn & Suites-Springfield 🅗
(417) 863-8400. **$95-$155.** 2715 N Glenstone Ave. I-44, exit 80A (Glenstone Ave), just s. Int corridors. **Pets:** Other species. Service with restrictions, supervision.
ASK ☒ ♿ 🛡 🖵 ⚊

▼▼ **Krystal Aire Inn & Suites-A Non-Smoking Hotel** H
(417) 869-0001. **$65-$95.** 2745 N Glenstone Ave. I-44, exit 80A, just sw. Ext/int corridors. **Pets:** Very small, dogs only. $10 daily fee/pet. Designated rooms, service with restrictions, supervision.

ASK ✕ 🛢 💻 🏊

▲ ▼▼ **Quality Inn & Suites** H
(417) 888-0898. **$79-$129.** 3930 S Overland Ave. US 60 (James River Expwy), exit Kansas Expwy, just n to Chesterfield Blvd, then just w. Int corridors. **Pets:** Small. $10 daily fee/pet. Service with restrictions, supervision.

SAVE ✕ &M 🛢 💻 🏊

▲ ▼▼ **Sleep Inn of Springfield** H
(417) 886-2464. **$75-$90.** 233 El Camino Alto. US 60 (James River Expwy), exit Campbell Ave, just se. Int corridors. **Pets:** Medium, other species. $20 one-time fee/room. Designated rooms, service with restrictions, supervision.

SAVE ✕ 🛢 💻 🏊

▼▼▼ **Springfield DoubleTree** H
(417) 831-3131. **$89-$179.** 2431 N Glenstone Ave. I-44, exit 80A, just s. Int corridors. **Pets:** Accepted.

✕ &M 💻 🍽 🏊

▲ ▼▼▼ **University Plaza Hotel and Convention Center** H
(417) 864-7333. **$159-$209.** 333 John Q Hammons Pkwy. 0.5 mi e on St. Louis St. Int corridors. **Pets:** Accepted.

SAVE ✕ &M 🛢 💻 🍽 🏊

SULLIVAN

▼▼ **Baymont Inn** H
(573) 860-3333. **$89.** 275 N Service Rd W. I-44, exit 225. Int corridors. **Pets:** Accepted.

ASK ✕ 🛢 💻 🏊

▲▲ ▼▼ **Comfort Inn** H ☘
(573) 468-7800. **$75-$95.** 736 S Service Rd W. I-44, exit 225, just sw. Int corridors. **Pets:** Medium. $10 daily fee/pet. Service with restrictions, supervision.

SAVE ✕ 🛢 💻 🏊

TRENTON

▼ **Trenton Knights Inn** H
(660) 359-2988. **$66-$79.** 1845A E 28th St. US 65, 1 mi n of jct SR 6 and US 65. Int corridors. **Pets:** $40 deposit/room, $10 one-time fee/room. Service with restrictions, supervision.

ASK ✕ 🛢

UNION

▼▼ **Super 8 Motel** H
(636) 583-8808. **Call for rates.** 1015 E Main St. I-44, exit 247 (US 50), 4.7 mi w; just w of jct SR 47. Int corridors. **Pets:** Accepted.

✕ &M 🛢 💻 🏊

WASHINGTON

▼▼ **Sleep Inn & Suites** H
(636) 390-8877. **$90-$160.** 2621 E 5th St. I-44, exit 251, 8.5 mi w on SR 100. Int corridors. **Pets:** Medium, dogs only. $25 daily fee/pet. Service with restrictions, supervision.

ASK ✕ 🛢 💻 🏊 ✕

▼ **Super 8 Washington** H
(636) 390-0088. **$76-$125.** 2081 Eckelkamp Ct. I-44, exit 251, 10 mi w on SR 100, just s of SR 100 and 47. Int corridors. **Pets:** Small, dogs only. $25 deposit/room, $10 daily fee/pet. Service with restrictions, supervision.

ASK ✕ 🛢 💻

WEST PLAINS

▼ **Super 8-West Plains** H
(417) 256-8088. **$55-$60.** 1210 Porter Wagoner Blvd. On US 63B, 0.8 mi s of jct US 63. Int corridors. **Pets:** Small, other species. $25 one-time fee/pet. Service with restrictions, supervision.

ASK ✕ 🛢 💻

MONTANA

ALBERTON

▼▼ The Ghost Rails Inn B & B BB
(406) 722-4990. **$59-$99, 3 day notice.** 702 Railroad Ave. Downtown. Int corridors. **Pets:** Accepted.
ASK ⊠ ₩ ⊠

BELGRADE

▼▼▼ Gallatin River Lodge CI ❖
(406) 388-0148. **$170-$450, 7 day notice.** 9105 Thorpe Rd. I-90, exit 298, 2.7 mi s on SR 85, 1 mi w on Valley Center Rd (gravel), then 0.5 mi s, follow sign. Int corridors. **Pets:** Dogs only. $20 one-time fee/pet. Designated rooms, service with restrictions, supervision.
⊠ ▣ 〒 ⊠

▲▲▲ ▼▼▼ Holiday Inn Express H
(406) 388-0800. **Call for rates.** 6261 Jackrabbit Ln. I-90, exit 298, just s on SR 85. Int corridors. **Pets:** Other species. $50 deposit/room. Service with restrictions, supervision.
SAVE ⊠ ♿ ♥ ▣ 〒

▲▲▲ ▼▼▼ La Quinta Inn & Suites Belgrade (Bozeman/Belgrade) H ❖
(406) 388-2222. **$59-$169.** 6445 Jackrabbit Ln. I-90, exit 298, just s on SR 85. Int corridors. **Pets:** Medium, other species. Service with restrictions, supervision.
SAVE ⊠ ♥ ▣ ➦ ⊠

▲▲▲ ▼▼▼ Super 8-Belgrade/Bozeman Airport H
(406) 388-1493. **$65-$117.** 6450 Jackrabbit Ln. I-90, exit 298, just s. Int corridors. **Pets:** Other species. $5 daily fee/pet. Designated rooms, service with restrictions, supervision.
SAVE ⊠ ♥ ▣ ➦

BIGFORK

▲▲▲ ▼▼▼ Mountain Lake Lodge H
(406) 837-3800. **$89-$285, 7 day notice.** 14735 Sylvan Dr. On US 35, 5 mi s. Ext corridors. **Pets:** $15 daily fee/pet. Designated rooms, service with restrictions, supervision.
SAVE ⊠ ♿ ♥ ▣ 〒 ➦ ⊠

▲▲▲ ▼▼ Timbers Motel M ❖
(406) 837-6200. **$58-$124, 7 day notice.** 8540 Hwy 35. Just n on US 35 from jct SR 209. Ext corridors. **Pets:** Other species. $10 daily fee/pet. Designated rooms, supervision.
SAVE ⊠ ▣ ➦

BIG SKY

▲▲▲ ▼▼▼▼ Buck's T-4 Lodge H ❖
(406) 995-4111. **$99-$199.** 46625 Gallatin Rd. US 191, 1 mi s of Big Sky entrance. Ext/int corridors. **Pets:** $10 daily fee/pet. Supervision.
SAVE ⊠ ♥ ▣ 〒 ⊠

▼▼▼▼ Rainbow Ranch Lodge RA
(406) 995-4132. **$185-$385.** 42950 Gallatin Rd. 5 mi s on US 191. Ext corridors. **Pets:** Accepted.
ASK ⊠ ♥ ▣ 〒 ⊠ ᴁ

BIG TIMBER

▼▼▼ Big Timber Super 8 H ❖
(406) 932-8888. **$70-$140.** 20A Big Timber Loop Rd. I-90, exit 367. Int corridors. **Pets:** Other species. $10 daily fee/pet. Designated rooms, service with restrictions, supervision.
ASK ⊠ ♿ ♥

▼▼ River Valley Inn H
(406) 932-4943. **$68-$90.** 600 W 2nd St. I-90, exit 367, just n, then 0.6 mi e. Int corridors. **Pets:** Accepted.
⊠ ♥

BILLINGS

▲▲▲ ▼▼▼▼ Best Western Clocktower Inn H ❖
(406) 259-5511. **$99-$149, 3 day notice.** 2511 1st Ave N. On I-90 business loop; downtown. Ext/int corridors. **Pets:** $15 daily fee/pet. Service with restrictions, supervision.
SAVE ⊠ ♥ ▣ 〒 ➦

▲▲▲ ▼▼▼▼ Best Western Kelly Inn & Suites H ❖
(406) 256-9400. **$110-$150.** 4915 Southgate Dr. I-90, exit 447, just w. Ext/int corridors. **Pets:** Other species. Designated rooms, service with restrictions, supervision.
SAVE ⊠ ♥ ▣ ➦

▼▼▼▼ Billings Hotel and Convention Center H
(406) 248-7151. **Call for rates.** 1223 Mullowney Ln. I-90, exit 446, just s. Int corridors. **Pets:** Accepted.
⊠ ♥ ▣ 〒 ➦ ⊠

▲▲▲ ▼▼▼ Billings Sleep Inn H
(406) 254-0013. **$60-$180.** 4904 Southgate Dr. I-90, exit 447, just w. Int corridors. **Pets:** Accepted.
SAVE ⊠ ♿ ♥ ▣

▼▼▼ Billings Super 8 H
(406) 248-8842. **$35-$81.** 5400 Southgate Dr. I-90, exit 447, just n on S Billings Blvd, 0.8 mi w on King Ave, then just s on Parkway Ln. Int corridors. **Pets:** Medium. $10 one-time fee/pet. No service, crate.
ASK ⊠ ♿ ♥ ▣

▲▲▲ ▼▼▼ Cherry Tree Inn H
(406) 252-5603. **$65.** 823 N Broadway. I-90, exit 450, 2 mi n on 27th St, then just w on 9th Ave. Int corridors. **Pets:** Accepted.
SAVE ⊠ ♥ ▣

▼▼▼ Clubhouse Inn & Suites H ❖
(406) 248-9800. **$89-$139.** 5610 S Frontage Rd. I-90, exit 446, just s. Ext/int corridors. **Pets:** Other species. Service with restrictions, supervision.
ASK ⊠ ♿ ♥ ▣ ➦

Comfort Inn by Choice Hotels 🅷
(406) 652-5200. **Call for rates.** 2030 Overland Ave. I-90, exit 446, 0.5 mi n, then just s. Int corridors. **Pets:** Accepted.

Days Inn 🅷
(406) 252-4007. **$61-$93.** 843 Parkway Ln. I-90, exit 447, just n on S Billings Blvd, 0.8 mi w on King Ave, then just s. Int corridors. **Pets:** Accepted.

Extended StayAmerica-Billings-West End 🅷
(406) 245-3980. **$69-$109.** 4950 Southgate Dr. I-90, exit 447, just w. Int corridors. **Pets:** Other species. $25 daily fee/pet. Service with restrictions, crate.

Hilltop Inn 🅷
(406) 245-5000. **$65-$75.** 1116 N 28th St. I-90, exit 450, 2 mi n on 27th St, just w on 11th Ave, then just n. Int corridors. **Pets:** Other species. $7 daily fee/pet. Designated rooms, service with restrictions, supervision.

Holiday Inn Grand Montana Billings 🅷
(406) 248-7701. **$129-$159.** 5500 Midland Rd. I-90, exit 446. Int corridors. **Pets:** Medium, other species. $25 one-time fee/room. Designated rooms, service with restrictions, supervision.

Kelly Inn 🅷
(406) 252-2700. **$69-$129.** 5425 Midland Rd. I-90, exit 446, just se. Ext/int corridors. **Pets:** Accepted.

La Quinta Inn & Suites 🅷 🐾
(406) 294-9090. **$89-$164.** 3040 King Ave W. I-90, exit 446, 3 mi n. Int corridors. **Pets:** Medium, other species. Service with restrictions, supervision.

Motel 6 #178 🅼
(406) 252-0093. **$49-$63.** 5400 Midland Rd. I-90, exit 446, just se. Ext corridors. **Pets:** Other species. Service with restrictions, supervision.

Quality Inn Homestead 🅷
(406) 652-1320. **Call for rates.** 2036 Overland Ave. I-90, exit 446, 0.5 mi n, then just s. Int corridors. **Pets:** Accepted.

Red Roof Inn #269 🅷
(406) 248-7551. **$59-$73.** 5353 Midland Rd. I-90, exit 446, just se. Int corridors. **Pets:** Accepted.

Residence Inn by Marriott 🅷
(406) 656-3900. **$134-$164.** 956 S 25th St W. I-90, exit 446, 1.5 mi w, just s on S 24th St, then just s; behind Home Depot. Int corridors. **Pets:** Other species. $75 one-time fee/room. Supervision.

Rimview Inn 🅼
(406) 248-2622. **$60-$75.** 1025 N 27th St. I-90, exit 450, 2 mi n. Ext/int corridors. **Pets:** Accepted.

Riverstone Billings Inn 🅷
(406) 252-6800. **$65-$75.** 880 N 29th St. I-90, exit 450, 2 mi n on 27th St, then just w on 9th Ave. Int corridors. **Pets:** Other species. $7 daily fee/pet. Designated rooms, service with restrictions, supervision.

Western Executive Inn 🅷
(406) 294-8888. **$60-$120.** 3121 King Ave W. I-90, exit 446, 2.5 mi w. Int corridors. **Pets:** Medium. $10 daily fee/pet.

BOZEMAN

AmericInn Lodge & Suites of Bozeman 🅷 🐾
(406) 522-8686. **$99-$189.** 1121 Reeves Rd W. I-90, exit 305, just n. Int corridors. **Pets:** Dogs only. $20 daily fee/pet. Designated rooms, service with restrictions, supervision.

Best Western GranTree Inn 🅷
(406) 587-5261. **$89-$159.** 1325 N 7th Ave. I-90, exit 306, just s. Int corridors. **Pets:** Service with restrictions, supervision.

Bozeman Days Inn & Suites 🅷 🐾
(406) 587-5251. **Call for rates.** 1321 N 7th Ave. I-90, exit 306, just s. Int corridors. **Pets:** Other species. $5 daily fee/pet. Supervision.

Bozeman Inn 🅼
(406) 587-3176. **$55-$95.** 1235 N 7th Ave. I-90, exit 306, just s. Ext corridors. **Pets:** Other species. $5 one-time fee/room. Service with restrictions.

Bozeman's Western Heritage Inn 🅷
(406) 586-8534. **$58-$118.** 1200 E Main St. I-90 business loop, exit 309, 0.5 mi w. Int corridors. **Pets:** Dogs only. $10 daily fee/room. Supervision.

Holiday Inn Bozeman 🅷
(406) 587-4561. **$79-$139.** 5 E Baxter Ln. I-90, exit 306, just s. Int corridors. **Pets:** Accepted.

Microtel Inn & Suites 🅷
(406) 586-3797. **$64-$115.** 612 Nikles Dr. I-90, exit 306, just ne. Int corridors. **Pets:** Accepted.

Rainbow Motel 🅼
(406) 587-4201. **$50-$75.** 510 N 7th Ave. I-90, exit 306, 0.8 mi s. Ext corridors. **Pets:** Medium, dogs only. $10 daily fee/pet. Designated rooms, service with restrictions, supervision.

Ramada Limited 🅷
(406) 585-2626. **$65-$125.** 2020 Wheat Dr. I-90, exit 306, just n, then just w. Ext/int corridors. **Pets:** Dogs only. $10 daily fee/pet. Supervision.

Rodeway Inn 🅷
(406) 585-7888. **$68-$115.** 817 Wheat Dr. I-90, exit 306, just n. Int corridors. **Pets:** Medium, other species. $5 one-time fee/pet. Supervision.

Royal "7" Budget Inn 🅼 🐾
(406) 587-3103. **$52-$64.** 310 N 7th Ave. I-90, exit 306, 0.8 mi s. Ext corridors. **Pets:** Medium, other species. $3 daily fee/pet. Designated rooms, supervision.

Super 8 🅷
(406) 586-1521. **$64-$99.** 800 Wheat Dr. I-90, exit 306, just n, then just w. Int corridors. **Pets:** Accepted.

BROWNING

Western Motel LLC M
(406) 338-7572. **$49-$160, 4 day notice.** 121 Central Ave E. On US 2; center. Ext corridors. **Pets:** Small, other species. $10 daily fee/pet. Service with restrictions, supervision.

SAVE ✕ 🅿

BUTTE

Best Western Butte Plaza Inn H
(406) 494-3500. **$105-$195.** 2900 Harrison Ave. I-90/15, exit 127 (Harrison Ave). Int corridors. **Pets:** Large, other species. $50 deposit/room. Designated rooms.

SAVE ✕ 🅿 💻 🍽 ⇔ ⊠

Butte War Bonnet Hotel H
(406) 494-7800. **$89-$179.** 2100 Cornell Ave. I-90/15, exit 127B (Harrison Ave), just n, then just e. Int corridors. **Pets:** Small. $25 deposit/room, $10 one-time fee/pet. Service with restrictions, supervision.

SAVE ✕ 🅿 💻 🍽 ⇔ ⊠

Comfort Inn of Butte H ✿
(406) 494-8850. **$105-$130.** 2777 Harrison Ave. I-90/15, exit 127 (Harrison Ave), just s. Int corridors. **Pets:** Large. $10 daily fee/pet. Service with restrictions, supervision.

SAVE ✕ 🅿 💻 ⇔ ⊠

Days Inn H
(406) 494-7000. **Call for rates.** 2700 Harrison Ave. I-90/15, exit 127 (Harrison Ave), just n. Int corridors. **Pets:** Accepted.

✕ 🅼 🅿 💻 ⇔

Rocker Inn M
(406) 723-5464. **$46-$57.** 122001 W Brown's Gulch Rd. I-90/15, exit 122 (Rocker Rd). Int corridors. **Pets:** Medium. $5 daily fee/room. Designated rooms, service with restrictions, supervision.

SAVE ✕ 🅿

Super 8 of Butte H
(406) 494-6000. **$70-$92.** 2929 Harrison Ave. I-90/15, exit 127 (Harrison Ave), just s. Int corridors. **Pets:** Large. $50 deposit/pet, $15 daily fee/pet. Designated rooms, service with restrictions, supervision.

SAVE ✕ 💻

CHINOOK

Chinook Motor Inn M ✿
(406) 357-2248. **$69-$79.** 100 Indiana St. On US 2. Int corridors. **Pets:** $5 daily fee/pet. Service with restrictions, supervision.

SAVE ✕

COLUMBUS

Super 8 of Columbus H
(406) 322-4101. **$77-$95.** 602 8th Ave N. I-90, exit 408, just s on SR 78. Int corridors. **Pets:** Accepted.

ASK ✕ 🅼 🅿 💻

CONRAD

Super 8 H
(406) 278-7676. **$70-$87.** 215 N Main St. I-15, exit 339, just w. Int corridors. **Pets:** Other species. $10 daily fee/pet. Service with restrictions, supervision.

ASK ✕ 🅿 💻

CUT BANK

Cut Bank Super 8 M ✿
(406) 873-5662. **$68-$88, 7 day notice.** 609 W Main St. On US 2, 0.3 mi w. Int corridors. **Pets:** Small, dogs only. $10 daily fee/pet. Designated rooms, service with restrictions, supervision.

SAVE ✕ 🅿 💻 ⇔

DEER LODGE

Rodeway Inn M
(406) 846-2370. **$70-$110.** 1150 N Main St. I-90, exit 184, 0.3 mi s. Int corridors. **Pets:** Other species. $10 one-time fee/room. Service with restrictions, supervision.

SAVE ✕ 🅿 💻

Western Big Sky Inn M
(406) 846-2590. **$50-$85.** 210 N Main St. I-90, exit 184, 1 mi w. Ext corridors. **Pets:** Other species. $10 daily fee/pet. Designated rooms, service with restrictions, supervision.

ASK ✕ 🅿 💻

DILLON

Best Western Paradise Inn H 🐾
(406) 683-4214. **$90-$140.** 650 N Montana St. I-15, exit 63, 0.3 mi s on SR 41. Ext corridors. **Pets:** Other species. $10 daily fee/room. Designated rooms, service with restrictions, supervision.

SAVE ✕ 🅿 💻 🍽 ⇔

Comfort Inn of Dillon H
(406) 683-6831. **$79-$130.** 450 N Interchange. I-15, exit 63. Int corridors. **Pets:** Large, other species. $10 daily fee/pet. Designated rooms, service with restrictions, supervision.

ASK ✕ 🅿 💻 ⇔

GuestHouse International Inns & Suites H
(406) 683-3636. **$79-$199.** 580 Sinclair St. I-15, exit 63. Int corridors. **Pets:** Accepted.

ASK ✕ 🅼 🅿 💻 ⇔

Super 8 Motel H
(406) 683-4288. **Call for rates.** 550 N Montana St. I-15, exit 63, just n on US 91. Int corridors. **Pets:** Accepted.

✕ 🅿

EAST GLACIER PARK

Dancing Bears Inn LLC M
(406) 226-4402. **$49-$160, 4 day notice.** 40 Montana Ave. Just off US 2, follow signs; center. Ext/int corridors. **Pets:** Small, other species. $10 daily fee/room. Service with restrictions, crate.

SAVE ✕ 🅿

EMIGRANT

Paradise Gateway Bed & Breakfast & Guest Cabins BB
(406) 333-4063. **$85-$350, 14 day notice.** Emigrant Mountain. I-90, exit 333 (US 89), 4.5 mi s of Emigrant; between MM 26 and 27, then 0.3 mi e on gravel road, follow signs. Ext/int corridors. **Pets:** Designated rooms, no service, supervision.

SAVE ✕ 🅿 💻

ENNIS

Riverside Motel & Outfitters M
(406) 682-4240. **$50-$145, 14 day notice.** 346 Main St. US 287, east of town. Ext corridors. **Pets:** Accepted.

ASK ✕ 🅿 💻 🅐

FORSYTH

Magnuson Hotels Sundowner Inn M
(406) 346-2115. **$80-$110.** 1018 Front St. I-94, exit 95, 0.5 mi nw on north frontage road. Ext corridors. **Pets:** Large. $10 daily fee/pet. Service with restrictions, supervision.

SAVE ✕ 🅿

Rails Inn Motel H
(406) 346-2242. **$62-$72, 3 day notice.** 290 Front St. I-94, exit 93, just n, then 0.5 mi e on frontage road. Int corridors. **Pets:** $6 daily fee/pet. Service with restrictions, supervision.

SAVE ✕ 🅿

AAA ▽ ◆ **Restwel Motel** **M**
(406) 346-2771. **$61-$73.** 810 Front St. I-94, exit 95, 0.8 mi nw on north frontage road. Ext corridors. **Pets:** Accepted.
[SAVE] [X] ⊟ [▭]

AAA ▽ ◆ **Westwind Motor Inn** **M**
(406) 346-2038. **$62-$72, 3 day notice.** 225 Westwind Ln. I-94, exit 93, 0.3 mi n. Int corridors. **Pets:** $6 daily fee/pet. Service with restrictions, supervision.
[SAVE] [X] ⊟ [▭]

GARDINER

AAA ▽ ◆◆◆ **Best Western by Mammoth Hot Springs** **M**
(406) 848-7311. **$80-$190, 3 day notice.** S Hwy 89. 0.5 mi n. Ext/int corridors. **Pets:** Accepted.
[SAVE] [X] ⊟ [▭] [Ⅱ] [≈] [⊠]

◆ **Yellowstone Park Travelodge** **M**
(406) 848-7520. **$125-$137, 3 day notice.** 109 Hellroaring St. North entrance, just s on US 89; 0.5 mi n of Yellowstone north gate. Ext corridors. **Pets:** Accepted.
[X] ⊟ [▭]

AAA ▽ ◆ **Yellowstone River Motel** **M**
(406) 848-7303. **$56-$100.** 14 E Park St. Just e of US 89. Ext corridors. **Pets:** Accepted.
[SAVE] [X] [&M] ⊟ [▭]

◆ ◆ **Yellowstone Super 8-Gardiner** **H**
(406) 848-7401. **$49-$149.** Hwy 89 S. On US 89. Int corridors. **Pets:** Other species. $10 daily fee/pet. Designated rooms, supervision.
[ASK] [X] ⊟ [▭] [≈]

GLASGOW

◆ ◆ **Cottonwood Inn** **H**
(406) 228-8213. **$77-$90.** 45 1st Ave NE. 0.5 mi e on US 2. Int corridors. **Pets:** Designated rooms, service with restrictions, supervision.
[ASK] [X] ⊟ [▭] [Ⅱ] [≈] [⊠]

GLENDIVE

AAA ▽ ◆ ◆ **Best Western Glendive Inn** **H**
(406) 377-5555. **$77-$106, 3 day notice.** 222 N Kendrick Ave. I-94, exit 215, on I-94 business loop; downtown. Ext/int corridors. **Pets:** Medium. $25 daily fee/room. Designated rooms, service with restrictions, supervision.
[SAVE] [X] ⊟ [▭] [≈]

◆ **Super 8 Glendive** **M**
(406) 365-5671. **$65-$90.** 1904 Merrill Ave. I-94, exit 215, just n. Int corridors. **Pets:** Other species. $5 one-time fee/room. Service with restrictions, supervision.
[ASK] [X] [▭]

GREAT FALLS

AAA ▽ ◆◆◆ **Best Western Heritage Inn** **H**
(406) 761-1900. **$109-$169, 3 day notice.** 1700 Fox Farm Rd. I-15, exit 278, 0.8 mi e on 10th Ave S and US 87/89 and SR 3/200. Int corridors. **Pets:** Large. $15 one-time fee/pet. Service with restrictions, supervision.
[SAVE] [X] ⊟ [▭] [Ⅱ] [≈] [⊠]

◆ ◆ **Comfort Inn by Choice Hotels** **H**
(406) 454-2727. **Call for rates.** 1120 9th St S. I-15, exit 278, 3 mi e on 10th Ave S and US 87/89 and SR 3/200, then just s. Int corridors. **Pets:** Accepted.
[X] [&M] ⊟ [▭] [≈]

AAA ▽ ◆◆◆ **Crystal Inn** **H**
(406) 727-7788. **$109-$129.** 3701 31st St SW. I-15, exit 277, just e. Int corridors. **Pets:** Accepted.
[SAVE] [X] ⊟ [▭] [≈]

◆ ◆ **Days Inn of Great Falls** **H**
(406) 727-6565. **$60-$95.** 101 14th Ave NW. I-15, exit 280 (Central Ave), 1.3 mi e on Central Ave/Business Rt I-15, 0.8 mi n on 3rd St NW, then just w. Int corridors. **Pets:** Dogs only. $5 daily fee/room. Designated rooms, supervision.
[ASK] [X] ⊟ [▭]

◆ ◆ **Extended StayAmerica-Great Falls-Missouri River** **H**
(406) 761-7524. **$65-$103.** 800 River Dr S. I-15, exit 278, 1.7 mi e on 10th Ave S, then 0.7 mi n. Int corridors. **Pets:** Other species. $25 daily fee/pet. Service with restrictions, crate.
[ASK] [X] [&M] ⊟ [▭]

AAA ▽ ◆ ◆ **The Great Falls Inn** **H** ❀
(406) 453-6000. **$75-$85.** 1400 28th St S. I-15, exit 278, 5.3 mi e on 10th Ave S, 0.3 mi s on 26th St S, then just e on 15th Ave S. Int corridors. **Pets:** Other species. $7 daily fee/pet. Designated rooms, service with restrictions, supervision.
[SAVE] [X] [&M] ⊟ [▭]

◆ ◆ ◆ **La Quinta Inn & Suites Great Falls** **H** ❀
(406) 761-2600. **$89-$139.** 600 River Dr S. I-15, exit 278, 1.7 mi e on 10th Ave S, then 0.8 mi n. Int corridors. **Pets:** Medium, other species. Service with restrictions, supervision.
[ASK] [X] [&M] ⊟ [▭] [≈] [⊠]

AAA ▽ ◆ **Motel 6 #4238** **M**
(406) 453-1602. **$63-$95.** 2 Treasure State Dr. I-15, exit 278, 0.8 mi e on 10th Ave S and US 87/89 and SR 3/200. Int corridors. **Pets:** Other species. Service with restrictions, supervision.
[SAVE] [X]

AAA ▽ ◆ ◆ **Quality Inn** **H**
(406) 761-3410. **$69-$99, 14 day notice.** 220 Central Ave. Downtown. Ext/int corridors. **Pets:** Small. Service with restrictions, supervision.
[SAVE] [X] ⊟ [▭] [≈]

HAMILTON

AAA ▽ ◆◆◆ **Best Western Hamilton Inn** **M**
(406) 363-2142. **$94.** 409 S 1st St (US 93). On US 93, south of city center. Ext corridors. **Pets:** Large, other species. Service with restrictions, crate.
[SAVE] [X] [&M] ⊟ [▭]

AAA ▽ ◆◆◆ **Town House Inns** **H** ❀
(406) 363-6600. **$60-$99.** 1113 N 1st St. On US 93, north of city center. Int corridors. **Pets:** Other species. $10 daily fee/pet. Designated rooms, service with restrictions, supervision.
[SAVE] [X] [&M] ⊟ [▭]

HARDIN

AAA ▽ ◆ **American Inn of Hardin** **H**
(406) 665-1870. **Call for rates.** 1324 N Crawford Ave. I-90, exit 495, just s on SR 47. Ext corridors. **Pets:** Large. $10 one-time fee/pet. Designated rooms, service with restrictions, supervision.
[SAVE] [X] ⊟ [▭] [≈]

◆ **Western Motel** **M**
(406) 665-2296. **$65-$95.** 830 W 3rd St. I-90, exit 495 eastbound, 1.3 mi s on SR 47 and CR 313, then just e; exit 497 westbound, 0.3 mi w on I-90 business loop, continue straight on 3rd St for 0.7 mi. Ext corridors. **Pets:** Accepted.
[X] ⊟

HARLOWTON

◆ **Countryside Inn** **M**
(406) 632-4119. **$52-$60.** 309 3rd St NE. US 12 E. Ext corridors. **Pets:** Large. $10 daily fee/room. Designated rooms, service with restrictions, supervision.
[ASK] [X] ⊟

HAVRE

▼▼ AmericInn Lodge & Suites of Havre 🅷 🐾
(406) 395-5000. **$78-$138.** 2520 Hwy 2 W. On US 2, west side of town. Int corridors. **Pets:** $20 one-time fee/room. Designated rooms, service with restrictions, supervision.
🗙 🛢 💻 🐾

HELENA

▼▼▼ Barrister Bed & Breakfast 🅱🅱 🐾
(406) 443-7330. **$119-$134, 4 day notice.** 416 N Ewing St. I-15, exit 192 (Prospect Ave), 1.5 mi sw via Prospect and Montana aves to 9th Ave, 0.8 mi w, then just s. Int corridors. **Pets:** Dogs only.
🄰🅂🄺 🗙 🐾

ⒶⒶⒶ ▼▼▼ Best Western Helena Great Northern Hotel 🅷
(406) 457-5500. **$105-$185.** 835 Great Northern Blvd. I-15, exit 193 (Cedar St), 2 mi w, just w on Lyndale Ave, then just s on Getchell St; downtown. Int corridors. **Pets:** Accepted.
🆂🅰🆅🅴 🗙 🌫 🛢 💻 🍴 🐾

ⒶⒶⒶ ▼▼ Days Inn Helena 🅷 🐾
(406) 442-3280. **$69-$149.** 2001 Prospect Ave. I-15, exit 192 (Prospect Ave), just w. Int corridors. **Pets:** Medium. $5 daily fee/pet. Designated rooms, service with restrictions, supervision.
🆂🅰🆅🅴 🗙 🌫 🛢 💻 🗙

ⒶⒶⒶ ▼▼ Elkhorn Mountain Inn 🅷
(406) 442-6625. **$66-$75.** 1 Jackson Creek Rd. I-15, exit 187 (Montana City), just w. Int corridors. **Pets:** Large, other species. $10 daily fee/pet. Service with restrictions.
🆂🅰🆅🅴 🗙 🌫 🛢 💻

ⒶⒶⒶ ▼▼ Helena Super 8 🅷
(406) 443-2450. **$55-$95.** 2200 11th Ave. I-15, exit 192B (capitol area) northbound; exit west business district southbound on US 12. Int corridors. **Pets:** $10 one-time fee/pet. Designated rooms, service with restrictions, supervision.
🆂🅰🆅🅴 🗙 🛢 💻

ⒶⒶⒶ ▼▼▼ Red Lion Colonial Hotel 🅷
(406) 443-2100. **$155.** 2301 Colonial Dr. I-15, exit 192 southbound; exit 192B northbound. Int corridors. **Pets:** Other species. $20 one-time fee/room. Service with restrictions, supervision.
🆂🅰🆅🅴 🗙 🛢 💻 🍴 🐾

▼▼▼ Wingate by Wyndham 🅷
(406) 449-3000. **$130-$150.** 2007 Oakes St. I-15, exit 193 (Cedar St), just sw. Int corridors. **Pets:** Accepted.
🄰🅂🄺 🗙 🌫 🛢 💻 🐾

HUNGRY HORSE

ⒶⒶⒶ ▼▼▼ Mini Golden Inns Motel Ⓜ
(406) 387-4313. **$86-$160, 30 day notice.** 8955 US 2 E. In Hungry Horse; east end of town. Ext corridors. **Pets:** Accepted.
🆂🅰🆅🅴 🗙 🌫 🛢 💻

KALISPELL

ⒶⒶⒶ ▼▼ Aero Inn 🅷
(406) 755-3798. **$49-$104.** 1830 US 93 S. 1.3 mi s on US 93 from jct US 2. Int corridors. **Pets:** Other species. $20 deposit/room. Designated rooms, service with restrictions, supervision.
🆂🅰🆅🅴 🗙 🛢 🐾

ⒶⒶⒶ ▼▼▼ Comfort Inn 🅷
(406) 755-6700. **$79-$159.** 1330 Hwy 2 W. 1 mi w on US 2 from jct US 93. Int corridors. **Pets:** Medium. $15 one-time fee/pet. Designated rooms, service with restrictions, supervision.
🆂🅰🆅🅴 🗙 🛢 💻 🍴 🐾

▼▼ Glacier Peaks Inn 🅷
(406) 756-3222. **Call for rates.** 1550 Hwy 93 N. 1.3 mi n on US 93 from jct US 2. Int corridors. **Pets:** Medium, other species. $10 daily fee/pet. Service with restrictions, supervision.
🗙 🛢

▼▼▼▼ Holiday Inn Express & Suites 🅷
(406) 755-7405. **$99-$199.** 275 Treeline Rd. 3 mi n on US 93 from jct US 2, just w. Int corridors. **Pets:** Accepted.
🗙 🌫 🛢 💻 🐾

▼▼ Kalispell/Glacier Int'l Airport area Super 8 🅷
(406) 755-1888. **Call for rates.** 1341 1st Ave E. 1.2 mi s on US 93 from jct US 2. Int corridors. **Pets:** Other species. $10 daily fee/room. Designated rooms, service with restrictions, supervision.
🗙 🌫 🛢 💻

▼▼ Kalispell Grand Hotel 🅷
(406) 755-8100. **$85-$150.** 100 Main St. On US 93; downtown. Int corridors. **Pets:** Other species. Service with restrictions, crate.
🄰🅂🄺 🗙 🍴

ⒶⒶⒶ ▼▼▼▼ La Quinta Inn & Suites Kalispell 🅷 🐾
(406) 257-5255. **$59-$199.** 255 Montclair Dr. Jct US 93 and 2, 1 mi e. Int corridors. **Pets:** Medium, other species. Service with restrictions, supervision.
🆂🅰🆅🅴 🗙 🌫 🛢 💻 🐾 🗙

ⒶⒶⒶ ▼▼▼▼ Red Lion Hotel Kalispell 🅷
(406) 751-5050. **Call for rates.** 20 N Main St. Just s on US 93 from jct of US 2; connected to Kalispell Center Mall. Int corridors. **Pets:** Other species. $20 one-time fee/room. Service with restrictions, supervision.
🆂🅰🆅🅴 🗙 🌫 🛢 💻 🍴 🐾 🗙

ⒶⒶⒶ ▼▼ Travelodge 🅷
(406) 755-6123. **$50-$119, 14 day notice.** 350 N Main St. US 93, just n of jct US 2. Ext/int corridors. **Pets:** Accepted.
🆂🅰🆅🅴 🗙 🛢 💻

LAKESIDE

▼▼ Bayshore Resort Motel Inc Ⓜ
(406) 844-3131. **$65-$185.** 616 Lakeside Blvd. On US 93; center. Ext corridors. **Pets:** $15 daily fee/room. Service with restrictions, supervision.
🗙 🛢 💻 🗙 🅰🅲

LAUREL

ⒶⒶⒶ ▼▼ Best Western Yellowstone Crossing 🅷
(406) 628-6888. **$85-$110, 6 day notice.** 205 SE 4th St. I-90, exit 434, just n, then just e. Int corridors. **Pets:** Medium. $10 daily fee/pet. Designated rooms, service with restrictions, supervision.
🆂🅰🆅🅴 🗙 🌫 🛢 💻 🐾

LEWISTOWN

ⒶⒶⒶ ▼▼ B & B Motel Ⓜ
(406) 535-5496. **$50-$80.** 520 E Main St. Downtown. Ext corridors. **Pets:** Accepted.
🆂🅰🆅🅴 🗙 🛢

LIBBY

▼▼ Caboose Motel and Sportsman Information Center Ⓜ
(406) 293-6201. **$55-$75.** 714 W 9th St. Just w on US 2 from jct SR 37. Ext corridors. **Pets:** Dogs only. $5 daily fee/pet. Supervision.
🄰🅂🄺 🗙 🛢 💻

ⒶⒶⒶ ▼▼ Rodeway Inn 🅷
(406) 293-2771. **$65-$80.** 448 US 2 W. Just w on US 2 from jct SR 37. Int corridors. **Pets:** $15 one-time fee/room. Service with restrictions, supervision.
🆂🅰🆅🅴 🗙 🛢 🐾

▼▼ Sandman Motel **M**
(406) 293-8831. **$55-$80.** 31901 US 2. Just w on US 2 from jct SR 37. Ext corridors. **Pets:** Accepted.
(ASK) ✕ ⊟

LINCOLN

◆◆ ▼ Leeper's Ponderosa Motel **M**
(406) 362-4333. **$64-$80.** Hwy 200 & 1st Ave. On SR 200, just w. Ext corridors. **Pets:** Other species. $5 daily fee/pet. Service with restrictions.
(SAVE) ✕ ⊟ ▦ ⊠

LIVINGSTON

◆◆ ▼▼ Best Western Yellowstone Inn & Conference Center **H** ☘
(406) 222-6110. **$89-$125.** 1515 W Park St. I-90, exit 333, just n. Int corridors. **Pets:** Large, other species. $10 daily fee/pet. Designated rooms, service with restrictions, supervision.
(SAVE) ✕ ⊟ ▦ ⊺ ⊠

▼▼ Livingston Rodeway Inn **M**
(406) 222-6320. **$70-$125, 10 day notice.** 102 Rogers Ln. I-90, exit 333, just n on US 89, then just w. Ext/int corridors. **Pets:** Accepted.
(ASK) ✕ ⊟ ▦ ⊺ ⊠

▼▼ Quality Inn **H** ☘
(406) 222-0555. **$69-$160.** 111 Rogers Ln. I-90, exit 333, just n on US 89, then just w. Int corridors. **Pets:** Other species. $10 daily fee/room. Service with restrictions, supervision.
(ASK) ✕ ⊠ ⊟ ▦ ⊠

LOLO

▼▼ Days Inn **H**
(406) 273-2121. **$80-$100.** 11225 US 93 S. North edge of town. Ext/int corridors. **Pets:** Dogs only. $10 daily fee/pet. Service with restrictions, supervision.
(ASK) ✕ ⊠ ⊟ ▦

MALTA

◆◆ ▼ Maltana Motel **M**
(406) 654-2610. **$69-$109.** 138 S 1st Ave W. Just s of US 2 via US 191, just w; downtown. Ext corridors. **Pets:** Dogs only. $10 one-time fee/pet. Designated rooms, service with restrictions, crate.
(SAVE) ✕ ⊟ ▦

MILES CITY

◆◆ ▼▼ Best Western War Bonnet Inn **H** ☘
(406) 234-4560. **$70-$200.** 1015 S Haynes Ave. I-94, exit 138 (Broadus), 0.3 mi n. Ext corridors. **Pets:** Large. $5 daily fee/pet. Designated rooms, service with restrictions, supervision.
(SAVE) ✕ ⊟ ▦ ⊠ ⊠

▼▼ GuestHouse International Inn & Suites **H** ☘
(406) 232-3661. **Call for rates.** 3111 Steel St. I-94, exit 138 (Broadus), just s. Int corridors. **Pets:** $15 daily fee/room. Service with restrictions, supervision.
✕ ⊠ ⊟ ▦ ⊠

MISSOULA

◆◆ ▼▼▼ Best Western Grant Creek Inn **H**
(406) 543-0700. **$119-$219.** 5280 Grant Creek Rd. I-90, exit 101 (Reserve St), just n. Int corridors. **Pets:** Small. $10 daily fee/pet. Designated rooms, service with restrictions, supervision.
(SAVE) ✕ ⊠ ⊟ ▦ ⊠ ⊠

◆◆ ▼▼▼ Broadway Inn Conference Center **H**
(406) 532-3300. **Call for rates.** 1609 W Broadway. I-90, exit 104 (Orange St), 0.5 mi s, then 1 mi w. Int corridors. **Pets:** Medium, dogs only. $10 daily fee/pet. Designated rooms, service with restrictions, supervision.
(SAVE) ✕ ⊟ ▦ ⊺ ⊠

▼▼ Campus Inn **M**
(406) 549-5134. **$70-$125.** 744 E Broadway. I-90, exit 105 (Van Buren St), just s to Broadway, then just w. Ext/int corridors. **Pets:** Large. $6 one-time fee/room. Designated rooms, service with restrictions, crate.
(ASK) ✕ ⊟ ▦ ⊠

▼▼▼ Comfort Inn **H**
(406) 542-0888. **$79-$169.** 4545 N Reserve St. I-90, exit 101 (Reserve St), 0.5 mi s. Int corridors. **Pets:** Medium, other species. $15 daily fee/room. Service with restrictions, supervision.
(ASK) ✕ ⊠ ⊟ ▦ ⊠

◆◆ ▼▼▼ Days Inn/Missoula Airport **H**
(406) 721-9776. **$80-$120.** 8600 Truck Stop Rd. I-90, exit 96, just n. Int corridors. **Pets:** Accepted.
(SAVE) ✕ ⊟ ▦

◆◆ ▼▼▼ Days Inn University **H**
(406) 543-7221. **$79-$109.** 201 E Main St. I-90, exit 104 (Orange St), 0.5 mi s to Broadway, 0.5 mi e to Washington, just s to Main St, then just w. Ext corridors. **Pets:** Small, dogs only. $20 daily fee/pet. Service with restrictions, supervision.
(SAVE) ✕ ⊟ ▦ ⊠

▼▼▼ Doubletree Hotel Missoula/Edgewater **H**
(406) 728-3100. **$89-$239.** 100 Madison St. I-90, exit 105 (Van Buren St), just s, then w on Front St. Int corridors. **Pets:** Medium. $30 one-time fee/room. Designated rooms, service with restrictions, supervision.
✕ ⊠ ▦ ⊺ ⊠

▼▼ Econo Lodge **H**
(406) 542-7550. **$75-$130.** 4953 N Reserve St. I-90 W, exit 101 (Reserve St), just s. Int corridors. **Pets:** Medium. $10 daily fee/pet. Designated rooms, crate.
(ASK) ✕ ⊟ ▦

◆◆ ▼ Family Inn **M** ☘
(406) 543-7371. **$64-$96.** 1031 E Broadway. I-90, exit 105 (Van Buren St), just s, then just e. Ext corridors. **Pets:** Large. $10 one-time fee/room. Service with restrictions, supervision.
(SAVE) ✕ ⊟ ⊠

▼▼▼ Hampton Inn **H**
(406) 549-1800. **$211.** 4805 N Reserve St. I-90, exit 101 (Reserve St), just s. Int corridors. **Pets:** Large. $10 one-time fee/room. Designated rooms, supervision.
✕ ⊠ ⊟ ▦ ⊠

◆◆ ▼▼▼ Holiday Inn Missoula-Downtown at the Park **H**
(406) 721-8550. **$139-$239.** 200 S Pattee St. I-90, exit 104 (Orange St), 0.5 mi s to Broadway, just e to Pattee St, then just s. Int corridors. **Pets:** Accepted.
(SAVE) ✕ ⊠ ⊟ ▦ ⊺ ⊠ ⊠

◆◆ ▼▼▼ La Quinta Inn **H** ☘
(406) 549-9000. **$59-$189.** 5059 N Reserve St. I-90, exit 101 (Reserve St), just s. Int corridors. **Pets:** Medium, other species. Service with restrictions, supervision.
(SAVE) ✕ ⊠ ⊟ ▦ ⊠

▼▼▼ Quality Inn & Conference Center **H**
(406) 251-2665. **$85-$150.** 3803 Brooks St. I-90, exit 101 (Reserve St), 5 mi s to Brooks St, then just w. Int corridors. **Pets:** Medium. $10 daily fee/pet. Designated rooms, crate.
(ASK) ✕ ⊠ ⊟ ▦

◆◆ ▼▼▼ Red Lion Inn **H**
(406) 728-3300. **$99-$179.** 700 W Broadway. I-90, exit 104 (Orange St), just s, then just w. Ext corridors. **Pets:** Other species. $20 one-time fee/room. Service with restrictions, supervision.
(SAVE) ✕ ⊟ ▦ ⊠

🐾 ▼▼▼ Redwood Lodge M
(406) 721-2110. **$60-$120.** 8060 Hwy 93 N. I-90, exit 96, just s. Ext corridors. **Pets:** Other species. $5 daily fee/pet. Service with restrictions, supervision.
SAVE ✕ 📶

🐾 ▼▼◆▼ Ruby's Inn & Convention Center H
(406) 721-0990. **$70-$125, 7 day notice.** 4825 N Reserve St. I-90, exit 101 (Reserve St), just s. Ext/int corridors. **Pets:** Accepted.
SAVE ✕ ♿M 📶 💻 ⇌ ✕

▼▼ Sleep Inn by Choice Hotels H
(406) 543-5883. **Call for rates.** 3425 Dore Ln. I-90, exit 101 (Reserve St), 5 mi s, then just e on Brooks St. Int corridors. **Pets:** Accepted.
✕ ♿M 📶 💻 ⇌

🐾 ▼▼▼ Southgate Inn H
(406) 251-2250. **$60-$125.** 3530 Brooks St. I-90, exit 101 (Reserve St), 5 mi s to Brooks St, then just e. Ext corridors. **Pets:** Other species. $10 daily fee/pet. Designated rooms, supervision.
SAVE ✕ 📶 ⇌ ✕

▼▼▼ Super 8-Brooks St H
(406) 251-2255. **$55-$100.** 3901 Brooks St. I-90, exit 101 (Reserve St), 5 mi s to Brooks St, then just w. Int corridors. **Pets:** Dogs only. $5 daily fee/pet. Designated rooms, service with restrictions, supervision.
ASK ✕ 📶

▼▼◆▼ Thunderbird Motel M
(406) 543-7251. **$60-$95.** 1009 E Broadway. I-90, exit 105 (Van Buren St), just s to Broadway, then just e. Ext/int corridors. **Pets:** Accepted.
ASK ✕ 📶 💻 ⇌

🐾 ▼▼ Travelers Inn Motel Inc M
(406) 728-8330. **$65-$85.** 4850 N Reserve St. I-90, exit 101 (Reserve St), just s. Ext corridors. **Pets:** Small, dogs only. $5 daily fee/pet. Designated rooms, service with restrictions, supervision.
SAVE ✕ 📶

POLSON

🐾 ▼▼◆▼ Best Western KwaTaqNuk Resort & Casino H ❀
(406) 883-3636. **$85-$161, 3 day notice.** 49708 US Hwy 93 E. Just s of downtown. Int corridors. **Pets:** Medium. $25 one-time fee/pet. Designated rooms, service with restrictions, supervision.
SAVE ✕ ♿M 📶 💻 ⇌ ✕

RED LODGE

▼▼▼ Comfort Inn of Red Lodge H
(406) 446-4469. **$60-$160.** 612 N Broadway. Jct US 212 and SR 78, north entrance. Int corridors. **Pets:** $15 one-time fee/pet. Designated rooms, service with restrictions, supervision.
ASK ✕ ♿M 📶 💻 ⇌

▼▼▼ Lu Pine Inn H
(406) 446-1321. **$69-$129.** 702 S Hauser Ave. 0.4 mi s, just w of US 212. Int corridors. **Pets:** Medium. Service with restrictions, supervision.
ASK ✕ 📶 💻 ⇌ ✕

▼▼ Yodeler Motel M
(406) 446-1435. **$55-$139.** 601 S Broadway. Just s on US 212. Ext corridors. **Pets:** Other species. $10 daily fee/pet. Designated rooms, supervision.
ASK ✕ 📶 💻

RONAN

▼▼ Starlite Motel M
(406) 676-7000. **$50-$74, 3 day notice.** 18 Main St SW. Just w of jct US 93 and Main St. Ext corridors. **Pets:** Large, dogs only. $10 daily fee/room. Designated rooms, supervision.
ASK ✕ 📶 💻

ST. IGNATIUS

▼▼ Sunset Motel M
(406) 745-3900. **$60-$80.** 333 Mountain View. Just s of downtown, exit US 93. Ext corridors. **Pets:** Dogs only. $5 daily fee/pet. Service with restrictions, supervision.
ASK ✕ 📶

ST. REGIS

🐾 ▼▼ Little River Motel M
(406) 649-2713. **$45-$80.** 50 Old US Hwy 10 W. I-90, exit 33, just n to flashing light, just w, then just sw. Ext corridors. **Pets:** Medium. $10 daily fee/pet. Designated rooms, service with restrictions, supervision.
SAVE ✕ 📶 🎞 ⇌

🐾 ▼▼▼ Super 8-St. Regis H
(406) 649-2422. **$75-$93.** 9 Old Hwy 10 E. I-90, exit 33, just n. Ext/int corridors. **Pets:** $20 deposit/room. Service with restrictions, supervision.
SAVE ✕ 📶 💻

SHELBY

▼▼ Comfort Inn of Shelby H
(406) 434-2212. **$99-$155.** 455 McKinley Ave. I-15, exit 363, just e, then just s. Int corridors. **Pets:** Accepted.
ASK ✕ 📶 💻 ✕

🐾 ▼▼ O'Haire Manor Motel M
(406) 434-5555. **$52-$80.** 204 2nd St S. Just s of Main St via Maple St. Ext/int corridors. **Pets:** $5 daily fee/pet. Designated rooms, service with restrictions, supervision.
SAVE ✕ 📶 💻

SHERIDAN

▼▼ Moriah Motel M
(406) 842-5491. **$62-$78.** 220 S Main St. On SR 287; center. Ext corridors. **Pets:** $10 one-time fee/pet. Service with restrictions, supervision.
ASK ✕ 📶

SIDNEY

🐾 ▼▼▼ Richland Motor Inn M
(406) 433-6400. **$94.** 1200 S Central Ave. 1.5 mi n of jct SR 200 and 16. Int corridors. **Pets:** Other species. $50 deposit/room, $5 one-time fee/pet. Service with restrictions, supervision.
SAVE ✕ 📶 💻

SUPERIOR

🐾 ▼▼▼ Budget Host Big Sky Motel M
(406) 822-4831. **$45-$77.** 103 4th Ave E. I-90, exit 47, just n. Ext corridors. **Pets:** $10 one-time fee/pet. Designated rooms, service with restrictions, supervision.
SAVE ✕ 📶

THOMPSON FALLS

🐾 ▼▼▼ The Riverfront M
(406) 827-3460. **$45-$125.** 4907 Hwy 200 W. 1 mi w of city center. Ext corridors. **Pets:** Medium, dogs only. $7 daily fee/pet. Service with restrictions, supervision.
SAVE ✕ 📶 💻

THREE FORKS

🐾 ▼▼ Broken Spur Motel M
(406) 285-3237. **$58-$119.** 124 W Elm (Hwy 2). I-90, exit 278 westbound, 1.3 mi sw; exit 274 eastbound, 1 mi s on SR 287 to jct SR 2, then 3 mi se. Ext corridors. **Pets:** Other species. $5 one-time fee/pet. Designated rooms, service with restrictions, supervision.
SAVE ✕ 📶

AAA **WW** **Fort Three Forks Motel & RV Park** **M**
(406) 285-3233. **$56-$120.** 10776 Hwy 287. I-90, exit 274. Ext corridors.
Pets: Accepted.
[SAVE] [X] [🛏] [💻]

VICTOR

AAA **WWW** **Wildlife Adventures Guest Ranch** **RA**
(406) 642-3262. **$125-$185, 7 day notice.** 1765 Pleasant View Dr. Jct
US 93 and Fifth St, 0.9 mi w, 3.2 mi s. Int corridors. **Pets:** Other species.
$10 daily fee/pet. Designated rooms, service with restrictions, supervision.
[SAVE] [X] [X] [K] [W] [Z]

WEST YELLOWSTONE

AAA **WWW** **Best Western Cross Winds Motor**
Inn **M** **❖**
(406) 646-9557. **$85-$166.** 201 Firehole Ave. Just w of US 191 and 287,
on US 20 at Dunraven St and Firehole Ave. Ext corridors. **Pets:** Designated
rooms, service with restrictions, supervision.
[SAVE] [X] [🛏] [💻] [≈]

AAA **WWWW** **Best Western Desert Inn** **H** **❖**
(406) 646-7376. **$75-$170.** 133 Canyon Ave. US 191 at US 20; corner of
Canyon and Firehole aves. Int corridors. **Pets:** Designated rooms, service
with restrictions, supervision.
[SAVE] [X] [&M] [🛏] [💻] [≈]

AAA **WWW** **Best Western Weston Inn** **M**
(406) 646-7373. **$130-$160.** 108 Gibbon Ave. US 191; jct Canyon Ave.
Ext/int corridors. **Pets:** Accepted.
[SAVE] [X] [🛏] [💻] [≈]

AAA **WW** **Brandin' Iron Inn** **M** **❖**
(406) 646-9411. **$79-$129, 3 day notice.** 201 Canyon Ave. Just w; n of
park entrance. Ext corridors. **Pets:** Other species. $15 one-time fee/room.
Designated rooms, service with restrictions, supervision.
[SAVE] [X] [&M] [🛏] [💻]

AAA **WW** **City Center Motel** **M** **❖**
(406) 646-7337. **$59-$89, 3 day notice.** 214 Madison Ave. W off US 191
at Madison Ave and Dunraven St; just nw of park entrance. Ext corridors.
Pets: $15 one-time fee/room. Designated rooms, service with restrictions,
supervision.
[SAVE] [X] [💻] [Z]

WWWW **ClubHouse Inn** **H**
(406) 646-4892. **Call for rates.** 105 S Electric St. Just sw of jct US 191,
187 and 20; just w of park entrance. Int corridors. **Pets:** Other species.
Designated rooms, service with restrictions, supervision.
[X] [&M] [🛏] [💻] [≈]

AAA **WWWW** **Holiday Inn SunSpree Resort West**
Yellowstone Conference Hotel **H**
(406) 646-7365. **$119-$249.** 315 Yellowstone Ave. Just w of park entrance.
Int corridors. **Pets:** Accepted.
[SAVE] [X] [&M] [🛏] [💻] [🍴] [≈] [⊠]

WW **Kelly Inn** **H**
(406) 646-4544. **$89-$209.** 104 S Canyon Ave. S of jct US 191, 287 and
20; just w of park entrance. Ext/int corridors. **Pets:** Other species. Designated rooms, service with restrictions, supervision.
[ASK] [X] [🛏] [💻] [≈]

AAA **WW** **Stage Coach Inn** **H**
(406) 646-7381. **$59-$189.** 209 Madison Ave. Corner of Dunraven St and
Madison Ave, just w of park entrance. Ext/int corridors. **Pets:** Other species.
Designated rooms, service with restrictions, crate.
[SAVE] [X] [🛏] [💻] [⊠]

AAA **WWW** **The Three Bear Lodge** **M**
(406) 646-7353. **$59-$179.** 217 Yellowstone Ave. Just w of park entrance.
Ext/int corridors. **Pets:** Other species. $10 daily fee/pet. Designated rooms,
service with restrictions, supervision.
[SAVE] [X] [🛏] [💻] [🍴] [≈] [⊠]

AAA **WW** **Yellowstone Lodge** **H** **❖**
(406) 646-0020. **$69-$169.** 251 S Electric St. Just w of park entrance. Int
corridors. **Pets:** Other species. $50 deposit/room. Designated rooms, serv-
ice with restrictions, crate.
[SAVE] [X] [🛏] [💻] [≈]

WHITEFISH

AAA **WWWW** **Best Western Rocky Mountain**
Lodge **H** **❖**
(406) 862-2569. **$92-$197.** 6510 Hwy 93 S. 1.3 mi s on US 93 from jct SR
487. Ext/int corridors. **Pets:** $20 one-time fee/room. Designated rooms,
service with restrictions, crate.
[SAVE] [X] [&M] [🛏] [💻] [≈] [⊠]

AAA **WWW** **Kristianna Mountain Homes** **CO** **❖**
(406) 862-2860. **$140-$1100, 30 day notice.** 331 Karrow Ave. Jct US 93
and SR 487, 2.4 mi n on SR 487, at flashing light go 5.2 mi on Big
Mountain Rd, just n on Gelande St, then just w on Kristanna Close. Ext/int
corridors. **Pets:** Small, dogs only. $20 daily fee/pet. Designated rooms,
service with restrictions.
[SAVE] [X] [🛏] [💻] [⊠] [K]

WWWW **North Forty Resort** **CA**
(406) 862-7740. **$119-$259, 14 day notice.** 3765 Hwy 40 W. 2.5 mi e on
SR 40 from jct US 93. Ext corridors. **Pets:** Accepted.
[X] [🛏] [💻] [⊠] [K]

AAA **WWWW** **Pine Lodge** **H**
(406) 862-7600. **$79-$170.** 920 Spokane Ave. 1 mi s on US 93. Int
corridors. **Pets:** Other species. Service with restrictions, supervision.
[SAVE] [X] [&M] [🛏] [💻] [≈]

WHITE SULPHUR SPRINGS

AAA **WW** **All Seasons Inn & Suites** **H** **❖**
(406) 547-8888. **$70-$140.** 808 3rd Ave SW. On US 89/12, south end of
town. Int corridors. **Pets:** $10 one-time fee/pet. Service with restrictions,
supervision.
[SAVE] [X] [&M] [🛏]

WIBAUX

AAA **WW** **Beaver Creek Inn & Suites** **M**
(406) 796-2666. **$78-$125.** 400 W 2nd Ave N. I-94, exit 241 westbound;
exit 242 eastbound. Int corridors. **Pets:** Other species. $8 daily fee/pet.
Designated rooms, service with restrictions, supervision.
[SAVE] [X] [🛏] [💻]

NEBRASKA

AINSWORTH

 Super 8 🄷
(402) 387-0700. **Call for rates.** 1025 E 4th St. 0.5 mi e on US 20. Int corridors. **Pets:** Accepted.
⊠ 🔌 💻

BEATRICE

Holiday Inn Express Hotel & Suites 🄷
(402) 228-7000. **$95.** 4005 N 6th St. 1 mi n on US 77. Int corridors. **Pets:** Other species.
ASK ⊠ ♿M 🔌 💻 ➰

New Victorian Inn 🄷
(402) 228-8808. **$49-$99.** 3721 N 6th St. 1 mi n on US 77. Int corridors. **Pets:** Accepted.
⊠ 🔌 ➰

BELLEVUE

Settle Inn and Suites 🄷
(402) 292-1155. **$69-$175.** 2105 Pratt Ave. US 75, exit Cornhusker, just w. Int corridors. **Pets:** Small, dogs only. $15 daily fee/room. Designated rooms, service with restrictions, supervision.
ASK ⊠ ♿M 🔌 💻 ➰

BROKEN BOW

Americas Best Value Inn & Suites 🄷
(308) 872-6428. **$66-$88.** 215 E South E St. SR 2/92, just e of town. Ext/int corridors. **Pets:** Medium, other species. $5 daily fee/pet. Designated rooms, service with restrictions, supervision.
ASK ⊠ 🔌 💻

The Arrow Hotel 🄷
(308) 872-6662. **$95-$150.** 509 S 9th Ave. On SR 2/92; downtown. Int corridors. **Pets:** $10 daily fee/pet. Designated rooms, service with restrictions, supervision.
SAVE ⊠ 🔌 💻 🍽

CENTRAL CITY

Super 8 🄷
(308) 946-5055. **$59-$65.** 1701 31st St. SR 14, 1 mi s of jct US 30. Ext/int corridors. **Pets:** Other species. $9 daily fee/pet. Supervision.
ASK ⊠ 🔌 💻

CHADRON

Best Western West Hills Inn 🄷
(308) 432-3305. **$70-$110.** 1100 W 10th St. Just s of jct US 385 and 20. Ext/int corridors. **Pets:** $15 daily fee/pet. Service with restrictions, crate.
SAVE ⊠ 🔌 💻 ➰

Grand Westerner Motel 🄼
(308) 432-5595. **$55-$64.** 1050 W Hwy 20. 0.8 mi w on US 20; just e of jct US 385. Ext corridors. **Pets:** Accepted.
ASK ⊠ 🔌

Motel 6 of Chadron #4259 🄷
(308) 432-3000. **Call for rates.** 755 Microtel Dr. Just s of jct US 385 and 20. Int corridors. **Pets:** Other species. Service with restrictions, supervision.
SAVE ⊠ 🔌 💻 ➰

Westerner Motel 🄼
(308) 432-5577. **$55-$64.** 300 Oak St. On US 20, 0.5 mi e of jct US 385 and SR 87. Ext corridors. **Pets:** Dogs only. $5 one-time fee/room. Service with restrictions, supervision.
SAVE ⊠ 🔌

COLUMBUS

Sleep Inn & Suites Hotel 🄷
(402) 562-5200. **$77-$130.** 303 23rd St. On US 30, 2 mi e of jct US 30 and 81; east side of town. Int corridors. **Pets:** Medium. $25 daily fee/pet. Service with restrictions.
ASK ⊠ ♿M 🔌 💻 ➰

Super 8-Columbus 🄷
(402) 563-3456. **$50-$56.** 3324 20th St. On US 30 and 81, just s. Int corridors. **Pets:** Small. $10 daily fee/pet. Designated rooms, no service, crate.
ASK ⊠ 🔌 💻

COZAD

Rodeway Inn 🄷
(308) 784-4900. **$50-$85.** 809 S Meridian. I-80, exit 222, just n. Int corridors. **Pets:** Other species. Service with restrictions, supervision.
ASK ⊠ 🔌

CRETE

Super 8 🄷
(402) 826-3600. **$55-$65.** 1880 W 12th St. 1.3 mi sw at jct SR 33/103; west end of town. Int corridors. **Pets:** Other species. $10 daily fee/pet. Designated rooms, service with restrictions, supervision.
ASK ⊠ 🔌 💻

GOTHENBURG

Gothenburg Super 8 🄷
(308) 537-2684. **$52-$72.** 401 Platte River Dr. I-80, exit 211 (SR 47), just n. Int corridors. **Pets:** Accepted.
SAVE ⊠ 🔌 💻 ➰

GRAND ISLAND

Holiday Inn-Interstate 80 🄷 🐾
(308) 384-7770. **$80-$130.** 7838 S US Hwy 281. I-80, exit 312 (US 281), just s. Int corridors. **Pets:** Medium, other species. $15 daily fee/room. Service with restrictions, supervision.
SAVE ⊠ ♿M 🔌 💻 🍽 ➰ ⊠

Super 8 🄷
(308) 384-4380. **Call for rates.** 2603 S Locust St. I-80, exit 314, 4.7 mi n. Int corridors. **Pets:** Accepted.
⊠ 🔌 💻 ➰

Travelodge 🄷
(308) 382-5003. **$56-$97.** 1311 S Locust St. I-80, exit 314, 5.2 mi n. Int corridors. **Pets:** Other species. $10 one-time fee/room. Service with restrictions, crate.
ASK ⊠ 🔌 💻

HASTINGS

Quality Hotel & Convention Center ⬛
(402) 463-6721. **Call for rates.** 2205 Osborne Dr E. Jct US 34 and 281, 2 mi n. Ext/int corridors. **Pets:** Accepted.

⊠ ⓂⓈ 🔋 🖥 🍴 ⊃ ⊠

⬥⬥⬥ Super 8 ⬛
(402) 463-8888. **$54-$84.** 2200 N Kansas Ave. Jct US 34 and 281, 2 mi n. Int corridors. **Pets:** Accepted.

SAVE ⊠ 🔋 🖥

HOLDREGE

⬥⬥ Super 8 ⬛
(308) 995-2793. **Call for rates.** 420 Broadway. US 183, 0.5 mi w on US 6/34. Int corridors. **Pets:** $10 daily fee/pet. Service with restrictions, supervision.

⊠ 🔋 🖥 ⊃

KEARNEY

⬥⬥⬥ AmericInn Lodge & Suites of Kearney ⬛
(308) 234-7800. **$85-$135.** 215 W Talmadge Rd. I-80, exit 272 (SR 44), just n. Int corridors. **Pets:** Medium, dogs only. $10 daily fee/pet. Designated rooms, service with restrictions, supervision.

SAVE ⊠ ⓂⓈ 🔋 🖥 ⊃ ⊠

⬥⬥⬥ Best Western Inn of Kearney ⬛ 🐾
(308) 237-5185. **$80-$105.** 1010 3rd Ave. I-80, exit 272 (SR 44), 1 mi n, then just w. Ext/int corridors. **Pets:** Other species. $10 one-time fee/room. Service with restrictions, supervision.

SAVE ⊠ 🔋 🖥 🍴 ⊃ ⊠

⬥⬥ Quality Inn by Choice Hotels ⬛
(308) 237-0838. **Call for rates.** 121 3rd Ave. I-80, exit 272 (SR 44), 0.3 mi n. Int corridors. **Pets:** Accepted.

⊠ 🔋 🖥 ⊃

⬥⬥ Rodeway Inn & Suites ⬛ 🐾
(308) 698-2810. **Call for rates.** 411 2nd Ave. I-80, exit 272 (SR 44), 0.8 mi n. Int corridors. **Pets:** Other species. $10 daily fee/room. Service with restrictions, supervision.

⊠ ⓂⓈ 🔋 🖥

⬥ Super 8 Motel Ⓜ
(308) 234-5513. **$54-$84.** 15 W 8th St. I-80, exit 272 (SR 44), 1 mi n, then just e. Int corridors. **Pets:** Accepted.

ASK ⊠ 🔋 🖥

KIMBALL

⬥⬥ Days Inn-Kimball Ⓜ
(308) 235-4671. **$70-$165.** 611 E 3rd St. I-80, exit 20, 1.5 ne on SR 71, then 0.5 mi e on US 30. Ext corridors. **Pets:** Other species. $10 daily fee/pet. Service with restrictions, supervision.

ASK ⊠ 🔋 🖥 ⊃

LEXINGTON

⬥⬥ Days Inn ⬛
(308) 324-6440. **$70-$99.** 2506 Plum Creek Pkwy. I-80, exit 237 (US 283), 0.6 mi n. Int corridors. **Pets:** Dogs only. $8 daily fee/pet. Designated rooms, service with restrictions, supervision.

ASK ⊠ 🔋 🖥

⬥⬥⬥⬥ Holiday Inn Express Hotel & Suites ⬛
(308) 324-9900. **$100-$150.** 2605 Plum Creek Pkwy. I-80, exit 237 (US 283), 0.5 mi n. Int corridors. **Pets:** Other species. $11 daily fee/room. Designated rooms, service with restrictions, supervision.

SAVE ⊠ ⓂⓈ 🔋 🖥 ⊃

LINCOLN

⬥⬥⬥ Candlewood Suites ⬛
(402) 420-0330. **$90-$140.** 4100 Pioneer Woods Dr. 4.6 mi e on SR 2, 2.2 mi n via 70th St, e on Pioneers Blvd, then just n. Int corridors. **Pets:** Large. $75 one-time fee/pet. Service with restrictions, crate.

ASK ⊠ ⓂⓈ 🔋 🖥

⬥⬥⬥⬥ Chase Suites Hotel ⬛
(402) 483-4900. **$109-$249.** 200 S 68th Pl. On US 34, 4.3 mi e, just s of jct 68th Pl. Ext corridors. **Pets:** Accepted.

SAVE ⊠ ⓂⓈ 🔋 🖥 ⊃ ⊠

⬥⬥ Comfort Suites ⬛
(402) 476-8080. **Call for rates.** 4231 Industrial Ave. I-80, exit 403 (27th St), 2.3 mi s. Int corridors. **Pets:** Large, other species. $10 daily fee/pet. No service, supervision.

⊠ ⓂⓈ 🔋 🖥 ⊃

⬥⬥⬥⬥ Country Inns & Suites By Carlson ⬛ 🐾
(402) 476-5353. **$99-$139.** 5353 N 27th St. I-80, exit 403 (27th St), 1.5 mi s. Int corridors. **Pets:** Medium. $15 daily fee/pet. Designated rooms, service with restrictions, supervision.

SAVE ⊠ ⓂⓈ 🔋 🖥 🍴 ⊃ ⊠

⬥⬥⬥⬥ Countryside Suites ⬛
(402) 742-7575. **$70-$85.** 6750 Wildcat Dr. I-80, exit 403 (27th St), just s, then e. Int corridors. **Pets:** Small, dogs only. $20 deposit/room, $10 daily fee/pet. Service with restrictions, supervision.

SAVE ⊠ ⓂⓈ 🔋 🖥 ⊃

⬥⬥⬥ Days Inn South ⬛
(402) 423-7111. **$53-$90.** 1140 Calvert St. 1.7 mi e on SR 2 from jct US 77. Ext/int corridors. **Pets:** Medium, dogs only. $5 daily fee/pet. Designated rooms, service with restrictions, supervision.

SAVE ⊠ 🔋 🖥

⬥⬥⬥⬥ Hampton Inn Lincoln Airport I-80 ⬛
(402) 474-2080. **$99-$199.** 1301 W Bond Cir. I-80, exit 399 (Airport), just e. Int corridors. **Pets:** Accepted.

⊠ ⓂⓈ 🔋 🖥 ⊃

⬥⬥⬥⬥ Holiday Inn Express ⬛ 🐾
(402) 435-0200. **$90-$100.** 1133 Belmont Ave. I-80, exit 401; exit 401A; 2 mi s on I-180, exit 2 (Cornhusker Hwy E), then just n on 11th St. Int corridors. **Pets:** Designated rooms, service with restrictions, supervision.

SAVE ⊠ ⓂⓈ 🔋 🖥 ⊃ ⊠

⬥⬥⬥ La Quinta Inn ⬛ 🐾
(402) 476-2222. **$69-$159.** 4433 N 27th St. I-80, exit 403 (27th St), 2.3 mi s. Int corridors. **Pets:** Medium, other species. Service with restrictions, supervision.

SAVE ⊠ ⓂⓈ 🔋 🖥 ⊃

⬥⬥⬥ Microtel Inn & Suites ⬛
(402) 476-2591. **$60-$159.** 2505 Fairfield St. I-80, exit 403 (27th St), 2.7 mi s, then just w. Int corridors. **Pets:** Other species. $10 daily fee/pet. Service with restrictions, supervision.

SAVE ⊠ ⓂⓈ 🔋 🖥 ⊃

⬥⬥ New Victorian Suites ⬛
(402) 464-4400. **$69-$149.** 216 N 48th St. 2.5 mi e on US 6 and 34; just ne of jct O St; entrance off 48th St. Int corridors. **Pets:** Accepted.

⊠ ⓂⓈ 🔋 ⊃

⬥⬥ Ramada Limited-South ⬛
(402) 423-3131. **$75-$95.** 1511 Center Park Rd. I-80, exit 397 (US 77), 5.7 mi s, then 1.7 mi ne on SR L55W. Int corridors. **Pets:** Accepted.

ASK ⊠ 🔋 🖥 ⊃

⬥⬥ Settle Inn & Suites ⬛
(402) 435-8100. **$69-$109.** 7333 Husker Cir. I-80, exit 403 (27th St), just s to Wildcat Dr, just e, then just n. Int corridors. **Pets:** Accepted.

⊠ ⓂⓈ 🔋 🖥 ⊃

WWW Staybridge Suites Lincoln-I-80 H
(402) 438-7829. **$121-$296.** 2701 Fletcher Ave. I-80, exit 403 (27th St), 0.4 mi s. Int corridors. **Pets:** Other species. $25 one-time fee/room. Service with restrictions, crate.
⊠ ᴹ̄ 🛏 💻 ⤚ ⊠

WWW Super 8-Lincoln/Cornhusker H 🐾
(402) 467-4488. **$49-$80.** 2545 Cornhusker Hwy. I-80, exit 403 (27th St), 3 mi s. Int corridors. **Pets:** Medium, dogs only. $10 one-time fee/pet. Service with restrictions, supervision.
ASK ⊠ ᴹ̄ 🛏 💻

WWW Super 8-Lincoln/West "O" Street H
(402) 476-8887. **$55-$67.** 2635 West O St. I-80, exit 396 eastbound, 0.5 mi e; exit 397 westbound, 0.5 mi w. Int corridors. **Pets:** $10 daily fee/room. Designated rooms, service with restrictions, crate.
ASK ⊠ ᴹ̄ 🛏 💻

MCCOOK

WW Days Inn-McCook H
(308) 345-7115. **$72-$84.** 901 N Hwy 83. Jct US 6 and 34, 0.3 mi n. Int corridors. **Pets:** Accepted.
ASK ⊠ 🛏 💻 ⤚

WWW Holiday Inn Express H
(308) 345-4505. **Call for rates.** 1 Holiday Bison Dr. On US 83, just n of jct US 6 and 34. Int corridors. **Pets:** Accepted.
⊠ ᴹ̄ 🛏 💻

MORRILL

WW Oak Tree Inn H
(308) 247-2111. **$59-$70.** 707 E Webster. 0.5 mi e on US 26. Ext/int corridors. **Pets:** $5 one-time fee/room. Service with restrictions, supervision.
ASK ⊠ ᴹ̄ 🛏 💻 🍴

NORFOLK

AAA WWWW Norfolk Lodge & Suites, an Ascend Collection hotel H
(402) 379-3833. **$90-$160.** 4200 W Norfolk Ave. On US 275 Bypass, 3 mi w of jct US 81. Ext/int corridors. **Pets:** Small, dogs only. $20 one-time fee/pet. Designated rooms, service with restrictions, crate.
SAVE ⊠ 🛏 💻 🍴 ⤚ ⊠

WW Super 8-Norfolk H
(402) 379-2220. **$45-$67.** 1223 Omaha Ave. Jct US 275 Bypass and 81. Int corridors. **Pets:** Other species. $10 one-time fee/pet. Service with restrictions, supervision.
ASK ⊠ 🛏 💻

NORTH PLATTE

AAA WW Americas Best Value Travelers Inn M
(308) 534-4020. **$40-$60.** 602 E 4th St. I-80, exit 177 (US 83), 1.5 mi n, then 0.3 mi e. Ext corridors. **Pets:** Medium, other species. Service with restrictions, supervision.
SAVE ⊠ 🛏 ⤚

WW Comfort Inn H
(308) 532-6144. **$70-$150.** 2901 S Jeffers St. I-80, exit 177 (US 83), just s. Int corridors. **Pets:** Small. $15 one-time fee/pet. Designated rooms, service with restrictions, supervision.
ASK ⊠ 🛏 💻

WWWW Holiday Inn Express Hotel & Suites H
(308) 532-9500. **Call for rates.** 300 Holiday Frontage Rd. I-80, exit 177 (US 83), just s. Int corridors. **Pets:** Accepted.
⊠ ᴹ̄ 🛏 💻 ⤚ ⊠

AAA WWWW La Quinta Inn & Suites H 🐾
(308) 534-0700. **$69-$159.** 2600 Eagles Wings Pl. I-80, exit 179, just n, then just w. Int corridors. **Pets:** Medium, other species. Service with restrictions, supervision.
SAVE ⊠ ᴹ̄ 🛏 💻 ⤚

AAA WWW Rodeway Inn M
(308) 532-2313. **$69-$89.** 920 N Jeffers St. I-80, exit 177 (US 83), 2 mi n on US 30 and 83. Ext corridors. **Pets:** Large. $7 daily fee/pet. Designated rooms, service with restrictions, supervision.
SAVE ⊠ 🛏 💻 ⤚

OGALLALA

AAA WWW Best Western Stagecoach Inn H 🐾
(308) 284-3656. **$70-$110, 3 day notice.** 201 Stagecoach Tr. I-80, exit 126 (US 26/SR 61), just n, then e on Frontage Rd. Ext corridors. **Pets:** Other species. $10 daily fee/pet. Designated rooms, service with restrictions, supervision.
SAVE ⊠ 🛏 💻 🍴 ⤚ ⊠

AAA WWW Days Inn M 🐾
(308) 284-6365. **$59-$89.** 601 Stagecoach Tr. I-80, exit 126 (US 26/SR 61), just n, then e on Frontage Rd. Int corridors. **Pets:** Dogs only. $6 one-time fee/room. Designated rooms, service with restrictions, supervision.
SAVE ⊠ 🛏 💻

WWWW Holiday Inn Express H
(308) 284-2266. **$94-$109, 10 day notice.** 501 Stagecoach Tr. I-80, exit 126 (US 26/SR 61), just n, then e on Frontage Rd. Ext/int corridors. **Pets:** Accepted.
⊠ 🛏 💻

OMAHA

WW Baymont Inn & Suites H
(402) 391-8129. **$74.** 3301 S 72nd St. I-80, exit 449 (72nd St), just n. Ext/int corridors. **Pets:** Large. $50 deposit/room, $10 daily fee/pet. Designated rooms, service with restrictions, supervision.
ASK ⊠ ᴹ̄ 🛏 💻

AAA WWWW Best Western Kelly Inn Omaha H 🐾
(402) 339-7400. **$114-$169.** 4706 S 108th St. I-80, exit 445 (L St E), 0.3 mi e, then just s. Int corridors. **Pets:** Other species. Service with restrictions, supervision.
SAVE ⊠ 🛏 💻 🍴 ⤚ ⊠

AAA WWW Best Western Settle Inn H 🐾
(402) 431-1246. **$79-$109.** 650 N 109th Ct. I-680, exit 3 (Dodge St W), 0.7 mi w to 108th St and N Old Mill Rd, then just w on Mill Valley Rd. Int corridors. **Pets:** Small, dogs only. $15 daily fee/room. Designated rooms, service with restrictions, supervision.
SAVE ⊠ 🛏 💻 ⤚ ⊠

WW Candlewood Suites H 🐾
(402) 758-2848. **Call for rates.** 360 S 108th Ave. I-680, exit 3 (Dodge St W), 0.7 mi to 108th St, then 0.8 mi s. Int corridors. **Pets:** Medium. $75 one-time fee/pet. Service with restrictions.
⊠ ᴹ̄ 🛏 💻

AAA WWWW Comfort Inn & Suites H
(402) 343-1000. **$85-$159.** 8736 W Dodge Rd. I-680, exit 3 (Dodge St E), 1.5 mi e. Int corridors. **Pets:** Medium. $30 one-time fee/pet. Designated rooms, service with restrictions, supervision.
SAVE ⊠ ᴹ̄ 🛏 💻 ⤚

WWWW Comfort Inn & Suites H 🐾
(402) 934-4900. **$86-$195.** 7007 Grover St. I-80, exit 449 (72nd St), just n, then e. Int corridors. **Pets:** $10 one-time fee/room. Service with restrictions, crate.
ASK ⊠ ᴹ̄ 🛏 💻 🍴 ⤚

AAA WWW Comfort Inn-Southwest H
(402) 593-2380. **$59-$200, 14 day notice.** 10728 L St. I-80, exit 445 (L St E), just n on 108th St, then e. Int corridors. **Pets:** Medium, other species. $10 daily fee/pet. Service with restrictions, supervision.
SAVE ⊠ ᴹ̄ 🛏 💻 ⤚

⬨ ▼▼▼ Countryside Suites Ⓜ
(402) 884-2644. **$70-$100.** 9477 S 142nd St. I-80, exit 440, just ne. Ext corridors. **Pets:** Other species. $10 daily fee/pet. Service with restrictions, supervision.
[SAVE] [✕] [&M] [🛏] [💻]

⬨ ▼▼▼▼ Crowne Plaza Hotel Ⓗ
(402) 496-0850. **Call for rates.** 655 N 108th Ave. I-680, exit 3 (Dodge St W), 0.7 mi to 108th St to 108th Ave and N Old Mill Rd exits, then just n. Int corridors. **Pets:** Large, other species. $150 deposit/room, $25 daily fee/pet. Service with restrictions, crate.
[SAVE] [✕] [🛏] [💻] [🍴] [🏊] [✕]

▼▼▼▼ DoubleTree Guest Suites Omaha Ⓗ
(402) 397-5141. **$100-$230.** 7270 Cedar St. I-80, exit 449 (72nd St), 1.3 mi n. Int corridors. **Pets:** Very small, dogs only. $50 one-time fee/room. Service with restrictions, supervision.
[✕] [&M] [🛏] [💻] [🍴] [🏊] [✕]

⬨ ▼▼▼▼ Hawthorn Suites Ⓗ
(402) 331-0101. **$119-$149.** 11025 M St. I-80, exit 445 (L St E), 0.3 mi e, just s on 108th St, then just w. Ext corridors. **Pets:** Medium. $6 daily fee/room. Service with restrictions.
[SAVE] [✕] [🛏] [💻] [🏊] [✕]

⬨ ▼▼▼▼ Hilton Omaha Ⓗ
(402) 998-3400. **$164-$314.** 1001 Cass St. Cass and 10th sts; downtown. Int corridors. **Pets:** Accepted.
[SAVE] [✕] [&M] [🛏] [💻] [🍴] [🏊] [✕]

▼▼▼▼ Holiday Inn Express Hotel & Suites-West Ⓗ 🐾
(402) 333-5566. **$111-$221.** 17677 Wright St. I-80, exit 445 (L St W), 5.5 mi w, then just s. Int corridors. **Pets:** Other species. $25 one-time fee/pet. Service with restrictions, supervision.
[ASK] [✕] [&M] [🛏] [💻] [🏊] [✕]

▼▼▼▼ Homewood Suites Ⓗ
(402) 397-7500. **$89-$199.** 7010 Hascall St. I-80, exit 449 (72nd St), just n, then just e. Ext/int corridors. **Pets:** Small, dogs only. $50 one-time fee/room. Designated rooms, service with restrictions, crate.
[✕] [🛏] [💻] [🏊]

▼▼ La Quinta Inn Omaha Ⓗ 🐾
(402) 493-1900. **$52-$99.** 3330 N 104th Ave. I-680, exit 4 (Maple St), just w to 108th St, just n to Bedford, then just e. Int corridors. **Pets:** Medium, other species. Service with restrictions, supervision.
[ASK] [✕] [🛏] [💻]

▼▼ La Quinta Inn Omaha Southwest Ⓗ 🐾
(402) 592-5200. **$52-$99.** 10760 M St. I-80, exit 445 (L St E), 0.3 mi e, s on 108th St, then just e. Int corridors. **Pets:** Medium, other species. Service with restrictions, supervision.
[ASK] [✕] [🛏] [💻]

⬨ ▼▼▼▼ Residence Inn by Marriott Ⓗ
(402) 553-8898. **$170-$208.** 6990 Dodge St. I-680, exit 3 (Dodge St E), 3 mi e. Ext corridors. **Pets:** Accepted.
[SAVE] [✕] [🛏] [💻] [🏊] [✕]

⬨ ▼▼▼ Satellite Motel Ⓜ
(402) 733-7373. **$45-$60.** 6006 L St. I-80, exit 450 (60th St), 0.8 mi s; just n of US 275 and SR 92. Ext/int corridors. **Pets:** Accepted.
[SAVE] [✕] [🛏] [💻]

▼▼ Sleep Inn & Suites Ⓗ
(402) 342-2525. **$72-$156.** 2525 Abbott Dr. I-480 E, exit 14th St (Cuming St), 2 mi n, follow signs. Int corridors. **Pets:** Small. $10 one-time fee/pet. Designated rooms, no service, crate.
[ASK] [✕] [🛏] [💻]

▼ Super 8-Omaha/Aksarben Ⓗ
(402) 390-0700. **$49-$85.** 7111 Spring St. I-80, exit 449 (72nd St), 0.3 mi n. Int corridors. **Pets:** Small. $10 daily fee/pet. Designated rooms, no service, crate.
[ASK] [✕] [🛏] [💻]

O'NEILL

▼ Elms Motel Ⓜ
(402) 336-3800. **$48-$105.** 414 E Hwy 20. 1 mi se on US 20/275. Ext corridors. **Pets:** Accepted.
[ASK] [✕] [🛏] [💻]

▼▼▼ Holiday Inn Express Hotel & Suites Ⓗ
(402) 336-4500. **$85-$105.** 1020 E Douglas St. 0.4 mi e on US 20/275. Int corridors. **Pets:** Other species. $10 daily fee/room. No service, supervision.
[ASK] [✕] [&M] [🛏] [💻] [🏊] [✕]

▼▼ Super 8-O'Neill Ⓗ
(402) 336-3100. **$50-$56.** 106 E Hwy 20. 0.5 mi e on US 20/275. Int corridors. **Pets:** Small. $10 daily fee/pet. Designated rooms, no service, crate.
[ASK] [✕] [&M] [🛏] [💻]

PAXTON

▼▼ Paxton Days Inn Ⓜ
(308) 239-4510. **Call for rates.** 851 Paxton Rd. I-80, exit 145, just n. Ext corridors. **Pets:** Accepted.
[✕] [🛏] [💻] [🍴]

ST. PAUL

⬨ ▼ Bel-Air Motel & RV Park Ⓜ
(308) 754-4466. **$49-$60.** 1158 Highway 281. On US 281, 1 mi s. Ext corridors. **Pets:** Accepted.
[SAVE] [✕] [🛏]

SCOTTSBLUFF

▼▼ Comfort Inn Ⓗ
(308) 632-7510. **$69-$109.** 1902 21st Ave. 1.8 mi e on US 26, just n. Ext/int corridors. **Pets:** Other species. $10 one-time fee/room. Service with restrictions, supervision.
[ASK] [✕] [🛏] [💻] [🏊]

▼ Lamplighter American Inn Ⓗ
(308) 632-7108. **Call for rates.** 606 E 27th St. US 26 business route, 0.5 mi e of jct SR 71, just s. Int corridors. **Pets:** Accepted.
[✕] [🛏] [💻] [🍴] [🏊]

▼▼ Scottsbluff Super 8 Ⓗ
(308) 635-1600. **Call for rates.** 2202 Delta Dr. 1.8 mi e on US 26. Int corridors. **Pets:** Dogs only. $10 one-time fee/pet. Designated rooms, service with restrictions, supervision.
[✕] [🛏] [💻] [🏊]

SIDNEY

⬨ ▼ Americas Best Value Inn & Suites Ⓜ
(308) 254-2081. **$56-$90.** 2115 W Illinois St. On US 30, west side of town. Int corridors. **Pets:** Accepted.
[SAVE] [✕] [🛏] [💻]

⬨ ▼▼▼ AmericInn Lodge & Suites of Sidney Ⓗ
(308) 254-0100. **$78-$144.** 645 Cabela Dr. I-80, exit 59, just nw. Int corridors. **Pets:** Accepted.
[SAVE] [✕] [&M] [🛏] [💻] [🏊]

⬨ ▼▼ Days Inn Ⓗ
(308) 254-2121. **$75-$125.** 3042 Silverberg Dr. I-80, exit 59, just n. Int corridors. **Pets:** Medium. $10 daily fee/pet. Designated rooms, service with restrictions, supervision.
[SAVE] [✕] [&M] [🛏] [💻] [🏊]

▼▼▼ Holiday Inn & Conference Center Ⓗ
(308) 254-2000. **$91-$125.** 664 Chase Blvd. I-80, exit 59, just s. Int corridors. **Pets:** Accepted.
[ASK] [✕] [&M] [🛏] [💻] [🍴] [🏊]

SOUTH SIOUX CITY

▼▼▼▼ **Marina Inn Conference Center** H
(402) 494-4000. **$99-$109.** 4th & B sts. I-29, exit 149 southbound; exit 148 northbound, on banks of Missouri River; e at stop light by Nebraska side of bridge. Int corridors. **Pets:** Accepted.
ASK ✕ ㅤ 🛗 🖥 ¶¶ ⇒

SYRACUSE

▼▼ **Sleep Inn & Suites** H
(402) 269-2700. **Call for rates.** 130 N 30th Rd. Jct SR 2, 1 mi n on SR 50. Int corridors. **Pets:** Accepted.
✕ ㅤ 🛗 🖥 ⇒

THEDFORD

AAA ▼▼▼ **Roadside Inn** H
(308) 645-2284. **$66-$95.** 39357 E Hwy 2. 1 mi e on SR 2, just w of US 83. Int corridors. **Pets:** Other species. $10 daily fee/room. Designated rooms, service with restrictions, supervision.
SAVE ✕ ㅤ 🛗 🖥

VALENTINE

▼▼▼ **Dunes Lodge & Suites** M
(402) 376-3131. **$49-$139.** 340 E Hwys 20 & 83. Jct US 20/83, 0.3 mi e. Ext corridors. **Pets:** Accepted.
ASK ✕ 🛗 🖥

AAA ▼▼▼ **Trade Winds Motel** M
(402) 376-1600. **$55-$84.** E Hwys 20 & 83. Jct US 20/83, 1 mi se. Ext corridors. **Pets:** $10 daily fee/pet. Service with restrictions, supervision.
SAVE ✕ 🛗 🖥 ⇒

WAHOO

▼▼▼ **Wahoo Heritage Inn** H
(402) 443-1288. **$58-$74.** 950 N Chestnut. On US 77 and SR 92, just nw of downtown. Ext/int corridors. **Pets:** Other species. $25 deposit/room, $5 daily fee/pet. Service with restrictions, crate.
ASK ✕ ㅤ 🛗 🖥

WAYNE

▼▼▼ **Super 8-Wayne** H
(402) 375-4898. **$52-$65.** 610 Tomar Dr. SR 35, 0.6 mi e of jct SR 15. Int corridors. **Pets:** Small. $10 daily fee/pet. Designated rooms, no service, crate.
ASK ✕ ㅤ 🛗 🖥

YORK

AAA ▼▼▼ **Americas Best Value Inn** M
(402) 362-5585. **$70-$95.** 2426 S Lincoln Ave. I-80, exit 353 (US 81), 1 mi n. Ext corridors. **Pets:** Other species. $10 daily fee/room. Designated rooms, service with restrictions, supervision.
SAVE ✕ 🛗 🖥 ⇒

▼▼▼ **Holiday Inn** H 🐾
(402) 362-6661. **Call for rates.** 4619 S Lincoln Ave. I-80, exit 353 (US 81), just s. Int corridors. **Pets:** Other species. $25 one-time fee/room. Designated rooms, service with restrictions, supervision.
✕ ㅤ 🛗 🖥 ¶¶ ⇒

AAA ▼▼▼ **Yorkshire Inn Motel** M
(402) 362-6633. **$42-$69, 7 day notice.** 3402 S Lincoln Ave. I-80, exit 353 (US 81), 0.5 mi n. Ext/int corridors. **Pets:** Accepted.
SAVE ✕ 🛗

NEVADA

BEATTY

Stagecoach Hotel Casino
(775) 553-2419. **$62-$77.** 900 E Hwy 95 N. North end of town; west side of US 95. Ext/int corridors. **Pets:** Medium. $10 deposit/pet, $5 one-time fee/pet. Designated rooms, service with restrictions, supervision.

CARLIN

Comfort Inn
(775) 754-6110. **$69.** 1018 Fir St. I-80, exit 280, just s, just e, then n. Int corridors. **Pets:** Accepted.

CARSON CITY

Days Inn
(775) 883-3343. **$50-$150.** 3103 N Carson St. US 395 N, north end of town. Ext corridors. **Pets:** Large. $10 daily fee/pet. Service with restrictions, supervision.

Holiday Inn Express & Suites
(775) 283-4055. **$110-$200.** 4055 N Carson St. US 395; north end of town. Int corridors. **Pets:** Other species. $20 one-time fee/pet. Service with restrictions, supervision.

The Plaza Hotel & Conference Center
(775) 883-9500. **$49-$79.** 801 S Carson St. South end of town. Ext/int corridors. **Pets:** Other species. $25 daily fee/room. Designated rooms.

ELKO

Gold Country Inn & Casino
(775) 738-8421. **$79-$159.** 2050 Idaho St. I-80, exit 303, just s. Ext corridors. **Pets:** Other species. $15 one-time fee/room. Designated rooms, service with restrictions, supervision.

Oak Tree Inn
(775) 777-2222. **Call for rates.** 95 Spruce Rd. I-80, exit 301, just n. Int corridors. **Pets:** Other species. $10 daily fee/pet. Service with restrictions, supervision.

Red Lion Hotel & Casino
(775) 738-2111. **$99-$259.** 2065 Idaho St. I-80, exit 303, just s. Int corridors. **Pets:** Other species. $20 one-time fee/room. Service with restrictions, supervision.

Rodeway Inn
(775) 738-7152. **$49-$129, 7 day notice.** 736 Idaho St. I-80, exit 301 or 303, 1 mi s. Ext corridors. **Pets:** Medium, dogs only. $15 daily fee/pet. Designated rooms, service with restrictions, supervision.

Shilo Inn

(775) 738-5522. **$90-$170.** 2401 Mountain City Hwy. I-80, exit 301, just n. Int corridors. **Pets:** Dogs only. $25 one-time fee/room. Designated rooms, service with restrictions, supervision.

Thunderbird Motel
(775) 738-7115. **$55-$100.** 345 Idaho St. I-80, exit 301 or 303, 1 mi s. Ext corridors. **Pets:** Accepted.

ELY

Best Western Park Vue Motel
(775) 289-4497. **$65-$95, 3 day notice.** 930 Aultman St. 0.8 mi w of jct US 50 and 93. Ext corridors. **Pets:** $20 one-time fee/pet. Service with restrictions, crate.

Historic Hotel Nevada & Gambling Hall
(775) 289-6665. **$49-$69.** 501 Aultman St. 1.1 mi w of jct US 50 and 93. Int corridors. **Pets:** Large, other species. $10 one-time fee/room. Supervision.

Ramada Inn-Copper Queen Casino
(775) 289-4884. **$94-$199.** 805 Great Basin Blvd. 0.3 mi s of jct US 6, 50 and 93. Ext/int corridors. **Pets:** Other species. Service with restrictions, supervision.

EUREKA

Best Western Eureka Inn
(775) 237-5247. **$100-$105.** 251 N Main St. On east side of Main St; center. Int corridors. **Pets:** Small. $15 daily fee/pet. Designated rooms, service with restrictions, supervision.

FALLON

Best Western Fallon Inn
(775) 423-6005. **$50-$149.** 1035 W Williams Ave. 0.4 mi W of jct US 50 and 95. Ext corridors. **Pets:** Accepted.

Comfort Inn
(775) 423-5554. **$70-$160.** 1830 W Williams Ave. 0.9 mi w of jct US 50 and 95. Int corridors. **Pets:** Medium. $15 daily fee/pet. Designated rooms, service with restrictions, supervision.

Motel 6 #4140
(775) 423-2277. **$43-$89.** 1705 S Taylor St. 0.8 mi s of jct US 50. Ext corridors. **Pets:** Other species. Service with restrictions, supervision.

Super 8 Motel
(775) 423-6031. **Call for rates.** 855 W Williams Ave. 0.4 mi w of jct US 50 and 95. Ext/int corridors. **Pets:** Accepted.

FERNLEY

AAA/ ▼▼◆ Best Western Fernley Inn M
(775) 575-6776. **$90-$118.** 1405 E Newlands Dr. I-80, exit 48, just sw. Ext corridors. **Pets:** $10 daily fee/pet. Designated rooms, service with restrictions, crate.
[SAVE] [✕] [&M] [📶] [▣] [⇌]

GARDNERVILLE

AAA/ ▼▼▼ Historian Inn M
(775) 783-1175. **$69-$99.** 1427 Hwy 395 N. Center. Ext corridors. **Pets:** Medium, other species. $10 daily fee/room. Service with restrictions, crate.
[SAVE] [✕] [&M] [📶] [▣]

AAA/ ▼▼ Topaz Lodge H
(775) 266-3338. **$49-$105.** 1979 US 395 S. US 395 S at Topaz Lake, 22 mi s. Ext corridors. **Pets:** Accepted.
[SAVE] [✕] [▣] [¶] [⇌]

AAA/ ▼ Westerner Motel M
(775) 782-3602. **$49-$99.** 1353 US 395. On US 395, south end of town. Ext corridors. **Pets:** Accepted.
[SAVE] [✕] [📶] [▣] [⇌]

JACKPOT

AAA/ ▼▼▼ Horseshu Hotel & Casino H
(775) 755-7777. **$37-$160.** 1385 Hwy 93. On US 93. Int corridors. **Pets:** Other species. Designated rooms, service with restrictions.
[SAVE] [✕] [▣] [¶] [⇌]

LAKE TAHOE AREA

STATELINE

▼▼▼ Harrah's Lake Tahoe H
(775) 588-6611. **Call for rates.** US 50. In casino center. Int corridors. **Pets:** Accepted.
[✕] [&M] [📶] [▣] [¶] [⇌] [✕]

AAA/ ▼▼▼ MontBleu Resort Casino & Spa H ✿
(775) 588-3515. **$79-$300.** 55 Lake Tahoe Blvd (US 50). 0.4 mi sw of jct SR 207. Int corridors. **Pets:** Medium. $35 one-time fee/room. Designated rooms, service with restrictions, crate.
[SAVE] [✕] [¶] [⇌] [✕]

ZEPHYR COVE

AAA/ ▼▼▼ Zephyr Cove Resort CA
(775) 589-4907. **Call for rates.** 760 Hwy 50. 4 mi n of state line. Ext/int corridors. **Pets:** Accepted.
[SAVE] [✕] [📶] [▣] [¶] [✕]

END AREA

LAS VEGAS METROPOLITAN AREA

BOULDER CITY

AAA/ ▼▼▼ Best Western Lighthouse Inn & Resort H
(702) 293-6444. **$70-$150.** 110 Ville Dr. Jct US 93. Ext corridors. **Pets:** Dogs only. $10 daily fee/pet. Designated rooms, service with restrictions, crate.
[SAVE] [✕] [📶] [▣] [⇌]

AAA/ ▼▼▼ Boulder Inn & Suites M
(702) 369-1000. **$79-$229.** 704 Nevada Way. On US 93. Ext corridors. **Pets:** Medium, dogs only. $10 daily fee/pet. Designated rooms, service with restrictions, supervision.
[SAVE] [✕] [📶] [▣] [¶] [⇌]

AAA/ ▼▼▼ El Rancho Boulder Motel M
(702) 293-1085. **$75-$120, 3 day notice.** 725 Nevada Way. On US 93. Ext corridors. **Pets:** Accepted.
[SAVE] [✕] [📶] [⇌]

AAA/ ▼ Sands Motel M ✿
(702) 293-2589. **$64-$99, 3 day notice.** 809 Nevada Way. On US 93. Ext corridors. **Pets:** Medium, dogs only. $10 one-time fee/pet. Designated rooms, service with restrictions, supervision.
[SAVE] [✕] [📶]

ECHO BAY

AAA/ ▼ Echo Bay Resort M
(702) 394-4000. **$70-$125, 3 day notice.** North Shore Rd. 4 mi e of SR 167; on Lake Mead. Int corridors. **Pets:** $50 deposit/room, $10 daily fee/pet. Service with restrictions, supervision.
[SAVE] [✕] [&M] [📶] [¶] [✕]

HENDERSON

AAA/ ▼▼▼▼ Green Valley Ranch H ✿
(702) 617-7777. **$150-$600.** 2300 S Paseo Verde Dr. I-215, exit Green Valley Pkwy, just s. Int corridors. **Pets:** Small, dogs only. $100 one-time fee/pet. Designated rooms, no service.
[SAVE] [✕] [&M] [▣] [¶] [⇌] [✕]

▼▼ Hawthorn Inn & Suites M
(702) 568-7800. **Call for rates.** 910 S Boulder Hwy. S of Lake Mead Pkwy. Int corridors. **Pets:** Accepted.
[✕] [📶] [▣] [⇌]

AAA/ ▼▼▼▼ Loews Lake Las Vegas Resort H ✿
(702) 567-6000. **Call for rates.** 101 Montelago Blvd. I-215, e to end, then n on Lake Las Vegas Pkwy. Int corridors. **Pets:** Other species. $25 one-time fee/pet. Designated rooms, service with restrictions.
[SAVE] [✕] [&M] [📶] [▣] [¶] [⇌] [✕]

▼▼◆▼ **Residence Inn-Green Valley** Ⓜ
(702) 434-2700. **$149-$169.** 2190 Olympic Ave. I-215, exit Green Valley Pkwy N, 3 mi n at Sunset Rd. Int corridors. **Pets:** Accepted.
☒ Ⓢᴹ 🛈 💻 ⇋ ⊠

▼▼◆▼ ▼▼◆▼ **The Ritz-Carlton, Lake Las Vegas** Ⓗ
(702) 567-4700. **$159-$399, 3 day notice.** 1610 Lake Las Vegas Pkwy. I-515, exit Lake Mead Pkwy, 6.3 mi ne, then 0.5 mi n. Int corridors. **Pets:** Accepted.
A$K ☒ Ⓢᴹ 🛈 💻 ⑪ ⇋ ⊠

LAS VEGAS

ⒶⒶⒶ ▼▼◆▼ **Best Western Main Street Inn** Ⓜ
(702) 382-3455. **$50-$200.** 1000 N Main St. I-15, exit 43E northbound; exit 44E southbound. Ext corridors. **Pets:** Medium, other species. $15 daily fee/pet. Service with restrictions, supervision.
SAVE ☒ 🛈 💻 ⑪ ⇋

ⒶⒶⒶ ▼▼◆▼ **Best Western Nellis Motor Inn** Ⓜ
(702) 643-6111. **$70-$110.** 5330 E Craig Rd. I-15, exit 48, 2.8 mi e; 0.3 mi from Nellis AFB. Ext corridors. **Pets:** Accepted.
SAVE ☒ 🛈 💻 ⇋

ⒶⒶⒶ ▼▼◆▼ **Best Western Parkview Inn** Ⓜ
(702) 385-1213. **$56-$200, 7 day notice.** 921 Las Vegas Blvd N. I-15, exit US 93/95, 0.3 mi n at Washington. Ext corridors. **Pets:** Large, other species. $8 daily fee/pet. Service with restrictions, supervision.
SAVE ☒ 🛈 💻 ⇋

▼▼ ▼▼ **Candlewood Suites** Ⓗ
(702) 836-3660. **Call for rates.** 4034 S Paradise Rd. I-15, exit E Flamingo Rd to Paradise Rd, just ne. Int corridors. **Pets:** Accepted.
☒ Ⓢᴹ 🛈 💻 ⇋

ⒶⒶⒶ ▼▼◆▼ **Comfort Inn** Ⓜ
(702) 399-1500. **$80-$300.** 910 E Cheyenne Ave. I-15, exit Cheyenne Ave W, just w. Int corridors. **Pets:** $10 daily fee/pet. Service with restrictions, supervision.
SAVE ☒ Ⓢᴹ 🛈 💻 ⇋

▼▼ ▼▼ **Extended StayAmerica-Valley View** Ⓗ
(702) 221-7600. **$84-$94.** 4270 S Valley View Blvd. I-15, exit W Flamingo Rd, just w, then just s. Ext corridors. **Pets:** Other species. $25 daily fee/pet. Service with restrictions, crate.
A$K ☒ 🛈 💻 ⇋

ⒶⒶⒶ ▼▼◆▼▼◆▼ **Four Seasons Hotel Las Vegas** Ⓗ 🐾
(702) 632-5000. **$295-$5000.** 3960 Las Vegas Blvd S. I-15, exit E Tropicana Ave, just s on the Strip. Int corridors. **Pets:** Small. Service with restrictions, supervision.
SAVE ☒ Ⓢᴹ 💻 ⑪ ⇋ ⊠

ⒶⒶⒶ ▼▼ **Highland Inn Motel** Ⓜ
(702) 896-4333. **$50-$130.** 8025 Dean Martin Dr. I-15, exit W Blue Diamond Rd, just w. Ext corridors. **Pets:** Very small, dogs only. $50 deposit/room, $10 daily fee/pet. Designated rooms, service with restrictions, supervision.
SAVE ☒ 🛈 💻

▼▼ ▼▼ **Homestead Studio Suites Hotel-Las Vegas/Midtown** Ⓜ
(702) 369-1414. **$89-$99.** 3045 S Maryland Pkwy. I-15, exit Sahara Ave E, 1.7 mi e, then 0.6 mi s. Int corridors. **Pets:** Other species. $25 daily fee/pet. Service with restrictions, crate.
A$K ☒ Ⓢᴹ 🛈 💻

▼▼◆▼ **La Quinta Inn & Suites Las Vegas (Convention Center)** Ⓜ 🐾
(702) 796-9000. **$79-$179.** 3970 Paradise Rd. I-15, exit E Flamingo Rd, 0.8 mi s of convention center; 0.5 mi e of the Strip. Int corridors. **Pets:** Medium, other species. Service with restrictions, supervision.
A$K ☒ Ⓢᴹ 🛈 💻 ⑪ ⇋

▼▼◆▼ **La Quinta Inn & Suites Las Vegas (Lakes/West)** Ⓜ 🐾
(702) 243-0356. **$92-$185.** 9570 W Sahara Ave. Just w of Fort Apache Rd. Int corridors. **Pets:** Medium, other species. Service with restrictions, supervision.
A$K ☒ Ⓢᴹ 🛈 💻 ⇋

▼▼◆▼ **La Quinta Inn & Suites Las Vegas (Summerlin Tech Center)** Ⓜ 🐾
(702) 360-1200. **$89-$169.** 7101 Cascade Valley Ct. US 95, exit W Cheyenne Ave. Int corridors. **Pets:** Medium, other species. Service with restrictions, supervision.
A$K ☒ Ⓢᴹ 🛈 💻 ⇋

ⒶⒶⒶ ▼▼◆▼ **La Quinta Inn Las Vegas (Nellis)** Ⓜ 🐾
(702) 632-0229. **$90-$170.** 4288 N Nellis Blvd. I-15, exit Craig Rd, e to N Las Vegas Blvd. Int corridors. **Pets:** Medium, other species. Service with restrictions, supervision.
SAVE ☒ Ⓢᴹ 🛈 💻 ⇋

ⒶⒶⒶ ▼▼ ▼▼ **La Quinta Inn Las Vegas (Tropicana)** Ⓜ 🐾
(702) 798-7736. **$85-$270.** 4975 S Valley View Blvd. I-15, exit Tropicana Ave W, just w. Int corridors. **Pets:** Medium, other species. Service with restrictions, supervision.
SAVE ☒ Ⓢᴹ 🛈 💻 ⇋

ⒶⒶⒶ ▼▼◆▼▼◆▼ **Red Rock Casino Resort & Spa** Ⓗ
(702) 797-7777. **$150-$600.** 11011 W Charleston Blvd. I-215, exit Charleston Blvd, just e. Int corridors. **Pets:** Accepted.
SAVE ☒ Ⓢᴹ ⑪ ⇋ ⊠

▼▼◆▼ **Residence Inn by Marriott Las Vegas South** Ⓗ
(702) 795-7378. **$149-$169.** 5875 Dean Martin Rd. I-15, exit Russell Rd, just sw. Int corridors. **Pets:** Accepted.
☒ Ⓢᴹ 🛈 💻 ⇋ ⊠

▼▼◆▼ **Residence Inn-Hughes Center** Ⓗ
(702) 650-0040. **$149-$179.** 370 Hughes Center Dr. I-15, exit Paradise Rd. Int corridors. **Pets:** Medium, other species. $100 one-time fee/room. Service with restrictions, supervision.
☒ Ⓢᴹ 🛈 💻 ⇋ ⊠

▼▼◆▼ **Residence Inn Las Vegas Convention Center** Ⓜ
(702) 796-9300. **$159-$189.** 3225 Paradise Rd. Opposite the convention center. Ext corridors. **Pets:** Accepted.
☒ Ⓢᴹ 🛈 💻 ⇋ ⊠

ⒶⒶⒶ ▼▼◆▼▼◆▼ **Skylofts at the MGM Grand Hotel** Ⓗ
(702) 891-3832. **Call for rates.** 3799 Las Vegas Blvd S. I-15, exit Tropicana Ave, 0.5 mi e to the Strip; atop the MGM Grand Hotel. Int corridors. **Pets:** Accepted.
SAVE 🛈 💻

▼▼ ▼▼ **Super 8 World Wide** Ⓜ
(702) 794-0888. **$50-$175.** 4250 Koval Ln. Jct Flamingo Rd and Koval Ln, just s. Int corridors. **Pets:** Other species. $15 daily fee/pet. Designated rooms, service with restrictions, supervision.
A$K ☒ 🛈 💻 ⇋

▼▼ ▼▼ **Trump International Hotel & Tower** Ⓗ
(702) 982-0000. **$199-$699, 3 day notice.** 2000 Fashion Show Dr. Just w of the Strip. Int corridors. **Pets:** Accepted.
☒ Ⓢᴹ 🛈 💻 ⑪ ⇋ ⊠

ⒶⒶⒶ ▼▼◆▼ **Westgate Flamingo Bay** Ⓒ🅞 🐾
(702) 251-3435. **$89-$319, 3 day notice.** 5625 W Flamingo Rd. I-15, exit E Flamingo Rd, just e of Jones Blvd. Ext corridors. **Pets:** Medium. $75 deposit/room. Designated rooms, service with restrictions, supervision.
SAVE ☒ Ⓢᴹ 🛈 💻 ⇋ ⊠

WWW The Westin Casuarina Las Vegas Hotel, Casino and Spa H ❀
(702) 836-5900. **$99-$149.** 160 E Flamingo Rd. I-15, exit Flamingo Rd E, 1.1 mi. Int corridors. **Pets:** $150 deposit/room, $35 one-time fee/room. Service with restrictions.
SAVE ✕ ⎙M 🛏 🖥 ⍢ ⊃ ✕

LAUGHLIN

WWW Don Laughlin's Riverside Resort Hotel & Casino H
(702) 298-2535. **$45-$750.** 1650 S Casino Dr. 2 mi s of Davis Dam. Int corridors. **Pets:** Accepted.
SAVE ✕ ⎙M 🛏 🖥 ⍢ ⊃ ✕

MESQUITE

WWW Best Western Mesquite Inn M
(702) 346-7444. **$69-$120.** 390 N Sandhill Blvd. I-15, exit 122. Ext corridors. **Pets:** Medium. $15 daily fee/pet. Designated rooms, service with restrictions, supervision.
SAVE ✕ 🛏 🖥 ⊃

WWW Falcon Ridge Hotel H
(702) 346-2200. **Call for rates.** 1030 W Pioneer Blvd. I-15, exit 120, just w. Int corridors. **Pets:** Accepted.
✕ ⎙M 🛏 🖥 ⊃ ✕

WW Virgin River Hotel Casino Bingo M
(702) 346-7777. **Call for rates.** 100 Pioneer Blvd. I-15, exit 122, just w. Ext corridors. **Pets:** Accepted.
✕ ⎙M 🛏 ⍢ ⊃

OVERTON

WWW Best Western North Shore Inn at Lake Mead M
(702) 397-6000. **$70-$90.** 520 N Moapa Valley Blvd. I-15, exit 93, 10 mi ne on SR 169. Int corridors. **Pets:** Medium, dogs only. $10 daily fee/room. Designated rooms, service with restrictions, supervision.
SAVE ✕ 🛏 🖥 ⊃

PAHRUMP

WWW Best Western Pahrump Station M ❀
(775) 727-5100. **$75-$130.** 1101 S Hwy 160. Downtown. Ext/int corridors. **Pets:** Dogs only. $8 deposit/pet. Designated rooms, service with restrictions, supervision.
SAVE ✕ ⎙M 🛏 🖥 ⍢ ⊃

WWW Saddle West Hotel & Casino M
(775) 727-1111. **Call for rates.** 1220 S Hwy 160. Downtown. Ext corridors. **Pets:** Dogs only. $100 deposit/pet, $10 daily fee/pet. Designated rooms, service with restrictions, supervision.
SAVE ✕ ⎙M 🛏 🖥 ⍢ ⊃

END METROPOLITAN AREA

MINDEN

WWW Best Western Minden Inn M
(775) 782-7766. **$80-$175.** 1795 Ironwood Dr. Just w of jct US 395. Ext corridors. **Pets:** Large, dogs only. $15 daily fee/pet. Designated rooms, service with restrictions, supervision.
SAVE ✕ ⎙M 🛏 🖥 ⊃

RENO

WWW Atlantis Casino Resort Spa Reno H
(775) 825-4700. **$69-$279.** 3800 S Virginia St. 3 mi s on US 395, exit 63, just w. Ext/int corridors. **Pets:** Accepted.
SAVE ✕ ⎙M 🛏 🖥 ⍢ ⊃ ✕

WWW Best Western Airport Plaza Hotel & Conference Center H
(775) 348-6370. **$80-$170, 3 day notice.** 1981 Terminal Way. US 395, exit 65A southbound (E Plumb Ln/Villanova Dr), just e on Villanova Dr; exit 65 northbound, just e on E Plumb Ln. Int corridors. **Pets:** Accepted.
SAVE ✕ ⎙M 🛏 🖥 ⍢ ⊃ ✕

WWW Days Inn M ❀
(775) 786-4070. **$40-$189.** 701 E 7th St. I-80, exit Wells Ave, just s. Ext corridors. **Pets:** Medium. $10 daily fee/pet. Designated rooms, service with restrictions.
SAVE ✕ 🛏 🖥 ⊃

WW Extended StayAmerica-Reno-South Meadows H
(775) 852-5611. **$100-$110.** 9795 Gateway Dr. US 395, exit 60 (S Meadows Pkwy), just e, then n. Int corridors. **Pets:** Other species. $25 daily fee/pet. Service with restrictions, crate.
ASK ✕ 🛏 🖥

WWW Grand Sierra Resort & Casino H
(775) 789-2000. **$69-$259.** 2500 E 2nd St. 0.5 mi s of jct I-80 and US 395; US 395, exit Mill St. Int corridors. **Pets:** Accepted.
SAVE ✕ ⎙M 🛏 ⍢ ⊃ ✕

WWW Holiday Inn-Downtown H
(775) 786-5151. **$69-$99.** 1000 E 6th St. I-80, exit Wells Ave, 2 blks e. Int corridors. **Pets:** $20 daily fee/room. Designated rooms, service with restrictions, supervision.
SAVE ✕ ⎙M 🛏 🖥 ⍢ ⊃

WWW La Quinta Inn Reno (Airport) M ❀
(775) 348-6100. **$49-$169.** 4001 Market St. US 395, exit 65A southbound (E Plumb Ln/Villanova Dr), just w on Villanova Dr; exit 65 northbound, just n, then just w on Villanova Dr. Ext corridors. **Pets:** Medium, other species. Service with restrictions, supervision.
ASK ✕ ⎙M 🛏 🖥 ⊃

WWW Quality Inn South H
(775) 329-1001. **$66-$139.** 1885 S Virginia St. US 395, exit Plumb Ln Villanova, 1 mi w. Ext/int corridors. **Pets:** Medium. $10 daily fee/room. Service with restrictions, supervision.
SAVE ✕ ⎙M 🛏 🖥 ⍢ ⊃

WWW Residence Inn by Marriott H
(775) 853-8800. **$166-$202.** 9845 Gateway Dr. US 395, exit S Meadows Pkwy, just e. Int corridors. **Pets:** Accepted.
✕ ⎙M 🛏 🖥 ⊃ ✕

WWW Seasons Inn M ❀
(775) 322-6000. **$59-$109, 3 day notice.** 495 West St. Corner of West and 5th sts; 1 blk w of casinos. Ext corridors. **Pets:** Small. $10 one-time fee/pet. Designated rooms, service with restrictions, supervision.
SAVE ✕

SPARKS

WWW Sparks Super 8 H
(775) 358-8884. **$50-$250.** 1900 E Greg St. I-80, exit 20, 0.6 mi n, then e. Int corridors. **Pets:** Small. $10 daily fee/pet. Service with restrictions, supervision.
SAVE ✕ 🛏 🖥 ⊃

TONOPAH

Best Western Hi-Desert Inn M ❀
(775) 482-3511. **$79-$159.** 320 Main St. On US 6 and 95. Int corridors. **Pets:** Dogs only. Designated rooms, service with restrictions, supervision.

Ramada Inn-Tonopah Station M
(775) 482-9777. **$75-$125.** 1100 Main St. On US 6 and 95. Int corridors. **Pets:** Accepted.

UNIONVILLE

Old Pioneer Garden BB ❀
(775) 538-7585. **Call for rates.** 2805 Unionville Rd. I-80, exit 149, 16 mi s, then 2.5 mi w. Int corridors. **Pets:** Designated rooms, no service, supervision.

WEST WENDOVER

Americas Best Value Inn M
(775) 664-2888. **Call for rates.** 1325 Wendover Blvd. I-80, exit 410, 0.5 mi w. Int corridors. **Pets:** Accepted.

WINNEMUCCA

Best Western Gold Country Inn H
(775) 623-6999. **$99-$189.** 921 W Winnemucca Blvd. I-80, exit 176 or 178, just s. Int corridors. **Pets:** Accepted.

Days Inn M
(775) 623-3661. **Call for rates.** 511 W Winnemucca Blvd. I-80, exit 176, just s. Ext corridors. **Pets:** Accepted.

Holiday Inn Express H
(775) 625-3100. **$99-$209.** 1987 W Winnemucca Blvd. I-80, exit 176, just s. Int corridors. **Pets:** Large, other species. $50 deposit/room, $20 daily fee/pet, $20 one-time fee/pet. Service with restrictions, supervision.

Red Lion Hotel & Casino H
(775) 623-2565. **$89-$149.** 741 W Winnemucca Blvd. I-80, exit 176 or 178, just s. Int corridors. **Pets:** Other species. $20 one-time fee/room. Service with restrictions, supervision.

Super 8 Motel H
(775) 625-1818. **Call for rates.** 1157 W Winnemucca Blvd. I-80, exit 176, 0.5 mi e. Int corridors. **Pets:** $50 deposit/pet, $10 one-time fee/pet. Designated rooms, service with restrictions, supervision.

Town House Motel M
(775) 623-3620. **$72-$80.** 375 Monroe St. I-80, exit 176 or 178, just s. Ext corridors. **Pets:** Small, dogs only. $5 daily fee/pet. Designated rooms, service with restrictions, supervision.

Winnemucca Holiday Motel M
(775) 623-3684. **$79-$149.** 670 W Winnemucca Blvd. I-80, exit 176 or 178, just s. Ext corridors. **Pets:** Other species. $25 deposit/room. Designated rooms, service with restrictions, supervision.

NEW HAMPSHIRE

CITY INDEX

ASHLAND

▼▼▼▼ Glynn House Inn BB ❀
(603) 968-3775. **$149-$289, 21 day notice.** 59 Highland St. I-93, exit 24 (SR 25 and US 3), 0.8 mi e to flag pole in center of town (Highland), then 0.3 mi nw. Ext/int corridors. **Pets:** Dogs only. $250 deposit/room. Designated rooms, service with restrictions.
⊠ ☎

BARTLETT

◈◈◈ ▼▼▼ The Bartlett Inn BB
(603) 374-2353. **$109-$248, 14 day notice.** 1477 US Rt 302. On US 302, 7 mi w of jct SR 16. Ext/int corridors. **Pets:** Dogs only. $15 one-time fee/pet. Designated rooms, supervision.
SAVE ⊠ 🛏 💻 ⊠ ☎

◈◈◈ ▼▼▼ The Villager Motel M
(603) 374-2742. **$49-$249, 10 day notice.** 1126 US 302. 1 mi e on US 302; 1.3 mi w of Attitash Mountain. Ext corridors. **Pets:** $10 daily fee/room. Service with restrictions, supervision.
SAVE ⊠ 🛏 💻 ➿ ⊠

BRETTON WOODS

▼▼▼▼ Bretton Arms Inn CI
(603) 278-1000. **$179-$389, 15 day notice.** US 302. Center. Int corridors. **Pets:** Accepted.
⊠ 🛏 💻 🍴 ⊠

▼▼▼▼ The Townhomes VH
(603) 278-2000. **$269-$1099, 21 day notice.** US 302. Center. Ext corridors. **Pets:** Accepted.
⊠ 🛏 ➿ ⊠

CAMPTON

◈◈◈ ▼▼▼ Days Inn Campton/Plymouth 🅷
(603) 536-3520. **$45-$149.** 1513 Daniel Webster Hwy. I-93, exit 27, just e, then just n. Int corridors. **Pets:** Accepted.
SAVE ⊠ 🛏 💻 ➿ ⊠

CHESTERFIELD

▼▼▼▼ Chesterfield Inn CI
(603) 256-3211. **$150-$320, 5 day notice.** 20 Cross Rd. I-91, exit 3, 2 mi e on SR 9. Ext/int corridors. **Pets:** Medium, other species. Designated rooms, service with restrictions, crate.
ASK ⊠ 🛏 💻 🍴

COLEBROOK

◈◈◈ ▼ Northern Comfort Motel M
(603) 237-4440. **$69-$89, 3 day notice.** 1 Trooper Scott Phillips Hwy. 1.5 mi s on US 3. Ext corridors. **Pets:** Accepted.
SAVE ⊠ 🛏 🏊 ⊠

CONCORD

▼▼ Concord Comfort Inn 🅷 ❀
(603) 226-4100. **$80-$289.** 71 Hall St. I-93, exit 13, just n on Main St, then 0.3 mi w. Int corridors. **Pets:** Dogs only. $15 daily fee/pet. Designated rooms, service with restrictions, crate.
ASK ⊠ 🖥 🛏 💻 ➿ ⊠

CONWAY

▼ White Deer Motel M
(603) 447-5366. **$89-$199.** 379 White Mountain Hwy. 2.1 mi s of jct US 302; 0.5 mi n of village center on SR 16. Ext/int corridors. **Pets:** $50 deposit/room, $10 daily fee/pet. Designated rooms, service with restrictions, supervision.
ASK ⊠ 🛏 💻

DIXVILLE NOTCH

◈◈◈ ▼▼▼▼ The Balsams Grand Resort Hotel 🅷
(603) 255-3400. **$278-$598, 7 day notice.** 1000 Cold Spring Rd.. Int corridors. **Pets:** Accepted.
SAVE ⊠ 🛏 🍴 ➿ ⊠

DOVER

▼▼ Days Inn M
(603) 742-0400. **$89-$179.** 481 Central Ave. Spaulding Tpke, exit 7, 2 mi n on SR 108; downtown. Ext/int corridors. **Pets:** Other species. $50 deposit/room, $10 daily fee/pet. Service with restrictions, supervision.
ASK ⊠ 🛏 💻 ➿

DURHAM

▼▼ Hickory Pond Inn CI
(603) 659-2227. **$99-$189, 3 day notice.** 1 Stagecoach Rd. 2.8 mi s on SR 108. Int corridors. **Pets:** Accepted.
ASK ⊠ ⊠

FRANCONIA

◈◈◈ ▼▼▼ Best Western White Mountain Resort 🅷
(603) 823-7422. **$80-$180, 3 day notice.** 87 Wallace Hill Rd. I-93, exit 38, just e. Int corridors. **Pets:** Accepted.
SAVE ⊠ 🛏 💻 ➿ ⊠

▼ Gale River Motel M ❀
(603) 823-5655. **$70-$200, 7 day notice.** 1 Main St. I-93, exit 38, 0.8 mi n on SR 18. Ext corridors. **Pets:** Other species. $10 one-time fee/pet. Designated rooms, service with restrictions, supervision.
⊠ 🛏 💻 ➿ ⊠

▼▼▼▼ Lovetts Inn by Lafayette Brook CI
(603) 823-7761. **Call for rates.** 1474 Profile Rd. I-93, exit 38, just w on Wallace Hill Rd, then 2.1 mi s on SR 18. Ext/int corridors. **Pets:** Dogs only. $25 one-time fee/room. Designated rooms, service with restrictions, crate.
⊠ 🛏 💻 🍴 ➿ ⊠ ☎

GILFORD

⚛ ▼▼▼ Fireside Resort Inn & Suites 🏠
(603) 293-7526. **$100-$260.** 17 Harris Shore Rd. Jct SR 11 and 11B, 2.5 mi e of jct US 3 N. Int corridors. **Pets:** Other species. $10 daily fee/pet. Designated rooms, service with restrictions, supervision.
🆂🅰🆅🅴 ✖ 🅼 🔌 📺 ⇆ ✖

GORHAM

▼ Moose Brook Motel Ⓜ
(603) 466-5400. **$49-$89, 7 day notice.** 65 Lancaster Rd. Jct SR 16, 0.5 mi w on US 2. Ext corridors. **Pets:** $5 one-time fee/pet. Designated rooms, service with restrictions, crate.
✖ 🔌 📺 ⇆

▼▼ Royalty Inn 🏠
(603) 466-3312. **$59-$159.** 130 Main St. On US 2 and SR 16; center. Ext/int corridors. **Pets:** Other species. $5 daily fee/pet. Designated rooms.
✖ 🅼 🔌 📺 🍽 ⇆ ✖

⚛ ▼▼ Top Notch Inn Ⓜ ✿
(603) 466-5496. **$49-$149.** 265 Main St. On US 2 and SR 16; center. Ext/int corridors. **Pets:** Medium, dogs only. Designated rooms, service with restrictions, supervision.
🆂🅰🆅🅴 ✖ 🔌 📺 ⇆

▼▼ Town & Country Motor Inn 🏠
(603) 466-3315. **$78-$148.** 20 SR 2. 0.5 mi e of jct SR 16. Ext/int corridors. **Pets:** $6 daily fee/pet. Designated rooms, service with restrictions, crate.
✖ 🔌 📺 🍽 ⇆ ✖

HAMPTON

⚛ ▼▼▼ Best Western The Inn at Hampton 🏠
(603) 926-6771. **$100-$225.** 815 Lafayette Rd. 0.5 mi n on US 1. Int corridors. **Pets:** Medium, other species. Designated rooms, supervision.
🆂🅰🆅🅴 ✖ 🅼 🔌 📺 ⇆ ✖

⚛ ▼▼▼ Lamie's Inn and The Old Salt Ⓒ
(603) 926-0330. **$99-$160, 3 day notice.** 490 Lafayette Rd. Jct SR 27 on US 1. Int corridors. **Pets:** Accepted.
🆂🅰🆅🅴 ✖ 🔌 🍽

HAMPTON FALLS

⚛ ▼▼▼ Hampton Falls Inn Ⓜ ✿
(603) 926-9545. **$79-$149.** 11 Lafayette Rd. I-95, exit 1, 0.5 mi e on SR 107, then 1 mi n on US 1. Int corridors. **Pets:** Medium, dogs only. $10 daily fee/room. Designated rooms, service with restrictions, supervision.
🆂🅰🆅🅴 ✖ 🔌 🍽 ⇆

HANCOCK

▼▼▼ The Hancock Inn Ⓒ
(603) 525-3318. **Call for rates.** 33 Main St. Jct SR 123 and 137; center. Int corridors. **Pets:** Accepted.
✖ 🍽

HARTS LOCATION

▼▼▼ Notchland Inn Ⓒ
(603) 374-6131. **$199-$395, 14 day notice.** US 302. On US 302, 6.4 mi w of town. Ext/int corridors. **Pets:** Accepted.
✖ 🔌 📺 🍽 ✖

HENNIKER

▼▼ Henniker Motel Ⓜ
(603) 428-3536. **$90-$149.** 61 Craney Pond Rd. I-89, exit 5, 6.5 mi w on US 202 and SR 9 to jct SR 114, 3 mi s on SR 114 to Flanders Rd, then 0.5 mi w, follow signs; adjacent to Pat's Peak. Ext/int corridors. **Pets:** Accepted.
🅰🆂🅺 ✖ 🔌 📺 ⇆

JEFFERSON

⚛ ▼▼▼ Jefferson Inn 🅱🅱 ✿
(603) 586-7998. **$95-$155, 14 day notice.** 6 Renaissance Ln. US 2, 0.5 mi e of SR 116. Int corridors. **Pets:** Dogs only. Designated rooms, crate.
🆂🅰🆅🅴 ✖ 🔌 ✖ 🅐 🕿

KEENE

⚛ ▼▼▼ Best Western Sovereign Hotel 🏠
(603) 357-3038. **$99-$289, 3 day notice.** 401 Winchester St. SR 10, just s of jct SR 12 and 101. Int corridors. **Pets:** Accepted.
🆂🅰🆅🅴 ✖ 🔌 📺 🍽 ⇆

▼▼▼ Holiday Inn Express 🏠 🐾
(603) 352-7616. **$120-$350.** 175 Key Rd. SR 101, just n, via Winchester St, 0.3 mi w. Int corridors. **Pets:** Medium, dogs only. $25 daily fee/pet. Designated rooms, service with restrictions, supervision.
🅰🆂🅺 ✖ 🅼 🔌 📺 ⇆

⚛ ▼▼▼ Super 8 Keene 🏠
(603) 352-9780. **$72-$249.** 3 Ashbrook Rd. Jct SR 9 and 12, just w. Int corridors. **Pets:** $20 one-time fee/room. Service with restrictions, supervision.
🆂🅰🆅🅴 ✖ 🅼 🔌 📺

LANCASTER

⚛ ▼▼▼ Coos Motor Inn 🏠
(603) 788-3079. **$49-$100.** 209 Main St. On US 2 and 3; center. Int corridors. **Pets:** Medium. $10 daily fee/pet. No service, supervision.
🆂🅰🆅🅴 ✖ 🔌 📺

LEBANON

⚛ ▼▼ Days Inn Ⓜ
(603) 448-5070. **$89-$159.** 135 SR 120. I-89, exit 18, 0.8 mi n. Ext/int corridors. **Pets:** Large. $20 one-time fee/room. Designated rooms, service with restrictions.
🆂🅰🆅🅴 ✖ 🔌 📺

▼▼▼ Residence Inn by Marriott-Lebanon 🏠
(603) 643-4511. **$189-$209.** 32 Centerra Pkwy. I-89, exit 18, 2.5 mi n on SR 120. Int corridors. **Pets:** Accepted.
✖ 🅼 🔌 📺 ⇆ ✖

LINCOLN

⚛ ▼▼▼ Comfort Inn & Suites 🏠 ✿
(603) 745-6700. **$99-$299, 3 day notice.** 21 Railroad St. I-93, exit 32, just e on SR 112; at Hobo Railroad. Int corridors. **Pets:** Other species. $15 daily fee/pet. Designated rooms, service with restrictions.
🆂🅰🆅🅴 ✖ 🅼 🔌 📺 ⇆ ✖

⚛ ▼▼▼ Econo Lodge Inn & Suites Ⓜ
(603) 745-3661. **$59-$299.** 381 US Rt 3. I-93, exit 33 (US 3), 0.3 mi ne. Ext/int corridors. **Pets:** Medium, dogs only. $15 daily fee/pet. Designated rooms, service with restrictions, crate.
🆂🅰🆅🅴 ✖ 🔌 📺 ⇆ ✖

⚛ ▼▼ Parker's Motel Ⓜ
(603) 745-8341. **$49-$89, 3 day notice.** 750 US Rt 3. I-93, exit 33 (US 3), 2 mi ne. Ext corridors. **Pets:** Medium. $5 daily fee/pet. Service with restrictions, supervision.
🆂🅰🆅🅴 ✖ 🔌 📺 ⇆ ✖

⚛ ▼▼▼ Woodward's Resort Ⓜ
(603) 745-8141. **$76-$145, 7 day notice.** 527 US 3. I-93, exit 33 (US 3), 1.4 mi ne. Ext/int corridors. **Pets:** Medium. Designated rooms, service with restrictions.
🆂🅰🆅🅴 ✖ 🔌 📺 🍽 ⇆ ✖

LITTLETON

⊕ ▼▼ Eastgate Inn, Bar & Grill M
(603) 444-3971. **$69-$119.** 335 Cottage St. I-93, exit 41, just e. Ext/int corridors. **Pets:** Accepted.
SAVE ☒ ▣ ⑪ ⟿ ☒

▼▼ Thayers Inn H
(603) 444-6469. **Call for rates.** 111 Main St. I-93, exit 42, 1.3 mi e on US 302 and SR 10; center. Int corridors. **Pets:** Accepted.
☒ ▮ ▣ ⑪

LOUDON

⊕ ▼▼ Red Roof Inn H
(603) 225-8399. **Call for rates.** 2 Staniels Rd. I-393, exit 3, 1.5 mi n. Int corridors. **Pets:** Large, other species. Designated rooms, no service, supervision.
SAVE ☒ ⅏ ▮ ▣

MANCHESTER

⊕ ▼▼ Comfort Inn H ✿
(603) 668-2600. **$89-$299, 14 day notice.** 298 Queen City Ave. I-293, exit 4, just w. Int corridors. **Pets:** Small. $25 one-time fee/room. Designated rooms, service with restrictions, supervision.
SAVE ☒ ▮ ▣ ⟿

▼▼▼ Holiday Inn Express Hotel & Suites–Manchester Airport H ✿
(603) 669-6800. **$99-$199.** 1298 S Porter St. I-293, exit 1. Int corridors. **Pets:** Medium, other species. $50 deposit/room. Service with restrictions, supervision.
ASK ☒ ⅏ ▮ ▣ ⟿

▼▼▼ Homewood Suites by Hilton H
(603) 668-2200. **$129-$299.** 1000 Perimeter Rd. I-293, exit 2, follow signs to Manchester Airport. Int corridors. **Pets:** Accepted.
☒ ⅏ ▮ ▣ ⟿ ☒

▼▼▼ Radisson Hotel Manchester H
(603) 625-1000. **$129-$199.** 700 Elm St. Jct Granite St; downtown. Int corridors. **Pets:** Accepted.
ASK ☒ ⅏ ▮ ▣ ⑪ ⟿ ☒

▼▼ TownePlace Suites by Marriott Manchester Airport H
(603) 641-2288. **$129-$149.** 686 Huse Rd. I-293, exit 1, 0.5 mi se on SR 28. Int corridors. **Pets:** Accepted.
☒ ⅏ ▮ ▣ ⟿

MEREDITH

▼▼▼ Church Landing at Mill Falls H
(603) 279-7006. **$239-$459, 3 day notice.** 281 Daniel Webster Hwy. Jct US 3 and SR 104, 0.6 mi n. Ext/int corridors. **Pets:** Accepted.
ASK ☒ ▮ ▣ ⑪ ⟿ ☒

▼▼▼ The Inn at Mill Falls H
(603) 279-7006. **$109-$289, 3 day notice.** 312 Daniel Webster Hwy. Jct US 3 and SR 25; center. Int corridors. **Pets:** Accepted.
ASK ☒ ▮ ▣ ⑪ ⟿

MERRIMACK

▼▼▼ Residence Inn by Marriott H
(603) 424-8100. **$149-$169.** 246 Daniel Webster Hwy. Everett Tpke, exit 11, just e, then 0.6 mi s on US 3. Ext/int corridors. **Pets:** Large, other species. $75 one-time fee/pet. Designated rooms.
☒ ⅏ ▮ ▣ ⟿ ☒

NASHUA

⊕ ▼▼ Best Western's Granite Inn H ✿
(603) 883-7700. **$85-$110, 3 day notice.** 10 St. Laurent St. US 3 (Everett Tpke), exit 7E, just e. Int corridors. **Pets:** Small. $25 one-time fee/pet. Designated rooms, service with restrictions, crate.
SAVE ☒ ▮ ▣ ⟿

▼▼ Extended StayAmerica-Boston-Nashua H
(603) 577-9900. **$62-$83.** 2000 Southwood Dr. US 3 (Everett Tpke), exit 8, just w. Int corridors. **Pets:** Other species. $25 daily fee/pet. Service with restrictions, crate.
ASK ☒ ⅏ ▮ ▣

▼▼▼ Holiday Inn Nashua H
(603) 888-1551. **Call for rates.** 9 Northeastern Blvd. US 3 (Everett Tpke), exit 4, just w, then 0.3 mi n. Int corridors. **Pets:** Accepted.
☒ ⅏ ▮ ▣

⊕ ▼▼ Red Roof Inn #7122 M
(603) 888-1893. **$67-$82.** 77 Spitbrook Rd. US 3 (Everett Tpke), exit 1, just e. Ext corridors. **Pets:** Medium, other species. Service with restrictions, supervision.
SAVE ☒ ⅏ ▮

NEWBURY

⊕ ▼▼ Best Western Sunapee Lake Lodge H
(603) 763-2010. **$129-$349, 14 day notice.** 1403 SR 103. Jct SR 103B, just e. Int corridors. **Pets:** Other species. $10 daily fee/pet. Designated rooms, supervision.
SAVE ☒ ⅏ ▮ ▣ ⟿ ☒

NEW CASTLE

⊕ ▼▼▼ Wentworth By The Sea Marriott Hotel & Spa H
(603) 422-7322. **$199-$339, 3 day notice.** 588 Wentworth Rd. On SR 1B, 2 mi e of SR 1A. Ext/int corridors. **Pets:** Accepted.
SAVE ☒ ▮ ▣ ⑪ ⟿ ☒

NORTH CONWAY

⊕ ▼▼ Best Western Red Jacket Mountain View and Conference Center H
(603) 356-5411. **$109-$249, 10 day notice.** 2251 White Mountain Hwy. 1 mi s on US 302/SR 16. Ext/int corridors. **Pets:** Accepted.
SAVE ☒ ⅏ ▮ ▣ ⑪ ⟿ ☒

⊕ ▼▼ Green Granite Inn and Conference Center H
(603) 356-6901. **$77-$306, 3 day notice.** 1515 White Mountain Hwy (Rt 16). 2.3 mi s on US 302/SR 16; village center. Ext/int corridors. **Pets:** Dogs only. $50 one-time fee/pet. Designated rooms, service with restrictions, supervision.
SAVE ☒ ▮ ▣ ⟿ ☒

⊕ ▼▼ Mt Washington Valley Inn H
(603) 356-5486. **$49-$199.** 1567 White Mountain Hwy. 2.5 mi s on US 302/SR 16; village center. Int corridors. **Pets:** Medium, dogs only. $50 deposit/room. Designated rooms, service with restrictions, supervision.
SAVE ☒ ▮ ▣ ⟿

▼▼▼ North Conway Hampton Inn & Suites H ✿
(603) 356-7736. **$169-$219.** 1788 White Mountain Hwy. Jct US 302/SR 16, 1 mi n. Int corridors. **Pets:** $50 one-time fee/room. Service with restrictions, supervision.
☒ ▮ ▣ ☒

⊕ ▼▼ North Conway Mountain Inn M
(603) 356-2803. **$79-$125, 3 day notice.** 2114 White Mountain Hwy. 1 mi s on US 302/SR 16. Ext corridors. **Pets:** $20 daily fee/pet. Crate.
SAVE ☒

White Trellis Motel M
(603) 356-2492. **$45-$199, 3 day notice.** 3245 White Mountain Hwy. 0.8 mi n on US 302/SR 16; village center. Ext corridors. **Pets:** Accepted.
⊠ 🖬 🖵

PITTSBURG

The Glen CA
(603) 538-6500. **$204-$266 (no credit cards), 7 day notice.** 118 Glen Rd. 9 mi n on US 3, from jct SR 145 to Varney Rd, then 0.3 mi s to Glen Rd, follow signs. Ext/int corridors. **Pets:** Accepted.
⊠ 🖬 🖵 🍴 ⊠ 🐾 🐾 🐾

PORTSMOUTH

Anchorage Inn & Suites H 🐾
(603) 431-8111. **$69-$189.** 417 Woodbury Ave. Jct US 1 and I-95; at Portsmouth Traffic Circle. Int corridors. **Pets:** Medium. $20 daily fee/room. Designated rooms, service with restrictions, supervision.
SAVE ⊠ 🖬 🏊 ⊠

Hampton Inn-Portsmouth H
(603) 431-6111. **$89-$209.** 99 Durgin Ln. I-95, exit 7, 1 mi w via Market St and Woodbury Ave to Durgin Ln, then 0.3 mi s. Int corridors. **Pets:** Accepted.
⊠ 🖬 🖬 🖵 🐾 ⊠

Hilton Garden Inn Portsmouth Downtown H
(603) 431-1499. **$129-$319.** 100 High St. Downtown. Int corridors. **Pets:** Accepted.
⊠ 🖬 🖬 🖵 🍴 🐾

Homewood Suites by Hilton H
(603) 427-5400. **$179-$259.** 100 Portsmouth Blvd. I-95, exit 7, 0.5 mi w, then 0.3 mi n. Int corridors. **Pets:** Accepted.
⊠ 🖬 🖬 🖵 🐾

Motel 6 Portsmouth #1424 M
(603) 334-6606. **$55-$85.** 3 Gosling Rd. I-95, exit 4 to Spaulding Tpke (US 4 and SR 16), exit 1, just e. Int corridors. **Pets:** Other species. Service with restrictions, supervision.
⊠ 🖬 🖬 🐾

Residence Inn by Marriott H
(603) 436-8880. **$159-$219.** 1 International Dr. SR 4/16, exit 1, just s. Int corridors. **Pets:** Accepted.
⊠ 🖬 🖬 🖵 🐾 ⊠

Sheraton Portsmouth Harborside Hotel & Conference Center H 🐾
(603) 431-2300. **Call for rates.** 250 Market St. Downtown. Int corridors. **Pets:** Large, dogs only. Designated rooms, supervision.
SAVE ⊠ 🖬 🖬 🖵 🍴 🐾 ⊠

ROCHESTER

Anchorage Inn M 🐾
(603) 332-3350. **$69-$139.** 13 Wadleigh Rd. Jct Spaulding Tpke and SR 125, exit 12. Ext corridors. **Pets:** $50 deposit/room, $15 daily fee/pet. Designated rooms, service with restrictions, supervision.
SAVE ⊠ 🖬 🐾

The Governor's Inn CI
(603) 332-0107. **$98-$168.** 78 Wakefield St. On SR 125 and 108, just n of monument; center. Int corridors. **Pets:** Accepted.
ASK ⊠ 🖬 🖵 🍴

SALEM

La Quinta Inn & Suites H 🐾
(603) 893-4722. **$49-$159.** 8 Keewaydin Dr. I-93, exit 2, just sw. Int corridors. **Pets:** Medium, other species. Service with restrictions, supervision.
ASK ⊠ 🖬 🖬 🖵 🐾

Red Roof Inn #7151 M
(603) 898-6422. **$66-$110.** 15 Red Roof Ln. I-93, exit 2, just se. Ext corridors. **Pets:** Medium, other species. Service with restrictions, supervision.
SAVE ⊠ 🖬 🖬

SNOWVILLE

Snowvillage Inn CI
(603) 447-2818. **$129-$269, 14 day notice.** 136 Stewart Rd. Jct SR 16, 5 mi s on SR 153, turn at Crystal Lake, then 1.5 mi s, follow signs. Ext/int corridors. **Pets:** Dogs only. $25 one-time fee/pet. Designated rooms, service with restrictions, supervision.
⊠ 🍴 ⊠ 🐾 🐾

SUGAR HILL

The Hilltop Inn BB 🐾
(603) 823-5695. **$110-$195, 8 day notice.** 9 Norton Ln. I-93, exit 38, 0.5 mi n on SR 18, then 2.8 mi w on SR 117. Int corridors. **Pets:** Dogs only. $10 daily fee/room.
⊠ 🖬 🐾 🐾

SUNAPEE

Dexter's Inn CI
(603) 763-5571. **Call for rates.** 258 Stagecoach Rd. Jct SR 103B and 11, 0.4 mi w on SR 11, 1.8 mi s (Winn Hill Rd). Ext/int corridors. **Pets:** Accepted.
⊠ 🖬 🖵 🍴 🐾 ⊠

THORNTON

Shamrock Motel M
(603) 726-3534. **$58-$85, 7 day notice.** 2913 US 3. I-93, exit 29, 2.3 mi n. Ext corridors. **Pets:** Accepted.
ASK ⊠ 🖬 🖵 🐾 🐾 🐾

TILTON

Black Swan Inn BB
(603) 286-4524. **$99-$170, 10 day notice.** 354 W Main St. I-93, exit 20 southbound, 1.5 mi w on SR 3 and 11. Int corridors. **Pets:** Accepted.
SAVE ⊠ 🖬 🖵

TROY

The Inn at East Hill Farm CI
(603) 242-6495. **$84-$126, 21 day notice.** 460 Monadnock St. Jct SR 12 and Monadock St, 2 mi e. Ext/int corridors. **Pets:** Other species. $10 daily fee/pet. Designated rooms, supervision.
SAVE ⊠ 🖬 🍴 🐾 ⊠ 🐾

WATERVILLE VALLEY

Best Western Silver Fox Inn H
(603) 236-3699. **$99-$169.** 70 Packards Rd. I-93, exit 28, 11 mi e on SR 49, then just n. Int corridors. **Pets:** Small. $20 one-time fee/room. Service with restrictions, supervision.
SAVE ⊠ 🖵

WEST LEBANON

Baymont Inn M 🐾
(603) 298-8888. **$80-$100.** 45 Airport Rd. I-89, exit 20 (SR 12A), just s, then just e. Int corridors. **Pets:** Large, other species. $10 one-time fee/pet. Service with restrictions, supervision.
SAVE ⊠ 🖬 🖬 🐾

Fireside Inn and Suites H
(603) 298-5900. **$120-$200.** 25 Airport Rd. I-89, exit 20 (SR 12A), just s. Int corridors. **Pets:** Dogs only. $10 daily fee/pet. Designated rooms, service with restrictions, supervision.
ASK ⊠ 🖬 🖵 🍴 🐾 ⊠

WOLFEBORO

▼ The Lake Motel [M]
(603) 569-1100. **$69-$159, 14 day notice.** 280 S Main St. 0.5 mi se on
SR 28. Ext/int corridors. **Pets:** Accepted.
⊠ 🖪 🖵 ⊠

WOODSVILLE

▲▲▲ ▼ All Seasons Motel [M]
(603) 747-2157. **$60-$105, 3 day notice.** 36 Smith St. I-91, exit 17, 4.1
mi e on US 302, then just s. Ext corridors. **Pets:** Accepted.
[SAVE] ⊠ 🖪 🖵 🖘

▲▲▲ ▼ ▼ Nootka Lodge [M]
(603) 747-2418. **$70-$210, 3 day notice.** 4982 Dartmouth College Hwy.
I-91, exit 17, 4.5 mi e on US 302. Ext corridors. **Pets:** Accepted.
[SAVE] ⊠ 🖪 🖘 ⊠

NEW JERSEY

CITY INDEX

ALLAMUCHY

🆎 ◆◆◆◆ The Inn at Panther Valley-A Clarion Collection Hotel Ⓗ
(908) 852-6000. **$124-$139.** 1627 SR 517. I-80, exit 19, 0.8 mi s. Ext/int corridors. **Pets:** Accepted.
[SAVE] ⊠ 🖥 💻 🍴

ATLANTIC CITY METROPOLITAN AREA

ABSECON

◆◆ Knights Inn-Atlantic City/ Absecon Ⓜ
(609) 407-1919. **Call for rates.** 531 Absecon Blvd. Garden State Pkwy, exit 40, 4.3 mi e on US 30 (White Horse Pike). Ext corridors. **Pets:** Accepted.
⊠ 🖥

ATLANTIC CITY

🆎 ◆◆◆◆ Sheraton Atlantic City Convention Center Hotel Ⓗ 🐾
(609) 344-3535. **$99-$399.** 2 Convention Blvd. Garden State Expwy, exit 38 to Atlantic City Expwy to Arctic Ave, just e to Michigan Ave, then just n. Int corridors. **Pets:** Medium, dogs only. Designated rooms, service with restrictions, supervision.
[SAVE] ⊠ 🖥 💻 🍴 🏊

BUENA

◆◆◆◆ Econo Lodge Ⓜ
(856) 697-9000. **$70-$89.** 102 Tuckahoe Rd. Corner of SR 40 and 54. Int corridors. **Pets:** Accepted.
[ASK] ⊠ 🖥 💻

SOMERS POINT

🆎 ◆◆◆◆ Residence Inn by Marriott Ⓗ 🐾
(609) 927-6400. **$239-$249.** 900 Mays Landing Rd. Garden State Pkwy, exit 30 southbound; exit 29 northbound, 1 mi e. Ext corridors. **Pets:** Other species. $100 one-time fee/room. Service with restrictions, supervision.
[SAVE] ⊠ 🖥 💻 🏊 ⊠

WEST ATLANTIC CITY

🆎 ◆◆◆◆ Quality Hotel Bayside Resort Ⓗ
(609) 641-3546. **$59-$299, 30 day notice.** 8029 Black Horse Pike. Garden State Pkwy, exit 38 (Atlantic City Expwy), 2 mi e to exit 5, 0.5 mi s on US 9 to US 40/322, then 1.8 mi e. Int corridors. **Pets:** Accepted.
[SAVE] ⊠ 🖥 💻 🍴 🏊 ⊠

🆎 ◆◆◆ Ramada-West Atlantic City Ⓗ
(609) 646-5220. **$59-$249.** 8037 Black Horse Pike. Garden State Pkwy, exit 38 (Atlantic City Expwy), 2 mi e to exit 5, 0.5 mi s on US 9 to US 40/322, then 1.8 mi e. Ext/int corridors. **Pets:** Accepted.
[SAVE] ⊠ 🖥 💻 🏊

END METROPOLITAN AREA

BASKING RIDGE

◆◆◆◆ Hotel Indigo Ⓗ
(908) 580-1300. **$99-$349.** 80 Allen Rd. I-78, exit 33, 0.3 mi n on CR 525, then 0.3 mi w. Int corridors. **Pets:** Accepted.
[ASK] ⊠ 🖥 💻 🍴

BEACH HAVEN

🆎 ◆◆◆ Engleside Inn Ⓗ 🐾
(609) 492-1251. **$99-$453, 30 day notice.** 30 Engleside Ave. 6.9 mi s of SR 72 Cswy to Engleside Ave, then just e. Ext corridors. **Pets:** Other species. $10 daily fee/pet. Service with restrictions, supervision.
[SAVE] ⊠ 🖥 💻 🍴 🏊

BRIDGEWATER

🆎 ◆◆◆◆ Hyatt Summerfield Suites Ⓗ
(908) 725-0800. **$99-$239.** 530 US 22 E. I-287, exit 14B northbound; exit 17 southbound to US 22 W, then 0.8 mi. Ext corridors. **Pets:** Accepted.
[SAVE] ⊠ 🔼 🖥 💻 🏊 ⊠

BUDD LAKE

◆◆◆ Extended StayAmerica Mt. Olive-Budd Lake Ⓗ
(973) 347-5522. **$71-$119.** 71 International Dr S. I-80, exit 25, just n, follow signs for International Trade Center; just e of jct US 46. Int corridors. **Pets:** Other species. $25 daily fee/pet. Service with restrictions, crate.
[ASK] ⊠ 🖥 💻

CAPE MAY

ᐁᐁ ᗯᗯᗯᗯ **Marquis de Lafayette Hotel** 🄷
(609) 884-3500. **$132-$545.** 501 Beach Ave. Between Decatur and Ocean sts. Ext/int corridors. **Pets:** Accepted.
🆂🅰🆅🅴 ⊠ 🛏 💻 🏊

ᐁᐁ ᗯᗯᗯ **Palace Hotel of Cape May** 🄷
(609) 898-8100. **$129-$329, 14 day notice.** 1101 Beach Ave. Jct Beach and Philadelphia aves. Int corridors. **Pets:** Other species. $25 daily fee/pet. Designated rooms, service with restrictions.
🆂🅰🆅🅴 ⊠ 🛏 💻

ᗯᗯᗯ **White Dove Cottage** 🄱🄱 🌸
(609) 884-0613. **$150-$280 (no credit cards), 21 day notice.** 619 Hughes St. Between Franklin and Ocean sts. Ext/int corridors. **Pets:** Medium, dogs only. Designated rooms.
🄰🅂🄺 ⊠ 🛏 💻 🗺

CAPE MAY COURT HOUSE

ᐁᐁ ᗯᗯᗯᗯ **The Doctors Inn** 🄱🄱
(609) 463-9330. **$100-$350, 14 day notice.** 2 N Main St. At Main (US 9) and Mechanic sts; just s of Garden State Pkwy. Int corridors. **Pets:** Small. $25 daily fee/pet. Service with restrictions, supervision.
🆂🅰🆅🅴 ⊠ 🛏

CLINTON

ᗯᗯᗯ **Hampton Inn** 🄷
(908) 713-4800. **$129-$159.** 16 Frontage Dr. I-78, exit 15, 0.3 mi s on CR 513, then left at next light. Int corridors. **Pets:** Accepted.
⊠ ♿ 🛏 💻 🏊

ᗯᗯᗯ **Holiday Inn-Clinton** 🄷 🌸
(908) 735-5111. **$139-$179.** 111 Rt 173. I-78, exit 15, just nw. Int corridors. **Pets:** $49 one-time fee/room. Service with restrictions, supervision.
🄰🅂🄺 ⊠ 🛏 💻 🍴 🏊

CRANBURY

ᗯᗯᗯ **Courtyard by Marriott Cranbury/South Brunswick** 🄷
(609) 655-9950. **$189-$209.** 420 Forsgate Dr. New Jersey Tpke, exit 8A to SR 32 W toward town, just w. Int corridors. **Pets:** Accepted.
⊠ ♿ 🛏 💻 🍴 🏊

ᗯᗯᗯ **Residence Inn by Marriott/Cranbury-South Brunswick** 🄷
(609) 395-9447. **$169-$179.** 2662 US 130. New Jersey Tpke, exit 8A to SR 32 W toward town, 2 mi w on S River Rd. Int corridors. **Pets:** Accepted.
⊠ ♿ 🛏 💻 🏊 🗺

ᗯᗯᗯ **Staybridge Suites/Cranbury** 🄷 🌸
(609) 409-7181. **$109-$249.** 1272 S River Rd. New Jersey Tpke, exit 8A to SR 32 toward Cranbury, 2 mi w. Int corridors. **Pets:** Other species. $75 one-time fee/room.
🄰🅂🄺 ⊠ 🛏 💻 🏊

EAST BRUNSWICK

ᗯ **Motel 6, East Brunswick #1083** 🄷
(732) 390-4545. **$69-$79.** 244 SR 18 N. New Jersey Tpke, exit 9 (SR 18) to SR 18 S, 1 mi, exit Edgeboro Rd, w at U-turn, then just e. Ext/int corridors. **Pets:** Other species. Service with restrictions, supervision.
⊠ ♿

ᗯᗯ **Studio 6 East Brunswick #6020** 🄷
(732) 238-3330. **$75-$85.** 246 Rt 18 at Edgeboro Rd. New Jersey Tpke, exit 9 (SR 18) to SR 18 S, 1 mi, exit Edgeboro Rd, w at U-turn, then just e. Int corridors. **Pets:** Other species. $10 daily fee/room. Service with restrictions, supervision.
⊠ ♿ 🛏 💻

EAST RUTHERFORD

ᗯᗯ **Homestead Studio Suites Hotel-Meadowlands/East Rutherford** 🄷
(201) 939-8866. **$104-$139.** 300 SR 3 E. New Jersey Tpke, exit 16W (from western spur), sports complex right after toll. Int corridors. **Pets:** Other species. $25 daily fee/pet. Service with restrictions, crate.
🄰🅂🄺 ⊠ ♿ 🛏 💻

ᗯᗯ **Residence Inn by Marriott Meadowlands–East Rutherford** 🄷
(201) 939-0020. **$249-$299.** 10 Murray Hill Pkwy. New Jersey Tpke, exit 16W to SR 3 W to SR 17 N, 1.5 mi n to Paterson Plank Rd (SR 120), then just e. Int corridors. **Pets:** Small. $100 one-time fee/room. Service with restrictions, supervision.
⊠ ♿ 🛏 💻 🏊 🗺

ᐁᐁ ᗯᗯᗯ **Sheraton Meadowlands Hotel & Conference Center** 🄷 🌸
(201) 896-0500. **$119-$399.** 2 Meadowlands Plaza. New Jersey Tpke, exit 16W (from western spur), sports complex right after toll to Sheraton Plaza Dr. Int corridors. **Pets:** $75 one-time fee/room. Designated rooms, service with restrictions, supervision.
🆂🅰🆅🅴 ⊠ ♿ 🛏 💻 🍴 🏊 🗺

EATONTOWN

ᗯᗯ **Staybridge Suites Hotel Eatontown-Tinton Falls** 🄷 🌸
(732) 380-9300. **$100-$270.** 4 Industrial Way E. Garden State Pkwy, exit 105, 0.7 mi e on SR 36, then 0.7 mi s on SR 35. Int corridors. **Pets:** Medium. $150 one-time fee/pet. Service with restrictions, supervision.
🄰🅂🄺 ⊠ ♿ 🛏 💻 🏊

EDISON

ᐁᐁ ᗯᗯᗯ **Comfort Inn** 🄷
(732) 287-0171. **$79-$120.** 831 US 1 S. 1.3 mi s of I-287. Int corridors. **Pets:** Accepted.
🆂🅰🆅🅴 ⊠ 🛏 💻

ᐁᐁ ᗯᗯᗯ **Courtyard by Marriott Edison/Woodbridge** 🄷
(732) 738-1991. **$184-$194.** 3105 Woodbridge Ave. New Jersey Tpke, exit 10, 0.5 mi se on CR 514, then just e. Int corridors. **Pets:** $75 one-time fee/pet. Designated rooms, service with restrictions, supervision.
🆂🅰🆅🅴 ⊠ ♿ 🛏 💻 🏊

ᗯᗯᗯ **Crowne Plaza Edison** 🄷
(732) 287-3500. **$159-$179.** 2055 Lincoln Hwy (SR 27). I-287, exit 2B (SR 27 S) northbound, 1 mi s; exit 3 (New Durham/Metuchen) southbound, 0.5 mi w, then 1 mi s on Talmadge Rd. Int corridors. **Pets:** Accepted.
🄰🅂🄺 ⊠ ♿ 🛏 💻 🍴

ᗯᗯ **Extended StayAmerica-Edison-Raritan Center** 🄷
(732) 346-9366. **$74-$114.** 1 Fieldcrest Ave. I-287, exit SR 514 to King Georges Post Rd, then just w. Int corridors. **Pets:** Other species. $25 daily fee/pet. Service with restrictions, crate.
🄰🅂🄺 ⊠ ♿ 🛏 💻

ᐁᐁ ᗯ **Red Roof Inn #7194** 🄼
(732) 248-9300. **$66-$100.** 860 New Durham Rd. I-287, exit 2A northbound, 0.3 mi w via Bridge St, then left; exit 3 southbound, just w. Ext corridors. **Pets:** Medium. Service with restrictions, supervision.
🆂🅰🆅🅴 ⊠ ♿ 🛏

ᐁᐁ ᗯᗯᗯ **Sheraton Edison** 🄷
(732) 225-8300. **$279.** 125 Raritan Center Pkwy. New Jersey Tpke, exit 10, 0.5 mi se on CR 514, keep right after tolls. Int corridors. **Pets:** Accepted.
🆂🅰🆅🅴 ⊠ ♿ 🛏 💻 🍴 🏊 🗺

ELIZABETH

▼▼▼ **Extended StayAmerica Elizabeth-Newark Airport** 🅷
(908) 355-4300. **$89-$129.** 45 Glimcher Realty Way. New Jersey Tpke, exit 13A, after toll follow signs to Jersey Garden Blvd; 1 mi, left on Kapkowski Rd, then just e. Int corridors. **Pets:** Other species. $25 daily fee/pet. Service with restrictions, crate.

(ASK) (✕) (&M) 🔋 (💻)

🔷🔷 ▼▼▼ **Hilton Newark Airport** 🅷
(908) 351-3900. **$99-$219.** 1170 Spring St. New Jersey Tpke, exit 13A, on US 1 and 9 N, U-turn on McClellan St. Int corridors. **Pets:** Medium. $75 one-time fee/room. Service with restrictions, crate.

(SAVE) (✕) (&M) 🔋 (💻) (🍴) (🏊)

▼▼▼ **Residence Inn by Marriott** 🅷
(908) 352-4300. **$194-$209.** 83 Glimcher Realty Way. New Jersey Tpke, exit 13A, after toll follow signs to Jersey Garden Blvd, 1 mi, left on Kapkowski Rd, then just e. Int corridors. **Pets:** Accepted.

(✕) (&M) 🔋 (💻) (🏊)

FAIRFIELD

▼▼▼ **La Quinta Inn & Suites Fairfield** 🅷 🐾
(973) 575-1742. **$59-$139.** 38 Two Bridges Rd. I-80, exit 52 westbound; exit 47B (Caldwells) eastbound, 7 mi e on US 46, exit Passaic Ave. Int corridors. **Pets:** Medium, other species. Service with restrictions, supervision.

(ASK) (✕) (&M) 🔋 (💻) (🏊)

FLEMINGTON

▼▼ **Ramada** Ⓜ
(908) 782-7472. **$74-$134.** 250 US 202 & SR 31. 0.5 mi s of the circle. Ext/int corridors. **Pets:** Medium. $10 daily fee/pet. Service with restrictions, supervision.

(ASK) (✕) 🔋 (💻) (🍴) (🏊)

HILLSBOROUGH

🔷🔷 ▼▼▼ **Days Inn Hillsborough Executive Inn** 🅷 🐾
(908) 685-9000. **$70-$130.** 118 Rt 206 S. 2.6 mi s of jct SR 28, US 202 and 206, at circle. Int corridors. **Pets:** $20 daily fee/pet. Service with restrictions, crate.

(SAVE) (✕) 🔋 (💻) (🍴) (🏊)

ISELIN

🔷🔷 ▼▼▼ **Renaissance Woodbridge Hotel** 🅷
(732) 634-3600. **$105-$189.** 515 Rt 1 S. Garden State Pkwy, exit 131A northbound, 0.7 mi e, s on Middlesex Essex Tpke, 0.4 mi to Gill Ln, then 1.5 mi w; exit 130 southbound, 0.7 mi on US 1 N to Gill Ln, then U-turn; diagonal to Woodbridge Center. Int corridors. **Pets:** Accepted.

(SAVE) (✕) 🔋 (💻) (🍴) (🏊)

LAWRENCEVILLE

▼ **Red Roof Inn-Princeton #7111** Ⓜ 🐾
(609) 896-3388. **$60-$100.** 3203 Brunswick Pike (US 1). I-295, exit 67A, just n. Ext corridors. **Pets:** Service with restrictions, supervision.

(ASK) (✕) 🔋

LEDGEWOOD

▼▼ **Quality Inn** 🅷
(973) 347-5100. **Call for rates.** 1691 US 46 W. I-80, exit 27, 2 mi e via US 206 N and 183 N. Int corridors. **Pets:** Accepted.

(✕) 🔋 (🍴) (🏊)

LONG BRANCH

▼▼▼ **Ocean Place Resort & Spa** 🅷
(732) 571-4000. **$125-$629, 7 day notice.** 1 Ocean Blvd. 2.5 mi e of jct SR 71, 0.5 mi s. Int corridors. **Pets:** $150 one-time fee/room. Designated rooms, service with restrictions, supervision.

(ASK) (✕) 🔋 (💻) (🍴) (🏊) (✕)

MAHWAH

▼▼▼ **Homewood Suites by Hilton** 🅷
(201) 760-9994. **$129-$209.** 375 Corporate Dr. I-287, exit 66, 1.7 mi on SR 17 S to MacArthur Blvd, then 0.4 mi w. Int corridors. **Pets:** Other species. $150 one-time fee/room. Service with restrictions.

(✕) 🔋 (💻)

🔷🔷 ▼▼▼ **Sheraton Mahwah Hotel** 🅷
(201) 529-1660. **$129-$289.** 1 International Blvd (Rt 17). I-287, exit 66, at SR 17 N. Int corridors. **Pets:** Accepted.

(SAVE) (✕) 🔋 (💻) (🍴) (🏊) (✕)

MIDDLETOWN

🔷🔷 ▼▼▼ **Comfort Inn Middletown** 🅷 🐾
(732) 671-3400. **$125-$189.** 750 Hwy 35 S. Garden State Pkwy, exit 114, 2 mi on Red Hill Rd, 1 mi s on King's Hwy to SR 35, then 0.3 mi s. Int corridors. **Pets:** $25 daily fee/room. Service with restrictions, supervision.

(SAVE) (✕) 🔋 (💻) (🏊)

MONMOUTH JUNCTION

▼▼ **Extended StayAmerica Princeton/South Brunswick** 🅷
(732) 438-5010. **$71-$119.** 4230 US 1 S. 0.5 mi s of jct US 1 and Raymond Rd. Int corridors. **Pets:** Other species. $25 daily fee/pet. Service with restrictions, crate.

(ASK) (✕) (&M) 🔋 (💻)

🔷🔷 ▼ **Red Roof Inn/North Princeton #7198** Ⓜ
(732) 821-8800. **$55-$100.** 208 New Rd. On US 1 S. Ext corridors. **Pets:** Large, other species. Service with restrictions, supervision.

(SAVE) (✕) 🔋

🔷🔷 ▼▼▼ **Residence Inn by Marriott** 🅷
(732) 329-9600. **$179-$219.** 4225 US 1 S. 0.5 mi s of Raymond Rd. Int corridors. **Pets:** Accepted.

(SAVE) (✕) (&M) 🔋 (💻) (🏊) (✕)

MORRIS PLAINS

▼▼ **Candlewood Suites Parsippany-Morris Plains** 🅷
(973) 984-9960. **Call for rates.** 100 Candlewood Dr. I-287, exit 39 northbound; exit 39B southbound, 2 mi w on SR 10. Int corridors. **Pets:** Accepted.

(✕) (&M) 🔋 (💻)

MORRISTOWN

🔷🔷 ▼▼▼ **Hyatt Summerfield Suites Morristown** 🅷
(973) 971-0008. **$89-$309.** 194 Park Ave. SR 24, exit 2A (Morristown), stay in far left lane. Int corridors. **Pets:** Medium. $150 one-time fee/room. Designated rooms, service with restrictions, crate.

(SAVE) (✕) (&M) 🔋 (💻) (🏊) (✕)

🔷🔷 ▼▼▼ **The Westin Governor Morris** 🅷 🐾
(973) 539-7300. **$129-$349.** 2 Whippany Rd. I-287, exit 36 southbound, left lane to light, left to stop, then left 1 mi; exit 36A northbound thru Morris Ave, 0.8 mi, follow signs. Int corridors. **Pets:** Medium, dogs only. $50 one-time fee/room. Service with restrictions.

(SAVE) (✕) 🔋 (💻) (🍴) (🏊)

MOUNT OLIVE

▼▼▼ **Residence Inn Mt Olive at the International Trade Center** 🅷
(973) 691-1720. **$180-$200.** 271 Continental Dr. I-80, exit 25, just n, follow signs for International Trade Center. Int corridors. **Pets:** Other species. $100 one-time fee/room. Service with restrictions.

(✕) 🔋 (💻) (🏊) (✕)

NEPTUNE

▼▼▼▼ Residence Inn by Marriott H
(732) 643-9350. **$179-$229.** 230 Jumping Brook Rd. Garden State Pkwy, exit 100B, 0.5 mi e on SR 33, then 0.5 mi n. Int corridors. **Pets:** Accepted.

NEWARK

(AAA) ▼▼▼▼ Sheraton Newark Airport Hotel H
(973) 690-5500. **Call for rates.** 128 Frontage Rd. New Jersey Tpke, exit 14 via Frontage Rd, 2nd right after toll booth. Int corridors. **Pets:** Accepted.

▼▼▼▼ SpringHill Suites by Marriott H ❀
(973) 624-5300. **$189-$199.** 652 Rt 1 & 9 S. I-95, exit 14, 1 mi sw via US 1 and 9 S. Int corridors. **Pets:** Large. $100 one-time fee/pet. Service with restrictions.

NORTH BERGEN

▼▼ Days Inn H
(201) 348-3600. **$139-$199.** 2750 Tonnelle Ave (US 1 & 9). Jct SR 3, 0.4 mi s. Int corridors. **Pets:** Medium. $100 deposit/pet. Designated rooms, service with restrictions, supervision.
[ASK] [X] [icons]

NORTH BRUNSWICK

▼▼▼ Holiday Inn Express Hotel & Suites H
(732) 297-7400. **Call for rates.** 2880 US 1 N. Between Finnegans and Black Horse lanes. Int corridors. **Pets:** Accepted.
[X] [icons]

PARAMUS

▼▼ La Quinta Inn H ❀
(201) 265-4200. **$89-$135.** 393 Rt 17 S. Garden State Pkwy, exit 163 northbound to SR 17 N, 0.6 mi to Midland Ave, then U-turn to SR 17 S; exit 165 southbound to Richwood Ave, 1 mi. Int corridors. **Pets:** Medium, other species. Service with restrictions, supervision.
[ASK] [X] [icons]

PARSIPPANY

▼▼▼▼ Embassy Suites H
(973) 334-1440. **$129-$279.** 909 Parsippany Blvd. I-80, exit 42 to US 202 N; just ne of jct US 202 and 46 W. Int corridors. **Pets:** Accepted.
[X] [icons]

(AAA) ▼▼▼ Red Roof Inn #7072 M
(973) 334-3737. **$64-$100.** 855 US 46 E. I-80, exit 47 westbound; exit 45 eastbound, 0.5 mi e. Ext corridors. **Pets:** Small. Service with restrictions, supervision.
[SAVE] [X] [icon]

▼▼▼▼ Residence Inn by Marriott Parsippany H ❀
(973) 984-3313. **$215-$263.** 3 Gatehall Dr. I-287, exit 39 northbound; exit 39B southbound, 2 mi w on SR 10. Int corridors. **Pets:** Other species. $100 one-time fee/room. Service with restrictions.
[X] [icons]

(AAA) ▼▼▼▼ Sheraton Parsippany Hotel H
(973) 515-2000. **$119-$385.** 199 Smith Rd. I-287, exit 41A northbound; exit 42 to US 46 E, 0.4 mi s. Int corridors. **Pets:** Accepted.
[SAVE] [X] [icons]

▼▼▼▼ Staybridge Suites Parsippany H ❀
(973) 334-2907. **$179-$269, 3 day notice.** 61 Interpace Pkwy. I-80, exit 42, 0.3 mi s on Cherry Hill Rd, then just w. Int corridors. **Pets:** Large, other species. $150 one-time fee/room. Designated rooms, service with restrictions, supervision.
[ASK] [X] [icons]

PHILADELPHIA METROPOLITAN AREA (NEARBY PENNSYLVANIA)

BORDENTOWN

(AAA) ▼▼▼ Days Inn-Bordentown M
(609) 298-6100. **$89-$129.** 1073 US 206 N. New Jersey Tpke, exit 7, 0.8 mi n. Ext corridors. **Pets:** Medium, other species. $10 daily fee/pet. Service with restrictions, supervision.
[SAVE] [X] [icons]

(AAA) ▼ Imperial Inn M
(609) 298-3355. **$60-$100.** 3312 US 206 S. New Jersey Tpke, exit 7, 0.8 mi s. Ext corridors. **Pets:** Medium, dogs only. $10 daily fee/pet. Service with restrictions, supervision.
[SAVE] [X] [icon]

CARNEYS POINT

▼▼▼ Comfort Inn & Suites H
(856) 299-8282. **Call for rates.** 634 Sodders Rd. I-295, exit 2B, just e on Pennsville-Auburn Rd, then 0.3 mi s. Int corridors. **Pets:** Accepted.
[X] [icons]

(AAA) ▼▼▼▼ Holiday Inn Express Hotel & Suites H
(856) 351-9222. **Call for rates.** 506 Pennsville-Auburn Rd. I-295, exit 2B, just e. Int corridors. **Pets:** Accepted.
[SAVE] [X] [icons]

CHERRY HILL

▼▼▼ Extended StayAmerica-Philadelphia-Cherry Hill H
(856) 616-1200. **$79-$129.** 1653 SR 70 (Marlton Pike). I-295, exit 34A, just e. Int corridors. **Pets:** Other species. $25 daily fee/pet. Service with restrictions, crate.
[ASK] [X] [icons]

(AAA) ▼▼▼▼ Holiday Inn Philadelphia-Cherry Hill H
(856) 663-5300. **$129-$169.** 2175 W Marlton Pike Rd. I-295, exit 34B, 2.5 mi w. Int corridors. **Pets:** Other species. $50 deposit/room. Service with restrictions, crate.
[SAVE] [X] [icons]

DEPTFORD

▼▼▼▼ Residence Inn by Marriott H
(856) 686-9188. **$150-$170.** 1154 Hurffville Rd. SR 42, exit Deptford, Woodbury, Runnemede to CR 544, just e to CR 415. Int corridors. **Pets:** Other species. $75 one-time fee/room. Service with restrictions, crate.

HADDONFIELD

▼▼▼▼ Haddonfield Inn BB ❖
(856) 428-2195. **$199-$369, 7 day notice.** 44 W End Ave. I-295, exit 28, 0.7 mi n on SR 168, 2.6 mi e on Kings Hwy, then just n. Int corridors. **Pets:** Dogs only. $35 daily fee/pet. Designated rooms, service with restrictions, supervision.

ASK ⊠ 🖥

MOUNT LAUREL

▼▼ Candlewood Suites H ❖
(856) 642-7567. **Call for rates.** 4000 Crawford Pl. New Jersey Tpke, exit 4, 1 mi s on SR 73 S. Int corridors. **Pets:** Large. $75 one-time fee/room. Service with restrictions, crate.

⊠ 🖥 🖵

▼▼ Extended StayAmerica Philadelphia-Mt. Laurel H
(856) 778-4100. **$77-$129.** 101 Diemer Dr. New Jersey Tpke, exit 4, 1 mi se on SR 73, just n on Crawford Pl, then just e. Int corridors. **Pets:** Other species. $25 daily fee/pet. Service with restrictions, crate.

ASK ⊠ 🖥 🖵

▼▼ Extended Stay Deluxe-Mt. Laurel H
(856) 608-9820. **$87-$144.** 500 Diemer Dr. New Jersey Tpke, exit 4, 1 mi se on SR 73, just n on Crawford Pl, then just e. Int corridors. **Pets:** Other species. $25 daily fee/pet. Service with restrictions, crate.

ASK ⊠ 🖥 🖵

▲▲▲ ▼▼▼▼ Hyatt Summerfield Suites-Mount Laurel H
(856) 222-1313. **$89-$199.** 3000 Crawford Pl. New Jersey Tpke, exit 4, 1 mi s on SR 73; I-295, exit 36A, 1.5 mi s on SR 73. Ext corridors. **Pets:** Accepted.

SAVE ⊠ ♨M 🖥 🖵 🏊 ⊠

▼▼▼▼ Philadelphia/Mount Laurel Homewood Suites by Hilton H
(856) 222-9001. **$89-$139.** 1422 Nixon Dr. I-295, exit 36B, follow ramp to end, then just n. Int corridors. **Pets:** Accepted.

⊠ ♨M 🖥 🖵 🏊 ⊠

▲▲▲ ▼▼ Red Roof Inn #7066 M
(856) 234-5589. **$60-$100.** 603 Fellowship Rd. New Jersey Tpke, exit 4, just nw on SR 73 to Fellowship Rd, then just s; I-295, exit 36A, just se on SR 73 to Fellowship Rd, then just s. Ext corridors. **Pets:** Medium. Service with restrictions, supervision.

SAVE ⊠ 🖥

▲▲▲ ▼▼▼▼ Residence Inn by Marriott Mount Laurel at Bishop's Gate H
(856) 234-1025. **$199-$219.** 1001 Sunburst Ln. I-295, exit 40A. Int corridors. **Pets:** Accepted.

SAVE ⊠ ♨M 🖥 🖵 🏊 ⊠

▲▲▲ ▼▼▼▼ Staybridge Suites H
(856) 722-1900. **$135-$185.** 4115 Church Rd. New Jersey Tpke, exit 4, 0.5 mi s on SR 73, then 0.5 mi w. Int corridors. **Pets:** Medium, other species. $75 one-time fee/pet. Service with restrictions, supervision.

SAVE ⊠ 🖥 🖵 🏊 ⊠

▲▲▲ ▼▼▼▼ Wyndham Mount Laurel H
(856) 234-7000. **$108-$136.** 1111 SR 73. New Jersey Tpke, exit 4; I-295, exit 36A, 0.5 mi se. Int corridors. **Pets:** Accepted.

SAVE ⊠ 🖥 🖵 ⍩ 🏊

WESTAMPTON

▲▲▲ ▼▼ Best Western Burlington Inn H
(609) 261-3800. **$134-$139, 3 day notice.** 2020 Burlington/Mt Holly Rd. New Jersey Tpke, exit 5, just n. Int corridors. **Pets:** Medium. $5 daily fee/pet. Designated rooms, service with restrictions, crate.

SAVE ⊠ 🖥 🖵 🏊

<hr/>

END METROPOLITAN AREA

PISCATAWAY

▼▼▼▼ Embassy Suites Hotel H ❖
(732) 980-0500. **$120-$230.** 121 Centennial Ave. I-287, exit 9 (Highland Park), just s to Centennial Ave. Int corridors. **Pets:** Medium. $50 one-time fee/room. Designated rooms, service with restrictions, crate.

⊠ 🖥 🖵 ⍩ 🏊

▼▼ Extended Stay Deluxe Piscataway-Rutgers University H
(732) 235-1000. **$99-$144.** 410 S Randolphville Rd. I-287, exit 7, 0.4 mi s. Int corridors. **Pets:** Other species. $25 daily fee/pet. Service with restrictions, crate.

ASK ⊠ ♨M 🖥 🖵 🏊

▼▼ Motel 6 Piscataway #1084 H
(732) 981-9200. **$65-$75.** 1012 Stelton Rd. I-287, exit 5, just e. Ext/int corridors. **Pets:** Other species. Service with restrictions, supervision.

▼▼▼▼ Radisson Hotel Piscataway H
(732) 980-0400. **Call for rates.** 21 Kingsbridge Rd. I-287, exit 9 (Highland Park) to Centennial Ave via River Rd S, then 0.4 mi s. Int corridors. **Pets:** Accepted.

⊠ 🖥 🖵 ⍩ 🏊

PLAINSBORO

▼▼▼▼ Courtyard by Marriott Princeton H
(609) 716-9100. **$188-$230.** 3815 US 1 S. 0.4 mi s of Scudders Mill Rd at Mapleton Rd. Int corridors. **Pets:** Accepted.

⊠ ♨M 🖥 🖵 🏊

POMPTON PLAINS

▲▲▲ ▼▼▼ Best Western Regency House Hotel H
(973) 696-0900. **$89-$119.** 140 SR 23 N. 6 mi n of jct I-80, US 46 and SR 23. Int corridors. **Pets:** Small. $20 daily fee/pet. Service with restrictions, supervision.

SAVE ⊠ 🖥 🖵 ⍩ 🏊

PRINCETON

▲▲▲ ▼▼▼▼ Clarion Hotel-The Palmer Inn H ❖
(609) 452-2500. **$119-$300, 3 day notice.** 3499 US 1 S. 2 mi s of jct CR 526 and 571. Ext/int corridors. **Pets:** Medium, other species. $20 daily fee/room. Service with restrictions, supervision.

SAVE ⊠ 🖥 🖵 ⍩ 🏊

▼▼ Extended StayAmerica Princeton-West Windsor H
(609) 919-9000. **$79-$119.** 3450 Brunswick Pike N. 0.5 mi s of Meadow Rd. Int corridors. **Pets:** Other species. $25 daily fee/pet. Service with restrictions, crate.

ASK ⊠ ♨M 🖥 🖵

▲▲▲ ▼▼▼ Holiday Inn Princeton H
(609) 520-1200. **$194.** 100 Independence Way. I-295, exit 67A (SR 1) northbound; exit 67 (SR 1) southbound, 7 mi n. Int corridors. **Pets:** Medium. $75 one-time fee/room. Designated rooms, service with restrictions, crate.

SAVE ⊠ 🖥 🖵 ⍩ 🏊 ⊠

WWWW Nassau Inn 🏨 🐾
(609) 921-7500. **$199-$245.** 10 Palmer Square. Center. Int corridors.
Pets: Medium. $75 one-time fee/room. Designated rooms, service with
restrictions, crate.
SAVE ☒ 🛏 🖵 🍽

**WWW Residence Inn by Marriott-Princeton at Carnegie
Center** 🏨
(609) 799-0550. **$242-$296.** 3563 US 1 S. 1.5 mi s of jct CR 527 and 571.
Int corridors. **Pets:** Accepted.
☒ 🅼 🛏 🖵 ⊃ ☒

WWW Staybridge Suites 🏨
(609) 951-0009. **Call for rates.** 4375 US 1 S. Just past Ridge Rd. Ext
corridors. **Pets:** Accepted.
☒ 🛏 🖵 ⊃ ☒

WWWW Westin Princeton at Forrestal Village 🏨
(609) 452-7900. **$109-$309.** 201 Village Blvd. On US 1 southbound, 1.5 mi
n of CR 571. Int corridors. **Pets:** Accepted.
SAVE ☒ 🅼 🛏 🖵 🍽 ⊃ ☒

RAMSEY

WWW Best Western-The Inn at Ramsey 🏨
(201) 327-6700. **$89-$119.** 1315 Rt 17 S. Jct I-287 and SR 17 S, 3 mi s.
Int corridors. **Pets:** Medium, dogs only. $20 daily fee/pet. Designated
rooms, service with restrictions, supervision.
SAVE ☒ 🛏 🖵 🍽

WW Extended StayAmerica Ramsey 🏨
(201) 236-9996. **$79-$139.** 112 SR 17 N. Just s of Lake St exit. Int
corridors. **Pets:** Other species. $25 daily fee/pet. Service with restrictions,
crate.
ASK ☒ 🅼 🛏 🖵

RED BANK

WW Extended StayAmerica Red Bank-Middletown 🏨
(732) 450-8688. **$84-$159.** 329 Newman Springs Rd. Garden State Pkwy,
exit 109, just e. Int corridors. **Pets:** Other species. $25 daily fee/pet. Service
with restrictions, crate.
ASK ☒ 🅼 🛏 🖵

ROCKAWAY

WWW Best Western at Rockaway 🏨
(973) 625-1200. **$139.** 14 Green Pond Rd. I-80, exit 37, just n. Int corridors.
Pets: Accepted.
SAVE ☒ 🛏 🖵 ⊃

RUTHERFORD

WW Extended StayAmerica-Meadowlands 🏨
(201) 635-0266. **$104-$154.** 750 Edwin L Ward Sr Memorial Hwy. I-95, exit
16W, 1.5 mi w on SR 3 to SR 17 N service road exit, then 0.5 mi e. Int
corridors. **Pets:** Other species. $25 daily fee/pet. Service with restrictions,
crate.
ASK ☒ 🛏 🖵

SECAUCUS

WW Extended StayAmerica-Secaucus-Meadowlands 🏨
(201) 617-1711. **$109-$154.** 1 Meadowlands Pkwy. Between eastern and
western spurs of New Jersey Tpke; exits 16E, 17, or 16W to SR 3, exit
Meadowlands Pkwy, just n. Int corridors. **Pets:** Other species. $25 daily
fee/pet. Service with restrictions, crate.
ASK ☒ 🅼 🛏 🖵

**WW Homestead Studio Suites
Hotel-Secaucus/Meadowlands** 🏨
(201) 553-9700. **$149-$204.** 1 Plaza Dr. New Jersey Tpke, exit 16E northbound; exit 17E southbound, 0.3 mi e. Int corridors. **Pets:** Other species.
$25 daily fee/pet. Service with restrictions, crate.
ASK ☒ 🅼 🛏 🖵 ⊃

WWWW La Quinta Inn & Suites Secaucus 🏨 🐾
(201) 863-8700. **$119-$249.** Between eastern and western spurs of New Jersey Tpke, exits 16E, 17 or 16W via SR 3 W and
Harmon Meadow Blvd; in Mill Creek Mall. Int corridors. **Pets:** Medium, other
species. Service with restrictions, supervision.
ASK ☒ 🛏 🖵 ⊃

WWW Red Roof Inn-Meadowlands #7150 Ⓜ
(201) 319-1000. **$84-$130.** 15 Meadowlands Pkwy. Between eastern and
western spurs of New Jersey Tpke, exits 16E, 17 or 16W to SR 3, exit
Meadowlands Pkwy. Ext corridors. **Pets:** Accepted.
ASK ☒ 🛏 ☒

SHORT HILLS

WWW WWW Hilton Short Hills 🏨
(973) 379-0100. **$194-$424.** 41 John F Kennedy Pkwy. I-78, exit 48 (SR
24), 2.5 mi to John F Kennedy Pkwy. Int corridors. **Pets:** Other species.
Service with restrictions, crate.
SAVE ☒ 🅼 🛏 🖵 🍽 ⊃ ☒

SOMERSET

WW Candlewood Suites 🏨
(732) 748-1400. **Call for rates.** 41 Worlds Fair Dr. I-287, exit 10 (CR 527),
left on Ramp (CR 527 S/Easton Ave), 0.3 mi, then 0.5 mi w. Int corridors.
Pets: Accepted.
☒ 🛏 🖵

WWW Crowne Plaza Somerset/Bridgewater 🏨
(732) 560-0500. **$80-$180.** 110 Davidson Ave. I-287, exit 10 (CR 527), just
n (direction Bound Brook) to Davidson Ave, then just sw. Int corridors.
Pets: Accepted.
ASK ☒ 🛏 🖵 🍽 ⊃ ☒

WW Extended StayAmerica-Somerset-Franklin 🏨
(732) 469-8080. **$79-$124.** 30 World Fair Dr. I-287, exit 10 (CR 527), left
on ramp (CR 527 S/Easton Ave), 0.3 mi, then 0.5 mi w. Int corridors.
Pets: Other species. $25 daily fee/pet. Service with restrictions, crate.
ASK ☒ 🛏 🖵

WWWW Holiday Inn-Somerset 🏨
(732) 356-1700. **$120-$149.** 195 Davidson Ave. I-287, exit 10 (CR 527),
just n (direction Bound Brook), then 0.5 mi sw. Int corridors. **Pets:** Other
species. $15 daily fee/pet. Service with restrictions, supervision.
SAVE ☒ 🅼 🛏 🖵 🍽 ⊃

WWW Homewood Suites by Hilton-Somerset 🏨
(732) 868-9155. **$119-$189.** 101 Pierce St. I-287, exit 10 (CR 527), left on
ramp (CR 527 S/Easton Ave), 0.3 mi, 0.7 mi w on World Fair Dr, then just
s. Int corridors. **Pets:** Accepted.
☒ 🅼 🛏 🖵 ⊃ ☒

WWW Residence Inn by Marriott-Somerset 🏨
(732) 627-0881. **$189-$199.** 37 World Fair Dr. I-287, exit 10 (CR 527), left
on ramp (CR 527 S/Easton Ave) 0.3 mi, then 0.5 mi w. Int corridors.
Pets: Other species. $100 one-time fee/room.
☒ 🅼 🛏 🖵 ⊃ ☒

WWW Staybridge Suites Somerset 🏨
(732) 356-8000. **Call for rates.** 260 Davidson Ave. I-287, exit 10 (CR 527),
just n (direction Bound Brook) to Davidson Ave, then 0.8 mi sw. Ext/int
corridors. **Pets:** Accepted.
☒ 🛏 🖵 ⊃ ☒

SPRINGFIELD

WWW Holiday Inn Springfield 🏨
(973) 376-9400. **$159.** 304 US 22 W. Garden State Pkwy, exit 140 north-
bound, 4 mi w; exit 140A southbound. Int corridors. **Pets:** Large. Service
with restrictions, supervision.
ASK ☒ 🛏 🖵 🍽 ⊃ ☒

TINTON FALLS

◆◆◆ ▼ Red Roof Inn #7211 M
(732) 389-4646. **$74-$120.** 11 Centre Plaza. Garden State Pkwy, exit 105, just right at 1st light after toll. Ext corridors. **Pets:** Medium. Service with restrictions, supervision.
[SAVE] [✕] [🕭M] [📱]

◆◆◆ ▼▼▼▼ Residence Inn by Marriott H
(732) 389-8100. **$152-$186.** 90 Park Rd. Garden State Pkwy, exit 105, 1st jughandle after toll, immediate left before Courtyard by Marriott, just n, then e. Ext corridors. **Pets:** Accepted.
[SAVE] [✕] [📱] [💻] [🏊] [✕]

TOMS RIVER

◆◆◆ ▼▼▼ Howard Johnson Hotel-Toms River H ✿
(732) 244-1000. **$99-$199.** 955 Hooper Ave. Garden State Pkwy, exit 82, 1 mi e on SR 37. Int corridors. **Pets:** $50 daily fee/pet. Designated rooms, service with restrictions.
[SAVE] [✕] [📱] [💻] [🍴] [🏊]

◆◆◆ ▼▼▼ Quality Inn H ✿
(732) 341-2400. **$129-$299.** 815 SR 37 W. Garden State Pkwy, exit 82A, 1.5 mi w. Int corridors. **Pets:** Medium, dogs only. $39 daily fee/pet. Service with restrictions, supervision.
[SAVE] [✕] [📱] [💻] [🏊]

VERNON

◆◆◆ ▼▼▼ Appalachian Motel M
(973) 764-6070. **$55-$125, 3 day notice.** 367 Rt 94 N. 1 mi n. Ext corridors. **Pets:** Small. $25 daily fee/pet. Designated rooms, service with restrictions, supervision.
[SAVE] [✕] [📱]

WANTAGE

▼ High Point Country Inn M ✿
(973) 702-1860. **$89.** 1328 SR 23 N. 1 mi n of Colesville Village Center. Ext corridors. **Pets:** Other species. $10 daily fee/pet. Designated rooms, service with restrictions.
[ASK] [✕] [📱] [🏊] [✕]

WARREN

▼▼▼▼ Somerset Hills Hotel H
(908) 647-6700. **Call for rates.** 200 Liberty Corner Rd. I-78, exit 33, just n on CR 525. Int corridors. **Pets:** Accepted.
[✕] [📱] [💻] [🍴] [🏊]

WAYNE

▼▼▼ La Quinta Inns & Suites H ✿
(973) 696-8050. **$67-$99.** 1850 SR 23. I-80, exit 53 (Butler-Verona) westbound to SR 23 N, 3 mi to Ratzer Rd (service road), then just n; exit 54 eastbound to Minisink Rd, U-turn for US 80 W, exit 53. Int corridors. **Pets:** Medium, other species. Service with restrictions, supervision.
[ASK] [✕] [🕭M] [📱] [💻] [🏊]

▼▼▼ Residence Inn by Marriott Wayne H
(973) 872-7100. **$199-$214.** 30 Nevins Rd. Jct CR 640 (Riverview Dr) and 681 (Valley Rd), 3.5 mi n, just w on Barbour Pond Dr, then just n. Int corridors. **Pets:** Accepted.
[✕] [📱] [💻] [🏊] [✕]

WEEHAWKEN

◆◆◆ ▼▼▼ Sheraton Suites On The Hudson H
(201) 617-5600. **$169-$579.** 500 Harbor Blvd. I-495 E toward Lincoln Tunnel, exit Weekawken/Hoboken, bear right at bottom of hill, then 0.4 mi e to Lincoln Harbor Complex; on 19th St. Int corridors. **Pets:** Accepted.
[SAVE] [✕] [📱] [💻] [🍴] [🏊]

WEST ORANGE

▼▼▼ Residence Inn by Marriott-West Orange H
(973) 669-4700. **$189-$204.** 107 Prospect Ave. I-280, exit 8B, 1 mi n on CR 577 (Prospect Ave). Int corridors. **Pets:** Accepted.
[✕] [📱] [💻] [🏊]

WHIPPANY

▼▼ Homestead Studio Suites Hotel-Hanover/Parsippany H
(973) 463-1999. **$69-$149.** 125 Rt 10 E. I-287, exit 39, 3.6 mi e. Int corridors. **Pets:** Other species. $25 daily fee/pet. Service with restrictions, crate.
[ASK] [✕] [🕭M] [📱] [💻]

◆◆◆ ▼▼▼▼ Hyatt Summerfield Suites Parsippany/Whippany H
(973) 605-1001. **$89-$309.** 1 Ridgedale Ave N. I-287, exit 39, just nw. Int corridors. **Pets:** Accepted.
[SAVE] [✕] [🕭M] [📱] [💻] [🏊]

WOODBRIDGE

▼▼ Homestead Studio Suites Hotel-Woodbridge-Newark H
(732) 442-8333. **$74-$114.** 1 Hoover Way. New Jersey Tpke, exit 11, 1.4 mi to US 9 N, then just w on King Georges Post Rd. Int corridors. **Pets:** Other species. $25 daily fee/pet. Service with restrictions, crate.
[ASK] [✕] [🕭M] [📱] [💻]

NEW MEXICO

CITY INDEX

ALAMOGORDO

▼▼ Quality Inn H
(575) 437-7100. **$67-$81.** 1401 S White Sands Blvd. 1.6 mi s of jct US 54/70 and 82. Int corridors. **Pets:** Accepted.
A$K ✕ 🛵ᴹ 🛏 🖥 ➔

▼▼ Super 8-Alamogordo H
(575) 434-4205. **Call for rates.** 3204 N White Sands Blvd. Just s of jct US 54/70 and 82. Int corridors. **Pets:** Other species. $10 daily fee/room. Service with restrictions, supervision.
✕ 🛏 🖥

ALBUQUERQUE

⟨AAA⟩ ▼▼▼ Best Western Airport InnSuites Albuquerque Hotel & Suites H
(505) 242-7022. **$79-$199.** 2400 Yale Blvd SE. I-25, exit 222 (Gibson Blvd) northbound; exit 222A southbound, 1 mi e, then just s. Int corridors. **Pets:** Accepted.
SAVE ✕ 🛏 🖥 ➔

⟨AAA⟩ ▼▼▼ Best Western Rio Grande Inn H
(505) 843-9500. **$105-$160.** 1015 Rio Grande Blvd NW. I-40, exit 157A (Rio Grande Blvd), just s. Int corridors. **Pets:** Medium. $25 one-time fee/room. Designated rooms, service with restrictions, supervision.
SAVE ✕ 🛏 🖥 🍴 ➔

⟨AAA⟩ ▼▼▼▼ Brittania & W E Mauger Estate Bed & Breakfast BB
(505) 242-8755. **$143-$179, 10 day notice.** 701 Roma Ave NW. I-25, exit 225, 1 mi w, then just s on 7th Ave. Int corridors. **Pets:** Dogs only. $30 one-time fee/room. Designated rooms, service with restrictions, crate.
SAVE ✕ 🛏 🖥

▼▼▼ Candlewood Suites H
(505) 888-3424. **$85-$190.** 3025 Menaul Blvd NE. I-40, exit 160, just n to Menaul Blvd, then 0.5 mi w. Int corridors. **Pets:** Large, other species. $75 one-time fee/room. Service with restrictions.
A$K ✕ 🛵ᴹ 🛏 🖥

⟨AAA⟩ ▼▼▼▼ ClubHouse Inn & Suites H
(505) 345-0010. **$89-$129.** 1315 Menaul Blvd NE. I-25, exit 227A Southbound, 1.5 mi s to Menaul Blvd, then just w; exit 225 northbound, 1.8 mi, then just w. Int corridors. **Pets:** Medium, other species. $10 daily fee/pet. Service with restrictions, crate.
SAVE ✕ 🛵ᴹ 🛏 🖥 ➔

⟨AAA⟩ ▼▼ Comfort Inn-Airport H
(505) 243-2244. **Call for rates.** 2300 Yale Blvd SE. I-25, exit 222A southbound; exit 222 (Gibson Blvd) northbound, 1 mi n, then just s. Ext/int corridors. **Pets:** Very small, dogs only. $10 daily fee/pet. Designated rooms, service with restrictions, supervision.
SAVE ✕ 🛵ᴹ 🛏 🖥 ➔

▼▼ Comfort Inn & Suites by Choice Hotels H
(505) 822-1090. **Call for rates.** 5811 Signal Ave NE. I-25, exit 233, just e via Alameda. Int corridors. **Pets:** Medium, other species. $15 one-time fee/pet. Designated rooms, service with restrictions, supervision.
✕ 🛵ᴹ 🛏 🖥 ➔

⟨AAA⟩ ▼▼▼ Comfort Inn East M
(505) 294-1800. **$59-$95.** 13031 Central Ave NE. I-40, exit 167 (Central Ave), just w. Ext corridors. **Pets:** Medium. $10 one-time fee/pet. Service with restrictions, crate.
SAVE ✕ 🛵ᴹ 🛏 🖥 🍴 ➔

▼▼▼ Country Inn & Suites Albuquerque Airport H
(505) 246-9600. **$69-$129.** 2601 Mulberry SE. I-25, exit 222 (Gibson Blvd), just e. Int corridors. **Pets:** Accepted.
A$K ✕ 🛏 🖥 ➔

⟨AAA⟩ ▼▼▼ Days Inn-Hotel Circle H
(505) 275-3297. **$50-$60.** 10321 Hotel Ave NE. I-40, exit 165 (Eubank Blvd), just n. Ext corridors. **Pets:** Accepted.
SAVE ✕ 🛏 🖥 ➔

▼▼▼▼ Drury Inn & Suites-Albuquerque H
(505) 341-3600. **$100-$159.** 4310 The 25 Way NE. I-25, Jefferson St NE; northwest quadrant of exchange. Int corridors. **Pets:** Other species. Service with restrictions, supervision.
A$K ✕ 🛵ᴹ 🛏 🖥 ➔

⟨AAA⟩ ▼ Econo Lodge East H
(505) 292-7600. **$45-$99.** 13211 Central Ave NE. I-40, exit 167 (Central Ave), just w. Ext corridors. **Pets:** Medium, other species. $7 one-time fee/pet. Service with restrictions, supervision.
SAVE ✕ 🛏

⟨AAA⟩ ▼ Econo Lodge Midtown H
(505) 880-0080. **$49-$99.** 2412 Carlisle Blvd NE. I-40, exit 160, just n. Ext corridors. **Pets:** Small. $15 one-time fee/pet. Service with restrictions, supervision.
SAVE ✕ 🛏

⟨AAA⟩ ▼▼▼ Econo Lodge Old Town H
(505) 243-8475. **$55-$140.** 2321 Central Ave NW. I-40, exit 157A, 0.6 mi s on Rio Grande Blvd, then 0.4 mi w. Ext corridors. **Pets:** Small, dogs only. $20 one-time fee/pet. Designated rooms, service with restrictions, supervision.
SAVE ✕ 🛏 🖥 ➔

⟨AAA⟩ ▼▼ Fairfield Inn Airport H
(505) 247-1621. **$59-$159.** 2300 Centre Ave SE. I-25, exit 222 (Gibson Blvd) northbound; exit 222A southbound, 1 mi e to Yale Blvd; northeast jct Gibson and Yale blvds. Int corridors. **Pets:** Accepted.
SAVE ✕ 🛵ᴹ 🛏 🖥 ➔

⟨AAA⟩ ▼▼ GuestHouse Inn & Suites H 🐾
(505) 271-8500. **$40-$99.** 10331 Hotel Ave NE. I-40, exit 165 (Eubank Dr), just n. Int corridors. **Pets:** Very small. $10 one-time fee/pet. Service with restrictions, supervision.
SAVE ✕ 🛏 🖥

⟨AAA⟩ ▼▼▼▼ Hacienda Antigua Inn BB 🐾
(505) 345-5399. **$139-$209, 10 day notice.** 6708 Tierra Dr NW. I-25, exit 230 (Osuna Dr), 2 mi w, then just n. Ext/int corridors. **Pets:** $30 one-time fee/pet. Service with restrictions, supervision.
SAVE ✕ 🛏 🖥 ➔

Hampton Inn-North
(505) 344-1555. **$79-$144.** 5101 Ellison NE. I-25, exit 231 (San Antonio Dr), just w. Ext corridors. **Pets:** Other species. Service with restrictions, supervision.

Hawthorn Inn & Suites
(505) 242-1555. **Call for rates.** 1511 Gibson Blvd SE. I-25, exit 222 (Gibson Blvd) northbound; exit 222A southbound, just e. Int corridors. **Pets:** Medium, other species. $25 daily fee/pet. Service with restrictions, supervision.

Hilton Albuquerque
(505) 884-2500. **$69-$159.** 1901 University Blvd NE. I-40, exit 160, just n to Menaul Blvd, then 1.1 mi w. Int corridors. **Pets:** Large. $75 one-time fee/room. Service with restrictions, supervision.

Holiday Inn Express
(505) 275-8900. **$95-$100.** 10330 Hotel Ave NE. I-40, exit 165 (Eubank Blvd), 2 blks n. Ext corridors. **Pets:** Large, other species. $25 one-time fee/pet. Designated rooms, service with restrictions, supervision.

The Hotel Blue
(505) 924-2400. **Call for rates.** 717 Central Ave NW. 8th St and Central Ave; downtown. Ext corridors. **Pets:** $15 daily fee/pet. Designated rooms, supervision.

Howard Johnson Express Inn
(505) 828-1600. **$75-$145.** 7630 Pan American Frwy NE. I-25, exit 231 (San Antonio Dr), 0.8 mi n on frontage road. Int corridors. **Pets:** Accepted.

La Quinta Inn Albuquerque (Airport)
(505) 243-5500. **$59-$149.** 2116 Yale Blvd SE. I-25, exit 222 (Gibson Blvd) northbound; exit 222A southbound, 1 mi e. Int corridors. **Pets:** Medium, other species. Service with restrictions, supervision.

La Quinta Inn Albuquerque (I-40 East)
(505) 884-3591. **$49-$119.** 2424 San Mateo Blvd NE. I-40, exit 161 westbound; exit 161B eastbound, just n. Ext corridors. **Pets:** Medium, other species. Service with restrictions, supervision.

La Quinta Inn Albuquerque (North)
(505) 821-9000. **$49-$119.** 5241 San Antonio Dr NE. I-25, exit 231 (San Antonio Dr), just e. Ext corridors. **Pets:** Medium, other species. Service with restrictions, supervision.

La Quinta Inn & Suites Albuquerque (West)
(505) 839-1744. **$59-$129.** 6101 Iliff Rd NW. I-40, exit 155, just sw. Int corridors. **Pets:** Medium, other species. Service with restrictions, supervision.

La Quinta Inn & Suites Northwest
(505) 345-7500. **$49-$129.** 7439 Pan American Frwy NE. I-25, exit 231 (San Antonio Dr), just w. Int corridors. **Pets:** Medium, other species. Service with restrictions, supervision.

La Quinta Suites Midtown/University
(505) 761-5600. **$89-$179.** 2011 Menaul Blvd. Jct University and Menaul blvds, just e. Int corridors. **Pets:** Medium, other species. Service with restrictions, supervision.

Motel 6 Albuquerque North #1290
(505) 821-1472. **$45-$58.** 8510 Pan American Frwy NE. I-25, exit 232, just n on Frontage Rd. Int corridors. **Pets:** Other species. Service with restrictions, supervision.

Nativo Lodge
(505) 798-4300. **Call for rates.** 6000 Pan American Frwy NE. I-25, exit 230, just e. Int corridors. **Pets:** Dogs only. $50 one-time fee/pet. Service with restrictions, supervision.

Plaza Inn Albuquerque
(505) 243-5693. **$89-$159.** 900 Medical Arts NE. I-25, exit 225, just e. Int corridors. **Pets:** Accepted.

Quality Inn & Suites Albuquerque Downtown
(505) 242-5228. **$59-$150.** 411 McKnight Ave NW. I-40, exit 159A, just s via 4th St S. Int corridors. **Pets:** $10 daily fee/pet. Designated rooms, service with restrictions, supervision.

Quality Suites
(505) 797-0850. **$70-$150.** 5251 San Antonio Dr NE. I-25, exit 231 (San Antonio Dr), just e. Int corridors. **Pets:** Medium. $10 daily fee/pet. Service with restrictions, supervision.

Ramada Limited
(505) 858-3297. **Call for rates.** 5601 Alameda Blvd NE. I-25, exit 233, just w. Int corridors. **Pets:** Accepted.

Residence Inn North by Marriott
(505) 761-0200. **$145-$177.** 4331 The Lane at 25 NE. I-25, exit 229 (Jefferson St), just w, just n to The Lane at 25 NE, then just e. Int corridors. **Pets:** Accepted.

Sandia Peak Inn
(505) 831-5036. **$50-$136.** 4614 Central Ave SW. I-40, exit 157A, just s, then 2 mi w. Ext corridors. **Pets:** Accepted.

Albuquerque Grand Airport Hotel
(505) 843-7000. **$99-$229.** 2910 Yale Blvd SE. I-25, exit 225 northbound; exit 222A southbound, 1 mi e on Gibson Blvd, then 0.5 mi s. Int corridors. **Pets:** Medium. $150 deposit/room. Designated rooms, service with restrictions, supervision.

Sheraton Albuquerque Uptown
(505) 881-0000. **$99-$399.** 2600 Louisiana Blvd NE. I-40, exit 162, 0.8 mi n. Int corridors. **Pets:** Medium. Service with restrictions, supervision.

Sleep Inn Airport
(505) 244-3325. **Call for rates.** 2300 International Ave SE. I-25, exit 222 (Gibson Blvd) northbound; exit 222A southbound, 1 mi e to Yale Blvd, then just n. Int corridors. **Pets:** Medium. $10 daily fee/pet. Service with restrictions, supervision.

Suburban Extended Stay Hotels
(505) 883-8888. **$79.** 2401 Wellsley Dr NE. I-40, exit 160, just n to Menaul Blvd, just w, then just s. Ext corridors. **Pets:** Accepted.

Super 8 East
(505) 271-4807. **Call for rates.** 450 Paisano NE. I-40, exit 166 (Juan Tabo Blvd), just n to Copper, then just s. Int corridors. **Pets:** Accepted.

▼▼▼ **Super 8 of Albuquerque** 🄷
(505) 888-4884. **$44-$74.** 2500 University Blvd NE. I-25, exit 225 northbound, 1.9 mi n on frontage road to Menaul Blvd, then just e; exit 227 (Comanche Rd) southbound, 0.9 mi s to Menaul Blvd, then just e. Int corridors. **Pets:** Accepted.
ASK ✕ 🛗 ▣

▼▼▼ **Super 8 West (Albuquerque)** 🄷
(505) 836-5560. **$44-$129.** 6030 Iliff Rd NW. I-40, exit 155, 0.5 mi s. Int corridors. **Pets:** Accepted.
ASK ✕ ▣

🆀 ▼▼▼▼ **TownePlace Suites by Marriott** 🄷 🐾
(505) 232-5800. **$59-$179.** 2400 Centre Ave SE. I-25, exit 222 (Gibson Blvd) northbound; exit 222A southbound, 1 mi e to Yale Blvd, at northeast jct of Gibson and Yale blvds, then just e. Int corridors. **Pets:** Medium, other species. Service with restrictions, crate.
SAVE ✕ 🛗 🛗 ▣ ⊇

ALGODONES

🆀 ▼▼▼▼ **Hacienda Vargas Bed and Breakfast Inn** 🅱🅱
(505) 867-9115. **$89-$169, 10 day notice.** 1431 SR 313 (El Camino Real). I-25, exit 248, 0.3 mi w, then 0.3 mi s. Int corridors. **Pets:** Accepted.
SAVE ✕ ✕ 🛅 🛐

ARROYO SECO

▼▼▼▼ **Adobe and Stars B & B** 🅱🅱
(575) 776-2776. **$95-$215, 31 day notice.** 584 State Hwy 150. 1.1 mi ne on SR 150 at Valdez Rd. Ext/int corridors. **Pets:** Medium. $50 deposit/room, $10 daily fee/pet. Designated rooms, service with restrictions, crate.
ASK ✕ 🛅 🛐

▼▼▼▼ **Cottonwood Inn Bed & Breakfast** 🅱🅱
(575) 776-5826. **$125-$275, 14 day notice.** 02 SR 230. On SR 150 at SR 230. Ext/int corridors. **Pets:** Dogs only. $20 one-time fee/pet. Designated rooms, service with restrictions, supervision.
ASK ✕ 🛅 ▣ ✕ 🛐 🛐

ARTESIA

🆀 ▼ **Artesia Inn** 🅼
(575) 746-9801. **$65-$90.** 1820 S 1st St. 1.5 mi s on US 285. Ext corridors. **Pets:** Other species. $11 one-time fee/room. Service with restrictions, supervision.
SAVE ✕ 🛅 ▣ ⊇

🆀 ▼▼▼▼ **Best Western Pecos Inn** 🄷
(575) 748-3324. **$95-$115, 3 day notice.** 2209 W Main. 1.5 mi w on US 82. Int corridors. **Pets:** Accepted.
SAVE ✕ 🛅 ▣ 🍴 ⊇ ✕

BERNALILLO

🆀 ▼▼ **Days Inn Bernalillo** 🄷
(505) 771-7000. **$40-$140.** 107 N Camino del Pueblo. I-25, exit 242, just w. Int corridors. **Pets:** Accepted.
SAVE ✕ ▣ ⊇

🆀 ▼▼▼▼ **Hyatt Regency Tamaya Resort and Spa** 🄷 🐾
(505) 867-1234. **$169-$445, 7 day notice.** 1300 Tuyuna Tr. I-25, exit 242, 1 mi w on SR 44 to Tamaya Rd, then 1 mi n, follow signs. Int corridors. **Pets:** Large. $50 one-time fee/room. Service with restrictions, supervision.
SAVE ✕ 🛗 🛅 ▣ 🍴 ⊇ ✕

▼▼▼ **La Hacienda Grande** 🅱🅱
(505) 867-1887. **$89-$129, 10 day notice.** 21 Barros Rd. I-25, exit 242, 0.3 mi w to Camino del Pueblo, then 0.5 mi n. Ext/int corridors. **Pets:** Designated rooms, crate.
ASK ✕ 🛐

🆀 ▼▼ **Quality Inn & Suites** 🄷
(505) 771-9500. **$55-$155.** 210 N Hill Rd. I-25, exit 242, just w. Int corridors. **Pets:** Medium. $10 one-time fee/pet. Service with restrictions, supervision.
SAVE ✕ 🛅 ▣

▼▼ **Super 8 Bernalillo** 🄷
(505) 771-4700. **$49-$150.** 265 E Hwy 550. I-25, exit 242, just w. Int corridors. **Pets:** Small. $20 deposit/pet, $10 daily fee/pet. Designated rooms, service with restrictions, supervision.
ASK ✕ 🛅 ▣

BLOOMFIELD

▼▼ **Super 8 Motel** 🅼
(505) 632-8886. **Call for rates.** 525 W Broadway Blvd. Jct of US 64 and 550. Int corridors. **Pets:** Other species. $15 one-time fee/room. Service with restrictions, supervision.
✕ ▣

CARLSBAD

🆀 ▼▼▼ **Best Western Stevens Inn** 🄷
(575) 887-2851. **$102-$116.** 1829 S Canal St. 1 mi s on US 62, 180 and 285. Ext corridors. **Pets:** Medium. $20 daily fee/pet. Designated rooms, service with restrictions, crate.
SAVE ✕ 🛅 ▣ 🍴 ⊇

🆀 ▼▼▼ **Carlsbad Inn** 🅼 🐾
(575) 887-1171. **$49-$69.** 2019 S Canal St. 1.5 mi s on US 62, 180 and 285. Ext corridors. **Pets:** Medium. $10 daily fee/pet. Designated rooms, no service, supervision.
SAVE ✕ 🛅 ⊇

🆀 ▼▼▼ **Continental Inn & Suites** 🅼
(575) 887-0341. **$49-$69.** 3820 National Parks Hwy. 3.5 mi sw on US 62 and 180. Ext corridors. **Pets:** Other species. $10 one-time fee/room. Designated rooms, service with restrictions, supervision.
SAVE ✕ 🛅 ⊇

🆀 ▼▼▼ **Days Inn of Carlsbad** 🄷
(575) 887-7800. **$89-$99.** 3910 National Parks Hwy. 3.5 mi sw on US 62 and 180. Ext corridors. **Pets:** Small, dogs only. $10 one-time fee/pet. Designated rooms, service with restrictions, supervision.
SAVE ✕ 🛗 🛅 ▣ ⊇

CHAMA

🆀 ▼▼▼ **Vista del Rio Lodge** 🅼
(575) 756-2138. **$60-$105, 3 day notice.** 2595 US Hwy 84/64. 0.5 mi s of SR 17. Ext corridors. **Pets:** Very small, dogs only. Service with restrictions, supervision.
SAVE ✕ 🛅 ▣ ✕ 🛐

CHIMAYO

▼▼ **Casa Escondida Bed & Breakfast** 🅱🅱 🐾
(505) 351-4805. **$99-$159, 14 day notice.** 64 CR 0100. Jct SR 76 and 98, just w on SR 76, then 0.5 mi ne on CR 100, follow signs. Ext/int corridors. **Pets:** Other species. $15 daily fee/pet. Designated rooms, service with restrictions, supervision.
✕ 🛅 ▣ 🛐 🛐

CIMARRON

🆀 ▼ **Cimarron Inn & RV Park** 🅼
(575) 376-2268. **$49-$60.** 212 10th St. On US 64. Ext corridors. **Pets:** Other species. Designated rooms, supervision.
SAVE ✕ 🛅 ▣

CLAYTON

Best Western Kokopelli Lodge H ❖
(575) 374-2589. **$105-$225.** 702 S 1st St. US 87, 0.5 mi se of jct US 56 and 64. Ext corridors. **Pets:** $5 daily fee/pet. Service with restrictions, supervision.
SAVE ⊠ 🛇 💻 ➰

Days Inn & Suites H
(575) 374-0133. **$89-$169.** 1120 S 1st St. US 87, 1 mi s of jct US 56 and 64. Int corridors. **Pets:** Medium. $15 daily fee/pet. Designated rooms, service with restrictions, supervision.
SAVE ⊠ 🛇 💻 ➰

Super 8 Motel M
(575) 374-8127. **Call for rates.** 1425 S 1st St. US 87, 1 mi se of jct US 56 and 64. Int corridors. **Pets:** Medium. $10 daily fee/pet. Service with restrictions, supervision.
⊠ 🛇 💻

CLOUDCROFT

The Lodge Resort H
(575) 682-2566. **$130-$365, 14 day notice.** 1 Corona Pl. US 82, 0.3 mi s on Curlew/Corona Pl. Int corridors. **Pets:** Accepted.
SAVE ⊠ 🛪 🛇 💻 🍴 ➰ 🗶

CLOVIS

Econo Lodge M
(575) 763-3439. **$59-$109.** 1400 E Mabry Dr. 0.5 mi e on US 60/70/84. Ext corridors. **Pets:** Accepted.
ASK ⊠ 🛇 💻 ➰

La Quinta Inn & Suites Clovis H ❖
(575) 763-8777. **$79-$109.** 4521 N Prince St. Jct US 60/84 and Prince St, 3 mi n. Int corridors. **Pets:** Medium, other species. Service with restrictions, supervision.
SAVE ⊠ 🛇 💻 ➰

Mabry Inn H
(575) 762-4491. **Call for rates.** 2700 E Mabry Dr. 1.5 mi e on US 60/70/84. Ext corridors. **Pets:** Accepted.
⊠ 🛪 🛇 💻 ➰ 🗶

DEMING

Best Western Mimbres Valley Inn H
(575) 546-4544. **$60-$120, 3 day notice.** 1500 W Pine St. I-10, exit 81, just e. Ext corridors. **Pets:** Other species. $15 daily fee/pet. Service with restrictions, supervision.
SAVE ⊠ 🛇 💻 ➰

Comfort Inn & Suites H
(575) 544-3600. **Call for rates.** 1010 W Pine St. I-10, exit 81, just e. Int corridors. **Pets:** Small, dogs only. $10 daily fee/pet. Service with restrictions, supervision.
⊠ 🛪 🛇 💻 ➰

Days Inn M ❖
(575) 546-8813. **$57-$80.** 1601 E Pine St. I-10, exit 85 westbound, 2 mi w on business loop; exit 81 eastbound, 1 mi e on business loop. Ext corridors. **Pets:** Small, other species. $5 daily fee/pet. Service with restrictions, supervision.
SAVE ⊠ 🛇 💻 ➰

Grand Motor Inn H ❖
(575) 546-2632. **$49-$54.** 1721 E Pine St. I-10, exit 85 westbound, 2 mi w on business loop; exit 82 eastbound, 1 mi e on business loop. Ext/int corridors. **Pets:** Medium. $5 one-time fee/room. Designated rooms, service with restrictions, supervision.
SAVE ⊠ 🛇 🍴 ➰

Holiday Inn H
(575) 546-2661. **$60-$90.** 4600 E Pine St. I-10, exit 85, just w. Ext corridors. **Pets:** Other species. Service with restrictions, supervision.
SAVE ⊠ 🛪 🛇 💻 🍴 ➰

La Quinta Inn & Suites H ❖
(575) 546-0600. **$79-$129.** 4300 E Pine St. I-10, exit 85, just w. Int corridors. **Pets:** Medium, other species. Service with restrictions, supervision.
SAVE ⊠ 🛪 🛇 💻 ➰

DULCE

Best Western Jircarilla Inn & Casino H
(505) 759-3663. **$85-$95.** US Hwy 64 Jicarilla Blvd. Center. Int corridors. **Pets:** Accepted.
SAVE ⊠ 🛇 💻 🍴

ELEPHANT BUTTE

Elephant Butte Inn & Spa H ❖
(575) 744-5431. **$79-$149.** 401 Hwy 195. I-25, exit 83, 4 mi e. Ext corridors. **Pets:** Medium, dogs only. $25 one-time fee/pet. Designated rooms, service with restrictions, supervision.
SAVE ⊠ 🛪 🛇 💻 🍴 ➰

ESPANOLA

Comfort Inn H
(505) 753-2419. **$59-$160.** 604-B S Riverside Dr. US 84 and 285, just s of jct SR 68. Int corridors. **Pets:** $10 daily fee/pet. Service with restrictions, supervision.
SAVE ⊠ 🛇 💻 ➰

Motel 6 #4343 M
(505) 753-5374. **$50-$100.** 811 S Riverside Dr. US 84 and 285, 0.5 mi s of jct SR 68. Int corridors. **Pets:** Accepted.
ASK ⊠ 🛇

FARMINGTON

Americas Best Value Inn H
(505) 325-2288. **$54-$79.** 600 E Broadway. 1 mi e; at Broadway and Scott Ave. Int corridors. **Pets:** Accepted.
SAVE ⊠ 🛇 💻 ➰ 🗶

Best Western Inn & Suites H
(505) 327-5221. **$99.** 700 Scott Ave. 1 mi e on SR 516 (Main St), just s. Int corridors. **Pets:** Accepted.
SAVE ⊠ 🛇 💻 🍴 ➰ 🗶

Comfort Inn H
(505) 325-2626. **$80-$130.** 555 Scott Ave. 1 mi e on SR 516 (Main St), just s. Int corridors. **Pets:** Accepted.
SAVE ⊠ 🛇 💻 ➰

Holiday Inn Express H
(505) 325-2545. **$99-$139.** 2110 Bloomfield Blvd. 1.6 mi e on US 64 (Bloomfield Blvd); just past jct Broadway; on Frontage Rd. Int corridors. **Pets:** Accepted.
ASK ⊠ 🛇 💻 ➰

La Quinta Inn Farmington H ❖
(505) 327-4706. **$59-$149.** 675 Scott Ave. 1 mi e on SR 516 (Main St), just s. Ext/int corridors. **Pets:** Medium, other species. Service with restrictions, supervision.
ASK ⊠ 🛇 💻 ➰

GALLUP

Americas Best Value Inn & Suites H
(505) 722-0757. **$52-$79.** 2003 Hwy 66 W. I-40, exit 20, 1 mi w. Ext/int corridors. **Pets:** Accepted.
ASK ⊠ 🛇 💻 🍴

♦♦ Best Western Inn & Suites ℍ
(505) 722-2221. **$70-$89.** 3009 US 66 W. I-40, exit 16, 1 mi e. Int corridors. **Pets:** Accepted.
[SAVE] [X] [🖥] [💻] [🍴] [🏊]

♦♦ Best Western Red Rock Inn ℍ
(505) 722-7600. **$70-$161, 3 day notice.** 3010 US 66 E. I-40, exit 26, 1 mi w. Int corridors. **Pets:** Accepted.
[SAVE] [X] [🖥] [💻] [🏊]

♦♦♦ Best Western Royal Holiday Motel Ⓜ
(505) 722-4900. **$55-$95.** 1903 W Hwy 66. I-40, exit 20, 0.5 mi s to US 66, then 0.8 mi w. Int corridors. **Pets:** Accepted.
[SAVE] [X] [🖥] [💻] [🏊]

♦♦ Comfort Inn Ⓜ
(505) 722-0982. **Call for rates.** 3208 US 66 W. I-40, exit 16, 0.3 mi e. Int corridors. **Pets:** Medium. $10 daily fee/room. Service with restrictions, supervision.
[X] [🖥] [💻] [🏊]

♦♦ Days Inn West Ⓜ
(505) 863-6889. **$56-$65.** 3201 W Hwy 66. I-40, exit 16, 0.3 mi e. Ext corridors. **Pets:** Accepted.
[ASK] [X] [🖥] [💻] [🏊]

♦♦ Economy Inn Ⓜ
(505) 863-9301. **Call for rates.** 1709 US 66 W. I-40, exit 20, s to US 66, then 0.5 mi w. Ext corridors. **Pets:** Accepted.
[SAVE] [X] [🖥]

♦♦♦ La Quinta Inn & Suites ℍ ☘
(505) 722-2233. **$69-$139.** 3880 Hwy 66 E. I-40, exit 26, just e. Int corridors. **Pets:** Medium, other species. Service with restrictions, supervision.
[ASK] [X] [🖥] [💻] [🏊] [🐾]

♦♦♦ Quality Inn & Suites ℍ
(505) 726-1000. **$69-$119.** 1500 W Maloney Ave. I-40, exit 20, just n on Munoz Dr, then just w. Ext/int corridors. **Pets:** Very small. $10 daily fee/pet. Designated rooms, service with restrictions, supervision.
[SAVE] [X] [🖥] [💻] [🏊]

♦♦ Ramada Limited ℍ
(505) 726-2700. **$79-$109.** 1440 W Maloney Ave. I-40, exit 20, 1 mi w. Int corridors. **Pets:** Accepted.
[ASK] [X] [🖥] [💻] [🏊]

♦♦ Red Roof Inn Ⓜ
(505) 722-7765. **$33-$60.** 3304 W Hwy 66. I-40, exit 16, just se. Ext corridors. **Pets:** Medium. Service with restrictions, supervision.
[SAVE] [X] [🖥] [💻] [🏊]

♦♦♦ Super 8 Motel Ⓜ
(505) 722-5300. **$50-$90 (no credit cards).** 1715 W US Hwy 66. I-40, exit 20, s to US 66, then 0.5 mi w. Int corridors. **Pets:** Medium. $10 daily fee/pet. Designated rooms, service with restrictions, supervision.
[SAVE] [X] [🖥] [💻] [🏊]

GRANTS

♦♦ Comfort Inn ℍ
(505) 287-8700. **$59-$109.** 1551 E Santa Fe Ave. I-40, exit 85, 0.3 mi n. Int corridors. **Pets:** Small. $20 one-time fee/pet. Service with restrictions, supervision.
[ASK] [X] [🖥] [💻] [🏊]

♦♦ Days Inn Ⓜ
(505) 287-8883. **$80.** 1504 E Santa Fe Ave. I-40, exit 85, 0.3 mi n. Ext corridors. **Pets:** Small. $15 one-time fee/pet. Service with restrictions, supervision.
[SAVE] [X] [🖥] [💻]

♦♦♦ Holiday Inn Express ℍ
(505) 285-4676. **$100-$129, 7 day notice.** 1496 E Sante Fe Ave. I-40, exit 85, 0.3 mi n. Int corridors. **Pets:** Small. $20 one-time fee/pet. Service with restrictions, supervision.
[SAVE] [X] [🖥] [💻] [🏊]

♦♦ Sands Motel Ⓜ
(505) 287-2996. **$31-$46.** 112 McArthur St. I-40, exit 85, 1.5 mi w on Business Loop 40 (Santa Fe Ave). Ext corridors. **Pets:** Other species. $5 one-time fee/pet. No service, crate.
[SAVE] [X]

HOBBS

♦♦♦ Best Western Executive Inn ℍ
(575) 397-7171. **$90-$95.** 309 N Marland Blvd. US 62, 180 and Snyder St. Ext corridors. **Pets:** Dogs only. $10 daily fee/pet. Service with restrictions, supervision.
[SAVE] [X] [🖥] [💻] [🏊]

♦♦ Days Inn Ⓜ
(575) 397-6541. **Call for rates.** 211 N Marland Blvd. 2 mi e on US 62 and 180. Ext corridors. **Pets:** Small. $10 daily fee/pet. Service with restrictions, supervision.
[X] [🖥] [💻] [🏊]

♦♦♦ Econo Lodge ℍ
(575) 397-3591. **$75-$85.** 619 N Marland Blvd. 2.5 mi e on US 62 and 180. Ext corridors. **Pets:** Accepted.
[SAVE] [X] [🖥] [💻] [🏊]

♦♦♦ Hobbs Family Inn ℍ
(575) 397-3251. **$60-$95.** 501 N Marland Blvd. 2.5 mi e on US 62 and 180. Ext/int corridors. **Pets:** Medium. $25 deposit/pet. No service.
[SAVE] [X] [🖥] [💻] [🍴] [🏊]

LAS CRUCES

♦♦♦ Best Western Mesilla Valley Inn ℍ
(575) 524-8603. **$72-$105.** 901 Avenida de Mesilla. I-10, exit 140, just n. Ext/int corridors. **Pets:** Accepted.
[SAVE] [X] [🖥] [💻] [🍴] [🏊]

♦♦♦ Best Western Mission Inn ℍ
(575) 524-8591. **$73.** 1765 S Main St. I-10, exit 142, 1 mi n. Ext corridors. **Pets:** Other species. $10 daily fee/pet. Service with restrictions, supervision.
[SAVE] [X] [🖥] [💻] [🍴] [🏊]

♦♦♦♦ Comfort Inn & Suites de Mesilla ℍ
(575) 527-1050. **$80-$125.** 1300 Avenida de Mesilla. I-10, exit 140, just s. Int corridors. **Pets:** Small. $10 daily fee/pet. Service with restrictions, crate.
[SAVE] [X] [&M] [🖥] [💻] [🏊]

♦♦ Comfort Inn of Las Cruces ℍ
(575) 527-2000. **$80-$130.** 2585 S Valley Dr. I-10, exit 142, just n. Int corridors. **Pets:** Small, dogs only. $20 one-time fee/pet. Designated rooms, service with restrictions, supervision.
[ASK] [X] [🖥] [💻] [🏊]

♦♦♦ Comfort Suites by Choice Hotels ℍ
(575) 522-1300. **Call for rates.** 2101 S Triviz. I-25, exit 1, just w on University Ave, then just n. Int corridors. **Pets:** Accepted.
[X] [&M] [🖥] [💻] [🏊]

♦♦♦ DreamCatcher Inn Bed & Breakfast de Las Cruces 🅱🅱 ☘
(575) 522-3035. **$125-$150, 5 day notice.** 10201 Starfly Rd. US 70 E to NASA/Baylor Canyon Rd, 0.5 mi s, then 0.5 mi w. Ext corridors. **Pets:** Other species. $25 one-time fee/room. Designated rooms.
[X] [&M]

♦♦♦ Hampton Inn ℍ
(575) 526-8311. **$62-$85.** 755 Avenida de Mesilla. I-10, exit 140. Ext corridors. **Pets:** Small. Service with restrictions, supervision.
[SAVE] [X] [🖥] [💻] [🏊]

▼▼▼▼ Hilltop Hacienda B & B 🅱🅱
(575) 382-3556. **$95-$135, 14 day notice.** 2600 Westmoreland Ave. I-25, exit 6 (US 70), just e to Del Rey Blvd, 3 mi n, then 1 mi e. Int corridors. **Pets:** Dogs only. $25 one-time fee/room. Supervision.
(A$K) ⊠ 🅰

▼▼▼ Hotel Encanto de Las Cruces 🅷
(575) 522-4300. **$98-$159.** 705 S Telshor Blvd. I-25, exit 3 (Lohman Ave), just e, then just s. Int corridors. **Pets:** Accepted.
(A$K) ⊠ 🛢 💻 🍴 🛬

▼▼▼▼ La Quinta Inn & Suites Las Cruces 🅷 🐾
(575) 523-0100. **$65-$139.** 1500 Hickory Dr. I-10, exit 140, just se of jct I-25 and Avenida de Mesilla. Int corridors. **Pets:** Medium, other species. Service with restrictions, supervision.
(A$K) ⊠ 🅰M 🛢 💻 🛬

▼▼▼▼ La Quinta Inn Las Cruces 🅷 🐾
(575) 524-0331. **$49-$139.** 790 Avenida de Mesilla. I-10, exit 140. Int corridors. **Pets:** Medium, other species. Service with restrictions, supervision.
(A$K) ⊠ 🅰M 🛢 💻 🛬

▼▼▼ Lundeen's Inn of the Arts 🅱🅱 🐾
(575) 526-3326. **$79-$125, 3 day notice.** 618 S Alameda Blvd. Jct Lohman Ave, just s; center. Int corridors. **Pets:** Medium. $15 one-time fee/pet. Designated rooms, service with restrictions, supervision.
(A$K) ⊠ 🛢 💻

▼▼ Quality Inn & Suites 🅷
(575) 524-4663. **$69-$159.** 2200 S Valley Dr. I-10, exit 142, 2 blks w. Ext corridors. **Pets:** Accepted.
(A$K) ⊠ 🅰M 🛢 💻 🛬

◈◈◈ ▼▼▼▼ Ramada Palms de Las Cruces 🅷
(575) 526-4411. **Call for rates.** 201 E University Ave. I-10, exit 142, just n. Int corridors. **Pets:** Accepted.
(SAVE) ⊠ 🅰M 🛢 💻 🍴 🛬

▼ Royal Host Motel 🅼
(575) 524-8536. **$47-$54.** 2146 W Picacho St. I-10, exit 139, 1 mi n on Motel Dr, then 0.5 mi e. Ext corridors. **Pets:** Medium. $10 one-time fee/pet. No service, supervision.
⊠ 🛢 🍴

▼▼ Sleep Inn by Choice Hotels 🅷
(575) 522-1700. **Call for rates.** 2121 S Triviz. I-25, exit 1, just w on University Ave, then just n. Int corridors. **Pets:** Medium. $15 one-time fee/room. Service with restrictions, supervision.
⊠ 🅰M 🛢 💻 🛬

▼▼▼ Staybridge Suites 🅷 🐾
(575) 521-7999. **$129-$199.** 2651 Northrise Dr. I-25, exit 6, just e. Int corridors. **Pets:** Medium, other species. $75 one-time fee/room. Designated rooms, service with restrictions, crate.
(A$K) ⊠ 🅰M 🛢 💻 🛬 ⊠

◈◈◈ ▼▼▼ Super 8 Motel 🅷
(575) 523-8695. **Call for rates.** 245 La Posada Ln. I-10, exit 142, just n on Valley Dr, then just e. Int corridors. **Pets:** Accepted.
(SAVE) ⊠ 🛢

LAS VEGAS

◈◈◈ ▼▼▼▼ Comfort Inn 🅷
(505) 425-1100. **$85-$125.** 2500 N Grand Ave. I-25, exit 347, just sw; US 85 and I-25 business route. Int corridors. **Pets:** Other species. $20 one-time fee/room. Designated rooms.
(SAVE) ⊠ 🛢 💻 🛬

◈◈◈ ▼ El Camino Motel 🅼
(505) 425-5994. **$45-$65.** 1152 N Grand Ave. I-25, exit 345, 0.3 mi w; US 85 and I-25 business route. Ext corridors. **Pets:** Accepted.
(SAVE) ⊠ 🛢 💻 🍴

◈◈◈ ▼▼▼▼ Plaza Hotel 🅷 🐾
(505) 425-3591. **$79-$153.** 230 Plaza St. I-25, exit 343 W, just w, follow signs to Old Town Plaza. Int corridors. **Pets:** $10 daily fee/pet. Service with restrictions.
(SAVE) ⊠ 🛢 💻 🍴

▼▼ Super 8 Motel-Las Vegas 🅼
(505) 425-5288. **$66-$159.** 2029 N Grand Ave. I-25, exit 347, 0.8 mi sw; US 85 and I-25 business route. Int corridors. **Pets:** Other species. $10 daily fee/pet. Service with restrictions, supervision.
(A$K) ⊠ 🛢 💻

LORDSBURG

▼▼ America's Best Value Inn-Lordsburg 🅷
(575) 542-3666. **$80.** 1408 S Main St. I-10, exit 22, just s. Ext corridors. **Pets:** Accepted.
(A$K) ⊠ 🅰M 🛢 💻 🛬

◈◈◈ ▼▼▼▼ Comfort Inn & Suites 🅷
(575) 542-3355. **$70-$120.** 400 W Wabash St. I-10, exit 22, just n, then w. Int corridors. **Pets:** Small. $10 daily fee/pet. Service with restrictions, supervision.
(SAVE) ⊠ 🅰M 🛢 💻 🛬 ⊠

LOS LUNAS

◈◈◈ ▼▼▼ Western Skies Inn & Suites 🅷
(505) 865-0001. **$65-$95.** 2258 Sun Ranch Village Loop. I-25, exit 203, just w. Int corridors. **Pets:** Large, other species. $50 deposit/room, $10 daily fee/pet. Designated rooms, service with restrictions, supervision.
(SAVE) ⊠ 🅰M 🛢 💻 🛬

LOVINGTON

◈◈◈ ▼▼▼ Lovington Inn 🅷
(575) 396-5346. **$59-$65.** 1600 W Ave D. Jct US 82 and SR 18, 1 mi w. Ext corridors. **Pets:** Accepted.
(SAVE) ⊠ 🛢 💻 🍴

MORIARTY

▼▼ Comfort Inn 🅷
(505) 832-6666. **$69-$109.** 119 Route 66 E. I-40, exit 196, just s, then just e. Int corridors. **Pets:** Accepted.
(A$K) ⊠ 🅰M 🛢 💻 🛬

◈◈◈ ▼ Days Inn 🅷
(505) 832-4451. **Call for rates.** 1809 Route 66 W. I-40, exit 194. Int corridors. **Pets:** Accepted.
(SAVE) ⊠ 🛢

◈◈◈ ▼▼▼ Holiday Inn Express 🅷
(505) 832-5000. **$88-$96.** 1507 Route 66. I-40, exit 194, 0.4 mi e. Int corridors. **Pets:** Medium, other species. $10 one-time fee/room. Designated rooms, service with restrictions, supervision.
(SAVE) ⊠ 🅰M 🛢 💻 🛬

◈◈◈ ▼▼▼ Luxury Inn 🅷
(505) 832-4457. **$52-$85.** 1316 Route 66 W. I-40, exit 194, 0.5 mi se on US 66 and I-40 business loop. Int corridors. **Pets:** Large, other species. $10 daily fee/pet. Service with restrictions, supervision.
(SAVE) ⊠ 🛢

◈◈◈ ▼▼▼ Super 8 🅷
(505) 832-6730. **$55-$89.** 1611 W Old Route 66. I-40, exit 194, 0.5 mi e on Central Ave. Int corridors. **Pets:** Large, other species. $10 daily fee/pet. Service with restrictions, supervision.
(SAVE) ⊠ 🛢

PINOS ALTOS

▼▼ ▼▼ Bear Creek Motel & Cabins ⬛
(575) 388-4501. **Call for rates.** 88 Main St. 1 mi n of Pinos Altos on SR 15. Ext corridors. **Pets:** Accepted.
⊠ 🛏 💻 🐾

POJOAQUE PUEBLO

▼▼ ▼▼ Cities of Gold Hotel 🅷
(505) 455-0515. **$79-$129.** 10A Cities of Gold Rd. On US 84/265, just n. Int corridors. **Pets:** $100 deposit/room. Designated rooms, service with restrictions, supervision.
ⒶⓈⓀ ⊠ ♿ 🛏 💻 🍴

RATON

▼▼▼ ▼▼▼ Best Western Sands Ⓜ
(575) 445-2737. **$73-$98, 7 day notice.** 300 Clayton Rd. I-25, exit 451, just w. Ext/int corridors. **Pets:** Accepted.
(SAVE) ⊠ 🛏 💻 🍴 🏊

▼▼▼ ▼▼▼ Budget Host Raton Ⓜ
(575) 445-3655. **$50-$70.** 136 Canyon Dr. I-25, exit 454, 0.8 mi s on I-25 business loop. Ext corridors. **Pets:** Medium. $5 daily fee/pet. Service with restrictions, supervision.
(SAVE) ⊠ ♿ 🛏

▼▼▼ Raton Pass Inn Ⓜ
(575) 445-3641. **$48-$64.** 308 Canyon Dr. I-25, exit 454, 0.8 mi s. Ext corridors. **Pets:** Dogs only. $2 daily fee/pet. Service with restrictions, supervision.
ⒶⓈⓀ ⊠ 🛏

RIO RANCHO

▼▼▼ ▼▼▼ Days Inn Rio Rancho 🅷
(505) 892-8800. **$59-$129.** 4200 Crestview Dr. I-25, exit 233 (Alameda Blvd), 8 mi w on SR 528; I-40, exit 155, 8 mi n on Coors Rd (SR 448). Ext corridors. **Pets:** Small. $15 one-time fee/pet. Service with restrictions, supervision.
(SAVE) ⊠ 🛏 🏊

▼▼▼ Extended StayAmerica Albuquerque-Rio Rancho Ⓜ
(505) 792-1338. **$57-$83.** 2608 The American Rd NW. Corner of SR 528 and Cottonwood, just n, then just w. Int corridors. **Pets:** Other species. $25 daily fee/pet. Service with restrictions, crate.
ⒶⓈⓀ ⊠ 🛏 💻

▼▼▼ ▼▼▼ Inn at Rio Rancho 🅷 🐾
(505) 892-1700. **$99-$139.** 1465 Rio Rancho Blvd. I-25, exit 233 (Alameda Blvd), 6.5 mi w; I-40, exit 155, 10 mi n on Coors Rd/Coors Bypass to SR 528, then 1 mi n. Ext corridors. **Pets:** Medium, other species. $10 daily fee/pet, $25 one-time fee/pet. Designated rooms, service with restrictions, crate.
(SAVE) ⊠ 🛏 💻 🍴 🏊

▼▼▼ Rio Rancho Super 8 🅷 🐾
(505) 896-8888. **Call for rates.** 4100 Barbara Loop SE. I-25, exit 233 (Alameda Blvd), 0.5 mi w, 3.8 mi nw on SR 528, then just e. Int corridors. **Pets:** Other species. $10 daily fee/pet. Service with restrictions, crate.
⊠

ROSWELL

▼▼▼ ▼▼▼ Best Western El Rancho Palacio 🅷
(575) 622-2721. **$70-$110, 3 day notice.** 2205 N Main St. 1.8 mi n on US 70 and 285. Ext corridors. **Pets:** Other species. No service.
(SAVE) ⊠ 🛏 💻 🏊

▼▼▼ ▼▼▼ Best Western Sally Port Inn & Suites 🅷
(575) 622-6430. **$90-$100.** 2000 N Main St. 1.5 mi n on US 70 and 285. Int corridors. **Pets:** Other species. $10 daily fee/pet. Designated rooms, service with restrictions, supervision.
(SAVE) ⊠ 🛏 💻 🍴 🏊 🐾

▼▼▼ ▼▼▼ Budget Inn-North Ⓜ 🐾
(575) 623-6050. **$45-$50.** 2101 N Main St. 1.8 mi n on US 70 and 285. Ext corridors. **Pets:** $5 daily fee/pet. Service with restrictions, supervision.
(SAVE) ⊠ 🛏 🏊

▼▼ ▼▼ Comfort Inn 🅷 🐾
(575) 623-4567. **$99-$159.** 3595 N Main St. On US 70 and 285, 3 mi n. Int corridors. **Pets:** Supervision.
(SAVE) ⊠ ♿ 🛏 💻 🏊

▼▼ ▼▼ Days Inn 🅷
(575) 623-4021. **$70-$90.** 1310 N Main St. 0.8 mi n on US 70 and 285. Ext corridors. **Pets:** Other species. Service with restrictions.
(SAVE) ⊠ 🛏 💻 🏊

▼▼▼ ▼▼▼ Holiday Inn Express 🅷
(575) 627-9900. **$120-$170.** 2300 N Main St. US 70. Int corridors. **Pets:** Medium. $10 daily fee/pet. Service with restrictions, supervision.
(SAVE) ⊠ ♿ 🛏 💻 🏊 🐾

▼▼▼ ▼▼▼ La Quinta Inn and Suites 🅷 🐾
(575) 622-8000. **$79-$159.** 200 E 19th St. Jct N Main and 19th St, 2 blks e. Int corridors. **Pets:** Medium, other species. Service with restrictions, supervision.
(SAVE) ⊠ ♿ 🛏 💻 🏊

▼▼▼ ▼▼▼ Leisure Inn 🅷
(575) 622-2575. **$48-$65.** 2700 W 2nd St. 2.5 mi w on US 70 and 380. Ext corridors. **Pets:** Small, dogs only. $5 one-time fee/pet. Designated rooms, service with restrictions, supervision.
(SAVE) ⊠ 🛏 💻 🏊 🐾

▼▼ ▼▼ Ramada Limited 🅷
(575) 623-9440. **$74-$85.** 2803 W 2nd St. 2.5 mi w on US 70 and 380. Ext/int corridors. **Pets:** $10 daily fee/pet. Service with restrictions, supervision.
ⒶⓈⓀ ⊠ 🛏 💻 🏊

▼▼ ▼▼ Western Inn Ⓜ
(575) 623-9425. **$47-$54.** 2331 N Main St. Jct US 70/285/380, 2.2 mi n. Ext corridors. **Pets:** Accepted.
⊠ 🛏 💻 🏊

RUIDOSO

▼▼▼ ▼▼▼ Dan Dee Cabins ⬛
(575) 257-2165. **$84-$199, 14 day notice.** 310 Main Rd. 0.8 mi w on Upper Canyon Rd. Ext corridors. **Pets:** $10 one-time fee/pet. No service, crate.
(SAVE) 🛏 💻 🐾

▼▼▼ ▼▼▼ The Lodge at Sierra Blanca 🅷 🐾
(575) 258-5500. **$109-$199.** 107 Sierra Blanca Dr. I-70 E, 3.5 mi w on SR 48 (Sudderth Dr), 2.2 mi n on SR 48 (Mechem Dr), then just e. Int corridors. **Pets:** Small. $50 one-time fee/pet. Service with restrictions, supervision.
(SAVE) ⊠ 🛏 💻 🏊 🐾

▼▼ ▼▼ Travelodge 🅷
(575) 378-4471. **$60-$180.** 159 W Hwy 70. Jct of US 70 and SR 48. Ext corridors. **Pets:** Small, other species. $10 daily fee/pet. Service with restrictions, supervision.
ⒶⓈⓀ ⊠ 🛏 💻 🏊

▼▼▼ ▼▼▼ The Village Lodge 🅲🅾 🐾
(575) 258-5442. **$89-$159, 7 day notice.** 1000 Mechem Dr. 2 mi n on SR 48. Ext corridors. **Pets:** Medium, other species. $10 one-time fee/pet. Crate.
(SAVE) ⊠ 🛏 💻

▼▼ ▼▼ Whispering Pine Cabins ⬛
(575) 257-4311. **$99-$265, 14 day notice.** 422 Main Rd. 0.9 mi w of jct SR 48 and Sudderth Dr. Ext corridors. **Pets:** Other species. $10 one-time fee/pet. No service.
⊠ 🛏 💻 🐾

RUIDOSO DOWNS

AAA ▼▼▼ **Best Western Pine Springs Inn** H
(575) 378-8100. **$80-$170, 7 day notice.** 1420 W Hwy 70. Just n; center. Ext corridors. **Pets:** Accepted.
SAVE ✕ 🛏 💻 ⚊

SANTA FE

AAA ▼▼▼ **Best Western Inn of Santa Fe** H
(505) 438-3822. **Call for rates.** 3650 Cerrillos Rd. I-25, exit 278, 2.8 mi n. Int corridors. **Pets:** Service with restrictions, supervision.
SAVE ✕ 🛏 💻 ⚊

AAA ▼▼▼ **Bishop's Lodge Ranch Resort & Spa** H
(505) 983-6377. **$299-$599, 3 day notice.** 1297 N Bishop's Lodge Rd. 3.5 mi n of jct Paseo de Peralta. Ext/int corridors. **Pets:** Accepted.
SAVE ✕ 🛏 💻 🍴 ⚊ ⚋

AAA ▼▼▼ **Comfort Inn Santa Fe** H
(505) 474-7330. **$69-$219.** 4312 Cerrillos Rd. I-25, exit 278, 1.6 mi n. Int corridors. **Pets:** Other species. $5 daily fee/pet. Designated rooms, service with restrictions, supervision.
SAVE ✕ 🛏 💻 ⚊

AAA ▼▼▼ **Econo Lodge** H
(505) 471-4000. **$55-$75.** 3470 Cerrillos Rd. I-25, exit 278, 3 mi n. Int corridors. **Pets:** $10 daily fee/pet. Service with restrictions.
SAVE ✕ 🛏M 🛏 💻 ⚊

AAA ▼▼▼ ▼▼▼ **Eldorado Hotel & Spa** H ❀
(505) 988-4455. **$139-$389, 3 day notice.** 309 W San Francisco St. Just w of The Plaza; at Sandoval St. Int corridors. **Pets:** Other species. $50 one-time fee/pet. Service with restrictions, crate.
SAVE ✕ 🛏M 💻 🍴 ⚊ ⚋

AAA ▼▼▼ **El Paradero Bed & Breakfast** BB
(505) 988-1177. **$95-$180, 14 day notice.** 220 W Manhattan Ave. 0.3 mi s on Cerrillos Rd, 1/2 blk e. Ext/int corridors. **Pets:** Dogs only. $20 daily fee/pet. Designated rooms, service with restrictions, supervision.
SAVE ✕ 🛏 💻

▼▼▼ **Hacienda Nicholas** BB ❀
(505) 986-1431. **$120-$240, 14 day notice.** 320 E Marcy St. Just e of jct Paseo de Paralta; 4 blks e of historic plaza. Ext/int corridors. **Pets:** Other species. $25 one-time fee/pet. Service with restrictions, crate.
ASK ✕

AAA ▼▼▼ **Hilton Santa Fe Historic Plaza** H ❀
(505) 988-2811. **$139-$379.** 100 Sandoval St. Just sw of The Plaza; between San Francisco and W Alameda sts. Ext/int corridors. **Pets:** Medium. $50 one-time fee/room. Service with restrictions, crate.
SAVE ✕ 🛏 💻 🍴 ⚊

▼▼▼ **Holiday Inn Express** H
(505) 474-7570. **$69-$199.** 3450 Cerrillos Rd. I-25, exit 278, 3 mi n. Int corridors. **Pets:** Accepted.
ASK ✕ 🛏M 🛏 💻 ⚊

AAA ▼▼▼ **Holiday Inn Santa Fe** H
(505) 473-4646. **$59-$159.** 4048 Cerrillos Rd. I-25, exit 278, 2.3 mi n; just n of Rodeo Dr. Int corridors. **Pets:** Medium. $50 one-time fee/room. Designated rooms, no service.
SAVE ✕ 🛏M 🛏 💻 🍴 ⚊ ⚋

▼▼▼ **Hotel Plaza Real** H
(505) 988-4900. **Call for rates.** 125 Washington Ave. Just ne of The Plaza; center. Ext/int corridors. **Pets:** Accepted.
✕ 🛏 💻 🍴

AAA ▼▼▼ **Hotel Santa Fe & The Hacienda at Hotel Santa Fe** H ❀
(505) 982-1200. **$129-$379.** 1501 Paseo de Peralta. At Cerrillos Rd, 0.6 mi s of The Plaza. Int corridors. **Pets:** Dogs only. $20 daily fee/pet. Service with restrictions, supervision.
SAVE ✕ 🛏 💻 🍴 ⚊ ⚋

▼▼▼ **The Inn & Spa at Loretto** H
(505) 988-5531. **$189-$499, 3 day notice.** 211 Old Santa Fe Tr. Just s of The Plaza. Int corridors. **Pets:** Medium, dogs only. $20 daily fee/pet. Designated rooms, service with restrictions, crate.
ASK ✕ 🛏M 💻 🍴 ⚊

▼▼▼ **Inn at Santa Fe** H
(505) 474-9500. **$89-$249.** 8376 Cerrillos Rd. I-25, exit 278, 0.3 mi n. Int corridors. **Pets:** Other species. $25 one-time fee/pet. Service with restrictions, supervision.
ASK ✕ 🛏M 🛏 💻 ⚊ ⚋

AAA ▼▼▼ ▼▼▼ **Inn of the Anasazi, a Rosewood Hotel** H ❀
(505) 988-3030. **$209-$1699.** 113 Washington Ave. Just ne of The Plaza. Int corridors. **Pets:** Other species. $50 daily fee/pet. Service with restrictions, supervision.
SAVE ✕ 💻 🍴

AAA ▼▼▼ **Inn On The Alameda** H ❀
(505) 984-2121. **$125-$390, 3 day notice.** 303 E Alameda St. Just e of The Plaza; at jct Paseo de Peralta. Ext/int corridors. **Pets:** Small, other species. $30 daily fee/pet. Designated rooms, service with restrictions.
SAVE ✕ 🛏 💻 ⚋

AAA ▼▼▼ ▼▼▼ **La Posada de Santa Fe Resort & Spa** H ❀
(505) 986-0000. **$232-$555, 3 day notice.** 330 E Palace Ave. Jct Paseo de Peralta and E Palace Ave. Ext corridors. **Pets:** $75 one-time fee/pet. Service with restrictions, crate.
SAVE ✕ 💻 🍴 ⚊ ⚋

▼▼▼ **La Quinta Inn Santa Fe** H ❀
(505) 471-1142. **$49-$159.** 4298 Cerrillos Rd. I-25, exit 278, 1.8 mi n. Ext/int corridors. **Pets:** Medium, other species. Service with restrictions, supervision.
ASK ✕ 🛏 💻 ⚊

AAA ▼▼▼ **Las Palomas** H
(505) 982-5560. **Call for rates.** 460 W San Francisco St. Just w of jct Guadalupe St. Ext corridors. **Pets:** Accepted.
SAVE ✕ 🛏 💻 ⚋

▼ **Motel 6–150** M
(505) 473-1380. **$45-$58.** 3007 Cerrillos Rd. I-25, exit 278, 3.8 mi n. Ext corridors. **Pets:** Other species. Service with restrictions, supervision.
✕ 🛏 ⚊

▼▼▼ **The Old Santa Fe Inn** M
(505) 995-0800. **$99-$390, 3 day notice.** 320 Galisteo St. Just sw of The Plaza; center. Ext/int corridors. **Pets:** Medium, dogs only. $20 daily fee/pet. Designated rooms, service with restrictions, supervision.
ASK ✕ 🛏 💻

▼▼ **Park Inn & Suites** H ❀
(505) 471-3000. **$69-$150.** 2907 Cerrillos Rd. I-25, exit 278, 7 mi n. Ext corridors. **Pets:** Medium, other species. $10 daily fee/pet. Service with restrictions, supervision.
ASK ✕ 🛏 💻 🍴 ⚊

AAA ▼▼▼ **Pecos Trail Inn** M
(505) 982-1943. **$89-$155.** 2239 Old Pecos Tr. I-25, exit 284, 0.8 mi n on CR 466 (Old Pecos Tr). Ext corridors. **Pets:** Service with restrictions.
SAVE ✕ 🛏 💻 🍴 ⚊ ⚌

▼▼▼ Quality Inn 🅷
(505) 471-1211. **$60-$200.** 3011 Cerrillos Rd. I-25, exit 278B, 3.8 mi n. Int corridors. **Pets:** Accepted.
SAVE ✕ 🔐 ▣ 🍽 ⊒

▼▼▼ Residence Inn by Marriott 🅷
(505) 988-7300. **$144-$209.** 1698 Galisteo St. I-25, exit 282, 1.7 mi n on St Francis Dr to St Michaels Dr, just e, then just n. Ext corridors. **Pets:** Accepted.
✕ 🔐 ▣ ⊒ ✕

▼▼▼ Sage Inn 🅼
(505) 982-5952. **$115-$160.** 725 Cerrillos Rd. 0.4 mi ne of St Francis Dr (US 84). Ext corridors. **Pets:** $25 one-time fee/pet. Designated rooms, supervision.
SAVE ✕ 🔐 ▣ ⊒

▼▼▼ Santa Fe Motel & Inn 🅼
(505) 982-1039. **$79-$199, 3 day notice.** 510 Cerrillos Rd. 4 blks sw of The Plaza. Ext corridors. **Pets:** $15 daily fee/pet. Designated rooms, supervision.
SAVE ✕ 🔐 ▣

▼▼▼ Santa Fe Plaza Travelodge 🅷
(505) 982-3551. **$50-$200.** 646 Cerrillos Rd. 0.8 mi sw of The Plaza. Ext/int corridors. **Pets:** Accepted.
SAVE ✕ 🔐 ▣ ⊒

▼▼▼ The Santa Fe Suites 🅼 ❄
(505) 989-3600. **$79-$99.** 3007 S St Francis Dr. 0.8 mi n on S St Francis Dr, just e on Zia Rd via access drive. Ext corridors. **Pets:** Other species. $10 daily fee/room. Designated rooms, service with restrictions, crate.
SAVE ✕ &M 🔐 ▣

SANTA ROSA

▼▼ Baymont Inn & Suites 🅷
(575) 472-5412. **$60-$135.** 3300 Historic Route 66. I-40, exit 277, 0.3 mi w. Int corridors. **Pets:** Small. $10 one-time fee/pet. Designated rooms, service with restrictions, supervision.
ASK ✕ 🔐 ▣ ⊒

▼▼ Best Western Adobe Inn 🅷
(575) 472-3446. **$58-$75.** 1501 Historic Route 66. I-40, exit 275. Ext corridors. **Pets:** Medium. Service with restrictions, supervision.
SAVE ✕ 🔐 ▣ ⊒

▼▼▼ Best Western Santa Rosa Inn 🅼
(575) 472-5877. **$55-$110.** 2491 Historic Route 66. I-40, exit 277, 0.5 mi w. Ext corridors. **Pets:** Medium, other species. $10 daily fee/pet. Designated rooms, service with restrictions.
SAVE ✕ 🔐 ▣ ⊒

▼▼▼ Comfort Inn 🅷 ❄
(575) 472-5570. **$70-$110.** 3343 E Historic Route 66. I-40, exit 277, 0.3 mi w. Ext corridors. **Pets:** Medium. $15 one-time fee/pet. Service with restrictions, supervision.
SAVE ✕ 🔐 ▣ ⊒

▼▼ Days Inn of Santa Rosa 🅷 ❄
(575) 472-5985. **Call for rates.** 1830 Historic Route 66. I-40, exit 275. Ext corridors. **Pets:** Medium. $5 daily fee/pet.
✕ 🔐 ▣

▼▼▼▼ Holiday Inn Express 🅷
(575) 472-5411. **$79-$199.** 3202 Historic Route 66. I-40, exit 277, 0.4 mi w. Int corridors. **Pets:** Accepted.
SAVE ✕ &M 🔐 ▣ ⊒ ✕

▼▼▼▼ La Quinta Inn-Santa Rosa 🅷 🐾
(575) 472-4800. **$75-$125.** 2277 Historic Route 66. I-40, exit 275, just e. Int corridors. **Pets:** Medium, other species. Service with restrictions, supervision.
SAVE ✕ 🔐 ▣ ⊒

▼ Motel 6–273 🅼
(575) 472-3045. **$43-$56.** 3400 Historic Route 66. I-40, exit 277, 0.3 mi w. Ext corridors. **Pets:** Other species. Service with restrictions, supervision.
✕ 🔐 ⊒

▼▼ Super 8 Motel-Santa Rosa 🅼
(575) 472-5388. **Call for rates.** 1201 Historic Route 66. I-40, exit 275, just w. Int corridors. **Pets:** Accepted.
✕ &M 🔐 ⊒

▼▼ Travelodge 🅷
(575) 472-3494. **$45-$85.** 1819 Historic Route 66. I-40, exit 275, just n. Ext corridors. **Pets:** Small. $5 one-time fee/pet. Designated rooms, service with restrictions, supervision.
SAVE ✕ 🔐 ▣

SILVER CITY

▼▼▼ Econo Lodge Silver City 🅷
(575) 534-1111. **$55-$129.** 1120 Hwy 180 E. 1.5 mi ne on US 180 and SR 90. Int corridors. **Pets:** Accepted.
SAVE ✕ &M 🔐 ▣ ⊒

▼▼▼▼ Holiday Inn Express 🅷 ❄
(575) 538-2525. **$114.** 1103 Superior St. 3 mi ne on US 180 and SR 90. Int corridors. **Pets:** Other species. Designated rooms, supervision.
SAVE ✕ 🔐 ▣

SOCORRO

▼▼▼▼ Best Western Socorro Hotel & Suites 🅷
(575) 838-0556. **$105, 7 day notice.** 1100 California Ave NE. Center. Ext/int corridors. **Pets:** Very small. $10 one-time fee/pet. Designated rooms, service with restrictions, crate.
SAVE ✕ &M 🔐 ▣ ⊒ ✕

▼▼▼▼ Comfort Inn & Suites 🅷
(575) 838-4400. **$85-$125.** 1259 Frontage Rd NW. I-25, exit 150, just w. Int corridors. **Pets:** Accepted.
ASK ✕ 🔐 ▣ ⊒

▼▼▼ Days Inn-Socorro 🅷
(575) 835-0230. **$55-$95.** 507 N California St. I-25, exit 147, 1.7 mi n; exit 150, just s. Ext corridors. **Pets:** Other species. $10 daily fee/pet. Service with restrictions, supervision.
SAVE ✕ 🔐 ▣ ⊒

TAOS

▼▼▼ American Artists Gallery House Bed & Breakfast 🅱🅱
(575) 758-4446. **$95-$225, 14 day notice.** 132 Frontier Ln. 1 mi s of jct US 64 and Taos Plaza, 0.3 mi e. Ext/int corridors. **Pets:** Dogs only. $25 one-time fee/pet. Designated rooms, service with restrictions, supervision.
SAVE ✕ 🔐 ▣ ✕ 🍴

▼▼▼ Burch Street Casitas 🅲🅰
(575) 737-9038. **$120-$150 (no credit cards), 21 day notice.** 310 Burch St. US 64, just e of jct SR 68, then just s. Ext corridors. **Pets:** Accepted.
SAVE ✕ 🔐 ▣ 🍴

▼▼▼▼ El Monte Sagrado Living Resort and Spa 🅷
(575) 758-3502. **$229-$839, 14 day notice.** 317 Kit Carson Rd. 0.5 mi e of jct US 64 and 68. Ext corridors. **Pets:** Accepted.
SAVE ✕ ▣ 🍽 ⊒

▼▼▼▼ Inn on La Loma Plaza 🅱🅱
(575) 758-1717. **$165-$450, 15 day notice.** 315 Ranchitos Rd. 0.3 mi sw on Ranchitos Rd, just w of Taos Plaza; in La Loma Plaza Historic District. Ext/int corridors. **Pets:** Accepted.
SAVE ✕ 🔐 ▣ ✕

⬥ ▼▼▼▼ Inn On The Rio 🆔
(575) 758-7199. **$100-$145, 14 day notice.** 910 Kit Carson Rd. US 64, 1.5 mi e of jct SR 68 and Taos Plaza. Ext corridors. **Pets:** Dogs only. $20 daily fee/pet. Designated rooms, service with restrictions, supervision.
SAVE ✕ 🖥 ➥ 🐾

⬥ ▼▼▼▼ La Posada de Taos 🆔 ❀
(575) 758-8164. **$134-$239, 10 day notice.** 309 Juanita Ln. From The Plaza, just w on Don Fernando St, just s on Manzanares St, then just w. Ext/int corridors. **Pets:** Medium, dogs only. $50 deposit/pet.
SAVE ✕ 🖥 🐾 🕿

⬥ ▼▼▼▼ Orinda Bed & Breakfast 🆔
(575) 758-8581. **$104-$169, 14 day notice.** 461 Valverde St. Just w from jct Don Fernando St and Camino de la Placita, then just s, follow signs. Ext/int corridors. **Pets:** Accepted.
SAVE ✕ 🖨 🖥

▼▼ Quality Inn 🆔
(575) 758-2200. **$75-$104.** 1043 Paseo del Pueblo Sur. SR 68, 2 mi sw of jct US 64 and Taos Plaza. Ext/int corridors. **Pets:** Accepted.
ASK ✕ 🖨 🖥 🍴 🐾

▼▼ Sagebrush Inn 🆔
(575) 758-2254. **$79-$219.** 1508 Paseo del Pueblo Sur. SR 68, 3 mi sw of jct US 64 and Taos Plaza. Ext corridors. **Pets:** Other species. $7 daily fee/pet. Designated rooms, service with restrictions, crate.
ASK ✕ 🖨 🖥 🍴 🐾

⬥ ▼▼▼▼ San Geronimo Lodge 🆔 ❀
(575) 751-3776. **$97-$169, 30 day notice.** 1101 Witt Rd. 1.3 mi e of jct SR 68 and Taos Plaza on US 64 (Kit Carson Rd), 0.6 mi s. Ext/int corridors. **Pets:** Large, dogs only. $15 one-time fee/room. Designated rooms, supervision.
SAVE ✕ 🖨 🐾 🐾

THOREAU

▼▼ Zuni Mountain Lodge 🆔
(505) 862-7616. **$115 (no credit cards), 7 day notice.** 40 W Perch Dr. I-40, exit 53, 13 mi s on SR 612, then w. Ext/int corridors. **Pets:** Medium, other species. Service with restrictions, supervision.
ASK ✕ 🐾 🕿 🕿

TRUTH OR CONSEQUENCES

▼▼▼ Comfort Inn & Suites 🆔
(575) 894-1660. **$65-$150.** 2250 N Date St. I-25, exit 79, just e. Int corridors. **Pets:** Other species. Designated rooms, service with restrictions, supervision.
ASK 🅢M 🖨 🖥 🐾

⬥ ▼▼▼ Hot Springs Inn 🅜
(575) 894-6665. **$60-$80.** 2270 N Date St. I-25, exit 79. Ext corridors. **Pets:** Accepted.
SAVE ✕ 🖨 🖥 🐾

▼▼▼ Sierra Grande Lodge & Spa 🆔
(575) 894-6976. **$99-$445.** 501 McAdoo St. Just w of Foch St; center. Ext/int corridors. **Pets:** Small. $25 one-time fee/room. Designated rooms, service with restrictions, supervision.
✕ 🖨 🖥

TUCUMCARI

⬥ ▼▼ Americana Motel 🅜
(575) 461-0431. **$28-$34.** 406 E Tucumcari Blvd. I-40, exit 332, 1.5 mi n on SR 18, then 0.5 mi e on Route 66. Ext corridors. **Pets:** Small. $5 daily fee/pet. Designated rooms, service with restrictions, supervision.
SAVE ✕ 🖨 🖥

⬥ ▼▼▼ Best Western Discovery Inn 🆔
(575) 461-4884. **$70-$80.** 200 E Estrella. I-40, exit 332. Ext corridors. **Pets:** Accepted.
SAVE ✕ 🖨 🖥 🐾

⬥ ▼▼ Budget Inn 🅜
(575) 461-4139. **Call for rates.** 824 W Tucumcari Blvd. I-40, exit 332, 1 mi n to Tucumcari Blvd, then 1 mi w. Ext corridors. **Pets:** Accepted.
SAVE ✕ 🖨

▼▼▼ Comfort Inn 🆔
(575) 461-4094. **$69-$99.** 2800 E Tucumcari Blvd. I-40, exit 335, 0.5 mi w. Ext corridors. **Pets:** $12 daily fee/room, $12 one-time fee/room. Designated rooms, no service, supervision.
ASK ✕ 🖨 🖥 🐾

▼▼ Days Inn 🆔
(575) 461-3158. **$60-$95.** 2623 S 1st St. I-40, exit 332, just n. Ext/int corridors. **Pets:** Accepted.
ASK ✕ 🖨 🖥

⬥ ▼▼▼ Econo Lodge 🆔
(575) 461-4194. **$50-$75.** 3400 Route 66 Blvd. I-40, exit 335, just n, then just w. Int corridors. **Pets:** Medium. $5 daily fee/pet. Designated rooms, service with restrictions, supervision.
SAVE ✕ 🖨

⬥ ▼▼▼ Microtel Inn-Tucumcari 🆔
(575) 461-0600. **$60-$90.** 2420 S 1st St. I-40, exit 332, just n. Int corridors. **Pets:** Small. $10 daily fee/pet. Designated rooms, no service, supervision.
SAVE ✕ 🖨 🖥 🐾

⬥ ▼▼▼ Quality Inn 🆔
(575) 461-3780. **$35-$55.** 3716 E Tucumcari Blvd. I-40, exit 335, 0.3 mi w on Route 66. Ext corridors. **Pets:** Accepted.
SAVE ✕ 🅢M 🖨 🖥 🍴 🐾 ⊠

▼▼ Super 8 Motel 🅜
(575) 461-4444. **Call for rates.** 4001 Old Route 66. I-40, exit 335, just w. Int corridors. **Pets:** Accepted.
✕ 🖨 🐾

⬥ ▼▼▼ Tucumcari Inn 🆔
(575) 461-0088. **$35-$55.** 1700 E Route 66 Blvd. I-40, exit 333, 0.5 mi n to Tucumcari Blvd, then just w. Ext corridors. **Pets:** Accepted.
SAVE ✕ 🖨 🐾

VAUGHN

⬥ ▼▼▼ Oak Tree Inn 🆔
(575) 584-8733. **$65-$75.** Hwy 54, 60 & 285. 1.5 mi e on US 54, 60 and 285. Ext/int corridors. **Pets:** Other species. $5 one-time fee/room.
SAVE ✕ 🅢M 🖨 🖥 🍴

NEW YORK

CITY INDEX

ALBANY

▼▼▼ CrestHill Suites �H
(518) 454-0007. **$119-$169.** 1415 Washington Ave. I-90, exit 2 westbound, just s on Fuller Rd, then just e; exit eastbound, just e. Int corridors. **Pets:** Accepted.
[ASK] [X] [&M] [🔒] [▦] [≈]

▼▼ Extended StayAmerica Albany �H
(518) 446-0680. **$74-$119.** 1395 Washington Ave. I-90, exit 2 westbound, just s on Fuller Rd, then 0.5 mi e; exit eastbound, just e. Int corridors. **Pets:** Other species. $25 daily fee/pet. Service with restrictions, crate.
[ASK] [X] [🔒] [▦]

▼▼▼ TownePlace Suites by Marriott �H
(518) 435-1900. **$130-$190.** 1379 Washington Ave. I-90, exit 2 westbound, just s on Fuller Rd, then 0.6 mi e; exit eastbound, just e. Int corridors. **Pets:** Accepted.
[X] [&M] [🔒] [▦] [≈]

ALLEGANY

▼▼ Microtel Inn & Suites-Olean/Allegany �H
(716) 373-5333. **$59-$119.** 3234 NYS Rt 417. I-86, exit 24, 2.1 mi e on SR 417 (State St). Int corridors. **Pets:** Large, other species. $15 daily fee/pet. Service with restrictions, supervision.
[ASK] [X] [&M] [🔒] [▦]

ANGELICA

▼▼ Angelica Inn B&B 🅱🅱
(585) 466-3063. **Call for rates.** 64 W Main St. I-86, exit 31, 0.5 mi w. Ext/int corridors. **Pets:** Accepted.
[X] [🔒] [▦] [🎟] [✍]

APALACHIN

▼▼ Quality Inn �H
(607) 625-4441. **$84-$209.** 7666 SR 434. SR 17, exit 66, just e. Int corridors. **Pets:** Other species. $10 daily fee/pet. Service with restrictions, supervision.
[ASK] [X] [🔒] [▦]

AUBURN

🆔 ▼▼▼ Holiday Inn-Auburn/Finger Lakes �H 🌿
(315) 253-4531. **$89-$159.** 75 North St. SR 34, just n of US 20/SR 5. Int corridors. **Pets:** Other species. $15 daily fee/room. Service with restrictions, crate.
[SAVE] [X] [&M] [🔒] [▦] [🍴] [≈]

▼▼ Inn at the Finger Lakes �H
(315) 253-5000. **$99-$179, 3 day notice.** 12 Seminary Ave. Jct SR 34/38, just e on US 20/SR 5; center. Int corridors. **Pets:** $20 one-time fee/pet. Designated rooms, service with restrictions, supervision.
[ASK] [X] [&M] [🔒] [▦]

AVERILL PARK

▼▼▼ La Perla at the Gregory House Country Inn & Restaurant 🆑
(518) 674-3774. **$120-$175, 7 day notice.** 3016 SR 43. Center. Int corridors. **Pets:** Small, dogs only. Service with restrictions, supervision.
[X] [🍴] [≈]

BALDWINSVILLE

🆔 ▼▼▼ Microtel Inn & Suites �H
(315) 635-9556. **$60-$150.** 131 Downer St. SR 690, exit SR 31 W, 0.4 mi e. Int corridors. **Pets:** Medium, other species. $10 daily fee/pet. Service with restrictions, supervision.
[SAVE] [X] [&M] [🔒] [▦]

▼▼▼ The Red Mill Inn �H
(315) 635-4871. **$92-$299.** 4 Syracuse St. Just w of jct SR 31 on SR 48; center. Int corridors. **Pets:** Medium. $50 one-time fee/room. Service with restrictions, supervision.
[ASK] [X] [🔒] [▦]

BATATIA

Budget Inn M
(585) 343-7921. **$49-$129.** 301 Oak St. I-90, exit 48, just n. Int corridors.
Pets: Medium, other species. $5 daily fee/pet. Designated rooms, service with restrictions, supervision.

Comfort Inn H
(585) 344-9999. **$59-$169.** 4371 Federal Dr. I-90, exit 48, just n on SR 98. Int corridors. **Pets:** Medium. $50 one-time fee/pet. Designated rooms, service with restrictions.

Days Inn H ❀
(585) 343-6000. **$59-$139.** 200 Oak St. I-90, exit 48, just s. Ext/int corridors. **Pets:** Large, other species. $10 one-time fee/pet. Designated rooms, service with restrictions, crate.

Holiday Inn-Darien Lake H
(585) 344-2100. **$69-$159.** 8250 Park Rd. I-90, exit 48, just w. Int corridors. **Pets:** $20 one-time fee/pet. Service with restrictions, supervision.

Quality Inn & Suites H ❀
(585) 344-7000. **$80-$135.** 8200 Park Rd. I-90, exit 48, just w. Int corridors. **Pets:** Other species. $10 daily fee/pet. Service with restrictions, supervision.

BATH

Bath Super 8 H
(607) 776-2187. **$56-$99, 3 day notice.** 333 W Morris St. I-86, exit 38, just n. Int corridors. **Pets:** Medium, other species. $10 one-time fee/pet. Service with restrictions, supervision.

Microtel Inn & Suites H
(607) 776-5333. **$59-$114.** 370 W Morris St. SR 17, exit 34. Int corridors. **Pets:** Accepted.

BINGHAMTON

Comfort Inn of Binghamton H
(607) 724-3297. **$99-$169.** 1000 Upper Front St. I-81, exit 5, 1 mi n on US 11 (Front St). Int corridors. **Pets:** Accepted.

Grand Royale Hotel-A Clarion Collection Hotel H
(607) 722-0000. **$73-$250.** 80 State St. Just n of jct Hawley St; downtown. Int corridors. **Pets:** Accepted.

Motel 6-1222 H
(607) 771-0400. **$45-$71.** 1012 Front St. I-81, exit 6 southbound, 2 mi s on US 11 (Front St); exit 5 northbound, 1 mi n on US 11 (Front St). Int corridors. **Pets:** Other species. Service with restrictions, supervision.

BOHEMIA

La Quinta Inn & Suites-Islip H ❀
(631) 881-7700. **$55-$169.** 10 Aero Rd. I-495, exit 57, 5.1 mi se on SR 454, just s on Johnson Ave, then just e. Int corridors. **Pets:** Medium, other species. Service with restrictions, supervision.

BOONVILLE

Headwaters Motor Lodge M
(315) 942-4493. **$68-$94.** 13524 Rt 12. Jct SR 12 and 120, 0.7 mi n. Int corridors. **Pets:** Medium. Service with restrictions, supervision.

BROCKPORT

Holiday Inn Express H
(585) 395-1000. **$85-$155.** 4908 Lake Rd S. Just s of jct SR 31, on SR 19 S. Int corridors. **Pets:** Accepted.

BUFFALO METROPOLITAN AREA

AMHERST

Comfort Inn University H ❀
(716) 688-0811. **$69-$149.** 1 Flint Rd. I-290, exit 5B, just n on SR 263 (Millersport Hwy), then just w. Int corridors. **Pets:** Large. $20 daily fee/pet. Service with restrictions, crate.

Homewood Suites Buffalo/Amherst H
(716) 833-2277. **$99-$179.** 1138 Millersport Hwy. I-290, exit 5A, just w. Int corridors. **Pets:** Small. $75 one-time fee/room. Service with restrictions, supervision.

Hotel Indigo Buffalo-Amherst H
(716) 689-4414. **Call for rates.** 10 Flint Rd. I-290, exit 5B, just n on SR 263 (Millersport Hwy). Int corridors. **Pets:** Accepted.

Lord Amherst Hotel M
(716) 839-2200. **$69-$135.** 5000 Main St. I-290, exit 7A, just w on SR 5. Ext/int corridors. **Pets:** Designated rooms, service with restrictions, supervision.

Motel 6 Buffalo-Amherst #1298 M
(716) 834-2231. **$55-$65.** 4400 Maple Rd. I-290, exit 5B, just n to Maple Rd, then 0.7 mi w. Int corridors. **Pets:** Other species. Service with restrictions, supervision.

Red Roof Inn #7104 M
(716) 689-7474. **$63-$105.** 42 Flint Rd. I-290, exit 5B, just n on SR 263 (Millersport Hwy). Ext corridors. **Pets:** Accepted.

BLASDELL

Clarion Hotel H
(716) 648-5700. **$69-$169.** 3950 McKinley Pkwy. I-90, exit 56, 0.4 mi e on SR 179, then 0.8 mi s. Int corridors. **Pets:** Accepted.

Econo Lodge South M
(716) 825-7530. **$49-$110.** 4344 Milestrip Rd. I-90, exit 56, just e on SR 179. Ext corridors. **Pets:** Medium. $10 daily fee/room. Designated rooms, service with restrictions, supervision.

BOWMANSVILLE

AAA ▼▼ **Red Roof Inn-Buffalo Airport #7137** **M**
(716) 633-1100. **$65-$100.** 146 Maple Dr. Just e of SR 78; just n of entrance to I-90 (New York State Thruway), exit 49. Ext corridors. **Pets:** Other species. Service with restrictions, supervision.
[SAVE] [X] [•]

BUFFALO

AAA ▼▼▼ **Best Western Inn-On The Avenue** **H**
(716) 886-8333. **$139-$179.** 510 Delaware Ave. Between Virginia and Allen sts; downtown. Int corridors. **Pets:** Medium, dogs only. $100 deposit/room. Designated rooms, service with restrictions.
[SAVE] [X] [•] [▣]

CHEEKTOWAGA

AAA ▼▼▼▼ **Comfort Inn-Cheektowaga** **H**
(716) 896-2800. **$89-$179.** 475 Dingens St. Just n of I-90, exit 53 (I-190); I-190, exit 1 (S Ogden St), just w. Int corridors. **Pets:** Medium, dogs only. $10 daily fee/pet. Service with restrictions, supervision.
[SAVE] [X] [&M] [•] [▣] [▥]

AAA ▼▼▼▼ **Comfort Suites-Buffalo Airport** **H**
(716) 633-6000. **$99-$159.** 901 Dick Rd. SR 33, exit Dick Rd, just sw. Int corridors. **Pets:** Medium. $10 daily fee/pet. Service with restrictions, supervision.
[SAVE] [X] [&M] [•] [▣] [▥]

▼▼▼▼ **Holiday Inn Express Hotel & Suites-Buffalo Airport** **H**
(716) 631-8700. **$150-$210.** 131 Buell Ave. I-90, exit 51 (SR 33), just e on Genesee St (SR 33), then just s. Int corridors. **Pets:** Accepted.
[X] [&M] [•] [▣] [▥] [▤]

AAA ▼▼▼▼ **Homewood Suites by Hilton** **H**
(716) 685-0700. **$109-$174.** 760 Dick Rd. SR 33, exit Dick Rd, 0.3 mi sw. Int corridors. **Pets:** $100 one-time fee/room. Service with restrictions, supervision.
[SAVE] [X] [•] [▣] [▥]

AAA ▼▼▼ **Oak Tree Inn** **H**
(716) 681-2600. **$69-$150.** 3475 Union Rd. I-90, exit 52, 0.3 mi e on Walden Ave, just n on SR 277 (Union Rd). Int corridors. **Pets:** Medium. $5 daily fee/pet. Service with restrictions, supervision.
[SAVE] [X] [&M] [•] [▣]

▼▼▼ **Residence Inn by Marriott** **H**
(716) 892-5410. **$160-$190.** 107 Anderson Rd. I-90, exit 52 westbound, stay to left off exit ramp. Int corridors. **Pets:** Accepted.
[X] [&M] [•] [▣] [▥] [▤]

CLARENCE

AAA ▼▼▼▼ **Asa Ransom House** **CI**
(716) 759-2315. **$115-$185, 7 day notice.** 10529 Main St. Jct SR 78 (Transit Rd), 5.3 mi e on SR 5 (Main St). Int corridors. **Pets:** Accepted.
[SAVE] [X] [&M] [•] [▣] [♨]

GRAND ISLAND

▼▼▼ **Cinderella Motel** **M**
(716) 773-2872. **$40-$89.** 2797 Grand Island Blvd. I-190, exit 19 northbound, 1.3 mi w on SR 324; exit 20B southbound, just e on SR 324. Ext corridors. **Pets:** Accepted.
[ASK] [X] [•] [▣] [✿]

AAA ▼▼▼ **Holiday Inn Grand Island Resort and Conference Center** **H**
(716) 773-1111. **$129-$199.** 100 Whitehaven Rd. I-190, exit 19, 4 mi e. Int corridors. **Pets:** $75 deposit/room, $25 one-time fee/room. Supervision.
[SAVE] [X] [•] [▣] [♨] [▥] [▤]

HAMBURG

AAA ▼▼ **Comfort Inn & Suites** **H**
(716) 648-2922. **$77-$179.** 3615 Commerce Pl. I-90, exit 57, just w. Int corridors. **Pets:** $20 daily fee/room. Service with restrictions, crate.
[SAVE] [X] [&M] [•] [▣] [▥]

AAA ▼▼ **Holiday Inn Buffalo-Hamburg** **H**
(716) 649-0500. **$110-$159.** 5440 Camp Rd. I-90, exit 57, 0.3 mi se on SR 75 (Camp Rd). Int corridors. **Pets:** Accepted.
[SAVE] [X] [•] [▣] [♨] [▥]

AAA ▼▼ **Red Roof Inn #7055** **M**
(716) 648-7222. **$60-$110.** 5370 Camp Rd. I-90, exit 57, just se on SR 75 (Camp Rd). Ext corridors. **Pets:** Medium, other species. Service with restrictions, supervision.
[SAVE] [X] [•]

KENMORE

▼▼ **Super 8-Buffalo/Niagara Falls** **H**
(716) 876-4020. **$44-$77.** 1288 Sheridan Dr. I-190, exit 15, 1.5 mi e on SR 324 (Sheridan Dr). Int corridors. **Pets:** Service with restrictions, supervision.
[X] [•]

LACKAWANNA

AAA ▼▼▼ **Best Western-The Inn of Lackawanna** **H**
(716) 821-0030. **$99-$189.** 2500 Hamburg Tpke. 3 mi s on SR 5; I-90 E, exit Milestrip Rd, 0.8 mi w on SR 179, then 1.5 mi n on SR 5 E; downtown. Int corridors. **Pets:** Accepted.
[SAVE] [X] [•] [▣] [▥]

SPRINGVILLE

▼▼ **Microtel Inn & Suites** **H**
(716) 592-3141. **$58-$90.** 270 S Cascade Dr. On US 219 S. Int corridors. **Pets:** Accepted.
[ASK] [X] [•] [▣]

TONAWANDA

AAA ▼▼ **Econo Lodge** **M**
(716) 694-6696. **$50-$300.** 2000 Niagara Falls Blvd. I-290, exit 3 (Niagara Falls Blvd), 0.5 mi n on US 62. Ext/int corridors. **Pets:** Accepted.
[SAVE] [X] [•] [▣]

WILLIAMSVILLE

▼▼ **La Quinta Inn–Buffalo Airport** **H** ✿
(716) 633-1011. **$60-$160.** 6619 Transit Rd. I-90, exit 49, just n. Int corridors. **Pets:** Medium, other species. Service with restrictions, supervision.
[ASK] [X] [•] [▣]

▼ **Microtel-Lancaster** **H**
(716) 633-6200. **$52-$139.** 50 Freeman Rd. I-90, exit 49, 0.4 mi n on Transit Rd (SR 78), just e. Int corridors. **Pets:** Dogs only. $10 one-time fee/pet. Service with restrictions, supervision.
[ASK] [X] [•]

▼▼▼ **Residence Inn by Marriott Buffalo/Amherst** H
(716) 632-6622. **$139-$169.** 100 Maple Rd. I-290, exit 5B, just n on Millersport Hwy, exit Maple Rd, then just e. Ext corridors. **Pets:** Accepted.
☒ ᯼ᴹ 🛏 🖵 ⊃ ☒

END METROPOLITAN AREA

CALCIUM

▼▼ **Microtel Inn Watertown** H
(315) 629-5000. **Call for rates.** 8000 Virginia Smith Dr. 4 mi e on SR 342; jct US 11. Int corridors. **Pets:** Accepted.
☒ 🛏

CANANDAIGUA

ⱯⱯⱯ⁄ ▼▼▼ **The Inn On The Lake** H
(585) 394-7800. **$119-$369.** 770 S Main St. I-90, exit 44 (Canandaigua/SR 332), just s across US 20 and SR 5. Int corridors. **Pets:** Medium. $25 daily fee/pet. Service with restrictions, supervision.
SAVE ☒ ᯼ᴹ 🛏 🖵 ⑪ ⊃ ☒

ⱯⱯⱯ⁄ ▼▼ **Red Carpet Inn** H
(585) 394-4140. **$40-$135.** 4232 Rt 5 & 20. 1 mi e of jct SR 332. Ext/int corridors. **Pets:** Accepted.
SAVE ☒ 🛏

▼▼ **Super 8** H
(585) 396-7224. **$72-$125.** 4450 Eastern Blvd. Jct SR 332, 5 and US 20, 0.5 mi e. Int corridors. **Pets:** Accepted.
ASK ☒ 🛏 🖵

CANASTOTA

▼▼ **Days Inn** H
(315) 697-3309. **$60-$200.** 377 N Peterboro St. I-90, exit 34 on SR 13. Int corridors. **Pets:** Large, other species. $15 one-time fee/room. Service with restrictions, supervision.
ASK ☒ 🛏 🖵

CHESTER

ⱯⱯⱯ⁄ ▼▼▼ **Holiday Inn Express Hotel & Suites** H ✿
(845) 469-3000. **$109-$209.** 2 Bryle Pl. SR 17, exit 126, just n on SR 94, then just w on SR 17M (Brookside Ave). Int corridors. **Pets:** Other species. $30 one-time fee/room. Designated rooms, service with restrictions.
SAVE ☒ ᯼ᴹ 🛏 🖵 ⊃ ☒

CLAY

▼▼▼ **Hampton Inn-Syracuse/Clay** H
(315) 622-3443. **$129-$189.** 3948 SR 31. Jct SR 481, exit 12, just w. Int corridors. **Pets:** Accepted.
☒ ᯼ᴹ 🛏 🖵 ⊃

CLAYTON

▼▼ **Fair Wind Lodge** M
(315) 686-5251. **Call for rates.** 38201 NYS Rt 12E. 2.3 mi sw. Ext corridors. **Pets:** Accepted.
☒ 🖵 ⊃ ⍨

CLINTON

▼▼▼ **Amidst the Hedges** BB ✿
(315) 853-3031. **$95-$200, 7 day notice.** 180 Sanford Ave. SR 412 (College St), 0.3 mi n on Elm St. Int corridors. **Pets:** Medium, dogs only. $100 deposit/pet. Designated rooms, no service, supervision.
☒ 🛏 🖵 ⊃

COBLESKILL

ⱯⱯⱯ⁄ ▼▼▼ **Best Western Inn of Cobleskill** H
(518) 234-4321. **$84-$166.** 121 Burgin Dr. I-88, exit 21 eastbound on SR 7, 0.8 mi e of jct SR 10; exit 22 westbound, 2.9 mi w on SR 27. Int corridors. **Pets:** $15 daily fee/room. Service with restrictions, supervision.
SAVE ☒ ᯼ᴹ 🛏 🖵 ⑪ ⊃

▼▼ **Super 8** H
(518) 234-4888. **Call for rates.** 955 E Main St. I-88, exit 22 westbound, 2.4 mi w on SR 7; exit 21 eastbound, 3.1 mi e on SR 7. Int corridors. **Pets:** Accepted.
☒ ᯼ᴹ

COLONIE

ⱯⱯⱯ⁄ ▼▼ **Cocca's Inn & Suites, Wolf Rd** M
(518) 459-2240. **$59-$149.** 2 Wolf Rd. I-87, exit 2E, just e. Ext/int corridors. **Pets:** $10 daily fee/pet. Service with restrictions, supervision.
SAVE ☒ 🛏 🖵

▼▼▼ **Holiday Inn Albany on Wolf Road** H
(518) 458-7250. **$179-$230.** 205 Wolf Rd. I-87, exit 4, 0.3 mi se. Int corridors. **Pets:** Accepted.
☒ ᯼ᴹ 🛏 🖵 ⑪ ⊃ ☒

▼▼▼ **Homewood Suites by Hilton–Albany** H
(518) 438-4300. **$129-$249.** 216 Wolf Rd. I-87, exit 4, 0.3 mi se. Int corridors. **Pets:** Accepted.
☒ ᯼ᴹ 🛏 🖵 ⊃ ☒

ⱯⱯⱯ⁄ ▼▼ **Red Roof Inn #7112** M
(518) 459-1971. **$70-$125.** 188 Wolf Rd. I-87, exit 4, just se to Wolf Rd, then just sw. Ext corridors. **Pets:** Other species. Service with restrictions.
SAVE ☒ ᯼ᴹ 🛏

CORNING

▼▼▼ **Staybridge Suites by Holiday Inn** H
(607) 936-7800. **$145-$240.** 201 Townley Ave. I-86/SR 17, exit 46, just s. Int corridors. **Pets:** Medium. $150 one-time fee/pet. Designated rooms, service with restrictions.
ASK ☒ ᯼ᴹ 🛏 🖵 ⊃ ☒

CORTLAND

▼▼ **Comfort Inn** H
(607) 753-7721. **Call for rates.** 2 1/2 Locust Ave. I-81, exit 11, just e off SR 13. Int corridors. **Pets:** Medium. $20 one-time fee/room. Service with restrictions, supervision.
☒ 🛏 🖵 ⑪

ⱯⱯⱯ⁄ ▼▼ **Econo Lodge** M
(607) 756-2856. **$55-$225.** 10 S Church St. I-81, exit 11, 0.8 mi s on SR 13/41 and US 11. Ext corridors. **Pets:** Small. $30 one-time fee/pet. Designated rooms, service with restrictions, supervision.
ASK ☒ 🛏 🖵

▼▼ **Quality Inn Cortland** H
(607) 756-5622. **$79-$199.** 188 Clinton Ave. I-81, exit 11, just n. Int corridors. **Pets:** Accepted.
ASK ☒ 🛏 🖵

AAA ▽▽▽ **Ramada Cortland** H
(607) 756-4431. **$69-$189.** 2 River St. I-81, exit 11, just s on SR 13. Int corridors. **Pets:** Other species. $15 daily fee/room. Service with restrictions, supervision.
SAVE ⊠ 🛏 💻 ¶| 🌊

CUBA

AAA ▽▽▽ **Cuba Econo Lodge** M
(585) 968-1992. **$49-$149.** 1 N Branch Rd. I-86, exit 28, just n to N Branch Rd, then e. Int corridors. **Pets:** Medium. $10 daily fee/pet. Service with restrictions, supervision.
SAVE ⊠ 🛏

DELHI

AAA ▽▽ **Buena Vista Motel** M
(607) 746-2135. **$69-$110.** 18718 State Hwy 28. Jct SR 10, 0.8 mi s. Ext corridors. **Pets:** Medium, dogs only. $15 daily fee/pet. Designated rooms, service with restrictions, supervision.
SAVE ⊠ 🛏

DEWITT

AAA ▽▽ **Econo Lodge** M
(315) 446-3300. **$80-$170, 3 day notice.** 3400 Erie Blvd E. I-481, exit 3, 1.2 mi w on SR 5; I-690, exit 17 S (Bridge St), just e on Erie Blvd (SR 5). Ext corridors. **Pets:** Medium. $10 daily fee/pet. Designated rooms, service with restrictions, supervision.
SAVE ⊠ 🛏 💻

DUNKIRK

AAA ▽▽▽ **Best Western Dunkirk/Fredonia** H
(716) 366-7100. **$90-$150.** 3912 Vineyard Dr. I-90, exit 59, just w. Int corridors. **Pets:** Medium, other species. $10 daily fee/pet. Service with restrictions, supervision.
SAVE ⊠ 🛏 💻 🌊

AAA ▽▽▽▽ **Comfort Inn** H
(716) 672-4450. **$79-$159.** 3925 Vineyard Dr. I-90, exit 59, just se on SR 75 (Camp Rd), then just w. Int corridors. **Pets:** Large. $10 daily fee/pet. Service with restrictions, supervision.
SAVE ⊠ 🛏 💻

EAST GREENBUSH

▽▽▽▽ **Residence Inn by Marriott** H
(518) 720-3600. **$169-$179.** 3 Tech Valley Dr. I-90, exit 9, just e. Int corridors. **Pets:** Large, other species. $75 one-time fee/room. Service with restrictions.
⊠ &M 🛏 💻 🌊 ⊠

EAST SYRACUSE

▽▽▽ **Candlewood Suites Syracuse** H
(315) 432-1684. **Call for rates.** 6550 Baptist Way. I-90, exit 35 (Carrier Cir) to SR 298 E to Old Collamer Rd, just n. Int corridors. **Pets:** Accepted.
⊠ &M 🛏 💻

▽▽ **Comfort Inn-Carrier Circle** H
(315) 437-0222. **$75-$149.** 6491 Thompson Rd S. I-90, exit 35 (Carrier Cir). Ext/int corridors. **Pets:** Large, other species. $30 one-time fee/room. Designated rooms, service with restrictions.
ASK ⊠ 🛏

▽▽▽ **CrestHill Suites** H
(315) 432-5595. **$109-$249.** 6410 New Venture Gear Dr. I-90, exit 35 (Carrier Cir) to SR 298 E, just s. Int corridors. **Pets:** Accepted.
ASK ⊠ 🛏 💻 🌊

▽▽ **Extended StayAmerica Hotels-Syracuse-Dewitt** H
(315) 463-1958. **$54-$83.** 6630 Old Collamer Rd S. I-90, exit 35 (Carrier Cir) to SR 298 E, just n. Int corridors. **Pets:** Other species. $25 daily fee/pet. Service with restrictions, crate.
ASK ⊠ 🛏 💻

▽▽▽ **Holiday Inn East-Carrier Circle** H 🐾
(315) 437-2761. **$109-$179.** 6555 Old Collamer Rd. I-90, exit 35 (Carrier Cir) to SR 298 E, just n. Ext/int corridors. **Pets:** $25 one-time fee/room. Service with restrictions, supervision.
ASK ⊠ 🛏 💻 ¶| 🌊 ⊠

▽▽ **Quality Inn Syracuse** H
(315) 432-9333. **$59-$139.** 6611 Old Collamer Rd S. I-90, exit 35 (Carrier Cir) to SR 298 E. Ext/int corridors. **Pets:** Accepted.
ASK ⊠ &M 🛏 💻 🌊

AAA ▽▽▽ **Red Roof Inn #7157** M
(315) 437-3309. **$58-$100.** 6614 N Thompson Rd. I-90, exit 35 (Carrier Cir), just n. Ext corridors. **Pets:** Medium. Supervision.
SAVE ⊠ 🛏

AAA ▽▽▽▽ **Residence Inn by Marriott** H
(315) 432-4488. **$170-$208.** 6420 Yorktown Cir. I-90, exit 35 (Carrier Cir) to SR 298, just e to Old Collamer Rd, then 0.5 mi n. Ext/int corridors. **Pets:** Accepted.
SAVE ⊠ &M 🛏 💻 🌊 ⊠

ELLICOTTVILLE

AAA ▽▽▽ **The Jefferson Inn of Ellicottville** BB 🐾
(716) 699-5869. **$79-$229, 30 day notice.** 3 Jefferson St. Western jct US 219 and SR 242, just n; eastern jct, 0.8 mi w; downtown. Ext/int corridors. **Pets:** Other species. $15 daily fee/pet. Designated rooms, no service.
SAVE ⊠ 🛏

▽▽▽▽ **Sugar Pine Lodge** BB
(716) 699-4855. **Call for rates.** 6158 Jefferson St, Rt 219 S. Jct US 219 and SR 242, 0.5 mi s on US 219. Ext/int corridors. **Pets:** Accepted.
⊠ 🛏 💻 🌊

ELMIRA

AAA ▽▽▽ **Coachman Motor Lodge** M
(607) 733-5526. **$90-$120.** 908 Pennsylvania Ave. SR 17, exit 56 (Church St), 0.7 mi w on SR 352, 0.5 mi s on Madison Ave (becomes Pennsylvania Ave), then 1.4 mi s. Ext corridors. **Pets:** Medium. Service with restrictions, supervision.
SAVE 🛏 💻

▽▽▽▽ **Holiday Inn-Elmira Riverview** H
(607) 734-4211. **$100-$250.** 760 E Water St. SR 17, exit 56 (Water St), 0.5 mi s. Ext/int corridors. **Pets:** Accepted.
ASK ⊠ 🛏 💻 ¶| 🌊 ⊠

FARMINGTON

AAA ▽▽▽ **Budget Inn** M
(585) 924-5020. **$49-$99, 3 day notice.** 6001 Rt 96. I-90, exit 44, 1 mi s on SR 332, then just e. Ext corridors. **Pets:** Accepted.
SAVE ⊠ 🛏 💻

FAYETTEVILLE

AAA ▽▽▽ **Craftsman Inn** H
(315) 637-8000. **$90-$207.** 7300 E Genesee St (SR 5). Across from Fayetteville Towne Center. Int corridors. **Pets:** Medium, dogs only. $25 one-time fee/pet. Designated rooms, service with restrictions, supervision.
SAVE ⊠ &M 🛏 💻 ¶|

FISHKILL

▽▽ **Extended StayAmerica-Fishkill-Poughkeepsie** H
(845) 896-0592. **$59-$129.** 55 W Merritt Blvd. I-84, exit 13, just n. Int corridors. **Pets:** Other species. $25 daily fee/pet. Service with restrictions, crate.
⊠ &M 🛏 💻

▼▼▼ Homestead Studio Suites
Hotel-Fishkill-Poughkeepsie H
(845) 897-2800. **$69-$139.** 25 Merritt Blvd. I-84, exit 13, just n. Int corridors. **Pets:** Other species. $25 daily fee/pet. Service with restrictions, crate.

⊗ ⬛ 🖵

▼▼ **Ramada Fishkill Poughkeepsie** H
(845) 896-4995. **$79-$169.** 20 Schuyler Blvd. I-84, exit 13, just n. Int corridors. **Pets:** Small. $25 daily fee/pet. Designated rooms, service with restrictions, supervision.

⊗ 🅼 ⬛ 🖵

◬◬◬ ▼▼▼ **Residence Inn by Marriott** H
(845) 896-5210. **$161-$197.** 14 Schuyler Blvd. I-84, exit 13, just n. Ext corridors. **Pets:** $100 one-time fee/room. Service with restrictions, supervision.

SAVE ⊗ 🅼 ⬛ 🖵 ⚓ ⊠

FREDONIA

◬◬◬ ▼▼▼ **Days Inn Dunkirk-Fredonia** H
(716) 673-1351. **$81-$143.** 10455 Bennett Rd. I-90, exit 59, just s on SR 60. Int corridors. **Pets:** Other species. $20 daily fee/pet. Designated rooms, service with restrictions, supervision.

SAVE ⊗ ⬛ 🖵 🍴 ⚓

◬◬◬ ▼▼▼ **The White Inn** CI
(716) 672-2103. **$79-$199.** 52 E Main St. I-90, exit 59, 0.5 mi s on SR 60, then 1.3 mi sw on US 20 (Main St); center. Int corridors. **Pets:** Medium, other species. $20 one-time fee/room. Designated rooms, service with restrictions, supervision.

SAVE ⊗ ⬛ 🍴

FULTON

▼▼ **Riverside Inn** H
(315) 593-2444. **$59-$159, 7 day notice.** 930 S 1st St. On SR 481. Int corridors. **Pets:** Other species. $100 deposit/room. Service with restrictions, supervision.

ASK ⊗ ⬛ 🖵 🍴 ⚓

GARDEN CITY

▼▼▼ **La Quinta Garden City** H 🐾
(516) 705-9000. **$165-$299.** 821 Stewart Ave. Meadowbrook Pkwy, exit 3, 0.5 mi w. Int corridors. **Pets:** Medium, other species. Service with restrictions, supervision.

ASK ⊗ 🅼 ⬛ 🖵

GATES

▼▼▼▼ **Holiday Inn-Rochester Airport** H
(585) 328-6000. **$149-$289, 14 day notice.** 911 Brooks Ave. I-390, exit 18A (SR 204), just e. Int corridors. **Pets:** Accepted.

ASK ⊗ ⬛ 🖵 🍴 ⚓ ⊠

◬◬◬ ▼▼▼ **Quality Inn-Rochester** H
(585) 464-8800. **$79-$159.** 1273 Chili Ave. I-390, exit 19, just off exit on SR 33. Int corridors. **Pets:** $25 deposit/pet. Designated rooms, service with restrictions, supervision.

SAVE ⊗ ⬛ 🖵 🍴 ⚓

GENESEO

▼▼▼▼ **Quality Inn Geneseo** H
(585) 243-0500. **$89-$159.** 4242 Lakeville Rd. I-390, exit 8, 3.4 mi w on SR 20A. Int corridors. **Pets:** Medium. $15 daily fee/pet. Designated rooms, service with restrictions, crate.

ASK ⊗ ⬛ 🖵 ⚓

GENEVA

◬◬◬ ▼▼▼ **Cobtree Vacation Rental Homes** VH 🐾
(315) 789-1144. **$120-$450, 90 day notice.** 440-450 Armstrong Rd. 3 mi n on SR 14. Ext corridors. **Pets:** $7 daily fee/pet. Designated rooms, no service.

SAVE ⊗ ⬛ 🖵

▼▼▼▼ **Ramada Geneva Lakefront** H
(315) 789-0400. **$92-$170.** 41 Lakefront Dr. Just e of SR 14, 5 and 20; downtown. Int corridors. **Pets:** Other species. $10 daily fee/pet. Service with restrictions, supervision.

ASK ⊗ ⬛ 🖵 🍴 ⚓ ⊠

GREAT NECK

▼▼▼▼ **The Andrew Hotel** H 🐾
(516) 482-2900. **$299-$309.** 75 N Station Plaza. Jct SR 25A, 0.8 mi n on Middle Neck Rd, just e. Int corridors. **Pets:** Medium, dogs only. $150 one-time fee/room. Service with restrictions.

ASK ⊗ ⬛ 🖵

◬◬◬ ▼▼▼▼ **Inn at Great Neck** H
(516) 773-2000. **$235-$285.** 30 Cutter Mill Rd. Jct SR 25A, 0.8 mi n on Middle Neck Rd, just w. Int corridors. **Pets:** Small, dogs only. $250 deposit/pet. Service with restrictions, supervision.

SAVE ⊗ ⬛ 🖵 🍴

GREECE

▼▼ **Extended StayAmerica-Rochester-Greece** H
(585) 663-5558. **$57-$88.** 600 Center Place Dr. I-390, exit 24A, just e on SR 104 (Ridge Rd), then just n on Buckman Rd. Int corridors. **Pets:** Other species. $25 daily fee/pet. Service with restrictions, crate.

ASK ⊗ 🅼 ⬛ 🖵

▼▼▼ **Hampton Inn-Rochester North** H
(585) 663-6070. **$119-$159.** 500 Center Place Dr. I-390, exit 24A, just e on SR 104 (Ridge Rd), then just n on Buckman Rd. Int corridors. **Pets:** Accepted.

⊗ 🅼 ⬛ 🖵 ⚓ ⊠

▼▼▼ **Residence Inn by Marriott-West** H
(585) 865-2090. **$197-$241.** 500 Paddy Creek Cir. I-390, exit 24A, just e on SR 104 (Ridge Rd), just s on Hoover Dr, then just w. Int corridors. **Pets:** Accepted.

⊗ ⬛ 🖵 ⚓ ⊠

GUILDERLAND

◬◬◬ ▼▼▼ **Best Western Sovereign Hotel Albany** H
(518) 489-2981. **$80-$140.** 1228 Western Ave. I-87/90, exit 24, follow signs to US 20 (Western Ave), then 1 mi e. Int corridors. **Pets:** Accepted.

SAVE ⊗ ⬛ 🖵 🍴 ⚓ ⊠

▼▼ **Days Inn-Albany/Guilderland** M
(518) 489-4423. **$84-$104.** 1230 Western Ave. I-90, exit 2, 0.7 mi s, follow signs to US 20 (Western Ave). Int corridors. **Pets:** Dogs only. $20 one-time fee/room. Service with restrictions, supervision.

ASK ⊗ 🅼 ⬛ 🖵

HANCOCK

▼▼ **Smith's Colonial Motel** M
(607) 637-2989. **$80-$130.** 23085 State Hwy 97. SR 17, exit 87, 2.7 mi s. Ext corridors. **Pets:** Accepted.

⊗ 🖵

HAUPPAUGE

▼▼▼ **Residence Inn by Marriott** H
(631) 724-4188. **$189-$199.** 850 Veterans Memorial Hwy. I-495, exit 57, 1.2 mi nw. Int corridors. **Pets:** Accepted.

⊗ 🅼 ⬛ 🖵 ⚓ ⊠

Sheraton Long Island Hotel H ❀
(631) 231-1100. **$109-$269.** 110 Vanderbilt Motor Pkwy. I-495, exit 53 (Wicks Rd), just n, then 0.3 mi e. Int corridors. **Pets:** Medium, dogs only. $150 deposit/room. Designated rooms, supervision.
SAVE ✕ ᏩM 🛆 🖵 ꟷ ꟷ ✕

HENRIETTA

Comfort Suites by Choice Hotels of Rochester H
(585) 334-6620. **$90-$166, 4 day notice.** 2085 Hylan Dr. I-390, exit 13, just e. Int corridors. **Pets:** Accepted.
ASK ✕ ᏩM 🛆 🖵

Homewood Suites by Hilton-Rochester H
(585) 334-9150. **$149-$199.** 2095 Hylan Dr. I-390, exit 13, just e. Int corridors. **Pets:** Accepted.
✕ ᏩM 🛆 🖵 ꟷ

Microtel-Rochester H
(585) 334-3400. **$65-$129.** 905 Lehigh Station Rd. I-390, exit 12 northbound; exit 12A southbound, just w on SR 253. Int corridors. **Pets:** Accepted.
ASK ✕ 🛆

Radisson Rochester Airport H
(585) 475-1910. **$129-$189, 3 day notice.** 175 Jefferson Rd. I-390, exit 14A southbound; exit 14 northbound, 3 mi w on SR 252 (Jefferson Rd). Int corridors. **Pets:** Accepted.
ASK ✕ ᏩM 🛆 🖵 ꟷꟷ ꟷ

Red Roof Inn-Henrietta #7042 M
(585) 359-1100. **$65-$100.** 4820 W Henrietta Rd. I-390, exit 12 northbound; exit 12A southbound, 0.5 mi w on SR 253, then just s on SR 15 (Henrietta Rd). Ext corridors. **Pets:** Large, other species. Designated rooms, service with restrictions, supervision.
SAVE 🛆

Residence Inn by Marriott H
(585) 272-8850. **$99-$179.** 1300 Jefferson Rd. I-390, exit 14A southbound, 0.5 mi e on SR 252 (Jefferson Rd); exit 14 northbound, just n on SR 15A, then 0.5 mi e on SR 252 (Jefferson Rd). Ext/int corridors. **Pets:** $100 one-time fee/pet. Service with restrictions, crate.
SAVE ✕ 🛆 🖵 ꟷ ✕

R I T Inn & Conference Center H
(585) 359-1800. **$109-$169.** 5257 W Henrietta Rd. I-390, exit 12 northbound; exit 12A southbound, 0.5 mi w on SR 253, then 0.7 mi s. Int corridors. **Pets:** Accepted.
ASK ✕ 🛆 🖵 ꟷꟷ ꟷ ✕

HERKIMER

Herkimer Motel M
(315) 866-0490. **$78-$98.** 100 Marginal Rd. I-90, exit 30, just n on SR 28. Ext/int corridors. **Pets:** Medium. $10 one-time fee/room. Service with restrictions, supervision.
SAVE ✕ 🛆 🖵 ꟷ

HIGHLAND

Super 8 M
(845) 691-6888. **$69-$108.** 3423 Rt 9W. Just s of jct SR 299 and US 9W. Int corridors. **Pets:** Other species. $20 daily fee/pet. Service with restrictions, crate.
ASK ✕ ᏩM 🛆 🖵

HUNTER

Hunter Inn H
(518) 263-3777. **$100-$320, 14 day notice.** Rt 23A. Jct SR 296, 1.9 mi e. Int corridors. **Pets:** Accepted.
✕ 🛆 ✕

HUNTINGTON STATION

Whitman Motor Lodge M
(631) 271-2800. **$109-$170.** 295 E Jericho Tpke. On SR 25 (Jericho Tpke), 0.6 mi e of SR 110. Ext/int corridors. **Pets:** Small. $100 deposit/room, $20 daily fee/pet. Service with restrictions, crate.
SAVE ✕ 🛆 🖵

INLET

Marina Motel M
(315) 357-3883. **$89-$180, 14 day notice.** 6 S Shore Rd. Center. Ext corridors. **Pets:** $50 deposit/room, $15 daily fee/pet. Designated rooms, crate.
SAVE ✕ 🛆

IRONDEQUOIT

Holiday Inn Express H
(585) 342-0430. **Call for rates.** 2200 Goodman St N. SR 104, exit Goodman St, just n. Int corridors. **Pets:** Other species. $25 one-time fee/room. Service with restrictions, supervision.
✕ 🛆 🖵 ꟷ

ITHACA

Best Western University Inn M ❀
(607) 272-6100. **$89-$234.** 1020 Ellis Hollow Rd. SR 79 E, 1 mi ne on Pine Tree Rd, just n; in East Hill Plaza. Int corridors. **Pets:** Other species. $10 daily fee/pet. Designated rooms, supervision.
SAVE ✕ 🛆 🖵 ꟷ

Comfort Inn H ❀
(607) 272-0100. **$89-$300.** 356 Elmira Rd. Jct SR 96, 89 and 79, 1.5 mi sw on SR 13. Int corridors. **Pets:** Dogs only. $25 one-time fee/room. Designated rooms, service with restrictions, supervision.
SAVE ✕ ᏩM 🛆 🖵

Hampton Inn H ❀
(607) 277-5500. **$129-$229.** 337 Elmira Rd. On SR 13. Int corridors. **Pets:** Medium, dogs only. $50 deposit/room. Designated rooms, service with restrictions, supervision.
SAVE ✕ ᏩM 🛆 🖵 ꟷ

Holiday Inn Ithaca Downtown H ❀
(607) 272-1000. **$169-$209.** 222 S Cayuga St. Just n of SR 96B. Int corridors. **Pets:** Large, other species. $25 one-time fee/room. Service with restrictions, crate.
ASK ✕ 🛆 🖵 ꟷꟷ ꟷ

La Tourelle Resort and Spa CI ❀
(607) 273-2734. **$125-$700, 3 day notice.** 1150 Danby Rd. 2.7 mi s on SR 96B. Int corridors. **Pets:** Dogs only. Designated rooms, service with restrictions, supervision.
ASK ✕ 🛆 🖵 ꟷꟷ ✕

Meadow Court Inn M
(607) 273-3885. **$65-$225.** 529 S Meadow St. 1.5 mi s on SR 13 and 96. Ext/int corridors. **Pets:** $10 daily fee/pet. Designated rooms, service with restrictions, crate.
SAVE ✕ ᏩM 🛆 🖵 ꟷꟷ

JAMESTOWN

Best Western Downtown Jamestown H ❀
(716) 484-8400. **$79-$168, 3 day notice.** 200 W 3rd St. I-86, exit 12, 2 mi s on SR 60 (Washington St). Int corridors. **Pets:** Other species. $25 one-time fee/room. Service with restrictions, supervision.
SAVE ✕ ᏩM 🛆 🖵 ꟷ

△△△ ▼▼▼▼ **Comfort Inn** H
(716) 664-5920. **$80-$160.** 2800 N Main St. I-86, exit 12, just s on SR 60. Int corridors. **Pets:** Other species. $5 one-time fee/pet. Service with restrictions, supervision.
[SAVE] [✕] [🔔] [💻]

△△△ ▼▼▼▼ **Radisson Hotel Jamestown** H
(716) 664-3400. **$90-$176.** 150 W 4th St. I-86, exit 12, 2 mi s on SR 60 (Washington St); center. Int corridors. **Pets:** Accepted.
[SAVE] [✕] [🔔] [💻] [🍴]

JOHNSON CITY

△△△ ▼▼▼▼ **Best Western of Johnson City** H
(607) 729-9194. **$90-$100.** 569 Harry L Dr. SR 17, exit 70N, 0.3 mi n. Int corridors. **Pets:** Large, other species. $10 daily fee/room. Designated rooms, service with restrictions, supervision.
[SAVE] [✕] [🔔] [💻]

△△△ ▼▼▼▼ **La Quinta Inn** H ✿
(607) 770-9333. **$80-$160.** 581 Harry L Dr. SR 17, exit 70, 0.3 mi n. Int corridors. **Pets:** Medium, other species. Service with restrictions, supervision.
[SAVE] [✕] [🔔] [💻]

△△△ ▼▼▼▼ **Red Roof Inn-Binghamton #7203** M
(607) 729-8940. **$68-$100.** 590 Fairview St. SR 17, exit 70, 0.3 mi n, then just n on Reynolds Rd. Ext corridors. **Pets:** Accepted.
[SAVE] [✕] [🔔]

JOHNSTOWN

▼▼▼▼ **Holiday Inn** H
(518) 762-4686. **$96-$160.** 308 N Comrie Ave. Jct SR 30A and 29 E, 1.3 mi n. Ext/int corridors. **Pets:** Accepted.
[ASK] [✕] [♿M] [🔔] [💻] [🍴] [➰]

KINGSTON

△△△ ▼▼▼▼ **Holiday Inn** H
(845) 338-0400. **$129-$199, 3 day notice.** 503 Washington Ave. I-87, exit 19, just e of traffic circle. Int corridors. **Pets:** Other species. $10 daily fee/room. Service with restrictions, supervision.
[SAVE] [✕] [🔔] [💻] [🍴] [➰] [✕]

LAKE GEORGE

▼▼ **Green Haven** M
(518) 668-2489. **$64-$139, 10 day notice.** 3136 Lake Shore Dr. I-87, exit 22, 0.8 mi n on SR 9N. Ext corridors. **Pets:** Dogs only. $20 one-time fee/pet. Service with restrictions, crate.
[ASK] [✕] [🔔] [💻] [➰] [✕]

▼▼ **Lake George Inn** M
(518) 668-4408. **$49-$139, 10 day notice.** 444 Canada St. I-87, exit 22, 0.3 mi s on US 9. Ext corridors. **Pets:** Accepted.
[ASK] [✕] [🔔] [💻] [➰]

▼▼ **Lake Haven Motel** M
(518) 668-2260. **$49-$132, 10 day notice.** 442 Canada St. I-87, exit 22, 0.4 mi s on US 9. Ext corridors. **Pets:** Accepted.
[✕] [🔔] [➰]

△△△ ▼▼▼ **Travelodge of Lake George** M
(518) 668-5421. **$69-$159.** 2011 SR 9. I-87, exit 21, just s. Ext corridors. **Pets:** Medium, other species. $20 daily fee/pet. Designated rooms, service with restrictions, supervision.
[SAVE] [✕] [🔔] [💻] [🍴] [➰]

LAKE LUZERNE

△△△ ▼▼ **Luzerne Court** M ✿
(518) 696-2734. **$75-$180, 14 day notice.** 508 Lake Ave. I-87, exit 21, 8.7 mi s on SR 9N. Ext corridors. **Pets:** Dogs only. Service with restrictions, supervision.
[SAVE] [✕] [🔔] [🍴] [➰] [✕]

LAKE PLACID

△△△ ▼▼▼▼ **Art Devlin's Olympic Motor Inn, Inc.** M
(518) 523-3700. **$68-$238, 14 day notice.** 2764 Main St. 0.5 mi e on SR 86. Ext corridors. **Pets:** Dogs only. $4 daily fee/pet. Designated rooms, supervision.
[SAVE] [✕] [🔔] [➰]

△△△ ▼▼▼▼ **Comfort Inn on Lake Placid** H
(518) 523-9555. **$95-$310.** 2125 Saranac Ave. 0.5 mi w on SR 86. Ext/int corridors. **Pets:** Other species. Service with restrictions, supervision.
[SAVE] [✕] [🔔] [💻] [🍴] [➰] [✕]

△△△ ▼▼▼▼ **Crowne Plaza Resort & Golf Club Lake Placid** H
(518) 523-2556. **$119-$309, 30 day notice.** 101 Olympic Dr. Downtown. Ext/int corridors. **Pets:** $10 daily fee/pet. Service with restrictions, supervision.
[SAVE] [✕] [🔔] [💻] [🍴] [➰] [✕]

△△△ ▼▼▼▼ **Golden Arrow Lakeside Resort** H ✿
(518) 523-3353. **$99-$299, 7 day notice.** 2559 Main St. On SR 86; center. Int corridors. **Pets:** Other species. $100 deposit/pet, $50 one-time fee/pet. Designated rooms, service with restrictions, supervision.
[SAVE] [✕] [🔔] [💻] [🍴] [➰] [✕]

▼▼▼▼ **High Peaks Resort** H
(518) 523-4411. **$109-$349.** 2384 Saranac Ave. 0.3 mi w on SR 86. Int corridors. **Pets:** Accepted.
[✕] [♿M] [🔔] [💻] [🍴] [➰] [✕]

△△△ ▼▼▼ **Swiss Acres Inn** H ✿
(518) 523-3040. **$59-$159, 7 day notice.** 1970 Saranac Ave. 1 mi w on SR 86. Ext/int corridors. **Pets:** $15 daily fee/pet. Service with restrictions, supervision.
[SAVE] [✕] [🔔] [💻] [🍴] [➰]

LANSING

△△△ ▼▼▼ **Econo Lodge** H ✿
(607) 257-1400. **$65-$209.** 2303 N Triphammer Rd. SR 13, exit Triphammer Rd. Int corridors. **Pets:** Large, other species. $15 daily fee/pet. Service with restrictions, supervision.
[SAVE] [✕] [🔔] [💻]

▼▼▼ **Homewood Suites by Hilton** H ✿
(607) 266-0000. **$94-$399.** 36 Cinema Dr. SR 13, exit Triphammer Rd, just e, then just n on Sheraton Dr (which becomes Cinema Dr). Int corridors. **Pets:** Other species. $100 one-time fee/room. Service with restrictions, supervision.
[✕] [♿M] [🔔] [💻] [➰] [✕]

▼▼ **Ramada Inn Executive Training & Conference Ctr** H
(607) 257-3100. **$109-$339.** 2310 N Triphammer Rd. Jct SR 13 and 34, 3.5 mi n on SR 13, exit Triphammer Rd, just w. Int corridors. **Pets:** Medium. $20 one-time fee/room. Designated rooms, service with restrictions, supervision.
[ASK] [✕] [🔔] [💻] [🍴] [➰] [✕]

LATHAM

△△△ ▼▼▼▼ **The Century House, a Clarion Hotel** H
(518) 785-0931. **Call for rates.** 997 New Loudon Rd. I-87, exit 7 (SR 7), just e, then 0.5 mi n on US 9. Int corridors. **Pets:** Accepted.
[SAVE] [✕] [🔔] [💻] [🍴] [➰]

ⒶⒶⒶ ▽▽▽ Comfort Inn Albany Airport & Conference Center 🅷
(518) 783-1900. **$109-$149.** 20 Airport Park Blvd. I-87, exit 4, 2.2 mi nw on Albany Shaker Rd. Int corridors. **Pets:** $15 daily fee/pet. Designated rooms, service with restrictions, crate.
[SAVE] [✕] [🛗] [▤]

▽▽▽ Hampton Inn-Latham 🅷
(518) 785-0000. **$119-$139.** 981 New Loudon Rd. I-87, exit 7 (SR 7), just e, then just n on US 9. Int corridors. **Pets:** Accepted.
[✕] [🛗] [▤] [≋]

▽▽▽ Hotel Indigo 🅷
(518) 869-9100. **$165-$195.** 254 Old Wolf Rd. I-87, exit 4, just w on Albany Shaker Rd. Int corridors. **Pets:** Accepted.
[ASK] [✕] [🛗] [▤] [ⓉⓎ]

ⒶⒶⒶ ▽▽▽▽ La Quinta Inn & Suites–Albany Airport 🅷 ❀
(518) 640-2200. **$90-$170.** 833 New Loudon Rd. I-87, exit 7 (SR 7), just s on US 9 to Latham Cir, then n on US 9. Int corridors. **Pets:** Medium, other species. Service with restrictions, supervision.
[SAVE] [✕] [🛗] [▤] [≋]

ⒶⒶⒶ ▽▽ Microtel Inn, Albany Airport 🅷
(518) 782-9161. **$50-$169.** 7 Rensselaer Ave. I-87, exit 6, just w. Int corridors. **Pets:** Accepted.
[SAVE] [✕] [🛗] [▤]

ⒶⒶⒶ ▽▽▽ Quality Inn & Suites 🅷
(518) 785-5891. **$89-$220.** 611 Troy-Schenectady Rd. I-87, exit 6, just w on SR 7. Ext/int corridors. **Pets:** Accepted.
[SAVE] [✕] [🛗] [▤] [≋]

▽▽▽ Residence Inn by Marriott Albany Airport 🅷
(518) 783-0600. **$189-$229.** 1 Residence Inn Dr. I-87, exit 6, 2 mi w on SR 7. Ext corridors. **Pets:** Accepted.
[✕] [▤] [≋] [✕]

ⒶⒶⒶ ▽▽▽ Travelodge Inn & Suites 🅷
(518) 785-6626. **$69-$139.** 831 New Loudon Rd. I-87, exit 6, just n of jct SR 2 and 9. Ext corridors. **Pets:** Accepted.
[SAVE] [✕] [🛗] [▤] [≋]

LITTLE FALLS

ⒶⒶⒶ ▽▽▽ Knights Inn of Little Falls 🅷
(315) 823-4954. **$75-$120, 3 day notice.** 20 Albany St. On SR 5 and 167. Int corridors. **Pets:** Other species. $10 one-time fee/pet. Service with restrictions, crate.
[SAVE] [✕] [▤] [ⓉⓎ]

LIVERPOOL

ⒶⒶⒶ ▽▽▽ Best Western Liverpool Grace Inn & Suites 🅷
(315) 701-4400. **$69-$219, 7 day notice.** 136 Transistor Pkwy. I-90, exit 37 (Electronics Pkwy), just n; I-81, exit 25 (7th North St), 1.3 mi w, just n on Electronics Pkwy, then just w. Int corridors. **Pets:** Small, other species. $25 daily fee/pet. Designated rooms, service with restrictions, supervision.
[SAVE] [✕] [🛗] [▤] [≋]

▽▽▽ Homewood Suites 🅷
(315) 451-3800. **$109-$199.** 275 Elwood Davis Rd. I-81, exit 25 (7th North St), 1 mi w; I-90, exit 36. Int corridors. **Pets:** Medium, other species. $100 one-time fee/room. Service with restrictions, crate.
[✕] [🛗] [▤] [≋] [✕]

ⒶⒶⒶ ▽▽▽ Knights Inn 🅜 ❀
(315) 453-6330. **$59-$189.** 430 Electronics Pkwy. I-90, exit 37 (Electronics Pkwy), just w; I-81, exit 25 (7th North St), 1.3 mi nw, then just w. Ext corridors. **Pets:** Medium. $20 daily fee/pet. Designated rooms, service with restrictions, crate.
[SAVE] [✕] [🛗]

ⒶⒶⒶ ▽▽ Super 8 Route 57 🅷
(315) 451-8550. **$59-$119, 3 day notice.** 7360 Oswego Rd. I-90, exit 38, 1 mi n on CR 57. Int corridors. **Pets:** Small, dogs only. $15 daily fee/pet. Service with restrictions, supervision.
[SAVE] [✕] [▤]

LONG LAKE

ⒶⒶⒶ ▽▽▽ Journey's End Cottages 🅒🅐
(518) 624-5381. **$125-$150, 60 day notice.** 941 Deerland Rd (Rt 30). On SR 30/28 N, 1 mi s. Ext corridors. **Pets:** Accepted.
[SAVE] [🛗] [▤] [✕] [Ⓚ] [☎]

▽▽ Quackenbush's Long View Lodge 🅒🅘
(518) 624-2862. **Call for rates.** 681 Deerland Rd. On SR 30/28 N, 2.2 mi s. Ext/int corridors. **Pets:** Accepted.
[✕] [🛗] [ⓉⓎ] [✕] [Ⓚ]

MALONE

▽▽ Econo Lodge of Malone 🅜
(518) 483-0500. **Call for rates.** 227 W Main St. Just w of jct US 11 and SR 30. Ext/int corridors. **Pets:** Accepted.
[✕] [🛗]

ⒶⒶⒶ ▽▽▽ Four Seasons Motel 🅜
(518) 483-3490. **$59-$99.** 206 W Main St. 1 mi w on US 11. Ext corridors. **Pets:** Medium. $10 daily fee/pet. Service with restrictions, supervision.
[SAVE] [✕] [🛗] [▤] [≋]

ⒶⒶⒶ ▽▽▽ Super 8 at Jons 🅷
(518) 483-8123. **$90-$150.** 42 Finney Blvd. On SR 30, just s of jct US 11. Int corridors. **Pets:** Other species. Designated rooms, service with restrictions, supervision.
[SAVE] [✕] [🛗] [▤]

MALTA

ⒶⒶⒶ ▽▽▽ Fairfield Inn & Suites by Marriott 🅷
(518) 899-6900. **$109-$249.** 101 Saratoga Village Blvd. I-87, exit 12, just e. Int corridors. **Pets:** Accepted.
[SAVE] [✕] [🛗] [▤] [≋]

MANCHESTER

ⒶⒶⒶ ▽ Scottish Inns 🅜
(585) 289-3811. **$49-$139.** 4078 Rt 96. I-90, exit 43, just s, then just w. Ext/int corridors. **Pets:** $10 daily fee/pet. Service with restrictions, supervision.
[SAVE] [✕] [🛗]

MASSENA

ⒶⒶⒶ ▽▽▽ Econo Lodge-Meadow View Motel 🅷
(315) 764-0246. **$72-$99.** 15054 SR 37. On SR 37, 2.7 mi sw. Int corridors. **Pets:** Accepted.
[SAVE] [✕] [🛗] [▤] [ⓉⓎ]

MAYVILLE

▽▽▽ Chautauqua Suites 🅷
(716) 269-7829. **$109-$169.** 215 W Lake Rd. Just s on SR 394. Int corridors. **Pets:** Accepted.
[ASK] [✕] [🛗] [▤] [ⓉⓎ]

MCGRAW

ⒶⒶⒶ ▽▽ Cortland Days Inn 🅷
(607) 753-7594. **$54-$149.** 3775 US Rt 11. I-81, exit 10 (McGraw/Cortland), just n. Int corridors. **Pets:** Small, other species. $15 daily fee/pet. Service with restrictions, supervision.
[SAVE] [✕] [🛗] [▤]

MELVILLE

▼▼ Extended StayAmerica-Long Island-Melville **H**
(631) 777-3999. **$119-$159.** 100 Spangnoli Rd. I-495, exit 49S eastbound, 0.5 mi e on south service road, then 1.1 mi s on SR 110; exit westbound, 1.5 mi s on SR 110. Int corridors. **Pets:** Other species. $25 daily fee/pet. Service with restrictions, crate.
(ASK) (✕) (ᵴᴹ) (🛏) (🖵)

MIDDLETOWN

◈◈◈ ▼▼ Microtel Inn & Suites **H**
(845) 692-0098. **$59-$149.** 19 Crystal Run Crossing. SR 17, exit 122, just nw. Int corridors. **Pets:** Accepted.
(SAVE) (✕) (ᵴᴹ) (🛏) (🖵) (¶)

MONTOUR FALLS

◈◈◈ ▼ Relax Inn **M**
(607) 535-7183. **$45-$159, 4 day notice.** 100 Clawson Blvd. Jct SR 14 and 224. Ext corridors. **Pets:** Small, dogs only. $10 daily fee/pet. Designated rooms, service with restrictions, supervision.
(SAVE) (✕) (🛏)

NEWARK

◈◈◈ ▼▼ Quality Inn Fingerlakes Region **H** ❀
(315) 331-9500. **$89-$189, 3 day notice.** 125 N Main St. Jct SR 31, just n on SR 88. Int corridors. **Pets:** Other species. $25 deposit/room. Service with restrictions.
(SAVE) (✕) (🛏) (🖵) (¶) (🏊)

NEWBURGH

▼▼ Super 8 **M**
(845) 564-5700. **$60-$145.** 1287 Rt 300. I-87, exit 17, just w; I-84, exit 6, 2 mi e. Int corridors. **Pets:** Accepted.
(ASK) (✕) (ᵴᴹ) (🛏) (🖵)

NEW HAMPTON

◈◈◈ ▼▼ Days Inn **M**
(845) 374-2411. **$79-$130.** 4939 Rt 17M. I-84, exit 3, 0.8 mi e on US 6 and SR 17M; SR 17, exit 123, 4 mi w. Ext/int corridors. **Pets:** Medium. $10 daily fee/pet. Designated rooms, service with restrictions, supervision.
(SAVE) (✕) (🛏) (🖵) (🏊)

NEW HARTFORD

▼▼▼ Holiday Inn Utica **H**
(315) 797-2131. **$89-$189, 7 day notice.** 1777 Burrstone Rd. I-90 (New York State Thruway), exit 31, 4.5 mi w on SR 5 W and 12 S, exit Burrstone Rd, then 1 mi nw. Int corridors. **Pets:** Accepted.
(ASK) (✕) (ᵴᴹ) (🛏) (🖵) (¶) (🏊) (🏊)

▼▼ Ramada **H**
(315) 735-3392. **$89-$149.** 141 New Hartford St. SR 8, 12 and 5, exit French Rd, just w, then just n. Int corridors. **Pets:** Medium. $20 daily fee/pet. Designated rooms, service with restrictions, supervision.
(ASK) (✕) (🛏) (🖵) (¶) (🏊)

NEW PALTZ

▼▼ Rodeway Inn & Suites **M**
(845) 883-7373. **$89-$219, 3 day notice.** 601 Main St (SR 299). I-87, exit 18, 0.5 mi e on SR 299. Ext/int corridors. **Pets:** Accepted.
(ASK) (✕) (🛏)

New York Metropolitan Area

ARMONK

▼▼▼ La Quinta Inn & Suites **H** ❀
(914) 273-9090. **$79-$189.** 94 Business Park Dr. I-684, exit 3S northbound; exit 3 southbound, 0.3 mi s on SR 22 to Business Park Dr. Int corridors. **Pets:** Medium, other species. Service with restrictions, supervision.
(ASK) (✕) (ᵴᴹ) (🛏) (🖵) (¶) (✕)

BROOKLYN

▼▼▼ Holiday Inn Express Brooklyn **H**
(718) 797-1133. **Call for rates.** 625 Union St. Between 3rd and 4th aves. Int corridors. **Pets:** Accepted.
(✕) (🛏) (🖵)

◈◈◈ ▼▼▼ Holiday Inn Express Brooklyn
Downtown **H** ❀
(718) 855-9600. **$189-$319.** 279 Butler St. In Park Slope; between 3rd Ave and Nevins St. Int corridors. **Pets:** Small. $50 one-time fee/room. Designated rooms, service with restrictions, crate.
(SAVE) (✕) (🛏) (🖵)

EAST ELMHURST

▼▼▼ Courtyard by Marriott New York/La Guardia
Airport **H**
(718) 446-4800. **$289-$379.** 90-10 Grand Central Pkwy. In East Elmhurst; Grand Central Pkwy, exit 6 (94th St) eastbound; exit 7 westbound, 0.5 mi s on 94th St to 23rd Ave, then just w to 90th St. Int corridors. **Pets:** Accepted.
(✕) (ᵴᴹ) (🛏) (🖵) (¶) (🏊)

ELMSFORD

▼▼ Extended StayAmerica-White Plains-Elmsford **H**
(914) 347-8073. **$99-$174.** 118 Tarrytown Rd. I-87, exit 8, just w. Int corridors. **Pets:** Other species. $25 daily fee/pet. Service with restrictions, crate.
(ASK) (✕) (ᵴᴹ) (🛏) (🖵)

FLUSHING

▼▼ Extended StayAmerica-NY City-Laguardia Airport **H**
(718) 357-3661. **$159-$259.** 18-30 Whitestone Expwy. In Flushing; I-678, exit 15, just w; in Whitestone. Int corridors. **Pets:** Other species. $25 daily fee/pet. Service with restrictions, crate.
(ASK) (✕) (🛏) (🖵)

◈◈◈ ▼▼▼ Sheraton La Guardia East Hotel **H**
(718) 460-6666. **$199-$219.** 135-20 39th Ave. In Flushing; Grand Central Pkwy to Northern Blvd, 1 mi e to Main St, 0.3 mi s to 39th Ave, then just w. Int corridors. **Pets:** Accepted.
(SAVE) (✕) (🛏) (🖵) (¶)

JAMAICA

▼▼▼ Crowne Plaza Hotel-JFK Airport **H**
(718) 489-1000. **Call for rates.** 151-20 Baisley Blvd. In Jamaica; Belt Pkwy E to Farmer's Blvd exit, just n to N Conduit Ave, then just w to Baisley Blvd; Van Wyck Expwy S, exit 2 (Rockaway Blvd), e to Baisley Blvd. Int corridors. **Pets:** Accepted.
(✕) (🛏) (🖵) (¶)

▼▼▼ Howard Johnson Express Inn-JFK Airport �H
(718) 723-6700. **$90-$200.** 153-95 Rockaway Blvd. In Jamaica; Belt Pkwy, exit 20, 0.4 mi e on service road, then just n; Van Wyck Expwy, s to exit 2 (Rockaway Blvd) service road, then just n. Int corridors. **Pets:** Accepted.
[ASK] [X] [🛏] [💻]

▼▼ Ramada Plaza Hotel at JFK �H
(718) 995-9000. **Call for rates.** Bldg 144/JFK International Airport. In Jamaica; Van Wyck Expwy at Belt Pkwy; southwest corner. Int corridors. **Pets:** Accepted.
[X] [🛏] [💻] [🍴]

MOUNT KISCO

▼▼▼ Holiday Inn �H ❀
(914) 241-2600. **Call for rates.** 1 Holiday Inn Dr. Saw Mill River Pkwy, exit 37, just e. Int corridors. **Pets:** $49 one-time fee/room. Service with restrictions, crate.
[X] [&M] [🛏] [💻] [🍴] [🏊]

NANUET

▼▼▼ Candlewood Suites �H
(845) 371-4445. **Call for rates.** 20 Overlook Blvd. I-287/87 (New York State Thruway), exit 14 (SR 59 W) to New Clarkstown Rd. Int corridors. **Pets:** Accepted.
[X] [🛏] [💻]

NEW YORK

🆎 ▼▼▼ 70 Park Avenue Hotel �H
(212) 973-2400. **$299-$795.** 70 Park Ave. At 38th St. Int corridors. **Pets:** Accepted.
[SAVE] [X] [&M] [🍴]

🆎 ▼▼▼ Affinia Dumont �H
(212) 481-7600. **$249-$689.** 150 E 34th St. Between Lexington and 3rd aves. Int corridors. **Pets:** Accepted.
[SAVE] [X] [🛏] [💻] [🍴]

🆎 ▼▼▼ Affinia 50 �H ❀
(212) 751-5710. **$189-$769.** 155 E 50th St. Between 3rd and Lexington aves. Int corridors. **Pets:** Other species. Service with restrictions, supervision.
[SAVE] [X] [🛏] [💻]

🆎 ▼▼▼ Affinia Gardens �H
(212) 355-1230. **$279-$769.** 215 E 64th St. Between 2nd and 3rd aves. Int corridors. **Pets:** Accepted.
[SAVE] [X] [🛏] [💻] [🏊]

🆎 ▼▼▼ Affinia Manhattan �H ❀
(212) 563-1800. **$189-$519.** 371 7th Ave. At 31st St. Int corridors. **Pets:** Other species. Service with restrictions, crate.
[SAVE] [X] [🛏] [💻] [🍴]

🆎 ▼▼▼ Affinia Shelburne �H
(212) 689-5200. **$179-$669.** 303 Lexington Ave. Between 37th and 38th sts. Int corridors. **Pets:** Accepted.
[SAVE] [X] [🛏] [💻] [🍴]

🆎 ▼▼▼ The Alex �H ❀
(212) 867-5100. **$350-$3700.** 205 E 45th St. At 3rd Ave. Int corridors. **Pets:** Large. $700 deposit/pet, $250 one-time fee/pet. Service with restrictions, crate.
[SAVE] [X] [🛏] [🍴] [🏊]

🆎 ▼▼▼ Algonquin Hotel �H ❀
(212) 840-6800. **$299-$950.** 59 W 44th St. Between 5th and 6th (Ave of the Americas) aves. Int corridors. **Pets:** Medium. Service with restrictions, supervision.
[SAVE] [X] [🛏] [🍴]

▼▼▼ Beekman Tower Hotel �H ❀
(212) 355-7300. **Call for rates.** 3 Mitchell Pl. Jct 49th St and 1st Ave. Int corridors. **Pets:** Other species. $150 deposit/room. Service with restrictions, crate.
[X] [🛏] [💻] [🍴]

🆎 ▼▼▼ ▼▼▼ The Benjamin Hotel �H ❀
(212) 715-2500. **$239-$869.** 125 E 50th St. Between Lexington and 3rd aves. Int corridors. **Pets:** Large, other species. Designated rooms, service with restrictions.
[SAVE] [X] [🛏] [💻] [🍴] [🏊]

🆎 ▼▼▼ ▼▼▼ The Carlyle, a Rosewood Hotel �H
(212) 744-1600. **$755-$1135.** 35 E 76th St. At Madison Ave. Int corridors. **Pets:** Accepted.
[SAVE] [X] [🛏] [💻] [🍴] [🏊]

🆎 ▼▼▼ Duane Street Hotel �H ❀
(212) 964-4600. **Call for rates.** 130 Duane St. Between Church and W Broadway. Int corridors. **Pets:** Dogs only. Service with restrictions, supervision.
[SAVE] [X] [🍴]

🆎 ▼▼▼ Eastgate Tower Hotel �H ❀
(212) 687-8000. **$179-$559.** 222 E 39th St. Between 2nd and 3rd aves. Int corridors. **Pets:** Other species. $200 deposit/pet. Service with restrictions, crate.
[SAVE] [X] [&M] [🛏] [💻] [🍴]

▼▼▼ ▼ Four Seasons Hotel New York �H
(212) 758-5700. **Call for rates.** 57 E 57th St. Between Park and Madison aves. Int corridors. **Pets:** Accepted.
[X] [&M] [🛏] [🍴] [🏊]

▼▼ The GEM Hotel-SoHo, an Ascend Collection hotel �H
(212) 358-8844. **Call for rates.** 135 E Houston St. Jct Forsythe; between 1st and 2nd aves. Int corridors. **Pets:** Accepted.
[X] [💻]

🆎 ▼▼▼ Hampton Inn-Madison Square Garden Area �H
(212) 947-9700. **$249-$307.** 116 W 31st St. Between 6th (Ave of the Americas) and 7th aves. Int corridors. **Pets:** Small, dogs only. $50 one-time fee/room. Service with restrictions, supervision.
[SAVE] [X] [🛏] [💻]

🆎 ▼▼▼ Hampton Inn-Manhattan/Chelsea �H
(212) 414-1000. **$301-$719.** 108 W 24th St. Between 6th (Ave of the Americas) and 7th aves. Int corridors. **Pets:** Other species. $40 one-time fee/pet. Service with restrictions.
[SAVE] [X] [🛏] [💻]

🆎 ▼▼▼ Hampton Inn-Manhattan/Seaport/Financial District �H
(212) 571-4400. **$314-$444.** 320 Pearl St. Between deck slip and Dover St. Int corridors. **Pets:** Small, dogs only. $40 one-time fee/pet. Supervision.
[SAVE] [X] [🛏] [💻]

▼▼▼ Hilton New York �H
(212) 586-7000. **$219-$669.** 1335 Ave of the Americas. Between 53rd and 54th sts. Int corridors. **Pets:** Accepted.
[X] [🛏] [💻] [🍴] [🏊]

🆎 ▼▼▼ Hilton Times Square �H
(212) 840-8222. **$299-$1499.** 234 W 42nd St. Between 7th and 8th aves. Int corridors. **Pets:** Accepted.
[SAVE] [X] [&M] [🛏] [💻] [🍴]

▼▼▼ Holiday Inn Express Fifth Ave �H
(212) 302-9088. **$249-$579.** 15 W 45th St. At 5th Ave. Int corridors. **Pets:** Medium, other species. $25 daily fee/pet. Service with restrictions.
[ASK] [X] [🛏] [💻]

Holiday Inn Express Manhattan/Madison Square Garden H
(212) 695-7200. **Call for rates.** 232 W 29th St. Between 7th and 8th aves. Int corridors. **Pets:** Accepted.
[SAVE] [X] [▭]

Hotel 373 Fifth Avenue H
(212) 213-3388. **$179-$399.** 373 Fifth Ave. Jct 35th St. Int corridors. **Pets:** Accepted.
[SAVE] [X]

Hotel Gansevoort H ❖
(212) 660-6700. **$395-$895, 3 day notice.** 18 9th Ave. At 13th St. Int corridors. **Pets:** Other species. $100 one-time fee/room. Service with restrictions.
[X] [&M] [▭] [▯] [⇌]

Hotel Plaza Athenee H
(212) 734-9100. **$695-$1250.** 37 E 64th St. Between Madison and Park aves. Int corridors. **Pets:** Accepted.
[X] [▭] [▯] [X]

Hotel Wales H
(212) 876-6000. **$299-$899.** 1295 Madison Ave. Between 92nd and 93rd sts E. Int corridors. **Pets:** Accepted.
[SAVE] [X] [▭] [▯] [X]

Jolly Hotel Madison Towers H
(212) 802-0600. **$237-$830.** 22 E 38th St. Between Park and Madison aves. Int corridors. **Pets:** Small. Service with restrictions, supervision.
[SAVE] [X] [▭]

Jumeirah-Essex House H
(212) 247-0300. **Call for rates.** 160 Central Park S. Between 6th (Ave of the Americas) and 7th aves. Int corridors. **Pets:** Accepted.
[X] [&M] [▭] [▯] [X]

La Quinta Inn Manhattan H ❖
(212) 736-1600. **$119-$510.** 17 W 32nd St. Between 5th Ave and Broadway. Int corridors. **Pets:** Medium, other species. Service with restrictions, supervision.
[SAVE] [X] [▭] [▭] [▯]

Le Parker Meridien New York H ❖
(212) 245-5000. **$199-$3000.** 118 W 57th St. Between 6th (Ave of the Americas) and 7th aves; vehicle entrance on 56th St. Int corridors. **Pets:** Large, other species. Service with restrictions.
[SAVE] [X] [▭] [▯] [⇌] [X]

Loews Regency Hotel H ❖
(212) 759-4100. **$489-$4500.** 540 Park Ave. At 61st St. Int corridors. **Pets:** Other species. $25 one-time fee/room.
[SAVE] [X] [&M] [▭] [▯]

The London NYC H
(212) 307-5000. **Call for rates.** 151 W 54th St. Between 6th (Ave of the Americas) and 7th aves. Int corridors. **Pets:** Accepted.
[SAVE] [X] [▯]

The Lowell Hotel H ❖
(212) 838-1400. **$625-$925.** 28 E 63rd St. Between Park and Madison aves. Int corridors. **Pets:** Medium, other species. $150 one-time fee/pet. Service with restrictions, supervision.
[ASK] [X] [▭] [▭] [▯] [X]

Mandarin Oriental, New York H
(212) 805-8800. **$955-$1435.** 80 Columbus Cir at 60th St. At 60th St. Int corridors. **Pets:** Accepted.
[SAVE] [X] [▯] [⇌]

Millenium Hilton H
(212) 693-2001. **$219-$609.** 55 Church St. Between Dey and Fulton sts. Int corridors. **Pets:** Accepted.
[SAVE] [X] [▭] [▭] [▯] [⇌] [X]

Millennium Broadway H
(212) 768-4400. **$499-$999.** 145 W 44th St. Between 6th (Ave of the Americas) and 7th aves; in Times Square. Int corridors. **Pets:** Accepted.
[ASK] [X] [&M] [▭] [▯] [X]

The Muse Hotel H
(212) 485-2400. **$299-$1800.** 130 W 46th St. Between 6th (Ave of the Americas) and 7th aves. Int corridors. **Pets:** Other species. $75 one-time fee/room. Service with restrictions.
[SAVE] [X] [▯] [X]

The New York Helmsley Hotel H ❖
(212) 490-8900. **$250-$525.** 212 E 42nd St. Between 2nd and 3rd aves. Int corridors. **Pets:** Other species. Service with restrictions.
[SAVE] [X] [▭] [▯]

New York Marriott Marquis H
(212) 398-1900. **$479-$679.** 1535 Broadway. Between 45th and 46th sts; motor entrance on 46th St. Int corridors. **Pets:** Accepted.
[X] [▭] [▭] [▯]

The New York Palace H
(212) 888-7000. **Call for rates.** 455 Madison Ave. Between 50th and 51st sts. Int corridors. **Pets:** Accepted.
[SAVE] [X] [&M] [▭] [▭] [▯] [X]

Novotel New York H
(212) 315-0100. **$209-$429.** 226 W 52nd St. At Broadway. Int corridors. **Pets:** Accepted.
[SAVE] [X] [▭] [▯]

Omni Berkshire Place H ❖
(212) 753-5800. **Call for rates.** 21 E 52nd St. Between Madison and 5th aves. Int corridors. **Pets:** Small. $50 one-time fee/pet.
[X] [&M] [▭] [▯] [X]

On The Ave Hotel H ❖
(212) 362-1100. **$199-$699.** 2178 Broadway. At 77th St. Int corridors. **Pets:** Medium, other species. $40 deposit/pet. Service with restrictions, crate.
[SAVE] [X] [▭] [▭] [▯]

The Peninsula New York H
(212) 956-2888. **$675-$975.** 700 5th Ave. At 55th St. Int corridors. **Pets:** Accepted.
[SAVE] [X] [▭] [▯] [⇌] [X]

Radisson Martinique on Broadway H
(212) 736-3800. **$229-$509.** 49 W 32nd St. Between Broadway and 5th Ave. Int corridors. **Pets:** Small, dogs only. $50 one-time fee/pet. Service with restrictions, supervision.
[SAVE] [X] [&M] [▭] [▭] [▯]

Renaissance New York Hotel Times Square H
(212) 765-7676. **$519-$719.** 2 Times Square, 7th Ave at W 48th St. Broadway and 7th Ave; auto access from 7th Ave, s of W 48th St. Int corridors. **Pets:** Medium, dogs only. $100 one-time fee/room. Service with restrictions, crate.
[SAVE] [X] [▭] [▯]

The Ritz Carlton-New York, Battery Park H
(212) 344-0800. **$395-$995.** Two West St. Jct Battery Park. Int corridors. **Pets:** Accepted.
[SAVE] [X] [&M] [▭] [▯]

The Ritz-Carlton New York, Central Park H ❖
(212) 308-9100. **Call for rates.** 50 Central Park S. Jct 59th St (Central Park S) and 6th Ave (Avenue of the Americas). Int corridors. **Pets:** $125 one-time fee/room.
[SAVE] [X] [&M] [▭] [▯] [X]

(AAA) ▼▼▼▼ Sheraton Manhattan at Times Square **H**
(212) 581-3300. **$229-$629, 3 day notice.** 790 7th Ave. Between 51st and 52nd sts. Int corridors. **Pets:** Accepted.
[SAVE] [✕] [点M] [🛏] [💻] [🍴] [🏊]

(AAA) ▼▼▼▼ Sheraton New York Hotel & Towers **H**
(212) 581-1000. **$229-$629, 3 day notice.** 811 7th Ave. At 52nd St. Int corridors. **Pets:** Accepted.
[SAVE] [✕] [点M] [🛏] [💻] [🍴] [✕]

(AAA) ▼▼▼ ▼▼▼ Sofitel New York **H**
(212) 354-8844. **$395-$3000.** 45 W 44th St. Between 5th and 6th (Ave of the Americas) aves. Int corridors. **Pets:** Service with restrictions, supervision.
[SAVE] [✕] [🛏] [🍴] [✕]

▼▼▼ ▼▼▼ The SoHo Grand Hotel **H**
(212) 965-3000. **Call for rates.** 310 W Broadway. In SoHo; jct Grand St. Int corridors. **Pets:** Accepted.
[✕] [🍴]

▼▼▼ ▼▼▼ The Time **H**
(212) 246-5252. **Call for rates.** 224 W 49th St. Between 8th Ave and Broadway. Int corridors. **Pets:** Medium. $50 daily fee/room. Service with restrictions, crate.
[✕] [🍴] [✕]

▼▼▼ ▼▼▼ Trump International Hotel & Tower **H** 🐾
(212) 299-1000. **$825-$875, 3 day notice.** 1 Central Park W. Jct Central Park S; at Columbus Circle. Int corridors. **Pets:** Small, dogs only. $250 one-time fee/room. Service with restrictions, supervision.
[✕] [🛏] [💻] [🍴] [✕]

(AAA) ▼▼▼ ▼▼▼ The Westin New York at Times Square **H**
(212) 201-2700. **$279-$899.** 270 W 43rd St. Corner of 8th Ave. Int corridors. **Pets:** Accepted.
[SAVE] [✕] [点M] [🛏] [💻] [🍴] [✕]

(AAA) ▼▼▼▼ W New York **H**
(212) 755-1200. **Call for rates.** 541 Lexington Ave. At 49th St. Int corridors. **Pets:** Accepted.
[SAVE] [✕] [点M] [🛏] [🍴]

(AAA) ▼▼▼ W New York Times Square **H**
(212) 930-7400. **Call for rates.** 1567 Broadway at 47th St. Corner of 47th St. Int corridors. **Pets:** Accepted.
[SAVE] [✕] [点M] [🛏] [🍴]

(AAA) ▼▼▼ ▼▼▼ W New York-Union Square **H** 🐾
(212) 253-9119. **Call for rates.** 201 Park Ave S. At 17th St. Int corridors. **Pets:** Medium. $25 daily fee/room, $100 one-time fee/room. Designated rooms, service with restrictions, supervision.
[SAVE] [✕] [点M] [🛏] [🍴] [✕]

ORANGEBURG

(AAA) ▼▼▼▼ Orangeburg Holiday Inn & Suites **H**
(845) 359-7000. **$109-$179.** 329 Rt 303. I-87/287, exit 12, 4 mi s on SR 303; 1 mi n of Palisades Interstate Pkwy, exit 5 northbound; 1 mi e of exit 6. Int corridors. **Pets:** Small, dogs only. $50 one-time fee/room. Designated rooms, service with restrictions, crate.
[SAVE] [✕] [🛏] [💻] [🍴] [🏊]

RYE BROOK

(AAA) ▼▼▼▼ Hilton Rye Town **H** 🐾
(914) 939-6300. **$139-$319.** 699 Westchester Ave. I-287 (Cross Westchester Expwy), exit 10 eastbound, 0.6 mi ne on SR 120A; exit westbound, 0.3 mi n on Webb Ave, then 0.4 mi ne on SR 120A. Int corridors. **Pets:** Small. $50 one-time fee/pet. Designated rooms, service with restrictions.
[SAVE] [✕] [点M] [🛏] [💻] [🍴] [🏊] [✕]

STATEN ISLAND

(AAA) ▼▼▼▼ Hilton Garden Inn Staten Island **H**
(718) 477-2400. **$149-$219.** 1100 South Ave. I-278, exit 6 (South Ave) westbound, just s; exit 5 eastbound to SR 440 S, exit South Ave, just s to South Ave, 1 mi n to Lois Ln, then just w. Int corridors. **Pets:** Accepted.
[SAVE] [✕] [🛏] [💻] [🍴] [🏊] [✕]

(AAA) ▼▼▼▼ The Staten Island Hotel **H**
(718) 698-5000. **$159-$208.** 1415 Richmond Ave. I-278, exit Richmond Ave, 0.5 mi se. Int corridors. **Pets:** Accepted.
[SAVE] [✕] [🛏] [💻] [🍴]

SUFFERN

(AAA) ▼▼▼▼ Holiday Inn-Suffern **H**
(845) 357-4800. **$108-$113.** 3 Executive Blvd. I-87 (New York State Thruway), exit 14B, just n. Int corridors. **Pets:** Accepted.
[SAVE] [✕] [🛏] [💻] [🍴] [🏊] [✕]

TARRYTOWN

(AAA) ▼▼▼▼ Sheraton Tarrytown Hotel **H** 🐾
(914) 332-7900. **$129-$319.** 600 White Plains Rd. I-87 (New York State Thruway), exit 9 northbound, 0.8 mi e on SR 119; exit southbound, just n on US 9, then 1 mi e on SR 119. Int corridors. **Pets:** Medium. $50 one-time fee/room. Supervision.
[SAVE] [✕] [点M] [💻] [🍴] [🏊]

(AAA) ▼▼▼▼ Westchester Marriott Hotel **H**
(914) 631-2200. **$289-$299.** 670 White Plains Rd. I-87 (New York State Thruway), exit 9 northbound, 0.8 mi e on SR 119; exit southbound, just n on US 9, then 1 mi e on SR 119. Int corridors. **Pets:** Accepted.
[SAVE] [✕] [🛏] [💻] [🍴] [🏊] [✕]

WHITE PLAINS

(AAA) ▼▼▼▼ Hyatt Summerfield Suites **H** 🐾
(914) 251-9700. **$99-$309.** 101 Corporate Park Dr. I-287 (Cross Westchester Expwy), exit 9A eastbound, 0.6 mi e on Westchester Ave, then 0.3 mi n; exit 9N-S westbound, 0.9 mi w on Westchester Ave. Int corridors. **Pets:** Medium. Service with restrictions.
[SAVE] [✕] [🛏] [💻] [🏊] [✕]

▼▼▼ ▼▼▼ The Ritz-Carlton, Westchester **H**
(914) 946-5500. **$239-$569.** 3 Renaissance Square. Jct SR 22, just w on Main St, then just n. Int corridors. **Pets:** Accepted.
[✕] [点M] [💻] [🍴] [🏊] [✕]

END METROPOLITAN AREA

NIAGARA FALLS METROPOLITAN AREA

LOCKPORT

ⒶⒶⒶ ▼▼▼ Comfort Inn 🅗
(716) 434-4411. **$59-$159.** 551 S Transit St. 1 mi s on SR 78. Int corridors.
Pets: $10 daily fee/pet. Service with restrictions, supervision.
[SAVE] [✕] [🅛ᴹ] [🖴] [💻]

ⒶⒶⒶ ▼▼▼ Holiday Inn Lockport 🅗
(716) 434-6151. **$89-$189.** 515 S Transit St. 1 mi s on SR 78. Int corridors.
Pets: Other species. $10 daily fee/pet. Service with restrictions, supervision.
[SAVE] [✕] [🅛ᴹ] [🖴] [💻] [🍴] [➳]

NEWFANE

▼ Lake Ontario Motel 🅜
(716) 778-5004. **$59-$100.** 3330 Lockport-Olcott Rd. 2.5 mi n of jct SR 104
on SR 78. Int corridors. **Pets:** $5 daily fee/room. Service with restrictions,
supervision.
[ASK] [✕] [🖴]

NIAGARA FALLS

ⒶⒶⒶ ▼▼▼ Howard Johnson Inn Closest to the
Falls 🅗 🐾
(716) 285-5261. **$59-$275.** 454 Main St. I-190, exit 21 (Robert Moses
Pkwy), exit City Traffic, just n to Rainbow Blvd, then just w. Int corridors.
Pets: Other species. $15 daily fee/pet. Designated rooms, service with
restrictions, crate.
[SAVE] [✕] [🅛ᴹ] [🖴] [💻] [➳]

▼▼▼ Quality Hotel and Suites "At the Falls" 🅗
(716) 282-1212. **$59-$399, 7 day notice.** 240 First St. I-190, exit 21
(Robert Moses Pkwy), eastbound to City Traffic exit, just w; downtown. Int
corridors. **Pets:** Medium. $30 daily fee/pet. Designated rooms, service with
restrictions, supervision.
[ASK] [✕] [🖴] [💻] [🍴] [➳]

END METROPOLITAN AREA

NORTH HORNELL

ⒶⒶⒶ ▼▼▼ Econo Lodge 🅜
(607) 324-0800. **$65-$85.** 7462 Seneca Rd. Jct I-86 and SR 36, exit 34,
just s to SR 21, just e to Seneca Rd, then just s. Ext/int corridors.
Pets: Other species. $10 daily fee/pet. Service with restrictions, supervision.
[SAVE] [✕] [🖴] [💻] [🍴]

NORTH SYRACUSE

ⒶⒶⒶ ▼ Budget Inn 🅜
(315) 458-3510. **$49-$120, 7 day notice.** 901 S Bay Rd. I-481, exit 10,
just n. Ext corridors. **Pets:** Small, dogs only. $10 daily fee/pet. Service with
restrictions, supervision.
[SAVE] [✕] [🖴] [💻]

▼▼▼ Candlewood Suites Syracuse Airport 🅗
(315) 454-8999. **$128-$148.** 5414 South Bay Rd. I-90, exit 36; I-81, exit 26
(Mattydale Rd), follow South Bay Rd signs, just n. Int corridors. **Pets:** Large,
other species. $25 one-time fee/room. Service with restrictions, crate.
[ASK] [✕] [🖴] [💻]

▼▼▼ Comfort Inn & Suites/Syracuse Airport 🅗
(315) 457-4000. **$109-$259.** 6701 Buckley Rd. I-81, exit 25 (7th North St),
just w. Int corridors. **Pets:** Medium. $10 daily fee/pet. Service with restric-
tions, supervision.
[ASK] [✕] [🖴] [💻] [➳] [X]

OGDENSBURG

ⒶⒶⒶ ▼▼▼ Quality Inn Gran-View 🅜
(315) 393-4550. **$99-$242.** 6765 State Hwy 37. On SR 37, 3 mi sw. Ext/int
corridors. **Pets:** Other species. $10 daily fee/pet. Designated rooms, service
with restrictions, crate.
[SAVE] [✕] [🖴] [💻] [🍴] [➳] [X]

ⒶⒶⒶ ▼▼▼ The Stonefence Resort & Motel 🅜
(315) 393-1545. **$69-$199.** 7191 SR 37. Jct SR 68, 0.5 mi w. Ext/int
corridors. **Pets:** Medium. $25 one-time fee/room. Designated rooms, serv-
ice with restrictions, supervision.
[SAVE] [✕] [🖴] [💻] [🍴] [➳] [X]

ⒶⒶⒶ ▼▼▼ Windjammer Lodge 🅜
(315) 393-6300. **$80-$110.** 5843 SR 37. On SR 37, 5 mi sw. Ext corridors.
Pets: Accepted.
[SAVE] [✕] [🖴] [💻] [➳]

OLD FORGE

▼▼ Adirondack Lodge Old Forge 🅜
(315) 369-6836. **$69-$209, 7 day notice.** 2752 SR 28. 0.3 mi s. Ext/int
corridors. **Pets:** Dogs only. $25 daily fee/room. Designated rooms, service
with restrictions, supervision.
[ASK] [✕] [🖴] [💻] [➳] [X]

ONEONTA

ⒶⒶⒶ ▼▼▼ Holiday Inn Oneonta/Cooperstown Area 🅗
(607) 433-2250. **$89-$209.** 5206 State Hwy 23. I-88, exit 15 (SR 23 and
28), 1.5 mi e. Int corridors. **Pets:** Accepted.
[SAVE] [✕] [🅛ᴹ] [🖴] [💻] [🍴] [➳] [X]

▼▼ Super 8 🅗
(607) 432-9505. **Call for rates.** 4973 SR 23. I-88, exit 15 (SR 23 and 28),
0.3 mi e. Int corridors. **Pets:** Service with restrictions, supervision.
[✕] [🅛ᴹ] [🖴] [💻]

OWEGO

ⒶⒶⒶ ▼ Sunrise Motel 🅜
(607) 687-5667. **$55-$65.** 3778 Waverly Rd. SR 17, exit 64 (SR 96 N),
across river, w to SR 17C, 2 mi w. Ext corridors. **Pets:** Accepted.
[SAVE] [✕]

PAINTED POST

ⒶⒶⒶ ▼▼ Americas Best Value Inn Lodge on the
Green 🅜 🐾
(607) 962-2456. **$76-$160.** 196 S Hamilton St. SR 17, exit 44B eastbound;
exit 44A westbound; US 15, exit 3, 1 mi n. Ext corridors. **Pets:** Dogs only.
$50 deposit/pet. Service with restrictions, crate.
[SAVE] [✕] [🖴] [💻]

▼▼ Corning Inn 🅗
(607) 937-5383. **Call for rates.** 255 S Hamilton St. SR 17, exit 44; US 15,
exit 3, 0.5 mi n. Int corridors. **Pets:** Accepted.
[✕] [🅛ᴹ] [🖴] [💻]

▼▼ Econo Lodge 🅗
(607) 962-4444. **$69-$109.** 200 Robert Dann Dr. I-86, exit 44, US 15 S,
exit 3, just n on S Hamilton St (SR 417), then just w. Int corridors. **Pets:** $10
daily fee/pet. Service with restrictions, supervision.
[ASK] [✕] [🅛ᴹ] [🖴] [💻]

Erwin Motel M ❀
(607) 962-7411. **$29-$99.** 806 Addison Rd. US 15, exit Erwin Addison, just e on SR 417. Ext corridors. **Pets:** Medium, dogs only. $10 daily fee/pet. Designated rooms, service with restrictions, supervision.
SAVE ✕ 🛏 ➰

PEMBROKE

Darien Lakes Econo Lodge H
(585) 599-4681. **$59-$159.** 8493 SR 77. I-90, exit 48A, just s. Int corridors. **Pets:** Accepted.
ASK ✕ 🛏

PENN YAN

Best Western Vineyard Inn & Suites H
(315) 536-8473. **$89-$189, 3 day notice.** 142 Lake St. I-90, exit 43, SR 14 S to SR 54 N; corner of SR 54 and 14A. Int corridors. **Pets:** Other species. $10 daily fee/pet. Supervision.
SAVE ✕ 🛏 ➾ ➰

PINE VALLEY

Best Western Marshall Manor M
(607) 739-3891. **$82-$114, 7 day notice.** 3527 Watkins Rd. I-86, exit 52B, 5 mi n on SR 14. Ext corridors. **Pets:** Large. $15 daily fee/pet. Designated rooms, service with restrictions, supervision.
SAVE ✕ 🛏 ➾ ➰

PLAINVIEW

Homewood Suites Long Island Melville H
(516) 293-4663. **$169-$459.** 1585 Round Swamp Rd. I-495, exit 48, just s. Int corridors. **Pets:** Accepted.
✕ ♿ 🛏 ➾ ➰ ✖

Residence Inn by Marriott H
(516) 433-6200. **$195-$215.** 9 Gerhard Rd. I-495, exit 44, 1.6 mi s on SR 135, exit 10, then just e on Old Country Rd. Int corridors. **Pets:** Accepted.
✕ ♿ 🛏 ➾ 🍴 ➰ ✖

PLATTSBURGH

Best Western The Inn at Smithfield H ❀
(518) 561-7750. **$70-$130.** 446 Rt 3. I-87, exit 37, just w. Int corridors. **Pets:** Other species. $25 one-time fee/room. Service with restrictions, supervision.
SAVE ✕ 🛏 ➾ 🍴 ➰

La Quinta Inn & Suites Plattsburgh H ❀
(518) 562-4000. **$62-$139.** 16 Plaza Blvd. I-87, exit 37, just w. Int corridors. **Pets:** Medium, other species. Service with restrictions, supervision.
ASK ✕ ♿ 🛏 ➾ ➰

Microtel Inn and Suites H
(518) 324-3800. **$79-$134.** 554 SR 3. I-87, exit 37, just w. Int corridors. **Pets:** Medium. $10 daily fee/room. Service with restrictions, supervision.
ASK ✕ ♿ 🛏 ➾

Super 8 M
(518) 562-8888. **$55-$90.** 7129 Rt 9 N. I-87, exit 39, just e, then just n. Int corridors. **Pets:** Accepted.
ASK ✕ ♿ 🛏 ➾ ➰

PORT JERVIS

Comfort Inn H
(845) 856-6611. **$69-$149.** 2247 Greenville Tpke. I-84, exit 1, just se. Int corridors. **Pets:** Accepted.
SAVE ✕ 🛏 ➾ ➰

POUGHKEEPSIE

Best Western Inn & Conference Center H
(845) 462-4600. **$100-$210.** 2170 South Rd (Rt 9). I-84, exit 13N, 4.7 mi s of Mid-Hudson Bridge. Int corridors. **Pets:** $50 deposit/pet. Service with restrictions, supervision.
SAVE ✕ 🛏 ➾ 🍴 ➰

Days Inn M
(845) 454-1010. **$69-$249.** 536 Haight Ave. 2 mi e of Mid-Hudson Bridge on US 44 and SR 55. Ext/int corridors. **Pets:** Accepted.
SAVE ✕ 🛏 ➾ ➰

Econo Lodge H
(845) 452-6600. **$70-$150.** 2625 US 9. I-84, exit 13N, 1.6 mi s of Mid-Hudson Bridge. Ext corridors. **Pets:** Medium. $100 deposit/pet, $25 daily fee/pet. Designated rooms, service with restrictions, supervision.
ASK ✕ ♿ 🛏

QUEENSBURY

Alpenhaus Motel M ❀
(518) 792-6941. **$49-$149.** 851 US 9. I-87, exit 19, 0.4 mi e, then just n. Ext corridors. **Pets:** Dogs only. $10 daily fee/pet. Service with restrictions.
ASK ✕ 🛏 ➾

RHINEBECK

Beekman Arms & Delamater Inn and Conference Center CI
(845) 876-7077. **$120-$300, 14 day notice.** 6387 Mill St (Rt 9). Jct US 9 and SR 308; center of village. Ext/int corridors. **Pets:** $15 daily fee/pet. Designated rooms, service with restrictions, crate.
✕ 🛏 ➾ 🍴

RIVERHEAD

Best Western East End H
(631) 369-2200. **$129-$299, 3 day notice.** 1830 SR 25. I-495, exit 72 (SR 25 E). Int corridors. **Pets:** Accepted.
SAVE ✕ 🛏 ➾ 🍴 ➰

Holiday Inn Express East End H
(631) 548-1000. **$179-$399, 3 day notice.** 1707 Old Country Rd (SR 58). I-495, exit 73, 0.5 mi e. Int corridors. **Pets:** Accepted.
ASK ✕ ♿ 🛏 ➾

ROCHESTER

Clarion Riverside Hotel H
(585) 546-6400. **$109-$199.** 120 E Main St. Downtown. Int corridors. **Pets:** Medium. $50 deposit/pet. Designated rooms, service with restrictions, supervision.
ASK ✕ ♿ 🛏 ➾ 🍴 ➾ ✖

Hyatt Regency Rochester H
(585) 546-1234. **$89-$319.** 125 E Main St. Jct South Ave; downtown. Int corridors. **Pets:** Accepted.
SAVE ✕ ♿ 🛏 ➾ 🍴 ➾

La Quinta Inn H ❀
(585) 254-1000. **$74-$139.** 1956 Lyell Ave. I-390, exit 21, just e. Int corridors. **Pets:** Medium, other species. Service with restrictions, supervision.
ASK ✕ 🛏 ➾

Strathallan Hotel H
(585) 461-5010. **Call for rates.** 550 East Ave. I-490, exit 17, 0.8 mi n on Goodman St, then just w. Int corridors. **Pets:** Accepted.
✕ ♿ 🛏 ➾ 🍴

ROCK HILL

The Lodge at Rock Hill H
(845) 796-3100. **$109-$259.** 283 Rock Hill Dr. SR 17, exit 109, just e. Int corridors. **Pets:** Medium. $25 one-time fee/room. No service, supervision.
SAVE ✕ 🛏 ➾ ➰

ROCKVILLE CENTRE

◇ ▽▽ **Best Western Mill River Manor** 🅷
(516) 678-1300. **$135-$144.** 173 Sunrise Hwy. On SR 27; between N Village and N Centre aves. Ext corridors. **Pets:** Accepted.
[SAVE] [✕] [&M] [🛗] [▣] [〒] [🏊]

ROME

▽ **Econo Lodge** 🅼
(315) 337-9400. **$60-$109.** 145 E Whitesboro St. Just s of jct SR 26 (Turin Rd) and 46. Ext corridors. **Pets:** Small. $25 one-time fee/pet. Service with restrictions, crate.
[ASK] [✕] [🛗] [▣]

◇ ▽▽▽ **Inn at the Beeches** 🅼
(315) 336-1775. **$89-$295.** 7900 Turin Rd. Jct SR 46, 2 mi n on SR 26 (Turin Rd). Ext corridors. **Pets:** Medium. $10 daily fee/pet. Designated rooms, service with restrictions, crate.
[SAVE] [✕] [🛗] [▣] [〒] [🏊]

◇ ▽▽▽ **Quality Inn of Rome** 🅷
(315) 336-4300. **$70-$200.** 200 S James St. On SR 49; downtown. Ext/int corridors. **Pets:** Other species. $25 daily fee/pet. Designated rooms, service with restrictions.
[SAVE] [✕] [🛗] [▣] [〒] [🏊]

ROSCOE

◇ ▽ **Roscoe Motel** 🅼
(607) 498-5220. **$60-$100, 7 day notice.** 2054 Old Rt 17. SR 17, exit 94, 0.5 mi n on SR 206, then just w. Ext corridors. **Pets:** $10 daily fee/pet. Service with restrictions, supervision.
[SAVE] [✕] [🛗] [▣]

ROTTERDAM

▽▽ **Super 8 Schenectady** 🅷 🐾
(518) 355-2190. **$75-$90.** 3083 Carman Rd. I-890, exit 9 (Curry Rd), 0.4 mi w; I-90, exit 25. Int corridors. **Pets:** Other species. $10 daily fee/pet. Service with restrictions, supervision.
[✕]

SACKETS HARBOR

▽▽ **Ontario Place Hotel** 🅷
(315) 646-8000. **$89-$370.** 103 General Smith Dr. Center. Int corridors. **Pets:** Accepted.
[ASK] [✕] [🛗] [▣]

SALAMANCA

▽▽▽ **Holiday Inn Express Hotel & Suites** 🅷
(716) 945-7600. **$134-$190.** 779 Broad St. I-86, exit 20, just n. Int corridors. **Pets:** Medium, other species. $50 deposit/room. Service with restrictions, supervision.
[ASK] [✕] [&M] [🛗] [▣] [🏊]

SARANAC LAKE

◇ ▽ **Adirondack Motel** 🅼
(518) 891-2116. **$75-$220.** 248 Lake Flower Ave. 0.7 mi e on SR 86. Ext corridors. **Pets:** Dogs only. $10 daily fee/pet. Service with restrictions, supervision.
[SAVE] [✕] [🛗] [▣] [✕]

◇ ▽▽▽ **Best Western Mountain Lake Inn** 🅷
(518) 891-1970. **$79-$205.** 487 Lake Flower Ave. 0.8 mi e on SR 86. Int corridors. **Pets:** Other species. $20 one-time fee/room. Designated rooms, service with restrictions, supervision.
[SAVE] [✕] [&M] [🛗] [▣] [〒] [🏊]

◇ ▽▽▽ **The Hotel Saranac** 🅷 🐾
(518) 891-2200. **$65-$225, 3 day notice.** 100 Main St. Center. Int corridors. **Pets:** Other species. $15 daily fee/pet. Service with restrictions, supervision.
[SAVE] [✕] [🛗] [▣] [〒]

▽ **Lake Flower Inn** 🅼
(518) 891-2310. **$68-$138, 14 day notice.** 234 Lake Flower Ave. 0.6 mi e on SR 86. Ext corridors. **Pets:** Dogs only. Designated rooms, supervision.
[✕] [🛗] [🏊] [✕]

▽ **Lake Side Motel** 🅼
(518) 891-4333. **$79-$159, 7 day notice.** 256 Lake Flower Ave. 0.6 mi e on SR 86. Ext corridors. **Pets:** Accepted.
[✕] [🛗] [🏊] [✕]

SARATOGA SPRINGS

◇ ▽▽▽ **Best Western Park Inn** 🅷
(518) 584-2350. **$99-$399.** 3291 S Broadway. I-87, exit 13N, 1.1 mi n on US 9. Int corridors. **Pets:** Large, dogs only. $20 daily fee/pet. Service with restrictions, supervision.
[SAVE] [✕] [🛗] [▣]

▽▽▽ **Holiday Inn** 🅷
(518) 584-4550. **$130-$560, 3 day notice.** 232 Broadway. On US 9, jct SR 50. Int corridors. **Pets:** Accepted.
[ASK] [✕] [🛗] [▣] [〒] [🏊]

▽▽▽ **Residence Inn by Marriott-Saratoga Springs** 🅷 🐾
(518) 584-9600. **$149-$319.** 295 Excelsior Ave. I-87, exit 15, just n, just s, then just e. Int corridors. **Pets:** Large. $75 one-time fee/room. Service with restrictions, crate.
[✕] [&M] [🛗] [▣] [🏊] [✕]

◇ ▽▽▽ **The Saratoga Hilton** 🅷 🐾
(518) 584-4000. **$89-$599.** 534 Broadway. I-87, exit 15, on SR 50. Int corridors. **Pets:** Medium. $25 daily fee/room. Service with restrictions, supervision.
[SAVE] [✕] [🛗] [▣] [〒] [🏊]

▽ **Saratoga Motel** 🅼
(518) 584-0920. **$79-$219, 14 day notice.** 440 Church St. On SR 9N, 2.3 mi w of jct US 9/SR 50. Ext corridors. **Pets:** Accepted.
[ASK] [✕] [▣]

▽▽▽ **Union Gables Bed & Breakfast** 🅱🅱
(518) 584-1558. **Call for rates.** 55 Union Ave. I-87, exit 14, 1.5 mi w. Int corridors. **Pets:** Accepted.
[✕] [🛗]

SAUGERTIES

◇ ▽▽ **Comfort Inn** 🅷 🐾
(845) 246-1565. **$89-$169.** 2790 SR 32. I-87, exit 20, just n. Int corridors. **Pets:** $10 daily fee/room. Service with restrictions, supervision.
[SAVE] [✕] [🛗] [▣]

SCHENECTADY

▽▽ **Days Inn** 🅷
(518) 370-3297. **$59-$109.** 167 Nott Terr. Jct State St (SR 5) and Nott Terr, 2 blks e; downtown. Int corridors. **Pets:** Small. $10 daily fee/pet. Designated rooms, no service, supervision.
[ASK] [✕] [🛗] [▣]

SCHOHARIE

▽▽▽ **Holiday Inn Express Hotel & Suites Schoharie** 🅷
(518) 295-6088. **$139-$169.** 160 Holiday Way. I-88, exit 23, just e to Park Pl, then just s. Int corridors. **Pets:** Dogs only. $17 daily fee/pet. Designated rooms, service with restrictions, supervision.
[ASK] [✕] [🛗] [▣]

SCHROON LAKE

Blue Ridge Motel M
(518) 532-7521. **Call for rates.** 2455 US Rt 9. I-87, exit 28, 4 mi n. Ext/int corridors. **Pets:** Accepted.
SAVE ⊠ 🛏 💻 ⊷ ☎

SKANEATELES

Skaneateles Suites M
(315) 685-7568. **$99-$175.** 4114 W Genesee St Rd. On US 20, 2 mi w. Ext corridors. **Pets:** Other species. $35 one-time fee/pet. Service with restrictions.
ASK ⊠ 🛏 💻

SOLVAY

Clarion Inn H
(315) 457-8700. **$72-$82.** 100 Farrell Rd. I-690, exit 4 (John Glenn Blvd). Int corridors. **Pets:** Small, other species. $25 daily fee/room. Crate.
ASK ⊠ 🛏 💻 🍴 ⊷

SOUTHAMPTON

Southampton Inn H
(631) 283-6500. **$149-$489.** 91 Hill St. 0.3 mi n from corner of Main St and Jobs Ln. Ext corridors. **Pets:** Small. $39 daily fee/pet. Designated rooms, service with restrictions, supervision.
SAVE ⊠ 🛁 🛏 🍴 ⊷ 🚫

SYLVAN BEACH

Cinderella's Cafe & Suites M
(315) 762-4280. **$59-$219, 15 day notice.** 1208 N Main St. On SR 13; center. Ext corridors. **Pets:** Accepted.
ASK ⊠ 🛏 💻 🍴

SYRACUSE

Renaissance Syracuse Hotel H
(315) 479-7000. **$188-$230.** 701 E Genesee St. Jct Almond St; downtown. Int corridors. **Pets:** Small, other species. $50 daily fee/room. Designated rooms, service with restrictions, supervision.
SAVE ⊠ 🛁 🛏 💻 🍴

Sheraton Syracuse University Hotel & Conference Center H 🐾
(315) 475-3000. **$119-$359.** 801 University Ave. I-81, exit 18. Int corridors. **Pets:** Medium, dogs only. Service with restrictions, supervision.
SAVE ⊠ 🛏 💻 🍴 ⊷ 🚫

TICONDEROGA

Circle Court Motel M
(518) 585-7660. **$63-$92.** 6 Montcalm St. SR 9N; at Liberty Monument traffic circle. Ext corridors. **Pets:** $10 daily fee/pet. Designated rooms, service with restrictions, supervision.
SAVE ⊠ 🛏 💻

TUPPER LAKE

Red Top Inn M
(518) 359-9209. **$50-$90, 7 day notice.** 1562 SR 30. 3 mi s. Ext/int corridors. **Pets:** Accepted.
SAVE ⊠ 🛏 💻

UTICA

Red Roof Inn #7180 M
(315) 724-7128. **$66-$116.** 20 Weaver St. I-90 (New York State Thruway), exit 31. Ext corridors. **Pets:** Other species. Service with restrictions, supervision.
SAVE ⊠ 🛏

VALATIE

Blue Spruce Inn & Suites M 🐾
(518) 758-9711. **$75-$105, 3 day notice.** 3093 Rt 9. I-90 (New York State Thruway), exit 12, 4 mi s on US 9 via New York State Thruway Extension, exit B1. Ext corridors. **Pets:** Large. Service with restrictions, supervision.
SAVE ⊠ 🛏 💻 🍴 ⊷

VESTAL

Quality Inn & Suites at Binghamton University H
(607) 729-6371. **$115-$250.** 4105 Vestal Pkwy E. SR 17, exit 70 westbound, 1 mi s on US 201 S, 0.5 mi w on SR 434 W; exit 67 eastbound, just s on SR 26, 2.5 mi e on SR 434. Int corridors. **Pets:** Accepted.
SAVE ⊠ 🛏 💻 🍴 ⊷

VICTOR

Hampton Inn and Suites-Rochester/Victor H
(585) 924-4400. **$139-$169.** 7637 SR 96. I-90 (New York State Thruway), exit 45, just n. Int corridors. **Pets:** Accepted.
SAVE ⊠ 🛏 💻 ⊷

Microtel Inn Victor H
(585) 924-9240. **$55-$100.** 7498 Main St Fischer Rd. I-90 (New York State Thruway), exit 45, just s on SR 96, then just w. Int corridors. **Pets:** Accepted.
ASK ⊠ 🛏 💻

WARRENSBURG

Super 8 Warrensburg/Lake George M
(518) 623-2811. **Call for rates.** 3619 SR 9. I-87, exit 23, just w. Int corridors. **Pets:** Accepted.
⊠

WATERLOO

Holiday Inn Waterloo-Seneca Falls H 🐾
(315) 539-5011. **$89-$189.** 2468 SR 414. I-90 (New York State Thruway), exit 41, 4 mi s; just n of jct SR 414/5 and US 20. Int corridors. **Pets:** Medium, other species. $10 daily fee/pet. Service with restrictions, supervision.
SAVE ⊠ 🛏 💻 🍴 ⊷ 🚫

Microtel Inn & Suites H
(315) 539-8438. **$56-$120.** 1966 Rt 5 & 20. I-90 (New York State Thruway), exit 41, 4 mi s on SR 414, then just e. Int corridors. **Pets:** Other species. $15 daily fee/room. Service with restrictions, supervision.
SAVE ⊠ 🛁 🛏 💻

WATERTOWN

Best Western Carriage House Inn & Conference Center H
(315) 782-8000. **$102-$116.** 300 Washington St. Center. Int corridors. **Pets:** Large, other species. $15 daily fee/pet. Designated rooms, service with restrictions, supervision.
SAVE ⊠ 🛏 💻 🍴 ⊷

Davidson's Motel M
(315) 782-3861. **$75-$110.** 26177 NYS Rt 3. From Town Square, 3.5 mi e. Ext corridors. **Pets:** Small. $5 daily fee/pet. Service with restrictions, supervision.
SAVE ⊠ 🛏 ⊷

Ramada H
(315) 788-0700. **$104-$109, 7 day notice.** 21000 NYS Rt 3. I-81, exit 45, just w. Int corridors. **Pets:** Accepted.
ASK ⊠ 🛏 💻 🍴 ⊷ 🚫

WATKINS GLEN

AAA ◆◆◆ Anchor Inn and Marina **M** ❀
(607) 535-4159. **$69-$169, 10 day notice.** 3425 Salt Point Rd. Just n on SR 14, 0.8 mi n. Ext corridors. **Pets:** $25 deposit/pet. Service with restrictions, supervision.
SAVE ✕ 🛏 ✕

AAA ◆◆◆ Chieftain Motel **M**
(607) 535-4759. **$69-$169, 10 day notice.** 3815 SR 14. 3 mi n of town; on west side of SR 14. Ext corridors. **Pets:** Accepted.
SAVE ✕ 🛏 ▣

WELLSVILLE

AAA ◆ Long Vue Inn & Suites **M**
(585) 593-2450. **$54-$129.** 5081 Rt 417 W. Jct SR 19, 3 mi w. Ext corridors. **Pets:** Medium. $5 daily fee/pet. Service with restrictions, supervision.
SAVE ✕ 🛏 ▣

◆◆ Microtel Inn & Suites **H**
(585) 593-3449. **Call for rates.** 30 W Dyke St. Just n off SR 19 and 417. Int corridors. **Pets:** Accepted.
✕ 🛏 ▣

WEST COXSACKIE

AAA ◆◆ Best Western New Baltimore Inn **H**
(518) 731-8100. **Call for rates.** 12600 Rt 9W. I-87 (New York State Thruway), exit 21B, 0.5 mi s. Int corridors. **Pets:** Medium. $10 daily fee/pet. Service with restrictions, crate.
SAVE ✕ 🛏 ▣ ⇶ ✕

WESTFIELD

◆◆◆ The William Seward Inn **CI** ❀
(716) 326-4151. **$100-$235, 7 day notice.** 6645 S Portage Rd. I-90 (New York State Thruway), exit 60, 4 mi se on SR 394. Int corridors. **Pets:** Dogs only. $25 daily fee/pet. Service with restrictions, crate.
ASK ✕ ¶

WESTMORELAND

AAA ◆ Carriage Motor Inn **M**
(315) 853-3561. **$35-$85, 5 day notice.** 5370 SR 233. I-90 (New York State Thruway), exit 32, just n. Ext corridors. **Pets:** Small, dogs only. $20 deposit/room, $15 daily fee/pet. Designated rooms, service with restrictions, supervision.
SAVE ✕ 🛏

WILMINGTON

◆◆◆ Green Mountain Lodge **M**
(518) 946-8232. **$69-$139, 7 day notice.** 5675 SR 86. Jct SR 86 and 431 (Whiteface Mt Hwy). Ext corridors. **Pets:** Medium, dogs only. $10 daily fee/pet. Designated rooms, service with restrictions, supervision.
✕ 🛏 ▣ ✕

AAA ◆◆◆ Hungry Trout Resort **M**
(518) 946-2217. **$69-$169, 7 day notice.** 5239 Rt 86. On SR 86, 2 mi w. Ext corridors. **Pets:** Accepted.
SAVE ✕ 🛏 ▣ ¶ ⇶ ✕

AAA ◆◆◆ Ledge Rock at Whiteface Mountain **M**
(518) 946-2379. **$79-$129, 10 day notice.** 5078 NYS Rt 86. On SR 86, 3 mi w. Ext corridors. **Pets:** $25 daily fee/pet. Service with restrictions.
SAVE ✕ 🛏 ▣ ≋ ✕

◆◆ Mountain Brook Lodge **M** ❀
(518) 946-2262. **$74-$89, 10 day notice.** 5712 Rt 86. Center. Ext corridors. **Pets:** $25 one-time fee/room. Service with restrictions, crate.
✕ 🛏 ▣ ⇶

AAA ◆◆◆ North Pole Inn **M**
(518) 946-7733. **$65-$199, 7 day notice.** 5636 NYS Rt 86. On SR 86, just w of jct CR 431. Ext corridors. **Pets:** Dogs only. $15 daily fee/room. Designated rooms, service with restrictions, supervision.
SAVE ✕ 🛏 ▣ ⇶ ✕

AAA ◆◆◆ Willkommen Hof Bed & Breakfast **BB** ❀
(518) 946-7669. **$70-$245, 14 day notice.** 5367 5367 Rt 86. On SR 86, 1.5 mi of jct CR 431. Int corridors. **Pets:** Large, other species. $50 deposit/room, $10 daily fee/pet. Designated rooms, service with restrictions, crate.
SAVE ✕ 🛏 ▣ ✕ ✎

WOODBURY

AAA ◆◆◆ Best Western Woodbury Inn **M**
(516) 921-6900. **Call for rates.** 7940 Jericho Tpke (SR 25). Jct SR 25 and 135, 0.9 mi e. Ext/int corridors. **Pets:** Accepted.
SAVE ✕ 🛏 ▣ ¶ ⇶

AAA ◆◆◆ Executive Inn at Woodbury **M** ❀
(516) 921-8500. **$99-$209.** 8030 Jericho Tpke (SR 25). Jct SR 25 and 135, 1 mi e. Ext corridors. **Pets:** Medium. $100 deposit/room, $50 one-time fee/room. Designated rooms, service with restrictions.
SAVE ✕ 🛏 ▣ ⇶

NORTH CAROLINA

CITY INDEX

ABERDEEN

▼ Motel 6-1234 Ⓜ
(910) 944-5633. **$43-$51.** 1408 Sandhills Blvd. Jct US 15/501 N, just s on US 1. Ext corridors. **Pets:** Other species. Service with restrictions, supervision.

⊠ 🛏 💻 🏊

▼▼ Sandhills Value Inn Ⓜ
(910) 944-2369. **$49-$129.** 1500 Sandhills Blvd. Jct US 15/501 N, just s on US 1. Ext corridors. **Pets:** Small, dogs only. $10 daily fee/pet. Service with restrictions, supervision.

(ASK) ⊠ 🛏 💻 🏊

ALBEMARLE

▼▼ Executive Inn Ⓗ
(704) 983-6990. **$65-$89.** 735 Hwy 24/27 Bypass. Jct US 52 S, 1.4 mi e. Ext corridors. **Pets:** Accepted.

(ASK) ⊠ 🛏 💻 🏊

ANDREWS

▼▼▼ Hawkesdene House Mountain Retreat ⒷⒷ
(828) 321-6027. **$179-$209, 7 day notice.** 381 Phillips Creek Rd. US 19 business route, 3.2 mi s on Cherry St, then 0.5 mi s. Ext/int corridors. **Pets:** Accepted.

(ASK) ⊠ 🛏 💻

ARCHDALE

◈ ▼▼ Best Western-High Point Ⓗ
(336) 861-3000. **$85-$199.** 1202 Liberty Rd. I-85, exit 113, just s on SR 62. Int corridors. **Pets:** $25 daily fee/pet. Designated rooms, no service, crate.

(SAVE) ⊠ 🛏 💻 🏊

◈ ▼▼▼ Comfort Inn Ⓗ
(336) 434-4797. **$175.** 10123 N Main St. I-85, exit 111, just n on US 311, then just sw on Balfour Dr. Int corridors. **Pets:** Small. $25 one-time fee/pet. No service, supervision.

(SAVE) ⊠ ♿ 🛏 💻 🏊

▼▼▼ Hampton Inn-High Point Ⓗ
(336) 434-5200. **$79-$109.** 10066 N Main St. I-85, exit 111, just n on US 311. Int corridors. **Pets:** Small. $25 one-time fee/pet. Designated rooms, no service, supervision.

(ASK) ⊠ 🛏 💻 🏊

▼▼▼ Holiday Inn Express Hotel & Suites Ⓗ
(336) 861-3310. **$93-$97, 3 day notice.** 10050 N Main St. I-85, exit 111, just n on US 311. Int corridors. **Pets:** Accepted.

(ASK) ⊠ 🛏 💻 🏊

▼▼ Innkeeper High Point Ⓜ
(336) 434-5151. **$55, 3 day notice.** 10002 S Main St. I-85, exit 111, just s on US 311. Ext/int corridors. **Pets:** Accepted.

(ASK) ⊠ 🛏 🏊

ARDEN

▼▼ Quality Inn & Suites Biltmore South Ⓗ 🐾
(828) 684-6688. **$70-$179.** 1 Skyline Inn Dr. I-26, exit 37. Int corridors. **Pets:** Large, other species. $25 one-time fee/room. Designated rooms, service with restrictions, crate.

(ASK) ⊠ 🛏 💻 🏊 ⊠

ASHEBORO

◈ ▼▼▼ Quality Inn Ⓗ
(336) 626-3680. **$75-$130.** 242 Lakecrest Rd. US 64, just nw on SR 42. Ext corridors. **Pets:** Small. $15 daily fee/pet. Service with restrictions, crate.

(SAVE) ⊠ 🛏 💻 🏊

ASHEVILLE

▼▼▼▼ 1889 WhiteGate Inn & Cottage ⒷⒷ
(828) 253-2553. **$169-$369, 14 day notice.** 173 E Chestnut St. I-240, exit 5B (Charlotte St), just n, then just w; in historic district. Ext/int corridors. **Pets:** Medium, dogs only. $50 one-time fee/room. Designated rooms, service with restrictions, supervision.

⊠ 🛏 💻

◈ ▼▼▼ 1891 Cedar Crest Inn ⒷⒷ
(828) 252-1389. **$145-$300, 14 day notice.** 674 Biltmore Ave. I-40, exit 50, 1.1 mi n. Ext/int corridors. **Pets:** Medium, dogs only. $50 one-time fee/pet. Designated rooms, crate.

(SAVE) ⊠ 🛏 💻

▼▼▼▼ 1900 Inn on Montford ⒷⒷ 🐾
(828) 254-9569. **$145-$625, 14 day notice.** 296 Montford Ave. I-240, exit 4C (Montford Ave/Haywood St), 0.7 mi n; in historic district. Ext/int corridors. **Pets:** Other species. Designated rooms, service with restrictions.

⊠ 🛏 💻

◈ ▼▼▼ Abbington Green Bed & Breakfast Inn ⒷⒷ
(828) 251-2454. **$150-$450, 30 day notice.** 46 Cumberland Cir. I-240, exit 4C (Montford Ave/Haywood St), n to W Chestnut St, just e to Cumberland Ave, then 0.3 mi n; in historic district. Ext/int corridors. **Pets:** Accepted.

(SAVE) ⊠ 🛏 💻 ⓩ

◇◇◇◇ Applewood Manor Inn Bed & Breakfast BB
(828) 254-2244. **$160-$225, 7 day notice.** 62 Cumberland Cir. I-240, exit 4C (Montford Ave/Haywood St), n on Montford Ave, e on W Chestnut St, n on Cumberland Ave, then ne; in historic district. Ext/int corridors. **Pets:** Dogs only. $35 daily fee/pet. Designated rooms.
SAVE ✕ 🖥 🖃

◇◇◇◇ Best Western of Asheville Biltmore East M
(828) 298-5562. **$49-$199, 3 day notice.** 501 Tunnel Rd. I-240, exit 7, 0.5 mi e on US 70 (Tunnel Rd). Ext corridors. **Pets:** Small, dogs only. $10 daily fee/pet. No service, supervision.
SAVE ✕ 🖥 🖃 ⇆

◇◇◇◇ Biltmore Village Inn BB ☙
(828) 274-8707. **$220-$325, 14 day notice.** 119 Dodge St. I-40, exit 50/50B (US 25 N), 0.5 mi n, just e on Lula St, just n on Reed St, just e on Warren Ave, then just s. Ext/int corridors. **Pets:** Medium, other species. $25 daily fee/pet. Designated rooms, crate.
SAVE ✕ 🖥 🖃

◇◇◇◇ Black Walnut B&B Inn BB ☙
(828) 254-3878. **$145-$295, 15 day notice.** 288 Montford Ave. I-240, exit 4C (Montford Ave/Haywood St), 0.5 mi n; in historic district. Ext/int corridors. **Pets:** Other species. Designated rooms, crate.
SAVE ✕ 🖃

◇◇ Carolina Bed & Breakfast BB
(828) 254-3608. **$120-$225.** 177 Cumberland Ave. I-240, exit 4C (Montford Ave/Haywood St), 0.5 mi n on Montford Ave, just e on Chestnut St, then just n. Ext/int corridors. **Pets:** Accepted.
✕ 🖥 🖃 🖃

◇◇◇ Comfort Suites-Biltmore Square Mall H
(828) 665-4000. **$69-$189.** 890 Brevard Rd. I-26, exit 33, 0.3 mi w. Int corridors. **Pets:** Large, other species. $20 daily fee/room. Designated rooms, service with restrictions.
ASK ✕ 🖥ᴹ 🖥 🖃 ⇆

◇◇◇ Crowne Plaza Resort H
(828) 254-3211. **$89-$179.** 1 Resort Dr. I-240, exit 3B (Resort Dr), just w. Int corridors. **Pets:** Accepted.
ASK ✕ 🖥 🖃 ❲❳ ⇆ ✕

◇◇◇ Days Inn-Asheville Mall M
(828) 252-4000. **$49-$249.** 201 Tunnel Rd. I-240, exit 6, 0.5 mi e, on south side of road. Ext corridors. **Pets:** Accepted.
SAVE ✕ 🖥 🖃 ⇆

◇◇◇ Days Inn-Biltmore East H
(828) 298-4000. **$42-$199.** 1435 Tunnel Rd. I-40, exit 55, just n. Int corridors. **Pets:** Small, dogs only. $10 daily fee/room. Service with restrictions, supervision.
SAVE ✕ 🖥 🖃 ⇆

◇◇ Extended StayAmerica H
(828) 253-3483. **$90-$120.** 6 Kenilworth Knoll. I-240, exit 6, 0.7 mi e on US 70 (Tunnel Rd), then just n. Int corridors. **Pets:** Other species. $25 daily fee/pet. Service with restrictions, crate.
ASK ✕ 🖥ᴹ 🖥 🖃

◇◇◇ Four Points by Sheraton Asheville Downtown H
(828) 253-1851. **Call for rates.** 22 Woodfin St. I-240, exit 5A (Merrimon Ave). Int corridors. **Pets:** Medium. $75 one-time fee/pet. Service with restrictions, supervision.
SAVE ✕ 🖥 🖃 ❲❳ ⇆

◇◇◇ Holiday Inn-Biltmore East at the Blue Ridge Parkway H
(828) 298-5611. **$69-$169.** 1450 Tunnel Rd. I-40, exit 55, just n. Int corridors. **Pets:** Accepted.
ASK ✕ 🖥 🖃 ❲❳ ⇆

◇◇◇ The Log Cabin Motor Court CA ☙
(828) 645-6546. **$55-$110, 14 day notice.** 330 Weaverville Hwy. US 19/23, exit 21 (New Stock Rd), 1 mi s on Weaverville Hwy. Ext corridors. **Pets:** Other species. $15 daily fee/pet. No service, crate.
SAVE ✕ 🖥 🖃 ❲❳ 🖃

◇◇ Quality Inn & Suites M
(828) 298-5519. **$55-$199.** 1430 Tunnel Rd. I-40, exit 55, just n. Ext corridors. **Pets:** Accepted.
ASK ✕ 🖥 🖃 ⇆

◇◇◇ Ramada H ☙
(828) 298-9141. **$74-$129, 7 day notice.** 800 Fairview Rd. I-240, exit 8; jct I-40 and US 74. Int corridors. **Pets:** Large, other species. $15 daily fee/pet. Designated rooms, service with restrictions, crate.
SAVE ✕ 🖥 🖃 ⇆ 🖃

◇◇ Red Roof Inn-West M ☙
(828) 667-9803. **$50-$90, 14 day notice.** 16 Crowell Rd. I-40, exit 44, just n on US 19 and 23, just w on Old Haywood Rd, then just s. Ext corridors. **Pets:** Large, other species. Service with restrictions, supervision.
SAVE ✕ 🖥

◇◇ Sleep Inn Biltmore H
(828) 277-1800. **$69-$180.** 117 Hendersonville Rd. I-40, exit 50 eastbound; exit 50B westbound, just n on US 25. Int corridors. **Pets:** Medium. $10 daily fee/pet. Designated rooms, no service, supervision.
ASK ✕ 🖥ᴹ 🖃

◇◇ Super 8 Motel Central M
(828) 667-8706. **Call for rates.** 8 Crowell Rd. I-40, exit 44, just n on US 19 and 23. Int corridors. **Pets:** Medium. $15 daily fee/pet. Designated rooms, service with restrictions, supervision.
✕ 🖥ᴹ 🖥 🖃

BANNER ELK

◇◇◇◇ The Banner Elk Inn B&B and Cottages BB ☙
(828) 898-6223. **$90-$250, 30 day notice.** 407 Main St E. Jct SR 184 and 194, 0.3 mi n on SR 194. Int corridors. **Pets:** Dogs only. Designated rooms, service with restrictions, supervision.
✕ 🖥 🖃

◇◇◇ Best Western Mountain Lodge at Banner Elk H ☙
(828) 898-4571. **$80-$210, 3 day notice.** 1615 Tynecastle Hwy. 1 mi se on SR 184. Ext corridors. **Pets:** Other species. Designated rooms, service with restrictions, crate.
SAVE ✕ 🖥ᴹ 🖥 🖃 ❲❳ ⇆

◇◇◇◇ Valle Crucis Bed & Breakfast BB
(828) 963-2525. **$139-$225, 7 day notice.** 2171 Broadstone Rd. Jct SR 321, 4.7 mi w on SR 105, then 2 mi n. Ext/int corridors. **Pets:** Accepted.
✕ 🖥 🖃

BLACK MOUNTAIN

◇◇◇ Inn On Mill Creek BB
(828) 668-1115. **$145-$200, 30 day notice.** 3895 Mill Creek Rd. I-40, exit 66, just n, 0.9 mi e on Ridgecrest Rd, 0.9 mi n on Yates Ave to white gate, then 1.5 mi n. Ext/int corridors. **Pets:** Accepted.
✕ 🖥 🖃 ✕ 🖃

BLOWING ROCK

◇◇ Hillwinds Inn M
(828) 295-7660. **$69-$359, 3 day notice.** 315 Sunset Dr. Just e of Main St. Ext/int corridors. **Pets:** Medium. $25 daily fee/pet. Service with restrictions, crate.
ASK ✕ 🖥 🖃

▼▼▼ The Village Inn **M**
(828) 295-3380. **$75-$359, 3 day notice.** 7876 Valley Blvd. On US 321 Bypass, just e of city park. Ext corridors. **Pets:** Medium. $25 daily fee/pet. Service with restrictions, crate.
(ASK) (X) (&M) (🛏) (💻)

BOONE

▼▼▼ La Quinta Inn & Suites **H** ❀
(828) 262-1234. **$69-$219.** 165 Hwy 105 Ext. US 321 NW, 1 mi n of jct US 321. Int corridors. **Pets:** Medium, other species. Service with restrictions, supervision.
(X) (&M) (🛏) (💻) (≈)

BREVARD

(AAA) ▼▼▼ Holiday Inn Express **H**
(828) 862-8900. **$89-$179.** 1570 Asheville Hwy. 3 mi e on US 64. Int corridors. **Pets:** $10 daily fee/pet. Service with restrictions, supervision.
(SAVE) (X) (&M) (🛏) (💻) (≈)

BURLINGTON

(AAA) ▼▼ Econo Lodge **H**
(336) 227-1270. **$46-$60, 10 day notice.** 2133 W Hanford Rd. I-40/85, exit 145, just s on SR 49, then just w. Int corridors. **Pets:** Accepted.
(SAVE) (X) (🛏) (≈)

▼ Motel 6–1257 **M**
(336) 226-1325. **$37-$45.** 2155 Hanford Rd. I-40/85, exit 145, just s on SR 49, then just w. Ext corridors. **Pets:** Other species. Service with restrictions, supervision.
(X) (≈)

(AAA) ▼▼▼ Quality Inn Burlington **H**
(336) 229-5203. **$50-$80.** 2444 Maple Ave. I-40/85, exit 145, just n. Int corridors. **Pets:** Large. $25 one-time fee/pet. Designated rooms, service with restrictions, supervision.
(SAVE) (X) (&M) (🛏) (💻) (≈)

CANDLER

(AAA) ▼▼ Days Inn West #6116 **M** ❀
(828) 667-9321. **$50-$140.** 2551 Smoky Park Hwy. I-40, exit 37, just w, then n. Ext corridors. **Pets:** Medium, other species. $10 daily fee/pet. Designated rooms, service with restrictions, supervision.
(SAVE) (X) (🛏) (💻) (≈)

(AAA) ▼▼▼ Owl's Nest Inn and Engadine Cabins **BB**
(828) 665-8325. **$145-$250, 14 day notice.** 2630 Smoky Park Hwy. I-40, exit 37, 0.5 mi w on SR 19/23. Ext/int corridors. **Pets:** Accepted.
(SAVE) (X) (🛏) (💻)

CANTON

▼▼ Days Inn **M**
(828) 648-0300. **Call for rates.** 1963 Champion Dr. I-40, exit 31. Ext corridors. **Pets:** Accepted.
(X) (🛏) (💻) (≈)

CARY

(AAA) ▼▼▼ Best Western Cary Inn & Extended Stay Suites **H**
(919) 481-1200. **$60-$130.** 1722 Walnut St. I-40, exit 293A, just s on US 1, exit 101A, then just e. Ext/int corridors. **Pets:** Accepted.
(SAVE) (X) (🛏) (💻) (≈) (X)

▼▼▼ Candlewood Suites-Raleigh/Cary **H** ❀
(919) 468-4222. **$93-$100.** 1020 Buck Jones Rd. I-40, exit 293A, just s on US 1, exit 101B, 0.5 mi nw; in Buck Jones Village. Int corridors. **Pets:** Large, other species. $15 daily fee/room. Service with restrictions, supervision.
(ASK) (X) (🛏) (💻)

▼▼▼ Comfort Suites Hotel **H**
(919) 852-4318. **$79-$129.** 350 Ashville Ave. US 1, exit 98A, 0.8 mi e on Tryon Rd, then just n. Int corridors. **Pets:** Accepted.
(ASK) (X) (&M) (🛏) (💻) (≈) (X)

▼▼ Days Inn **M**
(919) 481-4011. **Call for rates.** 1716 Walnut St. I-40, exit 293A, just s on US 1, exit 101A, then just e. Ext corridors. **Pets:** Accepted.
(X) (&M) (🛏) (≈)

▼▼ Extended StayAmerica-Raleigh/Cary **H**
(919) 468-5828. **$77-$87.** 1500 Regency Pkwy. US 1, exit 98A, 0.5 mi e on Tryon Rd, then just s. Int corridors. **Pets:** Other species. $25 daily fee/pet. Service with restrictions, crate.
(ASK) (X) (🛏) (💻)

▼▼ Extended Stay Deluxe Raleigh-Cary-Regency Parkway **H**
(919) 460-1161. **$92-$102.** 3100 Regency Pkwy. US 1, exit 98A, 0.5 mi e on Tryon Rd, then just s. Int corridors. **Pets:** Other species. $25 daily fee/pet. Service with restrictions, crate.
(ASK) (X) (🛏) (💻) (≈)

▼▼▼ La Quinta Inn & Suites Raleigh (Cary) **H** ❀
(919) 851-2850. **$79-$129.** 191 Crescent Commons Dr. US 1, exit 98A, 0.5 mi e on Tryon Rd, then just n. Int corridors. **Pets:** Medium, other species. Service with restrictions, supervision.
(ASK) (X) (&M) (🛏) (💻) (≈)

▼▼▼ Residence Inn **H** ❀
(919) 467-4080. **$172-$184.** 2900 Regency Pkwy. US 1, exit 98A, 0.5 mi e on Tryon Rd, then just s. Int corridors. **Pets:** $75 one-time fee/room. Service with restrictions.
(X) (&M) (🛏) (💻) (≈) (X)

▼▼ StudioPLUS-Harrison Ave **H**
(919) 677-9910. **$90-$100.** 600 Weston Pkwy. I-40, exit 287, 0.5 mi s on Harrison Ave, then just w. Int corridors. **Pets:** Other species. $25 daily fee/pet. Service with restrictions, crate.
(ASK) (X) (🛏) (💻) (≈)

(AAA) ▼▼▼ TownePlace Suites by Marriott–Raleigh/Cary/ Weston Parkway **H**
(919) 678-0005. **$182-$196.** 120 Sage Commons Way. I-40, exit 287, 0.5 mi s on Harrison Ave, 2.3 w on Weston Pkwy, then just n. Int corridors. **Pets:** Medium, other species. $100 one-time fee/room. Designated rooms, service with restrictions, crate.
(SAVE) (X) (&M) (🛏) (💻) (≈)

(AAA) ▼▼▼▼ The Umstead Hotel & Spa **H**
(919) 447-4000. **$199-$425.** 100 Woodland Pond Dr. I-40, exit 287, just s on Harrison Ave, just e on SAS Campus Dr, then just n. Int corridors. **Pets:** Accepted.
(SAVE) (X) (🍴) (≈) (X)

CASHIERS

(AAA) ▼▼▼ High Hampton Inn & Country Club **H**
(828) 743-2411. **$264-$369.** 1525 Hwy 107 S. Jct US 64, 1.5 mi s. Ext/int corridors. **Pets:** Accepted.
(SAVE) (X) (🛏) (💻) (🍴) (X) (X) (W) (Z)

▼▼ Laurelwood Mountain Inn **M**
(828) 743-9939. **$69-$99, 3 day notice.** 58 Hwy 107. Jct US 64, just n. Ext corridors. **Pets:** Accepted.
(ASK) (X) (&M) (🛏) (💻)

CHAPEL HILL

▼▼ Holiday Inn **H**
(919) 929-2171. **$99-$129.** 1301 N Fordham Blvd. I-40, exit 270, 2 mi s on US 15/501. Ext corridors. **Pets:** Accepted.
(X) (🛏) (💻) (🍴) (≈)

Residence Inn by Marriott-Chapel Hill H
(919) 933-4848. **$197-$211.** 101 Erwin Rd. I-40, exit 270, 1.2 mi s on US 15/501, then just w. Int corridors. **Pets:** Accepted.
SAVE ⊠ ⑤ⁿ ⊟ 🖥 ⋙ ⊠

The Siena Hotel H ✿
(919) 929-4000. **$119-$300.** 1505 E Franklin St. I-40, exit 270, 2 mi s on US 15/501, then 0.5 mi w. Int corridors. **Pets:** Dogs only. $75 one-time fee/room. Designated rooms, service with restrictions.
SAVE ⊠ ⑤ⁿ ⊟ ⑪

CHARLOTTE METROPOLITAN AREA

CHARLOTTE

Best Western-Airport Inn M
(704) 394-4111. **$69, 30 day notice.** 2625 Little Rock Rd. I-85, exit 32, just w. Ext corridors. **Pets:** $10 daily fee/pet. Service with restrictions, supervision.
SAVE ⊠ ⊟ 🖥 ⋙

Candlewood Suites–Charlotte University H
(704) 598-9863. **$77-$80.** 8812 University East Dr. I-85, exit 45A (W.T. Harris Blvd), 2.5 mi e on SR 24, then just s; in University East Business Park. Int corridors. **Pets:** Other species. $75 one-time fee/room.
ASK ⊠ ⊟ 🖥

Candlewood Suites-Executive Park H ✿
(704) 529-7500. **Call for rates.** 5840 Westpark Dr. I-77, exit 5 (Tyvola Rd), just e, then 0.5 mi s. Int corridors. **Pets:** Medium. $75 one-time fee/pet. Service with restrictions, crate.
⊠ ⑤ⁿ ⊟ 🖥

Comfort Inn-Executive Park H
(704) 525-2626. **$54-$84.** 5822 Westpark Dr. I-77, exit 5 (Tyvola Rd), just e, then 0.5 mi s. Int corridors. **Pets:** Large, other species. $25 one-time fee/pet. Service with restrictions, supervision.
SAVE ⊠ ⊟ 🖥 ⋙

Comfort Inn-UNCC H
(704) 598-0007. **$70-$159.** 5111 Equipment Dr. I-85, exit 41, just w, then just s. Int corridors. **Pets:** Accepted.
SAVE ⊠ ⊟ 🖥 ⋙

Comfort Suites-University H
(704) 547-0049. **$100-$200.** 7735 University City Blvd. I-85, exit 45A (W. T. Harris Blvd), 1 mi e on SR 24, then 0.5 mi s on SR 49. Int corridors. **Pets:** Accepted.
ASK ⊠ ⑤ⁿ ⊟ 🖥 ⋙

Country Inn & Suites-Charlotte University H
(704) 549-8770. **Call for rates.** 131 E McCullough Dr. I-85, exit 45A (W. T. Harris Blvd), 0.5 mi e on SR 24, 0.4 mi s on US 29 (N Tryon St), then just e. Int corridors. **Pets:** Accepted.
⊠ ⑤ⁿ ⊟ 🖥 ⋙ ⊠

Crowne Plaza–Charlotte H
(704) 372-7550. **$119-$289.** 201 S McDowell St. I-277, exit 2A, just w on 4th St, then just s. Int corridors. **Pets:** Medium. $50 one-time fee/room. Service with restrictions, supervision.
SAVE ⊠ ⊟ 🖥 ⑪ ⋙

DoubleTree Guest Suites-South Park H
(704) 364-2400. **$99-$289.** 6300 Morrison Blvd. I-77, exit 5 (Tyvola Rd), 3.3 mi e on Tyvola/Fairview rds, just n on Barclay Downs, then just e. Int corridors. **Pets:** Other species. Service with restrictions, crate.
SAVE ⊠ ⊟ 🖥 ⑪ ⋙

DoubleTree Hotel Charlotte-Gateway Village H
(704) 347-0070. **$89-$229.** 895 W Trade St. I-77, exit 10 or 10B, just e. Int corridors. **Pets:** Accepted.
SAVE ⊠ ⑤ⁿ ⊟ 🖥 ⑪ ⋙

Drury Inn & Suites-Charlotte North H
(704) 593-0700. **$90-$170.** 415 W WT Harris Blvd. I-85, exit 45A (W. T. Harris Blvd), just e on SR 24. Int corridors. **Pets:** Other species. Service with restrictions, supervision.
ASK ⊠ ⑤ⁿ ⊟ 🖥 ⋙

Extended StayAmerica-Charlotte-Pineville H
(704) 341-0929. **$85-$95.** 10930 Park Rd. I-485, exit 64A, just n on SR 51, then just e; behind Terraces at Park Place Shopping Center. Int corridors. **Pets:** Other species. $25 daily fee/pet. Service with restrictions, crate.
ASK ⊠ ⑤ⁿ ⊟ 🖥

Extended StayAmerica-Charlotte-University Place H
(704) 510-1636. **$80-$90.** 8211 University Executive Park Dr. I-85, exit 45A (W. T. Harris Blvd), 0.5 mi e on SR 24, then 0.5 mi s on US 29 (N Tryon St). Int corridors. **Pets:** Other species. $25 daily fee/pet. Service with restrictions, crate.
ASK ⊠ ⊟ 🖥

Extended Stay Deluxe-Charlotte/Pineville H
(704) 542-9521. **$99-$109.** 8405 Pineville-Matthews Rd. I-485, exit 64A, 0.7 mi n on SR 51. Int corridors. **Pets:** Other species. $25 daily fee/pet. Service with restrictions, crate.
ASK ⊠ ⊟ 🖥

Four Points by Sheraton-Charlotte H
(704) 522-0852. **Call for rates.** 315 E Woodlawn Rd. I-77, exit 6A, 0.5 mi e. Int corridors. **Pets:** Accepted.
SAVE ⊠ ⊟ 🖥 ⑪ ⋙

Holiday Inn Airport H
(704) 394-4301. **Call for rates.** 2707 Little Rock Rd. I-85, exit 32, just e. Int corridors. **Pets:** Accepted.
⊠ ⊟ 🖥 ⑪ ⋙

Holiday Inn at University Executive Park H
(704) 547-0999. **$99-$289.** 8520 University Executive Park Dr. I-85, exit 45A (W. T. Harris Blvd), just e on SR 24, then just s. Int corridors. **Pets:** Accepted.
ASK ⊠ ⑤ⁿ ⊟ 🖥 ⑪ ⋙

Holiday Inn-Billy Graham Parkway H
(704) 523-1400. **Call for rates.** 321 W Woodlawn Rd. I-77, exit 6B northbound, just w; exit southbound, just s on S Tryon St. Int corridors. **Pets:** Accepted.
⊠ ⑤ⁿ ⊟ 🖥 ⑪ ⋙ ⊠

Homestead Studio Suites Hotel-Charlotte/Airport M
(704) 676-0083. **$95-$105.** 710 Yorkmont Rd. I-77, exit 6B northbound, just w, just s on S Tryon St, then just w; exit southbound, just s on S Tryon St, then just w. Ext corridors. **Pets:** Other species. $25 daily fee/pet. Service with restrictions, crate.
ASK ⊠ ⊟ 🖥

Homewood Suites by Hilton Airport H
(704) 357-0500. **$69-$189.** 2770 Yorkmont Rd. I-77, exit 6B, 2 mi nw on Billy Graham Pkwy, exit Coliseum/Tyvola Rd, just se on Tyvola Rd, then just w. Int corridors. **Pets:** Accepted.
⊠ ⑤ⁿ ⊟ 🖥 ⋙

Hyatt Summerfield Suites H
(704) 525-2600. **$99-$299.** 4920 S Tryon St. I-77, exit 6B northbound, just w, then just s; exit southbound, just s. Int corridors. **Pets:** Medium. $5 daily fee/room, $150 one-time fee/room. Designated rooms, service with restrictions.

La Quinta Inn- Airport North H ❀
(704) 392-1600. **$59-$109.** 3127 Sloan Dr. I-85, exit 33, just w, then just s. Int corridors. **Pets:** Medium, other species. Service with restrictions, supervision.

La Quinta Inn & Suites Charlotte Airport South H ❀
(704) 523-5599. **$69-$129.** 4900 S Tryon St. I-77, exit 6B northbound, just w, then just s; exit southbound, just s. Int corridors. **Pets:** Medium, other species. Service with restrictions, supervision.

MainStay Suites H
(704) 521-3232. **Call for rates.** 7926 Forest Pine Dr. I-77, exit 3 southbound; exit 2 northbound, just e, then just s. Int corridors. **Pets:** Accepted.

Marriott-Charlotte SouthPark H
(704) 364-8220. **$217-$233.** 2200 Rexford Rd. I-77, exit 5 (Tyvola Rd), 3.6 mi e on Tyvola/Fairview rds, just n on Sharon Rd, just w on Morrison Blvd, just n on Roxborough Rd, then just w. Int corridors. **Pets:** $100 one-time fee/pet. Service with restrictions, crate.

Omni Charlotte Hotel H
(704) 377-0400. **$237-$267.** 132 E Trade St. I-77, exit 10 or 10B, 0.8 mi e; jct Tryon St. Int corridors. **Pets:** Small. $100 one-time fee/room. Service with restrictions, supervision.

Quality Inn & Suites Airport H
(704) 393-5306. **$70-$80, 14 day notice.** 3100 Queen City Dr. I-85, exit 33, just w, then just n. Ext/int corridors. **Pets:** Medium. $25 one-time fee/pet. Service with restrictions, supervision.

Ramada Conference Center "Airport South" H
(704) 525-8350. **Call for rates.** 212 W Woodlawn Rd. I-77, exit 6A, just e. Int corridors. **Pets:** Accepted.

Ramada Northeast M
(704) 596-2999. **$49-$54.** 5415 Equipment Dr. I-85, exit 41, just w, then 0.4 mi n. Ext/int corridors. **Pets:** Accepted.

Red Roof Inn-Airport M
(704) 392-2316. **Call for rates.** 3300 Queen City Dr. I-85, exit 33, just w, then just s. Ext corridors. **Pets:** Accepted.

Residence Inn by Marriott-Charlotte South H ❀
(704) 527-8110. **$172-$184.** 5816 Westpark Dr. I-77, exit 5 (Tyvola Rd), just e, then 0.4 mi s. Ext/int corridors. **Pets:** Other species. $75 one-time fee/room. Service with restrictions, crate.

Residence Inn by Marriott-Charlotte Uptown H
(704) 340-4000. **$267-$277.** 404 S Mint St. I-77, exit 10 or 10B, 0.6 mi e on Trade St, then just s. Int corridors. **Pets:** Accepted.

Residence Inn by Marriott-Piper Glen H
(704) 319-3900. **$217-$233.** 5115 Piper Station Dr. I-485, exit 59, just s on Rea Rd, then just e. Int corridors. **Pets:** Accepted.

Residence Inn by Marriott-University Research Park H
(704) 547-1122. **$159-$299.** 8503 N Tryon St. I-85, exit 45A (W. T. Harris Blvd), 0.5 mi e on SR 24, then just s on US 29 (N Tryon St). Ext corridors. **Pets:** Accepted.

Sheraton Charlotte Airport Hotel H
(704) 392-1200. **$99-$279.** 3315 Scott Futrell Dr. I-85, exit 33, just e, then just s. Int corridors. **Pets:** Accepted.

Sleep Inn H
(704) 549-4544. **$70-$170.** 8525 N Tryon St. I-85, exit 45A (W. T. Harris Blvd), 0.5 mi e on SR 24, just s on US 29 (N Tryon St). Int corridors. **Pets:** Large, other species. $25 one-time fee/room. Service with restrictions, supervision.

Sleep Inn-Yorkmont H
(704) 525-5005. **$80-$130, 14 day notice.** 701 Yorkmont Rd. I-77, exit 6B northbound, just w, just s on S Tryon St, then just w; exit southbound, just s on Tryon St, then just w. Int corridors. **Pets:** Small. $20 daily fee/pet. Designated rooms, service with restrictions, crate.

Staybridge Suites-Arrowood H
(704) 527-6767. **Call for rates.** 7924 Forest Pine Dr. I-77, exit 3 southbound; exit 2 northbound, just e, then just s. Int corridors. **Pets:** Large, other species. $100 one-time fee/room. Service with restrictions.

StudioPLUS-Tyvola H
(704) 527-1960. **$83-$93.** 5830 Westpark Dr. I-77, exit 5 (Tyvola Rd), just e, then 0.4 mi s. Int corridors. **Pets:** Other species. $25 daily fee/pet. Service with restrictions, crate.

TownePlace Suites by Marriott-Arrowood H
(704) 227-1040. **$133-$143.** 7805 Forest Point Blvd. I-77, exit 3 southbound; exit 2 northbound, just e. Int corridors. **Pets:** Other species. $75 one-time fee/room. Service with restrictions, supervision.

TownePlace Suites by Marriott–University H
(704) 548-0388. **$195-$205.** 8710 Research Dr. I-85, exit 45B, just w on SR 24, then just n. Int corridors. **Pets:** Accepted.

The Westin Charlotte H ❀
(704) 375-2600. **$119-$379.** 601 S College St. I-277, exit College St, just n; jct E Stonewall St. Int corridors. **Pets:** Medium, dogs only. Designated rooms, service with restrictions, crate.

CONCORD

Americas Best Value Inn M
(704) 788-8550. **$135, 3 day notice.** 2451 Kannapolis Hwy. I-85, exit 58, just s on US 29, then just w. Ext corridors. **Pets:** Small, dogs only. $25 one-time fee/pet. Designated rooms, service with restrictions, supervision.

Sleep Inn H
(704) 788-2150. **$70-$230.** 1120 Copperfield Blvd. I-85, exit 60, just e. Int corridors. **Pets:** Accepted.

CORNELIUS

Clarion Inn–Lake Norman H ❀
(704) 896-0660. **$80-$150.** 19608 Liverpool Pkwy. I-77, exit 28, just w, then s. Int corridors. **Pets:** Large, other species. $25 one-time fee/room. Designated rooms, service with restrictions, supervision.
SAVE ✕ 📶 🖵 ☞

Days Inn-Lake Norman H
(704) 892-9120. **$65-$139.** 19901 Holiday Ln. I-77, exit 28, just e, then just n. Ext corridors. **Pets:** Accepted.
ASK ✕ ⚕ 📶 🖵 🍴 ☞

Econo Lodge Lake Norman M
(704) 892-3500. **$69-$180.** 20740 Torrence Chapel Rd. I-77, exit 28, just w, then just n. Ext corridors. **Pets:** Other species. $15 daily fee/pet. Designated rooms, service with restrictions, supervision.
ASK ✕ 📶 🖵 ☞

HUNTERSVILLE

Candlewood Suites H
(704) 895-3434. **$110-$170.** 16530 Northcross Dr. I-77, exit 25, just w on SR 73, then just s. Int corridors. **Pets:** Medium. $75 one-time fee/pet. Service with restrictions, supervision.
ASK ✕ 📶 🖵

END METROPOLITAN AREA

CHEROKEE

Best Western Great Smokies Inn M
(828) 497-2020. **$49-$149.** 1636 Acquoni Rd. US 441 N, 2.5 mi n; downtown. Ext corridors. **Pets:** Accepted.
SAVE ✕ 📶 🖵 🍴 ☞

Holiday Inn M
(828) 497-9181. **$49-$169.** 37 Tsalagi Rd. 0.8 mi w on US 19 S. Ext corridors. **Pets:** Accepted.
SAVE ✕ 📶 🖵 🍴 ☞ ✕

Microtel Inn & Suites H ❀
(828) 497-7800. **Call for rates.** 674 Casino Tr. Jct US 441 and Business Rt US 441 S. Int corridors. **Pets:** Other species. $15 daily fee/room. Designated rooms, service with restrictions, crate.
SAVE ✕ ⚕ 📶 🖵 ☞

Pioneer Motel M
(828) 497-2435. **$48-$80, 3 day notice.** 122 Tsalagi Rd. 0.8 mi w on US 19 S. Ext corridors. **Pets:** Small, dogs only. $25 one-time fee/room. Designated rooms, service with restrictions.
SAVE ✕ ⚕ 📶 🖵 ☞ ✕

Two Rivers Lodge M ❀
(828) 488-2284. **$35-$120, 4 day notice.** 5280 Ela Rd. 5 mi e on US 19 S. Ext corridors. **Pets:** Large, dogs only. $15 one-time fee/room. Designated rooms, service with restrictions.
ASK ✕ 📶 🖵 ☞

CHIMNEY ROCK

Mountain Village Chalets CA
(828) 625-9783. **$67-$336, 14 day notice.** 950 Main St. 1 mi w on US 74A. Ext corridors. **Pets:** $50 one-time fee/pet. No service, supervision.
SAVE 📶 🖵 ✎

CLAREMONT

Super 8 Motel M
(828) 459-7777. **$66-$85.** 3054 N Oxford St. I-40, exit 135, just s. Ext/int corridors. **Pets:** Small, dogs only. $10 daily fee/pet. Service with restrictions, supervision.
SAVE ✕ 📶 🖵 ☞

CLAYTON

Sleep Inn H
(919) 772-7771. **Call for rates.** 105 Commerce Pkwy. I-40, exit 312, just w on SR 42, then just s. Int corridors. **Pets:** Accepted.
✕ ⚕ 📶 🖵 ☞

Super 8 H
(919) 661-1991. **$60-$70.** 101 Leone Ct. I-40, exit 312, just e on SR 42, then just s. Ext corridors. **Pets:** Medium. $5 daily fee/pet. Service with restrictions, supervision.
ASK ✕ 📶 🖵 ☞

CLEMMONS

The Village Inn Golf & Conference Center H
(336) 766-9121. **$68-$79, 3 day notice.** 6205 Ramada Dr. I-40, exit 184, just s, then just e. Int corridors. **Pets:** Accepted.
ASK ✕ 📶 🖵 🍴 ☞

COLUMBUS

Days Inn M
(828) 894-3303. **Call for rates.** 626 W Mills St. I-26, exit 67, just w on SR 108. Ext corridors. **Pets:** Accepted.
SAVE ✕ 📶 🖵 ☞

CONOVER

Days Inn M
(828) 465-2378. **$62-$140, 5 day notice.** 1710 Fairgrove Church Rd SE. I-40, exit 128, just s. Ext corridors. **Pets:** Medium, dogs only. $15 daily fee/pet. Designated rooms, service with restrictions, supervision.
SAVE ✕ ⚕ 📶 🖵 ☞

DUNN

Jameson Inn M
(910) 891-5758. **$83-$90.** 901 Jackson Rd. I-95, exit 73, just w, then just s. Ext corridors. **Pets:** Accepted.
ASK ✕ ⚕ 📶 🖵 ☞

Quality Inn H
(704) 892-6597. **$60-$169, 14 day notice.** 16825 Caldwell Creek Dr. I-77, exit 25, just e on SR 73, just n on US 21, then just w. Ext/int corridors. **Pets:** Medium, other species. $25 one-time fee/room. Designated rooms, service with restrictions, crate.
ASK ✕ 📶 🖵

Residence Inn by Marriott-Lake Norman H
(704) 584-0000. **$217-$233.** 16830 Kenton Dr. I-77, exit 25, 1 mi w on SR 73, then just n. Int corridors. **Pets:** Accepted.
✕ ⚕ 📶 🖵 ☞ ✕

MATTHEWS

Country Inn & Suites-Matthews H ❀
(704) 846-8000. **$99-$119.** 2001 Mount Harmony Church Rd. I-485, exit 51B, 0.5 mi e on US 74, just n on Independence Commerce Dr, then just w. Int corridors. **Pets:** $10 daily fee/room.
SAVE ✕ ⚕ 📶 🖵 ☞

DURHAM

Americas Best Value Carolina Duke Inn M
(919) 286-0771. **$55-$60.** 2517 Guess Rd. I-85, exit 175, just e. Ext corridors. **Pets:** Accepted.
[SAVE] [X] [🔧] [💻] [🏊]

Candlewood Suites H
(919) 484-9922. **Call for rates.** 1818 E NC Hwy 54. I-40, exit 278, just s, then just w. Int corridors. **Pets:** Accepted.
[X] [♿] [🔧] [💻]

Comfort Inn Medical Park H
(919) 471-6100. **$99-$139.** 1816 Hillandale Rd. I-85, exit 174, just w. Int corridors. **Pets:** Medium. $40 one-time fee/room. Service with restrictions, supervision.
[SAVE] [X] [🔧] [💻] [🏊] [X]

Durham Skyland Inn, a Magnuson Hotel M ❀
(919) 383-2508. **$59-$99.** 5400 US 70 W. I-85, exit 170, 0.3 mi e on US 70, then just n. Ext corridors. **Pets:** Other species. $15 daily fee/pet. Service with restrictions.
[ASK] [X] [🔧] [💻] [🏊]

Extended Stay Deluxe-Durham-RTP-Miami Blvd North H
(919) 941-2878. **$105-$115.** 4610 S Miami Blvd. I-40, exit 281, just n. Int corridors. **Pets:** Other species. $25 daily fee/pet. Service with restrictions, crate.
[ASK] [X] [🔧] [💻] [🏊]

Extended Stay Deluxe-RTP-Miami Blvd-South H
(919) 998-0400. **$110-$120.** 4919 S Miami Blvd. I-40, exit 281, just s. Int corridors. **Pets:** Other species. $25 daily fee/pet. Service with restrictions, crate.
[ASK] [X] [♿] [🔧] [💻] [🏊]

Four Points by Sheraton H ❀
(919) 806-8200. **Call for rates.** 7807 Leonardo Dr. I-40, exit 274, just s on SR 751. Int corridors. **Pets:** Large, other species. $50 one-time fee/room. Designated rooms.
[SAVE] [X] [🔧] [💻] [🍴] [🏊]

Holiday Inn Express H
(919) 313-3244. **$105-$114, 3 day notice.** 2516 Guess Rd. I-85, exit 175, just e. Int corridors. **Pets:** Small, other species. $10 daily fee/pet. Designated rooms, service with restrictions, crate.
[ASK] [X] [🔧] [💻] [🏊]

Holiday Inn Express Hotel & Suites-RTP H
(919) 474-9800. **$144-$154, 3 day notice.** 4912 S Miami Blvd. I-40, exit 281, just s. Int corridors. **Pets:** Accepted.
[ASK] [X] [♿] [🔧] [💻]

Homestead Studio Suites Hotel-Durham/University H
(919) 402-1700. **$77-$87.** 1920 Ivy Creek Blvd. I-40, exit 270, 2 mi n on US 15/501, exit 105B, then just e on Martin Luther King Jr Pkwy; in University Place. Ext corridors. **Pets:** Other species. $25 daily fee/pet. Service with restrictions, crate.
[ASK] [X] [🔧] [💻]

La Quinta Inn & Suites Raleigh (Durham-Chapel Hill) H ❀
(919) 401-9660. **$65-$129.** 4414 Durham Chapel Hill Blvd. I-40, exit 270, 1.7 mi n on US 15/501. Int corridors. **Pets:** Medium, other species. Service with restrictions, supervision.
[ASK] [X] [♿] [🔧] [💻] [🏊]

La Quinta Inn & Suites Raleigh (Research Triangle Park) H ❀
(919) 484-1422. **$59-$139.** 1910 W Park Dr. I-40, exit 278, just n on SR 55, then just e. Int corridors. **Pets:** Medium, other species. Service with restrictions, supervision.
[ASK] [X] [♿] [🔧] [💻] [🏊]

Quality Inn & Suites H ❀
(919) 382-3388. **$72-$77.** 3710 Hillsborough Rd. I-85, exit 173, just e on Cole Mill Rd, then just w on US 70 business route. Ext/int corridors. **Pets:** Large. $25 one-time fee/room. Designated rooms, service with restrictions, supervision.
[SAVE] [X] [🔧] [💻] [🏊]

Residence Inn by Marriott H
(919) 361-1266. **$197-$211.** 201 Residence Inn Blvd. I-40, exit 278, just s, then just w. Ext/int corridors. **Pets:** Other species. $75 one-time fee/room. Service with restrictions.
[SAVE] [X] [♿] [🔧] [💻] [🏊] [X]

Sleep Inn-RDU/RTP H
(919) 993-3393. **$79-$149.** 5208 Page Rd. I-40, exit 282, just s. Int corridors. **Pets:** Accepted.
[ASK] [X] [♿] [🔧] [💻]

Staybridge Suites of Durham H
(919) 401-9800. **$149-$299.** 3704 Mt. Moriah Rd. I-40, exit 270, just n on US 15/501, then just e. Int corridors. **Pets:** Accepted.
[ASK] [X] [♿] [🔧] [💻] [🏊]

StudioPLUS-Research Triangle Park H
(919) 361-1853. **$86-$96.** 2504 NC Hwy 54. I-40, exit 278, just s on SR 55, then just e. Int corridors. **Pets:** Other species. $25 daily fee/pet. Service with restrictions, crate.
[ASK] [X] [🔧] [💻] [🏊]

Wyndham Hotel-Research Triangle Park H
(919) 941-6066. **Call for rates.** 4620 S Miami Blvd. I-40, exit 281, just n. Int corridors. **Pets:** Accepted.
[X] [🔧] [💻] [🍴] [🏊]

EDEN

Hampton Inn H
(336) 627-1111. **$99-$111.** 724 S Van Buren Rd. Jct SR 700/770, 1.4 mi s on SR 87/14. Int corridors. **Pets:** Accepted.
[ASK] [X] [🔧] [💻] [🏊]

Jameson Inn M
(336) 627-0472. **$73-$78.** 716 Linden Dr. Jct SR 700/770, 1.4 mi s on SR 87/14, then just e. Ext corridors. **Pets:** $15 daily fee/room. Designated rooms, no service, supervision.
[ASK] [X] [♿] [🔧] [💻] [🏊]

FAYETTEVILLE

Comfort Inn Cross Creek H ❀
(910) 867-1777. **$99-$119.** 1922 Skibo Rd. All American Frwy, exit US 401 Bypass, 0.8 mi s. Int corridors. **Pets:** Medium. $49 one-time fee/room. Service with restrictions, crate.
[SAVE] [X] [🔧] [💻] [🏊]

Comfort Inn-Fayetteville M
(910) 323-8333. **$72-$99.** 1957 Cedar Creek Rd. I-95, exit 49, just w. Ext corridors. **Pets:** $10 one-time fee/pet. Designated rooms, no service, crate.
[ASK] [X] [🔧] [💻] [🏊]

Country Hearth Inn & Suites M ❀
(910) 438-0748. **$60-$90.** 1902 Cedar Creek Rd. I-95, exit 49, just w. Ext corridors. **Pets:** Medium. $10 daily fee/pet. Service with restrictions, crate.
[SAVE] [X] [♿] [🔧] [💻] [🏊]

Econo Lodge I-95 M
(910) 433-2100. **$60-$90.** 1952 Cedar Creek Rd. I-95, exit 49, just w. Ext corridors. **Pets:** Accepted.
[SAVE] [X] [🔧] [🏊]

Extended StayAmerica M
(910) 485-2747. **$99-$109.** 408 Owen Dr. Jct All American Frwy. Ext corridors. **Pets:** Other species. $25 daily fee/pet. Service with restrictions, crate.
[ASK] [X] [🔧] [💻]

◆◆◆ **Extended Stay Deluxe Fayetteville-Cross Creek Mall** 🅗
(910) 868-5662. **$109-$119.** 4105 Sycamore Dairy Rd. All American Frwy, exit Morganton Rd, just e, then just n. Int corridors. **Pets:** Other species. $25 daily fee/pet. Service with restrictions, crate.
(ASK) ⊗ 🖥 💻 ➰

◆◆◆ **Holiday Inn Bordeaux** 🅗 ✿
(910) 323-0111. **$99-$375.** 1707 Owen Dr. Jct I-95 business route/US 301 S, 2.3 mi w. Ext/int corridors. **Pets:** Small, other species. $50 one-time fee/pet. Service with restrictions.
⊗ 🖥 💻 🍽 ➰

◆◆◆◆ **Holiday Inn I-95** 🅗
(910) 323-1600. **$108-$120, 3 day notice.** 1944 Cedar Creek Rd. I-95, exit 49, just w. Ext/int corridors. **Pets:** $25 one-time fee/room. Designated rooms, service with restrictions, supervision.
(SAVE) ⊗ 🖥 💻 🍽 ➰

◆◆ **Innkeeper-Cross Creek** Ⓜ
(910) 867-7659. **$71, 3 day notice.** 1720 Skibo Rd. All American Frwy, exit US 401 Bypass, just s; enter thru Cross Creek Plaza entrance. Ext/int corridors. **Pets:** Accepted.
(ASK) ⊗ 🖥 ➰

◆◆◆◆ **Red Roof Inn** 🅗
(910) 321-1460. **$56-$85.** 1569 Jim Johnson Rd. I-95, exit 49, just w on SR 53, then just n. Int corridors. **Pets:** Medium. Service with restrictions, supervision.
(SAVE) ⊗ ⓛ 🖥 ➰

◆◆◆ **Residence Inn by Marriott-Fayetteville-Cross Creek-Ft. Bragg** 🅗
(910) 868-9005. **$147-$158.** 1468 Skibo Rd. Jct SR 24/87, just s on US 401 Bypass. Int corridors. **Pets:** Medium. $100 one-time fee/pet. Service with restrictions, crate.
⊗ ⓛ 🖥 💻 ➰ ⊗

FLAT ROCK

◆◆◆◆ **Highland Lake Inn** 🅗
(828) 693-6812. **$79-$259, 7 day notice.** 86 Lily Pad Ln. I-26, exit 53, 2.1 mi w. Ext/int corridors. **Pets:** Medium, dogs only. $25 daily fee/pet. Designated rooms, no service.
(ASK) ⊗ 🖥 💻 🍽 ➰ ⊗

FLETCHER

◆◆◆ **Holiday Inn Asheville-Airport** 🅗
(828) 684-1213. **$79-$169.** 550 Airport Rd. I-26, exit 40, just e. Int corridors. **Pets:** Accepted.
(ASK) ⊗ 🖥 💻 🍽 ➰

FOREST CITY

◆◆ **Jameson Inn** Ⓜ
(828) 287-8788. **$78-$85.** 164 Jameson Inn Dr. US 74 Bypass, exit 181, 1.8 mi nw on US 74A. Ext corridors. **Pets:** Accepted.
(ASK) ⊗ ⓛ 🖥 💻 ➰

FRANKLIN

◆ **The Franklin Motel** Ⓜ
(828) 524-4431. **$50-$70.** 17 W Palmer St. Jct US 441 Bypass, 1 mi n on US 441 business route; downtown. Ext corridors. **Pets:** Accepted.
(ASK) ⊗ 🖥 ➰

◆◆ **Microtel Inn & Suites** 🅗 ✿
(828) 349-9000. **$60-$130.** 81 Allman Dr. Jct US 441 Bypass, 0.4 mi s on US 441 and 23. Int corridors. **Pets:** Medium. $20 one-time fee/room. Designated rooms, service with restrictions.
(ASK) ⊗ 🖥 💻

GASTONIA

◆◆ **Knights Inn** Ⓜ
(704) 864-8744. **$49-$59.** 1400 E Franklin Blvd. I-85, exit 20, 0.5 mi s on SR 279, then just w on US 29/74. Ext corridors. **Pets:** Accepted.
(ASK) ⊗ 🖥 💻

GOLDSBORO

◆◆◆ ◆◆◆ **Best Western Goldsboro Inn** Ⓜ
(919) 735-7911. **$62-$180.** 801 US 70 E Bypass. US 70 E Bypass, exit Wayne Memorial Dr eastbound, just n, just w on Eleventh St, then 0.4 mi sw on service road; exit westbound, straight on Eleventh St, then 0.4 mi sw on service road. Ext corridors. **Pets:** Accepted.
(SAVE) ⊗ 🖥 💻 🍽 ➰

◆◆◆ **Comfort Suites** 🅗
(919) 759-0098. **Call for rates.** 2613 N Park Dr. US 70 E Bypass, exit Spence Ave, just n, then just e. Int corridors. **Pets:** Other species. $50 one-time fee/pet. Service with restrictions, crate.
⊗ ⓛ 🖥 💻 ➰

◆◆◆ **Country Inn & Suites by Carlson** 🅗
(919) 581-0503. **Call for rates.** 2302 Norwood Ave. US 70 Bypass, exit Wayne Memorial Dr, just n, just w on Eleventh St, then just sw on Lincoln Mercury Dr. Int corridors. **Pets:** Accepted.
⊗ ⓛ 🖥 💻 ➰

◆◆◆ ◆◆◆ **Hampton Inn** 🅗 🐾
(919) 778-1800. **$91-$111.** 905 N Spence Ave. US 70 E Bypass, exit Spence Ave, just s. Int corridors. **Pets:** Medium. Service with restrictions, supervision.
(SAVE) ⊗ 🖥 💻 ➰

◆◆◆ ◆◆◆ **Holiday Inn Express Goldsboro** 🅗 ✿
(919) 751-1999. **$105-$195.** 909 N Spence Ave. US 70 E Bypass, exit Spence Ave, just s. Int corridors. **Pets:** Other species. $20 one-time fee/room. Service with restrictions, crate.
(SAVE) ⊗ 🖥 💻 ➰

◆◆◆ **Jameson Inn** 🅗
(919) 778-9759. **$83-$90.** 1408 Harding Dr. US 70 E Bypass, exit Spence Ave, just n, then just e on North Park Dr. Int corridors. **Pets:** Accepted.
(ASK) ⊗ ⓛ 🖥 💻 ➰

GREENSBORO

◆◆◆ ◆◆◆ **Best Western Deep River** 🅗
(336) 454-0333. **$84-$189, 7 day notice.** 7800 National Service Rd. I-40, exit 210 (SR 68), just s, just w on Thorndike Rd, then just n. Int corridors. **Pets:** Small. $25 one-time fee/pet. Service with restrictions, supervision.
(SAVE) ⊗ 🖥 ➰

◆◆◆ **Candlewood Suites** 🅗
(336) 454-0078. **$90-$120.** 7623 Thorndike Rd. I-40, exit 210 (SR 68), just s, then just w. Int corridors. **Pets:** Accepted.
(ASK) ⊗ ⓛ 🖥 💻

◆◆◆ **Clarion Hotel-Airport** 🅗
(336) 299-7650. **$86-$115.** 415 Swing Rd. I-40 business route, exit 25, just n, then just w. Int corridors. **Pets:** Accepted.
(ASK) ⊗ 🖥 💻 🍽 ➰

◆◆◆ ◆◆◆ **Comfort Inn** 🅗 ✿
(336) 294-6220. **$68-$84, 7 day notice.** 2001 Veasley St. I-40 business route, exit 29, just s on High Point Rd, then just w. Int corridors. **Pets:** Other species. Service with restrictions, supervision.
(SAVE) ⊗ 🖥 💻 ➰

◆◆◆ **Comfort Suites Airport** 🅗
(336) 882-6666. **$99-$229.** 7619 Thorndike Rd. I-40, exit 210 (SR 68), just s, then just w. Int corridors. **Pets:** Small. $25 one-time fee/room. Designated rooms, crate.
⊗ ⓛ 🖥 💻 ➰

▼▼ ▼▼ **Crestwood Suites** 🄷
(336) 886-1250. **Call for rates.** 501 Americhase Dr. I-40, exit 210 (SR 68), 0.5 mi s. Int corridors. **Pets:** Accepted.

⊠ 🛢 🖵

▼▼▼▼ **Drury Inn & Suites-Greensboro** 🄷
(336) 856-9696. **$80-$145.** 3220 High Point Rd. I-40 business route, exit 29, just s. Int corridors. **Pets:** Other species. Service with restrictions, supervision.

A$K ⊠ 🛢 🖵 ⇌

▼▼ ▼▼ **Econo Lodge Inn & Suites** 🄼
(336) 275-9575. **$49-$159, 14 day notice.** 120 Seneca Rd. I-40/Business 85, exit 37, just s, then e. Ext/int corridors. **Pets:** Accepted.

A$K ⊠ 🛢 🖵

▼▼ ▼▼ **Extended StayAmerica-Greensboro-Wendover Ave** 🄼
(336) 299-0200. **$72-$82.** 4317 Big Tree Way. I-40 business route, exit 26 or 26B, just ne on Wendover Ave, then just w. Ext corridors. **Pets:** Other species. $25 daily fee/pet. Service with restrictions, crate.

A$K ⊠ 🛢 🖵 ⇌

▼▼ ▼▼ **Extended Stay Deluxe** 🄷
(336) 454-0080. **$100-$110.** 7617 Thorndike Rd. I-40, exit 210 (SR 68), just s, then just w. Int corridors. **Pets:** Other species. $25 daily fee/pet. Service with restrictions, crate.

A$K ⊠ 🛢 🖵 ⇌

▼▼▼▼ **Holiday Inn Express** 🄷
(336) 854-0090. **$99, 3 day notice.** 4305 Big Tree Way. I-40 business route, exit 26 or 26B, just ne on Wendover Ave, then just w. Int corridors. **Pets:** $10 daily fee/room. Designated rooms, service with restrictions, supervision.

A$K ⊠ 🔥M 🛢 🖵 ⇌

▼▼▼▼ **La Quinta Inn & Suites Greensboro** 🄷 🐾
(336) 316-0100. **$69-$129.** 1201 Lanada Rd. I-40 business route, exit 26 or 26A, just sw on Wendover Ave, then just e on Stanley Rd. Int corridors. **Pets:** Medium, other species. Service with restrictions, supervision.

A$K ⊠ 🔥M 🛢 🖵 ⇌

🅰🅰🅰 ▼▼▼▼ **Red Roof Inn Airport** 🄼
(336) 271-2636. **$50-$106.** 615 Regional Rd S. I-40, exit 210 (SR 68), just s, then just e. Ext corridors. **Pets:** Accepted.

SAVE ⊠ 🔥M 🛢 🖵

▼▼▼▼ **Residence Inn by Marriott-Greensboro Airport** 🄷
(336) 632-4666. **$147-$158.** 7616 Thorndike Rd. I-40, exit 210, just s on SR 68, then just w. Int corridors. **Pets:** Medium. $100 one-time fee/pet. Designated rooms, service with restrictions, supervision.

⊠ 🔥M 🛢 🖵 ⇌ ⊠

GREENVILLE

▼▼ ▼▼ **Baymont Inn & Suites** 🄷 🐾
(252) 355-2521. **$69-$109.** 3439 S Memorial Dr. Jct US 264 alternate route, just s on SR 11/903. Ext corridors. **Pets:** Medium, other species. $50 deposit/pet, $10 daily fee/pet. Designated rooms, service with restrictions, supervision.

A$K ⊠ 🛢 🖵 ⇌

▼▼ ▼▼ **Home-Towne Suites** 🄷
(252) 752-3411. **$59-$130.** 2111 W Arlington Blvd. Jct US 13/SR 11, 0.4 mi w on Stantonsburg Rd, then just s. Int corridors. **Pets:** Accepted.

A$K ⊠ 🛢 🛢

▼▼ ▼▼ **Jameson Inn** 🄼
(252) 752-7382. **$73-$78.** 920 Crosswinds St. Jct US 264 alternate route, just s on US 13/SR 11, then just w. Ext corridors. **Pets:** Accepted.

A$K ⊠ 🔥M 🛢 🖵 ⇌

HAYESVILLE

🅰🅰🅰 ▼▼▼▼ **Deerfield Inn** 🄼
(828) 389-8272. **$60-$100.** 40 Chatuge Ln. 3 mi e on US 64. Ext corridors. **Pets:** Medium. $10 daily fee/pet. Designated rooms, service with restrictions, supervision.

SAVE ⊠ 🔥M 🛢 🖵

HENDERSON

▼▼▼▼ **Econo Lodge** 🄼
(252) 438-8511. **$45-$75.** 112 Parham Rd. I-85, exit 215, just e on US 158. Ext corridors. **Pets:** Medium. $12 daily fee/pet. Service with restrictions.

A$K ⊠ 🛢 🖵 ⇌

▼▼▼▼ **Jameson Inn** 🄷
(252) 430-0247. **$78-$85.** 400 N Cooper Dr. I-85, exit 212, just w on Ruin Creek Rd, then just n. Int corridors. **Pets:** Accepted.

A$K ⊠ 🔥M 🛢 🖵 ⇌

▼▼▼▼ **Lamplight Inn B&B** 🄱🄱 🐾
(252) 438-6311. **$90-$120, 7 day notice.** 1680 Flemingtown Rd. I-85, exit 220, 1.5 mi nw. Int corridors. **Pets:** Medium, dogs only. Service with restrictions, supervision.

⊠ 🕿

🅰🅰🅰 ▼▼▼▼ **Sleep Inn** 🄷
(252) 433-9449. **$59-$85.** 18 Market St. I-85, exit 212, just w on Ruin Creek Rd, then just se on Zeb Robinson Rd. Int corridors. **Pets:** Small, other species. $15 daily fee/pet. Designated rooms, service with restrictions, supervision.

SAVE ⊠ 🛢 🖵

HENDERSONVILLE

🅰🅰🅰 ▼▼▼▼ **Best Western Hendersonville Inn** 🄼
(828) 692-0521. **$45-$160.** 105 Sugarloaf Rd. I-26, exit 49A, just e. Ext corridors. **Pets:** Small, other species. $10 daily fee/pet. Service with restrictions.

SAVE ⊠ 🛢 🖵 🍴 ⇌

🅰🅰🅰 ▼▼▼▼ **Comfort Inn** 🄷
(828) 693-8800. **$55-$149.** 206 Mitchell Dr. I-26, exit 49B, just w. Ext corridors. **Pets:** Large, other species. $15 daily fee/pet. Service with restrictions, supervision.

SAVE ⊠ 🛢 🖵 ⇌

HICKORY

▼▼▼▼ **Jameson Inn** 🄼
(828) 304-0410. **$78-$85.** 1120 13th Ave Dr SE. I-40, exit 125, just s, then 0.4 mi w. Ext corridors. **Pets:** Accepted.

A$K ⊠ 🔥M 🛢 🖵 ⇌

🅰🅰🅰 ▼▼ **Red Roof Inn Hickory** 🄼
(828) 323-1500. **$50-$80, 14 day notice.** 1184 Lenoir Rhyne Blvd. I-40, exit 125, just n. Ext corridors. **Pets:** Other species. Service with restrictions, supervision.

SAVE ⊠ 🛢

HIGHLANDS

🅰🅰🅰 ▼▼▼▼ **Mountain High Lodge** 🄼
(828) 526-2790. **$49-$189, 7 day notice.** 200 Main St. Just w on US 64; downtown. Ext corridors. **Pets:** Other species. Designated rooms, service with restrictions, supervision.

SAVE ⊠ 🔥M 🛢 🖵

HILLSBOROUGH

🅰🅰🅰 ▼▼▼▼ **Holiday Inn Express** 🄷
(919) 644-7997. **$95-$230.** 202 Cardinal Dr. I-85, exit 164, just e, then just s. Int corridors. **Pets:** Accepted.

SAVE ⊠ 🔥M 🛢 🖵 ⇌

JACKSONVILLE

Americas Best Value Inn 🅷
(910) 455-6888. **$70-$90.** 2149 N Marine Blvd. Jct Western Blvd, just n on US 17. Int corridors. **Pets:** Accepted.
SAVE ⊠ 🗐 📧 ⊅

Extended StayAmerica 🅷
(910) 347-7684. **$99-$169.** 20 McDaniel Dr. Jct Western Blvd, just n on US 17, then just w. Int corridors. **Pets:** Other species. $25 daily fee/pet. Service with restrictions, crate.
ASK ⊠ ♿ 🗐 📧

Hampton Inn 🅷
(910) 347-6500. **$79-$129.** 474 Western Blvd. Jct US 17, just n. Ext corridors. **Pets:** Small. Service with restrictions, crate.
SAVE ⊠ 🗐 📧 ⊅

Innkeeper 🅷
(910) 938-0800. **$80, 3 day notice.** 2139 N Marine Blvd. Jct Western Blvd, just n on US 17. Int corridors. **Pets:** Small, dogs only. $10 daily fee/pet. Service with restrictions, supervision.
ASK ⊠ 🗐 ⊅

JONESVILLE

Comfort Inn 🅼 ❖
(336) 835-9400. **$79-$150.** 1633 Winston Rd. I-77, exit 82, just w. Ext corridors. **Pets:** Medium. $10 one-time fee/pet. Service with restrictions, supervision.
SAVE ⊠ ♿ 🗐 📧 ⊅

Days Inn Jonesville-Elkin 🅼
(336) 526-6777. **$69-$109.** 1540 NC 67 Hwy. I-77, exit 82, 0.3 mi w. Ext corridors. **Pets:** Small, other species. $10 daily fee/pet. Designated rooms, no service, supervision.
SAVE ⊠ 🗐 📧 ⊅

Holiday Inn Express 🅷
(336) 835-6000. **$79-$99.** 1713 NC 67 Hwy. I-77, exit 82, just e. Int corridors. **Pets:** Small. $10 daily fee/pet. Designated rooms, service with restrictions, supervision.
ASK ⊠ ♿ 🗐 📧 ⊅

KENLY

Super 8 🅼
(919) 284-3800. **Call for rates.** 843 Johnston Pkwy. I-95, exit 106, just w, then just s. Ext corridors. **Pets:** Accepted.
⊠ ♿ ⊅

LAURINBURG

Jameson Inn 🅼
(910) 277-0080. **$73-$78.** 14 Jameson Inn Ct. Jct US 74 Bypass, just n on US 15/401 Bypass, just e. Ext corridors. **Pets:** Medium. $15 daily fee/pet. Service with restrictions, supervision.
ASK ⊠ 🗐 📧 ⊅

LENOIR

Days Inn 🅷
(828) 754-0731. **Call for rates.** 206 Blowing Rock Blvd. Jct US 321, just n of SR 18. Ext corridors. **Pets:** Accepted.
⊠ 🗐 📧

LEXINGTON

Comfort Suites of Lexington 🅷
(336) 357-2333. **Call for rates.** 1620 Cotton Grove Rd. I-85, exit 91, just s on SR 8, then just ne. Ext/int corridors. **Pets:** Accepted.
⊠ ♿ 🗐 📧 ⊅

Econo Lodge 🅼
(336) 249-0111. **$75-$125.** 418 Piedmont Dr. I-85, exit 96, 3.9 mi w on US 64. Ext corridors. **Pets:** Accepted.
SAVE ⊠ 🗐 📧 ⊅

LINCOLNTON

Days Inn 🅼
(704) 735-8271. **$50-$80.** 614 Clark Dr. US 321, exit 24, 1 mi w on SR 150, then just s on US 321 business route. Ext corridors. **Pets:** Other species. $10 daily fee/room. No service, supervision.
ASK ⊠ 🗐 📧 ⊅

LUMBERTON

Best Western Inn 🅼
(910) 618-9799. **$79-$149.** 201 Jackson Ct. I-95, exit 22, just e, then just s. Ext corridors. **Pets:** Medium. $10 daily fee/pet. Service with restrictions, supervision.
SAVE ⊠ 🗐 📧 ⊅

Quality Inn and Suites 🅷
(910) 738-8261. **$60-$99.** 3608 Kahn Dr. I-95, exit 20, just e, then just n. Ext/int corridors. **Pets:** Accepted.
SAVE ⊠ 🗐 📧 🍴 ⊅

MOCKSVILLE

Comfort Inn & Suites 🅷 ❖
(336) 751-5966. **$46-$200.** 629 Madison Rd. I-40, exit 170, just s on US 601, then just w. Int corridors. **Pets:** Small. $20 one-time fee/room. Service with restrictions, crate.
SAVE ⊠ ♿ 🗐 📧 ⊅

Quality Inn 🅷 ❖
(336) 751-7310. **$64-$80.** 1500 Yadkinville Rd. I-40, exit 170, just s on US 601. Ext corridors. **Pets:** $25 one-time fee/pet. Service with restrictions, supervision.
ASK ⊠ 🗐 📧 ⊅

MOREHEAD CITY

Holiday Inn Express Hotel & Suites 🅷
(252) 247-5001. **Call for rates.** 5063 Executive Dr. Jct US 70 and SR 24. Int corridors. **Pets:** Accepted.
⊠ 🗐 📧 ⊅

MORGANTON

Comfort Inn & Suites 🅷
(828) 430-4000. **$79-$169.** 1273 Burkemont Ave. I-40, exit 103, just s. Int corridors. **Pets:** Medium. $25 one-time fee/pet. Designated rooms, service with restrictions, supervision.
SAVE ⊠ ♿ 🗐 📧 ⊅

Holiday Inn-Morganton 🅷
(828) 437-0171. **$75-$89.** 2400 S Sterling St. I-40, exit 105 (SR 18), just s. Ext corridors. **Pets:** $25 one-time fee/room. Service with restrictions, supervision.
ASK ⊠ ♿ 🗐 📧 🍴 ⊅

Sleep Inn 🅷
(828) 433-9000. **Call for rates.** 2400A S Sterling St. I-40, exit 105 (SR 18), just s. Int corridors. **Pets:** Accepted.
⊠ 🗐 📧

MORRISVILLE

Extended StayAmerica-RDU Airport 🅼
(919) 380-1499. **$100-$110.** 2700 Slater Rd. I-40, exit 284 or 284A, 0.4 mi s on Airport Blvd, then just w. Ext corridors. **Pets:** Other species. $25 daily fee/pet. Service with restrictions, crate.
ASK ⊠ 🗐 📧

▼▼▼▼ Holiday Inn Express H
(919) 653-2260. **$124-$144, 3 day notice.** 1014 Airport Blvd. I-40, exit 284 or 284A, just s. Int corridors. **Pets:** Accepted.
ASK ✕ ♿ 🛏 💻 ⇝

▼▼▼▼ Holiday Inn–Raleigh-Durham Airport H
(919) 465-1910. **Call for rates.** 930 Airport Blvd. I-40, exit 284 or 284A, just s. Int corridors. **Pets:** Small. $10 one-time fee/pet. Service with restrictions, supervision.
✕ ♿ 🛏 💻 🍴 ⇝

▼▼▼▼ La Quinta Inn & Suites–Aerial Center Pkwy H ❖
(919) 481-3600. **$69-$129.** 1001 Aerial Center Pkwy. I-40, exit 284 or 284A, just s, then just e. Int corridors. **Pets:** Medium, other species. Service with restrictions, supervision.
ASK ✕ ♿ 🛏 💻 ⇝

▼▼▼▼ La Quinta Inn & Suites (Raleigh-Durham Int'l Airport) H ❖
(919) 461-1771. **$69-$149.** 1001 Hospitality Ct. I-40, exit 284 or 284A, just s, just e on Aerial Center Pkwy, then just ne; in Aerial Center Park. Int corridors. **Pets:** Medium, other species. Service with restrictions, supervision.
ASK ✕ ♿ 🛏 💻 ⇝

▼▼▼▼ Staybridge Suites Raleigh Durham Airport H
(919) 468-0180. **$159-$169, 3 day notice.** 1012 Airport Blvd. I-40, exit 284 or 284A, just s; enter between Hampton Inn and Holiday Inn Express. Int corridors. **Pets:** Accepted.
ASK ✕ ♿ 🛏 💻 ✕

MOUNT AIRY

▼▼▼ Quality Inn M
(336) 789-2000. **$69-$140.** 2136 Rockford St. Jct US 52, 0.6 mi s on US 601. Ext corridors. **Pets:** Medium, other species. $25 one-time fee/pet. Designated rooms, service with restrictions, supervision.
ASK ✕ 🛏 💻 ⇝

MURPHY

◆◆◆ ▼▼▼ Best Western of Murphy H ❖
(828) 837-3060. **$65-$119, 5 day notice.** 1522 Andrews Rd. US 74, 19 and SR 129, exit Andrews Rd. Ext corridors. **Pets:** Medium. Designated rooms.
SAVE ✕ 🛏 💻 ⇝

◆◆◆ ▼▼▼ Days Inn M
(828) 837-8030. **$59-$99.** 754 Hwy 64 W. US 64 W/19 S/74 W and 129 S. Ext corridors. **Pets:** Accepted.
SAVE ✕ 🛏 💻 ⇝

ORIENTAL

▼▼▼ Oriental Marina & Inn M
(252) 249-1818. **$89-$174.** 103 Wall St. Jct SR 55 (Broad St), just ne on Hodges St. Ext corridors. **Pets:** Other species. $50 one-time fee/room. Service with restrictions, supervision.
✕ 🛏 💻 🍴 ⇝

OUTER BANKS AREA

KILL DEVIL HILLS

▼▼▼▼ Clarion Oceanfront Hotel-Nags Head Beach H
(252) 441-6333. **$59-$249.** 1601 S Virginia Dare Tr. SR 12, at MM 9.5. Int corridors. **Pets:** Accepted.
ASK ✕ 🛏 💻 🍴 ⇝ ✕

▼▼▼ Quality Inn-John Yancey M
(252) 441-7141. **Call for rates.** 2009 S Virginia Dare Tr. SR 12, at MM 10.3. Ext/int corridors. **Pets:** Accepted.
✕ 🛏 💻 ⇝

▼▼▼ Ramada Plaza Nags Head Beach H ❖
(252) 441-2151. **$79-$259, 3 day notice.** 1701 S Virginia Dare Tr. SR 12, at MM 9.5. Int corridors. **Pets:** Other species. $20 daily fee/pet. Designated rooms, service with restrictions.
ASK ✕ 🛏 💻 🍴 ⇝ ✕

◆◆◆ ▼▼▼ Travelodge-Nags Head Beach H ❖
(252) 441-0411. **$39-$189, 3 day notice.** 804 N Virginia Dare Tr. SR 12, at MM 8.1. Ext/int corridors. **Pets:** Other species. Designated rooms, service with restrictions, crate.
SAVE ✕ 🛏 💻 ⇝

NAGS HEAD

▼▼▼ Comfort Inn Oceanfront South H ❖
(252) 441-6315. **Call for rates.** 8031 Old Oregon Inlet Rd. SR 12, at MM 17. Int corridors. **Pets:** $20 daily fee/room. Supervision.
✕ 🛏 💻 ⇝

OCRACOKE

◆◆◆ ▼▼▼ The Anchorage Inn M
(252) 928-1101. **$99-$299, 3 day notice.** 205 Irvin Garrish Hwy (SR 12). From Cedar Island Ferry, just n. Ext corridors. **Pets:** Other species. $25 daily fee/room. Designated rooms, service with restrictions, supervision.
SAVE ✕ 🛏 💻 ⇝ ✕

END AREA

PINEHURST

◆◆◆ ▼▼▼▼ Homewood Suites by Hilton H
(910) 255-0300. **$159.** 250 Central Park Ave. Jct SR 5 and 211; in Olmsted Village. Int corridors. **Pets:** Accepted.

SAVE ✕ ♿ 🛏 💻 ⇝

PINE KNOLL SHORES

▼▼▼ AmeriSuites Atlantic Beach H
(252) 247-5118. **$89-$279, 3 day notice.** 118 Salter Path Rd. SR 58, at MM 5. Int corridors. **Pets:** Accepted.
ASK ✕ ♿ 🛏 💻 ⇝

PLYMOUTH

▼▼▼▼ Holiday Inn Express 🅷
(252) 793-4700. **$90-$170.** 840 US Hwy 64 W. Jct SR 32 S, 1 mi w. Ext/int corridors. **Pets:** $25 one-time fee/pet. Designated rooms, service with restrictions, supervision.
A$K ☒ Ꮚᴹ 🛏 💻 ⊇

∰ ▼▼▼ Port-o Plymouth Inn 🅼
(252) 793-5006. **$50-$100.** 510 Hwy 64 E. On US 64. Ext corridors. **Pets:** Accepted.
SAVE ☒ 🛏 ⊇

RALEIGH

∰ ▼▼▼▼ Best Western Raleigh North 🅷
(919) 872-5000. **$65-$90.** 2715 Capital Blvd. I-440, exit 11 or 11B, just n on US 1. Int corridors. **Pets:** Accepted.
SAVE ☒ 🛏 💻 ⊇

▼▼▼▼ Candlewood Suites-Crabtree 🅷
(919) 789-4840. **$109.** 4433 Lead Mine Rd. I-440, exit 7 or 7B, just w, then just n. Int corridors. **Pets:** Accepted.
A$K ☒ Ꮚᴹ 🛏 💻

∰ ▼▼▼▼ Comfort Suites 🅷
(919) 876-2211. **$95-$150.** 4400 Capital Blvd. I-440, exit 11 and 11B, 2.5 mi n on US 1. Int corridors. **Pets:** Medium, other species. $10 daily fee/pet, $25 one-time fee/room. Designated rooms, service with restrictions, crate.
SAVE ☒ Ꮚᴹ 🛏 💻 ⊇

▼▼▼ Days Inn 🅼
(919) 878-9310. **$46-$69.** 3201 Wake Forest Rd. I-440, exit 10 (Wake Forest Rd), just n, then just w. Ext corridors. **Pets:** Accepted.
A$K ☒ 🛏 💻 ⊇

▼▼▼ Extended StayAmerica-North Raleigh 🅷
(919) 829-7271. **$76-$86.** 911 Wake Towne Dr. I-440, exit 10 (Wake Forest Rd), just s, then w. Int corridors. **Pets:** Other species. $25 daily fee/pet. Service with restrictions, crate.
A$K ☒ 🛏 💻

∰ ▼▼▼▼ Fairfield Inn & Suites by Marriott-Crabtree
(919) 881-9800. **$157-$169.** 2201 Summit Park Ln. I-440, exit 7 or 7B, just w on US 70, just s on Blue Ridge Rd, then just e. Int corridors. **Pets:** Accepted.
SAVE ☒ Ꮚᴹ 🛏 💻 ⊇

▼▼▼▼ Holiday Inn Crabtree Valley 🅷
(919) 782-8600. **Call for rates.** 4100 Glenwood Ave. I-440, exit 7 or 7B, just w on US 70. Int corridors. **Pets:** Accepted.
☒ Ꮚᴹ 🛏 💻 🍽 ⊇ ⌧

∰ ▼▼▼▼ Holiday Inn Raleigh-North 🅷
(919) 872-3500. **$120-$139.** 2805 Highwoods Blvd. I-440, exit 11 or 11B, just n on US 1, then just w. Int corridors. **Pets:** Accepted.
SAVE ☒ Ꮚᴹ 🛏 💻 🍽 ⊇ ⌧

▼▼▼▼ Homestead Studio Suites Hotel-Raleigh/Crabtree Valley 🅷
(919) 510-8551. **$76-$86.** 4810 Bluestone Dr. I-440, exit 7 or 7B, 1.6 mi w on US 70, then just s. Ext corridors. **Pets:** Other species. $25 daily fee/pet. Service with restrictions, crate.
A$K ☒ 🛏 💻

▼▼▼▼ Homestead Studio Suites Hotel-Raleigh/Northeast 🅷
(919) 807-9970. **$82-$92.** 2601 Appliance Ct. I-440, exit 11 or 11B, just n on US 1, then just e. Int corridors. **Pets:** Other species. $25 daily fee/pet. Service with restrictions, crate.
A$K ☒ 🛏 💻 ⊇

▼▼▼ Homestead Studio Suites Hotel-Raleigh/North Raleigh 🅼
(919) 981-7353. **$76-$86.** 3531 Wake Forest Rd. I-440, exit 10 (Wake Forest Rd), 0.5 mi n. Ext corridors. **Pets:** Other species. $25 daily fee/pet. Service with restrictions, crate.
A$K ☒ Ꮚᴹ 🛏 💻

▼▼▼▼ La Quinta Inn & Suites Raleigh (Crabtree) 🅷 ✿
(919) 785-0071. **$69-$149.** 2211 Summit Park Ln. I-440, exit 7 or 7B, just w on US 70, just s on Blue Ridge Rd, then just e. Int corridors. **Pets:** Medium, other species. Service with restrictions, supervision.
A$K ☒ Ꮚᴹ 🛏 💻 ⊇

▼▼▼ Red Roof Inn-South 🅷
(919) 833-6005. **$60-$75.** 1813 S Saunders St. I-40, exit 298B, just n. Int corridors. **Pets:** Large, other species. Designated rooms, service with restrictions, supervision.
SAVE ☒ Ꮚᴹ 🛏

∰ ▼▼▼▼ Residence Inn by Marriott Crabtree 🅷
(919) 279-3000. **$197-$211.** 2200 Summit Park Ln. I-440, exit 7 or 7B, just w on US 70, just s on Blue Ridge Rd, then just e. Int corridors. **Pets:** Accepted.
SAVE ☒ Ꮚᴹ 🛏 💻 ⊇ ⌧

∰ ▼▼▼ Residence Inn by Marriott-North Raleigh 🅷
(919) 878-6100. **$167-$179.** 1000 Navaho Dr. I-440, exit 10 (Wake Forest Rd), just n, then w. Ext corridors. **Pets:** Medium. $75 one-time fee/room. Service with restrictions, crate.
SAVE ☒ Ꮚᴹ 🛏 💻 ⊇ ⌧

REIDSVILLE

∰ ▼▼▼ Comfort Inn 🅼
(336) 634-1275. **$68-$199.** 2203 Barnes St. US 29, exit 150 (Barnes St), just e. Ext corridors. **Pets:** Small. $15 daily fee/pet. Designated rooms, service with restrictions, supervision.
SAVE ☒ Ꮚᴹ 🛏 💻 ⊇

RESEARCH TRIANGLE PARK

▼▼▼▼ Radisson Hotel in Research Triangle Park 🅷
(919) 549-8631. **$199-$239.** 150 Park Dr. I-40, exit 280, just s, then just w. Int corridors. **Pets:** Accepted.
A$K ☒ 🛏 💻 🍽 ⊇ ⌧

ROANOKE RAPIDS

▼▼▼ Jameson Inn 🅼
(252) 533-0022. **$83-$90.** 101 S Old Farm Rd. I-95, exit 173, 0.5 mi w on US 158, then just s. Ext corridors. **Pets:** Accepted.
A$K ☒ 🛏 ⊇

ROBBINSVILLE

▼▼▼ Microtel Inn & Suites 🅷
(828) 479-6772. **$59-$115.** 111 Rodney Orr Bypass (US 129). Center of downtown. Int corridors. **Pets:** Accepted.
A$K ☒ Ꮚᴹ 🛏 💻

ROCKY MOUNT

∰ ▼▼▼ Best Western Inn I-95 Gold Rock 🅼
(252) 985-1450. **$65-$95.** 7095 NC 4. I-95, exit 145, just e. Ext corridors. **Pets:** Medium. $20 daily fee/room. Supervision.
SAVE ☒ 🛏 💻 ⊇

∰ ▼▼▼ Best Western–Rocky Mount Inn 🅼
(252) 442-8101. **$60-$80.** 1921 N Wesleyan Blvd. US 64, exit 468A, 2.2 mi n on US 301 Bypass. Ext corridors. **Pets:** Medium, other species. $20 one-time fee/pet. Supervision.
SAVE ☒ 🛏 💻 ⊇

AAA ▼▼◆ Comfort Inn H
(252) 937-7765. **$86-$105.** 200 Gateway Blvd. I-95, exit 138, 1 mi e on US 64, exit Winstead Ave, then just s. Int corridors. **Pets:** Other species. $25 one-time fee/room. Service with restrictions.
SAVE ✕ 🐾 💻 ⇌

▼▼ Motel 6 #2009 H
(252) 984-0907. **$39-$48.** 1370 N Weslyan Blvd. Jct US 64 Bypass, 1.5 mi n on US 301. Int corridors. **Pets:** Other species. Service with restrictions, supervision.
✕ 🐾 ⇌

▼▼ Quality Inn Rocky Mount H
(252) 972-9400. **$59-$79.** 1200 Benvenue Rd. Jct US 301 Bypass, just n on SR 43/48. Ext/int corridors. **Pets:** Accepted.
ASK ✕ Ⓜ 🐾 ⇌

AAA ▼▼▼▼ Residence Inn by Marriott H ❀
(252) 451-5600. **$162-$174.** 230 Gateway Blvd. I-95, exit 138, 1 mi e on US 64, exit Winstead Ave, just s, then just e. Int corridors. **Pets:** Other species. $40 one-time fee/room. Service with restrictions.
SAVE ✕ Ⓜ 🐾 💻 ⇌ ✕

SALISBURY

▼▼◆◆ Hampton Inn H
(704) 637-8000. **$69-$129.** 1001 Klumac Rd. I-85, exit 75, just n on US 601, then just sw. Int corridors. **Pets:** Other species. Designated rooms, service with restrictions, supervision.
✕ 🐾 💻 ⇌

▼▼ Holiday Inn H
(704) 637-3100. **$89-$179, 30 day notice.** 530 Jake Alexander Blvd S. I-85, exit 75, 0.5 mi n on US 601. Ext/int corridors. **Pets:** Medium. $25 one-time fee/pet. Service with restrictions, supervision.
ASK ✕ Ⓜ 🐾 💻 🍴 ⇌ ✕

SALUDA

▼▼ The Oaks Bed & Breakfast BB
(828) 749-2000. **$129-$209, 7 day notice.** 339 Greenville St. I-26, exit 59, 1.1 mi sw, 0.3 mi w on US 176, then cross railway tracks. Ext/int corridors. **Pets:** Accepted.
ASK ✕ 🐾 💻 ☎

SANFORD

▼▼▼ Hampton Inn H
(919) 775-2000. **$93.** 1904 S Horner Blvd. Jct US 1, 3.2 mi s on US 421 and SR 87. Int corridors. **Pets:** Medium, other species. $35 one-time fee/pet. Designated rooms, service with restrictions, crate.
✕ Ⓜ 🐾 💻 ⇌

▼▼ Jameson Inn M ❀
(919) 708-7400. **$83-$90.** 2614 S Horner Blvd. Jct US 1, 4.1 mi s on US 421 and SR 87. Ext corridors. **Pets:** Small, dogs only. $15 daily fee/pet. Designated rooms, service with restrictions, supervision.
ASK ✕ Ⓜ 🐾 💻 ⇌

SCOTLAND NECK

AAA ▼▼▼ Best Western-Scotland Neck Inn M ❀
(252) 826-5141. **$70-$96.** 308 S Main St. Jct SR 125 S, just s on US 258. Int corridors. **Pets:** Other species. $25 daily fee/pet. Designated rooms, service with restrictions, supervision.
SAVE ✕ 🐾 💻 ⇌

SELMA

AAA ▼▼▼ Quality Inn M
(919) 965-5200. **$56-$99.** 1705 Industrial Park Dr. I-95, exit 97, just w, then just s. Ext corridors. **Pets:** Other species. $15 daily fee/room. Designated rooms, service with restrictions, supervision.
SAVE ✕ 🐾 💻 ⇌

SHELBY

AAA ▼▼▼ Super 8 M
(704) 484-2101. **$50-$80.** 1716 E Dixon Blvd. Jct SR 180, 0.4 mi w on US 74 Bypass. Ext corridors. **Pets:** Small. $10 daily fee/pet. Service with restrictions, crate.
SAVE ✕ 🐾 💻

SMITHFIELD

▼▼ Jameson Inn M
(919) 989-5901. **$78-$85.** 125 S Equity Dr. I-95, exit 95, just w, just n on Industrial Park Blvd, then just w. Ext corridors. **Pets:** Accepted.
ASK ✕ Ⓜ 🐾 💻 ⇌

AAA ▼▼▼ Log Cabin Motel M
(919) 934-1534. **$45-$52.** 2491 US 70 E (Business Route). I-95, exit 95, 0.5 mi e. Ext corridors. **Pets:** $10 daily fee/pet. Service with restrictions, crate.
SAVE ✕ 🐾 ⇌

AAA ▼▼▼ Super 8 H
(919) 989-8988. **$75-$120.** 735 Industrial Park Dr. I-95, exit 95, just w, then just n. Int corridors. **Pets:** Medium, other species. $10 daily fee/room. Designated rooms, service with restrictions, supervision.
SAVE ✕ Ⓜ 🐾 💻 ⇌

SOUTHERN PINES

AAA ▼▼◆◆ Best Western Pinehurst Inn H
(910) 692-0640. **$69-$119, 7 day notice.** 1675 US Hwy 1 S. Jct US 15/501, 0.5 mi n on US 1. Ext corridors. **Pets:** Medium, dogs only. $10 daily fee/pet. Service with restrictions, crate.
SAVE ✕ 🐾 💻 ⇌

▼▼ Econo Lodge Inn & Suites H
(910) 692-2063. **$60-$75.** 408 W Morganton Rd. US 1, exit Morganton Rd, just w. Int corridors. **Pets:** Other species. $20 daily fee/pet. Service with restrictions, crate.
ASK ✕ 🐾 💻

▼▼▼ Residence Inn by Marriott H
(910) 693-3400. **$187-$201.** 105 Brucewood Rd. Jct US 1, 1.2 mi n on US 15/501, then just e. Int corridors. **Pets:** Accepted.
✕ 🐾 💻 ⇌ ✕

SOUTHPORT

AAA ▼▼▼◆ Comfort Suites H
(910) 454-7444. **$89-$159.** 4963 Southport Supply Rd (SR 211). Jct SR 87, 1.8 mi n. Int corridors. **Pets:** Accepted.
SAVE ✕ 🐾 💻 ⇌

SPRING LAKE

▼▼ Super 8 Motel H
(910) 436-8588. **Call for rates.** 256 S Main St. Jct SR 210, just se on SR 24/87, just s. Int corridors. **Pets:** Accepted.
✕ 🐾 💻

SPRUCE PINE

AAA ▼▼▼▼ Richmond Inn BB
(828) 765-6993. **$85-$135, 10 day notice.** 51 Pine Ave. Exit off US 19 E and 226 to Oak Ave, just n on Walnut Ave, follow signs; center. Int corridors. **Pets:** $20 one-time fee/pet. Designated rooms, crate.
SAVE ✕ 🐾 💻 ☎

STATESVILLE

AAA ▼▼▼ Best Western Statesville Inn H
(704) 881-0111. **$75-$126.** 1121 Morland Dr. I-77, exit 49A, just e on US 70 E. Ext corridors. **Pets:** Small. $15 daily fee/pet. Designated rooms, service with restrictions, supervision.
SAVE ✕ 🐾 💻 ⇌

▼▼ Econo Lodge Inn & Suites Ⓜ ❀
(704) 872-4101. **$59-$99.** 740 Sullivan Rd. I-40, exit 151, just s. Ext corridors. **Pets:** Medium. $25 one-time fee/pet. Designated rooms, service with restrictions, supervision.

▼▼ Quality Inn & Suites Ⓗ
(704) 878-2721. **$70-$130.** 715 Sullivan Rd. I-40, exit 151, just s. Ext corridors. **Pets:** Medium. $10 one-time fee/pet. Designated rooms, service with restrictions, supervision.

SUNSET BEACH

ⒶⒶⒶ ▼▼▼▼ Sea Trail Golf Resort & Convention Center Ⓒⓞ
(910) 287-1100. **$75-$199, 3 day notice.** 211 Clubhouse Rd. US 17, 2.2 mi e on SR 904, then 1.5 mi s on SR 179. Ext corridors. **Pets:** Accepted.

THOMASVILLE

ⒶⒶⒶ ▼▼ Days Inn Ⓗ
(336) 472-6600. **$50-$70.** 895 Lake Rd. I-85, exit 102, just w, then just s. Int corridors. **Pets:** Small. $25 daily fee/pet. No service, supervision.

▼▼ Microtel Inn & Suites Ⓗ
(336) 474-4515. **$60-$130.** 959 Lake Rd. I-85, exit 102, just w, then just s. Int corridors. **Pets:** Small, dogs only. $10 daily fee/pet, $25 one-time fee/pet. Designated rooms, service with restrictions, supervision.

TRYON

ⒶⒶⒶ ▼▼▼▼ 1906 Pine Crest Inn & Restaurant Ⓒⓘ
(828) 859-9135. **$99-$399, 14 day notice.** 85 Pine Crest Ln. I-26, exit 67, 4 mi w on SR 108, just s on New Market Rd, then just e. Ext/int corridors. **Pets:** Accepted.

WASHINGTON

▼▼ Comfort Inn Ⓗ
(252) 946-4444. **$70-$150.** 1636 Carolina Ave. Jct US 264, 1 mi n on US 17. Int corridors. **Pets:** Medium. $20 daily fee/pet. Designated rooms, supervision.

WAYNESVILLE

▼▼ Days Inn-Waynesville Ⓜ
(828) 452-9009. **$50-$135.** 232 Phillips Rd. US 23/74, exit 102, just sw. Ext corridors. **Pets:** Accepted.

WELDON

ⒶⒶⒶ ▼▼ Days Inn Ⓜ
(252) 536-4867. **$55-$75.** 1611 Julian R Allsbrook Hwy. I-95, exit 173, just e on US 158. Ext corridors. **Pets:** Other species. $9 daily fee/pet. Designated rooms, no service, supervision.

WEST JEFFERSON

▼▼ Nation's Inn Ⓜ
(336) 246-2080. **Call for rates.** 107 Beaver Creek School Rd. Jct US 221, just n on SR 194, then just w. Ext corridors. **Pets:** Accepted.

WHITEVILLE

ⒶⒶⒶ ▼▼▼ Best Western Premiere Inn Ⓜ ❀
(910) 642-2378. **$77-$99.** 503 N J K Powell Blvd. Jct US 74/76, 1 mi s on US 701 Bypass. Ext corridors. **Pets:** Large. $20 daily fee/pet. Designated rooms, service with restrictions, supervision.

WILKESBORO

ⒶⒶⒶ ▼▼▼▼ Holiday Inn Express Ⓗ
(336) 838-1800. **$90-$137.** 1700 Winkler St. 2 mi n on US 421 and SR 16. Int corridors. **Pets:** Accepted.

WILLIAMSTON

▼▼▼ Hampton Inn Ⓗ
(252) 809-1100. **$69-$89.** 1099 Hampton Ct. US 64, exit 514, just s on US 17, then just w. Int corridors. **Pets:** Accepted.

▼▼▼ Holiday Inn Ⓗ
(252) 792-3184. **$89.** 101 East Blvd. US 64, exit 514, 1.5 mi n on US 17 business route. Ext/int corridors. **Pets:** Other species. No service, supervision.

WILMINGTON

▼▼ Baymont Inn Ⓜ
(910) 392-6767. **$71-$109, 14 day notice.** 306 S College Rd. Jct US 17 business route, just s on SR 132. Ext/int corridors. **Pets:** Accepted.

ⒶⒶⒶ ▼▼▼ Comfort Inn Wilmington Ⓗ
(910) 791-4841. **$70-$159.** 151 S College Rd. Jct US 17 business route, just s on SR 132. Int corridors. **Pets:** Large. $10 daily fee/pet. Designated rooms, service with restrictions, supervision.

▼▼ Days Inn Ⓜ
(910) 799-6300. **$42-$79.** 5040 Market St. Jct SR 132, 0.6 mi s on US 17 business route. Ext corridors. **Pets:** $15 daily fee/room. Designated rooms, no service, crate.

▼▼ Extended StayAmerica-Wilmington-New Centre Drive Ⓗ
(910) 793-4508. **$90-$105.** 4929 New Centre Dr. Jct SR 132, 0.4 mi s on US 17 business route, just e. Int corridors. **Pets:** Other species. $25 daily fee/pet. Service with restrictions, crate.

▼▼ Innkeeper Ⓗ
(910) 799-4292. **$85-$124, 3 day notice.** 5345 W Market St. Jct SR 132, just s on US 17 business route. Int corridors. **Pets:** $20 one-time fee/room. No service, supervision.

▼▼▼ Jameson Inn Ⓗ
(910) 452-5660. **$93-$102.** 5102 Dunlea Ct. Jct SR 132, 0.5 mi s on US 17 business route, just w on New Centre Dr. Int corridors. **Pets:** Medium, other species. $15 daily fee/pet. Designated rooms, service with restrictions, supervision.

▼▼▼ MainStay Suites Ⓗ
(910) 392-1741. **$89-$350, 7 day notice.** 5229 Market St. Jct SR 132, just s on US 17 business route. Int corridors. **Pets:** Accepted.

▼▼ Quality Inn Ⓜ
(910) 791-8850. **$60-$140, 3 day notice.** 4926 Market St. Jct SR 132, 0.9 mi s on US 17 business route. Ext corridors. **Pets:** Accepted.

WWW Residence Inn by Marriott-Landfall H ❀
(910) 256-0098. **$159-$179.** 1200 Culbreth Dr. Jct US 17 business route, 2.4 mi e on US 74, 0.4 mi n on Military Cutoff Rd, then just e. Int corridors. **Pets:** Medium. $75 one-time fee/room. Designated rooms, service with restrictions.
SAVE ⊠ ⓖM 🖥 💻 ⊇ ⊠

WILSON

WW Best Western-Wilson M
(252) 237-8700. **$60-$90.** 817-A Ward Blvd. US 264, exit 42, 2.6 mi n on Downing St, then just w. Ext corridors. **Pets:** Accepted.
SAVE ⊠ 🖥 💻 ⊇

WWW Days Inn H
(252) 291-2323. **$64-$89.** 1801 S Tarboro St. US 264, exit 40, 3.3 mi e on SR 42. Ext corridors. **Pets:** Accepted.
SAVE ⊠ 🖥 💻 ⊇

WWW Holiday Inn Express & Suites H ❀
(252) 246-1588. **$94.** 2308 Montgomery Dr. US 264, exit 40, 3.2 mi e on SR 42, then just n. Int corridors. **Pets:** Large, other species. $20 one-time fee/pet. Service with restrictions, supervision.
ASK ⊠ 🖥 💻 ⊇

WINDSOR

WWW The Inn at Grays Landing BB
(252) 794-2255. **$70-$140.** 401 S King St. US 17, just w on SR 308. Int corridors. **Pets:** $10 daily fee/room. Designated rooms, service with restrictions, crate.
ASK ⊠ 🖾

WINSTON-SALEM

WWWW Augustus T Zevely Inn BB ❀
(336) 748-9299. **$100-$245, 14 day notice.** 803 S Main St. I-40 business route, exit 5D eastbound, 0.5 mi s on Liberty St to Old Salem Rd, just e on Academy St, then just s; exit 5C westbound, just n on Cherry St, just e on 2nd St, 1 mi s on Liberty St to Old Salem Rd, just e on Academy St, then just s. Ext/int corridors. **Pets:** Medium, dogs only. $15 daily fee/pet. Designated rooms, service with restrictions, crate.
SAVE ⊠ 🖥

W Crossland Economy Studios M
(336) 759-7780. **$60-$70.** 7910 North Point Blvd. US 52, exit 115B, 2 mi s on University Pkwy, then just e. Ext corridors. **Pets:** Other species. $25 daily fee/pet. Service with restrictions, crate.
ASK ⊠ 🖥

WW Extended StayAmerica Winston-Salem-Hanes Mall Blvd M
(336) 768-0075. **$70-$80.** 1995 Hampton Inn Ct. I-40, exit 189 (Stratford Rd), just s, just e on Hanes Mall Blvd, then just n. Ext corridors. **Pets:** Other species. $25 daily fee/pet. Service with restrictions, crate.
ASK ⊠ 🖥 💻

WWWW The Hawthorne Inn & Conference Center H
(336) 777-3000. **$79-$165.** 420 High St. I-40 business route, exit 5C (Cherry St) eastbound, just e; exit westbound, just w on 1st St, then just s on Marshall St. Int corridors. **Pets:** Accepted.
SAVE ⊠ ⓖM 🖥 💻 ❚❘ ⊇

WW Innkeeper M
(336) 721-0062. **$52-$60, 3 day notice.** 2115 Peters Creek Pkwy. I-40, exit 192 (Peters Creek Pkwy), just e on SR 150. Ext/int corridors. **Pets:** Accepted.
ASK ⊠ 🖥 ⊇

WWWW La Quinta Inns & Suites Winston-Salem H ❀
(336) 765-8777. **$69-$139.** 2020 Griffith Rd. I-40, exit 189 (Stratford Rd), just s, just e on Hanes Mall Blvd, then just s. Int corridors. **Pets:** Medium, other species. Service with restrictions, supervision.
ASK ⊠ ⓖM 🖥 💻 ⊇

WWWW Quality Inn & Suites-Hanes Mall H
(336) 765-6670. **$69-$150.** 2008 S Hawthorne Rd. I-40 business route, exit 2A, 0.5 mi s on Silas Creek Pkwy, then just e. Ext corridors. **Pets:** Medium, other species. $25 one-time fee/pet. Service with restrictions.
SAVE ⊠ ⓖM 🖥 💻 ❚❘ ⊇

WWW Quality Inn-Coliseum H
(336) 767-8240. **$60-$130.** 531 Akron Dr. US 52, exit 112, just e. Int corridors. **Pets:** Small. $15 daily fee/pet. Designated rooms, service with restrictions, supervision.
SAVE ⊠ 🖥 💻 ❚❘ ⊇

WWW Quality Inn University H
(336) 767-9009. **Call for rates.** 5719 University Pkwy. US 52, exit 115B, 0.4 mi w. Ext corridors. **Pets:** Accepted.
SAVE ⊠ 🖥 💻 ⊇

WWW Residence Inn by Marriott H ❀
(336) 759-0777. **$177-$190.** 7835 North Point Blvd. US 52 N, exit 115B, 2 mi s on University Pkwy, then just e. Ext corridors. **Pets:** Medium. $75 one-time fee/room. Service with restrictions, supervision.
⊠ 🖥 ⊇ ⊠

WW Salem Inn & Suites H
(336) 725-8561. **Call for rates.** 127 S Cherry St. I-40 business route, exit 5C (Cherry St) eastbound, just e on High St, then just s; exit westbound, just w on 1st St, just s on Marshall St, just e on High St, then just s. Ext corridors. **Pets:** Accepted.
⊠ 🖥 💻 ⊇

WWW Sundance Plaza Hotel and Spa H ❀
(336) 723-2911. **$60-$150.** 3050 University Pkwy. I-40 business route, exit 5C (Cherry St), 3 mi n. Int corridors. **Pets:** Other species. Designated rooms, service with restrictions.
SAVE ⊠ 🖥 💻 ❚❘ ⊇

YADKINVILLE

WW Days Inn H
(336) 679-5000. **Call for rates.** 220 Sharon Dr. US 421, exit 257, just s on US 601, then just e. Int corridors. **Pets:** Accepted.
⊠ ⓖM 🖥 💻 ⊇

YANCEYVILLE

WW Days Inn M
(336) 694-9494. **$65-$170.** 1858 NC Hwy 86 N. Jct SR 62, 1.6 mi nw on US 158/SR 86. Ext corridors. **Pets:** Accepted.
ASK ⊠ 🖥 ⊇

NORTH DAKOTA

CITY INDEX

BEULAH

▼▼ AmericInn Lodge & Suites of Beulah 🄷
(701) 873-2220. **$85-$161.** 2100 2nd Ave NW. Jct SR 49/200, 1.2 mi s. Int corridors. **Pets:** $25 one-time fee/room. Service with restrictions, supervision.

BISMARCK

◈◈◈ ▼▼ Best Western Doublewood Inn Ⓜ
(701) 258-7000. **$70-$110.** 1400 E Interchange Ave. I-94, exit 159, just s on US 83. Int corridors. **Pets:** Dogs only. $10 one-time fee/pet. Designated rooms, service with restrictions, supervision.

◈◈◈ ▼▼▼ Best Western Ramkota Hotel 🄷
(701) 258-7700. **$109-$125.** 800 S 3rd St. Just s of jct I-94 business loop (Bismarck Expwy) and S 3rd St. Int corridors. **Pets:** Medium. $10 daily fee/room. Designated rooms, service with restrictions, supervision.

▼▼ Comfort Inn 🄷
(701) 223-1911. **$80-$90.** 1030 Interstate Ave. I-94, exit 159, 0.3 mi nw on US 83. Int corridors. **Pets:** Very small. Service with restrictions, supervision.

▼▼ Days Inn-Bismarck Ⓜ
(701) 223-9151. **Call for rates.** 1300 E Capitol Ave. I-94, exit 159, just s on US 83. Int corridors. **Pets:** Accepted.

▼▼ Expressway Inn 🄷
(701) 222-2900. **$75-$100.** 200 Bismarck Expwy. Jct I-94 business loop (Bismarck Expwy) and S 3rd St. Int corridors. **Pets:** Medium. $10 one-time fee/room. Designated rooms, service with restrictions, supervision.

▼▼ Kelly Inn Ⓜ
(701) 223-8001. **$67-$125.** 1800 N 12th St. I-94, exit 159, 0.3 mi s on US 83. Int corridors. **Pets:** $20 one-time fee/room. Designated rooms, service with restrictions, supervision.

◈◈◈ ▼▼▼ Radisson Hotel Bismarck 🄷
(701) 255-6000. **$99.** 605 E Broadway Ave. Jct 6th St; center. Int corridors. **Pets:** Other species. $20 one-time fee/pet. Service with restrictions, supervision.

◈◈◈ ▼▼ Ramada Limited Bismarck 🄷
(701) 221-3030. **$84-$105.** 3808 E Divide Ave. I-94, exit 161, just s on E Bismarck Expwy. Int corridors. **Pets:** Other species. $10 daily fee/room. Service with restrictions, crate.

◈◈◈ ▼ Select Inn Ⓜ
(701) 223-8060. **$53-$74.** 1505 Interchange Ave. I-94, exit 159, just se on US 83. Int corridors. **Pets:** $25 deposit/room, $5 daily fee/room. Designated rooms, service with restrictions, supervision.

CARRINGTON

▼▼ Carrington Inn & Suites Ⓜ
(701) 652-3982. **$60-$90.** 101 4th Ave S. Jct US 52 and 281, 0.5 mi e on US 52; just s of jct SR 200. Int corridors. **Pets:** Other species. $10 daily fee/pet. Designated rooms, supervision.

▼▼ Chieftain Conference Center Ⓜ
(701) 652-3131. **$60-$100.** 60 4th Ave S. Jct US 52 and 281, 0.5 mi e on US 52; just s of jct SR 200. Ext/int corridors. **Pets:** Small. $5 one-time fee/pet. Designated rooms, service with restrictions, supervision.

CASSELTON

◈◈◈ ▼▼ Governors' Inn and Conference Center 🄷
(701) 347-4524. **$89-$159.** 2050 Governors Dr. I-94, exit 331, just n on SR 18. Int corridors. **Pets:** $9 daily fee/pet. Designated rooms, service with restrictions, crate.

DEVILS LAKE

▼▼ Fireside Inn & Suites Ⓜ
(701) 662-6760. **$69-$89.** 215 Hwy 2 E. On US 2 at jct SR 20. Int corridors. **Pets:** Accepted.

DICKINSON

◈◈◈ ▼▼ AmericInn Motel & Suites of Dickinson 🄷
(701) 225-1400. **Call for rates.** 229 15th St W. I-94, exit 61 (SR 22), just n, then e. Int corridors. **Pets:** Accepted.

◈◈◈ ▼▼ Comfort Inn 🄷
(701) 264-7300. **Call for rates.** 493 Elks Dr. I-94, exit 61 (SR 22), just n, then w. Int corridors. **Pets:** $10 one-time fee/room. Service with restrictions, supervision.

◈◈◈ ▼▼ Hartfiel Inn 🄱🄱
(701) 225-6710. **$89-$109.** 509 3rd Ave W. I-94, exit 61 (SR 22), 0.8 mi s. Int corridors. **Pets:** Medium, dogs only. Designated rooms, supervision.

▼▼▼ Holiday Inn Express Hotel & Suites 🄷
(701) 456-8000. **$115-$170.** 103 14th St W. I-94, exit 61 (SR 22), just n, then just e. Int corridors. **Pets:** $10 one-time fee/room. Service with restrictions, supervision.

◈◈◈ ▼▼ Quality Inn & Suites-Dickinson 🄷
(701) 225-9510. **$60-$170.** 71 Museum Dr. I-94, exit 61 (SR 22), just s, then e. Int corridors. **Pets:** Accepted.

EDGELEY

▼▼ Prairie Rose Inn 🄷
(701) 493-2075. **$55-$80.** 111 Frontage Rd. Jct US 281 and SR 13. Ext/int corridors. **Pets:** Accepted.

FARGO

⟨AAA⟩ ◆◆◆ AmericInn Lodge & Suites of Fargo M
(701) 234-9946. **$78-$142.** 1423 35th St SW. I-29, exit 64, just e on 13th Ave SW, just s on 34th St SW, then just w on 14th Ave SW. Int corridors. **Pets:** Medium. $10 daily fee/pet. Designated rooms, service with restrictions, supervision.

SAVE ✕ 🛗 💻 🏊 ✖

⟨AAA⟩ ◆◆◆ Best Western Fargo Doublewood Inn & Conference Center H
(701) 235-3333. **$85-$99.** 3333 13th Ave S. I-29, exit 64, 0.3 mi e. Int corridors. **Pets:** Small, dogs only. Service with restrictions, supervision.

SAVE ✕ 🛗 🛗 💻 🍴 🏊 ✖

⟨AAA⟩ ◆◆◆ Best Western Kelly Inn & Suites H 🐾
(701) 282-2143. **$100-$130, 3 day notice.** 1767 44th St S. I-94, exit 348, just n on 45th St SW, then just e on 18th Ave. Ext/int corridors. **Pets:** Medium. Designated rooms, service with restrictions, supervision.

SAVE ✕ 🛗 🛗 💻 🏊 ✖

⟨AAA⟩ ◆◆◆ Candlewood Suites H
(701) 235-8200. **$109-$149.** 1831 NDSU Research Park Dr. I-29, exit 67 (19th Ave), 1.6 mi e. Int corridors. **Pets:** Other species. $150 one-time fee/room. Service with restrictions, supervision.

SAVE ✕ 🛗 🛗 💻

◆◆ Comfort Inn by Choice Hotels West H
(701) 282-9596. **Call for rates.** 3825 9th Ave SW. I-29, exit 64, just n on 13th Ave S, then just w. Int corridors. **Pets:** Accepted.

✕ 🛗 💻 🏊

◆◆◆ Comfort Inn Fargo East M
(701) 280-9666. **Call for rates.** 1407 35th St SW. I-29, exit 64, just e on 13th Ave SW, just s on 34th St SW, then just w on 14th Ave S. Int corridors. **Pets:** Accepted.

✕ 🛗 💻 🏊

◆◆◆ Comfort Suites M
(701) 237-5911. **Call for rates.** 1415 35th St SW. I-29, exit 64, just e on 13th Ave SW, just s on 34th St SW, then just w on 14th Ave S. Int corridors. **Pets:** $10 daily fee/room. Service with restrictions, supervision.

✕ 🛗 🛗 💻 🏊

⟨AAA⟩ ◆◆◆◆ Country Inn & Suites By Carlson H
(701) 234-0565. **Call for rates.** 3316 13th Ave S. I-29, exit 64 (13th Ave S), 0.3 mi e. Int corridors. **Pets:** Accepted.

SAVE ✕ 🛗 💻 🏊 ✖

◆◆ Econo Lodge M
(701) 232-3412. **Call for rates.** 1401 35th St SW. I-29, exit 64, just e on 13th Ave SW, just s on 34th St SW, then just w on 14th Ave SW. Int corridors. **Pets:** Accepted.

✕ 🛗 💻

◆◆◆◆ Holiday Inn of Fargo Convention Center H
(701) 282-2700. **$99-$169.** 3803 13th Ave S. I-29, exit 64, just nw. Int corridors. **Pets:** $10 one-time fee/room. Service with restrictions, supervision.

ASK ✕ 🛗 🛗 💻 🍴 🏊 ✖

◆◆◆ Kelly Inn M
(701) 281-9700. **$79-$129.** 3800 Main Ave. I-29, exit 65, just w on US 10. Ext/int corridors. **Pets:** Accepted.

ASK ✕ 🛗 💻 🍴 🏊 ✖

◆◆◆ Kelly Inn 13th Avenue M
(701) 277-8821. **$82-$126.** 4207 13th Ave SW. I-29, exit 64, 0.5 mi w. Ext/int corridors. **Pets:** Medium. Service with restrictions, supervision.

ASK ✕ 🛗 🛗 💻 🏊

⟨AAA⟩ ◆◆◆◆ MainStay Suites H
(701) 277-4627. **$85-$149.** 1901 44th St SW. I-94, exit 348, just n on 45th St SW, then just e on 19th Ave S. Int corridors. **Pets:** Accepted.

SAVE ✕ 🛗 🛗 💻 🏊 ✖

◆◆◆ Prairie Rose Inn & Conference Center M
(701) 235-3141. **Call for rates.** 1340 21st Ave S. I-94, exit 351, just s on University Dr, then just w. Ext/int corridors. **Pets:** Accepted.

✕ 🛗 🛗 💻 🍴 🏊 ✖

⟨AAA⟩ ◆◆◆ Select Inn M
(701) 282-6300. **$46-$51.** 1025 38th St SW. I-29, exit 64, just nw on 13th Ave S. Int corridors. **Pets:** Accepted.

SAVE ✕ 🛗 🛗

⟨AAA⟩ ◆◆◆ Sleep Inn M
(701) 281-8240. **$60-$99.** 1921 44 St SW. I-94, exit 348 (45th St SW), just n, then just e on 19th Ave S. Int corridors. **Pets:** Accepted.

SAVE ✕ 🛗 🛗 💻 🏊 ✖

⟨AAA⟩ ◆◆◆◆ Staybridge Suites H 🐾
(701) 281-4900. **$109-$299.** 4300 20th Ave S. I-94, exit 348 (45th St SW), just n, then e. Int corridors. **Pets:** Small. $50 one-time fee/pet. Service with restrictions, crate.

SAVE ✕ 🛗 🛗 💻 🏊 ✖

◆◆ Super 8 Motel & Suites-Fargo M
(701) 232-9202. **$55-$135.** 3518 Interstate Blvd. I-29, exit 64 (13th Ave S), just n on east frontage road via 35th St. Int corridors. **Pets:** Accepted.

ASK ✕ 🛗 💻 🏊

GRAFTON

◆◆ AmericInn Motel & Suites of Grafton H
(701) 352-2788. **Call for rates.** 1015 12th St W. SR 17, 1.2 mi w. Int corridors. **Pets:** Accepted.

✕ 🛗 🛗 💻 🏊 ✖

GRAND FORKS

⟨AAA⟩ ◆◆◆ Americas Best Value Inn of Grand Forks M
(701) 775-0555. **$42-$110.** 1000 N 42nd St. I-29, exit 141, just se on US 2 (Gateway Dr). Int corridors. **Pets:** Dogs only. $25 deposit/pet, $10 daily fee/pet. Designated rooms, service with restrictions, supervision.

SAVE ✕ 🛗

⟨AAA⟩ ◆◆◆ Days Inn–Grand Forks M
(701) 775-0060. **$79-$149.** 3101 34th St S. I-29, exit 138, 0.5 mi e on 32nd Ave S, then just n. Int corridors. **Pets:** Small. $8 daily fee/pet. Designated rooms, service with restrictions, supervision.

SAVE ✕ 🛗 💻 🏊

◆◆◆ GuestHouse International Townhouse M
(701) 746-5411. **$65-$115.** 710 1st Ave N. I-29, exit 140, 3 mi e on DeMers Ave; downtown. Int corridors. **Pets:** Large, other species. $15 daily fee/room. Designated rooms, service with restrictions, crate.

ASK ✕ 🛗 💻 🍴 🏊 ✖

⟨AAA⟩ ◆◆◆ Ramada Inn M
(701) 775-3951. **$59-$109.** 1205 N 43rd St. I-29, exit 141, just se on US 2 (Gateway Dr). Int corridors. **Pets:** Small. Designated rooms, service with restrictions, supervision.

SAVE ✕ 🛗 💻 🍴 🏊 ✖

⟨AAA⟩ ◆◆◆ Travelodge of Grand Forks M
(701) 772-8151. **$64-$114, 14 day notice.** 2100 S Washington St. I-29, exit 140, 2.5 mi e on Demers Ave, then 1.5 mi s. Int corridors. **Pets:** Medium, dogs only. $5 daily fee/room. Designated rooms, service with restrictions, supervision.

SAVE ✕ 🛗 💻 🏊 ✖

JAMESTOWN

◆◆ Comfort Inn Jamestown M 🐾
(701) 252-7125. **Call for rates.** 811 20th St SW. I-94, exit 258, just nw on US 281. Int corridors. **Pets:** $10 daily fee/pet. Designated rooms, service with restrictions, supervision.

✕ 🛗 💻 🏊

KENMARE

▼▼ ▼▼ Quilt Inn H
(701) 385-4100. **$60-$70.** 1232 Central Ave N. Just n on US 52. Int corridors. **Pets:** Accepted.
ASK ✕ 🛏 🌊

MANDAN

◈◈ ▼▼▼▼ Best Western Seven Seas Hotel & Waterpark H
(701) 663-7401. **$96-$106.** 2611 Old Red Tr. I-94, exit 152, just n on Sunset Dr, then just w. Int corridors. **Pets:** Accepted.
SAVE ✕ 🔊 🛏 💻 🍴 🌊 🗙

MEDORA

▼▼ ▼▼ AmericInn Motel & Suites of Medora H
(701) 623-4800. **Call for rates.** 75 E River Rd S. I-94, exit 24, just se of downtown. Int corridors. **Pets:** Accepted.
✕ 🔊 🛏 💻 🌊 🗙

MINOT

◈◈ ▼▼ ▼▼ Best Western Kelly Inn M
(701) 852-4300. **$90-$170.** 1510 26th Ave SW. US 2 and 52 Bypass, at 16th St SW. Ext/int corridors. **Pets:** Other species. Service with restrictions.
SAVE ✕ 🛏 💻 🌊 🗙

◈◈ ▼▼ ▼▼ Comfort Inn H
(701) 852-2201. **$90-$200.** 1515 22nd Ave SW. US 2 and 52 Bypass, at 16th St SW. Int corridors. **Pets:** Medium. $10 daily fee/room. Designated rooms, service with restrictions, supervision.
SAVE ✕ 🛏 💻 🌊 🗙

▼▼ Days Inn Minot M
(701) 852-3646. **Call for rates.** 2100 4th St SW. Jct US 2 and 52 Bypass, just n. Int corridors. **Pets:** Accepted.
✕ 🛏 💻 🌊

▼▼ ▼▼ Fairfield Inn by Marriott H
(701) 838-2424. **$75-$85.** 900 24th Ave SW. 0.5 mi e of jct US 2, 52 Bypass and 16th St SW. Int corridors. **Pets:** Other species. Service with restrictions, crate.
✕ 🔊 🛏 💻 🌊

◈◈ ▼▼▼▼ Sleep Inn & Suites H
(701) 837-3100. **$109-$199.** 2400 10th St SW. US 2 and 52 Bypass at 16th St SW. Int corridors. **Pets:** Very small. $25 daily fee/pet. Designated rooms, service with restrictions, supervision.
SAVE ✕ 🔊 🛏 💻 🌊 🗙

VALLEY CITY

◈◈ ▼▼ ▼▼ AmericInn Lodge & Suites of Valley City H
(701) 845-5551. **Call for rates.** 280 Winter Show Rd SE. I-94, exit 292, just ne. Int corridors. **Pets:** Accepted.
SAVE ✕ 🔊 🛏 💻 🌊 🗙

▼▼ Super 8-Valley City M
(701) 845-1140. **$66-$86.** 860 11th St SW. I-94, exit 292, just nw. Int corridors. **Pets:** Accepted.
ASK ✕ 🛏 💻

WAHPETON

▼▼ ▼▼ Rodeway Inn H
(701) 642-1115. **Call for rates.** 209 13th St S. SR 13, 0.3 mi e of jct SR 210 Bypass. Int corridors. **Pets:** Accepted.
✕ 🛏 💻 🌊

▼▼ Wahpeton Super 8 H
(701) 642-8731. **Call for rates.** 995 21st Ave N. 1.5 mi n on SR 210 Bypass. Int corridors. **Pets:** Accepted.
✕ 🛏 💻 🌊

WATFORD CITY

◈◈ ▼▼ McKenzie Inn M
(701) 444-3980. **$56-$110.** 132 SW 3rd St. US 85, just w. Ext corridors. **Pets:** Small, dogs only. $5 daily fee/pet. Designated rooms, service with supervision.
SAVE ✕ 🛏

◈◈ ▼▼ Roosevelt Inn & Suites H
(701) 842-3686. **$60-$72.** 600 2nd Ave SW. US 85, 0.3 mi w. Int corridors. **Pets:** Medium. $10 daily fee/pet, $10 one-time fee/pet. Service with restrictions, supervision.
SAVE ✕ 🛏 💻 🌊

WILLISTON

◈◈ ▼▼ ▼▼ El Rancho Motor Hotel H
(701) 572-6321. **$59-$89.** 1623 2nd Ave W. 1 mi n on US 2 and 85 N Bypass. Ext/int corridors. **Pets:** Accepted.
SAVE ✕ 🛏 💻 🍴

◈◈ ▼▼ ▼▼ Marquis Plaza & Suites H
(701) 774-3250. **$78-$127.** 1525 9th Ave NW. US 2 and 85, 4 mi e of jct US 85. Int corridors. **Pets:** Small. $10 daily fee/pet. Designated rooms, service with restrictions, supervision.
SAVE ✕ 🔊 🛏 💻 🌊

OHIO

AKRON

⬥⬥ ▼▼ ▼▼ Red Roof Inn-Akron South #0207 🅜
(330) 644-7748. $54-$80. 2939 S Arlington Rd. I-77, exit 120, just n. Ext corridors. Pets: Medium. Service with restrictions, crate.
SAVE ✖ 🛢

ALLIANCE

▼▼ ▼▼ Comfort Inn 🅗
(330) 821-5555. Call for rates. 2500 W State St. 2.5 mi w on US 62. Int corridors. Pets: Accepted.
✖ 🛢 💻 🏊

▼▼▼▼ Holiday Inn Express Hotel & Suites 🅗
(330) 821-6700. $99-$199, 14 day notice. 2341 W State St. 2 mi w on US 62. Int corridors. Pets: Medium. $10 one-time fee/pet. Designated rooms, service with restrictions, supervision.
ASK ✖ 🛢 💻 🏊

⬥⬥ ▼▼ ▼▼ Super 8 Motel 🅜
(330) 821-5688. $56-$95. 2330 W State St. 2 mi w on US 62. Ext corridors. Pets: Other species. $5 daily fee/pet. Service with restrictions.
SAVE ✖ 🛢 🏊

AMHERST

▼▼ ▼▼ Days Inn 🅜
(440) 985-1428. $45-$75. 934 N Leavitt Rd. SR 58, just n of SR 2. Ext/int corridors. Pets: Medium. $10 daily fee/pet, $10 one-time fee/pet. Designated rooms, service with restrictions, supervision.
ASK ✖ 🛢 💻 🏊

ASHLAND

▼▼ ▼▼ The Surrey Inn 🅗 🐾
(419) 289-7700. $59-$79. 1065 Claremont Ave. 1 mi s. Int corridors. Pets: Small, dogs only. $10 daily fee/room. Service with restrictions.
ASK ✖ 🛢 💻

ASHTABULA

⬥⬥ ▼▼ Cedars Motel 🅜 🐾
(440) 992-5406. $80. 2015 W Prospect Rd. Jct SR 11, 3 mi w on US 20. Ext corridors. Pets: Other species. $5 daily fee/pet. Service with restrictions, supervision.
SAVE ✖ 🛢

⬥⬥ ▼▼ Ho Hum Motel 🅜
(440) 969-1136. $55-$80. 3801 N Ridge Rd W. I-90, exit 223, 3 mi n on SR 45, then 1 mi e on SR 20. Ext corridors. Pets: Other species. $5 daily fee/pet. Service with restrictions, supervision.
SAVE ✖ 🛢

ATHENS

▼▼▼▼ The Ohio University Inn & Conference Center 🅗
(740) 593-6661. Call for rates. 331 Richland Ave. 1 mi w on US 33 and 50. Int corridors. Pets: Medium. $50 one-time fee/room. Designated rooms, service with restrictions, supervision.
✖ 🛢 💻 🍽 🏊

AUSTINBURG

▼▼▼ ◆ Comfort Inn-Ashtabula 🅗
(440) 275-2711. $80-$164. 1860 Austinburg Rd. I-90, exit 223, just n. Int corridors. Pets: Medium, other species. $15 daily fee/pet. Service with restrictions.
ASK ✖ 🛢 💻 🍽 🏊

AUSTINTOWN

⬥⬥ ▼▼ ▼▼ Austintown Super 8 Motel 🅜
(330) 793-7788. $54-$100. 5280 76 Dr. I-80, exit 223, just s on SR 46. Int corridors. Pets: $10 daily fee/pet. Service with restrictions, supervision.
SAVE ✖ 🛢 💻

⬥⬥ ▼▼ ▼▼ Best Western Meander Inn 🅗 🐾
(330) 544-2378. $69-$112, 7 day notice. 870 N Canfield-Niles Rd. I-80, exit 223, 0.3 mi s on SR 46. Int corridors. Pets: Other species. $10 daily fee/pet. Service with restrictions, supervision.
SAVE ✖ 🛢 💻 🍽 🏊

◆◆◆◆ Comfort Inn & Suites M
(330) 792-9740. **Call for rates.** 5425 Clarkins Dr. I-80, exit 223B, just n. Ext corridors. **Pets:** $10 daily fee/room. Designated rooms, service with restrictions, crate.

BEAVERCREEK

◆◆◆◆ Residence Inn by Marriott Beavercreek H
(937) 427-3914. **$150-$155.** 2779 Fairfield Commons. I-675, exit 17, just e, just s on New Germany-Trebein, then just e. Int corridors. **Pets:** Accepted.

BELLEFONTAINE

◆◆ Comfort Inn Bellefontaine M
(937) 599-5555. **$72-$89.** 260 Northview Dr. Jct US 33 and SR 68, just ne. Int corridors. **Pets:** Small, other species. $15 daily fee/pet. Service with restrictions, supervision.

BLUFFTON

◆◆◆ Comfort Inn H
(419) 358-6000. **$80-$109.** 117 Commerce Ln. I-75, exit 142, just w on SR 103. Int corridors. **Pets:** Medium, other species. $25 one-time fee/pet. Service with restrictions, supervision.

BOARDMAN

AAA ◆◆ Americas Best Value Inn & Suites H ✿
(330) 549-0157. **$49-$121.** 9988 Market St. 0.5 mi n on SR 7. Int corridors. **Pets:** Medium. $10 daily fee/room. Service with restrictions, supervision.

◆◆ Days Inn Boardman Youngstown H
(330) 758-1816. **Call for rates.** 7393 South Ave. Jct I-680 and US 224, 0.3 mi w. Int corridors. **Pets:** Accepted.

BOSTON HEIGHTS

AAA ◆◆◆ Comfort Inn M
(330) 650-2040. **$55-$99.** 6731 Industrial Pkwy. I-80/90, exit 180, 0.3 mi n on SR 8. Int corridors. **Pets:** Accepted.

BOTKINS

AAA ◆ Budget Host Inn M
(937) 693-6911. **$43-$75.** 505 E State St. I-75, exit 104 (SR 219), just w. Ext corridors. **Pets:** $40 deposit/room. Designated rooms, service with restrictions.

BRUNSWICK

◆◆ Sleep Inn H
(330) 273-1112. **Call for rates.** 1435 S Carpenter Rd. I-71, exit 226, just w. Ext corridors. **Pets:** Accepted.

BRYAN

AAA ◆◆◆ Colonial Manor Motel M
(419) 636-3123. **$73-$115.** 924 E High St. US 127, 0.8 mi e on SR 2/34. Ext corridors. **Pets:** Medium. Designated rooms, no service, crate.

CAMBRIDGE

◆◆ Baymont Inn & Suites H
(740) 439-1505. **$69-$109.** 61595 Southgate Pkwy. I-70, exit 178, just s on SR 209. Int corridors. **Pets:** Medium, other species. Designated rooms, service with restrictions, supervision.

◆ Budget Inn M
(740) 432-2304. **$30-$50.** 6405 Glenn Hwy. I-70, exit 176, just e on US 40. Ext/int corridors. **Pets:** Small. $10 daily fee/pet. Designated rooms, service with restrictions, supervision.

AAA ◆◆ Comfort Inn H
(740) 435-3200. **$79-$149.** 2327 Southgate Pkwy. I-70, exit 178, just n on SR 209. Int corridors. **Pets:** Accepted.

◆◆ Days Inn-Cambridge H
(740) 432-5691. **$59-$89, 3 day notice.** 2328 Southgate Pkwy. I-70, exit 178, just n on SR 209. Int corridors. **Pets:** Accepted.

CANTON

AAA ◆◆ Red Roof Inn #7019 M
(330) 499-1970. **$50-$80.** 5353 Inn Circle Ct NW. I-77, exit 109, just w on Everhard Rd. Ext corridors. **Pets:** Small. Service with restrictions, supervision.

◆◆ Residence Inn by Marriott H
(330) 493-0004. **$160-$170.** 5280 Broadmoor Cir NW. I-77, exit 109, 0.5 mi e on Everhard Rd. Int corridors. **Pets:** Accepted.

CARROLLTON

◆◆ Carrollton Days Inn H
(330) 627-9314. **$81-$130, 7 day notice.** 1111 Canton Rd. On SR 43, 0.5 mi n of SR 39. Int corridors. **Pets:** Medium. $20 one-time fee/pet. Service with restrictions, supervision.

CELINA

AAA ◆◆ Americas Best Value Inn-Celina M
(419) 586-4656. **$56-$125.** 1421 SR 703 E. Jct SR 29. Ext corridors. **Pets:** Small. $15 daily fee/room. Designated rooms, service with restrictions, supervision.

CHILLICOTHE

AAA ◆◆ Best Western Adena Inn H
(740) 775-7000. **$89-$179.** 1250 N Bridge St. US 35, exit Bridge St, 0.8 mi n. Int corridors. **Pets:** Accepted.

◆◆ Christopher Inn & Suites H
(740) 774-6835. **$83-$190.** 30 N Plaza Blvd. US 35, exit Bridge St, just n on US 23. Int corridors. **Pets:** Small, other species. $50 deposit/room. Service with restrictions, supervision.

CINCINNATI METROPOLITAN AREA

BATAVIA

▼▼ Ameristay Inn & Suites 🅷 ❖
(513) 735-4678. **$76-$139.** 2188 Winemiller Ln. I-275, exit 63B (SR 32), 7.3 mi e. Int corridors. **Pets:** $25 one-time fee/room. Service with restrictions, supervision.

🄰🄺 ⊠ 🛏 💻 ⇆

▼▼▼ Hampton Inn-Cincinnati Eastgate 🅷
(513) 752-8584. **$76-$99.** 858 Eastgate North Dr. I-275, exit 63B (SR 32), just e, just n on Gleneste Withamsville Rd, then just w; behind Longhorn Steak House. Int corridors. **Pets:** Medium, other species. Service with restrictions, supervision.

⊠ 🛏 💻 ⇆

▼▼▼ Holiday Inn-Cincinnati Eastgate 🅷
(513) 752-4400. **Call for rates.** 4501 Eastgate Blvd. I-275, exit 63B (SR 32), 0.5 mi e to Eastgate Mall exit, then 0.5 mi n. Int corridors. **Pets:** Accepted.

⊠ 🛏 💻 🍴 ⇆ 🗙

BLUE ASH

▼ Extended StayAmerica Blue Ash North 🅷
(513) 469-8900. **$54-$99.** 11145 Kenwood Rd. I-71, exit 15, 0.5 mi w on Pfeiffer Rd, then 1.3 mi n. Int corridors. **Pets:** Other species. $25 daily fee/pet. Service with restrictions, crate.

🄰🄺 ⊠ 🛏 💻

▼▼ Extended StayAmerica-Cincinnati-Blue Ash-South 🅷
(513) 793-6750. **$54-$99.** 4260 Hunt Rd. I-71, exit 14, 1.3 mi w on Ronald Reagan Hwy, exit Hunt Rd, then just e. Int corridors. **Pets:** Other species. $25 daily fee/pet. Service with restrictions, crate.

🄰🄺 ⊠ 🛏 💻 ⇆

⨁ ▼▼▼ Residence Inn by Marriott-Blue Ash 🅷
(513) 530-5060. **$179-$189.** 11401 Reed-Hartman Hwy. I-275, exit 47, 0.8 mi s. Ext/int corridors. **Pets:** Large, other species. $95 one-time fee/room. Service with restrictions.

🅂🄰🅅🄴 ⊠ 🄴🄼 🛏 💻 ⇆ 🗙

⨁ ▼▼ TownePlace Suites by Marriott Blue Ash 🅷 ❖
(513) 469-8222. **$139-$149.** 4650 Cornell Rd. I-275, exit 47, 0.9 mi s on Reed-Hartman Hwy, then just w. Int corridors. **Pets:** Medium, other species. $75 one-time fee/room. Service with restrictions.

🅂🄰🅅🄴 ⊠ 🛏 💻 ⇆

CHERRY GROVE

⨁ ▼▼ Best Western Clermont 🅼
(513) 528-7702. **$73-$100.** 4004 Williams Dr. I-275, exit 65, just w, then just s. Ext corridors. **Pets:** Small. $20 one-time fee/pet. Service with restrictions, supervision.

🅂🄰🅅🄴 ⊠ 🛏 💻 ⇆

CINCINNATI

⨁ ▼▼▼ Holiday Inn Express Cincinnati West 🅷
(513) 574-6000. **$110-$200.** 5505 Rybolt Rd. I-74, exit 11. Int corridors. **Pets:** Accepted.

🅂🄰🅅🄴 ⊠ 🄴🄼 🛏 💻 ⇆

⨁ ▼▼▼ Millennium Hotel Cincinnati 🅷
(513) 352-2100. **$79-$239.** 150 W 5th St. Between Elm and Race sts. Int corridors. **Pets:** Accepted.

🅂🄰🅅🄴 ⊠ 🛏 💻 🍴 ⇆

⨁ ▼▼▼▼ The Westin Cincinnati 🅷 ❖
(513) 621-7700. **$169-$339.** 21 E 5th St. Between Vine and Walnut sts. Int corridors. **Pets:** Medium, dogs only. Service with restrictions, supervision.

🅂🄰🅅🄴 ⊠ 🄴🄼 🛏 💻 🍴 ⇆ 🗙

FAIRFIELD

▼▼ Extended StayAmerica Cincinnati-Fairfield 🅷
(513) 860-5733. **$64-$109.** 9651 Seward Rd. I-275, exit 41, 1.7 mi n on SR 4. Int corridors. **Pets:** Other species. $25 daily fee/pet. Service with restrictions, crate.

🄰🄺 ⊠ 🛏 💻 ⇆

FOREST PARK

▼▼ SpringHill Suites by Marriott 🅷
(513) 825-9035. **$89-$219.** 12001 Chase Plaza Dr. I-275, exit 39, just s on Winton Rd, then just w. Int corridors. **Pets:** Accepted.

🄰🄺 ⊠ 🛏 💻 ⇆

HARRISON

▼▼ Comfort Inn 🅷
(513) 367-9666. **$79-$99.** 391 Comfort Dr. I-74, exit 1, just n on New Haven Rd, then just e. Int corridors. **Pets:** Accepted.

🄰🄺 ⊠ 🄴🄼 🛏 💻 ⇆

MASON

▼▼ La Quinta Inn & Suites 🅷 ❖
(513) 459-1111. **$49-$129.** 9918 Escort Dr. I-71, exit 19, just w, then just s. Int corridors. **Pets:** Medium, other species. Service with restrictions, supervision.

🄰🄺 ⊠ 🛏 💻 ⇆

▼▼ Microtel Inn & Suites Kings Island 🅷
(513) 754-1500. **$55-$169.** 5324 Beach Blvd. I-71, exit 25, just nw. Int corridors. **Pets:** Accepted.

🄰🄺 ⊠ 🄴🄼 🛏 💻

⨁ ▼▼ TownePlace Suites by Marriott 🅷
(513) 774-0610. **$139-$149.** 9369 Waterstone Blvd. I-71, exit 19, 0.5 mi e on Mason-Montgomery and Fields-Ertel rds, then 0.9 mi n. Int corridors. **Pets:** Accepted.

🅂🄰🅅🄴 ⊠ 🄴🄼 🛏 💻 ⇆

MIDDLETOWN

⨁ ▼▼▼ Best Western Regency Inn 🅷
(513) 424-3551. **$50-$110.** 6475 Culbertson Rd. I-75, exit 32. Int corridors. **Pets:** Accepted.

🅂🄰🅅🄴 ⊠ 🄴🄼 🛏 💻 🍴 ⇆

▼▼▼ Middletown Drury Inn & Suites 🅷
(513) 425-6650. **$70-$125.** 3320 Village Dr. I-75, exit 32, just w on SR 122. Int corridors. **Pets:** Other species. Service with restrictions, supervision.

🄰🄺 ⊠ 🄴🄼 🛏 💻 ⇆ 🗙

▼ Super 8 Middletown 🅷
(513) 422-4888. **$59-$69.** 3553 Commerce Dr. I-75, exit 32, just e, then just n. Int corridors. **Pets:** Medium, dogs only. $10 daily fee/pet. Designated rooms, service with restrictions, supervision.

🄰🄺 ⊠ 🛏 💻

MILFORD

▼▼▼ Homewood Suites by Hilton 🅷
(513) 248-4663. **$89-$129.** 600 Chamber Dr. I-275, exit 59 southbound; exit 59A northbound, 0.5 mi w on Milford Pkwy, then 0.5 mi s. Int corridors. **Pets:** Accepted.

⊠ 🄴🄼 🛏 💻 ⇆

MOUNT ORAB

AAA ▼▼▼▼ **Best Western Mount Orab Inn** H
(937) 444-6666. **$77-$129.** 100 Leininger St. Jct US 68 and SR 32, just n on US 68. Int corridors. **Pets:** Accepted.
[SAVE] [X] [日] [▯] [⇄]

SHARONVILLE

▼▼▼▼ **Drury Inn & Suites-Cincinnati North** H
(513) 771-5601. **$100-$186.** 2265 E Sharon Rd. I-75, exit 15, just e. Int corridors. **Pets:** Other species. Service with restrictions, supervision.
[ASK] [X] [&M] [日] [▯] [⇄] [X]

▼▼▼▼ **Homewood Suites by Hilton-Cincinnati North** H
(513) 772-8888. **$109-$179.** 2670 E Kemper Rd. I-275, exit 44, jct Mosteller Rd. Int corridors. **Pets:** Medium. $15 daily fee/pet. Service with restrictions, crate.
[X] [日] [▯] [⇄] [X]

▼▼▼▼ **La Quinta Inn & Suites** H ❀
(513) 771-0300. **$59-$139.** 11029 Dowlin Dr. I-75, exit 15, just e. Int corridors. **Pets:** Medium, other species. Service with restrictions, supervision.
[ASK] [X] [&M] [日] [▯] [⇄] [X]

AAA ▼▼▼▼ **Residence Inn by Marriott** H
(513) 771-2525. **$174-$189.** 11689 Chester Rd. I-75, exit 15, just w on Sharon Rd, then 1 mi n. Ext corridors. **Pets:** Accepted.
[SAVE] [X] [&M] [日] [▯] [⇄] [X]

AAA ▼▼▼▼ **Sheraton Cincinnati North Hotel** H ❀
(513) 771-2080. **$89-$219.** 11320 Chester Rd. I-75, exit 15, just w on Sharon Rd, then 0.5 mi n. Int corridors. **Pets:** Medium, dogs only. Service with restrictions, supervision.
[SAVE] [X] [&M] [日] [▯] [▮▮] [⇄] [X]

SPRINGDALE

▼▼◆ **La Quinta Inn** H ❀
(513) 671-2300. **$55-$119.** 12150 Springfield Pike. I-275, exit 41, just n on SR 4. Int corridors. **Pets:** Medium, other species. Service with restrictions, supervision.
[ASK] [X] [日] [▯]

WEST CHESTER

AAA ▼▼▼▼ **Staybridge Suites Cincinnati North** H
(513) 874-1900. **$99-$169.** 8955 Lakota Dr W. I-75, exit 19, just w on Union Centre Blvd, then just n. Int corridors. **Pets:** Accepted.
[SAVE] [X] [&M] [日] [▯] [⇄] [X]

WILMINGTON

▼▼ **Baymont Inn** H
(937) 383-3950. **Call for rates.** 201 Carrie Dr. Jct US 22 and 68, 1.5 mi e on US 22. Int corridors. **Pets:** Accepted.
[X] [日] [▯] [⇄] [X]

▼▼▼▼ **Holiday Inn Wilmington & Roberts Conference Centre** H
(937) 283-3200. **$89-$149.** 123 Gano Rd. I-71, exit 50, just w. Int corridors. **Pets:** Accepted.
[ASK] [X] [&M] [日] [▯] [▮▮] [⇄]

END METROPOLITAN AREA

CLEVELAND METROPOLITAN AREA

BEACHWOOD

▼▼ **Extended StayAmerica-Cleveland-Beachwood** H
(216) 595-9551. **$75-$91.** 3820 Orange Pl. I-271, exit Chagrin Blvd, just e. Int corridors. **Pets:** Other species. $25 daily fee/pet. Service with restrictions, crate.
[ASK] [X] [日] [▯]

AAA ▼▼▼▼ **Hilton Cleveland East/Beachwood** H
(216) 464-5950. **$99-$209.** 3663 Park East Dr. I-271, exit Chagrin Blvd, just w. Int corridors. **Pets:** Accepted.
[SAVE] [X] [日] [▯] [▮▮] [⇄] [X]

▼▼ **Homestead Studio Suites Hotel-Cleveland/Beachwood** H
(216) 896-5555. **$84-$102.** 3625 Orange Pl. I-271, exit Chagrin Blvd, just e. Int corridors. **Pets:** Other species. $25 daily fee/pet. Service with restrictions, crate.
[ASK] [X] [日] [▯]

AAA ◆▼▼▼ **Residence Inn by Marriott Cleveland-Beachwood** H
(216) 831-3030. **$129-$239.** 3628 Park East Dr. Jct US 422 and I-271, exit Chagrin Blvd, just w. Int corridors. **Pets:** Accepted.
[SAVE] [X] [&M] [日] [▯] [⇄] [X]

BROOKLYN

▼▼ **Extended StayAmerica Cleveland-Brooklyn** H
(216) 267-7799. **$67-$82.** 10300 Cascade Crossing. I-480, exit 13, just s. Int corridors. **Pets:** Other species. $25 daily fee/pet. Service with restrictions, crate.
[ASK] [X] [日] [▯]

BROOK PARK

▼▼ **Howard Johnson Cleveland Airport** M
(216) 676-5200. **Call for rates.** 16644 Snow Rd. I-71, exit 237, just e. Ext/int corridors. **Pets:** Accepted.
[X] [日] [▯] [⇄]

CLEVELAND

AAA ▼▼▼▼ **Cleveland Airport Marriott** H
(216) 252-5333. **$179-$199.** 4277 W 150th St. I-71, exit 240, just s. Int corridors. **Pets:** Accepted.
[SAVE] [X] [日] [▯] [▮▮] [⇄]

▼▼ **Comfort Inn Downtown Cleveland** H
(216) 861-0001. **$79-$199.** 1800 Euclid Ave. Corner of Euclid Ave and E 18th St. Int corridors. **Pets:** Small, other species. $250 deposit/room, $100 one-time fee/room. Designated rooms, service with restrictions, supervision.
[ASK] [X] [日] [▯]

▼▼▼ La Quinta Inn & Suites Cleveland Airport Ⓗ ❖
(216) 251-8500. $49-$119. 4222 W 150th St. I-71, exit 240, just n. Int corridors. Pets: Medium, other species. Service with restrictions, supervision.
Ⓐ$Ⓚ ⓧ 🖥 🖵

▼▼▼ Residence Inn by Marriott Ⓗ
(216) 443-9043. $129-$219. 527 Prospect Ave. Between E 9th St and Ontario. Int corridors. Pets: Accepted.
ⓧ 🖥 🖵

▼▼▼ ▼▼▼ The Ritz-Carlton, Cleveland Ⓗ
(216) 623-1300. $229-$399. 1515 W 3rd St. In Tower City Center (3rd St side). Int corridors. Pets: Accepted.
ⓧ 🖥 🍴 🏊 🈺

ⒶⒶⒶ▼ ▼▼▼ Sheraton Cleveland Airport Hotel Ⓗ ❖
(216) 267-1500. $99-$235. 5300 Riverside Dr. I-71, exit 237, just s of I-480 on SR 237, follow signs. Int corridors. Pets: Large. $300 deposit/room. Service with restrictions, supervision.
Ⓢ🅰🆅🅴 ⓧ ♿ 🖥 🖵 🍴 🏊 🈺

INDEPENDENCE

▼▼ La Quinta Inn Ⓗ ❖
(216) 447-1133. $49-$109. 6161 Quarry Ln. I-77, exit Rockside Rd, just e. Int corridors. Pets: Medium, other species. Service with restrictions, supervision.
Ⓐ$Ⓚ ⓧ 🖥 🖵

ⒶⒶⒶ▼ ▼▼▼ Red Roof Inn #7028 Ⓜ
(216) 447-0030. $56-$86. 6020 Quarry Ln. I-77, exit Rockside Rd, just e. Ext corridors. Pets: Accepted.
Ⓢ🅰🆅🅴 ⓧ 🖥

▼▼▼ Residence Inn by Marriott Ⓗ
(216) 520-1450. $170-$208. 5101 W Creek Rd. I-77, exit Rockside Rd, just w to W Creek Rd, then just n. Ext corridors. Pets: Accepted.
ⓧ 🖥 🖵 🏊 🈺

ⒶⒶⒶ▼ ▼▼▼ Sheraton Independence Hotel Ⓗ ❖
(216) 524-0700. $89-$229. 5300 Rockside Rd. I-77, exit Rockside Rd, just w. Int corridors. Pets: Medium. Service with restrictions.
Ⓢ🅰🆅🅴 ⓧ ♿ 🖵 🍴 🏊 🈺

LAKEWOOD

▼▼ Days Inn Ⓜ
(216) 226-4800. Call for rates. 12019 Lake Ave. I-90, exit 166, 1 mi n on W 117th St, then just w. Int corridors. Pets: Accepted.
ⓧ 🖥 🖵

▼▼ Travelodge Ⓜ
(216) 221-9000. Call for rates. 11837 Edgewater Dr. I-90, exit 166, 1 mi n on W 117th St, then just w. Int corridors. Pets: Accepted.
ⓧ 🖥 🖵

MACEDONIA

▼▼ Knights Inn-Cleveland/Macedonia Ⓜ
(330) 467-1981. Call for rates. 240 E Highland Rd. I-271, exit 18, just s; I-80/90 (Ohio Tpke), exit 180, 3 mi n. Ext corridors. Pets: Other species. $5 one-time fee/room. Service with restrictions, supervision.
ⓧ 🖥 🖵 🏊

▼▼▼ La Quinta Inn & Suites Cleveland-Macedonia Ⓗ ❖
(330) 468-5400. $45-$109. 268 E Highland Rd. I-271, exit 18, just s; I-80/90 (Ohio Tpke), exit 180, just n. Int corridors. Pets: Medium, other species. Service with restrictions, supervision.
Ⓐ$Ⓚ ⓧ ♿ 🖥 🖵 🏊

MAYFIELD HEIGHTS

ⒶⒶⒶ▼ ▼▼▼ Baymont Inn & Suites-Cleveland (Mayfield Heights) Ⓗ
(440) 442-8400. Call for rates. 1421 Golden Gate Blvd. I-271, exit 34, 0.3 mi w off US 322. Int corridors. Pets: Accepted.
Ⓢ🅰🆅🅴 ⓧ 🖥 🖵

MEDINA

▼▼▼ Holiday Inn Express Ⓗ
(330) 723-4994. $90-$100. 2850 Medina Rd. I-71, exit 218, just e. Int corridors. Pets: Accepted.
Ⓐ$Ⓚ ⓧ 🖥 🖵 🏊 🈺

▼▼ Motel 6 4112 Ⓗ
(330) 723-3322. $42-$65. 3122 Eastpointe Dr. I-71, exit 218, just w. Int corridors. Pets: Other species. Service with restrictions, supervision.
ⓧ 🏊

▼▼ Red Roof Inn Ⓜ
(330) 725-1395. $55-$77. 5021 Eastpointe Dr. I-71, exit 218, just w. Ext corridors. Pets: Accepted.
Ⓐ$Ⓚ ⓧ 🖥 🏊

MIDDLEBURG HEIGHTS

ⒶⒶⒶ▼ ▼▼▼ Comfort Inn-Cleveland Airport Ⓗ
(440) 234-3131. $109-$129. 17550 Rosbough Dr. I-71, exit 235, 0.3 mi w to Engle Rd, then 0.3 mi n. Int corridors. Pets: Medium, other species. $35 one-time fee/pet. Service with restrictions, supervision.
Ⓢ🅰🆅🅴 ⓧ ♿ 🖥 🖵 🏊

ⒶⒶⒶ▼ ▼▼▼ Days Inn Cleveland Airport South Ⓜ
(440) 243-2277. $69-$149. 7233 Engle Rd. I-71, exit 235, just w. Ext corridors. Pets: $10 daily fee/pet. Service with restrictions.
Ⓢ🅰🆅🅴 ⓧ 🖥 🖵 🏊

ⒶⒶⒶ▼ ▼▼▼ Red Roof Inn-Middleburg Heights #7060 Ⓗ
(440) 243-2441. $50-$80. 17555 Bagley Rd. I-71, exit 235, just w. Ext/int corridors. Pets: Medium. Service with restrictions, supervision.
Ⓢ🅰🆅🅴 ⓧ 🖥

▼▼▼ Residence Inn by Marriott Ⓗ ❖
(440) 234-6688. $129-$169. 17525 Rosbough Dr. I-71, exit 235, just w on Bagley Rd, then just n on Engle Rd. Ext/int corridors. Pets: Other species. $100 one-time fee/room. Service with restrictions, crate.
ⓧ 🖥 🖵 🈺

▼▼ StudioPLUS-Cleveland-Middleburg Heights Ⓗ
(440) 243-7024. $53-$65. 17552 Rosbough Dr. I-71, exit 235, 0.3 mi w to Engle Rd, then 0.3 mi n. Int corridors. Pets: Other species. $25 daily fee/pet. Service with restrictions, crate.
Ⓐ$Ⓚ ⓧ 🖥 🖵

ⒶⒶⒶ▼ ▼▼▼ TownePlace Suites Ⓗ ❖
(440) 816-9300. $139-$159. 7325 S Engle Rd. I-71, exit 235, just w on Bagley Rd. Int corridors. Pets: Other species. $75 one-time fee/pet.
Ⓢ🅰🆅🅴 ⓧ 🖥 🖵 🏊

NORTH OLMSTED

▼▼ Candlewood Suites Ⓗ
(440) 716-0584. $104. 24741 Country Club Blvd. I-480, exit 6B, just n on SR 252. Int corridors. Pets: Accepted.
Ⓐ$Ⓚ ⓧ 🖥 🖵

▼▼ Homestead Studio Suites Hotel-Cleveland/Airport/North Olmsted Ⓗ
(440) 777-8585. $59-$73. 24851 Country Club Blvd. I-480, exit 6B, just n on SR 252. Ext corridors. Pets: Other species. $25 daily fee/pet. Service with restrictions, crate.
Ⓐ$Ⓚ ⓧ ♿ 🖥 🖵

WWW **Radisson Hotel Cleveland Airport** H
(440) 734-5060. **$129-$199.** 25070 Country Club Blvd. I-480, exit 6B, just n on SR 252. Int corridors. **Pets:** Accepted.

(A$K) (X) (&M) (🍴) (📋) (🍴) (🏊) (X)

WW **StudioPLUS Cleveland-Airport-N Olmstead** H
(440) 716-2412. **$59-$73.** 25801 Country Club Blvd. I-480, exit 6B, just n on SR 252. Int corridors. **Pets:** Other species. $25 daily fee/pet. Service with restrictions, crate.

(A$K) (X) (🍴) (📋) (🏊)

RICHFIELD

WWW **Quality Inn & Suites** H
(330) 659-6151. **$79-$129.** 4742 Brecksville Rd. I-80, exit 173, just s. Int corridors. **Pets:** Accepted.

(A$K) (X) (🍴) (📋) (🍴) (🏊) (X)

SOLON

WWW **Hampton Inn** H
(440) 542-0400. **$109-$169.** 6035 Enterprise Pkwy. US 422, exit Harper Rd, 0.6 mi s, then 0.4 mi e. Int corridors. **Pets:** Other species. $50 one-time fee/room. Service with restrictions, crate.

(X) (&M) (🍴) (📋) (🏊)

STRONGSVILLE

(AAA) WWW **Super 8** M
(440) 238-0170. **$60-$86.** 15385 Royalton Rd. I-71, exit 231A, just e; I-76 (Ohio Tpke), exit 161, 1 mi s. Ext corridors. **Pets:** Small. $50 deposit/room, $25 daily fee/pet. Designated rooms, service with restrictions, supervision.

(SAVE) (X) (🍴) (📋)

TWINSBURG

(AAA) WWW **Comfort Suites-Twinsburg** H 🐾
(330) 963-5909. **$79-$139.** 2715 Creekside Dr. I-480, exit 37 (SR 91), just n. Int corridors. **Pets:** Dogs only. $5 daily fee/room, $15 one-time fee/room. Designated rooms, service with restrictions, crate.

(SAVE) (X) (&M) (🍴) (📋) (🏊)

WESTLAKE

WW **Extended Stay Deluxe Cleveland-Westlake** H
(440) 899-4160. **$63-$77.** 30360 Clemens Rd. I-90, exit 156, just n. Int corridors. **Pets:** Other species. $25 daily fee/pet. Service with restrictions, crate.

(A$K) (X) (🍴) (📋)

(AAA) WWW **Red Roof Inn-Westlake #7094** M 🐾
(440) 892-7920. **$56-$90.** 29595 Clemens Rd. I-90, exit 156, just n. Ext corridors. **Pets:** Medium, other species. Service with restrictions, supervision.

(SAVE) (X) (🍴)

WWW **Residence Inn by Marriott** H
(440) 892-2254. **$99-$179.** 30100 Clemens Rd. I-90, exit 156, just n. Ext corridors. **Pets:** Accepted.

(A$K) (X) (🍴) (📋) (🏊) (X)

WILLOUGHBY

(AAA) WWW **Red Roof Inn-East #7053** M
(440) 946-9872. **$50-$90.** 4166 SR 306. I-90, exit 193, just s. Ext corridors. **Pets:** Large, other species. Service with restrictions, supervision.

(SAVE) (X) (🍴)

END METROPOLITAN AREA

CLYDE

WW **Red Roof Inn** H
(419) 547-6660. **$59-$118.** 1363 W McPherson Hwy. 1 mi w on SR 20. Int corridors. **Pets:** Small, dogs only. $50 deposit/pet. Designated rooms, service with restrictions, supervision.

(A$K) (X) (&M) (🍴) (🏊)

COLUMBUS METROPOLITAN AREA

CIRCLEVILLE

WWWW **Holiday Inn Express Hotel & Suites** H
(740) 420-7711. **Call for rates.** 23911 US 23 S. Jct US 22, 1.2 mi s. Int corridors. **Pets:** Accepted.

(X) (&M) (🍴) (📋) (🏊)

COLUMBUS

WWW **Baymont Inn & Suites Columbus at Rickenbacker** H
(614) 491-4400. **Call for rates.** 2323 Rickenbacker Pkwy. I-270, exit 49, 3.4 mi s, then just w. Int corridors. **Pets:** Medium. $25 one-time fee/room. Supervision.

(X) (🍴) (🏊)

(AAA) WWW **Baymont Inn & Suites Columbus/OSU** M
(614) 267-4646. **$69-$149.** 3246 Olentangy River Rd. SR 315, exit N Broadway, 0.3 mi s. Ext corridors. **Pets:** Accepted.

(SAVE) (X) (📋) (🏊)

(AAA) WWWW **Best Western Columbus North** H
(614) 888-8230. **$90.** 888 E Dublin-Granville Rd. I-71, exit 117, 0.5 mi w on SR 161. Int corridors. **Pets:** Medium, other species. $25 deposit/room. No service, crate.

(SAVE) (X) (🍴) (📋) (🍴) (🏊) (X)

WWW **Candlewood Suites Polaris** H
(614) 436-6600. **Call for rates.** 8515 Lyra Dr. I-71, exit 121, 0.3 mi w on SR 750. Int corridors. **Pets:** Accepted.

(X) (&M) (🍴) (📋) (🏊) (X)

(AAA) WWW **Columbus Gatehouse Inn** H
(614) 864-8844. **$99-$199.** 2084 S Hamilton Rd. I-70, exit 107, just e. Ext corridors. **Pets:** Other species. $100 one-time fee/room. Service with restrictions.

(SAVE) (X) (🍴) (📋) (🏊) (X)

(AAA) WWW **Comfort Inn** H
(614) 228-6511. **$98.** 650 S High St. I-71, exit 100A, just s. Ext/int corridors. **Pets:** Medium. $25 daily fee/room. Service with restrictions, supervision.

(SAVE) (X) (🍴) (📋)

WWW **Comfort Inn** H 🐾
(614) 791-9700. **$79-$179.** 8400 Lyra Dr. I-71N, exit 121, just w. Int corridors. **Pets:** Medium. $25 one-time fee/room. Designated rooms, service with restrictions.

(A$K) (X) (🍴) (📋) (🏊) (X)

DoubleTree Columbus/Worthington H

(614) 885-3334. **$99-$179.** 175 Hutchinson Ave. I-270, exit 23, just n of jct US 23 N, just e on Dimension Dr, then just s on High Cross Blvd. Int corridors. **Pets:** Medium. $50 one-time fee/room. Service with restrictions, crate.

SAVE ☒ ☖M ⌨ ▦ ⑪ ⊿

DoubleTree Guest Suites H

(614) 228-4600. **$109-$209.** 50 S Front St. Corner of Front and State sts, just n. Int corridors. **Pets:** Accepted.

☒ ⌨ ▦ ⑪

Drury Inn & Suites-Columbus Convention Center H

(614) 221-7008. **$100-$180.** 88 E Nationwide Blvd. 0.3 mi n on US 23. Int corridors. **Pets:** Other species. Service with restrictions, supervision.

ASK ☒ ☖M ⌨ ▦ ⊿

Extended StayAmerica-Columbus-Easton H

(614) 428-6022. **$90-$110.** 4200 Stelzer Rd. I-270, exit 32, just w on Morse Rd, then just n. Int corridors. **Pets:** Other species. $25 daily fee/pet. Service with restrictions, crate.

ASK ☒ ⌨ ▦

Extended StayAmerica-Columbus-North H

(614) 431-0033. **$45-$55.** 6255 Zumstein Dr. I-71, exit 117, just nw. Int corridors. **Pets:** Other species. $25 daily fee/pet. Service with restrictions, crate.

ASK ☒ ⌨ ▦

Extended StayAmerica-Columbus-Worthington H

(614) 785-1006. **$58-$71.** 7465 High Cross Blvd. I-270, exit 23, just n on US 23, just e on Dimension Dr, then just s. Int corridors. **Pets:** Other species. $25 daily fee/pet. Service with restrictions, crate.

ASK ☒ ⌨ ▦

Extended Stay Deluxe Columbus/Polaris H

(614) 431-5522. **$81-$99.** 8555 Lyra Dr. I-71 N, exit 121, just w on Polaris Pkwy. Int corridors. **Pets:** Other species. $25 daily fee/pet. Service with restrictions, crate.

ASK ☒ ☖M ⌨ ▦ ⊿

Harrison House Bed & Breakfast BB

(614) 421-2202. **$129-$169.** 313 W 5th Ave. I-670, exit 3 (Neil Ave), 0.9 mi n, then just w. Int corridors. **Pets:** Accepted.

ASK ☒ ⊿

Holiday Inn Columbus Downtown Capitol Square H

(614) 221-3281. **$109, 5 day notice.** 175 E Town St. I-70, exit 100B, 0.3 mi n on 4th St. Int corridors. **Pets:** Accepted. ,

SAVE ☒ ⌨ ▦ ⑪ ⊿

Holiday Inn on the Lane H 🐾

(614) 294-4848. **$115-$135.** 328 W Lane Ave. 0.5 mi e of SR 315, exit Lane Ave. Int corridors. **Pets:** Designated rooms, service with restrictions, crate.

SAVE ☒ ☖M ⌨ ▦ ⑪ ⊿ ☒

Microtel Inn & Suites (West) H

(614) 851-1745. **$50-$90.** 5655 Feder Rd. I-70, exit 91A, just sw. Int corridors. **Pets:** Small, other species. $15 daily fee/pet. No service, supervision.

SAVE ☒ ⌨ ▦

Ramada North Columbus H

(614) 890-8111. **$80-$129.** 6767 Schrock Hill Ct. I-270, exit 27, n off Cleveland Ave; enter off Schrock Rd. Int corridors. **Pets:** Medium, other species. $10 daily fee/pet. Service with restrictions, supervision.

SAVE ☒ ⌨ ▦ ⊿

Red Roof Inn-Columbus Convention Center H

(614) 224-6539. **$85-$150.** 111 E Nationwide Blvd. Jct 3rd St. Int corridors. **Pets:** Small. Service with restrictions, supervision.

SAVE ☒ ☖M ⌨

Red Roof Inn-OSU #7121 M

(614) 267-9941. **$60-$130.** 441 Ackerman Rd. SR 315, exit Ackerman Rd, 0.3 mi e. Ext corridors. **Pets:** Other species. Service with restrictions, supervision.

ASK ☒ ☖M ⌨

Red Roof Inn-West #7009 M

(614) 878-9245. **$50-$80.** 5001 Renner Rd. I-70, exit 91 eastbound; exit 91B westbound, just nw. Ext corridors. **Pets:** Small, other species. Service with restrictions, supervision.

SAVE ☒ ☖M ⌨

Red Roof Inn-Worthington #7310 H

(614) 846-3001. **$50-$90.** 7480 N High St. I-270, exit 23, 0.3 mi n on US 23, just e on Dimension Dr, then just s on Vantage Dr. Ext/int corridors. **Pets:** Large, other species. Service with restrictions, supervision.

ASK ☒ ⌨

Residence Inn by Marriott H

(614) 222-2610. **$179-$219.** 36 E Gay St. Between High and S 3rd sts. Int corridors. **Pets:** Other species. $100 one-time fee/room. Service with restrictions.

☒ ☖M ⌨ ▦

Residence Inn by Marriott H

(614) 885-0799. **$149-$159.** 7300 Huntington Park Dr. I-270, exit 23, 0.4 mi n, 0.3 mi e on E Campus View Blvd, then 0.3 mi s. Int corridors. **Pets:** Accepted.

☒ ⌨ ▦ ⊿ ☒

Residence Inn by Marriott Easton H

(614) 414-1000. **$170-$208.** 3999 Easton Loop W. I-270, exit 33, 1 mi w, then just n. Int corridors. **Pets:** Accepted.

☒ ⌨ ▦ ⊿ ☒

Sheraton Suites Columbus H 🐾

(614) 436-0004. **$229-$259.** 201 Hutchinson Ave. I-270, exit 23, 0.3 mi n on US 23, just e on Dimension Dr, then 0.4 mi se on Vantage Dr. Int corridors. **Pets:** Large. No service, supervision.

SAVE ☒ ☖M ⌨ ▦ ⑪ ⊿

TownePlace Suites by Marriott H

(614) 885-1557. **$114-$119.** 7272 Huntington Park Dr. I-270, exit 23, 0.4 mi n, 0.3 mi e on E Campus View Blvd, then 0.3 mi s. Int corridors. **Pets:** Accepted.

☒ ⌨ ▦ ⊿

The Westin Columbus H 🐾

(614) 228-3800. **$99-$519.** 310 S High St. Corner of Main and High sts. Int corridors. **Pets:** Medium, other species. Service with restrictions.

SAVE ☒ ⌨ ▦ ⑪

DUBLIN

Chase Suite Hotel H

(614) 766-7762. **$99-$179.** 4130 Tuller Rd. I-270, exit 20, 0.3 mi s on Sawmill Rd via Village Pkwy and Dublin Center Dr. Ext corridors. **Pets:** Other species. $250 deposit/room, $10 daily fee/pet. Service with restrictions.

SAVE ☒ ⌨ ▦ ⊿

Drury Inn & Suites-Columbus Northwest H

(614) 798-8802. **$95-$145.** 6170 Parkcenter Cir. I-270, exit 15 (Tuttle Crossing Blvd), 0.3 mi e, then just n on Blazer Pkwy. Int corridors. **Pets:** Other species. Service with restrictions, supervision.

ASK ☒ ☖M ⌨ ▦ ⊿

▼▼▼▼ Dublin Homewood Suites by Hilton Ⓗ
(614) 791-8675. **$119-$149.** 5300 Parkcenter Ave. I-270, exit 15 (Tuttle Crossing Blvd), just e, just n on Blazer Pkwy, then just e. Int corridors. **Pets:** Accepted.

⊠ ⓜ 🛏 🖥 ⮑ ☒

▼▼ Extended StayAmerica-Columbus-Dublin Ⓗ
(614) 760-0053. **$67-$82.** 450 Metro Pl N. I-270, exit 17A, just e on SR 161, just s on Frantz Rd, then just n. Int corridors. **Pets:** Other species. $25 daily fee/pet. Service with restrictions, crate.

ⒶⓈⓀ ⊠ 🛏 🖥

▼▼ Extended StayAmerica Columbus-Sawmill Ⓗ
(614) 764-0159. **$63-$77.** 6601 Reflections Dr. I-270, exit 20, 0.7 mi s on Sawmill Rd, just e on SR 161, just s on Martin, then just se. Int corridors. **Pets:** Other species. $25 daily fee/pet. Service with restrictions, crate.

ⒶⓈⓀ ⊠ 🛏 🖥 ⮑

▼▼ Extended Stay Deluxe (Columbus/Tuttle) Ⓗ
(614) 760-0245. **$76-$93.** 5530 Tuttle Crossing Blvd. I-270, exit 15 (Tuttle Crossing Blvd), 0.5 mi w. Int corridors. **Pets:** Other species. $25 daily fee/pet. Service with restrictions, crate.

ⒶⓈⓀ ⊠ 🛏 🖥

▼▼ La Quinta Inn Ⓗ ❖
(614) 792-8300. **$55-$119.** 6145 Parkcenter Cir. I-270, exit 15 (Tuttle Crossing Blvd), just e, then just n on Blazer Pkwy. Int corridors. **Pets:** Medium, other species. Service with restrictions, supervision.

ⒶⓈⓀ ⊠ ⓜ 🛏 🖥

ⒶⒶⒶ ▼▼▼ Red Roof Inn-Dublin #7127 Ⓜ
(614) 764-3993. **$50-$80.** 5125 Post Rd. I-270, exit 17A, just ne. Ext corridors. **Pets:** Accepted.

Ⓢⓐⓥⓔ ⊠ ⓜ 🛏

▼▼▼▼ Residence Inn by Marriott Dublin Ⓗ
(614) 791-0403. **$149-$159.** 435 Metro Pl S. I-270, exit 17A, 0.5 mi e to Frantz Rd, then 0.5 mi s. Ext/int corridors. **Pets:** Accepted.

⊠ ⓜ 🛏 🖥 ⮑ ☒

▼▼▼ Staybridge Suites Ⓗ
(614) 734-9882. **Call for rates.** 6095 Emerald Pkwy. I-270, exit 15 (Tuttle Crossing Blvd), just w. Int corridors. **Pets:** Accepted.

⊠ ⓜ 🛏 🖥 ⮑ ☒

GAHANNA

▼▼ Candlewood Suites Columbus Airport Ⓗ
(614) 863-4033. **$103-$120.** 590 Taylor Rd. I-270, exit 37, just e, 0.6 mi s on Morrison Rd, then just e. Int corridors. **Pets:** Accepted.

ⒶⓈⓀ ⊠ 🛏 🖥

▼▼ TownePlace Suites by Marriott Columbus Airport Ⓗ
(614) 861-1400. **$116-$142.** 695 Taylor Rd. I-270, exit 37, just e, 0.6 mi s on Morrison Rd, then just e. Int corridors. **Pets:** Other species. $100 one-time fee/room. Service with restrictions, crate.

⊠ 🛏 🖥 ⮑

GROVE CITY

ⒶⒶⒶ ▼▼▼ Best Western Executive Inn Ⓜ
(614) 875-7770. **$64-$90.** 4026 Jackpot Rd. I-71, exit 100, just e. Ext corridors. **Pets:** Medium, dogs only. $10 daily fee/pet. Designated rooms, service with restrictions, crate.

Ⓢⓐⓥⓔ ⊠ 🛏 🖥 ⮑

▼▼▼▼ Drury Inn & Suites-Columbus South Ⓗ
(614) 875-7000. **$80-$186.** 4109 Parkway Centre Dr. I-71, exit 100, just e. Int corridors. **Pets:** Other species. Service with restrictions, supervision.

ⒶⓈⓀ ⊠ ⓜ 🛏 🖥 ⮑

ⒶⒶⒶ ▼▼▼▼ La Quinta Inn South Ⓗ ❖
(614) 539-6200. **$49-$134.** 3962 Jackpot Rd. I-71, exit 100, just e. Int corridors. **Pets:** Medium, other species. Service with restrictions, supervision.

Ⓢⓐⓥⓔ ⊠ 🛏 🖥 ⮑ ☒

▼▼ Red Roof Inn Columbus/Grove City Ⓜ ❖
(614) 871-9617. **$65.** 4055 Jackpot Rd. I-71, exit 100, just e. Ext corridors. **Pets:** Medium. $100 deposit/pet. Service with restrictions, supervision.

ⒶⓈⓀ ⊠ 🛏 🖥 ⮑

HEBRON

▼▼ Red Roof Inn Ⓗ
(740) 467-7663. **Call for rates.** 10668 Lancaster Rd SW. I-70, exit 126, just s. Int corridors. **Pets:** Service with restrictions, supervision.

⊠ ⓜ

HILLIARD

▼▼▼▼ Comfort Suites by Choice Hotels-Columbus Ⓗ
(614) 529-8118. **Call for rates.** 3831 Park Mill Run Dr. I-270, exit 13A northbound; exit 13 southbound, 0.3 mi e on Fishinger Blvd. Int corridors. **Pets:** Accepted.

⊠ ⓜ 🛏 🖥 ⮑

▼▼▼▼ Homewood Suites by Hilton-Columbus Ⓗ
(614) 529-4100. **$89-$189.** 3841 Park Mill Run Dr. I-270, exit 13 southbound; exit 13A northbound. Int corridors. **Pets:** Small, other species. $10 daily fee/room, $25 one-time fee/room. Service with restrictions, crate.

⊠ ⓜ 🛏 🖥 ⮑ ☒

MARYSVILLE

▼▼▼ Comfort Inn Ⓗ
(937) 644-0400. **$80-$90.** 16420 Allenby Dr. Jct US 33 and 36. Int corridors. **Pets:** Large, dogs only. $25 daily fee/pet. Service with restrictions.

ⒶⓈⓀ ⊠ 🛏 🖥 ⮑

NEWARK

ⒶⒶⒶ ▼▼▼▼ Cherry Valley Lodge Ⓗ
(740) 788-1200. **$118-$189.** 2299 Cherry Valley Rd. 3.5 mi w on SR 16, then 0.3 mi s. Int corridors. **Pets:** Other species. $150 deposit/room. Designated rooms, service with restrictions, crate.

Ⓢⓐⓥⓔ ⊠ ⓜ 🛏 🖥 🍴 ⮑ ☒

OBETZ

▼▼▼ Comfort Inn Obetz Rickenbacker Ⓗ
(614) 492-9000. **$59-$129.** 4870 Old Rathmell Ct. I-270, exit 49, just e. Int corridors. **Pets:** Other species. $20 daily fee/pet. Service with restrictions, crate.

ⒶⓈⓀ ⊠ ⓜ 🛏 🖥 ⮑

REYNOLDSBURG

ⒶⒶⒶ ▼▼▼ Days Inn & Suites Columbus East Ⓗ
(614) 864-1280. **$53-$85.** 2100 Brice Rd. I-70, exit 110 westbound; exit 110B eastbound, just n. Int corridors. **Pets:** Small, other species. $20 daily fee/pet. Service with restrictions, supervision.

Ⓢⓐⓥⓔ ⊠ 🛏 🖥 🍴 ⮑

▼▼ Extended StayAmerica-Columbus-East Ⓗ
(614) 759-1451. **$49-$60.** 2200 Lake Club Dr. I-70, exit 110 westbound; exit 110B eastbound, 0.5 mi n on Brice Rd, just w on Channingway, then just s. Int corridors. **Pets:** Other species. $25 daily fee/pet. Service with restrictions, crate.

ⒶⓈⓀ ⊠ 🛏 🖥 ⮑

▼▼▼ The Fairfield Inn & Suites Columbus East Ⓗ ❖
(614) 864-4555. **$98-$120.** 2826 Taylor Rd SW. I-70, 112B eastbound; 112 westbound, just n, then just e. Int corridors. **Pets:** Other species. $75 one-time fee/room. Service with restrictions, crate.

⊠ ⓜ 🛏 🖥 ⮑ ☒

▼▼▼▼ La Quinta Inn Columbus East 🅷 ☼
(614) 866-6456. **$39-$99.** 2447 Brice Rd. I-70, exit 110 westbound; exit 110B eastbound, 0.3 mi n. Int corridors. **Pets:** Medium, other species. Service with restrictions, supervision.
🆂🅺 ✕ 🛏 💻 ➿

▼▼ Super 8 Reynoldsburg 🅼
(614) 864-3880. **$50-$60.** 2055 Brice Rd. I-70, exit 110 westbound; exit 110B eastbound. Ext corridors. **Pets:** Accepted.
🆂🅺 ✕ 🛏 💻 ➿

WESTERVILLE

▼▼ Baymont Inn & Suites North East 🅼
(614) 890-1244. **Call for rates.** 909 S State St. I-270, exit 29, 0.3 mi n on SR 3. Ext corridors. **Pets:** Accepted.
✕ 🛏 💻 ➿

END METROPOLITAN AREA

CONNEAUT

▲▲▲ ▼▼▼ Days Inn of Conneaut 🅷
(440) 593-6000. **$65-$89.** 600 Days Blvd. I-90, exit 241, 0.3 mi n. Int corridors. **Pets:** Other species. $10 daily fee/pet. Designated rooms, service with restrictions, supervision.
🆂🅰🆅🅴 ✕ 🛏 💻 ➿

CUYAHOGA FALLS

▲▲▲ ▼▼▼▼ Sheraton Suites Akron-Cuyahoga Falls 🅷 ☼
(330) 929-3000. **$239-$439.** 1989 Front St. SR 8, exit Broad Blvd, just w. Int corridors. **Pets:** Medium. Designated rooms, service with restrictions, supervision.
🆂🅰🆅🅴 ✕ ⛷🅼 🛏 💻 🍽 ➿ ⊠

DAYTON

▼▼ Comfort Inn by Choice Hotels-North 🅷
(937) 890-9995. **Call for rates.** 7125 Miller Ln. I-75, exit 59 (Wyse Rd/Benchwood Rd), just w on Benchwood Rd, then 0.6 mi n. Int corridors. **Pets:** Accepted.
✕ ⛷🅼 🛏 💻 ➿

▲▲▲ ▼▼▼ Country Inn & Suites Dayton South 🅷
(937) 425-7400. **$89-$129.** 8277 Yankee St. I-675, exit 2, just e on SR 725, then just s; southbound, just s on Yankee St. Int corridors. **Pets:** Medium, other species. $20 one-time fee/pet. Designated rooms, supervision.
🆂🅰🆅🅴 ✕ ⛷🅼 🛏 💻 ➿ ⊠

▼▼▼▼ Dayton Marriott Hotel 🅷
(937) 223-1000. **$179-$189.** 1414 S Patterson Blvd. I-75, exit 51 (Edwin C Moses Blvd), 1.5 mi n, just e on Washington St, then 1 mi s. Int corridors. **Pets:** Accepted.
✕ 🛏 💻 🍽 ➿ ⊠

▼▼▼▼ Drury Inn & Suites-Dayton North 🅷
(937) 454-5200. **$87-$193.** 6616 Miller Ln. I-75, exit 59 (Wyse Rd/Benchwood Rd), just w on Benchwood Rd, then just n. Int corridors. **Pets:** Other species. Service with restrictions, supervision.
🆂🅺 ✕ ⛷🅼 🛏 💻 ➿

▼▼ Extended StayAmerica-Dayton North 🅷
(937) 898-9221. **$49-$95.** 6688 Miller Ln. I-75, exit 59 (Wyse Rd/Benchwood Rd), just w on Benchwood Rd, then just n. Int corridors. **Pets:** Other species. $25 daily fee/pet. Service with restrictions, crate.
🆂🅺 ✕ 🛏 💻 ➿

▼▼ Extended StayAmerica Dayton South 🅷
(937) 439-2022. **$53-$99.** 7851 Lois Cir. I-75, exit 44, just e on SR 725; opposite mall. Int corridors. **Pets:** Other species. $25 daily fee/pet. Service with restrictions, crate.
🆂🅺 ✕ 🛏 💻 ➿

▼▼▼▼ Hampton Inn-Dayton South 🅷
(937) 436-3700. **$109.** 8099 Old Yankee St. I-675, exit 2, just e on SR 725, then just s; southbound, just s. Int corridors. **Pets:** Accepted.
✕ ⛷🅼 🛏 💻 ➿

▲▲▲ ▼▼▼ Red Roof Inn-North #7023 🅼
(937) 898-1054. **$50-$70, 7 day notice.** 7370 Miller Ln. I-75, exit 59 (Wyse Rd/Benchwood Rd), just w on Benchwood Rd, then 0.8 mi n. Ext corridors. **Pets:** Accepted.
🆂🅰🆅🅴 ✕ 🛏

DOVER

▼▼ Americas Best Value Inn & Suites 🅼
(330) 364-7724. **$45-$100.** 889 Commercial Pkwy. I-77, exit 83, just e. Ext corridors. **Pets:** Accepted.
🆂🅺 ✕ 🛏 💻 ➿

ELYRIA

▼▼ Comfort Inn 🅷
(440) 324-7676. **$69-$139, 15 day notice.** 739 Leona St. I-80, exit 145, just n on SR 57, exit Midway Blvd. Int corridors. **Pets:** $10 daily fee/pet. Service with restrictions, supervision.
🆂🅺 ✕ 🛏 💻

▼▼▼ Red Roof Inn & Suites 🅷
(440) 324-4444. **$59-$99.** 621 Midway Blvd. I-80, exit 145, just n on SR 57, exit Midway Blvd. Int corridors. **Pets:** Medium, other species. Service with restrictions, supervision.
🆂🅺 ✕ ⛷🅼 🛏 💻 ➿

▼▼ Super 8 Motel 🅷
(440) 323-7488. **$59-$99.** 910 Lorain Blvd. I-80, exit 145, 0.5 mi s on SR 57. Ext corridors. **Pets:** Other species. $10 one-time fee/pet. Designated rooms, service with restrictions, supervision.
🆂🅺 ✕ 💻 ➿

ENGLEWOOD

▼▼▼▼ Holiday Inn-Dayton Northwest Airport 🅷
(937) 832-1234. **$95-$125.** 10 Rockridge Rd. I-70, exit 29, just n. Int corridors. **Pets:** Accepted.
🆂🅺 ✕ 💻 🍽 ➿

▼▼ Red Roof Inn-Dayton (Englewood) 🅼
(937) 836-8339. **Call for rates.** 9325 N Main St. I-70, exit 29, just s. Ext corridors. **Pets:** Large. Service with restrictions, supervision.
✕ 🛏 ➿

FAIRBORN

▼▼▼ Hawthorn Inn & Suites 🅷
(937) 754-9109. **$74-$149.** 730 E Xenia Dr. I-675, exit 22, 0.6 mi w. Int corridors. **Pets:** Medium. $75 one-time fee/room. Service with restrictions, supervision.
🆂🅺 ✕ 🛏 💻

▼▼▼ Holiday Inn Dayton/Fairborn/I-675 🅷
(937) 426-7800. **$109-$179.** 2800 Presidential Dr. I-675, exit 17 (N Fairfield Rd), just w on N Fairfield Rd. Int corridors. **Pets:** Accepted.
🆂🅺 ✕ ⛷🅼 🛏 💻 🍽 ➿

WWWW Homewood Suites by
Hilton-Fairborn/Dayton
(937) 429-0600. **$99-$159.** 2750 Presidential Dr. I-675, exit 17 (N Fairfield Rd), just w. Ext/int corridors. **Pets:** Large, other species. $100 one-time fee/room. Service with restrictions, supervision.

⊠ 🖥 🖵 ⇌ ⊠

ⒶⒶⒶ WWWW Ramada Limited & Suites-Fairborn
Ohio 🄷
(937) 490-2000. **$70-$100.** 2540 University Blvd. I-675, exit 15 (Colonel Glenn Hwy), 1.5 mi e, then just s. Int corridors. **Pets:** Accepted.

(SAVE) ⊠ 🖥 🖵 ⇌

ⒶⒶⒶ WWW Red Roof Inn-Fairborn #7205 🄷
(937) 426-6116. **$50-$70, 7 day notice.** 2580 Colonel Glenn Hwy. I-675, exit 17 (N Fairfield Rd), just w. Ext corridors. **Pets:** Accepted.

(SAVE) ⊠ 🖥

WW StudioPLUS Dayton-Fairborn 🄷
(937) 429-0140. **$52-$78.** 3131 Presidential Dr. I-675, exit 15 (Colonel Glenn Hwy), 1.5 mi e, then just s. Int corridors. **Pets:** Other species. $25 daily fee/pet. Service with restrictions, crate.

(ASK) ⊠ 🖥 🖵 ⇌

FAIRLAWN

ⒶⒶⒶ W Americas Best Value Inn 🄷
(330) 666-8887. **$38-$100.** 79 Rothrock Rd. I-77, exit 137A, just e. Int corridors. **Pets:** Accepted.

(SAVE) ⊠ 🖥 🖵

WW Extended StayAmerica Akron-Copley 🄷
(330) 668-9818. **$63-$77.** 185 W Montrose Ave. I-77, exit 137B, just w on SR 18. Int corridors. **Pets:** Other species. $25 daily fee/pet. Service with restrictions, crate.

(ASK) ⊠ 🖥 🖵

W Motel 6 Akron North #2000 Ⓜ
(330) 666-0566. **$45-$58.** 99 Rothrock Rd. I-77, exit 137A, just e. Ext corridors. **Pets:** Other species. Service with restrictions, supervision.

⊠

ⒶⒶⒶ WWWW The Residence Inn by Marriott 🄷
(330) 666-4811. **$149-$169.** 120 W Montrose Ave. I-77, exit 137B, just w. Ext corridors. **Pets:** Accepted.

(SAVE) ⊠ 🖥 🖵 ⇌ ⊠

WW StudioPLUS-Akron-Copley 🄷
(330) 666-3177. **$67-$82.** 170 W Montrose Ave. I-77, exit 137B, just w on SR 18. Int corridors. **Pets:** Other species. $25 daily fee/pet. Service with restrictions, crate.

(ASK) ⊠ 🖥 🖵 ⇌

FINDLAY

WWW Extended Stay Deluxe Findlay-Tiffin Ave 🄷
(419) 425-9696. **$63-$77.** 2355 Tiffin Ave. 3 mi e on US 224. Int corridors. **Pets:** Other species. $25 daily fee/pet. Service with restrictions, crate.

(ASK) ⊠ 🖥 🖵 ⇌ ⊠

ⒶⒶⒶ WW Quality Inn Ⓜ ❋
(419) 423-4303. **$65-$110.** 1020 Interstate Ct. I-75, exit 159, just w. Ext corridors. **Pets:** Dogs only. $15 daily fee/pet. Service with restrictions, supervision.

(SAVE) ⊠ 🖥 🖵 ⇌

WW Red Roof Inn Ⓜ
(419) 424-0466. **Call for rates.** 1951 Broad Ave. I-75, exit 159, 0.5 mi e. Ext corridors. **Pets:** Medium. $10 one-time fee/pet. No service, crate.

⊠ 🖥 ⇌

FOSTORIA

ⒶⒶⒶ WWW Best Western Fostoria Inn & Suites 🄷
(419) 436-3600. **$81-$125.** 1690 N County Line Rd. SR 12, 2 mi n on SR 23. Int corridors. **Pets:** Large, other species. $10 daily fee/pet. Designated rooms, service with restrictions, crate.

(SAVE) ⊠ 🖥ᴹ 🖥 🖵 ⇌

FREDERICKTOWN

WWW Heartland Country Resort 🄲🄰 ❋
(419) 768-9300. **$180-$240, 7 day notice.** 3020 Township Rd 190. I-71, exit 151, 2 mi e on SR 95, 0.6 mi s on SR 314, then 1.3 mi e. Ext corridors. **Pets:** Other species. $15 daily fee/room.

(ASK) ⊠ 🖥 🖵 ⊠

FREMONT

WWW Comfort Inn & Suites 🄷
(419) 355-9300. **$90-$250.** 840 Sean Dr. I-80/90, exit 91, 2 mi s on SR 53. Int corridors. **Pets:** Medium, other species. $25 one-time fee/pet. Service with restrictions, supervision.

(ASK) ⊠ 🖥 🖵 ⇌

WW Days Inn 🄷
(419) 334-9551. **$69-$129.** 3701 SR 53 N. I-80/90, exit 91, just n. Int corridors. **Pets:** Small, dogs only. $50 deposit/pet. Designated rooms, service with restrictions, supervision.

(ASK) ⊠ 🖵 🍴 ⇌

WW Holiday Inn-Fremont 🄷
(419) 334-2682. **Call for rates.** 3422 Port Clinton Rd. I-80/90, exit 91, just s. Int corridors. **Pets:** Accepted.

⊠ 🖥ᴹ 🖥 🖵 🍴 ⇌

GENEVA

ⒶⒶⒶ W Howard Johnson Express Inn 🄷
(440) 466-1168. **$60-$95.** SR 534. I-90, exit 218, just n. Ext/int corridors. **Pets:** Accepted.

(SAVE) ⊠ 🖥 🖵 ⇌

GENEVA-ON-THE-LAKE

ⒶⒶⒶ WWWW The Lodge & Conference Center at
Geneva-on-the-Lake 🄷 ❋
(440) 466-7100. **$89-$279, 3 day notice.** 4888 N Broadway. I-90, exit 218, 8 mi n. Ext corridors. **Pets:** Large. $25 one-time fee/pet. Designated rooms, service with restrictions, supervision.

(SAVE) ⊠ 🖥ᴹ 🖥 🖵 🍴 ⇌ ⊠

GREEN

ⒶⒶⒶ WWW Super 8 Motel 🄷
(330) 899-9888. **$66-$160.** 1605 Corporate Woods Pkwy. I-77, exit 118, just w. Ext/int corridors. **Pets:** Large. $10 daily fee/pet. Designated rooms, service with restrictions, supervision.

(SAVE) ⊠ 🖥 🖵 ⇌

GREENVILLE

ⒶⒶⒶ WW Greenville Inn 🄷
(937) 548-3613. **$65-$115.** 851 E Martin. Jct US 36 and 127, 0.3 mi w on SR 571. Int corridors. **Pets:** Other species. $10 daily fee/pet. Service with restrictions, supervision.

(SAVE) ⊠ 🖥 🖵 🍴

HOLLAND

ⒶⒶⒶ WWW Econo Lodge Ⓜ
(419) 866-6565. **$40-$80.** 1201 E Mall Dr. I-475, exit 8, just w on SR 2. Ext corridors. **Pets:** Accepted.

(SAVE) ⊠ 🖥 🖵 ⇌

Extended StayAmerica Toledo-Holland H
(419) 861-1133. **$54-$66.** 6155 Trust Dr. I-475, exit 8, just e to Holland-Sylvania Rd, then just n. Int corridors. **Pets:** Other species. $25 daily fee/pet. Service with restrictions, crate.
ASK ✕ 🛏 📼

Hawthorn Suites H
(419) 867-9555. **$79-$169.** 6101 Trust Dr. I-475, exit 8, just e to Holland-Sylvania Rd, then just n. Ext corridors. **Pets:** $125 one-time fee/room. Service with restrictions, crate.
SAVE ✕ 🛏 📼 ⊇ ✕

Quality Inn Toledo Airport M
(419) 867-1144. **$59-$149.** 1401 E Mall Dr. I-475, exit 8, just w on SR 2. Ext/int corridors. **Pets:** Other species. $10 daily fee/pet. Service with restrictions, crate.
SAVE ✕ 🛏 📼 ⊇

Red Roof Inn Toledo/Holland #7058 M
(419) 866-5512. **$49-$62.** 1214 Corporate Dr. I-475, exit 8, just e on Holland-Sylvania Rd, then just n to Trust Dr. Ext corridors. **Pets:** Accepted.
ASK ✕ 🛏

HUBER HEIGHTS

Holiday Inn Express Hotel & Suites H
(937) 235-2000. **$105-$150.** 5612 Merily Way. I-70, exit 36, just se on SR 202. Int corridors. **Pets:** $25 one-time fee/room. No service, crate.
ASK ✕ 🛏 📼 ⊇

HURON

Microtel Inn & Suites H
(419) 433-7829. **Call for rates.** 601 Rye Beach Rd. SR 2, exit Rye Beach, 2.5 mi w on US 6. Int corridors. **Pets:** Medium, other species. $10 daily fee/pet. Service with restrictions, crate.
✕ 🛏 📼 ⊇

JACKSON

Comfort Inn-Jackson H ❄
(740) 286-7581. **$80-$90, 30 day notice.** 605 E Main St. Jct SR 32, 0.5 mi n on SR 93. Int corridors. **Pets:** Medium. $20 one-time fee/room. Supervision.
SAVE ✕ 🛏 📼

Red Roof Inn H
(740) 288-1200. **$72-$82.** 1000 Acy Ave. US 35, exit McCarty Ln, just nw. Int corridors. **Pets:** Medium. $25 deposit/room. Service with restrictions, supervision.
SAVE ✕ 🛏

JEFFERSONVILLE

Quality Inn-Washington Court House H
(740) 426-6400. **$59-$170.** 10160 Carr Rd NW. I-71, exit 69 (SR 41), just w. Int corridors. **Pets:** Accepted.
ASK ✕ 🛏 📼 ⊇

KENT

Days Inn-Akron Kent M
(330) 677-9400. **$55-$69.** 4422 Edson Rd. I-76, exit 33. Ext corridors. **Pets:** Other species. $10 daily fee/pet. Service with restrictions, crate.
ASK ✕ 🛏 📼 ⊇

Super 8 Motel H
(330) 678-8817. **$59-$69, 14 day notice.** 4380 Edson Rd. I-76, exit 33. Int corridors. **Pets:** Medium, dogs only. $10 daily fee/pet. Service with restrictions, supervision.
ASK ✕ 🛏

LOGAN

Baymont Inn and Suites H
(740) 385-1700. **$69-$179, 7 day notice.** 12819 SR 664. Jct US 33, just n. Int corridors. **Pets:** Accepted.
SAVE ✕ 🛏 📼 ⊇

Holiday Inn Express Hocking Hills H
(740) 385-7700. **$109-$169.** 12916 Grey St. SR 664, just w to Lake Logan Rd, then just n. Int corridors. **Pets:** Small, dogs only. Designated rooms, service with restrictions, supervision.
SAVE ✕ 🛏 📼

The Inn & Spa At Cedar Falls CI ❄
(740) 385-7489. **$125-$289.** 21190 SR 374. 9.5 mi s on SR 664, 1 mi e. Int corridors. **Pets:** Dogs only. $30 daily fee/pet. Designated rooms, service with restrictions, crate.
ASK ✕ 🛏 📼 ⓘ ✕ W ⊠

LOUDONVILLE

Little Brown Inn M
(419) 994-5525. **$49-$79.** 940 S Market St. 1 mi s on SR 3. Int corridors. **Pets:** Medium. $10 daily fee/pet. Designated rooms, service with restrictions, supervision.
ASK ✕ 🛏

MANSFIELD

Best Western Richland Inn Mansfield H
(419) 756-6670. **$59-$159.** 180 E Hanley Rd. I-71, exit 169, jct SR 13. Int corridors. **Pets:** Medium. $25 one-time fee/room. No service, crate.
SAVE ✕ 🛏 📼 ⊇

Comfort Inn North H
(419) 529-1000. **$70-$160.** 500 N Trimble Rd. Jct US 30. Int corridors. **Pets:** Accepted.
ASK ✕ 🛏 📼 ⊇ ✕

La Quinta Inn Mansfield H 🐾
(419) 774-0005. **$55-$109.** 120 Stander Ave. I-71, exit 169. Int corridors. **Pets:** Medium, other species. Service with restrictions, supervision.
ASK ✕ 🛏 📼 ⊇

Super 8 Motel H
(419) 756-8875. **$60-$119.** 2425 Interstate Cir. I-71, exit 169. Int corridors. **Pets:** Accepted.
SAVE ✕ 🛏 📼

Travelodge M
(419) 756-7600. **$50-$100.** 90 W Hanley Rd. I-71, exit 169, just s. Ext corridors. **Pets:** Medium. $10 daily fee/pet. Service with restrictions, crate.
SAVE ✕ 🛏 📼

MARIETTA

Best Western Marietta M ❄
(740) 374-7211. **$66-$139.** 279 Muskingum Dr. I-77, exit 6, 3.5 mi sw on SR 821, then 1 mi s on SR 60. Ext corridors. **Pets:** Medium, other species. Service with restrictions, supervision.
SAVE ✕ 🛏 📼 ✕

Comfort Inn Marietta H ❄
(740) 374-8190. **$70-$150.** 700 Pike St. I-77, exit 1, just e. Int corridors. **Pets:** Medium, other species. $15 daily fee/pet. Designated rooms, service with restrictions, supervision.
SAVE ✕ 🛏 📼 ⓘ ⊇

The Lafayette Hotel H
(740) 373-5522. **$60-$185.** 101 Front St. Center. Int corridors. **Pets:** Other species. $50 deposit/room. Service with restrictions, crate.
ASK ✕ 🛏 📼 ⓘ

▼▼ **Super 8 Motel-Marietta** H
(740) 374-8888. **Call for rates.** 46 Acme St. I-77, exit 1, just w. Int corridors. **Pets:** Accepted.

MARION

▼▼ **Comfort Inn by Choice Hotels** H
(740) 389-5552. **Call for rates.** 256 James Way. Jct US 23 and SR 95, just w. Int corridors. **Pets:** Other species. $15 daily fee/pet. Service with restrictions, crate.

MAUMEE

▼▼▼ **Baymont Inn & Suites** H
(419) 865-9400. **Call for rates.** 6425 Kit Ln. I-475, exit 6, just w. Int corridors. **Pets:** Accepted.

▼▼ **Comfort Inn West Toledo/Maumee** H
(419) 893-2800. **$69-$105.** 1426 S Reynolds Rd. I-80/90, exit 59, just s. Int corridors. **Pets:** Other species. $10 daily fee/pet. Service with restrictions, supervision.

▼▼ **Days Inn-Toledo/Maumee** M
(419) 897-6900. **Call for rates.** 1704 Tollgate Dr. I-80/90, exit 59, just s. Ext corridors. **Pets:** Accepted.

▼▼▼ **Homewood Suites by Hilton-Toledo** H
(419) 897-0980. **$99-$159.** 1410 Arrowhead Rd. I-475, exit 6, just e. Int corridors. **Pets:** Accepted.

▼▼▼ **Red Roof Inn-Maumee #7046** M ✿
(419) 893-0292. **$50-$80.** 1570 S Reynolds Rd. I-80/90, exit 59, just s. Ext/int corridors. **Pets:** Other species. Service with restrictions, supervision.

▼▼▼ **Residence Inn by Marriott Maumee** H ✿
(419) 891-2233. **$149-$169.** 1370 Arrowhead Dr. I-475, exit 6, just e. Int corridors. **Pets:** $75 one-time fee/room. Service with restrictions, crate.

▼▼ **StudioPLUS-Toledo-Maumee** H
(419) 891-1211. **$76-$93.** 542 W Dussel Dr. I-475, exit 8, just e. Int corridors. **Pets:** Other species. $25 daily fee/pet. Service with restrictions, crate.

▼▼ **Super 8 Motel-Maumee/Toledo** H
(419) 897-3800. **Call for rates.** 1390 Arrowhead Rd. I-475, exit 6, just e. Int corridors. **Pets:** Accepted.

MENTOR

▼▼▼ **Best Western Lawnfield Inn & Suites** H
(440) 205-7378. **$75-$150.** 8434 Mentor Ave. I-90, exit 195, 1.5 mi n to SR 20 (Mentor Ave), then just e. Int corridors. **Pets:** Accepted.

▼▼▼ **Residence Inn by Marriott** H
(440) 392-0800. **$129-$219.** 5660 Emerald Ct. Jct SR 2 and Heisley Rd, just s. Int corridors. **Pets:** Other species. $75 one-time fee/room. Service with restrictions.

▼▼ **Studio 6 #6019** M
(440) 946-0749. **$59-$69.** 7677 Reynolds Rd. Just s of SR 2 on SR 306. Ext corridors. **Pets:** Other species. $10 daily fee/room. Service with restrictions, supervision.

▼▼ **Super 8 Motel** H
(440) 951-8558. **$49-$110.** 7325 Palisades Pkwy. On SR 306, just s of SR 2. Int corridors. **Pets:** Accepted.

MIAMISBURG

▼▼▼ **Hawthorn Suites Dayton South** H
(937) 434-7881. **Call for rates.** 155 Prestige Pl. I-75, exit 44, just e on SR 725, just se on Prestige Plaza Dr, then just s. Ext corridors. **Pets:** Other species. $100 one-time fee/room. Service with restrictions.

▼▼▼ **Holiday Inn-Dayton Mall** H
(937) 434-8030. **$89-$149.** 31 Prestige Plaza Dr. I-75, exit 44, just e on SR 725, then just s. Int corridors. **Pets:** Medium. $30 one-time fee/room. Service with restrictions, crate.

▼▼▼ **Homewood Suites by Hilton-Dayton South** H
(937) 432-0000. **$89-$149.** 3100 Contemporary Ln. I-75, exit 44, just e on SR 725, just se on Prestige Plaza Dr, then just s. Int corridors. **Pets:** Large, other species. $10 daily fee/room, $25 one-time fee/room. Service with restrictions, supervision.

▼▼▼ **Quality Inn Dayton South** H
(937) 865-0077. **$65-$99.** 250 Byers Rd. I-75, exit 44, just w on SR 725. Int corridors. **Pets:** Accepted.

▼▼▼ **Red Roof Inn-South #7006** M
(937) 866-0705. **$50-$70, 7 day notice.** 222 Byers Rd. I-75, exit 44, just w on SR 725. Ext corridors. **Pets:** Medium, other species. Service with restrictions, supervision.

MILAN

▼▼ **Motel 6–4016** H
(419) 499-8001. **$39-$139, 3 day notice.** 11406 US 250 Milan Rd. I-80/90, exit 118, 1.5 mi n. Int corridors. **Pets:** Other species. Service with restrictions, supervision.

▼▼ **Red Roof Inn** H
(419) 499-4347. **$49-$159.** 11303 Rt 250 Milan Rd. I-80/90, exit 118, 0.5 mi n. Int corridors. **Pets:** Small, dogs only. $50 deposit/pet. Designated rooms, service with restrictions, supervision.

▼▼ **Super 8 Motel** H
(419) 499-4671. **$44-$149.** 11313 US 250 Milan Rd. I-80/90, exit 118, 0.5 mi n on SR 250. Int corridors. **Pets:** Small, dogs only. $50 deposit/pet. Designated rooms, service with restrictions, supervision.

MILLERSBURG

▼▼▼ **Comfort Inn Millersburg** H
(330) 674-7400. **$69-$169.** 1102 Glen Dr. SR 39, 0.5 mi s on S Clay. Int corridors. **Pets:** Small, dogs only. $15 daily fee/pet. Designated rooms, service with restrictions, supervision.

▼ **Hotel Millersburg** H
(330) 674-1457. **$55-$179.** 35 W Jackson St. Downtown. Int corridors. **Pets:** Small. $10 daily fee/pet. Designated rooms, crate.

MONTPELIER

▼▼▼ Holiday Inn Express Hotel & Suites Bryan/
Montpelier H
(419) 485-0008. **$100, 3 day notice.** 13399 SR 15. I-80/90, exit 13, just s.
Int corridors. **Pets:** Large, other species. $10 daily fee/pet. Designated
rooms, service with restrictions.
ASK ✕ 🛏 🖥 🏊

▼▼▼ Ramada Inn & Suites H
(419) 485-5555. **$89-$129.** 13508 SR 15. I-80/90, exit 13, just s. Int corridors. **Pets:** Other species. Service with restrictions, crate.
✕ 🛏 🖥 🍴 🏊 ⊠

MORAINE

▼▼▼▼ Holiday Inn Hotel & Suites Dayton South H ❈
(937) 294-1471. **$95-$126.** 2455 Dryden Rd. I-75, exit 50A (Dryden Rd),
just nw. Int corridors. **Pets:** Large. $25 one-time fee/pet. Service with
restrictions, crate.
ASK ✕ 🛏 🖥 🍴 🏊 ⊠

MOUNT VERNON

▼▼ Comfort Inn H
(740) 392-6886. **$70-$150, 14 day notice.** 150 Howard St. Jct SR 13;
south of downtown. Int corridors. **Pets:** Other species. $10 daily fee/pet.
Service with restrictions, supervision.
ASK ✕ 🛏 🖥 🏊

▼▼▼ Holiday Inn Express H
(740) 392-1900. **$109-$139.** 11555 Upper Gilchrist Rd. 3 mi e on US 36,
then just s. Int corridors. **Pets:** Medium, other species. Designated rooms,
service with restrictions, crate.
ASK ✕ 🛏 🖥 🏊

NAPOLEON

◈◈◈ ▼▼▼ Best Western Napoleon Inn &
Suites H ❈
(419) 599-0850. **$69-$84.** 1290 Independence Dr. US 6/24, just se. Int
corridors. **Pets:** Other species. $12 daily fee/pet. Supervision.
SAVE ✕ 🛏 🖥 🏊 ⊠

NEWTON FALLS

◈◈◈ ▼▼▼ Econo Lodge M
(330) 872-0988. **$45-$99.** 4248 SR 5. I-80, exit 209, just w. Ext corridors.
Pets: Other species. $10 daily fee/room. Service with restrictions.
SAVE ✕ 🛏

NORTH LIMA

▼▼▼ Quality Inn and Suites H
(330) 549-9190. **Call for rates.** 10076 Market St. I-76, exit 232, 0.5 mi n.
Ext corridors. **Pets:** Accepted.
✕ 🛏 🖥

NORTHWOOD

▼▼▼ Baymont Inn & Suites H
(419) 662-1200. **$45-$95.** 2600 Lauren Ln. I-75, exit 198, just e on Wales
Rd, then just s on Oregon Rd. Int corridors. **Pets:** Accepted.
ASK ✕ ♿M 🛏 🖥 🏊

NORWALK

▼▼ Econo Lodge M
(419) 668-5656. **$44-$144.** 342 Milan Ave. 3 mi n on US 250; 6 mi s of
I-80/90 (Ohio Tpke). Ext corridors. **Pets:** Small, dogs only. $50 deposit/pet.
Designated rooms, service with restrictions, supervision.
ASK ✕ 🛏 🖥 🏊

OBERLIN

◈◈◈◈ Oberlin Inn CI
(440) 775-1111. **$109-$189.** 7 N Main St. On SR 58; jct College and Main
sts; center. Int corridors. **Pets:** Accepted.
ASK ✕ 🛏 🖥 🍴

OREGON

▼▼ Comfort Inn East H ❈
(419) 691-8911. **$75-$99, 7 day notice.** 2930 Navarre Ave. I-280, exit 7,
just n on access road, then 0.5 mi e on SR 2 (Navarre Ave). Int corridors.
Pets: Large. $10 one-time fee/room. Designated rooms, service with restric-
tions, supervision.
ASK ✕ 🛏 🖥 🏊

▼▼ Sleep Inn & Suites H
(419) 697-7800. **$79-$109, 7 day notice.** 1761 Meijer Cir. I-280, exit 6,
just w. Int corridors. **Pets:** Accepted.
ASK ✕ 🛏 🖥 🏊

PERRYSBURG

▼▼ Howard Johnson Inn Toledo South M ❈
(419) 837-5245. **$45-$99.** 3555 Hanley Rd. I-80/90, exit 71 to I-280, exit
1B. Ext/int corridors. **Pets:** Medium. $10 daily fee/room, $25 one-time fee/
room. Designated rooms, service with restrictions, supervision.
ASK ✕ 🛏 🖥 🏊

▼▼ La Quinta Inn & Suites Toledo-Perrysburg H ❈
(419) 872-0000. **$49-$105.** 1154 Professional Dr. I-75, exit 193, just w. Int
corridors. **Pets:** Medium, other species. Service with restrictions, supervision.
ASK ✕ 🛏 🖥

◈◈◈ ▼▼▼ Super 8 Motel-Toledo/Perrysburg/Millbury M
(419) 837-6409. **$39-$89.** 3491 Latcha Rd. I-80/90, exit 71 to I-280, exit
1B, just n. Ext corridors. **Pets:** Accepted.
SAVE ✕ 🛏

PIQUA

◈◈◈ ▼▼▼ Comfort Inn-Piqua H
(937) 778-8100. **$64-$89.** 987 E Ash St. I-75, exit 82, just w. Int corridors.
Pets: Medium, other species. $25 daily fee/pet. Service with restrictions,
crate.
SAVE ✕ 🛏 🖥 🏊 ⊠

▼▼ La Quinta Inn Piqua H ❈
(937) 615-0140. **$69-$102.** 950 E Ash St. I-75, exit 82, just w. Int corridors.
Pets: Medium, other species. Service with restrictions, supervision.
ASK ✕ 🛏 🖥 🏊

POLAND

▼▼ Red Roof Inn #7253 H
(330) 758-1999. **$46-$82.** 1051 Tiffany S. I-680, exit 11, just w. Int corridors. **Pets:** Accepted.
ASK ✕ 🛏 🖥

▼▼▼ Residence Inn by Marriott-Youngstown H
(330) 726-1747. **$126-$154.** 7396 Tiffany S. I-680, exit 11, just w. Int
corridors. **Pets:** Accepted.
✕ 🛏 🖥 🏊 ⊠

PORT CLINTON

◈◈◈ ▼▼▼ Best Western Port Clinton H
(419) 734-2274. **$49-$169.** 1734 E Perry St. 1.7 mi e on SR 163, w of jct
SR 2. Int corridors. **Pets:** Small, dogs only. $50 deposit/pet. Designated
rooms, service with restrictions, supervision.
SAVE ✕ 🖥 🏊

Commodore Perry Inn & Suites 🅷
(419) 732-2645. **$50-$190, 3 day notice.** 255 W Lakeshore Dr. Just n of bridge. Int corridors. **Pets:** Accepted.
[SAVE] ⊠ 🛎 💻 🍴 ⊇

Super 8 🅷
(419) 734-4446. **$49-$149.** 1704 E Perry St. 1.7 mi e on SR 163, w of jct SR 2. Int corridors. **Pets:** Small, dogs only. $50 deposit/pet. Designated rooms, service with restrictions, supervision.
[ASK] ⊠ 💻

RIO GRANDE

College Hill Motel 🄼
(740) 245-5326. **$69-$79.** 10987 State Rt 588. US 35, exit Rio Grande, just s on SR 325, then 0.7 mi e. Ext corridors. **Pets:** Accepted.
[ASK] ⊠ 🛎

ST. CLAIRSVILLE

Americas Best Value Inn St. Clairsville/Wheeling 🄼
(740) 695-5038. **$59-$129.** 51260 National Rd. I-70, exit 218, 0.5 mi ne on US 40. Ext corridors. **Pets:** Other species. $10 one-time fee/room. Service with restrictions, supervision.
[SAVE] ⊠ 🛎 💻 ⊇

Red Roof Inn #7101 🄼
(740) 695-4057. **$55-$85.** 68301 Red Roof Ln. I-70, exit 218, just n. Ext corridors. **Pets:** Medium, other species. Service with restrictions, crate.
[SAVE] ⊠ 🛎

ST. MARYS

Americas Best Value Inn St Marys 🅷 ❀
(419) 394-2341. **$58-$128.** 1321 Celina Rd. SR 66/29, 0.8 mi w on SR 703. Ext corridors. **Pets:** Medium, other species. $25 daily fee/pet. Designated rooms, service with restrictions.
[SAVE] ⊠ 🛎 💻 ⊇ ⊠

Country Hearth Inn and Suites 🅷
(419) 394-2710. **Call for rates.** 1410 Commerce Dr. Jct US 33 and SR 29, just e. Int corridors. **Pets:** Accepted.
[SAVE] ⊠ 🛎 💻 ⊇

SANDUSKY

Best Budget Inn 🄼
(419) 626-3610. **$39-$129.** 2027 Cleveland Rd. US 6, just e of Cedar Point Cswy. Ext/int corridors. **Pets:** Medium, dogs only. $50 deposit/pet. Designated rooms, service with restrictions, supervision.
[SAVE] ⊠ ⊇

Knights Inn Sandusky 🄼
(419) 621-9000. **$44-$139.** 2405 Cleveland Rd. US 6, 2 mi e of Cedar Point Cswy. Ext/int corridors. **Pets:** Small, dogs only. $25 deposit/room. Designated rooms, service with restrictions, supervision.
[ASK] ⊠ 🛎 💻 ⊇

La Quinta Inn 🄼 ❀
(419) 626-6766. **$59-$119.** 3304 Milan Rd. US 250, 2 mi n of SR 2. Int corridors. **Pets:** Medium, other species. Service with restrictions, supervision.
[ASK] ⊠ 🛎 💻 ⊇

SEAMAN

Comfort Inn 🅷
(937) 386-2511. **$79-$105.** 55 Stern Dr. Jct SR 32 and 247. Int corridors. **Pets:** $15 one-time fee/room. Service with restrictions, supervision.
[ASK] ⊠ 🛎 💻 ⊇

SEVILLE

Hawthorn Suites Ltd 🅷 ❀
(330) 769-5025. **$79-$129.** 5025 Park Ave W. I-76/SR 224, exit 2, just n. Int corridors. **Pets:** Medium. $75 one-time fee/room. Service with restrictions, crate.
[SAVE] ⊠ 🛎 💻 ⊇

Super 8 Motel-Seville 🅷
(330) 769-8880. **$59-$85.** 6116 Speedway Dr. Jct SR 224 and Lake Rd. Int corridors. **Pets:** Medium. $25 deposit/room, $25 one-time fee/pet. Service with restrictions, supervision.
[ASK] ⊠ ♿ 🛎 💻

SIDNEY

Comfort Inn 🅷
(937) 492-3001. **$80.** 1959 W Michigan Ave. I-75, exit 92, just sw of SR 47. Int corridors. **Pets:** Small. $25 one-time fee/pet. Service with restrictions, supervision.
[ASK] ⊠ 🛎 💻 ⊇

Quality Inn 🅷
(937) 492-1131. **$67-$75.** 400 Folkerth Ave. I-75, exit 92, just w. Int corridors. **Pets:** Accepted.
[ASK] ⊠ 🛎 💻 🍴 ⊇

SPRINGFIELD

Holiday Inn South Springfield Ohio 🅷
(937) 323-8631. **$89-$105.** 383 E Leffel Ln. I-70, exit 54, just n, then e. Int corridors. **Pets:** Accepted.
[ASK] ⊠ 🛎 💻 🍴 ⊇ ⊠

Ramada Limited 🅷
(937) 328-0123. **$60-$110.** 319 E Leffel Ln. I-70, exit 54, just n, then e. Int corridors. **Pets:** Medium. $10 daily fee/pet. Designated rooms, service with restrictions, supervision.
[SAVE] ⊠ 🛎 💻 ⊇

Red Roof Inn 🅷
(937) 325-5356. **$58-$105.** 155 W Leffel Ln. I-70, exit 54, just n, then w. Int corridors. **Pets:** Small, other species. Supervision.
[SAVE] ⊠ 🛎 💻 ⊇

STEUBENVILLE

Holiday Inn-Steubenville 🅷
(740) 282-0901. **$100-$120.** 1401 University Blvd. Jct US 22 and SR 7, 1 mi sw. Ext/int corridors. **Pets:** Small. $25 daily fee/pet. Service with restrictions, supervision.
[SAVE] ⊠ 🛎 💻 🍴 ⊇

STRASBURG

Ramada Limited Dover/Strasburg 🅷
(330) 878-1400. **$70-$140.** 509 S Wooster Ave. I-77, exit 87, 0.4 mi n on US 250 and SR 21. Int corridors. **Pets:** Dogs only. $15 daily fee/room. Service with restrictions, supervision.
[SAVE] ⊠ ♿ 🛎 💻 ⊇

STREETSBORO

Microtel Inn & Suites of Streetsboro 🅷
(330) 422-1234. **$54-$109.** 9371 SR 14. I-80, exit 187, 1.2 mi s. Int corridors. **Pets:** $15 daily fee/pet. Service with restrictions, supervision.
[SAVE] ⊠ 🛎 💻 ⊇

TownePlace Suites by Marriott 🅷
(330) 422-1855. **$119-$159.** 795 Mondial Pkwy. I-80, exit 187, 0.8 mi s. Int corridors. **Pets:** Accepted.
⊠ 🛎 💻 ⊇

SWANTON

AAA **WWW** Days Inn **H**
(419) 865-2002. **$49-$73.** 10753 Airport Hwy. I-80/90, exit 3A, just s, then e. Int corridors. **Pets:** Accepted.
SAVE **X** **P**

TIFFIN

WWWW Holiday Inn Express **H**
(419) 443-5100. **Call for rates.** 78 Shaffer Park Dr. Just w of mall. Int corridors. **Pets:** Other species. $20 daily fee/room. Service with restrictions, supervision.
X **B** **P** **≈**

TIPP CITY

AAA **WWWW** La Quinta Inn & Suites **H** **❀**
(937) 667-1574. **$59-$89.** 19 Weller Dr. I-75, exit 68, just w. Int corridors. **Pets:** Medium, other species. Service with restrictions, supervision.
SAVE **X** **B** **P** **≈**

TOLEDO

AAA **WWWW** Comfort Inn-North **M** **❀**
(419) 476-0170. **$73-$105.** 445 E Alexis Rd. I-75, exit 210, 2 mi w on SR 184; just e of jct US 24 and SR 184. Int corridors. **Pets:** Medium, other species. $15 deposit/room. Service with restrictions, supervision.
SAVE **X** **B** **P**

AAA **WWWWW** Hilton Toledo and Dana Conference
Center **H** **❀**
(419) 381-6800. **$99-$189.** 3100 Glendale Ave. I-475, exit 8 (SR 2/Airport Hwy), 3.3 mi e on SR 2, 0.8 mi s on Byrne Rd, then 0.5 mi e. Int corridors. **Pets:** Medium, other species. $50 one-time fee/pet. Designated rooms, no service, supervision.
SAVE **X** **B** **P** **↑↑** **≈** **X**

AAA **WWWW** Park Inn Hotel **H**
(419) 241-3000. **$138-$159.** 101 N Summit St. Between Jefferson and Monroe sts; downtown. Int corridors. **Pets:** Small, dogs only. Designated rooms, no service, supervision.
SAVE **X** **P** **↑↑**

WWW Red Roof Inn Toledo University #7196 **M**
(419) 536-0118. **$54-$71.** 3530 Executive Pkwy. I-475, exit 17, 0.5 mi s on Secor Rd, then just e. Ext corridors. **Pets:** Large. Service with restrictions, supervision.
ASK **X** **B**

TROY

WWWW Holiday Inn Express Hotel & Suites **H**
(937) 332-1700. **Call for rates.** 60 Troy Town Dr. I-75, exit 74, just w. Int corridors. **Pets:** Medium, other species. $25 one-time fee/pet. Service with restrictions, crate.
X **B** **P** **≈** **X**

WWWW Residence Inn By Marriott **H**
(937) 440-9303. **$125-$153.** 87 Troy Town Dr. I-75, exit 74, just w. Int corridors. **Pets:** Accepted.
X **B** **P** **≈** **X**

UHRICHSVILLE

AAA **WWW** Best Western Country Inn **M**
(740) 922-0774. **$59-$89, 3 day notice.** 111 McCauley Dr. US 250, exit McCauley Dr. Ext corridors. **Pets:** $5 daily fee/pet. Designated rooms, service with restrictions, crate.
SAVE **X** **B** **P**

UPPER SANDUSKY

AAA **WWW** Best Western **H**
(419) 294-3919. **Call for rates.** 1726 E Wyandot Ave. Jct US 23 and 30. Int corridors. **Pets:** Accepted.
SAVE **X** **&M** **B** **P** **≈**

VERMILION

WWWW Holiday Inn Express **H**
(440) 967-8770. **$85-$160.** 2417 SR 60. Jct SR 2 and 60. Int corridors. **Pets:** Medium, other species. $15 one-time fee/pet. Designated rooms, service with restrictions, supervision.
ASK **X** **B** **P** **≈**

WWW Motel Plaza **M**
(440) 967-3191. **$65-$89, 3 day notice.** 4645 Liberty Ave. On US 6, 2 mi e of SR 60. Ext corridors. **Pets:** Dogs only. $25 deposit/pet. Service with restrictions, supervision.
ASK **X** **B** **P**

WAPAKONETA

WWWW Holiday Inn Express **H**
(419) 738-2050. **$89-$109.** 1008 Lunar Dr. I-75, exit 111, just w. Int corridors. **Pets:** Accepted.
ASK **X** **&M** **B** **P** **≈**

WARREN

AAA **WWW** Americas Best Value Inn **M**
(330) 392-2515. **$60-$80, 3 day notice.** 777 Mahoning Ave. 0.3 mi n of Courthouse Square. Ext corridors. **Pets:** Other species. Supervision.
SAVE **X** **P** **≈**

AAA **WWWW** Comfort Inn **H**
(330) 393-1200. **$69-$109.** 136 N Park Ave. Downtown; east side of Courthouse Square. Int corridors. **Pets:** Medium. $10 daily fee/pet. Service with restrictions, supervision.
SAVE **X** **B** **P** **↑↑**

WAUSEON

AAA **WWWW** Best Western Del Mar **M**
(419) 335-1565. **$60-$125.** 8319 SR 108. I-80/90, exit 34, just s. Ext corridors. **Pets:** Other species. $15 one-time fee/pet. Service with restrictions.
SAVE **X** **B** **P** **≈**

WOOSTER

AAA **WWW** Econo Lodge **M**
(330) 264-8883. **$45-$99.** 2137 E Lincoln Way. US 30, 3 mi e. Ext corridors. **Pets:** Small, dogs only. $10 daily fee/pet. Designated rooms, service with restrictions, supervision.
SAVE **X** **B** **P** **≈**

XENIA

WWWW Holiday Inn-Xenia **H**
(937) 372-9921. **$79-$89, 30 day notice.** 300 Xenia Towne Square. On W Main St, 0.3 mi w. Int corridors. **Pets:** Dogs only. $10 daily fee/pet. Supervision.
ASK **X** **B** **P** **↑↑** **≈**

YOUNGSTOWN

AAA **WWW** Days Inn & Suites **M**
(330) 759-9820. **$50-$110, 3 day notice.** 1615 E Liberty St. I-80, exit 229, just s. Int corridors. **Pets:** $25 daily fee/pet. Designated rooms, no service, supervision.
SAVE **X** **B** **P** **≈**

ZANESVILLE

◈ ▼▼ Baymont Inn & Suites Zanesville H
(740) 454-9332. **$79-$129.** 230 Scenic Crest Dr. I-70, exit 155, just s. Int corridors. **Pets:** Medium. $25 one-time fee/pet. Service with restrictions, supervision.
SAVE ✕ 🔲 🖲 ⊇

◈ ▼▼ Best Western–B.R. Guest H ❀
(740) 453-6300. **$74-$134.** 4929 E Pike. I-70, exit 160, just s. Int corridors. **Pets:** Large, other species. $10 daily fee/pet. Service with restrictions, supervision.
SAVE ✕ ��&M 🔲 🖲 ⊇

◈ ▼▼▼ Comfort Inn H
(740) 454-4144. **$69-$199.** 500 Monroe St. I-70, exit 155 westbound; exit 7th St eastbound, e on Elberon to light, just n on Underwood. Int corridors. **Pets:** Medium, other species. $10 one-time fee/pet. Designated rooms, service with restrictions, supervision.
SAVE ✕ 🔲 🖲 ⊇

▼▼▼ Ramada Hotel & Conference Center H
(740) 453-0771. **$79-$140.** 4645 E Pike. I-70, exit 160, on US 22 and 40. Int corridors. **Pets:** Accepted.
ASK ✕ 🔲 🖲 🍴 ⊇ ✕

◈ ▼▼▼ Super 8 Motel-Zanesville H
(740) 455-3124. **$39-$99.** 2440 National Rd. I-70, exit 152, just n. Int corridors. **Pets:** Accepted.
SAVE ✕ 🔲 🖲

OKLAHOMA

ALTUS

Best Western Altus 🅷
(580) 482-9300. **$79-$99, 3 day notice.** 2804 N Main St. 2 mi n on US 283. Ext corridors. **Pets:** Accepted.
SAVE ✕ 🛆 💷 🌊 ✕

Hampton Inn & Suites 🅷 🐾
(580) 482-1273. **$104-$119.** 3601 N Main St.. Int corridors. **Pets:** Designated rooms, service with restrictions, supervision.
SAVE ✕ 🛆M 🛆 💷 🌊

ARDMORE

Holiday Inn 🅷
(580) 223-7130. **$97-$109.** 2705 W Broadway. I-35, exit 31A, just e. Ext corridors. **Pets:** Medium. $20 one-time fee/room. Designated rooms, service with restrictions, crate.
✕ 🛆 💷 🍴 🌊

La Quinta Inn Ardmore 🅷 🐾
(580) 223-7976. **$50-$90.** 2432 Veterans Blvd. I-35, exit 33, just e. Ext corridors. **Pets:** Medium, other species. Service with restrictions, supervision.
SAVE ✕ 🛆 💷 🌊

BARTLESVILLE

Microtel Inn & Suites of Bartlesville 🅷
(918) 333-2100. **$69-$99.** 2696 SE Washington Blvd. 1.4 mi s of jct US 60 E. Int corridors. **Pets:** Accepted.
ASK ✕ 🛆M 🛆 💷

BIG CABIN

Super 8-Big Cabin 🅼
(918) 783-5888. **Call for rates.** 30954 S Hwy 69. I-44, exit 283, just ne. Ext/int corridors. **Pets:** Accepted.
✕ 🛆 💷 🌊

BLACKWELL

Best Western Blackwell Inn 🅷
(580) 363-1300. **$88.** 4545 W White Ave. I-35, exit 222, just ne. Int corridors. **Pets:** Small. $10 daily fee/pet. Designated rooms, service with restrictions, supervision.
SAVE ✕ 🛆 💷 🌊

Comfort Inn 🅷
(580) 363-7000. **$49-$179.** 1201 N 44th St. I-35, exit 222, just ne. Int corridors. **Pets:** Small, dogs only. $10 daily fee/pet. Designated rooms, service with restrictions, supervision.
SAVE ✕ 🛆 💷 🌊

CHICKASHA

Best Western Inn 🅷
(405) 224-4890. **$69-$84, 3 day notice.** 2101 S 4th St. I-44, exit 80, just nw. Ext/int corridors. **Pets:** Accepted.
SAVE ✕ 🛆 💷 🍴 🌊 ✕

DURANT

Holiday Inn Express Hotel & Suites 🅷 🐾
(580) 924-8881. **Call for rates.** 2112 W Main St. Just e of jct US 75/69 and 70. Int corridors. **Pets:** Medium. $25 one-time fee/room. No service.
✕ 🛆 💷 🌊

ENID

Baymont Inn & Suites-Enid 🅷
(580) 234-6800. **$80-$90.** 3614 W Owen K Garriott Rd. Just off US 412, 2 mi w of US 81. Int corridors. **Pets:** Medium, dogs only. $100 deposit/pet, $10 daily fee/pet. Designated rooms, service with restrictions, supervision.
ASK ✕ 🛆M 🛆 💷 🌊

Holiday Inn Express Hotel & Suites 🅷
(580) 237-7722. **Call for rates.** 4702 W Owen K Garriott Rd. 2.3 mi w of jct US 81. Int corridors. **Pets:** Accepted.
✕ 🛆 💷 🌊

GROVE

Best Western Timber Ridge Inn 🅷
(918) 786-6900. **$87.** 120 W 18th St. Just w of jct US 59. Ext/int corridors. **Pets:** Medium, other species. $10 daily fee/pet. Designated rooms, service with restrictions, supervision.
SAVE ✕ 🛆 💷 🌊

GUYMON

Comfort Inn & Suites 🅷
(580) 338-0831. **$75-$115.** 501 5th St (Hwy 54 E). Just s of jct US 64. Int corridors. **Pets:** $15 daily fee/pet. Service with restrictions, supervision.
ASK ✕ 🛆 💷 🌊

Guymon Super 8 🅷
(580) 338-0507. **$70-$100.** 1201 Hwy 54 E. Jct US 54 and 64. Int corridors. **Pets:** Medium, dogs only. $7 daily fee/pet. Service with restrictions, supervision.
SAVE ✕ 🛆 💷

Western Townsman Inn 🅷
(580) 338-6556. **Call for rates.** 212 NE Hwy 54. 0.7 mi s of jct US 64. Ext corridors. **Pets:** Accepted.
✕ 🛆 💷 🌊

HENRYETTA

Green Country Inn 🅼
(918) 652-9988. **$45-$58.** 2004 Old Hwy 75 W. I-40, exit 237, just ne. Ext corridors. **Pets:** Small. $5 daily fee/pet. Designated rooms, service with restrictions, supervision.
SAVE ✕ 🛆 🌊

IDABEL

Comfort Suites 🅷
(580) 286-9393. **$89-$179.** 400 SE Lincoln Rd. Just s of jct US 70 and 259. Int corridors. **Pets:** Medium, other species. $15 one-time fee/pet. Service with restrictions, supervision.
ASK ✕ 🛆 💷 🌊

LAWTON

(AAA) ♦♦♦ Baymont Inn & Suites 🅷
(580) 353-5581. **$93.** 1203 NW 40th St. I-44, exit 39A, 3.7 mi w. Int corridors. **Pets:** Other species. $25 deposit/room. Service with restrictions, crate.
[SAVE] [✕] [🛏] [💻] [🐾]

(AAA) ♦♦♦ Best Western Hotel & Convention Center 🅷
(580) 353-0200. **$94-$105.** 1125 E Gore Blvd. I-44, exit 37, just e. Ext/int corridors. **Pets:** $40 one-time fee/pet. Service with restrictions, crate.
[SAVE] [✕] [🛏] [💻] [🍴] [🐾] [✕]

LOCUST GROVE

(AAA) ♦♦♦ Best Western Locust Grove Inn & Suites 🅷
(918) 479-8082. **$72-$250, 7 day notice.** 106 Holiday Ln. Just nw of jct US 412 and SR 82. Int corridors. **Pets:** Small. $40 one-time fee/pet. Designated rooms, service with restrictions, crate.
[SAVE] [✕] [🛏] [💻] [🐾]

LONE WOLF

(AAA) ♦♦♦ Quartz Mountain Resort Arts & Conference Center 🅷
(580) 563-2424. **$89-$129.** 22469 Lodge Rd. 1.4 mi w of jct SR 44 and 44A, 1.9 mi n. Int corridors. **Pets:** Other species. $25 one-time fee/pet. Service with restrictions, supervision.
[SAVE] [✕] [🛏] [💻] [🍴] [🐾] [✕]

MCALESTER

(AAA) ♦♦♦ Best Western Inn of McAlester 🅷
(918) 426-0115. **$90-$140.** 1215 George Nigh Expwy. 3 mi s on US 69. Ext corridors. **Pets:** Accepted.
[SAVE] [✕] [🛏] [💻] [🐾]

♦♦♦ Comfort Suites 🅷
(918) 302-0001. **Call for rates.** 650 George Nigh Expwy. 1.2 mi s on US 69. Int corridors. **Pets:** Accepted.
[✕] [🛏] [💻] [🐾]

MIAMI

(AAA) ♦♦♦ Microtel Inn & Suites 🅷
(918) 540-3333. **$61-$105.** 2015 E Steve Owens Blvd. I-44, exit 313, just w. Int corridors. **Pets:** Large, other species. $25 one-time fee/room. Service with restrictions, crate.
[SAVE] [✕] [🛏] [💻] [🐾]

MUSKOGEE

(AAA) ♦♦♦♦ La Quinta Inn & Suites Muskogee 🅷 🐾
(918) 687-9000. **$69-$129.** 3031 Military Blvd. Just se of jct US 62 and 69. Int corridors. **Pets:** Medium, other species. Service with restrictions, supervision.
[SAVE] [✕] [🛏] [💻] [🍴] [🐾]

OKLAHOMA CITY METROPOLITAN AREA

DEL CITY

♦♦ La Quinta Inn Oklahoma City East (Del City) 🅷 🐾
(405) 672-0067. **$59-$99.** 5501 Tinker Diagonal Rd. I-40, exit 156A (Sooner Rd), just nw. Ext/int corridors. **Pets:** Medium, other species. Service with restrictions, supervision.
[ASK] [✕] [🛏] [💻] [🐾]

EDMOND

(AAA) ♦♦♦ Best Western Edmond Inn & Suites 🅷
(405) 216-0300. **$91-$101, 14 day notice.** 2700 E 2nd St. I-35, exit 141, 1.1 mi w. Int corridors. **Pets:** Accepted.
[SAVE] [✕] [🛏] [💻] [🐾]

EL RENO

(AAA) ♦♦♦ Best Western Hensley's 🅷
(405) 262-6490. **$80-$99.** 2701 S Country Club Rd. I-40, exit 123, just s. Ext corridors. **Pets:** Accepted.
[SAVE] [✕] [🛏] [💻] [🐾]

(AAA) ♦♦ Motel 6 🅷
(405) 262-6060. **Call for rates.** 1506 Domino Dr. I-40, exit 123, just ne. Int corridors. **Pets:** Other species. Service with restrictions, supervision.
[SAVE] [✕] [🛏] [🐾]

GUTHRIE

(AAA) ♦♦♦ Best Western Territorial Inn 🅷
(405) 282-8831. **$84-$94.** 2323 Territorial Tr. I-35, exit 157, just sw. Int corridors. **Pets:** Small. Service with restrictions, supervision.
[SAVE] [✕] [🛏] [💻] [🐾]

MIDWEST CITY

♦♦♦ Hawthorn Suites 🅷
(405) 737-7777. **$105-$125, 3 day notice.** 5701 Tinker Diagonal Rd. I-40, exit 156A (Sooner Rd), just n. Int corridors. **Pets:** Small. $10 daily fee/pet. Designated rooms, service with restrictions, supervision.
[ASK] [✕] [⛄] [🛏] [💻] [🐾]

(AAA) ♦♦♦♦ Sheraton Midwest City Hotel at the Reed Conference Center 🅷
(405) 741-7333. **Call for rates.** 5750 Will Rogers Rd. I-40, exit 156A (Sooner Rd), just ne. Int corridors. **Pets:** Accepted.
[SAVE] [✕] [🛏] [💻] [🍴] [🐾] [✕]

MOORE

(AAA) ♦♦♦ Best Western Green Tree Inn & Suites 🅷
(405) 912-5066. **$81-$106, 3 day notice.** 1811 N Moore Ave. I-35, exit 118, just n on westbound frontage road. Int corridors. **Pets:** Very small, dogs only. $10 daily fee/pet. Service with restrictions, supervision.
[SAVE] [✕] [🛏] [💻] [🐾]

NORMAN

♦♦♦ La Quinta Inn & Suites Oklahoma City (Norman) 🅷 🐾
(405) 579-4000. **$89-$139.** 930 Ed Noble Dr. I-35, exit 108B (Lindsey St), just nw. Int corridors. **Pets:** Medium, other species. Service with restrictions, supervision.
[ASK] [✕] [⛄] [🛏] [💻] [🐾]

(AAA) ♦♦♦ Quality Inn 🅼
(405) 364-5554. **$80-$95.** 100 SW 26th Dr. I-35, exit 109 (Main St), just se. Ext corridors. **Pets:** Small. $5 daily fee/pet. Service with restrictions, supervision.
[SAVE] [✕] [💻]

Residence Inn by Marriott H
(405) 366-0900. **$125-$153.** 2681 Jefferson St. I-35, exit 108A, just se. Ext corridors. **Pets:** $150 one-time fee/room. Service with restrictions, crate.
SAVE ⊠ 🛏 💻 ➿ 🐾

OKLAHOMA CITY

Baymont Inn H
(405) 631-8661. **Call for rates.** 8315 I-35 S. I-35, exit 121A (82nd St), just sw. Ext corridors. **Pets:** Other species. Service with restrictions, crate.
⊠ 🛏 💻 ➿

Best Western Broadway Inn & Suites H
(405) 848-1919. **Call for rates.** 6101 N Santa Fe. I-44, exit 127, just e on 63rd St, then just s. Int corridors. **Pets:** Dogs only. $100 one-time fee/room. Service with restrictions, supervision.
SAVE ⊠ 🛏 💻 🍴 ➿

Best Western Memorial Inn & Suites H
(405) 286-5199. **$95-$110.** 1301 W Memorial Rd. John Kilpatrick Tpke, exit Western Ave, just nw. Int corridors. **Pets:** Medium. $10 daily fee/pet. Service with restrictions, supervision.
SAVE ⊠ 🛏 💻 ➿

Best Western Saddleback Inn & Conference Center H
(405) 947-7000. **$90-$130, 45 day notice.** 4300 SW 3rd St. I-40, exit 145 (Meridian Ave), just ne. Ext/int corridors. **Pets:** Small. $50 deposit/pet. Service with restrictions, crate.
SAVE ⊠ 🛏 💻 ➿ 🐾

Candlewood Suites Hotel H
(405) 680-8770. **Call for rates.** 4400 River Park Dr. I-40, exit 145 (Meridian Ave), 1.1 mi s. Int corridors. **Pets:** Accepted.
⊠ 🛏 💻

Comfort Inn H
(405) 943-4400. **$68-$88.** 4240 W I-40 Service Rd. I-40, exit 145 (Meridian Ave), just e on south frontage road. Ext/int corridors. **Pets:** Accepted.
SAVE ⊠ 🛏 💻 ➿

Comfort Inn North H
(405) 478-7282. **$69-$140.** 4625 NE 120th St. I-35, exit 137 (122nd St), just sw. Int corridors. **Pets:** Dogs only. $20 daily fee/pet. Service with restrictions, supervision.
SAVE ⊠ 🛏 💻 ➿

Country Inn & Suites By Carlson H
(405) 843-2002. **$79-$125.** 3141 Northwest Expwy. 0.4 mi e of jct SR 74 and 3. Int corridors. **Pets:** Accepted.
ASK ⊠ 🛏 💻 ➿

Courtyard by Marriott-Downtown/Bricktown H
(405) 232-2290. **$179-$219.** 2 W Reno Ave. Gaylord and Reno aves; downtown. Int corridors. **Pets:** Accepted.
SAVE ⊠ 🛏 💻 🍴 ➿

Courtyard by Marriott-NW H
(405) 848-0808. **$159-$169.** 1515 Northwest Expwy. I-44, exit 125C westbound; exit 125B eastbound, just e. Int corridors. **Pets:** Accepted.
⊠ 🛏 💻 🍴 ➿ 🐾

Econo Lodge H
(405) 478-0400. **Call for rates.** 12001 N I-35 Service Rd. I-35, exit 137, just sw. Ext corridors. **Pets:** Accepted.
⊠ 🛏 💻 ➿

Embassy Suites H
(405) 682-6000. **$110-$209.** 1815 S Meridian Ave. I-40, exit 145 (Meridian Ave), 1 mi s. Int corridors. **Pets:** Large. $50 one-time fee/room. Service with restrictions, crate.
⊠ 🛏 💻 🍴 ➿ 🐾

Four Points by Sheraton Oklahoma City H
(405) 681-3500. **Call for rates.** 6300 Terminal Dr. I-40, exit 145 (Meridian Ave), 4 mi s. Int corridors. **Pets:** Small. $30 one-time fee/room. Service with restrictions, supervision.
SAVE ⊠ 🛏 💻 🍴 ➿

Homewood Suites Oklahoma City-West H
(405) 789-3600. **$109-$149.** 6920 W Reno Ave. Just e of jct Rockwell Ave. Int corridors. **Pets:** Accepted.
⊠ 🛏 💻 ➿ 🐾

La Quinta Inn & Suites Oklahoma City (Northwest Expressway) H 🐾
(405) 773-5575. **$79-$119.** 4829 Northwest Expwy. 1.9 mi w of jct SR 3 and 74. Int corridors. **Pets:** Medium, other species. Service with restrictions, supervision.
ASK ⊠ 🛏 💻 ➿

La Quinta Inn and Suites-Quail Springs H 🐾
(405) 755-7000. **$89-$149.** 3003 W Memorial Rd. John Kilpatrick Tpke, exit May Ave, just nw. Int corridors. **Pets:** Medium, other species. Service with restrictions, supervision.
ASK ⊠ 🛏 💻 ➿ 🐾

La Quinta Inn Oklahoma City (Airport) H 🐾
(405) 942-0040. **$59-$99.** 800 S Meridian Ave. I-40, exit 145 (Meridian Ave), just se. Ext/int corridors. **Pets:** Medium, other species. Service with restrictions, supervision.
ASK ⊠ 🛏 💻 🍴 ➿

Quality Inn H
(405) 632-6666. **$75-$100.** 7800 CA Henderson Blvd. I-240, exit 2A, just s. Ext corridors. **Pets:** Small, dogs only. $20 one-time fee/room. Service with restrictions, supervision.
ASK ⊠ 🛏 💻 ➿

Residence Inn by Marriott H 🐾
(405) 601-1700. **$179-$219.** 400 E Reno Ave. Just se of jct Joe Carter Ave; in Bricktown. Int corridors. **Pets:** Medium. $100 one-time fee/room. Service with restrictions, crate.
SAVE ⊠ 🛏 💻 ➿ 🐾

Residence Inn by Marriott Oklahoma City South-Crossroads Mall H
(405) 634-9696. **$162-$198.** 1111 E I-240 Service Rd. I-240, exit 4C eastbound, 0.4 mi nw; exit 5 westbound, 0.8 mi nw. Int corridors. **Pets:** Accepted.
⊠ 🛏 💻 ➿ 🐾

Sheraton Oklahoma City H
(405) 235-2780. **Call for rates.** One N Broadway Ave. Sheridan and Broadway aves; downtown. Int corridors. **Pets:** Accepted.
SAVE ⊠ 🛏 💻 🍴 ➿

The Skirvin Hilton H 🐾
(405) 272-3040. **$129-$369.** 1 Park Ave. Just n of jct Robinson Ave; downtown. Int corridors. **Pets:** Medium. $75 one-time fee/room. Service with restrictions, supervision.
SAVE ⊠ 🛏 💻 🍴 ➿

Super 8 Bricktown M
(405) 677-1000. **Call for rates.** 3030 S I-35. I-35, exit 124B northbound; exit 125A southbound, just n on service road. Ext corridors. **Pets:** Accepted.
⊠ 🛏 💻 ➿

SHAWNEE

La Quinta Inn & Suites H 🐾
(405) 275-7930. **$79-$129.** 5401 Enterprise Ct. I-40, exit 186, just ne. Int corridors. **Pets:** Medium, other species. Service with restrictions, supervision.
SAVE ⊠ 🛏 💻 ➿

YUKON

△△△ ▼▼▼▼ **Best Western Inn & Suites Yukon** �H
(405) 265-2995. **$79-$139.** 11440 W I-40 Service Rd. I-40, exit 138, just sw. Ext/int corridors. **Pets:** Other species. $25 deposit/room, $6 daily fee/room. Designated rooms, service with restrictions, supervision.
🆂🅰🆅🅴 ⊠ 🛏 💻 🌊

△△△ ▼▼▼▼ **Comfort Suites** �H
(405) 577-6500. **$87-$150.** 11424 NW 4th St. I-40, exit 138, just nw. Int corridors. **Pets:** Small. $10 daily fee/pet. Designated rooms, service with restrictions, crate.
🆂🅰🆅🅴 ⊠ 🛏 💻 🌊

END METROPOLITAN AREA

OKMULGEE

△△△ ▼▼▼▼ **Best Western Okmulgee** �H
(918) 756-9200. **$82-$95.** 3499 N Wood Dr. Just n of jct US 75 and SR 56. Int corridors. **Pets:** Accepted.
🆂🅰🆅🅴 ⊠ 🛏 💻 🌊

PAULS VALLEY

▼▼▼▼ **Comfort Inn & Suites** �H
(405) 207-9730. **Call for rates.** 103 S Humphrey Blvd. I-35, exit 72, just e. Int corridors. **Pets:** Small. $25 deposit/pet. Designated rooms, service with restrictions, supervision.
⊠ 🛏 💻 🌊

△△△ ▼▼▼ **Days Inn** �H
(405) 238-7548. **$78.** 2606 W Grant Ave. I-35, exit 72, just e. Int corridors. **Pets:** Accepted.
🆂🅰🆅🅴 ⊠ 🛏 💻

PONCA CITY

△△△ ▼▼▼▼ **Comfort Inn & Suites** �H
(580) 765-2322. **$93-$160.** 3101 N 14th St. I-35, exit 214, 3 mi n on US 77. Int corridors. **Pets:** Small. $10 one-time fee/pet. Service with restrictions, crate.
🆂🅰🆅🅴 ⊠ 🗛 🛏 💻 🌊

PRYOR

△△△ ▼▼▼ **Microtel Inn & Suites** �H
(918) 476-4661. **$60-$99.** 315 Mid America Dr. 5.1 mi s on US 69. Int corridors. **Pets:** Accepted.
🆂🅰🆅🅴 ⊠ 🛏 💻

SALLISAW

▼▼▼ **Blue Ribbon Inn** �H
(918) 775-6294. **Call for rates.** 706 S Kerr Blvd (US 59). I-40, exit 308 (US 59), just n. Ext/int corridors. **Pets:** Accepted.
⊠ 🛏 💻 🌊

SAVANNA

△△△ ▼▼▼ **Candlelight Inn & Suites** �H
(918) 548-3676. **$75-$90, 3 day notice.** Hwy 69. 1.5 mi sw of jct US 69 and Indian Creek Tpke. Int corridors. **Pets:** Large, other species. Service with restrictions, supervision.
🆂🅰🆅🅴 ⊠ 🛏 💻

SAYRE

▼▼▼ **AmericInn Lodge & Suites of Sayre** �H
(580) 928-2700. **$85-$160, 7 day notice.** 2405 S El Camino Rd. I-40, exit 20, just n. Int corridors. **Pets:** Medium. $15 one-time fee/room. Designated rooms, service with restrictions, supervision.
🅰🆂🅺 ⊠ 🗛 🛏 💻 🌊

SEMINOLE

△△△ ▼▼▼▼ **Best Western Seminole Inn & Suites** �H
(405) 382-3139. **$97-$108.** 1525 N Milt Phillips Ave. 0.5 mi s of jct US 377, SR 9 and 99. Int corridors. **Pets:** Very small. $25 deposit/pet. Supervision.
🆂🅰🆅🅴 ⊠ 🛏 💻 🌊

THACKERVILLE

▼▼▼ **Winstar Microtel Inn and Suites** �H
(580) 276-4487. **$135-$300.** Rt 1, Box 682. I-35, exit 1, 1.2 mi n on E Service Rd. Int corridors. **Pets:** Small. $10 daily fee/pet. Service with restrictions, crate.
🅰🆂🅺 ⊠ 🛏 💻 🌊

TULSA METROPOLITAN AREA

BROKEN ARROW

▼▼▼▼ **Clarion Hotel** �H
(918) 258-7085. **$79-$199.** 2600 N Aspen Ave. Just s of jct SR 51. Int corridors. **Pets:** Accepted.
🅰🆂🅺 ⊠ 🛏 💻 🌊

▼▼▼▼ **Homewood Suites by Hilton Tulsa South** �H
(918) 392-7700. **$119-$169.** 4900 W Madison Pl. Just ne of jct 71st St and Garnett Ave. Int corridors. **Pets:** Small, other species. $75 one-time fee/pet. Service with restrictions, supervision.
⊠ 🗛 🛏 💻 🌊 ⊠

CLAREMORE

△△△ ▼▼ **Claremore Motor Inn** 🅼
(918) 342-4545. **$44-$89.** 1709 N Lynn Riggs Blvd. 1.2 mi n on SR 66. Ext/int corridors. **Pets:** Accepted.
🆂🅰🆅🅴 ⊠ 🛏

▼▼▼ **Days Inn Claremore** �H
(918) 343-3297. **$62-$95.** 1720 S Lynn Riggs Blvd. 1.6 mi s on SR 66. Int corridors. **Pets:** Accepted.
🅰🆂🅺 ⊠ 🛏 💻 🌊

▼▼▼ **Microtel Inn & Suites** �H
(918) 343-2868. **Call for rates.** 10600 E Mallard Lake Rd. 2.6 mi s on SR 66. Int corridors. **Pets:** Small, other species. $20 daily fee/pet. Designated rooms, service with restrictions, supervision.
⊠ 🛏 💻 🌊

△△△ ▼▼▼ **Super 8 Motel** �H
(918) 341-2323. **$59-$99.** 1100 E Will Rogers Blvd. I-44, exit 255, just w. Ext/int corridors. **Pets:** Small. $10 daily fee/pet. Designated rooms, service with restrictions, supervision.
🆂🅰🆅🅴 ⊠ 🛏 💻

GLENPOOL

△△△ ▼▼▼ **Best Western Glenpool/Tulsa** �H
(918) 322-5201. **$80-$90.** 14831 S Casper St. I-44, exit 224, 9.5 mi s on US 75. Ext corridors. **Pets:** $20 one-time fee/pet. No service, supervision.
🆂🅰🆅🅴 ⊠ 🛏 💻 🌊

TULSA

▼▼▼ Ambassador Hotel H
(918) 587-8200. **$259-$329.** 1324 S Main St. Jct 14th and Main sts. Int corridors. **Pets:** Accepted.
ASK ✕ 🛏 🖵 ⑪

▼▼ Baymont Inn & Suites Tulsa H
(918) 488-8777. **Call for rates.** 4530 E Skelly Dr. I-44, exit 229 (Yale Ave/SR 66), just s, then w. Int corridors. **Pets:** Accepted.
✕ 🛏 🖵 ⇀

AAA▸ ▼▼ Best Western Airport H
(918) 438-0780. **$75-$99.** 222 N Garnett Rd. I-244, exit 14 (Garnett Rd), just s. Ext corridors. **Pets:** Other species. $25 one-time fee/room. Service with restrictions, crate.
SAVE ✕ 🛏 🖵 ⇀

▼▼▼ Candlewood Suites H
(918) 294-9000. **Call for rates.** 10008 E 73rd St S. Just sw of jct 71st St and 101st E Ave. Int corridors. **Pets:** Accepted.
✕ ♿M 🛏 🖵

AAA▸ ▼▼▼ Crowne Plaza Tulsa H
(918) 582-9000. **$149-$189, 14 day notice.** 100 E 2nd St. Jct 2nd St and Boston; downtown. Int corridors. **Pets:** Accepted.
SAVE ✕ ♿M 🛏 🖵 ⑪ ⇀ ⊠

▼▼ Days Inn H
(918) 496-9300. **Call for rates.** 4724 S Yale Ave. I-44, exit 229 (Yale Ave/SR 66), just s. Ext corridors. **Pets:** Accepted.
✕ 🛏 🖵 ⇀

▼▼▼ DoubleTree Hotel At Warren Place H 🐾
(918) 495-1000. **$99-$209.** 6110 S Yale Ave. I-44, exit 229 (Yale Ave/SR 66), 1.3 mi s. Int corridors. **Pets:** Medium, other species. $50 deposit/room. Service with restrictions, crate.
✕ ♿M 🛏 🖵 ⑪ ⇀ ⊠

▼▼▼ DoubleTree Hotel Tulsa Downtown H
(918) 587-8000. **$109-$209.** 616 W 7th St. Jct 7th St and Houston. Int corridors. **Pets:** Accepted.
✕ 🛏 🖵 ⑪ ⇀ ⊠

▼▼▼ Embassy Suites Hotel H 🐾
(918) 622-4000. **$109-$169.** 3332 S 79th E Ave. I-44, exit 231 eastbound; exit 232 (Memorial Dr) westbound, just sw. Int corridors. **Pets:** Small, other species. $50 deposit/room. Service with restrictions, crate.
✕ 🛏 🖵 ⑪ ⇀

▼▼▼ Hilton Tulsa Southern Hills H
(918) 492-5000. **$99-$144.** 7902 S Lewis Ave. I-44, exit 227, 3 mi s. Int corridors. **Pets:** Medium, other species. $75 one-time fee/room. Service with restrictions, crate.
✕ 🛏 🖵 ⑪ ⇀

▼▼▼ Holiday Inn H
(918) 622-7000. **$129.** 5000 E Skelly Dr. I-44, exit 229 (Yale Ave/SR 66); on south frontage road. Ext/int corridors. **Pets:** Accepted.
ASK ✕ 🛏 🖵 ⑪ ⇀

▼▼▼ La Quinta Inn & Suites Tulsa Central H 🐾
(918) 665-2630. **$69-$119.** 6030 E Skelly Dr. I-44, exit 230, just s. Int corridors. **Pets:** Medium, other species. Service with restrictions, supervision.
ASK ✕ 🛏 🖵 ⇀

▼▼ Microtel Inn & Suites H
(918) 858-3775. **$63-$100, 30 day notice.** 4531 E 21st St. Just w of 21st St and Yale Ave. Int corridors. **Pets:** Other species. $25 one-time fee/room. Service with restrictions, supervision.
ASK ✕ 🛏 🖵

▼▼▼ Radisson Tulsa H
(918) 627-5000. **$119-$149.** 10918 E 41st St. Just e of US 169. Int corridors. **Pets:** Accepted.
ASK ✕ 🖵 ⑪ ⇀ ⊠

▼▼▼ Ramada Tulsa Airport East H
(918) 437-7660. **$89, 30 day notice.** 1010 N Garnett Rd. I-244, exit 14 (Garnett Rd), just n. Int corridors. **Pets:** Accepted.
ASK ✕ ♿M 🛏 🖵 ⑪ ⇀ ⊠

▼▼ Red Roof Inn M
(918) 622-6776. **$50-$100.** 4717 S Yale Ave. I-44, exit 229 (Yale Ave), just s. Ext corridors. **Pets:** Small. $15 daily fee/pet. Service with restrictions, supervision.
ASK ✕ 🛏 ⇀

AAA▸ ▼▼▼▼ Renaissance Tulsa Hotel & Convention Center H
(918) 307-2600. **$176-$215.** 6808 S 107th E Ave. Just ne of jct US 169 and 71st St. Int corridors. **Pets:** Accepted.
SAVE ✕ ♿M 🛏 🖵 ⑪ ⇀ ⊠

▼▼▼ Residence Inn by Marriott H
(918) 250-4850. **$144-$176.** 11025 E 73rd St. US 169, exit 71st St, just e. Int corridors. **Pets:** Accepted.
✕ 🛏 🖵 ⇀ ⊠

▼▼ Sleep Inn & Suites Tulsa Central H
(918) 663-2777. **$89-$159.** 8021 E 33rd St S. I-44, exit 231 eastbound; exit 232 (Memorial Dr) westbound, just sw. Int corridors. **Pets:** Accepted.
ASK ✕ 🛏 🖵 ⇀ ⊠

▼▼▼ Staybridge Suites H
(918) 461-2100. **$159.** 11111 E 73rd St. Just se of jct US 169 and 71st St. Int corridors. **Pets:** Small, other species. $75 one-time fee/pet. Designated rooms, service with restrictions, supervision.
ASK ✕ ♿M 🛏 🖵 ⇀ ⊠

END METROPOLITAN AREA

WOODWARD

AAA▸ ▼▼▼ Northwest Inn H
(580) 256-7600. **Call for rates.** Hwy 270 S & 1st St. 1.4 mi s of jct US 183, 270, SR 3 and 34. Ext/int corridors. **Pets:** Accepted.
SAVE ✕ 🛏 🖵 ⑪ ⇀

OREGON

ALBANY

Best Western Albany Inn H ❀
(541) 928-6322. **$65-$149.** 315 Airport Rd SE. I-5, exit 234B southbound; exit 234 northbound, just sw. Ext corridors. **Pets:** Medium. $10 daily fee/pet. Crate.
SAVE ✕ 🦮 💻 🏊

Comfort Suites H
(541) 928-2053. **$89-$159.** 100 Opal Ct NE. I-5, exit 234A southbound; exit 234 northbound, just se. Int corridors. **Pets:** Medium, dogs only. $15 one-time fee/pet. Service with restrictions, supervision.
SAVE ✕ 🦮 💻 🏊 ✕

Econo Lodge M
(541) 926-0170. **$54-$95.** 1212 SE Price Rd. I-5, exit 233, just e on Santiam Hwy (US 20), then just n. Ext corridors. **Pets:** Medium, dogs only. $10 daily fee/pet. Service with restrictions, supervision.
SAVE ✕ 🦮

Holiday Inn Express Hotel & Suites H
(541) 928-8820. **$99-$179.** 105 Opal Ct NE. I-5, exit 234A southbound; exit 234 northbound, just se. Int corridors. **Pets:** Medium, dogs only. $15 one-time fee/pet. Service with restrictions, supervision.
SAVE ✕ 🦮 🦮 💻 🏊 ✕

La Quinta Inn Albany H ❀
(541) 928-0921. **$65-$115.** 251 Airport Rd SE. I-5, exit 234B southbound; exit 234 northbound, just sw. Int corridors. **Pets:** Medium, other species. Service with restrictions, supervision.
ASK ✕ 🦮 💻 🏊 ✕

Motel 6 #4124 M
(541) 926-4233. **$62-$75.** 2735 E Pacific Blvd. I-5, exit 234B southbound; exit 234 northbound, 0.5 mi w. Ext corridors. **Pets:** Other species. Service with restrictions, supervision.
SAVE ✕ 🦮

Phoenix Inn Suites-Albany H
(541) 926-5696. **$79-$139.** 3410 Spicer Rd SE. I-5, exit 233, just se. Int corridors. **Pets:** Other species. $15 daily fee/pet. Service with restrictions, supervision.
SAVE ✕ 🦮 💻 🏊

Quality Inn H
(541) 928-5050. **$59-$150.** 1100 Price Rd SE. I-5, exit 233, just e on Santiam Hwy (US 20), then just n. Int corridors. **Pets:** Small, dogs only. $10 daily fee/pet. Designated rooms, service with restrictions, supervision.
SAVE ✕ 🦮 🦮 💻 🏊

ASHLAND

Ashland Chanticleer Inn BB
(541) 482-1919. **$125-$195, 31 day notice.** 120 Gresham St. Just se of downtown on Main St (SR 99), then just s. Int corridors. **Pets:** Medium, dogs only. $15 daily fee/pet, $20 one-time fee/pet. Designated rooms, service with restrictions, crate.
✕

Ashland Springs Hotel H
(541) 488-1700. **$89-$259.** 212 E Main St. Corner of 1st St; center. Int corridors. **Pets:** Medium, dogs only. $30 one-time fee/room. Designated rooms, service with restrictions, supervision.
ASK ✕ 🦮 🍴

Best Western Bard's Inn H
(541) 482-0049. **$90-$190.** 132 N Main St. Just nw on SR 99 (N Main St) from Downtown Plaza. Ext/int corridors. **Pets:** Accepted.
SAVE ✕ 🦮 💻 🏊

Best Western Windsor Inn H
(541) 488-2330. **$89-$189.** 2520 Ashland St. I-5, exit 14, just se on Ashland St (SR 66). Ext corridors. **Pets:** $15 daily fee/pet. Designated rooms, service with restrictions, supervision.
SAVE ✕ 🦮 💻 🏊

Cedarwood Inn M
(541) 488-2000. **$59-$119, 3 day notice.** 1801 Siskiyou Blvd. I-5, exit 11 northbound, 2.6 mi nw; exit 14 southbound, just w on Ashland St (SR 66), 0.6 mi s on Tolman Creek Rd, then 0.6 mi w. Ext corridors. **Pets:** Accepted.
SAVE ✕ 🦮 💻 🏊

Flagship Inn of Ashland M
(541) 482-2641. **$59-$119, 3 day notice.** 1193 Siskiyou Blvd. I-5, exit 14, 1.3 mi w on Ashland St (SR 66), then just n. Ext corridors. **Pets:** Small. $10 daily fee/pet. Designated rooms, service with restrictions, supervision.
SAVE ✕ 🦮 💻 🏊

La Quinta Inn & Suites Ashland H ❀
(541) 482-6932. **$69-$172.** 434 S Valley View Rd. I-5, exit 19, just sw. Int corridors. **Pets:** Medium, other species. Service with restrictions, supervision.
ASK ✕ 🦮 💻 🏊

Plaza Inn & Suites At Ashland Creek H ❀
(541) 488-8900. **$89-$289.** 98 Central Ave. From Downtown Plaza, just nw on N Main St (SR 99), just n on Water St, then just w. Int corridors. **Pets:** Medium. $25 daily fee/room. Designated rooms, service with restrictions, supervision.
SAVE ✕ 🦮 💻

ⓐⓐⓐ ▼▼▼ Timbers Motel of Ashland Ⓜ ❖
(541) 482-4242. **Call for rates.** 1450 Ashland St. I-5, exit 14, 1.2 mi w on Ashland St (SR 66). Ext corridors. **Pets:** Other species. Designated rooms, service with restrictions, crate.
[SAVE] [✕] [📶] [💻] [🏊]

ⓐⓐⓐ ▼▼▼▼ Village Suites at Ashland Hills Ⓗ ❖
(541) 482-8310. **$99-$149.** 2525 Ashland St. I-5, exit 14, just ne on Ashland St (SR 66). Int corridors. **Pets:** Other species. Designated rooms, service with restrictions, supervision.
[SAVE] [✕] [📶] [💻] [🚫]

ASTORIA

ⓐⓐⓐ ▼ Astoria Dunes Motel Ⓜ
(503) 325-7111. **$70-$130.** 288 W Marine Dr. Just e of Astoria Bridge on US 30. Ext corridors. **Pets:** Medium, dogs only. $15 daily fee/pet. Designated rooms, service with restrictions, supervision.
[SAVE] [✕] [📶] [💻] [🏊]

▼◆▼ Astoria Holiday Inn Express Hotel & Suites Ⓗ ❖
(503) 325-6222. **$119-$339.** 204 W Marine Dr. On US 30; west side of town. Int corridors. **Pets:** $15 daily fee/pet. Designated rooms, service with restrictions, supervision.
[ASK] [✕] [♿] [📶] [💻] [🏊] [🚫]

ⓐⓐⓐ ▼◆▼ Best Western Lincoln Inn Ⓗ ❖
(503) 325-2205. **$89-$399.** 555 Hamburg Ave. On US 101/30; at east end of Young's Bay Bridge. Int corridors. **Pets:** Medium, dogs only. $15 daily fee/pet. Designated rooms, service with restrictions, supervision.
[SAVE] [✕] [📶] [💻] [🏊] [🚫]

▼▼ Clementine's Bed & Breakfast ⒷⒷ
(503) 325-2005. **$95-$165, 7 day notice.** 847 Exchange St. At 8th and Exchange sts; in historic downtown. Int corridors. **Pets:** $15 one-time fee/room. Designated rooms, no service.
[✕] [📶] [💻] [🎬] [🚭]

ⓐⓐⓐ ▼▼▼ Crest Motel, P.C. Ⓜ
(503) 325-3141. **$62-$137.** 5366 Leif Erickson Dr. 4 mi e of Astoria Bridge on US 30. Ext corridors. **Pets:** Other species. Service with restrictions, supervision.
[SAVE] [✕] [📶] [💻] [🎬]

ⓐⓐⓐ ▼▼ Red Lion Inn Astoria Ⓜ
(503) 325-7373. **$99-$239.** 400 Industry St. Just w of Astoria Bridge on US 30, just n on Basin St (caution: do not turn onto Astoria-Megler Bridge). Ext corridors. **Pets:** Other species. $20 one-time fee/room. Service with restrictions, supervision.
[SAVE] [✕] [📶] [💻] [🎬]

BAKER CITY

ⓐⓐⓐ ▼▼▼▼ Best Western Sunridge Inn Ⓗ
(541) 523-6444. **$85-$95.** 1 Sunridge Ln. I-84, exit 304, just w. Int corridors. **Pets:** Accepted.
[SAVE] [✕] [📶] [💻] [🍴] [🏊]

▼▼▼▼ Geiser Grand Hotel Ⓗ ❖
(541) 523-1889. **$89-$229, 3 day notice.** 1996 Main St. I-84, exit 304, 0.9 mi w on Campbell St, then 0.3 mi s; downtown. Int corridors. **Pets:** Large, other species. $15 daily fee/pet. Service with restrictions, crate.
[ASK] [✕] [🍴]

ⓐⓐⓐ ▼▼▼ Super 8 Baker City Ⓗ
(541) 523-8282. **$65-$80.** 250 Campbell St. I-84, exit 304, just e. Int corridors. **Pets:** Other species. $10 daily fee/pet. Service with restrictions, supervision.
[SAVE] [✕] [♿] [📶] [💻] [🏊]

BANDON

ⓐⓐⓐ ▼▼▼ Bandon Inn Ⓜ ❖
(541) 347-4417. **$74-$139.** 355 Hwy 101. Center. Ext corridors. **Pets:** Medium. $15 daily fee/pet. Designated rooms, service with restrictions, supervision.
[SAVE] [✕] [📶] [💻] [🎬]

ⓐⓐⓐ ▼▼ Best Western Inn at Face Rock Ⓗ ❖
(541) 347-9441. **$110-$301.** 3225 Beach Loop Dr. 1 mi s on US 101, 0.8 mi w on Seabird Rd, then just s. Ext corridors. **Pets:** Medium. $25 one-time fee/pet. Designated rooms, service with restrictions, supervision.
[SAVE] [✕] [📶] [💻] [🍴] [🏊] [🚫] [🎬]

BEND

ⓐⓐⓐ ▼▼▼▼ Bend Inn & Suites Ⓗ
(541) 388-4114. **$79-$149.** 15 NE Butler Market Rd. US 97, exit 136 (Butler Market Rd), just n. Ext corridors. **Pets:** Medium. $15 daily fee/pet. Service with restrictions, supervision.
[SAVE] [✕] [📶] [💻] [🏊]

▼▼ Bend Riverside Motel Suites Ⓜ
(541) 389-2363. **$68-$159.** 1565 NW Wall St. US 97, exit 137 (Revere Ave), just s. Ext corridors. **Pets:** Accepted.
[ASK] [✕] [📶] [💻] [🏊]

ⓐⓐⓐ ▼▼▼ Best Western Inn & Suites of Bend Ⓗ
(541) 382-1515. **$72-$159.** 721 NE 3rd St. Jct US 20 and Business Rt US 97 (NE 3rd St), just s. Ext corridors. **Pets:** Accepted.
[SAVE] [✕] [📶] [💻] [🏊]

▼▼▼ Cricketwood Country Bed & Breakfast ⒷⒷ ❖
(541) 330-0747. **Call for rates.** 63520 Cricketwood Rd. US 97, exit 136 (NE Butler Market Rd), 3.2 mi ne on Butler Market Rd (becomes Hamehook Rd), 0.8 mi n on Hamehook Rd, just e on Repine Dr, then just n. Ext/int corridors. **Pets:** Dogs only. $10 daily fee/room. Designated rooms, no service.
[✕] [📶] [💻]

ⓐⓐⓐ ▼▼◆ Days Inn Ⓗ
(541) 383-3776. **Call for rates.** 849 NE 3rd St. Jct US 20 and Business Rt US 97 (NE 3rd St), just s. Ext corridors. **Pets:** Accepted.
[SAVE] [✕] [📶] [💻] [🏊]

ⓐⓐⓐ ▼ Dunes Motel Ⓜ
(541) 382-6811. **$39-$125.** 1515 NE 3rd St. Jct US 20 and Business Rt US 97 (NE 3rd St), just n. Ext corridors. **Pets:** Small. $6 daily fee/pet. Service with restrictions, supervision.
[SAVE] [✕] [📶] [💻]

ⓐⓐⓐ ▼▼▼ Fairfield Inn & Suites by Marriott Ⓗ
(541) 318-1747. **$99-$139.** 1626 NW Wall St. US 97, exit 137 (Revere Ave), just s; downtown. Int corridors. **Pets:** Other species. $75 one-time fee/room. Service with restrictions.
[SAVE] [✕] [♿] [📶] [💻] [🏊] [🚫]

ⓐⓐⓐ ▼▼▼ Holiday Inn Express Hotel & Suites Ⓗ
(541) 317-8500. **$99-$189.** 20615 Grandview Dr. On US 97; north end of town. Int corridors. **Pets:** Other species. $10 daily fee. Service with restrictions, supervision.
[SAVE] [✕] [♿] [📶] [💻] [🏊] [🚫]

▼▼ La Quinta Inn Bend Ⓗ ❖
(541) 388-2227. **$59-$129.** 61200 SE 3rd St (Business Rt US 97). From south end jct US 97 and Business Rt US 97, just n. Int corridors. **Pets:** Medium, other species. Service with restrictions, supervision.
[ASK] [✕] [📶] [💻] [🏊]

ⓐⓐⓐ ▼▼▼ Quality Inn Ⓗ
(541) 318-0848. **$89-$129.** 20600 Grandview Dr. On US 97; north end of town. Int corridors. **Pets:** Medium. $12 daily fee/pet. Designated rooms, service with restrictions, supervision.
[SAVE] [✕] [♿] [📶] [💻] [🏊]

AAA ◈◈◈◈ Red Lion Hotel Bend 🅗
(541) 382-7011. **$99-$196.** 1415 NE 3rd St. Jct US 20 and Business Rt US 97 (NE 3rd St), just n. Ext corridors. **Pets:** Other species. $20 one-time fee/room. Service with restrictions, supervision.
[SAVE] ⊠ 🔥M 🛏 💻 ➔

AAA ◈◈◈◈ The Riverhouse Hotel & Convention Center 🅗
(541) 389-3111. **$99-$219, 3 day notice.** 3075 N Business 97. US 97, exit 136 (Butler Market Rd) northbound, just n; exit 135B southbound. Ext/int corridors. **Pets:** Accepted.
[SAVE] ⊠ 🛏 💻 🍽 ➔ ⊠

AAA ◈◈◈ Shilo Inn Suites Hotel Bend 🅗 ❖
(541) 389-9600. **$112-$300.** 3105 OB Riley Rd. 1.5 mi n on US 97 from jct US 20 E. Ext corridors. **Pets:** Dogs only. $25 one-time fee/room. Designated rooms, service with restrictions, supervision.
[SAVE] ⊠ 🛏 💻 🍽 ➔ ⊠

BOARDMAN

AAA ◈◈◈ Rodeway Inn Ⓜ
(541) 481-2375. **$58-$129.** 105 SW Front St. I-84, exit 164, just sw. Ext corridors. **Pets:** Other species. Designated rooms, service with restrictions, supervision.
[SAVE] ⊠ 🛏 💻 ➔

BROOKINGS

AAA ◈◈◈ Best Western Beachfront Inn 🅗
(541) 469-7779. **$154-$295.** 16008 Boat Basin Rd. Jct US 101, 0.6 mi w on Benham Ln. Ext corridors. **Pets:** $10 daily fee/pet. Designated rooms, service with restrictions, supervision.
[SAVE] ⊠ 🔥M 🛏 💻 ➔ ⓚ

AAA ◈◈◈ Wild Rivers Motorlodge Ⓜ ❖
(541) 469-5361. **$69-$119.** 437 Chetco Ave. On US 101, just n of Chetco River Bridge. Ext corridors. **Pets:** $20 one-time fee/room. Service with restrictions, supervision.
[SAVE] ⊠ 🛏 💻

BURNS

AAA ◈◈◈ America's Best Inn Ⓜ
(541) 573-1700. **$60-$86.** 999 Oregon Ave (US 395/20). 1 mi w on US 395/20 from jct SR 78. Ext/int corridors. **Pets:** Small, dogs only. $10 daily fee/pet. Designated rooms, service with restrictions, supervision.
[SAVE] ⊠ 🛏 💻 ➔

AAA ◈◈◈ Silver Spur Motel Ⓜ
(541) 573-2077. **$42-$52.** 789 N Broadway. US 395/20; at north edge of town center. Ext corridors. **Pets:** Other species. $5 one-time fee/pet. Designated rooms, service with restrictions.
[SAVE] ⊠ 🛏 💻

CANNON BEACH

◈◈ Cannon Beach Ecola Creek Lodge Ⓜ
(503) 436-2776. **$55-$230, 3 day notice.** 208 5th St. 0.3 mi w of US 101 via north exit to Ecola State Park. Ext corridors. **Pets:** $20 daily fee/pet. Designated rooms, service with restrictions, supervision.
[ASK] ⊠ 🔥M 🛏 💻 ⓚ

◈◈◈◈ Inn at Cannon Beach 🅗
(503) 436-9085. **Call for rates.** 3215 S Hemlock St. US 101, exit Tolovana Park, just w, then just n. Ext corridors. **Pets:** Accepted.
⊠ 🛏 💻 ⓚ

◈◈◈◈ The Ocean Lodge 🅗 ❖
(503) 436-2241. **$199-$379, 7 day notice.** 2864 S Pacific St. US 101, exit Tolovana Park, just w on Warren Way, just n on S Hemlock St, just w on W Chisana St, then just n. Ext/int corridors. **Pets:** $15 daily fee/pet. Designated rooms, service with restrictions, supervision.
⊠ 🛏 💻

AAA ◈◈◈◈ Surfsand Resort at Cannon Beach 🅗 ❖
(503) 436-2274. **$179-$459, 7 day notice.** 148 W Gower St. US 101, exit Cannon Beach (2nd exit); downtown. Ext corridors. **Pets:** Other species. $15 daily fee/pet. Designated rooms, service with restrictions, supervision.
[SAVE] ⊠ 🛏 💻 ➔ ⊠

AAA ◈◈◈ Tolovana Inn Ⓒ🄾
(503) 436-2211. **$69-$429, 3 day notice.** 3400 S Hemlock St. US 101, exit Tolovana Park, just w on Warren Way, then just s. Ext corridors. **Pets:** Accepted.
[SAVE] ⊠ 🛏 💻 ➔ ⊠ ⓚ

CANYONVILLE

AAA ◈◈◈ Best Western Canyonville Inn & Suites 🅗
(541) 839-4200. **$80-$171.** 200 Creekside Dr. I-5, exit 99, just w. Int corridors. **Pets:** Small. $15 daily fee/pet. Designated rooms, service with restrictions, supervision.
[SAVE] ⊠ 🛏 💻 ➔

CASCADE LOCKS

AAA ◈◈◈ Best Western Columbia River Inn 🅗
(541) 374-8777. **$100-$180.** 735 WaNaPa St (US 30). I-84, exit 44 eastbound, 0.4 mi ne; westbound, 1.4 mi nw. Int corridors. **Pets:** Medium. $10 daily fee/pet. Service with restrictions, supervision.
[SAVE] ⊠ 🔥M 🛏 💻 ➔

CENTRAL POINT

◈◈◈ Super 8 Inn & Suites 🅗
(541) 664-5888. **$90-$135.** 4999 Biddle Rd. I-5, exit 33, 0.5 mi e. Int corridors. **Pets:** Other species. $25 daily fee/pet. Supervision.
[ASK] ⊠ 🔥M 🛏 💻 ➔

CLATSKANIE

AAA ◈◈◈ Clatskanie River Inn 🅗
(503) 728-9000. **$89-$149.** 600 E Columbia River Hwy (US 30). On US 30. Int corridors. **Pets:** Accepted.
[SAVE] ⊠ 🛏 💻 ➔

COOS BAY

AAA ◈◈◈ Best Western Holiday Motel 🅗
(541) 269-5111. **$99-$159.** 411 N Bayshore Dr. Just n of downtown on US 101. Ext/int corridors. **Pets:** Small, dogs only. $15 daily fee/pet. Service with restrictions, supervision.
[SAVE] ⊠ 🛏 💻 ➔

AAA ◈◈◈ Red Lion Hotel Coos Bay 🅗
(541) 267-4141. **$104-$156.** 1313 N Bayshore Dr. 0.5 mi n of downtown on US 101. Ext corridors. **Pets:** Other species. $20 one-time fee/room. Service with restrictions, supervision.
[SAVE] ⊠ 🔥M 🛏 💻 🍽 ➔

CORVALLIS

AAA ◈◈◈ Best Western Grand Manor Inn & Suites 🅗 ❖
(541) 758-8571. **$90-$200, 7 day notice.** 925 NW Garfield Ave. Jct SR 34 and US 20, just w on NW Harrison Blvd, 1.4 mi n on NW 9th St, then just w. Int corridors. **Pets:** Medium, dogs only. $10 daily fee/pet. Designated rooms, service with restrictions, supervision.
[SAVE] ⊠ 🔥M 🛏 💻 ➔

AAA ◈◈◈ Days Inn 🅗
(541) 754-7474. **$59-$169.** 1113 NW 9th St. Jct SR 34 and US 20, just w on NW Harrison Blvd, then 1 mi n. Int corridors. **Pets:** Accepted.
[SAVE] ⊠ 🛏 💻 ➔

Holiday Inn Express On The River H ❀
(541) 752-0800. **$70-$209.** 781 NE 2nd St. Jct SR 34 and US 20, 0.4 mi n. Int corridors. **Pets:** Other species. $25 daily fee/room. Designated rooms, service with restrictions.
[SAVE] [X] [🗋] [🖵] [≋] [⊠]

Motel 6 #4243 H
(541) 758-9125. **$55-$99.** 935 NW Garfield Ave. Jct SR 34 and US 20, just w on NW Harrison Blvd, 1.4 mi n on NW 9th St, then just w. Int corridors. **Pets:** Accepted.
[SAVE] [X] [🗋]

Super 8 H
(541) 758-8088. **Call for rates.** 407 NW 2nd St. US 20, just n of jct SR 34; downtown. Int corridors. **Pets:** Accepted.
[X] [⅙M] [🗋] [≋]

COTTAGE GROVE

Comfort Inn H
(541) 942-9747. **$64-$150.** 845 Gateway Blvd. I-5, exit 174, just w. Ext/int corridors. **Pets:** Large. $10 daily fee/pet. Designated rooms, service with restrictions, supervision.
[SAVE] [X] [🗋] [🖵] [≋]

Holiday Inn Express H
(541) 942-1000. **$99-$129.** 1601 Gateway Blvd. I-5, exit 174, just w. Int corridors. **Pets:** Medium, dogs only. $15 one-time fee/pet. Service with restrictions, supervision.
[SAVE] [X] [⅙M] [🗋] [🖵] [≋]

CRESWELL

Super 8 Creswell Inn M
(541) 895-3341. **$55-$80.** 345 E Oregon Ave. I-5, exit 182, just w. Ext corridors. **Pets:** Accepted.
[SAVE] [X] [🗋] [🖵] [≋]

DALLAS

Best Western Dallas Inn & Suites H
(503) 623-6000. **$90-$130.** 250 Orchard Dr. SR 223, just n. Int corridors. **Pets:** Small. $10 daily fee/pet. Designated rooms, service with restrictions, supervision.
[SAVE] [X] [⅙M] [🗋] [🖵]

DEPOE BAY

Crown Pacific Inn M
(541) 765-7773. **$75-$95.** 50 NE Bechill St. Just n of downtown. Ext/int corridors. **Pets:** Other species. $10 daily fee/pet. Designated rooms, service with restrictions, supervision.
[SAVE] [X] [🗋] [🖵] [Ⓚ]

Surfrider Resort H
(541) 764-2311. **$119-$199, 3 day notice.** 3115 NW US 101. 2 mi n of Depoe Bay. Ext corridors. **Pets:** Small. $20 one-time fee/pet. Designated rooms, no service, supervision.
[SAVE] [X] [🗋] [🖵] [🍴] [≋] [⊠] [Ⓚ]

ENTERPRISE

Ponderosa Motel M
(541) 426-3186. **$56-$79.** 102 E Greenwood St. Center. Ext corridors. **Pets:** Accepted.
[ASK] [X] [🗋] [🖵]

The Wilderness Inn M
(541) 426-4535. **Call for rates.** 301 W North St. Corner of NW 2nd St. Ext corridors. **Pets:** Medium, dogs only. $10 daily fee/pet. No service, supervision.
[X] [🗋] [🖵]

EUGENE

Americas Best Value Inn M
(541) 343-0730. **$49-$79.** 1140 W 6th Ave. I-5, exit 194B, 3 mi w on I-105, then just w on SR 99 N (6th Ave). Ext corridors. **Pets:** Large. $10 daily fee/pet. Designated rooms, service with restrictions, supervision.
[SAVE] [X] [🗋]

Best Western Greentree Inn H ❀
(541) 485-2727. **$105-$175, 3 day notice.** 1759 Franklin Blvd. I-5, exit 191 (Glenwood Blvd) southbound, 0.6 mi n, then 1.1 mi w; exit 192 northbound, 1 mi w. Ext/int corridors. **Pets:** $50 deposit/pet. Designated rooms, service with restrictions, supervision.
[SAVE] [X] [🗋] [🖵] [≋]

Best Western New Oregon Motel H ❀
(541) 683-3669. **$105-$175, 3 day notice.** 1655 Franklin Blvd. I-5, exit 194B southbound to I-105, exit University of Oregon, 0.9 mi e; exit 192 northbound, 1 mi w. Ext/int corridors. **Pets:** $50 deposit/pet. Service with restrictions, supervision.
[SAVE] [X] [🗋] [🖵] [≋] [⊠]

Eugene/Springfield Residence Inn by Marriott H
(541) 342-7171. **$189-$199.** 25 Club Rd. I-5, exit 194B, 1.3 mi w on I-105, exit 2 (Coburg Rd), straight through jct Coburg Rd to Southwood Ln, just w, then se on Country Club Rd; follow signs for Autzen Stadium. Int corridors. **Pets:** Accepted.
[X] [⅙M] [🗋] [🖵] [≋] [⊠]

Express Inn & Suites M
(541) 868-1520. **$65-$85, 3 day notice.** 990 W 6th Ave. I-5, exit 194B, 3 mi w on I-105, then just w on SR 99 N (6th Ave). Ext corridors. **Pets:** Small, dogs only. $10 daily fee/pet. Service with restrictions, supervision.
[SAVE] [X] [🗋]

Hilton Eugene H 🐾
(541) 342-2000. **$139-$249.** 66 E 6th Ave. At 6th Ave and Oak St; center. Int corridors. **Pets:** Large. $35 one-time fee/pet. Service with restrictions, supervision.
[X] [🗋] [🖵] [🍴] [≋] [⊠]

La Quinta Inn & Suites Waterfront H ❀
(541) 344-8335. **$99-$199.** 155 Day Island Rd. I-5, exit 194B, 1.3 mi w on I-105, exit 2 (Coburg Rd), straight through jct Coburg Rd to Southwood Ln, just w, then 0.5 mi se on Country Club Rd; follow signs for Autzen Stadium. Int corridors. **Pets:** Medium, other species. Service with restrictions, supervision.
[ASK] [X] [🗋] [🖵] [≋]

Motel 6–#36 M
(541) 687-2395. **$55-$65.** 3690 Glenwood Dr. I-5, exit 191, just sw. Ext corridors. **Pets:** Other species. Service with restrictions, supervision.
[X] [🗋] [≋]

Red Carpet Inn M
(541) 345-0579. **$55-$70, 7 day notice.** 1055 6th Ave. I-5, exit 194B, 3 mi w on I-105, then just w on SR 99N (6th Ave). Ext corridors. **Pets:** Accepted.
[SAVE] [X] [🗋]

Red Lion Hotel Eugene M
(541) 342-5201. **$129-$199.** 205 Coburg Rd. I-5, exit 194B, 1.3 mi w on I-105, exit 2 (Coburg Rd), then just n. Ext corridors. **Pets:** Other species. $20 one-time fee/room. Service with restrictions, supervision.
[SAVE] [X] [🗋] [🖵] [🍴] [≋] [⊠]

Valley River Inn H
(541) 743-1000. **$139-$249.** 1000 Valley River Way. I-5, exit 194B, 2.5 mi w on I-105, exit 1, follow Valley River Center signs. Int corridors. **Pets:** Accepted.
[ASK] [X] [🗋] [🖵] [🍴] [≋] [⊠]

FLORENCE

Best Western Pier Point Inn H
(541) 997-7191. **$124-$240.** 85625 US 101 S. Jct SR 126, 1.1 mi s. Ext corridors. **Pets:** Accepted.

Le Chateau Motel M
(541) 997-3481. **$54-$119.** 1084 US 101 N. Jct SR 126, just n. Ext corridors. **Pets:** Other species. $16 one-time fee/room. Designated rooms, service with restrictions, supervision.

Ocean Breeze Motel M
(541) 997-2642. **$59-$150.** 85165 US 101 S. Jct SR 126, 2 mi s. Ext corridors. **Pets:** Dogs only. $10 daily fee/pet. Designated rooms, service with restrictions, supervision.

Old Town Inn M
(541) 997-7131. **$65-$99.** 170 US 101 S. Jct SR 126, 0.4 mi s. Ext corridors. **Pets:** Accepted.

Park Motel M ❖
(541) 997-2634. **$55-$150, 7 day notice.** 85034 US 101 S. Jct SR 126, 2.2 mi s. Ext corridors. **Pets:** Other species. $10 daily fee/pet. Service with restrictions, supervision.

FOREST GROVE

Best Western University Inn & Suites H
(503) 992-8888. **$89-$199.** 3933 Pacific Ave. East end of town on SR 8. Int corridors. **Pets:** Medium, dogs only. $15 daily fee/pet. Designated rooms, service with restrictions, supervision.

GARIBALDI

Comfort Inn H
(503) 322-3338. **$89-$189.** 502 Garibaldi Ave. On US 101 at jct 5th St; center. Int corridors. **Pets:** Accepted.

GEARHART

Gearhart By The Sea CO
(503) 738-8331. **$89-$300, 3 day notice.** 1157 N Marion Ave. US 101, exit City Center, 1 mi w. Ext corridors. **Pets:** Medium. $11 daily fee/pet. Designated rooms, service with restrictions, supervision.

GLIDE

Illahee Inn and Restaurant M ❖
(541) 496-4870. **$75-$95.** 170 Wild Thyme Ln. Just n to SR 138, 2.5 mi e. Ext corridors. **Pets:** Medium. $10 one-time fee/pet. Service with restrictions, supervision.

Steelhead Run Bed & Breakfast and Fine Art Gallery BB ❖
(541) 496-0563. **$65-$139, 9 day notice.** 23049 N Umpqua Hwy (SR 138). Just n to SR 138, 3 mi e, then just e of MM 24. Ext/int corridors. **Pets:** Other species. $20 daily fee/room. Designated rooms.

GOLD BEACH

Gold Beach Inn M
(541) 247-7091. **$89-$169.** 29346 Ellensburg Ave. On US 101; center. Ext corridors. **Pets:** Accepted.

Inn of the Beachcomber M
(541) 247-6691. **$79-$184.** 29266 Ellensburg Ave. On US 101; south end of town. Ext/int corridors. **Pets:** Accepted.

Jot's Resort M ❖
(541) 247-6676. **$65-$230, 3 day notice.** 94360 Wedderburn Loop. Just w of US 101; north end of bridge. Ext corridors. **Pets:** Other species. $15 daily fee/pet. Service with restrictions, supervision.

Motel 6–4047 M
(541) 247-4533. **$61-$92.** 94433 Jerry's Flat Rd. Just e of jct US 101. Ext corridors. **Pets:** Other species. Service with restrictions, supervision.

GOVERNMENT CAMP

Mt. Hood Inn H
(503) 272-3205. **Call for rates.** 87450 E Government Camp Loop. 0.5 mi w of center. Int corridors. **Pets:** Dogs only. $10 daily fee/pet. Service with restrictions, supervision.

GRANTS PASS

Bestway Inn M
(541) 479-2952. **$55-$75.** 1253 NE 6th St. I-5, exit 58, 0.9 mi s on SR 99. Ext corridors. **Pets:** Small, dogs only. $5 daily fee/pet. Designated rooms, service with restrictions, supervision.

Best Western Grants Pass Inn H
(541) 476-1117. **$70-$142.** 111 NE Agness Ave. I-5, exit 55, just nw. Ext corridors. **Pets:** Accepted.

Best Western Inn at the Rogue H
(541) 582-2200. **$85-$110.** 8959 Rogue River Hwy. I-5, exit 48, just nw. Int corridors. **Pets:** Accepted.

Buona Sera Inn M
(541) 476-4260. **Call for rates.** 1001 NE 6th St. I-5, exit 58, 1.1 mi s on SR 99. Ext corridors. **Pets:** Accepted.

Comfort Inn H
(541) 479-8301. **$60-$130.** 1889 NE 6th St. I-5, exit 58, just s on SR 99. Int corridors. **Pets:** Large, other species. $100 deposit/room, $10 one-time fee/pet. Designated rooms, service with restrictions, supervision.

Holiday Inn Express H
(541) 471-6144. **$96-$169.** 105 NE Agness Ave. I-5, exit 55, just nw. Int corridors. **Pets:** Large, other species. $10 daily fee/pet. Designated rooms, service with restrictions, supervision.

Knights Inn Motel M
(541) 479-5595. **Call for rates.** 104 SE 7th St. I-5, exit 58, 1.7 mi s on SR 99, just e on G St, then just n. Ext corridors. **Pets:** Medium, dogs only. $5 one-time fee/pet. Service with restrictions, crate.

La Quinta Inn & Suites Grants Pass H ❖
(541) 472-1808. **$59-$119.** 243 NE Morgan Ln. I-5, exit 58, 0.4 mi s on SR 99, just e on Hillcrest Dr to SR 99 N, then just n. Int corridors. **Pets:** Medium, other species. Service with restrictions, supervision.

Motel 6–#253 M
(541) 474-1331. **$45-$55.** 1800 NE 7th St. I-5, exit 58, 0.3 mi s on SR 99. Ext corridors. **Pets:** Other species. Service with restrictions, supervision.

Redwood Motel M ❀
(541) 476-0878. **$60-$352.** 815 NE 6th St. I-5, exit 58, 1.2 mi s on SR 99. Ext corridors. **Pets:** Medium, dogs only. $10 daily fee/pet. Designated rooms, no service, supervision.
[SAVE] [✕] [♿M] [🛏] [💻] [🏊]

Riverside Inn H ❀
(541) 476-6873. **$125-$149, 3 day notice.** 986 SW 6th St. I-5, exit 58, 2.5 mi s on SR 99. Ext corridors. **Pets:** Large, other species. $10 daily fee/pet. Designated rooms, service with restrictions, supervision.
[SAVE] [✕] [♿M] [🛏] [💻] [🏊]

Shilo Inn H ❀
(541) 479-8391. **$75-$159.** 1880 NW 6th St. I-5, exit 58, 0.3 mi s on SR 99. Int corridors. **Pets:** Dogs only. $25 one-time fee/room. Designated rooms, service with restrictions, supervision.
[SAVE] [✕] [♿M] [🛏] [💻] [🏊]

Sunset Inn M
(541) 479-3305. **$55-$135.** 1400 NW 6th St. I-5, exit 58, 0.7 mi s on SR 99. Ext corridors. **Pets:** Accepted.
[SAVE] [✕] [🛏] [💻] [🏊]

Super 8–Grants Pass H
(541) 474-0888. **$55-$103.** 1949 NE 7th St. I-5, exit 58, 0.4 mi s on SR 99, just e on Hillcrest Dr to SR 99 N, then just n. Int corridors. **Pets:** Medium, dogs only. $25 deposit/room. Service with restrictions, supervision.
[SAVE] [✕] [♿M] [🛏] [💻] [🏊]

Sweet Breeze Inn M ❀
(541) 471-4434. **Call for rates.** 1627 NE 6th St. I-5, exit 58, 0.5 mi s on SR 99. Ext/int corridors. **Pets:** Small. $50 deposit/pet, $5 daily fee/pet, $5 one-time fee/pet. Designated rooms, service with restrictions, supervision.
[SAVE] [✕] [🛏]

Travelodge M ❀
(541) 479-6611. **Call for rates.** 1950 NW Vine St. I-5, exit 58, just s on SR 99. Ext corridors. **Pets:** Medium, other species. $10 daily fee/pet. Designated rooms, service with restrictions, crate.
[✕] [♿M] [🛏] [💻] [🏊]

HALSEY

Pioneer Villa Travelodge M
(541) 369-2804. **$72-$85.** 33180 SR 228. I-5, exit 216, just se. Ext corridors. **Pets:** $5 daily fee/pet. Service with restrictions, crate.
[ASK] [✕] [🛏] [💻] [🍴] [🏊]

HERMISTON

Comfort Inn & Suites Hermiston H
(541) 564-5911. **Call for rates.** 77514 SR 207. I-84, exit 182, just nw. Int corridors. **Pets:** Accepted.
[✕] [♿M] [🛏] [💻] [🏊]

Oak Tree Inn H
(541) 567-2330. **$69-$84.** 1110 SE 4th St. 0.4 mi s on US 395, then just w. Int corridors. **Pets:** Small. $10 daily fee/pet. Service with restrictions, supervision.
[SAVE] [✕] [🛏] [💻]

Oxford Suites H
(541) 564-8000. **$109-$119.** 1050 N 1st St. 0.5 mi n on US 395. Int corridors. **Pets:** Small, dogs only. $30 one-time fee/room. Service with restrictions, supervision.
[ASK] [✕] [♿M] [🛏] [💻] [🏊]

HINES

Best Western Rory & Ryan Inns H
(541) 573-5050. **$70-$145, 3 day notice.** 534 US 20 N. On US 20 (Central Oregon Hwy). Int corridors. **Pets:** Small, dogs only. $15 daily fee/pet. Designated rooms, service with restrictions, supervision.
[SAVE] [✕] [🛏] [💻] [🏊]

HOOD RIVER

Best Western Hood River Inn H ❀
(541) 386-2200. **$95-$179, 3 day notice.** 1108 E Marina Way. I-84, exit 64, just ne. Int corridors. **Pets:** Large, dogs only. $15 daily fee/pet. Designated rooms, service with restrictions, supervision.
[SAVE] [✕] [🛏] [💻] [🍴] [🏊] [✕]

Columbia Gorge Hotel CI ❀
(541) 386-5566. **$199-$399, 14 day notice.** 4000 Westcliff Dr. I-84, exit 62, just sw of overpass. Int corridors. **Pets:** Dogs only. $35 one-time fee/room. Designated rooms, service with restrictions, supervision.
[SAVE] [✕] [🛏] [🍴]

Vagabond Lodge M ❀
(541) 386-2992. **$54-$105.** 4070 Westcliff Dr. I-84, exit 62, 0.3 mi nw. Ext corridors. **Pets:** Medium. $5 one-time fee/pet. Designated rooms, service with restrictions, supervision.
[SAVE] [✕] [🛏] [💻]

JACKSONVILLE

Jacksonville Inn CI
(541) 899-1900. **$159-$465, 3 day notice.** 175 E California St. On California St (SR 238); between 3rd and 4th sts; center. Ext/int corridors. **Pets:** Designated rooms, service with restrictions, supervision.
[SAVE] [✕] [🛏] [💻] [🍴]

Jacksonville's Magnolia Inn BB ❀
(541) 899-0255. **$95-$165, 3 day notice.** 245 N 5th St. At 5th (SR 238) and D sts. Int corridors. **Pets:** Dogs only. $25 one-time fee/room. Designated rooms, supervision.
[SAVE] [✕] [♿M]

The Stage Lodge M ❀
(541) 899-3953. **$98-$175, 7 day notice.** 830 N 5th St. 0.5 mi ne of downtown. Ext corridors. **Pets:** Medium. $12 daily fee/pet. Designated rooms, service with restrictions, supervision.
[ASK] [✕] [🛏] [💻]

JOHN DAY

Best Western John Day Inn M
(541) 575-1700. **$90-$100.** 315 W Main St. Just w of jct US 26 and 395. Ext corridors. **Pets:** Other species. $15 daily fee/pet. Designated rooms, service with restrictions.
[SAVE] [✕] [🛏] [💻] [🏊]

Dreamers Lodge M ❀
(541) 575-0526. **$42-$99.** 144 N Canyon Blvd. Just n of jct US 26 and 395. Ext corridors. **Pets:** Medium, dogs only. $5 daily fee/pet. Service with restrictions, supervision.
[SAVE] [✕] [🛏] [💻]

KEIZER

Keizer Renaissance Inn H
(503) 390-4733. **$79-$99.** 5188 Wittenberg Ln N. I-5, exit 260B southbound; exit 260 northbound, 1.5 mi w via Chemawa Rd and Lockhaven Dr, just s on River Rd, just e on Claggett St NE, then just s. Int corridors. **Pets:** Dogs only. $10 daily fee/pet. Service with restrictions, supervision.
[SAVE] [✕] [♿M] [🛏] [💻] [🍴] [🏊] [✕]

KLAMATH FALLS

Best Western Klamath Inn M ❀
(541) 882-1200. **$89-$139.** 4061 S 6th St. Just w on 6th St (SR 140) from jct SR 140 E/39 S and SR 39 N/US 97 business route. Ext corridors. **Pets:** $10 daily fee/pet. Designated rooms, no service, supervision.
[SAVE] [✕] [🛏] [💻] [🏊]

Days Inn Klamath Falls M
(541) 882-8864. **$129.** 3612 S 6th St. 0.3 mi w on 6th St (SR 140) from jct SR 140 E/39 S and SR 39 N/US 97 business route. Ext corridors. **Pets:** Accepted.
[SAVE] [✕] [🛏] [💻] [🏊] [✕]

Econo Lodge M ❀
(541) 884-7735. **$35-$110.** 75 Main St. US 97, exit City Center Dr, 1.3 mi s. Ext corridors. **Pets:** $10 daily fee/pet. Designated rooms, no service, supervision.
SAVE X 🖥 💻

Golden West Motel M
(541) 882-1758. **$42-$68.** 6402 S 6th St. S 6th St (SR 140) at eastern edge of town. Ext corridors. **Pets:** Dogs only. $10 daily fee/pet. Designated rooms, service with restrictions, supervision.
SAVE X 🖥

Majestic Inn & Suites M
(541) 883-7771. **$35-$105.** 5543 S 6th St. 1 mi e on 6th St (SR 140) from jct SR 140 E/39 S and SR 39 N/US 97 business route. Ext corridors. **Pets:** Medium. $6 daily fee/pet. Designated rooms, service with restrictions, supervision.
SAVE X 🖥

Maverick Motel M
(541) 882-6688. **$39-$109.** 1220 Main St. US 97 N, exit City Center, 0.3 mi e. Ext corridors. **Pets:** Medium. $6 daily fee/pet. Designated rooms, service with restrictions, supervision.
SAVE X 🖥

Motel 6–226 M
(541) 884-2110. **$45-$55.** 5136 S 6th St. 0.5 mi e on 6th St E (SR 140) from jct SR 39/US 97 business route. Ext corridors. **Pets:** Other species. Service with restrictions, supervision.
X 🖥 💻

Oregon 8 Motel M ❀
(541) 883-3431. **$35-$99.** 5225 Hwy 97 N. Between MM 270 and 271; east side of highway. Ext corridors. **Pets:** $10 daily fee/pet. Designated rooms, no service, supervision.
SAVE X 🖥 💻

Quality Inn M ❀
(541) 882-4666. **$70-$145.** 100 Main St. Just e of US 97, exit City Center. Ext corridors. **Pets:** $10 daily fee/pet. Designated rooms, no service, supervision.
SAVE X 🖥 💻

The Running y Ranch H
(541) 850-5500. **$139-$199, 3 day notice.** 5500 Running y Rd. On 6th St (SR 140), 7.2 mi n from jct US 66 and SR 140. Int corridors. **Pets:** $25 one-time fee/room. Designated rooms, service with restrictions, supervision.
ASK X 🖥 💻

Shilo Inn Suites Hotel-Klamath Falls H ❀
(541) 885-7980. **$110-$220.** 2500 Almond St. North end of US 97. Int corridors. **Pets:** Dogs only. $25 one-time fee/room. Service with restrictions, supervision.
SAVE X 🖥 💻

Super 8 H
(541) 884-8880. **$74-$86.** 3805 Hwy 97. On US 97, 2 mi n. Int corridors. **Pets:** Other species. $25 deposit/room. Service with restrictions, supervision.
ASK X 🖥

LA GRANDE

Americas Best Value Sandman Inn H ❀
(541) 963-3707. **$80-$85.** 2410 E R Ave. I-84, exit 261, just s on Island Ave, then just n. Int corridors. **Pets:** Other species. $25 one-time fee/room. Designated rooms, service with restrictions, supervision.
SAVE X 🖥 💻

Royal Motor Inn M
(541) 963-4154. **$40-$59.** 1510 Adams Ave. I-84, exit La Grande; downtown. Ext corridors. **Pets:** Accepted.
SAVE X 🖥

Travelodge M ❀
(541) 963-7116. **$55-$65.** 2215 Adams Ave. I-84, exit La Grande; downtown. Ext corridors. **Pets:** Medium, other species. $10 one-time fee/pet. Designated rooms, service with restrictions, supervision.
X 🖥 💻

LAKEVIEW

Best Western Skyline Motor Lodge M
(541) 947-2194. **$79-$129, 7 day notice.** 414 N G St. Jct US 395 and SR 140. Ext corridors. **Pets:** Medium, other species. $15 daily fee/pet. Designated rooms, service with restrictions, supervision.
SAVE X 🖥 💻

LA PINE

Best Western Newberry Station H
(541) 536-5130. **$80-$100.** 16515 Reed Rd. North end of town; just off SR 97. Int corridors. **Pets:** Small, dogs only. $10 one-time fee/room. Service with restrictions, supervision.
SAVE X 🖥 💻

LINCOLN BEACH

Salishan Spa & Golf Resort H ❀
(541) 764-2371. **Call for rates.** 7760 US 101 N. Just e of US 101; center. Ext corridors. **Pets:** Other species. $35 one-time fee/room. Supervision.
SAVE X 🖥 💻 🍴 🏊 X 🎾

LINCOLN CITY

Ashley Inn & Suites H ❀
(541) 996-7500. **$69-$199.** 3430 NE US 101. Just n of downtown. Int corridors. **Pets:** Medium, dogs only. $25 one-time fee/pet. Designated rooms, service with restrictions, crate.
ASK X 🖥 💻 🏊 X

Coho Inn M ❀
(541) 994-3684. **$65-$290.** 1635 NW Harbor Ave. US 101, exit N 17th St, just w. Ext corridors. **Pets:** Medium. $15 one-time fee/pet. Designated rooms, service with restrictions, supervision.
SAVE X 🖥 💻 🏊 X 🎾

Comfort Inn & Suites H
(541) 994-8155. **$89-$299.** 136 NE US 101. N of D River. Int corridors. **Pets:** Small, dogs only. $20 daily fee/pet. Designated rooms, service with restrictions, supervision.
SAVE X 🖥 💻

Econo Lodge H
(541) 994-5281. **$52-$229.** 1713 NW 21st St. US 101, exit NW 21st St, just w. Int corridors. **Pets:** Small, dogs only. $15 one-time fee/pet. Designated rooms, service with restrictions, supervision.
SAVE X 🖥 💻 🎾

Lincoln City Inn H
(541) 996-4400. **$50-$130, 3 day notice.** 1091 SE 1st St. On US 101 at D River. Int corridors. **Pets:** Accepted.
SAVE X 🖥 💻

Looking Glass Inn M ❀
(541) 996-3996. **$84-$249, 3 day notice.** 861 SW 51st St. US 101, exit 51st St; south end of town. Ext corridors. **Pets:** Dogs only. $10 daily fee/pet. Designated rooms, service with restrictions, crate.
ASK X 🖥 💻 🎾

Motel 6–#4172 H
(541) 996-9900. **$46-$126.** 3517 NW US 101. North end of downtown. Int corridors. **Pets:** Accepted.
X 💻 🖥

(AAA) ▼▼▼▼ The O'dysius Hotel 🄷 ❀
(541) 994-4121. **$159-$365.** 120 NW Inlet Ave. On US 101 at D River; center. Int corridors. **Pets:** Small, dogs only. $25 daily fee/pet. Service with restrictions, supervision.
(SAVE) (X) (🛏) (🖳) (🔏)

(AAA) ▼▼▼▼ Palace Inn & Suites 🄷
(541) 996-9466. **$69-$209.** 550 SE US 101. Center. Int corridors. **Pets:** Medium, dogs only. $25 one-time fee/room. No service, supervision.
(SAVE) (X) (🛏) (🖳) (🚫)

MADRAS

(AAA) ▼▼▼ Best Western Madras Inn 🄼
(541) 475-6141. **$80-$130, 3 day notice.** 12 SW 4th St. On US 97/26 southbound, at B and 4th sts; downtown. Ext corridors. **Pets:** Large, other species. $20 daily fee/pet. Designated rooms, service with restrictions, supervision.
(SAVE) (X) (🛏) (🖳) (🌊)

(AAA) ▼ Budget Inn 🄼
(541) 475-3831. **$55-$99.** 133 NE 5th St. On US 97/26 N; downtown. Ext corridors. **Pets:** Medium, other species. $10 daily fee/pet. Service with restrictions, supervision.
(SAVE) (X) (🛏)

▼▼▼ Inn at Cross Keys Station 🄷 ❀
(541) 475-5800. **$76-$146.** 66 NW Cedar St. On US 26; north end of town. Int corridors. **Pets:** Medium, dogs only. $30 daily fee/pet. Designated rooms, service with restrictions, supervision.
(ASK) (X) (🛏) (🖳) (🌊)

MCMINNVILLE

(AAA) ▼▼▼ Best Western Vineyard Inn 🄷
(503) 472-4900. **$115-$120.** 2035 S SR 99 W. Jct SR 99 W and 18. Int corridors. **Pets:** $10 daily fee/pet. Designated rooms, service with restrictions, supervision.
(SAVE) (X) (🛏) (🖳) (🌊)

(AAA) ▼▼▼▼ Comfort Inn & Suites 🄷
(503) 472-1700. **$90-$162.** 2520 SE Stratus Ave. Jct SR 99 W, 3.6 mi e on SR 18. Int corridors. **Pets:** Medium, other species. $10 daily fee/pet. Service with restrictions, crate.
(SAVE) (X) (🛏) (🖳) (🌊)

(AAA) ▼▼▼▼ Red Lion Inn & Suites 🄷
(503) 472-1500. **$94-$122.** 2535 NE Cumulus Ave. Jct SR 99 W, 2.7 mi e on SR 18. Int corridors. **Pets:** Other species. $20 one-time fee/room. Service with restrictions, supervision.
(SAVE) (X) (🛏) (🖳) (🌊) (🚫)

(AAA) ▼ Safari Motor Inn 🄼
(503) 472-5187. **$70-$90.** 381 NE SR 99 W. North end of SR 99 W. Ext corridors. **Pets:** Small. $10 daily fee/pet. Designated rooms, service with restrictions, supervision.
(SAVE) (X) (🛏) (🖳)

MEDFORD

(AAA) ▼▼▼▼ Best Western Horizon Inn 🄷 ❀
(541) 779-5085. **$79-$109.** 1154 E Barnett Rd. I-5, exit 27 (Barnett Rd), just e. Ext corridors. **Pets:** Other species. $20 one-time fee/pet. Designated rooms, supervision.
(SAVE) (X) (🛏) (🖳) (🌊) (🚫)

(AAA) ▼▼▼ Candlewood Suites Medford Airport 🄷
(541) 772-2800. **$109-$149.** 3548 Heathrow Way. I-5, exit 33, 1.5 mi se via E Pine St and Biddle Rd, just w on O'Hare Pkwy, then just n. Int corridors. **Pets:** Other species. $10 daily fee/room. Service with restrictions, supervision.
(SAVE) (X) (🛏) (🖳)

(AAA) ▼ Cedar Lodge Motor Inn 🄼
(541) 773-7361. **$52-$75.** 518 N Riverside Ave. I-5, exit 27 (Barnett Rd), 0.3 mi w on Barnett Rd, then 1.2 mi n. Ext corridors. **Pets:** Medium. $5 daily fee/pet. Service with restrictions, supervision.
(SAVE) (X) (🛏) (🌊)

▼ Motel 6-Medford North–739 🄼
(541) 779-0550. **$55-$65.** 2400 Biddle Rd. I-5, exit 30 southbound, just ne on Crater Lake Hwy, follow signs to Biddle Rd/Airport, then just n; northbound, follow signs to Biddle Rd/Airport, then just n. Ext corridors. **Pets:** Other species. Service with restrictions, supervision.
(X) (🛏) (🌊)

▼ Motel 6-Medford South–#89 🄼
(541) 773-4290. **$49-$59.** 950 Alba Dr. I-5, exit 27 (Barnett Rd), just e on Barnett Rd, then just n. Ext corridors. **Pets:** Other species. Service with restrictions, supervision.
(X) (🛏) (🌊)

(AAA) ▼▼ Quality Inn & Suites 🄷
(541) 779-0050. **Call for rates.** 1950 Biddle Rd. I-5, exit 30 southbound, just ne on Crater Lake Hwy, follow signs to Biddle Rd/Airport, then just s; exit northbound, follow signs to Biddle Rd/Airport, then just s. Int corridors. **Pets:** Accepted.
(SAVE) (X) (🛏) (🖳) (🌊) (🚫)

(AAA) ▼▼▼▼ Red Lion Hotel Medford 🄷
(541) 779-5811. **$99-$139.** 200 N Riverside Ave. I-5, exit 27 (Barnett Rd), 0.3 mi w on Barnett Rd, then 1 mi n. Ext corridors. **Pets:** Other species. $20 one-time fee/room. Service with restrictions, supervision.
(SAVE) (X) (🛏) (🖳) (🍴) (🌊)

(AAA) ▼▼▼ Shilo Inn Medford 🄷 ❀
(541) 770-5151. **$85-$165.** 2111 Biddle Rd. I-5, exit 30 southbound, just ne on Crater Lake Hwy, follow signs to Biddle Rd/Airport, then just s; northbound, follow signs to Biddle Rd/Airport, then just s. Int corridors. **Pets:** Dogs only. $25 one-time fee/room. Service with restrictions, supervision.
(SAVE) (X) (🛏) (🖳) (🚫)

▼▼▼ TownePlace Suites by Marriott 🄷 ❀
(541) 842-5757. **$129-$139.** 1395 Center Dr. I-5, exit 27 (Barnett Rd) southbound to Stewart Ave, just s; northbound, just w on Barnett Rd, just s on Stewart Ave, then just s. Int corridors. **Pets:** Medium. $25 daily fee/room. Designated rooms, service with restrictions, crate.
(X) (🛏) (🖳) (🌊)

MERLIN

▼▼ Morrison's Rogue River Lodge 🄲🄰
(541) 476-3825. **$175-$440, 45 day notice.** 8500 Galice Rd. I-5, exit 61, 12 mi w on Merlin-Galice Rd. Ext/int corridors. **Pets:** Small. $10 daily fee/room, $15 one-time fee/room. Designated rooms, service with restrictions, supervision.
(X) (🛏) (🖳) (🍴) (🌊) (🚫)

MYRTLE POINT

(AAA) ▼ Myrtle Trees Motel 🄼
(541) 572-5811. **$60-$70, 5 day notice.** 1010 8th St (Hwy 42). On SR 42, 0.5 mi e. Ext corridors. **Pets:** Very small, dogs only. $15 daily fee/pet. Designated rooms, service with restrictions, supervision.
(SAVE) (X) (🛏) (🔏)

NEWBERG

(AAA) ▼▼▼ Shilo Inn Suites–Newberg 🄷 ❀
(503) 537-0303. **$80-$175.** 501 Sitka Ave. Northeast of center on Portland Rd (SR 99 W). Int corridors. **Pets:** Dogs only. $25 one-time fee/room. Service with restrictions, supervision.
(SAVE) (X) (🛏) (🖳) (🌊) (🚫)

NEWPORT

The Best Western Agate Beach Inn 🅷 🐾
(541) 265-9411. **$100-$225.** 3019 N Coast Hwy. Jct US 20, 1.5 mi n on US 101. Int corridors. **Pets:** $20 one-time fee/pet. Designated rooms, service with restrictions, supervision.

The Landing at Newport 🆑 🐾
(541) 574-6777. **$109-$229.** 890 SE Bay Blvd. Jct US 101, 0.5 mi e on US 20, then 0.3 mi s on John Moore Rd. Ext corridors. **Pets:** $75 deposit/room, $10 daily fee/room, $25 one-time fee/room. Designated rooms, service with restrictions, supervision.

La Quinta Inn & Suites Newport 🅷 🐾
(541) 867-7727. **$79-$129.** 45 SE 32nd St. US 101, just s of Yaquina Bay Bridge. Int corridors. **Pets:** Medium, other species. Service with restrictions, supervision.

Shilo Inn Suites Oceanfront Hotel–Newport 🅷 🐾
(541) 265-7701. **$105-$270.** 536 SW Elizabeth St. Jct US 20, 0.5 mi s on US 101, then just w on SW Falls St. Ext/int corridors. **Pets:** Dogs only. $25 one-time fee/room. Designated rooms, service with restrictions, supervision.

Waves of Newport Motel and Vacation Rentals 🅷
(541) 265-4661. **$68-$129, 3 day notice.** 820 NW Coast St. Jct US 20, 0.5 mi n on US 101, just w on NW 11th St, then just s on Spring St. Ext corridors. **Pets:** Large, other species. $10 daily fee/pet. Supervision.

The Whaler Motel 🅼 🐾
(541) 265-9261. **$99-$175.** 155 SW Elizabeth St. Jct US 20, just s on US 101, then just w on SW 2nd St. Ext corridors. **Pets:** Dogs only. $15 daily fee/pet. Service with restrictions, supervision.

NORTH BEND

Comfort Inn 🅼 🐾
(541) 756-3191. **$89-$179.** 1503 Virginia Ave. 0.5 mi w of US 101. Ext/int corridors. **Pets:** Small, dogs only. $15 daily fee/pet. Designated rooms, service with restrictions, supervision.

The Mill Casino & Hotel 🅷
(541) 756-8800. **$108-$135.** 3201 Tremont Ave. 0.7 mi n on US 101; downtown. Int corridors. **Pets:** Accepted.

OAKLAND

Best Western Rice Hill 🅼
(541) 849-3335. **$77, 3 day notice.** 621 John Long Rd. I-5, exit 148, just e. Ext corridors. **Pets:** Supervision.

OAKRIDGE

Best Western Oakridge Inn 🅼
(541) 782-2212. **$109-$146.** 47433 Hwy 58. West end of SR 58. Ext corridors. **Pets:** Small. $15 daily fee/pet. Designated rooms, service with restrictions, supervision.

Cascade Motel 🅼
(541) 782-2489. **$56-$75.** 47487 Hwy 58. Center. Ext corridors. **Pets:** Medium, dogs only. $10 daily fee/pet. Designated rooms, service with restrictions, supervision.

ONTARIO

Creek House Bed & Breakfast Inn 🅱🅱 🐾
(541) 823-0717. **$99-$139, 7 day notice.** 717 SW 2nd St. I-84, exit 376A, 0.8 mi w on Idaho Ave, then 0.4 mi s. Int corridors. **Pets:** Dogs only. $25 one-time fee/room. Supervision.

Holiday Inn-Ontario, OR 🅷
(541) 889-8621. **$79-$119.** 1249 Tapadera Ave. I-84, exit 376B, just nw. Int corridors. **Pets:** Accepted.

Rodeway Inn 🅼
(541) 889-9188. **$60-$78.** 615 E Idaho Ave. I-84, exit 376A, just sw. Ext corridors. **Pets:** Medium, other species. $5 daily fee/pet. Designated rooms, service with restrictions, supervision.

Sleep Inn 🅷
(541) 881-0007. **$59-$129.** 1221 SE 1st Ave. I-84, exit 376B, just ne. Int corridors. **Pets:** Dogs only. $10 daily fee/pet. Designated rooms, service with restrictions, supervision.

PACIFIC CITY

Inn at Cape Kiwanda 🅷 🐾
(503) 965-7001. **$99-$349.** 33105 Cape Kiwanda Dr. Just w on Pacific Ave, 1 mi n. Ext corridors. **Pets:** $20 daily fee/pet. Designated rooms, service with restrictions, supervision.

Pacific City Inn 🅼 🐾
(503) 965-6464. **$79-$99, 3 day notice.** 35280 Brooten Rd. Center. Ext corridors. **Pets:** Dogs only. $16 daily fee/pet. Designated rooms, service with restrictions, supervision.

PENDLETON

Americas Best Value Inn 🅼
(541) 276-1400. **$69-$99.** 201 SW Court Ave. I-84, exit 210 (SR 11), 0.7 mi ne on SE 3rd Dr, then 0.6 mi w. Ext corridors. **Pets:** Dogs only. $20 one-time fee/room.

Best Western Pendleton Inn 🅷
(541) 276-2135. **$95-$125.** 400 SE Nye Ave. I-84, exit 210 (SR 11), just se. Int corridors. **Pets:** Small. $10 one-time fee/pet. Service with restrictions, supervision.

Holiday Inn Express 🅷
(541) 966-6520. **$109-$149.** 600 SE Nye Ave. I-84, exit 210 (SR 11), just se. Int corridors. **Pets:** Other species. $10 daily fee/room. Service with restrictions, supervision.

Motel 6-#349 🅼
(541) 276-3160. **$51-$61.** 325 SE Nye Ave. I-84, exit 210 (SR 11), just se. Ext corridors. **Pets:** Other species. Service with restrictions, supervision.

Oxford Suites 🅷
(541) 276-6000. **$109-$149.** 2400 SW Court Pl. I-84, exit 209, just n on SW Emigrant Ave, just nw on SW 20th St, then just sw to SW Court Pl. Int corridors. **Pets:** Accepted.

Red Lion Hotel Pendleton 🅷
(541) 276-6111. **$109-$159.** 304 SE Nye Ave. I-84, exit 210 (SR 11), just sw. Ext/int corridors. **Pets:** Other species. $20 one-time fee/room. Service with restrictions, supervision.

W W Rugged Country Lodge H
(541) 966-6800. **Call for rates.** 1807 SE Court Ave. I-84, exit 210 (SR 11), 0.7 mi ne on SE 3rd Dr, then 0.4 mi e. Ext/int corridors. **Pets:** Accepted.
☒ 🖪 ▣

WW WWW Travelodge M ✿
(541) 276-7531. **$65-$80.** 411 SW Dorion Ave. I-84, exit 209, 0.9 mi ne on SW Frazer Ave, then just nw on SW 4th St. Ext corridors. **Pets:** Dogs only. $10 daily fee/pet. Designated rooms, service with restrictions.
SAVE ☒ 🖪 ▣

PORTLAND METROPOLITAN AREA

BEAVERTON

W W Comfort Inn & Suites H
(503) 643-9100. **$59-$159.** 13455 SW Tualatin Valley Hwy. SR 217, exit 2A (Canyon Rd/SR 8), 1 mi w. Int corridors. **Pets:** Accepted.
ASK ☒ 🖪 ▣ ⟲

WWWW Homewood Suites By Hilton H
(503) 614-0900. **$99-$179.** 15525 NW Gateway Ct. US 26, exit 65, just sw on NW Cornell Rd, just s on NW 158th Ave, just se on NW Waterhouse Ave, then just e. Int corridors. **Pets:** Accepted.
☒ ♿M 🖪 ▣ ⟲

AAA WWWW Phoenix Inn Suites-Beaverton H
(503) 614-8100. **$89-$149.** 15402 NW Cornell Rd. US 26, exit 65, just ne. Int corridors. **Pets:** Medium. $15 daily fee/pet. Designated rooms, service with restrictions, supervision.
SAVE ☒ ♿M 🖪 ▣ ⟲ ☒

AAA WWWW Shilo Inn Hotel &
Suites-Portland/Beaverton H ✿
(503) 297-2551. **$107-$187.** 9900 SW Canyon Rd. SR 217, exit 2A (Canyon Rd/Beaverton Hillsdale Hwy), 0.3 mi e on feeder road to SR 8 (Canyon Rd), then 0.6 mi e. Int corridors. **Pets:** Dogs only. $25 one-time fee/room. Designated rooms, service with restrictions, supervision.
SAVE ☒ 🖪 ▣ 🍴 ⟲

CLACKAMAS

AAA WWW Best Western Sunnyside Inn H ✿
(503) 652-1500. **$76-$106, 7 day notice.** 12855 SE 97th Ave. I-205, exit 14, follow signs for Sunnyside Rd E, just e on Sunnyside Rd, then just s. Ext corridors. **Pets:** Large, other species. $25 one-time fee/room. Designated rooms, service with restrictions, crate.
SAVE ☒ 🖪 ▣ ⟲

WWWW Comfort Suites H
(503) 723-3450. **$81-$108.** 15929 SE McKinley Ave. I-205, exit 12 northbound, exit 12B southbound, just w. Int corridors. **Pets:** Medium, other species. $30 one-time fee/room. Service with restrictions, supervision.
ASK ☒ 🖪 ▣ ⟲ ☒

GLADSTONE

WWWW Oxford Suites H
(503) 722-7777. **$95-$125.** 75 82nd Dr. I-205, exit 11, 0.3 mi sw. Int corridors. **Pets:** $25 one-time fee/room. Service with restrictions, supervision.
ASK ☒ 🖪 ▣ ⟲ ☒

GRESHAM

AAA WWWW Best Western Pony Soldier Inn H
(503) 665-1591. **$99-$169, 7 day notice.** 1060 NE Cleveland Ave. I-84, exit 14 (Fairview Pkwy), 0.9 mi s, 0.4 mi e on NE Glisan St, 1.2 mi s on NE 223rd Ave, 0.7 mi e on Burnside Rd, then just s. Int corridors. **Pets:** Accepted.
SAVE ☒ 🖪 ▣ ⟲ ☒

AAA WWW Days Inn & Suites H
(503) 465-1515. **$74-$114.** 24124 SE Stark St. I-84, exit 16, 1.5 mi s on NE 238th Dr/NE 242nd Dr, then just w. Int corridors. **Pets:** Dogs only. $10 daily fee/pet. Designated rooms, service with restrictions, supervision.
SAVE ☒ 🖪 ▣ ⟲

W W Days Inn-Portland East/Gresham H
(503) 618-8400. **$64-$100.** 2261 NE 181st Ave. I-84, exit 13, just sw. Int corridors. **Pets:** Accepted.
ASK ☒ ♿M 🖪 ▣ ⟲

WWWW Extended StayAmerica Portland/Gresham H
(503) 661-0226. **$80-$95.** 17777 NE Sacramento St. I-84, exit 13, 0.3 mi s on NE 181st Ave, just s on NE San Rafael St, then just n on NE 178th Ave. Int corridors. **Pets:** Other species. $25 daily fee/pet. Service with restrictions, crate.
ASK ☒ ♿M 🖪 ▣

WWWW Holiday Inn Portland/Gresham H
(503) 907-1777. **$95-$195.** 2752 NE Hogan Dr. I-84, exit 16, 1.8 mi s on 238th/Hogan drs. Int corridors. **Pets:** Accepted.
ASK ☒ ♿M 🖪 ▣ 🍴 ⟲

AAA WWWW Howard Johnson Gresham H
(503) 666-9545. **$49-$179.** 1572 NE Burnside Rd. I-84, exit 16, 2.7 mi s on NE 238th Dr, just w on Division St, then just se; I-205, exit 19, 5.5 mi e on Division St, then just se. Int corridors. **Pets:** Medium. $20 daily fee/pet. Designated rooms, service with restrictions, supervision.
SAVE ☒ 🖪 ▣ ⟲

AAA WWW Super 8 H
(503) 661-5100. **$64-$79.** 121 NE 181st Ave. I-84, exit 13, 1 mi s. Int corridors. **Pets:** Medium, dogs only. $10 daily fee/pet. Designated rooms, service with restrictions, supervision.
SAVE ☒ 🖪 ▣

HILLSBORO

W W Extended StayAmerica-Portland-Beaverton H
(503) 439-1515. **$88-$104.** 18665 NW Eider Ct. US 26, exit 64, 0.7 mi s on NW 185th Ave, then just w. Int corridors. **Pets:** Other species. $25 daily fee/pet. Service with restrictions, crate.
ASK ☒ 🖪 ▣

WWWW Extended Stay Deluxe-Portland-Hillsboro-NW Cornell Rd H
(503) 439-0706. **$108-$123.** 19311 NW Cornell Rd. US 26, exit 64, 0.5 mi s on NW 185th Ave, then 0.4 mi w. Int corridors. **Pets:** Other species. $25 daily fee/pet. Service with restrictions, crate.
ASK ☒ 🖪 ▣ ⟲

AAA WWWW Larkspur Landing Hillsboro/Portland H
(503) 681-2121. **$99-$171.** 3133 NE Shute Rd. US 26, exit 61, 1.1 mi s. Int corridors. **Pets:** Other species. $75 deposit/pet, $10 daily fee/pet. Service with restrictions, crate.
SAVE ☒ 🖪 ▣ ☒

WWWW Residence Inn by Marriott Portland West H
(503) 531-3200. **$179-$219.** 18855 NW Tanasbourne Dr. US 26, exit 64, just s on NW 185th Ave, then just w. Ext/int corridors. **Pets:** Accepted.
☒ ♿M 🖪 ▣ ⟲ ☒

WWWW TownePlace Suites by Marriott-Portland Hillsboro H
(503) 268-6000. **$170-$208.** 6550 NE Brighton St. US 26, exit 62A westbound; exit 62 eastbound, just s, 1 mi s on Cornelius Pass Rd, 0.7 mi w on Cornell Rd, just n on NW 229th Ave, then just w. Ext/int corridors. **Pets:** Accepted.
☒ 🖪 ▣ ⟲ ☒

KING CITY

◇◇◇ Best Western Northwind Inn & Suites 🏠
(503) 431-2100. **$120-$135.** 16105 SW Pacific Hwy. I-5, exit 292, just nw on SR 217, exit 6 (SR 99W), then 2.5 mi s. Int corridors. **Pets:** Medium. $20 daily fee/pet. Service with restrictions, supervision.
SAVE ☒ ♿M 🛄 🖵 🐾

LAKE OSWEGO

◇◇◇ Crowne Plaza Hotel 🏠 ☀
(503) 624-8400. **$79-$249.** 14811 Kruse Oaks Dr. I-5, exit 292B northbound; exit 292 southbound, just e on Kruse Way, then just s. Int corridors. **Pets:** Other species. $25 one-time fee/room. Service with restrictions, supervision.
SAVE ☒ ♿M 🛄 🖵 🍽 🐾 ☒

◇◇◇ Residence Inn by Marriott-Portland South 🏠
(503) 684-2603. **$169-$199.** 15200 SW Bangy Rd. I-5, exit 292B northbound; exit 292 southbound, just e, then 0.3 mi s. Ext corridors. **Pets:** Other species. $10 daily fee/room.
☒ ♿M 🛄 🖵 🐾 ☒

MILWAUKIE

◇◇ Econo Lodge Suites Inn Ⓜ
(503) 654-2222. **$59-$79.** 17330 SE McLoughlin Blvd. I-205, exit 9, 2.3 mi n on SR 99 E (McLoughlin Blvd). Ext corridors. **Pets:** Small, dogs only. $10 daily fee/pet. Designated rooms, service with restrictions, supervision.
SAVE ☒ 🛄 🐾

OREGON CITY

◇◇◇ Best Western Rivershore Hotel 🏠 ☀
(503) 655-7141. **$95-$115.** 1900 Clackamette Dr. I-205, exit 9, just n. Int corridors. **Pets:** Other species. $5 daily fee/pet. Designated rooms, service with restrictions, supervision.
SAVE ☒ ♿M 🛄 🖵 🍽 🐾 ☒

PORTLAND

◇◇ Americas Best Value Inn & Suites-Portland Airport 🏠
(503) 255-9771. **$54-$79.** 4911 NE 82nd Ave. I-84, exit 5 eastbound, 2 mi n; westbound, exit I-205 N to exit 23B (Killingsworth St), 0.5 mi w, then 0.6 mi s. Int corridors. **Pets:** Accepted.
☒ 🛄 🖵 🐾

◇◇◇ The Benson Hotel, a Coast Hotel 🏠 ☀
(503) 228-2000. **$129-$359.** 309 SW Broadway. At SW Broadway and Oak St. Int corridors. **Pets:** Other species. $75 one-time fee/pet. Service with restrictions, supervision.
SAVE ☒ ♿M 🖵 🍽

◇◇◇ Best Western Inn At The Meadows 🏠
(503) 286-9600. **$105-$141.** 1215 N Hayden Meadows Dr. I-5, exit 306B, just e. Int corridors. **Pets:** Medium, other species. $20 daily fee/room. Service with restrictions, supervision.
SAVE ☒ 🛄 🖵

◇◇◇ Best Western Pony Soldier Inn-Airport 🏠 ☀
(503) 256-1504. **$109-$209.** 9901 NE Sandy Blvd. I-205, exit 23A, just e. Int corridors. **Pets:** Small. Designated rooms, service with restrictions, crate.
SAVE ☒ ♿M 🛄 🖵 🐾 ☒

◇◇◇ Briarwood Suites Ⓜ
(503) 788-9394. **$64-$109.** 7740 SE Powell Blvd. I-205, exit 19, 1 mi w. Ext corridors. **Pets:** Accepted.
SAVE ☒ 🛄 🖵

◇◇◇ Days Inn-Portland 🏠 ☀
(503) 289-1800. **$72-$81.** 9930 N Whitaker Rd. I-5, exit 306B, just e. Int corridors. **Pets:** Other species. $15 one-time fee/room. Service with restrictions, supervision.
SAVE ☒ 🛄 🖵

◇◇◇◇ The Heathman Hotel 🏠 ☀
(503) 241-4100. **$259-$725, 3 day notice.** 1001 SW Broadway. At SW Broadway and Salmon St. Int corridors. **Pets:** Medium. $35 daily fee/pet. Designated rooms, service with restrictions, supervision.
SAVE ☒ ♿M 🖵 🍽

◇◇◇ Hilton Portland & Executive Tower 🏠 ☀
(503) 226-1611. **$139-$239.** 921 SW 6th Ave. I-405, exit 1B (6th Ave); at 6th Ave and Taylor St. Int corridors. **Pets:** Medium, other species. $50 one-time fee/room. Service with restrictions, supervision.
SAVE ☒ 🛄 🍽 🐾 ☒

◇◇◇ Holiday Inn Express-I-205 Stark 🏠
(503) 252-7400. **Call for rates.** 9707 SE Stark St. I-205, exit 21A southbound; exit 20 northbound, just e on Washington St, just n on SE 99th Ave, then just w. Int corridors. **Pets:** Accepted.
☒ ♿M 🛄 🖵

◇◇◇ Holiday Inn Portland Airport Hotel & Convention Center 🏠
(503) 256-5000. **$119-$229.** 8439 NE Columbia Blvd. I-205, exit 23B, 0.5 mi w. Int corridors. **Pets:** $25 one-time fee/room. Designated rooms, service with restrictions, supervision.
SAVE ☒ 🛄 🖵 🍽 🐾

◇◇◇ Hospitality Inn 🏠
(503) 244-6684. **$79-$129.** 10155 SW Capitol Hwy. I-5, exit 295 southbound; exit 294 northbound, just e. Int corridors. **Pets:** Small, dogs only. $10 daily fee/pet. Designated rooms, service with restrictions, supervision.
SAVE ☒ 🛄 🖵

◇◇◇ Hotel deLuxe 🏠 ☀
(503) 219-2094. **$169-$369.** 729 SW 15th Ave. I-5 to I-405, exit Salmon St northbound, just n on 14th Ave, w on Morrison St, then s; exit Couch/Burnside St southbound; at SW 15th Ave and Yamhill St. Int corridors. **Pets:** $65 one-time fee/room. Service with restrictions.
SAVE ☒ ♿M 🖵 🍽

◇◇◇ Hotel Fifty 🏠 ☀
(503) 221-0711. **$139-$289.** 50 SW Morrison St. At Morrison St and Naito Pkwy (formerly Front Ave). Int corridors. **Pets:** Medium, dogs only. $50 one-time fee/pet. Designated rooms, service with restrictions, supervision.
SAVE ☒ ♿M 🛄 🖵 🍽

◇◇◇ Hotel Lucia 🏠 ☀
(503) 225-1717. **$319.** 400 SW Broadway. At SW Broadway and Stark St. Int corridors. **Pets:** $45 one-time fee/pet. Designated rooms, service with restrictions, crate.
SAVE ☒ ♿M 🖵 🍽

◇◇◇ Hotel Monaco Portland 🏠 ☀
(503) 222-0001. **Call for rates.** 506 SW Washington St. At SW 5th Ave and SW Washington St. Int corridors. **Pets:** Other species. Crate.
SAVE ☒ ♿M 🖵 🍽 ☒

◇◇◇ Hotel Vintage Plaza 🏠
(503) 228-1212. **Call for rates.** 422 SW Broadway. At Broadway and Washington St. Int corridors. **Pets:** Accepted.
SAVE ☒ 🖵 🍽

◇◇◇ Howard Johnson Portland Airport 🏠 ☀
(503) 256-4111. **$65-$120.** 8247 NE Sandy Blvd. I-84, exit 5 eastbound, 1.5 mi n on 82nd Ave; exit I-205 N westbound; I-205, exit 23A southbound; exit 23B northbound (US 30 business route/Sandy Blvd W), 1 mi w. Ext/int corridors. **Pets:** Medium. $10 daily fee/pet. Designated rooms, service with restrictions, supervision.
SAVE ☒ 🛄 🖵 🐾

▼▼▼▼ La Quinta Inn & Suites Portland Airport ꞏ🏠 ꞏ✤
(503) 382-3820. **$69-$134.** 11207 NE Holman St. I-205, exit 24B north-bound; exit 24 southbound, 0.4 mi e on Airport Way, then just sw. Int corridors. **Pets:** Medium, other species. Service with restrictions, supervision.

ⒶⓈⓀ ⊠ ꞏ&M 🗋 🖃 🐾

▼▼ La Quinta Inn Portland Lloyd Center/Convention Center 🏠 ✤
(503) 233-7933. **$69-$120.** 431 NE Multnomah St. I-5, exit 302A, just e on NE Weidler St, just s on NE Martin Luther King Jr Blvd, then just e. Int corridors. **Pets:** Medium, other species. Service with restrictions, supervision.

ⒶⓈⓀ ⊠ 🗋 🖃 🐾

ⒶⒶⒶ ▼▼▼ The Mark Spencer Hotel 🏠 ✤
(503) 224-3293. **$99-$249.** 409 SW 11th Ave. At SW Stark St and SW 11th Ave. Int corridors. **Pets:** Other species. $10 daily fee/pet. Service with restrictions, supervision.

ⓈⒶⓋⒺ ⊠ 🗋 🖃

▼▼ Motel 6 North Portland #4198 🏠
(503) 247-3700. **Call for rates.** 1125 N Schmeer Rd. I-5, exit 306B, 0.4 mi s on N Whitaker Rd, then just e. Int corridors. **Pets:** Other species. Service with restrictions, supervision.

⊠ 🗋

ⒶⒶⒶ ▼▼▼▼ Oxford Suites 🏠 ✤
(503) 283-3030. **$139-$199.** 12226 N Jantzen Dr. I-5, exit 308, just e on Hayden Island Dr. Int corridors. **Pets:** $25 daily fee/pet. Service with restrictions, supervision.

ⓈⒶⓋⒺ ⊠ ꞏ&M 🗋 🖃 🐾 ⊠

ⒶⒶⒶ ▼▼▼▼ The Paramount Hotel, a Coast Hotel 🏠
(503) 223-9900. **$159-$199.** 808 SW Taylor St. At SW 8th Ave and SW Taylor St. Int corridors. **Pets:** Medium, dogs only. $50 one-time fee/room. Service with restrictions, crate.

ⓈⒶⓋⒺ ⊠ ꞏ&M 🗋 🖃 🍽

ⒶⒶⒶ ▼▼ Park Lane Suites 🅼
(503) 226-6288. **$129-$249.** 809 SW King Ave. I-405, exit Couch/Burnside St southbound, 0.5 mi w on Burnside St, then just s; exit Everett St northbound, 0.3 mi w on Glisan St, just s on NW 21st Ave, just w on Burnside St, then just s. Ext corridors. **Pets:** Accepted.

ⓈⒶⓋⒺ ⊠ ꞏ&M 🗋 🖃

ⒶⒶⒶ ▼▼ Ramada Portland 🏠
(503) 255-6511. **$69-$199.** 6221 NE 82nd Ave. I-205, exit 23B (Killingsworth St), just w on Columbia Blvd, then just n on 80th Ave. Int corridors. **Pets:** Small. $20 daily fee/pet. Service with restrictions, supervision.

ⓈⒶⓋⒺ ⊠ ꞏ&M 🗋 🖃 🍽 🐾 ⊠

ⒶⒶⒶ ▼▼▼ Red Lion Hotel on the River Jantzen Beach-Portland 🏠
(503) 283-4466. **$169.** 909 N Hayden Island Dr. I-5, exit 308, just ne. Int corridors. **Pets:** Other species. $20 one-time fee/room. Service with restrictions, supervision.

ⓈⒶⓋⒺ ⊠ ꞏ&M 🗋 🖃 🍽 🐾 ⊠

ⒶⒶⒶ ▼▼▼ Red Lion Hotel Portland Airport 🏠
(503) 255-6722. **Call for rates.** 7101 NE 82nd Ave. I-205, exit 24A northbound; exit 24 southbound, 1.3 mi w on NE Airport Way, then 0.5 mi s. Ext/int corridors. **Pets:** Other species. $20 one-time fee/room. Service with restrictions, supervision.

ⓈⒶⓋⒺ ⊠ 🗋 🖃 🍽 🐾 ⊠

ⒶⒶⒶ ▼▼▼ Red Lion Hotel Portland-Convention Center 🏠
(503) 235-2100. **$126-$170.** 1021 NE Grand Ave. I-5, exit 302A, just e on NE Weidler St, just s on NE Martin Luther King Jr Blvd, then just e. Int corridors. **Pets:** Other species. $20 one-time fee/room. Service with restrictions, supervision.

ⓈⒶⓋⒺ ⊠ 🗋 🖃 🍽

▼▼▼▼ Residence Inn by Marriott Portland Downtown/Lloyd Center 🏠
(503) 288-1400. **$174-$189.** 1710 NE Multnomah St. I-5, exit 302A, 0.8 mi e on Weidler St, then just s on 15th Ave; I-84, exit 1 (Lloyd Center) westbound, just n on 13th St, then just e. Ext corridors. **Pets:** Accepted.

⊠ ꞏ&M 🗋 🖃 ⊠

▼▼▼ Residence Inn by Marriott-Portland North Harbour 🏠 ✤
(503) 285-9888. **$149-$169.** 1250 N Anchor Way. I-5, exit 307, follow signs to Marine Dr E, then just n. Int corridors. **Pets:** Large. $75 one-time fee/room. Service with restrictions, supervision.

⊠ ꞏ&M 🗋 🖃 ⊠

ⒶⒶⒶ ▼▼▼▼ Residence Inn Portland Downtown at RiverPlace 🏠 ✤
(503) 552-9500. **$199-$209.** 2115 SW River Pkwy. At SW Moody Ave and SW River Pkwy; on the Willamette River Waterfront. Int corridors. **Pets:** Other species. $10 daily fee/pet. Service with restrictions.

ⓈⒶⓋⒺ ⊠ 🗋 🖃 🐾 ⊠

ⒶⒶⒶ ▼▼▼ ▼▼ RiverPlace, a Larkspur Collection Hotel 🏠 ✤
(503) 228-3233. **$239-$525.** 1510 SW Harbor Way. At Naito Pkwy (formerly Front Ave) and SW Harbor Way. Int corridors. **Pets:** Other species. $50 one-time fee/room.

ⓈⒶⓋⒺ ⊠ ꞏ&M 🗋 🖃 🍽 ⊠

ⒶⒶⒶ ▼▼▼▼ Sheraton Portland Airport Hotel 🏠 ✤
(503) 281-2500. **$97-$248.** 8235 NE Airport Way. I-205, exit 24A northbound; exit 24 southbound, 1.5 mi w. Int corridors. **Pets:** Medium. $25 one-time fee/room. Service with restrictions.

ⓈⒶⓋⒺ ⊠ ꞏ&M 🖃 🍽 🐾

ⒶⒶⒶ ▼▼ ▼ Shilo Inn-Portland/Rose Garden 🏠 ✤
(503) 736-6300. **$92-$200.** 1506 NE 2nd Ave. I-5, exit 302A, just e on NE Weidler St, then just s. Int corridors. **Pets:** Dogs only. $25 one-time fee/room. Designated rooms, service with restrictions, supervision.

ⓈⒶⓋⒺ ⊠ 🗋 🖃

▼▼▼ Staybridge Suites Portland-Airport 🏠 ✤
(503) 262-8888. **$115-$170.** 11936 NE Glenn Widing Dr. I-205, exit 24B northbound; exit 24 southbound, 0.7 mi e, then just nw. Int corridors. **Pets:** Large, other species. $75 one-time fee/pet. Service with restrictions, crate.

ⒶⓈⓀ ⊠ ꞏ&M 🗋 🖃 🐾 ⊠

ⒶⒶⒶ ▼▼▼ ▼▼ The Westin Portland 🏠 ✤
(503) 294-9000. **$119-$349.** 750 SW Alder St. At Park Ave and SW Alder St. Int corridors. **Pets:** Medium, dogs only. $200 deposit/room. Service with restrictions, supervision.

ⓈⒶⓋⒺ ⊠ ꞏ&M 🖃 🍽

TIGARD

ⒶⒶⒶ ▼▼▼ Embassy Suites Hotel-Portland Washington Square 🏠
(503) 644-4000. **$119-$209.** 9000 SW Washington Square Rd. SR 217, exit 4B (Progress/Scholls Ferry Rd), just ne on SW Scholls Ferry Rd, just e on SW Hall Blvd, then just s. Int corridors. **Pets:** Medium, dogs only. $49 one-time fee/room. Designated rooms, service with restrictions, supervision.

ⓈⒶⓋⒺ ⊠ ꞏ&M 🗋 🖃 🍽 🐾

▼▼ Homestead Studio Suites Hotel Portland-Tigard 🏠
(503) 670-0555. **$85-$100.** 13009 SW 68th Pkwy. I-5, exit 293 (Haines St) southbound, 0.5 mi s on SW 68th Ave; exit 293 northbound, just w on Atlanta Ave, then 0.7 mi s; SR 217, exit 7 (72nd Ave), just ne, just e on Hampton St, then just s. Ext corridors. **Pets:** Other species. $25 daily fee/pet. Service with restrictions, crate.

ⒶⓈⓀ ⊠ 🗋 🖃

AAA ▼▼ Shilo Inn-Tigard/Washington Square 🅷
(503) 620-4320. **$85-$125.** 10830 SW Greenburg Rd. SR 217, exit 5 (Greenburg Rd), just sw. Int corridors. **Pets:** Accepted.
[SAVE] [✕] [🛏] [🖵] [✕]

TROUTDALE

AAA ▼▼ Comfort Inn & Suites, Columbia Gorge West 🅷
(503) 669-6500. **$69-$159.** 477 NW Phoenix Dr. I-84, exit 17, south side of interstate, just s off Frontage Rd. Int corridors. **Pets:** Accepted.
[SAVE] [✕] [🛏] [🖵] [✕]

▼▼ Holiday Inn Express-Portland East 🅷
(503) 492-2900. **$89-$159.** 1000 NW Graham Rd. I-84, exit 17 eastbound, e on Frontage Rd, then just n; westbound, just n. Int corridors. **Pets:** Other species. $10 daily fee/room. Designated rooms, supervision.
[ASK] [✕] [🛏] [🖵] [✕]

▼ Motel 6-Portland Troutdale-407 🅼
(503) 665-2254. **$47-$55.** 1610 NW Frontage Rd. I-84, exit 17 eastbound, just sw; westbound, just w on Frontage Rd, then just sw. Ext corridors. **Pets:** Other species. Service with restrictions, supervision.
[✕] [🅜] [🛏] [🖵]

TUALATIN

AAA ▼▼▼ Comfort Inn & Suites 🅷 🐾
(503) 612-9952. **$99-$199.** 7640 SW Warm Springs St. I-5, exit 289, just w on Nyberg Rd, just s on Martinazzi Ave, then just e; just behind Fred Meyer. Int corridors. **Pets:** Small, dogs only. $15 daily fee/pet. Designated rooms, service with restrictions, supervision.
[SAVE] [✕] [🅜] [🛏] [🖵] [✕]

WILSONVILLE

▼▼▼ Best Western Willamette Inn 🅷
(503) 682-2288. **$96-$106, 7 day notice.** 30800 SW Parkway Ave. I-5, exit 283, just e on Wilsonville Rd, then 0.3 mi s. Int corridors. **Pets:** Small, other species. Designated rooms, service with restrictions, supervision.
[SAVE] [✕] [🛏] [🖵] [✕]

▼▼▼ Holiday Inn-Wilsonville 🅷
(503) 682-2211. **$109-$199.** 25425 SW 95th Ave. I-5, exit 286, just w on Boones Ferry Rd, then just se. Int corridors. **Pets:** Medium. $15 daily fee/room. Designated rooms, service with restrictions, crate.
[ASK] [✕] [🛏] [🖵] [🍴] [✕]

AAA ▼▼▼ La Quinta Inn Wilsonville 🅷 🐾
(503) 682-3184. **$70-$149.** 8815 SW Sun Pl. I-5, exit 286, just e on Elligsen Rd, just n on Parkway Ave, then just w. Int corridors. **Pets:** Medium, other species. Service with restrictions, supervision.
[SAVE] [✕] [🛏] [🖵] [✕]

▼▼▼ Wilsonville Inn & Suites 🅷
(503) 570-9700. **$69-$159.** 29769 SW Boones Ferry Rd. I-5, exit 283, just w on Wilsonville Rd, then just n. Int corridors. **Pets:** Accepted.
[ASK] [✕] [🅜] [🛏] [🖵] [✕] [✕]

END METROPOLITAN AREA

PORT ORFORD

AAA ▼ Castaway by the Sea 🅼
(541) 332-4502. **$65-$160, 3 day notice.** 545 W 5th St. Jct US 101, 1 blk w on Harbor Dr, then 1 blk n. Ext corridors. **Pets:** Accepted.
[SAVE] [✕] [🛏] [🖵] [🅺]

PRINEVILLE

AAA ▼▼▼ Best Western Prineville Inn 🅷
(541) 447-8080. **$76-$135, 3 day notice.** 1475 NE 3rd St. 0.8 mi e on US 26. Int corridors. **Pets:** Small, dogs only. $15 daily fee/room. Service with restrictions, supervision.
[SAVE] [✕] [🅜] [🛏] [🖵] [✕]

▼ Econo Lodge 🅷
(541) 447-6231. **Call for rates.** 123 NE 3rd St. Center; downtown. Int corridors. **Pets:** Dogs only. $10 one-time fee/pet. Service with restrictions, supervision.
[✕] [🛏] [🖵]

▼▼▼ Stafford Inn 🅷 🐾
(541) 447-7100. **$82-$117.** 1773 NE 3rd St. 1 mi e on US 26. Int corridors. **Pets:** $20 one-time fee/room. Service with restrictions, supervision.
[ASK] [✕] [🅜] [🛏] [🖵] [✕]

PROSPECT

▼▼ Prospect Historic Hotel-Motel & Dinner House 🅼 🐾
(541) 560-3664. **$70-$190.** 391 Mill Creek Dr. Jct SR 62, 0.3 mi s on 1st St (0.7 mi e of MM 43), just w. Ext/int corridors. **Pets:** Other species. $15 one-time fee/room. Designated rooms, service with restrictions, supervision.
[✕] [🛏] [🖵] [🍴] [✕]

REDMOND

▼▼▼ Comfort Suites-Redmond Airport 🅷
(541) 504-8900. **Call for rates.** 2243 SW Yew Ave. US 97, exit 124 (Yew Ave/Airport Way/Redmond Airport), just nw; 2 mi s of jct SR 126. Int corridors. **Pets:** Small, other species. $25 one-time fee/room. Supervision.
[✕] [🛏] [🖵] [✕]

▼▼ Eagle Crest Resort 🅷
(541) 923-2453. **Call for rates.** 1522 Cline Falls Rd. 4.5 mi w on SR 126, 1 mi s. Int corridors. **Pets:** Accepted.
[✕] [🅜] [🛏] [🖵] [🍴] [✕] [✕]

AAA ▼ Motel 6 Redmond-4076 🅷
(541) 923-2100. **$60-$100.** 2247 S Hwy 97. Jct SR 126, 1 mi s on US 97, then just w. Int corridors. **Pets:** Other species. Service with restrictions, supervision.
[SAVE] [✕] [🅜] [🛏]

AAA ▼▼ Redmond Inn 🅼
(541) 548-1091. **Call for rates.** 1545 S US 97. 0.5 mi s on US 97 from jct SR 126. Ext corridors. **Pets:** Accepted.
[SAVE] [✕] [🛏] [🖵] [✕]

▼▼ Redmond Super 8 🅷
(541) 548-8881. **Call for rates.** 3629 SW 21st Pl. US 97, exit 124 (Yew Ave/Airport Way/Redmond Airport), just ne; 2 mi s of jct SR 126. Int corridors. **Pets:** Accepted.
[✕] [🖵] [✕]

REEDSPORT

AAA ▼ Anchor Bay Inn 🅼
(541) 271-2149. **$50-$80.** 1821 Winchester Ave (US 101). Jct SR 38, 0.8 mi s. Ext corridors. **Pets:** Dogs only. $9 daily fee/pet. Designated rooms, service with restrictions, supervision.
[SAVE] [✕] [🛏] [🖵] [✕] [🅺]

◆◆◆ ▼▼◆ **Best Western Salbasgeon Inn** **M**
(541) 271-4831. **Call for rates.** 1400 US 101 S. Jct SR 38, 0.4 mi s. Ext corridors. **Pets:** Small, dogs only. $10 daily fee/pet. Designated rooms, service with restrictions, supervision.
[SAVE] [X] [🛏] [📺] [🏊]

◆◆◆ ▼◆ **Economy Inn** **M**
(541) 271-3671. **Call for rates.** 1593 US 101. Jct SR 38, 0.5 mi s. Ext corridors. **Pets:** Accepted.
[SAVE] [X] [🛏] [🏊] [🎮]

◆◆◆ ▼▼◆ **Salbasgeon Inn of the Umpqua** **M**
(541) 271-2025. **Call for rates.** 45209 SR 38. Jct US 101, 7.5 mi e. Ext corridors. **Pets:** $10 one-time fee/room. Designated rooms, supervision.
[SAVE] [X] [🛏] [📺] [🏊]

ROCKAWAY BEACH

▼◆ **Silver Sands Motel** **M**
(503) 355-2206. **Call for rates.** 215 S Pacific St. Just w off US 101, on S 2nd Ave, then just w. Ext corridors. **Pets:** Accepted.
[X] [🛏] [📺] [🏊] [🏊] [🎮]

◆◆◆ ▼▼◆ **Tradewinds Motel** **M** 🐾
(503) 355-2112. **$58-$169, 7 day notice.** 523 N Pacific St. Just w off US 101, on NW 6th Ave, then just s. Ext corridors. **Pets:** Medium, dogs only. $15 daily fee/pet. Designated rooms, service with restrictions, supervision.
[SAVE] [X] [🛏] [📺] [🎮]

ROSEBURG

◆◆◆ ▼▼◆ **Best Western Garden Villa Inn** **M**
(541) 672-1601. **$89-$139.** 760 NW Garden Valley Blvd. I-5, exit 125, just nw. Ext corridors. **Pets:** Accepted.
[SAVE] [X] [🛏] [📺] [🏊]

◆◆◆ ▼▼◆ **Holiday Inn Express** **H** 🐾
(541) 673-7517. **Call for rates.** 375 W Harvard Ave. I-5, exit 124, just se. Ext/int corridors. **Pets:** Other species. $10 daily fee/room. Designated rooms, supervision.
[SAVE] [X] [📶] [🛏] [📺] [🏊]

◆◆◆ ▼▼◆ **Motel 6 #4108** **H**
(541) 464-8000. **$49-$72.** 3100 NW Aviation Dr. I-5, exit 127, just se. Int corridors. **Pets:** Other species. Service with restrictions, supervision.
[SAVE] [X] [📶] [🛏]

◆◆◆ ▼▼◆ **Quality Inn** **M**
(541) 673-5561. **$65-$120.** 427 NW Garden Valley Blvd. I-5, exit 125, just se. Ext corridors. **Pets:** Dogs only. $50 deposit/room, $10 daily fee/room. Designated rooms, service with restrictions, supervision.
[SAVE] [X] [🛏] [📺] [🏊]

◆◆◆ ▼◆ **Roseburg Travelodge** **M**
(541) 672-4836. **$65-$109.** 315 W Harvard Ave. I-5, exit 124, just se. Ext corridors. **Pets:** Medium. $10 daily fee/room. Designated rooms, service with restrictions, supervision.
[SAVE] [X] [🛏] [📺] [🏊]

◆◆◆ ▼◆ **Shady Oaks Motel** **M**
(541) 672-2608. **$45-$69.** 2954 Old Hwy 99 S. I-5, exit 120, 0.5 mi n. Ext corridors. **Pets:** Dogs only. $8 daily fee/pet. Designated rooms, service with restrictions, supervision.
[SAVE] [X] [🛏]

▼▼◆ **Sleep Inn and Suites** **H**
(541) 464-8338. **$69-$109.** 2855 NW Edenbower Blvd. I-5, exit 127, just sw. Int corridors. **Pets:** Medium. $10 one-time fee/room. Service with restrictions, crate.
[ASK] [X] [🛏] [📺] [🏊]

▼▼◆ **Super 8** **H**
(541) 672-8880. **Call for rates.** 3200 NW Aviation Dr. I-5, exit 127, just ne. Int corridors. **Pets:** Other species. $10 one-time fee/room. Service with restrictions, supervision.
[X] [📶] [🛏] [🏊]

◆◆◆ ▼▼◆ **Windmill Inn of Roseburg** **H** 🐾
(541) 673-0901. **Call for rates.** 1450 NW Mulholland Dr. I-5, exit 125, just ne. Int corridors. **Pets:** Other species. Designated rooms, service with restrictions, supervision.
[SAVE] [X] [🛏] [📺] [🏊] [🏊]

ST. HELENS

◆◆◆ ▼▼▼▼ **Best Western Oak Meadows Inn** **H**
(503) 397-3000. **$89-$169, 3 day notice.** 585 S Columbia River Hwy. South end of town on US 30. Int corridors. **Pets:** $10 one-time fee/pet. Service with restrictions, supervision.
[SAVE] [X] [🛏] [📺] [🏊]

SALEM

◆◆◆ ▼▼◆▼ **Best Western Black Bear Inn** **M** 🐾
(503) 581-1559. **$90-$130, 7 day notice.** 1600 Motor Ct NE. I-5, exit 256, just e, then just s. Ext corridors. **Pets:** Medium. $10 daily fee/room. Designated rooms, service with restrictions, supervision.
[SAVE] [X] [🛏] [📺] [🏊] [🏊]

◆◆◆ ▼▼◆ **Best Western Mill Creek Inn** **H**
(503) 585-3332. **$112-$168.** 3125 Ryan Dr SE. I-5, exit 253, just w on Mission St (SR 22), just n on Hawthorn Ave, then just w. Int corridors. **Pets:** Small, dogs only. $20 daily fee/pet. Designated rooms, service with restrictions, supervision.
[SAVE] [X] [🛏] [📺] [🏊] [🏊]

◆◆◆ ▼▼◆ **Best Western Pacific Hwy Inn** **M**
(503) 390-3200. **Call for rates.** 4646 Portland Rd NE. I-5, exit 258, 0.3 mi e. Ext corridors. **Pets:** Accepted.
[SAVE] [X] [🛏] [📺] [🏊]

▼◆ **Crossland Studios Salem North** **M**
(503) 363-7557. **$69-$84.** 3535 Fisher Rd NE. I-5, exit 258, just e on Portland Rd NE, 0.4 mi s on Ward Dr, then 0.8 mi s. Ext corridors. **Pets:** Other species. $25 daily fee/pet. Service with restrictions, crate.
[ASK] [X] [🛏] [📺]

◆◆◆ ▼▼◆ **Howard Johnson Inn** **H**
(503) 375-7710. **$70-$110.** 2250 Mission St SE. I-5, exit 253, 1.4 mi w. Int corridors. **Pets:** Accepted.
[SAVE] [X] [🛏] [📺] [🏊]

◆◆◆ ▼▼◆▼ **Phoenix Inn Suites-North Salem** **H** 🐾
(503) 581-7004. **$79-$139.** 1590 Weston Ct NE. I-5, exit 256, just w, then just s. Int corridors. **Pets:** Small, other species. $15 daily fee/pet. Service with restrictions, supervision.
[SAVE] [X] [📶] [🛏] [📺] [🏊] [🏊]

◆◆◆ ▼▼◆▼ **Phoenix Inn Suites-South Salem** **H**
(503) 588-9220. **$79-$139.** 4370 Commercial SE. I-5, exit 252, 1.5 mi w on Kuebler Rd, then 0.7 mi n. Int corridors. **Pets:** Medium. $15 daily fee/pet. Designated rooms, service with restrictions, supervision.
[SAVE] [X] [📶] [🛏] [📺] [🏊] [🏊]

◆◆◆ ▼▼◆▼ **Red Lion Hotel Salem** **H**
(503) 370-7888. **$124-$169.** 3301 Market St NE. I-5, exit 256, just w. Int corridors. **Pets:** Other species. $20 one-time fee/room. Service with restrictions, supervision.
[SAVE] [X] [📶] [🛏] [📺] [🍴] [🏊]

▼▼◆▼ **Residence Inn by Marriott** **H** 🐾
(503) 585-6500. **$170-$180.** 640 Hawthorne Ave SE. I-5, exit 253, just w, then n. Int corridors. **Pets:** Medium. $100 one-time fee/room. Service with restrictions, supervision.
[X] [📶] [🛏] [📺] [🏊] [🏊]

WYY Shilo Inn Suites-Salem H ☀
(503) 581-4001. **$90-$180.** 3304 Market St NE. I-5, exit 256, just w. Int corridors. **Pets:** Dogs only. $25 one-time fee/room. Designated rooms, service with restrictions, supervision.
[SAVE] ✕ 🔒 💻 🐾 ✕

WY Super 8 Salem H
(503) 370-8888. **$70-$90.** 1288 Hawthorne Ave NE. I-5, exit 256, just w, then just s. Int corridors. **Pets:** Accepted.
[ASK] ✕ 🔒 🐾

WY Travelodge Salem Capital M
(503) 581-2466. **$57-$73.** 1555 State St. I-5, exit 253, just w on SR 22/99 (Mission St), 0.6 mi n on Airport Rd SE, then 1 mi w. Ext corridors. **Pets:** Medium. $10 daily fee/pet. Designated rooms, service with restrictions, supervision.
[SAVE] ✕ 🔒 💻 🐾

SANDY

WYY Best Western Sandy Inn H
(503) 668-7100. **$75-$110, 3 day notice.** 37465 US 26. West side of town. Int corridors. **Pets:** Medium, dogs only. $10 daily fee/pet. Service with restrictions, supervision.
[SAVE] ✕ 🔒ᴹ 🔒 💻 🐾

SEASIDE

WYY Best Western Ocean View Resort H ☀
(503) 738-3334. **$59-$489, 3 day notice.** 414 N Prom. US 101, exit 1st Ave, just w, just n on Necanicum Dr, then just w on 4th Ave. Ext/int corridors. **Pets:** $20 daily fee/pet. Designated rooms, service with restrictions, supervision.
[SAVE] ✕ 🔒 💻 🍴 🐾

WYY Comfort Inn & Suites by Convention Center/Boardwalk H
(503) 738-3011. **$89-$399.** 545 Broadway. US 101, just w on Ave A; downtown. Int corridors. **Pets:** Accepted.
[SAVE] ✕ 🔒ᴹ 🔒 💻 🐾

WYY Ebb-Tide Resort H
(503) 738-8371. **$60-$200, 3 day notice.** 300 N Prom. US 101, exit 1st Ave, 0.4 mi w, just n on Columbia St, then just w on 2nd Ave. Ext/int corridors. **Pets:** Accepted.
[SAVE] ✕ 🔒 💻 🐾 ✕

WYY Holiday Inn Express Hotel & Suites H ☀
(503) 717-8000. **$89-$399.** 34 Holladay Dr. US 101, exit Broadway St, just w, then just n. Int corridors. **Pets:** Medium, dogs only. $25 daily fee/pet. Designated rooms, service with restrictions, supervision.
[SAVE] ✕ 🔒ᴹ 🔒 💻 🐾 ✕

WY Inn at Seaside M ☀
(503) 738-9581. **$65-$209, 3 day notice.** 441 2nd Ave. US 101, exit 1st Ave, then just w. Ext/int corridors. **Pets:** Other species. $10 daily fee/pet. Designated rooms, service with restrictions, supervision.
[ASK] ✕ 🔒 💻 🐾

WY Inn At The Shore M ☀
(503) 738-3113. **Call for rates.** 2275 S Prom. US 101, exit Ave U, just w. Ext corridors. **Pets:** $20 one-time fee/pet. Designated rooms, supervision.
✕ 🔒 💻 🎬

WYY Rivertide Suites H
(503) 717-1100. **$95-$525, 3 day notice.** 102 N Holladay. US 101, just w on Broadway St, then just n. Int corridors. **Pets:** Medium. $25 daily fee/pet. Designated rooms, service with restrictions, supervision.
[SAVE] ✕ 🔒ᴹ 🔒 💻 🐾

WYY Seashore Inn...on the Beach M
(503) 738-6368. **$75-$249.** 60 N Prom. US 101, exit 1st Ave, 0.4 mi w. Ext/int corridors. **Pets:** Small. $20 daily fee/room. Designated rooms, service with restrictions, crate.
[SAVE] ✕ 🔒 💻 🐾 🎬

WY The Seaside Inn H
(503) 738-6403. **Call for rates.** 581 S Prom. US 101, exit Ave G, 0.6 mi w, then just n. Int corridors. **Pets:** Accepted.
✕ 🔒 🍴

WYY Shilo Inn Suites Oceanfront Hotel-Seaside H ☀
(503) 738-9571. **$100-$550.** 30 N Prom. US 101, exit Broadway St, 0.4 mi w. Ext corridors. **Pets:** Dogs only. $25 one-time fee/room. Designated rooms, service with restrictions, supervision.
[SAVE] ✕ 🔒 💻 🍴 🐾 ✕ 🎬

SISTERS

WYY Best Western Ponderosa Lodge M
(541) 549-1234. **$100-$270.** 500 Hwy 20 W. Just w on US 20 from jct SR 242; at Barclay Dr; west end of town. Ext corridors. **Pets:** Accepted.
[SAVE] ✕ 🔒 💻 🐾

WYY FivePine Lodge & Spa Resort CA
(541) 549-5900. **$159-$219, 7 day notice.** 1021 Desperado Tr. Jct SR 126 and US 20, just e on US 20; east end of town. Int corridors. **Pets:** Medium. $25 daily fee/pet. Designated rooms, service with restrictions, supervision.
✕ 🔒 💻 🍴 🐾 ✕

SPRINGFIELD

WYY Best Western Grand Manor Inn H
(541) 726-4769. **$93-$156.** 971 Kruse Way. I-5, exit 195A, just se. Int corridors. **Pets:** Dogs only. $100 deposit/room, $10 daily fee/pet. Designated rooms, service with restrictions, supervision.
[SAVE] ✕ 🔒ᴹ 🔒 💻 🐾

WYY Comfort Suites Eugene/Springfield H ☀
(541) 746-5359. **$99-$179.** 969 Kruse Way. I-5, exit 195A, just se. Int corridors. **Pets:** Medium, dogs only. $25 daily fee/pet. Designated rooms, service with restrictions, supervision.
[ASK] ✕ 🔒 💻 🐾

WYY Holiday Inn Express Hotel & Suites H
(541) 746-8471. **$109-$179.** 3480 Hutton St. I-5, exit 195A, just se. Int corridors. **Pets:** Small, dogs only. $10 daily fee/pet. Designated rooms, supervision.
[ASK] ✕ 🔒 💻 🐾

WY Motel 6 #418 M
(541) 741-1105. **$51-$61.** 3752 International Ct. I-5, exit 195A, just e on Beltline Rd, just nw on Gateway St, then just n. Ext corridors. **Pets:** Other species. Service with restrictions, supervision.
✕ 🔒ᴹ 🐾

WYY Super 8 H
(541) 746-1314. **Call for rates.** 3315 Gateway St. I-5, exit 195A, just e on Beltline Rd, then just s. Int corridors. **Pets:** $22 one-time fee/pet. Designated rooms, service with restrictions, supervision.
[SAVE] ✕ 🔒 💻

WYY Village Inn M
(541) 747-4546. **$79.** 1875 Mohawk Blvd. I-5, exit 194A, 2.5 mi e on SR 126, exit Mohawk Blvd, then just n. Ext corridors. **Pets:** Accepted.
[SAVE] ✕ 🔒 💻 🍴 🐾

SUNRIVER

AAA ▼▼▼ **Discover Sunriver Vacation Rentals** VH
(541) 593-2482. **$90-$140, 60 day notice.** Sunriver Village Mall, Bldg #9. US 97, exit 153 (S Century Dr), 2 mi w to Abbott Dr, then just n on Beaver Dr. Int corridors. **Pets:** Large, dogs only. $35 one-time fee/pet. Designated rooms, no service, supervision.
[SAVE] [X] [🛏] [💻] [⚓] [🚫]

AAA ▼▼▼ **Sunray Vacation Rentals** VH
(541) 593-3225. **$100-$800, 60 day notice.** 56890 Venture Ln. US 97, exit 153 (Century Dr), 2 mi w, follow signs to Mt Bachelor, just s on Century Dr, then just e;. Ext corridors. **Pets:** Accepted.
[SAVE] [X] [🛏] [💻] [⚓] [🚫]

AAA ▼▼▼ ▼▼▼ **Sunriver Resort** H ❀
(541) 593-1000. **$149-$274, 21 day notice.** 17600 Center Dr. US 97, exit 153 (S Century Dr), 2 mi w to Abbott Dr, then just w. Ext corridors. **Pets:** Other species. $75 one-time fee/room. Designated rooms.
[SAVE] [X] [🛏] [💻] [🍽] [⚓] [🚫]

SUTHERLIN

▼▼ **Microtel Inn** H ❀
(541) 459-6800. **Call for rates.** 1400 Hospitality Pl. I-5, exit 136, just se. Int corridors. **Pets:** Other species. Service with restrictions, supervision.
[X] [🛏] [💻]

SWEET HOME

AAA ▼▼ **Sweet Home Inn** M
(541) 367-5137. **$69-$99.** 805 Long St. Just e of jct US 20 and SR 228; just s on 10th Ave, then just w. Ext corridors. **Pets:** Medium, dogs only. $15 one-time fee/pet. Designated rooms, service with restrictions, supervision.
[SAVE] [X] [🛏] [💻]

THE DALLES

AAA ▼▼▼ **Comfort Inn Columbia Gorge** H
(541) 298-2800. **$85-$174.** 351 Lone Pine Dr. I-84, exit 87, just nw. Int corridors. **Pets:** Accepted.
[SAVE] [X] [🛏] [💻] [⚓] [🚫]

AAA ▼▼ **Cousins Country Inn** H ❀
(541) 298-5161. **Call for rates.** 2114 W 6th St. I-84, exit 83 eastbound, just nw; exit 84 westbound, just nw on W 2nd St, just sw on Webber St, then just n. Ext corridors. **Pets:** $10 one-time fee/pet. Designated rooms, service with restrictions, crate.
[SAVE] [X] [🔊M] [🛏] [💻] [🍽] [⚓]

▼▼ **The Dalles Inn** H
(541) 296-9107. **$79-$139.** 112 W 2nd St. I-84, exit 84 eastbound, just se; exit 85 westbound, 0.8 mi nw; at Liberty and W 2nd sts; downtown. Ext/int corridors. **Pets:** Accepted.
[ASK] [X] [🛏] [💻] [⚓]

▼▼ **Motel 6 #4268** H
(541) 296-1191. **Call for rates.** 2500 W 6th St. I-84, exit 83 eastbound, just nw exit 84 westbound, just nw on w 2nd St, just sw on Webber St, then just n. Int corridors. **Pets:** Other species. Service with restrictions, supervision.
[X] [🛏] [⚓]

AAA ▼▼▼ **Shilo Inn Suites Hotel-The Dalles** H ❀
(541) 298-5502. **Call for rates.** 3223 Bret Clodfelter Way. I-84, exit 87, just ne. Int corridors. **Pets:** Dogs only. $25 one-time fee/room. Service with restrictions, supervision.
[SAVE] [X] [🛏] [💻] [🍽] [⚓] [🚫]

▼▼ ▼▼ **Super 8 Motel** H
(541) 296-6888. **Call for rates.** 609 Cherry Heights Rd. I-84, exit 84 eastbound, just se on W 2nd St, then just sw; exit 84 westbound, just nw on W 2nd St, just sw on Webber St, then just se on W 8th St. Int corridors. **Pets:** Accepted.
[X] [🛏] [💻] [⚓]

TILLAMOOK

AAA ▼▼▼ **Best Western Inn & Suites** H
(503) 842-7599. **$98-$200, 7 day notice.** 1722 N Makinster Rd. 1 mi n on US 101. Int corridors. **Pets:** Accepted.
[SAVE] [X] [🛏] [💻] [⚓] [🚫]

▼ **Mar-Clair Inn** M ❀
(503) 842-7571. **$86-$106.** 11 Main Ave. US 101, just n of jct SR 6. Ext/int corridors. **Pets:** Small, dogs only. $10 one-time fee/pet. Service with restrictions, supervision.
[ASK] [X] [🛏] [💻] [🍽] [⚓] [🚗]

AAA ▼▼ ▼▼ **Shilo Inn Suites Hotel-Tillamook** H ❀
(503) 842-7971. **$95-$200.** 2515 Main Ave. 1 mi n on US 101. Int corridors. **Pets:** Dogs only. $25 one-time fee/room. Service with restrictions, supervision.
[SAVE] [X] [🛏] [💻] [🍽] [⚓] [🚫]

WARRENTON

AAA ▼▼ **Shilo Inn Suites**
Hotel–Warrenton/Astoria H ❀
(503) 861-2181. **$125-$250.** 1609 E Harbor Dr. On US 26/101; near west end of Young's Bay Bridge. Int corridors. **Pets:** Dogs only. $25 one-time fee/room. Designated rooms, service with restrictions, supervision.
[SAVE] [X] [🛏] [💻] [🍽] [🚫]

WELCHES

AAA ▼▼▼ **The Resort at the Mountain** H ❀
(503) 622-3101. **$139-$475, 3 day notice.** 68010 E Fairway Ave. 0.8 mi s of US 26 on E Welches Rd. Ext corridors. **Pets:** Dogs only. $50 one-time fee/pet. Service with restrictions, crate.
[SAVE] [X] [🛏] [💻] [🍽] [⚓] [🚫]

WHEELER

▼▼ **Wheeler on the Bay Lodge and Marina** M
(503) 368-5858. **$80-$155, 3 day notice.** 580 Marine Dr. On US 101; center. Ext corridors. **Pets:** Accepted.
[X] [🛏] [💻] [🚫] [🚗]

WINSTON

AAA ▼▼ **Sweet Breeze Inn II** M ❀
(541) 679-2420. **$49-$89, 3 day notice.** 251 NE Main St. I-5, exit 119, 3 mi w. Ext corridors. **Pets:** Small, dogs only. $10 daily fee/pet. Designated rooms, service with restrictions, supervision.
[SAVE] [X] [🛏]

WOODBURN

AAA ▼▼▼ **Best Western Woodburn Inn** H
(503) 982-6515. **$99-$229, 3 day notice.** 2887 Newburg Hwy. I-5, exit 271, just ne. Int corridors. **Pets:** Accepted.
[SAVE] [X] [🔊M] [🛏] [💻] [⚓]

▼▼▼ **La Quinta Inn & Suites Woodburn** H ❀
(503) 982-1727. **$59-$104.** 120 Arney Rd NE. I-5, exit 271, just nw. Int corridors. **Pets:** Medium, other species. Service with restrictions, supervision.
[ASK] [X] [🛏] [💻] [⚓]

YACHATS

AAA ▼▼▼ **The Adobe Resort** H ❀
(541) 547-3141. **$75-$405.** 1555 US 101. 0.5 mi n; just w of US 101. Int corridors. **Pets:** Other species. $10 one-time fee/pet. Designated rooms, service with restrictions.
[SAVE] [X] [🛏] [💻] [🍽] [⚓] [🚫] [🚗]

◆ **The Dublin House** Ⓜ
(541) 547-3703. **$49-$135.** 251 W 7th St. US 101 at 7th St; downtown. Ext corridors. **Pets:** Dogs only. $10 daily fee/pet. Designated rooms, supervision.
⊠ 🚫 💻 🏊 🐾

⟨AAA⟩ ◆◆ **Fireside Motel** Ⓜ 🐾
(541) 547-3636. **$60-$155.** 1881 US 101 N. 0.6 mi n; just w of US 101. Ext corridors. **Pets:** Other species. $10 daily fee/pet. Designated rooms, service with restrictions, supervision.
⟨SAVE⟩ ⊠ 🚫 💻 ⊠ 🐾

◆◆ **Shamrock Lodgettes** ⟨CA⟩
(541) 547-3312. **Call for rates.** 105 US 101 S. On US 101, just s. Ext corridors. **Pets:** Accepted.
⊠ 🚫 💻 ⊠ 🐾

PENNSYLVANIA

CITY INDEX

ABBOTTSTOWN

The Altland House 🆔
(717) 259-9535. **$105-$175.** Center Square Rt 30. Jct SR 194. Int corridors. **Pets:** Medium. $15 one-time fee/pet. Service with restrictions, supervision.

SAVE ✕ 🐾 💻 ⑪

ALLENTOWN

Allentown Howard Johnson Inn & Suites 🅷
(610) 439-4000. **$38-$99.** 3220 Hamilton Blvd. I-78, exit 54 (Hamilton Blvd), 0.8 mi n. Int corridors. **Pets:** $25 one-time fee/pet. Service with restrictions.

SAVE ✕ 🐾ᴹ 🐾 💻 ≋

Comfort Inn Lehigh Valley-West 🅷
(610) 391-0344. **$85-$130.** 7625 Imperial Way. I-78, exit 49B (SR 100), just n. Int corridors. **Pets:** Other species. $25 one-time fee/room. Service with restrictions, crate.

ASK ✕ 🐾 💻

Four Points by Sheraton Hotel & Suites Allentown Airport 🅷 ✿
(610) 266-1000. **$120-$140.** 3400 Airport Rd. On SR 987 N (Airport Rd), 0.5 mi n of jct US 22. Int corridors. **Pets:** Large. $25 one-time fee/pet. Designated rooms, service with restrictions, supervision.

SAVE ✕ 🐾ᴹ 🐾 💻 ⑪ ≋

Holiday Inn-Allentown Center City 🅷
(610) 433-2221. **Call for rates.** 904 Hamilton Blvd. 9th St and Hamilton Blvd; downtown. Int corridors. **Pets:** Accepted.

✕ 🐾 💻 ⑪ ≋

Microtel Inn 🅷
(610) 266-9070. **$61-$130.** 1880 Steelstone Rd. US 22, exit Airport Rd S. Int corridors. **Pets:** Small. $25 one-time fee/pet. Designated rooms, service with restrictions, supervision.

ASK ✕ 🐾ᴹ 🐾 💻

Quality Inn-Allentown 🅷
(610) 435-7880. **$49-$299.** 1715 Plaza Ln. US 22, exit 15th St, just n. Int corridors. **Pets:** Small. $30 daily fee/pet. Service with restrictions, supervision.

SAVE ✕ 🐾 💻

Staybridge Suites Allentown Airport Lehigh Valley 🅷
(610) 443-5000. **$149-$289.** 1787-A Airport Rd. US 22, exit Airport Rd S, 0.3 mi s. Int corridors. **Pets:** Large, other species. $50 one-time fee/room. Service with restrictions, crate.

ASK ✕ 🐾ᴹ 🐾 💻 ≋

ALTOONA

Motel 6 #1415 Ⓜ
(814) 946-7601. **$52-$62.** 1500 Sterling St. I-99/US 220, exit 31 (Plank Rd), just w. Ext corridors. **Pets:** Other species. Service with restrictions, supervision.

✕ 🐾ᴹ ≋

Quality Inn of Altoona 🅷
(814) 944-4581. **Call for rates.** 2915 Pleasant Valley Blvd. I-99/US 220, exit 32 (Frankstown Rd), 0.4 mi w, then 0.5 mi n. Ext corridors. **Pets:** Accepted.

✕ 🐾 💻 ⑪ ≋

Super 8 Altoona Ⓜ
(814) 942-5350. **$56-$89.** 3535 Fairway Dr. I-99/US 220, exit 32 (Frankstown Rd), just w. Int corridors. **Pets:** Medium. $10 daily fee/pet. Service with restrictions, supervision.

ASK ✕ 🐾ᴹ 🐾 💻

BARKEYVILLE

Comfort Inn-Barkeyville Ⓜ
(814) 786-7901. **$79-$140, 3 day notice.** 137 Gibb Rd. I-80, exit 29, just n on SR 8. Ext corridors. **Pets:** Medium. $10 one-time fee/room. Designated rooms, no service, supervision.

SAVE ✕ 🐾 💻

 Super 8-Barkeyville M
(814) 786-8375. **$60-$120.** 1010 Dholu Rd. I-80, exit 29, just n on SR 8. Int corridors. **Pets:** Medium, dogs only. $10 daily fee/pet. Service with restrictions, supervision.

[SAVE] [X] [H] [P]

BEDFORD

Bedford Springs Resort H
(814) 623-8100. **$199-$399, 3 day notice.** 2138 Business Rt 220. I-76, exit 146, 3.9 mi s. Int corridors. **Pets:** Accepted.

[SAVE] [X] [H] [P] [TI] [≈] [X]

Best Western Bedford Inn H
(814) 623-9006. **$77-$105.** 4517 Business Rt 220. I-70/76 (Pennsylvania Tpke), exit 146, 0.3 mi n. Ext/int corridors. **Pets:** $50 deposit/room, $10 daily fee/room. Service with restrictions, supervision.

[SAVE] [X] [H] [P] [TI] [≈] [X]

Budget Host Inn M
(814) 623-8107. **$35-$90.** 4378 Business Rt 220. I-70/76 (Pennsylvania Tpke), exit 146, just n. Ext corridors. **Pets:** $10 daily fee/pet. Service with restrictions, supervision.

[SAVE] [X] [≈]

Quality Inn Bedford H
(814) 623-5188. **$70-$161.** 4407 Business Rt 220 N. I-70/76 (Pennsylvania Tpke), exit 146, just n. Ext/int corridors. **Pets:** Medium, other species. $15 daily fee/room. Designated rooms, service with restrictions, supervision.

[SAVE] [X] [H] [P] [TI] [≈]

Relax Inn and Suites M
(814) 623-7800. **Call for rates.** 4271 Business Rt 220. I-70/76 (Pennsylvania Tpke), exit 146, just s. Ext/int corridors. **Pets:** Accepted.

[X] [H] [P]

Super 8 M
(814) 623-5880. **Call for rates.** 4498 Business Rt 220. I-70/76 (Pennsylvania Tpke), exit 146, 0.3 mi n. Int corridors. **Pets:** Accepted.

[X] [H]

BETHEL

Comfort Inn-Bethel/Midway H
(717) 933-8888. **$79-$150.** 41 Diner Dr. I-78, exit 16, just w. Int corridors. **Pets:** Other species. $10 daily fee/pet. Designated rooms, service with restrictions, crate.

[SAVE] [X] [H] [P] [≈]

BETHLEHEM

Best Western Lehigh Valley Hotel & Conference Center H
(610) 866-5800. **$89-$169.** 300 Gateway Dr. US 22, exit Center St and SR 512. Ext/int corridors. **Pets:** Accepted.

[SAVE] [X] [H] [P] [TI] [≈]

Comfort Inn H
(610) 865-6300. **$84-$159.** 3191 Highfield Dr. US 22, exit SR 191, just s. Ext/int corridors. **Pets:** Large, other species. $10 daily fee/pet. Service with restrictions, supervision.

[ASK] [X] [H] [P]

Comfort Suites H
(610) 882-9700. **$109-$229.** 120 W 3rd St. SR 378, exit 3rd St, at W 3rd and Brodhead sts; center. Int corridors. **Pets:** Medium. $10 daily fee/room. Designated rooms, service with restrictions.

[SAVE] [X] [H] [P] [TI]

Extended StayAmerica-Allentown/Bethlehem H
(610) 866-8480. **$69-$144.** 3050 Schoenersville Rd. US 22, exit SR 378/Schoenersville Rd, follow signs for Schoenersville Rd, just n. Int corridors. **Pets:** Other species. $25 daily fee/pet. Service with restrictions, crate.

[ASK] [X] [H] [P]

Historic Hotel Bethlehem H
(610) 625-5000. **$169-$259.** 437 Main St. SR 378 S, exit 3 (City Center), just n on 3rd Ave, 0.3 mi e on Union, then 0.3 mi s. Int corridors. **Pets:** $75 one-time fee/room. Designated rooms, supervision.

[SAVE] [X] [M] [H] [P] [TI]

Homewood Suites–Allentown/Bethlehem Airport H
(610) 264-7500. **$119-$189.** 2031 Avenue C. US 22, exit SR 378/Schoenersville Rd, follow signs for Schoenersville Rd, 0.7 mi n. Int corridors. **Pets:** Large, other species. $100 one-time fee/room. Service with restrictions.

[SAVE] [X] [M] [H] [P] [≈] [X]

Residence Inn by Marriott H
(610) 317-2662. **$161-$197.** 2180 Motel Dr. US 22, exit Airport Rd S, 0.8 mi se on Catasauqua Rd. Int corridors. **Pets:** Accepted.

[X] [H] [P] [≈] [X]

BLOOMSBURG

Econo Lodge at Bloomsburg H ✿
(570) 387-0490. **$65-$139.** 189 Columbia Mall Dr. I-80, exit 232, just n on SR 42. Int corridors. **Pets:** Medium, other species. $20 one-time fee/room. Service with restrictions, crate.

[SAVE] [X] [H] [P]

The Inn at Turkey Hill CI ✿
(570) 387-1500. **$125-$235.** 991 Central Rd. I-80, exit 236 eastbound; exit 236A westbound, just s. Ext/int corridors. **Pets:** Other species. $20 daily fee/room. Designated rooms, service with restrictions, supervision.

[ASK] [X] [H] [P] [TI]

BLUE MOUNTAIN

Kenmar Motel M
(717) 423-5915. **$70-$90.** 17788 Cumberland Hwy. I-76, exit 201, just e on SR 997 N. Ext corridors. **Pets:** Medium, dogs only. $10 one-time fee/pet. Designated rooms, service with restrictions, supervision.

[SAVE] [X] [H]

BRADFORD

Best Western Bradford Inn H
(814) 362-4501. **$105-$170.** 100 Davis St S. US 219, exit Forman St southbound, just w to Davis St, then 0.3 mi s; exit Elm St northbound, just w. Ext/int corridors. **Pets:** $10 daily fee/pet. Service with restrictions, crate.

[SAVE] [X] [H] [P] [TI] [≈]

Comfort Inn-Bradford H
(814) 368-6772. **$100-$110.** 76 Elm St. US 219, exit Forman St southbound, just w to Davis St, then 0.3 mi s; exit Elm St northbound, just w. Int corridors. **Pets:** Accepted.

[ASK] [X] [H] [P] [≈]

Glendorn CI ✿
(814) 362-6511. **Call for rates.** 1000 Glendorn Dr. US 219, exit Forman St, just s on Mechanic St, then 4.3 mi w on W Corydon. Ext/int corridors. **Pets:** Dogs only. $75 daily fee/pet. Designated rooms, service with restrictions, supervision.

[X] [H] [P] [TI] [≈] [X]

BREEZEWOOD

Best Western Plaza Inn M
(814) 735-4352. **$65-$95.** 16407 Lincoln Hwy. I-76 (Pennsylvania Tpke), exit 161, just w on US 30; I-70, exit 147. Ext corridors. **Pets:** Accepted.

[SAVE] [X] [H] [P] [≈]

Breezewood Ramada H
(814) 735-4005. **$54-$72, 7 day notice.** 16620 Lincoln Hwy. I-76 (Pennsylvania Tpke), exit 161, just e on US 30; I-70, exit 147, just e on US 30. Int corridors. **Pets:** Accepted.

[SAVE] [X] [H] [P] [TI] [≈] [X]

Howard Johnson of Breezewood M
(814) 735-2200. **$59-$89.** 16550 Lincoln Hwy. I-76 (Pennsylvania Tpke), exit 161, just w on US 30; I-70, exit 147, just e on US 30. Int corridors. **Pets:** Medium, other species. $10 daily fee/pet. Designated rooms, service with restrictions, supervision.

Wiltshire Motel M
(814) 735-4361. **$40-$49.** 140 S Breezewood Rd. I-76 (Pennsylvania Tpke), exit 161, just w on US 30; I-70, exit 147. Ext corridors. **Pets:** Other species. Service with restrictions, supervision.

BROOKVILLE

Budget Host Gold Eagle Inn M
(814) 849-7344. **$52-$85.** 250 W Main St. I-80, exit 78, 0.5 mi s on SR 36. Ext corridors. **Pets:** Service with restrictions, crate.

Quality Inn M
(814) 849-8381. **$70-$110, 10 day notice.** 235 Allegheny Blvd. I-80, exit 78, just s on SR 36. Int corridors. **Pets:** Other species. $20 one-time fee/pet. Service with restrictions, supervision.

Super 8 M
(814) 849-8840. **$60-$65.** 251 Allegheny Blvd. I-80, exit 78, just n on SR 36. Int corridors. **Pets:** $10 daily fee/pet. Service with restrictions, supervision.

CAMBRIDGE SPRINGS

The Riverside Inn CI ☼
(814) 398-4645. **$65-$180, 10 day notice.** 1 Fountain Ave. Just ne of center. Int corridors. **Pets:** $25 one-time fee/pet. Service with restrictions, crate.

CAMP HILL

Radisson Penn Harris Hotel & Convention Center H
(717) 763-7117. **$109-$174.** 1150 Camp Hill Bypass. Jct US 11, 15 and Erford Rd. Ext/int corridors. **Pets:** Small, dogs only. $25 one-time fee/room. Designated rooms, service with restrictions, crate.

CARLISLE

America's Best Inn M
(717) 245-2242. **$58-$179.** 1825 Harrisburg Pike. I-81, exit 52 (US 11) southbound, 0.5 mi n; exit 52A northbound; I-76 (Pennsylvania Tpke), exit 226, 1.2 mi n on US 11. Int corridors. **Pets:** Other species. $25 daily fee/room. Service with restrictions, supervision.

Comfort Suites Hotel H
(717) 960-1000. **$117-$209, 3 day notice.** 10 S Hanover St. I-81, exit 47, 0.8 mi n on SR 34, just s of the square; downtown. Int corridors. **Pets:** Medium. $10 daily fee/pet. Designated rooms, service with restrictions, crate.

Days Inn & Suites-Carlisle H
(717) 258-4147. **$79-$175, 14 day notice.** 101 Alexander Spring Rd. I-81, exit 45, just sw. Int corridors. **Pets:** Accepted.

Hampton Inn Carlisle H
(717) 240-0200. **$119-$204.** 1164 Harrisburg Pike. I-76, exit 226, just n; I-81, exit 52 (US 11) southbound; exit 52B northbound, 0.8 mi s. Int corridors. **Pets:** Small, other species. $25 one-time fee/pet. Designated rooms, service with restrictions, crate.

Holiday Inn Carlisle H ☼
(717) 245-2400. **$89-$175, 7 day notice.** 1450 Harrisburg Pike. I-81, exit 52 (US 11) southbound; exit 52A northbound, just se; I-76 (Pennsylvania Tpke), exit 226, 0.8 mi n. Int corridors. **Pets:** Small, other species. $10 daily fee/pet. Designated rooms, service with restrictions, supervision.

Hotel Carlisle & Embers Convention Center H
(717) 243-1717. **$85-$175, 30 day notice.** 1700 Harrisburg Pike. I-81, exit 52 (US 11) southbound; exit 52A northbound, 0.4 mi n; I-76 (Pennsylvania Tpke), exit 226, 1.2 mi n. Int corridors. **Pets:** Accepted.

Pheasant Field Bed & Breakfast BB
(717) 258-0717. **$119-$209, 3 day notice.** 150 Hickorytown Rd. I-76 (Pennsylvania Tpke), exit 226, 0.4 mi n on US 11, 2.3 mi se on S Middlesex Rd, 0.4 mi e on Ridge Dr, then just s (right turn). Ext/int corridors. **Pets:** Accepted.

Ramada Limited H ☼
(717) 243-8585. **$70-$170.** 1252 Harrisburg Pike. I-81, exit 52 (US 11) southbound; exit 52B northbound; I-76 (Pennsylvania Tpke), exit 226, 1 mi n on US 11. Ext/int corridors. **Pets:** Medium, dogs only. $10 daily fee/pet. Designated rooms, service with restrictions, supervision.

Residence Inn by Marriott Harrisburg Carlisle H ☼
(717) 610-9050. **$149-$189.** 1164 Harrisburg Pike. I-76, exit 226, just n; I-8, exit 52 (US 11) southbound; exit 52B northbound, 0.8 mi s. Int corridors. **Pets:** $75 one-time fee/room. Service with restrictions.

Sleep Inn Carlisle H
(717) 249-8863. **Call for rates.** 5 E Garland Dr. I-81, exit 47 northbound, just ne; exit 47A southbound. Int corridors. **Pets:** Other species. $10 daily fee/room. Designated rooms, service with restrictions, supervision.

Super 8/Carlisle South M
(717) 245-9898. **$45-$140.** 100 Alexander Spring Rd. I-81, exit 45, just se. Int corridors. **Pets:** Accepted.

Super 8/North Carlisle M
(717) 249-7000. **$39-$150, 3 day notice.** 1800 Harrisburg Pike. I-81, exit 52A northbound; exit 52 (US 11) southbound, 0.5 mi n; I-76 (Pennsylvania Tpke), exit 226, 1.3 mi n. Ext/int corridors. **Pets:** Accepted.

CHAMBERSBURG

Best Western Chambersburg H
(717) 262-4994. **$59-$159.** 211 Walker Rd. I-81, exit 16, just w on US 30, then just n. Int corridors. **Pets:** Accepted.

Comfort Inn-Chambersburg H
(717) 263-6655. **$63-$150.** 3301 Black Gap Rd. I-81, exit 20, just e, then just s on SR 997. Int corridors. **Pets:** Small. $25 one-time fee/pet. Designated rooms, no service, crate.

AAA ◆◆ Days Inn H
(717) 263-1288. **$60-$129.** 30 Falling Spring Rd. I-81, exit 16, just e on US 30. Int corridors. **Pets:** Medium. $10 daily fee/pet. Designated rooms, service with restrictions, supervision.
[SAVE] [X] [■] [▣] [≈]

◆◆ Econo Lodge M
(717) 264-8005. **Call for rates.** 1110 Sheller Ave. I-81, exit 14, just w on SR 316. Int corridors. **Pets:** Accepted.
[X] [■] [▣]

◆◆ Red Carpet Inn M
(717) 267-2323. **Call for rates.** 1175 Wayne Ave. I-81, exit 14, just e on SR 316. Ext corridors. **Pets:** Accepted.
[X] [■] [▣]

CLARION

◆◆ Comfort Inn-Clarion H
(814) 226-5230. **$59-$129.** 129 Dolby St. I-80, exit 62, 0.6 mi n on SR 68. Int corridors. **Pets:** $10 one-time fee/pet. Service with restrictions, supervision.
[ASK] [X] [■] [▣] [≈]

◆◆ Holiday Inn H
(814) 226-8850. **$109-$169.** 45 Holiday Inn Rd. I-80, exit 62, 0.5 mi n on SR 68. Int corridors. **Pets:** Large, other species. $10 daily fee/room. Service with restrictions, supervision.
[ASK] [X] [■] [▣] [⊤] [≈] [⊠]

◆◆ Microtel Inn & Suites-Clarion H
(814) 227-2700. **Call for rates.** 151 Hotel Dr. I-80, exit 62, just n on SR 68, then just e. Int corridors. **Pets:** Accepted.
[X] [■] [▣]

AAA ◆◆ Quality Inn & Suites Clarion M
(814) 226-8682. **$80.** 24 United Dr. I-80, exit 62, just n on SR 68. Int corridors. **Pets:** Other species. $5 daily fee/pet. Designated rooms, service with restrictions, supervision.
[SAVE] [X] [■] [▣] [⊤] [≈]

◆◆ Super 8-Clarion M ☙
(814) 226-4550. **$50-$75.** 135 Hotel Rd. I-80, exit 62, just n on SR 68. Ext corridors. **Pets:** Other species. $10 daily fee/pet. Service with restrictions, crate.
[ASK] [X] [■] [▣] [≈]

CLARKS SUMMIT

AAA ◆◆ Comfort Inn-Clarks Summit/Scranton H
(570) 586-9100. **$69-$159.** 811 Northern Blvd. I-81, exit 194, on US 6 and 11; I-476 (Pennsylvania Tpke), exit 131. Int corridors. **Pets:** Other species. $10 daily fee/pet. Service with restrictions, supervision.
[SAVE] [X] [■] [▣]

AAA ◆◆ Econo Lodge of Clarks Summit/Scranton North M
(570) 586-1211. **$44-$149.** 649 Northern Blvd. I-81, exit 194, on US 6 and 11 E; I-476 (Pennsylvania Tpke), exit 131, just e. Ext corridors. **Pets:** Medium. $10 daily fee/pet. Service with restrictions.
[SAVE] [X] [■] [▣]

CLEARFIELD

AAA ◆◆ Budget Inn M ☙
(814) 765-2639. **$31-$70.** 6321 Woodland Hwy (US 322 E). I-80, exit 120, 1.5 mi sw on SR 879, then 1.2 mi e. Ext/int corridors. **Pets:** $7 daily fee/pet. Designated rooms, service with restrictions, supervision.
[SAVE] [X] [■]

◆◆ Super 8-Clearfield M
(814) 768-7580. **Call for rates.** 14597 Clearfield/Shawville Hwy (Rt 879). I-80, exit 120, just s. Int corridors. **Pets:** Other species. $5 daily fee/room. Designated rooms, service with restrictions, supervision.
[X] [&M] [■] [▣]

DANVILLE

AAA ◆◆ Best Western Danville Inn H ☙
(570) 275-5750. **$79-$129.** 79 Old Valley School Rd. I-80, exit 224, just s. Int corridors. **Pets:** Medium. $15 daily fee/room. Service with restrictions, crate.
[SAVE] [X] [■] [▣] [≈]

AAA ◆◆ Quality Inn & Suites Danville M ☙
(570) 275-5100. **$69-$169, 3 day notice.** 15 Valley West Rd. I-80, exit 224, just n on SR 54. Int corridors. **Pets:** Medium, other species. $25 one-time fee/room. Designated rooms, service with restrictions, supervision.
[SAVE] [X] [■] [▣] [⊤] [≈]

DICKSON CITY

◆◆ Residence Inn by Marriott-Scranton H
(570) 343-5121. **$140-$160.** 947 Viewmont Dr. I-81, exit 190, just e, follow signs to Viewmont Dr. Int corridors. **Pets:** Accepted.
[X] [■] [▣] [≈] [⊠]

DU BOIS

AAA ◆◆ Best Western Inn & Conference Center H ☙
(814) 371-6200. **$79-$149, 3 day notice.** 82 N Park Pl. I-80, exit 97 eastbound, 2.5 mi e on DuBois Ave (US 219), then just s; exit 101 westbound, 2.7 mi w on DuBois Ave (SR 255), then just s on US 219. Int corridors. **Pets:** $10 daily fee/pet. Service with restrictions, supervision.
[SAVE] [X] [■] [▣] [⊠]

◆◆ Clarion Hotel DuBois H
(814) 371-5100. **Call for rates.** 1896 Rich Hwy. I-80, exit 97, just s. Int corridors. **Pets:** Other species. $10 daily fee/room. Service with restrictions, supervision.
[X] [&M] [■] [▣] [⊤] [≈]

DUNMORE

AAA ◆◆ Days Inn H
(570) 348-6101. **$59-$299.** 1226 O'Neill Hwy. I-81, exit 188 (Throop), just n at SR 347. Int corridors. **Pets:** Accepted.
[SAVE] [X] [■] [▣]

◆◆ Holiday Inn-Scranton East H
(570) 343-4771. **$79-$199.** 200 Tigue St. I-84/380, exit 1 (Tigue St), 0.3 mi e of jct I-81. Ext/int corridors. **Pets:** Other species. $10 daily fee/pet. Designated rooms, service with restrictions.
[ASK] [X] [■] [▣] [⊤] [≈] [⊠]

AAA ◆◆ Sleep Inn & Suites H
(570) 961-1116. **$89-$169.** 102 Monahan Ave. I-81, exit 188 (Throop), just e at SR 347 N (O'Neill Hwy), then just s. Int corridors. **Pets:** Medium. $10 daily fee/pet. Designated rooms, service with restrictions, supervision.
[SAVE] [X] [&M] [■] [▣] [≈] [⊠]

EASTON

◆◆ Comfort Inn H
(610) 253-0546. **Call for rates.** 2555 Nazareth Rd. US 22, exit 25th St, just e on N Service Rd. Int corridors. **Pets:** Medium. $20 daily fee/pet. Service with restrictions, supervision.
[X] [■]

◆◆ The Lafayette Inn BB ☙
(610) 253-4500. **$150-$250.** 525 W Monroe St. US 22, exit 4th St (SR 611), just n on 3rd St, 0.3 mi ne on College Ave, then 0.3 mi n on Cattell St to jct Monroe St. Ext/int corridors. **Pets:** $20 daily fee/room. Designated rooms, service with restrictions, supervision.
[X] [■] [▣]

EBENSBURG

▼▼▼ Comfort Inn 🄷
(814) 472-6100. **Call for rates.** 111 Cook Rd. Jct US 219, just e on US 22. Int corridors. **Pets:** Accepted.

⊠ ☒ 🛏 💻 ⊱

ERIE

▼▼▼▼ Comfort Inn at Splash Lagoon 🄷 ❖
(814) 866-6666. **Call for rates.** 8051 Peach St. I-90, exit 24, just s. Int corridors. **Pets:** Other species. $10 daily fee/pet. Service with restrictions.

⊠ 🛏 💻 ⊱

▼▼ Days Inn 🄷
(814) 868-8521. **$110-$190, 30 day notice.** 7415 Schultz Rd. I-90, exit 27, just n on SR 97. Int corridors. **Pets:** Other species. $10 daily fee/pet. Service with restrictions, supervision.

(ASK) ⊠ 🛏 💻 ⊱

▼▼▼▼ Homewood Suites by Hilton 🄷
(814) 866-8292. **$119-$169.** 2084 Interchange Rd. I-79, exit 180, just e; in Pavillion Marketplace. Int corridors. **Pets:** Medium, other species. $75 one-time fee/room. Service with restrictions, supervision.

⊠ ☒ 🛏 💻 ⊱

▼▼▼▼ La Quinta Inn & Suites 🄷 ❖
(814) 864-1812. **$59-$169.** 7820 Perry Hwy. I-90, exit 27, just n. Int corridors. **Pets:** Medium, other species. Service with restrictions, supervision.

(ASK) ⊠ 🛏 💻 ⊱

▼▼▼▼ Microtel Inn-Erie 🄼
(814) 864-1010. **$70-$130.** 8100 Peach St. I-90, exit 24, just s. Int corridors. **Pets:** Dogs only. $10 daily fee/pet. Designated rooms, service with restrictions, supervision.

(ASK) ⊠ 🛏 💻

🄰🄰🄰 ▼▼▼ Red Roof Inn #7054 🄼
(814) 868-5246. **$68-$110.** 7865 Perry Hwy. I-90, exit 27, just n on SR 97. Ext/int corridors. **Pets:** Other species. Service with restrictions, supervision.

(SAVE) ⊠ 🛏 💻

🄰🄰🄰 ▼▼▼▼ Sheraton Erie Bayfront Hotel 🄷 ❖
(814) 454-2005. **$119-$189.** 55 West Bay Dr. I-90, exit 22B to Bayfront Connector, I-79 to Bayfront Pkwy. Int corridors. **Pets:** Medium, dogs only. Designated rooms, service with restrictions, crate.

(SAVE) ⊠ ☒ 🛏 💻 🍽 ⊱ ⊠

▼▼▼▼ TownePlace Suites by Marriott 🄷 ❖
(814) 866-7100. **$110-$150.** 2090 Interchange Rd. I-79, exit 180, just e; in Pavillion Marketplace. Int corridors. **Pets:** Medium, other species. $100 one-time fee/room.

⊠ 🛏 💻 ⊱

▼▼▼▼ Wingate by Wyndham 🄷
(814) 860-3050. **Call for rates.** 8060 Old Oliver Rd. I-90, exit 24, just s on Peach St, just w, just n, then just e. Int corridors. **Pets:** Accepted.

⊠ ☒ 🛏 💻 ⊱

FOGELSVILLE

▼▼▼▼ Glasbern 🄲🄸
(610) 285-4723. **$150-$485, 7 day notice.** 2141 Packhouse Rd. I-78, exit 49B (SR 100), 0.3 mi n to 1st light, 0.3 mi w on Main St, 0.6 mi n on Church St, then 0.8 mi ne. Ext/int corridors. **Pets:** Accepted.

(ASK) ⊠ 🛏 💻 🍽 ⊱ ⊠

▼▼▼▼ Holiday Inn Conference Center 🄷
(610) 391-1000. **$139-$299.** 7736 Adrienne Dr. I-78, exit 49A, 0.3 mi s on SR 100. Int corridors. **Pets:** Accepted.

(ASK) ⊠ ☒ 🛏 💻 🍽 ⊱ ⊠

▼▼▼ Sleep Inn 🄷
(610) 395-6603. **$59-$159.** 327 Star Rd. I-78, exit 49A, 0.3 mi s on SR 100, left at 1st traffic light, then immediate left on service road. Int corridors. **Pets:** $15 daily fee/pet. Designated rooms, service with restrictions, supervision.

(ASK) ⊠ ☒ 🛏 💻

▼▼▼▼ Staybridge Suites-Allentown West 🄷
(610) 841-5100. **Call for rates.** 327 C Star Rd. I-78, exit 49A, 0.3 mi s on SR 100, e at traffic light, then n on service road. Int corridors. **Pets:** Accepted.

⊠ 🛏 💻 ⊱ ⊠

FRANKLIN

▼▼ Franklin Super 8 🄷
(814) 432-2101. **Call for rates.** 847 Allegheny Blvd. 2 mi on SR 8 N. Int corridors. **Pets:** Medium. $15 one-time fee/pet. Designated rooms, service with restrictions, crate.

⊠ 🛏 💻

GETTYSBURG

▼▼▼ 1863 Inn of Gettysburg 🄷 ❖
(717) 334-6211. **$94-$300.** 516 Baltimore St. Jct US 15 business route and SR 97. Ext/int corridors. **Pets:** Other species. $10 one-time fee/room. Designated rooms, service with restrictions, supervision.

(ASK) ⊠ 🛏 💻 🍽 ⊱

🄰🄰🄰 ▼▼▼ Americas Best Value Inn 🄼 ❖
(717) 334-1188. **$56-$155.** 301 Steinwehr Ave. 1 mi s on US 15 business route, just s of jct SR 134. Ext/int corridors. **Pets:** Other species. Service with restrictions, supervision.

(SAVE) ⊠ 🛏 ⊱

🄰🄰🄰 ▼▼▼▼ Battlefield Bed & Breakfast Inn 🄱🄱
(717) 334-8804. **$175-$349, 7 day notice.** 2264 Emmitsburg Rd. 4 mi s on Steinwehr Ave and Baltimore Pike. Int corridors. **Pets:** Accepted.

(SAVE) ⊠

▼▼ Comfort Inn-Gettysburg 🄼
(717) 337-2400. **$69-$145.** 871 York Rd. 1 mi e on US 30. Int corridors. **Pets:** $10 daily fee/pet. Designated rooms, no service, crate.

(ASK) ⊠ 🛏 💻 ⊱

🄰🄰🄰 ▼▼▼▼ Country Inn & Suites Gettysburg 🄷
(717) 337-9518. **$69-$165.** 1857 Gettysburg Village Dr. US 15, exit SR 97, just e. Int corridors. **Pets:** $20 daily fee/room. Service with restrictions, supervision.

(SAVE) ⊠ 🛏 💻 ⊱

▼▼ Gettysburg Travelodge 🄼
(717) 334-9281. **$69-$159.** 613 Baltimore St. On SR 97 at US 15 business route. Ext/int corridors. **Pets:** Other species. $25 one-time fee/room. Designated rooms, service with restrictions.

(ASK) ⊠ 🛏 💻

▼▼▼ Holiday Inn Express of Gettysburg 🄷
(717) 337-1400. **$76-$170.** 869 York Rd. 1 mi e on US 30. Int corridors. **Pets:** Service with restrictions, supervision.

(ASK) ⊠ ☒ 🛏 💻 ⊱

🄰🄰🄰 ▼▼▼▼ Wyndham Gettysburg 🄷 ❖
(717) 339-0020. **$89-$199.** 95 Presidential Cir. US 15, exit York St, just e on US 30. Int corridors. **Pets:** Medium, dogs only. $20 daily fee/pet. Service with restrictions, supervision.

(SAVE) ⊠ ☒ 🛏 💻 🍽 ⊱

GIRARD

▼▼ The Green Roof Inn 🄼 ❖
(814) 774-7072. **$57-$156.** 8790 Rt 18. I-90, exit 9, 1.9 mi s. Ext corridors. **Pets:** Other species. $10 daily fee/pet. Designated rooms, service with restrictions, supervision.

(ASK) ⊠ 🛏 💻

GRANTVILLE

Days Inn Grantville-Hershey M
(717) 469-0631. **$89-$140.** 252 Bow Creek Rd. I-81, exit 80. Ext corridors. **Pets:** $10 daily fee/pet. Service with restrictions, supervision.

Holiday Inn Harrisburg-Hershey Area, I-81 H
(717) 469-0661. **$109-$219.** 604 Station Rd. I-81, exit 80. Int corridors. **Pets:** $75 deposit/room, $25 one-time fee/room. Service with restrictions, supervision.

GREENCASTLE

Comfort Inn H
(717) 597-8164. **$62-$100.** 50 Pine Dr. I-81, exit 3, just s on US 11. Int corridors. **Pets:** Large, other species. $15 daily fee/pet. Designated rooms, service with restrictions, supervision.

GROVE CITY

Super 8 M
(724) 748-3000. **$49-$140.** 2001 Leesburg Grove City Rd. I-79, exit 113, just w on SR 208. Int corridors. **Pets:** Accepted.

HAMBURG

Microtel Inn & Suites H
(610) 562-4234. **$74-$150.** 50 Industrial Dr. I-78, exit 29B, 0.3 mi n on SR 61, then just e. Int corridors. **Pets:** Other species. $10 daily fee/pet. Service with restrictions, supervision.

HARRISBURG

Comfort Inn Harrisburg/Hershey H
(717) 540-8400. **$69-$169.** 7744 Linglestown Rd. I-81, exit 77, 0.5 mi w. Int corridors. **Pets:** Medium, other species. $10 daily fee/pet. Designated rooms, service with restrictions, supervision.

Comfort Inn Riverfront H ✿
(717) 233-1611. **$109-$199.** 525 S Front St. I-83, exit 43, 0.5 mi n. Int corridors. **Pets:** Small. $25 daily fee/pet. Designated rooms, service with restrictions, supervision.

Crowne Plaza Harrisburg-Hershey H
(717) 234-5021. **$129-$219.** 23 S 2nd St. Jct Chestnut St; downtown. Int corridors. **Pets:** Accepted.

Holiday Inn Express East H
(717) 561-8100. **$89-$179, 5 day notice.** 4021 Union Deposit Rd. I-83, exit 48, just w. Int corridors. **Pets:** Medium. $15 daily fee/pet. Service with restrictions, supervision.

Holiday Inn Express Hotel & Suites H
(717) 657-2200. **$69-$169.** 5680 Allentown Blvd. I-81, exit 72, just s on N Mountain Rd, then just w on US 22. Int corridors. **Pets:** Medium. $25 daily fee/room. Service with restrictions, crate.

Holiday Inn Harrisburg East-Airport H ✿
(717) 939-7841. **$140-$200.** 4751 Lindle Rd. I-283, exit 2, just e. Int corridors. **Pets:** Small, other species. $75 deposit/room, $25 one-time fee/room. Service with restrictions, crate.

Howard Johnson Inn H
(717) 540-9100. **$49-$109.** 7930 Linglestown Rd. I-81, exit 77. Int corridors. **Pets:** Small. $10 one-time fee/pet. Designated rooms, service with restrictions, supervision.

La Quinta Inn & Suites Harrisburg Airport H ✿
(717) 939-8000. **$49-$109.** 990 Eisenhower Blvd. I-283, exit 2, just se; I-76 (Pennsylvania Tpke), exit 247, 1 mi n. Int corridors. **Pets:** Medium, other species. Service with restrictions, supervision.

Red Roof Inn-North #7037 M ✿
(717) 657-1445. **$62-$103.** 400 Corporate Cir. I-81, exit 69, just n on Progress Ave. Ext/int corridors. **Pets:** Other species. Service with restrictions, supervision.

Red Roof Inn-South #7027 M
(717) 939-1331. **$70-$111.** 950 Eisenhower Blvd. I-283, exit 2, just e. Ext/int corridors. **Pets:** Accepted.

Residence Inn by Marriott Harrisburg-Hershey H
(717) 561-1900. **$170-$208.** 4480 Lewis Rd. US 322, exit Penhar Dr, just e. Ext corridors. **Pets:** $100 one-time fee/room. Designated rooms, service with restrictions, supervision.

Sheraton Harrisburg Hershey H
(717) 564-5511. **$139-$325.** 4650 Lindle Rd. I-283, exit 2, just e. Int corridors. **Pets:** Accepted.

Super 8-North M
(717) 233-5891. **$50-$129.** 4125 N Front St. I-81, exit 66, 0.8 mi n. Ext corridors. **Pets:** $10 daily fee/pet. Service with restrictions, supervision.

HAZLETON

Best Western Genetti Inn & Suites H
(570) 454-2494. **$81-$110, 3 day notice.** 1441 N Church St. I-80, exit 262, 6 mi s on SR 309. Ext/int corridors. **Pets:** $10 daily fee/pet. Service with restrictions, supervision.

Ramada Inn Hazleton H
(570) 455-2061. **Call for rates.** 1213 N Church St. I-80, exit 262, 6 mi s on SR 309; I-81, exit 145, 0.5 mi s on SR 93, 1 mi e on Airport Rd, then 0.7 mi s. Int corridors. **Pets:** Accepted.

HERSHEY

Best Western Inn-Hershey H
(717) 533-5665. **$99-$239, 3 day notice.** US 422 & Sipe Ave. Jct US 322, just e. Ext/int corridors. **Pets:** $25 daily fee/room. Designated rooms, no service.

Days Inn Hershey H ✿
(717) 534-2162. **$89-$269.** 350 W Chocolate Ave. On US 422; center. Int corridors. **Pets:** Medium, dogs only. $15 daily fee/pet. Designated rooms, service with restrictions, supervision.

Hampton Inn & Suites H
(717) 533-8400. **$89-$229.** 749 E Chocolate Ave. 0.9 mi e on US 422. Int corridors. **Pets:** Small. $10 daily fee/pet. Designated rooms, service with restrictions, crate.

Hershey Econo Lodge M
(717) 533-2515. **$59-$179.** 115 Lucy Ave. Jct US 322, just e on US 422. Ext corridors. **Pets:** Large, dogs only. $10 daily fee/pet. Designated rooms, crate.
SAVE X 🛏 💻

HUNTINGDON

Huntingdon Motor Inn M ❖
(814) 643-1133. **$51-$85.** 6920 Motor Inn Dr. On US 22 at SR 26. Ext corridors. **Pets:** $20 one-time fee/pet. Service with restrictions, supervision.
X 🛏 💻

INDIANA

Holiday Inn H
(724) 463-3561. **Call for rates.** 1395 Wayne Ave. US 422, exit Wayne Ave, 1 mi n. Ext/int corridors. **Pets:** Accepted.
X 🛏 💻 🍴 ⇌

JONESTOWN

Days Inn Lebanon/Lickdale H
(717) 865-4064. **$50-$179.** 3 Everest Ln. I-81, exit 90. Int corridors. **Pets:** Small, other species. $10 daily fee/pet. Designated rooms, service with restrictions, supervision.
ASK X 🛏 💻

Quality Inn Jonestown/Lebanon M
(717) 865-6600. **$55-$150.** 16 Marsanna Ln. I-81, exit 90, just w. Int corridors. **Pets:** Medium. $10 daily fee/pet. Service with restrictions, supervision.
ASK X 🛏 💻 ⇌

KITTANNING

Quality Inn Royle H
(724) 543-1159. **$55-$99.** 405 Butler Rd. SR 28, exit US 422 W (Belmont). Ext/int corridors. **Pets:** Accepted.
ASK X 🛏 💻 🍴

Rodeway Inn Kittanning M
(724) 543-1100. **$45-$65.** 13607 US 422. E of jct Business Rt US 422, SR 66 and 28. Ext corridors. **Pets:** Dogs only. $5 daily fee/pet. Service with restrictions.
ASK X 🛏 💻

LAUREL HIGHLANDS AREA

CHALK HILL

The Lodge at Chalk Hill M
(724) 438-8880. **$49-$110.** Rt 40 E. Just w. Ext corridors. **Pets:** Other species. $10 daily fee/pet. Designated rooms, service with restrictions.
SAVE X 🛏 💻 X

DONEGAL

Lesley's Mountain View Country Inn CI
(724) 593-6349. **$160-$210, 7 day notice.** 327 Mountain View Rd. I-76 (Pennsylvania Tpke), exit 91, 1 mi e, then 0.5 mi s. Ext/int corridors. **Pets:** Small. Designated rooms, supervision.
X 🍴

FARMINGTON

Historic Summit Inn H
(724) 438-8594. **$139-$299, 3 day notice.** 101 Skyline Dr. On US 40; center. Int corridors. **Pets:** Small, dogs only. $20 daily fee/pet. Service with restrictions, supervision.
ASK X 🛏 💻 🍴 ⇌ X

GREENSBURG

Four Points by Sheraton H
(724) 836-6060. **$105.** 100 Sheraton Dr. I-76 (Pennsylvania Tpke), exit 75, 5.6 mi on US 119 N, 3 mi e on US 30, then just n. Int corridors. **Pets:** Accepted.
SAVE X 🛏 💻 🍴 ⇌

Knights Inn-Greensburg H
(724) 836-7100. **$60-$80.** 1215 S Main St. I-76 (Pennsylvania Tpke), exit 75, 4 mi s on US 119; just s of US 30. Ext corridors. **Pets:** $10 daily fee/pet. Service with restrictions, supervision.
ASK X 🛏 💻 ⇌

JOHNSTOWN

Comfort Inn & Suites H
(814) 266-3678. **$109-$169.** 455 Theatre Dr. US 219, exit Elton (SR 756), just e. Int corridors. **Pets:** $15 daily fee/pet. Designated rooms, service with restrictions, supervision.
ASK X ⌖M 🛏 💻 ⇌

Econo Lodge M
(814) 536-1114. **$49-$149.** 430 Napoleon Pl. Jct SR 271 and 403; downtown. Int corridors. **Pets:** Large. $10 daily fee/room. Service with restrictions, supervision.
ASK X ⌖M 🛏 💻

Holiday Inn Downtown H ❖
(814) 535-7777. **Call for rates.** 250 Market St. Corner of Market and Vine sts; downtown. Int corridors. **Pets:** $25 one-time fee/room. Service with restrictions, crate.
X 🛏 💻 🍴 ⇌ X

Holiday Inn Express Johnstown M
(814) 266-8789. **$99-$139.** 1440 Scalp Ave. US 219, exit Windber (SR 56 E), just e. Int corridors. **Pets:** $25 one-time fee/room. Service with restrictions, supervision.
ASK X ⌖M 🛏 💻

Sleep Inn H
(814) 262-9292. **$89-$115.** 453 Theatre Dr. US 219, exit Elton (SR 756), just e. Int corridors. **Pets:** Accepted.
ASK X ⌖M 🛏 💻

Super 8 Johnstown H
(814) 535-5600. **$70-$90.** 627 Solomon Run Rd. US 219, exit Galleria Dr, just w. Int corridors. **Pets:** Medium, other species. $7 daily fee/pet. Service with restrictions, supervision.
SAVE X 🛏 💻

NEW STANTON

Days Inn New Stanton H
(724) 925-3591. **$50-$125, 7 day notice.** 127 W Byers Ave, Box K. I-76, exit 75, 0.5 mi sw; I-70, exit 57B westbound; exit 57 eastbound. Int corridors. **Pets:** Other species. $100 deposit/room, $10 daily fee/pet. Designated rooms, service with restrictions, supervision.
SAVE X 🛏 💻 🍴 ⇌

Howard Johnson Inn M
(724) 925-3511. **$49-$119.** 112 W Byers Ave. I-76, exit 75, 0.5 mi sw; I-70, exit 57B westbound; exit 57 eastbound. Ext/int corridors. **Pets:** Small, other species. $7 daily fee/pet. Designated rooms, service with restrictions.
SAVE X 🛏 💻 ⇌

 Super 8-New Stanton **M**
(724) 925-8915. **$53-$76.** 103 Bair Blvd. I-76, exit 75, 0.5 mi se; I-70, exit 57B westbound; exit 57 eastbound. Int corridors. **Pets:** Large. $10 daily fee/pet. Designated rooms, service with restrictions, supervision.

[SAVE] [X] [🐕] [💻]

SOMERSET

 Budget Host Inn **M**
(814) 445-7988. **$45-$95, 3 day notice.** 799 N Center Ave. I-70/76 (Pennsylvania Tpke), exit 110, 0.3 mi s. Ext corridors. **Pets:** Small. $7 daily fee/pet. No service, supervision.

[ASK] [X] [🐕]

 Dollar Inn **M**
(814) 445-2977. **$38-$85.** 1146 N Center Ave. I-70/76 (Pennsylvania Tpke), exit 110, 0.3 mi s, then just n on SR 601/N Central Ave; at top of hill. Ext corridors. **Pets:** Medium, other species. $7 daily fee/pet. Designated rooms, service with restrictions, crate.

[ASK] [X] [🐕]

 Glades Pike Inn **BB**
(814) 443-4978. **Call for rates.** 2684 Glades Pike Rd. I-70/76 (Pennsylvania Tpke), exit 110, 6 mi w on SR 31; exit 91, 13 mi e on SR 31. Int corridors. **Pets:** Accepted.

[X] [☎]

 Holiday Inn **H**
(814) 445-9611. **$94-$149.** 202 Harmon St. I-70/76 (Pennsylvania Tpke), exit 110, just s. Int corridors. **Pets:** Medium. $35 one-time fee/room. Designated rooms, service with restrictions, supervision.

[SAVE] [X] [💻] [🍴] [🏊]

 The Inn at Georgian Place **CI**
(814) 443-1043. **$105-$195, 7 day notice.** 800 Georgian Place Dr. I-70/76 (Pennsylvania Tpke), exit 110, 0.5 mi e, then 0.3 mi n on SR 601. Int corridors. **Pets:** Accepted.

[ASK] [X] [🍴]

 Quality Inn Somerset **H**
(814) 443-4646. **$69-$199.** 215 Ramada Rd. I-70/76 (Pennsylvania Tpke), exit 110, just s. Int corridors. **Pets:** Other species. $25 one-time fee/room. Designated rooms, service with restrictions, supervision.

[SAVE] [X] [🐕] [💻] [🍴] [🏊] [X]

 Super 8 **M**
(814) 445-8788. **$49-$125.** 125 Lewis Dr. I-70/76 (Pennsylvania Tpke), exit 110, just s. Int corridors. **Pets:** Accepted.

[ASK] [X] [🐕] [💻]

UNIONTOWN

 Uniontown Holiday Inn **H**
(724) 437-2816. **$99-$179.** 700 W Main St. 1.8 mi w on US 40. Int corridors. **Pets:** Accepted.

[ASK] [X] [🔥] [🐕] [💻] [🍴] [🏊] [X]

END AREA

LEBANON

 Berry Patch Bed and Breakfast **BB**
(717) 865-7219. **$125-$219, 14 day notice.** 115 Moore Rd. I-81, exit 90, 2.8 mi s on SR 72, 1 mi on New Bunker Hill St, 0.8 mi s on S Lancastor St, just e, then follow signs. Ext/int corridors. **Pets:** Large. $20 daily fee/pet. Designated rooms, service with restrictions, supervision.

[ASK] [X] [🐕]

 Quality Inn-Lebanon Valley **H**
(717) 273-6771. **$80-$169.** 625 Quentin Rd. Jct US 422, 0.5 mi s on SR 72. Ext/int corridors. **Pets:** Medium, other species. $10 daily fee/pet. Designated rooms, no service, supervision.

[SAVE] [X] [🔥] [🐕] [💻] [🍴] [🏊] [X]

LEWISBURG

 All Suites Inn **M**
(570) 523-8882. **$95-$225.** 4663 Westbranch Hwy (US 15). 0.5 mi s on US 15. Ext corridors. **Pets:** Dogs only. $100 deposit/pet, $15 daily fee/pet. Designated rooms, no service, crate.

[SAVE] [X] [🔥] [🐕] [💻] [🍴]

 Days Inn-Lewisburg **H**
(570) 523-1171. **$78-$100.** 409 N Derr Dr. 0.5 mi n of jct SR 45. Ext corridors. **Pets:** Other species. Service with restrictions.

[SAVE] [X] [🐕] [💻] [🏊]

LINCOLN FALLS

 Morgan Century Farm **BB**
(570) 924-4909. **$99-$145, 5 day notice.** 30-809 Rt 154. In village. Ext/int corridors. **Pets:** Medium. $10 one-time fee/pet. Designated rooms, service with restrictions, supervision.

[X] [🐕] [💻] [☎]

LOCK HAVEN

 Best Western-Lock Haven **H** ✿
(570) 748-3297. **$87-$149, 3 day notice.** 101 E Walnut St. US 220, exit SR 120 W, just w. Int corridors. **Pets:** Other species. $10 daily fee/pet. Service with restrictions.

[SAVE] [X] [🐕] [💻]

MANSFIELD

 Comfort Inn **H** ✿
(570) 662-3000. **$89-$140.** 300 Gateway Dr. Jct US 6 and 15. Int corridors. **Pets:** Other species. $15 one-time fee/room. Designated rooms, crate.

[SAVE] [X] [🐕] [💻] [X]

 Mansfield Inn **M**
(570) 662-2136. **$55-$80, 3 day notice.** 26 S Main St. Jct US 6, just s on Business Rt 15; downtown. Ext corridors. **Pets:** Dogs only. $5 one-time fee/pet. No service, crate.

[SAVE] [X] [🐕] [💻]

 West's Deluxe Motel **M**
(570) 659-5141. **$65-$80.** 2848 S Main St. SR 15, exit Covington and Canoe Camp, Business Rt 15, 0.8 mi s on SR 660 W (Main St). Ext corridors. **Pets:** Accepted.

[SAVE] [X] [🐕] [💻] [🏊]

MARIENVILLE

 The Forest Lodge & Campground **M** ✿
(814) 927-8790. **$40-$85, 14 day notice.** SR 66. 6 mi n of town. Ext/int corridors. **Pets:** $12 daily fee/pet. Designated rooms, service with restrictions, supervision.

[ASK] [X] [🐕] [💻]

 Microtel Inn & Suites **H**
(814) 927-8300. **Call for rates.** 252 Cherry St. 0.6 mi sw of center, on SR 66. Int corridors. **Pets:** Accepted.

[X] [🐕] [💻]

MEADVILLE

Quality Inn M ❀
(814) 333-8883. **$59-$109.** 17259 Conneaut Lake Rd. I-79, exit 147B, just w on US 322. Ext/int corridors. **Pets:** Dogs only. $10 daily fee/pet. Designated rooms, service with restrictions, supervision.
ASK ✕ 🛏 💻

MECHANICSBURG

Comfort Inn Capital City H ❀
(717) 766-3700. **$79-$129.** 1012 Wesley Dr. I-76 (Pennsylvania Tpke), exit 236 (US 15), 1 mi n to Wesley Dr exit, then just w. Int corridors. **Pets:** Large, other species. $25 daily fee/pet. Service with restrictions, crate.
SAVE ✕ 🛗 🛏 💻 🏊

Comfort Inn West H
(717) 790-0924. **$84-$160, 3 day notice.** 6325 Carlisle Pike. Jct Carlisle Pike and US 11, 1 mi w on US 11. Int corridors. **Pets:** Small, other species. $25 deposit/pet. Designated rooms, service with restrictions, supervision.
SAVE ✕ 🛏 💻

Hampton Inn-Harrisburg West H
(717) 691-1300. **$109-$159.** 4950 Ritter Rd. I-76 (Pennsylvania Tpke), exit 236 (US 15), 1 mi n to Rossmoyne Rd exit. Int corridors. **Pets:** Other species. Designated rooms, service with restrictions, supervision.
✕ 🛗 🛏 💻 🏊

Holiday Inn Harrisburg-West H
(717) 697-0321. **$119-$180.** 5401 Carlisle Pike. Jct Carlisle Pike and US 11, just w. Ext corridors. **Pets:** $25 one-time fee/room. Service with restrictions, crate.
ASK ✕ 🛏 💻 🍴 🏊 🐾

MERCER

Colonial Inn Motel M
(724) 662-5600. **$35-$49.** 383 N Perry Hwy (US 19). I-80, exit 15, 3.5 mi n; I-79, exit 121, 4.5 mi s on SR 62, then 0.5 mi n on US 19. Ext/int corridors. **Pets:** Other species. $5 daily fee/pet. Service with restrictions, supervision.
ASK ✕ 🛏 💻

Comfort Inn Mercer H
(724) 748-3030. **$69-$139.** 835 Perry Hwy. I-80, exit 15, just n on US 19. Int corridors. **Pets:** Other species. Designated rooms, service with restrictions, crate.
ASK ✕ 🛏 💻 🏊 🐾

Microtel Inn & Suites H
(724) 748-9920. **$79-$84.** 2049 Leesburg Grove City Rd. I-79, exit 113, 0.9 mi w on SR 208. Int corridors. **Pets:** Accepted.
SAVE ✕ 🛏 💻

MIFFLINVILLE

Super 8 M
(570) 759-6778. **$55-$150.** 450 W 3rd St. I-80, exit 242, just n on SR 339. Ext corridors. **Pets:** $10 one-time fee/room. Service with restrictions.
ASK ✕ 🛏 💻

MILROY

Best Western Nittany Inn H
(717) 667-9595. **$86-$96, 7 day notice.** 5 Commerce Dr. US 322, exit Milroy, just e. Int corridors. **Pets:** Very small, dogs only. $20 daily fee/pet. Service with restrictions, supervision.
SAVE ✕ 🛏 💻 🏊

MONTGOMERY

White Deer Motel M
(570) 547-1007. **Call for rates.** 6967 Rt 15 Hwy. Jct SR 54, 1.4 mi s. Ext corridors. **Pets:** Accepted.
SAVE ✕ 🛏 💻

MORGANTOWN

Holiday Inn H
(610) 286-3000. **$95-$119.** 6170 Morgantown Rd. I-76, exit 298, just s on SR 10. Int corridors. **Pets:** Medium. $20 daily fee/pet. Designated rooms, service with restrictions, supervision.
✕ 🛏 💻 🍴 🏊 🐾

NEW CASTLE

Comfort Inn-New Castle H
(724) 658-7700. **$59-$130.** 1740 New Butler Rd (US Business 422). Jct SR 65, 1 mi e on US 422, then 1 mi w on US 422 business route. Int corridors. **Pets:** Small. $10 one-time fee/pet. Designated rooms, no service, supervision.
ASK ✕ 🛏 💻

NEW COLUMBIA

Holiday Inn Express H
(570) 568-1100. **Call for rates.** 160 Commerce Park Dr. I-80, exit 210A (US 15/New Columbia), just s. Int corridors. **Pets:** Accepted.
SAVE ✕ 🛗 🛏 💻 🏊

New Columbia Comfort Inn H
(570) 568-8000. **$75-$140.** 330 Commerce Park Dr. I-80, exit 210A (US 15/New Columbia), just s. Int corridors. **Pets:** Other species.
SAVE ✕ 🛗 🛏 💻 🍴 🏊

NEW CUMBERLAND

Days Inn Harrisburg South H
(717) 774-4156. **$60-$130.** 353 Lewisberry Rd. I-83, exit 39A, just ne. Int corridors. **Pets:** Accepted.
SAVE ✕ 🛏 💻 🏊

Harrisburg Holiday Inn Hotel & Conference Center H
(717) 774-2721. **$99-$149.** 148 Sheraton Dr. I-83, exit 40A, just se. Int corridors. **Pets:** Accepted.
SAVE ✕ 🛏 💻 🍴 🏊

Quality Inn Harrisburg West H
(717) 774-6200. **$109-$131.** 175 Beacon Hill Blvd. I-83, exit 40A, just e, then just n. Ext/int corridors. **Pets:** Accepted.
SAVE ✕ 🛗 🛏 💻 🏊

PENNSYLVANIA DUTCH COUNTRY AREA

AKRON

 Boxwood Inn BB ❀
(717) 859-3466. **$110-$235, 7 day notice.** 1320 Diamond St. SR 272, 0.4 mi se on Main St to Diamond St, then 0.3 mi s. Ext/int corridors. **Pets:** Dogs only. $25 one-time fee/pet. Designated rooms, service with restrictions, crate.

ASK ✕ 🔒 💻

DENVER

 Black Horse Lodge and Suites H
(717) 336-7563. **$59-$199, 3 day notice.** 2180 N Reading Rd. I-76 (Pennsylvania Tpke), exit 286, 1 mi w to SR 272, then 0.3 mi n. Ext/int corridors. **Pets:** Other species. Service with restrictions.

SAVE ✕ 🔒 💻 🍴 🏊

Comfort Inn H
(717) 336-4649. **$80-$170, 3 day notice.** 2017 N Reading Rd. I-76 (Pennsylvania Tpke), exit 286, 1 mi w to SR 272, then just s. Int corridors. **Pets:** Medium, dogs only. $20 one-time fee/pet. Designated rooms, service with restrictions, supervision.

SAVE ✕ 🔒 💻

Holiday Inn-Lancaster County H
(717) 336-7541. **$109-$160.** 1 Denver Rd. I-76 (Pennsylvania Tpke), exit 286, 1 mi w to SR 272, then just s. Int corridors. **Pets:** $15 daily fee/pet. Service with restrictions, supervision.

ASK ✕ 🔒M 🔒 💻 🍴 🏊

GORDONVILLE

Motel 6-Lancaster #4174 M
(717) 687-3880. **$55-$100.** 2959 Lincoln Hwy E. On US 30; center. Int corridors. **Pets:** Other species. Service with restrictions, supervision.

SAVE ✕ 🔒M 🔒

LANCASTER

Americas Best Value Inn M
(717) 397-4911. **$40-$150.** 1320 Harrisburg Pike. US 30 (Lincoln Hwy), exit Harrisburg Pike, 0.6 mi s. Ext corridors. **Pets:** $10 daily fee/pet. Service with restrictions, supervision.

SAVE ✕ 🔒

Best Western Eden Resort & Suites H
(717) 569-6444. **$89-$229.** 222 Eden Rd. Jct US 30 (Lincoln Hwy) and SR 272 (Oregon Pike). Ext/int corridors. **Pets:** Small, other species. $15 daily fee/pet. Designated rooms, service with restrictions, crate.

SAVE ✕ 🔒M 🔒 💻 🍴 🏊 🏊

Hawthorn Inn & Suites H
(717) 290-7100. **$69-$159.** 2045 Lincoln Hwy E. Jct US 30 (Lincoln Hwy E). Int corridors. **Pets:** Medium, dogs only. $50 one-time fee/room. Designated rooms, service with restrictions, supervision.

SAVE ✕ 🔒 💻

Lancaster Host Resort & Conference Center H ❀
(717) 299-5500. **$99-$199.** 2300 Lincoln Hwy E. On US 30 (Lincoln Hwy), 5 mi e. Int corridors. **Pets:** Medium. $25 one-time fee/room. Service with restrictions, crate.

SAVE ✕ 🔒 💻 🍴 🏊 🏊

Red Roof Inn of Lancaster M ❀
(717) 299-9700. **$80-$98.** 2307 Lincoln Hwy E. On US 30 (Lincoln Hwy), 5 mi e. Ext/int corridors. **Pets:** Medium. Designated rooms, service with restrictions, supervision.

ASK ✕ 🔒M 🔒 🏊

LITITZ

Holiday Inn Express Hotel & Suites H ❀
(717) 625-2366. **$120-$240.** 101 Crosswinds Dr. 1.4 mi s on Lititz Pike/SR 501, then just w on Trolley Run Rd. Int corridors. **Pets:** Medium. $25 one-time fee/room. Service with restrictions, supervision.

SAVE ✕ 🔒M 🔒 💻 🏊

MOUNTVILLE

MainStay Suites H
(717) 285-2500. **$110-$210.** 314 Primrose Ln. US 30 (Lincoln Hwy), exit Mountville. Int corridors. **Pets:** Medium, other species. $100 deposit/room, $10 daily fee/room. Service with restrictions, crate.

SAVE ✕ 🔒M 🔒 💻 🏊

NEW HOLLAND

Comfort Inn H
(717) 355-9900. **$90-$190.** 626 W Main St. 0.5 mi w on SR 23. Int corridors. **Pets:** Medium. $20 daily fee/pet. Designated rooms, service with restrictions, supervision.

ASK ✕ 🔒 💻

STRASBURG

Carriage House Motor Inn M
(717) 687-7651. **$49-$109.** 144 E Main St. 0.3 mi e on SR 896 and 741. Ext corridors. **Pets:** Accepted.

SAVE ✕ 🔒

END AREA

PHILADELPHIA METROPOLITAN AREA

AUDUBON

Homewood Suites by Hilton H ❖
(610) 539-7300. **$119-$219.** 681 Shannondell Blvd. I-422, exit Trooper Rd, 1.2 mi n. Int corridors. **Pets:** Other species. $250 one-time fee/room. Service with restrictions, crate.

SAVE ✕ &M ❸ 🔲 ➴ ✕

BENSALEM

Extended StayAmerica-Philadelphia/Bensalem H
(215) 633-6900. **$79-$144.** 3216 Tillman Dr. I-95, exit 37 (PA 132/Street Rd), 2.5 mi w, then just s; I-276, exit 351, 0.9 mi on US 1, 1.4 mi e, then just s. Int corridors. **Pets:** Other species. $25 daily fee/pet. Service with restrictions, crate.

A$K ✕ &M ❸ 🔲

Holiday Inn-Philadelphia Northeast H ❖
(215) 638-1500. **$119-$149.** 3499 Street Rd. I-276 (Pennsylvania Tpke), exit 351, just s on US 1, then 0.3 mi e on SR 132. Ext/int corridors. **Pets:** Small, other species. $30 one-time fee/pet. Designated rooms, service with restrictions, crate.

SAVE ✕ ❸ 🔲 ¶ ➴

Sleep Inn & Suites-Bensalem H
(215) 244-2300. **Call for rates.** 3427 Street Rd. I-276 (Pennsylvania Tpke), exit 351, just s on US 1, then 0.3 mi e on SR 132. Int corridors. **Pets:** Accepted.

SAVE ✕ &M ❸ 🔲

BERWYN

Residence Inn by Marriott H ❖
(610) 640-9494. **$229-$239.** 600 W Swedesford Rd. US 202, exit Paoli/SR 252, 1 mi n. Ext corridors. **Pets:** Other species. $100 one-time fee/room. Service with restrictions, crate.

✕ &M ❸ 🔲 ➴ ✕

CHADDS FORD

Brandywine River Hotel H
(610) 388-1200. **$129-$179.** 1609 Baltimore Pike. Jct US 1 and SR 100, 2 mi w of US 202. Int corridors. **Pets:** Medium, dogs only. $150 deposit/room, $20 daily fee/pet. Designated rooms, service with restrictions, crate.

SAVE ✕ ❸ 🔲

CONSHOHOCKEN

Residence Inn by Marriott Philadelphia/Conshohocken H
(610) 828-8800. **$233-$285.** 191 Washington St. I-76 (Schuylkill Expwy), exit 332 (SR 23); I-476, exit 16 (SR 23), 0.3 mi over Fayette Bridge to Elm St, then just se along the river. Int corridors. **Pets:** Accepted.

✕ &M ❸ 🔲 ➴ ✕

EAST NORRITON

Hyatt Summerfield Suites-Plymouth Meeting H
(610) 313-9990. **$99-$229.** 501 E Germantown Pike. I-476, exit 20; I-276 (Pennsylvania Tpke), exit 333, 2.5 mi w. Int corridors. **Pets:** Medium. $5 daily fee/room, $150 one-time fee/pet. Service with restrictions, supervision.

SAVE ✕ ❸ 🔲 ➴

ERWINNA

Golden Pheasant Inn CI 🐾
(610) 294-9595. **$95-$225, 21 day notice.** 763 River Rd. SR 32, 0.5 mi n of jct Dark Hollow Rd. Ext/int corridors. **Pets:** Medium, other species. $25 daily fee/pet. Designated rooms, service with restrictions, supervision.

A$K ✕ ❸ 🔲 ¶ ✕

ESSINGTON

Motel 6 #1267 M
(610) 521-6650. **$75-$85.** 43 Industrial Hwy. I-95, exit 9A, 0.3 mi sw on SR 291. Ext corridors. **Pets:** Other species. Service with restrictions, supervision.

✕ &M

Red Roof Inn-Airport #7119 M
(610) 521-5090. **$80-$120.** 49 Industrial Hwy. I-95, exit 9A, 0.3 mi sw on SR 291. Ext corridors. **Pets:** Accepted.

SAVE ✕ &M ❸

FORT WASHINGTON

Hilton Garden Inn Philadelphia/Fort Washington H
(215) 646-4637. **$109-$199.** 530 Pennsylvania Ave. I-276 (Pennsylvania Tpke), exit 339. Int corridors. **Pets:** Medium, dogs only. $100 deposit/room, $25 daily fee/room. Service with restrictions, supervision.

✕ &M ❸ 🔲 ¶ ➴

Holiday Inn Fort Washington Hotel & Conference Center H ❖
(215) 643-3000. **$89-$99.** 432 Pennsylvania Ave. I-276 (Pennsylvania Tpke), exit 339 (SR 309 S), just w. Int corridors. **Pets:** $45 one-time fee/room. Service with restrictions, crate.

SAVE ✕ 🔲 ¶ ➴

GLEN MILLS

Sweetwater Farm Bed & Breakfast BB
(610) 459-4711. **Call for rates.** 50 Sweetwater Rd. US 1, 2 mi w on Valley Rd, then 0.6 mi s. Int corridors. **Pets:** Other species. $35 daily fee/pet. Designated rooms.

✕ ❸ 🔲 ➴ ✕

HORSHAM

Days Inn-Horsham/Willow Grove H
(215) 674-2500. **$109-$169.** 245 Easton Rd. I-276 (Pennsylvania Tpke), exit 343, 1 mi n. Int corridors. **Pets:** $10 daily fee/pet. Designated rooms, service with restrictions, supervision.

SAVE ✕ 🔲

Extended StayAmerica-Philadelphia/Horsham H
(215) 784-9045. **$69-$134.** 114 Welsh Rd. S toward Jenkintown, 0.6 mi w on Maryland Rd, 0.5 mi sw on Computer Ave, then just n. Int corridors. **Pets:** Other species. $25 daily fee/pet. Service with restrictions, crate.

A$K ✕ &M ❸ 🔲

Residence Inn by Marriott-Willow Grove H
(215) 443-7330. **$188-$230.** 3 Walnut Grove Dr. I-276 (Pennsylvania Tpke), exit 343, 1 mi n on SR 611 (Easton Rd), then 1.3 mi w on Dresher Rd; inside Pennsylvania Business Campus. Ext corridors. **Pets:** Accepted.

✕ &M ❸ 🔲 ➴ ✕

KING OF PRUSSIA

MainStay Suites H
(484) 690-3000. **$109-$159, 30 day notice.** 440 American Ave. I-76 (Pennsylvania Tpke), exit 326 (Valley Forge); Schuylkill Expwy, exit 328A (Mall Blvd), 1.3 mi n on N Gulph Rd, 1 mi ne on 1st Ave, then just e. Int corridors. **Pets:** Accepted.

SAVE ✕ &M ❸ 🔲 ➴

Park Ridge Hotel and Conference Center at Valley Forge H
(610) 337-1800. **$109-$309.** 480 N Gulph Rd. I-76 (Pennsylvania Tpke), exit 327 (Valley Forge), 0.3 mi w. Int corridors. **Pets:** Accepted.

SAVE ✕ &M ❸ 🔲 ¶ ➴ ✕

KULPSVILLE

Best Western-The Inn at Towamencin �H
(215) 368-3800. **$130-$140.** 1750 Sumneytown Pike. I-476, exit 31, just e. Int corridors. **Pets:** Accepted.
⧉ ✕ 🛏 ⬛ 🍴 🔌 ⊠

LANGHORNE

Residence Inn Langhorne �H
(215) 946-6500. **$189-$269.** 15 E Cabot Blvd. I-95, exit 46A (Oxford Valley Rd), just e off US 1 N; 0.5 mi n of Sesame Place. Int corridors. **Pets:** Medium. $100 one-time fee/room. Service with restrictions.
⧉ ✕ 🗲 🛏 ⬛ 🔌 ⊠

Sheraton Bucks County Hotel �H 🐾
(215) 547-4100. **$229-$332.** 400 Oxford Valley Rd. I-95, exit 46A (Oxford Valley Rd), 0.8 mi e, exit off US 1 N. Int corridors. **Pets:** Medium, dogs only. Service with restrictions, supervision.
⧉ ✕ 🗲 🛏 ⬛ 🍴 🔌 ⊠

LIONVILLE

Extended StayAmerica-Philadelphia/Exton �H
(610) 524-7185. **$79-$139.** 877 N Pottstown Pike (Rt 100). I-76, exit 312, 1.8 mi s on SR 100. Int corridors. **Pets:** Other species. $25 daily fee/pet. Service with restrictions, crate.
ASK ✕ 🛏 ⬛

Hampton Inn Exton �H
(610) 363-5555. **$149-$169.** 4 N Pottstown Pike. I-76 (Pennsylvania Tpke), exit 312, 0.5 mi s; jct SR 113 and 100. Int corridors. **Pets:** Large, other species. Service with restrictions, supervision.
✕ 🗲 🛏 ⬛ 🔌

Residence Inn by Marriott-Exton �H
(610) 594-9705. **$189-$199.** 10 N Pottstown Pike. I-76 (Pennsylvania Tpke), exit 312, 1 mi s on SR 100. Int corridors. **Pets:** Accepted.
✕ 🛏 ⬛ 🔌 ⊠

MALVERN

Extended StayAmerica-Philadelphia/Malvern �H
(610) 240-0455. **$79-$139.** 300 Morehall Rd (US 29). US 202, exit SR 29 N. Int corridors. **Pets:** Other species. $25 daily fee/pet. Service with restrictions, crate.
ASK ✕ 🗲 🛏 ⬛

Homestead Studio Suites Hotel Philadelphia-Malvern �H
(610) 695-9200. **$89-$154.** 8 E Swedesford Rd. Just w of US 202 and SR 29 N. Int corridors. **Pets:** Other species. $25 daily fee/pet. Service with restrictions, crate.
ASK ✕ 🛏 ⬛ 🔌

Homewood Suites by Hilton �H
(610) 296-3500. **$119-$209.** 12 E Swedesford Rd. US 202, exit SR 29, follow signs. Int corridors. **Pets:** Medium. $25 one-time fee/pet. Service with restrictions, crate.
✕ 🗲 🛏 ⬛ 🔌

Sheraton Great Valley Hotel �H 🐾
(610) 524-5500. **$169-$194.** 707 Lancaster Pike. Jct US 202 and 30 E. Int corridors. **Pets:** Medium, dogs only. Service with restrictions, supervision.
⧉ ✕ 🗲 🛏 ⬛ 🔌

Staybridge Suites �H
(610) 296-4343. **Call for rates.** 20 Morehall Rd. Jct US 30 and SR 29, just nw. Ext/int corridors. **Pets:** Accepted.
✕ 🛏 ⬛ 🔌 ⊠

MONTGOMERYVILLE

Quality Inn Conference Center �H
(215) 699-8800. **$94-$129.** 969 Bethlehem Pike. I-276 (Pennsylvania Tpke), exit 339, 8 mi n on SR 309. Ext corridors. **Pets:** Large. $25 daily fee/room. Designated rooms, service with restrictions, supervision.
ASK ✕ 🛏 ⬛

Residence Inn by Marriott �H
(267) 468-0111. **$207-$253.** 1110 Bethlehem Pike. I-276 (Pennsylvania Tpke), exit 339, 6.5 mi n on SR 309. Int corridors. **Pets:** Accepted.
✕ 🛏 ⬛ 🔌 ⊠

NEW HOPE

1870 Wedgwood Inn of New Hope BB 🐾
(215) 862-2570. **$90-$285, 10 day notice.** 111 W Bridge St (SR 179). 0.5 mi w of SR 32; downtown. Ext/int corridors. **Pets:** Medium, dogs only. $20 daily fee/pet. Service with restrictions, supervision.
✕ 🛏 ⬛

Aaron Burr House Inn & Conference Center BB 🐾
(215) 862-2520. **$95-$295, 10 day notice.** 80 W Bridge St (SR 179). 0.5 mi w of SR 32; at W Bridge and Chestnut sts. Int corridors. **Pets:** Medium, dogs only. $25 daily fee/pet. Service with restrictions, supervision.
✕ 🛏

PHILADELPHIA

Best Western Center City Hotel �H
(215) 568-8300. **$135-$165.** 501 N 22nd St. Just n of Benjamin Franklin Pkwy. Int corridors. **Pets:** Medium. $15 daily fee/pet. Service with restrictions.
⧉ ✕ 🛏 ⬛ 🍴 🔌

Extended StayAmerica-Philadelphia Airport �H
(215) 492-6766. **$84-$134.** 9000 Tinicum Blvd. I-95, exit 12B (airport), just n on Essington Ave, then just w on Bartram Ave. Int corridors. **Pets:** Other species. $25 daily fee/pet. Service with restrictions, crate.
ASK ✕ 🗲 🛏 ⬛

Four Points by Sheraton Philadelphia Airport �H
(215) 492-0400. **$100-$260.** 4101 Island Ave. Jct I-95 and SR 291, exit 13 northbound; exit 15 southbound. Int corridors. **Pets:** Medium. Service with restrictions, supervision.
⧉ ✕ 🛏 ⬛ 🍴 🔌

Four Points by Sheraton Philadelphia Northeast �H
(215) 671-9600. **$209-$219, 4 day notice.** 9461 Roosevelt Blvd. I-276 (Pennsylvania Tpke), exit 351, 5 mi s on US 1. Int corridors. **Pets:** Accepted.
⧉ ✕ 🛏 ⬛ 🍴 🔌

Four Seasons Hotel Philadelphia �H
(215) 963-1500. **$395-$505.** 1 Logan Square. Corner of 18th St and Benjamin Franklin Pkwy. Int corridors. **Pets:** Accepted.
⧉ ✕ 🗲 🛏 ⬛ 🍴 🔌 ⊠

Loews Philadelphia Hotel �H 🐾
(215) 627-1200. **$179-$299.** 1200 Market St. Corner of 12th and Market sts. Int corridors. **Pets:** Other species. $25 one-time fee/room. Service with restrictions.
⧉ ✕ 🗲 🛏 ⬛ 🍴 ⊠

Park Hyatt Philadelphia at The Bellevue �H
(215) 893-1234. **$199-$569, 3 day notice.** Broad & Walnut Sts. Broad St; between Walnut and Locust sts. Int corridors. **Pets:** Accepted.
⧉ ✕ 🛏 ⬛ 🍴 ⊠

▼▼▼ **Philadelphia Airport Residence Inn by Marriott** H
(215) 492-1611. **$239-$259.** 4630 Island Ave. I-95, exit 13 northbound; exit 15 southbound, 0.5 mi e; just e of SR 291. Ext/int corridors. **Pets:** Accepted.
(X) (&M) (🛏) (💻) (🛒) (🏋)

▼▼▼ **Philadelphia Downtown Marriott Hotel** H
(215) 625-2900. **$299-$329.** 1201 Market St. Between 12th and 13th sts. Int corridors. **Pets:** Accepted.
(X) (🛏) (💻) (🍴) (🛒) (🏋)

△△△ ▼▼▼ **The Radisson Plaza-Warwick Hotel Philadelphia** H ❖
(215) 735-6000. **$189-$389.** 1701 Locust St. Jct 17th and Locust sts. Int corridors. **Pets:** Large, dogs only. $60 one-time fee/room. Service with restrictions.
(SAVE) (X) (🛏) (💻) (🍴)

▼▼▼ **Residence Inn by Marriott Philadelphia City Center** H
(215) 557-0005. **$269-$299.** 1 E Penn Square. Jct Market and Juniper sts. Int corridors. **Pets:** Other species. $75 one-time fee/room. Service with restrictions.
(X) (🛏) (💻)

△△△ ▼▼▼▼ **The Rittenhouse Hotel and Condominium Residences** H ❖
(215) 546-9000. **$470-$510, 3 day notice.** 210 W Rittenhouse Square. On Rittenhouse Square. Int corridors. **Pets:** Service with restrictions, supervision.
(SAVE) (X) (&M) (🍴) (🛒) (🏋)

▼▼▼▼ **The Ritz-Carlton Philadelphia** H ❖
(215) 523-8000. **$399-$4000.** Ten Avenue of the Arts. On Broad St; between Market and Chestnut. Int corridors. **Pets:** $75 one-time fee/room. Service with restrictions.
(X) (💻) (🍴) (🏋)

△△△ ▼▼▼ **The Sheraton Philadelphia City Center Hotel** H
(215) 448-2000. **$359-$379.** 2 Franklin Plaza. Jct 17th and Race sts. Int corridors. **Pets:** Accepted.
(SAVE) (X) (🛏) (💻) (🍴) (🛒)

△△△ ▼▼▼▼ **Sheraton Philadelphia University City Hotel** H ❖
(215) 387-8000. **$185-$289, 3 day notice.** 36th & Chestnut Sts. I-76 (Pennsylvania Tpke), exit 345, 0.5 mi w. Int corridors. **Pets:** Medium, dogs only. Service with restrictions, crate.
(SAVE) (X) (&M) (🛏) (💻) (🍴) (🛒)

△△△ ▼▼▼ **Sheraton Society Hill** H ❖
(215) 238-6000. **$159-$329.** One Dock St. Just s of jct 2nd and Walnut sts. Int corridors. **Pets:** Medium, dogs only. Service with restrictions, supervision.
(SAVE) (X) (🛏) (💻) (🍴) (🛒) (🏋)

△△△ ▼▼▼ **Sheraton Suites Philadelphia Airport** H
(215) 365-6600. **$109-$289.** 4101 Island Ave. Jct I-95 and SR 291, exit 13 northbound; exit 15 southbound. Int corridors. **Pets:** Medium. Service with restrictions, supervision.
(SAVE) (X) (🛏) (💻) (🍴) (🛒)

▼▼▼ ▼▼▼ **Sofitel Philadelphia** H
(215) 569-8300. **Call for rates.** 120 S 17th St. Jct Sansom and 17th sts. Int corridors. **Pets:** Accepted.
(X) (&M) (🍴)

△△△ ▼▼▼ ▼▼▼ **The Westin Philadelphia** H
(215) 563-1600. **$499-$509.** 99 S 17th St at Liberty Pl. Between Market and Chestnut sts. Int corridors. **Pets:** Accepted.
(SAVE) (X) (💻) (🍴) (🏋)

PLYMOUTH MEETING

▼▼ ▼▼ **Extended StayAmerica-Philadelphia Plymouth Meeting** H
(610) 260-0488. **$89-$129.** 437 Irwins Ln. I-276 (Pennsylvania Tpke), exit 333, follow signs for Plymouth Rd (Norristown), just w on Plymouth Rd, then just n. Int corridors. **Pets:** Other species. $25 daily fee/pet. Service with restrictions, crate.
(ASK) (X) (&M) (🛏) (💻)

POTTSTOWN

△△△ ▼▼▼ **Best Western Pottstown Inn** H
(610) 327-3300. **Call for rates.** 1600 Industrial Hwy. US 422, exit Armand Hammer Blvd. Int corridors. **Pets:** Accepted.
(SAVE) (X) (&M) (🛏) (💻) (🛒)

△△△ ▼▼▼ **Comfort Inn & Suites** H
(610) 326-5000. **$104-$139.** 99 Robinson St. SR 100, 1 mi n of jct US 422. Int corridors. **Pets:** Other species. $15 daily fee/room. Designated rooms, service with restrictions, crate.
(SAVE) (X) (&M) (🛏) (💻) (🛒)

QUAKERTOWN

△△△ ▼▼▼ **Comfort Inn & Suites** H ❖
(215) 538-3000. **$89-$169.** 1905 John Fries Hwy (SR 663). I-476 (Pennsylvania Tpke), exit 44, just e. Ext corridors. **Pets:** Other species. $25 one-time fee/room. Service with restrictions, crate.
(SAVE) (X) (🛏) (💻)

▼▼▼ **Hampton Inn-Quakertown** H
(215) 536-7779. **$79-$159.** 1915 John Fries Hwy (SR 663). I-476 (Pennsylvania Tpke), exit 44, just e. Int corridors. **Pets:** Accepted.
(X) (&M) (🛏) (💻) (🛒)

TREVOSE

△△△ ▼▼▼ **Red Roof Inn #7185** M
(215) 244-9422. **$64-$100.** 3100 Lincoln Hwy. I-276 (Pennsylvania Tpke), exit 351, 0.5 mi s on US 1 at US 132. Ext corridors. **Pets:** Other species. Service with restrictions, supervision.
(SAVE) (X) (&M) (🛏)

UPPER BLACK EDDY

▼▼▼ **The Bridgeton House on the Delaware** BB
(610) 982-5856. **$169-$429.** 1525 River Rd. On SR 32; center. Int corridors. **Pets:** Small, dogs only. $100 deposit/pet. Designated rooms, service with restrictions, supervision.
(X) (🛏) (💻)

WEST CHESTER

△△△ ▼▼▼ **Microtel Inn & Suites** H
(610) 738-9111. **$79-$114.** 500 Willowbrook Ln. Just se of US 202, exit Matlack St. Int corridors. **Pets:** Accepted.
(SAVE) (X) (&M) (🛏)

END METROPOLITAN AREA

PHILIPSBURG

⚑ ⚑ Main Liner Motel M
(814) 342-2004. **$39-$75.** One Mile W (US 322 W) Hwy. 1 mi w of jct SR 53 N. Ext corridors. **Pets:** Medium. $10 daily fee/pet. Designated rooms, service with restrictions, supervision.
SAVE ☒ ✆

PINE GROVE

⚑ ⚑ Comfort Inn H
(570) 345-8031. **$79-$140.** SR 443. I-81, exit 100. Int corridors. **Pets:** Other species. $10 daily fee/room. Designated rooms, service with restrictions, crate.
ASK ☒ ⓛ ✆ ▯ ⇝

PITTSBURGH METROPOLITAN AREA

BEAVER FALLS

⚑⚑⚑ Holiday Inn H ✿
(724) 846-3700. **$139-$179.** 7195 Eastwood Rd. I-76 (Pennsylvania Tpke), exit 13, just n. Int corridors. **Pets:** Large. $35 one-time fee/pet. Service with restrictions, supervision.
ASK ☒ ⓛ ✆ ▯ ⇝ ☒

BETHEL PARK

⚑⚑ ⚑⚑⚑ Crowne Plaza Pittsburgh South H
(412) 833-5300. **$109-$299.** 164 Ft Couch Rd. 1 mi n on US 19. Int corridors. **Pets:** Medium. $25 daily fee/room. Designated rooms, service with restrictions, crate.
SAVE ☒ ⓛ ✆ ▯ ⇝

BUTLER

⚑⚑ Comfort Inn H
(724) 287-7177. **$80-$200.** 1 Comfort Ln. 4 mi s on SR 8. Int corridors. **Pets:** $20 daily fee/room. Service with restrictions.
ASK ☒ ⓛ ✆ ⇝

⚑⚑ Days Inn Butler H
(724) 287-6761. **$79-$84.** 139 Pittsburgh Rd. 2 mi s. Int corridors. **Pets:** Dogs only. $35 daily fee/pet. Service with restrictions, supervision.
ASK ☒ ⓛ ✆ ▯ ⇝ ☒

⚑⚑ Locust Brook Lodge BB
(724) 283-8453. **$85-$150.** 179 Eagle Mill Rd. 5 mi w on US 422 to jct Eagle Mill Rd, then 0.8 mi s; I-79, exit 99, 10 mi e on US 422 to jct Eagle Mill Rd, then 0.8 mi s. Ext/int corridors. **Pets:** Accepted.
ASK ☒

⚑⚑ Super 8 M
(724) 287-8888. **$62-$67.** 138 Pittsburgh Rd. 2 mi s. Int corridors. **Pets:** Medium. $10 daily fee/pet. Designated rooms, service with restrictions, supervision.
ASK ☒ ⓛ ✆

CANONSBURG

⚑⚑ Super 8 M
(724) 873-8808. **Call for rates.** 8 Curry Ave. I-79, exit 45, follow signs. Int corridors. **Pets:** Accepted.
☒ ⓛ ✆

CARNEGIE

⚑⚑ Extended StayAmerica-Pittsburgh-Carnegie H
(412) 278-4001. **$78-$92.** 520 N Bell Ave. I-279, exit 1B (Rosslyn exit), just se. Int corridors. **Pets:** Other species. $25 daily fee/pet. Service with restrictions, crate.
ASK ☒ ⓛ ⓛ ✆

CORAOPOLIS

⚑ Americas Best Value Inn-Pittsburgh Airport M
(412) 604-2378. **$55-$60.** 8858 University Blvd. 0.5 mi n of Business Rt SR 60. Ext corridors. **Pets:** Accepted.
ASK ☒ ⓛ

⚑⚑ ⚑⚑⚑ Crowne Plaza Hotel Pittsburgh International H
(412) 262-2400. **$99-$199.** 1160 Thorn Run Rd. Business Rt SR 60, exit Thorn Run Rd. Int corridors. **Pets:** Accepted.
SAVE ☒ ⓛ ✆ ▯ ⇝

⚑⚑ ⚑⚑ Days Inn Pittsburgh International Airport H
(412) 859-4000. **Call for rates.** 2500 Marketplace Blvd. SR 60, exit 2 (Montour Run Rd), 0.5 mi e, then 0.5 mi n. Int corridors. **Pets:** Accepted.
☒ ⓛ ✆ ⇝

⚑⚑ ⚑⚑⚑ Embassy Suites-Pittsburgh International Airport H
(412) 269-9070. **$129-$289.** 550 Cherrington Pkwy. Business Rt SR 60, exit Thorn Run Rd. Int corridors. **Pets:** Accepted.
SAVE ☒ ⓛ ⓛ ✆ ▯ ⇝ ☒

⚑⚑⚑ Hampton Inn Airport-Pittsburgh H
(412) 264-0020. **$79-$149.** 8514 University Blvd. Business Rt SR 60, 0.5 mi n. Int corridors. **Pets:** Accepted.
☒ ⓛ ✆

⚑⚑ ⚑⚑⚑ Holiday Inn-Pittsburgh Airport H
(412) 262-3600. **$99-$299.** 8256 University Blvd. Business Rt SR 60, 1 mi n. Int corridors. **Pets:** Accepted.
SAVE ☒ ⓛ ⓛ ✆ ▯ ⇝

⚑⚑ La Quinta Inn Pittsburgh (Airport) H ✿
(412) 269-0400. **$69-$119.** 8507 University Blvd. 1 mi n of Business Rt SR 60. Int corridors. **Pets:** Medium, other species. Service with restrictions, supervision.
ASK ☒ ⓛ ⓛ ✆

CRANBERRY TOWNSHIP

⚑⚑⚑ Holiday Inn Express H
(724) 772-1000. **Call for rates.** 20003 Rt 19. I-76 (Pennsylvania Tpke), exit 28, jct US 19 and I-76 (Pennsylvania Tpke); I-79, exit 76 northbound; exit 78 southbound, just s. Int corridors. **Pets:** Accepted.
☒ ⓛ ✆

⚑⚑⚑ Pittsburgh Marriott North H
(724) 772-3700. **$206-$252.** 100 Cranberry Woods Dr. I-79, exit 78 (SR 228) to Cranberry Woods Dr. Int corridors. **Pets:** Small. $75 one-time fee/room. Designated rooms, service with restrictions, crate.
☒ ⓛ ⓛ ✆ ▯ ⇝

⚑⚑ Red Roof Inn-Cranberry Township-Pittsburgh North #7079 M
(724) 776-5670. **$80-$98.** 20009 Rt 19. I-76 (Pennsylvania Tpke), exit 28; I-79, exit 76 northbound; exit 78 southbound. Ext corridors. **Pets:** Medium. Service with restrictions, supervision.
☒ ⓛ

⚑⚑⚑ Residence Inn Cranberry H
(724) 779-1000. **$143-$175.** 1308 Freedom Rd. I-76 (Pennsylvania Tpke), exit 28, 0.5 mi n on US 19, then 0.3 mi w; I-79, exit 78 southbound, 0.5 mi w. Int corridors. **Pets:** Accepted.
☒ ⓛ ✆ ⇝ ☒

DELMONT

▼▼ Super 8 M
(724) 468-4888. **Call for rates.** 180 Sheffield Dr. SR 66, just s of US 22. Int corridors. **Pets:** Other species. $10 one-time fee/pet. Service with restrictions, supervision.
⊠ 🐾M 🛏 💻

GIBSONIA

▼▼ Comfort Inn Gibsonia M
(724) 444-8700. **$69-$149.** 5137 Rt 8. I-76 (Pennsylvania Tpke), exit 39, just n. Ext corridors. **Pets:** Large, other species. $10 daily fee/pet. Service with restrictions, supervision.
ASK ⊠ 🛏 💻

GREEN TREE

▼▼▼ Hampton Inn Hotel Green Tree H
(412) 922-0100. **$114-$139.** 555 Trumbull Dr. I-279, exit 4A, northbound; exit 4B southbound, jct US 22 and 30, 1 mi nw via Mansfield Ave. Int corridors. **Pets:** Accepted.
⊠ 🛏 💻

▼▼ Quality Suites H
(412) 279-6300. **Call for rates.** 700 Mansfield Ave. I-279, exit 4A to jct US 22 and 30, 1.5 mi nw. Ext corridors. **Pets:** Accepted.
⊠ 🛏 💻 🏊 ⊠

⚠ ▼▼▼ The Radisson Hotel Pittsburgh/Green
Tree H ❀
(412) 922-8400. **$99-$359.** 101 Radisson Dr. I-279, exit 4A to jct US 22 and 30, 1.1 mi nw via Mansfield Ave. Int corridors. **Pets:** Other species. $100 deposit/room. Designated rooms, service with restrictions, supervision.
SAVE ⊠ 🐾M 🛏 💻 🍽 🏊 ⊠

MARS

▼▼ Comfort Inn Cranberry Township H
(724) 772-2700. **$74-$150.** 924 Sheraton Dr. I-76 (Pennsylvania Tpke), exit 28; I-79, exit 76 (US 19 N) northbound; exit 78 southbound, 0.5 mi s on US 19. Int corridors. **Pets:** Medium, dogs only. $10 one-time fee/pet. Designated rooms, service with restrictions, supervision.
ASK ⊠ 🛏 💻

MONACA

▼▼▼ Hampton Inn Beaver Valley/Pittsburgh H
(724) 774-5580. **$104-$124.** 202 Fairview Dr. SR 60, exit 12, just n. Int corridors. **Pets:** Medium, other species. Service with restrictions, supervision.
⊠ 🐾M 🛏 💻 🏊

▼▼▼ Holiday Inn Express Hotel & Suites-Center
Township H
(724) 728-5121. **$109.** 105 Stone Quarry Rd. SR 60, exit 12, just n. Int corridors. **Pets:** Accepted.
⊠ 🛏 💻 🏊

▼▼ The Inn H
(724) 728-9270. **$79-$99.** 1523 Old Brodhead Rd. SR 60, exit 12, 1 mi e. Int corridors. **Pets:** Small. $30 daily fee/room. Service with restrictions, supervision.
ASK ⊠ 🛏 💻

MONROEVILLE

▼▼▼ Comfort Inn Pittsburgh East H
(412) 244-1600. **$79-$159.** 699 Rodi Rd. I-376, exit 11, just n. Int corridors. **Pets:** Accepted.
ASK ⊠ 🛏 💻 🍽 🏊

▼▼ Days Inn-Monroeville M
(412) 856-1610. **$48-$99.** 2727 Mosside Blvd. I-76 (Pennsylvania Tpke), exit 57; I-376, exit 14A, 1 mi s on SR 48. Ext corridors. **Pets:** Dogs only. $10 daily fee/room. Service with restrictions, crate.
ASK ⊠ 🛏

▼▼ Extended StayAmerica-Pittsburgh-Monroeville H
(412) 856-8400. **$75-$97.** 3851 Northern Pike. I-76 (Pennsylvania Tpke), exit 57 (Monroeville), 1.2 mi w on Business Rt 22. Int corridors. **Pets:** Other species. $25 daily fee/pet. Service with restrictions, crate.
ASK ⊠ 🛏 💻

▼▼▼ Hampton Inn Monroeville/Pittsburgh H
(412) 380-4000. **$109-$139.** 3000 Mosside Blvd. I-76 (Pennsylvania Tpke), exit 57; I-376, exit 14A, 0.3 mi s on SR 48. Int corridors. **Pets:** Accepted.
⊠ 🛏 💻 🏊

⚠ ▼▼ Red Roof Inn-Monroeville #7174 M
(412) 856-4738. **$75-$86.** 2729 Mosside Blvd. I-76 (Pennsylvania Tpke), exit 57; I-376, exit 14A, 0.8 mi s on SR 48. Ext corridors. **Pets:** Service with restrictions, supervision.
SAVE ⊠ 🛏

▼▼ Super 8 Pittsburgh/Monroeville M ❀
(724) 733-8008. **$60-$130.** 1807 Rt 286. I-76 (Pennsylvania Tpke), exit 57; I-376, exit 14A, 2 mi e on US 22 E, then 2 mi e. Int corridors. **Pets:** Large, other species. $10 daily fee/pet. Service with restrictions, supervision.
ASK ⊠ 🛏

MOON RUN

▼▼ Extended Stay Deluxe Pittsburgh Airport H
(412) 490-0979. **$95-$105.** 200 Chauvet Dr. SR 60, exit 1, just s. Int corridors. **Pets:** Other species. $25 daily fee/pet. Service with restrictions, crate.
ASK ⊠ 🛏 💻 🏊

⚠ ▼▼▼ Four Points by Sheraton Pittsburgh
Airport H
(724) 695-0002. **$95-$205.** 1 Industry Ln. SR 60, exit 2 (Montour Run Rd). Int corridors. **Pets:** Medium. $50 one-time fee/room. Service with restrictions, supervision.
SAVE ⊠ 🛏 💻 🍽 🏊

⚠ ▼▼▼ Holiday Inn Express Pittsburgh Airport H
(412) 788-8400. **$89-$179.** 5311 Campbells Run Rd. US 22 and 30 W, exit SR 60 S (Crafton), just w. Int corridors. **Pets:** $15 daily fee/room. Service with restrictions, supervision.
SAVE ⊠ 🛏 💻 🏊

▼ Motel 6 Pittsburgh #657 M
(412) 922-9400. **$45-$55.** 211 Beecham Dr. I-79, exit 60A, just s on Steubenville Pike (SR 60), then e. Ext corridors. **Pets:** Other species. Service with restrictions, supervision.
⊠ 🐾M

⚠ ▼▼▼ Pittsburgh Airport Marriott H
(412) 788-8800. **$242-$296.** 777 Aten Rd. SR 60, exit 2 (Montour Run Rd). Int corridors. **Pets:** Accepted.
SAVE ⊠ 🛏 💻 🍽 🏊 ⊠

▼▼ Red Roof Inn South Airport #7030 M
(412) 787-7870. **$70-$90.** 6404 Steubenville Pike. I-79, exit 60A, 3.2 mi w on SR 60. Ext/int corridors. **Pets:** Accepted.
⊠ 🛏

▼▼▼ Residence Inn-Pittsburgh Airport H
(412) 787-3300. **$170-$208.** 1500 Park Lane Dr. SR 60, exit 2 (Montour Run Rd), just w on Cliff Mine Dr to Summit Park Dr, just s to Park Lane Dr, then just e. Int corridors. **Pets:** Accepted.
⊠ 🐾M 🛏 💻 🏊 ⊠

OAKDALE

Comfort Inn-Pittsburgh Airport ⊞
(412) 787-2600. **$85-$135.** 7011 Old Steubenville Pike. US 22 and 30, jct SR 60; 4 mi w of jct I-279 and 79. Ext/int corridors. **Pets:** Other species. $20 daily fee/pet. Designated rooms, service with restrictions, supervision.

PITTSBURGH

Hilton Pittsburgh ⊞
(412) 391-4600. **$99-$229.** 600 Commonwealth Pl. Jct I-279/376/SR 885; in Gateway Center. Int corridors. **Pets:** Accepted.

Omni William Penn Hotel ⊞
(412) 281-7100. **Call for rates.** 530 William Penn Pl. Jct 6th St and William Penn Pl. Int corridors. **Pets:** Small. $50 one-time fee/room. Service with restrictions, crate.

Residence Inn by Marriott Pittsburgh University/Medical Center ⊞ ❀
(412) 621-2200. **$224-$274.** 3896 Bigelow Blvd. On SR 380. Int corridors. **Pets:** Other species. $100 one-time fee/room. Service with restrictions, supervision.

Sheraton Station Square Hotel ⊞
(412) 261-2000. **Call for rates.** 300 W Station Square St. I-376, exit Grant St, south end of Smithfield St Bridge; across river. Int corridors. **Pets:** Accepted.

The Westin Convention Center Pittsburgh ⊞ ❀
(412) 281-3700. **$159-$335.** 1000 Penn Ave. Jct 10th St; at Liberty Center. Int corridors. **Pets:** Medium. Service with restrictions, crate.

WASHINGTON

Ramada Inn ⊞
(724) 225-9750. **$79-$135.** 1170 W Chestnut St. I-70, exit 15, 0.5 mi e on US 40. Ext/int corridors. **Pets:** Small. $35 one-time fee/room. Designated rooms, service with restrictions, crate.

Red Roof Inn #7048 Ⓜ
(724) 228-5750. **$54-$80.** 1399 W Chestnut St. I-70, exit 15, just e on US 40. Ext/int corridors. **Pets:** Medium. Service with restrictions, supervision.

WEST MIFFLIN

Extended StayAmerica-Pittsburgh-West Mifflin ⊞
(412) 650-9096. **$83-$98.** 1303 Lebanon Church Rd. 0.5 mi e of jct SR 51. Int corridors. **Pets:** Other species. $25 daily fee/pet. Service with restrictions, crate.

Holiday Inn Express Hotel & Suites ⊞
(412) 469-1900. **$125-$175.** 3122 Lebanon Church Rd. 1.5 mi e of jct SR 51. Int corridors. **Pets:** Large. $10 daily fee/pet. Service with restrictions, supervision.

END METROPOLITAN AREA

PITTSTON

Knights Inn-Scranton/Pittston Ⓜ
(570) 654-6020. **$45-$85.** 310 SR 315. I-81, exit 175 northbound, just s on SR 315; exit 175A southbound; I-476 (Northeast Extension Pennsylvania Tpke), exit 115. Ext corridors. **Pets:** Small, other species. Service with restrictions, supervision.

POCONO MOUNTAINS AREA

BLAKESLEE

Best Western Inn-Blakeslee/Pocono ⊞
(570) 646-6000. **$85-$175.** New Ventures Business Park. I-80, exit 284, just n. Int corridors. **Pets:** $50 deposit/room. Service with restrictions, crate.

EAST STROUDSBURG

Budget Inn & Suites ⊞
(570) 424-5451. **$67-$106, 3 day notice.** I-80, exit 308. I-80, exit 308, just se on Greentree Rd. Ext/int corridors. **Pets:** Large. Designated rooms, service with restrictions, supervision.

Super 8 Ⓜ
(570) 424-7411. **$58-$168.** 340 Greentree Dr. I-80, exit 308, just se. Int corridors. **Pets:** $100 deposit/room, $10 daily fee/pet. Designated rooms, service with restrictions, supervision.

HAMLIN

Comfort Inn ⊞
(570) 689-4148. **$79-$169.** 117 Twin Rocks Rd. I-84, exit 17, just n on SR 191. Int corridors. **Pets:** Other species. $15 daily fee/pet. Designated rooms, service with restrictions, supervision.

MARSHALLS CREEK

Value Inn Ⓜ
(570) 588-1100. **$45-$129.** 5219 Milford Rd, Rt 209. I-80, exit 309, 7.9 mi n on SR 209. Ext corridors. **Pets:** Small. $25 daily fee/pet. Designated rooms, service with restrictions, supervision.

MATAMORAS

Best Western Inn at Hunt's Landing ⊞
(570) 491-2400. **$90-$170.** 120 Rt 6 & 209. I-84, exit 53. Int corridors. **Pets:** Other species. $10 daily fee/pet. Designated rooms, service with restrictions, supervision.

MILFORD

♦♦♦♦ Cliff Park Inn Restaurant & Golf Course **CI** ❧
(570) 296-6491. **$150-$289, 14 day notice.** 155 Cliff Park Rd. I-84, exit
46, 2 mi e on US 6, just s on 6th St, 1.5 mi w on SR 2001, then 0.5 mi s.
Int corridors. **Pets:** Large, other species. $75 one-time fee/room. Desig-
nated rooms, service with restrictions.
[ASK] [X] [⟆]

♦♦♦♦ Hotel Fauchere **H** ❧
(570) 409-1212. **Call for rates.** 401 Broad St. Downtown; in historic
Milford. Int corridors. **Pets:** Large. $25 daily fee/pet. Designated rooms,
service with restrictions, crate.
[X] [⟆]

♦♦ Milford Motel **M** ❧
(570) 296-6411. **$45-$110, 3 day notice.** 591 Rt 6 & 209. US 6 and 209
N, 0.7 mi e. Ext corridors. **Pets:** Large, dogs only. $5 daily fee/pet. Desig-
nated rooms, service with restrictions, supervision.
[SAVE] [X] [🖥]

♦♦♦ Red Carpet Inn-Milford **M**
(570) 296-9444. **$55-$125, 7 day notice.** 106 Red Carpet Dr. I-84, exit
46, just s. Ext corridors. **Pets:** Medium. $10 daily fee/pet. Designated
rooms, no service, supervision.
[SAVE] [X] [🖥]

♦♦♦ Scottish Inns **M**
(570) 491-4414. **$50-$110.** 274 Rt 6 & 209. I-84, exit 53, 1 mi s. Ext
corridors. **Pets:** Accepted.
[SAVE] [X] [🖥] [🖥]

STARLIGHT

♦♦♦ The Inn at Starlight Lake **CI**
(570) 798-2519. **$115-$195, 14 day notice.** 289 Starlight Lake Rd. Off
SR 370, 1 mi n, follow signs. Ext/int corridors. **Pets:** Other species. $10
daily fee/room. Designated rooms, supervision.
[ASK] [X] [⟆] [X] [🎿] [W] [Z]

END AREA

PUNXSUTAWNEY

♦♦ Pantall Hotel **H**
(814) 938-6600. **$54-$99.** 135 E Mahoning St. On US 119/SR 36; downtown. Int corridors. **Pets:** $25 one-time fee/pet. Designated rooms, service
with restrictions, supervision.
[ASK] [X] [🖥] [⟆]

READING

♦♦ Quality Inn Airport **H**
(610) 736-0400. **$55-$150.** 2017 Bernville Rd. US 222, exit SR 183, 2 mi
s. Int corridors. **Pets:** Small, other species. $15 daily fee/pet. Designated
rooms, service with restrictions, supervision.
[ASK] [X] [🖥] [🖥]

ST. MARYS

♦♦ Comfort Inn **H**
(814) 834-2030. **Call for rates.** 195 Comfort Ln. 1.8 mi s of center on SR
255, just w. Int corridors. **Pets:** Other species. $15 daily fee/pet. Service
with restrictions, supervision.
[X] [🖥] [🖥] [⟆]

SAYRE

♦♦♦ Best Western Grand Victorian **H**
(570) 888-7711. **$119-$139.** 255 Spring St. SR 17, exit 61, just s. Int
corridors. **Pets:** Other species. $10 daily fee/pet. Service with restrictions.
[SAVE] [X] [🖥] [🖥] [⟆] [⟆] [X]

SCRANTON

♦♦ Clarion Hotel **H**
(570) 344-9811. **$79-$139.** 300 Meadow Ave. I-81, exit 184, just w. Int
corridors. **Pets:** Other species. $25 daily fee/room. Service with restrictions,
supervision.
[ASK] [X] [🖥] [🖥] [⟆] [⟆] [X]

♦♦♦ Hilton Scranton & Conference Center **H**
(570) 343-3000. **$99-$259.** 100 Adams Ave. I-81, exit 185, just w of jct
Lackawanna Ave, Jefferson Ave and Spruce St; downtown. Int corridors.
Pets: Accepted.
[X] [ᎭM] [🖥] [🖥] [⟆] [⟆]

SELINSGROVE

♦♦♦ Country Hearth Inn **H**
(570) 374-8880. **$79-$179.** 613 N Susquehanna Tr. On US 11 and 15, just
n of jct US 522. Int corridors. **Pets:** Medium, other species. $25 daily
fee/room. Designated rooms, service with restrictions, crate.
[SAVE] [X] [🖥] [🖥] [⟆] [⟆]

SHAMOKIN DAM

♦♦ Econo Lodge Inn & Suites **H**
(570) 743-1111. **$59-$169.** 3249 N Susquehanna Tr. US 11 and 15; just n
of jct SR 61. Ext corridors. **Pets:** Small, other species. $10 daily fee/pet.
Designated rooms, service with restrictions, supervision.
[ASK] [X] [🖥] [🖥] [⟆] [⟆]

♦♦♦ Hampton Inn **H** ❧
(570) 743-2223. **$119-$169.** 3 Stettler Ave. US 11 and 15, 1 mi s of jct SR
61. Int corridors. **Pets:** Other species. $25 one-time fee/room. Service with
restrictions, supervision.
[SAVE] [X] [ᎭM] [🖥] [🖥] [⟆]

SHICKSHINNY

♦♦ The Blue Heron Bed & Breakfast **BB**
(570) 864-3740. **$60-$90 (no credit cards), 7 day notice.** 1270 Bethel
Hill Rd. Jct US 11, 6.2 mi n on SR 239, then 2 mi n on CR 4016
(Harveyville/Bethel Hill Rd). Int corridors. **Pets:** Accepted.
[X] [W]

SHIPPENSBURG

♦♦♦ Best Western Shippensburg Hotel **H**
(717) 532-5200. **$55-$129.** 125 Walnut Bottom Rd. I-81, exit 29, 0.5 mi w
on SR 174. Int corridors. **Pets:** Medium, other species. $10 daily fee/pet.
Service with restrictions, supervision.
[SAVE] [X] [🖥] [🖥] [⟆] [X]

SOUTH WILLIAMSPORT

♦♦♦ Quality Inn Williamsport **H**
(570) 323-9801. **$59-$219.** 234 US Hwy 15. 0.8 mi s on US 15. Ext/int
corridors. **Pets:** Accepted.
[SAVE] [X] [🖥] [🖥] [⟆]

♦♦♦ Ridgemont Motel **M**
(570) 321-5300. **$49-$59.** 637 Rt 15 Hwy. 1.2 mi s on US 15. Ext corridors.
Pets: Accepted.
[SAVE] [X] [🖥] [🖥]

STATE COLLEGE

◆◆◆ The Autoport Motel & Restaurant 🅷
(814) 237-7666. **$72-$171.** 1405 S Atherton St. US 322 business route, 1.4 mi e of jct SR 26. Ext/int corridors. **Pets:** Accepted.

ASK ☒ 🛢 💻 🍽 🏊

◆◆◆ ◆◆◆ Days Inn Penn State 🅷
(814) 238-8454. **$69-$129.** 240 S Pugh St. Just e of SR 26 northbound; 0.4 mi n of jct US 322 business route; downtown. Int corridors. **Pets:** Other species. $10 daily fee/room. Designated rooms, service with restrictions, supervision.

SAVE ☒ 🛢 💻 🍽 🏊

◆◆◆ ◆ Nittany Budget Motel Ⓜ
(814) 238-0015. **$42-$195.** 2070 Cato Ave. SR 26, 2.6 mi s of jct US 322 business route. Ext corridors. **Pets:** Other species. $5 daily fee/pet. Service with restrictions, supervision.

SAVE ☒ 🛢

◆◆◆ ◆◆◆ Quality Inn Ⓜ
(814) 234-1600. **Call for rates.** 1274 N Atherton St. US 322 business route, 1 mi w of jct SR 26. Int corridors. **Pets:** Other species. Service with restrictions, supervision.

SAVE ☒ 🅼 🛢

◆◆◆◆ Residence Inn by Marriott 🅷
(814) 235-6960. **$129-$139.** 1555 University Dr. US 322 business route, 1.5 mi e of jct SR 26. Int corridors. **Pets:** Other species. $75 one-time fee/room.

☒ 🛢 💻 🏊 🏋

◆◆◆ ◆◆◆ Super 8 State College 🅷
(814) 237-8005. **$61-$99, 14 day notice.** 1663 S Atherton St. US 322 business route, 1.6 mi e of jct SR 26. Int corridors. **Pets:** $25 one-time fee/room. Service with restrictions, supervision.

SAVE ☒ 🛢 💻 🏋

◆◆◆ ◆◆◆◆ Toftrees Golf Resort & Conference Center 🅷
(814) 234-8000. **$69-$399.** One Country Club Ln. US 322 business route, exit Toftrees/Woodcrest, 0.7 mi ne; 4 mi w of jct SR 26. Int corridors. **Pets:** Accepted.

SAVE ☒ 🛢 💻 🍽 🏊 🏋

TOWN HILL

◆ Days Inn Breezewood 🅷
(814) 735-3860. **$53-$68, 3 day notice.** 9648 Old Rt 126. I-70, exit 156, just n. Int corridors. **Pets:** Accepted.

ASK ☒ 🛢 💻 🍽

WARREN

◆◆◆ ◆◆◆◆ Holiday Inn of Warren 🅷
(814) 726-3000. **$114.** 210 Ludlow St. Jct US 6, just n on Ludlow St (US 62 N). Int corridors. **Pets:** Accepted.

SAVE ☒ 🛢 💻 🍽 🏊

◆◆ ◆◆ Warren Super 8 🅷
(814) 723-8881. **$81-$82.** 204 Struthers St. 1.5 mi w on US 6, exit Ludlow St, w on Allegheny, then s. Ext/int corridors. **Pets:** Accepted.

ASK ☒ 🛢 💻

WAYNESBURG

◆◆◆ ◆ Econo Lodge Ⓜ
(724) 627-5544. **$69-$75.** 126 Miller Ln. I-79, exit 14, just w. Ext corridors. **Pets:** Accepted.

SAVE ☒ 🛢 💻

WELLSBORO

◆◆◆ ◆◆◆ Penn Wells Lodge Ⓜ
(570) 724-3463. **$60-$127.** 4 Main St. Just n on US 6 and SR 287. Ext/int corridors. **Pets:** $20 daily fee/room. Designated rooms, service with restrictions, supervision.

SAVE ☒ 🛢 💻 🏊 🏋

WEST HAZLETON

◆◆◆ ◆◆◆◆ Comfort Inn Hazleton/West Hazleton 🅷 🐾
(570) 455-9300. **$79-$169.** 58 SR 93. I-81, exit 145, 0.3 mi se; I-80, exit 256, 3.8 mi se. Int corridors. **Pets:** Other species. $10 daily fee/pet. Service with restrictions.

SAVE ☒ 🛢 💻 🍽

WEST MIDDLESEX

◆◆◆ ◆◆◆ Super 8-West Middlesex/Sharon 🅷
(724) 528-3888. **$59-$131.** 3369 New Castle Rd. I-80, exit 4B (SR 60), just w to SR 18, then just s. Int corridors. **Pets:** Small, other species. $15 daily fee/pet. Designated rooms, service with restrictions, supervision.

ASK ☒ 🛢 💻

WILKES-BARRE

◆◆◆ ◆◆◆ Best Western Genetti Hotel & Conference Center 🅷
(570) 823-6152. **$80-$110.** 77 E Market St. Jct Washington St; downtown. Int corridors. **Pets:** Accepted.

SAVE ☒ 🛢 💻 🍽 🏊

◆◆◆ ◆◆◆ Days Inn 🅷
(570) 826-0111. **$50-$175, 14 day notice.** 760 Kidder St. I-81, exit 170B, to exit 1 (SR 309 S business route), just w; I-76 (Pennsylvania Tpke), exit 105 to exit 1 (SR 115 N). Int corridors. **Pets:** Accepted.

SAVE ☒ 🛢

◆◆◆ ◆◆ Econo Lodge Arena 🅷 🐾
(570) 823-0600. **$59-$179, 3 day notice.** 1075 Wilkes-Barre Township Blvd. I-81, exit 165 southbound; exit 165B northbound, on SR 309 business route. Int corridors. **Pets:** Large, other species. $50 deposit/room, $10 daily fee/pet. Designated rooms, service with restrictions, supervision.

SAVE ☒ 🛢 💻

◆◆◆◆ Extended Stay Deluxe Wilkes Barre-Hwy 315 🅷
(570) 970-2500. **$84-$199.** 1067 PlainsTownship Blvd. I-81, exit 170B, 0.3 mi n. Int corridors. **Pets:** Other species. $25 daily fee/pet. Service with restrictions, crate.

ASK ☒ 🅼 🛢 💻

◆◆◆◆ Host Inn All Suites Hotel 🅷
(570) 270-4678. **Call for rates.** 860 Kidder St. I-81, exit 170B to exit 1 (SR 309 S business route) off expressway, then 0.5 mi w. Int corridors. **Pets:** Accepted.

☒ 🅼 🛢 💻 🏊

◆◆◆ ◆◆ Red Roof Inn #7139 Ⓜ
(570) 829-6422. **$66-$100.** 1035 Hwy 315. I-81, exit 170B, jct SR 115, 0.7 mi w, exit 1 (SR 309 S business route) to SR 315, then just n. Ext corridors. **Pets:** Accepted.

SAVE ☒ 🛢

◆◆◆◆ The Woodlands Inn & Resort 🅷 🐾
(570) 824-9831. **$119-$199.** 1073 Hwy 315. I-81, exit 170B to exit 1 (SR 309 S business route), then 0.3 mi n. Int corridors. **Pets:** $50 one-time fee/room. Service with restrictions, crate.

ASK ☒ 🛢 💻 🍽 🏊 🏋

WILLIAMSPORT

Best Western Williamsport Inn [H]
(570) 326-1981. **$69-$140.** 1840 E 3rd St. I-180, exit 25 (Faxon St), just e; 1 mi w of W 3rd St. Ext corridors. **Pets:** Accepted.

Candlewood Suites [H]
(570) 601-9100. **$89-$259, 14 day notice.** 1836 E 3rd St. I-180, exit 25 (Faxon St), 0.5 mi e. Int corridors. **Pets:** Accepted.

Genetti Hotel & Suites [H]
(570) 326-6600. **$80-$255, 7 day notice.** 200 W 4th St. Jct William St; downtown. Ext/int corridors. **Pets:** Accepted.

Holiday Inn Downtown Williamsport [H]
(570) 327-8231. **$99-$159.** 100 Pine St. Jct US 220 and SR 15 S; downtown. Int corridors. **Pets:** Accepted.

WIND GAP

Red Carpet Inn [M]
(610) 863-7782. **Call for rates.** 1395 Jacobsburg Rd. SR 33, exit Wind Gap/Bath SR 512 S, just s on Jacobsburg Rd, follow signs. Ext/int corridors. **Pets:** Small. $20 daily fee/pet. Service with restrictions, supervision.

WYOMISSING

Econo Lodge Inn and Suites [H]
(610) 378-5105. **$69-$140, 3 day notice.** 635 Spring St. Just off US 422, exit Papermill Rd. Int corridors. **Pets:** Small. $15 daily fee/pet. Service with restrictions, supervision.

Homewood Suites-Reading/Wyomissing [H]
(610) 736-3100. **$139-$194.** 2801 Papermill Rd. US 422, exit Papermill Rd, 1.8 mi nw; US 222, exit Spring Ridge Rd. Int corridors. **Pets:** Accepted.

The Inn at Reading [H]
(610) 372-7811. **$99-$149.** 1040 Park Rd. US 222, exit N Wyomissing Blvd, just n, then 0.3 mi e. Int corridors. **Pets:** Small. $10 daily fee/room. Designated rooms, service with restrictions, supervision.

Reading Crowne Hotel [H]
(610) 376-3811. **$259.** 1741 W Papermill Rd. US 422, exit Papermill Rd. Int corridors. **Pets:** Accepted.

WYSOX

Comfort Inn [H]
(570) 265-5691. **$115-$139.** US 6. On US 6; center. Int corridors. **Pets:** Other species. $25 one-time fee/room. Service with restrictions, supervision.

YORK

Budget Host Inn [M]
(717) 755-1068. **$54-$65.** 1162 Haines Rd. I-83, exit 18, just e on SR 124. Ext corridors. **Pets:** Dogs only. $25 deposit/pet. Service with restrictions, supervision.

Comfort Inn Corporate Gateway [H] ❖
(717) 699-1919. **$109-$169.** 2250 N George St. I-83, exit 22, just n. Int corridors. **Pets:** Medium, other species. $50 daily fee/pet. Designated rooms, service with restrictions, crate.

Holiday Inn Conference Center of York [H]
(717) 846-9500. **Call for rates.** 2000 Loucks Rd. I-83, exit 21B northbound, 2.5 mi w on US 30, then just n; exit 22 southbound, 0.5 mi s on SR 181, 2.2 mi w on US 30, then just n. Int corridors. **Pets:** Accepted.

Holiday Inn Express [H] 🐾
(717) 741-1000. **$100-$200.** 140 Leader Heights Rd. I-83, exit 14, just w on SR 182. Int corridors. **Pets:** Other species. $50 one-time fee/room. No service, supervision.

Red Roof Inn #315 [H]
(717) 843-8181. **Call for rates.** 125 Arsenal Rd. I-83, exit 21B northbound, 0.3 mi w on US 30; exit 21 southbound, 0.5 mi s on SR 181 to US 30. Int corridors. **Pets:** Medium. Service with restrictions, supervision.

The Yorktowne Hotel [H]
(717) 848-1111. **$149-$350.** 48 E Market St. SR 462 eastbound and I-83 business route, just e of square, follow signs. Int corridors. **Pets:** Accepted.

RHODE ISLAND

CITY INDEX

EAST PROVIDENCE

▼▼ Extended StayAmerica Providence-East Providence 🅷
(401) 272-1661. **$84-$139.** 1000 Warren Ave. I-195, exit 8 eastbound, just e; exit 6 westbound, 1.1 mi e via Warren Ave. Int corridors. **Pets:** Other species. $25 daily fee/pet. Service with restrictions, crate.
ⒶⓈⓀ ⊠ 🕭 🔋 🖵

MIDDLETOWN

▼ Econo Lodge 🅼
(401) 849-2718. **$45-$210.** 1359 W Main Rd. On SR 114, just n of jct SR 214. Int corridors. **Pets:** Other species. $100 deposit/room, $15 daily fee/ pet. Designated rooms, service with restrictions, supervision.
ⒶⓈⓀ ⊠ 🔋

▼▼▼ Howard Johnson Inn-Newport 🅷 🐾
(401) 849-2000. **$49-$254.** 351 W Main Rd. On SR 114, 0.3 mi s of jct SR 138. Int corridors. **Pets:** Other species. $10 daily fee/pet. Designated rooms, service with restrictions, supervision.
ⓈⒶⓋⒺ ⊠ 🕭 🔋 🖵 🍴 ⊷ ⊠

▼▼▼ Residence Inn by Marriott-Newport/Middletown 🅷 🐾
(401) 845-2005. **$119-$275, 3 day notice.** 325 W Main Rd. On SR 114, 0.3 mi s of jct SR 138. Int corridors. **Pets:** Other species. $100 one-time fee/room. Designated rooms, service with restrictions.
ⓈⒶⓋⒺ ⊠ 🕭 🔋 🖵 ⊷ ⊠

NEWPORT

▼▼▼ Beech Tree Inn 🅱🅱
(401) 847-9794. **$125-$350, 14 day notice.** 34 Rhode Island Ave. Just e of SR 114; 0.8 mi s of jct SR 138. Int corridors. **Pets:** Other species. $25 daily fee/room. No service.
ⓈⒶⓋⒺ ⊠ 🔋

▼▼▼ The Burbank Rose 🅱🅱
(401) 849-9457. **$89-$240, 7 day notice.** 111 Memorial Blvd W. Just e on SR 138A. Int corridors. **Pets:** Medium. $15 one-time fee/room. Designated rooms, no service, crate.
ⓈⒶⓋⒺ ⊠ 🔋 🖵 🇿

▼▼▼ The Hotel Viking 🅷
(401) 847-3300. **$109-$499, 7 day notice.** One Bellevue Ave. Corner of Kay and Church sts and Bellevue Ave. Int corridors. **Pets:** Accepted.
ⓈⒶⓋⒺ ⊠ 🔋 🖵 🍴 ⊷ ⊠

▼▼▼ Hyatt Regency Newport Hotel & Spa 🅷
(401) 851-1234. **$109-$449, 3 day notice.** 1 Goat Island. 0.8 mi w of America's Cup Ave, follow signs to Goat Island. Int corridors. **Pets:** $75 one-time fee/room. Designated rooms, service with restrictions.
ⓈⒶⓋⒺ ⊠ 🕭 🔋 🖵 🍴 ⊷ ⊠

NORTH KINGSTOWN

▼▼ Hamilton Village Inn 🅼
(401) 295-0700. **$79-$139, 7 day notice.** 642 Boston Neck Rd. SR 1A, 1.3 mi s of jct SR 102. Ext corridors. **Pets:** Other species. Designated rooms, service with restrictions, supervision.
⊠ 🔋 🖵 🍴

PROVIDENCE

▼▼▼ Hilton Providence 🅷
(401) 831-3900. **$119-$379.** 21 Atwells Ave. I-95, exit 21. Int corridors. **Pets:** Accepted.
⊠ 🔋 🖵 🍴 ⊷

▼▼▼ The Hotel Providence 🅷
(401) 861-8000. **Call for rates.** 311 Westminster St. I-95, exit 22A, 0.5 mi se on Memorial Blvd, then 0.3 mi sw; entrance on Mathewson St. Int corridors. **Pets:** Accepted.
ⓈⒶⓋⒺ ⊠ 🔋 🖵 🍴

▼▼▼ Marriott Providence Downtown 🅷 🐾
(401) 272-2400. **$209-$259.** One Orms St. I-95, exit 23 to state offices. Int corridors. **Pets:** Other species. $49 one-time fee/room. Designated rooms, service with restrictions, supervision.
ⓈⒶⓋⒺ ⊠ 🕭 🔋 🖵 🍴 ⊷

▼▼▼ The Westin Providence 🅷 🐾
(401) 598-8000. **$149-$509.** One W Exchange St. I-95, exit 22A; downtown. Int corridors. **Pets:** Medium, dogs only. $75 one-time fee/room. Service with restrictions, supervision.
ⓈⒶⓋⒺ ⊠ 🕭 🔋 🖵 🍴 ⊷ ⊠

WAKEFIELD

▼▼▼ The Kings' Rose Inn 🅱🅱 🐾
(401) 783-5222. **$150-$175, 7 day notice.** 1747 Mooresfield Rd (SR 138). I-95, exit 3A, 11 mi e on SR 138; 3.3 mi w of US 1. Int corridors. **Pets:** No service, supervision.
⊠

WARWICK

▼▼▼ Best Western Airport Inn 🅷
(401) 737-7400. **$99-$119.** 2138 Post Rd. I-95, exit 13, e to US 1, then just ne. Int corridors. **Pets:** Accepted.
ⓈⒶⓋⒺ ⊠ 🔋 🖵

▼▼▼ Crowne Plaza Hotel at the Crossings 🅷
(401) 732-6000. **$109-$159.** 801 Greenwich Ave. I-95, exit 12A southbound; exit 12 northbound, 0.3 mi se on SR 5. Int corridors. **Pets:** Accepted.
ⒶⓈⓀ ⊠ 🕭 🔋 🖵 🍴 ⊷ ⊠

▼▼ Extended StayAmerica Providence-Airport-Warwick 🅷
(401) 732-2547. **$74-$114.** 245 W Natick Rd. I-295, exit 2 northbound, just sw; exit 3A southbound, 1.1 mi e on SR 37, 2 mi s on SR 2, then just sw. Int corridors. **Pets:** Other species. $25 daily fee/pet. Service with restrictions, crate.
ⒶⓈⓀ ⊠ 🕭 🔋 🖵

▼▼▼ Hampton Inn & Suites Providence-Warwick Airport 🅷
(401) 739-8888. **$105-$175.** 2100 Post Rd. I-95, exit 13, e to US 1, then just n. Int corridors. **Pets:** Large. Service with restrictions, supervision.
ⓈⒶⓋⒺ ⊠ 🕭 🔋 🖵 ⊷

▼▼▼ Holiday Inn Express Hotel & Suites 🅷
(401) 736-5000. **$79-$159.** 901 Jefferson Blvd. I-95, exit 13, 0.4 mi on Airport Connector Rd, then exit Jefferson Blvd. Int corridors. **Pets:** Accepted.
ⒶⓈⓀ ⊠ 🕭 🔋 🖵 ⊷

 Homestead Studio Suites
Hotel-Providence/Airport/Warwick **H**
(401) 732-6667. **$84-$134.** 268 Metro Center Blvd. I-95, exit 12A, 0.4 mi e on SR 113, 0.4 mi n on SR 5, then 0.4 mi e. Int corridors. **Pets:** Other species. $25 daily fee/pet. Service with restrictions, crate.

La Quinta Inn & Suites **H** ❀
(401) 941-6600. **$65-$159.** 36 Jefferson Blvd. I-95, exit 15, just se. Int corridors. **Pets:** Medium, other species. Service with restrictions, supervision.

Residence Inn by Marriott **H**
(401) 737-7100. **$159-$169.** 500 Kilvert St. I-95, exit 13 to Jefferson Blvd, 0.4 mi n, then 0.6 mi w. Ext corridors. **Pets:** Accepted.

Sheraton Providence Airport Hotel **H** ❀
(401) 738-4000. **$99-$269.** 1850 Post Rd. I-95, exit 13, 0.6 mi n on US 1. Int corridors. **Pets:** Large. $30 deposit/pet. Service with restrictions, crate.

WEST GREENWICH

Residence Inn by Marriott Providence / Coventry **H**
(401) 828-1170. **$140-$200.** 755 Center of New England Blvd. I-95, exit 7, just ne; Center of New England Plaza. Int corridors. **Pets:** Accepted.

WEST WARWICK

Extended StayAmerica Providence-Airport-West Warwick **H**
(401) 885-3161. **$74-$114.** 1235 Division Rd. I-95, exit 8A northbound, just s on SR 2, then just w; exit 8 southbound, just s on SR 2, then just w. Int corridors. **Pets:** Other species. $25 daily fee/pet. Service with restrictions, crate.

WYOMING

Stagecoach House Inn **BB**
(401) 539-9600. **$100-$199.** 1136 Main St (SR 138). I-95, exit 3B northbound, 0.7 mi nw; exit southbound, 0.4 mi nw. Ext/int corridors. **Pets:** $25 one-time fee/room. Designated rooms, service with restrictions, supervision.

SOUTH CAROLINA

CITY INDEX

AIKEN

▼▼▼▼ Holiday Inn Express M
(803) 648-0999. **$81-$275.** 155 Colony Pkwy/Whiskey Rd. Jct US 1/78 and SR 19, 1.8 mi s on SR 19. Ext corridors. **Pets:** Large, other species. $45 one-time fee/room. Service with restrictions, crate.

(ASK) ⊠ 🛢 🖵 🛥 ⊠

▼▼▼ Quality Inn & Suites M
(803) 641-1100. **$55-$80.** 3608 Richland Ave W. Jct US 1/78 and SR 19, 2.9 mi w on US 1/78. Ext corridors. **Pets:** Large. $12 daily fee/pet. Service with restrictions, supervision.

(SAVE) ⊠ 🛢 🖵 🛥

▼▼ Super 8-Aiken H
(803) 641-8800. **$72-$270.** 2577 Whiskey Rd. Jct US 78 and SR 302/19 (Whiskey Rd), 1.7 mi s on SR 19. Int corridors. **Pets:** Accepted.

(ASK) ⊠ 🛢 🖵 🛥

ANDERSON

▼▼▼▼ Country Inn & Suites H
(864) 622-2200. **$90-$180.** 116 Interstate Blvd. I-85, exit 19B, just n, then just se. Int corridors. **Pets:** Small. $25 daily fee/pet. Designated rooms, service with restrictions, supervision.

(ASK) ⊠ 🛢ᴹ 🛢 🖵 🛥

▼▼ Days Inn M
(864) 375-0375. **$63-$150.** 1007 Smith Mill Rd. I-85, exit 19A, just se. Ext corridors. **Pets:** Accepted.

(ASK) ⊠ 🛢ᴹ 🛢 🖵 🛥

▼▼▼ Holiday Inn Express H
(864) 231-0231. **$75-$189.** 410 Alliance Pkwy. I-85, exit 27, just s on SR 81. Int corridors. **Pets:** Small, dogs only. $5 daily fee/pet, $25 one-time fee/room. Service with restrictions, supervision.

(SAVE) ⊠ 🛢ᴹ 🛢 🖵 🛥

▼▼ Jameson Inn M
(864) 375-9800. **$78-$85.** 128 Interstate Blvd. I-85, exit 19B, just n, then just se. Int corridors. **Pets:** Accepted.

(ASK) ⊠ 🛢ᴹ 🛢 🖵 🛥

▼▼ La Quinta Inn Anderson M 🐾
(864) 225-3721. **$49-$99.** 3430 Clemson Blvd. I-85, exit 19A, 2.9 mi se on US 76/SR 28; exit 21 southbound, 2.6 mi s on US 178. Ext corridors. **Pets:** Medium, other species. Service with restrictions, supervision.

(ASK) ⊠ 🛢 🖵 🛥

▼▼▼ Mainstay Suites H
(864) 226-1112. **Call for rates.** 151 Civic Center Blvd. I-85, exit 19A, 2.2 mi se on US 76, then 0.6 mi s. Int corridors. **Pets:** Accepted.

⊠ 🛢 🖵 🛥

BENNETTSVILLE

▲▲▲ ▼▼▼ Best Western Bennettsville M
(843) 479-1700. **$70-$139.** 213 US Hwy 15 & 401 Bypass E. 0.6 mi s of center, just ne on US 15/401/SR 9. Ext corridors. **Pets:** Large. $25 daily fee/room. Service with restrictions, supervision.

(SAVE) ⊠ 🛢 🖵 🛥

BLUFFTON

▼▼▼ Holiday Inn Express Hotel & Suites H
(843) 757-2002. **$89-$139.** 35 Bluffton Rd. Jct William Hilton Pkwy (US 278/Bluffton Rd US 46), just se. Int corridors. **Pets:** Medium. $50 one-time fee/room. Service with restrictions, supervision.

(ASK) ⊠ 🛢ᴹ 🛢 🖵 🛥

▼▼▼▼ The Inn at Palmetto Bluff CA 🐾
(843) 706-6500. **Call for rates.** 476 Mount Pelia Rd. Jct US 278/SR 170, 4.4 mi sw on SR 170 to SR 46, then 2.2 mi e to Palmetto Bluff Rd; check-in at gatehouse. Ext corridors. **Pets:** $75 one-time fee/room. Service with restrictions, supervision.

⊠ 🛢 🖵 🍴 🛥 ⊠

CAMDEN

▲▲▲ ▼▼▼ Colony Inn M
(803) 432-5508. **$65-$75.** 2020 W DeKalb St. Jct US 521/1/601, 1.6 mi w on US 1/601. Ext/int corridors. **Pets:** Medium. $10 one-time fee/room. Service with restrictions, supervision.

(SAVE) ⊠ 🛢 🖵 🍴 🛥

CAYCE

▲▲▲ ▼▼▼ Riverside Inn M
(803) 939-4688. **$62.** 111 Knox Abbott Dr. US 21, just w of Congaree River Bridge. Ext corridors. **Pets:** $20 one-time fee/room. Service with restrictions.

(SAVE) ⊠ 🛢 🖵 🛥 ⊠

CHARLESTON METROPOLITAN AREA

CHARLESTON

Best Western Charleston-Downtown ✦
(843) 722-4000. **$100-$250.** 250 Spring St. I-26, exit 221A (US 17 S), 1.2 mi sw; just e of Ashley River. Int corridors. **Pets:** Other species. $25 daily fee/room. Service with restrictions.

Best Western Sweetgrass Inn
(843) 571-6100. **$49-$199.** 1540 Savannah Hwy. US 17 S, 3.6 mi w of Ashley River Bridge; jct I-526 W (end) and US 17 N, 1.7 mi e. Ext corridors. **Pets:** Medium. $20 daily fee/room. Designated rooms, service with restrictions, supervision.

The Inn at Middleton Place ✦
(843) 556-0500. **Call for rates.** 4290 Ashley River Rd. I-526, exit 11 (Ashley River Rd/SR 61), then 10.3 mi on SR 61 N. Ext corridors. **Pets:** Medium, other species. $50 one-time fee/pet. Designated rooms, service with restrictions, crate.

La Quinta Inn Riverview ✦
(843) 556-5200. **$69-$159.** 11 Ashley Point Dr. US 17 S, just over Ashley River Bridge to Albermarle Rd, 0.4 mi s to Ashley Pointe Dr. Ext/int corridors. **Pets:** Medium, other species. Service with restrictions, supervision.

Residence Inn by Marriott
(843) 571-7979. **$147-$158.** 90 Ripley Point Dr. US 17 S, just over Ashley River Bridge to Albermarle Rd, just s. Int corridors. **Pets:** Other species. $100 one-time fee/room. Service with restrictions.

Town & Country Inn & Conference Center
(843) 571-1000. **Call for rates.** 2008 Savannah Hwy. US 17 S, 3.5 mi nw of Ashley River Bridge; jct I-526 W (end) and US 17 N, just se. Ext corridors. **Pets:** Accepted.

Vendue Inn ✦
(843) 577-7970. **$199-$459, 3 day notice.** 19 Vendue Range. Off E Bay St, 1 blk from Waterfront Park; in historic district. Int corridors. **Pets:** $50 one-time fee/pet. Service with restrictions, supervision.

FOLLY BEACH

Holiday Inn Folly Beach Oceanfront ✦
(843) 588-6464. **$109-$309, 3 day notice.** 1 Center St. Terminus of SR 171; center. Ext corridors. **Pets:** Large, other species. $75 one-time fee/room. Service with restrictions, supervision.

KIAWAH ISLAND

Kiawah Island Golf Resort–Courtside Villas
(843) 768-2121. **Call for rates.** 1401 Shipwatch Rd. Just e of main gate to Kiawah Beach Dr, then just s; in West Beach Village area. Ext corridors. **Pets:** Accepted.

Kiawah Island Golf Resort–Fairway Oaks Villas
(843) 768-2121. **Call for rates.** 1301 Kiawah Beach Dr. Just e of main gate, then just s; in West Beach Village area. Ext corridors. **Pets:** Accepted.

Kiawah Island Golf Resort–Mariners Watch Villas
(843) 768-2121. **Call for rates.** 4200 Sea Forest Dr. 1.6 mi e of main gate, then just s; in East Beach Village area. Ext corridors. **Pets:** Accepted.

Kiawah Island Golf Resort–Parkside Villas
(843) 768-2121. **Call for rates.** 4501 Park Lake Dr. 2 mi e of main gate, then just s; in East Beach Village area. Ext corridors. **Pets:** Accepted.

Kiawah Island Golf Resort–Seascape Villas
(843) 768-2121. **Call for rates.** 3510 Shipwatch Rd. Just e of main gate, then just s; in West Beach Village area. Ext corridors. **Pets:** Accepted.

Kiawah Island Golf Resort–Shipwatch Villas
(843) 768-2121. **Call for rates.** 2200 Shipwatch Rd. Just e of main gate, then just s; in West Beach Village area. Ext corridors. **Pets:** Accepted.

Kiawah Island Golf Resort–Tennis Club Villas
(843) 768-2121. **Call for rates.** 4659 Tennis Club Ln. 2.2 mi e of main gate, then just s; at Roy Barth Tennis Center. Ext corridors. **Pets:** Accepted.

Kiawah Island Golf Resort–Turtle Cove Villas
(843) 768-2121. **Call for rates.** 5501 Green Dolphin Way. 2.4 mi e of main gate, then just se; at Roy Barth Tennis Center. Ext corridors. **Pets:** Accepted.

Kiawah Island Golf Resort–Turtle Point Villas
(843) 768-2121. **Call for rates.** 4901 Green Dolphin Way. 2.4 mi e of main gate, then just se; at Roy Barth Tennis Center and Turtle Point Golf Club. Ext corridors. **Pets:** Accepted.

Kiawah Island Golf Resort–Windswept Villas
(843) 768-2121. **Call for rates.** 4300 Sea Forest Dr. 1.6 mi e of main gate, then just s; in East Beach Village area. Ext corridors. **Pets:** Accepted.

MOUNT PLEASANT

Days Inn Patriots Point
(843) 881-1800. **$69-$179, 3 day notice.** 261 Johnnie Dodds Blvd. Just e of base of Cooper River Bridge. Ext corridors. **Pets:** Small, dogs only. $10 daily fee/pet. Service with restrictions, supervision.

Extended StayAmerica-Charleston-Mount Pleasant
(843) 884-4453. **$85-$105.** 304 Wingo Way. Just e of Cooper River Bridge on US 17, then just n. Int corridors. **Pets:** Other species. $25 daily fee/pet. Service with restrictions, crate.

Homewood Suites by Hilton ✦
(843) 881-6950. **$101-$229.** 1998 Riviera Dr. I-526, exit 32 (Georgetown/US 17 N), 1.4 mi ne on US 17, 1 mi se on Isle of Palms connector (SR 517), then just sw. Int corridors. **Pets:** Dogs only. $75 one-time fee/room. Service with restrictions, crate.

Inn at River Crossing
(843) 884-5853. **$60-$120.** 310 Hwy 17 (Johnnie Dodds Blvd). US 17, 0.7 mi n of Cooper River Bridge. Ext corridors. **Pets:** Medium, other species. $30 one-time fee/room. Service with restrictions.

◆◆◆ ▼▼▼ **Red Roof Inn** M
(843) 884-1411. **$56-$140.** 301 Johnnie Dodds Blvd. Just e of base of Cooper River Bridge, on US 17 (Johnnie Dodds Blvd), then just s on McGrath-Darby Blvd. Ext corridors. **Pets:** Accepted.
[SAVE] [✕] [🔒] [⇆]

▼▼▼ **Residence Inn by Marriott** H ❖
(843) 881-1599. **$159-$239.** 1116 Isle of Palms Connector. I-526, exit 32 (Georgetown/US 17 N), 1.4 mi ne on US 17 to Isle of Palms connector (SR 517), then just se. Int corridors. **Pets:** Medium. $100 one-time fee/room. Service with restrictions.
[✕] [🔒] [💻] [⇆]

◆◆◆ ▼▼▼ **Sleep Inn Mt Pleasant** H
(843) 856-5000. **$79-$149, 14 day notice.** 299 Wingo Way. Just e of base of Cooper River Bridge, then just n at McGrath-Darby Blvd. Int corridors. **Pets:** Other species. $15 daily fee/room. Service with restrictions, crate.
[SAVE] [✕] [🔒M] [🔒] [💻] [⇆]

NORTH CHARLESTON

▼▼▼ **Candlewood Suites** H
(843) 797-3535. **$99-$185.** 2177 Northwoods Blvd. I-26, exit 209 (Ashley Phosphate Rd), just e, then just n. Int corridors. **Pets:** Medium. $12 daily fee/pet, $150 one-time fee/pet. Designated rooms, service with restrictions, crate.
[ASK] [✕] [🔒] [💻]

◆◆◆ ▼▼▼ **Comfort Suites Charleston/N Charleston, SC** H
(843) 725-5400. **$89-$169.** 2520 N Forest Dr. I-26, exit 209 (Ashley Phosphate Rd), just w of Northside Dr. Int corridors. **Pets:** Accepted.
[SAVE] [✕] [🔒M] [🔒] [💻]

▼▼ **Homestead Studio Suites Hotel-Charleston/Airport** H
(843) 740-3440. **$95-$110.** 5045 N Arco Ln. I-26, exit 213 westbound; exit 213A eastbound; enter through Tanger Outlet access roads. Int corridors. **Pets:** Other species. $25 daily fee/pet. Service with restrictions, crate.
[ASK] [✕] [🔒M] [🔒] [💻]

▼▼▼ **La Quinta Inn Charleston** H ❖
(843) 797-8181. **$49-$139.** 2499 La Quinta Ln. I-26, exit 209 (Ashley Phosphate Rd), just w. Ext/int corridors. **Pets:** Medium, other species. Service with restrictions, supervision.
[ASK] [✕] [🔒] [💻] [⇆]

▼ **Motel 6 #642** M
(843) 572-6590. **$39-$51.** 2551 Ashley Phosphate Rd. I-26, exit 209 (Ashley Phosphate Rd), just w. Ext corridors. **Pets:** Other species. Service with restrictions, supervision.
[✕] [⇆]

◆◆◆ ▼▼▼▼ **Quality Suites Convention Center** H ❖
(843) 747-7300. **$99-$179, 30 day notice.** 5225 N Arco Ln. I-26, exit 213 westbound; exit 213A eastbound; enter through Tanger Outlet access roads. Int corridors. **Pets:** Large. $49 one-time fee/room. Service with restrictions, supervision.
[SAVE] [✕] [🔒] [💻] [⇆]

◆◆◆ ▼▼▼▼ **Radisson Hotel Charleston Airport** H
(843) 744-2501. **$129-$169.** 5991 Rivers Ave. I-26, exit 211B (Aviation Ave), just ne. Int corridors. **Pets:** Medium. $50 one-time fee/pet. Designated rooms, service with restrictions.
[SAVE] [✕] [🔒] [💻] [🍽] [⇆]

◆◆◆ ▼▼▼ **Red Roof Inn** M
(843) 572-9100. **$50-$95.** 7480 Northwoods Blvd. I-26, exit 209 (Ashley Phosphate Rd), just e, then just n. Ext corridors. **Pets:** Medium, other species. Service with restrictions, supervision.
[SAVE] [✕] [🔒]

▼▼▼ **Residence Inn by Marriott** H ❖
(843) 572-5757. **$142-$162.** 7645 Northwoods Blvd. I-26, exit 209 (Ashley Phosphate Rd), just e, then n. Ext corridors. **Pets:** Other species. $100 one-time fee/room. Service with restrictions, crate.
[✕] [🔒] [💻] [⇆] [✕]

◆◆◆ ▼▼▼ **Residence Inn Charleston Airport** H ❖
(843) 266-3434. **$187-$201.** 5035 International Blvd. I-26, exit 213A eastbound, 0.4 mi s, then just w; exit westbound, 0.4 mi s, then just w; I-526, exit International Blvd, 0.8 mi e. Int corridors. **Pets:** Other species. $100 one-time fee/room. Service with restrictions.
[SAVE] [✕] [🔒M] [🔒] [💻] [⇆] [✕]

◆◆◆ ▼▼▼ **Sheraton Hotel North Charleston Convention Center** H
(843) 747-1900. **Call for rates.** 4770 Goer Dr. I-26, exit 213 westbound; exit 213B eastbound, just n. Int corridors. **Pets:** Accepted.
[SAVE] [✕] [🔒] [💻] [🍽] [⇆]

◆◆◆ ▼▼▼ **Sleep Inn Charleston North** H
(843) 572-8400. **$69-$159.** 7435 Northside Dr. I-26, exit 209 (Ashley Phosphate Rd), just w. Int corridors. **Pets:** Medium. $10 daily fee/room. Designated rooms, service with restrictions, crate.
[SAVE] [✕] [🔒] [💻]

▼▼ ▼ **StudioPlus** H
(843) 553-0036. **$95-$110.** 7641 Northwoods Blvd. I-26, exit 209 (Ashley Phosphate Rd), just e, then just n. Int corridors. **Pets:** Other species. $25 daily fee/pet. Service with restrictions, crate.
[ASK] [✕] [🔒] [💻] [⇆]

SUMMERVILLE

▼▼▼ **Country Inn & Suites** H
(843) 285-9000. **$99-$109.** 220 Holiday Dr. I-26, exit 199A, just w on US 17 alternate route to Holiday Dr, then just n. Int corridors. **Pets:** Medium, other species. $10 daily fee/pet. Service with restrictions, supervision.
[ASK] [✕] [🔒] [💻] [⇆]

◆◆◆ ▼▼▼ **Holiday Inn Express-Charleston/Summerville** H ❖
(843) 875-3300. **$78.** 120 Holiday Dr. I-26, exit 199A, just w. Int corridors. **Pets:** Other species. Service with restrictions, supervision.
[SAVE] [✕] [🔒M] [🔒] [💻] [⇆]

▼ **Summerville Econo Lodge** M
(843) 875-3022. **$79-$84.** 110 Holiday Dr. I-26, exit 199A, just w on US 17A, then just n. Ext corridors. **Pets:** Small. $10 daily fee/room. Service with restrictions, crate.
[ASK] [✕] [🔒] [💻]

◆◆◆ ▼▼▼▼ **Woodlands Resort & Inn** C ❖
(843) 875-2600. **$325-$890, 7 day notice.** 125 Parsons Rd. I-26, exit 199A, 2 mi s on US 17 alternate route, 1.5 mi w on W Richardson Ave (SR 165), then just s. Int corridors. **Pets:** $25 one-time fee/room. Service with restrictions.
[SAVE] [✕] [🍽] [⇆] [✕]

END METROPOLITAN AREA

CHARLOTTE METROPOLITAN AREA (NEARBY NORTH CAROLINA)

ROCK HILL

Baymont Inn & Suites H
(803) 329-1330. **$74-$115.** 1106 N Anderson Rd. I-77, exit 82B (US 21), 0.4 mi sw to US 21 Bypass, then just s. Int corridors. **Pets:** Medium. $10 daily fee/pet. Service with restrictions, supervision.

The Book & the Spindle BB
(803) 328-1913. **$90-$105, 10 day notice.** 626 Oakland Ave. I-77, exit 82B (US 21), 3.1 mi s; before Aiken. Int corridors. **Pets:** Small, other species. $15 deposit/pet. Designated rooms, service with restrictions, supervision.

Howard Johnson Inn M
(803) 329-7900. **Call for rates.** 911 Riverview Rd. I-77, exit 82B (US 21), just sw, then just s. Ext corridors. **Pets:** Accepted.

Super 8 H
(803) 980-0400. **$50-$60.** 888 Riverview Rd. I-77, exit 82B (US 21), just sw, then just s. Int corridors. **Pets:** Medium. $10 daily fee/pet. Designated rooms, service with restrictions, supervision.

END METROPOLITAN AREA

CHERAW

Days Inn M
(843) 537-5554. **$57-$110.** 820 Market St. Jct US 52/1/SR 9. Ext corridors. **Pets:** Accepted.

Jameson Inn M
(843) 537-5625. **$83-$88.** 885 Chesterfield Hwy. Jct US 1/52/SR 9, 1.6 mi w on SR 9. Ext corridors. **Pets:** Small. $15 daily fee/room. Service with restrictions, supervision.

CLEMSON

Comfort Inn-Clemson H
(864) 653-3600. **$85-$175.** 1305 Tiger Blvd. Jct SR 133 (College Ave) and US 76/123, 0.5 mi e. Int corridors. **Pets:** Other species. $10 daily fee/room. Designated rooms, service with restrictions.

CLINTON

Comfort Inn M
(864) 833-5558. **$59-$99.** 105 Trade St. I-26, exit 52, just n; behind truck stop. Ext corridors. **Pets:** Small. $10 daily fee/room. Designated rooms, service with restrictions, crate.

Days Inn M
(864) 833-6600. **$55-$99.** 12374 Hwy 56 N. I-26, exit 52, just s. Ext corridors. **Pets:** Accepted.

COLUMBIA

Chestnut Cottage Bed & Breakfast BB
(803) 256-1718. **$159-$229, 15 day notice.** 1718 Hampton St. SR 12 (Taylor St), just s; between Henderson and Barnwell sts; downtown. Int corridors. **Pets:** Accepted.

Econo Lodge M
(803) 772-7275. **$50-$125.** 773 St Andrews Rd. I-26, exit 106A westbound; exit 106 eastbound, just w. Ext corridors. **Pets:** Other species. $10 daily fee/pet. Service with restrictions, supervision.

Extended StayAmerica Columbia-Fort Jackson M
(803) 782-2025. **$85-$95.** 5430 Forest Dr. I-77, exit 12, just ne, then just s along service road; behind mall. Ext corridors. **Pets:** Other species. $25 daily fee/pet. Service with restrictions, crate.

Extended StayAmerica-Columbia-West H
(803) 251-7878. **$65-$75.** 450 Gracern Rd. I-126, exit Greystone Blvd, just n to Stoneridge Dr, just w to Gracern Rd, then s. Ext corridors. **Pets:** Other species. $25 daily fee/pet. Service with restrictions, crate.

Jameson Suites H
(803) 736-6666. **$103-$113.** 7525 Two Notch Rd. I-20, exit 74 (Two Notch Rd), just ne; I-77, exit 17 (Two Notch Rd), 0.5 mi sw. Int corridors. **Pets:** Accepted.

La Quinta Inn & Suites Columbia NE/Ft. Jackson Area H 🐾
(803) 736-6400. **$49-$109.** 1538 Horseshoe Dr. I-20, exit 74 (Two Notch Rd), just n; I-77, exit 17 (Two Notch Rd), 0.5 mi s. Int corridors. **Pets:** Medium, other species. Service with restrictions, supervision.

La Quinta Inn-Maingate Ft. Jackson H 🐾
(803) 783-5410. **$69-$129.** 7333 Garners Ferry Rd. I-77, exit 9A, just se. Int corridors. **Pets:** Medium, other species. Service with restrictions, supervision.

Motel 6 #1291 H
(803) 736-3900. **$43-$53.** 7541 Nates Rd. I-20, exit 74 (Two Notch Rd), just n, then just e; I-77, exit 17 (Two Notch Rd), 0.5 mi s, then e. Int corridors. **Pets:** Other species. Service with restrictions, supervision.

Quality Inn & Suites M
(803) 776-1700. **Call for rates.** 7251 Garners Ferry Rd. I-77, exit 9A, just se. Ext corridors. **Pets:** Accepted.

Radisson Hotel Columbia & Conference Center H
(803) 731-0300. **$89-$199.** 2100 Bush River Rd. I-20, exit 63 (Bush River Rd), just e; I-26, exit 108 (Bush River Rd), 0.7 mi w. Int corridors. **Pets:** $25 one-time fee/room. Designated rooms, service with restrictions, supervision.

Residence Inn by Marriott H 🐾
(803) 779-7000. **$157-$169.** 150 Stoneridge Dr. I-126, exit Greystone Blvd, just n, then just e. Ext corridors. **Pets:** Other species. $10 daily fee/room, $50 one-time fee/room.

▼▼▼▼ Residence Inn by Marriott ⊞
(803) 788-8850. **$137-$147.** 2320 Legrand Rd. I-77, exit 19 southbound, just ne on Farrow Rd to Rabon Rd, then just se; exit 18 northbound. Int corridors. **Pets:** $75 one-time fee/room. Service with restrictions, supervision.
⊠ 🖬 💻 🗢 ⊠

▼▼ StudioPLUS Greystone Columbia ⊞
(803) 771-0303. **$75-$85.** 180 Stoneridge Dr. I-126, exit Greystone Blvd, just n, then just e. Int corridors. **Pets:** Other species. $25 daily fee/pet. Service with restrictions, crate.
(ASK) ⊠ 🖬 💻 🗢

▲▲▲ ▼ Super 8 M
(803) 735-0008. **$70-$95.** 5719 Fairfield Rd. I-20, exit 70, just s. Ext corridors. **Pets:** Accepted.
(SAVE) ⊠ 🖬

▼▼▼▼ TownePlace Suites by Marriott ⊞
(803) 781-9391. **$133-$143.** 350 Columbiana Dr. I-26, exit 103 (Harbison Blvd), just sw to Columbiana Dr, then 0.7 mi nw. Int corridors. **Pets:** Accepted.
⊠ (ᵴᴹ) 🖬 💻 🗢

DUNCAN

▼▼ Jameson Inn M
(864) 433-8405. **$78-$83.** 1546 E Main St. I-85, exit 63, 0.4 mi se on SR 290. Ext corridors. **Pets:** Accepted.
(ASK) ⊠ 🖬 💻 🗢

EASLEY

▲▲▲ ▼▼ Comfort Inn M
(864) 859-7520. **$74-$79.** 5539 Calhoun Memorial Hwy. Jct US 123 and SR 93, just e on US 123. Ext corridors. **Pets:** Accepted.
(SAVE) ⊠ 🖬 💻 🗢

▼▼ Jameson Inn M
(864) 306-9000. **$78-$85.** 211 Dayton School Rd. Jct US 123 and SR 93, 0.6 mi e on US 123; jct US 123 and SR 153, 1.4 mi w. Ext corridors. **Pets:** Small, other species. $15 daily fee/pet. Service with restrictions, supervision.
(ASK) ⊠ 🖬 💻 🗢

FLORENCE

▲▲▲ ▼▼▼ Comfort Inn M
(843) 665-4558. **$59-$89.** 1916 W Lucas St. I-95, exit 164, just se. Ext/int corridors. **Pets:** Other species. $10 daily fee/pet. Designated rooms, service with restrictions, supervision.
(SAVE) ⊠ 🖬 💻 🗢

▲▲▲ ▼▼▼▼ Holiday Inn Hotel & Suites ⊞ 🐾
(843) 665-4555. **$85-$160.** 1819 W Lucas St. I-95, exit 164, just se. Ext corridors. **Pets:** $25 one-time fee/room. Designated rooms, service with restrictions, supervision.
(SAVE) ⊠ (ᵴᴹ) 🖬 💻 🍴 🗢

▲▲▲ ▼▼▼ Howard Johnson Express Inn & Suites M 🐾
(843) 664-9494. **$69, 60 day notice.** 3821 Bancroft Rd. I-95, exit 157, just ne on US 76. Ext corridors. **Pets:** Medium. $10 one-time fee/pet. Designated rooms, service with restrictions, supervision.
(SAVE) ⊠ 🖬 💻 🗢

▼▼ Motel 6 #1250 M
(843) 667-6100. **$35-$45.** 1834 W Lucas St. I-95, exit 164, just sw. Ext corridors. **Pets:** Other species. Service with restrictions, supervision.
⊠ 🗢

▲▲▲ ▼▼▼ Quality Inn & Suites M 🐾
(843) 664-2400. **$59-$100.** 150 Dunbarton Dr. I-95, exit 160A, just e, then just n. Ext corridors. **Pets:** Other species. $20 one-time fee/room. Designated rooms, service with restrictions, crate.
(SAVE) ⊠ 🖬 💻 🗢

▲▲▲ ▼▼▼ Red Roof Inn M
(843) 678-9000. **$45-$125.** 2690 David McLeod Blvd. I-95, exit 160A, just e on service road. Ext corridors. **Pets:** Accepted.
(SAVE) ⊠ (ᵴᴹ)

▲▲▲ ▼▼▼ Super 8 M
(843) 661-7267. **$56-$180.** 1832 1/2 W Lucas St. I-95, exit 164, just se. Ext corridors. **Pets:** Medium. $10 daily fee/pet. No service, supervision.
(SAVE) ⊠ 🖬 💻 🗢

GAFFNEY

▼▼ Jameson Inn M
(864) 489-0240. **$78-$85.** 101 Stuard St. I-85, exit 92, 0.5 mi se on SR 11/W Floyd Baker Blvd. Ext corridors. **Pets:** Very small, other species. $15 daily fee/pet. Service with restrictions, supervision.
(ASK) ⊠ 🖬 💻 🗢

▼▼ Sleep Inn ⊞ 🐾
(864) 487-5337. **$84-$90.** 834 Windslow Ave. I-85, exit 90, just se, then ne on frontage road. Int corridors. **Pets:** Large, other species. $5 daily fee/room, $25 one-time fee/room. Service with restrictions, supervision.
(ASK) ⊠ (ᵴᴹ) 🖬 💻 🗢

▲▲▲ ▼▼▼ Super 8 M
(864) 489-1699. **$54.** 100 Ellis Ferry Ave. I-85, exit 92, 0.7 mi se on SR 11/W Floyd Baker Blvd. Ext corridors. **Pets:** Accepted.
(SAVE) ⊠ 🖬 💻 🗢

THE GRAND STRAND AREA

GEORGETOWN

▼▼ Jameson Inn Georgetown M
(843) 546-6090. **$78-$95.** 120 Church St. Jct US 17/17 alternate route/701, 1.2 mi se on US 17; just w of ICW Bridge at Georgetown Landing. Ext corridors. **Pets:** Accepted.
(ASK) ⊠ 🖬 💻 🗢

LITTLE RIVER

▲▲▲ ▼▼▼ Holiday Inn Hotel & Suites-North Myrtle Beach ⊞
(843) 281-9400. **$49-$229.** 722 Hwy 17. Jct SR 9/US 17, 1 mi e; at Coquina Harbor. Int corridors. **Pets:** Medium. $20 daily fee/pet. Service with restrictions, crate.
(SAVE) ⊠ 🖬 💻 🍴 🗢

MYRTLE BEACH

▼▼▼▼ La Quinta Inn & Suites Myrtle Beach �H 🐾
(843) 916-8801. **$69-$189.** 1561 21st Ave N. Jct US 17 Bypass, just se. Int corridors. **Pets:** Medium, other species. Service with restrictions, supervision.
(A$K) (✕) (&M) 🛁 💻 🏊

▼▼▼▼ La Quinta Inn Myrtle Beach �H 🐾
(843) 449-5231. **$59-$199.** 4709 N Kings Hwy. Jct 48th Ave N and US 17 business route. Int corridors. **Pets:** Medium, other species. Service with restrictions, supervision.
(A$K) (✕) 🛁 💻 🏊

⚜ ▼▼▼ Sea Mist Oceanfront Resort �H 🐾
(843) 448-1551. **$32-$199, 14 day notice.** 1200 S Ocean Blvd. Jct 12th Ave S. Ext/int corridors. **Pets:** Large, other species. $50 one-time fee/pet. Designated rooms, service with restrictions, crate.
(SAVE) (✕) 🛁 💻 🍴 🏊 (✕)

▼▼▼▼ Staybridge Suites-Fantasy Harbour �H 🐾
(843) 903-4000. **$80-$280, 7 day notice.** 303 Hard Rock Pkwy. Jct US 17 Bypass, 0.7 mi n on US 501, exit River Oaks Rd/George Bishop Pkwy, just w on River Oaks Rd, then 0.4 mi s. Int corridors. **Pets:** Medium. $20 daily fee/room. Service with restrictions.
(A$K) (✕) 🛁 💻 🏊 (✕)

NORTH MYRTLE BEACH

▼▼ ▼▼ La Quinta Inn-North Myrtle Beach �H 🐾
(843) 280-4555. **$49-$169.** 1601-B US 17 N. Jct SR 9, just s. Int corridors. **Pets:** Medium, other species. Service with restrictions, supervision.
(A$K) (✕) 🛁 💻 🏊

PAWLEYS ISLAND

▼▼ Vista Inn & Suites Ⓜ
(843) 237-4261. **$59-$129.** 7903 Ocean Hwy. 2.6 mi sw on US 17. Ext corridors. **Pets:** Accepted.
(A$K) (✕) 🛁 💻 🍴 🏊

SURFSIDE BEACH

⚜ ▼▼▼ Holiday Inn Oceanfront �H
(843) 238-5601. **$69-$229, 3 day notice.** 1601 N Ocean Blvd. Jct 16th Ave N and N Ocean Blvd. Int corridors. **Pets:** $75 one-time fee/room. Service with restrictions, crate.
(SAVE) (✕) 🛁 💻 🍴 🏊 (✕)

END AREA

GREENVILLE

⚜ ▼▼▼ Best Western Greenville Airport Inn Ⓜ
(864) 676-1167. **$63-$72.** 5009 Pelham Rd. I-85, exit 54 (Pelham Rd), just se. Ext corridors. **Pets:** Small, other species. $10 daily fee/room. Service with restrictions, supervision.
(SAVE) (✕) 🛁 💻 🏊

▼▼▼▼ Crowne Plaza Hotel and Resort Greenville �H
(864) 297-6300. **$138-$179.** 851 Congaree Rd. I-385, exit 37, just s, then just nw. Int corridors. **Pets:** Accepted.
(A$K) (✕) (&M) 🛁 💻 🍴 🏊 (✕)

▼▼▼▼ Drury Inn & Suites-Greenville �H
(864) 288-4401. **$90-$175.** 10 Carolina Point Pkwy. I-85, exit 51A, just se; I-385, exit 35, 0.6 mi nw. Int corridors. **Pets:** Other species. Service with restrictions, supervision.
(A$K) (✕) 🛁 💻 🏊

▼▼▼ Extended StayAmerica-Greenville Airport �H
(864) 213-9698. **$81-$91.** 3715 Pelham Rd. I-85, exit 54 (Pelham Rd), 0.5 mi w. Int corridors. **Pets:** Other species. $25 daily fee/pet. Service with restrictions, crate.
(A$K) (✕) 🛁 💻

▼▼▼ Hawthorn Suites �H
(864) 297-0099. **Call for rates.** 48 McPrice Ct. I-385, exit 39 (Haywood Rd), just n, just e on Orchard Park Rd, then just s. Ext corridors. **Pets:** Accepted.
(✕) 🛁 💻 🏊 (✕)

▼▼▼ Holiday Inn Express Hotel & Suites �H 🐾
(864) 213-9331. **$99-$155.** 2681 Dry Pocket Rd. I-85, exit 54 (Pelham Rd), just w to The Parkway, just n to Parkway E, then just se. Int corridors. **Pets:** Other species. $15 daily fee/room. Designated rooms, service with restrictions.
(A$K) (✕) 🛁 💻 🏊 (✕)

▼▼▼ Holiday Inn I-85/Augusta Rd �H
(864) 277-8921. **$86-$119.** 4295 Augusta Rd. I-85, exit 46A, just s. Int corridors. **Pets:** $30 one-time fee/room. Service with restrictions, crate.
(A$K) (✕) (&M) 🛁 💻 🍴 🏊

▼▼▼ La Quinta Inn & Suites Greenville (Haywood) �H 🐾
(864) 233-8018. **$69-$109.** 65 W Orchard Park Dr. I-385, exit 39 (Haywood Rd), just n, then w. Int corridors. **Pets:** Medium, other species. Service with restrictions, supervision.
(A$K) (✕) 🛁 💻 🏊 (✕)

▼▼▼ La Quinta Inn Greenville (Woodruff Rd) Ⓜ 🐾
(864) 297-3500. **$49-$99.** 31 Old Country Rd. I-85, exit 51A, just nw on SR 146; I-385, exit 37, just sw on Roper Mountain Rd, then 0.9 mi se. Ext/int corridors. **Pets:** Medium, other species. Service with restrictions, supervision.
(A$K) (✕) 🛁 💻 🏊

▼▼ MainStay Suites-Greenville �H 🐾
(864) 987-5566. **$80-$126.** 2671 Dry Pocket Rd. I-85, exit 54 (Pelham Rd), just w to The Parkway, just n to Parkway E, then just se. Int corridors. **Pets:** Other species. $10 daily fee/pet. Service with restrictions, crate.
(A$K) (✕) 🛁 💻 🏊

▼▼ Microtel Inn & Suites �H
(864) 297-3811. **$56-$79, 7 day notice.** 1024 Woodruff Rd. I-85, exit 51A, 0.5 mi nw; I-385, exit 37, just nw on Roper Mountain Rd, then just se. Int corridors. **Pets:** Large, other species. $35 one-time fee/room. Service with restrictions, supervision.
(A$K) (✕) 🛁 💻

▼▼▼▼ The Phoenix Greenville's Inn �H
(864) 233-4651. **$89-$295, 3 day notice.** 246 N Pleasantburg Dr. I-385, exit 40B, 0.6 mi s on SR 291. Ext corridors. **Pets:** Other species. $25 one-time fee/room. Service with restrictions, crate.
(A$K) (✕) 🛁 💻 🍴 🏊

⚜ ▼▼▼ Quality Inn Executive Center Ⓜ 🐾
(864) 271-0060. **$66-$86.** 540 N Pleasantburg Dr. I-385, exit 40B, just s. Ext corridors. **Pets:** $15 daily fee/pet. Service with restrictions.
(SAVE) (✕) 🛁 💻 🏊

⚜ ▼▼▼ Red Roof Inn Ⓜ
(864) 297-4458. **$50-$100, 14 day notice.** 2801 Laurens Rd. I-85, exit 48A, just se to frontage road, then just e to end. Ext corridors. **Pets:** Medium, other species. Service with restrictions, supervision.
(SAVE) (✕) (&M) 🛁

Sleep Inn Palmetto Expo Center 🅗 ☙
(864) 240-2006. **$59-$109, 3 day notice.** 231 N Pleasantburg Dr (SR 291). I-385, exit 40B, 0.6 mi s on SR 291. Int corridors. **Pets:** Medium. $20 one-time fee/pet. Service with restrictions.
[SAVE] [X] [♿M] [🛏] [💻] [▨]

Staybridge Suites Greenville/Spartanburg 🅗
(864) 288-4448. **$86-$180.** 31 Market Point Dr. I-85, exit 51A (Woodruff Rd), 0.5 mi se to Miller Rd, 0.5 mi s to S Oak Forest Dr, then just nw; I-385, exit 35, nw to Miller Rd, 0.5 mi s to S Oak Forest Dr, then just nw. Int corridors. **Pets:** Accepted.
[ASK] [X] [🛏] [💻] [⇆]

StudioPLUS-Greenville-Haywwod Mall 🅗
(864) 288-4300. **$80-$90.** 530 Woods Lake Rd. I-385, exit 39, just s, then just w. Int corridors. **Pets:** Other species. $25 daily fee/pet. Service with restrictions, crate.
[ASK] [X] [🛏] [💻] [⇆]

GREENWOOD

Inn on the Square, a Clarion Collection 🅗
(864) 330-1010. **$95-$125.** 104 E Court Ave. Jct Main St, just s of center; downtown. Int corridors. **Pets:** Small. $10 daily fee/pet. Service with restrictions.
[SAVE] [X] [🛏] [💻] [▥] [⇆]

HARDEEVILLE

Sleep Inn Hardeeville 🅗
(843) 784-7181. **$59-$149, 7 day notice.** 16553 Whyte Hardee Blvd. I-95, exit 5 (US 17), just se. Int corridors. **Pets:** Small. $20 one-time fee/room. Service with restrictions, supervision.
[SAVE] [X] [♿M] [🛏] [💻] [⇆]

HILTON HEAD ISLAND

Beachwalk Hotel & Condominiums 🅗
(843) 842-8888. **$59-$149.** 40 Waterside Dr. Sea Pines Cir, 0.7 mi se on Pope Rd, just e. Ext corridors. **Pets:** Accepted.
[SAVE] [X] [🛏] [💻] [⇆]

Comfort Inn 🅗
(843) 842-6662. **$49-$199.** 2 Tanglewood Dr. Sea Pines Cir, 1.1 mi se on Pope Ave, just sw; at Coligny Plaza. Int corridors. **Pets:** Accepted.
[SAVE] [X] [🛏] [💻] [⇆]

Holiday Inn Oceanfront Resort 🅗
(843) 785-5126. **$79-$299.** 1 S Forest Beach Dr. Sea Pine Cir, 1.1 mi se on Pope Ave, just sw at Coligny Cir. Int corridors. **Pets:** Accepted.
[SAVE] [X] [♿M] [🛏] [💻] [▥] [⇆] [▨]

Park Lane Hotel & Suites 🅗
(843) 686-5700. **$89-$179.** 12 Park Ln. 10 mi of J Wilton Graves Bridge on US 278 business route. Int corridors. **Pets:** Accepted.
[SAVE] [X] [🛏] [💻] [⇆] [▨]

Quality Inn & Suites of Hilton Head Island 🅗
(843) 681-3655. **$59-$139.** 200 Museum St. 3.3 mi e of J Wilton Graves Bridge on US 278 business route. Ext corridors. **Pets:** Medium. $10 daily fee/room, $25 one-time fee/room. Designated rooms, service with restrictions, crate.
[ASK] [X] [🛏] [💻] [⇆]

Red Roof Inn-Hilton Head Ⓜ
(843) 686-6808. **$50-$105.** 5 Regency Pkwy. Over bridge, 9 mi e on US 278 business route; between Shipyard Plantation and Palmetto Dunes. Ext corridors. **Pets:** Accepted.
[SAVE] [X] [🛏] [⇆]

Westin Hilton Head Island Resort & Spa 🅗
(843) 681-4000. **$119-$489.** Two Grass Lawn Ave. 5.6 mi from J Wilton Graves Bridge on US 278 business route to Coggins Point Rd, then just e, follow signs. Int corridors. **Pets:** Accepted.
[SAVE] [X] [🛏] [💻] [▥] [⇆] [▨]

IRMO

Extended Stay Deluxe (Columbia-Harbison) 🅗
(803) 781-8590. **$95-$105.** 1170 Kinley Rd. I-26, exit 102B, just e, then n. Int corridors. **Pets:** Other species. $25 daily fee/pet. Service with restrictions, crate.
[ASK] [X] [♿M] [🛏] [💻] [⇆]

LANCASTER

Jameson Inn Ⓜ
(803) 283-1188. **$73-$78.** 114 Commerce Blvd. Jct SR 9 Bypass and US 521, 1.3 mi w on SR 9 Bypass. Ext corridors. **Pets:** Accepted.
[ASK] [X] [♿M] [🛏] [💻] [⇆]

LANDRUM

The Red Horse Inn Cottages 🅲🅐 ☙
(864) 895-4968. **$210-$400.** 45 Winstons Chase Ct. Jct SR 14/414, 1.5 mi w on SR 414 to Campbell Rd, then 0.7 mi n. Ext corridors. **Pets:** Medium. $25 one-time fee/pet. Designated rooms, service with restrictions, supervision.
[X] [🛏] [💻] [▨]

LUGOFF

Ramada Limited Ⓜ
(803) 438-1807. **$65.** 542 Hwy 601 S. I-20, exit 92 (US 601), just n. Ext corridors. **Pets:** $10 daily fee/pet. No service, supervision.
[X] [🛏] [💻] [⇆]

MANNING

Best Western Palmetto Inn Ⓜ
(803) 473-4021. **$63-$90.** 2825 Paxville Hwy. I-95, exit 119 (SR 261), just se. Ext corridors. **Pets:** Accepted.
[SAVE] [X] [🛏] [💻] [⇆]

Ramada Inn Ⓜ
(803) 473-5135. **Call for rates.** 2816 Paxville Hwy. I-95, exit 119 (SR 261), just se. Ext corridors. **Pets:** Accepted.
[X] [🛏] [💻] [⇆]

MAULDIN

Super 8 🅗
(864) 751-0003. **$75.** 310 W Butler Rd. I-85, exit 46C, 3.8 mi s on Old Mauldin Rd (which becomes W Butler Rd). Int corridors. **Pets:** Medium. $10 daily fee/pet. Service with restrictions, supervision.
[SAVE] [X] [♿M] [🛏] [💻] [⇆]

NEWBERRY

America's Best Value Inn Ⓜ
(803) 276-5850. **$65-$75.** 11701 S Carolina Hwy 34. I-26, exit 74 (SR 34), just ne. Ext corridors. **Pets:** Small. $10 daily fee/pet. Service with restrictions, supervision.
[SAVE] [X] [🛏] [💻] [⇆]

ORANGEBURG

Country Inn & Suites 🅗
(803) 928-5300. **$105-$190.** 731 Citadel Rd. I-26, exit 145B, just s. Int corridors. **Pets:** Medium. $10 daily fee/pet. No service, crate.
[ASK] [X] [♿M] [🛏] [💻] [⇆]

▼▼▼ Jameson Inn Orangeburg M
(803) 534-1611. **$78-$85.** 2350 Chestnut St NE. I-26, exit 145A (US 601), 3.9 mi sw to jct US 601 and 21/178 Bypass, then 2 mi nw. Ext corridors. **Pets:** Accepted.
(ASK) ⊠ 🛏 💻 ➰

₳₳₳⁷ ▼▼▼ Traveler's Inn M
(803) 531-2590. **$55-$150.** 3691 St Matthews Rd. I-26, exit 145A (US 601), just sw. Ext corridors. **Pets:** Other species. $15 daily fee/pet. Service with restrictions, supervision.
(SAVE) ⊠ 🛏 💻 ➰

RICHBURG

₳₳₳⁷ ▼▼▼ Super 8 M
(803) 789-7888. **$59-$89, 7 day notice.** 3085 Lancaster Hwy. I-77, exit 65, just w on SR 9. Ext corridors. **Pets:** Small, other species. $6 one-time fee/pet. Service with restrictions, supervision.
(SAVE) ⊠ 🛏 💻 ➰

RIDGELAND

₳₳₳⁷ ▼▼▼▼ Comfort Inn H
(843) 726-2121. **$79-$109.** Hwy 336 & I-95. I-95, exit 21 (US 336), just nw. Ext/int corridors. **Pets:** Dogs only. $10 one-time fee/pet. Service with restrictions, crate.
(SAVE) ⊠ 🛏 💻 ➰

ST. GEORGE

₳₳₳⁷ ▼▼▼ Comfort Inn M
(843) 563-4180. **$54-$110.** 139 Motel Dr. I-95, exit 77 (US 78), just e. Ext corridors. **Pets:** Accepted.
(SAVE) ⊠ 🛏 💻 ➰

₳₳₳⁷ ▼ Econo Lodge M
(843) 563-4195. **$55-$80.** 5971 W Jim Bilton Blvd. I-95, exit 77 (US 78), just e. Ext corridors. **Pets:** Small. $10 daily fee/pet. Service with restrictions, supervision.
(SAVE) ⊠ 🛏 💻 ➰

₳₳₳⁷ ▼▼▼ Quality Inn- St George M ❖
(843) 563-4581. **$54-$100.** 6014 W Jim Bilton Blvd. I-95, exit 77 (US 78), just e. Ext corridors. **Pets:** Medium. $10 daily fee/pet. Service with restrictions, supervision.
(SAVE) ⊠ 🔥M 🛏 💻 ➰

SANTEE

₳₳₳⁷ ▼▼▼ Baymont Inn & Suites M
(803) 854-3221. **$45-$75, 3 day notice.** 249 Britain St. I-95, exit 98 (SR 6), just nw, then just s. Ext corridors. **Pets:** Accepted.
(SAVE) ⊠ 🛏 💻 ➰

₳₳₳⁷ ▼▼▼ Holiday Inn Santee H
(803) 854-9800. **$62-$135.** 139 Bradford Blvd. I-95, exit 98 (SR 6), just nw, then just sw. Int corridors. **Pets:** Medium, other species. $20 daily fee/pet. Designated rooms, service with restrictions.
(SAVE) ⊠ 🔥M 🛏 💻 🍴 ➰

₳₳₳⁷ ▼▼▼ Howard Johnson Express Inn M ❖
(803) 854-3870. **$58-$63.** 9112 Old Hwy 6. I-95, exit 98 (SR 6), 0.4 mi se. Ext corridors. **Pets:** Medium. $10 one-time fee/pet. Service with restrictions, supervision.
(SAVE) ⊠ 🛏 💻 ➰

₳₳₳⁷ ▼▼▼ Super 8 M
(803) 854-3456. **$65-$75.** 9125 Old Hwy 6. I-95, exit 98 (SR 6), 0.4 mi se. Ext corridors. **Pets:** $10 daily fee/pet. Service with restrictions, crate.
(SAVE) ⊠ 🛏 💻 ➰

SENECA

▼▼ Jameson Inn M
(864) 888-8300. **$83-$90.** 226 Hi-Tech Rd. Jct SR 28 and US 76/123, 0.9 mi w on US 76/123, just se. Ext corridors. **Pets:** Accepted.
(ASK) ⊠ 🔥M 🛏 💻 ➰

SIMPSONVILLE

▼▼ Days Inn M
(864) 963-7701. **Call for rates.** 45 Ray E Talley Ct. I-385, exit 27, just s, then just e. Ext corridors. **Pets:** Accepted.
⊠ 🛏 💻 ➰

▼ Motel 6 #4266 H
(864) 962-8484. **$45-$55.** 3706 Grandview Dr. I-385, exit 27, just s, then just w. Int corridors. **Pets:** Other species. Service with restrictions, supervision.
(ASK) ⊠ 🔥M 🛏

₳₳₳⁷ ▼▼▼ Quality Inn M
(864) 963-2777. **$59-$89.** 3755 Grandview Dr. I-385, exit 27, just s. Ext corridors. **Pets:** Small. $10 daily fee/pet. Service with restrictions, supervision.
(SAVE) ⊠ 🛏 💻 ➰

SPARTANBURG

▼▼ Extended StayAmerica-Spartanburg-Asheville Hwy M
(864) 573-5949. **$70-$80.** 130 Mobile Dr. I-85 business route, exit 4/4B, just se, then just ne on service road. Ext corridors. **Pets:** Other species. $25 daily fee/pet. Service with restrictions, crate.
(ASK) ⊠ 🛏

▼▼▼ Holiday Inn Express Hotel & Suites H
(864) 699-7777. **Call for rates.** 895 Spartan Blvd. I-26, exit 21B (US 29), just e to Blackstock Rd, then 0.7 mi n; adjacent to Westgate Mall. Int corridors. **Pets:** Accepted.
⊠ 🔥M 🛏 💻 ➰

SUMMERTON

₳₳₳⁷ ▼▼▼ Days Inn of Summerton M
(803) 485-2865. **$34-$65.** 400 Bluff Blvd. I-95, exit 108, just n. Ext corridors. **Pets:** Other species. $10 daily fee/room. Service with restrictions.
(SAVE) ⊠ 🛏 💻 ➰

SUMTER

▼▼ Ramada Inn M
(803) 775-2323. **$69-$73.** 226 N Washington St. US 76 business route/521, just n. Ext corridors. **Pets:** $50 deposit/pet, $10 daily fee/pet. Designated rooms, service with restrictions, crate.
(ASK) ⊠ 🛏 💻 🍴 ➰ ⊠

₳₳₳⁷ ▼ Travelers Inn & Suites M
(803) 469-9210. **$59-$89.** 1210 Camden Rd. Jct US 521/US 76. Ext corridors. **Pets:** Medium. $10 daily fee/pet. Designated rooms, service with restrictions, supervision.
(SAVE) ⊠ 🛏 💻 ➰

TRAVELERS REST

▼▼ Sleep Inn H
(864) 834-7040. **Call for rates.** 110 Hawkins Rd. US 25, exit Hawkins Rd. Int corridors. **Pets:** Other species. $15 daily fee/room. Service with restrictions, supervision.
⊠ 🔥M 🛏 💻 ➰

WALTERBORO

₳₳₳⁷ ▼▼▼ Best Western of Walterboro H ❖
(843) 538-3600. **$69-$99, 3 day notice.** 1428 Sniders Hwy. I-95, exit 53 (SR 63), just e. Ext corridors. **Pets:** Small. $15 daily fee/pet. Designated rooms, service with restrictions, supervision.
(SAVE) ⊠ 🛏 💻 ➰

Econo Lodge M ✿
(843) 538-3830. **$49-$99.** 1145 Sniders Hwy. I-95, exit 53 (SR 63), just e. Ext corridors. **Pets:** $10 one-time fee/room. Service with restrictions.
SAVE ✕ 🛎 💻

Microtel Inn and Suites H
(843) 539-5656. **$59-$69, 10 day notice.** 130 Cane Branch Rd. I-95, exit 53 (SR 63), just w, then just s. Int corridors. **Pets:** Accepted.
SAVE ✕ 🛎 💻 ➤

Quality Inn & Suites M
(843) 538-5473. **$59-$89.** 1286 Sniders Hwy. I-95, exit 53 (SR 63), just e. Ext corridors. **Pets:** Small. $15 daily fee/pet. Service with restrictions, supervision.
ASK ✕ 🛎 💻 ➤

Ramada Inn of Walterboro H
(843) 538-5400. **$65.** 1245 Sniders Hwy. I-95, exit 53 (SR 63), just e. Ext corridors. **Pets:** Medium. $10 daily fee/pet. Designated rooms, service with restrictions, supervision.
ASK ✕ 🛎 💻 ➤

Rice Planters Inn M
(843) 538-8964. **$44.** 97 Ladson Ln. I-95, exit 53 (SR 63), just e. Ext corridors. **Pets:** Small, other species. $5 daily fee/pet. Service with restrictions, supervision.
SAVE ✕ ➤

Super 8 Motel M
(843) 538-5383. **$46-$61, 7 day notice.** 1972 Bells Hwy. I-95, exit 57 (SR 64), just nw. Ext corridors. **Pets:** Small. $10 daily fee/pet. Designated rooms, service with restrictions, supervision.
SAVE ✕ 🛎 💻 ➤

WINNSBORO

Days Inn M
(803) 635-1447. **$55.** 1894 US Hwy 321 Bypass. I-77, exit 34 (SR 34), 6.5 mi w; jct US 321/SR 34/213. Ext corridors. **Pets:** Small. $10 daily fee/pet. Designated rooms, service with restrictions, supervision.
ASK ✕ 🛎 💻 ➤

Fairfield Motel M
(803) 635-3458. **$50-$65.** 56 US 321 Bypass S. Jct SR 213/US 321 Bypass S, 1.8 mi n. Ext corridors. **Pets:** Small. $10 daily fee/pet. Service with restrictions, supervision.
SAVE ✕ 🛎 ➤

YEMASSEE

Best Western Point South M ✿
(843) 726-8101. **$60-$90.** 3536 Point South Dr. I-95, exit 33 (US17), just ne. Ext corridors. **Pets:** Medium. $15 daily fee/room. Designated rooms, service with restrictions, supervision.
SAVE ✕ 🛎 💻 ➤

Holiday Inn Express Point South/Yemassee H
(843) 726-9400. **$69-$139.** 138 Frampton Dr. I-95, exit 33 (US 17), just ne. Int corridors. **Pets:** Medium. $25 one-time fee/pet. Designated rooms, service with restrictions, crate.
ASK ✕ 🛎 🛎 💻 ➤

SOUTH DAKOTA

CITY INDEX

ABERDEEN

 Aberdeen East Super 8 🄷
(605) 229-5005. **$80-$125, 30 day notice.** 2405 6th Ave SE. 1.8 mi e on US 12. Int corridors. **Pets:** $6 daily fee/pet. Designated rooms, service with restrictions, supervision.

[ASK] [✕] [⛐M] [🛏] [🖵] [🏊] [✕]

🔻🔻 Aberdeen North Super 8 🄷
(605) 226-2288. **$80-$150, 30 day notice.** 1023 8th Ave NW. On US 281, 1.5 mi nw. Int corridors. **Pets:** Accepted.

[ASK] [✕] [🛏] [🖵]

🔻🔻 Aberdeen West Super 8 🄷
(605) 225-1711. **$80-$125, 30 day notice.** 714 S Hwy 281. Jct US 12 and 281. Int corridors. **Pets:** $6 daily fee/pet. Designated rooms, service with restrictions, supervision.

[ASK] [✕] [🛏] [🖵]

🅐🅐🅐 🔻🔻🔻 AmericInn Lodge & Suites of Aberdeen 🄷
(605) 225-4565. **$100-$250.** 310 Centennial St. 2.2 mi e on US 12, just n. Int corridors. **Pets:** Large, dogs only. $25 one-time fee/room. Service with restrictions, supervision.

[SAVE] [✕] [⛐M] [🛏] [🖵] [🏊] [✕]

🅐🅐🅐 🔻🔻🔻 Best Western Ramkota Hotel 🄷
(605) 229-4040. **$85-$100.** 1400 8th Ave NW. 1.5 mi nw on US 281. Ext/int corridors. **Pets:** Service with restrictions, crate.

[SAVE] [✕] [⛐M] [🛏] [🖵] [🍽] [🏊] [✕]

🔻🔻🔻 Comfort Inn 🄷
(605) 226-0097. **$84-$190, 7 day notice.** 2923 6th Ave SE. 2 mi e on US 12. Int corridors. **Pets:** Large, other species. $30 deposit/room. No service, crate.

[ASK] [✕] [⛐M] [🛏] [🖵] [🏊] [✕]

🔻🔻🔻 Holiday Inn Express Hotel & Suites 🄷 🐾
(605) 725-4000. **$104-$170.** 3310 7th Ave SE. 2.1 mi e on US 12. Int corridors. **Pets:** Dogs only. $20 one-time fee/room. Designated rooms, service with restrictions, supervision.

[✕] [⛐M] [🛏] [🖵] [🏊] [✕]

ARLINGTON

🔻🔻 Arlington Inn 🄷
(605) 983-4609. **$55-$98.** 402 S Hwy 81. 1 mi s on US 81. Int corridors. **Pets:** Other species. $15 one-time fee/pet. Designated rooms, service with restrictions, supervision.

[ASK] [✕] [🛏]

BLACK HILLS AREA

BELLE FOURCHE

🔻 Ace Motel Ⓜ
(605) 892-2612. **$48-$68.** 109 6th Ave. 0.5 mi n via US 85, just e; just s of US 212 Bypass. Ext corridors. **Pets:** Dogs only. $4 daily fee/pet. Designated rooms, service with restrictions, supervision.

[✕] [🛏]

CUSTER

🅐🅐🅐 🔻🔻 Bavarian Inn Motel 🄷
(605) 673-2802. **$59-$119, 3 day notice.** 907 N 5th St. 1 mi n on US 16 and 385. Ext/int corridors. **Pets:** Accepted.

[SAVE] [✕] [🛏] [🖵] [🍽] [🏊] [✕]

🔻🔻🔻 Rock Crest Lodge and Cabins Ⓒ🄰 🐾
(605) 673-4323. **$59-$129, 14 day notice.** 15 W Mt. Rushmore Rd. US 16, 0.5 mi w. Ext/int corridors. **Pets:** Medium, dogs only. $25 deposit/room, $10 daily fee/pet. Designated rooms, service with restrictions, crate.

[ASK] [✕] [🛏] [🖵] [🏊] [✕]

🅐🅐🅐 🔻 Rocket Motel Ⓜ
(605) 673-4401. **$45-$95.** 211 Mt. Rushmore Rd. On US 16; center. Ext corridors. **Pets:** Other species. $10 daily fee/pet. Designated rooms, service with restrictions, crate.

[SAVE] [✕] [🛏] [🖵]

🅐🅐🅐 🔻🔻🔻 Super 8 Custer 🄷
(605) 673-2200. **$59-$140.** 535 W Mt. Rushmore Rd. US 16, 0.8 mi w. Int corridors. **Pets:** $10 daily fee/pet. Service with restrictions, supervision.

[SAVE] [✕] [🛏] [🖵] [🏊]

DEADWOOD

🔻 Black Hills Inn & Suites Ⓜ
(605) 578-7791. **$43-$85, 3 day notice.** 206 Mountain Shadow Ln. 0.3 mi s of jct US 385 and 85. Ext/int corridors. **Pets:** Accepted.

[ASK] [✕] [🛏] [🖵] [🏊]

🅐🅐🅐 🔻🔻 Deadwood Gulch Resort 🄷 🐾
(605) 578-1294. **$59-$139.** 304 Cliff St. 0.7 mi s on US 85 S. Ext/int corridors. **Pets:** Small, dogs only. $25 one-time fee/pet. Designated rooms, supervision.

[SAVE] [✕] [🛏] [🖵] [🍽] [✕]

🅐🅐🅐 🔻🔻 First Gold Hotel & Gaming 🄷
(605) 578-9777. **$59-$299, 7 day notice.** 270 Main St. 0.7 mi n on US 85. Int corridors. **Pets:** Medium. $25 one-time fee/room. Designated rooms, service with restrictions, supervision.

[SAVE] [✕] [🖵] [🍽]

HILL CITY

🅐🅐🅐 🔻🔻🔻 Best Western Golden Spike Inn & Suites 🄷 🐾
(605) 574-2577. **$71-$155.** 106 Main St. Just n on US 16 and 385. Ext/int corridors. **Pets:** Large, other species. $10 daily fee/pet. Designated rooms, service with restrictions, supervision.

[SAVE] [✕] [🛏] [🖵] [🍽] [🏊] [✕]

◭◭◭ ▼▼▼ **Lantern Inn** 🅜
(605) 574-2582. **$54-$130.** 580 E Main St. On north side of town, on US 16 and 385. Ext corridors. **Pets:** Very small, other species. $6 daily fee/pet. Designated rooms, supervision.
[SAVE] [✕] [📋] [⇌]

◭◭◭ ▼▼▼▼ **The Lodge at Palmer Gulch** 🄷 🐾
(605) 574-2525. **$50-$695, 10 day notice.** 12620 SR 244. On SR 244, 5 mi w of Mt. Rushmore. Int corridors. **Pets:** Dogs only. $20 daily fee/pet. Service with restrictions, supervision.
[SAVE] [✕] [📋] [💻] [🍴] [⇌] [✕]

◭◭◭ ▼▼ **Whispering Winds Cottages** 🄲🄰
(605) 574-9533. **$80-$140, 3 day notice.** 12720 S Hwy 16. US 16 E, 5 mi e, then 1 mi s of US 385. Ext corridors. **Pets:** Accepted.
[SAVE] [✕] [📋]

HOT SPRINGS

◭◭◭ ▼▼▼ **Americas Best Value Inn By The River** 🅜
(605) 745-4292. **$40-$90.** 602 W River. On US 385; downtown. Ext corridors. **Pets:** Large. $10 daily fee/pet. Designated rooms, supervision.
[SAVE] [✕] [📋] [⇌]

◭◭◭ ▼▼▼ **Best Western Sundowner Inn** 🄷
(605) 745-7378. **$54-$200.** 737 S 6th St. 0.5 mi se off US 18 and 385. Int corridors. **Pets:** Medium, other species. Designated rooms, service with restrictions, supervision.
[SAVE] [✕] [♿M] [📋] [💻] [⇌] [✕]

◭◭◭ ▼▼▼ **Budget Host Hills Inn** 🅜
(605) 745-3130. **$49-$154.** 640 S 6th St. 0.5 mi se off US 18 and 385. Ext corridors. **Pets:** Medium. Designated rooms, service with restrictions, supervision.
[SAVE] [✕] [📋] [⇌]

◭◭◭ ▼▼▼▼ **Holiday Inn Express Hotel & Suites** 🄷
(605) 745-4411. **Call for rates.** 1401 Hwy 18. Jct US 18 and 385, 0.7 mi w on US 18 Bypass. Int corridors. **Pets:** Accepted.
[SAVE] [✕] [♿M] [📋] [💻] [✕]

▼▼ **Hot Springs Super 8** 🄷
(605) 745-3888. **Call for rates.** 800 Mammoth St. Jct US 18 and 385, 1 mi w on US 18 Bypass. Int corridors. **Pets:** Accepted.
[✕] [📋] [💻]

KEYSTONE

◭◭◭ ▼▼▼▼ **Best Western Four Presidents Lodge** 🄷
(605) 666-4472. **$79-$189, 3 day notice.** 24075 Hwy 16A. On US 16A, 1 mi n. Int corridors. **Pets:** Accepted.
[SAVE] [✕] [♿M] [📋] [💻] [⇌]

◭◭◭ ▼▼▼ **Holy Smoke Resort** 🄲🄰 🐾
(605) 666-4616. **$50-$145, 3 day notice.** 24105 Hwy 16A. On US 16A, 1 mi n. Ext corridors. **Pets:** Dogs only. $8 daily fee/pet. Designated rooms, service with restrictions, supervision.
[SAVE] [✕] [📋] [💻] [🍴] [🎿]

▼▼ **Mt. Rushmore's Washington Inn** 🄷
(605) 666-5070. **$39-$199, 3 day notice.** 231 Winter St. On US 16A; downtown. Ext/int corridors. **Pets:** Medium, other species. Designated rooms, service with restrictions, supervision.
[ASK] [✕] [♿M] [📋] [⇌]

▼▼ **Mt. Rushmore's White House Resort** 🄷
(605) 666-4917. **$39-$199, 3 day notice.** 115 Swanzey St. Jct US 16A and SR 40. Ext/int corridors. **Pets:** Medium, other species. Designated rooms, service with restrictions, supervision.
[ASK] [✕] [♿M] [📋] [🍴] [⇌] [✕]

◭◭◭ ▼▼▼ **Powder House Lodge** 🄲🄰
(605) 666-4646. **$70-$250, 3 day notice.** 24125 Hwy 16A. On US 16A, 1.5 mi n. Ext corridors. **Pets:** Accepted.
[SAVE] [📋] [💻] [🍴] [⇌]

LEAD

◭◭◭ ▼▼▼▼ **Spearfish Canyon Lodge** 🄷 🐾
(605) 584-3435. **$89-$169, 5 day notice.** 10619 Roughlock Falls Rd. I-90, exit 14 (Spearfish Canyon), 13 mi s. Int corridors. **Pets:** $25 daily fee/pet. Service with restrictions, supervision.
[SAVE] [✕] [📋] [💻] [🍴] [✕]

RAPID CITY

▼▼ **Americas Best Value Inn** 🄷
(605) 343-5434. **$59-$199.** 620 Howard St. I-90, exit 58, just nw of Haines Ave. Int corridors. **Pets:** Other species. $10 daily fee/room. Service with restrictions, supervision.
[ASK] [✕] [📋] [💻] [⇌]

◭◭◭ ▼▼▼ **AmericInn Lodge & Suites of Rapid City** 🄷
(605) 343-8424. **$69-$299.** 1632 Rapp St. I-90, exit 59 (LaCrosse St), just se. Int corridors. **Pets:** Accepted.
[SAVE] [✕] [♿M] [📋] [💻] [⇌] [✕]

◭◭◭ ▼▼▼▼ **Best Western Ramkota Hotel** 🄷
(605) 343-8550. **$100-$260.** 2111 N LaCrosse St. I-90, exit 59 (LaCrosse St), just n. Int/int corridors. **Pets:** Accepted.
[SAVE] [✕] [♿M] [📋] [🍴] [⇌] [✕]

◭◭◭ ▼▼▼ **Best Western Town & Country Inn** 🄷 🐾
(605) 343-5383. **$59-$159, 3 day notice.** 2505 Mt. Rushmore Rd. 1.3 mi s on US 16. Ext corridors. **Pets:** Medium, other species. $20 daily fee/pet. Service with restrictions, supervision.
[SAVE] [✕] [📋] [💻] [⇌]

◭◭◭ ▼▼ **Big Sky Lodge** 🅜 🐾
(605) 348-3200. **$59-$129.** 4080 Tower Rd. 3 mi s on US 16, 0.3 mi n on Skyline Dr, take service road off US 16. Ext corridors. **Pets:** Other species. $10 daily fee/room. Designated rooms, service with restrictions, supervision.
[SAVE] [✕] [📋] [💻] [🎿]

◭◭◭ ▼▼▼ **Country Inn & Suites By Carlson** 🄷
(605) 394-0017. **$59-$249.** 2321 N LaCrosse St. I-90, exit 59 (LaCrosse St), 0.3 mi n. Int corridors. **Pets:** Accepted.
[SAVE] [✕] [♿M] [📋] [💻] [⇌] [✕]

◭◭◭ ▼▼▼ **Days Inn I-90** 🄷
(605) 348-8410. **$59-$299.** 1570 N LaCrosse St. I-90, exit 59 (LaCrosse St), just s. Int corridors. **Pets:** Medium, other species. $10 daily fee/pet. Designated rooms, service with restrictions, crate.
[SAVE] [✕] [♿M] [📋] [💻] [⇌]

◭◭◭ ▼▼ **Fair Value Inn** 🅜
(605) 342-8118. **$45-$100.** 1607 LaCrosse St. I-90, exit 59 (LaCrosse St), 0.3 mi s. Ext corridors. **Pets:** Dogs only. Designated rooms, service with restrictions, supervision.
[SAVE] [✕] [📋] [💻]

◭◭◭ ▼▼▼ **Gold Star Motel** 🅜
(605) 341-7051. **$45-$78.** 801 E North. I-90, exit 60, 1.5 mi sw on I-90 business loop, 1.2 mi s, then just e, from exit 59 (LaCrosse St). Ext corridors. **Pets:** $5 daily fee/pet. Service with restrictions, supervision.
[SAVE] [✕] [📋]

▼▼▼ **GrandStay Residential Suites** 🄷
(605) 341-5100. **$84-$300.** 660 Disk Dr. I-90, exit 58C (Haines Ave), just n, then w. Int corridors. **Pets:** Medium. $50 daily fee/pet. Designated rooms, service with restrictions, supervision.
[ASK] [✕] [♿M] [📋] [💻] [⇌]

▼▼▼ **Holiday Inn Express Hotel & Suites, I-90** 🄷
(605) 355-9090. **$94-$269.** 645 E Disk Dr. I-90, exit 59 (LaCrosse St), just ne. Int corridors. **Pets:** Medium, other species. $10 daily fee/pet. Designated rooms, service with restrictions, supervision.
[ASK] [✕] [♿M] [📋] [💻] [⇌]

▼▼▼ Holiday Inn-Rushmore Plaza **H**
(605) 348-4000. **Call for rates.** 505 N 5th St. I-90, exit 58, 1.3 mi s on Haines. Int corridors. **Pets:** Accepted.
⊠ &M 🛇 🖳 ❌ 🏊 ⊠

AAA ▼▼▼ La Quinta Inn & Suites **H** ❀
(605) 718-7000. **$49-$149.** 1416 N Elk Vale Rd. I-90, exit 61 (Elk Vale Rd), just s, then just e. Int corridors. **Pets:** Medium, other species. Service with restrictions, supervision.
SAVE ⊠ &M 🛇 🖳 ❌ 🏊 ⊠

AAA ▼ Lazy U Motel **M**
(605) 343-4242. **$42-$72.** 2215 Mt. Rushmore Rd. 1 mi s on US 16. Ext corridors. **Pets:** Accepted.
SAVE ⊠ 🛇

AAA ▼▼ Microtel Inn & Suites **H**
(605) 348-2523. **$57-$369.** 1740 Rapp St. I-90, exit 59 (LaCrosse St), just se. Int corridors. **Pets:** Medium, dogs only. $10 daily fee/room. Service with restrictions, supervision.
SAVE ⊠ &M 🛇 🖳 🏊

AAA ▼▼▼ Quality Inn **H**
(605) 342-3322. **$50-$330.** 1902 N LaCrosse St. I-90, exit 59 (LaCrosse St), just s. Ext/int corridors. **Pets:** Medium, other species. $10 daily fee/pet. Service with restrictions, supervision.
SAVE ⊠ &M 🛇 🖳 ❌ 🏊 ⊠

AAA ▼▼▼ Super 8 LaCrosse St **H**
(605) 348-8070. **$49-$110.** 2124 LaCrosse St. I-90, exit 59 (LaCrosse St), just n. Int corridors. **Pets:** Medium, other species. $10 daily fee/pet. Service with restrictions, crate.
SAVE ⊠ &M 🛇 🖳

AAA ▼ Super 8 Motel-South **H** ❀
(605) 342-4911. **$35-$175.** 2520 Tower Rd. 1.4 mi s on US 16, then just e. Int corridors. **Pets:** Other species. Service with restrictions, supervision.
SAVE ⊠ 🛇 🖳

SPEARFISH

AAA ▼▼▼ Best Western Black Hills Lodge **H**
(605) 642-7795. **$59-$119.** 540 E Jackson Blvd. I-90, exit 12, just s. Ext/int corridors. **Pets:** Large, dogs only. $10 daily fee/pet. Designated rooms, service with restrictions, supervision.
SAVE ⊠ 🖳 🏊

▼▼ Days Inn **H** ❀
(605) 642-7101. **$65-$300.** 240 Ryan Rd. I-90, exit 10, 1.2 mi s. Ext/int corridors. **Pets:** Other species. $10 daily fee/pet. Designated rooms, service with restrictions, supervision.
ASK ⊠ 🛇 🖳

AAA ▼▼▼ Holiday Inn Hotel & Convention Center **H** ❀
(605) 642-4683. **$89-$139.** 305 N 27th St. I-90, exit 14 (Spearfish Canyon), just n. Ext/int corridors. **Pets:** $100 deposit/room, $25 one-time fee/pet. Designated rooms, service with restrictions, supervision.
SAVE ⊠ &M 🛇 🖳 ❌ 🏊 ⊠

▼▼ Howard Johnson Express Inn **H**
(605) 642-8105. **$55-$120.** 323 S 27th St. I-90, exit 14 (Spearfish Canyon), just s. Int corridors. **Pets:** Other species. $10 daily fee/pet. Service with restrictions, supervision.
ASK ⊠ 🛇 🖳 ❌ 🏊

▼▼ Spearfish Super 8 **H**
(605) 642-4721. **$54-$225.** 440 Heritage Dr. I-90, exit 14 (Spearfish Canyon), just s, then e, then s. Int corridors. **Pets:** Other species. $10 daily fee/pet. Designated rooms, service with restrictions, supervision.
ASK ⊠ 🛇 🖳 🏊

STURGIS

AAA ▼▼▼ Best Western of Sturgis **H**
(605) 347-3604. **$50-$130.** 2431 S Junction Ave. I-90, exit 32. Ext/int corridors. **Pets:** Other species. $10 daily fee/room. Designated rooms, service with restrictions, supervision.
SAVE ⊠ 🛇 🖳 ❌ 🏊

▼▼▼ Holiday Inn Express & Suites–Sturgis **H** ❀
(605) 347-4140. **$90-$500.** 2721 Lazelle St. I-90, exit 30 (US 14A), just s. Int corridors. **Pets:** Other species. $20 one-time fee/room. Designated rooms, service with restrictions, crate.
ASK ⊠ &M 🛇 🖳 🏊 ⊠

AAA ▼ Star Lite Motel **M**
(605) 347-2506. **$35-$80.** 2426 Junction Ave. I-90, exit 32, just n. Ext corridors. **Pets:** Small. $10 daily fee/pet. Designated rooms, service with restrictions, supervision.
SAVE ⊠ 🛇 🖳

END AREA

BRANDON

▼▼▼ Comfort Inn **H**
(605) 582-5777. **$89-$169.** 1105 N Splitrock Blvd. I-90, exit 406, just s. Int corridors. **Pets:** Accepted.
ASK ⊠ &M 🛇 🖳 🏊 ⊠

BROOKINGS

▼▼ Brookings Super 8 **H**
(605) 692-6920. **$66-$86.** 3034 Lefevre Dr. I-29, exit 132, just e. Int corridors. **Pets:** Accepted.
ASK ⊠ &M 🛇 🏊

AAA ▼▼ Fairfield Inn & Suites **H**
(605) 692-3500. **$85-$103.** 3000 Lefevre Dr. I-29, exit 132, just e. Int corridors. **Pets:** Accepted.
SAVE ⊠ &M 🛇 🖳 🏊 ⊠

▼▼▼ Holiday Inn Express Hotel & Suites **H**
(605) 692-9060. **$110-$150.** 3020 Lefevre Dr. I-29, exit 132, just se. Int corridors. **Pets:** $10 daily fee/pet. Service with restrictions, supervision.
⊠ &M 🛇 🖳 🏊 ⊠

BUFFALO

▼ Tipperary Lodge **M**
(605) 375-3721. **$52-$54.** 604 1st St W. 0.5 mi n on US 85, turn at sign. Int corridors. **Pets:** Other species. Designated rooms, service with restrictions, supervision.
ASK ⊠ 🛇

CANISTOTA

AAA ▼▼▼ Best Western U-Bar Motel **M**
(605) 296-3466. **$61-$97.** 130 Ash St. I-90, exit 368, 6 mi s, follow signs. Ext corridors. **Pets:** Very small, dogs only. Designated rooms, service with restrictions, supervision.
SAVE ⊠ 🛇 🖳

CHAMBERLAIN

▼▼ AmericInn Lodge & Suites of Chamberlain **H**
(605) 734-0985. **$60-$150.** 1981 E King St. I-90, exit 265, just e. Int corridors. **Pets:** Medium, other species. $10 daily fee/room. Designated rooms, service with restrictions, supervision.
ASK ⊠ &M 🛇 🖳 🏊 ⊠

◇◇ ▽ Bel Aire Motel M
(605) 734-5595. **$45-$70.** 312 E King St. On US 16 and I-90 business loop; downtown. Ext/int corridors. **Pets:** Accepted.
[SAVE] [✕] [■]

◇◇ ▽▽ Best Western Lee's Motor Inn H
(605) 734-5575. **$60-$95.** 220 W King St. US 16 and I-90 business loop; downtown. Ext/int corridors. **Pets:** Small, other species. Service with restrictions, supervision.
[SAVE] [✕] [▭] [≈] [✕]

◇◇ ▽▽▽ Cedar Shore Resort H
(605) 734-6376. **$90-$200.** 1500 Shoreline Dr. I-90, exit 260, 2.5 mi e on Business Rt I-90, then 1 mi ne on Mickelson county road, follow signs. Int corridors. **Pets:** $10 daily fee/room. Service with restrictions, supervision.
[SAVE] [✕] [&M] [■] [▭] [¶¶] [≈] [✕]

▽▽ Holiday Inn Express H
(605) 734-5593. **Call for rates.** 100 W Hwy 16. I-90, exit 260, just n. Int corridors. **Pets:** Accepted.
[✕] [&M] [▭]

◇◇ ▽▽ Oasis Inn H ❀
(605) 734-6061. **$59-$109.** 1100 E Hwy 16. I-90, exit 260, 0.4 mi e on US 16 and I-90 business loop. Ext/int corridors. **Pets:** Other species. Designated rooms, service with restrictions, supervision.
[SAVE] [✕] [&M] [■] [▭] [≈]

DELL RAPIDS

▽▽ Bilmar Inn & Suites H
(605) 428-4288. **$56-$110.** 510 N Hwy 77. I-29, exit 98 (SR 115), 3 mi e, then just n. Int corridors. **Pets:** Accepted.
[ASK] [✕] [&M] [■]

DE SMET

◇◇ ▽▽▽ De Smet Super Deluxe Inn & Suites H ❀
(605) 854-9388. **$65-$140.** 288 Hwy 14 E. US 14, just e. Int corridors. **Pets:** Other species. $10 daily fee/pet. Designated rooms, service with restrictions, supervision.
[SAVE] [✕] [■] [▭] [≈]

FAITH

◇◇ ▽▽ Prairie Vista Inn H
(605) 967-2343. **$66-$86.** Hwy 212 & E 1st. On US 212; at east city edge. Int corridors. **Pets:** Medium. $15 daily fee/pet. Designated rooms, service with restrictions, crate.
[SAVE] [✕] [■] [▭]

FAULKTON

▽▽ Super 8 H
(605) 598-4567. **Call for rates.** 700 Main St. On US 212; center. Int corridors. **Pets:** Accepted.
[✕] [■] [▭]

FLANDREAU

◇◇ ▽▽▽ Royal River Casino & Hotel H
(605) 997-3746. **$65-$199.** 607 S Veterans St. I-29, exit 114, 7 mi e, follow signs. Int corridors. **Pets:** Medium, dogs only. $50 deposit/room. Designated rooms, service with restrictions, supervision.
[SAVE] [✕] [&M] [■] [▭] [¶¶] [≈] [✕]

FORT PIERRE

▽▽ Fort Pierre Motel M
(605) 223-3111. **$58-$78, 3 day notice.** 211 S 1st St. On US 83, 1.2 mi s of jct US 14. Ext corridors. **Pets:** Accepted.
[✕] [■]

FREEMAN

▽▽▽ Freeman Country Inn H
(605) 925-4888. **$58-$75.** 1019 S Hwy 81. On US 81, just s. Int corridors. **Pets:** Other species. $20 daily fee/pet. Designated rooms, service with restrictions, supervision.
[ASK] [✕] [■]

HURON

◇◇ ▽▽▽ Best Western of Huron H
(605) 352-2000. **$81-$125.** 2000 Dakota Ave. 1.3 mi s on SR 37. Ext/int corridors. **Pets:** Dogs only. $10 daily fee/room. Service with restrictions, crate.
[SAVE] [✕] [&M] [■] [▭] [✕]

▽▽ Comfort Inn H
(605) 352-6655. **Call for rates.** 100 21st St SW. 1.3 mi s on SR 37. Ext/int corridors. **Pets:** Accepted.
[✕] [&M] [■] [▭] [✕]

INTERIOR

◇◇ ▽ Badlands Budget Host Inn M
(605) 433-5335. **$55-$67.** 900 SD Hwy 377. Jct SR 44 and 377, 2 mi s of Badlands National Park. Ext corridors. **Pets:** Other species. $5 daily fee/room. Service with restrictions, supervision.
[SAVE] [▭] [≈] [▨] [✓]

KADOKA

▽▽ Americas Best Value Inn M
(605) 837-2188. **$50-$130.** 401 SR 73. I-90, exit 150, just s. Int corridors. **Pets:** Accepted.
[✕] [■]

◇◇ ▽ Budget Host Sundowner Motor Inn M
(605) 837-2296. **$50-$145.** 510 SD Hwy 73. I-90, exit 150, just s. Ext corridors. **Pets:** Accepted.
[SAVE] [✕] [■] [≈]

◇◇ ▽▽▽ Rodeway Inn M 🐾
(605) 837-2287. **$59-$109.** 915 Hwy 248. 1.5 mi w on I-90 business route from exit 152, 1.3 mi e from exit 150. Ext corridors. **Pets:** Medium, other species. Service with restrictions, crate.
[SAVE] [✕] [&M] [▭] [¶¶] [≈] [✕]

MADISON

▽▽▽ AmericInn Lodge & Suites of Madison H
(605) 256-3076. **$74-$123.** 504 10th St SE. SR 34, 0.5 mi se; south side of town. Int corridors. **Pets:** Accepted.
[ASK] [✕] [&M] [■] [▭] [≈]

MITCHELL

◇◇ ▽▽▽ AmericInn Lodge & Suites of Mitchell H
(605) 996-9700. **$72-$135.** 1421 S Burr St. I-90, exit 332, just n. Int corridors. **Pets:** Medium, other species. $20 daily fee/room. Designated rooms, service with restrictions, supervision.
[SAVE] [✕] [&M] [■] [▭] [≈]

◇◇ ▽▽▽ Best Western Motor Inn M ❀
(605) 996-5536. **$40-$100.** 1001 S Burr St. I-90, exit 332, 0.6 mi n. Ext corridors. **Pets:** Large. Service with restrictions, supervision.
[SAVE] [✕] [■] [▭] [≈]

◇◇ ▽▽▽ Days Inn Mitchell H
(605) 996-6208. **$69-$109.** 1506 S Burr St. I-90, exit 332, just n. Int corridors. **Pets:** $25 deposit/pet, $10 daily fee/pet. Designated rooms, service with restrictions, supervision.
[SAVE] [✕] [&M] [■] [▭] [≈] [✕]

WWW Hampton Inn H ❀
(605) 995-1575. **$67-$123.** 1920 Highland Way. I-90, exit 332, just se. Int corridors. **Pets:** Dogs only. $20 one-time fee/room. Service with restrictions.
SAVE ✕ ᴴ 🍴 ▣ 🏊 ✕

WWW Kelly Inn & Suites H
(605) 995-0500. **$69-$130.** 1010 Cabela Dr. I-90, exit 332, just sw. Ext/int corridors. **Pets:** Other species. Service with restrictions, supervision.
SAVE ✕ 🍴 ▣ 🏊 ✕

WWW Ramada Inn & Suites Conference Center H ❀
(605) 996-6501. **Call for rates.** 1525 W Havens St. I-90, exit 330, 0.5 mi n. Ext/int corridors. **Pets:** Other species. $10 daily fee/room. Service with restrictions, crate.
SAVE ✕ ᴴ 🍴 ▣ 🍴 🏊 ✕

WWW Thunderbird Lodge M ❀
(605) 996-6645. **$49-$109.** 1601 S Burr St. I-90, exit 332, just n. Ext/int corridors. **Pets:** Medium. $10 daily fee/room. Designated rooms, service with restrictions, supervision.
SAVE ✕ ᴴ 🍴 ▣

MOBRIDGE

WW Wrangler Inn H
(605) 845-3641. **$65-$149.** 820 W Grand Crossing. 0.5 mi w on US 12. Ext/int corridors. **Pets:** Designated rooms, service with restrictions, supervision.
ASK ✕ 🍴 ▣ 🍴 🏊 ✕

MURDO

WWW Best Western Graham's M
(605) 669-2441. **$49-$129, 7 day notice.** 301 W 5th. On I-90 business loop, 0.5 mi w of jct US 83; I-90, exits 191 and 192. Ext corridors. **Pets:** Medium, other species. $10 one-time fee/room. Designated rooms, service with restrictions, supervision.
SAVE ✕ ▣ 🏊

WWW Days Inn Range Country H
(605) 669-2425. **$63-$150.** 302 W 5th. I-90 business loop, 0.5 mi w of jct US 83, exits 192 and 191. Ext/int corridors. **Pets:** Accepted.
SAVE ✕ ▣ 🏊

NORTH SIOUX CITY

WWWW Hampton Inn H ❀
(605) 232-9739. **$75-$110.** 101 S Sodrac Dr. I-29, exit 2, just w. Int corridors. **Pets:** Small. $10 one-time fee/room. Service with restrictions, supervision.
✕ ᴴ 🍴 ▣ 🏊 ✕

PICKSTOWN

WW Fort Randall Inn M
(605) 487-7801. **$65-$80.** 116 US Hwy 18. On US 18/281; just e of the dam. Ext corridors. **Pets:** Dogs only. $10 daily fee/room. Service with restrictions, crate.
ASK ✕ 🍴

PIERRE

WWW Best Western Ramkota Hotel H
(605) 224-6877. **$106-$121.** 920 W Sioux Ave. 1 mi w on US 14/83. Ext/int corridors. **Pets:** Other species. Service with restrictions, supervision.
SAVE ✕ 🍴 ▣ 🍴 🏊

WWW Comfort Inn of Pierre H
(605) 224-0377. **$65-$120.** 410 W Sioux Ave. 0.3 mi w on US 14/83 and SR 34. Int corridors. **Pets:** Dogs only. $10 daily fee/pet. Service with restrictions, supervision.
SAVE ✕ ᴴ 🍴 ▣ 🏊

WWW Governor's Inn H ❀
(605) 224-4200. **$70-$135.** 700 W Sioux Ave. 0.8 mi w on US 14/83 and SR 34. Ext/int corridors. **Pets:** Other species. $25 one-time fee/room. Supervision.
SAVE ✕ 🍴 ▣ 🏊

WWW River Lodge H
(605) 224-4140. **$62-$79.** 713 W Sioux Ave. 0.8 mi w on US 14/83. Int corridors. **Pets:** Accepted.
SAVE ✕ 🍴

PINE RIDGE

WWW Prairie Winds Casino & Hotel H
(605) 867-2683. **Call for rates.** HC 49 Box 10. On US 18, 13 mi e of US 385 on Pine Ridge Indian Reservation. Int corridors. **Pets:** Accepted.
SAVE ✕ ᴴ 🍴 ▣ 🍴 🏊 ✕

PLANKINTON

WW Smart Choice Inn & Suites H ❀
(605) 942-7722. **$40-$80.** 801 S Main St. I-90, exit 308, just n. Int corridors. **Pets:** Other species. $8 one-time fee/pet. Service with restrictions, supervision.
ASK ✕ 🍴

SIOUX FALLS

WW Baymont Inn H
(605) 362-0835. **$79-$145.** 3200 Meadow Ave. I-29, exit 77 (41st St), just w, then just n. Int corridors. **Pets:** Other species. $25 one-time fee/room. Service with restrictions, supervision.
ASK ✕ ᴴ 🍴 ▣ 🏊

WWW Best Western Empire Towers H ❀
(605) 361-3118. **$75-$130.** 4100 W Shirley Pl. I-29, exit 77 (41st St), just ne. Int corridors. **Pets:** Other species. $15 daily fee/room. Designated rooms, service with restrictions, supervision.
SAVE ✕ 🍴 ▣ 🏊

WWWW Best Western Ramkota Hotel & Conference Center H ❀
(605) 336-0650. **$120-$300.** 3200 W Maple. I-29, exit 81 (Airport/Russell St), just e. Ext/int corridors. **Pets:** Large, dogs only. Service with restrictions, supervision.
SAVE ✕ ᴴ 🍴 ▣ 🍴 🏊 ✕

WWWW ClubHouse Hotel & Suites H ❀
(605) 361-8700. **$139-$179.** 2320 S Louise Ave. I-29, exit 78 (26th St), just e. Ext/int corridors. **Pets:** Other species. Service with restrictions, supervision.
SAVE ✕ ᴴ 🍴 ▣ 🏊 ✕

WWW Comfort Inn by Choice Hotels South H
(605) 361-2822. **Call for rates.** 3216 S Carolyn Ave. I-29, exit 77 (41st St), just e, then n. Int corridors. **Pets:** Accepted.
✕ 🍴 ▣ 🏊

WWWW Comfort Suites by Choice Hotels H
(605) 362-9711. **Call for rates.** 3208 S Carolyn Ave. I-29, exit 77 (41st St), just e, then n. Int corridors. **Pets:** Accepted.
✕ 🍴 ▣ 🏊

WW Country Inn & Suites By Carlson H
(605) 373-0153. **$84-$159.** 200 E 8th St. Just e of Phillips Ave; downtown. Int corridors. **Pets:** Accepted.
ASK ✕ ᴴ 🍴 ▣ 🍴 🏊

W Days Inn Airport H
(605) 331-5959. **$59-$139.** 5001 N Cliff Ave. I-90, exit 399 (Cliff Ave), just s. Int corridors. **Pets:** $10 daily fee/pet. Designated rooms, no service.
✕ ᴴ 🍴 ▣

▼▼ Days Inn-Empire ⛔
(605) 361-9240. **$59-$139.** 3401 Gateway Blvd. I-29, exit 77 (41st St), just w. Int corridors. **Pets:** $10 daily fee/pet. Designated rooms, no service, supervision.
⊠ 🖥 💻

(AAA) ▼▼▼▼ Homewood Suites By Hilton ⛔ ☘
(605) 338-8585. **$69-$169.** 3620 W Avera Dr. I-229, exit 1C (Louise Ave), just s. Int corridors. **Pets:** Other species. $5 daily fee/room, $15 one-time fee/room. Service with restrictions.
SAVE ⊠ ⛎ 🖥 💻 ➥ ⊠

(AAA) ▼▼▼ Kelly Inn ⛔
(605) 338-6242. **$64-$99.** 3101 W Russell St. I-29, exit 81 (Airport/Russell St), 0.3 mi e. Ext/int corridors. **Pets:** Service with restrictions, crate.
SAVE ⊠ 🖥 💻 ➥

(AAA) ▼▼▼▼ Quality Inn & Suites ⛔ ☘
(605) 336-1900. **$89-$169.** 5410 N Granite Ln. I-29, exit 83 (SR 38), just e, then 0.3 mi n. Int corridors. **Pets:** Medium, other species. $10 daily fee/pet. Designated rooms, service with restrictions.
SAVE ⊠ ⛎ 🖥 💻 ➥

▼▼ Red Roof Inn ⛔
(605) 361-1864. **$43-$78, 7 day notice.** 3500 S Gateway Blvd. I-29, exit 77 (41st St), just w. Int corridors. **Pets:** Accepted.
ASK ⊠ 🖥

▼▼▼ Residence Inn by Marriott ⛔
(605) 361-2202. **$130-$150.** 4509 W Empire Pl. I-29, exit 77 (41st St), 0.5 mi se. Int corridors. **Pets:** Other species. $75 one-time fee/room. Service with restrictions, crate.
⊠ ⛎ 🖥 💻 ➥ ⊠

(AAA) ▼▼▼▼ Sheraton Sioux Falls ⛔ ☘
(605) 331-0100. **$79-$159.** 1211 N West Ave. I-29, exit 81 (Airport/Russell St), 1.3 mi e. Int corridors. **Pets:** Large, dogs only. Service with restrictions, supervision.
SAVE ⊠ ⛎ 🖥 💻 🍽 ➥ ⊠

(AAA) ▼▼▼▼ Staybridge Suites ⛔ ☘
(605) 361-2298. **$130-$230, 10 day notice.** 2505 S Carolyn Ave. I-29, exit 78, just se. Int corridors. **Pets:** Medium, other species. $25 daily fee/pet. Designated rooms, service with restrictions, supervision.
SAVE ⊠ ⛎ 🖥 💻 ➥ ⊠

(AAA) ▼▼▼ Super 8/I-90/Airport East ⛔ ☘
(605) 339-9212. **$50-$100, 3 day notice.** 4808 N Cliff Ave. I-90, exit 399 (Cliff Ave), 0.3 mi s. Int corridors. **Pets:** Medium, other species. $10 one-time fee/pet. No service, supervision.
SAVE ⊠ 🖥 💻

▼▼ Super 8-East ⛔
(605) 338-8881. **$80-$149.** 2616 E 10th St. I-229, exit 6, just e. Int corridors. **Pets:** Accepted.
ASK ⊠ ⛎ 🖥 💻 ➥

▼▼▼ TownePlace Suites by Marriott ⛔
(605) 361-2626. **$89-$99.** 4545 W Homefield Dr. I-29, exit 78 (26th St), just w. Int corridors. **Pets:** Medium, other species. $75 one-time fee/room. Service with restrictions, supervision.
⊠ ⛎ 🖥 💻 ➥ ⊠

SISSETON

(AAA) ▼▼▼ Sisseton Super 8 ⛔ ☘
(605) 742-0808. **$70-$110.** 2104 SD Hwy 10. I-29, exit 232 (SR 10), 1.5 mi w; just w of jct SR 127. Int corridors. **Pets:** Large, dogs only. Supervision.
SAVE ⊠ ⛎ 🖥 💻 ➥

SUMMERSET

▼▼ Ramada ⛔
(605) 787-4844. **Call for rates.** 7900 Stagestop Rd. I-90, exit 48, just s. Int corridors. **Pets:** Accepted.
⊠ ⛎ 🖥 💻 ➥

VERMILLION

(AAA) ▼▼▼ Comfort Inn ⛔
(605) 624-8333. **$79-$99.** 701 W Cherry St. I-29, exit 26 (SR 50), 7.5 mi w on Business Rt SR 50. Int corridors. **Pets:** Medium. $5 daily fee/pet. Service with restrictions, supervision.
SAVE ⊠ ⛎ 🖥 💻 ➥ ⊠

▼▼▼▼ Holiday Inn Express Hotel & Suites-Vermillion ⛔
(605) 624-7600. **Call for rates.** 1200 N Dakota St. I-29, exit 26, 7 mi w. Int corridors. **Pets:** Accepted.
⊠ ⛎ 🖥 💻 ➥

WALL

(AAA) ▼▼▼▼ Best Western Plains Motel Ⓜ
(605) 279-2145. **$60-$170.** 712 Glenn St. I-90, exit 110, just n. Ext corridors. **Pets:** Other species. $10 one-time fee/pet. Service with restrictions, supervision.
SAVE ⊠ 🖥 💻 ➥ ⊠

(AAA) ▼▼▼ Econo Lodge Ⓜ
(605) 279-2121. **$59-$179.** 804 Glenn St. I-90, exit 110, just n. Ext corridors. **Pets:** Medium. $10 one-time fee/pet. Designated rooms, service with restrictions, supervision.
SAVE ⊠ 🖥 💻 ➥

(AAA) ▼▼ Sunshine Inn Ⓜ
(605) 279-2178. **$49-$69.** 608 Main St. Downtown. Ext corridors. **Pets:** Other species. $5 one-time fee/room. Service with restrictions.
SAVE ⊠

WATERTOWN

(AAA) ▼▼▼▼ Best Western Ramkota Hotel ⛔ ☘
(605) 886-8011. **$96-$175.** 1901 9th Ave SW. I-29, exit 177 (US 212), 4 mi w. Int corridors. **Pets:** Medium, dogs only. Service with restrictions, supervision.
SAVE ⊠ ⛎ 🖥 💻 🍽 ➥ ⊠

(AAA) ▼▼▼ Comfort Inn ⛔
(605) 886-3010. **$75-$140.** 800 35th St Cir. I-29, exit 177 (US 212), just w. Ext/int corridors. **Pets:** Other species. $15 one-time fee/room. Designated rooms, service with restrictions, supervision.
SAVE ⊠ ⛎ 🖥 💻 ➥

(AAA) ▼▼▼ Country Inn & Suites By Carlson ⛔
(605) 886-8900. **$96-$140.** 3400 8th Ave SE. I-29, exit 177 (US 212), just w. Int corridors. **Pets:** $45 one-time fee/room. Designated rooms, service with restrictions, supervision.
SAVE ⊠ ⛎ 🖥 💻 ➥

(AAA) ▼▼▼ Days Inn ⛔
(605) 886-3500. **Call for rates.** 2900 9th Ave SE. I-29, exit 177 (US 212), 0.5 mi w. Ext/int corridors. **Pets:** Other species. $20 one-time fee/room. Service with restrictions, supervision.
SAVE ⊠ ⛎ 🖥 💻 ➥

(AAA) ▼▼▼▼ Holiday Inn Express Hotel & Suites ⛔
(605) 882-3636. **$104-$144.** 3901 9th Ave SE. I-29, exit 177 (US 212), just e. Int corridors. **Pets:** $10 one-time fee/room. Service with restrictions, supervision.
SAVE ⊠ ⛎ 🖥 💻 ➥ ⊠

▼▼ Super 8-Watertown ⛔
(605) 882-1900. **$56-$73.** 503 14th Ave SE. On US 81, 0.3 mi s of jct US 212. Int corridors. **Pets:** $10 daily fee/room. Designated rooms, service with restrictions, supervision.
ASK ⊠ 🖥 💻 ➥

◆◆ Travelers Inn Motel **H**
(605) 882-2243. **Call for rates.** 920 14th St SE. I-29, exit 177 (US 212), 1.5 mi w, then just s. Int corridors. **Pets:** Accepted.

◆◆ ◆ Travel Host Motel **M**
(605) 886-6120. **$45-$69.** 1714 9th Ave SW. I-29, exit 177 (US 212), 4 mi w. Int corridors. **Pets:** Dogs only. $5 one-time fee/pet. Designated rooms, no service, supervision.

WINNER

◆◆◆◆ Holiday Inn Express Hotel & Suites **H**
(605) 842-2255. **$89-$204.** 1360 E Hwy 44. Just ne of jct US 18 and 183. Int corridors. **Pets:** Very small, other species. $25 daily fee/pet. Service with restrictions, supervision.

YANKTON

◆◆ ◆◆ Best Western Kelly Inn-Yankton **H**
(605) 665-2906. **$79-$114, 3 day notice.** 1607 Hwy 50 E. On US 50, 1.8 mi e. Ext/int corridors. **Pets:** Other species. Service with restrictions, supervision.

◆◆ ◆◆ Days Inn **H**
(605) 665-8717. **$65-$110.** 2410 Broadway. US 81, 1.7 mi n. Int corridors. **Pets:** Medium, other species. $10 daily fee/pet. Service with restrictions, supervision.

◆◆ Lewis & Clark Resort **M**
(605) 665-2680. **Call for rates.** 43496 Shore Dr. 4 mi w on SR 52; in Lewis and Clark State Park, turn into park, just w of Marina. Ext corridors. **Pets:** Accepted.

TENNESSEE

ALCOA

Family Inns of America M
(865) 970-2006. **$49-$59.** 2450 Airport Hwy. US 129, just e. Ext corridors. **Pets:** Very small, dogs only. Service with restrictions, supervision.
[SAVE] [X] [🛏] [🏊]

Jameson Inn Alcoa H
(865) 984-6800. **$93-$100.** 206 Corporate Pl. US 129, just s. Int corridors. **Pets:** Accepted.
[ASK] [X] [🛏] [🛏] [🏊] [🏊]

MainStay Suites H
(865) 379-7799. **$114-$199.** 361 Fountain View Cir. US 129, just n on SR 35, just se on Associates Blvd, then just w. Int corridors. **Pets:** Small, other species. $100 one-time fee/room. Service with restrictions, supervision.
[SAVE] [X] [🛏] [🛏] [🏊]

ATHENS

Days Inn-Athens M
(423) 745-5800. **$60-$75, 3 day notice.** 2541 Decatur Pike. I-75, exit 49, 0.3 mi e. Ext corridors. **Pets:** Medium. $10 daily fee/pet. Service with restrictions, crate.
[ASK] [X] [🛏] [🛏] [🏊]

Travelodge H
(423) 745-1212. **Call for rates.** 115 CR 247. I-75, exit 52, just w. Ext corridors. **Pets:** Accepted.
[X] [🛏] [🛏] [🏊]

BRENTWOOD

Baymont Inn & Suites H 🐾
(615) 376-4666. **$90-$111.** 111 Penn Warren Dr. I-65, exit 74B, 1.5 mi w, then just s on West Park. Int corridors. **Pets:** Large, other species. $10 daily fee/pet. Designated rooms, service with restrictions.
[SAVE] [X] [🛏] [🛏] [🏊]

Candlewood Suites H
(615) 309-0600. **Call for rates.** 5129 Virginia Way. I-65, exit 74B, 0.5 mi w, 0.5 mi s on Franklin Rd (US 31), 1.2 mi w on Maryland Way, just s on Ward Cir, then just s. Int corridors. **Pets:** Accepted.
[X] [🛏] [🏊]

MainStay Suites-Brentwood H 🐾
(615) 371-8477. **Call for rates.** 107 Brentwood Blvd. I-65, exit 74B, 1 mi w. Int corridors. **Pets:** Small, other species. $10 daily fee/pet. Service with restrictions, crate.
[X] [🛏] [🛏] [🏊]

Residence Inn Brentwood H
(615) 371-0100. **$197-$211.** 206 Ward Cir. I-65, exit 74B, 0.3 mi s on Franklin Pike Cir (US 31 S), 0.5 mi w on Maryland Way. Ext/int corridors. **Pets:** Medium. $100 one-time fee/room.
[SAVE] [X] [🛏] [🛏] [🏊] [🏊]

Sleep Inn H
(615) 376-2122. **Call for rates.** 1611 Galleria Blvd. I-65, exit 69 northbound, 0.4 mi, then just n; exit 69W southbound, just n. Int corridors. **Pets:** Accepted.
[X] [🛏] [🛏] [🏊]

BULLS GAP

Best Western Executive Inn H
(423) 235-9111. **$80-$100.** 50 Speedway Ln. I-81, exit 23. Int corridors. **Pets:** Accepted.
[SAVE] [X] [🛏] [🛏] [🏊]

BUTLER

Iron Mountain Inn B&B and Creekside Chalet BB
(423) 768-2446. **$109-$350, 14 day notice.** 138 Moreland Dr. 1.6 mi w on Pine Orchard Rd from SR 67 at Stout Store, follow signs; 13 mi w on SR 67 from US 421 in Mountain City, follow sign at Stout Store area; 15.1 mi from Shell Station in Hampton to Pine Orchard, 1.6 mi to Moreland Dr. Ext/int corridors. **Pets:** Small, dogs only. $50 one-time fee/pet. Designated rooms, no service, supervision.
[ASK] [X] [🛏] [🛏] [🏊]

CARYVILLE

Budget Host Inn M
(423) 562-9595. **$33-$55, 7 day notice.** 115 Woods Ave. I-75, exit 134, just w. Ext corridors. **Pets:** Very small, dogs only. $10 daily fee/pet. Supervision.
[SAVE] [X] [🛏]

CHATTANOOGA

America's Best Inn-Hamilton Mall Area M
(423) 894-5454. **$49-$100.** 7717 Lee Hwy. I-75, exit 7B northbound; exit 7 southbound. Ext corridors. **Pets:** Accepted.
[ASK] [X] [🛏] [🛏] [🏊]

Baymont Inn & Suites-Chattanooga H
(423) 821-1090. **$60-$130.** 3540 Cummings Hwy. I-24, exit 174, 0.4 mi s. Int corridors. **Pets:** Medium, other species. $50 deposit/room, $10 daily fee/pet. Designated rooms, service with restrictions, supervision.
[SAVE] [X] [🛏] [🛏] [🏊]

Best Western Heritage Inn H
(423) 899-3311. **$49-$125.** 7641 Lee Hwy. I-75, exit 7B northbound; exit 7 southbound. Ext corridors. **Pets:** Small, dogs only. $10 daily fee/pet. Service with restrictions, crate.
[SAVE] [X] [🛏] [🛏] [🍽] [🏊]

Best Western Royal Inn H
(423) 821-6840. **$80-$120.** 3644 Cummings Hwy. I-24, exit 174, 0.4 mi s. Ext corridors. **Pets:** Small. $10 daily fee/pet. Service with restrictions, supervision.
[SAVE] [X] [🛏] [🛏] [🏊]

◆◆◆ Comfort Inn 🅷 ❖
(423) 499-1993. **$65-$99.** 7620 Hamilton Park Dr. I-75, exit 7B northbound; exit 7 southbound, just w to Lee Hwy, just s, then just e. Int corridors. **Pets:** Medium. $15 daily fee/pet. Designated rooms, service with restrictions, supervision.
[SAVE] 🅗 🖵 🐾

◆◆◆◆ Country Inn & Suites By Carlson-Chattanooga I-24 West 🅷
(423) 825-6100. **$99-$108.** 3725 Modern Industries Blvd. I-24, exit 174, just s. Int corridors. **Pets:** Small, dogs only. $25 one-time fee/room. Designated rooms, no service, crate.
[SAVE] [✕] [&M] 🅗 🖵 🐾

◆◆◆ Days Inn-Lookout Mountain Tiftonia West 🅷
(423) 821-6044. **$49-$89.** 3801 Cummings Hwy. I-24, exit 174, just n. Ext corridors. **Pets:** $10 daily fee/pet. Service with restrictions, supervision.
[SAVE] [✕] 🅗 🖵 🐾

◆◆ Extended StayAmerica-Chattanooga-Airport 🅷
(423) 892-1315. **$60-$70.** 6240 Airpark Dr. SR 153, exit 1 (Lee Hwy), 0.3 mi s to Vance Rd, then just w. Ext corridors. **Pets:** Other species. $25 daily fee/pet. Service with restrictions, crate.
[ASK] [✕] 🅗 🖵

◆◆◆ GuestHouse International Inn 🅷
(423) 510-0800. **$40-$65.** 2201 Park Dr. I-75, exit 5 (Shallowford Rd), 0.5 mi w. Ext corridors. **Pets:** Small. $10 daily fee/pet. Service with restrictions, supervision.
[SAVE] [✕] 🅗 🖵

◆◆◆◆ Holiday Inn Chattanooga Choo-Choo 🅷 ❖
(423) 266-5000. **$139-$159.** 1400 Market St. I-24, exit 178 (Broad St) eastbound, then E Main St; exit 178 (Market St) westbound, 0.5 mi n. Ext/int corridors. **Pets:** Medium. $25 one-time fee/room. Service with restrictions, supervision.
[SAVE] [✕] 🅗 🖵 🍴 🐾 [✕]

◆◆◆ La Quinta Inn Chattanooga 🅷 ❖
(423) 855-0011. **$39-$85.** 7015 Shallowford Rd. I-75, exit 5 (Shallowford Rd), just w. Ext corridors. **Pets:** Medium, other species. Service with restrictions, supervision.
[ASK] [✕] 🅗 🖵 🐾

◆◆◆◆ La Quinta Inn-Downtown 🅷 ❖
(423) 265-3151. **$59-$169.** 100 W 21st St. I-24, exit 178, US 11 to Lookout Mountain, w to 20th St, w to Williams St, then w. Int corridors. **Pets:** Medium, other species. Service with restrictions, supervision.
[SAVE] [&M] 🅗 🖵 🐾

◆◆◆◆ MainStay Suites-Chattanooga 🅷
(423) 485-9424. **$79-$109.** 7030 Amin Dr. I-75, exit 5 (Shallowford Rd), just w, then s. Int corridors. **Pets:** Medium, dogs only. $50 one-time fee/room. Designated rooms, service with restrictions, crate.
[ASK] [✕] 🅗 🖵

◆◆◆◆ Microtel Inn-Chattanooga 🅷
(423) 510-0761. **$43-$76.** 7014 McCutcheon Rd. I-75, exit 5 (Shallowford Rd), just w, 0.3 mi n on Shallowford Village Dr, then just w. Int corridors. **Pets:** Accepted.
[ASK] [✕] 🅗

◆◆◆ Motel 6 Downtown #4145 🅷
(423) 265-7300. **$40-$100.** 2440 Williams St. I-24, exit 178 (Market St). Int corridors. **Pets:** Other species. Service with restrictions, supervision.
[✕] 🅗

◆◆◆ Quality Inn 🅷
(423) 821-1499. **$69-$145.** 3109 Parker Ln. I-24, exit 175, just s. Ext corridors. **Pets:** Large. $15 daily fee/pet. Designated rooms, no service, supervision.
[SAVE] [✕] 🅗 🖵 🐾

◆◆◆ Quality Suites 🅷 ❖
(423) 892-1500. **$75-$99.** 7324 Shallowford Rd. I-75, exit 5 (Shallowford Rd), just e. Ext corridors. **Pets:** Medium. $15 daily fee/pet. Designated rooms, service with restrictions, supervision.
[SAVE] [✕] 🅗 🖵 🐾

◆◆◆◆ Ramada Limited-Lookout Mountain West 🅷
(423) 821-7162. **$40-$80.** 30 Birmingham Hwy. I-24, exit 174, just s. Ext/int corridors. **Pets:** Medium. $10 daily fee/pet. Service with restrictions, supervision.
[ASK] [✕] 🅗 🖵 🐾

◆◆◆◆ Red Roof Inn-Chattanooga 🅼
(423) 899-0143. **$40-$70, 14 day notice.** 7014 Shallowford Rd. I-75, exit 5 (Shallowford Rd), just w. Ext corridors. **Pets:** Accepted.
[ASK] [✕]

◆◆◆◆ Residence Inn by Marriott 🅷
(423) 266-0600. **$164-$184.** 215 Chestnut St. US 27, exit 1C (4th St), just n. Int corridors. **Pets:** Other species. $100 one-time fee/room. Service with restrictions.
[✕] [&M] 🅗 🖵 🐾

◆◆◆◆ The Sheraton Read House Hotel 🅷 ❖
(423) 266-4121. **$119-$299.** 827 Broad St. US 27, exit 1A, just e. Int corridors. **Pets:** Medium. $50 one-time fee/pet. Designated rooms, service with restrictions, supervision.
[SAVE] [✕] 🅗 🖵 🍴 🐾

◆◆◆◆ Staybridge Suites 🅷
(423) 267-0900. **$119-$389.** 1300 Carter St. US 27 N, exit 1A (Martin Luther King Blvd), just e to Carter St, then 0.3 mi s. Int corridors. **Pets:** Other species. $25 one-time fee/pet. Service with restrictions.
[ASK] [✕] [&M] 🅗 🖵 🐾

◆◆◆◆ Super 8 Motel 🅷
(423) 490-8560. **$40-$90.** 7024 McCutcheon Rd. I-75, exit 5 (Shallowford Rd), just w, then 0.3 mi n on Shallowford Village Dr. Int corridors. **Pets:** Accepted.
[SAVE] 🅗 🖵 🐾

◆◆◆ Super 8 Motel/Lookout Mountain 🅷
(423) 821-8880. **$46-$121.** 20 Birmingham Hwy. I-24, exit 174. Int corridors. **Pets:** Accepted.
[ASK] [✕] 🐾

CLARKSVILLE

◆◆◆ Candlewood Suites 🅷
(931) 906-0900. **$89-$129.** 3050 Clay Lewis Rd. I-24, exit 4, 0.3 mi s. Int corridors. **Pets:** Large, other species. $75 one-time fee/room. Service with restrictions, crate.
[ASK] [✕] [&M] 🅗 🖵

◆◆◆ Days Inn North 🅷
(931) 552-1155. **$50-$65, 3 day notice.** 130 Westfield Ct. I-24, exit 4, just s. Ext corridors. **Pets:** Accepted.
[ASK] [✕] [&M] 🅗 🖵 🐾

◆◆◆◆ Econo Lodge Inn & Suites 🅷
(931) 647-2002. **Call for rates.** 3065 Wilma Rudolph Blvd. I-24, exit 4, 0.3 mi w. Ext corridors. **Pets:** Small. $10 daily fee/pet. Designated rooms, service with restrictions, supervision.
[SAVE] [✕] 🅗 🖵 🐾

◆◆◆◆ Quality Inn-Exit 4 🅷
(931) 648-4848. **$90-$100.** 3095 Wilma Rudolph Blvd. I-24, exit 4, just e. Ext corridors. **Pets:** Medium, other species. $15 daily fee/room, $25 one-time fee/room. Service with restrictions.
[SAVE] [✕] 🅗 🖵 🍴 🐾 [✕]

◆◆◆ Red Roof Inn 🅷
(931) 905-1555. **$41-$79.** 197 Holiday Dr. I-24, exit 4, just se. Ext corridors. **Pets:** Medium. Service with restrictions, supervision.
[ASK] [✕] 🅗 🐾

CLEVELAND

America's Best Inn & Suites M
(423) 472-3281. **$40-$70.** 2655 Westside Dr NW. I-75, exit 25, just e. Ext corridors. **Pets:** Medium. $10 daily fee/pet. Service with restrictions, supervision.
SAVE ✕ 🖥 💻 🏊

Baymont Inn & Suites-Cleveland H
(423) 339-1000. **$59-$63.** 107 Interstate Dr NW. I-75, exit 25, just w. Int corridors. **Pets:** Accepted.
ASK ✕ 🖥 💻 🏊

Colonial Inn M
(423) 472-6845. **$35-$45, 7 day notice.** 1555 25th St. I-75, exit 25, 0.3 mi e. Ext corridors. **Pets:** Accepted.
✕ 🖥 💻 🏊

Douglas Inn & Suites H
(423) 559-5579. **$55-$115.** 2600 Westside Dr NW. I-75, exit 25, just e. Ext/int corridors. **Pets:** Medium, other species. $10 one-time fee/pet. Service with restrictions, supervision.
SAVE ✕ 🐾 🖥 💻

Holiday Inn Mountain View H
(423) 472-1500. **$85-$176.** 2400 Executive Park Dr. I-75, exit 25, just w. Ext/int corridors. **Pets:** Small. $25 one-time fee/room. Designated rooms, service with restrictions, supervision.
✕ 🖥 💻 🍴 🏊

Howard Johnson Chalet H
(423) 476-8511. **$65-$85.** 2595 Georgetown Rd. I-75, exit 25, just e. Ext corridors. **Pets:** Small. $25 daily fee/pet. No service, supervision.
SAVE ✕ 🖥 💻 🍴 🏊

Quality Inn H
(423) 478-5265. **$75-$125.** 153 James Asbury Dr. I-75, exit 27, just w. Ext/int corridors. **Pets:** Accepted.
SAVE ✕ 🖥 💻 🏊

Ramada Limited H
(423) 472-5566. **Call for rates.** 156 James Asbury Dr. I-75, exit 27, just w. Ext corridors. **Pets:** Accepted.
✕ 🖥 💻 🏊

Super 8 Motel H
(423) 476-5555. **Call for rates.** 163 Bernham Dr. I-75, exit 27, just w. Ext/int corridors. **Pets:** Accepted.
SAVE ✕ 🖥 💻 🏊

CLINTON

Super 8 Motel M
(865) 457-2311. **Call for rates.** 720 Park Pl. I-75, exit 122, just w. Ext corridors. **Pets:** Accepted.
✕ 🐾 🖥 💻 🏊

COLUMBIA

Americas Best Value Inn M
(931) 381-1410. **$66-$76.** 1548 Bear Creek Pike. I-65, exit 46, just w. Ext corridors. **Pets:** Other species. $7 daily fee/pet. Service with restrictions, supervision.
SAVE ✕ 🖥

Jameson Inn H
(931) 388-3326. **$93-$100.** 715 James M Campbell Blvd. 0.9 mi w jct SR 50 and US 31. Int corridors. **Pets:** Accepted.
ASK ✕ 🖥 💻 🏊

COOKEVILLE

Alpine Lodge & Suites H
(931) 526-3333. **$44-$68.** 2021 E Spring St. I-40, exit 290, just s. Int corridors. **Pets:** Medium. $5 daily fee/pet. Designated rooms, service with restrictions, supervision.
SAVE ✕ 🖥 💻 🏊

Baymont Inn & Suites Cookeville H
(931) 525-6668. **$81-$117.** 1151 S Jefferson Ave. I-40, exit 287, just s. Int corridors. **Pets:** Accepted.
ASK ✕ 🐾 🖥 💻 🏊

Best Western Thunderbird Motel H
(931) 526-7115. **$50-$100.** 900 S Jefferson Ave. I-40, exit 287, just n. Ext corridors. **Pets:** $15 daily fee/pet. Designated rooms, service with restrictions.
SAVE ✕ 🐾 🖥 💻 🏊

Clarion Inn H
(931) 526-7125. **$80-$95.** 970 S Jefferson Ave. I-40, exit 287, just n. Ext/int corridors. **Pets:** $25 one-time fee/pet. Designated rooms, service with restrictions, supervision.
ASK ✕ 🐾 💻 🍴 🏊

Country Hearth Inn & Suites H 🐾
(931) 528-1040. **$30-$104.** 1100 S Jefferson Ave. I-40, exit 287. Ext corridors. **Pets:** Large, other species. $10 daily fee/pet. Designated rooms, service with restrictions, supervision.
ASK ✕ 🖥 💻 🏊

Days Inn M
(931) 528-1511. **$55-$120.** 1296 S Walnut Ave. I-40, exit 287. Ext corridors. **Pets:** Small, dogs only. $10 daily fee/pet. Designated rooms, service with restrictions, supervision.
SAVE ✕ 🖥 💻 🏊

CORNERSVILLE

Econo Lodge M
(931) 293-2111. **$69-$79.** 3731 Pulaski Hwy. I-65, exit 22 at US 31A. Ext corridors. **Pets:** Accepted.
SAVE ✕ 🖥 💻 🏊

CROSSVILLE

La Quinta Inn-Crossville H 🐾
(931) 456-9338. **$59-$190.** 4038 Hwy 127 N. I-40, exit 317, just n. Int corridors. **Pets:** Medium, other species. Service with restrictions, supervision.
SAVE ✕ 🐾 🖥 💻 🏊

DANDRIDGE

Holiday Inn Express H 🐾
(865) 397-1910. **$69-$89.** 119 Sharon Dr. I-40, exit 417, just s. Int corridors. **Pets:** Medium, other species. $25 one-time fee/room. Designated rooms, service with restrictions, supervision.
SAVE ✕ 🐾 🖥 💻 🏊

Jefferson Inn H
(865) 940-5042. **$55-$60.** 127 Sharon Dr. I-40, exit 417, just s. Int corridors. **Pets:** Small, dogs only. $10 daily fee/pet. Service with restrictions, supervision.
ASK ✕ 🐾 🖥 💻 🏊

Super 8 Motel H
(865) 397-1200. **$60-$155.** 125 Sharon Dr. I-40, exit 417, just s. Int corridors. **Pets:** Accepted.
SAVE ✕ 🐾 🖥 💻 🏊

DECHERD

Jameson Inn H
(931) 962-0130. **$78-$83.** 1838 Decherd Blvd. Jct Main St and SR 41A, just s. Ext corridors. **Pets:** Accepted.

ASK X 🛏 💻 ⇨

DICKSON

Best Western Executive Inn H
(615) 446-0541. **$50-$80.** 2338 Hwy 46. I-40, exit 172, just n. Ext corridors. **Pets:** Small, dogs only. $10 daily fee/pet. Designated rooms, service with restrictions, supervision.

SAVE X 🛏 💻 ⇨

Econo Lodge Inn & Suites H
(615) 441-5252. **$49-$79.** 1025 E Christi Rd. I-40, exit 172, just s. Int corridors. **Pets:** Small, dogs only. $10 daily fee/pet. Designated rooms, service with restrictions, supervision.

SAVE X 🛏 💻 ⇨

Holiday Inn Express H
(615) 446-2781. **Call for rates.** 100 Barzani Blvd. I-40, exit 172, just n. Int corridors. **Pets:** Accepted.

X 🛗 🛏 💻 ⇨

Super 8 H
(615) 446-1923. **$50-$70.** 150 Suzanne Dr. I-40, exit 172, just n on SR 46, then just e. Int corridors. **Pets:** Accepted.

SAVE X 🛏 💻 ⇨

DYERSBURG

Best Western Dyersburg Inn H ❀
(731) 285-8601. **$69.** 770 Hwy 51 Bypass W. I-155, exit 13, 0.5 mi s; jct of US 51 Bypass and SR 78. Ext corridors. **Pets:** Small, other species. $20 daily fee/pet. Service with restrictions, supervision.

SAVE X 🛏 💻 🍴 ⇨

Executive Inn & Suites H
(731) 287-0044. **$45-$55.** 2331 Lake Rd. I-155, exit 13, 0.5 mi s. Ext corridors. **Pets:** Large. $10 daily fee/pet. Service with restrictions, supervision.

ASK X 🛏

Hampton Inn H
(731) 285-4778. **$69-$89.** 2750 Mall Loop Rd. I-155, exit 13, just s. Int corridors. **Pets:** Medium, other species. Service with restrictions, supervision.

X 🛗 🛏 💻 ⇨

EAST RIDGE

Americas Best Value Inn H
(423) 894-6110. **Call for rates.** 639 Camp Jordan Pkwy. I-75, 1A (Ringgold Rd) northbound; exit 1 southbound, just e. Ext/int corridors. **Pets:** Accepted.

X 🛏 💻 ⇨

Howard Johnson Plaza Hotel H
(423) 892-8100. **$50-$80.** 6700 Ringgold Rd. I-75, exit 1A (Ringgold Rd), just e. Int corridors. **Pets:** Accepted.

ASK X 🛏 💻 🍴 ⇨

Ramada Limited H ❀
(423) 894-1860. **$49-$79.** 6650 Ringgold Rd. I-75, 1A (Ringgold Rd) northbound; exit 1 southbound. Int corridors. **Pets:** Medium. $10 daily fee/pet. Designated rooms, service with restrictions, supervision.

SAVE X 🛏 💻 ⇨

Super 8 Motel M
(423) 894-6720. **Call for rates.** 6521 Ringgold Rd. I-75, exit 1B (Ringgold Rd), just w. Ext corridors. **Pets:** Accepted.

X 🛗 🛏 💻 ⇨

ETOWAH

Sleep Inn & Suites H
(423) 263-4343. **$69-$169.** 600 N Tennessee Ave (US 411). I-75, exit 49 (SR 30), jct US 411 and SR 30, just s. Int corridors. **Pets:** Accepted.

SAVE X 🛗 🛏 💻

FAIRVIEW

Deerfield Inn & Suites H
(615) 799-4700. **$60-$80.** 1407 Hwy 96 N. I-40, exit 182. Ext corridors. **Pets:** Accepted.

SAVE X 🛏 💻

FARRAGUT

Super 8-West M ❀
(865) 675-5566. **Call for rates.** 11748 Snyder Rd. I-40/75, exit 373 (Campbell Station Rd), just ne. Ext corridors. **Pets:** $10 daily fee/pet. Designated rooms, service with restrictions.

X 🛗 🛏 💻 ⇨

FAYETTEVILLE

Best Western-Fayetteville Inn H
(931) 433-0100. **$82-$120.** 3021 Thornton Taylor Pkwy. 0.7 mi e of US 431, on US 64 and 231 Bypass. Ext corridors. **Pets:** Accepted.

SAVE X 🛏 💻 🍴 ⇨

FRANKLIN

Best Western Franklin Inn H
(615) 790-0570. **$60-$100, 7 day notice.** 1308 Murfreesboro Rd. I-65, exit 65, just w. Ext corridors. **Pets:** $10 one-time fee/pet. Service with restrictions, supervision.

SAVE X 🛏 💻 ⇨

Days Inn H
(615) 790-1140. **$69-$99.** 4217 S Carothers Rd. I-65, exit 65, just e. Ext corridors. **Pets:** Small. $10 daily fee/pet. No service, supervision.

SAVE X 🛏 💻 ⇨

Homestead Studio Suites Hotel-Nashville/Franklin-Cool Springs H
(615) 771-7600. **$85-$95.** 680 Bakers Bridge Ave. I-65, exit 69 (Galleria Blvd), 0.3 mi e on Moore's Ln to Carothers Pkwy, 0.5 mi s, then 0.3 mi w. Ext corridors. **Pets:** Other species. $25 daily fee/pet. Service with restrictions, crate.

ASK X 🛏 💻

La Quinta Inn & Suites Nashville-Franklin M ❀
(615) 791-7700. **$59-$109.** 4207 Franklin Commons Ct. I-65, exit 65, just e. Int corridors. **Pets:** Medium, other species. Service with restrictions, supervision.

ASK X 🛏 💻 ⇨

GALLATIN

Jameson Inn H
(615) 451-4494. **$93-$100.** 1001 Village Green Crossing. 2 mi s on US 31. Ext corridors. **Pets:** Accepted.

ASK X 🛗 🛏 💻 ⇨

GATLINBURG

Cobbly Nob Rentals Inc CA ❀
(865) 436-5298. **$100-$1000, 30 day notice.** 3722 E Parkway. On US 321, 10.3 mi n of jct US 441. Ext corridors. **Pets:** Medium. $15 daily fee/pet. Designated rooms, crate.

SAVE X 🛏 💻 ⇨

Garden Plaza Hotel M ❀
(865) 436-9201. **$59-$129.** 520 Historic Nature Tr. 0.4 mi e of US 441 at traffic light 8. Ext/int corridors. **Pets:** Medium, other species. $15 one-time fee/pet. Designated rooms, service with restrictions, crate.

ASK X 🛗 🛏 💻 🍴 ⇨ 🐾

AAA ◆◆◆◆ Greenbrier Valley Resorts at Cobbly Nob 🄲🄰 🐾
(865) 436-2015. **$75-$1000, 30 day notice.** 3629 E Parkway. On US 321, 10.1 mi n of jct US 441. Ext corridors. **Pets:** Other species. $100 deposit/pet, $15 daily fee/pet. Designated rooms, no service, crate.
[SAVE] [✕] 🛏 💻 ➘

AAA ◆◆◆ Microtel Gatlinburg 🄷
(865) 436-0107. **$45-$159, 3 day notice.** 211 Historic Nature Tr. Just e of US 441 at traffic light 8. Int corridors. **Pets:** Small. $10 daily fee/pet. Designated rooms, service with restrictions, supervision.
[SAVE] [✕] 🄼 🛏 💻

AAA ◆◆◆◆ Outback Resort Rentals & Sales 🅅🄷
(865) 430-9385. **$120-$799, 30 day notice.** 902 Street of Dreams Way. SR 441 S, 2 mi e on Wiley Oakey, 2 mi e on N Woodland. Ext corridors. **Pets:** Small. $50 deposit/pet. Service with restrictions, crate.
[SAVE] [✕] 🛏 💻 ➘

◆◆◆ Terrace on the Water 🄼
(865) 436-4965. **$69-$105.** 396 Parkway. On US 441; between traffic lights 2 and 3. Ext corridors. **Pets:** Accepted.
[ASK] 🛏 💻 ➘

GREENEVILLE

AAA ◆◆◆◆ Comfort Inn of Greeneville 🄷 🐾
(423) 639-4185. **$70-$200.** 1790 E Andrew Johnson Hwy. US 11 E, 2.9 mi ne. Ext/int corridors. **Pets:** Other species. $10 daily fee/room. Service with restrictions, supervision.
[SAVE] [✕] 🛏 💻 ➘

AAA ◆◆◆ Days Inn 🄼
(423) 639-2156. **$44-$189, 7 day notice.** 935 E Andrew Johnson Hwy. US 11 E, 2 mi ne. Ext corridors. **Pets:** Large, other species. $10 daily fee/room. Designated rooms, service with restrictions.
[SAVE] [✕] 🛏 💻

◆◆◆◆ Jameson Inn 🄷
(423) 638-7511. **$83-$90.** 3160 E Andrew Johnson Hwy. US 11 E Bypass, 3.6 mi ne. Int corridors. **Pets:** Very small, other species. $15 daily fee/pet. Designated rooms, service with restrictions, crate.
[ASK] [✕] 🄼 🛏 💻 ➘

HARRIMAN

AAA ◆◆◆ Best Western Harriman Inn 🄼
(865) 882-6200. **$55-$100.** 120 Childs Rd. I-40, exit 347, just n. Ext corridors. **Pets:** Accepted.
[SAVE] [✕] 🄼 🛏 💻

HIXSON

◆◆◆ Home Away Extended Stay Studios 🄷
(423) 643-4663. **$58-$64.** 1949 North Point Blvd. Jct SR 153 and Hixson Pike, just w. Ext corridors. **Pets:** Other species. $10 one-time fee/pet. Service with restrictions, crate.
[ASK] [✕] 🛏 💻 ➘

HURRICANE MILLS

AAA ◆◆◆ Best Western of Hurricane Mills 🄼 🐾
(931) 296-4251. **$90-$140, 3 day notice.** 15542 Hwy 13 S. I-40, exit 143. Ext corridors. **Pets:** Large, other species. $10 daily fee/pet. Designated rooms, service with restrictions.
[SAVE] [✕] 🛏 💻 ➘

JACKSON

AAA ◆◆◆ Best Western Inn & Suites 🄷
(731) 664-3030. **$75-$95.** 1936 Hwy 45 Bypass. I-40, exit 80A, just s. Ext corridors. **Pets:** Small, dogs only. $15 daily fee/pet. Designated rooms, service with restrictions, supervision.
[SAVE] [✕] 🛏 💻 ➘

◆◆◆◆ Jackson Hampton Inn & Suites 🄷
(731) 427-6100. **$109-$129.** 150 Campbell Oaks Dr. I-40, exit 83. Int corridors. **Pets:** Accepted.
[✕] 🄼 🛏 💻 ➘

◆◆◆◆ Jameson Inn 🄷
(731) 660-8651. **$90-$120.** 1292 Vann Dr. I-40, exit 80B, 0.6 mi w. Int corridors. **Pets:** Accepted.
[ASK] [✕] 🛏 💻 ➘

◆◆◆◆ La Quinta Inn of Jackson 🄷 🐾
(731) 664-1800. **$55-$99.** 2370 N Highland Ave. I-40, exit 82A. Int corridors. **Pets:** Medium, other species. Service with restrictions, supervision.
[ASK] [✕] 🛏 💻 ➘

◆◆◆ Quality Inn 🄷
(731) 668-1400. **$65-$80, 3 day notice.** 535 Wiley Parker Rd. I-40, exit 80A, just s, then e on Carriage House Dr. Ext/int corridors. **Pets:** Small. $15 one-time fee/pet. Service with restrictions, supervision.
[ASK] [✕] 🛏 💻 ➘

JELLICO

AAA ◆◆ Americas Best Value Inn 🄼
(423) 784-7241. **$55.** 133 Holiday Ln. I-75, exit 160, just w. Ext corridors. **Pets:** Medium. $5 daily fee/pet. Designated rooms, service with restrictions, supervision.
[SAVE] [✕] 🄼 🛏 💻 ➘

◆◆◆ Days Inn 🄼
(423) 784-7281. **$62-$75.** US 25 W. I-75, exit 160, just w. Ext corridors. **Pets:** Medium. $8 daily fee/pet. Designated rooms, service with restrictions, supervision.
[ASK] [✕] 🄼 💻 🍴 ➘

JOHNSON CITY

◆◆◆ Comfort Inn of Johnson City 🄷
(423) 928-9600. **$60-$280.** 1900 S Roan St. I-26, exit 24, just w on US 321. Ext corridors. **Pets:** Large, other species. $15 daily fee/pet. Service with restrictions.
[ASK] [✕] 🛏 💻 ➘

◆◆◆◆ DoubleTree Hotel 🄷
(423) 929-2000. **$99-$449.** 211 Mockingbird Ln. I-26, exit 35 eastbound; exit 35B westbound, 0.6 mi e on N Roan St. Int corridors. **Pets:** Accepted.
[✕] 🛏 💻 🍴 ➘

◆◆◆ Holiday Inn-Johnson City 🄷 🐾
(423) 282-4611. **Call for rates.** 101 W Springbrook Dr. I-26, exit 20A westbound; exit 20 eastbound, just e on N Roan St, then just n. Int corridors. **Pets:** Large. $25 one-time fee/pet. Service with restrictions, supervision.
[✕] 🛏 💻 🍴 ➘

◆◆◆ Jameson Inn 🄷
(423) 282-0488. **$84-$91.** 119 Pinnacle Dr. I-26, exit 17, just w on CR 354, then just s. Ext corridors. **Pets:** Accepted.
[ASK] [✕] 🛏 💻 ➘

AAA ◆◆◆ Red Roof Inn-Johnson City 🄼
(423) 282-3040. **$50-$80, 14 day notice.** 210 Broyles Dr. I-26, exit 20A westbound; exit 20 eastbound, just w on N Roan St. Ext corridors. **Pets:** Large, other species. Service with restrictions, crate.
[SAVE] [✕] 🛏

◆◆◆ Sleep Inn & Suites 🄷
(423) 915-0081. **$74-$250.** 2020 Franklin Terrace Ct. I-26, exit 19, just w, then just n, follow signs; entrance on Oakland Ave at light. Int corridors. **Pets:** Small. $10 daily fee/pet. Service with restrictions, crate.
[ASK] [✕] 🄼 🛏 💻

KIMBALL

AAA⁷ ▼▼ Country Hearth Inn & Suites M
(423) 837-7185. **$45-$90, 5 day notice.** 395 Main St. I-24, exit 152, 0.5 mi n. Ext corridors. **Pets:** Accepted.
⟦SAVE⟧ ⟦✕⟧ ⟦🛏⟧ ⟦➤⟧

KINGSPORT

AAA ▼▼▼ Best Western Colonial Inn M
(423) 239-3400. **$65-$100.** 4234 Fort Henry Dr. I-81, exit 59, 0.7 mi n on SR 36. Ext corridors. **Pets:** Medium. $10 daily fee/pet. Designated rooms, service with restrictions, supervision.
⟦SAVE⟧ ⟦✕⟧ ⟦ᕁM⟧ ⟦🛏⟧ ⟦💻⟧

▼▼▼ Jameson Inn H
(423) 230-0534. **$83-$90.** 3004 Bay Meadow Pl. I-26, exit 4, just n. Int corridors. **Pets:** Accepted.
⟦ASK⟧ ⟦✕⟧ ⟦🛏⟧ ⟦💻⟧ ⟦➤⟧

▼▼▼▼ La Quinta Inn Kingsport H ❀
(423) 323-0500. **$65-$109.** 10150 Airport Pkwy. I-81, exit 63, just e. Int corridors. **Pets:** Medium, other species. Service with restrictions, supervision.
⟦ASK⟧ ⟦✕⟧ ⟦ᕁM⟧ ⟦🛏⟧ ⟦💻⟧ ⟦➤⟧

▼▼ Quality Inn & Conference Center H
(423) 245-0271. **$62-$300.** 1900 American Way. On US 11 W at SR 93. Ext corridors. **Pets:** Accepted.
⟦ASK⟧ ⟦✕⟧ ⟦🛏⟧ ⟦💻⟧ ⟦❙❙⟧ ⟦➤⟧

▼▼ Sleep Inn H
(423) 279-1811. **$72-$250.** 200 Hospitality Pl. I-81, exit 63, just s. Int corridors. **Pets:** Medium. $10 daily fee/pet. Service with restrictions, crate.
⟦ASK⟧ ⟦✕⟧ ⟦🛏⟧ ⟦💻⟧

KINGSTON

AAA⁷ ▼▼▼ Comfort Inn of Kingston M
(865) 376-4965. **$70-$90.** 905 N Kentucky St. I-40, exit 352, 0.3 mi s. Ext corridors. **Pets:** Small, other species. $10 daily fee/pet. Service with restrictions, supervision.
⟦SAVE⟧ ⟦✕⟧ ⟦🛏⟧ ⟦💻⟧

▼▼ Motel 6 M
(865) 376-2069. **$43-$90.** 495 Gallaher Rd. I-40, exit 356, just n. Ext corridors. **Pets:** Accepted.
⟦ASK⟧ ⟦✕⟧ ⟦🛏⟧ ⟦💻⟧ ⟦➤⟧

KINGSTON SPRINGS

AAA⁷ ▼▼◆ Best Western Harpeth Inn H
(615) 952-3961. **$49-$99, 3 day notice.** 116 Luyben Hills Rd. I-40, exit 188, just n. Ext corridors. **Pets:** Accepted.
⟦SAVE⟧ ⟦✕⟧ ⟦🛏⟧ ⟦💻⟧ ⟦➤⟧

KNOXVILLE

AAA⁷ ▼▼◆ Best Western Knoxville Suites H
(865) 687-9922. **$60-$150.** 5317 Pratt Rd. I-75, exit 108 (Merchants Dr), just e, then n. Int corridors. **Pets:** Accepted.
⟦SAVE⟧ ⟦✕⟧ ⟦ᕁM⟧ ⟦🛏⟧ ⟦💻⟧ ⟦➤⟧

▼▼ Candlewood Suites-Knoxville H
(865) 777-0400. **$89-$129.** 10206 Parkside Dr. I-40/75, exit 374 (Lovell Rd), 0.5 mi s, then 1 mi e. Int corridors. **Pets:** Medium. $75 one-time fee/room. Service with restrictions.
⟦ASK⟧ ⟦✕⟧ ⟦ᕁM⟧ ⟦🛏⟧ ⟦💻⟧

AAA⁷ ▼▼◆ The Clarion Inn H
(865) 687-8989. **$69-$99.** 5634 Merchants Center Blvd. I-75, exit 108 (Merchants Dr), just w, then just n. Int corridors. **Pets:** Accepted.
⟦SAVE⟧ ⟦✕⟧ ⟦ᕁM⟧ ⟦🛏⟧ ⟦💻⟧ ⟦➤⟧

▼▼▼▼ Crowne Plaza Knoxville H ❀
(865) 522-2600. **$134-$169.** 401 W Summit Hill Dr. Corner of Walnut St; downtown. Int corridors. **Pets:** Other species. $25 one-time fee/room. Service with restrictions.
⟦ASK⟧ ⟦✕⟧ ⟦ᕁM⟧ ⟦🛏⟧ ⟦💻⟧ ⟦❙❙⟧ ⟦➤⟧

AAA⁷ ▼▼▼ Econo Lodge Inn & Suites–East Knoxville M
(865) 932-1217. **$49-$129.** 7424 Strawberry Plains Pike. I-40, exit 398 (Strawberry Plains), just n. Ext corridors. **Pets:** Small, other species. $10 daily fee/room. Designated rooms, service with restrictions, supervision.
⟦SAVE⟧ ⟦✕⟧ ⟦🛏⟧ ⟦💻⟧ ⟦➤⟧

AAA⁷ ▼▼ Econo Lodge West M
(865) 693-6061. **$45-$129, 7 day notice.** 9240 Park West Blvd. I-40/75, exit 378 (Cedar Bluff Rd), just n to Park West Blvd, then just w. Ext corridors. **Pets:** Medium. $10 daily fee/pet. Designated rooms, service with restrictions, supervision.
⟦SAVE⟧ ⟦✕⟧ ⟦🛏⟧ ⟦💻⟧ ⟦➤⟧

▼▼ Extended StayAmerica Knoxville-Cedar Bluff M
(865) 769-0822. **$65-$75.** 214 Langley Pl. I-40/75, exit 378 (Cedar Bluff), just s, then 1 mi w on N Peters Rd. Ext corridors. **Pets:** Other species. $25 daily fee/pet. Service with restrictions, crate.
⟦ASK⟧ ⟦✕⟧ ⟦ᕁM⟧ ⟦🛏⟧ ⟦💻⟧

▼▼ Extended StayAmerica Knoxville-West Hills H
(865) 694-4178. **$70-$80.** 1700 Winston Rd. I-40/75, exit 380 (West Hills), just w on Kingston Pike, then just s. Int corridors. **Pets:** Other species. $25 daily fee/pet. Service with restrictions.
⟦ASK⟧ ⟦✕⟧ ⟦🛏⟧ ⟦💻⟧ ⟦➤⟧

▼▼▼▼ Hilton Knoxville Downtown H ❀
(865) 523-2300. **$89-$329.** 501 W Church Ave. Between Locust and Walnut sts; downtown. Int corridors. **Pets:** Medium. $25 one-time fee/room. Service with restrictions, supervision.
⟦✕⟧ ⟦ᕁM⟧ ⟦🛏⟧ ⟦💻⟧ ⟦❙❙⟧ ⟦➤⟧

▼▼▼▼ Holiday Inn Cedar Bluff H
(865) 693-1011. **$109-$159.** 304 Cedar Bluff Rd. I-40/75, exit 378 (Cedar Bluff Rd) eastbound; exit 378B westbound, just n to Executive Park Dr. Int corridors. **Pets:** Medium, other species. $50 one-time fee/room. Designated rooms, service with restrictions, supervision.
⟦ASK⟧ ⟦✕⟧ ⟦🛏⟧ ⟦💻⟧ ⟦❙❙⟧ ⟦➤⟧ ⟦✕⟧

AAA⁷ ▼▼▼▼ Holiday Inn-Central/Papermill Road H
(865) 584-3911. **$89-$189.** 1315 Kirby Rd. I-40/75, exit 383 (Papermill Rd), 0.5 mi e. Int corridors. **Pets:** Accepted.
⟦SAVE⟧ ⟦✕⟧ ⟦ᕁM⟧ ⟦🛏⟧ ⟦💻⟧ ⟦❙❙⟧ ⟦➤⟧

▼▼▼▼ Holiday Inn Express Knoxville-East H ❀
(865) 525-5100. **$99-$159.** 730 Rufus Graham Rd. I-40, exit 398 (Strawberry Plains), just n. Int corridors. **Pets:** Other species. $15 daily fee/pet. Designated rooms, service with restrictions, crate.
⟦ASK⟧ ⟦✕⟧ ⟦ᕁM⟧ ⟦🛏⟧ ⟦💻⟧ ⟦➤⟧

▼▼▼▼ Homewood Suites by Hilton H
(865) 777-0375. **$99-$159.** 10935 Turkey Dr. I-40/75, exit 374 (Lovell Rd), just s to Parkside Dr, then 0.5 mi n on Snow Goose. Int corridors. **Pets:** Accepted.
⟦✕⟧ ⟦ᕁM⟧ ⟦🛏⟧ ⟦💻⟧ ⟦➤⟧ ⟦✕⟧

▼▼▼▼ La Quinta Inn & Suites East H ❀
(865) 633-5100. **$49-$149.** 7210 Saddle Rack St. I-40, exit 398 (Strawberry Plains), just s, just e on Region Ln, then just se on Shumard Ave. Int corridors. **Pets:** Medium, other species. Service with restrictions, supervision.
⟦ASK⟧ ⟦✕⟧ ⟦ᕁM⟧ ⟦🛏⟧ ⟦💻⟧ ⟦➤⟧

▼▼ La Quinta Inn Knoxville (West) M ❀
(865) 690-9777. **$55-$105.** 258 N Peters Rd. I-40/75, exit 378 (Cedar Bluff Rd), just s, then just e. Ext corridors. **Pets:** Medium, other species. Service with restrictions, supervision.
⟦ASK⟧ ⟦✕⟧ ⟦ᕁM⟧ ⟦🛏⟧ ⟦💻⟧ ⟦➤⟧

▼ Motel 6–1252 M
(865) 675-7200. **$43-$55.** 402 Lovell Rd. I-40/75, exit 374 (Lovell Rd), just s. Ext corridors. **Pets:** Other species. Service with restrictions, supervision.
⊠ ⴲM ⇌

▼▼ Quality Inn M
(865) 342-3701. **$79-$99.** 117 Cedar Ln. I-75, exit 108 (Merchants Dr), just e. Ext corridors. **Pets:** Small, other species. Designated rooms, service with restrictions, supervision.
⊠ ⴲM ⊟ ⫿ ⇌

▼▼ Red Roof Inn M
(865) 688-1010. **$65-$99, 3 day notice.** 5334 Central Ave Pike. I-75, exit 108 (Merchants Dr), just e. Ext corridors. **Pets:** Small. Service with restrictions, supervision.
A$K ⊠ ⫿ ⇌

◈ ▼◈ Red Roof Inn-West M
(865) 691-1664. **$50-$100, 14 day notice.** 209 Advantage Pl. I-40/75, exit 378 (Cedar Bluff Rd), just s to N Peters Rd, then w. Ext corridors. **Pets:** Medium. Service with restrictions, supervision.
SAVE ⊠ ⴲM ⊟

LAKE CITY

▼▼ Days Inn M
(865) 426-2816. **$77-$98.** 221 Colonial Ln. I-75, exit 129, just w. Ext corridors. **Pets:** Large. $15 deposit/pet. Service with restrictions, supervision.
A$K ⊠ ⊟ ⫿ ⇌

LAWRENCEBURG

◈ ▼▼ Best Western Villa Inn H
(931) 762-4448. **$71-$100.** 2126 N Locust Ave. On US 43, 2.2 mi n of jct US 64. Ext corridors. **Pets:** Medium. $10 daily fee/pet. Designated rooms, service with restrictions, supervision.
SAVE ⊠ ⊟ ⫿ ⇌

LEBANON

▼▼ Americas Best Value Inn & Suites M
(615) 449-5781. **$46-$110.** 822 S Cumberland St. I-40, exit 238, just n. Ext corridors. **Pets:** Small. $12 daily fee/pet. Service with restrictions, crate.
A$K ⊠ ⊟ ⫿ ⇌

▼▼ Comfort Inn M 🐾
(615) 444-1001. **$49-$89.** 829 S Cumberland St. I-40, exit 238, just n. Ext corridors. **Pets:** Other species. $10 daily fee/pet. Designated rooms, service with restrictions, crate.
A$K ⊠ ⊟ ⫿ ⇌

◈ ▼◈▼ Sleep Inn & Suites-Lebanon/Nashville H
(615) 449-7005. **$75-$159.** 150 S Eastgate Ct. I-40, exit 232. Int corridors. **Pets:** Medium, other species. $25 one-time fee/room. Service with restrictions, crate.
SAVE ⊠ ⊟ ⫿ ⇌

LENOIR CITY

◈ ▼▼ Days Inn H
(865) 986-2011. **$60-$80.** 1110 Hwy 321 N. I-75, exit 81, just e. Ext corridors. **Pets:** Small. $10 daily fee/pet. Service with restrictions, supervision.
SAVE ⊠ ⊟ ⫿ ⇌

◈ ▼▼ Econo Lodge H
(865) 986-0295. **$52-$89.** 1211 Hwy 321 N. I-75, exit 81, just w. Ext corridors. **Pets:** Medium. $10 one-time fee/pet. Service with restrictions, supervision.
SAVE ⊠ ⊟ ⇌

LEWISBURG

▼▼ A Richland Inn Hotel H
(931) 359-1800. **$50-$70.** 723 E Commerce St. Jct US 431 and 31A, just w; just e of town. Ext corridors. **Pets:** Small, other species. Service with restrictions, supervision.
⊠ ⊟

LOUDON

◈ ▼ Americas Best Value Inn M
(865) 458-5855. **$55-$69.** 15100 Hwy 72. I-75, exit 72, just w. Ext corridors. **Pets:** Medium. $7 daily fee/pet. Service with restrictions, supervision.
SAVE ⊠ ⊟ ⇌

MANCHESTER

▼▼ Ambassador Inn H
(931) 728-2200. **$59-$89.** 925 Interstate Dr. I-24, exit 110, just n. Ext/int corridors. **Pets:** Small, dogs only. Designated rooms, service with restrictions, supervision.
A$K ⊠ ⊟ ⫿ ⇌

▼▼▼ Country Inn & Suites By Carlson H
(931) 728-7551. **Call for rates.** 126 Expressway Dr. I-24, exit 114, just w. Int corridors. **Pets:** Accepted.
⊠ ⴲM ⊟ ⫿ ⇌

◈ ▼▼ Days Inn & Suites M
(931) 728-9530. **$60-$65, 10 day notice.** 2259 Hillsboro Blvd. I-24, exit 114, just w. Ext corridors. **Pets:** Accepted.
SAVE ⊠ ⴲM ⊟ ⫿ ⇌

◈ ▼▼ Ramada Limited H
(931) 728-0800. **$69-$99.** 2314 Hillsboro Blvd. I-24, exit 114, just n. Ext corridors. **Pets:** Accepted.
SAVE ⊠ ⊟ ⫿ ⇌

MARTIN

◈ ▼▼ Days Inn H
(731) 587-9577. **$63-$199.** 800 University St. Jct US 431 and 43 Bypass. Ext corridors. **Pets:** Accepted.
SAVE ⊠ ⊟ ⫿ ⇌

MCKENZIE

◈ ▼▼ Best Western Inn McKenzie H
(731) 352-1083. **$62-$67.** 16180 N Highland Ave. Jct US 79 and SR 22, just s. Ext corridors. **Pets:** Small. $10 daily fee/pet. Designated rooms, service with restrictions, supervision.
SAVE ⊠ ⊟ ⫿ ⇌

MCMINNVILLE

◈ ▼▼ Best Western Tree City Inn H
(931) 473-2159. **$72-$78.** 809 Sparta Hwy. Jct US 70 S Bypass and Red Rd, 1 mi s, follow signs. Ext corridors. **Pets:** Small, dogs only. $25 daily fee/pet. Service with restrictions, supervision.
SAVE ⊠ ⊟ ⫿ ⇌

▼▼ McMinnville Inn M
(931) 473-7338. **Call for rates.** 2545 Sparta Hwy. I-24, exit 111, n on SR 55 to US 70 S Bypass. Ext corridors. **Pets:** Accepted.
⊠ ⊟ ⫿ ⇌

MEMPHIS METROPOLITAN AREA

COLLIERVILLE

▼▼▼▼ Hampton Inn Collierville 🅷
(901) 854-9400. **$89-$104.** 1280 W Poplar Ave. 0.9 mi w of jct CR 175 on US 72. Int corridors. **Pets:** Accepted.
⊠ 🌐ᴹ 🛗 🖵 🐾

CORDOVA

▼▼ Quality Suites-Wolfchase 🅷
(901) 386-4600. **Call for rates.** 8166 Varnavas Dr. I-40, exit 16, 0.3 mi s on Germantown Pkwy, then e. Int corridors. **Pets:** Accepted.
⊠ 🛗 🖵 🐾

▼▼ StudioPLUS-Cordova 🅷
(901) 754-4030. **$65-$75.** 8110 Cordova Centre Dr. I-40, exit 16, 0.8 mi s. Int corridors. **Pets:** Other species. $25 daily fee/pet. Service with restrictions, crate.
(A$K) 🌐ᴹ 🛗 🖵 🐾

GERMANTOWN

▼▼ Comfort Inn & Suites-Germantown 🅷 ❀
(901) 757-7800. **$79-$129.** 7787 Wolf River Blvd. I-40, exit 16, 5 mi s on Germantown Pkwy to Wolf River Blvd, then just w. Int corridors. **Pets:** $25 one-time fee/pet. Service with restrictions, supervision.
(A$K) ⊠ 🌐ᴹ 🛗 🖵 🐾

▼▼▼▼ Homewood Suites by Hilton-Germantown 🅷
(901) 751-2500. **$109-$159.** 7855 Wolf River Blvd. I-40, exit 16, 5.8 mi s on CR 177; at Germantown Pkwy and Wolf River Blvd. Int corridors. **Pets:** Medium. $50 one-time fee/room. Service with restrictions, supervision.
⊠ 🛗 🖵 🐾

▼▼▼▼ Residence Inn 🅷
(901) 752-0900. **$157-$169.** 9314 Poplar Pike. I-240, exit 15 (Poplar Ave), 7 mi e. Int corridors. **Pets:** Other species. $100 one-time fee/room. Service with restrictions, supervision.
⊠ 🌐ᴹ 🛗 🖵 🐾 ⊠

LAKELAND

▼▼ Super 8 Motel 🅷
(901) 372-4575. **Call for rates.** 9779 Huff Puff Rd. I-40, exit 20. Ext corridors. **Pets:** Accepted.
⊠ 🛗 🐾

MEMPHIS

▼▼▼▼ Baymont Inn & Suites Memphis East 🅷
(901) 377-2233. **Call for rates.** 6020 Shelby Oaks Dr. I-40, exit 12, just n. Int corridors. **Pets:** Medium. Service with restrictions, crate.
⊠ 🛗 🖵 🐾

(AAA) ▼▼ Best Western Executive Inn 🅷
(901) 312-7000. **$79.** 3105 Millbranch Rd. I-240, exit 24. Ext corridors. **Pets:** Accepted.
(SAVE) ⊠ 🛗 🖵 🐾

(AAA) ▼▼ Best Western Travelers Inn 🅷
(901) 363-8430. **$70-$90.** 5024 US Hwy 78. I-240, exit 21 (US 78), 6 mi s. Ext corridors. **Pets:** Small. $25 daily fee/pet. Designated rooms, service with restrictions, crate.
(SAVE) ⊠ 🛗 🖵 🐾

▼▼▼▼ Drury Inn & Suites-Memphis Northeast 🅷
(901) 373-8200. **$77-$135.** 1556 Sycamore View. I-40, exit 12, just n. Int corridors. **Pets:** Other species. Service with restrictions, supervision.
(A$K) ⊠ 🛗 🖵 🐾

▼▼ Extended StayAmerica 🅷
(901) 362-0338. **$75-$85.** 6520 Mt Moriah Rd. Jct SR 385 and Kirby Pkwy, just s. Int corridors. **Pets:** Other species. $25 daily fee/pet. Service with restrictions, crate.
(A$K) ⊠ 🌐ᴹ 🛗 🖵

▼▼ Extended StayAmerica-Poplar Ave 🅷
(901) 685-7575. **$85-$95.** 6325 Quail Hollow. I-240, exit 15 (Poplar Ave), 0.4 mi n, then just n on Briarcrest. Int corridors. **Pets:** Other species. $25 daily fee/pet. Service with restrictions, crate.
(A$K) ⊠ 🌐ᴹ 🛗 🖵

▼▼ Extended Stay Deluxe Memphis-Wolfchase Galleria 🅷
(901) 380-1525. **$85-$95.** 2520 Horizon Lake Dr. I-40, exit 16B, just n, then just w. Int corridors. **Pets:** Other species. $25 daily fee/pet. Service with restrictions, crate.
(A$K) ⊠ 🛗 🖵 🐾

▼▼ Homestead Studio Suites Hotel-Memphis/Airport 🅷
(901) 344-0010. **$75-$85.** 2541 Corporate Ave E. I-240, exit 23B (Airways Blvd S), just s to Democrat Rd, just w to Nonconnah Blvd, then 0.4 mi n to Corporate Ave, follow signs. Int corridors. **Pets:** Other species. $25 daily fee/pet. Service with restrictions, crate.
(A$K) ⊠ 🌐ᴹ 🛗 🖵

▼▼ Homestead Studio Suites Hotel-Memphis/Poplar Ave 🅷
(901) 767-5522. **$95-$105.** 6500 Poplar Ave. I-240, exit 15 (Poplar Ave), 1 mi e. Int corridors. **Pets:** Other species. $25 daily fee/pet. Service with restrictions, crate.
(A$K) ⊠ 🌐ᴹ 🛗 🖵

▼▼▼▼ Homewood Suites 🅷 ❀
(901) 763-0500. **$99-$189.** 5811 Poplar Ave. I-240, exit 15 (Poplar Ave). Ext/int corridors. **Pets:** Small, dogs only. $100 one-time fee/room. Service with restrictions, crate.
⊠ 🛗 🖵 🐾

▼▼▼▼ Homewood Suites by Hilton 🅷
(901) 758-5018. **$99-$119.** 3583 Hacks Cross Rd. I-240, exit 16, 4 mi e on SR 385, then 1 mi n. Int corridors. **Pets:** Accepted.
⊠ 🌐ᴹ 🛗 🖵 🐾

▼▼▼▼ La Quinta Inn & Suites Memphis (Primacy Parkway) 🅷 ❀
(901) 374-0330. **$69-$139.** 1236 Primacy Pkwy. I-240, exit 15 (Poplar Ave), 0.3 mi e, s on Ridgeway, just w, then just s. Int corridors. **Pets:** Medium, other species. Service with restrictions, supervision.
(A$K) ⊠ 🌐ᴹ 🛗 🖵 🐾

(AAA) ▼▼▼▼ La Quinta Inn & Suites Sycamore View-Memphis 🅷 ❀
(901) 381-0044. **$80-$137.** 6069 Macon Cove. I-40, exit 12, just s. Int corridors. **Pets:** Medium, other species. Service with restrictions, supervision.
(SAVE) ⊠ 🌐ᴹ 🛗 🖵 🐾

(AAA) ▼▼ Quality Inn 🅷
(901) 382-2323. **$69-$169.** 6068 Macon Cove Rd. I-40, exit 12, just s. Ext/int corridors. **Pets:** Small, other species. $10 daily fee/pet. Designated rooms, service with restrictions, supervision.
(SAVE) ⊠ 🌐ᴹ 🛗 🖵 🐾

(AAA) ▼▼ Quality Inn Airport/Graceland 🅷
(901) 345-3344. **$70-$140.** 1581 E Brooks Rd. I-55, exit 5A (Brooks Rd), 0.3 mi e. Ext corridors. **Pets:** Other species. $25 daily fee/pet. Service with restrictions, supervision.
(SAVE) ⊠ 🛗 🖵 🐾

▼▼▼ Residence Inn by Marriott Memphis Downtown 🅷
(901) 578-3700. **$256-$275.** 110 Monroe Ave. I-40, exit 1; I-55, exit Riverside Dr, 0.6 mi s, then just e. Int corridors. **Pets:** Accepted.
⊠ 🔥M 🖃 ⊠

▼▼ Sleep Inn 🅷
(901) 312-7777. **Call for rates.** 2855 Old Austin Peay Hwy. I-40, exit 8. Int
corridors. **Pets:** Medium. $15 daily fee/pet. Service with restrictions, super-
vision.
⊠ 🔥M 🖥 🖃 🏊

▼▼▼ Staybridge Suites 🅷
(901) 682-1722. **$99-$189.** 1070 Ridge Lake Blvd. I-240, exit 15 (Poplar
Ave), just e, then n under overpass. Int corridors. **Pets:** Medium. $75
one-time fee/room. Service with restrictions, supervision.
A$K ⊠ 🔥M 🖥 🖃 🏊 ⊠

▼▼▼ The Westin Memphis Beale St 🅷 ❀
(901) 334-5900. **Call for rates.** 170 Lt. George W. Lee Ave. Jct S 3rd St
and Lt. George W. Lee Ave. Int corridors. **Pets:** Medium, dogs only. $150
deposit/pet. Service with restrictions, supervision.
SAVE ⊠ 🔥M 🖃 🍴

END METROPOLITAN AREA

MONTEAGLE

▼▼▼ Best Western Smoke House Lodge 🅷
(931) 924-2091. **$60-$130, 14 day notice.** 850 W Main St. I-24, exit 134,
just s. Ext corridors. **Pets:** Accepted.
SAVE ⊠ 🖥 🖃 🍴 🏊 ⊠

▼▼ Edgeworth Inn 🅱🅱
(931) 924-4000. **$150-$200.** Monteagle Assembly, Cottage 23. I-24, exit
134, 0.4 mi e on US 41A, 2nd left through assembly gates, follow signs.
Ext/int corridors. **Pets:** Accepted.
A$K ⊠ 🖥 🖃 🗾

MORRISTOWN

▼▼▼ Days Inn 🅼
(423) 587-2200. **$42-$149.** 2512 E Andrew Johnson Hwy. I-81, exit 8, 6 mi
n on US 25 E to exit 2B (Greenville-Morristown), then just w. Ext corridors.
Pets: Small. $10 daily fee/pet. Service with restrictions, supervision.
SAVE ⊠ 🔥M 🖥 🖃 🏊

**▼▼▼ Holiday Inn Morristown Conference
Center** 🅷
(423) 587-2400. **$125-$289, 7 day notice.** 5435 S Davy Crockett Pkwy.
I-81, exit 8, just n. Int corridors. **Pets:** Medium. $25 one-time fee/room.
Designated rooms, service with restrictions, supervision.
SAVE ⊠ 🖥 🖃 🍴 🏊

▼▼▼ Ramada Morristown 🅷
(423) 581-8700. **$69-$200.** 3304 W Andrew Johnson Hwy. 2.5 mi w on US
11 E. Ext corridors. **Pets:** Other species. $10 one-time fee/pet. Service with
restrictions.
A$K ⊠ 🔥M 🖥 🖃 🍴 🏊

▼▼ Super 8 Motel 🅼
(423) 318-8888. **$40-$60.** 5400 S Davy Crockett Pkwy. I-81, exit 8, just n.
Int corridors. **Pets:** Medium. $9 daily fee/pet. Service with restrictions,
supervision.
A$K ⊠ 🔥M 🖥 🖃

MOUNT JULIET

▼▼▼ Quality Inn & Suites 🅷
(615) 773-3600. **$70-$120.** 1000 Hershel Dr. I-40, exit 226. Int corridors.
Pets: Medium. $25 one-time fee/room. No service, supervision.
SAVE ⊠ 🖥 🖃 🏊

MURFREESBORO

▼▼ Baymont Inn & Suites 🅼 ❀
(615) 896-1172. **$80-$140.** 2230 Armory Dr. I-24, exit 78B, just n. Ext
corridors. **Pets:** Large. $10 daily fee/pet. Designated rooms, service with
restrictions, supervision.
A$K ⊠ 🔥M 🖥 🖃 🏊

▼▼▼ Best Western Chaffin Inn 🅼
(615) 895-3818. **$71-$111, 3 day notice.** 168 Chaffin Pl. I-24, exit 78B.
Ext corridors. **Pets:** $15 daily fee/pet. No service, supervision.
SAVE ⊠ 🖥 🖃 🏊

▼▼▼ DoubleTree Hotel Murfreesboro 🅷 ❀
(615) 895-5555. **$189-$199.** 1850 Old Fort Pkwy. I-24, exit 78B. Int corridors. **Pets:** Large. $50 one-time fee/room. Designated rooms, service with
restrictions, crate.
⊠ 🖥 🖃 🍴 🏊

▼▼▼ Hampton Inn & Suites 🅷 ❀
(615) 890-2424. **$99-$309.** 325 N Thompson Ln. I-24, exit 78B, just n. Int
corridors. **Pets:** Other species. $20 daily fee/room. Service with restrictions,
supervision.
A$K ⊠ 🖥 🖃 🏊

▼▼▼ Howard Johnson Express Inn 🅷
(615) 896-5522. **$50-$100.** 2424 S Church St. I-24, exit 81A eastbound;
exit 81 westbound. Int corridors. **Pets:** Small. $10 daily fee/pet. Service with
restrictions, supervision.
SAVE ⊠ 🖥 🖃 🍴 🏊

▼▼▼ Quality Inn Murfreesboro 🅷
(615) 890-1006. **$75-$85.** 2135 S Church St. I-24, exit 81 westbound; exit
81B eastbound. Int corridors. **Pets:** Accepted.
SAVE ⊠ 🖥 🖃 🏊

▼▼▼ Ramada Limited 🅷 ❀
(615) 896-5080. **$50-$150.** 1855 S Church St. I-24, exit 81. Int corridors.
Pets: Large, other species. $10 daily fee/pet. Service with restrictions,
supervision.
SAVE ⊠ 🖥 🖃 🏊

▼▼▼ Vista Inn and Suites 🅷
(615) 848-9030. **$55-$200, 3 day notice.** 118 Westgate Blvd. I-24, exit
81A eastbound; exit 81 westbound. Int corridors. **Pets:** Small. $10 daily
fee/pet. Designated rooms, service with restrictions, crate.
SAVE ⊠ 🖥 🖃 🏊

NASHVILLE METROPOLITAN AREA

ANTIOCH

▼▼▼▼ Holiday Inn-The Crossings 🅷 ❀
(615) 731-2361. **$99-$119.** 201 Crossings Pl. I-24, exit 60, 0.5 mi e. Int corridors. **Pets:** Other species. Service with restrictions, crate.
ASK ✕ 📶 🛏 💻 ❌ 🏊

GOODLETTSVILLE

▥▼ ▼▼ Best Western Fairwinds Inn 🅷
(615) 851-1067. **$70-$90, 7 day notice.** 100 Northcreek Blvd. I-65, exit 97 (Long Hollow Pike), 0.5 mi e. Ext corridors. **Pets:** Accepted.
SAVE ✕ 🛏 💻 🏊

▼▼▼ Holiday Inn Express Hotel & Suites 🅷
(615) 851-1891. **$109-$179.** 120 Cartwright St. I-65, exit 97 (Long Hollow Pike), just w. Int corridors. **Pets:** Accepted.
✕ 📶 🛏 💻 🏊

▥▼ ▼▼ Rodeway Inn 🅼
(615) 859-1416. **$45-$70.** 650 Wade Cir. I-65, exit 96, just ne. Ext corridors. **Pets:** Small. $10 daily fee/pet. Designated rooms, service with restrictions, supervision.
SAVE ✕ 🛏 💻 🏊

NASHVILLE

▥▼ ▼▼ Airport Super 8 Nashville 🅷
(615) 889-8887. **$69-$92.** 720 Royal Pkwy. I-40, exit 216C (Donelson Pike N), 0.5 mi n, then just e. Int corridors. **Pets:** Accepted.
SAVE ✕ 📶 🛏 🏊

▥▼ ▼▼ Baymont Inn & Suites Nashville-West 🅷
(615) 353-0700. **$80-$100, 15 day notice.** 5612 Lenox Ave. I-40, exit 204. Int corridors. **Pets:** Accepted.
SAVE ✕ 🛏 💻 🏊

▥▼ ▼▼ Best Western Music City Inn 🅷
(615) 641-7721. **$60-$199, 3 day notice.** 13010 Old Hickory Blvd. I-24, exit 62. Ext corridors. **Pets:** Small. $25 one-time fee/room. Designated rooms, service with restrictions, supervision.
SAVE ✕ 🛏 💻 🏊

▥▼ ▼▼▼ Best Western Music Row 🅷
(615) 242-1631. **$90-$200.** 1407 Division St. I-40, exit 209B (Broadway), just w around circle, then just e. Int corridors. **Pets:** Small, other species. $10 daily fee/pet. Service with restrictions.
SAVE ✕ 🛏 💻 🏊

▼▼ Crossland Studios Nashville 🅷
(615) 366-0559. **$63-$73.** 1210 Murfreesboro Rd. I-40, exit 215 (Briley Pkwy), 2 mi s to exit 4, then 0.8 mi n. Ext corridors. **Pets:** Other species. $25 daily fee/pet. Service with restrictions, crate.
ASK ✕ 📶 🛏 💻

▼▼▼ Drury Inn & Suites-Nashville Airport 🅷
(615) 902-0400. **$80-$140.** 555 Donelson Pike. I-40, exit 216 (Donelson Pike). Int corridors. **Pets:** Other species. Service with restrictions, supervision.
ASK ✕ 📶 🛏 💻 🏊

▥▼ ▼▼▼ Days Inn 🅷
(615) 889-0090. **$60-$105.** 2460 Music Valley Dr. I-40, exit 215B (Briley Pkwy), 4 mi n to exit 11 (McGavock Pike). Int corridors. **Pets:** Accepted.
SAVE ✕ 💻 🏊

▼▼ Extended StayAmerica 🅷
(615) 383-7490. **$120-$130.** 3311 West End Ave. I-440, exit 1A, then just e. Int corridors. **Pets:** Other species. $25 daily fee/pet. Service with restrictions, crate.
ASK ✕ 📶 🛏 💻

▥▼ ▼▼ GuestHouse International Inn &
Suites 🅷 ❀
(615) 885-4030. **$109-$169.** 2420 Music Valley Dr. Briley Pkwy, exit 12, 0.3 mi w, then 0.3 mi n. Int corridors. **Pets:** Medium. $25 one-time fee/room. Designated rooms, service with restrictions, crate.
SAVE ✕ 🛏 💻 🏊

▥▼ ▼▼▼▼▼ The Hermitage Hotel 🅷
(615) 244-3121. **$239-$2500.** 231 6th Ave N. Corner of Union St; center. Int corridors. **Pets:** Accepted.
SAVE ✕ 📶 🛏 🍽 ❌

▼▼ Homestead Studio Suites Hotel-Nashville/Airport 🅷
(615) 316-9020. **$75-$85.** 727 McGavock Pike. I-40, exit 215B (Briley Pkwy), 1 mi n to exit 7 (Elm Hill Pike), then just e. Ext corridors. **Pets:** Other species. $25 daily fee/pet. Service with restrictions, crate.
ASK ✕ 📶 🛏 💻

▼▼▼ Homewood Suites by Hilton 🅷
(615) 884-8111. **$89-$149.** 2640 Elm Hill Pike. I-40, exit 216C (Donelson Pike). Int corridors. **Pets:** Accepted.
✕ 📶 🛏 💻 🏊

▼▼▼ Hotel Indigo-Nashville West End 🅷
(615) 329-4200. **$139-$299, 3 day notice.** 1719 West End Ave. I-40/65, exit 209B (Broadway), 0.4 mi w. Int corridors. **Pets:** Accepted.
✕ 📶 🛏 💻 🍽

▥▼ ▼▼▼ Hotel Preston 🅷
(615) 361-5900. **$89-$219, 3 day notice.** 733 Envious Ln. I-40, exit 215 (Briley Pkwy). Int corridors. **Pets:** Accepted.
SAVE ✕ 🛏 💻 🍽 🏊

▼▼▼▼ La Quinta Inn & Suites Nashville-Airport 🅷 ❀
(615) 885-3100. **$59-$119.** 531 Donelson Pike. I-40, exit 216C (Donelson Pike), 0.3 mi n. Int corridors. **Pets:** Medium, other species. Service with restrictions, supervision.
ASK ✕ 🛏 💻 🏊

▥▼ ▼▼▼ ▼▼▼ Loews Vanderbilt Hotel
Nashville 🅷 ❀
(615) 320-1700. **$169-$459.** 2100 West End Ave. I-40, exit 209B (Broadway), 1.3 mi w. Int corridors. **Pets:** Other species. $25 one-time fee/room. No service, supervision.
SAVE ✕ 🛏 💻 🍽 ❌

▥▼ ▼▼ Microtel Inn & Suites 🅷
(615) 662-0004. **$63-$94.** 100 Coley Davis Ct. I-40, exit 196. Int corridors. **Pets:** Small. $10 daily fee/room. Service with restrictions, supervision.
SAVE ✕ 🛏 💻 🏊

▥▼ ▼▼▼▼ Radisson Hotel Nashville Airport 🅷
(615) 889-9090. **$199.** 1112 Airport Center Dr. I-40, exit 216C (Donelson Pike N). Int corridors. **Pets:** Accepted.
SAVE ✕ 📶 🛏 💻 🍽 🏊

▥▼ ▼▼ Red Roof Inn Airport 🅼
(615) 872-0735. **$50-$90, 14 day notice.** 510 Claridge Dr. I-40, exit 216C (Donelson Pike), 0.3 mi n. Ext corridors. **Pets:** Medium, dogs only. Service with restrictions, supervision.
SAVE ✕ 🛏

▥▼ ▼▼▼ Residence Inn 🅷 ❀
(615) 889-8600. **$135-$155.** 2300 Elm Hill Pike. I-40, exit 215B (Briley Pkwy), 1.5 mi n. Ext corridors. **Pets:** Other species. $100 one-time fee/room. Service with restrictions, crate.
SAVE ✕ 🛏 💻 🏊

WWW Sheraton Music City Hotel 🅷 ❀
(615) 885-2200. **$99-$265.** 777 McGavock Pike. I-40, exit 215B (Briley Pkwy), 1 mi n to exit 7 (Elm Hill Pike), 0.5 mi e, then s. Int corridors. **Pets:** Large, other species. Service with restrictions, supervision.
SAVE ⊠ ⅏ 🛏 💻 ⑪ ⌲ ⌧

WWW Sheraton Nashville Downtown
Hotel 🅷 ❀
(615) 259-2000. **$139-$299.** 623 Union St. I-40, exit 209, just s of State Capitol. Int corridors. **Pets:** Medium. Service with restrictions, supervision.
SAVE ⊠ 🛏 💻 ⑪ ⌲ ⌧

WWW Sleep Inn 🅷
(615) 227-8686. **$39-$93, 3 day notice.** 3200 Dickerson Pike. I-65, exit 90A. Int corridors. **Pets:** Other species. $10 daily fee/pet. No service.
SAVE ⊠ ⅏ 🛏 💻 ⌲

WWW Super 8-West 🅷
(615) 356-6005. **$60-$180.** 6924 Charlotte Pike. I-40, exit 201. Ext corridors. **Pets:** Medium. $15 daily fee/pet. Service with restrictions, supervision.
SAVE ⊠ 🛏 💻

WW Thrifty Inn-Nashville South 🅷
(615) 834-4242. **$42-$61.** 343 Harding Pl. I-24, exit 56 (Harding Pl). Ext corridors. **Pets:** Other species. Service with restrictions, supervision.
ASK ⊠ 💻 ⌲

END METROPOLITAN AREA

NEWPORT

WWW Best Western Newport Inn Ⓜ
(423) 623-8713. **$45-$170, 14 day notice.** 1015 Cosby Hwy. I-40, exit 435, just w. Ext corridors. **Pets:** Accepted.
SAVE ⊠ ⅏ 🛏 💻 ⌲

WWW Comfort Inn 🅷
(423) 623-5355. **$54-$150.** 1149 Smokey Mountain Ln. I-40, exit 432B. Int corridors. **Pets:** Other species. $10 daily fee/pet. Designated rooms, service with restrictions, supervision.
SAVE ⊠ ⅏ 🛏 💻 ⌲

WW Holiday Inn 🅷
(423) 623-8622. **Call for rates.** 1010 Cosby Hwy. I-40, exit 435. Ext/int corridors. **Pets:** Accepted.
⊠ 🛏 💻 ⑪ ⌲ ⌧

WWW Motel 6-4090 Ⓜ
(423) 623-1850. **$35-$70.** 255 Heritage Blvd. I-40, exit 435. Int corridors. **Pets:** Other species. Service with restrictions, supervision.
SAVE ⊠ ⅏ 🛏 💻 ⌲

OAK RIDGE

WWW DoubleTree Oak Ridge 🅷
(865) 481-2468. **$104-$134.** 215 S Illinois Ave. 0.3 mi se of SR 95 on SR 62. Int corridors. **Pets:** Medium, other species. $50 one-time fee/room. Service with restrictions, supervision.
⊠ 🛏 💻 ⑪ ⌲

WWW Jameson Inn 🅷
(865) 483-6809. **$89-$94.** 216 S Rutgers Ave. Jct SR 95 and 62, 0.9 mi se on SR 62 to Rutgers Ave, then 0.7 mi n. Int corridors. **Pets:** Accepted.
ASK ⊠ 🛏 💻 ⌲

OOLTEWAH

WW Super 8 Motel Ⓜ
(423) 238-5951. **$45-$65.** 5111 Hunter Rd. I-75, exit 11, just w. Ext corridors. **Pets:** Medium. $10 daily fee/pet. Service with restrictions, supervision.
ASK ⊠ 🛏 💻

PICKWICK DAM

WWW Pickwick Landing State Resort Park Inn 🅷
(731) 689-3135. **$68-$82.** 220 Playground Loop. Intersection of US 57 and SR 128. Ext/int corridors. **Pets:** Medium. $10 daily fee/pet. Designated rooms, service with restrictions, supervision.
ASK ⊠ ⅏ 🛏 💻 ⑪ ⌲ ⌧

PIGEON FORGE

WWW Blackberry Ridge-Accommodations by Sunset
Cottage 🄲🄰
(865) 429-8478. **Call for rates.** 3630 S River Rd. Just e of jct US 441 at traffic light 8, just n. Ext corridors. **Pets:** Accepted.
⊠ 🛏 💻

WWW Briarstone Inn Ⓜ ❀
(865) 453-4225. **$40-$90.** 3626 Parkway. On US 441; between traffic lights 7 and 8. Ext corridors. **Pets:** Small, dogs only. $15 daily fee/pet. Designated rooms, service with restrictions.
SAVE ⊠ 🛏 💻 ⌲

WWWW Eden Crest Vacation Rentals 🄲🄰 ❀
(865) 774-0059. **$125-$395.** 652 Wears Valley Rd. US 321 to light 3, just w. Ext corridors. **Pets:** Small, dogs only. $150 one-time fee/pet. Service with restrictions, crate.
SAVE ⊠ 🛏 💻 ⌲

WWW Grand Resort Hotel & Convention Center 🅷
(865) 453-1000. **$50-$150, 3 day notice.** 3171 Parkway. On US 441 at traffic light 6. Ext/int corridors. **Pets:** Small, dogs only. $10 daily fee/room. Service with restrictions, supervision.
SAVE ⊠ ⅏ 🛏 💻 ⑪ ⌲

WWW Hampton Inn & Suites 🅷 ❀
(865) 428-1600. **$64-$219.** 2025 Parkway. On US 441 at traffic light 0. Int corridors. **Pets:** Medium. $20 daily fee/room. Service with restrictions, crate.
ASK ⊠ ⅏ 🛏 💻 ⌲

WW Holiday Inn Resort 🅷
(865) 428-2700. **$50-$180.** 3230 Parkway. On US 441; between traffic lights 6 and 7. Int corridors. **Pets:** Accepted.
ASK ⊠ 🛏 💻 ⑪ ⌲

WWWW La Quinta Inn 🅷 ❀
(865) 429-3010. **$40-$139.** 219 Emert St. Just w of jct US 441; between traffic lights 7 and 8. Int corridors. **Pets:** Medium, other species. Service with restrictions, supervision.
SAVE ⊠ ⅏ 🛏 💻 ⌲

WW Microtel Suites at Music Road 🅷
(865) 453-1116. **$35-$115.** 2045 Parkway. On US 441, just s of traffic light 0. Int corridors. **Pets:** Accepted.
ASK ⊠ ⅏ 🛏 💻 ⌲

WW Motel 6 #4021 Ⓜ
(865) 908-1244. **$29-$99.** 336 Henderson Chapel Rd. Jct US 441, just w at traffic light 1. Int corridors. **Pets:** Other species. Service with restrictions, supervision.
SAVE ⊠ ⅏ ⌲

⚛️ ◈◈ National Parks Resort Lodge 🅷
(865) 453-4106. **$30-$130.** 2385 Parkway. On US 441 at traffic light 1. Int corridors. **Pets:** $20 deposit/room, $20 one-time fee/pet. Designated rooms, service with restrictions, crate.
[SAVE] [X] [🛏] [💻] [🏊]

⚛️ ◈◈◈ Ramada Inn Ⓜ
(865) 453-1823. **$35-$149.** 4010 Parkway. On US 441; between traffic lights 8 and 10. Ext corridors. **Pets:** Accepted.
[SAVE] [X] [🛏] [💻]

⚛️ ◈◈ Smoky Shadows Motel & Conference Center 🅷
(865) 453-7155. **$39-$119, 3 day notice.** 4215 Parkway. On US 441, just n of traffic light 10. Ext/int corridors. **Pets:** Accepted.
[SAVE] [X] [🛏M] [🛏] [💻] [🏊]

⚛️ ◈◈◈ Starr Crest Resort Cabin Rentals ⒸⒶ
(865) 429-0156. **$89-$1209, 30 day notice.** 1431 Upper Middle Creek Rd. I-40, US 441, e at traffic light 8, 1.5 mi on Dollywood Ln. Ext corridors. **Pets:** Accepted.
[SAVE] [X] [🛏] [💻] [🏊]

⚛️ ◈◈ Super 8 Motel 🅷
(865) 428-2300. **$40-$140.** 215 Emert St. Just w of jct US 441; between traffic lights 7 and 8. Ext corridors. **Pets:** Accepted.
[SAVE] [X] [🛏M] [🛏] [💻] [🏊]

POWELL

⚛️ ◈◈ Super 8 Motel of Powell Ⓜ
(865) 938-5501. **$60-$130.** 323 E Emory Rd. I-75, exit 112. Ext corridors. **Pets:** Very small. $10 daily fee/pet. Service with restrictions, crate.
[SAVE] [X] [🛏] [💻] [🏊]

PULASKI

◈◈ Richland Inn 🅷
(931) 363-0006. **Call for rates.** 1020 W College St. On US 64, 1 mi w of jct US 31. Ext corridors. **Pets:** Accepted.
[X] [🛏] [💻]

⚛️ ◈ Super 8 Motel 🅷
(931) 363-4501. **$77-$120.** I-65 & Hwy 64, Exit 14 East. I-65, exit 14, just e. Ext corridors. **Pets:** Accepted.
[SAVE] [X] [🛏] [💻] [🏊]

ROGERSVILLE

◈◈◈ Comfort Inn & Suites 🅷
(423) 272-8700. **$110-$150.** 128 James Richardson Ln. US 11 W. Int corridors. **Pets:** Small. $25 one-time fee/pet. Designated rooms, no service, supervision.
[ASK] [X] [🛏M] [🛏] [💻] [🏊]

◈◈ Holiday Inn Express 🅷
(423) 272-1842. **Call for rates.** 7139 Hwy 11 W. Jct SR 66 and US 11, 0.5 mi sw. Int corridors. **Pets:** Other species. $10 one-time fee/pet. Service with restrictions, supervision.
[X] [🛏M] [🛏] [💻] [🏊]

SELMER

◈◈ America's Best Inn 🅷
(731) 645-8800. **$50-$65.** 644 Mulberry Ave. Jct SR 64 and 45, just s on SR 45. Ext corridors. **Pets:** Dogs only. $10 daily fee/pet. Designated rooms, service with restrictions.
[ASK] [X] [🛏] [💻] [🏊]

SEVIERVILLE

◈◈◈ Baymont Inn & Suites 🅷
(865) 933-9448. **$49-$149.** 2863 Winfield Dunn Pkwy. I-40, exit 407, 2.3 mi s on SR 66. Int corridors. **Pets:** Large. $10 daily fee/pet. Designated rooms, service with restrictions, crate.
[ASK] [X] [🛏M] [🛏] [💻] [🏊]

◈◈ Big Bear Extended Stay Suites 🅷
(865) 225-1719. **$49-$139.** 2162 Parkway. I-40, exit 407, just s on SR 66, then w. Ext corridors. **Pets:** Medium, other species. $10 daily fee/room. Service with restrictions.
[ASK] [X] [🛏] [💻]

⚛️ ◈◈◈ La Quinta Sevierville 🅷 🐾
(865) 933-3339. **$40-$170.** 2428 Winfield Dunn Pkwy. I-40, exit 407, 3.2 mi on SR 66. Int corridors. **Pets:** Medium, other species. Service with restrictions, supervision.
[SAVE] [X] [🛏M] [🛏] [💻] [🏊]

⚛️ ◈◈◈ Quality Inn Interstate Ⓜ
(865) 933-1719. **$50-$199.** 155 Dumplin Valley Rd. I-40, exit 407, just s on SR 66, then just w. Ext corridors. **Pets:** Medium, other species. $10 daily fee/room. Designated rooms, service with restrictions, supervision.
[SAVE] [X] [🛏M] [🛏] [💻] [🏊]

⚛️ ◈◈ Sleep Inn 🅷
(865) 429-0484. **$49-$129.** 1020 Parkway. On US 441, 1.2 mi s of jct US 411. Int corridors. **Pets:** Large, other species. $10 daily fee/room. Service with restrictions, crate.
[SAVE] [X] [🛏M] [🛏] [💻] [🏊]

SHELBYVILLE

⚛️ ◈◈ Best Western Celebration Inn & Suites 🅷
(931) 684-2378. **$75-$269, 3 day notice.** 724 Madison St. Jct SR 231 and US 41. Ext corridors. **Pets:** Medium. $15 daily fee/pet. Service with restrictions, supervision.
[SAVE] [X] [🛏] [💻] [🏊]

SWEETWATER

⚛️ ◈◈ Comfort Inn West 🅷
(423) 337-3353. **$60-$169.** 249 Hwy 68. I-75, exit 60, just e. Ext/int corridors. **Pets:** Accepted.
[SAVE] [X] [🛏] [💻] [🏊]

⚛️ ◈◈ Econo Lodge Ⓜ
(423) 337-6646. **$53-$100.** 731 S Main St. On US 11, jct SR 68. Ext/int corridors. **Pets:** Accepted.
[SAVE] [X] [🛏] [💻] [🏊]

◈◈ Magnuson Hotel 🅷
(423) 337-3541. **$69-$99.** 1421 Murray's Chapel Rd. I-75, exit 60, just w. Ext/int corridors. **Pets:** Small. $15 one-time fee/room. Designated rooms, service with restrictions, supervision.
[ASK] [X] [🛏] [💻] [🍽] [🏊]

⚛️ ◈◈◈ Quality Inn & Suites 🅷
(423) 337-4900. **$70-$153.** 1116 Hwy 68. I-75, exit 60, just w. Int corridors. **Pets:** Other species. $15 one-time fee/pet. Service with restrictions.
[SAVE] [X] [🛏M] [🛏] [💻] [🏊]

TOWNSEND

⚛️ ◈◈ Econo Lodge Ⓜ
(865) 448-9000. **$39-$189.** 7824 E Lamar Alexander Pkwy. On US 321, 0.7 mi s of jct SR 73. Ext corridors. **Pets:** Small. $20 daily fee/pet. Service with restrictions, supervision.
[SAVE] [X] [🛏M] [🛏] [💻] [🏊]

⚛️ ◈◈ Valley View Lodge Ⓜ
(865) 448-2237. **$45-$110, 3 day notice.** 7726 E Lamar Alexander Pkwy. On US 321, 1.1 mi s of jct SR 73. Ext corridors. **Pets:** Dogs only. $15 one-time fee/pet. Designated rooms, service with restrictions, supervision.
[SAVE] [X] [🛏M] [🛏] [💻] [🏊] [X]

TULLAHOMA

▼▼ Jameson Inn **H**

(931) 455-7891. **$83-$90.** 2113 N Jackson St. 3 mi n on SR 41A (N Jackson St). Ext corridors. **Pets:** Small. $15 daily fee/pet. No service, supervision.

ASK ✕ 🛗 💻 🏊

VONORE

▼▼▼ Grand Vista Hotel & Suites **H**

(423) 884-6200. **$99-$189.** 117 Grand Vista Dr. I-75, exit 172, 14 mi e. Int corridors. **Pets:** $10 daily fee/pet. Designated rooms, service with restrictions, crate.

ASK ✕ 🛗 🛗 💻 🏊

WHITE HOUSE

▼▼▼ Holiday Inn Express **H**

(615) 672-7200. **$89-$109.** 206 Knight Cir. I-65, exit 108, just e. Int corridors. **Pets:** Small. $25 daily fee/pet. Designated rooms, service with restrictions, crate.

ASK ✕ 🛗 🛗 💻 🏊

QUALITY INN

AAA ▼▼ Quality Inn **H**

(615) 672-7000. **$60-$80.** 354 Hester Ln. I-65, exit 108, just e. Ext corridors. **Pets:** Accepted.

SAVE ✕ 🛗 🛗 💻 🏊

WHITEVILLE

▼▼ Super 8 **H**

(731) 254-8884. **$50-$60.** 2040 Hwy 64. US 64 and SR 179. Ext corridors. **Pets:** $5 daily fee/pet. Service with restrictions, supervision.

ASK ✕ 🛗 🛗 💻

TEXAS

CITY INDEX

ABILENE

🔺 ▽▽▽ Americas Best Value Inn Ⓜ 🐾
(325) 673-5424. **Call for rates.** 1633 W Stamford St. S Frontage Rd off I-20 and US 80, exit 285 eastbound; exit 286A westbound. Ext corridors. **Pets:** Other species. $10 one-time fee/pet.
SAVE ✕ 🛡 💻

🔺 ▽▽▽ Best Western Mall South Ⓗ
(325) 695-1262. **$96-$100, 7 day notice.** 3950 Ridgemont Dr. US 83/84, exit Ridgemont Dr, just s. Ext corridors. **Pets:** Medium. $30 daily fee/pet. Designated rooms, service with restrictions, crate.
SAVE ✕ 🛡 💻 🏊

🔺 ▽▽▽ Budget Host Colonial Inn Ⓜ
(325) 677-2683. **$60-$100.** 3210 Pine St. Jct I-20 and US 83 business route, exit 286A. Ext/int corridors. **Pets:** Accepted.
SAVE ✕ 🛡 💻 🏊

▽▽ Civic Plaza Hotel Ⓗ
(325) 676-0222. **Call for rates.** 505 Pine St. Downtown. Ext corridors. **Pets:** Accepted.
✕ 🛡 💻 🍴 🏊

🔺 ▽▽▽▽ Comfort Suites University Ⓗ
(325) 672-0338. **$99-$129.** 1902 E Overland Tr. I-20, exit 288, on N Frontage Rd. Int corridors. **Pets:** $30 one-time fee/room. Designated rooms, service with restrictions, supervision.
SAVE ✕ 🛡M 🛡 💻 🏊

🔺 ▽▽▽ Holiday Inn Express Mall South Ⓗ
(325) 695-0500. **$99-$139.** 3112 S Clack. US 83/277 and Southwest Dr, just e to Catclaw, then just n. Int corridors. **Pets:** Accepted.
SAVE ✕ 🛡M 🛡 💻 🏊

▽▽▽▽ La Quinta Inn Abilene Ⓗ 🐾
(325) 676-1676. **$59-$119.** 3501 W Lake Rd. I-20, exit 286C. Ext corridors. **Pets:** Medium, other species. Service with restrictions, supervision.
ASK ✕ 🛡 💻 🏊

▽▽ Motel 6 Abilene #79 Ⓜ
(325) 672-8462. **$45-$56.** 4951 W Stamford St. I-20, exit 282, on eastbound frontage road. Ext corridors. **Pets:** Other species. Service with restrictions, supervision.
✕ 🛡 🏊

▽▽ Super 8 Abilene North Ⓜ
(325) 673-5251. **$70-$80.** 1525 E I-20. I-20, exit 288. Ext corridors. **Pets:** Accepted.
ASK ✕ 🛡 💻 🏊

ALAMO

▽▽▽ La Quinta Inn & Suites Ⓗ 🐾
(956) 783-6955. **$59-$119.** 909 E Frontage Rd. US 83, exit Alamo Rd. Int corridors. **Pets:** Medium, other species. Service with restrictions, supervision.
ASK ✕ 🛡M 🛡 💻 🏊

▼▼ **Super 8** ⚏
(956) 787-9444. **Call for rates.** 714 N Alamo Rd. US 83, exit FM 907, just n. Ext corridors. **Pets:** Accepted.
☒ ☷ ⊒

ALICE

▼ **Days Inn** ⚏
(361) 664-6616. **$75-$120.** 555 N Johnson St. On US 281 business route, n of Johnson St. Int corridors. **Pets:** Accepted.
🅰$🅺 ☒ ☷ ⊑ ⊒

ALPINE

◈◈ ▼▼ **Oak Tree Inn** ⚏
(432) 837-5711. **$65-$79.** 2407 E Holland (Hwy 90/67). US 90, 2 mi e. Int corridors. **Pets:** Other species. $10 daily fee/pet. Service with restrictions.
🆂🅰🆅🅴 ☒ ⚒ ☷ ⊑

ALVARADO

▼▼▼ **Super 8** ⚏
(817) 790-7378. **Call for rates.** 5445 S I-35W. I-35W, exit 27A (US 67), just e to 1st traffic light on US 67, then 0.4 mi n on access road. Int corridors. **Pets:** Accepted.
☒ ⚒ ☷ ⊑ ⊒

ALVIN

▼▼ **Americas Best Value Inn & Suites** Ⓜ
(281) 331-0335. **Call for rates.** 1588 S Hwy 35 Loop. SR 35 Bypass, 0.5 mi sw of SR 6. Ext corridors. **Pets:** Accepted.
☒ ☷ ⊑ ⊒

AMARILLO

◈◈ ▼▼ **Ambassador Hotel** ⚏ 🐾
(806) 358-6161. **$139-$169.** 3100 I-40 W. I-40, exit 68, just w on north frontage road. Int corridors. **Pets:** Large, other species. $50 one-time fee/pet. Designated rooms, service with restrictions, crate.
🆂🅰🆅🅴 ☒ ☷ ⊑ ⊟ ⊒ ☒

◈◈ ▼▼▼ **Baymont Inn & Suites** ⚏
(806) 356-6800. **Call for rates.** 3411 I-40 W. I-40, exit 67, 0.3 mi e on south frontage road. Int corridors. **Pets:** Other species. $10 daily fee/pet. Designated rooms, supervision.
🆂🅰🆅🅴 ☒ ☷ ⊑ ⊒

◈◈ ▼▼▼ **Best Western Amarillo Inn** ⚏
(806) 358-7861. **$80-$130.** 1610 Coulter Dr. I-40, exit 65 (Coulter Dr), 0.6 mi n. Ext/int corridors. **Pets:** Large, other species. $20 one-time fee/pet. Service with restrictions, supervision.
🆂🅰🆅🅴 ☒ ⊑ ⊒

◈◈ ▼▼▼ **Best Western Santa Fe** ⚏
(806) 372-1885. **$70-$100, 14 day notice.** 4600 I-40 E. I-40, exit 73 (Eastern St) eastbound; exit 73 (Bolton St) westbound, U-turn on south frontage road. Int corridors. **Pets:** Large, other species. $15 daily fee/pet. Service with restrictions, supervision.
🆂🅰🆅🅴 ☒ ☷ ⊑ ⊒

◈◈ ▼▼▼ **Big Texan Motel** Ⓜ
(806) 372-5000. **$59-$90, 7 day notice.** 7701 I-40 E. I-40, exit 75 (Lakeside Dr), 0.3 mi w on north frontage road. Ext corridors. **Pets:** Other species. $30 deposit/pet, $10 daily fee/pet. Designated rooms, service with restrictions, supervision.
🆂🅰🆅🅴 ☒ ☷ ⊟ ⊒

▼▼ **Days Inn East Amarillo** ⚏
(806) 379-6255. **Call for rates.** 1701 I-40 E. I-40, exit 71 (Ross-Osage), just w on north frontage road. Int corridors. **Pets:** Other species. $10 one-time fee/pet. Designated rooms, service with restrictions, supervision.
☒ ☷ ⊑ ⊒

▼▼ **Days Inn South** ⚏
(806) 468-7100. **Call for rates.** 8601 Canyon Dr. I-27, exit 116, just n on east service road. Int corridors. **Pets:** Medium, other species. $20 one-time fee/pet. Service with restrictions, supervision.
☒ ☷ ⊒

▼▼▼ **Drury Inn & Suites-Amarillo** ⚏
(806) 351-1111. **$95-$145.** 8540 W I-40. I-40, exit 64. Int corridors. **Pets:** Other species. Service with restrictions, supervision.
🅰$🅺 ☒ ⚒ ☷ ⊑ ⊒

▼▼ **Extended StayAmerica Amarillo West** ⚏
(806) 351-0117. **$65-$98.** 2100 Cinema Dr. I-40, exit 64, just n. Int corridors. **Pets:** Other species. $25 daily fee/pet. Service with restrictions, crate.
🅰$🅺 ☒ ☷ ⊑

◈◈ ▼▼▼ **Hampton Inn** ⚏
(806) 372-1425. **$84-$114.** 1700 I-40 E. I-40, exit 71 (Ross-Osage), just e on south frontage road. Int corridors. **Pets:** Other species. Service with restrictions, supervision.
🆂🅰🆅🅴 ☒ ☷ ⊑ ⊒

◈◈ ▼▼▼ **Holiday Inn-I-40** ⚏
(806) 372-8741. **Call for rates.** 1911 I-40 at Ross-Osage. I-40, exit 71 (Ross-Osage), on north frontage road. Int corridors. **Pets:** Other species. $25 one-time fee/room. Designated rooms, no service, supervision.
🆂🅰🆅🅴 ☒ ☷ ⊑ ⊟ ⊒

◈◈ ▼▼▼ **Howard Johnson** ⚏
(806) 374-2020. **$50-$63, 5 day notice.** 1620 I-40 E. I-40, exit 71 (Ross-Osage), just e on south frontage road. Ext corridors. **Pets:** Accepted.
🆂🅰🆅🅴 ☒ ☷ ⊑ ⊒

▼▼▼ **La Quinta Inn Amarillo (East/Airport Area)** ⚏ 🐾
(806) 373-7486. **$49-$89.** 1708 I-40 E. I-40, exit 71 (Ross-Osage), just e on south frontage road. Ext corridors. **Pets:** Medium, other species. Service with restrictions, supervision.
🅰$🅺 ☒ ☷ ⊑ ⊒

▼▼▼ **La Quinta Inn Amarillo (West/Medical Center)** ⚏ 🐾
(806) 352-6311. **$49-$89.** 2108 S Coulter Dr. I-40, exit 65 (Coulter Dr), just n. Ext corridors. **Pets:** Medium, other species. Service with restrictions, supervision.
🅰$🅺 ☒ ⚒ ☷ ⊑ ⊒

▼▼▼ **Microtel Inn & Suites** ⚏
(806) 372-8373. **$59-$119.** 1501 S Ross St. I-40, exit 71 (Ross-Osage), just n. Int corridors. **Pets:** $20 one-time fee/pet. Service with restrictions, supervision.
🆂🅰🆅🅴 ☒ ⚒ ☷ ⊑ ⊒

◈◈ ▼▼▼ **Quality Inn & Suites West** ⚏
(806) 358-7943. **$70-$140.** 6800 I-40 W. I-40, exit 66 (Bell St), 0.5 mi w on north frontage road. Ext corridors. **Pets:** Small. $20 one-time fee/pet. Service with restrictions, supervision.
🆂🅰🆅🅴 ☒ ☷ ⊑ ⊒

◈◈ ▼▼▼ **Quality Inn-East** ⚏
(806) 376-9993. **$69-$100.** 1515 I-40 E. I-40, exit 71 (Ross-Osage), just w on north frontage road. Ext corridors. **Pets:** Accepted.
🆂🅰🆅🅴 ☒ ☷ ⊑ ⊒

▼▼▼ **Residence Inn by Marriott** ⚏
(806) 354-2978. **$144-$176.** 6700 I-40 W. I-40, exit 66 (Bell St), 0.5 mi w on north frontage road. Int corridors. **Pets:** Other species. $50 one-time fee/room. Service with restrictions, supervision.
☒ ⚒ ☷ ⊑ ⊒ ☒

◈◈ ▼▼▼ **Travelodge West** ⚏
(806) 353-3541. **$55-$59.** 2035 Paramount Blvd. I-40, exit 68A (Paramount Blvd), just s. Ext corridors. **Pets:** Medium. $5 daily fee/pet. No service.
🆂🅰🆅🅴 ☒ ☷ ⊑ ⊒

ANGLETON

(AAA) ▼▼▼ Best Western Angelton Inn 🅗
(979) 849-5822. **$85-$95.** 1809 N Velasco St. Jct SR 35 and Business Rt SR 288, 1 mi n. Ext corridors. **Pets:** Small. $25 one-time fee/room. Service with restrictions, supervision.

[SAVE] [✕] 🄵 🖳 〰

ANTHONY

(AAA) ▼▼▼ Best Western Oasis of the Sun 🅗
(915) 886-3333. **$90-$100.** 9401 S Desert Blvd. I-10, exit 0, just s. Ext corridors. **Pets:** Very small. $25 daily fee/pet. Designated rooms, service with restrictions, supervision.

[SAVE] [✕] 🄼 🄵 🖳 〰 🄢

ARLINGTON

▼▼▼ Arlington TownePlace Suites by Marriott 🅗
(817) 861-8728. **$125-$153.** 1709 E Lamar Blvd. 2 mi w of SR 360. Int corridors. **Pets:** Medium, other species. $75 one-time fee/room. Service with restrictions, crate.

[✕] 🄼 🄵 🖳 〰

(AAA) ▼▼▼ Baymont Inn & Suites @ Six Flags Dr 🅗
(817) 633-2400. **Call for rates.** 2401 Diplomacy Dr. I-30, exit 30 (SR 360), 0.5 mi s; off SR 360, exit Six Flags Dr northbound; exit Ave H/Lamar Blvd southbound, on southbound service road. Int corridors. **Pets:** Accepted.

[SAVE] [✕] 🄼 🄵 🖳 〰

(AAA) ▼▼▼ Best Western Cooper Inn & Suites 🄼
(817) 784-9490. **$79-$109.** 4024 Melear Dr. I-20, exit 449B (Cooper St), just n to Melear Dr, then just w. Ext corridors. **Pets:** Other species. $10 daily fee/pet. No service, supervision.

[SAVE] [✕] 🄵 🖳 〰

▼▼▼ Country Inn & Suites By Carlson 🅗
(817) 261-8900. **$75-$160.** 1075 Wet N Wild Way. I-30, exit 28 (Collins St/FM 157), just e. Ext corridors. **Pets:** Accepted.

[ASK] [✕] 🄼 🄵 🖳 〰 🄢

(AAA) ▼▼▼ Days Inn Ranger Ballpark in Arlington/Six Flags 🅗
(817) 261-8444. **$57-$125, 3 day notice.** 910 N Collins St. I-30, exit 28 (Collins St/FM 157), 1 mi s. Int corridors. **Pets:** Medium, other species. $10 daily fee/pet. Service with restrictions, supervision.

[SAVE] [✕] 🄵 🖳 〰

▼▼▼ Hawthorn Suites 🅗
(817) 640-1188. **$69-$249.** 2401 Brookhollow Plaza Dr. I-30, exit 30 (SR 360), just n to Lamar Blvd, just w to Brookhollow Plaza Dr, then just n. Ext corridors. **Pets:** Accepted.

[ASK] [✕] 🄵 🖳 〰 🄢

▼▼▼ La Quinta Inn & Suites Dallas/Arlington North 🅗 🌸
(817) 640-4142. **$79-$189.** 825 N Watson Rd. I-30, exit 30 (SR 360), exit Six Flags Dr northbound; exit Ave H/Lamar Blvd southbound. Int corridors. **Pets:** Medium, other species. Service with restrictions, supervision.

[ASK] [✕] 🄵 🖳 〰

▼▼▼ La Quinta Inn & Suites Dallas/Arlington South 🅗 🌸
(817) 467-7756. **$89-$149.** 4001 Scott's Legacy Dr. I-20, exit 450 (Matlock Rd), on westbound service road. Int corridors. **Pets:** Medium, other species. Service with restrictions, supervision.

[ASK] [✕] 🄼 🄵 🖳 〰

(AAA) ▼▼▼ Microtel Inn 🅗
(817) 557-8400. **$55-$75.** 1740 Oak Village Blvd. I-20, exit 449 (Cooper St) westbound; exit 449A (Cooper St) eastbound, just s. Int corridors. **Pets:** Small, dogs only. $15 daily fee/pet. Service with restrictions, supervision.

[SAVE] [✕] 🄵 〰

(AAA) ▼▼▼ Sheraton Arlington Hotel 🅗
(817) 261-8200. **$119-$525.** 1500 Convention Center Dr. I-30, exit 29 (Ballpark Way) westbound; exit 28B (Nolan Ryan Expwy) eastbound, 0.4 mi e on Copeland Rd to Convention Center Dr, then just s. Int corridors. **Pets:** Accepted.

[SAVE] [✕] 🄼 🄵 🖳 🍴 〰

(AAA) ▼▼▼ Sleep Inn Main Gate-Six Flags 🅗
(817) 649-1010. **$50-$130.** 750 Six Flags Dr. I-30, exit 30 (SR 360), 0.5 mi s. Int corridors. **Pets:** Small, other species. $10 daily fee/pet, $35 one-time fee/pet. Service with restrictions, supervision.

[SAVE] [✕] 🄵 🖳 〰

▼▼ Studio 6-South Arlington #6036 🅗
(817) 465-8500. **$71-$81.** 1980 W Pleasant Ridge Rd. I-20, exit 449 (Cooper St), 0.3 mi n, then just w. Ext corridors. **Pets:** Other species. $10 daily fee/room. Service with restrictions, supervision.

[✕] 🄵 🖳

▼▼ StudioPLUS Dallas-Arlington 🅗
(817) 649-0021. **$55-$92.** 2420 E Lamar Blvd. I-30, exit 30 (SR 360), just n to Lamar Blvd; just w of SR 360. Int corridors. **Pets:** Other species. $25 daily fee/pet. Service with restrictions, crate.

[ASK] [✕] 🄵 🖳 〰

AUSTIN

▼▼▼ Baymont Inn Highland Mall 🅗
(512) 452-9401. **Call for rates.** 7100 I-35 N. I-35, exit 239, on west frontage road. Ext corridors. **Pets:** Accepted.

[✕] 🄵 🖳 〰

(AAA) ▼▼▼ Best Western Atrium North 🅗
(512) 339-7311. **$99-$129.** 7928 Gessner Dr. I-35, exit 240A, 0.4 mi w on Anderson Ln. Int corridors. **Pets:** Small, other species. $25 one-time fee/room. Service with restrictions.

[SAVE] [✕] 🄵 🖳 〰

(AAA) ▼▼▼ Best Western Austin–South 🅗
(512) 447-5511. **$80-$139, 7 day notice.** 4323 I-35 S. I-35, exit 230A (Stassney Rd) southbound; exit 230 (Ben White Blvd) northbound. Int corridors. **Pets:** Accepted.

[SAVE] [✕] 🄵 🖳 🍴 〰

▼▼▼ Candlewood Suites Austin Northwest 🅗
(512) 338-1611. **$114.** 9701 Stonelake Blvd. Jct SR 360 (Capital of Texas Hwy) and Stonelake Blvd, just s. Int corridors. **Pets:** Accepted.

[ASK] [✕] 🄼 🄵 🖳

▼▼▼ Candlewood Suites-South 🅗
(512) 444-8882. **$109-$159.** 4320 S I-35. I-35, exit 230 northbound; exit 230B southbound, on southbound frontage road. Int corridors. **Pets:** Accepted.

[ASK] [✕] 🄼 🄵 🖳

(AAA) ▼▼▼ Clarion Inn & Suites Conference Center 🅗
(512) 444-0561. **$119-$199.** 2200 S I-35. I-35, exit 232A (Oltorf Blvd), on west side access road. Ext/int corridors. **Pets:** Medium. $50 one-time fee/room. Service with restrictions, supervision.

[SAVE] [✕] 🄵 🖳 🍴 〰

▼▼▼ Comfort Suites Airport 🅗
(512) 386-6000. **Call for rates.** 7501 E Ben White Blvd. I-35, exit 230B (Ben White Blvd/SR 71), 3.6 mi e. Int corridors. **Pets:** Accepted.

[✕] 🄼 🄵 🖳

▼▼ Crossland Studios Austin West 🅗
(512) 331-4747. **$50-$84.** 12621 Hymeadow Rd. US 183 N, exit Lake Creek, just n, then just e. Ext corridors. **Pets:** Other species. $25 daily fee/pet. Service with restrictions, crate.

[ASK] [✕] 🄵 🖳

▼▼▼▼ **DoubleTree Guest Suites-Austin** H
(512) 478-7000. **$139-$329.** 303 W 15th St. Just nw of state capitol building. Int corridors. **Pets:** Accepted.
⊠ 🛏 🖵 🍴 🏊

AAA ▼▼▼▼ **The Driskill** H ❀
(512) 474-5911. **$199-$509.** 604 Brazos St. Jct 6th St. Int corridors. **Pets:** Small. $50 one-time fee/pet. Service with restrictions, supervision.
SAVE ⊠ 🍴

▼▼▼▼ **Drury Inn & Suites-Austin North** H
(512) 467-9500. **$90-$146.** 6711 I-35 N. I-35, exit 238A, on east frontage road. Int corridors. **Pets:** Other species. Service with restrictions, supervision.
ASK ⊠ 🛏 🖵 🏊

▼▼▼ **Econo Lodge** H
(512) 835-7070. **$60-$130.** 9102 Burnet Rd. US 183 and Burnet Rd; on northeast corner. Ext corridors. **Pets:** Small. $50 one-time fee/pet. Designated rooms, no service, supervision.
ASK ⊠ 🛏 🖵

▼▼▼ **Embassy Suites Austin North** H
(512) 454-8004. **$129-$209.** 5901 I-35 N. I-35, exit 238A, on east frontage road. Int corridors. **Pets:** Accepted.
⊠ 🛏 🖵 🍴 🏊

▼▼▼ **Embassy Suites Hotel-Downtown** H
(512) 469-9000. **$159-$269.** 300 S Congress Ave. Just s of Congress Ave Bridge. Int corridors. **Pets:** Accepted.
⊠ 🛏 🖵 🍴 🏊

▼▼▼ **Extended StayAmerica Austin Arboretum** H
(512) 231-1520. **$85-$120.** 10100 Capital of Texas Hwy. Jct Loop 1 (Mo-Pac) and Capital of Texas Hwy (SR 360), just w. Int corridors. **Pets:** Other species. $25 daily fee/pet. Service with restrictions, crate.
ASK ⊠ 🦮 🛏 🖵

▼▼▼ **Extended StayAmerica Austin Downtown** H
(512) 457-9994. **$125-$166.** 600 Guadalupe St. Jct 6th and Guadalupe sts; on northwest corner. Int corridors. **Pets:** Other species. $25 daily fee/pet. Service with restrictions, crate.
ASK ⊠ 🦮 🛏 🖵

▼▼▼ **Extended StayAmerica Austin Northwest Lakeline Mall** H
(512) 258-3365. **$65-$98.** 13858 US Hwy 183 N. Jct US 183 and SR 620; on southwest corner. Int corridors. **Pets:** Other species. $25 daily fee/pet. Service with restrictions, crate.
ASK ⊠ 🛏 🖵 🏊

▼▼▼ **Extended StayAmerica Austin Southwest** H
(512) 892-4272. **$90-$126.** 5100 US Hwy 290 W. I-35, exit 230, US 290 W to Brodie Ln exit, then 1 mi w. Int corridors. **Pets:** Other species. $25 daily fee/pet. Service with restrictions, crate.
ASK ⊠ 🛏 🖵

▼▼▼▼ **Extended StayAmerica Deluxe Austin-North Central** H
(512) 339-6005. **$80-$115.** 8221 N I-35. I-35, exit 241, on east frontage road. Int corridors. **Pets:** Other species. $25 daily fee/pet. Service with restrictions, crate.
ASK ⊠ 🛏 🖵 🏊

▼▼▼▼ **Extended Stay Deluxe Austin-Arboretum-North** H
(512) 833-0898. **$85-$115.** 2700 Gracy Farms Ln. 2 mi n of US 183 on Loop 1 (Mo-Pac Expwy), exit Burnet Rd (FM 1325). Int corridors. **Pets:** Other species. $25 daily fee/pet. Service with restrictions, crate.
ASK ⊠ 🛏 🖵 🏊

▼▼▼ **Extended Stay Deluxe Austin Metro** H
(512) 452-0880. **$80-$114.** 6300 US Hwy 290 E. Jct I-35 and US 290 E. Int corridors. **Pets:** Other species. $25 daily fee/pet. Service with restrictions, crate.
ASK ⊠ 🛏 🖵 🏊

▼▼▼ **Extended Stay Deluxe (Austin/Northwest/Research Park)** H
(512) 219-6500. **$80-$110.** 12424 Research Blvd. US 183, exit Oak Knoll, on eastbound frontage road. Int corridors. **Pets:** Other species. $25 daily fee/pet. Service with restrictions, crate.
ASK ⊠ 🦮 🛏 🖵 🏊

▼▼▼ **Fairfield Inn & Suites Austin NW** H
(512) 527-0734. **$125-$153.** 11201 N Mo-Pac Blvd. US 183 N, 1.5 mi n on Loop 1 (Mo-Pac Expwy) to Braker Ln exit, on east frontage road. Int corridors. **Pets:** Accepted.
⊠ 🦮 🛏 🖵 🏊 🏇

▼▼▼▼ **Four Seasons Hotel** H ❀
(512) 478-4500. **$440-$2500.** 98 San Jacinto Blvd. Bordering Town Lake. Int corridors. **Pets:** Very small. Service with restrictions, supervision.
⊠ 🛏 🖵 🍴 🏊 🏇

▼▼▼▼ **Hampton Inn Northwest** H
(512) 349-9898. **$109-$169.** 3908 W Braker Ln. 1 mi n of US 183 on Loop 1 (Mo-Pac Expwy) to Braker Ln exit. Int corridors. **Pets:** Accepted.
⊠ 🦮 🖵 🏊

AAA ▼▼▼ ▼▼▼ **Hilton Austin** H ❀
(512) 482-8000. **$109-$389.** 500 E 4th St. Jct 4th St and Neches. Int corridors. **Pets:** Medium. $75 one-time fee/room. Service with restrictions, supervision.
SAVE ⊠ 🦮 🖵 🍴 🏊 🏇

▼▼▼ **Holiday Inn Express Hotel & Suites** H
(512) 251-9110. **$130-$150.** 14620 N I-35. I-35, exit 247, on west frontage road. Int corridors. **Pets:** Medium. $50 one-time fee/pet. Service with restrictions, crate.
ASK ⊠ 🦮 🛏 🖵 🏊

▼▼ **Homestead Studio Suites Hotel-Austin/Arboretum-South** H
(512) 837-6677. **$55-$86.** 9100 Waterford Centre Blvd. US 183, exit Burnet Rd, on westbound frontage road. Ext corridors. **Pets:** Other species. $25 daily fee/pet. Service with restrictions, crate.
ASK ⊠ 🛏 🖵

▼▼▼ **Homestead Studio Suites Hotel-Austin/Downtown/Town Lake** H
(512) 476-1818. **$114-$155.** 507 S 1st St. I-35, exit 234B southbound; exit 234A northbound, 1.8 mi w on Cesar Chavez/E 1st St, then 0.5 mi s. Int corridors. **Pets:** Other species. $25 daily fee/pet. Service with restrictions, crate.
ASK ⊠ 🛏 🖵

▼▼▼ **Homewood Suites-Austin South** H
(512) 445-5050. **$109-$159.** 4143 Governor's Row. I-35, exit 231 (Ben White Blvd/SR 71) southbound; exit 229 northbound, at Ben White Blvd. Int corridors. **Pets:** Small, other species. $200 one-time fee/pet. Crate.
⊠ 🦮 🛏 🖵 🏊

▼▼▼ **Homewood Suites by Hilton Arboretum NW** H
(512) 349-9966. **$109-$199.** 10925 Stonelake Blvd. US 183 N to Loop 1 (Mo-Pac Expwy), 1.5 mi n to Braker Ln; on northwest corner. Int corridors. **Pets:** Accepted.
⊠ 🦮 🛏 🖵 🏊 🏇

AAA ▼▼▼ **Howard Johnson** H
(512) 462-9201. **$63-$80.** 2711 I-35 S. I-35, exit 231 (Woodward Ave) southbound; exit 232A (Oltorf St) northbound, on northbound frontage road; just n of jct I-35 and US 290/SR 71. Int corridors. **Pets:** Small. $100 deposit/room. Designated rooms, service with restrictions, supervision.
SAVE ⊠ 🛏 🖵 🏊

AAA ▼▼▼ ▼▼▼ **Hyatt Regency Austin** H ❀
(512) 477-1234. **$129-$399.** 208 Barton Springs Rd. At south end of Congress Ave Bridge; on south bank of Town Lake. Int corridors. **Pets:** Small. $50 daily fee/room. Designated rooms, service with restrictions, crate.
SAVE ⊠ 🦮 🛏 🖵 🍴 🏊 🏇

🏵 ▽▽▽ Hyatt Regency Lost Pines Resort and Spa 🅷 ☘
(512) 308-1234. **$169-$599, 3 day notice.** 575 Hyatt Lost Pines Rd. SR 71, 13 mi e of Austin Airport; 9 mi w of Bastrop. Int corridors. **Pets:** Large. $35 one-time fee/room. Designated rooms, service with restrictions, crate.
SAVE ⊠ 🅺 🔒 💻 ⏍ 🛳 ⊠

▽▽▽ La Quinta Inn & Suites 🅷 ☘
(512) 246-2800. **$69-$139.** 150 Parker Dr. I-35, exit 250, on west frontage road. Int corridors. **Pets:** Medium, other species. Service with restrictions, supervision.
ASK ⊠ 🅺 🔒 💻 🛳

▽▽▽ La Quinta Inn & Suites Austin (Airport) 🅷 ☘
(512) 386-6800. **$109-$175.** 7625 E Ben White Blvd. I-35, exit 230B (Ben White Blvd/SR 71), 3.8 mi e. Int corridors. **Pets:** Medium, other species. Service with restrictions, supervision.
ASK ⊠ 🅺 🔒 💻 🛳

▽▽▽ La Quinta Inn & Suites Austin (Mopac North) 🅷 ☘
(512) 832-2121. **$69-$159.** 11901 N Mo-Pac Expwy. US 183, 2 mi n on Loop 1 (Mo-Pac Expwy) to Duval exit. Int corridors. **Pets:** Medium, other species. Service with restrictions, supervision.
ASK ⊠ 🅺 🔒 💻 🛳

▽▽▽ La Quinta Inn & Suites Austin (Southwest at Mopac) 🅷 ☘
(512) 899-3000. **$115-$179.** 4424 S Loop 1 (Mo-Pac Expwy). Jct Loop 1 (Mo-Pac Expwy), US 290 and SR 71 E, on southbound frontage road. Int corridors. **Pets:** Medium, other species. Service with restrictions, supervision.
ASK ⊠ 🅺 🔒 💻 🛳

▽▽▽ La Quinta Inn Austin (Capitol) 🅷 ☘
(512) 476-1166. **$109-$180.** 300 E 11 St. Just e of state capitol building. Ext/int corridors. **Pets:** Medium, other species. Service with restrictions, supervision.
ASK ⊠ 🔒 💻 🛳

▽▽▽ La Quinta Inn Austin (Highland Mall) 🅷 ☘
(512) 459-4381. **$69-$139.** 5812 I-35 N. I-35, exit 238A, on west frontage road. Ext corridors. **Pets:** Medium, other species. Service with restrictions, supervision.
ASK ⊠ 🔒 💻 🛳

▽▽▽ La Quinta Inn Austin (I-35 South/Ben White) 🅷 ☘
(512) 443-1774. **$72-$139.** 4200 I-35 S. I-35, exit 231 (St. Edwards/Woodward Ave) southbound; exit 230 northbound, just s of jct I-35, US 290 and SR 71, on frontage road. Ext corridors. **Pets:** Medium, other species. Service with restrictions, supervision.
ASK ⊠ 🅺 🔒 💻 🛳

▽▽▽ La Quinta Inn Austin (Oltorf) 🅷 ☘
(512) 447-6661. **$79-$135.** 1603 E Oltorf Blvd. I-35, exit 232A (Oltorf Blvd), just s. Ext/int corridors. **Pets:** Medium, other species. Service with restrictions, supervision.
ASK ⊠ 🔒 💻 🛳

🏵 ▽▽▽ La Quinta Inn North 🅷 ☘
(512) 467-1701. **$79-$149.** 7622 N I-35 & 183. I-35, exit 240A, on west frontage road. Int corridors. **Pets:** Medium, other species. Service with restrictions, supervision.
SAVE ⊠ 🔒 💻 🛳

🏵 ▽▽▽ Mansion at Judge's Hill 🅷 ☘
(512) 495-1800. **$139-$399, 3 day notice.** 1900 Rio Grande. Jct Rio Grande and Martin Luther King Jr Blvd. Int corridors. **Pets:** Other species. $50 one-time fee/room. Service with restrictions, crate.
SAVE ⊠ 💻 ⏍

🏵 ▽▽▽ Northcross Suites 🅷
(512) 452-9391. **Call for rates.** 7685 Northcross Dr. Loop 1 (Mo-Pac Expwy), exit Anderson Rd, just e to Northcross Dr, then just s. Ext corridors. **Pets:** Accepted.
SAVE ⊠ 🔒 💻 🛳

▽▽▽ Omni Austin Hotel & Suites 🅷
(512) 476-3700. **$209-$379.** 700 San Jacinto Blvd. 8th St and San Jacinto Blvd. Int corridors. **Pets:** Accepted.
ASK ⊠ 🅺 🔒 💻 ⏍ 🛳 ⊠

🏵 ▽▽▽ Omni Austin Hotel Southpark 🅷 ☘
(512) 448-2222. **$109-$279.** 4140 Governor's Row. I-35, exit 230B southbound; exit 230 northbound, on east frontage road. Int corridors. **Pets:** Medium. $50 one-time fee/room. Service with restrictions, supervision.
SAVE ⊠ 🔒 💻 ⏍ 🛳 ⊠

▽▽▽ Ramada Austin Central 🅷
(512) 454-1144. **$86-$106.** 919 E Koenig Ln. I-35, exit 238A, on west frontage road. Int corridors. **Pets:** Accepted.
ASK ⊠ 🔒 💻 🛳

▽▽▽ Renaissance Austin Hotel 🅷
(512) 343-2626. **$278-$340.** 9721 Arboretum Blvd. Jct US 183 and Capital of Texas Hwy (SR 360); southwest corner. Int corridors. **Pets:** Accepted.
⊠ 🅺 🔒 💻 ⏍ 🛳 ⊠

▽▽▽ Residence Inn by Marriott Austin Airport/South 🅷
(512) 912-1100. **$152-$186.** 4537 S I-35. I-35, exit 229 (Stassney Rd) southbound; exit 230 (Ben White Blvd/SR 71) northbound, on northbound frontage road. Int corridors. **Pets:** Medium, other species. $100 one-time fee/room. Service with restrictions.
⊠ 🔒 💻 🛳 ⊠

▽▽▽ Residence Inn by Marriott Austin/Downtown/Convention Center 🅷
(512) 472-5553. **$239-$269.** 300 E 4th St. Between Trinity St and San Jacinto Blvd. Int corridors. **Pets:** Accepted.
⊠ 🔒 💻 ⏍ 🛳

▽▽▽ Residence Inn by Marriott-Austin North/Parmer Lane 🅷 ☘
(512) 977-0544. **$170-$208.** 12401 N Lamar Blvd. I-35, exit 245, just w. Int corridors. **Pets:** Other species. $100 one-time fee/room. Service with restrictions.
⊠ 🅺 🔒 💻 🛳 ⊠

▽▽▽ St. Michael Plaza Hotel 🅷
(512) 836-8520. **$89, 3 day notice.** 7800 I-35 N. I-35, exit 240A, on west frontage road at US 183. Int corridors. **Pets:** Accepted.
ASK ⊠ 🔒 💻 ⏍ 🛳

🏵 ▽▽▽ Sheraton Austin 🅷
(512) 478-1111. **$139-$379.** 701 E 11th St. I-35, exit 234B, 0.3 mi e. Int corridors. **Pets:** Accepted.
SAVE ⊠ 🔒 💻 ⏍ 🛳 ⊠

▽▽▽ Staybridge Suites Hotel 🅷
(512) 349-0888. **$169-$189.** 10201 Stonelake Blvd. Jct US 183 and Capital of Texas Hwy (SR 360); northwest corner. Int corridors. **Pets:** Medium. $75 one-time fee/pet. Service with restrictions, supervision.
ASK ⊠ 🅺 🔒 💻 🛳 ⊠

▽▽ Studio 6-Northwest #6032 Ⓜ
(512) 258-3556. **$66-$81.** 11901 Pavillon Blvd. US 183, exit Oak Knoll westbound; exit Duval/Balcones Woods eastbound, on eastbound frontage road. Ext corridors. **Pets:** Other species. $10 daily fee/room. Service with restrictions, supervision.
⊠ 🔒 💻

 **Super 8 Austin North** 🅷
(512) 339-1300. **$50-$80.** 8128 N I-35. I-35, exit 241, on west frontage road. Int corridors. **Pets:** Medium. $20 one-time fee/pet. Service with restrictions, supervision.
[SAVE] ⊠ 🗎 💻 🌊

 **Super 8 Central** 🅼
(512) 472-8331. **$75-$200.** 1201 N I-35. I-35, exit 234, at 12th St. Ext corridors. **Pets:** Accepted.
[SAVE] ⊠ 🗎 💻 🌊

🏆🏆🏆 **Wyndham Garden Hotel** 🅷 🐾
(512) 448-2444. **$119-$189.** 3401 I-35 S. I-35, exit 231 (Woodward St) southbound; exit 230 (Ben White Blvd/SR 71) northbound; on northbound frontage road. Ext/int corridors. **Pets:** $35 one-time fee/room. Designated rooms, service with restrictions.
[ASK] ⊠ 🔖 🗎 💻 🍴 🌊 ⊠

BASTROP

 **Days Inn Bastrop** 🅷
(512) 321-1157. **$60-$80.** 4102 Hwy 71 E. On SR 71, 2 mi e of river at Loop 150 E. Ext corridors. **Pets:** Other species. $25 daily fee/pet. Designated rooms, service with restrictions, supervision.
[SAVE] ⊠ 🗎 💻 🌊

BAY CITY

 **Best Western Matagorda Hotel & Conference Center** 🅷
(979) 244-5400. **$85-$96.** 407 7th St. SR 35 (7th St), 1 mi s of jct SR 35 and 60. Ext corridors. **Pets:** Accepted.
[SAVE] ⊠ 🗎 💻 🌊

BEAUMONT

 **Best Western Jefferson Inn** 🅷
(409) 842-0037. **$89-$119, 3 day notice.** 1610 I-10 S. I-10, exit 851 (College St), westbound service road; 0.5 mi s of jct US 90. Ext corridors. **Pets:** Accepted.
[SAVE] ⊠ 🗎 💻 🌊

🏆🏆🏆 **Holiday Inn Beaumont Midtown** 🅷
(409) 892-2222. **$90.** 2095 N 11th St. I-10, exit 853B (11th St), just n. Int corridors. **Pets:** Accepted.
⊠ 🔖 🗎 💻 🍴 🌊

🏆🏆🏆 **Holiday Inn Beaumont Plaza** 🅷
(409) 842-5995. **$109-$139.** 3950 I-10 S. I-10, exit 848 (Walden Rd), just n. Int corridors. **Pets:** Medium, other species. $25 daily fee/pet. Service with restrictions, crate.
[SAVE] ⊠ 🗎 💻 🍴 🌊

🏆🏆🏆 **La Quinta Inn & Suites** 🅷 🐾
(409) 842-0002. **$89-$155.** 5820 Walden Rd. I-10, exit 848, just n. Int corridors. **Pets:** Medium, other species. Service with restrictions, supervision.
[ASK] ⊠ 🔖 🗎 💻 🌊

🏆🏆 **La Quinta Inn Beaumont (Midtown)** 🅷 🐾
(409) 838-9991. **$49-$105.** 220 I-10 N. I-10, exit 852B (Calder Ave) eastbound; exit 852A (Laurel Ave) westbound, on eastbound service road. Ext corridors. **Pets:** Medium, other species. Service with restrictions, supervision.
[ASK] ⊠ 🗎 💻 🌊

BEDFORD

🏆🏆🏆 **Baymont Inn DFW West** 🅷
(817) 267-5200. **$69.** 1450 W Airport Frwy. SR 121/183, 0.3 mi e of jct Bedford Rd/Forest Ridge Dr. Ext corridors. **Pets:** Accepted.
[SAVE] ⊠ 🗎 💻 🌊

🏆🏆 **Comfort Inn DFW Airport West** 🅷
(817) 545-2555. **Call for rates.** 2904 Crystal Springs St. SR 121, exit Harwood Rd. Ext/int corridors. **Pets:** Accepted.
⊠ 🗎 💻

🏆🏆 **Extended Stay Deluxe Dallas-Bedford** 🅷
(817) 354-5210. **$60-$86.** 1908 Forest Ridge Dr. SR 183, exit Forest Ridge Dr, just n. Int corridors. **Pets:** Other species. $25 daily fee/pet. Service with restrictions, crate.
[ASK] ⊠ 🗎 💻 🌊

BEEVILLE

🏆🏆🏆 **Best Western Texan Inn** 🅷
(361) 358-9999. **$99-$110.** 2001 Hwy 59. US 181 at US 59, just e. Ext/int corridors. **Pets:** $10 daily fee/pet. Service with restrictions.
[SAVE] ⊠ 🗎 💻 🌊

🏆🏆 **Motel 6** 🅷
(361) 358-4000. **Call for rates.** 400 S US 181 Bypass. 0.3 mi s of jct US 59 and 181. Ext corridors. **Pets:** Other species. Service with restrictions, supervision.
⊠ 🗎 🌊

BELTON

🏆🏆🏆 **Budget Host Inn** 🅷 🐾
(254) 939-0744. **$49-$75, 3 day notice.** 1520 S I-35. I-35, exit 292 southbound; exit 293A northbound. Ext corridors. **Pets:** Small. $10 daily fee/pet. Service with restrictions, supervision.
[SAVE] ⊠ 🗎 💻 🌊

🏆🏆🏆 **La Quinta Inn & Suites** 🅷 🐾
(254) 939-2772. **$65-$150.** 229 W Loop 121. I-35, exit 292, just w. Int corridors. **Pets:** Medium, other species. Service with restrictions, supervision.
[ASK] ⊠ 🗎 💻 🌊

BENBROOK

🏆🏆🏆🏆 **Best Western Winscott Inn & Suites** 🅷
(817) 249-0076. **$100-$190.** 590 Winscott Rd. I-20, exit 429B. Int corridors. **Pets:** Small. $10 daily fee/pet. Designated rooms, no service, supervision.
[SAVE] ⊠ 🗎 💻 🌊

🏆🏆 **Motel 6-4051** 🅷
(817) 249-8885. **Call for rates.** 8601 Benbrook Blvd (Hwy 377 S). I-20, exit 429A, 0.7 mi s. Int corridors. **Pets:** Other species. Service with restrictions, supervision.
⊠ 🔖 🗎 🌊

BIG SPRING

🏆🏆🏆 **Comfort Inn** 🅷
(432) 267-4553. **Call for rates.** 2900 E I-20. I-20, exit 179. Ext corridors. **Pets:** Accepted.
[SAVE] ⊠ 🗎 💻 🌊

🏆🏆🏆 **Quality Inn & Suites** 🅷
(432) 264-7086. **$90-$130.** 300 Tulane Ave. I-20, exit 179, just s. Ext corridors. **Pets:** Small, other species. $20 daily fee/pet. Service with restrictions, supervision.
[SAVE] ⊠ 🔖 🗎 💻 🌊

🏆🏆 **Whitten Inn** 🅷
(432) 267-1601. **Call for rates.** 700 W I-20. I-20, exit 177, just n. Ext corridors. **Pets:** Accepted.
⊠ 🗎 💻 🌊

BOERNE

🏆🏆🏆 **Best Western Texas Country Inn** 🅷
(830) 249-9791. **$89-$112, 3 day notice.** 35150 I-10 W. I-10, exit 540 (SR 46), westbound access road. Ext corridors. **Pets:** Accepted.
[SAVE] ⊠ 🗎 💻 🌊

AAA ◈◈◈◈ Holiday Inn Express Hotel & Suites-Six Flags West Boerne H
(830) 249-6800. **Call for rates.** 35000 I-10 W. I-10, exit 540 (SR 46), just e to Norris Ln, then just s. Int corridors. **Pets:** $25 one-time fee/pet. Designated rooms, service with restrictions, supervision.
SAVE ⊠ ⊟ ▣ ≋

BONHAM

AAA ◈ Americas Best Value Inn M
(903) 583-3121. **$57-$67.** 1515 Old Ector Rd. Jct SR 56 W and 121 S. Ext corridors. **Pets:** $25 deposit/room. Designated rooms, service with restrictions, supervision.
SAVE ⊠ ⊟ ▣ ≋

BORGER

AAA ◈◈◈ Best Western Borger Inn H
(806) 274-7050. **$69-$130.** 206 S Cedar. Jct SR 136 and 207, just n. Int corridors. **Pets:** $10 one-time fee/pet. Service with restrictions, supervision.
SAVE ⊠ ⊟ ▣ ≋

BOWIE

AAA ◈◈ Americas Best Value Inn H
(940) 872-5426. **$65-$75.** 2436 S US 287. Jct SR 59. Ext corridors. **Pets:** Accepted.
SAVE ⊠ ⊟ ▣ ≋

AAA ◈ Park's Inn M
(940) 872-1111. **$60-$70.** 708 W Wise St. 0.5 mi n of jct SR 59; downtown. Ext corridors. **Pets:** Other species. $5 daily fee/pet. Service with restrictions, supervision.
SAVE ⊠ ⊟ ≋

BRADY

AAA ◈◈◈ Best Western Brady Inn H
(325) 597-3997. **$67-$90, 3 day notice.** 2200 S Bridge St. 1.1 mi s on US 87/377. Ext corridors. **Pets:** Very small. $10 daily fee/pet. Designated rooms, service with restrictions, supervision.
SAVE ⊠ ⊟ ▣ ≋

AAA ◈◈ Days Inn M
(325) 597-0789. **$59-$69.** 2108 S Bridge St. 1 mi s on US 87/377 at US 190. Ext corridors. **Pets:** Very small. $10 daily fee/pet. Designated rooms, service with restrictions, supervision.
SAVE ⊠ ⊟ ▣ ≋

BRENHAM

AAA ◈◈◈◈ Best Western Inn of Brenham H
(979) 251-7791. **$89-$99, 3 day notice.** 1503 Hwy 290 E. Eastbound, 0.7 mi w of jct US 290 E and SR 577; westbound, 1.3 mi e of jct SR 36 and US 290. Ext corridors. **Pets:** Small. $10 daily fee/pet. Service with restrictions, crate.
SAVE ⊠ ⊟ ▣ ¶ ≋

AAA ◈◈◈◈ Comfort Suites H
(979) 421-8100. **$79-$199.** 2350 S Day St. US 290, exit SR 36 S, just n on Business Rt SR 36. Int corridors. **Pets:** Small. $20 daily fee/pet. Service with restrictions, supervision.
SAVE ⊠ ⊟ ▣ ≋

◈◈◈◈ La Quinta Inn & Suites H ✿
(979) 836-5551. **$69-$159.** 2950 Woodridge Blvd. Jct US 290 and SR 36, just s. Int corridors. **Pets:** Medium, other species. Service with restrictions, supervision.
ASK ⊠ ⊞ ⊟ ▣ ≋

BROWNFIELD

AAA ◈◈ Best Western Caprock Inn H
(806) 637-9471. **$89-$102, 10 day notice.** 321 Lubbock Rd. Jct US 385 and 82, 2 blks n. Ext corridors. **Pets:** Accepted.
SAVE ⊠ ⊟ ▣ ≋

BROWNSVILLE

◈◈◈◈ La Quinta Inn & Suites H ✿
(956) 350-2118. **$75-$130.** 5051 N Expwy US 77. US 77, exit Alton Gloor Rd southbound; exit Stillman northbound U-turn; on southbound access road. Int corridors. **Pets:** Medium, other species. Service with restrictions, supervision.
ASK ⊠ ⊟ ▣ ≋

◈◈◈◈ Residence Inn by Marriott H
(956) 350-8100. **$152-$186.** 3975 N Expwy 77. US 77 and 83, exit Morrison Rd. Int corridors. **Pets:** Medium. $100 one-time fee/room. Service with restrictions, supervision.
⊠ ⊞ ⊟ ▣ ≋ ⊠

◈◈◈ Staybridge Suites H ✿
(956) 504-9500. **$99-$119.** 2900 Pablo Kisel Blvd. US 77 and 83 exit Ruben Torres Sr Blvd (FM 802), 0.8 mi n on access road to Pablo Kisel Blvd, then 0.5 mi e. Int corridors. **Pets:** Medium. $75 one-time fee/room. Service with restrictions, supervision.
ASK ⊠ ⊟ ▣ ≋ ⊠

BUFFALO

AAA ◈◈◈ Best Western Craig's Inn H
(903) 322-5831. **$90-$150, 7 day notice.** IH-45 & US 79. I-45, exit 178, just n on NW Frontage Rd. Ext/int corridors. **Pets:** Small, other species. $10 daily fee/pet. Designated rooms, service with restrictions, supervision.
SAVE ⊠ ⊟ ▣ ≋

BURKBURNETT

◈◈◈◈ Burkburnett Hampton Inn H
(940) 569-8109. **$113-$139.** 1008 Sheppard Rd. I-44, exit 12, just e. Int corridors. **Pets:** Accepted.
⊠ ⊞ ⊟ ▣ ≋

BURLESON

AAA ◈◈◈◈ Comfort Suites H
(817) 426-6666. **$100.** 321 S Burleson Blvd. I-35W, exit 34 southbound, 2 mi s to crossover, U-turn; exit 36 northbound, on northbound access road. Int corridors. **Pets:** Medium, other species. $25 daily fee/pet. Designated rooms, service with restrictions, supervision.
SAVE ⊠ ⊞ ⊟ ▣ ≋

BURNET

AAA ◈◈◈ Best Western Post Oak Inn M
(512) 756-4747. **$69-$115, 3 day notice.** 908 Buchanan Dr. Jct US 281 and FM 29, 1 mi w. Ext corridors. **Pets:** Small. $15 one-time fee/pet. Service with restrictions, supervision.
SAVE ⊠ ⊟ ▣ ≋

◈◈◈ Log Country Cove VH
(512) 756-9132. **Call for rates.** 617 Log Country Cove. Jct FM 1431 and 2342, 1 mi n; Park Rd 4 and FM 2342, 3 mi s. Ext corridors. **Pets:** Accepted.
⊠ ⊟ ▣ ⊠

CANTON

AAA ◈◈◈ Best Western Canton Inn H
(903) 567-6591. **$80-$170.** 2251 N Trade Days Blvd. Jct I-20 and SR 19, exit 527. Ext corridors. **Pets:** Accepted.
SAVE ⊠ ⊟ ▣ ≋

▼▼ Comfort Inn & Suites 🅗
(903) 567-0909. **Call for rates.** 2406 N Trade Days Blvd. I-20, exit 527. Ext corridors. **Pets:** Accepted.
⊠ 🔊ᴹ 🖶 💻 🕿

▼▼ Super 8 🅗
(903) 567-6567. **$63-$189, 3 day notice.** 17350 I-20. I-20, exit 527. Ext corridors. **Pets:** $10 daily fee/pet. Service with restrictions, supervision.
⊠ 🖶 💻 🕿

CANYON

⏱ ▼▼▼ Best Western Palo Duro Canyon 🅗
(806) 655-1818. **$80-$180.** 2801 4th Ave. I-27, exit 106, 1 mi w. Int corridors. **Pets:** Other species. $25 daily fee/room. No service, supervision.
ⓈⒶⓋⒺ ⊠ 🔊ᴹ 🖶 💻 🕿

⏱ ▼▼▼ Holiday Inn Express Hotel & Suites 🅗
(806) 655-4445. **$105-$160.** 2901 4th Ave. I-27, exit 106, 2 mi w. Int corridors. **Pets:** Accepted.
ⓈⒶⓋⒺ ⊠ 🔊ᴹ 🖶 💻 🕿

CEDAR PARK

⏱ ▼▼ Comfort Inn 🅗
(512) 259-1810. **$82-$117.** 300 E Whitestone Blvd. I-35, exit 256, 8 mi w on FM 1431. Int corridors. **Pets:** $10 daily fee/pet. Supervision.
ⓈⒶⓋⒺ ⊠ 🔊ᴹ 🖶 💻 🕿

CHILDRESS

⏱ ▼▼ Comfort Inn 🅗
(940) 937-6363. **$95-$159.** 1804 Ave F NW (Hwy 287). On US 287, just s of jct US 62/83. Ext corridors. **Pets:** Accepted.
ⓈⒶⓋⒺ ⊠ 🔊ᴹ 🖶 💻 🕿

▼ Rodeway Inn 🅗 ❀
(940) 937-3695. **$44-$62.** 1612 Ave F NW. On US 287, just s of jct US 62/83. Ext corridors. **Pets:** $5 daily fee/pet. Service with restrictions, crate.
Ⓐ$Ⓚ ⊠ 🖶 💻

⏱ ▼▼ Super 8 Childress Ⓜ
(940) 937-8825. **$60-$150.** 411 Ave F NE (Hwy 287 S). Jct US 83/287, 1.5 mi e. Ext corridors. **Pets:** $13 daily fee/pet. Service with restrictions, supervision.
ⓈⒶⓋⒺ ⊠ 🖶 💻 🕿

CISCO

▼▼ Americas Best Value Inn Ⓜ
(254) 442-3735. **Call for rates.** 1898 Hwy 206 W. I-20, exit 330. Ext corridors. **Pets:** Accepted.
⊠ 🖶 💻 🕿

CLARENDON

⏱ ▼▼▼ Best Western Red River Inn 🅗
(806) 874-0160. **$85-$115.** 902 W 2nd St. Jct US 287 and SR 70. Int corridors. **Pets:** Large. $10 daily fee/pet. Designated rooms, service with restrictions, crate.
ⓈⒶⓋⒺ ⊠ 🔊ᴹ 🖶 💻 🕿

⏱ ▼▼ Western Skies Motel Ⓜ
(806) 874-3501. **$45-$99.** 800 W 2nd St. 0.5 mi nw on US 287 and SR 70. Ext corridors. **Pets:** $5 daily fee/pet. Crate.
ⓈⒶⓋⒺ ⊠ 🖶 🕿

CLAUDE

⏱ ▼ L a Motel Ⓜ
(806) 226-4981. **$35-$65.** Hwy 287/200 E 1st St. 0.3 mi s. Ext corridors. **Pets:** Small. $5 one-time fee/room. Designated rooms, no service, supervision.
ⓈⒶⓋⒺ ⊠ 🖶 💻 🍴

CLEBURNE

▼▼ Budget Host Inn-Sagamar Inn Ⓜ
(817) 556-3631. **$75-$90, 3 day notice.** 2107 N Main St. US 67, exit SR 174, just e. Ext corridors. **Pets:** Small, dogs only. $15 daily fee/pet, $15 one-time fee/pet. Designated rooms, service with restrictions, supervision.
Ⓐ$Ⓚ ⊠ 🖶 💻 🕿

▼▼▼ Comfort Inn 🅗
(817) 641-4702. **$95-$175.** 2117 N Main St. On SR 174, just s of jct US 67. Int corridors. **Pets:** Other species. $10 daily fee/room. Designated rooms, service with restrictions, supervision.
Ⓐ$Ⓚ ⊠ 🔊ᴹ 🖶 💻 🕿

▼▼▼ La Quinta Inn & Suites 🅗 ❀
(817) 641-4455. **$65-$135.** 107 E Kilpatrick Ave. Just n of jct SR 171/174 and FM 4. Int corridors. **Pets:** Medium, other species. Service with restrictions, supervision.
Ⓐ$Ⓚ ⊠ 🔊ᴹ 🖶 💻 🕿

CLUTE

⏱ ▼▼▼ Best Western Clute Inn & Suites 🅗
(979) 388-0055. **$70-$120.** 900 Hwy 332. Just w of jct SR 288. Int corridors. **Pets:** Small, dogs only. $15 daily fee/pet. Service with restrictions, crate.
ⓈⒶⓋⒺ ⊠ 🖶 💻 🕿

▼▼ La Quinta Inn Clute/Lake Jackson Ⓜ ❀
(979) 265-7461. **$59-$109.** 1126 Hwy 332 W. On SR 288/332, just w of jct Business Rt SR 288. Ext corridors. **Pets:** Medium, other species. Service with restrictions, supervision.
Ⓐ$Ⓚ ⊠ 🖶 💻 🕿

▼▼▼ Mainstay Suites Clute/Lake Jackson 🅗
(979) 388-9300. **$119-$212.** 1003 W Hwy 332. Just w of jct SR 288. Int corridors. **Pets:** Accepted.
Ⓐ$Ⓚ ⊠ 🖶 💻 🕿

COLLEGE STATION

▼▼▼ Hilton College Station and Conference Center 🅗
(979) 693-7500. **$99-$249.** 801 University Dr E. SR 6, exit University Dr, 1.1 mi w. Int corridors. **Pets:** Medium, other species. Service with restrictions, crate.
⊠ 🖶 💻 🍴 🕿

▼▼▼ Homewood Suites--College Station 🅗
(979) 846-0400. **$84-$249.** 950 University Dr E. Jct SR 6 and 60 (Texas Ave), 1.5 mi e. Int corridors. **Pets:** Accepted.
⊠ 🔊ᴹ 🖶 💻 🕿 ⊠

⏱ ▼▼▼ Howard Johnson 🅗
(979) 693-6810. **$55-$150.** 3702 Hwy 6 S. SR 6 S, exit Rock Prairie Rd. Ext corridors. **Pets:** Small. $20 daily fee/pet. Designated rooms, no service.
ⓈⒶⓋⒺ ⊠ 🖶 💻 🕿

▼▼▼ La Quinta Inn College Station 🅗 ❀
(979) 696-7777. **$65-$149.** 607 Texas Ave. Just s on jct SR 60 and 6 business route to Live Oak St, then just e. Ext corridors. **Pets:** Medium, other species. Service with restrictions, supervision.
Ⓐ$Ⓚ ⊠ 🖶 💻 🕿

▼▼ Manor House Inn 🅗
(979) 764-9540. **$49-$145, 4 day notice.** 2504 Texas Ave S. 2.4 mi s of jct SR 60. Ext corridors. **Pets:** Accepted.
Ⓐ$Ⓚ ⊠ 🖶 💻 🕿

▼▼▼ TownePlace Suites By Marriott 🅗
(979) 260-8500. **$107-$131.** 1300 E University Dr. SR 6, exit University Dr, 1 mi w. Ext corridors. **Pets:** Other species. $100 one-time fee/room. Supervision.
⊠ 🖶 💻 🕿

COLUMBUS

Holiday Inn Express Hotel & Suites 🅗
(979) 733-9300. **$110-$130.** 4321 I-10. I-10, exit 696 (SR 71), just w on westbound service road. Int corridors. **Pets:** Other species. $25 daily fee/pet. Service with restrictions, supervision.
SAVE ⊠ 🛉 🖳 ⊅

CONWAY

Budget Host S & S Motel Ⓜ
(806) 537-5111. **Call for rates.** I-40 & SR 207. In Conway; I-40, exit 96 (SR 207), 0.3 mi w on southbound access road. Ext corridors. **Pets:** Accepted.
SAVE ⊠ 🛉 🍴

CORPUS CHRISTI

Best Western Garden Inn 🅗
(361) 241-6675. **$84-$109.** 11217 I-37. I-37, exit 11B (Violet Rd); on southbound access road. Ext corridors. **Pets:** Medium, other species. $15 daily fee/pet. Service with restrictions, supervision.
SAVE ⊠ ᴸᴹ 🛉 🖳 ⊅

Best Western Marina Grand Hotel 🅗
(361) 883-5111. **$109-$150, 3 day notice.** 300 N Shoreline Blvd. Center of downtown. Int corridors. **Pets:** Accepted.
SAVE ⊠ 🛉 🖳 ⊅

Best Western on the Island 🅗
(361) 949-2300. **$70-$180.** 14050 S Padre Island Dr. On Park Rd 22. Ext corridors. **Pets:** Medium. $50 deposit/room. Designated rooms, service with restrictions, supervision.
SAVE ⊠ 🛉 🖳 ⊅

Christy Estate Suites 🅒🅞
(361) 854-1091. **Call for rates.** 3942 Holly Rd. SR 358, exit Weber Rd, 0.5 mi s. Ext/int corridors. **Pets:** Accepted.
⊠ 🛉 🖳 ⊅

Days Inn Corpus Christi South 🅗
(361) 854-0005. **Call for rates.** 2838 S Padre Island Dr. On SR 358 westbound access road, 0.4 mi w, exit Kostoryz Rd. Ext corridors. **Pets:** Accepted.
⊠ 🛉 🖳 ⊅

Drury Inn-Corpus Christi 🅗
(361) 289-8200. **$70-$113.** 2021 N Padre Island Dr. I-37, exit SR 358, just se at Leopard St. Int corridors. **Pets:** Other species. Service with restrictions, supervision.
ASK ⊠ 🛉 🖳 ⊅

Econo Lodge Ⓜ
(361) 884-2485. **$60-$150.** 801 S Shoreline Blvd. I-37, exit Shoreline; between Park and Fuman aves. Ext corridors. **Pets:** Accepted.
ASK ⊠ 🛉 🖳 ⊅

Extended Stay Deluxe–Corpus Christi-Staples 🅗
(361) 991-1967. **$73-$103.** 6218 S Staples St. SR 358 soundbound, exit S Staples St, 0.3 mi, then 1.5 mi s. Int corridors. **Pets:** Other species. $25 daily fee/pet. Service with restrictions, crate.
ASK ⊠ ᴸᴹ 🛉 🖳 ⊅

Holiday Inn-Airport and Conference Center 🅗
(361) 289-5100. **$109-$179, 3 day notice.** 5549 Leopard St. Jct SR 358 and Leopard St, 5.5 mi w. Int corridors. **Pets:** Accepted.
SAVE ⊠ 🛉 🖳 🍴 ⊅

Holiday Inn-Emerald Beach 🅗
(361) 883-5731. **$125-$199.** 1102 S Shoreline Blvd. 1.5 mi s on bay from downtown marina. Ext/int corridors. **Pets:** Accepted.
ASK ⊠ ᴸᴹ 🛉 🖳 🍴 ⊅ ⊠

Homewood Suites by Hilton 🅗
(361) 854-1331. **$94-$149.** 5201 Crosstown Expwy (SR 286). I-37, exit SR 358 E (Greenwood Dr), 0.6 mi e on eastbound access road. Int corridors. **Pets:** Medium, other species. $100 one-time fee/pet. Crate.
⊠ 🛉 🖳 ⊅ ⊠

La Quinta Inn Corpus Christi (North) 🅗 🐾
(361) 888-5721. **$45-$129.** 5155 I-37 N. I-37, exit 3A (Navigation Blvd), on southbound access road. Ext corridors. **Pets:** Medium, other species. Service with restrictions, supervision.
ASK ⊠ 🛉 🖳 ⊅

La Quinta Inn Corpus Christi (South) 🅗 🐾
(361) 991-5730. **$59-$139.** 6225 S Padre Island Dr. SR 358, exit Airline Rd. Ext corridors. **Pets:** Medium, other species. Service with restrictions, supervision.
ASK ⊠ 🛉 🖳 ⊅

Motel 6 #231 Ⓜ
(361) 289-9397. **$45-$55.** 845 Lantana St. I-37, exit 4B (Lantana St), on southbound access road. Ext corridors. **Pets:** Other species. Service with restrictions, supervision.
⊠ ⊅

Omni Corpus Christi Hotel-Bayfront Tower 🅗
(361) 887-1600. **$189.** 900 N Shoreline Blvd. In town across from bay; downtown; in the marina district. Int corridors. **Pets:** Accepted.
SAVE ⊠ ᴸᴹ 🛉 🖳 🍴 ⊅ ⊠

Omni Corpus Christi Hotel-Marina Tower 🅗
(361) 887-1600. **$179.** 707 N Shoreline Blvd. Just n across from bay. Int corridors. **Pets:** Accepted.
ASK ⊠ 🛉 🖳 🍴 ⊅ ⊠

Quality Inn & Suites Sandy Shores 🅗
(361) 883-7456. **$79-$250, 3 day notice.** 3202 Surfside Blvd. 1 mi n on US 181; at north end of Harbor Bridge, exit Bridge St. Ext/int corridors. **Pets:** Small. $20 daily fee/pet. Designated rooms, service with restrictions, supervision.
ASK ⊠ 🛉 🖳 ⊅

Red Roof Inn 🅗
(361) 992-9222. **$39-$149.** 6805 S Padre Island Dr. SR 358, exit Nile Dr. Ext corridors. **Pets:** Accepted.
SAVE ⊠ 🛉 🖳 ⊅

Rodeway Inn 🅗
(361) 883-6161. **$69-$104.** 5224 I-37 (Navigation Blvd). I-37, exit 3A (Navigation Blvd), on northbound access road. Ext corridors. **Pets:** Medium. $25 one-time fee/room. Designated rooms, service with restrictions, supervision.
ASK ⊠ 🛉 🖳 ⊅

Surfside Condominiums 🅒🅞
(361) 949-8128. **$130-$215, 3 day notice.** 15005 Windward Dr. Park Rd 22 on N Padre Island Dr, jct Whitecap Blvd, 0.6 mi n to Winward Dr, then 0.8 mi w. Ext corridors. **Pets:** Small. $15 daily fee/pet. Designated rooms, service with restrictions, supervision.
SAVE ⊠ 🛉 🖳 ⊅

DALHART

Best Western Nursanickel Motel 🅗 🐾
(806) 244-5637. **$70-$109.** 102 Scott Ave (Hwy 87 S). Just s of jct US 54 and 87. Ext corridors. **Pets:** Large. $8 daily fee/pet. Service with restrictions, supervision.
SAVE ⊠ 🛉 🖳 ⊅

Budget Inn Ⓜ
(806) 244-4557. **$45-$55.** 415 Liberal St (Hwy 54). On US 54, just e of US 87 and 385. Ext corridors. **Pets:** Medium. $20 deposit/pet. Service with restrictions, supervision.
SAVE ⊠ 🛉

AAA ▽▽▽ **Days Inn** �H
(806) 244-5246. **$70-$130.** 701 Liberal St (Hwy 54). On US 54, 0.5 mi e. Int corridors. **Pets:** Other species. $15 one-time fee/room. Service with restrictions, supervision.
⟨SAVE⟩ ⊠ 📠 💻 ⌁

AAA ▽▽▽ **Rodeway Inn** M
(806) 249-8585. **Call for rates.** 1110 Liberal St (Hwy 54 E). 0.5 mi e of jct US 54 and 87. Ext corridors. **Pets:** Small, dogs only. Service with restrictions, supervision.
⟨SAVE⟩ ⊠ 📠 💻 ⌁

AAA ▽▽ **Sands Motel** M
(806) 244-4568. **$30-$60.** 301 Liberal St (Hwy 54). On US 54, just e of US 87 and 385. Ext corridors. **Pets:** Medium. Service with restrictions.
⟨SAVE⟩ ⊠ 📠

AAA ▽▽◇ **Super 8** M
(806) 249-8526. **$65-$95.** 403 Tanglewood Rd. Jct US 87 and 54, 0.5 mi e. Int corridors. **Pets:** Small. $25 deposit/pet. Designated rooms, service with restrictions, supervision.
⟨SAVE⟩ ⊠ 📠

DALLAS METROPOLITAN AREA

ADDISON

▽▽◇▽ **Homewood Suites by Hilton** �H
(972) 788-1342. **$79-$159.** 4451 Belt Line Rd. Just e of jct Belt Line and Midway rds. Ext/int corridors. **Pets:** Accepted.
⊠ &M 📠 💻 ⌁ ⊠

AAA ▽▽◇▽ **Hyatt Summerfield Suites-Addison** �H
(972) 661-3113. **$89-$209.** 4900 Edwin Lewis Dr. Just n of jct Belt Line Rd and Quorum Dr to Edwin Lewis Dr, then just w. Ext/int corridors. **Pets:** Small. $200 one-time fee/room. Service with restrictions, crate.
⟨SAVE⟩ ⊠ &M 📠 💻 ⌁ ⊠

▽▽◇▽ **La Quinta Inn & Suites Dallas (Addison-Galleria Area)** �H 🐾
(972) 404-0004. **$49-$139.** 14925 Landmark Blvd. Jct Belt Line Rd and Landmark Blvd, just s. Int corridors. **Pets:** Medium, other species. Service with restrictions, supervision.
⟨ASK⟩ ⊠ &M 📠 💻 ⌁

▽▽◇▽ **Quality Inn & Suites** �H
(972) 991-8888. **$60-$199.** 4103 Belt Line Rd. Between Midway Rd and Marsh Ln. Ext corridors. **Pets:** Medium. $50 one-time fee/pet. Service with restrictions, supervision.
⟨ASK⟩ ⊠ 📠 💻 ⌁

▽▽◇▽ **Residence Inn by Marriott-Addison** �H
(972) 866-9933. **$170-$208.** 14975 Quorum Dr. Just s of jct Beltline Rd and Quorum Dr. Int corridors. **Pets:** Accepted.
⊠ 📠 💻 ⌁ ⊠

ALLEN

▽▽ **Pyramids Hotel** �H
(972) 396-9494. **$99-$199.** 407 Central Expwy S. US 75, exit 33 (Bethany Dr). Int corridors. **Pets:** Other species. $30 one-time fee/room. Designated rooms, service with restrictions.
⟨ASK⟩ ⊠ 📠 💻 ⌁ ⊠

ATHENS

▽▽ **Inn on the Hill** �H
(903) 675-9214. **Call for rates.** 2050 Hwy 31 E. 2.6 mi e of jct SR 19 and 31 (city square). Ext corridors. **Pets:** Accepted.
⊠ 📠 💻 🍴 ⌁

BALCH SPRINGS

▽▽ **La Quinta Inn** �H 🐾
(972) 286-1010. **$45-$95.** 12875 Seagoville Rd. I-20, exit 481 (Seagoville Rd), just n. Int corridors. **Pets:** Medium, other species. Service with restrictions, supervision.
⟨ASK⟩ ⊠ 📠 💻 ⌁

CARROLLTON

▽▽◇ **Rodeway Inn** �H
(972) 245-9900. **Call for rates.** 1832 N I-35E. I-35E, exit 443C (Northside Dr) northbound; exit 443B southbound (Belt Line Rd), U-turn 1 mi n. Int corridors. **Pets:** Accepted.
⊠ 📠

COMMERCE

AAA ▽▽◇▽ **Holiday Inn Express Hotel & Suites** �H
(903) 886-4777. **$89-$159.** 2207 Culver St. 0.9 mi e of jct SR 224, 24 and 50. Int corridors. **Pets:** Small. $25 daily fee/pet. Designated rooms, service with restrictions, supervision.
⟨SAVE⟩ ⊠ &M 📠 💻 ⌁

DALLAS

▽▽◇▽ **Baymont Inn & Suites** �H
(214) 350-5577. **$65-$125.** 2370 W Northwest Hwy. I-35E, exit 436 Northwest Hwy (Loop 12), 0.8 mi e. Int corridors. **Pets:** Accepted.
⟨ASK⟩ ⊠ 📠 💻 ⌁

AAA ▽▽◇ **Candlewood Dallas Market Center** �H 🐾
(214) 631-3333. **$89-$109.** 7930 N Stemmons Frwy. I-35, exit 433B (Mockingbird Ln), on northbound frontage road. Int corridors. **Pets:** Medium. $75 daily fee/pet. Designated rooms, service with restrictions, supervision.
⟨SAVE⟩ ⊠ 📠 💻 ⌁

▽▽◇▽ **Candlewood Suites-Dallas by the Galleria** �H
(972) 233-6888. **$105-$125.** 13939 Noel Rd. Jct Dallas Pkwy and Spring Valley, just e to Noel Rd, then just s. Int corridors. **Pets:** Medium. $150 one-time fee/pet. Service with restrictions, crate.
⟨ASK⟩ ⊠ &M 📠 💻

▽▽◇▽ **Candlewood Suites Dallas North/Richardson** �H
(972) 669-9606. **Call for rates.** 12525 Greenville Ave. I-635, exit 18A (Greenville Ave), just n. Int corridors. **Pets:** Large, other species. $75 one-time fee/room. Service with restrictions.
⊠ &M 📠 💻

AAA ▽▽◇▽ **Comfort Inn & Suites Market Center** �H
(214) 461-2677. **$109-$149.** 7138 N Stemmons Frwy. I-35E, exit 433B (Mockingbird Ln) northbound; exit 432B (Commonwealth Dr) southbound, turn under freeway, 0.7 mi on north access road. Int corridors. **Pets:** Other species. $25 one-time fee/pet. Service with restrictions, supervision.
⟨SAVE⟩ ⊠ 📠 💻

▽▽◇▽ **Country Inn & Suites Dallas Park Central** �H
(972) 907-9500. **Call for rates.** 13185 N Central Expwy. US 75 N, exit 22 (Midpark Rd). Int corridors. **Pets:** Accepted.
⊠ 📠 💻 ⌁

AAA ▽▽◇▽ **Crowne Plaza Suites Hotel Dallas Park Central** �H
(972) 233-7600. **$169-$219.** 7800 Alpha Rd. I-635, exit 19C (Coit Rd) eastbound; exit 19B (Coit Rd) westbound, 0.3 mi nw of jct US 75. Int corridors. **Pets:** Medium, other species. $150 deposit/pet. Service with restrictions, crate.
⟨SAVE⟩ ⊠ 📠 💻 🍴 ⌁

▼▼ Extended StayAmerica Dallas-Richardson H
(972) 238-1133. **$55-$86.** 12270 Greenville Ave. I-635, exit 18A (Greenville Ave), just s. Int corridors. **Pets:** Other species. $25 daily fee/pet. Service with restrictions, crate.

ASK ☒ ⊟ ▦

▼▼ Extended Stay Delux Dallas-Market Center H
(214) 630-0154. **$65-$103.** 2979 N Stemmons Frwy. I-35E, exit 432B, on eastbound access road. Int corridors. **Pets:** Other species. $25 daily fee/pet. Service with restrictions, crate.

ASK ☒ ⊟ ▦ ⊸

▼▼ Extended Stay Deluxe Dallas-North-Park Central H
(972) 671-7722. **$50-$75.** 9019 Vantage Point Rd. I-635, exit 18A (Greenville Ave), just sw. Ext corridors. **Pets:** Other species. $25 daily fee/pet. Service with restrictions, crate.

ASK ☒ ⓜ ⊟ ▦

▼▼▼ Fairfield Inn by Marriott-Park Central H
(972) 437-9905. **$90-$110.** 9230 LBJ Frwy. I-635, exit 18A (Greenville Ave S), just s, then just e. Int corridors. **Pets:** Medium, other species. $75 one-time fee/pet. Service with restrictions, supervision.

☒ ⊟ ▦ ⊸

⊕⊕⊕ ▼▼▼▼ The Fairmont Dallas H
(214) 720-2020. **$129-$329.** 1717 N Akard St. Corner of Ross Ave and N Akard St. Int corridors. **Pets:** Accepted.

SAVE ☒ ⓜ ⊟ ▦ ⑪ ⊸

⊕⊕⊕ ▼▼▼▼ Hilton Anatole Dallas H
(214) 748-1200. **$119-$319.** 2201 Stemmons Frwy. I-35E, exit 430B (Market Center Blvd), just nw. Int corridors. **Pets:** Accepted.

SAVE ☒ ⓜ ⊟ ▦ ⊸ ☒

▼▼▼ Holiday Inn Select Dallas Central H
(214) 373-6000. **Call for rates.** 10650 N Central Expwy. US 75, exit 6 (Walnut Hill Ln/Meadow Rd), 0.5 mi n on northbound access road. Int corridors. **Pets:** Accepted.

☒ ⊟ ▦ ⑪ ⊸

▼▼ Homestead Studio Suites Hotel-Dallas/North Addison/Tollway H
(972) 447-1800. **$60-$86.** 17425 N Dallas Pkwy. North Dallas Tollway, exit Trinity Mills, just s of jct Trinity Mills and Dallas Pkwy, on southbound access road. Ext corridors. **Pets:** Other species. $25 daily fee/pet. Service with restrictions, crate.

ASK ☒ ⊟ ▦

▼▼▼ Homestead Studio Suites Hotel-Dallas/Plano H
(972) 248-2233. **$70-$103.** 18470 N Dallas Pkwy. North Dallas Tollway, exit Frankford, just ne. Int corridors. **Pets:** Other species. $25 daily fee/pet. Service with restrictions, crate.

ASK ☒ ⓜ ⊟ ▦ ⊸

▼▼▼ Homewood Suites by Hilton H 🐾
(214) 819-9700. **$99-$169.** 2747 N Stemmons Frwy. I-35E, exit 432A (Inwood Rd), just s. Int corridors. **Pets:** Medium. $100 one-time fee/room. Service with restrictions, supervision.

☒ ⓜ ⊟ ▦ ⊸

▼▼▼ Homewood Suites by Hilton-I-635 H
(972) 437-6966. **$99-$139.** 9169 Markville Dr. I-635, exit 18A (Greenville Ave S), just s, then just e. Int corridors. **Pets:** Accepted.

☒ ⊟ ▦ ⊸ ☒

▼▼▼ Hotel Indigo Dallas Downtown H
(214) 741-7700. **Call for rates.** 1933 Main St. Main and Harwood sts; northwest corner. Int corridors. **Pets:** Accepted.

☒ ⊟ ▦ ⑪

⊕⊕⊕ ▼▼▼▼ Hotel Lawrence H 🐾
(214) 761-9090. **$139-$189, 3 day notice.** 302 S Houston St. I-35E, exit 428A (Commerce St), 0.8 mi to Griffin, just s to Jackson St, then just w. Int corridors. **Pets:** Medium. $25 one-time fee/pet.

SAVE ☒ ▦ ⑪

⊕⊕⊕ ▼▼▼▼ Hotel Palomar H 🐾
(214) 520-7969. **$159-$359.** 5300 E Mockingbird Ln. US 75 and Mockingbird Ln; on southeast corner. Int corridors. **Pets:** Other species. Designated rooms, service with restrictions, crate.

SAVE ☒ ⓜ ⑪ ⊸ ☒

⊕⊕⊕ ▼▼▼▼ Hotel St. Germain CI 🐾
(214) 871-2516. **$290-$650, 7 day notice.** 2516 Maple Ave. I-35, exit 430A (Oak Lawn Ave), 0.5 mi e, then 1 mi s. Int corridors. **Pets:** Small, dogs only. $50 daily fee/pet. Designated rooms, service with restrictions, supervision.

SAVE ☒ ⑪

▼▼▼ Hotel ZaZa H 🐾
(214) 468-8399. **$275-$375.** 2332 Leonard St. Jct Maple Ave/Routh St and McKinney Ave, southeast corner. Int corridors. **Pets:** Medium. $50 one-time fee/room.

ASK ☒ ⓜ ⊟ ▦ ⑪ ⊸ ☒

▼▼▼ La Quinta Inn & Suites Dallas (North Central) H 🐾
(214) 361-8200. **$69-$139.** 10001 N Central Expwy. US 75, exit 6 (Walnut Hill Ln/Meadow Rd) northbound, 0.5 mi n to Meadow Rd, then U-turn under highway; exit 7 (Royal/Meadow Rd) southbound, 1 mi s on feeder. Int corridors. **Pets:** Medium, other species. Service with restrictions, supervision.

ASK ☒ ⓜ ⊟ ▦ ⊸

▼▼▼ La Quinta Inn & Suites Dallas Northwest H 🐾
(214) 904-9955. **$69-$139.** 2380 W Northwest Hwy. I-35, exit 436 Northwest Hwy (Loop 12), 0.8 mi e. Int corridors. **Pets:** Medium, other species. Service with restrictions, supervision.

ASK ☒ ⊟ ▦ ⊸

▼▼ La Quinta Inn Dallas (East) H 🐾
(214) 324-3731. **$49-$109.** 8303 E R L Thornton Frwy. I-30, exit 52A (Jim Miller Rd). Ext corridors. **Pets:** Medium, other species. Service with restrictions, supervision.

ASK ☒ ⓜ ⊟ ▦ ⊸

▼▼ La Quinta Inn Dallas Uptown H 🐾
(214) 821-4220. **$59-$129.** 4440 N Central Expwy. N off US 75, exit 2 (Henderson-Knox) northbound; exit 1B (Haskell/Blackburn) southbound. Ext corridors. **Pets:** Medium, other species. Service with restrictions, supervision.

ASK ☒ ⊟ ▦ ⊸

▼ Motel 6-560 H
(972) 620-2828. **$45-$57.** 2753 Forest Ln. I-635, exit 26 (Josey Ln) eastbound; exit 25 (Josey Ln) westbound, just s to Forest Ln, then just w. Ext corridors. **Pets:** Other species. Service with restrictions, supervision.

☒ ⊸

▼ Motel 6 Forest Lane-South #1119 H
(972) 484-9111. **$45-$57.** 2660 Forest Ln. I-635, exit 26 (Josey Ln) eastbound, 0.5 mi s to Forest Ln, then just w; exit 25 (Josey Ln) westbound, just s to Forest Ln, then just w. Ext corridors. **Pets:** Other species. Service with restrictions, supervision.

☒ ⊸

▼▼▼ Quality Inn & Suites-North Dallas H
(972) 484-3330. **$89-$129.** 2421 Walnut Hill Ln. I-35E, exit 438 (Walnut Hill Ln). Int corridors. **Pets:** Accepted.

ASK ☒ ⊟ ▦ ⊸

⊕⊕⊕ ▼▼▼ Radisson Dallas Love Field H 🐾
(214) 630-7000. **$104-$129.** 1241 W Mockingbird Ln. I-35E, exit 433B, just ne of jct I-35E and W Mockingbird Ln. Int corridors. **Pets:** Medium, other species. $25 one-time fee/pet. Service with restrictions, crate.

SAVE ☒ ⊟ ▦ ⑪ ⊸

⊕⊕⊕ ▼▼▼ Radisson Hotel Central/Dallas H
(214) 750-6060. **$109-$199.** 6060 N Central Expwy. US 75, exit 3 (Mockingbird Ln), on northbound frontage road. Int corridors. **Pets:** Accepted.

SAVE ☒ ⊟ ▦ ⑪ ⊸

Red Roof Inn Dallas (Richardson) #8474
(972) 234-1016. **Call for rates.** 13685 N Central Expwy. US 75 N, exit 22 (Midpark Rd). Ext/int corridors. **Pets:** Medium, other species. Service with restrictions, crate.

Red Roof Inn-Market Center
(214) 638-5151. **Call for rates.** 1550 Empire Central Dr. I-35E, exit 434A (Empire Central Dr), 0.3 mi e. Ext corridors. **Pets:** Accepted.

Renaissance Dallas Hotel
(214) 631-2222. **$224-$274.** 2222 Stemmons Frwy. I-35E, exit 430B (Market Center Blvd), 0.3 mi nw on access road. Int corridors. **Pets:** Accepted.

Residence Inn by Marriott at Dallas Central
(214) 750-8220. **$189-$200.** 10333 N Central Expwy. US 75, exit 6 (Walnut Hill Ln/Meadow Rd) northbound, 0.5 mi n to Meadow Rd, U-turn under highway; exit 7 (Royal/Meadow Rd) southbound, 1 mi s on access road. Ext corridors. **Pets:** Accepted.

Residence Inn by Marriott-Dallas Market Center
(214) 631-2472. **$161-$197.** 6950 N Stemmons Frwy. I-35E, exit 432B (Commonwealth Ln), 0.6 mi n on northbound frontage road. Ext/int corridors. **Pets:** Accepted.

Residence Inn by Marriott-Dallas Park Central
(972) 503-1333. **$188-$230.** 7642 LBJ Frwy. I-635, exit 20 (Hillcrest), just e, on eastbound access road. Int corridors. **Pets:** Accepted.

The Ritz-Carlton, Dallas
(214) 922-0200. **$249-$569.** 2121 McKinney Ave. SR 366 (Woodall Rodgers Frwy), exit Pearl St, just sw to Olive St, then just nw. Int corridors. **Pets:** Small. $125 one-time fee/room. Service with restrictions, supervision.

Rosewood Crescent Hotel
(214) 871-3200. **Call for rates.** 400 Crescent Ct. Corner of Crescent Ct and McKinney Ave; uptown. Int corridors. **Pets:** Other species. $100 one-time fee/pet. Service with restrictions.

Rosewood Mansion On Turtle Creek
(214) 559-2100. **$595-$2400.** 2821 Turtle Creek Blvd. 2 mi nw, entrance on Gillespie St, just e of jct Gillespie St and Oak Lawn Ave. Int corridors. **Pets:** Accepted.

Sheraton Suites Market Center-Dallas
(214) 747-3000. **Call for rates.** 2101 N Stemmons Frwy. Nw off I-35E and US 77, exit 430B (Market Center Blvd). Int corridors. **Pets:** Accepted.

Staybridge Suites Dallas Near The Galleria
(972) 391-0000. **$135-$171.** 7880 Alpha Rd. I-635, exit 19B (Coit Rd), 0.3 mi n, then just w. Int corridors. **Pets:** Accepted.

Staybridge Suites North Dallas
(972) 726-9990. **$89-$199.** 16060 N Dallas Pkwy. North Dallas Tollway northbound, exit Keller Springs, just n on north access road; exit Keller Springs southbound, just e to Noel Tr, then just s. Int corridors. **Pets:** Accepted.

Super 8
(972) 572-1030. **$70-$100.** 8541 S Hampton Rd. I-20, exit 465, 0.3 mi e to S Hampton Rd, then just s. Ext corridors. **Pets:** Accepted.

Warwick Melrose Hotel
(214) 521-5151. **$365.** 3015 Oak Lawn Ave. I-35E, exit 430 (Oak Lawn Ave), 0.8 mi n; entrance off Cedar Springs, just n. Int corridors. **Pets:** Medium. $50 one-time fee/pet. Service with restrictions, crate.

The Westin City Center, Dallas
(214) 979-9000. **$109-$409.** 650 N Pearl St. Between San Jacinto and Bryan St, 0.3 mi w of US 75 Central Expwy. Int corridors. **Pets:** Medium, dogs only. $200 one-time fee/pet. No service, supervision.

The Westin Galleria, Dallas
(972) 934-9494. **$169-$399.** 13340 Dallas Pkwy. Just n of jct I-635 and N Dallas Pkwy. Int corridors. **Pets:** Accepted.

Westin Park Central
(972) 385-3000. **Call for rates.** 12720 Merit Dr. I-635, exit 19C (Coit Rd) eastbound; exit 19B (US 75/Coit Rd) westbound; 0.3 mi w of jct US 75. Int corridors. **Pets:** Medium, other species. Service with restrictions, crate.

DENTON

La Quinta Inn Denton
(940) 387-5840. **$49-$119.** 700 Fort Worth Dr. I-35E, exit 465B (Fort Worth Dr), just n. Ext corridors. **Pets:** Medium, other species. Service with restrictions, supervision.

Motel 6 Denton #97
(940) 566-4798. **$45-$59.** 4125 I-35 N. I-35, exit 469. Ext corridors. **Pets:** Other species. Service with restrictions, supervision.

Quality Inn & Suites Denton
(940) 387-3511. **$65-$219.** 1500 Dallas Dr. 2 mi se of jct I-35E and US 77 business route, exit 464 westbound; exit 465A (Teasley Ln) eastbound, 0.4 mi n to Dallas Dr, then 0.5 mi e. Ext corridors. **Pets:** Large. $20 one-time fee/pet. Service with restrictions.

Super 8-Denton
(940) 380-8888. **$69-$75.** 620 S I-35E. I-35, exit 465A (Teasley Ln). Int corridors. **Pets:** Small. $25 daily fee/pet. Designated rooms, service with restrictions, supervision.

Travelodge
(940) 383-1471. **$59-$139.** 4211 I-35 N. Jct US 380 and I-35, exit 469, just n. Int corridors. **Pets:** Small. $50 deposit/room. Designated rooms, service with restrictions, supervision.

DESOTO

McM Grande Hotel
(972) 224-9100. **$89-$119.** 1515 N I-35E. I-35E, exit 416 (Wintergreen Rd), just s. Ext/int corridors. **Pets:** Medium, other species. Designated rooms, service with restrictions, supervision.

Red Roof Inn Dallas/DeSoto
(972) 224-7100. **$52-$90.** 1401 I-35E. I-35E, exit 416, just s. Ext/int corridors. **Pets:** Medium. Service with restrictions, crate.

DUNCANVILLE

▼ Motel 6–#1130
(972) 296-0345. **$45-$57.** 202 Jellison Blvd. I-20, exit 462A (Duncanville Rd) eastbound; exit 462B (Main St) westbound, just s to Camp Wisdom, just w to Duncanville Rd, just n to Jellison Blvd, then just w. Ext/int corridors. **Pets:** Other species. Service with restrictions, supervision.

⊠ 🛏 ⇌

ENNIS

▼▼▼ Baymont Inn & Suites Ennis H
(972) 875-3390. **Call for rates.** 100 S I-45. I-45, exit 251B. Ext/int corridors. **Pets:** Small. $10 deposit/pet. Designated rooms, service with restrictions, supervision.

SAVE ⊠ 🛏 💻 ⇌

FARMERS BRANCH

▼▼ Comfort Inn of North Dallas H
(972) 406-3030. **$59-$99.** 14040 Stemmons Frwy. I-35E, exit 442 (Valwood Pkwy). Int corridors. **Pets:** Small, other species. $10 daily fee/room. Service with restrictions, supervision.

ASK ⊠ 🛏 💻 ⇌

▼▼▼ Fairfield Inn & Suites by Marriott Dallas North H
(972) 661-9800. **$98-$120.** 13900 Parkside Center Blvd. I-635, exit 23, 0.9 mi n to Spring Valley, just w, then just s. Int corridors. **Pets:** Other species. $75 one-time fee/room. Service with restrictions.

⊠ 🛏 💻 ⇌

▼▼▼ Holiday Inn Select North Dallas H
(972) 243-3363. **$109-$129.** 2645 LBJ Frwy. I-635, exit 26 (Josey Ln) eastbound, just n; exit 25 westbound, 0.4 mi w. Int corridors. **Pets:** Accepted.

ASK ⊠ 🛏 💻 ¶¶ ⇌

▼▼ La Quinta Inn Dallas (NW-Farmers Branch) H 🐾
(972) 620-7333. **$39-$99.** 13235 Stemmons Frwy N. I-35E, exit 441 (Valley View Ln), on southbound frontage road. Ext corridors. **Pets:** Medium, other species. Service with restrictions, supervision.

ASK ⊠ 🛏 💻 ⇌

▼▼▼ Omni Dallas Hotel Park West H
(972) 869-4300. **$90-$207.** 1590 LBJ Frwy. Nw off I-635, 1.5 mi w of jct I-35E, exit 29 (Luna Rd). Int corridors. **Pets:** Accepted.

ASK ⊠ 🛏 💻 ¶¶ ⇌ ⊠

▼▼▼ Sheraton Dallas North by the Galleria H
(972) 661-3600. **$89-$249, 3 day notice.** 4801 LBJ Frwy. I-635, exit 22C (Inwood Rd) eastbound, then n; exit 22B (Dallas Pkwy) westbound. Int corridors. **Pets:** Accepted.

SAVE ⊠ 🛏 💻 ¶¶ ⇌ ⊠

▼▼ StudioPLUS Hotel Dallas-Farmers Branch H
(972) 385-6006. **$60-$92.** 4022 Parkside Center Blvd. I-635, exit 23 (Midway Rd), 0.9 mi n to Parkside Center Blvd. Int corridors. **Pets:** Other species. $25 daily fee/pet. Service with restrictions, crate.

ASK ⊠ 🛏 ⇌

FRISCO

▼▼▼ Sheraton Stonebriar Hotel H
(972) 668-8700. **$99-$419.** 5444 State Hwy 121. SR 121, exit Legacy Dr; northwest corner. Int corridors. **Pets:** Accepted.

SAVE ⊠ 🛏 💻 ¶¶

▼▼▼ The Westin Stonebriar Resort H
(972) 668-8000. **Call for rates.** 1549 Legacy Dr. 0.3 mi n of jct SR 121. Int corridors. **Pets:** Accepted.

SAVE ⊠ 🛏 💻 ¶¶ ⇌ ⊠

GARLAND

▼▼ Best Western Executive Inn H
(972) 613-5000. **$55-$70.** 12670 E Northwest Hwy. I-635, exit 11B, just s. Ext corridors. **Pets:** Accepted.

SAVE ⊠ 🛏 💻 ⇌

▼▼ Best Western Lakeview Inn H
(972) 303-1601. **$80-$90.** 1635 E I-30 at Bass Pro Rd. I-30, exit 62 (Chaha Rd). Ext corridors. **Pets:** Large. $10 daily fee/pet. Designated rooms, supervision.

SAVE ⊠ 🛏 💻 ⇌

▼▼ La Quinta Inn Dallas (Garland) H 🐾
(972) 271-7581. **$39-$99.** 12721 I-635. I-635, exit 11B, just nw. Ext/int corridors. **Pets:** Medium, other species. Service with restrictions, supervision.

ASK ⊠ 🛏 💻 ⇌

▼ Motel 6–0620 H
(972) 226-7140. **$43-$57.** 436 W I-30. I-30, exit 59 (Belt Line Rd). Ext corridors. **Pets:** Other species. Service with restrictions, supervision.

⊠ ⇌

▼▼▼ Radisson Hotel Dallas East H
(214) 341-5400. **$99-$109, 3 day notice.** 11350 LBJ Frwy. I-635, exit 13 (Jupiter/Kingsley rds), just sw. Int corridors. **Pets:** Accepted.

ASK ⊠ 🛏 💻 ¶¶ ⇌

GRAND PRAIRIE

▼▼ La Quinta Inn Dallas (Grand Prairie) H 🐾
(972) 641-3021. **$39-$109.** 1410 NW 19th St. I-30, exit 32, just e. Ext corridors. **Pets:** Medium, other species. Service with restrictions, supervision.

ASK ⊠ 🛏 💻 ⇌

▼ Motel 6–446 H
(972) 642-9424. **$40-$51.** 406 E Palace Pkwy. I-30, exit 34 (Belt Line Rd), just n to Safari Pkwy, then 0.6 mi w. Ext corridors. **Pets:** Other species. Service with restrictions, supervision.

⊠ 🛏 💻 ⇌

GREENVILLE

▼▼▼ Best Western Monica Royale Inn & Suites H
(903) 454-3700. **$99-$149, 7 day notice.** 3001 Mustang Crossing. I-30, exit 93A. Int corridors. **Pets:** Small, other species. $50 deposit/pet. Service with restrictions, supervision.

SAVE ⊠ 🛏 💻 ⇌

▼▼▼ Holiday Inn Express Hotel & Suites H
(903) 454-8680. **Call for rates.** 2901 Mustang Crossing. I-30, exit 93A. Int corridors. **Pets:** Accepted.

⊠ 🛏 💻 ⇌

▼▼ Quality Inn H
(903) 454-7000. **Call for rates.** 1215 E I-30. I-30, exit 94B, just e of jct I-30 and US 69. Int corridors. **Pets:** Small. $25 one-time fee/room. Service with restrictions, supervision.

⊠ 🛏 💻 ¶¶ ⇌

IRVING

▼▼▼ Candlewood Dallas/Las Colinas H
(972) 714-9990. **Call for rates.** 5300 Greenpark Dr. SR 114, exit Walnut Hill Ln, just s. Int corridors. **Pets:** Accepted.

⊠ 🛏 💻

▼▼ Days Inn DFW North H
(972) 621-8277. **$55.** 4325 W Hwy 114. SR 114, exit Belt Line Rd, on westbound service road. Ext corridors. **Pets:** Accepted.

ASK ⊠ 💻 ¶¶ ⇌

▼▼▼▼ Drury Inn & Suites-DFW Airport 🅷
(972) 986-1200. **$80-$140.** 4210 W Airport Frwy. SR 183, exit Esters Rd, on southbound access road. Int corridors. **Pets:** Other species. Service with restrictions, supervision.
ASK ✕ 🖥 💻 🐾

▼▼ Extended Stay Deluxe (Dallas-Las Colinas-Green Park Dr) 🅷
(972) 751-0808. **$75-$108.** 5401 Green Park Dr. SR 114, exit Walnut Hill Ln, just s. Int corridors. **Pets:** Other species. $25 daily fee/pet. Service with restrictions, crate.
ASK ✕ 🔬 🖥 💻 🐾

🔺🔺🔺 Four Seasons Resort and Club 🅷
(972) 717-0700. **$395-$2500.** 4150 N MacArthur Blvd. SR 114, exit MacArthur Blvd, 1.5 mi s. Int corridors. **Pets:** Accepted.
SAVE ✕ 🔬 🖥 💻 🍴 🐾 ✕

▼▼ Homestead Studio Suites Hotel-Dallas/DFW Airport North 🅷
(972) 929-3333. **$45-$75.** 7825 Heathrow Dr. SR 114, exit Freeport Pkwy; on eastbound service road, just w. Int corridors. **Pets:** Other species. $25 daily fee/pet. Service with restrictions, crate.
ASK ✕ 🖥 💻

🔺🔺 ▼▼▼ Hyatt Summerfield Suites-Las Colinas 🅷
(972) 831-0909. **$189-$259.** 5901 N MacArthur Blvd. SR 114, exit MacArthur Blvd, northwest corner. Ext/int corridors. **Pets:** Accepted.
SAVE ✕ 🔬 🖥 💻 🐾 ✕

▼▼▼▼ La Quinta Inn & Suites Dallas (DFW-Airport North) 🅷 ❖
(972) 915-4022. **$59-$149.** 4850 W John Carpenter Frwy. SR 114, exit Freeport Pkwy, on eastbound service road. Int corridors. **Pets:** Medium, other species. Service with restrictions, supervision.
ASK ✕ 🔬 🖥 💻 🐾

▼▼▼▼ La Quinta Inn & Suites Dallas DFW Airport South (Irving) 🅷 ❖
(972) 252-6546. **$59-$169.** 4105 W Airport Frwy. 3 mi nw off SR 183, exit Esters Rd; on northbound access road. Int corridors. **Pets:** Medium, other species. Service with restrictions, supervision.
ASK ✕ 🔬 🖥 💻 🐾

▼▼ Motel 6 #1274 DFW North Ⓜ
(972) 915-3993. **$51-$61.** 7800 Heathrow Dr. SR 114, exit Freeport Pkwy, just se. Int corridors. **Pets:** Other species. Service with restrictions, supervision.
✕ 🖥 🐾

▼▼▼▼ Omni Mandalay Hotel at Las Colinas 🅷 ❖
(972) 556-0800. **$129-$499.** 221 E Las Colinas Blvd. Nw off SR 114, exit O'Connor Rd. Int corridors. **Pets:** Small. $50 one-time fee/room. Service with restrictions, crate.
ASK ✕ 🖥 💻 🍴 🐾 ✕

🔺🔺 ▼▼ Red Roof Inn/DFW Airport North Ⓜ
(972) 929-0020. **Call for rates.** 8150 Esters Blvd. SR 114, exit Esters Blvd, just n. Ext corridors. **Pets:** Accepted.
SAVE ✕ 🖥

▼▼▼▼ Residence Inn by Marriott at Las Colinas 🅷
(972) 580-7773. **$179-$219.** 950 W Walnut Hill Ln. SR 114, exit MacArthur Blvd, 0.5 mi s, then just e. Ext corridors. **Pets:** Accepted.
✕ 🔬 🖥 💻 🐾 ✕

▼▼▼▼ Residence Inn by Marriott-DFW/Irving 🅷
(972) 871-1331. **$197-$241.** 8600 Esters Blvd. SR 114, exit Esters Blvd, 0.9 mi n. Int corridors. **Pets:** Accepted.
✕ 🔬 🖥 💻 🐾 ✕

🔺🔺 ▼▼▼▼ Sheraton Grand Hotel 🅷
(972) 929-8400. **$99-$359.** 4440 W John Carpenter Frwy. SR 114, exit Esters Blvd, just s. Int corridors. **Pets:** Accepted.
SAVE ✕ 🖥 💻 🍴 🐾 ✕

🔺🔺 ▼▼▼▼ Staybridge Suites Dallas-Las Colinas 🅷
(972) 465-9400. **$121-$181.** 1201 Executive Cir. SR 114, exit MacArthur Blvd, just s to W Walnut Hill Ln, then just w. Int corridors. **Pets:** Accepted.
SAVE ✕ 🖥 💻 🐾

🔺🔺 ▼▼▼▼ The Westin Dallas Fort Worth Airport 🅷
(972) 929-4500. **Call for rates.** 4545 W John Carpenter Frwy. Nw off SR 114, exit Esters Blvd. Int corridors. **Pets:** Accepted.
SAVE ✕ 🖥 💻 🍴 🐾

▼▼▼▼ Wyndham-Las Colinas 🅷
(972) 650-1600. **$89-$249.** 110 W John Carpenter Frwy. Sw off SR 114, exit O'Connor Rd. Int corridors. **Pets:** Accepted.
ASK ✕ 🖥 💻 🍴 🐾

KAUFMAN

🔺🔺 ▼▼ Best Western La Hacienda Inn Ⓜ
(972) 962-6272. **$65-$90.** 200 E Hwy 175. Just e of jct US 175 and SR 34. Ext corridors. **Pets:** Very small. $8 daily fee/pet. Service with restrictions, supervision.
SAVE ✕ 🖥 💻 🐾

LAKE DALLAS

🔺🔺 ▼▼▼ Best Western Lake Dallas Inn & Suites 🅷
(940) 497-1007. **$90-$170, 3 day notice.** 305 Swisher Rd. I-35E, exit 458 (Swisher Rd), 0.6 mi on N Frontage Rd. Int corridors. **Pets:** Medium. $25 one-time fee/pet. Service with restrictions, supervision.
SAVE ✕ 🖥 💻 🐾

LEWISVILLE

▼▼ Comfort Suites by Choice Hotels 🅷
(972) 315-6464. **$80-$110.** 755A Vista Ridge Mall Dr. I-35E, exit 448A (Round Grove Rd) southbound, 0.5 mi s of jct I-35 and Round Grove Rd on southbound service road to Vista Ridge Mall Dr, then just w; exit 447B northbound, just w on SR 121 Bypass. Int corridors. **Pets:** Small. $50 one-time fee/pet. Service with restrictions, crate.
ASK ✕ 🖥 💻 🐾

▼▼▼ Country Inn & Suites by Carlson 🅷
(972) 315-6565. **$75-$115.** 755B Vista Ridge Mall Dr. I-35E, exit 448A (Round Grove Rd) southbound, 0.5 mi s on service road to Vista Ridge Mall Dr, then just w; exit 447B northbound, just w on SR 121 Bypass. Int corridors. **Pets:** Other species. $100 one-time fee/room. Service with restrictions, supervision.
ASK ✕ 🖥 💻

▼▼ Extended StayAmerica Dallas-Lewisville 🅷
(972) 315-7455. **$45-$75.** 1900 Lake Pointe Dr. I-35E, exit 449 (Corporate Dr), just e to Lake Pointe Dr, then just s. Int corridors. **Pets:** Other species. $25 daily fee/pet. Service with restrictions, crate.
ASK ✕ 🖥 💻

▼▼ La Quinta Inn Dallas (Lewisville) 🅷 ❖
(972) 221-7525. **$45-$109.** 1657 S Stemmons Frwy. I-35E, exit 449 (Corporate Dr), just w. Int corridors. **Pets:** Medium, other species. Service with restrictions, supervision.
ASK ✕ 🔬 🖥 💻 🐾

▼▼ Motel 6–1288 🅷
(972) 436-5008. **$43-$55.** 1705 Lakepointe Dr. I-35E, exit 449 (Corporate Dr), just n on access road. Int corridors. **Pets:** Other species. Service with restrictions, supervision.
✕ 🐾

▼▼▼ Residence Inn by Marriott Dallas H
(972) 315-3777. **$175-$181.** 755C Vista Ridge Mall Dr. I-35E, exit 448A (Round Grove Rd), 0.5 mi s on service road; jct I-35 and Round Grove Rd to Vista Ridge Mall Dr, just w; exit 447B northbound, just w. Int corridors. **Pets:** Accepted.

[icons]

MCKINNEY

▼▼ Days Inn McKinney H
(972) 548-8888. **Call for rates.** 2104 N Central Expwy. US 75, 0.5 mi n of jct US 380, exit 41. Ext corridors. **Pets:** Accepted.

[icons]

▼▼ Super 8-McKinney H
(972) 548-8880. **Call for rates.** 910 N Central Expwy. US 75, exit 40A (Virginia St/Louisiana St), 0.5 mi n on northbound service road. Int corridors. **Pets:** Accepted.

[icons]

MESQUITE

▼▼▼ Comfort Inn H
(972) 285-6300. **Call for rates.** 923 Windbell Cir. I-635, exit 5, just e. Int corridors. **Pets:** Accepted.

[icons]

◯◯◯ ▼▼▼▼ La Quinta Inn and Suites H 🐾
(972) 216-7460. **$59-$129.** 118 E Hwy 80. US 80 E, exit Belt Line Rd. Int corridors. **Pets:** Medium, other species. Service with restrictions, supervision.

[icons]

▼▼ Super 8 H
(972) 289-5481. **Call for rates.** 121 Grand Junction Blvd. I-635, exit 4 (Military Pkwy). Ext corridors. **Pets:** Accepted.

[icons]

MIDLOTHIAN

◯◯◯ ▼▼▼ Americas Best Value Midlothian Inn H
(972) 775-1891. **$79-$110.** 220 N Hwy 67. On US 67, just n of jct US 287. Ext corridors. **Pets:** Medium, other species. $10 daily fee/pet. Service with restrictions, supervision.

[icons]

PLANO

◯◯◯ ▼▼▼▼ Best Western Park Suites Hotel H
(972) 578-2243. **$104-$109.** 640 Park Blvd E. US 75, exit 29A northbound, just e; exit 29 southbound, 0.5 mi s on access road, just e on 15th St, then 0.5 mi n on access road. Int corridors. **Pets:** Accepted.

[icons]

▼▼▼▼ Candlewood Suites-Plano H
(972) 618-5446. **$66-$142.** 4701 Legacy Dr. Jct SR 289 (Preston Rd) and Legacy Dr, just e. Int corridors. **Pets:** Medium. $75 one-time fee/pet. Service with restrictions.

[icons]

▼▼ Extended Stay Deluxe (Dallas/Plano) H
(972) 378-9978. **$85-$115.** 2900 Dallas Pkwy. Dallas Pkwy, exit Park Blvd northbound; exit Parker Rd southbound, on northbound service road. Int corridors. **Pets:** Other species. $25 daily fee/pet. Service with restrictions, crate.

[icons]

▼▼ Extended Stay Deluxe Dallas-Plano-Plano Parkway H
(972) 398-0135. **$75-$109.** 4636 W Plano Pkwy. Jct SR 289 (Preston Rd) and W Plano Pkwy, 0.4 mi e. Int corridors. **Pets:** Other species. $25 daily fee/pet. Service with restrictions, crate.

[icons]

▼▼▼ Holiday Inn Express Hotel & Suites Plano East H
(972) 881-1881. **$129-$139.** 700 Central Pkwy E. Just e of US 75; 0.3 mi ne of jct FM 544, exit 29A northbound; exit 29 southbound, 0.5 mi s on access road, just e on 15th St, then 0.5 mi n on access road. Int corridors. **Pets:** $50 one-time fee/room. Designated rooms, service with restrictions, supervision.

[icons]

▼▼▼ Homestead Studio Suites Hotel-Dallas/Plano Parkway H
(972) 596-9966. **$75-$109.** 4709 W Plano Pkwy. Just n of jct Plano Pkwy and SR 289 (Preston Rd), then just e. Int corridors. **Pets:** Other species. $25 daily fee/pet. Service with restrictions, crate.

[icons]

▼▼▼▼ Homewood Suites by Hilton H
(972) 758-8800. **$109-$179.** 4705 Old Shepherd Pl. Jct Plano Pkwy and SR 289 (Preston Rd), 0.4 mi n, then just e. Int corridors. **Pets:** Accepted.

[icons]

▼▼▼▼ La Quinta Inn & Suites Dallas (West Plano) H 🐾
(972) 599-0700. **$59-$159.** 4800 W Plano Pkwy. Just n of jct SR 289 (Preston Rd), then just e. Int corridors. **Pets:** Medium, other species. Service with restrictions, supervision.

[icons]

▼▼ La Quinta Inn Dallas (Plano) H 🐾
(972) 423-1300. **$39-$99.** 1820 N Central Expwy. US 75, exit 29A (Park Blvd), northbound, just ne; exit 29 southbound, 0.5 mi s on access road, just e on 15th St, then just n on northbound access road. Ext corridors. **Pets:** Medium, other species. Service with restrictions, supervision.

[icons]

▼▼ Motel 6–1121 H
(972) 578-1626. **$45-$57.** 2550 N Central Expwy. US 75, exit 29A (Park Blvd) northbound; exit 29 southbound, 1 mi n of jct Park Rd (SR 544), on east side of US 75. Ext/int corridors. **Pets:** Other species. Service with restrictions, supervision.

[icons]

▼▼▼ Red Roof Inn Dallas-Plano H
(972) 881-8191. **Call for rates.** 301 Ruisseau Dr. US 75, exit 30 (Parker Rd), 0.5 mi w to Premier, then just n. Ext/int corridors. **Pets:** Accepted.

[icons]

◯◯◯ ▼▼▼▼ Southfork Hotel H
(972) 578-8555. **$89-$99.** 1600 N Central Expwy. US 75, exit 29A northbound; exit 29 southbound, on northbound access road. Int corridors. **Pets:** Accepted.

[icons]

▼▼ Super 8-Plano H
(972) 423-8300. **$60-$70.** 1704 N Central Expwy. US 75, exit 29A (Park Blvd) northbound, just e; exit 29 southbound, 0.5 mi s on access road, just e on 15th St, then just n on access road. Int corridors. **Pets:** Accepted.

[icons]

▼▼ TownePlace Suites by Marriott H
(972) 943-8200. **$159-$169.** 5005 Whitestone Ln. North Dallas Tollway, exit Spring Creek Pkwy, 1.9 mi e, just n on SR 289 (Preston Rd), to Whitestone Ln, then just w. Int corridors. **Pets:** Accepted.

[icons]

RICHARDSON

▼▼▼ Homestead Studio Suites Hotel-Dallas/Richardson H
(972) 479-0500. **$65-$98.** 901 E Campbell Rd. US 75, exit 26 (Campbell Rd), just e. Int corridors. **Pets:** Other species. $25 daily fee/pet. Service with restrictions, crate.

[icons]

WWWW The Radisson Hotel Dallas North At
Richardson H
(972) 644-4000. **$129-$169.** 1981 N Central Expwy. US 75, exit 26 (Campbell Rd), 1.8 mi n; jct SR 5. Int corridors. **Pets:** Accepted.
ASK ⊠ &M 🛏 🖵 ¶¶ ≈

WWWW WWWW Renaissance Dallas-Richardson
Hotel H
(972) 367-2000. **$176-$215.** 900 E Lookout Dr. US 75, exit 27A (Gallatin Pkwy/Renner Rd) northbound; exit 26 (Gallatin Pkwy/Campbell Rd) southbound, just e. Int corridors. **Pets:** Medium, other species. Service with restrictions, crate.
SAVE ⊠ 🛏 🖵 ¶¶ ≈ ✕

WWWW Residence Inn by Marriott Richardson H
(972) 669-5888. **$170-$208.** 1040 Waterwood Dr. US 75, exit 26 (Campbell Rd), just e to Greenville Ave, 0.4 mi n to Glenville Rd, then just w. Int corridors. **Pets:** Accepted.
⊠ 🛏 🖵 ≈ ✕

ROANOKE

WWWW Comfort Suites Roanoke H
(817) 490-1455. **$90-$130.** 801 Byron Nelson Blvd. I-35, exit 70 (SR 114), 3.4 mi e, exit Rufe/Snow, then just se. Int corridors. **Pets:** Accepted.
ASK ⊠ &M 🛏 🖵 ≈

WWWW Speedway Sleep Inn & Suites H
(817) 491-3120. **$70-$109.** 13471 Raceway Dr. I-35, exit 70 (SR 114), just e, then just s. Int corridors. **Pets:** Medium, other species. $30 deposit/room. Service with restrictions, supervision.
SAVE ⊠ &M 🛏 🖵 ≈

ROCKWALL

WWWWW Hilton Bella Harbor on Lake Ray Hubbard H
(214) 771-3700. **$119-$349.** 2055 Summer Lee Dr. I-30 E, exit 67A (Horizon Rd), 0.5 mi s. Int corridors. **Pets:** Accepted.
⊠ 🛏 ¶¶ ≈

WWWW La Quinta Inn & Suites H ❀
(972) 771-1685. **$79-$169.** 689 E I-30. I-30, exit 67 westbound; exit 67B eastbound. Int corridors. **Pets:** Medium, other species. Service with restrictions, supervision.
SAVE ⊠ &M 🛏 🖵 ≈

ROWLETT

WWWW Comfort Suites Lake Ray Hubbard H
(972) 463-9595. **$95-$110.** 8701 E I-30. I-30, exit 64 (Dalrock Rd). Int corridors. **Pets:** Accepted.
SAVE ⊠ &M 🛏 🖵 ≈

TERRELL

WWW Best Western Country Inn H
(972) 563-1521. **$59-$89, 3 day notice.** 1604 Hwy 34 S. I-20, exit 501 (SR 34), just n. Ext corridors. **Pets:** Accepted.
SAVE ⊠ 🛏 🖵 ≈

UNIVERSITY PARK

WWWW Hotel Lumen H ❀
(214) 219-2400. **$159-$399.** 6101 Hillcrest Ave. Just n of jct Mockingbird Ln and Hillcrest Ave. Int corridors. **Pets:** Other species. Designated rooms, service with restrictions.
SAVE ⊠ 🛏 ¶¶

END METROPOLITAN AREA

DECATUR

WWW Best Western Decatur Inn M
(940) 627-5982. **$72-$90.** 1801 S Hwy 287. 0.6 mi s of jct Business Rt US 380. Ext corridors. **Pets:** Accepted.
SAVE ⊠ 🛏 🖵 ≈

WWWW Holiday Inn Express Hotel & Suites H
(940) 627-0776. **$117.** 1051 N Hwy 287. US 380, exit US 287 N, just n. Int corridors. **Pets:** Accepted.
ASK ⊠ 🛏 🖵 ≈

WWW Super 8 H
(940) 627-0250. **Call for rates.** 1600 US S 81/287. 0.4 mi s of jct Business Rt US 380. Int corridors. **Pets:** Accepted.
SAVE ⊠ 🛏 🖵 ≈

DEL RIO

WWW Best Western Inn of Del Rio H
(830) 775-7511. **$60-$130, 3 day notice.** 810 Veterans Blvd. In town. Ext corridors. **Pets:** Medium. $15 daily fee/pet. Service with restrictions, supervision.
SAVE ⊠ 🛏 🖵 ≈

WWW Comfort Inn & Suites H
(830) 775-2933. **$70-$129, 3 day notice.** 3616 Veterans Blvd. 3.2 mi nw on US 90. Ext/int corridors. **Pets:** Medium. $10 daily fee/pet. Service with restrictions, supervision.
SAVE ⊠ 🛏 🖵 ≈

WWWWW La Quinta Inn Del Rio H ❀
(830) 775-7591. **$59-$109.** 2005 Veterans Blvd. 1.8 mi nw on US 90, 277 and 377. Ext/int corridors. **Pets:** Medium, other species. Service with restrictions, supervision.
ASK ⊠ 🛏 🖵 ≈

WWW Motel 6 Del Rio #323 H
(830) 774-2115. **$39-$51.** 2115 Veterans Blvd. Jct US 90/277 and Garner Dr. Ext corridors. **Pets:** Other species. Service with restrictions, supervision.
⊠ ≈

WWWW Ramada Inn H ❀
(830) 775-1511. **$94-$114.** 2101 Veterans Blvd. 1.8 mi nw on US 90, 277 and 377. Ext/int corridors. **Pets:** Medium, other species. Designated rooms, service with restrictions, crate.
SAVE ⊠ 🛏 🖵 ¶¶ ≈ ✕

DONNA

WWWW Victoria Palms Inn & Suites H
(956) 464-4656. **Call for rates.** 602 N Victoria Rd. US 83, exit Victoria Rd. Ext corridors. **Pets:** Accepted.
⊠ 🛏 🖵 ¶¶ ≈ ✕

DUMAS

WWW Best Western Windsor Inn H
(806) 935-9644. **$69-$109.** 1701 S Dumas Ave. US 287, 2 mi s of US 87 and SR 152. Ext corridors. **Pets:** Accepted.
SAVE ⊠ 🛏 🖵 ≈ ✕

◇◇ ▼▼ Econo Lodge H
(806) 935-9098. **$63-$90.** 1719 S Dumas Ave. US 287, 2 mi s of US 87 and SR 152. Int corridors. **Pets:** Medium. $10 daily fee/pet. Service with restrictions, supervision.
SAVE ⊠ 🛢

▼▼▼ Holiday Inn Express H
(806) 935-4000. **Call for rates.** 1525 S Dumas Ave. US 287, 1.1 mi s of US 87 and SR 152. Int corridors. **Pets:** Other species. $25 daily fee/pet. Service with restrictions, supervision.
⊠ 🛢 🖵 ➤

▼▼ Super 8 M
(806) 935-6222. **$89-$119.** 119 W 17th St. US 287, 2 mi s of jct US 87 and SR 152. Ext corridors. **Pets:** $20 daily fee/pet. Service with restrictions, supervision.
ASK ⊠ 🛢 🖵

EAGLE PASS

◇◇ ▼▼ Americas Best Value Inn H
(830) 773-9531. **$61-$68.** 2150 N US Hwy 277. On US 277, 4 mi n. Ext corridors. **Pets:** Very small. Service with restrictions.
SAVE ⊠ 🛢 🖵 ➤

▼▼▼ La Quinta Inn Eagle Pass H ✿
(830) 773-7000. **$69-$109.** 2525 E Main St. US 57 and 277 at Loop 431. Ext corridors. **Pets:** Medium, other species. Service with restrictions, supervision.
ASK ⊠ 🛢 🖵 ➤

EASTLAND

▼▼ Super 8 Motel & RV Park M
(254) 629-3336. **$64-$69.** 3900 I-20 E. I-20, exit 343, on north service road. Ext corridors. **Pets:** $10 daily fee/pet.
ASK ⊠ 🛢 🖵 ➤

EDINBURG

◇◇ ▼▼ Best Western Edinburg H
(956) 318-0442. **$79-$109, 3 day notice.** 2708 S Bus Hwy 281. US 281, exit Canton Ave, 1 mi w to Bus Hwy 281. Ext corridors. **Pets:** Small. $15 daily fee/pet. Designated rooms, service with restrictions, supervision.
SAVE ⊠ ⅗M 🛢 🖵 ➤

◇◇ ▼▼▼ Comfort Inn Edinburg M
(956) 318-1117. **$65-$70.** 4001 Closner Blvd. US 281, exit Trenton Rd, just w, then just n on Business Rt US 281. Int corridors. **Pets:** Medium. $9 daily fee/pet. Designated rooms, service with restrictions, supervision.
SAVE ⊠ 🛢 🖵 ➤

▼▼ Super 8 H
(956) 381-8888. **$62-$80.** 1210 E Canton Rd. US 281, exit Canton Ave, just off southbound access road. Ext corridors. **Pets:** Accepted.
ASK ⊠ 🛢 🖵 ➤

▼▼ Super 8 H
(956) 381-1688. **$62-$80.** 202 N Hwy 281. US 281, exit University Dr. Ext/int corridors. **Pets:** Accepted.
ASK ⊠ 🛢 🖵 ➤

EL PASO

◇◇ ▼▼▼ Best Western Sunland Park Inn M
(915) 587-4900. **$60-$74, 7 day notice.** 1045 Sunland Park Dr. I-10, exit 13, just s. Ext corridors. **Pets:** Accepted.
SAVE ⊠ 🛢 🖵 ➤

◇◇ ▼▼▼ Chase Suites by Woodfin H
(915) 772-8000. **$150-$299.** 6791 Montana Ave. I-10, exit 25 (Airway Blvd), 1 mi n, then just e. Ext corridors. **Pets:** Accepted.
SAVE ⊠ 🛢 🖵 ➤

▼▼ Comfort Inn Airport East H
(915) 594-9111. **$85.** 900 Yarbrough Dr. I-10, exit 28B. Ext corridors. **Pets:** Accepted.
ASK ⊠ 🛢 🖵 ➤

▼▼ Econo Lodge M
(915) 778-3311. **Call for rates.** 6363 Montana Ave. I-10, exit 24 (Geronimo Dr) westbound; exit 24B eastbound, 0.5 mi n on Geronimo Dr, 0.5 mi e. Ext corridors. **Pets:** Accepted.
⊠ 🛢 🖵 ➤

▼▼ Extended StayAmerica-El Paso-Airport H
(915) 772-5754. **$60-$92.** 6580 Montana Ave. I-10, exit 24 (Geronimo Dr), westbound, exit 24B (Geronimo Dr) eastbound, 0.5 mi n, then 0.5 mi e. Ext corridors. **Pets:** Other species. $25 daily fee/pet. Service with restrictions, crate.
ASK ⊠ 🛢 🖵

▼▼▼ GuestHouse International Suites H
(915) 772-0395. **$95-$165.** 1940 Airway Blvd. I-10, exit 25 (Airport Blvd), 1.2 mi n. Int corridors. **Pets:** Small, other species. $100 deposit/room. Service with restrictions, supervision.
ASK ⊠ ⅗M 🛢 🖵 ➤

▼▼▼ Hawthorn Inn & Suites H
(915) 778-6789. **$117-$135.** 6789 Boeing Dr. I-10, exit 25 (Airport Blvd), 2 mi n, then just w. Int corridors. **Pets:** Accepted.
ASK ⊠ ⅗M 🛢 🖵 ➤

◇◇ ▼▼▼▼ Holiday Inn-Airport H ✿
(915) 778-6411. **$89-$209.** 6655 Gateway Blvd W. I-10, exit 25 (Airway Blvd). Ext/int corridors. **Pets:** Medium, other species. $49 one-time fee/room. Service with restrictions.
SAVE ⊠ 🛢 🖵 🍴 ➤

◇◇ ▼▼▼▼ Holiday Inn El Paso Sunland Park H
(915) 833-2900. **$100-$200.** 900 Sunland Park Dr. I-10, exit 13, just s. Ext corridors. **Pets:** Accepted.
SAVE ⊠ 🛢 🖵 🍴 ➤

▼▼ La Quinta Inn Airport East H ✿
(915) 593-8400. **$49-$99.** 9125 Gateway Blvd W. I-10, exit 28B westbound; exit 27 eastbound. Ext corridors. **Pets:** Medium, other species. Service with restrictions, supervision.
ASK ⊠ 🛢 🖵 ➤

▼▼ La Quinta Inn & Suites El Paso East H ✿
(915) 591-3300. **$65-$99.** 7944 Gateway Blvd E. I-10, exit 28B. Int corridors. **Pets:** Medium, other species. Service with restrictions, supervision.
ASK ⊠ ⅗M 🛢 🖵 ➤

▼▼ La Quinta Inn & Suites El Paso West H ✿
(915) 585-2999. **$59-$99.** 7620 N Mesa St. I-10, exit 11 (Mesa St), just ne. Int corridors. **Pets:** Medium, other species. Service with restrictions, supervision.
ASK ⊠ 🛢 🖵 ➤

▼▼ La Quinta Inn El Paso (Airport) M ✿
(915) 778-9321. **$49-$99.** 6140 Gateway Blvd E. I-10, exit 24B (Geronimo Dr) eastbound; exit 24 westbound. Ext corridors. **Pets:** Medium, other species. Service with restrictions, supervision.
ASK ⊠ 🛢 🖵 ➤

▼▼ La Quinta Inn El Paso (Lomaland) H ✿
(915) 591-2244. **$49-$99.** 11033 Gateway Blvd W. I-10, exit 29 eastbound; exit 30 westbound, 1 mi w. Ext corridors. **Pets:** Medium, other species. Service with restrictions, supervision.
ASK ⊠ ⅗M 🛢 🖵 ➤

▼▼ La Quinta Inn El Paso (West) M ✿
(915) 833-2522. **$49-$99.** 7550 Remcon Cir. I-10, exit 11 (Mesa St). Ext corridors. **Pets:** Medium, other species. Service with restrictions, supervision.
ASK ⊠ 🛢 🖵 ➤

▼▼ Microtel Inn & Suites West M
(915) 584-2026. **$68-$86.** 6185 S Desert Blvd. I-10, exit 8 (Artcraft Rd/Paseo del Norte), on eastbound frontage road. Int corridors. **Pets:** Large, other species. $100 deposit/room. Designated rooms, service with restrictions, crate.
[ASK] [✕] [&M] [🛏] [💻] [≈]

▼▼ Microtel Inn & Suites H
(915) 772-3650. **$78-$96.** 2001 Airway Blvd. I-10, exit 25 (Airway Blvd), 1.3 mi n. Int corridors. **Pets:** Small, other species. $100 deposit/pet. Service with restrictions, crate.
[✕] [&M] [🛏] [💻]

▼▼ Microtel Inn & Suites El Paso East H
(915) 858-1600. **$53-$71.** 12211 Gateway Blvd W. I-10, exit 34 (Joe Battle), on westbound frontage road. Int corridors. **Pets:** Large. $100 deposit/pet. Service with restrictions, supervision.
[ASK] [✕] [&M] [🛏] [💻] [≈]

▼▼▼ Quality Inn & Suites H
(915) 772-3300. **Call for rates.** 6099 Montana Ave. I-10, exit 24 (Geronimo Dr) westbound; exit 24B (Geronimo Dr) eastbound, 0.5 mi n. Ext corridors. **Pets:** Accepted.
[✕] [🛏] [💻] [🍴] [≈]

▲▲▲ ▼▼▼ Red Roof Inn West H
(915) 587-9977. **$60-$68.** 7530 Remcon Cir. I-10, exit 11 (Mesa St), just ne. Ext/int corridors. **Pets:** Accepted.
[SAVE] [✕] [&M] [≈]

▼▼▼ Residence Inn by Marriott El Paso H
(915) 771-0504. **$149-$182.** 6355 Gateway Blvd W. I-10, exit 24B (Geronimo Dr) eastbound, n to Edgemere, then just e; exit 25 (Airway Blvd) westbound, on westbound frontage road. Int corridors. **Pets:** Accepted.
[✕] [🛏] [💻] [≈] [✕]

▼▼▼ Sleep Inn by Choice Hotels H
(915) 585-7577. **Call for rates.** 953 Sunland Park Dr. I-10, exit 13. Int corridors. **Pets:** Small. $25 one-time fee/room. Service with restrictions, supervision.
[✕] [🛏] [💻] [≈]

▼▼ Studio 6 El Paso #6001 M
(915) 594-8533. **$60-$73.** 11049 Gateway Blvd W. I-10, exit 29 eastbound; exit 30 westbound. Ext corridors. **Pets:** Other species. $10 daily fee/room. Service with restrictions, supervision.
[✕] [🛏] [💻] [≈]

▼▼ Super 8 H
(915) 584-4030. **$60-$80.** 7840 N Mesa St. I-10, exit 11 (N Mesa), just s. Ext corridors. **Pets:** Accepted.
[ASK] [✕] [🛏] [💻] [≈]

▼▼▼ Wingate by Wyndham H
(915) 772-4088. **Call for rates.** 6351 Gateway Blvd W. I-10, exit 24B (Geronimo Dr) westbound; exit 25 (Airport Blvd) eastbound, U-turn, 0.5 mi. Int corridors. **Pets:** $150 deposit/room. Service with restrictions, supervision.
[✕] [&M] [🛏] [💻] [≈]

▼▼▼ Wyndham El Paso Airport H
(915) 778-4241. **$129-$172, 6 day notice.** 2027 Airway Blvd. I-10, exit 25 (Airway Blvd), 1.3 mi n. Int corridors. **Pets:** Small. $75 deposit/room. Designated rooms, service with restrictions, supervision.
[ASK] [✕] [🛏] [💻] [🍴] [≈] [✕]

EULESS

▼▼ La Quinta DFW Airport West-Euless H 🐾
(817) 540-0233. **$62-$92.** 1001 W Airport Frwy. SR 183, exit Industrial Blvd (FM 157). Ext corridors. **Pets:** Medium, other species. Service with restrictions, supervision.
[ASK] [✕] [🛏] [💻] [≈]

▼▼ Microtel Inn and Suites H
(817) 545-1111. **$54-$99.** 901 W Airport Frwy. SR 183, exit Industrial Blvd (FM 157), just e. Int corridors. **Pets:** Medium, dogs only. $25 one-time fee/room. Service with restrictions, supervision.
[ASK] [✕] [&M] [🛏] [💻] [≈]

▼▼ Motel 6-Euless #1345 H
(817) 545-0141. **$41-$55.** 110 Airport Frwy. SR 183, exit Euless/Main St, on westbound access road. Ext corridors. **Pets:** Other species. Service with restrictions, supervision.
[✕] [≈]

FORT DAVIS

▼▼ Historical Prude Guest Ranch RA
(432) 426-3202. **$51-$130, 3 day notice.** 6 mi n Hwy 118. 4.5 mi n of jct SR 118 and 17. Ext corridors. **Pets:** Very small. $10 daily fee/pet. No service, supervision.
[ASK] [✕] [🛏] [🍴] [≈] [✕] [W] [✕]

FORT STOCKTON

▲▲▲ ▼▼▼ Best Western Swiss Clock Inn H
(432) 336-8521. **$109-$129.** 3201 W Dickinson Blvd. I-10, exit 256, 0.5 mi e. Ext corridors. **Pets:** Accepted.
[SAVE] [✕] [🛏] [💻] [🍴] [≈]

▲▲▲ ▼▼▼ Days Inn H
(432) 336-7500. **$79-$140.** 1408 N US Hwy 285. I-10, exit 257, just s. Ext corridors. **Pets:** Accepted.
[SAVE] [✕] [🛏] [💻] [≈]

▼▼ La Quinta Inn Fort Stockton H 🐾
(432) 336-9781. **$89-$129.** 1537 N Hwy 285. I-10, exit 257. Ext corridors. **Pets:** Medium, other species. Service with restrictions, supervision.
[ASK] [✕] [🛏] [💻] [≈]

▲▲▲ ▼▼▼ Quality Inn H
(432) 336-5955. **$75-$135.** 1308 N US Hwy 285. I-10, exit 257, just s. Ext corridors. **Pets:** Accepted.
[SAVE] [✕] [🛏] [💻] [≈]

FORT WORTH

▼▼▼ ▼▼▼ The Ashton Hotel H 🐾
(817) 332-0100. **$290-$810.** 610 Main St. Jct 6th and Main sts; center. Int corridors. **Pets:** Medium, dogs only. $150 deposit/room. Service with restrictions, crate.
[ASK] [✕] [🍴]

▼▼▼ Candlewood Suites H
(817) 838-8229. **$89-$109.** 5201 Endicott Ave. I-820, exit 17B, just s. Int corridors. **Pets:** Accepted.
[ASK] [✕] [🛏] [💻]

▼▼ Comfort Inn-North H
(817) 834-8001. **Call for rates.** 4850 North Frwy. I-35W, exit 56A. Int corridors. **Pets:** Accepted.
[✕] [🛏] [💻] [≈]

▼▼▼ Comfort Suites Hotel H
(817) 731-9600. **$119-$169, 12 day notice.** 6851 West Frwy. I-30, exit 7B, 0.8 mi e to Green Oaks Rd. Int corridors. **Pets:** Accepted.
[ASK] [✕] [&M] [🛏] [💻] [≈]

▲▲▲ ▼▼▼▼ Country Inn & Suites By Carlson H
(817) 831-9200. **$109-$219.** 2200 Mercado Dr. I-35W, exit 53, just w. Int corridors. **Pets:** Small, other species. $25 one-time fee/pet. Service with restrictions, supervision.
[SAVE] [✕] [&M] [🛏] [💻] [≈]

W Crossland Economy Studios Fort Worth-Fossil Creek **H**
(817) 838-3500. **$50-$80.** 3804 Tanacross Dr. I-820, exit 17B (Beach St), just s. Ext corridors. **Pets:** Other species. $25 daily fee/pet. Service with restrictions, crate.
(ASK) ⊠ 🛢 💻

WW Extended StayAmerica Fort Worth-City View **H**
(817) 263-9006. **$75-$109.** 5831 Overton Ridge Blvd. I-20, exit 431 (Bryant Irvin Rd), 0.5 mi s to Overton Ridge Blvd. Int corridors. **Pets:** Other species. $25 daily fee/pet. Service with restrictions, crate.
(ASK) ⊠ 🛢 💻

WW Extended Stay Deluxe Fort Worth-City View **H**
(817) 263-8700. **$90-$126.** 4701 City Lake Blvd W. I-20, exit 431 (Bryant Irvin Rd), just e. Int corridors. **Pets:** Other species. $25 daily fee/pet. Service with restrictions, crate.
(ASK) ⊠ 🛢 💻 🏊

WW Extended Stay Deluxe Hotel Fort Worth-Fossil Creek **H**
(817) 232-1622. **$75-$103.** 3261 NE Loop 820. I-820, exit 17B (N Beach St), 0.5 mi w. Int corridors. **Pets:** Other species. $25 daily fee/pet. Service with restrictions, crate.
(ASK) ⊠ 🛢 💻 🏊

WWW Hampton Inn & Suites-FW Alliance Airport **H**
(817) 439-0400. **$99-$154.** 13600 North Frwy. I-35W, exit 66 (Westport Pkwy). Int corridors. **Pets:** Accepted.
⊠ &M 🛢 💻 🏊

WWW Historic Hilton Fort Worth **H** ❀
(817) 870-2100. **$129-$249.** 815 Main St. Northeast corner of Main and 8th sts; center. Int corridors. **Pets:** Medium. $50 one-time fee/pet. Designated rooms, service with restrictions.
⊠ &M 🛢 💻 🍴

WWW Holiday Inn Express Hotel & Suites **H** ❀
(817) 624-0303. **Call for rates.** 3541 NW Loop 820. I-820, exit 10A eastbound; exit 10B westbound. Int corridors. **Pets:** Small, other species. $15 daily fee/pet. Service with restrictions, supervision.
⊠ &M 🛢 💻

WWW Holiday Inn Express Hotel & Suites-Fort Worth West **H**
(817) 560-4200. **$117-$139.** 2730 Cherry Ln. I-30, exit 7A. Int corridors. **Pets:** Accepted.
(ASK) ⊠ 🛢 💻 🏊

WW Homestead Studio Suites Hotel-Fort Worth/Medical Center **H**
(817) 338-4808. **$74-$109.** 1601 River Run. I-30, exit 12 (University Dr), just s. Ext corridors. **Pets:** Other species. $25 daily fee/pet. Service with restrictions, crate.
(ASK) ⊠ 🛢 💻

AAA **WWW** Hotel Trinity InnSuites Forth Worth/DFW **H** ❀
(817) 534-4801. **$75-$125.** 2000 Beach St. I-30, exit 16C (Beach St), just s. Ext/int corridors. **Pets:** Other species. $50 one-time fee/room. Designated rooms, service with restrictions, crate.
(SAVE) ⊠ 🛢 💻 🏊 🐾

WWW La Quinta Inn & Suites Fort Worth (North) **H** ❀
(817) 222-2888. **$79-$149.** 4700 North Frwy. I-35W, exit 56A, just n. Int corridors. **Pets:** Medium, other species. Service with restrictions, supervision.
(ASK) ⊠ 🛢 💻 🏊

WWW La Quinta Inn & Suites Fort Worth (Southwest) **H** ❀
(817) 370-2700. **$89-$149.** 4900 Bryant Irvin Rd. I-20, exit 431 (Bryant Irvin Rd). Int corridors. **Pets:** Medium. Service with restrictions, supervision.
(ASK) ⊠ &M 🛢 💻 🏊

WW La Quinta Inn Fort Worth (West/Medical Center) **H** ❀
(817) 246-5511. **$49-$109.** 7888 I-30 W (W Freeway). I-30, exit 7A. Ext/int corridors. **Pets:** Medium, other species. Service with restrictions, supervision.
(ASK) ⊠ 🛢 💻 🏊

WW Microtel Inn & Suites **H**
(817) 222-3740. **Call for rates.** 3740 Tanacross Dr. I-820, exit 17B (Beach St), just s. Int corridors. **Pets:** Small. $20 daily fee/pet. No service, supervision.
⊠ 🛢 💻

WWW Quality Inn & Suites **H**
(817) 560-4180. **$90-$156.** 2700 Cherry Ln. I-30, exit 7A, just s. Ext corridors. **Pets:** Medium, other species. $75 deposit/pet, $35 one-time fee/pet. Designated rooms, service with restrictions, supervision.
(ASK) ⊠ 🛢 💻 🏊

WWWW The Renaissance Worthington Hotel **H** ❀
(817) 870-1000. **$260-$318.** 200 Main St. Northwest corner of 2nd and Main sts. Int corridors. **Pets:** $200 deposit/room. Service with restrictions, supervision.
⊠ 🛢 💻 🍴 🏊 🐾

WWWW Residence Inn-Alliance Airport **H**
(817) 750-7000. **$170-$208.** 13400 North Frwy. I-35W, exit 66. Int corridors. **Pets:** Other species. $75 one-time fee/room. Service with restrictions, crate.
⊠ 🛢 💻 🏊 🐾

WWWW Residence Inn by Marriott Fort Worth Cultural District **H**
(817) 885-8250. **$188-$230.** 2500 Museum Way. I-30, exit 12A, just e of jct University and 7th St, to Stayton St, just s. Int corridors. **Pets:** Accepted.
⊠ &M 🛢 💻 🏊 🐾

WWWW Residence Inn By Marriott Fort Worth-River Plaza **H**
(817) 870-1011. **$197-$241.** 1701 S University Dr. I-30, exit 12 (University Dr), 0.4 mi s. Ext corridors. **Pets:** Accepted.
⊠ &M 🛢 💻 🏊 🐾

WW TownePlace Suites by Marriott-Fort Worth **H**
(817) 732-2224. **$161-$197.** 4200 International Plaza Dr. I-820, exit 433. Int corridors. **Pets:** Other species. $100 one-time fee/room. Service with restrictions.
⊠ 🛢 💻 🏊

FREDERICKSBURG

AAA **WWW** Best Western Fredericksburg **H**
(830) 992-2929. **$69-$169.** 314 E Highway St. Jct US 87 and 290, 6 blks s. Int corridors. **Pets:** Small. $25 daily fee/pet. Service with restrictions, supervision.
(SAVE) ⊠ 🛢 💻 🏊

AAA **WWW** Comfort Inn & Suites **H**
(830) 990-2552. **$70-$180.** 723 S Washington St. W on Main St, then s. Int corridors. **Pets:** Small. $40 daily fee/pet. Designated rooms, service with restrictions, supervision.
(SAVE) ⊠ 🛢 💻 🏊

AAA **WWW** Dietzel Motel **M** ❀
(830) 997-3330. **$52-$99.** 1141 W US 290. 1 mi w on US 290 at US 87. Ext corridors. **Pets:** Other species. $10 daily fee/pet. Designated rooms, service with restrictions.
(SAVE) ⊠ 🛢 🏊

AAA **WWW** Fredericksburg Econo Lodge **M** ❀
(830) 997-3437. **$49-$109.** 810 S Adams St. Jct US 289 and SR 16 S, 1 mi s. Ext corridors. **Pets:** Other species. $10 daily fee/pet. Service with restrictions, crate.
(SAVE) ⊠ 🛢 💻 🏊

▼▼▼▼ **Fredericksburg Inn & Suites** 🅷 ❀
(830) 997-0202. **$99-$219.** 201 S Washington St. US 290 and 87, 3 blks s. Ext corridors. **Pets:** Small, dogs only. $35 one-time fee/room. Designated rooms, service with restrictions, supervision.
⊠ 🛢 💻 ⇌

▼▼▼▼ **Holiday Inn Express** 🅷
(830) 990-4200. **Call for rates.** 1220 N Hwy 87. 1 mi w on US 290 at US 87. Int corridors. **Pets:** Small, other species. $50 one-time fee/room. Service with restrictions, crate.
⊠ 🕭M 🛢 💻 ⇌

▼▼▼▼ **La Quinta Inn & Suites** 🅷 ❀
(830) 990-2899. **$89-$179.** 1465 E Main St. 1 mi e of downtown. Int corridors. **Pets:** Medium, other species. Service with restrictions, supervision.
🅰🆂🅺 ⊠ 🕭M 🛢 💻 ⇌

▼▼▼ **Quality Inn** 🅷
(830) 997-9811. **$80-$116.** 908 S Adams St. 0.8 mi sw on SR 16; 0.8 mi sw of jct US 87 and 290. Ext corridors. **Pets:** Accepted.
🅰🆂🅺 ⊠ 🛢 💻 ⇌

▼▼▼ **Sunday House Inn & Suites** 🅷
(830) 997-4484. **$99-$229.** 501 E Main St. 0.4 mi e on US 290. Ext corridors. **Pets:** Small. $15 daily fee/pet. Designated rooms, service with restrictions, supervision.
🅰🆂🅺 ⊠ 🛢 💻 ⇌

▲▲▲ ▼ **Sunset Inn** Ⓜ
(830) 997-9581. **$59-$75.** 900 S Adams St. 0.8 mi sw of jct US 290 and SR 16. Ext corridors. **Pets:** Small. Service with restrictions.
🆂🅰🆅🅴 ⊠ 🛢 💻 🍴

▲▲▲ ▼▼ **Super 8 Fredericksburg** Ⓜ
(830) 997-6568. **$63-$90.** 514 E Main St. US 290, just e of jct US 87. Ext corridors. **Pets:** Medium. $10 one-time fee/pet. Service with restrictions, supervision.
🆂🅰🆅🅴 ⊠ 🛢 💻 ⇌

FREER

▲▲▲ ▼◆▼ **Best Western Windwood Inn & Suites** Ⓜ
(361) 394-6200. **$90.** 1172 E Riley St. On US 59 and SR 44. Ext corridors. **Pets:** Accepted.
🆂🅰🆅🅴 ⊠ 🕭M 🛢 💻 ⇌

FULTON

▲▲▲ ▼◆▼ **Best Western Inn by the Bay** Ⓜ
(361) 729-8351. **$100-$161.** 3902 N Hwy 35. SR 35, 0.5 mi n of jct Business Rt SR 35 and FM 3063. Ext corridors. **Pets:** Accepted.
🆂🅰🆅🅴 ⊠ 🕭M 🛢 💻 ⇌

▼◆▼ **The Inn at Fulton Harbor** 🅷
(361) 790-5888. **$99-$275.** 215 N Fulton Beach Rd. Fulton Beach Rd at Cactus St. Ext corridors. **Pets:** Accepted.
🅰🆂🅺 ⊠ 🕭M 🛢 💻 ⇌

GAINESVILLE

▲▲▲ ▼ **Budget Host Inn** Ⓜ
(940) 665-2856. **$42-$50.** 1900 N I-35. I-35, exit 499 northbound; exit 498B southbound. Ext corridors. **Pets:** Accepted.
🆂🅰🆅🅴 ⊠

▲▲▲ ▼◆▼ **La Quinta Inn & Suites** 🅷 ❀
(940) 665-5700. **$79-$159.** 4201 N I-35. I-35, exit 501, just w on FM 1202, then just s on access road. Int corridors. **Pets:** Medium, other species. Service with restrictions, supervision.
🆂🅰🆅🅴 ⊠ 🕭M 🛢 💻 ⇌

▲▲▲ ▼▼ **Rodeway Inn** Ⓜ
(940) 665-7737. **$69-$89, 3 day notice.** 2103 N I-35. I-35, exit 499 northbound, 1.4 mi n on access road to S Frontage Rd; exit 498B southbound. Ext corridors. **Pets:** Small. $10 daily fee/pet. Service with restrictions, supervision.
🆂🅰🆅🅴 ⊠ 🛢 💻 ⇌

▲▲▲ ▼▼ **Super 8** 🅷
(940) 665-5599. **$55-$65.** 1936 I-35 N. I-35, exit 499 northbound, exit 498A southbound. Int corridors. **Pets:** Small. $50 deposit/room, $10 daily fee/pet. Designated rooms, service with restrictions, supervision.
🆂🅰🆅🅴 ⊠ 🛢 💻 ⇌

GALVESTON

▲▲▲ ▼▼▼ **Holiday Inn Resort** 🅷
(409) 740-3581. **Call for rates.** 5002 Seawall Blvd. Just e of jct Seawall Blvd and 53rd St. Ext corridors. **Pets:** Accepted.
🆂🅰🆅🅴 ⊠ 🛢 💻 🍴 ⇌

▼▼▼▼ **La Quinta Inn & Suites** 🅷 ❀
(409) 740-9100. **$59-$229.** 8710 Seawall Blvd. Jct Seawall Blvd and 87th St, just w. Int corridors. **Pets:** Medium, other species. Service with restrictions, supervision.
🅰🆂🅺 ⊠ 🕭M 🛢 💻 ⇌

GATESVILLE

▲▲▲ ▼▼▼ **Best Western Chateau Ville Motor Inn** 🅷
(254) 865-2281. **$76-$86, 14 day notice.** 2501 E Main St. Jct US 84 and SR 36, 0.5 mi w. Ext corridors. **Pets:** Small. Supervision.
🆂🅰🆅🅴 ⊠ 🛢 💻 ⇌

GEORGETOWN

▼▼▼▼ **La Quinta Inn Georgetown** 🅷 ❀
(512) 869-2541. **$69-$119.** 333 I-35 N. I-35, exit 264 northbound; exit 262 southbound; on west frontage road. Ext corridors. **Pets:** Medium, other species. Service with restrictions, supervision.
🅰🆂🅺 ⊠ 🛢 💻 ⇌

GEORGE WEST

▲▲▲ ▼◆▼ **Best Western George West Executive Inn** 🅷 ❀
(361) 449-3300. **$100-$120.** 208 N Nueces St. Just n of US 59 on SR 281. Ext corridors. **Pets:** $25 one-time fee/room. Service with restrictions.
🆂🅰🆅🅴 ⊠ 🛢 💻 ⇌

GIDDINGS

▲▲▲ ▼▼▼ **Executive Inn** Ⓜ
(979) 542-5791. **Call for rates.** 3556 E Austin St. 2 mi e on US 290. Ext corridors. **Pets:** Accepted.
🆂🅰🆅🅴 ⊠ 🛢 💻 ⇌

GLEN ROSE

▲▲▲ ▼◆▼ **Best Western Dinosaur Valley Inn & Suites** 🅷 ❀
(254) 897-4818. **$118-$375.** 1311 NE Big Bend Tr. On US 67. Int corridors. **Pets:** Medium. $5 daily fee/pet, $20 one-time fee/pet. Service with restrictions, supervision.
🆂🅰🆅🅴 ⊠ 🕭M 🛢 💻 ⇌ ⊠

GRANBURY

▲▲▲ ▼▼▼▼ **Best Western Granbury** 🅷
(817) 573-4239. **$110-$212.** 1517 N Plaza Dr. 2.2 mi n of jct SR 144 and US 377 Bypass; on US 377 Bypass. Int corridors. **Pets:** Other species. $25 daily fee/pet. Service with restrictions.
🆂🅰🆅🅴 ⊠ 🕭M 🛢 💻 ⇌

Comfort Inn H
(817) 573-2611. **$90-$140.** 1201 Plaza Dr N. 1.5 mi n of jct SR 144 and US 377 Bypass, on US 377 Bypass. Ext corridors. **Pets:** Small. $15 daily fee/pet. Service with restrictions, supervision.
SAVE X ☎ 💻 🏊

Plantation Inn on the Lake H
(817) 573-8846. **$75-$100.** 1451 E Pearl St. 0.3 mi w of Business Rt US 377 at US 377 Bypass. Ext/int corridors. **Pets:** Medium, dogs only. $10 daily fee/pet. Service with restrictions, supervision.
SAVE X ☎ 💻 🏊

GRAPEVINE

Embassy Suites Outdoor World H
(972) 724-2600. **$139-$299.** 2401 Bass Pro Dr. SR 121, exit Bass Pro Dr. Int corridors. **Pets:** Small. $50 one-time fee/room. Service with restrictions, crate.
SAVE X �CM ☎ 💻 🍴 🏊 ⊠

Homewood Suites by Hilton H
(972) 691-2427. **$134-$169.** 2214 Grapevine Mills Cir W. SR 121 N, exit Bass Pro Dr. Int corridors. **Pets:** Accepted.
X �CM ☎ 💻 🏊 ⊠

Hyatt Regency DFW H
(972) 453-1234. **$99-$399.** 2334 N International Pkwy. In Dallas-Fort Worth International Airport Terminal C area. Int corridors. **Pets:** Accepted.
SAVE X �CM ☎ 💻 🍴 🏊

Super 8 Motel-Grapevine H 🐾
(817) 329-7222. **$84-$104.** 250 E Hwy 114. SR 114, exit Main St. Int corridors. **Pets:** Other species. $10 daily fee/pet. Service with restrictions, supervision.
ASK X �CM ☎ 💻 🏊

GROOM

Chalet Inn M
(806) 248-7524. **$39-$60.** I-40 FM 2300. I-40, exit 113, just s. Ext corridors. **Pets:** Medium. $5 daily fee/pet. Designated rooms, service with restrictions, supervision.
SAVE X �CM

HARLINGEN

Country Inn & Suites By Carlson H
(956) 428-0043. **$85-$125, 3 day notice.** 3825 S Expwy 83. US 83 and 77, exit Ed Carey. Int corridors. **Pets:** Accepted.
ASK X ☎ 💻 🏊

La Quinta Inn Harlingen H 🐾
(956) 428-6888. **$45-$105.** 1002 S Expwy 83. US 83 and 77, exit M St. Ext corridors. **Pets:** Medium, other species. Service with restrictions, supervision.
ASK X �CM ☎ 💻 🏊

Super 8 H
(956) 412-8873. **$56-$100.** 1115 S Expwy 83. US 83 and 77, exit M St, just n. Int corridors. **Pets:** Medium, other species. $10 daily fee/pet. Supervision.
SAVE X ☎ 💻 🏊

HEARNE

Oak Tree Inn H
(979) 279-5599. **$95-$120, 3 day notice.** 1051 N Market St. 0.6 mi n of jct US 79 and SR 6. Ext/int corridors. **Pets:** Small. $10 daily fee/pet. Service with restrictions, supervision.
SAVE X ☎ 💻 🍴

HENDERSON

Best Western Inn of Henderson H
(903) 657-9561. **$79-$119.** 1500 Hwy 259 S. 2 mi s on US 259, 0.7 mi s of jct US 79 and 259 S. Ext/int corridors. **Pets:** Accepted.
SAVE X ☎ 💻 🏊

HEREFORD

Best Western Red Carpet Inn H
(806) 364-0540. **$69-$79.** 830 W 1st St. Just w of jct US 385 and 60. Ext corridors. **Pets:** Small. Service with restrictions, supervision.
SAVE X ☎ 💻 🏊

Holiday Inn Express H
(806) 364-3322. **Call for rates.** 1400 W 1st St. Jct US 385 and 60, just w. Int corridors. **Pets:** Accepted.
X �CM ☎ 💻 🏊

HILLSBORO

Best Western Hillsboro Inn H
(254) 582-8465. **$70-$100.** 307 I-35. I-35, exit 368A northbound; exit 368B southbound, just w. Ext corridors. **Pets:** Other species. $12 daily fee/room. Service with restrictions.
SAVE X ☎ 💻 🏊

Comfort Inn of Hillsboro H
(254) 582-3333. **Call for rates.** 1515 Old Brandon Rd. I-35, exit 368A northbound; exit 368B southbound, just w. Ext corridors. **Pets:** Medium. $20 daily fee/pet. Service with restrictions, supervision.
X �CM ☎ 💻 🏊

Motel 6–4136 H
(254) 580-9000. **Call for rates.** 1506 Hillview Dr. I-35, exit 368 southbound; exit 368A northbound. Int corridors. **Pets:** Other species. Service with restrictions, supervision.
X �CM ☎ 🏊

Super 8 H
(254) 580-0404. **Call for rates.** 1512 Hillview Dr. I-35, exit 368A northbound; 368 southbound, just e. Int corridors. **Pets:** Accepted.
X ☎ 💻 🏊

HONDO

Americas Best Value Inn M
(830) 426-3031. **$40-$90.** 401 Hwy 90 E. Jct SR 173. Ext corridors. **Pets:** Accepted.
SAVE X ☎ 🏊

Hondo Executive Inn M
(830) 426-2535. **$45-$95.** 102 E 19th St. On US 90 W. Ext corridors. **Pets:** $15 one-time fee/pet. Service with restrictions, supervision.
SAVE X ☎ 💻 🏊

HOUSTON METROPOLITAN AREA

BAYTOWN

▼▼▼ Comfort Suites Baytown 🅷
(281) 421-9764. **Call for rates.** 7209 Garth Rd. I-10, exit 792 (Garth Rd), just n. Int corridors. **Pets:** Accepted.
⊠ &M 🛡 🖵 🐾

▼▼ La Quinta Inn Baytown East 🅷 🐾
(281) 421-5566. **$49-$115.** 5215 I-10 E. I-10, exit 792 (Garth Rd). Int corridors. **Pets:** Medium, other species. Service with restrictions, supervision.
A$K ⊠ 🛡 🖵 🐾

CLEVELAND

▼▼ Super 8 Motel 🅷
(281) 432-8800. **Call for rates.** 427 W Southline. US 59, exit SR 105, just e to W Southline, then just s. Int corridors. **Pets:** Accepted.
⊠ 🛡 🖵

CONROE

▼▼▼ La Quinta Inn & Suites 🅷 🐾
(936) 228-0790. **$80-$145.** 4006 Sprayberry Ln. I-45, exit 91 (League Line Rd), just e. Int corridors. **Pets:** Medium, other species. Service with restrictions, supervision.
A$K ⊠ &M 🛡 🖵 🐾

HOUSTON

▼▼ Baymont Inn (I-45 North) 🅷
(281) 444-7500. **Call for rates.** 17111 North Frwy. I-45, exit 66, on southbound service road, 0.4 mi s of jct FM 1960 and I-45. Ext corridors. **Pets:** Other species. Service with restrictions, supervision.
⊠ 🛡 🖵 🐾

ΑΑΑ ▼▼▼ Best Western Westchase Mini Suites 🅷
(713) 782-1515. **$109, 3 day notice.** 2950 W Sam Houston Pkwy S. Just w of Sam Houston Pkwy (Beltway 8) and Westheimer Rd, on southbound frontage road. Int corridors. **Pets:** Small, other species. Service with restrictions, crate.
SAVE ⊠ &M 🛡 🖵 🐾

▼▼ Candlewood Suites Houston by the Galleria 🅷
(713) 839-9411. **$86.** 4900 Loop Central Dr. I-610, exit 7 (Furnace Rd) southbound; exit 7 (Westpark) northbound, on northbound frontage road. Int corridors. **Pets:** Accepted.
A$K ⊠ 🛡 🖵

▼▼▼ Candlewood Suites-Houston-Clear Lake 🅷 🐾
(281) 461-3060. **Call for rates.** 2737 Bay Area Blvd. I-45, exit 26 (Bay Area Blvd), 3.7 mi e. Int corridors. **Pets:** Medium. $75 one-time fee/room. Service with restrictions, crate.
⊠ 🛡 🖵

▼▼▼ Candlewood Suites-Town & Country 🅷
(713) 464-2677. **Call for rates.** 10503 Town & Country Way. I-10, exit 755 eastbound, 1.1 mi on frontage road to Town & Country Blvd, then 0.4 mi s; exit 756A westbound, U-turn under I-10, just e to Town & Country Blvd, then 0.4 mi s. Int corridors. **Pets:** Accepted.
⊠ &M 🛡 🖵

▼▼▼ Candlewood Suites-Westchase 🅷
(713) 780-7881. **Call for rates.** 4033 W Sam Houston Pkwy S. Sam Houston Pkwy (Beltway 8), exit Westpark, southeast corner of Westpark and Sam Houston Pkwy (Beltway 8) on northbound frontage road. Int corridors. **Pets:** Accepted.
⊠ &M 🛡 🖵

▼▼▼ Comfort Suites 🅷
(281) 440-4448. **$89-$94, 3 day notice.** 150 Overland Tr. I-45, exit 66 (FM 1960), on southbound frontage road. Int corridors. **Pets:** Small. $25 one-time fee/pet. Service with restrictions, supervision.
A$K ⊠ &M 🛡 🖵 🐾

ΑΑΑ ▼▼▼ Comfort Suites Galleria 🅷
(713) 787-0004. **$149-$239.** 6221 Richmond Ave. US 59, exit Hillcroft St, 1 mi n to Richmond Ave, then 0.6 mi e. Int corridors. **Pets:** Small. $50 one-time fee/room. Service with restrictions, supervision.
SAVE ⊠ 🛡 🖵 🐾

ΑΑΑ ▼▼▼ Country Inn & Suites Houston at Sugarland 🅷
(281) 498-9000. **$85-$140.** 11230 Southwest Frwy. US 59, exit Murphy Rd/Wilcrest Dr northbound, 1.4 mi n on frontage road, then U-turn under Sam Houston Pkwy (Beltway 8); exit Sam Houston Pkwy (Beltway 8) frontage road southbound, 1 mi on southbound frontage road. Int corridors. **Pets:** $50 daily fee/room. Designated rooms, service with restrictions, supervision.
SAVE ⊠ 🛡 🖵 🐾

▼▼ Crossland Economy Studios Houston-Northwest 🅷
(713) 934-7600. **$50-$80.** 5959 Guhn Rd. US 290, exit Fairbanks, just e on eastbound frontage road, then just s. Ext corridors. **Pets:** Other species. $25 daily fee/pet. Service with restrictions, crate.
A$K ⊠ &M 🛡 🖵

ΑΑΑ ▼▼▼ Crowne Plaza Northwest Hotel 🅷
(713) 462-9977. **$80-$179.** 12801 Northwest Frwy. Nw on US 290, exit Hollister Rd, 0.7 mi e on south service road. Ext/int corridors. **Pets:** Accepted.
SAVE ⊠ 🛡 🖵 🍴 🐾 ⊠

ΑΑΑ ▼▼▼ Crowne Plaza Suites–Houston–Sugarland Southwest 🅷 🐾
(713) 995-0123. **$89-$179.** 9090 Southwest Frwy. US 59, exit Beechnut/Gessner; on southbound frontage road. Int corridors. **Pets:** Medium, other species. $40 one-time fee/room. Designated rooms, service with restrictions, supervision.
SAVE ⊠ 🛡 🖵 🍴 🐾

ΑΑΑ ▼▼▼ DoubleTree Guest Suites Houston by the Galleria 🅷
(713) 961-9000. **$139-$299.** 5353 Westheimer Rd. I-610, exit 8C (Westheimer Rd) northbound; exit 9A (San Felipe Rd/Westheimer Rd) southbound, 0.8 mi w. Int corridors. **Pets:** Medium. $75 one-time fee/room. Designated rooms, service with restrictions, crate.
SAVE ⊠ 🛡 🖵 🍴 🐾 ⊠

▼▼▼ DoubleTree Houston Downtown 🅷
(713) 759-0202. **$119-$359.** 400 Dallas St. At Dallas and Bagby sts. Int corridors. **Pets:** Accepted.
⊠ 🛡 🖵 🍴

▼▼▼ Drury Inn & Suites-Houston Hobby 🅷
(713) 941-4300. **$80-$150.** 7902 Mosley Rd. I-45, exit 36 (Airport Blvd/College Rd) northbound, just w on Airport Blvd, then just n; exit southbound, follow frontage road to Mosley Rd. Int corridors. **Pets:** Other species. Service with restrictions, supervision.
A$K ⊠ &M 🛡 🖵 🐾

▼▼▼ Drury Inn & Suites-Houston Near the Galleria 🅷
(713) 963-0700. **$80-$211.** 1615 W Loop S. I-610, exit 9 (San Felipe Rd) northbound; exit 9A (San Felipe Rd/Westheimer Rd) southbound, on east service road. Int corridors. **Pets:** Other species. Service with restrictions, supervision.
A$K ⊠ &M 🛡 🖵 🐾

▼▼▼ Drury Inn & Suites-Houston West H

(281) 558-7007. **$80-$151.** 1000 N Hwy 6. I-10, exit 751 (Addicks Rd/SR 6), just n on SR 6. Int corridors. **Pets:** Other species. Service with restrictions, supervision.

[ASK] [X] [🛏] [▣] [🌊]

▼▼ Extended StayAmerica Houston-Greenway Plaza H

(713) 521-0060. **$75-$109.** 2330 Southwest Frwy. US 59, exit Greenbriar/ Shephard; on southbound frontage road. Int corridors. **Pets:** Other species. $25 daily fee/pet. Service with restrictions, crate.

[ASK] [X] [🛏] [▣]

▼◆ Extended Stay Deluxe Houston Medical Center/Reliant Park H

(713) 790-9753. **$80-$189.** 1303 La Concha. I-610, exit 1C (Kirby Dr), just n. Int corridors. **Pets:** Other species. $25 daily fee/pet. Service with restrictions, crate.

[ASK] [X] [🛏] [▣] [🌊]

▼▼ Extended Stay Deluxe Houston-Northwest H

(713) 895-0965. **$75-$109.** 5454 Hollister St. US 290, exit Tidwell/Hollister, just s. Int corridors. **Pets:** Other species. $25 daily fee/pet. Service with restrictions, crate.

[ASK] [X] [🛏] [▣] [🌊]

◆◆ ▼▼▼ Four Seasons Hotel Houston H 🐾

(713) 650-1300. **$350-$850.** 1300 Lamar St. Lamar and Austin sts. Int corridors. **Pets:** Small. Designated rooms, service with restrictions, crate.

[SAVE] [X] [🛏] [▣] [🍴] [🌊] [X]

◆◆ ▼▼▼ ▼▼ Hilton Americas-Houston H 🐾

(713) 739-8000. **$129-$386.** 1600 Lamar St. At George R Brown Convention Center; between Crawford and Avenida De Las Americas. Int corridors. **Pets:** Medium. $75 one-time fee/room. Service with restrictions, supervision.

[SAVE] [X] [♿] [🛏] [▣] [🍴] [🌊] [X]

◆◆ ▼▼▼ ▼▼ Hilton Houston Post Oak H 🐾

(713) 961-9300. **$139-$329.** 2001 Post Oak Blvd. I-610, exit 8C (Westheimer Rd) northbound, just w; exit 9A (San Felipe Rd/Westheimer Rd) southbound; between San Felipe and Westheimer rds. Int corridors. **Pets:** Large. $35 one-time fee/room. Service with restrictions, supervision.

[SAVE] [X] [🛏] [▣] [🍴] [🌊]

◆◆ ▼▼▼ Hilton Houston Southwest H

(713) 977-7911. **$179-$289.** 6780 Southwest Frwy. US 59, exit Hillcroft St, on southbound frontage road. Int corridors. **Pets:** Accepted.

[SAVE] [X] [🛏] [▣] [🍴] [🌊] [X]

◆◆ ▼▼▼ Holiday Inn Astrodome at Reliant Park H

(713) 790-1900. **$120-$180.** 8111 Kirby Dr. I-610, exit 1C (Kirby Dr), 0.3 mi n. Int corridors. **Pets:** Accepted.

[SAVE] [X] [🛏] [▣] [🍴] [🌊]

◆◆ ▼▼▼ Holiday Inn Express-FM 1960 H

(281) 444-5800. **$79-$168, 7 day notice.** 3555 FM 1960 W. I-45, exit 66 (FM 1960), 3.5 mi w. Int corridors. **Pets:** Large. $40 one-time fee/room. Service with restrictions, supervision.

[SAVE] [X] [▣] [🌊]

◆◆ ▼▼▼ Holiday Inn Express Hotel & Suites-Intercontinental H

(281) 372-1000. **$135.** 1330 N Sam Houston Pkwy E. Off Sam Houston Pkwy (Beltway 8), exit Aldine Westfield eastbound, 0.8 mi e on service road; exit Hardy Toll Rd westbound, U-turn, then 1 mi e on service road. Int corridors. **Pets:** Accepted.

[SAVE] [X] [🛏] [▣] [🌊]

◆◆ ▼▼▼ Holiday Inn Express Hotel & Suites Memorial Area H

(713) 688-2800. **$128-$171.** 7625 Katy Frwy. I-10, exit 762 (Silber Rd), on eastbound frontage road. Int corridors. **Pets:** Small. $25 one-time fee/pet. Service with restrictions, supervision.

[SAVE] [X] [♿] [🛏] [▣] [🌊]

◆◆◆ ▼▼▼ Holiday Inn Houston Hobby Airport H

(713) 946-8900. **$129-$169, 3 day notice.** 8611 Airport Blvd. I-45, exit 36 (Airport Blvd), 1.3 mi w. Int corridors. **Pets:** Medium. $50 one-time fee/pet. Service with restrictions, crate.

[SAVE] [X] [🛏] [▣] [🍴] [🌊]

▼▼▼ Holiday Inn Houston Intercontinental Airport H

(281) 449-2311. **$99-$209.** 15222 John F Kennedy Blvd. Jct N Sam Houston Pkwy (Beltway 8) E and John F Kennedy Blvd. Int corridors. **Pets:** Accepted.

[ASK] [X] [🛏] [▣] [🍴] [🌊] [X]

▼▼ Homestead Studio Suites Hotel-Houston/Galleria Area H

(713) 960-9660. **$85-$155.** 2300 W Loop S. Loop 610, exit 9A (San Felipe Rd) southbound; exit 9 (San Felipe Rd) northbound, on southbound frontage road. Int corridors. **Pets:** Other species. $25 daily fee/pet. Service with restrictions, crate.

[ASK] [X] [🛏] [▣]

▼▼▼ Homewood Suites by Hilton Intercontinental H

(281) 219-9100. **$89-$174.** 1340 N Sam Houston Pkwy E. Sam Houston Pkwy (Beltway 8), exit Aldine Westfield eastbound, 0.8 mi e on frontage road; exit Hardy Toll Rd westbound, U-turn, then 1 mi e on frontage road. Int corridors. **Pets:** Accepted.

[X] [♿] [🛏] [▣] [🌊] [X]

▼▼▼ Homewood Suites by Hilton-Westchase H

(713) 334-2424. **$119-$199.** 2424 Rogerdale Rd. Sam Houston Pkwy (Beltway 8), exit Westheimer Rd, just w to Rogerdale Rd, then just n. Int corridors. **Pets:** Small, other species. $175 one-time fee/pet. Supervision.

[X] [♿] [🛏] [▣] [🌊] [X]

▼▼▼ Homewood Suites by Hilton-Willowbrook H

(281) 955-5200. **$119-$199.** 7655 W FM 1960. Just e of jct SR 249 and FM 1960. Int corridors. **Pets:** Accepted.

[X] [♿] [▣] [🌊]

◆◆◆ ▼▼▼ Hotel Icon H

(713) 224-4266. **$99-$2050.** 220 Main St. Between Travis and Main sts; entrance on Congress St. Int corridors. **Pets:** Accepted.

[SAVE] [X] [🛏] [▣] [🍴]

▼▼ ▼▼ Hotel Za Za Houston Museum District H 🐾

(713) 526-1991. **$199-$2500.** 5701 Main St. US 59, exit Main St northbound, 0.5 mi s; exit Fannin southbound, 0.5 mi s to Ewing, then just w. Int corridors. **Pets:** Other species. $75 one-time fee/room. Crate.

[X] [♿] [🛏] [🍴] [🌊] [X]

▼▼▼ Houston Marriott Medical Center Hotel H

(713) 796-0080. **$279-$289.** 6580 Fannin St. I-610, exit 2 (Main St), 2.5 mi ne to Holcombe St, 0.3 mi e, then just n. Int corridors. **Pets:** Accepted.

[X] [♿] [🛏] [▣] [🍴] [🌊] [X]

▼▼▼ La Quinta Inn H 🐾

(713) 680-8282. **$49-$125.** 11130 Northwest Frwy. US 290 W, exit W 34th St, on southeast corner. Int corridors. **Pets:** Medium, other species. Service with restrictions, supervision.

[ASK] [X] [🛏] [▣] [🌊]

◆◆◆ ▼▼▼ La Quinta Inn & Suites H 🐾

(281) 784-1112. **Call for rates.** 415 FM 1960. I-45, exit 66 (FM 1960), just e. Int corridors. **Pets:** Medium, other species. Service with restrictions, supervision.

[SAVE] [X] [🛏] [▣] [🌊]

▼▼▼ La Quinta Inn & Suites Houston (Bush Intercontinental Airport) H 🐾

(281) 219-2000. **$59-$179.** 15510 John F Kennedy Blvd. Sam Houston Pkwy (Beltway 8), exit John F Kennedy Blvd/Vickery, just n. Int corridors. **Pets:** Medium, other species. Service with restrictions, supervision.

[ASK] [X] [♿] [🛏] [🌊]

▼▼▼▼ **La Quinta Inn & Suites Houston (Galleria Area)** 🏠 ❀
(713) 355-3440. **$69-$185.** 1625 W Loop S. I-610, exit 9 (San Felipe Rd) northbound; exit 9A (San Felipe Rd/Westheimer Rd) southbound, on northbound service road. Int corridors. **Pets:** Medium, other species. Service with restrictions, supervision.
(ASK) ⊠ 🗄 💻 🐾

▼▼▼▼ **La Quinta Inn & Suites Houston Hobby Airport** 🏠 ❀
(713) 490-1008. **$69-$159.** 8776 Airport Blvd. I-45, exit 36 (Airport/ College), 1.3 mi w. Int corridors. **Pets:** Medium, other species. Service with restrictions, supervision.
(ASK) ⊠ 🗄 💻 🐾

🔷 ▼▼▼▼ **La Quinta Inn & Suites Houston North Beltway** 🏠 ❀
(832) 554-5000. **$59-$159.** 10137 North Frwy. I-45, exit 59 (West Rd), on southbound frontage road. Int corridors. **Pets:** Medium, other species. Service with restrictions, supervision.
(SAVE) ⊠ 🗄 💻 🐾

▼▼▼▼ **La Quinta Inn & Suites Houston (Park 10)** 🏠 ❀
(281) 646-9200. **$65-$139.** 15225 Katy Frwy. I-10, exit 748 (Barker Cypress Rd) eastbound, 2.6 mi on eastbound service road; exit 751 (SR 6) westbound, just s to Grisby Rd, then 0.5 mi w. Int corridors. **Pets:** Medium, other species. Service with restrictions, supervision.
(ASK) ⊠ 🗄 💻 🐾

▼▼▼▼ **La Quinta Inn & Suites Westchase** 🏠 ❀
(281) 495-7700. **$79-$149.** 10850 Harwin Dr. Sam Houston Pkwy (Beltway 8), exit Bellaire/Harwin northbound; exit Westpark/Harwin southbound. Int corridors. **Pets:** Medium, other species. Service with restrictions, supervision.
(ASK) ⊠ 🗄 💻 🐾

▼▼▼▼ **La Quinta Inn & Suites–Willowbrook** 🏠 ❀
(281) 897-8868. **$79-$183.** 18828 State Hwy 249 (Tomball Pkwy). SR 249, exit Grant/Schroeder; on northbound frontage road. Int corridors. **Pets:** Medium, other species. Service with restrictions, supervision.
(ASK) ⊠ 🐾 🗄 💻 🐾

▼▼ ▼▼ **La Quinta Inn Houston (Cyfair)** 🏠 ❀
(281) 469-4018. **$59-$125.** 13290 FM 1960 W. Just w of jct US 290 and FM 1960. Ext corridors. **Pets:** Medium, other species. Service with restrictions, supervision.
(ASK) ⊠ 🗄 💻 🐾

▼▼ ▼▼ **La Quinta Inn Houston (East)** 🏠 ❀
(713) 453-5425. **$45-$105.** 11999 East Frwy. I-10, exit 778A (Federal Rd) eastbound; exit 776B (Holland Ave) westbound, just n. Ext corridors. **Pets:** Medium, other species. Service with restrictions, supervision.
(ASK) ⊠ 🗄 💻 🐾

▼▼ ▼▼ **La Quinta Inn Houston (Wilcrest)** 🏠 ❀
(713) 932-0808. **$49-$109.** 11113 Katy Frwy. I-10, exit 754 (Kirkwood Dr) westbound; exit 755 (Wilcrest Rd) eastbound, on eastbound service road. Ext corridors. **Pets:** Medium, other species. Service with restrictions, supervision.
(ASK) ⊠ 🗄 💻 🐾

🔷 ▼▼▼▼ **Marriott Houston Hobby Airport** 🏠
(713) 943-7979. **$170-$208.** 9100 Gulf Frwy. I-45, exit 36 (Airport Blvd/ College Rd) southbound; exit 38 (Monroe) northbound, on southbound frontage road. Int corridors. **Pets:** Accepted.
(SAVE) ⊠ 🗄 💻 🍴 🐾

🔷 ▼▼▼▼ **Omni Houston Hotel** 🏠
(713) 871-8181. **$324-$459.** Four Riverway. I-610, exit 10 (Woodway Dr), 0.3 mi w. Int corridors. **Pets:** Accepted.
(SAVE) ⊠ 🗄 💻 🍴 🐾 ⊠

🔷 ▼▼▼▼ **Omni Houston Hotel Westside** 🏠 ❀
(281) 558-8338. **$119-$339.** 13210 Katy Frwy. I-10, exit 753A (Eldridge St), just n. Int corridors. **Pets:** Small. $50 one-time fee/pet. Service with restrictions, crate.
(SAVE) ⊠ 🗄 💻 🍴 🐾

🔷 ▼▼▼▼ **Renaissance Houston Hotel Greenway Plaza** 🏠
(713) 629-1200. **$279-$289.** 6 Greenway Plaza E. US 59 (Southwest Frwy), exit Buffalo Speedway. Int corridors. **Pets:** Small. Service with restrictions, supervision.
(SAVE) ⊠ 🗄 💻 🍴 🐾 ⊠

▼▼▼▼ **Residence Inn by Marriott** 🏠
(832) 366-1000. **$260-$318.** 904 Dallas St. At Main St. Int corridors. **Pets:** Small, other species. $100 one-time fee/pet. Service with restrictions, crate.
⊠ 🐾 🗄 💻 🐾

▼▼▼▼ **Residence Inn by Marriott Houston by the Galleria** 🏠
(713) 840-9757. **$189-$231.** 2500 McCue Rd. I-610, exit 8C (Westheimer Rd) northbound; exit 9A (San Felipe Rd/Westheimer Rd) southbound, just w to McCue, then just n. Ext/int corridors. **Pets:** Accepted.
⊠ 🗄 💻 🐾

▼▼▼▼ **Residence Inn by Marriott Houston Westchase** 🏠
(713) 974-5454. **$197-$241.** 9965 Westheimer Rd. Sam Houston Pkwy (Beltway 8), exit Westheimer Rd, 0.7 mi e to Elmside Dr, then just s. Int corridors. **Pets:** Accepted.
⊠ 🗄 💻 🐾 ⊠

▼▼▼▼ **Residence Inn by Marriott-Medical Center/Reliant Park** 🏠
(713) 660-7993. **$179-$219.** 7710 Main St. I-610, exit 2 (S Main St/Buffalo Speedway), 1.5 mi n. Ext corridors. **Pets:** Accepted.
⊠ 🗄 💻 🐾 ⊠

▼▼▼▼ **Residence Inn by Marriott-West University** 🏠 ❀
(713) 661-4660. **$224-$274.** 2939 Westpark Dr. US 59, exit Kirby Dr, just s, then just w. Int corridors. **Pets:** Other species. $100 one-time fee/room. Service with restrictions, crate.
⊠ 🐾 🗄 💻 🐾 ⊠

▼▼▼▼ **Residence Inn by Marriott Willowbrook** 🏠
(832) 237-2002. **$180-$220.** 7311 W Greens Rd. SR 249, exit Greens Rd, just e. Int corridors. **Pets:** Accepted.
⊠ 🗄 💻 🐾 ⊠

▼▼▼▼ **Residence Inn-Houston Clear Lake** 🏠
(281) 486-2424. **$189-$199.** 525 Bay Area Blvd. I-45 S, exit 26 (Bay Area Blvd), 1.2 mi e. Ext/int corridors. **Pets:** Medium. $100 one-time fee/room. Supervision.
⊠ 🗄 💻 🐾 ⊠

🔷 ▼▼▼▼ **The St. Regis, Houston** 🏠 ❀
(713) 840-7600. **$245-$615.** 1919 Briar Oaks Ln. I-610, exit 9A (San Felipe Rd/Westheimer Rd), 0.3 mi e. Int corridors. **Pets:** Medium, dogs only. Supervision.
(SAVE) ⊠ 🗄 💻 🍴 🐾 ⊠

🔷 ▼▼▼▼ **Sheraton Houston Brookhollow** 🏠 ❀
(713) 688-0100. **$99-$300, 3 day notice.** 3000 N Loop W. I-610, exit 13C (TC Jester Blvd), on southbound frontage road. Int corridors. **Pets:** Other species. Service with restrictions.
(SAVE) ⊠ 🐾 🗄 💻 🍴 🐾 ⊠

🔷 ▼▼▼▼ **Sheraton North Houston Hotel** 🏠 ❀
(281) 442-5100. **Call for rates.** 15700 John F Kennedy Blvd. Sam Houston Pkwy (Beltway 8), exit John F Kennedy Blvd, just n. Int corridors. **Pets:** Medium. Service with restrictions, crate.
(SAVE) ⊠ 🐾 🗄 💻 🍴 🐾

Sheraton Suites Houston Near The Galleria H
(713) 586-2444. **Call for rates.** 2400 W Loop S. I-610, exit 9 (San Felipe Rd) northbound; exit 9A (San Felipe Rd/Westheimer Rd) southbound. Int corridors. **Pets:** Accepted.
[SAVE] [X] 🛁 💻 ¶¶ ➾

Staybridge Suites Houston-Near The Galleria H
(713) 355-8888. **$190-$195.** 5190 Hidalgo St. I-610, exit 9A (San Felipe Rd/Westheimer Rd) southbound; exit 8C (Westheimer Rd) northbound, 0.4 mi w to Sage Rd, then just s. Int corridors. **Pets:** Accepted.
[ASK] [X] 🔚 🛁 💻 ➾

TownePlace Suites by Marriott-Central H
(713) 690-4035. **$122-$149.** 12820 Northwest Frwy (US 290). US 290, exit Bingle/43rd St eastbound; exit Bingle/Pinemont/43rd St westbound, on westbound feeder. Int corridors. **Pets:** Accepted.
[X] 🔚 🛁 💻 ⊠

TownePlace Suites by Marriott-West H
(281) 646-0058. **$122-$149.** 15155 Katy Frwy. I-10, exit 751, just s on SR 6 to Grisby Rd, then w. Int corridors. **Pets:** Accepted.
[X] 🛁 💻 ➾

The Westin Galleria, Houston H
(713) 960-8100. **$189-$429.** 5060 W Alabama St. I-610, exit 8C (Westheimer Rd) northbound; exit 9A (San Felipe Rd/Westheimer Rd) southbound, 0.5 mi w on Westheimer Rd to Sage, just s, then just e. Int corridors. **Pets:** Accepted.
[SAVE] [X] 🔚 💻 ¶¶ ➾

The Westin Oaks, Houston H
(713) 960-8100. **Call for rates.** 5011 Westheimer Rd. I-610, exit 8C (Westheimer Rd) northbound; exit 9A (San Felipe Rd/Westheimer Rd) southbound, just w. Int corridors. **Pets:** Accepted.
[SAVE] [X] 💻 ¶¶ ➾

KATY

La Quinta Inn & Suites Katy H 🐾
(281) 392-9800. **$109-$189.** 22455 Katy Frwy (I-10). I-10, exit 743 (Grand Pkwy), on eastbound service road. Int corridors. **Pets:** Medium, other species. Service with restrictions, supervision.
[SAVE] [X] 🔚 🛁 💻 ➾

MONTGOMERY

Best Western Lake Conroe H
(936) 588-3030. **$80-$110.** 14643 Hwy 105 W. I-45, exit SR 105, 8.1 mi w. Ext corridors. **Pets:** Small. $25 daily fee/pet. Service with restrictions, crate.
[SAVE] [X] 🛁 💻 ➾

NASSAU BAY

Hilton Houston NASA Clear Lake H
(281) 333-9300. **$100-$210.** 3000 NASA Pkwy. I-45, exit 25 (NASA Rd One), 3.8 mi e. Int corridors. **Pets:** Accepted.
[X] 🛁 💻 ¶¶ ➾ ⊠

ROSENBERG

La Quinta Inn and Suites H 🐾
(832) 595-6111. **$80-$170.** 28332 Southwest Frwy. Jct US 59 and SR 36; on southbound Frontage Rd. Int corridors. **Pets:** Medium, other species. Service with restrictions, supervision.
[ASK] [X] 🛁 💻 ➾

SEABROOK

La Quinta Inn & Suites #618 H 🐾
(281) 326-7300. **$79-$229.** 3636 NASA Pkwy. I-45, exit 25 (NASA Rd One), 6 mi e; SR 146, 2 mi w. Int corridors. **Pets:** Medium, other species. Service with restrictions, supervision.
[ASK] [X] 🛁 💻 ➾

STAFFORD

La Quinta Inn Houston (Stafford/Sugarland) H 🐾
(281) 240-2300. **$59-$129.** 12727 Southwest Frwy. US 59 eastbound service road, exit Corporate Dr southbound; exit Airport Blvd/Kirkwood Rd northbound. Int corridors. **Pets:** Medium, other species. Service with restrictions, supervision.
[ASK] [X] 🛁 💻 ➾

Residence Inn by Marriott Houston/Sugar Land H
(281) 277-0770. **$162-$198.** 12703 Southwest Frwy. US 59, exit 90 (Corporate Dr) southbound; exit Airport Blvd/Kirkwood Rd northbound; on northbound service road. Int corridors. **Pets:** Accepted.
[X] 🛁 💻 ➾ ⊠

SUGAR LAND

Drury Inn & Suites-Houston/Sugar Land H
(281) 277-9700. **$85-$155.** 13770 Southwest Frwy. Sw on US 59, exit Dairy Ashford/Sugar Creek southbound; exit Dairy Ashford/Sugar Creek northbound, left under US 59. Int corridors. **Pets:** Other species. Service with restrictions, supervision.
[ASK] [X] 🛁 💻 ➾

THE WOODLANDS

Drury Inn & Suites-Houston/The Woodlands H
(281) 362-7222. **$90-$160.** 28099 I-45 N. I-45, exit 76 southbound; exit 77 northbound, on west service road. Int corridors. **Pets:** Other species. Service with restrictions, supervision.
[ASK] [X] 🔚 🛁 💻 ➾

Holiday Inn Express Hotel & Suites H
(281) 681-8088. **$109.** 24888 I-45 N. I-45, exit 73 (Rayford/Sawdust Rd), on northbound access road. Int corridors. **Pets:** Accepted.
[SAVE] [X] 🛁 💻 ➾ ⊠

Residence Inn by Marriott H
(281) 292-3252. **$153-$187.** 1040 Lake Front Cir. I-45, exit 78 southbound; exit 79 (SR 242) northbound, 0.8 mi s of jct I-45 and Research Forest Dr, just w. Int corridors. **Pets:** Accepted.
[X] 🛁 💻 ➾ ⊠

TOMBALL

Super 8 H
(281) 351-4114. **$94-$119.** 1437 Keefer St. SR 249 and FM 2920; northeast corner. Ext corridors. **Pets:** Medium. $25 one-time fee/pet. Designated rooms, service with restrictions, supervision.
[SAVE] [X] 🛁 💻 ➾

WEBSTER

Extended Stay Deluxe Houston NASA-Bay Area Blvd H
(281) 338-7711. **$95-$144.** 720 W Bay Area Blvd. I-45, exit 26 (Bay Area Blvd), just e. Int corridors. **Pets:** Other species. $25 daily fee/pet. Service with restrictions, crate.
[ASK] [X] 🛁 💻 ➾

La Quinta Inn & Suites Webster H 🐾
(281) 554-5290. **$89-$159.** 520 W Bay Area Blvd. I-45, exit 26 (Bay Area Blvd), just e. Int corridors. **Pets:** Medium, other species. Service with restrictions, supervision.
[ASK] [X] 🛁 💻 ➾

Super 8-Houston-Webster-NASA M
(281) 333-5385. **$70-$150, 3 day notice.** 18103 Kingsrow Rd. I-45, exit 25 (NASA Rd One), 1.5 mi e. Ext corridors. **Pets:** Medium. $25 daily fee/pet. Designated rooms, service with restrictions, supervision.
[SAVE] [X] 🛁 💻 ➾

WINNIE

▼▼ Days Inn & Suites ⊞
(409) 296-2866. **$59-$149.** 14932 FM 1663. I-10, exit 829, just n. Ext corridors. **Pets:** Small. $25 daily fee/pet. Service with restrictions, supervision.
ASK ✕ 🖶 💻 ⊇

▲▲▲ ▼▼▼ Winnie Inn & Suites ⊞
(409) 296-2947. **$50-$90.** 205 Spur 5, Hwy 124. I-10, exit 829, just s. Ext corridors. **Pets:** Accepted.
SAVE ✕ 🖶 💻 ⊇

END METROPOLITAN AREA

HUNTSVILLE

▼▼▼ Holiday Inn Express (Sam Houston) ⊞
(936) 293-8800. **Call for rates.** 201 W Hill Park Cir. I-45, exit 116, just w on US 190. Ext corridors. **Pets:** Accepted.
✕ 🅜 🖶 💻 ⊇

▼▼▼ La Quinta Inn Huntsville ⊞ 🐾
(936) 295-6454. **$59-$109.** 124 I-45 N. I-45, exit 116. Ext corridors. **Pets:** Medium, other species. Service with restrictions, supervision.
ASK ✕ 🖶 💻 ⊇

INGLESIDE

▲▲▲ ▼▼▼ Best Western Naval Station Inn ⊞
(361) 776-2767. **$75-$125.** 2025 State Hwy 361. 1 mi e of jct SR 1069. Ext corridors. **Pets:** Accepted.
SAVE ✕ 🖶 💻 ⊇

JACKSONVILLE

▼▼▼ Holiday Inn Express ⊞
(903) 589-8500. **Call for rates.** 1848 S Jackson St. On US 69, 2 mi s of jct US 69 and 79. Int corridors. **Pets:** Accepted.
✕ 🅜 🖶 💻 ⊇

JASPER

▲▲▲ ▼▼ Econo Lodge Ⓜ
(409) 384-2511. **$70.** 612 W Gibson St. US 190 and SR 63, 1.2 mi w of jct US 96. Ext corridors. **Pets:** Small. $35 deposit/pet, $12 daily fee/pet. Service with restrictions, supervision.
SAVE ✕ 🖶 ⊇

▼▼▼ Super 8 Motel ⊞
(409) 384-8600. **Call for rates.** 2100 N Wheeler. US 96, 1.8 mi n of jct US 190. Ext corridors. **Pets:** Accepted.
✕ 🖶 💻 ⊇

JUNCTION

▼▼ Days Inn ⊞
(325) 446-3730. **Call for rates.** 111 S Martinez St. I-10, exit 457, 0.3 mi s. Ext corridors. **Pets:** Accepted.
✕ 🖶 💻 ⊇

▲▲▲ ▼▼▼ Econo Lodge Ⓜ
(325) 446-2475. **$44-$79.** 311 S Segovia Access Rd. I-10, exit 465; on south access road. Ext corridors. **Pets:** Accepted.
SAVE ✕ 🖶 💻 ⊇

▼▼ The Hills Motel Ⓜ
(325) 446-2567. **Call for rates.** 1520 Main St. I-10, exit 456, 1.3 mi s on US 377. Ext corridors. **Pets:** Accepted.
✕ 🖶 ⊇

▼▼ Rodeway Inn ⊞
(325) 446-4588. **$55-$69.** 2343 N Main St. I-10, exit 456, just s on US 377. Ext corridors. **Pets:** Small, other species. $10 one-time fee/room. Service with restrictions, supervision.
ASK ✕ 🖶 💻 ⊇

▼▼ Sun Valley Motel Ⓜ
(325) 446-2505. **Call for rates.** 1611 Main St. I-10, exit 456 eastbound, 1 mi s on US 377; exit 460 westbound, 3 mi w on Loop 481 to jct US 377, then just n. Ext corridors. **Pets:** Medium. $5 daily fee/pet. Designated rooms, no service, crate.
✕ 🖶 ⊇

KERRVILLE

▲▲▲ ▼▼▼ Best Western Sunday House Inn ⊞
(830) 896-1313. **$80-$105.** 2124 Sidney Baker St. I-10, exit 508 (SR 16), just s. Ext corridors. **Pets:** Medium. $10 daily fee/pet. Designated rooms, service with restrictions, supervision.
SAVE ✕ 💻 🍴 ⊇

▼▼ Days Inn of Kerrville Ⓜ
(830) 896-1000. **$79-$149.** 2000 Sidney Baker St. I-10, exit 508 (SR 16), 0.5 mi s. Ext/int corridors. **Pets:** Accepted.
ASK ✕ 🖶 💻 ⊇

▲▲▲ ▼▼▼ Y. O. Ranch Resort Hotel & Conference Center ⊞
(830) 257-4440. **$109-$119.** 2033 Sidney Baker St. I-10, exit 508 (SR 16), 0.3 mi s. Ext/int corridors. **Pets:** Other species. $50 deposit/room. Service with restrictions, supervision.
SAVE ✕ 🖶 💻 🍴 ⊇ ✕

KILGORE

▲▲▲ ▼▼▼ Best Western Inn of Kilgore ⊞
(903) 986-1195. **$80-$120.** 1411 N Hwy 259. I-20, exit 589, 3.9 mi s. Ext corridors. **Pets:** Medium, dogs only. $20 one-time fee/pet. Service with restrictions, supervision.
SAVE ✕ 🖶 💻 ⊇

KILLEEN

▲▲▲ ▼▼▼ Holiday Inn Express ⊞
(254) 554-2727. **$70-$99.** 1602 E Central Texas Expwy. US 190, exit Trimmier Rd. Ext corridors. **Pets:** Large, other species. Service with restrictions, crate.
SAVE ✕ 🖶 💻

▼▼ La Quinta Inn Killeen ⊞ 🐾
(254) 526-8331. **$59-$109.** 1112 S Fort Hood St. US 190, exit Fort Hood St, on westbound access road. Ext corridors. **Pets:** Medium, other species. Service with restrictions, supervision.
ASK ✕ 🖶 💻 ⊇

▼▼▼ Residence Inn by Marriott ⊞
(254) 634-1020. **$125-$153.** 400 E Central Texas Expwy. US 190, exit Ft. Hood/Jasper (SR 195) on S Frontage Rd. Int corridors. **Pets:** Small. $100 one-time fee/pet. Service with restrictions.
✕ 🅜 🖶 💻 ⊇ ✕

▲▲▲ ▼▼▼▼ Shilo Inn Suites Hotel Killeen ⊞ 🐾
(254) 699-0999. **$125-$215.** 3701 S W S Young Dr. US 190, exit W S Young Dr, 1 mi s. Int corridors. **Pets:** Dogs only. $25 one-time fee/room. Designated rooms, service with restrictions, supervision.
SAVE ✕ 🅜 🖶 💻 🍴 ⊇ ✕

▼▼▼▼ **TownePlace Suites by Marriott** 🅗
(254) 554-8899. **$89-$109.** 2401 Florence Rd. US 190, exit Trimmer Rd to Jasper, on south access road go 1 blk e to Florence Rd, then just s. Int corridors. **Pets:** Medium, other species. $100 one-time fee/room. Service with restrictions, crate.
⊠ 🔊 🖪 🖵 🕬

KINGSVILLE

🔷 ▼▼▼ **Quality Inn** 🅗
(361) 592-5251. **$69-$89, 4 day notice.** 221 S Hwy 77 Bypass. On US 77, just s of jct SR 141. Ext corridors. **Pets:** Accepted.
ᔕᐯᕮ ⊠ 🖪 🖵 🕬

🔷 ▼▼▼ **Rodeway Inn** 🅗
(361) 595-5753. **$64-$69.** 3430 Hwy 77. 4.5 mi s on US 77. Ext corridors. **Pets:** Accepted.
ᔕᐯᕮ ⊠ 🖪 🖵 🕬

🔷 ▼▼▼ **Super 8** Ⓜ
(361) 592-6471. **$65-$90.** 105 S US Hwy 77 Bypass. 0.8 mi e on US 77. Ext corridors. **Pets:** Small. $20 one-time fee/pet. No service, supervision.
ᔕᐯᕮ ⊠ 🖪 🕬

LA GRANGE

🔷 ▼▼▼▼ **Best Western La Grange Inn and Suites** 🅗
(979) 968-6800. **Call for rates.** 600 E State Hwy 71 Bypass. Jct US 77 and SR 71, just e on N Frontage Rd. Int corridors. **Pets:** Medium. $15 daily fee/room. Crate.
ᔕᐯᕮ ⊠ 🖪 🖵 🕬

LAJITAS

▼▼▼ **Lajitas Resort and Spa** 🅗
(432) 424-5000. **Call for rates.** 1 Main St. Center. Ext/int corridors. **Pets:** $50 one-time fee/pet. Service with restrictions.
⊠ 🖪 🖵 🕬 🕬 ⊠

LAKE JACKSON

▼▼▼ **Cherotel Brazosport Hotel & Conference Center** 🅗
(979) 297-1161. **Call for rates.** 925 Hwy 332. On SR 228/332, just w of jct Business Rt SR 288. Int corridors. **Pets:** Accepted.
⊠ 🖪 🖵 🕬 🕬

LAMESA

🔷 ▼▼▼ **Shiloh Inn** Ⓜ
(806) 872-6721. **$63-$79, 3 day notice.** 1707 Lubbock Hwy. Jct US 87 and 180, 1 mi n. Ext corridors. **Pets:** Other species. $12 daily fee/pet. No service, supervision.
ᔕᐯᕮ ⊠ 🖪 🖵 🕬 🕬

LAREDO

▼▼ **Americas Best Value Inn** Ⓜ
(956) 723-3603. **$65-$85.** 5240 San Bernardo Ave. I-35, exit 3B (Mann Rd), on southbound access road. Ext corridors. **Pets:** Large. $20 one-time fee/pet. No service, supervision.
ⒶSK ⊠ 🖪 🕬

▼▼ **Days Inn & Suites** 🅗
(956) 724-8221. **$60-$159.** 7060 N San Bernardo Ave. I-35, exit 4 (San Bernardo Ave), just s on southbound access road. Ext/int corridors. **Pets:** Small. $10 daily fee/pet. Service with restrictions, supervision.
ⒶSK ⊠ 🖪 🖵 🕬 🕬

▼▼ **Extended StayAmerica Laredo-Del Mar** 🅗
(956) 724-1920. **$60-$92.** 106 W Village. I-35, exit 3B (Mann Rd), just n on northbound access road to W Village, then just e. Int corridors. **Pets:** Other species. $25 daily fee/pet. Service with restrictions, crate.
ⒶSK ⊠ 🖵

▼▼▼ **La Posada Hotel & Suites** 🅗
(956) 722-1701. **Call for rates.** 1000 Zaragoza St. I-35, exit downtown; just e of International Bridge. Ext/int corridors. **Pets:** Accepted.
⊠ 🔊 🖪 🖵 🕬 🕬

▼▼ **La Quinta Inn Laredo (I-35)** 🅗 ❀
(956) 722-0511. **$49-$105.** 3610 Santa Ursula Ave. I-35, exit 2 (US 59). Ext corridors. **Pets:** Medium, other species. Service with restrictions, supervision.
ⒶSK ⊠ 🖪 🖵 🕬

▼▼ **Motel 6 South-142** Ⓜ
(956) 725-8187. **$48-$59.** 5310 San Bernardo Ave. I-35, exit 3B (Mann Rd). Ext corridors. **Pets:** Other species. Service with restrictions, supervision.
⊠ 🔊 🕬

🔷 ▼▼▼ **Red Roof Inn Laredo** Ⓜ
(956) 712-0733. **$57-$80.** 1006 W Calton Rd. I-35, exit 3A, 0.3 mi w. Ext/int corridors. **Pets:** Large, other species. Service with restrictions, crate.
ᔕᐯᕮ ⊠ 🖪 🕬

▼▼▼ **Residence Inn by Marriott Laredo** 🅗
(956) 753-9700. **$134-$164.** 310 Lost Oaks Blvd. From airport, Loop 20 S to US 59 W to I-35 N, exit 3B, then right. Int corridors. **Pets:** Other species. $100 one-time fee/room. Service with restrictions, supervision.
⊠ 🔊 🖪 🖵 🕬

▼▼▼ **Staybridge Suites-Laredo** 🅗
(956) 722-0444. **Call for rates.** 7010 Bob Bullock Loop. US 83, exit onto Loop 20 (Bob Bullock Loop); hotel is on west side. Int corridors. **Pets:** Accepted.
⊠ 🖪 🖵 🕬 🕬

LLANO

🔷 ▼▼▼ **Best Western Llano** 🅗
(325) 247-4101. **$69-$100.** 901 W Young St. 1 mi w on SR 71 and 29. Ext corridors. **Pets:** Accepted.
ᔕᐯᕮ ⊠ 🖪 🕬

LONGVIEW

▼▼ **Baymont Inn** 🅗
(903) 757-3663. **Call for rates.** 502 S Access Rd. I-20, exit 595. Ext corridors. **Pets:** Accepted.
⊠ 🖪 🖵 🕬

▼▼▼ **Comfort Suites Longview South** 🅗
(903) 758-7848. **$90-$110.** 711 N Access Rd. I-20, exit 596, just w. Int corridors. **Pets:** Accepted.
ⒶSK ⊠ 🔊 🖪 🖵 🕬

▼▼ **Motel 6–158** Ⓜ
(903) 758-5256. **$45-$58.** 110 S Access Rd. I-20, exit 595A. Ext corridors. **Pets:** Other species. Service with restrictions, supervision.
⊠ 🕬

LUBBOCK

🔷 ▼▼▼ **Best Western Lubbock Windsor Inn** 🅗
(806) 762-8400. **$70-$180.** 5410 I-27. 3.5 mi s on I-27, exit 1B southbound; U-turn at exit 1A (50th St) northbound. Int corridors. **Pets:** Large. $15 daily fee/pet. Designated rooms, service with restrictions, supervision.
ᔕᐯᕮ ⊠ 🖪 🖵 🕬

▼▼ **Extended StayAmerica Lubbock Southwest** 🅗
(806) 785-9881. **$65-$98.** 4802 S Loop 289. S Loop 289, exit Slide Rd, on north access road. Int corridors. **Pets:** Other species. $25 daily fee/pet. Service with restrictions, crate.
ⒶSK ⊠ 🖪 🖵

▼▼▼ **La Quinta Inn and Suites** �H ❧
(806) 749-1600. **$80-$180.** 5006 Auburn St. Jct Loop 289 W and Quaker Ave, 1 mi s on W Frontage Rd. Int corridors. **Pets:** Medium, other species. Service with restrictions, supervision.
ASK ✕ 🔒 💻 ≈

▼▼▼ **La Quinta Inn and Suites Lubbock (West/Medical Center)** �H ❧
(806) 792-0065. **$79-$139.** 4115 Marsha Sharp Frwy. 3.3 mi sw; 2.5 mi ne of Loop 289 on US 62 and 82. Int corridors. **Pets:** Medium, other species. Service with restrictions, supervision.
ASK ✕ 🔒 💻 ≈

▼▼▼ **La Quinta Inn Lubbock** �H ❧
(806) 763-9441. **$59-$99.** 601 Ave Q. 0.8 mi nw on US 84 (Ave Q). Ext corridors. **Pets:** Medium, other species. Service with restrictions, supervision.
ASK ✕ 🔒 💻 ≈

▼▼ **Lubbock Super 8** Ⓜ
(806) 762-8726. **$40-$100, 3 day notice.** 501 Ave Q. 1 mi nw on US 84. Ext corridors. **Pets:** Other species. $8 one-time fee/pet. Service with restrictions.
ASK ✕ 🔒 💻

▼▼▼ **Residence Inn by Marriott** �H
(806) 745-1963. **$139-$149.** 2551 S Loop 289. Loop 289, exit University, 3 mi s, on south frontage road. Ext corridors. **Pets:** Accepted.
✕ 🔒 💻 ≈ ✕

▼▼▼ **Staybridge Suites** �H
(806) 765-8900. **Call for rates.** 2515 19th St. Jct University Ave and 19th St; on southwest corner. Int corridors. **Pets:** Large. $75 one-time fee/room. Designated rooms, service with restrictions, crate.
✕ 🔒 💻 ≈

▼▼▼ **TownePlace Suites by Marriott** �H
(806) 799-6226. **$108-$132.** 5310 W Loop 289. W Loop 289, exit US 62/82 (Brownfield Rd), 0.5 mi s on west frontage road. Int corridors. **Pets:** Accepted.
✕ 💵ᴹ 🔒 💻 ≈

LUFKIN

ⒶⒶⒶ ▼▼▼ **Best Western Crown Colony Inn & Suites** �H
(936) 634-3481. **$99-$119, 3 day notice.** 3211 S 1st St. 2 mi s of jct US 59 and Loop 287. Int corridors. **Pets:** Small. $25 one-time fee/room. No service, crate.
SAVE ✕ 🔒 💻 ≈

▼▼ **La Quinta Inn Lufkin** �H ❧
(936) 634-3351. **$59-$109.** 2119 S 1st St. US 59, exit Carriageway northbound, 0.3 mi s of jct S Loop 287 and US 59 business route. Ext corridors. **Pets:** Medium, other species. Service with restrictions, supervision.
ASK ✕ 🔒 💻 ≈

MADISONVILLE

ⒶⒶⒶ ▼▼▼ **Best Western Executive Inn & Suites** �H
(936) 349-1700. **$100.** 3307 E Main St. I-45, exit 142, just e. Int corridors. **Pets:** Accepted.
SAVE ✕ 💵ᴹ 🔒 💻 ≈

MANSFIELD

▼▼▼ **Comfort Inn** �H
(817) 453-8848. **$79-$139.** 175 N Hwy 287. US 287 S, exit E Broad St. Int corridors. **Pets:** Small, other species. $15 one-time fee/room. Service with restrictions, supervision.
ASK ✕ 💵ᴹ 🔒 💻 ≈

▼▼▼ **La Quinta Inn & Suites** �H ❧
(817) 453-5040. **$79-$109.** 1503 Breckenridge Rd. US 287, exit Walnut Creek/Debbie Ln, 1.2 mi n to Debbie Ln, then just e to Breckenridge Rd. Int corridors. **Pets:** Medium, other species. Service with restrictions, supervision.
ASK ✕ 💵ᴹ 🔒 💻 ≈

MARBLE FALLS

ⒶⒶⒶ ▼▼▼ **Best Western Marble Falls Inn** �H
(830) 693-5122. **$69-$139.** 1403 US Hwy 281. 0.4 mi n of jct SR 281 and FM 1431. Ext/int corridors. **Pets:** Medium. $10 daily fee/pet. Designated rooms, service with restrictions, supervision.
SAVE ✕ 🔒 💻 ≈

ⒶⒶⒶ ▼▼▼ **Quality Inn** �H
(830) 693-7531. **$69-$159.** 1206 Hwy 281 N. 0.3 mi n of jct SR 281 and FM 1431. Ext corridors. **Pets:** Medium. $10 one-time fee/pet. Designated rooms, service with restrictions, supervision.
SAVE ✕ 🔒 💻 ≈

MARSHALL

ⒶⒶⒶ ▼▼▼ **Best Western Executive Inn** �H
(903) 935-0707. **$89-$109.** 5201 E End Blvd S. I-20, exit 617, 0.4 mi n on US 59. Ext corridors. **Pets:** Medium. $25 daily fee/pet. Service with restrictions, supervision.
SAVE ✕ 🔒 💻 ≈

▼▼▼ **La Quinta Inn & East Texas Conference Center** �H ❧
(903) 927-0009. **$59-$129.** 5301 E End Blvd S. I-20, exit 617, just n on US 59. Int corridors. **Pets:** Medium, other species. Service with restrictions, supervision.
ASK ✕ 🔒 💻 ≈

▼ **Motel 6 Marshall #422** Ⓜ
(903) 935-4393. **$43-$56.** 300 I-20 E. I-20, exit 617, just e on access road. Ext corridors. **Pets:** Other species. Service with restrictions, supervision.
✕ 🔒 ≈

MCALLEN

▼▼▼ **Drury Inn-McAllen** �H
(956) 687-5100. **$90-$140.** 612 W Expwy 83. US 83, exit 2nd St, on northwest frontage road. Int corridors. **Pets:** Other species. Service with restrictions, supervision.
ASK ✕ 🔒 💻 ≈

▼▼▼ **Drury Suites-McAllen** �H
(956) 682-3222. **$96-$225.** 228 W Expwy 83. At US 83 and 6th St. Int corridors. **Pets:** Other species. Service with restrictions, supervision.
ASK ✕ 🔒 💻 ≈

▼▼▼ **Howard Johnson Plaza** �H
(956) 984-7900. **Call for rates.** 2721 S 10th St. 2.5 mi s on SR 336 (S 10th St). Int corridors. **Pets:** $200 one-time fee/pet. Designated rooms, service with restrictions, supervision.
✕ 💵ᴹ 🔒 💻 🍽 ≈ ✕

ⒶⒶⒶ ▼▼▼▼ **La Copa Hotel** �H
(956) 686-1741. **$69-$99.** 2000 S 10th St. US 83, exit 10th St, just s of US 83. Ext corridors. **Pets:** Accepted.
SAVE ✕ 🔒 💻 🍽 ≈

▼▼▼ **La Quinta Inn McAllen** �H ❧
(956) 687-1101. **$70-$84.** 1100 S 10th St. Just n of US 83. Ext corridors. **Pets:** Medium, other species. Service with restrictions, supervision.
ASK ✕ 🔒 💻 ≈

▼ **Motel 6 McAllen #212** Ⓜ
(956) 687-3700. **$48-$63.** 700 W Expwy 83. US 83, exit 2nd St, on northwest frontage road. Ext corridors. **Pets:** Other species. Service with restrictions, supervision.
✕ ≈

▼▼▼ Pear Tree Inn-McAllen 🄷
(956) 682-4900. **$80-$105.** 300 W Expwy 83. US 83, exit 2nd St, on northwest frontage road. Int corridors. **Pets:** Other species. Service with restrictions, supervision.
(ASK) (X) 🛢 💷 ⊸

▼▼ Posada Ana Inn 🄷
(956) 631-6700. **$62-$82.** 620 W Expwy 83. US 83, exit 2nd St, on northwest frontage road. Int corridors. **Pets:** Other species. Service with restrictions, supervision.
(ASK) (X) 💷

▼▼▼ Residence Inn by Marriott 🄷
(956) 994-8626. **$125-$153.** 220 W Expwy 83. US 83, exit 2nd St, just w, then just n on 2nd St. Int corridors. **Pets:** Accepted.
(X) 🛢 💷 ⊸ (X)

▼▼ Super 8 🄷
(956) 688-6666. **$55-$89.** 6420 S 23rd St. US 83, exit 23rd St, 3 mi s; jct W Military Hwy 1016. Ext corridors. **Pets:** Accepted.
(ASK) (X) 🛢 💷 ⊸

▼▼ Super 8 🄷
(956) 682-1190. **Call for rates.** 1420 E Jackson Ave. US 83, exit Jackson Ave/Sam Houston St, just s. Int corridors. **Pets:** Accepted.
(X) 🛢 ⊸

MEMPHIS

▼▼ Travelodge 🅼
(806) 259-3583. **Call for rates.** 1600 Boykin Dr. On US 287, 1.3 mi n of jct SR 256. Ext corridors. **Pets:** Accepted.
(X) 🛢 💷 🍴 ⊸

MIDLAND

🔺🔺🔺 ▼▼▼ Clarion Inn 🄷
(432) 694-7774. **$100.** 4300 W Wall St. I-20, exit 134 (Midkiff Rd), 1 mi n to I-20 business loop, then 0.7 mi w. Ext/int corridors. **Pets:** Accepted.
(SAVE) (X) 🛢 💷 🍴 ⊸ (X)

▼▼▼ Hilton Midland Plaza 🄷
(432) 683-6131. **$109-$359.** 117 W Wall St. Jct Wall and Loraine sts; downtown. Int corridors. **Pets:** Accepted.
(X) (&M) 🛢 💷 🍴 ⊸ (X)

▼▼▼ La Quinta Inn Midland 🄷 �
(432) 697-9900. **$59-$119.** 4130 W Wall St. I-20, exit 131, 0.9 mi n on Loop 250 to exit 1A; 1.2 mi e on I-20 business route. Ext corridors. **Pets:** Medium, other species. Service with restrictions, supervision.
(ASK) (X) 🛢 💷 ⊸

MINERAL WELLS

🔺🔺🔺 ▼▼▼ Best Western Clubhouse Inn & Suites 🄷
(940) 325-2270. **$129.** 4410 Hwy 180 E. Jct US 180 and SR 1195; in East Mineral Wells. Int corridors. **Pets:** Other species. $10 one-time fee/pet. Service with restrictions, supervision.
(SAVE) (X) (&M) 🛢 💷 ⊸

MISSION

▼▼▼ El Rocio Retreat 🄱🄱 �
(956) 584-7432. **$75-$315.** 2519 S Inspiration Rd. Jct US 83 at Inspiration Rd, 2 mi s. Ext/int corridors. **Pets:** Other species. $25 deposit/room. No service.
(ASK) (X)

▼▼▼ Hawthorn Suites 🄷 �
(956) 519-9696. **$99-$119.** 3700 Plantation Grove Blvd. US 83, exit Shary Rd, 2.1 mi s to Plantation Grove Blvd. Ext corridors. **Pets:** Medium, other species. $25 one-time fee/pet. Service with restrictions, supervision.
(ASK) (X) 🛢 💷 ⊸

MONAHANS

▼▼ Americas Best Value Colonial Inn 🅼
(432) 943-4345. **$100-$140.** 702 W I-20. I-20, exit 80, just s. Ext/int corridors. **Pets:** Accepted.
(ASK) (X) 🛢 💷 ⊸

MOUNT PLEASANT

🔺🔺🔺 ▼▼▼ Best Western Mt. Pleasant Inn 🅼
(903) 572-5051. **$72-$89.** 102 E Burton Rd. I-30, exit 162, just e. Ext corridors. **Pets:** Small. $10 daily fee/pet. Service with restrictions, supervision.
(SAVE) (X) 🛢 💷 ⊸

🔺🔺🔺 ▼▼▼ Comfort Inn 🄷
(903) 577-7553. **$75-$100.** 2515 W Ferguson Rd. I-30, exit 160. Ext corridors. **Pets:** Medium, other species. $10 daily fee/room. Service with restrictions, supervision.
(SAVE) (X) 🛢 💷 ⊸

▼▼▼ Holiday Inn Express Hotel & Suites 🄷
(903) 577-3800. **Call for rates.** 2306 Greenhill Rd. I-30, exit 162, just n. Int corridors. **Pets:** Service with restrictions, crate.
(X) (&M) 🛢 💷 ⊸

MOUNT VERNON

🔺🔺🔺 ▼▼▼ Super 8 of Mount Vernon 🄷
(903) 588-2882. **$60-$70.** 401 W I-30. I-30, exit 146 (SR 37). Ext corridors. **Pets:** Small. $10 daily fee/pet. Service with restrictions, supervision.
(SAVE) (X) 🛢 💷

NACOGDOCHES

🔺🔺🔺 ▼▼▼ Best Western Northpark Inn 🄷
(936) 560-1906. **$60-$120.** 4809 NW Stallings Dr. Jct US 59 N and Loop 224, exit Westward Dr. Ext corridors. **Pets:** Small. $15 daily fee/pet. Service with restrictions.
(SAVE) (X) 🛢 💷 ⊸

▼▼ La Quinta Inn Nacogdoches 🄷 �
(936) 560-5453. **$45-$105.** 3215 South St. US 59, jct Loop 224 and US 59 business route, south of town. Ext corridors. **Pets:** Medium, other species. Service with restrictions, supervision.
(ASK) (X) 🛢 💷 ⊸

NEW BOSTON

🔺🔺🔺 ▼▼▼ Best Western Inn of New Boston 🄷
(903) 628-6999. **$80-$90.** 1024 N Center. I-30, exit 201, on westbound access road. Ext corridors. **Pets:** Accepted.
(SAVE) (X) 🛢 💷 ⊸

NORTH RICHLAND HILLS

🔺🔺🔺 ▼▼▼ Best Western NE Mall Inn & Suites 🄷
(817) 656-8881. **$80-$130.** 8709 Airport Frwy. SR 121 and 183, 0.5 mi sw of FM 3029, Exit Precinct Line Rd, 0.5 mi e of I-820. Ext corridors. **Pets:** Small. $75 deposit/pet. Service with restrictions, supervision.
(SAVE) (X) 🛢 💷 ⊸

▼▼ Studio 6 #6034 🄷
(817) 788-6000. **$61-$75.** 7450 NE Loop 820. I-820, exit 21 (Holiday Ln), 0.4 mi e on south access road. Ext corridors. **Pets:** Other species. $10 daily fee/room. Service with restrictions, supervision.
(X) 🛢 💷

ODEM

🔺🔺🔺 ▼▼▼ Budget Inn-Odem 🅼
(361) 368-2166. **$55-$120, 3 day notice.** 1505 Voss Ave (US 77). US 77, 1 mi s of jct SR 631. Ext corridors. **Pets:** Accepted.
(SAVE) (X) 🛢 💷 ⊸

ODESSA

Best Western Garden Oasis H
(432) 337-3006. **Call for rates.** 110 W I-20. Jct I-20 and US 385, exit 116, just w. Ext/int corridors. **Pets:** Other species. Designated rooms, service with restrictions, supervision.
SAVE ✕ 🛏 💻 🍽 🏊 ⊠

Days Inn H
(432) 335-8000. **Call for rates.** 3075 E Business Loop 20. I-20, exit 121, 0.7 mi n on Loop 338, then 0.5 mi w. Int corridors. **Pets:** Accepted.
SAVE ✕ 🛏 💻 🏊

La Quinta Inn Odessa H ❀
(432) 333-2820. **$59-$129.** 5001 E Business Loop I-20. I-20, exit 121, 0.8 mi n on Loop 338, then just w. Ext corridors. **Pets:** Medium, other species. Service with restrictions, supervision.
ASK ✕ 🛏 💻 🏊

McM Grande Hotel H ❀
(432) 362-2311. **$95.** 6201 E Business Loop I-20. I-20, exit 121, 0.8 mi n on Loop 338, then 1 mi e. Ext/int corridors. **Pets:** Other species. $50 deposit/room. Designated rooms, service with restrictions, crate.
ASK ✕ 🛏 💻 🍽 🏊 ⊠

Motel 6 Odessa #439 M
(432) 333-4025. **$60-$75.** 200 E I-20 Service Rd. I-20, exit 116, on eastbound frontage road. Ext corridors. **Pets:** Other species. Service with restrictions, supervision.
✕ 🏊

Quality Inn & Suites H
(432) 333-3931. **Call for rates.** 3001 E Business Loop I-20. I-20, exit 121, 0.7 mi n on Loop 338, then 0.5 mi w. Ext/int corridors. **Pets:** Accepted.
✕ 🛏 💻 🏊 ⊠

OLMITO

La Quinta Inn H ❀
(956) 350-8855. **$60-$70.** 8280 North Expwy. US 77/83, exit SR 511, just e. Int corridors. **Pets:** Medium, other species. Service with restrictions, supervision.
ASK ✕ 🛏 💻 🏊

OZONA

Travelodge M
(325) 392-2656. **$65-$95.** 8 11th St. I-10, exit 368 westbound, 2 mi w; exit 365 eastbound to Loop 466, 1 mi e. Ext corridors. **Pets:** Other species. $20 daily fee/pet. Service with restrictions, supervision.
SAVE ✕ 🛏 💻 🏊

PALESTINE

Best Western Palestine Inn H
(903) 723-4655. **$79-$129.** 1601 W Palestine Ave. Jct US 287/SR 19, 0.7 mi sw on US 79. Ext corridors. **Pets:** Medium. $10 daily fee/pet. Designated rooms, service with restrictions, supervision.
SAVE ✕ 🛏 💻 🍽 🏊

PARIS

Best Western Inn of Paris H
(903) 785-5566. **$64-$84.** 3755 NE Loop 286. Jct US 82 and E Loop 286, just n. Ext corridors. **Pets:** Accepted.
SAVE ✕ 🛏 💻 🏊

Days Inn H
(903) 784-8164. **$75-$95, 14 day notice.** 2650 N Main St. NE Loop 286, exit US 271, just n. Ext corridors. **Pets:** Accepted.
SAVE ✕ 🛏 💻 🏊

Holiday Inn H
(903) 785-5545. **$81.** 3560 NE Loop 286. E Loop 286, 0.3 mi n of jct US 82. Ext corridors. **Pets:** Accepted.
SAVE ✕ 🛏 💻 🍽 🏊

PEARLAND

Best Western Pearland Inn H
(281) 997-2000. **$90-$130.** 1855 N Main St. Jct Loop 8 S and SR 35, 1.5 mi s. Ext corridors. **Pets:** Accepted.
SAVE ✕ 🛏 💻 🏊

La Quinta Inn & Suites H ❀
(281) 412-5454. **$80-$140.** 9002 Broadway. Jct SR 288 and 518, 1.6 mi e. Int corridors. **Pets:** Medium, other species. Service with restrictions, supervision.
ASK ✕ 🖥 🛏 💻 🏊

PEARSALL

Executive Inn M
(830) 334-3693. **$59-$99.** 613 N Oak. I-35, exit 104, 3 mi e. Ext corridors. **Pets:** $25 daily fee/pet. Service with restrictions, supervision.
ASK ✕ 🛏 💻

PECOS

Knights Inn Laura Lodge Motel & Suites M
(432) 445-4924. **$59-$99.** 1000 E Business I-20. I-20, exit 42 (US 285), 1 mi nw to Business Rt I-20, then 0.5 mi e. Ext corridors. **Pets:** Small. $10 daily fee/pet. Designated rooms, service with restrictions, supervision.
SAVE ✕ 🛏 💻 🏊

Oak Tree Inn H
(432) 447-0180. **$65-$79.** 22 N Frontage Rd. I-20, exit 42 (US 285), just w on north access road. Int corridors. **Pets:** Other species. $10 daily fee/pet. Service with restrictions.
SAVE ✕ 🛏 💻

PERRYTON

Best Western Perryton Inn H
(806) 434-2850. **$65-$120.** 3505 S Main St (US 83). US 83, just s of town. Int corridors. **Pets:** $10 one-time fee/pet. Service with restrictions, supervision.
SAVE ✕ 🛏 💻 🍽 🏊

PHARR

La Quinta Inn & Suites H ❀
(956) 787-2900. **$70-$110.** 4603 N Cage. US 281 northbound, exit Nolana Loop, just w. Int corridors. **Pets:** Medium, other species. Service with restrictions, supervision.
ASK ✕ 🖥 🛏 💻 🏊

PLAINVIEW

Best Western Conestoga H
(806) 293-9454. **$80-$93.** 600 N I-27. I-27, exit 49, just s of US 70, on eastbound access road. Ext corridors. **Pets:** Accepted.
SAVE ✕ 🛏 💻 🏊

PORT ARANSAS

Alister Square Inn M ❀
(361) 749-3000. **$59-$268.** 122 S Alister St. Just n of Ave C. Ext corridors. **Pets:** Other species. $25 daily fee/pet. Service with restrictions, supervision.
SAVE ✕ 🛏 🏊

Beachgate CondoSuites & Motel CO
(361) 749-5900. **$35-$365, 30 day notice.** 2000 On the Beach Dr. Beach access; between markers 8 and 9; street access on Anchor Rd off 11th St. Ext/int corridors. **Pets:** Small, dogs only. $15 daily fee/pet. Supervision.
✕ 🛏 💻 🏊

Best Western Ocean Villa H
(361) 749-3010. **$69-$179.** 400 E Ave G. Just se of S Alister St (SH 361). Int corridors. **Pets:** Accepted.
SAVE ✕ 🖥 🛏 💻 🏊

AAA ◆ Mariner Inn & Suites M
(361) 749-8200. **$59-$259, 3 day notice.** 2607 State Hwy 361. 0.6 mi n of Gulf Beach Rd. Ext corridors. **Pets:** Dogs only. $10 daily fee/pet. Designated rooms, service with restrictions.
SAVE ✕ 🖬 💻 ⌾

AAA ◆◆ Plantation Suites & Conference Center M
(361) 749-3866. **$59-$350.** 1909 Hwy 361. On SR 361, 0.4 mi s. Ext corridors. **Pets:** Large. $50 one-time fee/room. Service with restrictions, supervision.
SAVE ✕ 🖬 💻 ⌾

PORT LAVACA

AAA ◆◆ Best Western Port Lavaca Inn H
(361) 553-6800. **$89.** 2202 N Hwy 35. 1 mi e. Int corridors. **Pets:** Small. $25 one-time fee/pet. Service with restrictions, supervision.
SAVE ✕ 🖬 💻 ⌾

POST

AAA ◆◆ Best Western Post Inn H
(806) 495-9933. **$96-$146, 7 day notice.** 1011 N Broadway. 1 mi n on US 84. Int corridors. **Pets:** Accepted.
SAVE ✕ 🖬 💻 ⌾

QUANAH

AAA ◆◆◆ Best Western Quanah Inn & Suites H
(940) 663-5407. **$90-$120.** 1100 W 11th St (Hwy 287). On north end of town. Int corridors. **Pets:** Accepted.
SAVE ✕ 🚬 🖬 💻 ⌾

RAYMONDVILLE

◆◆ Americas Best Value Inn & Suites H
(956) 689-5900. **$39-$89.** 450 S Expwy 77/I-69. US 77/I-69, exit 186 (Raymondville), on frontage road. Ext corridors. **Pets:** Other species. $10 one-time fee/room. Service with restrictions, crate.
ASK ✕ 🖬 💻 ⌾

AAA ◆◆◆ Best Western Executive Inn Raymondville H
(956) 689-4141. **$65-$99.** 118 N Expwy 77. US 77, jct FM 186 on southbound access road. Ext corridors. **Pets:** Small. $20 one-time fee/room. Designated rooms, service with restrictions, supervision.
SAVE ✕ 🖬 💻 ⌾

ROBSTOWN

◆◆◆ Days Inn M
(361) 387-8600. **$70-$100.** 650 Hwy 77 S. Just n of jct CR 892 and US 77. Ext corridors. **Pets:** Accepted.
ASK ✕ 🖬 💻 ⌾

AAA ◆◆ Executive Inn H
(361) 387-9416. **$89.** 620 Hwy 77 S. On US 77, 1 mi s. Ext corridors. **Pets:** $10 daily fee/room. Supervision.
SAVE ✕ 🖬 ⌾

ROCKPORT

◆◆ Days Inn M
(361) 729-6379. **$59-$200.** 1212 Laurel St. Jct Laurel St and Business Rt SR 35; center. Ext corridors. **Pets:** Medium. $15 daily fee/pet. Service with restrictions, supervision.
ASK ✕ 🖬 💻 ⌾

AAA ◆◆◆ Hunt's Castle H
(361) 729-5002. **$99-$179.** 725 S Water St. Business Rt SR 35, jct Market St, 1.6 mi e to Water St, then just s. Ext corridors. **Pets:** Other species. $10 daily fee/pet. Service with restrictions.
SAVE ✕ 🖬 💻 ⌾

◆◆◆ Laguna Reef Hotel CO
(361) 729-1742. **$85-$135, 3 day notice.** 1021 Water St. 0.5 mi s, just e of Business Rt SR 35; entrance on S Austin St. Ext corridors. **Pets:** Accepted.
ASK ✕ 🚬 🖬 💻 ⌾ ⌾

ROUND ROCK

AAA ◆◆◆ Best Western Executive Inn H
(512) 255-3222. **$89-$123.** 1851 N I-35. I-35, exit 253 northbound; exit 253A (U-turn) southbound. Ext corridors. **Pets:** Very small, other species. Service with restrictions.
SAVE ✕ 🚬 🖬 💻 ⌾

◆◆◆ Candlewood Suites H
(512) 828-0899. **$99-$159.** 521 S I-35. I-35, exit 252A, just n on northbound frontage road. Int corridors. **Pets:** Medium, other species. $75 one-time fee/room. Service with restrictions, crate.
ASK ✕ 🖬 ⌾

◆◆◆ La Quinta Inn Austin (Round Rock) H 🐾
(512) 255-6666. **$75-$125.** 2004 I-35 N. I-35, exit 254, on west frontage road. Int corridors. **Pets:** Medium, other species. Service with restrictions, supervision.
ASK ✕ 🖬 💻 ⌾

◆◆◆ Residence Inn by Marriott Austin Round Rock H
(512) 733-2400. **$161-$197.** 2505 S I-35. I-35, exit 250 southbound; exit 251 northbound, on east frontage road. Int corridors. **Pets:** Accepted.
✕ 🚬 🖬 💻 ⌾ ⌾

◆◆◆ SpringHill Suites H
(512) 733-6700. **$125-$153.** 2960 Hoppe Tr. I-35, exit 256 southbound; exit 254 northbound, on West Frontage Rd. Int corridors. **Pets:** Small, dogs only. $75 daily fee/room. Service with restrictions, supervision.
✕ 🚬 🖬 💻 ⌾ ⌾

◆◆◆ Staybridge Suites Austin-Round Rock H
(512) 733-0942. **$149.** 520 I-35 S. I-35, exit 252B northbound; exit 252AB southbound, on west frontage road. Int corridors. **Pets:** Accepted.
ASK ✕ 🚬 🖬 💻 ⌾

SALADO

◆◆◆ Holiday Inn Express Salado H
(254) 947-4004. **$100.** 1991 N Stagecoach Rd. I-35, exit 286. Int corridors. **Pets:** $50 one-time fee/pet. Service with restrictions, supervision.
ASK ✕ 🚬 🖬 💻 ⌾

SAN ANGELO

AAA ◆◆◆ Americas Best Value Inn M
(325) 653-1323. **$53-$60.** 1601 S Bryant Blvd. US 87 and 277 at Ave L. Ext/int corridors. **Pets:** Accepted.
SAVE ✕ 🖬 💻 ⌾

AAA ◆◆◆ Best Western San Angelo H
(325) 223-1273. **$89-$99, 3 day notice.** 3017 W Loop 306. Loop 306, exit College Hills Blvd, just s. Ext corridors. **Pets:** Accepted.
SAVE ✕ 🖬 💻 ⌾

◆◆◆ Days Inn San Angelo H
(325) 658-6594. **Call for rates.** 4613 S Jackson St. Jct US 87 and Jackson St. Ext corridors. **Pets:** Small, dogs only. Service with restrictions, crate.
✕ 🖬 💻 🍴 ⌾

AAA ◆◆◆ Howard Johnson San Angelo H
(325) 653-2995. **$68-$86.** 415 W Beauregard Ave. Just w on US 67 business route at US 87 southbound. Ext/int corridors. **Pets:** Medium, other species. Designated rooms, service with restrictions, supervision.
SAVE ✕ 🖬 💻 🍴 ⌾

▼▼▼ La Quinta Inn San Angelo (Conference Center) ⊞ ❖
(325) 949-0515. **$49-$119.** 2307 Loop 306. Loop 306, exit Knickerbocker Rd, just s. Ext corridors. **Pets:** Medium, other species. Service with restrictions, supervision.
[A$K] [✕] [🛏] [💻] [🏊]

▼▼ Rodeway Inn ⊞
(325) 944-2578. **$75-$125.** 2502 Loop 306. Loop 306, exit Knickerbocker Rd. Ext corridors. **Pets:** Accepted.
[A$K] [✕] [🛏] [💻] [🏊]

▼▼▼ San Angelo Inn & Conference Center ⊞
(325) 658-2828. **$139-$159.** 441 Rio Concho Dr. US 87 to Concho Ave, 0.5 mi e; downtown. Int corridors. **Pets:** Accepted.
[A$K] [✕] [🛏] [💻] [🍴] [🏊]

▼▼▼ Staybridge Suites ⊞
(325) 653-1500. **Call for rates.** 1355 Knickerbocker Rd. US 87 S, 1 mi w. Int corridors. **Pets:** Accepted.
[✕] [🛏] [💻] [🏊]

SAN ANTONIO METROPOLITAN AREA

ELMENDORF

AAA ▼▼▼ Comfort Inn & Suites Braunig Lake ⊞
(210) 633-1833. **$90-$110.** 13800 I-37 S. I-37, exit 130 (Donop/Southton rds), on northbound access lane. Ext corridors. **Pets:** Medium, other species. $7 daily fee/pet. Service with restrictions, crate.
[SAVE] [✕] [🛏] [💻] [🏊]

FLORESVILLE

AAA ▼▼▼ Best Western Floresville Inn ⊞
(830) 393-0443. **$85-$150.** 1720 S 10th St. US 181, just s of downtown. Ext corridors. **Pets:** Medium. $12 daily fee/pet. Service with restrictions, supervision.
[SAVE] [✕] [🛏] [💻] [🏊]

LIVE OAK

▼▼▼ La Quinta Inn San Antonio (I-35 North at Toepperwein) ⊞ ❖
(210) 657-5500. **$69-$135.** 12822 I-35 N. I-35, exit 170B (Toepperwein), on northbound access road. Ext/int corridors. **Pets:** Medium, other species. Service with restrictions, supervision.
[A$K] [✕] [⚒M] [🛏] [💻] [🏊]

NEW BRAUNFELS

▼▼▼ Executive Inn & Suites ⊞
(830) 625-3932. **$49-$199.** 808 Hwy 46 S. I-35, exit 189, 0.4 mi e. Ext corridors. **Pets:** Small, dogs only. $25 daily fee/pet. Designated rooms, service with restrictions, supervision.
[A$K] [✕] [⚒M] [🛏] [💻] [🏊]

▼▼ Holiday Inn ⊞
(830) 625-8017. **Call for rates.** 1051 I-35 E. I-35, exit 189, on southbound access road. Ext corridors. **Pets:** Accepted.
[✕] [⚒M] [🛏] [💻] [🍴] [🏊]

▼▼▼ La Quinta Inn & Suites ⊞ ❖
(830) 627-3333. **$69-$169.** 365 Hwy 46 S. I-35, exit 189, just s on SR 46. Int corridors. **Pets:** Medium, other species. Service with restrictions, supervision.
[A$K] [✕] [⚒M] [🛏] [💻] [🏊]

▼▼▼ Quality Inn & Suites ⊞
(830) 643-9300. **$59-$400.** 1533 IH-35 N. I-35, exit 190, on southbound access road. Int corridors. **Pets:** Accepted.
[A$K] [✕] [🛏] [💻] [🏊]

AAA ▼▼▼ Rodeway Inn ⊞
(830) 629-6991. **$39-$150.** 1209 I-35 N. I-35, exit 189, on southbound access road. Ext corridors. **Pets:** Medium. $20 one-time fee/room. Service with restrictions, crate.
[SAVE] [✕] [🛏] [💻] [🏊]

▼▼ Super 8-New Braunfels M
(830) 629-1155. **$59-$199.** 510 Hwy 46 S. I-35, exit 189 (SR 46), just e. Ext corridors. **Pets:** Small. $25 daily fee/pet. Service with restrictions, supervision.
[A$K] [✕] [🛏] [💻] [🏊]

SAN ANTONIO

AAA ▼▼ Alamo Inn M ❖
(210) 227-2203. **$60-$150.** 2203 E Commerce St. I-37, exit 141A, at Commerce St and New Braunfels Ave. Ext corridors. **Pets:** Small. $25 deposit/pet, $10 daily fee/pet. Designated rooms, service with restrictions, crate.
[SAVE] [✕] [🛏] [💻]

AAA ▼▼▼▼ Arbor House Suites Bed & Breakfast BB
(210) 472-2005. **$129-$207, 14 day notice.** 109 Arciniega St. Just s of E Nueva; between S Presa and S St Marys sts; near La Villita Historic District. Ext/int corridors. **Pets:** Medium, other species. Service with restrictions, supervision.
[SAVE] [✕] [🛏] [💻]

▼▼▼ Baymont Inns & Suites ⊞
(210) 593-0338. **Call for rates.** 9542 I-10 W. I-10, exit Wurzbach Rd, just e on eastbound access road. Ext corridors. **Pets:** Accepted.
[✕] [🛏] [💻] [🏊]

AAA ▼▼▼ Best Western Casa Linda San Antonio Airport ⊞
(210) 366-1800. **$88-$128.** 8818 Jones Maltsberger Rd. I-410, exit 21B (Jones Maltsberger Rd), on westbound access road. Int corridors. **Pets:** Medium, other species. Service with restrictions.
[SAVE] [✕] [🛏] [💻] [🏊]

AAA ▼▼▼ Best Western-Garden Inn ⊞
(210) 599-0999. **$79-$250.** 11939 N I-35. I-35, exit 170, on southbound access road, 0.5 mi s to Judson Rd exit. Ext corridors. **Pets:** Very small. $25 daily fee/pet. Service with restrictions, supervision.
[SAVE] [✕] [🛏] [💻] [🏊]

AAA ▼▼▼ Best Western Posada Ana Inn-Medical Center ⊞
(210) 691-9550. **$94-$116.** 9411 Wurzbach Rd. I-10, exit 561 (Wurzbach Rd), on eastbound access road. Int corridors. **Pets:** Medium. Service with restrictions, crate.
[SAVE] [✕] [⚒M] [🛏] [💻] [🏊]

AAA ▼▼▼ Best Western Posada Ana Inn-San Antonio Airport ⊞
(210) 342-1400. **$89-$122.** 8600 Jones Maltsberger Rd. I-410, exit 21A (Jones Maltsberger Rd), 0.5 mi s. Int corridors. **Pets:** Small. Designated rooms, service with restrictions, supervision.
[SAVE] [✕] [🛏] [💻] [🏊]

▼▼▼ Brackenridge House B & B BB
(210) 271-3442. **$125-$300, 14 day notice.** 230 Madison St. Just s of S St. Marys St at Durango St. Ext/int corridors. **Pets:** Large, other species. Designated rooms, no service.
[✕] [🛏] [💻] [🏊]

▼▼▼ Candlewood Suites Hotel H ❀
(210) 615-0550. **Call for rates.** 9350 I-10 W. I-10 W, exit 561 (Wurzbach Rd), eastbound access road; between Wurzbach Rd and Callaghan. Int corridors. **Pets:** Medium. $75 one-time fee/room. Service with restrictions, crate.

⊠ 🖥 💻 ⊅

◈◈◈ ▼▼▼ Clarion Inn & Suites H
(210) 226-4361. **$109-$129, 7 day notice.** 3855 I-35 N. I-35, exit 162 (Binz-Engleman Rd) southbound; exit 161 northbound, on southbound access road. Ext corridors. **Pets:** Accepted.

SAVE ⊠ 🖥 💻 ¶¶ ⊅

◈◈◈ ▼▼▼ Comfort Inn & Suites Airport H
(210) 249-2000. **$99-$199.** 8640 Crownhill Blvd. I-410, exit Airport Blvd, just off I-410 eastbound access road; just e of Broadway Ave. Int corridors. **Pets:** Small. $25 one-time fee/pet. Service with restrictions, supervision.

SAVE ⊠ 🖥 💻 ⊅

◈◈◈ ▼▼ Comfort Inn-Fiesta M
(210) 696-4766. **$90-$100.** 6755 N Loop 1604 W. I-10, exit CR 1604 W, 0.5 mi w of La Cantera Blvd. Int corridors. **Pets:** Accepted.

SAVE ⊠ &M 🖥 💻 ⊅

◈◈◈ ▼▼ Comfort Inn Sea World H
(210) 684-8606. **$69-$159.** 4 Piano Pl. I-410, exit Evers Rd westbound, U-turn; exit 14 Callahan/Babocks Rd eastbound. Ext corridors. **Pets:** Accepted.

SAVE ⊠ 🖥 💻 ⊅

▼▼ Country Hearth Inn H
(210) 616-0030. **$69-$175, 7 day notice.** 7500 Louis Pasteur Dr. I-410, exit 14C (Babcock Rd), 1 mi nw on Babcock Rd, then 0.5 mi n on Louis Pasteur Dr. Int corridors. **Pets:** Accepted.

ASK ⊠ &M 🖥 💻

◈◈◈ ▼▼▼ Crowne Plaza San Antonio Riverwalk H
(210) 354-2800. **$189-$269.** 111 Pecan St E. Corner of Pecan and Soledad sts. Int corridors. **Pets:** Medium. $50 one-time fee/pet. Service with restrictions, supervision.

SAVE ⊠ 🖥 💻 ¶¶ ⊅ ⊠

◈◈◈ ▼▼▼ Days Inn Coliseum/AT&T Center H
(210) 225-4040. **$55-$130.** 3443 I-35 N. I-35, exit 160, on southbound access road. Ext corridors. **Pets:** Medium. $15 daily fee/pet. Service with restrictions, supervision.

SAVE ⊠ 🖥 💻 ⊅

◈◈◈ ▼▼▼ Days Inn Downtown Riverwalk Area H
(210) 271-3334. **$70-$150.** 1500 I-35 S. I-10/35, exit 154 (Laredo St). Ext/int corridors. **Pets:** Accepted.

SAVE ⊠ 💻 ⊅

▼▼▼▼ Drury Inn & Suites Northeast H
(210) 657-1107. **$90-$140.** 4900 Crestwind Dr. I-35, exit 165 (Walzem Rd), on northbound access road. Int corridors. **Pets:** Other species. Service with restrictions, supervision.

ASK ⊠ &M 🖥 💻 ⊅

▼▼▼▼ Drury Inn & Suites-San Antonio Airport H
(210) 308-8100. **$100-$168.** 95 NE Loop 410. I-410, exit 21A (Jones Maltsberger Rd), 1.8 mi w of airport. Int corridors. **Pets:** Other species. Service with restrictions, supervision.

ASK ⊠ &M 🖥 💻 ⊅

▼▼▼▼ Drury Inn & Suites-San Antonio North H
(210) 404-1600. **$103-$213.** 801 N Loop 1604 E. On FM 1604, 0.4 mi w on US 281. Int corridors. **Pets:** Other species. Service with restrictions, supervision.

ASK ⊠ 🖥 💻 ⊅

▼▼▼▼ Drury Inn & Suites-San Antonio Northwest H
(210) 561-2510. **$98-$311.** 9806 I-10 W. I-10, exit 561 (Wurzbach Rd), on southeast corner. Int corridors. **Pets:** Other species. Service with restrictions, supervision.

ASK ⊠ 🖥 💻 ⊅

▼▼▼▼ Drury Inn & Suites-San Antonio Riverwalk H
(210) 212-5200. **$125-$286.** 201 N St. Mary's St. Just s of College St. Int corridors. **Pets:** Other species. Service with restrictions, supervision.

ASK ⊠ 🖥 💻 ⊅

◈◈◈ ▼▼▼ Drury Plaza Hotel-San Antonio Riverwalk H
(210) 270-7799. **$135-$325.** 105 S St. Mary's St. Commerce and St. Mary's and Market sts. Int corridors. **Pets:** Other species. Service with restrictions, supervision.

SAVE ⊠ &M 🖥 💻 ⊅

◈◈◈ ▼▼ Econo Lodge Inn & Suites Fiesta Park M ❀
(210) 690-5500. **$39-$179.** 13575 I-10 W. I-10, exit 557, westbound access road. Ext corridors. **Pets:** Small, dogs only. $10 daily fee/room. Designated rooms, service with restrictions, supervision.

SAVE ⊠ 🖥 💻 ⊅

◈◈◈ ▼▼▼ ▼▼▼ Emily Morgan Hotel H
(210) 225-8486. **$239-$509, 3 day notice.** 705 E Houston St. On Houston St, just n of Bonham St. Int corridors. **Pets:** $75 one-time fee/room. Service with restrictions, supervision.

SAVE ⊠ &M 💻 ¶¶ ⊅ ⊠

▼▼▼▼ The Fairmount Hotel H
(210) 224-8800. **Call for rates.** 401 S Alamo St. Opposite convention center and Hemisfair Plaza. Ext/int corridors. **Pets:** Accepted.

⊠ 🖥 💻 ⊠

▼▼▼▼ Hampton Inn Six Flags Area H ❀
(210) 561-9058. **$100-$199.** 11010 I-10 W. I-10, exit 560 westbound; exit 559 (Huebner Rd) eastbound. Int corridors. **Pets:** Small. $75 one-time fee/pet. Designated rooms, service with restrictions, crate.

⊠ 🖥 💻 ⊅

▼▼▼▼ Hilton San Antonio Airport H ❀
(210) 340-6060. **$109-$450.** 611 NW Loop 410. I-410, exit San Pedro Ave, on westbound access road. Int corridors. **Pets:** Medium, dogs only. $75 one-time fee/room. Service with restrictions.

⊠ 🖥 💻 ¶¶ ⊅ ⊠

▼▼▼▼ Holiday Inn Express-San Antonio Airport H
(210) 308-6700. **$149-$184.** 91 NE Loop 410. I-410, exit 21A (Jones Maltsberger Rd) eastbound; exit 20B westbound, on westbound access road; between San Pedro Ave and Jones Maltsberger Rd. Int corridors. **Pets:** Accepted.

ASK ⊠ &M 🖥 💻 ⊅

◈◈◈ ▼▼▼ Holiday Inn Select H
(210) 349-9900. **$119-$209.** 77 NE Loop 410. I-410, exit 20B (McCullough St), on westbound access road. Int corridors. **Pets:** Large. $100 deposit/room, $25 one-time fee/room. Service with restrictions, supervision.

SAVE ⊠ &M 🖥 💻 ¶¶ ⊅

▼▼ ▼▼ HomeGate Studios & Suites H
(210) 342-4800. **$49-$99.** 11221 San Pedro Ave. I-410, exit US 281 (San Pedro Ave), 2.3 mi n on US 281, exit Nakoma, on west frontage road. Ext corridors. **Pets:** Accepted.

ASK ⊠ ⊅

▼▼ ▼▼ Homestead Studio Suites Hotel-San Antonio-Airport M
(210) 491-9009. **$65-$120.** 1015 Central Pkwy S. I-410, exit US 281 (San Pedro Ave), just n of Bitters Rd; on northbound access road. Ext corridors. **Pets:** Other species. $25 daily fee/pet. Service with restrictions, crate.

ASK ⊠ 🖥 💻

AAA ▼▼▼▼ ▼▼▼ Hotel Contessa 🄷 ☸
(210) 229-9222. **$179-$305.** 306 W Market. Market St at St. Mary's St. Int corridors. **Pets:** Medium, dogs only. $50 daily fee/room. Designated rooms, supervision.
[SAVE] [✕] [▣] [🍴] [⇌] [✕]

AAA ▼▼▼ Howard Johnson Lackland Inn & Suites 🄷
(210) 675-9690. **$69-$95.** 6815 Hwy 90 W. I-410, exit US 90 to Military Dr, 0.5 mi e on westbound access road. Ext corridors. **Pets:** Small, other species. $25 one-time fee/room. Service with restrictions, supervision.
[SAVE] [✕] [▤] [▣] [⇌]

▼▼ Inn on the Riverwalk 🄱🄱
(210) 225-6333. **$99-$309, 7 day notice.** 129 Woodward Pl. Just n of W Durango Blvd. Ext/int corridors. **Pets:** Other species. $20 daily fee/pet. Designated rooms, service with restrictions, supervision.
[ASK] [✕] [▤] [▣]

▼▼▼ La Quinta Inn 🄷 ☸
(210) 661-4545. **$70-$150.** 6075 IH 10 E Foster Rd. I-10, exit 583 (Foster Rd), on westbound access road. Int corridors. **Pets:** Medium, other species. Service with restrictions, supervision.
[ASK] [✕] [⬛M] [▤] [▣] [⇌]

▼▼▼ La Quinta Inn & Suites San Antonio (Convention Center) 🄷 ☸
(210) 222-9181. **$109-$249.** 303 Blum St. 0.5 mi ne. Ext/int corridors. **Pets:** Medium, other species. Service with restrictions, supervision.
[ASK] [✕] [▤] [▣] [⇌]

▼▼▼ La Quinta Inn Alamo Dome South 🄷 ☸
(210) 337-7171. **$85-$145.** 3180 Goliad Rd. I-37, exit 135 (Brooks City Base/SE Military Dr), just w of interstate. Int corridors. **Pets:** Medium, other species. Service with restrictions, supervision.
[ASK] [✕] [▤] [▣] [⇌]

▼▼▼ La Quinta Inn & Suites Medical Center 🄷 ☸
(210) 525-8090. **$99-$199.** 4431 Horizon Hill Blvd. I-10, exit 562, on eastbound access road; between Callaghan and Wurzbach rds. Int corridors. **Pets:** Medium, other species. Service with restrictions, supervision.
[ASK] [✕] [⬛M] [▤] [▣] [⇌]

▼▼▼ La Quinta Inn & Suites San Antonio Airport 🄷 ☸
(210) 342-3738. **$69-$149.** 850 Halm Blvd. I-410, exit US 281 S, southwest corner. Int corridors. **Pets:** Medium, other species. Service with restrictions, supervision.
[ASK] [✕] [⬛M] [▤] [▣] [⇌]

▼▼▼ La Quinta Inn & Suites San Antonio-Downtown 🄷 ☸
(210) 212-5400. **$99-$199.** 100 W Durango Blvd. I-35, exit 155B (Durango Blvd), 3 blks e of jct E Flores St. Int corridors. **Pets:** Medium, other species. Service with restrictions, supervision.
[ASK] [✕] [⬛M] [▤] [▣] [⇌]

▼▼▼ La Quinta Inn San Antonio (I-35 North @ Windsor Park Mall) 🄷 ☸
(210) 653-6619. **$65-$129.** 6410 I-35 N. I-35, exit 163B northbound, on I-35 northbound access road; between Rittiman and Eisenhauer rds; exit 164A (Rittiman Rd) southbound. Ext corridors. **Pets:** Medium, other species. Service with restrictions, supervision.
[ASK] [✕] [▤] [▣] [⇌]

▼▼▼ La Quinta Inn San Antonio (Lackland) 🄷 ☸
(210) 674-3200. **$69-$139.** 6511 Military Dr W. Sw of jct US 90 and Military Dr W. Ext corridors. **Pets:** Medium, other species. Service with restrictions, supervision.
[ASK] [✕] [▤] [▣] [⇌]

▼▼▼ La Quinta Inn San Antonio (Market Square) 🄷 ☸
(210) 271-0001. **$95-$219.** 900 Dolorosa St. I-10/35, exit Durango Blvd, just n on Santa Rosa St, then just w on Nueva St. Ext corridors. **Pets:** Medium, other species. Service with restrictions, supervision.
[ASK] [✕] [⬛M] [▤] [▣] [⇌]

▼▼▼ La Quinta Inn San Antonio (SeaWorld/Ingram Park) 🄷 ☸
(210) 680-8883. **$69-$155.** 7134 NW Loop 410. I-410, exit 10 (Culebra Rd), on eastbound access road. Ext corridors. **Pets:** Medium, other species. Service with restrictions, supervision.
[ASK] [✕] [▤] [▣] [⇌]

▼▼▼ La Quinta Inn San Antonio (South Park) 🄷 ☸
(210) 922-2111. **$69-$139.** 7202 S Pan American Expwy. I-35, exit 150A (Military Dr) northbound; exit 150B southbound, southeast of jct I-35 and Military Dr SW. Ext corridors. **Pets:** Medium, other species. Service with restrictions, supervision.
[ASK] [✕] [⬛M] [▤] [▣] [⇌]

▼▼▼ La Quinta Inn San Antonio (Vance Jackson) 🄷 ☸
(210) 734-7931. **$65-$135.** 5922 I-10 W. I-10, exit 565B eastbound; exit 565C (Vance Jackson Rd) westbound, on eastbound access road. Ext corridors. **Pets:** Medium, other species. Service with restrictions, supervision.
[ASK] [✕] [▤] [▣] [⇌]

▼▼▼ ▼▼▼ Marriott Plaza San Antonio 🄷 ☸
(210) 229-1000. **$189-$209.** 555 S Alamo St. Opposite convention center and Hemisfair Plaza. Int corridors. **Pets:** Medium. $50 one-time fee/room. Service with restrictions, crate.
[✕] [⬛M] [▣] [🍴] [⇌] [✕]

▼▼▼ Microtel Inn & Suites 🄷
(210) 404-1900. **$89-$109.** 15314 Hwy 281 N. US 281 N, exit Brook Hollow. Int corridors. **Pets:** Accepted.
[ASK] [✕] [▤] [▣] [⇌]

▼▼ Motel 6-1122 🄼
(210) 225-1111. **$51-$95.** 211 N Pecos St. I-10/35, exit 155B (Pecos St), on I-10 E/35 S access road. Ext corridors. **Pets:** Other species. Service with restrictions, supervision.
[✕] [▤] [⇌]

▼▼ Motel 6-134 🄼
(210) 650-4419. **$39-$63.** 9503 I-35 N. I-35, exit 167A (Randolf Blvd) southbound; exit 167 (Starlight Terr) northbound. Ext corridors. **Pets:** Other species. Service with restrictions, supervision.
[✕] [⇌]

▼▼ Motel 6-651 🄼
(210) 673-9020. **$41-$61.** 2185 SW Loop 410. I-410, exit 7 (Marbach Rd), 0.7 mi w; on westbound access road. Ext corridors. **Pets:** Other species. Service with restrictions, supervision.
[✕] [▤] [⇌]

▼▼ Motel 6 East #183 🄷
(210) 333-1850. **$41-$59.** 138 N WW White Rd. I-10, exit 580 (WW White Rd), just off westbound access road. Ext corridors. **Pets:** Other species. Service with restrictions, supervision.
[✕] [⇌]

▼▼ Motel 6 Fort Sam Houston #1350 🄼
(210) 661-8791. **$41-$55.** 5522 N PanAm Expwy. I-35/410, exit 164 (Rittiman Rd), just s on northbound access road; just off Goldfield St. Ext corridors. **Pets:** Other species. Service with restrictions, supervision.
[✕] [⇌]

AAA ▼▼▼ ▼▼▼ Omni La Mansion del Rio 🄷 ☸
(210) 518-1000. **$219-$379, 3 day notice.** 112 College St. Just s on the Riverwalk. Ext/int corridors. **Pets:** Small. $50 one-time fee/pet. Designated rooms, service with restrictions, crate.
[SAVE] [✕] [▤] [▣] [🍴] [⇌]

Omni San Antonio Hotel H
(210) 691-8888. **$149-$299.** 9821 Colonnade Blvd. I-10, exit Wurzbach Rd, 12 mi nw on westbound access road. Int corridors. **Pets:** Accepted.

Pear Tree Inn by Drury-San Antonio Northeast H
(210) 654-1144. **$73-$113.** 8300 I-35 N. I-35, exit 165 (Walzem Rd), northbound access road. Ext/int corridors. **Pets:** Other species. Service with restrictions, supervision.

Pear Tree Inn San Antonio Airport H
(210) 366-9300. **$83-$117.** 143 NE Loop 410. Loop 410 W, exit 21 (Jones Maltsberger Rd), on westbound access road; between Airport Blvd and Jones Maltsberger Rd. Int corridors. **Pets:** Other species. Service with restrictions, supervision.

Quality Inn M
(210) 927-4800. **$59-$119.** 606 Division Ave. I-35, exit 152 (Division Ave), on northbound access road. Ext corridors. **Pets:** Accepted.

Quality Inn & Suites H
(210) 359-7200. **$80-$100.** 222 S WW White Rd. I-10, exit 580 (WW White Rd), 0.4 mi s. Ext corridors. **Pets:** $10 daily fee/pet. Service with restrictions, supervision.

Quality Inn & Suites North Airport H
(210) 545-5400. **$80-$150.** 1505 Bexar Crossing. US 281, exit 1604 (Anderson Loop), 0.5 mi s on southbound access road. Int corridors. **Pets:** Small. $25 one-time fee/pet. Designated rooms, service with restrictions, supervision.

Radisson Downtown Market Square H
(210) 224-7155. **$99-$199.** 502 W Durango St. I-35, exit Durango St, 1 blk e. Int corridors. **Pets:** $75 one-time fee/pet. Service with restrictions, supervision.

Red Roof Inn H
(210) 333-9430. **$69-$99.** 4403 I-10 E. I-10, exit 580 (WW White Rd), on westbound access road. Ext corridors. **Pets:** Accepted.

Red Roof Inn Lackland H
(210) 675-4120. **$60-$140.** 6861 Hwy 90 W. Northeast jct of US 90 and Military Dr W; access via Renwick St, off Military Dr, just n of jct US 90. Ext corridors. **Pets:** Accepted.

Red Roof Inn-San Antonio Airport H
(210) 340-4055. **Call for rates.** 333 Wolfe Rd. On southbound access road, just s of US 281 at Isom Rd. Ext/int corridors. **Pets:** Small. Service with restrictions, supervision.

Red Roof Inn San Antonio (Downtown) M
(210) 229-9973. **$70-$200.** 1011 E Houston St. I-37, exit 141 northbound; exit 141B southbound. Int corridors. **Pets:** Small. Service with restrictions, supervision.

Red Roof Inn San Antonio (NW-SeaWorld) H
(210) 509-3434. **$50-$85.** 6880 NW Loop 410. I-410, exit 11 (Alamo Downs Pkwy), on eastbound access road. Ext/int corridors. **Pets:** Small. Service with restrictions, supervision.

Residence Inn Alamo Plaza H
(210) 212-5555. **$215-$263.** 425 Bonham St. I-37/281, exit Commerce St, just w to Bowie St, then 4 blks n. Int corridors. **Pets:** Accepted.

Residence Inn by Marriott San Antonio Downtown/Market Square H
(210) 231-6000. **$169-$189.** 628 S Santa Rosa Blvd. I-10/35, exit Durango St, 0.5 mi e. Int corridors. **Pets:** Medium, other species. $100 one-time fee/room. Service with restrictions, supervision.

Residence Inn North San Antonio H
(210) 490-1333. **$148-$180.** 1115 N SR 1604 E. Loop 1604, just w of US 281 on westbound access road. Int corridors. **Pets:** Accepted.

Residence Inn NW/Six Flags H
(210) 561-9660. **$143-$175.** 4041 Bluemel Rd. I-10, exit 561 (Wurzbach Rd), 0.3 mi w on eastbound access road. Ext corridors. **Pets:** Small, other species. $75 one-time fee/pet. No service, crate.

Residence Inn San Antonio-Airport H
(210) 805-8118. **$170-$208.** 1014 NE Loop 410. Loop 410, exit Broadway St, 0.4 mi e on eastbound access road. Ext corridors. **Pets:** Accepted.

Royal Hawaiian Continental Inn H
(210) 655-3510. **Call for rates.** 9735 I-35 N. I-35, exit 167 (Starlight Terr) northbound; exit 167A (Randolph Blvd) southbound; just n of Loop 410 NE; on southbound access road. Ext corridors. **Pets:** Accepted.

San Antonio Marriott Rivercenter H
(210) 223-1000. **$359-$439.** 101 Bowie St. Corner of Bowie and Commerce sts. Int corridors. **Pets:** Medium. $50 one-time fee/room. Service with restrictions, crate.

San Antonio Marriott Riverwalk H
(210) 224-4555. **$359-$439.** 889 E Market St. Opposite convention center and Hemisfair Plaza; across from Marriott River Center. Int corridors. **Pets:** Medium. $50 one-time fee/room. Service with restrictions, crate.

Sheraton Gunter H
(210) 227-3241. **Call for rates.** 205 E Houston St. Center. Int corridors. **Pets:** Medium, dogs only. $50 one-time fee/room. Designated rooms, service with restrictions, supervision.

Staybridge Suites San Antonio-Airport H
(210) 341-3220. **$149-$297.** 66 NE Loop 410. I-410, exit 20B (McCullough St), on eastbound access road; next to Texas Land & Cattle Restaurant. Int corridors. **Pets:** Accepted.

Staybridge Suites San Antonio NW-Colonnade H
(210) 558-9009. **$129-$289.** 4320 Spectrum One. I-10 W, exit 561 (Wurzbach Rd), follow westbound access road through light, then just n. Int corridors. **Pets:** Accepted.

Staybridge Suites Sunset Station H
(210) 448-5120. **Call for rates.** 123 Hoefgen. In historic downtown Sunset Station. Int corridors. **Pets:** Accepted.

Studio 6 #6046 M
(210) 691-0121. **$61-$75.** 11802 I-10 W. I-10, exit 558 (De Zavala Rd), 0.7 mi e on eastbound access road. Ext corridors. **Pets:** Other species. $10 daily fee/room. Service with restrictions, supervision.

AAA ▼▼▼ **Super 8 Downtown Riverwalk** **M**
(210) 222-8833. **$70-$150.** 1614 N St. Mary's St. I-35, exit 157B (Brooklyn/McCullough St), 4 blks n on Quincey. Ext corridors. **Pets:** Medium. $25 daily fee/pet. Service with restrictions, supervision.
[SAVE] [X] [&M] [▢] [⇆]

▼▼ **Super 8 on Roland** **H**
(210) 798-5500. **Call for rates.** 302 Roland Ave. I-10, exit 577 (Roland Ave) eastbound. Ext corridors. **Pets:** Accepted.
[X] [🛢] [▢] [⇆]

▼▼ **Super 8-Six Flags Fiesta** **H**
(210) 696-6916. **Call for rates.** 5319 Casa Bella. I-10, exit 557 westbound; exit 558 eastbound, on westbound access road. Int corridors. **Pets:** Accepted.
[X] [🛢] [⇆]

▼▼▼ **Towne Place Suites by Marriott San Antonio Northwest** **H**
(210) 694-5100. **$139-$149.** 5014 Prue Rd. I-10, exit Huebner Rd, 1 blk se to Fredericksburg Rd, then just n. Int corridors. **Pets:** Accepted.
[X] [&M] [🛢] [▢] [⇆]

AAA ▼▼▼▼ **Watermark Hotel & Spa** **H** ❀
(210) 396-5800. **$269-$509, 3 day notice.** 212 W Crockett. Between St. Mary's and Navarro sts; on the Riverwalk. Int corridors. **Pets:** Small. $50 one-time fee/pet. Designated rooms, service with restrictions, crate.
[SAVE] [X] [&M] [¶] [⇆] [⊠]

AAA ▼▼▼▼ **The Westin Riverwalk** **H**
(210) 224-6500. **$149-$549, 3 day notice.** 420 W Market St. 2 blks w of Navarro St. Int corridors. **Pets:** Accepted.
[SAVE] [X] [&M] [▢] [¶] [⇆] [⊠]

END METROPOLITAN AREA

SAN MARCOS

AAA ▼▼ **Days Inn** **H**
(512) 353-5050. **$49-$135.** 1005 I-35 N. I-35, exit 205 northbound; exit 204B southbound, on southbound frontage road, jct SR 80. Ext corridors. **Pets:** Dogs only. $10 one-time fee/pet. Designated rooms, service with restrictions, supervision.
[SAVE] [X] [🛢] [▢] [⇆]

AAA ▼▼ **Econo Lodge** **H**
(512) 353-5300. **$39-$120.** 811 S Guadalupe St. I-35, exit 204 northbound; exit 204A southbound, on west frontage road. Ext corridors. **Pets:** Small. $15 one-time fee/room. Service with restrictions, supervision.
[SAVE] [X] [🛢] [▢] [⇆]

▼▼▼ **La Quinta Inn San Marcos** **H** ❀
(512) 392-8800. **$69-$140.** 1619 I-35 N. I-35, exit 206 southbound, 0.5 mi s, on west frontage road; exit northbound, 1 mi n to turnaround to west frontage road, then 1.5 mi s. Ext/int corridors. **Pets:** Medium, other species. Service with restrictions, supervision.
[ASK] [X] [&M] [🛢] [▢] [⇆]

AAA ▼▼▼ **Ramada Limited** **H**
(512) 395-8000. **$55-$149.** 1701 I-35 N. I-35, exit 206 southbound, 0.4 mi s on west frontage road; exit northbound, 1 mi n to turnaround for west frontage road, then 1.4 mi s. Ext corridors. **Pets:** Small, dogs only. $20 daily fee/pet. Service with restrictions, supervision.
[SAVE] [X] [🛢] [▢] [⇆]

▼▼ **Rodeway Inn** **H**
(512) 353-8011. **$39-$149.** 1635 Aquarena Springs Dr. I-35, exit 206, 0.5 mi s. Ext corridors. **Pets:** Dogs only. $10 one-time fee/pet. Designated rooms, service with restrictions, supervision.
[X] [🛢] [⇆]

SEGUIN

▼▼▼▼ **La Quinta Inn & Suites** **H** ❀
(830) 372-0567. **$80-$160.** 1501 Hwy 46 N. I-10, exit 607 (SR 46). Int corridors. **Pets:** Medium, other species. Service with restrictions, supervision.
[ASK] [X] [🛢] [▢] [⇆]

▼▼ **Quality Inn** **H**
(830) 372-0860. **$88-$115.** 2950 N 123 Bypass. I-10, exit 610 (SR 123). Ext corridors. **Pets:** Small. $25 one-time fee/pet. Service with restrictions, supervision.
[ASK] [X] [🛢] [▢] [¶] [⇆]

▼▼ **Super 8 of Seguin** **H**
(830) 379-6888. **$59-$179.** 1525 N Hwy 46. I-10, exit 607 (SR 46), on eastbound access road. Int corridors. **Pets:** Medium. $15 daily fee/pet. Service with restrictions, supervision.
[ASK] [X] [🛢] [▢]

UNIVERSAL CITY

▼▼ **Hawthorn Suites-San Antonio Northeast** **H**
(210) 655-9491. **$89-$149.** 13101 E Loop, 1604 N. Loop 1604 at Pat Booker Rd; 0.8 mi e of I-35. Ext corridors. **Pets:** Accepted.
[ASK] [X] [🛢] [▢] [⇆]

SCHULENBURG

AAA ▼▼▼▼ **Best Western Shulenburg Inn & Suites** **H** ❀
(979) 743-2030. **$90-$140, 7 day notice.** 101 Huser Blvd. I-10, exit 674, just s. Int corridors. **Pets:** Small, other species. $15 daily fee/pet. Service with restrictions, supervision.
[SAVE] [X] [🛢] [▢] [⇆]

SHAMROCK

AAA ▼▼▼▼ **Best Western Shamrock Inn & Suites** **H**
(806) 256-1001. **$99-$139.** 1802 N Main St. I-40, exit 163, just n. Int corridors. **Pets:** Large, other species. $10 daily fee/pet. Designated rooms, service with restrictions, supervision.
[SAVE] [X] [&M] [🛢] [⇆]

AAA ▼▼ **Western Motel** **M**
(806) 256-3244. **$59-$99.** 104 E 12th St. Business Rt I-40 and US 83. Ext corridors. **Pets:** Medium. $5 daily fee/pet. Service with restrictions, supervision.
[SAVE] [X] [🛢] [¶]

SHERMAN

▼▼▼ **Comfort Suites of Sherman** **H**
(903) 893-0499. **$99-$145, 14 day notice.** 2900 US Hwy 75 N. US 75, exit 63, 0.3 mi s of jct US 82. Int corridors. **Pets:** Accepted.
[ASK] [X] [🛢] [▢] [⇆]

▼▼▼ **La Quinta Inn & Suites Sherman/Denison** **H** ❀
(903) 870-1122. **$79-$129.** 2912 US 75 N. US 75, exit 63, just sw of jct US 82. Int corridors. **Pets:** Medium, other species. Service with restrictions, supervision.
[ASK] [X] [🛢] [▢] [⇆]

SINTON

Best Western Sinton 📶
(361) 364-2882. **$69-$79.** 8108 US Hwy 77. US 77 at CR 36A. Ext corridors. **Pets:** Small, dogs only. $20 one-time fee/pet. Designated rooms, service with restrictions, supervision.
[SAVE] [X] [🖥] [▣] [🏊]

SMITHVILLE

Americas Best Value Inn & Suites 📶
(512) 237-2040. **Call for rates.** 1503 Dorothy Nichols Ln. Jct SR 71 and Dorothy Nichols Ln. Ext corridors. **Pets:** Other species. $25 one-time fee/room. Service with restrictions, supervision.
[X] [🖥] [▣] [🏊]

SNYDER

Purple Sage Motel Ⓜ ❁
(325) 573-5491. **$55-$75.** 1501 E Coliseum Dr. 1 mi w on US 180 from jct US 84. Ext corridors. **Pets:** Other species. Service with restrictions, crate.
[SAVE] [X] [🖥] [▣] [🏊]

SONORA

Americas Best Value Inn-Twin Oaks Motel Ⓜ
(325) 387-2551. **$45-$60.** 1009 N Crockett Ave. I-10, exit 400 westbound; exit 399 eastbound, 0.5 mi e, then 0.3 mi s on US 277. Ext corridors. **Pets:** Accepted.
[SAVE] [X] [🖥]

Best Western Sonora Inn 📶
(325) 387-9111. **$86-$95.** 270 Hwy 277 N. I-10, exit 400. Ext corridors. **Pets:** Small. $10 daily fee/pet. Designated rooms, service with restrictions, crate.
[SAVE] [X] [🖥] [▣] [🏊]

Holiday Host Motel Ⓜ
(325) 387-2532. **$45-$55.** 127 Loop 467 (Hwy 290). Loop 467, exit 404 westbound, 3 mi w; exit 399 eastbound, 3 mi e. Ext corridors. **Pets:** No service, supervision.
[SAVE] [X] [🖥] [🏊]

SOUTH PADRE ISLAND

Best Western La Copa Inn & Suites Beach Resort 📶
(956) 761-6000. **$49-$399, 3 day notice.** 350 Padre Blvd. Just s of Queen Isabella Cswy. Int corridors. **Pets:** Medium. $25 one-time fee/pet. Service with restrictions, supervision.
[SAVE] [X] [🖥] [▣] [🏊]

Fiesta Isles Hotel 📶
(956) 761-4913. **Call for rates.** 5701 Padre Blvd. 3 mi n of Queen Isabella Cswy. Ext corridors. **Pets:** Accepted.
[X] [🖥] [▣] [🏊]

Howard Johnson Inn 📶
(956) 761-5658. **$69-$299.** 1709 Padre Blvd. SR 100, 0.9 mi n at corner of W Palm St. Int corridors. **Pets:** Accepted.
[ASK] [X] [🖥M] [🖥] [▣] [🏊]

Inverness at South Padre ⒸⓄ
(956) 761-7919. **Call for rates.** 5600 Gulf Blvd. 2.7 mi n on SR 100 from Queen Isabella Cswy. Ext corridors. **Pets:** Large. $150 one-time fee/room. Service with restrictions, supervision.
[X] [🖥] [▣] [🏊]

La Quinta Inn and Suites South Padre Island 📶 ❁
(956) 772-7000. **$55-$270.** 7000 Padre Blvd. I-77, exit SR 100, over Queen Isabella Cswy, then 3 mi n. Int corridors. **Pets:** Medium, other species. Service with restrictions, supervision.
[ASK] [X] [🖥M] [🖥] [▣] [🏊] [X̄]

Motel 6 South Padre Island #1237 Ⓜ
(956) 761-7911. **$35-$89.** 4013 Padre Blvd. 2 mi n of Queen Isabella Cswy. Ext corridors. **Pets:** Other species. Service with restrictions, supervision.
[X] [🏊]

Ramada Limited 📶
(956) 761-4097. **$66-$309.** 4109 Padre Blvd. 2 mi n of Queen Isabella Cswy. Ext corridors. **Pets:** Medium. $10 one-time fee/pet. Service with restrictions, supervision.
[SAVE] [X] [🖥] [▣] [🏊]

South Padre Beach Resort 📶
(956) 761-5401. **Call for rates.** 100 Padre Blvd. Just s of Queen Isabella Cswy. Int corridors. **Pets:** Accepted.
[SAVE] [X] [🖥] [▣] [🍴] [🏊] [X̄]

Super 8 📶
(956) 761-6300. **$99-$249.** 4205 Padre Blvd. 2.7 mi n of Queen Isabella Cswy. Ext corridors. **Pets:** Very small, dogs only. $10 daily fee/room. Designated rooms, no service, supervision.
[ASK] [X] [🖥] [▣] [🏊]

Travelodge 📶
(956) 761-4744. **Call for rates.** 6200 Padre Blvd. 3 mi n of Queen Isabella Cswy. Ext corridors. **Pets:** Small. $10 daily fee/pet. Service with restrictions, supervision.
[X] [🖥M] [🖥] [▣] [🏊]

STEPHENVILLE

Best Western Cross Timbers 📶
(254) 968-2114. **$62-$90.** 1625 W South Loop (US 377). 1.8 mi sw on US 377 Bypass and 67. Ext corridors. **Pets:** Small. $20 daily fee/pet. Service with restrictions, supervision.
[SAVE] [X] [🖥] [▣] [🏊]

Quality Inn Near Tarleton State University 📶
(254) 968-5256. **Call for rates.** 2865 W Washington St. 1.5 mi s on US 377/167. Ext corridors. **Pets:** Accepted.
[X] [🖥] [▣] [🍴] [🏊]

SULPHUR SPRINGS

Best Western Trail Dust Inn & Suites 📶 ❁
(903) 885-7515. **$79-$99.** 1521 Shannon Rd. Jct I-30 and Loop 301, exit 127. Ext/int corridors. **Pets:** Small. $10 deposit/pet, $20 daily fee/pet, $15 one-time fee/pet. Designated rooms, supervision.
[SAVE] [X] [🖥] [▣] [🏊]

Comfort Suites 📶
(903) 438-0918. **$89.** 1521 E Industrial Dr. I-30, exit 127, just n. Int corridors. **Pets:** Accepted.
[ASK] [X] [🖥M] [🖥] [▣] [🏊]

SWEETWATER

Days Inn 📶
(325) 235-4853. **Call for rates.** 701 SW Georgia Ave. I-20, exit 244, just w on south frontage road. Ext corridors. **Pets:** Small. $15 daily fee/room. Service with restrictions, supervision.
[SAVE] [X] [🖥] [▣] [🍴] [🏊]

La Quinta Inn 📶 ❁
(325) 236-6887. **$65-$125.** 500 NW Georgia Ave. I-20, exit 244, just w of jct SR 70 on north access road. Ext/int corridors. **Pets:** Medium, other species. Service with restrictions, supervision.
[SAVE] [X] [🖥] [▣] [🏊]

Ranch House Motel & Restaurant 📶
(325) 236-6341. **$59-$89.** 301 SW Georgia Ave. I-20, exit 244, just w of jct SR 70 on south access road. Ext/int corridors. **Pets:** Medium, other species. Designated rooms, no service, supervision.
[SAVE] [X] [🖥] [▣] [🍴] [🏊]

▼▼ Super 8 H
(325) 235-5234. **$70-$139.** 216 SE Georgia Ave. I-20, exit 244. Ext corridors. **Pets:** Accepted.
(ASK) ⊠ 🛏 💻 ≈

TEMPLE

▼▼ La Quinta Inn Temple H ☀
(254) 771-2980. **$49-$109.** 1604 W Barton Ave. SR 53, just e; jct I-35 and US 81, exit 301. Ext/int corridors. **Pets:** Medium, other species. Service with restrictions, supervision.
(ASK) ⊠ 🛏 💻 ≈

▼▼ Residence Inn by Marriott H
(254) 773-8400. **$125-$153.** 4301 S General Bruce Dr. I-35, exit 298, on E Frontage Rd. Int corridors. **Pets:** Accepted.
⊠ 🛁 🛏 💻 ≈ ⊠

TERLINGUA

AAA▼ ▼▼ Big Bend Motor Inn M
(432) 371-2218. **$90-$150, 7 day notice.** Hwy 118/170. SR 118, 2 mi from entrance of Big Bend National Park. Ext corridors. **Pets:** Accepted.
(SAVE) ⊠ 🛏 💻

TEXARKANA

▼▼ La Quinta Inn H ☀
(903) 794-1900. **$49-$69.** 5201 State Line Ave. I-30, exit 223A, sw of jct US 59 and 71. Ext corridors. **Pets:** Medium, other species. Service with restrictions, supervision.
(ASK) ⊠ 🛏 💻 ≈

AAA▼ ▼▼ Rodeway Inn H
(903) 792-6688. **$52-$70.** 5105 N State Line Ave. I-30, exit 223A, just sw. Ext corridors. **Pets:** Accepted.
(SAVE) ⊠ 🛏 💻 ≈

THREE RIVERS

▼▼ Econo Lodge M
(361) 786-3563. **$59-$89.** 1401 N Harborth Ave. I-37, exit 72 (US 281), 3.8 mi s. Ext corridors. **Pets:** Accepted.
(ASK) ⊠ 🛏 💻 ≈

TULIA

▼▼ Select Inn of Tulia M
(806) 995-3248. **Call for rates.** 1591 I-27. I-27, exit 74. Ext corridors. **Pets:** Accepted.
⊠ 🛗 🛏

TYLER

AAA▼ ▼▼▼ Candlewood Suites H
(903) 509-4131. **$99-$129.** 315 E Rieck Rd. 1.1 mi s of jct Loop 323 and US 69 (S Broadway) to Rieck Rd, just e. Int corridors. **Pets:** Accepted.
(SAVE) ⊠ 🛗 🛏 💻

▼▼▼ Holiday Inn Select H
(903) 561-5800. **$109-$169.** 5701 S Broadway Ave. 1.1 mi s of jct Loop 323 and US 69 (S Broadway). Int corridors. **Pets:** Accepted.
⊠ 🛏 💻 ⑪ ≈ ⊠

▼▼ La Quinta Inn Tyler H ☀
(903) 561-2223. **$59-$95.** 1601 W SW Loop 323. 1 mi w of S US 69. Ext corridors. **Pets:** Medium, other species. Service with restrictions, supervision.
(ASK) ⊠ 🛏 💻 ≈

AAA▼ ▼▼ Ramada Tyler Conference Center H
(903) 593-3600. **Call for rates.** 3310 Troup Hwy. 0.3 mi n of jct E Loop 323 and SR 110. Ext corridors. **Pets:** Accepted.
(SAVE) ⊠ 🛏 💻 ⑪ ≈

▼▼▼ Residence Inn by Marriott H
(903) 595-5188. **$152-$186.** 3303 Troup Hwy. 0.3 mi n of jct E Loop 323 and SR 110. Ext corridors. **Pets:** $100 one-time fee/room. Service with restrictions.
⊠ 🛏 💻 ≈ ⊠

UVALDE

▼▼ Quality Inn of Uvalde H
(830) 278-4511. **$90-$112.** 920 E Main St. 0.5 mi e on US 90. Ext corridors. **Pets:** Medium. Designated rooms, service with restrictions, supervision.
(ASK) ⊠ 🛏 💻 ⑪ ≈

VAN HORN

AAA▼ ▼▼ Americas Best Value Inn M
(432) 283-2410. **$55-$120.** 1705 W Broadway St. I-10, exit 138, 0.3 mi e, then 1 mi w on US 80. Ext corridors. **Pets:** Accepted.
(SAVE) ⊠ 🛏 💻 ≈

AAA▼ ▼ Budget Inn M
(432) 283-2019. **$36-$40.** 1303 W Broadway St. I-10, exit 138, 0.7 mi e. Ext corridors. **Pets:** Accepted.
(SAVE) ⊠ 🛏

AAA▼ ▼▼ Days Inn M
(432) 283-1007. **$65-$105.** 600 E Broadway St. I-10, exit 140B, just w. Ext corridors. **Pets:** Accepted.
(SAVE) ⊠ 🛏 💻 ≈

AAA▼ ▼▼ Econo Lodge H
(432) 283-2211. **$60-$95.** 1601 W Broadway St. I-10, exit 138, 0.5 mi e on Business Rt I-10. Ext corridors. **Pets:** Medium, other species. $10 daily fee/pet. Designated rooms, service with restrictions, supervision.
(SAVE) ⊠ 🛏 💻 ≈

AAA▼ ▼ Economy Inn M
(432) 283-2754. **$38-$42.** 1500 W Broadway St. I-10, exit 138, 0.5 mi e on US 80. Ext corridors. **Pets:** Accepted.
(SAVE) ⊠ 🛏

▼▼▼ Holiday Inn Express H
(432) 283-7444. **$89-$109.** 1905 SW Frontage Rd. I-10, exit 138. Ext corridors. **Pets:** Accepted.
⊠ 🛗 🛏 💻 ≈

AAA▼ ▼▼▼ Knights Inn & Suites M
(432) 283-2030. **$55-$99.** 1309 W Broadway St. I-10, exit 138, 1 mi e. Ext corridors. **Pets:** Accepted.
(SAVE) ⊠ 🛏 💻 ≈

AAA▼ ▼ Motel 6–4024 M
(432) 283-2992. **$46-$56.** 1805 W Broadway St. I-10, exit 138. Ext corridors. **Pets:** Other species. Service with restrictions, supervision.
(SAVE) ⊠ 🛏 ≈

AAA▼ ▼▼ Ramada Inn H
(432) 283-2780. **Call for rates.** 200 Golf Course Dr. I-10, exit 138. Ext/int corridors. **Pets:** Other species. $10 daily fee/pet. Service with restrictions, crate.
(SAVE) ⊠ 🛏 💻 ≈

AAA▼ ▼▼▼ Van Horn Super 8 M
(432) 283-2282. **$65-$105.** 1807 E Service Rd. I-10, exit 138. Ext corridors. **Pets:** Accepted.
(SAVE) ⊠ 🛏 💻

VEGA

AAA▼ ▼▼▼ Best Western Country Inn M
(806) 267-2131. **$65-$79.** 1800 W Vega Blvd. 0.5 mi w on US 40 business loop. Ext corridors. **Pets:** Medium. $10 daily fee/pet. Designated rooms, service with restrictions, supervision.
(SAVE) ⊠ 🛏 💻 ≈

⟨AAA⟩ ▽▽▽▽ Comfort Inn 🅷
(806) 267-0126. **$69-$89.** 1005 S Main St. I-40, exit 36. Int corridors.
Pets: Small. $10 daily fee/pet. Service with restrictions, supervision.
[SAVE] [✕] [🛏] [💻] [🏊]

VERNON

⟨AAA⟩ ▽▽▽ Best Western Village Inn 🅷
(940) 552-5417. **$70-$105.** 1615 US Hwy 287 E. US 287, exit Main St, just
w. Ext/int corridors. **Pets:** Accepted.
[SAVE] [✕] [🛏] [💻] [🍴] [🏊]

▽▽▽▽ Holiday Inn Express Hotel and Suites 🅷 🐾
(940) 552-0200. **$99-$109.** 700 Hillcrest Dr. Jct US 287 and 70. Int corridors. **Pets:** Very small. $25 one-time fee/room. Service with restrictions,
supervision.
[ASK] [✕] [🗐] [🛏] [💻] [🏊]

VICTORIA

⟨AAA⟩ ▽▽▽▽ Best Western Victoria Inn and Suites 🅷
(361) 485-2300. **$81-$160, 7 day notice.** 8106 NE Zac Lenz Pkwy. Jct
Zac Lenz Pkwy and Invitational Dr. Int corridors. **Pets:** Accepted.
[SAVE] [✕] [🛏] [💻] [🏊]

▽▽▽▽ Howard Johnson 🅷
(361) 575-0251. **Call for rates.** 2705 E Houston Hwy (Business Rt 59).
On Business Rt US 59, 2.5 mi ne. Ext/int corridors. **Pets:** Accepted.
[✕] [🛏] [💻] [🍴] [🏊] [✕]

▽▽▽ La Quinta Inn Victoria 🅷 🐾
(361) 572-3585. **$59-$105.** 7603 N Navarro St (US 77 N). 4 mi n; at Loop
463. Ext corridors. **Pets:** Medium, other species. Service with restrictions,
supervision.
[ASK] [✕] [🛏] [💻] [🏊]

⟨AAA⟩ ▽▽▽ Lone Star Inn & Suites 🅷
(361) 579-0225. **$65-$90.** 1907 US 59 N. US 59, exit Bloomington (US
185); on northeast corner. Ext corridors. **Pets:** Small. $25 daily fee/pet.
Designated rooms, service with restrictions, supervision.
[SAVE] [✕] [🛏] [💻] [🏊]

▽▽▽ Motel 6 Victoria #225 Ⓜ
(361) 573-1273. **$49-$62.** 3716 Houston Hwy. On Business Rt US 59. Ext
corridors. **Pets:** Other species. Service with restrictions, supervision.
[✕] [🛏] [🏊]

▽▽▽ Quality Inn-Victoria 🅷
(361) 578-2030. **$75-$90, 7 day notice.** 3112 E Houston Hwy (Business
Rt 59). On Business Rt US 59, 2 mi ne. Ext corridors. **Pets:** Accepted.
[ASK] [✕] [🛏] [💻] [🏊]

VIDOR

▽▽▽ La Quinta Inn of Vidor 🅷 🐾
(409) 783-2600. **$80-$100.** 165 E Courtland St. I-10, exit 861A, just s. Int
corridors. **Pets:** Medium, other species. Service with restrictions, supervision.
[ASK] [✕] [🛏] [💻] [🏊]

WACO

⟨AAA⟩ ▽▽▽ Best Western Old Main Lodge 🅷 🐾
(254) 753-0316. **$86-$100.** I-35 & 4th St. I-35 and US 81, exit 335A
(4th-5th sts). Ext corridors. **Pets:** Small. Designated rooms, service with
restrictions, supervision.
[SAVE] [✕] [🛏] [💻] [🏊]

⟨AAA⟩ ▽▽▽ Days Inn 🅷
(254) 799-8585. **$69-$125.** 1504 I-35 N. I-35, exit 338B, just n. Ext corridors. **Pets:** Accepted.
[SAVE] [✕] [🛏] [💻] [🏊]

⟨AAA⟩ ▽▽▽ Hotel Waco 🅷
(254) 753-0261. **$69-$99, 7 day notice.** 1001 Martin Luther King Blvd.
I-35, exit 335C (Lake Brazos Dr), just n. Int corridors. **Pets:** Accepted.
[SAVE] [✕] [🛏] [💻] [🍴] [🏊]

▽▽▽ La Quinta Inn Waco (University) 🅷 🐾
(254) 752-9741. **$65-$129.** 1110 S 9th St. I-35, exit 334 (17th St) southbound; exit 334A (18th St) northbound. Ext corridors. **Pets:** Medium, other
species. Service with restrictions, supervision.
[ASK] [✕] [🛏] [💻] [🏊]

▽▽▽▽ Residence Inn by Marriott 🅷
(254) 714-1386. **$126-$154.** 501 S University Parks Dr. I-35, exit 335B, 0.3
mi w. Int corridors. **Pets:** Other species. $100 one-time fee/room. Service
with restrictions.
[✕] [🛏] [💻] [🏊] [✕]

▽▽▽ Super 8 Motel-Waco 🅷
(254) 754-1023. **Call for rates.** 1320 S Jack Kultgen Frwy. I-35, exit 334,
just e. Int corridors. **Pets:** Accepted.
[✕] [🛏] [💻]

⟨AAA⟩ ▽▽▽▽ Super 8 Motel Waco Mall 🅷
(254) 776-3194. **$60-$110.** 6624 Woodway Dr. Jct US 84 and SR 6, just w.
Ext corridors. **Pets:** Small. $10 one-time fee/pet. Service with restrictions,
supervision.
[SAVE] [✕] [🛏] [💻] [🏊]

WAXAHACHIE

▽▽▽ Super 8 🅷
(972) 938-9088. **$67-$99, 7 day notice.** 400 N I-35E. I-35E, exit 401B. Int
corridors. **Pets:** Small, other species. $15 daily fee/pet. No service, super-
vision.
[ASK] [✕] [🛏] [💻] [🏊]

WEATHERFORD

⟨AAA⟩ ▽▽▽ Best Western Santa Fe Inn 🅷
(817) 594-7401. **$94.** 1927 Santa Fe Dr. I-20, exit 409 (Clear Lake Rd/FM
2552), 0.3 mi nw. Ext corridors. **Pets:** Accepted.
[SAVE] [✕] [🛏] [💻] [🏊]

▽▽▽▽ Hampton Inn 🅷
(817) 599-4800. **$105-$129.** 2524 S Main St. I-20, exit 408. Int corridors.
Pets: Small. $10 daily fee/pet. Service with restrictions, supervision.
[ASK] [✕] [🛏] [💻] [🏊]

▽▽▽▽ Holiday Inn Express Hotel & Suites 🅷
(817) 599-3700. **$110-$200.** 2500 S Main St. I-20, exit 408. Ext/int corridors. **Pets:** Small. $10 daily fee/pet. Service with restrictions, supervision.
[ASK] [✕] [🗐] [🛏] [💻] [🏊]

▽▽▽▽ La Quinta Inn & Suites 🅷 🐾
(817) 594-4481. **$79-$129.** 1915 Wall St. I-20, exit 408, just se. Int corridors. **Pets:** Medium, other species. Service with restrictions, supervision.
[ASK] [✕] [🗐] [🛏] [💻] [🏊]

WEIMAR

⟨AAA⟩ ▽▽▽ Czech Inn 🅷 🐾
(979) 725-9788. **$61-$71.** 102 Townsend Ln. I-10, exit 682, just w on north
access road. Int corridors. **Pets:** Other species. $10 daily fee/room. Desig-
nated rooms, service with restrictions, supervision.
[SAVE] [✕] [🛏] [💻] [🏊]

WELLINGTON

▽▽▽ Cherokee Inn & Restaurant Ⓜ
(806) 447-2508. **$44-$80.** 1105 Houston St. US 83, just n of jct FM 338.
Ext corridors. **Pets:** Accepted.
[ASK] [✕] [🍴]

WESLACO

Best Western Palm Aire Hotel & Suites 🅷
(956) 969-2411. **$60-$90.** 415 S International Blvd. US 83, exit International Blvd, just s. Ext corridors. **Pets:** Accepted.

Super 8 🅷
(956) 969-9920. **Call for rates.** 1702 E Expwy 83. US 83, exit Airport Dr. Ext corridors. **Pets:** Accepted.

WICHITA FALLS

Best Western Northtown Inn 🅷
(940) 766-3300. **$69.** 1317 Kenley Ave. I-44, exit 2, just w. Int corridors. **Pets:** Medium, other species. $10 daily fee/pet. No service, supervision.

Best Western Wichita Falls Inn 🅷
(940) 766-6881. **$69-$89, 7 day notice.** 1032 Central Frwy. I-44, exit 2, just w. Ext corridors. **Pets:** Medium. $10 daily fee/pet. Service with restrictions, supervision.

Hawthorn Suites Limited 🅷
(940) 692-7900. **$99-$189.** 1917 Elmwood Ave N. US 281 S, exit Southwest Pkwy (CR 369), 2.3 mi w to Kemp Blvd, 2 blks n to Elmwood Ave, then just e. Int corridors. **Pets:** Other species. $50 one-time fee/room. Designated rooms, service with restrictions, crate.

Holiday Inn 🅷
(940) 761-6000. **Call for rates.** 100 Central Frwy. I-287, exit 1C, on west side access road. Int corridors. **Pets:** Accepted.

La Quinta Inn Wichita Falls 🅷 ❀
(940) 322-6971. **$52-$89.** 1128 Central Frwy N. I-44, exit 2, just w. Ext corridors. **Pets:** Medium, other species. Service with restrictions, supervision.

Motel 6 #130 Ⓜ
(940) 322-8817. **$43-$55.** 1812 Maurine St. I-44, exit 2, just e. Ext corridors. **Pets:** Other species. Service with restrictions, supervision.

Ramada Inn & Suites 🅷
(940) 687-2025. **$75-$175.** 4540 Maplewood Ave. Jct Southwest Pkwy (CR 369). Int corridors. **Pets:** Accepted.

Ramada Limited 🅷
(940) 855-0085. **$67-$74.** 3209 Northwest Frwy. US 287, exit Beverly (CR 11), just w. Ext corridors. **Pets:** $10 one-time fee/room. Service with restrictions, crate.

WOODWAY

Extended StayAmerica Waco-Woodway 🅷
(254) 399-8836. **$70-$103.** 5903 Woodway Dr. I-35, exit 330 (SR 6), 5 mi sw; Loop 340, exit 330 to jct SR 84. Int corridors. **Pets:** Other species. $25 daily fee/pet. Service with restrictions, crate.

Travelodge Waco 🅷
(254) 751-7400. **$75-$110, 14 day notice.** 7007 Woodway Dr. I-35, exit 330 (SR 6 N), 2.4 mi w to exit US 84, then 1.1 mi s. Int corridors. **Pets:** Medium. $25 one-time fee/room. Service with restrictions, supervision.

ZAPATA

Best Western Inn by the Lake 🅷
(956) 765-8403. **$100-$115.** 1896 S US Hwy 83. On US 83, 0.5 mi se. Ext corridors. **Pets:** Accepted.

UTAH

BEAVER

Best Western Butch Cassidy Inn M
(435) 438-2438. **$71-$90.** 161 S Main St. I-15, exit 109, 1.5 mi e. Ext corridors. **Pets:** Accepted.

Best Western Paradise Inn M
(435) 438-2455. **$80-$90, 14 day notice.** 314 W 1425 N. I-15, exit 112, just e; north end of town. Ext corridors. **Pets:** Medium, other species. $9 daily fee/room. Service with restrictions.

Quality Inn M
(435) 438-5426. **$55-$75.** 781 W 1800 S. I-15, exit 109, just w. Int corridors. **Pets:** Accepted.

BICKNELL

Aquarius Motel and Restaurant H
(435) 425-3835. **$52-$64.** 240 W Main St. SR 24, 9 mi w of Capitol Reef National Park; downtown. Ext/int corridors. **Pets:** Other species. $25 deposit/room, $5 daily fee/room. Service with restrictions, crate.

BLANDING

Four Corners Inn M
(435) 678-3257. **$55-$70.** 131 E Center St. On US 191. Ext corridors. **Pets:** Accepted.

Gateway Inn M
(435) 678-2278. **$55-$85.** 88 E Center St. East side on US 191. Ext corridors. **Pets:** Accepted.

BLUFF

Kokopelli Inn M
(435) 672-2322. **$59-$69.** 160 E Main St. On US 191. Int corridors. **Pets:** Small. $11 daily fee/pet. Service with restrictions, supervision.

Recapture Lodge M
(435) 672-2281. **$55-$74.** 220 E Main St. On US 191. Ext corridors. **Pets:** Other species. Service with restrictions, supervision.

BOULDER

Boulder Mountain Lodge H ❀
(435) 335-7460. **$75-$184, 14 day notice.** 20 N Hwy 12. Just n of jct SR 12 and Burr Trail Rd. Ext/int corridors. **Pets:** $15 daily fee/pet. Designated rooms, service with restrictions, supervision.

BRIGHAM CITY

Crystal Inn H
(435) 723-0440. **$94-$104.** 480 Westland Dr. I-15, exit 362, 1 mi e. Int corridors. **Pets:** Other species. $75 deposit/room. Designated rooms, service with restrictions, supervision.

BRYCE CANYON CITY

Best Western Ruby's Inn H
(435) 834-5341. **$69-$200.** 1000 S Hwy 63. On SR 63, 1 mi s of SR 12, 1 mi n of Bryce Canyon National Park entrance. Ext/int corridors. **Pets:** Other species. $10 daily fee/room. Designated rooms, service with restrictions, supervision.

Bryce View Lodge M
(435) 834-5180. **$60-$110.** 991 S SR 63. On SR 63, 1 mi s of SR 12; 1 mi n of Bryce Canyon National Park entrance. Ext corridors. **Pets:** Other species. $10 daily fee/room. Service with restrictions, supervision.

CEDAR CITY

Anniversary House Bed & Breakfast BB
(435) 865-1266. **$99-$139, 14 day notice.** 133 S 100 W. I-15, exit 59, 1 mi e to 100 W, then just s. Int corridors. **Pets:** Large, dogs only. Designated rooms, crate.

Cedar Rest Motel M
(435) 586-9471. **Call for rates.** 479 S Main St. I-15, exit 59, just e. Ext corridors. **Pets:** Accepted.

Comfort Inn & Suites H
(435) 865-0003. **$59-$179.** 1288 S Main St. I-15, exit 57, just e, then just n. Int corridors. **Pets:** Accepted.

Crystal Inn Cedar City H
(435) 586-8888. **$59-$99.** 1575 W 200 N. I-15, exit 59, just w. Ext/int corridors. **Pets:** Other species. $25 one-time fee/room. Designated rooms, service with restrictions.

Days Inn M
(435) 867-8877. **$64-$149.** 1204 S Main St. I-15, exit 57, 0.4 mi ne. Ext corridors. **Pets:** Small. $10 daily fee/pet. Designated rooms, service with restrictions, supervision.

Holiday Inn Express Hotel & Suites M
(435) 865-7799. **Call for rates.** 1555 S Old Hwy 91. I-15, exit 57, just e, then s. Int corridors. **Pets:** Accepted.

▼▼ **Motel 6 of Cedar City–4041** **M**
(435) 586-9200. **Call for rates.** 1620 W 200 N. I-15, exit 59, just w. Int corridors. **Pets:** Other species. Service with restrictions, supervision.
❌ 📧

▼▼ **Quality Inn** **M**
(435) 586-2082. **$59-$129.** 250 N 1100 W. I-15, exit 59, just e. Ext corridors. **Pets:** Other species. $10 daily fee/room. Designated rooms, service with restrictions, supervision.
ASK ❌ 📧 💻 ➴

▼▼ **Super 7 Motel** **M**
(435) 586-6566. **$35-$95.** 190 S Main St. I-15, exit 57, just e. Ext corridors. **Pets:** Accepted.
ASK ❌ 📧

▼▼ **Super 8 Motel** **M**
(435) 586-8880. **Call for rates.** 145 N 1550 W. I-15, exit 59, just w. Int corridors. **Pets:** Accepted.
❌ ♿ 📧 💻

COALVILLE

◆◆◆ ▼▼▼▼ **Best Western Holiday Hills** **H**
(435) 336-4444. **$89-$109, 3 day notice.** 210 S 200 W. I-80, exit 162, just w. Int corridors. **Pets:** Large, other species. $15 daily fee/pet. Designated rooms, service with restrictions, crate.
SAVE ❌ 📧 💻 ➴ ❎

DELTA

▼▼ **Days Inn** **M**
(435) 864-3882. **Call for rates.** 527 E Topaz Blvd. US 6, at US 50. Ext corridors. **Pets:** $15 one-time fee/pet. Designated rooms, service with restrictions, supervision.
❌ 📧 💻 ➴

ESCALANTE

▼▼ **Rainbow Country Bed & Breakfast** **BB**
(435) 826-4567. **$69-$99, 3 day notice.** 585 E 300 S. Just off SR 12; east end of town. Int corridors. **Pets:** $10 daily fee/pet. Service with restrictions, supervision.
ASK ❌ ♿ ✍

FILLMORE

◆◆◆ ▼▼▼ **Best Western Paradise Resort** **M**
(435) 743-6895. **$80-$85.** 905 N Main St. I-15, exit 167, just e. Ext corridors. **Pets:** Large, other species. Service with restrictions, supervision.
SAVE ❌ 📧 💻 🍴 ➴

▼▼ **Comfort Inn & Suites** **M** 🐾
(435) 743-4334. **$69-$100.** 940 S Hwy 99. I-15, exit 163, just e. Int corridors. **Pets:** $6 one-time fee/pet. Designated rooms, service with restrictions, supervision.
ASK ❌ 📧 💻 ➴

GARDEN CITY

▼▼ **Canyon Cove Inn** **M**
(435) 946-3565. **Call for rates.** 315 W Logan (Hwy 89). 0.5 mi w of jct US 89 and SR 30. Int corridors. **Pets:** Accepted.
❌ 📧 ➴

GLENDALE

▼▼ **Historic Smith Hotel Bed & Breakfast** **BB** 🐾
(435) 648-2156. **$60-$95.** 295 N Main St. US 89; north end of town. Int corridors. **Pets:** Other species. $5 one-time fee/pet. Designated rooms, no service, supervision.
ASK ❌ ✍

GREEN RIVER

◆◆◆ ▼▼▼▼ **Holiday Inn Express** **M**
(435) 564-4439. **$89-$124.** 1845 E Main St. I-70, exit 160, 2.6 mi ne. Int corridors. **Pets:** Accepted.
SAVE ❌ 📧 💻 ➴

▼▼ **Ramada Limited** **M**
(435) 564-8441. **$50-$120.** 2125 E Main St. I-70, exit 164, 1 mi nw. Ext/int corridors. **Pets:** Accepted.
ASK ❌ 📧 💻 ➴

◆◆◆ ▼▼▼ **Super 8** **M**
(435) 564-8888. **$55-$90.** 1248 E Main St. I-70, exit 160, 3.1 mi ne. Int corridors. **Pets:** Accepted.
SAVE ❌ 📧 💻 ➴

HATCH

▼ **Riverside Resort & RV Park** **M**
(435) 735-4223. **$60-$90, 10 day notice.** 594 US Hwy 89. On US 89, 1 mi n. Ext corridors. **Pets:** Other species. $50 deposit/room, $5 daily fee/pet. Designated rooms, service with restrictions, supervision.
ASK ❌ 📧 🍴 ❎ ✍

HEBER CITY

◆◆◆ ▼▼▼ **Swiss Alps Inn** **M**
(435) 654-0722. **$60-$110.** 167 S Main St. I-80, exit 146 (US 40), 15 mi s. Ext corridors. **Pets:** Service with restrictions, supervision.
SAVE ❌ 📧 💻 ➴ ❎

HUNTSVILLE

▼▼ **Jackson Fork Inn** **M**
(801) 745-0051. **$80-$140, 3 day notice.** 7345 E 900 S. I-15, exit 344 (12th St), 12 mi e on SR 39. Int corridors. **Pets:** Medium. $20 one-time fee/room. Designated rooms, supervision.
ASK ❌ 🍴 ✍

HURRICANE

▼▼ **Super 8** **M**
(435) 635-0808. **$49-$115.** 65 S 700 W. Just s of SR 9. Ext corridors. **Pets:** Accepted.
ASK ❌ 📧 💻 ➴

KANAB

◆◆◆ ▼▼▼ **Best Western Red Hills** **M**
(435) 644-2675. **$50-$130.** 125 W Center St. Center. Ext/int corridors. **Pets:** Other species. $10 one-time fee/room. Designated rooms, service with restrictions.
SAVE ❌ 📧 💻 ➴

◆◆◆ ▼▼▼ **Bob-Bon Inn** **M**
(435) 644-5094. **$45-$70, 3 day notice.** 236 Hwy 89 N. On US 89. Ext corridors. **Pets:** Accepted.
SAVE ❌ 📧 ➴

▼▼▼▼ **Clarion Collection-Victorian Charm Inn** **M**
(435) 644-8660. **$69-$159.** 190 N Hwy 89. North end of town. Int corridors. **Pets:** Accepted.
ASK ❌

◆◆◆ ▼▼▼▼ **Holiday Inn Express Hotel & Suites** **H**
(435) 644-3100. **$90-$179.** 217 S 100 E. On US 89; jct 200 S. Int corridors. **Pets:** Accepted.
SAVE ❌ 📧 💻 ➴

▼▼ **Parry Lodge** **M**
(435) 644-2601. **$62-$102.** 89 E Center St. On US 89; corner of 100 E; center. Ext/int corridors. **Pets:** Large, other species. $10 daily fee/pet. Designated rooms, service with restrictions, crate.
ASK ❌ 📧 💻 🍴 ➴

Quail Park Lodge M ❖
(435) 644-8700. **$59-$99.** 125 N 300 W (Hwy 89). On US 89. Ext corridors. **Pets:** Medium, dogs only. Designated rooms, service with restrictions, supervision.

Quality Inn M
(435) 644-8888. **$79-$159.** 815 E Hwy 89. On US 89, just e. Int corridors. **Pets:** Accepted.

Rodeway Inn M
(435) 644-5500. **$50-$150.** 70 S 200 W. Just s of US 89. Ext corridors. **Pets:** Accepted.

Shilo Inn Suites-Kanab H ❖
(435) 644-2562. **$80-$196.** 296 W 100 N. On US 89; n of downtown. Int corridors. **Pets:** Dogs only. $25 one-time fee/room. Designated rooms, service with restrictions, supervision.

LAKE POWELL

Defiance House Lodge-Bullfrog Marina H
(435) 684-3000. **$135-$155, 3 day notice.** Hwy 276. 1 mi from entrance at Bullfrog sign. Int corridors. **Pets:** Other species. $15 one-time fee/room. Designated rooms, service with restrictions, supervision.

LAYTON

Hampton Inn H
(801) 775-8800. **$79-$109.** 1700 Woodland Park Dr. I-15, exit 332 (Antelope Dr), 0.3 mi se. Int corridors. **Pets:** Accepted.

La Quinta Inn H ❖
(801) 776-6700. **$59-$109.** 1965 N 1200 W. I-15, exit 332 (Antelope Dr), just e. Int corridors. **Pets:** Medium, other species. Service with restrictions, supervision.

TownePlace Suites H
(801) 779-2422. **$116-$142.** 1743 Woodland Park Dr. I-15, exit 332 (Antelope Dr), 0.3 mi se. Int corridors. **Pets:** Accepted.

LEHI

Best Western Timpanogos Inn H
(801) 768-1400. **$60-$100.** 195 S 850 E. I-15, exit 279, just w, then just s. Int corridors. **Pets:** Accepted.

Super 8 M
(801) 766-8800. **Call for rates.** 125 S 850 E. I-15, exit 279, just w, then just s. Int corridors. **Pets:** Other species. $10 daily fee/pet. Service with restrictions, supervision.

LOGAN

Best Western Baugh Motel H
(435) 752-5220. **Call for rates.** 153 S Main St. On US 89 and 91. Ext corridors. **Pets:** Accepted.

Best Western Weston Inn H ❖
(435) 752-5700. **$80-$110, 7 day notice.** 250 N Main St. I-15, exit 362, on US 89 and 91; downtown. Ext corridors. **Pets:** Medium. $15 daily fee/room. Designated rooms, service with restrictions, supervision.

Super 8 M
(435) 753-8883. **$45-$86.** 865 S Hwy 89/91. I-15, exit 362, 2 mi s; south end of town. Int corridors. **Pets:** Other species. $10 daily fee/pet. Service with restrictions, supervision.

MANTI

Manti Country Village Motel M
(435) 835-9300. **$69-$99.** 145 N Main St. On US 89. Ext corridors. **Pets:** Medium, dogs only. $75 deposit/pet. Designated rooms, service with restrictions, supervision.

MEXICAN HAT

San Juan Inn & Trading Post M
(435) 683-2220. **$64-$85.** Hwy 163 & San Juan River. On US 163. Ext corridors. **Pets:** Dogs only. $10 one-time fee/pet. Designated rooms, no service, supervision.

MOAB

Apache Motel M
(435) 259-5727. **$39-$79.** 166 S 400 E. Jct US 191 and 100 S, just e, then just s. Ext corridors. **Pets:** Large, other species. Service with restrictions, supervision.

Big Horn Lodge M ❖
(435) 259-6171. **$39-$105.** 550 S Main St. South end of town. Ext corridors. **Pets:** Other species. $5 daily fee/pet. Designated rooms, service with restrictions, supervision.

Bowen Motel M
(435) 259-7132. **$50-$102.** 169 N Main St. Downtown. Ext corridors. **Pets:** Small. $10 daily fee/pet. Designated rooms, service with restrictions, supervision.

Cedar Breaks Condos CO
(435) 259-5125. **$100-$205, 14 day notice.** 400 East & Center St. Jct Main and Center sts, just e, then just s. Ext corridors. **Pets:** Other species. $10 daily fee/pet. Designated rooms, no service, supervision.

The Gonzo Inn M ❖
(435) 259-2515. **$98-$330.** 100 W 200 S. Downtown. Ext/int corridors. **Pets:** Other species. $30 daily fee/room. Service with restrictions.

La Quinta Inn Moab H ❖
(435) 259-8700. **$53-$232.** 815 S Main St. South end of town. Int corridors. **Pets:** Medium, other species. Service with restrictions, supervision.

Moab Valley Inn H
(435) 259-4419. **$70-$170.** 711 S Main St. 1 mi s on US 191. Int corridors. **Pets:** $10 daily fee/room. Designated rooms, service with restrictions, supervision.

Motel 6 Moab #4119 M
(435) 259-6686. **$59-$199.** 1089 N Main St. North end of town; west side of street. Int corridors. **Pets:** Medium. $20 one-time fee/pet. Designated rooms, service with restrictions, supervision.

Nichol's Lane Accommodations CO
(435) 259-5125. **$75-$150, 14 day notice.** 543 Nichol Ln. Jct Center and Main sts, e to 400 E, just s, then just e. Ext corridors. **Pets:** Other species. $10 daily fee/pet. Designated rooms, no service, supervision.

WWW Ramada of Downtown Moab M
(435) 259-7141. **$69-$199.** 182 S Main St. At 200 S; downtown. Ext/int corridors. **Pets:** Medium. $20 one-time fee/pet. Service with restrictions, supervision.
ASK ⊠ 🛗 💻 🍽 🏊

AAA WWWW Red Cliffs Adventure Lodge H
(435) 259-2002. **$99-$320, 30 day notice.** Milepost 14 Hwy 128. 2 mi n to jct US 191 and SR 128, 14.5 mi e. Ext corridors. **Pets:** Large. $20 daily fee/pet. Designated rooms, service with restrictions, supervision.
SAVE ⊠ 🛗 💻 🍽 🏊 ✕

AAA WWW Red Stone Inn M ✿
(435) 259-3500. **$39-$100.** 535 S Main St. Downtown. Ext/int corridors. **Pets:** $5 daily fee/pet. Designated rooms, service with restrictions, supervision.
SAVE ⊠ 🛗 💻

AAA WWW River Canyon Lodge, An Extended Stay Inn & Suites M
(435) 259-8838. **$59-$290.** 71 W 200 N. Jct 200 N and Main St, just w; downtown. Int corridors. **Pets:** Medium. $20 one-time fee/pet. Service with restrictions, supervision.
SAVE ⊠ 🛗 💻 🏊

WWW Riverside Inn H
(435) 259-8848. **$55-$135, 7 day notice.** 988 N Main St. 1 mi n on US 191. Int corridors. **Pets:** Accepted.
⊠ 🛗 🏊

AAA WW Silver Sage Inn M
(435) 259-4420. **$45-$90.** 840 S Main St. South end of town on US 191. Int corridors. **Pets:** $5 daily fee/pet. Service with restrictions.
SAVE ⊠ 🛗 💻

WW Sleep Inn H
(435) 259-4655. **$59-$189.** 1051 S Main St. South end of town. Int corridors. **Pets:** Large, other species. $50 deposit/room. Designated rooms, service with restrictions, supervision.
ASK ⊠ 🛗 💻 🏊

WW Super 8 Moab M
(435) 259-8868. **$59-$189.** 889 N Main St. US 191, 1 mi n. Int corridors. **Pets:** Medium. $20 one-time fee/pet. Service with restrictions, supervision.
ASK ⊠ 🛗 💻 🏊

MONTICELLO

AAA WWW Best Western Wayside Inn M
(435) 587-2261. **$65-$80, 7 day notice.** 197 E Central St. On US 491, just e of US 191. Ext corridors. **Pets:** Accepted.
SAVE ⊠ 🛗 💻 🏊

AAA WWW Rodeway Inn & Suites M
(435) 587-2489. **$40-$111.** 649 N Main St. On US 191; north end of town. Int corridors. **Pets:** Small. $10 daily fee/pet. Designated rooms, service with restrictions, supervision.
SAVE ⊠ 🛗 💻 🏊

MONUMENT VALLEY

AAA WWW Goulding's Trading Post & Lodge H
(435) 727-3231. **$80-$189, 3 day notice.** 1000 Main St. Just n of Arizona border; 2 mi w of US 163. Ext corridors. **Pets:** Accepted.
SAVE ⊠ 🛗 💻 🍽 🏊

NEPHI

AAA WWW Best Western Paradise Inn M
(435) 623-0624. **$75-$95.** 1025 S Main St. I-15, exit 222, 0.5 mi n. Ext corridors. **Pets:** Accepted.
SAVE ⊠ 🛗 💻 🏊

AAA WWW Safari Motel M
(435) 623-1071. **$55-$61.** 413 S Main St. I-15, exit 228, 3 mi s. Ext corridors. **Pets:** Other species. $3 one-time fee/pet.
SAVE ⊠ 🛗 🏊

WWW Super 8 M
(435) 623-0888. **$40-$90, 7 day notice.** 1901 S Main St. I-15, exit 222, just se. Int corridors. **Pets:** Accepted.
ASK ⊠ 🛗

OGDEN

AAA WWW Best Rest Inn H
(801) 393-8644. **$55-$105.** 1206 W 2100 S. I-15, exit 343 (21st St), just e. Ext corridors. **Pets:** Accepted.
SAVE ⊠ 🛗 💻 🍽 🏊

AAA WWWW Best Western High Country Inn H
(801) 394-9474. **$79-$109.** 1335 W 12th St. I-15, exit 344 (12th St), just e. Ext/int corridors. **Pets:** Accepted.
SAVE ⊠ 🛗 💻 🍽 🏊

WWW Comfort Suites of Ogden H
(801) 621-2545. **$79-$150.** 2250 S 1200 W. I-15, exit 343 (21st St), just e. Int corridors. **Pets:** Other species. $100 deposit/room. Service with restrictions, supervision.
ASK ⊠ 🛗 💻 🍽 🏊 ✕

WWW Holiday Inn Express Hotel & Suites H
(801) 392-5000. **$89-$129.** 2245 S 1200 W. I-15, exit 343 (21st St), just e. Int corridors. **Pets:** Other species. $75 deposit/room. Service with restrictions, supervision.
ASK ⊠ 🛗 💻 🏊

WWW Motel 6 #1082 M
(801) 627-2880. **Call for rates.** 1500 W Riverdale Rd. I-15 N, exit 339; I-15 S, exit 340. Ext/int corridors. **Pets:** Accepted.
⊠ 🛗 🏊

WW Sleep Inn M
(801) 731-6500. **$55-$75.** 1155 S 1700 W. I-15, exit 344 (12th St), just w. Int corridors. **Pets:** Accepted.
ASK ⊠ 🛗 🏊

AAA WWW Super 8 M ✿
(801) 731-7100. **$70-$100.** 1508 W 2100 S. I-15, exit 343 (21st St), just w. Int corridors. **Pets:** $10 daily fee/pet. Designated rooms, service with restrictions, supervision.
SAVE ⊠ 🛗

OREM

AAA WWW La Quinta Inn H ✿
(801) 235-9555. **$72-$162.** 1100 W 780 N. I-15, exit 272 (800 N), just e. Int corridors. **Pets:** Medium, other species. Service with restrictions, supervision.
SAVE ⊠ 🛗 💻 🏊

WWWW La Quinta Inn & Suites (University Parkway) H ✿
(801) 226-0440. **$69-$169.** 521 W University Pkwy. I-15, exit 269 (University Pkwy), 0.7 mi e. Int corridors. **Pets:** Medium, other species. Service with restrictions, supervision.
ASK ⊠ 🛗 💻 🏊

PANGUITCH

AAA WWW Color Country Motel M ✿
(435) 676-2386. **$34-$82.** 526 N Main St. On US 89. Ext corridors. **Pets:** Medium, other species. $10 one-time fee/room. Service with restrictions, supervision.
SAVE ⊠

▼▼ **Harold's Place Cabins** 🅒🅐
(435) 676-2350. **$85-$95.** 3066 Hwy 12. 1 mi e off US 89 at SR 12; 17 mi w of Bryce Canyon. Ext corridors. **Pets:** Medium, dogs only. $10 daily fee/room. Designated rooms, service with restrictions, crate.
A$K ✕ ➡ ⑪ 🖉

▼▼ **Harold's Place Inn** Ⓜ
(435) 676-2350. **$65-$85.** 3090 Hwy 12. 0.5 mi e off US 89 at SR 12. Int corridors. **Pets:** Medium. Designated rooms, service with restrictions, crate.
A$K ✕ 🖉

▼ **Horizon Motel** Ⓜ
(435) 676-2651. **$45-$79.** 730 N Main St. On US 89. Ext corridors. **Pets:** Small, dogs only. $10 daily fee/room. Designated rooms, service with restrictions, supervision.
A$K ✕ 🛢 ➡ 🖉

PARK CITY

🆀🆀 ▼▼▼ **Best Western Landmark Inn** 🄷 ❀
(435) 649-7300. **$69-$399.** 6560 N Landmark Dr. I-80, exit 145 (Kimball Jct), just s, then just w. Int corridors. **Pets:** Large, other species. $10 daily fee/pet. Designated rooms, service with restrictions, supervision.
SAVE ✕ 🛢 ➡ ➿ 🆇

▼▼◆ **Holiday Inn Express** 🄷
(435) 658-1600. **Call for rates.** 1501 W Ute Blvd. I-80, exit 145 (Kimball Jct), just s, then 0.3 mi w. Int corridors. **Pets:** Other species. $20 daily fee/pet. Service with restrictions, supervision.
✕ 🛢 ➡ ➿ 🆇

PRICE

🆀🆀 ▼▼◆ **Legacy Inn** Ⓜ ❀
(435) 637-2424. **$54-$125.** 145 N Carbonville Rd. US 6, exit 240, just e, then just n on Main St. Ext corridors. **Pets:** Medium, other species. $10 daily fee/pet. Designated rooms, service with restrictions, supervision.
SAVE ✕ 🛢 ➡

PROVO

🆀🆀 ▼▼ **Days Inn** Ⓜ
(801) 375-8600. **Call for rates.** 1675 N 200 W. I-15, exit 269 (University Pkwy), 3.7 mi e. Ext corridors. **Pets:** Accepted.
SAVE ✕ 🛢 ➡ ➿

▼▼ **Econo Lodge** Ⓜ
(801) 373-0099. **$69-$79.** 1625 W Center St. I-15, exit 265 (Center St) southbound, 0.3 mi w; exit 265B (Center St) northbound, 0.4 mi w. Ext corridors. **Pets:** Medium, other species. $10 daily fee/pet. No service, supervision.
A$K ✕ 🛢 ➡

▼▼◆ **La Quinta Inn (University Ave)** 🄷 ❀
(801) 374-9750. **$69-$169.** 1460 S University Ave. I-15, exit 263 (University Ave), 1 mi e, just n on 500 W, 0.3 mi e on 100 N. Int corridors. **Pets:** Medium, other species. Service with restrictions, supervision.
A$K ✕ 🛢 ➡ ⑪ ➿

▼▼ **Sleep Inn** Ⓜ
(801) 377-6597. **$55-$229.** 1505 S 40 E. I-15, exit 263 (University Ave), just e. Int corridors. **Pets:** Accepted.
A$K ✕ 🛢 ➡ ➿

🆀🆀 ▼▼ **Super 8** Ⓜ
(801) 374-6020. **$59-$200.** 1555 N Canyon Rd. I-15, exit 269 (University Pkwy), 4.2 mi e. Ext/int corridors. **Pets:** Small. $20 daily fee/pet. Designated rooms, service with restrictions, supervision.
SAVE ✕ 🛢 ➡ ➿

RICHFIELD

🆀🆀 ▼▼ **Best Western Richfield Inn** Ⓜ
(435) 893-0100. **$72-$100.** 1275 N Main St. I-70, exit 40, just s. Int corridors. **Pets:** Small. $15 daily fee/pet. Designated rooms, service with restrictions, supervision.
SAVE ✕ 🛢 ➡ ➿

🆀🆀 ▼▼▼ **Days Inn** 🄷
(435) 896-6476. **Call for rates.** 333 N Main St. I-70, exit 40, 1 mi s on US 89. Int corridors. **Pets:** Other species. $10 one-time fee/pet. Designated rooms, service with restrictions, supervision.
SAVE ✕ 🛢 ➡ ⑪ ➿

▼ **New West Motel 1** Ⓜ
(435) 896-4076. **$30-$42.** 447 S Main St. I-70, exit 37 or 40; downtown. Ext corridors. **Pets:** Other species. $5 daily fee/room. Service with restrictions, crate.
A$K ✕ 🛢 ➡

▼▼ **Richfield Travelodge** Ⓜ
(435) 896-9271. **Call for rates.** 647 S Main St. I-70, exit 37; south end of town. Int corridors. **Pets:** Other species. $10 one-time fee/room. Designated rooms, supervision.
✕ 🛢 ➡ ⑪ ➿

▼▼ **Super 8 Motel** Ⓜ
(435) 896-9204. **$64-$69, 7 day notice.** 1377 N Main St. I-70, exit 40, just s. Ext/int corridors. **Pets:** Accepted.
A$K ✕ 🛢 ➡

ROOSEVELT

▼▼ **Frontier Motel** Ⓜ
(435) 722-2201. **$94-$114.** 75 S 200 E. On US 40; center. Ext corridors. **Pets:** Accepted.
A$K ✕ 🛢 ⑪ ➿

ST. GEORGE

▼▼ **America's Best Inn & Suites** Ⓜ
(435) 652-3030. **Call for rates.** 245 N Red Cliffs Dr. I-15, exit 8, just e. Ext corridors. **Pets:** Accepted.
✕ 🛢 ➡ ➿

▼▼ **Americas Best Value Inn** Ⓜ
(435) 688-8383. **$44-$89.** 915 S Bluff St. I-15, exit 6 (Bluff St), just w. Int corridors. **Pets:** Accepted.
A$K ✕ 🛢 ➿

🆀🆀 ▼▼ **Budget Inn & Suites** 🄷
(435) 673-6661. **Call for rates.** 1221 S Main St. I-15, exit 6 (Bluff St), just w. Ext corridors. **Pets:** Accepted.
SAVE ✕ 🛢 ➡ ➿ 🆇

🆀🆀 ▼▼▼ **Crystal Inn St. George** 🄷
(435) 688-7477. **$82-$132.** 1450 S Hilton Dr. I-15, exit 6 (Bluff St), just w. Int corridors. **Pets:** Accepted.
SAVE ✕ 🛢 ➡ ⑪ ➿ 🆇

▼▼ **Econo Lodge** Ⓜ
(435) 673-4861. **$40-$120.** 460 E St. George Blvd. I-15, exit 8, cross streets 500 E and St. George Blvd; downtown. Ext corridors. **Pets:** Small. $10 daily fee/pet. Designated rooms, service with restrictions, supervision.
A$K ✕ ➡ ➿

🆀🆀 ▼▼ ▼▼ **The Green Valley Spa & Resort** 🄷
(435) 628-8060. **$112-$325, 30 day notice.** 1871 W Canyon View Dr. Bluff and S Main sts, 4 mi sw via Hilton Dr to Dixie Dr, then to Canyon View Dr. Ext corridors. **Pets:** Small, dogs only. $500 deposit/room, $25 daily fee/room. Service with restrictions, supervision.
SAVE ✕ �figM 🛢 ➡ ⑪ ➿ 🆇

Holiday Inn H
(435) 628-4235. **$90-$150.** 850 S Bluff St. I-15, exit 6 (Bluff St), just w. Ext/int corridors. **Pets:** Medium, other species. $25 one-time fee/pet. Designated rooms, service with restrictions, supervision.

La Quinta Inn & Suites–St. George H
(435) 674-2664. **$79-$169.** 91 E 2680 S. I-15, exit 4, just e on Brigham Rd. Int corridors. **Pets:** Medium, other species. Service with restrictions, supervision.

Red Cliffs Inn & Suites M
(435) 673-3537. **$50-$125.** 912 Red Cliffs Dr. I-15, exit 10, just e. Ext/int corridors. **Pets:** Accepted.

Rodeway Inn M
(435) 628-4271. **$39-$109.** 999 E Red Hills Pkwy. I-15, exit 8, just w, then right on 1000 E. Ext corridors. **Pets:** Accepted.

Seven Wives Inn BB
(435) 628-3737. **$99-$195, 7 day notice.** 217 N 100 W. I-15, exit 8, 2.1 mi w, then n. Ext/int corridors. **Pets:** $20 one-time fee/pet. Designated rooms, service with restrictions, supervision.

TownPlace Suites by Marriott H
(435) 986-9955. **$119-$139.** 251 S 1470 E. I-15, exit 8, just e. Int corridors. **Pets:** Small. $100 one-time fee/room. Designated rooms, service with restrictions, supervision.

SALINA

Scenic Hills Super 8 M
(435) 529-7483. **Call for rates.** 75 E 1500 S. I-70, exit 56, just n. Ext corridors. **Pets:** Accepted.

SALT LAKE CITY METROPOLITAN AREA

COTTONWOOD HEIGHTS

Candlewood Suites H
(801) 567-0111. **Call for rates.** 6990 S Park Centre Dr. I-15, exit 297 (7200 S), 2.8 mi e via 7200 S, then just s. Int corridors. **Pets:** Small. Service with restrictions, supervision.

Residence Inn by Marriott Cottonwood H
(801) 453-0430. **$169-$209.** 6425 S 3000 E. I-215, exit 6 (6200 S), 0.4 mi s, then just e. Int corridors. **Pets:** $100 one-time fee/pet. Service with restrictions.

DRAPER

Comfort Inn H
(801) 571-2511. **$79-$120, 14 day notice.** 12033 S Factory Outlet Dr. I-15, exit 291, just e, then just n. Int corridors. **Pets:** Small. $25 daily fee/pet. Designated rooms, service with restrictions, supervision.

Ramada Limited M
(801) 571-1122. **Call for rates.** 12605 S Minuteman Dr. I-15, exit 291, just e, then 0.5 mi s on Frontage Rd. Int corridors. **Pets:** $10 daily fee/room. Supervision.

MIDVALE

Best Western Executive Inn H
(801) 566-4141. **$70-$100, 14 day notice.** 280 W 7200 S. I-15, exit 297 (7200 S), just e. Int corridors. **Pets:** Accepted.

Extended StayAmerica M
(801) 567-0404. **$57-$77.** 7555 S Union Park Ave. I-215, exit 9 (Union Park Ave), 0.3 mi s. Int corridors. **Pets:** Other species. $25 daily fee/pet. Service with restrictions, crate.

La Quinta Inn H
(801) 566-3291. **$49-$109.** 7231 S Catalpa St. I-15, exit 297 (7200 S), just e. Int corridors. **Pets:** Medium, other species. Service with restrictions, supervision.

Motel 6 #476 M
(801) 561-0058. **$55-$68.** 7263 S Catalpa St. I-15, exit 297 (7200 S), just e, then just s. Ext corridors. **Pets:** Other species. Service with restrictions, supervision.

National 9 Discovery Inn M
(801) 561-2256. **$64-$94.** 380 W 7200 S. I-15, exit 297 (7200 S), just e. Ext/int corridors. **Pets:** Accepted.

Super 8 M
(801) 255-5559. **$69-$99.** 7048 S 900 E. I-15, exit 297 (7200 S), 1.5 mi e, then just n. Int corridors. **Pets:** $50 deposit/room. Service with restrictions, supervision.

MURRAY

Holiday Inn Express H
(801) 268-2533. **$90-$118.** 4465 S Century Dr. I-15, exit 301 (4500 S), just w, then just n. Int corridors. **Pets:** Large. $25 daily fee/pet. Designated rooms, service with restrictions.

Pavilion Inn H
(801) 506-8000. **Call for rates.** 5335 S 440 W. I-15, exit 300 (5300 S), 0.3 mi w. Int corridors. **Pets:** Accepted.

NORTH SALT LAKE

Best Western CottonTree Inn H
(801) 292-7666. **Call for rates.** 1030 N 400 E. I-15, exit 315 (Woods Cross), just e, then just s. Int corridors. **Pets:** Other species. $50 deposit/room. Service with restrictions, supervision.

SALT LAKE CITY

Best Western Airport Inn M
(801) 539-5005. **$90, 30 day notice.** 315 N Admiral Byrd Rd. I-80, exit 113 (5600 W), 0.6 mi n, then just e. Int corridors. **Pets:** Accepted.

Candlewood Suites Airport H
(801) 359-7500. **Call for rates.** 2170 W N Temple. 3 mi w of Temple Square. Int corridors. **Pets:** Accepted.

Chase Suite Hotel by Woodfin [H] ❖
(801) 532-5511. **$139-$169.** 765 E 400 S. Cross street 700 E. Ext corridors. **Pets:** Medium, other species. $10 daily fee/pet. Designated rooms, service with restrictions, crate.

City Creek Inn [M]
(801) 533-9100. **$58-$88.** 230 W N Temple St. Cross street 200 W; just w of Temple Square. Ext corridors. **Pets:** Small, dogs only. $100 deposit/pet. Service with restrictions, supervision.

Comfort Inn Airport [H]
(801) 746-5200. **$79-$199.** 200 N Admiral Byrd Rd. I-80, exit 113 (5600 W), 0.6 mi n, just e, then just s. Int corridors. **Pets:** Accepted.

Days Inn Airport [H] 🐾
(801) 539-1515. 1900 W N Temple. 2.6 mi w of Temple Square. Int corridors. **Pets:** Other species. $10 daily fee/pet. Designated rooms, service with restrictions, supervision.

Econo Lodge [M]
(801) 363-0062. **$60-$130.** 715 W N Temple. 0.8 mi w of Temple Square. Ext corridors. **Pets:** Accepted.

Hilton Salt Lake City Airport [H]
(801) 539-1515. **$79-$229.** 5151 Wiley Post Way. I-80, exit 114 (Wright Brothers Dr) westbound, 0.3 mi n, then 0.5 mi w; exit 113 (56th West) eastbound, 1.3 mi n to Amelia Earhart Dr, 0.3 mi e to Jimmy Doolittle Rd, 0.3 mi s to Wiley Post Way, then 0.3 mi e. Int corridors. **Pets:** Other species. $50 one-time fee/pet. Designated rooms, service with restrictions, crate.

Hilton Salt Lake City Center [H]
(801) 328-2000. **$119-$359.** 255 S W Temple. On W Temple, just s of Temple Square. Int corridors. **Pets:** Accepted.

Holiday Inn Express Airport East [H]
(801) 741-1500. **$139-$209.** 200 N 2100 W. I-80, exit 118 (Redwood Rd) westbound; exit 115 (N Temple) eastbound, 3.1 mi w of Temple Square. Int corridors. **Pets:** Accepted.

Holiday Inn Hotel & Suites-Airport West [H]
(801) 741-1800. **$99-$189.** 5001 W Wiley Post Way. I-80, exit 114 (Wright Brothers Dr) westbound, just n, then 0.3 mi w; exit 113 (56th W) eastbound, 0.6 mi n on 5600 W, just e on Amelia Earhard Dr, just s on Jimmy Doolittle Rd, then 0.5 mi e. Int corridors. **Pets:** Medium. $15 daily fee/room. Service with restrictions, supervision.

Homestead Studio Suites Sugar House [M]
(801) 474-0771. **$72-$94.** 1220 E 2100 S. I-80, exit 126 (1300 E), 0.5 mi n, then just w. Ext corridors. **Pets:** Other species. $25 daily fee/pet. Service with restrictions, crate.

Hotel Monaco [H]
(801) 595-0000. **$119-$299.** 15 W 200 S. Cross streets 200 S and Main St. Int corridors. **Pets:** Accepted.

Howard Johnson Express Inn [M]
(801) 521-3450. **$79-$99.** 121 N 300 W. 0.3 mi w of Temple Square. Ext/int corridors. **Pets:** Other species. $10 daily fee/room. Designated rooms, supervision.

Metropolitan Inn [M]
(801) 531-7100. **$79.** 524 SW Temple. Cross street 500 S. Ext corridors. **Pets:** Medium. $25 one-time fee/room. Designated rooms, service with restrictions, crate.

Peery Hotel [H]
(801) 521-4300. **$129-$300.** 110 W Broadway. W Temple and 300 S. Int corridors. **Pets:** Accepted.

Radisson Hotel Salt Lake City Downtown [H]
(801) 531-7500. **$109-$259.** 215 W South Temple. Opposite Delta Center. Int corridors. **Pets:** Small, other species. $25 one-time fee/room. Service with restrictions, crate.

Red Lion Hotel Salt Lake Downtown [H]
(801) 521-7373. **$80-$170.** 161 W 600 S. At W Temple and 600 S. Int corridors. **Pets:** Other species. $20 one-time fee/room. Service with restrictions, supervision.

Residence Inn by Marriott Airport [H]
(801) 532-4101. **$152-$186.** 4883 W Douglas Corrigon Way. I-80, exit 114 westbound, via Wright Brothers Dr; exit 113 eastbound, via Amelia Earhart and Wright Brothers drs, then 2.6 mi se. Int corridors. **Pets:** Accepted.

Residence Inn by Marriott City Center [H] ❖
(801) 355-3300. **$152-$186.** 285 W Broadway (300 S). Cross streets 300 W and 300 S. Int corridors. **Pets:** Medium. $100 one-time fee/pet. Service with restrictions, crate.

Sheraton City Centre [H] ❖
(801) 401-2000. **$109-$309.** 150 W 500 S. At 200 W and 500 S. Int corridors. **Pets:** Dogs only. Service with restrictions, supervision.

Shilo Inn Suites Hotel [H] ❖
(801) 521-9500. **$100-$296.** 206 S W Temple. Cross streets 200 S and W Temple. Int corridors. **Pets:** Dogs only. $25 one-time fee/room. Service with restrictions, supervision.

Super 8 Airport [M]
(801) 533-8878. **$60-$180.** 223 N Jimmy Doolittle Rd. I-80, exit 113 eastbound, 0.6 mi n, then e, then just s; exit 114 westbound, just n, 0.7 mi w, then just s. Int corridors. **Pets:** Accepted.

SANDY

Best Western CottonTree Inn [H]
(801) 523-8484. **$108-$167, 3 day notice.** 10695 S Auto Mall Dr. I-15, exit 293 (10600 S), 0.3 mi e. Int corridors. **Pets:** Medium. $10 one-time fee/room. Service with restrictions, supervision.

Comfort Inn [H]
(801) 255-4919. **$60-$160.** 8955 S 255 W. I-15, exit 295 (9000 S), just e, then just n. Int corridors. **Pets:** Large. $10 daily fee/pet. Designated rooms, service with restrictions, supervision.

Holiday Inn Express [H] ❖
(801) 495-1317. **$99-$169.** 10680 S Auto Mall Dr. I-15, exit 293 (10600 S), 0.3 mi e, then just s. Int corridors. **Pets:** Large, other species. $10 daily fee/room. Designated rooms, supervision.

WWW Residence Inn by Marriott [H]
(801) 561-5005. **$179-$199.** 270 W 10000 S. I-15, exit 293 (10600 S), from State St, 0.3 mi w. Int corridors. **Pets:** Accepted.
[X] [•] [▣] [≈] [X]

SOUTH JORDAN

WW Sleep Inn [M]
(801) 572-2020. **$50-$110.** 10676 S 300 W. I-15, exit 293 (10600 S), just w. Int corridors. **Pets:** Accepted.
[ASK] [X] [•] [▣] [≈]

WW Super 8 [M]
(801) 553-8888. **Call for rates.** 10722 S 300 W. I-15, exit 293 (10600 S), just w. Int corridors. **Pets:** Accepted.
[X] [•] [▣] [≈]

TAYLORSVILLE

WW Homestead Studio Suites [M]
(801) 269-9292. **$52-$72.** 5683 S Redwood Rd. I-215, exit 13, just n. Ext corridors. **Pets:** Other species. $25 daily fee/pet. Service with restrictions, crate.
[ASK] [X] [•] [▣]

WEST VALLEY CITY

WWW Baymont Inn & Suites [H]
(801) 886-1300. **$79-$119.** 2229 W City Center Ct. I-215, exit 18 (3500 S), just e, then just w. Int corridors. **Pets:** Accepted.
[ASK] [X] [•] [▣] [≈]

WWW Country Inn & Suites [H]
(801) 908-0311. **$109-$129.** 3422 S Decker Lake Dr. I-215, exit 18 (3500 S), just e, then just n. Int corridors. **Pets:** Large, other species. $50 deposit/room. Designated rooms, service with restrictions, crate.
[ASK] [X] [•] [▣] [≈]

WW La Quinta Inn [H] 🐾
(801) 954-9292. **$69-$93.** 3540 S 2200 W. I-215, exit 18 (3500 S), just e. Int corridors. **Pets:** Medium, other species. Service with restrictions, supervision.
[ASK] [X] [•] [▣] [≈]

WW Sleep Inn [M] 🐾
(801) 975-1888. **$60-$130.** 3440 S 2200 W. I-215, exit 18 (3500 S), just e, then just n. Int corridors. **Pets:** Small, other species. $20 deposit/pet. Service with restrictions, supervision.
[ASK] [X] [•] [▣]

WOODS CROSS

WWWW Hampton Inn [H]
(801) 296-1211. **$119-$144.** 2393 S 800 W. I-15, exit 315, just w, then just n. Int corridors. **Pets:** Small. Service with restrictions, supervision.
[X] [•] [▣] [≈]

END METROPOLITAN AREA

SCIPIO

WW Super 8 [M]
(435) 758-9188. **Call for rates.** 230 W 400 N. I-15, exit 188, just ne. Int corridors. **Pets:** Accepted.
[X] [•] [▣] [≈]

SPANISH FORK

AAA WW Western Inn [M]
(801) 798-9400. **$50-$80.** 632 Kirby Ln. I-15, exit 258 southbound, 0.5 mi e; exit 257 northbound, 1 mi ne. Int corridors. **Pets:** Dogs only. $50 deposit/room, $12 daily fee/pet. Designated rooms, service with restrictions, supervision.
[SAVE] [X] [•]

SPRINGDALE

AAA WWWW Best Western Zion Park Inn [M]
(435) 772-3200. **$70-$135, 7 day notice.** 1215 Zion Park Blvd. 2 mi s of park entrance. Int corridors. **Pets:** Medium. $25 one-time fee/room. Designated rooms, service with restrictions, supervision.
[SAVE] [X] [•] [▣] [†] [≈] [X]

WWW Canyon Ranch Motel [M]
(435) 772-3357. **$59-$109, 3 day notice.** 668 Zion Park Blvd. SR 9, just s of south gate to Zion National Park. Ext corridors. **Pets:** Accepted.
[X] [•] [▣] [≈]

AAA WWWW Driftwood Lodge & Suites [M] 🐾
(435) 772-3262. **$59-$199, 3 day notice.** 1515 Zion Park Blvd. SR 9, 2 mi s of south gate to Zion National Park. Ext corridors. **Pets:** Other species. $24 daily fee/pet. Designated rooms, service with restrictions, supervision.
[SAVE] [X] [•] [▣] [†] [≈]

SPRINGVILLE

AAA WWWW Best Western Mountain View Inn [H] 🐾
(801) 489-3641. **$75-$136, 3 day notice.** 1455 N 1750 W. I-15, exit 261, just e. Int corridors. **Pets:** Large. $10 daily fee/pet. Service with restrictions, crate.
[SAVE] [X] [•] [▣] [≈]

TOOELE

WWW Holiday Inn Express Hotel & Suites [H]
(435) 833-0500. **Call for rates.** 1531 N Main St. I-80, exit 99, 11 mi s on SR 36. Int corridors. **Pets:** Other species. $15 daily fee/room. Service with restrictions, supervision.
[X] [•] [▣] [≈]

TORREY

AAA WWW Affordable Inns @ Capital Reef [M] 🐾
(435) 425-3688. **$49-$125.** 600 E Hwy 24. 0.3 mi w of SR 12; 3.3 mi w of Capitol Reef National Park. Int corridors. **Pets:** Medium. $10 one-time fee/pet. Designated rooms, service with restrictions, supervision.
[SAVE] [X] [•] [≈]

AAA WWW Best Western Capitol Reef Resort [H]
(435) 425-3761. **$60-$140.** 2600 E Hwy 24. 2 mi e of jct SR 12 and 24, 1 mi w of Capitol Reef National Park. Ext corridors. **Pets:** Small. $10 daily fee/pet. Designated rooms, service with restrictions, supervision.
[SAVE] [X] [•] [▣] [†] [≈] [X]

WW Hidden Falls Hotel [H]
(435) 425-3866. **Call for rates.** 2424 E Hwy 24. 1.5 mi e of jct SR 12 and 24, 1.5 mi w of Capitol Rd. Ext corridors. **Pets:** Accepted.
[X] [•] [▣]

AAA WW Rim Rock Inn [M]
(435) 425-3398. **$59-$79.** 2523 E Hwy 24. 2.5 mi e of jct SR 12 and 24; east end of town. Ext corridors. **Pets:** Accepted.
[SAVE] [X] [†]

◆◆ ♦♦♦ Sandstone Inn & Restaurant H
(435) 425-3775. **$64-$125.** 875 E Hwy 24. Jct SR 12 and 24; 3 mi w of Capitol Reef National Park. Ext corridors. **Pets:** $10 daily fee/pet. Designated rooms, service with restrictions, crate.

SAVE ⊠ 🖶 ⟨⟩ ⤳

◆◆ ♦♦♦ Torrey Days Inn M
(435) 425-3111. **$70-$85.** 675 E Hwy 24. Jct SR 12 and 24. Int corridors.
Pets: Accepted.

SAVE ⊠ ⟨&M⟩ 🖶 ⟨💻⟩ ⤳

TREMONTON

◆◆ ♦♦ Sandman Motel M
(435) 257-7149. **$49-$66.** 585 W Main St. I-15/84 N, exit 376, 2.1 mi ne to 4-way stop, then 1.5 mi w; I-15 S, exit 381, 0.6 mi e to 4-way stop, s to Main St, then 0.5 mi e; I-84, exit 40, 1.5 mi e. Ext corridors. **Pets:** Other species. Designated rooms, service with restrictions, supervision.

SAVE ⊠

TROPIC

◆◆ ♦♦♦ Americas Best Value Inn & Suites-Bryce Valley Inn H
(435) 679-8811. **$50-$125.** 199 N Main St. SR 12, 10 mi e of Bryce Canyon Park. Ext/int corridors. **Pets:** Other species. $20 one-time fee/pet. Designated rooms, service with restrictions, crate.

SAVE ⊠ 🖶 ⟨💻⟩ ⟨⟩

VERNAL

♦♦ Sage Motel & Restaurant M
(435) 789-1442. **$95.** 54 W Main St. On US 40; center. Ext corridors.
Pets: Accepted.

ASK ⊠ 🖶 ⟨⟩

WASHINGTON

♦♦♦ Holiday Inn Express Hotel & Suites H
(435) 986-1313. **$99-$169.** 2450 N Town Center Dr. I-15, exit 16, just e. Int corridors. **Pets:** Accepted.

ASK ⊠ 🖶 ⟨💻⟩ ⤳

VERMONT

ALBURG

▽▽ Ransom Bay Inn & Restaurant 🅱🅱
(802) 796-3399. **$95-$105.** 4 Center Bay Rd. 0.5 mi s on US 2, from jct SR 78. Int corridors. **Pets:** Accepted.
🄰🅂🄺 ⊠ 🆆 ☎

BARRE

Ⓐ Ⓐ Ⓐ ▽▽▽ The Hollow Inn & Motel Ⓜ ❖
(802) 479-9313. **$80-$139, 3 day notice.** 278 S Main St. Jct US 302, 1 mi s on SR 14; I-89, exit 6, 4.3 mi e on SR 63, then 0.7 mi n on SR 14. Ext/int corridors. **Pets:** Medium. $100 deposit/pet, $20 daily fee/pet. Designated rooms, service with restrictions, supervision.
🆂🅰🆅🄴 ⊠ 🔋 ⬛ ∽ ⊠

Ⓐ Ⓐ Ⓐ ▽ Pierre Motel Ⓜ
(802) 476-3188. **$62-$95, 7 day notice.** 362 N Main St. I-89, exit 7, 4 mi e on SR 62; jct US 302. Ext corridors. **Pets:** Dogs only. $10 one-time fee/pet. Service with restrictions, supervision.
🆂🅰🆅🄴 ⊠ 🔋 ∽

BENNINGTON

Ⓐ Ⓐ Ⓐ ▽ Americas Best Value Inn Ⓜ
(802) 442-2322. **$69-$139, 3 day notice.** 357 US 7 S. Jct SR 9 and US 7, 1.2 mi s. Ext corridors. **Pets:** Dogs only. $10 daily fee/pet. Designated rooms, service with restrictions, supervision.
🆂🅰🆅🄴 ⊠ 🔋 ∽

Ⓐ Ⓐ Ⓐ ▽▽ Bennington Motor Inn Ⓜ
(802) 442-5479. **$69-$165, 3 day notice.** 143 W Main St. Jct US 7, 0.4 mi w on SR 9. Ext corridors. **Pets:** Accepted.
🆂🅰🆅🄴 ⊠ 🔋 ⬛

Ⓐ Ⓐ Ⓐ ▽ Harwood Hill Motel Ⓜ
(802) 442-6278. **$63-$95, 3 day notice.** 864 Harwood Hill Rd. Jct SR 9, 1.2 mi n on US 7, then 1.7 mi n on Historic Rt 7A. Ext corridors. **Pets:** Accepted.
🆂🅰🆅🄴 ⊠ 🔋 ⬛

▽ Knotty Pine Motel Ⓜ
(802) 442-5487. **$75-$130.** 130 Northside Dr (SR 7A). Jct SR 9, 1.2 mi n on US 7, then just n on Historic SR 7A. Ext corridors. **Pets:** Other species. Service with restrictions, supervision.
⊠ 🔋 ⬛ ∽

BOLTON VALLEY

▽▽▽ Black Bear Inn 🄲🄸 ❖
(802) 434-2126. **$89-$355, 21 day notice.** 4010 Bolton Access Rd. I-89, exit 10 northbound, 6.2 mi w on US 2, then 4 mi n; exit 11 southbound, 8.4 mi e on US 2, then 4 mi n. Ext/int corridors. **Pets:** Other species. $20 one-time fee/pet. Designated rooms, service with restrictions.
⊠ 🔋 ⬛ 🍴 ∽

BRANDON

Ⓐ Ⓐ Ⓐ ▽▽ Brandon Motor Lodge Ⓜ
(802) 247-9594. **$75-$145.** 2095 Franklin St. 2 mi s on US 7. Ext corridors. **Pets:** $10 one-time fee/room. Service with restrictions, supervision.
🆂🅰🆅🄴 ⊠ 🔋 ∽ ⊠

▽▽▽ The Lilac Inn 🄲🄸
(802) 247-5463. **$125-$330, 30 day notice.** 53 Park St. Just e on SR 73. Int corridors. **Pets:** Accepted.
🄰🅂🄺 ⊠ 🍴 ☎

BRATTLEBORO

▽▽ Colonial Motel & Spa 🄷
(802) 257-7733. **$79-$145.** 889 Putney Rd. I-91, exit 3, just e on SR 9, then 0.5 mi s on US 5. Ext corridors. **Pets:** Dogs only. $15 daily fee/room. Service with restrictions, supervision.
🄰🅂🄺 ⊠ 🔋 ⬛ ∽ ⊠

Ⓐ Ⓐ Ⓐ ▽▽ Econo Lodge Ⓜ
(802) 254-2360. **$45-$175.** 515 Canal St. I-91, exit 1, 0.3 mi n on US 5. Ext/int corridors. **Pets:** Accepted.
🆂🅰🆅🄴 ⊠ 🔋 ⬛ ∽

Ⓐ Ⓐ Ⓐ ▽▽ Super 8 Ⓜ
(802) 254-8889. **$50-$195.** 1043 Putney Rd. I-91, exit 3, just e on SR 9, then just s on US 5. Int corridors. **Pets:** Other species. $20 one-time fee/room.
🆂🅰🆅🄴 ⊠ 🆖🄼 🔋

CAVENDISH

▽▽▽ The Pointe at Castle Hill Resort & Spa 🄷
(802) 226-7688. **$109-$449, 14 day notice.** 2940 SR 103. On SR 103, just n of jct SR 131. Int corridors. **Pets:** Accepted.
🄰🅂🄺 ⊠ 🔋 ⬛ 🍴 ∽ ⊠

COLCHESTER

▽▽ Days Inn 🄷
(802) 655-0900. **$50-$135.** 124 College Pkwy. I-89, exit 15 northbound, just e on SR 15; exit 16 southbound, 1.1 mi s on US 7, then 1 mi e on SR 15. Int corridors. **Pets:** Dogs only. $10 daily fee/pet. Designated rooms, service with restrictions.
🄰🅂🄺 ⊠ 🆖🄼 🔋 ∽

▽▽▽ Hampton Inn & Conference Center 🄷 ❖
(802) 655-6177. **$119-$319.** 42 Lower Mountain View Dr. I-89, exit 16, just n on US 7. Int corridors. **Pets:** Other species. Designated rooms, service with restrictions, supervision.
⊠ 🆖🄼 🔋 ⬛ ∽

▽▽ Motel 6 #1407 🄷
(802) 654-6860. **$45-$65.** 74 S Park Dr. I-89, exit 16, just s on US 7. Int corridors. **Pets:** Other species. Service with restrictions, supervision.
⊠ 🔋 ∽

ESSEX JUNCTION

Ⓐ Ⓐ Ⓐ ▽▽▽ ▽▽▽ The Essex Resort & Spa 🄷
(802) 878-1100. **$169-$299, 7 day notice.** 70 Essex Way. SR 289, exit 10, 0.3 mi s. Int corridors. **Pets:** Accepted.
🆂🅰🆅🄴 ⊠ 🆖🄼 🔋 ⬛ 🍴 ∽ ⊠

◆◆◆ Handy Suites 🅷
(802) 872-5200. **$74-$249.** 27 Susie Wilson Rd. I-89, exit 15 northbound, 2 mi e, then just n. Int corridors. **Pets:** Medium, dogs only. $50 deposit/pet. Designated rooms, service with restrictions, crate.
(ASK) ⊠ (🖐M) 🗋 🖥 ⊇

FAIRLEE

◆◆◆ ◆◆◆ Silver Maple Lodge & Cottages 🅱🅱
(802) 333-4326. **$74-$109, 14 day notice.** 520 US 5 S. I-91, exit 15, 0.5 mi s. Ext/int corridors. **Pets:** Other species. Designated rooms.
(SAVE) ⊠ 🗋 🖥 (🆉)

FLETCHER

◆◆◆◆ The Inn at Buck Hollow Farm 🅱🅱 ❀
(802) 849-2400. **$93-$105, 14 day notice.** 2150 Buck Hollow Rd. 6.4 mi n of jct SR 104 via Buck Hollow Rd. Int corridors. **Pets:** $20 daily fee/pet. Designated rooms, crate.
(ASK) ⊠ ⊇ ⊠ (🆉)

JAMAICA

◆◆◆ ◆◆◆◆ Three Mountain Inn 🅲🅸 ❀
(802) 874-4140. **$165-$370, 21 day notice.** 3732 Main St. On SR 30; center. Ext/int corridors. **Pets:** Dogs only. $25 daily fee/pet. Designated rooms, service with restrictions, crate.
(SAVE) ⊠ (🍴) ⊇ ⊠

KILLINGTON

◆◆◆ ◆◆◆◆ The Cascades Lodge 🅷
(802) 422-3731. **$94-$299, 21 day notice.** 58 Old Mill Rd. 3.6 mi s on Killington Rd, from jct SR 100/US 4, then just e. Int corridors. **Pets:** $50 daily fee/pet. Service with restrictions, crate.
(SAVE) ⊠ 🗋 🖥 (🍴) ⊇ ⊠

LONDONDERRY

◆ Snowdon Motel 🅼
(802) 824-6047. **$55-$125, 7 day notice.** 4071 VT Rt 11. Jct SR 100, 2 mi e. Ext corridors. **Pets:** Medium, dogs only. $10 daily fee/room. Designated rooms, service with restrictions, supervision.
(ASK) ⊠ 🗋 (🆉)

LUDLOW

◆◆◆ ◆◆◆ All Seasons Motel 🅷
(802) 228-8100. **$70-$250, 14 day notice.** 112 Main St. On SR 103; center. Ext/int corridors. **Pets:** Small, dogs only. $25 daily fee/pet. Supervision.
(SAVE) ⊠ 🗋 🖥 ⊇

◆◆◆◆ The Andrie Rose Inn 🅱🅱
(802) 228-4846. **$110-$364, 20 day notice.** 13 Pleasant St. Corner of Depot St; center. Int corridors. **Pets:** Accepted.
⊠ 🗋 (🍴) (🆉)

◆◆◆ ◆◆◆◆ Best Western Ludlow Colonial Motel 🅷
(802) 228-8188. **$100-$350, 14 day notice.** 93 Main St. On SR 103; center. Ext/int corridors. **Pets:** Small, dogs only. $25 daily fee/pet. Supervision.
(SAVE) ⊠ 🗋 🖥 ⊇

◆◆◆ ◆◆◆◆ Timber Inn Motel 🅼
(802) 228-8666. **$79-$269, 14 day notice.** 112 Rt 103 S. On SR 103 S, 1 mi e. Ext corridors. **Pets:** Dogs only. $15 daily fee/pet. Designated rooms, service with restrictions.
(SAVE) ⊠ 🗋 🖥 ⊇ ⊠

MANCHESTER CENTER

◆◆◆ ◆◆◆ Casablanca Motel 🅲🅰 ❀
(802) 362-2145. **$70-$108, 7 day notice.** 5927 Main St (Rt 7A). Jct SR 11/30 N, 1 mi n on Historic SR 7A. Ext corridors. **Pets:** Other species. $15 daily fee/pet. Designated rooms, service with restrictions.
(ASK) ⊠ 🗋 ⊇

MANCHESTER VILLAGE

◆◆◆ ◆◆◆ ◆◆◆◆ The Equinox, a Luxury Collection Golf Resort & Spa 🅷
(802) 362-4700. **$209-$999, 21 day notice.** 3567 Main St. 1.3 mi s on Historic SR 7A, from jct SR 11/30. Int corridors. **Pets:** Medium, dogs only. $125 one-time fee/room. Designated rooms, no service, supervision.
(SAVE) ⊠ 🗋 🖥 (🍴) ⊇ ⊠

MENDON

◆◆◆ ◆◆◆ Econo Lodge-Killington Area 🅷
(802) 773-6644. **$49-$145.** 51 US 4. Jct US 7, 5.3 mi e. Int corridors. **Pets:** $12 daily fee/room. Designated rooms, service with restrictions, supervision.
(SAVE) ⊠ 🗋 🖥 ⊇

◆◆◆ Mendon Mountainview Lodge 🅷
(802) 773-4311. **$59-$269, 7 day notice.** 78 US 4. On US 4, 6 mi e of jct US 7. Int corridors. **Pets:** Accepted.
(ASK) ⊠ 🗋 ⊇ ⊠

MIDDLEBURY

◆◆◆ ◆◆◆◆ The Middlebury Inn 🅷
(802) 388-4961. **$119-$299, 3 day notice.** 14 Court Square. On US 7; center. Ext/int corridors. **Pets:** Accepted.
(SAVE) ⊠ 🗋 🖥 (🍴)

◆◆◆ ◆◆◆◆ Swift House Inn 🅲🅸 ❀
(802) 388-9925. **$120-$285, 14 day notice.** 25 Stewart Ln. 0.3 mi n on US 7 from jct SR 125 W. Ext/int corridors. **Pets:** Medium, dogs only. $50 daily fee/pet. Designated rooms, service with restrictions, crate.
(SAVE) ⊠ 🖥 (🍴) ⊠

MONTGOMERY CENTER

◆◆◆ ◆◆◆◆ Phineas Swann Bed & Breakfast 🅱🅱 ❀
(802) 326-4306. **$89-$395, 30 day notice.** 195 Main St. Center. Ext/int corridors. **Pets:** Dogs only. Designated rooms, crate.
(SAVE) ⊠ 🗋 ⊠

MORRISVILLE

◆◆◆ ◆◆◆ Sunset Motor Inn 🅼
(802) 888-4956. **$83-$182, 7 day notice.** 160 VT Rt 15 W. On SR 15, just w of jct SR 100. Ext/int corridors. **Pets:** Accepted.
(SAVE) ⊠ (🖐M) 🗋 ⊇

◆◆◆◆ Village Victorian Bed & Breakfast 🅱🅱
(802) 888-8850. **$80-$170, 15 day notice.** 107 Union St. From center, just e, then just n. Int corridors. **Pets:** Small, dogs only. $10 daily fee/pet. Designated rooms, supervision.
(ASK) ⊠ (🆉)

NORTH HERO

◆◆◆ ◆◆◆ Shore Acres Inn 🅷
(802) 372-8722. **$95-$235, 21 day notice.** 237 Shore Acres Dr. 0.5 mi s on US 2. Ext/int corridors. **Pets:** Dogs only. $15 daily fee/pet. Crate.
(SAVE) ⊠ 🗋 (🍴) ⊠ (🆉)

PUTNEY

▼▼ The Putney Inn �H ❖
(802) 387-5517. **$98-$198.** 57 Putney Landing Rd. I-91, exit 4, just e. Ext corridors. **Pets:** Large. $10 daily fee/pet. Designated rooms, service with restrictions, supervision.
(A$K) (✕) (▣) (¶)

RUTLAND

🖤 ▼▼▼ Comfort Inn at Trolley Square �H ❖
(802) 775-2200. **$89-$219.** 19 Allen St. On US 7, 1 mi s from jct US 4 W; 1.5 mi n from US 4 E. Int corridors. **Pets:** Medium. $35 one-time fee/pet. Designated rooms, service with restrictions, supervision.
(SAVE) (✕) (&M) (🖬) (▣) (🔁)

▼▼▼ Holiday Inn Rutland/Killington �H
(802) 775-1911. **$119-$249.** 476 US Rt 7 S. 2.4 mi s on US 7, from US 4 W; 0.4 mi n, US 7 from US 4 E. Int corridors. **Pets:** Accepted.
(A$K) (✕) (&M) (🖬) (▣) (¶) (🔁) (✕)

▼▼ Ramada Limited of Rutland �H
(802) 773-3361. **$59-$109.** 253 S Main St, US 7. 1.3 mi s on US 7, from US 4 W; 1.5 mi n on US 7, from US 4 E. Int corridors. **Pets:** Accepted.
(A$K) (✕) (🖬) (▣) (🔁)

🖤 ▼▼▼ Red Roof Inn Rutland-Killington �H
(802) 775-4303. **Call for rates.** 401 US Hwy 7 S. On US 7/4. Int corridors. **Pets:** Medium. Designated rooms, service with restrictions, supervision.
(SAVE) (✕) (🖬) (▣) (🔁)

🖤 ▼ Rodeway Inn 🅼
(802) 775-2575. **$49-$169, 5 day notice.** 138 N Main St. 0.5 mi n of jct US 4 E. Ext corridors. **Pets:** Accepted.
(SAVE) (✕) (🖬) (▣) (🔁)

🖤 ▼ Rodeway Inn 🅼
(802) 773-9176. **$49-$169.** 115 Woodstock Ave. Jct US 7, 0.5 mi e on US 4. Ext/int corridors. **Pets:** Very small, dogs only. $10 daily fee/pet. Designated rooms, service with restrictions, supervision.
(SAVE) (✕) (🖬) (▣) (🔁)

ST. ALBANS

🖤 ▼▼ Econo Lodge 🅼
(802) 524-5956. **$60-$200.** 287 S Main St. I-89, exit 19, 1 mi w to US 7, then 0.5 mi s. Ext/int corridors. **Pets:** Small. $25 daily fee/pet. Designated rooms, service with restrictions, supervision.
(SAVE) (✕) (🖬) (▣)

▼▼▼ La Quinta Inn & Suites �H ❖
(802) 524-3300. **$65-$179.** 813 Fairfax Rd. I-89, exit 19, just w, then just s on SR 104. Int corridors. **Pets:** Medium, other species. Service with restrictions, supervision.
(A$K) (✕) (&M) (🖬) (▣) (🔁)

ST. JOHNSBURY

▼▼ Fairbanks Inn 🅼
(802) 748-5666. **$95-$145.** 401 Western Ave. I-91, exit 21, 1 mi e on US 2. Ext corridors. **Pets:** Accepted.
(A$K) (✕) (🖬) (▣) (🔁)

SAXTONS RIVER

🖤 ▼▼▼ The Inn at Saxtons River 🖸
(802) 869-2110. **$99-$189, 10 day notice.** 27 Main St. Center. Int corridors. **Pets:** Accepted.
(SAVE) (✕) (🖬) (✕)

SHAFTSBURY

▼ Governor's Rock Motel 🅼
(802) 442-4734. **$55-$105.** 4325 Rt 7A. 3.3 mi n on Historic SR 7A, from jct SR 67. Ext corridors. **Pets:** Accepted.
(✕) (🖬) (▣)

▼▼ Hillbrook Motel 🅼
(802) 447-7201. **$65-$90, 3 day notice.** 2629 Rt 7A. SR 7, exit 2, 2 mi n. Ext corridors. **Pets:** Accepted.
(✕) (🖬) (▣) (🔁)

▼ Serenity Motel 🅲🅰
(802) 442-6490. **$65-$85.** 4379 Rt 7A. 3.3 mi n on Historic SR 7A, from jct SR 67. Ext corridors. **Pets:** Large. Designated rooms, service with restrictions, supervision.
(✕) (🖬) (▣)

SOUTH BURLINGTON

🖤 ▼▼ Best Western Windjammer Inn & Conference Center �H ❖
(802) 863-1125. **$99-$229.** 1076 Williston Rd. I-89, exit 14E, 0.3 mi e on US 2. Int corridors. **Pets:** Large. $10 daily fee/pet. Designated rooms, service with restrictions, supervision.
(SAVE) (✕) (&M) (🖬) (▣) (¶) (🔁) (✕)

🖤 ▼▼▼ DoubleTree Hotel Burlington �H ❖
(802) 658-0250. **$79-$239.** 1117 Williston Rd. I-89, exit 14E, just e on US 2. Int corridors. **Pets:** $50 deposit/room. Service with restrictions, supervision.
(SAVE) (✕) (&M) (🖬) (▣) (¶) (🔁)

▼▼▼ Green Mountain Suites �H
(802) 860-1212. **$149-$399, 3 day notice.** 401 Dorset St. I-89, exit 14E, just e on US 2, then 0.8 mi s. Int corridors. **Pets:** Large. $300 deposit/room, $25 daily fee/room. Designated rooms, service with restrictions, supervision.
(A$K) (✕) (&M) (🖬) (▣) (🔁)

▼▼▼ La Quinta Inn & Suites �H ❖
(802) 865-3400. **$55-$159.** 1285 Williston Rd. I-89, exit 14E, 0.5 mi e on US 2. Int corridors. **Pets:** Medium, other species. Service with restrictions, supervision.
(A$K) (✕) (&M) (🖬) (▣) (🔁)

🖤 ▼▼▼ Sheraton Burlington Hotel & Conference Center �H ❖
(802) 865-6600. **$139-$339.** 870 Williston Rd. I-89, exit 14W, just w on US 2. Int corridors. **Pets:** Service with restrictions, supervision.
(SAVE) (✕) (🖬) (▣) (¶) (🔁)

🖤 ▼▼▼ Smart Suites �H
(802) 860-9900. **$99-$179.** 1700 Shelburne Rd. I-89, exit 13 to US 7, then 1.5 mi s. Int corridors. **Pets:** Small, other species. $25 one-time fee/room. Designated rooms.
(SAVE) (✕) (🖬) (▣)

SOUTH WOODSTOCK

▼▼▼ Kedron Valley Inn 🖸 ❖
(802) 457-1473. **$135-$350, 14 day notice.** 10671 South Rd. Jct US 4, 5 mi s. Ext/int corridors. **Pets:** Other species. $15 daily fee/pet.
(A$K) (✕) (🖬) (¶) (✕) (📞)

SPRINGFIELD

▼▼▼ Holiday Inn Express �H
(802) 885-4516. **$110-$190.** 818 Charlestown Rd. I-91, exit 7. Int corridors. **Pets:** Medium. $25 one-time fee/pet. Service with restrictions, supervision.
(A$K) (✕) (&M) (🖬) (▣) (🔁)

STOWE

▼▼▼ 1066 Ye Olde England Inne 🖸 ❖
(802) 253-7558. **$109-$189, 15 day notice.** 433 Mountain Rd. 0.4 mi w on SR 108, from jct SR 100. Ext/int corridors. **Pets:** Large, other species. $20 daily fee/pet. Designated rooms, service with restrictions, crate.
(A$K) (✕) (🖬) (▣) (¶) (🔁) (✕)

⚛ ▼▼▼ Commodores Inn 🅷
(802) 253-7131. **$98-$198.** 823 S Main St. Jct SR 108, 0.8 mi s on SR 100. Int corridors. **Pets:** Other species. $10 one-time fee/pet. Designated rooms.
[SAVE] [X] [🛏] [🍽] [🏊] [X]

▼▼▼ Edson Hill Manor 🅲🅸
(802) 253-7371. **$179-$239, 15 day notice.** 1500 Edson Hill Rd. Jct SR 100, 3.5 mi w on SR 108, then 1.3 mi n. Ext/int corridors. **Pets:** Large. Designated rooms, service with restrictions.
[X] [🍽] [🏊] [X]

⚛ ▼▼▼ Golden Eagle Resort 🅼 🐾
(802) 253-4811. **$99-$389, 5 day notice.** 511 Mountain Rd. 0.5 mi w on SR 108, from jct SR 100. Ext corridors. **Pets:** Designated rooms, service with restrictions, supervision.
[SAVE] [X] [🛏] [🖥] [🍽] [🏊] [X]

⚛ ▼▼▼ Hob Knob Inn & Restaurant 🅼 🐾
(802) 253-8549. **$95-$300, 14 day notice.** 2364 Mountain Rd. Jct SR 100, 2.5 mi w on SR 108. Ext/int corridors. **Pets:** $20 daily fee/pet.
[ASK] [X] [🛏] [🖥] [🍽] [🏊]

⚛ ▼▼▼ Honeywood Country Lodge 🅼 🐾
(802) 253-4124. **$99-$149, 15 day notice.** 4527 Mountain Rd. Jct SR 100, 4.5 mi w on SR 108. Ext corridors. **Pets:** Dogs only. $10 daily fee/pet. Service with restrictions.
[SAVE] [X] [🛏] [🖥] [🏊] [X]

⚛ ▼▼▼ Innsbruck Inn at Stowe 🅼
(802) 253-8582. **$84-$199, 15 day notice.** 4361 Mountain Rd. 4.5 mi w on SR 108, from jct SR 100. Ext/int corridors. **Pets:** Accepted.
[SAVE] [X] [🛏] [🖥] [🏊] [X]

▼▼▼ The Mountain Road Resort at Stowe 🅼
(802) 253-4566. **Call for rates.** 1007 Mountain Rd. 1 mi w on SR 108, from jct SR 100. Ext corridors. **Pets:** Accepted.
[X] [🛏] [🖥] [🏊] [X]

▼▼▼ The Snowdrift Motel 🅼
(802) 253-7305. **$78-$150, 15 day notice.** 2135 Mountain Rd. Jct SR 100, 2.1 mi w on SR 108. Ext/int corridors. **Pets:** $10 daily fee/pet. Designated rooms, service with restrictions, supervision.
[X] [🛏] [🖥] [🏊] [X]

▼▼▼ Ten Acres Lodge 🅲🅸
(802) 253-7638. **$99-$249, 21 day notice.** 14 Barrows Rd. Jct SR 100, 2.1 mi w on SR 108, then 0.5 mi s on Luce Hill Rd. Ext/int corridors. **Pets:** Accepted.
[X] [🏊] [X]

⚛ ▼▼▼ Topnotch Resort and Spa 🅷 🐾
(802) 253-8585. **$300-$1600, 14 day notice.** 4000 Mountain Rd. 4.2 mi w on SR 108, from jct SR 100. Ext/int corridors. **Pets:** Dogs only. Designated rooms, service with restrictions, supervision.
[SAVE] [X] [🛏] [🖥] [🍽] [🏊] [X]

SUNDERLAND

▼▼▼ Arcady at the Sunderland 🅼 🐾
(802) 362-1176. **Call for rates.** 6249 Rt 7A. On Historic SR 7A, 6.3 mi s of jct SR 11. Ext corridors. **Pets:** $18 daily fee/pet. Designated rooms, service with restrictions, supervision.
[X] [🛏] [🖥] [🏊]

WEST BRATTLEBORO

▼ Molly Stark Motel 🅼
(802) 254-2440. **$45-$95.** 829 Marlboro Rd. I-91, exit 2, 3.3 mi w on SR 9. Ext corridors. **Pets:** Dogs only. $5 daily fee/pet. No service, crate.
[X] [🛏] [🖥]

WEST DOVER

⚛ ▼▼▼ Big Bear's Lodge 🅼
(802) 464-5591. **$75-$215, 15 day notice.** 344 Rt 100 N. 8.7 mi n on SR 100, from jct SR 9. Ext/int corridors. **Pets:** $10 daily fee/pet. Designated rooms, crate.
[SAVE] [X] [🏊] [X] [🐾] [🌀]

▼▼▼ The Gray Ghost Inn 🅷
(802) 464-2474. **$92-$169, 14 day notice.** 290 Rt 100 N. 7.8 mi n on SR 100, from jct SR 9. Int corridors. **Pets:** Dogs only. Service with restrictions, supervision.
[X] [🍽] [🏊] [🌀]

▼▼▼ Red Oak Inn 🅲🅸
(802) 464-8817. **$79-$149, 7 day notice.** 45 Rt 100. 5 mi n. Int corridors. **Pets:** Accepted.
[ASK] [X] [🛏] [🖥] [🏊] [X]

WESTMORE

▼▼▼▼ WilloughVale Inn on Lake Willoughby 🅲🅸
(802) 525-4123. **Call for rates.** 793 VT Rt 5A. Just s on SR 5A, from jct SR 16. Int corridors. **Pets:** Medium, dogs only. $20 daily fee/pet. Designated rooms, service with restrictions, crate.
[X] [🛏] [🖥] [🍽] [X]

WHITE RIVER JUNCTION

▼▼ Comfort Inn 🅷
(802) 295-3051. **$99-$229.** 56 Ralph Lehman Dr. I-91, exit 11, just e. Int corridors. **Pets:** Service with restrictions, supervision.
[ASK] [X] [♿] [🛏] [🖥] [🏊]

⚛ ▼▼▼ Econo Lodge 🅷 🐾
(802) 295-3015. **$59-$139.** 91 Ballardvale Dr. I-91, exit 11, just s on US 5. Int corridors. **Pets:** Medium, dogs only. $20 one-time fee/room. Designated rooms, service with restrictions, supervision.
[SAVE] [X] [🛏] [🖥] [🏊] [X]

▼▼ Super 8-White River Junction 🅷
(802) 295-7577. **$67-$119.** 442 N Hartland Rd. US 5, just w of jct I-89 and 91. Ext corridors. **Pets:** Other species. Service with restrictions, supervision.
[ASK] [X] [🏊]

WILLISTON

⚛ ▼▼▼ Residence Inn by Marriott 🅷
(802) 878-2001. **$139-$239.** 35 Hurricane Ln. I-89, exit 12, just s on SR 2A, then just e. Ext corridors. **Pets:** Accepted.
[SAVE] [X] [🛏] [🖥] [🏊] [X]

▼▼▼ TownePlace Suites by Marriott 🅷 🐾
(802) 872-5900. **$119-$129.** 66 Zephyr Rd. I-89, exit 12, 1.1 mi n on SR 2A. Int corridors. **Pets:** $75 one-time fee/room. Service with restrictions.
[X] [♿] [🖥] [🏊] [X]

WILMINGTON

⚛ ▼▼ Nordic Hills Lodge 🅷 🐾
(802) 464-5130. **$105-$219, 3 day notice.** 34 Look Rd. 2.5 mi n on SR 100, from jct SR 9, then 0.6 mi w on Colbrook Rd. Int corridors. **Pets:** Other species. $25 one-time fee/pet. Designated rooms, service with restrictions.
[SAVE] [X] [🍽] [🏊] [X]

WOODSTOCK

⚛ ▼ Braeside Motel 🅼
(802) 457-1366. **$88-$148, 15 day notice.** 432 US 4 E (Woodstock Rd). 1 mi e. Ext corridors. **Pets:** Accepted.
[SAVE] [X] [🛏] [🏊]

▼ Ottauquechee Motor Lodge 🅼
(802) 672-3404. **Call for rates.** 529 US Rt 4. US 4, 4.5 mi w. Ext/int corridors. **Pets:** Accepted.
[X] [🛏]

VIRGINIA

CITY INDEX

ABINGDON

◆◆◆◆ Holiday Inn Express 🅗
(276) 676-2829. **$89-$129.** 940 E Main St. I-81, exit 19 (US 11), just w. Int corridors. **Pets:** Medium. $25 one-time fee/room. Designated rooms, service with restrictions, supervision.
SAVE ✕ 🅢🅜 🛏 💻 🏊

◆ Super 8 of Abingdon 🅜
(276) 676-3329. **Call for rates.** 298 Towne Centre Dr. I-81, exit 17, just ne. Int corridors. **Pets:** Accepted.
✕ 🛏 💻

ALTAVISTA

◆◆◆ Comfort Inn 🅗
(434) 369-4000. **Call for rates.** 1558 Main St. US 29 business route, at jct US 29. Int corridors. **Pets:** Accepted.
✕ 🛏 💻 🏊 ✕

BIG STONE GAP

◆◆ ◆ Country Inn Motel 🅜
(276) 523-0374. **$46-$57.** 627 Gilley Ave. US 23, 1 mi w on US 23 business route and 58A. Ext corridors. **Pets:** Other species. $3 daily fee/pet. Service with restrictions, supervision.
SAVE ✕ 🛏

BLACKSBURG

◆◆◆◆ Comfort Inn 🅗 🐾
(540) 951-1500. **$80-$160, 7 day notice.** 3705 S Main St. 3.5 mi s on US 460, jct US 460 Bypass. Int corridors. **Pets:** Other species. Service with restrictions.
SAVE ✕ 🛏 💻 🏊

BRISTOL

◆◆◆ Econo Lodge 🅜
(276) 466-2112. **$69-$140.** 912 Commonwealth Ave. I-81, exit 3, 1.5 mi e. Ext corridors. **Pets:** Small, dogs only. $10 daily fee/pet. Designated rooms, service with restrictions, supervision.
SAVE ✕ 🛏 💻

◆◆◆ Holiday Inn Hotel & Suites 🅗
(276) 466-4100. **$104-$115.** 3005 Linden Dr. I-81, exit 7, just w. Int corridors. **Pets:** Accepted.
ASK ✕ 🅢🅜 🛏 💻 🍴 🏊

◆◆◆◆ La Quinta Inn Bristol 🅗 🐾
(276) 669-9353. **$49-$99.** 1014 Old Airport Rd. I-81, exit 7, just e. Ext corridors. **Pets:** Medium, other species. Service with restrictions, supervision.
ASK ✕ 🅢🅜 🛏 💻 🏊

◆ Motel 6 #4125 🅗
(276) 466-6060. **$58-$75.** 21561 Clear Creek Rd. I-81, exit 7, 0.3 mi w. Int corridors. **Pets:** Other species. Service with restrictions, supervision.
✕ 🅢🅜 🛏

◆◆◆ Super 8 🅗
(276) 466-8800. **$45-$280.** 2139 Lee Hwy. I-81, exit 5, just s. Int corridors. **Pets:** Other species. $10 daily fee/pet. Service with restrictions, supervision.
SAVE ✕ 🛏

BUCHANAN

◆◆◆◆ Wattstull Inn 🅗
(540) 254-1551. **$58-$75, 7 day notice.** 130 Arcadia Rd. I-81, exit 168, just e on SR 614. Ext corridors. **Pets:** Other species. $10 daily fee/pet. Designated rooms, service with restrictions, supervision.
SAVE ✕ 🛏 🍴 🏊

BURKEVILLE

◆◆◆◆ Comfort Inn Burkeville 🅗
(434) 767-3750. **$89-$135, 3 day notice.** 419 N Agnew St. On US 460, just e of jct US 360. Int corridors. **Pets:** Medium. $25 one-time fee/pet. Service with restrictions, supervision.
SAVE ✕ 🛏 💻 🍴 🏊

CHARLOTTESVILLE

◆◆◆ Comfort Inn 🅗 🐾
(434) 293-6188. **$79-$129.** 1807 Emmet St. Jct US 250 Bypass, just n on US 29. Int corridors. **Pets:** Other species. $10 one-time fee/pet. Service with restrictions, supervision.
SAVE ✕ 🛏 💻 🏊

◆◆◆◆ DoubleTree Hotel Charlottesville 🅗 🐾
(434) 973-2121. **$95-$279.** 990 Hilton Heights Rd. I-64, exit 118B (US 29), 4 mi n of jct US 250 Bypass. Int corridors. **Pets:** Medium. $35 one-time fee/room. Designated rooms, service with restrictions, crate.
SAVE ✕ 🛏 💻 🍴 🏊

◆◆◆ Fairfield Inn by Marriott 🅗
(434) 964-9411. **$89-$109.** 577 Branchlands Blvd. US 29 (Emmet St), 1.3 mi n of US 250 Bypass. Int corridors. **Pets:** Accepted.
✕ 🛏 💻 🏊

▼▼▼ Holiday Inn-Monticello/Charlottesville 🅷 ❀
(434) 977-5100. **Call for rates.** 1200 5th St SW. I-64, exit 120, just n on SR 631. Int corridors. **Pets:** Other species. $15 daily fee/pet. Supervision.
⊠ 🖥 💻 🍽 🏊

🔺 ▼▼▼ Omni Charlottesville Hotel 🅷 ❀
(434) 971-5500. **Call for rates.** 235 W Main St. I-64, exit 120, 2.3 mi n on SR 631; downtown. Int corridors. **Pets:** Small, dogs only. $50 one-time fee/pet. Service with restrictions.
🆂🅰🆅🅴 ⊠ 🖥 💻 🍽 🏊 ⊠

▼▼▼ Quality Inn-University Area 🅷
(434) 971-3746. **Call for rates.** 1600 Emmet St. US 29 (Emmet St), just n of jct US 250 Bypass, then just e on Holiday Dr. Ext corridors. **Pets:** Accepted.
⊠ 🖥 💻

🔺 ▼▼▼ Red Roof Inn of Charlottesville 🅷
(434) 295-4333. **Call for rates.** 1309 W Main St. US 29 (Emmet St), 1 mi e on US 250 (University Ave). Int corridors. **Pets:** Accepted.
🆂🅰🆅🅴 ⊠ 🖥

🔺 ▼▼▼ Residence Inn by Marriott 🅷 ❀
(434) 923-0300. **$139-$169.** 1111 Millmont St. I-64, exit 118B (US 29), 2.5 mi n on US 29/250 E, just s on Barracks Rd, then just se. Int corridors. **Pets:** Other species. $100 one-time fee/room.
🆂🅰🆅🅴 ⊠ 🖥 💻 🏊 ⊠

🔺 ▼▼▼ Sleep Inn & Suites Monticello 🅷
(434) 244-9969. **$89-$239.** 1185 5th St. I-64, exit 120, just n. Int corridors. **Pets:** $15 daily fee/pet. Service with restrictions, crate.
🆂🅰🆅🅴 ⊠ 🖥 💻 🏊

CHINCOTEAGUE

🔺 ▼▼▼ Americas Best Value Inn & Suites 🅼
(757) 336-6562. **$65-$199, 10 day notice.** 6151 Maddox Blvd. Just e on Maddox Blvd. Ext corridors. **Pets:** Medium, dogs only. $10 daily fee/pet. Designated rooms, service with restrictions, crate.
🆂🅰🆅🅴 ⊠ 🖥 💻 🏊

🔺 ▼▼▼ Quality Inn 🅷
(757) 336-6565. **$49-$299.** 6273 Maddox Blvd. Just e on Maddox Blvd. Ext corridors. **Pets:** Other species. $15 daily fee/pet. Service with restrictions, supervision.
🆂🅰🆅🅴 ⊠ 🖥 💻 🏊 ⊠

CHRISTIANSBURG

🔺 ▼▼▼ Econo Lodge 🅼
(540) 382-6161. **$49-$189.** 2430 Roanoke St. I-81, exit 118, just w on US 11/460. Ext corridors. **Pets:** Small. $10 daily fee/pet. Designated rooms, service with restrictions, supervision.
🆂🅰🆅🅴 ⊠ �figM 🖥 💻

🔺 ▼▼▼ Quality Inn 🅷
(540) 382-2055. **$74-$170.** 50 Hampton Blvd. I-81, exit 118C, just e. Ext corridors. **Pets:** Other species. $10 daily fee/room. Service with restrictions, crate.
🆂🅰🆅🅴 ⊠ 🖥 💻 🏊

▼ Super 8-Christiansburg West 🅷
(540) 382-5813. **Call for rates.** 55 Laurel St NE. I-81, exit 118, 1 mi w on US 11/460, then 3.5 mi nw on US 460 Bypass; jct SR 114. Int corridors. **Pets:** Accepted.
⊠ 🖥

CLARKSVILLE

🔺 ▼▼▼ Best Western On The Lake 🅷
(434) 374-5023. **$87-$107.** 103 Second St. Just n of US 58 business route. Int corridors. **Pets:** Other species. $100 deposit/pet, $20 daily fee/pet. Designated rooms, service with restrictions, supervision.
🆂🅰🆅🅴 ⊠ �figM 🖥 💻 🏊

COLLINSVILLE

🔺 ▼▼▼ Knights Inn 🅼
(276) 647-3716. **$55-$70.** 2357 Virginia Ave. Jct US 58, 3 mi n on US 220 business route. Ext corridors. **Pets:** Medium. $7 daily fee/room. Service with restrictions, supervision.
🆂🅰🆅🅴 ⊠ 🖥 🏊

▼▼▼ Quality Inn-Dutch Inn Hotel and Convention Center 🅷
(276) 647-3721. **$80-$300.** 2360 Virginia Ave. Jct US 58, 3 mi n on US 220 business route. Ext corridors. **Pets:** $10 daily fee/pet. Service with restrictions, crate.
🅰🆂🅺 ⊠ 🖥 💻 🍽 🏊

COVINGTON

🔺 ▼▼▼ Best Western Mountain View 🅷
(540) 962-4951. **Call for rates.** 820 E Madison St. I-64, exit 16, just n. Ext corridors. **Pets:** Service with restrictions, supervision.
🆂🅰🆅🅴 ⊠ 🖥 💻 🍽 🏊

🔺 ▼▼▼ Compare Inn & Suites 🅷
(540) 962-2141. **$98-$115.** 203 Interstate Dr. I-64, exit 16, just sw. Int corridors. **Pets:** Accepted.
🆂🅰🆅🅴 ⊠ 🖥 💻 🏊

CULPEPER

▼▼ Comfort Inn-Culpeper 🅷
(540) 825-4900. **$90-$100.** 890 Willis Ln. 2 mi s on US 29 business route; jct US 29, then just e. Ext corridors. **Pets:** Other species. $15 daily fee/pet. Service with restrictions, supervision.
🅰🆂🅺 ⊠ 🖥 💻 🏊

DALEVILLE

🔺 ▼▼▼ Howard Johnson Inn 🅷
(540) 992-1234. **$60-$85.** 437 Roanoke Rd. I-81, exit 150B, just nw on US 220. Ext corridors. **Pets:** Accepted.
🆂🅰🆅🅴 ⊠ 🖥 💻 🏊 ⊠

DANVILLE

▼▼▼ Comfort Inn & Suites 🅷 ❀
(434) 793-2000. **$79-$139, 14 day notice.** 100 Tower Dr. US 58, just w of jct US 29 business route. Int corridors. **Pets:** Medium. $10 daily fee/room. Designated rooms, service with restrictions, supervision.
🅰🆂🅺 ⊠ 🖥 💻 🍽 🏊

▼▼▼ Courtyard by Marriott 🅷
(434) 791-2661. **$98-$120.** 2136 Riverside Dr. On US 58, just w of jct US 29 business route. Int corridors. **Pets:** Medium. $10 daily fee/pet. Service with restrictions, supervision.
⊠ �figM 🖥 💻 🏊

▼▼ Holiday Inn Express Danville 🅷
(434) 793-4000. **$85-$104, 3 day notice.** 2121 Riverside Dr. US 58, 0.5 mi e of jct US 86 and 29. Ext/int corridors. **Pets:** Accepted.
🅰🆂🅺 ⊠ 🖥 💻 🏊

▼▼ Innkeeper Danville North 🅼
(434) 836-1700. **$50-$65, 3 day notice.** 1030 Piney Forest Rd. US 29 N business route, 0.5 mi n of US 58. Ext corridors. **Pets:** Accepted.
🅰🆂🅺 ⊠ 🖥 🏊

▼▼ Innkeeper Danville West 🅷
(434) 799-1202. **$50-$71, 3 day notice.** 3020 Riverside Dr. US 58 W, just w of jct US 29. Ext/int corridors. **Pets:** Accepted.
🅰🆂🅺 ⊠ 🖥 🏊

▼ Super 8 🅼
(434) 799-5845. **Call for rates.** 2385 Riverside Dr. On US 58, just e of jct US 29 business route. Int corridors. **Pets:** Large. $10 daily fee/pet. Service with restrictions, crate.
⊠ 🖥 💻

DISTRICT OF COLUMBIA METROPOLITAN AREA

ALEXANDRIA

◆◆◆ ▼◆▼ ◆◆◆ Comfort Inn Alexandria 🇭
(703) 922-9200. **$79-$119, 45 day notice.** 5716 S Van Dorn St. I-95/495, exit 173, 2 mi e of jct I-395 and 495. Int corridors. **Pets:** Large. $25 one-time fee/pet. Designated rooms, service with restrictions, supervision.
SAVE ⊠ 🛢 🖃 🍴 ⇌

◆ ◆ Extended StayAmerica-Washington, DC-Alexandria 🇲
(703) 941-9440. **$99-$199.** 205 N Breckinridge Pl. I-395, exit 3B, 0.3 mi w on SR 236, 0.4 mi ne on Beauregard St, just e on Gloucester Rd, then just s. Int corridors. **Pets:** Other species. $25 daily fee/pet. Service with restrictions, crate.
ASK ⊠ 🕭ᴹ 🛢 🖃

▼◆▼ ◆◆▼ Hawthorn Suites Alexandria 🇭
(703) 370-1000. **$180-$240.** 420 N Van Dorn St. I-395, exit 3A, 0.3 mi e on SR 236 to S Van Dorn St, then 0.5 mi n. Int corridors. **Pets:** Large, other species. $150 one-time fee/room.
ASK ⊠ 🛢 🖃 ⇌

▼◆▼ ◆◆▼ Holiday Inn Hotel & Suites-Historic District Alexandria 🇭
(703) 548-6300. **Call for rates.** 625 First St. George Washington Memorial Pkwy, just e of jct 1st and Washington sts. Int corridors. **Pets:** Medium, dogs only. $50 one-time fee/room. Service with restrictions, supervision.
⊠ 🛢 🖃 🍴 ⇌ 🗙

◆◆ ◆◆ Homestead Studio Suites Hotel-Alexandria 🇭
(703) 329-3399. **$89-$189.** 200 Bluestone Rd. I-95/495, exit 174 (Eisenhower Ave Connector), just n to Eisenhower Ave, then 1.2 mi e. Int corridors. **Pets:** Other species. $25 daily fee/pet. Service with restrictions, crate.
ASK ⊠ 🕭ᴹ 🛢 🖃

◆◆◆ ▼◆▼ ◆◆▼ Hotel Monaco Alexandria 🇭 🐾
(703) 549-6080. **$149-$459.** 480 King St. On SR 7; between S Pitt and S Royal sts; just sw of City Hall. Int corridors. **Pets:** Other species. Service with restrictions, supervision.
SAVE ⊠ 🍴 ⇌

◆◆◆ ▼◆▼ ◆◆▼ Morrison House 🇭
(703) 838-8000. **$169-$549, 3 day notice.** 116 S Alfred St. Jct King and S Alfred sts, just s. Int corridors. **Pets:** Accepted.
SAVE ⊠ 🛢 🍴

◆◆◆ ▼◆▼ ◆◆▼ Red Roof Inn-Alexandria 🇲
(703) 960-5200. **$83-$121.** 5975 Richmond Hwy. I-95/495, exit 177A, 0.5 mi s on US 1. Ext corridors. **Pets:** Accepted.
SAVE ⊠ 🕭ᴹ 🛢

▼◆▼ ◆◆▼ Residence Inn by Marriott Alexandria-Old Town 🇭
(703) 548-5474. **$279-$289.** 1456 Duke St. I-95/495, exit 176, 0.5 mi n on SR 241, then 0.7 mi e on SR 236. Int corridors. **Pets:** Accepted.
⊠ 🕭ᴹ 🛢 🖃 ⇌

◆◆◆ ▼◆▼ ◆◆▼ Sheraton Suites Old Town Alexandria 🇭 🐾
(703) 836-4700. **$119-$389.** 801 N St Asaph St. Just e of Washington St. Int corridors. **Pets:** Medium. Designated rooms, service with restrictions, supervision.
SAVE ⊠ 🛢 🖃 🍴 ⇌ 🗙

◆◆◆ ▼◆▼ ◆◆▼ Washington Suites-Alexandria 🇭
(703) 370-9600. **$159-$409.** 100 S Reynolds St. I-395, exit 3A, 0.8 mi e on SR 236 E (Duke St), then just s; near a shopping center. Int corridors. **Pets:** Medium. $20 daily fee/pet. Designated rooms, service with restrictions.
SAVE ⊠ 🕭ᴹ 🛢 🖃 🍴 ⇌ 🗙

◆◆◆ ▼◆▼ ◆◆▼ The Westin Alexandria 🇭 🐾
(703) 253-8600. **$129-$499.** 400 Courthouse Square. I-95/495, exit 176B, just n on Telegraph Rd (SR 241 N), 0.4 mi e on SR 236, then just s on Dulany St; opposite US Courthouse; in Carlyle area. Int corridors. **Pets:** Medium, dogs only.
SAVE ⊠ 🕭ᴹ 🛢 🖃 🍴 ⇌ 🗙

ARLINGTON

◆◆◆ ▼◆▼ ◆◆▼ Arlington Court Suites Hotel, a Clarion Collection 🇭
(703) 524-4000. **$109-$359.** 1200 N Courthouse Rd. 1.5 mi sw of Theodore Roosevelt Bridge on US 50. Int corridors. **Pets:** Medium, other species. $10 daily fee/pet, $75 one-time fee/room. Service with restrictions, crate.
SAVE ⊠ 🛢 🖃

◆◆◆ ▼◆▼ ◆◆▼ Palomar Arlington at Waterview 🇭
(703) 351-9170. **Call for rates.** 1121 N 19th St. I-66, exit 73, just sw of Key Bridge; in Rosslyn area. Int corridors. **Pets:** Accepted.
SAVE ⊠ 🕭ᴹ 🍴

▼◆▼ ◆◆▼ Residence Inn by Marriott Arlington At Rosslyn 🇭
(703) 812-8400. **$278-$340.** 1651 N Oak St. I-66, exit 73, 0.3 mi s on Fort Myer Dr, 0.3 mi w on Wilson Blvd to N Pierce St, then 2 blks e on Clarendon Blvd; 2 blks from Rosslyn Metro Station. Int corridors. **Pets:** Accepted.
⊠ 🛢 🖃

▼◆▼ ◆◆▼ Residence Inn by Marriott-Pentagon City 🇭
(703) 413-6630. **$279-$289.** 550 Army Navy Dr. I-395, exit 8C, just 1 mi s of 14th St Bridge. Int corridors. **Pets:** Accepted.
⊠ 🕭ᴹ 🛢 🖃 ⇌ 🗙

▼◆▼ ◆◆▼ The Ritz-Carlton, Pentagon City 🇭 🐾
(703) 415-5000. **Call for rates.** 1250 S Hayes St. 1 mi s of 14th St Bridge. Int corridors. **Pets:** Small, dogs only. $125 one-time fee/room. Designated rooms, service with restrictions.
⊠ 🕭ᴹ 🛢 🖃 🍴 ⇌ 🗙

◆◆◆ ▼◆▼ ◆◆▼ Sheraton Crystal City Hotel 🇭
(703) 486-1111. **$114-$499.** 1800 Jefferson Davis Hwy. I-395, exit 8C, 1.4 mi s of 14th St Bridge on US 1; hotel entrance, corner of Eads St. Int corridors. **Pets:** Accepted.
SAVE ⊠ 🛢 🖃 🍴 ⇌ 🗙

◆◆◆ ▼◆▼ ◆◆▼ Sheraton National Hotel 🇭
(703) 521-1900. **Call for rates.** 900 S Orme St. I-395, exit 8A, at SR 27 and 244; 1.3 mi s of 14th St Bridge. Int corridors. **Pets:** Accepted.
SAVE ⊠ 🛢 🖃 🍴 ⇌

◆◆◆ ▼◆▼ ◆◆▼ The Westin Arlington Gateway 🇭
(703) 717-6200. **$139-$600.** 801 N Glebe Rd. I-66, exit 71, just e on Fairfax Dr to Vermont Ave; just n of jct SR 120 and Wilson Blvd; 2 blks from metro station. Int corridors. **Pets:** Accepted.
SAVE ⊠ 🕭ᴹ 🛢 🖃 🍴 ⇌ 🗙

ASHBURN

◆◆◆ ▼◆▼ ◆◆▼ Homewood Suites by Hilton/Dulles North 🇭 🐾
(703) 723-7500. **$139-$269.** 44620 Waxpool Rd. 1.7 mi w of jct SR 28 and Waxpool Rd (SR 625); SR 7, 3.4 mi s on Loudoun County Pkwy (CR 607), 0.3 mi w. Int corridors. **Pets:** $20 daily fee/room. Designated rooms, service with restrictions, crate.
SAVE ⊠ 🕭ᴹ 🛢 🖃 ⇌

CENTREVILLE

▼▼ Extended StayAmerica-Centreville ⊞
(703) 988-9955. **$89-$155.** 5920 Fort Dr. I-66, exit 53, 0.9 mi s on SR 28; off SR 28, 0.3 mi s of jct US 29. Int corridors. **Pets:** Other species. $25 daily fee/pet. Service with restrictions, crate.
A$K ⊠ 🛡 🖵

CHANTILLY

▼▼ Extended StayAmerica Washington, DC-Dulles Airport-Chantilly ⊞
(703) 263-7173. **$89-$179.** 14420 Chantilly Crossing Ln. On US 50, 0.4 mi w of jct SR 28; at Chantilly Crossing Shopping Complex. Int corridors. **Pets:** Other species. $25 daily fee/pet. Service with restrictions, crate.
A$K ⊠ �ᵭM 🛡 🖵

▼▼ Extended Stay Deluxe Chantilly ⊞
(703) 263-7200. **$99-$189.** 4506 Brookfield Corporate Dr. I-66, exit 53, 3 mi n on SR 28; 1 mi s of jct SR 28 and US 50. Int corridors. **Pets:** Other species. $25 daily fee/pet. Service with restrictions, crate.
A$K ⊠ ᵭM 🛡 🖵 🏊 ⊠

▼▼ Residence Inn by Marriott Chantilly Dulles South ⊞
(703) 263-7900. **$259-$269.** 14440 Chantilly Crossing Ln. I-66, exit 57B, on US 50, just w of jct SR 28. Int corridors. **Pets:** Accepted.
⊠ 🛡 🖵 🏊 ⊠

𝔸𝔸𝔸 ▼▼▼ Staybridge Suites Hotel Chantilly/Dulles International Airport ⊞ ❀
(703) 435-8090. **$79-$249.** 3860 Centerview Dr. Jct SR 28, just e on US 50. Int corridors. **Pets:** Medium. $75 one-time fee/room. Designated rooms, service with restrictions, crate.
SAVE ⊠ ᵭM 🛡 🖵 🏊

▼▼ TownePlace Suites by Marriott-Chantilly ⊞
(703) 709-0453. **$179-$189.** 14036 Thunderbolt Pl. Jct SR 28, just e on US 50. Int corridors. **Pets:** Accepted.
⊠ 🛡 🖵 🏊 ⊠

▼▼▼ Wingate by Wyndham Dulles Airport-Chantilly ⊞
(571) 203-0999. **$145-$269.** 3940 Centerview Dr. Jct SR 28, just e on US 50. Int corridors. **Pets:** Medium. $75 one-time fee/room. Service with restrictions, supervision.
A$K ⊠ ᵭM 🛡 🖵 🏊

FAIRFAX

▼▼ Candlewood Suites Fairfax-Washington, D.C. ⊞
(703) 359-4490. **Call for rates.** 11400 Random Hills Rd. I-66, exit 57A, 0.5 mi e on US 50, just s on Waples Mill Rd, then 0.4 mi w. Int corridors. **Pets:** Accepted.
⊠ ᵭM 🛡 🖵

𝔸𝔸𝔸 ▼▼▼ Comfort Inn University Center ⊞ ❀
(703) 591-5900. **Call for rates.** 11180 Fairfax Blvd. I-66, exit 57A, 0.8 mi se on US 50, then 0.5 mi nw of jct US 29. Int corridors. **Pets:** Large. $25 one-time fee/pet. Service with restrictions, supervision.
SAVE ⊠ 🛡 🖵 ¶ 🏊 ⊠

▼▼ Extended Stay Deluxe Fairfax Ⓜ
(703) 359-5000. **$75-$189.** 3997 Fair Ridge Dr. I-66, exit 57B, 1.2 mi w on US 50. Int corridors. **Pets:** Other species. $25 daily fee/pet. Service with restrictions, crate.
A$K ⊠ ᵭM 🛡 🖵 🏊

▼▼ Homestead Studio Suites Hotel-Fair Oaks ⊞
(703) 273-3444. **$65-$175.** 12104 Monument Dr. I-66, exit 57B, 0.8 mi w on US 50, 0.3 mi s on SR 620 (West Ox Rd), then just se. Ext corridors. **Pets:** Other species. $25 daily fee/pet. Service with restrictions, crate.
A$K ⊠ ᵭM 🛡 🖵

▼▼ Homestead Studio Suites Hotel-Falls Church/Merrifield ⊞
(703) 204-0088. **$89-$189.** 8281 Willow Oaks Corporate Dr. I-495, exit 50A, just w on US 50 to Gallows Rd, then just s. Ext corridors. **Pets:** Other species. $25 daily fee/pet. Service with restrictions, crate.
A$K ⊠ ᵭM 🛡 🖵

▼▼▼ Residence Inn by Marriott-Fair Lakes ⊞
(703) 266-4900. **$239-$249.** 12815 Fair Lakes Pkwy. I-66, exit 55 (Fairfax County Pkwy N), just w. Int corridors. **Pets:** Accepted.
⊠ ᵭM 🛡 🖵 🏊 ⊠

FALLS CHURCH

▼▼▼ Homewood Suites by Hilton-Falls Church ⊞
(703) 560-6644. **$166-$229.** 8130 Porter Rd. I-495, exit 50A, just w to SR 650; 0.4 mi n of SR 650. Int corridors. **Pets:** Medium, dogs only. $100 one-time fee/room. Service with restrictions, crate.
⊠ ᵭM 🛡 🖵 🏊 ⊠

▼▼▼ Residence Inn by Marriott Fairfax-Merrifield ⊞
(703) 573-5200. **$269-$299.** 8125 Gatehouse Rd. I-495, exit 50A, just w to SR 640 N. Int corridors. **Pets:** Accepted.
⊠ ᵭM 🛡 🖵 🏊 ⊠

▼▼ TownePlace Suites by Marriott-Falls Church ⊞
(703) 237-6172. **$197-$241.** 205 Hillwood Ave. I-495, exit 50B, 2.5 mi e on US 50, 0.6 mi n on Annandale Rd (CR 649), then e; just s of US 29. Int corridors. **Pets:** Accepted.
⊠ ᵭM 🛡 🖵 🏊

𝔸𝔸𝔸 ▼▼▼ The Westin Tysons Corner ⊞
(703) 893-1340. **$89-$399.** 7801 Leesburg Pike. I-495, exit 47B, just e on SR 7. Int corridors. **Pets:** Accepted.
SAVE ⊠ 🛡 🖵 ¶ 🏊 ⊠

HERNDON

▼▼ Candlewood Suites Washington-Dulles Herndon ⊞ ❀
(703) 793-7100. **$207-$215.** 13845 Sunrise Valley Dr. SR 28, 0.4 mi e on Frying Pan Rd, 0.7 mi nw. Int corridors. **Pets:** Medium, other species. $150 one-time fee/pet. Service with restrictions, supervision.
A$K ⊠ ᵭM 🛡 🖵

▼▼ Extended StayAmerica-Herndon Ⓜ
(703) 481-5363. **$89-$179.** 1021 Elden St. 0.8 mi n on SR 657 from jct SR 267 (Dulles Toll Rd), exit 10. Int corridors. **Pets:** Other species. $25 daily fee/pet. Service with restrictions, crate.
⊠ ᵭM 🛡 🖵

𝔸𝔸𝔸 ▼▼▼ Hilton Washington Dulles Airport ⊞
(703) 478-2900. **$99-$359.** 13869 Park Center Rd. SR 267 (Dulles Toll Rd), exit 9, 3 mi s on SR 28; at McLearen Blvd (SR 668). Int corridors. **Pets:** Accepted.
SAVE ⊠ ᵭM 🛡 🖵 ¶ 🏊 ⊠

𝔸𝔸𝔸 ▼▼▼ Hyatt Summerfield Suites-Herndon ⊞
(703) 437-5000. **$195-$225.** 467 Herndon Pkwy. SR 267 (Dulles Toll Rd), exit 11 CR 7100 (Fairfax County Pkwy), just n to Spring St exit, just s to Herndon Pkwy (CR 606), just w on CR 606. Int corridors. **Pets:** Accepted.
SAVE ⊠ 🛡 🖵 🏊 ⊠

▼▼▼ Residence Inn by Marriott-Herndon/Reston ⊞
(703) 435-0044. **$269-$279.** 315 Elden St. 0.4 mi w on CR 606 from jct CR 7100 (Fairfax County Pkwy). Int corridors. **Pets:** Accepted.
⊠ 🛡 🖵 🏊 ⊠

▼▼▼ Staybridge Suites Herndon Dulles ⊞
(703) 713-6800. **$99-$284.** 13700 Coppermine Rd. SR 267 (Dulles Toll Rd), exit 10, 0.7 mi s on Centreville Rd (SR 657), then 0.4 mi w. Ext corridors. **Pets:** Medium. $150 one-time fee/room. Service with restrictions, supervision.
A$K ⊠ 🛡 🖵 🏊 ⊠

LEESBURG

AAA ▼▼▼ Best Western Leesburg Hotel & Conference Center ⊞ 🐾
(703) 777-9400. **$84-$144, 3 day notice.** 726 E Market St. 0.5 mi e on SR 7 business route. Int corridors. **Pets:** Medium. $10 one-time fee/room. Designated rooms, service with restrictions, supervision.
[SAVE] [✕] 🔒 🖵 ⇌

▼▼▼▼ Holiday Inn Leesburg at historic Carradoc Hall ⊞
(703) 771-9200. **$169-$189.** 1500 E Market St. 2 mi e on SR 7. Int corridors. **Pets:** Accepted.
[ASK] [✕] [♿] 🔒 🖵 [🍴] ⇌

LORTON

AAA ▼▼▼▼ Comfort Inn Gunston Corner ⊞
(703) 643-3100. **$99-$149.** 8180 Silverbrook Rd. I-95, exit 163, just w. Int corridors. **Pets:** Other species. $25 one-time fee/room. Designated rooms, service with restrictions.
[SAVE] [✕] 🔒 🖵 ⇌ [✕]

MANASSAS

AAA ▼▼▼ Best Western Battlefield Inn ⊞
(703) 361-8000. **$100-$175, 7 day notice.** 10820 Balls Ford Rd. I-66, exit 47A westbound; exit 47 eastbound, just s on SR 234 business route. Ext corridors. **Pets:** Accepted.
[SAVE] [✕] 🔒 🖵 [🍴] ⇌

▼▼▼▼ Comfort Suites Manassas ⊞
(703) 686-1100. **$99-$149.** 7350 Williamson Blvd. I-66, exit 47A westbound; exit 47 eastbound, 0.5 mi s on SR 234 business route, then just e. Int corridors. **Pets:** Accepted.
[ASK] [✕] 🔒 🖵 ⇌ [✕]

AAA ▼▼▼ Red Roof Inn-Manassas Ⓜ
(703) 335-9333. **$74-$100.** 10610 Automotive Dr. I-66, exit 47 eastbound; exit 47A westbound, just s on SR 234 business route, then just e on Balls Ford Rd. Ext corridors. **Pets:** Accepted.
[SAVE] [✕] [♿] 🔒

AAA ▼▼▼ Residence Inn by Marriott Manassas Battlefield ⊞
(703) 330-8808. **$130-$170.** 7345 Williamson Blvd. I-66, exit 47A westbound; exit 47 eastbound, 0.5 mi s on SR 234 business route, then just e. Int corridors. **Pets:** Accepted.
[SAVE] [✕] [♿] 🔒 🖵 ⇌ [✕]

MCLEAN

AAA ▼▼▼ Best Western Tysons Westpark Hotel ⊞
(703) 734-2800. **$89-$229.** 8401 Westpark Dr. I-495, exit 47A, 1.3 mi w on SR 7. Int corridors. **Pets:** Service with restrictions, crate.
[SAVE] [✕] [♿] 🔒 🖵 [🍴] ⇌

AAA ▼▼▼ Crowne Plaza Tysons Corner ⊞
(703) 893-2100. **$69-$369.** 1960 Chain Bridge Rd. I-495, exit 46A, 0.5 mi s on SR 123, just nw on International Dr, then just sw on Greensboro Dr. Int corridors. **Pets:** Accepted.
[SAVE] [✕] [♿] 🔒 🖵 [🍴] ⇌ [✕]

▼▼▼▼ Hilton McLean Tysons Corner ⊞
(703) 847-5000. **$99-$359.** 7920 Jones Branch Dr. I-495, exit 46A, 0.3 mi sw on SR 123, just nw on Tysons Blvd, 0.4 mi ne on Galleria/Westpark Dr, then just s. Int corridors. **Pets:** Accepted.
[✕] [♿] 🔒 🖵 [🍴] ⇌

▼▼▼▼▼ The Ritz-Carlton, Tysons Corner ⊞ 🐾
(703) 506-4300. **Call for rates.** 1700 Tysons Blvd. I-495, exit 46A, 0.3 mi sw on SR 123, then just nw. Int corridors. **Pets:** Small. $250 one-time fee/room.
[✕] [♿] 🔒 🖵 [🍴] ⇌ [✕]

AAA ▼▼▼ Staybridge Suites-McLean/Tysons Corner ⊞ 🐾
(703) 448-5400. **$239-$299.** 6845 Old Dominion Dr. I-495, exit 46B, 2 mi n on SR 123, then 0.3 mi e on SR 309. Int corridors. **Pets:** Medium. $100 one-time fee/room. Designated rooms.
[SAVE] [✕] [♿] 🔒 🖵 ⇌

RESTON

▼▼▼▼ Homestead Studio Suites Hotel-Reston ⊞
(703) 707-9700. **$109-$229.** 12190 Sunset Hills Rd. SR 267 (Dulles Toll Rd), exit 12 (Reston Pkwy), just n, then just w. Ext corridors. **Pets:** Other species. $25 daily fee/pet. Service with restrictions, crate.
[ASK] [✕] 🔒 🖵

AAA ▼▼▼ Sheraton Reston Hotel ⊞
(703) 620-9000. **$99-$429.** 11810 Sunrise Valley Dr. SR 267 (Dulles Toll Rd), exit 12 (Reston Pkwy), just s. Int corridors. **Pets:** Accepted.
[SAVE] [✕] [♿] 🔒 🖵 [🍴] ⇌

SPRINGFIELD

▼▼▼ Comfort Inn Washington DC/Springfield ⊞
(703) 922-9000. **Call for rates.** 6560 Loisdale Ct. I-95, exit 169A, just e on SR 644 E; jct I-395 and 495, 0.8 mi s. Int corridors. **Pets:** Accepted.
[✕] 🔒 🖵

▼▼▼ Extended StayAmerica-Washington, DC-Springfield ⊞
(703) 822-0992. **$99-$199.** 6800 Metropolitan Center Dr. I-95, exit 169A, just e on SR 644, 0.6 mi s on Loisdale Rd, then just e. Int corridors. **Pets:** Other species. $25 daily fee/pet. Service with restrictions, crate.
[ASK] [✕] [♿] 🔒 🖵 ⇌

▼▼▼▼ Hampton Inn Washington DC/Springfield ⊞
(703) 924-9444. **$119-$169.** 6550 Loisdale Ct. I-95, exit 169A, just e on SR 644 E; jct I-395 and 495, 0.8 mi s. Int corridors. **Pets:** Accepted.
[✕] [♿] 🔒 🖵 ⇌

AAA ▼▼▼ Red Roof Inn Springfield ⊞
(703) 644-5311. **Call for rates.** 6868 Springfield Blvd. I-95, exit 169B, just sw of SR 644; jct I-395 and 495, 0.8 mi s. **Pets:** Medium, other species. Service with restrictions, supervision.
[SAVE] [✕] [♿]

▼▼▼ TownePlace Suites by Marriott Springfield ⊞
(703) 569-8060. **$220-$230.** 6245 Brandon Ave. I-95, exit 169B, just nw of SR 644; jct I-395 and 495, 0.8 mi s. Int corridors. **Pets:** Other species. $75 one-time fee/room. Service with restrictions.
[✕] [♿] 🔒 🖵 ⇌

STERLING

AAA ▼▼▼ Best Western Dulles Airport Inn ⊞
(703) 471-8300. **$74-$154.** 45440 Holiday Dr. 1.7 mi n on SR 28 from jct SR 267 (Dulles Toll Rd), just e on CR 846, then just s on Shaw Rd. Ext corridors. **Pets:** Accepted.
[SAVE] [✕] 🔒 🖵

▼▼▼ Candlewood Suites Washington Dulles/Sterling ⊞
(703) 674-2288. **Call for rates.** 45520 E Severn Way. 1.6 mi s on SR 28 from jct SR 7, 0.3 mi e. Int corridors. **Pets:** Accepted.
[✕] [♿] 🔒 🖵

▼▼▼ Extended StayAmerica-Sterling ⊞
(703) 444-7240. **$89-$159.** 46001 Waterview Plaza. 1.3 mi e on SR 7 from jct SR 28. Int corridors. **Pets:** Other species. $25 daily fee/pet. Service with restrictions, crate.
[ASK] [✕] [♿] 🔒 🖵

Hampton Inn-Dulles/Cascades ℍ ❖
(703) 450-9595. **$79-$219.** 46331 McClellan Way. 1.7 mi e on SR 7, from jct SR 28, 0.5 mi n on CR 1794 (Cascades Pkwy) to Palisade Pkwy, just e, then 0.4 mi s on Whitfield Pl. Int corridors. **Pets:** $25 one-time fee/pet. Service with restrictions, crate.
SAVE ✕ 🛏 💻 ➴ 🐾

Holiday Inn Washington Dulles International Airport ℍ
(703) 471-7411. **$99-$279.** 45425 Holiday Dr. 1.7 mi n on SR 28 from jct SR 267 (Dulles Toll Rd), just e on CR 846, then just s on Shaw Rd. Ext/int corridors. **Pets:** Other species. $50 one-time fee/room. Designated rooms, service with restrictions, crate.
SAVE ✕ 🛎 🛏 💻 🍴 ➴ 🐾

Residence Inn by Marriott Dulles Airport @ Dulles 28 Center ℍ
(703) 421-2000. **$269-$279.** 45250 Monterey Pl. SR 28, exit CR 625 (Waxpool Rd), just w, just n on Pacific Blvd, then just e on Commercial Dr. Int corridors. **Pets:** Medium, other species. $150 one-time fee/room. Service with restrictions.
✕ 🛎 🛏 💻 ➴ 🐾

Suburban Extended Stay Hotel Washington-Dulles/Sterling ℍ
(703) 674-2299. **Call for rates.** 45510 Severn Way. 1.6 mi s on SR 28 from jct SR 7, 0.3 mi e. Int corridors. **Pets:** Accepted.
✕ 🛏 💻

TownePlace Suites by Marriott at Dulles Airport ℍ
(703) 707-2017. **$188-$230.** 22744 Holiday Park Dr. 1.7 mi n on SR 28 from jct SR 267 (Dulles Toll Rd), just e on CR 846, then just s on Shaw Rd. Int corridors. **Pets:** Accepted.
SAVE ✕ 🛏 💻 ➴

TownePlace Suites by Marriott Sterling ℍ
(703) 421-1090. **$169-$179.** 21123 Whitfield Pl. 1.7 mi e on SR 7 from jct SR 28, 0.5 mi n on SR 1794 (Cascades Pkwy) to Palisades Pkwy, just e, then just s. Int corridors. **Pets:** $100 one-time fee/room. Service with restrictions.
SAVE ✕ 🛏 💻 ➴

VIENNA

Comfort Inn Tysons Corner Ⓜ
(703) 448-8020. **$79-$199.** 1587 Spring Hill Rd. I-495, exit 47A, 1.8 mi w on SR 7, then just s; just e of jct SR 267 (Dulles Toll Rd). Ext corridors. **Pets:** Accepted.
SAVE ✕ 🛏 💻 ➴

Homestead Studio Suites Hotel-Tysons Corner ℍ
(703) 356-6300. **$99-$209.** 8201 Old Courthouse Rd. I-495, exit 47A, 0.6 mi w on SR 7, then just s on Gallows Rd. Int corridors. **Pets:** Other species. $25 daily fee/pet. Service with restrictions, crate.
ASK ✕ 🛎 🛏 💻

Residence Inn by Marriott-Tysons Corner ℍ
(703) 893-0120. **$242-$296.** 8616 Westwood Center Dr. I-495, exit 47A, 1.9 mi w on SR 7, then just s. Ext corridors. **Pets:** Accepted.
SAVE ✕ 🛏 💻 ➴ 🐾

Residence Inn by Marriott Tysons Corner Mall ℍ
(703) 917-0800. **$269-$329.** 8400 Old Courthouse Rd. I-495, exit 46A, 1.1 mi s on SR 123; 0.3 mi s of jct SR 7 and 123. Int corridors. **Pets:** Accepted.
✕ 🛎 🛏 💻 ➴ 🐾

Sheraton Premiere At Tysons Corner ℍ
(703) 448-1234. **Call for rates.** 8661 Leesburg Pike. SR 7, just e of jct SR 267 (Dulles Toll Rd). Int corridors. **Pets:** Accepted.
SAVE ✕ 🛏 💻 🍴 ➴ 🐾

WOODBRIDGE

Residence Inn by Marriott Potomac Mills ℍ
(703) 490-4020. **$169-$199.** 14301 Crossing Pl. I-95, exit 158B (Prince William Pkwy), 0.5 mi sw. Int corridors. **Pets:** Other species. $100 one-time fee/room. Service with restrictions, crate.
✕ 🛎 🛏 💻 ➴ 🐾

END METROPOLITAN AREA

EMPORIA

Best Western Emporia ℍ
(434) 634-3200. **$65-$83.** 1100 W Atlantic St. I-95, exit 11B, just w on US 58. Ext corridors. **Pets:** Accepted.
SAVE ✕ 🛏 💻 ➴

Days Inn-Emporia ℍ
(434) 634-9481. **$59-$80.** 921 W Atlantic St. I-95, exit 11B, just w on US 58. Ext corridors. **Pets:** $8 daily fee/pet.
SAVE ✕ 🛏 💻 ➴

Hampton Inn ℍ
(434) 634-9200. **$99.** 898 Wiggins Rd. I-95, exit 11B, just w. Int corridors. **Pets:** Accepted.
SAVE ✕ 🛎 🛏 💻 ➴

Quality Inn ℍ
(434) 348-8888. **Call for rates.** 1207 W Atlantic St. I-95, exit 11B, just w on US 58. Ext corridors. **Pets:** Medium. $7 daily fee/pet. Service with restrictions, supervision.
SAVE ✕ 🛏 💻 ➴

Sleep Inn ℍ
(434) 348-3900. **$69-$119.** 899 Wiggins Rd. I-95, exit 12A, just e on US 58, then just s. Int corridors. **Pets:** Medium. $10 one-time fee/pet. Designated rooms, service with restrictions, supervision.
SAVE ✕ 🛎 🛏 💻

Super 8 Ⓜ
(434) 348-3282. **$60-$79, 7 day notice.** 1411 Skippers Rd. I-95, exit 8, just e on US 301. Ext corridors. **Pets:** Medium, other species. $5 daily fee/pet. Designated rooms, service with restrictions, supervision.
SAVE ✕ 🛏 💻 ➴

EXMORE

Best Western Eastern Shore Inn ℍ
(757) 442-7378. **$70-$150.** 2543 Lankford Hwy. US 13, just n of SR 178. Ext/int corridors. **Pets:** Accepted.
SAVE ✕ 🛎 🛏 💻 ➴

FANCY GAP

Days Inn ℍ
(276) 728-5101. **$50-$75.** 142 Kelly Rd. I-77, exit 8, 0.3 mi w; on top of the hill. Ext/int corridors. **Pets:** Accepted.
ASK ✕ 🛏 💻

▼▼ **Doe Run Lodging at Groundhog Mountain** [CO] ❀
(276) 398-4099. **$99-$500, 3 day notice.** 27 Buck Hollar Rd. MM 189.2 on Blue Ridge Pkwy; 10 mi n from US 52. Ext corridors. **Pets:** Other species. $25 one-time fee/room. Designated rooms.
(ASK) [X] [B] [▭] [▯] [X]

FRANKLIN

▼ **Super 8** [M]
(757) 562-2888. **Call for rates.** 1599 Armory Dr. Jct US 58 Bypass and SR 671. Int corridors. **Pets:** Accepted.
[X] [B] [▭]

FREDERICKSBURG

◆◆◇ ▼▼ **Best Western Central Plaza** [M]
(540) 786-7404. **$69-$109.** 3000 Plank Rd. I-95, exit 130B on SR 3. Ext corridors. **Pets:** $10 daily fee/pet. Designated rooms, service with restrictions, crate.
(SAVE) [X] [&M] [B] [▭]

◆◆◇ ▼▼▼ **Best Western Fredericksburg** [H] ❀
(540) 371-5050. **$69-$109, 14 day notice.** 2205 Plank Rd. I-95, exit 130A, 0.3 mi e on SR 3. Ext corridors. **Pets:** $10 daily fee/pet. Designated rooms, service with restrictions, crate.
(SAVE) [X] [&M] [B] [▭] [▯]

◆◆◇ ▼▼▼ **Country Inn & Suites Fredericksburg** [H]
(540) 898-1800. **$98-$108.** 5327 Jefferson Davis Hwy. I-95, exit 126 southbound; exit 126A northbound; just n on US 1. Int corridors. **Pets:** Accepted.
(SAVE) [X] [B] [▭] [▯]

◆◆◇ ▼▼▼ **Fredericksburg Hospitality House Hotel & Conference Center** [H] ❀
(540) 786-8321. **$79-$169.** 2801 Plank Rd. I-95, exit 130B (SR 3). Int corridors. **Pets:** Small, other species. $25 one-time fee/pet. Designated rooms, service with restrictions, supervision.
(SAVE) [X] [&M] [B] [▭] [▯]

◆◆◇ ▼▼▼ **Holiday Inn-Fredericksburg North** [H]
(540) 371-5550. **$75-$119.** 564 Warrenton Rd. I-95, exit 133, just nw on US 17. Ext corridors. **Pets:** Medium. Service with restrictions.
(SAVE) [X] [B] [▭] [▯] [▯] [X]

◆◆◇ ▼▼▼ **Quality Inn Central Park** [H]
(540) 371-0330. **$75-$109.** 2310 Plank Rd. I-95, exit 130A on SR 3 E. Ext corridors. **Pets:** Accepted.
(SAVE) [X] [B] [▭] [▯]

▼▼ **Quality Inn Fredericksburg** [H] ❀
(540) 373-0000. **$59-$109.** 543 Warrenton Rd. I-95, exit 133, just n on US 17. Ext corridors. **Pets:** $25 daily fee/pet. Service with restrictions.
(ASK) [X] [B] [▭] [▯]

▼▼▼ **TownePlace Suites by Marriott** [H]
(540) 891-0775. **$80-$98.** 4700 Market St. I-95, exit 126 southbound; exit 126A northbound, just n on US 1, then just e. Int corridors. **Pets:** Accepted.
[X] [B] [▭] [▯]

FRONT ROYAL

◆◆◆ ▼▼ **Budget Inn** [M]
(540) 635-2196. **$45-$65.** 1122 N Royal Ave. I-66, exit 6, 2.2 mi s on US 340/522 and SR 55. Ext corridors. **Pets:** Small, dogs only. $8 daily fee/pet. Service with restrictions, supervision.
(SAVE) [X] [B]

◆◆◆ ▼▼ **Relax Inn** [M]
(540) 635-4101. **Call for rates.** 1801 Shenandoah Ave. I-66, exit 6, 1.5 mi s on US 340/522. Ext corridors. **Pets:** $10 daily fee/pet. Designated rooms, no service, supervision.
(SAVE) [X] [B] [▭] [▯]

◆◆◆ ▼▼ **Twi-Lite Motel** [M]
(540) 635-4148. **$39-$89.** 53 W 14th St. I-66, exit 6, 2.3 mi s on US 340/522. Ext corridors. **Pets:** Small. $9 daily fee/pet. Designated rooms, no service, supervision.
(SAVE) [X] [B] [▯]

GLADE SPRING

◆◆◆ ▼▼ **Swiss Inn Motel & Suites** [M]
(276) 429-5191. **$39-$160.** 33361 Lee Hwy. I-81, exit 29, just e. Ext corridors. **Pets:** Medium. $8 one-time fee/pet. Designated rooms, service with restrictions, supervision.
(SAVE) [X] [B]

GORDONSVILLE

◆◆◆ ▼▼▼ **Best Western Crossroads Inn & Suites** [H]
(540) 832-1700. **$99-$149.** 135 Wood Ridge Terr. I-64, exit 136, just n. Int corridors. **Pets:** Other species. $15 daily fee/pet. Designated rooms, service with restrictions, supervision.
(SAVE) [X] [B] [▭] [▯]

GREENVILLE

◆◆◆ ▼▼ **Budget Host-Historic Hessian House** [H]
(540) 337-1231. **$45-$75, 3 day notice.** 3554 Lee Jackson Hwy. I-81, exit 213, 0.3 mi e. Ext corridors. **Pets:** Accepted.
(SAVE) [X] [B]

GRUNDY

▼▼▼ **Comfort Inn** [H]
(276) 935-5050. **$74-$175.** 22006 Riverside Dr. On US 460, 0.5 mi e. Int corridors. **Pets:** Very small, dogs only. $30 one-time fee/pet. Designated rooms, service with restrictions, supervision.
(ASK) [X] [&M] [B] [▭]

HAMPTON ROADS AREA

CHESAPEAKE

▼▼▼ **Candlewood Suites** [H] ❀
(757) 405-3030. **$95-$104.** 4809 Market Pl. I-664, exit 11A (E Portsmouth Blvd/SR 337). Int corridors. **Pets:** Large. $75 one-time fee/pet. Service with restrictions, crate.
[X] [&M] [B] [▭]

▼▼ **Extended StayAmerica Chesapeake-Greenbrier Circle** [H]
(757) 523-7377. **$67-$103.** 809 Greenbrier Cir. I-64, exit 289A (Greenbrier Pkwy), just n. Int corridors. **Pets:** Other species. $25 daily fee/pet. Service with restrictions, crate.
(ASK) [X] [&M] [B] [▭]

▼▼ **Extended StayAmerica Hotel** [H]
(757) 483-9200. **$62-$88.** 3214 Churchland Blvd. I-664, exit 9B northbound; exit 8B southbound, 1 mi s on US 17. Int corridors. **Pets:** Other species. $25 daily fee/pet. Service with restrictions, crate.
(ASK) [X] [B] [▭]

▼▼▼ **Residence Inn by Marriott, Chesapeake-Greenbrier** [H]
(757) 502-7300. **$149-$179.** 1500 Crossways Blvd. I-64, exit 289B (Greenbrier Pkwy), just s to Jarman Rd (at Crossways Center) to Crossways Blvd, then 0.6 mi n. Int corridors. **Pets:** Accepted.
[X] [B] [▭] [▯] [X]

▼▼▼ Staybridge Suites Greenbrier 🅷 ❖
(757) 420-2525. $115-$139, 3 day notice. 709 Woodlake Dr. I-64, exit
289A (Greenbrier Pkwy), just n. Int corridors. Pets: Medium. $75 one-time
fee/room.
ASK ✕ 🅱 🖳 🏊

▼ Super 8 Motel 🅼 ❖
(757) 686-8888. $57-$100. 3216 Churchland Blvd. I-664, exit 9B, 1 mi s on
SR 17. Int corridors. Pets: Other species. $10 daily fee/room. Designated
rooms, service with restrictions, crate.
ASK ✕ 🅱 🖳

▼▼ TownePlace Suites By Marriott 🅷
(757) 523-5004. $129-$149. 2000 Old Greenbrier Rd. I-64, exit 289A
(Greenbrier Pkwy), just n. Int corridors. Pets: Accepted.
✕ 🅼 🅱 🖳 🏊

GLOUCESTER

▼▼▼ Comfort Inn Gloucester 🅷
(804) 695-1900. $84-$179. 6639 Forest Hill Ave. US 17, just s. Int corridors. Pets: Medium. $10 daily fee/pet. Service with restrictions, supervision.
ASK ✕ 🅱 🖳 🏊

HAMPTON

▼▼ Candlewood Suites 🅷
(757) 766-8976. $100-$140. 401 Butler Farm Rd. I-64, exit 261B (Hampton
Roads Center Pkwy) eastbound; exit 262B (Magruder Blvd) westbound,
then n. Int corridors. Pets: Medium, other species. $75 one-time fee/room.
Service with restrictions, crate.
ASK ✕ 🅼 🅱 🖳

🔷 ▼▼▼ Clarion Hotel-Hampton Roads Convention
Center 🅷 ❖
(757) 838-5011. $89-$199. 1809 W Mercury Blvd. I-64, exit 263B (Mercury
Blvd), jct SR 58. Int corridors. Pets: Other species. $25 one-time fee/pet.
Supervision.
SAVE ✕ 🅼 🅱 🖳 🍴 🏊

▼▼ Extended StayAmerica-Hampton Coliseum 🅼
(757) 896-3600. $62-$83. 1915 Commerce Dr. I-64, exit 263 (Mercury
Blvd), just n, then just e. Int corridors. Pets: Other species. $25 daily
fee/pet. Service with restrictions, crate.
ASK ✕ 🅼 🅱 🖳

▼▼▼ Holiday Inn Hampton Hotel & Conference
Center 🅷
(757) 838-0200. $104-$159. 1815 W Mercury Blvd. I-64, exit 263B (Mer-
cury Blvd) westbound; exit 263 eastbound. Ext/int corridors. Pets:
Accepted.
ASK ✕ 🅼 🅱 🖳 🍴 🏊 ✕

▼▼ Ramada Hampton Coliseum & Convention
Center 🅷
(757) 827-7400. $49-$149, 15 day notice. 1905 Coliseum Dr. I-64, exit
263 (Mercury Blvd) eastbound, just n, then just e towards Hampton Coliseum; exit 263B westbound. Ext/int corridors. Pets: Small. $10 daily fee/
pet. Service with restrictions, supervision.
ASK ✕ 🅱 🖳 🏊

▼ Super 8 Motel 🅼
(757) 723-2888. Call for rates. 1330 Thomas St. I-64, exit 265B westbound; exit 265C eastbound. Int corridors. Pets: Accepted.
✕ 🅱 🖳

NEWPORT NEWS

▼▼▼ Comfort Inn 🅷
(757) 249-0200. $109-$149, 5 day notice. 12330 Jefferson Ave. I-64, exit
255A, just s on Clarie Ln (mall parking lot). Int corridors. Pets: Accepted.
ASK ✕ 🅼 🅱 🖳 🏊

▼▼ Crestwood Suites 🅼
(757) 951-1017. Call for rates. 11 Old Oyster Point Rd. I-64, exit 256A,
just s on Oyster Point Rd to Canon Blvd, just e, then just n. Int corridors.
Pets: Accepted.
✕ 🅱 🖳

🔷 ▼▼▼ Days Inn-Oyster Point at City Center 🅷 ❖
(757) 873-6700. $89-$119, 3 day notice. 11829 Fishing Point Dr. I-64,
exit 255A, 2.5 mi s to Thimble Shoals Dr E, then 1 blk. Int corridors.
Pets: Medium, other species. $25 daily fee/room. Service with restrictions,
crate.
SAVE ✕ 🅱 🖳 🏊

▼▼ Extended StayAmerica Newport News-Oyster
Point 🅷
(757) 873-2266. $52-$82. 11708 Jefferson Ave. I-64, exit 258A (US 17), 1
mi s. Ext corridors. Pets: Other species. $25 daily fee/pet. Service with
restrictions, crate.
ASK ✕ 🅱 🖳

🔷 ▼▼▼ Mulberry Inn 🅷
(757) 887-3000. $79-$139. 16890 Warwick Blvd. I-64, exit 250A (SR
105/Ft Eustis Blvd S) s to US 60, then 0.3 mi w. Ext/int corridors.
Pets: Medium. $10 daily fee/pet, $50 one-time fee/pet. Designated rooms,
service with restrictions, supervision.
SAVE ✕ 🅱 🖳 🏊

▼▼▼ Omni Newport News Hotel 🅷
(757) 873-6664. $144-$164. 1000 Omni Blvd. I-64, exit 258A (US 17), just
s to Oyster Point Rd. Int corridors. Pets: Small, dogs only. $50 one-time
fee/room. Designated rooms, service with restrictions, supervision.
ASK ✕ 🅱 🖳 🍴 🏊

🔷 ▼▼▼ Point Plaza-Suites at City Center 🅷 ❖
(757) 599-4460. $69-$159, 7 day notice. 950 J Clyde Morris Blvd. I-64,
exit 258B (US 17), just n. Ext/int corridors. Pets: $50 one-time fee/room.
Designated rooms, service with restrictions, crate.
SAVE ✕ 🅱 🖳 🍴 🏊

▼▼ StudioPLUS-Newport News–I-64–Jefferson Ave 🅷
(757) 882-8847. $64-$103. 12359 Hornsby Ln. I-64, exit 255A, just s on
Jefferson Ave. Int corridors. Pets: Other species. $25 daily fee/pet. Service
with restrictions, crate.
ASK ✕ 🅱 🖳 🏊

NORFOLK

🔷 ▼▼▼ ▼▼▼ B & B @ Historic Page House
Inn 🅱🅱 ❖
(757) 625-5033. $145-$230, 7 day notice. 323 Fairfax Ave. I-264, exit 9,
1.4 mi n on Waterside Dr to Olney Rd, just w to Mowbray Arch, then just s;
in Ghent historic district. Int corridors. Pets: Medium. $25 daily fee/pet.
Service with restrictions, supervision.
SAVE ✕ 🅱 ✕

🔷 ▼▼▼ La Quinta Inn & Suites Norfolk
Airport 🅷 ❖
(757) 466-7001. Call for rates. 1387 N Military Hwy. I-64, exit 281 (Military
Hwy), just s. Int corridors. Pets: Medium, other species. Service with restric-
tions, supervision.
SAVE ✕ 🅱 🖳 🏊

🔷 ▼▼▼ Quality Suites Lake Wright 🅷 ❖
(757) 461-6251. $119-$169. 6280 Northampton Blvd. I-64, exit 282, just w
on US 13. Int corridors. Pets: Other species. $35 one-time fee/room. Serv-
ice with restrictions, supervision.
SAVE ✕ 🅼 🅱 🖳 🍴 🏊

▼▼▼ Residence Inn by Marriott Norfolk Airport 🅷 ❖
(757) 333-3000. $149-$179. 1590 N Military Hwy. I-64, exit 281B (Military
Hwy). Int corridors. Pets: Other species. $75 one-time fee/room. Service
with restrictions.
✕ 🅼 🅱 🖳 🏊 ✕

Sheraton Norfolk Waterside Hotel H
(757) 622-6664. **$99-$319.** 777 Waterside Dr. I-264, exit 9 (Waterside Dr); downtown. Int corridors. **Pets:** Accepted.

Sleep Inn Lake Wright H
(757) 461-1133. **$99-$139.** 6280 Northampton Blvd. I-64, exit 282, just w on US 13. Int corridors. **Pets:** Other species. $25 one-time fee/room. Service with restrictions, supervision.

Tazewell Hotel and Suites H
(757) 623-6200. **$79-$199, 3 day notice.** 245 Granby St. Jct Tazewell St; downtown. Int corridors. **Pets:** Accepted.

SUFFOLK

Quality Inn H
(757) 934-2311. **$89-$109.** 2864 Pruden Blvd. US 460 at jct US 58 Bypass. Ext corridors. **Pets:** Accepted.

TownePlace Suites by Marriott H
(757) 483-5177. **$119-$129.** 8050 Harbour View Blvd. I-664, exit 8A (College Dr), just n. Int corridors. **Pets:** Medium, other species. $100 one-time fee/room. Designated rooms, service with restrictions, supervision.

VIRGINIA BEACH

Candlewood Suites H
(757) 213-1500. **$69-$199, 3 day notice.** 4437 Bonney Rd. I-264, exit 17B (Independence Blvd/Pembroke Area), just n to Bonney Rd, then just e. Int corridors. **Pets:** Medium, other species. $150 one-time fee/room. Service with restrictions, crate.

DoubleTree Hotel Virginia Beach H
(757) 422-8900. **$59-$249.** 1900 Pavilion Dr. I-264, exit 22 (Birdneck Rd). Int corridors. **Pets:** Accepted.

Extended StayAmerica-Virginia Beach-Independence Blvd M
(757) 473-9200. **$57-$124.** 4548 Bonney Rd. I-264, exit 17B (Independence Blvd/Pembroke Area), just n to Bonney Rd, then just e. Ext corridors. **Pets:** Other species. $25 daily fee/pet. Service with restrictions, crate.

Holiday Inn-Executive Center H
(757) 499-4400. **$109-$189.** 5655 Greenwich Rd. I-64, exit 284B (Newtown Rd); jct I-64 and 264. Int corridors. **Pets:** Small, dogs only. $35 one-time fee/room. Designated rooms, service with restrictions, supervision.

Holiday Inn Surfside Hotel & Suites H
(757) 491-6900. **Call for rates.** 2607 Atlantic Ave. I-264, n of terminus; at Atlantic Ave and 26th St. Int corridors. **Pets:** Accepted.

La Quinta Inn & Suites H
(757) 428-2203. **$59-$199.** 2800 Pacific Ave. I-264, 0.5 mi n of terminus. Int corridors. **Pets:** Medium, other species. Service with restrictions, supervision.

La Quinta Inn Norfolk (Virginia Beach) H
(757) 497-6620. **$45-$149.** 192 Newtown Rd. I-64, exit 284B to I-264, exit Newtown Rd S. Int corridors. **Pets:** Medium, other species. Service with restrictions, supervision.

Red Roof Inn VA Beach (Norfolk Airport) M
(757) 460-6700. **$56-$190.** 5745 Northampton Blvd. I-64, exit 282, 1 mi n on US 13 (Northampton Blvd). Ext corridors. **Pets:** Large, dogs only. Designated rooms, service with restrictions, supervision.

Residence Inn Virginia Beach Oceanfront H
(757) 425-1141. **$178-$305, 3 day notice.** 3217 Atlantic Ave. I-264, 1.5 mi n of terminus; Atlantic Ave and 33rd St. Int corridors. **Pets:** Other species. $75 one-time fee/room.

Sheraton Oceanfront Hotel H
(757) 425-9000. **$109-$319, 3 day notice.** 3501 Atlantic Ave. I-264, 1 mi n of terminus; jct 36th St. Int corridors. **Pets:** Medium, dogs only. $75 deposit/pet. Designated rooms, service with restrictions, supervision.

TownePlace Suites By Marriott H
(757) 490-9367. **$129-$169.** 5757 Cleveland St. I-64, exit 284B to I-264 (Virginia Beach-Norfolk Expwy), exit Newtown Rd N. Int corridors. **Pets:** Accepted.

The Westin Virginia Beach Town Center H
(757) 557-0550. **Call for rates.** 4535 Commerce St. I-264, exit 17B (Independence Blvd), just n, then just e. Int corridors. **Pets:** Accepted.

END AREA

HARRISONBURG

Comfort Inn H
(540) 433-6066. **$84-$140.** 1440 E Market St. I-81, exit 247A, just e. Int corridors. **Pets:** Other species. $10 daily fee/pet. Service with restrictions, supervision.

Days Inn Harrisonburg H
(540) 433-9353. **$79-$140.** 1131 Forest Hill Rd. I-81, exit 245, just e. Int corridors. **Pets:** Small, dogs only. $10 daily fee/pet. Designated rooms, service with restrictions, supervision.

Harrisonburg Econo Lodge M
(540) 433-2576. **Call for rates.** 1703 E Market St. I-81, exit 247A, 0.5 mi e on US 33. Ext/int corridors. **Pets:** Small. $20 daily fee/pet. Designated rooms, service with restrictions, supervision.

Ramada H
(540) 434-9981. **$49-$129.** 1 Pleasant Valley Rd. I-81, exit 243, just w, then just n on US 11. Ext corridors. **Pets:** Accepted.

Super 8 M
(540) 433-8888. **$45-$89, 3 day notice.** 3330 S Main St. I-81, exit 243, just e, then just s on US 11. Int corridors. **Pets:** Small. $10 one-time fee/pet. Designated rooms, no service, supervision.

⟦SAVE⟧ ⟦X⟧ ⟦♨⟧ ⟦💻⟧

The Village Inn H ❀
(540) 434-7355. **$75-$80.** 4979 S Valley Pike. I-81, exit 240 southbound, 0.6 mi w on SR 257, then 1.5 mi n on US 11; exit 243 northbound, just w to US 11, then 1.7 mi s. Ext corridors. **Pets:** Other species. $10 daily fee/pet. Service with restrictions, crate.

⟦SAVE⟧ ⟦X⟧ ⟦♨⟧ ⟦💻⟧ ⟦🍴⟧ ⟦🏊⟧ ⟦X⟧

HILLSVILLE

Best Western Four Seasons South H
(276) 728-4136. **$81-$91, 3 day notice.** 57 Airport Rd. I-77, exit 14, just w on US 58 and 221. Ext corridors. **Pets:** $10 daily fee/room. Designated rooms, service with restrictions, supervision.

⟦SAVE⟧ ⟦X⟧ ⟦♨⟧ ⟦💻⟧ ⟦🏊⟧

Quality Inn H
(276) 728-2120. **$69-$169.** 85 Airport Rd. I-77, exit 14, just w on US 58 and 221. Ext corridors. **Pets:** Medium, other species. $10 daily fee/pet. Designated rooms, service with restrictions, supervision.

⟦SAVE⟧ ⟦X⟧ ⟦♨⟧ ⟦💻⟧ ⟦🏊⟧

HOPEWELL

Candlewood Suites H ❀
(804) 541-0200. **$159-$259.** 5113 Plaza Dr. I-295, exit 9B (SR 36), just w; adjacent to Oak Lawn Plaza. Int corridors. **Pets:** Medium. $75 one-time fee/pet. Service with restrictions, crate.

⟦SAVE⟧ ⟦X⟧ ⟦♨⟧ ⟦💻⟧

Fairfield Inn & Suites by Marriott H
(804) 458-2600. **$98-$120.** 3952 Courthouse Rd. I-295, exit 9A (SR 36), just e. Int corridors. **Pets:** Small. $20 daily fee/pet. Designated rooms, service with restrictions, crate.

⟦X⟧ ⟦♨⟧ ⟦💻⟧ ⟦🏊⟧

HUDDLESTON

Mariners Landing CO
(540) 297-4900. **$80-$260, 7 day notice.** 1217 Graves Harbor Tr. On SR 626; on Smith Mountain Lake. Ext/int corridors. **Pets:** Accepted.

⟦ASK⟧ ⟦X⟧ ⟦♨⟧ ⟦💻⟧ ⟦🍴⟧ ⟦🏊⟧ ⟦X⟧

IRVINGTON

The Tides Inn H ❀
(804) 438-5000. **$189-$375, 7 day notice.** 480 King Carter Dr. 0.3 mi w of CR 200. Ext/int corridors. **Pets:** Medium, other species. $25 daily fee/pet. Designated rooms, service with restrictions.

⟦SAVE⟧ ⟦X⟧ ⟦♨⟧ ⟦💻⟧ ⟦🍴⟧ ⟦🏊⟧ ⟦X⟧

KESWICK

Keswick Hall at Monticello H ❀
(434) 979-3440. **$275-$425, 7 day notice.** 701 Club Dr. I-64, exit 129, just n. Int corridors. **Pets:** Large. $75 one-time fee/pet. Designated rooms, service with restrictions, crate.

⟦SAVE⟧ ⟦X⟧ ⟦♨⟧ ⟦💻⟧ ⟦🍴⟧ ⟦🏊⟧ ⟦X⟧

LAWRENCEVILLE

Brunswick Mineral Springs B & B Circa 1785 BB
(434) 848-4010. **Call for rates.** 14910 Western Mill Rd. 5 mi e on US 58, 1 mi s on SR 712, then just e. Int corridors. **Pets:** Accepted.

⟦X⟧ ⟦♨⟧ ⟦💻⟧

LEBANON

Lebanon Super 8 H
(276) 889-1800. **$66-$150.** 71 Townview Dr. Just e on SR 654 from US 19 Bypass. Int corridors. **Pets:** Accepted.

⟦ASK⟧ ⟦X⟧ ⟦♨⟧ ⟦💻⟧

LEXINGTON

Best Western Inn at Hunt Ridge H
(540) 464-1500. **$59-$179.** 25 Willow Spring Rd. I-64, exit 55, just n on US 11 to SR 39; I-81, exit 191, 0.6 mi w. Int corridors. **Pets:** Large, other species. $25 one-time fee/room. Service with restrictions, supervision.

⟦SAVE⟧ ⟦X⟧ ⟦♨⟧ ⟦💻⟧ ⟦🍴⟧ ⟦🏊⟧

Best Western Lexington Inn H
(540) 458-3020. **$69-$150.** 850 N Lee Hwy. I-64, exit 55, just s on US 11; I-81, exit 191, 1.6 mi w. Ext corridors. **Pets:** Other species. $25 one-time fee/room. Service with restrictions, supervision.

⟦SAVE⟧ ⟦X⟧ ⟦♨⟧ ⟦💻⟧

Comfort Inn-Virginia Horse Center H
(540) 463-7311. **$64-$175.** 62 Comfort Way. I-64, exit 55, just s on US 11; I-81, exit 191, 0.6 mi w. Int corridors. **Pets:** Medium. $25 one-time fee/room. Designated rooms, service with restrictions, supervision.

⟦SAVE⟧ ⟦X⟧ ⟦♨⟧ ⟦💻⟧

Days Inn H
(540) 463-9131. **$60-$130.** 2809 N Lee Hwy. I-81, exit 195, just sw on US 11. Ext corridors. **Pets:** Medium. $10 daily fee/pet. Service with restrictions, supervision.

⟦SAVE⟧ ⟦X⟧ ⟦♨⟧ ⟦💻⟧ ⟦🍴⟧ ⟦🏊⟧

Econo Lodge M
(540) 463-7371. **$50-$150.** 65 Econo Ln. I-81, exit 191, just s on US 11. Ext corridors. **Pets:** Accepted.

⟦ASK⟧ ⟦X⟧ ⟦♨⟧ ⟦💻⟧

Holiday Inn Express H ❀
(540) 463-7351. **$99-$200.** 880 N Lee Hwy. I-64, exit 55, just s on US 11; I-81, exit 191, 1 mi w. Int corridors. **Pets:** Large, other species. $25 one-time fee/room. Service with restrictions, supervision.

⟦SAVE⟧ ⟦X⟧ ⟦♨⟧ ⟦💻⟧

Howard Johnson Inn H ❀
(540) 463-9181. **$50-$200.** 2836 N Lee Hwy. I-81, exit 195, just s on US 11. Int corridors. **Pets:** Other species. $12 daily fee/pet. Designated rooms, service with restrictions, supervision.

⟦SAVE⟧ ⟦X⟧ ⟦♨⟧ ⟦💻⟧ ⟦🏊⟧

Super 8 M
(540) 463-7858. **$57-$125.** 1139 N Lee Hwy. I-64, exit 55, just n. Int corridors. **Pets:** Accepted.

⟦ASK⟧ ⟦X⟧ ⟦♨⟧ ⟦💻⟧

LURAY

Days Inn-Luray H
(540) 743-4521. **$49-$159.** 138 Whispering Hill Rd. US 211 Bypass, 1.7 mi e of jct US 340. Ext/int corridors. **Pets:** Medium, other species. $10 daily fee/pet. Designated rooms, service with restrictions.

⟦ASK⟧ ⟦X⟧ ⟦♨⟧ ⟦💻⟧ ⟦🏊⟧ ⟦X⟧

The Mimslyn Inn H
(540) 743-5105. **$145-$325.** 401 W Main St. 0.3 mi w on US 211 business route. Int corridors. **Pets:** Accepted.

⟦SAVE⟧ ⟦X⟧ ⟦♨⟧ ⟦💻⟧ ⟦🍴⟧ ⟦🏊⟧ ⟦X⟧

LYNCHBURG

Econo Lodge M
(434) 847-1045. **$90-$160, 4 day notice.** 2400 Stadium Rd. US 29, exit 4 southbound; exit 6 northbound, just w on James St, then just n. Ext corridors. **Pets:** Very small. $25 daily fee/room. Designated rooms, service with restrictions.

⟦SAVE⟧ ⟦X⟧ ⟦♨⟧ ⟦💻⟧

▼▼ **Extended StayAmerica–University Blvd** Ⓜ
(434) 239-8863. **$62-$83.** 1910 University Blvd. US 460, exit Candlers Mountain Rd/University Blvd. Int corridors. **Pets:** Other species. $25 daily fee/pet. Service with restrictions, crate.

ⒶⓈⓀ ☒ ⓖⓂ 🅗 🖵

▼▼ **Hampton Inn** Ⓗ
(434) 237-2704. **$96-$99.** 5604 Seminole Ave. US 460, exit Candlers Mountain Rd, 0.3 mi w; US 29, exit Candlers Mountain Rd. Ext/int corridors. **Pets:** Accepted.

☒ ⓖⓂ 🅗 🖵

▼▼▼ **Holiday Inn Express** Ⓗ
(434) 237-7771. **$99-$104, 3 day notice.** 5600 Seminole Ave. US 460, exit Candlers Mountain Rd, 0.3 mi w; US 29, exit Candlers Mountain Rd. Int corridors. **Pets:** Accepted.

ⒶⓈⓀ ☒ 🅗 🖵 ⤳

▼▼ **Holiday Inn Select** Ⓗ
(434) 528-2500. **$119.** 601 Main St. US 29, exit 1 (Main St), just w; downtown. Int corridors. **Pets:** Accepted.

ⒶⓈⓀ ☒ 🅗 🖵 🍽 ⤳

▼▼ **Lynchburg Super 8** Ⓗ
(434) 846-1668. **Call for rates.** 3736 Candlers Mountain Rd. US 29, exit 8B, just e. Int corridors. **Pets:** $10 daily fee/pet. Designated rooms, service with restrictions, supervision.

☒ ⓖⓂ 🅗 🖵

ⒶⒶⒶ ▼▼▼ **Quality Inn** Ⓗ
(434) 847-9041. **$59-$99, 15 day notice.** 3125 Albert Lankford Dr. US 29, exit 7, just s. Int corridors. **Pets:** Other species. $25 one-time fee/room. Designated rooms, service with restrictions, supervision.

ⓈⒶⓋⒺ ☒ 🅗 🖵 ⤳

MARION

ⒶⒶⒶ ▼▼▼ **Best Western-Marion** Ⓗ
(276) 783-3193. **Call for rates.** 1424 N Main St. I-81, exit 47, 0.3 mi s on US 11. Ext corridors. **Pets:** Small. $7 daily fee/pet. Designated rooms, service with restrictions, supervision.

ⓈⒶⓋⒺ ☒ 🅗 🖵 🍽 ⤳

MARTINSVILLE

▼▼ **Best Lodge** Ⓜ
(276) 647-3941. **$48-$68.** 1985 Virginia Ave. Jct US 58, 2.5 mi n on US 220 business route. Ext corridors. **Pets:** Small. $10 one-time fee/pet. Designated rooms, service with restrictions, supervision.

ⒶⓈⓀ ☒ 🅗 🖵

ⒶⒶⒶ ▼▼▼▼ **Best Western Martinsville Inn** Ⓗ
(276) 632-5611. **$60-$65.** US 220 Business Rt S. Jct US 58, 2.3 mi n. Ext corridors. **Pets:** Accepted.

ⓈⒶⓋⒺ ☒ 🅗 🖵 🍽 ⤳

▼▼▼▼ **Hampton Inn** Ⓗ
(276) 647-4700. **$109-$249.** 50 Hampton Dr. Jct US 58, 2.5 mi n on US 220 business route. Int corridors. **Pets:** Accepted.

☒ 🅗 🖵 ⤳

▼▼▼▼ **Holiday Inn Express** Ⓗ
(276) 666-6835. **$76-$97, 3 day notice.** 1895 Virginia Ave. Jct US 58, 2.4 mi n on US 220 business route. Int corridors. **Pets:** Accepted.

ⒶⓈⓀ ☒ 🅗 🖵 ⤳

MIDDLETOWN

ⒶⒶⒶ ▼▼▼ **Super 8** Ⓗ
(540) 868-1800. **$59-$150.** 2120 Relaince Rd. I-81, exit 302. Int corridors. **Pets:** Accepted.

ⓈⒶⓋⒺ ☒ 🅗 🖵 ⤳

MINT SPRING

▼▼ **Days Inn-Staunton** Ⓜ
(540) 337-3031. **$65-$175.** 372 White Hill Rd. I-81, exit 217, just e on SR 654. Ext corridors. **Pets:** Accepted.

ⒶⓈⓀ ☒ 🅗 🖵 ⤳

MOUNT JACKSON

ⒶⒶⒶ ▼▼▼ **Super 8–Mt. Jackson** Ⓜ
(540) 477-2911. **Call for rates.** 250 Conicville Blvd. I-81, exit 273, just e. Ext corridors. **Pets:** Medium. $10 daily fee/pet. Designated rooms, service with restrictions, supervision.

ⓈⒶⓋⒺ ☒ 🅗 🖵 ⤳

▼▼▼▼ **The Widow Kip's** ⒷⒷ 🐾
(540) 477-2400. **$100-$135, 5 day notice.** 355 Orchard Dr. I-81, exit 273, 1.5 mi s on US 11, just w on SR 263, then just sw on SR 698. Int corridors. **Pets:** Other species. $20 daily fee/pet. Designated rooms, no service.

ⒶⓈⓀ ☒ 🅗 🖵 ⤳

NEW CHURCH

▼▼▼▼ **The Garden & The Sea Inn** ⒷⒷ 🐾
(757) 824-0672. **$95-$225, 10 day notice.** 4188 Nelson Rd. US 13, 0.3 mi n, just w on CR 710 (Nelson Rd). Int corridors. **Pets:** Accepted.

ⒶⓈⓀ ☒ 🅗 🖵 ⤳ ⓩ

NEW MARKET

ⒶⒶⒶ ▼▼ **Budget Inn** Ⓜ
(540) 740-3105. **$29-$69, 3 day notice.** 2192 Old Valley Pike. I-81, exit 264, 1 mi n on US 11. Ext corridors. **Pets:** Small. $10 one-time fee/pet. Designated rooms, no service, supervision.

ⓈⒶⓋⒺ ☒ 🅗

▼▼▼ **Days Inn** Ⓗ
(540) 740-4100. **Call for rates.** 9360 George Collins Pkwy. I-81, exit 264, just w on US 211. Ext corridors. **Pets:** Accepted.

☒ 🅗 🖵 ⤳

NORTON

▼▼ **Days Inn** Ⓗ
(276) 679-5340. **Call for rates.** 375 Wharton Ln. Jct US 58 and 23. Int corridors. **Pets:** Accepted.

☒ 🅗 🖵

ONANCOCK

ⒶⒶⒶ ▼▼▼ **1890 Spinning Wheel Bed & Breakfast** ⒷⒷ 🐾
(757) 787-7311. **$85-$125, 3 day notice.** 31 North St. Just n of jct Market (SR 179) and North sts. Int corridors. **Pets:** Large, other species. $10 daily fee/pet. Designated rooms, service with restrictions, supervision.

ⓈⒶⓋⒺ ☒ 🕅 ⓩ

PETERSBURG

ⒶⒶⒶ ▼▼▼ **Days Inn** Ⓗ
(804) 733-4400. **$56-$150.** 12208 S Crater Rd. I-95, exit 45, jct US 301. Ext corridors. **Pets:** Large. $10 daily fee/pet. Designated rooms, service with restrictions, supervision.

ⓈⒶⓋⒺ ☒ 🅗 🖵 ⤳

ⒶⒶⒶ ▼▼▼ **Howard Johnson Inn-Steven Kent** Ⓗ 🐾
(804) 733-0600. **$60-$66.** 12205 S Crater Rd. I-95, exit 45, jct US 301. Ext/int corridors. **Pets:** Other species. $10 daily fee/pet. Service with restrictions, crate.

ⓈⒶⓋⒺ ☒ 🅗 🖵 🍽 ⤳

ⒶⒶⒶ ▼▼▼ **Quality Inn** Ⓗ
(804) 732-2900. **Call for rates.** 11974 S Crater Rd. I-95, exit 45, just n. Ext corridors. **Pets:** $5 daily fee/pet. Designated rooms, service with restrictions, supervision.

ⓈⒶⓋⒺ ☒ 🅗 🖵 ⤳

POUNDING MILL

▼▼▼ Claypool Hill Holiday Inn Express Hotel &
Suites H
(276) 596-9880. **Call for rates.** 180 Clay Dr. 0.5 mi e of US 19/460. Int
corridors. **Pets:** Accepted.
⊠ 🖪 💻 ⇆

▼ Claypool Hill Super 8 H
(276) 964-9888. **$63-$125.** 12367 Governor GC Peery Hwy. 0.3 mi w on
US 19/460. Int corridors. **Pets:** Accepted.
ASK ⊠ 🖪 💻

RADFORD

▲▲▲ ▼▼▼▼ Best Western Radford Inn H
(540) 639-3000. **$69-$119.** 1501 Tyler Ave. I-81, exit 109, 2.7 mi nw on SR
177. Int corridors. **Pets:** Accepted.
SAVE ⊠ 🖪 💻 ¶¶ ⇆ ⊠

▼ Super 8-Radford M
(540) 731-9355. **Call for rates.** 1600 Tyler Ave. I-81, exit 109, just w. Int
corridors. **Pets:** Medium. $10 daily fee/pet. Service with restrictions, super-
vision.
⊠ 🖪 💻

RAPHINE

▲▲▲ ▼▼▼ Days Inn-Shenandoah Valley M
(540) 377-2604. **$60-$190.** 584 Oakland Cir. I-81, exit 205, just sw. Int
corridors. **Pets:** Medium. $10 daily fee/pet. Service with restrictions, super-
vision.
SAVE ⊠ 🖪 💻 ⇆

RICHMOND METROPOLITAN AREA

CHESTERFIELD

▲▲▲ ▼▼▼ La Quinta Inn H ✿
(804) 743-0770. **$69-$164.** 9040 Pams Ave. I-95, exit 64, just w. Int corridors. **Pets:** Medium, other species. Service with restrictions, supervision.
SAVE ⊠ ᴸᴹ 🖪 💻

COLONIAL HEIGHTS

▼▼▼ Candlewood Suites H
(804) 526-0111. **$79-$149.** 15820 Woods Edge Rd. I-95, exit 58 northbound; exit 58B southbound, just w. Int corridors. **Pets:** Accepted.
ASK ⊠ 🖪 💻

DOSWELL

▲▲▲ ▼▼▼ Best Western-Kings Quarters H
(804) 876-3321. **$59-$189, 3 day notice.** 16102 Theme Park Way. I-95,
exit 98, just e on SR 30; entrance to theme park. Ext corridors. **Pets:** Small,
other species. $25 deposit/room. Service with restrictions, supervision.
SAVE ⊠ 🖪 💻 ¶¶ ⇆ ⊠

GLEN ALLEN

▼▼▼ Candlewood Suites Richmond-West H
(804) 364-2000. **Call for rates.** 4120 Brookriver Dr. I-64, exit 178, just w
on W Broad St. Int corridors. **Pets:** Accepted.
⊠ ᴸᴹ 🖪 💻

▼▼▼ Holiday Inn Express H
(804) 934-9300. **$119-$134, 3 day notice.** 9933 Mayland Dr. I-64, exit
180B, just n to Mayland Dr, then just w. Int corridors. **Pets:** Medium. $10
daily fee/pet. Service with restrictions, crate.
ASK ⊠ ᴸᴹ 🖪 💻 ⇆

▼▼▼ Homewood Suites by Hilton Richmond West
End-Innsbrook H
(804) 217-8000. **$89-$189.** 4100 Innslake Dr. I-64, exit 178B, just e on W
Broad St to Cox Rd, then just n. Int corridors. **Pets:** Accepted.
⊠ ᴸᴹ 🖪 💻 ⇆

▼▼▼ Residence Inn by Marriott H
(804) 762-9852. **$161-$197.** 3940 Westerre Pkwy. I-64, exit 180, n on
Gaskins Rd to W Broad St. Int corridors. **Pets:** Accepted.
⊠ ᴸᴹ 🖪 💻 ⇆ ⊠

RICHMOND

▼▼ Candlewood Suites H
(804) 271-0016. **Call for rates.** 4301 Commerce Rd. I-95, exit 69, just n.
Int corridors. **Pets:** Accepted.
⊠ ᴸᴹ 🖪 💻

▲▲▲ ▼▼ Comfort Inn & Conference
Center-Midtown H
(804) 359-4061. **$80-$150.** 3200 W Broad St. Jct Broad St and I-95, just e.
Int corridors. **Pets:** Accepted.
SAVE ⊠ 🖪 💻 ⇆

▼▼ Extended StayAmerica-I-64-West Broad M
(804) 285-2065. **$47-$83.** 6811 Paragon Pl. I-64, exit 183C (W Broad St),
just w to Glenside Dr, just n. Ext corridors. **Pets:** Other species. $25 daily
fee/pet. Service with restrictions, crate.
ASK ⊠ 🖪 💻

▼▼ Extended Stay Deluxe Richmond H
(804) 285-7050. **$83-$119.** 6807 Paragon Pl. I-64, exit 183C (W Broad St),
just w to Glenside Dr, just n. Int corridors. **Pets:** Other species. $25 daily
fee/pet. Service with restrictions, crate.
ASK ⊠ 🖪 💻 ⇆

▼▼ Homestead Studio Suites
Hotel-Richmond/Midlothian H
(804) 272-1800. **$62-$108.** 241 Arboretum Pl. Jct Powhite Pkwy (US 76)
and Midlothian Tpke (US 60), just w. Int corridors. **Pets:** Other species. $25
daily fee/pet. Service with restrictions, crate.
ASK ⊠ ᴸᴹ 🖪 💻

▲▲▲ ▼▼▼▼▼ The Jefferson Hotel H
(804) 788-8000. **$265-$395.** 101 W Franklin St. Franklin and Adams sts;
center. Int corridors. **Pets:** Accepted.
SAVE ⊠ 🖪 ¶¶ ⇆

▼▼▼▼ Omni Richmond Hotel H
(804) 344-7000. **$169-$309.** 100 S 12th St. I-95, exit 74A; I-195, exit Canal
St. Int corridors. **Pets:** Accepted.
ASK ⊠ 🖪 💻 ¶¶ ⇆

▲▲▲ ▼▼◆ Quality Inn West End H
(804) 346-0000. **$70-$180.** 8008 W Broad St. I-64, exit 183C (W Broad St)
westbound; exit 183 eastbound, 1.5 mi w. Int corridors. **Pets:** Medium. $10
daily fee/pet, $35 one-time fee/room. Service with restrictions, crate.
SAVE ⊠ 🖪 💻

▲▲▲ ▼▼◆ Sheraton Park South Hotel H
(804) 323-1144. **$99-$249.** 9901 Midlothian Tpke. US 60, 1 mi w of
Powhite Pkwy (US 76). Int corridors. **Pets:** Accepted.
SAVE ⊠ ᴸᴹ 🖪 💻 ¶¶ ⇆ ⊠

▲▲▲ ▼▼▼▼ Sheraton Richmond West H
(804) 285-2000. **$79-$235.** 6624 W Broad St. I-64, exit 183 eastbound; exit
183B westbound. Int corridors. **Pets:** Accepted.
SAVE ⊠ ᴸᴹ 🖪 💻 ¶¶ ⇆ ⊠

Super 8 Ⓜ
(804) 262-8880. **$135-$140, 30 day notice.** 5615 Chamberlayne Rd. I-95, exit 82. Int corridors. **Pets:** Accepted.

ASK ⊠ 🗎 💻

SANDSTON

Red Roof Inn Ⓜ
(804) 440-5770. **$59-$79.** 5209 Williamsburg Rd. I-64, exit 195, 1.5 mi s to Williamsburg Rd, then just e. Ext corridors. **Pets:** Small. $20 one-time fee/pet. Service with restrictions, crate.

SAVE ⊠ 🗎 💻

END METROPOLITAN AREA

ROANOKE

Comfort Inn Airport 🅗
(540) 527-2020. **$79-$190.** 5070 Valley View Blvd. I-81, exit 143 to I-581, exit 3, e to Hershberger Rd. Int corridors. **Pets:** Medium, dogs only. $25 one-time fee/pet. Designated rooms, no service, supervision.

SAVE ⊠ 🗎 💻 ⇔

Days Inn 🅗
(540) 366-0341. **$60-$100.** 8118 Plantation Rd. I-81, exit 146, just e on SR 115. Ext/int corridors. **Pets:** $15 one-time fee/room. Service with restrictions, crate.

SAVE ⊠ 🗎 💻 ⇔

Extended StayAmerica Roanoke-Airport Ⓜ
(540) 366-3216. **$57-$83.** 2705 W Frontage Rd NW. I-581, exit 3W, just w to Ordway Dr, then 0.4 mi n via service frontage road. Ext corridors. **Pets:** Other species. $25 daily fee/pet. Service with restrictions, crate.

ASK ⊠ 🗎

Holiday Inn Hotel Tanglewood 🅗
(540) 774-4400. **$99-$149.** 4468 Starkey Rd. I-581, exit Franklin Rd/Salem, 0.8 mi n on SR 419. Int corridors. **Pets:** Accepted.

SAVE ⊠ 🗎 💻 🍽 ⇔

Holiday Inn Roanoke 🅗 🐾
(540) 362-4500. **$129-$149.** 3315 Ordway Dr. I-581, exit 3W, just w to Ordway Dr, then 0.6 mi n via service road. Int corridors. **Pets:** Large, other species. $25 one-time fee/room. Service with restrictions, supervision.

ASK ⊠ 🗎 💻 🍽 ⇔ ⊠

MainStay Suites Roanoke Airport 🅗
(540) 527-3030. **$99-$175.** 5080 Valley View Blvd. I-581, exit 3E, just n. Int corridors. **Pets:** Medium, dogs only. $40 one-time fee/room. Service with restrictions, supervision.

SAVE ⊠ 🗎 💻

Quality Inn Airport 🅗
(540) 366-8861. **Call for rates.** 6626 Thirlane Rd. I-581, exit 2 southbound, just s on SR 117 (Peters Creek Rd), then just w. Ext corridors. **Pets:** Small, dogs only. $25 daily fee/room. Designated rooms, service with restrictions, crate.

SAVE ⊠ 🗎 💻 🍽 ⇔ ⊠

Residence Inn Roanoke Airport 🅗
(540) 265-1119. **$179-$219.** 3305 Ordway Dr NW. I-581, exit 3W, just s. Int corridors. **Pets:** Medium, other species. $49 one-time fee/room. Service with restrictions, supervision.

⊠ ⚫M 🗎 💻 ⇔

Sleep Inn Tanglewood 🅗
(540) 772-1500. **$64-$140.** 4045 Electric Rd. I-581/US 220, exit Franklin Rd/Salem, 0.7 mi n on SR 419. Int corridors. **Pets:** Small, other species. $25 daily fee/pet. Designated rooms, service with restrictions, crate.

SAVE ⊠ 🗎 💻

Super 8 🅗
(540) 563-8888. **$58-$98, 7 day notice.** 6616 Thirlane Rd. I-581, exit 25, s on SR 117 (Peters Creek Rd), then just w. Int corridors. **Pets:** Small. $10 daily fee/pet. No service, supervision.

ASK ⊠ 🗎

ROCKY MOUNT

Franklin Motel Ⓜ
(540) 483-9962. **$45-$90.** 20281 Virgil H Goode Hwy. 6.5 mi n on US 220. Ext corridors. **Pets:** Very small. $10 daily fee/pet. Service with restrictions, supervision.

SAVE ⊠ 🗎

Rocky Mount Holiday Inn Express Hotel & Suites 🅗
(540) 489-5001. **$95-$175, 30 day notice.** 395 Old Franklin Tpke. US 220 S and SR 40, 0.3 mi e. Int corridors. **Pets:** Accepted.

ASK ⊠ 🗎 💻 ⇔

RUTHER GLEN

Comfort Inn & Suites 🅗
(804) 448-1144. **Call for rates.** 24058 Welcome Way Dr. I-95, exit 104 (SR 207), just w. Int corridors. **Pets:** Accepted.

⊠ ⚫M 🗎 💻 ⇔

Super 8-Ruther Glen Ⓜ
(804) 448-2608. **Call for rates.** 24011 Ruther Glen Rd. I-95, exit 104 (SR 207), just e on Rogers Clark Blvd. Ext corridors. **Pets:** Accepted.

⊠ 💻 ⇔

SALEM

Comfort Suites Inn at Ridgewood Farm 🅗
(540) 375-4800. **$80-$130.** 2898 Keagy Rd. I-81, exit 141, 4.7 mi s on SR 419, then just w. Int corridors. **Pets:** Accepted.

⊠ 🗎 💻 ⇔

Days Inn 🅗
(540) 986-1000. **$74-$89.** 1535 E Main St. I-81, exit 141, 2 mi s on SR 419, then just w on US 460. Ext/int corridors. **Pets:** Other species. $25 deposit/room. Service with restrictions.

SAVE ⊠ 🗎 💻

Econo Lodge-Roanoke/Salem Ⓜ
(540) 389-0280. **$34-$99.** 301 Wildwood Rd. I-81, exit 137, just e on SR 112. Ext corridors. **Pets:** Medium. $5 daily fee/pet. Service with restrictions, crate.

SAVE ⊠ 🗎 💻

La Quinta Inn 🅗 🐾
(540) 562-2717. **$80-$150.** 140 Sheraton Dr. I-81, exit 141, 0.5 mi se on SR 419. Int corridors. **Pets:** Medium, other species. Service with restrictions, supervision.

SAVE ⊠ 🗎 💻 ⇔

SOUTH BOSTON

Holiday Inn-Express 🅗
(434) 575-4000. **Call for rates.** 1074 Bill Tuck Hwy. Just e on US 58, from jct US 501. Int corridors. **Pets:** Accepted.

⊠ ⚫M 🗎 💻 ⇔

Quality Inn South Boston 🅗
(434) 572-4311. **$60-$100.** 2001 Seymour Dr. Jct US 58, 501 and 360, 1 mi e on US 360. Ext corridors. **Pets:** Accepted.

SAVE ⊠ 🗎 💻 ⇔

SOUTH HILL

AAA ♦♦♦ Comfort Inn H
(434) 447-2600. **$60-$90.** 918 E Atlantic St. I-85, exit 12B, just w. Ext corridors. **Pets:** Other species. $10 daily fee/pet. No service.
SAVE ✕ 🛗 💻

♦♦♦♦ Fairfield Inn & Suites H 🐾
(434) 447-6800. **$85-$103.** 150 Arnold Dr. I-85, exit 12A, just e on US 58. Int corridors. **Pets:** Other species. $75 one-time fee/room. Service with restrictions, crate.
✕ &M 🛗 💻 ⊇

♦♦ Super 8 H
(434) 447-2313. **$61-$155.** 250 Thompson St. I-85, exit 12A, just n. Int corridors. **Pets:** Accepted.
ASK ✕ &M 🛗

STAFFORD

AAA ♦♦♦♦ Best Western Aquia/Quantico Inn H 🐾
(540) 659-0022. **Call for rates.** 2868 Jefferson Davis Hwy. I-95, exit 143A, jct US 1 and SR 610. Ext corridors. **Pets:** Medium, other species. $10 daily fee/pet. Designated rooms, service with restrictions, supervision.
SAVE ✕ 🛗 💻 🍴 ⊇

♦♦♦♦ Holiday Inn Express H
(540) 657-5566. **$109-$149.** 28 Greenspring Dr. I-95, exit 143B, just w on Garrisonville Rd. Int corridors. **Pets:** Medium. $25 daily fee/pet. Service with restrictions, supervision.
ASK ✕ 🛗 💻

♦♦♦♦ TownePlace Suites by Marriott H
(540) 657-1990. **$89-$109.** 2772 Jefferson Davis Hwy. I-95, exit 143A, just s on US 1. Int corridors. **Pets:** Accepted.
✕ &M 🛗 💻 ⊇

STAUNTON

AAA ♦♦♦ Best Western Staunton Inn H 🐾
(540) 885-1112. **Call for rates.** 92 Rowe Rd. I-81, exit 222, just e on US 250. Int corridors. **Pets:** Large. Service with restrictions, supervision.
SAVE ✕ 🛗 💻 ⊇

AAA ♦♦♦ Comfort Inn H 🐾
(540) 886-5000. **$72-$135.** 1302 Richmond Ave. I-81, exit 222, just w on US 250. Int corridors. **Pets:** Other species. $10 daily fee/room. Designated rooms, service with restrictions, crate.
SAVE ✕ 🛗 💻

AAA ♦♦♦ Econo Lodge Staunton H
(540) 885-5158. **$45-$109, 3 day notice.** 1031 Richmond Ave. I-81, exit 222, 0.7 mi w on US 250. Ext/int corridors. **Pets:** Medium. $10 daily fee/pet. Service with restrictions, supervision.
SAVE ✕ 🛗 💻

AAA ♦♦♦♦ Holiday Inn Golf & Conference Center H
(540) 248-6020. **$100-$201.** 152 Fairway Ln. I-81, exit 225, 0.3 mi w on SR 275 (Woodrow Wilson Pkwy). Int corridors. **Pets:** $25 one-time fee/pet. Designated rooms, service with restrictions, supervision.
SAVE ✕ 🛗 💻 🍴 ⊇

♦♦ Quality Inn-Conference Center H
(540) 248-5111. **$59-$139.** 96 Baker Ln. I-81, exit 225, just e on SR 275 (Woodrow Wilson Pkwy). Ext corridors. **Pets:** Medium, dogs only. $10 daily fee/pet. Designated rooms, service with restrictions, supervision.
ASK ✕ 🛗 💻 ⊇

AAA ♦♦♦ Sleep Inn H 🐾
(540) 887-6500. **$69-$125.** 222 Jefferson Hwy. I-81, exit 222, just e on US 250. Int corridors. **Pets:** Large. Service with restrictions, supervision.
SAVE ✕ 🛗 💻

AAA ♦♦♦♦ Stonewall Jackson Hotel & Conference Center H
(540) 885-4848. **$112-$199.** 24 S Market St. Between Beverly and Johnson sts; downtown. Int corridors. **Pets:** $25 daily fee/room. No service, supervision.
SAVE ✕ 💻 🍴 ⊇ 🐾

STEPHENS CITY

AAA ♦♦♦ Comfort Inn-Stephens City H
(540) 869-6500. **$85-$125.** 167 Town Run Ln. I-81, exit 307, just se. Int corridors. **Pets:** Medium. $15 daily fee/pet. Service with restrictions, supervision.
SAVE ✕ 🛗 💻 ⊇

STONY CREEK

AAA ♦♦♦♦ Hampton Inn-Stony Creek H
(434) 246-5500. **$84-$119.** 10476 Blue Star Hwy. I-95, exit 33, 0.3 mi s on SR 301. Int corridors. **Pets:** Medium, other species. $15 daily fee/pet. Designated rooms, service with restrictions, supervision.
SAVE ✕ &M 🛗 💻 ⊇

AAA ♦♦♦♦ Sleep Inn & Suites H
(434) 246-5100. **$69-$149.** 11019 Blue Star Hwy. I-95, exit 33, 0.3 mi s on SR 301. Int corridors. **Pets:** Medium, other species. $15 daily fee/pet. Service with restrictions, supervision.
SAVE ✕ 🛗 💻 ⊇

STRASBURG

AAA ♦♦♦♦ Hotel Strasburg CI
(540) 465-9191. **$89-$190.** 213 S Holliday St. I-81, exit 298, 2.2 mi s on US 11, then just s. Int corridors. **Pets:** Medium, dogs only. $10 daily fee/pet. No service, supervision.
SAVE ✕ 🍴

♦♦ Ramada H
(540) 465-2444. **$65-$99.** 21 Signal Knob Dr. I-81, exit 298, just e. Int corridors. **Pets:** Accepted.
ASK ✕ 🛗 💻 🍴 ⊇ 🐾

TAPPAHANNOCK

♦♦♦ The Essex Inn BB
(804) 443-9900. **$159-$199, 7 day notice.** 203 Duke St. 0.3 mi s on US 17, then just e. Ext/int corridors. **Pets:** Medium, other species. Designated rooms, crate.
✕ 🛗 💻

♦♦ Super 8 M
(804) 443-3888. **$61-$87.** 1800 Tappahannock Blvd. US 17 and 360. Int corridors. **Pets:** $10 daily fee/pet. Service with restrictions, supervision.
ASK ✕ 🛗 💻

TROUTVILLE

AAA ♦♦♦♦ Comfort Inn Troutville H
(540) 992-5600. **$64-$125.** 2545 Lee Hwy S. I-81, exit 150A, just s on US 11. Int corridors. **Pets:** Accepted.
SAVE ✕ 🛗 💻 ⊇

VERONA

AAA ♦♦♦ Knights Inn H
(540) 248-8981. **$40-$69, 3 day notice.** 70 Lodge Ln. I-81, exit 227, just w, then just n. Ext corridors. **Pets:** Small. $10 one-time fee/pet. No service, supervision.
SAVE ✕ 🛗 💻 ⊇

WARRENTON

Comfort Inn M
(540) 349-8900. **$129-$179.** 7379 Comfort Inn Dr. 1.5 mi n on US 15/29, on service road. Ext/int corridors. **Pets:** Medium. $10 daily fee/pet. Designated rooms, service with restrictions, supervision.
[SAVE] [X] [fridge] [microwave] [pool]

WARSAW

Best Western Warsaw H
(804) 333-1700. **$84-$97.** 4522 Richmond Rd. US 360, just w of town. Int corridors. **Pets:** Small. $10 daily fee/pet. Service with restrictions, supervision.
[SAVE] [X] [fridge] [microwave] [pool]

WASHINGTON

Middleton Inn BB
(540) 675-2020. **$235-$595, 14 day notice.** 176 Main St. 0.5 mi w on US 211 business route. Ext/int corridors. **Pets:** Accepted.
[SAVE] [X] [fridge] [microwave]

WAYNESBORO

Days Inn Waynesboro H
(540) 943-1101. **$55-$120.** 2060 Rosser Ave. I-64, exit 94, 0.5 mi n on US 340. Ext corridors. **Pets:** Other species. $10 daily fee/room. Service with restrictions, supervision.
[SAVE] [X] [fridge] [microwave] [pool]

Quality Inn Waynesboro H
(540) 942-1171. **Call for rates.** 640 W Broad St. I-64, exit 96, 3 mi w on SR 624; jct US 250 and 340. Ext/int corridors. **Pets:** $10 daily fee/room.
[SAVE] [X] [fridge] [microwave] [pool]

Super 8 H
(540) 943-3888. **$54-$110.** 2045 Rosser Ave. I-64, exit 94, n on US 340 to Lew Dewitt Blvd, then just w to Apple Tree Ln. Int corridors. **Pets:** Small. $5 daily fee/pet. Service with restrictions, supervision.
[SAVE] [X] [fridge] [microwave]

WILLIAMSBURG, JAMESTOWN & YORKTOWN AREA

WILLIAMSBURG

Clarion Hotel Historic District Williamsburg Virginia H
(757) 229-4100. **Call for rates.** 351 York St. US 60 E, 0.3 mi se of jct SR 5 and 31. Ext/int corridors. **Pets:** Accepted.
[SAVE] [X] [access] [fridge] [microwave] [restaurant] [pool] [pets]

Crowne Plaza Williamsburg at Fort Magruder H
(757) 220-2250. **$69-$279.** 6945 Pocahontas Tr. US 60, 0.8 mi e of jct SR 5 and 31. Int corridors. **Pets:** Medium. $45 one-time fee/room. Designated rooms, service with restrictions, crate.
[ASK] [X] [fridge] [microwave] [restaurant] [pool] [pets]

Days Inn Colonial Downtown H
(757) 229-5060. **$39-$129.** 902 Richmond Rd. Just w of Colonial Williamsburg on US 60. Ext corridors. **Pets:** Small. $10 daily fee/pet. Designated rooms, no service, supervision.
[SAVE] [X] [fridge] [pool]

La Quinta Inn Williamsburg (Historic Area) H ❖
(757) 253-1663. **$49-$129.** 119 Bypass Rd. US 60 Bypass Rd, 0.3 mi e of Richmond Rd. Ext corridors. **Pets:** Medium, other species. Service with restrictions, supervision.
[SAVE] [X] [access] [fridge] [microwave] [pool]

Patrick Henry Inn H
(757) 229-9540. **Call for rates.** 249 York St. E on US 60 (Richmond Rd) at jct SR 5 and 31; 1 blk from Colonial Williamsburg. Int corridors. **Pets:** Accepted.
[SAVE] [X] [fridge] [microwave] [pool]

Residence Inn by Marriott Williamsburg H
(757) 941-2000. **$70-$89.** 1648 Richmond Rd. US 60, just w of jct Bypass Rd. Int corridors. **Pets:** Other species. $75 one-time fee/room. Service with restrictions, crate.
[SAVE] [X] [access] [fridge] [microwave] [pool] [pets]

Williamsburg Inn H ❖
(757) 220-7978. **$279-$799, 3 day notice.** 136 E Francis St. In Colonial Williamsburg restored area. Int corridors. **Pets:** Medium. $500 deposit/pet, $50 daily fee/pet. Designated rooms, crate.
[ASK] [X] [fridge] [restaurant] [pool] [pets]

YORKTOWN

Candlewood Suites-Yorktown H
(757) 952-1120. **Call for rates.** 329 Commonwealth Dr. I-64, exit 256B, just n, then just e. Int corridors. **Pets:** Medium, other species. $75 one-time fee/room. Service with restrictions, supervision.
[X] [access] [fridge] [microwave] [pool]

Days Inn H
(757) 283-1111. **$70-$100.** 4531 George Washington Memorial Hwy. I-64, exit 256B, 0.8 mi ne on Victory Blvd (SR 171), 2.4 mi n on US 17. Int corridors. **Pets:** $10 daily fee/pet. Designated rooms, service with restrictions, supervision.
[ASK] [X] [fridge] [microwave]

TownePlace Suites by Marriott H
(757) 874-8884. **$129-$159.** 200 Cybernetics Way. I-64, exit 256B, e to Kiln Creek Pkwy. Int corridors. **Pets:** Other species. $100 one-time fee/pet. Service with restrictions, supervision.
[SAVE] [X] [access] [fridge] [microwave] [pool]

END AREA

WINCHESTER

Best Western Lee-Jackson Inn & Conference Center H
(540) 662-4154. **$63-$74.** 711 Millwood Ave. I-81, exit 313B, just nw on US 50/522/17. Ext corridors. **Pets:** Large. $5 daily fee/pet. Designated rooms, service with restrictions, supervision.
[SAVE] [X] [fridge] [microwave] [restaurant] [pool]

Days Inn H
(540) 667-1200. **$58-$85.** 2951 Valley Ave. I-81, exit 310, just w, then 1.8 mi n on US 11. Ext/int corridors. **Pets:** Large, other species. $5 daily fee/pet. Designated rooms, service with restrictions.
[SAVE] [X] [fridge] [microwave]

The George Washington Hotel, a Wyndham Historic Hotel H
(540) 678-4700. **$139.** 103 E Piccadilly St. I-81, exit 313, between Cameron and Kent sts; in Olde Towne area. Int corridors. **Pets:** Medium, other species. $75 one-time fee/pet. Supervision.
[ASK] [X] [fridge] [microwave] [restaurant] [pool]

Quality Inn H
(540) 545-8121. **Call for rates.** 1017 Millwood Pike. I-81, exit 313 northbound; exit 313A southbound, just se on US 50/17, at US 522. Ext/int corridors. **Pets:** Large. $10 daily fee/room. Designated rooms, service with restrictions, supervision.
SAVE ✕ 🛗 💻 🍴 ⊰

Red Roof Inn H
(540) 667-5000. **$58-$73.** 991 Millwood Pike. I-81, exit 313 northbound; exit 313A southbound, just se on US 50/17. Ext corridors. **Pets:** Medium, other species. Service with restrictions, supervision.
SAVE ✕ 🛗

Super 8 H
(540) 665-4450. **Call for rates.** 1077 Millwood Pike. I-81, exit 313 northbound; exit 313A southbound, 0.3 mi se on US 50/17. Int corridors. **Pets:** Accepted.
SAVE ✕ 🛗 💻

Travelodge of Winchester H
(540) 665-0685. **$60-$90, 7 day notice.** 160 Front Royal Pike. I-81, exit 313 northbound; exit 313A southbound, just s on US 522. Int corridors. **Pets:** Dogs only. $15 daily fee/pet. Service with restrictions, supervision.
SAVE ✕ 🛗 💻 ⊰

WOODSTOCK

Comfort Inn Shenandoah H ❀
(540) 459-7600. **$72-$119.** 1011 Motel Dr. I-81, exit 283, just e. Int corridors. **Pets:** Other species. $10 daily fee/pet. Supervision.
SAVE ✕ 🛗 💻 ⊰

WYTHEVILLE

Best Western Wytheville Inn H
(276) 228-7300. **$50-$160, 3 day notice.** 355 Nye Rd. I-77, exit 41, just e. Int corridors. **Pets:** $6 daily fee/pet. Designated rooms, service with restrictions, supervision.
SAVE ✕ 🛗 💻 ⊰

Budget Host Inn/Interstate Inn M
(276) 228-8618. **Call for rates.** 705 Chapman Rd. I-77/81, exit 73, just w. Ext corridors. **Pets:** Small. $12 daily fee/pet. Service with restrictions, supervision.
✕ 🛗

Comfort Inn H
(276) 637-4281. **Call for rates.** 2594 E Lee Hwy. I-77/81, exit 80, just w. Int corridors. **Pets:** Accepted.
✕ ♿ 🛗 💻 ⊰

Days Inn H
(276) 228-5500. **$55-$85.** 150 Malin Dr. I-77/81, exit 73, just w. Ext corridors. **Pets:** Medium. $10 daily fee/room. Service with restrictions, supervision.
ASK ✕ 🛗 💻

La Quinta Inn H ❀
(276) 228-7400. **$75-$175.** 1800 E Main. I-77/81, exit 73, just w. Int corridors. **Pets:** Medium, other species. Service with restrictions, supervision.
SAVE ✕ 🛗 💻 ⊰

Ramada H ❀
(276) 228-6000. **$49-$79, 3 day notice.** 955 Peppers Ferry Rd. I-77, exit 41, just e. Ext corridors. **Pets:** $10 daily fee/pet, $10 one-time fee/pet. Service with restrictions, supervision.
SAVE ✕ 🛗 💻 🍴 ⊰

Red Carpet Inn M
(276) 228-5525. **$45-$90, 7 day notice.** 280 Lithia Rd. I-77/81, exit 73, just w. Ext corridors. **Pets:** Small. $10 daily fee/pet. Service with restrictions, supervision.
SAVE ✕ 🛗

Red Roof Inn & Suites H
(276) 223-1700. **$42-$139.** 1900 E Main St. I-77/81, exit 73, just w. Ext corridors. **Pets:** Service with restrictions, supervision.
SAVE ✕ 🛗 💻 ⊰

Super 8 H
(276) 228-6620. **Call for rates.** 130 Nye Cir. I-77, exit 41, just e. Ext corridors. **Pets:** Accepted.
✕ 🛗 💻

WASHINGTON

CITY INDEX

ABERDEEN

 **GuestHouse International Inn & Suites** 🅷
(360) 537-7460. **Call for rates.** 701 E Heron St. Just e on US 12, cross street to Kansas St; downtown. Int corridors. **Pets:** Accepted.
⊠ 🛏 💻 ⇌

AIRWAY HEIGHTS

▼▼▼ **Stratford Suites** 🅷 ❖
(509) 321-1600. **$129-$225.** 11808 W Center Ln. I-90, exit 277, 4 mi w on SR 2. Ext corridors. **Pets:** Large, other species. $15 daily fee/room. Service with restrictions, crate.
⊠ 🕭ᴹ 🛏 ⇌

ANACORTES

𝔸𝔸𝔻 ▼▼▼ **Anacortes Inn** 🅼
(360) 293-3153. **Call for rates.** 3006 Commercial Ave. Just s of downtown. Ext corridors. **Pets:** Accepted.
SAVE ⊠ 🛏 💻 ⇌

𝔸𝔸𝔻 ▼▼▼ **Anacortes Ship Harbor Inn** 🅼
(360) 293-5177. **Call for rates.** 5316 Ferry Terminal Rd. 0.3 mi s of ferry landing. Ext corridors. **Pets:** Medium. $10 daily fee/pet. Service with restrictions, supervision.
SAVE ⊠ 🛏 💻 🕸

𝔸𝔸𝔻 ▼▼▼ **Cap Sante Inn** 🅼 ❖
(360) 293-0602. **$68-$135.** 906 9th St. On 9th St, just e. Ext corridors. **Pets:** Dogs only. $10 daily fee/pet. Designated rooms, service with restrictions, supervision.
SAVE ⊠ 🛏 🕸

▼▼▼ **Fidalgo Country Inn & Suites** 🅷
(360) 293-3494. **$90-$400.** 7645 SR 20. Jct Fidalgo Bay Rd. Ext/int corridors. **Pets:** Accepted.
ASK ⊠ 🕭ᴹ 🛏 💻 ⇌

▼▼ **Islands Inn** 🅼
(360) 293-4644. **$79-$150.** 3401 Commercial Ave. Just s of downtown. Ext corridors. **Pets:** Accepted.
ASK ⊠ 🛏 💻 🍽 ⇌

𝔸𝔸𝔻 ▼▼▼ **Majestic Inn & Spa** 🅷
(360) 299-1400. **$189-$219.** 419 Commercial Ave. Downtown. Int corridors. **Pets:** Accepted.
SAVE ⊠ 🛏 💻 🍽 🕸

ASHFORD

▼▼▼ **Mountain Meadows Inn Bed & Breakfast** 🅱🅱
(360) 569-2788. **$99-$165, 14 day notice.** 28912 SR 706 E. West end of town. Ext/int corridors. **Pets:** Medium, other species. $10 daily fee/pet. Designated rooms, supervision.
⊠ 🛏 💻 🎿 🅿 🏊

BELLINGHAM

𝔸𝔸𝔻 ▼▼▼ **Best Western Heritage Inn** 🅷 ❖
(360) 647-1912. **$109-$149.** 151 E McLeod Rd. I-5, exit 256A, just e. Int corridors. **Pets:** $20 daily fee/pet. Designated rooms, supervision.
SAVE ⊠ 🛏 💻 ⇌

𝔸𝔸𝔻 ▼▼▼ **Best Western Lakeway Inn & Conference Center** 🅷
(360) 671-1011. **$99-$209.** 714 Lakeway Dr. I-5, exit 253 (Lakeway Dr), just se. Int corridors. **Pets:** Small. $25 daily fee/room. Designated rooms, service with restrictions, supervision.
SAVE ⊠ 🛏 💻 🍽 ⇌ 🕸

𝔸𝔸𝔻 ▼▼▼ **Econo Lodge Inn & Suites** 🅷
(360) 671-4600. **Call for rates.** 3750 Meridian St. I-5, exit 256A, just w. Ext corridors. **Pets:** Very small, dogs only. $10 one-time fee/pet. Designated rooms, service with restrictions, supervision.
SAVE ⊠ 🛏 🏊

▼▼▼ **GuestHouse Inn** 🅷 ❖
(360) 671-9600. **$79-$120.** 805 Lakeway Dr. I-5, exit 253 (Lakeway Dr), just ne. Int corridors. **Pets:** Small, dogs only. $10 daily fee/room. Designated rooms, service with restrictions, supervision.
ASK ⊠ 🛏 💻

𝔸𝔸𝔻 ▼▼▼ **Holiday Inn Express-Bellingham** 🅷 ❖
(360) 671-4800. **$107-$145.** 4160 Meridian St. I-5, exit 256A, 0.7 mi e. Int corridors. **Pets:** Medium. $15 one-time fee/pet. Service with restrictions, supervision.
SAVE ⊠ 🕭ᴹ 🛏 💻 ⇌

𝔸𝔸𝔻 ▼▼▼ **Hotel Bellwether** 🅷 ❖
(360) 392-3100. **$156-$710, 3 day notice.** One Bellwether Way. I-5, exit 253 (Lakeway Dr), 0.9 mi nw via Lakeway Dr and E Holly St, just w on Bay St, 0.6 mi n via W Chestnut St and Roeder Ave, then just w. Int corridors. **Pets:** Large. $20 daily fee/room. Designated rooms, service with restrictions, crate.
SAVE ⊠ 🛏 💻 🍽 🕸

◆◆◆ ▼▼▼ **La Quinta Inn Bellingham** 🅗 ❖
(360) 671-6200. **$59-$169.** 125 E Kellogg Rd. I-5, exit 256A, 1 mi ne via Meridian St. Int corridors. **Pets:** Medium, other species. Service with restrictions, supervision.
(SAVE) ⊠ 🛢 🔲 🐾

▼ **Motel 6–44** M
(360) 671-4494. **$55-$75.** 3701 Byron Ave. I-5, exit 252, just nw. Ext corridors. **Pets:** Other species. Service with restrictions, supervision.
⊠ ♿M 🛢 🐾

◆◆◆ ▼▼▼ **Quality Inn Baron Suites** 🅗 ❖
(360) 647-8000. **$85-$219.** 100 E Kellogg Rd. I-5, exit 256A, 1 mi ne via Meridian St. Ext/int corridors. **Pets:** Medium. $10 daily fee/pet. Designated rooms, service with restrictions, crate.
(SAVE) ⊠ 🛢 🔲 🐾

BLAINE

◆◆◆ ▼▼ ▼▼ **Semiahmoo Resort** 🅗
(360) 318-2000. **$119-$399, 3 day notice.** 9565 Semiahmoo Pkwy. I-5, exit 270, 9.5 mi nw on Semiahmoo Spit. Int corridors. **Pets:** Medium, dogs only. $50 one-time fee/pet. Designated rooms, service with restrictions, supervision.
(SAVE) ⊠ 🛢 🔲 🍴 🐾 ⊠

BURLINGTON

◆◆◆ ▼▼ **Cocusa Motel** 🅗 ❖
(360) 757-6044. **$63-$135.** 370 W Rio Vista. I-5, exit 230, just e. Ext corridors. **Pets:** $20 one-time fee/room. Designated rooms, service with restrictions, supervision.
(SAVE) ⊠ 🛢 🔲 🐾

CASHMERE

◆◆◆ ▼▼ **Village Inn Motel** M
(509) 782-3522. **$59-$94, 7 day notice.** 229 Cottage Ave. On Business Rt US 2 and 97; downtown. Ext corridors. **Pets:** Small, dogs only. $10 daily fee/pet. Designated rooms, no service, supervision.
(SAVE) ⊠ 🛢

CASTLE ROCK

◆◆◆ ▼▼▼ **Timberland Inn & Suites** M
(360) 274-6002. **$60-$200.** 1271 Mount St. Helens Way. I-5, exit 49, just ne. Ext corridors. **Pets:** Small, dogs only. $15 daily fee/pet. Designated rooms, service with restrictions, supervision.
(SAVE) ⊠ 🛢 🔲

CENTRALIA

▼ **Motel 6–394** M
(360) 330-2057. **$45-$55.** 1310 Belmont Ave. I-5, exit 82, just w on Harrison Ave, then just n. Ext corridors. **Pets:** Other species. Service with restrictions, supervision.
⊠ 🛢 🐾

CHEHALIS

◆◆◆ ▼▼▼ **Best Western Park Place Inn & Suites** 🅗 ❖
(360) 748-4040. **$91-$124, 3 day notice.** 201 SW Interstate Ave. I-5, exit 76, just se. Int corridors. **Pets:** Small, dogs only. $10 daily fee/pet. Designated rooms, service with restrictions, supervision.
(SAVE) ⊠ ♿M 🛢 🔲 🐾

CHELAN

◆◆◆ ▼▼▼▼ **Best Western Lakeside Lodge & Suites** 🅗
(509) 682-4396. **$100-$400, 7 day notice.** 2312 W Woodin Ave. West end of town. Ext corridors. **Pets:** Accepted.
(SAVE) ⊠ 🛢 🔲 🐾

CHEWELAH

◆◆◆ ▼▼▼ **Nordlig Motel** M
(509) 935-6704. **$58-$63.** W 101 Grant Ave. North edge of town on US 395. Ext corridors. **Pets:** Dogs only. $5 one-time fee/pet. Service with restrictions, supervision.
(SAVE) ⊠ 🛢

CLARKSTON

◆◆◆ ▼▼▼ **Best Western Rivertree Inn** 🅗 ❖
(509) 758-9551. **$99-$169.** 1257 Bridge St. 0.9 mi w of Snake River Bridge on US 12. Ext corridors. **Pets:** Medium, other species. $20 one-time fee/pet. Designated rooms, service with restrictions, supervision.
(SAVE) ⊠ ♿M 🛢 🔲 🐾 ⊠

▼ **Motel 6** M
(509) 758-1631. **Call for rates.** 222 Bridge St. Just w of Snake River Bridge. Ext corridors. **Pets:** Other species. Service with restrictions, supervision.
⊠ ♿M 🛢 🐾

CLE ELUM

◆◆◆ ▼▼ **Cascade Mountain Inn** M ❖
(509) 674-2380. **$49-$99.** 906 E 1st St. I-90, exit 85, 1 mi nw. Int corridors. **Pets:** Small, dogs only. $20 daily fee/pet. Designated rooms, supervision.
(SAVE) ⊠ ♿M 🛢 🔲

◆◆◆ ▼▼ **Cle Elum Travelers Inn** M
(509) 674-5535. **$60-$85.** 1001 E 1st St. I-90, exit 85, 1 mi w on SR 903. Ext/int corridors. **Pets:** Medium, dogs only. $5 daily fee/pet. Service with restrictions, supervision.
(SAVE) ⊠ 🛢

◆◆◆ ▼▼▼ **Stewart Lodge** M
(509) 674-4548. **$86-$99.** 805 W 1st St. I-90, exit 84 eastbound, just n; exit westbound, 0.6 mi w. Ext corridors. **Pets:** Medium. $10 daily fee/pet. Designated rooms, service with restrictions, crate.
(SAVE) ⊠ 🛢 🐾

▼▼ **Timber Lodge Inn** M
(509) 674-5966. **$70-$90.** 301 W 1st St. I-90, exit 84 eastbound, 1 mi ne; exit westbound, just w; downtown. Ext/int corridors. **Pets:** Medium, other species. $15 daily fee/pet. Designated rooms, service with restrictions, supervision.
(ASK) ⊠ ♿M 🛢

COLFAX

▼▼▼▼ **Wheatland Inn** 🅗
(509) 397-0397. **$99-$139.** 701 N Main. Downtown. Int corridors. **Pets:** Medium, dogs only. $10 daily fee/pet. Designated rooms, service with restrictions, supervision.
(ASK) ⊠ ♿M 🛢 🔲 🐾

CONCRETE

◆◆◆ ▼▼▼▼ **Ovenell's Heritage Inn B&B and Log Cabins** 🄲🄰
(360) 853-8494. **$105-$160, 3 day notice.** 46276 Concrete Sauk Valley Rd. 0.5 mi w of downtown on SR 20, 3 mi se. Ext/int corridors. **Pets:** Dogs only. $20 daily fee/pet. Designated rooms, service with restrictions, supervision.
(SAVE) ⊠ 🛢 🔲 ⊠

COULEE DAM

▼▼ ▼▼ **Coulee House Inn & Suites** M
(509) 633-1101. **$99-$199, 7 day notice.** 110 Roosevelt Way. Just e of river bridge. Ext corridors. **Pets:** Other species. $20 daily fee/room. Designated rooms, service with restrictions, supervision.
(ASK) ⊠ 🛢 🔲 🐾 ⊠

DAYTON

▼▼▼▼ The Weinhard Hotel **H**
(509) 382-4032. **$125-$180, 7 day notice.** 235 E Main St. Downtown. Int corridors. **Pets:** Dogs only. $20 one-time fee/pet. Supervision.
ASK ✕ &M

EAST WENATCHEE

▼▼▼▼ Cedars Inn, East Wenatchee **H**
(509) 886-8000. **$61-$190.** 80 Ninth St NE. Just e of SR 28. Int corridors. **Pets:** Accepted.
ASK ✕ &M 🛏 📺 🏊

EATONVILLE

◈◈◈ ▼▼▼ Mill Village Motel **M**
(360) 832-3200. **$80-$100.** 210 Center St E. Just e of jct SR 161; center. Ext corridors. **Pets:** Small, dogs only. $10 one-time fee/room. Service with restrictions, supervision.
SAVE ✕ 🛏 📺

ELLENSBURG

◈◈◈ ▼▼▼▼ Best Western Lincoln Inn & Suites **H** ❖
(509) 925-4244. **$99-$299.** 211 W Umptanum Rd. I-90, exit 109, just n, then just w. Int corridors. **Pets:** Medium, dogs only. $25 daily fee/pet. Designated rooms, service with restrictions, supervision.
SAVE ✕ &M 🛏 📺 🏊 ⊠

▼▼▼▼ Ellensburg Comfort Inn **H** ❖
(509) 925-7037. **$89-$139.** 1722 Canyon Rd. I-90, exit 109. Int corridors. **Pets:** Small. $10 daily fee/pet. Service with restrictions, supervision.
ASK ✕ 🛏 📺 🏊

▼▼▼▼ Holiday Inn Express **H**
(509) 962-9400. **$145-$175.** 1620 Canyon Rd. I-90, exit 109, just n. Int corridors. **Pets:** Small. $10 daily fee/room. Designated rooms, service with restrictions, supervision.
ASK ✕ 🛏 📺 🏊

◈◈◈ ▼▼▼ I-90 Inn Motel **M**
(509) 925-9844. **$64-$84.** 1390 Dollar Way N. I-90, exit 106, just n. Ext corridors. **Pets:** Accepted.
SAVE ✕ 🛏

▼▼▼ Nites Inn **M**
(509) 962-9600. **$58-$69.** 1200 S Ruby. I-90, exit 109, 0.5 mi n. Ext corridors. **Pets:** Other species. $9 one-time fee/pet. Service with restrictions, supervision.
ASK ✕ 🛏 📺

▼▼▼ Quality Inn & Conference Center **H**
(509) 925-9800. **Call for rates.** 1700 Canyon Rd. I-90, exit 109, just n. Int corridors. **Pets:** Accepted.
✕ 🛏 📺 🍴 🏊

ELMA

▼▼▼ Microtel Inn & Suites-Elma **H** ❖
(360) 482-6868. **Call for rates.** 800 E Main St. Just ne of jct US 12 and SR 8. Int corridors. **Pets:** Service with restrictions, supervision.
✕ 🛏 📺

EPHRATA

◈◈◈ ▼▼▼▼ Best Western Rama Inn **H**
(509) 754-7111. **$80-$150, 3 day notice.** 1818 Basin St SW. West end of town on SR 28. Int corridors. **Pets:** Other species. $25 one-time fee/room. Service with restrictions, supervision.
SAVE ✕ &M 🛏 📺 🏊

FERNDALE

▼▼▼ Ferndale Super 8 **H**
(360) 384-8881. **$70-$185.** 5788 Barrett Ave. I-5, exit 262, just ne. Int corridors. **Pets:** Other species. $15 one-time fee/room. Designated rooms, service with restrictions, supervision.
ASK ✕ &M 🛏 📺 🏊

◈◈◈◈ ▼▼▼▼ Silver Reef Hotel Casino & Spa **H** ❖
(360) 383-0777. **$116-$269.** 4876 Haxton Way. I-5, exit 260, 3.6 mi w. Int corridors. **Pets:** Small, other species. $15 one-time fee/pet. Designated rooms, service with restrictions.
SAVE ✕ 🛏 📺 🍴 🏊 ⊠

FORKS

◈◈◈ ▼▼▼ Forks Motel **M**
(360) 374-6243. **$57-$150.** 351 US 101 (S Forks Ave). Just s. Ext corridors. **Pets:** Medium. $15 deposit/pet. Service with restrictions, supervision.
SAVE ✕ 🛏 📺 🏊

▼▼▼ Manitou Lodge **BB** ❖
(360) 374-6295. **$99-$179, 14 day notice.** 813 Kilmer Rd. 7.7 mi sw on SR 110 (LaPush Rd), 0.7 mi w on Mora Rd, then 0.8 mi n. Ext/int corridors. **Pets:** Other species. $10 daily fee/room. Service with restrictions, supervision.
✕ 🛏 📺 🎿 📺 🐾

▼▼▼ Miller Tree Inn Bed & Breakfast **BB**
(360) 374-6806. **$95-$205, 7 day notice.** 654 E Division St. 0.3 mi e of US 101 (S Forks Ave). Ext/int corridors. **Pets:** Other species. $10 daily fee/pet. Designated rooms, service with restrictions.
✕ 🛏 📺 🎿 🐾

◈◈◈ ▼▼▼ Olympic Suites Inn **M** ❖
(360) 374-5400. **$49-$129.** 800 Olympic Dr. North end of town; just ne off US 101 (S Forks Ave). Ext corridors. **Pets:** Dogs only. $10 daily fee/pet. Designated rooms, service with restrictions, supervision.
SAVE ✕ 🛏 📺 🎿

GOLDENDALE

◈◈◈ ▼▼▼ Quality Inn & Suites **H**
(509) 773-5881. **$89-$149.** 808 E Simcoe Dr. US 97, exit Simcoe Dr, just sw. Ext corridors. **Pets:** Accepted.
SAVE ✕ 🛏 📺 🍴 🏊

ILWACO

◈◈◈ ▼▼ Heidi's Inn **M**
(360) 642-2387. **Call for rates.** 126 Spruce St. Downtown. Ext corridors. **Pets:** Small, dogs only. $6 one-time fee/pet. Designated rooms, service with restrictions, supervision.
SAVE ✕ 🛏 📺 🎿

KALALOCH

◈◈◈ ▼▼▼ Kalaloch Lodge **CA**
(360) 962-2271. **$99-$300, 3 day notice.** 157151 Hwy 101. In Kalaloch; at MM 157. Ext/int corridors. **Pets:** Other species. $15 daily fee/pet. Designated rooms.
SAVE ✕ 🛏 📺 🍴 🎿 🐾

KALAMA

◈◈◈ ▼▼ Kalama River Inn **M**
(360) 673-2855. **$53-$70.** 602 NE Frontage Rd. I-5, exit 30 northbound, 0.4 mi n; exit southbound, 0.4 mi s. Ext corridors. **Pets:** Small, dogs only. $5 daily fee/pet. No service, supervision.
SAVE ✕ 🛏

KELSO

◈◈◈ ▼▼▼ Best Western Aladdin **H**
(360) 425-9660. **$90-$120.** 310 Long Ave. I-5, exit 39, 1.1 mi w via Allen and W Main sts, then just n on 5th Ave NW. Int corridors. **Pets:** Accepted.
SAVE ✕ 🛏 📺 🏊

▼▼▼ **GuestHouse Inn & Suites** 🚹
(360) 414-5953. **Call for rates.** 501 Three Rivers Dr. I-5, exit 39, 0.3 mi w on Allen St, then 0.3 mi s. Int corridors. **Pets:** Accepted.
✕ 🏢 💻 🏊

▼ **Motel 6–43** 🅼
(360) 425-3229. **$55-$65.** 106 Minor Rd. I-5, exit 39, 0.3 mi ne. Ext corridors. **Pets:** Other species. Service with restrictions, supervision.
✕ 🏢 🏊

🐾 ▼▼▼ **Red Lion Hotel & Conference Center Kelso/Longview** 🚹
(360) 636-4400. **Call for rates.** 510 Kelso Dr. I-5, exit 39, 0.3 mi se. Int corridors. **Pets:** Other species. $20 one-time fee/room. Service with restrictions, supervision.
SAVE ✕ 🏢 💻 🍴 🏊

▼ ▼ **Super 8** 🚹
(360) 423-8880. **Call for rates.** 250 Kelso Dr. I-5, exit 39, just se. Int corridors. **Pets:** Other species. $10 daily fee/room. Service with restrictions, supervision.
✕ 🔧🅼 🏢 💻 🏊

KENNEWICK

🐾 ▼▼▼ **Best Western Kennewick Inn** 🚹
(509) 586-1332. **$100-$140.** 4001 W 27th Ave. I-82, exit 113 (US 395), 0.8 mi n. Int corridors. **Pets:** Small. $10 one-time fee/room. Service with restrictions, crate.
SAVE ✕ 🔧🅼 🏢 💻 🏊 ✕

▼ ▼ **Clover Island Inn** 🚹 🐾
(509) 586-0541. **$89-$349.** 435 Clover Island Dr. US 395, exit Port of Kennewick, 1 mi e on Columbia Dr, then just n. Int corridors. **Pets:** $10 one-time fee/room. Service with restrictions, supervision.
ASK ✕ 🏢 💻 🏊 ✕

▼▼▼ **Comfort Inn** 🅼
(509) 783-8396. **$85-$130.** 7801 W Quinault Ave. 0.5 mi s on Columbia Center Blvd from SR 240. Int corridors. **Pets:** Large. $10 daily fee/pet. Service with restrictions, supervision.
ASK ✕ 🔧🅼 🏢 💻 🏊

🐾 ▼ ▼ **Days Inn Kennewick** 🚹
(509) 735-9511. **$63-$130.** 2811 W 2nd Ave. Jct US 395 and Clearwater Ave, just s, just w. Ext/int corridors. **Pets:** Accepted.
SAVE ✕ 🏢 💻 🏊

▼▼▼ **Fairfield Inn by Marriott** 🚹
(509) 783-2164. **$134-$164.** 7809 W Quinault Ave. 0.5 mi s on Columbia Center Blvd from SR 240. Int corridors. **Pets:** Accepted.
✕ 🔧🅼 🏢 💻 🏊

🐾 ▼▼▼ **Guesthouse International Suites** 🚹
(509) 735-2242. **$72-$82.** 5616 W Clearwater Ave. US 395, 1.9 mi w. Int corridors. **Pets:** $10 one-time fee/pet. Designated rooms, service with restrictions, supervision.
SAVE ✕ 🔧🅼 🏢 💻

🐾 ▼ ▼ **Kennewick Super 8** 🚹
(509) 736-6888. **$71-$91, 10 day notice.** 626 N Columbia Center Blvd. 1.1 mi s of SR 240. Int corridors. **Pets:** Other species. $10 daily fee/room. Service with restrictions, supervision.
SAVE ✕ 🔧🅼 🏢 💻 🏊

▼▼▼ **La Quinta Inn & Suites Kennewick** 🚹 🐾
(509) 736-3326. **$69-$119.** 4220 W 27th Pl. I-82, exit 113 (US 395), 0.8 mi n. Int corridors. **Pets:** Medium, other species. Service with restrictions, supervision.
ASK ✕ 🔧🅼 🏢 💻 🏊 ✕

▼▼▼ **Quality Inn Kennewick** 🚹
(509) 735-6100. **$70-$90.** 7901 W Quinault Ave. 0.5 mi s on Columbia Center Blvd from SR 240. Int corridors. **Pets:** Accepted.
ASK ✕ 🔧🅼 🏢 💻 🏊

🐾 ▼▼▼ **Red Lion Hotel Columbia Center-Kennewick** 🚹
(509) 783-0611. **$130.** 1101 N Columbia Center Blvd. SR 240, 0.5 mi s. Int corridors. **Pets:** Other species. $20 one-time fee/room. Service with restrictions, supervision.
SAVE ✕ 🔧🅼 🏢 💻 🍴 🏊

LACEY

▼▼▼ **Candlewood Suites Olympia/Lacey** 🚹
(360) 491-1698. **$140-$186.** 4440 3rd Ave SE. I-5, exit 108 northbound, just n; exit 109 southbound, just s on Martin Ave E, just e on College Way, then just s. Int corridors. **Pets:** Medium. $75 one-time fee/room. Service with restrictions, supervision.
ASK ✕ 🏢 💻

🐾 ▼ ▼ **La Quinta Inn** 🚹 🐾
(360) 412-1200. **$80-$119.** 4704 Park Center Ave NE. I-5, exit 109, just sw. Int corridors. **Pets:** Medium, other species. Service with restrictions, supervision.
SAVE ✕ 🏢 💻 🏊

▼ ▼ **Quality Inn & Suites** 🚹 🐾
(360) 493-1991. **$65-$115, 30 day notice.** 120 College St SE. I-5, exit 109, just sw. Int corridors. **Pets:** Other species. $15 daily fee/pet. Designated rooms, service with restrictions, crate.
ASK ✕ 🏢 💻

LA CONNER

▼▼▼ **The Heron Inn & Watergrass Day Spa** 🅱🅱
(360) 466-4626. **Call for rates.** 117 Maple Ave. At Maple Ave and Morris St; northeast edge of town. Int corridors. **Pets:** Medium, dogs only. $25 one-time fee/pet. Service with restrictions, supervision.
✕ 🎾 🇿

🐾 ▼▼▼ **La Conner Country Inn** 🚹 🐾
(360) 466-3101. **$129-$239.** 107 S 2nd St. 2nd and Morris sts; downtown. Ext/int corridors. **Pets:** Other species. $50 one-time fee/room. Designated rooms, service with restrictions, supervision.
SAVE ✕ 🏢 💻 🍴

LANGLEY

▼▼▼ **The Inn at Langley** 🚹
(360) 221-3033. **Call for rates.** 400 1st St. Center. Ext corridors. **Pets:** Accepted.
✕ 🏢 💻 🎾

LEAVENWORTH

🐾 ▼▼▼ **Bavarian Ritz Hotel** 🚹
(509) 548-5455. **$89-$269, 3 day notice.** 633 Front St. Center. Ext/int corridors. **Pets:** Accepted.
SAVE ✕ 🏢 💻

🐾 ▼▼▼ **Der Ritterhof Motor Inn** 🚹 🐾
(509) 548-5845. **$70-$107, 3 day notice.** 190 US 2. 0.3 mi w. Ext corridors. **Pets:** Dogs only. $10 daily fee/pet. Service with restrictions, supervision.
SAVE ✕ 🔧🅼 🏢 💻 🏊

▼ **The Evergreen Inn** 🅼
(509) 548-5515. **Call for rates.** 1117 Front St. US 2, just s. Ext corridors. **Pets:** Accepted.
✕ 🏢 💻

▼ ▼ **Howard Johnson** 🅼
(509) 548-4326. **Call for rates.** 405 US 2. West end of town. Ext corridors. **Pets:** Accepted.
✕ 🔧🅼 🏢 💻 🏊

◆◆◆ ▽▽◆ Obertal Inn M
(509) 548-5204. **$79-$179.** 922 Commercial St. Off US 2; center. Ext corridors. **Pets:** Other species. $15 daily fee/pet. Service with restrictions.
[SAVE] [X] [🛏] [💻]

▽▽▽▽ Quality Inn & Suites H
(509) 548-7992. **Call for rates.** 185 US 2. 0.3 mi w. Ext corridors. **Pets:** Accepted.
[X] [&M] [🛏] [💻] [≈]

▽▽ River's Edge Lodge M
(509) 548-7612. **Call for rates.** 8401 US 2. 3.5 mi e. Ext corridors. **Pets:** Other species. $20 daily fee/pet. Designated rooms, service with restrictions, supervision.
[X] [🛏] [💻] [≈]

LIBERTY LAKE

◆◆◆ ▽▽▽▽ Best Western Peppertree Liberty Lake Inn H
(509) 755-1111. **$64-$219.** 1816 N Pepper Ln. I-90, exit 296. Int corridors. **Pets:** Accepted.
[SAVE] [X] [&M] [🛏] [💻] [≈]

◆◆◆ ▽▽▽ Cedars Inn Spokane at Liberty Lake H
(509) 340-3333. **$69-$110.** 2327 N Madson Rd. I-90, exit 296, 1 mi e on Appleway Ave, then just n. Int corridors. **Pets:** $15 daily fee/pet. Designated rooms, service with restrictions.
[SAVE] [X] [&M] [🛏] [💻] [≈]

LONG BEACH

▽▽▽ Anchorage Cottages CA
(360) 642-2351. **$70-$128, 30 day notice.** 2209 Boulevard N. Just w of SR 103. Ext corridors. **Pets:** Accepted.
[X] [🛏] [💻] [X] [Z]

◆◆◆ ▽▽▽ The Breakers CO 🐾
(360) 642-4414. **$68-$298, 20 day notice.** 210 26th St NW. North end of downtown. Ext corridors. **Pets:** Dogs only. $15 daily fee/room. Service with restrictions, supervision.
[SAVE] [X] [🛏] [💻] [≈] [X] [K]

▽▽ Our Place at the Beach H 🐾
(360) 642-3793. **Call for rates.** 1309 South Blvd. Just w of SR 103; south end of town. Ext corridors. **Pets:** Other species. Service with restrictions, supervision.
[X] [🛏] [💻] [X] [K]

◆◆◆ ▽▽◆ Rodeway Inn & Suites H
(360) 642-3714. **$63-$140.** 115 3rd St SW. Downtown. Ext corridors. **Pets:** Accepted.
[SAVE] [X] [🛏] [💻] [≈] [K]

◆◆◆ ▽▽▽ Super 8 H 🐾
(360) 642-8988. **$79-$199.** 500 Ocean Beach Blvd. On SR 103; downtown. Int corridors. **Pets:** Other species. $10 daily fee/pet. Supervision.
[SAVE] [X] [&M] [🛏] [💻] [K]

LONGVIEW

◆◆◆ ▽▽▽ Hudson Manor Inn & Suites M
(360) 425-1100. **$65-$90.** 1616 Hudson St. Downtown. Ext corridors. **Pets:** Medium, other species. $15 one-time fee/room. Service with restrictions, supervision.
[SAVE] [X] [🛏] [💻]

◆◆◆ ▽▽ Longview Travelodge M
(360) 423-6460. **$55-$75.** 838 15th Ave. Downtown; opposite Medical Center. Ext corridors. **Pets:** Dogs only. $15 daily fee/pet. Designated rooms, service with restrictions.
[SAVE] [X] [🛏] [💻]

▽▽▽ Quality Inn & Suites H
(360) 414-1000. **$80-$190.** 723 7th Ave. I-5, exit 36, 3 mi w on SR 432. Int corridors. **Pets:** Other species. $15 daily fee/room. Service with restrictions, crate.
[ASK] [X] [&M] [🛏] [💻] [≈]

◆◆◆ ▽▽ The Townhouse Motel M
(360) 423-7200. **$55-$95, 3 day notice.** 744 Washington Way. Downtown. Ext corridors. **Pets:** Large. $5 daily fee/pet. Supervision.
[SAVE] [X] [🛏] [💻] [≈]

MOCLIPS

◆◆◆ ▽▽▽ Ocean Crest Resort H
(360) 276-4465. **$79-$209, 7 day notice.** 4651 SR 109 N. South edge of town. Ext corridors. **Pets:** Other species. $18 daily fee/pet. Designated rooms, service with restrictions, supervision.
[SAVE] [X] [🛏] [💻] [¶] [≈] [X] [K]

MORTON

◆◆◆ ▽▽▽ The Seasons Motel M
(360) 496-6835. **$70-$100.** 200 Westlake Ave. On US 12; jct SR 7. Ext corridors. **Pets:** Small. $10 one-time fee/pet. Service with restrictions, supervision.
[SAVE] [X] [🛏] [💻]

MOSES LAKE

▽▽▽ AmeriStay Inn & Suites H
(509) 764-7500. **$89-$259.** 1157 N Stratford Rd. I-90, exit 179, 1 mi n to SR 17, 2.8 mi nw, exit Stratford Rd, just n, then just e. Int corridors. **Pets:** Accepted.
[ASK] [X] [&M] [🛏] [💻] [≈]

◆◆◆ ▽▽▽▽ Best Western Lake Front Hotel H 🐾
(509) 765-9211. **$80-$225.** 3000 Marina Dr. I-90, exit 176, just nw. Int corridors. **Pets:** Large. $20 daily fee/pet. Designated rooms, service with restrictions, supervision.
[SAVE] [X] [&M] [🛏] [💻] [¶] [≈] [X]

◆◆◆ ▽▽◆▽ Comfort Suites Moses Lake H
(509) 765-3731. **$99-$299.** 1700 E Kittleson Rd. I-90, exit 179, just nw. Int corridors. **Pets:** Accepted.
[SAVE] [X] [&M] [🛏] [💻] [≈]

▽▽▽ Inn at Moses Lake H
(509) 766-7000. **$69-$119.** 1745 E Kittleson Rd. I-90, exit 179, just n. Int corridors. **Pets:** Medium. $10 one-time fee/room. Designated rooms, service with restrictions, supervision.
[ASK] [X] [🛏] [💻] [≈]

◆◆◆ ▽▽▽ Moses Lake Super 8 H
(509) 765-8886. **Call for rates.** 449 Melva Ln. I-90, exit 176, just n. Int corridors. **Pets:** $10 daily fee/pet. Service with restrictions, supervision.
[SAVE] [X] [🛏] [≈]

◆◆◆ ▽▽▽ Shilo Inn Suites-Moses Lake H 🐾
(509) 765-9317. **$75-$170.** 1819 E Kittleson Rd. I-90, exit 179, just n. Int corridors. **Pets:** Dogs only. $25 one-time fee/room. Service with restrictions, supervision.
[SAVE] [X] [&M] [🛏] [💻] [≈] [X]

MOUNT VERNON

◆◆◆ ▽▽▽ Best Western College Way Inn H
(360) 424-4287. **$90-$120, 7 day notice.** 300 W College Way. I-5, exit 227, just w. Ext corridors. **Pets:** $20 daily fee/pet. Designated rooms, service with restrictions, supervision.
[SAVE] [X] [🛏] [💻]

Best Western CottonTree Inn & Convention Center H ✿
(360) 428-5678. **$99-$180.** 2300 Market St. I-5, exit 227, 0.3 mi e on College Way, then 0.5 mi n on Riverside Dr. Int corridors. **Pets:** Dogs only. $25 one-time fee/room. Designated rooms, service with restrictions, supervision.
SAVE ✕ &M ⟡ 💻 ⟿

Quality Inn-Mount Vernon H
(360) 428-7020. **$90-$179.** 1910 Freeway Dr. I-5, exit 227, just w on College Way, then just n. Ext corridors. **Pets:** Accepted.
SAVE ✕ ⟡ 💻 ⟿

Tulip Inn M
(360) 428-5969. **$65-$99.** 2200 Freeway Dr. I-5, exit 227, just w on College Way, then just n. Ext corridors. **Pets:** $10 one-time fee/pet. Designated rooms, service with restrictions, supervision.
SAVE ✕ ⟡ 💻

OAK HARBOR

Acorn Motor Inn H
(360) 675-6646. **$46-$109.** 31530 SR 20. On SR 20 at 300th Ave W (SE Barrington Dr). Int corridors. **Pets:** Other species. $10 daily fee/room. Designated rooms, service with restrictions, supervision.
SAVE ✕ ⟡

Candlewood Suites H
(360) 279-2222. **$99-$189.** 33221 SR 20. Just n of town. Int corridors. **Pets:** Medium, other species. $75 one-time fee/pet. Service with restrictions, supervision.
SAVE ✕ &M ⟡ 💻

Coachman Inn H
(360) 675-0727. **$84-$209.** 32959 SR 20. Jct Goldie Rd and Midway Blvd. Ext corridors. **Pets:** $8 daily fee/pet. Designated rooms, service with restrictions, supervision.
SAVE ✕ ⟡ 💻 ⟿ ✕

OCEAN PARK

Ocean Park Resort M
(360) 665-4585. **$65-$168, 10 day notice.** 25904 R St. Just e of SR 103; downtown. Ext corridors. **Pets:** Small. $7 daily fee/pet. Designated rooms, service with restrictions, supervision.
SAVE ✕ ⟡ 💻 ⟿ ✕ 🐾 ✉

OCEAN SHORES

Canterbury Inn CO
(360) 289-3317. **$82-$198.** 643 Ocean Shores Blvd NW. 0.3 mi s of Chance a La Mer Blvd. Int corridors. **Pets:** Large, dogs only. $150 deposit/room, $15 daily fee/pet. Designated rooms, service with restrictions, supervision.
SAVE ✕ ⟡ 💻 ⟿ 🐾

The Grey Gull Resort CO
(360) 289-3381. **Call for rates.** 651 Ocean Shores Blvd NW. Just s of Chance a La Mer Blvd. Ext corridors. **Pets:** Accepted.
✕ ⟡ 💻 ⟿ 🐾

The Polynesian Condominium Resort CO
(360) 289-3361. **$99-$239, 3 day notice.** 615 Ocean Shores Blvd NW. 0.3 mi s of Chance a La Mer Blvd. Ext/int corridors. **Pets:** Accepted.
SAVE ✕ ⟡ 💻 ⟦⟧ ⟿ ✕ 🐾

Shilo Inn Suites Oceanfront Hotel–Ocean Shores H ✿
(360) 289-4600. **$140-$330.** 707 Ocean Shores Blvd NW. Northwest corner of Chance a La Mer and Ocean Shores blvds NW. Int corridors. **Pets:** Dogs only. $25 one-time fee/room. Designated rooms, service with restrictions, supervision.
SAVE ✕ &M ⟡ 💻 ⟦⟧ ⟿ ✕

OKANOGAN

Okanogan Inn & Suites H ✿
(509) 422-6431. **$60-$65.** 1 Apple Way. SR 97, exit SR 20, just w. Int corridors. **Pets:** Other species. Designated rooms, supervision.
SAVE ✕ ⟡ ⟦⟧ ⟿

Ponderosa Motor Lodge M
(509) 422-0400. **Call for rates.** 1034 S 2nd Ave. 0.3 mi n on SR 215 from jct SR 20. Ext corridors. **Pets:** No service, supervision.
SAVE ✕ ⟡ 💻 ⟿

OLYMPIA

Clarion Hotel H
(360) 352-7200. **$84-$139.** 900 Capitol Way S. I-5, exit 105 (City Center) northbound; exit 105A southbound, 0.4 mi w on 14th Ave, then 0.5 mi n; downtown. Int corridors. **Pets:** Accepted.
SAVE ✕ &M ⟡ 💻 ⟦⟧ ⟿

Red Lion Hotel Olympia H
(360) 943-4000. **$179.** 2300 Evergreen Park Dr SW. I-5, exit 104, 0.7 mi n on US 101, just n on Cooper Point Rd N, 0.7 mi e on S Evergreen Park Dr SW, then just n on Lakeridge Way SW. Int corridors. **Pets:** Other species. $20 one-time fee/room. Service with restrictions, supervision.
ASK ✕ &M ⟡ 💻 ⟦⟧ ⟿

OLYMPIC NATIONAL PARK

Lake Crescent Lodge H
(360) 928-3211. **$75-$243, 7 day notice.** 416 Lake Crescent Rd. 22 mi w of Port Angeles on US 101. Ext/int corridors. **Pets:** Other species. $15 daily fee/pet. Designated rooms, no service, crate.
SAVE ✕ ⟡ 💻 ⟦⟧ ✕ 🐾 🐾 ✉

Log Cabin Resort CA
(360) 928-3325. **Call for rates.** 3183 E Beach Rd. 3.3 mi nw of US 101 (MM 232). Ext corridors. **Pets:** Accepted.
✕ ⟡ 💻 ⟦⟧ ✕ 🐾 🐾 ✉

OMAK

Best Western Peppertree Inn at Omak H
(509) 422-2088. **$89-$250.** 820 Koala Dr. US 97, just n of Riverside Dr. Int corridors. **Pets:** Very small, dogs only. $10 daily fee/pet. Supervision.
SAVE ✕ &M ⟡ 💻 ⟿

Omak Inn H
(509) 826-3822. **$75-$90.** 912 Koala Dr. On US 97, just n of Riverside Dr. Int corridors. **Pets:** $25 one-time fee/room. Designated rooms, service with restrictions, supervision.
SAVE ✕ ⟡ 💻 ⟿

OTHELLO

Best Western Othello Inn H ✿
(509) 488-5671. **$69-$129.** 1020 E Cedar St. Just off Main St at 10th and Cedar sts. Int corridors. **Pets:** Dogs only. $15 one-time fee/room. No service, supervision.
SAVE ✕ ⟡ 💻 ⟿

PACIFIC BEACH

Sandpiper Beach Resort CO
(360) 276-4580. **Call for rates.** 4159 SR 109. 1.8 mi s. Ext corridors. **Pets:** Accepted.
✕ ⟡ 💻 🐾 🐾 ✉

PACKWOOD

Cowlitz River Lodge M
(360) 494-4444. **Call for rates.** 13069 US 12. East end of town. Ext corridors. **Pets:** Small, dogs only. $10 daily fee/pet. Designated rooms, service with restrictions, crate.
✕ ⟡

AAA ▼▼ Crest Trail Lodge H
(360) 494-4944. **$70-$100.** 12729 US 12. Just w of town. Int corridors. **Pets:** Small. $10 one-time fee/room. Service with restrictions, supervision.
SAVE ⊠ ❚ 🖷 ➤

▼ Inn of Packwood M ☙
(360) 494-5500. **$79-$119.** 13032 US 12. Center. Ext corridors. **Pets:** Dogs only. $15 daily fee/pet. Designated rooms, no service, crate.
ASK ⊠ ❚ 🖷 ➤

PASCO

AAA ▼▼▼ Best Western Pasco Inn & Suites H
(509) 543-7722. **$120-$160.** 2811 N 20th Ave. I-182, exit 12B, just n. Int corridors. **Pets:** Small. $10 one-time fee/room. Service with restrictions, crate.
SAVE ⊠ &M ❚ 🖷 ➤

▼▼▼ Holiday Inn Express Pasco at TRAC H
(509) 543-7000. **Call for rates.** 4525 Convention Pl. I-182, exit 9 (Rd 68), just n, then just e. Int corridors. **Pets:** Medium, dogs only. $20 daily fee/room. Designated rooms, service with restrictions, supervision.
⊠ &M ❚ 🖷 ➤

▼ Motel 6-Pasco M
(509) 546-2010. **Call for rates.** 1520 N Oregon St. I-182, exit 14A (SR 395 S). Ext corridors. **Pets:** Accepted.
⊠ ❚ ➤

AAA ▼▼▼ Red Lion Hotel Pasco H
(509) 547-0701. **Call for rates.** 2525 N 20th Ave. I-182, exit 12B, just n. Int corridors. **Pets:** Other species. $20 one-time fee/room. Service with restrictions, supervision.
SAVE ⊠ &M ❚ 🖷 ⑪ ➤

AAA ▼▼ Sleep Inn H ☙
(509) 545-9554. **$80-$164.** 9930 Bedford St. I-182, exit 7, just ne. Int corridors. **Pets:** Medium. $10 daily fee/room. Designated rooms, service with restrictions, supervision.
SAVE ⊠ &M ❚ 🖷 ➤

PORT ANGELES

AAA ▼▼▼ Portside Inn H
(360) 452-4015. **$59-$119, 3 day notice.** 1510 E Front St. Front St at Alder St; on east side. Ext corridors. **Pets:** Medium, other species. $25 one-time fee/room. Designated rooms, service with restrictions, supervision.
SAVE ⊠ ❚ 🖷 ➤

AAA ▼▼▼ Quality Inn-Uptown M ☙
(360) 457-9434. **Call for rates.** 101 E 2nd St. At Laurel St, just w of US 101; on bluff. Ext corridors. **Pets:** Small, dogs only. $10 daily fee/pet. Designated rooms, service with restrictions, supervision.
SAVE ⊠ ❚ 🖷 🗚

AAA ▼▼▼ Red Lion Hotel Port Angeles H
(360) 452-9215. **$249.** 221 N Lincoln St. On US 101 westbound; at ferry landing. Ext/int corridors. **Pets:** Other species. $20 one-time fee/room. Service with restrictions, supervision.
SAVE ⊠ ❚ 🖷 ⑪ ➤

AAA ▼ Riviera Inn M
(360) 417-3955. **$59-$149.** 535 E Front St. On US 101 W; downtown. Ext corridors. **Pets:** Small, dogs only. $15 daily fee/pet. Designated rooms, service with restrictions, supervision.
SAVE ⊠ ❚ 🗚

▼ Super 8 M
(360) 452-8401. **Call for rates.** 2104 E 1st St. 1.8 mi e of downtown, just s of US 101. Int corridors. **Pets:** $15 daily fee/pet. Designated rooms, service with restrictions, supervision.
⊠ &M ❚ 🖷

PORTLAND METROPOLITAN AREA (NEARBY OREGON)

VANCOUVER

▼▼ Comfort Inn H
(360) 574-6000. **Call for rates.** 13207 NE 20th Ave. I-5, exit 7, just e; I-205, exit 36, just w. Int corridors. **Pets:** Other species. $15 daily fee/pet. Service with restrictions, supervision.
⊠ ❚ 🖷 ➤

▼▼ Extended StayAmerica-Portland-Vancouver H
(360) 604-8530. **$85-$100.** 300 NE 115th Ave. I-205, exit 28 (Mill Plain Blvd E), just ne. Int corridors. **Pets:** Other species. $25 daily fee/pet. Service with restrictions, crate.
ASK ⊠ ❚ 🖷

AAA ▼▼▼ Hilton Vancouver Washington and Vancouver Convention Center H ☙
(360) 993-4500. **$99-$219.** 301 W 6th St. I-5, exit 1C (Mill Plain Blvd) southbound, 0.3 mi w, then 0.3 mi s on W Columbia St; exit 1B northbound, 0.5 mi, follow signs to City Center/6th St. Int corridors. **Pets:** Medium. $35 one-time fee/room. Service with restrictions, crate.
SAVE ⊠ ❚ 🖷 ⑪ ➤ ⊠

▼▼▼ Homewood Suites by Hilton H ☙
(360) 750-1100. **$109-$179.** 701 SE Columbia Shores Blvd. SR 14, exit 1, just s. Ext/int corridors. **Pets:** Medium, other species. $10 daily fee/pet. Service with restrictions.
⊠ ❚ 🖷 ➤ ⊠

▼▼▼ La Quinta Inn & Suites H ☙
(360) 566-1100. **$89-$169.** 1500 NE 134th St. I-5, exit 7, just w; I-205, exit 36, 0.5 mi w. Int corridors. **Pets:** Medium, other species. Service with restrictions, supervision.
ASK ⊠ &M ❚ 🖷 ➤

AAA ▼▼▼ Phoenix Inn Suites-Vancouver H
(360) 891-9777. **$79-$149.** 12712 SE 2nd Cir. I-205, exit 28 (Mill Plain Blvd E), 0.8 mi e, then just n on SE 126th Ave. Int corridors. **Pets:** Medium. $15 daily fee/pet. Designated rooms, service with restrictions, supervision.
SAVE ⊠ ❚ 🖷 ➤ ⊠

AAA ▼▼▼ Quality Inn & Suites H
(360) 696-0516. **$69-$109.** 7001 NE Hwy 99. I-5, exit 4, 0.5 mi se. Int corridors. **Pets:** Other species. $10 daily fee/room. Service with restrictions, supervision.
SAVE ⊠ ❚ 🖷 ➤

▼▼▼ Red Lion Hotel Vancouver @ the Quay H
(360) 694-8341. **$129-$179.** 100 Columbia St. 0.5 mi s on dock at foot of Columbia St. Int corridors. **Pets:** Other species. $20 one-time fee/room. Service with restrictions, supervision.
ASK ⊠ &M ❚ 🖷 ⑪ ➤ ⊠

▼▼▼ Residence Inn Vancouver H ☙
(360) 253-4800. **$169-$189.** 8005 NE Parkway Dr. I-205, exit 30 (SR 500 W), 0.5 mi w to Thurston Way, just n to NE Parkway Dr, then just w. Ext corridors. **Pets:** Other species. $75 one-time fee/room. Service with restrictions.
⊠ &M ❚ 🖷 ➤ ⊠

△△△◇ ▽▽ Rodeway Inn & Suites H ☆
(360) 254-0900. **$79-$96.** 9201 NE Vancouver Mall Dr. I-205, exit 30 (SR 500 W), 0.6 mi w to Thurston Way, just n to Vancouver Mall Dr, then 0.5 mi e; southeast edge of Westfield Shopping Center. Int corridors. **Pets:** Large, other species. $25 one-time fee/pet. Designated rooms, service with restrictions, supervision.
SAVE ✕ ♿M ☎ 💻 ≈

△△△◇ ▽▽ Shilo Inn & Suites-Salmon Creek H ☆
(360) 573-0511. **$82-$190.** 13206 Hwy 99. I-5, exit 7, just e; I-205, exit 36, just w. Int corridors. **Pets:** Dogs only. $25 one-time fee/room. Service with restrictions, supervision.
SAVE ✕ ☎ 💻 ≈ 🐾

▽▽ Staybridge Suites Vancouver-Portland H ☆
(360) 891-8282. **$99-$186.** 7301 NE 41st St. I-205, exit 30 (SR 500 W), 1.5 mi w to NE Andresen Rd, just n to NE 40th St, just e to NE 72nd St, just n to NE 41st St, then just e. Int corridors. **Pets:** Medium. $75 one-time fee/room. Designated rooms, service with restrictions.
✕ ♿M ☎ 💻 ≈ 🐾

END METROPOLITAN AREA

PORT TOWNSEND

△△△◇ ▽▽▽▽ Bishop Victorian Hotel H
(360) 385-6122. **$110-$225, 3 day notice.** 714 Washington St. Corner of Washington and Quincy sts. Int corridors. **Pets:** Dogs only. $20 daily fee/pet. Supervision.
SAVE ✕ ☎ 💻 🐾

▽▽ Harborside Inn H
(360) 385-7909. **Call for rates.** 330 Benedict St. Just e of SR 20. Ext corridors. **Pets:** Accepted.
✕ ☎ 💻 ≈ 🐾

△△△◇ ▽▽ Palace Hotel H ☆
(360) 385-0773. **$59-$289.** 1004 Water St. Downtown. Int corridors. **Pets:** $10 one-time fee/pet. Designated rooms, supervision.
SAVE ✕ ☎ 💻 🐾

△△△◇ ▽▽ The Swan Hotel M
(360) 385-1718. **$100-$510, 3 day notice.** 216 Monroe St. Downtown. Ext corridors. **Pets:** Dogs only. $20 daily fee/pet. Supervision.
SAVE ✕ ☎ 💻 🐾

PROSSER

△△△◇ ▽▽▽▽ Best Western The Inn at Horse Heaven H
(509) 786-7977. **$99-$119.** 259 Merlot Dr. I-82, exit 80, just s. Int corridors. **Pets:** Dogs only. $10 one-time fee/pet. Designated rooms, service with restrictions, supervision.
SAVE ✕ ♿M ☎ 💻 ≈

PULLMAN

△△△◇ ▽▽▽▽ Hilltop Inn H ☆
(509) 332-0928. **$70-$199, 3 day notice.** 928 NW Olsen St. 1.6 mi e on SR 270 from US 195. Int corridors. **Pets:** Other species. $15 daily fee/pet. Designated rooms, service with restrictions, supervision.
SAVE ✕ ♿M ☎ 💻 ≈ 🐾

▽▽▽▽ Holiday Inn Express Hotel & Suites H ☆
(509) 334-4437. **$129.** SE 1190 Bishop Blvd. Jct US 195 business route, 0.5 mi s, 1 mi e on SR 270. Int corridors. **Pets:** Large, other species. Designated rooms, service with restrictions.
A$K ✕ ♿M ☎ 💻 ≈

△△△◇ ▽▽ Quality Inn Paradise Creek H
(509) 332-0500. **$85-$160, 3 day notice.** 1400 SE Bishop Blvd. Jct US 195 business route, just s, 1 mi e on SR 270. Int corridors. **Pets:** Designated rooms, service with restrictions, supervision.
SAVE ✕ ☎ 💻 ≈ 🐾

QUINAULT

△△△◇ ▽▽ Lake Quinault Lodge H
(360) 288-2900. **$129-$268, 3 day notice.** 345 S Shore Rd. 2 mi off US 101. Ext/int corridors. **Pets:** $25 daily fee/room. Designated rooms, supervision.
SAVE ✕ ☎ 💻 🍴 ≈ 🐾 🐾 🐾

QUINCY

▽▽ Traditional Inns M
(509) 787-3525. **$85-$149.** 500 F St SW. West end of town on SR 28. Ext corridors. **Pets:** Accepted.
A$K ✕ ☎ 💻

REPUBLIC

△△△◇ ▽▽ Prospector Inn H
(509) 775-3361. **$55-$175.** 979 S Clark Ave. Downtown. Int corridors. **Pets:** Other species. $12 daily fee/pet. Designated rooms, service with restrictions, supervision.
SAVE ✕ ☎ 💻 🐾

RICHLAND

▽▽▽▽ Clarion Hotel & Conference Center H
(509) 946-4121. **Call for rates.** 1515 George Washington Way. I-182, exit 5B, 2.5 mi n. Int corridors. **Pets:** Accepted.
✕ ♿M ☎ 💻 🍴 ≈ 🐾

△△△◇ ▽▽ Days Inn M ☆
(509) 943-4611. **$54-$76.** 615 Jadwin Ave. I-182, exit 5B, 0.9 mi n; just w of SR 240 business route; downtown. Ext corridors. **Pets:** Other species. $10 daily fee/pet. Service with restrictions.
SAVE ✕ ☎ 💻 ≈

▽▽▽▽ Holiday Inn Express Hotel & Suites H
(509) 737-8000. **Call for rates.** 1970 Center Pkwy. Just s on Columbia Center Blvd from SR 240, just w. Int corridors. **Pets:** Accepted.
✕ ♿M ☎ 💻 ≈

△△△◇ ▽▽▽▽ Red Lion Hotel Richland Hanford House H
(509) 946-7611. **$139.** 802 George Washington Way. I-182, exit 5B, 1.3 mi n on SR 240 business route. Ext/int corridors. **Pets:** Other species. $20 one-time fee/room. Service with restrictions, supervision.
SAVE ✕ ♿M ☎ 💻 🍴 ≈ 🐾

△△△◇ ▽▽▽▽ Shilo Inn Suites Hotel–Richland H ☆
(509) 946-4661. **$97-$180.** 50 Comstock St. I-182, exit 5B, 0.5 mi n. Ext corridors. **Pets:** Dogs only. $25 one-time fee/room. Designated rooms, service with restrictions, supervision.
SAVE ✕ ☎ 💻 🍴 ≈ 🐾

RITZVILLE

(AAA) ▽▽▽ Americas Best Value Inn- Colwell M ❀
(509) 659-1620. **$49-$79.** 501 W 1st Ave. I-90, exit 220, 0.9 mi n; downtown. Ext corridors. **Pets:** Medium, other species. $10 daily fee/pet. Service with restrictions, supervision.
[SAVE] [✕] [🔋] [💻] [≈]

(AAA) ▽▽▽ Best Western Bronco Inn H
(509) 659-5000. **$69-$199.** 105 W Galbreath Way. I-90, exit 221, cross overpass, then second left. Int corridors. **Pets:** Other species. $10 one-time fee/pet. Service with restrictions, supervision.
[SAVE] [✕] [🔋] [💻] [≈]

▽▽ La Quinta Inn Ritzville H ❀
(509) 659-1007. **$59-$149.** 1513 Smitty's Blvd. I-90, exit 221, just n. Int corridors. **Pets:** Medium, other species. Service with restrictions, supervision.
[ASK] [✕] [🔋M] [🔋] [💻] [≈] [✕]

▽ Top Hat Motel M ❀
(509) 659-1100. **$38-$64.** 210 E 1st Ave. I-90, exit 221, 1 mi ne via Division St. Ext corridors. **Pets:** Dogs only. Service with restrictions, supervision.
[ASK] [🔋]

SAN JUAN ISLANDS AREA

DEER HARBOR

▽▽ Deer Harbor Inn CI
(360) 376-4110. **Call for rates.** 33 Inn Ln. In Deer Harbor; 7 mi sw of ferry landing; 3.5 mi sw of Westsound. Ext/int corridors. **Pets:** Accepted.
[✕] [🔋] [💻] [🍴] [🎬] [✈]

FRIDAY HARBOR

▽▽ Argyle House Bed & Breakfast BB
(360) 378-4084. **$100-$250, 14 day notice.** 685 Argyle Ave. In Friday Harbor; 0.3 mi e of jct Spring St. Ext/int corridors. **Pets:** Dogs only. Supervision.
[✕] [🔋] [💻] [🎬] [✈]

▽▽ Elements Hotel & Spa H
(360) 378-4000. **$147-$407, 10 day notice.** 410 Spring St. In Friday Harbor; 0.5 mi w of ferry dock. Ext corridors. **Pets:** Accepted.
[ASK] [✕] [🔋] [💻] [≈] [✕]

(AAA) ▽◆◆◆◆ Lakedale Resort H
(360) 378-2350. **$179-$489, 7 day notice.** 4313 Roche Harbor Rd. 4 mi n of Friday Harbor via Tucker Ave. Ext/int corridors. **Pets:** Accepted.
[SAVE] [✕] [🔋] [💻] [✕] [🎬]

END AREA

SEATTLE METROPOLITAN AREA

AUBURN

▽▽ Auburn GuestHouse Inn H
(253) 735-9600. **$89-$99.** 9 14th Ave NW. SR 167, exit 15th St NW, 0.8 mi e, just s on a St NE, then just w. Int corridors. **Pets:** Medium, dogs only. $10 daily fee/room. Service with restrictions, supervision.
[ASK] [✕] [🔋] [💻]

(AAA) ▽▽▽ Best Western Peppertree Auburn Inn H ❀
(253) 887-7600. **$90-$220.** 401 8th St SW. SR 18, exit C St, just s, then just w. Int corridors. **Pets:** Small, dogs only. $10 daily fee/pet. Service with restrictions, supervision.
[SAVE] [✕] [🔋] [💻] [≈]

(AAA) ▽ Cedars Inn Auburn H
(253) 833-8007. **$55-$109.** 102 15th St NE. SR 167, exit 15th St NW, 0.8 mi e. Int corridors. **Pets:** Accepted.
[SAVE] [✕] [🔋]

(AAA) ▽▽▽ Travelodge Suites H ❀
(253) 833-7171. **Call for rates.** 9 16th St NW. SR 167, exit 15th St NW, 0.8 mi e, then just n on a St NE. Int corridors. **Pets:** Other species. $10 daily fee/pet. Service with restrictions, supervision.
[SAVE] [✕] [🔋M] [🔋] [💻]

BAINBRIDGE ISLAND

(AAA) ▽▽▽ Best Western Bainbridge Island Suites H ❀
(206) 855-9666. **$119-$169.** 350 NE High School Rd. 0.8 mi n of ferry dock on SR 305, then just w. Int corridors. **Pets:** Medium. $50 one-time fee/room. Supervision.
[SAVE] [✕] [🔋] [💻]

BELLEVUE

(AAA) ▽▽▽ Bellevue Club Hotel H ❀
(425) 454-4424. **$285-$655.** 11200 SE 6th St. I-405, exit 12, 0.4 mi nw. Int corridors. **Pets:** Small, dogs only. $30 one-time fee/pet. Service with restrictions, supervision.
[SAVE] [✕] [🔋M] [🔋] [🍴] [≈] [✕]

(AAA) ▽▽ Days Inn Bellevue H
(425) 643-6644. **$75-$120.** 3241 156th Ave SE. I-90, exit 11 westbound; exit 11A (156th Ave SE) eastbound, just ne. Ext corridors. **Pets:** Medium. $25 one-time fee/pet. Designated rooms, service with restrictions, supervision.
[SAVE] [✕] [🔋] [💻]

▽▽ Extended StayAmerica-Seattle-Bellevue H
(425) 453-8186. **$125-$143.** 11400 Main St. I-405, exit 13A, just se. Int corridors. **Pets:** Other species. $25 daily fee/pet. Service with restrictions, crate.
[ASK] [✕] [🔋] [💻]

▽▽ Homestead Studio Suites Hotel-Seattle-Bellevue M
(425) 865-8680. **$125-$143.** 3700 132nd Ave SE. I-90, exit 11A (156th Ave SE) westbound; exit 10B eastbound, 0.5 mi se. Ext corridors. **Pets:** Other species. $25 daily fee/pet. Service with restrictions, crate.
[ASK] [✕] [🔋] [💻]

(AAA) ▽▽ La Residence Suite Hotel H
(425) 455-1475. **$125-$199.** 475 100th Ave NE. I-405, exit 13B, 0.9 mi w on NE 8th St, then just s. Int corridors. **Pets:** Accepted.
[SAVE] [✕] [🔋] [💻]

(AAA) ▼▼▼▼ Larkspur Landing Bellevue/Seattle H
(425) 373-1212. **$169-$219.** 15805 SE 37th St. I-90, exit 11 westbound; exit 11A (156th Ave SE) eastbound, 0.9 mi se on south frontage road. Int corridors. **Pets:** Accepted.
[SAVE] [X] [🖥] [▥]

(AAA) ▼▼▼▼ Red Lion Hotel Bellevue H
(425) 455-5240. **Call for rates.** 11211 Main St. I-405, exit 12, 0.4 mi n on 114th St. Int corridors. **Pets:** Other species. $20 one-time fee/room. Service with restrictions, supervision.
[SAVE] [X] [🖥] [▥] [🍴] [➤]

▼▼▼▼ Residence Inn by Marriott, Bellevue-Redmond H
(425) 882-1222. **$215-$263.** 14455 NE 29th Pl. I-405, exit 14 (SR 520), 2.3 mi e to 148th Ave NE (north exit), then just nw. Ext corridors. **Pets:** Accepted.
[X] [🖥] [▥] [➤] [X]

(AAA) ▼▼▼▼ Sheraton Bellevue Hotel H
(425) 455-3330. **$119-$419.** 100 112th Ave NE. I-405, exit 12 northbound; exit 13 southbound, just s. Int corridors. **Pets:** Accepted.
[SAVE] [X] [⚒M] [🖥] [▥] [🍴]

(AAA) ▼▼▼▼ ▼▼ The Westin Bellevue H ❀
(425) 638-1000. **$149-$419.** 600 Bellevue Way NE. I-405, exit 13B, 1.5 mi w on NE 8th St. Int corridors. **Pets:** Small, dogs only. $75 deposit/room. Designated rooms, service with restrictions, supervision.
[SAVE] [X] [▥] [🍴] [➤]

BOTHELL

▼▼▼ Extended StayAmerica-Seattle-Bothell H
(425) 402-4252. **$110-$125.** 923 228th St SE. I-405, exit 26, just sw. Int corridors. **Pets:** Other species. $25 daily fee/pet. Service with restrictions, crate.
[ASK] [X] [🖥] [▥]

▼▼▼ Extended Stay Deluxe Seattle-Bothell H
(425) 482-2900. **$125-$140.** 22122 17th Ave SE. I-405, exit 26, just n on Bothell Everett Hwy, just e on Canyon Park Blvd SE, then just s. Int corridors. **Pets:** Other species. $25 daily fee/pet. Service with restrictions, crate.
[ASK] [X] [⚒M] [🖥] [▥] [➤]

▼▼▼ Residence Inn by Marriott Seattle NE H
(425) 485-3030. **$188-$230.** 11920 NE 195th St. I-405, exit 24, 0.4 mi ne. Ext corridors. **Pets:** Accepted.
[X] [🖥] [▥] [➤] [X]

BREMERTON

(AAA) ▼▼ Flagship Inn H
(360) 479-6566. **$75-$115.** 4320 Kitsap Way. 3.5 mi w of ferry terminal; SR 3, exit Kitsap Way, 0.5 mi e. Int corridors. **Pets:** Accepted.
[SAVE] [X] [🖥] [▥] [➤]

▼▼ Midway Inn H
(360) 479-2909. **Call for rates.** 2909 Wheaton Way. SR 303, 2 mi n. Int corridors. **Pets:** Accepted.
[X] [🖥] [▥]

(AAA) ▼▼ Oyster Bay Inn H
(360) 377-5510. **$84-$99.** 4412 Kitsap Way. 3.8 mi w of ferry terminal; SR 3, exit Kitsap Way, 0.5 mi e. Int corridors. **Pets:** $20 daily fee/room. Service with restrictions, crate.
[SAVE] [X] [🖥] [▥] [🍴]

▼▼ Super 8 H ❀
(360) 377-8881. **Call for rates.** 5068 Kitsap Way. 4.2 mi w of ferry terminal; SR 3, exit Kitsap Way, just ne. Int corridors. **Pets:** Other species. $10 one-time fee/room. Service with restrictions, supervision.
[X] [⚒M] [🖥] [▥]

EDMONDS

(AAA) ▼▼▼▼ Best Western Edmonds Harbor Inn H ❀
(425) 771-5021. **$109-$140.** 130 W Dayton St. Just s at Port of Edmonds. Ext/int corridors. **Pets:** Medium. $20 daily fee/pet. Designated rooms, service with restrictions, supervision.
[SAVE] [X] [🖥] [▥]

(AAA) ▼ K & E Motor Inn M
(425) 778-2181. **$60-$89, 3 day notice.** 23921 Hwy 99. I-5, exit 177, 1 mi w on SR 104, exit SR 99 (Aurora Ave), then just n. Ext corridors. **Pets:** Small. $10 daily fee/pet. Designated rooms, no service, supervision.
[SAVE] [X] [🖥]

(AAA) ▼▼ Travelodge Seattle/Edmonds H
(425) 771-8008. **$69-$109.** 23825 Hwy 99. I-5, exit 177, 1 mi w on SR 104, exit SR 99 (Aurora Ave), then just n. Ext corridors. **Pets:** Accepted.
[SAVE] [X] [🖥] [▥]

EVERETT

▼▼ Days Inn Seattle/Everett H
(425) 355-1570. **$80-$121.** 1602 SE Everett Mall Way. I-5, exit 189 northbound, 0.5 mi w on SR 527, then 0.5 mi s; exit southbound, 0.7 mi s. Ext corridors. **Pets:** Accepted.
[ASK] [X] [🖥] [▥] [➤]

▼▼ Extended StayAmerica-Seattle-Everett H
(425) 355-1923. **$110-$125.** 8410 Broadway. I-5, exit 189, follow signs to Broadway, just nw. Int corridors. **Pets:** Other species. $25 daily fee/pet. Service with restrictions, crate.
[ASK] [X] [🖥] [▥]

▼▼ Extended Stay Deluxe-Seattle-Everett H
(425) 337-1341. **$131-$146.** 1431 112th St SE. I-5, exit 189, 1.5 mi se on 19th Ave SE, then 0.3 mi w. Int corridors. **Pets:** Other species. $25 daily fee/pet. Service with restrictions, crate.
[ASK] [X] [🖥] [▥]

(AAA) ▼▼▼▼ Holiday Inn Downtown Everett H
(425) 339-2000. **Call for rates.** 3105 Pine St. I-5, exit 193 northbound; exit 194 southbound, just sw. Int corridors. **Pets:** Accepted.
[SAVE] [X] [🖥] [▥] [🍴] [➤]

(AAA) ▼▼▼▼ Inn at Port Gardner H
(425) 252-6779. **$139-$289.** 1700 W Marine View Dr. I-5, exit 193 northbound, 1.2 mi w on Pacific Ave, then 1.2 mi n; exit 194 southbound, 1.2 mi w on Everett Ave, then 1 mi n; in Everett Marina Village. Int corridors. **Pets:** Medium. $25 one-time fee/room. Service with restrictions, supervision.
[SAVE] [X] [🖥] [▥]

(AAA) ▼▼▼▼ La Quinta Inn Everett H ❀
(425) 347-9099. **Call for rates.** 12619 4th Ave W. I-5, exit 186, just w. Int corridors. **Pets:** Medium, other species. Service with restrictions, supervision.
[SAVE] [X] [🖥] [▥] [➤]

FEDERAL WAY

(AAA) ▼▼▼▼ Clarion Hotel Federal Way H
(253) 941-6000. **$75-$169.** 31611 20th Ave S. I-5, exit 143, 0.5 mi w on 320th St, then just n. Int corridors. **Pets:** Medium, dogs only. $25 daily fee/pet. Designated rooms, supervision.
[SAVE] [X] [🖥] [▥] [🍴] [➤]

(AAA) ▼▼▼ Days Inn Federal Way H
(253) 838-3164. **Call for rates.** 34827 Pacific Hwy S. I-5, exit 142B, 0.6 mi w. Ext corridors. **Pets:** Accepted.
[SAVE] [X] [🖥] [▥]

▼▼ ▼▼ **Extended StayAmerica-Seattle-Federal Way** **H**
(253) 946-0553. **$90-$115.** 1400 S 320th St. I-5, exit 143, 0.6 mi w. Int corridors. **Pets:** Other species. $25 daily fee/pet. Service with restrictions, crate.
(ASK) ⊠ 🔋 💻

▼▼ ▼▼ **Federal Way Super 8** **H**
(253) 838-8808. **$68-$100.** 1688 S 348th St. I-5, exit 142B, just w. Int corridors. **Pets:** Accepted.
(ASK) ⊠ 🔋

FIFE

▼▼ ▼▼ **Extended StayAmerica-Tacoma-Fife** **H**
(253) 926-6316. **$100-$115.** 2820 Pacific Hwy E. I-5, exit 136B north-bound; exit 136 southbound, just nw. Int corridors. **Pets:** Other species. $25 daily fee/pet. Service with restrictions, crate.
(ASK) ⊠ 🔋 💻

(AAA) ▼▼▼ **GuestHouse Royal Coachman, Fife** **H**
(253) 922-2500. **Call for rates.** 5805 Pacific Hwy E. I-5, exit 137, just ne. Ext corridors. **Pets:** Medium, dogs only. $10 daily fee/pet, $25 one-time fee/pet. Service with restrictions, supervision.
(SAVE) ⊠ 🔋 💻

(AAA) ▼▼▼ **Quality Inn** **M**
(253) 926-2301. **$75-$110.** 5601 Pacific Hwy E. I-5, exit 137, just ne. Ext corridors. **Pets:** Other species. $15 daily fee/pet. Designated rooms, service with restrictions, supervision.
(SAVE) ⊠ 🔋 💻

GIG HARBOR

(AAA) ▼▼▼▼ **Best Western Wesley Inn** **H** ✿
(253) 858-9690. **$159-$279, 3 day notice.** 6575 Kimball Dr. SR 16, exit City Center, just e on Pioneer Way, then 0.3 mi s. Int corridors. **Pets:** $10 daily fee/pet. Designated rooms, service with restrictions, supervision.
(SAVE) ⊠ 🔋M 🔋 💻 🏊

(AAA) ▼▼▼▼ **The Inn at Gig Harbor** **H** ✿
(253) 858-1111. **$171-$220, 3 day notice.** 3211 56th St NW. SR 16, exit Olympic Dr, just w, then 0.4 mi n. Int corridors. **Pets:** Large, other species. $25 one-time fee/room. Designated rooms, service with restrictions, super-vision.
(SAVE) ⊠ 🔋M 🔋 💻 🍴 🔲

KENT

▼▼▼▼ **Extended StayAmerica-Seattle-Kent** **H**
(253) 872-6514. **$90-$105.** 22520 83rd Ave S. SR 167, exit 84th Ave S, just nw. Int corridors. **Pets:** Other species. $25 daily fee/pet. Service with restrictions, crate.
(ASK) ⊠ 🔋 💻

▼▼▼▼ **Hawthorn Suites** **H**
(253) 395-3800. **$129-$199.** 6329 S 212th St. I-5, exit 152, 2.6 mi se via Orilla Rd and 212th St. Ext corridors. **Pets:** Accepted.
(ASK) ⊠ 🔋 💻 🏊 🔲

▼▼▼▼ **TownePlace Suites by Marriott-Seattle Southcenter** **H**
(253) 796-6000. **$170-$208.** 18123 72nd Ave S. I-405, exit 1 (SR 181), 1.6 mi s on W Valley Hwy, just e on S 180th St, then just s. Ext corridors. **Pets:** Other species. $10 daily fee/pet.
⊠ 🔋M 🔋 💻 🏊 🔲

KIRKLAND

(AAA) ▼▼▼▼ **The Heathman Hotel** **H**
(425) 284-5800. **$219-$399.** 220 Kirkland Ave. I-405, exit 18 (NE 85th St), 1 mi w, then just s on 3rd St. Int corridors. **Pets:** Accepted.
(SAVE) ⊠ 🔋M 💻 🍴

▼▼▼▼ **La Quinta Inn & Suites Seattle (Bellevue/Kirkland)** **H** ✿
(425) 828-6585. **$69-$169.** 10530 NE Northup Way. I-405, exit 14 (SR 520) via 108th Ave exit, n on 108th Ave, then just w. Int corridors. **Pets:** Medium, other species. Service with restrictions, supervision.
(ASK) ⊠ 🔋 💻 🏊

▼▼ **Motel 6-687** **M**
(425) 821-5618. **$75-$85.** 12010 120th Pl NE. I-405, exit 20B northbound; exit 20 southbound, just se. Ext corridors. **Pets:** Other species. Service with restrictions, supervision.
⊠ 🏊

(AAA) ▼▼▼ ▼▼▼ **Woodmark Hotel, Yacht Club & Spa** **H**
(425) 822-3700. **$279-$1800.** 1200 Carillon Point. On Lake Washington Blvd, 1 mi n of SR 520. Int corridors. **Pets:** Accepted.
(SAVE) ⊠ 💻 🍴 🔲

LAKEWOOD

▼▼▼▼ **La Quinta–Lakewood Inn & Suites** **H** ✿
(253) 582-7000. **$119-$139.** 11751 Pacific Hwy SW. I-5, exit 125, just nw. Int corridors. **Pets:** Medium, other species. Service with restrictions, super-vision.
⊠ 🔋 💻 🏊

(AAA) ▼▼▼ **Western Inn** **H**
(253) 588-5241. **$59-$78.** 9920 S Tacoma Way. I-5, exit 127 (S Tacoma Way), just w on SR 512, then just n. Ext corridors. **Pets:** Accepted.
(SAVE) ⊠ 🔋 💻

LYNNWOOD

(AAA) ▼▼▼▼ **Best Western Alderwood** **H** ✿
(425) 775-7600. **$109-$169.** 19332 36th Ave W. I-5, exit 181B northbound, just n on Poplar Way, just w on 196th St SW, then just n; exit 181 (SR 524 W) southbound, just nw. Int corridors. **Pets:** Very small, dogs only. $25 one-time fee/pet. Designated rooms, service with restrictions.
(SAVE) ⊠ 🔋 💻 🏊

▼▼ ▼▼ **Extended StayAmerica-Seattle-Lynnwood** **H**
(425) 670-2520. **$95-$110.** 3021 196th St SW. I-5, exit 181E southbound; exit 181B northbound, just ne. Int corridors. **Pets:** Other species. $25 daily fee/pet. Service with restrictions, crate.
(ASK) ⊠ 🔋 💻

(AAA) ▼▼▼▼ **La Quinta Inn Lynnwood** **H** ✿
(425) 775-7447. **$59-$169.** 4300 Alderwood Mall Blvd. I-5, exit 181A north-bound, just w; exit 181 (SR 524 W) northbound, 0.5 mi w on 196th St SW, just s on 44th Ave SW, then just e. Int corridors. **Pets:** Medium, other species. Service with restrictions, supervision.
(SAVE) ⊠ 🔋 💻 🏊

▼▼▼▼ **Residence Inn by Marriott-Seattle North/Lynnwood** **H**
(425) 771-1100. **$233-$285.** 18200 Alderwood Mall Pkwy. I-5, exit 183 southbound, just w on 164th St SW, then 1.5 mi se on 28th St W; exit 182 northbound on SR 525, exit 1, then just s; just n of Alderwood Mall Shop-ping Center. Ext corridors. **Pets:** $15 daily fee/room. Service with restric-tions, supervision.
⊠ 🔋 💻 🏊 🔲

MONROE

(AAA) ▼▼▼ **Best Western Sky Valley Inn** **H**
(360) 794-3111. **$99-$159.** 19233 US 2. West end of town. Int corridors. **Pets:** Accepted.
(SAVE) ⊠ 🔋 💻 🏊

(AAA) ▼▼▼ **GuestHouse International Inn & Suites** **H**
(360) 863-1900. **$114-$144.** 19103 US 2. West end of town. Int corridors. **Pets:** Accepted.
(SAVE) ⊠ 🔋 💻 🏊

MOUNTLAKE TERRACE

▼▼ ▼▼ Studio 6 #6042 **M**
(425) 771-3139. **$81-$91.** 6017 244th St SW. I-5, exit 177, just ne. Ext corridors. **Pets:** Other species. $10 daily fee/room. Service with restrictions, supervision.
✕ ☾M ⌖ ▣

MUKILTEO

▼▼ ▼▼ Extended StayAmerica-Seattle-Mukilteo **H**
(425) 493-1561. **$121-$136.** 3917 Harbour Pointe Blvd SW. Jct SR 526 and 525 (Mukilteo Speedway), 1.5 mi s, then just w. Int corridors. **Pets:** Other species. $25 daily fee/pet. Service with restrictions, crate.
ASK ✕ ⌖ ▣

▼▼▼▼ TownePlace Suites by Marriott-Mukilteo **H**
(425) 551-5900. **$143-$175.** 8521 Mukilteo Speedway. Just se of jct 84th St SW and SR 525 (Mukilteo Speedway). Ext corridors. **Pets:** Large, other species. $10 daily fee/pet. Service with restrictions.
✕ ☾M ⌖ ▣ ⇘ ✕

POULSBO

▼▼▼▼ Holiday Inn Express **H**
(360) 697-4400. **$99-$199.** 19801 NE 7th Ave. On SR 305. Int corridors. **Pets:** Small. $20 daily fee/pet. Service with restrictions, supervision.
ASK ✕ ⌖ ▣

▲▲▲ ▼▼▼▼ Poulsbo Inn & Suites **H**
(360) 779-3921. **$99-$130, 7 day notice.** 18680 SR 305. SR 3, 2.3 mi e. Ext corridors. **Pets:** Medium, other species. $15 daily fee/pet. Designated rooms, service with restrictions, crate.
SAVE ✕ ☾M ⌖ ▣ ⇘ ✕

PUYALLUP

▲▲▲ ▼▼▼▼ Best Western Park Plaza **H** ❀
(253) 848-1500. **$159-$169, 7 day notice.** 620 S Hill Park Dr. SR 512, exit S Hill Park Dr southbound, just w; exit 9th St SW northbound, just w. Int corridors. **Pets:** Dogs only. $25 one-time fee/room. Service with restrictions, supervision.
SAVE ✕ ☾M ⌖ ▣ ⇘

▼▼ Crossland Economy Suites-Tacoma-Puyallup **M**
(253) 445-5945. **$74-$89.** 2101 N Meridian. SR 512, exit Milton/Tacoma, just w on SR 167, then just n. Ext corridors. **Pets:** Other species. $25 daily fee/pet. Service with restrictions, crate.
ASK ✕ ☾M ⌖ ▣

▼▼▼▼ Holiday Inn Express Hotel & Suites Puyallup **H** ❀
(253) 848-4900. **$189-$239.** 812 S Hill Park Dr. SR 512, exit S Hill Park Dr southbound, just w; exit 9th St SW northbound, just w. Int corridors. **Pets:** Dogs only. $25 one-time fee/room. Service with restrictions, supervision.
ASK ✕ ⌖ ▣ ⇘

REDMOND

▼▼▼▼ Residence Inn by Marriott Redmond Town Center **H**
(425) 497-9226. **$259-$269.** 7575 164th Ave NE. I-405, exit 14 (SR 520), 4.5 mi e to W Lake Sammamish Pkwy, just n to Leary Way, just e to Bear Creek Pkwy, just s to NE 74th Ave, just w to 164th Ave NE, then just n; center. Int corridors. **Pets:** Accepted.
✕ ⌖ ▣ ⇘ ✕

RENTON

▼▼ ▼▼ Extended Stay Deluxe-Seattle **H**
(425) 228-2454. **$121-$136.** 1150 Oakesdale Ave SW. I-405, exit 1 southbound, just s; exit Renton northbound, just n on Interurban Ave, 0.6 mi e on SW Grady Way, then just n. Int corridors. **Pets:** Other species. $25 daily fee/pet. Service with restrictions, crate.
ASK ✕ ⌖ ▣ ⇘

▲▲▲ ▼▼ ▼▼ Guest House Inn & Suites **M**
(425) 228-2858. **$90-$110.** 4710 Lake Washington Blvd NE. I-405, exit 7, just ne. Ext corridors. **Pets:** Accepted.
SAVE ✕ ⌖ ▣

▲▲▲ ▼▼▼▼ Holiday Inn Seattle-Renton **H**
(425) 226-7700. **$79-$169.** One S Grady Way. I-405, exit 2 (SR 167/ Rainier Ave), jct SR 167 N. Int corridors. **Pets:** Other species. $25 deposit/ room. Designated rooms, service with restrictions, supervision.
SAVE ✕ ⌖ ▣ ❙❙ ⇘

▲▲▲ ▼▼▼▼ Larkspur Landing Renton/Seattle **H**
(425) 235-1212. **$149-$179.** 1701 E Valley Rd. SR 167, exit E Valley Rd, 1 mi nw. Int corridors. **Pets:** Accepted.
SAVE ✕ ⌖ ▣

▼▼▼▼ TownePlace Suites Seattle South/Renton **H**
(425) 917-2000. **$169-$179.** 300 SW 19th St. SR 167, exit E Valley Rd, 1 mi nw, then just w. Int corridors. **Pets:** Accepted.
✕ ☾M ⌖ ▣ ⇘

SEATAC

▼▼ ▼▼ Clarion Hotel **H**
(206) 242-0200. **$99-$119.** 3000 S 176th St. Just e of SR 99. Int corridors. **Pets:** Small. $20 daily fee/pet. Designated rooms, service with restrictions, supervision.
ASK ✕ ☾M ⌖ ▣ ❙❙ ⇘

▼▼▼▼ Doubletree Hotel Seattle Airport **H**
(206) 246-8600. **$119-$289.** 18740 International Blvd. On SR 99. Int corridors. **Pets:** Medium, other species. Designated rooms, service with restrictions, supervision.
✕ ⌖ ▣ ❙❙ ⇘

▼▼▼▼ Hilton Seattle Airport & Conference Center **H** ❀
(206) 244-4800. **$129-$299.** 17620 International Blvd. On SR 99. Int corridors. **Pets:** Medium. $75 one-time fee/room. Supervision.
✕ ▣ ❙❙ ⇘

▼▼▼▼ Holiday Inn Express Hotel & Suites-Seattle Sea-Tac Airport **H** ❀
(206) 824-3200. **Call for rates.** 19621 International Blvd. On SR 99. Int corridors. **Pets:** Other species. $75 deposit/room, $50 one-time fee/room. Service with restrictions, crate.
✕ ⌖ ▣

▲▲▲ ▼▼▼▼ Holiday Inn Seattle SeaTac International Airport **H**
(206) 248-1000. **Call for rates.** 17338 International Blvd. On SR 99. Int corridors. **Pets:** Small. $10 daily fee/pet. Designated rooms, service with restrictions, supervision.
SAVE ✕ ☾M ⌖ ▣ ❙❙ ⇘

▼▼▼▼ La Quinta Inn Seattle (Sea-Tac International) **H** ❀
(206) 241-5211. **$69-$169.** 2824 S 188th St. On SR 99. Int corridors. **Pets:** Medium, other species. Service with restrictions, supervision.
ASK ✕ ⌖ ▣ ⇘

▼▼ Motel 6-1332 **M**
(206) 246-4101. **$59-$69.** 16500 International Blvd. On SR 99. Ext corridors. **Pets:** Other species. Service with restrictions, supervision.
✕

▼▼ Motel 6-736 **M**
(206) 824-9902. **$55-$65.** 20651 Military Rd. I-5, exit 151, just se. Ext corridors. **Pets:** Other species. Service with restrictions, supervision.
✕ ⌖ ⇘

▼▼▼ **Red Lion Hotel Seattle Airport** 🅗
(206) 246-5535. **$99-$279.** 18220 International Blvd. On SR 99. Int corridors. **Pets:** Other species. $20 one-time fee/room. Service with restrictions, supervision.
A$K ✕ 🛢 💻 🍴 ⛱

▼▼ **Super 8 Sea-Tac** 🅗 ✿
(206) 433-8188. **$77-$97.** 3100 S 192nd St. Just e of SR 99. Int corridors. **Pets:** Other species. $25 deposit/room. Designated rooms, service with restrictions, crate.
A$K ✕ 💻

SEATTLE

🆎 ▼▼ ▼▼ **Alexis Hotel** 🅗
(206) 624-4844. **$139-$349.** 1007 1st Ave. Corner of Madison St and 1st Ave. Int corridors. **Pets:** Accepted.
SAVE ✕ 🛢 💻 🍴 ⊠

🆎 ▼▼▼ **Comfort Inn & Suites Seattle** 🅗
(206) 361-3700. **Call for rates.** 13700 Aurora Ave N. I-5, exit 175, 1.1 mi w on NE 145th St, then 0.3 mi s. Int corridors. **Pets:** Small, dogs only. $15 daily fee/pet. Designated rooms, service with restrictions, supervision.
SAVE ✕ 🛢 💻 ⊠

🆎 ▼▼▼ **Crowne Plaza Seattle-Downtown** 🅗
(206) 464-1980. **$169-$329.** 1113 6th Ave. Corner of 6th Ave and Seneca St. Int corridors. **Pets:** Large. $50 one-time fee/room. Service with restrictions.
SAVE ✕ 🛢 💻 🍴

🆎 ▼▼▼ **The Edgewater** 🅗 ✿
(206) 728-7000. **$459-$659.** 2411 Alaskan Way, Pier 67. On waterfront at Pier 67; at base of Wall St. Int corridors. **Pets:** Other species. Designated rooms, service with restrictions, crate.
SAVE ✕ 🛢 💻 🍴

▼▼ **Executive Hotel Pacific** 🅗
(206) 623-3900. **$159-$249.** 400 Spring St. Between 4th and 5th aves. Int corridors. **Pets:** Accepted.
A$K ✕ 💻

▼▼ **Extended StayAmerica-Seattle-Northgate** 🅗
(206) 365-8100. **$90-$110.** 13300 Stone Ave N. I-5, exit 175, 1 mi w on n 145th St, 0.5 mi s on Aurora Ave, then just e on 135th St. Int corridors. **Pets:** Other species. $25 daily fee/pet. Service with restrictions, crate.
A$K ✕ 🛢 💻

🆎 ▼▼▼ **The Fairmont Olympic Hotel** 🅗 ✿
(206) 621-1700. **$299-$469.** 411 University St. Corner of 4th Ave and University St. Int corridors. **Pets:** Medium. Service with restrictions, supervision.
SAVE ✕ 🛢 💻 🍴 ⛱ ⊠

▼▼▼ **Homewood Suites by Hilton-Seattle Downtown** 🅗
(206) 281-9393. **$159-$299.** 206 Western Ave N. I-5, exit 167 (Mercer St), 0.3 mi w, 0.5 mi s on Fairview Ave, 1.2 mi w on Denny Way, then just n. Int corridors. **Pets:** Medium, other species. $20 daily fee/pet.
✕ 🛢 💻

▼▼ ▼▼ **Hotel 1000** 🅗
(206) 957-1000. **$219-$439.** 1000 1st Ave. Northeast corner of 1st Ave and Madison St. Int corridors. **Pets:** Accepted.
A$K ✕ 🛢 💻 🍴

🆎 ▼▼ ▼▼ **Hotel Max** 🅗 ✿
(206) 728-6299. **$149-$269.** 620 Stewart St. Corner of 7th Ave and Stewart St. Int corridors. **Pets:** Medium. $40 one-time fee/room. Service with restrictions.
SAVE ✕ 🅜 🛢 💻 🍴

🆎 ▼▼ ▼▼ **Hotel Monaco** 🅗 ✿
(206) 621-1770. **$139-$349.** 1101 4th Ave. Corner of 4th Ave and Spring St. Int corridors. **Pets:** Other species.
SAVE ✕ 💻 🍴 ⊠

🆎 ▼▼ ▼▼ **Hotel Nexus Seattle** 🅗 ✿
(206) 365-0700. **$99-$159.** 2140 N Northgate Way. I-5, exit 173, just nw. Ext corridors. **Pets:** Other species. $50 one-time fee/pet. Service with restrictions, crate.
SAVE ✕ 🛢 💻 ⛱

🆎 ▼▼ ▼▼ **Hotel Vintage Park** 🅗
(206) 624-8000. **$139-$309.** 1100 5th Ave. Corner of Spring St and 5th Ave. Int corridors. **Pets:** Accepted.
SAVE ✕ 🍴 ⊠

▼▼▼ **La Quinta Inn & Suites Seattle Downtown** 🅗 ✿
(206) 624-6820. **$79-$169.** 2224 8th Ave. Corner of 8th Ave and Blanchard St. Int corridors. **Pets:** Medium, other species. Service with restrictions, supervision.
A$K ✕ 🛢 💻 ⊠

🆎 ▼▼ ▼▼ **Pan Pacific Hotel Seattle** 🅗
(206) 264-8111. **$169-$425.** 2125 Terry Ave. Just s of jct E Denny Way. Int corridors. **Pets:** Accepted.
SAVE ✕ 💻 🍴 ⊠

🆎 ▼▼ ▼▼ **Red Lion Hotel on Fifth Avenue-Seattle** 🅗
(206) 971-8000. **$329.** 1415 5th Ave. Between Pike and Union sts. Int corridors. **Pets:** Other species. $20 one-time fee/room. Service with restrictions, supervision.
SAVE ✕ 🛢 💻 🍴

🆎 ▼▼ ▼▼ **Residence Inn Marriott Seattle Downtown/ Lake Union** 🅗
(206) 624-6000. **$239-$299.** 800 Fairview Ave N. I-5, exit 167 (Mercer St); south end of Lake Union. Int corridors. **Pets:** Other species. $25 daily fee/pet.
SAVE ✕ 🛢 💻 ⛱ ⊠

🆎 ▼▼ ▼▼ **The Roosevelt, a Coast Hotel** 🅗
(206) 621-1200. **$159-$279.** 1531 7th Ave. Corner of 7th Ave and Pine St. Int corridors. **Pets:** Medium, dogs only. $50 one-time fee/pet. Service with restrictions, supervision.
SAVE ✕ 🛢 💻 🍴

🆎 ▼▼ ▼▼ **Sheraton Seattle Hotel** 🅗 ✿
(206) 621-9000. **$179-$399.** 1400 6th Ave. Corner of 6th Ave and Pike St. Int corridors. **Pets:** Medium, dogs only. Designated rooms, service with restrictions, supervision.
SAVE ✕ 🛢 💻 🍴 ⛱ ⊠

🆎 ▼▼ ▼▼ **The Sixth Avenue Inn** 🅗
(206) 441-8300. **Call for rates.** 2000 6th Ave. Jct Virginia St. Int corridors. **Pets:** Accepted.
SAVE ✕ 🛢 💻 🍴

🆎 ▼▼ ▼▼ **Sorrento Hotel** 🅗 ✿
(206) 622-6400. **Call for rates.** 900 Madison St. I-5, exit Madison St, just e; at 9th Ave and Madison St. Int corridors. **Pets:** Large. $60 one-time fee/room. Designated rooms, service with restrictions, supervision.
SAVE ✕ 💻 🍴 ⊠

▼▼ ▼▼ **University Inn** 🅗
(206) 632-5055. **$145-$185.** 4140 Roosevelt Way NE. I-5, exit 169, 0.5 mi e, then just s. Int corridors. **Pets:** Large, dogs only. $20 daily fee/room. Designated rooms, service with restrictions, supervision.
A$K ✕ 🛢 💻 🍴 ⛱

🆎 ▼▼ ▼▼ **The Westin Seattle** 🅗
(206) 728-1000. **$190-$399.** 1900 5th Ave. Corner of 5th Ave and Stewart St. Int corridors. **Pets:** Accepted.
SAVE ✕ 🅜 🛢 💻 🍴 ⛱

🆎 ▼▼ ▼▼ **W Seattle** 🅗
(206) 264-6000. **$239-$509.** 1112 4th Ave. Corner of 4th Ave and Seneca St. Int corridors. **Pets:** Accepted.
SAVE ✕ 🍴

SILVERDALE

▼▼ Oxford Inn H
(360) 692-7777. **$89.** 9734 NW Silverdale Way. SR 3, exit Newberry Hill Rd, just e, then 1.2 mi n. Int corridors. **Pets:** Medium, other species. $20 one-time fee/room. Designated rooms, supervision.

(ASK) (X) 🛏 💻

▼▼▼ Oxford Suites Silverdale H
(360) 698-9550. **$129-$189.** 9550 SW Silverdale Way. SR 3, exit Newberry Hill Rd, 1.5 mi. Int corridors. **Pets:** Accepted.

(ASK) (X) (&M) 🛏 💻 🏊 (X)

◈ ▼▼▼ Silverdale Beach Hotel H ❀
(360) 698-1000. **$115-$160.** 3073 NW Bucklin Hill Dr. SR 3, exit Newberry Hill Rd, just e, 1 mi n on Silverdale Way, then just e. Int corridors. **Pets:** $20 daily fee/room. Service with restrictions, crate.

(SAVE) (X) 🛏 💻 🍴 🏊 (X)

SNOHOMISH

◈ ▼▼▼ Inn At Snohomish M
(360) 568-2208. **$65-$130.** 323 2nd St. East end of town. Ext corridors. **Pets:** Other species. Service with restrictions, supervision.

(SAVE) (X) 🛏 💻

TACOMA

▼ Crossland Studios-Tacoma-Hosmer M
(253) 538-9448. **$74-$89.** 8801 S Hosmer St. I-5, exit 128 northbound, just se; exit 129 southbound, just e on 72nd St, then 1.0 mi s. Ext corridors. **Pets:** Other species. $25 daily fee/pet. Service with restrictions, crate.

(ASK) (X) 🛏 💻

◈ ▼▼ Extended StayAmerica-Tacoma-South H
(253) 475-6565. **$105-$115.** 2120 S 48th St. I-5, exit 130, 0.4 mi nw. Int corridors. **Pets:** Other species. $25 daily fee/pet. Service with restrictions, crate.

(ASK) (X) 🛏 💻

◈ ▼▼▼ Hotel Murano H
(253) 238-8000. **$189-$469.** 1320 Broadway Plaza. I-5, exit 133 (City Center) to I-705 N, exit a St, left on 11th St, then left; downtown. Int corridors. **Pets:** Accepted.

(SAVE) (X) 🛏 💻 🍴 (X)

▼▼▼ La Quinta Inn & Suites Tacoma (Conference Center) H ❀
(253) 383-0146. **$79-$169.** 1425 E 27th St. I-5, exit 135 southbound; exit 134 northbound, just n. Int corridors. **Pets:** Medium, other species. Service with restrictions, supervision.

(ASK) (X) 🛏 💻 🍴 🏊

◈ ▼▼▼ Red Lion Hotel Tacoma H
(253) 548-1212. **$109-$149.** 8402 S Hosmer St. I-5, exit 128 northbound, just ne; exit 129 southbound, just e on 72nd St, then 1 mi s. Int corridors. **Pets:** Other species. $20 one-time fee/room. Service with restrictions, supervision.

(SAVE) (X) 🛏 💻 🏊

◈ ▼▼▼ Shilo Inn & Suites -Tacoma H ❀
(253) 475-4020. **$112-$200.** 7414 S Hosmer St. I-5, exit 129, just se. Int corridors. **Pets:** Dogs only. $25 one-time fee/room. Designated rooms, service with restrictions, supervision.

(SAVE) (X) 🛏 💻 🏊 (X)

TUKWILA

▼▼ Extended StayAmerica-Seattle-Tukwila H
(206) 244-2537. **$85-$100.** 15451 53rd Ave S. I-5, exit 153 northbound, just n on Southcenter Pkwy, just n on 61st St, just w on Southcenter Blvd, then just sw; exit 154B (Southcenter Mall) southbound, just sw. Ext corridors. **Pets:** Other species. $25 daily fee/pet. Service with restrictions, crate.

(ASK) (X) 🛏 💻

▼▼▼ Homewood Suites by Hilton H
(206) 433-8000. **$99-$209.** 6955 Fort Dent Way. I-405, exit 1 (SR 181), just ne. Ext/int corridors. **Pets:** Accepted.

(X) 🛏 💻 🏊 (X)

▼▼▼ Ramada Limited Sea-Tac Airport H
(206) 244-8800. **$90-$100.** 13900 Tukwila International Blvd. I-5, exit 158 southbound, 2 mi s; exit 154A (SR 518 W) northbound, 1 mi n on SR 99. Int corridors. **Pets:** Accepted.

(ASK) (X) 🛏 💻

▼▼▼ Residence Inn by Marriott-Seattle South H
(425) 226-5500. **$188-$230.** 16201 W Valley Hwy. I-405, exit 1 (SR 181), just s. Ext corridors. **Pets:** Very small. $75 one-time fee/room. Service with restrictions, crate.

(X) (&M) 🛏 💻 🏊 (X)

VASHON

▼ The Swallow's Nest Guest Cottages CA ❀
(206) 463-2646. **Call for rates.** 6030 SW 248th St. North end Ferry Landing, 7.8 mi s on Vashon Hwy; south end (Tahlequah) Ferry Landing, 5.8 mi n on Vashon Hwy, 1.4 mi e on Quartermaster Dr, 1.5 mi s on Dockton Rd, 0.4 mi s on 75th Ave, then 1 mi e. Ext corridors. **Pets:** Other species. $15 daily fee/pet. Designated rooms, service with restrictions, supervision.

(X) 🛏 💻 (X)

END METROPOLITAN AREA

SEDRO-WOOLLEY

◈ ▼▼▼ South Bay Bed and Breakfast @ Lake Whatcom BB
(360) 595-2086. **$165-$185, 14 day notice.** 4095 S Bay Dr. I-5, exit 240, 5.5 mi ne via Lake Samish and Cain Lake rds, then 3.2 mi e. Int corridors. **Pets:** Accepted.

(SAVE) (X) (R) (X)

SEQUIM

◈ ▼▼▼ Juan de Fuca Cottages CA
(360) 683-4433. **$99-$275, 14 day notice.** 182 Marine Dr. From downtown, 7 mi n via Sequim Ave and E Anderson Rd. Ext corridors. **Pets:** Medium, dogs only. $20 daily fee/pet. Designated rooms, service with restrictions, supervision.

(SAVE) (X) 🛏 💻 (X) (Z)

◈ ▼▼▼ Quality Inn & Suites–Sequim H ❀
(360) 683-2800. **$80-$180.** 134 River Rd. US 101, exit River Rd, just nw. Int corridors. **Pets:** Dogs only. $10 daily fee/pet. Designated rooms, service with restrictions, supervision.

(SAVE) (X) 🛏 💻 🏊

◈ ▼▼▼ Sequim West Inn M
(360) 683-4144. **$54-$125, 3 day notice.** 740 W Washington St. US 101, exit River Rd, 0.9 mi ne via River Rd and W Washington St. Ext corridors. **Pets:** Small. $10 daily fee/pet. Service with restrictions, supervision.

(SAVE) (X) 🛏 💻

SHELTON

◈ ▼▼▼ Little Creek Casino Resort H ❀
(360) 427-7711. **$86-$519.** W W 91 SR 108. Jct US 101 and SR 108. Int corridors. **Pets:** Other species. $30 one-time fee/room. Service with restrictions.

(SAVE) (X) (&M) 🛏 💻 🍴 🏊

▼▼ **Super 8 of Shelton** 🅷 ❖

(360) 426-1654. **Call for rates.** 2943 Northview Cir. US 101, exit Wallace-Kneeland Blvd, just se. Int corridors. **Pets:** Dogs only. $10 daily fee/pet. Designated rooms, service with restrictions, supervision.

⊠ 🛢 🖵

SNOQUALMIE PASS

▼▼ **Summit Lodge at Snoqualmie Pass** 🅷

(425) 434-6300. **$119-$279, 3 day notice.** 603 SR 906. I-90, exit 52 eastbound, 0.3 mi e; exit 53 westbound, 0.3 mi w. Int corridors. **Pets:** Accepted.

ASK ⊠ 🛢 🖵 🍴 ⇌

SOAP LAKE

▼▼▼ **Inn at Soap Lake** Ⓜ

(509) 246-1132. **$59-$125.** 226 E Main Ave. Just w of SR 17. Ext/int corridors. **Pets:** $10 daily fee/pet. Designated rooms, service with restrictions, supervision.

⊠ 🛢 🖵 ⊠

▼▼▼ **Notaras Lodge** Ⓜ

(509) 246-0462. **$65-$135.** 236 E Main Ave. Just w of SR 17. Ext corridors. **Pets:** Accepted.

⊠ 🛢 🖵

SPOKANE

🅐🅐🅐 ▼▼ **Apple Tree Inn** Ⓜ

(509) 466-3020. **$49-$69.** 9508 N Division St. Jct US 2 and 395, just n. Ext/int corridors. **Pets:** Small, dogs only. $10 daily fee/pet. Designated rooms, service with restrictions, supervision.

SAVE ⊠ 🛢 ⇌

🅐🅐🅐 ▼▼▼ **Best Western Peppertree Airport Inn** 🅷

(509) 624-4655. **$89-$219.** 3711 S Geiger Blvd. I-90, exit 276, just n. Int corridors. **Pets:** Very small, dogs only. $10 daily fee/room. Service with restrictions, supervision.

SAVE ⊠ 🅼 🛢 🖵 ⇌ ⊠

▼▼ **Comfort Inn North** 🅷

(509) 467-7111. **Call for rates.** 7111 N Division St. I-90, exit 281 (Division St), 4.6 mi n. Int corridors. **Pets:** Accepted.

⊠ 🛢 🖵 ⇌ ⊠

🅐🅐🅐 ▼▼ **Comfort Inn University District/Downtown** 🅷 ❖

(509) 535-9000. **$89-$130.** 923 E 3rd Ave. I-90, exit 281 (Division St), just n to E 3rd Ave, then 0.7 mi e. Int corridors. **Pets:** Large, other species. $25 one-time fee/room. Service with restrictions, supervision.

SAVE ⊠ 🅼 🛢 🖵 ⇌

🅐🅐🅐 ▼▼▼▼ **The Davenport Hotel and Tower** 🅷 ❖

(509) 455-8888. **$169-$319.** 10 S Post St. Downtown. Int corridors. **Pets:** Designated rooms, supervision.

SAVE ⊠ 🅼 🛢 🍴 ⇌ ⊠

▼▼ **Days Inn City Center** 🅷

(509) 747-2011. **$54-$99.** 120 W 3rd Ave. I-90, exit 281 (Division St), just n, then just w on 2nd Ave. Ext corridors. **Pets:** Medium. $10 daily fee/pet. Service with restrictions, supervision.

ASK ⊠ 🛢 🖵 🍴 ⇌

🅐🅐🅐 ▼▼▼ **Doubletree Hotel Spokane City Center** 🅷 ❖

(509) 455-9600. **$124-$234.** 322 N Spokane Falls Ct. I-90, exit 281 (Division St), just n; downtown. Int corridors. **Pets:** $50 one-time fee/room. Service with restrictions, supervision.

SAVE ⊠ 🛢 🖵 🍴 ⇌ ⊠

▼▼▼ **Holiday Inn Express-Downtown** 🅷

(509) 328-8505. **Call for rates.** 801 N Division St. I-90, exit 281 (Division St), 0.8 mi n. Ext/int corridors. **Pets:** Dogs only. $50 deposit/room. Designated rooms, service with restrictions, supervision.

⊠ 🅼 🛢 🖵

▼▼▼ **Holiday Inn Spokane Airport** 🅷

(509) 838-1170. **Call for rates.** 1616 S Windsor Dr. I-90, exit 277 westbound; exit 277B eastbound, just w on US 2, then just s. Int corridors. **Pets:** Accepted.

⊠ 🅼 🛢 🖵 🍴 ⇌

▼▼ **Howard Johnson Inn** 🅷

(509) 838-6630. **$119-$199.** 211 S Division St. I-90, exit 281 (Division St), just n. Int corridors. **Pets:** Accepted.

ASK ⊠ 🛢 🖵

🅐🅐🅐 ▼▼ **Madison Inn** 🅷

(509) 474-4200. **$75-$90.** 15 W Rockwood Blvd. I-90, exit 281 (Division St) eastbound, just e to Cowley St, 0.4 mi s, then just w; exit westbound, just n to 2nd Ave, just w to Browne St, 0.5 mi s to 9th Ave, then just e. Int corridors. **Pets:** Other species. $10 daily fee/pet. Designated rooms, service with restrictions, supervision.

SAVE ⊠ 🅼 🛢 🖵

🅐🅐🅐 ▼▼ **Oxford Suites-Downtown Spokane** 🅷

(509) 353-9000. **Call for rates.** 115 W North River Dr. I-90, exit 281 (Division St), 1 mi n, then just n. Int corridors. **Pets:** Medium, dogs only. $25 one-time fee/room. Designated rooms, service with restrictions, supervision.

⊠ 🛢 🖵 ⇌ ⊠

🅐🅐🅐 ▼▼ **Ramada Limited** 🅷

(509) 838-8504. **$65-$150.** 123 S Post St. I-90, exit 280B (Lincoln St), just n to 1st Ave W, just e to Post St, then just s. Ext corridors. **Pets:** Very small. $25 daily fee/pet. Designated rooms, service with restrictions, crate.

SAVE ⊠ 🛢 🖵

🅐🅐🅐 ▼▼▼ **Ramada Limited Suites** 🅷

(509) 468-4201. **$80-$150.** 9601 N Newport Hwy. US 2 and 395, just n on US 2 (Newport Hwy). Int corridors. **Pets:** Accepted.

SAVE ⊠ 🅼 🛢 🖵 ⇌ ⊠

▼▼▼ **Ramada Spokane Airport & Indoor Waterpark** 🅷

(509) 838-5211. **$125-$130.** 8909 Airport Dr. I-90, exit 277B eastbound; exit 277 westbound, 3.4 mi n. Int corridors. **Pets:** Other species. $10 one-time fee/room. Designated rooms, service with restrictions, supervision.

ASK ⊠ 🛢 🖵 🍴 ⇌ ⊠

🅐🅐🅐 ▼▼▼ **Red Lion Hotel at the Park-Spokane** 🅷

(509) 326-8000. **$199.** 303 W North River Dr. I-90, exit 281 (Division St), 1.5 mi n on US 195, then just w. Int corridors. **Pets:** Other species. $20 one-time fee/room. Service with restrictions, supervision.

SAVE ⊠ 🛢 🖵 🍴 ⇌ ⊠

🅐🅐🅐 ▼▼▼ **Red Lion River Inn-Spokane** 🅷

(509) 326-5577. **$175.** 700 N Division St. I-90, exit 281 (Division St), 0.8 mi n; downtown. Int corridors. **Pets:** Other species. $20 one-time fee/room. Service with restrictions, supervision.

SAVE ⊠ 🅼 🛢 🖵 🍴 ⇌ ⊠

🅐🅐🅐 ▼▼▼ **Super 8 Airport West** 🅷 ❖

(509) 838-8800. **$60-$150.** 11102 W Westbow Blvd. I-90, exit 272 (Medical Lake Rd), just s. Int corridors. **Pets:** Other species. $15 one-time fee/room. Service with restrictions, supervision.

SAVE ⊠ 🅼 🛢 🖵 ⇌

▼▼ **Travelodge** 🅷 ❖

(509) 623-9727. **$89-$109.** W 33 Spokane Falls Blvd. I-90, exit 281 (Division St), 0.5 mi n, then just w. Int corridors. **Pets:** Other species. $10 daily fee/pet. Service with restrictions.

ASK ⊠ 🅼 🛢 🖵

SPOKANE VALLEY

▼▼ Comfort Inn Valley H
(509) 924-3838. **Call for rates.** 905 N Sullivan Rd. I-90, exit 291B, just s. Int corridors. **Pets:** Medium, dogs only. $10 one-time fee/pet. Service with restrictions, supervision.

▼ Crossland Studios-Spokane Valley H
(509) 928-5948. **$59-$74.** 12803 E Sprague Ave. I-90, exit 289, 1.1 mi s, just e. Ext corridors. **Pets:** Other species. $25 daily fee/pet. Service with restrictions, crate.

▼▼▼ Holiday Inn Express-Valley H
(509) 927-7100. **$109-$209.** 9220 E Mission Ave. I-90, exit 287, just s. Ext/int corridors. **Pets:** Other species. Designated rooms, service with restrictions, supervision.

▼▼▼ La Quinta Inn & Suites Spokane H ❖
(509) 893-0955. **$89-$159.** 3808 N Sullivan Rd. I-90, exit 291B, 1.3 mi n. Int corridors. **Pets:** Medium, other species. Service with restrictions, supervision.

◈ ▼▼▼ Mirabeau Park Hotel and Convention Center H ❖
(509) 924-9000. **$96-$169.** 1100 N Sullivan Rd. I-90, exit 291B, just s. Int corridors. **Pets:** Medium, other species. $25 one-time fee/room. Designated rooms, service with restrictions, crate.

◈ ▼▼▼▼ Oxford Suites Spokane Valley H ❖
(509) 847-1000. **$115-$199.** 15015 E Indiana Ave. I-90, exit 291A eastbound; exit 291B westbound, just nw. Int corridors. **Pets:** Small, dogs only. $25 one-time fee/pet. Service with restrictions, supervision.

◈ ▼▼▼ Pheasant Hill Inn & Suites H ❖
(509) 926-7432. **$80-$190.** 12415 E Mission Ave. I-90, exit 289, just se. Int corridors. **Pets:** $15 one-time fee/room. Service with restrictions, supervision.

▼▼▼ Quality Inn Valley Suites H
(509) 928-5218. **$89-$129.** 8923 E Mission Ave. I-90, exit 287. Int corridors. **Pets:** Medium, dogs only. $50 deposit/room. Service with restrictions, supervision.

▼▼▼ Residence Inn by Marriott H ❖
(509) 892-9300. **$139-$149.** 15915 E Indiana Ave. I-90, exit 291 westbound, just e; exit 291B eastbound, just n, then just e. Int corridors. **Pets:** Small. $75 one-time fee/room. Designated rooms, service with restrictions, crate.

◈ ▼▼ Rodeway Inn & Suites H
(509) 535-7185. **$49-$129, 7 day notice.** 6309 E Broadway. I-90, exit 286, just w. Ext/int corridors. **Pets:** Medium, dogs only. $10 daily fee/pet. Designated rooms, service with restrictions, supervision.

▼▼ Super 8 H
(509) 928-4888. **$62-$92.** N 2020 Argonne Rd. I-90, exit 287, just n. Int corridors. **Pets:** Large, other species. $25 deposit/room, $15 one-time fee/room. Designated rooms, service with restrictions, supervision.

STEVENSON

◈ ▼▼▼▼ Skamania Lodge H ❖
(509) 427-7700. **$129-$269, 5 day notice.** 1131 SW Skamania Lodge Way. 1 mi w on SR 14, just n on Rock Creek Dr, then just w. Int corridors. **Pets:** $50 one-time fee/room. Designated rooms, service with restrictions, supervision.

SULTAN

◈ ▼ Dutch Cup Motel M
(360) 793-2215. **$77-$96, 3 day notice.** 819 Main St. Jct US 2 and Main St. Ext corridors. **Pets:** Medium. $9 daily fee/room. Designated rooms, service with restrictions, supervision.

SUNNYSIDE

◈ ▼▼▼ Best Western Grapevine Inn H
(509) 839-6070. **$100-$210, 3 day notice.** 1849 Quail Ln. I-82, exit 69, just n, then just w. Int corridors. **Pets:** Small, dogs only. $20 one-time fee/room. Designated rooms, supervision.

◈ ▼ Country Inn & Suites M ❖
(509) 837-7878. **$45-$60.** 408 Yakima Valley Hwy. Downtown. Ext corridors. **Pets:** Medium. $10 daily fee/pet. Service with restrictions, supervision.

TOPPENISH

◈ ▼▼▼ Best Western Toppenish Inn H ❖
(509) 865-7444. **$90-$140.** 515 S Elm St. I-82, exit 50, 3.1 mi e. Int corridors. **Pets:** $10 daily fee/pet. Service with restrictions, supervision.

◈ ▼ Quality Inn & Suites H
(509) 865-5800. **$72-$120.** 511 S Elm St. I-82, exit 50, 3.2 mi e. Int corridors. **Pets:** Medium, dogs only. $10 daily fee/pet. Service with restrictions, supervision.

TUMWATER

◈ ▼▼ Best Western Tumwater Inn H
(360) 956-1235. **$103-$120.** 5188 Capitol Blvd. I-5, exit 102, just e. Int corridors. **Pets:** Other species. $15 daily fee/pet.

▼▼▼ Comfort Inn and Conference Center H ❖
(360) 352-0691. **$89-$120.** 1620 74th Ave SW. I-5, exit 101, just se. Int corridors. **Pets:** Small. $10 daily fee/pet. Service with restrictions, supervision.

▼▼ Extended StayAmerica-Olympia-Tumwater H
(360) 754-6063. **$90-$105.** 1675 Mottman Rd SW. I-5, exit 104, 0.4 mi nw on US 101, just s on Crosby Blvd, then just se. Int corridors. **Pets:** Other species. $25 daily fee/pet. Service with restrictions, crate.

▼▼ GuestHouse Inn & Suites H ❖
(360) 943-5040. **$89-$120.** 1600 74th Ave SW. I-5, exit 101, just se. Int corridors. **Pets:** Small. $10 daily fee/pet. Service with restrictions, supervision.

TWISP

▼▼ Idle-A-While Motel M
(509) 997-3222. **$50-$130.** 505 N SR 20. Just n of town. Ext corridors. **Pets:** Accepted.

UNION

▼▼▼▼ Alderbrook Resort & Spa H
(360) 898-2200. **$139-$529, 7 day notice.** 7101 E SR 106. Just e of town. Ext/int corridors. **Pets:** $25 daily fee/pet. Service with restrictions, supervision.
(ASK) (X) 🖥 💻 🍴 ➤ (X)

UNION GAP

🌢 ▼▼▼▼ Best Western Ahtanum Inn H
(509) 248-9700. **$89-$209.** 2408 Rudkin Rd. I-82, exit 36, just n. Int corridors. **Pets:** Medium. $10 daily fee/pet. No service, supervision.
(SAVE) (X) 🔵M 🖥 💻 ➤ (X)

🌢 ▼▼▼▼ Quality Inn-Yakima Valley M ❖
(509) 248-6924. **$69-$169.** 12 E Valley Mall Blvd. I-82, exit 36, just s. Ext corridors. **Pets:** Medium, dogs only. $10 daily fee/pet. Service with restrictions, supervision.
(SAVE) (X) 🔵M 🖥 💻 ➤

▼▼ ▼▼ Super 8 Motel Yakima H
(509) 248-8880. **$76-$110.** 2605 Rudkin Rd. I-82, exit 36, just s. Int corridors. **Pets:** Other species. $15 one-time fee/room. Designated rooms, service with restrictions, supervision.
(ASK) (X) 🔵M 🖥 💻 ➤

WALLA WALLA

🌢 ▼▼▼▼ Best Western Walla Walla Suites Inn H ❖
(509) 525-4700. **$110-$150.** 7 E Oak St. US 12, exit 2nd Ave, just s. Int corridors. **Pets:** Dogs only. $10 daily fee/pet. Service with restrictions, crate.
(SAVE) (X) 🔵M 🖥 💻 ➤

🌢 ▼▼ Budget Inn M
(509) 529-4410. **$55-$99.** 305 N 2nd Ave. US 12, exit 2nd Ave, 0.3 mi s. Ext corridors. **Pets:** Medium. $10 daily fee/pet. Designated rooms, service with restrictions, supervision.
(SAVE) (X) 🔵M 🖥 💻 ➤

▼▼▼▼ Holiday Inn Express H
(509) 525-6200. **$119-$129.** 1433 W Pine St. US 12, exit Pendleton/ Prescott. Int corridors. **Pets:** Accepted.
(ASK) (X) 🖥 💻 ➤ (X)

🌢 ▼▼▼▼ La Quinta Inn Walla Walla H ❖
(509) 525-2522. **$69-$139.** 520 N 2nd Ave. US 12, exit 2nd Ave, just s. Int corridors. **Pets:** Medium, other species. Service with restrictions, supervision.
(SAVE) (X) 🖥 💻 ➤ (X)

🌢 ▼▼▼▼ Marcus Whitman Hotel & Conference Center H ❖
(509) 525-2200. **$119-$349.** 6 W Rose St. Downtown. Int corridors. **Pets:** Medium. $20 daily fee/pet. Designated rooms, service with restrictions.
(SAVE) (X) 🖥 💻 🍴

▼▼▼ Walla Walla Super 8 H
(509) 525-8800. **Call for rates.** 2315 Eastgate St N. US 12, exit Wilbur Ave, just s. Int corridors. **Pets:** Accepted.
(X) 🔵M 🖥 ➤

🌢 ▼▼▼ Walla Walla Travelodge M
(509) 529-4940. **$55-$99.** 421 E Main St. US 12, exit 2nd Ave, 0.5 mi s, then just e. Ext/int corridors. **Pets:** Medium. $7 daily fee/pet. Service with restrictions, supervision.
(SAVE) (X) 🖥 💻 ➤

🌢 ▼▼▼ Walla Walla Vineyard Inn H
(509) 529-4360. **$59-$149.** 325 E Main St. US 12, exit 2nd Ave, 0.5 mi s, then just e. Ext/int corridors. **Pets:** Dogs only. $25 one-time fee/room. Service with restrictions, supervision.
(SAVE) (X) 🖥 💻 ➤ (X)

WENATCHEE

🌢 ▼▼ Avenue Motel M
(509) 663-7161. **$50-$76.** 720 N Wenatchee Ave. On US 2 business loop; just nw of downtown. Ext/int corridors. **Pets:** Accepted.
(SAVE) (X) 🖥 💻 ➤

🌢 ▼▼▼▼ Coast Wenatchee Center Hotel H
(509) 662-1234. **$79-$165.** 201 N Wenatchee Ave. Downtown. Int corridors. **Pets:** $10 one-time fee/room. Supervision.
(SAVE) (X) 🖥 💻 🍴 ➤

🌢 ▼▼ Comfort Inn H
(509) 662-1700. **$76-$140.** 815 N Wenatchee Ave. Downtown. Int corridors. **Pets:** Accepted.
(SAVE) (X) 🖥 💻 ➤

🌢 ▼▼ Econo Lodge M
(509) 663-7121. **$55-$120.** 232 N Wenatchee Ave. Downtown. Ext corridors. **Pets:** Small, dogs only. $10 daily fee/pet. Service with restrictions, supervision.
(SAVE) (X) 🖥 💻 ➤

▼▼▼ Holiday Inn Express H
(509) 663-6355. **$99-$189.** 1921 N Wenatchee Ave. Northwest side of town. Int corridors. **Pets:** Accepted.
(ASK) (X) 🔵M 🖥 💻 ➤

🌢 ▼▼▼▼ La Quinta Inn & Suites Wenatchee H ❖
(509) 664-6565. **$69-$139.** 1905 N Wenatchee Ave. West end of town. Int corridors. **Pets:** Medium, other species. Service with restrictions, supervision.
(SAVE) (X) 🔵M 🖥 💻 ➤ (X)

🌢 ▼▼▼▼ Red Lion Hotel Wenatchee H
(509) 663-0711. **$99-$180.** 1225 N Wenatchee Ave. Just nw of downtown. Int corridors. **Pets:** Other species. $20 one-time fee/room. Service with restrictions, supervision.
(SAVE) (X) 🖥 💻 🍴 ➤

🌢 ▼▼▼ Super 8 H ❖
(509) 662-3443. **$59-$129.** 1401 N Miller St. 1.5 mi n on US 2. Int corridors. **Pets:** $50 deposit/room, $10 daily fee/pet. Designated rooms, service with restrictions, supervision.
(SAVE) (X) 🖥 💻 ➤

🌢 ▼▼▼ Travelodge-Wenatchee M
(509) 662-8165. **$55-$95.** 1004 N Wenatchee Ave. Downtown. Ext corridors. **Pets:** Accepted.
(SAVE) (X) 🔵M 🖥 💻 ➤

WESTPORT

▼▼ Albatross Motel M
(360) 268-9233. **$49-$89, 3 day notice.** 200 E Dock St. Just s from boat basin. Ext corridors. **Pets:** Accepted.
(X) 🖥 (X)

🌢 ▼▼▼ Chateau Westport H
(360) 268-9101. **$89-$388.** 710 W Hancock St. Just w of SR 105 Spur N; 1.5 mi n of Twin Harbors State Park. Int corridors. **Pets:** Dogs only. $25 daily fee/room. Designated rooms, service with restrictions, supervision.
(SAVE) (X) 🔵M 🖥 💻 ➤ (X) (X)

WINTHROP

🌢 ▼▼▼ Americas Best Value Cascade Inn M
(509) 996-3100. **$70-$150, 3 day notice.** 1006 SR 20. 1 mi e. Ext corridors. **Pets:** Medium. $10 daily fee/pet. Designated rooms, service with restrictions, supervision.
(SAVE) (X) 🖥 💻 ➤

▼▼▼▼ River Run Inn M
(509) 996-2173. **$75-$145, 10 day notice.** 27 Rader Rd. 0.5 mi w on SR 20. Ext corridors. **Pets:** Accepted.
SAVE ✕ 🛏 🖵 🏊

▼▼▼ Winthrop Inn M ❀
(509) 996-2217. **$70-$125, 3 day notice.** 960 SR 20. 0.9 mi e. Int corridors. **Pets:** Dogs only. $10 daily fee/pet. Service with restrictions, supervision.
SAVE ✕ 🛏 🏊 ✕

▼▼▼ Winthrop Mtn View Chalets CA
(509) 996-3113. **$75-$125, 7 day notice.** 1120 SR 20. South end of town. Ext corridors. **Pets:** Dogs only. $30 daily fee/pet. Designated rooms, service with restrictions, supervision.
SAVE ✕ 🛏 🖵 ☎

WOODLAND

▼▼▼ Cedars Inn Woodland H
(360) 225-6548. **Call for rates.** 1500 Atlantic Ave. I-5, exit 21, just ne. Ext corridors. **Pets:** Other species. $10 daily fee/pet. Service with restrictions, supervision.
✕ 🛏 🏊

▼▼▼ Lewis River Inn M
(360) 225-6257. **$64-$110.** 1100 Lewis River Rd. I-5, exit 21, just e. Ext corridors. **Pets:** Accepted.
SAVE ✕ 🛏 🖵

YAKIMA

▼▼▼▼ Best Western Lincoln Inn H ❀
(509) 453-8898. **$99-$299.** 1614 N 1st St. I-82, exit 31, just s. Int corridors. **Pets:** Very small, dogs only. $25 daily fee/pet. Service with restrictions, supervision.
SAVE ✕ 🔊M 🛏 🖵 🏊

▼▼▼ Cedars Suites Yakima Downtown M
(509) 452-8101. **$55-$110.** 1010 E a St. I-82, exit 33B eastbound; exit 33 westbound, just w to 9th St, just n to a St, then just e. Ext corridors. **Pets:** Accepted.
SAVE ✕ 🛏

▼▼▼ Comfort Suites H ❀
(509) 249-1900. **Call for rates.** 3702 Fruitvale Blvd. US 12, exit 40th Ave, just s. Int corridors. **Pets:** Small, dogs only. $20 daily fee/pet. Designated rooms, service with restrictions, supervision.
SAVE ✕ 🔊M 🛏 🖵 🏊

▼▼ Days Inn Yakima H
(509) 248-3393. **$70-$130.** 1504 N 1st St. I-82, exit 31, 0.6 mi s. Int corridors. **Pets:** Other species. $15 daily fee/pet. Designated rooms, no service, supervision.
ASK ✕ 🔊M 🛏 🖵 🏊

▼▼▼▼ Fairfield Inn & Suites by Marriott H
(509) 452-3100. **$112-$136.** 137 N Fair Ave. I-82, exit 33A eastbound, just s; exit 33 westbound, just w to 9th St, just n to B St, then just e. Int corridors. **Pets:** Accepted.
✕ 🔊M 🛏 🖵 🏊

▼▼▼▼ Holiday Inn Express Yakima H ❀
(509) 249-1000. **$139-$169.** 1001 E a St. I-82, exit 33B eastbound; exit 33 westbound, just w to 9th St, just n to a St, then just e. Int corridors. **Pets:** Small. $20 daily fee/room. Designated rooms, service with restrictions, supervision.
SAVE ✕ 🔊M 🛏 🖵 🏊

▼▼▼ Howard Johnson Plaza Yakima Gateway H
(509) 452-6511. **$89-$129.** 9 N 9th St. I-82, exit 33 westbound; exit 33B eastbound, just s. Int corridors. **Pets:** Medium, dogs only. $15 deposit/pet. Designated rooms, service with restrictions, crate.
ASK ✕ 🔊M 🛏 🖵 🍴 🏊

▼▼▼ Oxford Inn H
(509) 457-4444. **$86-$96.** 1603 E Yakima Ave. I-82, exit 33, just e; exit 33B eastbound. Int corridors. **Pets:** Medium, other species. $20 one-time fee/room. Designated rooms.
ASK ✕ 🔊M 🛏 🖵 🏊 ✕

▼▼▼ Oxford Suites H
(509) 457-9000. **$105-$165.** 1701 E Yakima Ave. I-82, exit 33 westbound; exit 33B eastbound. Int corridors. **Pets:** Accepted.
ASK ✕ 🔊M 🛏 🖵 🏊

▼▼▼ Ramada Limited M
(509) 453-0391. **$60-$301.** 818 N 1st St. I-82, exit 31, 1.2 mi s. Ext corridors. **Pets:** Accepted.
ASK ✕ 🔊M 🛏 🖵 🏊 ✕

▼▼▼ Red Lion Hotel Yakima Center H
(509) 248-5900. **$85-$169.** 607 E Yakima Ave. I-82, exit 33 westbound; exit 33B eastbound, 0.8 mi w. Ext/int corridors. **Pets:** Other species. $20 one-time fee/room. Service with restrictions, supervision.
ASK ✕ 🛏 🖵 🍴 🏊

▼▼▼ Sun Country Inn M
(509) 248-5650. **$58-$70, 3 day notice.** 1700 N 1st St. I-82, exit 31, just s. Ext corridors. **Pets:** Other species. $8 daily fee/pet. Service with restrictions, supervision.
ASK ✕ 🔊M 🛏 🖵 🏊

ZILLAH

▼▼▼ Comfort Inn H
(509) 829-3399. **$104-$160.** 911 Vintage Valley Pkwy. I-82, exit 52, just n. Int corridors. **Pets:** Accepted.
ASK ✕ 🔊M 🛏 🖵 🏊

BARBOURSVILLE

Best Western Huntington Mall Inn
(304) 736-9772. **$79-$99.** 3441 US 60 E. I-64, exit 20A eastbound; exit 20 westbound, 0.3 mi s. Int corridors. **Pets:** Other species. $10 one-time fee/room. Service with restrictions, crate.

Comfort Inn by Choice Hotels
(304) 733-2122. **Call for rates.** 249 Mall Rd. I-64, exit 20, 0.4 mi n. Int corridors. **Pets:** Accepted.

BECKLEY

Best Western Four Seasons Inn
(304) 252-0671. **$67-$110.** 1939 Harper Rd. I-64/77, exit 44, just e on SR 3. Ext/int corridors. **Pets:** Other species. $5 daily fee/pet. Service with restrictions, supervision.

Country Inn & Suites By Carlson
(304) 252-5100. **$99-$199.** 2120 Harper Rd. I-64/77, exit 44, just w on SR 3. Int corridors. **Pets:** Accepted.

Econo Lodge
(304) 255-2161. **$49-$100.** 1909 Harper Rd. I-64/77, exit 44, 0.3 mi e on SR 3. Ext/int corridors. **Pets:** Other species. Service with restrictions, supervision.

Howard Johnson Express Inn
(304) 255-5900. **$49-$125.** 1907 Harper Rd. I-64/77, exit 44, 0.4 mi e on SR 3. Int corridors. **Pets:** Accepted.

Microtel Inn
(304) 256-2000. **$55-$129, 3 day notice.** 2130 Harper Rd. I-64/77, exit 44. Int corridors. **Pets:** Medium. $25 one-time fee/room. Service with restrictions, supervision.

Park Inn & Suites
(304) 255-9091. **Call for rates.** 134 Harper Park Dr. I-64/77, exit 44, just w on SR 3. Int corridors. **Pets:** Accepted.

Super 8
(304) 253-0802. **$69-$109.** 2014 Harper Rd. I-64/77, exit 44, just e. Int corridors. **Pets:** Small. $15 one-time fee/room. Designated rooms, service with restrictions, supervision.

BLUEFIELD

Holiday Inn Bluefield-On The Hill
(304) 325-6170. **Call for rates.** 3350 Big Laurel Hwy. I-77, exit 1, 3.8 mi nw via US 52/460. Int corridors. **Pets:** $25 daily fee/pet. Service with restrictions, supervision.

BRIDGEPORT

Holiday Inn Clarksburg-Bridgeport
(304) 842-5411. **$90-$140.** 100 Lodgeville Rd. I-79, exit 119, just e on US 50. Int corridors. **Pets:** Other species. $5 daily fee/pet. Service with restrictions, supervision.

Sleep Inn
(304) 842-1919. **$79.** 115 Tolley Dr. I-79, exit 119, just e on US 50. Int corridors. **Pets:** Other species. Supervision.

Super 8 Motel–Bridgeport
(304) 842-7381. **$54-$71.** 168 Barnett Run Rd. I-79, exit 121, just w. Ext corridors. **Pets:** Medium. $10 daily fee/room. Service with restrictions, crate.

CHARLESTON

Charleston Comfort Suites
(304) 925-1171. **$110-$130.** 107 Alex Ln. I-77, exit 95, just s on SR 61. Int corridors. **Pets:** Medium, other species. $25 one-time fee/room. Service with restrictions.

Country Inn & Suites By Carlson
(304) 925-4300. **$110-$130.** 105 Alex Ln. I-77, exit 95, just s on SR 61. Int corridors. **Pets:** Medium, other species. Service with restrictions.

Days Inn Charleston East
(304) 925-1010. **$55-$75.** 6400 MacCorkle Ave SE. I-77, exit 95, just s on SR 61. Int corridors. **Pets:** Small, dogs only. $15 daily fee/pet. Service with restrictions, supervision.

Knights Inn-Charleston East
(304) 925-0451. **$50-$65.** 6401 MacCorkle Ave SE. I-77, exit 95, just s on SR 61. Ext corridors. **Pets:** Small, dogs only. $10 daily fee/pet. Service with restrictions, supervision.

Red Roof Inn-Kanawha City
(304) 925-6953. **$48-$76.** 6305 SE MacCorkle Ave. I-77, exit 95, just s on SR 61. Ext corridors. **Pets:** Accepted.

CROSS LANES

Comfort Inn West Charleston
(304) 776-8070. **Call for rates.** 102 Racer Dr. I-64, exit 47, just s. Int corridors. **Pets:** Accepted.

DANIELS

The Resort at Glade Springs
(304) 763-2000. **$148-$342, 7 day notice.** 255 Resort Dr. I-64, exit 125, 1.5 mi w on SR 307, then 2.8 mi w on US 19. Ext/int corridors. **Pets:** Accepted.

DAVIS

⚛ ▼▼▼▼ Black Bear Resort 🅒🄰
(304) 866-4391. **$90-$510.** Cortland Rd, Canaan Valley. 4.5 mi s on SR 32. Ext corridors. **Pets:** Dogs only. $50 deposit/pet. Designated rooms, no service, supervision.
[SAVE] ☒ 🔋 🖳 🏊 ☒

DUNBAR

▼ Dunbar Super 8 Motel 🄷
(304) 768-6888. **$64-$75.** 911 Dunbar Ave. I-64, exit 53, just w. Int corridors. **Pets:** $10 daily fee/pet. Service with restrictions, supervision.
[ASK] ☒ 🔋 🖳

EDRAY

⚛ ▼▼▼ Marlinton Motor Inn 🄼 🐾
(304) 799-4711. **$65-$129, 3 day notice.** US 219 N. Center. Ext corridors. **Pets:** Medium. $12 daily fee/pet. Designated rooms, no service, supervision.
[SAVE] ☒ 🔋 🖳 🍴 🏊

ELKINS

⚛ ▼▼▼▼ Cheat River Lodge 🅒🄰
(304) 636-2301. **$73-$88.** Rt 1, Box 115, Faulkner Rd. 4.8 mi e on US 33, then 1.5 mi ne. Ext corridors. **Pets:** Dogs only. $20 daily fee/pet. Service with restrictions, supervision.
[SAVE] ☒ 🔋 🖳 🍴 ☒

▼ Econo Lodge 🄼
(304) 636-5311. **Call for rates.** US 33 E. 1 mi e. Ext/int corridors. **Pets:** Accepted.
☒ 🔋 🏊

▼▼▼ Elkins Super 8 🄷
(304) 636-6500. **Call for rates.** 350 Beverly Pike. 0.8 mi s on SR 219. Int corridors. **Pets:** Accepted.
☒ 🔋 🖳

FAIRMONT

⚛ ▼▼▼ Holiday Inn Fairmont 🄷
(304) 366-5500. **$75-$234.** 930 E Grafton Rd. I-79, exit 137, just e. Int corridors. **Pets:** Medium, other species. $25 one-time fee/room. Service with restrictions, crate.
[SAVE] ☒ 🄻🄼 🔋 🖳 🍴 🏊

▼▼▼ Super 8 🄷
(304) 363-1488. **$57-$106.** 2208 Pleasant Valley Rd. I-79, exit 133, just e. Int corridors. **Pets:** Medium. $10 daily fee/room. Service with restrictions, crate.
[ASK] ☒ 🔋 🖳

FALLING WATERS

▼▼▼ Holiday Inn Express Martinsburg North 🄷
(304) 274-6100. **Call for rates.** 1220 TJ Jackson Dr. I-81, exit 20, just w. Int corridors. **Pets:** Accepted.
☒ 🔋 🖳 🏊

FROST

▼▼▼ The Inn at Mountain Quest 🄲🄸
(304) 799-7267. **$130-$150.** Rt 92 Frost. On SR 92, 0.4 mi n. Ext corridors. **Pets:** Accepted.
[ASK] ☒ 🍴 ☒

HUNTINGTON

⚛ ▼▼▼ Red Roof Inn 🄷
(304) 733-3737. **$50-$75.** 5190 US Rt 60 E. I-64, exit 15, just s. Ext corridors. **Pets:** Medium, other species. Service with restrictions, supervision.
[SAVE] ☒ 🔋

JANE LEW

⚛ ▼▼▼ Plantation Inn & Suites 🄼
(304) 884-7806. **$65-$100.** 1322 Hackers Creek Rd. I-79, exit 105, just e. Ext corridors. **Pets:** Small. $10 one-time fee/pet. Service with restrictions, supervision.
[SAVE] ☒ 🔋 🖳

KEYSER

⚛ ▼▼▼ Keyser Inn 🄷
(304) 788-0913. **$55-$61.** Rt 220 S. On US 220, 2.3 mi s. Int corridors. **Pets:** Medium. $25 one-time fee/pet. Service with restrictions, supervision.
[SAVE] ☒ 🔋 🖳

LEWISBURG

⚛ ▼▼▼ Brier Inn 🄷
(304) 645-7722. **$64-$110.** 540 N Jefferson St. I-64, exit 169, just s on US 219. Ext corridors. **Pets:** Accepted.
[SAVE] ☒ 🔋 🖳 🍴 🏊

▼▼▼ Super 8 🄷
(304) 647-3188. **$67-$115, 30 day notice.** 550 N Jefferson St. I-64, exit 169, just s on US 219. Int corridors. **Pets:** $10 daily fee/pet. Service with restrictions, supervision.
[ASK] ☒ 🔋 🖳

LOGAN

▼ Super 8-Logan 🄼
(304) 752-8787. **Call for rates.** 316 Riverview Ave. 1.8 mi e on SR 73. Int corridors. **Pets:** Accepted.
☒ 🔋 🖳

MARTINSBURG

▼▼ Days Inn Martinsburg 🄷
(304) 263-1800. **Call for rates.** 209 Viking Way. I-81, exit 13, just e on W King St (CR 15). Ext/int corridors. **Pets:** Accepted.
☒ 🔋 🖳

▼▼ Econo Lodge 🄼
(304) 274-2181. **$60-$62.** 5595 Hammonds Mill Rd. I-81, exit 20, just e. Ext/int corridors. **Pets:** Other species. Service with restrictions, supervision.
[ASK] ☒ 🖳

▼▼▼ Holiday Inn Martinsburg 🄷
(304) 267-5500. **$109-$149.** 301 Foxcroft Ave. I-81, exit 13, just e on W King St (CR 15). Int corridors. **Pets:** Other species. $15 one-time fee/room. Designated rooms, service with restrictions, supervision.
[ASK] ☒ 🔋 🖳 🍴 🏊

⚛ ▼ Knights Inn-Martinsburg 🄼
(304) 267-2211. **$47-$95.** 1997 Edwin Miller Blvd. I-81, exit 16E, 0.4 mi e on SR 9. Ext corridors. **Pets:** Medium, other species. $10 daily fee/pet. Designated rooms, service with restrictions, crate.
[SAVE] ☒ 🔋

▼ Super 8-Martinsburg 🄷
(304) 263-0801. **Call for rates.** 2048 Edwin Miller Blvd. I-81, exit 16E, just e on SR 9. Int corridors. **Pets:** Accepted.
☒ 🔋

MORGANTOWN

▼▼▼ Comfort Inn-Morgantown 🄷
(304) 296-9364. **$69-$125.** 225 Comfort Inn Dr. I-68, exit 1, 0.3 mi n on US 119. Int corridors. **Pets:** Other species. $25 deposit/pet. Designated rooms, service with restrictions, supervision.
[ASK] ☒ 🔋 🖳 🍴 🏊

🏅 💎 Friends Inn Ⓜ
(304) 599-4850. **$50-$150, 14 day notice.** 452 Country Club Rd. I-79, exit 155, s on US 19 to SR 705, then e on University Ave. Ext corridors. **Pets:** Very small. $100 deposit/pet, $5 daily fee/pet. Designated rooms, no service, supervision.
ⓢ ⓧ ⊟

🏅 💎💎 Ramada Conference Center Ⓗ
(304) 296-3431. **$95-$150.** 20 Scott Ave. I-68, exit 1, 0.3 mi n. Int corridors. **Pets:** Other species. Service with restrictions, supervision.
ⓢ ⓧ ⊟ ⊡ 🍴 ⊉

💎💎💎 Residence Inn by Marriott Morgantown Ⓗ 🐾
(304) 599-0237. **$139-$144.** 1046 Willowdale Rd. I-79, exit 155, 2 mi s on US 19, then 0.9 mi e on SR 705. Int corridors. **Pets:** Small, other species. $75 one-time fee/room. Designated rooms, service with restrictions, supervision.
ⓧ 🏋 ⊟ ⊡ ⊉ ⊗

NITRO

💎 Econo Lodge Ⓜ
(304) 755-8341. **Call for rates.** 4115 1st Ave. I-64, exit 45, 0.8 mi e on SR 25. Ext corridors. **Pets:** Accepted.
ⓧ ⊟ ⊡

PARKERSBURG

💎💎💎 The Blennerhassett Ⓗ
(304) 422-3131. **Call for rates.** 320 Market St. Between Fourth and Fifth sts; downtown. Int corridors. **Pets:** Accepted.
ⓧ ⊡ 🍴

🏅 💎 Red Carpet Inn Ⓜ 🐾
(304) 485-1851. **$45-$65.** 6333 Emerson Ave. I-77, exit 179, 0.4 mi sw on SR 68. Ext corridors. **Pets:** Dogs only. $8 daily fee/pet. Service with restrictions, crate.
ⓢ ⓧ ⊟ ⊡

💎💎 Red Roof Inn Ⓜ
(304) 485-1741. **$49-$72.** 3714 E 7th St. I-77, exit 176, just w on US 50. Ext corridors. **Pets:** Medium, other species. Service with restrictions, supervision.
🅰️🆂🅺 ⓧ ⊟ ⊡

💎 Travelodge Parkersburg Ⓜ
(304) 424-5100. **Call for rates.** 3604 E 7th St. I-77, exit 176, just w. Ext corridors. **Pets:** Medium, other species. $5 daily fee/pet. Service with restrictions, supervision.
ⓧ ⊟ ⊡ ⊉

PHILIPPI

🏅 💎 Budget Inn Philippi Ⓜ
(304) 457-5888. **$49-$85.** Rt 4, Box 155. 2.5 mi s on US 250. Int corridors. **Pets:** $10 daily fee/pet. Service with restrictions, supervision.
ⓢ ⓧ 🏋 ⊟

PRINCETON

💎💎 Comfort Inn-Princeton Ⓗ
(304) 487-6101. **$65-$85.** 136 Ambrose Ln. I-77, exit 9, 0.3 mi w on US 460. Int corridors. **Pets:** Small. $10 daily fee/pet. Designated rooms, no service, crate.
🅰️🆂🅺 ⓧ ⊟ ⊡

🏅 💎💎 Days Inn Ⓗ 🐾
(304) 425-8100. **$63-$88.** 347 Meadowfield Ln. I-77, exit 9, 0.3 mi w on US 460, just s on Ambrose Ln, then just e. Ext corridors. **Pets:** Medium. $20 daily fee/pet. Designated rooms, service with restrictions, supervision.
ⓢ ⓧ ⊡ ⊉

🏅 💎💎 Holiday Inn Express Princeton Ⓗ 🐾
(304) 425-8156. **$85-$125.** 805 Oakvale Rd. I-77, exit 9, just w. Int corridors. **Pets:** Medium. $20 daily fee/pet. Designated rooms, service with restrictions, supervision.
ⓢ ⓧ ⊟ ⊡ ⊉

💎💎 Sleep Inn & Suites Ⓗ
(304) 431-2800. **$99-$225.** 1015 Oakvale Rd. I-77, exit 9, just w on US 460, then just n via service road. Int corridors. **Pets:** Supervision.
🅰️🆂🅺 ⓧ ⊟ ⊡ ⊉

RIPLEY

🏅 💎💎 Holiday Inn Express Ⓗ
(304) 372-5000. **$89.** 1 Hospitality Dr. I-77, exit 138, just w on SR 33, then 0.3 mi n. Ext/int corridors. **Pets:** Accepted.
ⓢ ⓧ ⊟ ⊡

🏅 💎💎 McCoys Inn & Conference Center Ⓗ 🐾
(304) 372-9122. **$90-$99.** 701 W Main St. I-77, exit 138, just e. Ext/int corridors. **Pets:** Medium. $15 daily fee/pet. Designated rooms, service with restrictions, supervision.
ⓢ ⓧ ⊡ 🍴 ⊉ ⊗

💎 Ripley Super 8 Ⓜ
(304) 372-8880. **$65-$105.** 102 Duke Dr. I-77, exit 138, just e on SR 33. Int corridors. **Pets:** Accepted.
🅰️🆂🅺 ⓧ ⊟ ⊡

SNOWSHOE

💎💎 Inn at Snowshoe Ⓗ
(304) 572-6520. **Call for rates.** SR 66. Jct US 219, 0.5 mi e, follow signs. Int corridors. **Pets:** Accepted.
ⓧ ⊟ ⊡ 🍴 ⊉ ⊗

SOUTH CHARLESTON

🏅 💎💎💎 Ramada Plaza Hotel Charleston Ⓗ
(304) 744-4641. **$89-$139.** 400 2nd Ave. I-64, exit 56, just nw. Int corridors. **Pets:** Accepted.
ⓢ ⓧ ⊟ ⊡ 🍴 ⊉

STAR CITY

🏅 💎 Econo Lodge-Coliseum Ⓗ
(304) 599-8181. **$64-$75.** 3506 Monongahela Blvd. I-79, exit 155, 1.4 mi s on US 119/SR 7. Ext corridors. **Pets:** Small, other species. $10 daily fee/pet. Service with restrictions, crate.
ⓢ ⓧ ⊟ ⊡

SUMMERSVILLE

🏅 💎💎 Best Western Summersville Lake Motor Lodge Ⓗ
(304) 872-6900. **$49-$100.** 1203 S Broad St. US 19 and Broad St; 0.6 mi s of jct SR 39. Ext corridors. **Pets:** Medium, other species. $10 daily fee/pet. Service with restrictions, supervision.
ⓢ ⓧ ⊟ ⊡

🏅 💎💎💎 Comfort Inn Ⓗ
(304) 872-6500. **$75-$180, 30 day notice.** 903 Industrial Dr N. US 19, 1.9 mi n of jct SR 39. Int corridors. **Pets:** Small, other species. $10 daily fee/pet. Designated rooms, service with restrictions, supervision.
ⓢ ⓧ ⊟ ⊡ ⊉ ⊗

💎💎💎 Hampton Inn Ⓗ
(304) 872-7100. **$96.** 5400 Webster Rd. Just s on SR 41 from US 19. Int corridors. **Pets:** Accepted.
ⓧ 🏋 ⊡ ⊉ ⊗

AAA ▼▼▼ Sleep Inn of Summersville H
(304) 872-4500. **$65-$155, 30 day notice.** 701 Professional Park Dr. US 19, 1.7 mi n of jct SR 39. Int corridors. **Pets:** Small, other species. $10 daily fee/pet. Designated rooms, service with restrictions, supervision.
SAVE ⊠ 🖥 💻 ≈

▼ Super 8-Summersville H
(304) 872-4888. **Call for rates.** 306 Merchants Walk. US 19, just n. Int corridors. **Pets:** Accepted.
⊠ 🖥

TRIADELPHIA

▼▼▼ Comfort Inn-Wheeling H
(304) 547-0610. **$79-$149.** 675 Fort Henry Rd. I-70, exit 11, just n. Int corridors. **Pets:** Accepted.
ASK ⊠ 🖥 💻 ≈

AAA ▼▼▼ Holiday Inn Express Wheeling East H
(304) 547-1380. **$79-$145.** 87 Jenkins Ln. I-70, exit 11. Int corridors. **Pets:** Small, dogs only. $25 daily fee/pet. Designated rooms, service with restrictions, supervision.
SAVE ⊠ 🖥 💻 ≈

WEIRTON

▼▼▼ Holiday Inn H
(304) 723-5522. **$105-$119.** 350 Three Springs Dr. 4.5 mi e on US 22, exit Three Springs Dr. Int corridors. **Pets:** $50 one-time fee/room. Designated rooms, service with restrictions, supervision.
⊠ 🖥 💻 ¶ ≈ ⊠

WESTON

AAA ▼▼▼ Comfort Inn H
(304) 269-7000. **$65-$130.** 2906 US Hwy 33 E. I-79, exit 99, just e. Ext corridors. **Pets:** Medium. $10 daily fee/room. Designated rooms, service with restrictions, supervision.
SAVE ⊠ 🖥 💻 ≈

▼▼ Holiday Inn Express Hotel & Suites H
(304) 269-3550. **$90-$140.** 215 Staunton Dr. I-79, exit 99, just e. Int corridors. **Pets:** $25 daily fee/room. Designated rooms, service with restrictions, crate.
ASK ⊠ 🖥 💻 ≈

▼▼ Weston Super 8 H
(304) 269-1086. **$69-$74.** 100 Market Place Mall, Suite 12. I-79, exit 99, just e. Int corridors. **Pets:** Very small, other species. $10 daily fee/pet. Service with restrictions, supervision.
ASK ⊠ 🖥 💻

WHEELING

▼▼ Wheeling Super 8 M
(304) 243-9400. **$67-$110.** 2400 National Rd. I-70, exit 5, just e. Int corridors. **Pets:** Accepted.
ASK ⊠ 🖥 💻

WHITE SULPHUR SPRINGS

AAA ▼▼▼▼ The Greenbrier H 🐾
(304) 536-1110. **$299-$650, 15 day notice.** 300 W Main St. I-64, exit 181 westbound, 1.8 mi w on US 60; exit 175 eastbound, just n, then 3.2 mi e on US 60. Ext/int corridors. **Pets:** Small. $150 one-time fee/pet. Designated rooms, service with restrictions, crate.
SAVE ⊠ 🛒 🖥 💻 ¶ ≈ ⊠

WILLIAMSTOWN

▼▼ Days Inn H 🐾
(304) 375-3730. **$45-$200.** 1339 Highland Ave. I-77, exit 185, just w on SR 31. Int corridors. **Pets:** Other species. $10 daily fee/pet, $40 one-time fee/pet. Designated rooms, service with restrictions, crate.
ASK ⊠ 🖥 💻 ≈

WISCONSIN

ABBOTSFORD

▼▼ Sleep Inn H
(715) 223-3337. $73-$83. 300 E Elderberry Rd. SR 29, exit 132 (SR 13), just se. Int corridors. Pets: Accepted.
ASK ✕ 🛏 ▣ 🌊

ALGOMA

AAA⁺ ▼ Algoma Beach Motel M
(920) 487-2828. $79-$159, 3 day notice. 1500 Lake St. Jct SR 54, 0.4 mi s on SR 42. Ext/int corridors. Pets: Accepted.
SAVE ✕ &M 🛏

▼ Scenic Shore Inn M
(920) 487-3214. $50-$68, 3 day notice. 2221 Lake St. Jct SR 54, 0.8 mi s on SR 42. Ext corridors. Pets: Medium, dogs only. Service with restrictions, supervision.
✕ 🛏 ▣

ANTIGO

▼▼ Days Inn H
(715) 623-0506. Call for rates. 525 Memory Ln. 0.4 mi n of jct SR 64 E and US 45, then just w. Int corridors. Pets: Accepted.
✕ 🛏 ▣ 🌊

▼▼ Super 8 Motel-Antigo H
(715) 623-4188. $59-$112. 535 Century Ave. On US 45 at SR 64 E. Int corridors. Pets: Dogs only. $15 daily fee/pet. Designated rooms, service with restrictions, supervision.
ASK ✕ 🛏 ▣ 🌊

APPLETON

AAA⁺ ▼▼ Best Western Midway Hotel H
(920) 731-4141. $89-$149. 3033 W College Ave. US 41, exit 137 (SR 125), 0.5 mi e. Int corridors. Pets: Medium. $10 daily fee/pet. Designated rooms, service with restrictions, supervision.
SAVE ✕ 🛏 ▣ ⊧ 🌊 🗙

▼▼ Candlewood Suites H 🐾
(920) 739-8000. $100-$145. 4525 W College Ave. Just w of US 41. Int corridors. Pets: Other species. $75 one-time fee/pet. Service with restrictions, crate.
ASK ✕ 🛏 ▣

▼▼▼ Comfort Suites Appleton Airport H
(920) 730-3800. $89-$149. 3809 W Wisconsin Ave. US 41, exit 138 (Wisconsin Ave), just e. Int corridors. Pets: Other species. $50 deposit/room, $10 one-time fee/room. Service with restrictions, crate.
ASK ✕ 🛏 ▣ 🌊 🗙

▼▼▼ Country Inn & Suites By Carlson H
(920) 830-3240. $99-$130. 355 Fox River Dr. US 41, exit 137 (SR 125), just nw. Int corridors. Pets: Small, other species. $20 one-time fee/room. Designated rooms, service with restrictions, supervision.
ASK ✕ 🛏 ▣ 🌊 🗙

AAA⁺ ▼ Days Inn M
(920) 733-5551. $55-$190. 210 Westhill Blvd. US 41, exit 137 (SR 125), just e. Int corridors. Pets: Accepted.
SAVE ✕ 🛏 ▣

▼▼ Extended StayAmerica-Appleton-Fox Cities H
(920) 830-9596. $60-$90. 4141 Boardwalk Ct. US 41, exit 137 (SR 125), just w on College Ave, then just s on Nicolet Rd. Int corridors. Pets: Other species. $25 daily fee/pet. Service with restrictions, crate.
ASK ✕ 🛏 ▣

▼▼ Fairfield Inn by Marriott H
(920) 954-0202. $90-$95. 132 Mall Dr. US 41, exit 137 (SR 125), just nw. Int corridors. Pets: Other species. $20 one-time fee/room. Service with restrictions, supervision.
✕ 🛏 ▣ 🌊

▼▼▼ La Quinta Inn & Suites College Ave H 🐾
(920) 734-7777. $79-$149. 3730 W College Ave. US 41, exit 137 (SR 125), just e. Int corridors. Pets: Medium, other species. Service with restrictions, supervision.
ASK ✕ 🛏 ▣ 🌊 🗙

▼▼ La Quinta Inn Appleton Fox River Mall Area M 🐾
(920) 734-6070. $49-$105. 3920 W College Ave. US 41, exit 137 (SR 125), just e. Ext/int corridors. Pets: Medium, other species. Service with restrictions, supervision.
ASK ✕ 🛏 ▣ 🌊

▼▼ Microtel Inn & Suites H
(920) 997-3121. Call for rates. 321 Metro Dr. US 41, exit 137 (SR 125), just nw. Int corridors. Pets: Accepted.
✕ 🛏 ▣

▼▼▼ Residence Inn by Marriott 🅗
(920) 954-0570. **$135-$165.** 310 Metro Dr. US 41, exit 137 (SR 125), just nw on Mall Dr. Int corridors. **Pets:** Other species. $100 one-time fee/room.
⊠ 🛏 🖵 ➰ ⊠

ARKDALE

▼▼▼ Northern Bay Golf Resort & Marina 🅒🅞
(608) 339-2090. **$136-$492, 7 day notice.** 1844 20th Ave. 2.9 mi nw on SR 21, 4 mi s on CR Z, then 1.5 nw via Dakota Ave and 20th Ave. Int corridors. **Pets:** Accepted.
🅐🆂🅚 ⊠ 🛏 🖵 🍴 ➰ ⊠ ☎

ASHLAND

🔷 ▼▼▼ AmericInn of Ashland 🅗
(715) 682-9950. **$79-$219.** 3009 Lake Shore Dr E. On US 2, 2.1 mi e of jct SR 13 S. Int corridors. **Pets:** Accepted.
🆂🅰🆅🅴 ⊠ 🛏 🖵 ➰ ⊠

▼ Ashland Motel 🅜
(715) 682-5503. **Call for rates.** 2300 W Lake Shore Dr. 1.8 mi w on US 2. Ext corridors. **Pets:** Other species. $5 daily fee/pet. Service with restrictions, supervision.
⊠ 🛏 🖵

🔷 ▼▼▼ Best Western Lake Superior Lodge 🅗
(715) 682-5235. **$100-$139.** 30600 US Hwy 2. 2.5 mi w. Ext/int corridors. **Pets:** $15 daily fee/room. Designated rooms, service with restrictions, crate.
🆂🅰🆅🅴 ⊠ 🖵 🍴 ➰

BALDWIN

▼▼ AmericInn Lodge & Suites of Baldwin 🅗 🐾
(715) 684-5888. **$70-$185.** 500 Baldwin Plaza Dr. I-94, exit 19 (US 63), just ne. Int corridors. **Pets:** Medium, dogs only. $10 daily fee/pet. Designated rooms, service with restrictions, supervision.
⊠ 🛏 🖵 ➰

▼▼ Super 8 🅗
(715) 684-2700. **$64-$149.** 2110 10th Ave. I-94, exit 19 (US 63), just se. Int corridors. **Pets:** Accepted.
⊠ 🛏 🖵 ➰

BARABOO

▼▼▼ Clarion Hotel & Conference Center 🅗
(608) 356-6422. **$67-$145, 3 day notice.** 626 W Pine St. On US 12, 0.3 mi n of SR 33. Int corridors. **Pets:** Small. $5 daily fee/pet. Designated rooms, service with restrictions, supervision.
🅐🆂🅚 ⊠ 🅖🅜 🛏 🖵 🍴 ➰ ⊠

BEAVER DAM

▼ Super 8 🅗
(920) 887-8880. **$68-$90.** 711 Park Ave. US 151, exit 132 (SR 33), just w. Int corridors. **Pets:** Large. $10 one-time fee/pet. Designated rooms, service with restrictions, supervision.
🅐🆂🅚 ⊠ 🛏 🖵

BELMONT

▼▼ Baymont Inn & Suites 🅗
(608) 762-6900. **$68.** 103 W Moundview Ave. US 151, exit 26, just w. Int corridors. **Pets:** Other species. $25 one-time fee/room.
🅐🆂🅚 ⊠ 🛏 🖵 ➰ ⊠

BELOIT

🔷 ▼▼▼ Americas Best Value Inn 🅗
(608) 365-8680. **$69-$89.** 3002 Milwaukee Rd. I-90, exit 185A, just sw at I-43 and SR 81. Int corridors. **Pets:** Accepted.
🆂🅰🆅🅴 ⊠ 🅖🅜 🛏 🖵

🔷 ▼▼▼ Beloit Inn 🅗 🐾
(608) 362-5500. **$89-$189.** 500 Pleasant St. Downtown. Int corridors. **Pets:** Other species. $100 deposit/room, $10 daily fee/pet. Service with restrictions, supervision.
🆂🅰🆅🅴 ⊠ 🛏 🖵 🍴

🔷 ▼▼▼ Comfort Inn of Beloit 🅗
(608) 362-2666. **$69-$99, 3 day notice.** 2786 Milwaukee Rd. I-90, exit 185A, just w at I-43 and SR 81. Int corridors. **Pets:** Medium. $10 daily fee/pet. Service with restrictions, supervision.
🆂🅰🆅🅴 ⊠ 🛏 🖵 ➰

🔷 ▼▼▼ Econo Lodge 🅜
(608) 364-4000. **$56-$80.** 2956 Milwaukee Rd. I-90, exit 185A, 0.3 mi w. Ext/int corridors. **Pets:** $6 daily fee/pet. Service with restrictions, crate.
🆂🅰🆅🅴 ⊠ 🛏 🖵 🍴

▼▼▼ Fairfield Inn & Suites 🅗 🐾
(608) 365-2200. **$94-$114.** 2784 Milwaukee Rd. I-90, exit 185A, just sw, at I-43 and SR 81. Int corridors. **Pets:** Medium. $15 daily fee/pet. Service with restrictions, supervision.
⊠ 🛏 🖵 ➰

BERLIN

🔷 ▼▼▼ Best Western Countryside 🅜
(920) 361-4411. **$89-$125.** 227 Ripon Rd. On SR 49, at CR F. Int corridors. **Pets:** Very small, dogs only. $10 one-time fee/pet. Designated rooms, service with restrictions, supervision.
🆂🅰🆅🅴 ⊠ 🛏 🖵

BIRCHWOOD

▼▼ Cobblestone Bed & Breakfast 🅱🅱
(715) 354-3494. **$87-$135, 8 day notice.** 319 S Main St. 0.8 mi e of jct SR 48 and Main St; center. Int corridors. **Pets:** Accepted.
🅐🆂🅚 ⊠

BLACK RIVER FALLS

🔷 ▼▼▼ Best Western-Arrowhead Lodge & Suites 🅗
(715) 284-9471. **$69-$189.** 600 Oasis Rd. I-94, exit 116, jct SR 54. Int corridors. **Pets:** Medium, other species. $50 deposit/room. Designated rooms, service with restrictions, supervision.
🆂🅰🆅🅴 ⊠ 🛏 🖵 🍴 ➰ ⊠

▼▼ Days Inn 🅗
(715) 284-4333. **$89-$110.** 919 Hwy 54 E. I-94, exit 116, just w. Int corridors. **Pets:** Medium, other species. $15 daily fee/pet. Designated rooms, service with restrictions, supervision.
🅐🆂🅚 ⊠ 🛏 🖵 ➰ ⊠

CADOTT

▼▼ Countryside Motel 🅜 🐾
(715) 289-4000. **$58-$95.** 545 Lavorata Rd. SR 29, exit 91 (SR 27), just s. Int corridors. **Pets:** Small, dogs only. $5 one-time fee/pet. Designated rooms, service with restrictions, supervision.
⊠

CHETEK

🔷 ▼▼▼ Super 8 🅗
(715) 924-4888. **$59-$72.** 115 Second St. US 53, exit 126 (CR-I), 0.5 mi e. Int corridors. **Pets:** Accepted.
🆂🅰🆅🅴 ⊠ 🖵 ➰

CHILTON

🔷 ▼▼▼ Best Western Stanton Inn 🅗 🐾
(920) 849-3600. **$80-$120, 3 day notice.** 1101 E Chestnut St. Jct US 151 and SR 32/57. Int corridors. **Pets:** Small, dogs only. $50 deposit/room. Designated rooms, supervision.
🆂🅰🆅🅴 ⊠ 🛏 🖵 ➰

CHIPPEWA FALLS

▼▼ AmericInn Motel & Suites of Chippewa Falls **H**
(715) 723-5711. **$85-$146.** 11 W South Ave. 2 mi s on SR 124, access via CR J. Int corridors. **Pets:** Dogs only. $10 daily fee/room. Service with restrictions, supervision.

(A$K) (X) (🛏) (🖵) (🏊) (X)

▼▼ Avalon Hotel & Conference Center **H**
(715) 723-2281. **$80-$125.** 1009 W Park Ave. Jct SR 124 and CR J. Ext/int corridors. **Pets:** Small, dogs only. $10 daily fee/pet. Designated rooms, service with restrictions.

(A$K) (X) (🛏) (🖵) (🍴) (🏊) (X)

CLINTONVILLE

▼▼ Cobblestone Inn & Suites **H**
(715) 823-2000. **$80-$110.** 175 Waupaca St. Jct US 45 and CR C. Int corridors. **Pets:** Accepted.

(A$K) (X) (🛏) (🖵)

COLUMBUS

▼▼ Super 8-Columbus **H**
(920) 623-8800. **$70-$118.** 219 Industrial Dr. US 151, exit 118 (SR 16/60), just ne. Int corridors. **Pets:** Medium, dogs only. $50 deposit/room, $10 one-time fee/room. Designated rooms, service with restrictions, crate.

(A$K) (X) (🛏) (🖵) (🏊)

CRANDON

▼ Four Seasons Motel **M**
(715) 478-3377. **$55-$80.** 304 W Glen St. 0.5 mi w on US 8. Ext/int corridors. **Pets:** Accepted.

(X) (🛏) (🖵)

DE FOREST

▼▼▼ Comfort Inn & Suites **H**
(608) 846-9100. **$89-$139, 3 day notice.** 5025 County Hwy V. I-90/94, exit 126 (CR V), just w. Int corridors. **Pets:** Accepted.

(A$K) (X) (🛏) (🖵) (🏊) (X)

▼▼▼ Holiday Inn Express **H**
(608) 846-8686. **$99-$129, 7 day notice.** 7184 Morrisonville Rd. I-90/94, exit 126 (CR V), just e. Int corridors. **Pets:** Accepted.

(A$K) (X) (🛏) (🖵) (🏊)

DELAVAN

▲▲▲ ▼▼ Super 8-Delavan **H**
(262) 728-1700. **$59-$249.** 518 Borg Rd. I-43, exit 21 (SR 50), just w. Int corridors. **Pets:** Small. $10 daily fee/pet. Service with restrictions, supervision.

(SAVE) (X) (🛏) (🖵)

DE PERE

▼▼▼ Kress Inn **H**
(920) 403-5100. **$109-$499.** 300 Grant St. US 41, exit 163 (Main Ave), 1 mi e, then just s on 3rd St. Int corridors. **Pets:** Accepted.

(A$K) (X) (🛏) (🖵)

DODGEVILLE

▲▲▲ ▼▼ Best Western Quiet House & Suites **H**
(608) 935-7739. **$99-$120.** 1130 N Johns St. On US 18, just e of jct SR 23. Int corridors. **Pets:** Accepted.

(SAVE) (X) (🛏) (🖵) (🏊)

▲▲▲ ▼ Pine Ridge Motel **M**
(608) 935-3386. **$30-$79.** 405 CR YZ. 0.5 mi e of jct SR 23. Ext corridors. **Pets:** Very small, dogs only. $50 deposit/pet. Designated rooms, service with restrictions, supervision.

(SAVE) (X) (🛏) (🖵)

▲▲▲ ▼▼ Super 8 of Dodgeville **H**
(608) 935-3888. **$60-$156, 14 day notice.** 1308 Johns St. Just n of US 18. Int corridors. **Pets:** $15 daily fee/pet. Supervision.

(SAVE) (X) (🛏) (🖵)

DOOR COUNTY AREA

EGG HARBOR

▲▲▲ ▼▼ The Shallows **M**
(920) 868-3458. **$75-$410, 30 day notice.** 7353 Horseshoe Bay Rd, Hwy G. On CR G, 2.5 mi s. Ext corridors. **Pets:** Medium, dogs only. $20 daily fee/pet. Service with restrictions, supervision.

(SAVE) (X) (🛏) (🖵) (🏊) (X)

FISH CREEK

▼ Julie's Park Cafe & Motel **M**
(920) 868-2999. **Call for rates.** 4020 Hwy 42. On SR 42, 0.3 mi n. Ext corridors. **Pets:** Large, other species. $15 daily fee/pet. Crate.

(X) (🛏) (🍴)

GILLS ROCK

▼▼ Harbor House Inn **BB** 🐾
(920) 854-5196. **$79-$199, 21 day notice.** 12666 SR 42. Center. Ext/int corridors. **Pets:** Dogs only. $10 daily fee/pet. Supervision.

(X) (🛏) (X) (☎)

▼ Maple Grove Motel **M**
(920) 854-2587. **$80-$100, 15 day notice.** 809 SR 42. On SR 42, 0.3 mi e; 1.5 mi w of car ferry. Ext corridors. **Pets:** Accepted.

(X) (🛏) (🖵) (☎)

STURGEON BAY

▼▼ AmericInn Lodge & Suites of Sturgeon Bay **H**
(920) 743-5898. **$69-$179.** 622 S Ashland Ave. On SR 42/57, 0.5 mi s of jct CR C/S. Int corridors. **Pets:** Accepted.

(A$K) (X) (🛏) (🖵) (🏊)

▲▲▲ ▼▼ Best Western Maritime Inn **H**
(920) 743-7231. **$65-$150.** 1001 N 14th Ave. 1 mi n on Business Rt SR 42/57. Int corridors. **Pets:** Accepted.

(SAVE) (X) (🛏) (🖵) (🏊)

▼ Super 8 **M**
(920) 743-9211. **Call for rates.** 409 Green Bay Rd. 1 mi s on Business Rt SR 42/57. Int corridors. **Pets:** Accepted.

(X) (🛏) (🖵) (🏊)

END AREA

EAGLE RIVER

Best Western Derby Inn H
(715) 479-1600. **$76-$200, 3 day notice.** 1800 Hwy 45 N. On US 45, 1 mi n. Int corridors. **Pets:** Medium. $50 deposit/room. Designated rooms, service with restrictions, supervision.

Days Inn H
(715) 479-5151. **$79-$104.** 844 Railroad St N. 0.5 mi n on US 45. Int corridors. **Pets:** Medium, other species. $15 one-time fee/pet. Designated rooms, service with restrictions, supervision.

Super 8 M
(715) 477-0888. **$59-$155.** 200 W Pine St. On SR 70; center. Int corridors. **Pets:** Medium, dogs only. $10 daily fee/pet. Designated rooms, service with restrictions, supervision.

EAST TROY

Country Inn & Suites by Carlson H
(262) 642-2100. **$89-$250, 14 day notice.** 2921 O'Leary Ln. I-43, exit 36, at jct SR 120. Int corridors. **Pets:** Large, dogs only. $25 one-time fee/room. Designated rooms, service with restrictions, supervision.

EAU CLAIRE

AmericInn Motel & Suites of Eau Claire H
(715) 874-4900. **$75-$175.** 6200 Texaco Dr. I-94, exit 59, jct US 12. Int corridors. **Pets:** Accepted.

Best Western Trail Lodge Hotel & Suites H
(715) 838-9989. **$81-$99.** 3340 Mondovi Rd. I-94, exit 65, just n. Int corridors. **Pets:** Accepted.

Comfort Inn H
(715) 833-9798. **$64-$129.** 3117 Craig Rd. I-94, exit 65, 1.3 mi n on SR 37; just s of jct US 12. Int corridors. **Pets:** Dogs only. $15 daily fee/pet. Designated rooms, service with restrictions, supervision.

Days Inn H
(715) 834-3193. **$46-$66.** 2305 Craig Rd. I-94, exit 65, 1.3 mi n on SR 37; just w of jct US 12. Int corridors. **Pets:** Accepted.

Econo Lodge H
(715) 833-8818. **Call for rates.** 4608 Royal Dr. I-94, exit 68, just n on SR 93, just w on Golf Rd, then just s. Int corridors. **Pets:** Accepted.

Grandstay Residential Suites H
(715) 834-1700. **$100-$169.** 5310 Prill Rd. I-94, exit 70, 0.8 mi n on US 53. Int corridors. **Pets:** Small. $50 daily fee/pet. Designated rooms, service with restrictions, crate.

Holiday Inn Campus Area H
(715) 835-2211. **$99-$149.** 2703 Craig Rd. I-94, exit 65, 1.3 mi n on SR 37; just w of jct US 12. Int corridors. **Pets:** Other species. $15 one-time fee/pet. Designated rooms, service with restrictions, crate.

The Plaza Hotel & Suites H
(715) 834-3181. **$70-$199.** 1202 W Clairemont Ave. I-94, exit 65, 1.3 mi n on SR 37; just w of jct US 12. Int corridors. **Pets:** Other species. $15 one-time fee/room. Service with restrictions, crate.

Ramada Convention Center H
(715) 835-6121. **Call for rates.** 205 S Barstow St. Jct S Barstow and Gibson sts; downtown. Int corridors. **Pets:** Accepted.

Rodeway Inn & Suites M
(715) 835-3600. **Call for rates.** 1828 S Hastings Way. I-94, exit 70 (US 53), 2 mi n. Int corridors. **Pets:** Accepted.

Sleep Inn & Suites Conference Center H 🐾
(715) 874-2900. **$85-$160.** 5872 N 33rd Ave. I-29, exit 69 (Hwy T), just s. Int corridors. **Pets:** Medium. $25 deposit/room, $10 daily fee/room. Service with restrictions, supervision.

EDGERTON

Comfort Inn H
(608) 884-2118. **$72-$139.** 11102 N Goede Rd. I-90, exit 163, just e. Int corridors. **Pets:** Accepted.

ELKHORN

AmericInn Lodge & Suites of Elk Horn H
(262) 723-7799. **$79-$109.** 210 E Commerce Ct. I-43, exit 25, just s. Int corridors. **Pets:** Medium. $25 one-time fee/pet. Service with restrictions, supervision.

FITCHBURG

Candlewood Suites H
(608) 271-3400. **$90-$130.** 5421 Caddis Bend. US 12/18, exit 260 (Fish Hatchery/CR D), 1.5 mi s. Int corridors. **Pets:** Medium, other species. $25 one-time fee/room. Service with restrictions, supervision.

Quality Inn & Suites H
(608) 274-7200. **Call for rates.** 2969 Cahill Main. US 12/18, exit 260 (Fish Hatchery/CR D), 1.5 mi s at CR PD (McKee Rd). Int corridors. **Pets:** Accepted.

FOND DU LAC

Comfort Inn Fond du Lac H
(920) 921-4000. **Call for rates.** 77 Holiday Ln. Sw of jct US 41 and 151. Int corridors. **Pets:** $10 one-time fee/pet. Service with restrictions, crate.

Executive Lodge of Fond du Lac H
(920) 923-2020. **$53-$89.** 649 W Johnson St. On SR 23, 0.3 mi e of jct US 41. Int corridors. **Pets:** Other species. $5 daily fee/pet. Designated rooms, service with restrictions, supervision.

Holiday Inn H
(920) 923-1440. **$99-$239.** 625 W Rolling Meadows Dr. On US 151, just sw of jct US 41. Int corridors. **Pets:** Accepted.

Microtel Inn & Suites H
(920) 929-4000. **$59-$80.** 920 S Military Rd. Jct US 41 and 151. Int corridors. **Pets:** Accepted.

Ramada Plaza Hotel H
(920) 923-3000. **$69-$299.** 1 N Main St. Downtown. Int corridors. **Pets:** Small, dogs only. $20 daily fee/room. Designated rooms, service with restrictions, crate.

▼▼ Super 8-FOND du LAC 🅗
(920) 922-1088. **$55-$200, 3 day notice.** 391 N Pioneer Rd. US 41, exit SR 23, just n on east frontage road (CR VV). Int corridors. **Pets:** Medium, dogs only. $15 daily fee/pet. Designated rooms, service with restrictions, supervision.
A$K ✕ 🛏 🖳

GRANTSBURG

◆◆◇ ▼ Wood River Motel Ⓜ
(715) 463-2541. **$68-$115, 3 day notice.** 703 W SR 70. 1 mi w on SR 70. Ext corridors. **Pets:** $10 one-time fee/pet. Supervision.
SAVE ✕ 🛁 🛏

GREEN BAY

▼▼ AmericInn Lodge & Suites of Green Bay West 🅗
(920) 434-9790. **$85-$170, 30 day notice.** 2032 Velp Ave. US 41, exit 170, 0.3 mi w. Int corridors. **Pets:** Small. $10 daily fee/pet. Designated rooms, service with restrictions, supervision.
A$K ✕ 🛁 🛏 🖳 ⇌

▼▼ Baymont Inn-Green Bay 🅗
(920) 494-7887. **$74-$159.** 2840 S Oneida St. US 41, exit 164 (Oneida St), just e. Int corridors. **Pets:** Accepted.
A$K ✕ 🛏 🖳

◆◆◇ ▼ Bay Motel Ⓜ
(920) 494-3441. **$49-$79.** 1301 S Military Ave. US 41, exit 167 (Lombardi Ave), 0.4 mi e to Marlee, then 0.6 mi n. Ext corridors. **Pets:** Accepted.
SAVE ✕ 🛏 🖳 ⑪

◆◆◇ ▼▼▼ Best Western Midway Hotel 🅗 ❀
(920) 499-3161. **$79-$280, 3 day notice.** 780 Armed Forces Dr. US 41, exit 167 (Lombardi Ave), 1.4 mi e to Holmgren Way, then just s. Int corridors. **Pets:** Small, dogs only. $35 one-time fee/room. Designated rooms, service with restrictions, supervision.
SAVE ✕ 🛏 🖳 ⑪ ⇌ ✕

▼▼ Candlewood Suites 🅗
(920) 430-7040. **$79-$199.** 1125 E Mason St. US 41, exit 168 (Mason St), 4 mi e. Int corridors. **Pets:** Other species. $75 one-time fee/pet. Service with restrictions, crate.
A$K ✕ 🛁 🛏 🖳

▼▼ Comfort Inn by Choice Hotels 🅗
(920) 498-2060. **Call for rates.** 2841 Ramada Way. US 41, exit 164 (Oneida St), just e to Ramada Way, then just n. Int corridors. **Pets:** Accepted.
✕ 🛏 🖳 ⇌

▼▼ Country Inn & Suites By Carlson 🅗
(920) 336-6600. **$99-$140.** 2945 Allied St. US 41, exit 164 (Oneida St), just nw. Int corridors. **Pets:** Accepted.
A$K ✕ 🛏 🖳 ⇌ ✕

◆◆◇ ▼▼▼ Days Inn-Lambeau Field 🅗
(920) 498-8088. **$59-$94.** 1978 Holmgren Way. US 41, exit 167 (Lombardi Ave), 1.4 mi e, then just s. Int corridors. **Pets:** Accepted.
SAVE ✕ 🛏 🖳 ⇌

▼▼ Holiday Inn City Centre 🅗
(920) 437-5900. **$89-$129.** 200 Main St. Downtown. Int corridors. **Pets:** Accepted.
✕ 🛏 🖳 ⑪ ⇌ ✕

▼▼ Quality Inn & Suites 🅗
(920) 437-8771. **$75-$290.** 321 S Washington St. On east side of Fox River, just s of Walnut St (SR 29); downtown. Int corridors. **Pets:** Accepted.
A$K ✕ 🛏 🖳 ⇌ ✕

▼▼ Ramada Plaza Hotel 🅗
(920) 499-0631. **$89-$309.** 2750 Ramada Way. US 41, exit 164 (Oneida St), just e. Int corridors. **Pets:** Large. $20 daily fee/pet. Designated rooms, service with restrictions, crate.
A$K ✕ 🛁 🛏 🖳 ⑪ ⇌ ✕

▼▼ Residence Inn by Marriott 🅗
(920) 435-2222. **$134-$164.** 335 W St Joseph St. SR 172, exit Riverside Dr, 1.1 mi n on SR 57, then just e. Ext corridors. **Pets:** Accepted.
✕ 🛏 🖳 ⇌ ✕

▼▼ Super 8 🅗
(920) 494-2042. **$75-$92.** 2868 S Oneida St. US 41, exit 164 (Oneida St), just e. Int corridors. **Pets:** $15 one-time fee/pet. Designated rooms, no service, supervision.
A$K ✕ 🛏 🖳 ✕

◆◆◇ ▼▼ Travelodge Green Bay/Lambeau 🅗
(920) 499-3599. **$52-$72.** 2870 Ramada Way. US 41, exit 164 (Oneida St), just e. Int corridors. **Pets:** Small. Designated rooms, service with restrictions, supervision.
SAVE ✕ 🛏 🖳

HAYWARD

▼▼ AmericInn of Hayward 🅗
(715) 634-2700. **$85-$195.** 15601 US Hwy 63. Just n of jct SR 77. Int corridors. **Pets:** Medium. $10 daily fee/pet. Designated rooms, service with restrictions, supervision.
A$K ✕ 🛏 🖳 ⇌

◆◆◇ ▼▼▼ Comfort Suites 🅗
(715) 634-0700. **$89-$189.** 15586 CR B. 0.5 mi s of jct SR 27. Int corridors. **Pets:** Accepted.
SAVE ✕ 🛁 🛏 🖳 ⇌ ✕

◆◆◇ ▼ Edelweiss Motel Ⓜ ❀
(715) 634-4679. **$55-$105.** Hwy 27 S & Park Rd. On SR 27, 1.8 mi s of jct US 63. Ext corridors. **Pets:** Other species. Designated rooms, supervision.
SAVE ✕ 🛏

▼ Northern Pine Inn 🅗
(715) 634-4959. **$59-$109.** 9966 N Hwy 27 S. On SR 27 S, 1.7 mi s of jct US 63. Ext/int corridors. **Pets:** Accepted.
A$K ✕ 🛏 🖳 ⇌ ✕

◆◆◇ ▼▼▼ Ramada-Hayward 🅗
(715) 634-4100. **$120-$145, 3 day notice.** 10290 Hwy 27 S. On SR 27 S, 0.7 mi s of jct US 63. Int corridors. **Pets:** Medium, dogs only. $15 one-time fee/room. Designated rooms, service with restrictions, supervision.
SAVE ✕ 🛏 🖳 ⑪ ⇌ ✕

▼▼ Super 8 🅗
(715) 634-2646. **$65-$120.** 10444 N SR 27. On SR 27, 0.3 mi s of jct US 63. Ext/int corridors. **Pets:** Accepted.
A$K ✕ 🛏 🖳 ⇌

HILLSBORO

◆◆◇ ▼▼ Hotel Hillsboro 🅗
(608) 489-3000. **$70-$110.** 1235 Water Ave (Hwy 33). SR 33 and 80/82, just w. Int corridors. **Pets:** $10 one-time fee/pet. Designated rooms, service with restrictions, supervision.
SAVE ✕ 🛏 🖳 ✕

HUDSON

▼▼ Comfort Inn 🅗
(715) 386-6355. **Call for rates.** 811 Dominion Dr. I-94, exit 2 (CR F), 1 mi w on south frontage road (Crestview Dr). Int corridors. **Pets:** Accepted.
✕ 🛏 🖳 ⇌

Super 8 of Hudson H
(715) 386-8800. **$70-$170.** 808 Dominion Dr. I-94, exit 2 (CR F), 1 mi w on south frontage road (Crestview Dr). Int corridors. **Pets:** Medium. $15 one-time fee/pet. Designated rooms, service with restrictions, supervision.

HURLEY

Days Inn of Hurley H
(715) 561-3500. **$84-$110.** 13355 N US Hwy 51. Jct US 2 and 51, 0.4 mi s on US 51. Int corridors. **Pets:** Large, other species. $15 daily fee/pet. Designated rooms, service with restrictions, supervision.

JANESVILLE

Best Western Janesville H
(608) 756-4511. **$75-$189, 3 day notice.** 3900 Milton Ave. I-90, exit 171A (SR 26), just e. Int corridors. **Pets:** Medium. $10 daily fee/pet. Designated rooms, service with restrictions, supervision.

Microtel Inn H ✿
(608) 752-3121. **$56-$80.** 3121 Wellington Pl. I-90, exit 171C (US 14), just se. Int corridors. **Pets:** Other species. $20 daily fee/pet. Service with restrictions, supervision.

JEFFERSON

Rodeway Inn M
(920) 674-4404. **Call for rates.** 1456 S Ryan Ave. On SR 26, 1.2 mi s of jct US 18. Int corridors. **Pets:** Accepted.

JOHNSON CREEK

Days Inn-Johnson Creek H ✿
(920) 699-8000. **Call for rates.** W4545 Linmar Ln. I-94, exit 267 (SR 26), just ne. Int corridors. **Pets:** Dogs only. $100 deposit/room, $10 daily fee/pet. Designated rooms, service with restrictions, supervision.

KENOSHA

Best Western Harborside Inn & Kenosha Convention Center H
(262) 658-3281. **$100-$200.** 5125 6th Ave. Just ne of jct SR 32 and 158; downtown. Int corridors. **Pets:** Small, other species. $25 one-time fee/pet. Designated rooms, service with restrictions, supervision.

Country Inn & Suites By Carlson H
(262) 857-3680. **$99-$140.** 7011 122nd Ave. I-94, exit 344 (SR 50), just nw. Int corridors. **Pets:** Small. $15 daily fee/pet. Designated rooms, service with restrictions, supervision.

LA CROSSE

Americas Best Value Inn H
(608) 781-3070. **$48-$110.** 2622 Rose St. I-90, exit 3, just s. Int corridors. **Pets:** Accepted.

Best Western-Midway Hotel Riverfront Resort H ✿
(608) 781-7000. **$74-$89, 30 day notice.** 1835 Rose St. I-90, exit 3, 1 mi s on US 53. Int corridors. **Pets:** Small, dogs only. $50 deposit/room, $15 one-time fee/pet. Designated rooms, service with restrictions, supervision.

Days Hotel & Conference Center H
(608) 783-1000. **$54-$99.** 101 Sky Harbour Dr. I-90, exit 2, just sw; on French Island. Int corridors. **Pets:** Accepted.

Econo Lodge H
(608) 781-0200. **$50-$130.** 1906 Rose St. I-90, exit 3, 0.9 mi s on US 53. Int corridors. **Pets:** Small, other species. $10 daily fee/pet. Designated rooms, service with restrictions, crate.

Grandstay Residential Suites of La Crosse H
(608) 796-1615. **$85-$179.** 525 Front St N. I-90, exit 3; downtown. Int corridors. **Pets:** Small. Designated rooms, service with restrictions, supervision.

Holiday Inn Hotel & Suites H
(608) 784-4444. **Call for rates.** 200 Pearl St. Downtown. Int corridors. **Pets:** Accepted.

Howard Johnson Hotel La Crosse H
(608) 781-0400. **Call for rates.** 2150 Rose St. I-90, exit 3, 0.8 mi s on US 53. Int corridors. **Pets:** Medium, other species. Designated rooms, service with restrictions, supervision.

Settle Inn H
(608) 781-5100. **$60-$100.** 2110 Rose St. I-90, exit 3, 0.9 mi s on US 53. Int corridors. **Pets:** Small, dogs only. $15 daily fee/pet. Designated rooms, service with restrictions, supervision.

Super 8-La Crosse H
(608) 781-8880. **Call for rates.** 1625 Rose St. I-90, exit 3, 1.2 mi s on US 53. Int corridors. **Pets:** Other species. $25 one-time fee/room. Designated rooms, service with restrictions.

LADYSMITH

AmericInn Motel & Suites of Ladysmith H
(715) 532-6650. **$72-$144, 3 day notice.** 800 W College Ave. On SR 27, 0.5 mi s of US 8. Int corridors. **Pets:** Other species. $15 daily fee/room. Designated rooms, service with restrictions, crate.

LAKE GENEVA

Budget Host Diplomat Motel M
(262) 248-1809. **$58-$106, 7 day notice.** 1060 Wells St. 1 mi s of SR 50. Ext corridors. **Pets:** Small, dogs only. Designated rooms, service with restrictions, supervision.

LAKE MILLS

Americas Best Value Inn H
(920) 648-3800. **Call for rates.** W 7614 Oasis Ln. I-94, exit 259 (SR 89), just n. Int corridors. **Pets:** Accepted.

LAND O'LAKES

Sunrise Lodge CA ✿
(715) 547-3684. **$85-$210, 21 day notice.** 5894 W Shore Dr. 2 mi s on US 45, 2.8 mi e on CR E, then 1 mi n. Ext corridors. **Pets:** Other species.

LODI

Best Western Countryside Inn 🏨 ✿
(608) 592-1450. **$80-$100.** W 9250 Prospect Dr. I-90/94, exit 119, just w. Int corridors. **Pets:** Medium. $10 daily fee/pet. Designated rooms, service with restrictions, supervision.
SAVE ✕ 🔥M 🖥 💻 ⌗ ✕

Lodi Valley Suites 🏨
(608) 592-7331. **$65-$85.** 1440 N Hwy 113. 1.5 mi n of jct SR 60. Int corridors. **Pets:** Accepted.
ASK ✕ 🖥 ⌗

LUCK

Luck Country Inn 🏨
(715) 472-2000. **$65-$149.** 10 Robertson Rd. Jct SR 35 and 48. Int corridors. **Pets:** Small. $5 daily fee/pet. Designated rooms, service with restrictions, supervision.
SAVE ✕ 🖥 💻 🍴 ⌗

MADISON

Baymont Inn & Suites 🏨
(608) 241-3861. **$53-$73.** 4202 E Towne Blvd. I-90/94, exit 135A (US 151), 0.5 mi w. Int corridors. **Pets:** Small, other species. Designated rooms, service with restrictions, crate.
SAVE ✕ 🖥 💻

Best Western East Towne Suites 🏨
(608) 244-2020. **$80-$190.** 4801 Annamark Dr. I-90/94, exit 135A southbound, exit 135C northbound, just sw on US 151. Int corridors. **Pets:** $25 one-time fee/pet. Service with restrictions, crate.
SAVE ✕ 🖥 💻

Best Western West Towne Suites 🏨 ✿
(608) 833-4200. **$85-$180.** 650 Grand Canyon Dr. US 12 and 14, exit 255 (Gammon Rd), just e on Odana Rd, then just sw. Int corridors. **Pets:** Medium. $15 daily fee/pet. Designated rooms, service with restrictions, supervision.
SAVE ✕ 🖥 💻

Clarion Suites Madison-Central 🏨 ✿
(608) 284-1234. **$99-$199.** 2110 Rimrock Rd. US 12 and 18, exit 262 (Rimrock Rd), just nw. Int corridors. **Pets:** $25 daily fee/pet. Designated rooms, service with restrictions, supervision.
SAVE ✕ 🖥 💻 ⌗

Comfort Suites-Madison 🏨
(608) 836-3033. **Call for rates.** 1253 John Q Hammons Dr. US 12 and 14, exit 252 (Greenway Blvd), just sw. Int corridors. **Pets:** Accepted.
✕ 🖥 💻 ⌗ ✕

Crowne Plaza Hotel Madison-East Towne 🏨 ✿
(608) 244-4703. **$139-$209.** 4402 E Washington Ave. I-90/94, exit 135A (US 151), 0.4 mi w. Int corridors. **Pets:** Other species. $25 one-time fee/room. Designated rooms, service with restrictions.
SAVE ✕ 🖥 💻 🍴 ⌗ ✕

Days Inn-Madison 🏨
(608) 223-1800. **$75-$165.** 4402 E Broadway Service Rd. US 12 and 18, exit 266 (US 51), just ne. Int corridors. **Pets:** Dogs only. $50 deposit/pet, $10 daily fee/pet. Service with restrictions, supervision.
SAVE ✕ 🖥 💻 ⌗

Econo Lodge of Madison 🏨
(608) 241-4171. **$65-$99, 30 day notice.** 4726 E Washington Ave. I-90/94, exit 135A (US 151), just w. Int corridors. **Pets:** Small. $10 daily fee/pet. Supervision.
SAVE ✕ 🖥 💻

ExtendedStay Deluxe 🏨
(608) 833-2121. **$80-$110.** 45 Junction Ct. SR 12, exit 253 (Old Sauk Rd), just w. Int corridors. **Pets:** Other species. $25 daily fee/pet. Service with restrictions, crate.
ASK ✕ 🖥 💻 ⌗

GrandStay Residential Suites 🏨
(608) 241-2500. **$99-$169.** 5317 High Crossing Blvd. I-90/94, exit 135C (US 151), 0.5 mi e. Int corridors. **Pets:** Accepted.
ASK ✕ 🔥M 🖥 💻 ⌗ ✕

Holiday Inn Express-Madison 🏨
(608) 255-7400. **Call for rates.** 722 John Nolen Dr. US 12 and 18, exit 263 (John Nolen Dr), just ne. Int corridors. **Pets:** Accepted.
✕ 🖥 💻 ⌗

Howard Johnson Plaza 🏨
(608) 244-2481. **$89-$149.** 3841 E Washington Ave. I-90/94, exit 135A (US 151), 1 mi w. Int corridors. **Pets:** $15 one-time fee/pet. Service with restrictions, crate.
ASK ✕ 🖥 💻 🍴 ⌗ ✕

La Quinta Inn & Suites 🏨 ✿
(608) 245-0123. **$69-$149.** 5217 E Terrace Dr. US 151, exit 98B (American Pkwy), just sw. Int corridors. **Pets:** Medium, other species. Service with restrictions, supervision.
ASK ✕ 🔥M 🖥 💻 ⌗

Microtel Inn & Suites 🏨 ✿
(608) 242-9000. **$59-$89.** 2139 E Springs Dr. I-90/94, exit 135A (US 151), just s, then 0.5 mi e. Int corridors. **Pets:** Small. $10 daily fee/pet. Designated rooms, service with restrictions, supervision.
SAVE ✕ 🖥 💻

Red Roof Inn-Madison #7052 Ⓜ ✿
(608) 241-1787. **$52-$90.** 4830 Hayes Rd. I-90/94, exit 135A (US 151), just sw. Ext corridors. **Pets:** Service with restrictions, supervision.
ASK ✕ 🔥M 🖥

Residence Inn by Marriott 🏨
(608) 244-5047. **$140-$160.** 4862 Hayes Rd. I-90/94, exit 135A (US 151), just sw to Hayes Rd, then just ne. Int corridors. **Pets:** Accepted.
✕ 🖥 💻 ⌗ ✕

Select Inn 🏨
(608) 249-1815. **$70-$105.** 4845 Hayes Rd. I-90/94, exit 135A (US 151), just sw. Int corridors. **Pets:** $25 deposit/pet, $10 daily fee/pet. Designated rooms, service with restrictions, supervision.
SAVE ✕ 🖥 💻 ✕

Sheraton Madison Hotel 🏨 ✿
(608) 251-2300. **$129-$269.** 706 John Nolen Dr. US 12/18, exit 263 (John Nolen Dr), just n. Int corridors. **Pets:** Large. Service with restrictions.
SAVE ✕ 🖥 💻 🍴 ⌗ ✕

Staybridge Suites 🏨
(608) 241-2300. **Call for rates.** 3301 City View Dr. I-90/94, exit 135C (US 151), just e on High Crossing Blvd. Int corridors. **Pets:** Accepted.
✕ 🖥 💻 ⌗ ✕

Super 8-Madison East 🏨
(608) 249-5300. **$54-$149, 7 day notice.** 4765 Hayes Rd. I-90/94, exit 135A (US 151), just sw to Hayes Rd, then 0.5 mi ne. Ext/int corridors. **Pets:** Accepted.
SAVE ✕ 🖥 💻 ⌗

Super 8-Madison 🏨
(608) 258-8882. **$60-$140.** 1602 W Beltline Hwy. US 12 and 18, exit 260B (CR D), just w on North Frontage Road. Int corridors. **Pets:** Medium, other species. $10 daily fee/room. Designated rooms, service with restrictions, supervision.
ASK ✕ 🖥 💻 ⌗

MANITOWOC

Best Western Lakefront Hotel H
(920) 682-7000. **$129-$199, 3 day notice.** 101 Maritime Dr. I-43, exit 152, 4.2 mi e on SR 42 N, then 1 mi s. Int corridors. **Pets:** Accepted.

Comfort Inn by Choice Hotels H
(920) 683-0220. **$70-$119.** 2200 S 44th St. I-43, exit 149, just e. Int corridors. **Pets:** Accepted.

Holiday Inn Manitowoc H
(920) 682-6000. **$105-$189.** 4601 Calumet Ave. I-43, exit 149, just e. Int corridors. **Pets:** Other species. $150 deposit/room. Service with restrictions, crate.

MARSHFIELD

Baymont Inn and Suites-Marshfield H
(715) 384-5240. **$69-$79.** 2107 N Central Ave. On SR 97; 1.6 mi n of SR 13. Int corridors. **Pets:** Other species. $10 daily fee/pet. Designated rooms, supervision.

Comfort Inn H
(715) 387-8691. **$59-$99.** 114 E Upham St. On SR 97; 0.8 mi n of jct SR 13. Int corridors. **Pets:** Accepted.

Holiday Inn & Conference Center H
(715) 486-1500. **$104-$134.** 750 S Central Ave. Jct SR 13 and 97, 0.5 mi s on Business Rt 13. Int corridors. **Pets:** Large, dogs only. $50 one-time fee/pet. Designated rooms, service with restrictions, supervision.

MAUSTON

Best Western Park Oasis Inn H
(608) 847-6255. **$80-$155.** W5641 Hwy 82 E. I-90/94, exit 69, just se. Int corridors. **Pets:** Medium. $50 deposit/room, $5 daily fee/pet. Service with restrictions, supervision.

Country Inn By Carlson H
(608) 847-5959. **$75-$91.** 1001 SR 82. I-90/94, exit 69, just ne. Int corridors. **Pets:** Accepted.

Super 8 M ❀
(608) 847-2300. **$63-$170.** 1001A Hwy 82 E. I-90/94, exit 69, just ne. Int corridors. **Pets:** Other species. $10 daily fee/pet. Service with restrictions, supervision.

MEDFORD

AmericInn Motel of Medford H
(715) 748-2330. **$74-$89.** 435 S 8th St. On SR 13, 0.5 mi s of jct SR 64. Int corridors. **Pets:** Accepted.

Woodlands Inn & Suites M
(715) 748-3995. **$75-$124.** 854 N 8th St. On SR 13, 0.6 mi n of jct SR 64. Int corridors. **Pets:** Accepted.

MENOMONIE

Comfort Inn H
(715) 233-1500. **$59-$200.** 1721 Plaza Dr NE. I-94, exit 45 (CR B), just sw. Int corridors. **Pets:** Medium. $10 one-time fee/room. Service with restrictions, supervision.

Menomonie Motel 6 #4109 H
(715) 235-6901. **$44-$63.** 2100 Stout St. I-94, exit 41 (SR 25), just se. Int corridors. **Pets:** Medium. Service with restrictions, supervision.

Super 8-Menomonie H
(715) 235-8889. **$60-$100.** 1622 N Broadway. I-94, exit 41 (SR 25), just s. Int corridors. **Pets:** Small. $10 daily fee/pet. Designated rooms, no service, crate.

MERRILL

AmericInn Lodge & Suites of Merrill H
(715) 536-7979. **$89-$149.** 3300 E Main St. US 51, exit 208, 0.5 mi w on SR 64. Int corridors. **Pets:** Large. $5 daily fee/pet. Service with restrictions, supervision.

Super 8 Motel H
(715) 536-6880. **Call for rates.** 3209 E Main St. US 51, exit 208, 0.5 mi w on SR 64. Int corridors. **Pets:** Accepted.

MIDDLETON

Country Inn & Suites H
(608) 831-6970. **$114-$169.** 2212 Deming Way. US 12/14, exit 251A, 0.3 mi w on University ave, then just n. Int corridors. **Pets:** Medium, dogs only. $35 daily fee/pet. Designated rooms, service with restrictions, supervision.

Marriott Madison West H ❀
(608) 831-2000. **$161-$197.** 1313 John Q Hammons Dr. US 12/14, exit 252 (Greenway Blvd), just w. Int corridors. **Pets:** Medium, other species. $50 one-time fee/room. Service with restrictions, supervision.

Residence Inn by Marriott-Madison West/Middleton H ❀
(608) 662-1100. **$152-$186.** 8400 Market St. US 12/14 (Beltline), exit 252 (Greenway Blvd), just w, then just n; in Greenway Station. Int corridors. **Pets:** Other species. $75 one-time fee/room. Service with restrictions.

Staybridge Suites by Holiday Inn H
(608) 664-5888. **$145-$250.** 7790 Elmwood Ave. US 12/14, exit 251 (University Ave), just nw. Int corridors. **Pets:** Medium, other species. $150 one-time fee/room.

MILWAUKEE METROPOLITAN AREA

BROOKFIELD

▽▽▽ Best Western Midway Hotel H
(262) 786-9540. **$120-$170.** 1005 S Moorland Rd. I-94, exit 301A (Moorland Rd), just s. Int corridors. **Pets:** Accepted.
SAVE ✕ ⊟ ⬛ ⊞ ⇔ ✕

▽▽▽ Country Inn & Suites Milwaukee West H
(262) 782-1400. **$109-$249.** 1250 S Moorland Rd. I-94, exit 301A (Moorland Rd), just se. Int corridors. **Pets:** Accepted.
SAVE ✕ ⊟ ⬛ ⊞ ⇔ ✕

▽▽ Homestead Studio Suites
Hotel-Milwaukee/Brookfield H
(262) 782-9300. **$80-$115.** 325 N Brookfield Rd. I-94, exit 297, 1.1 mi e on US 18, then just e. Int corridors. **Pets:** Other species. $25 daily fee/pet. Service with restrictions, crate.
ASK ✕ Ⓜ ⊟ ⬛

▽▽ La Quinta Inn H ❀
(262) 782-9100. **$49-$119.** 20391 W Bluemound Rd. I-94, exit 297, just e on US 18. Int corridors. **Pets:** Medium, other species. Service with restrictions, supervision.
ASK ✕ ⊟ ⬛

▽▽▽ Sheraton Milwaukee Brookfield H ❀
(262) 786-1100. **$129-$349, 3 day notice.** 375 S Moorland Rd. I-94, exit 301B (Moorland Rd), just n. Int corridors. **Pets:** Medium, dogs only. Designated rooms, service with restrictions, supervision.
SAVE ✕ Ⓜ ⊟ ⬛ ⊞ ⇔

▽▽ TownePlace Suites by Marriott H
(262) 784-8450. **$155-$160.** 600 N Calhoun Rd. I-94, exit 297 eastbound, 2.1 mi e on US 18; exit 301B (Moorland Rd) westbound, 1.5 mi n, then 0.4 mi w on US 18. Int corridors. **Pets:** Accepted.
✕ ⊟ ⬛ ⇔

BROWN DEER

▽▽▽ Candlewood Suites H
(414) 355-3939. **$117-$169.** 4483 W Schroeder Dr. Just nw of SR 100 and 57. Int corridors. **Pets:** Medium. $25 daily fee/pet. Service with restrictions, crate.
✕ Ⓜ ⊟ ⬛

DELAFIELD

▽▽ La Quinta Inn & Suites Milwaukee-Delafield H ❀
(262) 646-8500. **$69-$199.** 2801 Hillside Dr. I-94, exit 287, just s on SR 83, then just e. Int corridors. **Pets:** Medium, other species. Service with restrictions, supervision.
ASK ✕ Ⓜ ⊟ ⬛ ⇔

GERMANTOWN

▽▽ Holiday Inn Express Milwaukee NW-Germantown H
(262) 255-1100. **Call for rates.** W 177 N9675 Riversbend Ln. US 41 and 45, exit CR Q (County Line Rd), then just w. Int corridors. **Pets:** Accepted.
✕ Ⓜ ⊟ ⬛ ⇔ ✕

▽▽ Super 8-Germantown/Milwaukee H
(262) 255-0880. **$70-$159.** N96 W17490 County Line Rd. US 41 and 45, exit CR Q (County Line Rd), then just w. Int corridors. **Pets:** $10 daily fee/pet. Service with restrictions, supervision.
SAVE ✕ ⊟ ⬛ ⇔ ✕

GLENDALE

▽▽▽ La Quinta Inn & Suites-Bayshore Town
Center H ❀
(414) 962-6767. **$79-$179.** 5423 N Port Washington Rd. I-43, exit 78A (Silver Spring Dr), just se. Int corridors. **Pets:** Medium, other species. Service with restrictions, supervision.
ASK ✕ ⊟ ⬛ ⇔ ✕

▽▽▽ Residence Inn by Marriott H
(414) 352-0070. **$149-$179.** 7275 N Port Washington Rd. I-43, exit 80 (Good Hope Rd), just e. Ext corridors. **Pets:** Accepted.
✕ ⊟ ⬛ ⇔ ✕

▽▽▽ Super 8 Hotel of Milwaukee North H
(414) 961-7272. **Call for rates.** 5485 N Port Washington Rd. I-43, exit 78A (Silver Spring Dr), just se. Int corridors. **Pets:** Accepted.
SAVE ✕ ⬛

GRAFTON

▽▽ Baymont Inn & Suites Milwaukee-Grafton H
(262) 387-1180. **$76-$130.** 1415 Port Washington Rd. I-43, exit 92 (SR 60), just w, then just s. Int corridors. **Pets:** Medium. $10 one-time fee/pet. Designated rooms, service with restrictions, supervision.
ASK ✕ ⊟ ⬛ ⇔

JACKSON

▽▽ Comfort Inn & Suites of Jackson H
(262) 677-1133. **$80-$130.** W227 N16890 Tillie Lake Ct. Nw of jct US 45 and SR 60. Int corridors. **Pets:** Medium. $30 one-time fee/pet. Designated rooms, service with restrictions, crate.
ASK ✕ ⊟ ⬛ ⇔ ✕

MEQUON

▽▽▽ Best Western Quiet House & Suites H ❀
(262) 241-3677. **$85-$225.** 10330 N Port Washington Rd. I-43, exit 85 (Mequon Rd), just w on SR 167, then 1 mi s. Int corridors. **Pets:** $15 daily fee/pet. Designated rooms, service with restrictions, supervision.
SAVE ✕ Ⓜ ⊟ ⬛ ⇔

▽▽ The Chalet Motel of Mequon M ❀
(262) 241-4510. **$62-$159.** 10401 N Port Washington Rd. I-43, exit 85 (Mequon Rd), just w on SR 167, then 1 mi s. Ext corridors. **Pets:** Other species. $10 daily fee/room. Designated rooms, service with restrictions, crate.
ASK ✕ ⊟ ⬛ ⊞

MILWAUKEE

▽▽▽ Best Western Inn Towne Hotel H
(414) 224-8400. **$70-$140, 3 day notice.** 710 N Old World 3rd St. Corner of Wisconsin Ave and N Old World 3rd St. Int corridors. **Pets:** Accepted.
SAVE ✕ ⊟ ⬛ ⊞

▽▽▽ Comfort Suites at Park Place H
(414) 979-0250. **$100-$500.** 10831 W Park Pl. I-41/45, exit 47B (Good Hope Rd), then right. Int corridors. **Pets:** Medium, dogs only. $15 daily fee/pet. Designated rooms, service with restrictions, supervision.
ASK ✕ Ⓜ ⊟ ⬛ ⇔ ✕

▽▽▽ Country Inn & Suites By Carlson H
(414) 762-6018. **$99-$140.** 6200 S 13th St. I-94, exit 319, just e on College Ave (CR ZZ). Int corridors. **Pets:** Small, dogs only. $15 daily fee/pet. Designated rooms, service with restrictions, supervision.
ASK ✕ ⊟ ⬛ ⇔ ✕

▼▼▼▼ Holiday Inn Express Hotel & Suites Milwaukee Airport ⊞
(414) 563-4000. **Call for rates.** 1400 W Zellman Ct. I-94, exit 319, 0.4 mi e on College Ave (CR 22) to S 13th St, then cont s. Int corridors. **Pets:** Accepted.
⊠ &M ⊞ ⊑ ⤳ ⊠

ⓐ ▼▼▼▼ Holiday Inn Hotel and Suites ⊞ ❖
(414) 482-4444. **Call for rates.** 545 W Layton Ave. I-94, exit 317, 1.3 mi e. Int corridors. **Pets:** $25 one-time fee/pet. Service with restrictions, supervision.
(SAVE) ⊠ ⊞ ⊑ ⑪ ⤳ ⊠

ⓐ ▼▼▼▼ Hotel Metro-Milwaukee ⊞
(414) 272-1937. **$219-$359.** 411 E Mason St. Corner of Mason and Milwaukee sts. Int corridors. **Pets:** Other species. $25 one-time fee/pet. Designated rooms, service with restrictions, crate.
(SAVE) ⊠ &M ⊑ ⑪ ⊠

ⓐ ▼▼▼▼ ▼▼▼▼ The Pfister Hotel ⊞
(414) 273-8222. **$145-$2000, 3 day notice.** 424 E Wisconsin Ave. Corner of E Wisconsin Ave and Jefferson St. Int corridors. **Pets:** Small. $200 one-time fee/room. Designated rooms, service with restrictions, crate.
(SAVE) ⊠ &M ⊞ ⊑ ⑪ ⤳ ⊠

NEW BERLIN

▼▼▼▼ La Quinta Inn & Suites ⊞ ❖
(262) 717-0900. **$49-$149.** 15300 W Rock Ridge Rd. I-43, exit 57 (Moorland Rd), just se. Int corridors. **Pets:** Medium, other species. Service with restrictions, supervision.
(ASK) ⊠ &M ⊞ ⊑ ⤳

OAK CREEK

▼▼▼▼ Comfort Suites Milwaukee Airport ⊞
(414) 570-1111. **$99-$159.** 6362 S 13th St. I-94, exit 319 (College Ave), just e on CR 22, then just s. Int corridors. **Pets:** Medium. $10 daily fee/pet. Service with restrictions, crate.
(ASK) ⊠ &M ⊞ ⊑ ⤳ ⊠

ⓐ ▼▼ Days Inn of Milwaukee South ⊞
(414) 764-1776. **$56-$79.** 1201 W College Ave. I-94, exit 319 (College Ave), just e. Int corridors. **Pets:** Medium, other species. $75 deposit/room. Service with restrictions.
(SAVE) ⊠ ⊞ ⊑

ⓐ ▼▼ La Quinta Inn & Suites Milwaukee-Airport ⊞ ❖
(414) 762-2266. **$59-$109.** 7141 S 13th St. I-94, exit 320 (Rawson Ave), just se. Int corridors. **Pets:** Medium, other species. Service with restrictions, supervision.
(ASK) ⊠ ⊞ ⊑

ⓐ ▼▼▼▼ MainStay Suites Oak Creek ⊞
(414) 571-8800. **$70-$190.** 1001 W College Ave. I-94, exit 319 (College Ave), just e. Int corridors. **Pets:** Medium. $75 one-time fee/room. Service with restrictions, crate.
(SAVE) ⊠ ⊞ ⊑

▼▼ Red Roof Inn-Milwaukee #7031 Ⓜ
(414) 764-3500. **$67-$82.** 6360 S 13th St. I-94, exit 319 (College Ave), just e. Ext corridors. **Pets:** Service with restrictions, supervision.
(ASK) ⊠ ⊞

OCONOMOWOC

ⓐ ▼▼▼▼ Olympia Resort, Spa & Conference Center ⊞ ❖
(262) 369-4999. **$149.** 1350 Royale Mile Rd. I-94, exit 282 (SR 67), 1 mi n. Int corridors. **Pets:** Other species. $10 daily fee/room. Service with restrictions, supervision.
(SAVE) ⊠ ⊞ ⊑ ⑪ ⤳ ⊠

PORT WASHINGTON

ⓐ ▼▼▼▼ Holiday Inn Harborview ⊞
(262) 284-9461. **$79-$229.** 135 E Grand Ave. On SR 33; waterfront of Lake Michigan; downtown. Int corridors. **Pets:** Accepted.
(SAVE) ⊠ &M ⊞ ⊑ ⑪ ⤳ ⊠

SAUKVILLE

ⓐ ▼▼▼ Saukville Super 8 ⊞
(262) 284-9399. **$60-$125.** 180 Foster Rd. I-43, exit 96, just s. Int corridors. **Pets:** Other species. $15 one-time fee/pet. Supervision.
(SAVE) ⊠ ⊞ ⊑ ⊠

WAUKESHA

ⓐ ▼▼▼ Best Western Waukesha Grand ⊞
(262) 524-9300. **$78-$195.** 2840 N Grandview Blvd. I-94, exit 293, just s on CR T. Int corridors. **Pets:** $20 one-time fee/pet. Service with restrictions, supervision.
(SAVE) ⊠ &M ⊞ ⊑ ⤳

▼▼▼ Extended StayAmerica-Milwaukee-Waukesha ⊞
(262) 798-0217. **$65-$95.** 2520 Plaza Ct. I-94, exit 297, just e on SR 18, then just s. Int corridors. **Pets:** Other species. $25 daily fee/pet. Service with restrictions, crate.
(ASK) ⊠ ⊞ ⊑

ⓐ ▼▼▼ Super 8-Waukesha ⊞
(262) 786-6015. **$50-$170.** 2510 Plaza Ct. I-94, exit 297, just w on CR JJ (Bluemound Rd). Int corridors. **Pets:** Medium. $10 daily fee/pet. Designated rooms, service with restrictions, supervision.
(SAVE) ⊠ ⊞ ⊑

WAUWATOSA

▼▼▼ Holiday Inn Express-Medical Center ⊞
(414) 778-0333. **$79-$149, 7 day notice.** 11111 W North Ave. US 45, exit 42A, just n on SR 100, then just w. Int corridors. **Pets:** Accepted.
(ASK) ⊠ ⊞ ⊑

ⓐ ▼▼▼ Super 8 of Milwaukee West ⊞
(414) 257-0140. **Call for rates.** 115 N Mayfair Rd. I-94, exit 304B, just n on SR 100. Int corridors. **Pets:** Small, other species. $100 deposit/room. Designated rooms, service with restrictions, crate.
(SAVE) ⊠ ⊞ ⊑

END METROPOLITAN AREA

MINERAL POINT

▼▼▼ Comfort Inn ⊞
(608) 987-4747. **$60-$150.** 1345 Business Park Rd. On US 151; 0.6 mi n of jct SR 23 and 39. Int corridors. **Pets:** Medium. $10 daily fee/pet. Service with restrictions, supervision.
(ASK) ⊠ ⊞ ⊑ ⤳

MINOCQUA

ⓐ ▼▼▼ AmericInn of Minocqua ⊞ ❖
(715) 356-3730. **$64-$129.** 700 Hwy 51. On US 51; downtown. Int corridors. **Pets:** Other species. $10 daily fee/room. Designated rooms, service with restrictions, supervision.
(SAVE) ⊠ &M ⊞ ⊑ ⤳ ⊠

◇◇◇ Best Western Concord Inn 🅷
(715) 356-1800. **$74-$140, 21 day notice.** 320 Front St. On US 51; downtown. Int corridors. **Pets:** Medium, dogs only. $10 daily fee/pet. Designated rooms, service with restrictions, supervision.
🆂🅰🆅🅴 ✖ ⚐M 🛏 💻 🐾 ✖

◇◇ Comfort Inn-Minocqua 🅷
(715) 358-2588. **$61-$115.** 8729 Hwy 51 N. On Hwy 51 at SR 70 W. Int corridors. **Pets:** Other species. $10 daily fee/pet. Crate.
🅰🆂🅺 ✖ 🛏 💻 🐾

◇◇ Super 8 🅼 ❀
(715) 356-9541. **$60-$140, 3 day notice.** 8730 Hwy 51 N. On US 51 at SR 70 W. Ext/int corridors. **Pets:** Large. $10 one-time fee/room. Designated rooms, service with restrictions, supervision.
🆂🅰🆅🅴 ✖

◇◇◇ The Waters of Minocqua 🅷
(715) 358-4000. **$69-$225.** 8116 Hwy 51 S. On US 51, 1 mi s. Int corridors. **Pets:** Medium. $10 daily fee/pet. Service with restrictions, crate.
🅰🆂🅺 ✖ ⚐M 🛏 💻 🍽 🐾 ✖

MONONA

◇◇ AmericInn of Madison South/Monona 🅷 ❀
(608) 222-8601. **$99-$199.** 101 W Broadway. US 12/18, exit 265 (Monona Dr), just nw. Int corridors. **Pets:** Other species. $5 daily fee/room. Service with restrictions.
🅰🆂🅺 ✖ 🛏 💻 🐾 ✖

◇◇◇ Country Inn & Suites By Carlson 🅷
(608) 221-0055. **$99-$140.** 400 River Pl. US 12/18, exit 265 (Monona Dr), just nw. Int corridors. **Pets:** Small. $20 daily fee/pet. Designated rooms, service with restrictions.
🅰🆂🅺 ✖ 🛏 💻 🐾 ✖

MONROE

◇◇◇ Gasthaus Motel 🅼
(608) 328-8395. **$59-$99.** 685 30th St. 1.5 mi s on SR 69. Ext corridors. **Pets:** Other species. $10 daily fee/pet. Designated rooms, service with restrictions, supervision.
🆂🅰🆅🅴 ✖ ⚐M 🛏 💻

◇◇ Super 8 of Monroe 🅷
(608) 325-1500. **$59-$79.** 500 6th St. On SR 69 S, 0.5 mi s of jct SR 81/11. Int corridors. **Pets:** Accepted.
🅰🆂🅺 ✖ 🛏 💻

NEILLSVILLE

◇◇ Super 8 Motel-Neillsville 🅷
(715) 743-8080. **Call for rates.** 1000 E Division St. US 10, jct Boon and Division St. Int corridors. **Pets:** Accepted.
✖ 🛏 💻 🐾

NEW GLARUS

◇◇◇ Chalet Landhaus Inn 🅷
(608) 527-5234. **$99-$225.** 801 Hwy 69. On SR 69. Int corridors. **Pets:** $35 daily fee/pet. Service with restrictions, supervision.
🆂🅰🆅🅴 ✖ 🛏 💻 🍽 🐾 ✖

◇◇ Swiss Aire Motel 🅷
(608) 527-2138. **$59-$99.** 1200 Hwy 69. Just s of jct SR 39/69. Ext/int corridors. **Pets:** Other species. $10 daily fee/pet. Designated rooms, service with restrictions, supervision.
🆂🅰🆅🅴 ✖ 🛏 💻

NEW LISBON

◇◇◇ Travelers Inn of New Lisbon 🅷
(608) 562-5141. **$58-$159.** 1700 E Bridge St. I-90/94, exit 61 (SR 80), just ne. Int corridors. **Pets:** Other species. Service with restrictions, supervision.
🆂🅰🆅🅴 ✖ 🛏 💻 🐾

NEW LONDON

◇ Americas Best Value Inn New London 🅷
(920) 982-5820. **$49-$115.** 1409 N Shawano St. US 45, exit US 54, just n. Int corridors. **Pets:** Accepted.
🅰🆂🅺 ✖ 🛏 💻 🐾

◇◇◇ AmericInn Lodge & Suites of New London 🅷 ❀
(920) 982-5700. **$69-$189.** 1404 N Shawano St. US 45, exit US 54, just n. Int corridors. **Pets:** Medium, other species. $10 one-time fee/room. Service with restrictions, supervision.
🆂🅰🆅🅴 ✖ ⚐M 🛏 💻 🐾

NEW RICHMOND

◇◇ AmericInn Motel & Suites of New Richmond 🅷
(715) 246-8800. **$69-$95.** 1020 S Knowles Ave. Just s on SR 65. Int corridors. **Pets:** Small, dogs only. $15 one-time fee/pet. Designated rooms, service with restrictions, supervision.
🅰🆂🅺 ✖ 🛏 💻 🐾 ✖

◇◇ Super 8 🅷
(715) 246-7829. **Call for rates.** 1561 Dorset Ln. Just s on SR 65. Int corridors. **Pets:** Accepted.
✖ 🛏 💻

ONALASKA

◇◇ Baymont Inn & Suites LaCrosse-Onalaska 🅷
(608) 783-7191. **$55-$189.** 3300 Kinney Coulee Rd N. I-90, exit 5, just ne. Int corridors. **Pets:** Small, other species. $15 one-time fee/pet. Service with restrictions, supervision.
🅰🆂🅺 ✖ ⚐M 🛏 💻 🐾

◇◇ Comfort Inn by Choice Hotels 🅷 ❀
(608) 781-7500. **Call for rates.** 1223 Crossing Meadows Dr. I-90, exit 4, just e on SR 157, then w on CR SS. Int corridors. **Pets:** Service with restrictions, supervision.
✖ 🛏 💻 🐾

◇◇◇ Holiday Inn Express 🅷
(608) 783-6555. **$80-$140.** 9409 Hwy 16. I-90, exit 5, 1 mi e. Int corridors. **Pets:** Service with restrictions, supervision.
🅰🆂🅺 ✖ 🛏 💻 🐾

◇◇ Microtel Inn 🅷
(608) 783-0833. **$60-$70.** 3240 N Kinney Coulee Rd. I-90, exit 5, just ne. Int corridors. **Pets:** Accepted.
🅰🆂🅺 ✖ 🛏 💻

OSCEOLA

◇◇ River Valley Inn 🅷
(715) 294-4060. **$75-$135.** 1030 Cascade St. Just n on SR 35. Int corridors. **Pets:** Small. $10 daily fee/pet. Designated rooms, service with restrictions, supervision.
🅰🆂🅺 ✖ 🛏 💻 🐾

OSHKOSH

◇◇◇ Comfort Suites 🅷
(920) 230-7378. **$90-$270.** 400 S Koeller St. US 41, exit 117 (9th Ave), just e. Int corridors. **Pets:** Dogs only. $15 daily fee/room. Designated rooms, service with restrictions.
🅰🆂🅺 ✖ ⚐M 🛏 💻 🐾

◇◇ Fairfield Inn by Marriott 🅷
(920) 233-8504. **$75-$90.** 1800 S Koeller St. US 41, exit 117 (9th Ave), 0.8 mi s on east frontage road. Int corridors. **Pets:** Accepted.
✖ 🛏 💻 🐾

Hawthorn Inn & Suites H
(920) 303-1133. **$109-$449.** 3105 S Washburn St. US 41, exit 116 (SR 44), just w, then just s. Int corridors. **Pets:** Medium, dogs only. $15 daily fee/room. Designated rooms, service with restrictions, supervision.

Holiday Inn Express Hotel & Suites H
(920) 303-1300. **Call for rates.** 2251 Westowne Ave. US 41, exit 119, 0.4 mi w of jct SR 21. Int corridors. **Pets:** Accepted.

La Quinta Inn Oshkosh H
(920) 233-4190. **$49-$115.** 1950 Omro Rd. US 41, exit 119, jct SR 21. Int corridors. **Pets:** Medium, other species. Service with restrictions, supervision.

PLATTEVILLE

Mound View Inn H
(608) 348-9518. **$65-$95, 3 day notice.** 1755 E Business Hwy 151. On US 151, exit 21, just w. Int corridors. **Pets:** Accepted.

Super 8 H
(608) 348-8800. **$60-$94.** 100 Hwy 80/81 S. Jct US 151 and SR 80. Int corridors. **Pets:** Other species. $10 daily fee/pet.

PLEASANT PRAIRIE

Holiday Inn Express Hotel & Suites H
(262) 942-6000. **Call for rates.** 7887 94th Ave. I-94, exit 344 (SR 50), 1.5 mi e, then 0.3 mi s. Int corridors. **Pets:** Accepted.

La Quinta Inn-Pleasant Prairie H
(262) 857-7911. **$49-$119.** 7540 118th Ave. I-94, exit 344 (SR 50), just e. Int corridors. **Pets:** Medium, other species. Service with restrictions, supervision.

PLOVER

AmericInn of Plover H
(715) 342-1244. **$69-$109.** 1501 American Dr. I-39, exit 153 (CR B), just nw. Int corridors. **Pets:** Medium, dogs only. $15 one-time fee/room. Service with restrictions, supervision.

Comfort Inn H
(715) 342-0400. **Call for rates.** 1560 American Dr. I-39, exit 153 (CR B), just w. Int corridors. **Pets:** Accepted.

Hampton Inn-Plover H
(715) 295-9900. **$89-$149.** 3090 Village Park Dr. I-39, exit 153 (CR B), just sw. Int corridors. **Pets:** Accepted.

PORTAGE

Comfort Suites H
(608) 745-4717. **$79-$149.** N5780 Kinney Rd. I-90/94, exit 108A (SR 78). Int corridors. **Pets:** Medium, dogs only. $10 daily fee/pet. Service with restrictions, supervision.

Super 8-Portage H
(608) 742-8330. **$55-$85.** 3000 New Pinery Rd. I-39, exit 92, just s. Int corridors. **Pets:** Other species. $10 daily fee/pet. Service with restrictions, supervision.

PRAIRIE DU CHIEN

Best Western Bluffview Inn & Suites H
(608) 326-4777. **$86-$170.** 37268 US Hwy 18 S. On US 18, 1.9 mi e of jct SR 27 N. Ext/int corridors. **Pets:** Very small. $15 daily fee/pet. Designated rooms, service with restrictions, supervision.

Bridgeport Inn H
(608) 326-6082. **Call for rates.** Hwy 18, 35 & 60 S. On US 18, 2.2 mi e of jct SR 27 N. Int corridors. **Pets:** Accepted.

Brisbois Motor Inn M
(608) 326-8404. **$49-$109.** 533 N Marquette Rd. On SR 35 N, 0.5 mi n of jct US 18/SR 35 S and 27 N. Ext/int corridors. **Pets:** Accepted.

Country Inn & Suites By Carlson H
(608) 326-5700. **$80-$149.** 1801 Cabela's Dr. On SR 35, 2 mi n of jct US 18/SR 35 S and 27 N. Int corridors. **Pets:** Large, other species. $20 daily fee/pet. Designated rooms, service with restrictions, supervision.

Holiday Motel M
(608) 326-2448. **$35-$160.** 1010 S Marquette Rd. On US 18, 1 mi e of jct SR 27 N. Ext corridors. **Pets:** Accepted.

Super 8-Prairie Du Chien H
(608) 326-8777. **$60-$100.** 1930 S Marquette Rd. On US 18, 1.9 mi e of jct SR 27 N. Ext/int corridors. **Pets:** Very small. $15 daily fee/pet. Designated rooms, service with restrictions, supervision.

RACINE

Racine Marriott Hotel H
(262) 886-6100. **$179-$219.** 7111 Washington Ave. I-94, exit 333, 4 mi e on SR 20. Int corridors. **Pets:** Medium. $30 deposit/pet. Designated rooms, service with restrictions, supervision.

REEDSBURG

Copper Springs Motel M
(608) 524-4312. **Call for rates.** E7278 Hwy 23 & 33. On SR 23 and 33, 2 mi e. Ext corridors. **Pets:** Accepted.

Quality Inn H
(608) 524-8535. **Call for rates.** 2115 E Main St. 1.5 mi e on SR 23 and 33. Int corridors. **Pets:** Accepted.

RHINELANDER

Americas Best Value Inn M
(715) 369-5880. **$66-$71.** 667 W Kemp St. On Business Rt US 8, just e of jct SR 47. Int corridors. **Pets:** $10 daily fee/pet. Service with restrictions, supervision.

Best Western Claridge Motor Inn H
(715) 362-7100. **$84-$160.** 70 N Stevens St. Between Davenport and Rives sts; downtown. Int corridors. **Pets:** Large. $10 daily fee/pet. Designated rooms, service with restrictions, supervision.

Comfort Inn M
(715) 369-1100. **$70-$160.** 1490 Lincoln St. On Business Rt US 8, 2.6 mi e of jct SR 47. Int corridors. **Pets:** Accepted.

▼▼ Holiday Acres Resort H
(715) 369-1500. **$69-$149.** 4060 S Shore Dr. 4.5 mi e on Business Rt US 8, 2.3 mi n on W Lake George Rd. Ext/int corridors. **Pets:** Accepted.

(ASK) (X) 🛏 💻 🍴 🌊 (X)

▼▼ Quality Inn H ❀
(715) 369-3600. **$76-$176.** 668 W Kemp St. On Business Rt US 8, just e of jct SR 47. Int corridors. **Pets:** $10 one-time fee/pet. Service with restrictions, supervision.

(ASK) (X) (&M) 🛏 💻 🌊 (X)

RICE LAKE

▼▼ Microtel Inn & Suites H
(715) 736-2010. **$60-$90.** 2771 Decker Dr. US 53, exit 140 (CR O), just ne. Int corridors. **Pets:** Accepted.

(ASK) (X) 🛏 💻

RICHLAND CENTER

▼▼ The Center Lodge H
(608) 647-8988. **$70-$90, 10 day notice.** 100 Foundry Dr. 0.9 mi e on US 14. Int corridors. **Pets:** Accepted.

(ASK) (X) 🛏 💻 🌊

RIPON

▼▼ AmericInn Lodge & Suites of Ripon H
(920) 748-7578. **$69-$185.** 1219 W Fond du Lac St. 1.8 mi w on SR 23. Int corridors. **Pets:** Accepted.

(ASK) (X) 🛏 💻 🌊 (X)

▼▼▼ Comfort Suites at Royal Ridges H
(920) 748-5500. **$69-$179.** 2 Westgate Dr. 2 mi w on SR 23. Int corridors. **Pets:** Medium. $15 daily fee/room. Designated rooms, service with restrictions, supervision.

(ASK) (X) 🛏 💻 🌊 (X)

ROTHSCHILD

▼▼ Candlewood Suites–Wausau H
(715) 355-8900. **$99-$129.** 803 Industrial Park Dr. I-39, exit 185 (business route US 51), just se. Int corridors. **Pets:** Accepted.

(ASK) (X) (&M) 🛏 💻

▼▼ Comfort Inn H 🐾
(715) 355-4449. **$69-$120.** 1510 County Hwy XX. I-39, exit 185 (Business Rt US 51), just se. Int corridors. **Pets:** Medium, dogs only. $10 daily fee/pet. Designated rooms, service with restrictions, supervision.

(ASK) (X) 🛏 💻 🌊

▼▼ Rodeway Inn H
(715) 355-3030. **$65-$69.** 904 Industrial Park Ave. I-39, exit 185 (Business Rt US 51), just se. Int corridors. **Pets:** Small. $10 daily fee/room. Designated rooms, supervision.

(ASK) (X) 🛏 💻 🌊 (X)

SHAWANO

▼ Super 8-Shawano M
(715) 526-6688. **$46-$90.** 211 Waukechon St. 1.2 mi e on SR 29 business route; SR 29, exit 227, 1.8 mi n. then 1.1 mi w. Int corridors. **Pets:** Other species. $25 deposit/pet. Service with restrictions, supervision.

(ASK) (X) 🛏 💻

SHEBOYGAN

(AAA) ▼ Americas Best Value Inn-Sheboygan H ❀
(920) 458-8080. **$79-$99.** 3402 Wilgus Rd. I-43, exit 126, just ne. Int corridors. **Pets:** Dogs only. $15 one-time fee/room. Service with restrictions, supervision.

(SAVE) (X) 🛏 💻

▼▼▼▼ Grandstay Residential Suites Hotel H
(920) 208-8000. **$99-$181.** 708 Niagara Ave. Downtown. Int corridors. **Pets:** Medium, dogs only. $50 one-time fee/room. Designated rooms, service with restrictions, supervision.

(ASK) (X) (&M) 🛏 💻 🌊

▼▼ La Quinta Inn Sheboygan H ❀
(920) 457-2321. **$59-$169.** 2932 Kohler Memorial Dr. I-43, exit 126, 1 mi n on SR 23. Int corridors. **Pets:** Medium, other species. Service with restrictions, supervision.

(ASK) (X) 🛏 💻

SHEBOYGAN FALLS

▼▼ Days Inn & Suites H
(920) 467-4314. **$50-$170.** 600 Hwy 32 N. SR 23, exit 32 (Sheboygan Falls/Howards Grove), just w. Int corridors. **Pets:** Accepted.

(ASK) (X) (&M) 🛏 💻 🌊 (X)

SIREN

(AAA) ▼▼▼ The Lodge at Crooked Lake H
(715) 349-2500. **$89-$265.** 24271 SR 35 N. On SR 35, 0.5 mi n of jct SR 70. Int corridors. **Pets:** Dogs only. $50 deposit/room, $10 daily fee/pet. Service with restrictions, supervision.

(SAVE) (X) 🛏 💻 🍴 🌊 (X)

▼ Pine Wood Motel M
(715) 349-5225. **$35-$65.** 23862 Hwy 35 S. On SR 35, 0.3 mi s of jct SR 70 W and CR B E. Ext corridors. **Pets:** Accepted.

(ASK) (X) 🛏 💻

SPARTA

(AAA) ▼ Best Nights Inn M
(608) 269-3066. **$39-$139.** 303 W Wisconsin St. I-90, exit 25 (SR 27), 0.5 mi n; exit 28 (SR 16), 1 mi w. Ext corridors. **Pets:** Accepted.

(SAVE) (X) 🛏 💻 🌊

(AAA) ▼▼▼ Best Western Sparta Trail Lodge H
(608) 269-2664. **$99-$129.** 4445 Theatre Rd. I-90, exit 28 (US 16), just w. Int corridors. **Pets:** Medium. $20 one-time fee/pet. Service with restrictions, supervision.

(SAVE) (X) (&M) 🛏 💻 🍴 🌊 (X)

▼▼ Country Inn By Carlson H ❀
(608) 269-3110. **$79-$180.** 737 Avon Rd. I-90, exit 25 (SR 27), just n. Int corridors. **Pets:** Other species. $10 daily fee/pet. Service with restrictions, supervision.

(ASK) (X) (&M) 🛏 💻

▼▼ Super 8 Sparta H
(608) 269-8489. **$70-$175.** 716 Avon Rd. I-90, exit 25 (SR 27), just n. Int corridors. **Pets:** Other species. $10 daily fee/pet. Service with restrictions, supervision.

(ASK) (X) 🛏 💻

SPOONER

(AAA) ▼▼ Best Western American Heritage Inn H ❀
(715) 635-9770. **$89-$169.** 101 W Maple St. On SR 70, just e of US 63, 1 mi w of US 53. Int corridors. **Pets:** Small, other species. $15 daily fee/pet. Designated rooms, service with restrictions, supervision.

(SAVE) (X) 🛏 💻 🌊 (X)

(AAA) ▼▼ Country House Motel & RV Park M
(715) 635-8721. **$55-$109.** 717 River St. On US 63, 0.5 mi s of jct SR 70. Ext/int corridors. **Pets:** Other species. $5 daily fee/pet. Designated rooms, service with restrictions, supervision.

(SAVE) (X) (&M) 🛏 💻 🌊

▽ Inn Town Motel M
(715) 635-3529. **$40-$71, 3 day notice.** 801 River St. 0.8 mi n of jct US 63 and SR 70. Ext corridors. **Pets:** Other species. $10 daily fee/pet. Service with restrictions, supervision.
⊠ 🖪

STEVENS POINT

∞ ▽ Americas Best Value Inn �H ❖
(715) 341-8888. **$60-$80.** 247 N Division St. I-39, exit 161 (US 51 business route), 0.6 mi s. Int corridors. **Pets:** Dogs only. $15 one-time fee/room. Service with restrictions, supervision.
SAVE ⊠ 🖪 💻

▽▽▽ Country Inn & Suites By Carlson H
(715) 345-7000. **$79-$149.** 301 Division St N. I-39, exit 161 (US 51 business route), 0.6 mi s. Int corridors. **Pets:** Other species. $25 one-time fee/room. No service, supervision.
ASK ⊠ 🖪 💻 ≈

▽ Fairfield Inn by Marriott H
(715) 342-9300. **$72-$88.** 5317 Hwy 10 E. I-39, exit 158A (US 10), just se. Int corridors. **Pets:** Other species. $50 one-time fee/room. Service with restrictions, supervision.
⊠ 🖪 💻 ≈

▽▽▽ Holiday Inn Express H
(715) 344-0000. **$104.** 1100 Amber Ave. I-39, exit 158 (US 10), 1 mi e, then just n. Int corridors. **Pets:** Other species. $25 daily fee/room. Service with restrictions, supervision.
⊠ ᴸM 🖪 💻 ≈

▽▽ La Quinta Inn & Suites Stevens Point H ❖
(715) 344-1900. **$45-$119.** 4917 Main St. I-39, exit 158B (US 10), just sw. Int corridors. **Pets:** Medium, other species. Service with restrictions, supervision.
ASK ⊠ 🖪 💻 ≈

▽ Point Motel M
(715) 344-8312. **$35-$80.** 209 Division St. I-39, exit 161 (US 51 business route), 0.7 mi s. Ext corridors. **Pets:** $5 daily fee/pet. Designated rooms, service with restrictions, supervision.
ASK ⊠ 🖪 💻

▽ Stay Inn & Suites H
(715) 341-9090. **$45-$120.** 159 Division St N. I-39, exit 161 (US 51 business route), 0.6 mi s. Int corridors. **Pets:** Accepted.
ASK ⊠ 🖪

STURTEVANT

∞ ▽▽▽ Grandview Inn H
(262) 886-0385. **$70-$135.** 910 S Sylvania Ave. I-94, exit 333 (SR 20), just s on west frontage road. Int corridors. **Pets:** Accepted.
SAVE ⊠ 🖪 💻 ≈

SUN PRAIRIE

∞ ▽▽▽ AmeriHost Inn & Suites-Sun Prairie H
(608) 834-9889. **$74-$149.** 105 Business Park Dr. US 151, exit 103 (CR N), just n. Int corridors. **Pets:** Medium, dogs only. $10 daily fee/pet. Service with restrictions, supervision.
SAVE ⊠ ᴸM 🖪 💻 ≈

∞ ▽ McGovern's Motel & Suites M
(608) 837-7321. **$59-$92.** 820 W Main St. On US 151, exit 101, 1.2 mi ne. Ext/int corridors. **Pets:** Dogs only. $10 daily fee/pet. Designated rooms, service with restrictions, supervision.
SAVE ⊠ 🖪 💻 🍴

SUPERIOR

∞ ▽▽ Barkers Island Inn H
(715) 392-7152. **$100-$190.** 300 Marina Dr. Just ne of US 2/53; on Barkers Island. Int corridors. **Pets:** Medium. $10 daily fee/room. Service with restrictions, crate.
SAVE ⊠ 🖪 💻 🍴 ≈ ⊠

∞ ▽▽▽ Best Western Bay Walk Inn H
(715) 392-7600. **$60-$140.** 1405 Susquehanna Ave. Just e of US 2 on Belknap St. Int corridors. **Pets:** Service with restrictions, supervision.
SAVE ⊠ 🖪 💻 ≈ ⊠

∞ ▽▽▽ Best Western Bridgeview Motor Inn H
(715) 392-8174. **$59-$169.** 415 Hammond Ave. 0.8 mi n at south end of Blatnik Bridge. Int corridors. **Pets:** Accepted.
SAVE ⊠ 🖪 💻 ≈ ⊠

∞ ▽▽▽ Superior Inn H
(715) 394-7706. **$45-$165.** 525 Hammond Ave. 0.8 mi n; south end of Blatnik Bridge. Int corridors. **Pets:** Other species. Designated rooms, service with restrictions, supervision.
SAVE ⊠ 🖪 💻 ≈

THORP

▽▽ AmericInn Lodge & Suites of Thorp H
(715) 669-5959. **$74-$84.** 203 1/2 W Hill St. US 29, exit 108 (SR 73), just nw. Int corridors. **Pets:** Accepted.
ASK ⊠ 🖪 💻 ≈

TOMAH

▽▽ AmericInn Lodge & Suites of Tomah H ❖
(608) 372-4100. **$69-$159.** 750 Vandervort St. I-94, exit 143 (SR 21), just e. Int corridors. **Pets:** Small. $25 one-time fee/room. Service with restrictions, supervision.
ASK ⊠ 🖪 💻 ≈

▽▽ Comfort Inn by Choice Hotels H
(608) 372-6600. **$70-$119.** 305 Wittig Rd. I-94, exit 143 (SR 21), just w. Int corridors. **Pets:** $10 daily fee/pet. Service with restrictions, supervision.
ASK ⊠ 🖪 💻 ≈

▽▽▽ Cranberry Country Lodge Convention Center and Water Park H
(608) 374-2801. **Call for rates.** 319 Wittig Rd. I-94, exit 143 (SR 21), just w. Int corridors. **Pets:** Accepted.
⊠ 🖪 💻 ≈ ⊠

▽▽ Econo Lodge H
(608) 372-9100. **$60-$150.** 2005 N Superior Ave. I-94, exit 143 (SR 21), just w. Ext/int corridors. **Pets:** $10 daily fee/pet. Service with restrictions, supervision.
ASK ⊠ 🖪 💻 ≈

▽▽ Holiday Inn H
(608) 372-3211. **$99-$119.** 1017 E McCoy Blvd. I-94, exit 143 (SR 21), just e. Int corridors. **Pets:** Accepted.
ASK ⊠ 🖪 💻 🍴 ≈ ⊠

∞ ▽▽▽ Lark Inn M ❖
(608) 372-5981. **$59-$125.** 229 N Superior Ave. I-94, exit 143 (SR 21), 1.5 mi s on US 12; I-90, exit 41, 2 mi n on US 12. Ext/int corridors. **Pets:** Medium, dogs only. $7 daily fee/pet. Designated rooms, service with restrictions, supervision.
SAVE ⊠ 🖪 💻

▽▽ Microtel Inn & Suites H
(608) 374-2050. **$60-$90.** 115 W Andres St. I-94, exit 143 (SR 21), just nw. Int corridors. **Pets:** Medium. $10 daily fee/room. Service with restrictions, supervision.
ASK ⊠ ᴸM 🖪 💻

▼▼ ▼▼ Super 8-Tomah 🅷
(608) 372-3901. **$50-$120.** 1008 E McCoy Blvd. I-94, exit 143 (SR 21), just e. Int corridors. **Pets:** Small. $10 daily fee/pet. Designated rooms, no service, supervision.
ASK ⊠ 🔌 🖵

TOMAHAWK

▼▼▼▼ Rodeway Inn & Suites 🅷
(715) 453-8900. **$70-$130.** 1738 E Comfort Dr. US 51, exit 229, just nw. Int corridors. **Pets:** $25 one-time fee/room. Service with restrictions, supervision.
ASK ⊠ 🔌 🖵 ⇌ ⊠

▼▼ ▼▼ Super 8 Motel-Tomahawk 🅷
(715) 453-5210. **$65-$125.** 108 W Mohawk Dr. On US 51 business route, 0.6 mi n of downtown. Int corridors. **Pets:** Other species. $25 deposit/pet. Designated rooms, service with restrictions, supervision.
ASK ⊠ 🔌 🖵 ⇌

TWO RIVERS

▼▼ ▼▼ Lighthouse Inn on Lake Michigan 🅷
(920) 793-4524. **$89-$151.** 1515 Memorial Dr. 0.3 mi s on SR 42. Int corridors. **Pets:** Medium, dogs only. $50 deposit/room. Designated rooms, service with restrictions, supervision.
ASK ⊠ 🔌 🖵 🍴 ⇌ ⊠

VERONA

▲▲▲ ▼▼▼▼ Holiday Inn Express Hotel & Suites Madison-Verona 🅷
(608) 497-1200. **$110-$200.** 515 W Verona Ave. Business 51, exit 81, 1.8 mi w. Int corridors. **Pets:** Other species. $13 daily fee/pet. Designated rooms, service with restrictions, supervision.
SAVE ⊠ 🔌 🖵 ⇌

VIROQUA

▼▼ Hickory Hill Motel Ⓜ
(608) 637-3104. **$54-$75.** US 14 S 3955. 1.8 mi se on US 14 and SR 27 and 82. Ext corridors. **Pets:** Other species. $10 daily fee/pet. Designated rooms, service with restrictions, supervision.
ASK ⊠ 🔌 ⇌

WATERFORD

▼▼▼▼ Baymont Inns & Suites-Waterford 🅷
(262) 534-4100. **$84-$169.** 750 Fox Ln. On SR 36, 1 mi s of jct SR 164. Int corridors. **Pets:** Accepted.
ASK ⊠ 🔌 🖵 ⇌

WATERTOWN

▼▼ ▼▼ Super 8 🅷
(920) 261-1188. **$65-$120.** 1730 S Church St. On SR 26, 1.5 mi s of jct SR 19. Int corridors. **Pets:** Accepted.
ASK ⊠ 🔌 🖵 ⇌

WAUPACA

▲▲▲ ▼▼▼▼ Best Western Grand Seasons Hotel 🅷 ❀
(715) 258-9212. **$79-$139.** 110 Grand Seasons Dr. Jct US 10 and SR 54 W. Int corridors. **Pets:** Medium. $50 deposit/room. Designated rooms, supervision.
SAVE ⊠ 🔌 🖵 ⇌ ⊠

WAUPUN

▼▼ Inn Town Motel Ⓜ
(920) 324-4211. **$49-$94.** 27 S State St. US 151, exit 146 (SR 49), 1 mi w on Main St, then just s. Ext corridors. **Pets:** Small, dogs only. $6 daily fee/pet. Service with restrictions, supervision.
ASK ⊠ 🔌 🖵

WAUSAU

▲▲▲ ▼▼ ▼▼ Best Western Midway Hotel 🅷
(715) 842-1616. **$80-$110, 3 day notice.** 2901 Hummingbird Rd. I-39, exit 190 (CR NN), just sw. Int corridors. **Pets:** Medium. $20 one-time fee/room. Designated rooms, service with restrictions, supervision.
SAVE ⊠ 🔌 🖵 🍴 ⇌ ⊠

▲▲▲ ▼▼ ▼▼ Days Inn Ⓜ
(715) 842-0641. **$51-$71.** 116 S 17th Ave. I-39, exit 192, just ne. Int corridors. **Pets:** Other species. $5 deposit/room. Designated rooms, service with restrictions, supervision.
SAVE ⊠ 🔌 🖵

▲▲▲ ▼▼ ▼▼ Days Inn & Suites Wausau 🅷
(715) 355-5501. **$60-$120.** 4700 Rib Mountain Dr. I-39, exit 188, just ne. Int corridors. **Pets:** Dogs only. $10 daily fee/pet. Designated rooms, service with restrictions, supervision.
SAVE ⊠ 🔌 🖵 ⇌

▼▼▼▼ Jefferson Street Inn 🅷 ❀
(715) 845-6500. **$149-$269, 7 day notice.** 201 Jefferson St. Just w of jct 6th St; center. Int corridors. **Pets:** $20 daily fee/room. Service with restrictions, supervision.
SAVE ⊠ 🔌 🖵 🍴 ⇌ ⊠

▼▼ ▼▼ La Quinta Inn-Wausau 🅷 ❀
(715) 842-0421. **$49-$105.** 1910 Stewart Ave. I-39, exit 192, just se. Int corridors. **Pets:** Medium, other species. Service with restrictions, supervision.
ASK ⊠ 🔌 🖵 ⇌

▼▼ ▼▼ Rib Mountain Inn 🅷
(715) 848-2802. **$69-$499, 3 day notice.** 2900 Rib Mountain Way. I-39, exit 190 (CR NN), 1 mi w on N Mountain Rd (CR NN), then just s. Ext/int corridors. **Pets:** Accepted.
ASK 🔌 🖵 ⇌

▼▼▼▼ Stewart Inn Bed and Breakfast 🅱🅱 ❀
(715) 849-5858. **$150-$215, 10 day notice.** 521 Grant St. Just n on N 6th St (SR 52), then just w. Int corridors. **Pets:** Other species. Crate.
⊠

▲▲▲ ▼▼ ▼▼ Super 8 Wausau 🅷
(715) 848-2888. **$62-$80.** 2006 Stewart Ave W. I-39, exit 192, just se. Int corridors. **Pets:** Dogs only. $10 daily fee/pet. Service with restrictions, supervision.
SAVE ⊠ 🔌 🖵 ⇌

WAUTOMA

▼▼▼▼ AmericInn Lodge & Suites of Wautoma 🅷
(920) 787-5050. **$78-$158.** W7696 SR 21/73. On SR 21 and 73, 1.2 mi e. Int corridors. **Pets:** Dogs only. $10 one-time fee/room. Service with restrictions, supervision.
ASK ⊠ 🔌 🖵 ⇌

▼▼▼▼ Super 8-Wautoma 🅷
(920) 787-4811. **$70-$95.** W7607 SR 21/73. On SR 21 and 73, 1.5 mi e. Int corridors. **Pets:** Large, other species. $10 one-time fee/pet. Designated rooms, service with restrictions, supervision.
⊠ 🔌 🖵 ⇌

WEST SALEM

▼▼ ▼▼ AmericInn Motel & Suites of West Salem 🅷
(608) 786-3340. **$83-$153.** 125 Buol Rd. I-90, exit 12, just sw on CR C. Int corridors. **Pets:** Accepted.
ASK ⊠ 🔌 🖵 ⇌ ⊠

WHITEWATER

 Baymont Inn & Suites 🅷
(262) 472-9400. **$69-$109.** 1355 W Main St. On US business 12, 0.5 mi w of jct SR 59 W. Int corridors. **Pets:** Medium, other species. $10 daily fee/pet. Service with restrictions, supervision.
SAVE ⊠ ㊗ 🏠 🖥 ≈

WINDSOR

▼▼ Days Inn 🅷
(608) 846-7473. **$62-$110.** 6311 Rostad Cir. I-90/94, exit 131 (SR 19). Int corridors. **Pets:** Medium, dogs only. $10 daily fee/pet. Designated rooms, service with restrictions, supervision.
A$K ⊠ ㊗ 🏠 🖥 ≈ ⊠

WISCONSIN DELLS

 Americas Best Value Day's End Motel 🅼
(608) 254-8171. **$34-$152, 3 day notice.** N 604 Hwy 12-16. I-90/94, exit 85 (US 12), 0.8 mi nw. Ext corridors. **Pets:** Other species. $7 daily fee/pet. Designated rooms, service with restrictions, crate.
SAVE ⊠ 🏠 🖥 ≈ ⊠

▼ Black Hawk Motel 🅼 ❀
(608) 254-7770. **$39-$179, 3 day notice.** 720 Race St. I-90/94, exit 87 (SR 13), 2 mi e on SR 13, 16 and 23. Ext corridors. **Pets:** Small, other species. $10 daily fee/pet. Designated rooms, service with restrictions, supervision.
SAVE ⊠ 🏠 🖥 ≈ ⊠

▼ Bridge View Motel 🅼
(608) 254-6114. **$49-$118, 3 day notice.** 1020 River Rd. Just n of SR 13; center. Ext corridors. **Pets:** Medium. $10 daily fee/pet. Designated rooms, service with restrictions, crate.
A$K ⊠ 🏠 🖥 ≈

▼▼▼ Days Inn of Wisconsin Dells 🅷
(608) 254-6444. **$48-$159, 3 day notice.** 944 Hwy 12 N. I-90/94, exit 87 (SR 13), 1 mi n at jct US 12 and SR 16. Int corridors. **Pets:** Medium, dogs only. $50 deposit/pet, $10 daily fee/pet. Designated rooms, service with restrictions, supervision.
SAVE ⊠ 🏠 🖥 ≈

▼▼▼ Econo Lodge 🅷
(608) 253-4343. **$55-$135.** 350 W Munroe Ave. I-90/94, exit 89 (SR 23 N), 0.4 mi e. Int corridors. **Pets:** Accepted.
SAVE ⊠ ㊗ 🏠 🖥 ≈

▼▼ Super 8-Wisconsin Dells 🅷
(608) 254-6464. **$40-$200.** 800 CR H. I-90/94, exit 87 (SR 13), just e. Int corridors. **Pets:** Medium, other species. $10 daily fee/pet. Designated rooms, service with restrictions, supervision.
⊠ 🏠 🖥 ≈ ⊠

WISCONSIN RAPIDS

 Americas Best Value Inn 🅷 ❀
(715) 423-8080. **$60-$80.** 3410 8th St S. 1.9 mi s on SR 13 of jct SR 54 W. Int corridors. **Pets:** Dogs only. $15 one-time fee/room. Service with restrictions, supervision.
SAVE ⊠ 🏠 🖥

▼▼▼ Hotel Mead 🅷
(715) 423-1500. **$89-$250.** 451 E Grand Ave. Just e of downtown. Int corridors. **Pets:** Medium. $25 one-time fee/pet. Designated rooms, service with restrictions, supervision.
SAVE ⊠ 🏠 🖥 🍴 ≈ ⊠

▼▼ Quality Inn 🅷
(715) 423-5506. **$70-$85.** 3120 8th St S. 1.5 mi s on SR 13. Int corridors. **Pets:** Accepted.
A$K ⊠ 🏠 🖥 ≈

▼▼▼ Sleep Inn & Suites 🅷
(715) 424-6800. **$90-$155.** 4221 8th St S. I-39, exit 136 (SR 73), 16.6 mi w; 3.5 mi n on SR 13. Int corridors. **Pets:** Medium, dogs only. $15 daily fee/room. Designated rooms, service with restrictions, supervision.
A$K ⊠ ㊗ 🏠 🖥 ≈

WITTENBERG

▼▼▼ Best Western Red Oak Inn 🅷 ❀
(715) 253-3755. **$69-$100, 3 day notice.** W17267 Red Oak Ln. US 29, exit 198, just se. Int corridors. **Pets:** Medium. $20 one-time fee/pet. Designated rooms, service with restrictions, supervision.
SAVE ⊠ ㊗ 🏠 🖥 ≈ ⊠

WYOMING

AFTON

The Corral Motel [CA]
(307) 885-5424. **$60-$110, 6 day notice.** 161 Washington St (US 89). On US 89; center. Ext corridors. **Pets:** Accepted.
[ASK] [X] [H]

Lazy B Motel [M]
(307) 885-3187. **$75-$95.** 219 Washington St (US Hwy 89). On US 89; center. Ext corridors. **Pets:** Large, dogs only. Service with restrictions, supervision.
[SAVE] [X] [H] [D] [≈]

BUFFALO

Best Western Crossroads Inn [H]
(307) 684-2256. **$69-$190.** 75 N Bypass Rd. I-25, exit 299 (US 16), just w. Ext/int corridors. **Pets:** Accepted.
[SAVE] [X] [H] [D] [T] [≈]

Comfort Inn [H]
(307) 684-9564. **$69-$165.** 65 Hwy 16 E. I-25, exit 299 (US 16 E), just e; I-90, exit 58, 1.3 mi w. Ext/int corridors. **Pets:** Large. $10 daily fee/pet. Designated rooms, service with restrictions, supervision.
[X] [&M] [H] [D] [≈]

The Occidental Hotel [H]
(307) 684-0451. **$50-$210, 14 day notice.** 10 N Main St. Center. Int corridors. **Pets:** Accepted.
[ASK] [X] [H] [T] [Z]

Super 8 of Buffalo [H]
(307) 684-2531. **$60-$140.** 655 E Hart St. I-25, exit 299 (US 16), just w; I-90, exit 58, 1.3 mi w. Int corridors. **Pets:** Other species. $11 daily fee/pet. Designated rooms, service with restrictions, supervision.
[SAVE] [X] [H] [D]

WYO Motel [M] 🐾
(307) 684-5505. **$49-$169.** 610 E Hart St. I-25, exit 299 (US 16), just w; I-90, exit 58, 1.3 mi w. Ext corridors. **Pets:** Medium. $5 one-time fee/pet. Service with restrictions, supervision.
[SAVE] [X] [H] [D] [≈]

CASPER

Best Western Ramkota [H]
(307) 266-6000. **$90-$130, 3 day notice.** 800 N Poplar St. I-25, exit 188B, just e. Int corridors. **Pets:** Other species. $50 deposit/pet. Designated rooms, service with restrictions, crate.
[SAVE] [X] [&M] [H] [D] [T] [≈] [X]

Days Inn Casper [H]
(307) 234-1159. **Call for rates.** 301 E 'E' St. I-25, exit 188A, just s. Int corridors. **Pets:** Accepted.
[X] [H] [D] [≈]

La Quinta Inn [H] 🐾
(307) 265-1200. **$134.** 400 W 'F' St. I-25, exit 188A, just e. Int corridors. **Pets:** Medium, other species. Service with restrictions, supervision.
[X] [&M] [H] [D] [≈] [X]

Parkway Plaza Hotel & Convention Centre [H]
(307) 235-1777. **$90-$129.** 123 W 'E' St. I-25, exit 188A, just w. Ext/int corridors. **Pets:** $50 deposit/room. Designated rooms, service with restrictions.
[SAVE] [X] [H] [D] [T] [≈] [X]

Quality Inn & Suites [H] 🐾
(307) 266-2400. **$90-$200.** 821 N Poplar St. I-25, exit 188B, just e. Int corridors. **Pets:** Large, dogs only. $10 deposit/room. Service with restrictions, supervision.
[SAVE] [X] [H] [D]

Ramada Plaza [H]
(307) 235-2531. **$90-$129.** 300 W 'F' St. I-25, exit 188A, just e. Int corridors. **Pets:** $25 deposit/room. Designated rooms, service with restrictions, crate.
[SAVE] [X] [&M] [H] [D] [T] [≈] [X]

The Royal Inn [M]
(307) 234-3501. **$55-$70.** 440 E 'A' St. I-25, exit 188A, just s to 'A' St, then just e. Ext corridors. **Pets:** Small, dogs only. $25 one-time fee/room. Designated rooms, service with restrictions, supervision.
[SAVE] [X] [H] [D] [≈]

Skyler Inn [H]
(307) 232-5100. **$77-$119.** 111 S Wilson St. I-25, exit 186, 0.5 mi s to Yellowstone Hwy, then 1 mi w, jct 1st St. Int corridors. **Pets:** Accepted.
[SAVE] [X] [H] [D]

Super 8 [H]
(307) 266-3480. **$99-$109.** 3838 CY Ave. I-25, exit 188B, 1.7 mi w on S Poplar St (SR 220), then 1.8 mi n. Int corridors. **Pets:** Accepted.
[X] [H] [D]

CHEYENNE

Cheyenne Super 8 Motel [M]
(307) 635-8741. **$69-$99.** 1900 W Lincolnway. I-25, exit 9, 0.7 mi e. Int corridors. **Pets:** Accepted.
[ASK] [X] [&M] [H] [D]

Comfort Inn of Cheyenne [H]
(307) 638-7202. **$79-$209.** 2245 Etchepare Dr. I-25, exit 7, just w. Int corridors. **Pets:** Accepted.
[SAVE] [X] [&M] [H] [D] [≈]

Days Inn Cheyenne [H] 🐾
(307) 778-8877. **Call for rates.** 2360 W Lincolnway. I-25, exit 9, just e. Int corridors. **Pets:** Large, other species. $5 one-time fee/pet. Service with restrictions, supervision.
[SAVE] [X] [H] [D] [X]

Historic Plains Hotel [H]
(307) 638-3311. **$109-$359.** 1600 Central Ave. I-80, exit 362, 1 mi n on I-180/I-25 business loop/US 85/87 business route, then just w on I-80 business loop/US 30; downtown. Int corridors. **Pets:** Accepted.
[SAVE] [X] [H] [D] [T]

▼▼ La Quinta Inn Cheyenne 🅷 ❖
(307) 632-7117. **$59-$199.** 2410 W Lincolnway. I-25, exit 9, just e. Int corridors. **Pets:** Medium, other species. Service with restrictions, supervision.
A$K ✕ &M 🛏 💻 ⊠

AAA ▼▼▼▼ Nagle Warren Mansion B & B 🅱🅱 ❖
(307) 637-3333. **$158-$192, 3 day notice.** 222 E 17th St. I-80, exit 362, 1.2 mi n on I-25 business loop/US 85/87 business route, then just e; jct House St; downtown. Int corridors. **Pets:** Medium, other species. $25 daily fee/room. Designated rooms, service with restrictions, supervision.
SAVE ✕ ⊠

AAA ▼ Oak Tree Inn 🅷
(307) 778-6620. **$59-$79.** 1625 Stillwater Ave. 1.2 mi e of jct Dell Range Blvd and Yellowstone Rd, 0.4 mi s. Ext/int corridors. **Pets:** Accepted.
SAVE ✕ 🛏 💻 🍴

▼▼ Porch Swing Bed & Breakfast 🅱🅱 ❖
(307) 778-7182. **$75-$95.** 502 E 24th St. I-80, exit 362, 1.8 mi n on I-25 business loop/US 85/87 business route, then just e; downtown. Int corridors. **Pets:** Other species. No service, supervision.
✕ 🐾

▼▼ Windy Hills Guest House 🅱🅱
(307) 632-6423. **$137-$310, 3 day notice.** 393 Happy Jack Rd. I-25, exit 10B, 22 mi w on SR 210 (Happy Jack Rd), then 1 mi s on private gravel road. Ext corridors. **Pets:** Accepted.
✕ 🛏 💻 🐾 🐾

CODY

AAA ▼▼▼ Best Western Sunset Motor Inn 🅼
(307) 587-4265. **$69-$189.** 1601 8th St. 0.8 mi w on US 14/16/20. Ext corridors. **Pets:** Small, dogs only. $25 one-time fee/pet. Designated rooms, service with restrictions, supervision.
SAVE ✕ 🛏 💻 🍴 🐾 🐾

AAA ▼ Big Bear Motel 🅼 ❖
(307) 587-3117. **$49-$109.** 139 W Yellowstone Ave. 2 mi w on US 14/16/20, from city center. Ext corridors. **Pets:** Other species. $10 daily fee/pet. Designated rooms, supervision.
SAVE ✕ 🛏 💻 🐾 🐾

AAA ▼ Cody Motor Lodge 🅼 ❖
(307) 527-6291. **$75-$125, 12 day notice.** 1455 Sheridan Ave. Just w on US 14/16/20 and SR 120. Int corridors. **Pets:** Other species. Designated rooms, service with restrictions, supervision.
SAVE ✕ 💻

▼▼ Green Gables Inn 🅼
(307) 587-6886. **$59-$129.** 1636 Central Ave. Just e on US 14/16/20 and SR 120. Ext corridors. **Pets:** Small, dogs only. Designated rooms, service with restrictions, crate.
A$K ✕ 🛏 💻

AAA ▼▼▼ Sunrise Motor Inn 🅼 ❖
(307) 587-5566. **$59-$170.** 1407 8th St. 0.8 mi w on US 14/16/20. Ext corridors. **Pets:** Medium, dogs only. $15 one-time fee/room. Designated rooms, service with restrictions, supervision.
SAVE ✕ 🛏 💻 🐾

DOUGLAS

AAA ▼▼▼ Best Western Douglas Inn & Conference Center 🅷 ❖
(307) 358-9790. **$95-$120, 3 day notice.** 1450 Riverbend Dr. I-25, exit 140, 0.8 mi e. Int corridors. **Pets:** $10 daily fee/pet. Designated rooms, service with restrictions, supervision.
SAVE ✕ &M 🛏 💻 🍴 🐾 🐾

AAA ▼▼▼▼ Holiday Inn Express Hotel & Suites 🅷 ❖
(307) 358-4500. **$120-$190.** 900 W Yellowstone Hwy. I-25, exit 140, 0.5 mi e. Int corridors. **Pets:** Small. $50 one-time fee/pet. Designated rooms, service with restrictions, supervision.
SAVE ✕ &M 🛏 💻 🐾

DUBOIS

AAA ▼ Branding Iron Inn 🅲🅰
(307) 455-2893. **$55-$112.** 401 W Ramshorn St. 0.3 mi w on US 26 and 287. Ext corridors. **Pets:** Other species. Service with restrictions, supervision.
SAVE ✕ 🛏 💻 🐾

AAA ▼▼ Longhorn RV & Motel 🅼 ❖
(307) 455-2337. **$52-$99.** 5810 US Hwy 26. 3 mi e on US 26 and 287. Ext corridors. **Pets:** Dogs only. $10 daily fee/room. Service with restrictions, supervision.
SAVE ✕ 🛏 💻 🐾

▼ Rocky Mountain Lodge 🅼
(307) 455-2844. **$60-$100, 3 day notice.** 1349 W Ramshorn St. 1.6 mi w on US 26 and 287. Ext corridors. **Pets:** Accepted.
A$K ✕ 🛏 💻 🐾

AAA ▼▼ Stagecoach Motor Inn 🅼 ❖
(307) 455-2303. **$58-$98.** 103 Ramshorn St. On US 26 and 287; center. Ext corridors. **Pets:** Small, dogs only. $10 daily fee/pet. Designated rooms, service with restrictions, supervision.
SAVE ✕ 🛏 💻 🐾 🐾 🐾

EVANSTON

▼▼ Comfort Inn 🅷
(307) 789-7799. **$75-$135.** 1931 Harrison Dr. I-80, exit 3 (Harrison Dr), just n. Int corridors. **Pets:** Accepted.
A$K ✕ 🛏 💻 🐾

AAA ▼▼ Days Inn 🅷
(307) 789-0783. **$69-$109.** 1983 Harrison Dr. I-80, exit 3 (Harrison Dr), just n. Int corridors. **Pets:** Small. $10 daily fee/pet. No service, supervision.
SAVE ✕ 🛏 💻 🐾

AAA ▼ Prairie Inn 🅼
(307) 789-2920. **$65-$90.** 264 Bear River Dr. I-80, exit 6, 0.3 mi n. Ext/int corridors. **Pets:** Small. $10 one-time fee/pet. Designated rooms, service with restrictions, supervision.
SAVE ✕ 🛏

EVANSVILLE

▼▼ Comfort Inn by Choice Hotels-Casper 🅷
(307) 235-3038. **Call for rates.** 480 Lathrop Rd. I-25, exit 185, just e. Int corridors. **Pets:** Other species. $10 daily fee/pet. Designated rooms, service with restrictions, supervision.
✕ &M 🛏 💻 🐾

▼▼▼ Sleep Inn & Suites 🅷
(307) 235-3100. **$80-$160.** 6733 Bonanza. I-25, exit 182, n on Hat Six Rd, then w. Int corridors. **Pets:** Large. $10 daily fee/room. Service with restrictions, supervision.
A$K ✕ 🛏 💻 🐾

▼▼▼ Super 8 East Casper 🅷 ❖
(307) 237-8100. **$99-$119.** 269 Miracle Dr. I-25, exit 185, just e. Int corridors. **Pets:** Other species. Service with restrictions, supervision.
A$K ✕ &M 🛏 💻 🐾

GILLETTE

AAA ▼▼▼▼ Best Western Tower West Lodge 🅷
(307) 686-2210. **$90-$230, 30 day notice.** 109 N US Hwy 14-16. I-90, exit 124, just n. Int corridors. **Pets:** Accepted.
SAVE ✕ 🛏 💻 🍴 🐾 🐾

(AAA)◆ � Budget Inn Express M
(307) 686-1989. **$69-$199.** 2011 Rodgers Dr. I-90, exit 124, just n. Int corridors. **Pets:** Small. $10 daily fee/pet. Designated rooms, supervision.
[SAVE] [X] [🛏] [🌊]

☆☆☆ Comfort Inn & Suites of Gillette H
(307) 685-2223. **$89-$300, 7 day notice.** 1607 W 2nd Ave. I-90, exit 124, just ne. Int corridors. **Pets:** Small. $15 daily fee/pet. Designated rooms, service with restrictions, supervision.
[ASK] [X] [🅼] [🛏] [💻] [🌊]

☆☆☆ Holiday Inn Express Hotel & Suites H ❖
(307) 686-9576. **$159-$239.** 1908 Cliff Davis Dr. I-90, exit 126. Int corridors. **Pets:** Designated rooms, service with restrictions, supervision.
[ASK] [X] [🅼] [🛏] [💻] [🌊]

GREEN RIVER

(AAA)◆ ☆☆ Oak Tree Inn H ❖
(307) 875-3500. **$90-$100.** 1170 W Flaming Gorge Way. I-80, exit 89, just s. Ext/int corridors. **Pets:** Large. $5 daily fee/pet. Service with restrictions, crate.
[SAVE] [X] [🅼] [🛏] [💻] [🍴]

GREYBULL

(AAA)◆ ☆☆ Yellowstone Motel M
(307) 765-4456. **$55-$99.** 247 Greybull Ave. 0.4 mi e on US 14. Ext corridors. **Pets:** Accepted.
[SAVE] [X] [🛏] [🌊]

GUERNSEY

(AAA)◆ ☆☆ The Bunkhouse Motel M
(307) 836-2356. **$65-$139, 7 day notice.** 350 W Whalen St. On US 26; center. Ext corridors. **Pets:** Other species. $10 one-time fee/room. Service with restrictions, supervision.
[SAVE] [X] [🛏] [💻]

HULETT

(AAA)◆ ☆☆☆ Best Western Devil's Tower Inn H
(307) 467-5747. **$70-$170.** 229 Hwy 24. Center. Int corridors. **Pets:** Large, other species. $25 one-time fee/pet. Designated rooms, service with restrictions, supervision.
[SAVE] [X] [🛏] [💻] [🌊]

(AAA)◆ ☆☆ Hulett Motel M
(307) 467-5220. **$65-$85.** 202 Main St. SR 24; at north end of town. Ext corridors. **Pets:** Dogs only. $20 one-time fee/room. Designated rooms, service with restrictions, supervision.
[SAVE] [X]

JACKSON HOLE AREA

ALPINE

(AAA)◆ ☆☆ Alpen Haus Resort Hotel H
(307) 654-7545. **$67-$170.** 50 W Hwy 26. Jct US 26 and 89. Int corridors. **Pets:** Small, dogs only. $10 daily fee/pet. Designated rooms, service with restrictions, supervision.
[SAVE] [X] [🛏] [🍴]

☆☆☆ Flying Saddle Resort M
(307) 654-4422. **Call for rates.** 118878 Jct US 26 & 89. 0.5 mi e of jct US 26 and 89. Ext corridors. **Pets:** Accepted.
[X] [🛏] [💻] [🍴] [🌊] [🐾]

GRAND TETON NATIONAL PARK

(AAA)◆ ☆☆☆ Flagg Ranch Resort H
(307) 543-2861. **Call for rates.** Hwy 89. US 89 and 191; 2 mi s of Yellowstone National Park south entrance; 5 mi n of Grand Teton National Park north entrance. Ext corridors. **Pets:** Accepted.
[SAVE] [X] [🅼] [💻] [🍴] [🐾] [🐕] [🅿]

☆☆☆ Jackson Lake Lodge H
(307) 543-2811. **$219-$319, 7 day notice.** US 89 and 287. 5 mi nw of Moran. Ext/int corridors. **Pets:** Accepted.
[X] [🅼] [🛏] [💻] [🍴] [🌊] [🐾] [🅿]

(AAA)◆ ☆☆☆ Signal Mountain Lodge H ❖
(307) 543-2831. **$130-$315, 7 day notice.** Inner Park Rd. Teton Park Rd, 2 mi s of US 89, 191 and 287. Ext corridors. **Pets:** Other species. $10 daily fee/room. Designated rooms, service with restrictions, supervision.
[SAVE] [X] [🛏] [💻] [🍴] [🐾] [🐕] [🅿]

☆☆ Togwotee Mountain Lodge CA
(307) 543-2847. **$89-$259, 7 day notice.** 27655 Hwy US 26 & 287. 16.5 mi e of Moran at jct US 26 and 287. Ext/int corridors. **Pets:** Accepted.
[X] [🛏] [💻] [🍴] [🐾]

JACKSON

(AAA)◆ ☆☆☆☆ 49'er Inn and Suites (Quality Inn and Suites) H
(307) 733-7550. **$79-$169, 14 day notice.** 330 W Pearl St. Just w; just s of town square. Ext/int corridors. **Pets:** Service with restrictions, supervision.
[SAVE] [X] [🛏] [💻] [🐾]

(AAA)◆ ☆☆☆ Antler Inn H
(307) 733-2535. **$72-$220.** 43 W Pearl St. Just s of town square. Ext/int corridors. **Pets:** Dogs only. Service with restrictions, supervision.
[SAVE] [X] [🛏] [💻] [🐾]

(AAA)◆ ☆☆☆ Cowboy Village Resort CA ❖
(307) 733-3121. **$86-$258.** 120 S Flat Creek Dr. 0.3 mi w on Broadway to Flat Creek Dr, just s; downtown. Ext corridors. **Pets:** Dogs only. Service with restrictions, supervision.
[SAVE] [X] [🛏] [💻] [🌊] [🐾]

(AAA)◆ ☆☆☆ Elk Country Inn M ❖
(307) 733-2364. **$76-$220, 14 day notice.** 480 W Pearl St. Just w, then just s of town square. Ext/int corridors. **Pets:** Other species. Designated rooms, service with restrictions, supervision.
[SAVE] [X] [🛏] [💻] [🐾]

☆☆☆ Homewood Suites by Hilton H
(307) 739-0808. **$249-$329.** 260 N Millward St. Just nw of town square, n on Millward St or w on Mercil Ave, from US 26/89/191 (Broadway). Int corridors. **Pets:** Medium. $100 one-time fee/room. No service, supervision.
[X] [🅼] [🛏] [💻] [🐾]

(AAA)◆ ☆☆☆ Jackson Hole Lodge H
(307) 733-2992. **$94-$319, 15 day notice.** 420 W Broadway. 0.3 mi w on US 26/89/191. Ext corridors. **Pets:** Medium. $50 deposit/room. Designated rooms, service with restrictions, supervision.
[SAVE] [X] [🛏] [💻] [🌊] [🐾]

◐◐◐ ▽▽▽▽ Snow King Resort 🅷
(307) 733-5200. **$150-$760, 3 day notice.** 400 E Snow King Ave. Just se of town square. Ext/int corridors. **Pets:** Accepted.
[SAVE] [✕] 🖥 💻 [¶] 🏊 [✕]

◐◐◐ ▽▽▽ Inn at Jackson Hole 🅷 ❀
(307) 733-2311. **$89-$549, 7 day notice.** 3345 W Village Dr. Center. Ext corridors. **Pets:** $10 daily fee/room. Service with restrictions, supervision.
[SAVE] [✕] 🖥 💻 [¶] 🏊 [✕]

TETON VILLAGE

◐◐◐ ▽▽▽▽ Four Seasons Resort Jackson Hole 🅷
(307) 732-5000. **Call for rates.** 7680 Granite Loop Rd. Located at the base of Jackson Hole Mountain Resort. Int corridors. **Pets:** Very small, dogs only. Service with restrictions, supervision.
[SAVE] [✕] [♿M] 🖥 💻 [¶] 🏊 [✕]

END AREA

LANDER

◐◐◐ ▽▽ Holiday Lodge 🅜
(307) 332-2511. **$60-$75.** 210 McFarlane Dr. Just e of jct US 287 and SR 789. Ext corridors. **Pets:** Dogs only. $10 daily fee/pet. Designated rooms, service with restrictions, crate.
[SAVE] [✕] 🖥

LARAMIE

▽▽ Days Inn 🅷
(307) 745-5678. **$99-$130.** 1368 McCue St. I-80, exit 310 (Curtis St), just e. Int corridors. **Pets:** Small. $17 daily fee/pet. Service with restrictions, supervision.
[ASK] [✕] [♿M] 🖥 💻 🏊

◐◐◐ ▽▽ Gas Lite Inn Motel 🅜
(307) 742-6616. **$56-$68.** 960 N 3rd St. I-80, exit 313, 1.6 mi n on US 287; downtown. Ext corridors. **Pets:** Other species. $5 daily fee/room. Service with restrictions, supervision.
[SAVE] [✕] 🖥

▽▽▽ Holiday Inn-Laramie-University of Wyoming 🅷
(307) 721-9000. **Call for rates.** 204 30th St. I-80, exit 316 (Grand Ave), 2.5 mi w; jct 30th St. Int corridors. **Pets:** Accepted.
[✕] [♿M] 🖥 💻 [¶] 🏊

◐◐◐ ▽▽ Travelodge Downtown 🅜
(307) 742-6671. **$65-$170.** 165 N 3rd St. I-80, exit 313, 1 mi n on US 287; downtown. Ext corridors. **Pets:** Large, other species. $50 deposit/pet. Designated rooms, service with restrictions, supervision.
[SAVE] [✕] 🖥 💻

LUSK

◐◐◐ ▽▽▽ Best Western Pioneer 🅜 ❀
(307) 334-2640. **$80-$190.** 731 S Main St. Just n of jct US 20/85. Ext corridors. **Pets:** $20 one-time fee/pet. Designated rooms, supervision.
[SAVE] [✕] 🖥 💻 🏊

▽▽ Town House Motel 🅜
(307) 334-2376. **$54-$105.** 525 S Main St. Just n of jct US 20/85. Ext corridors. **Pets:** Other species. $5 one-time fee/pet. Designated rooms, service with restrictions.
[ASK] [✕] 🖥 💻

NEWCASTLE

◐◐◐ ▽▽ Auto Inn Motel 🅜
(307) 746-2734. **$59-$175.** 2503 W Main St. West end of town on US 16. Ext corridors. **Pets:** $6 daily fee/pet. Designated rooms, service with restrictions, supervision.
[SAVE] [✕] 🖥 💻

◐◐◐ ▽ Sage Motel 🅜
(307) 746-2724. **$50-$75, 3 day notice.** 1227 S Summit Ave. 0.3 mi s of jct US 16 on US 85, just w. Ext corridors. **Pets:** Small, dogs only. $10 daily fee/pet. Designated rooms, service with restrictions, supervision.
[SAVE] [✕] 🖥 💻

PAINTER

▽ Hunter Peak Ranch 🆁🅰 ❀
(307) 587-3711. **$150-$220.** 4027 Crandall Rd. SR 296, 5 mi s of US 212; 40 mi n of SR 120. Ext corridors. **Pets:** Dogs only. $15 daily fee/pet. Designated rooms, no service, supervision.
[✕] 🖥 💻 [¶] [✕] [♿] [✕] [✕]

PINEDALE

▽▽ Baymont Inn & Suites 🅷 ❀
(307) 367-8300. **Call for rates.** 1624 W Pine St. 1 mi n on US 191. Int corridors. **Pets:** Large, dogs only. $50 deposit/pet, $10 daily fee/pet. Service with restrictions, supervision.
[✕] [♿M] 🖥 💻 🏊

◐◐◐ ▽▽▽ Best Western Pinedale Inn 🅷
(307) 367-6869. **$99-$179, 3 day notice.** 850 W Pine St. 0.5 mi n on US 191. Int corridors. **Pets:** Designated rooms, service with restrictions, supervision.
[SAVE] [✕] 🖥 💻 🏊

◐◐◐ ▽▽▽ The Lodge at Pinedale 🅷
(307) 367-8800. **$72-$139.** 1054 W Pine St. 0.7 mi n on US 191. Int corridors. **Pets:** $10 daily fee/room. Designated rooms, service with restrictions, supervision.
[SAVE] [✕] 🖥 💻 🏊

▽▽ Sun Dance Motel 🅜
(307) 367-4336. **Call for rates.** 148 E Pine St. US 191; city center. Ext corridors. **Pets:** Accepted.
[✕] 🖥 💻

POWELL

◐◐◐ ▽▽▽ Americas Best Value Inn 🅜
(307) 754-5117. **$78-$150.** 777 E 2nd St. 0.3 mi e on US 14A. Ext corridors. **Pets:** Accepted.
[SAVE] [✕] 🖥 💻 🏊

RAWLINS

◐◐◐ ▽▽▽ Best Western CottonTree Inn 🅷
(307) 324-2737. **$130-$170, 5 day notice.** 2221 W Spruce St. I-80, exit 211, just n. Ext/int corridors. **Pets:** Accepted.
[SAVE] [✕] 🖥 💻 [¶] 🏊 [✕]

▽▽▽ Hampton Inn 🅷
(307) 324-2320. **$125-$153.** 406 Airport Rd. I-80, exit 215 (Cedar St), just n. Int corridors. **Pets:** Dogs only. Designated rooms, service with restrictions, supervision.
[✕] [♿M] 🖥 💻 🏊

▼▼▼▼ Holiday Inn Express 🅷
(307) 324-3760. **$159-$189.** 201 Airport Rd. I-80, exit 215, just w. Int corridors. **Pets:** Accepted.
(ASK) ⊠ (ᴸᴹ) 🛢 🖵 ⊇

▼▼ Microtel Inn & Suites 🅷
(307) 324-5588. **$79-$139.** 812 Locust St. I-80, exit 214, just n. Int corridors. **Pets:** Medium. $15 daily fee/pet. Designated rooms, service with restrictions, supervision.
⊠ (ᴸᴹ) 🛢 🖵

⧫⧫⧫ ▼▼▼ Oak Tree Inn 🅷
(307) 324-4700. **$79-$129.** 2005 E Daley St. I-80, exit 215, 0.5 mi w, then just n on US 287. Int corridors. **Pets:** Large, other species. $10 daily fee/room. Service with restrictions, supervision.
(SAVE) ⊠ (ᴸᴹ) 🛢 🖵 🍴

RIVERTON

▼▼ Comfort Inn & Suites 🅷
(307) 856-8900. **$89-$139.** 2020 N Federal Blvd. 1.5 mi ne on US 26/SR 789. Int corridors. **Pets:** Accepted.
(ASK) ⊠ 🛢 🖵 ⊇

▼▼ Days Inn 🅼
(307) 856-9677. **$70-$150.** 909 W Main St. 0.5 mi nw on US 26. Ext corridors. **Pets:** Small. $10 daily fee/pet. Designated rooms, service with restrictions, supervision.
(ASK) ⊠ 🛢 🖵

⧫⧫⧫ ▼▼▼ Holiday Inn Convention Center 🅷
(307) 856-8100. **$99-$149.** 900 E Sunset Dr. 0.8 mi ne on US 26/SR 789. Int corridors. **Pets:** Accepted.
(SAVE) ⊠ (ᴸᴹ) 🛢 🖵 🍴 ⊇

▼ Super 8 🅼
(307) 857-2400. **$60-$150, 7 day notice.** 1040 N Federal Blvd. 1 mi ne on US 26/SR 789. Int corridors. **Pets:** Small. $10 daily fee/pet. No service, supervision.
(ASK) ⊠ 🛢 🖵

ROCK SPRINGS

▼▼▼▼ Hampton Inn 🅷 🐾
(307) 382-9222. **$139-$159.** 1901 Dewar Dr. I-80, exit 102 (Dewar Dr), 1 mi s. Int corridors. **Pets:** Large, other species. Service with restrictions, supervision.
⊠ 🛢 🖵 ⊇

▼▼▼▼ Holiday Inn 🅷 🐾
(307) 382-9200. **$135.** 1675 Sunset Dr. I-80, exit 102 (Dewar Dr), 0.3 mi sw. Ext/int corridors. **Pets:** Other species. $10 daily fee/room. Designated rooms, service with restrictions, supervision.
(ASK) ⊠ 🛢 🖵 🍴 ⊇

▼▼ La Quinta Inn 🅷 🐾
(307) 362-1770. **$109-$179.** 2717 Dewar Dr. I-80, exit 102 (Dewar Dr), just n. Int corridors. **Pets:** Medium, other species. Service with restrictions, supervision.
(ASK) ⊠ 🛢 🖵 ⊇

▼ Motel 6–#395 🅼
(307) 362-1850. **$65-$91.** 2615 Commercial Way. I-80, exit 102 (Dewar Dr), n to Foothills Blvd, then just e. Ext corridors. **Pets:** Other species. Service with restrictions, supervision.
⊠ 🛢 ⊇

▼▼ Quality Inn 🅼
(307) 382-9490. **$109-$149.** 1670 Sunset Dr. I-80, exit 102 (Dewar Dr), 0.3 mi s, then just w. Ext corridors. **Pets:** Other species. $10 daily fee/pet. Service with restrictions, supervision.
(ASK) ⊠ 🛢 🖵 ⊇ ⊠

SARATOGA

▼ Hacienda Motel 🅼
(307) 326-5751. **$79-$89, 7 day notice.** 1500 S First St. 0.5 mi s on SR 130. Int corridors. **Pets:** $10 daily fee/pet. Designated rooms, service with restrictions, supervision.
(ASK) ⊠ 🛢

SHERIDAN

⧫⧫⧫ ▼ Americas Best Value Inn 🅼 🐾
(307) 672-9757. **$54-$97.** 580 E 5th St. I-90, exit 23, 0.4 mi w. Ext corridors. **Pets:** Other species. Service with restrictions, supervision.
(SAVE) ⊠ 🛢 🖵

⧫⧫⧫ ▼▼▼▼ Best Western Sheridan Center 🅷
(307) 674-7421. **$80-$150.** 612 N Main St. I-90, exit 23 (5th St), 1 mi w, then just s. Ext/int corridors. **Pets:** Medium, other species. $25 one-time fee/room. Service with restrictions, supervision.
(SAVE) ⊠ 🛢 🖵 🍴 ⊇

⧫⧫⧫ ▼ Budget Host Inn 🅼
(307) 674-7496. **$70-$200.** 2007 N Main St. I-90, exit 20, 0.7 mi s; on I-90 business loop. Ext corridors. **Pets:** Small, other species. $10 daily fee/pet. Designated rooms, service with restrictions, supervision.
(SAVE) ⊠ 🛢 🖵

▼▼ Candlewood Suites 🅷
(307) 675-2100. **Call for rates.** 1709 Sugarland Dr. I-90, exit 25, just w, then just n. Int corridors. **Pets:** Accepted.
⊠ (ᴸᴹ) 🛢 🖵

⧫⧫⧫ ▼▼▼▼ Holiday Inn Atrium & Convention Center 🅷 🐾
(307) 672-8931. **$108-$126.** 1809 Sugarland Dr. I-90, exit 25, 0.3 mi nw. Int corridors. **Pets:** Other species. $50 deposit/room. Service with restrictions, supervision.
(SAVE) ⊠ 🛢 🖵 🍴 ⊇ ⊠

⧫⧫⧫ ▼▼▼▼ Mill Inn 🅼 🐾
(307) 672-6401. **$65-$130.** 2161 Coffeen Ave. I-90, exit 25, 0.3 mi w. Ext/int corridors. **Pets:** Medium. $15 daily fee/room. Service with restrictions, crate.
(SAVE) ⊠ 🛢 🖵

SUNDANCE

⧫⧫⧫ ▼▼ Best Western Inn at Sundance 🅷
(307) 283-2800. **$65-$200.** 2719 E Cleveland Ave. I-90, exit 189, just n, then just w on I-90 business loop. Int corridors. **Pets:** Medium, other species. $10 daily fee/pet. Designated rooms, service with restrictions, supervision.
(SAVE) ⊠ 🖵 ⊇

⧫⧫⧫ ▼ Budget Host Arrowhead Motel 🅼
(307) 283-3307. **$49-$79.** 214 Cleveland Ave. I-90 business loop and US 14. Ext corridors. **Pets:** Dogs only. $10 daily fee/room. Service with restrictions, supervision.
(SAVE) ⊠ 🛢

THERMOPOLIS

▼▼ Days Inn 🅷 🐾
(307) 864-3131. **$93-$149.** 115 E Park St. In Hot Springs State Park. Ext/int corridors. **Pets:** $50 deposit/pet, $15 daily fee/pet. Service with restrictions, supervision.
(ASK) ⊠ 🖵 🍴 ⊇ ⊠

▼▼▼ Hot Springs Super 8 🅷
(307) 864-5515. **Call for rates.** Lane 5, Hwy 20 S. On US 20, just se. Int corridors. **Pets:** Accepted.
⊠ (ᴸᴹ) 🛢 🖵 ⊇

TORRINGTON

◆◆ **Holiday Inn Express Hotel & Suites** H
(307) 532-7600. **$90-$210.** 1700 E Valley Rd. US 85, e on US 26. Int corridors. **Pets:** Accepted.
⊠ 🔊 🖥 🖵 ⌿

UCROSS

◆◆◇ ◆◆◆ **The Ranch at Ucross** RA
(307) 737-2281. **$229-$300, 3 day notice.** 2673 US Hwy 14 E. Jct US 14/16, 0.5 mi w. Ext/int corridors. **Pets:** Accepted.
SAVE ⊠ ¶¶ ⌿ ⊠ 📶

WAPITI

◆◆◇ ◆◆ **Green Creek Inn** M ❖
(307) 587-5004. **$65-$180, 5 day notice.** 2908 Northford Hwy. 2.8 mi w on US 14/16/20. Ext corridors. **Pets:** Medium, other species. $15 daily fee/pet. Service with restrictions, supervision.
SAVE ⊠ 🖥 🐾

◆◆ **Yellowstone Valley Inn** M
(307) 587-3961. **$59-$169, 21 day notice.** 3324 Yellowstone Park Hwy. 3.3 mi w on US 14/16/20. Ext corridors. **Pets:** Accepted.
A$K ⊠ 🖥 🖵 ¶¶ ⌿ ⊠ 🐾

WHEATLAND

◆◆◇ ◆◆◆ **Best Western Torchlite Motor Inn** H ❖
(307) 322-4070. **$80-$150.** 1809 N 16th St. I-25, exit 78, just e; 1.5 mi n on US 87/I-25 business loop (16th St). Ext corridors. **Pets:** Large, other species. Service with restrictions, supervision.
SAVE ⊠ 🖥 🖵 ⌿

YELLOWSTONE NATIONAL PARK

◆◆◇ ◆◆ **Elephant Head Lodge** CA
(307) 587-3980. **$150-$350, 30 day notice.** 1170 Yellowstone Hwy. 11.7 mi e of Yellowstone National Park East Gate on US 14/16/20. Ext corridors. **Pets:** $20 one-time fee/pet. Designated rooms, service with restrictions, supervision.
SAVE ⊠ 🖥 🖵 ¶¶ ⊠ 🐾 📶 🐾

◆◆ **Shoshone Lodge** CA ❖
(307) 587-4044. **$100-$325, 30 day notice.** 349 Yellowstone Hwy. 3.5 mi e of Yellowstone National Park East Gate on US 14/16/20. Ext corridors. **Pets:** $10 daily fee/pet. Designated rooms, service with restrictions, supervision.
⊠ 🖥 🖵 ¶¶ ⊠ 🐾 🐾

Canadian Lodgings

ALBERTA

BANFF

◆◆◆◆◆ Banff Rocky Mountain Resort 🆔
(403) 762-5531. **$170-$385, 3 day notice.** 1029 Banff Ave. Banff Ave and Tunnel Mountain Rd; just s of Trans-Canada Hwy 1. Ext corridors. **Pets:** Accepted.

◆◆◆ Best Western Siding 29 Lodge 🆔
(403) 762-5575. **$100-$350.** 453 Marten St. 0.6 mi (1 km) ne, just off Banff Ave. Int corridors. **Pets:** Other species. $10 daily fee/pet. Service with restrictions, supervision.

◆◆ Castle Mountain Chalets 🆔
(403) 762-3868. **$150-$345, 14 day notice.** Bow Valley Pkwy (Hwy 1A). 20 mi (32 km) w on Trans-Canada Hwy 1, jct Castle, 0.6 mi (1 km) ne on Hwy 1A (Bow Valley Pkwy). Ext corridors. **Pets:** Accepted.

◆◆◆◆ Douglas Fir Resort & Chalets 🆔
(403) 762-5591. **$115-$459.** 525 Tunnel Mountain Rd. From centre, 1 mi (1.6 km) ne. Ext/int corridors. **Pets:** Accepted.

◆◆◆◆ The Fairmont Banff Springs 🆔 ❀
(403) 762-2211. **$233-$593, 3 day notice.** 405 Spray Ave. Just s on Banff Ave over the bridge, 0.3 mi (0.5 km) e. Int corridors. **Pets:** Medium. $25 daily fee/room. Service with restrictions, supervision.

◆◆ Hidden Ridge Resort 🆔
(403) 762-3544. **Call for rates.** 901 Hidden Ridge Way. 1.5 mi (2.4 km) ne at Tunnel Mountain Rd. Ext corridors. **Pets:** Accepted.

◆◆◆ Johnston Canyon Resort 🆔
(403) 762-2971. **$119-$314, 3 day notice.** Hwy 1A. 15 mi (24 km) nw on Hwy 1A (Bow Valley Pkwy). Ext corridors. **Pets:** Accepted.

◆◆◆◆ The Juniper 🆔
(403) 762-2281. **$160-$260, 3 day notice.** 1 Juniper Way. Trans-Canada Hwy 1, exit Mt. Norquay Rd, just n. Int corridors. **Pets:** Accepted.

◆◆◆ Red Carpet Inn 🆔
(403) 762-4184. **$75-$169.** 425 Banff Ave. N of Rabbit St. Ext/int corridors. **Pets:** Other species. $10 daily fee/pet. Designated rooms, service with restrictions, supervision.

BROOKS

◆◆◆◆ Best Western Brooks Inn 🆔 ❀
(403) 363-0080. **$120-$125, 5 day notice.** 115 Fifteenth Ave W. Just s off Trans-Canada Hwy 1. Ext/int corridors. **Pets:** $10 one-time fee/pet. Designated rooms, service with restrictions, supervision.

◆◆◆ Heritage Inn 🆔 ❀
(403) 362-6666. **$105-$169.** 1217 2nd St W. Trans-Canada Hwy 1, exit Hwy 873, 0.5 mi (0.8 km) s. Int corridors. **Pets:** Medium. $10 daily fee/pet. Designated rooms, service with restrictions, supervision.

◆◆◆ Lakeview Inns & Suites 🆔
(403) 362-7440. **$119-$179.** 1307 2nd St W. Trans-Canada Hwy 1, exit Hwy 873, 0.5 mi (0.8 km) s. Int corridors. **Pets:** Accepted.

◆◆◆ Travelodge Brooks 🆔
(403) 362-8000. **$92-$119.** 1240 Cassils Pl E. Trans-Canada Hwy 1, just sw on SR 542, exit E Brooks. Ext/int corridors. **Pets:** Accepted.

CALGARY METROPOLITAN AREA

AIRDRIE

◆◆◆◆ Ramada Inn & Suites 🆔
(403) 945-1288. **$149-$289.** 191 E Lake Crescent. Hwy 2, exit E Airdrie. Int corridors. **Pets:** Medium, other species. $20 daily fee/pet. Designated rooms, service with restrictions, supervision.

◆◆◆ Super 8 Airdrie 🆔
(403) 948-4188. **$109-$155.** 815 E Lake Blvd. Hwy 2, exit E Airdrie, 0.5 mi (0.8 km) e on Hwy 587 E. Int corridors. **Pets:** Accepted.

CALGARY

◆◆◆ 5 Calgary Downtown Suites 🆔
(403) 263-0520. **$99-$299.** 618 5th Ave SW. Corner of 5th Ave SW and 5th St SW. Int corridors. **Pets:** Other species. $10 daily fee/pet. Service with restrictions.

◆◆◆ Blackfoot Inn 🆔
(403) 252-2253. **$205-$335.** 5940 Blackfoot Tr SE. At 58th Ave SE; access to property from 58th Ave only. Int corridors. **Pets:** Large, other species. $30 one-time fee/room. Service with restrictions, crate.

Calgary Marriott Hotel
(403) 266-7331. **$299-$349.** 110 9th Ave SE. Jct 9th Ave and Centre St; adjacent to Telus Convention Centre. Int corridors. **Pets:** Small, dogs only. Service with restrictions, crate.

Calgary Westways Guest House
(403) 229-1758. **$110-$180, 4 day notice.** 216 25th Ave SW. 1.1 mi (1.7 km) s on Hwy 2A (MacLeod Tr S), 0.2 mi (0.5 km) w. Int corridors. **Pets:** Large, other species. $8 daily fee/pet.

Carriage House Inn
(403) 253-1101. **$149-$229.** 9030 MacLeod Tr S. On Hwy 2A (MacLeod Tr); corner of 90th Ave SW. Int corridors. **Pets:** $10 daily fee/pet. Service with restrictions, crate.

Coast Plaza Hotel & Conference Centre
(403) 248-8888. **$139-$304.** 1316 33rd St NE. Just s of jct 16th Ave (Trans-Canada Hwy 1) and 36th St NE, just w on 12th Ave NE. Int corridors. **Pets:** Accepted.

Delta Bow Valley
(403) 266-1980. **$159-$469.** 209 4th Ave SE. 1st St SE and 4th Ave SE. Int corridors. **Pets:** Small. $35 one-time fee/room. Designated rooms, service with restrictions, supervision.

Delta Calgary Airport
(403) 291-2600. **$159-$550.** 2001 Airport Rd NE. At Calgary International Airport. Int corridors. **Pets:** Accepted.

Delta Calgary South
(403) 278-5050. **$389-$399.** 135 Southland Dr SE. On Hwy 2A (MacLeod Tr); corner of Southland Dr. Int corridors. **Pets:** Medium, other species. $35 one-time fee/pet. Designated rooms, no service.

Econo Lodge South
(403) 252-4401. **$89-$209.** 7505 MacLeod Tr SW. Corner of Hwy 2A (MacLeod Tr) and 75th Ave. Ext/int corridors. **Pets:** Medium, other species. $10 one-time fee/pet. Designated rooms, service with restrictions, supervision.

Executive Royal Inn North Calgary
(403) 291-2003. **$130-$325.** 2828 23rd St NE. Barlow Tr NE, just w; at 27th Ave NE. Int corridors. **Pets:** Other species. $20 one-time fee/room. Supervision.

The Fairmont Palliser
(403) 262-1234. **$129-$529.** 133 9th Ave SW. 9th Ave SW and 1st St SW. Int corridors. **Pets:** Accepted.

Holiday Inn Express Hotel & Suites Calgary Downtown
(403) 269-8262. **Call for rates.** 1020 8th Ave SW. 8th Ave at 10th St SW. Int corridors. **Pets:** Small, other species. $25 one-time fee/room. Designated rooms, service with restrictions, supervision.

Holiday Inn Express Hotel & Suites Calgary-South
(403) 225-3000. **$130-$190, 3 day notice.** 12025 Lake Fraser Dr SE (MacLeod Tr S). Hwy 2 (Deerfoot Tr), exit Anderson Rd W, just s on MacLeod Tr, just e on Lake Fraser Gate, then just n. Int corridors. **Pets:** Other species. $20 one-time fee/pet. Designated rooms, service with restrictions, crate.

Hotel Arts
(403) 266-4611. **$139-$319.** 119 12th Ave SW. At 1st St SW; centre. Int corridors. **Pets:** Accepted.

Lakeview Signature Inn
(403) 735-3336. **$139-$309.** 2622 39th Ave NE. Barlow Tr NE, just e. Int corridors. **Pets:** Small. $100 one-time fee/pet. Service with restrictions, crate.

Radisson Hotel Calgary Airport
(403) 291-4666. **Call for rates.** 2120 16th Ave NE. Just e of jct 16th Ave NE (Trans-Canada Hwy 1) and Hwy 2 (Deerfoot Tr). Int corridors. **Pets:** Accepted.

Sandman Hotel Downtown Calgary
(403) 237-8626. **$189-$218.** 888 7th Ave SW. Corner of 7th Ave SW and 8th St SW. Int corridors. **Pets:** Small. $10 one-time fee/pet. Designated rooms, service with restrictions, crate.

Sandman Hotel Suites & Spa Calgary Airport
(403) 219-2475. **$199.** 25 Hopewell Way NE. Just n of jct Barlow Tr and McKnight Blvd. Int corridors. **Pets:** $10 daily fee/room. Service with restrictions.

Sheraton Cavalier Hotel
(403) 291-0107. **$139-$469, 3 day notice.** 2620 32nd Ave NE. Barlow Tr at 32nd Ave NE. Int corridors. **Pets:** Medium. Service with restrictions, supervision.

Sheraton Suites Calgary Eau Claire
(403) 266-7200. **$179-$739.** 255 Barclay Parade SW. At 3rd St SW and 2nd Ave SW. Int corridors. **Pets:** Small, dogs only. Designated rooms, service with restrictions, supervision.

Travelodge Calgary Macleod Trail
(403) 253-7070. **$119-$219.** 9206 MacLeod Tr S. On MacLeod Tr just s of 90th Ave SW. Int corridors. **Pets:** Medium. $25 one-time fee/room. Designated rooms, service with restrictions, supervision.

Travelodge Calgary University
(403) 289-6600. **$98-$199.** 2227 Banff Tr NW. 16th Ave NW (Trans-Canada Hwy 1) and Banff Tr NW. Int corridors. **Pets:** Accepted.

Travelodge Hotel Calgary Airport
(403) 291-1260. **$119-$219.** 2750 Sunridge Blvd NE. Just se of jct 32nd Ave NE and Barlow Tr NE. Int corridors. **Pets:** $10 one-time fee/pet. Service with restrictions, supervision.

The Westin Calgary
(403) 266-1611. **Call for rates.** 320 4th Ave SW. Corner of 4th Ave SW and 3rd St. Int corridors. **Pets:** Service with restrictions, supervision.

Wingate Inn
(403) 514-0099. **$147-$225, 4 day notice.** 400 Midpark Way SE. Hwy 2A (MacLeod Tr), 0.3 mi (0.5 km) e on Sun Valley, just n on Midpark Way, then just s. Int corridors. **Pets:** Accepted.

COCHRANE

⊕ ▼▼▼ Best Western Harvest Country Inn ⊞
(403) 932-1410. **Call for rates.** 11 West Side Dr. Hwy 1A, 0.6 mi (1 km) sw on Hwy 22. Ext/int corridors. **Pets:** Accepted.
[SAVE] [X] [⊟] [▭]

▼▼▼ Super 8-Cochrane ⊞
(403) 932-6355. **Call for rates.** 10 Westside Dr. Hwy 1A, 0.6 mi (1 km) sw on Hwy 22. Int corridors. **Pets:** Accepted.
[X] [⊟] [▭] [▭] [X]

▼▼ Travelodge Cochrane ⊞
(403) 932-5588. **$99-$169.** 5 West Side Dr. Hwy 1A, 0.6 mi (1 km) sw on Hwy 22. Int corridors. **Pets:** Accepted.
[ASK] [X] [⊟] [▭] [▭]

OKOTOKS

▼▼▼ Lakeview Inns & Suites ⊞ ❁
(403) 938-7400. **$129-$149, 14 day notice.** 22 Southridge Dr. Hwy 2, exit 2A, 2.5 mi (4 km) s to Southridge Dr. Int corridors. **Pets:** Other species. $10 daily fee/pet. Designated rooms, service with restrictions, supervision.
[ASK] [X] [⊟] [▭]

STRATHMORE

⊕ ▼▼▼ Best Western Strathmore Inn ⊞
(403) 934-5777. **$100-$140, 3 day notice.** 550 Hwy 1. Trans-Canada Hwy 1, jct SR 817; centre. Int corridors. **Pets:** Medium. $10 one-time fee/room. Designated rooms, service with restrictions.
[SAVE] [X] [⊟] [▭] [▭]

▼▼▼ Travelodge Strathmore ⊞
(403) 901-0000. **$134-$154.** 350 Ridge Rd. Just n of Trans-Canada Hwy 1 at Ridge Rd. Int corridors. **Pets:** Medium, other species. $10 daily fee/room. Designated rooms, service with restrictions, supervision.
[ASK] [X] [⊟] [▭] [▭] [X]

END METROPOLITAN AREA

CAMROSE

▼▼ Norsemen Inn ⊞
(780) 672-9171. **$95-$99.** 6505 48th Ave. Hwy 13 (48th Ave) at 65th St; west end of town. Int corridors. **Pets:** Accepted.
[ASK] [X] [⊟] [▭] [¶]

CANMORE

⊕ ▼▼▼ Banff Boundary Lodge ⊙
(403) 678-9555. **$89-$239, 3 day notice.** 1000 Harvie Heights Rd. Just e of Banff National Park east gate, parallel to Trans-Canada Hwy 1, exit Harvie Heights Rd. Ext corridors. **Pets:** Other species. $15 daily fee/pet. Designated rooms, no service, supervision.
[SAVE] [X] [⊟] [▭] [Æ]

⊕ ▼▼▼▼ Best Western Pocaterra Inn ⊞
(403) 678-4334. **$109-$209.** 1725 Mountain Ave. 3.6 mi (5.8 km) e of Banff National Park east gate on Hwy 1A (Bow Valley Tr). Int corridors. **Pets:** Medium. $15 one-time fee/pet. Designated rooms, service with restrictions, supervision.
[SAVE] [X] [⊾M] [⊟] [▭] [▭] [X]

⊕ ▼▼▼ Canadian Rockies Chalets ⊙
(403) 678-3799. **$79-$275, 3 day notice.** 1206 Bow Valley Tr. Trans-Canada Hwy 1, exit 86, 1.4 mi (2.2 km) se on Bow Valley Tr; across from hospital. Ext corridors. **Pets:** Accepted.
[SAVE] [X] [⊟] [▭] [Æ]

▼▼▼▼ Canmore Inn & Suites ⊞
(403) 609-4656. **$82-$252.** 1402 Bow Valley Tr. 3.5 mi (5.6 km) e of Banff National Park east gate on Hwy 1A (Bow Valley Tr); Trans-Canada Hwy 1, exit Canmore. Int corridors. **Pets:** $15 daily fee/pet. Designated rooms, service with restrictions.
[ASK] [X] [⊟] [▭] [▭] [X]

▼▼▼ The Lodges at Canmore ⊞
(403) 678-9350. **Call for rates.** 107 Montane Rd. Trans-Canada Hwy 1, exit 1A (Bow Valley Tr), 0.6 mi (1.6 km) w to Montane Rd. Int corridors. **Pets:** Accepted.
[X] [⊟] [▭] [▭]

▼▼▼ Mystic Springs Chalets & Hot Pools ⊙ ❁
(403) 609-0333. **$245-$369.** 140 Kananaskis Way. Trans-Canada Hwy 1, exit 1A (Bow Valley Tr), 0.6 mi (1 km) w, then n at Montane Dr. Ext corridors. **Pets:** Small, other species. $20 daily fee/pet. Designated rooms, service with restrictions, crate.
[ASK] [X] [⊟] [▭] [▭] [X]

⊕ ▼▼▼ Radisson Hotel & Conference Centre ⊞
(403) 678-3625. **$169-$249.** 511 Bow Valley Tr. Trans-Canada Hwy 1, exit Canmore, just e. Ext/int corridors. **Pets:** Accepted.
[SAVE] [X] [⊟] [▭] [¶] [▭] [X]

⊕ ▼▼▼ Rocky Mountain Ski Lodge ⋈ ❁
(403) 678-5445. **$125-$215.** 1711 Bow Valley Tr. Trans-Canada Hwy 1, exit Canmore; 3 mi (4.8 km) e of Banff National Park east gate on Hwy 1A (Bow Valley Tr). Ext corridors. **Pets:** Large, other species. $10 daily fee/pet. Designated rooms, service with restrictions.
[SAVE] [X] [⊟] [▭] [X]

⊕ ▼▼▼ Rundle Mountain Lodge ⋈ ❁
(403) 678-5322. **$75-$210, 7 day notice.** 1723 Bow Valley Tr. Trans-Canada Hwy 1, exit Canmore; 3 mi (4.8 km) e of Banff National Park east gate on Hwy 1A (Bow Valley Trail). Ext corridors. **Pets:** Other species. $20 daily fee/pet. Designated rooms, service with restrictions, crate.
[SAVE] [X] [⊟] [▭] [▭]

⊕ ▼▼▼ Windtower Lodge & Suites ⊙
(403) 609-6600. **$149-$429, 3 day notice.** 160 Kananaskis Way. Trans-Canada Hwy 1, exit 1A (Bow Valley Tr), 0.6 mi (1 km) w, then n at Montane Dr. Int corridors. **Pets:** $20 daily fee/pet. Designated rooms, service with restrictions, supervision.
[SAVE] [X] [⊟] [▭] [¶] [Æ]

CLAIRMONT

⊕ ▼▼▼▼ Ramada Inn & Suites ⊞ ❁
(780) 814-7448. **$169-$299.** 7201 99 St. Jct Hwy 43 and 2, 0.7 mi (1.2 km) n, then just e, 0.7 mi (1.2 km) s. Int corridors. **Pets:** Other species. $25 one-time fee/room. Service with restrictions, crate.
[SAVE] [X] [⊟] [▭]

CLARESHOLM

▼▼ Bluebird Motel Ⓜ
(403) 625-3395. **$84-$94.** 5505 1st St W. 0.3 mi (0.5 km) n on Hwy 2. Ext corridors. **Pets:** Other species. Designated rooms, service with restrictions, supervision.

☒ 🛇 💻

▼▼ Motel 6 Claresholm Ⓗ 🐾
(403) 625-4646. **$75-$125.** 11 Alberta Rd (Hwy #2). North end of town. Int corridors. **Pets:** Other species. Service with restrictions, supervision.

ASK ☒ 🛇

DRAYTON VALLEY

▼▼ Lakeview Inns & Suites Ⓗ
(780) 542-3200. **$113-$150.** 4302 50th St. Hwy 22, exit Drayton Valley, 1.5 mi (2.4 km) n; east end of town. Int corridors. **Pets:** Accepted.

☒ 🛇 💻 🍽 🗙

DRUMHELLER

ⒶⒶ ▼▼▼ Best Western Jurassic Inn Ⓗ
(403) 823-7700. **Call for rates.** 1103 Hwy 9 S. Hwy 9, southeast access to town. Ext/int corridors. **Pets:** Accepted.

SAVE ☒ 🛇 💻 🍽 🐾

EDMONTON METROPOLITAN AREA

EDMONTON

ⒶⒶ ▼▼▼ Best Western Cedar Park Inn Ⓗ
(780) 434-7411. **$129-$199, 14 day notice.** 5116 Gateway Blvd. Hwy 2 (Gateway Blvd) at 51st Ave. Int corridors. **Pets:** Other species. $25 daily fee/room. Designated rooms, service with restrictions, crate.

SAVE ☒ 🛇 💻 🍽 🐾

▼▼ Coast Edmonton House ⒸⓄ
(780) 420-4000. **Call for rates.** 10205 100th Ave. Just se of jct 102nd St and 100th Ave. Int corridors. **Pets:** Accepted.

☒ 🛇 💻 🍽 🐾

ⒶⒶ ▼▼ Comfort Inn West Ⓗ
(780) 484-4415. **$109-$154.** 17610 100th Ave. At 176th St. Int corridors. **Pets:** Medium. $10 daily fee/pet. Service with restrictions, supervision.

SAVE ☒ 🛇 💻 🍽

ⒶⒶ ▼▼ Continental Inn Ⓗ
(780) 484-7751. **$110-$145, 6 day notice.** 16625 Stony Plain Rd. On Hwy 16A (Stony Plain Rd) at 166th St. Int corridors. **Pets:** Accepted.

SAVE ☒ 🛇 💻 🍽

▼▼▼ Courtyard by Marriott Edmonton Ⓗ
(780) 423-9999. **$197-$241.** 1 Thornton Ct. Just off Jasper Ave (101 Ave); between 99th and 97th sts. Int corridors. **Pets:** Accepted.

☒ ⒧ 🛇 💻 🍽 🐾

▼▼▼ Delta Edmonton Centre Suite Hotel Ⓗ
(780) 429-3900. **$99-$449.** 10222 102nd St. At 102nd St at 103rd Ave. Int corridors. **Pets:** Accepted.

☒ 🛇 💻 🍽 🗙

▼▼▼ Delta Edmonton South Hotel and Conference Centre Ⓗ 🐾
(780) 434-6415. **$160-$270.** 4404 Gateway Blvd. Jct Calgary Tr (Hwy 2) and Whitemud Dr. Int corridors. **Pets:** Other species. $35 one-time fee/ room. Service with restrictions, supervision.

ASK ☒ 🛇 💻 🍽 🐾

▼▼ Executive Royal Inn West Edmonton Ⓗ
(780) 484-6000. **$120.** 10010 178th St. Corner of 178th St and 100th Ave. Int corridors. **Pets:** Accepted.

ASK ☒ 🛇 💻 🍽

ⒶⒶ ▼▼ Inn and Spa at Heartwood Ⓑ Ⓑ
(403) 823-6495. **$99-$280, 3 day notice.** 320 N Railway Ave E. Downtown. Ext/int corridors. **Pets:** Other species. $25 daily fee/room. Designated rooms, supervision.

SAVE ☒ 🛇 💻

▼▼▼ Ramada Inn & Suites Ⓗ
(403) 823-2028. **Call for rates.** 680 2nd St SE. Off Hwy 9. Ext/int corridors. **Pets:** Accepted.

☒ 🛇 💻 🐾 🗙

▼▼ Super 8 Ⓗ
(403) 823-8887. **$139-$179.** 600-680 2nd St SE. Off Hwy 9. Ext/int corridors. **Pets:** Accepted.

ASK ☒ 🛇 💻 🐾 🗙

ⒶⒶ ▼▼▼ ▼▼▼ The Fairmont Hotel Macdonald Ⓗ 🐾
(780) 424-5181. **$159-$489.** 10065 100th St. Just s of Jasper Ave. Int corridors. **Pets:** $25 daily fee/pet. Supervision.

SAVE ☒ ⒧ 💻 🍽 🐾 🗙

ⒶⒶ ▼▼▼ Four Points by Sheraton Edmonton South Ⓗ
(780) 465-7931. **Call for rates.** 7230 Argyll Rd. Hwy 2 (Gateway Blvd), 2.3 mi (3.7 km) e at 63rd Ave (which becomes Argyll Rd); at 75th St. Int corridors. **Pets:** Small. $250 deposit/room, $10 daily fee/pet. Designated rooms, service with restrictions, supervision.

SAVE ☒ 🛇 💻 🍽 🐾

ⒶⒶ ▼▼▼ Holiday Inn Express Edmonton-Downtown Ⓗ
(780) 423-2450. **$132-$142, 7 day notice.** 10010 104th St. Corner of 100th Ave; centre. Int corridors. **Pets:** Small. $25 one-time fee/pet. Designated rooms, service with restrictions, supervision.

SAVE ☒ 🛇 💻 🐾 🗙

ⒶⒶ ▼▼▼ Mayfield Inn & Suites at West Edmonton Ⓗ
(780) 484-0821. **$150-$225.** 16615 109th Ave. 1 mi (1.6 km) n of jct Hwy 2 (Gateway Blvd) and 16A on Mayfield Rd. Int corridors. **Pets:** Accepted.

SAVE ☒ 🛇 💻 🍽 🐾 🗙

▼▼▼ Metterra Hotel on Whyte Ⓗ
(780) 465-8150. **$170-$350.** 10454 82nd Ave (Whyte Ave). Just e of 105th St. Int corridors. **Pets:** Small. $10 daily fee/room. Designated rooms, service with restrictions, supervision.

ASK ☒ 💻

ⒶⒶ ▼▼▼ Radisson Hotel Edmonton South Ⓗ
(780) 437-6010. **$165-$200.** 4440 Gateway Blvd NW. Between Whitemud Dr and 45th Ave. Int corridors. **Pets:** Accepted.

SAVE ☒ 🛇 💻 🍽 🐾 🗙

ⒶⒶ ▼▼▼ Rosslyn Inn & Suites Ⓗ 🐾
(780) 476-6241. **$113.** 13620 97th St. Hwy 16 (Yellowhead Tr), exit 97th St, 1 mi (1.6 km) n. Int corridors. **Pets:** Medium. $10 daily fee/pet. Designated rooms, service with restrictions, supervision.

SAVE ☒ 🛇 💻 🍽

▼▼▼ Sawridge Inn–Edmonton South 🅷
(780) 438-1222. **$129-$159, 14 day notice.** 4235 Gateway Blvd. Just s of Whitemud Dr. Int corridors. **Pets:** Medium, other species. $10 daily fee/room. Designated rooms, service with restrictions, crate.
(A$K) (X) (🛏) (💻) (🍴) (🚫)

ⓒ ▼▼ Super 8 Edmonton South 🅷
(780) 433-8688. **$129-$149.** 3610 Gateway Blvd. Jct 36th Ave. Int corridors. **Pets:** Accepted.
(SAVE) (X) (&M) (🛏) (💻) (🏊)

▼▼▼ The Sutton Place Hotel, Edmonton 🅷
(780) 428-7111. **$325-$355.** 10235 101st St. 102nd Ave at 101st St. Int corridors. **Pets:** Small. $185 deposit/room, $35 one-time fee/room. Service with restrictions, supervision.
(A$K) (X) (🛏) (💻) (🍴) (🏊) (🚫)

ⓒ ▼▼ Travelodge Edmonton West 🅷 🐾
(780) 483-6031. **$109-$159.** 18320 Stony Plain Rd. Hwy 16A (Stony Plain Rd) at 184th St. Int corridors. **Pets:** Small. $50 deposit/room. Designated rooms, service with restrictions, supervision.
(SAVE) (X) (🛏) (💻) (🍴) (🏊) (🚫)

▼▼▼ Varscona Hotel on Whyte 🅷
(780) 434-6111. **$160-$350.** 8208 106th St. Corner of 82nd Ave (Whyte Ave) and 106th St. Int corridors. **Pets:** Small. $10 daily fee/room. Designated rooms, service with restrictions, supervision.
(A$K) (X) (🛏) (💻) (🍴)

ⓒ ▼▼▼ The Westin Edmonton 🅷 🐾
(780) 426-3636. **Call for rates.** 10135 100th St. 101st Ave at 100th St. Int corridors. **Pets:** Medium. Service with restrictions, supervision.
(SAVE) (X) (💻) (🍴) (🏊) (🚫)

▼▼▼ Wingate Inn Edmonton West 🅷
(780) 443-1000. **$139-$160.** 18220 100th Ave. 100th Ave at 182nd St. Int corridors. **Pets:** Accepted.
(A$K) (X) (&M) (🛏) (💻) (🏊) (🚫)

FORT SASKATCHEWAN

▼▼▼ Lakeview Inns & Suites 🅷
(780) 998-7888. **$125-$179.** 10115 88th Ave. Just w of Hwy 15/21 and 101st St. Int corridors. **Pets:** Other species. $10 daily fee/room. Service with restrictions.
(A$K) (X) (🛏) (💻) (🍴)

SHERWOOD PARK

ⓒ ▼▼ Franklin's Inn 🅷
(780) 467-1234. **$105-$149, 3 day notice.** 2016 Sherwood Dr. At Granada Blvd. Int corridors. **Pets:** Other species. $5 daily fee/pet. Designated rooms, service with restrictions, supervision.
(SAVE) (X) (🛏) (💻) (🍴)

ⓒ ▼▼ Ramada Sherwood Park 🅷
(780) 467-6727. **Call for rates.** 30 Broadway Blvd. Hwy 16, exit Broadmoor Blvd, 1.2 mi (2 km) s. Int corridors. **Pets:** Accepted.
(SAVE) (X) (&M) (🛏) (💻)

▼▼ Roadking Inns 🅷
(780) 464-1000. **$129-$149.** 26 Strathmoor Dr. Hwy 16, exit Broadmoor Blvd, just sw. Int corridors. **Pets:** Medium, other species. $39 one-time fee/room. Designated rooms, service with restrictions, supervision.
(A$K) (X) (🛏) (💻) (🍴)

STONY PLAIN

▼▼ Motel 6 Stony Plain 🅷 🐾
(780) 968-5123. **Call for rates.** 66 Boulder Blvd. Just off Hwy 16A. Int corridors. **Pets:** Very small, dogs only. $100 deposit/room. Designated rooms, service with restrictions, supervision.
(🛏)

ⓒ ▼▼▼ Ramada Inn & Suites 🅷
(780) 963-0222. **$90-$175.** 3301 43rd Ave. Hwy 16A, exit S Park Dr, just s. Ext/int corridors. **Pets:** Medium, other species. $15 daily fee/room. Designated rooms, service with restrictions, supervision.
(SAVE) (X) (🛏) (💻) (🍴) (🏊)

END METROPOLITAN AREA

EDSON

ⓒ ▼▼▼ Best Western High Road Inn 🅷
(780) 712-2378. **$119-$129, 3 day notice.** 300 52nd St. On 2nd Ave; centre. Int corridors. **Pets:** Accepted.
(SAVE) (X) (🛏) (💻) (🍴) (🏊) (🚫)

ⓒ ▼▼ Guest House Inn & Suites 🅼
(780) 723-4486. **$101-$124.** 4411 4th Ave. 0.6 mi (1 km) e on Hwy 16. Ext/int corridors. **Pets:** Small. Designated rooms, service with restrictions, supervision.
(SAVE) (X) (🛏) (💻) (🍴) (🚫)

▼▼ Lakeview Inns & Suites 🅷
(780) 723-2500. **$120.** 4300 2nd Ave. 0.6 mi (1.1 km) e on Hwy 16. Int corridors. **Pets:** Accepted.
(A$K) (X) (🛏) (💻)

FORT MACLEOD

ⓒ ▼ Sunset Motel 🅼
(403) 553-4448. **$54-$78.** 104 Hwy 3 W. 0.6 mi (1 km) w on Hwy 2 and 3. Ext corridors. **Pets:** Other species. Service with restrictions, supervision.
(SAVE) (X) (🛏) (💻)

GRANDE CACHE

ⓒ ▼▼▼ Best Western Grande Mountain Getaways & Hotel 🅷
(780) 827-3303. **Call for rates.** 9901 100th St. Hwy 40 (100th St); south end of town. Int corridors. **Pets:** Small, dogs only. $10 daily fee/pet. Designated rooms, service with restrictions, supervision.
(SAVE) (X) (🛏) (💻) (🍴) (🚫)

GRANDE PRAIRIE

ⓒ ▼▼▼ Best Western Grande Prairie Hotel & Suites 🅷
(780) 402-2378. **$190-$200, 14 day notice.** 10745 117th Ave. Corner of Hwy 43 and 117th Ave. Int corridors. **Pets:** Medium. $25 one-time fee/room. Service with restrictions, supervision.
(SAVE) (X) (🛏) (💻) (🍴) (🏊)

ⓒ ▼▼▼ Pomeroy Inn & Suites, Grande Prairie 🅷
(780) 831-2999. **$179-$189.** 11710 102nd St. 102nd St at 117th Ave. Int corridors. **Pets:** Accepted.
(SAVE) (X) (🛏) (💻) (🏊) (🚫)

ⓒ ▼▼ Quality Hotel & Conference Centre Grande Prairie 🅷
(780) 539-6000. **$203-$300.** 11201 100th Ave. 1.8 mi (2.9 km) w on Hwy 2. Int corridors. **Pets:** Other species. $25 daily fee/pet. Designated rooms, service with restrictions, supervision.
(SAVE) (X) (🛏) (💻) (🍴)

▼▼ Service Plus Inns and Suites H
(780) 538-3900. **$159-$300.** 10810 107th a Ave. 1.4 mi (2.2 km) w on Hwy 2, just n. Int corridors. **Pets:** Medium. $10 one-time fee/pet. Designated rooms, service with restrictions, supervision.

⊠ 🖪 💻 ⇌ ⊠

▼▼ Stanford Inn H
(780) 539-5678. **$129-$149.** 11401 100th Ave. 1.8 mi (2.8 km) w on Hwy 2. Ext/int corridors. **Pets:** Accepted.

ASK ⊠ 🖪 💻 ⑴

▼▼ Super 8 H
(780) 532-8288. **Call for rates.** 10050 116 Ave. 102nd St at 117th Ave. Int corridors. **Pets:** Accepted.

⊠ 🖪 💻 ⇌ ⊠

HANNA

▼▼ Hanna Inn H
(403) 854-2400. **$130-$140.** 113 Palliser Tr. Hwy 9, just n. Ext/int corridors. **Pets:** Accepted.

ASK ⊠ 🖪 💻 ⇌

HIGH PRAIRIE

▼▼▼ Pomeroy Inn & Suites High Prairie H ✻
(780) 523-2398. **$149-$169.** 3905 51st Ave. Just n of Hwy 2, east end of town. Int corridors. **Pets:** Other species. $25 daily fee/room. Supervision.

ASK 🖪 💻 ⑴ ⇌ ⊠

HIGH RIVER

▼▼ Heritage Inn H ✻
(403) 652-3834. **$124-$249.** 1104 11th Ave SE. Trans-Canada Hwy 2, exit 23, 0.5 mi (0.8 km) w of Hwy 2. Int corridors. **Pets:** Medium. $10 daily fee/pet. Designated rooms, service with restrictions, supervision.

ASK ⊠ 🖪 💻 ⑴ ⇌

▼▼▼ Super 8 H
(403) 652-4448. **$140-$250.** 1601 13th Ave SE. Trans-Canada Hwy 2, exit High River, just w. Int corridors. **Pets:** Accepted.

⊠ ⑤ᴹ 🖪 💻 ⇌ ⊠

HINTON

ⒶⒶ ▼▼ Best Western White Wolf Inn H
(780) 865-7777. **$160-$200, 7 day notice.** 828 Carmichael Ln. At west end of town; just off Hwy 16. Ext corridors. **Pets:** Small. $15 daily fee/room. Designated rooms, service with restrictions, supervision.

SAVE ⊠ 🖪 💻

▼▼ Super 8 H
(780) 817-2228. **Call for rates.** 284 Smith St. 1 mi (1.6 km) e on Hwy 16. Int corridors. **Pets:** Other species. $15 one-time fee/room. Designated rooms, service with restrictions, supervision.

⊠ 🖪 💻 ⇌

JASPER

ⒶⒶ ▼▼ Amethyst Lodge H ✻
(780) 852-3394. **$85-$285.** 200 Connaught Dr. 0.3 mi (0.5 km) e. Ext/int corridors. **Pets:** $10 daily fee/room. Service with restrictions, crate.

SAVE ⊠ 🖪 💻 ⑴

ⒶⒶ ▼▼ The Coast Pyramid Lake Resort H
(780) 852-4900. **$125-$368, 3 day notice.** Pyramid Lake Rd. Jct Connaught Dr and Cedar St, 3.75 mi (6 km) nw via Pyramid Lake Rd. Ext corridors. **Pets:** $25 one-time fee/pet. Designated rooms, service with restrictions, supervision.

SAVE ⊠ 🖪 💻 ⑴ ⊠ Ⓐ

ⒶⒶ ▼▼▼ The Fairmont Jasper Park Lodge H ✻
(780) 852-3301. **Call for rates.** Lodge Rd. 3 mi (4.8 km) ne via Hwy 16; 2 mi (3.2 km) se off highway via Maligne Rd, follow signs. Ext corridors. **Pets:** Large. $50 daily fee/pet. Service with restrictions, supervision.

SAVE ⊠ ⑤ᴹ 🖪 💻 ⑴ ⇌ ⊠ Ⓐ

ⒶⒶ ▼▼▼▼ Jasper Inn Alpine Resort H ✻
(780) 852-4461. **$111-$414, 3 day notice.** 98 Geikie St. Corner of Geikie and Bonhomme sts. Ext/int corridors. **Pets:** Other species. $25 daily fee/room. Designated rooms, service with restrictions, supervision.

SAVE ⊠ 🖪 💻 ⑴ ⇌ ⊠ Ⓐ

ⒶⒶ ▼▼▼▼ Lobstick Lodge H ✻
(780) 852-4431. **$99-$255.** 94 Geikie St. Corner of Geikie and Juniper sts. Int corridors. **Pets:** $10 daily fee/room. Service with restrictions, crate.

SAVE ⊠ 🖪 💻 ⑴ ⇌ Ⓐ

▼▼ Maligne Lodge M ✻
(780) 852-3143. **$99-$400.** 900 Connaught. 0.6 mi (1 km) sw. Ext/int corridors. **Pets:** Other species. $25 one-time fee/room. Service with restrictions, crate.

ASK ⊠ 🖪 💻 ⑴ ⇌

ⒶⒶ ▼▼ Marmot Lodge M ✻
(780) 852-4471. **$89-$255.** 86 Connaught Dr. 1 mi (1.6 km) ne. Ext corridors. **Pets:** $10 daily fee/room. Service with restrictions, crate.

SAVE ⊠ ⑤ᴹ 🖪 💻 ⑴ ⇌

▼▼ Patricia Lake Bungalows ⒸⒶ
(780) 852-3560. **$75-$325, 7 day notice.** Pyramid Lake Rd. 3 mi (4.8 km) nw via Pyramid Lake Rd. Ext corridors. **Pets:** Medium, dogs only. $10 daily fee/pet. Designated rooms, service with restrictions, supervision.

⊠ 🖪 💻 ⊠ Ⓐ Ⓩ

ⒶⒶ ▼▼ The Sawridge Inn and Conference Centre H
(780) 852-5111. **$139-$289, 3 day notice.** 82 Connaught Dr. 1.1 mi (1.7 km) e. Int corridors. **Pets:** Accepted.

SAVE ⊠ ⑤ᴹ 🖪 💻 ⇌ ⊠

ⒶⒶ ▼▼ Sunwapta Falls Resort M
(780) 852-4852. **$99-$389, 7 day notice.** Hwy 93. 34.75 mi (55 km) s on Icefields Pkwy (Hwy 93). Ext corridors. **Pets:** Accepted.

SAVE ⊠ 🖪 💻 ⑴ ⊠ Ⓐ Ⓩ

▼▼ Tonquin Inn M
(780) 852-4987. **$135-$309, 3 day notice.** 100 Juniper St. Corner of Juniper and Geikie sts. Ext/int corridors. **Pets:** Accepted.

ASK ⊠ 🖪 💻 ⑴ ⇌ ⊠

KANANASKIS

▼▼▼ Delta Lodge at Kananaskis H ✻
(403) 591-7711. **$139-$309, 3 day notice.** Kananaskis Village. Trans-Canada Hwy 1, 14.7 mi (23.5 km) s on Hwy 40 (Kananaskis Tr), then 1.8 mi (3 km) on Kananaskis Village access road, follow signs. Int corridors. **Pets:** Medium. $35 daily fee/room. Designated rooms, service with restrictions, supervision.

ASK ⊠ 🖪 💻 ⑴ ⇌ ⊠

LAKE LOUISE

ⒶⒶ ▼▼ ▼▼ The Fairmont Chateau Lake Louise H ✻
(403) 522-3511. **$249-$1899, 3 day notice.** 111 Lake Louise Dr. 1.8 mi (3 km) up the hill from the village. Int corridors. **Pets:** Dogs only. $25 one-time fee/room. Service with restrictions, supervision.

SAVE ⊠ 💻 ⑴ ⇌ ⊠

▼▼ Lake Louise Inn H
(403) 522-3791. **$149-$489, 7 day notice.** 210 Village Rd. Just w of 4-way stop. Ext/int corridors. **Pets:** Accepted.

ASK ⊠ 🖪 💻 ⑴ ⇌ ⊠

LETHBRIDGE

▼▼ Comfort Inn H
(403) 320-8874. **Call for rates.** 3226 Fairway Plaza Rd S. Mayor Magrath Dr, exit Scenic Dr northbound; southeast end of city. Int corridors. **Pets:** Accepted.

⊠ 🖪 💻 ⇌

▼▼▼ Days Inn Lethbridge �H
(403) 327-6000. **$105-$185.** 100 3rd Ave S. Corner of 3rd Ave and Scenic Dr; centre. Ext/int corridors. **Pets:** Accepted.
(ASK) (✕) 🛏 🖵 🏊

ⒸⒶ ▼▼▼▼ Holiday Inn Express Hotel & Suites Lethbridge �H
(403) 394-9292. **$149-$249.** 120 Stafford Dr S. Hwy 3, exit Stafford Dr, just s; downtown. Int corridors. **Pets:** Other species. $45 one-time fee/room. Designated rooms, service with restrictions, supervision.
(SAVE) (✕) 🛏 🖵 🏊 (✕)

ⒸⒶ ▼▼▼▼ Lethbridge Lodge Hotel and Conference Centre �H
(403) 328-1123. **$119-$199.** 320 Scenic Dr. Scenic Dr at 4th Ave S; centre. Int corridors. **Pets:** $15 daily fee/pet. Designated rooms, service with restrictions, supervision.
(SAVE) (✕) 🛏 🖵 🍴 🏊

ⒸⒶ ▼▼▼▼ Quality Inn & Suites �H
(403) 331-6440. **$135-$230.** 4040 2nd Ave S. Hwy 3 (Crownsnest Hwy), just s on W.T. Hill Blvd, then just e. Int corridors. **Pets:** Other species. $10 daily fee/pet. Designated rooms, service with restrictions, supervision.
(SAVE) (✕) 🛏 🖵 🏊 (✕)

▼▼▼▼ Ramada Lethbridge �H 🐾
(403) 380-5050. **$140-$160.** 2375 Mayor Magrath Dr S. 2.6 mi (4.5 km) se on Hwy 4 and 5, exit Mayor Magrath Dr S. Int corridors. **Pets:** Other species. $20 one-time fee/room. Designated rooms, service with restrictions.
(ASK) (✕) 🛏 🖵 🏊 (✕)

▼▼ Sandman Hotel Lethbridge �H
(403) 328-1111. **$109-$159.** 421 Mayor Magrath Dr S. Hwy 3, exit Mayor Magrath Dr, just s. Int corridors. **Pets:** Other species. $10 daily fee/pet. Designated rooms, service with restrictions, crate.
(ASK) (✕) 🛏 🖵 🍴 🏊

MEDICINE HAT

ⒸⒶ ▼▼▼▼ Best Western Inn �H
(403) 527-3700. **$99-$249.** 722 Redcliff Dr. On Trans-Canada Hwy 1, 0.3 mi (0.4 km) w of jct Hwy 3, access 7th St SW. Ext/int corridors. **Pets:** Accepted.
(SAVE) (✕) 🛏 🖵 🏊 (✕)

▼▼▼▼ Medicine Hat Lodge Resort, Casino & Spa �H
(403) 529-2222. **$139-$166.** 1051 Ross Glen Dr SE. East end approach to city on Trans-Canada Hwy 1, at Dunmore Rd. Int corridors. **Pets:** Other species. $10 daily fee/room. Designated rooms, service with restrictions, supervision.
(ASK) (✕) 🛏 🖵 🍴 🏊 (✕)

▼▼ Motel 6-Medicine Hat #5700 �H
(403) 527-1749. **$80-$95.** 20 Strachan Ct SE. Trans-Canada Hwy 1, exit Dunmore Rd, just sw. Int corridors. **Pets:** Other species. Service with restrictions, supervision.
(✕) 🛏

▼▼ Super 8 �H
(403) 528-8888. **$82-$89.** 1280 Trans-Canada Way SE. Trans-Canada Hwy 1 at 13 Ave SE; just n off Trans-Canada Hwy 1. Ext/int corridors. **Pets:** $10 daily fee/pet. Designated rooms, service with restrictions, supervision.
(ASK) (✕) 🛏 🖵 🏊

PINCHER CREEK

▼▼ Heritage Inn �H 🐾
(403) 627-5000. **$120-$289.** 919 Waterton Ave (Hwy 6). Hwy 3, 2.9 mi (4.7 km) s. Int corridors. **Pets:** Medium. $10 daily fee/pet. Designated rooms, service with restrictions, supervision.
(ASK) (✕) 🛏 🖵 🍴

▼▼▼ Ramada Inn & Suites �H
(403) 627-3777. **$150-$250.** 1132 Table Mountain St. Hwy 3, just s on Hwy 6. Ext/int corridors. **Pets:** Accepted.
(✕) 🛏 🖵 🏊 (✕)

RED DEER

ⒸⒶ ▼▼▼▼ Best Western Red Deer Inn & Suites �H
(403) 346-3555. **$120-$160.** 6839 66th St. Hwy 2, exit 67th St, just e. Int corridors. **Pets:** Accepted.
(SAVE) (✕) 🛁 🛏 🖵 🏊

ⒸⒶ ▼▼▼▼ Comfort Inn & Suites �H
(403) 348-0025. **$99-$149.** 6846 66th St. Hwy 2, exit 67th St, just e. Int corridors. **Pets:** Accepted.
(SAVE) (✕) 🛁 🛏 🖵 🏊 (✕)

▼▼ Motel 6-Red Deer �H
(403) 340-1749. **$65-$85.** 900-5001 19th St. Hwy 2, exit 394 (Gaetz Ave), just n, then just w; in Southpointe Common Shopping District. Int corridors. **Pets:** Accepted.
(ASK) (✕) 🛏

▼▼▼ Sandman Hotel Red Deer �H
(403) 343-7400. **Call for rates.** 2818 Gaetz Ave. 1 mi (1.6 km) n on Hwy 2A (Gaetz Ave). Int corridors. **Pets:** Accepted.
(✕) 🛁 🛏 🖵 🍴 🏊

ROCKY MOUNTAIN HOUSE

ⒸⒶ ▼▼▼▼ Best Western Rocky Mountain House �H 🐾
(403) 844-3100. **$109-$199.** 4407 41st Ave. Hwy 11 and 22, just w on 42nd Ave, then just s; east end of town. Int corridors. **Pets:** Other species. $10 daily fee/pet. Designated rooms, service with restrictions, supervision.
(SAVE) (✕) 🛏 🖵 🏊 (✕)

ⒸⒶ ▼▼▼ Holiday Inn Express Rocky Mountain House �H
(403) 845-2871. **$119-$129.** 4715 45th St. Hwy 11 and 22, just e on 47th Ave, then just n. Int corridors. **Pets:** $15 daily fee/pet. Service with restrictions, supervision.
(SAVE) (✕) 🛏 🖵

▼▼▼ Super 8 �H
(403) 846-0088. **$114-$140.** 4406 41st Ave. Hwy 11 and 22, just w on 42nd Ave, then just s; east end of town. Int corridors. **Pets:** Accepted.
(ASK) (✕) 🛏 🖵 🏊 (✕)

SLAVE LAKE

▼▼▼▼ Lakeview Inn & Suites �H
(780) 849-9500. **Call for rates.** 1550 Holmes Tr SE. Just n of Hwy 2, east end of town. Int corridors. **Pets:** Accepted.
(✕) 🛏 🖵

STETTLER

ⒸⒶ ▼▼▼▼ Best Western Crusader Inn �H
(403) 742-3371. **$129.** 6020 50th Ave. Hwy 12 (50th Ave); at 61st St. Ext/int corridors. **Pets:** Accepted.
(SAVE) (✕) 🛁 🛏 🖵 🍴 🏊 (✕)

TABER

▼▼ Heritage Inn �H 🐾
(403) 223-4424. **$95-$129.** 4830 46th Ave. 0.6 mi (1 km) e of jct Hwy 3 and 36 S, on Hwy 3. Int corridors. **Pets:** Medium. $10 daily fee/pet. Designated rooms, service with restrictions, supervision.
(ASK) (✕) 🛏 🖵 🍴 (✕)

▼▼ Super 8, Taber �H
(403) 223-8181. **$89.** 5700 46th Ave. Hwy 3, west end of town. Ext/int corridors. **Pets:** Accepted.
(✕) 🛏 🖵

THREE HILLS

CAA ▼▼▼▼ **Best Western Diamond Inn** H
(403) 443-7889. **Call for rates.** 351 7th Ave N. From Hwy 21 and 27, 1.1 mi (1.9 km) w. Int corridors. **Pets:** Accepted.

SAVE ✕ 📞 💻 🍴

VALLEYVIEW

CAA ▼▼▼ **Western Valley Inn** M
(780) 524-4000. **$109-$159.** 5402 Highway St. Just w of jct Hwy 43 and 49. Ext corridors. **Pets:** Dogs only. $20 daily fee/pet. Supervision.

SAVE ✕ 📞 💻

WATERTON PARK

CAA ▼▼▼ **Bayshore Inn** M
(403) 859-2211. **$119-$249, 3 day notice.** 111 Waterton Ave. Centre. Ext/int corridors. **Pets:** Other species. $20 daily fee/pet. Designated rooms, service with restrictions.

SAVE ✕ &M 📞 💻 🍴

CAA ▼▼▼▼ **Waterton Lakes Resort** H
(403) 859-2150. **$120-$215, 3 day notice.** 101 Clematis Ave. Centre. Ext/int corridors. **Pets:** $20 daily fee/pet. Designated rooms, service with restrictions, supervision.

SAVE ✕ 📞 💻 🍴 ⇌ ✕

WESTEROSE

▼▼ ▼▼ **Village Creek Country Inn** H
(780) 586-0006. **Call for rates.** 15 Village Dr, RR2. Hwy 2, exit 482, 17.5 mi (28 km) w on Hwy 13; in Village at Pigeon Lake. Ext/int corridors. **Pets:** Accepted.

✕ 📞 💻

WETASKIWIN

CAA ▼▼ ▼▼ **Best Western Wayside Inn** H
(780) 312-7300. **$120-$140.** 4103 56th St. On Hwy 2A, just n of jct Hwy 13 W. Int corridors. **Pets:** Medium. $100 deposit/room. Designated rooms, service with restrictions, crate.

SAVE ✕ 📞 💻 🍴

WHITECOURT

CAA ▼▼ ▼▼ **Super 8** H
(780) 778-8908. **$129-$139.** 4121 Kepler St. On Hwy 43, just e of Hwy 32. Int corridors. **Pets:** $25 one-time fee/room. Designated rooms, service with restrictions, supervision.

SAVE ✕ 📞 💻

BRITISH COLUMBIA

CITY INDEX

100 MILE HOUSE

▼▼▼ 100 Mile House Super 8 ⓜ
(250) 395-8888. **$100-$150, 7 day notice.** 989 Alder Ave. 0.6 mi (1 km) s on Hwy 97. Ext corridors. **Pets:** Accepted.
(ASK) ⊠ 🛡 🖵

▼▼ Ramada Limited ⓜ
(250) 395-2777. **$80-$179.** 917 Alder Ave. 0.6 mi (1 km) s on Hwy 97. Int corridors. **Pets:** Other species. Designated rooms, service with restrictions, supervision.
(ASK) ⊠ 🛡 🖵

▼▼ Red Coach Inn ⒣
(250) 395-2266. **Call for rates.** 170 Cariboo Hwy N. On Hwy 97, on north end of town. Ext/int corridors. **Pets:** Accepted.
⊠ 🛳 🛡 🖵 🍽 ⇴

108 MILE HOUSE

ⒶⒶ ▼▼▼ 108 Resort & Conference Centre ⒣
(250) 791-5211. **$95-$135.** 4816 Telqua Dr. From Hwy 97, 1 mi (1.6 km) nw on access road, follow signs. Ext corridors. **Pets:** Accepted.
(SAVE) ⊠ 🛳 🛡 🍽 ⇴ ⊠

ABBOTSFORD

ⒶⒶ ▼▼▼ Best Western Bakerview Inn ⓜ ❀
(604) 859-1341. **$110-$159, 7 day notice.** 1821 Sumas Way. Trans-Canada Hwy 1, exit 92 (Town Centre), just n on Hwy 11. Ext corridors. **Pets:** Other species. Service with restrictions, crate.
(SAVE) ⊠ 🛡 🖵 🍽 ⇴

▼▼▼ Coast Abbotsford Hotel & Suites ⒣
(604) 853-1880. **$99-$260, 3 day notice.** 2020 Sumas Way. Trans-Canada Hwy 1, exit 92 (Town Centre), just n on Hwy 11. Int corridors. **Pets:** Accepted.
(ASK) ⊠ 🛳 🛡 🖵 🍽 ⇴

ⒶⒶ ▼▼▼ Super 8 Abbotsford ⒣
(604) 853-1141. **$99-$399.** 1881 Sumas Way. Trans-Canada Hwy 1, exit 92 (Town Centre), just n on Hwy 11. Ext/int corridors. **Pets:** Accepted.
(SAVE) ⊠ 🛳 🛡 🖵 ⇴ ⊠

BLUE RIVER

▼▼▼ Glacier Mountain Lodge ⓜ
(250) 673-2393. **$99-$209.** 869 Shell Rd. On Hwy 5 (Yellowhead Hwy); at Shell Rd, follow signs. Int corridors. **Pets:** Other species. $15 one-time fee/room. Designated rooms, service with restrictions, supervision.
⊠ 🛡

BOWEN ISLAND

▼▼ Wildwood Lane Cottages ⒸⒶ
(604) 947-2253. **Call for rates.** 1321 Adams Rd. From ferry terminal, 3.5 mi (5.6 km) w on Grafton Rd, then 0.6 mi (1 km) n. Ext corridors. **Pets:** Accepted.
⊠ 🛡 🖵 🐾

CACHE CREEK

ⒸⒶ ▼▼▼ Bonaparte Motel ⓜ
(250) 457-9693. **$49-$120.** 1395 Hwy 97 N. Just n of jct Trans-Canada Hwy 1. Ext corridors. **Pets:** Small, dogs only. $10 daily fee/pet. Designated rooms, service with restrictions, supervision.
(SAVE) ⊠ 🛡 ⇴

CAMPBELL RIVER

ⒸⒶ ▼▼▼ Anchor Inn & Suites ⒣
(250) 286-1131. **$119-$289.** 261 Island Hwy. On Island Hwy 19A, 1.3 mi (2 km) s. Int corridors. **Pets:** Accepted.
(SAVE) ⊠ 🛡 🖵 🍽 ⇴ 🐾

ⒸⒶ ▼▼▼ Best Western Austrian Chalet ⓜ
(250) 923-4231. **$114-$175.** 462 S Island Hwy. 2 mi (3.2 km) s on Island Hwy 19A. Ext/int corridors. **Pets:** Small, other species. $25 daily fee/room. Designated rooms, service with restrictions, supervision.
(SAVE) ⊠ 🛳 🛡 🖵 ⇴ 🐾

ⒸⒶ ▼▼ Campbell River Lodge Fishing & Adventure Resort ⓜ 🐾
(250) 287-7446. **$74-$124, 3 day notice.** 1760 N Island Hwy. On Island Hwy 19A, 1.3 mi (2 km) nw of downtown; just e from Hwy 19 and 28. Ext/int corridors. **Pets:** $10 daily fee/pet. Service with restrictions, supervision.
(SAVE) ⊠ 🛡 🖵 🍽 🐾

ⒸⒶ ▼▼▼ Ocean Resort ⓜ ❀
(250) 923-4281. **$99-$185.** 4834 S Island Hwy. 11 mi (18 km) s on Hwy 19A. Int corridors. **Pets:** Small. $20 daily fee/room. Designated rooms, service with restrictions, supervision.
(SAVE) ⊠ 🛡 🐾

▼▼ Town Centre Inn ⓜ ❀
(250) 287-8866. **$74-$99.** 1500 Dogwood St. Follow Island Hwy 19A through town, watch for signs, just e on Dogwood St; corner of 16th Ave. Ext corridors. **Pets:** Small. $5 one-time fee/room. Designated rooms, service with restrictions, supervision.
(ASK) ⊠ 🛡 🖵 🐾

Travelodge Campbell River M
(250) 286-6622. **$80-$115.** 340 S Island Hwy. 1.9 mi (3 km) s on Island Hwy 19A. Int corridors. **Pets:** Accepted.
ASK ✕ ᴹ 🛏 💻 ≈

CASTLEGAR

Quality Inn Castlegar H
(250) 365-2177. **$100-$180.** 1935 Columbia Ave. Jct Hwy 3A and 3B, just s. Ext/int corridors. **Pets:** Medium. $10 daily fee/pet. Designated rooms, service with restrictions, supervision.
ASK ✕ 🛏 💻 ⑾

Super 8 Motel-Castlegar H
(250) 365-2700. **$125-$299.** 651 18th St. Hwy 3, exit city centre. Int corridors. **Pets:** Medium, other species. $10 daily fee/pet. Designated rooms.
ASK ✕ ᴹ 🛏 💻 ⑾ ≈

CHASE

Chase Country Inn Motel M
(250) 679-3333. **$75-$109.** 576 Coburn St. Trans-Canada Hwy 1 and Coburn St. Ext corridors. **Pets:** Medium, dogs only. $10 daily fee/pet. Designated rooms, service with restrictions, supervision.
ASK ✕ 🛏 💻

Talking Rock Resort and Quaaout Lodge H
(250) 679-3090. **Call for rates.** 1663 Little Shuswap Lake Rd W. Trans-Canada Hwy 1, exit Squilax Bridge, 1.5 mi (2.5 km) w on Little Shuswap Rd. Int corridors. **Pets:** Dogs only. $25 daily fee/pet. Designated rooms, service with restrictions, supervision.
✕ ᴹ 🛏 💻 ⑾ ≈ ⊠

CHEMAINUS

Best Western Chemainus Festival Inn H ❀
(250) 246-4181. **$133-$154, 3 day notice.** 9573 Chemainus Rd. Trans-Canada Hwy 1, exit Henry Rd, 0.9 mi (1.4 km) e. Int corridors. **Pets:** Medium, other species. $15 daily fee/room, $25 one-time fee/room. Designated rooms, service with restrictions, supervision.
SAVE ✕ ᴹ 🛏 💻 ≈

CHETWYND

Lakeview Inns & Suites H
(250) 788-3000. **$129.** 4820 N Access Rd. Hwy 29 and 97, just n on 48th St, then just e. Int corridors. **Pets:** Medium, dogs only. $25 daily fee/room. Designated rooms, supervision.
ASK ✕ 🛏 💻

Pomeroy Inn & Suites H
(250) 788-4800. **$149-$199.** 5200 N Access Rd. Hwy 29 and 97, just n on 52nd St. Int corridors. **Pets:** Accepted.
ASK ✕ 🛏 💻 ≈ ⊠

CHILLIWACK

Best Western Rainbow Country Inn H
(604) 795-3828. **$95-$249.** 43971 Industrial Way. Trans-Canada Hwy 1, exit 116 (Lickman Rd). Int corridors. **Pets:** Accepted.
SAVE ✕ ᴹ 🛏 💻 ⑾ ≈

Chilliwack Travelodge H
(604) 792-4240. **$91-$121.** 45466 Yale Rd W. Trans-Canada Hwy 1, exit 119, just n. Int corridors. **Pets:** Accepted.
SAVE ✕ ♿ 🛏 💻 ⑾ ≈

Comfort Inn M
(604) 858-0636. **$100-$450.** 45405 Luckakuck Way. Trans-Canada Hwy 1, exit 119, s on Vedder Rd, then 0.6 mi (1 km) w. Int corridors. **Pets:** Medium. $5 daily fee/room. Designated rooms, service with restrictions, supervision.
ASK ✕ ᴹ 💻

CHRISTINA LAKE

New Horizon Motel M
(250) 447-9312. **$105-$190.** 2037 Hwy 3. Just e. Ext corridors. **Pets:** Accepted.
✕ ᴹ 🛏 💻

CLEARWATER

Clearwater Valley Resort & KOA Kampground CA
(250) 674-3909. **$92-$147.** 373 Clearwater Valley Rd. Jct Hwy 5 (Yellowhead Hwy) and Clearwater Valley Rd. Ext corridors. **Pets:** $10 daily fee/pet. Designated rooms, service with restrictions, supervision.
SAVE ✕ 🛏 💻 ⑾ ≈ ⊠

Loons at The Lakeshore Motel M
(250) 674-3345. **Call for rates.** 57 E Old N Thompson Hwy. 0.6 mi (1 km) w on Old N Thompson Hwy, just off Hwy 5 (Yellowhead Hwy). Ext corridors. **Pets:** Accepted.
✕ 🛏 💻 ᴢ

COMOX

Port Augusta Inn & Suites M ❀
(250) 339-2277. **$85-$165.** 2082 Comox Ave. From Hwy 19A (Cliffe Ave), follow signs to Comox Ave, then 2.5 mi (4 km) e. Ext/int corridors. **Pets:** Very small, dogs only. $10 daily fee/pet. Designated rooms, service with restrictions, supervision.
SAVE ✕ ᴹ 🛏 💻 ⑾ ≈

COURTENAY

Best Western The Westerly Hotel H
(250) 338-7741. **$144-$209.** 1590 Cliffe Ave. Corner of Cliffe Ave and Island Hwy 19A N. Int corridors. **Pets:** Large. $10 daily fee/pet. Service with restrictions, supervision.
SAVE ✕ ᴹ 🛏 💻 ⑾ ≈ ⊠

Kingfisher Oceanside Resort & Spa H ❀
(250) 338-1323. **Call for rates.** 4330 S Island Hwy. 3.8 mi (6 km) s on Island Hwy 19A S, watch for signs. Ext corridors. **Pets:** $25 daily fee/room.
✕ ᴹ 🛏 💻 ⑾ ≈ ⊠ ⚓

Travelodge Courtenay M ❀
(250) 334-4491. **$93-$118.** 2605 Cliffe Ave. 0.8 mi (1.2 km) s on Island Hwy 19A S. Ext corridors. **Pets:** $10 daily fee/pet. Designated rooms, service with restrictions, supervision.
SAVE ✕ 🛏 💻 ≈

CRANBROOK

Best Western Cranbrook Hotel H
(250) 417-4002. **$139-$199.** 1019 Cranbrook St N. Hwy 3 and 95; centre. Int corridors. **Pets:** Very small. $200 deposit/room, $20 daily fee/pet. Designated rooms, service with restrictions, supervision.
SAVE ✕ 🛏 💻 ≈ ⊠

Days Inn Cranbrook H ❀
(250) 426-6683. **Call for rates.** 600 Cranbrook St N. Corner of 6th St and Cranbrook St N. Int corridors. **Pets:** Small, other species. $20 one-time fee/pet. Designated rooms, service with restrictions, supervision.
✕ 🛏 💻 ⑾ ≈

Heritage Inn H ❀
(250) 489-4301. **$130-$229.** 803 Cranbrook St N. Hwy 3 and 95; centre. Int corridors. **Pets:** Medium. $10 daily fee/pet. Designated rooms, service with restrictions, supervision.
ASK ✕ 🛏 💻 ⑾ ≈

St. Eugene Golf Resort & Casino H
(250) 420-2000. **$125-$192.** 7731 Mission Rd. Hwy 3, exit Kimberley/Airport (Hwy 95A) to Mission Rd, 2.8 mi (4.5 km) n. Int corridors. **Pets:** $25 daily fee/room. Designated rooms, service with restrictions, supervision.
SAVE ✕ 🛏 💻 ⑾ ≈ ⊠

▼▼ Super 8 **H** ❖
(250) 489-8028. **$95-$115.** 2370 Cranbrook St N. Just w of jct Hwy 93 and 95. Int corridors. **Pets:** Large. $10 daily fee/pet. Designated rooms, service with restrictions, supervision.
(ASK) (X) (H)

CRESTON

▼ Downtowner Motor Inn **M**
(250) 428-2238. **$55-$80.** 1218 Canyon St. Corner of 12th Ave N. Int corridors. **Pets:** Accepted.
(X) (H)

(CAA) ▼▼ Skimmerhorn Inn **M** ❖
(250) 428-4009. **$87-$157.** 2711 Hwy 3. On Hwy 3, 0.5 mi (0.8 km) e. Ext corridors. **Pets:** Dogs only. $10 daily fee/pet. Designated rooms, service with restrictions, supervision.
(SAVE) (X) (H) (📶) (≋)

(CAA) ▼▼ Sunset Motel **M**
(250) 428-2229. **$79-$109.** 2705 Canyon St (Hwy 3 E). On Hwy 3, 0.6 mi (1 km). Ext corridors. **Pets:** Accepted.
(SAVE) (X) (H) (📶) (≋)

DAWSON CREEK

(CAA) ▼▼▼ Best Western Dawson Creek Hotel & Suites **H** ❖
(250) 782-6226. **$179, 3 day notice.** 500 Hwy 2. 1.8 mi (3 km) e of center. Int corridors. **Pets:** Medium, other species. $25 daily fee/room. Service with restrictions, supervision.
(SAVE) (X) (H) (📶) (≋)

(CAA) ▼▼▼ Dawson Creek Days Inn **H**
(250) 782-8887. **$117-$144.** 640 122nd Ave. Hwy 49, just n on 122nd Ave; midway through town. Int corridors. **Pets:** Accepted.
(SAVE) (X) (H) (📶)

(CAA) ▼▼▼ Dawson Creek Super 8 **H**
(250) 782-8899. **$133-$220.** 1440 Alaska Ave. Just s of jct Hwy 97 S (Hart Hwy) and 97 N (Alaska Hwy). Int corridors. **Pets:** $25 daily fee/room. Designated rooms, service with restrictions, supervision.
(SAVE) (X) (H) (📶) (📶)

DUNCAN

(CAA) ▼▼ Best Western Cowichan Valley Inn **H**
(250) 748-2722. **$131-$191.** 6474 Trans-Canada Hwy 1. 1.8 mi (3 km) n. Int corridors. **Pets:** Accepted.
(SAVE) (X) (H) (📶) (📶) (≋)

▼ Falcon Nest Motel **M**
(250) 748-8188. **$58-$84.** 5867 Trans-Canada Hwy 1. 0.9 mi (1.5 km) n. Ext corridors. **Pets:** Accepted.
(X) (H) (📶) (≋)

▼▼ Travelodge Silver Bridge Inn Duncan **H**
(250) 748-4311. **$119-$209.** 140 Trans-Canada Hwy 1. Just n of Silver Bridge. Ext corridors. **Pets:** Other species. $10 daily fee/pet. Designated rooms.
(ASK) (X) (H) (📶) (📶)

FERNIE

(CAA) ▼▼▼ Best Western Fernie Mountain Lodge **H**
(250) 423-5500. **$135-$185.** 1622 7th Ave. Jct Hwy 3 and 7th Ave; east end of town. Int corridors. **Pets:** Accepted.
(SAVE) (X) (H) (📶) (📶) (≋)

(CAA) ▼▼▼ Park Place Lodge **H**
(250) 423-6871. **$114-$254.** 742 Hwy 3. At 7th St. Int corridors. **Pets:** Other species. Designated rooms, supervision.
(SAVE) (X) (H) (📶) (📶) (≋) (📶)

▼▼▼ Stanford Hotels & Resorts **CO**
(250) 423-5000. **$99-$608, 30 day notice.** 100 Riverside Way. From centre, 1.2 mi (2 km) on Hwy 3. Ext/int corridors. **Pets:** Accepted.
(ASK) (X) (H) (📶) (📶) (≋) (📶)

▼▼ Super 8-Fernie **H**
(250) 423-6788. **Call for rates.** 2021 Hwy 3. On Hwy 3; west end of town. Int corridors. **Pets:** Accepted.
(X) (H)

FORT ST. JOHN

(CAA) ▼▼▼ Best Western Coachman Inn **H**
(250) 787-0651. **$150.** 8540 Alaska Rd. 1.2 mi (2 km) s on Hwy 97 (Alaska Hwy). Int corridors. **Pets:** Other species. $15 daily fee/pet. Designated rooms, service with restrictions, supervision.
(SAVE) (X) (H) (📶) (📶) (📶)

(CAA) ▼▼▼ Lakeview Inn & Suites **H**
(250) 787-0779. **$96-$106.** 10103 98th Ave. Corner of 100th Ave; centre of downtown. Int corridors. **Pets:** Medium. $10 one-time fee/pet. Designated rooms, service with restrictions, supervision.
(SAVE) (X) (H) (📶) (📶)

▼▼ Pomeroy Inn & Suites **H** ❖
(250) 262-3030. **Call for rates.** 9304 Alaska Rd. Just s on Hwy 97 (Alaska Hwy). Int corridors. **Pets:** Other species. $25 daily fee/pet. Crate.
(X) (📶) (H) (📶)

▼▼▼ Quality Inn Northern Grand **H**
(250) 787-0521. **$156-$189, 30 day notice.** 9830 100th Ave. Centre. Int corridors. **Pets:** Accepted.
(ASK) (X) (H) (📶) (📶) (≋) (📶)

(CAA) ▼▼▼ Super 8-Fort St. John **H**
(250) 785-7588. **$160-$180.** 9500 Alaska Hwy. Just s on Hwy 97 (Alaska Hwy). Int corridors. **Pets:** $25 daily fee/pet. Service with restrictions, supervision.
(SAVE) (X) (📶) (H) (📶) (📶) (≋) (📶)

FORT STEELE

▼▼ Bull River Guest Ranch **RA**
(250) 429-3760. **$165-$1000.** 2975 Bull River Rd. Hwy 95, 12.9 mi (21.4 km) se of town on Ft Steele-Wardner Rd, 7.2 mi (12 km) ne on gravel road; Hwy 3 W, 24.6 mi (41 km) e of Cranbrook, 5 mi (8.2 km) n on Ft Steele-Wardner Rd, 7.2 mi (12 km) ne on gravel road. Ext corridors. **Pets:** Dogs only. No service, supervision.
(X) (H) (📶) (📶) (📶) (📶) (📶)

GIBSONS

▼▼▼ Bonniebrook Lodge Oceanfront Inn **CI**
(604) 886-2887. **$169-$299, 7 day notice.** 1532 Ocean Beach Esplanade. Hwy 101, 3.8 mi (6 km) s on Veterans Rd to Fichett St, just sw to King St, 0.6 mi (1 km) sw to Chaster, then 5 mi (8 km) sw to Gowers Pt Rd, follow signs. Ext/int corridors. **Pets:** Accepted.
(ASK) (X) (H) (📶) (📶) (📶)

(CAA) ▼▼▼ Cedars Inn Hotel & Convention Centre **M**
(604) 886-3008. **$94-$156.** 895 Gibsons Way. Hwy 101 and Shaw Rd; 3.8 mi (6 km) n from ferry terminal. Ext/int corridors. **Pets:** $15 daily fee/pet. Designated rooms, service with restrictions.
(SAVE) (X) (H) (📶) (≋) (📶)

GOLD BRIDGE

▼▼▼ Morrow Chalets **CA**
(250) 238-2462. **$250-$350, 30 day notice.** Tyaughton Lake Rd. 5 mi (8 km) n from the Tyaughton Lake turnoff, follow signs. Ext corridors. **Pets:** Other species. Supervision.
(X) (H) (📶) (📶)

▼▼ Tyax Mountain Lake Resort 🔢
(250) 238-2221. **$169-$203, 45 day notice.** Tyaughton Lake Rd. 5 mi (8 km) n from the Tyaughton Lake turnoff, follow signs. Int corridors. **Pets:** Accepted.
⊠ 🔋 🍴 🔀 🐾

GOLDEN

▼▼▼▼ Best Western Mountain View Inn 🔢
(250) 344-2333. **$129-$189.** 1024 11th St N. Just w of jct Hwy 95 and Trans-Canada Hwy 1; on S Service Rd. Int corridors. **Pets:** Small, dogs only. $20 daily fee/room. Designated rooms, service with restrictions, supervision.
SAVE ⊠ 🔋 💻 🐾

▼▼ Golden Rim Motor Inn 🅼
(250) 344-2216. **$79-$185.** 1416 Golden View Rd. On Trans-Canada Hwy 1, 1 mi (1.6 km) e of jct Hwy 95. Ext corridors. **Pets:** Small, dogs only. $10 daily fee/pet. Designated rooms, service with restrictions, supervision.
ASK ⊠ 🔋 💻 🍴 🐾

▼▼▼▼ Hillside Lodge & Chalets 🅲🅰
(250) 344-7281. **$138-$225, 5 day notice.** 1740 Seward Frontage Rd. 9.4 mi (15 km) w on Hwy 1, follow signs n off highway. Ext corridors. **Pets:** Accepted.
SAVE ⊠ 🔋 💻 🔀 🐾 📞

GRAND FORKS

▼▼ Ramada Limited 🅼
(250) 442-2127. **Call for rates.** 2729 Central Ave. West end of town on Hwy 3. Ext corridors. **Pets:** Accepted.
⊠ 🔋 💻 🍴 🐾

▼▼ Western Traveller Motel 🅼
(250) 442-5566. **$64-$139.** 1591 Central Ave. West end of town on Hwy 3. Ext corridors. **Pets:** Small, dogs only. $7 one-time fee/pet. Designated rooms, no service, supervision.
SAVE ⊠ 🔋 💻

GULF ISLANDS NATIONAL PARK RESERVE AREA

GALIANO ISLAND

▼▼▼ Galiano Oceanfront Inn & Spa 🔢
(250) 539-3388. **$199-$425, 7 day notice.** 134 Madrona Dr. From Sturdies Bay ferry terminal, just ne on Sturdies Bay Rd. Ext/int corridors. **Pets:** Accepted.
ASK ⊠ 🔋 💻 🍴 🐾

PENDER ISLAND

▼▼▼▼ Poets Cove Resort & Spa 🔢
(250) 629-2100. **Call for rates.** 9801 Spalding Rd, South Pender Island. From Otter Bay Ferry Terminal, follow signs to South Pender Island, then 10 mi (16 km) s; Otter Bay Rd to Bidwell Harbour Rd to Canal Rd. Ext/int corridors. **Pets:** Accepted.
SAVE ⊠ 🅶🅼 🔋 💻 🍴 🐾 🔀 🐾

QUADRA ISLAND

▼▼ Taku Resort & Marina 🅼 🐾
(250) 285-3031. **$89-$300, 15 day notice.** 616 Taku Rd. From Campbell River ferry terminal, 4.1 mi (6.6 km) n on West Rd, then just e on Heriot Bay Rd, follow signs to Heriot Bay. Ext corridors. **Pets:** $15 daily fee/pet. Designated rooms, service with restrictions, supervision.
⊠ 🔋 💻 🔀 🐾 📞

SALT SPRING ISLAND

▼▼ Harbour House 🔢
(250) 537-5571. **$69-$295.** 121 Upper Ganges Rd. 0.6 mi (1 km) n on Lower Ganges Rd, then just e, towards Long Harbour ferry terminal. Ext/int corridors. **Pets:** Accepted.
ASK ⊠ 🅶🅼 💻 🍴 🐾

▼▼ Seabreeze Inne 🅼
(250) 537-4145. **$69-$159, 3 day notice.** 101 Bittancourt Rd. From Ganges Township, 0.6 mi (1 km) s on Fulford-Ganges Rd. Ext corridors. **Pets:** Accepted.
⊠ 🔋 💻

END AREA

HARRISON HOT SPRINGS

▼▼▼▼ Harrison Beach Hotel 🔢 🐾
(604) 796-1111. **$99-$249.** 160 Esplanade Ave. Just w; on lakefront. Int corridors. **Pets:** Small, dogs only. $150 deposit/room, $15 daily fee/pet. Designated rooms, service with restrictions, supervision.
SAVE ⊠ 🅶🅼 🔋 💻 🍴 🐾

▼▼▼▼ Harrison Hot Springs Resort & Spa 🔢
(604) 796-2244. **$139-$599, 3 day notice.** 100 Esplanade Ave. Just w; on lakefront. Int corridors. **Pets:** Accepted.
SAVE ⊠ 🔋 💻 🍴 🐾 🔀

HOPE

▼▼▼ Alpine Motel 🅼
(604) 869-9931. **$78-$115.** 505 Old Hope-Princeton Way. Trans-Canada Hwy 1, exit 173 westbound; exit 170 eastbound, just n from lights. Ext corridors. **Pets:** Accepted.
SAVE ⊠ 🔋 💻

▼▼ Best Continental Motel 🅼
(604) 869-9726. **$59-$125.** 860 Fraser Ave. Trans-Canada Hwy 1, exit 170 to downtown; at Fort St. Ext corridors. **Pets:** Dogs only. $10 daily fee/pet. No service, supervision.
SAVE ⊠ 🔋 💻

▼▼ Quality Inn 🅼
(604) 869-9951. **$75-$145.** 350 Old Hope-Princeton Way. Trans-Canada Hwy 1, exit 173 westbound; exit 170 eastbound, just n from lights. Int corridors. **Pets:** Medium. Service with restrictions, supervision.
SAVE ⊠ 🅶🅼 🔋 💻 🐾

INVERMERE

▼▼▼ Best Western Invermere Inn 🔢
(250) 342-9246. **$129-$209, 3 day notice.** 1310 7th Ave. Hwy 93 and 95, exit Invermere, 1.8 mi (3 km) w; centre. Int corridors. **Pets:** Accepted.
SAVE ⊠ 🔋 💻 🍴

KAMLOOPS

ⓐ ▼▼▼ Accent Inns 🅼
(250) 374-8877. **$109-$179.** 1325 Columbia St W. Trans-Canada Hwy 1, exit 369 (Columbia St) eastbound, at Notre Dame Dr; exit 370 (Summit Dr) westbound, at Notre Dame Dr. Ext corridors. **Pets:** Accepted.
(SAVE) ⊠ 🅖🅜 🗄 💻 ⇌ 🗙

ⓐ ▼▼▼ Best Western Kamloops 🅗 🐾
(250) 828-6660. **$140-$185.** 1250 Rogers Way. Trans-Canada Hwy 1, exit 368 (Hillside Ave), just s. Int corridors. **Pets:** Medium, other species. $20 one-time fee/room. Designated rooms, service with restrictions, supervision.
(SAVE) ⊠ 🅖🅜 🗄 💻 🍴 ⇌ 🗙

ⓐ ▼▼▼ Econo Lodge Inn & Suites 🅼 🐾
(250) 372-8533. **$59-$129.** 1773 Trans-Canada Hwy E. 1.5 mi (2.4 km) e on Trans-Canada Hwy 1, south side of service access road. Ext corridors. **Pets:** $100 deposit/room. Designated rooms, service with restrictions, supervision.
(SAVE) ⊠ 🗄 💻 ⇌

ⓐ ▼▼ Grandview Motel 🅼
(250) 372-1312. **$55-$110.** 463 Grandview Terr. Trans-Canada Hwy 1, exit 369 (Columbia St) eastbound, 1.3 mi (2 km) n; exit 370 (Summit Dr) westbound to Columbia St, via City Centre. Ext corridors. **Pets:** Accepted.
(SAVE) ⊠ 🗄 💻 ⇌

ⓐ ▼▼▼ Hampton Inn by Hilton Kamloops 🅗 🐾
(250) 571-7897. **$110-$180.** 1245 Rogers Way. Trans-Canada Hwy 1, exit 368 (Hillside Ave), just s via Hillside Way. Int corridors. **Pets:** Dogs only. $20 daily fee/pet. Designated rooms, service with restrictions, supervision.
(SAVE) ⊠ 🅖🅜 🗄 💻 ⇌ 🗙

▼▼ Kamloops Super 8 🅼
(250) 374-8688. **Call for rates.** 1521 Hugh Allan Dr. Trans-Canada Hwy 1, exit 367 (Pacific Way). Int corridors. **Pets:** Accepted.
⊠ 🅖🅜 🗄 💻

▼▼ Ranchland Motel 🅼
(250) 828-8787. **$59-$99.** 2357 Trans-Canada Hwy E. 2.8 mi (4.5 km) e on Trans-Canada Hwy 1, exit River Rd, then just w along service access road. Ext corridors. **Pets:** Medium. $10 daily fee/pet. Designated rooms, no service, supervision.
(ASK) ⊠ 🗄 💻

ⓐ ▼▼▼ Scott's Inn & Restaurant 🅼 🐾
(250) 372-8221. **$80-$120.** 551 11th Ave. Trans-Canada Hwy 1, exit 369 (Columbia St) eastbound, 3.1 mi (5 km) n; exit City Centre westbound, 1 mi (1.6) km s on Columbia St. Ext corridors. **Pets:** Small. $6 daily fee/pet. Designated rooms, service with restrictions, supervision.
(SAVE) ⊠ 🗄 💻 🍴 ⇌

KIMBERLEY

ⓐ ▼▼▼▼ Trickle Creek Lodge 🅗
(250) 427-5175. **$130-$134.** 500 Stemwinder Dr. From Gerry Sorensen Way, follow signs. Int corridors. **Pets:** Accepted.
(SAVE) ⊠ 🗄 💻 🍴 ⇌ 🗙

LUND

ⓐ ▼▼ The Historic Lund Hotel 🅗
(604) 414-0474. **$95-$225, 3 day notice.** 1436 Hwy 101. End of Hwy 101; on Sunshine Coast. Ext/int corridors. **Pets:** Accepted.
(SAVE) ⊠ 🗄 💻 🍴

MADEIRA PARK

▼▼▼▼ Sunshine Coast Resort & Marina 🅲🅞 🐾
(604) 883-9177. **$95-$495, 21 day notice.** 12695 Sunshine Coast Hwy. Just n of Madeira Park Rd, follow signs. Ext/int corridors. **Pets:** Other species. $20 daily fee/pet. Service with restrictions, supervision.
⊠ 🅖🅜 🗄 💻 🗙

MANNING PARK

ⓐ ▼▼▼ Manning Park Resort 🅗 🐾
(250) 840-8822. **$130-$174, 14 day notice.** 7500 Hwy 3. Crowsnest Hwy 3; between Hope and Princeton. Ext/int corridors. **Pets:** Dogs only. $25 one-time fee/room. Designated rooms, service with restrictions.
(SAVE) ⊠ 🗄 💻 🍴 ⇌ 🗙 🝙

MCBRIDE

ⓐ ▼▼▼ North Country Lodge 🅼
(250) 569-0001. **$84-$99, 3 day notice.** 868 Frontage Rd N. Just w of village main exit, on Hwy 16 north service road. Ext corridors. **Pets:** Other species. $10 daily fee/pet. Designated rooms, service with restrictions, supervision.
(SAVE) ⊠ 🗄 💻 🍴

MERRITT

ⓐ ▼▼▼ Best Western Nicola Inn 🅗
(250) 378-4253. **$82-$179.** 4025 Walters St. Hwy 5, exit 290, 0.6 mi (1 km) w. Ext corridors. **Pets:** Accepted.
(SAVE) ⊠ 🗄 💻 🍴 ⇌

▼▼▼ Super 8 Merritt 🅼
(250) 378-9422. **$95-$130.** 3561 Voght St. Hwy 5, exit 290, just w. Ext corridors. **Pets:** Accepted.
(ASK) ⊠ 🗄 💻 🍴 ⇌

NAKUSP

ⓐ ▼▼▼ The Selkirk Inn 🅼
(250) 265-3666. **$59-$95.** 210 W 6th Ave. Centre. Int corridors. **Pets:** Small. $20 deposit/room, $10 daily fee/pet. Designated rooms, service with restrictions, supervision.
(SAVE) ⊠ 🅖🅜 🗄 💻

NANAIMO

ⓐ ▼▼▼ Best Western Dorchester Hotel 🅗 🐾
(250) 754-6835. **$110-$200, 3 day notice.** 70 Church St. Hwy 19A (Island Hwy) to Comox Rd; downtown. Int corridors. **Pets:** Medium, dogs only. $15 daily fee/pet. Designated rooms, service with restrictions, supervision.
(SAVE) ⊠ 🗄 💻 🍴

ⓐ ▼▼▼ Best Western Northgate Inn 🅗 🐾
(250) 390-2222. **$94-$142, 3 day notice.** 6450 Metral Dr. Hwy 19A (Island Hwy), just w on Aulds Rd, then just s. Int corridors. **Pets:** Small, other species. $20 daily fee/room. Designated rooms, service with restrictions, supervision.
(SAVE) ⊠ 🗄 💻 🍴 🗙

▼▼ Days Inn Nanaimo Harbourview 🅗 🐾
(250) 754-8171. **$104-$134.** 809 Island Hwy S. On Island Hwy 1, 1.3 mi (2 km) s. Int corridors. **Pets:** Medium, dogs only. $10 daily fee/pet. Designated rooms, service with restrictions, supervision.
(ASK) ⊠ 🗄 💻 🍴 ⇌

ⓐ ▼▼▼ Inn on Long Lake 🅗 🐾
(250) 758-1144. **$109-$249.** 4700 Island Hwy N. 3.1 mi (5 km) n on Hwy 19A (Island Hwy) from Departure Bay ferry terminal. Ext corridors. **Pets:** Other species. $20 one-time fee/pet. Designated rooms, service with restrictions, supervision.
(SAVE) ⊠ 🅖🅜 🗄 💻 🗙

ⓐ ▼▼▼ Travelodge Nanaimo 🅼
(250) 754-6355. **$120-$146.** 96 Terminal Ave N. Jct Terminal Ave and Island Hwy 19A. Int corridors. **Pets:** Medium. $15 one-time fee/pet. Designated rooms, supervision.
(SAVE) ⊠ 🗄 💻

NELSON

(CAA) ▼▼▼ **Best Western Baker Street Inn & Convention Centre** H
(250) 352-3525. **$109-$259.** 153 Baker St. Jct Hwy 6 and 3A. Int corridors. **Pets:** Accepted.
SAVE ⊠ &M 🛎 ▣ ⊞

NEW DENVER

▼▼ **Sweet Dreams Guesthouse** BB
(250) 358-2415. **$65-$95, 14 day notice.** 702 Eldorado St. Just w of Hwy 6 on Slocan Ave. Int corridors. **Pets:** Dogs only. Service with restrictions, crate.
ASK ⊠ K W Z

OKANAGAN VALLEY AREA

ENDERBY

(CAA) ▼▼▼ **Howard Johnson Inn Fortunes Landing** H
(250) 838-6825. **$79-$109.** 1510 George St. 0.6 mi (1 km) n on Hwy 974. Ext corridors. **Pets:** Other species. $10 daily fee/pet. Service with restrictions.
SAVE ⊠ 🛎 ▣ ⊞ ⇌

KELOWNA

(CAA) ▼▼▼ **Accent Inns** H
(250) 862-8888. **$99-$189.** 1140 Harvey Ave. Corner of Hwy 97 N (Harvey Ave) and Gordon Dr. Ext corridors. **Pets:** $15 daily fee/room. Designated rooms, service with restrictions, supervision.
SAVE ⊠ &M 🛎 ▣ ⊞ ⇌ ⊠

(CAA) ▼▼▼▼ **Best Western Inn-Kelowna** H ❀
(250) 860-1212. **$150-$220.** 2402 Hwy 97 N. 0.6 mi (1 km) s of jct Hwy 33 and 97 N (Harvey Ave); corner of Leckie Rd. Ext/int corridors. **Pets:** Medium. $25 daily fee/pet. Designated rooms, crate.
SAVE ⊠ &M 🛎 ▣ ⊞ ⇌ ⊠

(CAA) ▼▼▼ **Comfort Inn Kelowna-Westside** H
(250) 769-2355. **$99-$189.** 1655 Westgate Rd. Jct Hwy 97 (Harvey Ave) and Bartley Rd, s to Ross Rd. Int corridors. **Pets:** Medium. $10 daily fee/pet. Designated rooms, service with restrictions, supervision.
SAVE ⊠ &M 🛎 ▣ ⊞ ⇌

(CAA) ▼▼ **Days Inn** M
(250) 868-3297. **$99-$179.** 2649 Hwy 97 N. Jct Hwy 97 (Harvey Ave) and 33, just n. Ext/int corridors. **Pets:** Medium. $10 one-time fee/pet. Designated rooms, service with restrictions, supervision.
SAVE ⊠ &M 🛎 ▣ ⇌

▼▼▼ **Delta Grand Okanagan Resort and Conference Centre** H
(250) 763-4500. **$189-$569.** 1310 Water St. Hwy 97 (Harvey Ave), 0.6 mi (1 km) w along Water St. Int corridors. **Pets:** Accepted.
⊠ &M 🛎 ▣ ⊞ ⇌ ⊠

▼▼▼ **Fairfield Inn & Suites by Marriott Kelowna** H ❀
(250) 763-2800. **$129-$209.** 1655 Powick Rd. Just s of Jct Hwy 97 N and 33 W. Int corridors. **Pets:** Other species. $15 daily fee/pet. Designated rooms, service with restrictions.
⊠ &M 🛎 ▣ ⇌ ⊠

▼▼▼ **Ramada Hotel & Conference Centre** H ❀
(250) 860-9711. **$99-$189.** 2170 Harvey Ave. Hwy 97 N (Harvey Ave) at Dilworth Dr. Ext/int corridors. **Pets:** Other species. $15 daily fee/room. Designated rooms, supervision.
ASK ⊠ &M 🛎 ▣ ⊞ ⇌

(CAA) ▼▼▼ **Recreation Inn & Suites** M
(250) 860-3982. **$89-$179.** 1891 Parkinson Way. From Hwy 97 N (Harvey Ave), just w on Spall Rd. Ext corridors. **Pets:** Accepted.
SAVE ⊠ 🛎 ▣ ⇌

(CAA) ▼▼▼ **The Royal Anne Hotel** H
(250) 763-2277. **$89-$189.** 348 Bernard Ave. Corner of Pandosy and Bernard Ave; downtown. Int corridors. **Pets:** $20 daily fee/room. Service with restrictions, supervision.
SAVE ⊠ 🛎 ▣

(CAA) ▼▼▼ **Vineyard Inn** M
(250) 860-5703. **$84-$189.** 2486 Hwy 97 N. Southwest corner of jct Hwy 97 (Harvey Ave) and 33. Ext corridors. **Pets:** Very small, dogs only. $15 daily fee/pet. Service with restrictions, supervision.
SAVE ⊠ 🛎 ▣ ⇌ ⊠

NARAMATA

▼▼ **The Village Motel** M
(250) 496-5535. **$90-$145, 14 day notice.** 244 Robinson Dr. 8.8 mi (14 km) n on Naramata Rd from Penticton. Ext corridors. **Pets:** Accepted.
⊠ 🛎 ▣ K Z

OSOYOOS

(CAA) ▼▼▼ **Best Western Sunrise Inn** H
(250) 495-4000. **$99-$299, 3 day notice.** 5506 Main St. Jct Hwy 97, 1.9 mi (3 km) on Hwy 3 (Main St). Int corridors. **Pets:** Accepted.
SAVE ⊠ &M 🛎 ▣ ⊞ ⇌

▼▼▼ **Spirit Ridge Vineyard Resort & Spa** CO
(250) 495-5445. **$215-$429.** 1200 Rancher Creek Rd. Hwy 97 S, e on Hwy 3 (Main St), cross bridge, left on 45th St, 0.9 mi (1.5 km) e. Ext/int corridors. **Pets:** Accepted.
ASK ⊠ &M 🛎 ▣ ⊞ ⇌ ⊠

PENTICTON

(CAA) ▼▼▼ **Best Western Inn at Penticton** H ❀
(250) 493-0311. **$90-$300.** 3180 Skaha Lake Rd. 2.5 mi (4 km) s. Ext corridors. **Pets:** Medium, dogs only. $10 daily fee/pet. Designated rooms, service with restrictions, supervision.
SAVE ⊠ 🛎 ▣ ⊞ ⇌

▼▼▼ **Days Inn & Conference Centre Penticton** H
(250) 493-6616. **$99-$299.** 152 Riverside Dr. Hwy 97, just n. Int corridors. **Pets:** Accepted.
ASK ⊠ &M 🛎 ▣ ⊞ ⇌

(CAA) ▼▼▼ **Penticton Lakeside Resort, Convention Centre & Casino** H ❀
(250) 493-8221. **$165-$235, 7 day notice.** 21 Lakeshore Dr W. Main St at Lakeshore Dr W. Int corridors. **Pets:** $15 daily fee/room. Designated rooms, service with restrictions, supervision.
SAVE ⊠ &M 🛎 ▣ ⊞ ⇌ ⊠

(CAA) ▼▼▼ **Ramada Inn & Suites** H ❀
(250) 492-8926. **$89-$269.** 1050 Eckhardt Ave W. 0.8 mi (1.2 km) w on Hwy 97. Ext/int corridors. **Pets:** Other species. $15 daily fee/pet. Designated rooms, service with restrictions, supervision.
SAVE ⊠ &M 🛎 ▣ ⇌

(CAA) ▼▼ **Spanish Villa Resort** M
(250) 492-2922. **$68-$350, 14 day notice.** 890 Lakeshore Dr W. Corner of Power St and Lakeshore Dr W. Ext corridors. **Pets:** Accepted.
SAVE ⊠ 🛎 ▣ ⇌

▼▼ **Super 8 Penticton** M
(250) 492-3829. **$90-$200.** 1706 Main St. Jct Main St and Industrial. Ext/int corridors. **Pets:** Medium, dogs only. $20 daily fee/pet. Designated rooms, service with restrictions, supervision.
ASK ⊠ &M 🛎 ▣ ⇌

SUMMERLAND

(CAA) ▼▼ **Summerland Motel** [M]
(250) 494-4444. **$80-$150, 10 day notice.** 2107 Tait St. 3.1 mi (5 km) s on Hwy 97. Ext corridors. **Pets:** $10 daily fee/room. Designated rooms, service with restrictions, supervision.
[SAVE] [X] [🛏] [💻] [🏊] [🐾]

VERNON

(CAA) ▼▼ **Best Western Vernon Lodge & Conference**
Centre [H] ❀
(250) 545-3385. **$109-$194.** 3914 32nd St. 1 mi (1.5 km) n on Hwy 97 (32nd St). Int corridors. **Pets:** $15 daily fee/room. Designated rooms, service with restrictions, supervision.
[SAVE] [X] [ᏀM] [🛏] [💻] [🍴] [🏊]

(CAA) ▼▼ **Best Western Villager Motor Inn** [M]
(250) 549-2224. **$96-$141.** 5121 26th St. 1.5 mi (2.5 km) n on 27th St. Ext corridors. **Pets:** Large, other species. $15 one-time fee/pet. Service with restrictions, supervision.
[SAVE] [X] [ᏀM] [🛏] [💻] [🏊]

(CAA) ▼▼▼ **Holiday Inn Express Hotel & Suites**
Vernon [H]
(250) 550-7777. **$119-$199.** 4716 34th St. Hwy 97 (32nd St) northbound at 48th Ave. Int corridors. **Pets:** $20 one-time fee/pet. Designated rooms, service with restrictions, supervision.
[SAVE] [X] [🛏] [💻] [🏊]

▼ **Vernon Travelodge** [M]
(250) 545-2161. **$79-$159.** 3000 28th Ave. Hwy 97 (32nd St), just e on 28th Ave. Ext corridors. **Pets:** Medium, dogs only. $10 daily fee/pet. Designated rooms, service with restrictions, supervision.
[ASK] [X] [🛏] [💻] [🏊]

WESTBANK

(CAA) ▼▼▼ **The Cove Lakeside Resort** [H] ❀
(250) 707-1800. **$145-$300, 3 day notice.** 4205 Gellatly Rd. Hwy 97 (Dobbin Rd), 1 mi (1.6 km) s, follow signs. Int corridors. **Pets:** Dogs only. $20 daily fee/room. Service with restrictions, supervision.
[SAVE] [X] [ᏀM] [🛏] [💻] [🍴] [🏊] [🐾]

END AREA

PARKSVILLE

▼▼▼ **Oceanside Village Resort** [CA] ❀
(250) 248-8961. **$110-$310, 30 day notice.** 1080 Resort Dr. Island Hwy 19, exit 46 (Parksville), 1.8 mi (2.5 km) n on Hwy 19A. Ext corridors. **Pets:** Designated rooms, service with restrictions, supervision.
[X] [🛏] [💻] [🏊] [🐾]

(CAA) ▼▼▼ **Quality Resort Bayside** [H] ❀
(250) 248-8333. **$119-$259.** 240 Dogwood St. Island Hwy 19, exit 51 (Parksville/Coombs), 1.3 mi (2 km) e, then 0.6 mi (1 km) n on Hwy 19A. Int corridors. **Pets:** Dogs only. $20 daily fee/pet. Service with restrictions, supervision.
[SAVE] [X] [ᏀM] [💻] [🍴] [🏊]

▼ **Skylite Motel** [M]
(250) 248-4271. **$69-$129.** 459 E Island Hwy. Island Hwy 19, exit 46 (Parksville), 2.2 mi (3.5 km) n on Hwy 19A. Ext corridors. **Pets:** Accepted.
[ASK] [X] [🛏]

▼▼▼ **Tigh-Na-Mara Seaside Spa Resort & Conference**
Center [H] ❀
(250) 248-2072. **$119-$359, 5 day notice.** 1155 Resort Dr. Island Hwy 19, exit 46 (Parksville), 1.3 mi (2 km) n on Hwy 19A. Ext corridors. **Pets:** Medium. $30 one-time fee/room. Designated rooms, service with restrictions, supervision.
[ASK] [X] [🛏] [💻] [🍴] [🏊] [🐾] [🐾]

▼▼ **Travelodge Parksville** [H]
(250) 248-2232. **$128-$208.** 424 W Island Hwy. Island Hwy 19, exit 51 (Parksville/Coombs), 1.3 mi (2 km) e, then just n on Hwy 19A. Int corridors. **Pets:** Accepted.
[ASK] [X] [ᏀM] [🛏] [💻] [🏊]

(CAA) ▼▼ **V.I.P. Motel** [M]
(250) 248-3244. **$69-$169.** 414 W Island Hwy. Island Hwy 19, exit 51 (Parksville/Coombs), 1.3 mi (2 km) e, then just n on Hwy 19A. Ext corridors. **Pets:** Medium. $10 one-time fee/pet. Service with restrictions, supervision.
[SAVE] [X] [🛏] [💻]

PARSON

▼▼ **Alexa Chalets-Timber Inn & Restaurant** [H]
(250) 348-2228. **Call for rates.** 3483 Hwy 95. Just off Hwy 95; 21.3 mi (34 km) s of Golden. Ext/int corridors. **Pets:** Accepted.
[X] [🛏] [💻] [🍴] [X] [🐾] [🏊] [🐾]

PEMBERTON

▼▼▼ **Pemberton Valley Lodge** [H] ❀
(604) 894-2000. **$139-$409.** 1490 Portage Rd. Just e on Hwy 99 from Pioneer Junction. Int corridors. **Pets:** Medium, dogs only. $45 one-time fee/room. Designated rooms, service with restrictions, supervision.
[ASK] [X] [ᏀM] [🛏] [💻] [🏊]

PORT ALBERNI

(CAA) ▼▼▼ **Best Western Barclay Hotel** [H]
(250) 724-7171. **$109-$159.** 4277 Stamp Ave. Johnston Rd (Hwy 4), just s on Gertrude St. Int corridors. **Pets:** Accepted.
[SAVE] [X] [🛏] [💻] [🍴] [🏊] [🐾]

▼▼ **The Hospitality Inn** [H]
(250) 723-8111. **$129-$155.** 3835 Redford St. 2 mi (3.2 km) sw of jct Hwy 4 via City Centre/Port Alberni South Route. Int corridors. **Pets:** Other species. $10 daily fee/pet. Designated rooms, supervision.
[ASK] [X] [💻] [🍴] [🏊]

(CAA) ▼ **Riverside Motel** [M]
(250) 724-9916. **$79-$99.** 5065 Roger St. Johnston Rd (Hwy 4), just s on Gertrude St, then just w. Ext corridors. **Pets:** Accepted.
[SAVE] [X] [🛏] [💻]

▼▼ **Somass Motel** [M]
(250) 724-3236. **$70-$125.** 5279 River Rd. 2 mi (3.2 km) on River Rd (Hwy 4) from Johnston Rd. Ext corridors. **Pets:** Large, other species. $10 daily fee/room. Service with restrictions, crate.
[X] [🛏] [💻] [🏊]

PORT HARDY

▼▼ **Glen Lyon Inn** [H]
(250) 949-7115. **$105-$180, 3 day notice.** 6435 Hardy Bay Rd. Hwy 19, 0.9 mi (1.5 km) n, follow signs. Ext corridors. **Pets:** Medium. $10 daily fee/room. Designated rooms, service with restrictions, supervision.
[ASK] [X] [🛏] [💻] [🍴] [🐾]

POWELL RIVER

▼▼ **Powell River Town Centre Hotel** [H]
(604) 485-3000. **$135-$180.** 4660 Joyce Ave. 0.5 mi (0.8 km) e on Duncan St (BC ferry terminal), then 0.6 mi (1 km) n. Int corridors. **Pets:** Accepted.
[ASK] [X] [ᏀM] [💻] [🍴]

PRINCE GEORGE

Best Western City Centre M ☘
(250) 563-1267. **$99-$150, 30 day notice.** 910 Victoria St. Just n of Victoria St (Hwy 16) and Patricia Blvd; downtown. Ext corridors. **Pets:** Large, other species. $25 daily fee/room. Designated rooms, service with restrictions, supervision.
[SAVE] [X] [♿] [🖵] [¶] [🏊]

Four Points by Sheraton Prince George H ☘
(250) 564-7100. **Call for rates.** 1790 Hwy 97 S. Hwy 97, exit Spruce northbound; exit city centre via Queensway southbound. Int corridors. **Pets:** Medium, dogs only. $10 daily fee/room. Designated rooms.
[SAVE] [X] [♿M] [♿] [🖵] [¶] [🏊]

P.G. Hi-Way Motel M
(250) 564-6869. **$60-$90.** 1737 20th Ave. Jct Hwy 97, 0.7 mi (1.2 km) e on Trans-Canada Hwy 16 (Yellowhead Hwy). Ext corridors. **Pets:** Accepted.
[SAVE] [X] [♿] [🖵]

PRINCE RUPERT

Aleeda Motel M
(250) 627-1367. **$65-$105.** 900 3rd Ave W. Corner of 3rd Ave W and 8th St. Int corridors. **Pets:** Other species. $5 daily fee/pet. Designated rooms, service with restrictions.
[SAVE] [X] [♿] [🖵] [🎿]

The Coast Prince Rupert Hotel H
(250) 624-6711. **$116-$197.** 118 6th St. Between 1st and 2nd aves W. Int corridors. **Pets:** Accepted.
[ASK] [X] [♿M] [🖵] [¶]

Inn on the Harbour M
(250) 624-9107. **$85-$145.** 720 1st Ave W. Corner of 6th St. Int corridors. **Pets:** Accepted.
[ASK] [X] [♿M] [♿] [🖵] [🎿]

Totem Lodge Motel M
(250) 624-6761. **$69-$99, 7 day notice.** 1335 Park Ave. 1 mi (1.6 km) w on Hwy 16 (2nd Ave W) from downtown. Int corridors. **Pets:** Very small, dogs only. $10 daily fee/pet. Designated rooms, no service, supervision.
[SAVE] [X] [♿] [🖵] [🎿]

PRINCETON

Best Western Princeton Inn M
(250) 295-3537. **$99-$139.** 169 Hwy 3. On Hwy 3. Ext corridors. **Pets:** Accepted.
[SAVE] [X] [♿] [🖵] [🏊]

Villager Inn M
(250) 295-6996. **$69-$95.** 244 4th St. Just off Hwy 3. Ext corridors. **Pets:** $10 daily fee/pet. Service with restrictions, supervision.
[SAVE] [X] [♿] [🖵] [🏊]

QUALICUM BEACH

Old Dutch Inn (By The Sea) H
(250) 752-6914. **$80-$140.** 2690 Island Hwy W. Hwy 19, exit 60 (Qualicum Beach/Port Alberni), 2.5 mi (4 km) on Memorial Ave at jct Hwy 19A. Int corridors. **Pets:** Accepted.
[ASK] [X] [♿] [🖵] [¶] [🏊] [🎿]

QUESNEL

Talisman Inn M
(250) 992-7247. **$69-$149.** 753 Front St. Hwy 97, 0.6 mi (1 km) n of Carson Ave. Int corridors. **Pets:** Small. $10 daily fee/pet. Designated rooms, service with restrictions, supervision.
[SAVE] [X] [♿] [🖵]

RADIUM HOT SPRINGS

Chalet Europe M
(250) 347-9305. **$89-$189, 7 day notice.** 5063 Madsen Rd. Hwy 95, just w on Hwy 93, then 0.4 mi (0.7 km) s, up the hill. Ext corridors. **Pets:** Accepted.
[X] [♿] [🖵] [🎿]

Lido Motel M
(250) 347-9533. **$65-$95, 7 day notice.** 4876 McKay St. Jct Hwy 93 and 95, just e, just s along Main St, then just e. Ext corridors. **Pets:** $10 daily fee/pet. Supervision.
[X] [♿] [🖵] [🏊]

REVELSTOKE

The Coast Hillcrest Resort Hotel H ☘
(250) 837-3322. **$159-$239.** 2100 Oak Dr. 2.7 mi (4.3 km) e on Trans-Canada Hwy 1, 0.6 mi (0.9 km) sw. Int corridors. **Pets:** $15 daily fee/room. Designated rooms, service with restrictions, supervision.
[SAVE] [X] [♿] [🖵] [¶] [🎿]

Days Inn & Suites H
(250) 837-2191. **$89-$199.** 301 Wright St. South side of Trans-Canada Hwy 1, just e of Columbia River Bridge at Victoria Rd, then just se on Wright St. Ext/int corridors. **Pets:** Accepted.
[ASK] [X] [♿M] [♿] [🖵] [🎿]

Monashee Lodge M
(250) 837-6778. **$79-$99.** 1601 3rd St W. South side of Trans-Canada Hwy 1, just e of Columbia River Bridge at Victoria Rd, then just se on Wright St. Ext corridors. **Pets:** Small, dogs only. $10 daily fee/pet. Designated rooms, service with restrictions.
[SAVE] [X] [♿] [🖵]

Sandman Hotel H
(250) 837-6161. **Call for rates.** 1901 LaForme Blvd. North side of Trans-Canada Hwy 1, at intersection nearest east end of Columbia River Bridge. Ext/int corridors. **Pets:** Accepted.
[X] [♿M] [♿] [🖵] [¶] [🏊]

Swiss Chalet Motel M
(250) 837-4650. **$89-$149.** 1101 Victoria Rd. 0.6 mi (1 km) s from Trans-Canada Hwy 1. Ext corridors. **Pets:** Accepted.
[SAVE] [X] [♿] [🖵]

SALMON ARM

Best Western Salmon Arm Inn M
(250) 832-9793. **$110-$220.** 61 10th St SW. From centre, 0.7 mi (1.1 km) w on Trans-Canada Hwy 1. Ext corridors. **Pets:** Accepted.
[SAVE] [X] [♿] [🖵] [🏊]

Holiday Inn Express Hotel & Suites Salmon Arm H
(250) 832-7711. **$139-$299.** 1090 22nd St NE. 0.5 mi (0.8 km) e on Trans-Canada Hwy 1. Int corridors. **Pets:** Medium. $10 daily fee/pet. Designated rooms, service with restrictions, supervision.
[ASK] [X] [♿M] [♿] [🖵] [🏊] [🎿]

SICAMOUS

Sicamous Super 8 M
(250) 836-4988. **Call for rates.** 1120 Riverside Ave. Trans-Canada Hwy 1, s on Hwy 97A, just w on Main St to traffic circle, then just s. Ext corridors. **Pets:** Medium. $10 daily fee/pet. No service, supervision.
[X] [♿M] [♿] [🖵]

SILVERTON

William Hunter Cabins CA ☘
(250) 358-2844. **Call for rates.** 303 Lake Ave. Centre. Ext corridors. **Pets:** Other species. $15 one-time fee/pet. Supervision.
[X] [♿] [🖵] [🎿] [🏊]

SMITHERS

♥♥ Aspen Inn & Suites M
(250) 847-4551. **Call for rates.** 4628 Yellowhead Hwy. 0.9 mi (1.5 km) w on Hwy 16 (Yellowhead Hwy). Ext corridors. **Pets:** Accepted.
⊠ 🛇 🖬 💻 ⑪ ⇌

SQUAMISH

♥♥♥ Executive Suites Garibaldi Springs Golf Resort H
(604) 815-0048. **$119-$389.** 40900 Tantalus Rd. Hwy 99, just e on Garibaldi Way, then just n 0.6 mi (1 km). Int corridors. **Pets:** Accepted.
A$K ⊠ 🛇 🖬 💻 ⑪ ⇌ 🛇

♥♥♥ Mountain Retreat Hotel & Suites H
(604) 815-0883. **$130-$140.** 38922 Progress Way. 0.9 mi (1.5 km) n on Hwy 99 at Industrial Way. Int corridors. **Pets:** $29 daily fee/room. Designated rooms, supervision.
SAVE ⊠ 🛇 🖬 💻 ⑪ ⇌ 🛇

SUN PEAKS

♥♥♥♥ Delta Sun Peaks Resort H ❄
(250) 578-6000. **$105-$335.** 3240 Village Way. Hwy 5, 19.4 mi (31 km) ne on Todd Mountain Rd, follow signs to village. Int corridors. **Pets:** Medium, dogs only. $35 one-time fee/room. Designated rooms, service with restrictions, supervision.
SAVE ⊠ 🛇 🖬 💻 ⑪ ⇌ 🛇

TERRACE

♥♥♥ Best Western Terrace Inn H
(250) 635-0083. **$108-$225, 14 day notice.** 4553 Greig Ave. Hwy 16, just e on Greig Ave, follow City Centre signs. Int corridors. **Pets:** Other species. $10 daily fee/room. Designated rooms, supervision.
SAVE ⊠ 🖬 💻 ⑪

TOFINO

♥♥♥ Best Western Tin Wis Resort Lodge H
(250) 725-4445. **$145-$260.** 1119 Pacific Rim Hwy. 1.8 mi (3.5 km) s on Hwy 4. Ext corridors. **Pets:** $25 daily fee/pet. Designated rooms, service with restrictions, supervision.
SAVE ⊠ 🖬 💻 ⑪ 🛇 🖉

♥♥♥ Long Beach Lodge Resort H
(250) 725-2442. **Call for rates.** 1441 Pacific Rim Hwy. 4.7 mi (7.5 km) s on Hwy 4. Ext/int corridors. **Pets:** Accepted.
⊠ 🛇 🖬 💻 ⑪ 🖉

♥♥♥ Pacific Sands Beach Resort H ❄
(250) 725-3322. **$175-$585.** 1421 Pacific Rim Hwy. 4.7 mi (7.5 km) s on Hwy 4. Ext corridors. **Pets:** $35 one-time fee/pet. Designated rooms, service with restrictions, supervision.
SAVE ⊠ 🛇 🖬 💻 🖉

♥♥♥ Wickaninnish Inn H ❄
(250) 725-3100. **$280-$1500, 14 day notice.** Osprey Ln at Chesterman Beach. 2.7 mi (4.3 km) e on Hwy 4. Int corridors. **Pets:** Dogs only. $40 daily fee/pet. Designated rooms, service with restrictions, supervision.
SAVE ⊠ 🛇 💻 ⑪ 🛇 🖉

VALEMOUNT

♥♥♥ Best Western Valemount Inn & Suites H
(250) 566-0086. **$110-$246.** 1950 Hwy 5 S. 0.9 mi (1.5 km) s on Hwy 5 (Yellowhead Hwy). Int corridors. **Pets:** Other species. $35 one-time fee/ room. Designated rooms, service with restrictions, supervision.
SAVE ⊠ 🛇 🖬 💻 ⑪ ⇌ 🛇

♥♥♥ Canoe Mountain Lodge H
(250) 566-9171. **Call for rates.** 1465 5th Ave. Just e of Hwy 5 (Yellowhead Hwy). Int corridors. **Pets:** Accepted.
SAVE ⊠ 🖬 💻

♥♥♥ Chalet Continental Motel H
(250) 566-9787. **$79-$149.** 1450 5th Ave. Off Hwy 5 (Yellowhead Hwy), just e. Int corridors. **Pets:** Medium, dogs only. $10 daily fee/pet. Designated rooms, service with restrictions, supervision.
SAVE ⊠ 🖬 💻 ⇌ 🛇

VANCOUVER METROPOLITAN AREA

ALDERGROVE

♥♥♥ Best Western Country Meadows H ❄
(604) 856-9880. **$89-$179.** 3070 264th St. Trans-Canada Hwy 1, exit 73 (264th St/Aldergrove), 3.1 mi (5 km) s on 264th St (Hwy 13). Int corridors. **Pets:** Small. $15 daily fee/room. Designated rooms, service with restrictions, supervision.
SAVE ⊠ 🛇 🖬 💻 ⑪ ⇌

BURNABY

♥♥ Accent Inns M ❄
(604) 473-5000. **$119-$179.** 3777 Henning Dr. Trans-Canada Hwy 1, exit 28 (Grandview Hwy), just n on Boundary Rd. Ext corridors. **Pets:** Small, dogs only. $15 daily fee/pet. Designated rooms, service with restrictions, supervision.
SAVE ⊠ 🛇 🖬 💻 ⑪ 🛇

♥♥♥ Best Western Kings Inn and Conference Centre H
(604) 438-1383. **$119-$199, 3 day notice.** 5411 Kingsway. Trans-Canada Hwy 1, exit 29 (Willingdon Ave), 1.9 mi (3 km) s to Kingsway, then 1.2 mi (2 km) e. Ext corridors. **Pets:** Small. $15 daily fee/room. Service with restrictions, crate.
SAVE ⊠ 🖬 💻 ⑪ ⇌

♥♥♥ Hilton Vancouver Metrotown H ❄
(604) 438-1200. **$109-$229.** 6083 McKay Ave. Trans-Canada Hwy 1, exit 29 (Willingdon Ave), 1.8 mi (3 km) s to Kingsway, then just e. Int corridors. **Pets:** $29 one-time fee/room. Service with restrictions, crate.
SAVE ⊠ 🛇 🖬 💻 ⑪ ⇌

♥♥♥ Lake City Inn & Suites M
(604) 294-5331. **$89-$199.** 5415 Lougheed Hwy. Trans-Canada Hwy 1, exit 29 (Willingdon Ave), just n, 0.6 mi (1 km) e on Lougheed Hwy, just n on Springer Ave, then just e on Broadway. Ext corridors. **Pets:** Accepted.
SAVE ⊠ 🖬 💻 ⇌

COQUITLAM

♥♥ Ramada Coquitlam H
(604) 931-4433. **$90-$150.** 631 Lougheed Hwy. Trans-Canada Hwy 1, exit 44 (Coquitlam), 1.9 mi (3 km) w on Lougheed Hwy (Hwy 7). Ext/int corridors. **Pets:** Other species. $10 daily fee/pet. Designated rooms, service with restrictions, supervision.
A$K ⊠ 🛇 🖬 💻 ⑪ ⇌

DELTA

Ⓐ ▼▼▼▼ **The Coast Tsawwassen Inn** 🅷 ❖
(604) 943-8221. **$124-$264.** 1665 56th St. Hwy 99, exit 28 (Tsawwassen Ferries), 5 mi (8 km) w on Hwy 17; 3.1 mi (5 km) from the BC ferry terminal. Int corridors. **Pets:** Medium. $10 daily fee/pet. Service with restrictions, supervision.
SAVE ☒ ⅗M 🖥 🖵 🍴 ⩳ ☒

▼▼▼ **River Run Cottages** 🅱🅱
(604) 946-7778. **$149-$225, 21 day notice.** 4551 River Rd W. Hwy 17, 1.6 mi (2.5 km) n on Ladner Trunk Rd (which becomes 47A St, then becomes River Rd W). Ext corridors. **Pets:** Accepted.
A$K ☒ 🖥 🖵 🎿 🕅 ⬚

LANGLEY

Ⓐ ▼▼ **Best Value Westward Inn** 🅼
(604) 534-9238. **$75-$95.** 19650 Fraser Hwy. Trans-Canada Hwy 1, exit 58 (200th St/Langley City), 3.1 mi (5 km) s on 200th St, 0.6 mi (1 km) w on Hwy 10, then just w. Ext corridors. **Pets:** Service with restrictions, supervision.
SAVE ☒ 🖥 🖵

Ⓐ ▼▼▼▼ **Best Western Langley Inn** 🅷
(604) 530-9311. **$119-$139.** 5978 Glover Rd. Trans-Canada Hwy 1, exit 66 (232nd St), 6 km s, follow signs. Int corridors. **Pets:** Small, dogs only. $15 daily fee/pet. Designated rooms, service with restrictions, supervision.
SAVE ☒ 🖥 🖵 🍴 ⩳

Ⓐ ▼▼▼▼ **Coast Hotel & Convention Centre** 🅷
(604) 530-1500. **$125-$175.** 20393 Fraser Hwy. Trans-Canada Hwy 1, exit 58 (200th St/Langley City), 3.9 mi (6.3 km) s on 200th St, then just e. Int corridors. **Pets:** Accepted.
SAVE ☒ ⅗M 🖵 🍴

Ⓐ ▼▼▼▼ **Holiday Inn Express Hotel & Suites Langley** 🅷
(604) 882-2000. **$124-$154.** 8750 204th St. Trans-Canada Hwy 1, exit 58 (200th St/Langley City), just e on 88th Ave. Int corridors. **Pets:** Accepted.
SAVE ☒ ⅗M 🖥 🖵 ⩳ ☒

▼▼▼ **Sandman Hotel Langley** 🅷
(604) 888-7263. **$125-$200.** 8855 202nd St. Trans-Canada Hwy 1, exit 58 (200th St/Langley City), just e on 88th Ave. Int corridors. **Pets:** Accepted.
A$K ☒ 🖥 🖵 🍴

▼▼▼ **Super 8 Langley/Aldergrove** 🅼
(604) 856-8288. **$109-$169.** 26574 Gloucester Way. Trans-Canada Hwy 1, exit 73 (264th St/Aldergrove), just e on 56th Ave. Int corridors. **Pets:** Small, other species. $15 daily fee/room. Designated rooms, service with restrictions, supervision.
A$K ☒ ⅗M 🖥 🖵 ⩳ ☒

MAPLE RIDGE

Ⓐ ▼▼▼ **Best Western Maple Ridge** 🅷
(604) 463-5111. **$89-$129.** 21735 Lougheed Hwy. 1.2 mi (2 km) w on Lougheed Hwy (Hwy 7). Ext corridors. **Pets:** Accepted.
SAVE ☒ ⅗M 🖥 🖵 🍴

Ⓐ ▼▼ **Travelodge Maple Ridge** 🅼
(604) 467-1511. **$90-$150.** 21650 Lougheed Hwy. 1.2 mi (2 km) w on Lougheed Hwy (Hwy 7). Int corridors. **Pets:** Accepted.
SAVE ☒ ⅗M 🖥 🖵 ☒

MISSION

Ⓐ ▼▼▼▼ **Best Western Mission City Lodge** 🅷 ❖
(604) 820-5500. **$99-$125, 15 day notice.** 32281 Lougheed Hwy. Just w of Hwy 11; corner of Lougheed Hwy (Hwy 7) and Hurd St. Int corridors. **Pets:** Small. $15 daily fee/room. Designated rooms, service with restrictions, supervision.
SAVE ☒ ⅗M 🖥 🖵 🍴 ⩳ ☒

NORTH VANCOUVER

Ⓐ ▼▼▼ **Holiday Inn Hotel & Suites North Vancouver** 🅷 ❖
(604) 985-3111. **$209-$350.** 700 Old Lillooet Rd. Trans-Canada Hwy 1, exit 22 (Mt Seymour Pkwy), follow signs. Int corridors. **Pets:** Small, dogs only. $25 daily fee/pet. Designated rooms, service with restrictions, supervision.
SAVE ☒ ⅗M 🖥 🖵 🍴 ⩳ ☒

▼▼ **Lionsgate Travelodge** 🅼 ❖
(604) 985-5311. **Call for rates.** 2060 Marine Dr. Trans-Canada Hwy 1, exit 14 (Capilano Rd), 0.9 mi (1.5 km) s, then just w; from north end of Lions Gate Bridge, just e. Ext corridors. **Pets:** $100 deposit/room. Designated rooms.
☒ 🖥 🖵 ⩳

Ⓐ ▼▼▼ **North Vancouver Hotel** 🅼
(604) 987-4461. **$99-$349.** 1800 Capilano Rd. Trans-Canada Hwy 1, exit 14 (Capilano Rd), 0.9 mi (1.5 km) s; from north end of Lions Gate Bridge, 0.6 mi (1 km) e on Marine Dr, then just n. Ext corridors. **Pets:** Medium, other species. $20 daily fee/room. Designated rooms.
SAVE ☒ ⅗M 🖥 🖵 ⩳

RICHMOND

Ⓐ ▼▼▼ **Accent Inns** 🅷 ❖
(604) 273-3311. **$99-$179.** 10551 St Edwards Dr. Hwy 99, exit 39 (Bridgeport/Airport) northbound to St Edwards Dr; exit 39A (Richmond/Airport) southbound to St Edwards Dr. Ext corridors. **Pets:** Medium. $15 daily fee/room. Designated rooms, service with restrictions, crate.
SAVE ☒ ⅗M 🖥 🖵 🍴

Ⓐ ▼▼▼ **Best Western Abercorn Inn** 🅷
(604) 270-7576. **$100-$240.** 9260 Bridgeport Rd. Hwy 99, exit 39 (Bridgeport/Airport) northbound; exit 39A (Richmond/Airport) southbound. Int corridors. **Pets:** Accepted.
SAVE ☒ ⅗M 🖥 🖵 🍴

Ⓐ ▼▼▼▼ **Best Western Richmond Hotel & Convention Center** 🅷 ❖
(604) 273-7878. **$179-$279.** 7551 Westminster Hwy. Corner of Minoru Blvd and Westminster Hwy. Int corridors. **Pets:** Medium. $20 daily fee/room. Designated rooms, service with restrictions, crate.
SAVE ☒ ⅗M 🖥 🖵 🍴 ⩳ ☒

Ⓐ ▼▼▼ **Delta Vancouver Airport** 🅷
(604) 278-1241. **$159-$329.** 3500 Cessna Dr. Corner of Russ Baker Way and Cessna Dr; near Moray Bridge. Int corridors. **Pets:** Large. $35 one-time fee/pet. Designated rooms, service with restrictions, supervision.
SAVE ☒ ⅗M 🖵 🍴 ⩳

Ⓐ ▼▼▼▼ **The Fairmont Vancouver Airport** 🅷 ❖
(604) 207-5200. **$319-$429.** 3111 Grant McConachie Way. In Vancouver International Airport. Int corridors. **Pets:** Other species. $25 daily fee/pet. Designated rooms, service with restrictions, supervision.
SAVE ☒ ⅗M 🖵 🍴 ⩳ ☒

Ⓐ ▼▼▼ **Holiday Inn Express Vancouver-Airport** 🅷 ❖
(604) 273-8080. **$115-$179.** 9351 Bridgeport Rd. Hwy 99, exit 39 (Bridgeport Rd/Airport) northbound; exit 39A (Richmond/Airport) southbound. Int corridors. **Pets:** Small. $15 daily fee/room. Designated rooms, service with restrictions, supervision.
SAVE ☒ ⅗M 🖥 🖵

Ⓐ ▼▼▼ **Holiday Inn International Vancouver Airport** 🅷 ❖
(604) 821-1818. **$115-$179.** 10720 Cambie Rd. Hwy 99, exit 39A (Bridgeport Rd/Airport) northbound to St. Edwards Dr, just 0.6 mi (1 km) n; exit 39B (No 4 Rd) southbound, just e. Int corridors. **Pets:** Small. $15 daily fee/room. Designated rooms, service with restrictions, supervision.
SAVE ☒ ⅗M 🖥 🖵 🍴

⚌ ▼▼ ▼▼ River Rock Casino Resort 🅷
(604) 247-8900. **$189-$449.** 8811 River Rd. Hwy 99, exit 39 (Bridgeport Rd/Airport) northbound; exit 39A (Richmond/Airport) southbound, just w on Bridgeport Rd, then just n on Great Canadian Way. Int corridors. **Pets:** Other species. $25 daily fee/pet.
SAVE ✕ ₆M 🖳 ⑪ 🏊 ⊠

▼▼ ▼▼ Sandman Hotel Vancouver Airport 🅷
(604) 303-8888. **$99-$159.** 3233 St Edwards Dr. Hwy 99, exit 39 (Bridgeport Rd/Airport) northbound to St Edwards Dr; exit 39A (Richmond/Airport) southbound. Int corridors. **Pets:** Accepted.
ASK ✕ ₆M 🖥 🖳 ⑪ 🏊

⚌ ▼▼ ▼▼ Vancouver Airport Marriott 🅷
(604) 276-2112. **$219-$259.** 7571 Westminster Hwy. Corner of Minoru Blvd and Westminster Hwy. Int corridors. **Pets:** Other species. $60 one-time fee/pet. Service with restrictions, crate.
SAVE ✕ ₆M 🖥 🖳 ⑪ 🏊

SURREY

⚌ ▼▼ ▼▼ Compass Point Inn 🅷
(604) 588-9511. **$99-$129.** 9850 King George Hwy. Jct Fraser Hwy (Hwy 1A) and Hwy 99A (King George Hwy). Int corridors. **Pets:** Small. $20 daily fee/pet. Designated rooms, service with restrictions, crate.
SAVE ✕ ₆M 🖥 🖳 ⑪ 🏊

▼▼ ▼▼ Ramada Hotel & Suites Surrey/Guildford 🅷
(604) 930-4700. **$99-$159.** 10410 158th St. Trans-Canada Hwy 1, exit 50 (160th St), just w on 104th Ave. Int corridors. **Pets:** Other species. $10 daily fee/pet. Service with restrictions, crate.
✕ ₆M 🖥 🖳 ⑪ 🏊

⚌ ▼▼ ▼▼ Ramada Inn Langley-Surrey 🅷 ❀
(604) 576-8388. **$119-$169.** 19225 Hwy 10. Trans-Canada Hwy 1, exit 58 (200th St/Langley City), 3.1 mi (5 km) s on 200th St, then 1.2 mi (2 km) w on Rt 10; corner of 192nd St and Rt 10. Int corridors. **Pets:** Medium, dogs only. $15 daily fee/pet. Designated rooms, service with restrictions, crate.
SAVE ✕ ₆M 🖥 🖳 ⑪ 🏊

▼▼ ▼▼ Sheraton Vancouver Guildford Hotel 🅷
(604) 582-9288. **$119-$209.** 15269 104th Ave. Trans-Canada Hwy 1, exit 48 eastbound, 0.6 mi (1 km) s on 152nd St, then just e; exit 50 westbound, 104th Ave, then just w. Int corridors. **Pets:** Accepted.
SAVE ✕ ₆M 🖥 🖳 ⑪ 🏊

VANCOUVER

⚌ ▼▼ 2400 Motel Ⓜ
(604) 434-2464. **$78-$199.** 2400 Kingsway. 4.5 mi (7.2 km) se on Hwy 1A and 99A (Kingsway and 33rd Ave). Ext corridors. **Pets:** $15 daily fee/pet. Designated rooms, service with restrictions, supervision.
SAVE ✕ 🖥 📖

⚌ ▼▼ ▼▼ Best Western Chateau Granville 🅷
(604) 669-7070. **$99-$259.** 1100 Granville St. Between Davie and Helmcken sts. Int corridors. **Pets:** Accepted.
SAVE ✕ ₆M 🖥 🖳 ⑪

⚌ ▼▼ ▼▼ Best Western Sands 🅷 ❀
(604) 682-1831. **$129-$269.** 1755 Davie St. Between Bidwell and Denman sts. Int corridors. **Pets:** Other species. $15 daily fee/pet. Designated rooms, service with restrictions, supervision.
SAVE ✕ 🖥 🖳 ⑪

⚌ ▼▼ ▼▼ Delta Vancouver Suites 🅷
(604) 689-8188. **$159-$299.** 550 W Hastings St. Between Seymour and Richards sts; entrance in alley way. Int corridors. **Pets:** Accepted.
SAVE ✕ ₆M 🖳 ⑪

▼▼ ▼▼ The Fairmont Hotel Vancouver 🅷 ❀
(604) 684-3131. **$249-$429.** 900 W Georgia St. Corner of Burrard at W Georgia St; enter from Hornby St. Int corridors. **Pets:** $25 daily fee/room. Service with restrictions, supervision.
✕ ₆M 🖳 ⑪ 🏊 ⊠

⚌ ▼▼ ▼▼ The Fairmont Waterfront 🅷
(604) 691-1991. **$249-$429.** 900 Canada Place Way. Howe St at Cordova St. Int corridors. **Pets:** Accepted.
SAVE ✕ ₆M 🖳 ⑪ 🏊 ⊠

⚌ ▼▼ ▼▼ Four Seasons Hotel Vancouver 🅷 ❀
(604) 689-9333. **$240-$820.** 791 W Georgia St. Between Howe and Granville sts. Int corridors. **Pets:** Other species. Designated rooms, service with restrictions, supervision.
SAVE ✕ ₆M ⑪ 🏊 ⊠

⚌ ▼▼ ▼▼ The Georgian Court Hotel 🅷 ❀
(604) 682-5555. **$179-$419.** 773 Beatty St. Between Georgia and Robson sts. Int corridors. **Pets:** Small. $20 daily fee/pet. Designated rooms, service with restrictions, supervision.
SAVE ✕ ₆M 🖳 ⑪ ⊠

⚌ ▼▼ ▼▼ Granville Island Hotel 🅷 ❀
(604) 683-7373. **$160-$525.** 1253 Johnston St. Granville Island; below the bridge, follow signs. Int corridors. **Pets:** Medium, other species. $25 daily fee/pet. Designated rooms, service with restrictions, supervision.
SAVE ✕ ₆M 🖳 ⑪ ⊠

⚌ ▼▼ ▼▼ Holiday Inn Express Vancouver 🅷 ❀
(604) 254-1000. **$119-$309.** 2889 E Hastings St. Between Renfrew and Kaslo sts. Int corridors. **Pets:** Medium. $15 daily fee/pet. Designated rooms, service with restrictions, crate.
SAVE ✕ ₆M 🖥 🖳

⚌ ▼▼ ▼▼ ▼▼ Hotel Le Soleil 🅷
(604) 632-3000. **$375-$475.** 567 Hornby St. Between Dunsmuir and Pender sts. Int corridors. **Pets:** Accepted.
SAVE ✕ ₆M 🖳 ⑪

⚌ ▼▼ ▼▼ Howard Johnson Hotel Downtown Vancouver 🅷
(604) 688-8701. **$79-$279.** 1176 Granville St. Between Davie and Helmcken sts. Int corridors. **Pets:** Medium. $250 deposit/room, $25 daily fee/pet. Designated rooms, service with restrictions, supervision.
SAVE ✕ 🖥 🖳 ⑪

⚌ ▼▼ ▼▼ Hyatt Regency Vancouver 🅷
(604) 683-1234. **$149-$429.** 655 Burrard St. Between W Georgia and Melville sts. Int corridors. **Pets:** Medium, dogs only. $50 one-time fee/room. Service with restrictions, supervision.
SAVE ✕ ₆M 🖳 ⑪ 🏊

⚌ ▼▼ ▼▼ L'Hermitage Hotel 🅷 ❀
(778) 327-4100. **$229-$599.** 788 Richards St. Between Robson and W Georgia sts. Int corridors. **Pets:** $25 daily fee/room. Service with restrictions.
SAVE ✕ ₆M 🖥 🖳 🏊 ⊠

⚌ ▼▼ ▼▼ Pacific Palisades Hotel 🅷 ❀
(604) 688-0461. **$225-$420.** 1277 Robson St. Between Jervis and Bute sts. Int corridors. **Pets:** Other species.
SAVE ✕ ₆M 🖥 🖳 ⑪ 🏊 ⊠

⚌ ▼▼ ▼▼ Pan Pacific Vancouver 🅷 ❀
(604) 662-8111. **$179-$449.** 300-999 Canada Place. Motor entrance off Burrard St. Int corridors. **Pets:** Medium. $30 daily fee/room. Supervision.
SAVE ✕ ₆M 🖥 🖳 ⑪ 🏊 ⊠

▼▼ ▼▼ Quality Hotel Downtown-The Inn at False Creek 🅷
(604) 682-0229. **$89-$209.** 1335 Howe St. Between Drake and Pacific sts. Int corridors. **Pets:** Medium, other species. $15 daily fee/pet. Designated rooms.
ASK ✕ ₆M 🖥 🖳 ⑪ 🏊

⚌ ▼▼ ▼▼ Ramada Inn & Suites Downtown Vancouver 🅷
(604) 685-1111. **$89-$489.** 1221 Granville St. Between Davie and Drake sts. Int corridors. **Pets:** Other species. $20 daily fee/room. Service with restrictions, supervision.
SAVE ✕ 🖥 🖳 ⑪

Ⓒ ▼▼▼▼ Renaissance Vancouver Hotel
   Harbourside 🅷
(604) 689-9211. **$219-$339.** 1133 W Hastings St. Between Bute and Thurlow sts. Int corridors. **Pets:** Accepted.
[SAVE] [✕] [&M] [📶] [💻] [🍴] [🏊] [✕]

Ⓒ ▼▼▼▼ Residence Inn by Marriott Vancouver
   Downtown 🅷
(604) 688-1234. **$189-$289.** 1234 Hornby St. Between Drake and Davie sts. Int corridors. **Pets:** $75 one-time fee/room. Service with restrictions.
[SAVE] [✕] [&M] [📶] [💻] [🍴] [🏊]

▼▼ ▼▼ Sandman Hotel Vancouver City Center 🅷
(604) 681-2211. **$109-$209.** 180 W Georgia St. Between Cambie and Beatty sts. Int corridors. **Pets:** Accepted.
[ASK] [✕] [💻] [🍴] [🏊]

Ⓒ ▼▼▼▼▼ Sheraton Vancouver Wall Centre
   Hotel 🅷
(604) 331-1000. **$199-$469.** 1088 Burrard St. Between Helmcken and Nelson sts. Int corridors. **Pets:** Accepted.
[SAVE] [✕] [&M] [📶] [💻] [🍴] [🏊] [✕]

Ⓒ ▼▼▼▼▼ The Sutton Place Hotel 🅷 🐾
(604) 682-5511. **$169-$599.** 845 Burrard St. Between Smithe and Robson sts. Int corridors. **Pets:** Other species. $150 one-time fee/room. Supervision.
[SAVE] [✕] [&M] [💻] [🍴] [🏊] [✕]

▼▼ ▼▼ Sylvia Hotel 🅷 🐾
(604) 681-9321. **$120-$500, 30 day notice.** 1154 Gilford St. Beach Ave and Gilford St; across from English Bay. Int corridors. **Pets:** Other species. Service with restrictions, supervision.
[✕] [📶] [💻] [🍴] [🎿]

Ⓒ ▼▼▼▼ Vancouver Marriott Pinnacle
   Downtown 🅷
(604) 684-1128. **$219-$339.** 1128 W Hastings St. Between Thurlow and Bute sts. Int corridors. **Pets:** Accepted.
[SAVE] [✕] [&M] [📶] [💻] [🍴] [🏊] [✕]

Ⓒ ▼▼▼▼ The Westin Bayshore Vancouver 🅷 🐾
(604) 682-3377. **$195-$460.** 1601 Bayshore Dr. W Georgia and Cardero sts. Int corridors. **Pets:** Medium. Service with restrictions, supervision.
[SAVE] [✕] [&M] [📶] [💻] [🍴] [🏊] [✕]

Ⓒ ▼▼▼▼ The Westin Grand, Vancouver 🅷
(604) 602-1999. **$169-$759.** 433 Robson St. Between Homer and Richards sts. Int corridors. **Pets:** Accepted.
[SAVE] [✕] [&M] [💻] [🍴] [🏊] [✕]

WHITE ROCK

Ⓒ ▼▼▼▼ Ocean Promenade Hotel 🅷
(604) 542-0102. **$129-$469.** 15611 Marine Dr. Hwy 99, exit 2B southbound; exit 2 (White Rock/8th Ave) northbound, 1.3 mi (2 km) w. Ext/int corridors. **Pets:** Accepted.
[SAVE] [✕] [&M] [📶] [💻]

END METROPOLITAN AREA

VICTORIA METROPOLITAN AREA

MALAHAT

Ⓒ ▼▼▼ ▼▼▼ The Aerie Resort & Spa 🅲 🐾
(250) 743-7115. **$139-$900.** 600 Ebadora Ln. 20 mi (32 km) n of Victoria off Trans-Canada Hwy 1, use Spectacle Lake turn off, follow signs. Int corridors. **Pets:** Small, dogs only. $35 daily fee/room. Designated rooms, service with restrictions, supervision.
[SAVE] [✕] [💻] [🍴] [✕]

▼▼ Malahat Bungalows Motel 🅼
(250) 478-3011. **$62-$500, 3 day notice.** 300 Trans-Canada Hwy. Trans-Canada Hwy 1, 16.3 mi (26 km) n of Victoria, follow signs. Ext corridors. **Pets:** Medium, other species. $10 daily fee/pet. Service with restrictions, supervision.
[✕] [📶] [🎿] [📠]

SAANICH

▼▼▼▼ Howard Johnson Hotel & Suites 🅷
(250) 704-4656. **$117-$153.** 4670 Elk Lake Dr. Blanshard St (Hwy 17), just w on Royal Oak Dr, then just n. Ext/int corridors. **Pets:** Accepted.
[ASK] [✕] [&M] [📶] [💻] [🍴] [🏊]

SAANICHTON

Ⓒ ▼▼ ▼▼ Quality Inn Waddling Dog 🅷
(250) 652-1146. **$99-$169.** 2476 Mt Newton Crossroad. Corner of Blanshard St (Hwy 17) and Mt Newton Crossroad. Int corridors. **Pets:** Accepted.
[SAVE] [✕] [💻] [🍴]

Ⓒ ▼▼ ▼▼ Victoria Airport Super 8 🅷
(250) 652-6888. **$99-$199.** 2477 Mt Newton Crossroad. Just e of Blanshard St (Hwy 17). Int corridors. **Pets:** Medium. $100 deposit/pet, $25 daily fee/pet. Service with restrictions, supervision.
[SAVE] [✕] [&M] [💻]

SIDNEY

Ⓒ ▼▼▼▼ Best Western Emerald Isle Motor Inn 🅷 🐾
(250) 656-4441. **$109-$299.** 2306 Beacon Ave. Hwy 17, exit Sidney, just e. Int corridors. **Pets:** Other species. $15 daily fee/pet. Designated rooms, service with restrictions, supervision.
[SAVE] [✕] [&M] [📶] [💻] [🍴] [✕]

Ⓒ ▼▼▼▼ The Cedarwood Inn & Suites 🅷
(250) 656-5551. **$89-$225.** 9522 Lochside Dr. Hwy 17, just e on McTavish Rd, then 0.8 mi (1.4 km) n. Ext corridors. **Pets:** Medium, other species. $15 daily fee/pet. Designated rooms, service with restrictions, supervision.
[SAVE] [✕] [📶] [💻] [🎿]

▼▼▼▼ Miraloma on the Cove 🅷
(250) 656-6622. **Call for rates.** 2326 Harbour Rd. Beacon Ave, 1.3 mi (2 km) n on Resthaven Dr, then 0.6 mi (1 km) e. Int corridors. **Pets:** Accepted.
[✕] [&M] [📶] [💻] [🍴] [✕] [🎿]

(AA) ▼▼▼▼ **The Sidney Pier Hotel & Spa** **H**
(250) 655-9445. **$109-$649.** 9805 Seaport Pl. From Hwy 17, 0.6 mi (1 km) e on Beacon Ave. Int corridors. **Pets:** Dogs only. $30 one-time fee/room. Designated rooms, supervision.
[SAVE] [X] [&M] [H] [P] [TI] [X]

(AA) ▼▼▼ **Victoria Airport Travelodge Sidney** **H**
(250) 656-1176. **$99-$199.** 2280 Beacon Ave. Just e of Hwy 17, exit Sidney. Int corridors. **Pets:** Large, other species. $10 daily fee/room. Designated rooms, service with restrictions, supervision.
[SAVE] [X] [&M] [H] [P] [≈]

SOOKE

▼▼ **Ocean Wilderness Inn** **BB**
(250) 646-2116. **$130-$220, 7 day notice.** 9171 W Coast Rd. 8.6 mi (14 km) w on Hwy 14. Ext/int corridors. **Pets:** $25 daily fee/pet. Designated rooms, service with restrictions, supervision.
[ASK] [X] [H] [AC] [W] [∅]

(AA) ▼▼▼ **Sooke Harbour House** **CI**
(250) 642-3421. **$305-$650, 7 day notice.** 1528 Whiffen Spit Rd. 1.2 mi (2 km) w on Hwy 14. Ext/int corridors. **Pets:** Accepted.
[SAVE] [X] [H] [P] [TI] [AC] [W]

VICTORIA

▼▼▼▼ **Abbeymoore Manor Bed & Breakfast Inn** **BB** ❖
(250) 370-1470. **$109-$249, 14 day notice.** 1470 Rockland Ave. Blanshard St (Hwy 17), 1.2 mi (2 km) e on Fort St, just s on St. Charles St, then just w. Ext/int corridors. **Pets:** Medium, dogs only. $15 daily fee/pet. Designated rooms.
[X] [H] [P] [AC]

(AA) ▼▼▼ **Abigail's Hotel** **H**
(250) 388-5363. **$169-$399, 7 day notice.** 906 McClure St. Blanshard St (Hwy 17), just e on Fairfield Rd, then just n on Vancouver St. Int corridors. **Pets:** Accepted.
[SAVE] [X] [H] [P]

(AA) ▼▼▼ **Accent Inns** **H** ❖
(250) 475-7500. **$99-$189.** 3233 Maple St. 1.9 mi (3 km) n on Blanshard St (Hwy 17); corner of Blanchard St and Cloverdale Ave. Ext corridors. **Pets:** Medium. $15 daily fee/room. Designated rooms, service with restrictions, supervision.
[SAVE] [X] [&M] [H] [P] [TI]

(AA) ▼▼▼ **Admiral Inn** **M**
(250) 388-6267. **$99-$269.** 257 Belleville St. Corner of Belleville and Quebec sts. Ext corridors. **Pets:** Accepted.
[SAVE] [X] [H] [P]

(AA) ▼▼▼ **Best Western Carlton Plaza Hotel** **H** ❖
(250) 388-5513. **$89-$259.** 642 Johnson St. Between Douglas and Broad sts. Int corridors. **Pets:** $10 daily fee/pet. Service with restrictions, supervision.
[SAVE] [X] [&M] [H] [P] [TI]

(AA) ▼▼▼ **Blue Ridge Inns** **M**
(250) 388-4345. **$69-$129.** 3110 Douglas St. Between Finlayson St and Speed Ave. Ext corridors. **Pets:** Small. $15 daily fee/room. Designated rooms, service with restrictions, supervision.
[SAVE] [X] [H] [P] [TI] [≈] [AC]

▼▼▼▼ **Chateau Victoria Hotel and Suites** **H** ❖
(250) 382-4221. **$95-$229.** 740 Burdett Ave. Between Douglas and Blanshard sts. Int corridors. **Pets:** Dogs only. $15 deposit/pet. Designated rooms, service with restrictions, crate.
[ASK] [X] [H] [P] [TI] [≈]

(AA) ▼▼▼ **Comfort Inn & Suites** **M** ❖
(250) 388-7861. **$89-$299.** 101 Island Hwy. Douglas St, 3.1 mi (5 km) w on Gorge Rd, then just s on Admirals Rd. Ext/int corridors. **Pets:** Small, dogs only. $15 daily fee/pet. Designated rooms, service with restrictions, supervision.
[SAVE] [X] [H] [P] [≈]

(AA) ▼▼▼ **Days Inn Victoria on the Harbour** **H** ❖
(250) 386-3451. **$79-$213.** 427 Belleville St. Between Oswego and Menzies sts. Int corridors. **Pets:** Other species. $10 daily fee/room. Designated rooms, service with restrictions.
[SAVE] [X] [H] [P] [TI] [≈] [AC]

(AA) ▼▼▼ ▼▼▼ **Delta Victoria Ocean Pointe Resort &**
Spa **H** ❖
(250) 360-2999. **$159-$398.** 45 Songhees Rd. Just w of Johnson St Bridge, Esquimalt at Tyee Rd. Int corridors. **Pets:** Small. $35 one-time fee/room. Designated rooms, service with restrictions, supervision.
[SAVE] [X] [&M] [H] [P] [TI] [≈] [X]

(AA) ▼▼▼ **Executive House Hotel** **H**
(250) 388-5111. **$195-$215.** 777 Douglas St. Between Blanshard and Douglas sts; downtown. Int corridors. **Pets:** Medium, other species. $15 daily fee/pet. Service with restrictions, supervision.
[SAVE] [X] [H] [P] [TI] [X] [AC]

▼▼▼▼ **The Fairmont Empress** **H**
(250) 384-8111. **$169-$569, 3 day notice.** 721 Government St. Between Belleville and Humboldt sts. Int corridors. **Pets:** Accepted.
[ASK] [X] [&M] [H] [P] [TI] [≈] [X] [AC]

(AA) ▼▼▼ ▼▼ **Harbour Towers Hotel & Suites** **H** ❖
(250) 385-2405. **$94-$450.** 345 Quebec St. Between Oswego and Pendray sts. Int corridors. **Pets:** Small. $23 daily fee/pet. Designated rooms, service with restrictions.
[SAVE] [X] [&M] [H] [P] [TI] [≈] [X] [AC]

(AA) ▼▼▼ ▼▼ **Hotel Grand Pacific** **H**
(250) 386-0450. **$149-$329.** 463 Belleville St. Between Oswego and Menzies sts. Int corridors. **Pets:** Accepted.
[SAVE] [X] [&M] [P] [TI] [≈] [X]

(AA) ▼▼▼ **Howard Johnson Hotel Victoria** **H**
(250) 382-2151. **$59-$159.** 310 Gorge Rd E. From Douglas St, 0.6 mi (1.4 km) w; between Jutland St and Washington Ave. Int corridors. **Pets:** Medium, dogs only. $25 one-time fee/room. Service with restrictions, supervision.
[SAVE] [X] [H] [P] [TI] [≈]

(AA) ▼▼▼ ▼▼ **Huntingdon Hotel & Suites** **H**
(250) 381-3456. **$99-$389.** 330 Quebec St. Between Oswego and Pendray sts. Int corridors. **Pets:** Large. $15 daily fee/pet. Designated rooms, service with restrictions, crate.
[SAVE] [X] [H] [P] [TI]

(AA) ▼▼▼ ▼▼ **The Magnolia Hotel & Spa** **H** ❖
(250) 381-0999. **$175-$335.** 623 Courtney St. Corner of Courtney and Gordon sts. Int corridors. **Pets:** $80 one-time fee/room. Designated rooms, service with restrictions, crate.
[SAVE] [X] [&M] [P] [TI] [X]

(AA) ▼▼▼ ▼▼ **Marriott Victoria Inner Harbour** **H** ❖
(250) 480-3800. **$229-$359.** 728 Humboldt St. Between Blanshard and Douglas sts. Int corridors. **Pets:** Small. $50 one-time fee/room. Designated rooms, service with restrictions, crate.
[SAVE] [X] [&M] [H] [P] [TI] [≈] [X]

(AA) ▼▼▼ **The Oswego Hotel** **H** ❖
(250) 294-7500. **$179-$699.** 500 Oswego St. Between Kingston and Quebec sts. Int corridors. **Pets:** Other species. $25 daily fee/room. Designated rooms, service with restrictions.
[SAVE] [X] [&M] [H] [P] [TI] [AC]

(AA) ▼▼ ▼▼ **Prior House B&B Inn** BB ❀
(250) 592-8847. **$159-$309, 14 day notice.** 620 St. Charles St. Blanshard St (Hwy 17), 1.2 mi (2 km) e on Fort St, then just s. Int corridors. **Pets:** Medium, dogs only. $20 one-time fee/room. Designated rooms, service with restrictions, crate.
SAVE ☒ 🛏 🖵 ᗑ

(AA) ▼▼▼▼ **Quality Inn Downtown** H
(250) 385-6787. **$69-$169.** 850 Blanshard St. Between Courtney St and Burnett Ave; downtown. Int corridors. **Pets:** Accepted.
SAVE ☒ 🛏 🖵 ⊤⊤ ᗑ ☒ ᗑ

▼▼▼▼ **Ramada Victoria** H
(250) 386-1422. **$59-$185.** 123 Gorge Rd E. From Douglas St, 1.2 mi (2.4 km) w. Int corridors. **Pets:** Small, dogs only. $15 daily fee/room. Designated rooms, supervision.
ASK ☒ 🛏 🖵 ⊤⊤ ᗑ

(AA) ▼▼ ▼▼ **Robin Hood Motel** M
(250) 388-4302. **$66-$109.** 136 Gorge Rd E. Douglas St, 1.2 mi (2.4 km) w. Ext corridors. **Pets:** Dogs only. $5 daily fee/pet. Designated rooms, service with restrictions, supervision.
SAVE ☒ 🛏 🖵

(AA) ▼▼ ▼ **Travelodge Victoria** H
(250) 388-6611. **$79-$189.** 229 Gorge Rd E. From Douglas St, 1.2 mi (2 km) w on Gorge Rd E; at Washington Ave. Ext corridors. **Pets:** Medium. $10 daily fee/pet. Designated rooms, service with restrictions.
SAVE ☒ 🛏 🖵 ⊤⊤ ᗑ

(AA) ▼▼▼ ▼▼ **The Westin Bear Mountain Victoria Golf Resort & Spa** H ❀
(250) 391-7160. **$169-$559.** 1999 Country Club Way. Trans-Canada Hwy 1, exit 14 (Highlands), 1.1 mi (1.7 km) n on Millstream Rd, then 1.9 mi (3 km) ne on Bear Mountain Pkwy, follow signs. Int corridors. **Pets:** Small, dogs only. $60 one-time fee/room. Designated rooms, service with restrictions, supervision.
SAVE ☒ ᗑM 🛏 🖵 ⊤⊤ ᗑ ☒

END METROPOLITAN AREA

WHISTLER

(AA) ▼▼▼▼ **Best Western Listel Whistler Hotel** H
(604) 932-1133. **$99-$249, 30 day notice.** 4121 Village Green. Hwy 99, just e on Village Gate Blvd, then follow Whistler Way. Int corridors. **Pets:** Accepted.
SAVE ☒ 🛏 🖵 ⊤⊤ ᗑ

(AA) ▼▼▼▼ **Crystal Lodge** H ❀
(604) 932-2221. **$141-$1049.** 4154 Village Green. Hwy 99, just e on Village Gate Blvd, then follow Whistler Way. Int corridors. **Pets:** Dogs only. $20 daily fee/pet. Service with restrictions, supervision.
SAVE ☒ ᗑM 🛏 🖵 ⊤⊤ ᗑ ☒

▼▼▼▼ **Delta Whistler Village Suites** H ❀
(604) 905-3987. **$99-$399, 45 day notice.** 4308 Main St. Hwy 99, just e on Village Gate Blvd, just n on Northlands Blvd, then just e. Int corridors. **Pets:** Other species. $35 one-time fee/pet. Service with restrictions, crate.
ASK ☒ ᗑM 🛏 🖵 ⊤⊤ ᗑ ☒

(AA) ▼▼▼ **Edgewater Lodge** M ❀
(604) 932-0688. **$124-$225, 14 day notice.** 8020 Alpine Way. 2.5 mi (4 km) n of Whistler Village via Hwy 99, then e. Ext corridors. **Pets:** Dogs only. $25 one-time fee/room. Service with restrictions, supervision.
SAVE ☒ ⊤⊤ ᗑ

(AA) ▼▼▼ ▼▼ **The Fairmont Chateau Whistler** H
(604) 938-8000. **$179-$900, 3 day notice.** 4599 Chateau Blvd. Hwy 99, 0.6 mi (1 km) e on Lorimer Rd (Upper Village), just w on Blackcomb Way. Int corridors. **Pets:** Accepted.
SAVE ☒ ᗑM 🖵 ⊤⊤ ᗑ ☒

(AA) ▼▼▼▼ ▼▼ **Four Seasons Resort Whistler** H ❀
(604) 935-3400. **$255-$3200, 30 day notice.** 4591 Blackcomb Way. Hwy 99, 0.6 mi (1 km) e on Lorimer Rd (Upper Village). Int corridors. **Pets:** No service, supervision.
SAVE ☒ ᗑM 🛏 🖵 ⊤⊤ ᗑ ☒

(AA) ▼▼▼▼ ▼▼ **Hilton Whistler Resort & Spa** H ❀
(604) 932-1982. **$185-$929.** 4050 Whistler Way. Hwy 99, just e on Village Gate Blvd, then follow Whistler Way. Int corridors. **Pets:** $25 daily fee/room. Service with restrictions, supervision.
SAVE ☒ ᗑM 🛏 🖵 ⊤⊤ ᗑ ☒

(AA) ▼▼▼▼ **Nita Lake Lodge** H
(604) 966-5700. **$179-$699, 30 day notice.** 2131 Lake Placid Rd. 1.8 mi (3 km) s on Hwy 99, just w. Int corridors. **Pets:** Accepted.
SAVE ☒ ᗑM 🛏 🖵 ⊤⊤ ☒

▼▼▼▼ **Pan Pacific Whistler Village Centre** H
(604) 966-5500. **$169-$1139, 7 day notice.** 4299 Blackcomb Way. Hwy 99, just e on Village Gate Blvd. Int corridors. **Pets:** Accepted.
☒ ᗑM 🛏 🖵 ᗑ ☒

▼▼▼▼ **Residence Inn by Marriott** CO
(604) 905-3400. **$129-$399.** 4899 Painted Cliff Rd. Hwy 99, 0.6 mi (1 km) e on Lorimer Rd (Upper Village), just se on Blackcomb Way, then just w, follow road all the way to the end. Int corridors. **Pets:** Accepted.
☒ 🛏 🖵 ᗑ ᗑ

▼▼▼ **Tantalus Resort Lodge** CO ❀
(604) 932-4146. **$129-$829.** 4200 Whistler Way. Hwy 99, just e on Village Gate Blvd, then follow Whistler Way to the end. Int corridors. **Pets:** Medium. $35 one-time fee/room. Designated rooms, service with restrictions, supervision.
ASK ☒ 🛏 🖵 ᗑ ☒ ᗑ

(AA) ▼▼▼▼ ▼▼ **The Westin Resort & Spa** H
(604) 905-5000. **$149-$5999, 60 day notice.** 4090 Whistler Way. Hwy 99, just e on Village Gate Blvd, then s. Int corridors. **Pets:** Accepted.
SAVE ☒ ᗑM 🛏 🖵 ⊤⊤ ᗑ ☒

WILLIAMS LAKE

▼▼ **Drummond Lodge Motel** M
(250) 392-5334. **$72-$140.** 1405 Cariboo Hwy. 0.6 mi (1 km) s on Hwy 97. Ext corridors. **Pets:** Accepted.
☒ 🛏 🖵

(AA) ▼▼ ▼▼ **Williams Lake Super 8** M
(250) 398-8884. **$82-$120.** 1712 Broadway Ave S. 1.2 mi (2 km) s on Hwy 97. Int corridors. **Pets:** Accepted.
SAVE ☒ ᗑM 🛏 🖵

MANITOBA

BEAUSEJOUR

◆◆ Superior Inn 🄷
(204) 268-9050. **$94-$99.** 1055 Park Ave. Jct Hwy 44, 12 and 302. Int corridors. **Pets:** Other species. $10 daily fee/room. Designated rooms, service with restrictions, supervision.

BRANDON

Ⓐ ◆◆◆ Canad Inns-Brandon 🄷
(204) 727-1422. **$105-$230.** 1125 18th St. On Hwy 10 (18th St) at jct Brandon Ave. Int corridors. **Pets:** Accepted.

◆◆ Colonial Inn 🄷
(204) 728-8532. **$62-$89.** 1944 Queens Ave. Jct Hwy 10 (18th St), just w. Ext/int corridors. **Pets:** Accepted.
Ⓐ𝖲𝖪 ✕ 🛏 🖥 🍽 ⋙

◆◆ Comfort Inn 🄷
(204) 727-6232. **$98-$130.** 925 Middleton Ave. Northside Trans-Canada Hwy 1 service road; between Hwy 10 (18th St) N and 10 S; just e of McDonald's Restaurant. Int corridors. **Pets:** Other species. $10 daily fee/room. Service with restrictions, supervision.
Ⓐ𝖲𝖪 ✕ 🄼 🛏 🖥

Ⓐ ◆◆ Days Inn 🄷
(204) 727-3600. **$109-$124.** 2130 Currie Blvd. Jct Trans-Canada Hwy 1, 5 mi (8 km) s on Hwy 10 S (18th St). Int corridors. **Pets:** $10 daily fee/pet. Designated rooms, supervision.
𝖲𝖠𝖵𝖤 ✕ 🛏 🖥 ⋙

◆◆ Royal Oak Inn & Suites 🄷
(204) 728-5775. **$115-$125.** 3130 Victoria Ave. 3 mi (5 km) s of Trans-Canada Hwy 1; 0.9 mi (1.4 km) w of jct Hwy 10 (18th St) and 1A (Victoria Ave). Int corridors. **Pets:** $10 daily fee/pet. Designated rooms, service with restrictions, crate.
Ⓐ𝖲𝖪 ✕ 🛏 🖥 🍽 ⋙ ✕

◆◆ Super 8 Motel Brandon 🄷
(204) 729-8024. **$90-$105.** 1570 Highland Ave. On Trans-Canada Hwy 1, south service road, just e of Hwy 10 (18th St). Int corridors. **Pets:** Medium. $10 one-time fee/pet. Service with restrictions, supervision.
Ⓐ𝖲𝖪 ✕ 🄼 🛏 🖥 ⋙

◆◆ Victoria Inn 🄷
(204) 725-1532. **$103-$199.** 3550 Victoria Ave. 3 mi (5 km) s of Trans-Canada Hwy 1; 1.1 mi (1.8 km) w of jct Hwy 10 (18th St) and 1A (Victoria Ave). Int corridors. **Pets:** Accepted.
Ⓐ𝖲𝖪 ✕ 🛏 🖥 🍽 ⋙ ✕

CHURCHILL

◆◆ Polar Inn & Suites 🄼
(204) 675-8878. **$116-$245.** 153 Kelsey Blvd. Centre. Int corridors. **Pets:** Service with restrictions.
Ⓐ𝖲𝖪 ✕ 🛏 🖥 🐾

◆◆ The Tundra Inn 🄷
(204) 675-8831. **$95-$205.** 34 Franklin St. Centre. Int corridors. **Pets:** Accepted.
Ⓐ𝖲𝖪 ✕ 🛏 🖥 🍽 🐾

FLIN FLON

◆◆ Victoria Inn North 🄷
(204) 687-7555. **Call for rates.** 160 Hwy 10A N. Jct Hwy 10 and 10A, 0.6 mi (1 km) nw (eastern approach to city). Int corridors. **Pets:** Accepted.
✕ 🛏 🖥 🍽 ⋙

HECLA

◆◆ Radisson Hecla Oasis Resort 🄷
(204) 279-2041. **$149-$309, 7 day notice.** Hwy 8. On Hwy 8, follow signs. Int corridors. **Pets:** Accepted.
Ⓐ𝖲𝖪 ✕ 🛏 🖥 🍽 ⋙ ✕

◆◆ Solmundson Gesta Hus 🄱🄱
(204) 279-2088. **$75-$90.** Village on Hecla Island. On Hwy 8. Int corridors. **Pets:** Accepted.
Ⓐ𝖲𝖪 ✕ 🖀

NEEPAWA

◆◆ Bay Hill Inns & Suites 🄷
(204) 476-8888. **$90-$115.** 160 Main St W. Hwy 16, just w of jct Rt 5. Int corridors. **Pets:** Accepted.
Ⓐ𝖲𝖪 ✕ 🛏 🖥 🍽 ⋙

PORTAGE LA PRAIRIE

◆◆ Super 8 🄷
(204) 857-8883. **$86-$92.** 2668 Hwy 1A W. 0.9 mi (1.5 km) w on Trans-Canada Hwy 1A. Int corridors. **Pets:** Accepted.
✕ 🛏 🖥 ⋙

◆◆ Westgate Inn Motel 🄼
(204) 239-5200. **$60-$89.** 1010 Saskatchewan Ave E. 0.6 mi (1 km) e on Trans-Canada Hwy 1A. Ext corridors. **Pets:** Small. Service with restrictions, supervision.
Ⓐ𝖲𝖪 ✕ 🛏 🖥

RUSSELL

Ⓐ ◆◆◆ The Russell Inn Hotel & Conference Centre 🄷
(204) 773-2186. **$89-$178, 14 day notice.** Hwy 16 Russell. 0.8 mi (1.2 km) se on Hwy 16 and 83. Ext/int corridors. **Pets:** Accepted.
𝖲𝖠𝖵𝖤 ✕ 🛏 🖥 🍽 ⋙ ✕

STEINBACH

◆◆ Days Inn 🄷
(204) 320-9200. **Call for rates.** 75 Hwy 12 N. Jct Trans-Canada Hwy 1 and 12, 12.5 mi (20 km) s. Int corridors. **Pets:** Small, other species. $20 daily fee/pet. Designated rooms, service with restrictions, supervision.
✕ 🛏 🖥 ⋙ ✕

THE PAS

◆◆ Kikiwak Inn 🄷
(204) 623-1800. **Call for rates.** Hwy 10 N. On Hwy 10, 0.4 mi (0.6 km) n. Int corridors. **Pets:** Accepted.
✕ 🛏 🖥 🍽 ⋙

▼▼ Super 8 🅷
(204) 623-1888. **Call for rates.** 1717 Gordon Ave. At southern approach to town. Int corridors. **Pets:** Accepted.

⊠ 🛢 🖭 🌊

ⓒ ▼ Wescana Inn 🅷
(204) 623-5446. **$86-$91.** 439 Fischer Ave. On Hwy 10; centre. Ext/int corridors. **Pets:** Other species. Designated rooms, service with restrictions, supervision.

🆂🆅 ⊠ 🛢 🖭 🍴

THOMPSON

▼▼ Country Inn & Suites By Carlson 🅷
(204) 778-8879. **$108.** 70 Thompson Dr N. Just w of Hwy 6. Int corridors. **Pets:** Accepted.

🅰🆂🅺 ⊠ 🛢 🖭

WINNIPEG METROPOLITAN AREA

WINNIPEG

ⓒ ▼▼ Best Western Pembina Inn & Suites 🅷
(204) 269-8888. **$100-$108, 3 day notice.** 1714 Pembina Hwy. 0.6 mi (1 km) n of jct Bishop Grandin Blvd. Int corridors. **Pets:** Accepted.

🆂🆅 ⊠ 🛢 🖭 🌊 🗷

ⓒ ▼▼▼ Canad Inns Polo Park 🅷
(204) 775-8791. **$97-$299.** 1405 St. Matthews Ave. Just e of St James St. Int corridors. **Pets:** Accepted.

🆂🆅 ⊠ 🛢 🖭 🍴 🌊 🗷

▼▼▼ Clarion Hotel & Suites 🅷 🐾
(204) 774-5110. **$159-$299.** 1445 Portage Ave. Jct Empress St. Int corridors. **Pets:** $15 one-time fee/pet. Service with restrictions, crate.

🅰🆂🅺 ⊠ 🛢 🖭 🍴 🌊 🗷

▼▼ Comfort Inn Airport 🅷
(204) 783-5627. **$109-$149.** 1770 Sargent Ave. At Sargent Ave and King Edward St. Int corridors. **Pets:** Accepted.

🅰🆂🅺 ⊠ 🗛 🛢 🖭

ⓒ ▼▼ Comfort Inn South 🅷
(204) 269-7390. **$105-$149.** 3109 Pembina Hwy. Just n of jct Perimeter Hwy 100 and 75. Int corridors. **Pets:** Medium. $10 daily fee/room. Designated rooms, service with restrictions, supervision.

🆂🆅 ⊠ 🛢 🖭

▼▼ Country Inn & Suites By Carlson 🅷 🐾
(204) 783-6900. **$99-$125, 4 day notice.** 730 King Edward St. Just s of jct Wellington Ave. Int corridors. **Pets:** Large. $25 one-time fee/room. Service with restrictions, supervision.

🅰🆂🅺 ⊠ 🗛 🛢 🖭

▼▼ Days Inn Winnipeg 🅷
(204) 586-8525. **$119-$139.** 550 McPhillips St. Just n of Logan Ave. Int corridors. **Pets:** Medium, other species. $10 one-time fee/pet. Designated rooms, service with restrictions, supervision.

🅰🆂🅺 ⊠ 🛢 🖭 🍴 🌊

ⓒ ▼▼▼ Delta Winnipeg 🅷 🐾
(204) 942-0551. **$89-$399.** 350 St. Mary Ave. At Hargrave St. Int corridors. **Pets:** Medium, other species. $35 one-time fee/room. Service with restrictions, crate.

🆂🆅 ⊠ 🗛 🛢 🖭 🍴 🌊 🗷

▼▼▼ The Fairmont Winnipeg 🅷
(204) 957-1350. **$143-$431.** 2 Lombard Pl. Just e of corner Portage Ave and Main St. Int corridors. **Pets:** Accepted.

🅰🆂🅺 ⊠ 🛢 🖭 🍴 🌊 🗷

▼▼▼ Greenwood Inn & Suites 🅷
(204) 775-9889. **Call for rates.** 1715 Wellington Ave. Wellington Ave at Century St. Int corridors. **Pets:** Accepted.

⊠ 🛢 🖭 🍴 🌊 🗷

ⓒ ▼▼▼ Hilton Suites Winnipeg Airport 🅷
(204) 783-1700. **$139-$209.** 1800 Wellington Ave. At Berry St. Int corridors. **Pets:** Accepted.

🆂🆅 ⊠ 🗛 🛢 🖭 🍴 🌊 🗷

ⓒ ▼▼▼ Holiday Inn Winnipeg-South 🅷 🐾
(204) 452-4747. **$120-$140.** 1330 Pembina Hwy. At McGillivray Blvd. Int corridors. **Pets:** Other species. Service with restrictions, supervision.

🆂🆅 ⊠ 🛢 🖭 🍴 🌊 🗷

▼▼ The Marlborough Hotel 🅷
(204) 942-6411. **$77-$179.** 331 Smith St. Just n off Metro Rt 85 (Portage Ave). Int corridors. **Pets:** Accepted.

🅰🆂🅺 ⊠ 🛢 🖭 🍴 🌊 🗷

▼▼ Place Louis Riel Suite Hotel 🅷 🐾
(204) 947-6961. **$125-$400.** 190 Smith St. At St. Mary Ave. Int corridors. **Pets:** $25 daily fee/room. Designated rooms, service with restrictions, supervision.

🅰🆂🅺 ⊠ 🗛 🛢 🖭 🍴 🗷

▼▼ Quality Inn & Suites 🅷 🐾
(204) 453-8247. **$80-$270, 30 day notice.** 635 Pembina Hwy. Jct Grant Ave, just s. Int corridors. **Pets:** Large, other species. $15 daily fee/pet. Crate.

🅰🆂🅺 ⊠ 🛢 🖭 🍴

▼▼▼ Radisson Hotel Winnipeg Downtown 🅷 🐾
(204) 956-0410. **$120-$182.** 288 Portage Ave. At Smith St. Int corridors. **Pets:** Large, other species. $30 one-time fee/room. Designated rooms, service with restrictions, crate.

🅰🆂🅺 ⊠ 🛢 🖭 🍴 🌊 🗷

ⓒ ▼▼ Travelodge 🅷 🐾
(204) 255-6000. **$82-$159.** 20 Alpine Ave. Just e of jct Fermor Ave and St. Anne's Rd. Int corridors. **Pets:** Medium, other species. $10 daily fee/room. Service with restrictions, supervision.

🆂🆅 ⊠ 🛢 🖭 🍴 🌊 🗷

▼▼▼ Victoria Inn Hotel & Convention Centre 🅷
(204) 786-4801. **$125-$155.** 1808 Wellington Ave. At Berry St. Int corridors. **Pets:** Accepted.

🅰🆂🅺 ⊠ 🛢 🖭 🍴 🌊 🗷

END METROPOLITAN AREA

NEW BRUNSWICK

BATHURST

▼▼ **Atlantic Host Hotel** 🅷
(506) 548-3335. **$99-$120.** 1450 Vanier Blvd. Rt 11, exit 310 (Vanier Blvd).
Int corridors. **Pets:** Accepted.
⊠ 🖵 🍴 ⊐ ⊠

▼▼ **Comfort Inn** 🅷
(506) 547-8000. **Call for rates.** 1170 St Peter's Ave. 2.1 mi (3.4 km) n on
Rt 134 (St Peter's Ave). Int corridors. **Pets:** Accepted.
⊠ 🖵 🖵

▼▼ **Danny's Inn & Conference Centre** 🅷 🐾
(506) 546-6621. **$84-$153.** Rt 134. Rt 11, exit 310 (Vanier Blvd) northbound to Rt 134 (St Peter's Ave), 2.5 mi (4 km) n; exit 318 southbound to
Rt 134 (St Peter's Ave), 2.3 mi (3.8 km) s. Ext/int corridors. **Pets:** $100
deposit/room. Designated rooms, service with restrictions, crate.
(ASK) ⊠ 🖵 🖵 🍴 ⊐ ⊠

▼▼ **Lakeview Inns & Suites** 🅷
(506) 548-4949. **$100-$112.** 777 St Peter's Ave. 1.8 mi (3 km) n on Rt 134
(St Peter's Ave). Int corridors. **Pets:** Small, dogs only. $25 daily fee/pet.
Designated rooms, service with restrictions, supervision.
(ASK) ⊠ 🔄M 🖵 🖵

BOUCTOUCHE

▼▼ **Auberge Bouctouche Inn & Suites** 🅷
(506) 743-5003. **$79-$159.** 50 Industrielle St. Rt 11, exit 32A/B. Int corridors. **Pets:** Accepted.
⊠ 🔄M 🖵

CAMPBELLTON

▼▼ **Comfort Inn** 🅷
(506) 753-4121. **$110-$160.** 111 chemin Val D'Amour. Hwy 11, exit 415,
0.6 mi (1 km) e on Sugarloaf St W. Ext/int corridors. **Pets:** Other species.
Service with restrictions, supervision.
(ASK) ⊠ 🖵 🖵

(CAA) ▼▼ **Howard Johnson** 🅷
(506) 753-4133. **$119-$139.** 157 Water St. Hwy 134; in City Centre Complex. Int corridors. **Pets:** Accepted.
(SAVE) ⊠ 🖵 🖵 🍴

▼▼ **Super 8 Motel-Campbellton** 🅷
(506) 753-8080. **$69-$279.** 26 Duke St. Just s of Roseberry St; jct George
and Duke sts; downtown. Ext/int corridors. **Pets:** $20 one-time fee/room.
Designated rooms, service with restrictions, supervision.
(ASK) ⊠ 🔄M 🖵 🖵 ⊐ ⊠

CARAQUET

▼▼▼ **Super 8** 🅷
(506) 727-0888. **Call for rates.** 9 Carrefour Ave. Just e of jct Rt 11 and St
Pierre Blvd E. Int corridors. **Pets:** Accepted.
⊠ 🔄M 🖵 🖵 ⊐ ⊠

COCAGNE

▼▼ **Cocagne Motel** Ⓜ
(506) 576-6657. **Call for rates.** 1718 Rt 535. Rt 11, exit 15, 0.6 mi (1 km)
n on Rt 535. Ext corridors. **Pets:** Accepted.
🖵 🏊

DALHOUSIE

(CAA) ▼▼▼ **Best Western Manoir Adelaide** 🅷
(506) 684-5681. **$110-$120, 3 day notice.** 385 Adelaide St. Centre. Int
corridors. **Pets:** Accepted.
(SAVE) ⊠ 🖵 🖵 🍴

DOAKTOWN

▼▼▼ **The Ledges Inn** 🅲🅸
(506) 365-1820. **$100-$150.** 30 Ledges Inn Ln. On Rt 8; centre. Int corridors. **Pets:** Accepted.
(ASK) ⊠ 🍴

EDMUNDSTON

▼▼ **Auberge Les Jardins Inn** 🅷
(506) 739-5514. **$99-$169.** 60 Principale St. Trans-Canada Hwy 2, exit 8.
Ext/int corridors. **Pets:** Accepted.
(ASK) ⊠ 🖵 🖵 🍴 ⊐

(CAA) ▼▼▼ **Chateau Edmundston Hotel & Suites** 🅷
(506) 739-7321. **$110-$160.** 100 rue Rice. Trans-Canada Hwy 2, exit 18
(Hebert Blvd), 1 mi (1.6 km) sw, then just w on Church Rd. Int corridors.
Pets: Accepted.
(SAVE) ⊠ 🖵 🖵 🍴 ⊐

▼▼▼ **Comfort Inn** 🅷
(506) 739-8361. **$89-$199.** 5 Bateman Ave. Trans-Canada Hwy 2, exit 18
(Hebert Blvd). Int corridors. **Pets:** Other species. Service with restrictions,
crate.
(ASK) ⊠ 🖵 🖵

▼▼▼ **Quality Inn** 🅷
(506) 735-5525. **$72-$135.** 919 Canada Rd. Trans-Canada Hwy 2, exit
13B eastbound; exit 13BA westbound. Ext/int corridors. **Pets:** Accepted.
(ASK) ⊠ 🔄M 🖵 🍴 ⊐ ⊠

FREDERICTON

▼▼ **Auberge Wandlyn Inn** 🅷
(506) 462-4444. **$90-$120.** 958 Prospect St. Rt 8, exit 3 (Hanwell Rd)
eastbound; exit 5 (Smythe St) westbound. Ext/int corridors. **Pets:** Accepted.
(ASK) ⊠ 🖵 🖵 🍴 ⊐ ⊠

▼▼ **City Motel** 🅷
(506) 450-9900. **Call for rates.** 1216 Regent St. Trans-Canada Hwy 2,
exit 285A and B eastbound; exit 285B westbound, 2 mi (3.3 km) n on Rt
101 (Regent St). Int corridors. **Pets:** Accepted.
⊠ 🖵 🖵 🍴

(CAA) ▼▼▼ **Comfort Inn** 🅷 🐾
(506) 453-0800. **$109-$199.** 797 Prospect St. Rt 8, exit 3 (Hanwell Rd)
eastbound; exit 5 (Smythe St) westbound. Int corridors. **Pets:** Other species. Designated rooms, service with restrictions, supervision.
(SAVE) ⊠ 🖵 🖵

(CAA) ▼▼▼ **Crowne Plaza Fredericton Lord
Beaverbrook** 🅷 🐾
(506) 455-3371. **$159-$279.** 659 Queen St. Corner of Regent St. Int
corridors. **Pets:** Designated rooms, service with restrictions.
(SAVE) ⊠ 🖵 🍴 ⊐ ⊠

Ⓐ ♦♦♦ **Delta Fredericton** 🄷
(506) 457-7000. **$164-$294.** 225 Woodstock Rd. 1 mi (1.6 km) n on Rt 102; downtown. Int corridors. **Pets:** Accepted.
⟨SAVE⟩ ⟨✕⟩ ⟨&M⟩ ⟨📶⟩ ⟨💻⟩ ⟨¶¶⟩ ⟨🏊⟩ ⟨✕⟩

Ⓐ ♦♦♦ **Lakeview Inns & Suites-Fredericton** 🄷
(506) 459-0035. **$107-$137.** 665 Prospect St. Rt 8, exit 3 (Hanwell Rd) eastbound; exit 5 (Smythe St) westbound. Int corridors. **Pets:** Accepted.
⟨SAVE⟩ ⟨✕⟩ ⟨📶⟩ ⟨💻⟩

Ⓐ ♦♦♦♦ **Ramada Hotel Fredericton** 🄷
(506) 460-5500. **$109-$149.** 480 Riverside Dr. On Rt 105 at the north end of Princess Margaret Bridge. Int corridors. **Pets:** Accepted.
⟨SAVE⟩ ⟨✕⟩ ⟨📶⟩ ⟨💻⟩ ⟨¶¶⟩ ⟨🏊⟩ ⟨✕⟩

Ⓐ ♦♦♦♦ **Riverside Resort & Conference Centre** 🄷 ❀
(506) 363-5111. **$95-$171.** 35 Mactaquac Rd (Hwy 102). Trans-Canada Hwy 2, exit 258 eastbound, 7 mi (11 km) e; exit 294 westbound, 19 mi (30 km) w. Ext/int corridors. **Pets:** Other species. Designated rooms, service with restrictions.
⟨SAVE⟩ ⟨✕⟩ ⟨&M⟩ ⟨📶⟩ ⟨💻⟩ ⟨¶¶⟩ ⟨🏊⟩ ⟨✕⟩

GRAND FALLS

Ⓐ ♦♦♦ **Best Western Grand Sault Hotel & Suites** 🄷 ❀
(506) 473-6200. **$124-$250, 3 day notice.** 187 Ouellette St. Trans-Canada Hwy 2, exit 79. Int corridors. **Pets:** Medium, other species. $25 daily fee/room. Designated rooms, service with restrictions, crate.
⟨SAVE⟩ ⟨✕⟩ ⟨&M⟩ ⟨📶⟩ ⟨💻⟩ ⟨🏊⟩

♦♦ **Quality Inn Grand Falls** 🄷
(506) 473-1300. **$105-$175.** 10039 Rt 144. Trans-Canada Hwy 2, exit 75, just w. Ext/int corridors. **Pets:** Very small. Designated rooms, service with restrictions, supervision.
⟨ASK⟩ ⟨✕⟩ ⟨&M⟩ ⟨📶⟩ ⟨💻⟩ ⟨¶¶⟩ ⟨🏊⟩ ⟨✕⟩

MIRAMICHI

Ⓐ ♦♦♦ **Canadas Best Value Inn & Suites** 🄷 ❀
(506) 622-1215. **$79-$127.** 201 Edward St. 0.6 mi (1 km) w on Rt 8. Int corridors. **Pets:** Dogs only. $8 one-time fee/pet. Supervision.
⟨SAVE⟩ ⟨✕⟩ ⟨📶⟩ ⟨💻⟩

♦♦ **Lakeview Inns & Suites** 🄷
(506) 627-1999. **$84-$114, 7 day notice.** 333 King George Hwy. 1.1 mi (1.8 km) w on Rt 8. Int corridors. **Pets:** Small, other species. $50 deposit/pet. Designated rooms, service with restrictions, supervision.
⟨ASK⟩ ⟨✕⟩ ⟨📶⟩ ⟨💻⟩

♦♦ **Park Inn & Suites** 🄷
(506) 622-0302. **$99-$129.** 1 Jane St. Just s off King George Hwy on Bridge St. Int corridors. **Pets:** Other species. $15 daily fee/room. Service with restrictions, supervision.
⟨ASK⟩ ⟨✕⟩ ⟨📶⟩ ⟨💻⟩ ⟨¶¶⟩

♦♦♦ **Rodd Miramichi River-A Rodd Signature Hotel** 🄷 ❀
(506) 773-3111. **$116-$180.** 1809 Water St. Hwy 11, exit 120, 0.4 mi (0.6 km) e. Int corridors. **Pets:** Large, other species. $10 daily fee/room. Designated rooms, service with restrictions, supervision.
⟨ASK⟩ ⟨✕⟩ ⟨&M⟩ ⟨📶⟩ ⟨💻⟩ ⟨¶¶⟩ ⟨🏊⟩ ⟨✕⟩

MONCTON

Ⓐ ♦♦ **Beacon Light Motel** Ⓜ
(506) 384-1734. **$75-$125.** 1062 Mountain Rd. Trans-Canada Hwy 2, exit 454 (Mapleton Rd), 1.7 mi (2.8 km) to Rt 126 (Mountain Rd), then just s. Ext/int corridors. **Pets:** Accepted.
⟨SAVE⟩ ⟨✕⟩ ⟨📶⟩ ⟨💻⟩ ⟨¶¶⟩ ⟨🏊⟩

Ⓐ ♦♦♦ **Coastal Inn Champlain** 🄷
(506) 857-9686. **$115-$149.** 502 Kennedy St. At Paul St; opposite Champlain Place Shopping Centre. Ext/int corridors. **Pets:** Small, other species. Designated rooms, service with restrictions, supervision.
⟨SAVE⟩ ⟨✕⟩ ⟨📶⟩ ⟨💻⟩ ⟨¶¶⟩ ⟨🏊⟩

♦♦ **Colonial Inns** 🄷
(506) 382-3395. **$89-$178.** 42 Highfield St. 1 blk n of Main St; centre. Ext/int corridors. **Pets:** Medium. $25 one-time fee/room. Designated rooms, service with restrictions, supervision.
⟨ASK⟩ ⟨✕⟩ ⟨📶⟩ ⟨¶¶⟩ ⟨🏊⟩

Ⓐ ♦♦♦ **Comfort Inn** 🄷 ❀
(506) 859-6868. **$95-$295.** 20 Maplewood Dr. Trans-Canada Hwy 2, exit 459A on Hwy 115 S, left on Rt 134 E (Lewisville Rd). Int corridors. **Pets:** Other species. Service with restrictions.
⟨SAVE⟩ ⟨✕⟩ ⟨📶⟩ ⟨💻⟩

♦♦ **Comfort Inn** 🄷
(506) 384-3175. **$99-$349.** 2495 Mountain Rd. Trans-Canada Hwy 2, exit 450. Int corridors. **Pets:** Accepted.
⟨ASK⟩ ⟨✕⟩ ⟨📶⟩ ⟨💻⟩

♦♦ **Country Inn & Suites By Carlson** 🄷 ❀
(506) 852-7000. **$89-$200.** 2475 Mountain Rd. Trans-Canada Hwy 2, exit 450. Int corridors. **Pets:** Small, other species. $25 one-time fee/room. Service with restrictions, supervision.
⟨ASK⟩ ⟨✕⟩ ⟨📶⟩ ⟨💻⟩

Ⓐ ♦♦♦♦ **Crowne Plaza Moncton Downtown** 🄷
(506) 854-6340. **$189-$399.** 1005 Main St. Highfield and Main sts; downtown. Int corridors. **Pets:** Other species. $10 one-time fee/room. Service with restrictions, crate.
⟨SAVE⟩ ⟨✕⟩ ⟨📶⟩ ⟨💻⟩ ⟨¶¶⟩ ⟨🏊⟩ ⟨✕⟩

♦♦♦ **Delta Beausejour** 🄷
(506) 854-4344. **Call for rates.** 750 Main St. Main and Bacon sts; downtown. Int corridors. **Pets:** Accepted.
⟨✕⟩ ⟨📶⟩ ⟨💻⟩ ⟨¶¶⟩ ⟨🏊⟩

♦♦♦ **Future Inns Moncton Hotel & Conference Centre** 🄷
(506) 852-9600. **$129-$189.** 40 Lady Ada Blvd. Trans-Canada Hwy 2, exit 454. Int corridors. **Pets:** Accepted.
⟨ASK⟩ ⟨✕⟩ ⟨&M⟩ ⟨💻⟩ ⟨¶¶⟩

Ⓐ ♦♦♦ **Hampton Inn & Suites Moncton** 🄷 ❀
(506) 855-4819. **$109-$145.** 700 Mapleton Rd. Trans-Canada Hwy 2, exit 454. Int corridors. **Pets:** Designated rooms, service with restrictions, supervision.
⟨SAVE⟩ ⟨✕⟩ ⟨&M⟩ ⟨📶⟩ ⟨💻⟩ ⟨🏊⟩

Ⓐ ♦♦♦ **Holiday Inn Express Hotel & Suites Moncton** 🄷
(506) 384-1050. **$109-$219.** 2515 Mountain Rd. Trans-Canada Hwy 2, exit 450. Ext/int corridors. **Pets:** Accepted.
⟨SAVE⟩ ⟨✕⟩ ⟨&M⟩ ⟨📶⟩ ⟨💻⟩ ⟨🏊⟩ ⟨✕⟩

Ⓐ ♦♦♦♦ **Residence Inn by Marriott Moncton** 🄷
(506) 854-7100. **$203-$248.** 600 Main St. At Assomption Blvd. Int corridors. **Pets:** Accepted.
⟨SAVE⟩ ⟨✕⟩ ⟨&M⟩ ⟨📶⟩ ⟨💻⟩ ⟨¶¶⟩ ⟨🏊⟩

♦♦♦ **Rodd Park House Inn** 🄷
(506) 382-1664. **$119-$155.** 434 Main St. On Rt 106 (Main St) at King St. Ext/int corridors. **Pets:** Large, other species. $10 daily fee/room. Service with restrictions, supervision.
⟨ASK⟩ ⟨✕⟩ ⟨💻⟩ ⟨¶¶⟩ ⟨🏊⟩

♦♦♦ **Super 8 Moncton/Dieppe** 🄷
(506) 858-8880. **Call for rates.** 370 Dieppe Blvd. Hwy 15, exit 16, 0.6 mi (1 km) s. Int corridors. **Pets:** Accepted.
⟨✕⟩ ⟨&M⟩ ⟨📶⟩ ⟨💻⟩ ⟨🏊⟩ ⟨✕⟩

OROMOCTO

(CAA) ▼▼▼ Days Inn Oromocto 🅷 ❀
(506) 357-5657. **$108-$126.** 60 Brayson Blvd. Trans-Canada Hwy 2, exit 301 eastbound; exit 303 westbound, just s to Pioneer Ave, then 1 mi (1.6 km) w. Int corridors. **Pets:** Medium, other species. $15 daily fee/pet. Designated rooms, service with restrictions, supervision.
[SAVE] [✕] [&M] [🖶] [🛏] [🍽] [🛍]

PERTH-ANDOVER

(CAA) ▼▼▼ The Castle Inn 🆑
(506) 273-9495. **$150-$250.** 21 Brentwood Dr. Trans-Canada Hwy 2, exit 115, follow signs over St. John River. Int corridors. **Pets:** Accepted.
[SAVE] [✕] [🖶] [🍽]

ROTHESAY

▼▼▼ Shadow Lawn Inn 🆑
(506) 847-7539. **$119-$195, 3 day notice.** 3180 Rothesay Rd. Hwy 1, exit 137B eastbound; exit 137A westbound, follow signs for Rothesay Rd and Rt 100, 1 mi (1.6 km) left on Old Hampton Rd (Rt 100), then left on Rt 100. Int corridors. **Pets:** $10 daily fee/room. Service with restrictions, supervision.
[ASK] [✕] [🛏] [🖶] [🍽]

SACKVILLE

▼▼ Coastal Inn Sackville 🅷
(506) 536-0000. **$112-$132.** 15 Wright St. Trans-Canada Hwy 2, exit 504. Int corridors. **Pets:** Accepted.
[ASK] [✕] [🛏]

(CAA) ▼▼▼ Marshlands Inn 🆑
(506) 536-0170. **$95-$205.** 55 Bridge St. On Hwy 106; centre. Int corridors. **Pets:** Accepted.
[SAVE] [✕] [🍽]

ST. ANDREWS

(CAA) ▼▼▼ The Fairmont Algonquin 🅷 ❀
(506) 529-8823. **$119-$569, 3 day notice.** 184 Adolphus St. Off Hwy 127. Int corridors. **Pets:** $29 daily fee/pet. Service with restrictions, supervision.
[SAVE] [✕] [🛏] [🖶] [🍽] [🛏] [🛍]

▼▼▼ St. Andrews Cottages 🅲🅰
(506) 529-8555. **$95-$139, 14 day notice.** 3889 Rt 127. On Rt 127, 1.5 mi (2.5 km) n. Ext corridors. **Pets:** Accepted.
[✕] [🛏] [🖶] [🛏] [🅇]

SAINT JOHN

(CAA) ▼▼ Colonial Inn Saint John 🅷
(506) 652-3000. **$95-$118.** 175 City Rd. Hwy 1, exit 123. Ext/int corridors. **Pets:** Accepted.
[SAVE] [✕] [🛏] [🍽] [🏊] [🛍]

▼▼ Comfort Inn 🅷
(506) 674-1873. **Call for rates.** 1155 Fairville Blvd. Hwy 1, exit 117 westbound; exit 119 eastbound, turn left. Int corridors. **Pets:** Accepted.
[✕] [🛏] [🖶]

▼▼ Country Inn & Suites 🅷 ❀
(506) 635-0400. **$99-$154.** 1011 Fairville Blvd. Hwy 1, exit 119B eastbound, left on Catherwood Dr, left at lights; exit 119A westbound. Int corridors. **Pets:** Other species. $10 daily fee/pet. Service with restrictions.
[ASK] [✕] [🛏] [🖶]

▼▼▼ Delta Brunswick 🅷 ❀
(506) 648-1981. **$99-$199.** 39 King St. Centre of downtown; in Brunswick Square Mall. Int corridors. **Pets:** Medium, other species. $35 one-time fee/room. Designated rooms, service with restrictions, supervision.
[ASK] [✕] [&M] [🖶] [🍽] [🛏] [🛍]

(CAA) ▼▼▼ Fort Howe Hotel and Convention Centre 🅷
(506) 657-7320. **$109-$149, 30 day notice.** 10 Portland St. Hwy 1, exit 121 eastbound off Harbour Bridge; exit 123 westbound. Int corridors. **Pets:** $10 one-time fee/room. Service with restrictions, supervision.
[SAVE] [✕] [🛏] [🖶] [🍽] [🛏]

(CAA) ▼▼▼ Hampton Inn & Suites 🅷
(506) 657-4600. **$99-$129.** 51 Fashion Dr. Hwy 1, exit 129, 1 mi (1.6 km) e on Rothesay Ave to Retail Dr; behind Home Depot. Int corridors. **Pets:** Accepted.
[SAVE] [✕] [&M] [🛏] [🖶] [🛏] [🛍]

(CAA) ▼▼▼ Hilton Saint John 🅷
(506) 693-8484. **$99-$185.** 1 Market Square. Hwy 1, exit 122, at Market Square. Int corridors. **Pets:** Accepted.
[SAVE] [✕] [🖶] [🍽] [🛏] [🛍]

(CAA) ▼▼▼ Holiday Inn Express Hotel & Suites 🅷
(506) 642-2622. **$109-$199.** 400 Main St/Chesley Dr. 0.6 mi (1 km) w on Hwy 1; north end of Chesley Dr, exit 121; off Harbour Bridge. Int corridors. **Pets:** Accepted.
[SAVE] [✕] [🛏] [🖶] [🛏]

(CAA) ▼▼▼ Hotel Courtenay Bay 🅷
(506) 657-3610. **$73-$129, 30 day notice.** 350 Haymarket. At Crown and Waterloo sts; downtown. Int corridors. **Pets:** Accepted.
[SAVE] [✕] [🖶] [🍽] [🛏]

(CAA) ▼▼▼ Inn on the Cove and Spa 🆑
(506) 672-7799. **$145-$225, 7 day notice.** 1371 Sand Cove Rd. Hwy 1, exit 119A, just s on Bleury St to Sand Cove Rd, then 3.2 mi (2 km) w. Int corridors. **Pets:** Accepted.
[SAVE] [✕] [&M] [🖶] [🍽]

ST-LEONARD

(CAA) ▼▼▼ Daigle's Motel 🅷
(506) 423-6351. **$78-$99.** 68 rue DuPont. Hwy 17, 0.6 mi (1 km) s of Trans-Canada Hwy 2, exit 58. Ext corridors. **Pets:** Accepted.
[SAVE] [✕] [🍽] [🛏]

ST. STEPHEN

(CAA) ▼ St. Stephen Inn 🅷 ❀
(506) 466-1814. **$55-$130.** 99 King St. On Hwy 1; centre. Ext/int corridors. **Pets:** Large. $10 daily fee/pet. Designated rooms, service with restrictions, supervision.
[SAVE] [✕] [🛏] [🍽]

SHEDIAC

▼▼ Gaudet Chalets & Motel 🅼
(506) 533-8877. **$55-$119, 30 day notice.** 14 Bellevue Heights. On Rt 133, 1.4 mi (2.4 km) w of Rt 15, exit 37. Ext corridors. **Pets:** Accepted.
[✕] [🛏] [🖶]

SUSSEX

▼ All Seasons Inn 🅼 ❀
(506) 433-2220. **$95-$125.** 1015 Main St. Hwy 1, exit 192 eastbound; exit 198 westbound, left towards Sussex Corner; centre. Ext corridors. **Pets:** Other species. $10 daily fee/pet. Service with restrictions, crate.
[ASK] [✕] [🍽]

▼▼ Fairway Inn 🅷
(506) 433-3470. **$100-$175.** 216 Roachville Rd. Hwy 1, exit 193. Ext/int corridors. **Pets:** Small. $10 daily fee/pet. Designated rooms, service with restrictions, supervision.
[ASK] [✕] [🛏] [🍽] [🛏]

▼ Pine Cone Motel 🅼
(506) 433-3958. **$55-$95.** 12808 Rt 114. Hwy 1, exit 198, 1.2 mi (2 km) e on Rt 114 towards Penobsquis. Ext corridors. **Pets:** Accepted.
[ASK] [✕]

WOODSTOCK

CAA ▼▼▼ **Best Western Woodstock Inn & Suites** H ❀

(506) 328-2378. **Call for rates.** 123 Gallop Ct. Trans-Canada Hwy 2, exit 185. Int corridors. **Pets:** Small, other species. $25 one-time fee/room. Designated rooms, service with restrictions, supervision.

SAVE ✖ 🖥 🖵 ≈

▼▼ **Econo Lodge** H ❀

(506) 328-8876. **Call for rates.** 168 Rt 555. Trans-Canada Hwy 2, exit 188 (Houlton Rd). Ext/int corridors. **Pets:** Medium. $10 daily fee/pet. Service with restrictions, supervision.

✖ 🖵 ❙❙ ≈

▼▼ **Howard Johnson Inn** H ❀

(506) 328-3315. **$90-$150.** 159 Rt 555, exit 188 TCH. Trans-Canada Hwy 2, exit 188 (Houlton Rd). Ext/int corridors. **Pets:** Medium. $10 daily fee/pet. Service with restrictions, supervision.

ASK ✖ 🖥 🖵 ❙❙ ≈

YOUNGS COVE ROAD

▼ **McCready's Motel** M

(506) 362-2916. **Call for rates.** 10995 Rt 10. Trans-Canada Hwy 2, exit 365, just w. Ext corridors. **Pets:** Accepted.

✖ ❙❙ 🐾 ☎

NEWFOUNDLAND AND LABRADOR

CHANNEL-PORT-AUX-BASQUES

▼▼ Hotel Port Aux Basques ⊞
(709) 695-2171. **$99-$120.** 1 Grand Bay Rd. Jct Trans-Canada Hwy 1. Int corridors. **Pets:** Accepted.
ⓐⓢⓚ ⊠ 🛏 💻 ⑾

▼▼ St. Christopher's Hotel ⊞
(709) 695-7034. **$85-$120.** 146 Caribou Rd. Trans-Canada Hwy 1, exit Port Aux Basques (downtown), follow signs 1.2 mi (2 km). Int corridors. **Pets:** Accepted.
ⓐⓢⓚ ⊠ 🛏 💻 ⑾

CLARENVILLE

▼ Restland Motel ⊞
(709) 466-7636. **$95-$110.** 262 Memorial Dr. Centre. Ext/int corridors. **Pets:** Accepted.
ⓐⓢⓚ ⊠ 🛏 ⑾ Ⓚ

▼▼ St. Jude Hotel ⊞
(709) 466-1717. **$90-$125.** 247 Trans-Canada Hwy. On Trans-Canada Hwy 1; centre. Int corridors. **Pets:** Accepted.
ⓐⓢⓚ ⊠ 🛏 💻 ⑾

CORNER BROOK

▼▼ Comfort Inn ⊞
(709) 639-1980. **$118-$138.** 41 Maple Valley Rd. Trans-Canada Hwy 1, exit 5 eastbound; exit 6 westbound, via Confederation Ave. Int corridors. **Pets:** Accepted.
ⓐⓢⓚ ⊠ 🛏 💻 ⑾

▼▼▼ Glynmill Inn ⊞
(709) 634-5181. **$118-$195.** 1B Cobb Ln. Centre. Int corridors. **Pets:** Accepted.
⊠ 🛏 💻 ⑾

▼▼▼ Greenwood Inn & Suites-Corner Brook ⊞
(709) 634-5381. **Call for rates.** 48 West St. At Chestnut St; centre. Int corridors. **Pets:** Accepted.
⊠ 🛏 💻 ⑾ 🏊

▼▼ Mamateek Inn ⊞
(709) 639-8901. **Call for rates.** 64 Maple Valley Rd. Trans-Canada Hwy 1, exit 5 eastbound; exit 6 westbound, via Confederation Ave. Int corridors. **Pets:** Accepted.
⊠ 💻 ⑾

COW HEAD

▼▼ Shallow Bay Motel & Cabins ⊞
(709) 243-2471. **$95-$125.** Rt 430, The Viking Tr. Hwy 430, 2.5 mi (4 km) w towards the ocean, follow signs. Ext/int corridors. **Pets:** Other species. Designated rooms, no service, supervision.
⊠ 🛏 💻 ⑾ 🏊 ⊠

GANDER

▼▼ Albatross Hotel ⊞
(709) 256-3956. **Call for rates.** Trans-Canada Hwy. On Trans-Canada Hwy 1. Ext/int corridors. **Pets:** Accepted.
⊠ 💻 ⑾

▼▼ Comfort Inn ⊞
(709) 256-3535. **Call for rates.** 112 Trans-Canada Hwy 1. Centre. Ext/int corridors. **Pets:** Accepted.
⊠ 🛏 💻 ⑾

▼▼ Sinbad's Hotel & Suites ⊞
(709) 651-2678. **$94-$248.** Bennett Dr. Centre; opposite Gander Mall. Ext corridors. **Pets:** Small, other species. Designated rooms, service with restrictions.
ⓐⓢⓚ ⊠ 🛏 💻 ⑾

GRAND FALLS-WINDSOR

▼▼ Mount Peyton Hotel ⊞
(709) 489-2251. **Call for rates.** 214 Lincoln Rd. 0.6 mi (1 km) ne on Trans-Canada Hwy 1. Ext/int corridors. **Pets:** Accepted.
⊠ 🛏 💻 ⑾

LABRADOR CITY

▼▼ Carol Inn ⊞
(709) 944-7736. **Call for rates.** 215 Drake Ave. Centre. Int corridors. **Pets:** Accepted.
⊠ 🛏 💻 ⑾

L'ANSE AU CLAIR

▼▼ Northern Light Inn ⊞
(709) 931-2332. **Call for rates.** Rt 510. Centre. Int corridors. **Pets:** Accepted.
⊠ 🛏 ⑾

ST. JOHN'S

▼▼▼ Capital Hotel ⊞
(709) 738-4480. **$123-$126.** 208 Kenmount Rd. Trans-Canada Hwy 1, exit 45, 4 mi (6.4 km) s on Team Gushue Hwy to Kenmount Rd. Int corridors. **Pets:** Small, other species. Service with restrictions, supervision.
⊠ 🛏 💻 ⑾

▼▼ Comfort Inn Airport ⊞
(709) 753-3500. **$129-$149.** 106 Airport Rd. Trans-Canada Hwy 1, exit 47A, 0.6 mi (1 km) n on Rt 40 (Portugal Cove Rd). Int corridors. **Pets:** Accepted.
ⓐⓢⓚ ⊠ 🛏 💻 ⑾

ⓒⒶⒶ ▼▼▼ Delta St. John's Hotel and Conference Centre ⊞
(709) 739-6404. **Call for rates.** 120 New Gower St. At Barter's Hill Rd; centre. Int corridors. **Pets:** Accepted.
ⓢⓐⓥⓔ ⊠ ♿ 💻 ⑾ 🏊 ⊠

▼▼ The Guv'nor Inn ⊞
(709) 726-0092. **Call for rates.** 389 Elizabeth Ave. 2 blks n of Freshwater Rd. Ext/int corridors. **Pets:** Accepted.
⊠ 🛏 💻 ⑾

▼▼▼ Holiday Inn St. John's-Govt Centre ⊞
(709) 722-0506. **$135-$165.** 180 Portugal Cove Rd. Trans-Canada Hwy 1, exit 47A, 0.9 mi (1.4 km) s. Ext/int corridors. **Pets:** Accepted.
ⓐⓢⓚ ⊠ ♿ 🛏 💻 ⑾ 🏊

Ⓐ ▼▼▼▼ Ramada St. John's Ⓗ
(709) 722-9330. **$109-$139, 3 day notice.** 102 Kenmount Rd. Trans-Canada Hwy 1, exit 45, 1 mi (1.6 km) s on Team Gushue Hwy to Kenmount Rd. Int corridors. **Pets:** Accepted.
SAVE ✕ 🖥 🖵 ｜｜

▼▼▼▼ Sheraton Hotel Newfoundland Ⓗ
(709) 726-4980. **$161-$495.** 115 Cavendish Square. At Duckworth and Ordnance sts; centre. Int corridors. **Pets:** Accepted.
✕ 🖵 ｜｜ ⤳ ✕

▼▼▼▼ Super 8 Ⓗ 🐾
(709) 739-8888. **$99-$149.** 175 Higgins Line. Trans-Canada Hwy 1, exit 47A, just s on Rt 40 (Portugal Cove Rd). Int corridors. **Pets:** Medium. Designated rooms, service with restrictions, supervision.
ASK ✕ 🖥M 🖥 🖵 ⤳

Ⓐ ▼▼ ▼▼ Travellers Inn St. John's Ⓗ
(709) 722-5540. **$89-$129.** 199 Kenmount Rd. Trans-Canada Hwy 1, exit 45, 1 mi (1.6 km) s on Team Gushue Hwy to Kenmount Rd. Ext/int corridors. **Pets:** Accepted.
SAVE ✕ 🖥 🖵 ｜｜ ⤳

STEPHENVILLE

▼▼ ▼▼ Holiday Inn Stephenville Ⓗ 🐾
(709) 643-6666. **$140-$158.** 44 Queen St. Centre. Int corridors. **Pets:** Other species. Service with restrictions, supervision.
ASK ✕ 🖥 🖵 ｜｜

NORTHWEST TERRITORIES

YELLOWKNIFE

(CAA) ▼▼▼▼ **Chateau Nova Hotel & Suites** [H]
(867) 873-9700. **$199.** 4401 50th Ave. Downtown. Int corridors.
Pets: Medium, other species. $20 daily fee/room. Service with restrictions, supervision.
[SAVE] [✕] [☐] [💻] [🍴] [✕]

▼▼▼▼ **Coast Fraser Tower** [H] 🐾
(867) 873-8700. **Call for rates.** 5303 52nd St. Corner of 52nd St and 53rd Ave. Int corridors. **Pets:** Large. $10 daily fee/room. Designated rooms, service with restrictions, supervision.
[✕] [☐] [💻] [Ж]

▼▼▼▼ **The Explorer Hotel** [H]
(867) 873-3531. **$185-$205.** 4825 49th Ave. Downtown. Int corridors.
Pets: Accepted.
[ASK] [✕] [☐] [💻] [🍴]

▼▼ **Yellowknife Super 8** [M]
(867) 669-8888. **$169-$199.** 308 Old Airport Rd. 1.2 mi (2 km) s on Franklin, 0.6 mi (1 km) w; in WalMart Plaza. Int corridors. **Pets:** $25 daily fee/room. Designated rooms, service with restrictions.
[ASK] [✕] [☐] [💻]

NOVA SCOTIA

AMHERST

▼▼ ▼▼ Auberge Wandlyn Inn H
(902) 667-3331. **Call for rates.** 1539 S Hampton St. Trans-Canada Hwy 104, exit 3, 0.6 mi (1 km) w. Ext/int corridors. **Pets:** Accepted.

✕ 🔒 💻 🍴 🏊

▼▼ ▼▼ Comfort Inn H
(902) 667-0404. **$117-$177.** 143 Albion St S. Trans-Canada Hwy 104, exit 4, 1 mi (1.6 km) n on Rt 2. Int corridors. **Pets:** Medium. Service with restrictions, supervision.

ASK ✕ 🔒 💻

▼▼▼ ▼ Super 8 H ❀
(902) 660-8888. **$89-$249.** 40 Lord Amherst Dr. Trans-Canada Hwy 104, exit 4. Int corridors. **Pets:** Medium. $10 daily fee/pet. Service with restrictions, supervision.

ASK ✕ 🔒M 🔒 💻 🏊

ANNAPOLIS ROYAL

▼▼ ▼▼ Annapolis Royal Inn M
(902) 532-2323. **$89-$150, 30 day notice.** 3924 Hwy 1. 0.6 mi (1 km) w. Ext corridors. **Pets:** Accepted.

ASK ✕ 💻

▼▼ ▼▼ Champlain Motel M
(902) 532-5473. **Call for rates.** RR 2. 2.5 mi (4.2 km) w on Rt 1. Ext corridors. **Pets:** Accepted.

✕ 🔒 💻 🏊

CAA ▼▼▼ ▼ Hillsdale House Inn BB ❀
(902) 532-2345. **$79-$149.** 519 St George St. Just e of Rt 1; centre. Int corridors. **Pets:** $25 one-time fee/pet. Service with restrictions.

SAVE ✕

▼▼▼ ▼ The King George Inn BB ❀
(902) 532-5286. **$80-$160.** 548 Upper St George St. Jct Rt 1 and 8, just e on Rt 8. Int corridors. **Pets:** Other species. Service with restrictions, crate.

ASK ✕ 💻

ANTIGONISH

CAA ▼▼ ▼▼ Maritime Inn Antigonish H ❀
(902) 863-4001. **$105-$175.** 158 Main St. Centre. Ext/int corridors. **Pets:** Other species. Designated rooms, supervision.

SAVE ✕ 💻 🍴

AULD'S COVE

CAA ▼▼ ▼▼ The Cove Motel & Restaurant/Gift
Shop M ❀
(902) 747-2700. **$99-$118.** 227 Cove Rd. 0.6 mi (1 km) n off Trans-Canada Hwy 104; 1.9 mi (3 km) w of Canso Cswy. Ext corridors. **Pets:** Medium. Designated rooms, service with restrictions, supervision.

SAVE ✕ 🔒 💻 🍴 ✕

BADDECK

▼▼ ▼▼ The Ceilidh Country Lodge M ❀
(902) 295-3500. **Call for rates.** 357 Shore Rd. Trans-Canada Hwy 105, exit 8, 1 mi (1.6 km) e on Rt 205 (Shore Rd). Ext/int corridors. **Pets:** Large, other species. $10 daily fee/room. Designated rooms, service with restrictions, supervision.

✕ 🔒 💻

CAA ▼▼ ▼▼ Hunter's Mountain Chalets CA
(902) 295-3392. **$78-$138, 4 day notice.** 562 Cabot Tr. Trans-Canada Hwy 105, exit 7, 1.6 mi (2.6 km) n. Ext corridors. **Pets:** Small, dogs only. $10 daily fee/pet. No service, supervision.

SAVE ✕ 🔒 🅰C 🕿

CAA ▼▼▼ ▼ Inverary Resort H ❀
(902) 295-3500. **$109-$189, 3 day notice.** 368 Shore Rd. Trans-Canada Hwy 105, exit 8, 1 mi (1.6 km) e on Rt 205 (Shore Rd). Ext/int corridors. **Pets:** Large, other species. $10 daily fee/room. Designated rooms, service with restrictions, supervision.

SAVE ✕ 🔒 💻 🍴 🏊 ✕

CAA ▼▼ ▼▼ McIntyre's Housekeeping Cottages CA
(902) 295-1133. **$72-$350, 4 day notice.** 8908 Hwy 105. Trans-Canada Hwy 105, 3 mi (5 km) w. Ext corridors. **Pets:** Other species. $8 daily fee/pet. Designated rooms, service with restrictions, supervision.

SAVE ✕ 🔒 💻

CAA ▼▼ ▼▼ Silver Dart Lodge & MacNeil House H
(902) 295-2340. **$99-$265.** 257 Hwy 205 (Shore Rd). Trans-Canada Hwy 105, exit 8, 0.6 mi (1 km) e on Rt 205 (Shore Rd). Ext/int corridors. **Pets:** Service with restrictions, supervision.

SAVE ✕ 🔒 💻 🍴 🏊 ✕

BAYFIELD

▼▼ ▼▼ Sea'Scape Cottages CA
(902) 386-2825. **$105-$130, 30 day notice.** Bayfield Antigonish Civil 6. Trans-Canada Hwy 104, exit 36, 3.2 mi (5.3 km) n on Sunrise Tr, then 1.1 mi (1.8 km) w. Ext corridors. **Pets:** Accepted.

ASK ✕ 🔒 💻 ✕ 🅰C 🕿

BLACK POINT

▼▼ Grand View Motel and Cottages M
(902) 857-9776. **Call for rates.** 8414 Hwy 3. Hwy 103, exit 5 westbound, 1.2 mi (2 km) s to Rt 3, then 9 mi (15 km) w; exit 6 eastbound to Rt 3, then 5.4 mi (9 km) e. Ext corridors. **Pets:** Accepted.

✕ 🔒 🅰C 🕿

BRIDGETOWN

▼▼ ▼▼ Bridgetown Motor Inn H
(902) 665-4403. **$72-$85.** 396 Granville St. Hwy 101, exit 20, 0.6 mi (1 km) w on Rt 1. Ext corridors. **Pets:** Accepted.

ASK ✕ 🔒 🏊

BRIDGEWATER

▼▼▼ Auberge Wandlyn Inn 🅗
(902) 543-7131. **Call for rates.** 50 North St. Hwy 103, exit 12, 1.1 mi (1.7 km) s on Rt 10. Int corridors. **Pets:** Accepted.
🗙 🛢 💻 ⑪ 🛋

▼▼ Bridgewater Bogan Villa Inn 🅗
(902) 543-8171. **Call for rates.** 35 High St. Hwy 103, exit 13, just e. Int corridors. **Pets:** Accepted.
🗙 💻 🛋

▼▼ Comfort Inn 🅗
(902) 543-1498. **Call for rates.** 49 North St. Hwy 103, exit 12, 1.1 mi (1.7 km) s on Rt 10. Int corridors. **Pets:** Accepted.
🗙 🔓 🛢 💻

CHESTER

▼▼ Windjammer Motel 🅜
(902) 275-3567. **$55-$85.** 4070 Rt 3. 0.6 mi (1 km) w. Ext corridors. **Pets:** Other species. Service with restrictions, supervision.
(ASK) 🗙 🛢

CHETICAMP

▼▼ Cabot Trail Sea & Golf Chalets 🅒🅐
(902) 224-1777. **$129-$169, 7 day notice.** 71 Fraser Doucet Ln. Centre. Ext corridors. **Pets:** Medium. $15 daily fee/pet. Service with restrictions, supervision.
(ASK) 🗙 🛢 💻 🗙 🐾 🅩

ⓒⒶ ▼▼▼ Laurie's Motor Inn 🅗
(902) 224-2400. **$85-$169, 3 day notice.** 15456 Laurie Rd. Centre. Ext/int corridors. **Pets:** Service with restrictions, crate.
(SAVE) 🗙 🛢 ⑪

ⓒⒶ ▼▼ Parkview Motel, Dining Room & Lounge 🅜
(902) 224-3232. **$69-$109, 7 day notice.** 16546 Cabot Tr. 4.5 mi (7.2 km) n at West Gate Cape Breton Highlands National Park. Ext corridors. **Pets:** Accepted.
(SAVE) 🗙 🛢 💻 ⑪ 🅩

CHURCH POINT

▼▼ Le Manoir Samson 🅜
(902) 769-2526. **$80-$110.** 1768 Rt 1. On Hwy 1; centre. Ext corridors. **Pets:** Medium. No service, crate.
🗙 🛢 🐾

DARTMOUTH

ⓒⒶ ▼▼▼ Comfort Inn 🅗 🐾
(902) 463-9900. **$130-$180.** 456 Windmill Rd. Hwy 111, exit Shannon Park. Int corridors. **Pets:** Service with restrictions, supervision.
(SAVE) 🗙 🛢 💻

▼▼ Country Inn & Suites By Carlson 🅗 🐾
(902) 465-4000. **$105-$200.** 101 Yorkshire Ave Ext. Hwy 111, exit Princess Margaret Blvd; at toll booths for A. Murray Mackay Bridge. Int corridors. **Pets:** Small. $150 deposit/room, $25 one-time fee/pet. Designated rooms, service with restrictions, supervision.
(ASK) 🗙 🛢 💻

ⓒⒶ ▼▼ Days Inn 🅗 🐾
(902) 465-6555. **Call for rates.** 20 Highfield Park Dr. From A. Murray Mackay Bridge, 0.8 mi (1.2 km) n on Hwy 111, exit 3 (Burnside Dr). Ext/int corridors. **Pets:** Other species. Designated rooms, service with restrictions.
(SAVE) 🗙 🔓 🛢 💻 ⑪

ⓒⒶ ▼▼▼ Holiday Inn Halifax-Harbourview 🅗
(902) 463-1100. **$115-$199.** 101 Wyse Rd. Adjacent to Angus L Mac-Donald Bridge. Int corridors. **Pets:** Accepted.
(SAVE) 🗙 🛢 💻 ⑪ 🛋

ⓒⒶ ▼▼▼ Park Place Hotel & Conference Centre Ramada Plaza 🅗 🐾
(902) 468-8888. **$109-$209.** 240 Brownlow Ave. From A. Murray Mackay Bridge, 0.7 mi (1.2 km) n on Hwy 111, exit 3 (Burnside Dr). Int corridors. **Pets:** Small. $50 deposit/pet, $25 one-time fee/pet. Designated rooms, service with restrictions, supervision.
(SAVE) 🗙 🛢 💻 ⑪ 🛋 🗙

▼▼ Quality Inn Halifax/Dartmouth 🅗 🐾
(902) 469-5850. **$80-$180.** 313 Prince Albert Rd. Hwy 111, exit 6A, 1 blk s. Int corridors. **Pets:** Medium. Designated rooms, service with restrictions, supervision.
(ASK) 🗙 🛢 💻 ⑪

ⓒⒶ ▼▼▼ Super 8 Hotel-Dartmouth 🅗 🐾
(902) 463-9520. **Call for rates.** 65 King St. Corner of King and Queen sts; centre of downtown. Int corridors. **Pets:** Large, other species. Service with restrictions, crate.
(SAVE) 🗙 🛢 💻

DIGBY

ⓒⒶ ▼▼▼ Admiral Digby Inn 🅗
(902) 245-2531. **$75-$129.** 441 Shore Rd. Hwy 101, exit 26, 1.5 mi (2.5 km) n, follow St John Ferry signs, 3 mi (5 km) w on Victoria Rd, just e of ferry terminal. Ext corridors. **Pets:** $100 deposit/room. Designated rooms, service with restrictions, supervision.
(SAVE) 🗙 🛢 💻 ⑪ 🛋

ⓒⒶ ▼▼▼ Seawinds Motel 🅜
(902) 245-2573. **$74-$134.** 90 Montague Row. Centre. Ext corridors. **Pets:** $10 one-time fee/pet. Supervision.
(SAVE) 🗙 🛢 💻

ⓒⒶ ▼▼▼ Thistle Down Country Inn 🅒🅘
(902) 245-4490. **$75-$135.** 98 Montague Row. Centre. Ext/int corridors. **Pets:** Designated rooms, supervision.
(SAVE) 🗙 🛢 💻 🛋

ECONOMY

▼▼▼▼ Four Seasons Retreat 🅒🅐
(902) 647-2628. **Call for rates.** 320 Cove Rd. 3 mi (5 km) e on Rt 2. Ext corridors. **Pets:** Accepted.
🗙 🛢 💻 🛋 🗙 🐾 🅩

HALIFAX

ⓒⒶ ▼▼▼▼ Best Western Chocolate Lake Hotel 🅗 🐾
(902) 477-5611. **$99-$289, 3 day notice.** 20 St. Margaret's Bay Rd. 0.4 mi (0.7 km) e of Armdale Rotary. Ext/int corridors. **Pets:** Other species. Service with restrictions, supervision.
(SAVE) 🗙 🛢 💻 ⑪ 🛋 🗙

ⓒⒶ ▼▼▼▼ Cambridge Suites Hotel 🅗
(902) 420-0555. **$129-$149.** 1583 Brunswick St. Corner of Brunswick and Sackville sts. Int corridors. **Pets:** Service with restrictions, supervision.
(SAVE) 🗙 🔓 🛢 💻 ⑪ 🗙

▼▼ Chebucto Inn 🅗
(902) 453-4330. **$85-$145.** 6151 Lady Hammond Rd. Jct Hwy 111 and Rt 2 (Bedford Hwy), 0.4 mi (0.7 km) e. Ext corridors. **Pets:** Accepted.
(ASK) 🗙 ⑪

ⓒⒶ ▼▼▼▼ Citadel Halifax Hotel 🅗 🐾
(902) 422-1391. **$124-$311.** 1960 Brunswick St. Between Cogswell and Duke sts. Int corridors. **Pets:** Large, other species. Designated rooms, service with restrictions, supervision.
(SAVE) 🗙 🛢 💻 ⑪ 🛋 🗙

ⓒⒶ ▼▼▼ Comfort Inn Halifax 🅗 🐾
(902) 443-0303. **$79-$199.** 560 Bedford Hwy. On Rt 2 (Bedford Hwy), 6 mi (9.6 km) w. Int corridors. **Pets:** $10 one-time fee/pet. Service with restrictions, supervision.
(SAVE) 🗙 🔓 🛢 💻 ⑪ 🛋

Ⓐ ◆◆◆◆ **Delta Barrington** 🏨 🐾
(902) 429-7410. **$209-$259, 14 day notice.** 1875 Barrington St. Between Cogswell and Duke sts. Int corridors. **Pets:** Medium, other species. $35 one-time fee/room. Service with restrictions, crate.
SAVE ✕ 🖭 🍴 ➳ ✕

Ⓐ ◆◆◆◆ **Delta Halifax** 🏨 🐾
(902) 425-6700. **$115-$209.** 1990 Barrington St. Corner of Cogswell and Barrington sts. Int corridors. **Pets:** Medium, other species. $35 one-time fee/room. Service with restrictions, crate.
SAVE ✕ 🖭 🍴 ➳ ✕

Ⓐ ◆◆ **Esquire Motel** Ⓜ 🐾
(902) 835-3367. **$79-$155.** 771 Bedford Hwy. Hwy 102, exit 4A, 3.3 mi (5.3 km) e on Rt 2 (Bedford Hwy). Ext corridors. **Pets:** Medium. $10 one-time fee/pet. Service with restrictions, supervision.
SAVE ✕ 🛡 ➳ ✕

◆◆ **Future Inns Halifax** 🏨
(902) 443-4333. **$119-$179.** 30 Fairfax Dr. Hwy 102, exit 2A. Int corridors. **Pets:** Accepted.
✕ ♿ 🛡 🖭 🍴

Ⓐ ◆◆◆◆ **Halifax Marriott Harbourfront** 🏨
(902) 421-1700. **$189-$239.** 1919 Upper Water St. Adjacent to historic properties and Casino Nova Scotia. Int corridors. **Pets:** Accepted.
SAVE ✕ 🛡 🖭 🍴 ➳ ✕

Ⓐ ◆◆◆◆ **Holiday Inn Express Halifax/Bedford** 🏨 🐾
(902) 445-1100. **$109-$179, 14 day notice.** 133 Kearney Lake Rd. Hwy 102, exit 2. Int corridors. **Pets:** Medium. $25 one-time fee/room. Designated rooms, service with restrictions, supervision.
SAVE ✕ ♿ 🛡 🖭 ➳

Ⓐ ◆◆◆◆ **Holiday Inn Halifax Centre** 🏨
(902) 423-1161. **$135-$199.** 1980 Robie St. Jct Quinpool St. Int corridors. **Pets:** Accepted.
SAVE ✕ 🛡 🖭 🍴 ➳ ✕

◆◆ **Lakeview Inns & Suites** 🏨 🐾
(902) 450-3020. **$139-$299.** 98 Chain Lake Dr. Hwy 102, exit 2A eastbound; Hwy 103, exit 2. Int corridors. **Pets:** $100 deposit/room. Service with restrictions, crate.
ASK ✕ ♿ 🛡 🖭 ➳

Ⓐ ◆◆◆◆ **The Lord Nelson Hotel & Suites** 🏨 🐾
(902) 423-6331. **$135-$245.** 1515 S Park St. Corner of Park St and Spring Garden Rd; centre. Int corridors. **Pets:** Service with restrictions.
SAVE ✕ ♿ 🛡 🖭 🍴

Ⓐ ◆◆◆◆ **The Prince George Hotel** 🏨 🐾
(902) 425-1986. **$155-$279.** 1725 Market St. Between Prince and Carmichael sts. Int corridors. **Pets:** $20 one-time fee/room. Service with restrictions, supervision.
SAVE ✕ ♿ 🖭 🍴 ➳ ✕

◆◆◆ **Quality Inn & Suites Halifax** 🏨 🐾
(902) 444-6700. **$119-$169.** 980 Parkland Dr. Hwy 102, exit 2. Int corridors. **Pets:** Service with restrictions, crate.
ASK ✕ ♿ 🛡 🖭 ➳ ✕

◆◆◆ **Quality Inn Halifax Airport** 🏨
(902) 873-3000. **$119-$179.** 60 Sky Blvd. Hwy 102, exit 6. Int corridors. **Pets:** Service with restrictions, crate.
ASK ✕ 🛡 🖭 🍴 ➳ ✕

◆◆◆ **Residence Inn by Marriott** 🏨
(902) 422-0493. **$169-$209.** 1599 Grafton St. Corner of Sackville St. Int corridors. **Pets:** $100 one-time fee/room. Service with restrictions.
✕ ♿ 🛡 🖭

◆◆ **Travelers Motel** Ⓜ
(902) 835-3394. **Call for rates.** 773 Bedford Hwy. Hwy 102, exit 4A, 3.3 mi (5.3 km) e on Rt 2 (Bedford Hwy). Ext corridors. **Pets:** Accepted.
✕ 🛡 ⚿

Ⓐ ◆◆◆◆ **The Westin Nova Scotian** 🏨
(902) 421-1000. **$119-$325.** 1181 Hollis St. Between Barrington and Lower Water sts. Int corridors. **Pets:** Accepted.
SAVE ✕ 🖭 🍴 ➳ ✕

INGONISH BEACH

Ⓐ ◆◆◆◆ **Keltic Lodge Resort & Spa** 🏨 🐾
(902) 285-2880. **$177-$276, 3 day notice.** Middle Head Peninsula. In Cape Breton Highlands National Park; off Cabot Tr. Ext/int corridors. **Pets:** Other species. Designated rooms, service with restrictions, supervision.
SAVE ✕ 🛡 🖭 🍴 ➳ ✕

KEMPTVILLE

Ⓐ ◆◆◆◆ **Trout Point Lodge** Ⓒ
(902) 482-8360. **$185-$325, 21 day notice.** 189 Trout Point Rd. 6.6 mi (11 km) e on Rt 203, 2.1 mi (3.5 km) n on gravel entry road. Ext corridors. **Pets:** Accepted.
SAVE ✕ 🍴 ✕ ⚿ 🎇

KENTVILLE

◆◆ **Sun Valley Motel** Ⓜ
(902) 678-7368. **$68-$90.** 843 Park St. Hwy 101, exit 14, 0.5 mi (0.8 km) e on Rt 1. Ext corridors. **Pets:** Accepted.
✕ 🛡 🖭 ⚿ ⌨

KINGSTON

Ⓐ ◆◆ **Best Western Aurora Inn** 🏨 🐾
(902) 765-3306. **$116-$125.** 831 Main St. Hwy 101, exit 17 to Rt 1, follow signs. Ext corridors. **Pets:** $10 one-time fee/pet. Supervision.
SAVE ✕ 🛡 🖭 🍴

LISCOMB

Ⓐ ◆◆◆◆ **Liscombe Lodge Resort & Conference Centre** 🏨
(902) 779-2307. **$155-$175, 3 day notice.** 2884 Hwy 7 (RR 1). On Hwy 7. Ext/int corridors. **Pets:** Accepted.
SAVE ✕ 🛡 🖭 🍴 ➳ ✕

LOWER ARGYLE

Ⓐ ◆◆◆◆ **Ye Olde Argyler Lodge** Ⓒ
(902) 643-2500. **$100-$215, 14 day notice.** Rt 3. Hwy 103, exit 32, 4.5 mi (7.5 km) e. Int corridors. **Pets:** Accepted.
SAVE ✕ 🍴

LUNENBURG

◆◆◆ **Boscawen Inn** Ⓒ
(902) 634-3325. **Call for rates.** 150 Cumberland St. Centre. Int corridors. **Pets:** Accepted.
✕ 🖭

◆◆ **The Homeport Motel** Ⓜ
(902) 634-8234. **$75-$150.** 167 Victoria Rd. 0.6 mi (1 km) w on Rt 3. Ext corridors. **Pets:** Accepted.
✕ 🛡 🖭

◆◆◆ **Lunenburg Arms Hotel & Spa** 🏨
(902) 640-4040. **Call for rates.** 94 Pelham St. Corner of Pelham and Duke sts; centre. Int corridors. **Pets:** Accepted.
✕ ♿ 🛡 🖭 🍴

MAHONE BAY

◆◆◆ Bayview Pines Country Inn BB ✿
(902) 624-9970. **$90-$150, 5 day notice.** 678 Oakland Rd. Hwy 103, exit 10, 1.2 mi (2 km) w on Rt 3 to Kedy's Landing, 3.6 mi (6 km) e of Mahone Bay. Ext/int corridors. **Pets:** Medium, dogs only. Designated rooms, service with restrictions, supervision.
⊠ 🛅 💻 🔏 ☎

MAVILLETTE

◆ Cape View Motel & Cottages M
(902) 645-2258. **$80.** 124 John Doucette Rd. Rt 1, 19.2 mi (32 km) ne of Yarmouth; centre. Ext corridors. **Pets:** Service with restrictions, supervision.
A$K ⊠ 🛅 💻 🔏 ☎

MIDDLETON

◆◆ Mid-Valley Motel H
(902) 825-3433. **Call for rates.** 121 Main St. Hwy 101, exit 18, 0.6 mi (1 km) w on Rt 1. Ext corridors. **Pets:** Accepted.
⊠ 🛅 🍽 ≈

MUSQUODOBOIT HARBOUR

(AA) ◆◆◆ The Elephant's Nest Bed &
                Breakfast BB ✿
(902) 827-3891. **$95-$145, 3 day notice.** 127 Pleasant Dr. Jct Hwy 107 and 7, 1.8 mi (3 km) w, follow signs. Ext/int corridors. **Pets:** Dogs only. Designated rooms, supervision.
SAVE ⊠ ☒ 🔏

NEW GLASGOW

◆◆ Comfort Inn H
(902) 755-6450. **$109-$179.** 740 Westville Rd. On Hwy 289, just e of jct Trans-Canada Hwy 104, exit 23. Int corridors. **Pets:** Service with restrictions, supervision.
A$K ⊠ 🛅 💻

◆◆ Country Inn & Suites By Carlson H ✿
(902) 928-1333. **$134-$137.** 700 Westville Rd. On Hwy 289, just e of jct Trans-Canada Hwy 104, exit 23. Int corridors. **Pets:** Large. $25 one-time fee/room. Designated rooms, service with restrictions, crate.
A$K ⊠ 🛅 💻

NEW HARBOUR

◆◆◆ Lonely Rock Seaside Bungalows CA
(902) 387-2668. **$90-$230, 14 day notice.** 150 New Harbour Rd. Rt 316, 0.4 mi (0.7 km) s. Ext corridors. **Pets:** Dogs only. $5 daily fee/pet. Designated rooms, no service, supervision.
⊠ 🛅 ☒ 🔏

NORTH SYDNEY

(AA) ◆◆◆ Clansman Motel H
(902) 794-7226. **$89-$125.** 9 Baird St. Hwy 125, exit 2, just e on King St. Ext/int corridors. **Pets:** Accepted.
SAVE ⊠ 🛅 💻 🍽 ≈

PARRSBORO

(AA) ◆◆◆ Gillespie House Inn BB ✿
(902) 254-3196. **$90-$129.** 358 Main St. On Rt 2; centre. Int corridors. **Pets:** Dogs only. $25 daily fee/room. Designated rooms, service with restrictions, supervision.
SAVE ⊠ 🖴 🔏 🔏 ☎

◆ The Sunshine Inn M
(902) 254-3135. **$82-$150.** Rt 2. 2 mi (3.2 km) n. Ext corridors. **Pets:** Accepted.
A$K ⊠ 🛅 ☒ ☎

PICTOU

(AA) ◆◆◆ Pictou Lodge Resort H ✿
(902) 485-4322. **$140-$435, 3 day notice.** 172 Lodge Rd. 4.3 mi (7 km) nw on Braeshore Rd; midway between Pictou and PEI ferry terminal at Caribou. Ext corridors. **Pets:** Large. $30 daily fee/pet. Service with restrictions, supervision.
SAVE ⊠ 🛅 💻 🍽 ≈ ☒

◆◆ Willow House Inn BB ✿
(902) 485-5740. **$60-$120.** 11 Willow St. Corner of Willow and Church sts; centre. Int corridors. **Pets:** Dogs only. Supervision.
⊠

PORT DUFFERIN

◆◆ Marquis of Dufferin Seaside Inn M ✿
(902) 654-2696. **$94.** 25658 Hwy 7, RR 1. On Hwy 7. Ext corridors. **Pets:** Other species. Designated rooms, service with restrictions.
⊠ 🍽 ☒ 🔏 ☎

PORT HASTINGS

◆ Cape Breton Causeway Inn H
(902) 625-0460. **$75-$115.** 21 Old Victoria Rd. E of Canso Cswy on Trans-Canada Hwy 105 rotary; entrance through north side of church. Ext/int corridors. **Pets:** Accepted.
⊠ 🛅 💻 🍽

◆◆ Econo Lodge MacPuffin M
(902) 625-0621. **$89-$139.** 373 Hwy 4. 1 mi (1.6 km) n on Hwy 4; 1 mi (1.6 km) s of Canso Cswy. Ext corridors. **Pets:** Other species. Designated rooms, service with restrictions, crate.
A$K ⊠ 💻 ≈

PORT HAWKESBURY

(AA) ◆◆ Maritime Inn Port Hawkesbury H
(902) 625-0320. **$117-$199.** 717 Reeves St. 4.2 mi (6.4 km) e of Canso Cswy on Hwy 4. Ext/int corridors. **Pets:** Accepted.
SAVE ⊠ 🛅 💻 🍽 ≈

SCOTSBURN

◆◆◆ Stonehame Lodge & Chalets CA
(902) 485-3468. **$85-$225, 14 day notice.** RR 3. Rt 256, 7.5 mi (12 km) w of Pictou via Rt 376, last 1.2 mi (2 km) on gravel entry road. Ext corridors. **Pets:** Accepted.
A$K ⊠ 🛅 💻 ≈ ☒

SMITHS COVE

(AA) ◆◆◆ Harbourview Inn BB ✿
(902) 245-5686. **$94-$149, 7 day notice.** 25 Harbourview Rd. Hwy 101, exit 25 eastbound; exit 24 westbound. Ext/int corridors. **Pets:** Medium, dogs only. Supervision.
SAVE ⊠ 🛅 💻 ≈ ☒

◆◆ Hedley House Inn By The Sea M
(902) 245-2500. **$75-$169.** RR 1. Hwy 101, exit 25 eastbound; exit 24 westbound. Ext corridors. **Pets:** Accepted.
A$K ⊠ 🛅 💻 🔏 ☎

◆◆ Mountain Gap Inn H
(902) 245-5841. **Call for rates.** 217 Hwy 1, Smiths Cove. Hwy 101, exit 25 eastbound; exit 24 westbound. Ext corridors. **Pets:** Accepted.
⊠ 🛅 💻 🍽 ≈ ☒

STELLARTON

(AA) ◆◆◆ Holiday Inn Express Stellarton-New
                Glasgow H
(902) 755-1020. **$126-$154, 15 day notice.** 86 Lawrence Blvd. Hwy 104, exit 24, just s, then 0.6 mi (1 km) w. Int corridors. **Pets:** Medium. $25 one-time fee/room. Designated rooms, no service, supervision.
SAVE ⊠ 🔏M 🛅 💻 ≈ ☒

SYDNEY

Cambridge Suites Hotel H
(902) 562-6500. **$119-$145.** 380 Esplanade. Hwy 4, 3.1 mi (5 km) e of jct Hwy 125, exit 6E; downtown. Int corridors. **Pets:** Accepted.

Comfort Inn H
(902) 562-0200. **$109-$189.** 368 Kings Rd. Hwy 4, 2.1 mi (3.5 km) e of jct Hwy 125, exit 6E. Int corridors. **Pets:** Other species. Service with restrictions, supervision.

Days Inn Sydney H
(902) 539-6750. **$89-$119.** 480 Kings Rd. Hwy 4, 1.7 mi (2.8 km) e of jct Hwy 125, exit 6E. Int corridors. **Pets:** Large. Designated rooms, service with restrictions, supervision.

Delta Sydney H
(902) 562-7500. **Call for rates.** 300 Esplanade. At Prince St; centre. Int corridors. **Pets:** Accepted.

Quality Inn Sydney H
(902) 539-8101. **$117-$135.** 560 Kings Rd. Hwy 4, 2 mi (3.3 km) e of jct Hwy 125. Int corridors. **Pets:** Accepted.

SYDNEY MINES

Gowrie House Country Inn CI
(902) 544-1050. **Call for rates.** 840 Shore Rd. Hwy 105, exit 21E, 1.9 mi (3 km) n on Rt 305. Ext/int corridors. **Pets:** Accepted.

TRURO

Comfort Inn H
(902) 893-0330. **$109-$199.** 12 Meadow Dr. Hwy 102, exit 14. Int corridors. **Pets:** Accepted.

Holiday Inn Truro Hotel & Convention Centre H
(902) 895-1651. **Call for rates.** 437 Prince St. Centre. Int corridors. **Pets:** Accepted.

The Palliser Motel M
(902) 893-8951. **$85-$95.** 103/104 Tidal Bore Rd. Hwy 102, exit 14. Ext corridors. **Pets:** Medium. Service with restrictions, supervision.

Super 8 H
(902) 895-8884. **Call for rates.** 85 Treaty Tr. Hwy 102, exit 13A. Int corridors. **Pets:** Accepted.

WESTERN SHORE

Oak Island Resort H
(902) 627-2600. **$114-$169.** 36 Treasure Dr. Hwy 103, exit 9 or 10, follow signs on Rt 3; 6 mi (10 km) e of Mahone Bay. Int corridors. **Pets:** Accepted.

WHITE POINT

White Point Beach Resort H
(902) 354-2711. **$100-$190, 3 day notice.** 75 White Point Rd 2. Hwy 103, exit 20A westbound, 5 mi (8 km) w on Rt 3; exit 20 eastbound, 6 mi (10 km) e on Rt 3. Ext/int corridors. **Pets:** Other species. Designated rooms.

WHYCOCOMAGH

Keltic Quay Bayfront Lodge & Cottages CA
(902) 756-1122. **$149-$299, 3 day notice.** 90 Main St. Just se off Trans-Canada Hwy 105; centre. Ext corridors. **Pets:** No service, supervision.

WINDSOR

Super 8 H
(902) 792-8888. **$99-$117.** 63 Cole Dr. Hwy 101, exit 5A, just s. Int corridors. **Pets:** Accepted.

YARMOUTH

Best Western Mermaid M
(902) 742-7821. **$79-$170.** 545 Main St. Corner of Main St and Starrs Rd. Ext corridors. **Pets:** Accepted.

Comfort Inn H
(902) 742-1119. **$95-$149.** 96 Starrs Rd. Jct Hwy 101 E and 3. Int corridors. **Pets:** Accepted.

Lakelawn Motel M
(902) 742-3588. **$74-$84.** 641 Main St. 0.6 mi (1 km) n on Hwy 1. Ext/int corridors. **Pets:** Medium, dogs only. Service with restrictions, supervision.

Rodd Colony Harbour Inn H
(902) 742-9194. **$96-$143.** 6 Forest St. At ferry terminal. Int corridors. **Pets:** $10 deposit/pet.

Rodd Grand Yarmouth-A Rodd Signature Hotel H
(902) 742-2446. **$131-$183.** 417 Main St. Near centre of downtown. Int corridors. **Pets:** $10 daily fee/pet.

Voyageur Motel M
(902) 742-7157. **$79-$99, 3 day notice.** RR #1. 3 mi (4.8 km) ne on Hwy 1. Ext corridors. **Pets:** Accepted.

CITY INDEX

AJAX

◆◆◆ Super 8-Ajax H
(905) 428-6884. **Call for rates.** 210 Westney Rd S. Jct Bayly St from Hwy 401, exit Westney Rd, 0.6 mi (1 km) s. Int corridors. **Pets:** Accepted.

ALGONQUIN PROVINCIAL PARK

◆◆◆ Killarney Lodge CA
(705) 633-5551. **$318-$638, 3 day notice.** Hwy 60-Lake of Two Rivers-Algonquin. On Hwy 60; 21 mi (33 km) into park from west gate; 14 mi (23 km) from east gate. Ext corridors. **Pets:** Medium, dogs only. $25 daily fee/pet. Designated rooms, service with restrictions, supervision.

ARNPRIOR

CAA ◆◆◆ Country Squire Motel M
(613) 623-6556. **$59-$120.** 111 Staye Court Dr. Hwy 17, exit White Lake Rd N. Ext corridors. **Pets:** Medium, dogs only. $15 daily fee/pet. Service with restrictions, supervision.

CAA ◆◆◆ Quality Inn H
(613) 623-7991. **$129-$149.** 70 Madawaska Blvd. Hwy 17, exit CR 29 N, 0.5 mi (0.8 km) to Madawaska Blvd, then 1.5 mi (2.4 km) w. Int corridors. **Pets:** $10 daily fee/pet. Service with restrictions, crate.

BANCROFT

CAA ◆◆◆ Best Western Sword Motor Inn M
(613) 332-2474. **$119-$128.** 146 Hastings St. On Hwy 62 N; centre. Ext/int corridors. **Pets:** Small, dogs only. $10 one-time fee/pet. Designated rooms, service with restrictions, supervision.

BARRIE

CAA ◆◆◆ Comfort Inn H
(705) 722-3600. **$106-$147, 30 day notice.** 75 Hart Dr. Hwy 400, exit 96A E (Dunlop St). Int corridors. **Pets:** Accepted.

CAA ◆◆◆ Comfort Inn & Suites H
(705) 721-1122. **$89-$129.** 210 Essa Rd. Hwy 400, exit 94 (Essa Rd), just e. Int corridors. **Pets:** Other species. Designated rooms, service with restrictions, supervision.

◆◆◆ Days Inn Barrie H
(705) 733-8989. **$110-$160.** 60 Bryne Dr. Hwy 400, exit 94 (Essa Rd), just s, then just e. Int corridors. **Pets:** Other species. $10 daily fee/pet. Designated rooms, service with restrictions, supervision.

CAA ◆◆◆ Holiday Inn Barrie-Hotel & Conference Centre H
(705) 728-6191. **$119-$189.** 20 Fairview Rd. Hwy 400, exit 94 (Essa Rd), just e. Int corridors. **Pets:** Accepted.

CAA ◆◆◆ Holiday Inn Express Hotel & Suites Barrie H
(705) 725-1002. **$117-$185.** 506 Bryne Dr. Hwy 400, exit 90 (Mapleview Dr), just sw. Int corridors. **Pets:** Medium. $15 one-time fee/room. Service with restrictions, supervision.

◆◆◆ Super 8 H
(705) 814-8888. **$126-$181.** 441 Bryne Dr. Hwy 400, exit 90 (Mapleview Dr), just nw. Int corridors. **Pets:** Large. $15 daily fee/pet. Designated rooms, service with restrictions, supervision.

CAA ◆◆◆ Travelodge Barrie H
(705) 734-9500. **$90-$120, 14 day notice.** 55 Hart Dr. Hwy 400, exit 96A E (Dunlop St). Int corridors. **Pets:** Medium. $50 deposit/room. Designated rooms, no service, crate.

BARRY'S BAY

◆◆◆ Mountain View Motel M
(613) 756-2757. **$75-$175, 7 day notice.** 18508 Hwy 60 E. On Hwy 60, 2.5 mi (4 km) e. Ext corridors. **Pets:** Accepted.

BAYFIELD

CAA ◆◆◆◆ The Little Inn of Bayfield CI
(519) 565-2611. **$192-$275, 4 day notice.** 26 Main St. Hwy 21, exit Main St, jct Catherine St. Int corridors. **Pets:** Medium, dogs only. $50 one-time fee/room. Designated rooms, service with restrictions, supervision.

CAA ◆◆◆ The Martha Ritz House CI
(519) 565-2325. **$125, 4 day notice.** 27 Main St. Hwy 21, exit Main St, jct Catherine St. Int corridors. **Pets:** Accepted.

BELLEVILLE

Best Western Belleville H
(613) 969-1112. **$99-$145.** 387 N Front St. Hwy 401, exit 543A, 0.3 mi (0.5 km) s on Hwy 62 (N Front St). Int corridors. **Pets:** Accepted.

Comfort Inn H
(613) 966-7703. **Call for rates.** 200 N Park St. Hwy 401, exit 543A, 0.6 mi (1 km) s on Hwy 62 (N Front St). Int corridors. **Pets:** Medium, other species. Service with restrictions, supervision.

Ramada Inn on the Bay H
(613) 968-3411. **$120-$169.** 11 Bay Bridge Rd. Hwy 2, 0.3 mi (0.5 km) s. Int corridors. **Pets:** $10 daily fee/room. Service with restrictions, supervision.

BLIND RIVER

Lakeview Inn M
(705) 356-0800. **$95-$110, 3 day notice.** 143 Causley St. On Hwy 17, just e of Hwy 557. Ext corridors. **Pets:** Accepted.

BRACEBRIDGE

Travelodge Bracebridge M
(705) 645-2235. **$80-$159.** 320 Taylor Rd. Hwy 11, exit 189 (Hwy 42/Taylor Rd), 0.6 mi (1 km) w. Ext corridors. **Pets:** Accepted.

BRAMPTON

Motel 6 Brampton #1902 H
(905) 451-3313. **$65-$71.** 160 Steelwell Rd. Hwy 410, exit Steeles Ave E, s on Tomken, then just w. Int corridors. **Pets:** Other species. Service with restrictions, supervision.

BRANTFORD

Comfort Inn H
(519) 753-3100. **Call for rates.** 58 King George Rd. Just s of jct Hwy 403 and 24. Int corridors. **Pets:** Accepted.

Days Inn H
(519) 759-2700. **$86-$140.** 460 Fairview Dr. Hwy 403, exit Wayne Gretzky Pkwy, 0.5 mi (0.8 km) n. Int corridors. **Pets:** Dogs only. $15 one-time fee/room. Designated rooms, service with restrictions, crate.

Quality Inn & Suites H
(519) 758-9999. **$94-$114.** 664 Colborne St. Hwy 403, exit Wayne Gretzky Pkwy, 1.3 mi (2 km) s to Colborne St, then just w. Int corridors. **Pets:** Small. $10 daily fee/pet. Designated rooms, service with restrictions, supervision.

BROCKVILLE

Comfort Inn H
(613) 345-0042. **$144-$234.** 7777 Kent Blvd. Hwy 401, exit 696, just nw. Int corridors. **Pets:** $15 daily fee/pet. Designated rooms, service with restrictions, crate.

Travelodge H
(613) 345-3900. **Call for rates.** 7789 Kent Blvd. Hwy 401, exit 696, just nw. Int corridors. **Pets:** Accepted.

BURLINGTON

Comfort Inn H
(905) 639-1700. **$105-$155.** 3290 S Service Rd. QEW, exit Walker's Line Rd westbound, just s to Harvester Rd, then just w; exit Guelph Line Rd eastbound, just s to Harvester Rd, then just e. Int corridors. **Pets:** Other species. Designated rooms, service with restrictions, supervision.

Homewood Suites by Hilton H
(905) 631-8300. **$119-$189.** 975 Syscon Rd. QEW, exit Burloak Dr S, w on Harvester Rd. Int corridors. **Pets:** Accepted.

Motel 6 Burlington #1900 H
(905) 331-1955. **$65-$75.** 4345 N Service Rd. QEW, exit Walker's Line Rd N to N Service Rd, then 0.9 mi (1.4 km) e. Int corridors. **Pets:** Other species. Service with restrictions, supervision.

Travelodge Hotel Burlington on the Lake H
(905) 681-0762. **Call for rates.** 2020 Lakeshore Rd. Corner of Brant St; downtown. Int corridors. **Pets:** $10 daily fee/pet. Service with restrictions, crate.

CAMBRIDGE

Cambridge Hotel and Conference Centre H
(519) 622-1505. **$124-$369.** 700 Hespeler Rd. Hwy 401, exit 282, just s. Int corridors. **Pets:** Other species. $150 one-time fee/room. Service with restrictions.

Comfort Inn H
(519) 658-1100. **$122-$164.** 220 Holiday Inn Dr. Hwy 401, exit 282, just n to Groh Ave. Int corridors. **Pets:** Other species. Service with restrictions.

Homewood Suites by Hilton Cambridge/Waterloo H
(519) 651-2888. **$124-$154.** 800 Jamieson Pkwy. Hwy 401, exit 286 (Townline Rd), just n. Int corridors. **Pets:** Accepted.

Langdon Hall Country House Hotel & Spa CI
(519) 740-2100. **$229-$629, 3 day notice.** 1 Langdon Dr. Hwy 401, exit 275, 0.8 mi (1.3 km) se on Fountain St, then 0.6 mi (1 km) s on Blair Rd, follow signs. Ext/int corridors. **Pets:** Accepted.

CHAPLEAU

Riverside Motel M
(705) 864-0440. **Call for rates.** 116 Cherry St. Corner of Grey and Cherry sts. Ext corridors. **Pets:** Accepted.

CHATHAM

Comfort Inn H
(519) 352-5500. **$104-$134.** 1100 Richmond St. Hwy 401, exit 81 (Bloomfield Rd), 3.1 mi (5 km) n. Int corridors. **Pets:** Other species. Service with restrictions, supervision.

Super 8 Motel-Chatham M
(519) 354-3366. **$70-$110.** 25 Michener Rd. 3.1 mi (5 km) e on Hwy 2. Int corridors. **Pets:** Accepted.

CHATSWORTH

▼▼ Key Motel M
(519) 794-2350. **$60-$85.** 317051 Hwy 6/10. On Hwy 6 and 10. Ext/int corridors. **Pets:** Accepted.

⊠ 🖪 🐾 ⊠

COBOURG

ⓒ ▼▼▼ Best Western Cobourg Inn and Convention Centre H ✿
(905) 372-2105. **$149-$294.** 930 Burnham St. Hwy 401, exit 472 (Burnham St S). Int corridors. **Pets:** Service with restrictions, supervision.

SAVE ⊠ 🖪 💷 ⊺¶ 🐾

▼▼ Comfort Inn H
(905) 372-7007. **Call for rates.** 121 Densmore Rd. Hwy 401, exit 474, just se. Int corridors. **Pets:** Accepted.

⊠ 🖪 💷

CORNWALL

ⓒ ▼▼▼ Best Western Parkway Inn & Conference Centre H
(613) 932-0451. **$130-$230.** 1515 Vincent Massey Dr. Hwy 401, exit 789 (Brookdale Ave), 1.8 mi (2.8 km) s, then just w. Int corridors. **Pets:** Medium. $10 daily fee/room. Designated rooms, service with restrictions, supervision.

SAVE ⊠ 🖪 💷 ⊺¶ 🐾

▼▼ Comfort Inn-Cornwall H
(613) 937-0111. **$79-$129.** 1625 Vincent Massey Dr. Hwy 401, exit 789 (Brookdale Ave), 1.8 mi (2.8 km) s, then 0.4 mi (0.7 km) w. **Pets:** Accepted.

ASK ⊠ 🖪 💷 🐾

ⓒ ▼ Econo Lodge H
(613) 936-1996. **$59-$110.** 1142 Brookdale Ave. Hwy 401, exit 789 (Brookdale Ave), 1.9 mi (3 km) s. Ext/int corridors. **Pets:** Very small, other species. $20 deposit/pet, $20 daily fee/pet, $20 one-time fee/pet. Designated rooms, service with restrictions, supervision.

SAVE ⊠ 🖪

DRYDEN

ⓒ ▼▼▼ Best Western Motor Inn H
(807) 223-3201. **$115-$150.** 349 Government St. On Hwy 17. Ext/int corridors. **Pets:** Medium. Service with restrictions, crate.

SAVE ⊠ 🖪 💷 ⊺¶ 🐾 ⊠

▼▼ Comfort Inn M
(807) 223-3893. **$117-$136.** 522 Government St. On Hwy 17. Int corridors. **Pets:** Accepted.

ASK ⊠ 🖪 💷

FONTHILL

▼ Hipwell's Motel M
(905) 892-3588. **$45-$75.** 299 Reg Rd 20 W. 1 mi (1.6 km) w; centre. Ext corridors. **Pets:** $5 daily fee/pet. Service with restrictions, supervision.

ASK ⊠ 🖪 🐾

FORT FRANCES

▼▼ Super 8 H ✿
(807) 274-4945. **Call for rates.** 810 Kings Hwy. On Hwy 11. Int corridors. **Pets:** Medium. $10 one-time fee/pet. Designated rooms, service with restrictions, supervision.

⊠ 🖪 💷 🐾 ⊠

FRENCH RIVER

ⓒ ▼ French River Trading Post Motel M
(705) 857-2115. **$72-$85.** 20112 Hwy 69. Trans-Canada Hwy 69, 0.6 mi (1 km) n of French River Bridge. Ext corridors. **Pets:** Accepted.

SAVE ⊠ 🖪 💷 ⊺¶ 🐾 ⊠

GANANOQUE

ⓒ ▼▼▼ Best Western Country Squire Resort H
(613) 382-3511. **$90-$195.** 715 King St E. Hwy 401, exit 647 eastbound; exit 648 westbound, 0.6 mi (1 km) w on Hwy 2 (King St). Ext/int corridors. **Pets:** Medium. $20 daily fee/pet. Designated rooms, service with restrictions, supervision.

SAVE ⊠ 🖪 💷 ⊺¶ 🐾 ⊠

ⓒ ▼▼ Clarion Inn & Conference Centre 1000 Islands H
(613) 382-7272. **$69-$249.** 50 Main St. Corner of Hwy 2 (King St); centre. Int corridors. **Pets:** Large. $15 daily fee/pet. Designated rooms, service with restrictions, crate.

SAVE ⊠ 🖪 💷 ⊺¶ 🐾

ⓒ ▼▼▼ Comfort Inn 1000 Islands M
(613) 382-4728. **$59-$249.** 785 King St E. Hwy 401, exit 647 eastbound; exit 648 westbound, 0.3 mi (0.5 km) w on Hwy 2 (King St). Ext/int corridors. **Pets:** Large. $15 daily fee/pet. Designated rooms, service with restrictions, crate.

SAVE ⊠ 🖪 💷 🐾

ⓒ ▼▼▼ Holiday Inn Express & Suites 1000 Islands H
(613) 382-8338. **$99-$299.** 777 King St E. Just w of jct Hwy 2 (King St), 401 and 1000 Islands Pkwy. Int corridors. **Pets:** Small. $15 one-time fee/pet. Designated rooms, service with restrictions.

SAVE ⊠ 🖪 💷 🐾

ⓒ ▼▼▼ Quality Inn & Suites 1000 Islands M
(613) 382-1453. **$79-$249.** 650 King St E. Hwy 401, exit 647 eastbound; exit 648 westbound, 0.6 mi (1 km) w on Hwy 2 (King St). Ext corridors. **Pets:** Large. $15 daily fee/pet. Designated rooms, service with restrictions, crate.

SAVE ⊠ 🖪 💷 ⊺¶ 🐾

▼▼▼ Trinity House Inn CI
(613) 382-8383. **$99-$250, 7 day notice.** 90 Stone St S. Corner of Pine St; centre. Int corridors. **Pets:** Other species. Designated rooms, service with restrictions, supervision.

⊠ 🖪 💷 ⊺¶ 🅩

GRIMSBY

ⓒ ▼▼▼ Super 8-Grimsby H
(905) 309-8800. **$99-$169.** 11 Windward Dr. QEW, exit 74 (Casablanca N). Int corridors. **Pets:** Medium, other species. $10 daily fee/room. Service with restrictions, supervision.

SAVE ⊠ 🖪 💷 🐾

GUELPH

ⓒ ▼▼▼ Comfort Inn Guelph H ✿
(519) 763-1900. **$118-$148.** 480 Silvercreek Pkwy. Jct Hwy 6 and 7. Int corridors. **Pets:** Designated rooms, service with restrictions.

SAVE ⊠ 🖪 💷

▼▼▼ Delta Guelph Hotel and Conference Centre H ✿
(519) 780 3700. **$119-$219.** 50 Stone Rd W. Jct Gordon St. Int corridors. **Pets:** $35 daily fee/room. Service with restrictions, supervision.

ASK ⊠ 🕮 🖪 💷 ⊺¶

ⓒ ▼▼▼ Holiday Inn Guelph H
(519) 836-0231. **$129-$199.** 601 Scottsdale Dr. Jct Hwy 6 N and Stone Rd E; 5 mi (8 km) n of jct Hwy 401. Int corridors. **Pets:** Accepted.

SAVE ⊠ 🖪 💷 ⊺¶ 🐾 ⊠

ⓒ ▼▼ Ramada Guelph H
(519) 836-1240. **$106-$169.** 716 Gordon St. Jct Stone Rd; 5 mi (8 km) n of Hwy 401 via Brock Rd. Int corridors. **Pets:** Medium. $12 daily fee/room. Designated rooms, service with restrictions, crate.

SAVE ⊠ 🖪 💷 ⊺¶ 🐾

Ⓐ ▼▼▼ Staybridge Suites H ☙
(519) 767-3300. **$129-$199.** 11 Corporate Ct. Jct Hwy 6 and Laird St, just e. Int corridors. **Pets:** Large, other species. $35 one-time fee/room.
[SAVE] [✕] [M] [🛏] [💻] [🏊]

Ⓐ ▼▼ Super 8-Guelph M
(519) 836-5850. **$89-$199.** 281 Woodlawn Rd W. Jct Hwy 6 and 7. Ext/int corridors. **Pets:** Very small, dogs only. $15 daily fee/pet. Designated rooms, service with restrictions, supervision.
[SAVE] [✕] [🛏] [💻] [🍴]

HALIBURTON

▼▼ Lakeview Motel M
(705) 457-1027. **$100-$205, 5 day notice.** 4951 CR 21. Jct Hwy 118, 1.6 mi (2.5 km) w. Ext corridors. **Pets:** Medium. $10 daily fee/pet. Designated rooms, service with restrictions.
[✕] [🛏] [💻] [🍴] [🏊]

HAMILTON

Ⓐ ▼▼▼ Sheraton Hamilton H ☙
(905) 529-5515. **$139-$339.** 116 King St W. Between Bay and James sts; downtown. Int corridors. **Pets:** Small, dogs only. Service with restrictions, crate.
[SAVE] [✕] [M] [🛏] [💻] [🍴] [🏊]

▼▼▼ Staybridge Suites H
(905) 577-9000. **Call for rates.** 118 Market St. Hwy 403, exit King St, then e across from Jackson Square; jct Caroline St. Int corridors. **Pets:** Accepted.
[✕] [🛏] [💻] [🏊]

▼▼ Super 8-Hamilton Airport/Mount Hope H
(905) 679-3355. **Call for rates.** 2975 Homestead Dr. Jct Hwy 6 S (Upper James St) and Homestead Dr. Int corridors. **Pets:** Accepted.
[✕] [🛏] [💻]

HUNTSVILLE

▼▼ Comfort Inn H ☙
(705) 789-1701. **$99-$149.** 86 King William St. Jct Hwy 60. Int corridors. **Pets:** Other species. Designated rooms, service with restrictions, supervision.
[ASK] [✕] [🛏] [💻]

Ⓐ ▼▼ HV Hidden Valley Resort H
(705) 789-2301. **$89-$239,** 1755 Valley Rd. Jct Hwy 11, 4 mi (6.5 km) e on Hwy 60 to Canal, follow signs. Int corridors. **Pets:** Medium, dogs only. $35 one-time fee/room. Service with restrictions, supervision.
[SAVE] [✕] [🛏] [💻] [🍴] [🏊] [✕]

▼▼ King William Inn M
(705) 789-9661. **$69-$129.** 23 King William St. Hwy 60, 0.6 mi (1 km) s. Ext corridors. **Pets:** Medium, dogs only. Designated rooms, service with restrictions, supervision.
[ASK] [✕] [🛏] [💻]

▼▼ Motel 6-Huntsville H ☙
(705) 787-0118. **$65-$130.** 70 Howland Dr. Jct Hwy 11 and 60, just se. Int corridors. **Pets:** Medium. Designated rooms, service with restrictions, crate.
[ASK] [✕] [🛏] [🏊]

▼ Tulip Inn M
(705) 789-4001. **$60-$130, 3 day notice.** 211 Arrowhead Park Rd. Hwy 11, exit 226 (Muskoka Rd 3), follow signs for Arrowhead Park. Ext corridors. **Pets:** Accepted.
[ASK] [✕] [🛏] [💻]

INGERSOLL

▼▼▼ Comfort Inn & Suites H
(519) 425-1100. **Call for rates.** 20 Samnah Cres. Hwy 401, exit 216 (Culloden Rd). Int corridors. **Pets:** Accepted.
[✕] [🛏] [💻] [🏊]

Ⓐ ▼▼▼ Elm Hurst Inn and Country Spa CI
(519) 485-5321. **$185, 3 day notice.** 415 Harris St. Jct Hwy 401 and 19 N. Int corridors. **Pets:** Accepted.
[SAVE] [✕] [🛏] [💻] [🍴] [✕]

KAPUSKASING

▼▼ Comfort Inn H
(705) 335-8583. **Call for rates.** 172 Government Rd E. Hwy 11; corner of Brunelle Rd. Int corridors. **Pets:** $10 one-time fee/room. Designated rooms, service with restrictions, supervision.
[✕] [🛏] [💻]

KENORA

Ⓐ ▼▼▼ Best Western Lakeside Inn & Conference
                          Centre H
(807) 468-5521. **$115-$160.** 470 First Ave S. Centre. Int corridors. **Pets:** Accepted.
[SAVE] [✕] [🛏] [💻] [🍴] [🏊]

▼▼ Comfort Inn M
(807) 468-8845. **$108-$135.** 1230 Hwy 17 E. 0.9 mi (1.5 km) e. Int corridors. **Pets:** Accepted.
[ASK] [✕] [🛏] [💻]

▼▼ Days Inn H
(807) 468-2003. **$101.** 920 Hwy 17 E. 0.6 mi (1 km) e. Ext/int corridors. **Pets:** Accepted.
[ASK] [✕] [🛏] [💻] [🍴] [🏊] [✕]

Ⓐ ▼▼ Kenora Travelodge H
(807) 468-3155. **$95-$160.** 800 Hwy 17 E. 0.6 mi (1 km) e. Int corridors. **Pets:** Other species. $10 daily fee/pet. Service with restrictions, supervision.
[SAVE] [✕] [🛏] [💻] [🏊] [✕]

KILLALOE

▼▼▼ Annie's Inn Bed & Breakfast BB
(613) 757-0950. **$65-$200 (no credit cards), 7 day notice.** 67 Roche St. Hwy 60, exit Maple St, 1 blk to Roche St, then w; driveway entrance is at the end of the street. Int corridors. **Pets:** Accepted.
[ASK] [✕] [🛏] [✎]

KINGSTON

Ⓐ ▼▼ Comfort Inn H
(613) 546-9500. **$100-$185.** 55 Warne Cres. Hwy 401, exit 617 (Division St), just s to Dalton Ave. Int corridors. **Pets:** Service with restrictions, crate.
[SAVE] [✕] [🛏] [💻]

▼▼ Comfort Inn H ☙
(613) 549-5550. **$90-$160.** 1454 Princess St. Hwy 401, exit 613 (Sydenham Rd), 2.5 mi (4 km) se. Int corridors. **Pets:** Large, other species. Service with restrictions, supervision.
[ASK] [✕] [🛏] [💻]

▼▼ Confederation Place Hotel H ☙
(613) 549-6300. **$89-$209.** 237 Ontario St. Centre of downtown. Int corridors. **Pets:** Medium. $15 daily fee/pet. Designated rooms, service with restrictions, supervision.
[ASK] [✕] [🛏] [💻] [🍴] [🏊]

Ⓐ ▼▼ The Executive Inn & Suites M
(613) 549-1620. **$99-$149, 3 day notice.** 794 Hwy 2 E. Hwy 401, exit 623, 5 mi (8 km) s, then 1.3 mi (2 km) e. Ext corridors. **Pets:** Accepted.
[SAVE] [✕] [🛏] [💻] [🏊]

Ⓐ ▼▼▼ Holiday Inn Kingston-Waterfront H ☙
(613) 549-8400. **$129-$320.** 2 Princess St. Corner of Ontario St; centre of downtown. Int corridors. **Pets:** Other species. $20 daily fee/room. Designated rooms, service with restrictions, supervision.
[SAVE] [✕] [M] [🛏] [💻] [🍴] [🏊] [✕]

KIRKLAND LAKE

▼▼ Comfort Inn 🏨 ✿
(705) 567-4909. **$115-$215.** 455 Government Rd W. Rt 66, just w of centre. Int corridors. **Pets:** Other species. Service with restrictions.

ASK ⊠ 🛏 💻

KITCHENER

ⒸⒶⒶ ▼▼▼▼ Delta Kitchener-Waterloo 🏨
(519) 744-4141. **Call for rates.** 105 King St E. Corner of King and Benton sts; downtown. Int corridors. **Pets:** Other species. $35 one-time fee/room. Service with restrictions.

SAVE ⊠ 🛏 💻 🍴 🏊 ⊠

ⒸⒶⒶ ▼▼▼▼ Radisson Hotel Kitchener-Waterloo 🏨
(519) 894-9500. **$119-$179.** 2960 King St E. Hwy 401, exit 278, 3.8 mi (6 km) w on Hwy 8, exit Weber St. Int corridors. **Pets:** Accepted.

SAVE ⊠ 🛏 💻 🍴 🏊

▼▼▼ Sunbridge Crescent B&B 🅱🅱
(519) 743-4557. **$100-$125.** 11 Sunbridge Cres. Hwy 85 N, exit University E, 0.6 mi (1 km) e to Bridge St, 0.3 mi (0.5 km) s to Bridal Tr, then 0.5 mi (0.9 km) e. Int corridors. **Pets:** Very small. Designated rooms, service with restrictions, supervision.

ASK ⊠ 🛏 💻 🏊 🗶

▼▼▼ Walper Terrace Hotel 🏨
(519) 745-4321. **$99-$179.** 1 King St W. Corner of King and Queen sts; downtown. Int corridors. **Pets:** Accepted.

ASK ⊠ 🛏 💻 🍴

LEAMINGTON

▼▼ Comfort Inn 🏨 ✿
(519) 326-9071. **$93-$142.** 279 Erie St S. 0.6 mi (1 km) s of jct Talbot and Erie sts; on direct route to Point Pelee National Park. Int corridors. **Pets:** $10 daily fee/room. Designated rooms, service with restrictions, supervision.

ASK ⊠ 🛏 💻

ⒸⒶⒶ ▼▼▼ Ramada Leamington 🏨
(519) 325-0260. **$90-$300, 3 day notice.** 201 Erie St N. 0.6 mi (1 km) n of Talbot St. Int corridors. **Pets:** Medium. $15 daily fee/pet. Designated rooms, service with restrictions, supervision.

SAVE ⊠ 🛏 💻 🏊 ⊠

LONDON

▼▼▼ Airport Inn & Suites 🏨
(519) 457-1200. **$99.** 2230 Dundas St E. Hwy 401, exit Airport Rd, 4.8 mi (7.7 km) n; corner of Airport Rd and Dundas St E. Int corridors. **Pets:** Medium, other species. $15 daily fee/pet. Designated rooms, service with restrictions, crate.

ASK ⊠ 🛏 💻

ⒸⒶⒶ ▼▼▼ Best Western Lamplighter Inn & Conference Centre 🏨
(519) 681-7151. **$149-$219.** 591 Wellington Rd S. 2.3 mi (3.7 km) n off Hwy 401, exit 186 (Wellington Rd). Int corridors. **Pets:** Medium, other species. $10 daily fee/pet. Designated rooms, service with restrictions, supervision.

SAVE ⊠ 🛏 💻 🍴 🏊 ⊠

ⒸⒶⒶ ▼▼ Comfort Inn 🏨 ✿
(519) 685-9300. **$97-$120.** 1156 Wellington Rd. Hwy 401, exit 186B (Wellington Rd), just n. Int corridors. **Pets:** Service with restrictions, crate.

SAVE ⊠ 🛏 💻

ⒸⒶⒶ ▼▼▼ Days Inn London 🏨
(519) 681-1240. **$65-$129.** 1100 Wellington Rd S. Hwy 401, exit 186B (Wellington Rd), 0.9 mi (1.5 km) n. Int corridors. **Pets:** Other species.

SAVE ⊠ 🛏 💻 🍴 🏊

ⒸⒶⒶ ▼▼▼▼ Delta London Armouries 🏨
(519) 679-6111. **$119-$239.** 325 Dundas St. Between Wellington and Waterloo sts. Int corridors. **Pets:** Large. $35 one-time fee/room. Service with restrictions, supervision.

SAVE ⊠ 🛏 💻 🍴 🏊 ⊠

ⒸⒶⒶ ▼▼▼▼ Hilton London Ontario 🏨
(519) 439-1661. **$119-$229.** 300 King St. Jct King St and Wellington Rd. Int corridors. **Pets:** Accepted.

SAVE ⊠ 🔥 🛏 💻 🍴 🏊 ⊠

ⒸⒶⒶ ▼▼▼▼ Holiday Inn Hotel & Suites-London 🏨
(519) 680-0077. **$129.** 864 Exeter Rd. Hwy 401, exit 186 (Wellington Rd) westbound; exit 186B eastbound. Int corridors. **Pets:** Accepted.

SAVE ⊠ 🛏 💻 🍴 🏊

ⒸⒶⒶ ▼▼▼▼ Homewood Suites by Hilton London 🏨
(519) 686-7700. **$109-$159.** 45 Bessemer Rd. Hwy 401, exit 186 (Wellington Rd). Int corridors. **Pets:** Accepted.

SAVE ⊠ 🔥 🛏 💻 🏊

▼▼ Motel 6 🏨
(519) 680-0900. **$76-$110.** 810 Exeter Rd. Hwy 401, exit 186 (Wellington Rd), just n. Int corridors. **Pets:** Accepted.

ASK ⊠ 🛏 🏊

ⒸⒶⒶ ▼▼▼▼ Quality Suites 🏨
(519) 680-1024. **$99-$180.** 1120 Dearness Dr. Hwy 401, exit 186B (Wellington Rd), 1 mi (1.6 km) n. Int corridors. **Pets:** Accepted.

SAVE ⊠ 🛏 💻

ⒸⒶⒶ ▼▼▼▼ Radisson Hotel and Suites London 🏨 ✿
(519) 668-7900. **$99-$169.** 855 Wellington Rd S. Jct Wellington and Southdale rds. Int corridors. **Pets:** Other species. $35 one-time fee/room. Service with restrictions, supervision.

SAVE ⊠ 🛏 💻 🍴 🏊

▼▼▼▼ Residence Inn by Marriott London Downtown 🏨
(519) 433-7222. **$157-$191.** 383 Colborne St. Jct King St. Int corridors. **Pets:** Accepted.

⊠ 🛏 💻 ⊠

ⒸⒶⒶ ▼▼▼▼ StationPark All Suite Hotel 🏨
(519) 642-4444. **$129-$194.** 242 Pall Mall St. Hwy 401, exit 186B (Wellington Rd), 5.6 mi (9 km) n. Int corridors. **Pets:** Accepted.

SAVE ⊠ 💻 🍴 ⊠

ⒸⒶⒶ ▼▼▼▼ Staybridge Suites 🏨
(519) 649-4500. **$129-$169.** 824 Exeter Rd. Hwy 401, exit 186 (Wellington Rd). Int corridors. **Pets:** Accepted.

SAVE ⊠ 🔥 🛏 💻 🏊

MARATHON

ⒸⒶⒶ ▼▼ Peninsula Inn Ⓜ
(807) 229-0651. **$88-$99, 6 day notice.** Hwy 17. 1.5 mi (2.4 km) w of jct Hwy 626. Ext corridors. **Pets:** Medium. $10 one-time fee/pet. Designated rooms, service with restrictions, supervision.

SAVE ⊠ 🛏 🍴

▼▼ Travelodge Marathon 🏨
(807) 229-1213. **$95-$110.** Hwy 17. On Hwy 17, jct Peninsula Rd. Int corridors. **Pets:** Accepted.

ASK ⊠ 🛏 💻

MASSEY

ⒸⒶⒶ ▼ Mohawk Motel Canada Ⓜ
(705) 865-2722. **$75-$155.** 335 Sable St. Centre. Ext/int corridors. **Pets:** Large. $6 daily fee/pet. Designated rooms, service with restrictions, supervision.

SAVE ⊠ 🛏 💻

MCKELLAR

Ⓐ ▼▼▼▼ The Inn at Manitou ⊞
(705) 389-2171. **$598-$998, 30 day notice.** 81 The Inn Rd. Hwy 124, exit McKellar Centre Rd, 5 mi (8 km) s, follow signs. Ext corridors. **Pets:** Medium. Designated rooms, service with restrictions.
[SAVE] [✕] [♿] [📶] [¶] [⚓] [✕]

MIDLAND

▼▼ Comfort Inn ⊞
(705) 526-2090. **$100-$170.** 980 King St. Jct Hwy 12 and King St. Int corridors. **Pets:** Accepted.
[ASK] [✕] [♿] [📶]

MILTON

Ⓐ ▼▼▼▼ Best Western Milton Inn ⊞
(905) 875-3818. **$109-$179.** 161 Chisholm Dr. Jct Hwy 401 and 25 S. Int corridors. **Pets:** $20 daily fee/pet. Designated rooms, service with restrictions, crate.
[SAVE] [✕] [♿] [📶] [¶] [⚓]

MINDEMOYA

▼▼ Mindemoya Motel Ⓜ
(705) 377-4779. **$82-$109, 3 day notice.** 6375 Hwy 542. In Mindemoya; 0.6 mi (1 km) w of jct Hwy 551 and 542. Ext corridors. **Pets:** Accepted.
[ASK] [✕] [♿] [📶]

MISSISSAUGA

Ⓐ ▼▼ ▼▼ Comfort Inn Airport West ⊞ ❀
(905) 624-6900. **$119-$169.** 1500 Matheson Blvd. Hwy 401, exit Dixie Rd, then s. Int corridors. **Pets:** Designated rooms, service with restrictions, supervision.
[SAVE] [✕] [♿] [📶] [¶]

Ⓐ ▼▼▼▼ Delta Meadowvale Resort and Conference Centre ⊞
(905) 821-1981. **$99-$299.** 6750 Mississauga Rd. Hwy 401 W, exit 336 (Mississauga Rd), just s. Int corridors. **Pets:** $35 one-time fee/room. Service with restrictions, crate.
[SAVE] [✕] [♿M] [♿] [📶] [¶] [⚓] [✕]

Ⓐ ▼▼▼▼ Delta Toronto Airport West ⊞
(905) 624-1144. **$99-$219.** 5444 Dixie Rd. 0.6 mi (1 km) s of jct Hwy 401 and Dixie Rd. Int corridors. **Pets:** Accepted.
[SAVE] [✕] [♿] [📶] [¶] [⚓] [✕]

▼▼ ▼▼ Econo Lodge Inn & Suites Toronto Airport ⊞
(905) 677-7331. **Call for rates.** 6355 Airport Rd. 1.3 mi (2 km) s of Derry Rd. Ext/int corridors. **Pets:** Accepted.
[✕] [♿] [📶] [¶]

Ⓐ ▼▼▼▼ Four Points by Sheraton Mississauga Meadowvale ⊞
(905) 858-2424. **$90-$210.** 2501 Argentia Rd. Hwy 401 exit 336, just s on Erin Mills Pkwy, then 1 mi (1.6 km) w. Int corridors. **Pets:** Accepted.
[SAVE] [✕] [♿M] [♿] [📶] [¶] [⚓]

Ⓐ ▼▼▼▼ Hilton Toronto Airport ⊞
(905) 677-9900. **$109-$309.** 5875 Airport Rd. Hwy 401, exit Dixon Rd, 2.2 mi (3.5 km) w. Int corridors. **Pets:** Accepted.
[SAVE] [✕] [♿M] [📶] [¶] [⚓]

▼▼▼▼ Holiday Inn Toronto-Mississauga ⊞
(905) 855-2000. **$99-$149.** 2125 N Sheridan Way. QEW, exit Erin Mills Pkwy. Int corridors. **Pets:** Accepted.
[ASK] [✕] [♿] [📶] [¶] [⚓]

▼▼ ▼▼ Motel 6 Mississauga #1910 ⊞
(905) 814-1664. **$65-$75.** 2935 Argentia Rd. Hwy 401, exit 333 (Winston Churchill Blvd), just s. Int corridors. **Pets:** Other species. Service with restrictions, supervision.
[✕] [♿M] [♿]

Ⓐ ▼▼▼▼ Novotel Toronto Mississauga Centre ⊞ ❀
(905) 896-1000. **$299.** 3670 Hurontario St. Hwy 403, exit 344, 0.8 mi s (1.2 km) on Hwy 10 (Hurontario St); at Burnhamthorpe Rd. Int corridors. **Pets:** Other species. Service with restrictions, crate.
[SAVE] [✕] [♿] [📶] [¶] [⚓] [✕]

▼▼▼▼ Residence Inn by Marriott ⊞
(905) 567-2577. **$167-$204.** 7005 Century Ave. Hwy 401, exit Erin Mills Pkwy/Mississauga Rd, s to Argentia Rd. Int corridors. **Pets:** Accepted.
[✕] [♿M] [♿] [📶] [⚓]

▼▼▼▼ Residence Inn by Marriott Mississauga Airport Corporate Centre West ⊞
(905) 602-7777. **$170-$208.** 5070 Creekbank Rd. Hwy 401 W, exit Dixie Rd S, 0.9 mi (1.5 km) to Eglinton Ave, then 0.6 mi (1 km). Int corridors. **Pets:** Accepted.
[✕] [♿] [📶] [⚓] [✕]

Ⓐ ▼▼▼▼ Sandalwood Suites Hotel Toronto Airport ⊞
(905) 238-9600. **$89-$159.** 5050 Orbitor Dr. Jct Eglinton Ave and Renforth Dr, 1.4 mi (2.3 km) w on Eglinton Ave. Int corridors. **Pets:** Accepted.
[SAVE] [✕] [♿] [📶]

Ⓐ ▼▼▼▼ Sheraton Gateway Hotel in Toronto International Airport ⊞ ❀
(905) 672-7000. **$129-$349.** Terminal 3, Toronto AMF. In Lester B Pearson International Airport. Int corridors. **Pets:** Small. Service with restrictions, supervision.
[SAVE] [✕] [♿M] [♿] [📶] [¶] [⚓] [✕]

Ⓐ ▼▼▼▼ Staybridge Suites Mississauga ⊞
(905) 564-6892. **$129-$299.** 6791 Hurontario St. Hwy 401 W, exit Hwy 10 (Hurontario St), then 0.9 mi (1.5 km) n; just s of Derry Rd. Int corridors. **Pets:** Accepted.
[SAVE] [✕] [♿] [📶] [⚓]

▼▼ Studio 6 Mississauga #1908 Ⓜ
(905) 502-8897. **$90-$100.** 60 Britannia Rd E. Hwy 401, exit Hwy 10 (Hurontario St). Int corridors. **Pets:** Other species. $10 daily fee/room. Service with restrictions, supervision.
[✕] [♿] [📶]

MONETVILLE

▼▼ Memquisit Lodge ⒸⒶ
(705) 898-2355. **Call for rates.** 506 Memquisit Rd. 13 mi (20.8 km) ne on west arm of Lake Nipissing, on Hwy 64 and Memquisit Lodge Rd; 23 mi (36.8 km) sw off Hwy 17, on Hwy 64. Ext corridors. **Pets:** Accepted.
[♿] [📶] [¶] [✕] [Ⓚ] [Ⓩ]

MORRISBURG

Ⓐ ▼▼ ▼▼ The McIntosh Country Inn & Conference Centre ⊞
(613) 543-3788. **$69-$129.** 12495 Hwy 2 E. Hwy 401, exit 750, 1.2 mi (2 km) s on Rt 31, then 0.6 mi (1 km) e. Int corridors. **Pets:** Medium. $10 one-time fee/pet. Service with restrictions, supervision.
[SAVE] [✕] [♿] [📶] [¶] [⚓] [✕]

NEWMARKET

▼▼ Comfort Inn ⊞
(905) 895-3355. **$115-$158.** 1230 Journey's End Cir. Hwy 404, exit 51 (Davis Dr), just w on Davis Dr, then just n on Harry Walker Pkwy. Int corridors. **Pets:** Other species. Service with restrictions.
[ASK] [✕] [♿] [📶]

NIAGARA FALLS METROPOLITAN AREA

FORT ERIE

ⒶⒶ ▼▼▼▼ Holiday Inn Fort Erie/Niagara-Convention Centre Ⓗ
(905) 871-8333. **$109-$299, 14 day notice.** 1485 Garrison Rd. QEW, exit Gilmore Rd. Int corridors. **Pets:** Medium. $30 daily fee/pet. Designated rooms, service with restrictions, supervision.
SAVE ✕ 🛏 💻 🍴 🏊 ⊠

LINCOLN

ⒶⒶ ▼▼▼ Best Western Beacon Harbourside Inn & Conference Centre Ⓗ
(905) 562-4155. **$90-$220, 3 day notice.** 2793 Beacon Blvd. QEW, exit 55. Int corridors. **Pets:** Accepted.
SAVE ✕ 🛏 💻 🍴 🏊 ⊠

ⒶⒶ ▼▼▼ Prudhommes Inn Ⓗ ✿
(905) 562-4101. **$60-$100.** 3305 N Service Rd. QEW, exit 57. Int corridors. **Pets:** $10 daily fee/pet. Designated rooms, service with restrictions, supervision.
SAVE ✕ 🛏 💻 🏊

NIAGARA FALLS

ⒶⒶ ▼▼▼ Best Western Fallsview Ⓗ ✿
(905) 356-0551. **$99-$599, 3 day notice.** 6289 Fallsview Blvd. Jct Niagara River Pkwy, just n on Murray St. Ext/int corridors. **Pets:** Large. $20 daily fee/pet. No service, supervision.
SAVE ✕ 💻 🍴 🏊

ⒶⒶ ▼▼▼▼ Crowne Plaza Niagara Falls-Fallsview Ⓗ
(905) 374-4447. **$99-$499.** 5685 Falls Ave. Entrance to Rainbow Bridge on Hwy 20; just n of the falls. Int corridors. **Pets:** Accepted.
SAVE ✕ 🛏 💻 🍴 🏊 ⊠

ⒶⒶ ▼▼▼ Falls Manor Motel Ⓜ ✿
(905) 358-3211. **$49-$129.** 7104 Lundy's Ln. 2.1 mi (3.4 km) w on Hwy 20. Ext corridors. **Pets:** Dogs only. $100 deposit/pet, $10 daily fee/pet. Designated rooms, service with restrictions, supervision.
SAVE ✕ 🛏 🍴 🏊

ⒶⒶ ▼▼▼ Howard Johnson Express Inn Ⓜ
(905) 358-9777. **$40-$200, 30 day notice.** 8100 Lundy's Ln. QEW, exit Hwy 20, 3.1 mi (5 km) w. Ext corridors. **Pets:** Accepted.
SAVE ✕ 🛏 💻 🏊

ⒶⒶ ▼▼▼ Howard Johnson Hotel by the Falls Ⓗ ✿
(905) 357-4040. **$59-$349.** 5905 Victoria Ave. On Hwy 20; 0.4 mi (0.6 km) from the falls. Int corridors. **Pets:** Small. $15 daily fee/pet. Designated rooms, service with restrictions, crate.
SAVE ✕ 🛏 💻 🍴 🏊 ⊠

ⒶⒶ ▼▼ Motel 6 Niagara Falls Ⓗ
(905) 356-6696. **Call for rates.** 5700 Stanley Ave. Just n of Hwy 20, just s of Hwy 420. Int corridors. **Pets:** Accepted.
SAVE ✕ 🛗 🛏 🏊

ⒶⒶ ▼▼ Niagara Parkway Court Motel Ⓜ
(905) 295-3331. **$39-$149.** 3708 Main St (Niagara Pkwy S). 1.6 mi (2.5 km) s of the falls. Ext corridors. **Pets:** $15 daily fee/pet. Designated rooms, service with restrictions, crate.
SAVE ✕ 🛏 💻

ⒶⒶ ▼▼▼▼ Peninsula Inn & Resort Ⓗ
(905) 354-8812. **$59-$339.** 7373 Niagara Square Dr. QEW, exit McLeod Rd, just w. Int corridors. **Pets:** Small. $10 daily fee/pet. Designated rooms, service with restrictions, crate.
SAVE ✕ 🛗 🛏 💻 🍴 🏊 ⊠

ⒶⒶ ▼▼▼▼ Sheraton on the Falls Ⓗ
(905) 374-4445. **$129-$999.** 5875 Falls Ave. Entrance to Rainbow Bridge on Hwy 20. Int corridors. **Pets:** Accepted.
SAVE ✕ 🛏 💻 🍴 🏊

ⒶⒶ ▼▼ Stanley Motor Inn Ⓜ
(905) 358-9238. **$55-$125, 4 day notice.** 6220 Stanley Ave. 2 blks from the falls; w of Skylon Tower. Ext/int corridors. **Pets:** Medium, dogs only. $10 daily fee/pet. Service with restrictions, crate.
SAVE ✕ 🛏 🏊 ✒

NIAGARA-ON-THE-LAKE

▼▼▼ Gate House Hotel Ⓒ
(905) 468-3263. **$145-$245.** 142 Queen St. Jct Gate St. Int corridors. **Pets:** Accepted.
✕ 🍴

▼▼▼▼ Harbour House Hotel Ⓗ ✿
(905) 468-4683. **$199-$475, 10 day notice.** 85 Melville St. Jct Ricardo St. Int corridors. **Pets:** Dogs only. $25 daily fee/room. Designated rooms, supervision.
ASK ✕ 💻

ⒶⒶ ▼▼▼▼ The Oban Inn and OSpa Ⓗ
(905) 468-2165. **$150-$410, 7 day notice.** 160 Front St. Jct Gate St. Ext/int corridors. **Pets:** Small. $50 daily fee/pet. Designated rooms, crate.
SAVE ✕ 💻 🍴 🏊 ⊠

▼▼▼ Old Bank House Ⓑ Ⓑ
(905) 468-7136. **$149-$249, 28 day notice.** 10 Front St. Corner of King and Front sts; centre. Int corridors. **Pets:** Small, dogs only. $25 daily fee/pet. Designated rooms, supervision.
ASK ✕ ✒

ⒶⒶ ▼▼▼▼ The Pillar and Post Hotel Ⓒ
(905) 468-2123. **Call for rates.** 48 John St. Just n on Hwy 55 (Mississauga St), then just e; 13 mi from QEW. Ext/int corridors. **Pets:** Accepted.
SAVE ✕ 🛏 💻 🍴 🏊 ⊠

ⒶⒶ ▼▼▼▼ Prince of Wales Hotel Ⓗ
(905) 468-3246. **$150-$420.** 6 Picton St. Jct Picton and King sts; 9 mi (14.4 km) e of jct QEW and Hwy 55, via Hwy 55. Ext/int corridors. **Pets:** Small. $35 deposit/room. Designated rooms, service with restrictions, crate.
SAVE ✕ 🛏 💻 🍴 🏊 ⊠

ⒶⒶ ▼▼▼▼ Queen's Landing Hotel Ⓗ
(905) 468-2195. **$150-$550.** 155 Byron St. Just n on King St, then just e. Int corridors. **Pets:** Very small. $100 daily fee/room. Designated rooms, crate.
SAVE ✕ 🛏 💻 🍴 🏊 ⊠

▼▼▼▼ Shaw Club Hotel and Spa Ⓗ ✿
(905) 468-5711. **Call for rates.** 92 Picton St. Jct Wellington St. Int corridors. **Pets:** Dogs only. $25 daily fee/room. Designated rooms, supervision.
✕ 🛏 💻 🍴

ST. CATHARINES

ⒶⒶ ▼▼▼ Comfort Inn Ⓗ
(905) 687-8890. **$89-$179.** 2 Dunlop Dr. QEW, exit 46 (Lake St); between Lake and Geneva sts. Int corridors. **Pets:** Designated rooms, service with restrictions, supervision.
SAVE ✕ 🛗 🛏 💻 🍴

ⒶⒶ ▼▼▼ Days Inn St. Catharines Niagara Ⓗ
(905) 934-5400. **$89-$289.** 89 Meadowvale Dr. QEW, exit 46 (Lake St). Int corridors. **Pets:** Large. $10 one-time fee/room. Designated rooms, service with restrictions, supervision.
SAVE ✕ 🛏 💻 🍴 🏊 ⊠

(CAA) ♦♦♦ Holiday Inn St. Catharines/Niagara 🅗
(905) 934-8000. **Call for rates.** 2 N Service Rd. QEW, exit 46 (Lake St),
just e. Int corridors. **Pets:** Accepted.
[SAVE] [X] [♦] [💻] [Y¶] [⇌] [X]

(CAA) ♦♦♦♦ Quality Hotel Parkway Convention Centre 🅗
(905) 688-2324. **$110-$230.** 327 Ontario St. QEW, exit 47 (Ontario St), 0.5
mi (0.8 km) s. Int corridors. **Pets:** $10 one-time fee/room. Designated
rooms, service with restrictions, crate.
[SAVE] [X] [♦] [💻] [Y¶] [⇌] [X]

(CAA) ♦♦♦ The Travelodge St. Catharines Ⓜ
(905) 688-1646. **$70-$179.** 420 Ontario St. QEW, exit 47 (Ontario St). Ext
corridors. **Pets:** Other species. $10 daily fee/pet. Service with restrictions,
crate.
[SAVE] [X] [♦] [💻] [⇌]

WELLAND

(CAA) ♦♦♦ Comfort Inn-Niagara Falls/Welland 🅗
(905) 732-4811. **$50-$150.** 870 Niagara St. 1.5 mi (2.5 km) n. Int corridors.
Pets: Other species. $15 daily fee/pet. Service with restrictions, crate.
[SAVE] [X] [♦] [💻] [⇌]

END METROPOLITAN AREA

NORTH BAY

(CAA) ♦♦♦ Best Western North Bay Hotel and Conference
Centre 🅗 ❀
(705) 474-5800. **$119-$189.** 700 Lakeshore Dr. Hwy 11, exit Lakeshore Dr,
2.5 mi (4 km) n on Hwy 11B. Int corridors. **Pets:** Large, other species.
Service with restrictions, crate.
[SAVE] [X] [♦] [💻] [Y¶] [⇌] [X]

(CAA) ♦♦♦ Clarion Resort Pinewood Park 🅗
(705) 472-0810. **$119-$199.** 201 Pinewood Park Dr. Hwy 11, exit Lakeshore Dr, immediately turn s on Pinewood Park Dr, then 0.4 mi (0.7 km). Int
corridors. **Pets:** Other species. Designated rooms, service with restrictions,
supervision.
[SAVE] [X] [♦] [💻] [Y¶] [⇌] [X]

♦♦ Comfort Inn 🅗
(705) 494-9444. **$92-$129.** 676 Lakeshore Dr. Hwy 11B, exit Lakeshore Dr;
2.5 mi (4 km) n of jct Hwy 11. Int corridors. **Pets:** Accepted.
[ASK] [X] [♦] [💻]

(CAA) ♦♦♦ Comfort Inn-Airport 🅗
(705) 476-5400. **$115-$165.** 1200 O'Brien St. 1.8 mi (3 km) e on Hwy 11
and 17 Bypass; at O'Brien St exit. Int corridors. **Pets:** Medium. Designated
rooms, service with restrictions, supervision.
[SAVE] [X] [♦] [💻]

♦♦ Super 8 North Bay 🅗
(705) 495-4551. **$100-$140.** 570 Lakeshore Dr. Hwy 11, exit Lakeshore Dr,
2.8 mi (4.5 km) n on Hwy 11B. Int corridors. **Pets:** $100 deposit/room.
Service with restrictions, supervision.
[ASK] [X] [♦] [💻]

(CAA) ♦♦♦ Travelodge 🅗
(705) 472-7171. **$85-$105.** 718 Lakeshore Dr. Hwy 11B, exit Lakeshore Dr,
2.2 mi (3.5 km) n of jct Hwy 11. Int corridors. **Pets:** Large, other species.
Designated rooms, service with restrictions, supervision.
[SAVE] [X] [♦] [💻]

(CAA) ♦♦♦ Travelodge-Airport 🅗
(705) 495-1133. **$109-$189.** 1525 Seymour St. Jct Hwy 11, 17 and Seymour St. Int corridors. **Pets:** Accepted.
[SAVE] [X] [♦] [💻] [⇌]

OAKVILLE

(CAA) ♦♦♦ Holiday Inn Oakville Centre 🅗 ❀
(905) 842-5000. **$109-$169.** 590 Argus Rd. QEW, exit 118 (Trafalgar Rd),
just s. Int corridors. **Pets:** $15 daily fee/room. Designated rooms, service
with restrictions, supervision.
[SAVE] [X] [&M] [♦] [💻] [Y¶] [⇌] [X]

(CAA) ♦♦♦ Staybridge Suites Oakville Burlington 🅗
(905) 847-2600. **$139-$199.** 2511 Wyecroft Rd. QEW, exit 111 (Bronte
Rd/Hwy 25), 0.3 mi (0.5 km) s, then just e. Int corridors. **Pets:** Medium. $50
one-time fee/room. Designated rooms, service with restrictions, supervision.
[SAVE] [X] [♦] [💻] [⇌]

ORILLIA

♦♦ Comfort Inn 🅗
(705) 327-7744. **$121-$148.** 75 Progress Dr. Hwy 11 N, exit Hwy 12, s on
Memorial Ave; corner of Progress Dr and Memorial Ave. Int corridors.
Pets: Medium. $10 daily fee/room. Designated rooms, no service, supervi-
sion.
[ASK] [X] [♦] [💻]

OSHAWA

♦♦ Comfort Inn 🅗
(905) 434-5000. **$100-$170, 10 day notice.** 605 Bloor St W. Hwy 401,
exit 416 (Park Rd), s to Bloor St, then 0.5 mi (0.8 km) w. Int corridors.
Pets: Accepted.
[ASK] [X] [♦] [💻]

(CAA) ♦♦♦ Holiday Inn Oshawa Whitby Conference
Centre 🅗 ❀
(905) 576-5101. **$139-$199.** 1011 Bloor St E. Hwy 401, exit 419 (Harmony
Rd). Int corridors. **Pets:** $15 daily fee/pet. Designated rooms, service with
restrictions, crate.
[SAVE] [X] [♦] [💻] [Y¶] [⇌] [X]

♦♦♦ Oshawa Travelodge 🅗
(905) 436-9500. **$99-$139.** 940 Champlain Ave. Hwy 401, exit 412 (Thickson Rd N). Int corridors. **Pets:** Accepted.
[ASK] [X] [♦] [💻] [⇌]

OTTAWA METROPOLITAN AREA

OTTAWA

(CAA) ♦♦♦ Best Western Barons Hotel & Conference
Centre 🅗
(613) 828-2741. **Call for rates.** 3700 Richmond Rd. Hwy 417, exit 130,
1.3 mi (2 km) s. Int corridors. **Pets:** Accepted.
[SAVE] [X] [♦] [💻] [Y¶] [⇌] [X]

♦♦♦ Bostonian Executive Suites 🅗
(613) 594-5757. **Call for rates.** 341 MacLaren St. Between Bank and
O'Connor sts. Int corridors. **Pets:** Accepted.
[X] [♦] [💻]

(CAA) ▼▼▼▼ **Brookstreet** 🅷
(613) 271-1800. **$149-$399.** 525 Legget Dr. Hwy 417, exit 138 (March Rd), 2.3 mi (3.7 km) n, just e on Solandt Dr to Legget Dr, then just n. Int corridors. **Pets:** Small. $250 deposit/pet, $25 daily fee/pet. Designated rooms, service with restrictions, supervision.
[SAVE] ⊠ 🖪 🖵 ⁤🍴 ⇌ ⊠

(CAA) ▼▼ ▼ **Cartier Place Suite Hotel** 🅷
(613) 236-5000. **$149-$229.** 180 Cooper St. Between Elgin and Cartier sts. Int corridors. **Pets:** Other species. $25 daily fee/room. Service with restrictions.
[SAVE] ⊠ 🖪 🖵 🍴 ⇌ ⊠

(CAA) ▼▼ ▼ **Comfort Inn** 🅷
(613) 744-2900. **$109-$189.** 1252 Michael St. Hwy 417, exit 115 (St. Laurent Blvd), just ne. Int corridors. **Pets:** Other species. Designated rooms, service with restrictions, supervision.
[SAVE] ⊠ 🖪 🖵

(CAA) ▼▼▼ **Comfort Inn Ottawa West** 🅷 🐾
(613) 592-2200. **$129-$159.** 222 Hearst Way. Hwy 417, exit 138 (Eagleson Rd), 0.4 mi (0.6 km) s, then just w on Katimavik Rd. Int corridors. **Pets:** Medium, other species. Designated rooms, no service, crate.
[SAVE] ⊠ 🖪 🖵

(CAA) ▼▼▼▼ **Crowne Plaza Ottawa** 🅷
(613) 237-3600. **$119-$199.** 101 Lyon St. Entrance at corner of Albert St. Int corridors. **Pets:** Accepted.
[SAVE] ⊠ 🖪 🖵 🍴 ⇌ ⊠

(CAA) ▼▼▼ **Days Inn-Downtown Ottawa** 🅷
(613) 789-5555. **$115-$169.** 319 Rideau St. Between Nelson St and King Edward Ave. Ext/int corridors. **Pets:** Medium. Designated rooms, service with restrictions, supervision.
[SAVE] ⊠ 🖪 🖵 🍴

▼▼ ▼ **The Days Inn Ottawa West** 🅷
(613) 726-1717. **$130-$210.** 350 Moodie Dr. Hwy 417, exit 134, 0.9 mi (1.5 km) s. Int corridors. **Pets:** Accepted.
[ASK] ⊠ 🖪 🖵 🍴

(CAA) ▼▼▼▼ **Delta Ottawa Hotel and Suites** 🅷
(613) 238-6000. **$290-$350.** 361 Queen St. Corner of Lyon St. Int corridors. **Pets:** Medium, other species. $35 one-time fee/pet. Service with restrictions, supervision.
[SAVE] ⊠ 🖪 🖵 🍴 ⇌ ⊠

▼▼ ▼ **Extended Stay Deluxe Ottawa Downtown** 🅷
(613) 236-7500. **$101-$179.** 141 Cooper St. Between Elgin and Cartier sts. Int corridors. **Pets:** Other species. $25 daily fee/pet. Service with restrictions, crate.
[ASK] ⊠ 🖪 🖵 🍴 ⊠

(CAA) ▼▼▼ ▼▼ **Fairmont Chateau Laurier** 🅷
(613) 241-1414. **$179-$409.** 1 Rideau St. Just e of Parliament buildings. Int corridors. **Pets:** Accepted.
[SAVE] ⊠ 🅛Ⓜ 🖪 🖵 🍴 ⇌ ⊠

(CAA) ▼▼▼▼ **Holiday Inn Hotel & Suites Ottawa Downtown** 🅷 🐾
(613) 238-1331. **$138-$183.** 111 Cooper St. Corner of Cartier St. Int corridors. **Pets:** Other species. Designated rooms, service with restrictions.
[SAVE] ⊠ 🖪 🖵 🍴

▼▼▼▼ **Hotel Indigo Ottawa** 🅷 🐾
(613) 231-6555. **$179-$259.** 123 Metcalfe St. Corner of Laurier Ave W. Int corridors. **Pets:** Medium. $75 one-time fee/room. Service with restrictions, supervision.
[ASK] ⊠ 🖪 🖵 🍴 ⇌ ⊠

(CAA) ▼▼▼▼ **Les Suites Hotel Ottawa** 🅷
(613) 232-2000. **$149-$259.** 130 Besserer St. Between Nicholas and Waller sts. Int corridors. **Pets:** Medium. $35 daily fee/pet. Designated rooms, service with restrictions, supervision.
[SAVE] ⊠ 🅛Ⓜ 🖪 🖵 🍴 ⇌ ⊠

▼▼▼ **Lord Elgin Hotel** 🅷
(613) 235-3333. **$129-$259.** 100 Elgin St. Between Laurier Ave and Slater St. Int corridors. **Pets:** Small, other species. Designated rooms, service with restrictions, supervision.
[ASK] ⊠ 🖪 🖵 🍴 ⇌ ⊠

(CAA) ▼▼▼ ▼▼ **Marriott Ottawa Hotel** 🅷
(613) 238-1122. **$199-$259.** 100 Kent St. Corner of Queen St. Int corridors. **Pets:** Other species. Service with restrictions, crate.
[SAVE] ⊠ 🖪 🖵 🍴 ⇌ ⊠

(CAA) ▼▼▼ **Monterey Inn Resort & Conference Centre** 🅷
(613) 288-3500. **$109-$139.** 2259 Prince of Wales Dr. 0.5 mi (0.8 km) s of Hunt Club Rd. Ext corridors. **Pets:** $10 daily fee/room. Designated rooms, service with restrictions.
[SAVE] ⊠ 🖪 🖵 🍴 ⇌ ⊠

(CAA) ▼▼▼▼ **Novotel Ottawa Hotel** 🅷 🐾
(613) 230-3033. **$159-$259.** 33 Nicholas St. Corner of Daly Ave. Int corridors. **Pets:** Service with restrictions, crate.
[SAVE] ⊠ 🖪 🖵 🍴 ⇌ ⊠

(CAA) ▼▼▼ **Quality Hotel Ottawa, Downtown** 🅷
(613) 789-7511. **$159-$169.** 290 Rideau St. Corner of King Edward Ave. Int corridors. **Pets:** Accepted.
[SAVE] ⊠ 🖪 🖵 🍴

(CAA) ▼▼▼▼ **Radisson Hotel Ottawa Parliament Hill** 🅷
(613) 236-1133. **$129-$179.** 402 Queen St. Corner of Bay and Queen sts. Int corridors. **Pets:** Other species. Service with restrictions, crate.
[SAVE] ⊠ 🖪 🖵 🍴

▼▼▼▼ **Residence Inn by Marriott** 🅷
(613) 231-2020. **$197-$241.** 161 Laurier Ave W. Corner of Elgin St. Int corridors. **Pets:** Large. $100 one-time fee/room. Service with restrictions, crate.
⊠ 🖪 🖵 ⇌ ⊠

(CAA) ▼▼▼ **Rideau Heights Motor Inn** Ⓜ
(613) 226-4152. **$99-$129.** 72 Rideau Heights Dr. Hwy 16 (Prince of Wales Dr), 0.3 mi (0.5 km) n of Hunt Club Rd. Ext corridors. **Pets:** Small. $10 daily fee/pet. Designated rooms, service with restrictions, supervision.
[SAVE] ⊠ 🖪 🖵

(CAA) ▼▼▼▼ **Sheraton Ottawa Hotel** 🅷
(613) 238-1500. **$149-$299.** 150 Albert St. Corner of O'Connor St. Int corridors. **Pets:** Accepted.
[SAVE] ⊠ 🖪 🖵 🍴 ⇌

(CAA) ▼▼▼▼ **Southway Inn of Ottawa** 🅷 🐾
(613) 737-0811. **$155-$170.** 2431 Bank St. On Hwy 31; corner of Hunt Club Rd. Int corridors. **Pets:** Medium, other species. $30 daily fee/pet. Designated rooms, service with restrictions, supervision.
[SAVE] ⊠ 🖪 🖵 🍴 ⇌ ⊠

(CAA) ▼▼ ▼ **Travelodge Ottawa East** 🅷
(613) 745-1133. **$109-$149.** 1486 Innes Rd. Hwy 417, exit 112 (Innes Rd), just e. Int corridors. **Pets:** Accepted.
[SAVE] ⊠ 🖪 🖵 🍴 ⇌

(CAA) ▼▼▼ **Travelodge Ottawa Hotel & Conference Centre** 🅷
(613) 722-7600. **$129-$149.** 1376 Carling Ave. Just e of jct Kirkwood Ave. Int corridors. **Pets:** Accepted.
[SAVE] ⊠ 🖪 🖵 🍴 ⊠

(AA) ▼▼ Webb's Motel M
(613) 728-1881. **$85-$125.** 1705 Carling Ave. Hwy 417, exit 126, 0.3 mi (0.5 km) n on Maitland Ave, then 0.3 mi (0.5 km) e. Ext/int corridors. **Pets:** Accepted.
SAVE ⊠ 🛏

▼▼ WelcomINNS H ❖
(613) 748-7800. **$105-$125.** 1220 Michael St. Hwy 417, exit 115 (St. Laurent Blvd), just ne. Int corridors. **Pets:** Medium. $20 deposit/room. Designated rooms, service with restrictions, supervision.
ASK ⊠ 🛏 💻 ⊠

(AA) ▼▼▼▼ The Westin Ottawa H
(613) 560-7000. **$179-$449.** 11 Colonel By Dr. Corner of Rideau St. Int corridors. **Pets:** Accepted.
SAVE ⊠ 💻 🍴 ≈ ⊠

END METROPOLITAN AREA

OWEN SOUND

▼▼ Comfort Inn H
(519) 371-5500. **$90-$200.** 955 9th Ave E. Jct Hwy 6, 10, 21 and 26. Int corridors. **Pets:** Other species. Service with restrictions, supervision.
ASK ⊠ 🛏 💻

▼▼▼▼ Days Inn and Conference Centre H
(519) 376-1551. **Call for rates.** 950 6th St E. Jct Hwy 6 and 10. Int corridors. **Pets:** Accepted.
⊠ 🛏 💻 🍴 ≈ ⊠

▼▼ Owen Sound Inn H
(519) 371-3011. **Call for rates.** 485 9th Ave E. Jct Hwy 6, 10, 26 and 21; follow Hwy 6 and 10, 0.6 mi (1 km) s. Int corridors. **Pets:** Accepted.
⊠ 🛏 💻

PARRY SOUND

▼▼ Comfort Inn H
(705) 746-6221. **Call for rates.** 120 Bowes St. Hwy 69, exit 224 (Bowes St), just w. Int corridors. **Pets:** Accepted.
⊠ 🛏 💻

▼▼ Microtel Inn & Suites H
(705) 746-2700. **Call for rates.** 292 Louisa St. Hwy 69, exit 224 (Bowes St), just w. Int corridors. **Pets:** Accepted.
⊠ 🛏 💻

▼▼ Resort Tapatoo H
(705) 378-2208. **Call for rates.** Otter Lake Rd. Hwy 69, exit 217, 3.9 mi (6.2 km) sw. Ext/int corridors. **Pets:** Accepted.
⊠ 🛏 💻 🍴 ≈ ⊠

PEMBROKE

▼ Colonial Fireside Inn M
(613) 732-3623. **$59-$120.** 1350 Pembroke St W. Jct Hwy 17, 3.1 mi (5 km) n on Forest Lea Rd, just e. Ext corridors. **Pets:** Accepted.
ASK ⊠ 🛏 💻 ≈

▼▼ Comfort Inn H ❖
(613) 735-1057. **$109-$225.** 959 Pembroke St E. 1 mi (1.6 km) e on Old Hwy 17. Int corridors. **Pets:** Designated rooms, service with restrictions, supervision.
ASK ⊠ 🛏 💻

PETAWAWA

(AA) ▼▼▼▼ Petawawa River Inn & Suites H
(613) 687-4686. **$110-$200.** 3520 Petawawa Blvd. Hwy 17, exit Paquette Rd, 1.5 mi (2.4 km) e, then just s. Int corridors. **Pets:** Large, other species. $10 daily fee/pet. Designated rooms, service with restrictions, supervision.
SAVE ⊠ 🛏 💻

PETERBOROUGH

▼▼ King Bethune House, Guest House & Spa BB ❖
(705) 743-4101. **$115-$399, 14 day notice.** 270 King St. From Charlotte and George sts (clock tower), 1 blk s on George St to King St, then just w. Int corridors. **Pets:** Other species. $25 daily fee/pet. Supervision.
⊠ 🛏 💻

▼▼▼ Motel 6–Peterborough H
(705) 748-0550. **$69-$109.** 133 Landsdowne St E. 1.6 mi (2.6 km) e of The Parkway. Int corridors. **Pets:** Medium. Designated rooms, service with restrictions, supervision.
ASK ⊠ 🛏

(AA) ▼▼ Quality Inn H
(705) 748-6801. **$92-$120.** 1074 Lansdowne St W. 1.9 mi (3 km) from jct Hwy 115. Int corridors. **Pets:** Other species. Designated rooms, service with restrictions, crate.
SAVE ⊠ 🛏 💻

PICKERING

▼▼ Comfort Inn H
(905) 831-6200. **$99-$165.** 533 Kingston Rd. Hwy 401, exit 394 N (White's Rd) to Hwy 2, 0.3 mi (0.5 km) w. Int corridors. **Pets:** Designated rooms, service with restrictions.
ASK ⊠ 🛏 💻

PLANTAGENET

▼▼ Motel de Champlain M
(613) 673-5220. **$64-$110.** 5999 Hwy 17. Jct CR 9. Ext/int corridors. **Pets:** Accepted.
ASK ⊠ 🛏 🍴

PORT CARLING

▼▼▼ Delta Sherwood Inn H
(705) 765-3131. **Call for rates.** 1090 Sherwood Rd. Hwy 169, just n of jct Hwy 118; on Lake Joseph. Ext/int corridors. **Pets:** Accepted.
⊠ 🛏 💻 🍴 ⊠

PORT HOPE

▼▼ Comfort Inn H
(905) 885-7000. **$109-$149.** Hwy 401 & 28. Hwy 401, exit 464, just n. Int corridors. **Pets:** Accepted.
ASK ⊠ 🛏 💻

PROVIDENCE BAY

(AA) ▼ Huron Sands Motel M
(705) 377-4616. **$80-$150, 3 day notice.** 5216 Hwy 551. In Providence Bay; on Hwy 551; centre. Ext corridors. **Pets:** $10 daily fee/room. Service with restrictions, supervision.
SAVE ⊠ 🛏 🐾

RENFREW

(CAA) ▽▽ Best Western-Renfrew Inn and Conference Centre H
(613) 432-8109. **$140-$165.** 760 Gibbons Rd. Hwy 17, exit O'Brien Rd. Int corridors. **Pets:** Accepted.
[SAVE] [✕] [🛏] [💻] [🍴] [🏊] [🐾]

▽ The Rocky Mountain Lodge M
(613) 432-5801. **Call for rates.** 409 Stewart St N. Jct Bruce St. Ext corridors. **Pets:** Accepted.
[✕] [🛏] [💻] [🍴]

ROSSPORT

▽▽ The Willows Inn Bed & Breakfast BB
(807) 824-3389. **$100-$110, 10 day notice.** 116 Main St. Centre. Int corridors. **Pets:** $15 one-time fee/room. Designated rooms, service with restrictions, supervision.
[✕] [K] [🐾]

ST. THOMAS

(CAA) ▽▽ Comfort Inn H
(519) 633-4082. **$100-$140.** 100 Centennial Ave. 4.1 mi (6.5 km) e on Hwy 3. Int corridors. **Pets:** Other species. $20 one-time fee/room. Service with restrictions, supervision.
[SAVE] [✕] [🛏] [💻]

SARNIA

▽▽▽ Holiday Inn Sarnia-Point Edward H
(519) 336-4130. **$115-$230.** 1498 Venetian Blvd. E of Bluewater Bridge. Int corridors. **Pets:** Other species. Designated rooms, service with restrictions, supervision.
[ASK] [✕] [🛏] [💻] [🍴] [🏊] [🐾]

▽▽ Super 8-Sarnia H
(519) 337-3767. **$85-$105.** 420 Christina St N. Between Exmouth and London rds. Ext/int corridors. **Pets:** Accepted.
[ASK] [✕] [⚙M] [🛏] [💻] [🍴]

SAULT STE. MARIE

▽ Adams Motel M
(705) 254-4345. **$69-$99.** 647 Great Northern Rd. 2.8 mi (4.4 km) n on Hwy 17B. Ext corridors. **Pets:** Accepted.
[ASK] [✕] [🛏] [💻]

(CAA) ▽▽▽ Algoma's Water Tower Inn H
(705) 949-8111. **$120-$155.** 360 Great Northern Rd. Jct Hwy 17 and Second Line. Int corridors. **Pets:** Accepted.
[SAVE] [✕] [🛏] [💻] [🍴] [🏊] [🐾]

▽ Ambassador Motel M
(705) 759-6199. **$59-$89.** 1275 Great Northern Rd. 4 mi (6.4 km) n on Hwy 17. Ext corridors. **Pets:** Accepted.
[✕] [🛏] [💻] [🏊] [🐾]

(CAA) ▽ Bel-Air Motel M
(705) 945-7950. **$55-$99.** 398 Pim St. 1.3 mi (2 km) n on Hwy 17B. Ext corridors. **Pets:** Small. $5 daily fee/pet. Designated rooms, no service.
[SAVE] [✕] [🛏] [💻]

(CAA) ▽ Catalina Motel M
(705) 945-9260. **$95-$140.** 259 Great Northern Rd. 2 mi (3.2 km) n on Hwy 17B. Ext corridors. **Pets:** $11 daily fee/pet. No service, crate.
[SAVE] [✕] [🛏] [💻]

(CAA) ▽▽ City Centre Travelodge H
(705) 759-1400. **$99-$139.** 332 Bay St. Opposite Station Mall. Int corridors. **Pets:** Medium. Designated rooms, service with restrictions, supervision.
[SAVE] [✕] [🛏] [💻] [🍴]

(CAA) ▽▽▽ Comfort Inn H
(705) 759-8000. **$105-$160.** 333 Great Northern Rd. 2.3 mi (3.6 km) n on Hwy 17B. Ext/int corridors. **Pets:** Large. $10 daily fee/pet. Designated rooms, service with restrictions, supervision.
[SAVE] [✕] [🛏] [💻]

▽▽ Glenview Cottages CA ❀
(705) 759-3436. **$109-$150.** 2611 Great Northern Rd. 6 mi (9.6 km) n on Hwy 17. Ext corridors. **Pets:** $10 daily fee/room. Designated rooms, crate.
[ASK] [✕] [🛏] [💻] [🏊] [🐾]

▽ Holiday Motel M
(705) 759-8608. **$55-$75.** 435 Trunk Rd. Jct Hwy 17 and 17B, just e. Ext corridors. **Pets:** Other species. Service with restrictions, supervision.
[✕] [🛏] [💻]

(CAA) ▽ Northlander Motel M
(705) 254-6452. **$55-$80.** 243 Great Northern Rd. 1.9 mi (3 km) n on Hwy 17B. Ext corridors. **Pets:** Other species. Service with restrictions, supervision.
[SAVE] [✕] [🛏] [💻]

▽ Satelite Motel M
(705) 759-2897. **$55-$95.** 248 Great Northern Rd. 1.9 mi (3 km) n on Hwy 17B. Ext corridors. **Pets:** Medium, other species. $4 daily fee/room. Service with restrictions, crate.
[✕] [🛏] [💻]

(CAA) ▽ Skyline Motel M
(705) 942-1240. **$65-$85, 5 day notice.** 232 Great Northern Rd. 1.9 mi (3 km) n on Hwy 17B. Ext corridors. **Pets:** Accepted.
[SAVE] [✕] [🛏] [💻]

▽▽ Sleep Inn H
(705) 253-7533. **$79-$139.** 727 Bay St. Between East and Church sts; downtown. Int corridors. **Pets:** Accepted.
[ASK] [✕] [🛏] [💻] [🐾]

(CAA) ▽▽▽ Super 8 H
(705) 254-6441. **$75-$135.** 184 Great Northern Rd. 1.3 mi (2 km) n on Hwy 17B. Int corridors. **Pets:** Accepted.
[SAVE] [✕] [🛏] [💻]

▽ Villa Inn Motel M
(705) 942-2424. **$55-$80.** 724 Great Northern Rd. 2.9 mi (4.6 km) n on Hwy 17B. Ext corridors. **Pets:** Other species. Service with restrictions.
[✕] [🛏] [💻]

SIMCOE

(CAA) ▽▽▽ Best Western Little River Inn H
(519) 426-2125. **$99-$260.** 203 Queensway W. Jct Hwy 24, just w on Hwy 3. Int corridors. **Pets:** Other species. Service with restrictions.
[SAVE] [✕] [🛏] [💻] [🍴] [🏊]

▽▽ Comfort Inn H
(519) 426-2611. **$94-$180.** 85 Queensway E. 0.3 mi (0.5 km) e on Hwy 3. Int corridors. **Pets:** Other species. Designated rooms, service with restrictions, supervision.
[ASK] [✕] [🛏] [💻]

SMITHS FALLS

(CAA) ▽▽ Best Western Colonel By Inn H
(613) 284-0001. **$80-$175.** 88 Lombard St. 1.2 mi (1.8 km) s on Hwy 15. Ext/int corridors. **Pets:** Other species. $10 daily fee/pet. Designated rooms, no service, supervision.
[SAVE] [✕] [🛏] [💻] [🏊]

SOUTH BAYMOUTH

(AA) ▼ **Huron Motor Lodge** 🄷
(705) 859-3131. **$95-$155.** 24 Water St N. In South Baymouth; centre; opposite ferry terminal. Ext corridors. **Pets:** Medium, other species. $10 daily fee/pet. Designated rooms, service with restrictions, supervision.
[SAVE] [✕] [🛆] [🕿] [Ⓧ] [☎]

STRATFORD

▼▼▼ **Arden Park Hotel** 🄷
(519) 275-2936. **$139-$199.** 552 Ontario (Hwy 7 & 8). Jct Romeo St. Int corridors. **Pets:** Accepted.
[✕] [⚹M] [🛆] [🕿] [🍴] [☎]

▼▼▼ **The River Garden Inn** 🄷
(519) 271-4650. **$95-$213.** 10 Romeo St N. Just n of Ontario St. Ext/int corridors. **Pets:** Small, dogs only. $45 one-time fee/room. Service with restrictions, supervision.
[✕] [🛆] [🕿] [☎]

STURGEON FALLS

▼▼▼ **Comfort Inn** 🄷
(705) 753-5665. **Call for rates.** 11 Front St. On Hwy 17 at western approach to town. Int corridors. **Pets:** Accepted.
[✕] [🛆] [🕿] [☎]

SUDBURY

(AA) ▼▼ **Best Western Downtown Sudbury Centre-Ville** 🄷
(705) 673-7801. **$110-$160.** 151 Larch St. Centre. Int corridors. **Pets:** Medium. $15 daily fee/pet. Service with restrictions, supervision.
[SAVE] [✕] [🛆] [🕿] [🍴]

(AA) ▼▼ **Comfort Inn** 🄷
(705) 522-1101. **$114-$164.** 2171 Regent St S. 3 mi (5 km) s on Hwy 46. Int corridors. **Pets:** Designated rooms, service with restrictions.
[SAVE] [✕] [🛆] [🕿]

(AA) ▼▼ **Comfort Inn East** 🄷
(705) 560-4502. **$109-$179.** 440 Second Ave N. Kingsway Hwy at Second Ave. Int corridors. **Pets:** Accepted.
[SAVE] [✕] [⚹M] [🛆] [🕿]

▼▼ **Days Inn-Sudbury** 🄷
(705) 674-7517. **$110-$150.** 117 Elm St. Centre of downtown. Int corridors. **Pets:** Medium. $20 daily fee/room. Designated rooms, service with restrictions, supervision.
[ASK] [✕] [🛆] [🕿] [🍴] [☎]

(AA) ▼▼▼▼ **Holiday Inn Hotel Sudbury** 🄷
(705) 522-3000. **$109-$152.** 1696 Regent St S. Hwy 69 (Regent St), just n of Paris St. Ext/int corridors. **Pets:** Accepted.
[SAVE] [✕] [🛆] [🕿] [🍴] [☎] [Ⓧ]

(AA) ▼▼▼ **Quality Inn & Conference Centre** 🄷
(705) 675-1273. **$114-$164, 30 day notice.** 390 Elgin St S. Jct Kingsway Hwy and Paris St, 0.3 mi (0.5 km) s, just e. Int corridors. **Pets:** Accepted.
[SAVE] [✕] [🛆] [🕿] [🍴] [☎]

▼▼▼ **Radisson Hotel, Sudbury** 🄷
(705) 675-1123. **$135-$175.** 85 St. Anne Rd. Jct St. Anne Rd and Notre Dame Ave; downtown. Int corridors. **Pets:** Accepted.
[ASK] [✕] [🛆] [🕿] [☎]

(AA) ▼▼ **Travelodge Hotel Sudbury** 🄷 🐾
(705) 522-1100. **$109-$189.** 1401 Paris St. 0.9 mi (1.5 km) n of jct Hwy 69 (Regent St). Int corridors. **Pets:** Other species. Designated rooms, service with restrictions.
[SAVE] [✕] [🛆] [🕿] [🍴] [☎]

THESSALON

(AA) ▼ **Carolyn Beach Motor Inn** 🄼
(705) 842-3330. **$92-$128.** 1 Lakeside Dr. Just w on Hwy 17; jct Hwy 17B. Ext corridors. **Pets:** $12 daily fee/pet. Service with restrictions, supervision.
[SAVE] [✕] [🛆] [🕿] [🍴] [Ⓧ]

THUNDER BAY

(AA) ▼▼ **Best Western Crossroads Motor Inn** 🄷
(807) 577-4241. **$129-$160, 3 day notice.** 655 W Arthur St. Jct Hwy 61, 17 and 11, just e. Int corridors. **Pets:** Accepted.
[SAVE] [✕] [🛆] [🕿]

(AA) ▼▼ **Best Western Nor'Wester Resort Hotel** 🄷
(807) 473-9123. **$119-$159, 3 day notice.** 2080 Hwy 61. 5.8 mi (9.2 km) sw of jct Hwy 11, 17 and 61, exit Loch Lomond Rd. Int corridors. **Pets:** Accepted.
[SAVE] [✕] [🛆] [🕿] [🍴] [🛆] [Ⓧ]

(AA) ▼▼ **Comfort Inn** 🄼
(807) 475-3155. **$95-$155.** 660 W Arthur St. Jct Hwy 11, 17 and 61, just e. Int corridors. **Pets:** Other species. Service with restrictions, supervision.
[SAVE] [✕] [🛆] [🕿]

(AA) ▼▼ **Super 8** 🄷
(807) 344-2612. **$80-$125.** 439 Memorial Ave. Jct Hwy 11, 17 and Harbour Expwy, 1.9 mi (3 km) e on Harbour Expwy, 1.3 mi (2 km) n. Int corridors. **Pets:** Accepted.
[SAVE] [✕] [🛆] [🕿]

▼▼ **Victoria Inn** 🄷
(807) 577-8481. **$115.** 555 W Arthur St. 0.5 mi (0.8 km) e of jct Hwy 11B, 17B and 61 (western access to town). Int corridors. **Pets:** Other species. $10 daily fee/pet. Service with restrictions, supervision.
[ASK] [✕] [🛆] [🕿] [🍴] [🛆] [Ⓧ]

TILLSONBURG

(AA) ▼▼ **Super 8-Tillsonburg** 🄷
(519) 842-7366. **$110-$140.** 92 Simcoe St. Hwy 19, just e. Int corridors. **Pets:** $10 daily fee/pet. Service with restrictions, supervision.
[SAVE] [✕] [🛆] [🕿] [🍴]

TIMMINS

▼▼ **Comfort Inn** 🄷
(705) 264-9474. **Call for rates.** 939 Algonquin Blvd E. Hwy 101, 0.3 mi (0.5 km) e of Hwy 655. Int corridors. **Pets:** Accepted.
[✕] [🛆] [🕿]

▼▼ **Travelodge** 🄷
(705) 360-1122. **Call for rates.** 1136 Riverside Dr. Hwy 101, 2.8 mi (4.4 km) w on Hwy 655. Int corridors. **Pets:** Accepted.
[✕] [🛆] [🕿]

TOBERMORY

▼ **Coach House Inn** 🄼
(519) 596-2361. **$59-$120.** 7189 Hwy 6. Hwy 6, 1.2 mi (2 km) s of ferry docks. Ext corridors. **Pets:** Accepted.
[✕] [🛆] [🕿] [Ⓧ] [☎]

TORONTO METROPOLITAN AREA

MARKHAM

▼▼▼ Comfort Inn ⊞
(905) 477-6077. **$109-$129.** 8330 Woodbine Ave. Hwy 401, exit 375, 5.6 mi (9 km) n; Hwy 404, exit Hwy 7, just e, then s. Int corridors. **Pets:** Accepted.
[ASK] [✕] [🛏] [💻] [≈] [✕]

▼▼▼ Delta Markham ⊞ ❖
(905) 477-2010. **$99-$199.** 50 E Valhalla Dr. Hwy 404, exit Hwy 7, then e. Int corridors. **Pets:** Medium, other species. $35 one-time fee/room. Crate.
[ASK] [✕] [🛏] [💻] [†] [≈] [✕]

CAA ▼▼▼ ▼▼▼ Hilton Suites Toronto/Markham Conference Centre & Spa ⊞
(905) 470-8500. **$129-$279.** 8500 Warden Ave. Hwy 404, exit Hwy 7, 2 mi (3.2 km) e. Int corridors. **Pets:** Medium, dogs only. $75 one-time fee/room. Service with restrictions, crate.
[SAVE] [✕] [🛏] [💻] [†] [≈] [✕]

CAA ▼▼▼ Holiday Inn Hotel & Suites-Markham ⊞
(905) 474-0444. **Call for rates.** 7095 Woodbine Ave. Just n of Steeles Ave. Int corridors. **Pets:** Accepted.
[SAVE] [✕] [🛏] [💻] [†] [≈]

▼▼▼ Homewood Suites by Hilton Toronto/Markham ⊞
(905) 477-4663. **$179.** 50 Bodrington Ct. Hwy 407, exit 84 (Woodbine Ave), just ne. Int corridors. **Pets:** Accepted.
[✕] [ᴸᴹ] [🛏] [💻] [≈]

CAA ▼▼▼ Howard Johnson Hotel Toronto-Markham ⊞
(905) 479-5000. **$99-$169.** 555 Cochrane Dr. Hwy 404 N, exit Hwy 7 E to E Valhalla Dr. Int corridors. **Pets:** $50 deposit/room. Service with restrictions, supervision.
[SAVE] [✕] [🛏] [💻] [†] [≈] [✕]

▼▼▼ Residence Inn by Marriott Toronto-Markham ⊞
(905) 707-7933. **$179-$189.** 55 Minthorn Blvd. Hwy 404, exit Hwy 7, 0.7 mi (1.1 km) w. Int corridors. **Pets:** Accepted.
[✕] [🛏] [💻] [≈] [✕]

▼▼▼ Staybridge Suites Toronto-Markham ⊞
(905) 771-9333. **$130-$184.** 355 S Park Rd. Hwy 404, exit Hwy 27, 0.9 mi (1.4 km) w, 0.3 mi (0.5 km) s on Commerce Valley Dr W, then just e. Int corridors. **Pets:** Medium, other species. $75 one-time fee/room. Service with restrictions, crate.
[ASK] [✕] [🛏] [💻] [≈]

RICHMOND HILL

CAA ▼▼▼ ▼▼▼ Sheraton Parkway Toronto North Hotel, Suites & Conference Centre ⊞
(905) 881-2121. **$109-$139.** 600 Hwy 7 E. Hwy 404, exit 27, 0.6 mi (1 km) w. Int corridors. **Pets:** Accepted.
[SAVE] [✕] [🛏] [💻] [†] [≈] [✕]

TORONTO

CAA ▼▼▼ Best Western Roehampton Hotel & Suites ⊞
(416) 487-5101. **$109-$159.** 808 Mt. Pleasant Rd. Just n of Eglinton Ave. Int corridors. **Pets:** Small. $35 one-time fee/room. Service with restrictions, supervision.
[SAVE] [✕] [🛏] [💻] [†] [≈]

▼▼ Carlingview Airport Inn ⊞
(416) 675-3303. **$95.** 221 Carlingview Dr. QEW, exit Hwy 427 N to Dixon Rd E, 0.6 mi (1 km) to Carlingview Dr, then just s. Ext/int corridors. **Pets:** $15 one-time fee/room. Designated rooms, service with restrictions, supervision.
[ASK] [✕] [🛏] [💻] [†]

CAA ▼▼▼ Comfort Inn ⊞
(416) 736-4700. **$100.** 66 Norfinch Dr. Hwy 400, exit Finch Ave E, just n. Int corridors. **Pets:** Accepted.
[SAVE] [✕] [🛏] [💻]

CAA ▼▼▼ Cosmopolitan Toronto Hotel & Spa ⊞
(416) 350-2000. **$179-$460.** 8 Colborne St. Between King and Wellington sts. Int corridors. **Pets:** Medium. $25 daily fee/room, $75 one-time fee/room. Service with restrictions, supervision.
[SAVE] [✕] [🛏] [💻] [†]

CAA ▼▼▼ Crowne Plaza Toronto Airport ⊞
(416) 675-1234. **$119-$184.** 33 Carlson Ct. Just w of jct Hwy 27, n of Dixon Rd. Int corridors. **Pets:** Accepted.
[SAVE] [✕] [🛏] [💻] [†] [≈] [✕]

CAA ▼▼▼ Crowne Plaza Toronto Don Valley ⊞ ❖
(416) 449-4111. **$114-$169.** 1250 Eglinton Ave E. Don Valley Pkwy, exit 375 (Wynford Dr). Int corridors. **Pets:** Medium. $25 deposit/pet. Service with restrictions, supervision.
[SAVE] [✕] [🛏] [💻] [†] [≈] [✕]

CAA ▼▼ Days Hotel & Conference Centre-Toronto Downtown ⊞
(416) 977-6655. **$119-$189.** 30 Carlton St. Adjacent to Maple Leaf Gardens. Int corridors. **Pets:** Accepted.
[SAVE] [✕] [🛏] [💻] [†] [≈] [✕]

CAA ▼▼▼ Delta Chelsea Hotel ⊞
(416) 595-1975. **$119-$429.** 33 Gerrard St W. Just w of Yonge St; just s of College St. Int corridors. **Pets:** Medium. $35 daily fee/room. Service with restrictions, supervision.
[SAVE] [✕] [🛏] [💻] [†] [≈] [✕]

▼▼▼ Delta Toronto East ⊞
(416) 299-1500. **$119-$299.** 2035 Kennedy Rd. Just ne of jct Hwy 401 and Kennedy Rd, exit 379. Int corridors. **Pets:** Small. $35 daily fee/pet. Designated rooms, service with restrictions, supervision.
[ASK] [✕] [🛏] [💻] [†] [≈] [✕]

CAA ▼▼▼ DoubleTree by Hilton Toronto Airport ⊞
(416) 244-1711. **$109-$209.** 655 Dixon Rd. Jct Hwy 27 N, just w of jct Hwy 401. Int corridors. **Pets:** Small. Service with restrictions, supervision.
[SAVE] [✕] [ᴸᴹ] [🛏] [💻] [†] [≈] [✕]

CAA ▼▼▼ The Fairmont Royal York ⊞ ❖
(416) 368-2511. **$189-$389.** 100 Front St W. QEW/Gardiner Expwy, exit n on York or Bay sts; entrance on Wellington St. Int corridors. **Pets:** $25 daily fee/room. Service with restrictions, crate.
[SAVE] [✕] [ᴸᴹ] [🛏] [💻] [†] [≈] [✕]

CAA ▼▼▼ Four Seasons Hotel ⊞ ❖
(416) 964-0411. **$345-$3900.** 21 Avenue Rd. Corner of Avenue Rd and Cumberland Ave. Int corridors. **Pets:** Large. Designated rooms, service with restrictions, supervision.
[SAVE] [✕] [🛏] [💻] [†] [≈] [✕]

▼▼▼ Gloucester Square Inns of Toronto BB
(416) 966-0013. **$159-$269, 14 day notice.** 512-514 Jarvis St. Jct Gloucester St. Int corridors. **Pets:** Accepted.
[ASK] [✕]

CAA ▼▼▼ Hilton Toronto ⊞
(416) 869-3456. **$209-$399.** 145 Richmond St W. Jct University Ave. Int corridors. **Pets:** Accepted.
[SAVE] [✕] [🛏] [💻] [†] [≈] [✕]

(CAA) ▼▼▼▼ Holiday Inn Express Toronto Downtown H
(416) 367-5555. **$119-$199.** 111 Lombard St. Gardiner Expwy, exit Jarvis St, 0.6 mi (1 km) n, then just w; between Adelaide and Richmond sts;. Int corridors. **Pets:** Small. Service with restrictions, supervision.
SAVE ✕ 🛏 🖃

(CAA) ▼▼▼▼ Holiday Inn Express Toronto-North York H
(416) 665-3500. **$119-$169.** 30 Norfinch Dr. Hwy 400, exit Finch Ave E. Int corridors. **Pets:** Large. $25 one-time fee/room. Service with restrictions, supervision.
SAVE ✕ ⚅ 🛏 🖃

▼▼▼▼ Hotel Le Germain Toronto H
(416) 345-9500. **Call for rates.** 30 Mercer St. Between John St and Blue Jays Way. Int corridors. **Pets:** Accepted.
✕ ⚅ 🖃 🍴

(CAA) ▼▼▼ ▼▼▼ InterContinental Toronto Centre H ❀
(416) 597-1400. **Call for rates.** 225 Front St W. Between Spadina and University aves. Int corridors. **Pets:** $50 one-time fee/room. Crate.
SAVE ✕ 🛏 🖃 🍴 🛥 ✕

(CAA) ▼▼▼ ▼▼▼ InterContinental Toronto Yorkville H ❀
(416) 960-5200. **$229-$3000.** 220 Bloor St W. Just w of Avenue Rd. Int corridors. **Pets:** $25 daily fee/pet, $50 one-time fee/pet. Designated rooms, supervision.
SAVE ✕ 🛏 🖃 🍴 🛥 ✕

(CAA) ▼▼▼ ▼▼▼ Le Meridien King Edward Hotel H ❀
(416) 863-9700. **$425.** 37 King St E. Just e of Yonge St. Int corridors. **Pets:** Large, other species. Service with restrictions.
SAVE ✕ 🛏 🍴

(CAA) ▼▼▼ Metropolitan Hotel H
(416) 977-5000. **$155-$285.** 108 Chestnut St. Just s of Dundas St. Int corridors. **Pets:** Medium. Supervision.
SAVE ✕ 🛏 🖃 🍴 🛥 ✕

▼▼ ▼▼ Montecassino Hotel & Event Venue H
(416) 630-8100. **$105-$145.** 3710 Chesswood Dr. Jct Sheppard Ave. Int corridors. **Pets:** Accepted.
ASK ✕ 🖃

(CAA) ▼▼▼▼ Novotel Toronto Centre H
(416) 367-8900. **$155-$335.** 45 The Esplanade. Just ne of Gardiner Expwy via Yonge St. Int corridors. **Pets:** Accepted.
SAVE ✕ 🛏 🖃 🍴 🛥 ✕

(CAA) ▼▼▼▼ Novotel Toronto North York H ❀
(416) 733-2929. **$145-$335.** 3 Park Home Ave. Hwy 401, exit Yonge St, 1.1 mi (1.7 km) n, then just w. Int corridors. **Pets:** Large, other species. Service with restrictions, supervision.
SAVE ✕ 🛏 🖃 🍴 🛥

(CAA) ▼▼▼ ▼▼▼ Pantages Hotel Toronto Centre H ❀
(416) 362-1777. **$179-$440.** 200 Victoria St. Jct Shuter St. Int corridors. **Pets:** Medium. $25 daily fee/room, $75 one-time fee/room. Service with restrictions, supervision.
SAVE ✕ 🛏 🖃 🍴

(CAA) ▼▼▼ ▼▼▼ Park Inn Toronto H
(416) 743-9997. **$89-$99.** 30 Vice Regent Blvd. Hwy 27, just s of Rexdale Blvd. Int corridors. **Pets:** Accepted.
SAVE ✕ 🛏 🖃

(CAA) ▼▼▼ ▼▼▼ Quality Hotel & Suites Toronto Airport East H
(416) 240-9090. **Call for rates.** 2180 Islington Ave. Hwy 401, exit 356, just s. Int corridors. **Pets:** $12 daily fee/pet. Designated rooms, service with restrictions, crate.
SAVE ✕ 🛏 🖃 🍴

(CAA) ▼▼▼▼ Quality Suites Toronto Airport H
(416) 674-8442. **$164-$187.** 262 Carlingview Dr. 0.6 mi (1 km) w of jct Hwy 27 N and Dixon Rd. Int corridors. **Pets:** Accepted.
SAVE ✕ 🛏 🖃 🍴

(CAA) ▼▼▼▼ Radisson Admiral Hotel Toronto-Harbourfront H
(416) 203-3333. **$159-$309.** 249 Queens Quay W. QEW E to Gardiner Expwy, exit Bay St S. Int corridors. **Pets:** Accepted.
SAVE ✕ 🛏 🖃 🍴 🛥

(CAA) ▼▼▼▼ Radisson Hotel Toronto East H
(416) 493-7000. **$149-$275.** 55 Hallcrown Pl. Hwy 401, exit Victoria Park N to Consumers Rd, then w. Int corridors. **Pets:** Small. $25 daily fee/pet. Designated rooms, service with restrictions, crate.
SAVE ✕ ⚅ 🛏 🖃 🍴 🛥

(CAA) ▼▼▼ ▼▼▼ Radisson Suite Hotel Toronto Airport H
(416) 242-7400. **$129-$189.** 640 Dixon Rd. Just e of jct Hwy 27; just w of jct Hwy 401. Int corridors. **Pets:** Small, other species. $7 daily fee/pet, $30 one-time fee/room. Designated rooms, service with restrictions, crate.
SAVE ✕ 🖃 🍴

(CAA) ▼▼▼ ▼▼▼ Renaissance Toronto Airport Hotel and Conference Centre H
(416) 675-6100. **$242-$296.** 801 Dixon Rd. Jct Hwy 27 N and Dixon Rd. Int corridors. **Pets:** Accepted.
SAVE ✕ ⚅ 🛏 🖃 🍴 🛥

(CAA) ▼▼▼ ▼▼▼ Renaissance Toronto Hotel Downtown H
(416) 341-7100. **$269-$329.** 1 Blue Jays Way. Jct Front St. Int corridors. **Pets:** $50 one-time fee/room. Service with restrictions, crate.
SAVE ✕ 🛏 🖃 🍴 🛥 ✕

▼▼▼ ▼▼▼ Residence Inn by Marriott Downtown Toronto/ Entertainment District H
(416) 581-1800. **$188-$230.** 255 Wellington St W. Jct Blue Jays Way. Int corridors. **Pets:** Accepted.
✕ 🛏 🖃 🛥

▼▼▼ ▼▼▼ Residence Inn by Marriott Toronto Airport H 🐾
(416) 798-2900. **$170-$208.** 17 Reading Ct. Just w of jct Hwy 27 and Dixon Rd. Int corridors. **Pets:** Small. $100 one-time fee/room. Designated rooms, service with restrictions, supervision.
✕ ⚅ 🛏 🖃 🛥 ✕

(CAA) ▼▼▼ ▼▼▼ The Sheraton Centre Toronto Hotel H ❀
(416) 361-1000. **$350-$459.** 123 Queen St W. Opposite Toronto Civic Centre and City Hall. Int corridors. **Pets:** Large, dogs only. Service with restrictions, supervision.
SAVE ✕ ⚅ 🛏 🖃 🍴 🛥 ✕

(CAA) ▼▼▼ ▼▼▼ SoHo Metropolitan Hotel H
(416) 599-8800. **$250-$895.** 318 Wellington St W. Jct Blue Jays Way. Int corridors. **Pets:** Accepted.
SAVE ✕ 🛏 🖃 🍴 🛥 ✕

(CAA) ▼▼▼ ▼▼▼ Super 8 Downtown Toronto H
(647) 426-8118. **$120-$240.** 222 Spadina Ave. At Dundas St; at Chinatown Center. Int corridors. **Pets:** Small. $15 daily fee/room. Service with restrictions, supervision.
SAVE ✕ 🛏 🖃

(CAA) ▼▼▼ ▼▼▼ The Sutton Place Hotel H
(416) 924-9221. **$174-$550.** 955 Bay St. Jct Wellesley St. Int corridors. **Pets:** Other species. $200 deposit/room, $50 one-time fee/room. Service with restrictions, crate.
SAVE ✕ 🛏 🖃 🍴 🛥 ✕

Toronto Airport Marriott Hotel [H]
(416) 674-9400. **$251-$307.** 901 Dixon Rd. Corner of Carlingview Dr. Int corridors. **Pets:** Small, dogs only. $30 one-time fee/room. Service with restrictions, supervision.

[SAVE] [X] [&M] [i] [=] [Y] [=] [X]

Toronto Marriott Bloor Yorkville [H]
(416) 961-8000. **$259-$309.** 90 Bloor St E. Just e of Yonge St. Int corridors. **Pets:** Accepted.

[SAVE] [X] [&M] [i] [=] [Y] [X]

Travelodge Hotel Toronto Airport (Dixon Road) [H]
(416) 674-2222. **$109-$189.** 925 Dixon Rd. Corner of Carlingview Dr. Int corridors. **Pets:** Accepted.

[SAVE] [X] [i] [=] [Y] [=]

Travelodge Toronto East [H]
(416) 299-9500. **Call for rates.** 20 Milner Business Ct. Jct Hwy 401 and Markham Rd, just n on Markham Rd. Int corridors. **Pets:** Accepted.

[SAVE] [X] [i] [=] [Y] [=]

Travelodge Toronto North (North York) [H] ✿
(416) 663-9500. **$109-$169.** 50 Norfinch Dr. Hwy 400, exit 25 (Finch Ave E). Int corridors. **Pets:** Large, other species. Designated rooms, service with restrictions.

[SAVE] [X] [i] [=] [Y] [=]

The Westin Bristol Place Toronto Airport [H]
(416) 675-9444. **$99-$390.** 950 Dixon Rd. 1.6 mi (2.6 km) w of jct Hwy 401. Int corridors. **Pets:** Accepted.

[SAVE] [X] [=] [Y] [=]

The Westin Harbour Castle [H] ✿
(416) 869-1600. **$319-$519.** One Harbour Sq. At the foot of Bay St; on shore of Lake Ontario. Int corridors. **Pets:** Medium. Service with restrictions.

[SAVE] [X] [i] [=] [X]

The Westin Prince Toronto [H]
(416) 444-2511. **$129-$429.** 900 York Mills Rd. Just s of Hwy 401 via Leslie St exit to York Mills Rd E. Int corridors. **Pets:** Accepted.

[SAVE] [X] [&M] [=] [Y] [=] [X]

Windsor Arms Hotel [H]
(416) 971-9666. **$295.** 18 St. Thomas St. Just s of Bloor St. Int corridors. **Pets:** Accepted.

[SAVE] [X] [Y] [=] [X]

VAUGHAN

Holiday Inn Express Hotel & Suites Vaughan-Southwest [H]
(905) 851-1510. **$142-$151.** 6100 Hwy 7. Jct Hwy 27. Int corridors. **Pets:** $25 one-time fee/room. Service with restrictions, crate.

[ASK] [X] [i] [=] [=]

Residence Inn by Marriott Toronto/Vaughan [H]
(905) 695-4002. **$179-$189.** 11 Interchange Way. Hwy 400 , exit 29 (Hwy 7), 0.6 mi (1 km) e. Int corridors. **Pets:** Accepted.

[X] [&M] [i] [=] [=] [X]

END METROPOLITAN AREA

TRENTON

Comfort Inn [H] ✿
(613) 965-6660. **$90-$160.** 68 Monogram Pl. Hwy 401, exit 526 (Glen Miller Rd), just s. Int corridors. **Pets:** Medium, other species. Designated rooms, service with restrictions, supervision.

[ASK] [X] [&M] [i] [=]

Holiday Inn Trenton [H]
(613) 394-4855. **$107-$130.** 99 Glen Miller Rd. Hwy 401, exit 526 (Glen Miller Rd), just s. Int corridors. **Pets:** Other species. $5 daily fee/room. Designated rooms, service with restrictions, supervision.

[SAVE] [X] [i] [=] [Y] [=]

Travelodge [H]
(613) 965-6789. **$90-$150.** 598 Old Hwy 2. Hwy 401, exit 538 (Wallbridge/ Loyalist Rd), 1.3 mi (2 km) s to Old Hwy 2, then 3.8 mi (6 km) w. Int corridors. **Pets:** Accepted.

[SAVE] [X] [i] [=]

TWEED

Park Place Motel [M]
(613) 478-3134. **$85-$110, 4 day notice.** 43 Victoria St. Hwy 37, 0.3 mi (0.5 km) s of centre. Ext corridors. **Pets:** Large. $10 daily fee/pet. Designated rooms, service with restrictions, supervision.

[ASK] [X] [i]

WALLACEBURG

Days Inn Wallaceburg [H]
(519) 627-0781. **Call for rates.** 76 McNaughton Ave. On Hwy 40 (McNaughton Ave), south side of town. Int corridors. **Pets:** Accepted.

[SAVE] [X] [i] [=]

WATERLOO

Comfort Inn [H]
(519) 747-9400. **$104-$179.** 190 Weber St N. Jct University Ave; just s. Int corridors. **Pets:** Accepted.

[SAVE] [X] [i] [=] [Y]

The Waterloo Inn Conference Hotel [H]
(519) 884-0220. **$179-$209.** 475 King St N. 1.9 mi (3 km) n on King St, jct Hwy 85. Int corridors. **Pets:** Large. $15 daily fee/pet. Designated rooms, service with restrictions, supervision.

[X] [&M] [i] [=] [Y] [=] [X]

WAWA

Best Northern [M]
(705) 856-7302. **$60-$95.** 150 Hwy 17 S. Hwy 17, 3.3 mi (5.3 km) s of jct Hwy 101. Ext corridors. **Pets:** Accepted.

[X] [i] [=] [Y] [X] [K]

The Mystic Isle Motel [M]
(705) 856-1737. **$70-$90.** 153 Hwy 17 S. On Hwy 17, 3.3 mi (5.2 km) s of jct Hwy 101. Ext corridors. **Pets:** Accepted.

[ASK] [X] [i] [=] [X] [K]

Northern Lights Motel & Breakfast [M] ✿
(705) 856-1900. **$79-$109.** 1014 Hwy 17. On Hwy 17, 5 mi (8 km) n of jct Hwy 101. Ext corridors. **Pets:** Other species. Supervision.

[SAVE] [X] [i] [=] [K]

Parkway Motel [M]
(705) 856-7020. **$89-$105.** 232 Hwy 17 S. Hwy 17, 2.5 mi (4 km) s of jct Hwy 101. Ext corridors. **Pets:** Large. $10 daily fee/room. Designated rooms, service with restrictions, supervision.

[SAVE] [X] [i] [=] [K]

▼ **Sportsman's Motel** Ⓜ
(705) 856-2272. **$85.** 171 Mission Rd. Hwy 101, 1.5 mi (2.4 km) e of jct Hwy 17. Ext corridors. **Pets:** $5 daily fee/room. Service with restrictions, supervision.
☒ ⊟ ⊑

WHITBY

ⒸⒶ ▼▼ **Canadiana Inn** Ⓜ
(905) 668-3686. **$75-$120.** 732 Dundas St E (Hwy 2). Hwy 401, exit 410 (Brock St/Hwy 12), 1 mi (1.6 km) n to Dundas St, then 0.6 mi (1 km) e. Ext corridors. **Pets:** Small, dogs only. Service with restrictions, supervision.
ⓈⒶⓋ ☒ ⊟ ⊑ ⌇

▼▼ **Motel 6 Whitby #1907** Ⓗ
(905) 665-8883. **$71-$85.** 165 Consumers Dr. Hwy 401, exit 410 (Brock St/Hwy 12), just ne. Int corridors. **Pets:** Other species. Service with restrictions, supervision.
☒ ⊟

ⒸⒶ ▼▼▼ **Quality Suites** Ⓗ
(905) 432-8800. **$119-$219, 10 day notice.** 1700 Champlain Ave. Hwy 401, exit 412 (Thickson Rd), 0.3 mi (0.5 km) n to Champlain Ave, then 0.6 mi (1 km) e. Int corridors. **Pets:** Accepted.
ⓈⒶⓋ ☒ ⊟ ⊑

ⒸⒶ ▼▼▼ **Residence Inn by Marriott** Ⓗ
(905) 444-9756. **$143-$175.** 160 Consumers Dr. Hwy 401, exit 410 (Brock St/Hwy 12). Int corridors. **Pets:** Medium, other species. Service with restrictions.
ⓈⒶⓋ ☒ ⓀⓂ ⊟ ⊑ ⌇

WIARTON

ⒸⒶ ▼▼ **Glen Miller Motel** Ⓜ
(519) 534-0175. **$70-$130.** 143 Hwy 6. 1.6 mi (2.5 km) n of town; centre. Ext corridors. **Pets:** Accepted.
ⓈⒶⓋ ☒ ⊟ ⊑ ⌧

WINDSOR

▼▼ **Comfort Inn** Ⓗ
(519) 966-7800. **$99-$139.** 2955 Dougall Ave. 3.3 mi (5.3 km) s on Hwy 3B, off Hwy 401 via Detroit-Windsor Tunnel exit. Int corridors. **Pets:** Accepted.
ⒶⓈⓀ ☒ ⊟ ⊑

▼▼ **Comfort Inn** Ⓗ
(519) 972-1331. **$99-$169, 14 day notice.** 2765 Huron Church Rd. West side of Huron Church Rd; 0.5 mi (0.8 km) s of EC Row Expwy. Int corridors. **Pets:** Medium. Service with restrictions, supervision.
ⒶⓈⓀ ☒ ⊟ ⊑ ⑪

ⒸⒶ ▼▼▼ **Comfort Suites Downtown** Ⓗ 🐾
(519) 971-0505. **$110-$170.** 500 Tuscarora St. Jct Glengarry and Wyandotte sts E. Int corridors. **Pets:** Medium, other species. $20 daily fee/pet. Service with restrictions, supervision.
ⓈⒶⓋ ☒ ⊟ ⊑

▼▼▼ **Hampton Inn and Suites** Ⓗ
(519) 972-0770. **$139-$194.** 1840 Huron Church Rd. 0.9 mi (1.5 km) n of EC Row Expwy. Int corridors. **Pets:** Accepted.
☒ ⓀⓂ ⊟ ⊑ ⌇

ⒸⒶ ▼▼▼ **Hilton Windsor** Ⓗ
(519) 973-5555. **$129-$249.** 277 Riverside Dr W. 0.6 mi (1 km) w of Detroit-Windsor Tunnel; 0.6 mi (1 km) e of Ambassador Bridge; downtown. Int corridors. **Pets:** Accepted.
ⓈⒶⓋ ☒ ⊑ ⑪ ⌇ ⌧

▼▼▼▼ **Holiday Inn Downtown Windsor** Ⓗ
(519) 256-4656. **$129-$299.** 430 Ouellette Ave. 0.3 mi (0.5 km) s of Riverside Dr at Park St W. Int corridors. **Pets:** Accepted.
 ⒶⓈⓀ ☒ ⓀⓂ ⊟ ⊑ ⑪ ⌇

ⒸⒶ ▼▼▼ **Holiday Inn Windsor (Ambassador Bridge)** Ⓗ 🐾
(519) 966-1200. **$135-$169.** 1855 Huron Church Rd. Jct Huron Church and Malden rds; 0.9 mi (1.5 km) n of EC Row Expwy. Int corridors. **Pets:** Other species. Service with restrictions, crate.
ⓈⒶⓋ ☒ ⊟ ⊑ ⑪ ⌇ ⌧

ⒸⒶ ▼▼▼ **Ivy Rose Motor Inn Ltd.** Ⓜ
(519) 966-1700. **$74-$99.** 2885 Howard Ave. 3 mi (4.8 km) s of downtown; just n of Devonshire Shopping Mall. Ext corridors. **Pets:** Accepted.
ⓈⒶⓋ ☒ ⊟ ⑪ ⌇

ⒸⒶ ▼▼▼ **Quality Suites Windsor** Ⓗ 🐾
(519) 977-9707. **$129-$249.** 250 Dougall Ave. Jct Chatham St; downtown. Int corridors. **Pets:** Service with restrictions, supervision.
ⓈⒶⓋ ☒ ⓀⓂ ⊟ ⊑

ⒸⒶ ▼▼▼ **Radisson Riverfront Hotel** Ⓗ 🐾
(519) 977-9777. **$139-$199.** 333 Riverside Dr W. 0.6 mi (1 km) w of Detroit-Windsor Tunnel; 0.6 mi (1 km) e of Ambassador Bridge; downtown. Int corridors. **Pets:** Medium, other species. Service with restrictions, crate.
ⓈⒶⓋ ☒ ⊟ ⊑ ⑪ ⌇ ⌧

ⒸⒶ ▼▼▼ **Travelodge Hotel Downtown Windsor** Ⓗ
(519) 258-7774. **$119-$169.** 33 Riverside Dr E. Jct Ouellette Ave; downtown. Int corridors. **Pets:** Medium. Service with restrictions, supervision.
ⓈⒶⓋ ☒ ⊟ ⊑ ⌇

ⒸⒶ ▼▼▼ **Travelodge Windsor Ambassador Bridge** Ⓗ
(519) 972-1100. **$92-$125.** 2330 Huron Church Rd. N of EC Row Expwy. Int corridors. **Pets:** Medium. Service with restrictions, supervision.
ⓈⒶⓋ ☒ ⊟ ⊑ ⌇

WOODSTOCK

ⒸⒶ ▼▼▼ **Quality Hotel and Suites** Ⓗ
(519) 537-5586. **$89-$269.** 580 Bruin Blvd. Hwy 401, exit 232, just n; w of Hwy 59. Int corridors. **Pets:** Other species. Service with restrictions, crate.
ⓈⒶⓋ ☒ ⊟ ⊑ ⑪ ⌇ ⌧

▼▼ **Super 8** Ⓗ
(519) 421-4588. **Call for rates.** 560 Norwich Ave. Jct Hwy 401 and 59, exit 232, just n. Int corridors. **Pets:** Accepted.
☒ ⊟ ⊑

PRINCE EDWARD ISLAND

ALBERTON

▼▼ Briarwood Inn, Cottages & Lodge M
(902) 853-2518. **$60-$125.** 253 Matthews Ln. 1.9 mi (3 km) e on Rt 12. Ext/int corridors. **Pets:** Accepted.
[ASK] [✕] [🛏] [💻] [🐾]

CAVENDISH

▼▼ Bay Vista Motel M
(902) 963-2225. **$59-$125.** 9517 Cavendish Rd. Jct Rt 13, 2.8 mi (4.8 km) w on Rt 6. Ext corridors. **Pets:** Small. Designated rooms, service with restrictions, supervision.
[✕] [🛏] [🌊] [🏊]

▼▼ Cavendish Bosom Buddies Cottages & Suites CA
(902) 963-3449. **$85-$295, 14 day notice.** RR 1. Jct Rt 6 and 13, 0.4 mi (0.7 km) e on Rt 6. Ext corridors. **Pets:** $10 deposit/pet. Supervision.
[✕] [🛏] [💻] [🌊] [🏊]

CAA ▼▼▼ Cavendish Maples Cottages CA
(902) 963-2818. **$75-$295, 30 day notice.** 73 Avonlea Blvd. Jct Rt 6 and 13, 1.5 mi (2.5 km) w on Rt 6. Ext corridors. **Pets:** Accepted.
[SAVE] [✕] [🛏] [💻] [🌊] [🏊]

CHARLOTTETOWN

CAA ▼▼▼ Best Western Charlottetown H ❀
(902) 892-2461. **$99-$209.** 238 Grafton St. Centre. Int corridors. **Pets:** Medium, other species. Designated rooms, service with restrictions, supervision.
[SAVE] [✕] [⛑M] [🛏] [💻] [🍴] [🌊] [🏊]

▼▼ Comfort Inn H
(902) 566-4424. **$110-$190.** 112 Trans-Canada Hwy 1. Trans-Canada Hwy 1, 2.8 mi (4.5 km) w. Int corridors. **Pets:** Other species. Service with restrictions, supervision.
[ASK] [✕] [🛏] [💻]

CAA ▼▼▼ Delta Prince Edward H
(902) 566-2222. **$115-$318.** 18 Queen St. At Water and Queen sts. Int corridors. **Pets:** Accepted.
[SAVE] [✕] [💻] [🍴] [🌊] [🏊]

▼▼ Econo Lodge M
(902) 368-1110. **$89-$199.** 20 Lower Malpeque Rd. Jct Trans-Canada Hwy 1 and Lower Malpeque Rd, 2.8 mi (4.5 km) w. Ext/int corridors. **Pets:** Accepted.
[ASK] [✕] [🛏] [💻] [🌊]

CAA ▼▼▼ Holiday Inn Express Hotel & Suites Charlottetown H ❀
(902) 892-1201. **$99-$319.** 200 Trans-Canada Hwy. On Trans-Canada Hwy 1, 3 mi (5 km) w. Int corridors. **Pets:** Other species.
[SAVE] [✕] [⛑M] [🛏] [💻] [🌊]

▼▼▼ Quality Inn on the Hill H
(902) 894-8572. **$119-$273.** 150 Euston St. Just e of University Ave. Int corridors. **Pets:** Accepted.
[ASK] [✕] [🛏] [💻] [🍴]

▼▼▼ Rodd Charlottetown-A Rodd Signature Hotel H
(902) 894-7371. **$117-$232.** 75 Kent St. Corner of Kent and Pownal sts. Int corridors. **Pets:** Large, other species. $10 daily fee/room. Designated rooms, service with restrictions.
[ASK] [✕] [🛏] [💻] [🍴] [🌊] [🏊]

▼▼ Rodd Confederation Inn & Suites M
(902) 892-2481. **$81-$141.** Trans-Canada Hwy 1. On Trans-Canada Hwy 1, 2.5 mi (4 km) w. Ext/int corridors. **Pets:** Other species. $10 daily fee/room. Service with restrictions, supervision.
[ASK] [✕] [🛏] [💻] [🍴] [🌊]

▼▼ Rodd Royalty Inn & Suites H
(902) 894-8566. **$102-$180.** Intersection Hwy 1 & 2. 2.5 mi (4 km) w on Trans-Canada Hwy 1. Ext/int corridors. **Pets:** Medium. $10 daily fee/room. Designated rooms, service with restrictions.
[ASK] [✕] [🛏] [💻] [🍴] [🌊]

CORNWALL

▼▼▼ Howard Johnson Hotel H
(902) 566-2211. **$89-$170.** 100 Trans-Canada Hwy. On Hwy 1, 4.3 mi (7 km) w of Charlottetown. Ext/int corridors. **Pets:** Accepted.
[ASK] [✕] [🛏] [💻] [🍴] [🌊] [🏊]

▼▼ Sunny King Motel M
(902) 566-2209. **$54-$116, 3 day notice.** Trans-Canada Hwy. On Hwy 1; centre. Ext corridors. **Pets:** Accepted.
[✕] [🛏] [💻] [🌊] [🏊]

CAA ▼▼▼ Super 8 H
(902) 892-7900. **$89-$160.** 15 York Point Rd. On Hwy 1, 3.7 mi (6 km) w of Charlottetown. Int corridors. **Pets:** Accepted.
[SAVE] [✕] [🛏] [💻] [🌊]

MAYFIELD

▼▼ Cavendish Gateway Resort by Clarion Collection M
(902) 963-2213. **$99-$199.** 6596 Rt 13. On Rt 13, 3.6 mi (6 km) w of Cavendish; centre. Ext/int corridors. **Pets:** Accepted.
[ASK] [✕] [🛏] [💻] [🌊]

MORELL

CAA ▼▼▼▼ Rodd Crowbush Golf & Beach Resort H
(902) 961-5600. **$151-$283, 3 day notice.** Rt 350 Lakeside. 3 mi (5 km) w on Rt 2, follow signs. Ext/int corridors. **Pets:** Accepted.
[SAVE] [✕] [🛏] [💻] [🍴] [🌊] [🏊]

RICHMOND

CAA ▼▼▼ Caernarvon Cottages & Gardens CA
(902) 854-3418. **$80-$125, 30 day notice.** 4697 Hwy 12, RR 1. Jct Hwy 2 and Rt 131, 6 mi (10 km) e. Ext/int corridors. **Pets:** No service, supervision.
[SAVE] [🛏] [💻] [🐾]

ROSENEATH

▼▼▼ Rodd Brudenell River-A Rodd Signature Resort H
(902) 652-2332. **$140-$249, 3 day notice.** Rt 3. Jct Rt 4, 3.3 mi (5.5 km) e. Ext/int corridors. **Pets:** Other species. $10 daily fee/room. Service with restrictions, supervision.
[ASK] [✕] [🛏] [💻] [🍴] [🌊] [🏊]

ST. PETERS

ⓐ ◈◈◈◈ The Inn at St. Peters 🆑 ❀
(902) 961-2135. **$255-$330, 7 day notice.** 1668 Greenwich Rd. Jct Rt 16 and 313, 0.6 mi (1 km) w on Rt 313. Ext corridors. **Pets:** Large. Service with restrictions.

🆂🅰🆅🅴 ☒ ⭫ 🍴 ▤ 🖥 🍴

SUMMERSIDE

◈◈◈ Econo Lodge 🅷
(902) 436-9100. **$90-$155.** 80 All Weather Hwy. Jct Hwy 1A and 2, 3.1 mi (5 km) w on Hwy 2. Int corridors. **Pets:** Accepted.

🅰🆂🅺 ☒ ⭫ 🖥 🍴 ⊶

ⓐ ◈◈◈ Quality Inn & Suites 🅷
(902) 436-2295. **$89-$279.** 618 Water St. 1 mi (1.6 km) e on Hwy 11. Ext/int corridors. **Pets:** $10 one-time fee/pet. Designated rooms, no service, supervision.

🆂🅰🆅🅴 ☒ ⭫ 🖥 ⊶ ⊠

ⓐ ◈◈◈ Slemon Park Hotel & Conference Centre 🅷
(902) 432-1780. **$99-$121.** 12 Redwood Ave. On Rt 2, 3 mi (5 km) w at Summerside Airport. Int corridors. **Pets:** Small. $150 deposit/room. Designated rooms, service with restrictions, crate.

🆂🅰🆅🅴 ☒ ⭫ 🍴 ⭫ 🖥 🍴

WOODSTOCK

◈◈◈ Rodd Mill River Resort 🅷
(902) 859-3555. **$102-$164, 3 day notice.** Rt 136. On Rt 136, just e of jct Rt 2. Int corridors. **Pets:** Accepted.

🅰🆂🅺 ☒ ⭫ 🖥 🍴 ⊶ ⊠

CITY INDEX

ALMA

🔷🔷 Comfort Inn 🅷
(418) 668-9221. **Call for rates.** 870 ave du Pont S. On Hwy 169; centre of town. Int corridors. **Pets:** Accepted.
⊠ 🔋 💻

BAIE-COMEAU

🔷🔷 Comfort Inn 🅷
(418) 589-8252. **$117-$131.** 745 boul Lafleche. On Rt 138. Int corridors. **Pets:** Accepted.
ASK ⊠ 🔋 💻

🔷🔷 Econo Lodge Baie-Comeau Ⓜ
(418) 589-7835. **Call for rates.** 1060 boul Lafleche. On Rt 138; centre. Ext corridors. **Pets:** Designated rooms, service with restrictions, supervision.
⊠ 🔋 💻

🔷🔷🔷 Hotel Le Manoir 🅷 🐾
(418) 296-3391. **$109-$119.** 8 ave Cabot. Rt 138, 2.6 mi (4.4 km) e, follow signs. Int corridors. **Pets:** Large. Designated rooms, service with restrictions, crate.
ASK ⊠ 💻 🍽 🏊

BAIE-ST-PAUL

Ⓒ 🔷🔷 Hotel Baie-Saint-Paul 🅷
(418) 435-3683. **Call for rates.** 911 boul Mgr-de-Laval. On Rt 138, 0.3 mi (0.5 km) e of Rt 362. Int corridors. **Pets:** Accepted.
SAVE ⊠ 🔋 💻 🍽 🏊

BERTHIERVILLE

🔷🔷 Days Inn Berthierville 🅷 🐾
(450) 836-1621. **$75-$165, 7 day notice.** 760 rue Gadoury. Hwy 40, exit 144. Ext/int corridors. **Pets:** Other species. $10 daily fee/room. Designated rooms, service with restrictions, supervision.
ASK ⊠ 🔋 💻

BROMONT

🔷🔷 Hotel Le Menhir 🅷
(450) 534-3790. **$98-$195.** 125 boul Bromont. Hwy 10, exit 78, 1.6 mi (2.7 km) s. Ext/int corridors. **Pets:** Accepted.
ASK ⊠ 🔋 💻 🍽 🏊

CARLETON-ST-OMER

🔷🔷 Hostellerie Baie Bleue Ⓜ
(418) 364-3355. **$70-$133.** 482 boul Perron. On Hwy 132. Ext corridors. **Pets:** Accepted.
ASK ⊠ 🔋 💻 🍽 🏊 🏊

CHICOUTIMI

Ⓒ 🔷🔷🔷 Centre de Congres et Hotel La Sagueneenne 🅷 🐾
(418) 545-8326. **$118-$172.** 250 des Sagueneens. Just w of jct Rt 175 (boul Talbot); in Saguenay sector. Int corridors. **Pets:** Small. $25 one-time fee/room. Designated rooms, service with restrictions, supervision.
SAVE ⊠ 🔋M 🔋 💻 🍽 🏊 🏊

🔷🔷 Comfort Inn 🅷
(418) 693-8686. **Call for rates.** 1595 boul Talbot. Jct Rt 170, 1.8 mi (2.8 km) n. Int corridors. **Pets:** Accepted.
⊠ 🔋 💻

COWANSVILLE

🔷🔷 Days Inn-Cowansville 🅷
(450) 263-7331. **$99-$134.** 111 Place Jean-Jacques Bertrand. Hwy 10, exit 68, 9.9 mi (15.9 km) s on Rt 139. Int corridors. **Pets:** Accepted.
ASK ⊠ 🔋 💻 🍽

DRUMMONDVILLE

Ⓒ 🔷🔷🔷 Best Western Hotel Universel 🅷
(819) 478-4971. **$115-$160.** 915 rue Hains. Hwy 20, exit 177, just s on boul St-Joseph, then just e. Int corridors. **Pets:** Other species. Designated rooms, supervision.
SAVE ⊠ 🔋 💻 🍽 🏊

🔷🔷 Comfort Inn 🅷
(819) 477-4000. **Call for rates.** 1055 rue Hains. Hwy 20, exit 177, 0.3 mi (0.5 km) s on boul St-Joseph, then just w. Int corridors. **Pets:** Accepted.
⊠ 🔋 💻

🔷🔷🔷 Quality Suites 🅷
(819) 472-2700. **$110-$220.** 2125 rue Canadien. Hwy 20, exit 175, just s. Int corridors. **Pets:** $25 one-time fee/room. Designated rooms, service with restrictions, supervision.
ASK ⊠ 🔋 💻 🏊

FORESTVILLE

🔷🔷 Econo Lodge Ⓜ
(418) 587-2278. **$89-$109.** 5 Rt 138 est. On Rt 138; centre. Ext/int corridors. **Pets:** Small. Supervision.
ASK ⊠ 🔋 💻 🍽

GATINEAU

Ⓒ 🔷🔷 Comfort Inn Gatineau 🅷
(819) 243-6010. **$101-$179.** 630 boul La Gappe. Hwy 50, exit 140, 1.1 mi (1.9 km) e. Int corridors. **Pets:** Other species. $25 one-time fee/room. Designated rooms, service with restrictions, supervision.
SAVE ⊠ 💻

(AA) ▼▼▼▼ Four Points by Sheraton Hotel & Conference Centre Gatineau-Ottawa ⬚
(819) 778-6111. **$99-$180.** 35 rue Laurier. Corner of rue Victoria, across from Canadian Museum of Civilization; in Hull sector. Int corridors. **Pets:** Service with restrictions, crate.
[SAVE] ⊠ 🔒 💻 🍴 ⊇

(AA) ▼▼▼▼▼▼ Hilton Lac Leamy ⬚
(819) 790-6444. **$190-$340.** 3 boul du Casino. In Casino du Lac Leamy; in Hull sector. Int corridors. **Pets:** Accepted.
[SAVE] ⊠ [🏋M] 🔒 💻 🍴 ⊇ ⊠

(AA) ▼▼▼▼▼▼ Holiday Inn Plaza La Chaudiere Gatineau-Ottawa ⬚
(819) 778-3880. **Call for rates.** 2 rue Montcalm. 0.5 mi (0.8 km) w of Portage Bridge at Rt 148 and rue Montcalm; in Hull sector. Int corridors. **Pets:** Accepted.
[SAVE] ⊠ 🔒 💻 🍴 ⊇ ⊠

GRENVILLE-SUR-LA-ROUGE

(AA) ▼▼▼▼▼▼ Hotel du Lac Carling ⬚
(450) 533-9211. **Call for rates.** 2255 Rt 327 nord. 3.1 mi (5 km) n. Int corridors. **Pets:** Accepted.
[SAVE] ⊠ 🔒 💻 🍴 ⊇ ⊠

LAC-BROME (KNOWLTON)

▼▼▼ Auberge Knowlton ⬤
(450) 242-6886. **$130-$160.** 286 chemin Knowlton. Corner of Hwy 104 and Rt 243; centre. Int corridors. **Pets:** Accepted.
⊠ 🍴

(AA) ▼▼▼▼ Auberge Quilliams Inn ⬤
(450) 243-0404. **$159-$350, 3 day notice.** 572 chemin Lakeside. Hwy 10, exit 90, 3.1 mi (4.9 km) s on Rt 243. Int corridors. **Pets:** Medium. $10 daily fee/room. Service with restrictions.
[SAVE] ⊠ 🔒 💻 🍴 ⊇ ⊠

LA MALBAIE

(AA) ▼▼▼▼▼▼ Fairmont Le Manoir Richelieu ⬚
(418) 665-3703. **$139-$269.** 181 rue Richelieu. On Rt 362, 2.6 mi (4.1 km) w of jct Rt 138. Int corridors. **Pets:** Accepted.
[SAVE] ⊠ 🔒 💻 🍴 ⊇ ⊠

▼▼▼▼ La Pinsonniere ⬤
(418) 665-4431. **$285-$485, 15 day notice.** 124 rue St-Raphael. Just off Rt 138, follow signs; in Cap-a-L'Aigle sector. Int corridors. **Pets:** Dogs only. $15 daily fee/pet. Designated rooms, supervision.
⊠ 💻 🍴 ⊇ ⊠

LA POCATIERE

▼▼ Motel Le Pocatois ⓜ
(418) 856-1688. **Call for rates.** 235 Rt 132. Hwy 20, exit 439, 0.5 mi (0.8 km) s. Ext/int corridors. **Pets:** Accepted.
⊠ 🔒 💻 🍴

LOUISEVILLE

▼▼▼ Gite du Carrefour et Maison historique J.L.L. Hamelin 🅱🅱
(819) 228-4932. **$65-$90 (no credit cards), 15 day notice.** 11 ave St-Laurent ouest. On Rt 138; Hwy 40, exit 174 westbound; exit 166 eastbound; centre. Int corridors. **Pets:** Very small. No service, supervision.
⊠ [✗] [✗] ⊇

MONTEBELLO

(AA) ▼▼▼▼▼▼ Fairmont Le Chateau Montebello ⬚
(819) 423-6341. **$199-$289, 3 day notice.** 392 rue Notre-Dame. On Rt 148. Int corridors. **Pets:** $35 daily fee/pet. Service with restrictions, supervision.
[SAVE] ⊠ 🔒 💻 🍴 ⊇ ⊠

MONTMAGNY

▼▼▼ Manoir des Erables ⬤
(418) 248-0100. **$89-$250, 10 day notice.** 220 boul Tache est (Rt 132). Hwy 20, exit 376, 1.4 mi (2.2 km) e on Rt 228, 0.9 mi (1.5 km) e. Ext/int corridors. **Pets:** $35 daily fee/room. Designated rooms, service with restrictions.
⊠ 💻 🍴 ⊇ ⊠

MONTREAL METROPOLITAN AREA

BROSSARD

▼▼▼▼▼ Alt Hotel Quartier Dix 30 ⬚
(450) 443-1030. **$129-$149.** 6500 boul de Rome. Jct Hwy 10 and 30, just w on Hwy 30, exit boul de Rome; in Quartier Dix 30 Mall. Int corridors. **Pets:** Accepted.
⊠ 💻

▼▼ Comfort Inn ⬚
(450) 678-9350. **$100-$122.** 7863 boul Taschereau. Rt 134, 0.9 mi (1.5 km) w of Hwy 10, exit boul Taschereau ouest. Int corridors. **Pets:** Accepted.
[ASK] ⊠ 🔒 💻

▼▼ Econo Lodge Montreal–Brossard ⓜ
(450) 466-2186. **$90-$165.** 8350 boul Taschereau. Rt 134, 1.4 mi (2.3 km) w of Hwy 10, exit boul Taschereau ouest. Ext/int corridors. **Pets:** Very small. $10 daily fee/pet. Service with restrictions, supervision.
[ASK] ⊠ 🔒 💻

DORVAL

(AA) ▼▼▼▼ aloft Montreal Airport ⬚ ❀
(514) 633-0900. **Call for rates.** 500 boul McMillan. Just n of Hwy 520 on north side service road at airport entrance. Int corridors. **Pets:** Medium. Service with restrictions, supervision.
[SAVE] ⊠ [🏋M] 🔒 💻 ⊇

(AA) ▼▼▼ Comfort Inn Dorval ⬚
(514) 636-3391. **$121-$158.** 340 ave Michel-Jasmin. Hwy 520, exit 2 eastbound; exit 1 westbound, just e along service road to ave Marshall, follow to ave Michel-Jasmin. Int corridors. **Pets:** Accepted.
[SAVE] ⊠ 🔒 💻

(AA) ▼▼▼▼ Hampton Inn & Suites ⬚
(514) 633-8243. **$225.** 1900 Rt Transcanadienne (Hwy 40). Hwy 40, exit 55, 0.5 mi (0.8 km) e of boul des Sources on south side service road. Int corridors. **Pets:** Accepted.
[SAVE] ⊠ [🏋M] 🔒 💻 ⊇

(AA) ▼▼▼▼ Hilton Montreal Aeroport ⬚
(514) 631-2411. **$195-$215.** 12505 boul Cote-de-Liesse. Just n of Hwy 520 on northside service road at airport entrance. Int corridors. **Pets:** Accepted.
[SAVE] ⊠ [🏋M] 🔒 💻 🍴 ⊇ ⊠

(AA) ▼▼▼ Travelodge Aeroport Montreal-Trudeau Airport ⬚
(514) 631-4537. **$99-$225, 4 day notice.** 1010 chemin Herron. Hwy 20, exit 54 westbound, just s on boul Fenelon to ave Dumont, follow to chemin Herron; exit 56 eastbound, 1.1 mi (1.7 km) along service road. Int corridors. **Pets:** $100 deposit/room. Designated rooms, service with restrictions, supervision.
[SAVE] ⊠ 🔒 💻 ⊠

LAVAL

⊛ ▼▼▼▼ Best Western Chateauneuf Laval 🄷
(450) 681-9000. **$100-$199.** 3655 Autoroute des Laurentides. Hwy 15, exit 10, just n on east side service road. Int corridors. **Pets:** Service with restrictions, supervision.
SAVE ⊠ 🛏 🖥 🍴 ⇝

▼▼ Comfort Inn 🄷
(450) 686-0600. **$109-$139.** 2055 Autoroute des Laurentides. Hwy 15, exit 8 (boul St-Martin), e on boul St-Martin, 0.4 mi (0.7 km) n on boul Le Corbusier, then w on boul Tessier. Int corridors. **Pets:** Medium. Designated rooms, service with restrictions, supervision.
ASK ⊠ 🛏 🖥 🍴

▼▼ Econo Lodge 🄷
(450) 681-6411. **$74-$124.** 1981 boul Cure-Labelle. Hwy 15, exit 8 (boul St-Martin) northbound; exit 10 southbound, 1.3 mi (2 km) w on boul St-Martin ouest, then 0.3 mi (0.5 km) n. Ext/int corridors. **Pets:** Accepted.
ASK ⊠ ⇝

⊛ ▼▼▼▼ Hampton Inn & Suites-Laval 🄷
(450) 687-0010. **$129-$149.** 1961 boul Cure-Labelle. Hwy 15, exit 8 (boul St-Martin) northbound; exit 10 southbound, 1.4 mi (2.3 km) w on boul St-Martin ouest, then just n. Int corridors. **Pets:** Small. Service with restrictions, supervision.
SAVE ⊠ 🛏 🖥 ⇝

⊛ ▼▼▼ Quality Suites Laval 🄷
(450) 686-6777. **$125-$159.** 2035 Autoroute des Laurentides. Hwy 15, exit 8 (boul St-Martin), 0.4 mi (0.7 km) n on boul Le Corbusier, w on boul Tessier. Int corridors. **Pets:** Medium. Designated rooms, service with restrictions, supervision.
SAVE ⊠ 🛏 🖥

⊛ ▼▼▼▼ Sheraton Laval Hotel 🄷 ❀
(450) 687-2440. **$129-$520.** 2440 Autoroute des Laurentides. Hwy 15, exit 10. Int corridors. **Pets:** Medium, dogs only. Designated rooms, service with restrictions, supervision.
SAVE ⊠ 🛏 🖥 🍴 ⇝ ⊠

MONTREAL

⊛ ▼▼▼▼ Candlewood Suites 🄷
(514) 667-5002. **$119-$400.** 191 boul Rene-Levesque est. Corner of rue Hotel-de-ville. Int corridors. **Pets:** Other species. Service with restrictions, crate.
SAVE ⊠ 🛏 🖥

⊛ ▼▼▼▼ Chateau Versailles Hotel 🄷 ❀
(514) 933-3611. **$169-$375.** 1659 rue Sherbrooke ouest. Corner rue St-Mathieu. Int corridors. **Pets:** Medium, other species. $25 daily fee/room. Designated rooms, service with restrictions, supervision.
SAVE ⊠ 🖥

⊛ ▼▼▼▼ Crowne Plaza Montreal Airport 🄷
(514) 344-1999. **$119-$250.** 6600 Cote-de-Liesse. Hwy 520, exit 5 eastbound on south side service road; exit westbound to rue Ness, follow signs for rue Hickmore and Hwy 520 E; in St-Laurent sector. Int corridors. **Pets:** Medium. $35 one-time fee/room. Service with restrictions, crate.
SAVE ⊠ 🛏 🖥 🍴 ⇝ ⊠

⊛ ▼▼▼▼ Days Hotel Montreal 🄷
(514) 938-4611. **$109-$179.** 1005 rue Guy. Just s of boul Rene-Levesque. Int corridors. **Pets:** Small. $15 daily fee/pet. Service with restrictions, crate.
SAVE ⊠ 🛏 🖥 🍴 ⇝ ⊠

⊛ ▼▼▼▼ Delta Montreal 🄷
(514) 286-1986. **$145-$322.** 475 ave President-Kennedy. Corner of rue City Councillors. Int corridors. **Pets:** $40 one-time fee/room. Designated rooms, service with restrictions, supervision.
SAVE ⊠ 🛏 🖥 🍴 ⇝ ⊠

⊛ ▼▼▼▼ Embassy Suites Montreal par/by Hilton 🄷
(514) 288-8886. **$170-$289.** 208 rue St-Antoine ouest. Corner of rue St-Francois-Xavier. Int corridors. **Pets:** Small, other species. $35 one-time fee/room. Service with restrictions, supervision.
SAVE ⊠ 🛏 🖥 🍴 ⇝

⊛ ▼▼▼▼ Fairmont The Queen Elizabeth 🄷 ❀
(514) 861-3511. **$159-$419.** 900 boul Rene-Levesque ouest. Between rue University and Mansfield. Int corridors. **Pets:** Small. $25 daily fee/pet. Service with restrictions, supervision.
SAVE ⊠ ⚿M 🛏 🖥 🍴 ⇝ ⊠

⊛ ▼▼▼▼ Four Points by Sheraton Montreal Centre-Ville
(514) 842-3961. **$125-$199.** 475 rue Sherbrooke ouest. Between rue Durocher and Aylmer. Int corridors. **Pets:** Other species. Service with restrictions.
SAVE ⊠ 🛏 🖥 🍴

⊛ ▼▼▼▼ Grand Plaza Montreal Centre-Ville 🄷
(514) 842-8581. **$109-$329.** 505 rue Sherbrooke est. Between rue Berri and St-Hubert. Int corridors. **Pets:** $35 one-time fee/room. Service with restrictions, supervision.
SAVE ⊠ 🖥 🍴 ⇝

⊛ ▼▼▼▼ Hilton Montreal Bonaventure 🄷
(514) 878-2332. **$185-$350.** 900 rue de la Gauchetiere ouest. Corner of Mansfield and de la Gauchetiere. Int corridors. **Pets:** Accepted.
SAVE ⊠ ⚿M 🛏 🖥 🍴 ⇝

⊛ ▼▼▼▼ Holiday Inn Express Hotel & Suites Montreal Centre-Ville 🄷 ❀
(514) 448-7100. **$119-$400.** 155 boul Rene-Levesque est. Corner de Bullion. Int corridors. **Pets:** $50 one-time fee/room. Designated rooms, service with restrictions, supervision.
SAVE ⊠ 🛏 🖥

⊛ ▼▼▼▼ Holiday Inn Montreal-Airport 🄷
(514) 739-3391. **$109-$169.** 6500 Cote-de-Liesse. Hwy 520, exit 5 eastbound on south side service road; exit westbound to rue Ness, follow signs for rue Hickmore and Hwy 520 E; in St-Laurent sector. Ext/int corridors. **Pets:** Small. $35 one-time fee/pet. Designated rooms, service with restrictions, supervision.
SAVE ⊠ ⚿M 🛏 🖥 🍴 ⇝ ⊠

⊛ ▼▼▼▼ Holiday Inn Montreal-Midtown 🄷
(514) 842-6111. **$119-$179.** 420 rue Sherbrooke ouest. Between rue Bleury and City Councillors. Int corridors. **Pets:** Medium. $35 one-time fee/room. Designated rooms, service with restrictions, supervision.
SAVE ⊠ 🛏 🖥 🍴 ⇝ ⊠

▼▼▼ Hotel Gault 🄷
(514) 904-1616. **Call for rates.** 449 rue Ste-Helene. Just s of rue Notre-Dame. Int corridors. **Pets:** Accepted.
⊠ 🛏 🖥 🍴

⊛ ▼▼▼▼ Hotel InterContinental Montreal 🄷 ❀
(514) 987-9900. **$189-$389.** 360 rue St-Antoine ouest. Corner of rue St-Pierre. Int corridors. **Pets:** Medium. $75 one-time fee/pet. Service with restrictions, supervision.
SAVE ⊠ 🛏 🖥 🍴 ⇝ ⊠

⊛ ▼▼▼ Hotel La Tour Centre-Ville 🄲🄾
(514) 866-8861. **$106-$350.** 400 boul Rene-Levesque ouest. Corner of rue de Bleury. Int corridors. **Pets:** Very small. $10 daily fee/room. Designated rooms, service with restrictions, supervision.
SAVE ⊠ 🛏 🖥 🍴 ⇝

▼▼▼ Hotel Le Germain 🄷 ❀
(514) 849-2050. **$230-$295.** 2050 rue Mansfield. Corner of ave President-Kennedy. Int corridors. **Pets:** $30 daily fee/room. Service with restrictions, supervision.
⊠ 🛏 🖥 🍴

▼▼▼ ▼▼▼ **Hotel Le St-James** H
(514) 841-3111. **Call for rates.** 355 rue St-Jacques ouest. Corner of rue St-Pierre. Int corridors. **Pets:** Accepted.

⊠ 🖭 ¶¶ ⊠

⒜ ▼▼▼ ▼▼▼ **Hotel Omni Mont-Royal** H ❖
(514) 284-1110. **$139-$279.** 1050 rue Sherbrooke ouest. Corner of rue Peel. Int corridors. **Pets:** Small. $50 one-time fee/room. Service with restrictions, supervision.

SAVE ⊠ 🛢 🖭 ¶¶ ⇛ ⊠

▼▼▼ **Hotel St-Paul** H
(514) 380-2222. **$189-$279.** 355 rue McGill. Corner of rue St-Paul. Int corridors. **Pets:** Accepted.

ASK ⊠ 🖭 ¶¶

▼▼ ▼ **Hotel Terrasse Royale** H
(514) 739-6391. **Call for rates.** 5225 chemin Cote-des-Neiges. Just n of chemin Queen Mary. Int corridors. **Pets:** Accepted.

⊠ 🛢 🖭 ¶¶

⒜ ▼▼▼ **Hotel Travelodge Montreal Centre** H
(514) 874-9090. **$99-$260.** 50 boul Rene-Levesque ouest. Between rue Clark and St-Urbain. Int corridors. **Pets:** $10 daily fee/pet. Service with restrictions, supervision.

SAVE ⊠ 🛢 🖭 ¶¶

⒜ ▼▼▼ ▼ **L'Appartement Hotel** CO
(514) 284-3634. **$115-$245.** 455 rue Sherbrooke ouest. Corner of rue Durocher. Int corridors. **Pets:** Designated rooms, service with restrictions, crate.

SAVE ⊠ 🛢 🖭 ⇛

▼▼▼ **La Presidence Hotel and Suites** CO
(514) 842-9988. **$149-$229.** 505 rue Sherbrooke est. Between rue Berri and St-Hubert. Int corridors. **Pets:** $35 one-time fee/room. Service with restrictions, supervision.

ASK ⊠ 🛢 🖭 ¶¶ ⇛

⒜ ▼▼▼ ▼▼▼ **Le Centre Sheraton** H ❖
(514) 878-2000. **$179-$649.** 1201 boul Rene-Levesque ouest. Between rue Drummond and Stanley. Int corridors. **Pets:** Medium. Service with restrictions, supervision.

SAVE ⊠ 🛢 🖭 ¶¶ ⇛ ⊠

⒜ ▼▼▼ ▼▼▼ **Le Meridien Versailles-Montreal** H ❖
(514) 933-8111. **$159-$375.** 1808 rue Sherbrooke ouest. Corner of rue St-Mathieu. Int corridors. **Pets:** Other species. $25 daily fee/room. Designated rooms, service with restrictions, crate.

SAVE ⊠ 🛢 🖭 ¶¶

⒜ ▼▼▼ ▼▼▼ **Le Saint-Sulpice Hotel Montreal** H ❖
(514) 288-1000. **$179-$539.** 414 rue St-Sulpice. Just n of rue St-Paul. Int corridors. **Pets:** Medium. $50 daily fee/room. Supervision.

SAVE ⊠ 🛢 🖭 ¶¶ ⊠

⒜ ▼▼▼ **Le Square Phillips Hotel & Suites** H
(514) 393-1193. **$141-$323.** 1193 Place Phillips. Between rue Ste-Catherine and boul Rene-Levesque. Int corridors. **Pets:** Service with restrictions, supervision.

SAVE ⊠ 🛢 🖭 ¶¶ ⇛

⒜ ▼▼▼ ▼▼▼ **Loews Hotel Vogue** H ❖
(514) 285-5555. **$199-$499.** 1425 de la Montagne. Between rue Ste-Catherine and boul de Maisonneuve. Int corridors. **Pets:** $25 one-time fee/room. Designated rooms, service with restrictions.

SAVE ⊠ 🛢 🖭 ¶¶ ⊠

▼▼▼ **Marriott Residence Inn Montreal Airport** H
(514) 336-9333. **$179-$219.** 6500 Place Robert-Joncas. Hwy 40, exit 65 (boul Cavendish), 0.3 mi (0.5 km) w on north side service road, then just n on rue Beaulac. Int corridors. **Pets:** Accepted.

⊠ 🛢ᴹ 🛢 🖭 ¶¶ ⇛ ⊠

⒜ ▼▼▼ **Marriott Residence Inn-Montreal Centre-ville/Downtown** H ❖
(514) 982-6064. **$175-$475.** 2045 rue Peel. Between rue Sherbrooke and boul de Maisonneuve. Int corridors. **Pets:** Medium. $100 one-time fee/room. Service with restrictions, crate.

SAVE ⊠ 🛢 🖭

⒜ ▼▼▼ ▼▼▼ **Novotel Montreal** H
(514) 337-3222. **$119-$329.** 2599 boul Alfred-Nobel. Hwy 40, exit 60 (boul Alfred-Nobel); in St-Laurent Technoparc, just s of south side service road; in St-Laurent sector. Int corridors. **Pets:** Accepted.

SAVE ⊠ 🛢 🖭 ¶¶ ⇛

⒜ ▼▼▼ ▼▼▼ **Novotel Montreal Centre** H
(514) 861-6000. **$109-$450.** 1180 rue de la Montagne. Between rue Ste-Catherine and boul Rene-Levesque. Int corridors. **Pets:** Small. Designated rooms, service with restrictions, supervision.

SAVE ⊠ 🖭 ¶¶

▼▼▼ **Opus Hotel Montreal** H
(514) 843-6000. **$269-$349.** 10 rue Sherbrooke ouest. Corner of boul St-Laurent. Int corridors. **Pets:** Accepted.

ASK ⊠ 🛢 🖭 ¶¶

▼◆▼ **Quality Hotel Dorval** H
(514) 731-7821. **Call for rates.** 7700 Cote-de-Liesse. Hwy 520, exit 4 eastbound, on south side service road; exit 4 (Montee-de-Liesse) westbound; in St-Laurent sector. Int corridors. **Pets:** Accepted.

⊠ 🛢 🖭 ¶¶ ⇛ ⊠

⒜ ▼▼▼ **Quality Hotel Downtown Montreal** H
(514) 849-1413. **$99-$450.** 3440 ave du Parc. Between rue Sherbrooke and Milton. Int corridors. **Pets:** Dogs only. $25 one-time fee/pet. Service with restrictions, supervision.

SAVE ⊠ 🛢 🖭 ¶¶

⒜ ▼▼▼ **Residence Inn by Marriott Montreal Westmount** H
(514) 935-9224. **$139-$159.** 2170 ave Lincoln. Just e of rue Atwater. Int corridors. **Pets:** Small. $75 one-time fee/room. Service with restrictions, supervision.

SAVE ⊠ 🛢ᴹ 🛢 🖭 ⇛

⒜ ▼▼▼ ▼▼▼ **Sofitel Montreal** H
(514) 285-9000. **$400-$800.** 1155 rue Sherbrooke ouest. Corner of rue Stanley. Int corridors. **Pets:** Service with restrictions, supervision.

SAVE ⊠ 🛢 ¶¶ ⊠

⒜ ▼▼▼ ▼▼▼ **W Montreal** H ❖
(514) 395-3100. **$189-$709.** 901 Square Victoria. Corner of rue St-Antoine. Int corridors. **Pets:** Medium, other species. $25 daily fee/room. Service with restrictions.

SAVE ⊠ 🛢ᴹ 🖭 ¶¶

▼▼▼ **XIXe siecle Hotel Montreal** H
(514) 985-0019. **$150-$325.** 262 rue St-Jacques ouest. Between rue St-Jean and St-Pierre. Int corridors. **Pets:** Accepted.

ASK ⊠ 🛢 ¶¶

POINTE-CLAIRE

⒜ ▼▼▼ **Comfort Inn** H
(514) 697-6210. **$89-$149.** 700 boul St-Jean. Hwy 40, exit 52, just s. Int corridors. **Pets:** Service with restrictions, supervision.

SAVE ⊠ 🛢 🖭

⒜ ▼▼▼ **Quality Suites Montreal Aeroport, Pointe-Claire** H
(514) 426-5060. **$99-$385.** 6300 Rt Transcanadienne. Hwy 40, exit 52 eastbound, south side service road; westbound, follow signs for boul St-Jean sud and Hwy 40 est to access south side service road. Int corridors. **Pets:** Accepted.

SAVE ⊠ 🛢ᴹ 🛢 🖭 ¶¶

ROSEMERE

▼▼▼ Hotel Le Rivage 🄷
(450) 437-2171. **Call for rates.** 125 boul Cure-Labelle. Hwy 15, exit 14, 2.4 mi (4 km) e. Int corridors. **Pets:** Accepted.
⊠ 🖬 🖵 🏊 🗶

ST-JEROME

🄬 ▼▼▼ Super 8 St-Jerome 🄷
(450) 438-4388. **$109-$139.** 3 boul J. F. Kennedy. Hwy 15, exit 41 southbound, just n; on west side of autoroute. Int corridors. **Pets:** $10 daily fee/pet. Designated rooms, service with restrictions, supervision.
SAVE ⊠ 🖬 🖵 🏊 🗶

ST-LAURENT

🄬 ▼▼ Park Inn Montreal 🄷
(514) 733-8818. **$125-$198.** 7300 Cote-de-Liesse. Hwy 520, exit 4 eastbound on southside service road; exit 4 (Montee-de-Liesse) westbound; in St-Laurent sector. Int corridors. **Pets:** Designated rooms, service with restrictions, supervision.
SAVE ⊠ 🖬 🖵 🍴 🏊

TERREBONNE

🄬 ▼▼▼ Super 8 Hotel Lachenaie Terrebonne 🄷
(450) 582-8288. **$89-$149.** 1155 ave Yves-Blais. Hwy 640, exit 50, just s on Montee des Pionniers, then just e; in Lachenaie sector. Int corridors. **Pets:** Medium. $15 daily fee/pet. Designated rooms, service with restrictions.
SAVE ⊠ 🖫 🖬 🖵 🏊 🗶

VAUDREUIL-DORION

🄬 ▼▼▼▼ Chateau Vaudreuil Suites Hotel 🄷 🌻
(450) 455-0955. **$159-$195.** 21700 Trans-Canada Hwy 40. Hwy 40, exit 36 westbound; exit 35 eastbound. Int corridors. **Pets:** Medium, other species. Crate.
SAVE ⊠ 🖬 🖵 🍴 🏊 🗶

END METROPOLITAN AREA

MONT-TREMBLANT CENTRE DE VILLEGIATURE

🄬 ▼▼▼▼ Fairmont Tremblant 🄷 🌻
(819) 681-7000. **$159-$619, 7 day notice.** 3045 chemin de la Chapelle. In Mont-Tremblant Resort centre. Int corridors. **Pets:** Small. $25 daily fee/room.
SAVE ⊠ 🖫 🖵 🍴 🏊 🗶

🄬 ▼▼▼▼ Le Grand Lodge Mont-Tremblant 🄷
(819) 425-2734. **$119-$299, 8 day notice.** 2396 rue Labelle. On Rt 327, 0.3 mi (0.4 km) s of Montee Ryan. Int corridors. **Pets:** Accepted.
SAVE ⊠ 🖬 🖵 🍴 🏊 🗶

🄬 ▼▼▼▼ Le Westin Resort & Spa, Tremblant 🄷
(819) 681-8000. **$165-$629, 30 day notice.** 100 chemin Kandahar. Hwy 117 N, exit 119 (Montee Ryan), 6 mi (10 km) e, follow signs; in Mont-Tremblant Resort centre. Int corridors. **Pets:** Accepted.
SAVE ⊠ 🖬 🖵 🍴 🏊 🗶

NEW RICHMOND

▼▼▼ Hotel Le Francis 🄷
(418) 392-4485. **Call for rates.** 210 chemin Pardiac. Just s of Rt 132. Ext/int corridors. **Pets:** Accepted.
⊠ 🖬 🖵 🍴 🏊 🗶

PERCE

▼ Au Pic de l'Aurore 🄲🄰
(418) 782-2151. **$69-$250, 15 day notice.** 1 Rt 132. 1.2 mi (2 km) e from village. Ext corridors. **Pets:** Medium. $25 one-time fee/pet. Designated rooms, service with restrictions, supervision.
⊠ 🖬 🖵

▼▼▼ Hotel La Normandie 🄷
(418) 782-2112. **$79-$239.** 221 Rt 132 ouest. Centre. Int corridors. **Pets:** Medium. $30 one-time fee/room. Designated rooms, service with restrictions, crate.
⊠ 🖬 🖵 🍴 🄚

▼▼▼ Hotel/Motel Le Mirage 🄼
(418) 782-5151. **$72-$198.** 288 Rt 132 ouest. On Rt 132. Ext corridors. **Pets:** Very small, dogs only. $25 one-time fee/pet.
ASK ⊠ 🖬 🍴 🏊

▼▼ Hotel Motel Manoir de Perce 🄷
(418) 782-2022. **$66-$168.** 212 Rt 132. Centre. Int corridors. **Pets:** Dogs only. $25 one-time fee/room. Supervision.
⊠ 🖬 🍴

QUEBEC METROPOLITAN AREA

BEAUPRE

🄬 ▼▼▼ Chateau Mont Sainte-Anne 🄷 🌻
(418) 827-5211. **$109-$499, 14 day notice.** 500 boul du Beau-Pre. Hwy 360, 2.3 mi (3.7 km) ne from jct Hwy 138. Int corridors. **Pets:** $20 daily fee/room. Designated rooms, service with restrictions, crate.
SAVE ⊠ 🖬 🍴 🏊 🗶

🄬 ▼▼▼ Hotel Val des Neiges 🄷
(418) 827-5711. **$92-$249.** 201 rue Val-des-Neiges. Just off Hwy 360. Int corridors. **Pets:** Large, dogs only. $10 deposit/pet. Designated rooms, service with restrictions, supervision.
SAVE ⊠ 🖬 🖵 🍴 🏊 🗶

BOISCHATEL

🄬 ▼▼ Econo Lodge 🄷
(418) 822-4777. **$90-$145.** 5490 boul Ste-Anne. On Rt 138. Int corridors. **Pets:** Medium. $15 daily fee/pet. Designated rooms, service with restrictions, supervision.
SAVE ⊠ 🖬

L'ANCIENNE-LORETTE

▼▼ Comfort Inn 🄷
(418) 872-5900. **$109-$169.** 1255 boul Duplessis. Jct boul Duplessis and Wilfrid-Hamel (Hwy 138). Int corridors. **Pets:** Medium. $25 one-time fee/room. Service with restrictions, supervision.
ASK ⊠ 🖬 🖵

LEVIS

▼▼ Comfort Inn 🅷
(418) 835-5605. **$99-$169.** 10 du Vallon est. Hwy 20, exit 325S eastbound; exit 325 westbound. Int corridors. **Pets:** Medium. $25 one-time fee/room. Designated rooms, service with restrictions, supervision.

🄰🄢🄺 ⊠ 🛢 🖵

ⒸⒶⒶ ▼▼▼ Comfort Inn & Suites Rive-Sud Quebec 🅷
(418) 836-3336. **$99-$209.** 495 Rte-du-Pont. Hwy 20, exit 311, just ne on Rt 116; in St-Nicolas sector. Int corridors. **Pets:** Very small. $20 one-time fee/pet. No service, crate.

🅂🄰🅅🄴 ⊠ ♿ 🛢 🖵 ♒

▼▼ Hotel Kennedy 🅷
(418) 837-0233. **Call for rates.** 129 Rte du President-Kennedy. Hwy 20, exit 325N, just n. Ext/int corridors. **Pets:** Accepted.

⊠ 🛢 🖵

QUEBEC

▼▼▼ ALT Hotel-Quebec 🅷 🌸
(418) 658-1224. **$129-$195.** 1200 ave Germain-des-Pres. Just n of boul Laurier; in Ste-Foy sector. Int corridors. **Pets:** $30 daily fee/room. Supervision.

⊠ 🖵 🍽

▼▼ Appartements La Pergola 🅲🅾
(418) 681-1428. **Call for rates.** 405 boul Rene-Levesque ouest. Between aves Moncton and des Erables. Int corridors. **Pets:** Accepted.

🛢 🖵

ⒸⒶⒶ ▼▼▼▼ Auberge Saint-Antoine 🅷 🌸
(418) 692-2211. **$159-$399.** 8 rue St-Antoine. Corner of rue Dalhousie. Int corridors. **Pets:** Other species. $150 one-time fee/room. Service with restrictions, supervision.

🅂🄰🅅🄴 ⊠ 🛢 🖵 🍽 🅇

▼▼▼ Chateau Bonne Entente 🅷
(418) 653-5221. **$189-$499.** 3400 chemin Ste-Foy. Hwy 540 (Autoroute Duplessis), exit chemin Ste-Foy, just w; in Ste-Foy sector. Int corridors. **Pets:** Accepted.

🅂🄰🅅🄴 ⊠ ♿ 🖵 🍽 ♒ 🅇

▼▼ Comfort Inn 🅷
(418) 666-1226. **$99-$199.** 240 boul Ste-Anne. Hwy 440, exit Francois-de-Laval. Int corridors. **Pets:** Large. $15 one-time fee/pet. Service with restrictions, supervision.

🄰🄢🄺 ⊠ 🛢 🖵

▼▼ Comfort Inn de l'Aeroport-Hamel 🅷
(418) 872-5038. **$96-$159.** 7320 boul Wilfrid-Hamel. Hwy 138, 0.9 mi (1.5 km) w of boul Duplessis. Int corridors. **Pets:** Medium, other species. $25 one-time fee/pet. Service with restrictions, supervision.

🄰🄢🄺 ⊠ 🛢 🖵

ⒸⒶⒶ ▼▼▼ Delta Quebec 🅷
(418) 647-1717. **$100-$270.** 690 boul Rene-Levesque est. Just w of boul Honore-Mercier. Int corridors. **Pets:** Accepted.

🅂🄰🅅🄴 ⊠ 🛢 🖵 🍽 ♒

ⒸⒶⒶ ▼▼▼▼ Fairmont Le Chateau Frontenac 🅷
(418) 692-3861. **$145-$499.** 1 rue des Carrieres. In Old Quebec. Int corridors. **Pets:** Accepted.

🅂🄰🅅🄴 ⊠ 🛢 🖵 🍽 ♒ 🅇

▼▼ Gite du Vieux-Bourg 🅱🅱
(418) 661-0116. **$80-$95, 7 day notice.** 492 ave Royale. Hwy 440, exit Francois-de-Laval, just n, then 0.3 mi (0.5 km) e; in Beauport sector. Int corridors. **Pets:** Accepted.

⊠ 🛢 🖵 ♒

ⒸⒶⒶ ▼▼▼ ▼▼▼ Hilton Quebec 🅷 🌸
(418) 647-2411. **$109-$339.** 1100 boul Rene-Levesque est. Corner of ave Honore-Mercier. Int corridors. **Pets:** Small. $25 one-time fee/room. Service with restrictions, supervision.

🅂🄰🅅🄴 ⊠ 🛢 🖵 🍽 ♒ 🅇

ⒸⒶⒶ ▼▼▼▼ Hotel Clarion Quebec 🅷
(418) 653-4901. **$99-$400.** 3125 boul Hochelaga. Hwy 73, exit 136 (Hochelaga ouest); in Ste-Foy sector. Int corridors. **Pets:** Accepted.

🅂🄰🅅🄴 ⊠ 🛢 🖵 🍽 ♒

▼▼▼ Hotel Dominion 1912 🅷 🌸
(418) 692-2224. **$179-$385.** 126 rue St-Pierre. Corner rue St-Paul. Int corridors. **Pets:** Dogs only. $30 daily fee/room. Service with restrictions, supervision.

⊠ 🖵

▼▼▼ Hotel Gouverneur Quebec-Sainte-Foy 🅷
(418) 651-3030. **Call for rates.** 3030 boul Laurier. Corner of rue Lavigerie; in Ste-Foy sector. Ext/int corridors. **Pets:** Accepted.

⊠ 🛢 🖵 🍽 ♒

ⒸⒶⒶ ▼▼ ▼▼ Hotel Quality Suites Quebec 🅷 🌸
(418) 622-4244. **$115-$210.** 1600 rue Bouvier. Hwy 40, exit 312N (Pierre-Bertrand nord), 1.3 mi (2 km) w of jct Rt 358. Int corridors. **Pets:** Other species. $25 one-time fee/room. Designated rooms, service with restrictions, supervision.

🅂🄰🅅🄴 ⊠ 🛢 🖵

ⒸⒶⒶ ▼▼▼ Hotel Quartier 🅷 🌸
(418) 650-1616. **$100-$350.** 2955 boul Laurier. Just e of Hwy 73; in Ste-Foy sector. Int corridors. **Pets:** $30 daily fee/pet. Service with restrictions, supervision.

🅂🄰🅅🄴 ⊠ 🛢 🖵 🍽 ♒

ⒸⒶⒶ ▼▼▼ Hotel Super 8 Quebec Ste-Foy 🅷
(418) 877-6888. **$81-$200.** 7286 boul Wilfred Hamel. Hwy 138, 0.7 mi (1.1 km) w of boul Duplessis; in Ste-Foy sector. Int corridors. **Pets:** Accepted.

🅂🄰🅅🄴 ⊠ 🛢 🖵 ♒ 🅇

ⒸⒶⒶ ▼▼ ▼▼ L'Hotel du Vieux Quebec 🅷 🌸
(418) 692-1850. **$98-$326.** 1190 rue St-Jean. Corner of rue de l'Hotel-Dieu. Int corridors. **Pets:** $25 daily fee/room. Designated rooms, service with restrictions, supervision.

🅂🄰🅅🄴 ⊠ 🛢 🖵 🍽

ⒸⒶⒶ ▼▼▼ ▼▼▼ Loews Le Concorde 🅷 🌸
(418) 647-2222. **$119-$359.** 1225 Cours du General-de-Montcalm. Corner of Grande Allee est. Int corridors. **Pets:** Other species. $25 one-time fee/room. Designated rooms, service with restrictions, supervision.

🅂🄰🅅🄴 ⊠ 🛢 🖵 🍽 ♒ 🅇

ST-FERREOL-LES-NEIGES

▼▼ Chalets Montmorency Condominiums
Mont-Sainte-Anne Quebec 🅲🅾
(418) 826-2600. **$99-$159.** 1768 ave Royale. On Hwy 360. Ext corridors. **Pets:** Accepted.

🄰🄢🄺 ⊠ 🛢 🖵 ♒ 🅇

▼▼ **Chalets-Village Mont-Sainte-Anne** 🄲🄰
(418) 826-3331. **$300-$3000, 60 day notice.** 1815 boul Les Neiges. On north side of Hwy 360; village centre. Ext corridors. **Pets:** Other species. $100 one-time fee/room. No service, supervision.
🗙 🛄 🛇

END METROPOLITAN AREA

RIGAUD

▼▼ **Howard Johnson** 🄷
(450) 458-7997. **Call for rates.** 93 Rt 201. Hwy 40, exit 17, just ne. Int corridors. **Pets:** Accepted.
🗙 🛄 🖵

RIMOUSKI

▼▼ **Comfort Inn** 🄷
(418) 724-2500. **$115-$155.** 455 boul St-Germain ouest. On Rt 132. Int corridors. **Pets:** Accepted.
🄰🅂🄺 🗙 🛄 🖵

▼▼ **Hotel Rimouski** 🄷
(418) 725-5000. **$115-$145, 15 day notice.** 225 boul Rene-Lepage est. On Rt 132, corner of rue Julien-Rehel. Int corridors. **Pets:** Accepted.
🄰🅂🄺 🗙 🦽🄼 🛄 🖵 🍴 🌊 🛇

RIVIERA-DU-LOUP

▼▼ **Comfort Inn** 🄷
(418) 867-4162. **$99-$179.** 85 boul Cartier. Hwy 20, exit 507, just se; Hwy 85, exit 96 (Fraserville); follow signs. Int corridors. **Pets:** Accepted.
🄰🅂🄺 🗙 🛄 🖵

🄰🄰 ▼▼▼ **Days Inn Riviere-du-Loup** 🄷
(418) 862-6354. **$99-$195.** 182 rue Fraser. Hwy 20, exit 503, 0.6 mi (1 km) e on Rt 132. Ext corridors. **Pets:** Accepted.
🅂🄰🅅🄴 🗙 🛄 🖵 🌊

ROBERVAL

▼▼▼ **Hotel Chateau Roberval** 🄷
(418) 275-7511. **Call for rates.** 1225 boul Marcotte. On Hwy 169; centre. Int corridors. **Pets:** Accepted.
🗙 🛄 🖵 🍴 🌊 🛇

ROUYN-NORANDA

▼▼ **Comfort Inn** 🄷
(819) 797-1313. **Call for rates.** 1295 rue Lariviere. On Rt 117, 2.5 mi (4 km) s from town centre. Int corridors. **Pets:** Accepted.
🗙 🛄 🖵

ST-ANTOINE-DE-TILLY

▼▼ **Manoir de Tilly** 🄲🄸
(418) 886-2407. **Call for rates.** 3854 chemin de Tilly. Jct Hwy 20, exit 291, 5.3 mi (8.5 km) n on Rt 273; centre. Int corridors. **Pets:** Accepted.
🗙 🍴

ST-FAUSTIN-LAC-CARRE

▼▼ **Motel Tremblant sur la Colline** 🄼
(819) 688-2102. **$89-$129, 7 day notice.** 357 Rt 117. On Rt 117, 2.5 mi (4 km) n of exit for city. Ext/int corridors. **Pets:** Accepted.
🄰🅂🄺 🗙 🛄 🖵 🌊

ST-HONORE-DE-TEMISCOUATA

▼ **Motel Jasper** 🄼
(418) 497-2322. **$58-$72.** 657 Rt 185. On Rt 185. Ext corridors. **Pets:** Accepted.
🗙 🛄 🍴

ST-HYACINTHE

▼▼▼ **Hotel des Seigneurs Saint-Hyacinthe** 🄷
(450) 774-3810. **$188-$240.** 1200 rue Johnson. Hwy 20, exit 130S, just e on rue Gauvin from boul Laframboise. Int corridors. **Pets:** Accepted.
🄰🅂🄺 🗙 🛄 🖵 🍴 🌊 🛇

ST-JEAN-PORT-JOLI

▼▼ **Auberge du Faubourg** 🄼
(418) 598-6455. **$99-$220, 10 day notice.** 280 ave de Gaspe ouest (Rt 132). 1.4 mi (2.4 km) w on Rt 132 from jct Rt 204; Hwy 20, exit 414. Ext corridors. **Pets:** $35 daily fee/room. Designated rooms, service with restrictions.
🄰🅂🄺 🗙 🛄 🖵 🍴 🌊 🄶

ST-JEAN-SUR-RICHELIEU

▼▼ **Holiday Inn Express** 🄷
(450) 359-4466. **$119-$169.** 700 rue Gadbois. Hwy 35, exit 9, e on rue Pierre-Caisse. Int corridors. **Pets:** $250 deposit/room. Designated rooms, service with restrictions, supervision.
🄰🅂🄺 🗙 🛄 🖵 🌊

STE-AGATHE-DES-MONTS

🄰🄰 ▼▼▼ **Super 8 Hotel Ste-Agathe** 🄷
(819) 324-8880. **$88-$149.** 500 rue Leonard. Hwy 15, exit 86, just w on Rt 117 to rue Leonard, then 0.3 mi (0.5 km) s. Int corridors. **Pets:** Medium, other species. $15 daily fee/room. Designated rooms, service with restrictions, supervision.
🅂🄰🅅🄴 🗙 🛄 🖵 🌊 🛇

STE-ANNE-DE-BEAUPRE

🄰🄰 ▼▼ **Manoir Ste-Anne** 🄼
(418) 827-8383. **$65-$125.** 9776 boul Ste-Anne. On Hwy 138. Ext corridors. **Pets:** Accepted.
🅂🄰🅅🄴 🗙 🛄 🖵

STE-EULALIE

🄰🄰 ▼▼ **Motel Marie-Dan** 🄼
(819) 225-4604. **$50-$80.** 311 rue des Bouleaux (Rt 161). Hwy 20, exit 210, follow signs to Rt 161, then just s. Ext corridors. **Pets:** Accepted.
🅂🄰🅅🄴 🗙 🛄 🌊

STE-MARTHE

▼▼▼ **Auberge des Gallant** 🄲🄸
(450) 459-4241. **$160-$250, 7 day notice.** 1171 chemin St-Henri. 5.3 mi (8.5 km) w on chemin St-Henri from Hwy 201. Int corridors. **Pets:** Medium. $25 daily fee/pet. Service with restrictions.
🗙 🖵 🍴 🌊 🛇

SHAWINIGAN

▼▼ **Auberge Escapade Inn** 🄷
(819) 539-6911. **$92-$175.** 3383 rue Garnier. Hwy 55, exit 217, then 0.3 mi (0.5 km) n on Rt 351. Ext/int corridors. **Pets:** Accepted.
🄰🅂🄺 🗙 🛄 🍴

(AAA) ♦♦♦ **Auberge Gouverneur & Centre de Congres Shawinigan** H
(819) 537-6000. **$103-$148.** 1100 Promenade-du-St-Maurice. Hwy 55 N, exit 211, 2.8 mi (4.4 km) n on Hwy 153, follow signs. Int corridors. **Pets:** Designated rooms, service with restrictions, supervision.
SAVE ✕ 🛏 💻 ⑪ ⇌ ✕

♦♦♦ **Comfort Inn & Suites** H
(819) 536-2000. **$79-$152.** 500 boul du Capitaine. Hwy 55 N, exit 211, 2.8 mi (4.4 km) n on Hwy 153, then 1.3 mi (2 km) s on Rt 157. Int corridors. **Pets:** $25 daily fee/room. Designated rooms, service with restrictions, crate.
ASK ✕ 🛏 💻

SHERBROOKE

♦♦ **Comfort Inn** H
(819) 564-4400. **$104-$136.** 4295 boul Bourque. Hwy 410, exit 4W, 0.9 mi (1.5 km) w on Rt 112. Ext/int corridors. **Pets:** Small. $25 one-time fee/pet. Designated rooms, service with restrictions, supervision.
ASK ✕ 🛏 💻

♦♦♦ **Delta Sherbrooke Hotel and Conference Centre** H
(819) 822-1989. **$104-$279.** 2685 rue King ouest. Hwy 410, exit 4W, 0.6 mi (1 km) e on Rt 112. Int corridors. **Pets:** Accepted.
ASK ✕ 🛏 💻 ⑪ ⇌ ✕

THETFORD MINES

♦♦ **Comfort Inn** H ❀
(418) 338-0171. **$128-$138.** 123 boul Frontenac ouest. On Rt 112. Int corridors. **Pets:** Other species. Service with restrictions, crate.
ASK ✕ 🛏 💻

TROIS-RIVIERES

♦♦ **Comfort Inn** H
(819) 371-3566. **Call for rates.** 6255 rue Corbeil. Hwy 55, exit 183 (boul Jean XXIII); 1.3 mi (2 km) n of Laviolette Bridge, then 0.3 mi (0.5 km) e. Int corridors. **Pets:** Accepted.
✕ 🛏 💻

(AAA) ♦♦♦ **Days Inn** H
(819) 377-4444. **$80-$170.** 3155 boul Saint-Jean. Hwy 55, exit 183 (boul Jean XXIII), 0.3 mi (0.5 km) w, then 0.3 mi (0.4 km) n. Int corridors. **Pets:** Accepted.
SAVE ✕ 🛏 💻

(AAA) ♦♦♦ **Delta Trois-Rivieres Hotel and Conference Center** H ❀
(819) 376-1991. **$107-$260.** 1620 rue Notre-Dame Centre. Corner of rue St-Roch; centre. Int corridors. **Pets:** Medium. $35 one-time fee/room. Service with restrictions, supervision.
SAVE ✕ 💻 ⑪ ⇌ ✕

(AAA) ♦♦♦ **Super 8 Hotel Trois-Rivieres** H
(819) 377-5881. **$109-$169.** 3185 boul St-Jean. Hwy 55, exit 183 (boul Jean XXIII), just nw. Int corridors. **Pets:** Small. $20 daily fee/pet. Designated rooms, supervision.
SAVE ✕ 🛏 💻 ⇌ ✕

VAL-D'OR

♦♦ **Comfort Inn** H
(819) 825-9360. **Call for rates.** 1665 3ieme Ave. In town centre. Int corridors. **Pets:** Accepted.
✕ 🛏 💻

(AAA) ♦♦♦ **Motel L'Escale Hotel Suite** H
(819) 824-2711. **$96-$126.** 1100 rue L'Escale. In town centre. Ext/int corridors. **Pets:** Service with restrictions, supervision.
SAVE ✕ 🛏 💻 ⑪

SASKATCHEWAN

CARONPORT

▼▼ The Pilgrim Inn 🄷
(306) 756-5002. **Call for rates.** Hwy 1 W. Jct Main Access; on Trans-Canada Hwy 1. Int corridors. **Pets:** Accepted.
⊠ 🛢 💻

ESTEVAN

Ⓒ ▼▼▼ Perfect Inns & Suites 🄷
(306) 634-8585. **$89-$120.** 134 2nd Ave. Just n of jct Hwy 39 E and 2nd Ave. Ext/int corridors. **Pets:** Accepted.
SAVE ⊠ 🛢 💻

KINDERSLEY

▼▼ Nova Inn 🄷
(306) 463-4687. **Call for rates.** 100 12th Ave NW. Jct of Hwy 7 and 21. Ext/int corridors. **Pets:** Accepted.
⊠ 🛢 💻 🍴

MOOSE JAW

▼▼ Comfort Inn 🄷
(306) 692-2100. **Call for rates.** 155 Thatcher Dr W. Just w of jct Main St. Int corridors. **Pets:** Accepted.
⊠ 🛢 💻

Ⓒ ▼▼▼ Days Inn–Moose Jaw 🄷
(306) 691-5777. **$105-$205.** 1720 Main St N. Jct Trans-Canada Hwy 1, just s. Int corridors. **Pets:** $13 daily fee/pet. Designated rooms, service with restrictions, supervision.
SAVE ⊠ 🛢 💻 🏊 🚫

▼▼ Heritage Inn 🄷 🐾
(306) 693-7550. **$100-$195.** 1590 Main St N. 0.9 mi (1.5 km) s of jct Trans-Canada Hwy 1 and 2; access from Hwy 2 via Thatcher Dr. Int corridors. **Pets:** Medium. $10 daily fee/pet. Designated rooms, service with restrictions, supervision.
ASK ⊠ 🛢 💻 🍴 🏊

▼▼ Prairie Oasis Motel 🄼
(306) 692-4894. **$86-$96.** 955 Thatcher Dr E. Just s of jct Trans-Canada Hwy 1 and Thatcher Dr E. Ext corridors. **Pets:** Dogs only. Designated rooms, service with restrictions, crate.
ASK ⊠ 🛢 💻 🏊 🚫

▼▼ Super 8 Motel-Moose Jaw 🄷
(306) 692-8888. **$109.** 1706 Main St N. 0.9 mi (1.5 km) s of jct Trans-Canada Hwy 1; access from Hwy 2 via Thatcher Dr. Int corridors. **Pets:** Accepted.
ASK ⊠ 🕎 🛢 💻

NORTH BATTLEFORD

▼▼ Super 8 Motel 🄷
(306) 446-8888. **$95-$115.** 1006 Hwy 16 Bypass. 0.3 mi (0.5 km) nw of jct Hwy 16. Int corridors. **Pets:** Other species. $25 one-time fee/room. Service with restrictions, supervision.
ASK ⊠ 🛢

▼▼ Tropical Inn 🄷
(306) 446-4700. **Call for rates.** 1001 Hwy 16 Bypass. Corner of Battleford Rd and Hwy 16 Bypass. Int corridors. **Pets:** Accepted.
⊠ 🛢 💻 🍴 🏊 🚫

PRINCE ALBERT

Ⓒ ▼▼▼ Best Western Marquis Inn & Suites 🄷
(306) 922-9595. **$99, 3 day notice.** 602 36th St E. Jct Hwy 3 (6th Ave E) and Marquis Rd. Int corridors. **Pets:** Other species. $25 deposit/pet. Designated rooms, supervision.
SAVE ⊠ 🛢 💻 🍴

▼▼ Comfort Inn 🄷 🐾
(306) 763-4466. **$114-$119.** 3863 2nd Ave W. 1.6 mi (2.6 km) s on Hwy 2. Int corridors. **Pets:** Other species. Service with restrictions, supervision.
ASK ⊠ 🛢 💻

Ⓒ ▼▼▼ Ramada South Hill Inn 🄷
(306) 922-1333. **$119.** 3245 2nd Ave W. 1.2 mi (2.0 km) s on Hwy 2. Ext/int corridors. **Pets:** Accepted.
SAVE ⊠ 🛢 💻 🍴

▼▼ Super 8 🄷
(306) 953-0088. **$90-$95.** 4444 2nd Ave W. 1.7 mi (2.7 km) s on Hwy 2. Int corridors. **Pets:** Small. $10 one-time fee/room. Service with restrictions, supervision.
ASK ⊠ 🛢 💻

▼▼ Travelodge-Prince Albert 🄷
(306) 764-6441. **$101-$175.** 3551 2nd Ave W. 1.4 mi (2.2 km) s on Hwy 2. Ext/int corridors. **Pets:** Medium. Service with restrictions, supervision.
ASK ⊠ 🛢 💻 🍴

REGINA

Ⓒ ▼▼▼ Best Western Seven Oaks Inn 🄷
(306) 757-0121. **$131-$183.** 777 Albert St. Jct 2nd Ave. Int corridors. **Pets:** $10 one-time fee/room. Supervision.
SAVE ⊠ 🛢 💻 🍴 🏊 🚫

Ⓒ ▼▼▼ Comfort Inn 🄷
(306) 789-5522. **$109-$159.** 3221 E Eastgate Dr. Trans-Canada Hwy 1, 1.3 mi (2 km) e of Ring Rd; at eastern approach to city. Int corridors. **Pets:** Accepted.
SAVE ⊠ 🛢 💻

▼▼ Country Inn & Suites By Carlson 🄷 🐾
(306) 789-9117. **$110-$145, 3 day notice.** 3321 Eastgate Bay. Trans-Canada Hwy 1, 1.3 mi (2 km) e of Ring Rd; at eastern approach to city. Int corridors. **Pets:** Other species. $100 deposit/room, $20 one-time fee/room. Service with restrictions, crate.
ASK ⊠ 🕎 🛢 💻

▼▼ Delta Regina 🄷
(306) 525-5255. **$165-$230.** 1919 Saskatchewan Dr. At Rose St; centre. Int corridors. **Pets:** Accepted.
ASK ⊠ 🛢 💻 🍴 🏊 🚫

Ⓒ ▼▼▼ Holiday Inn Express Hotel & Suites Regina 🄷
(306) 569-4600. **$145.** 1907 11th Ave. Corner of Rose St; centre of downtown. Int corridors. **Pets:** Small. $15 daily fee/room. Designated rooms, service with restrictions, supervision.
SAVE ⊠ 🛢 💻

▼▼▼ Holiday Inn Hotel & Suites 🄷
(306) 789-3883. **$150-$200.** 1800 Prince of Wales Dr. Jct Trans-Canada Hwy 1, just n; at eastern approach to city. Int corridors. **Pets:** $40 daily fee/pet. Designated rooms, service with restrictions, supervision.
⊠ 🛢 💻 🍴 🏊 🚫

(AA) ▼▼▼ **Howard Johnson Inn** ℍ
(306) 565-0455. **Call for rates.** 1110 Victoria Ave E. Trans-Canada Hwy 1, just w of Ring Rd; at eastern approach to city. Int corridors. **Pets:** Accepted.
SAVE ✕ 🏢 💻 ≋

▼▼▼ **Quality Hotel** ℍ
(306) 569-4656. **$109-$169.** 1717 Victoria Ave. Just e of Broad St; downtown. Int corridors. **Pets:** Accepted.
ASK ✕ 🏢 💻 ⑪

(AA) ▼▼▼ ▼▼▼ **Radisson Plaza Hotel Saskatchewan** ℍ
(306) 522-7691. **$169-$280.** 2125 Victoria Ave. Victoria Ave at Scarth St; centre. Int corridors. **Pets:** Accepted.
SAVE ✕ ⑤ᴹ 🏢 💻 ⑪ ⊠

▼▼▼ **Ramada Hotel & Convention Centre** ℍ
(306) 569-1666. **$124-$194.** 1818 Victoria Ave. Victoria Ave and Broad St; centre of downtown. Int corridors. **Pets:** Accepted.
ASK ✕ 🏢 💻 ⑪ ≋ ⊠

(AA) ▼▼▼ **Regina Inn Hotel & Conference Centre** ℍ
(306) 525-6767. **$119-$195.** 1975 Broad St. Jct Victoria Ave; centre of downtown. Int corridors. **Pets:** Medium. $35 one-time fee/room. Service with restrictions, crate.
SAVE ✕ 🏢 💻 ⑪

▼▼▼▼ **Sandman Hotel Suites and Spa** ℍ
(306) 757-2444. **$139-$189.** 1800 Victoria Ave E. Just e of Ring Rd; at eastern approach to city. Int corridors. **Pets:** Accepted.
ASK ✕ 🏢 💻 ≋

▼▼ **Super 8 Motel** ℍ
(306) 789-8833. **Call for rates.** 2730 Victoria Ave E. Trans-Canada Hwy 1, 1 mi (1.6 km) e of Ring Rd; at eastern approach to city. Int corridors. **Pets:** Accepted.
✕ ⑤ᴹ 🏢 💻

(AA) ▼▼▼▼ **Wingate by Wyndham** ℍ 🐾
(306) 584-7400. **$162-$200.** 1700 Broad St. Corner of Saskatchewan Dr; centre of downtown. Int corridors. **Pets:** Medium. $25 daily fee/pet. Service with restrictions, supervision.
SAVE ✕ ⑤ᴹ 🏢 💻

SASKATOON

(AA) ▼▼▼ **Best Western Harvest Inn** ℍ
(306) 244-5552. **$128-$210, 3 day notice.** 1715 Idylwyld Dr N. 1.6 mi (2.6 km) n on Hwy 11 (Idylwyld Dr). Ext/int corridors. **Pets:** Small, dogs only. $25 one-time fee/room. Designated rooms, service with restrictions, supervision.
SAVE ✕ 🏢 💻 ⑪

(AA) ▼▼▼ **Colonial Square Motel & Suites** ℍ
(306) 343-1676. **$99-$129, 7 day notice.** 1301 8th St E. Just w of Cumberland Ave. Ext/int corridors. **Pets:** Accepted.
SAVE ✕ 🏢 💻

(AA) ▼▼▼ **Comfort Inn** ℍ
(306) 934-1122. **$100-$109, 7 day notice.** 2155 Northridge Dr. 1.9 mi (3 km) n; just ne of jct Hwy 11 (Idylwyld Dr) and Circle Dr. Int corridors. **Pets:** Other species. $10 daily fee/pet. Service with restrictions.
SAVE ✕ ⑤ᴹ 🏢 💻

▼▼▼ **Country Inn & Suites By Carlson** ℍ 🐾
(306) 934-3900. **$106-$116.** 617 Cynthia St. Just w of jct Hwy 11 (Idylwyld Dr) and Circle Dr. Int corridors. **Pets:** $25 one-time fee/room. Service with restrictions, crate.
ASK ✕ ⑤ᴹ 🏢 💻

▼▼▼▼ **Delta Bessborough** ℍ
(306) 244-5521. **$122-$340.** 601 Spadina Crescent E. At 21st St E; centre of downtown. Int corridors. **Pets:** Accepted.
ASK ✕ 🏢 💻 ⑪ ≋ ⊠

▼▼▼▼ **Holiday Inn Express Hotel & Suites** ℍ
(306) 384-8844. **$149.** 315 Idylwyld Dr N. Jct 25th St W. Int corridors. **Pets:** Accepted.
ASK ✕ ⑤ᴹ 🏢 💻 ≋

▼▼ **Motel 6 Saskatoon** ℍ
(306) 665-6688. **$81-$102.** 231 Marquis Dr. Jct Trans-Canada Hwy 16 W (Yellowhead Hwy). Int corridors. **Pets:** Other species. Designated rooms, service with restrictions, crate.
ASK ✕ 🏢 ≋

▼▼ **Sandman Hotel** ℍ
(306) 477-4844. **$114-$154.** 310 Circle Dr W. Jct Ave C N. Int corridors. **Pets:** Accepted.
ASK ✕ 🏢 💻 ⑪ ≋

(AA) ▼▼▼▼ **Sheraton Cavalier** ℍ
(306) 652-6770. **Call for rates.** 612 Spadina Crescent E. At 21st St E; centre of downtown. Int corridors. **Pets:** Accepted.
SAVE ✕ 💻 ⑪ ≋ ⊠

▼▼ **Super 8** ℍ
(306) 384-8989. **$110-$122.** 706 Circle Dr E. 1.3 mi (2 km) e of jct Hwy 11 (Idylwyld Dr). Ext/int corridors. **Pets:** Medium. $5 one-time fee/room. Service with restrictions, supervision.
ASK 🏢 💻

▼▼ **Travelodge Hotel-Saskatoon** ℍ
(306) 242-8881. **Call for rates.** 106 Circle Dr W. 1.9 mi (3 km) n, then just w of jct Hwy 11 (Idylwyld Dr). Int corridors. **Pets:** Accepted.
✕ 🏢 💻 ⑪ ≋ ⊠

SHAUNAVON

▼▼ **Hidden Hilten Motel** Ⓜ
(306) 297-4166. **$67-$83.** 352 5th St W. 0.3 mi (0.5 km) e from jct Hwy 13 and 37, just n. Ext corridors. **Pets:** Accepted.
ASK ✕ 🏢 💻

SWIFT CURRENT

▼▼ **Comfort Inn** ℍ
(306) 778-3994. **$103-$144.** 1510 S Service Rd E. Trans-Canada Hwy 1, just w of 22nd Ave NE. Int corridors. **Pets:** Accepted.
ASK ✕ 🏢 💻

(AA) ▼▼ **Safari Inn Motel** Ⓜ
(306) 773-4608. **$65-$70.** 810 S Service Rd E. 0.6 mi (1 km) e of jct Hwy 1 and 4 (Central Ave). Ext corridors. **Pets:** Medium. $10 daily fee/pet. Designated rooms, service with restrictions, supervision.
SAVE ✕ 🏢 💻

▼▼ **Super 8 Motel** ℍ
(306) 778-6088. **Call for rates.** 405 N Service Rd E. Just e of Hwy 4 (Central Ave). Int corridors. **Pets:** Accepted.
✕ 🏢 💻 ≋

WEYBURN

(AA) ▼▼▼ **Perfect Inns & Suites** Ⓜ
(306) 842-2691. **$64-$140.** 238 Sims Ave. 0.3 mi (0.5 km) w of jct Hwy 35 and 39. Ext/int corridors. **Pets:** Accepted.
SAVE ✕ 🏢 💻

YORKTON

▼▼▼ **Comfort Inn & Suites** ℍ
(306) 783-0333. **Call for rates.** 22 Dracup Ave. Just w of jct Hwy 9, 10 and 16 (Yellowhead Hwy). Int corridors. **Pets:** Accepted.
✕ 🏢 💻 ≋

(AA) ▼▼▼ **Ramada** ℍ
(306) 783-9781. **Call for rates.** 100 Broadway St E. On Hwy 9, 10, and 16 (Yellowhead Hwy); downtown. Int corridors. **Pets:** $10 daily fee/pet. Service with restrictions.
SAVE ✕ 🏢 💻 ⑪ ≋ ⊠

YUKON TERRITORY

DAWSON CITY

◈ Bonanza Gold Motel M
(867) 993-6789. **$89-$189.** Bonanza Creek Rd. 1.5 mi (2.4 km) s on Hwy 2. Ext corridors. **Pets:** Other species. $20 one-time fee/room. Designated rooms, service with restrictions, supervision.

[✕] [🔌] [💻] [🍴]

◈◈ Klondike Kate's Cabins CA ❀
(867) 993-6527. **$100-$160.** 1103 3rd Ave & King St. Corner of 3rd Ave and King St. Ext corridors. **Pets:** $25 one-time fee/room. Service with restrictions.

[✕] [🔌] [💻] [🍴] [✂]

ⒶⒶ ◈◈ Westmark Inn Dawson City M
(867) 993-5542. **$154-$164.** 5th St & Harper. At 5th and Harper sts; downtown. Ext/int corridors. **Pets:** Accepted.

[SAVE] [✕] [💻] [🍴]

HAINES JUNCTION

ⒶⒶ ◈◈ Alcan Motor Inn M
(867) 634-2371. **Call for rates.** Alaska & Haines Hwys. Jct Hwy 1 (Alaska Hwy) and 3 (Haines Hwy). Ext corridors. **Pets:** Accepted.

[SAVE] [✕] [🔌] [💻] [🍴]

WHITEHORSE

ⒶⒶ ◈◈ High Country Inn H
(867) 667-4471. **$129-$259, 3 day notice.** 4051 4th Ave. 0.4 mi (0.6 km) e of Main St. Int corridors. **Pets:** $15 daily fee/room. Designated rooms, supervision.

[SAVE] [✕] [🔌] [💻] [🍴]

ⒶⒶ ◈◈ Westmark Whitehorse Hotel & Conference Centre H
(867) 393-9700. **$159-$179.** 201 Wood St. At 2nd Ave; centre. Int corridors. **Pets:** Accepted.

[SAVE] [✕] [♿M] [🔌] [💻] [🍴] [✂]

Pet-Friendly Campgrounds

United States
Canada

United States

Alabama

CHILDERSBURG — DESOTO CAVERNS PARK CAMP-GROUND. (256) 378-7252. **$26-$30.** 5181 DeSoto Caverns Pkwy. On SR 76, 5 mi e.

PELHAM — BIRMINGHAM SOUTH CAMPGROUND. (205) 664-8832. **2P $36-$42, XP: $2.** 222 Hwy 33. I-65, exit 242, 0.5 mi w on CR 52, then 0.3 mi n.

Arizona

AMADO — DE ANZA TRAILS RV RESORT. (520) 398-8628. **Call for rates.** 2869 E Frontage Rd. I-19, exit 48, just e, then 1.6 mi s. (HC 65, Box 381, TUMACACORI, 85640).

ANTHEM — PIONEER RV PARK. (623) 465-7465. **2P $33, XP: $3.** 36408 N Black Canyon Hwy. I-17, exit 225, 0.3 mi w, follow signs.

APACHE JUNCTION — SUPERSTITION SUNRISE LUXURY RV RESORT. (480) 986-4524. **2P $50. (no credit cards).** 702 S Meridian Rd. US 60, exit 193 (Signal Butte Rd), 0.4 mi n to Southern, 1 mi e, then 0.5 mi n.

BENSON — BUTTERFIELD RV RESORT. (520) 586-4400. **2P $28-$35, XP: $2.** 251 S Ocotillo Rd. I-10, exit 304 (Ocotillo Rd), 0.6 mi s.

BENSON — COCHISE TERRACE RV RESORT. (520) 586-0600. **2P $23-$34, XP: $2.** 1030 S Barrel Cactus Ridge. I-10, exit 302, 1 mi s on SR 90, then just w.

BENSON — PATO BLANCO LAKES RV RESORT. (520) 586-8966. **$38.** 635 E Pearl St. I-10, exit 306, just s, 0.7 mi w on Frontage Rd, then 0.4 mi n on County Rd.

BENSON — SAN PEDRO RESORT COMMUNITY. (520) 586-9546. **2P $27, XP: $2.** 1110 S Hwy 80, Box 1. I-10, exit 304 (Ocotillo Ave), 0.5 mi s, 1 mi e on 4th St, then 1.3 mi se.

CAMP VERDE — DISTANT DRUMS RV RESORT. (928) 554-8000. **2P $20-$38, XP: $5.** 583 W Middle Verde Rd. I-17, exit 289, just sw.

CASA GRANDE — FIESTA GRANDE-RV RESORT. (520) 836-7222. **Call for rates.** 1511 E Florence Blvd. I-10, exit 194, 2 mi w.

CASA GRANDE — PALM CREEK GOLF AND RV RESORT. (520) 421-7000. **2P $30-$59, XP: $2-$5.** 1110 N Henness Rd. I-10, exit 194, 1 mi w, then just n.

ELOY — DESERT VALLEY RV RESORT. (520) 466-4500. **2P $32, XP: $3.** 4555 W Tonto Rd. I-10, exit 203 (Toltec Rd), 0.5 mi n on Toltec Rd, then 0.5 mi w.

FORT MCDOWELL — EAGLE VIEW RV RESORT AT FT MCDOWELL. ⓐⓐⓐ (480) 789-5310. **4P $43-$47, XP: $10.** 9605 N Ft McDowell Rd. Jct Shea Blvd, 2 mi ne on SR 87, 0.5 mi se.

GOLD CANYON — CANYON VISTAS RV RESORT. (480) 288-8844. **2P $20-$39, XP: $3.** 6601 E US Hwy 60. 1.2 mi w of Kings Ranch Rd; between MM 202 and 201.

HUACHUCA CITY — TOMBSTONE TERRITORIES RV PARK. ⓐⓐⓐ (520) 457-2584. **2P $30-$34, XP: $1.** 2111 E Hwy 82. Jct SR 90, 7.7 mi e; between MM 59 and 60.

LAKE HAVASU CITY — CRAZY HORSE CAMPGROUNDS. (928) 855-4033. **Call for rates. (no credit cards).** 1534 Beachcomber Blvd. 0.7 mi w of London Bridge/US 95 on McCulloch Blvd, just w.

LAKE HAVASU CITY — HAVASU RV RESORT. (928) 764-2020. **2P $46-$50, XP: $5.** 1905 Victoria Farms Rd. From London Bridge, 5.3 mi n on SR 95, just e on Chenoweth Dr, then 0.4 mi n.

LAKE HAVASU CITY — ISLANDER RV RESORT. (928) 680-2000. **2P $44-$89, XP: $4-$6.** 751 Beachcomber Blvd. Jct Lake Havasu Blvd, 1.7 mi sw on McCulloch Blvd.

LAKE HAVASU CITY — PROSPECTOR'S RV RESORT. (928) 764-2000. **Call for rates.** 4750 London Bridge Rd N. 7.6 mi n of London Bridge; 1.5 mi sw of jct SR 95.

MESA — APACHE WELLS RV RESORT. (480) 832-4324. **2P $20-$39, XP: $3.** 2656 N 56th St. Jct N Higley Rd, 0.4 mi e on E McDowell Rd, just s.

MESA — GOOD LIFE RV RESORT. ⓐⓐⓐ (480) 832-4990. **2P $30-$40, XP: $3.** 3403 E Main St. US 60, exit 184 (Val Vista Dr), 2 mi n, then just w.

MESA — MESA REGAL RV RESORT. (480) 830-2821. **Call for rates. (no credit cards).** 4700 E Main St. Just e of Greenfield Rd.

MESA — MESA SPIRIT RV RESORT. ⓐⓐⓐ (480) 832-1770. **2P $19-$48, XP: $4.** 3020 E Main St. US 60, exit 184 (Val Vista Dr), 2 mi n to Main St, then 0.8 mi w.

MESA — MONTE VISTA VILLAGE RESORT. (480) 833-2223. **Call for rates.** 8865 E Baseline Rd. US 60, exit 191 (Ellsworth), 0.6 mi s, then just w.

MESA — SUN LIFE VACATION RESORT. (480) 981-9500. **Call for rates. (no credit cards).** 5055 E University Dr. Just w of Higley Rd.

MESA — TOWERPOINT RV RESORT. 🟦 (480) 832-4996. **2P $30-$40, XP: $3.** 4860 E Main St. US 60, exit 186 (Higley Rd), 2 mi n, then just w.

MESA — VAL VISTA VILLAGE. (480) 832-2547. **2P $20-$65, XP: $3.** 233 N Val Vista Dr. US 60, exit 184 (Val Vista Dr), 2.2 mi n.

MESA — VALLE DEL ORO RV RESORT. (480) 984-1146. **Call for rates.** 1452 S Ellsworth Rd. US 60, exit 191, just n.

MESA — VIEWPOINT RV & GOLF RESORT. (480) 373-8700. **2P $35-$79, XP: $3-$6.** 8700 E University Dr. 2.4 mi e of Power Rd.

PHOENIX — DESERT SHADOWS RV RESORT. 🟦 (623) 869-8178. **2P $34, XP: $3.** 19203 N 29th Ave. I-17, exit 214A (Union Hills) northbound, 0.3 mi w, then 0.4 mi n; exit 214 A&B southbound, 0.5 mi s, 0.3 mi w on Union Hills, then 0.4 mi n.

PICACHO — PICACHO PEAK RV RESORT. (520) 466-7841. **2P $30, XP: $2.** 17065 E Peak Ln. I-10, exit 219, 0.7 mi s on frontage road. (PO Box 300, 85241).

SHOW LOW — VOYAGER AT JUNIPER RIDGE. 🟦 (928) 532-3456. **2P $24-$37, XP: $2.** 1993 Juniper Ridge Resort. Jct US 60, 7.3 mi n on SR 77 to White Mountain Lake Rd, then 3 mi e.

SUN CITY — PARADISE RV RESORT. 🟦 (623) 977-0344. **Call for rates.** 10950 W Union Hills Dr. Loop 101, exit 15 (Union Hills Dr), 3.8 mi w.

TONOPAH — SADDLE MOUNTAIN RV PARK. (623) 386-3892. **2P $28, XP: $2.** 3607 N 411th Ave. I-10, exit 94, 0.6 mi s.

TUCSON — BEAUDRY RV RESORT. (520) 239-1300. **4P $25-$59.** 5151 S Country Club. I-10, exit 264B (Palo Verde and Irvington), just n to Irvington, 0.5 mi w, then just s.

TUCSON — VOYAGER RV RESORT. 🟦 (520) 574-5000. **4P $32-$54, XP: $5.** 8701 S Kolb Rd. I-10, exit 270, 0.7 mi s.

YUMA — ARABY ACRES RV RESORT. (928) 344-8666. **2P $40-$53, XP: $2.** 6649 E 32nd St. I-8, exit 7 (Araby Rd), just s, then just e.

YUMA — BONITA MESA RV RESORT. (928) 342-2999. **2P $35, XP: $5.** 9400 N Frontage Rd. I-8, exit 12 (Fortuna Rd), just n, then 1.6 mi w.

YUMA — COCOPAH RV & GOLF RESORT. (928) 343-9300. **2P $32-$37, XP: $2.** 6800 Strand Ave. I-8, exit Winterhaven/4th Ave eastbound, 0.5 mi s on 4th Ave, 2.4 mi w on 1st St, just s on Ave C, 1.4 mi w on Riverside, then 0.9 mi nw.

YUMA — DEL PUEBLO RV PARK & TENNIS RESORT. (928) 341-2100. **Call for rates. (no credit cards).** 14794 Ave 3 E. I-8, exit 3 (Ave 3 E/SR 280 S), 5.3 mi s.

YUMA — HIDDEN SHORES RV VILLAGE. (928) 539-6700. **6P $54-$84.** 10300 Imperial Dam Rd. I-8, exit 12 (Fortuna Rd), 1.9 mi n, 10.4 mi n on US 95, then 6.5 mi w; Yuma Proving Ground Base.

YUMA — LAS QUINTAS OASIS RESORT. (928) 305-9005. **2P $35, XP: $2.** 10442 E Frontage Rd. I-8, exit 12 (Fortuna Rd), just n, then 0.6 mi w; north side of interstate.

YUMA — SUN VISTA RV RESORT. 🟦 (928) 726-8920. **2P $46, XP: $3.** 7201 E 32nd St (Business 8). I-8, exit 7 (Araby Rd), just s, then 0.5 mi e.

YUMA — WESTWIND RV & GOLF RESORT. 🟦 (928) 342-2992. **2P $32-$50, XP: $3.** 9797 E 32nd St (S Frontage Rd). I-8, exit 12 (Fortuna Rd) on south side, 1 mi w.

California

AGUANGA — OUTDOOR RESORTS RANCHO CALIFORNIA. (951) 767-0848. **Call for rates.** 45525 Hwy 79 S. I-15, exit 58 (SR 79 S), 14 mi e; just e of SR 371.

BIG BEAR LAKE — BIG BEAR SHORES RV RESORT & YACHT CLUB. (909) 866-4151. **6P $60-$140.** 40751 North Shore Ln. SR 18, 5 mi e of the dam on SR 38 (North Shore Dr), 1.2 mi se. (PO Box 1572, 92315).

BUELLTON — FLYING FLAGS RV PARK & CAMPGROUND. 🟦 (805) 688-3716. **2P $22-$98, XP: $3.** 180 Ave of the Flags. Just w of US 101, exit 140A (SR 246).

CASTAIC — VALENCIA TRAVEL VILLAGE. 🟦 (661) 257-3333. **2P $55-$60, XP: $2.** 27946 Henry Mayo Rd. I-5, exit SR 126, 1.3 mi w.

CATHEDRAL CITY — OUTDOOR RESORTS/PALM SPRINGS. (760) 324-4005. **Call for rates.** 69-411 Ramon Rd. I-10, exit 126 (Date Palm Dr), 2.2 mi s, then 0.5 mi e.

CHULA VISTA — CHULA VISTA RV RESORT. (619) 422-0111. **4P $45-$75, XP: $3.** 460 Sandpiper Way. I-5, exit 7B (J St/Marina Pkwy), 4 mi w, then 0.5 mi n.

CHULA VISTA — SAN DIEGO METRO KOA. (619) 427-3601. **4P $35-$235, XP: $4.** 111 N 2nd Ave. I-5, exit 8B (E St), 1 mi e to 2nd Ave, then 1 mi n; I-805, exit E St, 1 mi w, then just n.

COLOMA — COLOMA RESORT. (530) 621-2267. **2P $40-$45, XP: $7.** 6921 Mt. Murphy Rd. E off SR 49 on Mt. Murphy Rd; on South Fork of American River. (PO Box 516, 95613).

DESERT HOT SPRINGS — SKY VALLEY RESORT. (760) 329-2909. **2P $35-$44, XP: $5.** 74-711 Dillon Rd. I-10, exit Palm Dr, 3.3 mi n, then 8.5 mi e.

EL CENTRO — DESERT TRAILS RV PARK. (760) 352-7275. **2P $22-$39, XP: $3.** 225 Wake Ave. I-8, exit 115 (4th St/SR 86), just s, then just e.

EL CENTRO — SUNBEAM LAKE RV RESORT. (760) 352-7154. **Call for rates.** 1716 W Sunbeam Lake Dr. I-8, exit 107 (Drew Rd), 0.5 mi n.

FORTUNA — RIVERWALK RV PARK & CAMPGROUND. (707) 725-3359. **2P $22-$65, XP: $5.** 2189 Riverwalk Dr. W of US 101, exit Kenmar Rd.

GARBERVILLE — BENBOW VALLEY RV RESORT & GOLF COURSE. (707) 923-2777. **2P $42-$60, XP: $6.** 7000 Benbow Dr. US 101, exit Benbow Dr, 2 mi s.

HEMET — GOLDEN VILLAGE PALMS RV RESORT. (951) 925-4123. **2P $42-$60, XP: $10.** 3600 W Florida Ave. SR 79 N (San Jacinto St), 3 mi w.

INDIO — INDIAN WELLS RV PARK. (760) 347-0895. **2P $46-$56, XP: $3-$5.** 47-340 Jefferson St. I-10, exit 139 (Jefferson St/Indio Blvd), 3 mi s.

INDIO — OUTDOOR RESORTS INDIO-THE ULTIMATE MOTOR-COACH RESORT. (760) 775-7255. **4P $40-$80, XP: $5.** 80-394 48th Ave. I-10, exit 139 (Jefferson St/Indio Blvd), 3.5 mi s, then just e.

JACKSON — JACKSON RANCHERIA RV PARK. (209) 223-8358. **$30-$55.** 12222 New York Ranch Rd. 2.5 mi e from jct SR 49 and 88, then just 1 mi n.

JULIAN — PINEZANITA TRAILER RANCH & CAMPGROUND. (760) 765-0429. **2P $25-$32, XP: $2-$4.** 4446 SR 79. On SR 79, 3.6 mi s of SR 78. (PO Box 2380, 92036).

LODI — FLAG CITY RV RESORT. (209) 339-8300. **2P $44, XP: $2.** 6120 W Banner St. I-5, exit SR 12 E, s on Star St, then just e.

NEWPORT BEACH — NEWPORT DUNES WATERFRONT RV RESORT. (949) 729-3863. **6P $60-$350.** 1131 Back Bay Dr. SR 73, exit 15 (Jamboree Rd) southbound, 3 mi s, then just n on SR 1; exit 13 (Bison Ave) northbound, just w to MacArthur Blvd, 2.5 mi s to SR 1, then 1.5 mi n.

NILAND — FOUNTAIN OF YOUTH SPA. (760) 354-1340. **2P $18-$43, XP: $2-$5.** 10249 Coachella Canal Rd. 14 mi nw on SR 111, then 2.3 mi ne on Hot Mineral Spa Rd.

ORANGE — ORANGELAND RECREATION VEHICLE PARK. (714) 633-0414. **8P $60-$75, XP: $2.** 1600 W Struck Ave. SR 57, exit 2 (Katella Ave), 0.5 mi e, then just s.

PASO ROBLES — WINE COUNTRY RV RESORT. (805) 238-4560. **2P $39-$79, XP: $3-$5.** 2500 Airport Rd. US 101, exit 231B (SR 46/Fresno/Bakersfield), 2 mi e, then just n. (PO Box 2552, 93447).

PETALUMA — SAN FRANCISCO NORTH/PETALUMA CAMP-GROUNDS. (707) 763-1492. **2P $42-$240, XP: $5-$10.** 20 Rainsville Rd. US 101, exit Penngrove, just w to Stony Point Rd, then 0.5 mi n.

PISMO BEACH — PACIFIC DUNES RANCH RV PARK. (805) 489-7787. **6P $43-$55, XP: $5.** 1205 Silver Spur Pl. In Oceano; SR 1, exit 22nd St, 0.3 mi s, then 0.4 mi w.

PISMO BEACH — PISMO COAST VILLAGE RV RESORT. (805) 773-1811. **6P $38-$56, XP: $2.** 165 S Dolliver St. 0.5 mi s on SR 1.

PLYMOUTH — FAR HORIZONS 49'ER VILLAGE. (209) 245-6981. **Call for rates.** 18265 Hwy 49. On SR 49, 0.3 mi s.

RED BLUFF — DURANGO RV RESORT. (530) 527-5300. **Call for rates. (no credit cards).** 100 Lake Ave. I-5, exit 649 (SR 36/Antelope Rd), just w, just ne on Belle Mill Rd, n on East Ave, then just ne.

REDDING — PREMIER RV RESORTS. (530) 246-0101. **2P $34-$45, XP: $3.** 280 N Boulder Dr. I-5, exit 380, SR 299 E (Burney-Alturas/Lake Blvd), just w on Lake Blvd, then just n.

SAN DIEGO — CAMPLAND ON THE BAY. (858) 581-4260. **Call for rates.** 2211 Pacific Beach Dr. I-5, exit 23A (Grand Ave) northbound, 1 mi w to Olney, then 0.3 mi s; exit 23 (Balboa/Garnet) southbound, s on Mission Bay Dr to Grand Ave, then 1 mi w to Olney.

SAN DIMAS — EAST SHORE RV PARK. (909) 599-8355. **2P $44-$49, XP: $3.** 1440 Camper View Rd. I-10, exit 44 (Fairplex Dr), 0.6 mi n, 0.6 mi w on Via Verde, then 0.6 mi n; in Frank G Bonelli Regional Park.

SAN JUAN BAUTISTA — BETABEL RV RESORT. (831) 623-2202. **2P $38, XP: $4.** 9664 Betabel Rd. US 101, exit Betabel Rd, just w.

SANTA BARBARA — OCEAN MESA AT EL CAPITAN. (805) 685-3887. **4P $40-$90, XP: $10.** 11560 Calle Real. US 101, exit 117 (El Capitan State Beach), just n to El Capitan Canyon sign, then e. (101 El Captain Terrance Ln, 93117).

SHAVER LAKE — CAMP EDISON. (559) 841-3134. **Call for rates.** 42696 Tollhouse Rd. Just ne; lakeside. (PO Box 600, 93664).

TEMECULA — PECHANGA RV RESORT. ⚫ (951) 770-2658. **$42-$52.** 45000 Pechanga Pkwy. I-15, exit 58 (SR 79 S), 1 mi e, then 2 mi s. 🅰 ⚓ 🚫

TEMECULA — VAIL LAKE RESORT. (951) 303-0173. **Call for rates.** 38000 Hwy 79 S. I-15, exit 58 (SR 79 S), 9 mi se. 🆂 ⚓ 🚫

TRINIDAD — EMERALD FOREST OF TRINIDAD. ⚫ (707) 677-3554. **2P $26-$42, XP: $3.** 753 Patricks Point Dr. US 101, exit Patricks Point Dr W. (PO Box 870, 95570). 🆂 🚫

WEAVERVILLE — TRINITY LAKE RESORTS AT PINEWOOD COVE RV PARK & CAMPGROUND. (530) 286-2201. **2P $20-$38, XP: $4-$5.** 45110 State Hwy 3. 14 mi ne of town. ⚓ 🚫

WILLITS — WILLITS-UKIAH KOA. (707) 459-6179. **2P $30-$75, XP: $4-$10.** 1600 Hwy 20. 1.5 mi w on SR 20, from jct US 101. (PO Box 946, 95490). ⚓ 🚫

WINTERHAVEN — RIVER'S EDGE RV RESORT. (760) 572-5105. **2P $28, XP: $2.** 2299 Winterhaven Dr. I-8, exit 170 (Winterhaven Dr), 0.5 mi e. 🅰 ⚓ 🚫

Colorado

BRECKENRIDGE — TIGER RUN RESORT. (970) 453-9690. **$37-$67.** 85 Tiger Run Rd. I-70, exit 203, 6 mi s on SR 9, then just e on Revette Dr. 🅰 ⚓ 🚫

FORT COLLINS — FORT COLLINS LAKESIDE KOA. (970) 484-9880. **2P $30-$75, XP: $3-$10.** 1910 N Taft Hill Rd. I-25, exit 269B, 6 mi w to Taft Hill, then 2.2 mi n. ⚓ 🚫

GOLDEN — DAKOTA RIDGE RV PARK. (303) 279-1625. **2P $39-$48, XP: $5.** 17800 W Colfax Ave. I-70, exit 262 (W Colfax Ave), 1.8 mi w on US 40. 🅰 ⚓ 🚫

GRAND LAKE — WINDING RIVER RESORT INC. ⚫ (970) 627-3215. **2P $30-$42, XP: $4-$5.** 1447 CR 491. 1.5 mi ne on US 34 to CR 491, then 1.5 mi w. (PO Box 629, 80447). 🚫

LOVELAND — JOHNSON'S CORNER RV RETREAT. (970) 669-8400. **4P $34-$38, XP: $3.** 3618 SE Frontage Rd. I-25, exit 254, 0.3 mi se; adjacent to Great Colorado Marketplace. 🅰 ⚓ 🚫

Florida

ARCADIA — LITTLE WILLIES RV RESORT. (863) 494-2717. **Call for rates. (no credit cards).** 5905 NE Cubitus Ave. 3.8 mi n on US 17, just w on NE McKay St, then 1.4 mi n. 🅰 ⚓ 🚫 ♿

ARCADIA — TOBY'S RV RESORT. (863) 494-1744. **2P $25-$48.** 3550 NE Hwy 70. On SR 70, 2.7 mi e. 🅰 ⚓ 🚫

BRADENTON — HORSESHOE COVE RV RESORT. (941) 758-5335. **2P $30-$60, XP: $3.** 5100 60th St E. I-75, exit 217 southbound; exit 217B northbound, 1.7 mi w on SR 70, then just n on Caruso Rd. 🅰 ⚓ 🚫

BRADENTON — MANATEE ENCORE RV RESORT. (941) 745-2600. **$27-$67.** 800 Kay Rd NE. I-75, exit 220 southbound; exit 220B northbound, 0.6 mi w on SR 64, then 0.8 mi n on Cypress Creek Blvd (merges to Kay Rd NE). 🆂 ⚓ 🚫

CHOKOLOSKEE — OUTDOOR RESORTS OF AMERICA OF CHOKOLOSKEE. (239) 695-2881. **Call for rates.** 100 CR 29 S. On CR 29; center. (PO Box 39, 34138). 🅰 ⚓ 🚫

CRYSTAL RIVER — CRYSTAL ISLES RV RESORT. (352) 795-3774. **Call for rates.** 11419 W Fort Island Tr. Jct US 19, 4.5 mi w on SR 44 W. ⚓ 🚫

CRYSTAL RIVER — CRYSTAL RIVER RV PARK. (352) 685-1900. **Call for rates.** 275 S Rock Crusher Rd. 1.5 mi s of SR 44. ⚓ 🚫

DAVENPORT — DEER CREEK RV RESORT. (863) 424-2839. **2P $45-$65.** 42749 Hwy 27. I-4, exit 55, 1 mi se. ⚓ 🚫 ♿

DAVENPORT — FORT SUMMIT KOA. ⚫ (863) 424-1880. **2P $44-$78, XP: $4.** 2525 Frontage Rd. Jct US 27 and I-4, exit 55, on frontage road; behind Best Western. ⚓ 🚫

DEBARY — HIGH BANKS MARINA & CAMP RESORT. (386) 668-4491. **2P $45-$65, XP: $5.** 488 W Highbanks Rd. 2.7 mi w of US 17-92. ⚓ 🚫

DESTIN — DESTIN RV BEACH RESORT. (850) 837-3529. **Call for rates.** 362 Miramar Beach Dr. 4.1 mi e of SR 293 (Mid-Bay Bridge), just s. 🅰 ⚓

FORT MYERS — SIESTA BAY RV RESORT. ⚫ (239) 466-8988. **2P $32-$49, XP: $4.** 19333 Summerlin Rd. 1.6 mi sw of jct US 41 on Gladiolus Dr (CR 865), 4.8 mi s on CR 869. 🅰 ⚓ 🚫

FORT MYERS BEACH — GULF WATERS RV RESORT. ⚫ (239) 437-5888. **Call for rates.** 11301 Summerlin Square Rd. 2.6 mi nw of jct Matanzas Pass Bridge, 0.4 mi e on Summerlin Rd, just s on Pine Ridge Rd, then just w. 🅰 ⚓ 🚫 ♿

FORT MYERS BEACH — INDIAN CREEK PARK RV RESORT & MANUFACTURED HOME COMMUNITY. ⚫ (239) 466-6060. **2P $47-$49, XP: $5.** 17340 San Carlos Blvd. 2.4 mi nw of jct Matanzas Pass Bridge on SR 865. 🅰 ⚓ 🚫

FORT OGDEN — LIVE OAK RV RESORT. (863) 993-4014. **2P $26-$45, XP: $2.** 12865 SW Hwy 17. On US 17, 3.3 mi s. 🅰 ⚓ 🚫 ♿

FORT PIERCE — TREASURE COAST RV RESORT. (772) 468-2099. **4P $39-$46.** 2550 Crossroads Pkwy. I-95, exit 129 (SR 70), just w, then just n. 🅰 ⚓ 🚫 ♿

JACKSONVILLE — **FLAMINGO LAKE RV RESORT.** ▲▲▲ (904) 766-0672. **2P $42-$75, XP: $3.** 3640 Newcomb Rd. I-295, exit 32, just nw on SR 115.

JENNINGS — **JENNINGS OUTDOOR RESORT CAMPGROUND.** (386) 938-3321. **2P $27-$32, XP: $2.** 2039 Hamilton Ave. I-75, exit 467, just w on SR 143.

JENSEN BEACH — **NETTLES ISLAND.** ▲▲▲ (772) 229-1300. **$50-$80.** 9803 S Ocean Dr. On SR A1A, 2.3 mi n of jct SR 732 (Jensen Beach Cswy); on S Hutchinson Island.

KISSIMMEE — **OUTDOOR RESORTS AT ORLANDO.** (863) 424-1407. **Call for rates.** 9000 W US 192. On US 192, 1 mi e of jct US 27; jct I-4, exit 64B, 6.3 mi w.

KISSIMMEE — **TROPICAL PALMS RV RESORT.** ▲▲▲ (407) 396-4595. **6P $39-$79.** 2650 Holiday Tr. I-4, exit 64, 1.5 mi e on US 192, then 0.8 mi s.

LA BELLE — **WHISPER CREEK RV RESORT.** ▲▲▲ (863) 675-6888. **2P $35. (no credit cards).** 3745 N SR 29 SW. On SR 29, 1.8 mi n of jct SR 80.

LAKE BUENA VISTA — **DISNEY'S FORT WILDERNESS RESORT & CAMPGROUND.** ▲▲▲ (407) 934-7639. **10P $43-$116.** 4510 N Fort Wilderness Tr. In Walt Disney World. (PO Box 10000, 32830-1000).

LAKELAND — **LAKELAND CAREFREE RV RESORT.** (863) 687-6146. **2P $32-$38, XP: $3.** 900 Old Combee Rd. I-4, exit 33 eastbound, 1 mi ne on SR 33, then just w; exit 38 westbound, 5 mi sw on SR 33, then just nw.

LAKELAND — **SANLAN RV PARK.** ▲▲▲ (863) 665-1726. **2P $18-$45, XP: $3.** 3929 US 98 S. I-4, exit 32, 8.7 mi s on US 98; just s of SR 570 (exit 10).

LEESBURG — **HOLIDAY TRAVEL RESORT.** ▲▲▲ (352) 787-5151. **4P $37, XP: $5.** 28229 CR 33. 3.5 mi s via US 27, 0.5 mi w.

MELBOURNE BEACH — **OUTDOOR RESORTS MELBOURNE BEACH LUXURY RV RESORT.** (321) 724-2600. **4P $57-$72, XP: $3.** 214 Horizon Ln. 2.5 mi s.

MIMS — **SEASONS IN THE SUN MOTOR COACH RESORT.** (321) 385-0440. **Call for rates.** 2400 Seasons In The Sun Blvd. I-95, exit 223, 0.5 mi w on SR 46.

NAPLES — **NEAPOLITAN COVE RV RESORT.** (239) 793-0091. **2P $30-$60.** 3729 Neapolitan Cir. On US 41; 1.1 mi n of jct CR 864 (Rattlesnake Hammock Rd).

NOKOMIS — **ENCORE ROYAL COACHMEN RESORT ON DONA BAY.** (941) 488-9674. **Call for rates.** 1070 Laurel Rd E. I-75, exit 195, 1.9 mi w (CR 762).

OCALA — **OCALA RV CAMP RESORT.** (352) 237-2138. **2P $30-$46, XP: $2-$4.** 3200 SW 38th Ave. I-75, exit 350, just w on SR 200, just n on SW 38th Ct, then 0.5 mi e.

OKEECHOBEE — **OKEECHOBEE KOA RESORT & GOLF COURSE.** (863) 763-0231. **Call for rates.** 4276 Hwy US 441 S. On US 98 and 441, 3 mi s of jct SR 70; 0.3 mi n of Lake Okeechobee and jct SR 78.

OLD TOWN — **YELLOW JACKET CAMPGROUND RESORT.** (352) 542-8365. **2P $32-$120, XP: $6-$10.** 55 SE 503 Ave. 10.7 mi s on SR 349, then 1.2 mi on dirt road.

PANAMA CITY BEACH — **EMERALD COAST RV BEACH RESORT.** ▲▲▲ (850) 235-0924. **2P $53-$80, XP: $3-$4.** 1957 Allison Ave. US 98/98A and Allison Ave, 1.5 mi w of Hathaway Bridge.

PORT CHARLOTTE — **ENCORE HARBOR LAKES RV RESORT.** (941) 624-4511. **Call for rates.** 3737 El Jobean Rd. On SR 776, 4.6 mi w of jct US 41.

PORT CHARLOTTE — **RIVERSIDE RV RESORT & CAMPGROUND.** ▲▲▲ (863) 993-2111. **4P $38-$55, XP: $2-$3.** 9770 SW CR 769. I-75, exit 170, 4.5 mi ne on Kings Hwy.

REDDICK — **OCALA NORTH RV PARK.** (352) 591-1723. **$27-$33.** 16905 NW CR 225. I-75, exit 368, just w on CR 318, then 0.8 mi s.

RIVER RANCH — **RIVER RANCH RV RESORT.** (863) 692-1116. **4P $55-$85, XP: $2.** 3400 River Ranch Blvd. 3.5 mi s of SR 60; 25 mi e of US 27; 23 mi w of Florida Tpke and US 441; just w of the Kissimmee River. (30529 River Ranch Blvd, 33867).

ROCKLEDGE — **SPACE COAST RV RESORT.** (321) 636-2873. **2P $55, XP: $3.** 820 Barnes Blvd. I-95, exit 195 (Fiske Blvd), just e, then just s on CR 502.

SARASOTA — **SUN-N-FUN RV RESORT.** ▲▲▲ (941) 371-2505. **4P $30-$75, XP: $7.** 7125 Fruitville Rd. I-75, exit 210, 1.2 mi e on SR 780.

SEBASTIAN — **ENCORE RV PARK-VERO BEACH.** (772) 589-7828. **2P $33-$56, XP: $5.** 9455 108th Ave. I-95, exit 156, just e on CR 512.

SEBRING — **BUTTONWOOD BAY RV RESORT.** ▲▲▲ (863) 655-1122. **2P $29-$39, XP: $5.** 10001 US 27 S. 1.5 mi s of SR 98.

SILVER SPRINGS — **THE SPRINGS RV RESORT.** (352) 236-5250. **2P $29, XP: $3.** 2950 NE 52nd Ct. On SR 40, 0.5 mi w of Silver Springs attraction, 0.5 mi n.

SILVER SPRINGS — **WILDERNESS RV PARK ESTATES.** (352) 625-1122. **$32, XP: $3.** 10313 E Hwy 40. On SR 40, 4.5 mi e of Silver Springs attraction.

ST. PETERSBURG — ST. PETERSBURG-MADEIRA BEACH RESORT KOA. (727) 392-2233. **Call for rates.** 5400 95th St N. Jct 38th Ave N, 1.4 mi n on Tyrone/Bay Pines Blvd (Alternate Rt US 19), 0.5 mi e.

SUMTERVILLE — SHADY BROOK GOLF & RV RESORT. (352) 568-2244. **Call for rates.** 178 N US 301. I-75, exit 321, 2.5 mi e on CR 470, then 0.7 mi n. (PO Box 130, 33585).

TAMPA — BAY BAYOU RV RESORT. 🆔 (813) 855-1000. **2P $39-$52.** 12622 Old Memorial Hwy. Jct SR 580 (Hillsborough Ave W), 0.4 mi n on Countryway Blvd, then 0.8 mi w.

TITUSVILLE — THE GREAT OUTDOORS RV & GOLF RESORT. (321) 269-5004. **2P $39-$55, XP: $3.** 125 Plantation Dr. I-95, exit 215, 0.5 mi w on SR 50, 1.8 mi s on paved entrance road.

UMATILLA — OLDE MILL STREAM RV RESORT. 🆔 (352) 669-3141. **2P $25-$35, XP: $3.** 1000 N Central Ave. 0.8 mi n on SR 19.

Georgia

PINE MOUNTAIN — PINE MOUNTAIN RV RESORT. (706) 663-4329. **Call for rates.** 8804 Hamilton Rd. I-185, exit 42, 8 mi s on US 27.

STONE MOUNTAIN — STONE MOUNTAIN PARK CAMPGROUND. (770) 498-5710. **Call for rates.** Stone Mountain Park. On east side of Stone Mountain; in Stone Mountain Memorial Park. (PO Box 778, 30086).

Idaho

CASCADE — ARROWHEAD R.V. PARK ON THE RIVER. 🆔 (208) 382-4534. **2P $18-$25, XP: $1-$2.** 955 S Hwy 55. South end of town. (PO Box 337, 83611).

COEUR D'ALENE — BLACKWELL ISLAND RV RESORT. (208) 665-1300. **2P $38-$48, XP: $3-$5.** 800 S Marina Dr. I-90, exit 12, 1.5 mi s on US 95.

KAMIAH — LEWIS-CLARK RESORT RV PARK. (208) 935-2556. **Call for rates.** 4243 Hwy 12. On US 12, 1.5 mi e.

WHITE BIRD — SWIFTWATER RV PARK. 🆔 (208) 839-2700. **2P $15-$30, XP: $5.** 3154 Salmon River Ct. Just n of Milepost 222, exit Hammer Creek Recreational area, 0.8 mi nw. (PO Box 150, 83554).

Illinois

LEE CENTER — MHC O'CONNELL'S YOGI BEAR JELLYSTONE PARK. 🆔 (815) 857-3860. **2P $38-$60, XP: $15-$20.** 970 Greenwing Rd. I-39, exit 87 (US 30), 12.8 mi w to CR 1955 E, then 3.3 mi se, follow signs. (PO Box 200, AMBOY, 61310).

MILLBROOK — YOGI BEAR'S JELLYSTONE PARK CAMP RESORT. 🆔 (630) 553-5172. **2P $45-$57, XP: $10-$15.** 8574 Millbrook Rd. 1.5 mi n of jct SR 71. (PO Box 306, 60536).

Indiana

CRAWFORDSVILLE — CRAWFORDSVILLE KOA. (765) 362-4190. **Call for rates.** 1600 Lafayette Rd. I-74, exit 34, 2 mi s on US 231.

FREMONT — YOGI BEAR'S JELLYSTONE PARK CAMP RESORT. 🆔 (260) 833-1114. **5P $30-$60, XP: $10.** 140 Ln, 201 Barton Lake. I-69, exit 157 southbound; exit 154 northbound, 3 mi w on SR 120, then 0.5 mi n on CR 300 W; Toll Rd, exit 144 to SR 120.

GRANGER — SOUTH BEND EAST KOA. (574) 277-1335. **2P $29-$51, XP: $3-$4.** 50707 Princess Way. I-80/90, exit 83, just w on SR 331, 2 mi n on SR 23 (Adams Rd), then just w.

MONTICELLO — INDIANA BEACH CAMPGROUND. (574) 583-8306. **Call for rates.** 5224 E Indiana Beach Rd. 0.5 mi w on US 24, 3.5 mi n on W Shafer Dr (6th St).

MONTICELLO — YOGI BEAR'S JELLYSTONE PARK AT INDIANA BEACH. (574) 583-8646. **Call for rates.** (no credit cards). 2882 NW Shafer Dr. 0.5 mi w on US 24, then 3.5 mi n.

PIERCETON — YOGI BEAR'S JELLYSTONE PARK CAMP-RESORT. (574) 594-2124. **5P $38-$60, XP: $6.** 1916 N 850 E. US 30, 4.3 mi n on SR 13, 1.3 mi e on CR 200.

SANTA CLAUS — LAKE RUDOLPH CAMPGROUND & RV RESORT. (812) 937-4458. **8P $25-$50.** 78 N Holiday Blvd. I-64, exit 63, 7.9 mi s on SR 162. (PO Box 98, 47579).

Louisiana

CARENCRO — BAYOU WILDERNESS RV RESORT. (337) 896-0598. **4P $39-$42, XP: $5.** 201 St Clair Rd. I-49, exit 2, 2.5 mi e on SR 98, then 1 mi n on Wilderness Tr.

HAMMOND — CALLOWAY RV & CAMPGROUND. (985) 542-8094. **Call for rates.** 14154 Club De Luxe Rd. I-12 to I-55 S, exit 28, 1 blk n, then 0.7 mi w.

KINDER — COUSHATTA CASINO RV RESORT. (337) 738-1200. **$19-$22.** 777 Pow Wow Pkwy. N of jct US 190 and 165, 4.5 mi on US 165. (PO Box 1240, 70648).

ROBERT — YOGI BEAR'S JELLYSTONE PARK CAMP-RESORT. (985) 542-1507. **Call for rates.** 46049 Hwy 445 N. I-12, exit 47, 3 mi n. (PO Box 519, 70455).

SCOTT — KOA KAMPGROUND OF LAFAYETTE. (337) 235-2739. **4P $27-$49, XP: $5-$6.** 537 Apollo Rd. I-10, exit 97, 0.5 mi s.

VIDALIA — RIVER VIEW RV PARK. ⒶⒶⒶ (318) 336-1400. **2P $30-$40, XP: $2.** 100 River View Pkwy. Jct US 65/84, 0.8 mi s on SR 131.

Maine

CASCO — POINT SEBAGO RESORT. (207) 655-3821. **4P $35-$86, XP: $5-$35.** 261 Point Sebago Rd. Jct SR 121, 3.7 mi n on US 302, then 1 mi w, follow signs.

DAMARISCOTTA — LAKE PEMAQUID CAMPGROUND. ⒶⒶⒶ (207) 563-5202. **4P $24-$46, XP: $5-$10.** 100 Twin Cove Ln. 0.8 mi n on US 1 business route, 2 mi e on Biscay Rd, then 0.3 mi n on Egypt Rd. (PO Box 967, 04543).

NORTH WATERFORD — PAPOOSE POND RESORT & CAMPGROUND. (207) 583-4470. **6P $24-$74, XP: $5-$10.** 700 Norway Rd. 1.9 mi w on SR 118 from jct SR 37; from Norway, 10 mi w on SR 118.

OLD ORCHARD BEACH — POWDER HORN FAMILY CAMPING RESORT. (207) 934-4733. **2P $29-$63, XP: $4-$10.** 48 Cascade Rd (SR 98). 1 mi nw on SR 98; jct US 1, 1.8 mi se on SR 98. (PO Box 366, 04064).

ORLAND — SHADY OAKS CAMPGROUND & CABINS. (207) 469-7739. **2P $30-$45, XP: $5.** 32 Leaches Pt. Jct US 1 and SR 175, sharp right, then 0.3 mi.

SCARBOROUGH — BAYLEY'S CAMPING RESORT. ⒶⒶⒶ (207) 883-6043. **2P $31-$86, XP: $5-$8.** 275 Pine Point Rd. Jct US 1, 2 mi e via SR 9 (Pine Point Rd), watch for sign.

WELLS — WELLS BEACH RESORT CAMPGROUND. ⒶⒶⒶ (207) 646-7570. **2P $34-$75, XP: $8.** 1000 Post Rd (US 1). Jct SR 109/9, 1.3 mi s.

Maryland

BERLIN — FRONTIER TOWN CAMPGROUND. (410) 641-0880. **2P $27-$84, XP: $6-$12.** 8428 Stephen Decatur Hwy. Jct SR 50, 4 mi s on SR 611. (PO Box 691, OCEAN CITY, 21843).

COLLEGE PARK — CHERRY HILL PARK. ⒶⒶⒶ (301) 937-7116. **2P $55-$65, XP: $5.** 9800 Cherry Hill Rd. I-95, exit 29B, 1 mi w on SR 212 (Powder Mill Rd), then 1 mi s; I-495, exit 25, just s to Cherry Hill Rd, then 1 mi nw.

FLINTSTONE — HIDDEN SPRINGS CAMPGROUND. (814) 767-9676. **4P $27-$31, XP: $2.** I-68, exit 50 to Rocky Gap State Park, 3.5 mi n on Pleasant Valley Rd. (PO Box 190, 21530).

FREELAND — MORRIS MEADOWS RECREATION FARM. ⒶⒶⒶ (410) 329-6636. **2P $28-$55, XP: $5-$10.** 1523 Freeland Rd. I-83, exit 36 (SR 439), w to jct SR 45, 1 mi n, then 3 mi w, follow signs.

WILLIAMSPORT — YOGI BEAR'S JELLYSTONE PARK CAMP RESORT HAGERSTOWN. (301) 223-7117. **Call for rates.** 16519 Lappans Rd. I-81, exit 1, 1.2 mi e on SR 68.

Massachusetts

BRIMFIELD — QUINEBAUG COVE CAMPGROUND. (413) 245-9525. **Call for rates.** 49 E Brimfield-Holland Rd. I-84, exit 3B, 3.8 mi w on US 20, then 0.3 mi s.

FOXBORO — NORMANDY FARMS CAMPGROUND. (508) 543-7600. **2P $33-$72, XP: $5-$10.** 72 West St. I-495, exit 14A, 1 mi n on US 1, then 1.3 mi e on Thurston and West sts.

OAKHAM — PINE ACRES FAMILY CAMPING RESORT. (508) 882-9509. **2P $33-$75, XP: $7-$15.** 203 Bechan Rd. Jct SR 122, 2 mi sw on SR 148, then just s via Spencer Rd.

SAVOY — SHADY PINES CAMPGROUND. (413) 743-2694. **Call for rates.** 547 Loop Rd. On SR 8A and 116, 3.1 mi se.

Michigan

BAY VIEW — PETOSKEY KOA RV & CABIN RESORT. (231) 347-0005. **Call for rates.** 1800 N US 31. US 31, 1 mi n of SR 119.

PORT HURON — PORT HURON KOA KAMPGROUND. (810) 987-4070. **8P $20-$75, XP: $5.** 5111 Lapeer Rd. I-94, exit 262, 8 mi n on Wadhams Rd, then 0.3 mi e; I-69, exit 196, 0.4 mi n on Wadhams Rd, then 0.3 mi e.

PORT SANILAC — LAKE HURON CAMPGROUND. (810) 622-0110. **2P $21-$68, XP: $5-$7.** 2353 N Lakeshore Rd (M25). Jct SR 25 and 46, 5 mi n.

Minnesota

AUSTIN — BEAVER TRAILS CAMPGROUND AND RV PARK. ⒶⒶⒶ (507) 584-6611. **2P $30-$50, XP: $3-$5.** 21943 630th Ave. I-90, exit 187 (SR 20), just sw.

CALEDONIA — DUNROMIN' PARK. (507) 724-2514. **2P $30-$45, XP: $4-$6.** 12757 Dunromin Dr. Jct SR 44, 2.8 mi s on SR 76 S, 0.5 mi e.

CASS LAKE — STONY POINT RESORT, TRAILER PARK CAMP-GROUNDS. ⒶⒶⒶ (218) 335-6311. **2P $24-$35, XP: $3.** 5510 US 2 NW. On US 2, 2 mi e of jct SR 371. (PO Box 518, 56633).

COKATO — COKATO LAKE CAMPING & RV RESORT. (320) 286-5779. **Call for rates.** 2945 CR 4 SW. 2.8 mi n of jct SR 12.

HINCKLEY — GRAND CASINO HINCKLEY RV RESORT & CHA-LETS. ⚠️ (320) 384-4886. **$15-$23.** 1326 Fire Monument Rd. I-35, exit 183, 1 mi e on SR 48.

PARK RAPIDS — BREEZE CAMPING & RV RESORT ON EAGLE LAKE. (218) 732-5888. **Call for rates.** 25824 CR 89. 9 mi n on US 71 from jct SR 34.

PARK RAPIDS — VAGABOND VILLAGE CAMPGROUND. (218) 732-5234. **Call for rates. (no credit cards).** 23801 Green Pines Rd. 2 mi e on SR 34, 5.7 mi n on CR 4, just w on CR 40, then 0.5 mi w via signs.

PRIOR LAKE — DAKOTAH MEADOWS RV PARK. ⚠️ (952) 445-8800. **Call for rates.** 2341 Park Pl. Just w of CR 83.

RICHMOND — EL RANCHO MANANA CAMPGROUND & RIDING STABLE. ⚠️ (320) 597-2740. **Call for rates.** 27302 Ranch Rd. Jct SR 23 and 24, 4 mi n on CR 9, 2 mi ne on Manana and Ranch rds; 9 mi s of jct I-94, exit 153, via CR 9.

WALKER — SHORES OF LEECH LAKE CAMPGROUND & MARINA. (218) 547-1819. **$45, XP: $8.** 6166 Morriss Point Rd. 2.8 mi nw on SR 371 and 200 from jct SR 34, 0.5 mi e, follow signs.

Mississippi

BILOXI — MAJESTIC OAKS RV RESORT. (228) 436-4200. **$39-$44.** 1750 Pass Rd. I-110, exit 46A, 3.1 mi w on US 90, 0.6 mi n on Rodenberg Ave, then just w.

OCEAN SPRINGS — CAMP JOURNEY'S END. (228) 875-2100. **2P $38, XP: $5.** 7501 Hwy 57. I-10, exit 57, 0.5 mi n.

PELAHATCHIE — YOGI ON THE LAKE. ⚠️ (601) 854-6859. **$17-$59, XP: $5.** 143 Campground Rd. I-20, exit 68, 2 mi n on SR 43, 0.5 mi w on Lake Rd, then just n.

PICAYUNE — SUN ROAMERS RV RESORT. ⚠️ (601) 798-5818. **2P $26-$36, XP: $3.** 41 Mississippi Pines Blvd. I-59, exit 4, 0.8 mi e on SR 43 S, then 0.5 mi s on Stafford Rd.

TOOMSUBA — MERIDIAN EAST/TOOMSUBA KOA. (601) 632-1684. **Call for rates.** 3953 KOA Campground Rd. I-20/59, exit 165, 1.5 mi s, follow signs.

TUNICA — GRAND CASINO TUNICA RV RESORT. (662) 363-2788. **Call for rates.** 111 Resort Village Rd. US 61, just w to Grand Casino Pkwy S.

VICKSBURG — MAGNOLIA RV PARK RESORT. ⚠️ (601) 631-0388. **4P $24-$27, XP: $3.** 211 Miller St. I-20, exit 1B, 1.1 mi s on US 61, just w.

Missouri

BRANSON — THE WILDERNESS AT SILVER DOLLAR CITY LOG CABINS AND RV'S. (417) 338-8189. **2P $25-$35, XP: $3-$5.** 5125 SR 265. 0.5 mi s of jct SR 76.

EUREKA — YOGI BEAR'S JELLYSTONE PARK CAMP-RESORT. (636) 938-5925. **2P $26-$52, XP: $4.** 5300 Fox Creek Rd. I-44, exit 261, 0.5 mi w. (PO Box 626, 63025).

KANSAS CITY — WORLDS OF FUN VILLAGE. (816) 453-7280. **6P $30-$40, XP: $2.** 8000 Parvin Rd. I-435, exit 54, just se. (4545 Worlds of Fun Ave, 64161).

MONROE CITY — MARK TWAIN LANDING RV RESORT. (573) 735-9422. **4P $35-$45, XP: $5.** 42819 Landing Ln. Jct US 36 and SR J, 8.2 mi s.

PLATTE CITY — BASSWOOD RESORT. (816) 858-5556. **Call for rates.** 15880 Interurban Rd. I-29, exit 18, just e, 3.5 mi e on SR 92 to Winan Rd, then 1.9 mi n, follow signs.

Montana

MISSOULA — JELLYSTONE RV RESORT. (406) 543-9400. **2P $28-$34, XP: $3-$4.** 9900 Jellystone Ave. I-90, exit 96 (west side entry), 0.9 mi n.

POLSON — POLSON MOTOR COACH & RV RESORT/KOA. (406) 883-2151. **2P $39-$65, XP: $3-$5.** 200 Irvine Flats Rd. 1 mi n on US 93, 0.3 mi w.

WEST GLACIER — WEST GLACIER KOA. (406) 387-5341. **2P $30-$51, XP: $5-$6.** 355 Halfmoon Flats Rd. 2.5 mi w on US 2, 1 mi s. (PO Box 215, 59936).

Nebraska

NORTH PLATTE — HOLIDAY RV PARK & CAMPGROUND. ⚠️ (308) 534-2265. **$20-$34, XP: $2.** 601 Halligan Dr. I-80, exit 177, just n on US 83, immediate right turn on frontage road (Halligan Dr), then 0.5 mi e.

Nevada

BOULDER CITY — BOULDER OAKS RV RESORT. (702) 294-4425. **4P $37, XP: $3.** 1010 Industrial Rd. Jct US 93, just w. (PO Box 62364, 89006).

CARSON CITY — COMSTOCK COUNTRY RV RESORT. ⟨AAA⟩ (775) 882-2445. **2P $30-$50, XP: $2.** 5400 S Carson St (US 395). Just s of jct US 50 W.

LAS VEGAS — OASIS LAS VEGAS RV RESORT. ⟨AAA⟩ (702) 260-2020. **4P $39-$71, XP: $2.** 2711 W Windmill Ln. I-15, exit 33 (Blue Diamond Rd), 0.5 mi e.

MESQUITE — DESERT SKIES RESORT. (928) 347-6000. **2P $50, XP: $3.** 350 E Hwy 91. I-15, exit 122, 1.5 mi ne via Hillside Dr. (PO Box 3780, 89024).

MINDEN — CARSON VALLEY RV RESORT & CASINO. (775) 782-9711. **4P $22-$35, XP: $6.** 1639 US 395 N. Center.

MINDEN — SILVER CITY RV RESORT. ⟨AAA⟩ (775) 267-3359. **2P $35, XP: $4.** 3165 US 395. 6 mi s of Carson City; 3 mi s of jct US 50 W.

PAHRUMP — PAHRUMP DESERT RETREAT KOA. ⟨AAA⟩ (775) 751-1174. **2P $28-$55, XP: $5-$10.** 301 W Leslie St. 10 mi n of SR 160 and 372, jct SR 160.

PAHRUMP — TERRIBLE'S LAKESIDE CASINO & RV RESORT. ⟨AAA⟩ (775) 751-7770. **6P $27-$39, XP: $2.** 5870 S Homestead Rd. SR 160, 3.5 mi s.

ZEPHYR COVE — ZEPHYR COVE RESORT RV PARK & CAMPGROUND. ⟨AAA⟩ (775) 589-4907. **6P $25-$65.** 760 Hwy 50. US 50, 4 mi n of state line. (PO Box 830, 89448).

New Hampshire

BARRINGTON — AYERS LAKE FARM CAMPGROUND. ⟨AAA⟩ (603) 335-1110. **4P $33-$47, XP: $5-$7. (no credit cards).** 557 US 202. Spaulding Tpke, exit 13, 4.5 mi w.

BARRINGTON — BARRINGTON SHORES CAMPGROUND. ⟨AAA⟩ (603) 664-9333. **5P $36-$50, XP: $3-$12.** 70 Hall Rd. Jct SR 125 and US 4, 2.5 mi w on US 4, then 3 mi n.

CHICHESTER — HILLCREST CAMPGROUND. (603) 798-5124. **2P $29-$35, XP: $5-$12.** 78 Dover Rd. I-93, exit 15, 8 mi e on SR 4; jct SR 28 and 4, 2 mi w on SR 4.

FREEDOM — DANFORTH BAY CAMPING & RV RESORT. ⟨AAA⟩ (603) 539-2069. **Call for rates.** 196 Shawtown Rd. Jct SR 25/153, 1 mi n on SR 153, then 3 mi w on Ossipee Lake Rd.

HAMPTON FALLS — WAKEDA CAMPGROUND LLC. (603) 772-5274. **2P $32-$70, XP: $10.** 294 Exeter Rd (SR 88). SR 88, 3.8 mi w of jct US 1.

LACONIA — PAUGUS BAY CAMPGROUND. (603) 366-4757. **4P $30-$41, XP: $3-$6. (no credit cards).** 96 Hilliard Rd. Jct US 3 and SR 11B, 0.5 mi n on US 3, then w.

MEREDITH — CLEARWATER CAMPGROUND. (603) 279-7761. **Call for rates.** 26 Campground Rd (SR 104). I-93, exit 23, 3 mi e.

MEREDITH — MEREDITH WOODS 4 SEASON CAMPING AREA. (603) 279-5449. **Call for rates.** 26 Campground Rd. I-93, exit 23, 3 mi e.

MILTON — MI-TE-JO LAKESIDE FAMILY CAMPGROUND. ⟨AAA⟩ (603) 652-9022. **2P $40-$45, XP: $8. (no credit cards).** 111 Mi-Te Jo Rd. SR 16, exit 17 northbound, 0.8 mi e on SR 75, 3.3 mi n on SR 125, then 1 mi e on Townhouse Rd; exit southbound, 3.3 mi on SR 125, then 1 mi e on Townhouse Rd. (PO Box 830, 03851).

NEW HAMPTON — TWIN TAMARACK FAMILY CAMPING & RV RESORT. ⟨AAA⟩ (603) 279-4387. **2P $33-$38, XP: $1-$8.** 41 Twin Tamarack Rd. I-93, exit 23, 2.5 mi e on SR 104.

SOUTH WEARE — COLD SPRINGS CAMP RESORT. (603) 529-2528. **Call for rates.** 62 Barnard Hill Rd. Jct SR 77/149, 1.5 mi se, 0.3 mi n on sign posted road; 10 mi nw of jct SR 114/101. (22 Wildlife Dr, 03281).

TAMWORTH — CHOCORUA CAMPING VILLAGE KOA. ⟨AAA⟩ (603) 323-8536. **2P $27-$70, XP: $6-$8.** 893 White Mountain Hwy. SR 16, 2.5 mi n of jct SR 25. (PO Box 484, CHOCORUA, 03817).

TWIN MOUNTAIN — TWIN MOUNTAIN KOA KAMP-GROUND. ⟨AAA⟩ (603) 846-5559. **2P $30-$53, XP: $7-$10.** 372 SR 115. Jct US 302, 2.1 mi n on US 3, then 0.8 mi ne. (PO Box 148, 03595).

WOODSTOCK — BROKEN BRANCH KOA. (603) 745-8008. **Call for rates.** 1000 Eastside Rd (SR 175). I-93, exit 31, 2 mi s, follow signs. (PO Box 6, 03293).

New Jersey

CAPE MAY — BEACHCOMBER CAMPING RESORT. (609) 886-6035. **2P $28-$45, XP: $5-$8.** 462 Seashore Rd. Garden State Pkwy, exit 4A (SR 47 N), w to 3rd traffic light, then 1 mi s; Railroad Ave and Seashore Rd.

CAPE MAY — HOLLY SHORES CAMPGROUND. ⟨AAA⟩ (609) 886-1234. **2P $31-$58, XP: $5-$8.** 491 US 9. Garden State Pkwy, exit 4A (SR 47 N) to 2nd traffic light, 1 mi s.

CAPE MAY — SEASHORE CAMPSITES INC. ⟨AAA⟩ (609) 884-4010. **4P $24-$56, XP: $3-$5.** 720 Seashore Rd. Garden State Pkwy, exit 4A (SR 47 N), 1 mi n to CR 626, then 2.7 mi s.

CAPE MAY COURT HOUSE — BIG TIMBER LAKE CAMP-ING RESORT. ⟨AAA⟩ (609) 465-4456. **4P $43-$64, XP: $3-$10.** 116 Swainton Goshen Rd. Garden State Pkwy, exit 13 southbound, 0.5 mi w on paved road, 1 mi s on US 9, then 1 mi w (CR 646). (PO Box 366, 08210).

OCEAN VIEW — OCEAN VIEW RESORT CAMPGROUND. ⬣
(609) 624-1675. **4P $39-$72, XP: $7.** 2555 Rt 9. US 9, 0.8 mi nw of
Garden State Pkwy, exit 17 southbound; exit northbound, use service
area turnaround. (PO Box 607, 08230).

New Mexico

ALBUQUERQUE — ALBUQUERQUE CENTRAL KOA. (505)
296-2729. **Call for rates.** 12400 Skyline Rd NE. I-40, exit 166, just s,
then 0.4 mi e.

ALBUQUERQUE — AMERICAN RV PARK OF ALBUQUER-
QUE. ⬣ (505) 831-3545. **4P $29-$37, XP: $5.** 13500 Central Ave
SW. I-40, exit 149, just s, then w.

BERNALILLO — ALBUQUERQUE NORTH/BERNALILLO KOA.
(505) 867-5227. **Call for rates.** 555 S Hill Rd. I-25, exit 240. (PO Box
758, 87004).

DEMING — LITTLE VINEYARD RV PARK. ⬣ (575) 546-3560.
2P $24, XP: $2. 2901 E Pine St. I-10, exit 85, 1 mi w.

GALLUP — USA RV PARK. ⬣ (505) 863-5021. **2P $21-$29, XP:
$2.** 2925 W Hwy 66. I-40, exit 16, 1 mi e.

LAS CRUCES — HACIENDA RV RESORT. ⬣ (575) 528-5800.
2P $39-$49, XP: $2. 740 Stern Dr. I-10, exit 140, just e.

SILVER CITY — SILVER CITY KOA. (575) 388-3351. **$23-$41, XP:
$4-$5.** 11824 E Hwy 180. 4.9 mi e on US 180 and SR 90.

New York

BATH — HICKORY HILL CAMPING RESORT. (607) 776-4345. **$40-
$56.** 7531 CR 13. SR 17, exit 38, 1 mi n on SR 54, then at fork, 2 mi
n on Haverling St (CR 13).

DEWITTVILLE — CHAUTAUQUA HEIGHTS CAMPING
RESORT CAMPGROUND. (716) 386-3804. **4P $21-$39, XP: $4-$8.**
5652 Thumb Rd. I-86, exit 10 westbound, 5 mi on CR 430 W; I-90, exit
60 to Mayville, 2.4 mi on CR 430 E, then just e.

FARMINGTON — CANANDAIGUA/ROCHESTER KOA CAMP-
GROUND. (585) 398-3582. **2P $28-$40, XP: $3-$5.** 5374 Farmington
Townline Rd. I-90, exit 44, 3.2 mi s on SR 332, then 1 mi e.

GARDINER — YOGI BEAR'S JELLYSTONE PARK CAMP-
RESORTS AT LAZY RIVER. (845) 255-5193. **4P $42-$65, XP: $4-$10.**
50 Bevier Rd. 2.5 mi w on US 44 and SR 55, just s on Albany Post,
then just e.

GARRATTSVILLE — YOGI BEAR'S JELLYSTONE PARK AT
CRYSTAL LAKE. (607) 965-8265. **4P $18-$63, XP: $5-$10.** 111 E
Turtle Lake Rd. Jct SR 80, 6.2 mi s on CR 16, 0.7 mi n on CR 51, then
1.1 mi w on CR 17.

GREENFIELD PARK — SKYWAY CAMPING RESORT. (845)
647-5747. **2P $54-$65, XP: $10.** 99 Mountaindale Rd. Jct US 209 and
SR 52, 5.2 mi w on SR 52, then 1.1 mi sw.

GREENFIELD PARK — YOGI BEAR'S JELLYSTONE PARK
CAMP-RESORT AT BIRCHWOOD ACRES. (845) 434-4743. **4P $38-
$67, XP: $7-$14.** 85 Martinfeld Rd. Jct US 209 and SR 52, 8 mi w on
SR 52, then 0.5 mi s. (PO Box 482, WOODRIDGE, 12789).

LAKE GEORGE — LAKE GEORGE ESCAPE. (518) 623-3207.
2P $24-$74, XP: $6. 175 E Schroon River Rd. I-87, exit 23, 0.4 mi e on
Diamond Point Rd, then 0.8 mi n. (PO Box 431, 12845).

LAKE GEORGE — LAKE GEORGE RV PARK. (518) 792-3775.
2P $48-$72, XP: $8. 74 SR 149. I-87 (New York State Thruway), exit
20, 0.5 mi n on US 9, then 0.4 mi e.

NORTH JAVA — YOGI BEAR'S JELLYSTONE PARK OF WNY.
(585) 457-9644. **5P $20-$69, XP: $3-$10.** 5204 Youngers Rd. 3 mi s on
SR 98, 1.3 mi e on Pee-Dee Rd, then 0.8 mi s.

OLD FORGE — OLD FORGE CAMPING RESORT. (315) 369-
6011. **Call for rates.** 3347 SR 28. 1 mi n of town. (PO Box 51, 13420).

PLATTEKILL — NEWBURGH/NEW YORK CITY NORTH KOA.
⬣(845) 564-2836. **2P $32-$59, XP: $5-$7.** 119 Freetown Hwy. 1.5 mi
n on SR 32, 3 mi s of jct US 44 and SR 55, 0.5 mi e, follow signs.

PULASKI — BRENNAN BEACH RV RESORT. ⬣ (315) 298-
2242. **Call for rates.** 80 Brennan Beach. I-81, exit 36, 4 mi w on SR
13, 1 mi n on SR 3.

VERONA — THE VILLAGES AT TURNING STONE. (315) 361-
7275. **Call for rates.** 5065 SR 365. I-90, exit 33, 1.3 mi w. (PO Box 126,
13478).

WATKINS GLEN — WATKINS GLEN-CORNING KOA KAMP-
GROUND. (607) 535-7404. **2P $34-$160, XP: $3-$8.** 1710 SR 414. SR
414, 4.5 mi s of jct SR 14. (PO Box 228, 14891).

North Carolina

BOONE — KOA-BOONE. (828) 264-7250. **2P $34-$38, XP: $2-$6.**
123 Harmony Mt Ln. Jct US 221 and 421, 3 mi n on SR 194, then 1 mi
w on Ray Brown Rd.

CANDLER — KOA ASHEVILLE WEST. (828) 665-7015. **2P $25-
$60, XP: $3-$4.** 309 Wiggins Rd. I-40, exit 37, just s, 0.5 mi w on US
19/23, then 0.3 mi n.

CEDAR MOUNTAIN — BLACK FOREST CAMPING
RESORT. (828) 884-2267. **2P $25-$36, XP: $3-$5.** 100 Summer Rd.
On US 276, 12.6 mi s of Brevard. (PO Box 709, 28718).

CHEROKEE — CHEROKEE GREAT SMOKIES KOA. (828) 497-9711. **2P $32-$199, XP: $5.** 410 Big Cove Rd. 4 mi n on Big Cove Rd. (92 KOA Campground Rd, 28719).　⊇ ⊗

MARION — YOGI BEAR'S JELLYSTONE PARK. ⚠ (828) 652-7208. **4P $40-$57, XP: $5.** 1210 Deacon Dr. I-40, exit 86, just n on SR 226, 1 mi e on Fairview Dr, then 1.3 mi se.　⊇ ⊗ ♿

North Dakota

BISMARCK — BISMARCK KOA. (701) 222-2662. **2P $24-$43, XP: $3.** 3720 Centennial Rd. I-94, exit 161, 1 mi n.　⊇ ⊗

Ohio

BROOKVILLE — DAYTON TALL TIMBERS RESORT KOA. (937) 833-3888. **2P $31-$56, XP: $2-$5.** 7796 Wellbaum Rd. I-70, exit 24, 0.3 mi n on SR 49, 0.5 mi w on Pleasant Plain Rd, then 0.3 mi s.　⊇ ⊗

LATHAM — LONG'S RETREAT FAMILY RESORT. (937) 588-3725. **2P $22-$32, XP: $5.** 50 Bell Hollow Rd. 4.3 mi e on SR 124 from jct SR 41.　⊗

SHELBY — SHELBY/MANSFIELD KOA. (419) 347-1392. **2P $31-$69, XP: $5-$15.** 6787 Baker 47. 4 mi nw on SR 39, then 4.5 mi n, follow signs.　⊇ ⊗

Oklahoma

GORE — MARVAL RESORT. ⚠ (918) 489-2295. **4P $19-$196, XP: $5.** Rt 3, Box 60 Gore. I-40, exit 287, 6 mi n on SR 100, then just e.　⊇ ⊗

Oregon

BEND — CROWN VILLA RV RESORT. (541) 388-1131. **4P $34-$94, XP: $3.** 60801 Brosterhous Rd. South end of jct US 97 and Business Rt US 97, just n on SE 3rd St (Business Rt US 97) 1 mi e on Murphy Rd, then just s.　⚠ ⊗

CANNON BEACH — RV RESORT AT CANNON BEACH. ⚠ (503) 436-2231. **Call for rates.** 340 Elk Creek Rd. US 101, exit Sunset Blvd, just ne. (PO Box 1037, 97110).　⚠ ⊇ ⊗ ♿

CANYONVILLE — SEVEN FEATHERS RV RESORT. (541) 839-3599. **6P $36-$44.** 325 Creekside Dr. I-5, exit 99 southbound, just w; exit northbound, just nw.　⚠ ⊇ ⊗ ♿

COBURG — PREMIER RV RESORT OF EUGENE. (541) 686-3152. **2P $39-$45, XP: $3.** 33022 Van Duyn Rd. I-5, exit 199, just e on Van Duyn Rd, then just s.　⚠ ⊇ ⊗ ♿

HAMMOND — ASTORIA/WARRENTON/SEASIDE KOA. ⚠ (503) 861-2606. **2P $30-$48, XP: $7.** 1100 NW Ridge Rd. 4.6 mi nw of jct US 101, follow signs to Fort Stevens State Park.　⊇ ⊗

LEBANON — MALLARD CREEK GOLF & RV RESORT. (541) 259-0070. **$37.** 31958 Bellinger Scale Rd. 4.6 mi se on US 20, 1.4 mi ne on Waterloo Rd, just e on Berlin Rd, then 0.7 mi n.　⚠ ⊗

NETARTS — NETARTS BAY RV PARK & MARINA. (503) 842-7774. **4P $24-$35, XP: $5.** 2260 Bilyeu. Just w. (PO Box 218, 97143).　⚠ ⊗

NEWPORT — OUTDOOR RESORTS PACIFIC SHORES MOTORCOACH RESORT. (541) 265-3750. **6P $50-$90, XP: $5.** 6225 N Coast Hwy 101. Jct US 20, 3.4 mi n on US 101, then just w.　⚠ ⊇ ⊗ ♿

PORTLAND — COLUMBIA RIVER RV PARK. ⚠ (503) 285-1515. **2P $30-$32, XP: $3.** 10649 NE 13th Ave. I-5, exit 307, follow signs for Marine Dr E, 1.5 mi e, then just s.　⚠

SALEM — PHOENIX RV PARK. ⚠ (503) 581-2497. **2P $28-$33, XP: $2.** 4130 Silverton Rd NE. I-5, exit 256, 0.3 mi e on Market, 1.3 mi n on Lancaster, then just e.　⚠ ⊗

SALEM — SALEM PREMIER RV RESORT. (503) 364-7714. **2P $34-$45, XP: $3.** 4700 Salem-Dallas Hwy 22. I-5, exit 260A (Salem Pkwy), follow signs to city center; 3 mi sw to Commercial St NE, then 1.4 mi s to Marion St; 4.7 mi sw from Marion St Bridge via SR 22; 4.3 mi e of jct SR 22 and 99 W.　⚠ ⊇ ⊗ ♿

SISTERS — SISTERS/BEND KOA. (541) 549-3021. **2P $48-$58, XP: $4-$6.** 67667 Hwy 20 W. On US 20, 3.5 mi e.　⚠ ⊇ ⊗

WARM SPRINGS — KAHNEETA HIGH DESERT RESORT & CASINO RV PARK. (541) 553-1112. **3P $25-$55, XP: $10.** 6823 Hwy 8. 11 mi ne off US 26; on Warm Springs Indian Reservation. (PO Box 1240, 97761).　⚠ ⊇ ⊗

WELCHES — MT. HOOD VILLAGE VACATION COTTAGES & RV RESORT. ⚠ (503) 622-4011. **6P $27-$47.** 65000 E US 26. On US 26, 2 mi w.　⊇ ⊗

WILSONVILLE — PHEASANT RIDGE RV RESORT. ⚠ (503) 682-7829. **2P $37-$45, XP: $1.** 8275 SW Elligsen Rd. I-5, exit 286, just e.　$⊗ ⚠ ⊇ ⊗ ♿

Pennsylvania

BAKERSVILLE — PIONEER PARK CAMPGROUND. (814) 445-6348. **2P $24-$36, XP: $3.** 273 Trent Rd. Just e on SR 31, 0.5 mi s, follow signs.　⊇ ⊗

BEDFORD — FRIENDSHIP VILLAGE CAMPGROUND. ⚠ (814) 623-1677. **2P $22-$35, XP: $3.** 348 Friendship Village Rd. 1.3 mi w on US 30 from jct US 220, 0.5 mi n via signs.　⊇ ⊗

BELLEFONTE — BELLEFONTE/STATE COLLEGE KOA. ⚫ (814) 355-7912. **2P $22-$60, XP: $3-$6.** 2481 Jacksonville Rd. I-80, exit 161, 2 mi ne on SR 26.

BOWMANSVILLE — LAKE IN WOOD CAMPGROUND. (717) 445-5525. **2P $30-$57, XP: $5-$7.** 576 Yellow Hill Rd. SR 23, 4.5 mi n on SR 625, 1 mi ne on Oaklyn Dr, then 1.5 mi e, follow signs.

BOWMANSVILLE — OAK CREEK CAMPGROUND. ⚫ (717) 445-6161. **4P $25-$43, XP: $7.** 400 E Maple Grove Rd. SR 625, 1.5 mi e. (PO Box 128, 17507).

BOWMANSVILLE — SUN VALLEY CAMPGROUND. (717) 445-6262. **Call for rates.** 451 E Maple Grove Rd. SR 625, 1.9 mi e. (PO Box 129, 17507).

CLAY — STARLITE CAMPING RESORT. (717) 733-9655. **2P $35-$40, XP: $1-$5.** 1500 Furnace Hill Rd. US 322, 1.1 mi n on Clay Rd, 2.4 mi ne, follow signs.

COOKSBURG — KALYUMET CAMPGROUND. (814) 744-9622. **4P $27-$38, XP: $5.** 8630 Miola Rd. I-80, exit 62, 2 mi e on SR 68 E to light at Clarion Courthouse, go straight for 9.5 mi.

FARMINGTON — BENNER'S MEADOW RUN CAMPING & CABINS. (724) 329-4097. **4P $31-$49, XP: $7-$10.** 315 Nelson Rd. 2.5 mi n of US 40, follow signs.

GARDNERS — MOUNTAIN CREEK CAMPGROUND. (717) 486-7681. **2P $27-$37, XP: $5.** 349 Pine Grove Rd. 2 mi w of SR 34, follow signs.

GETTYSBURG — GETTYSBURG CAMPGROUND. ⚫ (717) 334-3304. **4P $30-$49, XP: $1-$3.** 2030 Fairfield Rd. 3 mi w on SR 116 W.

GETTYSBURG — GETTYSBURG KOA KAMPGROUND. ⚫ (717) 642-5713. **Call for rates.** 20 Knox Rd. 3 mi w on US 30, 3 mi s on Knoxlyn Rd, follow signs.

GETTYSBURG — GRANITE HILL CAMPING RESORT. ⚫ (717) 642-8749. **2P $30-$50, XP: $2-$8.** 3340 Fairfield Rd. 5.8 mi w on SR 116.

GETTYSBURG — ROUND TOP CAMPGROUND. (717) 334-9565. **Call for rates.** 180 Knight Rd. 3 mi s on SR 134 at US 15.

HARRISVILLE — KOZY REST KAMPGROUND. ⚫ (724) 735-2417. **4P $23-$35, XP: $2-$5.** 449 Campground Rd. Jct SR 8/SR 58, 0.5 mi e on SR 58 to Campground Rd, then 1.9 mi ne.

HERSHEY — HERSHEY HIGHMEADOW CAMPGROUND. (717) 534-8999. **2P $32-$48, XP: $4.** 1200 Matlack Rd. 0.5 mi n on SR 39 W from jct US 322 and 422. (PO Box 866, 17033).

HOLTWOOD — MUDDY RUN RECREATION PARK. (717) 284-5850. **6P $23, XP: $3.** 172 Bethesda Church Rd W. 1.8 mi ne on SR 372.

JONESTOWN — JONESTOWN KOA. (717) 865-2526. **2P $28-$63, XP: $5.** 145 Old Rt 22. 2 mi e on US 22 from jct SR 72, 0.5 mi s; I-81, exit 90, 5 mi se; I-78, exit 6, 5 mi w, follow signs. (PO Box 867, 17038).

KNOX — WOLFS CAMPING RESORT. ⚫ (814) 797-1103. **Call for rates.** 308 Timberwolf Run. I-80, exit 53.

LANCASTER — OLD MILL STREAM CAMPGROUND. (717) 299-2314. **4P $33-$43, XP: $3.** 2249 Lincoln Hwy E. 5 mi e on US 30.

LENHARTSVILLE — ROBIN HILL CAMPING RESORT. (610) 756-6117. **2P $42-$50, XP: $1-$4.** 149 Robin Hill Rd. I-78, exit 40 (Krumsville) or exit 35 (Lenhartsville) for 3 mi, follow signs.

LICKDALE — LICKDALE CAMPGROUND. (717) 865-6411. **4P $25-$37, XP: $3-$7.** 11 Lickdale Rd. I-81, exit 90, just e.

LIVERPOOL — FERRY BOAT CAMPSITES. ⚫ (717) 444-3200. **$36-$42, XP: $3.** 32 Ferry Ln. 2 mi s on US 11/15.

MANHEIM — PINCH POND FAMILY CAMPGROUND & RV PARK. ⚫ (717) 665-7640. **Call for rates.** 3075 Pinch Rd. I-76 (Pennsylvania Tpke), exit 266, 1 mi s on SR 72, 0.5 mi w on Cider Press Rd, then 1 mi n.

MANSFIELD — BUCKTAIL CAMPING RESORT. (570) 662-2923. **4P $19-$57, XP: $8-$11.** 130 Bucktail Rd. US 15, exit US 6, just e, 1.5 mi n on Lambs Creek Rd, then 1 mi w.

MARSHALLS CREEK — OTTER LAKE CAMP RESORT. ⚫ (570) 223-0123. **2P $36-$59, XP: $4-$8.** 4805 Marshalls Creek Rd. I-80, exit 309, 3 mi n on US 209, just n on SR 402, then 7 mi w on Marshalls Creek Rd. (PO Box 850, 18335).

MCKEAN — ERIE KOA KAMPGROUNDS. (814) 476-7706. **2P $29-$68, XP: $3-$6.** 6624 West Rd. I-90, exit 18, 1.3 mi s on SR 832, then 0.8 mi e; I-79, exit 174, 1.5 mi w. (6645 West Rd, 16426).

MEADVILLE — BROOKDALE FAMILY CAMPGROUND. (814) 789-3251. **4P $26-$43, XP: $4-$6.** 25164 State Hwy 27. On SR 27, 8 mi e.

MERCER — MERCER-GROVE CITY KOA. (724) 748-3160. **2P $35-$65, XP: $5.** 1337 Butler Pike. I-79, exit 113, 3 mi n on SR 258, follow signs.

MERCER — ROCKY SPRINGS CAMPGROUND. (724) 662-4415. **Call for rates. (no credit cards).** 84 Rocky Spring Rd, Rt 318. I-80, exit 15 westbound, 2 mi n on US 19 to Butler St (SR 318), then 4.5 mi w; exit eastbound, jct I-80 and exit 4A (SR 318), 6.5 mi ne.

MERCERSBURG — SAUNDEROSA PARK INC. (717) 328-2216. **Call for rates.** 5909 Little Cove Rd. 4.8 mi w on SR 16, 2.5 mi s on SR 456.

MEXICO — BUTTONWOOD CAMPGROUND. (717) 436-8334. **4P $26-$36, XP: $3.** River Rd. US 322, exit 24 (Port Royal), 0.6 mi s on SR 75 S, 0.8 mi se on Old US 322, then 0.4 mi s. (PO Box 223, 17056).

MILL RUN — YOGI BEAR'S JELLYSTONE PARK CAMP RESORT. (724) 455-2929. **4P $20-$60, XP: $3-$10.** 839 Mill Run Rd. Just s on SR 381. (PO Box 91, 15464).

NEW COLUMBIA — WILLIAMSPORT SOUTH/NITTANY MOUNTAIN KOA KAMPGROUND. (570) 568-5541. **2P $28-$46, XP: $3-$5.** 2751 Millers Bottom Rd. I-80, exit 210A, 0.5 mi s on US 15, 4.5 mi w on New Columbia Rd, then 0.4 mi nw.

NEW HOLLAND — SPRING GULCH RESORT. (717) 354-3100. **2P $35-$63, XP: $2-$6.** 475 Lynch Rd. Jct SR 23 and 897, 4 mi s on SR 897.

NORTHUMBERLAND — SPLASH MAGIC CAMPGROUND & RV RESORT. (570) 473-8021. **4P $35-$49, XP: $5-$7.** 213 Yogi Blvd. I-80, exit 224, 2 mi e on SR 54, 8 mi s on US 11; 2.5 mi n on US 11.

PINE GROVE — PINE GROVE KOA AT TWIN GROVE PARK. ⚠️ (717) 865-4602. **2P $25-$50, XP: $4-$6.** 1445 Suedburg Rd. I-81, exit 100, 5 mi w on SR 443.

PORTERSVILLE — BEAR RUN CAMPGROUND. ⚠️ (724) 368-3564. **2P $25-$50, XP: $10.** 184 Badger Hill Rd. I-79, exit 96, 0.8 mi n on SR 488.

PORTLAND — DRIFTSTONE ON THE DELAWARE. ⚠️ (570) 897-6859. **2P $32-$44, XP: $5-$8.** SR 611, Portland exit, 4 mi s on River Rd, slight left at split. (2731 River Rd, MOUNT BETHEL, 18343).

QUARRYVILLE — YOGI BEAR'S JELLYSTONE PARK. (717) 786-3458. **2P $46-$102, XP: $3-$25.** 340 Blackburn Rd. 2.7 mi s on US 222, 1.5 mi se, follow signs.

ROBESONIA — ADVENTURE BOUND CAMPING RESORTS AT EAGLES PEAK. (610) 589-4800. **4P $28-$54, XP: $4-$10.** 397 Eagles Peak Rd. 1.6 mi s on SR 419 from jct US 422, just s on Main St, 0.5 mi w on Memorial Blvd, then 1.1 mi s on Sheridan Rd, follow signs for Eagles Peak.

ROSE POINT — COOPER'S LAKE. (724) 368-8710. **2P $20, XP: $10.** 205 Currie Rd. I-79, exit 99, 0.8 mi w on US 422, then 1 mi n.

SANDY LAKE — GODDARD PARK VACATION LAND CAMPGROUND. (724) 253-4645. **2P $24-$35, XP: $2-$3.** 867 Georgetown Rd. I-79, exit 130, 0.3 mi w on SR 358, then 3.5 mi n, follow signs.

SHARTLESVILLE — MOUNTAIN SPRINGS CAMPING RESORT INC & ARENA. (610) 488-6859. **Call for rates.** 3450 Mountain Rd. I-78, exit 23, 1 mi n. (PO Box 365, 19554).

SIGEL — CAMPERS PARADISE CAMPGROUNDS & CABINS. (814) 752-2393. **2P $28-$38, XP: $5-$7.** 37 Steele Dr. On SR 949 N, 3 mi n of SR 36.

STRASBURG — WHITE OAK CAMPGROUND. ⚠️ (717) 687-6207. **2P $26-$32, XP: $3.** 3156 White Oak Rd. 3.7 mi s of Centre Square on S Decatur St/May Post Office Rd, then 0.3 mi e. (PO Box 90, 17579).

UPPER BLACK EDDY — COLONIAL WOODS FAMILY CAMPING RESORT. (610) 847-5808. **Call for rates.** 545 Lonely Cottage Dr. 1.5 mi e on Marienstein Rd from jct SR 611, then 1 mi n, follow signs.

WATERFORD — SPARROW POND FAMILY CAMPGROUND AND RECREATION FACILITY. ⚠️ (814) 796-6777. **4P $28-$50, XP: $3-$5.** 11103 Route 19 N. I-90, exit 24, 10 mi s on US 19 (Peach St).

South Carolina

HILTON HEAD ISLAND — HILTON HEAD HARBOR RV RESORT & MARINA. (843) 681-3256. **4P $45-$59, XP: $3.** 43A Jenkins Rd. 0.9 mi se of Intracoastal Waterway Bridge off US 278, 0.4 mi n, follow signs. (PO Box 21585, 29925).

HILTON HEAD ISLAND — HILTON HEAD ISLAND MOTORCOACH RESORT. ⚠️ (843) 785-7699. **4P $55-$65, XP: $2.** 133 Arrow Rd. 5.6 mi e on Cross Island Pkwy (US 278 toll), then just w. (PO Box 6037, 29938).

MYRTLE BEACH — APACHE FAMILY CAMPGROUND AND OCEANFRONT PIER. (843) 449-7323. **4P $30-$60, XP: $5.** 9700 Kings Rd. Jct SR 22, 1.3 mi sw on US 17, then 0.8 mi e on Lake Arrowhead Rd.

MYRTLE BEACH — LAKEWOOD CAMPING RESORT. ⚠️ (843) 238-5161. **Call for rates.** 5901 S Kings Hwy. Jct SR 544, 0.5 mi ne on US 17 business route.

MYRTLE BEACH — MYRTLE BEACH TRAVEL PARK. (843) 449-3714. **4P $34-$63, XP: $4.** 10108 Kings Rd. Jct US 17 business route/SR 22, 1.3 mi s.

MYRTLE BEACH — OCEAN LAKES FAMILY CAMPGROUND. ⚠️ (843) 238-5636. **$29-$66.** 6001 S Kings Hwy. Jct SR 544 and US 17 business route.

MYRTLE BEACH — PIRATELAND FAMILY CAMPING RESORT. (843) 238-5155. **Call for rates.** 5401 S Kings Hwy. Jct SR 544, 1.2 mi ne on US 17 business route.

South Dakota

CHAMBERLAIN — CEDAR SHORE CAMPGROUND. ⟨AAA⟩ (605) 734-5273. **$25-$35.** 1400 Shoreline Dr. I-90, exit 260, 2.5 mi e on US 16 and I-90 business loop, then 1 mi ne on Mickelson country road, follow signs. (PO Box 308, 57325).

⟨image⟩ ⟨image⟩

DEADWOOD — WHISTLER GULCH CAMPGROUND & RV PARK. (605) 578-2092. **$22-$38.** 235 Cliff St. 0.7 mi s on US 85.

⟨image⟩ ⟨image⟩

HILL CITY — RAFTER J BAR RANCH CAMPGROUND. ⟨AAA⟩ (605) 574-2527. **Call for rates.** 12325 Rafter J Rd. 3.3 mi s on US 16 and 385 at SR 87/244. (PO Box 128, 57745).

⟨image⟩ ⟨image⟩ ⟨image⟩

INTERIOR — BADLANDS WHITE RIVER KOA. ⟨AAA⟩ (605) 433-5337. **2P $26-$43, XP: $4.** 20720 SD Hwy 44. 4 mi e of jct SR 377.

⟨image⟩ ⟨image⟩ ⟨image⟩

MITCHELL — MITCHELL KOA. (605) 996-1131. **2P $33-$47, XP: $3.** 41255 SD Hwy 38. I-90, exit 335, 0.5 mi n, then 0.3 mi w.

⟨image⟩ ⟨image⟩

NORTH SIOUX CITY — SIOUX CITY NORTH KOA. (605) 232-4519. **2P $24-$42, XP: $2-$4.** 675 Streeter Dr. I-29, exit 2 northbound, 1 mi n on west service road; exit 4 southbound, 1 mi w on west service road.

⟨image⟩ ⟨image⟩

SIOUX FALLS — YOGI BEAR CAMP RESORT. (605) 332-2233. **2P $21-$42, XP: $3.** 26014 478th Ave. I-90, exit 402, just n.

⟨image⟩ ⟨image⟩

SPEARFISH — ELKHORN RIDGE RV PARK & CAMPGROUND. ⟨AAA⟩ (605) 722-1800. **6P $12-$44.** 20189 US 85. I-90, exit 17 (US 85), 0.5 mi s.

⟨image⟩ ⟨image⟩ ⟨image⟩

Tennessee

EAST RIDGE — BEST HOLIDAY TRAV-L-PARK/ CHATTANOOGA. (706) 891-9766. **2P $25-$35, XP: $3.** 1709 Mack Smith Rd. I-75, exit 1 southbound; exit 1B northbound, 0.3 mi w, then 1 mi s.

⟨image⟩ ⟨image⟩

GATLINBURG — OUTDOOR RESORTS OF GATLINBURG. (865) 436-5861. **Call for rates.** 4229 Parkway E. 11.5 mi e on US 321 N.

⟨image⟩ ⟨image⟩

PIGEON FORGE — RIVEREDGE RV PARK. (865) 453-5813. **2P $27-$37, XP: $4.** 4220 Huskey St. Just off US 441 at traffic light 10.

⟨image⟩ ⟨image⟩ ⟨image⟩

TOWNSEND — TOWNSEND/GREAT SMOKIES KOA. (865) 448-2241. **Call for rates.** 8533 State Hwy 73. On SR 73, 0.4 mi w of entrance to Great Smoky Mountain National Park.

⟨image⟩ ⟨image⟩ ⟨image⟩

Texas

ABILENE — KOA-ABILENE. (325) 672-3681. **Call for rates.** 4851 W Stamford St. I-20, exit 282 (Shirley Rd), 0.5 mi w of US 83-277, follow signs.

⟨image⟩

AMARILLO — AMARILLO RV RANCH. ⟨AAA⟩ (806) 373-4962. **2P $31-$33, XP: $2.** 1414 Sunrise Dr. I-40, exit 74 (Whitaker Rd), 0.3 mi w on north frontage road.

⟨image⟩ ⟨image⟩ ⟨image⟩

AMARILLO — FORT AMARILLO RV RESORT. (806) 331-1700. **2P $33, XP: $2.** 10101 Amarillo Blvd W. I-40, exit 64 westbound, 0.3 mi n on Soncy to Amarillo Blvd, then 1 mi w; exit 62B eastbound, 0.7 mi e.

⟨image⟩ ⟨image⟩ ⟨image⟩

AUSTIN — AUSTIN LONE STAR CAREFREE RV RESORT. (512) 444-6322. **$28-$50.** 7009 I-35 S. I-35, exit 226B/227 (Slaughter/S Congress aves) southbound; exit 228/229 (Wm Cannon Dr) northbound, on N Frontage Rd.

⟨image⟩ ⟨image⟩ ⟨image⟩

BEAUMONT — GULF COAST RV RESORT. (409) 842-2285. **2P $35, XP: $4-$6.** 5175 Brooks Rd. I-10, exit 846 westbound; exit 845 eastbound, follow blue signs.

⟨image⟩ ⟨image⟩ ⟨image⟩

BOERNE — ALAMO FIESTA RV RESORT. ⟨AAA⟩ (830) 249-4700. **$33-$40, XP: $3.** 33000 IH-10 W. I-10, exit 543, 1 mi w on westbound access road.

⟨image⟩ ⟨image⟩ ⟨image⟩ ⟨image⟩

DONNA — VICTORIA PALMS RESORT. (956) 464-7801. **Call for rates.** 602 N Victoria Rd. Just s of jct US 83.

⟨image⟩ ⟨image⟩ ⟨image⟩

GALVESTON — JAMAICA BEACH RV PARK. (409) 632-0200. **2P $44-$59, XP: $2-$3.** 17200 FM 3005. Jct 61st St and Seawall Blvd, 11 mi w.

⟨image⟩ ⟨image⟩ ⟨image⟩ ⟨image⟩

GOODLETT — OLE TOWNE COTTON GIN RV PARK. (940) 674-2477. **Call for rates.** 230 Market St. US 287, 1 blk e; in town.

⟨image⟩ ⟨image⟩

HARLINGEN — PARADISE PARK. (956) 425-6881. **Call for rates.** 1201 N Expwy 77. US 77 Expwy N, exit Wilson Rd, 0.5 mi s on W Frontage Rd.

⟨image⟩ ⟨image⟩ ⟨image⟩

KERRVILLE — GUADALUPE RIVER RV RESORT. (830) 367-5676. **Call for rates.** 2605 Junction Hwy. I-10, exit 505 (Harper Rd), 2.5 mi s, then 2.5 mi w on SR 27.

⟨image⟩ ⟨image⟩ ⟨image⟩

KERRVILLE — KERRVILLE KOA. (830) 895-1665. **Call for rates.** 2400 Goat Creek Rd. I-10, exit 501, 1.5 mi s on FM 1338.

⟨image⟩ ⟨image⟩

LUBBOCK — LUBBOCK KOA. (806) 762-8653. **Call for rates.** 5502 CR 6300. 2.5 mi nw of Loop 289 on US 84.

⟨image⟩ ⟨image⟩

LUBBOCK — LUBBOCK RV PARK. ⟨AAA⟩ (806) 747-2366. **2P $28-$30, XP: $2.** 4811 N I-27. I-27, exit 9, 2 mi n of Loop 289. (PO Box 597, 79403).

⟨image⟩ ⟨image⟩

MERCEDES — LLANO GRANDE LAKE PARK RESORT AND COUNTRY CLUB. (956) 565-2638. **2P $28-$36, XP: $2.** 489 Yolanda. On Mile 2 W Rd, 1.8 mi s of jct US 83.

MERCEDES — PARADISE SOUTH R.V. RESORT. (956) 565-2044. **2P $34, XP: $2.** 9099 N Mile 2 Rd W. On Mile 2 W Rd, just n of US 83.

PORT ISABEL — LONG ISLAND VILLAGE. (956) 943-6449. **3P $46-$52, XP: $3. (no credit cards).** 900 S Garcia St. On SR 100, turn right before crossing causeway. (PO Box 695, 78578).

SAN ANTONIO — ADMIRALTY RV RESORT. (210) 647-7878. **2P $36-$45, XP: $3.** 1485 N Ellison Dr. Jct Loop 1604 and SR 151, 1.3 mi nw on SR 151 to Military Dr, just w to Ellison Dr, then 0.7 mi n.

SAN ANTONIO — BLAZING STAR RV RESORT. (210) 680-7827. **2P $45-$60, XP: $3-$5.** 1120 W Loop 1604 N. Just s of Military Dr.

SAN ANTONIO — SAN ANTONIO KOA KAMPGROUND. (210) 224-9296. **2P $37-$41, XP: $4.** 602 Gembler Rd. I-35, exit AT&T Center Pkwy, 0.5 mi s, then 0.8 mi e; I-10, exit WW White Rd, 0.3 mi n, then 1 mi w.

SAN BENITO — FUN-N-SUN RV RESORT. (956) 399-5125. **Call for rates.** 1400 Zillock Rd. 4 mi nw from US 83 and 77, exit Paso Real Rd, 0.4 mi s.

UVALDE — QUAIL SPRINGS RV PARK. (830) 278-8182. **2P $27, XP: $3.** 2727 E Main St. 2.2 mi e on US 90.

WICHITA FALLS — WICHITA FALLS RV PARK. (940) 723-1532. **2P $25-$28, XP: $3.** 2944 Seymour Hwy (Business 277 S). I-44, exit 1A, 1.2 mi s.

Utah

BRYCE CANYON CITY — RUBY'S INN CAMPGROUND TRAILER PARK. (435) 834-5301. **2P $35-$40, XP: $2.** 1280 S Hwy 63. On SR 63, 1 mi n of Bryce Canyon National Park entrance. (PO Box 640022, 84764).

CANNONVILLE — CANNONVILLE-BRYCE VALLEY KOA. (435) 679-8988. **2P $25-$150, XP: $3.** Hwy 12 at Redrock Rd. On SR 12; north end of town. (PO Box 50, 84718).

FRUIT HEIGHTS — CHERRY HILL CAMPING RESORT. (801) 451-5379. **2P $20-$38, XP: $2.** 1325 S Main St. I-15, exit 324 (US 89) northbound, then exit 397, just e; exit 328 southbound, just e, then 2 mi s.

MOAB — MOAB VALLEY RV RESORT. (435) 259-4469. **$39-$75, XP: $5.** 1773 N Hwy 191. 2 mi n, just s of Colorado River Bridge.

ST. GEORGE — MCARTHUR'S TEMPLE VIEW RV RESORT. (435) 673-6400. **2P $28-$41, XP: $3.** 975 S Main St. I-15, exit 6 (Bluff St), 0.5 mi w, then just n.

VIRGIN — ZION RIVER RESORT RV PARK & CAMPGROUND. (435) 635-8594. **4P $45-$55, XP: $3.** 730 E Hwy 9. I-15, exit 16 (SR 16) northbound, 22 mi ne; exit 27 southbound, 12 mi ne. (PO Box 790219, 84779).

Virginia

BIG ISLAND — WILDWOOD CAMPGROUND. (434) 299-5228. 2P **$30-$35, XP: $3-$5.** SR 130, 1.3 mi e from jct Blue Ridge Pkwy, 14 mi w of SR 29. (6252 Elon Rd, MONROE, 24574).

CHARLOTTESVILLE — CHARLOTTESVILLE KOA. (434) 296-9881. **2P $29-$40, XP: $3-$5.** 3825 Red Hill Rd. US 29 (s of I-64), 4.2 mi e on CR 708; SR 20, 1.4 mi w on CR 708.

CHERITON — CHERRYSTONE FAMILY CAMPING RESORT. (757) 331-3063. **Call for rates.** 1511 Townfields Dr. 1.5 mi w on SR 680 from jct US 13. (PO Box 545, 23316).

FRONT ROYAL — FRONT ROYAL RV CAMPGROUND. (540) 635-2741. **$30-$65, XP: $2-$5.** 585 KOA Dr. I-66, exit 6 or 13, 2 mi s on US 340 S. (PO Box 274, 22630).

LURAY — LURAY RV RESORT COUNTRY WAYE. (540) 743-7222. **2P $38-$43, XP: $3-$6.** 3402 Kimball Rd. Jct US 211, 2 mi n on US 340, then 0.3 mi e on SR 658.

LURAY — YOGI BEAR'S JELLYSTONE PARK. (540) 743-4002. **2P $35-$60, XP: $3-$6.** 2250 Hwy 211 E. On US 211, 3 mi e. (PO Box 191, 22835).

MADISON — SHENANDOAH HILLS CAMPGROUND. (540) 948-4186. **2P $29-$45, XP: $3-$5.** 110 Campground Ln. 2 mi s on US 29.

MINT SPRING — WALNUT HILLS CAMPGROUND. (540) 337-3920. **2P $28-$38, XP: $4.** 484 Walnut Hills Rd. I-81, exit 217, 0.7 mi w to US 11, 1.5 mi s, then 1.2 mi e on SR 655.

NATURAL BRIDGE — NATURAL BRIDGE KOA KAMPGROUND. (540) 291-2770. **2P $24-$117, XP: $3-$5.** 214 Kildeer Ln. I-81, exit 180 northbound; exit 180B southbound, just nw on US 11. (PO Box 148, 24578).

TOPPING — GREY'S POINT CAMP. (804) 758-2485. **Call for rates.** 3601 Grey's Point Rd. On US 3; just s of Rappahannock River Bridge. (PO Box 8, 23169).

URBANNA — BETHPAGE CAMP RESORT. (804) 758-4349. **4P $39-$72, XP: $4.** 679 Brown's Ln. 1 mi n of town on CR 602. (PO Box 178, 23175).

VIRGINIA BEACH — HOLIDAY TRAV-L-PARK. ⒶⒶⒶ (757) 425-0249. **2P $28-$72, XP: $3-$6.** 1075 General Booth Blvd. I-264 terminus to Pacific Ave, 2.5 mi s. 🔲 🛶 🍴

VIRGINIA BEACH — OUTDOOR RESORTS/VIRGINIA BEACH. (757) 721-2020. **Call for rates.** 3665 S Sandpiper Rd. I-264 terminus to Pacific Ave, 2 mi s to Rudee Inlet Bridge/General Booth Blvd, 5.6 mi s to Princess Anne Rd, 0.8 mi e to Sandbridge Rd, 5.5 mi e to Sandpiper Rd, then 3.5 mi s. 🛶 🍴

Washington

BURLINGTON — BURLINGTON KOA. (360) 724-5511. **2P $24-$45, XP: $3-$4.** 6397 N Green Rd. I-5, exit 232, 3.5 mi n on Old US 99. 🔲 🛶 🍴

CHENEY — PONDEROSA FALLS RV RESORT. (509) 747-9415. **6P $27-$45, XP: $5.** 7520 S Thomas Mallen Rd. I-90, exit 272, 1.4 mi s. 🛶 🍴

CLARKSTON — GRANITE LAKE PREMIER RV RESORT. ⒶⒶⒶ (509) 751-1635. **Call for rates.** 306 Granite Lake Dr. Just w of Snake River Bridge on US 12, just n on 5th St. 🔲 🍴

COULEE CITY — SUN LAKES PARK RESORT. (509) 632-5291. **Call for rates.** 34228 Park Lake Rd NE. US 2, 4 mi s on SR 17. 🛶 🍴

EPHRATA — STARS AND STRIPES RV PARK & DRIVING RANGE. (509) 787-1062. **Call for rates.** 5707 US 28 W. 5 mi w. 🛶 🍴

LYNDEN — LYNDEN KOA. (360) 354-4772. **2P $30-$70, XP: $5.** 8717 Line Rd. 1.7 mi n of downtown on SR 539 (Guide Meridian Rd), 3 mi e on SR 546 (E Badger Rd), then 0.5 mi s. 🛶 🍴

MOSSYROCK — HARMONY LAKESIDE RV PARK. ⒶⒶⒶ (360) 983-3804. **2P $29-$52, XP: $5.** 563 SR 122. I-5, exit 68, 21 mi e on US 12, then 5.7 mi n. 🔲 🍴

OAK HARBOR — NORTH WHIDBEY RV PARK. (360) 675-9597. **$30, XP: $3.** 565 W Cornet Bay Rd. On SR 20, 1 mi s of Deception Pass Bridge; 8 mi n of town. 🍴

PORT ANGELES — PORT ANGELES/SEQUIM KOA. (360) 457-5916. **2P $22-$76, XP: $3-$5.** 80 O'Brien Rd & US 101 E. 7 mi e on US 101; 8 mi w of Sequim on US 101; just e of US 101, MM 255. 🛶 🍴

SPOKANE — ALDERWOOD RV RESORT. (509) 467-5320. **2P $27-$37, XP: $3.** 14007 N Newport Hwy. I-90, exit 287, 8 mi₂ n to SR 206, then 1.5 mi w. 🛶 🍴

SPOKANE VALLEY — SPOKANE KOA. (509) 924-4722. **Call for rates.** 3025 N Barker Rd. I-90, exit 293, 1.5 mi n. 🛶 🍴

West Virginia

HARPERS FERRY — HARPERS FERRY/CIVIL WAR BATTLE-FIELDS KOA. ⒶⒶⒶ (304) 535-6895. **2P $35-$54, XP: $5-$6.** 343 Campground Rd. 1 mi sw on US 340 from Shenandoah River Bridge, 0.3 mi s, follow signs. 🛶 🍴

MILTON — HUNTINGTON/FOX FIRE KOA. (304) 743-5622. **4P $25-$50, XP: $1-$6.** 290 Fox Fire Rd. I-64, exit 28, 0.3 mi s on US 60, then 2.7 mi w on Fox Fire Rd. 🛶 🍴

Wisconsin

BAGLEY — YOGI BEAR'S JELLYSTONE PARK CAMP RESORT. (608) 996-2201. **$22-$48, XP: $3-$6.** 11354 CR X. 1.3 mi n. 🛶 🍴

ELKHART LAKE — PLYMOUTH ROCK CAMPING RESORT. (920) 892-4252. **8P $37-$50, XP: $6-$12.** N7271 Lando St. 3 mi s on SR 67, 4 mi n of Plymouth. (PO Box 445, 53020). 🛶 🍴

FORT ATKINSON — JELLYSTONE PARK OF FORT ATKINSON. (920) 568-4100. **4P $21-$41, XP: $5-$9.** N 551 Wishing Well Dr. 5 mi s on SR 26 from jct US 12, 0.8 mi w on Koshkonong Lake Rd, then just s. 🛶 🍴

FREMONT — YOGI BEAR'S JELLYSTONE PARK CAMP RESORT. (920) 446-3420. **Call for rates.** E 6506 Hwy 110. On SR 110 S, 1.5 mi w. (PO Box 497, 54940). 🛶 🍴

WISCONSIN DELLS — CHRISTMAS MOUNTAIN CAMPGROUND. (608) 253-1000. **Call for rates. (no credit cards).** 944 S Christmas Mountain Rd. I-90/94, exit 87 (SR 13), 0.4 mi ne to CR H, 4 mi sw, then just s. 🛶 🍴

WISCONSIN DELLS — YOGI BEAR'S JELLYSTONE PARK CAMP-RESORT. ⒶⒶⒶ (608) 254-2568. **4P $19-$109, XP: $5-$10.** S 1915 Ishnala Rd. I-90/94, exit 89 eastbound; exit 92 (US 12) westbound, follow signs. (PO Box 510, 53965). 🛶 🍴

Canada

Alberta

EDMONTON — GLOWING EMBERS TRAVEL CENTRE & RV PARK. ⒸⒶⒶ (780) 962-8100. **2P $36-$42, XP: $1.** 26309 Hwy 16A. 1.9 mi (3 km) w of city limits; 1.1 mi (1.8 km) sw of Devon exit (Hwy 60 S), follow signs.

HINTON — HINTON/JASPER KOA. ⒸⒶⒶ (780) 865-5062. **2P $27-$42, XP: $3-$5.** 50409B Hwy 16. On Hwy 16, 2.5 mi (4 km) w. (4720 Vegas Rd NW, CALGARY, T3A 1W3).

PINE LAKE — LEISURE CAMPGROUNDS. (403) 886-4705. **Call for rates.** On Hwy 42, 14.7 mi (24.6 km) e of Hwy 2. (PO Box 68, T0M 1S0).

SUNDRE — TALL TIMBER LEISURE PARK. (403) 638-3555. **Call for rates.** 0.6 mi (1 km) e of Centre St on Main Ave E (Hwy 27 E). (PO Box 210, T0M 1X0).

British Columbia

BURNABY — BURNABY CARIBOO R.V. PARK. ⒸⒶⒶ (604) 420-1722. **2P $36-$55, XP: $3-$5.** 8765 Cariboo Pl. Trans-Canada Hwy 1, exit 37 (Gaglardi Way), follow signs.

CAMPBELL RIVER — RIPPLE ROCK RV PARK. (250) 287-7108. **2P $23-$42, XP: $3.** 15011 Browns Bay Rd. Jct Hwy 19A, 28 and 19, 12 mi (19 km) n on Hwy 19, then 2.8 mi (4.5 km) e.

FAIRMONT HOT SPRINGS — FAIRMONT HOT SPRINGS RV PARK. (250) 345-6033. **$20-$49.** 5225 Fairmont Resort Rd. 1 mi (1.6 km) e off Hwy 93 and 95; adjacent to Fairmont Hot Springs Resort.

MALAHAT — VICTORIA WEST KOA. (250) 478-3332. **2P $34-$48, XP: $4-$6.** On Trans-Canada Hwy 1 (Malahat Dr), 15.9 mi (25.6 km) n of Victoria. (PO Box 103, V0R 2L0).

NORTH VANCOUVER — CAPILANO RV PARK. ⒸⒶⒶ (604) 987-4722. **2P $31-$50, XP: $4.** 295 Tomahawk Ave. Trans-Canada Hwy 1, exit 14 (Capilano Rd), 1 mi (1.6 km) s to Marine Dr, follow signs.

OLIVER — DESERT GEM RV AND RESORT INC. ⒸⒶⒶ (250) 498-5544. **2P $25-$38, XP: $5.** 34037 Hwy 97. Just s of 340th Ave. (PO Box 1920, V0H 1T0).

SURREY — PEACE ARCH RV PARK. (604) 594-7009. **Call for rates.** 14601 40th Ave. Hwy 99, exit 10, follow signs.

WHISTLER — RIVERSIDE RV RESORT AND CAMPGROUND. (604) 905-5533. **2P $20-$55, XP: $5.** 8018 Mons Rd. Hwy 99, from Upper Village, 0.9 mi (1.5 km) n, exit Blackcomb Way, follow signs.

New Brunswick

WOODSTOCK — YOGI BEAR'S JELLYSTONE PARK AT KOZY ACRES. (506) 328-6287. **5P $35-$40, XP: $8.** 174 Hemlock St. Trans-Canada Hwy 2, exit 191 (Beardsley Rd). (PO Box 9004, E7M 6B5).

Ontario

BRADFORD — YOGI BEAR'S JELLYSTONE PARK & CAMP-RESORT. ⒸⒶⒶ (905) 775-1377. **2P $35-$55, XP: $6-$8.** 3666 Simcoe Rd 88. Hwy 400, exit 64B; jct Hwy 400 and Simcoe Rd 88. (RR 1, L3Z 2A4).

FOREST — OUR PONDEROSA RV RESORT & GOLF RESORT. (519) 786-2031. **Call for rates.** 9338 W Ipperwash Rd. Jct CR 7, 1.9 mi (3 km) n. (RR 2, N0N 1J0).

KINCARDINE — FISHERMAN'S COVE TENT & TRAILER PARK LTD. (519) 395-2757. **2P $42-$50, XP: $3.** 13 Southline Ave. Jct Hwy 21 and 9, 10.6 mi (17.7 km) e to Kinloss, then 1.9 mi (3 km) s; follow signs. (RR 4, N2Z 2X5).

KITCHENER — BINGEMANS. (519) 744-1002. **6P $35-$55.** 425 Bingemans Centre Dr. 3.5 mi (5.6 km) on Hwy 7; 1 mi (1.6 km) e of jct Hwy 7 and Conestoga Pkwy (Hwy 86).

NIAGARA FALLS — CAMPARK RESORTS. ⒸⒶⒶ (905) 358-3873. **2P $36-$52, XP: $3-$5.** 9387 Lundy's Ln. 3.9 mi (6.3 km) w of falls on Hwy 20.

NIAGARA FALLS — NIAGARA FALLS KOA KAMPGROUND. (905) 356-2267. **2P $39-$89, XP: $6-$12.** 8625 Lundy's Ln. 3.5 mi (5.6 km) w on Hwy 20.

NIAGARA FALLS — YOGI BEAR'S JELLYSTONE PARK CAMP-RESORT. ⒸⒶⒶ (905) 354-1432. **2P $34-$57, XP: $3-$5.** 8676 Oakwood Dr. QEW, exit 27 (McLeod Rd), 1.5 mi (2.4 km) se.

SAUBLE BEACH — CARSON'S CAMP LTD.. (519) 422-1143. **2P $27-$42, XP: $3-$10. (no credit cards).** 110 Southampton Pkwy. 0.6 mi (1 km) s on CR 13. (Rt 1, N0H 2G0).

SAUBLE BEACH — WOODLAND PARK. (519) 422-1161. **2P $32-$49, XP: $2-$20.** 47 Sauble Falls Pkwy, RR 1. 0.6 mi (1 km) n on CR 13.

Quebec

FRELIGHSBURG — LE CAMPING DES CHUTES HUNTER. (450) 298-5005. **Call for rates.** 18 chemin des Chutes. Jct Rt 237, just w on chemin du Moulin a Scie.

LEVIS — KOA-QUEBEC CITY. (AA) (418) 831-1813. **2P $26-$60, XP: $3-$5.** 684 chemin Olivier. Hwy 20, exit 311, 0.9 mi (1.5 km) w, northside service road; in St-Nicolas sector.

ST-MATHIEU-DE-BELOEIL — CAMPING ALOUETTE. (AA) (450) 464-1661. **2P $34-$42, XP: $3.** 3449 de l'Industrie. Hwy 20, exit 105, follow signs.

STE-SABINE — CAMPING CARAVELLE. (450) 293-7637. **2P $26-$32. (no credit cards).** 180 Rang de la Gare. Jct Rt 104, 2.9 mi (4.7 km) s on Rt 235, then 0.5 mi (0.8 km) w on Rang de la Gare; 3.6 mi (6 km) s of Farnham.

❧ Pet-Friendly Travel Notes ❧